OXFORD LIBRARY OF PSYCHOLOGY

The Oxford Handbook of Adolescent Substance Abuse

Edited by

Robert A. Zucker

Sandra A. Brown

OXFORD

UNIVERSITY PRESS

OXFORD
UNIVERSITY PRESS

Oxford University Press is a department of the University of Oxford. It furthers
the University's objective of excellence in research, scholarship, and education
by publishing worldwide. Oxford is a registered trade mark of Oxford University
Press in the UK and certain other countries.

Published in the United States of America by Oxford University Press
198 Madison Avenue, New York, NY 10016, United States of America.

Library of Congress Cataloging-in-Publication Data
Names: Zucker, Robert A., editor. | Brown, Sandra A., editor.
Title: The Oxford handbook of adolescent substance abuse /
edited by Robert A. Zucker and Sandra A. Brown.
Description: New York, NY : Oxford University Press, [2019] |
Includes bibliographical references and index.
Identifiers: LCCN 2019004320 (print) | LCCN 2019006946 (ebook) |
ISBN 9780190673864 (UPDF) | ISBN 9780190673871 (EPUB) | ISBN 9780199735662 (hardcover)
Subjects: LCSH: Teenagers—Substance use. | Substance abuse.
Classification: LCC HV4999.Y68 (ebook) | LCC HV4999.Y68 O94 2019 (print) |
DDC 362.290835—dc23
LC record available at https://lccn.loc.gov/2019004320

9 8 7 6 5 4 3 2 1

Printed by Sheridan Books, Inc., United States of America

LIST OF CONTRIBUTORS

Kristen G. Anderson, PhD
Department of Psychology
Reed College

Amelia M. Arria, PhD
Center on Young Adult Health and
Development
University of Maryland School of
Public Health

Andria Botzet, MA, LAMFT
Department of Psychiatry
University of Minnesota

Maya M. Boustani, PhD
Department of Psychology
Loma Linda University

J. Wesley Boyd, MD, PhD
Center for Bioethics
Harvard Medical School

Kristen E. L. Briggs
Department of Psychology
Villanova University

Sandra A. Brown, PhD
Department of Psychology
University of San Diego

Brittany A. Bugbee, MPH
Center on Young Adult Health and
Development
University of Maryland School of
Public Health

Alison R. Burns, PhD
Child and Family Psychological
Services, PLLC

Tatiana Buynitsky, MS

Aimee Chabot, MA
Fuqua School of Business
Duke University

Tammy Chung, PhD
Department of Psychiatry
University of Pittsburgh School of
Medicine

Mairav Cohen-Zion, PhD
Department of Behavioral Sciences
The Academic College of Tel Aviv-Jaffa

Sarah Copelas, BA
College of Osteopathic Medicine
University of New England

Courtney Cronley, PhD
School of Social Work
University of Texas at Arlington

Elizabeth J. D'Amico, PhD
RAND Corporation

Jorge Delva, MSW, PhD
Communities Engagement Program
Michigan Institute on Clinical and Health
Research

Sabrina E. Des Rosiers, PhD
Department of Psychology
Barry University

John E. Donovan, PhD
Department of Psychiatry
University of Pittsburgh

Tamara Fahnhorst, MA
Department of Psychiatry
University of Minnesota

Sarah W. Feldstein Ewing, PhD
Division of Clinical Psychology
School of Medicine
Oregon Health & Science University

Lawrence W. Green, PhD
Department of Epidemiology & Biostatistics
University of California, San Francisco

Claudette L. Grinnell-Davis, PhD
Anne and Henry Zarrow School of Social
Work
University of Oklahoma

Christian Grov, PhD
Department of Community Health and
Social Sciences
The CUNY Institute for Implementation
Science and Population Health

Erin Harrop, PhD
School of Social Work
University of Washington

Craig E. Henderson, PhD
Department of Psychology and Philosophy
Sam Houston State University

Brian M. Hicks, PhD
Addiction Center
Department of Psychiatry
University of Michigan

Harold D. Holder, PhD
Alcohol Policy Panel of San Diego

Noelle Hurd, PhD
Department of Psychology
University of Virginia

Andrea M. Hussong, PhD
Department of Psychology and
Neuroscience
University of North Carolina
at Chapel Hill

Padmini Iyer, PhD
Danish Refugee Council
Danish Demining Group
Department of Anthropology
Rutgers University

Kristina M. Jackson, PhD
Department of Behavioral and Social
Sciences
Center for Alcohol and Addiction Studies
Brown University

Megan Janoff, BA
Psychiatrist
New Haven, CT

Deborah Jones, PhD
Department of Psychology &
Neuroscience
University of North Carolina–Chapel Hill

John F. Kelly, PhD
Recovery Research Institute
Massachusetts General Hospital
Harvard Medical School

Jason R. Kilmer, PhD
University of Washington

John R. Knight, MD
Boston Children's Hospital
Harvard Medical School

Christine M. Lee, PhD
Psychiatry & Behavioral Sciences
University of Washington

Sharon Levy, MD, MPH
Adolescent Substance Use and Addiction
Program
Harvard Medical School

Nehama Lewis, PhD
Department of Communication
University of Haifa

Howard A. Liddle, EdD, ABPP
Department of Public Health Sciences
University of Miami

Dana M. Litt, PhD
Health Behavior and Health Systems
University of North Texas Health
Science Center

Laura MacPherson, PhD
Greenebaum Cancer Center
University of Maryland

Jennifer L. Maggs, PhD
Human Development and Family Studies
Pennsylvania State University

Meghan E. Martz, PhD
University of Michigan Addiction Center

Julie Maslowsky, PhD
Department of Kinesiology and Health
Education
University of Texas at Austin

Denis M. McCarthy, PhD
Department of Psychological Sciences
University of Missouri

Kayleigh N. McCarty, MA
Department of Psychological Sciences
University of Missouri

Matt McGue, PhD
Department of Psychology
University of Minnesota

Meghan McGurk, MPH
Office of Public Health Studies
University of Hawai'i at Manoa

Laura G. McKee, PhD
Department of Psychology
Georgia State University

Sandra L. Momper, PhD
School of Social Work
University of Michigan

Mark G. Myers, PhD
Mental Health Service
V.A. San Diego Healthcare System
Department of Psychiatry
University of California, San Diego

Ursula S. Myers, PhD
  University of California, San Diego
Ali Nicholson Stockness, BA
  Department of Psychiatry
  University of Minnesota
Sonya B. Norman, PhD
  Department of Psychiatry
  University of California, San Diego
Patrick M. O'Malley, PhD
  Institute for Social Research
  University of Michigan
Mark B. Padilla, PhD
  Department of Global and Sociocultural
    Studies
  School of International and
    Public Affairs
  Florida International University
Megan E. Patrick, PhD
  Institute for Translational Research and
    Institute of Child Development
  University of Minnesota
Eric R. Pedersen, PhD
  RAND Corporation
Sarah J. Peterson, MS
  Department of Psychology
  University of Kentucky
Marianne Pugatch, PhD, MSW
  Center for Healthcare Organization &
    Implementation Research (CHOIR)
  VA Boston Healthcare System
Danielle E. Ramo, PhD
  Department of Psychiatry
  Helen Diller Family Comprehensive
    Cancer Center
  University of California, San Francisco
Carie Rodgers, PhD, ABPP
  VA Center of Excellence in Stress and
    Mental Health
  University of California, San Diego
Kelly L. Rulison, PhD
  Department of Public Health Education
  University of North Carolina–Greensboro
Miriam Schizer, MD, MPH
  Harvard Medical School
John Schulenberg, PhD
  Center for Human Growth and
    Development
  University of Michigan

Seth J. Schwartz, PhD
  Public Health Sciences
  University of Miami
Julia Shadur, PhD
  School of Integrative Studies
    (Childhood Studies)
  Human Development and
    Family Science
  George Mason University
Gregory T. Smith, PhD
  Department of Psychology
  University of Kentucky
Jessica Solis, PhD
  Department of Psychiatry and Behavioral
    Sciences
  Duke University School of Medicine
Linda Patia Spear, PhD
  Department of Psychology
  Binghamton University, SUNY
Gabriela Livas Stein, PhD
  Department of Psychology
  University of North Carolina–Greensboro
Randy Stinchfield, PhD
  Department of Psychiatry
  University of Minnesota
Steve Sussman, PhD
  Institute for Health Promotion & Disease
    Prevention
  Krek School of Medicine
  University of Southern California
Natali Svirsky, PhD
  Department of Behavioral Sciences
  The Academic College of Tel Aviv-Jaffa
José Szapocznik, PhD
  Clinical Translational Science Institute
  University of Miami
Susan F. Tapert, PhD
  Department of Psychiatry
  University of California, San Diego
Jennifer B. Unger, PhD
  Institute for Health Promotion & Disease
    Prevention
  Krek School of Medicine
  University of Southern California
Eric F. Wagner, PhD
  Stempel College of Public Health &
    Social Work
  Florida International University

Elissa R. Weitzman, ScD, MSc
Department of Pediatrics
Harvard Medical School

Reagan R. Wetherill, PhD
Perelman School of Medicine
University of Pennsylvania

Helene Raskin White, PhD
Center of Alcohol Studies
Sociology Department
Rutgers University

Kendall C. Browne, PhD
Department of Psychiatry
and Behavioral Sciences,
University of Washington

Thomas A. Wills, PhD
Cancer Epidemiology Program
University of Hawaii Cancer Center

Jeffrey J. Wilson, MD
Carilion Clinic Psychiatry
Roanoke, VA

Michael Windle, PhD
Rollins School of Public Health
Emory University

Ken C. Winters, PhD
Oregon Research Institute,
Eugene, OR

Matthew J. Worley, PhD
Department of Psychiatry
University of California, San Diego

Julie Yeterian, PhD
Department of Clinical Psychology
William James College

Marc Zimmerman, PhD
Department of Health Behavior and
Health Education
School of Public Health
University of Michigan

Robert A. Zucker, PhD, ABPP
Department of Psychology
University of Michigan

CONTENTS

The Oxford Handbook of Adolescent Substance Abuse

Introduction to the Field and the Issues

Robert A. Zucker *and* Sandra A. Brown

Abstract

This volume provides a comprehensive overview of the origins, development, and course of substance use as it emerges and unfolds in adolescence, a period where great change at genetic, neurobiological, behavioral, and social-environmental levels is taking place. The volume also provides reviews of clinical symptomatology and the multiple methods for intervention that have developed to address this major set of public health problems. This chapter provides a brief overview of these areas; it includes sections on epidemiology, similarities and differences among the different drugs of abuse, etiology and course, clinical symptomatology and comorbidity, intervention methods, and social policy. These summaries, covering multiple levels of analysis, provide a comprehensive description of a field that is still developing, but that has already achieved a substantial level of maturity.

Key Words: adolescent substance use, development, cross-level effects, substance use variations, mechanistic structures

Adolescence is not just a pass-through interval between childhood and adulthood. It is a time of emergence, of rapid change, of consolidation. It is also a time of awkwardness for some and flowering for others. It is a period of dynamic interaction of the individual with the social world, at the same time as it is one where significant biological change, at multiple levels, is taking place. Reward seeking and reward responsivity are at their height at the same time that rational, evaluative, self-control processes are still maturing (Zucker et al., 2008). Thus, short-term decision making may not be modulated by a broader, longer term consideration of consequences (Spear, 2000). This imbalance drives the development of behaviors that have the potential to create danger to self and others at the same time that they bring pleasure to the adolescent.

Simultaneously, from a sociocultural perspective, adolescence is a time when the privileges of adult status begin to be conferred, albeit with considerable time variation across cultures. One of these privileges is the right to use psychoactive substances.

This is an activity that, in substance-using families, has been evident to the child even from the very first years of life (Mennella & Beauchamp, 1998). So as he or she grows older, she or he becomes aware, in a more nuanced way, that this is an activity people sometimes turn to for celebration, for relaxation, and also for escape from the world they live in. It also is an activity that can be seen when negative emotions are strong, at times of anger, and it sometimes also appears at times of loss. For all these reasons, it is not surprising that beginning substance use would be anticipated as the early adolescent youth becomes increasingly tuned in to the world of his or her older peers. And for the reasons just described, it also is a behavior that has the potential to be carried on in a heavier and, and for some, an out-of-control manner, as adolescence proceeds.

This account is all about growing up in families and subcultures that use psychoactive drugs. But not all do so. Approximately 10% of adults in the United States have never used psychoactive substances (Center for Behavioral Health Statistics and Quality, 2016). The experience of children growing up in such families has an impact in both direct and indirect ways. It is an experience of being a minority in a culture where the dominant pattern is one of use, thus leading to the possibility that these youths may to some degree be estranged from their peers. Conversely, to the extent that there is estrangement between parent and child in circumstances where the family is in conflict, substance use is likely to be an activity that unmonitored youth will encounter in their peers (Fosco et al., 2012; Trucco et al., 2014). Moreover, they may find such activity attractive because it distantiates them from their parents.

Our goal for this Handbook was to address these issues in detail, at a time when there is ever-increasing public sensitivity to the magnitude of substance use problems among youth, and where there is continuing public dialogue about the desirability, or not, of increasing legalized access to marijuana. Our net of chapter content was spread to provide not just a comprehensive overview of the broad field involving adolescent substance use and abuse but also one that delved into the mechanistic underpinnings of the behavior at multiple levels of analysis. Because the causal network of this behavior is so large, and its impact is so powerful, both at the time of use as well as in terms of the long-term outcomes and complications of use, the domains we cover spread from infancy to adulthood, and from molecular genetics to social policy. We saw this as an opportunity to define a new field at a time where there has been an extraordinary growth of interest in it, and a recognition that a great many of the outcomes, social, and personal costs of later years of substance use have their origins from, and are in some instances a derivative of, what takes place during these early years. Although to date there has been a small number of other handbooks focused on this developmental time period, most have had a more specialized focus, either via the lens of a specific discipline such as pharmacology (Pagliaro & Pagliaro, 2012) or adolescent psychiatry (Rosner, 2013), or with a specific functional goal (e.g., to summarize the prevention and/or intervention literature (Leukefeld, Gullotta, & Staton-Tindall, 2009; Scheier, 2015). We are aware of only one considerably shorter volume that has some elements in common with the present work (Liddle & Rowe, 2006), but that collection was published a decade ago and did not have a developmental focus. Authors here all shared this developmental perspective, understanding that the emergence of substance use and abuse during this time interval is a process of unfolding, of a moving target, taking place while a great many other changes are taking place as well. All of the authors similarly reflect and make recommendations about where the science should focus next, and they discuss the major questions the field needs to address.

The present compendium comes at a historically important time in the history of adolescent substance abuse research. It has only been within the past generation that a more conscious awareness has existed, in both clinical and scientific communities, of the critical nature of this developmental period (Masten et al., 2008; Moss, Chen, & Yi, 2014; Substance Abuse and Mental Health Services Administration, 2009), and it has only been within the past decade that the field has embraced a cross-level analytic conceptualization of the phenomenon and produced the data to begin to map the cross-level connections (Steinberg et al., 2006). This is an intriguing albeit daunting playing field to describe, given the ultimate relevance the scientific work on this behavior has on the everyday life of the community. A special effort has been made, both in terms of the selection of Handbook chapter content and also within each chapter, to anchor the work in both arenas. Each of the authors is an authority in the area he or she reviews. Each author's goal is to provide a comprehensive overview, by summarizing and synthesizing the research knowledge base, identifying the critical issues in each area covered, and setting the agenda for future research.

The Handbook is organized into eight sections. It begins with a review of the conceptual framework and background for this era of beginning and early use.

Section I: Conceptual Framework and Background (Chapters 2 and 3)

We have already indicated why a developmental framework is essential in understanding the adolescent period. The two chapters here—by Schuenberg, Maslowsky, Patrick, and Martz (Chapter 2) and Jackson (Chapter 3)—review these issues in detail and developmentally link them not only to their precursors but also to their destinations, the period of emerging adulthood. They also make it very clear that normative pathways of development will only account for a portion of developmental variance; the changing demands of context and individual differences in risk potential—often detectable prior to adolescence—also play a significant role (Hicks et al., 2014). The importance of this multifaceted perspective as a key to understanding the phenomenon cannot be emphasized enough. It was only a decade ago that this was acknowledged at the National Instittutes of Health level (Li, 2004). And although it is now the underlying framework for virtually all substance abuse research on adolescence, this paradigm is far from common in the adult literature (Zucker, 2000).

Section II: Epidemiology (Chapters 4 and 5)

The two chapters here present summaries of the data on demographic (Patrick & O'Malley) and cultural variation (Delva, Momper, Grinell-Davis, & Padilla) in substance use and abuse. In Chapter 4, Patrick and O'Malley provide the epidemiologic data on magnitude, age, and demographic variation in the frequency of use in the various drugs of abuse; document the significant variations in population preference for the different drugs; provide a concrete picture of the public health burden; and also—again from a developmental perspective, albeit one in historical time—describe how national patterns of use have varied across the years. In Chapter 5, "Cultural Variations and Relevance to Etiology," Delva, Momper, Grinell-Davis, and Padilla provide a detailed account of the great within-culture as well as across-culture variation in patterns of use and abuse that exists among ethnic minority subpopulations, and they provide a carefully disaggregated description of the role that culture plays in determining population variability. The authors make the point that cultural variation is ultimately an individual phenomenon rather than an attribute of a group, and it is a function of the integration of multiple identities assimilated into an individual identity, crafted from the multiple dimensions of role, pressure, and the presence of within- and between-culture heterogeneity, all of which impinge upon the person. They also note that "cultural identity" involves developmental variation at the individual level, but it also changes with historical change.

Section III: Drugs of Abuse: Similarities and Differences (Chapters 6–10)

This group of chapters articulates how substance use/abuse is only in some ways a unitary entity. But given the large differences in pharmacology, availability, cultural variation in patterns of use, attitudes, and consequences of use among drugs, in other ways it very clearly is not. Chapter 6 on smoking/nicotine dependence (Myers & McPherson), Chapter 7 on alcohol (Chung & Jackson), Chapter 8 on marijuana (Litt, Kilmer, Tapert, & Lee), Chapter 9 on other illicit drugs (Ramo), and Chapter 10 on prescription drug abuse (Arria & Bugbee) provide the detail. All describe patterns of onset and course for each of these drug classes, the likelihood that dependence will or will not rapidly follow, the substantial individual differences among heavier users of the different drug types, the differences in peer association patterns associated with heavy use, and the differences in subcultures of use. And within the constraint that these substances vary in how long there has been a history of use and scientific scrutiny, similarities and differences in the neuropharmacological action of the drugs is also reviewed.

Section IV: Etiology and Course in the Context of Adolescent Development (Chapters 11–17)

The challenge to understanding the etiologic process at the stage where the science is now is that it requires understanding across multiple levels of analysis, and within level, it requires understanding different, albeit to some degree overlapping, mechanistic structures. This section summarizes this work across a diverse set of scientific disciplines, all of which are actively pursuing the question of what models best predict developmental course and the developmental heterogeneity that is known to be very much a part of it. The core domains we have selected for review involve etiology at genetic, neural, behavioral, cognitive, and social contextual levels of analysis.

The section opens with Chapter 11, Spear's overview of current animal models of adolescent substance abuse. Work here, over more than a decade, has been substantial, and in a number of domains it has existed long before human models of were developed. Adolescent laboratory animals share many of the traits of human adolescents, but the time course for their passage from early childhood to adulthood allows the researcher to examine, and test drug effects, and observe life span consequences within a truncated timeline that allows continued revision and hypothesis testing in a manner that would be impossible with human subjects. Spear's review of this work, much of which is her own, has provided a substantial basis for the affirmation that repeated use by adolescents of some of the most common drugs of abuse, in particular alcohol, nicotine, and the cannabinoids, produces alterations in cognitive and social functioning and emotional processing, which appear to have long-term effects on the neurocircuitry of reward, emotional, social, and cognitive processing (Nigg, 2017). This work has had substantial impact in driving some of the early neuroimaging studies and identifying the most likely targets for substance abuse effects.

In Chapter 12, McGue and Hicks review the evidence for familial aggregation of adolescent substance use as a function of the relative contributions of genetic and environmental influences. They focus on the issue of whether the relative magnitude of their respective effects changes between adolescence and early adulthood. The limited evidence for this variation at the specific gene level is also summarized. Their account indicates a special sensitivity to the fact that all behavior from a developmental standpoint is a moving target, and they observe that the shared environmental influences of adolescence have considerably more of an effect than is true as youth move into early adulthood. Conversely, genetic effects on substance use in adolescence shift qualitatively as well as quantitatively as they transition into early adulthood, becoming stronger but also becoming much more substance specific. The data they review continue to demonstrate the dynamic and unique nature of the adolescent period, as well as the importance of factoring time variation into the etiologic matrix.

Wetherill and Tapert's chapter on neural circuitry and neurocognitive development (Chapter 13) summarizes the changes in composition and structural organization of the brain over the course of later childhood and adolescence. They describe the developmental course of the complex of neural networks that link the different brain regions and allow them to both interact, as well as functionally adapt, over the course of adolescence. They also review the effects of processes operating at other levels of system that have direct impact upon the brain's ability to self-regulate. These are sleep, and sex hormone changes, both of which also have major impact upon the process of regulation/dysregulation and are significantly affected by the physiological and behavioral changes of adolescence that take place during puberty.

In the behavioral arena (Chapters 14 and 15), research summaries are presented for behavioral undercontrol (Windle) and internalizing symptomatology (Hussong and colleagues) the two most common, non-drug-specific behavioral pathways that have strong etiologic linkages to substance use onset and course. Because they are so well known and have such a large amount of research focused upon them, it is feasible to present a multilayered view of their pathways' component structures. Each of these chapters does so, albeit focusing upon different issues. Windle's review (Chapter 14) emphasizes the multiple levels of analysis that are embedded within the undercontrol construct and challenges the reader to disaggregate the etiology into a set of parallel, albeit linked systems, whose interaction needs to be much better understood.

In contrast, the etiologic linkage between internalizing symptomatology and substance use/abuse has been a much more contested one, and the challenge is to explain why some studies have established an unequivocal connection and others have not. This conundrum has led many to posit that the relationship does not exist, in spite of considerable evidence of a robust connection, albeit often later than adolescence (Hussong et al., 2011; Meier et al., 2013; Zucker, 1994). In Chapter 15, Hussong and colleagues address this problem by focusing on the developmental linkages between risk and social experience. They make the point that, in contrast to the more unitary linkage between externalizing behavior and substance use, a cascade of threatening or fear-arousing social interactions is commonly part of the early high-risk etiologic picture. With repeated exposure to such circumstances, the ability to dampen the negative affective response is impaired, and a propensity for more intense experience of the stress develops. Over time this results in a greater sensitivity to experience negative emotionality without the ability to dampen it or move on into other affective states when the arousal experience subsides. Although there are undoubtedly some individuals who have a genetic vulnerability for this sensitivity, a considerable proportion of those with the symptomatology in youth and thereafter develop it by way of risk aggregation.

Donovan's chapter on Socialization (Chapter 16) reviews the voluminous literature on the role of the proximal (family, peers) and distal (media) social environments in prompting, shaping, and directing the emergence of substance use and abuse. At least superficially these essential etiologic elements appear to operate solely at the behavioral level. The literature clearly indicates some nesting effects are operating, in the sense that parental use is linked to poor parenting, which in turn is linked to low parental monitoring, leading to greater freedom from parental supervision, more opportunity to make contact with peers from similar social backgrounds, a greater opportunity to obtain access to drugs, and a greater opportunity to utilize drugs without the interference of parental discipline. In other words, heavier use is embedded in a social network that progressively leads into use, with a low probability of curbing. The association between self-use and sibling use is simply another facet in this network. However, the organizing analytic model that Donovan presents shows that what at first glance is a behavioral process is in fact a network of social influence processes involving bonding (between parent and child as well as within the social network of peers) and social control, which shapes the internal process of identification that leads to modeling and solidification of use. Social media effects appear to be largely independent of the proximal influencing structure, but the fact that they are social influences suggests there is a similar underlying mechanistic structure responsible for their effect.

The utilization of substances of abuse involves both cognitive processing and action (i.e., behavior). In a carefully thought out and mechanistically detailed account of the scientific work underlying the theory of action, Peterson and Smith (Chapter 17) summarize the role of these cognitions—known as expectancies—in developing, sustaining, and/or changing the course of substance use. Although expectancies are not frequently discussed as motivational concepts, they share a similar structure (Reich & Goldman, 2015). It involves awareness of the object and awareness of the object's functional significance; the latter invariably has an emotional valence attached to it. Expectancies conceptualize the action sequence linking the cognition with an action component involving a propensity toward or away from the object. The linkage of object to action is a function of the kinds of rewards (or punishments) anticipated when the action is fulfilled. Thus, expectancies serve as implicit guiders and directors of pathways to or away from action, and they are an essential component of adaptive behavior.

Expectancy research has a long history of linkage with basic research on the theory of behavior, which in turn provides the means to deconstruct action sequences into component pieces whose operations are closer to the mechanistic structure underlying the action. Expectancy constructs such as reward, avoidance, memory, appetitive valence and strength, and attentional focus are all significantly closer to neurobehavioral operations than are concepts such as knowing, wishing, and craving. This provides a more straightforward linkage between behavioral

function and neural substrate than is the case with more molar behavioral concepts. Furthermore, at the behavioral level of analysis, evidence indicates that expectancies mediate the relationship between knowledge/familiarity with drugs and awareness and action (Goldman et al., 2006; Reich et al., 2010; Wiers & Stacy, 2006). They have the advantage, therefore, as behavioral targets, of being more discrete elements to manipulate in the development of new prevention and treatment programming. Although this is only a hypothesis at this point, it offers a set of concrete next-step operations that can be tested.

Section V: Developmental Tasks and Substance Abuse (Chapters 18–23)

The five chapters in this section focus on some of the core processes and experiences of adolescence, within an organizational framework that acknowledges the multiple levels of input that shape course, and takes account of the potential for different rates of change in different experiential domains. The domains we have selected for review are those most often associated with the adolescent experience, albeit at different levels of analysis. These include Peer Relationships, Sexual Relationships, Driving, and the changing capacity for Self-Regulation. The last two chapters in this section address the relationship between Self and Environment albeit in significantly different ways; one is the course of Identity Development. The other addresses the issue of Resilience, the challenging question of what the processes are that lead one who is subject to a high-risk heritage to develop in a way that escapes that heritage.

Peer Relationships

The arguably most common exhortation that youth become involved in drugs because of their involvement with substance-using peers is also a simplistic one. In a well-documented and carefully reasoned chapter on the development of peer influences across adolescence and the linkage of this process with the use of substances of abuse, in Chapter 18, Rulison, Patrick, and Maggs make the point that the peer influence construct is in fact a set of multiple operations. These operations take place both interpersonally *and* intrapersonally, and it is through these multiple processes that "social" influence creates its effect on use. Modeling, that is, imitating the behavior of another, is one such example. Normative regulation, the individual's creation of perceived social norms, is another. In addition, at the interpersonal level, peers structure the opportunities in which substance use can occur, and they also stimulate social motives to engage in a shared activity. Selection processes also shape network dynamics and lead youth to move in cohorts that differ in patterns of use. All of these processes are operating, albeit some are more common at one developmental way point than at another.

Sexual Relations

The relationship between romance and substance use, and in particular with alcohol, has a long history. Given that the onset of both sexual activity and substance use normatively takes place in adolescence, the romantic connection, or some variant thereof, is clearly of developmentally long standing, However, this association is a far from innocent one; it takes place at a developmental interval where both of the activities are regarded as illicit, hence requiring a certain amount of secrecy and/or privacy in order for them to occur. Although much work remains to be done, a good deal of evidence supports the view that the relationship between substance use and sexual involvement is bidirectional. Use tends to precede sexual initiation, with heavier users being more likely to initiate sex earlier. They also are more likely to engage in risky sex (more frequent, more often casual, more often without condom use), and rates of unplanned pregnancy are higher. From the other direction, the use of substances, in particular alcohol, is more likely to continue and even increase among those actively dating, while substance use drops off among those in committed relationships or those not seeking any relationship at all. Studies have suggested there are expectancy effects here, in part driven by media messages, that lead youth to believe that substance use is more likely to be arousing, and also simply that use is more likely to lead to sexual involvement, both of which tend to drive consumption. At the same time, as Norman and colleagues point out in Chapter 19, despite these myriad associations, the field still lacks an overarching model that would account for the diversity of findings documented by a large number of relatively narrowly focused studies. The chapter effectively summarizes this large array of work, and the authors begin to work toward an integrative framework that can be useful both as an organizing framework for the diversity and also can be useful in the development of preventive intervention strategies to alleviate the problems.

Driving

Although driving and substance use are not what one would typically call developmental tasks of adolescence, the fact is that they are viewed as indicators of transitioning into adulthood. Moreover, the significant parallelism between risky driving and the problem use of alcohol and/or other drugs is more than a passing one. Both are emergent phenomena that reflect the risky part of the developmental transition away from the home and into a network of relationships and activities that are developmentally associated with the broader challenge of creating an adult identity. To engage in either is to affirm one's changed status. These connections are articulated and reviewed in Chapter 20 by McCarty and McCarthy.

The authors' data very clearly indicate that the differences in patterning of substance use are reflective of historical trends (e.g., recent greater prevalence of marijuana-impaired driving than alcohol-impaired driving) and also cultural variations (e.g., differences in joint occurrence of these behaviors as a function of gender, ethnic group membership, etc.). Their review also provides information on the socialization forces that the family exerts on this learning—forces that influence both substance use and driving misbehavior. Their review additionally outlines the individual differences that exist in the adolescent-to-adult transition for ethnic and gender subgroups. This transition is not the same experience for all adolescents, a fact that is a sine qua non of the developmental challenge involved in moving toward adulthood; it is also a fact that is rarely considered applicable for these two very practical skill sets.

In the latter part of their chapter the authors also review the types and effectiveness of safeguards that society has put into place to shape the behavior taking place during this risky developmental stage. For substance abuse, this involves setting a minimum legal drinking age, as well as enforcing laws about the utilization of illicit drugs. For driving, a graded set of experiences is required, which hopefully will create a successful and accident-free transition to fully licensed driver status. In a way, the content of this chapter is more clearly illustrative than any of the other chapters in this volume about the tension that exists between activity focused solely on scientific understanding of the mechanistic basis for behavior, and activity seeking to provide a developmentally relevant guide to society in the practical negotiation of a critical and sometimes perilous developmental life stage.

Self-Regulation and Decision Making

In Chapter 21, Anderson and Briggs present a highly detailed and step-by-step account of the development of the multiple cognitive control systems responsible for both self-regulation and decision making over the course of adolescence. The challenge for youth, in terms of making rational decisions that will not lead them into trouble, is that they are moving through a period of time when social relationships increase in involvement, which in turn frequently provides a strong push toward the use of alcohol and other drugs. Decision making on the basis of feelings (i.e., hot decision making) is also more likely to take place. Other factors in adolescence (e.g., lack of sleep, increasing awareness of positive expectancies about alcohol and other drug use, increasing autonomy) tend to make self-regulation a more difficult task, and they also make it more likely that choices will be driven by short-term reward motivations without consideration of the longer term consequences of the actions. Their careful detailing of the multiple processes involved in developing self-regulatory capacity also provides the background for some suggestions for more cognitively focused intervention strategies that might be effective in reducing risk for poor substance use decision making during this period.

Identity Development

In Chapter 22, Wills, Sussman, and McGurk focus on the internal experience of self that changes and emerges during the critical period of adolescence. The authors make the important distinction between self-concept and identity, the former being a cognitive schema of the different attributes of self (e.g., intelligence, social competence, physical appearance), the latter being a superordinate construct integrating a number of more differentiated facets, including cultural values, peer group identification, ethnic and religious identity, and gender identity, as well as self-concept. They note the importance of understanding that identity content changes as development proceeds, and also that the salience of substance use and the direction of influence are not the same across all facets. The most direct influences are those involving religious and ethnic identity, which typically have specific strictures about use and level of use, and thus play a causal role even to the extent of influencing whether onset is appropriate, and if it is, how early in adolescence use is considered to be appropriate Peer group identification also plays a powerful role at a mechanistically quite different level, involving proximal social influence processes, size, and quality of peer networks that drive the youth into or away from involvement with some peers and not others. These influences sometimes operate protectively, by way of the norms and activities fostered by the group, and sometimes create greater risk, as a function of their different norms and activities.

One issue that is far from settled is the extent to which substance use itself has an impact on identity; or, conversely, is the direction of impact primarily the other way? One line of research indicates that level of self-esteem (low) may drive one into heavier use. Other research indicates the obverse, that substance use itself can become an identify facet, in which case it may be harder to change. It is likely that both of these mechanisms operate, but the circumstances where each of these processes might operate remains to be articulated (Hicks et al., 2014; Schulenberg & Maggs, 2002).

Resilience

Although less often a focus among researchers interested in the development of the pathology of abuse, the individual, social, and community processes that lead to the dilution of risk and those that independently foster a successful social adaptation are also essential components of the etiologic matrix. To the extent these positive features are present, they create a challenge to the view that risk, if in place long enough, is tantamount to damaged outcome. Moreover, the considerably heavier emphasis in the resilience literature on development as a transactional process that takes place between individual, proximal social environment, and community is a reminder that the developmental field in which the organism is unfolding is an essential component of the etiologic process, and that resilience processes are as important to document and understand as are risk factors. In Chapter 23, Hurd and Zimmerman address these issues, and the chapter is included here explicitly because this is an essential—albeit typically ignored—component of etiology. In a very comprehensive and broad-ranging review, Hurd and Zimmerman describe existing findings at each of the three levels of operation. In contrast to some of the other areas reviewed in this Handbook, the work in this area is heavily theory based, and investigators are conscious of what domains of influence they have not examined along with describing the effects in those they have. At the individual level, work has focused on enhancement of positive behaviors that are individual strength enhancing/asset building at the same time as they operate to negate whatever negative forces the youth is subject to. These include building positive mood, enhancing academic achievement goals, enhancing competence skills, and strengthening racial identity, to name just a few. At the proximal social level, most of the work has been done on functioning within the family, at a significant number of content foci involving enhancement of family attachment, parental involvement, social supports, and effective family functioning. At the community level, recent work has focused on the development of positive role models in the community and the fostering of adult/neighbor mentoring of youth with whom they have some contact. The development of increased community resources for youth and their families is another modality that has also received attention.

Section VI: Comorbidity in Adolescent Substance Abuse: Chapters 24–27

All of the chapters in this section address a common theme, namely, that there is a high rate of comorbidity between drug and alcohol abuse/dependence and other mental disorders, and that adolescence is the time of greatest co-occurrence. In Chapter 24, Wilson and Janoff provide an overview of most of the multiple behavioral/psychiatric comorbidities associated with alcohol and drug use. Antisocial/delinquent "comorbidity," the topic of Chapter 25, by White, Cronley, and Iyer, focuses on the most highly concurrent relationship between substance abuse and other behavior, and one that is also the source of the greatest damage to self and to others. The visibility, impact, and long-term individual and social cost of this comorbidity warrant a chapter of their own. Chapter 26, by Schizer, Weitzman, and Levy, provides an overview of the common linkages between substance use and the medical/physical health issues of adolescence, as they show up in primary care. The chapter also describes the special role and opportunity for the primary care provider to make contact with and help substance-abusing youth who would not otherwise receive the benefits of contact with a knowledgeable and caring health professional. A separate chapter has been devoted to sleep impairment (Chapter 27) and its linkages to substance use. Sleep impairment is the one health issue for which the entire population is potentially at risk. It also has high prevalence

and can become manifest very early in development and at any point thereafter. When it does, its effects are visible (and sometimes intrusive) to the family, and the impairment itself has major ramifications in many areas of youth behavior. It is especially an issue among youth at risk for substance use (Wong et al., 2004, 2009). The obverse is also true: Persons with sleep difficulties are also more likely to have alcohol and other drug problems (Brower et al., 2001). Chapter 26, by Cohen-Zion and Svirsky, is specifically devoted to a review of these linkages. Each of the chapters also addresses the issue of treatment/intervention, given that those with these comorbidities are typically more difficult to engage at the same time that they are more likely to need treatment.

Comorbidity in Adolescent Substance Abuse and Disorder

In their well-documented chapter (Chapter 24), Wilson and Janoff provide a comprehensive clinical review of the many comorbid disorders associated with substance abuse/disorder in adolescence. In parallel with the etiologic literature, they note that the two major clusters of co-occurrence involve externalizing symptomatology (e.g., conduct disorder, oppositional defiant disorder, and attention-deficit disorders) and internalizing symptomatology (e.g., major depressive disorder, posttraumatic stress disorder, and anxiety disorder). They also make the point that comorbidity is more common among those with substance use and disorder in adolescence than it is with those in adulthood, indicating the special vulnerability of adolescence to negative outcomes. This is a risk that parents tend largely to be unaware of. And as is true in etiologic studies, the pathway of effect is most commonly from the comorbidity to the substance use and disorder. But particularly for those with a clinical level of symptomatology, the direction of effect is not always that way. For example, an extensive literature has documented how marijuana use is precursive to psychosis as well as subsyndromal symptomatology.

Wilson and Janoff also articulate many of the treatment challenges of adolescents with co-occurring disorders, of which the first is simply recognizing that such a situation exists. They advocate always for the construction of an integrated treatment plan that addresses both disorders, and they review a rich literature on the complexities of formulating such a plan. Their constant use of clinical examples will make their account valuable to the practicing clinician, while at the same time they outline for researchers the many treatment-regimen-related questions still requiring answers.

Risks for Delinquent Behavior

The Child Behavior Checklist and its adolescent Youth Self-Report Form (Achenbach, 1991) are two of the most commonly used child and adolescent behavioral assessment instruments. One of the major components of psychopathology that they measure is the broadband Externalizing Behavior domain. The externalizing construct, also sometimes referred to as behavioral undercontrol (Zucker, Heitzeg, & Nigg, 2011), involves disinhibitory, impulsive, and sensation-seeking behavior, as well as rule breaking. Some elements of extraversive behavioral style are also present. The construct is highly predictive of both substance use onset and substance abuse, and it is recognized as one of the strongest precursive risk factors in the development of both of these behaviors (Zucker et al., 2011). Its relationship with substance use/abuse is extensively reviewed by Windle in Chapter 14. From a psychometric standpoint, the externalizing broadband scale is a dimensional measure that incorporates two narrow band subscales, delinquent behavior and aggressive behavior. Delinquent behavior is related to, but by no means identical with, the delinquency subscale component of the externalizing/behavioral undercontrol construct. It is differentiated in several ways: (a) The delinquency subscale/component is both a personality/temperament dimension and a dimension of clinical symptomatology. (b) In contrast, delinquent behavior is an action that is a social behavior, that always involves rule breaking, also always has some negative consequence(s) associated with it. Intentions are not part of the domain. (c) Furthermore, delinquent behavior does or does not take place. It is not scalar; therefore, a high score simply indicates a high likelihood that such behavior will occur, but a low score is not the obverse. It is simply a low propensity for delinquent activity. In short, the arena of activity covered here is a separate and differentiated, albeit related construct to the behavioral undercontrol domain. The coassociation of alcohol and other drug use with delinquent behavior in adolescence is a large one. Moreover, although the prevalence of delinquent activity at this developmental period does not equal that of substance use, it is still a significant problem in its own right. Utilizing the community sample of the Pittsburgh Youth Study (Loeber et al., 2008), and weighting sample characteristics to approximate those in the community

at large, estimates are that 54% of boys between 12 and 18 had committed minor theft (stealing less than $5, or shoplifting), half had been involved in larceny or dealing in stolen property, and 18% had committed serious theft (burglary or motor vehicle theft). The urban nature of the Pittsburgh sample as well as some other demographic restrictions would suggest these figures are probably a bit higher than in the overall US population; but they nonetheless indicate that in the adolescent era, delinquent activity—like substance abuse—is a far from rare occurrence. Thus, the question of what the causal relationship is between these two behaviors is an important one for the community at large, especially if the evidence suggests there is a synergy between these two domains. In their in-depth review (Chapter 25), White and colleagues consider this issue in detail. They note the substantial acute and longer term developmental associations between the two behaviors, and they examine the issue of whether this relationship is causal (and, if so, in which direction) or simply correlational. They also probe the issue of whether these relationships are the same across all levels, or whether they might be different at higher levels of use and delinquent activity. They also summarize the work examining whether the coassociations are the same across all drugs of abuse or not (e.g., between alcohol and marijuana, etc.). In many instances they are, but in some specific areas, involving the use of marijuana versus alcohol, they are not. The authors close their review with some observations about the multiple influences that enhance risk for delinquency and for substance abuse, both individually and jointly, and also make some suggestions about the matrix of domains that needs to be addressed in order to have impact on this highly problematic set of behaviors.

Medical Issues and Role of the Primary Care Physician

Substance use in adolescence is not always detected by parents. The primary health care system is another pass-through point for large numbers of adolescents, where the opportunity also exists to notice and respond to the problems that alcohol and other drug use provides. This is especially so for young adolescents, who may have gone far out of their way to keep their use, and the contexts in which it is occurring, out of the purview of their family. In Chapter 26, Schizer, Weitzman, and Levy provide an exceptionally detailed and erudite as well as practical guide to contact with adolescents where substance use problems are (or should be) a significant part of the encounter. Because so many youths encounter health care providers as part of their life experience, the primary care physician has the potential to prevent, delay, early detect, reduce harm, refer, and diagnose important, nonpsychiatric comorbid conditions that would be especially vulnerable to the effects of alcohol and other drugs. They also have the potential to help parents in negotiating the delicate conversation that may need to take place with their child about the child's use. Their special role, as neutral confidante, also has the potential to open up a dialogue with their adolescent patients about the level of risk they may be incurring by using or by hanging out with friends who are significant users. And last, they are the gentle entry point for referral for more expert assessment and/or treatment when it becomes clear that the level of use is of sufficient magnitude to be of diagnostic significance. In addition to discussing the different conditions of such an encounter, the chapter extensively reviews the guidelines for next-step action. These include protocols for screening, advice giving, brief intervention, and follow-up. As such, it is likely to be useful to primary care physicians, pediatricians, and other caregivers who have a professional/helping relationship with adolescents.

Sleep

Sleep is an essential component in the maintenance of health, and its disruption creates health and behavioral difficulties in a variety of domains. It shows up as a significant component in the development of attentional problems and impulsivity, as well as the development of substance use and substance use problems in adolescence (Wong et al., 2004, 2009). In each of these areas it contributes independent variance to the problem behavior. Within the specific context of the present volume, Cohen-Zion and Svirsky (Chapter 27) review the recent work addressing the ways that sleep operates in the development of substance use, as well as the ways that substance abuse contributes to the development of the sleep difficulties.

As the authors document in a number of different studies, one of the significant dilemmas relating to these effects is that they occur during a time where the social structural demands of early school start time and late night peer group activity have an impact on an organism that is going through developmental changes in the sleep cycle that call for increased rather than decreased sleep time. The environmental demands make it more difficult to satisfy the biologically driven need for more sleep, even though increased sleep would operate as a reparative process facilitating the maturation of the sleep regulatory system (Crowley, Acebo, & Carskadon, 2007; Taylor, Jenni, Acebo, & Carskadon, 2005). The unfortunate consequence of this is increased difficulty in mood regulation and greater proneness to risk-taking behavior, including a greater likelihood of involvement with alcohol, marijuana, and other drugs of abuse. The risk proneness and mood regulation difficulty, in turn, would be anticipated to facilitate the movement into substance problems instead of facilitating a judgement call of desistance, or at least careful and moderated use.

The evidence for these effects is substantial, and it utilizes both objective physiological measures of sleep as well as self-report. The authors also document how these invasive processes appear to heighten use of both alcohol and marijuana, although the long-term negative consequences are different, and even the negative consequences following cessation vary. Chapter 27 closes with a brief review of the effectiveness of the currently quite small number of intervention/prevention programs, and it calls for considerably more work to address this significant and highly visible set of developmental/social issues.

Section VII: Assessment and Intervention (Chapters 28–34)

The seven chapters in this section review the literature on assessment and intervention methods at multiple levels of system, ranging from the individual to the cultural/sociopolitical. They also illustrate that intervention at different developmental waypoints in the evolution of substance abuse requires attention at different levels of system, with attention focused more on macro-level systems of operation earlier in the development of patterns of use/abuse, and with focus more on individual behavior as problems become more entrenched and damaging to self and others in later phases.

Winters and colleagues' chapter on assessing adolescent alcohol and other drug abuse (Chapter 28) is a comprehensive and thoughtful review of some of the most important issues needing consideration when a clinical assessment measure is being selected. These go well beyond the obvious concern with psychometric characteristics; they include the need to evaluate the measure's capacity to cover short-term as compared to longer term patterns of intake and problems, the justification for and validity of self-report as compared to other measures of use (e.g., biological samples, observer reports, information from collaterals, etc.), the difference between assessment of treatment outcome parameters and more summative indicators of use and problems, and so on. In the process, commentary is offered about the usefulness of different measures and about the content parameters likely to be most important for different clinical assessment needs. Within these multiple evaluation contexts, 21 different assessment measures are reviewed. The chapter is likely to be highly useful as a first step for any investigator with a need to assess substance use and misuse in adolescence, and it should be equally helpful for clinicians seeking to develop a new screening or clinical evaluation battery.

D'Amico and Feldstein-Ewing, in their chapter on prevention and intervention (Chapter 29), embrace a broad framework within which to review and understand the early problem use of substances of abuse in adolescence, and they relate that to the design of differentiated intervention programming. Their review very much embraces the framework within which this Handbook was conceived; they take special pains to differentiate the settings in which prevention and early intervention activity take place, they emphasize the essential point that all programming needs to take account of the particular neurodevelopmental stage within which it is targeted, be aware of the embeddedness of substance-using behavior in its particular cultural and community context, and understand the constraints and freedoms that will be present for both youth and the community that will affect the likelihood of success for the intervention program being offered. They illustrate the special tailoring that the best programs have designed to take these factors into account, take note of the success such tailoring produces in terms of intervention outcomes, and more generally advocate for this as a standard for the field. Their take-away message is that all youthful substance use needs to be understood as an activity that is part of a developmental process that is an embedded manifestation of individual culture, lifestyle, and community reinforcers and constraints. Intervention—whether it be preventive in focus, early screening, or treatment after problem use has begun—needs to take account of this. This would produce a significant increase in the availability of focused programs, utilizing individualized methods that recognize the variety of forms that adolescent substance abuse can take. The empirical studies support this perspective, and in fact, the most successful ones form the backdrop for the propositions the authors articulate.

Targeted Prevention Approaches

It would be unheard of for a patient to visit a physician's office showing a well-demarcated symptom pattern and then be offered a nonspecific cure-all treatment. Yet that is the situation for the vast majority of school- and community-based intervention programs, and for the pronouncements that pediatric primary care providers offer their adolescent and young adult patients. At the same time, in Chapter 30, Wagner and Lewis show in considerable detail that a significant evidence base now exists for the effectiveness of two different kinds of targeted programs that are the antithesis of "one size fits all." They have different target populations and use different methodologies because of their goals, and they form the basis for an empirically validated strategy to impact substance use during the developmental interval when it is emerging, and where it is presenting the largest public health challenge of any segment of the life cycle.

Their review focuses on two different kinds of targeted prevention: one is message tailoring in health campaigns. This programming works to influence trends in health improvement information by identifying specific, high-risk target populations, thus creating the potential for greater information impact. The challenge is developing the methodology to create increasingly more well-defined audience segmentation, which in turn allows for the creation of messaging that resonates by way of its very specific appeal. The other body of work is developing specialized intervention programming to impact selected higher risk individuals. Such differentiated selectivity allows for fine-tuning based on traits/characteristics known to be present in the high-risk subgroup. This model has the potential to be more clinically effective at the same time that it becomes more cost effective. As the authors note, the next step work in both of these areas is to continue the fine-tuning and develop better understanding of the mechanistic substructure of the work.

Family-Based Treatments

As our earlier commentary has already made clear, despite the temptation to view the consumption of substances with abuse potential as individual acts, the reality is that they are very much behaviors embedded within a set of multiple overlapping systems. Intervention programming that has impact upon these structures is therefore more likely to be effective both in the near term and over time. Boustani, Henderson, and Liddle, in Chapter 31 on family-based treatment, provide an exhaustive summary of this increasingly burgeoning field, describing 36 randomized trials and providing an extraordinarily detailed account of what works and what doesn't, as well as a commentary on the putative underlying mechanisms producing the effects. It thus provides a detailed reference and guide to the evidence-based family treatment literature. It will serve as a major summarization resource of this field for some time to come. It will also serve as a go-to guide for clinicians who want to ascertain the usefulness of particular components of their own work, and a first-step resource for researchers interested in designing next-step studies of the mechanistic structures underlying treatment effectiveness.

Adolescent Cultural Contexts for Substance Abuse

One of the major influences of culture upon daily life is the manner in which it influences day-to-day patterns of living. Some of these patterns simply reflect lifestyle variation, but some are the direct outcome of differences in access to the opportunity structure of the larger culture, which, as an end result, create disparities in education, in wealth, and even in health status. Chapter 32 on cultural contexts by Schwartz, Des Rosiers, Unger, and Szapocznik focuses specially on the issue of health disparities, and although substance abuse is one set of behaviors where such disparity is evident, they focus their discourse at a more general level—on how to understand the health disparities that exist across cultures. Thereafter, they move to the specific level of how to create intervention programming that will effectively address these disparities.

Drawing upon research on Hispanics for concrete examples, their exposition notes that population-level data on health status across cultural groups have repeatedly documented the existence of disparities in health prevalence that are not explainable by individual- and even neighborhood-level variation. One must turn to population-level processes, in particular those relating to differences in social dominance between cultures, along with system-level justifications, for the disparity, as the active elements leading to unequal allocation of social resources. They therefore advocate for interventions to combat the social/cultural differences that operate at all these levels. Without the addition of population-level, probably policy-level activity,

effects produced at the lower levels will at best be modest and, at worst, will simply wash out over time. Although it remains unsaid, the authors' exposition is clear: Culture operates not only to produce health disparity, but by way of internalized norms and values, it also operates to sustain disparity within the group or groups that are free from the social burden.

Twelve-Step Approaches

Twelve-step approaches, both professionally led and peer led, are an important and effective part of the adult treatment armamentarium. The more than 80-year existence of Alcoholic Anonymous as a peer organization, to say nothing of related programs (e.g., Narcotics Anonymous) that have proliferated over these years, attests to the effectiveness of this method. It is, therefore, a logical extension to consider that the method would also be effective in helping younger patients conquer their addiction. In Chapter 33, Kelly, Worley, and Yeterian, in their extensive review of 12-step approaches for adolescents, detail the ways that such programs have an effect but also describe the many issues that make the method more difficult to implement with this age group. For one, the depth of the addiction tends to be less severe among adolescents, so they may be more likely to see some of the 12-step life-change-focused principles as less relevant. For another, to the extent that connections are made to ongoing groups, youth may discover that the issues members discuss do not fit with their own struggles with addiction because members are older, and the particular actions needed to maintain sobriety are often different. Another impediment is that 12-step groups vary in their level of "youth friendliness." For these and other reasons, adolescents tend not to continue as long in their 12-step involvement. Relatedly, given the greater substance use of youth in later adolescence and early adulthood, involvement with more sobriety-focused peers is a more difficult locational task so that the adolescent's social experiences can be more conflictual than is the case for adult 12-step users.

Despite these impediments, the weight of empirical evidence indicates that more 12-step involvement is consistently related to better long-term outcomes. The challenge for the field is therefore to articulate those practices that will facilitate that outcome, and that at the same time are user-friendly to the rest of the adolescent's life. The authors describe more recent practices that satisfy these criteria and that appear to be clinically effective, but research is needed to validate their utility. Given the importance of early intervention in arresting long-term trajectories of abuse, this is clearly a high-priority item for the adolescent clinical research agenda.

INPATIENT AND OUTPATIENT MODELS

Historically, the only interventions existing to treat substance use disorder in adolescence were offshoots of adult treatment programming, were primarily based in adult treatment settings, and were largely inpatient in structure. Attention to less severe forms of problem use was relegated to counselors, often based within the educational system. The formal education system was also utilized as a setting in which opinions about use could ostensibly be changed. The focus was on nonuse as the only appropriate stance, with a heavy emphasis on awareness of prevention of damage to self and others. Formal intervention was relegated to those youth who made contact with the juvenile justice system, or as noted earlier, had symptomatology sufficiently severe that they needed a secure structure in order to be able to address their difficulties in a sustained way.

As the earlier chapters in this section indicate, in more recent years a number of effective earlier stage interventions have emerged, with the focus on prevention, early identification of problem behavior, and rapid attention to problem use as it emerges. At the same time, the more formal substance abuse treatment community has developed differentiated programming, both outpatient and inpatient, for adolescents with the more severe problems that the first line interventions did not remediate. In some instances, these formal programs are also the first therapeutic encounters for youth who have systematically denied any need for the help these earlier intervention programs might offer. In other, more economically compromised communities where preventive health-focused programs provided by the educational system or the community are lacking, formal outpatient or inpatient substance abuse treatment may also be the point of first therapeutic contact. In Chapter 34, Knight and colleagues set the context for these interventions by reviewing the developmental variations that exist in the way substance use disorder displays itself. They are also very explicit in noting that—in contrast to earlier practices where youth treatment took place in primarily adult treatment programs—age specialization of care during this period is essential because of the differences in developmental needs of younger as compared to older adolescents, and they discuss the variations in inpatient and outpatient intervention that are called for by this. The remainder of the chapter provides (a) a review of the evidence-based outcome literature for both outpatient and inpatient programming (the literature indicates clear, albeit small to moderate effect sizes, across both modalities) and (b) a discussion of what the essential components should be for a good adolescent treatment program. On both these counts, the chapter serves an eminently practical function, by providing guidance for professionals who are reviewing the effectiveness of their own programs, and by providing aid for lay persons, whether family or other professionals, about what they need to look for when searching out an appropriate referral for a family member or a patient of theirs.

Section VIII: Social Policy
Public Health Policy and Prevention

Holder and Green's chapter on public policy and prevention (Chapter 35) presents an exhaustive review of the multilevel structure of policy and prevention efforts, and the research studies evaluating these efforts. They note a reality that is often ignored by behavioral and neuroscientists, namely, that legal and public health policy is a major, demonstrably effective strategy for the reduction of youth substance use and problems, even though its formulations are not at the individual level. Their review is organized by type of drug (alcohol, tobacco, other drugs) because public policy and preventive programming operate at that drug-specific level. It also pays special attention to the specific qualities of adolescence and how they may be differentially affected by policy. To give but one example, it is essential for effectiveness with adolescents that tobacco control efforts be interdependent and synergistic across modalities. Thus, the mass media need to provide a backdrop of content that is consistent with prevention/nonuse messages received in school education programs and/or from parents. The policy-level programming does not work well when glamorous depictions of smokers or heavy drinkers—in the movies—are inconsistent with the messages the teenager receives at school or at home. These inconsistencies across modalities are much more likely to be noticed by youth and exploited as an example that "there are really no right or wrong policies here; it's just your opinion." More generally, the evidence is clear, across drugs of abuse, that policy actions need to be multifaceted to have significant impact, operating at the levels of government regulation of availability (and imposition of penalties when that is transgressed), to media messaging, to education and monitoring/regulation at the community and family levels.

The highly focused nature of Holder and Green's review does not easily provide a place to address the basic question of where policy-level activity fits into a multilevel mechanistic model of substance use. At this juncture, however, as we conclude this summary of the multiple facets involved in the etiology, development, and control of adolescent substance use and abuse, it is appropriate to ask that question. The obvious answer is that policy-level interventions change the social control structure; they are a distal set of social context characteristics that have the capability to elicit penalties if policy is transgressed.

They operate at another level as well. Although they are distal from the individual, they operate at the individual level by way of their modification of the availability of environmental cues. Given the importance of cueing presence to substance use, they affect cognitions about use. When policy changes availability, such cognitions will not be triggered. In that sense also, they have an indirect effect upon drug use expectancies. Without the visible social presence of a drug, expectancies about use are less likely to be formed (Zucker et al., 1995).

References

Achenbach, T. M. (1991). *Manual for the Child Behavior Checklist/4–18 and 1991 Profile*. Burlington, VT: University of Vermont Department of Psychiatry.

Brower, K. J., Aldrich, M. S., Robinson, E. A., Zucker, R. A., & Greden, J. F. (2001). Insomnia, self-medication, and relapse to alcoholism. *American Journal of Psychiatry, 158*, 399–404. doi:10.1176/appi.ajp.158.3.399. PMID: 11229980.

Center for Behavioral Health Statistics and Quality. (2016). *2015 National Survey on Drug Use and Health: Detailed Tables*. Rockville, MD: Substance Abuse and Mental Health Services Administration. https://www.samhsa.gov/data/sites/default/files/NSDUH-DetTabs-2015/NSDUH-DetTabs-2015/NSDUH-DetTabs-2015.pdf

Crowley, S. J., Acebo, C., & Carskadon, M. A. (2007). Sleep, circadian rhythms, and delayed phase in adolescence. [Review]. *Sleep Medicine, 8*(6), 602–612.

Fosco, G. M., Stormshak, E. A., Dishion, T. J., & Winter, C. (2012). Family relationships and parental monitoring during middle school as predictors of early adolescent problem behavior. *Journal of Clinical Child and Adolescent Psychology, 41*(2), 202–213. http://doi.org/10.1080/15374416.2012.651989

Goldman, M. S., Reich, R. R., & Darkes, J. (2006). Expectancy as a unifying construct in alcohol related cognition. In A. Stacy & R. Weirs (Eds.), *Implicit cognition and addiction* (pp. 105–121). New York, NY: Sage.

Hicks, B. M., Iacono, W. G., & McGue, M. (2014). Identifying childhood characteristics that underlie premorbid risk for substance use disorders: Socialization and boldness. *Development and Psychopathology, 26*(1), 141–157.

Hicks, B. M., Johnson, W., Durbin, C. E., Blonigen, D. M., Iacono, W. G., & McGue, M. (2014). Delineating selection and mediation effects among childhood personality and environmental risk factors in the development of adolescent substance abuse. *Journal of Abnormal Child Psychology, 42*(5), 845–859.

Hussong, A. M., Jones, D. J., Stein, G. L., Baucom, D. H., & Boeding, S. (2011). An internalizing pathway to alcohol use and disorder. *Psychology of Addictive Behaviors, 25*, 390–404. doi:10.1037/a0024519

Leukefeld, C. G., Gullotta, T. P., & Staton-Tindall, M. (Eds.). (2009). *Adolescent substance abuse: Evidence-based approaches to prevention and treatment*. New York, NY: Springer.

Li, K. T. (2004, June 10). Alcohol abuse increases, dependence declines across decade. Young adult minorities emerge as high-risk subgroups. *NIH News*.

Liddle, H. A., & Rowe, C. L. (Eds.) (2006). *Adolescent substance abuse: Research and clinical advances*. New York, NY: Cambridge University Press.

Loeber, R., Farrington, D. P., Stouthamer-Loeber, M., & White, H. R. (2008). *Violence and serious theft: Developmental course and origins from childhood to adulthood*. New York, NY: Routledge Press.

Masten, A. S., Faden, V. B., Zucker, R. A., & Spear, L. P. (2008). Underage drinking: A developmental framework. *Pediatrics, 121* (Supplement 4), S235–S251. doi:10.1542/peds.2007–2243A

Meier, M. H., Caspi, A., Houts, R., Slutske, W. S., Harrington, H. L., Jackson, K. M., . . . Moffitt, T. E. (2013). Prospective developmental subtypes of alcohol dependence from age 18 to 32 years: Implications for nosology, etiology, and intervention. *Development and Psychopathology, 25*(3), 785–800. doi:10.1017/S0954579413000175

Mennella, J. A., & Beauchamp, G. K. (1998). The infant's response to scented toys: Effects of exposure. *Chemical Senses, 23*, 11–17.

Moss, H. B., Chen, C. M., & Yi, H-Y. (2014). Early adolescent patterns of alcohol, cigarettes, and marijuana polysubstance use and young adult substance use outcomes in a nationally representative sample. *Drug and Alcohol Dependence, 136*, 51–62.

Nigg, J. T. (2017, in press). Self-regulation, behavioral inhibition, and risk for alcoholism and substance use disorders. In H. E. Fitzgerald & L. I. Puttler (eds.), *Alcohol use disorders: A developmental science approach to etiology, conception to adolescence*. New York, NY: Oxford University Press.

Pagliaro, L. A., & Pagliaro, A. M. (2012) *Handbook of child and adolescent drug and substance abuse: Pharmacological, developmental, and clinical considerations*. New York, NY: John Wiley.

Reich, R. R., Below, M. C., & Goldman, M. S. (2010). Explicit and implicit measures of expectancy and related alcohol cognitions: A meta-analytic comparison. *Psychology of Addictive Behaviors, 24*(1), 13–25. doi:10.1037/a0016556

Reich, R. R., & Goldman, M. S. (2015). Decision making about alcohol use: The case for scientific convergence. *Addictive behaviors, 44*, 23–28.

Rosner, R. (Ed.) (2013). *Clinical handbook of adolescent addiction*. Chichester, UK: Wiley-Blackwell.

Scheier, L. M. (Ed.) (2015). *Handbook of adolescent drug use prevention: Research, intervention strategies, and practice*. Washington, DC: American Psychological Association.

Schulenberg, J. E., & Maggs, J. L. (2002). A developmental perspective on alcohol use and heavy drinking during adolescence and the transition to young adulthood. *Journal of Studies on Alcohol, Supplement, 14,* 54–70.

Spear, L. P. (2000). The adolescent brain and age-related behavioral manifestations. *Neuroscience and Biobehavioral Reviews, 24,* 417–463.

Steinberg, L., Dahl, R. E., Keating, D., Kupfer, D. J., Masten, A. S., & Pine, D. S. (2006). Psychopathology in adolescence: integrating affective neuroscience with the study of context. In D. Cicchetti and D. J. Cohen (eds.), *Developmental psychopathology, Vol 2. Developmental neuroscience* (2nd ed., pp. 710–741). New York, NY: Wiley.

Substance Abuse and Mental Health Services Administration Office of Applied Studies. (2009). *The NSDUH Report: Young Adults' Need for and Receipt of Alcohol and Illicit Drug Use Treatment: 2007.* Rockville, MD: Author.

Taylor, D. J., Jenni, O. G., Acebo, C., & Carskadon, M. A. (2005). Sleep tendency during extended wakefulness: insights into adolescent sleep regulation and behavior. *J Sleep Res, 14*(3), 239–244.

Trucco, E. M., Colder, C. R., Wieczorek, W. F., Lengua, L. J., & Hawk, L. W. (2014). Early adolescent alcohol use in context: How neighborhoods, parents, and peers impact youth. *Development and Psychopathology, 26*(2), 425–436.

Wiers, R. W., & Stacy, A. W. (2006). Implicit cognition and addiction. *Current Directions in Psychological Science, 15,* 292–296. doi:10.1111/j.1467–8721.2006.00455.x t

Wong, M. M., Brower, K. J., Fitzgerald, H. E., & Zucker, R. A. (2004). Sleep problems in early childhood and early onset of alcohol and other drug use in adolescence. *Alcoholism: Clinical and Experimental Research, 28*(4), 578–587. doi:10.1097/01.ALC.0000121651.75952.39. PMID:15100609.

Wong, M. M., Brower, K. J., & Zucker, R. A. (2009). Childhood sleep problems, early onset of substance use, and behavioral problems in adolescence. *Sleep Medicine, 10*(7), 787–796.

doi:10.1016/j.sleep.2008.06.015. PMID:19138880. PMCID:PMC2716423.

Zucker, R. A. (1994). Pathways to alcohol problems and alcoholism: A developmental account of the evidence for multiple alcoholisms and for contextual contributions to risk. In Zucker, R. A., Howard, J., & Boyd, G. M. (Eds.), *The development of alcohol problems: Exploring the biopsychosocial matrix of risk* (NIAAA Research Monograph No. 26) (pp. 255–289). Rockville, MD.: U.S. Department of Health and Human Services. [Chapter 13] (213)

Zucker, R. A. (2000). Alcohol involvement over the life course. In *National Institute on Alcohol Abuse and Alcoholism, Tenth Special Report to the U.S. Congress on Alcohol and Health: Highlights from Current Research* (pp. 28–53). Washington, DC: US Department of Health and Human Services.

Zucker, R. A., Donovan, J. E., Masten, A. S., Mattson, M. E., & Moss, H. (2008). Early developmental processes •and the continuity of risk for underage drinking and problem drinking. *Pediatrics, 121*(Suppl. 4), S252–S272. doi:10.1542/peds.2007-2243B. PMID: 18381493. PMCID: PMC2581879.

Zucker, R. A., Heitzeg, M. M., & Nigg, J. T. (2011). Parsing the undercontrol-disinhibition pathway to substance use disorders: A multilevel developmental problem. *Child Development Perspectives, 5*(4), 248–255. doi:10.1111/j.1750–8606.2011.00172.x

Zucker, R. A., Kincaid, S. B., Fitzgerald, H. E., & Bingham, C. R. (1995). Alcohol schema acquisition in preschoolers: Differences between children of alcoholics and children of nonalcoholics. *Alcoholism: Clinical and Experimental Research, 19*(4), 1011–1017. doi:10.1111/j.1530-0277.1995.tb00982.x. PMID: 7485810

PART 1

Conceptual Framework and Background

Substance Use in the Context
of Adolescent Development

John Schulenberg, Julie Maslowsky, Megan E. Patrick, *and* Meghan Martz

Abstract

Adolescence is a prime time for substance use onset and escalation. Key developmental concepts regarding continuity, discontinuity, transitions, and tasks are identified. For many young people, substance use reflects a cascading effect whereby earlier difficulties contribute to substance use onset and escalation, which then cascades into other difficulties. In contrast, this cascading flow can get interrupted, resulting in ontogenetic discontinuity whereby substance use and other risky behaviors during adolescence are more the result of developmentally proximal individual and contextual characteristics than distal ones. This discontinuity can reflect either a temporary developmental disturbance or a turning point, a permanent change in course. Substance use is intertwined with the many developmental changes of adolescence, providing some developmentally functional experiences while posing serious risks to health and well-being that can reverberate into adulthood.

Key Words: adolescence, substance use, development, continuity, discontinuity

When the infamous criminal Willie Sutton was asked why he robbed banks, he allegedly said, "Because that's where the money is!" Similarly, for those of us interested in the etiology, epidemiology, and prevention of substance use, we focus on adolescence because that's where the drugs are. Rarely is substance use initiated prior to or after the second decade of life. Clearly, there are critical developmental antecedents of adolescent substance use initiation and escalation that occur earlier in development (Zucker, Donovan, Masten, Mattson, & Moss, 2008), and some individuals do manage to delay substance use initiation until adulthood (and many avoid it altogether), but with adolescence comes the often overwhelming opportunity and incentive for alcohol and other drug use. Why is this? That is, what is it about adolescence that ignites substance use onset and escalation? Our purpose in this chapter is to address this question.

Adolescence is second only to infancy in terms of the rapid pace and pervasiveness of physical,

biological, and neurocognitive changes (Steinberg et al., 2006; Susman & Dorn, 2009). Of course, compared to infants, adolescents are hyperaware of these individual changes, and for adolescents, these individual changes are layered in with pervasive social context changes. With the manifestation and progression of puberty come the often visible changes in all biological systems. Neurological changes are rapid and not necessarily internally in sync (Casey & Jones, 2010; Pfeifer & Allen, 2012). In a few short years, cognition and decision-making capabilities develop from childlike to adult-like. Sensation seeking increases, as does boredom. Self-awareness heightens, along with concerns about concurrent and future identity. Image management often becomes acute. Peer focus and social integration loom large, often with quests for more independence and time away from parents and increases in desire and opportunity for more free time with peers (Brown & Larson, 2009; Osgood, Wilson, O'Malley, Bachman, &

Johnston, 1996; Patrick, Schulenberg, Maggs, & Maslowsky, 2014). Sexual interest and curiosity heighten. Educational experiences are transformed from the typically cozy context of primary school to the often chaotic, brusque, and consequential context of middle and high school (Eccles & Roeser, 2009; Wigfield, Eccles, Mac Iver, Reuman, & Midgley, 1991). Amidst all of this developmental change, we think that it is no coincidence that interest in and opportunity for substance use begin for most young people. Although substance use is not a recommended practice whatsoever because of the many serious risks involved, alcohol and other drug use can serve numerous positively perceived purposes for some adolescents. Alcohol and other drug use can be a way to cope with stresses large and small; a way to facilitate distance from parents and social integration with peers; and a way to experiment, gather new sensations, and create and manage new self-images (e.g., Chassin, Presson, & Sherman, 1989; Crosnoe, 2011; Schulenberg & Maggs, 2002).

In this chapter, we offer a broad perspective about the connection between adolescence and substance use, the contextual and individual characteristics, changes, and experiences that set the stage for engaging in or avoiding substance use. We begin with the identification and discussion of key developmental concepts as they relate to substance use onset and escalation during adolescence. We then discuss developmental considerations of risk and protective factors for, and short- and long-term consequences of, adolescent substance use. We conclude with a consideration of implications and future directions.

Developmental Conceptualizations
What It Means to Take a Developmental Perspective on Adolescent Substance Use

There are several interrelated meanings of taking a developmental perspective on adolescent substance use. Five meanings are relevant to our approach. First, and most obviously, a developmental perspective means an emphasis on stability and change over time, an emphasis well suited to the fits and starts that likely characterize adolescent substance use onset and escalation. Understanding the "age curve" of substance use during adolescence is essential for both epidemiological and etiological purposes. This helps target prevention and intervention efforts and lets us know the "normativeness" of use at a given age. At the population level, most all forms of substance use increase across adolescence (except

for the use of inhalants, which decreases from 8th to 12th grade; Johnston, O'Malley, Bachman, Schulenberg, & Miech, 2015). Second, taking a developmental perspective means attending to heterogeneity in the age curve, describing and explaining individual trajectories of substance use that represent intraindividual change as well as interindividual differences in the rate and shape of change (Schulenberg, Wadsworth, O'Malley, Bachman, & Johnston, 1996). This includes emphasis on age of onset and rate of escalation. Age of onset has proven to be important in distinguishing more problematic substance use (earlier onset) from more developmentally limited substance use (later onset) (King & Chassin, 2007; Moffitt, 1993; Moffitt & Caspi, 2001; Walters, 2011; Zucker, 1994). Faster increase in use typically reflects more difficulties (Bryant, Schulenberg, O'Malley, Bachman, & Johnston, 2003; D'Amico et al., 2001; Lynne-Landsman, Bradshaw, & Ialongo, 2010; Schulenberg & Maggs, 2001). Especially during adolescence, when experimentation is common and much is in flux, it is essential to view substance use as a moving target across multiple waves. These two meanings— focusing on the age curve of substance use and heterogeneity about the age curve—provide a foundation for our developmental perspective.

A third meaning of taking a developmental perspective involves embedding substance use trajectories within the context of the life span. Doing so entails attending to childhood and early adolescent roots of later adolescent substance use, as well as the short- and long-term consequences of adolescent substance use on later functioning and adjustment (Brown et al., 2008; Schulenberg, Patrick, Maslowsky, & Maggs, 2014). Of course, not all substance use fits so neatly into this "continuity" view. That is, not all adolescent substance use has strong roots in childhood; nor does it always lead to major consequences going forward into adulthood. This highlights the importance, from a developmental perspective, of distinguishing the extent to which adolescent substance use reflects continuity or discontinuity across the life span, a topic central to our developmental framework as discussed in section below.

A fourth meaning of taking a developmental perspective concerns embedding substance use trajectories within the multitude of individual and social context transitions and developmental tasks of adolescence. Nearly every domain of adolescent development, ranging from neurocognitive changes to changing peer relations, is connected to substance use. The search for risk factors, covariates, and consequences of substance use spans the entirety of adolescence. This brings in the emphasis on the meaning and purpose of substance use for the individual, especially in terms of how it relates to various developmental tasks and transitions concurrently and into the future, a key aspect of our developmental framework that we highlight in section below next.

A final meaning for us of taking a developmental perspective on adolescent substance use involves attending to the sociocultural context that structures adolescents' lives, ranging from sociodemographic characteristics to the broader macrosystem and chronosystem (Bronfenbrenner, 1979; Tomasik & Silbereisen, 2012). There are clear differences in typical substance use trajectories as a function of, for example, gender, race/ethnicity, and family socioeconomic status (SES); substance use tends to start earlier for lower SES than higher SES youth, it tends to start later for Black than White youth, and it tends to escalate faster for boys than girls (Johnston et al., 2015; Schulenberg et al., 2014). At the population level, rates of and attitudes toward substance use shift historically, with documented wide fluctuations regarding most substances over the past four decades (Johnston et al., 2015); typically, changes in attitudes precede changes in use (Keyes et al., 2011, 2012). Furthermore, the experience of adolescent substance use tends to vary by country. For example, US adolescents currently have lower rates of alcohol and cigarette use, but higher rates of illicit drug use, compared to most European countries (Hibell et al., 2012). These macro and time-varying trends in behaviors and supporting attitudes set the context for individual substance use trajectories, making some trajectories more or less likely. In the United States, adolescent rates of many substances have declined since the middle to late 1990s, more so for younger than older students (Johnston et al., 2015). These changes have resulted in a population age curve that now starts later but increases more rapidly across adolescence (Schulenberg et al., 2014). Furthermore, this slower start but faster increase pattern also applies to rates of alcohol and marijuana use across the transition to adulthood, with more recent cohorts showing lower rates in their senior year but rates that rise faster through the middle-20s (Jager, Schulenberg, O'Malley, & Bachman, 2013). Thus, at the broader sociocultural level, the experience of substance use during adolescence appears to be shifting toward later onset but more rapid escalation. More generally, not only is substance use during adolescence best viewed as a moving target, the broader sociocultural context that structures adolescent development in general and substance use in particular is also best viewed as a moving target. That is, substance use etiology and epidemiology must go hand in hand (Compton, Thomas, Conway, & Colliver, 2005; Maslowsky & Schulenberg, 2013; Schulenberg et al., 2014; Tarter, 2010).

Thus, to take a developmental perspective on adolescent substance use means to focus on the age curve of substance use across adolescence as well as on the heterogeneity about the age curve in terms of individual substance use trajectories. It means to be concerned with how adolescent substance use trajectories are linked with upstream childhood and early adolescent characteristics and experiences and downstream later adolescence and adulthood functioning and adjustment, as well as with the many developmental tasks and transitions of adolescence; our chapter is centered on these meanings. Finally, it means to view adolescent substance use trajectories as embedded within the sociodemographic and broader sociocultural context. We next consider key developmental conceptualizations concerning developmental continuity and discontinuity, transitions, and tasks.

Developmental Continuity and Discontinuity

Continuity and discontinuity are essential concepts for the understanding of development (Kagan, 1980; Werner, 1957), and in our view, they are essential for understanding substance use etiology. Through a series of conceptual papers and chapters, we have elaborated a developmental framework regarding substance use during adolescence and the transition to adulthood that emphasizes continuity and discontinuity, as well as developmental transitions, tasks, and trajectories (e.g., Maggs & Schulenberg, 2005; Patrick et al., 2014; Patrick & Schulenberg, 2013; Schulenberg & Maggs, 2002; Schulenberg, Maggs, & O'Malley, 2003; Schulenberg & Maslowsky, 2009; Schulenberg & Patrick, 2012; Schulenberg et al., 2014; Schulenberg, Sameroff, & Cicchetti, 2004; Schulenberg & Zarrett, 2006). This framework draws from broad interdisciplinary developmental science and developmental-contextual perspectives that highlight multilevel and multidirectional change and dynamic person–context interactions (Cairns, 2000; Elder & Shanahan, 2006; Lerner, 2006; Sameroff, 2010). In our developmental framework, we view individuals and contexts as playing strong active roles in the process of development, highlighting the importance of the person–context match—that is, the connection between what the developing individual needs and what the context provides. Individuals select available contexts and activities based on opportunities and personal characteristics; selected contexts then provide additional opportunities (and limit other opportunities represented by contexts not selected) for continued socialization and further selection. This progressive mutual selection and accommodation underscore coherence and continuity in development. But in our view, with dynamic person–context interactions and multidirectional change come the potential for discontinuity; development does not necessarily follow a smooth and progressive function, and early experiences do not always have strong or lasting effects (e.g., Cairns, 2000; Lewis, 1999; Rutter, 1996). Thus, both continuity and discontinuity are expected across the life span.

The concepts of continuity and discontinuity have multiple meanings in the literature. Continuity is sometimes viewed as synonymous with stability, meaning the extent to which individuals maintain relative rank ordering over time; but among developmental scientists, continuity is typically viewed in broader terms, pertaining to the course of intraindividual trajectories and underlying structures over time (e.g., Cicchetti & Rogosch, 2002; Liben, 2008). In terms of ongoing trajectories of substance use, continuity suggests, for example, a flat trajectory or even a smooth change consistent with the normative course; in contrast, discontinuity suggests a sharp change in level or direction (Schulenberg, Maggs, Steinman, & Zucker., 2001; Schulenberg & Patrick, 2012). As summarized next, two conceptualizations of continuity and discontinuity are particularly relevant to understanding the etiology of substance use (Schulenberg et al., 2003; Schulenberg & Zarrett, 2006).

In the first conceptualization, continuity and discontinuity pertain to causative linkages across the life span (e.g., Lewis, 1999; Masten, 2001), defined as ontogenetic continuity and discontinuity. Ontogenetic continuity reflects progression and individual coherence over time, with earlier developmentally distal events and experiences essentially causing future outcomes (Caspi, 2000). Not surprisingly, ontogenetic continuity tends to prevail across the life span; indeed, a developmental perspective would not be justified if this were not

true. Despite the formative influence of ontogenetic continuity, later functioning is not always a direct effect of earlier functioning (Cicchetti & Rogosch, 2002; Lewis, 1999; Martin & Martin, 2002). Instead, the effects of early experiences may be amplified, neutralized, or reversed by later experiences (Schulenberg & Zarrett, 2006). Such developmentally proximal influences reflect ontogenetic discontinuity, whereby current functioning is due more to recent and current contexts and experiences than to earlier ones (Lewis, 1999).

The distinction between ontogenetic continuity and discontinuity is important when examining the etiology of substance use. Much of adolescent substance use is appropriately viewed as "the result" of earlier difficulties and family socialization experiences (e.g., Dodge et al., 2009; Zucker et al., 2008), reflecting ontogenetic continuity (e.g., life-course-persistent antisocial behavior in Moffitt & Caspi, 2001). And consistent with the concept of ontogenetic continuity, adolescent substance use can have direct consequences on later functioning and adjustment. In other cases, however, the roots of substance use do not go that far into the past, but rather into current social contexts and developmental tasks and transitions (Schulenberg & Maslowsky, 2009), reflecting ontogenetic discontinuity (e.g., adolescence-limited antisocial behavior in Moffitt & Caspi, 2001; see also Zucker, 1994). Likewise, due to postadolescent experiences that serve to neutralize or even reverse potential consequences of adolescent substance use (e.g., employment, marriage, becoming a parent), adolescent substance use does not always have long-term consequences (Schulenberg et al., 2003).

The second conceptualization of continuity and discontinuity important for the understanding of substance use etiology draws the distinction between the descriptive level (pertaining to manifest behaviors) and the explanatory level (pertaining to underlying purposes, functions, and meanings) (Kagan, 1969; Lerner, 2006). This conceptualization draws from organismic developmental theories where discontinuity is viewed as reflecting qualitative or underlying structural-level change, such as the emergence of new structure or meaning (Reese & Overton, 1970; Werner, 1957). Homotypic continuity refers to continuity at both the descriptive and explanatory levels (Kagan, 1969) whereby both a given behavior (e.g., alcohol use) and the underlying purpose of that behavior (e.g., having fun with friends) remain continuous over time. Heterotypic continuity refers to when behaviors vary across time (descriptive discontinuity) while the underlying purpose or meaning of those varying behaviors remains the same (explanatory continuity). For example, the desire to be successful in peer relations may be continuous from childhood into adolescence, but what it takes to be successful with peers can shift over time and may cross into deviant behaviors during adolescence (Allen, Porter, McFarland, Marsh, & McElhaney, 2005). Functional discontinuity, which can be viewed as the opposite of heterotypic continuity, combines descriptive continuity with explanatory discontinuity. That is, the manifest behavior appears unchanged, but the underlying function or meaning of that behavior changes over time. For example, a high school student may first use marijuana to experiment and fit in with her friends; several years later, she may still use marijuana, but now as a means of coping with stress (Patrick & Schulenberg, 2011; Patrick, Schulenberg, O'Malley, Johnston, & Bachman, 2011). As we summarize later, we find such developmental shifts in reasons for substance use as well as substance use behaviors.

Developmental Transitions

Developmental transitions include transformations in individuals, their contexts, and the relations between individuals and their contexts across the life course (e.g., Bronfenbrenner, 1979; Schulenberg & Maggs, 2002). Often, developmental transitions are viewed globally, like the transitions into adolescence and into adulthood, though they are also viewed more specifically in terms of intraindividual transitions (e.g., biological) and socially based external ones (e.g., school and work related) (Rutter, 1996). The period between the end of childhood and the beginning of adulthood is dense with such internally and externally based transitions. The power of these interlinked transitions on the course of substance use during adolescence can be understood in relation to the concepts of continuity and discontinuity discussed earlier. Schulenberg and colleagues (e.g., Schulenberg & Maggs, 2002; Schulenberg & Zarrett, 2006) summarize numerous ways in which transitions can contribute to substance use onset, escalation, and desistence. For example, consistent with Coleman's (1989) focal theory, multiple transitions can serve to overwhelm coping capacities. Transitions can place young people in new contexts, putting them at increased risk for chance events, good or bad, through exposure to new situations and opportunities. And transitions can alter the person–context match, resulting in improved or decreased health and well-being.

Turning first to discontinuity, internal and external transitions can have proximal effects on developmental trajectories that counteract developmentally distal effects. Such transitions may introduce ontogenetic discontinuity through the presentation of novel contexts that alter the person–context match. The transitions into middle and high school, for example, constitute important developmental transitions that can have an impact in escalating difficulties, including substance use (e.g., Eccles & Roeser, 2009; Guo, Collins, Hill, & Hawkins, 2000; Jackson & Schulenberg, 2013). As we have discussed as part of our evolving developmental framework, this discontinuity in ongoing trajectories can take the form of turning points or developmental disturbances. Turning points reflect long-term changes in course (Elder & Shanahan, 2006; Ronka, Oravala, & Pulkkinen, 2002; Rutter, 1996), such as lasting change in direction or shape of ongoing trajectories. In contrast to the "permanent change" associated with turning points, developmental disturbances reflect more momentary perturbations (Schulenberg & Zarrett, 2006). Once individuals are given time to adjust, they might resume their prior, ongoing trajectory. That is, consistent with the notion of homeorhesis in systems theories of developmental psychopathology (Sameroff, 2010), the individuals would return to the original ongoing trajectory (not the original static point). In such cases, a transition may simply result in short-term deviance (e.g., an escalation in binge drinking, experimenting with illicit drugs) that subsides and thus may not have long-term effects on developmental course or predict later functioning in adulthood (Schulenberg et al., 2003; Schulenberg & Zarrett, 2006). Although we have focused on discontinuity in terms of increased difficulties, transition-inspired discontinuity can also reflect increased health and well-being. For example, a school transition may result in a better person–context match in terms of appropriate level of challenge and contribute to improved health and well-being.

Developmental transitions also can contribute to continuity, not just discontinuity. Much of developmental psychology is built on the notion of ontogenetic continuity (Cairns, 2000; Lewis, 1999). Therefore, it might be easy to believe that continuity occurs automatically as part of development and that transitions have no place in fostering continuity. But when one embraces a strong person–context interaction perspective on development, continuity is not viewed as automatic. Instead, transitions become important mechanisms for both discontinuity *and* continuity. Transitions contribute to continuity by serving, for example, as proving grounds that help consolidate and strengthen ongoing behavioral and adjustment trajectories for better and worse (Schulenberg & Zarrett, 2006). Individuals tend to rely on intrinsic tendencies and known behavioral and coping repertoires in novel and ambiguous situations (e.g., Caspi, 2000; Dannefer, 1987), suggesting that young people already experiencing difficulties may have trouble negotiating new transitions and fall further behind their well-functioning peers. In contrast, those already doing well have the resources to deal successfully with new transitions and climb further ahead of their age-mates having difficulties (Schulenberg et al., 2014). Thus, during major transitions such as the transition into middle school or high school, ongoing salutary and deviant trajectories may become more solidified, highlighting the role of transitions in perpetuating ontogenetic continuity.

Developmental Tasks

Developmental tasks are culturally defined, socially and biologically influenced psychosocial tasks to be accomplished during specific times in the life span (Havighurst, 1952; Tomasik & Silbereisen, 2012). They are distinct from developmental transitions in that tasks pertain to accomplishments, whereas transitions pertain more to the actual process of change (Schulenberg & Maggs, 2002). The two are related and often overlapping (e.g., the task of finding a romantic partner and the transition to a committed relationship), and both follow socially and biologically prescribed timelines (Heckhausen, 1999).

Developmental tasks can contribute to continuity and discontinuity in substance use in ways similar to those summarized earlier regarding developmental transitions. Attempting to accomplish tasks can serve, for example, to increase stress or alter person–context relationships, potentially resulting in onset and changes in the course of substance use. In turn, substance use can contribute to difficulties, as well as successes, in accomplishing developmental tasks (e.g., Schulenberg & Maggs, 2002; Schulenberg & Zarrett, 2006). During adolescence and the transition to adulthood, important tasks include forming stronger peer bonds and exploring one's identity (Brown & Larson, 2009; Cote, 2009; Erikson, 1968; Patrick et al., 2014). Although not ideal, these two tasks can sometimes be facilitated by substance use and, in turn, encourage further use

(Schulenberg & Maggs, 2002). That is, substance use can be developmentally functional, with reasons for use including social integration and identity exploration.

As adolescents individuate from parents, peers take center stage, and peer bonding and social integration become important developmental tasks. Peers can either facilitate or mitigate substance use, depending on their characteristics (Brown & Larson, 2009; Patrick et al., 2014). Between childhood and adolescence, the repertoire of acceptable/sought after behaviors in peers tends to move toward risk taking that might include substance use (e.g., Allen et al., 2005; Crosnoe, 2011). This suggests both heterotypic continuity, where the underlying motivation of peer success remains continuous and the behaviors to accomplish this success shift toward more risky behaviors, and functional discontinuity, where the underlying purpose of a consistent behavior (substance use) shifts from deviancy to social integration. Perceptions of social norms are strong predictors of substance use; adolescents who believe their friends engage in more substance use are more likely to engage themselves (Bauman & Ennett, 1996; Dishion & Owen, 2002; Patrick & Schulenberg, 2010; Windle, 2000). In addition, pertaining to the potential positive functions of alcohol and other drug use, adolescents often report that reasons for engaging in substance use include social motivations such as fitting in and having a good time with their friends (Patrick, Schulenberg, O'Malley, Maggs, et al., 2011; Patrick, Schulenberg, O'Malley, Johnston, et al., 2011).

The task of identity exploration can also relate to substance use during adolescence (Arnett, 2005; Barber, Eccles, & Stone, 2001; Jones & Hartmann, 1988; Schulenberg & Maggs, 2002). As young people try out new activities and groups such as athletics, arts, service groups, and academic honor societies, they also become exposed to and consider joining peer crowds that often have distinct norms regarding substance use behaviors. Adolescent peer crowds in the United States include labels such as "jocks," "brains," "preps," and "druggies" (Barber et al., 2001; La Greca, Prinstein, & Fetter, 2001; Sussman, Pokhrel, Ashmore, & Brown, 2007). Membership in these crowds has obvious implications for both identity formation and substance use, in addition to physical appearance, interests, and other behaviors. Beyond the influence of peers, coping with difficulties in identity exploration and commitment (e.g., identity diffusion) can set the stage for substance use (Arnett, 2005), which may then exacerbate identity difficulties; in contrast, making identity commitments is associated with reductions in substance use and other risk behaviors (Maggs, Schulenberg, & Hurrelmann, 1997; Marcia, 1994; Schulenberg & Maggs, 2002). Thus, substance use can sometimes be used to help negotiate social and identity developmental tasks and at other times impede successful negotiation of such tasks.

Developmental Perspective on Risk and Protective Factors

For decades, our science has been aware of the multiple risk and protective factors of adolescent substance use, spanning nearly every aspect of adolescents' lives and ranging from biological- to cultural-level influences (e.g., Brown et al., 2008; Hawkins, Catalano, & Miller, 1992; Jessor, 1987; Sloboda, Glantz, & Tarter, 2012; Windle et al., 2008). Looking to the future, major advances in understanding the etiology of substance use are unlikely to come in the form of new risk or protective factors, but rather in the form of interrelations among risk and protective factors across levels of influence and across time. In this section, we summarize key questions and approaches regarding risk and protective factors that follow from taking a developmental perspective.

Multiple Pathways

Given that risk and protective factors are probabilistic in their relations to substance use, none is necessary and each is sufficient. In other words, having a given risk factor is not required for substance use involvement, and having just one given risk factor can set the stage. This means that there are multiple pathways to substance use, demonstrating the notion of equifinality, which describes the presence of several distinct routes to a common outcome. Equifinality poses two notable challenges for understanding substance use etiology. First, when we list the possible risk factors evident across multiple samples, we likely end up with a description of everyone in general and no one in particular. Second, what are found to be "causes" for some young people may simply be correlates or even consequences for others.

A developmental perspective that highlights multiple trajectories and pathways can be used to bring some needed order to the seemingly messy etiological processes leading to substance use. Longitudinal research is a powerful tool for distinguishing timing, ordering, and developmental specificity of risk factors, correlates, and consequences. Although there are multiple pathways into substance use, it is likely that some pathways are more common than others. For example, Dodge et al. (2009) identified a common pathway into substance use that begins with early childhood factors such as child's temperament and parenting behaviors, progresses into difficulties in childhood behavior and peer relations, and culminates in adolescent behavior problems and deviant peer associations, known proximal risk factors for adolescent substance use. Describing and explaining common pathways can capture most but not all of the ways adolescents become involved with substance use. This enables a systematic approach to studying multiple pathways into substance use; those who do not follow a common pathway can then be identified, and their unique pathways into substance use can provide a more nuanced understanding of substance use etiology.

Interactive Effects

Often, risk and protective factors are viewed in isolation in their relation to substance use outcomes. Although useful, such approaches leave open questions about how risk and protective factors work together—and sometimes in competition—to predict substance use. Indeed, much of the innovative new research on adolescent substance use demonstrates how established risk factors interact with each other, such as the interactive relationship among conduct problems and depressive symptoms in predicting substance use (Maslowsky & Schulenberg, 2013), and the moderating effect of parent substance abuse on the association of adolescent depression with subsequence substance abuse (Gorka, Shankman, Seeley, & Lewinsohn, 2013).

As typically used in research, protective factors are at the opposite side of the same continuum as risk factors. Having academic difficulties is a risk factor and academic success is a protective factor. But as sometimes conceptualized, protective factors come into play only when one is otherwise at risk; that is, protective factors only work in interaction with risk factors. In the latter case, the term *promotive factor* is used to describe a salutary influence that pertains to all in general, whereas the term *protective factor* is used to describe a salutary influence that pertains only to those at risk (Gutman, Sameroff, & Cole, 2003). For example, among national samples of 8th and 10th graders, Dever et al. (2012) found that parental monitoring was both a promotive factor in that it predicted lower substance use for all, and a protective factor in that it had an especially powerful positive effect for youth high at risk (due to being especially high on sensation seeking).

One important methodological aspect of highlighting interaction effects among risk factors is the need for representative samples. If effects are moderated by sociodemographic and other risk and protective factors, the demands on sample size and representativeness to avoid contradictory findings are high. Studies are often powered only to detect hypothesized main effects. Detecting interactions requires study designs that anticipate interactions between multiple risk and protective factors and a sample size adequate to detect those interactions. If moderation of risk and protective processes by sociodemographic characteristics is anticipated, sampling frames should also take into account how to achieve adequate representation among subgroups in order to test for and detect subgroup differences. Survey research is particularly well suited to this task.

Of course, survey research cannot, by itself, get at interactions involving substance use risk factors operating at levels not subject to self-report, including biological and situation-specific factors. For example, in both animal and human models, the adolescent brain differs structurally and functionally from the adult brain (Spear, 2000). Dramatic neural transformations occur in the adolescent brain, and according to the differential maturity mismatch hypothesis, the interaction between an early maturing reward-seeking limbic system and a slower maturing cognitive control system in the prefrontal cortex contribute to increased risk taking (Bava & Tapert, 2010; Casey & Jones, 2010; Steinberg et al., 2008; see Pfeifer & Allen, 2012, for alternative view). Neural changes and risk-taking behaviors may also interact bidirectionally. Not only do characteristics of the developing adolescent brain contribute to susceptibility for risk taking and substance use, but also the use of substances (particularly at high or frequent levels) during adolescence may hinder cognitive functioning and structural neural development (Squeglia, Jacobus, & Tapert, 2009). In addition, hormonal shifts initiated during puberty, and the influence of pubertal hormones on neural circuitry within the adolescent brain, may interact to drive the propensity for risk taking (Sisk & Zehr, 2005; Spear, 2000; Steinberg et al., 2008). An exciting direction for future research is the combination of survey and laboratory-based techniques in order to assess interactions among risk factors measured at multiple levels of analysis, from biological to cultural, and to approach an integrated picture of risk and protective processes for adolescent substance use.

Developmental Arrays of Risk and Protective Factors

Building on the multiple pathways and interactive characteristics of risk and protective factors is the idea of risk and protective factors being arrayed developmentally. There are several interconnected issues under the heading of developmental arrays, beginning with cascading effects, where earlier difficulties in one domain contribute to difficulties in other domains, eventually substance use (Dodge et al., 2009; Masten, Faden, Zucker, & Spear, 2008; Zucker et al., 2008). Such cascades could be used to model heterotypic continuity, with common underlying mechanisms such as externalizing behaviors manifesting in different, developmentally appropriate forms over the course of childhood and adolescence (e.g., Dodge et al., 2009). Alternatively, they may capture the accumulation of risk factors over time that eventually leads to substance use (e.g., Rutter & Garmezy, 1983).

In addition, the developmental array of risk factors is important when attempting to distinguish developmentally distal and proximal effects. In general, proximal risk factors should be more powerful because they are temporally closer to the outcome, but central to much developmental metatheory is the idea of sensitive periods and powerful developmentally distal effects (Lerner, 2006). For example, although temporally distal, early childhood risk factors such as child temperament and family stress can strongly relate to substance use in adolescence (Burk et al., 2011; Dodge et al., 2009). Similarly, early-emerging mental health symptoms have been shown to be a stronger risk factor for substance use than later-emerging but more proximal symptoms (Maslowsky, Schulenberg, & Zucker, 2014). Thus, the etiology of adolescent substance use is further specified by the identification of developmental windows—sensitive periods—at which key predictors are most influential on the development of substance use. Describing such periods is also important for informing the design of developmentally appropriate substance use prevention and intervention programs for adolescents.

Another issue regarding the developmental array of risk and protective factors pertains to the prediction of substance use onset versus substance use escalation (Jackson & Schulenberg, 2013). Studies that predict both the incidence and the extent of alcohol use often find different effects of risk and protective factors (e.g., Capaldi, Stoolmiller, Kim, & Yoerger, 2009; D'Amico & McCarthy, 2006). In addition, the likelihood and frequency of drinking have been shown to be differentially affected by intervention programs (Brown, Catalano, Fleming, Haggerty, & Abbott, 2005; Wood et al., 2010). The two—initiation and escalation—are obviously connected, and in fact, early onset in adolescence contributes to later escalation (e.g., Lynskey et al., 2003); but the etiologic processes underlying initiation and escalation are likely distinct, with the risk factors associated with onset during adolescence being of different magnitude and perhaps even different type compared to risk factors associated with escalating use during adolescence (e.g., Donovan, 2004). Providing information on the timing and content of these different risk factors can assist in more clearly specifying the underlying etiologic processes for onset and escalation. Understanding the prediction of onset versus escalation brings us to our final subsection concerning risk and protective factors of substance use.

Predicting Trajectories

Substance use at one point of time, especially during adolescence, may tell us little about etiology. Studies that focus on a single point or limited period of time give us little insight into the developmental array of risk factors discussed earlier, and they may not be able to distinguish short-lived versus chronic substance use. Focusing instead on longer term trajectories of substance use can provide some needed leverage on etiologic mechanisms and process. Distinguishing substance use from abuse is a fundamental purpose of etiologic research (Newcomb & Bentler, 1989). Among the many issues involved in defining substance abuse, in contrast to use, is developmental course. A trajectory of earlier and heavier use is likely to reflect abuse, whereas a trajectory of later onset and lighter use is likely to reflect experimental use (Chassin, Pitts, & Prost, 2002; Hill, White, Chung, Hawkins, & Catalano, 2000). The necessity of a developmental approach here is twofold: It can be used to map both pathways into substance use and the trajectories of actual use onto developmental space and time. Using a developmentally informed study design, one can model trajectories of use, identify the most severe (in terms of levels of use, abuse, and chronicity), and look backward to identify early predictors of severe use, such as early age of substance use onset, which has been shown to predict

a greater likelihood of substance use disorder in numerous studies (Grant & Dawson, 1997; Tarter, 2010; Wagner & Anthony, 2002). Developmentally informed designs also help to contextualize the substance use within the developmental period in which it occurs. As discussed earlier, substance use, particularly alcohol use, becomes normative and sometimes functional in later adolescence, and thus it may be less associated with risk factors—that is, a trajectory of use that reflects a developmental disturbance, described earlier as a common period of time-limited deviance, may not be especially predictable in advance. A final point regarding the developmental context of risk factors for trajectories of substance use pertains to the measurement of the trajectory: During times when rapid change is expected, such as major transitions, more and finer-grained trajectories (e.g., measurement bursts) are needed.

Developmental Perspective on Consequences

It is fair to say that attempts over the past few decades to isolate the long-term consequences of adolescent alcohol and other drug use have not met with limited success. And perhaps we should expect it to be this way—life tends to be far too complicated to reliably attribute later problems to a single set of earlier difficulties. Furthermore, adolescent substance use is a multivariate construct (or perhaps better thought of as multiple constructs), and adulthood functioning and adjustment also consist of multiple constructs covering the wide expanse of life domains. Building on the developmental perspective that we have advocated in this chapter can help attend to the various complexities of conceptualizing and examining long-term connections across the life span (Schulenberg et al., 2003). In this section, we summarize some key issues and approaches regarding substance use consequences that follow from taking a developmental perspective.

Issues of Causality and Endogeneity

Obviously, issues of causality loom large when attempting to determine consequences of adolescent substance use. One key aspect in attempts to isolate adolescent substance use, as a causative factor for later functioning and adjustment, is the consideration of contemporaneous and more upstream characteristics and experiences that contribute to both adolescent substance use and later difficulties. Without the possibility of random assignment, we need to be able to control for selection effects, wherein individuals who are more prone to experience adolescent substance use are also more prone to experience later adulthood difficulties. Long-term longitudinal studies are becoming more common, allowing for better leverage on potential consequences of adolescent substance use. With such data, within-person multilevel longitudinal analyses provide an effective strategy for isolating potential causal effects of substance use. By controlling for all time-stable individual characteristics (e.g., early-life risk factors), such techniques can provide some controls for selection effects and show the extent to which within-person changes in substance use are associated with subsequent functioning. Studies employing this method have demonstrated, for example, that within-person increases in symptoms of alcohol abuse and depression contribute to increased likelihood of diagnosis with major depressive disorder (Fergusson, Boden, & Horwood, 2009), and within-person increases in smoking behavior contribute to higher levels of depressive symptoms (Duncan & Rees, 2005). Also useful are propensity score matching analyses, whereby respondents are matched on numerous upstream and contemporaneous characteristics with the exception of substance use; this helps control for selection effects and thus can determine the contribution of substance use on later functioning and adjustment. For example, using this type of analysis with Monitoring the Future longitudinal data, Maggs et al. (2015) found that frequent marijuana use in adolescence contributed to less educational attainment at age 26.

Multiple Outcomes and Multiple Patterns of Use

Multifinality refers to multiple endpoints resulting from the same starting point (Cicchetti & Rogosch, 1996); in this case, there is likely a full range of negative, null, and sometimes even positive consequences of the initial starting point, adolescent substance use. Although substance use is probabilistically related to a range of negative health, social, and achievement consequences, only a subset of those who engage in normative and even problematic substance use experience its potential negative consequences. What are the factors that distinguish those whose substance use is less costly from those who develop an addiction, become sick or injured, or experience social and achievement difficulties as a result of their substance use? Obviously, heavier use is likely more consequential than lighter use; and given that neither adolescent substance use nor

adulthood functioning is a unitary construct, much depends on the type of substance used and adulthood domains considered. But beyond these obvious points, a developmental perspective can help tame some of the complexity by focusing attention on multiple patterns and reasons for use.

First, the trajectory of substance use during adolescence—including timing of onset and escalation—matters in terms of consequences. Early initiation and ongoing use of alcohol and marijuana are well known predictors of later substance use disorders (Grant & Dawson, 1997; Lynskey et al., 2003; Schulenberg & Patrick, 2012; Wagner & Anthony, 2002). Redirecting risky trajectories by delaying initiation of substance use in adolescence has been shown to reduce problematic substance use in young adulthood (Kellam & Anthony, 1998; Spoth, Trudeau, Guyll, Shin, & Redmond, 2009). But heavy use over a relatively short period of time, especially during late adolescence and early adulthood, may carry relatively few consequences. That is, consistent with the notion of developmental disturbance discussed earlier, some short-term heavy substance use may reflect a temporary deviation from the given individual's ongoing pattern and such temporary deviations, especially during a time in life when substance use is more normative, may not be predictive of later functioning and adjustment (Schulenberg et al., 2003). For example, Newcomb, Scheier, and Bentler (1993) found that a trajectory of increasing polysubstance use from adolescence into young adulthood predicted serious mental health problems such as psychoticism and suicidality in adulthood, whereas polysubstance use that lasted only during adolescence had no association with adult mental health. Similarly, focusing on college students from the Monitoring the Future study, Schulenberg and Patrick (2012) found that a "fling" pattern of frequent binge drinking (i.e., frequent binge drinking that starts with transition to college and then subsides after a few years) showed no association with a full range of psychosocial outcomes 10 to 15 years later; a cautionary aspect of this finding, however, is that those who followed the fling pattern, compared to those who followed an "infrequent" pattern, were at heightened risk for an alcohol use disorder at age 35. Thus, based on community and national studies, it appears that adolescent substance use consequences depend to some extent on whether substance use continues into adulthood. Of course, at the individual level, any heavy substance use, regardless of ongoing pattern, can increase the likelihood of personal or legal tragedies that indeed can have long-term consequences (Newcomb & Bentler, 1988; Schulenberg & Maggs, 2002).

Second, adolescent substance use consequences depend to some extent on with what substance use is interacting. Polysubstance use, or use of multiple substances, is generally associated with more severe consequences and developmental outcomes than use of a single substance (Agrawal, Lynskey, Madden, Bucholz, & Heath, 2006). Indeed, studies have shown that polysubstance use confers elevated risk for a range of adverse health behaviors and conditions in adolescence and adulthood, including risky sexual behavior, addiction, and suicidality (Connell, Gilreath, & Hansen, 2009; Newcomb & Bentler, 1988; Wu, Pilowsky, & Schlenger, 2005). Comorbidity of substance use with mental health problems is another consistent indicator of likelihood of severe and problematic substance use (Jackson, Sher, & Schulenberg, 2008; Maslowsky & Schulenberg, 2013; Maslowsky, Schulenberg, O'Malley, & Kloska, 2013; Stenbacka, 2003). More generally, the same attention given to the interaction of risk factors for adolescent substance use discussed earlier should be given to understanding the interaction of adolescent substance use with other individual and contextual risk factors in the prediction of adulthood functioning and adjustment.

And third, why one uses substances can matter in terms of the consequences of adolescent substance use. Self-reported reasons for engaging in substance use reflect the perceived functions of substance use in meeting the individual's needs, or what the individual gains by his or her substance use (Boys et al., 2001; Cooper, 1994; Cox & Klinger, 1988; Kuntsche, Knibbe, Gmel, & Engels, 2005). The majority of self-reported reasons for using alcohol and marijuana (such as to have fun with friends) decrease from adolescence to young adulthood; and some reasons that are less common among adolescents increase with the transition to adulthood (e.g., to relax, using alcohol to sleep) (Patrick, Schulenberg, O'Malley, Maggs, et al., 2011). These underlying motives for substance use have implications for current and continued use and consequences of use. Reasons associated with the lowest levels of use during adolescence include to experiment and to fit in with peers (Patrick, Schulenberg, O'Malley, Maggs, et al., 2011). Drinking alcohol to get high and because of boredom are reasons most strongly associated with increases in binge drinking from ages 18 to 22, and those who continue to use alcohol to get away from their problems are most likely to continue with higher rates of binge drinking after age 22 (Patrick & Schulenberg, 2011). Adolescents who use substances such as alcohol and marijuana to regulate emotions may be at increased risk for substance use problems decades later, well into adulthood (Patrick, Schulenberg, O'Malley, Johnston, & Bachman, 2011).

Distinguishing Short- and Long-Term Effects

Finally, building on the issues of causality and patterns of use, a developmentally informed approach includes an emphasis on both short- and long-term consequences of adolescent substance use. No doubt, continuities in consequences are to be expected over time. Within, say, a cascading model, short- and long-term consequences of adolescent substance use should go hand in hand, where initial negative consequences in one domain (e.g., cognitive) cascade into negative consequences in another (e.g., education). But discontinuities in consequences are also to be expected over time. Just as risk factors temporally closer to the outcome tend to be more powerful than developmentally distal risk factors, it is reasonable to expect that short-term consequences of substance use are more powerful than long-term ones. Negative effects of adolescent substance use may wear off with age as other life experiences and major life transitions occur and as levels of substance use wane or individuals get better at managing their substance use—that is, as the multifinality mentioned earlier becomes manifest.

In contrast, there are also reasons to expect that long-term effects would be more powerful than short-term ones. For example, some effects of substance use may not be apparent initially, but only appear as life wears on and there is increased heterogeneity in interindividual differences in the extent to which substance use impacts other life domains (Schulenberg et al., 2003). Resilience, coping ability, or social integration compensatory mechanisms may suffice for a period in order to avoid initial negative consequences of substance use (Fergus & Zimmerman, 2005); these mechanisms may fade in the face of accumulated health and social effects of earlier substance use. For example, adolescents who use substances are more likely to associate with peers who do the same (Kandel, 1985; Patrick et al., 2014), and adult substance users are more likely to marry other substance users (Grant et al., 2007), each of which likely serves to reduce any initial negative social consequences of substance use; but over time, this positive function of substance use may fade as other negative consequences ascend. Indeed, given the perceived positive functions of alcohol and other drug use discussed earlier in terms of social integration and identity development during adolescence, it is possible that there are "positive" short-term consequences in some domains followed by negative long-term consequences in the same or other domains. Ultimately, how substance use consequences are manifest in the short and long term and whether such consequences take different forms in different developmental periods are empirical questions most appropriately addressed with a developmentally informed approach and long-term longitudinal data.

Conclusions and Implications

Substance use during adolescence is not inevitable, and most young people manage to negotiate the adolescent years without serious substance use difficulties. But, as witnessed by decades of etiologic research, if substance use is going to occur in one's lifetime, it is most likely to occur during the second decade of life. In this chapter, our focus has been on why adolescence is a key time for substance use onset and escalation. In fact, as we reviewed here, it would be difficult to find aspects of adolescence that do not relate to substance use.

Broad-based concepts regarding developmental continuity, discontinuity, transitions, and tasks help highlight the dynamic aspect of functioning and adjustment during adolescence and make the case for considering developmentally distal and proximal effects on adolescent substance use. For many young people, substance use during adolescence reflects a cascading effect whereby earlier difficulties in a variety of domains contribute to substance use onset and escalation, which then cascades into other difficulties (Dodge et al., 2009; Masten et al., 2008). In contrast, partly as a function of the numerous individual and social context transitions during adolescence, this cascading flow can get interrupted or diverted, resulting in ontogenetic discontinuity whereby, for example, substance use and other risky behaviors during adolescence are more the result of developmentally proximal individual and contextual characteristics than distal ones (Moffitt & Caspi, 2001). This can be understood in terms of the peer and social integration benefits of substance use and other risky behaviors, illustrating heterotypic continuity in which the purpose of being successful in peer relations remains consistent over time, but the behaviors to meet this purpose shift. In some cases, this discontinuity may prove to be a developmental disturbance (Schulenberg &

Zarrett, 2006), and more salutary behavior trajectories are expected to eventually resume. But in other cases, this detour that may come with the multiple transitions of adolescence is best understood as a turning point—discontinuity that reflects a profound and permanent change in course (Rutter, 1996). Thus, understanding substance use from a developmental perspective requires acknowledging the important transitions in multiple domains of adolescents' lives and the developmental tasks that are central to them. Substance use is intertwined with the many developmental changes of adolescence, providing some developmental functional experiences while posing serious risks to health and well-being that can reverberate into adulthood.

We began this chapter by asking what it means to take a developmental perspective. The increased emphasis in the literature over the past few decades on the developmental aspects of adolescent substance use has resulted in substantial progress in our understanding of distal and proximal risk factors for substance use, developmental specificity of both risk for and consequences of substance use, and important subgroup differences in processes leading up to substance use. Building on these advances, we believe that the future of substance use research from a developmental perspective will involve the integration of multiple levels of analysis (Cicchetti & Dawson, 2002; Crone & Dahl, 2012), from brain and biology to behavior and social context, and their effects on the health and well-being of the population. Advances in the neuroscience and genetics of substance use increasingly indicate that biological risk factors are as dynamic and interactive as social and behavioral factors (e.g., Sloboda et al., 2012; Zucker et al., 2008). Due to the complexity of neural, biological, psychological, and social aspects of adolescent development, multidisciplinary collaborations between neuroscientists, psychologists, sociologists, and other related disciplines will likely prove most productive in giving us a truer view of substance use etiology during adolescence. Developmental science has long advocated such multilevel approaches, and it provides a needed developmental framework for a multilevel approach (e.g., Cairns, 2000). Such multilevel developmental approaches can be especially useful to gain a better understanding of which multilevel configurations of developmentally distal and proximal risk factors differentiate more experimental use from more chronic use, keeping the emphasis on common and unique trajectories. And such approaches can help to more fully address pressing questions about the extent to which adolescent substance use and other risky behaviors "matter" in terms of adulthood functioning and adjustment. That is, for whom and under what conditions do the experiences of adolescence matter the most in terms of long-term health and well-being? Imagine the possibilities if we could answer this question, especially regarding the implications for comprehensive interventions and educational and social policies. For us, this is the ultimate benefit of taking a developmental perspective on adolescent substance use.

References

Agrawal, A., Lynskey, M. T., Madden, P. A. F., Bucholz, K. K., & Heath, A. C. (2006). A latent class analysis of illicit drug abuse/dependence: Results from the National Epidemiological Survey on Alcohol and Related Conditions. *Addiction, 102*(1), 94–104.

Allen, J. P., Porter, M. R., McFarland, F. C., Marsh, P., & McElhaney, K. B. (2005). The two faces of adolescents' success with peers: Adolescent popularity, social zadaptation, and deviant behavior. *Child Development, 76*, 747–760.

Arnett, J. J. (2005). The developmental context of substance use in emerging adulthood. *Journal of Drug Issues, 35*, 235–253.

Barber, B. L., Eccles, J. S., & Stone, M. R. (2001). Whatever happened to the jock, the brain, and the princess? Young adult pathways linked to adolescent activity involvement and social identity. *Journal of Adolescent Research, 16*(5), 429–455.

Bauman, K. E., & Ennett, S. T. (1996). On the importance of peer influence for adolescent drug use: Commonly neglected considerations. *Addiction, 91*(2), 185–198.

Bava, S., & Tapert, S. F. (2010). Adolescent brain development and the risk for alcohol and other drug problems. *Neuropsychology Review, 20*(4), 398–413.

Boys, A., Marsden, J., & Strang, J. (2001). Understanding reasons for drug use among young people: A functional perspective. *Health Education Research, 16*, 457–469.

Bronfenbrenner, U. (1979). *The ecology of human development: Experiments by nature and design.* Cambridge, MA: Harvard University Press.

Brown, B. B., & Larson, J. (2009). Peer relationships in adolescence. In R. M. Lerner & L. Steinberg (Eds.), *Handbook of adolescent psychology* (3rd ed., pp. 74–103). Hoboken, NJ: Wiley.

Brown, E. C., Catalano, R. F., Fleming, C. B., Haggerty, K. P., & Abbott, R. D. (2005). Adolescent substance use outcomes in the raising healthy children project: A two-part latent growth curve analysis. *Journal of Consulting and Clinical Psychology, 73*, 699–710.

Brown, S. A., McGue, M., Maggs, J. L., Schulenberg, J. E., Hingson, R., Swartzwelder, S., . . . Murphy, S. (2008). A developmental perspective on alcohol and youths 16 to 20 years of age. *Pediatrics, 121*, S290–S310.

Bryant, A., Schulenberg, J., O'Malley, P. M., Bachman, J. G., & Johnston, L. D. (2003). How academic achievement, attitudes, and behaviors relate to the course of substance use during adolescence: A six-year multi-wave national longitudinal study. *Journal of Research on Adolescence, 13*, 361–397.

Burk, L. R., Armstrong, J. M., Goldsmith, H. H., Klein, M. H., Strauman, T. J., Costanzo, P., & Essex, M. J. (2011).

Sex, temperament, and family context: How the interaction of early factors differentially predict adolescent alcohol use and are mediated by proximal adolescent factors. *Psychology of Addictive Behaviors, 25*(1), 1–15.

Cairns, R. B. (2000). Developmental science: Three audacious implications. In L. R. Bergman, R. B. Cairns, L-G. Nilsson, & L. Nystedt (Eds.), *Developmental science and the holistic approach* (pp. 49–62). Mahwah, NJ: Erlbaum.

Capaldi, D. M., Stoolmiller, M., Kim, H. K., & Yoerger, K. (2009). Growth in alcohol use in at-risk adolescent boys: Two-part random effects prediction models. *Drug and Alcohol Dependence, 105*, 109–117.

Casey, B. J, & Jones, R. M. (2010). Neurobiology of the adolescent brain and behavior: Implications for substance use disorders. *Journal of American Academy of Child and Adolescent Psychiatry, 49*(12), 1189–1201.

Caspi, A. (2000). The child is father of the man: Personality continuities from childhood to adulthood. *Journal of Personality and Social Psychology, 78*, 158–172.

Chassin, L., Pitts, S. C., & Prost, J. (2002). Binge drinking trajectories from adolescence to emerging adulthood in a high-risk sample: Predictors and substance abuse outcomes. *Journal of Consulting and Clinical Psychology, 70*(1), 67–78.

Chassin, L., Presson, C. C., & Sherman, S. J. (1989). "Constructive" vs. "destructive" deviance in adolescent health-related behaviors. *Journal of Youth and Adolescence, 18*, 245–262.

Cicchetti, D., & Dawson, G. (2002). Multiple levels of analysis. *Development and Psychopathology, 14*(3), 417–420.

Cicchetti, D., & Rogosch, F. A. (1996). Equifinality and multifinality in developmental psychopathology. *Development and Psychopathology, 8*(4), 597–600.

Cicchetti, D., & Rogosch, F. A. (2002). A developmental psychopathology perspective on adolescence. *Journal of Consulting and Clinical Psychology, 70*, 6–20.

Coleman, J. C. (1989). The focal theory of adolescence: A psychological perspective. In K. Hurrelmann & U. Engel (Eds.), *The social world of adolescents: International perspectives* (pp. 43–56). New York, NY: Walter de Gruyter.

Compton, W. M., Thomas, Y., Conway, K. P., & Colliver, J. D. (2005). Developments in the epidemiology of drug use and drug use disorders. *American Journal of Psychiatry, 162*(8), 1494–502.

Connell, C., Gilreath, T., & Hansen, N. (2009). A multiprocess latent class analysis of the co-occurrence of substance use and sexual risk behavior among adolescents. *Journal of Studies on Alcohol and Drugs, 70*, 943–951.

Cooper, M. L. (1994). Motivations for alcohol use among adolescents: Development and validation of a four-factor model. *Psychological Assessment, 6*, 117–128.

Cote, J. E. (2009). Identity formation and self development in adolescence. In R. M. Lerner & L. Steinberg (Eds.), *Handbook of adolescent psychology* (3rd ed., pp. 266–304). Hoboken, NJ: Wiley.

Cox, W. M., & Klinger, E. (1988). A motivational model of alcohol use. *Journal of Abnormal Psychology, 97*, 168–180.

Crone, E. A., & Dahl, R. E. (2012). Understanding adolescence as a period of social-affective engagement and goal flexibility. *Nature Reviews Neuroscience, 13*, 636–650.

Crosnoe R. (2011). *Fitting in, standing out: Navigating the social challenges of high school to get an education.* New York, NY: Cambridge University Press.

D'Amico, E. J., & McCarthy, D. M. (2006). Escalation and initiation of younger adolescents' substance use: The impact of perceived peer use. *Journal of Adolescent Health, 39*(4), 481–487.

D'Amico, E. J., Metrik, J., McCarthy, D. M., Frissell, K. C., Appelbaum, M., & Brown, S. A. (2001). Progression into and out of binge drinking among high school students. *Psychology of Addictive Behaviors, 15*(4), 341–349.

Dannefer, D. (1987). Aging as intracohort differentiation: Accentuation, the Matthew effect, and the life course. *Sociological Forum, 2*, 211–236.

Dever, B. V., Schulenberg, J. E., Dworkin, J. B., O'Malley, P. M., Kloska, D. D., & Bachman, J. G. (2012). Predicting risk-taking with and without substance use: The effects of parental monitoring, school bonding, and sports participation. *Prevention Science, 13*(6), 605–615.

Dishion, T. J., & Owen, L. D. (2002). A longitudinal analysis of friendships and substance use: Bidirectional influence from adolescence to adulthood. *Developmental Psychology, 38*(4), 480.

Dodge, K. A., Malone, P. S., Lansford, J. E. Miller, S., Pettit, G. S., & Bates, J. E. (2009). A dynamic cascade model of the development of substance use onset. *Monographs of the Society for Research in Child Development, 74*(3), 1–120.

Donovan, J. E. (2004). Adolescent alcohol initiation: A review of psychosocial risk factors. *Journal of Adolescent Health, 35*, 7–18.

Duncan, B., & Rees, D. I. (2005). Effect of smoking on depressive symptomatology: A reexamination of data from the National Longitudinal Study of Adolescent Health. *American Journal of Epidemiology, 162*(5), 461–470.

Eccles, J. S., & Roeser, R. W. (2009). Schools, academic motivation, and stage-environment fit. In R. M. Lerner & L. Steinberg (Eds.), *Handbook of adolescent psychology* (3rd ed., pp. 404–434). Hoboken, NJ: Wiley.

Elder, G. H., Jr., & Shanahan, M. J. (2006). The life course and human development. In W. Damon & R. M. Lerner (Series Eds.), R. M. Lerner (Vol. Ed.),. *Handbook of child psychology, Vol. 1. Theoretical models of human development* (6th ed., pp. 665–715). Hoboken, NJ: Wiley.

Erikson, E. H. (1968). *Identity: Youth and crisis.* New York, NY: Norton.

Fergus, S., & Zimmerman, M. A. (2005). Adolescent resilience: A framework for understanding healthy development in the face of risk. *Annual Review of Public Health, 26*(1), 399–419.

Fergusson, D. M., Boden, J. M., & Horwood, L. J. (2009). Tests of causal links between alcohol abuse or dependence and major depression. *Archives of General Psychiatry, 66*(3), 260–266.

Gorka, S. M., Shankman, S. A., Seeley, J. R., & Lewinsohn, P. M. (2013). The moderating effect of parental illicit substance use disorders on the relation between adolescent depression and subsequent illicit substance use disorders. *Drug and Alcohol Dependence, 128*(1–2), 1–7.

Grant, B. F., & Dawson, D. A. (1997). Age at onset of alcohol use and its association with DSM-IV alcohol abuse and dependence: Results from the National Longitudinal Alcohol Epidemiologic Survey. *Journal of Substance Abuse, 9*, 103–110.

Grant, J. D., Heath, A. C., Bucholz, K. K., Madden, P. A. F., Agrawal, A., Statham, D. J., & Martin, N. G. (2007). Spousal concordance for alcohol dependence: Evidence for assortative mating or spousal interaction effects? *Alcoholism, Clinical and Experimental Research, 31*(5), 717–728.

Guo, J., Collins, L. M., Hill, K. G., & Hawkins, J. D. (2000). Developmental pathways to alcohol abuse and dependence in young adulthood. *Journal of Studies on Alcohol, 61*, 799–808.

Gutman, L. M., Sameroff, A. J., & Cole, R. (2003). Academic growth curve trajectories from 1st grade to 12th grade: Effects of multiple social risk factors and preschool child factors. *Developmental Psychology, 39*, 777–790.

Havighurst, R. (1952). *Developmental tasks and education.* New York, NY: McKay.

Hawkins, J. D., Catalano, R. F., & Miller, J. Y. (1992). Risk and protective factors for alcohol and other drug problems in adolescence and early adulthood: Implications for substance abuse prevention. *Psychological Bulletin, 112*, 64–105.

Heckhausen, J. (1999). *Developmental regulation in adulthood: Age-normative and sociostructural constraints as adaptive challenges.* New York, NY: Cambridge University Press.

Hibell, B., Gufformsson, U., Ahlström, S., Balakireva, O., Bjarnasson, T., Kokkevi, A., & Kraua, L. (2012). *The 2011 ESPAD report (The European School Survey Project on Alcohol and Other Drugs): Substance use among students in 36 European countries.* Stockholm, Sweden: The Swedish Council for Information on Alcohol and Other Drugs, The European Monitoring Centre for Drugs and Drug Addiction, the Council of Europe, and the Co-operation Group to Combat Drug Abuse and Illicit Trafficking in Drugs.

Hill, K. G., White, H. R., Chung, I. J., Hawkins, J. D., & Catalano, R. F. (2000). Early adult outcomes of adolescent binge drinking: Person- and variable-centered analyses of binge drinking trajectories. *Alcoholism, Clinical and Experimental Research, 24*(6), 892–901.

Jackson, K. M., & Schulenberg, J. E. (2013). Alcohol use during the transition from middle school to high school: National panel data on prevalence and moderators. *Developmental Psychology, 49*(11), 2147–2158.

Jackson, K. M., Sher, K. J., & Schulenberg, J. E. (2008). Conjoint developmental trajectories of young adult substance use. *Alcoholism: Clinical and Experimental Research, 32*(5), 723–737.

Jager, J., Schulenberg, J. E., O'Malley, P. M., & Bachman, J. G. (2013). Historical variation in rates of change in substance use across the transition to adulthood: The trend towards lower intercepts and steeper slopes. *Development and Psychopathology, 25*(2), 527–543.

Jessor, R. (1987). Problem-behavior theory, psychosocial development, and adolescent problem drinking. *British Journal of Addiction, 82*, 331–342.

Johnston, L. D., O'Malley, P. M., Bachman, J. G., Schulenberg, J. E. & Miech, R. A. (2015). *Monitoring the Future national survey results on drug use, 1975–2014: Vol 2, College students and adults ages 19–55.* Ann Arbor: Institute for Social Research, University of Michigan.

Jones, R. M., & Hartmann, B. R. (1988). Ego identity: Developmental differences and experimental substance use among adolescents. *Journal of Adolescence, 11*(4), 347–360.

Kagan, J. (1969). The three faces of continuity in human development. In D. A. Goslin (Ed.), *Handbook of socialization theory and research* (pp. 983–1002). Chicago, IL: Rand McNally.

Kagan, J. (1980). Perspectives on continuity. In O. G. Brim, Jr., & J. Kagan (Eds.), *Constancy and change in human development* (pp. 26–74). Cambridge, MA: Harvard University Press.

Kandel, D. B. (1985). On processes of peer influences in adolescent drug use: A developmental perspective. *Advances in Alcohol and Substance Abuse, 4*, 139–163.

Kellam, S. G., & Anthony, J. C. (1998). Targeting early antecedents to prevent tobacco smoking: Findings from an epidemiologically based randomized field trial. *American Journal of Public Health, 88*(10), 1490–1495.

Keyes, K. M., Schulenberg, J. E., O'Malley, P. M., Johnston, L. D., Bachman, J. G., Li, G., & Hasin, D. (2011). The social norms of birth cohorts and adolescent marijuana use in the United States, 1976-2007. *Addiction, 10*, 1790–1800. doi:10.1111/j.1360-0443.2011.03485.x. PMC3174352

Keyes, K. M., Schulenberg, J. E., O'Malley, P. M., Johnston, L. D., Bachman, J. G., Li, G., & Hasin, D. (2012). Birth cohort effects on adolescent alcohol use: The influence of social norms from 1976–2007. *Archives of General Psychiatry, 69(12),* 1304–1313.

King, K. M., & Chassin, L. (2007). A prospective study of the effects of age of initiation of alcohol and drug use on young adult substance dependence. *Journal of Studies on Alcohol, 68*, 256–265.

Kuntsche, E., Knibbe, R., Gmel, G., & Engels, R. (2005). Why do young people drink? A review of drinking motives. *Clinical Psychology Review, 25*, 841–861.

La Greca, A. M., Prinstein, M. J., & Fetter, M. D. (2001). Adolescent peer crowd affiliation: Linkages with health-risk behaviors and close friendships. *Journal of Pediatric Psychology, 26*(3), 131–143.

Lerner, R. M. (2006). Developmental science, developmental systems, and contemporary theories of human development. In W. Damon & R. M. Lerner (Series Eds.), R. M. Lerner (Vol. Ed.), *Handbook of child psychology, Vol. 1. Theoretical models of human development* (6th ed., pp. 1–17). Hoboken, NJ: Wiley.

Lewis, M. (1999). Contextualism and the issue of continuity. *Infant Behavior and Development, 22*, 431–444.

Liben, L. S. (2008). Continuities and discontinuities in children and scholarship. *Child Development, 79*(6), 1600–1605.

Lynne-Landsman, S. D., Bradshaw, C. P., & Ialongo, N. S. (2010). Testing a developmental cascade model of adolescent substance use trajectories and young adult adjustment. *Development and Psychopathology, 22*(4), 933–948.

Lynskey, M. T., Heath, A. C., Bucholz, K. K., Slutske, W. S., Madden, P. A. F., Nelson, E. C., . . . Martin, N. G. (2003). Escalation of drug use in early-onset cannabis users vs co-twin controls. *Journal of the American Medical Association, 289*(4), 427–433.

Maggs, J. L., & Schulenberg, J. E. (2005). Trajectories of alcohol use during the transition to adulthood. *Alcohol Research and Health, 28*, 195–211.

Maggs, J., Schulenberg, J., & Hurrelmann, K. (1997). Developmental transitions during adolescence: Health promotion implications. In J. Schulenberg, J. Maggs, & K. Hurrelmann (Eds.), *Health risks and developmental transitions during adolescence* (pp. 522–546). New York, NY: Cambridge University Press.

Maggs, J. L., Staff, J., Kloska, D. D., Patrick, M. E., O'Malley, P. M., & Schulenberg, J. E. (2015). Predicting young adult degree attainment by late adolescent marijuana use.

Journal of Adolescent Health, 57(2), 205–211. doi:10.1016/j.jadohealth.2015.04.028. PMC4514914

Marcia, J. (1994). Identity and psychotherapy. In S. L. Archer (Ed.), *Interventions for adolescent identity development* (pp. 29–46). Thousand Oaks, CA: Sage.

Martin, P., & Martin, M. (2002). Proximal and distal influences on development: The model of developmental adaptation. *Developmental Review, 22*, 78–96.

Maslowsky, J., & Schulenberg, J. E. (2013). Interaction matters: Quantifying conduct problem x depressive symptoms interaction and its association with adolescent alcohol, cigarette, and marijuana use in a national sample. *Development and Psychopathology, 25*(4), 1029–1043.

Maslowsky, J., Schulenberg, J. E., O'Malley, P. M., & Kloska, D. D. (2013). Depressive symptoms, conduct problems, and risk for polysubstance use among adolescents: Results from US national surveys. *Mental Health and Substance Use, 7*(2), 157–169.

Maslowsky, J., Schulenberg, J., & Zucker, R. A. (2014). Influence of conduct problems and depressive symptomatology on adolescent substance use: Developmentally proximal versus distal effects. *Developmental Psychology, 50*, 1179–1189.

Masten, A. S. (2001). Ordinary magic: Resilience processes in development. *American Psychologist, 56*, 227–238.

Masten, A. S., Faden, V. B., Zucker, R. A., & Spear, L. P. (2008). Underage drinking: A developmental framework. *Pediatrics, 121*, S235–S251.

Moffitt, T. E. (1993). Adolescence-limited and life-course-persistent antisocial behavior: A developmental taxonomy. *Psychological Review, 100*(4), 674–701.

Moffitt, T. E., & Caspi, A. (2001). Childhood predictors differentiate life-course persistent and adolescent-limited antisocial pathways among males and females. *Development and Psychopathology, 13*, 355–375.

Newcomb, M., & Bentler, P. (1988). Impact of adolescent drug use and social support on problems of young adults: A longitudinal study. *Journal of Abnormal Psychology, 97*, 64–75.

Newcomb, M. D., & Bentler, P. M. (1989). Substance use and abuse among children and teenagers. *American Psychologist, 44*(2), 242.

Newcomb, M. D., Scheier, L. M., & Bentler, P. M. (1993). Effects of adolescent drug use on adult mental health: A prospective study of a community sample. *Experimental and Clinical Psychopharmacology, 1*(1–4), 215–241.

Osgood, D. W., Wilson, J. K., O'Malley, P. M., Bachman, J. G., & Johnston, L. D. (1996). Routine activities and individual deviant behaviors. *American Sociological Review, 61*, 635–655.

Patrick, M. E., & Schulenberg, J. E. (2010). Alcohol use and heavy episodic drinking prevalence and predictors among national samples of American 8th and 10th grade students. *Journal of Studies on Alcohol and Drugs, 71*, 41–45.

Patrick, M. E., & Schulenberg, J. E. (2011). How trajectories of reasons for alcohol use relate to trajectories of binge drinking: National panel data spanning late adolescence to early adulthood. *Developmental Psychology, 47*, 311–317.

Patrick, M. E., & Schulenberg, J. E. (2013). Prevalence and predictors of adolescent alcohol use and binge drinking in the United States. *Alcohol Research: Current Reviews, 35*(2), 193–200.

Patrick, M. E., Schulenberg, J. E., Maggs, J. L., & Maslowsky, J. (2014). Substance use and peers during adolescence and the transition to adulthood: Selection, socialization, and development. In K. Sher (Ed.), *The Oxford handbook of* substance use disorders, Volume 1. New York: Oxford University Press. doi:10.1093/oxfordhb/9780199381678.013.004

Patrick, M. E., Schulenberg, J. E., O'Malley, P. M., Johnston, L., & Bachman, J. (2011). Adolescents' reported reasons for alcohol and marijuana use as predictors of substance use and problems in adulthood. *Journal of Studies on Alcohol and Drugs, 72,* 106–116.

Patrick, M. E., Schulenberg, J. E., O'Malley, P. M., Maggs, J. L., Kloska, D. D., Johnston, L., & Bachman, J. (2011). Age-related changes in reasons for using alcohol and marijuana from ages 18 to 30 in a national sample. *Psychology of Addictive Behaviors, 25,* 330–339.

Pfeifer, J. H., & Allen, N. (2012). Arrested development? Reconsidering dual-systems models of brain function in adolescence and disorders. *Trends in Cognitive Sciences, 16*(6), 322–329.

Reese, H. W., & Overton, W. F. (1970). Models of development and theories of development. In L. R. Goulet & P. B. Baltes (Eds.), *Life-span developmental psychology: Research and theory* (pp. 116–145). New York, NY: Academic Press.

Ronka, A., Oravala, S., & Pulkkinen, L. (2002). "I met this wife of mine and things got on a better track:" Turning points in risk development. *Journal of Adolescence, 25,* 47–63.

Rutter, M. (1996). Transitions and turning points in developmental psychopathology: As applied to the age span between childhood and mid-adulthood. *International Journal of Behavioral Development, 19,* 603–626.

Rutter, M., & Garmezy, N. (1983). Developmental psychopathology. In P. H. Mussen & E. M. Hetherington (Eds.), *Handbook of child psychology, Vol. 4. Socialization, personality and social development* (pp. 775–911). New York, NY: Wiley.

Sameroff, A. (2010). A unified theory of development: A dialectic integration of nature and nurture. *Child Development, 81,* 6–22.

Schulenberg, J., & Maggs, J. L. (2001). Moving targets: Modeling developmental trajectories of adolescent alcohol misuse, individual and peer risk factors, and intervention effects. *Applied Developmental Science, 5,* 237–253.

Schulenberg, J. E., & Maggs, J. L. (2002). A developmental perspective on alcohol use and heavy drinking during adolescence and the transition to young adulthood. *Journal of Studies on Alcohol Supplement, 14,* 54–70.

Schulenberg, J. E., Maggs, J. L., & O'Malley, P. M. (2003). How and why the understanding of developmental continuity and discontinuity is important: The sample case of long-term consequences of adolescent substance use. In J. T. Mortimer & M. J. Shanahan (Eds.), *Handbook of the life course* (pp. 413–436). New York, NY: Plenum.

Schulenberg, J., Maggs, J. L., Steinman, K., & Zucker, R. A. (2001). Development matters: Taking the long view on substance abuse etiology and intervention during adolescence. In P. M. Monti, S. M. Colby, & T. A. O'Leary (Eds.), *Adolescents, alcohol, and substance abuse: Reaching teens through brief intervention* (pp. 19–57). New York, NY: Guilford Press.

Schulenberg, J. E., & Maslowsky, J. (2009). Taking substance use and development seriously: Developmentally distal and proximal influences on adolescent drug use. *Monographs of the Society for Research in Child Development, 74,* 121–130.

Schulenberg, J. E., & Patrick, M. E. (2012). Historical and developmental patterns of alcohol and drug use among college students: Framing the problem. In H. R. White & D. Rabiner (Eds.), *College drinking and drug use* (pp. 13–35). New York, NY: Guilford Press.

Schulenberg, J. E., Patrick, M. E., Maslowsky, J., & Maggs, J. L. (2014). The epidemiology and etiology of adolescent substance use in developmental perspective. In M. Lewis & K. Rudolph (Eds.), *Handbook of developmental psychopathology* (3rd ed., pp. 601–620). New York, NY: Springer.

Schulenberg, J. E., Sameroff, A. J., & Cicchetti, D. (2004). Editorial: The transition to adulthood as a critical juncture in the course of psychopathology and mental health. *Development and Psychopathology, 16,* 799–806.

Schulenberg, J. E., Wadsworth, K. N., O'Malley, P. M., Bachman, J. G., & Johnston, L. D. (1996). Adolescent risk factors for binge drinking during the transition to young adulthood: Variable- and pattern-centered approaches to change. *Developmental Psychology, 32,* 659–674.

Schulenberg, J. E., & Zarrett, N. R. (2006). Mental health during emerging adulthood: Continuity and discontinuity in courses, causes, and functions. In J. J. Arnett & J. L. Tanner (Eds.), *Emerging adults in America: Coming of age in the 21st century* (pp. 135–172). Washington, DC: American Psychological Association.

Squeglia, L. M., Jacobus, J., & Tapert, S. F. (2009). The influence of substance use on adolescent brain development. *Clinical EEG and Neuroscience, 40*(1), 31–38.

Sisk, C. L., & Zehr, J. L. (2005). Pubertal hormones organize the adolescent brain and behavior. *Frontiers in Neuroendocrinology, 26*(3), 163–174.

Sloboda, Z., Glantz, M. D., & Tarter, R. E. (2012). Revisiting the concepts of risk and protective factors for understanding the etiology and development of substance use and substance use disorders: implications for prevention. *Substance Use and Misuse, 47*(8–9), 944–962.

Spear, L. P. (2000). The adolescent brain and age-related behavior manifestations. *Neuroscience and Biobehavioral Reviews, 24,* 417–463.

Spoth, R., Trudeau, L., Guyll, M., Shin, C., & Redmond, C. (2009). Universal intervention effects on substance use among young adults mediated by delayed adolescent substance initiation. *Journal of Consulting and Clinical Psychology, 77*(4), 620–632.

Steinberg, L., Albert, D., Cauffman, E., Banich, M., Graham, S., & Woolard, J. (2008). Age differences in sensation seeking and impulsivity as indexed by behavior and self-report: Evidence for a dual systems model. *Developmental Psychology, 44,* 1764–1778.

Steinberg, L., Dahl, R., Keating, D., Kupfer, D. J., Masten, A. S., & Pine, D. S. (2006). Psychopathology in adolescence: Integrating affective neuroscience with the study of context. In D. Cicchetti & D. Cohen (Eds.), *Developmental psychopathology, Vol. 2. Developmental neuroscience* (2nd ed., pp. 710–741). New York, NY: Wiley.

Stenbacka, M. (2003). Problematic alcohol and cannabis use in adolescence—risk of serious adult substance abuse? *Drug and Alcohol Review, 22*(3), 277.

Susman, E. J., & Dorn, L. D. (2009). Puberty: Its role in development. In R. M. Lerner & L. Steinberg (Eds.), *Handbook of adolescent psychology* (3rd ed., pp. 116–151). Hoboken, NJ: Wiley.

Sussman, S., Pokhrel, P., Ashmore, R. D., & Brown, B. B. (2007). Adolescent peer group identification and characteristics: A review of the literature. *Addictive Behaviors, 32*(8), 1602–1627.

Tarter, R. E. (2010). Etiology of adolescent substance abuse: A developmental perspective. *American Journal on Addictions, 11*(3), 171–191.

Tomasik, M. J., & Silbereisen, R. K. (2012). Social change and adolescent developmental tasks: The case of postcommunist Europe. *Child Development Perspectives, 6*, 326–334.

Wagner, F. A., & Anthony, J. C. (2002). From first drug use to drug dependence: Developmental periods of risk for dependence upon marijuana, cocaine, and alcohol. *Neuropsychopharmacology, 26*(4), 479–488.

Walters, G. D. (2011). The latent structure of life-course-persistent antisocial behavior: Is Moffitt's developmental taxonomy a true taxonomy? *Journal of Consulting and Clinical Psychology, 79*(1), 96–105.

Werner, H. (1957). The concept of development from a comparative and organismic point of view. In D. B. Harris (Ed.), *The concept of development: An issue in the study of human behavior* (pp. 125–148). Minneapolis: University of Minnesota Press.

Wigfield, A., Eccles, J. S., Mac Iver, D., Reuman, D. A., & Midgley, C. (1991). Transitions during early adolescence: Changes in children's domain-specific self-perceptions and general self-esteem across the transition to junior high school. *Developmental Psychology, 27*, 552–565.

Windle, M. (2000). Parental, sibling, and peer influences on adolescent substance use and alcohol problems. *Applied Developmental Science, 4*(2), 98–110.

Windle, M., Spear, L. P., Fuligni, A. J., Angold, A., Brown, J. D., Pine, D., . . . Dahl, R. E. (2008). Transitions into underage and problem drinking: Developmental processes and mechanisms between 10 and 15 years of age. *Pediatrics, 121*, S273–S289.

Wood, M. D., Fairlie, A. M., Fernandez, A. C., Borsari, B., Capone, C., Laforge, R., & Carmona-Barros, R. (2010). Brief motivational and parent interventions for college students: A randomized factorial study. *Journal of Consulting and Clinical Psychology, 78*, 349–361.

Wu, L., Pilowsky, D., & Schlenger, W. (2005). High prevalence of substance use disorders among adolescents who use marijuana and inhalants. *Drug and Alcohol Dependence, 78*, 23–32.

Zucker, R. A. (1994). Pathways to alcohol problems and alcoholism: A developmental account of the evidence for multiple alcoholisms and for contextual contributions to risk. In R. A. Zucker, J. Howard, & G. M. Boyd (Eds.), *The development of alcohol problems: Exploring the biopsychosocial matrix of risk* (pp. 255–289). Rockville, MD: National Institute on Alcohol Abuse and Alcoholism.

Zucker, R. A., Donovan, J. E., Masten, A. S., Mattson, M. E., & Moss, H. B. (2008). Early developmental processes and the continuity of risk for underage drinking and problem drinking. *Pediatrics, 121*(Suppl. 4), S252–S272.

A Developmental Perspective on Substance Involvement From Adolescence to Emerging Adulthood

Kristina M. Jackson

Abstract

Substance use is a developmental disorder, with clear age-graded trends reflecting initiation in adolescence, increased use through emerging adulthood, and a decline thereafter. A developmental framework places substance use behavior both within the context of normal development and in relation to the interplay between environmental and person-specific characteristics, where underlying risk may manifest as a substance use problem in the face of an enabling environment. Individuals have changing vulnerabilities to substance use and related problems that are due to chronological aging as well as attributable to the normative developmental tasks and role transitions that may serve as a turning point directing an individual toward or away from substance use. Against the backdrop of normative patterns are distinct developmental trajectories that are likely linked to different etiological pathways and that, through valid testing of developmental theory, can inform the content and timing of prevention programs targeted to reach high-risk subgroups.

Key Words: developmental, substance use, course, initiation, progression

Alcohol, tobacco, and illicit drug use and related adverse consequences remain a substantial public health problem. Alcohol consumption is the third leading cause of death in the United States (Mokdad, Marks, Stroup, & Gerberding, 2004), and tobacco use remains the chief preventable cause of illness and death in our society (Centers for Disease Control and Prevention [CDC], 2009). Tobacco use is responsible for nearly half a million deaths annually, including at least 30% of all cancer deaths, most deaths from chronic obstructive pulmonary disease (COPD), and early cardiovascular disease and deaths (CDC, 2009) and the impact of cigarette smoking and other tobacco use on chronic disease accounts for 75% of American spending on health care (Anderson, 2010). Both substances are associated with economic losses to society and are responsible for a substantial burden on the US medical and mental health care systems and are

responsible each year for millions of years of potential life lost, in part because of the impact upon the very young (Bouchery, Harwood, Sacks, Simon, & Brewer, 2011; CDC, 2009). In addition, in 2007, the most recent year for which data are available, the cost of illicit drug use totaled more than $193 billion (National Drug Intelligence Center, 2011).

Early substance use is highly associated with a host of short- and long-term adverse outcomes. Early onset of alcohol use is associated with higher rates of depression (Buydens-Branchey, Branchey, & Noumair, 1989), risky sexual behaviors (Stueve & O'Donnell, 2005), and lower school achievement (McGue, Iacono, Legrand, Malone, & Elkins, 2001a). Alcohol use contributes to the three leading causes of death among underage drinkers, unintentional injury (Hingson, Heeren, Jamanka, & Howland, 2000), violence (Hingson, Heeren, & Zakocs, 2001; Swahn, Bossarte, & Sullivent, 2008), and suicidality (Cho, Hallfors, & Iritani, 2007; Swahn et al., 2008; Swahn & Bossarte, 2007), in part due to the highly opportunistic nature of underage drinking characterized by infrequent yet heavy use. Early alcohol consumption is particularly concerning, as alcohol use has acute and prolonged neurobiological effects specific to the adolescent brain (Brown, Tapert, Granholm, & Delis, 2000; Monti et al. 2005).

Alcohol affects the developing brain structures that regulate behavior (Clark, Thatcher, & Tapert, 2008), and research in neuroscience supports adolescence as a vulnerable period for exposure to addictive substances (Chambers, Taylor, & Potenza, 2003; Crews, He, & Hodge 2007; Nixon & McClain, 2010). Thus, substance use–related risk may operate through the effects of alcohol on neurocognitive functioning (Squeglia, Spadoni, Infante, Myers, & Tapert, 2009; Tapert & Brown, 1999) and brain structure and function (Tapert et al., 2004).

Half of all long-term regular smokers who begin smoking during adolescence die prematurely from tobacco-related diseases, with the greatest risk for those who start smoking regularly when teenagers (Fagerström, 2002). Early cigarette smoking is associated with lung cancer, respiratory diseases such as COPD, and early-onset cardiovascular disease in adulthood (Fagerström, 2002; Gold et al., 1996; US Department of Health and Human Services [USDHHS], 2012). Smoking in adolescence and young adulthood is associated with reduced lung function and impaired lung growth as well as asthma during childhood and adolescence (Gold et al., 1996; USDHHS, 2012). In addition, it is associated in the short term with less physical fitness and overall diminished physical health (USDHHS, 2012).

Marijuana is the most commonly used illicit drug in the United States, and it is associated with a multitude of adverse outcomes (Budney, Moore, & Vandrey, 2008; Hall & Degenhardt, 2009). Early marijuana use is associated with involvement in crime (Fergusson, Horwood, & Swain-Campbell, 2002) and with poor academic achievement and low, socioeconomic status (Green & Ensminger, 2006; Horwood et al., 2010; Fergusson & Boden, 2008). Early-onset marijuana users also are more likely than late or never users to experience psychiatric problems such as depression and anxiety (D. Brook, J. Brook, Zhang, Cohen, & Whiteman, 2002; Fairman & Anthony, 2012; Fergusson et al., 2002), to develop psychotic illness (Arseneault,

Cannon, Witton, & Murray, 2004; Moore, Zammit, & Lingford-Hughes, 2007), and to have subsequent neuropsychological deficits (Gruber, Sagar, Dahlgren, Racine, & Lukas, 2012). The early use of illicit substances other than marijuana also is associated with adverse long-term outcomes such as diminished overall health for stimulant use (Garrity et al., 2007).

Many of these associations between adverse outcomes and early alcohol, tobacco, and illicit drug use hold when controlling for demographic factors, personal and family history of substance involvement, and normative influences. Some research, however, suggests the association between early-onset substance use may be a manifestation of general vulnerability to behavioral deviance (e.g., King & Chassin, 2007; McGue et al., 2001a, 2001b; Prescott & Kendler, 1999), and there is still debate regarding whether these associations are causal, as opposed to a marker of early-onset problem behaviors.

Substance use in general during adolescence also can interfere with normative developmental tasks (Maggs & Schulenberg, 2005; Schulenberg, Maggs, & O'Malley, 2003), and it can impede the development of skills necessary to negotiate the transition to adulthood (Schulenberg & Maggs, 2002). It is also associated with poorer interpersonal communication and conflict resolution skills, possibly serving as a developmental "snare" that hinders the normative desistance in antisocial behavior frequently observed as adolescents develop into young adults (Hussong, Curran, Moffitt, Caspi, & Carrig, 2004; Moffitt, 1993). These concerns combined with the short-term acute harms and long-term chronic health outcomes resulting from the use of alcohol, tobacco, and illicit drugs make it important to examine the course of substance use using a longitudinal, developmental framework.

Epidemiology

The literature consistently supports strong age-graded trends in the use of alcohol, tobacco, and illicit drugs. Adolescence is the peak period of risk for initiation of all substances, with rates rising steadily throughout the adolescent years, generally peaking around age 20–21, and declining thereafter (e.g., Chen & Jacobson, 2012; Chen & Kandel, 1995; Dawson, Grant, Stinson, & Chou, 2004; Jackson, Sher, Cooper, & Wood, 2002; Johnstone, Leino, Ager, Ferrer, & Fillmore, 1996; Wittchen et al., 2008). Substance use shows a strong downward trend in the 20s, with tobacco use tapering off more gradually and marijuana being the most developmentally limited in nature. Smoking may be more persistent because it is most addictive and is relatively compatible with adult daily functioning (Chassin, Presson, Rose, & Sherman, 1996).

Figure 3.1 presents age trends in past-month alcohol (top panel) and illicit drug use (bottom panel) based on 2011–2012 National Survey on Drug Use and Health data (NSDUH; Substance Abuse and Mental Health Services Administration; SAMHSA, 2013a, 2013b). The 2012 data are shown for heavy alcohol use (five or more drinks on the same occasion on each of 5 or more days), "binge" alcohol use (five or more drinks on the same occasion), and current alcohol use, and both 2011 and 2012 data are shown for illicit drug use. Clear age-related trends are noted for both alcohol and drug use, with rapid escalation throughout adolescence and peak prevalence observed in the age group 19–20 for heavy alcohol use (but not current use) and age group 21–25 for illicit drug use.

Although these data are suggestive of age trends in alcohol involvement, prospective data are necessary to rule out age effects that are attributable to birth cohort differences. Prospective data from four waves of the National Longitudinal Survey of Adolescent Health (AddHealth) indicate that drunkenness, smoking, and marijuana use increase in frequency over the course of adolescence and into the early 20s, and decline (drunkenness and marijuana use) or level off (smoking) in young adulthood (Mahalik et al., 2013). Substance use panel data from the 2013 Monitoring the Future survey (MTF; Johnston, O'Malley, Bachman, Schulenberg, & Miech, 2014a) are presented in Figures 3.2–3.6. As shown in Figure 3.2, current (30-day) and annual use of alcohol increase rapidly over late adolescence, peaking around ages 25–26. Figure 3.3 indicates that heavy drinking increases during late adolescence, declines over young adulthood, and levels off by the fourth decade of life. In contrast, consumption of alcohol on a daily basis increases over this same time interval. Cigarette use (Figure 3.4) shows an annual decline over the life course, but heavy use (daily use, and particularly smoking at least a half-pack of cigarettes per day) increases over adulthood. Annual and current illicit drug use are relatively stable over ages 18–22 years, with a decline through adulthood (Figure 3.5); use of marijuana specifically shows similar trends (Figure 3.6).

Against the backdrop of these normative trends, there is a subset of users who initiate substance use at an early age, with high rates of use observed during early adolescence. Drinking prevalence even among very young adolescents aged 9–12 years ("tweens") is alarmingly high, with 9.8%, 16.1%, and 29.4% of fourth, fifth, and sixth graders, respectively, reporting having tried more than a sip of alcohol (Donovan et al., 2004). Monitoring the Future data from 2013 (Johnston, O'Malley, Bachman, Schulenberg, & Miech, 2014b) indicate that even as early as eighth grade, nearly one third (28%) had ever tried alcohol and 12% had ever been drunk. One quarter (24%) of eighth graders reported current (past-year) alcohol use, and 9% reported being drunk in the past year. One in six (15%) had ever tried cigarettes, and 1 in 22 (4.5%) had already become a current (past-month) smoker. In addition, 17% of eighth graders had tried marijuana (7% in the past month), 11% reported ever trying inhalants, and 4% had ever tried amphetamines.

A recent report by Eaton et al. (2012) summarized results from the 2011 national Youth Risk Behavior Survey (YRBS), which includes data from state and urban school district surveys conducted among students in grades 9–12. Nationwide, 70.8% of students in grades 9–12 had ever drank alcohol (other than a few sips), 38.7% of students reported past 30-day (current) alcohol use, and 21.9% had consumed five or more drinks of alcohol in a row in the past 30 days. In addition, 44.7% of students in grades 9–12 reported ever trying cigarette smoking (even one or two puffs), 10.2% of students ever smoked cigarettes daily, and 18.1% of students had past 30-day (current) smoking. Finally, 39.9% of these students ever used marijuana, with past 30-day use at 23.1%.

Several studies have surveyed the prevalence of youth who reported initiation of substance use at a young age (prior to the teen years). The 2011 YRBS data indicate that nationwide, one fifth of students in grades 9–12 had drunk alcohol for the first time before age 13 years, one out of 10 had smoked a whole cigarette for the first time by age 13, and 8.1% of students had tried marijuana for the first time before age 13 years (Eaton et al., 2012). According to 2013 YRBS data (Kann et al., 2014), 19% of students report lifetime alcohol use (other than a few sips) by age 13; 9% had smoked a whole cigarette for the first time before age 13 years, and 9% reported lifetime marijuana use by age 13. Given the high prevalence at such a young age, it is critical to consider early initiation as well as normative patterns of use when studying changes in substance involvement across the lifespan.

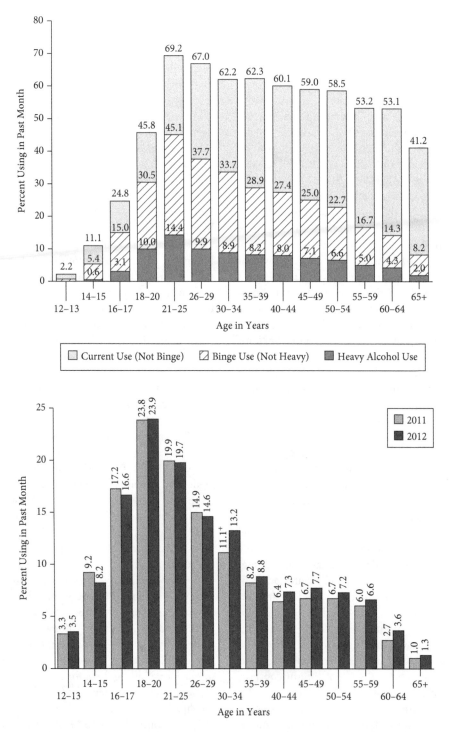

Figure 3.1 Past-month alcohol use (top panel) and illicit drug use (bottom panel) among persons aged 12 or older, by age group, based on data from the National Survey on Drug Use and Health (NSDUH; SAMHSA, 2013a, 2013b). 2012 NSDUH data are shown for alcohol, and 2011 and 2012 data are shown for illicit drug use. For alcohol use, the bar is divided into three sections corresponding to three types of alcohol use: (1) current alcohol use, which does not include binge use or heavy use; (2) binge alcohol use (five or more drinks on the same occasion); and (3) heavy alcohol use (five or more drinks on the same occasion on each of 5 or more days).

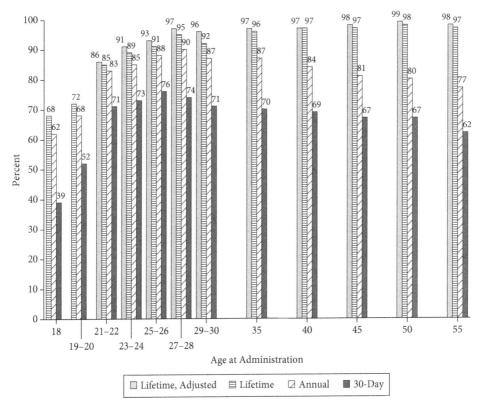

Figure 3.2 Lifetime, annual, and 30-day prevalence of alcohol use among respondents of modal ages 18 through 55, by age group, based on 2013 Monitoring the Future national survey results on drug use, 1975–2013 (Johnston et al., 2014a).

Taking a Developmental Perspective
Chronological Age-Related Development

As shown in the epidemiological data presented earlier, substance use, related problems, and abuse/dependence show clear age-graded patterning, with increases throughout adolescence and a leveling off around the early 20s. Because of these age-related trends, substance abuse has been referred to as a developmental disorder (Sher & Gotham, 1999; Tarter & Vanyukov, 1994). Although development is related to age, it is more than just getting older (Masten, Faden, Zucker, & Spear, 2008). As noted by Zucker (2006), time can be cultural (e.g., changes in availability of alcohol in a given culture, norms about drinking in different age cohorts), social (e.g., changes in roles or relationships at different life stages), or biological (e.g., the "turning on/off" of systems over the course of aging). Age per se is not an explanation for change but rather an index of psychosocial experiences and events, as well as biological maturation and neurocognitive changes, that can lead to substance initiation and problem use (Rutter, 1996; Zucker, 2006).

The peak of substance use coincides with the developmental stage of "emerging adulthood" (Arnett, 2005), the transitional period from high school to young adulthood that is marked by frequent change and exploration, and movement toward the assumption of adult roles and responsibilities. Emerging adulthood has become a distinct period in the life course in industrialized societies, attributable to factors such as a delay in the ages of marriage and parenthood due to extended higher education, the invention of the birth control pill and changing standards of sexual morality, changes in women's roles, and an increased desire for independence and freedom among youth (Arnett, 2005). The developmental changes that take place during emerging adulthood can lead to a rise in substance use because of the increased freedom and the delay of adult responsibilities that allow emerging adults to experiment with different substances. Emerging adults also may use substances as a way of dealing with greater stress or of relieving their identity confusion (Arnett, 2005). Also, the increases that occur in drinking behavior during the early part of emerging adulthood may be due to the freedom to legally

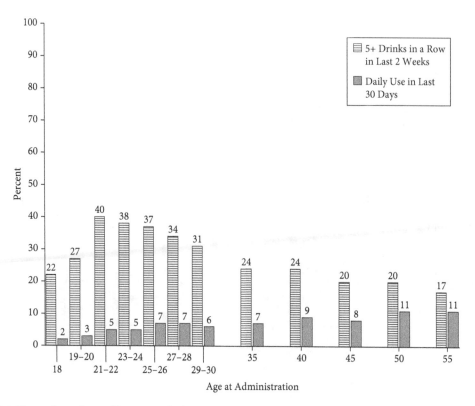

Figure 3.3 Two-week prevalence of five or more drinks in a row and 30-day prevalence of daily alcohol use among respondents of modal ages 18 through 55, by age group, based on 2013 Monitoring the Future national survey results on drug use, 1975–2013 (Johnston et al., 2014a).

purchase alcohol (Bachman, Wadsworth, O'Malley, Johnston, & Schulenberg, 1997), although this would not explain the age-graded trends observed for use of other substances.

The gradual decline following peak substance involvement in emerging adulthood is frequently referred to as "maturing out" (Donovan, Jessor, & Jessor, 1983; Jochman & Fromme, 2010). The processes involved in maturation may explain the decrease in prevalence: Individuals enter into adult roles such as spouse, parent, and employee that are incompatible with drinking (see section on "Developmental Tasks/Transitions"). The normative declines in impulsivity and negative emotionality and the increase in conscientiousness that occur as individuals reach young adulthood also may contribute to the maturing-out effect (Littlefield, Sher, & Wood, 2009; Littlefield, Sher, & Steinley, 2010). In addition, cognitive processing and self-regulation improve significantly at the end of adolescence and early young adulthood (Williams, Ponesse, Schachar, Logan, & Tannock, 1999). Some of the normative decline in high-risk behavior may be due to learning how to deal with these substances and

how to acquire responsible, moderate consumption (Brodbeck, Bachmann, Croudace, & Brown, 2013). Finally, whereas adolescents may partake in substance use as a way to imitate what they perceive to be an adult role (Crosnoe & Riegle-Crumb, 2007), emerging adults may no longer need to rely on engagement in health risk behaviors in order to feel like adults (Mahalik et al., 2013). It is important to note, however, that although the normative desistence in substance use is attributed to maturing out, a recent study using data from the National Epidemiologic Survey on Alcohol and Related Conditions (NESARC) found that most of the decrease in prevalence of alcohol and drug use disorders across the life span appears to be attributable to less onset (decreasing incidence) and lower rates of recurrence, and that rates of persistence were actually relatively stable over the life span (Vergés et al., 2012, 2013).

Stage-Related Development

Substance use itself is developmental in nature, moving across different stages ranging from initiation of use, regular or heavy use, and either

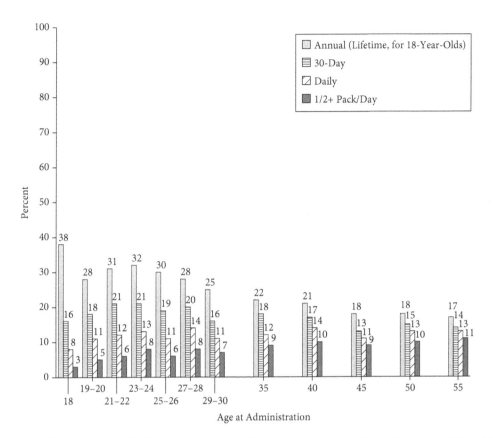

Figure 3.4 Annual, 30-day, daily, and half-pack-a-day prevalence of cigarette use among respondents of modal ages 18 through 55, by age group, based on 2013 Monitoring the Future national survey results on drug use, 1975–2013 (Johnston et al., 2014a).

maintenance or remission/offset. Although stage of drinking and age are associated, they are not synonymous (Colder, Chassin, Lee, & Villalta, 2010). The developmental progression to substance use may begin with relatively minor deviant behaviors and proceed to experimentation with different substances, and for some youth, serious delinquency and drug-related problems and use disorders (Elliott, Huizinga, & Menard, 1989).

Substance use emerges through a series of stages that set an individual on a pathway of use, with the most basic stages being marked by report of any use ("use" versus "nonuse"), on the basis of recency of use (current use, lifetime use), or by degree of use (e.g., light drinking, heavy drinking). For alcohol involvement, a drinking career is marked by milestones which can include first sip, first full drink, first intoxication, first heavy episodic drinking, first alcohol problem, and so on. These milestones are supported by item response theory (IRT) studies showing an ordered progression of alcohol involvement along a severity dimension (Kahler, Strong, Read, Palfai, & Wood, 2004; Krueger et al., 2004).

The idea of "milestones" also has been applied to smoking behaviors. In a study on the natural course of adolescent smoking, Gervais, O'Loughlin, Meshefedjian, Bancej, and Tremblay (2006) studied the ordering of and time to attainment of 12 smoking milestones such as first inhalation, first full cigarette, first regular (monthly/weekly/daily) smoking, and first physical addiction. Findings suggested that nicotine dependence symptoms develop even during experimentation with cigarettes; interestingly, ordering of the milestones did not differ as a function of prior smoking experience.

Stage theory is commonly used in the smoking literature (e.g., Flay, Hu, & Richardson, 1998; Kaufman et al., 2002; Kremers, Mudde, & de Vries, 2004; Leventhal & Cleary, 1980; Lloyd-Richardson, Papandonatos, Kazura, Stanton, & Niaura, 2002; Mayhew, Flay, & Mott, 2000; Novak & Clayton, 2001; Sun, Unger, & Sussman, 2005), with stages characterized by smoking frequency and intensity, for example, nonsmoking, experimentation, and regular/daily smoking. Both Flay et al. (1998) and Lloyd-Richardson et al. (2002) identify

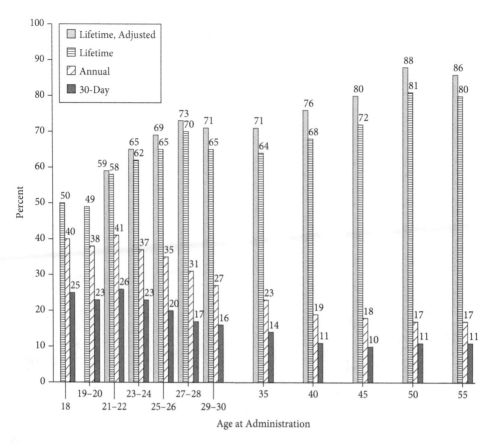

Figure 3.5 Lifetime, annual, and 30-day prevalence of illicit drug use among respondents of modal ages 18 through 55, by age group, based on 2013 Monitoring the Future national survey results on drug use, 1975–2013 (Johnston et al., 2014a).

an intermediate stage between nonsmoker and experimenter, "triers," who report smoking part of a cigarette or one cigarette in their lifetime. In addition, susceptibility to smoking, a proximal indicator of likelihood of future smoking, is featured in some stage-based smoking acquisition models (e.g., Choi, Gilpin, Farkas, & Pierce, 2001; Pierce, Choi, Gilpin, Farkas, & Merritt, 1996).

One stage theory that has received a great deal of attention is that of the gateway theory, which posits that tobacco and alcohol can be considered as gateway substances to heavier drug use (Kandel, 1975). This theory was derived on the basis of findings showing that use of tobacco and alcohol seems to increase the chances of the subsequent use of cannabis, which in turn leads to involvement in other illicit drugs (Kandel, 1975). Many study findings have supported this stage-like temporal progression (Lee & Abdel-Ghany, 2004; Wagner & Anthony, 2002b). Although the typical sequence of alcohol and tobacco initiation followed first by cannabis use and then other illicit drugs is the most

frequently observed sequence, recent studies have demonstrated that the use of licit substances before illicit substances is not universal (Degenhardt et al., 2009; Patton, Coffey, Carlin, Sawyer, & Lynskey, 2005). Suris, Akre, Berchtold, Jeannin, and Michaud (2007) determined that up to one fifth of young cannabis users had never smoked a cigarette. Deviation from the cannabis–hard drug sequence, however, is rare (Fergusson, Boden, & Horwood, 2006; Yamaguchi & Kandel, 1984).

Developmental Tasks/Transitions

Human development involves periods of continuity and orderly change as well as intervals of discontinuity and transformation (Masten et al., 2008). Important life transitions can contribute to "turning points" in behavioral trajectories (Elder & Shanahan, 2006; Rutter, 1996; Schulenberg & Maggs, 2002) and thus are a predictable time of discontinuity (Cicchetti & Rogosch, 2002; Rutter, Kim-Cohen, & Maughan, 2006). The literature provides evidence for an increase in substance use

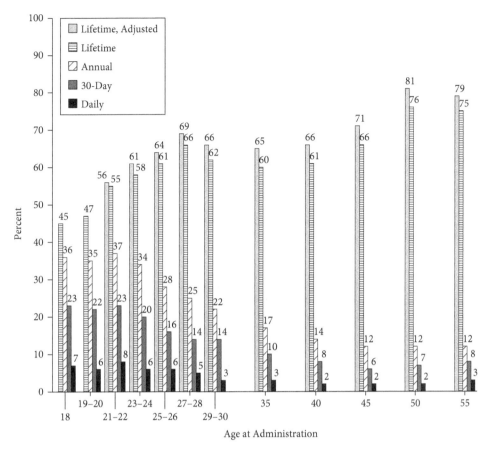

Figure 3.6 Lifetime, annual, and 30-day prevalence of marijuana use among respondents of modal ages 18 through 55, by age group, based on 2013 Monitoring the Future national survey results on drug use, 1975–2013 (Johnston et al., 2014a).

following important transitions which commonly occur in adolescence and emerging adulthood. Youth face significant developmental tasks such as academic performance, establishing autonomy, and assuming adult roles (Steinberg, 1989). Difficulty accomplishing these developmental milestones may negatively affect cognitive and social factors that elicit substance use and related problems.

During adolescence, dropping out of high school (Crum, Ensminger, Ro, & McCord, 1998; Harford, Yi, & Hilton, 2006), paid employment during the school year (Mortimer & Staff, 2004; Safron, Schulenberg, & Bachman, 2001), attaining a driver's license (McCarthy & Brown, 2004), and pubertal development (Dick, Rose, Pulkkinen, & Kaprio, 2001; Tschann et al., 1994) all are important transitions associated with substance use and/or problem behaviors. These may be in part perhaps because of new opportunities for use through affiliation with older peers and greater access to alcohol,

and less monitoring of behavior by parents or other adults.

The period of emerging adulthood is associated with the adoption of new roles and statuses, including completing school, beginning a full-time job, getting married, and starting a family (Macmillan & Eliason, 2003; Oesterle, Hawkins, & Hill, 2011). The normative timing of these social role transitions corresponds to the increases and declines in substance use and misuse during the young adult years (Bachman et al., 1997), perhaps because of lifestyle changes due to new adult responsibilities (Gotham, Sher, & Wood, 2003; Schulenberg & Maggs, 2002). Role incompatibility theory posits that the role of a substance user is incompatible with the acquisition of typical and normative adult roles (Yamaguchi & Kandel, 1984).

Marriage, pregnancy, and parenthood are shown to be associated with reduced alcohol and marijuana use and, to a lesser degree, cigarette smoking during young adulthood (Bachman et al., 1997; Bailey, Hill, Hawkins, Catalano, & Abbott, 2008; Curran, Muthen, & Harford, 1998; Merline, Schulenberg, O'Malley, Bachman, & Johnston, 2008). The transitions of marriage and parenthood are clearly associated with a reduction in alcohol use and problems (Bachman et al., 1997; Curran et al., 1998; Labouvie, 1996; Sadava & Pak, 1994; Yamaguchi, 1990). Lee, Chassin, and MacKinnon (2010) demonstrated role socialization effects of marriage on subsequent declines in heavy drinking that were mediated by decreased involvement in social activities. In addition, marriage or being in a committed relationship appears to be associated with quitting smoking, remaining an ex-smoker, and not adopting smoking (McDermott, Dobson, & Owen, 2009), and establishing stable relationships with romantic partners and becoming a parent are strong predictors of cessation of marijuana use (Chen & Kandel, 1998; Hammer & Vaglum, 1990) as well as decreased persistence, new onset, and recurrence of drug use disorders (Vergés et al., 2013). Merline et al. (2008) showed that whereas the decline in heavy drinking that occurs with entry into marriage accelerates with time, marriage effects level off for smoking and marijuana use. In addition, the evident decreases in substance use appeared to be larger for those who were more frequent users before marriage.

Evidence is conflicting regarding the relationship between workforce entry and alcohol involvement, although workforce entry was associated with decreased postcollege drinking in Gotham, Sher, and Wood (1997). Muthén and Muthén (2000) observed increased alcohol-related problems at age 37 for those who dropped out of high school in contrast to a decline for those who completed high school or college. In addition, Hammer and Vaglum (1990) found that those with a high unemployment rate had a higher probability of continued cannabis use. Arria et al. (2013) showed that heavy substance use impacts on opportunities to secure gainful employment after college, in part because of decreased educational attainment, but this was also true for college attendees.

Kandel (1980) hypothesized that the adoption of adult roles is associated with reduced substance use due to role socialization and role selection. Indeed, research shows support for both; whereas Gotham et al. (2003) concluded that there is greater support for role socialization, in which alcohol involvement interfered with developmental task completion, Merline et al. (2008) found evidence of role

selection in the form of choosing a marital partner (assortative mating). Dawson and colleagues tested for role socialization versus role selection effects on remission from alcohol dependence and found that the associations with certain role transitions, namely completion of school and start of full-time employment, are reflective of role selection, whereas others, including getting married, becoming a parent, and getting divorced, reflect role socialization (Dawson, Grant, Stinson, & Chou, 2006).

Interventionists can take advantage of transitions (e.g., the start of school, adolescence, leaving home, college, marriage, parenthood), as these "unstable systems" offer greater opportunity for change. However, it is important to note that there is a great deal of heterogeneity with regard to the timing and context of transitions. The degree of association between problem substance use and role transitions may depend on certain characteristics of that transition, for example, in the case of marriage, marital satisfaction and substance use habits of the spouse (Merline et al., 2008). Although some transitions are predictable and socially desirable, others are nonnormative, such as early or late pubertal development (Brooks-Gunn & Reiter, 1990) or premature role entry (pseudomaturity; Newcomb, 1996) such as marriage (Martino, Collins, & Ellickson, 2004) or parenthood (Oesterle et al. 2011) at an early age. In addition, although turning points could be singular, important life events such as marriage and parenthood, or even rare events such as school transitions or serving in the military during wartime, are often repeating in nature and may have different implications depending on the context surrounding the transition (Sampson & Laub, 2005).

Initiation and Progression of Substance Use

The developmental periods with greatest change in substance use correspond to the transition into use and the remission/desistence of use and related problems. The following section focuses on these phases of substance use, which generally correspond to the stages of adolescence and emerging adulthood.

Initiation

Initiation of substance use is greater during adolescence than at any other time during development. Although the legal drinking age is 21, initiation of alcohol use generally occurs well before then. The prevalence of initiating drinking at age 12 or younger ranges from 23% to 37% across national surveys (Newes-Adeyi, Chen, Williams, & Faden, 2004). Initiation of smoking predominately takes place in adolescence, although there are some studies indicating onset of smoking during young adulthood (generally during college) (Myers, Doran, Trinidad, Klonoff, & Wall, 2009; Tercyak, Rodriguez, & Audrain-McGovern, 2007; Wetter et al., 2004). Finally, initiation of marijuana use typically occurs between 14 and 20 years of age (Behrendt, Wittchen, Hofler, Lieb, & Beesdo, 2009; von Sydow et al., 2001), with 18 being the peak age of risk for first use (Chen & Kandel, 1995; Wagner & Anthony, 2002a). Very few individuals begin to use marijuana in their mid to late 20s (Chen & Kandel, 1995; Wagner & Anthony, 2002a).

Data from the 2011 NSDUH study indicate that the mean age of first use among past-year initiates (for individuals aged 12 or older) was age 17.3 for alcohol, age 17.8 for cigarette smoking, and age 18.0 for marijuana use (SAMHSA, 2014). Using data from the National Comorbidity Survey, Wagner and Anthony (2007) found that the peak risk for initiation of drug use was estimated to occur at ages 18–19 for marijuana and alcohol and around age 21–22 for cocaine. Risk for initiating alcohol use was evident across the life span, with risk spread across a much longer period for alcohol use than for marijuana and cocaine use. Risk of initiating marijuana and cocaine was very small beyond age 25, with risk for alcohol initiation not diminishing until around age 40.

There is inconsistency in the meaning of "first use," particularly for alcohol. First drink has been operationalized in many ways, including *any* use/trying of alcohol including just a sip (e.g., D'Amico & McCarthy, 2006; Gruber, DiClimente, Anderson, & Lodico, 1996; Jackson, Ennett, Dickinson, & Bowling, 2012), alcohol use beyond a sip or a few sips/taste (e.g., Malone Northrup, Masyn, Lamis, & Lamont, 2012; Mason et al., 2011; Warner & White, 2003), first intoxication (Clapper, Buka, Goldfield, Lipsitt, & Tsuang, 1995), and first regular drinking (Grant, Stinson, & Harford, 2001). Some definitions consider the context behind the first drinking experience; for example, requiring use without parental permission (e.g., Sung, Erkanli, Angold, & Costello, 2004; Trucco, Colder, & Wieczorek, 2011) or use other than at a religious ceremony (Morean, Corbin, & Fromme, 2012).

Along similar lines, although cigarette smoking generally refers to first whole cigarette, some studies have examined ever having puffed on a cigarette (Brady, Song, & Halpern-Felsher, 2008; Okoli, Richardson, Ratner, & Johnson, 2009), smoking one or two puffs (Hu, Griesler, Schaffran, Wall, & Kandel, 2012), or smoking "a puff or more" (O'Loughlin et al., 2003), or ever inhaled on a cigarette (DiFranza et al., 2007). Most studies on cannabis use simply assess any use of marijuana, perhaps because quantifying cannabis use can be challenging due to different means of administration and different dosage/potency (Zeisser et al,. 2012).

In addition, age of onset often is categorized as early versus late based on an arbitrary age threshold, for example, alcohol use by age 13 (Hingson, Heeren, & Winter, 2006), age 14 (Dawson, Grant, & Li, 2007), or age 15 (Chou & Pickering, 1992). Ellickson, D'Amico, Collins, and Klein (2005) note that using dichotomous outcomes such as initiation of marijuana use prior to age 16 (e.g., Green & Ritter, 2000) makes it difficult to distinguish between use in early, middle, and late adolescence.

Those who initiate use of a substance at a young age tend to initiate other substances early. Younger age at first alcohol use and a younger age at first nicotine use are associated with a younger age at first cannabis use (Behrendt et al., 2012). Furthermore, early onset of more than one substance contributes greater risk for initiation of subsequent drugs. Agrawal et al. (2006) found that women who initiated cigarette, alcohol, or cannabis use at an early age were at elevated risk for early experimentation with each subsequent drug class. Kandel and Chen (2000) found that age of onset into alcohol and cigarettes differentiated between marijuana trajectories that were distinguished by early versus late onset, irrespective of degree of involvement.

Progression: Transition and Uptake

Studies using adolescent and young adult samples indicate substantial forward movement in alcohol involvement, with an ordered progression from nonuse to normative drinking to high-risk drinking to problem drinking (Power, Stewart, Hughes, & Arbona, 2005). There is, however, some evidence of backward movement (regression), even among adolescents (Jackson & Schulenberg, 2013; Windle, 1996). Stability seems to be greatest among abstainers and light drinkers as compared to heavier drinkers (Kerr, Fillmore, & Bostrom, 2002; Pape & Hammer, 1996; Power et al., 2005; Webb, Redman, Gibberd, & Sanson-Fisher, 1991; Windle, 1996). However, heavy drinkers are still likely to occupy the same relative position over time (Pape & Hammer, 1996).

Heavy and problematic alcohol use peak around age 21 or 22, and the hazard of onset of alcohol dependence peaks by age 18 years, with rapidly declining onsets after age 25 (Li, Hewitt, & Grant, 2004). Data from a nationally representative sample (NESARC) indicated that time to progression from initiation of drinking to onset of alcohol dependence averaged about 5 years (Alvanzo et al., 2011). In an adolescent treatment sample, there was an ordered progression from first drink of alcohol to first time consuming five or more drinks daily, with an average of 1.3 years between first drink and first time drunk, and less than 5 months from first drunk to first monthly drinking (Jackson, 2010).

For the most part the acquisition of smoking behavior is progressive and unidirectional with escalation to higher level use and little receding (Blitstein, Robinson, Murray, Klesges, & Zbikowski, 2003), but with support for the transition from ex-smoker back to regular smoker (Kremers, Mudde, & deVries, 2001; 2004; Lloyd-Richardson et al., 2002). Wellman, DiFranza, Savageau, and Dussault (2004) found discontinuous progression from infrequent smoking to more frequent smoking, with many interspersed periods of not smoking, and greater transition to daily smoking among those who had developed dependence symptoms.

The uptake process from experimentation to regular smoking typically lasts 2–3 years (USDHHS, 2004). Progression to regular smoking seems to be associated with a pleasurable initial experience with the first cigarette (Pomerleau, Pomerleau, Mehringer, Snedecor, & Cameron, 2005; Sartor et al. 2010). Anthony, Warner, and Kessler (1994) estimated that nearly one third of individuals who smoked tobacco, even once, will develop tobacco dependence. Nicotine dependence generally develops in adolescence, with 22%–40% of adolescent smokers meeting criteria for full nicotine dependence (DiFranza et al., 2007; Gervais et al., 2006; Kandel et al., 2005; Kandel, Hu, Griesler, & Schaffran, 2007). Using retrospective data from the National Comorbidity Survey, Breslau, Johnson, Hiripi, and Kessler (2001) found that the onset of DSM-IIIR nicotine dependence typically occurred at least 1 year after the onset of daily smoking.

Yet symptoms of dependence may develop relatively quickly following first cigarette and at very low levels of smoking (DiFranza et al., 2002, 2007). Kandel et al. (2007) found that one quarter of smokers reached DSM-IV nicotine dependence within 2 years of first tobacco use, and one fifth experienced their first dependence criterion (generally tolerance, impaired control, or withdrawal) within 3 months of tobacco use onset. Kandel, Hu, and Yamaguchi (2009) also showed rapid progression from onset of tobacco use to first dependence criterion (ranging from 10 months to 14 months). This line of research holds that it takes very little smoking experience for a teenager to get "hooked" on cigarettes. Even nonsmokers (youth who never smoked a cigarette, not even a few puffs) have reported feeling addicted (Okoli et al., 2009) or having symptoms of nicotine dependence (Racicot, McGrath, Karp, & O'Loughlin, 2012), presumably due to exposure to peer smoking (social contagion).

Risk for dependence on marijuana peaks between 15 and 18 years of age and drops dramatically in the late 20s (von Sydow et al., 2001; Wagner & Anthony, 2002a). Chen, O'Brien, and Anthony (2005) found that about 4% of cannabis users developed a cannabis dependence syndrome within the 24-month interval after the first use; Wagner and Anthony (2002a) found similar rates using retrospective data from the National Comorbidity Survey (NCS). von Sydow and colleagues (2001) found mean transition times of 2 and 2.4 years for initiation of cannabis use to abuse and dependence, respectively, in a longitudinal community sample of adolescents and young adults. Most cases of cannabis dependence occur within 10 years of first use (Behrendt et al., 2009; Van Etten & Anthony, 1999). Wittchen et al. (2008) found that approximately half of individuals who had experimented with marijuana went on to become regular users and that 40% of these individuals made the transition to regular use within 2 years of initiation. Similarly, half of those who met criteria for cannabis abuse developed the disorder within 2 years of onset of use, and two thirds of those who went on to develop dependence did so within 2 years.

Several studies have made explicit comparisons of progression times for different substances. Transitions to regular alcohol use and disorders occur more slowly than nicotine or cannabis disorders. Behrendt et al. (2009) found that the transition to dependence is faster for marijuana than for alcohol or nicotine. One study calculated lengths of time for transitions to regular use, problems due to substance use, and first dependence criteria, for alcohol, tobacco, and illicit drug use (Ridenour, Lanza, Donny, & Clark, 2006). Transitions in tobacco use tended to occur more rapidly than transitions for drinking, but they were slower than cannabis, cocaine, and opiates. For example, the transition time between first use and regular use (9.6 months), between first use and problem use (22.4 months), and between regular use and dependence (31.1 months) for tobacco exceeded that for alcohol (18.7 months, 28.4 months, and 38.4 months, respectively) but was much slower than that for cocaine (2.7 months, 3.5 months, and 4.5 months, respectively) or opiates (1.7 months, 1.5 months, and 1.5 months, respectively). Differences in the speed of transition from use to dependence may be related to the addictive liability of the substances as well as their availability and social acceptability (Lopez-Quintero et al., 2011). In addition, an individual's progression to greater involvement in marijuana use tends to parallel his or her progression through stages of other substance use. For example, transition to regular marijuana use is significantly associated with progression to regular drinking, and progression to cannabis dependence is significantly associated with onset of alcohol dependence (Ridenour et al., 2006).

Association Between First Use and Progression to Heavier Use

Considerable research supports early age of first alcohol, tobacco, and marijuana use as elevating risk for substance use–related problems and use disorders. Early onset of drinking is associated with greater and earlier risky drinking, alcohol-related problems, and alcohol use disorders (Dawson, 2000; Dawson et al., 2007; Grant & Dawson, 1997; Hingson et al., 2006; Kraus, Bloomfield, Augustin, & Reese, 2000; Labouvie, Bates, & Pandina, 1997; Pedersen & Skrondal, 1998; Stueve

& O'Donnell, 2005; Wagner & Anthony, 2007). Using data from the 1992 National Longitudinal Alcohol Epidemiologic Survey (NLAES), Grant and Dawson (1997) showed that those who started drinking at age 14 or younger were more likely to be diagnosed with lifetime (*DSM-IV*) alcohol dependence (40%) than those who began at age 21 or 22 (10%). For each additional year that passed before initiation of drinking, the risk for developing alcohol dependence and abuse declined 14% and 8%, respectively. Figure 3.7 portrays a reduction in the percentage with past-year alcohol dependence or abuse as a function of age at first use of alcohol using NSDUH data.

Similarly, the likelihood of daily smoking, frequent smoking, and nicotine dependence are higher for those with an early reported age of first cigarette (Breslau, Fenn, & Peterson, 1993; Everett et al., 1999; Hu, Davies, & Kandel, 2006; Taioli & Wynder, 1991) or an early age of first regular smoking (Stanton, 1995). In all, 88% of adult smokers who are daily smokers report that they started smoking by the age of 18 years (USDHHS, 2012). Likewise, heavy marijuana use and rates of cannabis dependence are elevated in early initiators (Anthony & Petronis, 1995; Behrendt et al., 2009; Chen, Storr, & Anthony, 2009; Gruber, Sagar, Dahlgren, Racine, & Lukas, 2012; King & Chassin, 2007; Sung et al., 2004; Wagner & Anthony, 2007; Winters & Lee, 2008), although Kandel and Chen (2000) found that persistent and heavy marijuana users did not necessarily initiate marijuana use at the earliest ages. In addition, stability of marijuana

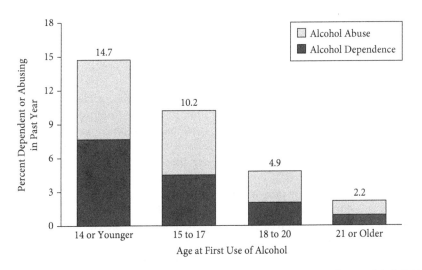

Figure 3.7 Alcohol dependence or abuse in the past year among adults aged 21 or older, by age at first use of alcohol: 2012, based on data from the National Survey on Drug Use and Health (NSDUH; SAMHSA, 2013c).

use is greater among youth who began use before late adolescence (Perkonigg et al., 2008).

Similar associations are observed for cross-substance associations, with early initiation of a given substance connoting risk for other substance use and dependence. Early onset of alcohol use predicts tobacco and illicit drug use, abuse, and dependence (McGue et al., 2001a; Robins & Przybeck, 1985; Windle, 1991), and alcohol and marijuana use are associated with rapid progression from first cigarette to onset of regular smoking (Sartor, Xian et al., 2008). Early smoking also is associated with alcohol consumption and alcohol use disorders (Grant, 1998) and illicit drug use and dependence (Hanna & Grant, 1999; Vega & Gil, 2005), although Mayet, Legleye, Chau, and Falissard (2011) did not find that the risk of transition to daily cannabis use was related to the initiation of smoking (or vice versa). Van Leeuwen et al. (2011) demonstrated that adolescents who reported early-onset comorbid use of both tobacco and alcohol had a higher likelihood of initiating cannabis use than adolescents who tried either tobacco or alcohol. Finally, early-onset marijuana users are at elevated risk for nicotine and alcohol dependence as well as regular smoking and other illicit drug use, abuse, and dependence (Agrawal, Madden, Martin, & Lynskey, 2013; Behrendt et al., 2012; Ellickson et al., 2005; Grant et al., 2010; Lynskey et al., 2003; Timberlake et al., 2007). For example, Kandel (2002) found that the earlier the age of first cannabis use, the more likely the individual was to use heroin and cocaine. Agrawal et al. (2013) demonstrated that cigarette smokers were at 1.87 increased odds of smoking marijuana within a week of their initial marijuana use compared to never smokers. Even the opportunity to use marijuana at a young age is elevated in users of alcohol or tobacco (Agrawal et al., 2013; Wagner & Anthony, 2002b), perhaps due to the presence of deviant peers who facilitate both cigarette and marijuana use, or related to a genetic vulnerability to drug use or general disinhibition. Windle and Windle (2012), however, found strongest predictive utility with substance-specific prediction (e.g., early cocaine use was the strongest predictor of cocaine disorders).

The longitudinal course of substance use itself appears to vary as a function of age of onset. Although one might expect early onset of substance use to be associated with a more rapid uptake, as suggested by work indicating common influences underlying onset and heavy or problematic substance use (Donovan, Jessor, & Costa, 1999; Jessor & Jessor, 1977; Prescott & Kendler, 1999), research seems to indicate that for alcohol and tobacco use (but not marijuana use), progression tends to be slower in those with early age of initiation, perhaps due to limited social and physical availability at a young age. Progression from first full drink to alcohol dependence is shown to be slower for those with early age of first drink in high-risk (Sartor, Lynskey, Heath, Jacob, & True, 2007) and community samples (Behrendt et al., 2008). In a sample of adolescents prospectively ascertained through early adulthood, Hussong, Bauer, and Chassin (2008) observed greater "telescoping" from first drink to alcohol use disorder among those who began drinking by age 14. One study indicated that although a more rapid escalation to alcohol use disorders occurred for those with an earlier age of onset (age 11–14), those under age 11 actually showed a slower progression (DeWit, Adlaf, Offord, & Ogborne, 2000). Similar findings have been observed for progression from first drink to the milestones of drunk, monthly drinking, weekly consumption of five or more drinks/day, and daily consumption of five or more drinks/day, with earlier initiates showing slower progression in a clinical adolescent sample (Jackson, 2010).

Along these same lines, several studies show that progression to nicotine dependence is slower among early-onset users, and this is the case for both early smokers and early initiates of alcohol use (Breslau et al, 1993; Sartor, Xian et al., 2008). Grant (1998) found that smoking initiation by age 13 was associated with greater lag time (4.3 years) to daily smoking than smoking initiation between the ages of 14 and 16 (2.3 years) and after the age of 17 (1.7 years). Related, a sizeable portion of smokers with later initiation (during young adulthood) go on to progress to established smoking at a more rapid rate than do adolescent initiates (Myers et al., 2009).

Together, these studies on speed of progression to more severe use of alcohol and tobacco as well as alcohol and tobacco use disorders suggest a developmental period of risk that is independent from timing of exposure (Sartor et al., 2007; Sher, 2007). Although early onset may indicate some sort of propensity for problematic alcohol involvement, this propensity may not manifest itself until conducive conditions are present later in adolescence (Sher, 2007). The delay in progression to heavier alcohol involvement among early drinkers may be due to limited opportunity to obtain and consume alcohol. Risky alcohol use and problems in youth are associated with alcohol availability, especially access through social sources such as parents, siblings, and friends (Harrison, Fulkerson, & Park, 2000), which may be greater for later-onsetting (i.e., older) youth. Similarly, Grant (1998) suggests that the lack of a supportive or permissive social environment for smoking among younger adolescents may be an important factor that accounts for slower progression to daily smoking. Importantly, there may be more risk involved for individuals who initiate late but show rapid increases in substance use because these individuals have less experience with drinking (or other substance use-related) situations and more risk is involved (Schulenberg & Maggs, 2002).

The differences in findings for likelihood of initiating substance use versus rate of progression imply the existence of within-individual processes underlying different transitions along the pathway to substance use disorders (McGue, 2007). Sartor, Xian et al. (2008) suggest that distinct mechanisms may underlie different stages of smoking behaviors based on their finding that only a subset of experimenters go on to become daily smokers or to develop nicotine dependence.

There seems to be a different association between onset and progression for marijuana use. Data from Behrendt et al. (2009) showed that the speed of transition to cannabis dependence was *not* slower among early- versus later-onset users, and DeWit, Hance, Offord, and Ogborne (2000) found that early initiators of marijuana use progressed rapidly to problem use. In addition, Chen et al. (2005) found that there was greater escalation to cannabis dependence when cannabis use begins before late adolescence (age 18+ years) and Chen et al. (2009) observed greater risk for drug dependence problems among new users of cannabis and other illicit drugs when they were adolescents versus those who were adults. This may be due to a difference in accessibility between marijuana use and licit drugs: Initial access to alcohol and tobacco (although sporadic) may be relatively easy, compared to access to marijuana, which is more effortful, but maintaining regular access is less challenging once a source is identified, allowing for a more rapid progression to heavy and problem use (Jackson & Sartor, 2014).

One issue to consider is that age of onset is confounded with duration of the substance use career (DeWit, Adlaf et al., 2000; Gruber et al., 1996; Kraus et al., 2000): Young users are exposed to risk for developing problems for a longer period. Risk behavior places people at risk because it becomes ingrained early in life and carries through to adulthood (Mahalik et al., 2013). Time since onset may be more important than age of initiation (Yamaguchi, 1990), but once age is controlled (critical for outcomes with differential likelihood of occurrence across the life span), it is impossible to separate age of onset from length of substance-using career.

Developmental Trajectories of Substance Use

An important part of studying development is characterizing and understanding heterogeneity in change. According to developmental psychopathology, we can learn the most by studying the abnormal population that fails to conform to the dominant trend or pathway (Cairns, Cairns, Cairns, Rodkin, & Xie, 1998; Cicchetti & Rogosch, 2002), making it important to consider specific trajectories of substance use which likely are linked to different etiological pathways (Colder et al., 2001). Development in adolescent problem behavior, including alcohol and other substance use, has been characterized by varying developmental tracks suggestive of multiple developmental pathways or a mixture of two or more subpopulations (Li, Duncan, & Hops, 2001). Trajectory approaches permit researchers to empirically identify homogeneous developmental pathways based on a pattern of responses over time (Maggs & Schulenberg, 2004/2005); these pathways are determined on the basis of age of onset, direction and speed of change, and degree of instability versus persistence over time. Although present-day trajectory approaches are largely empirically based, they build on prior work that took a developmental perspective to characterize substance use and problem behavior, including Moffitt's (1993) work subtyping antisocial behavior into life-course persistent versus adolescent-limited offending groups and Zucker's (1987) influential etiological model which proposed a Developmentally Limited Alcoholism type, which presents as severe alcohol-related problems and externalizing behavior limited to the adolescent stage (along with three additional typologies defined on the basis of antisocial features and negative affectivity). In addition, some researchers have derived typologies of change on a conceptual basis for both smoking (Chassin, Presson, Sherman, & Edwards, 1991; Juon, Ensminger, & Syndor, 2002) and alcohol use (Pape & Hammer, 1996; Sher, Gotham, & Watson, 2004; Stice, Myers, & Brown, 1998) such as escalator versus de-escalator; increased versus stable versus declined; or stable nonsmoker, late-onset smoker, stable smoker, and quitter.

Recent work has embraced methods that empirically derive latent (unknown) groups using general growth mixture modeling techniques (GGMM; Muthén, 2004; Muthén & Shedden, 1999; Nagin, 1999, 2005). Dozens of studies exist that characterize trajectories of substance use over adolescence, and across young adulthood (see Jackson & Sartor, 2014). These studies are primarily concentrated in the alcohol and smoking fields, but a handful of studies have charted the courses of marijuana use. Longitudinal trajectories tend to be distinguished on the basis of both onset (early vs. later) and chronicity (stable versus transient), as opposed to falling along a severity dimension. Several prototypical courses have been identified, including a low- or nonusing course (generally with the largest prevalence, even in high-risk and clinical samples), a stable chronic high course, and one or more courses defined by direction/rate of change (e.g., increasing vs. decreasing; steep vs. shallow slope) (see Sher, Jackson, & Steinley, 2011). Not surprisingly, the definition and meaning of the trajectory groups tend to vary by the age of the sample, with studies focusing on adolescents generally finding one or more "increasing" trajectories marked by early onset and more or less rapid escalation but (in contrast to studies on young adult populations) failing to detect "decreasing" trajectories. Clearly, it is essential to collect prospective data along the full span of adolescence and early adulthood in order to shed light on the processes that help explain why some individuals remit/reduce their substance use and others consistently engage in substance use at high and potentially harmful levels.

There are quite a few studies that apply trajectory models to data from long-term prospective studies that chart the full course of alcohol involvement from mid-adolescence to emerging adulthood (e.g., Bennett, McCrady, Johnson, & Pandina, 1999; Chassin, Pitts, & Prost, 2002; Flory, Lynam, Milich, Leukefeld, & Clayton, 2004; Lee et al., 2012; Mitchell & Beals, 2006; Sher, Jackson, & Steinley, 2011; Tucker, Orlando, & Ellickson, 2003; Tucker, Ellickson, Orlando, Martino, & Klein, 2005; Warner, White, & Johnson, 2007; White, Johnson, & Buyske 2000; Windle, Mun, & Windle, 2005) or from late adolescence (age 18/college freshmen) to emerging adulthood (e.g., Casswell, Pledger, & Pratap, 2002; Costanzo et al., 2007; Finlay, White, Mun, Cronley, & Lee, 2012; Jackson & Sher, 2005; 2008; Jackson, Sher, & Schulenberg, 2008; Muthén & Muthén, 2000; Schulenberg, O'Malley, Bachman, Wadsworth, &

Johnston, 1996). These studies have modeled a wide array of indices of alcohol involvement, including heavy drinking, frequency of use, quantity of use, and alcohol problems/consequences. Interestingly, few of these studies have identified a "fling trajectory" that mirrors the normative trajectory observed by epidemiological data (Schulenberg, O'Malley et al., 1996; Tucker et al., 2003; Windle et al., 2005), suggesting that there is a great deal of variability in patterns of use over time such that very few individuals display substance use that resembles the "average" pattern of growth.

There are also many studies examining trajectories of smoking that chart the full course from mid-adolescence to emerging adulthood (e.g., Brook et al., 2008; Brook, Ning, & Brook, 2006; Brook, Pahl, & Ning, 2006; Caldeira et al., 2012; Costello, Dierker, Jones, & Rose, 2008; Guo et al., 2002; Hu et al., 2012; Lessov-Schlaggar et al., 2008; Orlando, Tucker, Ellickson, & Klein, 2004; Riggs, Chou, Li, & Pentz, 2007; Tucker, Ellickson, Orlando, & Klein, 2006; White et al., 2000; White, Pandina, & Chen, 2002). Most studies have modeled smoking quantity or a composite of quantity and frequency, with a few modeling the probability of (any) smoking. Whereas the research on trajectories of alcohol use (as well as marijuana use) tend to show groups that decline at the point of emerging adulthood, this is less true for cigarette smoking, likely because tobacco is far more addictive than the other substances. On the other hand, unlike with alcohol and marijuana use, a group of experimenters or "chippers" (Shiffman, 1989) with lighter but stable cigarette use often is identified.

With regard to marijuana use, several studies have charted the course of frequency of use using samples that were initially ascertained in school and followed beyond high school (e.g., Brook, Lee, Brown, Finch, & Brook, 2011; Brown, Flory, Lynam, Leukefeld, & Clayton, 2004; Martino, Collins, & Ellickson, 2004; Flory et al., 2004; Schulenberg et al. 2005; Wanner, Vitaro, Ladouceur, Brendgen, & Tremblay, 2006); findings from these studies often closely parallel the groups observed for alcohol involvement. In fact, some studies have identified trajectories of multiple substances (Guo et al., 2002; Jackson et al., 2008; Tucker et al., 2005) and show that smoking, drinking, and marijuana use tend to track each other over time, with roughly equal concordance between trajectories of marijuana and tobacco use and between trajectories of alcohol and tobacco use.

Identification of distinct developmental patterns of substance use permits testing of more precise theories, identification of predictors of specific developmental patterns of use, and development of prevention programs targeted to reach high-risk subgroups (Maggi, Hertzman, & Vaillancourt, 2007). Distinct longitudinal patterns may reveal different optimal ages for the implementation of prevention programs across subgroups, and specific subgroups of youth may respond well to prevention programs with content tailored to stage of use (Colder et al., 2001; Soldz, 2005; Soldz & Cui, 2002). For example, whereas harm-reduction programs may suffice for adolescent-limited users, adolescents on a life-course-persistent trajectory would require prevention efforts that ideally would already have started in childhood (Silbereisen, 1998). Intervening on early-stage risk factors will increase the likelihood of changing a youth's trajectory away from problems and toward positive behaviors (Ialongo, Poduska, Werthamer, & Kellam, 2001).

Developmental Specificity of Risk Factors

A major objective of developmental science is to describe how, when, and why individuals' behaviors change over time (Nesselroade & Baltes, 1979). An important characteristic of research in developmental psychopathology concerns the degree to which individual development affects both the course of a behavior and moderates the influence of a given risk factor on the behavior. That is, we move beyond simply describing group differences between normative and nonnormative groups and instead focus on examining how these group differences evolved over the course of development (Cicchetti & Rogosch, 2002). Researchers conducting longitudinal research in substance use aim to identify constructs that explain individual differences in stability and change (interindividual variability in intra-individual change). Moreover, the influence of these risk factors can vary over time—that is, individual development can moderate the effect of a given risk factor.

Developmental Timing

Substance use literature suggests there is developmental specificity with regard to the influence of risk factors, not only over age but also over developmental stage, by age of onset, and across important life transitions, as discussed next.

ACROSS AGE

Research on substance use supports age-related patterns with differential prediction for younger versus older individuals. For example, the influence of parental monitoring decreases and peer influence increases as youth progress through adolescence and into young adulthood (Latendresse et al., 2008). Van Ryzin, Fosco, and Dishion (2012) examined substance use over age 12 to age 23 and found that parental monitoring was more influential in early adolescence and family relationship quality was more influential in middle and late adolescence, whereas peers were the only significant influence on early adult use. Sampson and Laub (2005) proposed an "age-graded" theory suggesting that social controls are manifested in shifting ways as individuals age; for example, social controls may be manifested as parenting and emotional attachment to parents in childhood, as school attachment and peers in adolescence, and as marital stability and employment in adulthood. Bricker, Andersen, Rajan, Sarason, and Peterson (2007) found that classmate smoking has a greater influence on the smoking initiation and progression to monthly smoking for older than for younger adolescents. In contrast, there is evidence that the associations between perceived peer norms and alcohol initiation and intensity of use are pronounced in younger adolescents (Kelly et al., 2012). The relative magnitude of peer selection and socialization effects on substance use also may vary across age, with stronger socialization influences during adolescence and selection influences greater during adulthood (Haller, Handley, Chassin, & Bountress, 2010).

The structure and importance of substance use–related cognitions are particularly influenced by chronological development. For example, drinking cognitions (both positive and negative) are more developed for sixth graders relative to third graders (Bekman, Goldman, Worley & Anderson, 2011), and with age, expectancies about the effects of alcohol shift from negative to positive (Dunn & Goldman, 1998; Hipwell et al., 2005). Pomery and colleagues (2009) found that willingness was a better predictor of change in substance use during early adolescence, but behavioral intention was a better predictor by middle adolescence. Together, these studies suggest there are age differences in the degree to which risk factors support substance use experience and help to determine its trajectory.

ACROSS STAGE OF ALCOHOL INVOLVEMENT

The theory underlying processes that predict progression from initial to heavier involvement is less developed than factors that predict initiation (Pedersen & Skrondal, 1998). There are many common influences underlying onset and heavier use of substances, especially in the domains of delinquency and externalizing disorders (e.g., Clark & Cornelius, 2004; Dierker, Avenevoli, Goldberg, & Glantz, 2004; Donovan et al., 1999; Jessor & Jessor, 1977; King, Iacono, & McGue, 2004; Prescott & Kendler, 1999; Van Den Bree, Whitmer, & Pickworth, 2004), but it is more likely that risk factors for initiation differ from risk factors for other transitions along the dimension of adolescent substance involvement (Donovan, 2004). Sartor and colleagues have suggested that risk factors for progression to early stages along the pathway to nicotine dependence (e.g., disinhibition manifested by alcohol or marijuana use) may not be the same as those factors that place one at risk for later transitions (e.g., anxiety-prone or depressed youth) (Sartor, Xian et al., 2008).

Substance use–related cognitions seem to be related to onset but not growth in heavy drinking (Colder, Chassin, Stice, & Curran, 1997). Aas, Leigh, Anderssen, and Jakobsen (1998) suggest that expectancy–behavior relationships are stronger when youth have less experience with alcohol; once experienced, expectancies may influence subsequent consumption indirectly through current drinking patterns. Automatic implicit processes, in particular, may be more important earlier in a drinking career, as opposed to more habitual processes in later phases of addiction (Wiers et al., 2007). Willner (2001) found that negative expectancies deter or delay initiation of marijuana use, but once initiated, positive expectancies become more salient (and more predictive of frequency of use). Reasons for not drinking have different salience at different phases of drinking engagement, with greater prediction of initiation and current drinking than of heavy episodic drinking or problems (Anderson, Grunwald, Bekman, Brown, & Grant, 2011; Bekman, Cummins, & Brown, 2010). Similarly, certain smoking attributions (e.g., curiosity about smoking, autonomy, coping, social image) appear to be more important at the earlier stages of smoking, whereas other attributions (e.g., engagement, mental enhancement) are more important at more advanced stages of smoking (Guo et al., 2010; 2012).

Bernat, Klein, and Forster (2012) showed that having friends who smoke appears to be influential for smoking initiation but not progression, and this appears to be true for both adolescents and young adults, supporting the idea that although stage of use and age are associated, they are not synonymous (Colder et al., 2010). Correlates of initiation tend to be situational or contextual variables such as peer substance use or substance availability, whereas correlates of heavier use and chronicity of use are more stable and fixed (e.g., Flay et al., 1998; McMaster & Wintre, 1996; Wilsnack, Klassen, Schur, & Wilsnack, 1991). Behavior genetic work indicates that shared environmental factors are stronger for initiation, whereas genetic influences are stronger for maintenance or progression of substance use (e.g., Agrawal & Lynskey 2008; Fowler et al., 2007; Maes et al. 1999; Pagan et al., 2006). Consistent with these findings, Jackson, Sher, Gotham, and Wood (2001) found that individuals with a family history of alcoholism were less likely to regress from high- to moderate-effect drinking than those without such a history, but there was no family history effect on initial status. Likewise, the impact of familial smoking behaviors seems to increase in later smoking-stage transitions (Bricker, Peterson, Sarason, Andersen, & Rajan, 2007; Dierker, Avenevoli, Merikangas, Flaherty, & Stolar, 2001; Flay et al., 1998; Robinson et al. 2006). In addition, internalizing disorders and negative affect appear to be predictive of progression but not onset for both alcohol use (Colder & Chassin, 1999) and tobacco use (Patton et al., 2005), again supporting the idea that correlates of progression tend to be less situational and more stable than correlates of initiation.

In addition, genetic influence predominates in *rate* of progression to regular drinking, problem use, and alcohol dependence (Sartor, Agrawal et al., 2008; Stallings, Hewitt, Beresford, Heath, & Eaves, 1999) and rate from first cigarette use to regular (daily/heavy) cigarette use (Stallings et al., 1999). Viken, Kaprio, Koskenvuo, and Rose (1999) noted that this was true for both drinking frequency and intoxication, stressing the importance of contextual factors in initiation of each new stage of use.

ACROSS AGE OF FIRST USE

Research supports age of first drink as a moderator of influences on substance use, with depression, behavioral undercontrol, and life-event stress more predictive of substance use for those with early debut (Dawson et al., 2007; Robins & Przybeck, 1985), and smoking as more predictive of illicit drug use for those with later onset (Robins & Przybeck, 1985). Agrawal et al. (2009) found age at first drink to moderate genetic and environmental influences such that later age at first drink protected against a familial predisposition to alcohol dependence. In addition, early onset corresponds to a longer period of time with developmental cascades ("snowball" effects) potentiating alcohol use, in turn leading to poor adaptation and coping (Buchmann et al., 2009). Profiles of risk for youth with early onset also may be related to neurocognitive deficits associated with early exposure to alcohol (Alfonso-Loeches & Guerri, 2011).

ACROSS DEVELOPMENTAL TRANSITIONS

Finally, the magnitude and strength of risk factors may vary across important developmental transitions such as puberty or school transition. Jackson and Schulenberg (2013) found different factors to predict pre–high school versus post–high school drinking. For example, whereas no sex differences were observed prior to the transition, girls were more likely to transition from non-drinking to light drinking, whereas boys were more likely to transition to heavy drinking. One might expect that the protective influence of religiosity on substance use would lessen during the college years, against the backdrop of an environment that promotes substance use.

The timing of a transition is also important. Externalizing behaviors occur more among early-maturing youth than on-time or late-maturing youth (Lynne, Graber, Nichols, Brooks-Gunn, & Botvin, 2007). Early-maturing girls may be at risk for drinking due to affiliation with older boys (peer influence), and the impact of pubertal timing appears to be magnified when early-developing youth associate with mixed-sex friends (Ge, Conger, & Elder, 1996; Stattin & Magnusson, 1990). Given that susceptibility to peer influence is particularly salient during the transition to middle school and early puberty is a known risk factor for alcohol use initiation in girls (Dick, Rose, Viken, & Kaprio, 2000; Tschann et al., 1994), prevention programs reaching out to girls who have attained puberty early may be an important component of reducing peer influences on drinking.

Correlates of Developmental Trajectories

Trajectory research enables better understanding of etiological processes, in that it permits identification of risk factors that differentiate among courses that have similar starting points but then diverge over time. For example, a non/low-using class has identical initial levels of substance use as a late-onsetting class, but over time their substance use patterns diverge. Within the field of developmental psychopathology, two important concepts are equifinality and multifinality (Cicchetti & Rogosch,

1996; Sroufe, 1997). Multifinality posits that an early risk factor may lead to different outcomes, perhaps by redirecting a drinker to an emergent risk factor that comes into play at a later developmental stage. Group-based trajectory models are well suited for identifying divergences in the developmental courses of resilient versus vulnerable cases; these divergences may correspond to turning points in development (Cairns et al., 1998; Nagin & Tremblay, 2005a). As an example of multifinality, Flory et al (2004) found that although the nonuser, late-onset, and early-onset trajectory groups had virtually identical (low) levels of drinking at sixth grade, peer pressure resistance measured at the same time was significantly different across the three groups, with greatest resistance among nonusers and lowest among early-onset users. A similar finding was observed by Hill, White, Chung, Hawkins, and Catalano (2000), who found that baseline externalizing was greatest for early-onset increasers, followed by late onsetters, and with nonbingers the lowest. In another illustration of multifinality, Connell, Dishion, and Deater-Deckard (2006) found that parental monitoring distinguished between a low/rare substance-using group and group with initial low use followed by steep onset of substance use; notably, this onset coincided with the transition to high school in ninth grade.

Equifinality posits that psychopathology may develop in different individuals through different developmental processes; that is, multiple, differing etiological pathways may exist that lead ultimately to the same outcome. For example, drinking initiation in one individual may be largely a function of a sensation-seeking personality, whereas for another, childhood environment plays a large role. Examining two distinct substance use trajectories that converge into nonuse (e.g., nonuse and "fling" trajectories) can be informative for pinpointing the contextual/environmental factors that elevate (or mitigate) risk by identifying the critical period at which these trajectories are divergent. Schulenberg, Wadsworth, O'Malley, Bachman, and Johnston (1996) found in their study that the fling and rare trajectories were virtually indistinguishable on baseline factors, suggesting that a time-limited fling with frequent binge drinking may be due to time-varying situational factors more so than to any long-standing individual characteristics.

A study by Brook et al. (2011) illustrates the concepts of both equifinality and multifinality. Although two courses, stable non/low marijuana users and maturing-out users, had virtually identical responses at ages 14 and 29, they diverged quite a bit around ages 19–20. Interestingly, they did not differ on young adulthood marital status or work achievement, suggesting that individuals who use marijuana during emerging adulthood but remit out are still able to successfully negotiate the normative role transitions of young adulthood, although those who matured out of marijuana use reported lower marital harmony and satisfaction with partners than stable nonusers. The maturing-out users also were more likely than the non/low users to display anxiety symptoms and to have an increased likelihood of engaging in young adult criminal behavior, even controlling for criminal behavior in early adolescence, indicating that their substance use behavior in the early 20s had long-term influences over young adulthood.

The Interplay Between the Individual and the Environment

Human development is thought to be embedded within and shaped by historical and place contexts. Developmental outcomes are the result of interactions between intrapersonal variables and the environment (Kandel & Davies, 1992; Schulenberg & Maggs, 2002). The environment can be an important trigger for problem behavior, where nonspecific risk such as difficult temperament evolves into deviant behavior in the face of an enabling environment (Rutter, 1994; Zucker, 2006). Developmental psychopathology places problem behavior both within the context of normal development and in relation to the interplay between environmental and person-specific characteristics (Cicchetti & Rogosch, 2002). The individual actively selects behaviors within the constraints and opportunities of the immediate environment (Windle & Zucker, 2010). For example, a favorable environment (e.g., available alcohol) provides an opportunity for intraindividual risk to be manifested as drinking (Clark, 2004; Sher, 2007), and a cue such as the presence of alcohol activates existing expectancies (Zucker, 2006). As another example, one might hypothesize that with recent antismoking legislation, there are fewer enabling environments, and underlying susceptibility to cigarette smoking is less likely to be manifested as tobacco dependence due to this nonsmoking environment.

Life course theory suggests that development is cumulative, whereby prior experience matters for subsequent development (Elder, 1998). Early success can promote cumulating advantages, whereas early challenges can have serious long-term consequences. Involvement in substance use behavior in young adulthood is based on earlier risk for substance use that results from the reciprocal interplay between individual behavior and social influences across several domains (family, schools, communities) from early childhood to adult years (Conger, 1997). The way an individual reacts to these environmental influences is affected by his or her own emotional, biological, and cognitive processes that emerge even as early as childhood. For example, Burdzovic Andreas and Watson (2007, 2010) found greater likelihood of alcohol use among adolescents living in poorer quality neighborhoods; this effect was magnified for youth with high sensation-seeking temperaments.

Furthermore, when considering development, we must recognize the dynamic interplay of processes across level of analysis and context as well as across time. Individuals' interactions with their environment, and interactions between various contexts, shape human development. That is, the initiation and progression of substance use results from interactions of systems both within an individual and between individual and other external systems. Bronfenbrenner's seminal model of child development (Bronfenbrenner, 1979, 1986) conceptualizes the environment in terms of nested systems. The individual is embedded in the microsystem, which is shaped by interpersonal environmental influences such as family, peers, and school. The mesosystemic environment entails interactions between microsystems; the exosystem consists of formal and informal institutions that shape opportunities and constraints within mesosystems and microsystems (e.g., neighborhoods, mass media); and the macrosystem is the cultural or ideological patterns that are concretely manifested in the lower systemic levels (e.g., national alcohol or tobacco control policy). Finally, the chronosystem encompasses the dimension of time as it relates to a child's environment. Thus, this model emphasizes the importance of the context for understanding individual development.

The social context is part of a dynamic process where the reciprocal interplay between individual characteristics and contextual influences varies across the adolescent and young adult years. Developmental cascade models suggest a progression from early family risk to early onset of disordered behavior to adjustment problems within school and peer contexts; these then have cascading effects leading to the onset and progression of substance use in adolescence and subsequent adjustment problems in young adulthood (Lynne-Landsman, Bradshaw, & Ialongo, 2010). For example, Haller et al. (2010) found that the influence of parental alcoholism on adult drug use disorders was mediated by developmental cascades among substance use, affiliation with substance use promoting peers, and academic achievement over an 18-year period. There was support for stable within-domain (alcohol/drug use, peer use) impairment over time as well as spillover into other domains (school), leading to subsequent impaired functioning over time.

Substance use can be time limited and situational. For example, emerging adults are responsive to environments that promote drinking, such as heavy-drinking college campuses (Presley, Meilman, & Leichliter, 2002; Slutske et al. 2004), particularly for those living in residence halls or in independent off-campus housing (Harford & Muthen, 2001). White, Labouvie, and Papadaratsakis (2005) found that college status was related to lower levels of alcohol and marijuana problems at age 18, greater increases from ages 18 to 21, and greater decreases from ages 21 to 30 even after controlling for level and growth in use. In contrast, smoking and drug use are more common among non–college students than among college students (White et al., 2005), suggesting specificity in substance use–related norms on the college campus.

Greek organizations, in particular, provide a heavy-drinking culture. One study showed that student members of Greek organizations drank more than non–fraternity members during college, but that the effects were short lived (Sher, Bartholow, & Nanda, 2001). Park, Sher, Wood, and Krull (2009) found that students selected into the Greek system on the basis of preexisting major personality traits, including impulsivity/novelty seeking, extraversion, and neuroticism; in turn, Greek affiliation was associated with higher levels of perceived peer drinking norms and alcohol availability. Park et al. (2009) cite their findings as evidence of an "accentuation effect" of individual– environment interactions (Feldman & Newcomb, 1969), where individuals select into a high-risk environment on the basis of individual differences, and the environment then exerts further influence on drinking.

Methodological Considerations in Longitudinal Substance Use Research
Importance of Prospective Data
When studying developmental change, prospective studies that follow a group of people over

time are essential. In addition, most theories on substance use posit within-person processes (e.g., negative affect regulation), and there is growing recognition that prospective (within-subject) data are critical for testing these hypotheses (Collins, 2006). However, research examining developmental timing often examines development itself with between-person designs (e.g., by age, or stage of drinking, or whether one has reached a given milestone, regardless of when). Yet using between-person comparisons to make within-person inferences is a logical fallacy, and the distinction between between-person and within-person associations has important implications for identifying optimal intervention strategies (targeting a type of person vs. targeting the right time to intervene). Thus, within-person data are critical for research questions about initiation and progression of substance use involvement: Does use change before versus after a milestone within the same person? Does an individual's profile of risk vary as a function of whether he is merely experimenting, whether he has begun using on a regular basis, or whether he is experiencing symptoms of dependence—and how quickly he progressed to these symptoms? Prospective data permit us to unconfound the different aspects of development (e.g., teasing apart stage of use from chronological age) as well as posit interactions between different aspects of development (e.g., the influence of a developmental transition on individual development may vary based on where people are in their lives at the time; Nagin, Pagani, Tremblay, & Vitaro, 2003).

Many studies, including the majority of national surveys, in the substance use field are cross-sectional, with participants assessed only once—that is, different age cohorts are observed at the same point in time. However, cross-sectional designs confound age with birth cohort, as opposed to longitudinal or prospective studies, which track the same people over time. Cross-sectional data are also prone to retrospection bias (Brewin, Andrews, & Gotlib, 1993), and retrospective report of event frequencies and event dates can be poor (Henry, Moffitt, Caspi, Langley, & Silva, 1994). In addition, forward telescoping is a concern when using cross-sectional data. Several studies have demonstrated that self-reported age of onset increases with age (Engels, Knibbe, & Drop, 1997; Johnson & Mott, 2001; Parra, O'Neill, & Sher, 2003). Finally, although cross-sectional studies can identify average developmental trends in alcohol use, they can mask individual differences in timing and pace of development (Masten et al.,

2008). This makes them less effective at predicting one person's future drinking patterns (Masten et al., 2008). Fortunately, longitudinal designs are becoming increasingly common.

On the other hand, prospective designs can be quite costly both financially and logistically, and attrition is a concern. A major disadvantage of conducting longitudinal research is the amount of time it takes to complete a study. Cohort sequential designs combine the strengths of cross-sectional and prospective designs (Bell, 1953; Nesselroade & Baltes, 1979). A prospective study is conducted for several birth cohorts to obtain a longer window of assessment. Although these designs are frequently used, many studies fail to model them appropriately. Individuals often vary substantially in age at baseline, with the range of ages often wider than the follow-up interval (Hertzog & Nesselroade, 2003). For researchers interested in developmental change, modeling age is more informative than modeling wave.

Temporal Considerations

When designing prospective research studies, the researcher must determine the interval at which participants will be assessed, which will depend on both the construct of interest and the developmental stage under study. If observations are spaced too far apart, there will be less precision with respect to a given stage of development, and important developmental change may be missed (Faden et al., 2004; Windle & Davies 1999). For example, studies with long assessment intervals may not adequately capture the milestones that progressively follow first drink of alcohol such as first time intoxicated or first heavy drinking experience. Yet it is neither practical nor efficient in terms of logistics and cost to space observations too close together (Collins & Graham, 2002) and too-frequent assessments have the potential to shape the behaviors being studied. Assessing respondents too frequently may be futile if substance use rates are too low and might even serve as a natural intervention by changing behavior. Ideally, the research design would capture rare events (e.g., any drinking in 10- to 12-year-olds; alcohol dependence symptoms in older adolescents) in a feasible manner without evoking reactivity, yet still have the temporal resolution to chart fine-grained behavior change.

Researchers are increasingly conducting studies using daily self-monitoring or real-time self-assessment of substance use behavior, often using Internet surveys or mobile technologies. These methods, often referred to as ecological momentary assessment (Stone & Shiffman, 1994) or experience sampling (Reis & Gable, 2000), involve fine-grained repeated sampling of behavior and allow for the capture of low–base rate events. Daily process data minimize biases (e.g., current state of the person, retroactive reconstruction) that are inherent to retrospective recall and maximize ecological validity by measuring respondents' experiences in natural settings (Shiffman & Hufford, 2002; Stone & Shiffman, 1994). However, these studies are usually limited to a short window of development (e.g., a few weeks or months) and are thus better suited for testing psychological processes than for articulating developmental change.

(Dis) continuity of Substance Use Behavior Over Time

Few theories of development posit simple linear change, and this is particularly true of substance use, where typical trends include escalation during adolescence followed by an asymptote and gradual decline over the course of young adulthood. Development may exhibit a discontinuous rate of change, such as the transition from middle school to high school or high school to college. This corresponds to the concept of turning points, the external events or behaviors that provoke change (Rutter, 1996). Modeling developmental transitions can offer vantage points for addressing issues of continuity and discontinuity (Schulenberg & Maslowsky, 2009). The timing of a turning point is important, too, with the influence of an event on individual development varying based on where people are in their lives at the time (Nagin et al., 2003). For example, Little, Handley, Leuthe, and Chassin (2009) found that individuals who became parents as emerging adults showed declines in alcohol consumption, whereas those who became parents during adolescence showed a role-related rise in subsequent alcohol consumption. Likewise, there may be different profiles of risk for a high school transition for prepubescent versus fully matured youth.

Continuities and discontinuities in alcohol use cannot always be described with simple chronological age models. Indeed, if the form of growth is nonlinear, then standard growth models may produce biased estimates of the average change function and individual differences in the shapes of that function (Mehta & West, 2000). Quadratic or higher order polynomials can be incorporated into the model (e.g., a positive quadratic term to indicate the deceleration of use occurs in later adolescence). Piecewise models, in particular, are useful for making comparisons in growth rates based on distinct developmental stages. Growth trajectories are broken into linear components with separate growth parameters (Raudenbush & Bryk, 2002), such as growth in middle school versus growth in high school. Two linear segments are joined at a "knot" representing the timing of a critical event (Cudeck & Klebe, 2002). Recent analytic models permit examination of whether the shift from one segment to another occurs at different times for different individuals (e.g., Cudeck & Klebe, 2002; Marceau, Ram, Houts, Grimm, & Susman, 2011), which would be expected when modeling the effect of developmental transitions such as puberty on substance use outcomes.

Measurement

Longitudinal research in social science is grounded in the notion of developmental continuity. Most critical is the idea of heterotypic continuity, which posits that the manifestation of a behavior changes over time despite continuity in underlying purpose or function (Nesselroade et al., 2007; Schulenberg & Maslowsky, 2009). Measured variables are often merely proxies for more theoretically interesting latent variables that cannot be measured directly (Hertzog & Nesselroade, 2003). This general issue is discussed in the measurement equivalence literature (Meredith & Horn, 2001; Nesselroade & Estabrook, 2009), which tests whether a construct has equivalent measurement properties at different ages or times. Without equivalence, true change over time is confounded with changes in measure reliability or validity and researchers cannot separate differences in the scales from changes in the constructs.

Moreover, it is often reasonable for a researcher to add or eliminate items in an effort to better capture certain phenomena of each developmental period. This issue is illustrated by the measure of risky alcohol use. Alcohol involvement manifests differently across the life span (Chung, Martin, & Winters, 2005); use of any alcohol is a valid indicator of risky drinking for 11-year-olds, versus a measure of frequent heavy drinking for 18-year-olds. With age, any use becomes a less precise indicator of problem drinking. Alcohol use and problems decouple due to changes in social norms and consequences. In addition, the average blood alcohol concentrations (BACs) attained by children and adolescents are much higher than those seen among adults, suggesting that the same dose of alcohol can result in likely acute risks stemming from high BACs in youth than in adults (Donovan, 2009), which complicates studies that examine changes in BAC over time.

The assumption of measurement equivalence can be empirically tested using structural equation models (Leite, 2007; McArdle, Grimm, Hamagami, Bowles, & Meredith, 2009). When items do vary over wave, one solution is to use within-occasion rescoring; however, this approach removes the means, so it is not possible to evaluate growth. Several analytic models have been proposed that handle nonidentical constructs that overlap across waves (Ferrer, Balluerka, & Widaman, 2008; Hancock, Kuo, & Lawrence, 2001; Pettit et al., 2007).

Mismatch Between Theory and Method

Quantitative researchers have advocated for better integration of developmental theory and analytic models (Hertzog & Nesselroade, 2003; Ram & Grimm, 2007; Sterba & Bauer, 2010), as our ability to test developmental theory validly is threatened if our statistical models fail to correspond to our theoretical models (Curran & Willoughby, 2003). Cross-sectional (between-person) data are not well suited to examine the within-person processes often posited by psychological theories (Curran & Bauer, 2011); for example, theories of affect regulation (Cox & Klinger, 2002) are most appropriately tested using repeated measures data. Although there is increasing recognition of the value of prospective data with regard to minimizing retrospection bias and establishing directionality, models that explicitly test between-person versus within-person effects are rare (Curran & Bauer, 2011).

A distinct minority of longitudinal studies carefully model growth (Khoo, West, Wu, & Kwok, 2006); meanwhile, researchers are asking more complex questions about the size and form of relationships. Cutting-edge models potentially provide better answers to traditional questions in longitudinal research—and may even lead researchers to formulate the question itself in a more appropriate way. They also permit researchers to raise interesting questions that were rarely, if ever, considered within the traditional analytic frameworks. Over the past decade, a host of powerful methods have been developed that allow for empirical testing of developmental theories (Curran, Obeidat, & Losardo, 2010). Computing resources are increasingly powerful, and readily available specialized software enables scientists to apply new sophisticated analyses in their work (Collins, 2006). It is encouraging to see the upsurge of published research studies that apply sensitive longitudinal models to answer important questions related to the progression of substance use, especially in terms of understanding the processes underlying the development of substance use problems and abuse/dependence.

Approaches to Modeling Covariates

Longitudinal research on substance use seeks to identify constructs that explain individual differences in stability and change. These constructs can be classified as either time invariant or time varying. Time-invariant covariates are assumed to be independent of the passage of time. These factors can be distal (e.g., sex) or proximal (e.g., motivations to use substances), with proximal risk factors serving as mediators for more distal risk (e.g., cognitive beliefs mediating social influences on drinking). For the most part, studies on substance use treat covariates as time invariant (e.g., prospectively predicting substance use from some risk factor assessed at baseline).

If the magnitude and/or direction of a covariate is expected to vary as a function of time, a time-varying effect is modeled. Another way to think about this is that individual development can moderate the influence of a given risk factor (Collins, 2006). As discussed earlier, risk factors for substance use can show age-related patterns, with some exerting stronger influences at different developmental stages than others. Developmental theory may posit that explanatory variables themselves vary over time; for example, there are clear age-related shifts in alcohol cognitions (Dunn & Goldman, 1998; Hipwell et al., 2005; Nicolai, Moshagen, & Demmel, 2012). Expectancies and alcohol use are shown to "travel together" (Mitchell, Beals, & Kaufman, 2006) in adolescence. Similarly, substance use and the number of substance-using friends appear to increase together linearly during adolescence (Simons-Morton & Chen, 2006). Declines in alcohol problems in the transition to young adulthood are associated with changes in personality traits associated with negative affectivity and self-regulation (Littlefield et al., 2009, 2010); there are similar findings for changes in tobacco use (Welch & Poulton, 2009) and drug use (Johnson, Hicks, McGue, & Iacono, 2007).

In addition, a researcher may want to consider the interplay of developmental processes in two constructs over time, as in the developmental cascade models that posit that early levels and changes in functioning in one domain (e.g.,

parenting difficulties) impact functioning in a different domain (e.g., substance use) (Dodge et al., 2009; Masten & Cicchetti, 2010). Constructs may exert a mutual influence on each other over time (travel together), over and above concurrent temporal covariation between them and over and above temporal stability in each. Sher et al. (2004) proposed that there are different patterns of time-varying covariates, or "dynamic predictors," and found empirical support for five types. For example, course trackers such as reasons for drinking and peer alcohol use differentiated individuals with or without an alcohol use disorder and covaried with symptomatology over time. Co-occurring use of multiple substances may also be a type of course tracker; for example, research shows that drinking, smoking, and marijuana use show corresponding courses over time (e.g., Brook, Lee, Finch, Brown, 2010; Jackson, Sher, Rose, & Kaprio, 2009; Jackson, Sher, & Schulenberg, 2008). Another type of dynamic predictor proposed by Sher et al. (2004) was the developmentally specific dynamic predictor, which predicted course only at certain ages (e.g., elevated performance enhancement alcohol expectancies among those consistently diagnosing with alcohol dependence during the college years but not during young adulthood). Other types of dynamic predictors included stable vulnerability indicators that remain consistently different in individuals with disorder from those without disorder (e.g., stable indices of temperament; indices of behavioral undercontrol); developmental lag markers that reflect slowed or inhibited normative developmental changes (e.g., generalized distress); and course-referenced variables that represent different constructs at different stages in the course of a disorder (drinking restraint). Modeling the longitudinal associations between time-varying predictors and outcomes is critical for gaining insights into the nature of the relationship between a substance use disorder and important etiological covariates.

Trajectory Modeling

Although trajectory approaches are ideal for studying the course of substance use involvement, caution must be taken to ensure that these trajectories not be reified (Jackson & Sher, 2005; Nagin & Tremblay, 2005a, 2005b). The number and nature of trajectory groups are not fixed properties of the individuals making up a sample. A seminal article by Bauer and Curran (2003) advises caution when interpreting trajectory models, as single-class models fit to nonnormal data cannot be distinguished from a multiple-class model fit to a mixture of normal distributions (although see Muthén, 2003, and Rindskopf, 2003). In addition, identification of trajectories can be affected by several design factors such as the definition of the measure (Jackson & Sher, 2005) and the numbers of and intervals between assessments (Chassin, Curran, Presson, Sherman, & Wirth, 2009; Hu, Muthén, Schaffran, Griesler, & Kandel, 2008; Hu et al., 2012; Jackson & Sher, 2008).

It is critical to bear in mind that substantive research questions are of greater importance to the substance use researcher than the class solution itself, and the existence of a true number of groups is irrelevant for the model to be useful in practice (Cudeck & Henly, 2003). Trajectory analyses can be thought of as "tools" to address substantive questions, particularly for developmental research, which moves beyond examining normative development (e.g., substance use increases over adolescence) to describing change at the level of the individual (e.g., there are distinct patterns of substance use over time) to the understanding of the processes that determine how substance use unfolds over the life span.

Conclusion

Substance use is a developmental disorder, with clear age-graded trends reflecting initiation in adolescence, increased use through emerging adulthood, and a decline thereafter. Individuals have changing vulnerabilities to substance use and related problems over the course of adolescence and young adulthood that are due to chronological aging as well as attributable to the normative developmental tasks and role transitions that may serve as a turning point that directs an individual toward or away from substance use. The examination of substance use development with respect to progressive stages of use is critical for understanding the relative influence of dynamic risk factors at varying points along the course of use. For example, certain factors, such as genetic liability to substance use disorders, are influential at all stages of substance use, whereas others are developmentally stage specific, thus calling for stage-specific intervention strategies.

A developmental framework places substance use behavior both within the context of normal development and in relation to the interplay between environmental and person-specific characteristics, where an underlying risk may manifest as a substance use problem in the face of an enabling environment. Against the backdrop of normative patterns of substance use, there are homogeneous developmental trajectories that are very likely linked to different etiological pathways and that can aid in the development of prevention programs targeted to reach high-risk subgroups. Determining the content and timing of these programs, however, requires valid testing of developmental theory using statistical models that correspond to our theoretical models, and the importance of carefully attending to the methodological challenges inherent in the longitudinal study of substance use in adolescence and young adulthood cannot be overstated.

Future Directions

1. Research consistently supports early age of onset as a risk factor for a wide array of adverse consequences in the realms of substance use and beyond, but there is a gap in our understanding of the nature of progression from first drink to heavier use. It is important that future research determine the factors that distinguish those adolescents who progress rapidly from first experience with a substance to heavier substance involvement from those who show a stable pattern of nonuse or light use across adolescence.

2. Whereas there is a good deal of longitudinal research in substance use that seeks to identify constructs that explain individual differences in stability and change (interindividual variability in intraindividual change), there is a lack of research that examines how individual development can moderate the effect of a given risk factor. It will be critical to turn our attention to examining the developmental specificity of risk factors, and importantly, to attempt to uncouple chronological age and stage of use when modeling development of substance use.

3. Although a great deal of etiological research in the past few decades has informed the design of prevention programs, the best timing for intervening on substance use across the life span is less well understood.

4. Longitudinal studies play an important role in developmental research, and these designs are becoming increasingly common; researchers are asking more complex questions about the size and form of relationships. However, there needs to be a better connection between what is considered to be "best practice" in the statistical methodology literature and "actual practice" in the field. As astutely stated by Curran et al. (2010), "Consistent with the old adage be careful for what you ask— you might just get it, once longitudinal data are

obtained, they must then be thoughtfully and rigorously analyzed" (pp. 121–122).

References

Aas, H., Leigh, B. C., Anderssen, N., & Jakobsen, R. (1998). Two-year longitudinal study of alcohol expectancies and drinking among Norwegian adolescents. *Addiction, 93,* 373–384.

Agrawal, A., Grant, J. D., Waldron, M., Duncan, A. E., Scherrer, J. F., Lynskey, M. T., . . . Heath, A. C. (2006). Risk for initiation of substance use as a function of age of onset of cigarette, alcohol, and cannabis use: Findings in a Midwestern female twin cohort. *Preventive Medicine, 43,* 125–128.

Agrawal, A., & Lynskey, M. T. (2008). Are there genetic influences on addiction: evidence from family, adoption and twin studies. *Addiction, 103,* 1069–1081.

Agrawal. A., Madden, P. A., Martin, N. G., & Lynskey, M. T. (2013). Do early experiences with cannabis vary in cigarette smokers? *Drug and Alcohol Dependence, 128,* 255–259.

Agrawal, A., Sartor, C. E., Lynskey, M. T., Grant, J. D., Pergadia, M. L., Grucza, R., . . . Heath, A. (2009). Evidence for an interaction between age at first drink and genetic influences on DSM-IV alcohol dependence symptoms. *Alcoholism: Clinical and Experimental Research, 33,* 2047–2056.

Alfonso-Loeches, S., & Guerri, C. (2011). Molecular and behavioral aspects of the actions of alcohol on the adult and developing brain. *Critical Reviews in Clinical Laboratory Sciences, 48,* 19–47.

Alvanzo, A. A. H., Storr, C. L., La Flair, L. Green, K. M. Wagner, F. A., & Crum, R. M. (2011). Race/ethnicity and sex differences in progression from drinking initiation to the development of alcohol dependence. *Drug and Alcohol Dependence, 118,* 375–382.

Anderson. G. (2010). Chronic care: Making the case for ongoing care. Princeton, NJ: Robert Wood Johnson Foundation. www.rwjf.org/pr/product.jsp?id=50968.

Anderson, K. G., Grunwald, I., Bekman, N., Brown, S. A., & Grant, A. (2011). To drink or not to drink: Motives and expectancies for use and nonuse in adolescence. *Addictive Behaviors, 36,* 972–979.

Anthony, J. C., & Petronis, K. R. (1995). Early-onset drug use and risk of later drug problems. *Drug and Alcohol Dependence, 40,* 9–15.

Anthony, J. C., Warner, L. A., & Kessler, R. C. (1994). Comparative epidemiology of dependence on tobacco, alcohol, controlled substances, and inhalants: Basic findings from the National Comorbidity Survey. *Experimental and Clinical Psychopharmacology, 2,* 244–268.

Arnett, J. J. (2005). The developmental context of substance use in emerging adulthood. *Journal of Drug Issues, 35,* 235–253.

Arria, A. M., Garnier-Dykstra, L. M., Cook, E. T., Caldeira, K. M., Vincent, K. B., Baron, R. A., & O'Grady, K. E. (2013). Drug use patterns in young adulthood and post-college employment. *Drug and Alcohol Dependence, 127,* 23–30.

Arseneault, L., Cannon, M., Witton, J., & Murray, R. M. (2004). Causal association between cannabis and psychosis: Examination of the evidence. *The British Journal of Psychiatry, 184,* 110–117.

Bachman, J. G., Wadsworth, K. N., O'Malley, P. M., Johnston, L. D., & Schulenberg, J. E. (1997). *Smoking, drinking, and drug use in young adulthood: The impacts of new freedoms and new responsibilities.* Mahwah, NJ: Erlbaum.

Bailey, J. A., Hill, K. G., Hawkins, J. D., Catalano, R. F., & Abbott, R. D. (2008). Men's and women's patterns of substance use around pregnancy. *Birth: Issues in Perinatal Care, 35,* 50–59.

Bauer, D. J., & Curran, P. J. (2003). Distributional assumptions of growth mixture models: Implications for over-extraction of latent trajectory classes. *Psychological Methods, 8,* 338–363.

Behrendt, S., Beesdo-Baum, S., Höfler, M., Perkonigg, A., Bühringer, G., Lieb, R., & Wittchen, H.-U. (2012). The relevance of age at first alcohol and nicotine use for initiation of cannabis use and progression to cannabis use disorders. *Drug and Alcohol Dependence, 123,* 48–56.

Behrendt, S., Wittchen, H.-U., Höfler, M., Lieb, R., Low, N. C. P., Rehm, J., & Beesdo, K. (2008). Risk and speed of transitions to first alcohol dependence symptoms in adolescents: A 10-year longitudinal community study in Germany. *Addiction, 103,* 1638–1647.

Behrendt, S., Wittchen, H.-U., Hofler, M., Lieb, R., & Beesdo, K. (2009). Transitions from first substance use to substance use disorders in adolescence: Is early onset associated with rapid escalation? *Drug and Alcohol Dependence, 99,* 68–78.

Bekman, N. M., Cummins, K., & Brown, S. A. (2010). Affective and personality risk and cognitive mediators of initial adolescent alcohol use. *Journal of Studies on Alcohol and Drugs, 71*(4), 570–580.

Bekman, N. M., Goldman, M. S., Worley, M. J., & Anderson, K. G. (2011). Pre-adolescent alcohol expectancies: Critical shifts and associated maturational processes. *Experimental and Clinical Psychopharmacology, 19,* 420–432.

Bell, R. Q. (1953). Convergence: An accelerated longitudinal approach. *Child Development, 24,* 145–152.

Bennett, M. E., McCrady, B. S., Johnson, V., & Pandina, R. J. (1999). Problem drinking from young adulthood to adulthood: Patterns, predictors and outcomes. *Journal of Studies on Alcohol, 60,* 605–614.

Bernat, D. H., Klein, E. G., & Forster, J. L. (2012). Smoking initiation during young adulthood: A longitudinal study of a population-based cohort. *Journal of Adolescent Health, 51,* 497–502.

Blitstein, J. L., Robinson, L. A., Murray, D. M., Klesges, R. C., & Zbikowski, S. M. (2003). Rapid progression to regular cigarette smoking among nonsmoking adolescents: Interactions with gender and ethnicity. *Preventive Medicine: An International Journal Devoted to Practice and Theory, 36,* 455–463.

Bouchery, E. E., Harwood, H. J., Sacks, J. J., Simon, C. J., & Brewer, R. D. (2011). Economic costs of excessive alcohol consumption in the U.S., 2006. *American Journal of Preventive Medicine, 41,* 516–524.

Brady, S. S., Song, A. V., & Halpern-Felsher, B. L. (2008). Adolescents report both positive and negative consequences of experimentation with cigarette use. *Preventive Medicine, 46,* 585–590.

Breslau, N., Fenn, N., & Peterson, E. (1993). Early smoking initiation and nicotine dependence in a cohort of young adults. *Drug and Alcohol Dependence, 33,* 129–237.

Breslau, N., Johnson, E., Hiripi, E., & Kessler, R. (2001). Nicotine dependence in the United States: Prevalence, trends, and smoking persistence. *Archives of General Psychiatry, 58,* 810–816.

Brewin, C. R., Andrews, B., & Gotlib, I. H. (1993). Psychopathology and early experience: A reappraisal of retrospective reports. *Psychological Bulletin, 113,* 82–98.

Bricker, J. B., Andersen, M. R., Rajan, K. B., Sarason, I. G. & Peterson, A. V. (2007). The role of schoolmates' smoking and non-smoking in adolescents' smoking transitions: A longitudinal study. *Addiction, 102*, 1665–1675.

Bricker, J. B., Peterson, A. V., Jr., Sarason, I. G., Andersen, M. R., & Rajan, K. B. (2007). Changes in the influence of parents' and close friends' smoking on adolescent smoking transitions. *Addictive Behaviors, 32*, 740–757.

Brodbeck, J., Bachmann, M. S., Croudace, T. J., & Brown, A. (2013). Comparing growth trajectories of risk behaviors from late adolescence through young adulthood: An accelerated design. *Developmental Psychology*. Advance online publication. *49*(9), 1732. doi: 10.1037/a0030873

Bronfenbrenner, U. (1979). *The ecology of human development*. Cambridge, MA: Harvard University Press.

Bronfenbrenner, U. (1986). Ecology of the family as a context for human development: Research perspectives. *Developmental Psychology, 22*, 723–742.

Brook, D. W., Brook, J. S., Zhang, C., Cohen, P., & Whiteman, M. (2002). Drug use and the risk of major depressive disorder, alcohol dependence, and substance use disorders. *Archives of General Psychiatry, 59*, 1039–1044.

Brook, D. W., Brook, J. S., Zhang, C., Whiteman, M., Cohen, P., & Finch, S. J. (2008). Developmental trajectories of cigarette smoking from adolescence to the early thirties: Personality and behavioral risk factors. *Nicotine & Tobacco Research, 10*, 1283–1291.

Brook, J. S., Lee, J. Y., Brown, E. N., Finch, S. J., & Brook, D. W. (2011). Developmental trajectories of marijuana use from adolescence to adulthood: Personality and social role outcomes. *Psychological Reports, 108*, 339–357.

Brook, J. S., Lee, J. Y., Finch, S. J., & Brown, E. N. (2010). Course of comorbidity of tobacco and marijuana use: Psychosocial risk factors. *Nicotine and Tobacco Research, 12*, 474–482.

Brook, J. S., Ning, Y., & Brook, D. W. (2006). Personality risk factors associated with trajectories of tobacco use. *The American Journal on Addictions, 15*, 426–433.

Brook, J. S., Pahl, K., & Ning, Y. (2006). Peer and parental influences on longitudinal trajectories of smoking among African Americans and Puerto Ricans. *Nicotine & Tobacco Research, 8*, 639–651.

Brooks-Gunn, J., & Reiter, E. O. (1990). The role of pubertal processes. In S. S. Feldman & G. R. Elliott (Eds.), *At the threshold: The developing adolescent* (pp. 16–53). Cambridge, MA: Harvard University Press.

Brown, S. A., Tapert, S. F., Granholm, E., & Delis, D. C. (2000). Neurocognitive functioning of adolescents: Effects of protracted alcohol use. *Alcoholism: Clinical and Experimental Research, 24*, 164–171.

Brown, T. L., Flory, K. Lynam, D. R., Leukefeld, C. & Clayton, R. R. (2004). Comparing the developmental trajectories of marijuana use of African American and Caucasian adolescents: Patterns, antecedents, and consequences. *Experimental and Clinical Psychopharmacology, 12*, 47–56.

Buchmann, A. F., Schmid, B., Blomeyer, D., Becker, K., Treutlein, J., Zimmermann, U.S., . . . Laucht, M. (2009). Impact of age at first drink on vulnerability to alcohol-related problems: Testing the marker hypothesis in a prospective study of young adults. *Journal of Psychiatric Research, 43*, 1205–1212.

Budney, A. J., Moore, B. A., & Vandrey, R. (2008). Health consequences of marijuana use. In J. Brick (Ed.), *Handbook of the medical consequences of drug abuse* (pp. 171–218). Binghamton, NY: Haworth Press.

Burdzovic Andreas, J., & Watson, M. W. (2007). Exposure to neighborhood violence and substance use in adolescents: Moderating effects of positive family characteristics. Society for Research in Child Development (SRCD), Biennial Meeting, April 2007, Boston, MA.

Burdzovic Andreas, J., & Watson, M. W. (2010). Timing of adolescent smoking, drinking, and marijuana use initiation as a function of neighborhood quality: A survival analysis approach. Life History Research Society Bi-Annual Meeting, October 2010, Montreal, Canada.

Buydens-Branchey, L., Branchey, M. H., Noumair, D. (1989). Age of alcoholism onset: I. Relationship to psychopathology. *Archives of General Psychiatry, 46*, 225–230.

Cairns, R. B., Cairns, B. D., Rodkin, P. & Xie, H. (1998). New directions in developmental research: Models and methods. In R. Jessor (Ed.), *New perspectives on adolescent risk behavior* (pp. 13–40). New York, NY: Cambridge University Press.

Caldeira, K. M., O'Grady, K. E., Garnier-Dykstra, L. M., Vincent, K. B., Pickworth, W. B., & Arria, A. M. (2012). Cigarette smoking among college students: Longitudinal trajectories and health outcomes. *Nicotine & Tobacco Research, 14*. 777–785.

Casswell, S., Pledger, M., & Pratap, S. (2002). Trajectories of drinking from 18 to 26 years: Identification and prediction. *Addiction, 97*, 1427–1437.

Centers for Disease Control and Prevention (CDC). (2009, Jan 22). State-specific smoking-attributable mortality and years of potential life lost—United States, 2000-2004, *Morbidity and Mortality Weekly Report, 58*(2). Retrieved May 11, 2013, from http://www.cdc.gov/mmwr/preview/mmwrhtml/mm5745a3.htm.

Chambers, R. A., Taylor, J. R., & Potenza, M. N. (2003). Developmental neurocircuitry of motivation in adolescence: A critical period of addiction vulnerability. *American Journal of Psychiatry, 160*, 1041–1052.

Chassin, L., Curran, P. J., Presson, C. C., Sherman, S. J., & Wirth, R. J. (2009). Developmental trajectories of cigarette smoking from adolescence to adulthood (pp. 187–244). *NCI Tobacco Control Monograph 22: Phenotypes, Endophenotypes, and Genetic Studies of Nicotine Dependence*.

Chassin, L., Pitts, S. C., & Prost, J. (2002). Binge drinking trajectories from adolescence to emerging adulthood in a high-risk sample: Predictors and substance abuse outcomes. *Journal of Consulting and Clinical Psychology, 70*, 67–78.

Chassin, L., Presson, C. C., Rose, J. S., & Sherman, S. J. (1996). The natural history of cigarette smoking from adolescence to adulthood: Demographic predictors of continuity and change. *Health Psychology, 15*, 478–484.

Chassin, L., Presson, C. C., Sherman, S. J., & Edwards, D. A. (1991). Four pathways to young-adult smoking status: Adolescent social-psychological antecedents in a Midwestern community sample. *Health Psychology, 10*, 409–418.

Chen, C. Y., O'Brien, M. S., & Anthony, J. C. (2005). Who becomes cannabis dependent soon after onset of use? Epidemiological evidence from the United States: 2000-2001. *Drug and Alcohol Dependence, 79*, 11–22.

Chen, C. Y., Storr, C. L., & Anthony, J. C. (2009). Early-onset drug use and risk for drug dependence problems. *Addictive Behaviors, 34*, 319–322.

Chen, K., & Kandel, D. B. (1995). The natural history of drug use from adolescence to the mid-thirties in a general population sample. *American Journal of Public Health, 85*, 41–47.

Chen, K., & Kandel, D. B. (1998). Predictors of cessation of marijuana use: An event history analysis. *Drug and Alcohol Dependence, 50*, 109–121.

Chen, P., & Jacobson, K. C. (2012). Developmental trajectories of substance use from early adolescence to young adulthood: Gender and racial/ethnic differences. *Journal of Adolescent Health, 50*, 154–163.

Cho, H., Hallfors, D. D., & Iritani, B. J. (2007). Early initiation of substance use and subsequent risk factors related to suicide among urban high school students. *Addictive Behaviors, 32*, 1628–1639.

Choi, W. S., Gilpin, E. A., Farkas, A. J., & Pierce, J. P. (2001). Determining the probability of future smoking among adolescents. *Addiction, 2*, 313–323.

Chou, S. P., & Pickering, R. P. (1992). Early onset of drinking as a risk factor for lifetime alcohol-related problems. *British Journal of Addiction, 87*, 1199–1204.

Chung, T., Martin, C. S., & Winters, K. C. (2005). Diagnosis, course and assessment of alcohol abuse and dependence in adolescents. In M. Galanter (Ed.), *Alcohol problems in adolescents and young adults: Epidemiology, neurobiology, prevention, and treatment* (pp. 5–27). New York, NY: Springer Science.

Cicchetti, D., & Rogosch, F. A. (1996). Equifinality and multifinality in developmental psychopathology. *Development and Psychopathology, 89*, 597–600.

Cicchetti, D., & Rogosch, F. A. (2002). A developmental psychopathology perspective on adolescence. *Journal of Consulting and Clinical Psychology, 70*, 6–20.

Clapper, R. L., Buka, S. L., Goldfield, E. C., Lipsitt, L. P., & Tsuang, L. P. (1995). Adolescent problem behaviors as predictors of adult alcohol diagnoses. *International Journal of the Addictions, 30*, 507–523.

Clark, D. B. (2004). The natural history of adolescent alcohol use disorders. *Addiction, 99*(S2), 5–22.

Clark, D. B., & Cornelius, J. (2004). Child psychopathology and adolescent cigarette smoking: A prospective survival analysis in children at high risk for substance use disorders. *Addictive Behaviors, 29*, 837–841.

Clark, D. B., Thatcher, D. L., & Tapert, S. F. (2008). Alcohol, psychological dysregulation, and adolescent brain development. *Alcoholism: Clinical and Experimental Research, 32*, 375–385.

Colder, C. R., & Chassin, L. (1999). The psychosocial characteristics of alcohol users versus problem users: Data from a study of adolescents at risk. *Development and Psychopathology, 11*, 321–348.

Colder, C. R., Chassin, L., Lee, M. R., & Villalta, I. K. (2010). Developmental perspectives: Affect and adolescent substance use. In J. D. Kassel (Ed.), *Substance abuse and emotion*. Washington, D.C: American Psychological Association.

Colder, C. R., Chassin, L., Stice, E. M., & Curran, P. J. (1997). Alcohol expectancies as potential mediators of parent alcoholism effects on the development of adolescent heavy drinking. *Journal of Research on Adolescence, 7*(4), 349–374.

Colder, C. R., Mehta, P., Balanda, K., Campbell, R. T., Mayhew, K. P., Stanton, W. R., Pentz, M. A., & Flay, B. R. (2001). Identifying trajectories of adolescent smoking: An application of latent growth mixture modeling. *Health Psychology, 20*, 127–135.

Collins, L. M. (2006). Analysis of longitudinal data: The integration of theoretical models, design, and statistical model. *Annual Review of Psychology, 57*, 505–528.

Collins, L. M., & Graham, J. W. (2002). The effect of the timing and temporal spacing of observations on statistical results in longitudinal studies. *Drug and Alcohol Dependence, 68*, S85–S96.

Conger, R. D. (1997). *The social context of substance abuse: A developmental perspective.* http://www.nida.nih.gov/PDF/Monographs/Monograph168/Download168.html.

Connell, A. M., Dishion, T. J., & Deater-Deckard, K. (2006). Variable- and person-centered approaches to the analysis of early adolescent substance use: Linking peer, family, and intervention effects with developmental trajectories (Special issue: Person-centered and variable-centered approaches to longitudinal data). *Merrill-Palmer Quarterly, 52*, 421–448.

Costanzo, P. R., Malone, P. S., Belsky, D., Kertesz, S., Pletcher, M., & Sloan, F. A. (2007). Longitudinal differences in alcohol use in early adulthood. *Journal of Studies on Alcohol and Drugs, 68*, 727–737.

Costello, D. M., Dierker, L. C., Jones, B. L., & Rose, J. S. (2008). Trajectories of smoking from adolescence to early adulthood and their psychosocial risk factors. *Health Psychology, 27*, 811–818.

Cox, W. M., & Klinger, E. (2002). Motivational structure: Relationships with substance use and processes of change. *Addictive Behaviors, 27*, 925–940.

Crews, F., He, J., & Hodge, C. (2007). Adolescent cortical development: A critical period of vulnerability for addiction. *Pharmacology Biochemistry and Behavior, 86*, 189–199.

Crosnoe, R., & Riegle-Crumb, C. (2007). A life course model of education and alcohol use. *Journal of Health and Social Behavior, 48*, 267–282.

Crum, R. M., Ensminger, M. E., Ro, M. J., & McCord, J. (1998). The association of educational achievement and school dropout with risk of alcoholism: A twenty-five-year prospective study of inner-city children. *Journal of Studies on Alcohol, 59*(3), 318–326.

Cudeck, R., & Henly, S. J. (2003). A realistic perspective on pattern representation in growth data: Comment on Bauer and Curran (2003). *Psychological Methods, 8*, 378–383.

Cudeck, R. & Klebe, K. J. (2002). Multiphase mixed-effects models for repeated measures data. *Psychological Methods, 7*, 41–63.

Curran, P. J., & Bauer, D. J. (2011). The disaggregation of within-person and between-person effects in longitudinal models of change. *Annual Review of Psychology, 62*, 583–619.

Curran, P. J., Muthen, B., O., & Harford, T. C. (1998). The influence of changes in marital status on developmental trajectories of alcohol use in young adults. *Journal of Studies on Alcohol, 59*, 647–658.

Curran, P. J., Obeidat, K., & Losardo, D. (2010). Twelve frequently asked questions about growth curve modeling. *Journal of Cognition and Development, 11*, 121–136.

Curran, P. J., & Willoughby, M. T. (2003). Implications of latent trajectory models for the study of developmental psychopathology. *Development and Psychopathology, 15*, 581–612.

D'Amico, E. J., & McCarthy, D. M. (2006). Escalation and initiation of younger adolescents' substance use: The impact of perceived peer use. *Journal of Adolescent Health, 39*, 481–487.

Dawson, D. A. (2000). The link between family history and early onset alcoholism: Earlier initiation of drinking or more rapid development of dependence? *Journal of Studies on Alcohol, 61*, 637–646.

Dawson, D. A., Grant, B. F., Stinson, F. S., & Chou, P. S. (2004). Another look at heavy episodic drinking and alcohol use disorders among college and noncollege youth. *Journal of Studies on Alcohol, 65*, 477–488.

Dawson, D. A., Grant, B. F., Stinson, F. S. & Chou, P. S. (2006). Estimating the effect of help-seeking on achieving recovery from alcohol dependence. *Addiction, 101*, 824–834.

Dawson, D. A., Grant, B. F., & Li, T.-K. (2007). Impact of age at first drink on stress-reactive drinking. *Alcoholism: Clinical and Experimental Research, 31*, 69–77.

Degenhardt, L., Chiu, W. T., Conway, K., Dierker, L., Glantz, M., Kalaydijan, A., . . . Kessler, R. C. (2009). Does the "gateway" matter? Associations between the order of drug use initiation and the development of drug dependence in the National Comorbidty Study Replication. *Psychcological Medicine, 39*, 157–167.

DeWit, D. J., Adlaf, E. M., Offord, D. R., & Ogborne, A. C. (2000). Age at first alcohol use: A risk factor for the development of alcohol disorders. *American Journal of Psychiatry, 157*, 745–750.

DeWit, D. J. Hance, J., Offord, D. R., & Ogborne, A. (2000). The influence of early and frequent use of marijuana on the risk of desistance and of progression to marijuana-related harm. *Preventive Medicine: An International Journal Devoted to Practice and Theory, 31*, 455–464.

Dick, D. M., Rose, R. J., Pulkkinen, L., & Kaprio (2001). Measuring puberty and understanding its impact: A longitudinal study of adolescent twins. *Journal of Youth and Adolescence, 30*, 385–400.

Dick, D. M., Rose, R. J., Viken, R. J., & Kaprio, J. (2000). Pubertal timing and substance use: Associations between and within families across late adolescence. *Developmental Psychology, 36*, 180–189.

Dierker, L. C., Avenevoli, S., Goldberg, A., & Glantz, M. (2004). Defining subgroups of adolescents at risk for experimental and regular smoking. *Prevention Science, 5*, 169–183.

Dierker, L. C., Avenevoli, S., Merikangas, K. R., Flaherty, B. P., & Stolar, M. (2001). Association between psychiatric disorders and the progression of tobacco use behaviors. *Journal of the American Academy of Child and Adolescent Psychiatry, 40*, 1159–1167.

DiFranza, J. R., Savageau, J. A., Fletcher, K., O'Loughlin, J., Pbert, L., Ockene, J. K., . . . Wellman, R. J. (2007). Symptoms of tobacco dependence after brief intermittent use—The development and assessment of nicotine dependence in youth-2 study. *Archives of Pediatrics & Adolescent Medicine, 161*, 704–710.

Di Franza, J. R., Savageau, J. A., Rigotti, N. A., Fletcher, K., Ockene, J., McNeill, A. D., . . . Wood, C. (2002). Development of symptoms of tobacco dependence in youths: 30 month follow up data from the DANDY study. *Tobacco Control, 11*, 228–235.

Dodge, K. A., Malone, P. S., Lansford, J. E., Miller, S., Pettit, G. S., & Bates, J. E., (2009). A dynamic cascade model of the development of substance-use onset. *Monographs of the Society for Research in Child Development, 74*, 1–130.

Donovan, J. E. (2004). Adolescent alcohol initiation: a review of psychosocial risk factors. *Journal of Adolescent Health, 35*, 7–18.

Donovan, J. E. (2009). Estimated blood alcohol concentrations for child and adolescent drinking and their implications for screening instruments. *Pediatrics, 123*(6), e975–e981.

Donovan, J. E., Jessor, R., & Costa, F. M. (1999). Adolescent problem drinking: Stability of psychosocial and behavioral correlates across a generation. *Journal of Studies on Alcohol, 60*, 352–361.

Donovan, J. E., Jessor, R., & Jessor, L. (1983). Problem drinking in adolescence and young adulthood: A follow-up study. *Journal of Studies on Alcohol, 44*, 109–137.

Donovan, J. E., Leech, S. L., Zucker, R. A., Loveland-Cherry, C. J., Jester, J. M., . . . Looman, W. S. (2004). Really underage drinkers: Alcohol use among elementary students. *Alcoholism: Clinical and Experimental Research, 28*, 341–349.

Dunn, M. E., & Goldman, M. S. (1998). Age and drinking-related differences in the memory organization of alcohol expectances in 3rd-, 6th-, 9th-, and 12th-grade children. *Journal of Consulting and Clinical Psychology, 66*, 579–585.

Eaton, D. K., Kann, L., Kinchen, S., Shanklin, S., Flint, K. H., Hawkins, J., . . . Centers for Disease, Control, & Prevention (2012). Youth risk behavior surveillance—United States, 2011. *Mmwr Surveillance Summary, 61*, 1–162.

Elder, G. H. Jr. (1998). The life course as developmental theory. *Child Development, 69*, 1–12.

Elder, G. H. Jr., & Shanahan, M. J. (2006). The life course and human development. In Lerner, R. M. (Ed.), Vol. 1, *Theoretical models of human development. The Handbook of child psychology* (6th ed.). Hoboken, NJ: John Wiley & Sons.

Ellickson, P. L., D'Amico, E. J., Collins, R. L., & Klein, D. J. (2005). Marijuana use and later problems: When frequency of recent use explains age of initiation effects (and when it does not). *Substance Use & Misuse, 40*, 343–359.

Elliott, D. S., Huizinga, D., & Menard, S. (1989). *Multiple problem youth: Delinquency, substance abuse, and mental health problems.* New York, NY: Springer Verlag.

Engels, R. C. E., Knibbe, R. J., & Drop, M. J. (1997). Inconsistencies in adolescents' self-reports of initiation of alcohol and tobacco use. *Addictive Behaviors, 22*, 613–623.

Everett, S. A., Warren, C. W., Sharp, D., Kann, L., Husten, C., & Gossett, L. S. (1999). Initiation of cigarette smoking and subsequent smoking behavior among U.S. high school students. *Preventive Medicine, 29*, 327–333.

Faden, V. B., Day, N. L., Windle, M., Windle, R., Grube, J. W., Molina, B. S. G., . . . Sher, K. J. (2004). Collecting longitudinal data through childhood, adolescence, and young adulthood: Methodological challenges. *Alcoholism: Clinical Experimental Research, 28*, 330–340.

Fagerström, K. (2002). The epidemiology of smoking: Health consequences and benefits of cessation. *Drugs, 2002; 62*, 1–9.

Fairman, B. J., & Anthony, J. C. (2012). Are early-onset cannabis smokers at an increased risk of depression spells? *Journal of Affective Disorders, 138*, 54–62.

Feldman, K., & Newcomb, T. (1969). The impact of college on students. San Francisco, CA: Jossey-Bass.

Fergusson, D. M., & Boden, J. M. (2008). Cannabis use and later life outcomes. *Addiction, 103*, 969–976.

Fergusson, D. M., Boden, J. M., & Horwood, L. J. (2006). Cannabis use and other illicit drug use: Testing the cannabis gateway hypothesis. *Addiction 101*, 556–569.

Fergusson, D. M., Horwood, L. J., & Swain-Campbell, N. (2002). Cannabis use and psychosocial adjustment in adolescence and young adulthood. *Addiction, 97*, 1123–1135.

Ferrer, E., Balluerka, N., & Widaman, K. F. (2008). Factorial invariance and the specification of second-order latent growth models. *Methodology: European Journal of Research Methods for the Behavioral and Social Sciences, 4*, 22–36.

Finlay, A. K., White, H. R., Mun, E.-Y., Cronley, C. C., & Lee, C. (2012). Racial differences in trajectories of heavy drinking and regular marijuana use from ages 13 to 24 among African-American and White males. *Drug and Alcohol Dependence, 121*, 118–123.

Flay, B. R., Hu, F. B., & Richardson, J. (1998). Psychosocial predictors of different stages of cigarette smoking among high school students. *Preventive Medicine: An International Journal Devoted to Practice and Theory, 27*, A9–A18.

Flory, K., Lynam, D., Milich, R., Leukefeld, C., & Clayton, R. (2004). Early adolescent through young adult alcohol and marijuana use trajectories: Early predictors, young adult outcomes, and predictive utility. *Development & Psychopathology, 16*, 193–213.

Fowler, T., Lifford, K., Shelton, K., Rice, F., Thapar, A., Neale, M. C., . . . Van den Bree, M. B. (2007). Exploring the relationship between genetic and environmental influences on initiation and progression of substance use. *Addiction, 101*, 413–422.

Garrity, T. F., Leukefeld, C. G., Carlson, R. G., Falck, R. S., Wang, J., & Booth, B. M. (2007). Physical health, illicit drug use, and demographic characteristics in rural stimulant users. *The Journal of Rural Health, 23*, 99–107.

Ge, X., Conger, R. D., & Elder, G. H. (1996). Coming of age too early: Pubertal influences on girls' vulnerability to psychological distress. *Child Development, 67*, 3386–3400.

Gervais, A., O'Loughlin, J., Meshefedjian, G., Bancej, C., & Tremblay, M. (2006). Milestones in the natural course of onset of cigarette use among adolescents. *Canadian Medical Association Journal, 175*, 255–265.

Gold, D. R., Wang, X., Wypij, D., Speizer, F. E., Ware, J. H., & Dockery, D. W. (1996). Effects of cigarette smoking on lung function in adolescent boys and girls. *New England Journal of Medicine, 335*, 931–937.

Gotham, H. J., Sher, K. J., & Wood, P. K. (1997). Predicting stability and change in frequency of intoxication from the college years to beyond: Individual difference and role transition variables. *Journal of Abnormal Psychology, 106*, 619–629.

Gotham, H. J., Sher, K. J., & Wood, P. K. (2003). Alcohol involvement and developmental task completion during young adulthood. *Journal of Studies on Alcohol, 64*, 32–42.

Grant, B. F. (1998). Age at smoking onset and its association with alcohol consumption and DSM-IV alcohol abuse and dependence: Results from the National Longitudinal Alcohol Epidemiologic Survey. *Journal of Substance Abuse, 10*, 59–73.

Grant, B. F., & Dawson D. A. (1997). Age at onset of alcohol use and its association with DSM-IV drug abuse and dependence: Results from the national longitudinal alcohol Epidemiologic Survey. *Journal of Substance Abuse, 10*, 163–173.

Grant, B. F., Stinson, F. S., & Harford, T. (2001). The 5-year course of alcohol abuse among young adults. *Journal of Substance Abuse, 13*, 229–238.

Grant, J. D., Lynskey, M. T., Scherrer, J. F., Agrawal, A., Heath, A. C., & Bucholz, K. K. (2010). A cotwin-control analysis of drug use and abuse/dependence risk associated with early-onset cannabis use. *Addictive Behaviors, 35*, 35–41.

Green, B. E., & Ritter, C. (2000). Marijuana use and depression. *Journal of Health and Social Behavior, 41*, 40–49.

Green, K. M., & Ensminger, M. E. (2006). Adult social behavioral effects of heavy adolescent marijuana use among African Americans. *Developmental Psychology, 42*, 1168–1178.

Gruber, E., DiClimente, R. J., Anderson, M. M., & Lodico, M. (1996). Early drinking onset and its association with alcohol use and problem behavior in late adolescence. *Preventive Medicine, 25*, 293–300.

Gruber, S. A., Sagar, K. A., Dahlgren, M. K., Racine, M., & Lukas, S. E. (2012). Age of onset of marijuana use and executive function. *Psychology of Addictive Behaviors, 26*, 496–506.

Guo, J., Chung, I. J., Hill, K. G., Hawkins, J. D., Catalano, R. F., & Abbott, R. D. (2002). Developmental relationships between adolescent substance use and risky sexual behavior in young adulthood. *Journal of Adolescent Health, 31*, 354–362.

Guo, J., Ick-Joong, C., Hill, K. (2002). Developmental relationship between adolescent substance use and risky sexual behavior in young adulthood. *Journal of Adolescent Health, 31*, 354–362.

Guo, Q., Unger, J. B., Azen, S. P., Li, C., Spruijt-Metz, D., Palmer, P. H., . . . Johnson, C. A. (2010). Cognitive attributions for smoking among adolescents in China. *Addictive Behaviors, 35*, 95–101.

Guo, Q., Unger, J. B., Azen, S. P. MacKinnon, D. P., & Johnson, C. A. (2012). Do cognitive attributions for smoking predict subsequent smoking development? *Addictive Behaviors, 37*, 273–279.

Hall, W., & Degenhardt, L. (2009). Adverse health effects of non-medical cannabis use. *Lancet, 374*, 1383–1391.

Haller, M., Handley, E., Chassin, L., & Bountress, K. (2010). Developmental cascades: Linking adolescent substance use, affiliation with substance use promoting peers, and academic achievement to adult substance use disorders. *Development and Psychopathology, 22*, 899–916.

Hammer, T., & Vaglum, P. (1990). Initiation, continuation or discontinuation of cannabis use in a general population. *British Journal of Addiction, 85*, 899–909.

Hancock, G. R., Kuo, W, -L., & Lawrence, F. R. (2001). An illustration of second-order latent growth models. *Structural Equation Modeling, 8*, 470–489.

Hanna, E. Z., & Grant, B. F. (1999). Parallels to early onset alcohol use in the relationship of early onset smoking with drug use and DSM-IV drug and depressive disorders: Findings from the National Longitudinal Epidemiological Survey. *Alcoholism: Clinical & Experimental Research, 23*, 513–522.

Harford, T. C., & Muthen, B. O. (2001). Alcohol use among college students: The effects of prior problem behaviors and change of residence. *Journal of Studies on Alcohol, 62*, 306–312.

Harford, T. C., Yi, H., & Hilton, M. E. (2006). Alcohol abuse and dependence in college and noncollege samples: A ten-year prospective follow-up in a national survey. *Journal of Studies on Alcohol, 67*(6), 803–809.

Harrison, P. A., Fulkerson, J. A., & Park, E. (2000). The relative importance of social versus commercial sources in youth access to tobacco, alcohol, and other drugs. *Preventive Medicine, 31*, 39–48.

Henry, B., Moffitt, T. E., Caspi, A., Langley, J. & Silva, P. A. (1994). On the "remembrance of things past": A longitudinal evaluation of the retrospective method. *Psychological Assessment, 6*, 92–101.

Hertzog, C., & Nesselroade, J. R. (2003). Assessing psychological change in adulthood: An overview of methodological issues. *Psychology and Aging, 18,* 639–657.

Hill, K. G., White, H. R., Chung, I., Hawkins, J. D., & Catalano, R. F. (2000). Early adult outcomes of adolescent binge drinking: Person- and variable-centered analyses of binge drinking trajectories. *Alcoholism: Clinical and Experimental Research, 24,* 892–901.

Hingson, R. W., Heeren, T., Jamanka, A., & Howland, J. (2000). Age of drinking onset and unintentional injury involvement after drinking. *Journal of the American Medical Association, 284,* 1527–1533.

Hingson, R. W., Heeren, T., & Winter, M. R. (2006). Age at drinking onset and alcohol dependence, age at onset, duration, and severity. *Archives of Pediatric and Adolescent Medicine, 160,* 739–746.

Hingson, R. W., Heeren, T., & Zakocs, R. (2001). Age of drinking onset and involvement in physical fights after drinking. *Pediatrics, 108,* 872–877.

Hipwell, A. E., White, H. R., Loeber, R., Stouthamer-Loeber, M., Chung, T., & Sembower, M. A. (2005). Young girls' expectancies about the effects of alcohol, future intentions and patterns of use. *Journal of Studies on Alcohol, 66,* 630–639.

Horwood, J. L., Fergusson, D. M., Hayatbakhsh, M. R., Najman, J. M., Coffey, C., Patton, G. C., . . . Hutchinson, D. M. (2010). Cannabis use and educational achievement: Findings from three Australasian cohort studies. *Drug and Alcohol Dependence, 110,* 247–253.

Hu, M. C., Davies, M., & Kandel, D. B. (2006). Epidemiology and correlates of daily smoking and nicotine dependence among young adults in the United States. *American Journal of Public Health, 96,* 299–308.

Hu, M. C., Griesler, P. C., Schaffran, C., Wall, M. M., & Kandel, D. B. (2012). Trajectories of criteria of nicotine dependence from adolescence to early adulthood. *Drug and Alcohol Dependence, 125,* 283–289.

Hu, M. C., Muthén, B., Schaffran, C., Griesler, P. C., & Kandel, D. B. (2008). Developmental trajectories of criteria of nicotine dependence in adolescence. *Drug and Alcohol Dependence, 98,* 94–104.

Hussong, A., Bauer, D., & Chassin, L. (2008). Telescoped trajectories from alcohol initiation to disorder in children of alcoholic parents. *Journal of Abnormal Psychology, 117,* 63–78.

Hussong, A. M., Curran, P. J., Moffitt, T. E., Caspi, A., & Carrig, M. M. (2004). Substance abuse hinders desistance in young adults' antisocial behavior. *Development and Psychopathology, 16,* 1029–1046.

Ialongo, N., Poduska, J., Werthamer, L., & Kellam, S. (2001). The distal impact of two first-grade preventive interventions on conduct problems and disorder in early adolescence. *Journal of Emotional and Behavioral Disorders, 9,* 146–160.

Jackson, C., Ennett, S. T., Dickinson, D. M., & Bowling, J. M. (2012). Letting children sip: Understanding why parents allow alcohol use by elementary school-aged children. *Archives of Pediatric and Adolescent Medicine,* Sept 17: 1–5. doi: 10.1001/archpediatrics.2012.1198.

Jackson, K. M. (2010). Progression through early drinking milestones in an adolescent treatment sample. *Addiction, 105,* 438–449.

Jackson, K. M., & Sartor, C. E. (2014). The natural course of substance use and dependence. In *The Oxford handbook of substance use disorders.* New York: Oxford University Press. http://dx.doi.org/10.1093/oxfordhb/9780199381678.013.007.

Jackson, K. M., & Schulenberg, J. E. (2013). Alcohol use during the transition from middle school to high school: National panel data on prevalence and moderators. *Developmental Psychology, 49,* 2147–2158.

Jackson, K. M., & Sher, K. J. (2005). Similarities and differences of longitudinal phenotypes across alternate indices of alcohol involvement: A methodologic comparison of trajectory approaches. *Psychology of Addictive Behaviors, 19,* 339–351.

Jackson, K. M., & Sher, K. J. (2008). Comparison of longitudinal phenotypes based on alternate heavy drinking cut scores: A systematic comparison of trajectory approaches III. *Psychology of Addictive Behaviors, 22,* 198–209.

Jackson, K. M., Sher, K. J., Cooper, M. L., & Wood, P. K. (2002). Adolescent alcohol and tobacco use: Onset, persistence and trajectories of use across two samples. *Addiction, 97,* 517–531.

Jackson, K. M., Sher, K. J., Gotham, H. J., & Wood, P. K. (2001). Transitioning into and out of large-effect drinking in young adulthood. *Journal of Abnormal Psychology, 110,* 378–391.

Jackson, K. M., Sher, K. J., Rose, R. J., & Kaprio, J. (2009). Trajectories of tobacco use from adolescence to adulthood: Are the most informative genotypes tobacco specific? (pp. 289–386). *NCI Tobacco Control Monograph 22: Phenotypes, Endophenotypes, and Genetic Studies of Nicotine Dependence.* Bethesda, MD: U.S. Department of Health and Human Services, National Institutes of Health, National Cancer Institute. NIH Publication No. 09-6366.

Jackson, K. M., Sher, K. J., & Schulenberg, J. E. (2008). Conjoint developmental trajectories of young adult substance use. *Alcoholism: Clinical and Experimental Research, 32,* 723–737.

Jessor, R., & Jessor, S. L. (1977). *Problem behavior and psychosocial development: A longitudinal study of youth.* San Diego, CA: Academic Press.

Jochman, K. A., & Fromme, K. (2010). Maturing out of substance use: The other side of etiology (pp. 565–578). In L. Scheier (Ed.), *Handbook of drug use etiology: Theory, methods, and empirical findings.* Washington, DC: American Psychological Association.

Johnson, T. P., & Mott, J. A. (2001). The reliability of self-reported age of onset of tobacco, alcohol and illicit drug use. *Addiction, 96,* 1187–1198.

Johnson, W., Hicks, B. M., McGue, M., & Iacono, W. G. (2007). Most of the girls are alright, but some aren't: Personality trajectory groups from ages 14 to 24 and some associations with outcomes. *Journal of Personality and Social Psychology, 93,* 266–284.

Johnston, L. D., O'Malley, P. M., Bachman, J. G., Schulenberg, J. E. & Miech, R. A. (2014a). *Monitoring the future national survey results on drug use, 1975–20 13: Volume 2, College students and adults ages 19-55.* Ann Arbor: Institute for Social Research, The University of Michigan. http://monitoringthefuture.org/pubs/monographs/mtf-vol2_2013.pdf.

Johnston, L. D., O'Malley, P. M., Bachman, J. G., Schulenberg, J. E. & Miech, R. A. (2014b). *Monitoring the future national survey results on drug use, 1975–2013: Volume I, Secondary school students.* Ann Arbor: Institute for Social Research, The University of Michigan. http://www.monitoringthefuture.org/pubs/monographs/mtf-vol1_2013.pdf.

Johnstone, B. M., Leino, E. V., Ager, C. R., Ferrer, H., & Fillmore, K. M. (1996). Determinants of life-course variation in the frequency of alcohol consumption: Meta-analysis of studies from the collaborative alcohol- related longitudinal project. *Journal of Studies on Alcohol, 57*, 494–506.

Juon, H., Ensminger, M. E., & Syndor, K. D. (2002). A longitudinal study of developmental trajectories to young adult cigarette smoking. *Drug and Alcohol Dependence, 66*, 303–314.

Kahler, C. W., Strong, D. R., Read, J. P., Palfai, T. P., & Wood, M. D. (2004). Mapping the continuum of alcohol problems in college students: A Rasch model analysis. *Psychology of Addictive Behaviors, 18*, 322–333.

Kandel, D. B. (1975). Stages in adolescent involvement in drug use. *Science, 190*, 912–914.

Kandel, D. B. (1980). Drug and drinking behavior among youth. *Annual Review of Sociology, 6*, 235–285.

Kandel, D. B. (2002). Stages and pathways of drug involvement: Examining the gateway hypothesis. New York, NY: Cambridge University Press.

Kandel, D. B., & Chen, K. (2000). Types of marijuana users by longitudinal course. *Journal of Studies on Alcohol, 61*, 367–378.

Kandel, D. B., & Davies, M. (1992). Progression to regular marijuana involvement: Phenomenology and risk factors for near-daily use. In M. D. Glantz & R. W. Pickens (Eds.), *Vulnerability to drug abuse* (pp. 211–253). Washington, DC: American Psychological Association.

Kandel, D. B., Hu, M., Griesler, P., & Schaffran, C. (2007). On the development of nicotine dependence in adolescence. *Drug and Alcohol Dependence, 91*, 26–39.

Kandel, D. B., Hu, M., & Yamaguchi, K. (2009). Sequencing of DSM-IV criteria of nicotine dependence. *Addiction, 104*, 1393–1402.

Kandel, D. B., Schaffran, C., Griesler, P., Samuolis, J., Davies, M., & Galanti, R. (2005). On the measurement of nicotine dependence in adolescence: Comparisons of the mFTQ and a DSM-IV-Based Scale. *Journal of Pediatric Psychology, 30*, 319–332.

Kann, L., Kinchen, S., Shanklin, S. L, Flint, K. H., Kawkins, J., Harris, W. A., . . . Centers for Disease Control and Prevention (CDC). (2014). Youth Risk Behavior Surveillance–United States, 2013. *Morbidity and Mortality Weekly Report (MMWR), 63*(4), 1–168.

Kaufman, N. J., Castrucci, B. C., Mowery, P. D., Gerlach, K. K., Emont, S., & Orleans, T. (2002). Predictors of change on the smoking uptake continuum among adolescents. *Archives of Pediatrics and Adolescent Medicine, 156*, 581–587.

Kelly, A. B., Chan, C. K., Toumbourou, J. W., O'Flaherty, M., Homel, R., Patton, G. C., & Williams, J. (2012). Very young adolescents and alcohol: Evidence of a unique susceptibility to peer alcohol use. *Addictive Behaviors, 37*, 414–419.

Kerr, W. C., Fillmore, K. M., & Bostrom, A. (2002). Stability of alcohol consumption over time: Evidence from three longitudinal surveys from the United States. *Journal of Studies on Alcohol, 63*, 325–333.

Khoo, S.-T., West, S. G., Wu, W., & Kwok, O.-M. (2006). Longitudinal methods. In M. Eid & E. Diener (Eds.), *Handbook of psychological measurement: A multimethod perspective*. Washington, DC: American Psychological Association books.

King, K. M., & Chassin, L. (2007). A prospective study of the effects of age of initiation of alcohol and drug use on young adult substance dependence. *Journal of Studies on Alcohol and Drugs, 68*, 256–265.

King, S. M., Iacono, W. G., & McGue, M. (2004). Childhood externalizing and internalizing psychopathology in the prediction of early substance use. *Addiction, 9*, 1548–1559.

Kraus, L., Bloomfield, K., Augustin, R., & Reese, A. (2000). Prevalence of alcohol use and the association between onset of use and alcohol-related problems in a general population sample in Germany. *Addiction, 95*, 1389–1401.

Kremers, S. P. J., Mudde, A. N., & de Vries, H. (2001). "Kicking the initiation": Do adolescent ex-smokers differ from other groups within the initiation continuum? *Preventive Medicine: An International Journal Devoted to Practice and Theory, 33*, 392–401.

Kremers, S. P., Mudde, A. N., & de Vries, H. (2004). Development and longitudinal test of an instrument to measure behavioral stages of smoking initiation. *Substance Use and Misuse, 39*, 225–252.

Krueger, R. F., Nichol, P. E., Hicks, B. M., Markon, K. E., Patrick, C. J., Iacono, W. G., & McGue, M. (2004). Using latent trait modeling to conceptualize an alcohol problems continuum. *Psychological Assessment, 16*, 107–119.

Labouvie, E. (1996). Maturing out of substance use: Selection and self-correction. *Journal of Drug Issues, 26*, 457–476.

Labouvie, E., Bates, M. E., & Pandina, R. J. (1997). Age of first use: Its reliability and predictive utility. *Journal of Studies on Alcohol, 58*, 638–643.

Latendresse, S. J., Rose, R. J., Viken, R. J., Pulkkinen, L., Kaprio, J., & Dick, D. M. (2008). Parenting mechanisms in links between parents' and adolescents' alcohol use behaviors. *Alcoholism: Clinical and Experimental Research, 32*, 322–330.

Lee, Y. G., & Abdel-Ghany, M. (2004). American youth consumption of licit and illicit substances. *International Journal of Consumer Studies, 28*, 454–465.

Lee, M., Chassin, L., & MacKinnon, D. (2010). The effect of marriage on young adult heavy drinking and its mediators: Results from two methods of adjusting for selection effects. *Psychology of Addictive Behaviors, 24*, 712–718.

Lee, J. O., Hill, K. G., Guttmannova, K. Bailey, J. A., Hartigan, L. A., Hawkins, J. D., & Catalano, R. F. (2012). The effects of general and alcohol-specific peer factors in adolescence on trajectories of alcohol abuse disorder symptoms from 21 to 33 years. *Drug and Alcohol Dependence, 121*, 213–219.

Leite, W. L. (2007). A comparison of latent growth models for constructs measured by multiple items. *Structural Equation Modeling, 14*, 581–610.

Lessov-Schlaggar, C. N., Hops, H., Brigham, J., Hudmon, K. S., Andrews, J. A., Tildesley, E., . . . Swan, G. E. (2008). Adolescent smoking trajectories and nicotine dependence. *Nicotine & Tobacco Research, 10*, 341–351.

Leventhal, H., & Cleary, P. D. (1980). The smoking problem: A review of the research and theory in behavioral risk modification. *Psychological Bulletin, 88*, 370–405.

Li, F., Duncan, T. E., & Hops, H. (2001). Examining developmental trajectories in adolescent alcohol use using piecewise growth mixture modeling analysis. *Journal of Studies on Alcohol, 62*, 199–210.

Li, T–K., Hewitt, B. G., & Grant, B. F. (2004). Alcohol use disorders and mood disorders: A National Institute on Alcohol Abuse and Alcoholism perspective. *Biological Psychiatry, 56*, 718–720.

Little, M., Handley, E., Leuthe, E., & Chassin, L. (2009). The impact of parenthood on alcohol consumption trajectories: Variations as a function of timing of parenthood, familial alcoholism, and gender. *Development and Psychopathology, 21,* 661–682.

Littlefield, A. K., Sher, K. J., & Steinley, D. (2010). Developmental trajectories of impulsivity and their association with alcohol use and related outcomes during emerging and young adulthood I. *Alcoholism: Clinical and Experimental Research, 34,* 1409–1416.

Littlefield, A. K., Sher, K. J., & Wood, P. K. (2009). Is "maturing out" of problematic alcohol involvement related to personality change? *Journal of Abnormal Psychology, 118,* 360–374.

Lloyd-Richardson, E. E., Papandonatos, G., Kazura, A., Stanton, C., & Niaura, R. (2002). Differentiating stages of smoking intensity among adolescents: Stage-specific psychological and social influences. *Journal of Consulting and Clinical Psychology, 70,* 998–1009.

Lopez-Quintero, C., Cobos, J. P. Hasin, D. S., Okuda, M., Wang, S., Grant, B. F., & Blanco, C., (2011). Probability and predictors of transition from first use to dependence on nicotine, alcohol, cannabis, and cocaine: Results of the National Epidemiologic Survey on Alcohol and Related Conditions (NESARC). *Drug and Alcohol Dependence, 115,* 120–130.

Lynne, S. D., Graber, J. A., Nichols, T. R., Brooks-Gunn, J., & Botvin, G. J. (2007). Links between pubertal timing, peer influences, and externalizing behaviors among urban students followed through middle school. *Journal of Adolescent Health, 40,* 181.e7–181.e13.

Lynne-Landsman, S. D., Bradshaw, C. P., & Ialongo, N. S. (2010). Testing a developmental cascade model of adolescent substance use trajectories and young adult adjustment. *Development and Psychopathology, 22,* 933–948.

Lynskey, M. T., Heath, A. C., Bucholz, K. K., Slutske, W. S., Madden, P. A. F., Nelson, E. C., . . . Martin, N. G. (2003). Escalation of drug use in early-onset cannabis users vs. co-twin controls. *Journal of the American Medical Association, 289,* 427–433.

Macmillan, R., & Eliason, S. R. (2003). Characterizing the life course as role configurations and pathways: A latent structure approach. In J. T. Mortimer & M. J. Shanahan (Eds.), *Handbook of the life course* (pp. 529–554). New York, NY: Kluwer Academic/Plenum.

Maes, H. H., Woodard, C. E., Murrelle, L., Meyer, J. M., Silberg, J. L., Hewitt, J. K., . . . Eaves, L. J. (1999). Tobacco, alcohol and drug use in eight- to sixteen-year-old twins: The Virginia Twin Study of Adolescent Behavioral Development. *Journal of Studies on Alcohol, 60,* 293–305.

Maggi, S., Hertzman, C., & Vaillancourt, T. (2007). Changes in smoking behaviors from late childhood to adolescence: Insights from the Canadian National Longitudinal Survey of Children and Youth. *Health Psychology, 26,* 232–240.

Maggs, J. L., & Schulenberg, J. E. (2005). Initiation and course of alcohol consumption among adolescents and young adults. In M. Galanter (Ed.), *Recent developments in alcoholism: Volume 17: Alcohol problems in adolescents and young adults,* (pp. 29–47). New York, NY: Kluwer Academic/Plenum Publishers.

Maggs, J. L., & Schulenberg, J. E. (2004–2005). Trajectories of alcohol use during the transition to adulthood. *Alcohol Research & Health, 28,* 195–201.

Mahalik, J. R., Levine Coley, R., McPherran Lombardi, C., Doyle Lynch, A., Markowitz, A. J., & Jaffee, S. R. (2013,

March 11). Changes in health risk behaviors for males and females from early adolescence through early adulthood. *Health Psychology.* Advance online publication. doi: 10.1037/a0031658.

Malone, P. S., Northrup, T. F., Masyn, K. E., Lamis, D. A., & Lamont, A. E. (2012). Initiation and persistence of alcohol use in United States Black, Hispanic, and White male and female youth. *Addictive Behaviors, 37,* 299–305.

Marceau, K., Ram, N., Houts, R. M., Grimm, K. J., & Susman, E. J. (2011). Individual differences in boys' and girls' timing and tempo of puberty: Modeling development with nonlinear growth models. *Developmental Psychology, 47,* 1389–1409.

Martino, S. C., Collins, R. L. and Ellickson, P. L. (2004), Substance use and early marriage. *Journal of Marriage and Family, 66,* 244–257.

Mason, W. A., Toumbourou, J. W., Herrenkohl, T. I., Hemphill, S. A., Catalano, R. F., & Patton, G. C. (2011). Early age alcohol use and later alcohol problems in adolescents: Individual and peer mediators in a bi-national study. *Psychology of Addictive Behaviors, 25,* 625–633.

Masten, A. S., & Cicchetti, D. (2010). Developmental cascades. *Development and Psychopathology, 22, Special issue: Developmental cascades: Part 1,* 491–495.

Masten, A. S., Faden, V. B., Zucker, R. A., & Spear, L. P. (2008). Underage drinking: A developmental framework. *Pediatrics, 121*(Suppl 4), S235–S251.

Mayet, A., Legleye, S., Chau, N., & Falissard, B. (2011). Transitions between tobacco and cannabis use among adolescents: A multi-state modeling of progression from onset to daily use. *Addictive Behaviors, 36,* 1101–1105.

Mayhew, K., Flay, B. R., & Mott, J. A. (2000). Stages in the development of adolescent smoking. *Drug and Alcohol Dependence, 59*(Suppl 1), S61–S81.

McArdle, J. J., Grimm, K. J., Hamagami, F., Bowles, R. P., & Meredith, W. (2009). Modeling life-span growth curves of cognition using longitudinal data with multiple samples and changing scales of measurement. *Psychological Methods, 14,* 126–149.

McCarthy, D. M., & Brown, S. A. (2004). Changes in alcohol involvement, cognitions and drinking and driving behavior after obtaining a driver's license. *Journal of Studies on Alcohol, 65,* 289–296.

McDermott, L., Dobson, A., & Owen, N. (2009). Determinants of continuity and change over 10 years in young women's smoking. *Addiction, 104,* 478–487.

McGue, M. (2007). Early drinking and the development of alcoholism: A commentary on Sartor et al. (2007). *Addiction, 102,* 188.

McGue, M., Iacono, W. G., Legrand, L. N., Malone, S., & Elkins, I. (2001a). Origins and consequences of age at first drink: I. Associations with substance-use disorders, disinhibitory behavior and psychopathology, and P3 amplitude. *Alcoholism: Clinical and Experimental Research, 25,* 1156–1165.

McGue, M., Iacono, W. G., Legrand, L. N., & Elkins, I. (2001b). Origins and consequences of age at first drink: II. Familial risk and heritability. *Alcoholism: Clinical and Experimental Research, 25,* 1166–1173.

McMaster, L. E., & Wintre, M. G. (1996). The relations between perceived parental reciprocity, perceived parental approval, and adolescent substance use. *Journal of Adolescent Research, 11,* 440–460.

Mehta, P. D., & West, S. G. (2000). Putting the individual back into individual growth curves. *Psychological Methods, 5*, 23–43.

Meredith, W., & Horn, J. L. (2001). The role of factorial invariance in modeling growth and change. In L. M. Collins & A. G. Sayer (Eds.), *New methods for the analysis of change* (pp. 203–240). Washington, DC: American Psychological Association.

Merline, A. C., Schulenberg, J. E., O'Malley, P. M., Bachman, J. G., & Johnston, L. D. (2008). Substance use in marital dyads: Premarital assortment and change over time. *Journal of Studies on Alcohol and Drugs, 69*, 352–361.

Mitchell, C., M., & Beals, J. (2006). The development of alcohol use and outcome expectancies among American Indian young adults: A growth mixture model. *Addictive Behaviors, 31*, 1–14.

Mitchell, C. M., Beals, J., & Kaufman, C. E. (2006). Alcohol use, outcome expectancies, and HIV risk status among American Indian youth: A latent growth curve model with parallel processes. *Journal of Youth and Adolescence, 35*, 729–740.

Moffitt, T. E. (1993). "Life-course persistent" and "adolescence-limited" antisocial behavior: A developmental taxonomy. *Psychological Review, 100*, 674–701.

Mokdad, A. H., Marks, J. S., Stroup, D. F., & Gerberding, J. L. (2004). Actual causes of death in the United States, 2000. *JAMA, 291*, 1238–1245.

Monti, P. M., Miranda, R. Jr., Nixon, K., Sher, K. J., Swartzwelder, H. S., Tapert, S. F., . . . Crews, F. T (2005). Adolescence: Booze, brains, and behavior. *Alcoholism: Clinical and Experimental Research, 29*, 207–220.

Moore, T. H., Zammit, S., & Lingford-Hughes, A. (2007). Cannabis use and risk of psychotic or affective mental health outcomes: a systematic review. *Lancet, 370*, 319–328.

Morean, M. E., Corbin, W. R., & Fromme, K. (2012). Age of first use and delay to first intoxication in relation to trajectories of heavy drinking and alcohol-related problems during emerging adulthood. *Alcoholism: Clinical and Experimental Research, 36*, 1991–1999.

Mortimer, J. T., & Staff, J. (2004). Early work as a source of developmental discontinuity during the transition to adulthood. *Development and Psychopathology, 16*, 1047–1070.

Muthén, B. (2004). Latent variable analysis: Growth mixture modeling and related techniques for longitudinal data. In D. Kaplan (ed.), *Handbook of quantitative methodology for the social sciences* (pp. 345–368). Newbury Park, CA: Sage Publications.

Muthén, B. O. (2003). Statistical and substantive checking in growth mixture modeling: Comment on Bauer and Curran. *Psychological Methods, 8*, 369–377.

Muthén, B., & Shedden, K. (1999). Finite mixture modeling with mixture outcomes using the EM algorithm. *Biometrics, 55*, 463–469.

Myers, M. G., Doran, N. M., Trinidad, D. R., Klonoff, E. A. & Wall, T. L. (2009). A prospective study of cigarette smoking initiation during college: Chinese and Korean American students. *Health Psychology, 28*, 448–456.

Nagin, D. S. (1999). Analyzing developmental trajectories: A semiparametric, group-based approach. *Psychological Methods, 4*, 139–157.

Nagin, D. (2005). *Group-based modeling of development.* Cambridge, MA: Harvard University Press.

Nagin, D. S., Pagani, L. S., Tremblay, R. E., & Vitaro, F. (2003). Life course turning points: The effect of grade retention on physical aggression. *Development and Psychopathology, 15*, 343–361.

Nagin, D. S., & Tremblay, R. E. (2005a). What has been learned from group-based trajectory modeling? Examples from physical aggression and other problem behaviors. *Annals of the American Academy of Political and Social Science, 602*, 82–117.

Nagin, D. S., & Tremblay, R. E. (2005b). Developmental trajectory groups: Fact or a useful statistical fiction? *Criminology: An Interdisciplinary Journal, 43*, 873–904.

National Drug Intelligence Center (2011). The economic impact of illicit drug use on American society. Washington, DC: United States Department of Justice.

Nesselroade, J. R., & Baltes, P. B. (1979). *Longitudinal research in the study of behavior and development.* San Diego, CA: Academic Press.

Nesselroade, J. R., & Estabrook, R. (2009). Factor invariance, measurement, and studying development over the lifespan. In C. K. Hertzog & H. Bosworth (Eds.), *Aging and cognition: Research methodologies and empirical advances* (pp. 39–52). Washington, DC: American Psychological Association.

Nesselroade, J. R., Gerstorf, D., Hardy, S. A., & Ram, N. (2007). Idiographic filters for psychological constructs. *Measurement: Interdisciplinary Research and Perspectives, 5*, 217–235.

Newcomb, M. D. (1996). Pseudomaturity among adolescents: Construct validation, sex differences, and associations in adulthood. *Journal of Drug Issues, 26*, 477–504.

Newes-Adeyi, G., Chen, C. M., Williams, G. D., & Faden, V. B. (2004). Trends in underage drinking in the United States, 1991–2003 (surveillance report #74). National Institute on Alcohol Abuse and Alcoholism, Division of Epidemiology and Prevention Research, Alcohol Epidemiologic Data System. http://pubs.niaaa.nih.gov/publications/surveillance74/Underage03.htm.

Nicolai, J., Moshagen, M., & Demmel, R. (2012). Patterns of alcohol expectancies and alcohol use across age and gender. *Drug and Alcohol Dependence, 126*, 347–353.

Nixon, N. & McClain, J. A. (2010). Adolescence as a critical window for developing an alcohol use disorder: Current findings in neuroscience. *Current Opinions in Psychiatry, 23*, 227–232.

Novak, S. P., & Clayton, R. R. (2001). The influence of school environment and self-regulation on transitions between stages of cigarette smoking: A multilevel analysis. *Health Psychology, 20*, 196–207.

Oesterle, S., Hawkins, J. D., & Hill, K. G. (2011). Men's and women's pathways to adulthood and associated substance misuse. *Journal of Studies on Alcohol and Drugs, 72*, 763–773.

Okoli, C. T. C., Richardson, C. G., Ratner, P. A., & Johnson, J. L. (2009). Non-smoking youths' "perceived" addiction to tobacco is associated with their susceptibility to future smoking. *Addictive Behaviors, 34*, 1010–1016.

O'Loughlin, J., DiFranza, J., Tyndale, R. F., Meshefedjian, G., Millan-Davey, E., Clarke, P. B., . . . Paradis, G. (2003). Nicotine-dependence symptoms are associated with smoking frequency in adolescen. *American Journal of Preventive Medicine, 25*, 219–225.

Orlando, M., Tucker, J. S., Ellickson, P. L., & Klein, D. J. (2004). Developmental trajectories of cigarette smoking and their correlates from early adolescence to young adulthood. *Journal of Consulting and Clinical Psychology, 27*, 400–410.

Pagan, J. L., Rose, R. J., Viken, R. J., Pulkkinen, L., Kaprio, J., & Dick, D. M. (2006). Genetic and environmental influences on stages of alcohol use across adolescence and into young adulthood. *Behavioral Genetics, 36*, 483–497.

Pape, H., & Hammer, T. (1996). How does young people's alcohol consumption change during the transition to early adulthood? A longitudinal study of changes at aggregate and individual level. *Addiction, 91*, 1345–1357.

Park, A., Sher, K. J., Wood, P. K., & Krull, J. L. (2009). Dual mechanisms underlying accentuation of risky drinking via fraternity/sorority affiliation: The role of personality, peer norms, and alcohol availability. *Journal of Abnormal Psychology, 118*, 241–255.

Parra, G. R., O'Neill, S. E., & Sher, K. J., (2003). Reliability of self-reported age of substance involvement onset. *Psychology of Addictive Behaviors, 17*, 211–218.

Patton, G. C., Coffey, C., Carlin, J. B., Sawyer, S. M., & Lynskey, M. (2005). Reverse gateways? Frequent cannabis use as a predictor of tobacco initiation and nicotine dependence. *Addiction, 100*, 1518–1525.

Pedersen W., & Skrondal A. (1998). Alcohol consumption debut: Predictors and consequences. *Journal of Studies on Alcohol, 59*, 32–42.

Perkonigg, A., Goodwin, R. D., Fiedler, A., Behrendt, S., Beesdo, K., Lieb, R., & Wittchen, H. -U. (2008). The natural course of cannabis use, abuse and dependence during the first decades of life. *Addiction, 103*, 439–449.

Pettit, G. S., Keiley, M. K., Laird, R. D., Bates, J. E., & Dodge, K. A. (2007). Predicting the developmental course of mother-reported monitoring across childhood and adolescence from early proactive parenting, child temperament, and parents' worries. *Journal of Family Psychology, 21*, 206–217.

Pierce, J. P., Choi, W. S., Gilpin, E. A., Farkas, A. J., & Merritt, R. K. (1996). Validation of susceptibility as a predictor of which adolescents take up smoking in the United States. *Health Psychology, 15*, 355–361.

Pomerleau, O. F., Pomerleau, C. S., Mehringer, A. M., Snedecor, S. A., & Cameron, O. G. (2005). Validation of retrospective reports of early experiences with smoking. *Addictive Behaviors, 30*, 607–611.

Pomery, E. A. Gibbons, F. X., Reis-Bergan, M., & Gerrard, M. (2009). From willingness to intention: Experience moderates the shift from reactive to reasoned behavior. *Personality and Social Psychology Bulletin, 35*, 894–908.

Power, T. G., Stewart, C. D., Hughes, S. O., & Arbona, C. (2005). Predicting patterns of adolescent alcohol use: A longitudinal study. *Journal of Studies on Alcohol, 66*, 74–81.

Prescott, C. A., & Kendler, K. S. (1999). Age at first drink and risk for alcoholism: A noncausal association. *Alcoholism: Clinical and Experimental Research, 23*, 101–107.

Presley, C. A., Meilman, P. W., & Leichliter, J. S. (2002). College factors that influence drinking. *Journal of Studies on Alcohol, Suppl 14, Special issue: College drinking, what it is, and what do to about it: Review of the state of the science*, 82–90.

Racicot, S., McGrath, J. J., Karp, I., & O'Loughlin, J. (2012). Predictors of nicotine dependence symptoms among never-smoking adolescents: A longitudinal analysis from the nicotine dependence in teens study. *Drug and Alcohol Dependence, 130*, 38–44.

Ram, N., & Grimm, K. J. (2007). Using simple and complex growth models to articulate developmental change: Matching method to theory. *International Journal of Behavioral Development, 31*, 303–316.

Raudenbush, S. W., & Bryk, A. S. (2002). *Hierarchical linear models: Applications and data analysis methods* (2nd ed.). Thousand Oaks, CA: Sage.

Reis, H. T., & Gable, S. L. (2000). Event-sampling and other methods for studying everyday experience. In H. T. Reis & C. M. Judd (Eds.), *Handbook of research methods in social and personality psychology* (pp. 190–222). New York, NY: Cambridge University Press.

Ridenour, T. A., Lanza, S. T., Donny, E. C., & Clark, D. B. (2006). Different lengths of times for progressions in adolescent substance involvement. *Addictive Behaviors, 31*, 962–983.

Riggs, N. R., Chou, C., Li, C., & Pentz, M. A. (2007). Adolescent to emerging adulthood smoking trajectories: When do smoking trajectories diverge, and do they predict early adulthood nicotine dependence? *Nicotine & Tobacco Research, 9*, 1147–1154.

Rindskopf, D. (2003). Mixture or homogeneous? Comment on Bauer and Curran. *Psychological Methods, 8*, 364–368.

Robins, L. N., & Przybeck, T. R. (1985). Age of onset of drug use as a factor in drug and other disorders. Etiology of Drug Abuse: Implications for Prevention. NIDA Research Monograph, Number 56 (pp. 178–192). Rockville, MD: NIDA.

Robinson, L. A., Murray, D. M., Alfano, C. M. Zbikowski, S. M., Blitstein, J. L., & Klesges, R. C. (2006). Ethnic differences in predictors of adolescent smoking onset and escalation: A longitudinal study from 7th to 12th grade. *Nicotine & Tobacco Research, 8*, 297–307.

Rutter, M. (1994). Beyond longitudinal data: Causes, consequences, changes, and continuity. *Journal of Consulting and Clinical Psychology, 62*(5), 928–940.

Rutter, M. (1996). Transitions and turning points in developmental psychopathology: As applied to the age span between childhood and mid-adulthood. *International Journal of behavioral Development, 19*, 603–626.

Rutter, M., Kim-Cohen, J., & Maughan, B. (2006). Continuities and discontinuities in psychopathology between childhood and adult life. *Journal of Child Psychology and Psychiatry, 47*, 276–295.

Sadava, S. W., & Pak, A. W. (1994). Problem drinking and close relationships during the third decade of life. *Psychology of Addictive Behaviors, 8*, 251–258.

Safron, D. H., Schulenberg, J. E., & Bachman, J. G. (2001). Part-Time Work and Hurried Adolescence: The Links Among Work Intensity, Social Activities, Health Behaviors, and Substance Use. *Journal of Health & Social Behavior, 42*, 425–449.

Sampson, R. J., & Laub, J. H. (2005). Seducations of method: Rejoinder to Nagin and Tremblay's "Developmental trajectory groups: Fact or fiction." *Criminology, 43*, 905–913.

Sartor, C. E., Xian, H., Scherrer, J. F., Lynskey, M. T., Duncan, A. E., Haber, J. R., . . . Jacob, T. (2008). Psychiatric and familial predictors of transition times between smoking stages: Results from an ofspring-of-twins study. *Addictive Behaviors, 33*, 235–251.

Sartor, C. E., Agrawal, A., Lynskey, M. T., Bucholz, K. K., & Heath, A. C. (2008). Genetic and environmental influences on the rate of progression to alcohol dependence in young women. *Alcoholism: Clinical and Experimental Research, 32*, 632–638.

Sartor, C. E., Lessov-Schlaggar, C. N., Scherrer, J. F., Bucholz, K. K., Madden, P. A. F., Pergadia, M. L., . . . Xian, H. (2010). Initial response to cigarettes predicts rate of progression to regular smoking: Findings from an offspring-of-twins design. *Addictive Behaviors, 35*, 771–778.

Sartor, C. E., Lynskey, M. T., Heath, A. C., Jacob, T., & True, W. (2007). The role of childhood risk factors in initiation of alcohol use and progression to alcohol dependence. *Addiction, 102*, 216–225.

Schulenberg, J. E., & Maggs, J. L. (2002). A developmental perspective on alcohol use and heavy drinking during adolescence and the transition to young adulthood. *Journal of Studies on Alcohol, S14*, 54–70.

Schulenberg, J. E., Maggs, J. L., & O'Malley, P. M. (2003). How and why the understanding of developmental continuity and discontinuity is important: The sample case of long-term consequences of adolescent substance use. In J. T. Mortimer and M. J. Shanahan (Eds.), *Handbook of the life course* (pp. 413–436). New York, NY: Kluwer Academic/Plenum Publishers.

Schulenberg, J. E., & Maslowsky, J. (2009). Taking substance use and development seriously: Developmentally distal and proximal influences on adolescent drug use. *Monographs of the Society for Research in Child Development, 74*, 121–130.

Schulenberg, J. E., Merline, A. C., Johnston, L. D., O'Malley, P. M., Bachman, J. G., & Laetz, V. B. (2005). Trajectories of marijuana use during the transition to adulthood: The big picture based on national panel data. *Journal of Drug Issues, 35*, 255–280.

Schulenberg, J., O'Malley, P. M., Bachman, J. G., Wadsworth, K. N., & Johnston, L. D. (1996). Getting drunk and growing up: Trajectories of frequent binge drinking during the transition to young adulthood. *Journal of Studies on Alcohol, 57*, 289–304.

Schulenberg, J., Wadsworth, K. N., O'Malley, P. M., Bachman, J. G., & Johnston, L. D. (1996). Adolescent risk factors for binge drinking during the transition to young adulthood: Variable- and pattern-centered approaches to change. *Developmental Psychology, 32*, 659–674.

Sher, K. J. (2007). Road to alcohol dependence: A commentary on Sartor et al. *Addiction, 102*, 185–187.

Sher, K. J., Bartholow, B. D., & Nanda, S. (2001). Short- and long-term effects of fraternity and sorority membership on heavy drinking: A social norms perspective. *Psychology of Addictive Behaviors, 15*, 42–51.

Sher, K. J., & Gotham, H. J. (1999). Pathological alcohol involvement: A developmental disorder of young adulthood. *Development and Psychopathology, 11*, 933–956.

Sher, K. J., Gotham, H. J., & Watson, A. (2004). Trajectories of dynamic predictors of disorder: Their meanings and implications. *Development and Psychopathology, 16*, 825–856.

Sher, K. J., Jackson, K. M., & Steinley, D. (2011). Alcohol use trajectories and the ubiquitous cat's cradle: Cause for concern? *Journal of Abnormal Psychology, 120*, 322–335.

Shiffman, S. (1989). Tobacco "Chippers": Individual differences in tobacco dependence. *Psychopharmacology, 97*, 539–547.

Shiffman, S., & Hufford, M. (2002). Methods of measuring patient experience: Paper vs. electronic patient diaries. White paper series, invivodata, Inc. www.invivodata.com.

Silbereisen, R. K. (1998). Lessons we learned—Tasks still to be solved. In R. Jessor (Ed.), *New perspectives on adolescent risk behavior* (pp. 518–543). New York: Cambridge University Press.

Simons-Morton, B., & Chen, R. S. (2006). Over time relationships between early adolescent and peer substance use. *Addictive Behaviors, 31*, 1211–1223.

Slutske, W. S., Hunt-Carter, E. E., Nabors-Oberg, R. E., Sher, K. J., Bucholz, K. K., Madden, . . . Heath, A. C. (2004). Do college students drink more than their non-college-attending peers? Evidence from a population-based longitudinal female twin study. *Journal of Abnormal Psychology, 113*, 530–540.

Soldz, S. (2005). Editorial: Pathways and prevention in tobacco use. *Addiction, 100*, 733–734.

Soldz, S., & Cui, X. (2002). Pathways through adolescent smoking: A 7-year longitudinal grouping analysis. *Health Psychology, 21*, 495–504.

Squeglia, L. M., Spadoni, A. D., Infante, M. A., Myers, M. G., & Tapert, S. F (2009). Initiating moderate to heavy alcohol use predicts changes in neuropsychological functioning for adolescent girls and boys. *Psychology of Addictive Behaviors, 23*, 715–722.

Sroufe, L. A. (1997). Psychopathology as an outcome of development. *Development and Psychopathology, 9*, 251–268.

Stallings, M. C., Hewitt, J. K., Beresford, T., Heath, A. C., & Eaves, L. J. (1999). A twin study of drinking and smoking onset and latencies from first use to regular use. *Behavior Genetics, 29*, 409–421.

Stanton, W. R. (1995). DSM-III—R tobacco dependence and quitting during late adolescence. *Addictive Behaviors, 20*, 595–603.

Stattin, H., & Magnusson, D. (1990). *Paths through life: Vol. 2. Pubertal maturation in female development.* Hillsdale, NJ: Erlbaum.

Steinberg, L. (1989). Pubertal maturation and parent-adolescent distance: An evolutionary perspective. In G. R. Adams, R. Montemayor, T. P. Gullotta (Eds.), *Biology of adolescent behavior and development* (pp. 71–97). Thousand Oaks, CA: Sage Publications, Inc.

Sterba, S. K. & Bauer, D. J. (2010). Matching method with theory in person-oriented developmental psychopathology research. *Development & Psychopathology, 22*, 239–254.

Stice, E., Myers, M. G., & Brown, S. A. (1998). Relations of delinquency to adolescent substance use and problem use: A prospective study. *Psychology of Addictive Behaviors, 12*, 136–146.

Stone, A. A., & Shiffman, S. (1994). Ecological momentary assessment (EMA) in behavioral medicine. *Annals of Behavioral Medicine, 16*, 199–202.

Stueve, A., & O'Donnell, L. N. (2005). Early alcohol initiation and subsequent sexual and alcohol risk behaviors among urban youths. *American Journal of Public Health, 95*, 887–893.

Substance Abuse and Mental Health Services Administration (2013a). *Results from the 2012 National Survey on Drug Use and Health: Summary of National Findings*, NSDUH Series H-46, HHS Publication No. (SMA) 13-4795. Rockville, MD: Substance Abuse and Mental Health Services Administration, 2013. http://www.samhsa.gov/data/NSDUH/2012SummNatFindDetTables/NationalFindings/NSDUHresults2012.htm#fig3.1.

Substance Abuse and Mental Health Services Administration (2013b). *Results from the 2012 National Survey on Drug Use and Health: Summary of National Findings*, NSDUH Series H-46, HHS Publication No. (SMA) 13-4795. Rockville, MD: Substance Abuse and Mental Health Services Administration, 2013. http://www.samhsa.gov/data/NSDUH/2012SummNatFindDetTables/NationalFindings/NSDUHresults2012.htm#fig2.5.

Substance Abuse and Mental Health Services Administration (2013c). *Results from the 2012 National Survey on Drug Use and Health: Summary of National Findings*, NSDUH Series H-46, HHS Publication No. (SMA) 13-4795. Rockville, MD: Substance Abuse and Mental Health Services Administration, 2013. http://www.samhsa.gov/data/NSDUH/2012SummNatFindDetTables/NationalFindings/NSDUHresultsAlts2012.htm#fig7.4.

Substance Abuse and Mental Health Services Administration (2014). *Results from the 2013 National Survey on Drug Use and Health: Summary of National Findings*, NSDUH Series H-48, HHS Publication No. (SMA) 14-4863. Rockville, MD: Substance Abuse and Mental Health ServicesAdministration.

Sun, P., Unger, J., & Sussman, S. (2005). A new measure of smoking initiation and progression among adolescents. *American Journal of Health Behavior, 29*, 3–11.

Sung, M., Erkanli, A., Angold, A., Costello, E. J. (2004). Effects of age at first substance use and psychiatric comorbidity on the development of substance use disorders. *Drug and Alcohol Dependence, 75*, 287–299.

Suris, J. C., Akre, C., Berchtold, A., Jeannin, A., & Michaud, P. A. (2007). Some go without a cigarette: Characteristics of cannabis users who have never smoked tobacco. *Archives of Pediatrics & Adolescent Medicine, 161*, 1042–1047.

Swahn, M. H., & Bossarte, R. M. (2007). Gender, early alcohol use, and suicide ideation and Attempts: Findings from the 2005 Youth Risk Behavior Survey. *Journal of Adolescent Health, 41*, 175–181.

Swahn, M. H., Bossarte, R. M., & Sullivent, E. (2008). Age of alcohol use initiation, suicidal behavior, and peer and dating violence victimization and perpetration among high-risk, seventh-grade adolescents. *Pediatrics, 121*, 297–305.

Taioli, E., & Wynder, E. L. (1991). The importance of age of starting smoking. *New England Journal of Medicine, 325*, 968–969.

Tapert, S. F., & Brown, S. A. (1999). Neuropsychological correlates of adolescent substance abuse: Four-year outcomes. *Journal of the International Neuropsychological Society, 5*, 481–493.

Tapert, S. F., Schweinsburg, A. D., Barlett, V. C., Brown, S. A., Frank, L. R., Brown, G. G., & Meloy, M. J. (2004). Blood oxygen level dependent response and spatial working memory in adolescents with alcohol use disorders. *Alcoholism: Clinical and Experimental Research, 28*, 1577–1586.

Tarter, R. E., & Vanyukov, M. (1994). Alcoholism: A developmental disorder. *Journal of Consulting and Clinical Psychology, 62*, 1096–1107.

Tercyak, K. P., Rodriguez, D., & Audrain-McGovern, J. (2007). High school seniors' smoking initiation and progression 1 year after graduation. *American Journal of Public Health, 97*, 1–2.

Timberlake, D. S., Haberstick, B. C., Hopfer, C. J., Bricker, J., Sakai, J. T., Lessem, J. M., & Hewitt, J. K. (2007). Progression from marijuana use to daily smoking and nicotine dependence in a national sample of U.S. adolescents. *Drug and Alcohol Dependence, 88*, 272–281.

Trucco, E. M., Colder, C. R., & Wieczorek, W. F. (2011). Vulnerability to peer influence: A moderated mediation study of early adolescent alcohol use initiation. *Addictive Behaviors, 36*, 729–736.

Tschann, J. M., Adler, N. E., Irwin, C. E., Millstein, S. G., Turner, R. A., & Kegeles, S. M. (1994). Initiation of substance use in early adolescence: The roles of pubertal timing and emotional distress. *Health Psychology, 13*, 326–333.

Tucker, J. S., Ellickson, P. L. Orlando, M. & Klein, D. J. (2006). Cigarette smoking from adolescence to young adulthood: Women's developmental trajectories and associated outcomes. *Women's Health Issues, 16*, 30–37.

Tucker, J. S., Ellickson, P. L., Orlando, M., Martino, S. C., & Klein, D. J. (2005). Substance use trajectories from early adolescence to emerging adulthood: A comparison of smoking, binge drinking, and marijuana use. *Journal of Drug Issues, 35*, 307–332.

Tucker, J. S., Orlando, M., & Ellickson, P. L. (2003). Patterns and correlates of binge drinking trajectories from early adolescence to young adulthood. *Health Psychology, 22*, 79–87.

US Department of Health and Human Services (USDHHS) (2004). *The health consequences of smoking: A report of the Surgeon General*. Atlanta, GA: Department of Health and Human Services, Centers for Disease Control and Prevention, National Center for Chronic Disease Prevention and Health Promotion, Office on Smoking and Health.

US Department of Health and Human Services (USDHHS) (2012). *Preventing tobacco use among youth and young adults: A report of the surgeon general*. Atlanta, GA: US Department of Health and Human Services, Centers for Disease Control and Prevention, National Center for Chronic Disease Prevention and Health Promotion, Office on Smoking and Health.

Van Den Bree, M. B. M., Whitmer, M. D., & Pickworth, W. B. (2004). Predictors of smoking development in a population-based sample of adolescents: A prospective study. *Journal of Adolescent Health, 35*, 172–181.

Van Etten, M. L., & Anthony J. C. (1999). Comparative epidemiology of initial drug opportunities and transitions to first use: marijuana, cocaine, hallucinogens and heroin. *Drug and Alcohol Dependence, 54*, 117–125.

Van Leeuwen, A. P., Verhulst, F. C., Reijneveld, S. A. Vollebergh, W. A. M., Ormel, J., & Huizink, C. (2011). Can the gateway hypothesis, the common liability model and/or, the route of administration model predict initiation of cannabis use during adolescence? A survival analysis—The trails study. *Journal of Adolescent Health, 48*, 73–78.

Van Ryzin, M. J., Fosco, G. M., & Dishion, T. J. (2012). Family and peer predictors of substance use from early adolescence to early adulthood: An 11-year prospective analysis. *Addictive Behaviors, 37*, 1314–1324.

Vega, W. A., & Gil, A. G. (2005). Revisiting drug progression: Long-range effects of early tobacco use. *Addiction, 100*, 1358–1369.

Vergés, A., Haeny, A. M., Jackson, K. M., Bucholz, K., Grant, J. D., Trull, T. J., . . . Sher, K. J. (2013). Refining the notion of maturing out: Results from the National Epidemiologic Survey on Alcohol and Related Conditions. *American Journal of Public Health, 103*, e67–e73.

Vergés, A., Jackson, K. M., Bucholz, K., Grant, J. D., Trull, T. J., Wood, P. K., & Sher, K. J. (2012). Deconstructing the age-prevalence curve of alcohol use disorders: Why "maturing out" is only a small piece of the puzzle. *Journal of Abnormal Psychology, 121*, 511–523.

Viken, R. J., Kaprio, J., Koskenvuo, M. & Rose, R. J. (1999). Longitudinal analyses of the determinants of drinking and of drinking to intoxication in adolescent twins. *Behavior Genetics, 29*, 455–461.

von Sydow, K., Lieb, R., Pfister, H., Hofler, M., Sonntag, H., & Wittchen, H-U. (2001). The natural course of cannabis use, abuse and dependence over four years: A longitudinal community study of adolescents and young adults. *Drug and Alcohol Dependence, 64*, 347–361.

Wagner, F. A., & Anthony, J. C. (2002a). From first drug use to drug dependence: developmental periods of risk for dependence upon marijuana, cocaine, and alcohol. *Neuropsychopharmacology, 26*, 479–488.

Wagner, F. A. &, Anthony, J. C. (2002b). Into the world of illegal drug use: Exposure opportunity and other mechanisms linking the use of alcohol, tobacco, marijuana, and cocaine. *American Journal of Epidemiology, 155*, 918–925.

Wagner, F. A., & Anthony, J. C. (2007). Male–female differences in the risk of progression from first use to dependence upon cannabis, cocaine, and alcohol. *Drug and Alcohol Dependence, 86*, 191–198.

Wanner, B., Vitaro, F., Ladouceur, R., Brendgen, M., & Tremblay, R. E. (2006). Joint trajectories of gambling, alcohol and marijuana use during adolescence: A person- and variable-centered developmental approach. *Addictive Behaviors, 31*, 566–580.

Warner, L. A., & White, H. R. (2003). Longitudinal effects of age at onset and first drinking situations on problem drinking. *Substance Use and Misuse, 38*, 1983–2016.

Warner, L. A., White, H. R., & Johnson, V. (2007). Alcohol initiation experiences and family history of alcoholism as predictors of problem drinking trajectories. *Journal of Studies on Alcohol and Drugs, 68*, 56–65.

Webb, G. R., Redman, S., Gibberd, R. W., & Sanson-Fisher, R. W. (1991). The reliability and stability of a quantity-frequency method and a diary method of measuring alcohol consumption. *Drug and Alcohol Dependence, 27*, 223–231.

Welch, D., & Poulton, R. (2009). Personality influences on change in smoking behavior. *Health Psychology, 28*, 292–299.

Wellman, R. J., DiFranza, J. R., Savageau, J. A., & Dussault, G. F. (2004). Short term patterns of early smoking acquisition. *Tobacco Control, 13*, 251–257.

Wetter, D. W., Kenford, S. L., Welsch, S. K., Smith, S. S., Fouladi, R. T., Fiore, M. C., & Baker, T. B. (2004). Prevalence and predictors of transitions in smoking behavior among college students. *Health Psychology, 23*, 168–177.

White, H. R., Johnson, V., & Buyske, S. (2000). Parental modeling and parenting behavior effects on offspring alcohol and cigarette use: A growth curve analysis. *Journal of Substance Abuse, 12*, 287–310.

White, H. R., Labouvie, E. W., & Papadaratsakis, V. (2005). Changes in substance use during the transition to adulthood: A comparison of college students and their noncollege age peers. *Journal of Drug Issues, 35*, 281–305.

White, H. R., Pandina, R. J. & Chen, P. (2002). Developmental trajectories of cigarette use from early adolescence into young adulthood. *Drug and Alcohol Dependence, 65*, 167–178.

Wiers, R. W., Bartholow, B. D., van den Wildenberg, E., Thush, C., Engels, R. C., Sher, K. J., . . . Stacy, A. W. (2007). Automatic and controlled processes and the development of addictive behaviors in adolescents: A review and a model. *Pharmacology Biochemistry and Behavior, 86*, 263–283.

Williams, B. R., Ponesse, J. S., Schachar, R. J., Logan, G. D., & Tannock, R. (1999). Development of inhibitory control across the life span. *Developmental Psychology, 35*, 205–213.

Willner, P., 2001. A view through the gateway: Expectancies as a possible pathway from alcohol to cannabis. *Addiction 96*, 691–703.

Wilsnack, S. C., Klassen, A. D., Schur, B. E., & Wilsnack, R. W. (1991). Predicting onset and chronicity of women's problem drinking: A five-year longitudinal analysis. *American Journal of Public Health, 81*, 305–318.

Windle, M. (1991). Alcohol use and abuse: Some findings from the National Adolescent Student Health Survey. *Alcohol Health & Research World, 15*, 5–10.

Windle, M. (1996). An alcohol involvement typology for adolescents: Convergent validity and longitudinal stability. *Journal of Studies on Alcohol, 57*, 627–637.

Windle, M., & Davies, P. T. (1999). Developmental theory and research. In K. E. Leonard and H. T. Blane (Eds.), *Psychological theories of drinking and alcoholism* (2nd ed.), (pp. 164–202). New York, NY: Guilford Press.

Windle, M., Mun, E. Y., & Windle, R. C. (2005). Adolescent-to-young adulthood heavy drinking trajectories and their prospective predictors. *Journal of Studies on Alcohol, 66*, 313–322.

Windle, M, & Windle, R. C. (2012). Early onset problem behaviors and alcohol, tobacco, and other substance use disorders in young adulthood. *Drug and Alcohol Dependence, 121*, 152–158.

Windle, M., & Zucker, R. A. (2010). Reducing underage and young adult drinking how to address critical drinking problems during this developmental period. *Alcohol Research and Health, 33*, 29–44.

Winters, K. C., & Lee, C-Y. S. (2008). Likelihood of developing an alcohol and cannabis use disorder during youth: Association with recent use and age. *Drug and Alcohol Dependence, 92*, 239–247.

Wittchen, H-U., Behrendt, S., Hofler, M., Perkonigg, A., Lieb, R., Buhringer, G., & Beesdo, K. (2008). What are the high risk periods for incident substance use and transitions to abuse and dependence? Implications for early intervention and prevention. *International Journal of Methods in Psychiatric Research, 17*, S16–S29.

Yamaguchi, K. (1990). Drug use and its social covariates from the period of adolescence to young adulthood: Some implications from longitudinal studies. In M. Galanter (Ed.), *Recent developments in alcoholism, Vol. 8: Combined alcohol and other drug dependence* (pp. 125–143). New York, NY: Plenum Press.

Yamaguchi, K., & Kandel, D. B. (1984). Patterns of drug use from adolescence to young adulthood: III. Predictors of progression. *American Journal of Public Health, 74*, 673–681.

Zeisser, C., Thompson, K., Stockwell, T., Duff, C., Chow, C., Vallance, K., . . . Lucas, P. (2012). A "standard joint"? The role of quantity in predicting cannabis-related problems. *Addiction Research & Theory, 20*, 82–92.

Zucker, R. A. (1987). The four alcoholisms: A developmental account of the etiologic process. In P. C. Rivers (Ed.), *Alcohol and addictive behaviors: Nebraska symposium on motivation, 34* (pp. 27–83). Lincoln, NE: University of Nebraska Press.

Zucker, R. A. (2006). Alcohol use and the alcohol use disorders: A developmental biopsychosocial systems formulation covering the life course. In D. Cicchetti & D. J. Cohen (Eds.), *Developmental psychopathology* (2nd ed.), *Vol. 3: Risk, disorder, and adaptation* (pp. 620–656). Hoboken, NJ: Wiley.

PART 2

Epidemiology

The Epidemiology of Substance Use Among Adolescents in the United States

Megan E. Patrick *and* Patrick M. O'Malley

Abstract

This chapter describes the epidemiology of substance use among adolescents in the United States, with a primary focus on rates of use of illicit and licit drugs among nationally representative samples of adolescents in 8th, 10th, and 12th grades in the Monitoring the Future study. Prevalence rates of alcohol use, tobacco use, marijuana use, other illegal drug use, nonmedical use of prescription drugs, and use of unregulated substances (e.g., synthetic marijuana, inhalants) are reported. Subgroup differences by grade, gender, race/ethnicity, parental education, and college plans are examined. In addition, historical trends in substance use and attitudes regarding substance use are described. Documenting the rates of substance use in the adolescent population and monitoring historical changes in public health and behavior are critical for understanding the public health burden of adolescent substance use.

Key Words: substance abuse, public health, gender, race/ethnicity, adolescent substance abuse, drug use, marijuana, United States

This chapter describes the epidemiology of substance use among adolescents in the United States. Epidemiology was originally the science of epidemics, investigating the source, spread, and control of communicable diseases (Rogers, 1965). The definition has broadened with time to encompass not just communicable diseases, but almost any health-related behavior or condition. One current definition of epidemiology is the study of the incidence, prevalence, causes, and consequences of health problems in human populations. In this chapter, we deal primarily with the health problem of substance use among adolescents. The primary focus is on rates of use of illicit and licit drugs among nationally representative samples of adolescents. The term "licit drugs" includes alcohol and tobacco, which are legally available to adults but not to adolescents under age 18 (for tobacco, in most states) or age 21 (for alcohol). The term "illicit drugs" includes controlled substances, both those that are essentially illegal for everyone (such

as heroin, LSD, and marijuana, which has some exceptions regarding its legality) and those that are available by prescription (for example, tranquilizers). In addition, inhalants will be considered; although the substances themselves may not be illegal, they are used for the purpose of getting intoxicated (and are a serious problem among adolescents).

In assessing the epidemiology of substance use among adolescents, the chapter relies heavily on self-reports of use. Although biological indicators of drug use are often thought to be more valid than self-reports, they are subject to some important limitations. Compared to self-reports, they are considerably more complicated and more expensive to implement, more restricted in the amount and time frame of use they can detect, and may provoke less cooperation from potential respondents. Consequently, self-report methods are often more practical and more desirable. It is therefore fortunate that self-report measures have been shown to be generally reliable and valid when gathered under the proper conditions (Johnston & O'Malley, 1985; Johnston, O'Malley, Bachman, & Schulenberg, 2013b; O'Malley, Bachman, & Johnston, 1983). These conditions include clear and understandable interview procedures and questionnaires, confidence by the respondent that responses will be kept confidential, and some degree of willingness by the respondent to provide accurate information. However, under other conditions, for example when arrestees or pregnant women are being questioned about recent drug use, self-reports are likely to be far less valid.

In the United States, high-quality data on the epidemiology of adolescent substance use are available, based largely on three main studies. The National Survey on Drug Use and Health (NSDUH; Substance Abuse and Mental Health Services Administration, n.d.) is an annual survey funded by the Substance Use and Mental Health Services Administration (SAMHSA) and is designed to provide nationwide and state-specific estimates on the prevalence of substance use and mental health in the United States. NSDUH is based on a random sample of US households, with in-person computer-assisted interviews conducted in the respondents' household. Persons ages 12 and older living in the household may be selected to participate (SAMHSA, n.d.). NDSUH presents results on adolescents, for example by reporting prevalence rates for behaviors among youth ages 12 to 17 (SAMHSA, 2011).

Second, the Youth Risk Behavior Surveillance System (YRBSS; Centers for Disease Control and Prevention, n.d.) is designed to monitor several categories of health risk behaviors, including a limited number of substance use measures. YRBSS data are gathered from both a national school-based survey administered by the Centers for Disease Control and Prevention (CDC), as well as other surveys conducted by education and health agencies (CDC, 2013). The nationally representative surveys of students in grades 9–12 are conducted every 2 years, since 1991.

Third, Monitoring the Future (MTF; National Institute on Drug Abuse, 2013) is an investigator-initiated study funded by the National Institute on Drug Abuse (NIDA) and is designed to study prevalence rates and historical changes in beliefs, attitudes, and behaviors of adolescents in the United States, with a particular focus on substance use. MTF includes annual in-school assessments of 8th- and 10th-grade students

(since 1991), and 12th-grade students (since 1975). The design yields nationally representative samples of US 8th, 10th, and 12th graders (Bachman, Johnston, O'Malley, & Schulenberg, 2011; Johnston et al., 2013b). In addition, an annual subsample of 12th-grade students is invited to complete questionnaires every 2 years through age 30 and every 5 years thereafter (Johnston, O'Malley, Bachman, & Schulenberg, 2012), although these follow-up data are not a focus of the current chapter.

While the three surveys make unique contributions to understanding the epidemiology of adolescent substance use, they also share commonalities that provide support for the findings. Over the years, there have been several attempts at identifying the unique and common contributions of the three surveys. One notable effort culminated in a special issue of the *Journal of Drug Issues* in 2001 (Hennessy & Ginsberg, 2001). A more recent effort was undertaken by the Substance Abuse and Mental Health Services Administration (2012). A principal conclusion from both of these extensive reviews was that, although the surveys provided somewhat different levels of estimates, the broad trends and patterns were sufficiently similar to allow for considerable confidence in the findings.

The purpose of this chapter is to describe the epidemiology of substance use among adolescents in the United States. We draw mainly from MTF as a source of empirical data on prevalence rates, developmental differences across adolescence, and historical changes. Among the three primary surveys, MTF provides the longest period of time with consistent measurement of trends. We begin by summarizing the prevalence rates for substance use among adolescents with a focus on alcohol, cigarettes, marijuana, other illegal drugs, and nonmedical use of prescription opioids; we review trends based on 38 years (1975–2012) of national surveys for 12th graders (modal age 18) and 22 years (1991–2012) for 8th graders (modal age 14) and for 10th graders (modal age 16). Second, we review the prevalence of attitudes toward substance use and perceived risks of substance use. Third, we describe documented developmental patterns in adolescent substance use. Finally, we report observed differences in substance use across sociodemographic subgroups, including gender, race/ethnicity, parental education (as a proxy for socioeconomic status), and plans to attend a 4-year college.

Prevalence of Substance Use Among Adolescents: 1976–2012

Most MTF measures of substance use provide data for three time periods: lifetime, last 12 months, and last 30 days. We focus first on use in the last 12 months, also referred to as annual use, or use in the past year. Prevalence rates for annual use of alcohol, marijuana, and illicit drug use other than marijuana are shown for 8th, 10th, and 12th graders in Figures 4.1–4.3. Past 30-day cigarette use and past 2-week binge drinking are shown in Figures 4.4 and 4.5. Substantial but varying portions of American adolescents report using alcohol, marijuana, and illicit drugs in the past 12 months. Among 12th graders in 2012, 64% reported using alcohol, 36% reported using marijuana, and 17% reported using illegal drugs other than marijuana (including LSD, other hallucinogens, crack, other cocaine, or heroin; or any use of other narcotics other than heroin, amphetamines, sedatives/barbiturates, or tranquilizers not under a doctor's orders) in the past year. Lifetime rates of substance use by 12th graders in 2012 showed that 69% reported ever using alcohol, 40% reported ever using cigarettes, 45% reported ever using marijuana, and 24% reported ever using illegal drugs other than marijuana in their lifetime. In the past 30 days, 28%

of 12th graders reported being drunk and 17% reported using cigarettes. Historical variations in use of each of these substances are clear, and rates and trends in each substance are described later in this chapter (see also Johnston, O'Malley, Bachman, & Schulenberg, 2013a; Johnston et al., 2013b; Patrick & O'Malley, 2015).

Alcohol

Alcohol is the most commonly used of these substances. The MTF survey asks about "alcoholic beverages, including beer, wine, liquor, and any other beverage that contains alcohol." In 2012, 42% of 12th graders reported drinking in the past 30 days, and 28% reported being drunk in the past 30 days. Consuming five or more drinks in a row on at least one occasion in the past 2 weeks (referred to as "binge" drinking) was reported by about 24% of 12th graders in 2012. Previous analyses have shown that it is more common for students to report binge drinking multiple times (i.e., two or more times) in the past 2 weeks than to report binge drinking only once in the past 2 weeks (Johnston et al., 2013b; Patrick & Schulenberg, 2010). This observation suggests a rapid transition to frequent heavier drinking for many young people. In addition, MTF measures

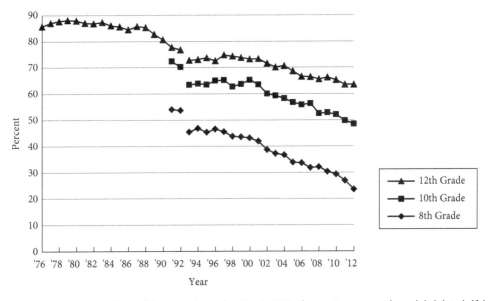

Figure 4.1 Trends in annual prevalence of alcohol use by grade. *Note*: In 1993, the question text was changed slightly in half the forms to indicate a drink meant more than a few sips. The 1993 data are based on the changed forms only. In 1994 the remaining forms were changed in a like manner. Data are based on all forms beginning in 1994. In 2004, the question text was changed slightly in half the forms. An examination of the data did not show any effect from the wording change. The remaining forms were changed in a like manner in 2005.

Source: The Monitoring the Future study, the University of Michigan.

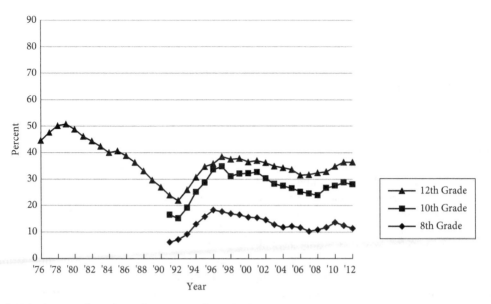

Figure 4.2 Trends in annual prevalence of marijuana use by grade. *Source*: The Monitoring the Future study, the University of Michigan.

rates of extreme binge drinking (see Patrick et al., 2013), or consuming 10 or more and 15 or more drinks in a row, which were reported by 16% and 8% of 12th graders in 2012, respectively.

Overall, alcohol use among adolescents has declined to historically low levels in recent years. Trends from 1976 to 2012 in the use of any alcohol use in the past year are shown in Figure 4.1;

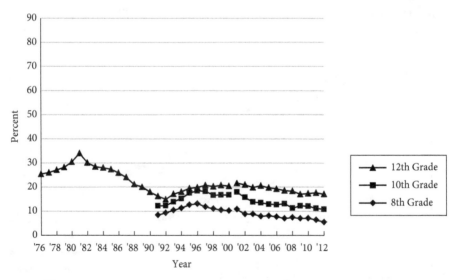

Figure 4.3 Trends in annual prevalence of use of any illicit drug other than marijuana by grade. *Notes*: For 12th grade only: Use of "any illicit drug other than marijuana" includes any use of LSD, other hallucinogens, crack, other cocaine, or heroin; or any use of other narcotics other than heroin, amphetamines, sedatives (barbiturates), methaqualone (excluded since 1990), or tranquilizers not under a doctor's orders. For 8th and 10th graders only: The use of narcotics other than heroin and sedatives (barbiturates) has been excluded because these younger respondents appear to overreport use (perhaps because they include the use of nonprescription drugs in their answers). For 12th graders only: Beginning in 1982, the question about stimulant use (i.e., amphetamines) was revised to get respondents to exclude the inappropriate reporting of nonprescription stimulants. The prevalence rate dropped slightly as a result of this methodological change. Beginning in 2001, revised sets of questions on other hallucinogens and tranquilizers were introduced. Data for any illicit drug other than marijuana are affected by these changes. From 2001 on, data points are based on the revised questions.

Source: The Monitoring the Future study, the University of Michigan.

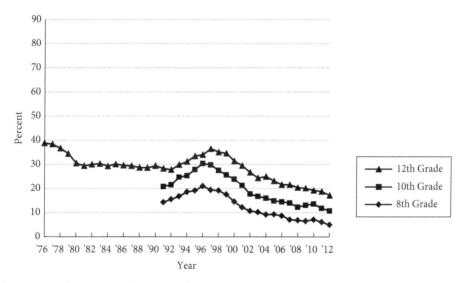

Figure 4.4 Trends in 30-day prevalence of cigarette use by grade. *Source*: The Monitoring the Future study, the University of Michigan.

trends in binge drinking in the past 2 weeks are shown in Figure 4.5. Similar trends have been observed for alcohol use in the past 30 days and drunkenness in the past 30 days. In the late 1970s, about 88% of 12th graders reported consuming alcohol in the past year. Levels remained similarly high until the late 1980s, when there was a precipitous drop, followed by a small increase from 1993 through the late 1990s, and then further decline to the present day. Binge drinking, or consuming five or more drinks in a row in the past 2 weeks, was reported by about 40% of 12th graders in the late 1970s and early 1980s, and by about 24% of 12th graders in 2012. These historical shifts in alcohol use can be attributed to multiple influences, including changes in various alcohol control policies and in perceived social norms. An important influence is the minimum legal drinking age, which has been demonstrated to lower drinking among youth (O'Malley & Wagenaar, 1991; Wagenaar & Toomey, 2002). Other policies that affect youth drinking include zero-tolerance underage drunk driving laws (that is, any alcohol detected in blood in a driver under the age of 21 is grounds for a

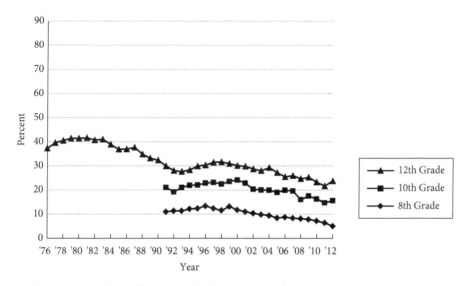

Figure 4.5 Trends in 2-week prevalence of five or more drinks in a row by grade. *Source*: The Monitoring the Future study, the University of Michigan.

"drunk driving" conviction) and beer taxes (higher taxes result in less drinking by youth; Carpenter, Kloska, O'Malley, & Johnston, 2007). Keyes et al. (2012) demonstrated that individuals who matured in birth cohorts with more restrictive social norms (for example, being more disapproving of alcohol use) were less likely to use alcohol compared with individuals who matured in cohorts with more permissive norms.

Cigarettes and Tobacco

Tobacco remains the leading cause of preventable death in the United States (CDC, 2012), despite declines in use. Trends in cigarette smoking in the past 30 days from 1976 to 2012 are shown in Figure 4.4. Following a decline in cigarette use among 12th graders in the late 1970s, smoking rates remained stable at about 30% through the 1980s. Cigarette use then escalated across the 1990s to a high in 1997, when 37% of 12th graders reported smoking in the past 30 days. After this peak in the late 1990s, cigarette use in all three grade levels fell dramatically, to 5% of 8th graders, 11% of 10th graders, and 17% of 12th graders smoking in the past 30 days in 2012. Roughly half of those who smoked in the past 30 days reported daily use: 2% of 8th graders, 6% of 10th graders, and 9% of 12th graders. Although cigarette smoking is at historically low rates, other forms of tobacco use are prevalent. For example, 20% of 12th graders reported smoking small cigars in the past 12 months, and 18% reported smoking tobacco with a hookah. Similarly, the CDC's National Youth Tobacco Survey found that, in 2011, 7% of middle school students and 23% of high school students reported currently using a tobacco product, with 4% of middle schoolers and 16% of high schoolers currently using cigarettes (CDC, 2012).

Marijuana

Marijuana is the most commonly used illicit drug among adolescents. MTF surveys include questions about use of marijuana (with the instruction that "marijuana is sometimes called weed, pot, dope") and hashish ("sometimes called hash, hash oil"). Figure 4.2 shows the annual prevalence of marijuana use by year since 1991 for 8th and 10th graders and since 1976 for 12th graders. The peak level of annual marijuana use among 12th graders was 51% in 1979. Prevalence fell thereafter, to a low of 22% in 1992, representing a dramatic drop of more than half. There was a sharp increase in marijuana use across the 1990s (mirroring trends in other

substance use during that time), with marijuana use nearly doubling among 8th, 10th, and 12th graders. Following a slow decline in rates from 1997 to 2006, marijuana use has shown increases again in recent years, to 36% of 12th graders reporting use in the past year in 2012. The use of marijuana on a daily or almost daily basis (i.e., 20 or more occasions in the past 30 days) reached the highest level in the past 30 years, at 6.6% of 12th graders, in 2011 (though still below the peak of 10.7% reached in 1978). In 2012, daily or almost daily marijuana use was reported by 6.5% of 12th graders.

Other Illegal Drugs

Although detailed information about a range of specific drugs is available (see Johnston et al., 2013b), a combined trend for use of illegal drugs other than marijuana is also created to describe general trends (shown in Figure 4.3). For 12th graders, this includes LSD, other hallucinogens, crack, other cocaine, heroin, other narcotics, amphetamines, sedatives (barbiturates), and tranquilizers, all without a doctor's orders. Use of illegal drugs other than marijuana peaked in 1981 at 34% of 12th graders using in the past year, before declining until about 1991. Rates of use of most types of drugs increased across the 1990s, with the prevalence of illicit drugs other than marijuana increasing from 15% in 1992 to 20% in 2000 among 12th graders, for example. Since 2001, rates of use of illegal drugs other than marijuana fell before leveling off. Rates of illegal drug use other than marijuana among 8th graders have fallen by about half since the mid-1990s. In 2012, 6% of 8th graders, 11% of 10th graders, and 17% of 12th graders reported use of illicit drugs other than marijuana in the past year.

SPECIFIC ILLEGAL DRUGS

As noted earlier, a wealth of detailed information on use of specific substances, subgroup differences, and historical changes is available elsewhere (Johnston et al., 2013b). Here, we provide a broad overview of adolescent use of several specific substances that have gained attention from sources such as media coverage or public concern. *LSD* use peaked in 1996 at 8.8% of 12th graders reporting past-year use, with very low rates since then (2.4% of 12th graders in 2012). Annual use of *ecstasy* (MDMA) peaked in 2001 at 9.2% of 12th graders, after more than doubling in the 3 years prior. In 2012, 3.8% of 12th graders reported using ecstasy in the past year. *Methamphetamine* use has been tracked in MTF since 1999, and declines in use across all grades have been noted since then (to 1.1% of 12th graders in 2012 using methamphetamines in the past year). *Crystal meth (ice)* questions were added in 1990 and captured increases across the decade, but annual use remained at relatively low levels (e.g., 3.0% of 12th graders in 2002) and has declined since then (to 0.8% of 12th graders in 2012). *Crack cocaine* use increased rapidly in the 1980s. It was first measured by MTF in 1986, at its highest level of 4.1% of 12th graders reporting use in the past year. Since then, use of crack cocaine has fallen, to 1.2% of 12th graders in 2012. *Heroin* use has decreased across the past decades (with the exception of some increase along with other illegal drugs in the 1990s) and adolescents reported consistently low rates of past-year use (0.6% of 12th graders) in 2012. *Club drugs*, including Rohypnol (added in 1996), ketamine (added in 2000), and GHB (added in 2000), have had very low rates, with 1.5%, 1.5%, and 1.4% of 12th graders in 2012 reporting past-year use, respectively.

Nonmedical Use of Prescription Drugs

Concern over the nonmedical use of prescription drugs has been mounting (NIDA, 2012b). The MTF study examines the nonmedical use (defined as use without a doctor's orders) of the general classes of amphetamines, sedatives (barbiturates), narcotics other than heroin, and tranquilizers. In 2012, 21% of 12th graders reported nonmedical use of prescription drugs in their lifetime, and 15% reported use in the past year. Questions have been added regarding the specific amphetamines Ritalin (at 5.1% in 2001, when it was added, and declining to 2.6% of 12th graders in 2012 reporting use in the past year) and Adderall (added in 2009, with little change in the past few years; 7.6% of 12th graders in 2012). The specific narcotics Vicodin and OxyContin have been tracked since 2002. Vicodin use in the past year peaked in 2003 (10.5% of 12th graders) and has seen some decreases since then to 7.5% of 12th graders in 2012. OxyContin use remains near its highest levels (4.3% of 12th graders in 2012, compared to the peak of 5.5% in 2005). In 2001, the tranquilizers question was revised to include Xanax, although rates have dropped to 5.3% of 12th graders reporting past-year use in 2012.

Other Substances Not Regulated

Over time, additional substances that are sometimes not yet regulated by the Food and Drug Administration are added to the MTF study as they emerge. *Synthetic marijuana* is one such substance and was measured for the first time in 2011. Synthetic marijuana is the second most popular drug, after natural marijuana, with 11% of 12th graders using in the past year in 2012. In addition, *inhalants* are an ongoing concern (NIDA, 2012a). Fumes or gases released from common household substances such as glues, aerosols, butane, and solvents are inhaled to get high. In MTF, participants are asked how often they have "sniffed glue, or breathed the contents of aerosol spray cans, or inhaled any other gases or sprays in order to get high." In 2012, 6.2% of 8th graders, 4.1% of 10th graders, and 2.9% of 12th graders reported past-year inhalant use. (This is the only substance that tends to be used by younger students more than by older students.) *Energy drinks* are also associated with increasing levels of concern (Reissig, Strain, & Griffiths, 2009). MTF defines energy drinks as "non-alcoholic beverages that usually contain high amounts of caffeine, including such drinks as Red Bull, Full Throttle, Monster, and Rockstar. They are usually sold in 8- or 16-ounce cans or bottles." Students were asked how many (if any) energy drinks they typically consumed each day. In 2012, 33.7% of 8th graders, 26.5% of 10th graders, and 20.9% of 12th graders reported drinking more than zero energy drinks per day, on average. A separate question asks about energy shots, defined as energy drinks sold as small "shots" of usually 2 or 3 ounces. Rates of energy shot use were about one third the rates for energy drinks; 10.5% of 8th graders, 7.6% of 10th graders, and 10.2% of 12th graders reported using more than zero energy shots per day, on average.

Substance Use Attitudes and Perceived Risks

Attitudes regarding substance use and perceptions of use are powerful correlates and predictors of substance use behavior. A main contribution of the MTF study has been to show how, over time and at the population level, changes in perceptions of risk about and disapproval of substance use precede and predict changes in substance use (Bachman, Johnston, O'Malley, 1990, 1998; Bachman, Johnston, O'Malley, & Humphrey, 1988; Johnston, 1985; Johnston et al., 2013b; Keyes et al., 2011). These dynamics have also been documented in other studies (SAMHSA, 2013b).

With regard to perceived risks of substance use, high school seniors surveyed by MTF generally agree that regular use of illicit drugs would be harmful to the user, although rates vary. The vast majority (89%) of 12th graders in 2012 reported that regular use of heroin would cause great harm to the user, although only 44% believed that regular use of marijuana would cause great harm to the user. Smoking one or more packs of cigarettes per day was judged to cause great harm to the user by 78% of 12th graders in 2012. About half (49%) of 12th graders reported that binge drinking at least weekly, defined as consuming five or more drinks once or twice each weekend, would cause great harm to the user. Consumption of four or five drinks nearly every day was rated as posing great risk by only 64% of 12th graders in 2012.

The perceived availability of various drugs has been examined over time. Overall, the trends show that when drugs are more widely used by adolescents they are also perceived as more available, as would be expected. Alcohol and marijuana are perceived as very accessible. In 2012, 58% of 8th graders, 78% of 10th graders, and 91% of 12th graders said it would be fairly easy or very easy to get alcohol, despite being below the legal drinking age of 21 years. Despite the illegality of marijuana in all states at the time, 37% of 8th graders, 69% of 10th graders, and 82% of 12th graders said that marijuana would be fairly easy or very easy to get. Other drugs are perceived as less available overall, although 50% of 12th graders reported that it would fairly or very easy to obtain narcotics other than heroin and 45% reported it would be fairly or very easy to get amphetamines. Sizeable portions of the 12th grade class of 2012 also perceived it would be fairly or very easy to get hallucinogens other than LSD (38%), ecstasy (MDMA, 36%), cocaine (30%), sedatives (barbiturates, 29%), LSD (28%), cocaine powder (25%), crack (22%), heroin (20%), crystal methamphetamine (ice, 15%), tranquilizers (15%), and PCP (15%).

Perceptions of friends' disapproval of substance use are also examined in MTF. The vast majority of 12th graders in 2012 reported that their friends would disapprove or strongly disapprove of them using drugs like crack, cocaine, and LSD. About three quarters (73%) thought their close friends would disapprove of them smoking marijuana *regularly*, although just over half (53%) thought their close friends would disapprove of them *experimenting* with marijuana. Perceived friends' disapproval was reported by 62% for weekend binge drinking, by 84% for daily heavy drinking, and by 83% for regular (a pack or more per day) cigarette use.

Differences by Grade, Gender, Race/Ethnicity, Parent Education, and College Plans

Table 4.1 provides 2012 prevalence estimates of alcohol use in the past year, binge drinking in the past 2 weeks, cigarette use in the last 30 days, marijuana use in the past year, and other illicit drug use in the past year. Prevalence estimates are given in percentages by grade (8th, 10th, and 12th), gender, race/ethnicity (White, Black, and Hispanic), parent education, and plans to attend 4-year college.

Grade Level

Developmental or age-graded changes in substance use across adolescence and young adulthood have received considerable research attention, and they are only briefly considered here. As shown and described earlier in this chapter and elsewhere, prevalence rates of substance use differ substantially by grade in MTF (Johnston et al., 2013b). For all measures of alcohol use, cigarette use, marijuana use, and the composite measure of the use of any illicit drug other than marijuana, 8th graders have the lowest prevalence and 12th graders have the highest prevalence. In other words, there are age-graded increases in substance use across adolescence. (The one exception is inhalant use [not tabled], for which 8th graders tend to report a higher prevalence than 12th graders.) This reflects the fact that 12th graders generally use substances at higher rates than 10th graders, who use at higher rates than 8th graders. Although mostly age graded, the differences are almost surely understated because high school dropouts are not included in the 12th-grade sample. MTF 12th graders represent a national sample of 12th graders so high school dropouts are not included, although most eventual dropouts are included in the lower grades, particularly the 8th grade. A natural question to ask is what effect the exclusion of dropouts from the MTF sample has on estimation of prevalence and trends for the entire age cohort. For an extensive discussion of the likely impact of exclusion of dropouts, see Johnston et al. (2013b, Appendix A). The impact is actually likely to be minimal on *trends*, because dropout rates have not changed very much. The impact on prevalence is likely not very large, because dropouts represent a relatively small portion of the entire age cohort, perhaps about 15%. Based on analysis of NSDUH data, which include both dropouts and seniors, the difference in

Table 4.1 Prevalence (in percentages) of Use of Alcohol in Past Year, 5+ Binge Drinking in Past 2 Weeks, Use of Cigarettes in Past 30 Days, Use of Marijuana in Past Year, Use of Any Illicit Drug Other Than Marijuana in Past Year for 8th, 10th, and 12th Graders by Selected Subgroups in 2012

	Alcohol in Past Year	5+ Drinks in Past 2 Weeks[a]	Cigarettes in Past 30 Days	Marijuana in Past Year	Any Illicit Drug Other Than Marijuana[b] in Past Year
8th Graders					
Total	23.6	5.1	4.9	11.4	5.5
Gender					
Boys	22.3	4.6	4.6	12.2	4.8
Girls	24.7	5.5	4.9	10.4	6.0
College plans					
None or under 4 years	38.8	15.3	17.3	28.4	13.0
Complete 4 years	22.4	4.4	3.9	10.1	4.9
Race/ethnicity[c]					
White	23.5	4.9	5.8	10.0	5.6
African American	22.4	4.3	4.0	12.4	3.9
Hispanic	33.4	9.9	5.5	17.2	8.1
Parental education[d]					
No college	30.7	8.0	7.1	17.2	7.2
Some college or higher	22.0	4.0	4.0	9.4	4.9
10th Graders					
Total	48.5	15.6	10.8	28.0	10.8
Gender					
Boys	47.8	16.4	12.0	31.0	11.3
Girls	49.2	14.8	9.6	25.3	10.4
College plans					
None or under 4 years	62.7	25.9	27.6	43.6	24.5
Complete 4 years	47.2	14.6	9.0	26.5	9.4
Race/ethnicity[c]					
White	50.9	16.3	12.9	27.5	11.5
African American	41.0	8.2	6.7	29.1	5.8
Hispanic	51.1	17.1	8.3	31.8	12.6

(*continued*)

Table 4.1 Continued

	Alcohol in Past Year	5+ Drinks in Past 2 Weeks[a]	Cigarettes in Past 30 Days	Marijuana in Past Year	Any Illicit Drug Other Than Marijuana[b] in Past Year
Parental education[d]					
No college	51.8	18.1	14.5	33.5	13.2
Some college or higher	48.4	15.3	9.8	26.9	10.1
12th Graders					
Total	63.5	23.7	17.1	36.4	17.0
Gender					
Boys	63.7	27.2	19.3	40.8	18.4
Girls	62.9	19.7	14.5	31.3	14.9
College plans					
None or under 4 years	67.2	27.5	27.9	41.5	19.4
Complete 4 years	62.4	22.6	14.7	34.8	16.1
Race/ethnicity[c]					
White	66.3	25.7	21.2	36.6	19.6
African American	52.4	11.3	8.6	33.2	7.6
Hispanic	64.0	21.8	13.2	37.3	13.6
Parental education[d]					
No college	65.1	24.1	18.2	38.7	17.4
Some college or higher	63.3	23.6	16.7	35.7	16.9

Note: For 8th graders, the approximate weighted N is 15,100. For 10th graders, the approximate weighted N is 15,000. For 12th graders, the approximate weighted N is 13,700.

[a] This measure refers to having five or more drinks in a row in the last 2 weeks.

[b] For 12th graders only: Use of "any illicit drug other than marijuana" includes any use of LSD, other hallucinogens, crack, other cocaine, or heroin, or any use of narcotics other than heroin, amphetamines, sedatives (barbiturates), or tranquilizers not under a doctor's orders. For 8th and 10th graders only: The use of narcotics other than heroin and sedatives (barbiturates) has been excluded because these younger respondents appear to overreport use (perhaps because they include the use of nonprescription drugs in their answers).

[c] To derive percentages for each racial subgroup, data for the specified year and the previous year have been combined to increase subgroup sample sizes and thus provide more stable estimates.

[d] Parental education is a combination of mother's education and father's education. Missing data are allowed on one of the two variables. If either parent has some college education or more, it is coded as "Some college or higher."

Source: The Monitoring the Future study, the University of Michigan.

prevalence of lifetime marijuana use in 2002 when dropouts were included was less than 3% (42% for seniors and 45% when dropouts were included). The difference in prevalence of lifetime cocaine use was about 2% (6% for seniors and 8% when dropouts were included) (Johnston et al., 2013b).

Gender

Overall, males tend to use substances more frequently and at higher levels than females, especially at heavier levels of use and among 12th graders as compared to among younger adolescents. In 8th grade, girls tend to have somewhat higher rates of alcohol use than boys. For example, 25% of 8th-grade girls and 22% of 8th-grade boys report using alcohol in the past year. By 12th grade, boys tend to use substances at higher rates than girls: 27% of 12th-grade boys and 20% of 12th-grade girls report binge drinking (i.e., consuming 5+ drinks in a row) in the past 2 weeks. There is some indication that gender differences in substance use have narrowed; for example, differences between males and females in alcohol use have decreased over the past decade. Among 12th graders the gender difference in past 30-day use of alcohol was 9.6% in 2001 (with 54.7% of boys and 45.1% of girls reporting use) and 5.0% in 2012 (with 43.8% of boys and 38.8% of girls reporting use). In 12th grade, boys also use other substances at higher levels: 19% of boys and 15% of girls smoked cigarettes in the past 30 days, 41% of boys and 31% of girls used marijuana in the past year, and 18% of boys and 15% of girls used an illicit drug other than marijuana in the past year. Gender differences continue into adulthood, with men consistently using substances at higher rates than women (Johnston et al., 2012; SAMHSA, 2011).

Race/Ethnicity

Racial/ethnicity comparisons are discussed here for African Americans, Hispanics, and Whites. Although the MTF design, like the designs of YRBS and NSDUH, is nationally representative, other racial/ethnic groups are too small to allow accurate estimates for any given year. Combining data across multiple years allows for some estimates for other racial/ethnic groups, including subcategories of Hispanics, and results can be found in other publications (for example, see Bachman et al., 1991; Delva et al., 2005; Wallace et al., 2002, 2009). (Also see Chapters 5 [Cultural variations and relevance to etiology, Delva et al.] and 32 [Adolescent cultural contexts, Schwartz] in this volume, which address these variations in considerable depth.)

In general, White teens have the highest prevalence of substance use overall, although Hispanics tend to have the highest rates at younger ages. For example, in 2012 in 8th grade, 17% of Hispanics, 12% of African Americans, and 10% of Whites report using marijuana in the past year. By the 12th grade, however, the order has changed such that 37% of Whites, 37% of Hispanics, and 33% of African Americans report past-year marijuana use. In 12th grade, 20% of Whites, 14% of Hispanics, and 8% of African Americans report past-year use of illicit drugs other than marijuana. African Americans tend to have lower rates of drug and alcohol use than

Whites or Hispanics. Some, but not all, of the race/ethnicity differences among 12th graders are attributable to differential high school dropout rates among the different groups, given that dropout rates tend to be higher among youth of color, and alcohol and substance use tends to be higher among school dropouts than among those staying in school (Bachman et al., 2008; SAMHSA, 2013a).

Parent Education

Parent education is used as a proxy for socioeconomic status and has similar relationships with substance use as wealth and income have (Patrick, Wightman, Schoeni, & Schulenberg, 2012). In Table 4.1, parental education is coded as parent(s) having attended no college versus parent(s) having attended at least some college. In 8th and 10th grades, adolescents whose parents did not attend any college report higher levels of use of all substances. Differences in substance use based on parent education are small for 12th graders; much of the change between the lower grades and 12th grade is likely due to dropouts being absent from 12th grade.

College Plans

Plans to attend and graduate from college are an important marker for academic success and substance use. In 8th, 10th, and 12th grades, students who intend to graduate from a 4-year college engage in less substance use than students who do not intend to graduate from a 4-year college. However, these differences narrow over the grades. This is partly due to the fact that high school dropouts are more likely to be included in the estimates for 8th and 10th graders. In 8th grade, 15% of those who do not intend to graduate from a 4-year college and 4% of those who do intend to graduate from a 4-year college have engaged in binge drinking in the past 2 weeks. By 12th grade, 28% of those who do not intend to graduate from college and 23% of those who do intend to graduate from college have engaged in binge drinking in the past 2 weeks. In 8th grade, 13% of those who do not and 5% of those who do intend to graduate from a 4-year college report illicit drug use in the past year; in 12th grade, 19% of those who do not and 16% of those who do intend to graduate from college report illicit drug use.

Overall Subgroup Differences

It is also possible to examine how rates of substance use differ across the following six combined subgroups for boys and across the following six groups for boys and for the same six groups for

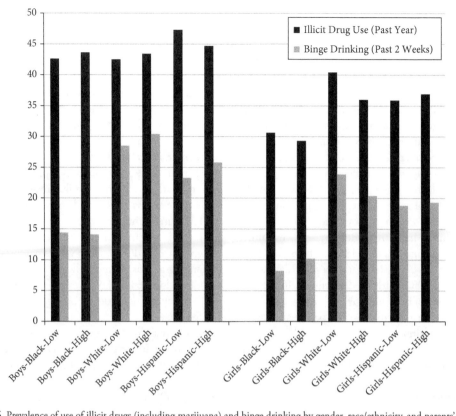

Figure 4.6 Prevalence of use of illicit drugs (including marijuana) and binge drinking by gender, race/ethnicity, and parents' education in 2011 and 2012 combined. *Note*: Low parental education = high school degree or less. High parental education = some college education or more.

girls: Black students with parents with lower education (i.e., high school degree or less), Black students with parents with higher education (i.e., some college or more), White students with parents with lower education, White students with parents with higher education, Hispanic students with parents with lower education, and Hispanic students with parents with higher education (see Figure 4.6). For 12th-grade boys in 2011 and 2012, the highest prevalence rate for use of illicit drugs including marijuana in the past year (44.2%) was among Hispanic boys whose parents had low education. Rates of binge drinking in the past 2 weeks (30.4%) were highest for White boys whose parents had higher levels of education. Lowest levels of illicit substance use among 12th-grade boys were among Black and White boys whose parents had lower education (42.5–42.6%). Lowest levels of binge drinking in the past 2 weeks were among Black boys whose parents had higher (14.1%) and lower (14.4%) levels of education. Among 12th-grade girls in 2011 and 2012, the highest prevalence rates for use of illicit drugs, including marijuana in the past year (40.4%) and

for binge drinking in the past 2 weeks (23.9%), were among White girls whose parents had lower levels of education. Lowest levels of past-year illicit drug use (27.7%) were among Black girls whose parents had higher levels of education and lowest levels of binge drinking in the past 2 weeks (8.2%) were among Black girls whose parents had lower levels of education. These patterns by race/ethnicity and parent education are complex and have been investigated in greater detail elsewhere (Bachman, O'Malley, Johnston, Schulenberg, & Wallace, 2011).

Conclusions

Documenting the rates of substance use in the population and monitoring historical changes in public health and behavior are critical for understanding the public health burden of adolescent substance use. In addition, research that captures attitudes toward substance use and perceived risks of using substances provides markers for individual behavior and leading indicators of historical change. Perceptions of drugs, such as subjective interpretations of harmfulness, may translate into behaviors that support those beliefs. In this way, adolescents who disapprove of drug use and who perceive consequences of use as harmful may be less likely to use substances than adolescents who view those drugs more positively and in relation to more favorable outcomes. Furthermore, examining historical trends in attitudes toward and perceptions of substance use may shed light on these changes over time and substance-using behaviors may reflect more widescale approval or disapproval of particular substances. Increases in use of a certain substance may be presaged by declines in the perception of that drug as harmful. Generally speaking, the demonstration in the 1980s that attitudes and beliefs appeared to be more important predictors of use than actual availability led to a national policy shift away from a policy only of reducing supply toward a policy that also emphasized reducing demand.

Grade-level differences speak to the developmental changes in substance use across adolescence, with a progression toward higher frequency and quantity of use. Differences by sociodemographic groups highlight subgroups at highest risk for use of alcohol, tobacco, marijuana, and other illicit drugs in the US population. Analyses of developmental changes and subgroup differences in substance use inform policy about adolescent substance use. They also provide important information for targeting prevention efforts and reaching the teens who may be at greatest risk.

Although not considered in this chapter, it should be noted that multiple factors play a role in determining substance use. Price is an obvious factor and tax policies are important levers that can be employed to influence price. This is, of course, most relevant to legal substances like alcohol and tobacco (Chaloupka, 2013). State and federal policies and regulations can also have significant influence, such as in curbing the misuse of prescription drugs. Recently certain anabolic steroids were added to the list of controlled substances, limiting access to these drugs for nonmedical use. Another federal intervention is the reformulation of OxyContin to reduce the abuse potential of the drug (FDA, 2013).

The complexity of factors playing a role in adolescent substance use suggests that a variety of research targets and approaches are necessary for understanding the issues involved. Major studies such as MTF document the prevalence rates and key correlates of substance use in adolescence, and therefore frame the scope of the problem and provide the background and foundation for continued research in the field of adolescent substance use.

References

Bachman, J. G., Johnston, L. D., & O'Malley, P. M. (1990). Explaining the recent decline in cocaine use among young adults: Further evidence that perceived risks and disapproval lead to reduced drug use. *Journal of Health and Social Behavior, 31*, 173–184.

Bachman, J. G., Johnston, L. D., & O'Malley, P. M. (1998). Explaining the recent increases in students' marijuana use: The impacts of perceived risks and disapproval from 1976 through 1996. *American Journal of Public Health, 88*, 887–892.

Bachman, J. G., Johnston, L. D., O'Malley, P. M., & Humphrey, R. H. (1988). Explaining the recent decline in marijuana use: Differentiating the effects of perceived risks, disapproval, and general lifestyle factors. *Journal of Health and Social Behavior, 29*, 92–112.

Bachman, J. G., Johnston, L. D., O'Malley, P. M. & Schulenberg, J. E. (2011). *The Monitoring the Future project after thirty-seven years: Design and procedures* (Monitoring the Future Occasional Paper No. 76). Ann Arbor, MI: Institute for Social Research, University of Michigan.

Bachman, J. G., O'Malley, P. M., Johnston, L. D., Schulenberg, J. E., & Wallace, J. M., Jr. (2011). Racial/ethnic differences in the relationship between parental education and substance use among U.S. 8th-, 10th-, and 12th-grade students: Findings from the Monitoring the Future project. *Journal of Studies on Alcohol and Drugs, 72*, 279–285.

Bachman, J. G., O'Malley, P. M., Schulenberg, J. E., Johnston, L. D., Freedman-Doan, P., & Messersmith, E. E. (2008). *The education-drug use connection: How successes and failures in school relate to adolescent smoking, drinking, drug use, and delinquency.* New York, NY: Erlbaum /Taylor & Francis.

Bachman, J. G., Wallace, J. M., Jr., O'Malley, P. M., Johnston, L. D., Kurth, C. L., & Neighbors, H. W. (1991). Racial/ethnic differences in smoking, drinking, and illicit drug use among American high school seniors, 1976–1989. *American Journal of Public Health, 81*, 372–377.

Carpenter, C. S., Kloska, D. D., O'Malley, P. M., & Johnston, L. D. (2007). Alcohol control policies and youth alcohol consumption: Evidence from 28 years of Monitoring the Future. *The B. E. Journal of Economic Analysis & Policy, 7*(1 Topics), Article 25.

Centers for Disease Control and Prevention (CDC). (n.d.). Youth Risk Behavior Surveillance System (YRBSS) Overview. Retrieved November 2015, from http://www.cdc.gov/healthyyouth/data/yrbs/overview.htm

Centers for Disease Control and Prevention. (2012). Current tobacco use among middle and high school students—United States, 2011. *Morbidity and Mortality Weekly Report, 62*(31), 581–585. Retrieved November 2015, from http://www.cdc.gov/mmwr/preview/mmwrhtml/mm6131a1.htm?s_cid=mm6131a1_w

Centers for Disease Control and Prevention. (2013). Methodology of the Youth Risk Behavior Surveillance System. *Morbidity and Mortality Weekly Report, 62*(1). Retrieved November 2015, from http://www.cdc.gov/mmwr/pdf/rr/rr6201.pdf

Chaloupka, F. J. (2013). Maximizing the public health impact of alcohol and tobacco taxes. *American Journal of Preventive Medicine, 44*(5), 561–562.

Delva, J., Wallace, J. M., Jr., O'Malley, P. M., Bachman, J. G., Johnston, L. D., & Schulenberg, J. E. (2005). The epidemiology of alcohol, marijuana, and cocaine use among Mexican

American, Puerto Rican, Cuban American, and other Latin American 8th-grade students in the United States: 1991–2002. *American Journal of Public Health, 95,* 696–702.

Food and Drug Administration (FDA). (2013). FDA approves abuse-deterrent labeling for reformulated OxyContin. *FDA News Release,* April 16, 2013. Retrieved November 2015, from http://www.fda.gov/NewsEvents/Newsroom/PressAnnouncements/ucm348252.htm

Hennessy, K., & Ginsberg, C. (2001). Introduction to Special Issue. *Journal of Drug Issues, 31*(3), 595–598.

Johnston, L. D., & O'Malley, P. M. (1985). Issues of validity and population coverage in student surveys of drug use. In B. A. Rouse, N. J. Kozel, & L. G. Richards (Eds.), *Self-report methods of estimating drug use: Meeting current challenges to validity* (NIDA Research Monograph 57, pp. 31–54). Washington, DC: National Institute on Drug Abuse.

Johnston, L. D., O'Malley, P. M., Bachman, J. G., & Schulenberg, J. E. (2012). *Monitoring the Future national survey results on drug use, 1975-2011, Vol. 2. College students and adults ages 19-50.* Ann Arbor: Institute for Social Research, University of Michigan.

Johnston, L. D., O'Malley, P. M., Bachman, J. G., & Schulenberg, J. E. (2013a). *Monitoring the Future national results on adolescent drug use: Overview of key findings, 2012.* Ann Arbor: Institute for Social Research, University of Michigan.

Johnston, L. D., O'Malley, P. M., Bachman, J. G., & Schulenberg, J. E. (2013b). *Monitoring the Future national survey results on drug use, 1975-2012, Vol. 1. Secondary school students.* Ann Arbor: Institute for Social Research, University of Michigan.

Johnston, L. D. (1985). The etiology and prevention of substance use: What can be learned from recent historical changes? In C. L. Jones & R. J. Battjes (Eds.), *The etiology of drug abuse: Implications for prevention* (NIDA Research Monograph No. 56, pp. 155–177). Washington, DC: US Government Printing Office.

Keyes, K. M., Schulenberg, J. E., O'Malley, P. M., Johnston, L. D., Bachman, J. G., Li, G., & Hasin, D. (2011). The social norms of birth cohorts and adolescent marijuana use in the United States, 1976-2007. *Addiction, 106,* 1790–1800.

Keyes, K., Schulenberg, J. E., O'Malley, P. M., Johnston, L. D., Bachman, J. G., Li, G., & Hasin, D. (2012). Birth cohort effects on adolescent alcohol use: The influence of social norms 1976–2007. *Archives of General Psychiatry, 69*(12), 1304–1313.

National Institute on Drug Abuse (NIDA). (2012a). *Inhalant abuse* (Research Report Series, NIH Publication Number 12-3818). Rockville, MD: National Institute on Drug Abuse. Retrieved November 2015, from http://www.drugabuse.gov/drugs-abuse/inhalants

National Institute on Drug Abuse. (2013). Monitoring the Future. Retrieved November 2015, from http://www.drugabuse.gov/related-topics/trends-statistics/monitoring-future

National Institute on Drug Abuse. (2012b). Prescription drug abuse: Young people at risk. Retrieved November 2015, from http://www.drugabuse.gov/related-topics/trends-statistics/infographics/prescription-drug-abuse-young-people-risk

O'Malley, P. M., Bachman, J. G., & Johnston, L. D. (1983). Reliability and consistency of self-reports of drug use. *International Journal of the Addictions, 18,* 805–824.

O'Malley, P. M., & Wagenaar, A. C. (1991). Effects of minimum drinking age laws on alcohol use, related behaviors,

and traffic crash involvement among American youth: 1976–1987. *Journal of Studies on Alcohol, 52,* 478–491.

Patrick, M. E., & O'Malley, P. M. (2015). Trends in drug use among youth in the United States. In L. M. Scheier (Ed.), *Handbook of adolescent drug use prevention: Research, intervention strategies, and practice* (p. 51–65). Washington, DC: American Psychological Association.

Patrick, M. E., & Schulenberg, J. E. (2010). Alcohol use and heavy episodic drinking prevalence and predictors among national samples of American eighth- and tenth-grade students. *Journal of Studies on Alcohol and Drugs, 71,* 41–45.

Patrick, M. E., Schulenberg, J. E., Martz, M. E., Maggs, J. L., O'Malley, P. M., & Johnston, L. (2013). Extreme binge drinking among American 12th-grade students: Prevalence and predictors. *JAMA Pediatrics, 167,* 1019–1025.

Patrick, M. E., Wightman, P., Schoeni, R. F., & Schulenberg, J. E. (2012). Socioeconomic status and substance use among young adults: A comparison across constructs and drugs. *Journal of Studies on Alcohol and Drugs, 73,* 772–782.

Reissig, C. J., Strain, E. C., & Griffiths, R. R. (2009). Caffeinated energy drinks—a growing problem. *Drug and Alcohol Dependence, 99,* 1–10.

Rogers, F. B. (Ed.). (1965). *Studies in epidemiology.* New York, NY: Putnam Press.

Substance Abuse and Mental Health Services Administration (SAMHSA). (2012). *Comparing and evaluating youth substance use estimates from the National Survey on Drug Use and Health and other surveys* (HHS Publication No. SMA 12-4727, Methodology Series M-9). Rockville, MD: Author.

Substance Abuse and Mental Health Services Administration. (n.d.). National Survey on Drug Use and Health (NSDUH). Retrieved November 2015, from http://www.samhsa.gov/data/population-data-nsduh

Substance Abuse and Mental Health Services Administration. (2011). Results from the National Survey on Drug Use and Health: Summary of national findings. Retrieved November 2015, from http://www.samhsa.gov/data/NSDUH/2k11Results/NSDUHresults2011.htm

Substance Abuse and Mental Health Services Administration. (2013a). Substance use among 12th grade aged youths by dropout status. *The NSDUH Report,* February 12, 2013. Retrieved November 2015, from http://www.samhsa.gov/data/2k13/NSDUH036/SR036SubstanceUseDropouts.htm

Substance Abuse and Mental Health Services Administration. (2013b). Trends in adolescent substance use and perception of risk of substance use. *The NSDUH Report,* January 3, 2013. Retrieved November 2015, from http://www.samhsa.gov/data/2k13/NSDUH099a/sr099a-risk-perception-trends.pdf

Wagenaar, A. C., & T. L. Toomey (2002). Effects of minimum drinking age laws: Review and analyses of the literature from 1960 to 2000. *Journal of Studies on Alcohol, 14,* 206–225.

Wallace, J. M., Jr., Bachman J. G., O'Malley, P. M., Johnston, L. D., Schulenberg, J. E., & Cooper, S. M. (2002). Tobacco, alcohol, and illicit drug use: Racial and ethnic differences among U.S. high school seniors, 1976–2000. *Public Health Reports, 117*(Suppl. 1), S67–S75.

Wallace, J. M., Jr., Vaughn, M. G., Bachman, J. G., O'Malley, P. M., Johnston, L. D., & Schulenberg, J. E. (2009). Race/ethnicity, socioeconomic factors, and smoking among early adolescent girls in the United States. *Drug and Alcohol Dependence, 104*(Suppl. 1), S42–S49.

CHAPTER 5

Cultural Variations and Relevance to Etiology

Jorge Delva, Sandra L. Momper, Claudette L. Grinnel-Davis, *and* Mark B. Padilla

Abstract

This chapter begins with a description of the role of culture on the etiology of substance use, misuse, and disorders among youth in the United States. This is followed by a discussion of how present constructions of majority-minority groups oversimplify the tremendous diversity individuals experience and how they tend to negate individual agency and fail to critique the structural forces that impact individuals' drug-using behaviors. The chapter concludes with the thesis that a critical intersectionality framework is necessary to understand how substance use disorders vary as a function of individuals' multiple dimensions, including how these are manifested and impacted by societies' social and structural forces.

Key Words: substance use, critical theory, intersectionality, culture, youth, identities

The purpose of this chapter is to discuss the potential role of culture on the etiology of substance use, misuse, and disorders among youth in the United States. We focus this chapter on US youth, as opposed to youth from other countries, for three reasons. First, the rich ethnocultural diversity that exists in the United States allows for an in-depth discussion of the subject of substance use, misuse, and disorders from a cultural perspective. Second, the literature in the United States has generated an important scholarly debate about how to understand the processes and communities involved in drug use in a diverse immigrant society. Unfortunately, much cultural research in the United States has divided the population into static communities with stereotypical cultural attributions. Quite often, comparisons are made between individuals, families, and communities that fall into a "mainstream and dominant" culture (usually represented by people who are categorized as White) and those that fall into a nondominant, nonmainstream group or groups categorized as immigrants and racial and ethnic minority populations. It is presumed that those categorized as minority populations experience stressors associated with assimilation and/or acculturation (Noemi, Velez, & Ungemack, 1995); and/or discrimination because of language, country of origin, phenotypes that are different from the mainstream group (Delva, Allen-Meares, & Momper, 2010; Gee, Delva, & Takeuchi, 2007; Guthrie, Young, Williams, Boyd, & Kintner, 2002); and an overall struggle to be recognized, accepted, and valued by the majority group (Gray, 2004; Suleiman, 2004; Walters & Simoni, 2002). Although such constructions of the world into dominant versus minority categories do reflect some aspects of how society is organized and experienced by people (how these individuals see themselves and how they are perceived and treated by others), these constructions oversimplify the tremendous diversity individuals experience and they tend to negate individual agency.

The contemporary cultural study of substance use, misuse, and disorders presents numerous challenges (Canino, Lewis-Fernandez, & Bravo, 1997; Nichter, 2003). Some of these primary challenges include the difficulties inherent in defining culture(s) separate from the concepts of society, nationality, and race and ethnicity, when the tendency is to use the latter two labels as proxies for cultural backgrounds. We believe that one of the reasons there is a rich and growing literature attempting to describe and understand substance-using behaviors among diverse racial and ethnic groups is that, indeed, it appears more straightforward to study substance-using behaviors as a function of a person's presumably fixed racial and/or ethnic background or nationality or ethnic identity than attempting to account for the complexity of the multiple and dynamic influences of culture on human experience (Delva et al., 2005).

We take issue with approaches to drug use that equate sociodemographic or presumably fixed individual characteristics such as nationality, immigrant status, socioeconomic position, and race/ethnicity with culture. Although we agree with other critiques of the tendency to ignore the intersectionality of these characteristics and other identities (i.e., gender, religiosity, sexual identity), our critique goes beyond this. We have entered a century in which it is increasingly important to understand the multiple identities individuals hold and how the juxtaposition of these characteristics is practiced in particular times and places (Cole, 2009; Delva et al., 2010; Goodman & Carey, 2004; Phillips, 2007; Rojas, 2009; Shields, 2008). In this age of tremendous global interconnectedness, cultural hybridity, and population mobility, it is increasingly difficult to think of individuals as embedded within clearly and distinctly separate cultural artifacts and normative environments. Contemporary social theory, particularly that influenced by transnationalism and globalization, has contributed to critical advances by refocusing scholarly attention to the ways that culture functions as dynamic systems whose shape is emergent, innovative, and contingent, rather than existing as a set of relatively fixed "cultural artifacts" (Basch, Glick Schiller, & Szanton Blanc, 1994; Boyne, 1990; García Canclini, 1995; Hall, 1991; Harvey, 1990; Wolf, 1982). Yet, while such theoretical discussions have advanced discussions in the social sciences since the 1990s, this more dynamic approach to culture and human behavior has rarely been applied in the health sciences, nor has it been dominant in discussions of drug-using behaviors. We believe this is an error in the contemporary scientific research on substance use, leaving much of the contemporary scholarship devoid of the conceptual tools necessary to apprehend the dynamic processes and situated experiences that shape drug-using behaviors.

Much of the existing literature on drug-using behaviors describes cultural influences as dimensions of identity, referring to factors such as racial and ethnic background, sex and gender, sexual identity, religious practices, social economic position, and nativity. To these identities we stress the need to examine additional factors that are much more variable and contextually contingent—such as economic uncertainty, the local meanings or normative climate of drug use, and social stigma or discrimination—in order to understand how multiple dimensions of individual identity are manifested at particular times and places (Schulenberg, Maggs, & Hurrelmann, 1997; Zucker, Boyd, & Howard, 1994). Furthermore, we also posit that the way identities and social factors operate depend heavily on changes in societies' drug production, distribution patterns, and population trends (Agar, 2003, 2006; Courtwright, 2001; Inciardi, 1992; Jonnes, 1996; Kluger, 1997; Musto, 1999). Essentially, we argue that individuals may take on one or more identities under certain contexts and at a particular point in time, leading to drug-using behaviors that may potentially manifest quite differently under different circumstances or points in time.

Finally, while our review focuses on US youth due to the work primarily conducted by the coauthors of this chapter and the difficulty of discussing cultural influences on health in a global context, we believe that our overall conceptual approach could be easily applied to studies of the cultural aspects of substance use, misuse, and disorders among youth in any other country. Given the rapid growth and diversification of cosmopolitan urban environments globally, we believe it is essential for contemporary scholarship to avoid the dichotomization of groups into presumably discrete cultural groups, a practice that is usually accompanied by ethnocentric attitudes that neglect the extensive heterogeneity within a culture and the considerable amount of shared cultural experience between "different" cultural groups. Therefore, even though our focus is on US populations, we believe the perspective we offer in this chapter may serve to inform cultural understanding of substance use, misuse, and disorders globally.

In this chapter we first discuss the concepts of culture, intersectionality, and identity development. We posit that the latter two concepts may be more useful in helping to understand substance use, misuse, and substance use disorders among youth than the concept of culture. We concur with Trimble (2010), who suggests that the term "culture" has probably become "the most misunderstood construct in behavioral and social science" (p. 244). In a humorous manner, ethnographer Michael Agar highlights the problem of using the term "culture" indiscriminately by saying, "Culture is a hindrance posing as a helper. It is now promiscuously used to pretend that something has been described or explained when in fact it has only been squashed with a label like an insect with a flyswatter" (Agar, 2010, p. 4). Although we do not advocate for entirely discarding discussions of culture, we are concerned about its tendency to reify and essentialize individuals and communities rather than disentangle the complex, situated practices that shape drug use behaviors.

We follow the discussion of culture, intersectionality, and identity development with an example of how our framework contributes to the analysis of the drug-using experiences among American Indians which illustrates the interplay of developmental transitions, youth identities, familial environment, historical context, and institutional and structural factors associated with the use and misuse of substances by American Indian youth. We conclude the chapter with a summary of the topics discussed and provide recommendations for future research.

Culture, Intersectionality, Identity Development, and Substance Use

Inherent in our introduction is our desire to take extreme caution in applying cultural labels to explain individuals' behaviors and attributing these practices to culture. More accurately, we view these behaviors theoretically as the result of a creative combination of identities and situated cultural experiences. For example, as a result of observing differences in beliefs and attitudes toward drugs between Hispanic and White non-Hispanic boys, one may conclude there are strong ethnic differences (Delva et al., 2005). By extension, these differences may be construed as proxies for cultural differences between these groups. However, it is plausible that the differences observed are the result of the different social and economic contexts in which individuals live (i.e., Hispanics being more recent immigrants and experiencing bigotry and discrimination) rather than cultural differences per se. This point is well argued by Phillips (2007), who after examining the "cultural" practice of female genital cutting in several countries concluded, "in

many of the contexts where culture is involved, there turn out to be noncultural accounts" (p. 46). Hispanic children are more likely to live in poverty, in neighborhoods where interactions with gangs and drug dealers are more common, and to experience prejudice, discrimination, bigotry, housing and school segregation, and outright racism than non-Hispanic Whites. It is therefore entirely plausible that differences observed between Hispanic and White children in the United States are largely determined by the effect of institutional and structural factors and less about something presumably inherent in their cultural makeup or racial and ethnic background. In fact, if indeed these differences reflected "cultural" practices, beliefs, and attitudes, one would expect drug use rates to be higher in their native countries, but this is not the case. Consistently, school surveys of substance use in Latin American countries point to lower rates of drug use among these youth in their home countries than among Spanish-speaking-origin populations in the United States (Organization of American States, 2008). Unfortunately, those surveys do not include information on socioeconomic status, racial and ethnic minorities, or information on youth sexual identity for the corresponding countries to allow for the proper examination of substance use patterns among more socioeconomically disadvantaged populations (Black minorities in Spanish-speaking dominant countries, indigenous populations, sexual minorities) as compared to the more dominant groups (individuals of European descent, heterosexual populations).

As a precursor to the arguments detailed later, we offer a few definitions of terms utilized in this chapter. By *substance use* we mean the consumption of mood-altering substances that are legal for adults (cigarettes and alcohol), that can be prescribed (tranquilizers), and those that are illegal for all ages (marijuana, cocaine). We also include inhalant products (solvents, gases). We note that the large number of substances individuals may elect to use adds a considerable amount of complication to the topic discussed in this chapter because each substance may have a different link to cultural practices or perhaps more important, the use of each substance may have different pathways depending on the combination and intersections of multiple identities for a given individual at a particular time and place.

The notion of drug "misuse" is complicated in any discussion of culture, since cultural variations in the social definition of substances, appropriate and inappropriate uses, and the institutional climate regulating substance use practices is widely variable and cannot be presumed to be universal. We seek to acknowledge this variability while providing some operational definitions for the sake of our discussion. By *misuse* we refer to the use of substances with sufficient frequency and quantity to increase the possibilities that the user will encounter negative social and health consequences, and that persistent use will further increase the chances of causing such problems in multiple domains of the individual's life, such as family, education, and employment. By "substance use disorders," we refer to the diagnostic criteria as defined by *The Diagnostic Statistical Manual of Mental Disorders*, fourth edition, text revision (*DSM-IV-TR*) of the American Psychiatric Association (American Psychiatric Association, 2000).

Many definitions of culture have been proposed in the social science literature. In their book *Culture: A Critical Review of Concepts and Definitions*, Kluckhohn and Kroeber (1952) provided over 150 definitions and Lorner and Malpass (1994) suggest there are about 175 definitions. For the purpose of this chapter we use the definition offered by Marsella and Kameoka (1989) that reads as follows:

> Culture is shared learned behavior that is transmitted from one generation to another for purposes of human adjustment, adaptation, and growth. Culture has both external and internal referents. External referents include artifacts, roles, and institutions. Internal referents include attitudes, values, beliefs, expectations, epistemologies, and consciousness. (p. 233)

We also concur with Marsella and Kameoka (1989) when they indicate that "Culture is something that mediates and shapes virtually all aspects of human behavior. It is the way in which human beings define and experience reality" (p. 233), or, as Kelly (1955) indicates, it is the construction of collective experiences resulting from the shared experiences within a group.

While we agree with the aforementioned definitions of culture, we bring a different perspective to the present discussion, a perspective we believe can better account for the complexity of the changes experienced by contemporary societies. The perspective is called intersectionality, and it arose primarily from feminist researchers (Collins, 1990; Crenshaw, 1991). It refers to the multiple identities that human beings adopt and/or are imposed on

them by the larger society, and to the idea that multiple dimensions of race, gender, sexuality, and class are experienced simultaneously in varying degrees according to the particular contexts in which individuals find themselves, fluctuating in salience, and differentially impacting individuals who are variously positioned in the social system. Traditionally, the intersectionality perspective has been utilized to study gender and sexual identities, but less focus has been placed on using this perspective to understand substance-using behaviors, with the exception of recent medical anthropological research on syndemics (Kurtz, 2008; Milstein, 2008; Romero-Daza, Weeks, & Singer, 2003; Singer et al., 2006; Stall, Friedman, & Catania, 2008).

In taking an intersectionality perspective we do not abandon the idea that cultural groups do exist and that some maintain internal and external referents that span centuries (e.g., Quechuas in Peru) while others are more recent (e.g., the shared values and behaviors by youth and adults who participate in rave parties). As we discussed in the beginning of the chapter, culture is inherently wrapped up in issues of identity, and as such, it is often interpreted as something internalized, intrinsic to the individual, and the individual's self-identification (Erikson, 1968). This perspective acknowledges the fact that people do follow cultural norms, which in turn tends to bind them in ways that may distinguish them socially from other groups. However, it also downplays a more nuanced reflection on the within-culture heterogeneity that exists as a result of the multiple identities that individuals inhabit and the ways these intersect with other contextual factors, such as moment in the life span (e.g., youth versus adults) or social position in society (e.g., lower versus higher socioeconomic position). This point is not to make the case for cultural relativism but rather to allow for greater acceptance or consideration of the multiplicity of cultural experiences, or perhaps more appropriately, to acknowledge that people experience life through multiple layers of cultural experiences. Every individual, whether adolescent or adult, simultaneously occupies various social identities, claiming membership in multiple social groups that together work to create the individual's self-concept (Tajfel, 1981). All of these identities contribute to individual behaviors and all are dimensions of "culture," a point that Nichter (2003) emphasizes. Some of these identities might be based on socioeconomic or demographic factors such as income level, wealth, educational level, occupational status, racial and ethnic makeup, sex, gender, sexual identity, immigration, intergenerational status, and religion. In our attempts to be culturally sensitive, we strive to avoid the problem that we have identified in some of our prior research: "Researchers can make sweeping generalizations and attach labels to groups studied that may be not only incorrectly attributed to culture but also that are static and take on essentialist characteristics" (Delva et al., 2010, p. 5). For example, referring to groups as "religious and/or spiritual," "fatalistic or future oriented," "individually or collectively oriented," or "family centered" results in essentialist models of groups of individuals that are simplistic, fixed, ahistorical, and apolitical.

To better illustrate our point, we include a hypothetical graphical representation of the distribution of behaviors, attitudes, values, and beliefs that individuals, families, and communities may have as a function of cultural elements and those of other identities (i.e., immigration status, age, gender, sexual identity, religion, racial and ethnic background, educational level, and occupational status), including their intersections (see Figure 5.1).

For example, if we allow the x-axis to represent children's scores on high-risk-taking behaviors, we see that the likelihood a child will misuse substances (area under the curve) will vary according to where the child is positioned on the graph, the position being dependent on the type and degree of the multiple identities and contexts experienced by the child. We argue that this perspective frees us from viewing the world from an essentialist, static, or unchanging perspective.

At the same time, researchers must also not make the mistake of assuming chasms of difference between groups as a result of different configurations of these multiple identities. Cole's (2009) recommended guidelines for conducting

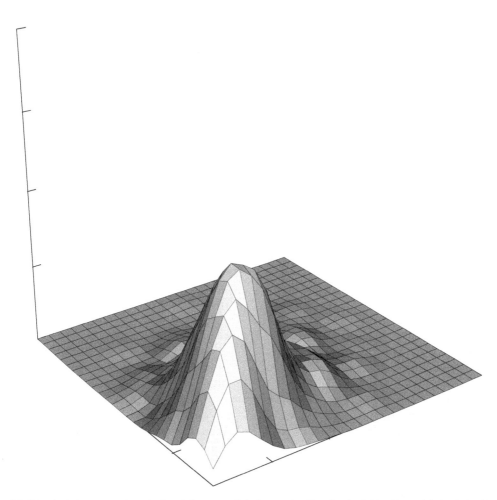

Figure 5.1 Hypothetical representation of cultural elements and the intersectionality of multiple identities and their relationship to substance misuse.

	No Identification with Dominant Culture	Identification with Dominant Culture
No Identification with Culture of Origin	**Marginalization**	**Assimilation**
Identification with Culture of Origin	**Separation**	**Integration**

Figure 5.2 Berry's (1990) model of identity management strategies.

research on intersecting identities point to the idea that we need to be as sensitive to the similarities between social identities as we are to the differences; just because a label is different does not mean that the values of the identities are necessarily different or socially meaningful.

This may be as true when looking at intraindividual behavioral (in)consistency as it is for studying demographically based group differences. The more identities a person has to negotiate, the more values have to be negotiated and understood in relationship to each other. A useful model of identity negotiation is that presented by Berry (1990), which focuses on purely the presence or absence of identification with varying identities (see Figure 5.2).

Berry's work primarily emphasizes the negotiation of ethnic identities (as does the vast majority of this research) and deals largely with two cultures in the context of immigration, one of which is referred to as the "dominant" culture and the other as the "culture" of origin. Despite the oversimplification of cultural experiences, that is, the dichotomizing of diverse and overlapping groups into two "static" cultural groups, the premises of Barry's framework are still useful. People who identify equally with both cultures can integrate into both settings, while people who identify with neither are marginalized.

However, this model does not account for what leads an individual to identify (or not) with either the dominant culture or the culture of origin, does not take into account the plurality of cultural experiences, and minimizes within-culture heterogeneity of experiences.

Another model, one presented by Roccas and Brewer (2002), by contrast, focuses not on the presence or absence of identification, but on the conflict that exists between identities and the strategies used to negotiate these conflicts. Figure 5.3 provides both the model and examples of conflict resolution. Some of these strategies are much easier to implement if the values of the two identities are similar. However,

for other combinations of identities, too much conflict may exist between the value sets to facilitate use of these strategies. For example, the identity set "gay Catholic" is considered by many Catholics to be an incompatible paradox due to the Church's official theological stance that homosexual behavior is a mortal sin. Merger (the reconciliation of these conflicting identities) is a significant challenge in this instance, although the pursuit of merger clearly motivates some groups to advocate full inclusion for the Lesbian Gay Bisexual transgender and Queer (LGBTQ) population in the Catholic Church. Or one could lead an apparently double life and alternate between identities, depending on whether one is at Mass or with friends (*compartmentalization*), while also being accused of hypocrisy by members of both groups. One may find other gay Catholics and find a supportive community there (*intersection*). Or one may have to come to a decision and take one of two routes: leave the Catholic Church and live openly as a gay person, or submit to the Church's guidelines and make sexual abstinence a spiritual discipline (*dominance*).

Some people are able more effectively than others to negotiate value differences. These people are said to have high *identity integration*—that is, they are more able to see their multiples identities as compatible with each other (Darling, Molina, Sanders, Lee, & Zhao, 2008). By contrast, people with low identity integration identify strongly with their multiple identities but see them as largely incompatible with each other and alternate back and forth between their identities depending on their context. This is similar to the compartmentalization strategy Roccas and Brewer (2002) identify.

Negotiating multiple identities has its risks and benefits. Group processes may be improved by contributing diverse opinions and ideas (Gurin, Dey, Gurin, & Hurtado, 2003; Mannix & Neale, 2005). But it could do so at a cost to individuals and their overall mental health. For instance, individuals who perceive themselves as being either a "token"

Intersection*	Dominance
The creation of a new separate identity based upon elements of both identities.	The choice of one identity to the exclusion of the other identity.
Suppose a male gay Latino youth. A person who negotiates identities this way would identify only with other gay male Latinos.	In this case, a male gay Latino youth may only identify with the Latino community and hide/repress his gay identity.
	On the other hand, another male gay Latino youth may only identify with other gay youth in ways that his Latino identity is put aside.

Merger	Compartmentalization
The willingness and ability to identify with both identities simultaneously.	The alternating salience of either identity depending on what the external situation demands or indicates.
A male gay Latino youth simultaneously and freely identifies with both gay males and Latinos.	A male gay Latino youth identifies with either his gay or Latino identity at a particular point in time depending on the context of his interactions.

Figure 5.3 Roccas and Brewer (2002) strategies for negotiating multiple identities.

* The meaning of the concept of 'intersection' used by Roccas and Brewer is different from the one we use in this Chapter and that stems from feminist research which refers to the existence of and negotiation among the multiple identities people experience or that are ascribed to them.

representative or occupying a "solo status" in relationship to the larger group are more likely to experience mental health struggles and perform worse than others in the group and therefore may reinforce stereotypes or lead the individual to think they are misrepresenting their identity groups (Steele, 1997; Thompson & Sekaquaptewa, 2002).

This is not to say that there are not individual benefits to navigating multiple identities as well. People with high identity integration in educational or in technological development settings are able to draw on more information across multiple disciplines and as a result have higher levels of productivity (Cheng, Sanchez-Burks, & Lee, 2008). People with higher levels of identity integration also have stronger, larger, and more interconnected social support systems than people with low identity integration (Mok, Morris, Benet-Martinez, & Karakitapoglu-Aygun, 2007).

Much of the identity integration literature, however, has been completed either on adults (Cheng, Sanders, et al., 2008; Darling et al., 2008), who may be assumed to be further along the path of identity development, or on college undergraduates, who are now largely considered "emerging adults" (Arnett, 2004) and may be at the time Waterman (1992) identifies as the point of ideological identity development. Can the identity integration literature

be translated for application to younger adolescents, for whom substance abuse has become an increasing social problem? Can we talk about negotiating and integrating social identities in a population for whom self-concept is still highly fluid?

In reality the adolescent development literature and the identity integration literature are not that far apart. Marcia's (1980, 1994) work on navigating adolescence describes the identity-building process as a pattern of crises and commitments, events that call for a response (crisis) and the action taken as a result (commitment). These alternations between what Marcia called *identity moratorium* and *identity achievement* are not that different from the process by which adults negotiate new roles and identities in the face of preexisting ones. But for a certain section of the population, particularly those with memberships in disenfranchised populations, these negotiations are more challenging. Research indicates that adolescents who come from non-White backgrounds or who are not exclusively heterosexual have more "cultural work" to do than other adolescents (Brown, 1989; Ontal-Grzebik & Raffaelli, 2004; Phinney, 1989). The values that have to be interpreted and negotiated in this cultural work are wide and varied. For example, it affects how people view their outward appearances, as Black females recognize that dominant standards of beauty do not apply to them (Phinney, 1989).

Likewise, the construct of *familismo*, which is utilized to describe the strong value of family interconnectedness shown by some Latino populations, is a stark contrast to the highly nuclear and individualist notions of White family functioning and can in turn affect decisions Latinos and Latinas make about extracurricular activities, job options, and higher education (Comas-Diaz, 2001; Steidel & Contreras, 2003). However, the influence of "*familism*" is probably just one of numerous aspects that inform a person's decision making.

So how might the interaction of social identities contribute to the tendency of adolescents to use or misuse substances? We know that in adults, high levels of identity integration have been found to have positive effects on overall well-being (Darling et al., 2008). We also know that Black American, Latino, and Asian American adolescents who identify positively with their ethnic groups do better in school and get into fewer fights than their peers (Bracey, Bámaca, & Umaña-Taylor, 2004). But, on the other hand, it appears that the stress of negotiating identities leads to the use of substances as a coping mechanism (Sodowsky & Lai, 1997; Yee & Thu, 1997). Furthermore, because adolescents are less likely to have the full sophistication required to negotiate perceived conflicts in value systems, adolescents negotiating multiple identities may have more stress resulting from longer periods of identity moratorium or lower levels of identity integration, either of which can contribute to lower levels of mental health. Finally, the stressor of racism may lead to higher levels of substance use (Freeman, 1990).

Darling et al. (2008) theorize a model of identity integration and professional achievement that may be applicable to the relationship between identity integration and substance use. As shown in Figure 5.4, an adolescent's ability to negotiate multiple identities may be processed through affective, relational, cognitive, and behavioral processes that affect decisions about substance use, abuse, and misuse.

Research on adolescent substance use and multicultural identity negotiation does not specifically use the identity integration framework. However, similarities in framework do exist and can be evaluated. One study looking at both HIV risk behaviors and substance abuse with Latino/a youth from an eco-developmental framework (Prado et al., 2010) identifies a macrosystem-level variable called "parent adolescent Americanism gap" that is indirectly related to substance use in early adolescence. While this study does not offer a peek at intraindividual conflict, it does outwardly represent the potential for internal values negotiation.

Overall, the literature on ethnic identity and substance use indicates that the link between cultural negotiation, ethnic identity, and substance use is a complicated and at times contradictory picture. For example, despite the positive benefits that ethnic identity has, it may also be positively correlated with the tendency to use alcohol and cigarettes in Latino adolescents (Zamboanga, Schwartz, Jarvis, & VanTyne, 2009). But here again, a variable of "acculturation stress" points to negotiation of identity and values as a complex interaction worthy of further analysis. Likewise, the mediating effect

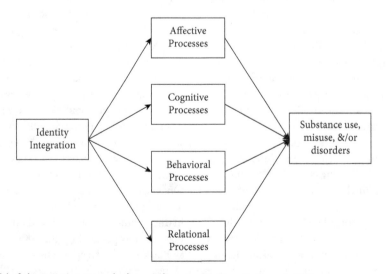

Figure 5.4 A model of identity integration and substance abuse (modified from Darling et al., 2008).

between immigrant and nonimmigrant populations on ethnic identity may also be important to overall substance use/misuse outcomes (Marsiglia, Kulis, Luengo, Nieri, & Villar, 2008; Ndiaye, Hecht, Wagstaff, & Elek, 2009). The stress of second-language acquisition or bilinguality does not help to clarify matters. In a study on Latino adolescents in the American Southwest, while ethnic identity in general was positively related to the tendency to use drugs and alcohol, primary use of English over other languages was also positively connected to substance use (Marsiglia, Kulis, Hecht, & Sills, 2004).

A brief overview of the relationship between ethnic identity and adolescent substance use appears to indicate that the examination of identity integration as a mediating factor is warranted and worthwhile. Because the ambiguity of the literature overall appears to point to layers of conflict and negotiation, looking at the degree to which an adolescent recognizes himself or herself as an integrated set of identities may provide further insight on a complicated body of work.

In this section we provided an in-depth discussion of the problems of using the concept of "culture" to explain substance-using behaviors and provided an alternative perspective that includes incorporating an intersectionality lens. In the next section we use the experiences of American Indians to further illustrate the ways by which historical, cultural, institutional, and structural factors; identity development; and the concept of intersectionality need to be taken into account when attempting to understand patterns of substance use, misuse, and disorders among youth (though we argue among adults as well).

Integrating Historical, Cultural, Institutional, and Structural Factors; Intersectionality; and Identity Development: The Experiences of American Indians

Substance Use Among American Indians

There are 3.1 million people who report being American Indian or Alaska Native (AI/AN) and 4.9 million people report being AI/AN and another race/ethnicity (US Census Bureau, 2009). There are 565 federally recognized tribal nations, Alaska Native villages, and corporations that range in membership from less than 100 to more than 350,000 people (Bureau of Indian Affairs [BIA], 2002; US Department of the Interior, 2011). More tribes are recognized only by individual states, and numerous tribes, bands, and AI villages are not formally

recognized by the federal government. Recognized tribes are in 35 states and reportedly 200 different languages are spoken (Fleming, 1992). Tremendous heterogeneity exists among tribes. A common stereotype depicts AIs/ANs as residents of reservations, but the majority (64%) live in urban environments and the rest live on reservations or tribal trust lands (US Census Bureau, 2000). Additionally about 33% of the AI/AN population is under age 18, compared with 26% of the total population. American Indian tribal groups report that the percentage of youth under 18 ranges from 26% to 39%, and the Alaska Native tribes report the population under 18 years of age to range from 32% to 40% (US Census Bureau, 2000). American Indians/Alaska Natives' median age of 29 is 6 years younger than the national US median age of 35 years.

Substance use and abuse disorders are frequently cited as one of the most serious public health issues in AI/AN communities (Baezconde-Garbanati, Beebe, & Perez-Stable, 2007; Beauvais, 1996; Burgess et al., 2007; Doolan & Froelicher, 2006; French, 2000; Hawkins, Cummins, & Marlatt, 2004). The American Indian Services Utilization, Psychiatric Epidemiology, Risk and Protective Factors Project (AI-SUPERPFP) study reported that AIs have high rates of substance use and abuse disorders (Mitchell, Beals, Novins, Spicer, & AI-SUPERPFP Team, 2003). Compared to non-American Indian youth, American Indian youth initiate substance use at a younger age, are more likely to continue use after initial use, and have higher rates of polysubstance use (Beauvais, 1992a; US Congress, Office of Technology Assessment [OTA], 1990). Regional variations in drug use figure prominently when comparing AI youth to others, with AI youth reporting significantly higher lifetime use of some substances in certain regions (Kulis, Okamoto, & Soma-Sen, 2006; Plunkett & Mitchell, 2000). When controlling for geographic region, drug use rates of AI youth are significantly higher than those of other groups for three of seven substances—alcohol, marijuana, and cocaine (Plunkett & Mitchell, 2000).

American Indians also have the highest prevalence of smoking among all racial and ethnic minority groups (Baezconde-Garbanati et al., 2007; Burgess et al., 2007; Doolan & Froelicher, 2006). Substance Abuse and Mental Health Services Administration (SAMHSA) (2002) reports that AI/AN youth aged 12 to 17 years are more likely than youths from other racial/ethnic groups to smoke cigarettes during the past month. American Indian youth from all regions of the country have the highest number of smokers among all racial groups (about 40% for both genders) (Henderson, Jacobsen, & Beals, 2005; Steinman & Hu, 2007), and about 46% of AI high school seniors are smokers (Fagan, Moolchan, Lawrence, Fernander, & Ponder, 2007). LeMaster, Connell, Mitchell, and Manson (2002) used data from the Voices of Indian Teens Project to determine the prevalence of cigarette and smokeless tobacco use among Indian adolescents in a sample of 2,390 youth ages 13 to 20 years attending high schools in five Indian communities west of the Mississippi, and approximately 50% of the youth reported having smoked cigarettes, with 30% smoking "once in a while."

American Indians used tobacco in many aspects of everyday life. In general tobacco was used for traditional spiritual and medicinal practices. Tobacco leaves were chewed, smoked in pipes, or used in cigars or cigarettes (Winter, 2000). Federal and institutional policies of the 19th and 20th centuries disallowed the practice of traditional ceremonies, and some believe this led to the use of tobacco in the form of cigarettes, instead of tobacco leaves, as a way to practice traditions without being "caught" (Forster, Rhodes, Poupart, Baker, & Davey, 2007). Forster et al. (2007) believe that the use of cigarettes instead of loose tobacco may have led to a higher prevalence of smoking cigarettes and recreational tobacco use among American Indians. American Indians are a heterogeneous population and smoking within this ethnic group differs by region, age, gender, and tribal group. For example, urban Indians have higher rates of smoking than rural Indians (Fagan et al., 2007; Indian Health Service, 2004). American Indian adults and youth from all regions have the highest rate of smoking among all racial groups (Henderson et al., 2005; Steinman & Hu, 2007). Although smoking rates have declined in other racial and ethnic minority groups, rates among American Indians appear to be rising, and, when compared to these groups, they still have the highest prevalence of cigarette smoking (Baezconde-Garbanati et al., 2007; Burgess et al., 2007).

Among American Indians, pipe smoking for ceremonies is distinguished from the nontraditional smoking of pipes. When smoking sacred tobacco in a pipe, small puffs of smoke are taken and held in the mouth, and deep inhaling is not the norm as the smoke is not for enjoyment but a symbolic gesture to cleanse the air, the heart, and the mind (Hodge, 2001). If the receiver of the pipe does not want to inhale any smoke, he or she holds the pipe and just pulls a hand toward the face along the stem of the pipe as a way to participate without inhaling the tobacco. Pipe smoking is a way to communicate with the creator so that a peaceful exchange occurs and prayers can be heard (Hodge, 2001). Consequently, in American Indian populations, cigarette use needs to be viewed within the larger context of tobacco use among American Indians since its inception.

Most studies have reported that rates of alcohol use are elevated among AI youth. While American Indians and Alaska Natives have experienced social and cultural devastation that can be directly attributed to alcohol use, it is important to recognize the large variance in actual rates of alcohol use and alcohol use–related problems experienced in Indian country. Accurate prevalence rates of alcohol use and abuse are difficult to assess, given the diversity of tribes, the diversity of settings (urban and rural), inaccurate record keeping, and the lack of research focusing on specific tribal groups using diverse and tribally specific methodologies (Szlemko, Wood, & Jumper-Thurman, 2006). Consequently, alcohol use rates across age groups and tribes are immensely variable, and data collected are often misleading (Beals et al., 2003; May, 1996; Spicer et al., 2003; Welty, 2002). For example, some researchers in Indian country report that alcohol use is extremely common among AI youth, but it may not be the first substance used or the primary drug of choice (Beauvais, Oetting, Wolf, & Edwards, 1989; Novins, Beals, & Mitchell, 2001). Also, other research notes that there is a sizeable population of AIs (adults and youth) who do not drink or who are nonproblem drinkers (Mail & Johnson, 1993; Myers, Kagawa-Singer, Kumanyika, Lex, & Markides, 1995).

Since 1975 the Tri-Ethnic Center located at Colorado State University has conducted annual surveys of 7th–12th graders on reservations and then combined the data for analysis into a single sample (Szlemko et al., 2006). In 1993, 73% of this sample of AI youth reported ever having used alcohol (Beauvais, 1998). AI male and female teens experience drinking problems at equally high rates (Beauvais, 1992b; Cockerham, 1975; Oetting & Beauvais, 1989), and in a sample of urban AI youth, gender may not have influenced which youth abused alcohol (Walker, 1992). Beauvais (1992a) compared drinking rates for reservation AI youth, off-reservation AI youth, and White students in the 8th and 12th grades. Off-reservation AI 8th graders were more likely to report lifetime alcohol use (80%) than reservation AIs (70%) or White (73%) 8th graders. AI youth drink larger amounts and experience more negative consequences than other youth as life on reservations, boarding school attendance, and dropping out of school contribute to these higher rates (Beauvais, 1996, 1998; Dick, Manson, & Beals, 1993; Oetting & Beauvais, 1989; Szlemko et al., 2006).

AI/AN youth aged 12 years or older are more likely than members of other racial groups to be current (past month) illicit drug users (12.6% vs. 8.0%) (SAMHSA, 2008).

Beauvais, Jumper-Thurman, and Burnside (2008) followed the trends of drug use among reservation youth for 30 years. Exposure to marijuana, stimulants, sedatives, PCP, psychedelics, and inhalants is declining while methamphetamine use has remained unchanged, and AI youth have the highest rate of use among all racial/ethnic groups (Beauvais et al., 2008; Kronk & Thompson, 2007).

Marijuana use is the most widely used illegal substance among all adolescents, although higher among AI adolescents (Ehlers, Slutske, Gilder, & Lau, 2007; Whitesell et al., 2007). A study using data from the Voices of Indian Teens Project sampled 9th to 12th graders in seven predominantly American Indian schools in four western communities (Novins & Mitchell, 1998). Results indicated that of 1,464 youth, 55.7% of AI teens reported using marijuana at least once during their lifetime, and 40.0% had used marijuana in the past month (Novins & Mitchell, 1998). Ehlers et al. (2007) surveyed 525 AIs between the ages of 18 and 70 years from eight southwestern reservations about marijuana use and found that 87% had ever used marijuana, 33% met criteria for a lifetime diagnosis of marijuana dependency, and 11% for marijuana abuse. They found several risk factors for marijuana dependence among AI adolescents including being male and having an external diagnosis (conduct disorder or antisocial personality disorder). Whitesell et al. (2007) found that peak risk ages for AI marijuana use begins at 12 years of age and rises steeply to age 16, where risk remains high until age 18 and declines sharply through age 24.

At this time little is known about prescription drug use and abuse among AIs; however, in 2004 the National Drug Threat Survey indicated a high percentage of state and local law enforcement agencies in the Midwest region (where many reservations exist) report that oxycodones (Oxycontin, Percocet, and Percodan) (60.9%) and hydrocodones (Lorcet and Vicodin) (51.8%) are commonly diverted and abused in their jurisdictions (US Department of Justice, 2004b). In a 2007 study of Oxycontin use and abuse on a Midwestern AI reservation, Momper, Delva, and Glover-Reed (2011) reported increased levels of the use of prescription drugs and, in particular, Oxycontin. For example, one participant in a Talking Circle stated: "I say there are more pills than anything around here than what it used to be. I always thought everybody used to be into weed. But then it started to grow into pills and coke. What really got bad around here is Oxycontin."

Consequences for Youth

The consequence of substance use and abuse is thought to directly impact the high rates of morbidity and mortality among AI adolescents. American Indian youth (ages 15 to 24 years) have a mortality rate 2.1 times higher than that of the general population (196.5 vs. 95.3 per 100,000 population) and 2.3 times higher than that of Whites, the group with the lowest rate (196.5 vs. 84.3 per 100,000 population) (Hawkins et al., 2004; Indian Health Service, Office of Public Health, Program Statistics Team, 1999). Of the 10 leading causes of death for AI teens, at least 3 are related to heavy alcohol use: accidents, suicide, and homicide (Hawkins et al., 2004; Indian Health Service [IHS], Office of Public Health, Program Statistics Team, 1999). The alcoholism death rate for Indian youth who receive services at IHS was 11.3 times higher than the combined all-races rate (IHS, Office of Public Health, Program Statistics Team, 1999). However, while risk-taking behavior levels continue to be higher than the general population, long-term trends in a BIA study of AI high school youth show some improvement, and as AI/AN youth mature, their participation in high-risk behaviors tends to diminish (Shaughnessy, Branum, & Everett-Jones, 2001).

Historical, Cultural, Institutional, and Structural Considerations

To better understand the consequences of American Indian youth using and misusing substances, it is critical to investigate historical and traumatic events and cultural practices that have contributed to these problems in these communities (Duran & Duran, 1995). For example, specific historical factors have been associated with increased substance use among AIs, including the provision of alcohol in the fur trading business, boarding school, urban relocation, and ethnic dislocation movements (Hawkins et al., 2004; May, 1982; Oetting, Beauvais, & Velarde, 1982; Trimble, Padilla, & Bell-Bolek, 1987), acculturation stress

(LaFromboise, 1988), alienation from the larger culture (Moncher, Holden, & Trimble, 1990), historical trauma (Weaver & Brave Heart, 1999), poverty, fewer employment and educational opportunities (Beauvais, 1992b, 1998), and an excessive amount of unstructured time on reservations where drinking and prescription drug use among youth is often a response to boredom (Edwards & Edwards, 1988; Momper et al., 2011). The concept of historical trauma refers to cumulative wounding across as well as during one's current life span (Weaver & Brave Heart, 1999). Historical policies and events for AI/ANs have led to a disruption in socialization processes for Indian families (Boyd, Ball, & Dishion, 2006; Institute for Government Research Studies in Administration, 1928; Nies, 1996). Under colonization, the structural context for socialization and development was constrained and regulated by the exploitative relationships with US military and civil authorities, conditions of social marginalization in the wider society, and the actions of social and state institutions. For example, many AI/AN families experienced an interruption in the intergenerational transmission of traditional culture which was imposed by the AI boarding school movement, which separated generations of AI youth from their tribes and families. To this day these programs continue to have a detrimental effect on AI families. These policies resulted in the disorganization of tribal structures and effectively replaced AI socialization with practices and beliefs inherent to the boarding school system (Boyd-Ball & Dishion, 2006). As a result of boarding school, AI women missed out on the role modeling of AI nurturing and childrearing (Ing, 1991). Descendents of boarding school attendees report a history of neglect and abuse as well as being unable to parent adequately or experiencing confusion as to how to raise healthy children (Brave Heart, 1998, 1999). Consequently, this has resulted in impaired culturally normative parenting, a process that is likely to increase youth risk of using substances (Brave Heart, 1999) among both the parents and the children.

Additionally many AI families continue to feel alienated from mainstream educational institutions which reduce their involvement in the education of their children (Cummins, 1989). AI students who are confronted with racist threats on a regular basis in the school environment often lose a positive sense of cultural identity and begin a process of "downshifting," which eventually leads to dropping out (Caine & Caine, 1997). The after-effects of parenting and school difficulties are described in a report by SAMHSA that examined three categories of risk factors for substance use (individual/peers, family, and school) (2004). When comparing these risk factors for AI/AN youth to other racial and ethnic groups, AI/AN youth were *more* likely than other youths to perceive moderate to no risk associated with substance use, to perceive their parents as not strongly disapproving of their substance use, to believe that all or most of the students in their school get drunk at least once a week, and were *less* likely than other youths to participate in youth activities or regularly attend religious services (SAMHSA, 2004). AI/AN parents were about as likely as other youth to talk to their child about the dangers of substance use, to let them know they had done a good job, to tell their youth they were proud of something they had done, and to make their youth do chores around the house or to limit TV watching (SAMHSA, 2004). However, parents were less likely to provide help with school homework or to limit the time out with friends on school nights (SAMHSA, 2004).

To understand substance use, misuse, and disorders among AI/AN youth properly, it is imperative to take into account the history and present-day social, economic, and political conditions of AIs/ANs. Many AI/AN youth live in communities that continue to experience long-term economic and social problems. Many AI adolescents experience life stress at rates exceeding those of adolescents in the general US population. For example, AI teens experience high rates of child abuse and neglect, suicide, poverty, and violent crime, with alcohol a factor (National Vital Statistics Report, 2001; US Census Bureau, 2001; US Department of Justice, 2004a). The 2008 poverty rate for AI/AN was 24.2% (US Census Bureau, 2008). With unemployment often being associated with substance abuse, of note is that between 2003 and 2005 the unemployment rate for AIs/ANs remained unchanged at 49% with some communities reporting rates as high as 83% (US Department of the Interior, 2005).

Intersectionality and Identity Development

Identity integration research has as a presupposition that people identify simultaneously with both the dominant culture and their own identities. It says nothing about people who neither want nor are unable to identify with the culture at large, people who are either perpetually excluded or who are ideologically opposed to the dominant culture. One pan-ethnic group for whom this may be true is American Indians. Each one of the hundreds of federally recognized tribes has a different history in relationship to the federal government, but frequently the history between the dominant culture and the tribe's values is one that recalls a long history of genocide.

In the United States it was expected that American Indians would eventually totally assimilate into mainstream society, but this has not occurred. Yet assimilation or acculturation continues to be a challenge for rural and urban AIs/ANs as they struggle to maintain their cultural heritage and identity in the face of a society that colonized them, took their land, and does not always tolerate or seek to understand their values or perspectives (Beauvais & LaBoueff, 1985). The strain created by these historical experiences is thought by many Indians and social science researchers to be the primary cause of the many social problems faced by Indian communities, particularly with respect to substance abuse (Akins, Mosher, Rotolo, & Griffin, 2003; Beauvais, 1998; Beauvais & La Boueff, 1985). In fact, studies of the effect of biculturalism (the ability to function well in both tribal Indian society and the modern Western world) on the use and abuse of substances among AI youth have shown varying results. For example, Oetting and Beauvais (1990) found that AI youth with a bicultural ethnic identity were less likely to use drugs, but they did not find this relationship in a second subsequent study (Oetting & Beauvais, 1991). Novins and Mitchell (1998) did not find any relationship between ethnic identity and marijuana use among AI adolescents in four distinct rural AI communities. Future research needs to take into account acculturation, enculturalism (the process of selectively preserving or acquiring the values, practices, and beliefs of their own culture), and biculturalism when investigating substance use and abuse within tribal or urban communities. This is particularly important, as evidence shows that 4.9 million AIs/ANs have identified with two races (US Census Bureau, 2009). Future research on AI/AN substance abuse needs to focus on the cultural, historical, and structural contexts of the community and the ways that substance use is shaped by the contradictory imperatives of acculturation in the context of systematic exploitation and marginalization (Galliher, Evans, & Weiser, 2007).

Nascent research on gay, lesbian bisexual, and transgender American Indian populations points to the importance of incorporating sexual identities into research on substance use, misuse, and disorders. Cassells, Pearson, Walters, Simoni, and Morris (2010) used data from the first national study of gay, lesbian, bisexual, and transgender American Indian and Alaska Natives to examine HIV prevalence and risk behaviors. They found extremely high rates of HIV (22%). The corresponding rates of HIV for men who have sex with men, men who have sex with men and women, and women who have sex with women and men were 36%, 19%, and 15%, respectively. They also found high rates of concurrent sexual partnerships, levels that are comparable to those found in sub-Saharan Africa, and found considerable variation in assortative/dissasortative mating. These findings and those of other studies of "Two Spirit" Native populations (Chae & Walters, 2009; Walters, Evans-Campbell, Simoni, Ronquillo, & Bhuyan, 2006) point to the importance of incorporating sexual identity into research if one is to further contribute to understanding substance use behaviors among at-risk, vulnerable, and historically neglected populations.

Directions for Future Research

The most significant challenge posed in understanding how culture(s) can contribute to the etiology of substance abuse disorders in adolescents is in breaking away from demography-based models of culture and unpacking the multiple layers of identities that coexist and interact within individuals. One may wonder if it is even possible to speak of culture or cultural artifacts from an etiological perspective without indeed reducing one's focus to studying one or two identities at a time while selecting one or two spheres of influences (contexts). The traditional quantitative method to dealing with multiple identities has been through the creation of interaction terms in either factorial ANOVA or multiple regression analyses. However, this method has as its assumption that these identities are all orthogonal constructions and that one can, for example, understand the complexity of being a gay Black man by mathematically adding or multiplying the effect of being gay to the effect of being a black male. Modern statistical advances now allow for more complexity for modeling consumption patterns and trajectories that approximate causality, including the influence of various social identities (i.e., hierarchical linear models, structural equations models, latent class models, spatial analysis, complex systems). However, a drawback to these models is that, in order to maintain any real statistical power, large samples of people are needed. Besides, running more sophisticated statistical models is not helpful if one's conceptual study remains limited to one or two identities (age, sex, race/ethnicity, parental education); neglects others (e.g., sexual identity, immigration status, religiosity and spirituality, socioeconomic position); and does not take into account historical issues (e.g., historical trauma), institutional context (e.g., K-12 educational practices that neglect or stereotype at-risk populations), and structural forces (i.e., housing and employment practices that keep populations marginalized and disenfranchised).

On the other hand, qualitative methods, particularly ethnography, provide a means to further study the way multiple identities intersect. Unfortunately, many of the benefits of the ethnographic approach have been impeded by the misuses of the culture concept as it has been applied historically to populations in colonial or developing country settings. By reifying and representing American Indians with cultural stereotypes that do not give adequate consideration to their internal heterogeneity or the dynamism of Native cultures, some anthropological work has done little more than reinforce stereotypes about Native populations. This misuse of the culture concept leads Walters and Simoni (2002) to suggest that not taking into consideration the multiple contexts and identities of AIs/ANs can result in "pathologized perceptions of Natives [that] reinforce and perpetuate paternalism and dependency," a perspective that is echoed by Phillips (2007), who concludes that such neglect may result in "Culture as a falsely homogenizing reification" (p. 14). Their statements, though specifically made in reference to their own topics of research and populations, we believe provide a warning against the oversimplification and reification of the culture concept. Nevertheless, it bears mentioning that some of the most innovative approaches to understanding substance use behaviors, particularly among socially and economically marginalized groups, has been produced by critical anthropologists conducting ethnography (Bourgois, 1996; Bourgois, Lettiere, & Quesada, 1997; Singer & Clair, 2003; Singer et al., 2006). Yet much of the important conceptual contributions of this literature have been its clear departure from a static notion of culture, examining instead the ways that multiple forces and complex identities are negotiated by individuals in their struggles to survive.

For anyone with gestalt sympathies and who believes that individuals are greater than the sum of their parts, or for scholars concerned with utilizing critical theory or intersectional frameworks such as those utilized in critical race theory, feminist theory, or queer theory, traditional approaches to the culture concept are no longer an option. How does one study the whole if the whole is much more than the sum of its parts? A kaleidoscope ceases to be one if the various interconnected and overlapping shapes that give form, structure, and identity to it are taken apart and presumed to separately represent the whole. The scholarly objective is to find the means to examine the influence of cultural variations on specific practices, such as substance use, while avoiding the oversimplification and reification of populations that has tended to contribute to, rather than alleviate, the social conditions fostering drug use in the first place.

We acknowledge this project is an ongoing challenge for which we do not have a clear or final answer. However, we do believe that an essential first step is to acknowledge this tension. We warn against continued scholarly work that neglects the multilayered complexity of individuals' experiences and attempts to understand substance use, misuse, and disorders without paying attention to individuals' multiple identities and their multiple contexts. One step we recommend is to incorporate an intersectionality perspective into work on these issues, whether the research uses quantitative or qualitative methods, and regardless of the theoretical orientation. We encourage substance use researchers to more systematically set out to incorporate intersectional approaches into their research designs and to be open to examining commonly neglected identities, contexts, or factors in their research. For example, the role that religiosity and spirituality plays in youth drug involvement is a seriously neglected area of research worldwide, despite the fact that people from all walks of life have beliefs, attitudes, and engage in behaviors that can be considered religious or spiritual. Likewise, given what we are beginning to learn about differential risk and consequences of substance use among lesbian, gay, bisexual, transgendered, and queer (LGBTQ) populations and the deleterious effect of being exposed to violence and microaggressions, it is imperative that researchers incorporate questions that assess LGBTQ experiences and the violence and microaggression experiences that LGBTQ and racial and ethnic minorities constantly endure (Gee, Delva, & Takeuchi, 2007; Gibbons, Gerrard, Cleveland, Wills, & Bordy, 2004; Sue et al., 2007; Williams, Neighbors, & Jackson, 2003).

Finally, we believe it is more helpful to study "if" and "how" between- and within-group variations in values, beliefs, attitudes, behaviors may be associated with substance use patterns than making sweeping generalizations about groups such as "In that group family members are highly valued" or "In this group we value interdependence." This is not to say that there is not heterogeneity in how different populations differ on values, beliefs, practices, and behaviors. Rather, the idea we suggest is that these statements by themselves are not helpful in understanding substance use behaviors. More scientifically interesting is to examine if variations in these attributes between populations contribute to our understanding of drug involvement and to examine the extent to which there is within-group variations in these attributes, and to describe how these variations may serve to explain within-group variations in drug involvement.

References

Agar, M. (2003). The story of crack: Towards a theory of illicit drugs trends. *Addiction Research & Theory, 11*, 3–29.

Agar, M. (2006). *Dope double agent: The naked emperor on drugs.* Lexington, MA: Lulubooks.

Agar, M. H. (2010). Culture: An upgrade. Preliminary draft can be found at http://www.ethknoworks.com/files/Culture_Upgrade_Chapter_1.pdf. Unpublished manuscript. Manuscript last accessed on August 24, 2010.

Akins, S., Mosher, C., Rotolo, T., & Griffin, R. (2003). Patterns and correlates of substance use among American Indians in Washington State. *Journal of Drug Issues, 33*, 45–72.

American Psychiatric Association. (2000). *Diagnostic and Statistical Manual of Mental Disorders, fourth edition, text revision (DSM-IV-TR).* Arlington, VA: Author.

Arnett, J. J. (2004). *Emerging adulthood.* New York, NY: Oxford University Press.

Baezconde-Garbanati, L., Beebe, L. A., & Perez-Stable, E. J. (2007). Building capacity to address tobacco-related disparities among American Indian and Hispanic/Latino communities: Conceptual and systemic considerations. *Society for the Study of Addiction, 102*(2), 112–122.

Basch, L., Glick Schiller, N., & Szanton Blanc, C. (1994). *Nations unbound: Transnational projects, postcolonial predicaments, and deterritorialized nation-states.* Amsterdam: Gordon and Breach.

Beals, J., Spicer, P., Mitchell, C. M., Novins, D. K., Manson, S. M., & The AI-SUPERPFP Team. (2003). Racial disparities in alcohol use: Comparison of two American Indian reservation populations with national data. *American Journal of Public Health, 93*, 1683–1685.

Beauvais, F. (1992a). Trends in Indian adolescent drug and alcohol use. *American Indian and Alaska Native Mental Health Research, 5*, 1–12.

Beauvais, F. (1992b). The consequences of drug and alcohol use for Indian youth. *American Indian and Alaska Native Mental Health Research, 5*, 32–37.

Beauvais, F. (1996). Trends in drug use among American Indian students and dropouts, 1975 to 1994. *American Journal of Public Health, 8*, 1594–1598.

Beauvais, F. (1998). American Indians and alcohol. *American Health and Research World, 22*, 253–259.

Beauvais, F., Jumper-Thurman, P., & Burnside, M. (2008). The changing patterns of drug use among American Indian

students over the past thirty years. *American Indian and Alaska Native Mental Health Research, 15*(2), 15–24.

Beauvais, F., & LaBoueff, S. (1985). Drug and alcohol abuse intervention in American Indian communities. *International Journal of the Addictions, 20*, 139–171.

Beauvais, F., Oetting, E. R., Wolf, W., & Edwards, R. W. (1989). American Indian youth and drugs, 1976–1987: A continuing problem. *American Journal of Public Health, 79*, 634–636.

Berry, J. W. (1990). Psychology of acculturation. In J. Berman (Ed.), *Cross-cultural perspectives; Nebraska symposium on motivation* (pp. 201–234). Lincoln, NE: University of Nebraska Press.

Bourgois, P. (1996). *In search of respect: Selling crack in El Barrio.* Cambridge, England: Cambridge University Press.

Bourgois, P., Lettiere, M., & Quesada, J. (1997). Social misery and the sanctions of substance abuse: Confronting HIV risk among homeless heroin addicts in San Francisco. *Social Problems, 44*, 155–173.

Boyd-Ball, A. J., & Dishion, T. J. (2006). Family-centered treatment for American Indian adolescent substance abuse: Toward a culturally and historically informed strategy. In H. A. Liddle, & C. L. Rowe (Eds.), *Adolescent substance abuse: Research and clinical advances* (pp. 424–448). Cambridge, England: Cambridge University Press.

Boyne, R. (1990). Culture and the world-system. In M. Featherstone (Ed.), *Global culture: Nationalism, globalization and modernity* (pp. 57–62). London: Sage.

Bracey, J. R., Bámaca, M. Y., & Umaña-Taylor, A. J. (2004). Examining ethnic identity among biracial and monoracial adolescents. *Journal of Youth and Adolescence, 33*, 123–132.

Brave Heart, M. Y. H. (1998). The return to the sacred path: Healing the historical trauma and historical unresolved grief response among the Lakota. *Smith College Studies in Social Work, 68*(3), 287–305.

Brave Heart, M. Y. H. (1999). Oyate Ptayela: Rebuilding the Lakota Nation through addressing historical trauma among Lakota parents. Examining two facets of American Indian identity: Exposure to other cultures and the influence of historical trauma. In H. N. Weaver (Ed.), *Voices of First Nations people: Human service considerations* (pp. 109–126). New York, NY: Haworth Press.

Brown, L. S. (1989). New voices, new visions: Toward a lesbian/gay paradigm for psychology. *Psychology of Women Quarterly, 13*, 445–458.

Bureau of Indian Affairs. (2002, July 12). Indian entities recognized and eligible to receive services from the United States Bureau of Indian Affairs. *Federal Register, 67*.

Burgess, D., Fu, S. S., Joseph, A. M., Hatsukami, D. K., Soloman, J., & van Ryn, M. (2007). Beliefs and experiences regarding smoking cessation among American Indians. *Nicotine & Tobacco Research, 9*(1), 19–28.

Caine, R. N., & Caine, G. (1997). *Education on the edge of possibility.* Alexandria, VA: Association for Supervision and Curriculum Development.

Canino, G., Lewis-Fernandez, R., & Bravo, M. (1997). Methodological challenges in cross-cultural mental health research. *Transcultural Psychiatry, 34*, 163–184.

Cassells, S., Pearson, C. Walters, K., Simoni, J. M., & Morris, M. (2010). Sexual partner concurrency and sexual risk among gay, lesbian, bisexual, and transgender American Indian/Alaska Natives. *Sexually Transmitted Diseases, 37*, 1–7.

Chae, D. H., & Walters, K. (2009). Racial discrimination and racial identity attitudes in relation to self-rated health and physical pain and impairment among two-spirit American Indian/Alaska Natives. *American Journal of Public Health, 99,* S144–S151.

Cheng, C., Sanchez-Burks, J., & Lee, F. (2008). Taking advantage of differences: Increasing team innovation through identity-integration. In M. Neale & E. Mannix (Eds.), *Research on managing groups and teams, Vol. 11: Diversity and groups* (pp. 55–73). New York, NY: Elsevier.

Cheng, C., Sanders, M., Sanchez-Burks, J., Molina, K., Lee, F., Darling, E., & Zhao, Y. (2008). Reaping the rewards of diversity: The role of identity integration. *Social and Personality Compass, 2/3,* 1182–1198.

Cockerham, W. C. (1975). Drinking attitudes and practices among Wind River reservation Indian youth. *Journal of Studies on Alcohol, 36,* 321–326.

Cole, E. R. (2009). Intersectionality and research in psychology. *American Psychologist, 64,* 170–180.

Collins, P. H. (1990). *Black feminist thought: Knowledge, consciousness, and the politics of empowerment.* New York, NY: Routledge.

Comas-Diaz, L. (2001). Hispanics, Latinos, or Americanos: The evolution of identity. *Cultural Diversity and Ethnic Minority Psychology, 7,* 115–120.

Courtwright, D. T. (2001). *Forces of habit: Drugs and the making of the modern world.* Cambridge, MA: Harvard University Press.

Crenshaw, K. (1991). Mapping the margins: Intersectionality, identity politics, and violence against women of color. *Stanford Law Review, 43*(6), 1241–1299.

Cummins, J. (1989). *Empowering minority students.* Sacramento, CA: California Association for Bilingual Education.

Darling, E., Molina, K., Sanders, M., Lee, F., & Zhao, Y. (2008). Belonging and achieving: The role of identity integration. *Social Psychological Perspectives: Advances in Motivation and Achievement, 15,* 241–273.

Delva, J., Allen-Meares, P., & Momper, S. (2010). *Cross-cultural research.* New York, NY: Oxford University Press.

Delva, J., Wallace, J. M., Bachman, J., O'Malley, P. M., Johnston, L. D., & Schulenberg, J. (2005). The epidemiology of alcohol, cigarettes, and illicit drugs among Mexican American, Puerto Rican, Cuban American, other Latin American youth in the US: 1991–2002. *American Journal of Public Health, 95,* 696–702.

Dick, R., Manson, S., & Beals, J. (1993). Alcohol use among male and female Native American adolescents: Patterns and correlates of student drinking in a boarding school. *Journal of Studies on Alcohol, 54,* 172–177.

Doolan, D. M., & Froelicher, E. S. (2006). Efficacy of smoking cessation intervention among special populations: Review of the literature from 2000 to 2005. *Nursing Research, 55*(Suppl. 4), 29–37.

Duran, E., & Duran, B. (1995). *Native American postcolonial psychology.* Albany, NY: State University of New York Press.

Edwards, E. D., & Edwards, M. E. (1988). Alcoholism prevention treatment and Native American youth: A community approach. *Journal of Drug Issues, 18,* 103–115.

Ehlers, C. L., Slutske, W. S., Gilder, D. A., & Lau, P. (2007). Age of first marijuana use and the occurrence of marijuana use disorders in Southwest California Indians. *Pharmacology, Biochemistry and Behavior, 86,* 290–296.

Erikson, E. (1968), *Identity: Youth and crisis.* New York, NY: W.W. Norton

Fagan, P., Moolchan, E. T., Lawrence, D., Fernander, A., & Ponder, P. K. (2007). Identifying health disparities across the tobacco continuum. *Addiction, 102*(Suppl. 2), 5–29.

Fleming, C. M. (1992). The next twenty years of prevention in Indian country: Visionary, complex, and practical. *American Indian and Alaska Native Mental Health Research, 4,* 85–88.

Forster, J. L., Rhodes, K. L., Poupart, J., Baker, L. O., & Davey, C. (2007). Report for the American Indian Community Tobacco Project Steering Council. Patterns of tobacco use in a sample of American Indians in Minneapolis-St. Paul. *Nicotine & Tobacco Research, 9*(S1), S29–S37.

Freeman, E. M. (1990). Social competence as a framework for addressing ethnicity and teenage alcohol problems. In A. R. Stiffman & L. E. Davis (Eds.), *Ethnic issues in adolescent mental health* (pp. 247–266). Thousand Oaks, CA: Sage.

French, L. A. (2000). *Addictions and Native Americans.* Westport, CT: Praeger.

Galliher, R. V., Evans, C. M., & Weiser, D. (2007). Social and individual predictors of substance use for Native American youth. *Journal of Child & Adolescent Substance Abuse, 16*(3), 1–16.

García Canclini, N. (1995). *Hybrid cultures: Strategies for entering and leaving modernity.* Minneapolis: University of Minnesota Press.

Gee, G. C., Delva, J., & Takeuchi, D. (2007). Relationships between self-reported unfair treatment and prescription medication use, illicit drug use, and alcohol dependence among Filipino Americans. *American Journal of Public Health, 97,* 933–940.

Gibbons, F. X., Gerrard, M., Cleveland, M. J., Wills, T. A., & Bordy, G. H. (2004). Perceived discrimination and substance use in African American parents and their children: A panel study. *Journal of Personality and Social Psychology, 86,* 517–529.

Goodman, G. S., & Carey, K. (Eds). (2004). *Critical multicultural conversations.* Cresskill, NJ: Hampton Press.

Gray, M. L. (2004). Finding pride and the struggle for freedom to assemble: The case of Queer youth in US schools. In G. Goodman & K. Carey (Eds.), *Critical multicultural conversations* (pp. 39–62). Cresskill, NJ: Hampton Press.

Gurin, P. Y., Dey, E. L., Gurin, G., & Hurtado, S. (2003). How does racial/ethnic diversity promote education? *Journal of Black Studies, 27,* 20–29.

Guthrie, B. J, Young, A. M., Williams, D. R., Boyd, C. J., & Kintner, E. K. (2002). African American girls' smoking habits and day-to-day experiences with racial discrimination. *Nursing Research, 51,* 183–190.

Hall, S. (1991). The local and the global: Globalization and ethnicity. In A. King (Ed.), *Culture, globalization, and the world system* (pp. 19–30). Binghamton, NY: State University of New York.

Harvey, D. (1990). *The condition of postmodernity.* Cambridge, England: Blackwell.

Hawkins, E. H., Cummins, L. H., & Marlatt, G. A. (2004). Preventing substance abuse in American Indian and Alaska Native youth: Promising strategies for healthier communities. *Psychological Bulletin, 130* (2), 304–323.

Henderson, P. N., Jacobsen, C., & Beals, J. (2005). Correlates of cigarette smoking among selected southwest and northern plains tribal groups: The AI-SUPERPFP study. *American Journal of Public Health, 95*(5), 867–872.

Hodge, F. S. (2001). American Indian and Alaska Native teen cigarette smoking: A review. In National Cancer Institute (Ed.),

Changing adolescent and smoking prevalence (Monograph 14, pp. 255–260). Bethesda, MD: National Cancer Institute.

Inciardi, J. (1992). *The War on Drugs II: The continuing epic of heroin, cocaine, crack, crime, AIDS, and Public Policy.* Mt. View, CA: Mayfield.

Indian Health Service, Office of Public Health, Program Statistics Team. (1999). *Trends in Indian health: 1998–99.* Rockville, MD: US Department of Health and Human Services.

Indian Health Service. (2004). *Trends in Indian Health: 2000–2002 Edition.* Washington, DC: US Dept of Health and Human Services.

Ing, N. R. (1991). The effects of residential schools on Native child-rearing practices. *Canadian Journal of Native Education, 18*(Suppl.), 65–118.

Institute for Government Research Studies in Administration. (1928). The problem of Indian administration: Report of a survey made at the request of Honorable Hubert Work, Secretary of the Interior. [Submitted February 21, 1928]. Retrieved August 10, 2010 from http://www.alaskool.org/native_ed/research_reports/IndianAdmin/Indian_Admin_Problms.html

Jonnes, J. (1996). *Hep-cats, narcs, and pipe dream: A history of America's romance with illegal drugs.* New York, NY: Villard/Strivers Row.

Kelly, G. A. (1955). *The psychology of personal constructs, Vols. I and II.* New York, NY: W.W. Norton.

Kluckhohn, C., & Kroeber, R. (1952). *Culture: A critical review of concepts and definitions.* New York, NY: Vintage Press.

Kluger, R. (1997). *Ashes to ashes: America's hundred-year cigarette war, the public health, and the unabashed triumph of Philip Morris.* New York, NY: Vintage Press.

Kronk, E., & Thompson, H. (2007). Modern realities of the "jurisdictional maze" in Indian Country: Case studies on methamphetamine use and the pressures to ensure homeland security. *The Federal Lawyer,* March/April, 48–52.

Kulis, S., Okamoto, S. K., & Soma Sen, A. D. R. (2006). Social contexts of drug offers among American Indian youth and their relationship to substance use: An exploratory study. *Cultural Diversity and Ethnic Minority Psychology, 12*(1), 30–44.

Kurtz, S. P. (2008). Arrest histories of high-risk gay and bi-sexual men in Miami: Unexpected additional evidence for syndemic theory. *Journal of Psychoactive Drugs, 40,* 513–521.

LaFromboise, T. D. (1988). American Indian mental health policy. *American Psychologist, 43,* 388–397.

LeMaster, P. L., Connell, C. M., Mitchell, C. M., & Manson, S. M. (2002). Tobacco use among American Indian adolescents: Protective and risk factors. *Journal of Adolescent Health, 30,* 426–432.

Lorner, W. J., & Malpass, R. S. (1994). *When psychology and culture meet: An introduction to cross-cultural psychology.* Upple Saddle River, NJ: Pearson.

Mail, P. D., & Johnson, S. (1993). Boozing, sniffing, and toking: An overview of the past, present, and future of substance use by American Indians. *American Indian and Alaska Native Mental Health Research, 5,* 1–33.

Mannix, E., & Neale, M. A. (2005). What differences make a difference? The promise and reality of diverse teams in organizations. *Psychological Science in the Public Interest, 6,* 31–55.

Marcia, J. (1980). Ego identity development. In J. Adelson (Ed.), *Handbook of adolescent psychology.* New York, NY: Wiley.

Marcia, J. (1994). The empirical study of ego identity. In H. A. Bosma, T. L. G. Graafsma, H. D. Grotevant, & D. J. DeLevita (Eds.), *Identity and development: An interdiscioplinary approach* (pp. 281-321). Newbury Park, CA: Sage.

Marsella, A. J., & Kameoka, V. (1989). Ethnocultural issues in the assessment of psychopathology. In S. Wetzler (Ed.), *Measuring mental illness: Psychiatric assessment for clinicians* (pp. 231–256). Washington, DC: American Psychiatric Press.

Marsiglia, F. F., Kulis, S., Hecht, M. L., & Sills, S. (2004). Ethnicity and ethnic identity as predictors of drug norms and drug use among preadolescents in the US Southwest. *Substance Use & Misuse, 39*(7), 1061–1094.

Marsiglia, F. F., Kulis, S., Luengo, M. A., Nieri, T., & Villar, P. (2008). Immigrant advantage? Substance use among Latin American immigrant and native-born youth in Spain. *Ethnicity & Health, 13*(2), 149–170.

May, P. A. (1982). Substance abuse and American Indians: Prevalence and susceptibility. *International Journal of the Addictions, 17,* 1185–1209.

May, P. A. (1996). Overview of alcohol abuse epidemiology for American Indian populations. In G. D. Sandefur, R. R. Rindfuss, & B. Cohen (Eds.), *Changing numbers, changing needs: American Indian demography and health* (pp. 235–261). Washington, DC: National Academy Press.

Milstein, B. (2008). *Hygeia's constellation: Navigating health futures in a dynamic and democratic world.* Atlanta, GA: Centers for Disease Control and Prevention, Syndemics Prevention Network.

Mitchell, C. M., Beals, J., Novins, D. K., Spicer, P., & AI-SUPERPFP Team (2003). Drug use among two American Indian populations: Prevalence of lifetime use and DSM-IV substance disorders. *Drug Alcohol Dependency, 69,* 26–41.

Mok, A., Morris, M., Benet-Martinez, V., & Karakitapoglu-Aygun, Z. (2007). Embracing American culture: Structures of social identity and social networks among first-generation biculturals. *Journal of Cross-Cultural Psychology, 38,* 629–635.

Momper, S. L., Delva, J., & Glover-Reed, B. G. (2011). Oxycontin abuse on a reservation: Qualitative reports by American Indians in talking circles. *Substance Use and Misuse, 46*(11), 1372-1379.

Moncher, M. S., Holden, G. W., & Trimble, J. E. (1990). Substance abuse among Native-American youth. *Journal of Consulting and Clinical Psychology, 58,* 408–415.

Musto, D. F. (1999). *The American disease: Origins of narcotic control* (3rd ed.). New York, NY: Oxford University Press.

Myers, H. F., Kagawa-Singer, M., Kumanyika, S. K., Lex, B. W., & Markides, K. S. (1995). Panel III: Behavioral risk factors related to chronic diseases in ethnic minorities. *Health Psychology, 14,* 613–621.

National Vital Statistics Report. (2001). *Deaths: Leading causes for 1999.* Washington, DC: Author.

Ndiaye, K., Hecht, M. L., Wagstaff, D. A., & Elek, E. (2009). Mexican-heritage preadolescents' ethnic identification and perceptions of substance use. *Substance use & Misuse, 44,* 1160–1182.

Nichter, M. (2003). Smoking: what does culture have to do with it? *Addiction, 98*(S1), 139–145

Nies, J. (1996). *Native American history: A chronology of a culture's vast achievements and their links to world events.* New York, NY: Ballantine.

Noemi Velez, C., & Ungemack, J. A. (1995). Psychosocial correlates of drug use among Puerto Rican youth: Generational status differences. *Social Science & Medicine, 40,* 91–103.

Novins, D. K., Beals, J., & Mitchell, C. M. (2001). Sequences of substance use among American Indian adolescents. *Journal of the American Academy of Child & Adolescent Psychiatry, 40*, 1168–1174.

Novins, D. K., & Mitchell, C. M. (1998). Factors associated with marijuana use among American Indian adolescents. *Addiction, 93*, 1693–1702.

Oetting, E. R., & Beauvais, F. (1989). Epidemiology and correlates of alcohol use among Indian adolescents living on reservations. In D. Spiegler, D. Tate, S. Aitken, & C. Christian (Eds.), *Alcohol use among US ethnic minorities* (NIAAA Research Monograph No. 18, pp. 239–267). Rockville, MD: National Institute on Alcohol Abuse and Alcoholism.

Oetting, E. R., & Beauvais, F. (1990–1991). Orthogonal cultural identification theory: The cultural identification of minority adolescents. *International Journal of Addictions, 25*, 655–685.

Oetting, E. R., Beauvais, F., & Velarde, J. (1982). Marijuana use by reservation Native American youth. *Listening Post Indian Health Services, 4*, 25–28.

Ontal-Grzebik, L. L., & Raffaelli, M. (2004). Individual and social influences on ethnic identity among Latino young adults. *Journal of Adolescent Research, 19*, 559–575.

Organization of American States (2008). Subregional system of information and research on drugs in Argentina, Chile, Bolivia, Ecuador, Peru, and Uruguay: First comparative study on drug use and associated factors in the general population 15–64 years of age. Inter-American Observatory on Drugs (OID) and the United Nations Office on Drugs and Crime. Available from http://www.cicad.oas.org/oid/default.asp. Accessed on November 10, 2010.

Phillips, A. (2007). *Multiculturalism without culture.* Princeton, NJ: Princeton University Press.

Phinney, J. S. (1989). Stages of ethnic identity development in minority group adolescents. *Journal of Early Adolescence, 9*, 34–49.

Plunkett, M., & Mitchell, C. M. (2000). Substance use rates among American Indian adolescents: Regional comparisons with monitoring the future high school seniors. *Journal of Drug Issues, 30*, 575–591.

Prado, G., Huang, S., Maldonado-Molina, M., Bandiera, F., Schwartz, S. J., de la Vega, P., . . . Pantin, H. (2010). An empirical test of ecodevelopmental theory in predicting HIV risk behaviors among Hispanic youth. *Health Education and Behavior, 37*(1), 97–114.

Roccas, S., & Brewer, M. B. (2002). Social identity complexity. *Personality and Social Psychology Review, 6*, 88–106.

Rojas, M. (2009). *Women of color and feminism.* Berkeley, CA: Seal Press.

Romero-Daza, N., Weeks, M., & Singer, M. (2003). "Nobody gives a damn if I live or die": Violence, drugs, and street-level prostitution in inner-city Hartford, Connecticut. *Medical Anthropologist, 22*, 233–259.

Schulenberg, J., Maggs, J. L., & Hurrelmann, K. (Eds.). (1997). *Health risks and developmental transitions during adolescence.* Cambridge, UK: Cambridge University Press.

Shaughnessy, L., Branum, C., & Everett-Jones, S. (2001). *2001 youth risk behavior survey of high school students attending Bureau funded schools.* Washington, DC: Bureau of Indian Affairs Office of Indian Education Programs.

Shields, S. A. (2008). Gender: An intersectionality perspective. *Sex Roles, 59*, 301–311.

Singer, M., & Clair, S. (2003). Syndemics and public health: Reconceptualizing disease in bio-social context. *Medical Anthropology Quarterly, 17*, 423–441.

Singer, M. C., Erickson, P. I., Badiane, L., Diaz, R., Ortiz, D., Abraham, T., & Nicolaysen, A. M. (2006). Syndemics, sex and the city: Understanding sexually transmitted diseases in social and cultural context. *Social Science & Medicine, 63*, 2010–2021.

Sodowsky, G. R., & Lai, W. M. (1997). Asian immigrant variables and structural models of cross cultural distress. In A. Booth, A. Crouter, & N. Landale (Eds.), *Immigration and the family: Research and policy on US Immigrants* (pp. 211–234). Mahwah, NJ: Erlbaum.

Spicer, P., Beals, J., Croy, C. D., Mitchell, C. M., Novins, D. K., Moore, L., . . . American Indian Service Utilization, Psychiatric Epidemiology, Risk and Protective Factors Project Team. (2003). The prevalence of DSM–III–R alcohol dependence in two American Indian reservation populations. *Alcoholism: Clinical and Experimental Research, 27*, 1785–1797.

Stall, R., Friedman, M., & Catania, J. (2008). Interacting epidemics and gay men's health: A theory of syndemic production among urban gay men. In R. J. Wolitski, R. Stall, and R. O. Valdiserri (Eds.), *Unequal opportunity: Health disparities affecting gay and bisexual men in the United States* (pp. 251–274). New York, NY: Oxford University Press.

Steele, C. (1997). A threat in the air: How stereotypes shape intellectual identity and performance. *American Psychologist, 52*, 613–629.

Steidel, A. G., & Contreras, J. M. (2003). A new familism scale for use with Latino populations. *Hispanic Journal of Behavioral Sciences, 25*, 312–330.

Steinman, K. J., & Hu, Y. (2007). Substance use among American Indian youth in an eastern city. *Journal of Ethnicity in Substance Abuse, 6*(1), 15–29.

Substance Abuse and Mental Health Services Administration, Office of Applied Studies. (January 25, 2002). *The NSDUH report: Cigarette use among American Indian/Alaska Native youths: 1999 to 2000.* Rockville, MD. Retrieved March 10, 2009 from http://archive.samhsa.gov/data/2k2/YouthIndianCigs/YouthIndianCigs.htm

Substance Abuse and Mental Health Services Administration, Office of Applied Studies. (September 24, 2004). *The NSDUH Report: Risk and Protective Factors for Substance Use Among American Indian and Alaska Native Youths: 2002 and 2003.* Rockville, MD: US Department of Health and Human Services. Retrieved August 10, 2010 from http://archive.samhsa.gov/data/2k4/AmIndianYouthRF/AmIndianYouthRF.htm

Substance Abuse and Mental Health Services Administration. (2008). Results from the 2007 National Survey on Drug Use and Health: National Findings (Office of Applied Studies, NSDUH Series H-34, DHHS Publication No. SMA 08-4343). Rockville, MD Retrieved March 8, 2009 from http://www.dpft.org/resources/NSDUHresults2007.pdf

Sue, D. W., Capodilupa, C. M., Torino, G. C., Bucceri, J. M., Holder, A. M., Nadal, K. L., & Esquilin, M. (2007). Racial microaggressions in everyday life: Implications for clinical practice. *American Psychologist, 62*, 271–286.

Suleiman, M. (2004). Image making and invisible minorities: A case of Arab American students. In G. Goodman and K. Carey (Eds.), *Critical multicultural conversations* (pp. 79–91). Cresskill, NJ: Hampton Press.

Szlemko, W. J., Wood, J. W., & Jumper-Thurman, P. (2006). Native Americans and alcohol: Past, present and future. *The Journal of General Psychology, 133*(4), 435–451.

Tajfel, H. (1981). *Human groups and social categories; Studies on social psychology*. Cambridge, England: Cambridge University Press

Thompson, M., & Sekaquaptewa, D. (2002). When being different is detrimental: Solo status and the performance of women and racial minorities. *Analyses of Social Issues and Public Policy, 2*, 183–203.

Trimble, J. E. (2010). The virtues of cultural resonance, competence, and relational collaboration with Native American Indian communities: A synthesis of the counseling and psychotherapy literature. *The Counseling Psychologist, 38*, 243–256.

Trimble, J. E., Padilla, A., & Bell-Bolek, C. (1987). *Drug abuse among ethnic minorities* (NIDA Office of Science Monograph, DHHS Publication No. ADM 87-1474). Washington, DC: US Government Printing Office.

U. S. Census Bureau. (2000). Ogunwole, S. U. We the People: American Indians and Alaska Natives in the United States. Census 2000 Special Reports. [Issued 2006, February]. Retrieved August 10, 2010 from http://www.census.gov/prod/2006pubs/censr-28.pdf

US Census Bureau. (2001). *Poverty in the United States: 2000*. Washington, DC: Author.

US Census Bureau. (2008). American Fact Finder fact sheet. American Indians: Census Facts. Retrieved August 13, 2010 from http://www.infoplease.com/spot/aihmcensus1.htm

US Census Bureau. (2009). General Demographic Characteristics: 2009 Population Estimates [Data File]. Available from http://factfinder.census.gov

US Congress, Office of Technology Assessment. (1990). *Indian adolescent mental health*. Washington, DC: US Government Printing Office.

US Department of the Interior Bureau of Indian Affairs. (2005). *American Indian Population and Labor Force Report*. Washington, DC: Author. Retrieved January 6, 2011, from http://www.bia.gov/cs/groups/public/documents/text/idc-001719.pdf

US Department of the Interior Bureau of Indian Affairs. (2011). What we do. Retrieved January 6, 2011 from http://www.bia.gov/WhatWeDo/ServiceOverview/index.htm

US Department of Justice. (2004a). *American Indians and Crime*. Washington, DC: Author.

US Department of Justice. (November, 2004b). *National Drug Intelligence Center: Pharmaceuticals Drug threat Assessment*. Washington, DC: Author.

Walker, R. D. (1992). *Preliminary results: Alcohol abuse in urban Indian adolescents and women, R01-AA07103*. Seattle: University of Washington.

Walters, K. L., Evans-Campbell T., Simoni, J. M., Ronquillo, T., & Bhuyan, R. (2006). "My spirit in my heart": Identity experiences and challenges among American Indian two-spirit women. *Journal of Lesbian Studies, 10*, 125–149.

Walters, K. L., & Simoni, J. M. (2002). Reconceptualizing Native women's health: An "indigenist" stress-coping model. *American Journal of Public Health, 92*, 520–524.

Waterman, A. S. (1992). Identity as an aspect of optimal psychological functioning. In G. R. Adams, T. P. Gullotta, & R. Montemayor (Eds.), *Adolescent identity formation* (pp. 50–72). Thousand Oaks, CA: Sage.

Weaver, H. N., & Brave Heart, M. Y. H. (1999). Examining two facets of American Indian identity: Exposure to other cultures and the influence of historical trauma. In H. N. Weaver (Ed.), *Voices of First Nations people: Human service considerations* (pp. 19–33). New York, NY: Haworth Press.

Welty, T. K. (2002). The epidemiology of alcohol use and alcohol-related health problems among American Indians. In P. D. Mail, S. Heurtin-Roberts, S. E. Martin, & J. Howard (Eds.), *Alcohol use among American Indians and Alaska Natives: Multiple perspectives on a complex problem* (pp. 49–70). Bethesda, MD: National Institutes of Health.

Whitesell, R. N., Beals, J., Mitchell, C. M., Novins, D. K., Spicer, P., & O'Connell, J. (2007). Marijuana initiation in two American Indian reservation communities: Comparison with a national sample. *Journal of Public Health, 97*(7), 1311–1318.

Williams, D. R., Neighbors, H. W., & Jackson, J. S. (2003). Racial/ethnic discrimination and health: findings from community studies. *American Journal of Public Health, 93*, 200–2008.

Winter, J. C. (2000). *Tobacco use by Native North Americans: Sacred smoke and silent killer*. Norman, OK: University of Oklahoma Press

Wolf, E. R. (1982). *Europe and the people without history*. University of California Press. Los Angeles.

Yee, B., & Thu, N. (1997). Correlates of drug use and abuse among Indochinese refugees: Mental health implications. *Journal of Psychoactive Drugs, 19*, 77–83.

Zamboanga, B., Schwartz, S., Jarvis, L., & VanTyne, K. (2009). Acculturation and substance use among Hispanic early adolescents: Investigating the mediating roles of acculturative stress and self-esteem. *Journal of Primary Prevention, 30*, 315–333.

Zucker, R., Boyd, G., & Howard, J. (Eds). (1994). *The development of alcohol problems: Exploring the biopsychosocial matrix of risk* (NIH Publication No. 94–3495). Rockville, MD: US Department of Human Health and Services HHS.

PART 3

The Drugs of Abuse: Similarities and Differences

Cigarette Smoking and Nicotine Dependence in Adolescence

Mark G. Myers *and* Laura MacPherson

Abstract

Despite declines in adolescent cigarette smoking prevalence, rates remain high, with approximately 11% of high school seniors reporting current cigarette smoking. Moreover, use of other tobacco products has soared, with prevalence of electronic cigarettes and little cigars exceeding that of cigarettes. The present chapter reviews patterns of adolescent cigarette use, other tobacco use, adolescent nicotine dependence, factors associated with the etiology of cigarette smoking, and smoking cessation. Despite decades of research on adolescent smoking cessation, the development and progression of nicotine dependence are just beginning to be understood. Similarly, little is known regarding adolescent smoking cessation. Significant progress has been made in addressing and preventing adolescent cigarette use. However, critical gaps exist in the current knowledge base that must be addressed in order to improve efforts at halting the progression of adolescent nicotine dependence and enhancing interventions for smoking cessation.

Key Words: adolescent, nicotine dependence, cigarette smoking, smoking cessation, tobacco use

Adolescent cigarette smoking prevalence has declined substantially in the last decade, yet tobacco use remains a significant public health problem. Approximately one in nine high school seniors report current cigarette smoking; this in contrast with approximately one in five in 2009 (Johnston, O'Malley, Miech, Bachman, & Schulenberg, 2016). However, cigarette smoking is no longer the most prevalent form of tobacco used, having been supplanted by electronic or "e-" cigarettes and little cigars (Johnston, O'Malley, Miech, Bachman, & Schulenberg, 2015). Thus, despite lower cigarette smoking rates, exposure to tobacco products may in fact be increasing. The concern remains that cigarette and other tobacco use behaviors may persist into adulthood (Pierce & Gilpin, 1996). The considerable investment in the prevention of adolescent cigarette smoking has yielded a wealth of knowledge regarding smoking initiation. In contrast, less is known about influences on and correlates of smoking progression and cessation, as well as the

nature of adolescent nicotine dependence. Research on adolescent smoking cessation, in particular, is in its early stages. Although adolescents frequently report a desire to quit and often engage in cessation efforts (Bancej, O'Loughlin, Platt, Paradis, & Gervais, 2007), these attempts typically end in failure, even when state-of-the-art smoking cessation treatments are administered (A. Stanton & Grimshaw, 2013; Sussman, Sun, & Dent, 2006). Sufficient work has been done to indicate that adolescent smoking cessation treatment is effective, but challenges remain for improving long-term outcomes, reaching vulnerable adolescent populations, and addressing the increasing use of other tobacco products.

Patterns of Youth Smoking in the United States

Youth cigarette smoking prevalence has fluctuated over the past four decades. Results from Monitoring the Future (MTF), a national study that has surveyed U.S. 12th graders since 1975, and 8th and 10th graders since 1991, provide a long-term view of cigarette smoking prevalence over time (Johnston et al., 2016). Other U.S. surveys that assess youth tobacco use include the Youth Risk Behavior Survey (YRBS) and the National Youth Tobacco Survey (NYTS), both conducted by the Centers for Disease Control and Prevention. The highest levels of smoking among 12th graders were observed in the 1970s, with 39% reporting any smoking in the past 30 days (current smoking) in 1976, and 29% reporting daily smoking in 1976 and 1977. Prevalence decreased through the 1980s, with high school seniors reporting monthly smoking rates between 29% and 30% from 1980 until 1993. A period of increased smoking followed in the 1990s, with past 30-day smoking by 12th graders reaching 37% in 1997 and declining thereafter to 11% in 2015.

As suggested by Curry and her colleagues (Curry, Mermelstein, & Sporer, 2009), increased smoking in the 1990s may have been a consequence of lower cigarette prices and increased marketing targeted at youth (e.g., the Joe Camel campaign; Fischer, Schwartz, Richards, Goldstein, & Rojas, 1991). The declines in youth smoking in the early 2000s are attributed to the 1998 Master Settlement between the tobacco industry and states attorneys general (Eckhart, 2004), which placed limits on advertising and yielded significant funds used for programs focused on preventing youth tobacco use (e.g., the Truth Campaign; Curry et al., 2009). However, the rates of decline observed in the early to middle 2000s have diminished in recent years.

In the most recent available survey (Johnston et al., 2016), approximately one in nine (11%) high school seniors reported smoking in the past month. Of those who did smoke, slightly less than one half (48%) were daily smokers and less than one fifth (18%) smoked 10 or more cigarettes per day. This issue is of significant concern given the persistence of adolescent smoking into adulthood (Pierce & Gilpin, 1996; USDHHS, 1994), suggesting that many of today's adolescent smokers are at risk for the serious negative health effects of cigarette smoking (USDHHS, 1989).

Use and Availability of Other Tobacco Products

Although historically less common than cigarette smoking, the use of other forms of tobacco has grown rapidly in recent years. For decades the most frequently used other tobacco product was smokeless or chewing tobacco. However, this form of tobacco has been displaced by several others. Most notably, findings from the 2015 MTF report indicate that current use (past 30 days) by high school seniors of e-cigarettes (17%) and flavored little cigars (12%) exceeds cigarette use. Furthermore, current use of regular little cigars (7%) and large cigars (6%) approaches that of chewing tobacco (8%). In addition, other tobacco products have been introduced and/or grown in popularity in recent years, most notably hookah and snus (finely ground tobacco in small packets that are placed in the mouth). The MTF survey has only recently assessed these products, with hookah added in 2010 and snus in 2011. Use of these products is currently only assessed for past-year prevalence among 12th-grade students. Findings from 2015 indicate that in the past year 23% of high school seniors had used hookah and 8% snus. Of particular concern is that other tobacco products are targeted at youth and may be perceived as less harmful than cigarettes, thus increasing risk for addiction to nicotine (Alpert, Koh, & Connolly, 2008). These concerns are borne out by the rapid increases in use of other tobacco products, particularly e-cigarettes and hookah (Johnston et al., 2015).

Of these other tobacco products, e-cigarettes are the focus of greatest attention because they have become adopted at a rapid rate and are heavily marketed. These battery-operated devices are shaped like cigarettes (cig-alikes) or take on various forms that include refillable tanks (vapes), and they vaporize a nicotine-containing solution that creates a mist to be inhaled by the user (Kuschner, Reddy, Mehrotra, & Paintal, 2011). Concerns have been voiced regarding the potential risk for youth adoption because e-cigarettes are promoted heavily online (Ayers, Ribisl, & Brownstein, 2011), have a high-tech design, are readily available, and are offered in various flavors, all of which may enhance their appeal (FDA, 2009). The extent to which e-cigarettes pose a health hazard is not fully understood. The U.S. Food and Drug Administration (FDA) has identified a number of toxins in e-cigarette nicotine solution (Westenberger, 2009), and inhaled vapor contains toxic chemicals and compounds (Grana, Benowitz, & Glantz, 2014). Possibly of greater concern is that use of e-cigarettes may pose a risk for the development or escalation of nicotine dependence (McMillen, Maduka, & Winickoff, 2012). Formal surveillance data on prevalence of youth e-cigarette use are currently scant. However, available evidence indicates that e-cigarette use is rapidly increasing among adolescents (Johnston et al., 2015) and adoption is reported by youth who have never smoked cigarettes (Carroll, Chapman & Wu, 2014; Durmowicz, 2014). Highlighting these concerns, recent research provides evidence that use of e-cigarettes leads to increased subsequent initiation of conventional cigarettes (Leventhal et al., 2015). These issues indicate the critical importance of increased public health and research attention to the adolescent adoption of e-cigarettes and its relationship with conventional cigarette use.

Adolescent Subgroups at High Risk for Smoking
Demographic Subgroups

As with adults, prevalence of adolescent cigarette use varies by age, gender, and race/ethnicity. Early to mid-adolescence is the period of greatest initiation to cigarette smoking (Edelen, Tucker, & Ellickson, 2007; Wills, Resko, Ainette, & Mendoza, 2004), as reflected by the significant differences in prevalence across grade levels in the MTF. For example, compared with 19% of high school seniors, in 2011 12% of 10th graders and 6% of 8th graders reported smoking cigarettes in the past month (Johnston et al., 2016). As with adults, males are more likely to smoke cigarettes than female adolescents. The gap in smoking prevalence by gender increased with age such that prevalence of monthly smoking was comparable for 8th-grade boys and girls (approximately 6% each), 3% higher for 10th-grade boys (13% versus 10%), and 7% higher for 12th-grade boys (22% versus 15%) (Johnston et al., 2016). Finally, rates of smoking differ across racial and ethnic groups, with Whites reporting substantially higher prevalence of cigarette use than Hispanic and African American youth (22%, 11%, and 7%, respectively) (Johnston et al., 2016).

Adolescent Alcohol and Other Drug Users

Research consistently demonstrates a link between adolescent smoking and alcohol and other drug (AOD) use problems (R. A. Brown, Lewinsohn, Seeley, & Wagner, 1996). In particular, adolescent cigarette smoking is strongly associated with alcohol and illicit drug use (Eckhardt, Woodruff, & Elder, 1994; Vega, Chen, & Williams, 2007) and disruptive behavior disorders (R. A. Brown et al., 1996; Upadhyaya, Deas, Brady, & Kruesi, 2002). Evidence indicates that adolescent current smokers are at significantly higher risk for use of alcohol and other drugs, violent behaviors, and academic problems than nonsmokers (Austin, McCarthy,

Slade, & Bailey, 2007). Highlighting this relationship, a recent study found that tobacco use was the strongest substance-specific predictor of subsequent AOD use problems (Palmer et al., 2009). In addition to more frequent use of alcohol and illicit drugs, youth who consistently smoke throughout adolescence are at significantly greater risk for marijuana and other drug abuse or dependence (Vega & Gil, 2005). Much of the research in this area has focused on concurrent use of cigarettes and alcohol, which predicts a variety of problems, both during adolescence and beyond. For example, it has been found that youth who smoke and drink have an increased risk of having difficulties at school, delinquency, and use of other drugs (Hoffman, Welte, & Barnes, 2001). Adolescents who report consistent smoking and drinking have higher rates of deviant behavior and violence and are more likely to have legal and AOD use problems in their 20s than those who consistently drink but do not regularly smoke (Orlando, Tucker, Ellickson, & Klein, 2005). Thus, adolescent smokers who engage in problem behaviors are at high risk for persistent smoking as well as other serious behavior problems.

Research examining smoking among clinical samples of adolescents treated for AOD use disorders reveals a high prevalence and persistence of smoking (Chun, Guydish, & Chan, 2007). Our previous research indicates that over 80% of youth treated for AOD use disorders reported current smoking at the time of treatment, of whom over 60% smoked 10 or more cigarettes per day (Myers & Brown, 1994; Shelef, Diamond, Diamond, & Myers, 2009). In addition to heavy smoking at the time of treatment, substantial persistence of smoking exists. In an initial study we found that 80% of those who smoked at the time of treatment were still smoking 4 years later (Myers & Brown, 1997). More recently, we examined patterns of smoking in relation to alcohol use trajectories over 8 years following adolescent AOD use disorder treatment (Myers, Doran, & Brown, 2007), at which time participants were on average 24 years of age. Observed patterns of cigarette use for subjects who smoked at the time of treatment were such that approximately one quarter had quit smoking for over a year by the final time point assessed. However, smoking rates remained very high when compared with the general population. Notably, three quarters of those who continued to drink frequently and over half of those with little or no posttreatment alcohol use reported current smoking at 8 years following treatment.

Adolescents With Psychiatric Symptoms and Disorders

Psychiatric symptoms and disorders are associated with increased adolescent smoking prevalence. Cross-sectional studies with adolescents have shown relationships between depressive symptoms and smoking (Covey & Tam, 1990; Hawkins, Catalano, & Miller, 1992; Patton et al., 1998) and psychiatric disorders and smoking (Kashani et al., 1987). Prospective studies have shown depression to both precede (Breslau, Peterson, Schultz, Chilcoat, & Andreski, 1998; McKenzie, Olsson, Jorm, Romaniuk, & Patton, 2010; Rohde, Kahler, Lewinsohn, & Brown, 2004; Rohde, Lewinsohn, Brown, Gau, & Kahler, 2003) and follow (Breslau et al., 1998; Brook, Cohen, & Brook, 1998; Brook, Schuster, & Zhang, 2004) cigarette smoking. In a study examining relationships between cigarette smoking and psychopathology in adolescents (aged 14 to 18 years) (R. A. Brown et al., 1996), smoking was prospectively found to increase the risk of developing an episode of major depressive disorder or drug abuse/dependence, and major depressive disorder was found to significantly predict smoking onset. Overall, 67% of the adolescent smokers had a history of psychiatric disorder compared to 33% in the nonsmokers. In another prospective study, adolescent smokers with high symptoms of depression and anxiety were significantly more likely to progress to heavier smoking in early adulthood than those with low symptom levels (McKenzie et al., 2010). Thus, evidence suggests that adolescent smoking progression is facilitated by the presence of psychiatric symptoms. Although the direction of causality between smoking and psychiatric symptoms is not established, it is clear that adolescents with high levels of psychiatric symptoms or with psychiatric disorders are at elevated risk for smoking initiation and progression.

Available research thus consistently demonstrates that youth engaged in alcohol and other substance use and who experience psychiatric symptoms smoke at elevated rates and are at higher risk for smoking progression into adulthood. As such, there is a particular need to address and intervene with tobacco use in these populations in order to prevent tobacco-related health consequences.

Adolescent Nicotine Dependence

Nicotine dependence has long been considered to play an essential role in the maintenance of smoking behavior (Berrettini & Lerman, 2005) as well as in cessation outcomes (Shiffman & Sayette,

2005) among adults. However, not until the early 1990s was it considered that adolescents who smoke could become dependent on nicotine. Initial seminal reviews highlighted the dearth of valid assessment instruments and lack of a clear conceptualization of nicotine dependence among adolescents (Colby, Tiffany, Shiffman, & Niaura, 2000a, 2000b). In contrast, the past decade has seen a proliferation of research with an eye toward advancing our understanding of the defining features, developmental course, and clinical implications of youth nicotine dependence.

Conceptualization of Nicotine Dependence in Adolescents

Models of adolescent nicotine dependence have primarily been based on conceptualizations developed with adults (Colby et al., 2000a). Although lacking universal consensus (Piper et al., 2004), nicotine dependence is generally considered to be a "syndrome" composed of a constellation of features that include behavioral, cognitive, core physiological, and psychological symptoms that occur surrounding the use of the drug (Shadel, Shiffman, Niaura, Nichter, & Abrams, 2000; Shiffman, Waters, & Hickcox, 2004). An assumption of this approach is that nicotine dependence is a complex multidimensional construct for which numerous theoretical frameworks exist that may vary in the features on which they place the greatest conceptual focus (Shadel et al., 2000; Tiffany, Conklin, Shiffman, & Clayton, 2004). Current theories of addiction also suggest that nicotine dependence is a process, rather than a state, that evolves over time (Tiffany et al., 2004). Moreover, as with most complex constructs, heterogeneity likely exists both within and across youth regarding (1) expression of dependence features (Strong, Schonbrun, Schaffran, Griesler, & Kandel, 2012); (2) the time at which nicotine dependence features begin to emerge following initial tobacco use (Y. Zhan et al., 2012); and (3) which features emerge first (Kandel, Hu, & Yamaguchi, 2009). However, these latter three points have only begun to receive empirical attention.

Adolescent Nicotine Dependence Assessment

Before advancing to discussion of the growing developmental literature on nicotine dependence, we begin with brief descriptions of the most commonly used assessments. Because no current gold standard measure of adolescent nicotine dependence exists, the field has benefited by incorporating assessments that vary to some extent in their focus or content and yet also provide complementary aspects of symptom evaluation (Strong et al., 2012).

DSM-IV CRITERIA

The *Diagnostic and Statistical Manual of Mental Disorders*, fourth edition (*DSM-IV*; American Psychiatric Association, 2000) presents a diagnosis of substance dependence intended to be used for alcohol and all categories of drugs. The seven symptoms of nicotine dependence in the *DSM-IV* include increased tolerance to the drug, a characteristic withdrawal syndrome, impaired control over drug use, desire/unsuccessful efforts to cut down or control use, increased narrowing of a behavioral repertoire surrounding drug use, increased focus on drug use over other life activities, and persistent use despite physical/psychological consequences (American Psychiatric Association, 2000). A number of well-validated, semistructured and brief interview-based measures have been developed to target *DSM-IV* nicotine dependence criteria among youth (Cohen, Myers, & Kelly, 2002; Colby et al., 2000a, 2000b; Kandel et al., 2005), allowing for a total sum of symptoms present (0–7), as well as examination of each symptom separately, rather than solely relying on the categorical diagnosis (Strong, Kahler, Colby, Griesler, & Kandel, 2009). Criticisms of the *DSM-IV* conceptualization of substance dependence in its application to youth include that it was not originally developed to assess dependence on tobacco in adolescence (Crowley, 2006), and that it is by definition intended to be descriptive rather than focused on explanatory mechanisms of dependence (Piper et al., 2004).

Despite these criticisms, *DSM-IV* models have been used effectively to further refine our understanding of the latent construct of nicotine dependence in youth (Rose, Dierker, & Donny, 2010; Strong et al., 2007, 2009), and there are large, well-designed longitudinal studies examining the natural course of the development of *DSM-IV* nicotine dependence symptoms across adolescence (Kandel, Hu, Griesler, & Schaffran, 2007).

With the publication of the *DSM-5* in 2013, the *DSM*-based nicotine dependence syndrome has been reformulated into a nicotine use disorder, which comprises the previous *DSM-IV* dependence criteria as well as the abuse criteria, with the exclusion of legal consequences, and the addition of a criterion assessing craving (APA, 2013). The considerable increase in the number of potential symptoms, including symptoms of abuse not previously applied to nicotine, in combination with a lowering of the threshold required to meet the diagnosis, may result in a higher prevalence of young smokers meeting a diagnosis that has only modest concurrent validity (Chung, Martin, Maisto, Cornelius, & Clark, 2012). Moreover, the results of Chung and colleagues also raise questions regarding the utility of abuse symptoms for purposes of assessing consequences of nicotine use. Future studies will need to identify the extent to which new *DSM-5* criteria can be applied successfully to our understanding of the nicotine dependence syndrome in youth.

NDSS

The Nicotine Dependence Syndrome Scale (NDSS; Shiffman et al., 2004), a relatively new measure, was developed based on Edwards and Gross's (1976) conceptualization of dependence, which was also in part the basis for *DSM-IV* substance dependence criteria. The NDSS is a self-report measure that includes symptoms across five domains, each of which was originally represented as a single factor: (1) Drive (craving and withdrawal), (2) Tolerance (reduced sensitivity to nicotine effects), (3) Continuity (smoking regularity), (4) Priority (behavioral preference for smoking over other activities), and (5) Stereotypy (smoking patterns are not disturbed by internal or external events). Clark and colleagues (2005) conducted a factor analysis of the NDSS in a large sample of adolescent daily smokers with alcohol use disorders recruited from both clinical and community settings, and derived a four-factor structure of the measure in which Drive and Tolerance loaded on a single factor that comprised the majority of the items on the NDSS, with all other factors similar to those with adults. The merging of the Drive and Tolerance scales may indicate that tolerance and withdrawal are more closely tied together at this earlier stage in a smoking career, even among a sample of youth with daily smoking patterns (Clark et al., 2005). The total NDSS score demonstrated incremental predictive validity in relation to continued smoking as well as smoking quantity/frequency. Modified short versions of the NDSS have been adapted for epidemiological and etiological studies of youth dependence (e.g., Dierker & Mermelstein, 2010; Rose et al., 2010) with demonstrated sound psychometrics. In particular, these adapted versions of the NDSS have also included developmentally modified items by taking into consideration contexts in which youth smoke, as well as constraints that exist around adolescents' autonomy over their own smoking behavior (Sterling et al., 2009).

The modified Fagerstrom Tolerance Questionnaire (mFTQ; Prokhorov, Koehly, Pallonen, & Hudmon, 1998) is an adapted version of the self-report questionnaire (FTQ; Fagerstrom, 1978) that was originally developed to assess behavioral indicators of a physical tolerance-dependence process among adult smokers. Notably, the original FTQ was not intended to directly correspond with diagnostically determined nicotine dependence, but rather to provide a continuously scaled measure of severity of physical tolerance (Fagerstrom, 1978). The original FTQ has been widely used; however, there are well-established concerns with the psychometric properties of the scale, including low internal consistency and likely multidimensional structure (e.g., Heatherton, Kozlowski, Frecker, & Fagerstrom, 1991). In the mFTQ, which possesses similar psychometric limitations, symptoms were modified so as to assess the lower levels of smoking behavior typically observed in adolescents, avoidance of physiological effects of nicotine deprivation, and perceived difficulty in refraining from smoking in situations when one is not able to do so (Prokhorov et al., 1998). Despite these limitations, the mFTQ has been demonstrated to prospectively predict smoking quantity and frequency, smoking persistence, and briefer abstinence duration among adolescent smokers with more established smoking patterns (e.g., Cohen et al., 2002; Kandel et al., 2005).

HONC

The Hooked on Nicotine Checklist (HONC; DiFranza et al., 2002) is a self-report measure proposed to assess the onset of nicotine dependence among youth, based on a concept of "loss of autonomy" over tobacco use which is hypothesized to be the core of dependence. The first six items on the HONC represent primarily cognitive and behavioral aspects of the construct, while the remaining four items inquire about perceived withdrawal symptoms when a youth is unable to smoke or is trying to stop smoking. DiFranza and colleagues (DiFranza et al., 2002, 2007) specifically argue that the onset of dependence, in this case "loss of autonomy," can occur with very minimal smoking exposure and stipulate that endorsement of even one item on the HONC is an indicator of dependence. Despite the rising popularity of the HONC, considerable debate exists over the validity of this approach (Dar & Frenk, 2010; Hughes & Shiffman, 2008), and Strong and colleagues (2012) raise the issue that utilizing such a low threshold may indeed mask "phenotypic variability" in a latent nicotine dependence construct. However, the HONC has been found related to smoking frequency as well as quantity and age of first use among youth (DiFranza et al., 2002; O'Loughlin, Tarasuk, Difranza, & Paradis, 2002).

Understanding Nicotine Dependence in Adolescents

Although the four measurement approaches outlined earlier generally possess acceptable validity and a range of psychometric properties, model-based approaches, specifically those based in item response theory (IRT; c.f. Lord, 1980), provide researchers a means of establishing a common metric across disparate scales, and thus a direct comparison of all individual symptoms to a common latent construct of nicotine dependence.

Recent studies have compared symptoms as assessed by the *DSM*, mFTQ, HONC, and NDSS, indicating that combining items from these measures provides complementary information and hence broader coverage of the nicotine dependence construct (MacPherson, Strong, & Myers, 2008; Strong et al., 2007, 2009, 2012). In addition, results generally converge across studies, indicating that behavioral and cognitive symptoms of dependence (e.g., unsuccessful efforts to cut down/control use, tolerance) occurred in the lowest range of nicotine dependence; core physiological symptoms (e.g., craving, smoking within 30 minutes of waking) in the middle range of nicotine dependence; and symptoms reflecting organization of behavior around smoking (e.g., neglecting important activities) and more severe physical dependence (e.g., smoking more in the first 2 hours of the day) observed at the highest end of the continuum (MacPherson et al., 2008; Strong et al., 2007, 2009, 2012). Such findings can offer insight into symptom patterns expected to be observed within various levels of nicotine dependence as well as a potential progression from lower to higher levels of severity of dependence among youth.

In sum, these are just a few examples of an approach to understanding where along the latent nicotine dependence continuum assessment coverage is adequate, where there may be gaps in which we need to consider assessing novel dependence symptoms, and how to enrich our concepts of nicotine dependence in youth as well as improve our assessment of the nicotine dependence phenotype (Strong et al., 2009, 2012).

Developmental Course of Nicotine Dependence in Adolescents

Little is known regarding the developmental course of nicotine dependence symptoms across adolescence. Longitudinal studies provide the most robust examination of the patterns and growth of nicotine dependence in adolescents, and recent well-designed research programs provide new insights (Kandel et al., 2007). The majority of this work has focused on adolescents who have recently initiated smoking or who were "at risk" to begin smoking at the inception of the study so as to examine this process in proximity with initial tobacco exposure. For example, in determining latency to first dependence symptom (based on *DSM-IV*) in a sample of 6th–10th graders drawn from a large public school system in a multiwave study spanning 3 years, Kandel and colleagues (2007) reported that 25% of youth who had initiated smoking in the past year reported experiencing their first dependence symptom within 5 months. Shorter latency to first symptom was associated with progression to a diagnosable level of dependence. Notably pleasant initial sensitivity to tobacco and number of cigarettes smoked in prior months predicted both outcomes. More recent findings from this prospective study also indicate a reciprocal relationship between cigarette consumption and nicotine dependence symptoms over time, although the direction of this relationship appears more robust for cigarette consumption to predict greater levels of subsequent nicotine dependence (Hu, Griesler, Wall, & Kandel, 2014). In another well-designed prospective cohort study of 9th- to 10th-grade adolescent novice smokers followed over 2 years, Mermelstein and colleagues examined cumulative probability of onset of nicotine dependence symptoms (assessed with the NDSS) among those who had subsequently become established smokers (i.e., had smoked 100 cigarettes) and for those who had never reached that mark by the final assessment (Zhan, Dierker, Rose, Selya, & Mermelstein, 2012). Although not surprising, each NDSS symptom was more likely to be reported among those who eventually met the established smoker criterion. Across both groups, findings were consistent with previous studies (Rose et al., 2010; Strong et al., 2009) in that the most rapidly emerging symptoms were related to tolerance and irritability upon not smoking, both of which are relatively low-severity dependence symptoms, whereas improved functioning in the morning, a relatively high-severity dependence symptom, was much slower to emerge.

In a more complex examination of the sequencing of *DSM-IV* nicotine dependence symptoms, Kandel and colleagues (Kandel et al., 2009) examined the cumulative progression across tolerance, impaired control, withdrawal, and unsuccessful attempts to quit. Overall findings indicated that for novice smokers, tolerance and impaired control appeared first, preceding withdrawal, and that impaired control preceded attempts to quit. Such findings allow for a prospective examination of the extent to which there is a fixed sequence of the onset of specific symptoms. Interestingly, these patterns varied across gender and across racial groups, even controlling for relevant covariates. For example, among males, tolerance appeared first or in some instances withdrawal on its own preceded impaired control, whereas for girls, withdrawal was experienced last, suggesting that progression pathways may vary in important ways across demographic variables.

In summary, significant progress has been made in the assessment and elucidation of adolescent nicotine dependence. Greater understanding of the progression of dependence, as well as the sequence of symptom emergence, has resulted from prospective studies such as those reviewed earlier. These studies have provided important insights into some of the individual and interpersonal factors associated with the emergence of nicotine dependence among adolescent smokers.

Etiology of Adolescent Cigarette Use

Adolescent cigarette smoking is influenced by a complex interplay between individual, interpersonal, and environmental factors (Curry et al., 2009; Flay, Petraitis, & Hu, 1999; Turner, Mermelstein, & Flay, 2004). The existing literature has examined a broad range of variables as correlates and predictors of adolescent smoking acquisition (Turner et al., 2004; Tyas & Pederson, 1998), and the present brief review will discuss only a subset of these. Individual factors include genetics, biology, temperament, and other personal characteristics. Peers and parents represent the key social influences on adolescent smoking. Environmental factors include cultural, community, and media influences as well as legislation and tobacco control policies. Studies of adolescent smoking have demonstrated that predictors and correlates of smoking vary across stages of smoking acquisition (Choi et al.,, 1997; Flay, Hu, & Richardson, 1998; Hirschman, Leventhal, & Glynn, 1984; Wang et al., 1999). As such, key influences on initiation to smoking may differ from those for smoking progression and cessation.

Individual Influences on Smoking

A variety of individual characteristics play a role in adolescent smoking initiation and progression. Individual characteristics such as gender, ethnicity, socioeconomic status (SES), and education are consistently linked with smoking, such that males, Whites, and individuals with lower SES and less education are more likely to smoke (Turner et al., 2004; Tyas & Pederson, 1998). Beyond demographic characteristics, evidence suggests a genetic component to cigarette smoking. Estimates of genetic influence from twin studies suggest that additive genetic factors account for the majority of influence on initiation and persistence of smoking (Bergen & Caporaso, 1999). However, when examined prospectively, evidence indicates some genetic influences operate indirectly (e.g., through influencing choice of peers), and environmental factors may have a greater role than genetics in accounting for the variability of smoking during adolescence (White, Hopper, Wearing, & Hill, 2003). Genetic influences on smoking may be expressed as individual differences in reinforcement experienced from smoking, such as initial sensitivity to nicotine (Pomerleau, 1995). For example, it has been found that individuals who become smokers are more likely to report pleasurable experiences when first smoking a cigarette smoked than ex-smokers or never smokers (Pomerleau, Pomerleau, & Namenek, 1998), which may reflect genetic differences in sensitivity to the positive effects of nicotine (Pomerleau, 1995).

Another individual difference associated with adolescent smoking is the strong association between cigarette use and negative mood states. Teens who smoke anticipate that a cigarette will help them manage anxiety, anger, and depression (Myers, McCarthy, MacPherson, & Brown, 2003; Wahl, Turner, Mermelstein, & Flay, 2005). In addition, adolescents report smoking in stressful situations and to control mood states (Chassin, Presson, Rose, & Sherman, 2007; Kassel, Stroud, & Paronis, 2003). As such, tobacco use is considered a means for regulating and coping with negative affective states, with both pharmacologic and cognitive mechanisms contributing to these effects (Brandon, 1994). These observations have led to the hypothesis that smoking is used as a form of self-medication to alleviate negative mood states (Curry et al., 2009; Lerman et al., 1996), which is supported by findings that adolescent smoking is significantly related with symptoms of anxiety and depression (McKenzie et al., 2010).

Interpersonal Influences on Smoking

Interpersonal influences are powerful predictors of adolescent smoking initiation (Forrester, Biglan, Severson, & Smolkowski, 2007) and progression (Bricker et al., 2006). These influences operate in a number of ways, including modeling and reinforcement of smoking, providing access to tobacco, and providing contexts that may foster the behavior. Although many studies find a link between having friends who smoke and adolescent smoking (Chassin, Presson, & Sherman, 1984; Kobus, 2003), the role of peers in adolescent smoking initiation is complex and is not readily explained by the popular notion of "peer pressure" (Arnett, 2007; Kobus, 2003). Recent studies have distinguished peer selection (i.e., how friends are chosen) from peer influence (perceived and explicit expectations of engaging in smoking behavior), suggesting that these are reciprocal processes and each accounts for part of the relationship between peers and adolescent smoking (Arnett, 2007; Mercken, Candel, Willems, & de Vries, 2007). These approaches suggest that factors involved in friend selection (e.g., similarity in gender, ethnicity, age, and grade in school, attitudes, substance use behaviors) may place individual adolescents at higher or lower risk for engaging in smoking (Kobus, 2003). Choice of friends, in turn, affects social contexts that can influence the likelihood of smoking initiation through perceived norms surrounding smoking, exposure to smoking, and perceived social identity as a smoker (Arnett, 2007).

Evidence also exists for family influences on youth smoking. In contrast with peer influences, which appear to be strongest for initiation, parental influences may be stronger than peers for later stages of smoking progression (Bricker, Peterson, Sarason, Andersen, & Rajan, 2007; Flay et al., 1998). Overall, peer, parent, and sibling smoking appear to have similar levels of influence on adolescent smoking (Bricker et al., 2006).

Environmental Influences on Smoking

Environmental factors such as protobacco and antitobacco marketing and media influences, tobacco regulation and policies, and pricing play an important role in adolescent smoking initiation and progression. Environmental factors influence tobacco use in part by shaping perceptions of the anticipated effects of tobacco use and attitudes toward tobacco (Turner et al., 2004). For example, adolescents who held the lowest perceptions of short- or long-term risk from smoking were substantially more likely to initiate smoking than those who held the highest risk perceptions (Song et al., 2009). Policies, including smoking restrictions and pricing, also play a role in adolescent smoking. For example, evidence indicates that higher cigarette prices reduce initiation to smoking (Carpenter & Cook, 2008; Cawley, Markowitz, & Tauras, 2004). Similarly, tobacco control efforts such as antitobacco advertising and restrictions on smoking behavior are found to influence adolescent smoking initiation (Emery et al., 2005) and progression (Siegel, Albers, Cheng, Biener, & Rigotti, 2005).

Adolescent Smoking Cessation and Relapse

Prior to the increased prevalence of youth smoking observed in the 1990s (Johnston et al., 2016), relatively few intervention or research efforts targeted youth smoking cessation (USDHHS, 1994). The past few years have seen increased attention toward the development and implementation of interventions targeted at adolescent smokers (Backinger, Fagan, Matthews, & Grana, 2003; Sussman et al., 2006). However, although many teens report attempts to stop smoking, these typically result in failure, and few utilize tobacco cessation programs (Myers, MacPherson, Jones, & Aarons, 2007; W. R. Stanton, Lowe, Fisher, Gillespie, & Rose, 1999).

Smoking Cessation Treatment

Increased attention to the issue of adolescent smoking cessation has led to a growing number of treatment outcome studies. Three reviews with meta-analyses of existing research have been published since 2005 (Fiore, Jaen, & Baker, 2008; A. Stanton & Grimshaw, 2013; Sussman et al., 2006). Sussman and colleagues (Sussman et al., 2006) included 48 controlled studies of adolescent smoking cessation treatment and concluded that "teen smoking cessation programming is effective" (p. 549). Another review, the 2008 update to the Clinical Practice Guideline for Treating Tobacco Use and Dependence (Fiore et al., 2008), included a meta-analysis of seven youth treatment studies that met inclusion criteria. Findings were interpreted to indicate that counseling appears to improve abstinence for youth who smoke; however, treatment effects are smaller than observed for adult smokers. The most recently published review (A. Stanton & Grimshaw, 2013) applied more stringent selection criteria, including nonrandomized trials only if baseline conditions were assessed, and found comparable across groups, yielding a total of 28 studies. Employing a conservative meta-analytic approach, the authors concluded that complex multicomponent interventions addressing various aspects of youth smoking showed promise. Approaches that showed some evidence of persistent abstinence were those that addressed motivational factors and incorporated cognitive-behavioral approaches. Thus, existing interventions for adolescent smoking cessation show promise; however, much work remains to be done in this arena (Curry et al., 2009).

Self-Change Smoking Cessation Efforts

Information regarding naturally occurring efforts to change smoking behaviors suggests that adolescent smokers frequently consider quitting smoking, and as such they may be amenable to intervention. Studies of general population and school samples consistently find that adolescents often want to stop smoking, frequently attempt smoking cessation, yet seldom succeed in maintaining long-term abstinence. We examined smoking cessation among youth in treatment for substance abuse (Myers & MacPherson, 2004). The majority (63%) of adolescents in our study had previously attempted to quit smoking, yet reported difficulties staying quit: 70% had returned to smoking within a month of quitting. The frequency and duration of smoking cessation efforts for this substance-abusing sample were comparable to findings with adolescent smokers from community-based studies (e.g., Burt & Peterson, 1998; Pierce et al., 1998). Overall, adolescents tend to return to smoking relatively soon following cessation attempts, indicating the potential value of tobacco-focused interventions to enhance and support abstinence from smoking.

To date, most research on adolescent addictive behavior self-change has focused on smoking cessation. Investigations to date find that the majority of adolescent smokers report intentions to quit smoking and cessation attempts (Ershler et al., 1989; Sargent et al., 1998; W. R. Stanton, Lowe, & Gillespie, 1996;

Sussman, Dent, Severson, Burton, & Flay, 1998). In particular, studies have consistently found that more than half of adolescent smokers reported cessation attempts during the previous year (Burt & Peterson, 1998; Myers & MacPherson, 2004; Sargent et al., 1998; W. R. Stanton et al., 1996; Sussman, Dent, Severson, et al., 1998).

Cross-sectional data on duration of adolescent abstinence following smoking cessation attempts demonstrate a frequent and rapid return to smoking (Myers & MacPherson, 2004; Pierce et al., 1998). For example, Pierce and his colleagues (Pierce et al., 1998) found that 44% of adolescents who reported making a quit attempt had resumed smoking within the first week and 80% within a month. Thus, despite frequent cessation attempts, few adolescents appear to achieve prolonged abstinence from smoking. The apparent difficulty youth experience in maintaining abstinence serves to highlight the potential value of identifying factors that influence this phase of the self-change process. Improved smoking cessation rates among adolescent smokers may be attained by gaining a better understanding of the factors that motivate cessation attempts, support abstinence following a quit attempt, and underlie a return to smoking following quit attempts (Colby & Gwaltney, 2007; Gwaltney, Bartolomei, Colby, & Kahler, 2008; Myers & MacPherson, 2008, 2009; Myers, MacPherson, et al., 2007).

SELF-CHANGE MOTIVES

Health concerns have consistently been identified as motivating adolescent smoking cessation efforts (Dozois, Farrow, & Miser, 1995; Myers & MacPherson, 2004; W. R. Stanton et al., 1999; Stone & Kristeller 1992; Sussman, Dent, Nezami, et al., 1998). Other reasons included pressure from peers, expense, participation in sports, smoking being a "nasty habit," pressure from parents, and being addicted. In our prior longitudinal study of smoking self-change in which we developed a measure of reasons for quitting, subscales reflecting social consequences and concern about smoking in the future prospectively predicted cessation attempts (Myers & MacPherson, 2008). These initial data provide evidence for the types of reasons that may lead to self-change efforts. Further study of this issue will provide guidance for the design of interventions to motivate adolescent smoking cessation.

SELF-CHANGE METHODS AND STRATEGIES

Identifying what adolescents do in the course of attempts to change cigarette smoking is likely to prove invaluable to informing intervention design. In particular, determining which strategies and methods of smoking self-change are perceived as acceptable and helpful and specifying those associated with better outcomes hold promise for improving existing adolescent cigarette smoking intervention programs. At the present time limited research addresses this topic. Overall, previous studies on adolescent methods for quitting smoking (Balch, 1998; R. A. Brown et al., 2003; Fisher, Stanton, & Lowe, 1999; Myers & MacPherson, 2004) consistently found that stopping abruptly was the most commonly reported approach. Gradual reduction and quitting with friends were other strategies identified across studies. We described initial findings from our measure of adolescent cessation strategies (Myers, MacPherson, et al., 2007). The most frequently reported cessation methods included avoidance, reduction, and distraction strategies. In particular, reducing the quantity of cigarettes smoked and limiting exposure to smoking situations were oft cited. These, along with social support strategies, received the highest helpfulness ratings. Consistent with other studies, formal intervention approaches were the least frequently employed strategies and were also rated as least helpful. In addition, utilizing more social support and smoking reduction strategies was significantly correlated with longer abstinence duration.

Coping With Temptations to Smoke

Resisting temptations to smoke is one of the key challenges encountered by individuals who attempt smoking cessation. Circumstances that increase the risk for a lapse to smoking for adults include being in the presence of cigarettes, alcohol consumption, and experiencing negative affect (Bliss, Garvey, Heinold, & Hitchcock, 1989; O'Connell & Martin, 1987; Shiffman, 1984; Shiffman et al., 1996). A well-developed body of research among adults has demonstrated that coping efforts in the face of temptations to smoke play an important role in the outcome of these situations. Evidence for the self-regulation function of temptation-coping is supported by research demonstrating that such coping may support abstinence by reducing the strength of urges to smoke (O'Connell, Hosein, Schwartz, & Leibowitz, 2007).

Little research has addressed temptation-coping for adolescent smoking. A single published report was identified in which self-reported coping strategies were assessed for participants in a school-based smoking cessation program (Jannone &

O'Connell, 2007). Consistent with adult studies, coping efforts were significantly associated with successful abstinence in the face of temptation to smoke. More recently, we examined a brief measure of adolescent coping with temptations to smoke in the face of social pressure (Myers & MacPherson, 2009). The coping scale was composed of items reflecting cognitive and behavioral strategies for managing temptations to smoke. Results indicated that higher scores on the coping scale significantly predicted length of abstinence for adolescents who had tried to quit. The findings suggest that assessing coping with temptations in response to a social situation may be useful for predicting teen smoking cessation outcomes. In particular, this result highlights the potential importance of social situations in adolescent cessation efforts.

Adolescent Smoking Relapse

As with coping strategies, little is known regarding the characteristics of adolescent relapse-risk situations. The few relevant studies indicate that exposure to smoking is a frequent adolescent relapse-risk situation (Falkin, Fryer, & Mahadeo, 2007) and that availability of cigarettes is linked to lapse (Burris & O'Connell, 2003). We previously published a study examining characteristics of situations in which adolescents returned to smoking following a cessation attempt (Myers et al., 2011). The typical lapse situation occurred at home in the evening while socializing with friends. The adolescents commonly endorsed experiencing social pressure to smoke and urges or cravings for a cigarette in these situations. The most frequently reported situational influence was desire for a cigarette, followed by thoughts about smoking and negative emotions. The findings indicate that a broad range of factors appear to influence adolescent smoking lapse. Specifically, the results suggest the value of including treatment content relevant to managing social and emotional cues, strategies to avoid asking for a cigarette, and preparing youth for anticipated difficulties of not smoking.

Studies of adult smokers find that alcohol use following a smoking cessation attempt increases the likelihood of relapse (Humfleet, Munoz, Sees, Reus, & Hall, 1999). In particular, alcohol consumption is a frequent precipitant of a return to smoking following cessation (Shiffman, 1986). Alcohol use may also play a role in adolescent smoking cessation efforts, as suggested by consistent evidence that youth cigarette smoking and alcohol use are closely related (Ellickson, Tucker, & Klein, 2001; Foster, Richter, & Keneipp, 2007; Myers & Kelly, 2006). For example, a study of adolescents found that 54% of smokers reported same-day use of alcohol and cigarettes (Duhig, Cavallo, McKee, George, & Krishnan-Sarin, 2005). Despite the well-developed literature documenting the link between youth smoking and alcohol use, few studies have examined the potential influence of drinking on adolescent smoking cessation efforts. In reviewing this literature, only a single study was identified that examined alcohol use in relation to smoking outcomes from an adolescent cessation trial (Jaszyna-Gasior, Schroeder, & Moolchan, 2007). Consistent with findings from adult research, postcessation alcohol consumption was associated with lower rates of abstinence for these adolescent smokers. However, a recent examination of characteristics of adolescent relapse following an attempt to quit smoking found that situations where teens returned to smoking were characterized by social and emotional factors, with very few lapses occurring in the presence of alcohol or other drug use (Myers et al., 2011).

Conclusion

Driven by increased prevalence of teen smoking in the 1990s, concern regarding adolescent smoking cessation and nicotine dependence has led to a substantial growth in our understanding of the complex factors linked to smoking-related processes. In particular, the past two decades have yielded seminal work in conceptualizing and examining the emergence of adolescent nicotine dependence. It is now clear that youth who smoke develop dependence on nicotine, and significant insights have been achieved into the characteristics and course of this process. Similarly, our knowledge of adolescent smoking cessation has evolved significantly, with a sufficient body of research to inform the effectiveness of interventions. Unfortunately, the initiation of cigarette smoking and other tobacco products by adolescents continues at substantial rates, indicating the need for continued attention and focus on this topic.

Future Directions

A number of issues are of importance to informing efforts to prevent and intervene with adolescent cigarette use. Especially relevant to prevention of cigarette smoking and nicotine dependence is the role of nicotine delivery products whose prevalence and popularity appear to be increasing.

Emerging evidence indicates that e-cigarettes and little cigars appeal to youth and are being used by more adolescents than are conventional cigarettes. Accordingly, research indicates significant rates of polyuse or concurrent use of more than one tobacco product (Creamer, Portillo, Clendennen, & Perry, 2016), a pattern of use that could increase the risks for nicotine dependence. However, the emergence of these products is a relatively recent phenomenon, and only limited data are available to characterize their use. Therefore, at this time little is known regarding factors that influence adoption of these products, patterns of their use, and the extent to which they may play a role in smoking initiation and progression. Of significant concern, initial evidence demonstrates that use of e-cigarettes increases the likelihood of subsequent cigarette smoking initiation (Leventhal et al., 2015). Thus, the adoption of these other tobacco products may serve to undermine recent declines in cigarette use and contribute to increased prevalence of youth nicotine dependence. These are all critical questions for better informing prevention-related policy and prevention programming.

Recent years have seen impressive contributions to our understanding of adolescent nicotine dependence, yet much work remains to better inform prevention and interventions targeted at cigarettes and other nicotine delivery products. A fundamental issue is the disconnect between currently employed measures of dependence (mFTQ, DSM, etc.) and basic models of addiction put forth to explain motivated smoking behavior. At this point there is a need to establish dependence measures that correspond more closely with emerging theoretical models to better elucidate the nature and development of adolescent nicotine dependence.

Despite significant advances in the field of adolescent smoking cessation, treatment remains in its early stages. Research to date has identified effective components of treatment but indicates many remaining challenges, not the least of which is effective engagement of youth in treatment (Curry et al., 2009). One avenue for addressing this issue is to develop novel approaches for engaging youth who smoke and assisting their efforts to quit. For example, developmentally focused interventions to addressing alcohol use have recently been developed that incorporate approaches, content, and marketing that appeal to youth (S. A. Brown, 2001, 2005). Adaptation of these strategies for the design of smoking and other tobacco product cessation

programs is a promising area for future work. In addition, there is a need for further information to guide the development of efficacious interventions. To this end, naturalistic studies that identify factors associated with successful adolescent tobacco use in self-change efforts can suggest treatment context and content (Mermelstein et al., 2002). Prospective investigation of the self-change process in the context of adolescent development can provide valuable knowledge regarding when and how to intervene with adolescents. Finally, only a small proportion of adolescents are likely to seek formal assistance for addictive behavior change (Balch et al., 2004; Barker et al., 2006; S. A. Brown, 2001; Wagner, Brown, Monti, Myers, & Waldron, 1999). Naturalistic studies can thus serve to suggest secondary prevention or low-intensity interventions intended to facilitate adolescent self-change efforts (S. A. Brown, 2005; D'Amico et al., 2006; D'Amico, McCarthy, Metrik, & Brown, 2004).

References

Alpert, H. R., Koh, H., & Connolly, G. N. (2008). Free nicotine content and strategic marketing of moist snuff tobacco products in the United States: 2000–2006. *Tobacco Control, 17*(5), 332–338.

American Psychiatric Association. (2000). *Diagnostic and statistical manual of mental disorders* (4th ed.). Washington DC: American Psychiatric Association.

Arnett, J. J. (2007). The myth of peer influence in adolescent smoking initiation. *Health Education and Behavior, 34*(4), 594–607.

Austin, G., McCarthy, W., Slade, S., & Bailey, J. (2007). *Links between smoking and substance use, violence, and school problems.* Retrieved from http://surveydata.wested.org/resources/hksc-surveyreader.pdf

Ayers, J. W., Ribisl, K. M., & Brownstein, J. S. (2011). Tracking the rise in popularity of electronic nicotine delivery systems (electronic cigarettes) using search query surveillance. *American Journal of Preventive Medicine, 40*(4), 448–453.

Backinger, C. L., Fagan, P., Matthews, E., & Grana, R. (2003). Adolescent and young adult tobacco prevention and cessation: Current status and future directions. *Tobacco Control, 12*(Suppl. 4), IV46–IV53.

Balch, G. I. (1998). Exploring perceptions of smoking cessation among high school smokers: Input and feedback from focus groups. *Preventive Medicine, 27*, A55–A63.

Balch, G. I., Tworek, C., Barker, D. C., Sasso, B., Mermelstein, R., & Giovino, G. A. (2004). Opportunities for youth smoking cessation: Findings from a national focus group study. *Nicotine and Tobacco Research, 6*(1), 9–17.

Bancej, C., O'Loughlin, J., Platt, R. W., Paradis, G., & Gervais, A. (2007). Smoking cessation attempts among adolescent smokers: A systematic review of prevalence studies. *Tobacco Control, 16*(6), e8. doi:10.1136/tc.2006.018853

Barker, D. C., Giovino, G., Malarcher, A., Gable, J., Donohue, K., Mowery, P., . . . Orleans, C. T. (2006). *How young smokers* approach quitting: Cohort data from the National Youth Smoking Cessation Survey. Presented at the Annual Meeting of the American Public Health Association, Boston, MA, November, 2006.

Bergen, A. W., & Caporaso, N. (1999). Cigarette smoking. Journal of the National Cancer Institute, 91(16), 1365–1375.

Berrettini, W. H., & Lerman, C. E. (2005). Pharmacotherapy and pharmacogenetics of nicotine dependence. American Journal of Psychiatry, 162(8), 1441–1451.

Bliss, R. E., Garvey, A. J., Heinold, J. W., & Hitchcock, J. L. (1989). The influence of situation and coping on relapse crisis outcomes after smoking cessation. Journal of Consulting Clinical Psychology, 57(3), 443–449.

Brandon, T. H. (1994). Negative affect as motivation to smoke. Current Directions in Psychological Science, 3(2), 33–37.

Breslau, N., Peterson, E. L., Schultz, L. R., Chilcoat, H. D., & Andreski, P. (1998). Major depression and stages of smoking. A longitudinal investigation. Archives of General Psychiatry, 55(2), 161–166.

Bricker, J. B., Peterson, A. V., Andersen, M. R., Leroux, B. G., Rajan, K. B., & Sarason, I. G. (2006). Close friends', parents', and older siblings' smoking: Reevaluating their influence on children's smoking. Nicotine and Tobacco Research, 8(2), 217–226.

Bricker, J. B., Peterson, A. V., Sarason, I. G., Andersen, M. R., & Rajan, K. B. (2007). Changes in the influence of parents' and close friends' smoking on adolescent smoking transitions. Addictive Behaviors, 32(4), 740–757.

Brook, J. S., Cohen, P., & Brook, D. W. (1998). Longitudinal study of co-occurring psychiatric disorders and substance use. Journal of the American Academy of Child and Adolescent Psychiatry, 37(3), 322–330.

Brook, J. S., Schuster, E., & Zhang, C. (2004). Cigarette smoking and depressive symptoms: A longitudinal study of adolescents and young adults. Psychological Reports, 95(1), 159–166.

Brown, R. A., Lewinsohn, P. M., Seeley, J. R., & Wagner, E. F. (1996). Cigarette smoking, major depression, and other psychiatric disorders among adolescents. Journal of the American Academy of Child Adolescent Psychiatry, 35(12), 1602–1610.

Brown, R. A., Ramsey, S. E., Strong, D. R., Myers, M. G., Kahler, C. W., Lejuez, C. W., . . . Abrams, D. B. (2003). Effects of motivational interviewing on smoking cessation in adolescents with psychiatric disorders. Tobacco Control, 12(Suppl. 4), iv3–iv10.

Brown, S. A. (2001). Facilitating change for adolescent alcohol problems: A multiple options approach. In E. F. Wagner & H. B. Waldron (Eds.), Innovations in adolescent substance abuse (pp. 169–187). Oxford, UK: Elsevier.

Brown, S. A. (2005). Facilitating youth self-change through school-based intervention. Addictive Behaviors, 30(9), 1797–1810.

Burris, R. F., & O'Connell, K. A. (2003). Reversal theory states and cigarette availability predict lapses during smoking cessation among adolescents. Research in Nursing and Health, 26(4), 263–272.

Burt, R. D., & Peterson, A. V. (1998). Smoking cessation among high school seniors. Preventive Medicine, 27, 319–327.

Carpenter, C., & Cook, P. J. (2008). Cigarette taxes and youth smoking: New evidence from national, state, and local Youth Risk Behavior Surveys. Journal of Health Economics, 27(2), 287–299.

Carroll Chapman, S. L., & Wu, L. T. (2014). E-cigarette prevalence and correlates of use among adolescents versus adults: A review and comparison. Journal of Psychiatric Research, 54, 43–54. doi:10.1016/j.jpsychires.2014.03.005

Cawley, J., Markowitz, S., & Tauras, J. (2004). Lighting up and slimming down: The effects of body weight and cigarette prices on adolescent smoking initiation. Journal of Health Economics, 23(2), 293–311.

Chassin, L., Presson, C. C., Rose, J., & Sherman, S. J. (2007). What is addiction? Age-related differences in the meaning of addiction. Drug and Alcohol Dependence, 87(1), 30–38.

Chassin, L., Presson, C. C., & Sherman, S. J. (1984). Cognitive and social influence factors in adolescent smoking cessation. Addictive Behaviors, 9, 383–390.

Choi, W. S., Pierce,. P., Gilpin, E. A., Farkas, A. J., Berry, C. C. (1997). Which adolescent experimenters progress to established smoking in the United States. American Journal of Preventive Medicine, 13(5), 385–391.

Chun, J., Guydish, J., & Chan, Y-F. (2007). Smoking among adolescents in substance abuse treatment: A study of programs, policy, and prevalence. Journal of Psychoactive Drugs, 39(4), 443–449.

Chung, T., Martin, C. S., Maisto, S. A., Cornelius, J. R., & Clark, D. B. (2012). Greater prevalence of proposed DSM-5 nicotine use disorder compared to DSM-IV nicotine dependence in treated adolescents and young adults. Addiction, 107(4), 810–818. doi:10.1111/j.1360-0443.2011.03722.x

Clark, D. B., Wood, D. S., Martin, C. S., Cornelius, J. R., Lynch, K. G., & Shiffman, S. (2005). Multidimensional assessment of nicotine dependence in adolescents. Drug and Alcohol Dependence, 77(3), 235–242.

Cohen, L. M., Myers, M. G., & Kelly, J. F. (2002). Assessment of nicotine dependence among substance abusing adolescent smokers: A comparison of the DSM-IV criteria and the modified Fagerström Tolerance Questionnaire. Journal of Psychopathology and Behavioral Assessment, 24(4), 225–233.

Colby, S. M., & Gwaltney, C. J. (2007). Pharmacotherapy for adolescent smoking cessation. Journal of the American Medical Association, 298(18), 2182–2184.

Colby, S. M., Tiffany, S., Shiffman, S., & Niaura, R. S. (2000a). Are adolescent smokers dependent on nicotine? A review of the evidence. Drug and Alcohol Dependence, 59(Suppl. 1), S83–S95.

Colby, S. M., Tiffany, S., Shiffman, S., & Niaura, R. S. (2000b). Measuring nicotine dependence among youth: A review of available approaches and instruments. Drug and Alcohol Dependence, 59(Suppl. 1), S23–S39.

Covey, L. S., & Tam, D. (1990). Depressive mood, the single-parent home, and adolescent cigarette smoking. American Journal of Public Health, 80(11), 1330–1333.

Creamer, M. R., Portillo, G. V., Clendennen, S. L., & Perry, C. L. (2016). Is adolescent poly-tobacco use associated with alcohol and other drug use? American Journal of Health Behavior, 40(1), 117–122. doi:10.5993/AJHB.40.1.13

Crowley, T. J. (2006). Adolescents and substance-related disorders: Research agenda to guide decisions on Diagnostic and statistical manual of mental disorders, fifth edition (DSM-V). Addiction, 101(Suppl. 1), 115–124.

Curry, S. J., Mermelstein, R. J., & Sporer, A. K. (2009). Therapy for specific problems: Youth tobacco cessation. Annual Review of Psychology, 60(1), 229–255. doi:10.1146/annurev.psych.60.110707.163659

D'Amico, E. J., Anderson, K. G., Metrik, J., Frissell, K. C., Ellingstad, T. P., & Brown, S. A. (2006). Adolescent self-selection of service formats: Implications for Secondary interventions targeting alcohol use. *American Journal on Addictions, 15*(S1), 58–66.

D'Amico, E. J., McCarthy, D. E., Metrik, J., & Brown, S. A. (2004). Alcohol-related services: Prevention, secondary intervention, and treatment preference of adolescents. *Journal of Child and Adolescent Substance Abuse, 14,* 61–80.

Dar, R., & Frenk, H. (2010). Can one puff really make an adolescent addicted to nicotine? A critical review of the literature. *Harm Reduction Journal, 7,* 28.

Dierker, L., & Mermelstein, R. (2010). Early emerging nicotine-dependence symptoms: A signal of propensity for chronic smoking behavior in adolescents. *Journal of Pediatrics, 156*(5), 818–822.

DiFranza, J. R., Savageau, J. A., Fletcher, K., O'Loughlin, J., Pbert, L., Ockene, J. K., . . . Wellman, R. J. (2007). Symptoms of tobacco dependence after brief intermittent use: The Development and Assessment of Nicotine Dependence in Youth-2 study. *Archives of Pediatrics and Adolescent Medicine, 161*(7), 704–710.

DiFranza, J. R., Savageau, J. A., Fletcher, K., Ockene, J. K., Rigotti, N. A., McNeill, A. D., . . . Wood, C. (2002). Measuring the loss of autonomy over nicotine use in adolescents: The DANDY (Development and Assessment of Nicotine Dependence in Youths) study. *Archives of Pediatrics and Adolescent Medicine, 156*(4), 397–403. doi:poa10271 [pii]

Dozois, D. N., Farrow, J. A., & Miser, A. (1995). Smoking patterns and cessation motivations during adolescence. *International Journal of the Addictions, 30,* 1485–1498.

Duhig, A. M., Cavallo, D. A., McKee, S. A., George, T. P., & Krishnan-Sarin, S. (2005). Daily patterns of alcohol, cigarette, and marijuana use in adolescent smokers and nonsmokers. *Addictive Behaviors, 30*(2), 271–283.

Durmowicz, E. L. (2014). The impact of electronic cigarettes on the paediatric population. *Tobacco Control, 23*(Suppl. 2), ii41–46. doi:10.1136/tobaccocontrol-2013-051468

Eckhart, D. (2004). *The tobacco master settlement agreement: Enforcement of marketing restrictions.* Retrieved March 2016, from http://publichealthlawcenter.org/sites/default/files/resources/tclc-syn-marketing-2004.pdf

Eckhardt, L., Woodruff, S. I., & Elder, J. P. (1994). A longitudinal analysis of adolescent smoking and its correlates. *Journal of School Health, 64,* 67–72.

Edelen, M. O., Tucker, J. S., & Ellickson, P. L. (2007). A discrete time hazards model of smoking initiation among West Coast youth from age 5 to 23. *Preventive Medicine, 44*(1), 52–54.

Edwards, G., & Gross, M. M. (1976). Alcohol dependence: Provisional description of a clinical syndrome. *British Medical Journal, 1*(6017), 1058–1061.

Ellickson, P. L., Tucker, J. S., & Klein, D. J. (2001). High-risk behaviors associated with early smoking: Results from a 5-year follow-up. *Journal of Adolescent Health, 28*(6), 465–473.

Emery, S., Wakefield, M. A., Terry-McElrath, Y., Saffer, H., Szczypka, G., O'Malley, P. M., . . . Flay, B. (2005). Televised state-sponsored antitobacco advertising and youth smoking beliefs and behavior in the United States, 1999–2000. *Archives of Pediatrics and Adolescent Medicine, 159*(7), 639–645.

Ershler, J., Leventhal, H., Fleming, R., Glynn, K. (1989). The quitting experience for smokers in sixth through twelfth grades. *Addictive Behaviors, 14,* 365–378.

Fagerstrom, K. O. (1978). Measuring degree of physical dependence to tobacco smoking with reference to individualization of treatment. *Addictive Behaviors, 3*(3–4), 235–241.

Falkin, G. P., Fryer, C. S., & Mahadeo, M. (2007). Smoking cessation and stress among teenagers. *Qualitative Health Research, 17*(6), 812–823.

FDA. (2009, July). FDA and public health experts warn about electronic cigarettes. Retrieved March 2016, from http://www.fda.gov/NewsEvents/Newsroom/PressAnnouncements/ucm173222.htm

Fiore, M. C., Jaen, C. R., & Baker, T. B. (2008). *Treating tobacco use and dependence: 2008 update.* Rockville, MD: US Department of Health and Human Services, Public Health Service.

Fischer, P. M., Schwartz, M. P., Richards, J. W., Jr., Goldstein, A. O., & Rojas, T. H. (1991). Brand logo recognition by children aged 3 to 6 years. Mickey Mouse and Old Joe the Camel. *Journal of the American Medical Association, 266*(22), 3145–3148.

Fisher, K. J., Stanton, W. R., & Lowe, J. B. (1999). Healthy behaviors, lifestyle, and reasons for quitting smoking among out-of-school youth. *Journal of Adolescent Health, 25*(4), 290–297.

Flay, B. R., Hu, F. B., & Richardson, J. (1998). Psychosocial predictors of different stages of smoking among high school students. *Preventive Medicine, 27,* A9–A18.

Flay, B. R., Petraitis, J., & Hu, F. B. (1999). Psychosocial risk and protective factors for adolescent tobacco use. *Nicotine and Tobacco Research, 1,* S59–S65.

Forrester, K., Biglan, A., Severson, H. H., & Smolkowski, K. (2007). Predictors of smoking onset over two years. *Nicotine and Tobacco Research, 9*(12), 1259–1267.

Foster, S. E., Richter, L., & Keneipp, K. (2007). *Tobacco: The smoking gun.* Retrieved March 2016, from http://www.centeronaddiction.org/addiction-research/reports/tobacco-smoking-gun

Grana, R., Benowitz, N., & Glantz, S. A. (2014). E-cigarettes: A scientific review. *Circulation, 129*(19), 1972–1986. doi:10.1161/CIRCULATIONAHA.114.007667

Gwaltney, C. J., Bartolomei, R., Colby, S. M., & Kahler, C. W. (2008). Ecological momentary assessment of adolescent smoking cessation: A feasibility study. *Nicotine and Tobacco Research, 10*(7), 1185–1190.

Hawkins, J. D., Catalano, R. F., & Miller, J. Y. (1992). Risk and protective factors for alcohol and other drug problems in adolescence and early adulthood: Implications for substance abuse prevention. *Psychological Bulletin, 112*(1), 64–105.

Heatherton, T. F., Kozlowski, L. T., Frecker, R. C., & Fagerstrom, K. (1991). The Fagerstrom Test for Nicotine Dependence: A revision of the Fagerstrom Tolerance Questionnaire. *British Journal of Addiction, 86,* 1119–1127.

Hirschman, R. S., Leventhal, H., & Glynn, K. (1984). The development of smoking behavior: Conceptualization and supportive cross-sectional survey data. *Journal of Applied Social Psychology, 14*(3), 184–206.

Hoffman, J. H., Welte, J. W., & Barnes, G. M. (2001). Co-occurrence of alcohol and cigarette use among adolescents. *Addictive Behaviors, 26*(1), 63–78.

Hu, M. C., Griesler, P. C., Wall, M. M., & Kandel, D. B. (2014). Reciprocal associations between cigarette consumption and

DSM-IV nicotine dependence criteria in adolescent smokers. *Addiction, 109*(9), 1518–1528. doi:10.1111/add.12619

Hughes, J. R., & Shiffman, S. (2008). Conceptualizations of nicotine dependence: A response to DiFranza. *Nicotine and Tobacco Research, 10*(12), 1811–1812.

Humfleet, G., Munoz, R., Sees, K., Reus, V., & Hall, S. (1999). History of alcohol or drug problems, current use of alcohol or marijuana, and success in quitting smoking. *Addictive Behaviors, 24*(1), 149–154. doi:S0306-4603(98)00057-4 [pii]

Jannone, L., & O'Connell, K. A. (2007). Coping strategies used by adolescents during smoking cessation. *Journal of School Nursing, 23*(3), 177–184.

Jaszyna-Gasior, M., Schroeder, J. R., & Moolchan, E. T. (2007). Alcohol use and tobacco abstinence among adolescents in cessation treatment: Preliminary findings. *Addictive Behaviors, 32*(3), 617–621.

Johnston, L. D., O'Malley, P. M., Miech, R. A., Bachman, J. G., & Schulenberg, J. E. (2015). *Monitoring the Future national survey results on drug use, 1975–2014, Vol. 1. Secondary school students.* Ann Arbor, MI: Institute for Social Research, University of Michigan.

Johnston, L. D., O'Malley, P. M., Miech, R. A., Bachman, J. G., & Schulenberg, J. E. (2016). *Monitoring the Future national results on adolescent drug use: Overview of key findings, 2015.* Ann Arbor, MI: Institute for Social Research, University of Michigan.

Kandel, D. B., Hu, M-C., Griesler, P. C., & Schaffran, C. (2007). On the development of nicotine dependence in adolescence. *Drug and Alcohol Dependence, 91*(1), 26–39.

Kandel, D. B., Hu, M-C., & Yamaguchi, K. (2009). Sequencing of DSM-IV criteria of nicotine dependence. *Addiction, 104*(8), 1393–1402.

Kandel, D. B., Schaffran, C., Griesler, P., Samuolis, J., Davies, M., & Galanti, R. (2005). On the measurement of nicotine dependence in adolescence: Comparisons of the mFTQ and a DSM-IV-Based Scale. *Journal of Pediatric Psychology, 30*(4), 319–332.

Kashani, J. H., Beck, N. C., Hoeper, E. W., Fallahi, C., Corcoran, C. M., McAllister, J. A., . . . Reid, J. C. (1987). Psychiatric disorders in a community sample of adolescents. *American Journal of Psychiatry, 144*(5), 584–589.

Kassel, J. D., Stroud, L. R., & Paronis, C. A. (2003). Smoking, stress, and negative affect: Correlation, causation, and context across stages of smoking. *Psychological Bulletin, 129*(2), 270–304.

Kobus, K. (2003). Peers and adolescent smoking. *Addiction, 98*, 37–55.

Kuschner, W. G., Reddy, S., Mehrotra, N., & Paintal, H. S. (2011). Electronic cigarettes and thirdhand tobacco smoke: Two emerging health care challenges for the primary care provider. *International Journal of General Medicine, 4*, 115–120.

Lerman, C., Audrain, J., Orleans, C. T., Boyd, R., Gold, K., Main, D., & Caporaso, N. (1996). Investigation of mechanisms linking depressed mood to nicotine dependence. *Addictive Behaviors, 21*(1), 9–19.

Leventhal, A. M., Strong, D. R., Kirkpatrick, M. G., Unger, J. B., Sussman, S., Riggs, N. R., . . . Audrain-McGovern, J. (2015). Association of electronic cigarette use With initiation of combustible tobacco product smoking in early adolescence. *Journal of the American Medical Association, 314*(7), 700–707. doi:10.1001/jama.2015.8950

Lord, F. (1980). *Applications of item response theory to practical testing problems.* Hillsdale, NJ: Erlbaum.

MacPherson, L., Strong, D. R., & Myers, M. G. (2008). Using an item response model to examine the nicotine dependence construct as characterized by the HONC and the mFTQ among adolescent smokers. *Addictive Behaviors, 33*(7), 880–894.

McKenzie, M., Olsson, C. A., Jorm, A. F., Romaniuk, H., & Patton, G. C. (2010). Association of adolescent symptoms of depression and anxiety with daily smoking and nicotine dependence in young adulthood: Findings from a 10-year longitudinal study. *Addiction, 105*(9), 1652–1659.

McMillen, R., Maduka, J., & Winickoff, J. (2012). Use of emerging tobacco products in the United States. *Journal of Environmental and Public Health, 2012*, 989474.

Mercken, L., Candel, M., Willems, P., & de Vries, H. (2007). Disentangling social selection and social influence effects on adolescent smoking: The importance of reciprocity in friendships. *Addiction, 102*(9), 1483–1492.

Mermelstein, R., Colby, S. M., Patten, C., Prokhorov, A. V., Brown, R. A., Myers, M., . . . McDonald, P. (2002). Methodological issues in measuring treatment outcome in adolescent smoking cessation studies. *Nicotine and Tobacco Research, 4*(4), 395–403.

Myers, M. G., & Brown, S. A. (1994). Smoking and health in substance-abusing adolescents: A two-year follow-up. *Pediatrics, 93*(4), 561–566.

Myers, M. G., & Brown, S. A. (1997). Cigarette smoking four years following treatment for adolescent substance abuse. *Journal of Child and Adolescent Substance Abuse, 7*(1), 1–15.

Myers, M. G., Doran, N. M., & Brown, S. A. (2007). Is cigarette smoking related to alcohol use during the 8 years following treatment for adolescent alcohol and other drug abuse? *Alcohol and Alcoholism, 42*(3), 226–233.

Myers, M. G., Gwaltney, C. J., Strong, D. R., Ramsey, S. E., Brown, R. A., Monti, P. M., & Colby, S. M. (2011). Adolescent first lapse following smoking cessation: Situation characteristics, precipitants and proximal influences. *Addictive Behaviors, 36*(12), 1253–1260.

Myers, M. G., & Kelly, J. F. (2006). Cigarette smoking among adolescents with alcohol and other drug use problems. *Alcohol Research and Health, 29*(3), 221–227.

Myers, M. G., & MacPherson, L. (2004). Smoking cessation efforts among substance abusing adolescents. *Drug and Alcohol Dependence, 73*, 209–213.

Myers, M. G., & MacPherson, L. (2008). Adolescent reasons for quitting smoking: Initial psychometric evaluation. *Psychology of Addictive Behaviors, 22*(1), 129–134.

Myers, M. G., & MacPherson, L. (2009). Coping with temptations and adolescent smoking cessation: An initial investigation. *Nicotine and Tobacco Research, 11*(8), 940–944.

Myers, M. G., MacPherson, L., Jones, L. R., & Aarons, G. A. (2007). Measuring adolescent smoking cessation strategies: Instrument development and initial validation. *Nicotine and Tobacco Research, 9*(11), 1131–1138.

Myers, M. G., McCarthy, D. M., MacPherson, L., & Brown, S. A. (2003). Constructing a short form of the Smoking Consequences Questionnaire with adolescents and young adults. *Psychological Assessment, 15*(2), 163–172.

O'Connell, K. A., Hosein, V. L., Schwartz, J. E., & Leibowitz, R. Q. (2007). How does coping help people resist lapses during smoking cessation? *Health Psychology, 26*(1), 77–84.

O'Connell, K. A., & Martin, E. J. (1987). Highly tempting situations associated with abstinence, temporary lapse, and relapse among participants in smoking cessation programs. *Journal of Consulting and Clinical Psychology, 55*(3), 367–371.

O'Loughlin, J., Tarasuk, J., Difranza, J., & Paradis, G. (2002). Reliability of selected measures of nicotine dependence among adolescents. *Annals of Epidemiology, 12*(5), 353–362.

Orlando, M., Tucker, J. S., Ellickson, P. L., & Klein, D. J. (2005). Concurrent use of alcohol and cigarettes from adolescence to young adulthood: An examination of developmental trajectories and outcomes. *Substance Use and Misuse, 40*(8), 1051–1069.

Palmer, R. H. C., Young, S. E., Hopfer, C. J., Corley, R. P., Stallings, M. C., Crowley, T. J., & Hewitt, J. K. (2009). Developmental epidemiology of drug use and abuse in adolescence and young adulthood: Evidence of generalized risk. *Drug and Alcohol Dependence, 102*(1–3), 78–87.

Patton, G. C., Carlin, J. B., Coffey, C., Wolfe, R., Hibbert, M., & Bowes, G. (1998). Depression, anxiety, and smoking initiation: A prospective study over 3 years. *American Journal of Public Health, 88*(10), 1518–1522.

Pierce, J. P., & Gilpin, E. A. (1996). How long will today's new adolescent smoker be addicted to cigarettes? *American Journal of Public Health, 86*, 253–256.

Pierce, J. P., Gilpin, E. A., Emery, S. L., Farkas, A. J., Zhu, S. H., Choi, W. S., . . . Navarro, A. (1998). Tobacco control in California: Who's winning the war? An evaluation of the Tobacco Control Program, 1989–1996. *A report to the California Department of Health Services*. Retrieved March 2016, from http://libraries.ucsd.edu/ssds/pub/CTS/cpc00004/1996FullReport.pdf

Piper, M. E., Piasecki, T. M., Federman, E. B., Bolt, D. M., Smith, S. S., Fiore, M. C., & Baker, T. B. (2004). A multiple motives approach to tobacco dependence: The Wisconsin Inventory of Smoking Dependence Motives (WISDM-68). *Journal of Consulting and Clinical Psychology, 72*(2), 139–154.

Pomerleau, O. F. (1995). Individual differences in sensitivity to nicotine: Implications for genetic research on nicotine dependence. *Behavior Genetics, 25*(2), 161–177.

Pomerleau, O. F., Pomerleau, C. S., & Namenek, R. J. (1998). Early experiences with tobacco among women smokers, ex-smokers, and never-smokers. *Addiction, 93*(4), 595–599.

Prokhorov, A. V., Koehly, L. M., Pallonen, U. E., & Hudmon, K. S. (1998). Adolescent nicotine dependence measured by the modified Fagerstrom Tolerance Questionnaire at two time points. *Journal of Child and Adolescent Substance Abuse, 7*(4), 35–47.

Rohde, P., Kahler, C. W., Lewinsohn, P. M., & Brown, R. A. (2004). Psychiatric disorders, familial factors, and cigarette smoking: II. Associations with progression to daily smoking. *Nicotine and Tobacco Research, 6*(1), 119–132.

Rohde, P., Lewinsohn, P. M., Brown, R. A., Gau, J. M., & Kahler, C. W. (2003). Psychiatric disorders, familial factors and cigarette smoking: I. Associations with smoking initiation. *Nicotine and Tobacco Research, 5*(1), 85–98.

Rose, J. S., Dierker, L. C., & Donny, E. (2010). Nicotine dependence symptoms among recent onset adolescent smokers. *Drug and Alcohol Dependence, 106*(2–3), 126–132.

Sargent, J. D., Mott, L. A., & Stevens, M. (1998). Predictors of smoking cessation in adolescents. *Archives of Pediatrics and Adolescent Medicine, 152*(4), 388–393.

Shadel, W. G., Shiffman, S., Niaura, R., Nichter, M., & Abrams, D. B. (2000). Current models of nicotine dependence: What is known and what is needed to advance understanding of tobacco etiology among youth. *Drug and Alcohol Dependence, 59(Suppl. 1)*, S9–S22.

Shelef, K., Diamond, G. S., Diamond, G. M., & Myers, M. G. (2009). Changes in tobacco use among adolescent smokers in substance abuse treatment. *Psychology of Addictive Behaviors, 23*(2), 355–361.

Shiffman, S. (1984). Coping with temptations to smoke. *Journal of Consulting and Clinical Psychology, 52*(2), 261–267.

Shiffman, S. (1986). A cluster-analytic classification of smoking relapse episodes. *Addictive Behaviors, 11*, 295–307.

Shiffman, S., Gnys, M., Richards, T. J., Paty, J. A., Hickcox, M., & Kassel, J. D. (1996). Temptations to smoke after quitting: A comparison of lapsers and maintainers. *Health Psychol, 15*(6), 455–461.

Shiffman, S., & Sayette, M. A. (2005). Validation of the nicotine dependence syndrome scale (NDSS): A criterion-group design contrasting chippers and regular smokers. *Drug and Alcohol Dependence, 79*(1), 45–52.

Shiffman, S., Waters, A., & Hickcox, M. (2004). The nicotine dependence syndrome scale: A multidimensional measure of nicotine dependence. *Nicotine and Tobacco Research, 6*(2), 327–348.

Siegel, M., Albers, A. B., Cheng, D. M., Biener, L., & Rigotti, N. A. (2005). Effect of local restaurant smoking regulations on progression to established smoking among youths. *Tobacco Control, 14*(5), 300–306.

Song, A. V., Morrell, H. E. R., Cornell, J. L., Ramos, M. E., Biehl, M., Kropp, R. Y., & Halpern-Felsher, B. L. (2009). Perceptions of smoking-related risks and benefits as predictors of adolescent smoking initiation. *American Journal of Public Health, 99*(3), 487–492.

Stanton, A., & Grimshaw, G. M. (2013). Tobacco cessation interventions for young people. *Cochrane Database of Systematic Reviews, (8)*, CD003289.

Stanton, W. R., Lowe, J. B., Fisher, K. J., Gillespie, A. M., & Rose, J. M. (1999). Beliefs about smoking cessation among out-of-school youth. *Drug and Alcohol Dependence, 54*, 251–258.

Stanton, W. R., Lowe, J. B., & Gillespie, A. M. (1996). Adolescents' experiences of smoking cessation. *Drug and Alcohol Dependence, 43*, 63–70.

Sterling, K. L., Mermelstein, R., Turner, L., Diviak, K., Flay, B., & Shiffman, S. (2009). Examining the psychometric properties and predictive validity of a youth-specific version of the Nicotine Dependence Syndrome Scale (NDSS) among teens with varying levels of smoking. *Addictive Behaviors, 34*(6–7), 616–619.

Stone, S. L., & Kristeller, J. L. (1992). Attitudes of adolescents toward smoking cessation. *American Journal of Preventive Medicine, 8*, 221–225.

Strong, D. R., Kahler, C. W., Abrantes, A. M., MacPherson, L., Myers, M. G., Ramsey, S. E., & Brown, R. A. (2007). Nicotine dependence symptoms among adolescents with psychiatric disorders: Using a Rasch model to evaluate symptoms expression across time. *Nicotine and Tobacco Research, 9*(5), 557–569.

Strong, D. R., Kahler, C. W., Colby, S. M., Griesler, P. C., & Kandel, D. (2009). Linking measures of adolescent nicotine dependence to a common latent continuum. *Drug and Alcohol Dependence, 99*(1–3), 296–308.

Strong, D. R., Schonbrun, Y. C., Schaffran, C., Griesler, P. C., & Kandel, D. (2012). Linking measures of adult nicotine dependence to a common latent continuum and a comparison with adolescent patterns. *Drug and Alcohol Dependence, 120*(1–3), 88–98.

Sussman, S., Dent, C. W., Nezami, E., Stacy, A. W., Severson, H. H., Burton, D., & Flay, B. R. (1998). Reasons for quitting and smoking temptation among adolescent smokers: Gender differences. *Substance Use and Misuse, 33*, 2705–2722.

Sussman, S., Dent, C. W., Severson, H. H., Burton, D., & Flay, B. R. (1998). Self-initiated quitting among adolescent smokers. *Preventive Medicine, 27*, A19–A28.

Sussman, S., Sun, P., & Dent, C. W. (2006). A meta-analysis of teen cigarette smoking cessation. *Health Psychology, 25*(5), 549–557.

Tiffany, S. T., Conklin, C. A., Shiffman, S., & Clayton, R. R. (2004). What can dependence theories tell us about assessing the emergence of tobacco dependence? *Addiction, 99*(Suppl. 1), 78–86.

Turner, L., Mermelstein, R., & Flay, B. (2004). Individual and contextual influences on adolescent smoking. *Annals of the New York Academy of Science, 1021*, 175–197. doi:10.1196/annals.1308.023 1021/1/175 [pii]

Tyas, S. L., & Pederson, L. L. (1998). Psychosocial factors related to adolescent smoking: A critical review of the literature. *Tobacco Control, 7*(4), 409–420.

Upadhyaya, H. P., Deas, D., Brady, K. T., & Kruesi, M. (2002). Cigarette smoking and psychiatric comorbidity in children and adolescents. *Journal of the American Academy of Child and Adolescent Psychiatry, 41*(11), 1294–1305.

US Department of Health and Human Services. (1989). *Reducing the health consequences of smoking: 25 years of progress. A report of the surgeon General.* Bethesda, MD: National Institutes of Health.

US Department of Health and Human Services. (1994). *Preventing tobacco use among young people: A report of the Surgeon General.* Washington, DC: Author.

Vega, W. A., Chen, K. W., & Williams, J. (2007). Smoking, drugs, and other behavioral health problems among multiethnic adolescents in the NHSDA. *Addictive Behaviors,* 32(9), 1949–1956. doi:S0306-4603(06)00402-3 [pii] 10.1016/j.addbeh.2006.12.022

Vega, W. A., & Gil, A. G. (2005). Revisiting drug progression: Long-range effects of early tobacco use. *Addiction, 100*(9), 1358–1369.

Wagner, E. F., Brown, S. A., Monti, P. M., Myers, M. G., & Waldron, H. B. (1999). Innovations in adolescent substance abuse treatment and prevention. *Alcoholism: Clinical and Experimental Research, 23*, 236–249.

Wahl, S. K., Turner, L. R., Mermelstein, R. J., & Flay, B. R. (2005). Adolescents' smoking expectancies: Psychometric properties and prediction of behavior change. *Nicotine and Tobacco Research, 7*(4), 613–623.

Wang, M. Q., Fitzhugh, E. C., Green, B. L., Turner, L. W., Eddy, J. M., & Westerfield, R. C. (1999). Prospective social-psychological factors of adolescent smoking progression. *Journal of Adolescent Health, 24*(1), 2–9.

Westenberger, B. J. (2009). *Evaluation of e-cigarettes.* St. Louis, MO: US Food and Drug Administration. Retrieved from http://www.fda.gov/downloads/Drugs/Drugs/ScienceResearch/UCM173250.pdf

White, V. M., Hopper, J. L., Wearing, A. J., & Hill, D. J. (2003). The role of genes in tobacco smoking during adolescence and young adulthood: A multivariate behaviour genetic investigation. *Addiction, 98*(8), 1087–1100.

Wills, T. A., Resko, J. A., Ainette, M. G., & Mendoza, D. (2004). Smoking onset in adolescence: A person-centered analysis with time-varying predictors. *Health Psychology, 23*(2), 158–167.

Zhan, W., Dierker, L. C., Rose, J. S., Selya, A., & Mermelstein, R. J. (2012). The natural course of nicotine dependence symptoms among adolescent smokers. *Nicotine and Tobacco Research, 14*(12), 1445–1452. doi:10.1093/ntr/nts031

Zhan, Y., Cao, Z., Bao, N., Li, J., Wang, J., Geng, T., . . . Lu, C. (2012). Low-frequency ac electroporation shows strong frequency dependence and yields comparable transfection results to dc electroporation. *Journal of Controlled Release, 160*(3), 570–576.

Adolescent Alcohol Use

Tammy Chung *and* Kristina M. Jackson

Abstract

Alcohol is the substance most commonly used by youth. Problematic alcohol use can be considered a developmental disorder, which typically has its origins in an individual's genetic liability, temperament, and experiences in childhood and adolescence. To provide a context for the emergence of alcohol use in adolescence, this chapter briefly reviews biological substrates of risk that include genetic liability and processes of developmental maturation (e.g., puberty, brain development). The chapter then addresses the prevalence of alcohol use and alcohol-related problems in adolescence, trajectories of youth alcohol use, and internalizing and externalizing behavior pathways associated with adolescent alcohol use. Risk and protective factors influencing adolescent alcohol use are discussed as targets to guide developmentally informed prevention and intervention.

Key Words: alcohol, adolescent, binge drinking, trajectories, alcohol use disorder, risk factors, protective factors

Alcohol is the substance most commonly used by adolescents in the United States (Johnston, O'Malley, Bachman, Schulenberg, & Miech, 2014a; Substance Abuse and Mental Health Services Administration, 2013). For many youth, alcohol consumption signifies adult status and, particularly for older adolescents, has positive associations with celebratory and social events. Adolescent alcohol involvement, however, can derail or delay the achievement of milestones, such as high school graduation, and precociously hasten the onset of other signifiers of adulthood, such as pregnancy and parenthood (Brown et al., 2008). Early onset of alcohol use also robustly predicts subsequent development of alcohol-related problems (e.g., DeWit, Adlaf, Offord, & Ogborne, 2000; Grant & Dawson, 1997). Although the prevalence of alcohol-related problems peaks in young adulthood, the origins of these problems can typically be traced back to adolescence. The high personal, as well as social and economic, costs of underage drinking compel the coordination of prevention and intervention efforts across multiple levels and channels of influence (e.g., national drug control policy, schools and families) in order to reduce alcohol involvement in youth and to promote healthy transitions into adulthood.

The adolescent developmental period (roughly ages 12–18 years) is characterized by peak physical health, as well as increased risk for a variety of psychiatric conditions, such as depression and conduct problems, and initiation to substance use (Dahl, 2004; Giedd, Keshavan, & Paus, 2008; Paus, Keshavan, & Giedd, 2008). The rapid changes that occur in physical, cognitive, and affective domains during adolescence contribute to a drive for adult status and autonomy, increased intensity and lability of emotions, as well as elevated feelings of stress associated with the transition to adult roles and responsibilities. Physical maturation during adolescence also facilitates the expansion of a youth's social environment, which can lead to greater access to alcohol through, for example, increased opportunity to associate with older peers and obtaining a driver's license. Risk-taking behavior tends to increase in adolescence, and it occurs in the context of continuing maturation of self-regulatory ability, a phenomenon that has been compared to "starting the car without a skilled driver at the wheel" (Steinberg, 2008). This temporary, developmentally normative and on-going maturation of self-regulatory ability relative to social and emotional reactivity heightens risk for certain mental health conditions in adolescence, particularly when support systems (e.g., parental monitoring) are not available or are compromised (Dahl, 2004). These developmental changes are specific to adolescence and result in a convergence of increased risk and an expansion of opportunities to engage in substance use, particularly for subgroups of vulnerable youth.

This chapter takes a life-span developmental systems approach to understanding adolescent alcohol involvement. The life-span approach proposes that multiple systems, operating at multiple levels, across development, and historically over time, interact to influence adolescent alcohol use (Bronfenbrenner, 1979; Brown et al., 2008; Flay & Petraitis, 1994; Sameroff, 2000; Windle, 2010). Primary systems influencing alcohol use include the individual (e.g., genetic liability, neurocognition, sensitivity to alcohol), family (e.g., parental and sibling alcohol use), neighborhood (e.g., alcohol use among students at a school), country (e.g., national alcohol control policy), and historical time period (e.g., changes in national legal drinking age). These systems are organized in a nested, hierarchical structure (e.g., individual nested within family) and represent more proximal (e.g., individual factors) versus distal (e.g., neighborhood enforcement of underage drinking law) influences that interact with one another to determine risk for adolescent alcohol involvement. The life-span approach also recognizes variability across individuals in the onset and course of alcohol use, as well as in the timing and duration of contextual factors, such as co-occurring psychopathology (e.g., depression, conduct problems) and stressful life events. Development reflects a nonlinear process, which includes periods of continuity and gradual change, alternating with periods of discontinuous transformation (Masten, Faden, Zucker, & Spear, 2008). In this model, risk and protective factors interact dynamically to influence development. The life-span approach further specifies that the individual actively selects behaviors within the constraints and opportunities of the immediate environment (Windle, 2010). In brief, the life-span approach proposes a multisystem, multilevel, dynamic, and probabilistic model of person–environment transactions that influence the course of adolescent alcohol use.

Although the focus of this chapter is on adolescent alcohol use, a key task in reducing alcohol-related harm among youth involves the identification of *common versus substance-specific* mechanisms underlying the initiation, escalation, maintenance, and desistance from alcohol use. Addiction to alcohol and other drugs involves a common genetic diathesis (Goldman, Oroszi, & Ducci, 2006), engages a common neurocognitive reward pathway involving the mesolimbic dopamine system (Goldstein & Volkow, 2002), and results in similar clinical symptoms (American Psychiatric Association, 2013). Furthermore, adolescence is the common developmental period of risk for onset and escalation of use for more widely used substances (e.g., alcohol, tobacco, marijuana). These common characteristics provide the rationale for using a unified developmental approach to studying risk and protection across substances.

Important cross-drug differences, however, require investigation of substance-specific mechanisms influencing use. For example, US national drug control policy stipulates different legal ages of purchase for alcohol (age 21 years) and tobacco (age 18 years), and it currently deems marijuana an illicit substance, although several states have either decriminalized or legalized recreational marijuana use. Legislation reflects societal attitudes toward a substance, and it impacts availability, particularly with regard to licit versus illicit status and differences in legal purchase age for licit substances. Other substance-specific factors include, for example, specificity of pharmacologic effects, genetic risk associated with alcohol metabolism (e.g., Li, 2000), and alcohol-specific sites of action in the brain (e.g., Aryal, Dvir, Choe, & Slesinger, 2009). The similarities and differences between alcohol and other drugs have implications for understanding the common and substance-specific etiology of substance involvement, as well as informing the content of alcohol-specific interventions for youth.

Overview

Problematic alcohol involvement is a developmental disorder, which typically has origins in an individual's genetic liability, temperament, and childhood and adolescent experiences (Zucker, 2006, 2014). Alcohol involvement spans a continuum of severity ranging from no lifetime use, initiation, experimentation, occasional use, regular use, heavy use, alcohol-related problems, and alcohol use disorder. Transitions to higher levels of use tend to occur with increasing age, but progression is not inevitable, movement across levels of use (in both directions) is probabilistic, and rate of progression varies across individuals. In this developmental context, the chapter starts with a brief review of biological substrates of risk, focusing on genetic liability and processes of developmental maturation associated with adolescent alcohol use. Next, the development of alcohol-related cognitions and peak ages of risk for alcohol initiation are reviewed. The sections that follow summarize the prevalence and characteristics of adolescent alcohol use. After a review of cross-sectional prevalence data, results of longitudinal research on trajectories of adolescent alcohol use, and developmental subtypes of alcohol use are reviewed. Next, the prevalence of alcohol-related problems and alcohol use disorder in youth is summarized. Adverse consequences of adolescent alcohol use are also described. The chapter then discusses risk and protective factors influencing adolescent alcohol involvement. Among general risk factors, two major pathways of risk for heavy alcohol use, involving behavioral disinhibition (externalizing) and negative emotionality (internalizing), are described. These risk and protective factors serve as targets to guide prevention and intervention efforts. Finally, directions for future research are discussed.

Genetic Liability for Alcohol Involvement

Heritable influences account for roughly 40%–60% of the variance in risk for alcohol dependence (e.g., Heath et al., 1997; Li & Burmeister, 2009; Rietschel & Treutlein, 2013). Variability in risk across studies may be due to differences in phenotype examined (e.g., heavy drinking versus *DSM-IV* dependence), population variability (e.g., variation in allele frequencies across racial subgroups), and population-specific environmental factors (e.g., alcohol availability) (Falconer & MacKay, 1996; Lynskey, Agrawal, & Heath, 2010). Furthermore, alcohol use disorders represent complex and heterogeneous phenotypes, in which no single symptom is considered pathognomonic of the illness (Kalsi, Prescott, Kendler, & Riley, 2008). Genetic influence may be specific to alcohol (e.g., Li, 2000) or reflect liability to substance involvement more generally (Goldman & Bergen, 1998; Kreek, Nielsen, & LaForge, 2004). Alcohol-specific genetic liability generally involves genes associated with alcohol metabolism (e.g., ALDH2; Li, 2000; Morozova, Mackay, & Anholt, 2014) and response to alcohol

(e.g., low response to alcohol; Morozova et al., 2014; Schuckit, Smith, & Kalmijn, 2004).

Common genetic liability for substance involvement is thought to involve genes associated with brain reward pathways (e.g., dopaminergic system genes), which, in turn, tend to be linked with certain types of co-occurring psychopathology, such as conduct problems, and a high level of trait disinhibition (Kreek et al., 2004). Trait behavioral disinhibition (e.g., Dick et al., 2005; 2010), which is evident in childhood, prior to the onset of alcohol and other substance use, appears to provide a behavioral and psychological substrate for common genetic liability across various types of substance use (Dick et al., 2009a; Hicks, Iacono, & McGue, 2012; Tarter et al., 2003). In support of this hypothesis, genes associated with, for example, regulation of the serotonin (e.g., 5-HTTLPR, MAOA promoter), dopamine (e.g., DAT1, DRD4), and GABA (e.g., GABRA2) systems have been associated with both externalizing behaviors and alcoholism (Kreek et al., 2004). In addition, certain substances may share pharmacologically based pathways. For example, the frequent co-occurrence of alcohol and tobacco use suggests common genetic influence, particularly for these two substances (Koopmans, van Doornen, & Boomsma, 1997; Madden, Bucholz, Martin, & Heath, 2000) possibly due to a shared pharmacologic pathway involving nicotinic acetylcholine receptor genes (Ehringer et al., 2007; Hendrickson, Guildford, & Tapper, 2013).

Genetic influence on problem drinking appears to be stronger in adults (Goldman et al., 2006), compared to adolescents (Hopfer, Crowley, & Hewitt, 2003; Rhee et al., 2003), a developmental difference that may be related to greater environmental influence on use and milder severity of alcohol-related problems in youth, compared to adults. The extent to which genetic factors influence the initiation and progression of alcohol use differs across studies. Some studies have observed genetic influences on age of alcohol initiation (e.g., Sartor et al., 2009; Schlaepfer et al., 2008), whereas others suggest strong environmental influence on alcohol onset (e.g., Pagan et al., 2006; Prescott & Kendler, 1999). Compared to onset of use, genetic influence appears to be stronger for the transition to regular drinking (e.g., Fowler et al., 2007; Stallings, Hewitt, Beresford, Heath, & Eaves, 1999) and for the transition from regular use to alcohol dependence (e.g., Agrawal & Lynskey, 2006; Sartor, Agrawal, Lynskey, Bucholz, & Heath, 2008; Sartor et al., 2009).

Environmental factors, ranging from the availability of alcohol in the home to enforcement of underage drinking laws, have been shown to amplify or dampen genetic risk for alcohol involvement (Dick et al., 2009b). Thus, environmental context, including gene–environment correlation (e.g., niche-seeking propensity), influences the expression of genetic variation (Bagot & Meaney, 2010; Lynskey et al., 2010). Given the interaction of genetic variation with environmental context, behavioral and environmental approaches continue to provide a foundation for the prevention and intervention (Brody et al., 2013). In this regard, a microtrial approach, which examines gene x behavioral intervention interactions to better identify for "whom" and "how" interventions work, holds some promise (Brody et al., 2013).

Genetic research has used candidate gene and genome-wide association approaches to determine risk for substance involvement, based on a common disease–common gene variant model, in which commonly occurring conditions, such as alcohol dependence, result from additive or interacting effects of common genetic variants (McCarroll, Feng, & Hyman, 2014). However, the common variant approach has resulted in small effect sizes associated with common variants (e.g., odds ratio of ~1.5), which make replication of results difficult, and identification of genetic markers that do not appear to have functional significance (McClellan & King, 2010). Technological advances, including sequencing of an individual's entire genome, provide the opportunity for the identification of rare variants of severe effect on risk for addiction and other conditions (Gratten, Wray, Keller, & Visscher, 2014; McCarroll et al., 2014). Gene-hunting efforts will need to combine the study of common and rare variants, and employ systems biology methods (e.g., characterizing gene networks, analysis of "big data") and cross-disciplinary approaches to advance understanding of how combinations of genes dynamically interact in ways that correspond to "phenotypes" of interest (e.g., high negative emotionality) (McCarroll et al., 2014).

In addition, epigenetic effects, in which environmental factors (e.g., exposure to trauma, prenatal substance exposure) can have long-lasting and potentially heritable influence on genetic effects, without change to the nucleotide sequence, warrant further study (Bagot & Meaney, 2010; Harlaar & Hutchison, 2013). Epigenetic effects may help to explain plasticity of behavior in response to environmental factors, particularly reduced plasticity as the result of chronic drug exposure (Nestler, 2014; Tuesta & Zhang, 2014). In sum, genetic influences on biological pathways and processes leading to heavy substance use need to be considered in the context of epigenetic and environmental factors that modify genetic liability.

Developmental Maturation During Adolescence and Risk for Alcohol Involvement

Several biologically based aspects of development foster conditions conducive to alcohol use in adolescence: early pubertal maturation, continuing brain development, and adolescent sensitivity to drug effects. Increased knowledge of how these biologically based aspects of development influence risk for adolescent alcohol use provides the basis for the design and strategic implementation of interventions to reduce adolescent alcohol use.

The timing and pace of pubertal maturation have important implications for an adolescent's social environment and risk for early alcohol use. Specifically, early maturers may experience a dyssynchrony in development whereby the maturation of cognitive and interpersonal skills lags behind precocious physical development (Dahl, 2004). This "maturity gap" involves an increase in emotional intensity and lability, in the context of relatively immature cognitive control systems (Dahl, 2004). Another factor associated with pubertal maturation and risk for early alcohol use involves a shift in circadian rhythm and a normative adolescent preference for later bedtimes (i.e., delayed circadian rhythm of "night owls"). Aberrations in circadian rhythm (e.g., extreme delay in bedtime, sleep difficulties) may indicate dysregulation of a basic biological function (Hasler & Clark, 2013), which has been associated with risk for alcohol involvement (e.g., Pieters, Van Der Vorst, Burk, Wiers, & Engels, 2010a; Wong, Brower, Fitzgerald, & Zucker, 2004).

Some gender and ethnic differences in puberty-related risk for early alcohol use have been observed. For girls, in particular, early pubertal maturation can facilitate relationships with older male romantic partners, placing a girl in a situation that may be beyond her ability to effectively handle, such as refusing an alcoholic beverage (Amaro, Blake, Schwartz, & Flinchbaugh, 2001). Among boys, early physical maturation appears to be less of a risk factor for early alcohol use, compared to girls (e.g., Costello, Sung, Worthman, & Angold, 2007), but it can provide opportunities to associate with older, more deviant peers (Mendle & Ferrero, 2012). Also in contrast to females, for males, same-gender peers tend to foster initiation to substance use and delinquent behavior (Dishion, Capaldi, Spracklen, & Fuzhong, 1995). With regard to ethnic differences, despite generally earlier onset of puberty among Black, compared to White, youth (Sun et al., 2002), protective factors (e.g., less positive alcohol expectancies) appear to be operating among Black youth to account for their lower rates of alcohol use during adolescence (Chung, Pedersen, Kim, Hipwell, & Stepp, 2013). Given that gender and ethnicity moderate the impact of early pubertal maturation on risk for alcohol use, there may be different pathways of risk and protection among subgroups of youth.

Continuing brain development during adolescence includes reduction in cortical gray matter through processes such as dendritic pruning, and increases in cortical white matter and functional connectivity between brain regions (Blakemore, 2012; Giedd et al., 2006, 2008). In tandem with continuing development of brain structure, the ability to reason logically, make sound decisions, and process emotional information increases into young adulthood (Simmonds, Hallquist, Asato, & Luna, 2014). In addition, the mesocorticolimbic dopamine system undergoes alterations and includes a peak in dopamine binding during adolescence (Ernst, Pine, & Hardin, 2009; Spear, 2010), which may underlie adolescent sensitivity to reward relative to children and adults (Geier, 2013).

Developmental brain changes in adolescence result in an earlier maturation of neural systems associated with affective response (a strong motivator of behavior), relative to on-going maturation of cognitive control over behavior (Ernst et al., 2009). This normative developmental shift toward increased sensitivity to reward and social stimuli results in a developmentally specific adolescent increase in risk-taking and sensation-seeking behavior, such as substance use (Ernst et al., 2009). Because adolescents (particularly after age 14 years) appear to be comparable to adults in the logical assessment of risk based on tasks completed in a lab environment, the difference in risk-taking behavior may be due to developmental differences in the processing of real-world social and emotional cues (Geier, 2013; Reyna & Farley, 2006), and possibly greater impact of contextual cues on behavior in adolescence (Crone & Dahl, 2012). Critically, initiation and escalation of alcohol use tends to occur among peers, in an emotionally heightened environment that may compromise logical decision-making processes (Chein, Albert, O'Brien, Uckert, & Steinberg,

2011; Steinberg, 2008). With maturation, the prefrontal cortex increases efficiency in inhibitory control over limbic structures, such as the amygdala, which contributes to the general reduction in risk-taking behaviors in adulthood (Geier, 2013; Luna, Garver, Urban, Lazar, & Sweeney, 2004). The normative neurocognitive changes that occur during adolescence can have significant impact on early alcohol use, in the context of a social environment that is supportive of underage drinking.

Adolescents and adults differ in their sensitivity to alcohol's effects, suggesting an adolescent-specific period of risk for heavy episodic drinking. Alcohol effects follow a biphasic pattern, with positive or stimulant effects (e.g., feel energized, sociable) predominating as blood alcohol concentration increases to roughly .06%, after which point more negative or sedative effects (e.g., feel tired, sluggish, slurred speech) predominate. Animal model research indicates that adolescents, compared to adults, are less sensitive to the sedative effects of alcohol, which may serve as a cue to limit intake (Spear & Varlinskaya, 2005). Animal models further suggest that adolescents, compared to adults, are more sensitive to alcohol's stimulant and social facilitation effects, as well as to alcohol's effects on the disruption of spatial memory (Spear & Varlinskaya, 2005). A study of human adolescents reported attenuated sensitivity to alcohol's sedative effects (Behar et al., 1983), findings that were supported in a study using ecological momentary assessment to examine subjective effects of alcohol among adolescent (ages 15–19 years) problem drinkers (Miranda et al., 2014). In brief, adolescents' lower sensitivity to alcohol's sedative effects helps to explain the pattern of heavy episodic ("binge") drinking typically observed among adolescents in both animal models and humans (Spear, 2010).

Another example of a developmentally specific impact of alcohol, based on animal model research, involves "sensitization" to alcohol, particularly when alcohol use is initiated before or during adolescence. Animal model research suggests that early "sensitization" to alcohol can result in long-lasting changes that are associated with greater alcohol consumption into adulthood (e.g., McBride et al., 2005), possibly through long-term alteration of gene expression (e.g., Pascual, Boix, Felipo, & Guerri, 2010).

These biologically based aspects of development, involving early pubertal maturation, relative immaturity of cognitive control systems, and adolescent sensitivity to alcohol effects, foster conditions that are conducive to a developmentally specific peak in risk for initiation to alcohol and other substance use. These biologically based changes occur together with changes in the social environment, such as transitions in school environment (e.g., from junior high to high school, high school to college), exposure to older peers, greater independence from the family, and changes in social roles (e.g., dating, entering the workforce), which can further facilitate alcohol use. The biologically driven events that occur during adolescence, within a specific developmental social context, emphasize the importance of strategically timed interventions, possibly for high-risk subgroups (e.g., early-maturing girls), that support the development of cognitive control over behavior in an environment with limited access to alcohol.

Cognitive Precursors of Alcohol Use

Prior to the onset of alcohol use, cognitive precursors of alcohol use or alcohol schemas signal an individual's increasing readiness to initiate alcohol use (Lang & Stritzke, 1993). Some children, as young as age 3 years, have developed schemas for alcohol that, in part, reflect parental drinking behavior (Zucker, Kincaid, Fitzgerald, & Bingham, 1995). Patterns of alcohol use in the household, particularly parents' drinking behavior, play a key role in a child's early development of alcohol-related schemas and attitudes toward drinking behavior (Zucker et al., 1995). Particularly for children of alcoholic parents, transmission of risk may occur through heritable liability, as well as family socialization processes and access to alcohol in the household.

Alcohol schemas can be implicit (i.e., not directly accessible through conscious thought) or explicit. Much more is known about explicit, than implicit, alcohol expectancies. Explicit alcohol use expectancies refer to self-reported thoughts regarding the anticipated positive (e.g., feel relaxed) and negative (e.g., feel sad) effects of alcohol use (Dunn & Goldman, 1996). Alcohol expectancies are thought to be shaped by a child's observations of alcohol use in the immediate environment (family and peer use) and drinking contexts (e.g., family dinner, unsupervised party) that help to shape early alcohol schemas, and actual drinking experiences (Ouellette, Gerrard, Gibbons, & Reis-Bergan, 1999). Cognitive beliefs and attitudes about drinking also may be influenced by portrayals of alcohol use in the media (e.g., television, books, movies) (Roberts, Foehr, Rideout, & Brodie, 1999), including social media interactions

(Moreno et al., 2010). Research indicates that over 90% of films contain alcohol content (Sargent, Wills, Stoolmiller, Gibson, & Gibbons, 2006), and nearly 50% of G-rated movies have references to alcohol use (Thompson & Yokota, 2001). Most of these films portray favorable images of drinking and few depict hazards of drinking (Everett, Schnuth, & Tribble, 1998; Stern, 2005). Expectancies about alcohol's effects appear to account, in part, for the association between adolescent alcohol use and exposure to alcohol in movies (Wills, Sargent, Gibbons, Gerrard, & Stoolmiller, 2009).

With regard to possible social media influences on alcohol use, alcohol-related photos and postings positively correlate with self-reported alcohol use and problem drinking (Moreno et al., 2010; Moreno, Christakis, Egan, Brockman, & Becker, 2012; Ridout, Campbell, & Ellis, 2012). In addition, among adolescents, experimentally manipulated norms about drinking on social media sites predict willingness to use alcohol (Litt & Stock, 2011), and focus group research (Moreno, Briner, Williams, Walker, & Christakis, 2009) suggests that adolescents perceive alcohol references on social networking sites as representative of actual alcohol use.

During middle childhood and early adolescence, alcohol expectancies shift from predominantly negative to more positive (Dunn & Goldman, 1996, 1998; Hipwell et al., 2005). Likewise, through age 14, most youth tend to have a negative attitude toward drinking, and correspondingly, few report an intention to drink in the near future (e.g., Gaines, Brooks, Maisto, Dietrich, & Shagena, 1988). Even in the absence of a conscious intention to drink in the near future, some youth may be at risk for early alcohol use due to favorable images of alcohol users (Dal Cin et al., 2009), and a "willingness" to engage in alcohol use, should the opportunity arise (Andrews, Hampson, & Peterson, 2011). Starting in early adolescence, the shift to more positive alcohol expectancies and attitudes toward alcohol may be linked to physical maturation triggered by pubertal onset and transitions in school context (e.g., transition to high school). These developmental events can provide an adolescent with increased opportunity to affiliate with older youth, who may facilitate access to alcohol and model drinking behavior. Positive expectancies for alcohol use predict transitions across most stages of use, including initiation, regular use, and problem use (e.g., Christiansen, Smith, Roehling, & Goldman, 1989; Donovan, 2004). In contrast, negative expectancies appear to play a greater role in decisions to not use or to discontinue use (Cameron, Stritzke, & Durkin, 2003).

Implicit alcohol-related cognitions have been assessed, for example, using tasks that prompt an individual to report the first word that comes to mind when presented with an ambiguous term (e.g., "shot" can refer to a shot of liquor or gun shot) or that assess the strength of association between two concepts in terms of reaction time (e.g., Implicit Association Task), such that a shorter time indicates a stronger association (e.g., association between "alcohol" and "happy" versus "alcohol" and "sad") (Wiers et al., 2007). Implicit alcohol-related cognitions have been found to account for unique variance in alcohol use after controlling for explicit cognitions (Jajodia & Earleywine, 2003; Pieters, Van Der Vorst, Engels, & Wiers, 2010b; Thush et al., 2008). Implicit alcohol-related cognitions appear to have stronger associations with alcohol consumption among individuals with lower levels of working memory capacity or executive functioning (Pieters, Burk, Van Der Vorst, Engels, & Wiers, 2014; Thush et al., 2008). Both explicit and implicit alcohol-related cognitions have been associated with alcohol use, but their relative importance in relation to current and future drinking behavior may be moderated by individual differences in, for example, executive functioning.

Reasons for Abstaining or Limiting Drinking

Reasons for abstaining or limiting drinking also affect the decision whether or not to drink (Cox & Klinger, 2004; Epler, Sher, & Piasecki, 2009) and are particularly relevant for an age group that is initiating and experimenting with alcohol. Different types of motives are predictive of drinking quantity (fear of negative consequences) versus frequency (indifference, family constraints) (Stritzke & Butt, 2001). One study found that motivations to not engage in alcohol use were cross-sectionally associated with adolescent alcohol involvement, but failed to prospectively predict alcohol outcomes over and above measures of disinhibition, harm avoidance, and consumption (Anderson, Briggs, & White, 2013).

Initiation of Alcohol Use
Sipping and Tasting

Alcohol is typically the first psychoactive substance that an individual consumes (Kandel, 2002). Initial exposure to alcohol often involves sips or tastes of alcohol supervised by a parent or other adult in the context of a family event (e.g., dinner, celebration) or religious ceremony. Studies estimate that by age 10, roughly 10% of children have consumed alcohol (Donovan, 2004). Almost one third of 11- to 12-year-olds have sipped or tasted alcohol (Donovan & Molina, 2008), with the proportion of sippers escalating to 67% by age 12.5 years (Donovan & Molina, 2013).

Relatively little is known about correlates of sipping and tasting (Ward, Snow, & Aroni, 2009). Some research conducted in the United States suggests that childhood sipping and tasting is less often the result of a deliberate process of early socialization to alcohol use, or of a child's own propensity for conduct problems and deviant behavior, than a result of parental alcohol use, parental tolerance of a child's exposure to alcohol, and availability of alcohol in the home (Donovan et al., 2004; Donovan & Molina, 2008; Jackson, Colby, Barnett, & Abar, 2015). These household conditions could set the stage for a child's positive attitudes toward alcohol use, which are associated with early sipping and tasting (Donovan & Molina, 2008). Peer norms supporting drinking and lower school engagement also appear to be predictive of sipping in children (Donovan & Molina, 2008; Jackson et al., 2015). Importantly, sipping appears to be predictive of later alcohol use: Youth who reported sipping or tasting alcohol by age 10 were significantly more likely than nonsippers to initiate drinking (not just a sip or taste) by age 14 (Donovan & Molina, 2011). These findings suggest the utility of parent-based prevention efforts in childhood to delay drinking onset.

Peak Ages of Risk for Alcohol Initiation: "First Full Drink"

Peak risk for the initiation of alcohol use, generally defined as consuming at least one full standard drink (definition: a drink that contains ~14 grams of pure alcohol; for example: a can of beer [12 oz, ~5% alcohol content], a glass of wine [5 oz, ~12% alcohol content], a shot of 80-proof liquor [1.5 oz, ~40% alcohol content]), occurs during early adolescence, between ages 13 and 14 years (Faden, 2006). National surveys (i.e., Monitoring the Future [MTF], National Survey on Drug Use and Health [NSDUH], Youth Risk Behavior Surveillance System [YRBSS]) report that more than 40% of youth have initiated alcohol use by age 16 years, and 80% have initiated alcohol use by age 18 (Faden, 2006). Data from the 2011 Youth Risk Behavior Surveillance (YRBS) survey indicate that nationwide, one fifth of students in grades 9–12 drank alcohol for the first time before age 13 years (Eaton et al., 2012). These statistics are cause for concern, given that early onset of alcohol use, typically defined as starting before ages 14–15 years, has been associated with greater likelihood of using other drugs (McGue, Iacono, Legrand, Malone, & Elkins, 2001) and of developing an alcohol use disorder (Hingson, Heeren, & Winter, 2006).

Time trend data for age of alcohol onset indicate an increase in the age of alcohol onset in the past decade, largely due to legislation in the mid-1980s that raised the legal drinking age from 18 to 21 years (Faden, 2006). Time trend data also suggest some race/ethnic (e.g., non-Hispanic White youth had earlier onset than Black youth) and gender (e.g., males had earlier onset than females) differences in age of initiation, but in recent years, fewer differences in age of onset by race/ethnicity and gender have been observed (Faden, 2006).

Early Initiation as a Predictor of Drinking Progression

Although first use of alcohol (more than a sip or taste) prior to ages 14–15 years has been associated with greater risk for later alcohol use disorder (e.g., Grant & Dawson, 1997; Hingson et al., 2006), very early alcohol use (e.g., prior to age 10) is less predictive of progression to alcohol-related problems than use that starts in early adolescence (Gruber, DiClimente, Anderson, & Lodico, 1996). Very early initiation of alcohol use may represent an isolated, opportunistic episode of alcohol use, rather than the onset of an acutely escalating pattern of use (Jackson, 2010). The link between early onset of alcohol use and later problems appears to be developmentally specific, that is, more narrowly located to use that typically begins in adolescence (rather than childhood), when conditions, such as opportunities to drink and access to alcohol, are more conducive to progression of alcohol use (Sartor, Lynskey, Heath, Jacob, & True, 2007; Sher, 2007). The association between early initiation and adverse outcomes may be explained, in part, by a temperamental trait of behavioral deviance more generally (McGue et al., 2001), and other shared risk factors, such as a family history of alcoholism (Prescott & Kendler, 1999; Sartor et al., 2007).

In certain subgroups, early age of onset is associated with accelerated course of alcohol use. In particular, progression from age of first drink to onset of alcohol use disorder was more rapid among youth who started drinking at or after age 14, and among children of an alcoholic parent, compared

to matched controls (Hussong, Bauer, & Chassin, 2008a). Both developmental specificity of alcohol onset (onset age ≥14) and externalizing behavior predicted rapid escalation ("telescoping") of alcohol milestones (Hussong et al., 2008a). In addition, girls may show accelerated course of drinking in the interval from first drink to heavy consumption (Jackson, 2010). These findings indicate that early initiation in itself may represent an isolated opportunity to drink, and that the timing of initial use, in addition to temperamental and contextual (e.g., availability and access) characteristics, predict progression and rate of escalation of alcohol use. Efforts to reduce underage drinking can target delay in age of alcohol initiation. However, given the available data, interventions that target youth with externalizing behaviors (e.g., conduct problems) and that focus on halting the progression of alcohol use soon after initiation (Jackson & Sartor, 2014) are indicated.

Initial Response to Alcohol Effects and Risk for Progression of Use

Another factor, possibly genetically influenced, that predicts early progression of use involves an individual's subjective response to initial drinking episodes (e.g., Joslyn et al., 2008; Schuckit et al., 2007). Individuals who report needing to consume a larger number of drinks to feel sedative effects (e.g., sleepy) during early drinking episodes are hypothesized to have low response to alcohol, and they have been found to be at greater risk for alcohol problems (King, Houle, de Wit, Holdstock, & Schuster, 2002; Schuckit et al., 2007). In a sample of 12-year-old youth, prospective data indicated that report of alcohol effects during the first five drinking experiences predicted alcohol use at 2-year follow-up (Schuckit et al., 2008). In combination with a general decrease in sensitivity to alcohol's sedative effects during adolescence (relative to adulthood), individual differences in alcohol sensitivity also contribute to risk for a subgroup of youth. These findings suggest that low subjective response to alcohol during early drinking episodes in youth can signal risk for progression to heavy alcohol use.

Initiation of Alcohol Use in Relation to the Onset of Other Substance Use

According to the "gateway hypothesis" (Kandel, 2002), which proposes a fairly predictable, causal sequence of initiation to various substances, the earliest substances to be used are typically alcohol (peak ages of initiation: 13–14 years) and tobacco (peak ages of initiation: 12–13 years). By comparison, peak age for onset of marijuana is ages 13–17 years, and for other illicit drugs it is ages 16–18 years (Wagner & Anthony, 2002). Support for the causal model of initiation described by the gateway hypothesis has been debated (e.g., Morral, McCafrey, & Paddock, 2002; Vanyukov et al., 2012), because race/ethnic differences in the sequence have been observed (e.g., White, Jarrett, Valencia, Loeber, & Wei, 2007), and environmental factors constrain drug availability and accessibility (Degenhardt et al., 2010; Patton, Coffey, Carlin, Sawyer, & Lynskey, 2005). Research on substance use initiation highlights the effect of availability (e.g., raising the legal drinking age, availability in the immediate environment) on the sequence in which use is initiated across substances.

Prevalence of Adolescent Alcohol Use

In the past 20 years, alcohol use by adolescents in the United States has declined, with a peak in the early 1990s (Johnston et al., 2014a). Developmentally, the prevalence of alcohol use in childhood is low, increases between ages 12 and 21 years, stabilizes in young adulthood (ages 22–25 years), then declines thereafter (Johnston et al., 2014a; PRIDE surveys, 2014; SAMHSA, 2013). According to a large school-based survey (2009–2010) of youth ages 9–12 years, 4% of fourth graders, 5% of fifth graders, and 8% of sixth graders reported "some" alcohol use in the past year (PRIDE surveys, 2010). National survey data for 2012 indicate that 4% of 12-year-olds reported past-year use of alcohol ("full drink"), with a doubling of the prevalence at age 13 years (9%) and again at age 14 years (20%), and increasing prevalence of alcohol use through age 21 years (84%) (SAMHSA, 2013). This increasing prevalence of alcohol use into young adulthood coincides with a normative developmental increase in risk-taking and sensation-seeking behavior (Dahl, 2004), with individuals who show steeper increases in these constructs demonstrating greater substance involvement (MacPherson, Magidson, Reynolds, Kahler, & Lejuez, 2010).

At ages 22–25 years, 2012 national survey data indicate that alcohol use prevalence tends to stabilize at 83%–86%, with age 30 marking the start of a decline in the prevalence of past-year alcohol use with age (SAMHSA, 2013). The stabilization and reduction in alcohol use prevalence in the mid-20s generally appears to reflect a "maturing out"

of alcohol use (Lee, Chassin, & Villalta, 2013), as part of a developmental shift associated with, for example, establishing a career and starting a family.

Heavy Episodic or "Binge" Drinking

An important developmental difference in pattern of alcohol use is that, compared to adults, adolescents drink less often but typically consume a larger quantity per occasion (SAMHSA, 2013). Drinking in this age group tends to be opportunistic, whereby youth take advantage of a favorable environment (e.g., available alcohol; low parental monitoring) (Clark, 2004). Adolescents' generally lower sensitivity to alcohol's sedative effects, based on animal model (Spear & Varlinskaya, 2005) and some human research (Miranda et al., 2014), also may explain episodes of high-volume alcohol consumption in this age group. Most of the alcohol consumed among 12- to 17-year-olds involves episodes of heavy or "binge" drinking (Johnston, O'Malley, Miech, Bachman, & Schulenberg, 2014b; SAMHSA, 2013). A common definition of heavy episodic drinking (HED) or "binge drinking" is consumption of five or more drinks per occasion (e.g., Johnston et al., 2014b), although some HED definitions specify different quantity thresholds for males and females (i.e., 5+ and 4+, respectively; NIAAA, 2004). Among young children (ages 9–13 years), HED may be defined by 3+ drinks per occasion (Donovan, 2009). HED is a particularly risky pattern of alcohol use that has been associated with adverse effects on mental and physical health, violence, and crime (Miller, Naimi, Brewer, & Jones, 2007).

Beginning in the 1970s, adolescent alcohol use and HED in the United States declined, in part due to increased public awareness and efforts to reduce alcohol-related driving fatalities, and to the increase in legal drinking age from 18 to 21 years in the mid-1980s (Faden & Fay, 2004). Absolute prevalence of HED in youth, however, remains cause for concern. In 2012, national survey data (SAMHSA, 2013) indicated that 12% of 16-year-olds reported HED in the past 30 days, with the largest increases in prevalence of HED occurring between ages 17 (18%) and 18 (26%). Almost half (47%) of 21-year-olds reported HED in the past 30 days (SAMHSA, 2013). Similar to the prevalence of alcohol use, prevalence of HED levels off in the early 20s (SAMHSA, 2013). Longitudinal data also support observations of an increase in heavy-drinking prevalence during adolescence, followed by a decline in young adulthood (Johnston et al., 2014a).

Gender Differences in Alcohol Use

Although studies have robustly found that males drink more than females across all indices of alcohol involvement, in recent years, the gender gap in alcohol use prevalence has narrowed, with females catching up to males (Zhong & Schwartz, 2010). For example, starting in 2002, eighth-grade girls in the MTF study had higher 30-day prevalence of alcohol use compared to their male counterparts, a difference that continued through 2012, although this gender difference has decreased in recent years (11.6% females, 10.3% males) (Johnston, O'Malley, Bachman, & Schulenberg, 2013). Among 10th and 12th graders in MTF, however, males had higher 30-day prevalence of alcohol use compared to females (Johnston et al., 2013). In a 2012 national household survey, among 12- to 17-year-olds, the proportion of current (use in the past month) drinkers was similar for males and females (25.5% and 27.1%, respectively) (SAMHSA, 2013). Despite the narrowing gender gap in rates of alcohol use, heavy drinking still is more likely to be reported by males, than by females, particularly among older adolescents. For example, in a 2012 national school-based survey, 10th- and 12th-grade males were more likely than females to report HED in the past 2 weeks (e.g., among 12th graders: 27.2% vs. 19.7%, respectively) (Johnston et al., 2013).

Socioeconomic Status and Adolescent Alcohol Use

MTF data indicate that socioeconomic status (SES) is more strongly associated with alcohol use among younger adolescents than older adolescents (Johnston et al., 2014a). Specifically, among eighth graders, higher prevalence of alcohol use was found among lower SES youth. However, by 12th grade, higher SES youth surpass lower SES peers in prevalence of alcohol use and intoxication (Johnston et al., 2014a). These findings suggest that pathways of alcohol use differ by SES in terms of onset and escalation of drinking behavior.

Race/Ethnic Differences in Alcohol Use in the United States

Race/ethnic differences in alcohol use prevalence have been observed, and they may occur as a result of multiple factors (e.g., differences in socioeconomic status, neighborhood conditions, cultural norms regarding alcohol use, subgroup differences in sensitivity to alcohol) (Chartier et al., 2014). By the 12th grade, school-based survey data from 2012 indicated that White students had the highest annual prevalence of HED (25.7%), relative to Black (11.3%) and Hispanic (21.8%) students (Johnston et al., 2013). National survey data collected in 2012 also indicate that among 12- to 17-year-olds, White (14.6%), Hispanic (12.8%), and multiracial (11.7%) youth had the highest rates of alcohol use in the past month, followed by American Indian (10.0%) and Black (9.3%) youth, with Asian (4.9%) youth reporting the lowest prevalence (SAMHSA, 2013). Race/ethnic differences in the prevalence of alcohol use suggest subgroup differences in risk and protective factors for alcohol use (Chung et al., 2013; Tobler, Livingston, & Komro, 2011), and the potential utility of culturally tailored prevention and intervention efforts (Chartier et al., 2014; Gil, Wagner, & Tubman, 2004).

Cross-National Data on Adolescent Alcohol Use

Internationally, regardless of variation across countries in legal purchase ages, drinking to intoxication is more often observed in adolescents than older adults, and adolescents' pattern of episodic high-volume consumption tends to be associated with risk for a variety of alcohol-related problems (Ahlstrom & Osterberg, 2004). Countries with lower legal drinking ages tended to have higher rates of HED among youth (e.g., Simons-Morton, Pickett, Boyce, terBogt, & Vollebergh, 2010), suggesting the impact of national alcohol control policy on prevalence of adolescent HED. In this regard, lifetime and annual rates of alcohol use are higher in Europe compared to the United States and Canada (Beccaria & White, 2012). For example, data from participating countries in the 2011 European School Survey Project on Alcohol and Other Drugs (ESPAD) indicated that 37% of 15- to 16-year-olds reported being drunk in the past year, compared to 29% of 10th graders in the United States (Beccaria & White, 2012). ESPAD data, however, need to be interpreted in the context of differences in prevalence rates across participating countries, and methodological differences between European and US studies of alcohol use prevalence in youth (Beccaria & White, 2012). The narrowing gender gap in rates of alcohol use has been observed in both European and US surveys of adolescents (Beccaria & White, 2012). Cross-cultural similarities in developmental patterns of alcohol use point to common features of adolescence that may contribute to risk for HED in youth (Ahlstrom & Osterberg, 2004).

Contexts and Reasons for Early Adolescent Alcohol Use

Initial alcohol use episodes, particularly those that occur prior to adolescence, tend to occur in a family context (Donovan & Molina, 2008; Warner & White, 2003). By adolescence, however, research indicates that older youth were less likely to drink with parents or other adults, and more likely to drink in someone else's home or in a public area, such as a park or street, and with large groups of similar-age peers (Goncy & Mrug, 2013; Hellandsjo Bu, Watten, Foxcroft, Ingebrigtsen, & Relling, 2002; Mayer, Forster, Murray, & Wagenaar, 1998). These findings suggest that prior to early adolescence, prevention efforts would ideally focus on parenting behaviors associated with risk for early alcohol use, whereas during adolescence, interventions need to address both family and peer risk factors for adolescent HED (Goncy & Mrug, 2013; Lopez, Schwartz, Prado, Campo, & Pantin, 2008).

Through late childhood, reasons for alcohol use (e.g., social, coping reasons) are relatively undifferentiated (Kuntsche, Knibbe, Gmel, & Engels, 2005, 2006), and among inexperienced drinkers, may overlap with alcohol use expectancies. However, starting in early adolescence, two to three common reasons or motives for alcohol use (i.e., to enhance positive feelings, to facilitate social interaction, to cope with negative emotions) have been identified, with youth most often endorsing social or enhancement reasons for drinking (Kuntsche et al., 2006, 2014). Among younger adolescents (ages 11–13 years), social motives were more strongly associated with drunkenness than coping motives (Kuntsche et al., 2014). Among older adolescents, HED tends to be associated with endorsement of enhancement and coping reasons for use (Kuntsche et al., 2005, 2006), which may be associated with behavioral disinhibition and negative affect pathways of alcohol use, respectively. There is some indication that heritable influences (e.g., temperament) may be associated with predispositions to drink to cope with negative affect or to drink for social reasons (Mackie, Conrod, Rijsdijk, & Eley, 2011).

During adolescence, gender differences in drinking motives emerge, with boys showing a greater increase in social and enhancement motives compared to girls (e.g., Cooper, 1994), especially among older (ages 14–19 years) adolescents (Kuntsche et al., 2014). Although there are some cross-national differences in youth drinking motives, there appear to be few differences in drinking motives across ethnic groups within European countries (Kuntsche et al., 2006, 2014). Subgroup differences in drinking motives suggest the potential utility of motivation-based alcohol use interventions that target, for example, adolescent males with externalizing problems who endorse enhancement reasons for alcohol use versus adolescent females with symptoms of negative affect who endorse coping reasons for alcohol use (e.g., Conrod, Castellanos, & Mackie, 2008; Stewart et al., 2005).

Trajectories of Alcohol Use

Whereas cross-sectional studies indicate an age–school grade increase in alcohol use that begins in adolescence, longitudinal studies are essential to characterizing individual trajectories of alcohol use. Trajectory analyses have been used to identify developmentally normative and modal patterns of alcohol involvement, and to capture individual differences in alcohol initiation, the timing of turning points in use (e.g., escalation, desistance), and level of alcohol use. Trajectories also effectively illustrate the developmental concepts of multifinality, in which individuals with similar risk profiles have different outcomes, and equifinality, whereby different pathways lead to a similar outcome (Cicchetti & Rogosch, 1996, 2002). Ideally, trajectory analyses aid the identification of discrete developmental pathways of alcohol use, which can be linked to distinct, time-invariant (e.g., gender, ethnicity) and time-varying (e.g., parental alcohol use) etiologic mechanisms that influence the course of alcohol involvement (Zucker, 2006).

The prototypical alcohol use trajectories identified in studies involving community samples, which have followed youth into adulthood, include stable low, chronic high, adolescent-limited, and later onset trajectories with an escalating pattern of use into adulthood (Brown et al., 2008; Jackson, 2016; Jackson & Sartor, 2014; Maggs & Schulenberg, 2005). In community surveys, the modal trajectory for alcohol use during adolescence involves light or experimental to moderate use of alcohol. Some studies have identified a developmentally limited pattern of alcohol use, which involves a time-limited increase in alcohol use during adolescence, followed by a reduction in use during adulthood. Only a minority of individuals (generally <10%) in community surveys show a pattern of chronic, heavy drinking from adolescence into young adulthood. Some studies have identified an early-onset decreasing trajectory (<10% of youth), in which alcohol use declines during or shortly after the high school years (e.g., Schulenberg, O'Malley, Bachman, Wadsworth, & Johnston, 1996). The contrast between the early-onset decreasing trajectory and the chronic heavy drinking trajectory provides an example of multifinality, a contrast that implies the operation of distinct mechanisms (e.g., stability versus change in peer social environment; individual differences in the level and chronicity of externalizing behaviors) that underlie the divergence in course for these two groups. A trajectory representing late adolescent onset and rapid escalation to heavy drinking (<10% of youth) also has been identified (e.g., Schulenberg et al., 1996).

These prototypical alcohol use trajectories have substantial heuristic value in characterizing heterogeneity in the course of alcohol involvement, including the depiction of turning points in course, patterns of continuity and desistance, and the possible impact of time-specific effects on alcohol use. However, an important caveat is that the trajectory groups are only approximations of any individual's actual pattern of use over time, and the number and nature of the groups identified depend on, for example, the alcohol use indicator examined (e.g., frequency of alcohol use versus frequency of heavy drinking), ages and time-frames covered, and number of time points analyzed (Jackson & Sher, 2005, 2006, 2008; Sher, Jackson, & Steinley, 2011).

Some studies have examined the association of alcohol trajectory types with gender and race/ethnicity. With regard to gender, males are more likely to be represented in early-onset and chronic heavy alcohol use trajectories, compared to females (e.g., Chassin, Pitts, & Prost, 2002; Greenbaum, Del Boca, Darkes, Wang, & Goldman, 2005; Hill, White, Chung, Hawkins, & Catalano, 2000). Decreasing trajectory groups are more likely to be identified for females than males (e.g., Wiesner, Weichold, & Silbereisen, 2007; Windle, Mun, & Windle, 2005). The few studies that have examined race/ethnic differences in alcohol use trajectories have found that, in accord with cross-sectional epidemiologic data, White adolescents are more likely to be in chronic heavy drinking trajectory classes than Asian or Black youth, who are more likely to be in nonuser low alcohol use classes (e.g., Finlay, White, Mun, Cronley, & Lee, 2012; Tucker, Orlando, & Ellickson, 2003). Some studies have found that Black youth tend to have later onset of alcohol use, and reach peak rates of alcohol use

later, compared to White youth, although heavy alcohol use tends to persist longer during adulthood among Blacks, compared to Whites (Caetano & Clark, 1998; Jackson, Sher, Cooper, & Wood, 2002). These race/ethnic and gender differences in alcohol use trajectories suggest distinct mechanisms of influence on drinking patterns for specific youth subgroups.

More research is needed to identify specific developmental influences and contexts associated with "turning points" (e.g., escalation, desistance) in alcohol use trajectories (e.g., Hussong, Curran, Moffitt, & Caspi, 2008b; Sher, Gotham, & Watson, 2004). For example, transitions in school context (e.g., middle school to high school, and high school to college) have been identified as critical junctures of risk for alcohol use progression (Jackson & Sartor, 2014). These relatively abrupt changes in social context may involve extensive restructuring of peer relationships, which may provide an adolescent with greater access to alcohol or increased opportunities to engage in alcohol use (for those youth who select to associate with alcohol-using peers, or who may be influenced by deviant peers). Rapid changes (increase or decrease) in use may be tied to discontinuities in the adolescent's social environment and access to alcohol (e.g., placement in a controlled treatment environment).

Alcohol use trajectory types have been linked to distinct outcomes. Youth in alcohol trajectories reflecting no to low alcohol involvement into young adulthood generally report the best outcomes across domains such as educational achievement, interpersonal relations, mental and physical health, and employment status (e.g., Chassin et al., 2002; Tucker et al., 2003). In contrast, youth in chronic heavy alcohol use trajectories that extend into adulthood tend to report greater substance involvement (e.g., K. Hill et al., 2000) and more alcohol-related impairment in multiple areas of functioning, such as worse perceptions of one's own competence (e.g., Chassin, Pitts, & DeLucia, 1999), poorer physical health (e.g., greater likelihood of sexually transmitted infection), greater legal involvement, increased risk for mental health conditions (e.g., depression, conduct problems), and problematic interpersonal relations (e.g., Berg et al., 2013; Flory, Lynam, Milich, Leukefeld, & Clayton, 2004; Tucker, Ellickson, Orlando, Martino, & Klein, 2005; Windle et al., 2005). Particularly for youth in chronic heavy alcohol use trajectories, reciprocal (bidirectional) influences of heavy alcohol and other drug use on psychosocial functioning may exacerbate both alcohol use and adverse outcomes.

When alcohol use trajectories have been examined in relation to trajectories of other substance use in community samples, research suggests that the trajectories for alcohol, cigarette smoking, and marijuana use generally tend to change together over time, although there is typically a lag in onset of marijuana use relative to alcohol and tobacco (Jackson & Sartor, 2014). For example, abstainers and low users of one substance, such as alcohol, are likely to be abstainers and low users of other substances, such as tobacco and marijuana (e.g., Tucker et al., 2005). Likewise, chronic heavy drinkers are likely to show chronic patterns of tobacco and marijuana involvement (e.g., Chassin, Flora, & King, 2004). In addition, frequent alcohol and marijuana use trajectories tend to have similar correlates, such as high levels of externalizing behavior (e.g., Flory et al., 2004). However, exceptions in the generally parallel trajectories across substances have been observed. For example, a study found that a number of alcohol users reported abstinence from marijuana (Flory et al., 2004), and another study reported that a proportion of youth smoked cigarettes, but abstained from marijuana (Audrain-McGovern et al., 2007). Trajectory shapes across substances may be similar, but absolute level of use may differ across substances (e.g., stability of alcohol and marijuana use, but greater frequency of using alcohol relative to marijuana). Furthermore, although there is a tendency for alcohol and marijuana use to decline in adulthood, some individuals who cut down on these two substances do not reduce cigarette use (e.g., Labouvie, Pandina, & Johnson, 1991).

The tendency for substance use trajectories to track one another over time suggests common risks and shared underlying mechanisms across substances (e.g., Jessor & Jessor, 1977). However, subgroups of youth who report regular use of one substance (e.g., tobacco), but not another (e.g., marijuana), and continued use of a substance (e.g., tobacco), despite decline in use of others (e.g., alcohol, marijuana), again suggest that substance-specific mechanisms (e.g., licit versus illicit status, addictive potential, availability) also play a role in determining use of a given substance.

Developmental Alcohol Use Subtypes

Trajectory models depict multiple pathways or subtypes of alcohol involvement, which can be linked to distinct etiologic mechanisms influencing course (Zucker, 2006). Historically, two main subtypes or risk pathways (Type I/II, Cloninger, 1987; Type A/B, Babor et al., 1992) have been described, based primarily on work with adult alcoholic patients (Leggio, Kenna, Fenton, Bonefant, & Swift, 2009). The first subtype involves later onset and slower progression of alcohol problems, with moderate heritability (Cloninger Type I, Babor Type A); whereas the second involves early onset of alcohol problems, high heritability, and antisocial features (Cloninger Type II, Babor Type B).

A particularly heuristic model, based on consideration of epidemiologic panel data, integrates features of the subtypes described earlier and proposes six developmental subtypes (Zucker, 1994, 2006). Three subtypes are distinguished by co-occurring psychiatric conditions: *antisocial alcoholism*, which is similar to Type B and Type II; *negative affect alcoholism*, which is proposed to be more common in women and tends to have a later onset; and *developmentally limited* alcoholism, in which alcohol-related problems and externalizing behavior are limited to adolescence. Three other subtypes do not have significant psychiatric comorbidity but differ in course, which may be highly influenced by environmental factors: *isolated alcohol abuse* may occur in response to isolated stressors (e.g., job loss), *episodic alcoholism* may occur in response to intermittent stressors, and *developmentally cumulative alcoholism*, which bears some resemblance to Type A and Type I subtypes.

Features of Zucker's developmental alcohol subtypes have been supported by alcohol trajectory studies (e.g., number and shape of proposed trajectories, trajectory correlates), but work remains to be done to better specify distinct neurobiological pathways and developmentally specific events that influence the shape of the main trajectory subtypes in predicting individual differences in alcohol use. For example, research suggests that the GABRA2 gene, which has been associated with risk for alcohol dependence, is associated with elevated trajectories of externalizing behavior in adolescents, and that this association is reduced under conditions of high parental monitoring (Dick et al., 2009a). Increased understanding of distinct mechanisms of risk and their association with specific trajectory types and developmental turning points can inform the content and timing of selective prevention and intervention efforts for specific subgroups of youth.

Alcohol-Related Problems and Alcohol Use Disorder

Adverse Consequences of Adolescent Alcohol Involvement

Alcohol-related problems among adolescents can occur as a result of inexperience with alcohol (e.g., vomiting, alcohol poisoning, blackout), and because underage drinking is a status offense. Adolescents' tendency to consume a high volume of alcohol per occasion (HED), compared to adults, also increases risk for acute alcohol-related harm. One study of youth (average age, 16 years) found that among those who reported alcohol use in the past 6 months, 75% experienced an alcohol-related problem (e.g., 48% reported "did something I regretted the next day") (Windle & Windle, 2005). Although most alcohol-related harm is relatively minor (e.g., hangover), other harms include increased risk for sexually transmitted infection, alcohol-related violence, suicide, and mortality (e.g., driving when intoxicated) (Centers for Disease Control and Prevention, 2014; Miller et al., 2007). Underage drinking predicts unintentional injury (Hingson & Kenkel, 2004; Hingson, Heeren, Jamanka, & Howland, 2000), and violence and suicidality (Swahn, Bossarte, & Sullivent, 2008), even while controlling for factors such as demographics, family history of substance involvement, and normative influences. Importantly, adolescents do not necessarily perceive negative consequences as such, highlighting the potential utility of interventions such as personalized feedback and motivational interviewing techniques that target personal cognitive appraisals of one's consequences (Merrill, Read, & Barnett, 2013).

Adolescent alcohol use can interfere with the normative developmental tasks of adolescence that are necessary to negotiate the transition to adulthood (Maggs & Schulenberg, 2005). For many youth, substance use has adverse effects on peer relations and school performance, which in turn hinders the development of skills and behavior such as intellectual growth, social competence, and coping with stressors (Schulenberg & Maggs, 2002). Alcohol use may be seen as a "shortcut" to attaining adult status that eliminates the need to develop competencies necessary for healthy adult functioning (Brown et al., 2008). Yet it is important to note that use of alcohol during later adolescence may serve constructive functions with regard to peer bonding and identity formation (Schulenberg & Maggs, 2002).

Alcohol Use Disorder

The *Diagnostic and Statistical Manual of Mental Disorders*, fifth edition (*DSM-5*; APA, 2013) uses 11 symptoms to diagnose a substance use disorder (SUD), which can be classified as mild (2–3 symptoms), moderate (4–5 symptoms), or severe (6 or more symptoms). SUD symptoms include recurrent alcohol-related problems in interpersonal relations (e.g., arguments with family members due to drinking), school or work performance (e.g., poor academic performance due to drinking), and use in a hazardous situation (e.g., driving while intoxicated); as well as symptoms associated with a compulsive pattern of use, including tolerance, withdrawal, craving, difficulties in controlling use, spending a lot of time drinking, and experiencing repeated negative psychological or physical consequences due to use.

DSM SUD criteria were developed based primarily on clinical experience and research with adult alcoholic patients (Saunders & Schuckit, 2006), and they have been applied across substances, and to youth, with little to no modification of criteria or thresholds. Although there are common features of dependence across substances, cross-drug differences exist in the manifestation of certain symptoms. In addition, there are developmental differences in the likelihood of experiencing certain symptoms, such that alcohol withdrawal is less likely to be reported by adolescent, compared to adult, drinkers (Chung, Martin, Armstrong, & Labouvie, 2002). Alcohol-related symptoms (e.g., blackout, passing out) commonly reported by youth are underrepresented by *DSM-5* criteria, resulting in possible underestimation of alcohol-related problems as defined by *DSM-5* among youth. Despite some cross-drug differences in symptom presentation and the applicability of some symptoms across substances, *DSM-IV* and *DSM-5* SUD criteria provide a widely used operational definition of problematic substance use that has shown some reliability and validity in adolescent samples (Chung, Martin, & Winters, 2005). Revisions resulting in *DSM-5* SUD criteria, including replacing the legal problems criterion with a craving symptom, warrant study with regard to reliability and validity of *DSM-5* AUD diagnosis in adolescent drinkers.

Similar to the increasing prevalence of alcohol use into young adulthood, the prevalence of alcohol use disorder (AUD) increases with age through adolescence, reaches a peak in young adulthood (ages 18–20 years), remains high through ages 21–24 years, then declines thereafter (SAMHSA, 2013; Wagner & Anthony, 2002). In 2012, 3.4% of 12- to 17-year-olds met AUD criteria in the past year, compared to 14.3% of 18-to 25-year-olds. Many more youth experience alcohol-related problems but do not meet criteria for an AUD (Pollock & Martin, 1999). Up to an additional 17% of youth are estimated to be "diagnostic orphans," who reported substance-related problems but fall short of meeting criteria for an AUD (Chung et al., 2002). Of some concern, adolescents who report alcohol-related problems that are sub-threshold for a diagnosis of abuse or dependence may be at risk for progression to AUD (e.g., Harford, Yi, & Grant, 2010), and may benefit from early intervention to halt the escalation of alcohol-related problems. From 2002 to 2012, time trend data indicate that the prevalence of alcohol abuse or dependence among 12- to 17-year-olds has declined (from 5.9% in 2002 to 3.4% in 2012) (SAMHSA, 2013).

Gender has been associated with differences in the timing and type of alcohol-related symptoms reported (Wagner, Lloyd, & Gil, 2002). Girls tend to have an earlier mean age of AUD onset compared to boys (14.6 vs. 16.1 years, respectively; Lewinsohn, Rohde, & Seeley, 1996). In accord with this finding, among youth ages 12–17 years, 2012 national survey data indicate slightly higher prevalence of past-year AUD among females (3.6%), compared to males (3.2%). However, among those ages 18–25 years, the gender difference in past-year AUD prevalence reverses, such that prevalence is higher among males (16.7%), compared to females (11.9%), and remains higher among males through adulthood (SAMHSA, 2013). Higher AUD prevalence among adolescent females, compared to males, may reflect females' greater vulnerability to alcohol-related problems, given similar prevalence of alcohol use by gender at those ages.

With regard to race/ethnic differences in AUD prevalence, there has been a recent shift involving Hispanic youth, such that in the 2012 NSDUH survey, American Indian (4.6%) and Hispanic youth (4.1%) had higher rates of past-year AUD compared to White (3.7%) and Black (1.6%) youth; whereas in the 2008 NSDUH survey, Hispanic (5.2%) youth had slightly lower rates of AUD compared to White (5.6%) youth (SAMHSA, 2009b). The recent shift in the relative prevalence of past-year AUD involving Hispanic youth reflects a small, yet alarming, increase in AUD prevalence in this fast-growing ethnic subgroup in the United States that warrants monitoring to prevent further escalation.

Although individuals vary in the probability of symptom progression, and the speed of symptom development, there is some regularity in the emergence of AUD symptoms in youth. For many adolescents, the transition from initial use to the first alcohol-related problem occurs within 2–3 years after first use (Ridenour, Lanza, Donny, & Clark, 2006; SAMHSA, 2013). Among adolescent regular drinkers, alcohol-related interpersonal problems tend to emerge first, within the first 2 years of regular drinking, followed by other alcohol-related consequences and symptoms of dependence, and withdrawal generally emerging last (Wagner et al., 2002). Among adolescents with an AUD, the majority (55%–62%) had an AUD at young adult follow-up (Clark, DeBellis, Lynch, Cornelius, & Martin, 2003), suggesting that while some youth remit, others experience more chronic alcohol problems.

Neurotoxic Consequences of Alcohol on the Developing Brain

The adverse effects of chronic, heavy alcohol use on the adult human brain, particularly on frontolimbic and striatal structures and cognitive functioning, have been well documented (Oscar-Berman & Marinkovic, 2007). Much less is known regarding the effects of adolescent alcohol use on the developing human brain. A growing literature involving human adolescents suggests neurotoxic effects of heavy alcohol use (particularly "binge" or HED episodes) on brain structure, functioning, and cognition (Hermens et al., 2013; Jacobus & Tapert, 2013; Maurage, Petit, & Campanella, 2013). For example, regular alcohol use in mid- to late adolescence has been associated with deviations from normative brain structural development (Luciana, Collins, Muetzel, & Lim, 2013). Heavy alcohol use has been associated with reduced hippocampal volume (De Bellis et al., 2000; Medina et al., 2008; Nagel, Schweinsburg, Phan, & Tapert, 2005) and damage to white matter tracts (McQueeny et al., 2009).

Adolescent heavy drinkers also tend to show subtle impairments in cognitive functioning (e.g., Schweinsburg, McQueeny, Nagel, Eyler, & Tapert, 2010; Tapert & Schweinsburg, 2005; White & Swartzwelder, 2005) and protracted effects on cognition over time (Brown, Tapert, Granholm, & Delis, 2000; Tapert & Brown, 1999). Among young adults whose total alcohol quantity in a week was similar, but who differed in dose per occasion (i.e., "moderate": 3–5 drinks 5–7 times per week [15–29 drinks/week] versus "binge": 5–12 drinks 2–3 times per week [15–29 drinks/week]), "binge" drinkers had greater impairments indicated by ERPs during a cognitive task than "moderate" drinkers (Maurage et al., 2012), suggesting specific risks associated with a "binge" drinking pattern. Importantly, alcohol effects on adolescent brain structure and functioning may contribute to impaired control over alcohol use, potentially exacerbating alcohol's neurotoxic effects (Clark, Thatcher, & Tapert, 2008).

Although these findings are suggestive of alcohol's effects on the developing human brain, the extent to which these deficits or impairments existed prior to heavy drinking, and were exacerbated by heavy alcohol and other substance use, warrants further study. Prospective, naturalistic, longitudinal research is needed to investigate the extent to which exposure to alcohol, in terms of timing, dose, and duration, impacts the developing human brain and cognitive functioning during adolescence. In this regard, the multisite National Consortium on Alcohol and Neurodevelopment in Adolescence (NCANDA) study (Brown et al., 2015) will provide a prospective examination of the possible effects on alcohol on the developing brain.

Risk, Promotive, and Protective Factors

Risk factors (e.g., substance-using peers) predict onset and progression of use, whereas promotive factors represent the more positive part of the risk factor continuum (e.g., non-substance-using peers) (Sameroff, 2000). Protective factors (e.g., parental monitoring) act as modifiers (or "moderators") that increase or decrease relative risks (Sameroff, 2000). Models of risk, promotive, and protective factors that predict adolescent substance use cover phenomena and contexts ranging from "neurons to neighborhoods" (Shonkoff & Phillips, 2000). Some predictors may be *specific* to a certain substance (e.g., positive attitudes toward alcohol use), whereas others may increase risk or protection across substances more *generally* (e.g., parental neglect). The primary domains or systems of influence include the individual (e.g., genetic liability, prenatal substance exposure), family (e.g., parental substance use), and broader social environment (e.g., peers, school, neighborhood, media). These domains may interact with one another over time in a cascade model of risk (e.g., Masten et al., 2005).

Factors influencing substance use are organized in a *hierarchical, nested structure* (Wilcox, 2003). Interacting systems (e.g., an individual nested within a family) operate at *multiple levels* in influencing an adolescent's risk for substance involvement (e.g., national underage drinking legislation influences rates of adolescent drinking, which, in turn, influences a youth's norms for teenage drinking behavior). The nested nature of influences on substance use can result in greater stability and clustering of risk factors across levels of influence for a subgroup of youth (Zucker, 2006). For example, an adolescent living with an alcoholic parent may have greater access to alcohol, and this family may live in a neighborhood with erratic enforcement of public drunkenness and underage drinking laws. Risks also can cluster within a system (e.g., family system: parental alcoholism, modeling of drinking behavior, access to alcohol in the home). The study of *macro-* (e.g., prevalence of alcohol use in school) and nested *micro-environmental effects* (e.g., alcohol use by household members) on an adolescent's risk for alcohol use also needs to take into account niche-seeking behavior, that is, an individual's tendency to actively seek out certain environments and peers (Patrick, Schulenberg, Maggs, & Maslowsky, 2014). The nested, hierarchical structure of risk suggests a concentration of risk in a subgroup of youth, who may benefit from early, targeted intervention.

Models of risk and protection also make a distinction between more *proximal and distal influences*, and recognize dynamic relations among risk and protection across development. More proximal factors typically involve those related to the individual (e.g., attitudes toward substance use) and are generally more strongly predictive of use than more distal social (e.g., family, peer group) and neighborhood contexts within which the adolescent is nested. Due to the nested structure of risk, distal factors can influence proximal factors, and the impact of distal factors on substance use can be mediated or moderated by proximal factors.

As a further layer of complexity, risk and protective factors *interact dynamically* over time to influence adolescent substance use. For example, risk and protective factors can *change over time* (e.g., parental monitoring may decrease with age; exposure to risk domains tends to increase with age, broadening from a family focus to greater influence of peer and neighborhood contexts), can have *developmentally specific effects* (e.g., becoming a parent as a teenager versus in adulthood has different effects on alcohol use; Little, Handley, Leuthe, & Chassin, 2009) or *persistent effects* (e.g., sequelae of sexual or physical abuse), can be *differentially salient* at certain points in development (e.g., increasing salience of peers, relative to family, with age; Newcomb, 1995), and can *reciprocally influence* one another (e.g., reciprocity of negative affect expressed by alcoholic fathers and offspring; Eiden, Leonard, Hoyle, & Chavez, 2004). The factors that predict transitions between levels of use (i.e., increase or decrease) may differ (e.g., social reasons for use may predict early onset of use, whereas coping reasons for use may predict progression to heavy use; Cooper et al., 2008). Among youth who have experienced adversity (e.g., poverty, trauma), increasing attention has been paid to factors associated with "resilience" and positive outcomes, with some evidence indicating that family-strengthening interventions can facilitate positive youth outcomes (e.g., Kumpfer & Summerhays, 2006). In brief, the timing, sequencing, chronicity (i.e., frequency, duration), and interaction of risk and protective factors over time can impact the course of substance use.

Most risk factors for substance use initiation tend to emerge immediately prior to and peak in adolescence, with a decline in the number of new risk factors following adolescence (e.g., Soldz & Cui, 2002), again pointing to the developmental specificity of risk for substance use. The *cumulative number and duration* of risk factors, more than any specific type of risk factor, predicts level of substance involvement in adolescents (e.g., Cleveland, Feinberg, Bontempo, & Greenberg, 2008; Hawkins et al., 1997). However, similar risk exposure can result in different outcomes, pointing to the importance of protective, buffering factors as moderators of risk effects (Masten et al., 2008). Gender and race/ethnic differences in the type, timing, and operation of risk and protective factors also need to be considered in understanding etiology and enhancing intervention efforts. For example, although Black youth are more likely to be exposed to contextual risk factors (e.g., neighborhood disorganization, lower socioeconomic status), they are less likely to engage in alcohol use, compared to White youth, who are more likely to report more proximal individual and interpersonal risk factors that increase risk for alcohol and other drug use (Chung, Hipwell, Loeber, White, & Stouthamer-Loeber, 2008; Chung, White, Hipwell, Stepp, & Loeber, 2010; Chung et al., 2013; Wills, Gibbons, Gerrard, & Brody, 2000). Subgroup differences highlight how mechanisms of risk differ depending on characteristics such as race/ethnicity and gender.

For some youth, a cascading pattern of risk can emerge, in which a prior risk factor may increase the likelihood of experiencing other types of risk; and beyond the cumulative effects of risk, the timing, duration, and chronicity of risk factors influence outcomes (Cox, Mills-Koonce, Propper, & Gariepy, 2010; Masten et al., 2005). For example, genetic liability to heavy substance use may be expressed in the context of prenatal substance exposure, which subsequently increases risk for early difficult temperament and subtle impairments in neurocognitive functioning, depending on the timing and degree of prenatal exposure (Spadoni, McGee, Fryer, & Riley, 2007). A test of a developmental risk cascade model in youth followed from pre-kindergarten through 12th grade examined temporally specific (i.e., childhood, adolescence) ways in which multiple risk domains (e.g., biological factors, family and peer environment, conduct problems) interacted sequentially and dynamically over time to predict early onset of substance use (Dodge et al., 2009). Cascade model research suggests multiple modest effects across risk domains, the importance of early developmental processes on outcomes, and the identification of potential targets for intervention in each domain at certain points in development (Dodge et al., 2009; Lynne-Landsman, Bradshaw, & Ialongo, 2010; Sitnick, Shaw, & Hyde, 2014).

General Risk Factors for Substance Use

Most of the risk and protective factors that influence the course of alcohol use also generally predict risk for other types of substance involvement (e.g., Elkins, McGue, & Iacono, 2007; Gillespie, Neale, Jacobson, & Kendler, 2009; Hawkins, Catalano, & Miller, 1992). Cross-drug similarities in risk and protection suggest a common, rather than substance-specific vulnerability to substance use. The following section briefly reviews factors in domains representing the individual, family, and broader social environment (e.g., peers, school, media) that act as general risk factors for adolescent substance involvement.

Among factors in the individual domain, genetic liability, prenatal substance exposure, temperament and co-occurring psychopathology, neurocognitive functioning, and response to stressful life events represent key influences on substance use trajectories. Efforts are underway to characterize pathways of risk for substance involvement that originate in biological processes (e.g., genetic influence on response to alcohol), which are then linked to neurocognitive mechanisms (e.g., activation of the mesolimbic dopamine system in the brain in response to reward) and broader psychological constructs (e.g., temperament) (e.g., Schumann et al., 2010; Whelan et al., 2014; Zucker, 2014).

Early difficult temperament, typically indicated by childhood problems in self-regulation of behavior and emotion (e.g., Tarter et al., 2003), is a key individual risk factor that is hypothesized to precede the emergence of two main pathways of risk for early substance use: externalizing (e.g., behavioral undercontrol, disinhibition) and internalizing (e.g., negative emotionality, depression and anxiety) pathways to heavy alcohol use (e.g., King, Iacono, & McGue, 2004; Sher & Gotham, 1999). In adolescent samples, greater novelty seeking and behavioral disinhibition have been robustly associated with problematic alcohol and drug use trajectories (e.g., Chassin et al., 2002, 2004; Jackson & Sher, 2005; Zucker, Heitzeg, & Nigg, 2011). Although the association between externalizing symptoms and alcohol involvement is robust (Iacono, Malone, & McGue, 2008), externalizing behavior is a heterogeneous construct, which needs to be parsed into more genetically and neurobiologically informative components in relation to substance use (Dick et al., 2010). A greater orientation to novelty seeking, which is often associated with externalizing behavior, also may predispose a youth to more positive attitudes toward and willingness to engage in substance use (Smith & Anderson, 2001). Hicks and colleagues (2010) propose that this pathway of behavioral disinhibition is expressed as disruptive behaviors in childhood, followed by early onsetting and rapidly progressing substance use and antisocial behavior in adolescence, and ultimately manifesting itself as substance use disorders and antisocial personality disorder in adulthood.

The second main pathway of risk, the internalizing pathway, proposes an association between negative emotionality and alcohol involvement (Hussong, Jones, Stein, Baucom, & Boeding, 2011). However, findings have been mixed, with some studies reporting an association between negative affectivity and course of adolescent alcohol involvement (e.g., Colder, Campbell, Ruel, Richardson, & Flay, 2002), and other studies not finding an association (e.g., Brook, Whiteman, Gordon, Nomura, & Brook, 1985; Stice, Myers, & Brown, 1998). Further research is needed to test specific mechanisms underlying the negative affect pathway (e.g., depression reduces risk by limiting contact with drinking peers; Capaldi, Stoolmiller, Kim, & Yoerger, 2009), and the magnitude of the negative affect association with alcohol involvement in specific subgroups (e.g., females; Marmorstein,

2009). For a more extensive review of the evidence for this pathway, see the chapter by Hussong in this volume (Hussong et al, Chapt. 15). In addition, other types of psychiatric comorbidity (Armstrong & Costello, 2002), which may emerge in adolescence (e.g., binge eating, sequelae of trauma), also can influence the course of adolescent substance use (e.g., Clark et al., 2003). In youth with both externalizing and internalizing symptoms, the syndromes appear to have an additive effect on risk for substance involvement (e.g., Marmorstein, 2009; Tarter et al., 2003), although more complex relations between internalizing and externalizing features across development are possible and need to be tested (Hussong et al., 2011).

Deficits in neurocognitive functioning are closely tied to behavioral and emotional dysregulation, and represent a different level of analysis of individual risk for alcohol use. Impairment and developmental delays in neurocognitive functioning (e.g., attentional control, inhibitory response, working memory) have been identified as a risk factor for substance use (e.g., Tarter et al., 2003) and consequence of heavy use (Jacobus & Tapert, 2013). Specifically, youth at high risk for substance use due to parental substance use disorder demonstrate impairments in executive cognitive functioning (e.g., effective inhibition of response, cognitive flexibility in shifting a mental set, ability to plan and follow-through on goal completion) prior to substance use (e.g., Heitzeg, Nigg, Yau, Zubieta, & Zucker, 2010; Nigg et al., 2006). These deficits appear to be related primarily to facets of impulsivity, which include response inhibition (Nigg et al., 2006), dysregulation of reward circuitry; and to deficits in affect regulation (e.g., S. Hill, Tessner, Wang, Carter, & McDermott, 2010). In addition, reduced P300 amplitude, an indicator of attention allocation capacity, has been found in offspring of an alcoholic parent and youth with externalizing symptoms (Hill, Shen, Lowers, & Locke, 2000; Iacono, Malone, & McGue, 2003; Porjesz et al., 2005). Other work suggests that deficits in social information processing may indicate impairment in emotional regulation among high-risk youth (e.g., Heitzeg, Nigg, Yau, Zubieta, & Zucker, 2008). These types of neurocognitive impairment may predict poor school performance, signaling risk for substance use (Hawkins et al., 1992).

Although stressful life events and trauma can be considered environmental events, an individual's reaction to stress is subjective, and depends on the nature, timing (e.g., early versus late adolescence), frequency and severity, and duration of a stressor. Robust associations between experience of physical and sexual trauma with risk for substance use (e.g., Clark et al., 2003), as well as heavy drinking trajectories into young adulthood (e.g., Shin, Miller, & Teicher, 2013), have been identified. Chronic child adversities, and particularly parental criminal behavior, are associated with alcohol use among 12- to 18-year-olds (Benjet, Borges, Medina-Mora, & Mendez, 2013). Alcohol and other substances may be used to reduce negative affect resulting from trauma (Hussong et al., 2011). Early use of substances to regulate emotions, however, can result in disrupted or delayed development of more effective coping responses.

Family factors (beyond heritable risk, discussed earlier) that can influence the course of adolescent substance use include, for example, household composition (e.g., single-parent household; step-parent; step-, half-, and full siblings), parental psychopathology (e.g., family history of addiction, antisociality in father, depression in mother), family environment (e.g., ongoing conflict and strain, domestic violence, sibling substance use), and parenting behaviors (e.g., low parental monitoring, inconsistent discipline) (Hawkins et al., 1992; Windle et al., 2008). Alcohol-specific family risk factors are reviewed next. With regard to parenting behavior, greater parental neglect, less monitoring and supervision, lower warmth, inconsistent or lax discipline (including tolerance of adolescent substance use), and punishing discipline style have been associated with increased risk for youth substance involvement (Windle et al., 2008). Importantly, parenting behavior in childhood may have downstream effects on an adolescent's peer selection and decision-making processes. As noted earlier, the correlated nature of familial risk factors (e.g., parental psychopathology, less consistent supervision, parental neglect) suggests a high concentration of risk in a subgroup of adolescents.

A youth's social environment also includes relations with peers, exposure to media, as well as school, neighborhood, and national environmental contexts that influence an individual's norms and attitudes toward substance use. In particular, an adolescent's perceptions of peer substance use robustly predict an adolescent's own substance use (Hawkins et al., 1992). By adolescence, peer substance use is generally a more robust predictor of substance use than family factors (e.g., Bush, Weinfurt, & Iannotti, 1994; Patrick & Schulenberg, 2010). Youth with a high clustering of familial risk for substance use

may become more reliant on peer relations as a potential source of social support (Fuligni & Eccles, 1993), but they also may be more likely to associate with deviant peers, who increase risk for substance use (Fergusson, Swain-Campbell, & Horwood, 2002). Many underage youth participate in social networks that include of-age youth (Gruenewald et al., 2010), who can facilitate access to and availability of substances (e.g., tobacco, alcohol). In addition, reduced parental monitoring may permit association with deviant peers, which in turn is associated with substance use and escalation (Chassin, Pillow, Curran, Molina, & Barrera, 1993).

Peer influence may facilitate youth alcohol use through multiple mechanisms that include peer selection, various forms of peer influence such as modeling drinking behavior or striving to match a peer's drinking behavior, and social facilitation effects of alcohol use (Patrick et al., 2014). In general, there is some evidence that high-risk youth select deviant youth as peers, and through a process of reciprocal socialization reinforce one another's positive attitudes toward substance use (Curran, Stice, & Chassin, 1997; Parra, Sher, Krull, & Jackson, 2007). This selection and reinforcement can include online peer relations through social media (Huang, Soto, Fujimoto, & Valente, 2014). An adolescent's close friends play an important role in shaping attitudes and norms regarding substance use, particularly among youth residing in an unhealthy family environment, who may look outside the family for support (Hoffmann & Su, 1998). Peer influence may be particularly salient in the context of unstructured leisure activities, which tend to be poorly supervised and provide opportunities for experimentation with alcohol and other substances (Trainor, Delfabbro, Anderson, & Winefield, 2010).

As relatively more distal influences, media exposure, and school and neighborhood contexts also play roles in determining youth risk for alcohol use. Mass media (e.g., TV channels aimed to youth and young adults, movies, magazines, websites, music) has been described as a "super peer" that provides information on norms and contexts for alcohol and other drug use (Anderson, DeBrujn, Angus, Gordon, & Hastings, 2009). Of some concern, the negative consequences associated with alcohol use are rarely depicted (Stern, 2005), which can leave the impression of substance use as a generally "risk-free" activity. Media portrayals of substance use, particularly for alcohol, can contribute to overestimation of peer substance use. Research supports social influence and affiliation with substance-using peers as mediators of the association between movie exposure and alcohol use (Song, Ling, Neilands, & Glantz, 2007; Wills et al., 2009); this seems particularly true for the alcohol use of friends (versus "kids your age") (Dal Cin et al., 2009). Alternatively, mass media also can effectively provide important corrective information regarding substance use norms and risks associated with use (e.g., Perkins, Linkenbach, Lewis, & Neighbors, 2010).

School-level effects on substance use include findings that a school environment in which the majority of youth disapprove of heavy drinking is associated with lower rates of alcohol use (Kumar, O'Malley, Johnston, Schulenberg, & Bachman, 2002), and similarly, that schools with fewer substance users provide less opportunity for students to pick niches that provide exposure to substance use (Cleveland & Wiebe, 2003). Substance use also may be affected by neighborhood-level economic deprivation (Buu et al., 2009; Jones-Webb, Snowden, Herd, Short, & Hannan, 1997), with youth in disadvantaged neighborhoods having a greater likelihood of being offered alcohol (Crum, Lillie-Blanton, & Anthony, 1996). For example, youth living in zip codes with lower median household income reported greater drinking frequency relative to youth living in other zip codes (Chen, Grube, & Remer, 2010). Similarly, youth substance use, alcohol dependence, and alcohol and drug arrests are associated with neighborhood disorganization (Duncan, Duncan, & Strycker, 2002; Winstanley et al., 2008). Disorganized neighborhoods with impoverished social and physical community resources may not be able to exert social controls over youth problem behaviors (Buu et al., 2009). In sum, these findings suggest the potential impact of school, neighborhood, and societal contexts on shaping norms and potentially limiting opportunities for youth to engage in substance use.

Alcohol-Specific Risk Factors

In addition to more general risk for substance use, alcohol-specific risk factors in each risk domain (i.e., individual, family, and broader social environment) impact an adolescent's drinking trajectory. For example, a family history of alcoholism may contribute to alcohol-specific risk through genetic liability, and risks associated with parental alcohol use (e.g., availability of alcohol in the home, modeling of drinking behavior, shaping a child's attitudes toward alcohol, providing norms favoring alcohol use). Once alcohol consumption starts, genetic liability may manifest in an individual

through low initial sensitivity to sedative effects of alcohol, a risk factor for progression to heavy drinking (e.g., Schuckit et al., 2007). Alternatively, individuals with reduced ability, due to genetic liability (ALDH), to efficiently metabolize alcohol may be at lower risk for heavy drinking (Li, 2000). Greater positive expectancies related to alcohol use (e.g., feel happy when drinking) predict alcohol use in youth (e.g., Christiansen et al., 1989; Hipwell et al., 2005; Schell, Martino, Ellickson, Collins, & McCaffrey, 2005), whereas reporting more reasons for abstaining or limiting drinking predicts less drinking behavior in youth (Cox & Klinger, 2004; Epler et al., 2009). Some research suggests that explicit alcohol expectancies may be modifiable, and they can be targeted for intervention, but effects may not be sustained over time (Scott-Sheldon, Carey, Elliott, Garey, & Carey, 2014).

Adolescent alcohol use is highly related to a greater number of alcohol-using friends (e.g., Curran et al., 1997), and peer encouragement and tolerance of alcohol use (Li, Duncan, Duncan, & Hops, 2001). In fact, growth in alcohol use over adolescence tends to closely track changes in adolescents' perceptions of peer alcohol use (e.g., Capaldi et al., 2009; Ennett et al., 2008; Martino, Ellickson, & McCaffrey, 2009). Although some researchers advocate parent–child communication as a means to reduce adolescents' alcohol use, there is little support for an association between alcohol-specific communication among parents and their children and the alcohol use of the adolescents (Ennett, Bauman, Foshee, Pemberton, & Hicks, 2001; Van Der Vorst, Burk, & Engels, 2010).

Greater perceived availability of alcohol (e.g., Chung et al., 2013; Johnston et al., 2014a; Komro, Maldonado-Molina, Tobler, Bonds, & Muller, 2007) is also associated with greater alcohol involvement. Although access to alcohol among adolescents primarily involves social sources (e.g., peers) (Harrison, Fulkerson, & Park, 2000), the density of alcohol outlets in the surrounding neighborhood has been associated with adolescent alcohol use (Chen et al., 2010; Huckle, Huakau, Sweetsur, Huisman, & Casswell, 2008; Reboussin, Song, & Wolfson, 2011; Todd, Grube, & Gruenewald, 2007). Specifically, areas with high density of off-premise alcohol outlets were associated with increased likelihood of purchase attempts by minors (Reboussin et al., 2011). Alcohol outlet densities also may increase youth access to alcohol from social sources by increasing friends' and family members' ease of access to alcohol (Freisthler, Byrnes, & Gruenewald, 2009). In addition, an important alcohol-specific societal-level factor concerns the legal age of alcohol use in the United States. The increase in legal drinking age from age 18 years to age 21 years resulted in lower alcohol-related mortality and prevalence of alcohol use among adolescents (Hingson, 2009). To maximize effectiveness in reducing underage drinking, alcohol-specific risk factors, in conjunction with more general risk for substance use, need to be addressed in interventions provided to adolescents.

Protective Factors: General and Alcohol Specific

Protective factors typically act to moderate risk. For example, greater parental warmth, lower perceived stress, and lower externalizing behavior mitigate risk for substance use (Windle et al., 2008). Parental warmth and responsiveness may reduce risk for substance use by increasing a youth's self-regulatory capacity and coping skills (Hawkins et al., 1997). Greater religiosity, which can reflect strong positive ties to the community, also has been associated with decreased risk for heavy adolescent substance use (Windle et al., 2008). Importantly, the effects of early adversity can be reversed or minimized with enriched environments (e.g., school programs) and positive social supports (Masten et al., 2008). Support provided by parents, family members, mentors, and community organizations (e.g., faith-based groups, recreation centers) can provide experiences that offset risks and support healthy transitions.

At a broader level, alcohol-control policies at national, state, and local levels, which restrict the supply and availability of alcohol to youth, can help to protect youth from early alcohol use and reduce alcohol-related harms. Effective alcohol control policies to reduce underage drinking include, for example, setting the minimum legal drinking age at 21 years in the United States, the use of alcohol excise taxes to increase purchase price, limiting alcohol outlet density and marketing, and strict enforcement of drunk-driving and underage drinking laws (e.g., Cook & Moore, 2002; Wagenaar & Toomey, 2002). Similar to the nested structure of risk, societal alcohol-control policies appear to have the most impact when they operate as part of nested influences across levels that include national, community, and school-based prevention programs, and active parental monitoring (Spoth, Greenberg, & Turrisi, 2008; Spoth et al., 2013).

Implications for Prevention, Screening, Outreach, and Treatment

Given that risks for adolescent alcohol use operate at multiple levels (e.g., individual, family, community) across development, prevention and intervention efforts need to strategically address risks through national and local alcohol control policies, universal and indicated (i.e., target specific subgroups) prevention programs, alcohol screening and brief intervention, and a continuum of alcohol treatment services for youth and their families. Many prevention and intervention efforts focus on the individual drinker and have downplayed ecological conditions (Maggs, Schulenberg, & Hurrelmann, 1997), which puts the burden for health behavior change upon individuals and fails to embed a program into a supportive structural context (Lerner, Ostrom, & Freel, 1997). Coordinated efforts across multiple levels of influence and types of resources, which mutually reinforce beneficial protective effects, are needed to reduce underage drinking and support healthy transitions into adulthood (Spoth et al., 2008). The timing and content of prevention and intervention efforts need to take into account critical periods of transition (e.g., middle to high school), specific targets for intervention (e.g., an adolescent's parents and peers), and content tailored to maximize effects in specific subgroups (e.g., females vs males).

Prevention

Efforts in this area aim to delay the onset of alcohol use by increasing protective factors, and minimizing or reversing risk factors. A secondary prevention goal is to halt the progression of drinking behavior once initiated. Universal prevention efforts are provided to all individuals in a given setting (e.g., a community or school), whereas targeted prevention focuses on intervening with specific subgroups who are at high risk for early initiation of alcohol use (e.g., youth with conduct problems, child of an alcoholic parent). High-risk youth (e.g., youth with high levels of externalizing behaviors and conduct problems), in particular, may benefit from early, continuing intervention and support to reduce risk for early alcohol use. The finding that 8% of sixth graders reported some alcohol use in the past year (PRIDE surveys, 2014) suggests that prevention efforts would ideally begin in grade school, well before most youth initiate alcohol use. Given that interventions to delay age of first drink have shown limited effectiveness (Spoth et al., 2008), efforts to target factors that slow the progression to heavy drinking (e.g., limiting youth access to alcohol) may provide greater protective effects.

Key features of effective prevention involve using developmentally appropriate and culturally sensitive prevention messages and activities, combined child-centered (e.g., developing peer resistance skills) and family-based (e.g., enhancing parent–child communication, developing parenting skills) prevention activities that are provided over the course of development, and leveraging a community's resources (e.g., community recreation centers, media campaigns, enforcement of underage drinking legislation) to support healthy outcomes (Lopez et al., 2008; Nation et al., 2003; Spoth et al., 2008). Ideally, interventions would be sequenced and timed to specific developmental needs, such as greater focus on family-based prevention in childhood, with a shift to more child-centered prevention activities that address risks in the youth's social environment that become more important influences during adolescence (Lopez et al., 2008). "Booster" prevention activities provided throughout childhood and adolescence can be used to reinforce prevention messages, particularly during high-risk developmental transitions (e.g., shift from junior high to high school). In contrast, prevention efforts provided in early adolescence that focus solely on the rational aspects of decision making and that neglect the social-ecological context in which risky behaviors tend to occur (e.g., peer alcohol use, sexual behavior) may have limited effectiveness, due to developmental constraints on a youth's ability to make sound decisions in a highly charged, typically social, context (Chein et al., 2011; Lopez et al., 2008).

Screening and Brief Intervention

To aid the early identification of youth with a risky pattern of alcohol use (e.g., HED), the American Academy of Pediatrics recommends routine annual screening for alcohol use among youth (American Academy of Pediatrics, 2010). Brief alcohol screening conducted by a health care provider can occur in a variety of contexts (e.g., pediatrician's office, juvenile justice setting, school-based clinic). In this regard, the National Institute on Alcohol Abuse and Alcoholism has developed a guide for youth alcohol screening and brief intervention in primary care (NIAAA, 2011), which uses a two-item alcohol risk screen based on frequency of drinking in the past year and the youth's perception of peer alcohol use.

Youth who report a risky pattern of use and alcohol-related problems can benefit from brief advice and motivational interviewing interventions that aim to stop underage drinking, particularly among older adolescents (American Academy of Pediatrics, 2010). Motivational interviewing techniques involve a nonconfrontational discussion of the pros and cons of drinking as a way of increasing an adolescent's readiness to reduce drinking behavior, and to focus on achieving positive life goals (Miller & Rollnick, 2002). Motivational interventions show some promise in reducing underage drinking (e.g., Jensen et al., 2011; Walton et al., 2010), particularly among older adolescents (Monti et al., 1999), but further research on its effectiveness with adolescents is needed (Clark & Moss, 2010).

Treatment

Among individuals who meet criteria for an AUD, there is high unmet treatment need; the majority (~90%) of individuals who report an AUD have received no treatment for alcohol-related problems (SAMHSA, 2013). Although many youth are able to reduce alcohol use on their own, youth who escalate to a more persistent pattern of regular heavy drinking and alcohol-related problems warrant formal intervention. Based on the severity of alcohol and other drug involvement, and extent of co-occurring psychopathology, youth are matched to an appropriate level of care. Treatment services cover a continuum that includes brief interventions (e.g., 20-minute feedback and advice to stop drinking), outpatient, intensive outpatient, partial hospitalization, inpatient, and residential placement. Most youth who receive treatment for substance use are placed at the outpatient level of care (SAMHSA, 2009a). Given the need to address an adolescent's problems in multiple areas (e.g., legal, psychiatric, school, family), adolescent treatment programs typically include components that involve the adolescent's family, and consultation with psychiatric and medical specialists.

Among adolescents who initiate substance use treatment, receipt of some treatment is associated with better substance use and psychosocial outcomes over follow-up compared to no treatment (e.g., wait list comparison group) (Williams & Chang, 2000). There is little evidence, however, to suggest that any particular type of treatment content (e.g., cognitive-behavioral treatment, 12-step [Alcoholics Anonymous, Narcotics Anonymous]) or format (e.g., individual, group, family) is superior to another, or optimal for all youth (Black & Chung, 2014; Waldron & Turner, 2008; Williams &

Chang, 2000). In general, greater, and more stable improvements in multiple areas of an adolescent's functioning (e.g., alcohol use, school performance) were associated with longer duration and completion of the recommended course of treatment, and family involvement in treatment (Chung & Maisto, 2006). On average, treated adolescents report decreased substance use and criminal activity, and improved health, in the year following treatment (Waldron & Turner, 2008).

Although treatment can initiate and maintain an adolescent's motivation to reduce alcohol use, the posttreatment environment (e.g., family and peers) plays a key role in determining longer term treatment outcomes (Williams & Chang, 2000). Posttreatment factors (e.g., use of abstinence-related coping, time spent with nonusing peers) generally account for more of the variance in adolescents' clinical outcomes through 1-year follow-up than pre- and during-treatment factors (Winters, Stinchfield, Opland, Weller, & Latimer, 2000). Long-term positive outcomes may require more than one episode of treatment (Chung & Maisto, 2006), and they can be facilitated by participation in a continuing program of care (e.g., Garner, Godley, Funk, Dennis, & Godley, 2007).

Summary

To reduce alcohol-related harm during childhood and adolescence, the timing, coordination, and integration of prevention and intervention services across multiple levels is essential. Community- and school-based prevention programs need to be initiated early in childhood and continued through adolescence to reinforce developmentally appropriate prevention messages. Outreach efforts that include screening for problem drinking of adolescents and their parents need to be instituted to enhance the early detection of youth who may benefit from intervention. Targeted intervention with youth and parents to address youth conduct problems and reduce affiliation with deviant peers can help to reduce risk for underage drinking. If formal treatment for an adolescent's alcohol use is indicated, a continuing care model, which includes periodic check-ups and boosters, can provide the foundation for stable recovery. The coordination of prevention and intervention services across multiple levels of influence can provide the support to youth and their families that is needed to delay the onset of alcohol use and to reduce alcohol-related harm during the transition to young adulthood.

Agenda for Future Research

A life-span, developmental systems model proposes that developmental contexts and changes in biological, psychological, and social domains that are unique to adolescence influence the emergence and progression of alcohol involvement. These multiple, nested systems of influence (e.g., individual, family, school), which operate across distinct levels of analysis (e.g., molecular, psychological, interpersonal, geographic), promote and constrain transitions across stages and levels of alcohol use (Zucker, 2006). Next steps in understanding the etiology of adolescent alcohol involvement and developing more effective alcohol prevention and intervention programs for youth involve delineating causal chains and developmental cascades underlying adolescent alcohol involvement and identifying mechanisms associated with escalation and desistance. Pathways involving genes, brain systems, behavior, and social-environmental systems leading to specific patterns of alcohol involvement in youth have only begun to be mapped (Whelan et al., 2014; Zucker, 2014). The following sections briefly review possible future directions in mapping links among component processes, and using this knowledge to guide public health initiatives and interventions for youth.

Core Features of Alcohol Use Disorder

Fundamental questions remain regarding the definition and core features of "alcohol use disorder" and "addiction" more generally (Martin, Langenbucher, Chung, & Sher, 2014; Saunders & Schuckit, 2006). It is unclear whether a single definition of substance use disorder can serve all purposes equally well (e.g., clinical, research, legal, insurance reimbursement), across all types of potentially addictive behaviors (e.g., alcohol and tobacco, gambling, sun tanning, binge eating), in both animal and human models, across national boundaries, and into the future (e.g., application to yet-to-be developed addictive substances). Mixed findings across studies with regard to genetic influence associated with specific alcohol phenotypes suggest the need for improved conceptualization and assessment of the core features of an alcohol use disorder (Martin et al., 2014). Research examining specific components of addiction (e.g., tolerance, withdrawal, impaired control over alcohol use) may be a more fruitful approach for certain purposes. Some have suggested that a neuroscience approach can help to identify a neurocognitive signature of "addiction," including its core features and boundary conditions (Charney et al., 2002; Schutz, 2012).

Advances in Assessment of Externalizing and Internalizing Behavior

Problems of "definition" and conceptualization also extend to the two main pathways (externalizing and internalizing) to problematic substance use and to environmental factors that constrain or foster symptom expression. There is a need to parse the components of behavioral disinhibition, especially in uncovering links across levels of biology and environment that constrain and foster the expression of disinhibitory behavior (Dick et al., 2010). Novel lab-based methods, such as virtual reality paradigms, can supplement questionnaire and interview assessments, providing a standardized method of assessing specific behavioral responses (e.g., attention capacity, social skills) "in the moment" (Parsons, Bowerly, Buckwalter, & Rizzo, 2007; Paschall, Fishbein, Hubal, & Eldreth, 2005).

Improved Assessment of Micro- and Macro-Level Environmental Contexts

Measures of relevant environmental features also need to be better specified at macro- (e.g., school level) and micro-levels (e.g., personal social network level) (Sher et al., 2010). Toward this goal, Internet- and mobile phone–based assessment can provide fine-grained, "real-time" data that link contextual and situational factors to changes in alcohol use (e.g., Miranda et al., 2014; Reimuller, Shadur, & Hussong, 2011). In particular, characteristics of the adolescent's social environment (e.g., alcohol-related postings on personal social network sites) and social cognitive processes (e.g., influence of peers on adolescent risk-taking behavior) warrant greater attention in relation to risk for alcohol involvement to better understand the effects of peer selection and peer influence, norm narrowing in the adolescent's personal network, and the "spread" of health behaviors versus "contagion" of negative influence (e.g., Huang et al., 2014; Valente, 2010). Emerging research on content analysis of adolescents' references to alcohol use on personal social network sites suggests the potentially powerful role of Internet-based social networks in shaping adolescents' attitudes and beliefs toward alcohol use (e.g., Moreno et al., 2010, 2012).

Advances in Genetics and Epigenetics

A key task involves the delineation of pathways and links among genes, behavior, and social-environmental contexts that contribute to adolescent alcohol involvement (Zucker, 2014). Greater attention needs to be given to genetic influence on specific aspects of alcohol involvement (e.g., alcohol craving), rather than on more global indicators of alcohol dependence, such as *DSM*-based diagnosis. In addition, studies have begun to examine gene x environment (e.g., Dick et al., 2009a, 2009b) and gene x intervention (Brody et al., 2009a; Brody, Chen, Beach, Philibert, & Kogan, 2009b; Brody et al., 2013) effects on trajectories of alcohol use. However, research is needed to better understand mechanisms by which a dynamically changing environment (e.g., proximal social network influences on health behaviors and more distal national alcohol control policies) can trigger, enhance, or dampen genetic risk (e.g., small effects from a large number of common variants) for heavy alcohol involvement (Hofer, 2005).

Technological advancements also provide new tools for "gene hunting" that include whole-genome sequencing of individuals and fine mapping (e.g., Wang, Yang, Ma, Payne, & Li, 2014), studies of how DNA variation affects expression of messenger RNA in specific tissues, and studies of protein expression, as well as methods to model the action of gene networks (Hudziak & Faraone, 2010). The field of epigenetics (e.g., Harlaar & Hutchison, 2013), which focuses on alterations to the genome (e.g., DNA methylation and histone modifications) that do not involve permanent changes to the DNA sequence, is also rapidly gaining attention due to increasing feasibility of epigenomic profiling of the genome (Wong, Hudson, & McPherson, 2011). There is some evidence from animal model research that repeated drug exposure can result in long-lasting changes in gene expression that maintain a compulsive pattern of substance use (Nestler, 2014; Wong et al., 2011). Emerging findings also suggest a developmentally specific impact of alcohol use in adolescence on potentially long-lasting changes in gene expression that increase risk for heavy alcohol use (e.g., Coleman, He, Lee, Styner, & Crews, 2011; Pascual et al., 2010).

Potential Contributions of Neuroimaging

Although there is some consensus that response to reward, response inhibition, and affective response are key intermediate phenotypes to be studied in neuroimaging paradigms (Clark et al., 2008; Hardin & Ernst, 2009; S. Hill et al., 2010; Nigg et al., 2006; Whelan et al., 2014; Zucker, 2014), work remains to be done in understanding how brain functioning in these areas changes during adolescence, in relation to ongoing changes in brain structure, and in relation to the timing and dose of alcohol use. Again, technological developments will permit greater spatial and temporal resolution of neuroimaging data, and also will provide improved methods for examining brain structure (e.g., diffusion spectrum imaging), instrinsic (resting state) connectivity, and the synchronization of activation in brain areas in relation to changing task demands. The integration of genetic markers with neuroimaging results also represents a key, yet complex, link in understanding pathways of risk for alcohol involvement (e.g., Goldberg & Weinberger, 2009; Pine, Ernst, & Leibenluft, 2010).

In this regard, the IMAGEN study, a large-scale, longitudinal genetic-neuroimaging study of 2000 14-year-old European adolescents aims to examine individual differences in impulsivity, reward response, and emotional reactivity as risk factors for psychiatric disorders, including substance use disorders (Schumann et al., 2010; Whelan et al., 2014). Multicenter studies of adolescents recruited from the community and followed over time, such as IMAGEN (Schumann et al., 2010) and NCANDA (Brown et al., 2015), and single-site studies, such as the Michigan Longitudinal Study (Zucker, 2014), hold promise for increasing knowledge of neurobiological factors that predict risk for and examine consequences of heavy substance use in adolescence. Studies of brain functioning, in particular, might usefully inform the development of protocols for cognitive rehabilitation that can help to build capacity for more effective response inhibition (e.g., Bickel, Yi, Landes, Hill, & Baxter, 2011; Feldstein-Ewing, Filbey, Sabbineni, Chandler, & Hutchison, 2011), particularly in highly charged, risky situations (e.g., presence of peers) that are conducive to alcohol use.

Improving Prevention and Treatment

Findings from neuroscience, particularly related to developmental constraints on youths' ability to consistently inhibit risky behaviors, are increasingly being used to inform the timing and content of interventions (Clark et al., 2013; Lopez et al., 2008). With the onset of puberty and adolescence, prevention and intervention efforts need to address family, peer, and media influences in minimizing risk for early alcohol use, possibly targeting high-risk youth (e.g., high behavioral disinhibition) for early, tailored interventions. Personal communication devices (e.g., mobile phone) and the Internet (e.g., social networking sites, monitored chat rooms) also provide methods that could facilitate dissemination of health education and prevention messages, as well as methods that could be used to facilitate ongoing treatment and continuing care for adolescent alcohol use.

With regard to substance use treatment, research with adults suggests the utility of adaptive treatment protocols (also "dynamic treatment regimes"), which provide for greater personalization in the timing, choice, and sequencing of interventions (Lagoa, Bekiroglu, Lanza, & Murphy, 2014; Murphy, Collins, & Rush, 2007), an approach that could be used to boost treatment effectiveness for high-risk subgroups (e.g., youth with conduct problems). Adoption of a continuing care model of alcohol treatment, similar to the treatment model for diabetes, is needed to provide ongoing support to an individual during recovery and to minimize the likelihood of returning to heavy use (e.g., for adult patients: Gustafson et al., 2014). Computer or Web-based interventions, tested mainly with adults (e.g., Bickel et al., 2011; Carroll et al., 2014; Riper et al., 2014), also show some promise as stand-alone or adjunct resources to help maintain treatment gains. Other approaches include monitored chatrooms and virtual reality programs, which could be used to practice new behaviors in support of recovery. These technology-based methods, while not yet tested with adolescents, may be particularly promising, given this age group's interest and facility with technology. The integration of findings from a developmental neuroscience perspective with advances in communications technologies holds promise for greater targeted impact and dissemination of prevention and intervention efforts.

Social Ecological Models

By and large, research has neglected to jointly consider the roles of different levels of influence on adolescent alcohol involvement. Although youth inhabit many different social contexts, including peer, family, school, neighborhood, and media worlds (Wilcox, 2003), many studies on underage drinking consider only a single level (or context), that of the individual. There has been a renewed interest in exploring the impact of environment- and community-level factors on health behaviors (Leventhal & Brooks-Gunn, 2000; Winstanley et al., 2008), in part because relatively recent advances in methods for analyzing multilevel influences permit differentiation between effects at different levels (Scribner, Cohen, & Fisher, 2000). It is critical to understand the basic mechanisms by which the environment exerts harmful or protective effects on health behavior. Research is needed that identifies the micro-processes through which the environment exerts influence on adolescent alcohol use.

Public Health Initiatives

Although progress has been made to coordinate systems of care (e.g., primary care, school-based health services, juvenile justice, family court, welfare system), much work remains to be done to address what some describe as a patchwork of service providers. In this regard, the use of geographic information systems that map community resources (e.g., hospitals, treatment facilities) and liabilities (e.g., hot spots for drug-related traffic accidents) in a region can provide policymakers with information regarding community-specific targets for change (e.g., Chilenski & Greenberg, 2009). As a complementary approach, electronic medical records can facilitate integration of care and referrals to treatment in the context of a patient's "medical home." In moving toward integrated health care, the US Office of National Drug Control Policy is working toward a national system of prevention that cuts across levels of influence from national drug control policy to schools and neighborhoods. The National Institute on Alcohol Abuse and Alcoholism's Underage Drinking Initiative is, for example, working to enable routine screening for adolescent alcohol use in pediatric offices (NIAAA, 2011), establish the evidence base for public policy regarding underage alcohol use (e.g., Wagenaar & Toomey, 2002), and disseminate evidence-based alcohol interventions.

Conclusion

The agenda for future research outlined earlier does not begin to cover all of the promising areas for further study and progress, and it provides only a glimpse of some intriguing possibilities for scientific discovery that can be translated into health-promoting interventions. In translating research to practice, it is essential to understand individuals in a dynamically changing developmental context and

in relation to the multiple nested systems influencing health outcomes. Implications for prevention and treatment include the need for a coordinated national system of prevention and health care, and interventions across macro- and micro-levels of influence that address proximal risks for early alcohol use during adolescence. Investigation of the links between genes, brain, behavior, and environment holds promise for minimizing risks and amplifying protective factors in efforts to reduce adolescent alcohol use.

References

Agrawal, A., & Lynskey, M. T. (2006). The genetic epidemiology of cannabis use, abuse and dependence: A review. *Addiction*, *101*, 801–812.

Ahlstrom, S. K., & Osterberg, E. L. (2004). International perspectives on adolescent and young adult drinking. *Alcohol Research and Health*, *28*, 258–268.

Amaro, H., Blake, S. M., Schwartz, P. M., & Flinchbaugh, L. J. (2001). Developing theory-based substance abuse prevention programs for young adolescent girls. *Journal of Early Adolescence*, *3*, 256–293.

American Academy of Pediatrics Committee on Substance Abuse. (2010). Policy statement—Alcohol use by youth and adolescents: A pediatric concern. *Pediatrics*, *125*, 1078–1087.

American Psychiatric Association. (2013). *Diagnostic and statistical manual of mental disorders* (5th ed.). Arlington, VA: Author.

Anderson, K. G., Briggs, K. E. L., & White, H. R. (2013). Motives to drink or not to drink: Longitudinal relations among personality, motives, and alcohol use across adolescence and early adulthood. *Alcoholism: Clinical and Experimental Research*, *37*, 860–867.

Andrews, J. A., Hampson, S., & Peterson, M. (2011). Early adolescent cognitions as predictors of heavy alcohol use in high school. *Addictive Behaviors*, *36*, 448–455.

Anderson, P., DeBrujn, A., Angus, K., Gordon, R., & Hastings, G. (2009). Impact of alcohol advertising and media exposure on adolescent alcohol use: A systematic review of longitudinal studies. *Alcohol and Alcoholism*, *44*, 229–243.

Armstrong, T. D., & Costello, E. J. (2002). Community studies on adolescent substance use, abuse, or dependence and psychiatric comorbidity. *Journal of Consulting and Clinical Psychology*, *70*, 1224–1239.

Aryal, P., Dvir, H., Choe, S., & Slesinger, P. A. (2009). A discrete alcohol pocket involved in GIRK channel activation. *Nature Neuroscience*, *12*, 988–995.

Audrain-McGovern, J., Rodriguez, D., Tercyak, K. P., Cuevas, J., Rodgers, K., & Patterson, F. (2007). Identifying and characterizing adolescent smoking trajectories. *Cancer Epidemiology, Biomarkers, and Prevention*, *13*, 2023–2034.

Babor, T. F., Hofmann, M., Del Boca, F., Hesselbrock, V., Meyer, R., Dolinsky, Z., & Rounsaville, B. (1992). Types of alcoholics, I: Evidence for an empirically derived typology based on indicators of vulnerability and severity. *Archives of General Psychiatry*, *49*, 599–608.

Bagot, R. C., & Meaney, M. C. (2010). Epigenetics and the biological basis of gene x environment interactions. *Journal of* the *American Academy of Child and Adolescent Psychiatry, 49,* 752–771.

Beccaria, F., & White, H. R. (2012). Underage drinking in Europe and North America. In P. De Witte & M. C. Mitchell, Jr. (Eds.), *Underage drinking: A report on drinking in the second decade of life in Europe and North America* (pp. 21–78). Leuven, Belgium: Presses universitaires de Louvain.

Behar, D., Berg, C. J., Rapoport, J. L., Nelson, W., Linnoila, M., Cohen, M., . . . Marshall, T. (1983). Behavioral and physiological effects of ethanol in high-risk and control children: A pilot study. *Alcoholism: Clinical and Experimental Research, 7,* 404–410.

Benjet, C., Borges, G., Medina-Mora, M. E., & Méndez, E. (2013). Chronic childhood adversity and stages of substance use involvement in adolescents. *Drug and Alcohol Dependence, 131,* 85–91.

Berg, N., Kiviruusu, O., Karvonen, S., Kestila, L., Lintonen, T., Rahkonen, O., & Huure, T. (2013). A 26-year follow-up of heavy drinking trajectories from adolescence to mid-adulthood and adult disadvantage. *Alcohol and Alcoholism, 48,* 452–457.

Bickel, W. K., Yi, R., Landes, R. D., Hill, P. F., & Baxter, C. (2011). Remember the future: Working memory training decreases delay discounting among stimulant addicts. *Biological Psychiatry, 69,* 260–265.

Black, J. J., & Chung, T. (2014). Mechanisms of change in adolescent substance use treatment: How does treatment work? *Substance Abuse, 35*(4), 344–355.

Blakemore, S. J. (2012). Imaging brain development: The adolescent brain. *NeuroImage, 61,* 397–406.

Brody, G. H., Beach, S. R., Hill, K. G., Howe, G. W., Prado, G., & Fullerton, S. M. (2013). Using genetically informed, randomized prevention trials to test etiological hypotheses about child and adolescent drug use and psycholpathology. *American Journal of Public Health, 103,* S19–S24.

Brody, G. H., Beach, S. R., Philibert, R. A., Chen, Y. F., Lei, M. K., Murry, V. M., & Brown, A. C. (2009a). Parenting moderates a genetic vulnerability factor in longitudinal increases in youths' substance use. *Journal of Consulting and Clinical Psychology, 77,* 1–11.

Brody, G. H., Chen, Y. F., Beach, S. R., Philibert, R. A., & Kogan, S. M. (2009b). Participation in a family centered prevention program decreases genetic risk for adolescents' risky behaviors. *Pediatrics, 124,* 911–917.

Bronfenbrenner, U. (1979). *The ecology of human development. Experiments by nature and design.* Cambridge, MA: Harvard University Press.

Brook, J. S., Whiteman, M., Gordon, A. S., Nomura, C., & Brook, D. (1985). Onset of adolescent drinking: A longitudinal study of intrapersonal and interpersonal antecedents. *Advances in Alcohol and Substance Abuse, 5,* 91–110.

Brown, S. A., Brumback, T., Tomlinson, K., Cummins, K., Thompson, W. K., Nagel, B. J., . . . Tapert, S. F. (2015). The National Consortium on Alcohol and NeuroDevelopment in Adolescence (NCANDA): A multi-site study of adolescent development and substance use. *Journal of Studies on Alcohol and Drugs, 76*(6), 895–908. doi: 10.15288/jsad.2015.76.895

Brown, S. A., McGue, M., Maggs, J., Schulenberg, J., Hingson, R., Swartzwelder, S., Martin, C., . . . Murphy, S. (2008). A developmental perspective on alcohol and youths 16 to 20 years of age. *Pediatrics, 121,* S290–S310.

Brown, S. A., Tapert, S. F., Granholm, E., & Delis, D. C. (2000). Neurocognitive functioning of adolescents: Effects of protracted alcohol use. *Alcoholism: Clinical and Experimental Research, 24,* 164–171.

Bush, P. J., Weinfurt, K. P., & Iannotti, R. J. (1994). Families versus peers: Developmental influences on drug use from grade 4-5 to grade 7-8. *Journal of Applied Developmental Psychology, 15,* 437–456.

Buu, A., DiPiazza, C., Wang, J., Puttler, L. I., Fitzgerald, H. E., & Zucker, R. A. (2009). Parent, family, and neighborhood effects on the development of child substance use and other psychopathology from preschool to the start of adulthood. *Journal of Studies on Alcohol and Drugs, 70,* 489–498.

Caetano, R., & Clark, C. L. (1998). Trends in alcohol consumption patterns among whites, blacks and Hispanics: 1984 and 1995. *Journal of Studies on Alcohol, 59,* 659–668.

Cameron, C. A., Stritzke, W. G., & Durkin, K. (2003). Alcohol expectancies in late childhood: An ambivalence perspective on transitions toward alcohol use. *Journal of Child Psychology and Psychiatry, 44,* 687–698.

Capaldi, D. M., Stoolmiller, M., Kim, H. K., & Yoerger, K. (2009). Growth in alcohol use in at risk adolescent boys: Two-part random effects prediction models. *Drug and Alcohol Dependence, 105,* 109–117.

Carroll, K. M., Kiluk, B. D., Nich, C., Gordon, M. A., Portnoy, G. A., Marino, D. R., & Ball, S. A. (2014). Computer-assisted delivery of cognitive-behavioral therapy: Efficacy and durability of CBT4CBT among cocaine-dependent individuals maintained on methadone. *American Journal of Psychiatry, 171,* 436–444.

Centers for Disease Control and Prevention. (2014). Youth Risk Behavior Surveillance- United States, 2013. Surveillance summaries. *Morbidity and Mortality Weekly Report, 63*(4).

Charney, D., Barlow, D., Botteron, K., Cohen, J., Goldman, D., Gur, R., . . . Zalcman, S. (2002). Neuroscience research agenda to guide development of a pathophysiologically based classification system. In D. Kupfer, M. First, & D. Regier (Eds.), *A research agenda for DSM-V* (pp. 31–84). Washington, DC: American Psychiatric Association.

Chartier, K. G., Scott, D. M., Wall, T. L., Covault, J., Karriker-Jaffe, K. J., Mills, B. A., . . . Arroyo, J. A. (2014). Framing ethnic variations in alcohol outcomes from biological pathways to neighborhood context. *Alcoholism: Clinical and Experimental Research, 38,* 611–618.

Chassin, L., Flora, D. B., & King, K. M. (2004). Trajectories of alcohol and drug use and dependence from adolescence to adulthood: The effects of parent alcoholism and personality. *Journal of Abnormal Psychology, 113,* 483–498.

Chassin, L., Pillow, D. R., Curran, P. J., Molina, B. S., & Barrera, M. (1993). Relation of parental alcoholism to early adolescent substance use: A test of three mediating mechanisms. *Journal of Abnormal Psychology, 102,* 3–19.

Chassin, L., Pitts, S. C., & DeLucia, C. (1999). The relation of adolescent substance use to young adult autonomy, positive activity involvement, and perceived competence. *Development and Psychopathology, 11,* 915–932.

Chassin, L., Pitts, S. C., & Prost, J. (2002). Binge drinking trajectories from adolescence to emerging adulthood in a high-risk sample: Predictors and substance abuse outcomes. *Journal of Consulting and Clinical Psychology, 70,* 67–78.

Chein, J., Albert, D., O'Brien, L., Uckert, K., & Steinberg, L. (2011). Peers increase adolescent risk taking by enhancing activity in the brain's reward circuitry. *Developmental Science, 14,* F1–F10.

Chen M-J., Grube, J. W., & Remer, L. G. (2010). Community alcohol outlet densities and underage drinking and related problems. *Addiction, 105*, 270–278.

Chilenski, S. M., & Greenberg, M. T. (2009). The importance of community context in the epidemiology of early adolescent substance use and delinquency in a rural sample. *American Journal of Community Psychology, 44*, 287–301.

Christiansen, B. A., Smith, G. T., Roehling, P. V., & Goldman, M. S. (1989). Using alcohol expectancies to predict adolescent drinking behavior after one year. *Journal of Consulting and Clinical Psychology, 57*, 93–99.

Chung, T., Hipwell, A., Loeber, R., White, H. R., & Stouthamer-Loeber, M. (2008). Ethnic differences in positive alcohol expectancies during childhood: The Pittsburgh Girls Study. *Alcoholism: Clinical and Experimental Research, 32*, 966–974.

Chung, T., & Maisto, S. A. (2006). Relapse to alcohol and other drug use in treated adolescents: Review and reconsideration of relapse as a change point in clinical course. *Clinical Psychology Review, 26*, 149–161.

Chung, T., Martin, C. S., Armstrong, T. D., & Labouvie, E. W. (2002). Prevalence of DSM-IV alcohol diagnoses and symptoms in adolescent community and clinical samples. *Journal of the American Academy of Child and Adolescent Psychiatry, 41*, 546–554.

Chung, T., Martin, C. S., & Winters, K. C. (2005). Diagnosis, course and assessment of alcohol abuse and dependence in adolescents. In M. Galanter (Ed). *Alcohol problems in adolescents and young adults: Epidemiology, neurobiology, prevention, and treatment* (pp. 5–27). New York, NY: Springer Science.

Chung, T., Pedersen, S., Kim, K., Hipwell, A., & Stepp, S. (2013). Racial differences in type of alcoholic beverage consumed during adolescence in the Pittsburgh Girls Study. *Alcoholism: Clinical and Experimental Research, 38*, 285–293.

Chung, T., White, H. R., Hipwell, A. E., Stepp, S. D., & Loeber, R. (2010). A parallel process model of the development of positive smoking expectancies and smoking behavior during early adolescence in Caucasian and African American girls. *Addictive Behaviors, 35*, 647–650.

Cicchetti, D., & Rogosch, F. A. (1996). Equifinality and multifinality in developmental psychopathology. *Development and Psychopathology, 89*, 597–600.

Cicchetti, D., & Rogosch, F. A. (2002). A developmental psychopathology perspective on adolescence. *Journal of Consulting and Clinical Psychology, 70*, 5–20.

Clark, D. B. (2004). The natural history of adolescent alcohol use disorders. *Addiction, 99* (S2), 5–22.

Clark, D. B., Chung, T., Pajtek, S., Zhai, Z., Long, E., & Hasler, B. (2013). Neuroimaging methods for adolescent substance use disorder prevention science. *Prevention Science, 14*, 300–309.

Clark, D. B., DeBellis, M., Lynch, K., Cornelius, J., & Martin, C. (2003). Physical and sexual abuse, depression and alcohol use disorders in adolescents: Onsets and outcomes. *Drug and Alcohol Dependence, 69*, 51–60.

Clark, D. B., & Moss, H. B. (2010). Providing alcohol-related screening and brief interventions to adolescents through health care systems: Obstacles and solutions. *PLoS Med, 7*, e1000214.

Clark, D. B., Thatcher, D. L., & Tapert, S. F. (2008). Alcohol, psychological dysregulation, and adolescent brain development. *Alcoholism: Clinical and Experimental Research, 32*, 375–385.

Cleveland, H. H., & Wiebe, R. P. (2003). The moderation of adolescent-to-peer similarity in tobacco and alcohol use by school levels of substance use. *Child Development, 74*, 279–291.

Cleveland, M. J., Feinberg, M. E., Bontempo, D. E., & Greenberg, M. T. (2008). The role of risk and protective factors in substance use across adolescence. *Journal of Adolescent Health, 43*, 157–164.

Cloninger, C. R. (1987). A systematic method for clinical description and classification of personality variants. *Archives of General Psychiatry, 44*, 573–588.

Colder, C. R., Campbell, R. T., Ruel, E., Richardson, J. L., & Flay, B. R. (2002). A finite mixture model of growth trajectories of adolescent alcohol use: Predictors and consequences. *Journal of Consulting and Clinical Psychology, 70*, 976–985.

Coleman, L. G., He, J., Lee, J., Styner, M., & Crews, F. T. (2011). Adolescent binge drinking alters adult brain neurotransmitter gene expression, behavior, brain regional volumes, and neurochemistry in mice. *Alcohol and Clinical Experimental Research, 35*, 671–688.

Conrod, P., Castellanos, N., & Mackie, C. (2008). Personality-targeted interventions delay the growth of adolescent drinking and binge drinking. *Journal of Child Psychology and Psychiatry, 49*, 181–190.

Cook, P. J., & Moore, M. J. (2002). The economics of alcohol abuse and alcohol-control policies. *Health Affairs, 21*, 120–133.

Cooper, M. L. (1994). Motivations for alcohol use among adolescents: Development and validation of a four-factor model. *Psychological Assessment, 6*, 117–128.

Cooper, M. L., Krull, J. L, Agocha, V. B., Flanagan, M., Grabe, S. A, Orcutt, H. K., . . . Dermen, K. H. (2008). Motivational pathways to alcohol use and abuse among black and white adolescents. *Journal of Abnormal Psychology, 117*, 485–501.

Costello, E. J., Sung, M., Worthman, C., & Angold, A. (2007). Pubertal maturation and the development of alcohol use and abuse. *Drug and Alcohol Dependence, 88S*, S50–S59.

Cox, M. J., Mills-Koonce, R., Propper, C., & Gariepy, J-L. (2010). Systems theory and cascades in developmental psychopathology. *Development and Psychopathology, 22*, 497–506.

Cox, W. M., & Klinger, E. (2004). A motivational model of alcohol use: Determinants of use and change. In W. M. Cox & E. Klinger (Eds.). *Handbook of motivational counseling* (pp. 121–138). Chichester, UK: Wiley.

Crone, E. A., & Dahl, R. E. (2012). Understanding adolescence as a period of social-affective engagement and goal flexibility. *Nature Reviews: Neuroscience, 13*, 636–650.

Crum, R. M., Lillie-Blanton, M., & Anthony, J. C. (1996). Neighborhood environment and opportunity to use cocaine and other drugs in late childhood and early adolescence. *Drug and Alcohol Dependence, 43*, 155–161.

Curran, P. J., Stice, E., & Chassin, L. (1997). The relation between adolescent alcohol use and peer alcohol use: A longitudinal random coefficients model. *Journal of Consulting and Clinical Psychology, 65*, 130–140.

Dahl, R. E. (2004). Adolescent brain development: A period of vulnerabilities and opportunities. Keynote address. *Annals of the New York Academy of Sciences, 1021*, 1–22.

Dal Cin, S., Worth, K. A., Gerrard, M., Gibbons, F. X., Stoolmiller, M., Wills, T. A., & Sargent, J. D. (2009). Watching and drinking: Expectancies, prototypes, and friends' alcohol use mediate the effect of exposure to alcohol use in movies on adolescent drinking. *Health Psychology, 28,* 473–483.

DeBellis, M. D., Clark, D. B., Beers, S. R., Soloff, P., Boring, A. M., Hall, J., . . . Keshavan, M. S. (2000). Hippocampal volume in adolescent onset alcohol use disorders. *American Journal of Psychiatry, 157,* 737–744.

Degenhardt, L., Dierker, L., Chiu, W. T., Medina-Mora, M. E., Neumark, Y., Sampson, N., . . . Kessler, R. C. (2010). Evaluating the drug use "gateway" theory using cross-national data: Consistency and associations of the order of initiation of drug use among participants in the WHO World Mental Health Surveys. *Drug and Alcohol Dependence, 108,* 84–97.

DeWit, D. J., Adlaf, E. M., Offord, D. R., & Ogborne, A. C. (2000). Age at first alcohol use: A risk factor for the development of alcohol disorders. *American Journal of Psychiatry, 157,* 745–750.

Dick, D., Latendresse, S., Lansford, J. E., Budde, J., Goate, A., Dodge, K. A., . . . Bates, J. E. (2009a) Role of GABRA2 in trajectories of externalizing behavior across development and evidence of moderation by parental monitoring. *Archives of General Psychiatry, 66,* 649–657.

Dick, D., Smith, G., Olausson, P., Mitchell, S., Leeman, R., O'Malley, S., & Sher, K. (2010). Understanding the construct of impulsivity and its relationship to alcohol use disorders. *Addiction Biology, 15,* 217–226.

Dick, D. M., Bernard, M., Aliev, F., Viken, R., Pulkkinen, L., Kaprio, J., & Rose, R. J. (2009b). The role of socioregional factors in moderating genetic influences on early adolescent behavior problems and alcohol use. *Alcoholism: Clinical and Experimental Research, 33,* 1739–1748.

Dick, D. M., Bierut, L., Hinrichs, A. L., Fox, L., Bucholz, K. K., Kramer, J., . . . Foroud, T. (2005). The role of GABRA2 in risk for conduct disorder and alcohol and drug dependence across developmental stages. *Behavioral Genetics, 36,* 577–590.

Dishion, T. J., Capaldi, D., Spracklen, K. M., & Fuzhong, L. (1995). Peer ecology of male adolescent drug use. *Development and Psychopathology, 7,* 803–824.

Dodge, K. A., Malone, P. S., Lansford, J. E., Miller, S., Pettit, G. S., & Bates, J. E. (2009). A dynamic cascade model of the development of substance use onset. *Monographs of the Society for Research on Child Development, 74,* vii–119.

Donovan, J. E. (2004). Adolescent alcohol initiation: A review of psychosocial risk factors. *Journal of Adolescent Health, 35,* 529.e7–529.e18.

Donovan, J. E. (2009). Estimated blood alcohol concentrations for child and adolescent drinking and their implications for screening instruments. *Pediatrics, 123,* e975–e981.

Donovan, J. E., & Molina, B. S. G. (2008). Children's introduction to alcohol use: Sips and tastes. *Alcoholism: Clinical and Experimental Research, 32,* 108–119.

Donovan, J. E., & Molina, B. S. G. (2011). Childhood risk factors for early onset drinking. *Journal of Studies on Alcohol and Drugs, 72,* 741–751.

Donovan, J. E., & Molina, B. S. G. (2013). Types of alcohol use experience from childhood through adolescence. *Journal of Adolescent Health, 53,* 453–459.

Donovan, J. E., Leech, S. L., Zucker, R. A., Loveland-Cherry, C. J., Jester, J. M., Fitzgerald, H. E., . . . Looman, W. S. (2004). Really underage drinkers: Alcohol use among elementary students. *Alcoholism: Clinical and Experimental Research, 28,* 341–349.

Duncan, S. C., Duncan, T. E., & Strycker, L. A. (2002). A multi-level analysis of neighborhood context and youth alcohol and drug problems. *Prevention Science, 3,* 125–133.

Dunn, M. E., & Goldman, M. S. (1996). Empirical modeling of an alcohol expectancy memory network in elementary school children as a function of grade. *Experimental and Clinical Psychopharmacology, 4,* 209–217.

Dunn, M. E., & Goldman, M. S. (1998). Age and drinking-related differences in the memory organization of alcohol expectancies in 3rd, 6th, 9th, and 12th grade. *Journal of Consulting and Clinical Psychology, 66,* 579–585.

Eaton, D. K., Kann, L., Kinchen, S., Shanklin, S., Flint, K. H., Hawkins, J., . . . Centers For Disease Control & Prevention. (2012). Youth Risk Behavior Surveillance—United States, 2011. *MMWR Surveillance, 61,* 1–162.

Ehringer, M. A., Clegg, H. V., Collins, A. C., Corley, R. P., Crowley, T., Hewitt, J. K., . . . Zeiger, J. S. (2007). Association of the neuronal nicotinic receptor beta2 subunit gene (CHRNB2) with subjective responses to alcohol and nicotine. *American Journal of Medical Genetics Part B: Neuropsychiatric Genetics, 144B,* 596–604.

Eiden, R. D., Leonard, K. E., Hoyle, R. H., & Chavez, F. (2004). A transactional model of parent-infant interactions in alcoholic families. *Psychology of Addictive Behaviors, 18,* 350–361.

Elkins, I. J., McGue, M., & Iacono, W. G. (2007). Prospective effects of attention deficit/hyperactivity disorder, conduct disorder, and sex on adolescent substance use and abuse. *Archives of General Psychiatry, 64,* 1145–1152.

Ennett, S. T., Bauman, K. E., Foshee, V. A., Pemberton, M., & Hicks, K. A. (2001). Parent—child communication about adolescent tobacco and alcohol use: What do parents say and does it affect youth behavior? *Journal of Marriage and the Family, 63,* 48–62.

Ennett, S. T., Foshee, V. A., Bauman, K. E., Hussong, A., Cai, L., Reyes, H. L., . . . Durant, R. (2008). The social ecology of adolescent alcohol misuse. *Child Development, 79,* 1777–1791.

Epler, A., Sher, K. J., & Piasecki, T. (2009). Reasons for abstaining or limiting drinking: A developmental perspective. *Psychology of Addictive Behaviors, 23,* 428–442.

Ernst, M., Pine, D. S., & Hardin, M. (2009). Triadic model of the neurobiology of motivated behavior in adolescence. *Psychological Medicine, 36,* 299–312.

Everett, S. A., Schnuth, R. L., & Tribble, J. L. (1998). Tobacco and alcohol use in top grossing American films. *Journal of Community Health, 23,* 317–324.

Faden, V. B. (2006). Trends in initiation of alcohol use in the United States 1975 to 2003. *Alcoholism: Clinical and Experimental Research, 30,* 1011–1022.

Faden, V. B., & Fay, M. P. (2004). Trends in drinking among Americans age 18 and younger: 1975–2002. *Alcohol and Clinical Experimental Research, 28,* 1388–1395.

Falconer, D. S., & MacKay, T. F. C. (1996). *Introduction to quantitative genetics* (4th ed.). London, UK: Longman.

Feldstein-Ewing, S. W., Filbey, F. M., Sabbineni, A., Chandler, L. D., & Hutchison, K. E. (2011). How psychosocial alcohol interventions work: A preliminary look at what fMRI can tell us. *Alcohol and Clinical Experimental Research, 35,* 643–651.

Fergusson, D., Swain-Campbell, N., & Horwood, L. J. (2002). Deviant peer affiliations, crime and substance use: A fixed effects regression analysis. *Journal of Abnormal Child Psychology, 30,* 419–430.

Finlay, A. K., White, H. R., Mun, E. Y., Cronley, C. C., & Lee, C. (2012). Racial differences in trajectories of heavy drinking and regular marijuana use from ages 13 to 24 among African-American and white males. *Drug and Alcohol Dependence*, *121*, 118–123.

Flay, B. R., & Petraitis, J. (1994). The theory of triadic influence: A new theory of health behavior with implications for preventive intetrventions. *Advances in Medical Sociology*, *4*, 19–44.

Flory, K., Lynam, D., Milich, R., Leukefeld, C., & Clayton, R. (2004). Early adolescent through young adult alcohol and marijuana use trajectories: Early predictors, young adult outcomes, and predictive utility. *Development and Psychopathology*, *16*, 193–213.

Fowler, T., Lifford, K., Shelton, K., Rice, F., Thapar, A., Neale, M. C., . . . Van Den Bree, M. B. M. (2007). Exploring the relationship between genetic and environmental influences on initiation and progression of substance use. *Addiction*, *102*, 413–422.

Freisthler, B., Byrnes, H. F., & Gruenewald, P. J. (2009). Alcohol outlet density, parental monitoring, and adolescent deviance: A multilevel analysis. *Children and Youth Services Review*, *31*, 325–330.

Fuligni, A. J., & Eccles, J. E. (1993). Perceived parent-child relationships and early adolescents' orientation towards peers. *Developmental Psychology*, *29*, 622–632.

Gaines, L. S., Brooks, P. H., Maisto, S., Dietrich, M., & Shagena, M. (1988). The development of children's knowledge of alcohol and the role of drinking, *Journal of Applied and Developmental Psychology*, *9*, 441–457.

Garner, B., Godley, M., Funk, R., Dennis, M., & Godley, S. (2007). The impact of continuing care adherence on environmental risks, substance use, and substance-related problems following adolescent residential treatment. *Psychology of Addictive Behaviors*, *21*, 488–497.

Geier, C. F. (2013). Adolescent cognitive control and reward processing: Implications for risk taking and substance use. *Hormones and Behavior*, *64*, 333–342.

Giedd, J. N., Clasen, L. S., Lenroot, R., Greenstein, D., Wallace, G. L., Ordaz, S., . . . Chrousos, G. (2006). Puberty-related influences on brain development. *Molecular and Cellular Endocrinology*, *254–255*, 154–162.

Giedd, J. N., Keshavan, M., & Paus, T. (2008). Why do many psychiatric disorders emerge during adolescence? *Nature Reviews Neuroscience*, *9*, 947–957.

Gil, A. G., Wagner, E. F., & Tubman, J. G. (2004). Culturally sensitive substance abuse intervention for Hispanics and African-American adolescents: Empirical examples from the ATTAIN project. *Addiction*, *99*, 140–150.

Gillespie, N. A., Neale, M. C., Jacobson, K., & Kendler, K. S. (2009). Modeling the genetic and environmental association between peer group deviance and cannabis use in male twins. *Addiction*, *104*, 420–429.

Goldberg, T., & Weinberger, D. (2009). *The genetics of cognitive neuroscience*. Boston, MA: MIT Press.

Goldman, D., & Bergen, A. (1998). General and specific inheritance of substance abuse and alcoholism. *Archives of General Psychiatry*, *55*, 964–965.

Goldman, D., Oroszi, G., & Ducci, F. (2006). The genetics of addictions: Uncovering the genes. *Focus*, *4*, 401–415.

Goldstein, R. Z., & Volkow, N. (2002). Drug addiction and its underlying neurobiological basis: Neuroimaging evidence for the involvement of the frontal cortex. *American Journal of Psychiatry*, *159*, 1642–1652.

Goncy, E. A., & Mrug, S. (2013). Where and when adolescents use tobacco, alcohol, and marijuana: Comparisons by age, gender, and race. *Journal of Studies on Alcohol and Drugs*, *74*, 288–300.

Grant, B. F., & Dawson, D. A. (1997). Age at onset of alcohol use and its association with DSM-IV drug abuse and dependence: Results from the national longitudinal alcohol epidemiologic survey. *Journal of Substance Abuse*, *10*, 163–173.

Gratten, J., Wray, N. R., Keller, M. C., & Visscher, P. M. (2014). Large-scale genomics unveils the genetic architecture of psychiatric disorders. *Nature Neuroscience*, *17*, 782–790.

Greenbaum, P. E., Del Boca, F. K., Darkes, J. Wang, C-P., & Goldman, M. S. (2005). Variation in drinking trajectories of freshmen college students. *Journal of Consulting and Clinical Psychology*, *73*, 229–238.

Gruber, E., DiClimente, R. J., Anderson, M. M., & Lodico, M. (1996). Early drinking onset and its association with alcohol use and problem behavior in late adolescence. *Preventive Medicine*, *25*, 293–300.

Gruenewald, P. J., Freisthler, B., Remer, L., LaScala, E. A., Treno, A. J., & Ponicki, W. R. (2010). Ecological associations of alcohol outlets with underage and young adult injuries. *Alcoholism: Clinical and Experimental Research*, *34*, 519–527.

Gustafson, D. H., McTavish, F. M., Chih, M-Y., Atwood, A. K., Johnson, R. A., Boyle, M. G., . . . Shah, D. (2014). A smartphone application to support recovery from alcoholism: A randomized clinical trial. *JAMA Psychiatry*, *71*, 566–572.

Hardin, M. G., & Ernst, M. (2009). Functional brain imaging of development-related risk and vulnerability for substance use in adolescents. *Journal of Addiction Medicine*, *3*, 47–54.

Harford, T., Yi, H-Y., & Grant, B. (2010). The five-year diagnostic utility of "diagnostic orphans" for alcohol use disorders in a national sample of young adults. *Journal of Studies on Alcohol and Drugs*, *71*, 410–417.

Harlaar, N., & Hutchison, K. E. (2013). Alcohol and the methylome: Design and analysis considerations for research using human samples. *Drug and Alcohol Dependence*, *133*, 305–316.

Harrison, P. A., Fulkerson, J. A., & Park, E. (2000). The relative importance of social versus commercial sources in youth access to tobacco, alcohol, and other drugs. *Preventive Medicine*, *31*, 39–48.

Hasler, B. P., & Clark, D. B. (2013). Circadian misalignment, reward-related brain function, and adolescent alcohol involvement. *Alcoholism: Clinical and Experimental Research*, *37*, 558–565.

Hawkins, J. D., Catalano, R. F., & Miller, J. Y. (1992). Risk and protective factors for alcohol and other drug problems in adolescence and early adulthood: Implications for substance abuse prevention. *Psychological Bulletin*, *112*, 64–105.

Hawkins, J. D., Graham, J. W., Maguin, E., Abbott, R., Hill, K. G., & Catalano, R. F. (1997). Exploring the effects of age alcohol use initiation and psychosocial risk factors on subsequent alcohol misuse. *Journal of Studies on Alcohol*, *58*, 280–290.

Heath, A. C., Bucholz, K. K., Madden, P. A., Dinwiddie, S. H., Slutske, W. S., Bierut, L. J., . . . Martin, N. G. (1997). Genetic and environmental contributions to alcohol dependence risk in a national twin sample: Consistency of findings in women and men. *Psychological Medicine*, *27*, 1381–1396.

Heitzeg, M. M., Nigg, J. T., Yau, W. Y., Zubieta, J. K., & Zucker, R. A. (2008). Affective circuitry and risk for alcoholism in late adolescence: Differences in frontostriatal responses between vulnerable and resilient children of alcoholic parents. *Alcoholism: Clinical and Experimental Research, 32,* 414–426.

Heitzeg, M. M., Nigg, J. T., Yau, W. Y., Zucker, R. A., & Zubieta, J. K. (2010). Striatal dysfunction marks preexisting risk and medial prefrontal dysfunction is related to problem drinking in children of alcoholics. *Biological Psychiatry, 68,* 287–95.

Hellandsjo Bu, E. T., Watten, R. G., Foxcroft, D. R., Ingebrigtsen, J. E., & Relling, G. (2002). Teenage alcohol and intoxication debut: The impact of family socialization factors, living area and participation in organized sports. *Alcohol and Alcoholism, 37,* 74–80.

Hendrickson, L. M., Guildford, M. J., & Tapper, A. R. (2013). Neuronal nicotinic acetylcholine receptors: Common molecular substrates of nicotine and alcohol dependence. *Frontiers in Psychiatry, 4,* article 29. doi: 10.3389/fpsyt.2013.00029

Hermens, D. F., Lagopoulos, J., Tobias-Webb, J., De Regt, T., Dore, G., Juckes, L., . . . Hickie, I. B. (2013). Pathways to alcohol-induced brain impairment in young people: A review. *Cortex, 49,* 3–17.

Hicks, B. M., Iacono, W. G., & McGue, M. (2010). Consequences of an adolescent onset and persistent course of alcohol dependence in men: Adolescent risk factors and adult outcomes. *Alcoholism: Clinical and Experimental Research, 34,* 819–833.

Hicks, B. M., Iacono, W. G., & McGue, M. (2012). Index of the transmissible common liability to addition: Heritability and prospective associations with substance abuse and related outcomes. *Drug and Alcohol Dependence, 123S,* S18–S23.

Hill, K. G., White, H. R., Chung, I., Hawkins, J. D., & Catalano, R. F. (2000). Early adult outcomes of adolescent binge drinking: Person- and variable-centered analyses of binge drinking trajectories. *Alcoholism: Clinical and Experimental Research, 24,* 892–901.

Hill, S. Y., Shen, S., Lowers, L., & Locke, L. (2000). Factors predicting the onset of adolescent drinking in families at high risk for developing alcoholism. *Biological Psychiatry, 48,* 265–275.

Hill, S. Y., Tessner, K., Wang, S., Carter, H., & McDermott, M. (2010). Temperament at 5 years of age predicts amygdala and orbitofrontal volume in the right hemisphere in adolescence. *Psychiatry Research, 182,* 14–21.

Hingson, R. (2009). The legal drinking age and underage drinking in the United States. *Archives of Pediatric and Adolescent Medicine, 163,* 598–600.

Hingson, R., Heeren, T., & Winter, M. R. (2006). Age at drinking onset and alcohol dependence: Age at onset, duration, and severity. *Archives of Pediatric and Adolescent Medicine, 160,* 739–746.

Hingson, R., & Kenkel, D. (2004). Social, health, and economic consequences of underage drinking. In R. J. Bonnie & M. E. O'Connell (Eds.), *Reducing underage drinking: A collective responsibility* (pp. 351–382). Washington, DC: National Academies Press.

Hingson, R. W., Heeren, T., Jamanka, A., & Howland, J. (2000). Age of drinking onset and unintentional injury involvement after drinking. *Journal of the American Medical Association, 284,* 1527–1533.

Hipwell, A. E., White, H. R., Loeber, R., Stouthamer-Loeber, M., Chung, T., & Sembower, M. A. (2005). Young girls' expectancies about the effects of alcohol, future intentions and patterns of use. *Journal of Studies on Alcohol, 66,* 630–639.

Hofer, M. A. (2005). The psychobiology of early attachment. *Clinical Neuroscience Research, 4,* 291–300.

Hoffmann, J. P., & Su, S. S. (1998). Stressful life events and adolescent substance use and depression: Conditional and gender differentiated effects. *Substance Use and Misuse, 33,* 2219–2262.

Hopfer, C. J., Crowley, T. J., & Hewitt, J. K. (2003). Review of twin and adoption studies of adolescent substance use. *Journal of the American Academy of Child and Adolescent Psychiatry, 42,* 710–719.

Huang, G. C., Soto, D., Fujimoto, K., & Valente, T. W. (2014). The interplay of friendship networks and social networking sites: Longitudinal analysis of selection and influence effects on adolescent smoking and alcohol use. *American Journal of Public Health, 104,* e51–e59.

Huckle, T., Huakau, J., Sweetsur, P., Huisman, O., & Casswell, S. (2008). Density of alcohol outlets and teenage drinking: Living in an alcogenic environment is associated with higher consumption in a metropolitan setting. *Addiction, 103,* 1614–1621.

Hudziak, J., & Faraone, S. (2010). The new genetics in child psychiatry. *Journal of the American Academy of Child and Adolescent Psychiatry, 49,* 729–735.

Hussong, A. M. (in press), Internalizing pathways. In S. Brown & R. A. Zucker (Eds.), *The Oxford handbook of adolescent substance abuse.* New York, NY: Oxford University Press.

Hussong, A. M., Bauer, D., & Chassin, L. (2008a). Telescoped trajectories from alcohol initiation to disorder in children of alcoholic parents. *Journal of Abnormal Psychology, 117,* 63–78.

Hussong, A. M., Curran, P. J., Moffitt, T. E., & Caspi, A. (2008b). Testing turning points using latent growth curve models: Competing models of substance abuse and desistance in young adulthood. In P. Cohen (Ed.), *Applied data analytic techniques for turning points research* (pp. 81–104). New York, NY: Routledge.

Hussong, A. M., Jones, D. J., Stein, G. L., Baucom, D. H., & Boeding, S. (2011). An internalizing pathway to alcohol use and disorder. *Psychology of Addictive Behaviors, 25,* 390–404.

Iacono, W. G., Malone, S. M., & McGue, M. (2008). Behavioral disinhibition and the development of early onset addiction: Common and specific influences. *Annual Review of Clinical Psychology, 4,* 325–348.

Iacono, W. G., Malone, S. M., & McGue, M. (2003). Substance use disorders, externalizing psychopathology, and P300 event-related potential amplitude. *International Journal of Psychophysiology, 48,* 147–178.

Jackson, K. M. (2010). Progression through early drinking milestones in an adolescent treatment sample. *Addiction, 105,* 438–449.

Jackson, K. M. (2016). A longitudinal perspective on substance involvement over the interval from adolescence to young adulthood. In S. Brown & R. A. Zucker (Eds.), *The Oxford handbook of adolescent substance abuse.* New York, NY: Oxford University Press.

Jackson, K. M., Colby, S. M., Barnett, N. P., & Abar, C. C. (2015). Prevalence and correlates of sipping alcohol in a prospective middle school sample. *Psychology of Addictive Behaviors, 29,* 766–778.

Jackson, K. M., & Sartor, C. E. (2014). The natural course of substance use and dependence. In K. Sher (Ed.), *The Oxford handbook of substance use disorders.* New York, NY: Oxford Press. doi: 10.1093/oxfordhb/9780199381678.013.007

Jackson, K. M., & Sher, K. J. (2005). Similarities and differences of longitudinal phenotypes across alternate indices of alcohol involvement: A methodologic comparison of trajectory approaches. *Psychology of Addictive Behaviors, 19*, 339–351.

Jackson, K. M., & Sher, K. J. (2006). Comparison of longitudinal phenotypes based on number and timing of assessments: A systematic comparison of trajectory approaches II. *Psychology of Addictive Behaviors, 20*, 373–384.

Jackson, K. M., & Sher, K. J. (2008). Comparison of longitudinal phenotypes based on alternate heavy drinking cut scores: A systematic comparison of trajectory approaches III. *Psychology of Addictive Behaviors, 22*, 198–209.

Jackson, K. M., Sher, K. J., Cooper, M. L., & Wood, P. K. (2002). Adolescent alcohol and tobacco use: Onset, persistence and trajectories of use across two samples. *Addiction, 97*, 517–531.

Jacobus, J., & Tapert, S. F. (2013). Neurotoxic effects of alcohol in adolescence. *Annual Review of Clinical Psychology, 9*, 703–721.

Jajodia, A., & Earleywine, M. (2003). Measuring alcohol expectancies with the implicit association test. *Psychology of Addictive Behaviors, 17*, 126–133.

Jensen, C. D., Cushing, C. C., Aylward, B. S., Craig, J. T., Sorell, D. M., & Steele, R. G. (2011). Effectiveness of motivational interviewing interventions for adolescent substance use behavior change: A meta-analytic review. *Journal of Consulting and Clinical Psychology, 79*, 433–440.

Jessor, R., & Jessor, S. L. (1977). *Problem behavior and psychosocial development: A longitudinal study of youth*. San Diego, CA: Academic Press.

Johnston, L. D., O'Malley, P. M., Bachman, J. G., & Schulenberg, J. E. (2013). *Demographic subgroup trends among adolescents for fifty-one classes of licit and illicit drugs, 1975-2012* (Monitoring the Future Occasional Paper No. 79). Ann Arbor, MI: Institute for Social Research.

Johnston, L. D., O'Malley, P. M., Bachman, J. G., Schulenberg, J. E., & Miech, R. A. (2014a). *Monitoring the Future national survey results on drug use, 1975-2013: Vol. 1. Secondary school students*. Ann Arbor: Institute for Social Research, University of Michigan.

Johnston, L. D., O'Malley, P. M., Miech, R. A., Bachman, J. G., & Schulenberg, J. E. (2014b). *Monitoring the Future national results on drug use: 1975-2013: Overview, Key Findings on Adolescent Drug Use*. Ann Arbor: Institute for Social Research, University of Michigan.

Jones-Webb, R. Snowden, L., Herd, D., Short, B., & Hannan, P. (1997). Alcohol-related problems among black, Hispanic, and white men: The contribution of neighborhood poverty. *Journal of Studies on Alcohol, 58*, 539–545.

Joslyn, G., Brush, G., Robertson, M., Smith, T. L., Kalmijn, J., Schuckit, M., & White, R. L. (2008). Chromosome 15q25.1 genetic markers associated with level of response to alcohol in humans. *Proceedings of the National Academy of Science USA, 105*, 20368–20373.

Kalsi, G., Prescott, C. A., Kendler, K. S., & Riley, B. P. (2008). Unraveling the molecular mechanisms of alcohol dependence. *Trends in Genetics, 25*, 49–55.

Kandel, D. B. (2002). *Stages and pathways of drug involvement: Examining the gateway hypothesis*. Cambridge, UK: Cambridge University Press.

King, A. C., Houle, T., de Wit, H., Holdstock, L., & Schuster, A. (2002). Biphasic alcohol response differs in heavy versus light drinkers. *Alcoholism: Clinical and Experimental Research, 26*, 827–835.

King, S. M., Iacono, W. G., & McGue, M. (2004). Childhood externalizing and internalizing psychopathology in the prediction of early substance use. *Addiction, 9*, 1548–1559.

Komro, K. A., Maldonado-Molina, M. M., Tobler, A. L., Bonds, J. R., & Muller, K. E. (2007). Effects of home access and availability of alcohol on young adolescents' alcohol use. *Addiction, 102*, 1597–1608.

Koopmans, J. R., van Doornen, L. J. P., & Boomsma, D. I. (1997). Association between alcohol use and smoking in adolescent and young adult twins: A bivariate genetic analysis. *Alcoholism: Clinical and Experimental Research, 21*, 537–546.

Kreek, M. J., Nielsen, D. A., & LaForge, K. S. (2004). Genes associated with addiction: Alcoholism, opiate and cocaine addiction. *NeuroMolecular Medicine, 5*, 85–108.

Kumar, R., O'Malley, P. M., Johnston, L. D., Schulenberg, J. E., & Bachman, J. G. (2002). Effects of school-level norms on student substance use. *Prevention Science, 3*, 105–124.

Kumpfer, K. L., & Summerhays, J. F. (2006). Prevention approaches to enhance resilience among high-risk youth: Comments on the papers of Dishion & Connell and Greenberg. *Annals of the New York Academy of Sciences, 1094*, 151–163.

Kuntsche, E., Gabhainn, S. N., Roberts, C., Windlin, B., Vieno, A., Bendtsen, P., . . . Wicki, M. (2014). Drinking motives and links to alcohol use in 13 European countries. *Journal of Studies on Alcohol, 75*, 428–437.

Kuntsche, E., Knibbe, R., Gmel, G., & Engels, R. (2005). Why do young people drink? A review of drinking motives. *Clinical Psychology Review, 25*, 841–861.

Kuntsche, E., Knibbe, R., Gmel, G., & Engels, R. (2006). Who drinks and why? A review of socio-demographic, personality, and contextual issues behind the drinking motives in young people. *Addictive Behaviors, 31*, 1844–1857.

Labouvie, E. W., Pandina, R. J., & Johnson, V. (1991). Developmental trajectories of substance use in adolescence: Differences and predictors. *International Journal of Behavioral Development, 14*, 305–328.

Lagoa, C. M., Bekiroglu, K., Lanza, S. T., & Murphy, S. A. (2014). Designing adaptive intensive interventions using methods from engineering. *Journal of Consulting and Clinical Psychology, 82*, 868–878.

Lang, A., & Stritzke, W. (1993). Children and alcohol: Young children's knowledge, attitudes, and expectations about alcohol. In M. Galanter (Ed.), *Recent developments in alcoholism: Ten years of progress* (Vol. 11, pp. 73–85). New York, NY: Plenum Press.

Lee, M. R., Chassin, L., & Villalta, I. K. (2013). Maturing out of alcohol involvement: Transitions in latent drinking statuses from late adolescence into adulthood. *Development and Psychopathology, 25*, 1137–1153.

Leggio, L., Kenna, G. A., Fenton, M., Bonefant, E., & Swift, R. M. (2009). Typologies of alcohol dependence: From Jellinek to genetics and beyond. *Neuropsychology Review, 19*, 115–129.

Lerner, R. M., Ostrom, C. W., & Freel, M. A. (1997). Preventing health-compromising behaviors among youth and promoting their positive development: A developmental contextual perspective. In J. Schulenberg, J. L. Maggs, & K. Hurrelmann (Eds.), *Health risks and developmental transitions during adolescence* (pp. 498–521). New York, NY: Cambridge University Press.

Leventhal, T., & Brooks-Gunn, J. (2000). The neighborhoods they live in: The effects of neighborhood residence on child and adolescent outcomes. *Psychological Bulletin, 126,* 309–337.

Lewinsohn, P. M., Rohde, P., & Seeley, J. R. (1996). Alcohol consumption in high school adolescents: Frequency of use and dimensional structure of associated problems. *Addiction, 91,* 375–390.

Li, F., Duncan, T. E., Duncan, S. C., & Hops, H. (2001). Piecewise growth mixture modeling of adolescent alcohol use data. *Structural Equation Modeling, 8,* 175–204.

Li, M. D., & Burmeister, M. (2009). New insights into the genetics of addiction. *Nature Reviews Genetics, 10,* 225–231.

Li, T. K. (2000). Pharmacogentics of responses to alcohol and genes that influence alcohol drinking. *Journal of Studies on Alcohol, 61,* 5–12.

Litt, D. M., & Stock, M. L. (2011). Adolescent alcohol-related risk cognitions: The roles of social norms and social networking sites. *Psychology of Addictive Behaviors, 25,* 708–713.

Little, M., Handley, E., Leuthe, E., & Chassin, L. (2009). The impact of parenthood on alcohol consumption trajectories: Variations as a function of timing of parenthood, familial alcoholism, and gender. *Development and Psychopathology, 21,* 661–682.

Lopez, B., Schwartz, S. J., Prado, G., Campo, A., & Pantin, H. (2008). Adolescent neurological development and its implications for adolescent substance use prevention. *Journal of Primary Prevention, 29,* 5–35.

Luciana, M., Collins, P. F., Muetzel, R. L., & Lim, K. O. (2013). Effects of alcohol use initiation on brain structure in typically developing adolescents. *American Journal of Drug and Alcohol Abuse, 39,* 345–355.

Luna, B., Garver, K. E., Urban, T. A., Lazar, N. A., & Sweeney, J. A. (2004). Maturation of cognitive processes from late childhood to adulthood. *Child Development, 75,* 1357–1372.

Lynne-Landsman, S. D., Bradshaw, C. P., & Ialongo, N. S. (2010). Testing a developmental cascade model of adolescent substance use trajectories and young adult adjustment. *Development and Psychopathology, 22,* 933–948.

Lynskey, M. T., Agrawal, A., & Heath, A. C. (2010). Genetically informative research on adolescent substance use: Methods, findings, and challenges. *Journal of the American Academy of Child and Adolescent Psychiatry, 49,* 1202–1214.

Mackie, C. J., Conrod, P. J., Rijsdijk, F., & Eley, T. C. (2011). A systematic evaluation and validation of subtypes of adolescent alcohol use motives: Genetic and environmental contributions. *Alcoholism: Clinical and Experimental Research, 35,* 420–430.

MacPherson, L., Magidson, J. F., Reynolds, E. K., Kahler, C. W., & Lejuez, C. W. (2010). Changes in sensation seeking and risk taking propensity predict increases in alcohol use among early adolescents. *Alcoholism: Clinical and Experimental Research, 34,* 1400–1408.

Madden, P. A. F., Bucholz, K. K., Martin, N. G., & Heath, A. C. (2000). Smoking and genetic contribution to alcohol-dependence risk. *Alcohol Research and Health, 24,* 209–214.

Maggs, J. L., & Schulenberg, J. E. (2005). Initiation and course of alcohol consumption among adolescents and young adults. In M. Galanter (Ed.), *Recent developments in alcoholism, Vol. 17. Alcohol problems in adolescents and young adults* (pp. 29–47). New York, NY: Kluwer Academic/Plenum Publishers.

Maggs, J. L., Schulenberg, J., & Hurrelmann, K. (1997). Developmental transitions during adolescence: Health promotion implications. In: J. Schulenberg, J. L. Maggs, J. L., & K. Hurrelmann (Eds.) *Health risks and developmental transitions during adolescence* (pp. 522–546). New York, NY: Cambridge University Press.

Marmorstein, N. (2009). Longitudinal associations between alcohol problems and depressive symptoms: Early adolescence through early adulthood. *Alcoholism: Clinical and Experimental Research, 33,* 49–59.

Martin, C. S., Langenbucher, J. W., Chung, T., & Sher, K. (2014). Truth or consequences in the diagnosis of substance use disorder. *Addiction, 109,* 1773–1778.

Martino, S. C., Ellickson, P. L., & McCaffrey, D. F. (2009). Multiple trajectories of peer and parental influence and their association with the development of adolescent heavy drinking. *Addictive Behaviors, 34,* 693–700.

Masten, A. S., Faden, V. B., Zucker, R. A., & Spear, L. P. (2008). Underage drinking: A developmental framework. *Pediatrics, 121*(Suppl. 4), S235–S251.

Masten, A. S., Roisman, G. I., Long, J. D., Burt, K. B., Obradovic, J., Riley, J. R., . . . Tellegen, A. (2005). Developmental cascades: Linking academic achievement and externalizing and internalizing symptoms over 20 years. *Developmental Psychology, 41,* 733–746.

Maurage, P., Joassin, F., Speth, A., Modave, J., Philippot, P., & Campanella, S. (2012). Cerebral effects of binge drinking: Respective influences of global alcohol intake and consumption pattern. *Clinical Neurophysiology, 123,* 892–901.

Maurage, P., Petit, G., & Campanella, S. (2013). Pathways to alcohol-induced brain impairment in young people: A review by Hermens et al., 2013. *Cortex, 49,* 1155–1159.

Mayer, R. R., Forster, J. L., Murray, D. M., & Wagenaar, A. C. (1998). Social settings and situations of underage drinking. *Journal of Studies on Alcohol, 59,* 207–215.

McBride, W. J., Kerns, R. T., Rodd, Z. A., Strother, W. N., Edenberg, H. J., Hashimoto, J. G., . . . Miles, M. F. (2005). Alcohol effects on central nervous system gene expression in genetic animal models. *Alcoholism: Clinical and Experimental Research, 29,* 167–175.

McCarroll, S. A., Feng, G., & Hyman, S. E. (2014). Genome-scale neurogenetics: Methodology and meaning. *Nature Neuroscience, 17,* 756–763.

McClellan, J., & King, M. (2010). Genetic heterogeneity in human disease. *Cell, 141,* 210–217.

McGue, M., Iacono, W. G., Legrand, L. N., Malone, S., & Elkins, I. (2001). Origins and consequences of age at first drink: I. Associations with substance-use disorders, disinhibitory behavior and psychopathology, and P3 amplitude. *Alcoholism: Clinical and Experimental Research, 25,* 1156–1165.

McQueeny, T., Schweinsburg, B. C., Schweinsburg, A. D., Jacobus, J., Bava, S., Frank, L. R., & Tapert, S. F. (2009). Altered white matter integrity in adolescent binge drinkers. *Alcoholism: Clinical and Experimental Research, 33,* 1278–1285.

Medina, K. L., McQueeny, T., Nagel, B. J., Hanson, K. L., Schweinsburg, A. D., & Tapert, S. F. (2008). Prefrontal cortex volumes in adolescents with alcohol use disorders: Unique gender effects. *Alcoholism: Clinical and Experimental Research, 32,* 386–394.

Mendle, J., & Ferrero, J. (2012). Detrimental psychological outcomes associated with pubertal timing in adolescent boys. *Developmental Review, 32,* 49–65.

Merrill, J. E., Read, J. P., & Barnett, N. P. (2013). The way one thinks affects the way one drinks: Subjective evaluations of alcohol consequences predict subsequent change in drinking behavior. *Psychology of Addictive Behaviors, 27*, 42–51.

Miller, J. W., Naimi, T. S., Brewer, R. D., & Jones, S. E. (2007). Binge drinking and associated health risk behaviors among high school students. *Pediatrics, 119*, 76–85.

Miller, W., & Rollnick, S. (2002). *Motivational interviewing: Preparing people for change* (2nd ed.). New York, NY: Guilford Press.

Miranda, R., Monti, P. M., Ray, L., Treolar, H., Reynolds, E. K., Ramirez, J., . . . Magill, M. (2014). Characterizing subjective responses to alcohol among adolescent problem drinkers. *Journal of Abnormal Psychology, 123*, 117–129.

Monti, P. M., Spirito, A., Myers, M., Colby, S., Barnett, N., Rohsenow, D., . . . Lewander, W. (1999). Brief intervention for harm reduction with alcohol-positive older adolescents in a hospital emergency department. *Journal of Consulting and Clinical Psychology, 67*, 989–994.

Moreno, M. A., Briner, L. A., Williams, A., Brockman, L., Walker, L., & Christakis, D. A. (2010). A content analysis of displayed alcohol references on a social networking web site. *Journal of Adolescent Health, 47*, 168–175.

Moreno, M. A., Briner, L. R., Williams, A., Walker, L., & Christakis, D. A. (2009). Real use or "real cool": Adolescents speak out about displayed alcohol references on social networking websites. *Journal of Adolescent Health, 45*, 420–422.

Moreno, M. A., Christakis, D. A., Egan, K. G., Brockman, L. N., & Becker, T. (2012). Associations between displayed alcohol references on Facebook and problem drinking among college students. *Archives of Pediatrics and Adolescent Medicine, 166*(2), 157–163.

Morozova, T., Mackay, T. F. C., & Anholt, R. R. H. (2014). Genetics and genomics of alcohol sensitivity. *Molecular Genetics and Genomics, 289*, 253–269.

Morral, A. R., McCafrey, D. F., & Paddock, S. M. (2002). Evidence does not favor marijuana gateway effects over a common-factor interpretation of drug use initiation: Responses to Anthony, Kenkel & Mathios and Lynskey. *Addiction, 97*, 1509–1510.

Murphy, S. A., Collins, L. M., & Rush, A. J. (2007). Customizing treatment to the patient: Adaptive treatment strategies. *Drug and Alcohol Dependence, 88*, S1–S72.

Nagel, B. J., Schweinsburg, A., Phan, V., & Tapert, S. F. (2005). Reduced hippocampal volume among adolescents with alcohol use disorders without psychiatric comorbidity. *Psychiatry Research, 139*, 181–190.

Nation, M., Crusto, C., Wandersman, A., Kumpfer, K. L., Seybolt, D., Morrissey-Kane, E., & Davino, K. (2003). What works in prevention: Principles of effective prevention programs. *American Psychologist, 58*, 449–456.

National Institute on Alcohol Abuse and Alcoholism. (2004). NIAAA council approves definition of binge drinking. *NIAAA Newsletter, 3*, 3.

National Institute on Alcohol Abuse and Alcoholism. (2011). *Alcohol screening and brief intervention for youth: A practitioner's guide*. Bethesda, MD: Author.

Nestler, E. J. (2014). Epigenetic mechanisms of drug addiction. *Neuropharmacology, 76*, 259–268.

Newcomb, M. D. (1995). Drug use etiology among ethnic minority adolescents: Risk and protective factors. In G. J. Botvin, S. Schinke, & M. A. Orlandi (Eds.), *Drug abuse prevention with multiethnic youth* (pp. 105–129). Thousand Oaks, CA: Sage.

Nigg, J. T., Wong, M. M., Martel, M. M., Jester, J. M., Puttler, L. I., Glass, J. M., . . . Zucker, R. A. (2006). Poor response inhibition as a predictor of problem drinking and illicit drug use in adolescents at risk for alcoholism and other substance use disorders. *Journal of the American Academy of Child and Adolescent Psychiatry, 45*, 468–475.

Oscar-Berman, M. M., & Marinkovic, K. (2007). Alcohol: Effects on neurobehavioral functions and the brain. *Neuropsychology Review, 17*, 239–257.

Ouellette, J. A., Gerrard, M., Gibbons, F. X., & Reis-Bergan, M. (1999). Parents, peers, and prototypes: Antecedents of adolescent alcohol expectancies, alcohol consumption, and alcohol-related life problems in rural youth. *Psychology of Addictive Behaviors, 13*, 183–197.

Pagan, J. L., Rose, R. J., Viken, R. J., Pulkkinen, L., Kaprio, J., & Dick, D. M. (2006). Genetic and environmental influences on stages of alcohol use across adolescence into young adulthood. *Behavior Genetics, 36*, 483–497.

Parra, G. R., Sher, K. J., Krull, J. L., & Jackson, K. M. (2007). Frequency of heavy drinking and perceived peer alcohol involvement: Comparison of influence and selection mechanisms from a developmental perspective. *Addictive Behaviors, 32*, 2211–2225.

Parsons, T. D., Bowerly, T., Buckwalter, J., & Rizzo, A. (2007). A controlled clinical comparison of attention performance in children with ADHD in a virtual reality classroom compared to standard neuropsychological methods. *Child Neuropsychology, 13*, 363–381.

Paschall, M., Fishbein, D. H., Hubal, R., & Eldreth, D. (2005). Psychometric properties of virtual reality vignette performance measures: A novel approach for assessing adolescents' social competency skills. *Health Education Research, 20*, 61–70.

Pascual, M., Boix, J., Felipo, V., & Guerri, C. (2010). Repeated alcohol administration during adolescence causes changes in the mesolimbic dopaminergic and glutamatergic systems and promotes alcohol intake in the adult rat. *Journal of Neurochemistry, 108*, 920–931.

Patrick, M. E., & Schulenberg, J. E. (2010). Alcohol use and heavy episodic drinking prevalence and predictors among national samples of American 8th and 10th grade students. *Journal of Studies on Alcohol and Drugs, 71*, 41–45.

Patrick, M. E., Schulenberg, J. E., Maggs, J. L., & Maslowsky, J. (2014). Substance use and peers during adolescence and emerging/early adulthood: Socialization, selection, and developmental transitions. In K. Sher (Ed.), *Handbook of substance use disorders*. Oxford, UK: Oxford University Press. doi: 10.1093/oxfordhb/9780199381678.013.004

Patton, G., Coffey, C., Carlin, J., Sawyer, S., & Lynskey, M. (2005). Reverse gateways? Frequent cannabis use as a predictor of tobacco initiation and nicotine dependence. *Addiction, 100*, 1518–1525.

Paus, T., Keshavan, M., & Giedd, J. (2008). Why do many psychiatric disorders emerge during adolescence? *Nature Reviews Neuroscience, 9*, 947–957.

Perkins, H. W., Linkenbach, J. W., Lewis, M. A., & Neighbors, C. (2010). Effectiveness of social norms media marketing in reducing drinking and driving: A statewide campaign. *Addictive Behaviors, 35*, 866–874.

Pieters, S., Burk, W. J., Van Der Vorst, H., Engels, R. C. M. E., & Wiers, R. (2014). Impulsive and reflective processes related to alcohol use in young adolescents. *Frontiers in Psychiatry, 5*, article 56. doi: 10.3389/fpsyt.2014.00056

Pieters, S., Van Der Vorst, H., Burk, W. J., Wiers, R., & Engels, R. C. M. E. (2010a). Puberty-dependent sleep regulation and alcohol use in early adolescents. *Alcoholism: Clinical and Experimental Research, 34*, 1512–1518.

Pieters, S., Van Der Vorst, H., Engels, R. C. M. E., & Wiers, R. W. (2010b). Implicit and explicit cognitions related to alcohol use in children. *Addictive Behaviors, 35*, 471–478.

Pine, D. S., Ernst, M., & Leibenluft, E. (2010). Imaging-genetics applications in child psychiatry. *Journal of the American Academy of Child and Adolescent Psychiatry, 49*, 772–782.

Pollock, N. K., & Martin, C. S. (1999). Diagnostic orphans: Adolescents with alcohol symptoms who do not qualify for DSM-IV abuse or dependence diagnoses. *American Journal of Psychiatry, 156*, 897–901.

Porjesz, B., Rangaswamy, M., Kamarajan, C., Jones, K. A., Padmanabhapillai, A., & Begleiter, H. (2005). The utility of neurophysiological markers in the study of alcoholism. *Clinical Neurophysiology, 11*, 993–1018.

Prescott, C. A., & Kendler, K. S. (1999). Age at first drink and risk for alcoholism: A noncausal association. *Alcoholism: Clinical and Experimental Research, 23*, 101–107.

PRIDE Surveys. (2010). 2009-10 National summary—Grade 4 thru 6. Retrieved July 2014, from http://www.pridesurveys.com/customercenter/ue09ns.pdf

PRIDE Surveys. (2014). 2011-12 National summary—Grade 6 thru 12. Retrieved July 2014, from http://www.pridesurveys.com/customercenter/us11ns.pdf

Reboussin, B. A., Song, E-Y., & Wolfson, M. (2011). The impact of alcohol outlet density on the geographic clustering of underage drinking behaviors within census tracts. *Alcoholism: Clinical and Experimental Research, 35*, 1541–1549.

Reimuller, A., Shadur, J., & Hussong, A. M. (2011). Parental social support as a moderator of self-medication in adolescents. *Addictive Behaviors, 36*, 203–208.

Reyna, V., & Farley, F. (2006). Risk and rationality in adolescent decision making. *Psychological Science in the Public Interest, 7*, 1–44.

Rhee, S. H., Hewitt, J. K., Young, S. E., Corley, R. P., Crowley, T. J., & Stallings, M. C. (2003). Genetic and environmental influences on substance initiation, use, and problem use in adolescents. *Archives of General Psychiatry, 60*, 1256–1264.

Ridenour, T. A., Lanza, S. T., Donny, E. C., & Clark, D. B. (2006). Different lengths of times for progressions in adolescent substance involvement. *Addictive Behaviors, 31*, 962–983.

Ridout, B., Campbell, A., & Ellis, L. (2012). "Off your Face(book)": Alcohol in online social identity construction and its relation to problem drinking in university students. *Drug and Alcohol Review, 31*, 20–26.

Rietschel, M., & Treutlein, J. (2013). The genetics of alcohol dependence. *Annals of the New York Academy of Sciences, 1282*, 39–70.

Riper, H., Blankers, M., Hadiwijaya, H., Cunningham, J., Clarke, S., Wiers, R., . . . Cuijpers, P. (2014). Effectiveness of guided and unguided low-intensity internet interventions for adult alcohol misuse: a meta-analysis. *PLoS One, 9*(6), e99912.

Roberts, D. F., Foehr, U. G., Rideout, V. J., & Brodie, M. (1999). *Kids and media @ the new millenium: A comprehensive national analysis of children's media use.* Menlo Park, CA: Kaiser Family Foundation.

Sameroff, A. (2000). Developmental systems and psychopathology. *Development and Psychopathology, 12*, 297–312.

Sargent, J. D., Wills, T. A., Stoolmiller, M., Gibson, J., & Gibbons, F. X. (2006). Alcohol use in motion pictures and its relation with early onset teen drinking. *Journal of Studies on Alcohol, 67*, 54–65.

Sartor, C. E., Agrawal, A., Lynskey, M. T., Bucholz, K. K., & Heath, A. C. (2008). Genetic and environmental influences on the rate of progression to alcohol dependence in young women. *Alcoholism: Clinical and Experimental Research, 32*, 632–638.

Sartor, C. E., Lynskey, M. T., Bucholz, K. K., Madden, P. A. F., Martin, N. G., & Heath, A. C. (2009). Timing of first alcohol use and alcohol dependence: Evidence of common genetic influences. *Addiction, 104*, 1512–1518.

Sartor, C. E., Lynskey, M. T., Heath, A. C., Jacob, T., & True, W. (2007). The role of childhood risk factors in initiation of alcohol use and progression to alcohol dependence. *Addiction, 102*, 216–225.

Saunders, J., & Schuckit, M. (2006). The development of a research agenda for substance use disorders diagnosis in the Diagnostic and Statistical Manual of Mental Disorders, fifth edition (DSM-V). *Addiction, 101*(Suppl. 1), 1–5.

Schell, T. L., Martino, S. C., Ellickson, P. L., Collins, R. L., & McCaffrey, D. (2005). Measuring developmental changes in alcohol expectancies. *Psychology of Addictive Behaviors, 19*, 217–220.

Schlaepfer, I. R., Hoft, N. R., Collins, A. C., Corley, R. P., Hewitt, J. K., Hopfer, C. J., . . . Ehringer, M. A. (2008). The CHRNA5/A3/B4 gene cluster variability as an important determinant of early alcohol and tobacco initiation in young adults. *Biological Psychiatry, 63*(11), 1039–1046.

Schuckit, M. A., Smith, T. L., Danko, G. P., Pierson, J., Hesselbrock, V., Bucholz, K. K., . . . Chan, G. (2007). The ability of the Self-Rating of the Effects of Alcohol (SRE) scale to predict alcohol-related outcomes five years later. *Journal of Studies on Alcohol and Drugs, 68*, 371–378.

Schuckit, M. A., Smith, T. L., & Kalmijn, J. A. (2004). The search for genes contributing to the low level of response to alcohol: Patterns of findings across studies. *Alcoholism: Clinical and Experimental Research, 28*, 1449–1458.

Schuckit, M. A., Smith, T. L., Trim, R., Heron, J., Horwood, J., Davis, J., Hibbeln, J., & ALSPAC Study Team. (2008). The self-rating of the effects of alcohol questionnaire as a predictor of alcohol-related outcomes in 12-year-old subjects. *Alcohol and Alcoholism, 43*, 641–646.

Schulenberg, J., & Maggs, J. L. (2002). A developmental perspective on alcohol use and heavy drinking during adolescence and the transition to young adulthood. *Journal of Studies on Alcohol*, Supplement No. 14, 54–70.

Schulenberg, J., O'Malley, P. M., Bachman, J. G., Wadsworth, K. M., & Johnston, L. D. (1996). Getting drunk and growing up: Trajectories of frequent binge drinking during the transition to young adulthood. *Journal of Studies on Alcohol, 57*, 289–304.

Schumann, G., Loth, E., Banaschewski, T., Barbot, A., Barker, G., Buchel, C., . . . IMAGEN Consortium. (2010). The IMAGEN study: Reinforcement-related behavior in normal brain function and psychopathology. *Molecular Psychiatry, 15*, 1128–1139.

Schutz, C. G. (2012). DSM-V, RDoC and diagnostic approaches in addiction research and therapy. *Journal of Addiction Research and Therapy, 3*, 2.

Schweinsburg, A., McQueeny, T., Nagel, B., Eyler, L. T., & Tapert, S. F. (2010). A preliminary study of functional magnetic resonance imaging response during verbal encoding among adolescent binge drinkers. *Alcohol, 44,* 111–117.

Scott-Sheldon, L. A., Carey, K. B., Elliott, J. C., Garey, L., & Carey, M. P. (2014). Efficacy of alcohol interventions for first-year college students: A meta-analytic review of randomized controlled trials. *Journal of Consulting and Clinical Psychology, 82,* 177–188.

Scribner, R. A., Cohen, D. A., & Fisher, W. (2000). Evidence of structural effect for alcohol outlet density: A multilevel analysis. *Alcoholism: Clinical and Experimental Research, 24,* 188–195.

Sher, K. J. (2007). The road to alcohol dependence: Comment on Sartor et al., (2007). *Addiction, 102,* 185–187.

Sher, K. J., & Gotham, H. J. (1999). Pathological alcohol involvement: A developmental disorder of young adulthood. *Development and Psychopathology, 11,* 933–956.

Sher, K. J., Dick, D. M., Crabbe, J., Hutchison, K., O'Malley, S., & Heath, A. (2010). Consilient research approaches in studying gene x environment interactions in alcohol research. *Addiction Biology, 15,* 200–216.

Sher, K. J., Gotham, H. J., & Watson, A. (2004). Trajectories of dynamic predictors of disorder: Their meanings and implications. *Development and Psychopathology, 16,* 825–856.

Sher, K. J., Jackson, K. M., & Steinley, D. (2011). Alcohol use trajectories and the ubiquitous cat's cradle: Cause for concern? *Journal of Abnormal Psychology, 120,* 322–335.

Shin, S. H., Miller, D. P., & Teicher, M. H. (2013). Exposure to childhood neglect and physical abuse and developmental trajectories of heavy episodic drinking from early adolescence into young adulthood. *Drug and Alcohol Dependence, 127,* 31–38.

Shonkoff, J., & Phillips, D. (Eds.). (2000). *From neurons to neighborhoods: The science of early childhood development.* Washington, DC: National Academy Press.

Simmonds, D. J., Hallquist, M. N., Asato, M., & Luna, B. (2014). Developmental stages and sex differences of white matter and behavioral development through adolescence: A longitudinal diffusion tensor imaging (DTI) study. *Neuroimage, 92,* 356–368.

Simons-Morton, B., Pickett, W., Boyce, W., ter Bogt, T. F. M., & Vollebergh, W. (2010). Cross-national comparison of adolescent drinking and cannabis use in the United States, Canada, and the Netherlands. *International Journal of Drug Policy, 21,* 64–69.

Sitnick, S. L., Shaw, D. S., & Hyde, L. W. (2014). Precursors of adolescent substance use from early childhood and early adolescence: Testing a developmental cascade model. *Development and Psychopathology, 26,* 125–140.

Smith, G. T., & Anderson, K. G. (2001). Adolescent risk for alcohol problems as acquired preparedness: A model and suggestions for intervention. In P. M. Monti, S. M. Colby, & T. A. O'Leary (Eds.), *Adolescents, alcohol, and substance abuse: Reaching teens through brief interventions* (pp. 109–141). New York, NY: Guilford Press.

Soldz, S., & Cui, X. (2002). Pathways through adolescent smoking: A 7-year longitudinal grouping analysis. *Health Psychology, 21,* 495–504.

Song, A. V., Ling, P. M., Neilands, T. B., & Glantz, S. A. (2007). Smoking in movies and increased smoking among young adults. *American Journal of Preventive Medicine, 33,* 396–403.

Spadoni, A. D., McGee, C. L., Fryer, S. L., & Riley, E. P. (2007). Neuroimaging and fetal alcohol spectrum disorders. *Neuroscience and Biobehavioral Reviews, 31,* 239–245.

Spear, L. P. (2010). *The behavioral neuroscience of adolescence.* New York, NY: WW Norton.

Spear, L. P., & Varlinskaya, E. I. (2005). Adolescence: Alcohol sensitivity, tolerance, and intake. In M. Galanter (Ed.), *Recent developments in alcoholism, Vol. 17. Alcohol problems in adolescents and young adults: Epidemiology, neurobiology, prevention, treatment* (pp. 143–159). New York, NY: Springer.

Spoth, R., Greenberg, M., & Turrisi, R. (2008). Preventive interventions addressing underage drinking: State of the evidence and steps toward public health impact. *Pediatrics, 121,* S311–S336.

Spoth, R., Rohrbach, L. A., Greenberg, M., Leaf, P., Brown, C. H., Fagan, A., . . . Society for Prevention Research Type 2 Translational Task Force Members and Contributing Authors. (2013). Addressing core challenges for the next generation of type 2 translation research and systems: The Translation Science to Population Impact (TSci Impact) Framework. *Prevention Science, 14,* 319–351.

Stallings, M. C., Hewitt, J. K., Beresford, T., Heath, A. C., & Eaves, L. J. (1999). A twin study of drinking and smoking onset and latencies from first use to regular use. *Behavioral Genetics, 29,* 409–421.

Steinberg, L. (2008). A social neuroscience perspective on adolescent risk-taking. *Developmental Review, 28,* 78–106.

Stern, S. R. (2005). Messages from teens on the big screen: Smoking, drinking, and drug use in teen-centered films. *Journal of Health Communication, 10,* 331–346.

Stewart, S. H., Conrod, P. J., Marlatt, G. A., Comeau, M. N., Thush, C., & Krank, M. (2005). New developments in prevention and early intervention for alcohol abuse in youths. *Alcoholism: Clinical and Experimental Research, 29,* 278–286.

Stice, E., Myers, M. G., & Brown, S. A. (1998). Relations of delinquency to adolescent substance use and problem use: A prospective study. *Psychology of Addictive Behaviors, 12,* 136–146.

Stritzke, W. G. K., & Butt, J. C. M. (2001). Motives for not drinking alcohol among Australian adolescents: Development and initial validation of a five-factor scale. *Addictive Behaviors, 26,* 633–649.

Substance Abuse and Mental Health Services Administration (SAMHSA), Office of Applied Studies. (2009a). *Treatment Episode Data Set (TEDS). Highlights—2007.* (National Admissions to Substance Abuse Treatment Services, DASIS Series: S-45, DHHS Publication No. SMA 09-4360). Rockville, MD: Author.

Substance Abuse and Mental Health Services Administration (SAMHSA). (2009b). *Results from the 2008 National Survey on Drug Use and Health: National Findings* (Office of Applied Studies, NSDUH Series H-36, HHS Publication No. SMA 09-4434). Rockville, MD: Author.

Substance Abuse and Mental Health Services Administration (SAMHSA). (2013). *Results from the 2012 National Survey on Drug Use and Health: Summary of National Findings* (NSDUH Series H-46, HHS Publication No. SMA 13-4795). Rockville, MD: Author.

Sun, S., Schubert, C., Chumlea, W., Roche, A., Kulin, H., Lee, P., . . . Ryan, A. (2002). National estimates of the timing of sexual maturation and racial differences among US children. *Pediatrics, 110,* 911–919.

Swahn, M. H., Bossarte, R. M., & Sullivent, E. (2008). Age of alcohol use initiation, suicidal behavior, and peer and dating violence victimization and perpetration among high-risk, seventh-grade adolescents. *Pediatrics, 121,* 297–305.

Tapert, S. F., & Brown, S. A. (1999). Neuropsychological correlates of adolescent substance use: Four-year outcomes. *Journal of the International Neuropsychological Society, 5,* 481–493.

Tapert, S. F., & Schweinsburg, A. D. (2005). The human adolescent brain and alcohol use disorders. In M. Galanter (Ed.), *Recent developments in alcoholism, Vol. 17. Research on alcohol problems in adolescents and young adults* (pp. 349–364). Norwell, MA: Kluwer Academic.

Tarter, R. E., Kirisci, L., Mezzich, A., Cornelius, J. R., Pajer, K., Vanyukov, M., . . . Clark, D. B. (2003). Neurobehavioral disinhibition in childhood predicts early age at onset of substance use disorder. *American Journal of Psychiatry, 160,* 1078–1085.

Thompson, K. M., & Yokota, F. (2001). Depiction of alcohol, tobacco, and other substances in G-rated animated feature films. *Pediatrics, 107,* 1369–1374.

Thush, C., Wiers, R., Ames, S. L., Grenard, J. L., Sussman, S., & Stacy, A. W. (2008). Interactions between implicit and explicit cognition and working memory capacity in the prediction of alcohol use in at-risk adolescents. *Drug and Alcohol Dependence, 94,* 116–124.

Tobler, A. L., Livingston, M. D., & Komro, K. A. (2011). Racial/ethnic differences in the etiology of alcohol use among urban adolescents. *Journal of Studies on Alcohol and Drugs, 72,* 799–810.

Todd, M., Grube, J. W., & Gruenewald, P. J. (2007). Alcohol outlet density and youth drinking trajectories. *Alcoholism: Clinical and Experimental Research, 114A,* 37.

Trainor, S., Delfabbro, P., Anderson, S., & Winefield, A. (2010). Leisure activities and adolescent psychological well-being. *Journal of Adolescence, 33,* 173–186.

Tucker, J. S., Ellickson, P. L., Orlando, M., Martino, S. C., & Klein, D. J. (2005). Substance use trajectories from early adolescence to emerging adulthood: A comparison of smoking, binge drinking, and marijuana use. *Journal of Drug Issues, 35,* 307–332.

Tucker, J. S., Orlando, M., & Ellickson, P. L. (2003). Patterns and correlates of binge drinking trajectories from early adolescence to young adulthood. *Health Psychology, 22,* 79–87.

Tuesta, L. M., & Zhang, Y. (2014). Mechanisms of epigenetic memory and addiction. *EMBO Journal, 33,* 1091–1103.

Valente, T. (2010). *Social networks and health: Models, methods, and applications.* Oxford, UK: Oxford University Press.

Van Der Vorst, H., Burk, W. J., & Engels, R. C. M. E. (2010). The role of parental alcohol specific communication in early adolescents' alcohol use. *Drug and Alcohol Dependence, 111,* 183–190.

Vanyukov, M. M., Tarter, R. E., Kirillova, G. P., Kirisci, L., Reynolds, M. D., Kreek, M. J., . . . Ridenour, T. A. (2012). Common liability to addiction and "gateway hypothesis": Theoretical, empirical and evolutionary perspective. *Drug and Alcohol Dependence, 123*(Suppl. 1), S3–S17.

Wagenaar, A. C., & Toomey, T. L. (2002). Effects of minimum drinking age laws: Review and analyses of the literature from 1960 to 2000. *Journal of Studies on Alcohol,* Suppl. 14, 206–225.

Wagner, E. F., Lloyd, D. A., & Gil, A. G. (2002). Racial/ethnic and gender differences in the incidence and onset age of DSM-IV alcohol use disorder symptoms among adolescents. *Journal of Studies on Alcohol, 63,* 609–619.

Wagner, F. A., & Anthony, J. C. (2002). From first drug use to drug dependence: Developmental periods of risk for dependence upon marijuana, cocaine, and alcohol. *Neuropsychopharmacology, 26,* 479–488.

Waldron, H., & Turner, C. (2008). Evidence-based psychosocial treatments for adolescent substance abuse: A review and meta-analysis. *Journal of Clinical Child and Adolescent Psychology, 37,* 1–24.

Walton, M. A., Chermack, S. T., Shope, J. T., Bingham, C. R., Zimmerman, M. A., Blow, F. C., & Cunningham, R. M. (2010). Effects of a brief intervention for reducing violence and alcohol misuse among adolescents: A randomized controlled trial. *Journal of the American Medical Association, 304,* 527–535.

Wang, S., Yang, Z., Ma, J. Z., Payne, T. J., & Li, M. D. (2014). Introduction to deep sequencing and its application to drug addiction research with a focus on rare variants. *Molecular Neurobiology, 49,* 601–614.

Ward, B., Snow, P., & Aroni, R. (2009). Children's alcohol initiation: An analytic overview. *Drugs, Education, Prevention and Policy, 17,* 270–277.

Warner, L. A., & White, H. R. (2003). Longitudinal effects of age at onset and first drinking situations on problem drinking. *Substance Use and Misuse, 38,* 1983–2016.

Whelan, R., Watts, R., Orr, C. A., Althoff, R. R., Artiges, E., Banaschewski, T., . . . the IMAGEN Consortium. (2014). Neuropsychosocial profiles of current and future adolescent alcohol misusers. *Nature.* doi: 10.1038/nature13402

White, A. M., & Swartzwelder, S. (2005). Age-related effects of alcohol on memory and memory-related brain function in adolescents and adults. In M. Galanter (Ed.), *Recent developments alcoholism, Vol. 17. Alcohol problems in adolescents and young adults: Epidemiology, neurobiology, prevention, treatment* (pp. 161–176). New York, NY: Springer.

White, H. R., Jarrett, N., Valencia, E. Y., Loeber, R., & Wei, E. (2007). Stages and sequences of initiation and regular substance use in a longitudinal cohort of black and white male adolescents. *Journal of Studies on Alcohol and Drugs, 68,* 173–181.

Wiers, R. W., Bartholow, B. D., van den Wildenberg, E., Thush, C., Engels, R. C. M. E., Sher, K. J., . . . Stacy, A. W. (2007). Automatic and controlled processes and the development of addictive behaviors in adolescents: A review and model. *Pharmacology, Biochemistry, and Behavior, 86,* 263–283.

Wiesner, M., Weichold, K., & Silbereisen, R. K. (2007). Trajectories of alcohol use among adolescent boys and girls: Identification, validation, and sociodemographic characteristics. *Psychology of Addictive Behaviors, 21,* 62–75.

Wilcox, P. (2003). An ecological approach to understanding youth smoking trajectories: Problems and prospects. *Addiction, 98*(Suppl. 1), 57–77.

Williams, R., & Chang, S. (2000). A comprehensive and comparative review of adolescent substance abuse treatment outcome. *Clinical Psychology: Science and Practice, 7,* 138–166.

Wills, T. A., Gibbons, F. X., Gerrard, M., & Brody, G. H. (2000). Protection and vulnerability processes relevant for early onset of substance use: A test among African-American children. *Health Psychology, 19,* 253–263.

Wills, T. A., Sargent, J. D., Gibbons, F. X., Gerrard, M., & Stoolmiller, M. (2009). Movie exposure to alcohol cues and adolescent alcohol problems: A longitudinal analysis in a national sample. *Psychology of Addictive Behaviors, 23*, 23–35.

Windle, M. (2010). A multilevel developmental contextual approach to substance use and addiction. *BioSocieties, 5*, 124–136.

Windle, M., Mun, E. Y., & Windle, R. C. (2005). Adolescent-to-young adulthood heavy drinking trajectories and their prospective predictors. *Journal of Studies on Alcohol, 66*, 313–322.

Windle, M., Spear, L. P., Fuligni, A. J., Angold, A., Brown, J. D., Pine, D., . . . Dahl, R. E. (2008). Transitions into underage and problem drinking: Developmental processes and mechanisms between 10 and 15 years of age. *Pediatrics, 121*, S273–S289.

Windle, M., & Windle, R. (2005). Alcohol consumption and its consequences among adolescents and young adults. In M Galanter (Ed.), *Recent developments in alcoholism, Vol. 17. Research on alcohol problems in adolescents and young adults* (pp. 67–83). Norwell, MA: Kluwer Academic.

Winstanley, E. L., Steinwachs, D. M., Ensminger, M. E., Latkin, C. A., Stitzer, M. L., & Olsen, Y. (2008). The association of self-reported neighborhood disorganization and social capital with adolescent alcohol and drug use, dependence, and access. *Drug and Alcohol Dependence, 92*, 173–182.

Winters, K. C., Stinchfield, R. D., Opland, E., Weller, C., & Latimer, W. W. (2000). The effectiveness of the Minnesota Model approach in the treatment of adolescent drug abusers. *Addiction, 95*, 601–612.

Wong, K. M., Hudson, T. J., & McPherson, J. D. (2011). Unraveling the genetics of cancer: genome sequencing and beyond. *Annual Review of Genomics and Human Genetics, 12*, 407–430.

Wong, M. M., Brower, K. J., Fitzgerald, H. E., & Zucker, R. A. (2004). Sleep problems in early childhood and early onset of alcohol and other drug use in adolescence. *Alcoholism: Clinical and Experimental Research, 28*, 578–587.

Zhong, H., & Schwartz, J. (2010). Exploring gender-specific trends in underage drinking across adolescent age groups and measures of drinking: Is girls' drinking catching up with boys'? *Journal of Youth and Adolescence, 39*, 911–926.

Zucker, R. A. (1994). Pathways to alcohol problems and alcoholism: A developmental account of the evidence for multiple alcoholisms and for contextual contributions to risk. In R. A. Zucker, B. J. Howard, & G. M. Boyd (Eds.), *The development of alcohol problems: Exploring the biopsychosocial matrix of risk* (pp. 255–289). Rockville, MD: National Institute on Alcohol Abuse and Alcoholism.

Zucker, R. A. (2006). Alcohol use and the alcohol use disorders: A developmental biopsychosocial systems formulation covering the life course. In D. Cicchetti & D. J. Cohen (Eds.), *Developmental psychopathology, Vol. 3. Risk, disorder, and adaptation* (2nd ed., pp. 620–656). Hoboken, NJ: Wiley.

Zucker, R. A. (2014). Genes, brain, behavior, and context: The developmental matrix of addictive behavior. In S. F. Stoltenberg (Ed.), *Genes and the motivation to use substances, Nebraska Symposium on Motivation, 61*, 51–69. doi 10.1007/978-1-4939-0653-6_4

Zucker, R. A., Heitzeg, M. M., & Nigg, J. T. (2011). Parsing the undercontrol-disinhibition pathway to substance use disorders: A multilevel developmental problem. *Child Development Perspectives, 5*, 246–255.

Zucker, R. A., Kincaid, S. B., Fitzgerald, H. E., & Bingham, C. R. (1995). Alcohol schema acquisition in preschoolers: Differences between children of alcoholics and children of nonalcoholics, *Alcoholism: Clinical and Experimental Research, 19*, 1011–1017.

Marijuana Use and Abuse in Adolescence

Dana M. Litt, Jason R. Kilmer, Susan F. Tapert, *and* Christine M. Lee

Abstract

This chapter reviews the extant literature surrounding adolescent marijuana use and abuse. Other than alcohol, marijuana is the most prevalent psychoactive substance used by adolescents. While recent progress has been made in understanding and identifying risk and protective factors of adolescent marijuana use, as well as short and longer term outcomes of use, the field is still in its infancy. The present chapter aims to summarize the prevalence, etiology, trajectories of use, motivations and reasons for use, and the physical and psychological consequences of marijuana use in adolescence. Finally, this chapter highlights the need for future research given the changing landscape of marijuana decriminalization in the United States and beyond.

Key Words: marijuana, adolescence, epidemiology, etiology, trajectories, motivations

Despite its illicit status, in 2012, almost half (45.2%) of high school seniors had tried marijuana, as had over one third of 10th graders (33.8%) and one sixth of 8th graders (15.2%). Past-year use is reported by 36.4% of 12th graders, 28% of 10th graders, and 11.4% of 8th graders; for each grade, past-month marijuana use is 22.9%, 17%, and 6.5%, respectively. For all categories of school-age participants (i.e., 8th grade, 10th grade, and 12th grade), daily use of marijuana (defined as use on 20 or more occasions in the past 30 days) has increased in each of the past 2 years. In fact, approximately one in fifteen high school seniors (6.5%) now reports daily use (Johnston, O'Malley, Bachman, & Schulenberg, 2013).

Marijuana accounted for more cases of dependence or abuse (4.5. million) in 2010 than any other illicit drug, and 1 million people over the age of 12 indicated that they had received treatment for marijuana use (Substance Abuse and Mental Health Services Administration [SAMHSA], 2011a). One in 8 people (12.8%) who first tried marijuana at age 14 or younger meet criteria for illicit drug

dependence or abuse, compared to 2.6% of those who first used after the age of 18 (SAMHSA, 2011a). Thus, because early onset of use is associated with greater risk of a substance use disorder, efforts to delay the onset of use could be an important topic of and target for prevention. A study of high school students (ninth through twelfth grade) from six high schools in New Jersey with lifetime drug use rates similar to the national norms indicated that 13.4% of the sample met past-year criteria for marijuana abuse or dependence (Chen, Sheth, Elliott, & Yeager, 2004). Specifically, 9% of students met criteria for dependence, with tolerance being the most prevalent symptom of marijuana dependence for males (endorsed by 32.5%) and using more than intended being the most prevalent dependence symptom endorsed by females (endorsed by 28.4%).

The Drug Abuse Warning Network (DAWN) statistics from 2009 suggest that approximately 2.1 million visits to emergency departments involved drug misuse or abuse (SAMHSA, 2011b). Almost half (47%) involved an illicit drug taken alone or in combination with pharmaceuticals, alcohol, or both; of these, 38.7% (376,467 visits) involved marijuana. The rate of marijuana involvement was highest for those between the ages of 18 and 20 (64,050 visits), followed by those between the ages of 21 and 24 (61,961 visits). For adolescents between the ages of 12 and 17, 45,088 visits to emergency departments involved marijuana. When drugs were taken with alcohol, almost one quarter of the time (24.1%), marijuana was one of the substances being combined. In drug-related suicide attempts, illicit drugs were involved 17.9% of the time, and marijuana was involved 7.1% of the time (second behind cocaine) (SAMHSA, 2011b).

Gender, Ethnic/Racial, and Geographic Differences in Adolescent Marijuana Use

Examination of gender differences in adolescent marijuana use is a particularly understudied area, underscoring the need for further investigations. However, in general, males appear to be more likely to use marijuana, with National Survey on Drug Use and Health (NSDUH) data indicating that 17% of adolescent males and 15% of females had used marijuana over their lifetime (SAMSHA, 2009). Three large national surveys—the Youth Risk Behavior Survey, Monitoring the Future, and the NSDUH—have found significant racial/ethnic differences in marijuana consumption rates among adolescents (e.g., Johnston et al., 2009; SAMHSA, 2002; Wallace et al., 2002). For example, among youths ages 12–17, Hispanics (19%) and Caucasians (17%) reported a higher lifetime prevalence of marijuana use, compared with African Americans (15%) (SAMHSA, 2002). Additional work by Schepis and colleagues (2011) found significant interactions between gender and ethnicity on past marijuana use. Specifically, the research indicated that African American males, but not females, were at greater odds of lifetime marijuana use, whereas Caucasian females were at greater odds of lifetime use than were males. Additionally, being of Asian or other descent was protective for females, but it was not associated with male use.

In addition to gender and racial/ethnic differences in marijuana use, there is also evidence that adolescent marijuana use in the United States varies as a function of geographical region. The results of the 2010–2011 NSDUH survey indicated that states in the Western United States such as Colorado, Montana, New Mexico, Oregon, and Washington as well as states in New England including Massachusetts, New Hampshire, Rhode Island, and Vermont had the highest rates of adolescent marijuana use (ages 12 and older) with up to 15% of adolescents reporting last month use (SAMHSA, 2012). In contrast, marijuana use was lowest among states primarily in the Southern US states such as Alabama, Arkansas, Louisiana, Mississippi, and Tennessee (SAMHSA, 2012).

Trajectories and Patterning of Marijuana Use

Longitudinal research has consistently shown different pathways, or trajectories, of marijuana use from adolescence into young adulthood, with various trajectories associated with different developmental outcomes and functioning in young adulthood. While the number of trajectories differs by study, sample, gender, and race/ethnicity, there appears to be consistency across studies indicating significant variability in timing of initiation and course of marijuana use across adolescence and young adulthood (e.g., Brown, Flory, Lynam, Leukefeld, & Clayton, 2004; Windle & Wiesner, 2004). Common trajectories of adolescent marijuana use tend to be characterized by those who are nonusers/abstinent, experimental or occasional light user, increasers in use across adolescence, high users early who decrease use across adolescence, quitters (those who increased use during adolescence but ceased use in young adulthood), and those who have chronic/heavy marijuana use across adolescence (e.g., Brook, Lee, Brown, Finch, & Brook, 2011; Brown et al., 2004; Ellickson, Martino, & Collins, 2004; Finlay, White, Mun, Cronley, & Lee, 2012; Flory, Lynam, Milich, Leukefeld, & Clayton, 2004; Juon, Fothergill, Green, Doherty, & Ensminger, 2011; Pahl, Brook & Koppel, 2011; Schulenberg et al., 2005; Windle & Wiesner, 2004). Several of these studies also examined adolescent risk factors or predictors of different trajectory groups. Not surprisingly, abstainers or nonuser trajectories tended to have the lowest risk factors for use, while earlier users and heavier more chronic users had highest risk factors. For example, Flory et al. (2004) found that youth who initiated marijuana use before age 11–12 were more likely to have lower school performance and commitment, self-esteem, family relations, perceptions of peer pressure resistance and higher on expectancies, while those in the nonusers tended to be lower in expectancies and higher on other factors. Windle and Wiesner (2004) found that trajectories associated with the high chronic use group had highest levels of delinquency, more stressful life events, lower academic achievement, and more friends who use drugs. In a study following sixth graders through age 20, Brown et al. (2004) found race differences in patterns of use among Caucasian and African American adolescents. While antecedents of substance use did not differ by race, Brown et al. (2004) did find that earlier users were higher in risk factors for substance use (i.e., lower church involvement, lower peer pressure resistance, higher sensation seeking and marijuana expectancies) than other groups, consistent with other studies.

Findings in general indicate that trajectories with earlier initiation of marijuana use are associated with worse young adult outcomes, including other drug and polydrug use, arrests, lower academic achievement, and lower psychological adjustment (e.g., Brown et al., 2004; Ellickson et al., 2004; Flory et al., 2004; Pahl et al., 2011). Pahl et al. (2011) found that women who increased their marijuana use through adolescence and young adulthood reported worse psychological adjustment in young adulthood, including more depressive symptoms and anger/hostility, and were at greater risk for substance use disorders than nonusers at age 32. Some research suggests that developmental outcomes in young adulthood might differ based on race and timing of onset; for example, Brown et al. (2004) found that early onset among Caucasian and mid-onset among African American adolescents evidenced worse outcomes at age 20.

Trajectories with chronic or heavy use across adolescence tend to be associated with engagement in criminal behavior and delinquent activity, lower academic aspirations and achievement, having more drug-using friends, and being higher in sensation seeking (e.g., Brook et al., 2011; Flory et al., 2004; Windle & Wiesner, 2004). Using data from 18 cohorts participating in the Monitoring the Future study from high school through young adulthood, Schulenberg and colleagues (2005) found that approximately 25% engaged in frequent marijuana use at some point during young adulthood (defined as using 3+ times/month or 20+ times/year), with approximately 5% (of total sample) engaging in chronic use throughout young adulthood. Chronic frequent users were at greater risk for using marijuana to cope; associating with others who use marijuana; and engaging in binge drinking, cigarette use, theft, and property damage, interpersonal aggression, and risk taking by age 23/24 (Schulenberg et al., 2005). Furthermore, chronic frequent marijuana use was related to less likelihood of graduating college or getting married, while being

related to increased likelihood of experiencing unemployment (Schulenberg et al., 2005). Tucker and colleagues (2005) found similar trajectories and those who increased their marijuana use throughout adolescence and into young adulthood were less likely to graduate from college, report poorer physical and mental health, and more likely to have a history of drug problems by age 23 compared to occasional light users and/or abstainers (Tucker, Ellickson, Orlando, Martino, & Klein, 2005). Further problems resulting from continued marijuana use through young adulthood can influence later outcomes such as prevalence of substance use disorders, incarceration, and marriage into mid-adulthood (Juon et al., 2011).

Marijuana's Influence on Other Substance Use: A Gateway Drug?

In addition to the possible health and cognitive consequences related to adolescent marijuana use, there has long been a concern that marijuana may serve as a "gateway" to experimentation and/or regular use of other illicit substances. The gateway hypothesis is actually comprised of three related but unique assertions (Van Gundy & Rebellon, 2010). First, the gateway hypothesis suggests that individuals rarely use illicit substances, such as heroin or cocaine, without first having used "gateway" substances, such as marijuana. Second, it suggests that using substances earlier in that typical sequence is associated with an increased risk of using other illicit substances later. Third, it suggests that the association between the use of marijuana and the later use of other illicit substances is causal. Whereas much research supports the first and second assertions (Kandel, 2002), far less research supports a causal link between marijuana use and the use and abuse of other illicit substances (Kandel & Jessor, 2002).

There is strong and consistent evidence that the use of marijuana almost invariably precedes the use of other illicit drugs. For example, Kandel and Yamaguchi (2002), using data from a national cross-sectional sample, found that although most marijuana users did not proceed to use cocaine and heroin, 90% of cocaine users had used marijuana prior to using cocaine. Golub and Johnson (2002), in a study of serious drug abusers, found that roughly 90% began their illicit drug use with marijuana. Similarly, Kandel, Yamaguchi, and Chen (1992) found that between 86% and 90% of people using both marijuana and other illicit drugs reported having used marijuana prior to the use of other illicit drugs. A strong temporal sequence was also reported in a study by Fergusson and Horwood (2000). This work indicated that of those individuals who used both marijuana and other illicit drugs, fewer than 1% used other illicit drugs prior to using marijuana. Furthermore, in a review of longitudinal studies assessing marijuana use, MacLeod and colleagues (2004) concluded that the association between marijuana use and later illicit substance use was significant, even when controlling for a variety of other factors such as novelty-seeking, self-esteem, risk-taking tendencies, conduct problems, and peer affiliations (MacLeod et al., 2004).

Despite the consistent findings associating marijuana use with subsequent illicit drug use, the interpretation of these results is still somewhat controversial. There are thought to be three possible mechanisms that explain the gateway pattern, all with varying levels of empirical support. First, some have argued that the gateway pattern arises because the pharmacological effects of marijuana increase the likelihood of using other illicit drugs later on (Hall & Lynskey, 2003; Schenk, 2002). A second hypothetical mechanism, arising from problem behavior theory (Donovan & Jessor, 1985; Jessor & Jessor, 1977) assumes that the association arises because of common factors that predispose young people to use both marijuana and other illicit drugs (Fergusson, Boden, & Horwood, 2006). A third explanation posits that the associations between marijuana use and other illicit drug use results from an individual learning process whereby individuals first experiment with marijuana and learn that the drug has pleasurable effects and low rates of adverse side effects. These experiences then lead to further experimentation with other illicit drugs. However, there is little direct evidence to support this explanation. A fourth mechanism proposed to account for the gateway effect of marijuana supposes that the regular social interaction with other drug-using peers increases the likelihood of further illicit drug use initiation (e.g., Degenhardt, Hall, & Lynskey, 2001). Currently, it is still unclear which, if any, of the aforementioned theories adequately explains the apparent gateway role of marijuana.

Consequences of Marijuana Use

The effects of marijuana are influenced by the dose received, how the person uses, past experience with the drug, expectancies, attitudes, mood, and the setting in which it is used (Hall & Degenhardt, 2009). The "high" that is likely seen as attractive to those who make the choice to use marijuana results

from the effect of delta-9-tetrahydrocannabinol (THC) (Cooper & Haney, 2009). If smoked, effects are promptly felt; if consumed orally through food or beverage, there is more of a delay in the onset of psychoactive effects. Relative to other substances, marijuana use is among the strongest antecedents of accidents, injuries, and emergency room visits (SAMHSA, 2003, 2005). Short-term or acute effects of marijuana can include feeling euphoric or "high," decreased cognitive functioning, respiratory problems, and increased heart rate (NIDA, 2002; Taylor et al., 2000; Hall & Solowij, 1998). Marijuana use can impair driving, certainly noteworthy for adolescents, up to 3 hours after use (Grotenhermen et al., 2007). Marijuana use is also associated with poor school performance and attendance (Lynskey & Hall, 2000; Roebuck et al., 2004) and violence against others (Moore & Stuart, 2005). Longer term harms often associated with marijuana use, including concern about long-term cognitive problems and cancer risk, are often harder to document. For example, questions of cancer risk due to carcinogen exposure often arise, but they are hard to measure when people use marijuana and tobacco simultaneously (e.g., a "blunt") or when marijuana users also report tobacco use (Hall & Degenhardt, 2009). However, from a general health standpoint, it is worth noting that debate remains surrounding some of the harms associated with marijuana (Copeland & Swift, 2009).

Cognitive Effects

With so many adolescents and young adults in school (or preparing to leave school for the workforce), any impact on cognitive functioning would presumably be of interest to parents, health educators, and, potentially, the students themselves. Marijuana use in adolescence is associated with altered brain structure, function, and neuropsychological performance. In general, adolescents who are heavy users of marijuana have been found to perform worse than nonusing youth on neuropsychological tests of problem solving (Lane, Cherek, Tcheremissine, Steinberg, & Sharon, 2007), attention, memory, and learning (Harvey, Sellman, Porter, & Frampton, 2007). Use of marijuana by adolescents is associated with poor school performance, disliking school, and school absences (Gruber & Pope, 2002). Marijuana use has been shown to be associated with deficits in attention and executive functioning even a day after last use (Pope & Yurgelun-Todd, 1996), in addition to problems with memory, time estimation, and psychomotor speed (Hanson, Winward, et al., 2010). Specific to adolescents, however, many of these issues are evident even once use subsides. Medina, Hanson, and colleagues (2007) demonstrated that even after controlling for alcohol use and depressive symptoms, adolescent marijuana users following approximately 1 month of abstinence nevertheless showed poorer attention, planning and sequencing, verbal story memory, and psychomotor speed than their non-marijuana-using peers. In fact, frequent, persistent marijuana use with onset in adolescence has been linked to neurocognitive performance disadvantages, even after controlling for years of education (Meier et al., 2012). This highlights the need to inform adolescents and parents about these potential harms.

In adults who smoke marijuana daily and initiate abstinence, memory deficits are still evident 1 week after quitting, though no significant difference compared to controls is evident after abstaining for 4 weeks (Pope, Gruber, Hudson, Huestis, & Yurgelun-Todd, 2001). However, the adolescent brain may be more susceptible to lingering difficulties after stopping. In teens followed at three time points over 3 weeks of abstinence from marijuana use, deficits in verbal learning were evident 3 days after abstinence (though no longer evident at 2 weeks and 3 weeks of abstinence), deficits in verbal working memory were still seen at 2 weeks of abstinence (though no longer evident at 3 weeks of abstinence), and deficits on an attention/vigilance task persisted even at 3 weeks of abstinence compared to a control group of nonusing adolescents (Hanson, Winward, et al., 2010). The authors conclude that teens using marijuana might be unaware of the cognitive issues they are experiencing, yet nevertheless be affected and experience an impact in academic, behavioral, or occupational functioning (Hanson, Winward, et al., 2010). In some studies cessation of use did not appear to fully restore cognitive performance among adolescent-onset marijuana users (Meier et al., 2012).

Influence on Brain Development

Neuroimaging approaches have revealed some structural and functional abnormalities, suggesting the possibility that heavy adolescent marijuana use could potentially adversely affect adolescent neuromaturation. Studies examining white matter show differences in white matter integrity among adolescent marijuana users compared to nonusers, particularly in fronto-parietal circuitry and pathways connecting the frontal and temporal lobes

(Bava et al., 2009). Earlier age of onset of marijuana use (i.e., adolescent onset) was related to poorer frontal white matter integrity in chronic adult marijuana users, which was in turn associated with increased impulsivity (Gruber, Silveri, Dahlgren, & Yurgelun-Todd, 2011).

Heavy marijuana use in the second decade of life has been associated with differences in cortical volumes. Marijuana-using adolescents have shown larger cerebellar volumes than nonusers (Medina, Nagel, & Tapert, 2010), and female marijuana users have larger prefrontal cortex volumes than same-gender nonusers (Medina et al., 2009), suggesting the possibility of attenuation of the typical cortical thinning that occurs during this phase in life. However, another study showed smaller right medial orbital prefrontal cortex volumes in marijuana-abusing adolescents than nonusers, and earlier initiation was linked to less medial and orbital PFC volume (Churchwell, Lopez-Larson, & Yurgelun-Todd, 2010). One study examined whether structural brain alterations were present before the onset of marijuana use. Right orbitofrontal cortex (but not amygdala, hippocampus, or anterior cingulate cortex volumes) at age 12 predicted initiation of marijuana use at age 16, even after controlling for other substance use, suggesting brain abnormalities as a risk factor for early marijuana use (Cheetham et al., 2012).

Besides alterations in white matter integrity and volume, brain response patterns in adolescent marijuana users have shown specific features. Heavy marijuana-using adolescents show differences in blood oxygen level–dependent response contrast, as compared to nonusers, during tasks of spatial working memory (Schweinsburg et al., 2005; Schweinsburg, McQueeny, Nagel, Eyler, & Tapert, 2010), inhibitory processing (Tapert et al., 2007), and verbal memory (Jacobsen, Pugh, Constable, Westerveld, & Mencl, 2007). Most studies suggest that adolescent marijuana users show a brain activation pattern that appears less efficient compared to nonusers during tasks of verbal learning and cognitive control (Schweinsburg et al., 2008, 2010; Tapert et al., 2007). Moreover, adolescent marijuana users show an altered cerebral blood flow compared to controls (Jacobus et al., 2012), which appears to remit after 4 weeks of monitored abstinence.

To examine the neuropsychological effects of alcohol and marijuana use among adolescents, most studies describe the influence of alcohol or marijuana separately. However, alcohol and marijuana are often used together. Concomitant users of marijuana and alcohol also show differences in brain structure and function, as well as a poorer performance on neuropsychological functioning. Animal studies have showed that THC administration alone did not result in neurodegeneration, but the same amount of THC combined with a small dose of ethanol induced neuronal cell death in the developing brain (Hansen et al., 2008), an effect similar to that observed with high doses of ethanol alone. Similarly, a comparison of hippocampal volumes between adolescent drinkers, drinkers who also use marijuana, and controls (Medina, Schweinsburg, Cohen-Zion, Nagel, & Tapert, 2007) showed that drinkers had smaller hippocampal volumes and abnormal hippocampal asymmetry than controls, but this was not the case for those reporting both alcohol and marijuana use. Another study showed more coherent white matter tracts in binge-drinking adolescents who also use marijuana, compared to binge drinking alone (Jacobus et al., 2009). A neuropsychological study found that alcohol hangover symptoms in nonusers of marijuana predicted worse verbal learning and memory scores, whereas this was not the case for adolescents who both use alcohol and marijuana (Mahmood, Jacobus, Bava, Scarlett, & Tapert, 2010).

Conversely, other studies showed a diminished cognitive performance in adolescents using both marijuana and alcohol, with alcohol and marijuana use associated with differences in prefrontal, cerebellar, and hippocampal volumes, less white matter microstructural integrity, and atypical brain activation patterns (Bava et al., 2009; Hanson, Medina, et al., 2010; Jacobsen et al., 2007; Medina, Nagel, & Tapert, 2010; Schweinsburg et al., 2005, 2008; Tapert et al., 2001, 2004, 2007). Adolescents who use both alcohol and marijuana have shown diminished performances on tasks of attention, information processing, spatial skills, learning and memory, and planning and problem solving even after 28 days of sustained abstinence (Medina, Hanson, et al., 2007; Tapert & Brown, 1999; Tapert, Granholm, Leedy, & Brown, 2002). It is important to note that relatively less is known about the effects of marijuana use without concomitant alcohol use. However, studies are underway that will be able to evaluate the long-term effects of marijuana use on the adolescent brain, as it is moving toward the same or similar legal status as alcohol in some US states and other countries.

Family Influences on Adolescent Marijuana Use
Genetic Factors

Research on family influences of marijuana use, abuse, and dependence indicate both genetic components, as well as environmental factors, such as parental monitoring and family environment. Numerous studies involving adult samples have been consistently indicating a genetic or heritable component to substance use, abuse, and dependence (e.g., Gruber & Pope, 2002; Hopfer, Stallings, Hewitt, & Crowley, 2003; Lynskey, Agrawal, & Heath, 2010 for reviews). Specific to marijuana/cannabis, research utilizing adult twin samples indicates that genetic factors are strong influences in risk for marijuana dependence (Kendler & Prescott, 1998; Kendler, Karkowski, Neale, & Prescott, 2000), while others suggest genetic factors are more influential in the etiology of use rather than dependence (Lynskey et al., 2002). For example, among a sample of female twins, genetic factors were found to have a moderate impact on marijuana initiation and strong impact in the course from regular use and more severe and problematic use (Kendler & Prescott, 1998). It has been estimated that approximately 45%–62% (depending on gender and study) of variance in risk for dependence may be attributed to genetic factors (Kendler & Prescott, 1998; Kendler et al., 2000; Lynskey et al., 2002).

The extent to which genetic factors contribute to adolescent marijuana misuse and problems appears to be less well understood compared to adult marijuana use and dependence (Young, Rhee, Stallings, Corley, & Hewitt, 2006). Findings from several adolescent twin studies show that genetic influences are less influential in experimental marijuana use during adolescence, suggesting that genetic and environmental factors are both important (Fowler et al., 2007; Maes et al., 1999; McGue et al., 2000; Miles et al., 2001; Miles, van den Bree, & Pickens, 2002). However, others have found strong genetic influences for adolescent marijuana use and problem use (Young et al., 2006) or just heavier use (Fowler et al., 2007). Furthermore, gender differences have been found regarding the extent to which genetic and environmental factors influence individual marijuana use, with things such as common environmental factors shared between twins to be more influential among females (e.g., being raised by same parents, same neighborhood; Miles et al., 2002).

Parental Factors

Numerous studies have found that parents have both direct and indirect influences on adolescent marijuana use. Parental monitoring, parent–child relationships, parental management styles and practices, and parent–child communication have all been associated with adolescent marijuana initiation and use (e.g., Brook, Kessler, & Cohen, 1999; Butters, 2002; Gutman, Eccles, Peck, & Malanchuk, 2011; Kosterman et al., 2000; Marti, Stice, & Springer, 2010, see Lac & Crano, 2009 for review). For example, Kosterman et al. (2000) found proactive family management strategies or practices, such as having better monitoring and firm rules, were associated with a decreased likelihood of starting or initiating marijuana use. Another study found that adolescents who had moderate to good relationships with their fathers also were more likely to model the father's marijuana use (Andrews, Hops, & Duncan, 1997). Cleveland, Gibbons, Gerrard, Pomery, and Brody (2005) found that parental monitoring, communication about substances, and warmth were related to substance use 5 years later, primarily through two indirect pathways: risk images and behavioral willingness.

In a longitudinal study of early adolescent youth, teens who had decreasing or inconsistent parental communication were associated with greater marijuana use (Tobler & Komro, 2010). While changes in parental monitoring and communication may be developmentally appropriate as teens grow, early or inconsistent change has found to be associated with marijuana initiation and use. Children who had more parent supervision and monitoring during middle childhood were less likely to initiate marijuana and other drug use during adolescence (Chilcoat & Anthony, 1996). Dishion, Nelson, and Bullock (2004) found parents of antisocial boys tended to alter their parenting styles between early to mid-adolescence, often by decreasing family management characterized by less positive parenting, having poorer parent–child relationships and less parental monitoring, compared to parents of well-adjusted boys who maintained high levels of family management. Furthermore, antisocial boys who also had more deviant friendships in adolescence and decreased family management were at greater risk for marijuana use at age 18.

Peer Influences on Adolescent Marijuana Use

One of the most commonly supported factors leading to all forms of adolescent substance use, including marijuana, is peer influence (Chassin, Presson, Sherman, Montello, & McGrew, 1986; Conrad, Flay, & Hill, 1992; Duncan, Duncan, & Hops, 1994). Peer influence may be overt in the form of actual encouragement or discouragement to engage in a behavior, or subtle and indirect in the form of adolescent perceptions about group norms, expectations, social acceptance, and status associated with the behavior. Both overt and indirect influences have been widely supported as risk factors for adolescent marijuana use.

Socialization Versus Selection

Affiliation with substance-using peers has long been cited as a prominent correlate of illicit drug use in adolescence (Dishion & Owen, 2002; Jessor & Jessor, 1977; Oetting & Beauvais, 1986). The adolescent literature has consistently shown similarity in substance use between adolescent peers (e.g., Ennett & Bauman, 1991, 1994; Urberg, Degirmencioglu, & Pilgrim, 1997). This similarity in substance use behavior has been generally attributed to two processes: socialization, wherein the peer group influences the substance use behavior of the individual; and selection, wherein individuals associate with peers who are similar to them in their substance use behavior (Andrews, Tildesley, Hops, & Li, 2002). Results from several longitudinal studies have shown both the effects of socialization (Ennett & Bauman, 1991, 1994; Schulenberg et al., 1999; Urberg et al., 1997; Wills & Cleary, 1999) and selection (Ennett & Bauman, 1994; Fisher & Bauman, 1988; Kandel, 1978). Both selection and socialization has been further supported by theoretical research examining peer clustering and peer normative influence.

Peer Clustering

According to peer cluster theory, the single dominant variable in adolescent drug use is the influence provided by the peers with whom an adolescent chooses to associate (Oetting & Beauvais, 1986). Research coming out of this tradition presupposes that drug use is nearly always directly linked to peer relationships such that peers shape attitudes about drugs, provide drugs, provide the social contexts for drug use, and share ideas and beliefs that become the rationales for drug use (Oetting & Beauvais, 1987). Based on shared substance use, peer groups form that use drugs together. These groups may consist of a large or small group of friends, or they may be dyads such as best friends (Andrews et al., 2002). These close and highly influential groups are referred to as peer clusters, and within drug-using peer clusters, drugs play an important part in defining the group, shaping its typical behaviors, and maintaining the group identity and structure (Oetting & Beauvais, 1986). Put simply, individuals inclined toward risks tend to identify and associate with others who are similarly inclined toward risks (Bauman & Ennett, 1996). Therefore, friends have similar drug behavior when their friendships are formed on the basis of common drug behavior. In these cases, selection rather than socialization produces the association between friend and adolescent drug use. Selection has multiple mechanisms: Drug users choose other users to be friends, nonusers choose other nonusers to be friends, friendships dissolve when the drug behavior of friends becomes dissimilar, and peer groups restrict membership to people with drug behaviors like their own. The strength of the clustering effect is usually quite high, with the association with deviant peers accounting for up to 50% of the variance in substance use (Dishion, Capaldi, Spracklen, & Li, 1995; Dishion & Owen, 2002). Overall, the research in this area has found that one of the strongest correlates of adolescent substance use, including marijuana, is the tendency to cluster into peer groups that use substances (Dishion & Owen, 2002; Jessor & Jessor, 1977; Oetting & Beauvais, 1987, 1990).

Popularity

Decades of research have focused on youth experiencing social difficulties as targets for substance use prevention efforts. However, recent work has suggested that adolescents who fare particularly well among peers may be at increased risk for substance use, including marijuana use. It is possible that popular adolescents represent a high-risk group and that individuals who aspire to be popular may begin to engage in the risky behavior in order to conform to the popular group norms (Prinstein, Choukas-Bradley, Helms, Brechwald, & Rancourt, 2011). A recent study indicated that among males, higher levels of popularity (peer-nominated) were associated with higher levels of marijuana use, whereas there was no significant relationship for females (Prinstein et al., 2011), perhaps in part due to differences in social expectations for males and females. Other studies have found that peer-nominated popularity is associated with recent marijuana use among middle school students (Ennett et al., 2006) and that self-rated popularity is associated with marijuana use among

high school seniors (Diego, Field, & Sanders, 2003). However, a recent study found that whereas both peer-nominated and self-rating of popularity were associated with lifetime marijuana use, only the latter was associated with current marijuana use (Tucker et al., 2011).

Research has also indicated interesting gender differences for the relationship between popularity and marijuana use. Among males, higher levels of popularity have been associated with higher levels of later marijuana use, after controlling for prior marijuana use (Tucker et al. 2011). However, the same study found no significant results for females. It is possible that as boys' level of popularity increases, several related factors also may increase, such as access to social gatherings at which illegal substances are available and used, and expectations to engage in risky or "mature" behaviors (Moffitt, 1997). Additionally, research suggests that members of popular crowds may be more likely to come from wealthier families, and this access to wealth may lead to increased access to, and opportunities to, engage in substance use (Mayeux, Sandstrom, & Cillessen, 2008). Although popularity in adolescent females is likely accompanied by similar access, expectations, and pressure, risk behaviors may signal different social messages, such that marijuana use may be considered acceptable (i.e., "cool") more for boys than girls (Warner, Weber, & Albanes, 1999).

Norms

Despite the fairly robust research indicating that direct peer influence such as peer clustering and selection impacts adolescent marijuana use, several investigators (Bauman & Ennett, 1996; Bauman & Fisher, 1986; Kandel, 1996; Kobus, 2003) have argued that findings derived from many of these studies are limited because they reflect respondents' projections of their own behavior onto their friends. Studies that have used network analysis and friend reports of their own behavior have found somewhat smaller effects than those using perceptions of peer use, leading to the suggestion that adolescents routinely overestimate actual peer use (Bauman & Ennett, 1994, 1996; Bauman & Fisher, 1986; Eiser & Van der Pligt, 1984; Fisher & Bauman, 1988; Kandel, 1996). As a result, a wealth of research has argued that adolescents' perceptions of substance use prevalence are more important in predicting substance use than direct influences such as peer clustering.

The social norms approach (e.g. Perkins, 2003) posits that indirect peer influence, in the form of normative perceptions, acts on an individual's personal behavior, regardless of the accuracy of the perceived norms. Normative perceptions are routinely divided into two distinct categories: descriptive and injunctive. Descriptive norms refer to the perception of others' actual behavior (i.e., the quantity and frequency of marijuana use) and are based largely on observations of how people consume marijuana in discrete situations. Injunctive norms, on the other hand, refer to the perceived approval of a behavior and represent perceived moral rules of the peer group (Cialdini, Reno, & Kallgren, 1990). Despite the wealth of literature studying the impact of social norms on alcohol use (see Borsari & Carey, 2003), less is known regarding the impact of marijuana-specific normative perceptions on behaviors. In one study assessing both descriptive and injunctive norms in adolescents, the authors found a positive relationship between both descriptive and injunctive norms on personal marijuana use. Additionally, the relationship between descriptive norms and personal marijuana use behavior was stronger when friends were also perceived as approving (injunctive norms) of use (Neighbors, Geisner, & Lee, 2008). Another study found that the odds of marijuana escalating to riskier levels for both males and females were significantly reduced for those adolescents who believed that fewer of their friends used drugs (Butters, 2004). Additionally, this particular relationship was stronger among females than males, indicating a potentially greater role of "others" for adolescent females when considering marijuana use. In addition to gender differences, a recent study found that perceived peer norms increased over the transition from middle school to high school, and that the increases in normative perceptions were associated with growth in adolescents' own marijuana use (Duan, Chou, Andreeva, & Pentz, 2009).

Marijuana Outcome Expectancies and Motivations for Use

Marijuana Outcome Expectancies

Cognitive and social learning theories suggest behavior is influenced by an individual's attitudes and expectations about the effects or consequences of a particular behavior (Ajzen, 1991; Bandura, 1977; Fishbein & Ajzen, 1975). Attitudes can be viewed as resulting from rational decisions made by examining the competing outcome evaluations with the perceived likelihood of each happening, motivating behavior in either direction. In the additions area, most of the work on substance use and outcome expectancies has been done with alcohol use (e.g.,

Jones, Corbin, & Fromme, 2002; Maisto, Carey & Bradizza, 1999 for review). Substantial work has shown that alcohol outcome expectancies may be for positive or negative effects and are formed as a result of both direct and vicarious experiences with alcohol (e.g., Goldman, Brown, Christiansen & Smith, 1991; Maisto, Carey, & Bradizza, 1999; Oei & Baldwin, 1994).

More recently, research has begun examining marijuana outcome expectancies; however, limited work has occurred with adolescents. Consistent with alcohol literature, Alfonso and Dunn (2007) found that adolescents who tend to believe in positive marijuana outcomes, such as making one more relaxed, happy, or funny, were more likely to have used marijuana compared to adolescents who endorsed more negative psychological or physiological harms of marijuana. Changes in expectancies to favorable, more positive outcomes from marijuana has been associated with positive increases in intentions to use marijuana among adolescents, as well as associated with later initiation (Skenderian, Siegel, Crano, Alvaro, & Lac, 2008).

Among adolescents and college students, expectations of marijuana as having social and sexual facilitation, tension reduction, and cognitive and perceptual enhancement effects, as well as cognitive and behavioral impairment, general negative effects, craving and physical effects from marijuana have been found (Aarons, Brown, Stice, & Coe, 2001; Schafer & Brown, 1991). Furthermore, differences in expectancies are evident when comparing differences by level of marijuana use. Never-using adolescents and past users have higher expectations for adverse negative consequences than present users, and frequent users report lower expectations for cognitive and behavioral impairment (Aarons et al., 2001). Similarly among young adults, frequent marijuana users hold more positive expectations (Morrison et al., 2002; Schafer & Brown, 1991), and these attitudes are directly related to intentions to use (Morrison, Golder, Keller, & Gillmore, 2002) and actual use (Schafer & Brown, 1991).

Motivations for Use

Motivational models of substance use suggest that behavior is motivated by different reasons (e.g., social enhancement and affect regulation), leading to theoretically distinct behaviors that are important for helping to understand the context and circumstances of behavior. Motives may influence when or where one will use a substance, how frequently or how much one will use, and what consequences may occur (Cooper, 1994). Recent empirical work on motives for using marijuana with incoming first-year college students indicates the most frequently cited reasons for using marijuana are enjoyment/fun, conformity, experimentation, social enhancement, boredom, and relaxation (Lee, Neighbors, Hendershot, & Grossbard, 2009; Lee, Neighbors, & Woods, 2007). Consistent with other literature (Newcomb, Chou, Bentler, & Huba, 1988; Simons, Correia, Carey, & Borsari, 1998), these findings suggest using marijuana to cope with negative affect, facilitate social opportunities, regulate or enhance positive emotions, and avoid social rejection are positively related to marijuana use and negative consequences. In adult samples, coping motives have been found to both moderate and mediate mental health functioning and marijuana use (e.g. Brodbeck, Matter, Page, & Moggi, 2007; Buckner, Bonn-Miller, Zvolensky & Schmidt, 2007).

Adolescent Marijuana Use and Mental Health

A robust line of research has indicated that for adolescents, the co-occurrence of substance use disorders and mental health problems is relatively high (SAMSHA, 2002). A majority of the research in this area has supported the notion that psychiatric disorders precede substance use, and therefore this explanation will be the primary focus of the present section. Mental health problems are routinely classified in two distinct categories. Problems in adolescence related to anxiety, fear, shyness, low self-esteem, sadness, and depression have been given the generic label of internalizing disorders (Ollendick & King, 1994). In contrast to the emotional basis of internalizing disorders, externalizing disorders are characterized by noncompliance, aggression, attention problems, destructiveness, impulsivity, hyperactivity, and antisocial behavior. These behaviors demonstrate a high degree of continuity from early childhood through adolescence and adulthood, and are a frequent correlate of substance use disorders (McMahon, 1994).

Internalizing Behavior Problems

Several theoretical models have been proposed to explain the association between adolescent substance use and internalizing symptoms (Brook, Cohen, & Brook, 1998; Fergusson & Horwood, 1997). Among the most commonly mentioned, self-medication models propose that adolescents

with preexisting emotional distress use alcohol and drugs to cope with internalizing symptoms associated with their psychopathology (Johnson & Kaplan, 1990; Sher, 1991). Another model has been proposed whereby substance use may lead to a developmental lag wherein adolescents do not develop healthy interpersonal, self-regulatory, and coping skills, which makes them less able to cope with the demands of adulthood and more likely to experience internalizing symptoms (Baumrind & Moselle, 1985). Finally, there is evidence that marijuana use is associated with detrimental effects on brain development, brain functioning, and neuropsychological performance in adults. This could heighten the risk for adult internalizing problems due to difficulties in school or work that are attributable to deficits in learning and memory.

Despite the theoretical models proposed, the evidence supporting internalizing disorder's associations with marijuana use is inconsistent. Significant associations between internalizing behavior problems and marijuana use have been reported (Babor, Webb, Burleson, & Kaminer, 2002; Wittchen et al., 2007) across several studies, but it should be noted that there is some inconsistency in the literature such that some studies have found that in adolescence, internalizing was not associated with significantly elevated odds of marijuana use (Tarter, Kirisci, Ridenour, & Vanyukov, 2008), whereas others have suggested that the internalizing pathway for substance problems may not be operating until late adolescence (Chassin, Pitts, DeLucia, & Todd, 1999; Zucker, 1994).

Externalizing Behavior Problems

Externalizing behavior problems have been consistently associated with early marijuana use and marijuana use disorders (Dobkin, Chabot, Maliantovitch, & Craig, 1998; King, Iacono, & McGue, 2004; Winters & Lee, 2008). In several landmark studies, the prevalence of adolescents with externalizing behavior problems, namely conduct disorder, among those with drug disorders has varied from one in three to more than 50% (Greenbaum, Prange, Friedman, & Silver, 1991; Keller, Lavori, Beardslee, & Wunder, 1992). The results of several studies indicated that externalizing psychopathology substantially elevates the risk for early initiation of marijuana use (Falls et al., 2011; King, Iacono, & McGue, 2004). Furthermore, the King study found that externalizing psychopathology was a relatively stronger predictor of marijuana use than for alcohol or marijuana (King et al.,

2004). The stronger effect found for marijuana use in King's study is consistent with findings from a longitudinal, community-based study, which demonstrated that conduct disorder was associated with relatively greater effects for marijuana compared to alcohol or nicotine (Boyle, Offord, Racine, & Szatmari, 1992). Additional research has indicated that conduct problems precede early marijuana use with children who displayed early conduct problems, even at subclinical levels, being significantly more likely to engage in adolescent marijuana use (Fergusson & Lynskey, 1998; Pederson, Mastekaasa, & Wichstrom, 2001).

In addition to conduct disorders (the most widely studied externalizing behavior problem related to marijuana use), early studies indicated that children with attention-deficit/hyperactivity disorder (ADHD) reported increased rates of drug use and substance use disorders (SUDs) by adolescence (August, Stewart, & Holmes, 1983; Barkley, Fischer, Edelbrock, & Smallish, 1990; Gittelman, Mannuzza, Shenker, & Bonagura, 1985; Hartsough & Lambert, 1987). However, the results of several more recent studies have suggested that the connection between ADHD and substance use disorders previously found is almost entirely due to a comorbid diagnosis of conduct disorder. One study found that independent of conduct disorder, a diagnosis of ADHD had little effect on substance use and abuse outcomes (Disney, Elkins, McGue, & Iacono, 1999).

Risk Perception
Perceptions of Risk

Perceived risk is a key concept of behavioral theories used to predict substance use among youth and a core component of many drug use prevention interventions (Ajzen, 2001; Gibbons, Gerrard, & Lane, 2003; Pechmann, 2001). Perceived risk refers to perceptions of the negative effects from engaging in a behavior, such as marijuana use. Given the importance of the perceived risk construct in predicting health behaviors, a growing literature has examined marijuana-specific risk perceptions. In recent years, fewer teens report seeing much danger associated with its use, even with regular use (Johnston, O'Malley, Bachman, & Schulenberg, 2012). US national trends show that perceived risk related to marijuana use has been falling rather sharply over the past 5 years (Johnston et al., 2012). For example, twelfth graders' perceived risk of harm from regular marijuana use has declined in recent years, with 52% of US high school seniors in 2008 and 2009 reporting that they thought that there was a great risk of harm from smoking marijuana regularly, which is down from 58% in 2006 (Johnston et al., 2012). Another recent US national survey found that nearly 34% of adolescents ages 12–17 generally do not perceive great risk associated with smoking marijuana at least once per month (SAMHSA, 2009). Furthermore, research has indicated that the percentage of adolescents who perceived great risk associated with regular marijuana use decreases with age (SAMHSA, 2009; MORI, 1999).

It should be noted that there are several possible domains of risk related to marijuana use. The area of perceived risk that is most commonly studied is physical effects. Research has routinely found that adolescents who believe that drugs are not physically harmful are more likely to experiment with marijuana (e.g., Duitsman & Colbry, 1995; Johnston et al., 2012). Other studies have focused on social consequences (Kilmer, Hunt, Lee, & Neighbors, 2007) and legal consequences (Como-Lesko, Primavera, & Szesko, 1994; Hemmelstein, 1995). Furthermore, a study by O'Callaghan, Reid, and Copeland (2006) indicated that risk perception varies considerably across problem domains. Results indicated that whereas a larger proportion of individuals perceived physical addiction to be a great risk (approximately 60%), far fewer indicated legal problems (25%) and acute adverse effects such as anxiety (12.3%).

Relationship to Personal Behavior

A wealth of research has found a significant association between perceived risk and personal marijuana use. For example, findings from the Monitoring the Future survey over the past 30 years have routinely indicated that there is an inverse association between perceived risk and drug use. One recent study examining national data from 2002 to 2007 found that youth age 12 to 17 who perceived great risk from smoking marijuana once a month were much less likely to have used marijuana in the past month than those who perceived moderate to no risk (SAMHSA, 2009).

It should be noted that research in this area has typically focused on health risks alone and generally have not acknowledged risk perception in relation to actually having experienced a consequence. As such, several limitations to interpreting relationships between risk perception and risk behaviors have been posed, including the difficulty of interpreting the temporal relationship of risk perception and a person's current behavior (e.g., risk perception may reflect a person's current behavior correctly, or, because of high risk perception, a person may adopt precautions to reduce a risk) and drawing conclusions from cross-sectional analyses comparing perceptions of vulnerability and precautionary behavior (Gerrard, Gibbons, & Bushman, 1996; Weinstein & Nicolich, 1993). In a study designed to investigate risk perception in the context of marijuana use and related consequences, results indicated that perceived risk for academic and social consequences was greater among nonusers of marijuana than those who reported use of marijuana and, in theory, the participants were more likely to actually experience a drug-related consequence (Kilmer et al., 2007). Furthermore, among those who reported having used marijuana, there were no differences in risk perception between those who had and had not experienced a consequence.

Conclusions and Future Directions

Other than alcohol, marijuana is the most prevalent psychoactive substance used by adolescents. Among adolescents surveyed in the Monitoring the Future study, marijuana use appears to be rising recently after having seen a decade of declining rates. It is important to note that as use has been increasing, perceived risk for and disapproval of use of marijuana have both been declining (Johnston et al., 2012). Longitudinal research has shown there are long-term developmental consequences associated with marijuana use during adolescence, particularly for those individuals who are early initiates and those who tend to use more chronically or heavily through adolescence. While recent progress has been made in understanding and identifying risk and protective factors of adolescent marijuana use, as well as short and longer term outcomes of use, the field is still in its infancy, relative to other substances such as alcohol or cigarette use.

As states consider decriminalization or legalization of marijuana, or even approve initiatives legalizing marijuana for recreational purposes, it will be important to monitor the impact on youth and adolescents, particularly if these legal decisions send a message about perceived risk or harm (i.e., Do advertisements for or new laws surrounding legalization or decriminalization send the unintended message that adults think marijuana is not that harmful?). With the historic initiatives legalizing possession of marijuana for recreational purposes approved by voters in Washington and Colorado in 2012, there are many questions that remain to be answered that may impact initiation and use rates among adolescents (Kilmer & Lee, 2013). Future questions and directions in this area could include the following:

• *Marijuana and driving.* With adolescents becoming legal drivers and presumably wanting to do everything possible to avoid legal concerns that would threaten keeping their driver's license, more research is clearly needed to inform decisions about driving for those who make the choice to use marijuana. How long after use is driving still affected? How long after use can THC be detected in the blood (e.g., in Washington any positive amount of THC per milliliter of blood is grounds for a DUI for those under 21 years of age)?

• *New laws and their impact.* What impact will changing laws surrounding medical use or outright legalization have on adolescent attitudes, perceptions of risks, outcome expectancies, and social norms? How will these impact timing of initiation, rates of initiation, and overall use? For states like Washington that set up state-run stores, how will increased outlet density, exposure, and availability similarly impact attitudes, perceptions, and use?

• *Prevention messages.* With most of the research findings about adolescence and brain development primarily disseminated through scientific journals, how could these be "translated" for use in prevention and intervention efforts? What are the best messages for parents to be giving adolescents about marijuana use?

• *Marijuana and athletic performance.* For adolescents who see participation in sports as important (or even an avenue toward attending college), what are the ways in which marijuana use could impact athletic performance? Future studies are needed to provide specific information within this domain.

• *Continuing research on brain development and functioning.* With clear research suggesting that marijuana can cause attention problems, how many adolescents struggling with attention problems (and even seeking treatment for things like ADHD) are having their problems caused or exacerbated by marijuana use? Studies show the impact on cognitive functioning for those using with some frequency, but how long after a single use might there still be measurable cognitive deficits?

• *Guidelines for reducing risks or harms.* For alcohol, the most efficacious prevention and intervention programs focus on harm reduction—for those who make the choice to drink, strategies on ways to do so in a less dangerous or less risky way are explored (Marlatt et al., 1998). What, if any, are the guidelines for less risky marijuana use? If there are guidelines, incorporation into prevention programs can be explored; if there are not low-risk ways of using, appropriate messaging also needs to be determined.

It is clear that there are many adolescents that use marijuana at problematic levels. As a field, research can continue documenting developmentally relevant health and psychological effects, as well as prevention and intervention strategies for best addressing marijuana use and problem use. While not a focus of the present chapter, there have been important advances in the development of prevention programs; however, most are aimed at younger children or early adolescents. As adolescents may begin experimentation or more regular use, the development and identification of programs to best serve the needs of these adolescents are warranted.

References

Aarons, G. A., Brown, S. A., Stice, E., & Coe, M. T. (2001). Psychometric evaluation of the Marijuana and Stimulant Effect Expectancy Questionnaires for adolescents. *Addictive Behaviors, 26*, 219–236. doi: 10.1016/S0306-4603(00)00103-9

Ajzen, I. (1991). The theory of planned behavior. *Organizational Behavior and Human Decision Processes, 50*, 179–211. doi: 10.1016/0749-5978(91)90020-T

Ajzen, I. (2001). Nature and operation of attitudes. *Annual Review of Psychology, 52*, 27–58.

Alfonso, J., & Dunn, M. E. (2007). Differences in the marijuana expectancies of adolescents in relation to marijuana use. *Substance Use and Misuse, 42*(6), 1009–1025. doi: 10.1080/10826080701212386

Andrews, J. A., Hops, H., & Duncan, S. C. (1997). Adolescent modeling of parent substance use: The moderating effect of the relationship with the parent. *Journal of Family Psychology, 11*, 259–270. doi: 10.1037/0893-3200.11.3.259

Andrews, J. A., Tildesley, E., Hops, H., & Li, F. (2002). The influence of peers on young adult substance use. *Health Psychology, 21*(4), 349–357.

August, G. J., Stewart, M. A., & Holmes, C. S. (1983). A four-year follow-up of hyperactive boys with and without conduct disorder. *British Journal of Psychiatry, 143*, 192–198.

Babor, T. F., Webb, C., Burleson, J. A., & Kaminer, Y. (2002). Subtypes for classifying adolescents with marijuana use disorders: Construct validity and clinical implications. *Addiction, 97*(Suppl. 1), 58–69.

Bandura, A. (1977). *Social learning theory.* Oxford, UK: Prentice-Hall.

Barkley, R. A., Fischer, M., Edelbrock, C. S., & Smallish, L. (1990). The adolescent outcome of hyperactive children diagnosed by research criteria, I: An 8-year prospective follow-up study. *Journal of the American Academy of Child and Adolescent Psychiatry, 29*(4), 546–557.

Bauman, K. E., & Ennett, S. T. (1994). Peer influence on adolescent drug use. *American Psychologist, 49*(9), 820–822.

Bauman, K. E., & Ennett, S. T. (1996). On the importance of peer influence for adolescent drug use: Commonly neglected considerations. *Addiction, 91*, 185–198.

Bauman, K. E., & Fisher, L. A. (1986). On the measurement of friend behavior in research on friend influence and selection: Findings from longitudinal studies of adolescent smoking and drinking. *Journal of Youth and Adolescence, 15*, 345–353.

Baumrind, D., & Moselle, K. A. (1985). A developmental perspective on adolescent drug abuse. *Advances in Alchohol and Substance Abuse, 4*(3–4), 41–67.

Bava, S., Frank, L. R., McQueeny, T., Schweinsburg, B. C., Schweinsburg, A. D., & Tapert, S. F. (2009). Altered white matter microstructure in adolescent substance users. *Psychiatry Research: Neuroimaging, 173*(3), 228–237.

Borsari, B., & Carey, K. B. (2003). Descriptive and injunctive norms in college drinking: A meta-analytic integration. *Journal of Studies on Alcohol, 64*(3), 331–341.

Boyle, M. H., Offord, D. R., Racine, Y. A., & Szatmari, P. (1992). Predicting substance abuse in late adolescence: Results from the Ontario Child Health Study follow-up. *American Journal of Psychiatry, 149*(6), 761–767.

Brodbeck, J., Matter, M., Page, J., & Moggi, F. (2007). Motives for cannabis use as a moderator variable of distress among young adults. *Addictive Behaviors 32*: 1537–1545.

Buckner, J. D., Bonn-Miller, M. O., Zvolensky, M. J., & Schmidt, N. B. (2007). Marijuana use motives and social anxiety among marijuana-using young adults. *Addictive Behaviors, 32*, 2238–2252.

Brook, J. S., Cohen, P., & Brook, D. W. (1998). Longitudinal study of co-occurring psychiatric disorders and substance use. *Journal of the American Academy of Child and Adolescent Psychiatry, 37*(3), 322–330.

Brook, J. S., Kessler, R. C., & Cohen, P. (1999). The onset of marijuana use from preadolescence and early adolescence to young adulthood. *Development and Psychopathology, 11*, 901–914. doi: 10.1017/S0954579499002370

Brook, J. S., Lee, J., Brown, E., Finch, S. J., & Brook, D. W. (2011). Developmental trajectories of marijuana use from adolescence to adulthood: Personality and social role outcomes. *Psychological Reports, 108*(2), 339–357. doi: 10.2466/10.18.PR0.108.2.339-357

Brown, T. L., Flory, K., Lynam, D. R., Leukefeld, C., & Clayton, R. R. (2004). Comparing the developmental trajectories of marijuana use of African American and Caucasian American adolescents: Patterns, antecedents, and consequences. *Experimental and Clinical Psychopharmacology, 12*, 47–56.

Butters, J. E. (2002). Family stressors and adolescent cannabis use: A pathway to problem use. *Journal of Adolescence, 25*, 645–654. doi: 10.1006/jado.2002.0514

Butters, J. E. (2004). The impact of peers and social disapproval on high-risk cannabis use: Gender differences and implications for drug education. *Drugs: Education, Prevention and Policy, 11*(5), 381–390.

Chassin, L., Pitts, S. C., DeLucia, C., & Todd, M. (1999). A longitudinal study of children of alcoholics: Predicting young adult substance use disorders, anxiety, and depression. *Journal of Abnormal Psychology, 108*(1), 106–119.

Chassin, L., Presson, C. C., Sherman, S. J., Montello, D., & McGrew, J. (1986). Changes in peer and parent influence during adolescence: Longitudinal versus cross-sectional perspectives on smoking initiation. *Developmental Psychology, 22*(3), 327–334.

Cheetham, A., Allen, N. B., Whittle, S., Simmons, J. G., Yucel, M., & Lubman, D. I. (2012). Orbitofrontal volumes in early adolescence predict initiation of cannabis use: A 4-year longitudinal and prospective study. *Biological Psychiatry, 71*(8), 684–692.

Chen, K., Sheth, A. J., Elliott, D. K., & Yeager, A. (2004). Prevalence and correlates of past-year substance use, abuse, and dependence in a suburban community sample of high-school students. *Addictive Behaviors, 29*, 413–423.

Chilcoat, H. D., & Anthony, J. C. (1996). Impact of parent monitoring on initiation of drug use through late childhood. *Journal of the American Academy of Child and Adolescent Psychiatry, 35*, 91–100. doi: 10.1097/00004583-199601000-00017.

Churchwell, J. C., Lopez-Larson, M., & Yurgelun-Todd, D. A. (2010). Altered frontal cortical volume and decision making in adolescent cannabis users. *Frontiers in Psychology, 1*, 225.

Cialdini, R. B., Reno, R. R., & Kallgren, C. A. (1990). A focus theory of normative conduct: Recycling the concept of norms to reduce littering in public places. *Journal of Personality and Social Psychology, 58*(6), 1015–1026.

Cleveland, M. J., Gibbons, F. X., Gerrard, M., Pomery, E. A., & Brody, G. H. (2005). The impact of parenting on risk cognitions and risk behavior: A study of mediation and moderation in a panel of African American adolescents. *Child Development, 76*, 900–916. doi: 10.1111/j.1467-8624.2005.00885.x

Como-Lesko, N., Primavera, L. H. & Szesko, P. R. (1994). Marijuana usage in relation to harmfulness ratings, perceived likelihood of negative consequences, and defense mechanisms in high school students. *American Journal of Drug and Alcohol Abuse, 20*, 301–315.

Conrad, K. M., Flay, B. R., & Hill, D. (1992). Why children start smoking cigarettes: Predictors of onset. *British Journal of Addiction, 87*(12), 1711–1724.

Cooper, M. (1994). Motivations for alcohol use among adolescents: Development and validation of a four-factor model. *Psychological Assessment, 6*, 117–128. doi: 10.1037/1040-3590.6.2.117

Cooper, Z. D., & Haney, M. (2009). Actions of delta-9-tetrahydrocannabinol in cannabis: Relation to use, abuse, dependence. *International Review of Psychiatry, 21*, 104–112.

Copeland, J., & Swift, W. (2009). Cannabis use disorder: Epidemiology and management. *International Review of Psychiatry, 21*(2), 96–103.

Degenhardt, L., Hall, W., & Lynskey, M. (2001). The relationship between cannabis use and other substance use in the general population. *Drug and Alcohol Dependence, 64*, 319–327.

Diego, M. A., Field, T. M., & Sanders, C. E. (2003). Academic performance, popularity, and depression predict adolescent substance use. *Adolescence, 38*, 35–42.

Dishion, T. J., Capaldi, D., Spracklen, K. M., & Li, F. (1995). Peer ecology of male adolescent drug use. *Development and Psychopathology, 7*(4), 803–824.

Dishion, T. J., Nelson, S. E., & Bullock, B. (2004). Premature adolescent autonomy: Parent disengagement and deviant peer process in the amplification of problem behaviour. *Journal of Adolescence, 27*, 515–530. doi: 10.1016/j.adolescence.2004.06.005

Dishion, T. J., & Owen, L. D. (2002). A longitudinal analysis of friendships and substance use: Bidirectional influence from adolescence to adulthood. *Developmental Psychology, 38*(4), 480–491.

Disney, E. R., Elkins, I. J., McGue, M., & Iacono, W. G. (1999). Effects of ADHD, conduct disorder, and gender on substance use and abuse in adolescence. *American Journal of Psychiatry, 156*, 1515–1521.

Dobkin, P. L., Chabot, L., Maliantovitch, K., & Craig, W. (1998). Predictors of outcome in drug treatment of adolescent inpatients. *Psychological Reports, 83*(1), 175–186.

Donovan, J. E., & Jessor, R. (1985). Structure of problem behavior in adolescence and young adulthood. *Journal of Counseling and Clinical Psychology, 53*, 890–904.

Duan, L., Chou, C., Andreeva, V., & Pentz, M. (2009). Trajectories of peer social influences as long-term predictors of drug use from early to late adolescence. *Journal of Youth and Adolescence, 38*, 454–465.

Duitsman, D. M., & Colbry, S. L. (1995). Perceived risk and use as predictors of substance use among college students. *Health Values, 19*, 44–52.

Duncan, T. E., Duncan, S. C., & Hops, H. (1994). The effects of family cohesiveness and peer encouragement on the development of adolescent alcohol use: A cohort-sequential approach to the analysis of longitudinal data. *Journal of Studies on Alcohol, 55*(5), 588–599.

Eiser, J., & Van der Pligt, J. (1984). Attitudinal and social factors in adolescent smoking: In search of peer group influence. *Journal of Applied Psychology, 14*(4), 348–363.

Ellickson, P. L., Martino, S. C., & Collins, R. L. (2004). Marijuana use from adolescence to young adulthood: Multiple developmental trajectories and their associated outcomes. *Health Psychology, 23*(3), 299–307. doi: 10.1037/0278-6133.23.3.299

Ennett, S. T., & Bauman, K. E. (1991). Mediators in the relationship between parental and peer characteristics and beer drinking by early adolescents. *Journal of Applied Social Psychology, 21*, 1699–1711.

Ennett, S. T., & Bauman, K. E. (1994). The contribution of influence and selection to adolescent peer group homogeneity: The case of adolescent cigarette smoking. *Journal of Personality and Social Psychology, 67*, 653–663.

Ennett, S. T., Bauman, K. E., Hussong, A., Faris, R., Foshee, V. A., Cai, L., & DuRant, R. H. (2006). The peer context of adolescent substance use: Findings from social network analysis. *Journal of Research on Adolescence, 16*(2), 159–186.

Falls, B. J., Wish, E. D., Garnier, L. M., Caldeira, K. M., O'Grady, K. E., Vincent, K. B., & Arria, A. M. (2011). The association between early conduct problems and early marijuana use in college students. *Journal of Child and Adolescent Substance Abuse, 20*(3), 221–236.

Fergusson, D. M., Boden, J. M., & Horwood, L. (2006). Cannabis use and other illicit drug use: Testing the cannabis gateway hypothesis. *Addiction, 101*, 556–569.

Fergusson, D. M., & Horwood, L. (1997). Early onset cannabis use and psychosocial adjustment in young adults. *Addiction, 92*(3), 279–296.

Fergusson, D. M., & Horwood, L. (2000). Does cannabis use encourage other forms of illicit drug use? *Addiction, 97*, 1123–1135.

Fergusson, D. M., & Lynskey, M. T. (1998). Conduct problems in childhood and psychosocial outcomes in young adulthood: A prospective study. *Journal of Emotional and Behavioral Disorders, 6*, 2–18.

Finlay, A. K., White, H. R., Mun, E., Cronley, C. C., & Lee, C. (2012). Racial differences in trajectories of heavy drinking and regular marijuana use from ages 13 to 24 among African-American and white males. *Drug and Alcohol Dependence, 121*(1–2), 118–123. doi: 10.1016/j.drugalcdep.2011.08.020

Fishbein, M., & Ajzen, I. (1975). *Belief, attitude, intention, and behavior: An introduction to theory and research.* Reading, MA: Addison-Wesley.

Fisher, L. A., & Bauman, K. E. (1988). Influence and selection in the friend–adolescent relationship: Findings from studies of adolescent smoking and drinking. *Journal of Applied Social Psychology, 18*(4, Pt 2), 289–314.

Flory, K., Lynam, D., Milich, R., Leukefeld, C., & Clayton, R. (2004). Early adolescent through young adult alcohol and marijuana use trajectories: Early predictors, young adult outcomes, and predictive utility. *Development and Psychopathology, 16*(1), 193–213. doi: 10.1017/S0954579404044475

Fowler, T., Lifford, K., Shelton, K., Rice, F., Thapar, A., Neale, M. C., . . . van den Bree, M. M. (2007). Exploring the relationship between genetic and environmental influences on initiation and progression of substance use. *Addiction, 102*(3), 413–422. doi: 10.1111/j.1360-0443.2006.01694.x

Gerrard, M., Gibbons, F. X., & Bushman, B. J. (1996). Relation between perceived vulnerability to HIV and precautionary sexual behavior. *Psychological Bulletin, 119*, 390–409.

Gibbons, F. X., Gerrard, M., & Lane, D. J. (2003). A social reaction model of adolescent health risk. In J. Suls & K. A. Wallston (Eds.), *Social psychological foundations of health and illness* (pp. 107–136). Malden, MA: Blackwell.

Gittelman, R., Mannuzza, S., Shenker, R., & Bonagura, N. (1985). Hyperactive boys almost grown up. I: Psychiatric status. *Archives of General Psychiatry, 42*, 937–947.

Goldman, M. S., Brown, S. A., Christiansen, B. A., & Smith, G. T. (1991). Alcoholism and memory: Broadening the scope of alcohol-expectancy research. *Psychological Bulletin, 110*, 137–146.

Golub, A., & Johnson, B. D. (2002). The misuse of the "gateway theory" in US policy on drug abuse control: A secondary analysis of the muddled detection. *International Journal of Drug Policy. 13*, 5–19.

Greenbaum, P. E., Prange, M. E., Friedman, R. M., & Silver, S. E. (1991). Substance abuse prevalence and comorbidity with other psychiatric disorders among adolescents with severe emotional disturbances. *Journal of the American Academy of Child and Adolescent Psychiatry, 30*(4), 575–583.

Grotenhermen, F., Leson, G., Berghaus, G., Drummer, O. H., Kruger, H., Longo, M., . . . Tunbridge, R. (2007). Developing limits for driving under cannabis. *Addiction, 102*, 1910–1917.

Gruber, A. J., & Pope, H. G., Jr. (2002). Marijuana use among adolescents. *Pediatric Clinics of North America, 49*, 389–413.

Gruber, S. A., Silveri, M. M., Dahlgren, M. K., & Yurgelun-Todd, D. (2011). Why so impulsive? White matter alterations are associated with impulsivity in chronic marijuana smokers. *Experimental and Clinical Psychopharmacology, 19*(3), 231–242.

Gutman, L., Eccles, J. S., Peck, S., & Malanchuk, O. (2011). The influence of family relations on trajectories of cigarette and alcohol use from early to late adolescence. *Journal of Adolescence, 34*, 119–128. doi: 10.1016/j.adolescence.2010.01.005

Hall, W., & Degenhardt, L. (2009). Adverse health effects of non-medical cannabis use. *Lancet, 374*(9698), 1383–1391.

Hall, W., & Lynskey, M. (2003). Testing hypotheses about the relationship between the use of cannabis and the use of other illicit drugs. *Drugs and Alcohol Review, 22*, 125–133.

Hall, W., & Solowij, N. (1998). Adverse effects of cannabis. *The Lancet, 352*, 1611–1616.

Hansen, H. H., Krutz, B., Sifringer, M., Stefovska, V., Bittigau, P., Pragst, F., . . . Ikonomidou, C. (2008). Cannabinoids enhance susceptibility of immature brain to ethanol neurotoxicity. *Annals of Neurology, 64*(1), 24–52.

Hanson, K. L., Medina, K., Nagel, B. J., Spadoni, A. D., Gorlick, A., & Tapert, S. F. (2010). Hippocampal volumes in adolescents with and without a family history of alcoholism. *American Journal of Drug and Alcohol Abuse, 36*(3), 161–167.

Hanson, K. L., Winward, J. L., Schweinsburg, A. D., Medina, K., Brown, S. A., & Tapert, S. F. (2010). Longitudinal study of cognition among adolescent marijuana users over three weeks of abstinence. *Addictive Behaviors, 35*(11), 970–976.

Hartsough, C. S., & Lambert, N. M. (1987). Pattern and progression of drug use among hyperactives and controls: A prospective short-term longitudinal study. *Journal of Child Psychology and Psychiatry, 28*(4), 543–553.

Harvey, M. A., Sellman, J. D., Porter, R. J., & Frampton, C. M. (2007). The relationship between non-acute adolescent cannabis use and cognition. *Drug and Alcohol Review, 26*(3), 309–319.

Hemmelstein, N. (1995). Adolescent marijuana use and perception of risk. *Journal of Alcohol and Drug Education, 41*, 1–15.

Hopfer, C. J., Stallings, M. C., Hewitt, J. K., & Crowley, T. J. (2003). Family transmission of marijuana use, abuse, and dependence. *Journal of the American Academy of Child and Adolescent Psychiatry, 42*, 834–841. doi: 10.1097/01.CHI.0000046874.56865.85

Jacobsen, L. K., Pugh, K. R., Constable, R. T., Westerveld, M., & Mencl, W. E. (2007). Functional correlates of verbal memory deficits emerging during nicotine withdrawal in abstinent adolescent cannabis users. *Biological Psychiatry, 61*(1), 31–40.

Jacobus, J. J., McQueeny, T. T., Bava, S. S., Schweinsburg, B. C., Frank, L. R., Yang, T. T., & Tapert, S. F. (2009). White matter integrity in adolescents with histories of marijuana use and binge drinking. *Neurotoxicology and Teratology, 31*(6), 349–355.

Jacobus, J., Goldenberg, D., Wierenga, C. E., Tolentino, N. J., Liu, T. T., & Tapert, S. F. (2012). Altered cerebral blood flow and neurocognitive correlates in adolescent cannabis users. *Psychopharmacology, 222*(4), 675–684.

Jessor, R., & Jessor, S. L. (1977). *Problem behavior and psychosocial development: A longitudinal study of youth.* New York, NY: Academic Press.

Johnson, R. J., & Kaplan, H. B. (1990). Stability of psychological symptoms: Drug use consequences and intervening processes. *Journal of Health and Social Behavior, 31*(3), 277–291.

Johnston, L. D., O'Malley, P. M., Bachman, J. G., & Schulenberg, J. E. (2009). *Monitoring the Future national results on adolescent drug use: Overview of key findings, 2009.* Ann Arbor: Institute for Social Research, University of Michigan, 83 pp.

Johnston, L. D., O'Malley, P. M., Bachman, J. G., & Schulenberg, J. E. (2013). *Monitoring the Future national results on adolescent drug use: Overview of key findings, 2012.* Ann Arbor: Institute for Social Research, University of Michigan, 78 pp.

Johnston, L. D., O'Malley, P. M., Bachman, J. G., & Schulenberg, J. E. (2012). *Monitoring the Future national results on adolescent drug use: Overview of key findings, 2011.* Ann Arbor: Institute for Social Research, University of Michigan, 78 pp.

Jones, B. T., Corbin, W., & Fromme, K. (2002). A review of expectancy theory and alcohol consumption. *Addiction, 96*(1), 57–72.

Juon, H., Fothergill, K. E., Green, K. M., Doherty, E. E., & Ensminger, M. E. (2011). Antecedents and consequences of marijuana use trajectories over the life course in an African American population. *Drug and Alcohol Dependence, 118*(2–3), 216–223. doi: 10.1016/j.drugalcdep.2011.03.027

Kandel, D. B. (1978). Similarity in real-life adolescent friendship pairs. *Journal of Personality and Social Psychology, 36*(3), 306–312.

Kandel, D. B. (1996). The parental and peer contexts of adolescent deviance: An algebra of interpersonal influence. *Journal of Drug Issues, 26,* 289–315.

Kandel, D. B. (2002). Examining the gateway hypothesis: Stages and pathways of drug involvement. In D. B. Kandel (Ed.), *Stages and pathways of drug involvement: Examining the gateway hypothesis* (pp. 3–15). New York, NY: Cambridge University Press.

Kandel, D. B., & Jessor, R. (2002). The gateway hypothesis revisited. In D. B. Kandel (Ed.), *Stages and pathways of drug involvement: Examining the gateway hypothesis* (pp. 365–372). New York, NY: Cambridge University Press.

Kendler, K. S., Karkowski, L. M., Neale, M. C., & Prescott, C. A. (2000). Illicit psychoactive substance use, heavy use, abuse, and dependence in a US population-based sample of male twins. *Archives of General Psychiatry, 57,* 261–269. doi: 10.1001/archpsyc.57.3.261

Kendler, K. S., & Prescott, C. A. (1998). Cannabis use, abuse, and dependence in a population-based sample of female twins. *American Journal of Psychiatry, 155,* 1016–1022.

Kandel, D. B., & Yamaguchi, K. (2002). Stages of drug involvement in the U.S. population. In D. B. Kandel (Ed.), *Stages and pathways of drug involvement: Examining the gateway hypothesis* (pp. 65–89). Cambridge, UK: Cambridge University Press.

Kandel, D. B., Yamaguchi, K., & Chen, K. (1992). Stages of progression in drug involvement from adolescence to adulthood: Further evidence for the gateway theory. *Journal of Studies on Alcohol, 53,* 447–457.

Keller, M. B., Lavori, P. W., Beardslee, W. R., & Wunder, J. (1992). The disruptive behavioral disorder in children and adolescents: Comorbidity and clinical course. *Journal of the American Academy of Child and Adolescent Psychiatry, 31*(2), 204–209.

Kilmer, J. R., Hunt, S. B., Lee, C. M., & Neighbors, C. (2007). Marijuana use, risk perception, and consequences: Is perceived risk congruent with reality? *Addictive Behaviors, 32,* 3026–3033.

Kilmer, J. R., & Lee, C. M. (2013). Research questions in a shifting legal climate. *Addictions Newsletter, 20,* 10–11.

King, S. M., Iacono, W. G., & McGue, M. (2004). Childhood externalizing and internalizing psychopathology in the prediction of early substance use. *Addiction, 99*(12), 1548–1559.

Kobus, K. (2003). Peers and adolescent smoking. *Addiction, 98,* S37–S55.

Kosterman, R., Hawkins, J., Guo, J., Catalano, R. F., & Abbott, R. D. (2000). The dynamics of alcohol and marijuana initiation: Patterns and predictors of first use in adolescence. *American Journal of Public Health, 90,* 360–366. doi: 10.2105/AJPH.90.3.360

Lac, A., & Crano, W. D. (2009). Monitoring matters: Meta-analytic review reveals the reliable linkage of parental monitoring with adolescent marijuana use. *Perspectives on Psychological Science, 4*(6), 578–586. doi: 10.1111/j.1745-6924.2009.01166.x

Lane, S. D., Cherek, D. R., Tcheremissine, O. V., Steinberg, J. L., & Sharon, J. L. (2007). Response perseveration and adaptation in heavy marijuana-smoking adolescents. *Addictive Behaviors, 32*(5), 977–990.

Lee, C. M., Neighbors, C., Hendershot, C. S., & Grossbard, J. (2009). Development and preliminary validation of a Comprehensive Marijuana Motives Questionnaire. *Journal of Studies on Alcohol and Drugs, 70,* 279–287.

Lee, C. M., Neighbors, C., & Woods, B. (2007). Marijuana motives: Young adults' reasons for using marijuana. *Addictive Behaviors, 32,* 1384–1394.

Lynskey, M. T., Agrawal, A., & Heath, A. C. (2010). Genetically informative research on adolescent substance use: Methods, findings, and challenges. *Journal of the American Academy of Child and Adolescent Psychiatry, 49,* 1202–1214. doi: 10.1016/j.jaac.2010.09.004

Lynskey, M. T., & Hall, W. (2000). The effects of adolescent cannabis use on educational attainment: A review. *Addiction, 95,* 1621–1630.

Lynskey, M. T., Heath, A. C., Nelson, E. C., Bucholz, K. K., Madden, P. F., Slutske, W. S., . . . Martin, N. G. (2002). Genetic and environmental contributions to cannabis dependence in a national young adult twin sample. *Psychological Medicine, 32,* 195–207. doi: 10.1017/S0033291701005062

Macleod, J., Oakes, R., Copello, A., Crome, I., Egger, M., Hickman, M., . . . Davey Smith, G. (2004). Psychological and social sequelae of cannabis and other illicit drug use by young people: A systematic review of longitudinal, general population studies. *Lancet, 363,* 1579–1588.

Maes, H. H., Woodard, C. E., Murrelle, L., Meyer, J. M., Silberg, J. L., Hewitt, J. K., . . . Eaves, L. J. (1999). Tobacco, alcohol and drug use in eight-to-sixteen-year-old twins: The Virginia twin study of adolescent behavioral development. *Journal of Studies on Alcohol, 60,* 293–305.

Mahmood, O. M., Jacobus, J., Bava, S., Scarlett, A., & Tapert, S. F. (2010). Learning and memory performances in adolescent users of alcohol and marijuana: Interactive effects. *Journal of Studies on Alcohol and Drugs, 71*(6), 885–894.

Maisto, S. A., Carey, K. B., & Bradizza, C. M. (1999). Social learning theory. In K. E. Leonard & H. T. Blane (Eds.), *Psychological theories of drinking and alcoholism* (2nd ed., pp. 107–163). New York, NY: Guilford Press.

Marlatt, G. A., Baer, J. S., Kivlahan, D. R., Dimeff, L. A., Larimer, M. E., Quigley, L. A., . . . Williams, E. (1998). Screening and brief intervention for high-risk college student drinkers: Results from a two-year follow-up assessment. *Journal of Consulting and Clinical Psychology, 66*(4), 604–615.

Marti, C., Stice, E., & Springer, D. W. (2010). Substance use and abuse trajectories across adolescence: A latent trajectory analysis of a community-recruited sample of girls. *Journal of Adolescence, 33,* 449–461. doi: 10.1016/j.adolescence.2009.06.005

Mayeux, L., Sandstrom, M. J., & Cillessen, A. H. N. (2008). Is being popular a risky proposition? *Journal of Research on Adolescence, 18,* 49–74.

McGue, M., Elkins, I., & Iacono, W. G. (2000). Genetic and environmental influences on adolescent substance use and abuse. *American Journal of Medical Genetics, 96,* 671–677. doi: 10.1002/1096-8628(20001009)96:5<671::AID-AJMG14>3.0.CO;2-W

McMahon, R. J. (1994). Diagnosis, assessment, and treatment of externalizing problems in children: The role of longitudinal data. *Journal of Consulting and Clinical Psychology, 62,* 901–917.

Medina, K. L., Hanson, K. L., Schweinsburg, A. D., Cohen-Zion, M., Nagel, B. J., & Tapert, S. F. (2007). Neuropsychological functioning in adolescent marijuana users: Subtle deficits detectable after a month of abstinence. *Journal of the International Neuropsychological Society, 13,* 807–820.

Medina, K. L., McQueeny, T., Nagel, B. J., Hanson, K. L., Yang, T. T., & Tapert, S. F. (2009). Prefrontal cortex morphometry in abstinent adolescent marijuana users: Subtle gender effects. *Addiction Biology, 14*(4), 457–468.

Medina, K. L., Nagel, B. J., & Tapert, S. F. (2010). Abnormal cerebellar morphometry in abstinent adolescent marijuana users. *Psychiatry Research: Neuroimaging, 182*(2), 152–159.

Medina, K. L., Schweinsburg, A. D., Cohen-Zion, M., Nagel, B. J., & Tapert, S. F. (2007). Effects of alcohol and combined marijuana and alcohol use during adolescence on hippocampal volume and asymmetry. *Neurotoxicology and Teratology, 29,* 141–152.

Meier, M. H., Caspi, A., Ambler, A., Harrington, H., Houts, R., Keefe, R. S. E., . . . Moffitt, T. E. (2012). Persistent cannabis users show neuropsychological decline from childhood to midlife. *Proceedings of the National Academy of Sciences USA, 109*(40), E2657–E2664.

Miles, D. R., van den Bree, M. B., Gupman, A. E., Newlin, D. B., Glants M. D., & Pickrens, R. W. (2001). A twin study on sensation seeking, risk taking behavior and marijuana use. *Drug and Alcohol Dependence, 62,* 57–68. doi: 10.1016/S0376-8716(00)00165-4

Miles, D. R., van den Bree, M. B., & Pickens, R. W. (2002). Sex differences in shared genetic and environmental influences between conduct disorder symptoms and marijuana use in adolescents. *American Journal of Medical Genetics, 114,* 159–168. doi: 10.1002/ajmg.10178

Moffitt, T. E. (1997). Adolescence-limited and life-course-persistent offending: A complementary pair of developmental theories. In T. P. Thornberry (Ed.), *Developmental theories of crime and delinquency* (pp. 11–54). Piscataway, NJ: Transaction Publishers.

Moore, T. M., & Stuart, G. L. (2005). A review of the literature on marijuana and interpersonal violence. *Aggression and Violent Behavior, 10,* 171–192.

MORI Social Research. (1999). *Drugs report: A research study among 11–16 year olds. Research study conducted for the Police Foundation, January-February.* London, UK: MORI.

Morrison, D. M., Golder, S., Keller, T. E., & Gillmore, M. (2002). The theory of reasoned action as a model of marijuana use: Tests of implicit assumptions and applicability to high-risk young women. *Psychology of Addictive Behaviors, 16,* 212–224. doi: 10.1037/0893-164X.16.3.212

National Institute on Drug Abuse (2002). *Research report series: Marijuana.* NIDA Research Report Series (NIH Publication No. 15-3859). Bethesda, MD: Author.

Neighbors, C., Geisner, I., & Lee, C. M. (2008). Perceived marijuana norms and social expectancies among entering college student marijuana users. *Psychology of Addictive Behaviors, 22,* 433–438.

Newcomb, M. D., Chou, C., Bentler, P. M., & Huba, G. J. (1988). Cognitive motivations for drug use among adolescents: Longitudinal tests of gender differences and predictors of change in drug use. *Journal of Counseling Psychology, 35,* 426–438. doi: 10.1037/0022-0167.35.4.426

O'Callaghan, F., Reid, A., & Copeland, J. (2006). Risk perception and cannabis use in a sample of young adults. *Journal of Substance Use, 11*(2), 129–136.

Oei, T. P. S., & Baldwin, A. R. (1994). Expectancy theory: A two-process model of alcohol use and abuse. *Journal of Studies on Alcohol, 55,* 525–534.

Oetting, E. R., & Beauvais, F. (1986). Peer cluster theory: Drugs and the adolescent. *Journal of Counseling and Development, 65*(1), 17–22.

Oetting, E. R., & Beauvais, F. (1987). Peer cluster theory, socialization characteristics, and adolescent drug use: A path analysis. *Journal of Counseling Psychology, 34,* 205–213.

Oetting, E. R., & Beauvais, F. (1990). Adolescent drug use: Findings of national and local surveys. *Journal of Consulting and Clinical Psychology, 58*(4), 385–394.

Ollendick, T. H., & King, N. J. (1994). Diagnosis, assessment, and treatment of internalizing problems in children: The role of longitudinal data. *Journal of Consulting and Clinical Psychology, 62,* 918–927.

Pahl, K. K., Brook, J. S., & Koppel, J. J. (2011). Trajectories of marijuana use and psychological adjustment among urban African American and Puerto Rican women. *Psychological Medicine, 41*(8), 1775–1783. doi: 10.1017/S0033291710002345

Pechmann, C. (2001). A comparison of health communication models: Risk learning versus stereotype priming. *Media Psychology, 3*(2), 189–210.

Pederson, W., Mastekaasa, A., & Wichstrom, L. (2001). Conduct problems and early cannabis initiation: A longitudinal study of gender differences. *Addiction, 96,* 415–431.

Perkins, H. W. (2003). The emergence and evolution of the social norms approach to substance abuse. In H. W. Perkins (Ed.), *The social norms approach to preventing school and college age substance abuse: A handbook for educators, counselors, and clinicians.* San Francisco, CA: Jossey-Bass.

Pope, H. G., Jr., Gruber, A. J., Hudson, J. I., Huestis, M. A., & Yurgelun-Todd, D. (2001). Neuropsychological performance in long-term cannabis users. *Archives of General Psychiatry, 58,* 909–915.

Pope, H. G., Jr., & Yurgelun-Todd, D. (1996). The residual cognitive effects of heavy marijuana use in college students. *Journal of the American Medical Association, 275*(7), 521–527.

Prinstein, M. J., Choukas-Bradley, S. C., Helms, S. W., Brechwald, W. A., & Rancourt, D. (2011). High peer popularity longitudinally predicts adolescent health risk behavior, or does it? An examination of linear and quadratic associations. *Journal of Pediatric Psychology, 36,* 980–990.

Roebuck, M. C., French, M. T., & Dennis, M. L. (2004). Adolescent marijuana use and school attendance. *Economics of Education Review, 23,* 133–141.

Schafer, J., & Brown, S. A. (1991). Marijuana and cocaine effect expectancies and drug use patterns. *Journal of Consulting and Clinical Psychology*, *59*, 558–565. doi: 10.1037/0022-006X.59.4.558

Schenk, S. (2002). Sensitization as a process underlying the progression of drug use via gateway drugs. In D. Kandel (Ed.), *Stages and pathways of drug involvement: Examining the gateway hypothesis* (pp. 318–336). New York, NY: Cambridge University Press.

Schepis, T. S., Desai, R. A., Cavallo, D. A., Smith, A. E., McFetridge, A., Liss, T. B. . . . Krishnan-Sarin, S. (2011). Gender differences in adolescent marijuana use and associated psychosocial characteristics. *Journal of Addiction Medicine*, *5*, 65–73.

Schulenberg, J., Maggs, J. L., Dielman, T. E., Leech, S. L., Kloska, D. D., Shope, J. T., & Laetz, V. B. (1999). On peer influences to get drunk: A panel study of young adolescents. *Merrill-Palmer Quarterly*, *45*, 108–142.

Schulenberg, J. E., Merline, A. C., Johnston, L. D., O'Malley, P. M., Bachman, J. G., & Laetz, V. B. (2005). Trajectories of marijuana use during the transition to adulthood: The big picture based on national panel data. *Journal of Drug Issues*, *35*, 255–280.

Sher, K. J. (1991). *Children of alcoholics: A critical appraisal of theory and research*. Chicago, IL: University of Chicago Press.

Simons, J., Correia, C. J., Carey, K. B., & Borsari, B. E. (1998). Validating a five-factor marijuana motives measure: Relations with use, problems, and alcohol motives. *Journal of Counseling Psychology*, *45*, 265–273.

Skenderian, J. J., Siegel, J. T., Crano, W. D., Alvaro, E. E., & Lac, A. (2008). Expectancy change and adolescents' intentions to use marijuana. *Psychology of Addictive Behaviors*, *22*, 563–569. doi: 10.1037/a0013020

Schweinsburg, A. D., McQueeny, T., Nagel, B. J., Eyler, L. T., & Tapert, S. F. (2010). A preliminary study of functional magnetic resonance imaging response during verbal encoding among adolescent binge drinkers. *Alcohol*, *44*(1), 111–117.

Schweinsburg, A. D., Nagel, B. J., Schweinsburg, B. C., Park, A., Theilmann, R. J., & Tapert, S. F. (2008). Abstinent adolescent marijuana users show altered fMRI response during spatial working memory. *Psychiatry Research: Neuroimaging*.

Schweinsburg, A. D., Schweinsburg, B. C., Cheung, E. H., Brown, G. G., Brown, S. A., & Tapert, S. F. (2005). fMRI response to spatial working memory in adolescents with comorbid marijuana and alcohol use disorders. *Drug and Alcohol Dependence*, *79*(2), 201–210.

Substance Abuse and Mental Health Services Administration. (2002). *Adolescent marijuana use by race/ethnicity in three national surveys (National Evaluation Data Services [NEDS] Fact Sheet 122)*. Rockville, MD: Center for Substance Abuse Treatment.

Substance Abuse and Mental Health Services Administration, Office of Applied Studies. (2002). *Emergency department trends from the Drug Abuse Warning Network, Final estimates 1995-2002 (DAWN series: D-24, DHHS Publication No. (SMA) 03-3780)*. Rockville, MD: Author.

Substance Abuse and Mental Health Services Administration, Office of Applied Studies. (2005). *Drug Abuse Warning Network, 2003: Area profiles of drug-related mortality (DAWN series: D-27, DHHS Publication No. (SMA) 05-4023)*. Rockville, MD: Center for Substance Abuse Treatment.

Substance Abuse and Mental Health Services Administration, Office of Applied Studies. (2009, January 8). *The NSDUH Report: Marijuana Use and Perceived Risk of Use among Adolescents: 2002 to 2007*. Rockville, MD: Author.

Substance Abuse and Mental Health Services Administration. (2011a). *Results from the 2010 National Survey on Drug Use and Health: Summary of national findings* (NSDUH Series H-41, HHS Publication No. [SMA] 11-4658). Rockville, MD: Author.

Substance Abuse and Mental Health Services Administration (2011b). *Drug Abuse Warning Network, 2009: National estimates of drug-related emergency department visits* (HHS Publication No. [SMA] 11-4659, DAWN Series D-35). Rockville, MD: Author.

Substance Abuse and Mental Health Services Administration (2012). *Results from the 2012 National Survey on Drug Use and Health: Summary of national findings* (NSDUH Series H-46, HHS Publication No. (SMA) 13-4795). Rockville, MD: Author.

Tapert, S. F., & Brown, S. A. (1999). Neuropsychological correlates of adolescent substance abuse: Four-year outcomes. *Journal of the International Neuropsychological Society*, *5*(6), 481–493.

Tapert, S. F., Brown, G. G., Kindermann, S. S., Cheung, E. H., Frank, L. R., & Brown, S. A. (2001). fMRI measurement of brain dysfunction in alcohol-dependent young women. *Alcoholism: Clinical and Experimental Research*, *25*(2), 236–245.

Tapert, S. F., Granholm, E., Leedy, N. G., & Brown, S. A. (2002). Substance use and withdrawal: Neuropsychological functioning over 8 years in youth. *Journal of the International Neuropsychological Society*, *8*(7), 873–883.

Tapert, S. F., Schweinsburg, A. D., Barlett, V. C., Brown, S. A., Frank, L. R., Brown, G. G., & Meloy, M. J. (2004). Blood oxygen level dependent response and spatial working memory in adolescents with alcohol use disorders. *Alcoholism: Clinical and Experimental Research*, *28*(10), 1577–1586.

Tapert, S. F., Schweinsburg, A. D., Drummond, S. P., Paulus, M. P., Brown, S. A., Yang, T. T., & Frank, L. R. (2007). Functional MRI of inhibitory processing in abstinent adolescent marijuana users. *Psychopharmacology (Berl)*, *194*(2), 173–183.

Tarter, R. E., Kirisci, L., Ridenour, T., & Vanyukov, M. (2008). Prediction of cannabis use disorder between childhood and young adulthood using the Child Behavior Checklist. *Journal of Psychopathology and Behavioral Assessment*, *30*(4), 272–278.

Taylor, D. R., Poulton, R., Moffit, T. E., Ramankutty, P., & Sears, M. R. (2000). The respiratory effects of cannabis dependence in young adults. *Addiction*, *95*, 1669–1677.

Tobler, A. L., & Komro, K. A. (2010). Trajectories or parental monitoring and communication and effects on drug use among urban young adolescents. *Journal of Adolescent Health*, *46*, 560–568. doi: 10.1016/j.jadohealth.2009.12.008

Tucker, J. S., Ellickson, P. L., Orlando, M., Martino, S. C., & Klein, D. J. (2005). Substance use trajectories from early adolescence to emerging adulthood: A comparison of smoking, binge drinking, and marijuana use. *Journal of Drug Issues*, *35*, 307–332.

Tucker, J. S., Green, H. D., Zhou, A. J., Miles, J. N. V., Shih, R., & D'Amico, E. J. (2011). Substance use among middle school students: Associations with self-rated and peer-rated popularity. *Journal of Adolescence*, *34*, 513–519.

Urberg, K. A., Degirmencioglu, S. M., & Pilgrim, C. (1997). Close friend and group influence on adolescent cigarette smoking and alcohol use. *Developmental Psychology, 33*, 834–844.

Van Gundy, K., & Rebellon, C. J. (2010). A life-course perspective on the "gateway hypothesis." *Journal of Health and Social Behavior, 51*, 244–259.

Wallace, J. M., Bachman, J. G., O'Malley, P. M., Johnston, L. D., Schulenberg, J. E., & Cooper, S. M. (2002). Tobacco, alcohol, and illicit drug use: racial and ethnic differences among U.S. high school seniors, 1976-2000. *Public Health Reports, 117*(Suppl. 1), S67–S75.

Warner, J., Weber, T. R., & Albanes, R. (1999). "Girls are retarded when they're stoned." Marijuana and the construction of gender roles among adolescent females. *Sex Roles, 40*, 25–43.

Weinstein, N. D., & Nicolich, M. (1993). Correct and incorrect interpretations of correlations between risk perceptions and risk behaviors. *Health Psychology, 12*, 235–245.

Wills, T. A., & Cleary, S. D. (1999). Peer and adolescent substance use among 6th–9th graders: Latent growth analyses of influence versus selection mechanisms. *Health Psychology, 18*, 453–463.

Windle, M., & Wiesner, M. (2004). Trajectories of marijuana use from adolescence to young adulthood: Predictors and outcomes. *Development and Psychopathology, 16*(4), 1007–1027. doi: 10.1017/S0954579404040118

Winters, K. C., & Lee, C. S. (2008). Likelihood of developing an alcohol and cannabis use disorder during youth: Association with recent use and age. *Drug and Alcohol Dependence, 92*(1–3), 239–247.

Wittchen, H., Fröhlich, C., Behrendt, S., Günther, A., Rehm, J., Zimmermann, P., . . . Perkonigg, A. (2007). Cannabis use and cannabis use disorders and their relationship to mental disorders: A 10-year prospective-longitudinal community study in adolescents. *Drug and Alcohol Dependence, 88*, S60–S70.

Young, S. E., Rhee, S., Stallings, M. C., Corley, R. P., & Hewitt, J. K. (2006). Genetic and environmental vulnerabilities underlying adolescent substance use and problems: General or specific? *Behavior Genetics, 36*, 603–615. doi: 10.1007/s10519-006-9066-7

Zucker, R. A. (1994). *Pathways to alcohol problems and alcoholism: A developmental account of the evidence for multiple alcoholisms and for contextual contributions to risk. In The development of alcohol problems: Exploring the biopsychosocial matrix of risk* (NIAAA Research Monograph No. 26; NIH Publication No. 94-3495, pp. 255–289). Rockville, MD: Department of Health and Human Services.

Other Illicit Drugs of Abuse in Adolescence

Danielle E. Ramo *and* Christian Grov

Abstract

Illicit drugs other than marijuana have a unique and important place in the picture of adolescent substance use and associated problems. Large, epidemiological studies have revealed that, although the use of individual drugs (other than marijuana) may fluctuate widely, the proportion of adolescents using any of them has been more stable in the decade between 2000 and 2010, compared to decades prior. In this chapter, we give an overview of illicit substance use in adolescence, including cocaine/crack, methamphetamine, heroin, ecstasy, MDMA, LSD, and GHB. We review epidemiological patterns of use among youth, including modes of use and common trajectories of use. We discuss cognitive, behavioral, and social contexts of other drug use in adolescence, and we review demographic patterns of use. We conclude by reviewing similarities and differences between substances.

Key Words: cocaine, crack, methamphetamine, heroin, ecstasy, MDMA, LSD, acid, GHB

Illicit drugs other than marijuana have a unique and important place in the picture of adolescent substance use and associated problems. Large, epidemiological studies have revealed that, although the use of individual drugs (other than marijuana) may fluctuate widely, the proportion of adolescents using any of them has been more stable in the decade between 2000 and 2010, compared to decades prior. For example, the Monitoring the Future study reported that in 1975 over one third (36%) of 12th graders had tried some illicit drug other than marijuana (Johnston, O'Malley, Bachman, & Schulenberg, 2011a). This figure rose to 43% by 1981 and then declined for a long period to a low of 25% in 1992. Some increase followed in the 1990s as the use of a number of drugs rose steadily, and it reached 30% by 1997. The use of any illicit drug other than marijuana has since fallen some, to 24% in 2009 and then to 25% in 2010. The National Survey of Drug Use and Health, another epidemiological survey of substance use in adolescents ages 12 years and older throughout the United States reports that the rate of current illicit drug use among youths aged 12 to 17 years remained similar from 2009 to 2010 (10.0% vs. 10.1%), but higher than the rate in 2008 (9.3%). Between 2002 and 2008, the rate declined from 11.6% to 9.3% (Substance Abuse and Mental Health Services Administration [SAMHSA], 2011c).

The usage rate for each individual drug, on the other hand, reflects many more rapidly changing determinants specific to that drug: how widely its psychoactive potential is recognized, how favorable the reports of its supposed benefits are, how risky its use is seen to be, how acceptable it is in the peer group, how accessible it is, and so on. In this chapter we focus on adolescents' use of, and factors associated with, cocaine (crack), methamphetamine, heroin, ecstasy, LSD, and GHB. This review reflects the state of the literature through 2011. We consider each substance independently, while highlighting some of the uniformity in illicit substance use among adolescents.

Cocaine (Crack)

Cocaine is a central nervous system (CNS) stimulant made from the leaves of the coca plant. Typically in powder form, the drug is often snorted, smoked, or diluted and injected. Crack, emerging and proliferating in the 1980s, is cocaine hydrochloride powder that has been processed to form a rock crystal that is then usually smoked. Street names for cocaine include coke, C, snow, flake, blow, candy, Charlie, toot, and rock.

Cocaine works primarily through influencing the dopamine neurotransmitter system in regions of the brain that are involved in experiencing pleasure (e.g., food, sex, many drugs of abuse). One neural system that appears to be most affected by cocaine originates in a region of the midbrain called the ventral tegmental area (VTA). Nerve fibers originating in the VTA extend to the nucleus accumbens, one of the brain's key areas involved in reward. Animal studies show that rewards increase levels of dopamine, thereby increasing neural activity in the nucleus accumbens (Koob & Bloom, 1988). Cocaine influences the communication process of dopamine in the brain's pleasure centers by blocking the reuptake of dopamine from the synapse, which results in accumulation of dopamine and an amplified signal to the receiving neurons. This is what causes the initial euphoria commonly reported by cocaine abusers. With repeated exposure to cocaine, the brain starts to adapt, and the reward pathway becomes less sensitive to natural reinforcers and to the drug itself (King, Joyner, Lee, Kuhn, & Ellinwood, 1992). Tolerance may develop—this means that higher doses and/or more frequent use of cocaine is needed to register the same level of pleasure experienced during initial use. At the same time, users can also become more sensitive (sensitization) to cocaine's anxiety-producing, convulsant, and other toxic effects (Robinson & Berridge, 2003).

Cocaine's effects include increased energy, reduced fatigue, and mental alertness, and the intensity is dependent upon the route of administration and amount of drug consumed. The faster cocaine is absorbed into the bloodstream and delivered to the brain, the more intense the high. Injecting or smoking cocaine produces a quicker, stronger high than snorting. On the other hand, faster absorption usually means shorter duration of action: The high from snorting cocaine may last 15 to 30 minutes, but the high from smoking may last only 5 to 10 minutes. To sustain the high, a cocaine abuser has to administer the drug again. For this reason, cocaine is sometimes abused in binges—taken repeatedly within a relatively short period of time, at increasingly higher doses.

Rates of cocaine use among adolescents have remained stable between 2009 and 2010, with 0.2% of youth ages 12 to 17 years using cocaine in the past month and less than 0.1% using crack cocaine in the past month (SAMHSA, 2011b). The Monitoring the Future survey shows that cocaine use among adolescents peaked in 1999 and has declined steadily over the decade since. In 2010, 1.6% of 8th graders, 2.2% of 10th graders, and 2.9% of 12th graders had abused cocaine in any form and 1.0% of 8th graders, 1.0% of 10th graders, and 1.4% of 12th graders had abused crack at least once in the year prior to being surveyed (Johnston et al., 2011a).

Considering admissions to treatment programs in 2007 from the Treatment Episode Data Set (TEDS), for all patients admitted for having smoked cocaine, 1.7% were under 19 years old. For all patients admitted for administering cocaine via other routes, 7.2% were under 19 years old. 1.4% of all those under 19 years old were admitted for smoking cocaine, and 2.3% were admitted for administering cocaine via other routes (SAMHSA, 2009).

There is a general pattern of using alcohol, marijuana, and/or inhalants prior to the use of cocaine and other illicit drugs among adolescents (Novins, Beals, & Mitchell, 2001). Like adults, teens tend to use cocaine in social settings (e.g., homes, or bars or clubs in areas where it is legal) in conjunction with another substance, most commonly alcohol (e.g., van der Poel, Rodenburg, Dijkstra, Stoele, & van de Mheen, 2009). In a study of risk factors for the transition from cocaine use to first crack use as well as snorting powder cocaine to a new route of administration (e.g., smoking, injecting) in adolescents, identified factors for both progressions included older age, recent use of several drugs of abuse, and not having a substance use disordered parent (Paquette, Roy, Petit, & Boivin, 2010).

Like most substances of abuse (licit and illicit), cocaine use among adolescents is associated with lower academic achievement (e.g., Jeynes, 2006). In a study of correlates of cocaine use among adolescent boys in jail in New York City, Kang and colleagues (1994) found that cocaine/crack users were more likely to use alcohol, marijuana, and intranasal heroin; to have multiple previous arrests; to be out of school; to be psychologically distressed;

to have been sexually molested as a child; to have substance-abusing parents; and to have cocaine/crack-using friends. They were also more likely to have frequent sex with girls, to be gay or bisexual, and to engage in anal intercourse. Protective factors against cocaine use include living in a household with both parents (Delva et al., 2005), optimism, coping, self-efficacy, educational aspirations, and church attendance (Grunbaum, Tortolero, Weller, & Gingiss, 2000).

Crack use is associated with a low level of psychosocial functioning compared to adolescents who use other illicit drugs, including problems with school and family, health and psychological symptoms, and delinquent behavior (Kandel & Davies, 1996). For crack use, there is evidence of a cycle of marginalization such that teens who eventually use crack are more likely to have problems at home and school, and the use of crack further marginalizes them through reducing their nonusing social network, increasing participation in illegal activities (e.g., selling drugs), and potentially contributing to homelessness (van der Poel & van de Mheen, 2006).

There are ethnic differences in adolescent cocaine use. White teens use cocaine at higher rates than those of other ethnicities (Grunbaum et al., 2000). In 2010, lifetime cocaine use was the same for males and females, and American Indian or Hispanic youth had the highest rates of use while African American and Asian youth had the lowest use (SAMHSA, 2011g). There is also evidence of ethnic differences in cocaine involvement in teens who committed suicide, with White teens more likely to have cocaine in their system upon death than African American teens (Garlow, Purselle, & Heninger, 2007).

There is a high prevalence of *Diagnostic and Statistical Manual of Mental Disorders*, fourth edition (*DSM-IV*) Axis I psychiatric disorders among youth who use cocaine. For example, in a study of teens age 14 to 17 years with cocaine dependence, treated in an inpatient drug treatment in South Carolina, Kilgus and Pumariega (2009) found that 68% were diagnosed with at least one other Axis I psychiatric disorder other than conduct disorder or other substance use disorders, and the prevalence of anxiety disorders was slightly higher than in other adolescent substance use disorder samples. Cocaine use poses a risk for engagement in HIV risk behaviors, with one study estimating that crack or cocaine use increased the risk of inconsistent condom use six-fold (Tolou-Shams, Ewing, Tarantino, & Brown, 2010). Psychiatric symptoms such as depressive symptoms are also found more often among teens who use cocaine compared to those who do not (Grunbaum et al., 2000).

Methamphetamine

Methamphetamine is a drug that acts as a stimulant on the CNS. It is classified as a Schedule II drug with limited medical uses. Many of the chemicals necessary to manufacture methamphetamine can be found in the typical home. As a result, US legislators passed a law in 2006 limiting the sale and recording the purchases of pseudoephedrine (a chemical found in over-the-counter decongestants), which is a primary ingredient needed to manufacture methamphetamine (National Institute on Drug Abuse [NIDA], 2010b).

Pure methamphetamine it is a white, odorless, bitter-tasting crystalline powder that easily dissolves in water or alcohol and is taken orally, intranasally (snorting the powder), by needle injection, or by smoking. Adulterants and other impurities introduced in the manufacturing of methamphetamine may alter its texture, odor, and potency.

Street names for the drug include Crystal Meth, Speed, Tina, and Ice.

Similar to cocaine, methamphetamine acts on the brain by increasing both the release and uptake of dopamine; however, methamphetamine creates a stronger and longer-lasting response. Dopamine is involved in reward, motivation, the experience of pleasure, and motor function. The resulting effect is a feeling of intense euphoria or rush. In contrast to cocaine, the duration of a methamphetamine high is more prolonged. Depending upon the route of administration, users can remain high for several hours after a single dose, and they can sustain this high for several days if repeatedly dosing (often without need for sleep). The price of methamphetamine varies by region, but it is typically in the range of $25 to $100. Because of its prolonged high, methamphetamine is often viewed as a more affordable drug than cocaine because users can get more "bang for their buck."

Some of methamphetamine's effects include increased wakefulness, attention, physical activity, and decreased appetite. These facets may make methamphetamine a more attractive option for adolescents who are looking for a drug that can facilitate study activities, productivity, energy, and weight loss. There are many other negative effects that methamphetamine use can have, including severe dental problems resulting from smoking (deterioration of tooth enamel and subsequent tooth decay), anxiety, confusion, insomnia, mood disturbances, and violent behavior. Chronic methamphetamine abusers can also display psychotic features such as paranoia, visual and auditory hallucinations, and delusions (for example, the sensation of insects crawling under the skin) (NIDA, 2010b).

According to the Monitoring the Future study (Johnston, O'Malley, Bachman, & Schuelenberg, 2010), methamphetamine use among adolescents has dropped significantly in recent years. Between 2000 and 2010, lifetime use among 8th graders declined from 4.2% to 1.8%, 6.9% to 2.5% among 10th graders, and 7.9% to 2.3% among 12th graders. Past-year use mirrored this decline: 2.5% in 2000 to 1.2% in 2010 among 8th graders, 4.0% to 1.6% among 10th graders, and 4.3% to 1.0% among 12th graders.

In a study of adolescents 12 to 17 years old, methamphetamine use was correlated with mental health treatment utilization and use of marijuana and other illegal drugs (Herman-Stahl, Krebs, Kroutil, & Heller, 2007). It has also been connected with antisocial behavior, peer use of methamphetamine, having friends who engaged in deviant behavior, self-reported alcohol use (Embry, Hankins, Biglan, & Boles, 2009), aggressive behavior and depression (Pluddemann, Flisher, McKetin, Parry, & Lombard, 2010), and suicidal ideation (Rawson, Gonzales, McCann, & Obert, 2005).

There are some gender differences in variables associated with methamphetamine use—females and adolescents who reported low religiosity, binge drinking, and selling drugs were more likely to use methamphetamine than were males or individuals who did not report these attitudes or behaviors (Herman-Stahl et al., 2007). There have been some mixed findings in gender differences in rates of methamphetamine use. Embry et al. (2009) found greater use among 11th-grade girls (6.0%) than boys (5.6%), whereas Springer et al. (2007), using data from the 2003 Youth Risk Behavior Survey (n = 15,240), reported that males had higher use than females (8.3% v. 6.8%).

Adolescent females seem to report differential consequences of methamphetamine use than males (Rawson, Gonzales, McCann, & Ling, 2007). For example, females are more likely to be admitted into treatment programs compared to males, and methamphetamine-abusing girls reported higher levels of depression and suicidal tendencies than did methamphetamine-abusing boys (Rawson et al.,

2005). Another study of Taiwanese adolescents found females displayed higher rates of mood and eating disorders than boys (Yen & Chong, 2006).

Data from the 2003 Youth Risk Behavior Survey noted that use was more than twice as high for White (8.1%) and Hispanic (8.2%) adolescents compared to Black adolescents (3.1%) (Springer et al., 2007). Similar patterns have been identified by others (Herman-Stahl et al., 2007).

Methamphetamine use also appears to be connected to risky sexual behavior and early onset of sexual behavior (i.e., sexual debut) in adolescents (Rawson et al., 2007; Springer et al., 2007). Users are more likely to have had a greater total number of sexual partners and were more likely to have had unplanned sex under the influence of alcohol (Yen, 2004). Yen also reported that high-frequency methamphetamine use was associated with increased tendencies to engage in unprotected sex and to use methamphetamine before sexual intercourse. Meanwhile, Springer et al. (2007) found that heavy methamphetamine users were more likely to report having had sexual intercourse before age 13 years, sex with multiple partners, and having been/gotten someone pregnant compared to those who used methamphetamine once or twice. Given these associations, methamphetamine use may be particularly problematic for adolescent gay and bisexual men, who are more likely to come into contact with HIV from their male partners (Mustanski, Newcomb, Du Bois, Garcia, & Grov, 2011). For HIV-positive individuals, methamphetamine use appears to interfere with the efficacy of HIV medications (Boddiger, 2005; Jernigan et al., 2005).

Finally, there is ample evidence that high doses of methamphetamine over an extended period of time can have toxic effects on the human brain (Chang, Alicata, Ernst, & Volkow, 2007). For adolescents, whose brains are still developing, there is potential for this to result in a variety of long-term neurological and psychiatric consequences (Rawson et al., 2007; Sowell, Thompson, Holmes, Jernigan, & Toga, 1999).

Heroin

Heroin is an illicit drug that is processed from morphine and usually appears as a white or brown powder or as a black, sticky substance. It is injected, snorted, or smoked. Street names for heroin include Smack, H, ska, and junk. The short term-effects of heroin are similar for teens and adults and include a surge of euphoria and clouded thinking followed by alternately wakeful and drowsy states.

Heroin depresses breathing; thus, an overdose can be fatal. Users who inject the drug risk exposure to infectious diseases such as HIV and hepatitis. With regular heroin use, tolerance develops, in which the user's physiological (and psychological) response to the drug decreases, and more heroin is needed to achieve the same intensity of effect. Heroin users are at high risk for addiction—it is estimated that about 23% of individuals who use heroin become dependent on it (Anthony, Warner, & Kessler, 1994). Opioid use among adolescents is a fairly new but established public health concern (Compton & Volkow, 2006). According to the Monitoring the Future study, heroin use rose in the mid- and late 1990s, along with the use of most drugs; it reached peak levels in 1996 among 8th graders (1.6%), in 1997 among 10th graders (1.4%), and in 2000 among 12th graders (1.5%). Since those peak levels, use has declined, with annual prevalence in all three grades fluctuating between 0.7% and 0.9% from 2005 through 2009 (Johnston et al., 2011a). Most of the decrease in use since the recent peak levels has been due to decreasing use of heroin without a needle. Use with a needle has fluctuated less over time, though in 2010, 12th graders showed a significant increase to 0.7%.

The National Survey of Drug Use and Health reported in 2010 that 46,000 youth ages 12 to 17 years had used heroin in their lifetime, which is lower than the 56,000 reported in 2009 (SAMHSA, 2011d, e, f, l). However, a large proportion of new heroin users are adolescents and young adults. Among the estimated 14,000 persons using heroin for the first time in 2010, 16% were under the age of 18 years, and another 59% were 18–25 years (SAMHSA, 2011h, i, j). The Treatment Episode Data Set (TEDS), a large national database of subjects in treatment programs that tracks admissions to publicly funded substance abuse treatment settings, reports an increase in heroin admissions to substance abuse facilities for youth under 20, rising from 8,230 in 1999 to 9,877 in 2009 (SAMHSA, 2011m). The 2008 Drug Abuse Warning Network (DAWN), which collects data on drug-related hospital emergency department (ED) episodes from 21 metropolitan areas, reported that in 2008, heroin-related ED episodes numbered 1,724 (SAMHSA, 2011k). Emergency room mentions of heroin rose from 1,353 to 1,749 among 12- to 17-year-olds; and from 29,214 to 50,220 among 18- to 24-year-olds between 2004 and 2009 (Drug Abuse Warning Network, 2009).

While most teens start to use heroin by snorting the drug, the large majority of teens who go on to have problems with heroin report injecting the drug at some point (Eaves, 2004). Teens who are in treatment for heroin use tend to have more severe substance use and psychosocial problems than their non-heroin-using peers. In a study comparing adolescent heroin users to nonusers who were also in drug and alcohol treatment, Clemmey and colleagues (Clemmey, Payne, & Fishman, 2004) reported that heroin users reported more days of drug use, days high, and days not meeting responsibilities and had more substance abuse and dependence symptoms than nonusers. Other correlates of heroin use among youth in substance use disorder youth include polysubstance dependence (Hopfer, Khuri, Crowley, & Hooks, 2002; Hopfer, Mikulich, & Crowley, 2000; Perry & Hedges Duroy, 2004), experiences of child abuse, having friends with illicit drug use, poor school attendance, early age of drug initiation (Chiang, Chen, Sun, Chan, & Chen, 2006), and lower self-efficacy for addiction treatment (Perry & Hedges Duroy, 2004). There is also a high rate of psychiatric comorbidity among youth who use heroin, including conduct disorders and anxiety disorders, compared to teens who use other substances (Chiang et al., 2006). Although adolescent heroin users appear to represent a distinct subpopulation with multiple indicators of heightened severity, they respond to treatment with significant reductions in drug use, psychological symptoms, illegal activities, and overall psychosocial impairment. Furthermore, adolescent heroin users appear to respond to treatment in the same remitting/relapsing pattern as nonheroin users, yet their higher severity persists in the period following treatment (e.g., 1 year; Clemmey et al., 2004).

There is some evidence that heroin users differ from teens who use nonheroin opiates, such as prescription opiates. Heroin users have been found to be more likely to have dropped out of school, be dependent on opioids, and inject drugs using needles, while prescription opioid-using youth were more likely to meet criteria for multiple substance use disorders (including prescription sedatives and psychostimulants), be diagnosed with attention-deficit/hyperactivity disorder, and report selling drugs; and they more likely to be court ordered to current treatment and report prior psychiatric treatment (Subramaniam & Stitzer, 2009).

There are gender and ethnic differences in patterns of teen heroin use. In 2010, the prevalence rate of heroin among 12th-grade males was twice as high as for females (1.1% vs. 0.5%). Heroin has been reported to be less prevalent among African American teens than among Caucasian teens (lifetime prevalence: 0.8% vs. 1.4%). Currently, Hispanic 12th graders have the second highest lifetime and annual prevalence rates for heroin (1.2% and 0.6%; Johnston, O'Malley, Bachman, & Schulenberg, 2011b). Reports of teens in treatment for heroin use have roughly equal distributions of boys and girls, with boys using more heroin per day than girls (Gordon, Mulvaney, & Rowan, 2004). A notable difference has been found in route of administration, with girls in treatment for heroin addiction more likely to report injecting as the primary route of administration than boys (with one study reporting 32.3% for girls and 18.3% for boys; Substance Abuse Management Information System, 1997). However, studies of teens in treatment for substance abuse report that those using heroin are more likely to be female, older, and Caucasian compared to their peers who do not use heroin (Clemmey et al., 2004).

Ecstasy

Ecstasy (3,4 methylenedioxymethamphetaine; MDMA, also called Adam, E, X, XTC eccie, hug drug, or a Roll/Rolling) is a synthetic, psychoactive drug that is chemically similar to the stimulant methamphetamine and the hallucinogen mescaline. Ecstasy produces feelings of euphoria, increased energy, emotional warmth, and distortions in time, perception, and tactile experiences. MDMA, the primary chemical found in ecstasy pills, was developed in Germany in the early 1900s as a parent compound to be used to synthesize other pharmaceuticals. MDMA first started becoming available on the street as "Ecstasy" in the early 1980s, and in 1985, the U.S. Drug Enforcement Administration (DEA) placed it on its list of Schedule I drugs, corresponding to those substances with no proven therapeutic value. In the 1990s there was a resurgence of Ecstasy use, with use proliferating in dance clubs and rave scenes. Ecstasy became known as a "club drug," and it was one of the most commonly used drugs of this type. According to large, epidemiological studies, recent users of Ecstasy tend to be young adults aged 18–21 years and residents of metropolitan areas (Wu, Schlenger, & Galvin, 2006).

Ecstasy is taken orally, usually as a capsule or tablet. Tablets, which typically contain from 50 mg to 150 mg of the active drug MDMA, are usually imprinted with a popular icon such as a cartoon character, animal, or corporate logos (e.g., Mitsubishi, Motorola). Users sometimes refer to the drug by these imprints (e.g., "a blue dolphin pill"). Pills can vary in color, white being the mode. Ecstasy is typically purchased in the setting where it will be used, most commonly at bars, nightclubs, or raves, although it is increasingly used in more conventional settings such as house parties. Prices range from $20 to $40 per tablet, and it is not uncommon for tablets to be adulterated with other chemicals, including aspirin, caffeine, dextromethorphan, pseudoephedrine, amphetamine, and heroin. Although MDMA tends to be the primary substance found in "Ecstasy" pills, less than half of tablets are comprised of MDMA only, while most tablets contain either MDMA and other substances or only substances other than MDMA. Depending on a variety of factors (including the pill's content, other adulterants, and user's metabolism), the high from Ecstasy typically begins within 30 minutes to an hour after consumption and lasts between 4 and 6 hours.

MDMA affects the brain by increasing the activity of the monoamine neurotransmitters serotonin, dopamine, and norepinephrine. Like other amphetamines, MDMA causes an increase in neurotransmitter activity in that more of these neurotransmitters are released from their storage sites in neurons. Compared to methamphetamine, MDMA causes greater serotonin release and somewhat lesser dopamine release. The serotonin system plays an important role in regulating mood, aggression, sexual activity, sleep, and sensitivity to pain. The excess release of serotonin by MDMA likely causes the mood-elevating effects experienced by Ecstasy users. However, by releasing large amounts of serotonin, Ecstasy causes a depletion of this neurotransmitter, likely contributing to the negative behavioral and psychological after-effects that users often experience for several days after taking MDMA.

Ecstasy use increased among young people throughout the 1990s in the United States, peaking in 2001. Initiation of Ecstasy use began rising in 1993 when there were 168,000 new users. By 2000, there were 1.9 million new users, but that number decreased to 642,000 new users in 2003 and has steadily increased since then (SAMHSA, 2011c). In the early 2000s, there was a widespread public safety campaign to warn young people about the dangers of Ecstasy as a party drug, but that effort declined as use dropped off. Current (past-month) use of Ecstasy declined from 0.5% in 2002 to 0.3%

in 2004 through 2007. In 2009, there was a resurgence of Ecstasy use in the United States, with reported use in "mainstream" settings such as bars and homes in addition to clubs and raves. In 2010, current use was estimated at 0.5% and lifetime use was 2.5% among 12- to 17-year-olds (SAMHSA, 2011c).

In 2010 there were an estimated 937,000 million new users of Ecstasy, further suggesting that it has once again gained popularity. In 2010, the average age of initiation of Ecstasy was 19.4 years, and the number of first-time, past-year Ecstasy users who initiated use prior to the age of 18 was 382,000, suggesting that initiation starts relatively young (SAMHSA, 2011c). The Monitoring the Future study reported that annual prevalence of Ecstasy use increased significantly in 8th and 10th grades between 2009 and 2010 (from 1.3% to 2.4% in 8th grade and from 3.7% to 4.7% in 10th grade; Johnston et al., 2011a). Furthermore, in recent years, there have been declines in perceived risk of Ecstasy use in all three grades, declines in disapproval of Ecstasy use among grades 8 and 10, and declines in perceived availability of Ecstasy in all three grades until a leveling in 2010.

Ecstasy use can produce psychedelic and stimulant side effects such as anxiety attacks, tachycardia, hypertension, and hyperthermia. The variety and severity of adverse reactions associated with Ecstasy use can increase when the drug is used in combination with other substances of abuse—a common occurrence among Ecstasy users. The Drug Abuse Warning Network (DAWN) study of hospital emergency visits indicates that visits involving the illicit drug Ecstasy increased from 10,220 in 2004 to 17,865 visits in 2008—a 74.8% increase (SAMHSA, 2011a). Notably, 17.9% of these visits involved adolescents aged 12 to 17 years.

For some young people, Ecstasy can be addictive. A survey of young adult and adolescent Ecstasy users found that 43% of those who reported Ecstasy use met the accepted diagnostic criteria for dependence, as evidenced by continued use despite knowledge of physical or psychological harm, withdrawal effects, and tolerance (or diminished response with continued use of the same amount; Cottler, Womack, Compton, & Ben-Abdallah, 2001). These results are consistent with those from similar studies in other countries that suggest a high rate of dependence among teen Ecstasy users (Stone, Storr, & Anthony, 2006). Although Ecstasy is currently classified as a type of hallucinogen and its withdrawal is not recognized in *DSM-IV*, there is evidence

for the association of withdrawal symptoms with Ecstasy abstinence. Ecstasy abstinence-associated withdrawal symptoms include fatigue, loss of appetite, depressed feelings, and trouble concentrating. Findings from latent class analysis indicate that Ecstasy users have a significantly higher risk of dependence than lysergic acid diethylamide (LSD) users (Stone et al., 2006). Of the Ecstasy users who met criteria for dependence, "use despite knowledge of physical or psychological harm" was the most prevalent dependence criterion (63%), while withdrawal and tolerance were also commonly reported dependence criteria. In this sample, 34% met criteria for abuse, and "hazardous use" was the most commonly reported abuse symptom. Only 23% of the Ecstasy-using sample did not meet criteria for either abuse or dependence (Cottler et al., 2001).

Because Ecstasy is primarily used by young people, some work has examined its use among adolescents who are in substance abuse treatment. Lifetime rates of Ecstasy are approximately 32%, and it is the second most commonly used club drug after LSD (Hopfer, Mendelson, Van Leeuwen, Kelly, & Hooks, 2006).

Like other illicit substances, there tends to be some variation in ecstasy use by gender and ethnicity. While males and females tend to use Ecstasy at similar rates, some studies have suggested that females are more likely to report negative health consequences related to the use of club drugs— specifically Ecstasy. One explanation posits that this gender difference is related to the more intense subjective effects of Ecstasy reported by women. Some research also suggests that females are more likely than males to report recent use of multiple club drugs (Liechti, Gamma, & Vollenweider, 2001; Topp, Hando, Dillon, Roche, & Solowij, 1999).

White young adults are more likely than others to use Ecstasy, and among those who do use, Whites tend to use more of the drug more often (Wu, Schlenger, & Galvin, 2006). Furthermore, White and younger individuals are more likely to use a variety of other drugs compared to those of other ethnicities and older Ecstasy users (Kelly, Parsons, & Wells, 2006).

The overwhelming majority of Ecstasy users also take a range of other psychoactive compounds, most commonly alcohol, marijuana, and stimulants (amphetamines and cocaine; Scholey et al., 2004; Winstock, Griffiths, & Stewart, 2001). The DAWN study of emergency hospital visits indicated that, in 2009, 77.8% of the emergency department visits involving Ecstasy use also involved the use of at least one or more other substances of abuse (SAMHSA, 2011a). Using these other substances is associated with greater likelihood that youth and young adults will initiate Ecstasy use. Data from the National Survey of Parents and Youth (NSPY), a longitudinal, nationally representative household survey of youth and their parents, indicates that initiation of Ecstasy use is predicted by an adolescent's early initiation of smoking, drinking, or marijuana use (Wu, Liu, & Fan, 2010). In particular, early initiation either of marijuana use, or of both smoking and drinking, increases a child's risk for Ecstasy use initiation. Data from the NSDUH has pointed to a "gateway" phenomenon whereby earlier marijuana initiation is associated with subsequent Ecstasy initiation, which in turn is associated with later cocaine and heroin initiation (Martins, Ghandour, & Chilcoat, 2007). While there are multiple routes in and out of substance use initiation, Ecstasy initiation seems to play a role in the subsequent initiation of cocaine and heroin.

As with other illicit substances, a common correlate of Ecstasy use is mental health problems. Ecstasy users endorse more symptoms of general distress than nonusers (Falck, Carlson, Wang, & Siegal, 2006; Keyes, Martins, & Hasin, 2008; Pisetsky, Chao, Dierker, May, & Striegel-Moore, 2008). The overlap between Ecstasy use and antisocial personality disorder (ASPD) is likely due, at least in part, to the common underlying personality trait of sensation seeking, which predicts both Ecstasy use and conduct disorder and ASPD symptoms (Falck, Carlson et al., 2006). Comparing the age of first Ecstasy use with the age of onset for selected psychiatric disorders revealed that for most participants, disorders preceded use (Falck, Carlson et al., 2006). Furthermore, those who had used Ecstasy more than 50 times were more likely to have experienced a lifetime disorder (Falck, Carlson et al., 2006).

There is a neurobiological relationship between Ecstasy use and depression, as MDMA can cause serotonin depletion as well as serotonergic neurodegradation that may result in depression among users of the drug (Falck, Wang, Carlson, & Siegal, 2006). It is also possible that those who are susceptible to mental health problems are more vulnerable to using Ecstasy (Martins, Mazzotti, & Chilcoat, 2006). One suggested mechanism is the desire in those who have mood disorders to regulate mood through the use of mood-altering drugs such as Ecstasy (i.e., self-medicate).

A number of behavioral correlates of Ecstasy use have been identified, including engaging in deviant behaviors (Martins et al., 2006), having more friends who use the drug (Strote, Lee, & Wechsler, 2002; Wu, Holzer, Breitkopf, Grady, & Berenson, 2006), and having risky sex (Sterk, Klein, & Elifson, 2008). A number of studies have identified reasons why Ecstasy users initiate use or maintain using once they have started. Positive attitudes toward drug use are associated with initiation of Ecstasy use among adolescents (Wu et al., 2010). Common reasons why young people say they started using Ecstasy include "to experiment," while reasons they maintain use tend to be to feel good or high and to have a good time with friends. Other common reasons for using are for their stimulant properties (e.g., to increase energy, to stay awake), to enhance the effect of another drug, to seek insight, or to relax and relieve tension. Less common reasons for using tend to be to get away from their problems, being "hooked," to get through the day, or because of anger or frustration.

Motivational factors play a role in maintaining Ecstasy use. Psychological models emphasize internal regulatory cues that motivate drug use and play a contributory role in dependence (Abdallah, Scheier, Inciardi, Copeland, & Cottler, 2007). Motivational cues tend to be strong predictors of both Ecstasy use and dependence in users. For example, female Ecstasy users report they are more willing to use drugs in the future compared to non-Ecstasy users (Wu, Holzer, et al., 2006). Other cognitive correlates of Ecstasy use are low risk perception and high perceived behavioral control of obtaining Ecstasy (being able to obtain it in a short period of time) (Abdallah et al., 2007; Leung, Ben Abdallah, Copeland, & Cottler, 2010; Wu, Holzer, et al., 2006).

A number of parental or familial correlates of Ecstasy use have been identified. Ecstasy users report more childhood experiences of physical abuse, emotional neglect, and physical neglect than non-Ecstasy users. Parent drug use has been identified as a significant predictor of child initiation of Ecstasy use. Living with both parents and close parental monitoring are negatively associated with Ecstasy use initiation, and they may be protective against it. Current Ecstasy users report experiencing greater difficulties with family relationships than non-Ecstasy users. Peer correlates of Ecstasy use include close associations with deviant peers and close friends' drug use. Current Ecstasy users report greater difficulties with peer relationships then nonusers (Wu et al., 2010).

LSD

LSD (d-lysergic acid diethylamide), often called "acid," is a Schedule I potent psychedelic mood-altering chemical. It was discovered in 1938 and is manufactured from lysergic acid, which is found in ergot, a fungus that grows on rye and other grains (NIDA, 2009).

LSD is sold in tablets, capsules, and, occasionally, liquid form; thus, it is usually taken orally. It is colorless and odorless, but bitter in taste. LSD is often added to absorbent paper, which is then divided into pieces, each equivalent to one dose. The high from LSD, often referred to as "trips," usually begins within 1 hour and can last between 8 and 12 hours. Users experience a variety of delusions and hallucinations—it significantly alters perception, mood, and psychological processes, and it can impair motor coordination and skills. It also alters perceptions of the passage of time. Physical effects include increased body temperature, heart rate, and blood pressure; sleeplessness; and loss of appetite. It has low dependence potential and low overdose potential. LSD does, however, produce tolerance, so some users who take the drug repeatedly must take progressively higher doses to achieve the state of intoxication that they had previously achieved.

In part because of the prolonged duration of the high experience, coupled with the intense delusions and hallucinations, users can sometimes become depressed, agitated, confused, panicked, or otherwise overwhelmed. This is often referred to as a "bad trip." Positive effects of LSD use include elation and increased energy; negative effects include confusion, anxiety, and feelings of uncertainty (Parrott & Stuart, 1997). Some users experience hallucinogen persisting perception disorder (or "flashbacks") whereby they "re-experience" events while not under the influence of the drug. Flashbacks occur suddenly, often without warning, and may do so within a few days or more than a year after LSD use. These flashbacks tend to occur in more frequent users of LSD or other hallucinogens (Batzer, Ditzler, & Brown, 1999; Markel, Lee, Holmes, & Domino, 1994).

LSD use among adolescents peaked in the 1990s (Schwartz, 1995). Because of its psychedelic and hallucinatory properties, LSD has been deeply connected to the dance and rave scene in the 1990s and early 2000s (Kelly, 2005). To date, it remains connected to subcultural dance/club scenes (Grov, Kelly, & Parsons, 2009; Parsons, Grov, & Kelly, 2009) and classified in the group of substances known as "club drugs." The drug may be popular among dance club patrons due to the intensifying effects that LSD has on sensations. Some users experience synesthesia, in which a person "feels" colors and sounds (NIDA, 2001); thus, for some, lights and music are integral facts of the LSD high. LSD may help its users to maintain high energy levels for dancing and to enhance an altered state of consciousness (Koesters, Rogers, & Rajasingham, 2002).

The dance and rave "electronic music" scene, particularly the underground scene (in nontraditional and unlicensed venues such as warehouses and abandoned lots), has historically been connected to adolescents and young adults—the two go hand in hand, thus providing a link between LSD use and adolescents. Furthermore, because of its hallucinatory and "outer body experience" properties, LSD may be particularly attractive to adolescents and emerging adults who are navigating various facets of their own self-discovery. That being said, LSD use generally decreases over time, as users age into adulthood. Data from the Monitoring the Future study of 8th, 10th, and 12th graders have shown stable rates of lifetime use in the past few years. In 2008, 1.9% of 8th graders, 2.6% of 10th graders, and 4.0% of 12th graders had used LSD at one point in their lives. However, the perceived risk of harm from taking LSD regularly decreased among 12th graders (from 67.3% in 2007 to 63.6% in 2008). NIDA notes that changes in attitudes among youth could signal a subsequent increase in use, an outcome that would be concerning after the large decreases seen since the mid-1990s, when LSD use was at its height (NIDA, 2009).

A cross-sectional survey of 904 women aged 14 to 26 years found, controlling for age, race, and ethnicity, distinct profiles for those who reported using LSD. These included being drunk at least 10 times during the last year, regular smoking of at least half a pack of cigarettes, and identification as a high-sexual-risk taker. Furthermore, LSD users, as compared to nonusers, were more likely to be White (vs. non-White), be 17 or younger (as compared to at least 18 years), report a history of physical abuse, and report severe depressive symptomology (Rickert, Siqueira, Dale, & Wiemann, 2003).

Using the 2002 NSDUH data on 16- to 23-year-olds (n = 19,084), Wu, Schlenger, and Galvin (2006) found Whites (17.3%), Native Americans (19.8%), and those of mixed racial and ethnic backgrounds (17.4%) were the most likely to have ever used LSD, while Black (1.6%), Asian (5.3%), and Hispanic (8.8%) were the least likely. LSD users were very likely to have used other drugs; 70.8% had used two or more club drugs. Virtually all LSD users had prior experience with alcohol (99.4%) and marijuana (98.4%). More than half of LSD users had prior experience with inhalants (51.6%) and crack/cocaine (61.1%). Past-year LSD use was unrelated to gender, employment status, or population density where they currently resided.

There are limited data on how sexual orientation is related to LSD use in adolescents. Parsons, Grov, and Kelly (2009) compared patterns of LSD use in a sample of club-going, drug-using emerging adults (18 to 29 years) in New York City and found that heterosexual men (71.0%) were more likely to have used LSD than heterosexual women (51.0%) and gay and bisexual men (50.0%). Patterns in recent use (past 4 months) were similar, with heterosexual men (38.0%) being significantly higher than lesbian and bisexual women (18.0%), heterosexual women (12.0%), and gay and bisexual men (10.0%).

GHB

Gamma hydroxybutyrate (GHB) is a synthesized central nervous system depressant that was first used in human research in the 1960s; however, it gained popularity for recreational use in the 1990s. In 2002, the Food and Drug Administration approved it for limited use in the treatment of narcolepsy (NIDA, 2010a). It is manufactured from its precursor, gamma-butyrolactone (GBL), which is a solvent also found in cleaning products, nail polish, and superglue removers. GHB is also a metabolite of the inhibitory neurotransmitter gamma-aminobutyric acid (GABA). GHB exists naturally in the brain, but at much lower concentrations than those found when the drug is abused. GHB also has anabolic effects, stimulating the synthesis of protein, and has been used by bodybuilders to aid in muscle building (NIDA, 2010a).

GHB is also known as G, Gina, Liquid Ecstasy, and grievous bodily harm.

GHB is usually ingested orally, either in liquid or powder form. Due to its salty taste, it is often added to a flavored beverage, sometimes alcoholic drinks. When combined with alcohol (also a CNS depressant), the effects of GHB can be exacerbated. Because it is a CNS depressant, it has the ability to sedate and incapacitate. It can produce anterograde amnesia, such that users may not remember experiences while under the influence of the drug.

As a result, it has been used to commit sexual assaults (drugging an unsuspecting victim); thus, it has been labeled by some as a "date rape" drug.

GHB users report positive effects similar to other CNS depressants (like alcohol), such as euphoria, sociability, inebriation, and disinhibition.

Depending on how it is manufactured, the concentration of GHB may be difficult to know. GHB has a steep dosage curve and thus it is easy for users to accidently overdose. Its effect typically occurs within 20–30 minutes after being ingested and lasts between 1.5 and 3 hours—longer if it is mixed with alcohol (NIDA, 2010a).

In high doses, GHB's sedative effects may result in sleep, coma, or death. High doses or combined use with other drugs such as alcohol can result in nausea, vomiting, and breathing difficulties. During an overdose, and due to the inability to wake oneself up, it is possible for a user to suffocate on one's own vomit. Repeated use of GHB may lead to withdrawal effects, including insomnia, anxiety, tremors, and sweating.

GHB has a myriad of neurological effects. It binds to GABA-B receptors in the brain, inhibits noradrenaline release in the hypothalamus, and mediates the release of an opiatelike substance in the striatum. GHB has a biphasic effect on dopamine response, with more neurotoxicity at lower doses, but less toxicity at higher doses. There is limited research on the long-term effects that GHB has on the brain, particularly a developing adolescent brain. In research on rats, GHB has been shown to impair spatial and working learning and memory (Pedraza, Garcia, & Navarro, 2009; Sircar & Basak, 2004; Sircar, Basak, & Sircar, 2008).

GHB use is most common among younger adults and adolescents, though relative to other drugs (like marijuana and cocaine), use is much lower. Much like Ecstasy and LSD, GHB has also been connected to the dance/rave scene. It is often considered among the group of drugs called "club drugs." Although GHB has been abused by body builders, there is little evidence to suggest this may be a motivating factor for use among adolescents. The Monitoring the Future study began tracking GHB use in 2000. In 2009, 0.7% of 8th-grade and 1.1% of 12th-grade students reported past-year use, which is significantly lower than its peak-year use of 1.2% in 2000 for 8th graders and in 2004 for 12th graders at 2.0% (Johnston, O'Malley, & Bachman, 2011).

There is scant research on psychosocial factors associated with GHB use among adolescents.

Much work is focused on adult subgroups (e.g., drug users, gay/bisexual men, college students, and club-going participants). Researchers have noted that gay and bisexual men are particularly likely to use GHB, in the range of 25%–30% having used (Halkitis & Palamar, 2006), though it is uncertain when use is initiated. Researchers using data on 16- to 23-year-olds from NSDUH (n = 19,084) found GHB use was unassociated with age or race/ethnicity. GHB users were very likely to have experience with other drugs and alcohol—100% of GHB users had also previously used alcohol, marijuana, and hallucinogens. A majority of GHB users had used tranquilizers (94.7%), nonmedical use of prescription pain relievers (87.0%), and inhalants (85.3%; Wu, Schlenger, & Galvin, 2006).

Conclusion

Adolescent drug use is clearly heterogeneous, with use differing markedly by specific drug and fluctuating with availability and perceptions of use. Patterns of use also differ by gender and ethnicity. For example, although White adolescents tend to use cocaine, ecstasy, and LSD in greater amounts than adolescents of other ethnicities, methamphetamine and heroin are used most often by White and Hispanic adolescents, crack is used most often by African Americans, and GHB has not shown differences in use by ethnicity. A greater understanding of the cultural, social, economic, environmental, and individual factors contributing to these patterns can help to explain some of these variations in use. Nevertheless, etiological factors associated with youth substance use are relatively uniform across substances, an area further developed in later chapters in this text. Although illicit substance use experimentation is not a prescription for addition, all substances discussed in this chapter have addition potential and therefore can lead to detrimental consequences when use continues into adulthood. Furthermore, earlier onset of illicit substance use is associated with drug problems in adulthood (Anthony & Petronis, 1995; Chen, Storr, & Anthony, 2009; D. Kandel & Yamaguchi, 1993). However, clinical course depends on many factors, including the availability of effective treatments for youth to prevent the escalation of use once experimentation occurs. Research and treatment efforts should continue to focus on how the adolescent substance use experience is unique compared to that of adults and how treatments can meet the needs of young people.

Future Directions

Epidemiological patterns of substance use are indicating that multiple substance use ("polysubstance use") is an increasingly normal pattern among adolescents who use any illicit drugs. Future research should seek to understand factors associated with polysubstance use and how treatment can be tailored for these patterns.

There is limited work on the role of sexual orientation in other drug use. Findings suggest that those who self-identify as lesbian, gay, or bisexual are more likely to have experiences with drugs. This may be related to factors associated with caustic homophobic environments in school and the home; however, this is an area for future research.

There is limited work investigating motivations to use illicit substances. We know "after the fact" differences between users and nonusers (such as demographic and behavioral), but it would be useful to understand motivation as this may be an intervention point to prevent drug abuse among adolescents.

References

Abdallah, A. B., Scheier, L. M., Inciardi, J. A., Copeland, J., & Cottler, L. B. (2007). A psycho-economic model of ecstasy consumption and related consequences: A multi-site study with community samples. *Substance Use and Misuse*, *42*(11), 1651–1684. doi:10.1080/10826080701208905

Anthony, J. C., & Petronis, K. R. (1995). Early-onset drug use and risk of later drug problems. *Drug and Alcohol Dependence*, *40*(1), 9–15. doi:10.1016/0376-8716(95)01194-3

Anthony, J. C., Warner, L. A., & Kessler, R. C. (1994). Comparative epidemiology of dependence on tobacco, alcohol, controlled substances, and inhalants: Basic findings from the National Comorbidity Survey. *Experimental and Clinical Psychopharmacology*, *2*(3), 244–268. doi:10.1037/1064-1297.2.3.244

Batzer, W., Ditzler, T., & Brown, C. (1999). LSD use and flashbacks in alcoholic patients. *Journal of Addictive Diseases*, *18*(2), 57–63. doi:10.1300/J069v18n02_06

Boddiger, D. (2005). Methamphetamine use linked to rising HIV transmission. *Lancet*, *365*(9466), 1217–1218. doi:10.1016/S0140-6736(05)74794-2

Chang, L., Alicata, D., Ernst, T., & Volkow, N. (2007). Structural and metabolic brain changes in the striatum associated with methamphetamine abuse. *Addiction*, *102*(Suppl. 1), 16–32. doi:10.1111/j.1360-0443.2006.01782.x

Chen, C.-Y., Storr, C. L., & Anthony, J. C. (2009). Early-onset drug use and risk for drug dependence problems. *Addictive Behaviors*, *34*(3), 319–322. doi:10.1016/j.addbeh.2008.10.021

Chiang, S-C., Chen, S-J., Sun, H-J., Chan, H-Y., & Chen, W. J. (2006). Heroin use among youths incarcerated for illicit drug use: Psychosocial environment, substance use history, psychiatric comorbidity, and route of administration. *American Journal on Addictions*, *15*(3), 233–241. doi:10.1080/10550490600626473

Clemmey, P., Payne, L., & Fishman, M. (2004). Clinical characteristics and treatment outcomes of adolescent heroin users. *Journal of Psychoactive Drugs*, *36*(1), 85–94. doi:10.1080/02791072.2004.10399726

Compton, W. M., & Volkow, N. D. (2006). Abuse of prescription drugs and the risk of addiction. *Drug and Alcohol Dependence*, *83*(Suppl. 1), S4–S7. doi:10.1016/j.drugalcdep.2005.10.020

Cottler, L. B., Womack, S. B., Compton, W. M., & Ben-Abdallah, A. (2001). Ecstasy abuse and dependence among adolescents and young adults: Applicability and reliability of DSM-IV criteria. *Human Psychopharmacology*, *16*(8), 599–606. doi:10.1002/hup.343

Delva, J., Wallace, J. M., Jr., O'Malley, P. M., Bachman, J. G., Johnston, L. D., & Schulenberg, J. E. (2005). The epidemiology of alcohol, marijuana, and cocaine use among Mexican American, Puerto Rican, Cuban American, and other Latin American eighth-grade students in the United States: 1991–2002. *American Journal of Public Health*, *95*(4), 696–702. doi:10.2105/AJPH.2003.037051

Drug Abuse Warning Network. (2009). *National estimates of drug-related emergency department visits, 2004–2009—Illicit drug visits* [Data file]. Retrieved from http://www.samhsa.gov/data/emergency-department-data-dawn/reports?tab=26

Eaves, C. S. (2004). Heroin use among female adolescents: The role of partner influence in path of initiation and route of administration. *American Journal of Drug and Alcohol Abuse*, *30*(1), 21–38. doi:10.1081/ADA-120029864

Embry, D., Hankins, M., Biglan, A., & Boles, S. (2009). Behavioral and social correlates of methamphetamine use in a population-based sample of early and later adolescents. *Addictive Behaviors*, *34*(4), 343–351. doi:10.1016/j.addbeh.2008.11.019

Falck, R. S., Carlson, R. G., Wang, J., & Siegal, H. A. (2006). Psychiatric disorders and their correlates among young adult MDMA users in Ohio. *Journal of Psychoactive Drugs*, *38*(1), 19–29. doi:10.1080/02791072.2006.10399824

Falck, R. S., Wang, J., Carlson, R. G., & Siegal, H. A. (2006). Prevalence and correlates of current depressive symptomatology among a community sample of MDMA users in Ohio. *Addictive Behaviors*, *31*(1), 90–101. doi:10.1016/j.addbeh.2005.04.017

Garlow, S. J., Purselle, D. C., & Heninger, M. (2007). Cocaine and alcohol use preceding suicide in African American and white adolescents. *Journal of Psychiatric Research*, *41*(6), 530–536. doi:10.1016/j.jpsychires.2005.08.008

Gordon, S. M., Mulvaney, F., & Rowan, A. (2004). Characteristics of adolescents in residential treatment for heroin dependence. *American Journal of Drug and Alcohol Abuse*, *30*(3), 593–603. doi:10.1081/ADA-200032300

Grov, C., Kelly, B. C., & Parsons, J. T. (2009). Polydrug use among club-going young adults recruited through time-space sampling. *Substance Use and Misuse*, *44*(6), 848–864.

Grunbaum, J. A., Tortolero, S., Weller, N., & Gingiss, P. (2000). Cultural, social, and intrapersonal factors associated with substance use among alternative high school students. *Addictive Behaviors*, *25*(1), 145–151. doi:10.1016/S0306-4603(99)00006-4

Halkitis, P. N., & Palamar, J. J. (2006). GHB use among gay and bisexual men. *Addictive Behaviors*, *31*(11), 2135–2139. doi:10.1016/j.addbeh.2006.01.009

Herman-Stahl, M. A., Krebs, C. P., Kroutil, L. A., & Heller, D. C. (2007). Risk and protective factors for methamphetamine use and nonmedical use of prescription stimulants among young adults aged 18 to 25. *Addictive Behaviors*, *32*(5), 1003–1015. doi:10.1016/j.addbeh.2006.07.010

Hopfer, C., Mendelson, B., Van Leeuwen, J. M., Kelly, S., & Hooks, S. (2006). Club drug use among youths in treatment for substance abuse. *American Journal on Addictions*, *15*(1), 94–99. doi:10.1080/10550490500419144

Hopfer, C. J., Khuri, E., Crowley, T. J., & Hooks, S. (2002). Adolescent heroin use: A review of the descriptive and treatment literature. *Journal of Substance Abuse Treatment*, *23*(3), 231–237. doi:10.1016/S0740-5472(02)00250-7

Hopfer, C. J., Mikulich, S. K., & Crowley, T. J. (2000). Heroin use among adolescents in treatment for substance use disorders. *Journal of the American Academy of Child and Adolescent Psychiatry*, *39*(10), 1316–1323. doi:10.1097/00004583-200010000-00021

Jernigan, T. L., Gamst, A. C., Archibald, S. L., Fennema-Notestine, C., Mindt, M. R., Marcotte, T. D., . . . Grant, I. (2005). Effects of methamphetamine dependence and HIV infection on cerebral morphology. *American Journal of Psychiatry*, *162*(8), 1461–1472. doi:10.1176/appi.ajp.162.8.1461

Jeynes, W. H. (2006). Adolescent religious commitment and their consumption of marijuana, cocaine, and alcohol. *Journal of Health and Social Policy*, *21*(4), 1–20. doi:10.1300/J045v21n04_01

Johnston, L. D., O'Malley, P. M., & Bachman, J. G. (2011). *Monitoring the Future national survey results on drug use, 1975–2010. Vol. 1: Secondary school students*. Ann Arbor: Institute for Social Research, The University of Michigan.

Johnston, L. D., O'Malley, P. M., Bachman, J. G., & Schuelenberg, J. E. (2010). *Marijuana use is rising; ecstasy use is beginning to rise; and alcohol use is declining among U.S. teens* [Press release]. Retrieved December 2015, from http://www.monitoringthefuture.org/pressreleases/10drugpr_complete.pdf

Johnston, L. D., O'Malley, P. M., Bachman, J. G., & Schulenberg, J. E. (2011a). *Monitoring the Future national results on adolescent drug use: Overview of key findings, 2010*. Retrieved December 2015, from http://www.monitoringthefuture.org/pubs/monographs/mtf-overview2010.pdf

Johnston, L. D., O'Malley, P. M., Bachman, J. G., & Schulenberg, J. E. (2011b). *Monitoring the Future national survey results on drug use, 1975–2010: Vol. 1, Secondary school students*. Retrieved December 2015, from http://www.monitoringthefuture.org/pubs/monographs/mtf-vol1_2010.pdf

Kandel, D., & Yamaguchi, K. (1993). From beer to crack: Developmental patterns of drug involvement. *American Journal of Public Health*, *83*(6), 851–855. doi:10.2105/AJPH.83.6.851

Kandel, D. B., & Davies, M. (1996). High school students who use crack and other drugs. *Archives of General Psychiatry*, *53*(1), 71–80.

Kang, S. Y., Magura, S., & Shapiro, J. L. (1994). Correlates of cocaine/crack use among inner-city incarcerated adolescents. *American Journal of Drug and Alcohol Abuse*, *20*(4), 413–429. doi:10.3109/00952999409109181

Kelly, B. C. (2005). Conceptions of risk in the lives of club drug-using youth. *Substance Use and Misuse*, *40*(9–10), 1443–1459. doi:10.1081/JA-200066812

Kelly, B. C., Parsons, J. T., & Wells, B. E. (2006). Prevalence and predictors of club drug use among club-going young adults in New York City. *Journal of Urban Health: Bulletin of the New York Academy of Medicine, 83*(5), 884–895. doi:10.1007/s11524-006-9057-2

Keyes, K. M., Martins, S. S., & Hasin, D. S. (2008). Past 12-month and lifetime comorbidity and poly-drug use of ecstasy users among young adults in the United States: Results from the National Epidemiologic Survey on Alcohol and Related Conditions. *Drug and Alcohol Dependence, 97*(1–2), 139–149. doi:10.1016/j.drugalcdep.2008.04.001

Kilgus, M. D., & Pumariega, A. J. (2009). Psychopathology in cocaine-abusing adolescents. *Addictive Disorders and Their Treatment, 8*(3), 138–144. doi:10.1097/ADT.0b013e3181825a0a

King, G. R., Joyner, C., Lee, T., Kuhn, C., & Ellinwood, E. H., Jr. (1992). Intermittent and continuous cocaine administration: Residual behavioral states during withdrawal. *Pharmacology, Biochemistry and Behavior, 43*(1), 243–248. doi:10.1016/0091-3057(92)90664-2

Koesters, S. C., Rogers, P. D., & Rajasingham, C. R. (2002). MDMA ("ecstasy") and other "club drugs". The new epidemic. *Pediatric Clinics of North America, 49*(2), 415–433.

Koob, G. F., & Bloom, F. E. (1988). Cellular and molecular mechanisms of drug dependence. *Science, 242*(4879), 715–723. doi:10.1126/science.2903550

Leung, K. S., Ben Abdallah, A., Copeland, J., & Cottler, L. B. (2010). Modifiable risk factors of ecstasy use: Risk perception, current dependence, perceived control, and depression. *Addictive Behaviors, 35*(3), 201–208. doi:10.1016/j.addbeh.2009.10.003

Liechti, M. E., Gamma, A., & Vollenweider, F. X. (2001). Gender differences in the subjective effects of MDMA. *Psychopharmacology, 154*(2), 161–168. doi:10.1007/s002130000648

Markel, H., Lee, A., Holmes, R. D., & Domino, E. F. (1994). LSD flashback syndrome exacerbated by selective serotonin reuptake inhibitor antidepressants in adolescents. *Journal of Pediatrics, 125*(5 Pt. 1), 817–819. doi:10.1016/S0022-3476(06)80189-7

Martins, S. S., Ghandour, L. A., & Chilcoat, H. D. (2007). Pathways between ecstasy initiation and other drug use. *Addictive Behaviors, 32*(7), 1511–1518. doi:10.1016/j.addbeh.2006.11.003

Martins, S. S., Mazzotti, G., & Chilcoat, H. D. (2006). Recent-onset ecstasy use: Association with deviant behaviors and psychiatric comorbidity. *Experimental and Clinical Psychopharmacology, 14*(3), 275–286. doi:10.1037/1064-1297.14.3.275

Mustanski, B., Newcomb, M. E., Du Bois, S. N., Garcia, S. C., & Grov, C. (2011). HIV in young men who have sex with men: A review of epidemiology, risk and protective factors, and interventions. *Annual Review of Sex Research, 48*(2–3), 218–253.

National Institute on Drug Abuse. (2001). *Hallucinogens and dissociative drugs (NIH Publication No. 01–4209)*. Retrieved December 2015, from http://www.drugabuse.gov/PDF/RRHalluc.pdf

National Institute on Drug Abuse. (2009). *NIDA InfoFacts: Hallucinogens: LSD, peyote, psilocybin, and PCP*. Retrieved from https://www.drugabuse.gov/drugs-abuse/club-drugs

National Institute on Drug Abuse. (2010a). *NIDA InfoFacts: Club drugs (GHB, ketamine, and rohypnol)*. Retrieved from https://www.drugabuse.gov/drugs-abuse/club-drugs

National Institute on Drug Abuse. (2010b). *NIDA InfoFacts: Methamphetamine*. Retrieved from http://www.drugabuse.gov/drugs-abuse/club-drugs

Novins, D. K., Beals, J., & Mitchell, C. M. (2001). Sequences of substance use among American Indian adolescents. *Journal of the American Academy of Child and Adolescent Psychiatry, 40*(10), 1168–1174. doi:10.1097/00004583-200110000-00010

Paquette, C., Roy, E., Petit, G., & Boivin, J. F. (2010). Predictors of crack cocaine initiation among Montreal street youth: A first look at the phenomenon. *Drug and Alcohol Dependence, 110*(1–2), 85–91. doi:10.1016/j.drugalcdep.2010.02.010

Parrott, A. C., & Stuart, M. (1997). Ecstasy (MDMA), amphetamine, and LSD: Comparative mood profiles in recreational polydrug users. *Human Psychopharmacology, 12*(5), 501–504. doi:10.1002/(SICI)1099-1077(199709/10)12:5<501::AID-HUP913>3.0.CO;2-V

Parsons, J. T., Grov, C., & Kelly, B. C. (2009). Club drug use and dependence among young adults recruited through time-space sampling. *Public Health Reports, 124*(2), 246–254. Retrieved from http://www.publichealthreports.org/

Pedraza, C., Garcia, F. B., & Navarro, J. F. (2009). Neurotoxic effects induced by gammahydroxybutyric acid (GHB) in male rats. *International Journal of Neuropsychopharmacology, 12*(9), 1165–1177. doi:10.1017/S1461145709000157

Perry, P. D., & Hedges Duroy, T. L. (2004). Adolescent and young adult heroin and non heroin users: A quantitative and qualitative study of experiences in a therapeutic community. *Journal of Psychoactive Drugs, 36*(1), 75–84. doi:10.1080/02791072.2004.10399725

Pisetsky, E. M., Chao, Y. M., Dierker, L. C., May, A. M., & Striegel-Moore, R. H. (2008). Disordered eating and substance use in high-school students: Results from the Youth Risk Behavior Surveillance System. *International Journal of Eating Disorders, 41*(5), 464–470. doi:10.1002/eat.20520

Pluddemann, A., Flisher, A. J., McKetin, R., Parry, C., & Lombard, C. (2010). Methamphetamine use, aggressive behavior and other mental health issues among high-school students in Cape Town, South Africa. *Drug and Alcohol Dependence, 109*(1–3), 14–19. doi:10.1016/j.drugalcdep.2009.11.021

Rawson, R. A., Gonzales, R., McCann, M., & Ling, W. (2007). Use of methamphetamine by young people: Is there reason for concern? *Addiction, 102*(7), 1021–1022. doi:10.1111/j.1360-0443.2007.01899.x

Rawson, R. A., Gonzales, R., McCann, M. J., & Obert, J. L. (2005). Methamphetamine use among treatment-seeking adolescents in Southern California: Participant characteristics and treatment response. *Journal of Substance Abuse Treatment, 29*(2), 67–74. doi:10.1016/j.jsat.2005.04.001

Rickert, V. I., Siqueira, L. M., Dale, T., & Wiemann, C. M. (2003). Prevalence and risk factors for LSD use among young women. *Journal of Pediatric and Adolescent Gynecology, 16*(2), 67–75. doi:10.1016/S1083-3188(03)00012-3

Robinson, T. E., & Berridge, K. C. (2003). Addiction. *Annual Review of Psychology, 54*, 25–53. doi:10.1146/annurev.psych.54.101601.145237

Scholey, A. B., Parrott, A. C., Buchanan, T., Heffernan, T. M., Ling, J., & Rodgers, J. (2004). Increased intensity of ecstasy and polydrug usage in the more experienced recreational ecstasy/MDMA users: A WWW study. *Addictive Behaviors, 29*(4), 743–752. doi:10.1016/j.addbeh.2004.02.022

Schwartz, R. H. (1995). LSD. Its rise, fall, and renewed popularity among high school students. *Pediatric Clinics of North America, 42*(2), 403–413.

Sircar, R., & Basak, A. (2004). Adolescent gamma-hydroxybutyric acid exposure decreases cortical N-methyl-D-aspartate receptor and impairs spatial learning. *Pharmacology, Biochemistry and Behavior, 79*(4), 701–708. doi:10.1016/j.pbb.2004.09.022

Sircar, R., Basak, A., & Sircar, D. (2008). Gamma-hydroxybutyric acid-induced cognitive deficits in the female adolescent rat. *Annals of the New York Academy of Sciences, 1139*, 386–389. doi:10.1196/annals.1432.044

Sowell, E. R., Thompson, P. M., Holmes, C. J., Jernigan, T. L., & Toga, A. W. (1999). In vivo evidence for post-adolescent brain maturation in frontal and striatal regions. *Nature Neuroscience, 2*(10), 859–861. doi:10.1038/13154

Springer, A. E., Peters, R. J., Shegog, R., White, D. L., & Kelder, S. H. (2007). Methamphetamine use and sexual risk behaviors in U.S. high school students: Findings from a National Risk Behavior Survey. *Prevention Science, 8*(2), 103–113. doi:10.1007/s11121-007-0065-6

Sterk, C. E., Klein, H., & Elifson, K. W. (2008). Young adult ecstasy users and multiple sexual partners: Understanding the factors underlying this HIV risk practice. *Journal of Psychoactive Drugs, 40*(3), 237–244. doi:10.1080/02791072.2008.10400638

Stone, A. L., Storr, C. L., & Anthony, J. C. (2006). Evidence for a hallucinogen dependence syndrome developing soon after onset of hallucinogen use during adolescence. *International Journal of Methods in Psychiatric Research, 15*(3), 116–130. doi:10.1002/mpr.188

Strote, J., Lee, J. E., & Wechsler, H. (2002). Increasing MDMA use among college students: Results of a national survey. *Journal of Adolescent Health, 30*(1), 64–72. doi:10.1016/S1054-139X(01)00315-9

Subramaniam, G. A., & Stitzer, M. A. (2009). Clinical characteristics of treatment-seeking prescription opioid vs. heroin-using adolescents with opioid use disorder. *Drug and Alcohol Dependence, 101*(1–2), 13–19. doi:10.1016/j.drugalcdep.2008.10.015

Substance Abuse and Mental Health Services Administration. (2009). *Treatment Episode Data Set (TEDS). Highlights—2007. National admissions to substance abuse treatment services* (DASIS Series S-45, DHHS Publication No. SMA 09–4360). Retrieved December 2015, from http://www.samhsa.gov/data/TEDS2k7highlights/TEDSHigh2k7.pdf

Substance Abuse and Mental Health Services Administration. (2011a). *Drug Abuse Warning Network, 2009: National Estimates of Drug-Related Emergency Department Visits* (DAWN Series D-35, DHHS Publication No. SMA 11–4659). Retrieved December 2015, from http://www.samhsa.gov/data/2k11/DAWN/2k9DAWNED/PDF/DAWN2k9ED.pdf

Substance Abuse and Mental Health Services Administration. (2011b). *Results from the 2010 National Survey on Drug Use and Health: Detailed tables.* Retrieved December 2015, from http://www.samhsa.gov/data/NSDUH/2k10ResultsTables/Web/PDFW/Cover.pdf

Substance Abuse and Mental Health Services Administration. (2011c). *Results from the 2010 National Survey on Drug Use and Health: Summary of national findings* (NSDUH Series H-41, DHHS Publication No. SMA 11–4658). Retrieved December 2015, from http://www.samhsa.gov/data/NSDUH/2k10Results/Web/PDFW/2k10Results.pdf

Substance Abuse and Mental Health Services Administration. (2011d). *Table 1.2A—Types of illicit drug use in lifetime, past year, and past month among persons aged 12 or 13: Number in thousands, 2009 and 2010.* Retrieved December 2015, from http://www.samhsa.gov/data/NSDUH/2k10ResultsTables/Web/PDFW/Sect1peTabs1to10.pdf

Substance Abuse and Mental Health Services Administration. (2011e). *Table 1.3A—Types of illicit drug use in lifetime, past year, and past month among persons aged 14 or 15: Number in thousands, 2009 and 2010.* Retrieved December 2015, from http://www.samhsa.gov/data/NSDUH/2k10ResultsTables/Web/PDFW/Sect1peTabs1to10.pdf

Substance Abuse and Mental Health Services Administration. (2011f). *Table 1.4A—Types of illicit drug use in lifetime, past year, and past month among persons aged 16 or 17: Number in thousands, 2009 and 2010.* Retrieved December 2015, from http://www.samhsa.gov/data/NSDUH/2k10ResultsTables/Web/PDFW/Sect1peTabs1to10.pdf

Substance Abuse and Mental Health Services Administration. (2011g). *Table 1.30B—Cocaine use in lifetime, past year, and past month among persons aged 12 to 17, by demographic characteristics: Percentages, 2009 and 2010.* Retrieved December 2015, from http://www.samhsa.gov/data/NSDUH/2k10ResultsTables/Web/PDFW/Sect1peTabs29to33.pdf

Substance Abuse and Mental Health Services Administration. (2011h). *Table 4.5B—Past year initiation of substance use among persons aged 12 or older, persons aged 12 or older at risk for initiation of substance use, and past year substance users aged 12 or older: Number in thousands and percentages, 2009 and 2010.* Retrieved December 2015, from http://www.samhsa.gov/data/NSDUH/2k10ResultsTables/Web/PDFW/Sect4peTabs5to8.pdf

Substance Abuse and Mental Health Services Administration. (2011i). *Table 4.6B—Past year initiation of substance use among persons aged 12 to 17, persons aged 12 to 17 at risk for initiation of substance use, and past year substance users aged 12 to 17: Number in thousands and percentages, 2009 and 2010.* Retrieved December 2015, from http://www.samhsa.gov/data/NSDUH/2k10ResultsTables/Web/PDFW/Sect4peTabs5to8.pdf

Substance Abuse and Mental Health Services Administration. (2011j). *Table 4.7B—Past year initiation of substance use among persons aged 18 to 25, persons aged 18 to 25 at risk for initiation of substance use, and past year substance users aged 18 to 25: Number in thousands and percentages, 2009 and 2010.* Retrieved December 2015, from http://www.samhsa.gov/data/NSDUH/2k10ResultsTables/Web/PDFW/Sect4peTabs5to8.pdf

Substance Abuse and Mental Health Services Administration. (2011k). *Table 5. ED visits involving illicit drugs, by patient demographics, 2008* (DHHS Publication No. SMA 11–4618). Retrieved December 2015, from http://www.samhsa.gov/data/2k11/DAWN/ED/DAWN2k8ED.pdf

Substance Abuse and Mental Health Services Administration. (2011l). *Table 8.8A—Numbers (in thousands) of persons aged 12 or older, by youth and adult age groups and geographic characteristics: 2009 and 2010.* Retrieved December 2015, from http://www.samhsa.gov/data/NSDUH/2k10ResultsTables/Web/PDFW/Sect8peTabs6to9.pdf

Substance Abuse and Mental Health Services Administration. (2011m). *Treatment Episode Data Set (TEDS). 1999—2009. National admissions to substance abuse treatment services* (DASIS Series S-56, DHHS Publication No. SMA 11–4646). Retrieved December 2015, from http://www.samhsa.gov/data/DASIS/teds09st/teds2009stweb.pdf

Substance Abuse Management Information System, Maryland Alcohol and Drug Abuse Administration. (1997). *Annual data from the Substance Abuse Management Information System*. Baltimore, MD: Author.

Tolou-Shams, M., Ewing, S. W. F., Tarantino, N., & Brown, L. K. (2010). Crack and cocaine use among adolescents in psychiatric treatment: Associations with HIV risk. *Journal of Child and Adolescent Substance Abuse, 19*(2), 122–134. doi:10.1080/10678281003634926

Topp, L., Hando, J., Dillon, P., Roche, A., & Solowij, N. (1999). Ecstasy use in Australia: Patterns of use and associated harm. *Drug and Alcohol Dependence, 55*(1–2), 105–115. doi:10.1016/S0376-8716(99)00002-2

van der Poel, A., Rodenburg, G., Dijkstra, M., Stoele, M., & van de Mheen, D. (2009). Trends, motivations and settings of recreational cocaine use by adolescents and young adults in the Netherlands. *International Journal of Drug Policy, 20*(2), 143–151. doi:10.1016/j.drugpo.2008.02.005

van der Poel, A., & van de Mheen, D. (2006). Young people using crack and the process of marginalization. *Drugs: Education, Prevention and Policy, 13*(1), 45–59. doi:10.1080/09687630500402891

Winstock, A. R., Griffiths, P., & Stewart, D. (2001). Drugs and the dance music scene: A survey of current drug use patterns among a sample of dance music enthusiasts in the UK. *Drug and Alcohol Dependence, 64*(1), 9–17. doi:10.1016/S0376-8716(00)00215-5

Wu, L-T., Schlenger, W. E., & Galvin, D. M. (2006). Concurrent use of methamphetamine, MDMA, LSD, ketamine, GHB, and flunitrazepam among American youths. *Drug and Alcohol Dependence, 84*(1), 102–113. doi:10.1016/j.drugalcdep.2006.01.002

Wu, P., Liu, X., & Fan, B. (2010). Factors associated with initiation of ecstasy use among US adolescents: Findings from a national survey. *Drug and Alcohol Dependence, 106*(2-3), 193–198. doi:10.1016/j.drugalcdep.2009.08.020

Wu, Z. H., Holzer, C. E., Breitkopf, C. R., Grady, J. J., & Berenson, A. B. (2006). Patterns and perceptions of ecstasy use among young, low-income women. *Addictive Behaviors, 31*(4), 676–685. doi:10.1016/j.addbeh.2005.05.051

Yen, C-F. (2004). Relationship between methamphetamine use and risky sexual behavior in adolescents. *Kaohsiung Journal of Medical Sciences, 20*(4), 160–165. doi:10.1016/S1607-551X(09)70101-9

Yen, C-F., & Chong, M-Y. (2006). Comorbid psychiatric disorders, sex, and methamphetamine use in adolescents: A case-control study. *Comprehensive Psychiatry, 47*(3), 215–220. doi:10.1016/j.comppsych.2005.07.006

Prescription Drug Abuse in Adolescence

Amelia M. Arria *and* Brittany A. Bugbee

Abstract

Nonmedical use of prescription drugs can pose a variety of serious public health threats. Rapid increases in the use of prescription drugs were observed at the turn of the 21st century and prompted new research and several actions by communities and policymakers. Adolescents and young adults are at heightened risk for this type of substance use. The evidence suggests that nonmedical use of prescription drugs overlaps significantly with alcohol and other drug problems, and it might be a sign of more severe involvement with illicit substance use. This chapter describes the epidemiology, availability and sources, motives, risk factors, and consequences of nonmedical prescription drug use among adolescents and young adults. Special topics include nonmedical use of prescription stimulants and academic performance, associations with attention-deficit/hyperactivity disorder and mental health, and diversion behavior. Future directions for research and strategies for demand and supply reduction are described.

Key Words: nonmedical use, medications, diversion, stimulants, analgesics, sedatives, tranquilizers, anxiolytics, medications, academic performance

Terminology and Measurement Issues

Although the use of prescription drugs without proper medical supervision is not a new phenomenon (Schuster, 2006), much ambiguity still exists when describing this complex behavior (Barrett, Meisner, & Stewart, 2008). Confusion exists for several reasons. First, prescription drugs encompass a variety of drug classes (e.g., analgesics, stimulants, etc.). Within those classes are different formulations of medications that are prescribed for a variety of symptoms and conditions. Therefore, terms such as "prescription drug abuse" are problematic because they ignore the differences between drug classes or formulations. It is far more preferable to refer specifically to the type of medication that is being used nonmedically.

Second, there are many ways in which prescription drugs can be used outside of medical supervision. The definition used in US national surveys is "using medications (excluding over-the-counter drugs) that were not prescribed for you or that you took only for the experience or feeling they caused" (Substance Abuse and Mental Health Services Administration, 2012a). For example, an individual can be prescribed a drug but use it in a way that is inconsistent with medical advice (e.g., use leftover pain medication that was originally prescribed for a toothache to medicate a shoulder injury). Alternatively, one might have a prescription for pain medication for a toothache but ingest doses in excess of what was recommended or after the pain has subsided simply to experience euphoria. Other individuals with leftover medication might not be experiencing any symptoms but still use it for some other purpose, such as in the case of prescription stimulants, which are used nonmedically to stay awake longer to study or get high.

Another set of scenarios involves individuals who do not have a prescription. In these cases, nonmedical use might be initiated in the presence of symptoms (e.g., pain, sleeping problems), but rather than obtaining a prescription, the drug is obtained from a friend or through some other means. Disentangling the different contexts in which prescription drugs are used and the motives for which they are used has led to many debates about proper terminology and proposals for subtyping (McCabe, Boyd, & Teter, 2009). A great deal of heterogeneity exists with regard to motives for use. For example, Young and colleagues found that while half of adolescent nonmedical prescription opioid users had evidence of behavioral disinhibition and rule breaking, the other half reported that their primary motive was to "self-treat" a variety of mental health issues (Young, McCabe, Cranford, Ross-Durow, & Boyd, 2012).

Third, multiple terms have been used to describe these various scenarios, including "misuse," "overuse," "abuse," "extra-medical use," and "nonmedical use" (Arria, Caldeira, O'Grady, Vincent, Johnson, et al., 2008; Kaye & Darke, 2012; McCabe et al., 2011; Meier, Troost, & Anthony, 2012). In the United States, the term "nonmedical use" is preferred to describe the behavior because it is not confused with the *DSM-IV* criteria for substance use disorders (American Psychiatric Association, 2000) and because it is used by the US federally sponsored National Survey on Drug Use and Health (NSDUH) (Substance Abuse and Mental Health Services Administration, 2012b). For the remainder of this chapter we will use the term "nonmedical use" and refer to abuse, dependence, and disorder when referring to studies that specifically assessed *DSM* criteria.

Measuring the nature and extent of nonmedical prescription drug use is challenging to researchers. In addition to standard issues of bias resulting from socially desirable responding or problems with recall, another potential problem with estimating nonmedical prescription drug use stems from the difficulty of conveying the meaning of nonmedical use to research participants. Prescription drug classes are known by a variety of names and slang terms that can sometimes be confusing to research participants (e.g., anxiolytics vs. analgesics). To reduce confusion, definitions are provided and photographs of pills are sometimes presented to respondents. While the use of self-report questionnaires is advantageous for cost and brevity, there is always the possibility of participants misunderstanding nonmedical use, which can then lead to inaccurate estimates of prevalence. And although personal interview methods can help clarify the definition of nonmedical use, substantially more time is required to extensively train interviewers and to administer interviews to maximize the veracity of the data collected.

Classes of Prescription Drugs Used Nonmedically

Table 10.1 summarizes the four most common types of prescription drugs with psychoactive properties that are used nonmedically. The complex and changing nature of prescription drugs that are available for medical use complicates the assessment and measurement of nonmedical prescription drug use. For example, the variety of medications available and the formulations of the same medications to treat attention-deficit/hyperactivity disorder (ADHD) have changed over time and appear to carry different risks (DuPont, Coleman, Bucher, & Wilford, 2008; Kollins, 2008; Teter, McCabe, LaGrange, Cranford, & Boyd, 2006). New formulations of oxycodone are currently being evaluated for their abuse-resistant potential (Severtson et al., 2013).

National Trends in Nonmedical Use of Prescription Drugs

After alcohol and marijuana use, nonmedical use of prescription drugs ranks third in prevalence for adolescents and young adults residing in the United States (Johnston, O'Malley, Bachman, & Schulenberg, 2013b). In 2011, 7.0% or 1.7 million 12- to 17-year-olds and 12.7% or 4.4 million 18- to 25-year-olds used at least one type of prescription drug nonmedically in the past year. Users from more recent birth cohorts appear to be at increased risk for dependence compared with earlier cohorts (Martins, Keyes, Storr, Zhu, & Grucza, 2010).

Adolescents (12- to 17-Year-Olds)

Figure 10.1 shows the trends in past-year nonmedical use of four classes of prescription drugs among 12- to 17-year-olds surveyed annually from 2002 to 2011 through the nation's largest epidemiologic surveillance system for monitoring alcohol and drug consumption—NSDUH. A downward trend is evident, driven mainly by decreases in pain reliever use, from a high of 7.7% in 2003 to a low of 5.9% in 2011. The prevalence estimates for other prescription drug classes are substantially lower than pain relievers, and the trend lines are somewhat flatter, with the exception of stimulants, which has decreased from a high of 2.7% in 2002 to a present low of 1.2% (Substance Abuse and Mental Health Services Administration, 2012a).

Another major source of data on nonmedical use of prescription drugs is the Monitoring the Future (MTF) study (Johnston, O'Malley, Bachman,

Table 10.1 Types of Prescription Drugs Used Nonmedically

Drug Class	Uses	Common Conditions	Examples
Opioids, analgesics, or pain relievers	Relieve acute or chronic pain	Postoperative pain	Codeine, Oxycontin®, Percocet®, Vicodin®
Stimulants	Treat attention difficulties to improve focus	Attention-deficit/hyperactivity disorder, narcolepsy	Adderall®, Concerta®, Provigil®, Ritalin®
Benzodiazepines, tranquilizers, or muscle relaxers	Relieve anxiety or tension, relax muscle spasms, treat sleep difficulties	Anxiety disorders, insomnia, epilepsy, muscle spasms	Ativan®, Klonopin®, Valium®, Xanax®
Sedatives	Treat sleep difficulties	Insomnia	Ambien®, Lunesta®, Sonata®

& Schulenberg, 2013a), an annual survey of US schoolchildren in grades 8–12 that began in 1975 and continues through the present. Various questions regarding lifetime, past-year, and past-30-day use of nonmedical use of prescription drugs have been asked, and the data are useful for understanding prevalence, perceived availability, harmfulness of these drugs, and changes over time among children who attend school in the United States. In 2012, 21.2% of 12th graders surveyed had used a prescription drug of any kind nonmedically in their lifetime. A slight decrease in this estimate is apparent since 2005 (24.0%), when the study began reporting this data. Past-year and past-month use—better indicators of current use—are estimated to be 14.8% and 7.0%, respectively, for 12th graders, both of which have also decreased slightly since 2005.

The extent to which prescription drugs are used nonmedically varies significantly by drug class and formulation. With respect to specific types of prescription analgesics, 7.9% of 12th graders used a "narcotic other than heroin" nonmedically in the past year, with 4.3% using OxyContin® and 7.5%

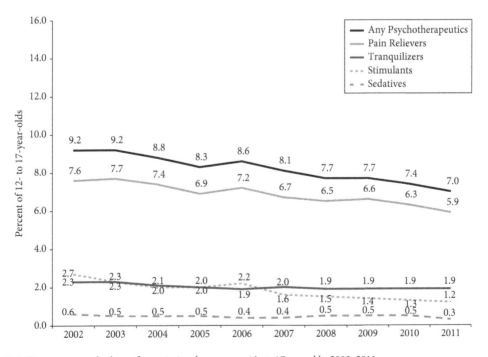

Figure 10.1 Past-year nonmedical use of prescription drugs among 12- to 17-year-olds, 2002–2011.

Table 10.2 Percentage of Secondary School Students Reporting Lifetime Medical and Nonmedical Use of Any Prescription Drugs

Lifetime Prescription Drug Use Status	Percent of Sample
Nonuser	47.4
Medical use only	31.5
Medical/nonmedical use	17.5
Nonmedical use only	3.3

Source: McCabe et al. (2007).

using Vicodin® (Johnston et al., 2013b). Past-year prevalence of nonmedical stimulant use was similar, with 7.6% of 12th graders using Adderall® and 2.6% using Ritalin®. A smaller proportion of 12th graders surveyed in the MTF used tranquilizers (5.3%) or sedatives (4.5%) nonmedically. For some prescription drug classes, past-year use among 8th and 10th graders is reported. Younger age groups have consistently lower estimates. For example, 1.8% of 8th graders used a tranquilizer in the past year, and 4.5% of 10th graders used Adderall® nonmedically. Notably, Adderall® is the only prescription drug for which recent increases can be seen in nonmedical use among 12th graders. In contrast, the percentage of 12th graders using Vicodin® nonmedically in the past year has declined from its peak in 2003 of 10.5% to its current prevalence estimate of 7.5%.

In addition to studies that utilize the aforementioned national data sources, several studies have been conducted on smaller geographically focused samples of adolescents. Prevalence estimates vary depending on region, methods used to recruit respondents, and operationalization of variables. These types of studies can examine in a more in-depth way the correlates, predictors, and outcomes of nonmedical use of prescription drugs. Collins et al. (2011) studied a sample of more than 1,000 adolescents ascertained from the Appalachian region of Tennessee. In this study, 35% of 12- to 17-year-olds had used a prescription medication nonmedically at least once in their lifetime, an estimate that was higher than cigarettes or marijuana. They identified several significant correlates of nonmedical use, including permissive community norms, high perceived availability, low perceived risk, high level of peer use, and low school commitment. Youth whose parents disapproved of nonmedical use were less likely to use.

Several studies conducted by a team of investigators at the University of Michigan have advanced our understanding of the nature of nonmedical use of prescription drugs among adolescents (Boyd, McCabe, Cranford, & Young, 2007; McCabe, Teter, & Boyd, 2004; McCabe, Boyd, & Young, 2007; McCabe et al., 2011). This set of studies utilized web-based methods to describe the correlates of nonmedical use of opioids, stimulants, tranquilizers, and sedatives among cohorts of school-children living in Michigan. Importantly, these and other studies documented the overlap between medical and nonmedical use of various prescription drugs. Table 10.2 shows the distribution of individuals who only used prescription drugs under the guidance of a physician (medical use), those who used both medically and nonmedically, and those who were only nonmedical users (McCabe, Boyd, & Young, 2007). In this study, nonmedical use of any prescription drug in conjunction with medical use was significantly more common than nonmedical use alone, although nearly half of the students studied had never used any of the four classes either nonmedically or medically.

Young Adults (18- to 25-Year-Olds)

Nonmedical prescription drug use is more common among young adults (18- to 25-year-olds) than both younger and older age groups. As can be seen in Figure 10.2, the prevalence of past-year analgesic use among 18- to 25-year-olds reached a peak in 2006 (12.5%), and it has been declining, most dramatically in the past 3 years, to a current low of 9.8% (Substance Abuse and Mental Health Services Administration, 2012a). Similar to what was observed for adolescents, the trend lines are somewhat flatter for stimulants, sedatives, and tranquilizers and among all classes of drugs used nonmedically than for analgesics, and sedatives are the least commonly used.

The NSDUH data show that the prevalence of past-month use of prescription drugs among young adults varies quite dramatically by college attendance (Herman-Stahl, Krebs, Kroutil, & Heller, 2007; Substance Abuse and Mental Health Services Administration, 2012a). Figure 10.3 compares past-month use among full-time college students with their similarly aged counterparts who are not enrolled full-time in college. Nonmedical analgesic use is lower among college students, whereas nonmedical tranquilizer use is only slightly less prevalent among college students. As was the case for 12- to 17-year-olds, sedatives were the least

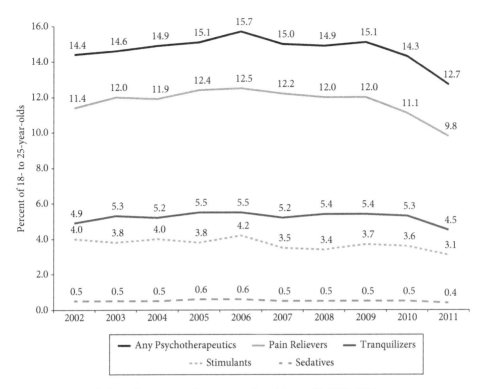

Figure 10.2 Past-year nonmedical use of prescription drugs among 18- to 25-year-olds, 2002–2011.

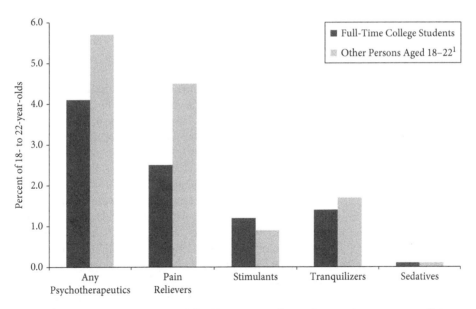

[1]Other persons aged 18–22 are defined by NSDUH as "respondents aged 18 to 22 not enrolled in school, enrolled in college part time, enrolled in other grades either full or part time, or enrolled with no other information available."

Figure 10.3 Past-month nonmedical use of prescription drugs among 18- to 22-year-olds, by college enrollment.

commonly used prescription drug among both subgroups. In contrast, owing in part to their purported value for increasing academic performance, nonmedical prescription stimulant use is somewhat higher among full-time college students. Later in this chapter, research is described that has shed light on the nature of prescription stimulant use among college students.

Since 1980, MTF has collected data on nonmedical use of prescription drugs among college students (Johnston, O'Malley, Bachman, & Schulenberg, 2012). Lifetime prevalence estimates of "narcotics other than heroin" have been irregular overall, but were fairly stable from 1980 to 1999 (ranging from a high of 8.9% in 1980 to a low of 5.1% in 1994). In 2000, the prevalence estimate rose again to 8.9% and reached a peak of 14.6% in 2006. Since 2006, the estimate has declined to the current 2011 estimate of 12.4%. Lifetime nonmedical sedative use has varied over time with a high of 8.1% in 1980 to a present estimate of 3.6%. Nonmedical tranquilizer use in 1980 was 15.2%, then declined and again reached a peak in 2005 of 11.9%, and has since declined to 7.1%. Lifetime prevalence of nonmedical stimulant use among college students is not reported, but from past-year estimates, stimulants are the most commonly used class of prescription drugs by college students, with 9.8% using Adderall® nonmedically and 2.3% using Ritalin®. Nonmedical use of prescription analgesics ranks second among college students, with 5.8% using Vicodin® and 2.4% using OxyContin® in the past year. The prevalence of past-year nonmedical tranquilizer and sedative use is estimated to be 4.2% and 1.7%, respectively.

Several other investigations have reported the prevalence of nonmedical use of prescription drugs among college students (Ford & Arrastia, 2008; McCabe, Knight, Teter, & Wechsler, 2005; McCabe, Teter, Boyd, Knight, & Wechsler, 2005). Some have focused on a particular drug class such as stimulants (Babcock & Byrne, 2000; Barrett, Darredeau, Bordy, & Pihl, 2005; Carroll, McLaughlin, & Blake, 2006; DeSantis, Webb, & Noar, 2008; Garnier-Dykstra, Caldeira, Vincent, O'Grady, & Arria, 2012; Hall, Irwin, Bowman, Frankenberger, & Jewett, 2005; Kaloyanides, McCabe, Cranford, & Teter, 2007; Novak, Kroutil, Williams, & Van Brunt, 2007) or opioids (McCabe, Cranford, Boyd, & Teter, 2007; McCabe, Teter, et al., 2005). Fewer studies have focused specifically on benzodiazepines (McCabe, 2005). A few qualitative studies have been conducted (DeSantis et al., 2008; Quintero, 2009).

The College Life Study (CLS) is a prospective study of 1,253 traditional-age college students who were originally assessed during their first year of college and assessed annually thereafter via personal interviews regardless of continued college attendance (Arria, Caldeira, O'Grady, Vincent, Fitzelle, et al., 2008; Vincent et al., 2012). Several findings about nonmedical use of prescription drugs among college students have emanated from the CLS and are discussed throughout this chapter (Arria et al., 2007; Arria, Garnier-Dykstra, Caldeira, Vincent, & O'Grady, 2011; Garnier et al., 2009; Garnier-Dykstra et al., 2012).

Because college students appear to be at particular risk for nonmedical prescription stimulant use (Herman-Stahl et al., 2007), several studies have focused on describing the patterns and correlates of stimulant use in this population. Lifetime prevalence estimates vary depending on assessment methods and the characteristics of students studied (DeSantis et al., 2008; Low & Gendaszek, 2002). Using data from 119 colleges and universities who participated in the 2001 College Alcohol Study, McCabe, Knight, et al. (2005) found significant variation in the prevalence of nonmedical prescription stimulant use across colleges, and they found that rates were higher among colleges in the Northeast, more selective colleges, and those that had residential housing options.

Numerous studies have observed that nonmedical use is much higher among students affiliated with Greek organizations than students who are not affiliated with a sorority or fraternity (DeSantis et al., 2008; McCabe, Knight, et al., 2005; McCabe, Teter, & Boyd, 2006a). One study documented that 55.4% of men sampled from a fraternity who did not have ADHD used prescription stimulants nonmedically at least once in their lifetime (DeSantis, Noar, & Webb, 2009). Individuals who belong to sororities and fraternities perceive a much higher prevalence of nonmedical prescription stimulant use (McCabe, 2008a).

Catalano et al. (2011) reported findings from an analysis of a longitudinal study that assessed a sample of adolescents ascertained from the community and assessed through the transition to young adulthood. Approximately one third of the sample used prescription opioids nonmedically at some point over the 5 years studied. Approximately half of nonmedical users who used in high school continued to use at ages 19 and 20 years, with only 6.1% using prescription opiates nonmedically for the first time after high school.

Adolescents and Young Adults Receiving Addiction Treatment

In contrast to the wealth of information available regarding the prevalence of nonmedical use of prescription drugs in the general population and non-treatment-seeking samples, little is known about the nonmedical prescription drug use history of adolescents receiving addiction treatment services. Williams and colleagues (2004) reported that 23% of adolescents attending a treatment center in Alberta, Canada had used a prescription stimulant nonmedically at some point in their life. Characterizing adolescents in treatment with respect to nonmedical prescription drug use is important because a better understanding of the individual's drug use patterns can inform more personalized treatment planning. Furthermore, following discharge, the widespread availability of these drugs might raise the risk of relapse. Therefore, efforts should be made to assess nonmedical use and incorporate reduction of nonmedical use of prescription drugs during treatment and after discharge as part of a continuing care plan.

Patterns of Nonmedical Use, Route of Administration, and Drug Abuse and Dependence

Although many research studies have documented the prevalence of use, few have described the patterns or persistence of use within individuals across time. Boyd, Teter, et al. (2009) analyzed two waves of a nationally representative sample of adults and observed that 85% of females and 79% of males who reported nonmedical use of prescription opioids at Wave 1 did not report use at Wave 2, suggesting that persistence of use is not common among the general population. Another study examined patterns of persistence of nonmedical prescription stimulant use during college and observed that despite the fairly high annual prevalence observed, only a small proportion (3.4%) of the sample used all 4 years of the study.

With respect to frequency of use, the available data suggest that nonmedical use of prescription stimulants among adolescents and young adults is sporadic. For example, DuPont et al. (2008) reported that one third of prescription stimulant users in college used only once in the past year,

45% used 2–10 times, and the remaining 18% used 11–50 times. Similarly, White, Becker-Blease, and Grace-Bishop (2006) observed that 15.5% of college students who used prescription stimulants nonmedically used them two or three times weekly. In that sample, half reported using only 2–3 times per year. Little information is available regarding the frequency with which adolescents or young adults use opioids nonmedically.

Oral ingestion is the most common route of administration for prescription stimulants among college students, but a substantial minority also report crushing and snorting or inhaling the drug. The prevalence of snorting varies depending on the sample studied and methodology (Babcock & Byrne, 2000; Garnier-Dykstra et al., 2012; Hall et al., 2005; Teter et al., 2006; Teter, Falone, Cranford, Boyd, & McCabe, 2010; White et al., 2006). Teter et al. (2010) reported that 41.5% of a college student sample reported nonoral routes of administration and observed a significant association with depressed mood. In a 4-year longitudinal study of college students, Garnier-Dykstra et al. (2012) found that 12.8%–16.6% of stimulant users in any 1 year reported snorting prescription stimulants.

The proportion of adolescent and young adult users meeting *DSM-IV* criteria for abuse and dependence on prescription drugs has been documented in several studies. In general, 18- to 34-year-olds are more likely than other age groups to meet criteria (Martins et al., 2010). Schepis and Krishnan-Sarin (2008) examined a nationally representative sample of 12- to 17-year-old nonmedical users from the 2005 NSDUH. While 8.2% of the sample reported past-year nonmedical use, 3.0% of the sample experienced at least one symptom of substance use disorder related to any form of nonmedical use, comprising 36.0% of past-year users. The proportion of the full sample meeting criteria for substance abuse and dependence was 0.6% and 0.8%, respectively. Importantly, they estimated that 17.4% of past-year users met *DSM-IV* criteria for substance use disorder. Similar findings were observed by Ghandour, Martins, and Chilcoat (2008), who found that 18.3% of past-year users met criteria for past-year dependence, and Simoni-Wastila, Yang, and Lawler (2008), who reported that 15.3% of past-year users met criteria for problematic nonmedical use.

Cotto and colleagues (2010) reported interesting gender differences with respect to meeting criteria for abuse and dependence on prescription drugs.

Among 18- to 25-year-olds, males were more likely to use and meet criteria for abuse, while females were more likely to meet criteria for dependence. Among 12- to 17-year-olds, females were more likely to be users and be dependent.

Ghandour et al. (2008) used statistical techniques to derive classes of individuals with different patterns of *DSM-IV* symptoms related to nonmedical use of opioid medications. Four classes were identified, ranging from Class 1 (least likely to experience symptoms of dependence) to Class 4 (the most likely to experience dependence symptoms). Classes 2 and 3 had similar probabilities of reporting some symptoms, but individuals in Class 3 were more likely to experience withdrawal, continue use despite problems, and giving up important activities due to use. Ghandour et al. observed that the vast majority of users (84.3%) belonged to Class 1, the lowest probability of dependence. Interestingly, adolescents were overrepresented in Class 3. The authors speculated that adolescents might not view their experiences as problems and/or overestimate the extent to which they have their use under control. Because this was a cross-sectional study, it did not inform about possible changes in symptom profiles over time. More research is needed to understand how problems associated with dependence escalate over time, especially among individuals who initiate during adolescence.

Availability and Sources for Obtaining Prescription Drugs for Nonmedical Use

There are documented increases in the number of prescriptions written for adolescents to treat a variety of symptoms and conditions (Fortuna, Robbins, Caiola, Joynt, & Halterman, 2010), which many believe have fueled increases in nonmedical drug use, at least for opioids (Kuehn, 2007; Manchikanti, Fellows, Ailinani, & Pampati, 2010) more so than stimulants (Kaye & Darke, 2012). Numerous studies have documented how young people obtain prescription drugs for nonmedical use and the perceived ease of access. A majority of adolescents and young adults believe that these drugs are widely available (Carroll et al., 2006; Johnston et al., 2012; Weyandt et al., 2009).

Studies have consistently demonstrated that adolescent and young adult users most commonly obtain prescription drugs from friends and acquaintances who have legitimate prescriptions, followed by family members (Barrett et al., 2005; Garnier-Dykstra et al., 2012; McCabe & Boyd, 2005). The findings from these studies are consistent with national data on the

sources of obtaining prescription drugs for nonmedical use (see Figure 10.4). National data also suggest that receiving prescription drugs from friends or family for free is more common than taking from a friend or relative without asking, particularly among 18- to 25-year-olds (Substance Abuse and Mental Health Services Administration, 2012a). Seldom do nonmedical users purchase these drugs on the Internet, despite the proliferation of Internet-based pharmacies (Forman, Woody, McLellan, & Lynch, 2006; Schepis, Marlowe, & Forman, 2008).

Demographic Correlates of Nonmedical Use of Prescription Drugs
Race and Ethnicity

In general, most studies have observed that racial and ethnic minority groups are at lower risk for nonmedical prescription drug use as compared to Whites. Among the general population, African American, Asian American, and Hispanic adults appear to have lower rates of nonmedical prescription drug use than White adults (Sees, Di Marino, Ruediger, Sweeney, & Shiffman, 2005), but Native Americans are at higher risk (Huang et al., 2006).

Among 12- to 17-year-olds in the general population, mixed findings have been observed with respect to racial differences, but overall, nonmedical use of prescription drugs, particularly stimulants, appears to be less common among racial minorities (Herman-Stahl et al., 2007; Nakawaki & Crano, 2012). Among the college student population, White students appear to have higher rates of nonmedical prescription stimulant and opioid use compared to Asian and African American students, but they do not significantly differ from Hispanics (DuPont et al., 2008; McCabe et al., 2006a; McCabe, Knight, et al., 2005; McCabe, Morales, et al., 2007; Teter et al., 2006). In one study, White college students were more likely to be offered the opportunity to use stimulants and analgesics nonmedically than other racial groups (Arria, Caldeira, Vincent, O'Grady, & Wish, 2008). Being White was also a risk factor for persistent nonmedical stimulant use (Arria, Garnier-Dykstra, Caldeira, Vincent, O'Grady, et al., 2011). In another study, Hispanic college students, compared to non-Hispanics, had lower rates of nonmedical opioid use (McCabe, Teter, et al., 2005).

Racial disparities in nonmedical use might be influenced by cultural differences or by health insurance and prescription coverage disparities (Bloom & Cohen, 2007; Hoagwood, Jensen, Feil, Vitiello, & Bhatara, 2000; Mulye et al., 2009). Hispanic and

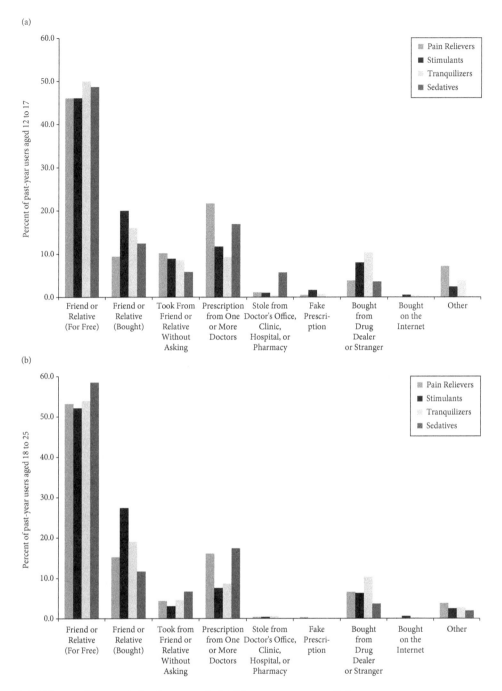

Figure 10.4 (a) Source where prescription drugs were obtained for most recent nonmedical use among past-year users (12- to 17-year-olds). (b) Source where prescription drugs were obtained for most recent nonmedical use among past-year users (18-to 25-year-olds).

African American children are significantly more likely to be uninsured or to have public health insurance, such as Medicaid, than White children (Berdahl, Friedman, McCormick, & Simpson, 2013). National data have shown that children with private health insurance or no insurance coverage are less likely to use a regular prescription medication than children who are covered by a public health insurance such as Medicaid (Bloom & Cohen, 2007), while another study found that children who had health insurance were more likely to use prescribed stimulants than children who did not have insurance coverage (Hoagwood et al., 2000). McCabe, Teter, and Boyd (2006b) reported that Asian American college students were less likely than others to medically use medications to treat sleep problems, anxiety, or pain. More research is needed to understand how the medical availability of prescribed medications might influence the risk of nonmedical use.

Sex

Several research studies have investigated whether males and females differ with respect to nonmedical prescription drug use. In general, sex differences are more apparent in younger age groups than among adults (Cotto et al., 2010). Some studies find that adolescent females are at higher risk than males for nonmedical use of prescription opioids, sedatives, and tranquilizers (McCabe, Boyd, & Young, 2007; Nakawaki & Crano, 2012; Wu, Pilowsky, & Patkar, 2008). In general, fewer sex differences are found with respect to nonmedical use of prescription stimulants (Simoni-Wastila, Ritter, & Strickler, 2004). Two studies have found that sex differences in nonmedical use are no longer apparent once statistical adjustment is made for other factors (Schepis & Krishnan-Sarin, 2008; Sung, Richter, Vaughan, Johnson, & Thom, 2005). Controlling for other factors, Simoni-Wastila, Yang, and Lawler (2008) observed that adolescent females were more likely to use tranquilizers and develop abuse and dependence on opiates than males. McCabe, Morales, et al. (2007) observed that after controlling for race, female college students did not differ from males with respect to nonmedical use of prescription drugs, and males had a greater likelihood of using other types of illicit drugs.

Based on data from the 2012 MTF, the annual prevalence for any type of prescription drug for females in the 12th grade is 13.7% versus 15.5% for males. With respect to different drug classes, annual prevalence estimates for Vicodin®, Oxycontin®, Ritalin®, and Adderall® are higher for males than females, and roughly equivalent for sedatives and tranquilizers (Johnston et al., 2013b). Slightly different conclusions are drawn from Figure 10.5, which displays data from the NSDUH on gender differences in the past-year nonmedical use of prescription drugs among 12- to 17-year-olds. Estimates for past-year use for all four drug classes are higher for females than males, although NSDUH does not report the statistical significance of these differences.

Complicating these findings are gender disparities in the medical use of prescription medications.

McCabe et al. (2006b) found that female undergraduates were more likely to be medical users of all classes of prescription drugs with the exception of stimulants. However, conflicting findings exist with respect to sex differences in nonmedical use of prescription stimulants among college students, with some studies finding higher rates among men (Low & Gendaszek, 2002) and others finding no difference among colleges students who had never been medically prescribed stimulants (Arria, Caldeira, O'Grady, Vincent, Johnson, et al., 2008).

Some research has suggested that sex differences exist regarding motivations for nonmedical use. Female college students have reported using prescription stimulants to lose weight (Low & Gendaszek, 2002; Teter et al., 2006) and "self-treat" somatic complaints with opioid, sedative, and anxiety medications nonmedically more often than males.

Socioeconomic Status

Interesting relationships exist between nonmedical use of prescription drugs and socioeconomic status. Compared to nonusers, adolescent and young adult users of prescription stimulants appear to have parents with higher levels of education and greater family income (Arria, O'Grady, Caldeira, Vincent, & Wish, 2008). In contrast, lower socioeconomic status appears to be related to nonmedical use of prescription opioids (Sung et al., 2005).

Motives for Nonmedical Prescription Drug Use

There are a variety of purported motives for using prescription drugs nonmedically. While the most commonly reported reasons for nonmedical prescription analgesic use are to relax, to relieve pain, or get high (Lord, Brevard, & Budman, 2011; McCabe, Cranford, et al., 2007), stimulants are used nonmedically to stay awake longer to study, especially among college students (Barrett et al., 2005; Carroll et al., 2006; DeSantis et al., 2008; Low & Gendaszek, 2002; Teter, McCabe, Cranford, Boyd, & Guthrie, 2005) (see section on "Nonmedical Use of Prescription Stimulants and Academic Performance in College"). Importantly, motives are not mutually exclusive; 24% of individuals in one study who reported using stimulants to study also reported motives related to partying or getting high (Arria et al., 2013). A study using MTF data found that approximately 75% of 12th graders had more than one motive for using prescription drugs nonmedically (McCabe & Cranford, 2012).

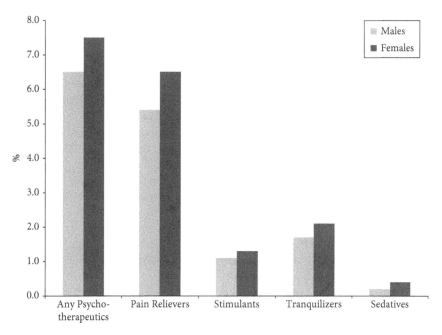

Figure 10.5 Past-year nonmedical use of prescription drugs, among 12- to 17-year-olds, by gender. *Source*: Substance Abuse and Mental Health Services Administration. (2012a). *Results from the 2011 National Survey on Drug Use and Health: Detailed Tables*. Rockville, MD: United States Department of Health and Human Services, Office of Applied Studies.

Some motives, such as experimentation, relaxation, getting high, and affect regulation, were identified for all three classes of prescription drugs included in the study (opioids, tranquilizers, and stimulants). However, some motives were unique to the drug class; weight loss and enhancing energy were only identified for prescription stimulants, while sleeping was only identified as a motive for prescription tranquilizers. Rozenbroek and Rothstein (2011) reported a variety of reasons why college students used various types of prescription drugs nonmedically. Interestingly, in that study, 21.6% of students reported taking central nervous system depressants to study and/or perform better academically.

A minority of college students (19.3%) reported using stimulants in combination with alcohol to stay awake longer to drink more (Low & Gendaszek, 2002). Additional motives for use have been reported, including to improve athletic performance or to counteract the effects of other drugs (Low & Gendaszek, 2002; Teter et al., 2005).

Associations Between Nonmedical Use of Prescription Drugs and Alcohol and Other Drug Use

One of the most consistent findings from research on nonmedical use of prescription drugs is that adolescent and young adult users are likely to have had histories of alcohol and other drug involvement and/or be current users of other substances, including alcohol (Fleary, Heffer, & McKyer, 2011; Lookatch, Dunne, & Katz, 2012; Schepis & Krishnan-Sarin, 2008; Teter et al., 2005) and marijuana (Arria, Caldeira, O'Grady, Vincent, Johnson, et al., 2008; Catalano et al., 2011; DeSantis et al., 2009; McCabe, Boyd, & Young, 2007; McCabe, Knight, et al., 2005; Sung et al., 2005; Teter, McCabe, Boyd, & Guthrie, 2003). McCabe, Knight, et al. (2005) reported that students who use prescription stimulants nonmedically were more than 10 times more likely to have used cannabis during the past year than nonusers. Other studies have reported that nonmedical users are much more likely to meet *DSM-IV* criteria for alcohol or cannabis use disorder than nonusers (Huang et al., 2006; McCabe, Cranford, & West, 2008; Schepis & Krishnan-Sarin, 2008). Moreover, nonmedical stimulant users have experienced more negative primary and secondary consequences of alcohol or other drug-related use than either individuals who have a prescription for stimulants or nonusers (Teter et al., 2003).

Several studies have observed significant associations between nonmedical use of prescription drugs and an array of other high-risk behaviors, including binge drinking, partying on a weekly basis, having multiple sexual partners, and driving after drinking (McCabe, Knight, et al., 2005; Teter et al., 2003). Moreover, having friends that engage in delinquent behavior is significantly associated with nonmedical use of tranquilizers, opioids, and stimulants (Fleary et al., 2011). Taken together, these findings lend support to problem behavior theory (Donovan & Jessor, 1985), which posits that risk-taking behaviors tend to cluster together in individuals who have a general propensity for deviance.

Risk and Protective Factors for Nonmedical Use of Prescription Drugs

Availability and access play a major role in nonmedical prescription drug use, which has implications for prevention (see section on "Future Directions for Research and Policy"). In addition to availability, other individual-level risk factors have been identified for nonmedical prescription drug use. Because of the significant overlap with other forms of adolescent drug use, it is not surprising that they share many common risk and protective factors. No less important, but less studied, are social risk factors that might heighten the availability, desire, or acceptability of using prescription drugs nonmedically, such as peer use, having opportunities to share drugs because of close living arrangements (e.g., college residence halls), and the impact of social media use (Mackey, Stewart, Connolly, Tapert, & Paulus, 2013).

Sensation Seeking

Sensation seeking, or the tendency to seek out novel experiences, is a well-known risk factor for substance use in adolescence (Donohew, Helm, Lawrence, Shatzer, & Watson, 1990; Herman-Stahl et al., 2007; Palmgreen, Donohew, Lorch, & Rogus, 1991; Reyna & Farley, 2006; Zuckerman, Neary, & Brustman, 1970; Zuckerman, 1994). Sensation seeking appears to peak during adolescence, and high levels of sensation seeking can reduce a young person's ability to accurately judge risk (Romer & Hennessy, 2007). Moreover, sensation seeking increases the chance of affiliation with drug-using peers, thereby amplifying the desire to engage in risky behavior (Romer & Hennessy, 2007). A few studies have found that nonmedical users are more likely than nonusers to score high on measures of sensation seeking (Lookatch et al., 2012; Low & Gendaszek, 2002). Whether or not sensation-seeking influences the risk of prescription drug use

over and above use of other types of drugs remains to be seen.

Perceived Harmfulness

Believing that the use of a particular drug is not associated with a great deal of risk—sometimes referred to as low levels of perceived harmfulness—is an important risk factor for illicit drug use (Bachman, Johnston, & O'Malley, 1998). Only a few studies have examined perceived harm in relation to nonmedical use of prescription drugs (Arria, Caldeira, Vincent, et al., 2008; Quintero, 2009). In one study of college students, approximately one quarter rated occasional use of nonmedical prescription stimulants as having "great risk," similar to prescription analgesics (27.8%). In comparison, 72.2% rated cocaine as having "great risk," whereas only 7.2% rated occasional marijuana use as having "great risk" (Arria, Caldeira, Vincent, et al., 2008). Therefore, the degree of perceived risk of nonmedical prescription drug use appears to fall between marijuana and cocaine, which contradicts the notion that young people automatically assume prescription drugs are safer or have less addictive potential than illicit drugs simply because they are medically available (Friedman, 2006).

One study examined the interaction effects of perceived risk and sensation seeking (Arria, Caldeira, Vincent, et al., 2008). College students who had low or moderate levels of sensation seeking were particularly susceptible to the influence of high perceived harmfulness. On the other hand, perceptions of risk did not seem to influence nonmedical use among those high in sensation seeking. These findings suggest that imparting educational messages related to risk might not be a viable drug prevention strategy for adolescents who purposely seek out novel and risky experiences.

Perceptions of Widespread Use and Expectancies Related to Beneficial Effects

Other types of beliefs held by adolescents and young adults can influence their risk for use. As mentioned earlier, a majority of adolescents report knowing someone who used a prescription drug nonmedically. For example, 71.4% of a sample of college students reported nonmedical stimulant use among their peers, in contrast to the fact that only 9.2% used these drugs (Carroll et al., 2006). In another study, 60% of college students knew someone who used and 50% reported that the drugs would be easy to obtain (Weyandt et al., 2009). Overestimating the degree to which these drugs are being used is related to the likelihood of using (McCabe, 2008a). Other studies have shown that having positive expectancies related to the effects of the drug will increase risk of use (Lookatch et al., 2012). More research is needed to understand the degree to which correcting misperceptions, especially with regard to peer use and the purported neuro-enhancing effects of prescription stimulants (Farah, Haimm, Sankoorikal, & Chatterjee, 2009; Looby & Earleywine, 2011; Lucke, Bell, & Partridge, 2011; Volkow et al., 2008), can help reduce the risk of nonmedical use.

Consequences of Nonmedical Use of Prescription Drugs

As with other types of drug use, risk for addiction is a paramount concern with prescription drugs. Addiction potential is a function of the interplay between an individual's developmental stage, one's biological propensity for addiction, the frequency and quantity of drug consumed, and characteristics of the drug itself (Compton & Volkow, 2006). The degree to which a drug is reinforcing depends on pharmacokinetics (Miller, 2004; Swanson & Volkow, 2003) and can be influenced by the context in which the drug is used (Compton & Volkow, 2006). Finally, there is some evidence to suggest that co-ingestion of other substances, either simultaneously or concurrently, can affect the development of addiction (Compton & Volkow, 2006), but more research is warranted to fully understand the impact of these interactions.

Health problems associated with nonmedical use vary significantly by drug class, with nonmedical use of prescription opioids carrying the most serious risk for addiction, overdoses, and other complications. Another concern is that the route of administration might change in nonmedical users of prescription opioids (from oral use to sniffing and then injecting) as the need for larger doses to

sustain a high increases. There is also the risk of transitioning from nonmedical use of prescription opioid to sniffing or injecting heroin (Lankenau et al., 2012; Mars, Bourgois, Karandinos, Montero, & Ciccarone, 2014; Young & Havens, 2012).

The number of emergency department (ED) visits related to the misuse or abuse of prescription drugs increased 114% between 2004 and 2011. Data from the Drug Abuse Warning Network (DAWN) presented in Table 10.3 show that ED visits as a result of the misuse or abuse of prescription drugs among adolescents and young adults is highest for persons aged 21 to 24 years. Because of the lower prevalence of nonmedical use among adolescents aged 12 to 17 years, they are also less likely than 21- to 24-year-olds to visit the ED as a result of nonmedical use of both narcotic pain relievers and anti-anxiety and insomnia medications.

Deaths due to prescription drug overdoses have increased steadily over the past 20 years, with a rise in prescription opioid-related deaths being a major contributor to the increase (Paulozzi, 2012). Risk factors of prescription drug overdose deaths include being male, being White, having a lower socioeconomic status, and being from a rural area. The majority of prescription drug overdose deaths are unintentional, particularly among younger age groups. Rates of prescription drug overdose deaths are higher among people who have conditions for which the medication may be prescribed. For example, a history of chronic pain is common among people who die from an overdose of prescription opioids.

Table 10.4 shows prescription opioid overdose deaths by age (Paulozzi, Jones, Mack, & Rudd, 2011). The majority of deaths occur among older individuals, with the highest rate of drug overdose deaths occurring among 45- to 54-year olds. For 15- to 24-year-olds, the rate of overdose deaths due to prescription drugs is double the rate of deaths

Table 10.3 Rates of Emergency Department Visits per 100,000 Population, 2011

	12- to 17-Year-Olds	18- to 20-Year-Olds	21- to 24-Year-Olds
Narcotic pain relievers*	38.4	157.2	306.2
Anti-anxiety and insomnia medications*	73.3	179.7	318.5

* The difference between 12- to 17-year-old and 21- to 24-year-old patients was statistically significant ($p < .05$).

Source: Drug Abuse Warning Network. (2013). Highlights of the 2011 Drug Abuse Warning Network (DAWN) findings on drug-related emergency department visits. The DAWN Report (pp. 1–5). Rockville, MD: Substance Abuse and Mental Health Services Administration, Center for Behavioral Health Statistics and Quality.

Table 10.4 Age-Adjusted Rates of Drug Overdose Deaths by Age Group, per 100,000 Population, 2008

Age Group (years)	All Drugs	Prescription Drugs	Pain Relievers	Illicit Drugs
0 to 14	0.2	0.2	0.1	—*
15 to 24	8.2	4.5	3.7	2.2
25 to 34	16.5	8.8	7.1	4.4
35 to 44	20.9	11.0	8.3	5.3
45 to 54	25.3	13.8	10.4	6.0
55 to 64	13.0	7.3	5.0	2.5
65 or older	4.1	3.0	1.0	0.3

Note. Rate per 100,000 population was age-adjusted to the 2000 US standard population using the vintage 2008 population. Because deaths might involve both prescription and illicit drugs, some deaths are included in both categories.

* Rate is not presented when the estimate is unstable because the number of deaths is less than 20.

Source: Paulozzi et al. (2011).

due to illicit drugs. For all age groups, the rate of overdose deaths due to prescription pain relievers is higher than the rate of deaths due to illicit drugs.

Nonmedical use of prescription stimulants is associated with a number of adverse health complications, albeit less serious compared to opioids, including cardiovascular failure, jitteriness, hyperthermia, seizures, and anxiety (Drug Abuse Warning Network, 2006; Morgan, Frost-Pineda, & Gold, 2006; National Institute on Drug Abuse, 2013).

Our current understanding of the acute and long-term physiological effects of nonmedical prescription drug use is incomplete. More research is needed to understand adverse drug reactions based on individual vulnerability and pre-existing conditions, as well as co-ingestion with alcohol and other drugs (Garnier et al., 2009; Saxe, 1986; Weathermon & Crabb, 1999). Moreover, future research should be aimed at understanding the ways in which adolescent and young adult substance use can compromise long-term health and well-being.

Nonmedical Use of Prescription Stimulants and Academic Performance in College

One of the most commonly reported motives for using prescription stimulants nonmedically is to potentially improve academic performance (Clegg-Kraynok, McBean, & Montgomery-Downs, 2011; DeSantis et al., 2009; DeSantis, Noar, & Webb, 2010; DeSantis et al., 2008; Garnier-Dykstra et al., 2012; Low & Gendaszek, 2002; Rabiner et al., 2009; Teter et al., 2005, 2006; White et al., 2006).

The use of stimulants appears to be motivated by a desire or need to stay awake longer to study for tests or to complete assignments, and to improve one's attentional capacity while performing such tasks. The existence of these purported motives has led to perhaps a misguided conclusion that the motives reflect the true effects of the drug—that nonmedical users are able to increase their concentration and achieve superior grades in school. In the media, stimulants used nonmedically have been labeled "brain steroids" or "smart drugs" (Carey, 2008; Talbot, 2009). Examining the research tells quite a different story. Cross-sectional studies have not supported the notion that nonmedical users of prescription stimulants achieve better grades. In fact, compared to their nonusing counterparts, users tend to have lower grade point averages (GPAs) (Clegg-Kraynok et al., 2011; McCabe et al., 2006a; McCabe, Knight, et al., 2005). Other studies have shown that nonmedical prescription stimulant use is associated with other behaviors that are likely to compromise academic performance, such as spending less time studying and skipping more classes (Arria, O'Grady, et al., 2008). And while students might initially believe that stimulants might help them achieve better grades, only 14% of users in one study said that using prescription stimulants did help them in the long run (Hall et al., 2005).

A recent prospective study has shed light on the processes that might underlie nonmedical prescription stimulant use to improve grades among college students (Arria et al., 2013). Students enrolled in the College Life Study (Arria, Caldeira, O'Grady,

Vincent, Fitzelle, et al., 2008; Vincent et al., 2012) were assessed annually during their time in college and asked questions about their use of alcohol and other drugs, and skipping classes. Administrative data was used to collect their GPAs. Employing latent variable growth curve modeling (Duncan, Duncan, & Strycker, 2006), and adjusting for several potentially confounding variables, the study results found significant relationships between cannabis and alcohol use disorder, skipping class, and GPA. Namely, cannabis use disorder predicted increases in skipping class, which in turn predicted decreases in GPA. Nonmedical prescription stimulant use for studying occurred in association with these cannabis-related declines in academic performance. Similar results were found for alcohol use disorder. In short, the research confirmed that academically struggling students with a history of other drug involvement are likely to use prescription stimulants as way to compensate for declining grades. Rather than suggesting that nonmedical users are high performers trying to gain an even greater academic edge, this research suggests that nonmedical use of prescription stimulants is a "red flag" for academic problems related to alcohol consumption and other drug use during college. Whether similar relationships exist among younger adolescents is a potential area for further research inquiry.

Nonmedical Prescription Stimulant Use and Attention-Deficit/Hyperactivity Disorder

Attention-deficit/hyperactivity disorder (ADHD) typically presents in childhood and is characterized by inattention, behavioral problems, and functional impairment commonly manifested as difficulties with schoolwork, and an inability to focus in the classroom and at home (Realmuto et al., 2009). Left untreated, ADHD, depending on severity, can lead to increased risk in a wide array of psychosocial problems and substance use (Klein et al., 2012; Wilens, Faraone, Biederman, & Gunawardene, 2003). On the other hand, the research evidence supports that initiation of medically supervised pharmacologic treatment for ADHD reduces the risk of later substance use problems (Biederman, Wilens, Mick, Spencer, & Faraone, 1999; McCabe et al., 2006a). Medications used to manage ADHD can be diverted from patients with prescriptions to other individuals for nonmedical use (see "Diversion of Prescription Drugs").

Researchers have speculated that untreated ADHD may be a possible risk factor underlying nonmedical use of prescription stimulants. One motive for using these drugs among college students is to improve attention and reduce hyperactivity (White et al., 2006). Rabiner and colleagues (2009) observed that nonmedical users of prescription stimulants scored higher on measures of inattention and hyperactivity-impulsivity than nonusers. Furthermore, they found that attention problems were associated with starting to use nonmedical prescription stimulants, but not other types of prescription drugs. Answering the question of whether or not nonmedical users are engaged in some form of "self-treatment" for ADHD is challenging for several reasons. First, nonmedical use often presents in late adolescence or early adulthood, and therefore determining a diagnosis of ADHD would require adequate recall of childhood behaviors and difficulties. Moreover, because nonmedical users often are current users of alcohol and other drugs, it can be clinically difficult to ascertain whether attention or concentration difficulties presaged or are the result of other substance use. In these cases, clinicians suggest that a diagnosis of ADHD can only be made following documented and prolonged abstinence from substance use.

In an attempt to answer this question by partially controlling for the potentially confounding influence of other drug use on attention problems, Arria, Garnier-Dykstra, Caldeira, Vincent, O'Grady, et al. (2011) compared three groups of individuals on a standardized assessment of ADHD: (1) nonmedical users of prescription stimulants; (2) marijuana users who had not used prescription stimulants nonmedically; and (3) nonusers of both prescription stimulants and marijuana. Nonmedical users reported significantly more problems with inattention than either comparison group, suggesting that untreated ADHD might be a risk factor for nonmedical use. The researchers cautioned against overinterpretation of the findings due to the small sample size and the lack of a comprehensive clinical diagnostic assessment of ADHD symptoms.

Nonmedical Use of Prescription Drugs and Mental Health Problems

Substance use and mental health problems often coexist (Kessler, Nelson, McGonagle, & Liu, 1996; Swendsen et al., 1998), and the nature of the relationship is complex. In some cases, mental health problems can precede the onset of substance use, and in others, alcohol or other drug use can be the precipitating factor. There appears to be a significant association between psychiatric symptoms and disorders with nonmedical use of prescription drugs among adults (Huang et al., 2006), and a few research studies have observed this relationship among adolescents (Schepis & McCabe, 2012; Subramaniam & Stitzer, 2009) and young adults (Herman-Stahl et al., 2007). Significant associations between lifetime major depression and nonmedical prescription drug use (irrespective of drug class) have been observed in a general population sample of adolescents (Schepis & McCabe, 2012). In that study, major depression was more common among nonmedical users who experienced disorder symptoms than users who did not experience symptoms. Others have identified significant relationships between nonmedical sedative/anxiolytic users and psychiatric symptoms of somatization, depression, anxiety, and phobic anxiety (Hall, Howard, & McCabe, 2010).

Anecdotal clinical evidence suggests that nonmedical prescription stimulant users often report "crashing" after discontinuing stimulant use, prompting an investigation into the possibility that stimulant use precipitates depressed mood and/or major depressive episodes. Teter et al. (2010) observed that depressed mood was associated with not only more frequent use of nonmedical prescription stimulants but also non-oral administration. Roughly half (51.4%) of individuals who used prescription stimulants three or more times reported experiencing depressed mood, compared to 25.8% of undergraduates who were nonusers. Aside from a biological explanation, depressed mood could also result from a failure to achieve personal academic goals, leading to the nonmedical use of prescription stimulants in an attempt to improve academic performance. Some support for this hypothesis was found by Ford and Schroeder (2009).

Other studies have suggested that stimulants are used nonmedically to cope with symptoms of depression or anxiety, especially in females (Lord et al., 2011). Novak et al. (2009) found that mood disorders and antisocial personality disorders were more likely to be associated with clinically problematic nonmedical use of prescription drugs, whereas anxiety disorders were linked to less severe involvement with prescription drugs. Longer term prospective studies are needed to disentangle the temporal relationship between depressed mood and nonmedical prescription stimulant use.

With regard to prescription opioids, Dowling et al. (2006) observed that respondents reporting mental and/or emotional problems were more than twice as likely as individuals without those problems to be recent-onset users. Significant associations were also observed between nervousness, hyperactivity, hopelessness, depression, and panic attacks and nonmedical use of prescription opioids. The authors speculated that somatic pain might be an indicator of more severe mental health problems. Others have linked nonmedical use of prescription opioids with an increase in the risk for suicide attempts (Kuramoto, Chilcoat, Ko, & Martins, 2012).

The available evidence suggests that nonmedical drug users should be screened for mental health problems to identify the temporal sequencing of symptoms. Moreover, a comprehensive assessment of substance use, including nonmedical use of prescription drugs, is warranted when working with youth and young adults who present in clinical settings with mental health problems.

Diversion Behavior

Unlike other forms of substance use, nonmedical prescription drug use involves the transfer of medications from a legitimate source to a person who does not have a prescription. More research is needed to understand diversion behavior (Kaye & Darke, 2012), but descriptive studies of adolescents and young adults have been useful in understanding the extent to which prescriptions are shared, sold, or traded. Most often, these drugs are diverted at little or no cost to the recipient (Garnier-Dykstra et al., 2012; White et al., 2006). One study reported that 14.7% of high school students with a prescription for stimulant medication gave their medication away for free and 7.3% sold it (Poulin, 2001).

Boyd et al. (2007) documented the prevalence of medical use of prescription drugs among a sample of high school students. One third was prescribed some type of psychoactive drug during the past 12 months (53% for analgesics, 9% for sleep medications, 3% for stimulants to treat ADHD, and 3% for anxiolytics or sedatives). They then described how often these drugs were traded or given away. Nearly one quarter of students with a legal prescription had given away or loaned a prescription medication. This was most prevalent for pain medications, and the most common recipients of prescription medications were female friends, followed by parents and male friends. Trading and selling prescription medication was much less prevalent.

In college, stimulant drugs appear to be the most commonly diverted medications, most likely because of their perceived benefit related to improving academic performance. In one study of college students, about one fourth (26%) who had been prescribed an analgesic medication in the past year had been *approached* to sell, trade, or give away their medication, in contrast to over half of individuals with a prescription for stimulant medication (54%) (McCabe et al., 2006b). In another study measuring diversion behavior among college students, 61.7% with a prescription for stimulants, 35.1% of students with a prescription for analgesics, and 13.8% with a prescription for other psychotropic medications diverted their medication (Garnier et al., 2010). Diversion was fairly infrequent among this sample, with many college students only sharing once or twice in their lifetime.

Research studies have identified factors that are associated with the likelihood to divert medications. Among college students, these risk factors include living off-campus, being a heavy drinker or drug user, and having a childhood history of conduct problems (Garnier et al., 2010).

Future Directions for Research and Policy

Additional research aimed at elucidating the etiology of substance use in general will inform our understanding of nonmedical prescription drug use because it has several features in common with other forms of substance use. Although much has been learned about the extent and nature of nonmedical prescription drug use, the research designs employed have been largely descriptive, and thus, our ability to draw conclusions about the processes underlying the onset of prescription drug use and escalation of problems resulting from use is limited. Employing more sophisticated research methods that allow for more frequent assessments of behavior and the contexts under which prescription drugs are used might advance our understanding of how nonmedical use is related to alcohol consumption and other illicit drug use behaviors.

To date, our understanding of individual biological vulnerability to addiction on prescription medications is incomplete. New research on genetically driven responses to prescription drugs (Foltin & Fischman, 1991; Lott, Soo-Jeong, Cook Jr, & de Wit, 2005; Stein et al., 2005) and gene–environment interactions that explain problematic substance use and addiction risk (Brody et al., 2009; Dick & Kendler, 2012) will undoubtedly shed light on the reasons why some individuals have persistent patterns of use while others cease soon after initiating. Such research efforts can be the foundation for designing new universal prevention strategies, identifying youth at particularly high risk for substance use, and intervening in the earliest stages of involvement (Greydanus, 2006; Sussman, 2013).

Research should also be directed at understanding how to engage more adolescents with prescription drug problems into intervention services given that few access treatment (Wu, Blazer, Li, & Woody, 2011). Moreover, comprehensive intervention and treatment approaches for adolescents and young adults who are facing the multiple challenges associated with polydrug use should be refined and tailored for adolescents with prescription drug problems (Hser, 2001; Winters, Botzet, & Fahnhorst, 2011). Research studies on the effectiveness of new interventions to reduce substance use problems in general, and nonmedical prescription drug use in particular—especially when frequent and severe—are needed.

More research is needed to clarify the extent to which mental health issues precede or are the consequence of nonmedical prescription drug use. This kind of research can help us better understand the natural history and course of substance use, and it will lead ultimately to improved intervention strategies. Regardless of the temporal association, it is prudent for clinicians to recognize that a comprehensive evaluation of mental health problems in patients presenting with substance use problems is warranted and vice versa.

Strategies to reduce nonmedical prescription drug use will require concerted efforts to reduce both demand and supply. Several research-informed prevention strategies should be evaluated for their impact on reducing demand. First, correcting misperceptions about the widespread nature of prescription drug abuse is a viable option. Adolescents significantly overestimate the proportion of their peers who are taking prescription drugs nonmedically, and adjusting these beliefs might cast the behavior as a more socially deviant behavior, and thus less desirable (McCabe, 2008b).

Second, parents can influence risk for adolescent substance use in multiple ways. Prevention efforts targeted at improving parenting practices, such as increasing the degree of parental monitoring of child behaviors and supervising activities, hold promise for reducing alcohol and other drug use (Chen, Storr, & Anthony, 2005) and, in turn, might have a protective effect against initiation of nonmedical prescription drug use. Parental disapproval of alcohol use has also been linked to reduced risk of adolescent substance use and related problems (Nash, McQueen, & Bray, 2005; Ryan, Jorm, & Lubman, 2010). Creating and disseminating tools to help parents impart these messages, improve parent–child communication, and reduce family conflict could be useful ways to empower parents.

Specific to nonmedical use of prescription stimulants, parents can help by dispelling the myth that this behavior is an acceptable way of improving academic performance in both secondary school and later in college. Moreover, parents can potentially reduce their child's risk of nonmedical use by not condoning it and certainly not facilitating access to prescription drugs that are not clinically indicated. Given the high degree of overlap between prescription drugs and use of other illicit drugs (Barrett et al., 2005; Herman-Stahl, Krebs, Kroutil, & Heller, 2006; McCabe, Knight, et al., 2005; Teter et al., 2003), parents should regard discovery of nonmedical use of prescription drugs as a warning sign for more serious illicit drug involvement.

On the other hand, when prevention efforts are unsuccessful and children start to use, parents can and should facilitate early intervention to address a nonmedical prescription drug problem. Early signs of adolescent drug use might include precipitous drops in academic performance; shifts in peer networks; gradual or sudden changes in mood, behavior, and sleeping patterns; and increasing disinterest in activities that were once normally enjoyed. Parents should consider comprehensive assessments of possible ADHD and other mental health problems and initiate proper interventions if indicated. Monitoring of alcohol and other substance use should be part of a comprehensive ongoing intervention. Easy-to-use tools and resources for parents that can help them recognize and respond to signs of emerging mental health and drug problems are needed and should be evaluated.

As mentioned earlier, the advent of the latest prescription drug use epidemic coincides with the increases in availability of prescription drugs to treat pain and other conditions, including ADHD. Therefore, supply reduction should be an integral part of any prevention strategy to reduce nonmedical use of prescription drugs. The critical challenge is to reduce availability of these drugs for nonmedical use, while at the same time ensuring access for individuals who need them for medical purposes. Systems to monitor access to and utilization of medications among clinical populations can detect these potentially adverse downstream effects of any supply reduction strategy.

The pharmaceutical industry has an important role to play in reducing nonmedical use by developing and testing abuse-resistant formulations of prescription medications and helping to educate health care professionals about proper prescribing practices and the risks of diversion. Educating physicians on an ongoing basis about proper dosing of pain medications (Arria, Garnier-Dykstra, Caldeira, Vincent, & O'Grady, 2011; McLellan & Turner, 2010) and proper clinical management of ADHD (Kollins, 2008; Wilens, Spencer, Biederman, & Brown, 2000), anxiety and other mental health conditions, and sleep problems are other sensible supply reduction strategies. Moreover, physicians and other health professionals should be vigilant regarding the risk for addiction to prescription opioids in particular (Compton & Volkow, 2006) and the possibility of diversion (Garnier et al., 2010). They should also discuss the risks of combining medications with alcohol, and they should be encouraged to have these sorts of conversations with patients (and perhaps parents of adolescent patients) to reduce the chances of sharing, selling, and trading prescribed medications (Lessenger & Feinberg, 2008). Such strategies need to be evaluated and redesigned based on evaluations to achieve the best balance between time burden and effectiveness. New evidence from a systematic review (Minozzi, Amato, & Davoli, 2012) that proper medically supervised treatment of chronic pain conditions does not necessarily carry increases in risk for addiction is encouraging.

Psychiatrists who manage ADHD in adolescent and young adult populations should be especially aware of research showing that nonmedical use and diversion is more likely among young people prescribed short-acting stimulant medications than controlled-release formulations (Bright, 2008; Greenhill et al., 2002; Sepúlveda et al., 2011; Wilens, Gignac, Swezey, Monutaux, & Biederman, 2006) and individuals with a history of conduct problems (Garnier et al., 2008; Wilens et al., 2008). More research is needed to identify additional risk factors for diversion among adolescents. Physicians should impart messages about the legal and medical consequences of diverting a prescription to counteract beliefs by young people that they are being helpful to a friend by sharing their medication.

In addition to the role they play in prevention and intervention, parents of adolescents also have a role to play in reducing supply of prescription medication for nonmedical use in at least two ways. First, they can encourage their adolescent child who has been prescribed a medication about the importance of proper medication adherence. Not only does medication adherence help reduce the chances of diversion, but it also improves the chances that the medication will have intended therapeutic benefits. Second, parents can role-model the proper use of prescription medications by only using medications that are prescribed to them and not sharing prescription medications with family members. They can also model the proper disposal of leftover prescription medications.

In addition to messages imparted by parents and physicians, other innovative methods for encouraging medication adherence and discouraging diversion among adolescents and young adults are needed. Young people should encourage their peers to seek professional help rather than sharing or trading medications. Prevention strategies that go beyond simply conveying messages about risks of diversion and nonmedical use are needed, because it is well known that adolescents and young adults are not likely to change their behavior simply because they are told it is risky.

Prescription drug monitoring programs (PDMPs) are an important policy option to be considered to reduce the likelihood of "doctor shopping." The implementation of state-level PDMPs in the United States has been associated with decreases in the supply of available prescription opioids and stimulants, admissions to addiction treatment programs for prescription opioid abuse, and claims to pharmaceutical insurance companies for prescription opioids (Curtis et al., 2006; Simeone & Holland, 2006). Another study found that emergency department physicians altered their plans for prescribing opioids in nearly half of cases after reviewing a patient's data in a state-level PDMP. In cases where the clinical plans were changed, physicians most frequently chose to prescribe less opioid medication than previously planned (Baehren et al., 2010). However, Paulozzi and colleagues (Paulozzi, Kilbourne, & Desai, 2011) found that PDMPs did not decrease the prescription drug overdose death rate and had no effect on the consumption of prescription opioids. These authors cautioned that because PDMPs only monitor Schedule II drugs (i.e., drugs with accepted medical uses but a high potential for abuse, such as codeine and oxycodone), nonmedical users might instead seek lower schedule drugs to avoid being caught. They also suggested that PDMPs should use the collected data more effectively to further evaluate the impact of the programs. There has been little research on PDMPs at the national level, and ongoing evaluations of PDMPs are required to assess their effectiveness in reducing nonmedical use.

Given that college students appear to be at heightened risk for nonmedical use of prescription stimulants, higher educational professionals should be involved in dialogues to prevent and discourage this behavior. Campuses should develop specific action plans to reduce nonmedical prescription stimulant use that could include increasing the awareness and enforcement of specific sanctions against sharing, selling, or trading prescription medications. Academic advisors should be educated regarding the possibility of nonmedical use of prescription stimulants to improve academic performance. In these settings, students should be encouraged to reconsider heavy workloads early in their college career and, instead, build up mastery of study skills and time management techniques required to be academically successful. Research indicates that even infrequent nonmedical prescription stimulant use is associated with underlying alcohol and other drug involvement, skipping class, and decreased GPA (Arria, Caldeira, O'Grady, Vincent, Johnson, et al., 2008; Arria, O'Grady, et al., 2008; Catalano et al., 2011; Clegg-Kraynok et al., 2011; McCabe et al., 2006a; McCabe, Knight, et al., 2005; Sung et al., 2005; Teter et al., 2003). Therefore, students who are academically struggling and who are either mandated or self-referred to campus academic assistance centers might benefit from a comprehensive evaluation of the reasons underlying their academic difficulties. Such an evaluation could include a confidential assessment of substance use patterns and mental health. Counseling focused on helping students self-reflect on how untreated mental health disorders and substance use might be impacting their academic performance and interfere in the long term with achievement of academic and career goals might also be beneficial.

Finally, it is important to continue monitoring nonmedical drug use trends through standardized epidemiologic surveillance systems to monitor the impact of new prevention strategies as well as to detect emerging patterns of use. For example, if nonmedical drug use becomes even more normalized than it is currently, increases might be expected in the proportion of "substance-naïve" initiates—namely, young people for whom their first substance use experience involves nonmedical prescription drug use rather than alcohol or other drugs. Surveillance systems should inquire about possible new patterns of drug use, including the use of the most current formulations of medications to treat pain, ADHD, anxiety, and sleep problems, as well as gather information about combining prescription drugs with alcohol and other drugs.

References

American Psychiatric Association. (2000). *Diagnostic and statistical manual of mental disorders* (4th ed.). Arlington, VA: Author.

Arria, A. M., Caldeira, K. M., Vincent, K. B., O'Grady, K. E., & Wish, E. D. (2007). *Nonmedical prescription stimulant use: Results of a longitudinal study of college students*. Paper presented at the American Academy of Child and Adolescent Psychiatry. Boston, MA: October 23-28.

Arria, A. M., Caldeira, K. M., O'Grady, K. E., Vincent, K. B., Fitzelle, D. B., Johnson, E. P., & Wish, E. D. (2008). Drug exposure opportunities and use patterns among college students: Results of a longitudinal prospective cohort study. *Substance Abuse*, 29(4), 19–38. doi:10.1080/08897070802418451

Arria, A. M., Caldeira, K. M., O'Grady, K. E., Vincent, K. B., Johnson, E. P., & Wish, E. D. (2008). Nonmedical use of prescription stimulants among college students: Associations with attention-deficit-hyperactivity disorder and poly-drug use. *Pharmacotherapy*, 28(2), 156–169. doi:10.1592/phco.28.2.156

Arria, A. M., Caldeira, K. M., Vincent, K. B., O'Grady, K. E., & Wish, E. D. (2008). Perceived harmfulness predicts nonmedical use of prescription drugs among college students: Interactions with sensation-seeking. *Prevention Science*, 9(3), 191–201. doi:10.1007/s11121-008-0095-8

Arria, A. M., Garnier-Dykstra, L. M., Caldeira, K. M., Vincent, K. B., O'Grady, K. E., & Wish, E. D. (2011). Persistent nonmedical use of prescription stimulants among college students: Possible association with attention deficit hyperactivity disorder symptoms. *Journal of Attention Disorders*, 15(5), 347–356. doi:10.1177/1087054710367621

Arria, A. M., Garnier-Dykstra, L. M., Caldeira, K. M., Vincent, K. B., & O'Grady, K. E. (2011). Prescription analgesic use among young adults: Adherence to physician instructions and diversion. *Pain Medicine*, 12(6), 898–903. doi:10.1111/j.1526-4637.2011.01107.x.

Arria, A. M., O'Grady, K. E., Caldeira, K. M., Vincent, K. B., & Wish, E. D. (2008). Nonmedical use of prescription stimulants and analgesics: Associations with social and academic behaviors among college students. *Journal of Drug Issues*, 38(4), 1045–1060. doi:10.1177/002204260803800406

Arria, A. M., Wilcox, H. C., Caldeira, K. M., Vincent, K. B., Garnier-Dykstra, L. M., & O'Grady, K. E. (2013). Dispelling the myth of "smart drugs": Cannabis and alcohol use problems predict nonmedical use of prescription stimulants for studying. *Addictive Behaviors*, 38(3), 1643–1650. doi:10.1016/j.addbeh.2012.10.002

Babcock, Q., & Byrne, T. (2000). Student perceptions of methylphenidate abuse at a public liberal arts college. *Journal of American College Health*, 49(3), 143–145. doi:10.1080/07448480009596296

Bachman, J. G., Johnston, L. D., & O'Malley, P. M. (1998). Explaining recent increases in students marijuana use: Impacts of perceived risks and disapproval 1976–1996.

American Journal of Public Health, 88, 887–892. doi:10.2105/AJPH.88.6.887

Baehren, D. F., Marco, C. A., Droz, D. E., Sinha, S., Callan, E. M., & Akpunonu, P. (2010). A statewide prescription monitoring program affects emergency department prescribing behaviors. *Annals of Emergency Medicine*, 56(1), 19–23. doi:10.1016/j.annemergmed.2009.12.011

Barrett, S. P., Darredeau, C., Bordy, L. E., & Pihl, R. O. (2005). Characteristics of methylphenidate misuse in a university student sample. *Canadian Journal of Psychiatry*, 50(8), 457–461.

Barrett, S. P., Meisner, J. R., & Stewart, S. H. (2008). What constitutes prescription drug misuse? Problems and pitfalls of current conceptualizations. *Current Drug Abuse Reviews*, 1(3), 255–262. doi:10.2174/1874473710801030255

Berdahl, T. A., Friedman, B. S., McCormick, M. C., & Simpson, L. (2013). Annual report on health care for children and youth in the United States: Trends in racial/ethnic, income, and insurance disparities over time, 2002–2009. *Academic Pediatrics*, 13(3), 191–203. doi:10.1016/j.acap.2013.02.003

Biederman, J., Wilens, T., Mick, E., Spencer, T., & Faraone, S. V. (1999). Pharmacotherapy of attention-deficit/hyperactivity disorder reduces risk for substance use disorder. *Pediatrics*, 104(2), e20–e20. doi:10.1542/peds.104.2.e20

Bloom, B., & Cohen, R. A. (2007). *Summary health statistics for U.S. children: National Health Interview Survey, 2006. Vital and Health Statistics*. Hyattsville, MD: National Center for Health Statistics.

Boyd, C., Teter, C., West, B., Morales, M., & McCabe, S. E. (2009). Non-medical use of prescription analgesics: A three-year national longitudinal study. *Journal of Addictive Diseases*, 28(3), 232–242. doi:10.1080/10550880903028452

Boyd, C. J., McCabe, S. E., Cranford, J. A., & Young, A. (2007). Prescription drug abuse and diversion among adolescents in a Southeast Michigan school district. *Archives of Pediatrics and Adolescent Medicine*, 161(3), 276–281. doi:10.1001/archpedi.161.3.276

Bright, G. M. (2008). Abuse of medications employed for the treatment of ADHD: Results from a large-scale community survey. *Medscape Journal of Medicine*, 10(5), 111–111.

Brody, G. H., Beach, S. R. H., Philibert, R. A., Chen, Y-F., Lei, M-K., Murry, V. M., & Brown, A. C. (2009). Parenting moderates a genetic vulnerability factor in longitudinal increases in youths' substance use. *Journal of Consulting and Clinical Psychology*, 77(1), 1–11. doi:10.1037/a0012996

Carey, B. (2008, March 9). Brain enhancement is wrong, right? *New York Times*, p. 1.

Carroll, B. C., McLaughlin, T. J., & Blake, D. R. (2006). Patterns and knowledge of nonmedical use of stimulants among college students. *Archives of Pediatrics and Adolescent Medicine*, 160(5), 481–485. doi:10.1001/archpedi.160.5.481

Catalano, R. F., White, H. R., Fleming, C. B., & Haggerty, K. P. (2011). Is nonmedical prescription opiate use a unique form of illicit drug use? *Addictive Behaviors*, 36(1–2), 79–86. doi:10.1016/j.addbeh.2010.08.028

Chen, C., Storr, C. L., & Anthony, J. C. (2005). Influences of parenting practices on the risk of having a chance to try cannabis. *Pediatrics*, 115(6), 1631–1639. doi:10.1542/peds.2004-1926

Clegg-Kraynok, M. M., McBean, A. L., & Montgomery-Downs, H. E. (2011). Sleep quality and characteristics of college students who use prescription psychostimulants nonmedically. *Sleep Medicine*, *12*(6), 598–602. doi:10.1016/j.sleep.2011.01.012

Collins, D., Abadi, M. H., Johnson, K., Shamblen, S., & Thompson, K. (2011). Non-medical use of prescription drugs among youth in an Appalachian population: Prevalence, predictors, and implications for prevention. *Journal of Drug Education*, *41*(3), 309–326. doi:10.2190/DE.41.3.e

Compton, W. M., & Volkow, N. D. (2006). Abuse of prescription drugs and the risk of addiction. *Drug and Alcohol Dependence*, *83*, S4–S7. doi:10.1016/j.drugalcdep.2005.10.020

Cotto, J. H., Davis, E., Dowling, G. J., Elcano, J. C., Staton, A. B., & Weiss, S. R. B. (2010). Gender effects on drug use, abuse, and dependence: A special analysis of results from the National Survey on Drug Use and Health. *Gender Medicine*, *7*(5), 402–413. doi:10.1016/j.genm.2010.09.004

Curtis, L. H., Stoddard, J., Radeva, J. I., Hutchison, S., Dans, P. E., Wright, A., . . . Schulman, K. A. (2006). Geographic variation in the prescription of Schedule II opioid analgesics among outpatients in the United States. *Health Services Research*, *41*(3 Pt 1), 837–855. doi:10.1111/j.1475-6773.2006.00511.x

DeSantis, A., Noar, S. M., & Webb, E. (2009). Nonmedical ADHD stimulant use in fraternities. *Journal of Studies on Alcohol and Drugs*, *70*(6), 952–954.

DeSantis, A., Noar, S. M., & Webb, E. M. (2010). Speeding through the frat house: A qualitative exploration of non-medical ADHD stimulant use in fraternities. *Journal of Drug Education*, *40*(2), 157–171. doi:10.2190/DE.40.2.d

DeSantis, A. D., Webb, E. M., & Noar, S. M. (2008). Illicit use of prescription ADHD medications on a college campus: A multimethological approach. *Journal of American College Health*, *57*(3), 315–323. doi:10.3200/JACH.57.3.315-324

Dick, D. M., & Kendler, K. S. (2012). The impact of gene-environment interaction on alcohol use disorders. *Alcohol Research: Current Reviews*, *34*(3), 318–324.

Donohew, L., Helm, D. M., Lawrence, P., & Shatzer, M. J. (1990). Sensation seeking, marijuana use, and responses to prevention messages: Implications for public health campaigns. In R. R. Watson (Ed.), *Drug and Alcohol Abuse Prevention* (First ed., pp. 73–93). Totowa, NJ: Humana Press.

Donovan, J. E., & Jessor, R. (1985). Structure of problem behavior in adolescence and young adulthood. *Journal of Consulting and Clinical Psychology*, *53*(6), 890–904. doi:10.1037/0022-006X.53.6.890

Dowling, K., Storr, C. L., & Chilcoat, H. D. (2006). Potential influences on initiation and persistence of extramedical prescription pain reliever use in the US population. *Clinical Journal of Pain*, *22*(9), 776–783. doi:10.1097/01.ajp.0000210926.41406.2c

Drug Abuse Warning Network. (2006). *Emergency department visits involving ADHD stimulant medications*. The DAWN Report. Rockville, MD: Office of Applied Studies (OAS) Substance Abuse and Mental Health Services Administration (SAMHSA).

Duncan, T. E., Duncan, S. C., & Strycker, L. A. (2006). *An introduction to latent variable growth curve modeling: Concepts, issues, and applications (2nd ed.)*. Mahwah, NJ: Erlbaum.

DuPont, R. L., Coleman, J. J., Bucher, R. H., & Wilford, B. B. (2008). Characteristics and motives of college students who engage in nonmedical use of methylphenidate. *American Journal on Addictions*, *17*(3), 167–171. doi:10.1080/10550490802019642

Farah, M. J., Haimm, C., Sankoorikal, G., & Chatterjee, A. (2009). When we enhance cognition with Adderall, do we sacrifice creativity? A preliminary study. *Psychopharmacology*, *202*(1–3), 541–547. doi:10.1007/s00213-008-1369-3

Fleary, S. A., Heffer, R. W., & McKyer, E. L. J. (2011). Dispositional, ecological and biological influences on adolescent tranquilizer, Ritalin, and narcotics misuse. *Journal of Adolescence*, *34*(4), 653–663. doi:10.1016/j.adolescence.2010.09.007

Foltin, R. W., & Fischman, M. W. (1991). Assessment of abuse liability of stimulant drugs in humans: A methodological survey. *Drug and Alcohol Dependence*, *28*(1), 3–48. doi:10.1016/0376-8716(91)90052-Z

Ford, J. A., & Arrastia, M. C. (2008). Pill-poppers and dopers: A comparison of non-medical prescription drug use and illicit/street drug use among college students. *Addictive Behaviors*, *33*(7), 934–941. doi:10.1016/j.addbeh.2008.02.016

Ford, J. A., & Schroeder, R. D. (2009). Academic strain and non-medical use of prescription stimulants among college students. *Deviant Behavior*, *30*(1), 26–53. doi:10.1080/01639620802049900

Forman, R. F., Woody, G. E., McLellan, T., & Lynch, K. G. (2006). The availability of web sites offering to sell opioid medications without prescriptions. *American Journal of Psychiatry*, *163*(7), 1233–1238. doi:10.1176/appi.ajp.163.7.1233

Fortuna, R. J., Robbins, B. W., Caiola, E., Joynt, M., & Halterman, J. S. (2010). Prescribing of controlled medications to adolescents and young adults in the United States. *Pediatrics*, *126*(6), 1108–1116. doi:10.1542/peds.2010-0791

Friedman, R. A. (2006). The changing face of teenage drug abuse—The trend toward prescription drugs. *New England Journal of Medicine*, *354*(14), 1448–1450. doi:10.1056/NEJMp068010

Garnier-Dykstra, L. M., Caldeira, K. M., Vincent, K. B., O'Grady, K. E., & Arria, A. M. (2012). Nonmedical use of prescription stimulants during college: Four-year trends in exposure opportunity, use, motives, and sources. *Journal of American College Health*, *60*(3), 226–234. doi:10.1080/07448481.2011.589876

Garnier, L. M., Arria, A. M., Caldeira, K. M., Vincent, K. B., O'Grady, K. E., & Wish, E. D. (2008). Diversion of medically prescribed stimulants and analgesics by college students. Paper presented at the College on Problems of Drug Dependence. San Juan, Puerto Rico: June 14-19.

Garnier, L. M., Arria, A. M., Caldeira, K. M., Vincent, K. B., O'Grady, K. E., & Wish, E. D. (2009). Nonmedical prescription analgesic use and concurrent alcohol consumption among college students. *American Journal of Drug and Alcohol Abuse*, *35*(5), 334–338. doi:10.1080/00952990903075059

Garnier, L. M., Arria, A. M., Caldeira, K. M., Vincent, K. B., O'Grady, K. E., & Wish, E. D. (2010). Sharing and selling of prescription medications in a college student sample. *Journal of Clinical Psychiatry*, *71*(3), 262–269. doi:10.4088/JCP.09m05189ecr

Ghandour, L. A., Martins, S. S., & Chilcoat, H. D. (2008). Understanding the patterns and distribution of opioid analgesic dependence symptoms using a latent empirical approach. *International Journal of Methods in Psychiatric Research*, *17*(2), 89–103. doi:10.1002/mpr.232

Greenhill, L., Beyer, D. H., Finkleson, J., Shaffer, D., Biederman, J., Conners, C. K., . . . Volkow, N. (2002). Guidelines and algorithms for the use of methylphenidate in children with attention-deficit/hyperactivity disorder. *Journal of Attention Disorders*, 6(Supp. 1), S89–100.

Greydanus, D. E. (2006). *Stimulant misuse: Strategies to manage a growing problem.* Hanover, MD: American College Health Association.

Hall, K. M., Irwin, M. M., Bowman, K. A., Frankenberger, W., & Jewett, D. C. (2005). Illicit use of prescribed stimulant medication among college students. *Journal of American College Health*, 53(4), 167–174. doi:10.3200/JACH.53.4.167-174

Hall, M. T., Howard, M. O., & McCabe, S. E. (2010). Subtypes of adolescent sedative/anxiolytic misusers: A latent profile analysis. *Addictive Behaviors*, 35(10), 882–889. doi:10.1016/j.addbeh.2010.05.006

Herman-Stahl, M. A., Krebs, C. P., Kroutil, L. A., & Heller, D. C. (2006). Risk and protective factors for nonmedical use of prescription stimulants and methamphetamine among adolescents. *Journal of Adolescent Health*, 39(3), 374–380. doi:10.1016/j.jadohealth.2006.01.006

Herman-Stahl, M. A., Krebs, C. P., Kroutil, L. A., & Heller, D. C. (2007). Risk and protective factors for methamphetamine use and nonmedical use of prescription stimulants among young adults aged 18 to 25. *Addictive Behaviors*, 32(5), 1003–1015. doi:10.1016/j.addbeh.2006.07.010

Hoagwood, K., Jensen, P. S., Feil, M., Vitiello, B., & Bhatara, V. S. (2000). Medication management of stimulants in pediatric practice settings: A national perspective. *Journal of Developmental and Behavioral Pediatrics*, 21(5), 322–331. doi:10.1097/00004703-200010000-00002

Hser, Y-I. (2001). An evaluation of drug treatments for adolescents in 4 US cities. *Archives of General Psychiatry*, 58(7), 689–695. doi:10.1001/archpsyc.58.7.689

Huang, B., Dawson, D. A., Stinson, F. S., Hasin, D. S., Ruan, W. J., Saha, T. D., . . . Grant, B. F. (2006). Prevalence, correlates, and comorbidity of nonmedical prescription drug use and drug use disorders in the United States: Results of the National Epidemiologic Survey on Alcohol and Related Conditions. *Journal of Clinical Psychiatry*, 67(7), 1062–1073. doi:10.4088/JCP.v67n0708

Johnston, L. D., O'Malley, P. M., Bachman, J. G., & Schulenberg, J. E. (2012). *Monitoring the future: National survey results on drug use, 1975-2011, Vol. II. College students and adults ages 19-50.* Ann Arbor, MI: Institute for Social Research, University of Michigan. Retrieved October 2015, from http://www.monitoringthefuture.org/pubs/monographs/mtf-vol2_2011.pdf

Johnston, L. D., O'Malley, P. M., Bachman, J. G., & Schulenberg, J. E. (2013a). *Monitoring the future: National results on adolescent drug use: 2012 overview: Key findings on adolescent drug use.* Ann Arbor, MI: Institute for Social Research, University of Michigan.

Johnston, L. D., O'Malley, P. M., Bachman, J. G., & Schulenberg, J. E. (2013b). *Monitoring the future: National survey results on drug use, 1975-2012, Vol. I. Secondary school students.* Ann Arbor, MI: Institute for Social Research, University of Michigan.

Kaloyanides, K. B., McCabe, S. E., Cranford, J. A., & Teter, C. J. (2007). Prevalence of illicit use and abuse of prescription stimulants, alcohol, and other drugs among college students: Relationship with age at initiation of prescription stimulants. *Pharmacotherapy*, 27(5), 666–674. doi:10.1592/phco.27.5.666

Kaye, S., & Darke, S. (2012). The diversion and misuse of pharmaceutical stimulants: What do we know and why should we care? *Addiction*, 107(3), 467–477. doi:10.1111/j.1360-0443.2011.03720.x

Kessler, R. C., Nelson, C. B., McGonagle, K. A., & Liu, J. (1996). Comorbidity of DSM-III—R major depressive disorder in the general population: Results from the US National Comorbidity Survey. *British Journal of Psychiatry Supplement*, 168(30), 17–30.

Klein, R. G., Mannuzza, S., Olazagasti, M. A. R., Roizen, E., Hutchison, J. A., Lashua, E. C., & Castellanos, F. X. (2012). Clinical and functional outcome of childhood attention-deficit/hyperactivity disorder 33 years later. *Archives of General Psychiatry*, 69(12), 1295–1303. doi:10.1001/archgenpsychiatry.2012.271

Kollins, S. H. (2008). ADHD, substance use disorders, and psychostimulant treatment: Current literature and treatment guidelines. *Journal of Attention Disorders*, 12(2), 115–125. doi:10.1177/1087054707311654

Kuehn, B. M. (2007). Opioid prescriptions soar: Increase in legitimate use as well as abuse. *Journal of the American Medical Association*, 297(3), 249–251. doi:10.1001/jama.297.3.249

Kuramoto, S. J., Chilcoat, H. D., Ko, J., & Martins, S. S. (2012). Suicidal ideation and suicide attempt across stages of nonmedical prescription opioid use and presence of prescription opioid disorders among U.S. adults. *Journal of Studies on Alcohol And Drugs*, 73(2), 178–184.

Lankenau, S. E., Teti, M., Silva, K., Bloom, J. J., Harocopos, A., & Treese, M. (2012). Initiation into prescription opioid misuse amongst young injection drug users. *International Journal of Drug Policy*, 23(1), 37–44. doi:10.1016/j.drugpo.2011.05.014

Lessenger, J. E., & Feinberg, S. D. (2008). Abuse of prescription and over-the-counter medications. *Journal of the American Board of Family Medicine*, 21(1), 45–54. doi:10.3122/jabfm.2008.01.070071

Looby, A., & Earleywine, M. (2011). Expectation to receive methylphenidate enhances subjective arousal but not cognitive performance. *Experimental and Clinical Psychopharmacology*, 19(6), 433–444. doi:10.1037/a0025252

Lookatch, S. J., Dunne, E. M., & Katz, E. C. (2012). Predictors of nonmedical use of prescription stimulants. *Journal of Psychoactive Drugs*, 44(1), 86–91. doi:10.1080/02791072.2012.662083

Lord, S., Brevard, J., & Budman, S. (2011). Connecting to young adults: An online social network survey of beliefs and attitudes associated with prescription opioid misuse among college students. *Substance Use and Misuse*, 46(1), 66–76. doi:10.3109/10826084.2011.521371

Lott, D. C., Soo-Jeong, K., Cook, E. H., Jr., & de Wit, H. (2005). Dopamine transporter gene associated with diminished subjective response to amphetamine. *Neuropsychopharmacology*, 30(3), 602–609. doi:10.1038/sj.npp.1300637

Low, K. G., & Gendaszek, A. E. (2002). Illicit use of psychostimulants among college students: A preliminary study. *Psychology, Health and Medicine*, 7(3), 283–287. doi:10.1080/13548500220139386

Lucke, J. C., Bell, S., & Partridge, B. (2011). Deflating the neuroenhancement bubble. *American Journal of Bioethics: Neuroscience*, 2(4), 38–43. doi:10.1080/21507740.2011.611122

Mackey, S., Stewart, J. L., Connolly, C. G., Tapert, S. F., & Paulus, M. P. (2013). A voxel-based morphometry study of young occasional users of amphetamine-type stimulants and cocaine. *Drug and Alcohol Dependence*, 135(1), 104–111. doi:10.1016/j.drugalcdep.2013.11.018

Manchikanti, L., Fellows, B., Ailinani, H., & Pampati, V. (2010). Therapeutic use, abuse, and nonmedical use of opioids: a ten-year perspective. *Pain Physician*, 13(5), 401–435.

Mars, S. G., Bourgois, P., Karandinos, G., Montero, F., & Ciccarone, D. (2014). "Every 'never' I ever said came true": Transitions from opioid pills to heroin injecting. *International Journal of Drug Policy*, 25(2), 257–266. doi:10.1016/j.drugpo.2013.10.004

Martins, S. S., Keyes, K. M., Storr, C. L., Zhu, H., & Grucza, R. A. (2010). Birth-cohort trends in lifetime and past-year prescription opioid-use disorder resulting from nonmedical use: Results from two national surveys. *Journal of Studies on Alcohol and Drugs*, 71(4), 480–487.

McCabe, S. E. (2005). Correlates of nonmedical use of prescription benzodiazepine anxiolytics: Results from a national survey of U.S. college students. *Drug and Alcohol Dependence*, 79(1), 53–62. doi:10.1016/j.drugalcdep.2004.12.006

McCabe, S. E. (2008a). Misperceptions of non-medical prescription drug use: A web survey of college students. *Addictive Behaviors*, 33(5), 713–724. doi:10.1016/j.addbeh.2007.12.008

McCabe, S. E. (2008b). Screening for drug abuse among medical and nonmedical users of prescription drugs in a probability sample of college students. *Archives of Pediatrics and Adolescent Medicine*, 162(3), 225–231. doi:10.1001/archpediatrics.2007.41

McCabe, S. E., & Boyd, C. J. (2005). Sources of prescription drugs for illicit use. *Addictive Behaviors*, 30(7), 1342–1350. doi:10.1016/j.addbeh.2005.01.012

McCabe, S. E., Boyd, C. J., & Teter, C. J. (2009). Subtypes of nonmedical prescription drug misuse. *Drug and Alcohol Dependence*, 102(1–3), 63–70. doi:10.1016/j.drugalcdep.2009.01.007

McCabe, S. E., Boyd, C. J., & Young, A. (2007). Medical and nonmedical use of prescription drugs among secondary school students. *Journal of Adolescent Health*, 40(1), 76–83. doi:10.1016/j.jadohealth.2006.07.016

McCabe, S. E., & Cranford, J. A. (2012). Motivational subtypes of nonmedical use of prescription medications: Results from a national study. *Journal of Adolescent Health*, 51(5), 445–452. doi:10.1016/j.jadohealth.2012.02.004

McCabe, S. E., Cranford, J. A., Boyd, C. J., & Teter, C. J. (2007). Motives, diversion and routes of administration associated with nonmedical use of prescription opioids. *Addictive Behaviors*, 32(3), 562–575. doi:10.1016/j.addbeh.2006.05.022

McCabe, S. E., Cranford, J. A., & West, B. T. (2008). Trends in prescription drug abuse and dependence, co-occurrence with other substance use disorders, and treatment utilization: Results from two national surveys. *Addictive Behaviors*, 33(10), 1297–1305. doi:10.1016/j.addbeh.2008.06.005

McCabe, S. E., Knight, J. R., Teter, C. J., & Wechsler, H. (2005). Non-medical use of prescription stimulants among US college students: Prevalence and correlates from a national survey. *Addiction*, 99(1), 96–106. doi:10.1111/j.1360-0443.2005.00944.x

McCabe, S. E., Morales, M., Cranford, J. A., Delva, J., McPherson, M. D., & Boyd, C. J. (2007). Race/ethnicity and gender differences in drug use and abuse among college students. *Journal of Ethnicity in Substance Abuse*, 6(2), 75–95. doi:10.1300/J233v06n02-06

McCabe, S. E., Teter, C. J., & Boyd, C. J. (2004). The use, misuse and diversion of prescription stimulants among middle and high school students. *Substance Use and Misuse*, 39(7), 1095–1116. doi:10.1081/JA-120038031

McCabe, S. E., Teter, C. J., & Boyd, C. J. (2006a). Medical use, illicit use and diversion of prescription stimulant medication. *Journal of Psychoactive Drugs*, 38(1), 43–56. doi:10.1080/02791072.2006.10399827

McCabe, S. E., Teter, C. J., & Boyd, C. J. (2006b). Medical use, illicit use, and diversion of abusable prescription drugs. *Journal of American College Health*, 54(5), 269–278. doi:10.3200/JACH.54.5.269-278

McCabe, S. E., Teter, C. J., Boyd, C. J., Knight, J. R., & Wechsler, H. (2005). Nonmedical use of prescription opioids among U.S. college students: Prevalence and correlates from a national survey. *Addictive Behaviors*, 30(4), 789–805. doi:10.1016/j.addbeh.2004.08.024

McCabe, S. E., West, B. T., Cranford, J. A., Ross-Durow, P., Young, A., Teter, C. J., & Boyd, C. J. (2011). Medical misuse of controlled medications among adolescents. *Archives of Pediatrics and Adolescent Medicine*, 165(8), 729–735. doi:10.1001/archpediatrics.2011.114.

McLellan, A. T., & Turner, B. J. (2010). Chronic noncancer pain management and opioid overdose: Time to change prescribing practices. *Annals of Internal Medicine*, 152(2), 123–124. doi:10.7326/0003-4819-152-2-201001190-00012

Meier, E. A., Troost, J. P., & Anthony, J. C. (2012). Extramedical use of prescription pain relievers by youth aged 12 to 21 years in the United States. *Archives of Pediatric and Adolescent Medicine*, 166(9), 1–5.

Miller, N. S. (2004). Prescription opiate medications: Medical uses and consequences, laws and controls. *Psychiatric Clinics of North America*, 27, 689–708.

Minozzi, S., Amato, L., & Davoli, M. (2012). Development of dependence following treatment with opioid analgesics for pain relief: A systematic review. *Addiction*, 108(4), 688–698. doi:10.1111/j.1360-0443.2012.04005.x

Morgan, D., Frost-Pineda, K., & Gold, M. S. (2006). Medical and nonmedical use of prescription opioids: Epidemiology and prevalence. *Psychiatric Annals*, 36(6), 404–409.

Mulye, T. P., Park, M. J., Nelson, C. D., Adams, S. H., Irwin, C. E., Jr., & Brindis, C. D. (2009). Trends in adolescent and young adult health in the United States. *Journal of Adolescent Health*, 45(1), 8–24. doi:10.1016/j.jadohealth.2009.03.013

Nakawaki, B., & Crano, W. D. (2012). Predicting adolescents' persistence, non-persistence, and recent onset of nonmedical use of opioids and stimulants. *Addictive Behaviors*, 37(6), 716–721. doi:10.1016/j.addbeh.2012.02.011

Nash, S. G., McQueen, A., & Bray, J. H. (2005). Pathways to adolescent alcohol use: Family environment, peer influence, and parental expectations. *Journal of Adolescent Health*, 37(1), 19–28. doi:10.1016/j.jadohealth.2004.06.004

National Institute on Drug Abuse. (2013). Health effects. Retrieved July 2013, from http://www.drugabuse.gov/drugs-abuse/commonly-abused-drugs/health-effects

Novak, S. P., Herman-Stahl, M., Flannery, B., & Zimmerman, M. (2009). Physical pain, common psychiatric and substance use disorders, and the non-medical use of prescription analgesics in the United States. *Drug and*

Alcohol Dependence, *100*(1–2), 63–70. doi:10.1016/j.drugalcdep.2008.09.013

Novak, S. P., Kroutil, L. A., Williams, R. L., & Van Brunt, D. L. (2007). The nonmedical use of prescription ADHD medications: Results from a national internet panel. *Substance Abuse Treatment, Prevention, and Policy*, *2*(32), 32–49. doi:10.1186/1747-597X-2-32

Palmgreen, P., Donohew, L., Lorch, E. P., & Rogus, M. (1991). Sensation seeking, message sensation value, and drug use as mediators of PSA effectiveness. *Health Communication*, *3*(4), 217–227. doi:10.1207/s15327027hc0304_4

Paulozzi, L. J. (2012). Prescription drug overdoses: A review. *Journal of Safety Research*, *43*(4), 283–289. doi:10.1016/j.jsr.2012.08.009

Paulozzi, L. J., Jones, C. M., Mack, K. A., & Rudd, R. A. (2011). Vital signs: Overdoses in prescription opioid pain relievers-United States, 1999-2008. *Morbidity and Mortality Weekly Report*, *60*(43), 1487–1492.

Paulozzi, L. J., Kilbourne, E. M., & Desai, H. A. (2011). Prescription drug monitoring programs and death rates from drug overdose. *Pain Medicine*, *12*(5), 747–754. doi:10.1111/j.1526-4637.2011.01062.x

Poulin, C. (2001). Medical and nonmedical stimulant use among adolescents: From sanctioned to unsanctioned use. *Canadian Medical Association Journal*, *165*(8), 1039–1044.

Quintero, G. (2009). Rx for a party: A qualitative analysis of recreational pharmaceutical use in a collegiate setting. *Journal of American College Health*, *58*(1), 64–72. doi:10.3200/JACH.58.1.64-72

Rabiner, D. L., Anastopoulos, A. D., Costello, E. J., Hoyle, R. H., McCabe, S. E., & Swartzwelder, H. S. (2009). Motives and perceived consequences of nonmedical ADHD medication use by college students: Are students treating themselves for attention problems? *Journal of Attention Disorders*, *13*(3), 259–270. doi:10.1177/1087054708320399

Realmuto, G., Winters, K. C., August, G. J., Lee, S., Botzet, A. M., & Fahnhorst, T. (2009). Psychosocial functioning of a community derived sample of adolescents with childhood ADHD. *Journal of Adolescence*, *18*(2), 172–192. doi:10.1080/10678280902724176

Reyna, V. F., & Farley, F. (2006). Risk and rationality in adolescent decision making: Implications for theory, practice, and public policy. *Psychological Science in the Public Interest*, *7*(1), 1–44. doi:10.1111/j.1529-1006.2006.00026.x

Romer, D., & Hennessy, M. (2007). A biosocial-affect model of adolescent sensation seeking: The role of affect evaluation and peer-group influence in adolescent drug use. *Prevention Science*, *8*(2), 89–101. doi:10.1007/s11121-007-0064-7

Rozenbroek, K., & Rothstein, W. G. (2011). Medical and nonmedical users of prescription drugs among college students. *Journal of American College Health*, *59*(5), 358–363. doi:10.1080/07448481.2010.512044

Ryan, S. M., Jorm, A. F., & Lubman, D. I. (2010). Parenting factors associated with reduced adolescent alcohol use: A systematic review of longitudinal studies. *Australian and New Zealand Journal of Psychiatry*, *44*(9), 774–783. doi:10.1080/00048674.2010.501759

Saxe, T. G. (1986). Drug-alcohol interactions. *American Family Physician*, *33*(4), 159–162.

Schepis, T. S., & Krishnan-Sarin, S. (2008). Characterizing adolescent prescription misusers: A population-based study. *Journal of the American Academy of Child and Adolescent Psychiatry*, *47*(7), 745–754. doi:10.1097/CHI.0b013e318172ef0d

Schepis, T. S., Marlowe, D. B., & Forman, R. F. (2008). The availability and portrayal of stimulants over the internet. *Journal of Adolescent Health*, *42*(5), 458–465. doi:10.1016/j.jadohealth.2007.11.140

Schepis, T. S., & McCabe, S. E. (2012). Exploring age of onset as a causal link between major depression and nonmedical use of prescription medications. *Drug and Alcohol Dependence*, *120*(1–3), 99–104. doi:10.1016/j.drugalcdep.2011.07.002

Schuster, C. R. (2006). History and current perspectives on the use of drug formulations to decrease the abuse of prescription drugs. *Drug and Alcohol Dependence*, *83*(Supp. 1), S8–S14. doi:10.1016/j.drugalcdep.2006.01.006

Sees, K. L., Di Marino, M. E., Ruediger, N. K., Sweeney, C. T., & Shiffman, S. (2005). Non-medical use of OxyContin tablets in the United States. *Journal of Pain and Palliative Care Pharmacotherapy*, *19*(2), 13–23. doi:10.1300/J354v19n02_04

Sepúlveda, D. R., Thomas, L. M., McCabe, S. E., Cranford, J. A., Boyd, C. J., & Teter, C. J. (2011). Misuse of prescribed stimulant medication for ADHD and associated patterns of substance use: Preliminary analysis among college students. *Journal of Pharmacy Practice*, *24*(6), 551–560. doi:10.1177/0897190011426558

Severtson, S. G., Bartelson, B. B., Davis, J. M., Munoz, A., Schneider, M. F., Chilcoat, H., . . . Dart, R. C. (2013). Reduced abuse, therapeutic errors, and diversion following reformulation of extended-release Oxycodone in 2010. *Journal of Pain*, *14*(10), 1122–1130. doi:10.1016/j.jpain.2013.04.011

Simeone, R., & Holland, L. (2006). *An evaluation of prescription drug monitoring programs*. Albany, NY: Simeone. Retrieved October 2015, from http://www.simeoneassociates.com/index.php?id=8

Simoni-Wastila, L., Ritter, G., & Strickler, G. (2004). Gender and other factors associated with the nonmedical use of abusable prescription drugs. *Substance Use and Misuse*, *39*(1), 1–23. doi:10.1081/JA-120027764

Simoni-Wastila, L., Yang, H-W. K., & Lawler, J. (2008). Correlates of prescription drug nonmedical use and problem use by adolescents. *Journal of Addiction Medicine*, *2*(1), 31–39. doi:10.1097/ADM.0b013e31815b5590

Stein, M. A., Waldman, I. D., Sarampote, C. S., Seymour, K. E., Robb, A. S., Conlon, C., . . . Cook, E. H., Jr. (2005). Dopamine transporter genotype and methylphenidate dose response in children with ADHD. *Neuropsychopharmacology*, *30*(7), 1374–1382. doi:10.1038/sj.npp.1300718

Subramaniam, G. A., & Stitzer, M. A. (2009). Clinical characteristics of treatment-seeking prescription opioid vs. heroin-using adolescents with opioid use disorder. *Drug and Alcohol Dependence*, *101*(1–2), 13–19. doi:10.1016/j.drugalcdep.2008.10.015

Substance Abuse and Mental Health Services Administration. (2012a). *Results from the 2011 National Survey on Drug Use and Health: Detailed tables*. Rockville, MD: United States Department of Health and Human Services, Office of Applied Studies.

Substance Abuse and Mental Health Services Administration. (2012b). *Results from the 2011 National Survey on Drug Use and Health: Summary of national findings* (NSDUH Series H-44). Rockville, MD: Office of Applied Studies.

Sung, H-E., Richter, L., Vaughan, R., Johnson, P. B., & Thom, B. (2005). Nonmedical use of prescription opioids among teenagers in the United States: Trends and correlates. *Journal of Adolescent Health*, *37*(1), 44–51. doi:10.1016/j.jadohealth.2005.02.013

Sussman, S. (2013). A lifespan developmental-stage approach to tobacco and other drug abuse prevention. *ISRN Addiction*. doi:10.1155/2013/745783

Swanson, J. M., & Volkow, N. D. (2003). Serum and brain concentrations of methylphenidate: Implications for use and abuse. *Neuroscience and Biobehavioral Reviews*, *27*(7), 615–621. doi:10.1016/j.neubiorev.2003.08.013

Swendsen, J. D., Merikangas, K. R., Canino, G. J., Kessler, R. C., Rubio-Stipec, M., & Angst, J. (1998). The comorbidity of alcoholism with anxiety and depressive disorders in four geographic communities. *Comprehensive Psychiatry*, *39*(4), 176–184. doi:10.1016/S0010-440X(98)90058-X

Talbot, M. (2009, April 27). Brain gain: The underground world of "neuroenhancing" drugs. *The New Yorker*. 32–43.

Teter, C. J., Falone, A. E., Cranford, J. A., Boyd, C. J., & McCabe, S. E. (2010). Nonmedical use of prescription stimulants and depressed mood among college students: Frequency and routes of administration. *Journal of Substance Abuse Treatment*, *38*(3), 292–298. doi:10.1016/j.jsat.2010.01.005

Teter, C. J., McCabe, S. E., Boyd, C. J., & Guthrie, S. K. (2003). Illicit methylphenidate use in an undergraduate student sample: Prevalence and risk factors. *Pharmacotherapy*, *23*(5), 609–617. doi:10.1592/phco.23.5.609.34187

Teter, C. J., McCabe, S. E., Cranford, J. A., Boyd, C. J., & Guthrie, S. K. (2005). Prevalence and motives for illicit use of prescription stimulants in an undergraduate student sample. *Journal of American College Health*, *53*(6), 253–262. doi:10.3200/JACH.53.6.253-262

Teter, C. J., McCabe, S. E., LaGrange, K., Cranford, J. A., & Boyd, C. J. (2006). Illicit use of specific prescription stimulants among college students: Prevalence, motives, and routes of administration. *Pharmacotherapy*, *26*(10), 1501–1510. doi:10.1592/phco.26.10.1501

Vincent, K. B., Kasperski, S. J., Caldeira, K. M., Garnier-Dykstra, L. M., Pinchevsky, G. M., O'Grady, K. E., & Arria, A. M. (2012). Maintaining superior follow-up rates in a longitudinal study: Experiences from the College Life Study. *International Journal of Multiple Research Approaches*, *6*(1), 56–72. doi:10.5172/mra.2012.6.1.56

Volkow, N. D., Fowler, J. S., Wang, G-J., Telang, F., Logan, J., Wong, C., . . . Swanson, J. M. (2008). Methylphenidate decreased the amount of glucose needed by the brain to perform a cognitive task. *PLoS ONE*, *3*(4), e2017–e2017. doi:10.1371%2Fjournal.pone.0002017

Weathermon, R., & Crabb, D. W. (1999). Alcohol and medication interactions. *Alcohol Research and Health*, *23*(1), 40–54.

Weyandt, L. L., Janusis, G., Wilson, K. G., Verdi, G., Paquin, G., Lopes, J., . . . Dussault, C. (2009). Nonmedical prescription stimulant use among a sample of college students: Relationship with psychological variables. *Journal of Attention Disorders*, *13*(3), 284–296. doi:10.1177/1087054709342212

White, B. P., Becker-Blease, K. A., & Grace-Bishop, K. (2006). Stimulant medication use, misuse, and abuse in an undergraduate and graduate student sample. *Journal of American College Health*, *54*(5), 261–268. doi:10.3200/JACH.54.5.261-268

Wilens, T. E., Adler, L. A., Adams, J., Sgambati, S., Rotrosen, J., Sawtelle, R., . . . Fusillo, S. (2008). Misuse and diversion of stimulants prescribed for ADHD: A systematic review of the literature. *Journal of the American Academy of Child and Adolescent Psychiatry*, *47*(1), 21–31. doi:10.1097/chi.0b013e31815a56f1

Wilens, T. E., Faraone, S. V., Biederman, J., & Gunawardene, S. (2003). Does stimulant therapy of attention-deficit/hyperactivity disorder beget later substance abuse? A meta-analytic review of the literature. *Pediatrics*, *111*(1), 179–185. doi:10.1542/peds.111.1.179

Wilens, T. E., Gignac, M., Swezey, A., Monutaux, M. C., & Biederman, J. (2006). Characteristics of adolescents and young adults with ADHD who divert or misuse their prescribed medications. *Journal of the American Academy of Child and Adolescent Psychiatry*, *45*(4), 408–414. doi:10.1097/01.chi.0000199027.68828.b3

Wilens, T. E., Spencer, T. J., & Biederman, J. (2000). Pharmacotherapy of attention-deficit/hyperactivity disorder. In T. E. Brown (Ed.), *Attention-deficit disorders and comorbidities in children, adolescents, and adults* (pp. 509–535). Arlington, VA: American Psychiatric Publishing.

Williams, R. J., Goodale, L. A., Shay-Fiddler, M. A., Gloster, S. P., & Chang, S. Y. (2004). Methylphenidate and dextroamphetamine abuse in substance-abusing adolescents. *American Journal on Addictions*, *13*(4), 381–389. doi:10.1080/10550490490483053

Winters, K. C., Botzet, A. M., & Fahnhorst, T. (2011). Advances in adolescent substance abuse treatment. *Current Psychiatry Reports*, *13*(5), 416–421. doi:10.1007/s11920-011-0214-2

Wu, L., Pilowsky, D. J., & Patkar, A. A. (2008). Non-prescribed use of pain relievers among adolescents in the United States. *Drug and Alcohol Dependence*, *94*(1–3), 1–11. doi:10.1016/j.drugalcdep.2007.09.023

Wu, L. T., Blazer, D. G., Li, T. K., & Woody, G. E. (2011). Treatment use and barriers among adolescents with prescription opioid use disorders. *Addictive Behaviors*, *36*(12), 1233–1239. doi:10.1016/j.addbeh.2011.07.033

Young, A., McCabe, S. E., Cranford, J. A., Ross-Durow, P., & Boyd, C. J. (2012). Nonmedical use of prescription opioids among adolescents: Subtypes based on motivation for use. *Journal of Addictive Diseases*, *31*(4), 332–341. doi:10.1080/10550887.2012.735564

Young, A. M., & Havens, J. R. (2012). Transition from first illicit drug use to first injection drug use among rural Appalachian drug users: A cross-sectional comparison and retrospective survival analysis. *Addiction*, *107*(3), 587–596. doi:10.1111/j.1360-0443.2011.03635.x

Zuckerman, M. (1994). *Behavioral expressions and biosocial bases of sensation seeking*. New York, NY: Cambridge University Press.

Zuckerman, M., Neary, R. S., & Brustman, B. A. (1970). Sensation-Seeking Scale correlates in experience (smoking, drugs, alcohol, "hallucinations," and sex) and preference for complexity (designs). *Proceedings of the Annual Convention of the American Psychological Association*, *5*(1), 317–318.

PART 4

Etiology and Course in the Context of Adolescent Development

A Developmental Biological Perspective of Adolescent Substance Abuse: Animal Models

Linda Patia Spear

Abstract

Studies using animal models of adolescence have shown lasting consequences of adolescent exposure to alcohol, nicotine, and cannabinoids, including increases in later drug self-administration in some instances, along with alterations in cognitive and socioemotional functioning. In the case of alcohol, some evidence has also emerged for retention of immature, adolescent-typical alcohol sensitivities into adulthood. Neural alterations include relatively long-lasting changes in later neural functioning and gene expression in the neurocircuitry processing rewards, social and emotional stimuli, and cognition. Thus, although at this early stage, other aged exposure groups have not always been included to determine whether adolescence represents an especially vulnerable period, convincing data has nevertheless emerged that repeated exposure to drugs during adolescence often exerts relatively long-lasting alterations in later neurobehavioral function.

Key Words: animal models, adolescent, alcohol, nicotine, cannabinoids, stimulants, substance abuse, rewards, aversions, self-administration

Studying contributors to substance use and abuse among young people and consequences of that use are beset by a number of challenges. There are ethical constraints limiting the experimental administration of such drugs to underaged youth, as well as difficulties in interpreting whether observed correlations between prior drug use and measures of interest in cross-sectional data reflect cause, consequence, or coincidence. Moreover, despite exciting progress in imaging technology that has permitted noninvasive imaging of the developing brain, many questions about the brain of the adolescent are still challenging to address in human studies. For instance, consider the smallest unit of analysis used in imaging studies: the voxel, a cube with a volume of 1 mm^3 or more. Each voxel has been estimated to represent the combined activity of some 45,000 neurons and 450–500 million synaptic connections (Scheff, Price, & Sparks, 2001), providing a challenging diversity of pooled data from which to extract information about normal and drug-induced changes at the neural level. Some of these challenges can potentially be circumvented through use of simple animal models of adolescent drug exposure. Indeed, much of what is currently known about the intricacies of brain development, neural substrates of drug use/abuse, and adolescent responsiveness to alcohol, nicotine, and other drugs of abuse has been obtained in laboratory animals. Before considering the results of such studies, though, it is important first to reflect on the appropriateness, value, and limitations of animal models in the study of substance abuse and adolescence.

Use of Animal Models

The potential usefulness of an animal model depends on the question under examination—that is, what aspect of human behavior is to be modeled. Whereas certain specific elements of adolescent neurobehavioral function and substance abuse appear amenable to study using animal models, other aspects are not. A few examples include issues regarding the impact of self-esteem, culture, media, and parenting styles on adolescent substance use. Yet, even in these instances, animal models may provide some potentially relevant information. For instance, animal studies of the neural substrates and environmental modulators of cue conditioning, context conditioning, cue-related relapse, and their ontogeny may help inform studies of media influences on the development, escalation, and/or persistence of substance abuse among adolescents.

The validity of animal models is typically assessed using three evaluation criteria (see Willner, 1991, for discussion of these criteria within a context of animal models of human psychopathology). *Face validity* addresses whether the phenomenon under study in the model resembles the target construct in humans in terms of its behavioral, cognitive, and physiological features. Yet things that appear similar are not necessarily homologous—that is, they may not share similar underlying mechanisms. This issue is addressed when assessing *construct validity*, a measure of validity that focuses on the relevance of the phenomenon under investigation in the animal model to the concept being modeled. Construct validity is investigated via determining how similar the animal model is to what is being modeled in terms of its biological foundation and neural underpinnings, as well as the impact exerted by experiences, the environment, and other moderators. *Predictive validity* is used to reflect the efficacy of the animal model for forecasting outcomes—that is, for predicting experimental findings or treatment outcomes in humans.

In the case of adolescent substance abuse research, it can sometimes be challenging to assess these types of validity for many of the same reasons underlying the need for animal models in the first place—for example, ethical constraints on giving alcohol or other drugs to underage youth, limitations in the extent to which currently available imaging techniques can be used to study cellular and molecular underpinnings of adolescent neurodevelopment and the neurobiology of addiction, and the high cost and limited number of human longitudinal studies critical for disentangling neurobehavioral contributors to versus consequences of adolescent alcohol/drug use. Nevertheless, as discussed later, studies available to date using animal models of adolescence and of substance use/abuse have provided reasonable support for the judicious use of animal models in studies of adolescent alcohol/drug abuse. Assessment of validity is an ongoing process, with progressively stronger assessments of validity possible as the data in this rapidly escalating field

emerge in studies of both human adolescents and in animal models of this developmental transition. Ultimately, the validity of animal models is determined by their contribution to understanding the phenomena under investigation and for developing and testing hypotheses leading to improved prevention and treatment of adolescent substance abuse.

Animal Models in Substance Abuse Research

In studies using simple rodent models of drug use, animals have been shown to voluntarily self-administer most of the drugs that are used or abused in humans for their rewarding effects. For instance, in operant situations rodents will avidly learn to press a lever or emit another operant response to obtain intravenous (i.v.) infusions of drugs such as cocaine, heroin, nicotine, and benzodiazepines (see Koob & LeMoal, 2006, for review and references). Likewise, rodents often orally self-administer substantial amounts of alcohol, particularly when drinking was initiated using beer or sweetened alcohol solutions (not unlike the situation in humans—who often begin to drink consuming similar substances). When drug access is limited, rats typically regulate their intake, compensating for lower drug concentrations by self-administering the drug more frequently than at higher concentrations. Reminiscent of advanced cases of drug abuse in humans, laboratory animals given unrestricted access to drugs such as cocaine often develop signs of overdose characterized by rapid deterioration of health that can lead to death if drug access is not terminated (e.g., Fitch & Roberts, 1993).

Laboratory animals not only generally self-administer the same drugs of use/abuse as do humans, but they also show similar behavioral and cognitive responses to acute drug administration as well. For instance, stimulant drugs such as amphetamine and cocaine induce behavioral activation characterized by increases in arousal, alertness, and motor activity, with stereotypic behaviors emerging at high doses; such psychomotor stimulation is evident in both humans and laboratory animals. Alcohol is another example, with studies in laboratory animals effectively modeling a broad diversity of alcohol effects seen in humans, ranging from euphoria and social stimulation produced at low blood alcohol levels to intoxicating, motor-impairing, sedative, and memory-impairing (e.g., "blackout") effects emerging at higher doses (e.g., see Spear & Varlinskaya, 2005).

As is the case with humans, laboratory animals exposed chronically to drugs such as heroin, nicotine, and alcohol can become addicted—physically dependent—on the drug, characterized by dysphoria and physical signs of withdrawal when chronic access to the drug is terminated. These withdrawal signs tend to be opposite those associated with acute drug exposure and are reasonably similar across species. For instance, in both humans and rodent models of alcohol dependence, withdrawal is characterized by hyperexcitability (tremor, anxiety, insomnia, dysphoria, and in extreme cases, seizures), presumably related to rebound increases in excitability following the suppression in neural activity associated with chronic exposure to high amounts of alcohol (e.g., see Koob & Le Moal, 2006). Physical dependence is also characterized by the tendency to relapse back into taking the drug after withdrawal, relapse that can be precipitated by drug re-exposure and stressors, as well as contextual and other cues previously associated with the drug. In humans, these cues can elicit cravings for the drug—"wanting" of the drug that has been modeled using a number of experimental paradigms in laboratory animals (e.g., Berridge & Robinson, 2003). Yet, even at drug exposure levels far less than those required to produce physical dependence, laboratory animals often develop a preference for contextual cues associated with drug effects via a form of classical conditioning known as conditioned place preference (CPP). Studies using techniques such as CPP and drug self-administration in simple rodent models have revealed substantial information about processes leading to the initiation and maintenance of drug use, the production of dependence, and the propensity to relapse post withdrawal (see Koob & LeMoal, 2006).

Indeed, much of what is known about the brain substrates mediating drug reinforcement and addiction has been obtained in rodent studies (see Koob & LeMoal, 2006, for review). This work has revealed surprising complexities in the neural systems activated by and mediating effects of drugs of abuse that go far beyond the simple notion of dopamine (DA) reward systems commonly discussed in even the popular media. Although many details are still being explored and debated (e.g., see Berridge, 2007), from the work to date it is clear that brain structures and neurochemical systems underlying the reinforcing effects of addictive drugs are separable in part from those critical for the production of dependence, and from those mediating drug craving and relapse (e.g., Gardner, 2011). Although comparable data are sparse in humans and in the past had been restricted largely to autopsy data,

advances in imaging techniques are providing increasingly sophisticated assessments of regional brain activation patterns in dependent individuals (e.g., Parvaz et al., 2011). From such studies, initial encouraging signs of across-species similarities in the neural substrates underlying varying effects of these drugs have emerged with, for instance, evidence for importance of DA systems and brain regions such as the nucleus accumbens emerging in studies of the neurobiology of drug self-administration and dependence in both humans and other animals (e.g., Willuhn, Wanat, Clark, & Phillips, 2010; Volkow, Wang, Fowler, Tomasi, & Telang, 2011).

Collectively, these across-species similarities in propensity for drug self-administration, acute drug effects, dependence and withdrawal, and their neural substrates provide reasonable face and construct validity to support the use of animal models in studies exploring neural and environmental factors contributing to substance abuse. Yet, at the same time, it is recognized that no animal model will be able to examine the full complexity of contributors to substance abuse in humans during adolescence, or at any other age.

Animal Models of Adolescence

It has occasionally been argued that adolescence is uniquely human (e.g., Bogin, 1994). Yet, if adolescence is defined as the transition from dependence on parents to the relative independence of adulthood, this developmental shift is a transition that all developing mammals undergo. Across mammalian species, adolescents are faced with similar goals: gaining the skills necessary for survival in adulthood as well as for reproductive success, thereby passing on one's genes to the next generation. During the adolescent transition, similar biological changes are seen across a wide variety of mammalian species. Some of these physiological changes are associated with puberty, a relatively restricted developmental event that occurs sometime within the broader adolescent period and that includes neural and hormonal changes necessary for sexual maturation, along with the emergence of secondary sexual characteristics. Other hormonal and physiological changes are also evident, including increases in growth hormone release and a notable growth spurt.

Among the considerable biological changes of adolescence are those occurring in the brain (see Spear, 2010, for review and references). Some of these adolescent-associated neural alterations are regressive, including regionally specific reductions in the number of synaptic connections between neurons as well as reductions in the relative volume of certain cortical and subcortical areas enriched in neurons (gray matter). Speed of information flow across distant brain regions is enhanced during adolescence with the continued development of myelin that serves to insulate axonal processes and thereby speed the electrical flow of information along them. Associated in part with the reduction in numbers of energetically costly synapses along with the increases in energy-efficient myelinated axons, overall brain energy utilization declines through adolescence until the high brain efficiency characteristic of adulthood is reached.

Among the brain regions undergoing notable change during adolescence are subcortical areas such as the amygdala and nucleus accumbens that receive DA input and that are critically involved in the processing of affective/socioemotional stimuli and rewards; these regions often react differently, and sometimes in an exaggerated way, to motivational stimuli during adolescence (e.g., Ernst & Fudge, 2009; Spear, 2011). In contrast, maturation of cognitive control regions in the prefrontal cortex (PFC) and other frontal regions occurs only gradually during adolescence. These maturational dissociations are thought to contribute to increased risk taking, exploratory drug use, and other adolescent-characteristic behaviors (e.g., Casey & Jones, 2010). Importantly for our discussion here, to the extent that across-species data are available, relative analogous changes and their temporal sequencing are typically expressed across species ranging from rats to humans, despite the substantially greater structural and functional complexity of relatively late-maturing areas such as the frontal cortex in humans (see Spear, 2000, 2011, for review).

Given these regional brain changes and their similarity across species, it should not be surprising that adolescents differ from more mature individuals in various aspects of their behavior, socioemotional functioning, and cognition, with certain commonalities evident across species. These include adolescent-typical elevations in peer-directed social interactions, risk taking and sensation seeking, and the greater per episode use of alcohol that is often seen in human adolescents as well as in organisms undergoing this developmental transition from other species as well (see Spear, 2000, for review). For instance, even in a simple rodent model, adolescent rats show more peer-directed social interactions, novelty-seeking/ risk-taking, and consummatory behavior; find social stimuli, novelty, and pleasant tastes particularly reinforcing; and voluntarily consume 2–3 times more alcohol than their adult counterparts (e.g., see Spear, 2000, 2007; Doremus, Brunell, Rajendran, & Spear, 2005; Doremus-Fitzwater, Varlinskaya, & Spear, 2010, for review). Such across-species similarities are speculated to have been conserved during evolution because of their adaptive significance, with for instance adolescent-associated increases in risk-taking propensities and affiliations with peers thought to facilitate the transition to maturity as well as to encourage emigration away from genetically related individuals, thereby avoiding inbreeding and the associated decreases in viability associated with expression of recessive genes (see Steinberg & Belsky, 1996; Spear, 2000, for review). According to this perspective, the propensities of human adolescents to engage in risk-taking, drug use, and other age-typical behaviors may be tethered in part by biological roots deeply embedded in the evolutionary past.

Even apart from such evolutionary considerations, though, across-species similarities in adolescent neurobehavioral characteristics provide reasonable face and construct validity for the judicious use of animal models of adolescence, keeping in mind again that the appropriateness of animal models depends on the questions being addressed. Studying adolescence in animal models does present a variety of unique challenges, including the relatively brief length of adolescence in rodents and other species with a short life span. For instance, although the absolute boundaries of adolescence are as blurred in other species as they are in human youth, the length of adolescence in the rat has been suggested to subsume somewhere from a conservative 2 weeks (e.g., postnatal days [P] 28 to P42; see Spear, 2000) to a broader 4-week period (P25-55; see Vetter-O'Hagen & Spear, 2011). Notable modifications are often required to adapt operant drug self-administration and other test procedures typically conducted over months in adult rodents for application during the restricted time window of adolescence (see Anderson & Spear, 2013, for a recent example). Nevertheless, judicious use of animal models—where appropriate and adaptable to the temporal and other constraints intrinsic in animal research—can be used to complement studies of human substance-abusing youth and address questions that are not ethically or technically amenable to study in human adolescents.

Self-Administration and Acute Drug Sensitivity in Animal Models of Adolescence

Drugs of abuse exert their psychoactive effects largely through direct action on the brain. The developing adolescent brain provides different substrates for drug action than the mature brain, thereby perhaps influencing the nature of acute drug responses and propensity for drug self-administration. These topics are the focus of this section, with a particular emphasis on the two drugs most commonly used by adolescents: alcohol and nicotine.

Alcohol

As discussed in detail in other chapters, experimentation with alcohol becomes normative during adolescence in the United States, with significant numbers of these adolescents exhibiting binge drinking. Indeed, adolescent patterns of alcohol use differ from those seen in adults, with adolescents drinking more than twice as much on average per drinking episode as do adults (SAMHSA survey data, 2006). Although there are obviously many factors that contribute to elevated alcohol consumption during adolescence, one key contributor is likely biological, given that even in simple rodent models, adolescents often voluntarily consume 2–3 times more alcohol than do adults (e.g., Brunell & Spear, 2005; Doremus et al., 2005; Hargreaves, Monds, Gunasekaran, Dawson, & McGregor, 2009; Vetter, Doremus-Fitzwater, & Spear, 2007; but see also Bell et al., 2006; Siegmund, Vengeliene, Singer, & Spanagel, 2005). Like their human counterparts, adolescent alcohol intake in rats is particularly notable in males (Vetter-O'Hagen, Varlinskaya, & Spear, 2009) and when using beer or sweetened alcohol solutions (Doremus et al., 2005; Hargreaves et al., 2009), although elevated ethanol consumption has also been reported under some conditions with unsweetened ethanol as well (e.g., see Vetter et al., 2007). Importantly, the elevated consumption of alcohol in adolescence is not just associated with normal elevations in intake of food and fluids during this time of rapid growth. For example, the greater preference for a sweetened solution containing ethanol seen among adolescents relative to adults depends on the presence of ethanol and is not merely related to its caloric properties or to the sweetener alone (e.g., Doremus et al., 2005; Vetter et al., 2007).

Along with greater alcohol intake, adolescents also often differ from adults in their sensitivity to the effects of alcohol. The directionality of these differences, however, varies notably with the effect targeted. On one hand, adolescents are often resistant to many undesired effects of alcohol that may serve as cues to limit intake. These effects begin at moderate doses of alcohol and include aversive properties of alcohol (Anderson, Varlinskaya, & Spear, 2010; Schramm-Sapyta et al., 2010; Vetter-O'Hagen et al., 2009; although see also Pautassi, Myers, Spear, Molina, & Spear, 2011), motor impairment (Ramirez, Varlinskaya, & Spear, 2011; Silveri & Spear, 2001; White et al., 2002), social inhibition (e.g., Varlinskaya & Spear, 2002), and sedation (Moy, Duncan, Knapp, & Breese, 1998; Silveri & Spear, 1998). Adolescents may even be less sensitive than adults to "hangover" effects (acute withdrawal) following exposure to moderate or high doses of alcohol, at least when indexed via withdrawal-related anxiety (Doremus-Fitzwater & Spear, 2007; Varlinskaya & Spear, 2004). Although data are very limited due to ethical concerns, available alcohol challenge data in human adolescents suggest similar adolescent alcohol insensitivities. In a 1983 study where Behar and colleagues gave 8- to 15-year-old boys a moderate dose of alcohol prior to a variety of objective and subjective measures of intoxication and motor impairment, they noted that they "were impressed by how little gross behavioral change occurred in the children . . . after a dose of alcohol which had been intoxicating in an adult population" (p. 407).

One factor that appears to contribute to attenuated alcohol sensitivities during adolescence is the propensity of the adolescent brain to quickly adapt to the presence of alcohol within a single alcohol exposure period—an adaptation termed "acute tolerance" (Mellanby, 1919). This rapidly emerging, within-session adaptation to alcohol has been shown to be notably more pronounced in younger organisms than adults to a variety of alcohol effects, including sedative, motor-impairing, and social-suppressing effects (e.g., Silveri & Spear, 1998; Spear & Varlinskaya, 2005). These rapid adaptations appear related in part to developmentally heightened activity of n-methyl-d-aspartate (NMDA) receptor systems associated with the major excitatory neurotransmitter in the brain (glutamate) and that have been suggested to play important roles in learning and brain plasticity (Ramirez et al., 2011; Silveri & Spear, 2004). Although a likely contributor to the resistance that adolescents show to alcohol intoxication, acute tolerance alone is insufficient to account for these age differences, given that blocking expression of acute tolerance does not eliminate expression of ontogenetic differences in alcohol sensitivity (e.g., Silveri & Spear, 2004). Indeed, as discussed in more detail later, the general adolescent insensitivity to aversive effects of alcohol is not specific to alcohol and is also evident with some other drugs (and non-drug substances) as well, hence perhaps reflecting in part the ontogeny of neural substrates underlying the processing of and responding to aversive stimuli.

Another possible contributor to the insensitivity that adolescents show to these various effects of alcohol is pharmacokinetic—that is, how quickly alcohol gets into and out of the systems of adolescents relative to adults. Indeed, general metabolic rate tends to be elevated in adolescence, with adolescent animals occasionally (Brasser & Spear, 2002; Hollstedt, Olsson, & Rydberg, 1977), but not consistently (Kelly, Bonthius, & West, 1987; Silveri & Spear, 2000; Zorzano & Herrera, 1989) exhibiting significantly (albeit slightly) faster rates of alcohol metabolism than adults. Even when present, though, these modest elevations in metabolic rate have not generally been of sufficient magnitude to account for the attenuated alcohol sensitivities of adolescents (e.g., see Little, Kuhn, Wilson, & Swartzwelder, 1996; Silveri & Spear, 2000). The tendency for adolescents to show slightly elevated alcohol metabolism than adults is also inconsistent with the *increased* sensitivity that adolescents exhibit to certain other alcohol effects.

Indeed, in contrast to the resistance that adolescents often show to intoxicating effects of alcohol, studies in laboratory animals have found adolescents to be more sensitive than adults to the social facilitating and rewarding effects of alcohol, as well as to alcohol-related disruptions in cognition and brain plasticity. For instance, juvenile and adolescent rats have been shown to be more vulnerable than adults to alcohol-related impairment in brain plasticity when indexed via "long-term potentiation"—that is, adaptive increases in neural reactivity induced by prior electrical stimulation of activity in that region (Pyapali, Turner, Wilson, & Swartzwelder, 1999). Adolescent rats were also found to be more sensitive than adults to alcohol-induced memory deficits on a spatial task, the Morris water maze, when rats were trained to learn the position of a hidden platform in a large tub of water (Markwiese, Acheson, Levin, Wilson, & Swartzwelder, 1998). Greater adolescent vulnerabilities to alcohol-related memory deficits were also reported in a study with humans comparing of-age individuals in their early versus late 20s, thereby avoiding ethical constraints associated with administering alcohol to underage youth. In this study by Acheson et al. (1998), the 21- to 24-year-olds showed greater vulnerability to alcohol-induced memory disruptions on both verbal and nonverbal memory tasks than 25- to 29-year-olds, findings reminiscent of the age differences seen in research with laboratory animals.

The other effects of alcohol to which adolescents appear particularly sensitive are its social facilitating and rewarding effects. The best documented of these effects is ethanol-induced social facilitation. Adolescent rats, like their human counterparts (e.g, Beck, Thombs, & Summons, 1993), are especially prone to alcohol-related stimulation of social behavior, showing notable increases in peer-directed social interactions that are not evident in adult rats following exposure to low doses of alcohol in a familiar, non-anxiety-provoking setting (e.g., Varlinskaya & Spear, 2002; see Spear & Varlinskaya, 2005, for review). Evidence is also beginning to emerge that adolescents may also be more sensitive than adults to the rewarding effects of alcohol, although this has been less well characterized than other alcohol effects, due in part to challenges associated with assessing alcohol preference in rats using CPP. When using second-order conditioning, however, a procedure that involves pairing a previously neutral stimulus (CS1) with alcohol, followed by the pairing of that CS1 with another stimulus (CS2), adolescent rats were found to express a preference for the CS2 that was not evident in control age-mates receiving unpaired exposure to the stimuli and alcohol; adults, in contrast, expressed no significant second-order conditioning to alcohol under these same training and test conditions (Pautassi, Myers, Spear, Molina, & Spear, 2008). Additional data supporting the suggestion that adolescents are more sensitive to the rewarding effects of alcohol than adults were obtained using assessment of alcohol-induced heart rate increases (tachycardia), an autonomic measure shown to be positively correlated with subjective measures of alcohol's rewarding effects and DA release in humans (e.g., Boileau et al., 2003; Conrod, Pihl, & Vassileva, 1998). In this study, only adolescent rats, and not their adult counterparts, were found to drink enough alcohol to induce increases in heart rate above that induced by consumption of the control solution alone (Ristuccia & Spear, 2008). Together, these studies hint that adolescents may find alcohol to be generally more rewarding than adults, although the findings to date are mixed (see

Dickinson, Kashawny, Thiebes, & Charles, 2009) and more work in this area is needed.

To the extent that these adolescent-typical accentuated and attenuated sensitivities to alcohol revealed largely in studies with laboratory animals are also characteristic of human adolescents, they would represent an unfortunate combination. Enhanced sensitivity to rewarding and social facilitating effects of alcohol during adolescence could encourage high levels of use—elevated consumption levels that may be more tolerated than in adulthood due to the relative insensitivity of adolescents to intoxicating effects of alcohol that normally serve as feedback cues to terminate consumption. At the same time, such enhanced consumption would seemingly exacerbate further the already greater vulnerability of adolescents to alcohol-related memory impairments and disruptions in brain plasticity.

Nicotine

Most smokers begin to smoke during adolescence. About 75% of adult tobacco users began their use between 11 and 17 years of age (Eissenberg & Balster, 2000), with those individuals showing the earliest onset of use progressing to dependence more rapidly (Colby, Tiffany, Shiffman, & Niaura, 2000). Animal models of nicotine self-administration have found adolescents to self-administer nicotine at least as readily as adults, although there is substantial disagreement regarding age differences in these effects. In some studies, adolescent rats (especially female rats) were found to self-administer notably more intravenously (i.v.) administered nicotine (Chen, Matta, & Sharp, 2007; Levin, Rezvani, Montoya, Rose, & Swartzwelder, 2003; Levin et al., 2007, 2011) or nicotine in conjunction with the cigarette smoke additive acetaldehyde (Belluzzi, Wang, & Leslie, 2005) than adults. In other work, however, under low operant demands, adolescent and adult rats were reported to self-administer similar amounts of nicotine i.v., with higher operant requirements resulting in greater self-administration among adults than adolescents (Shram, Funk, Li, & Le, 2008a; Shram, Li, & Le, 2008b). Although the critical contributors to these across laboratory differences are unknown, among the possibilities are differences in cues paired with the nicotine infusion, with for instance nicotine infusions generally paired with a cue light in studies finding greater self-administration in adults than adolescents, but not in the studies finding greater self-administration during adolescence. Indeed, as discussed later, in studies in both humans and laboratory animals, adolescents have been often found to differ in complex and still poorly delineated ways from adults in their response to reward-related cues (see Spear, 2011, for review), including cues paired with nicotine (e.g., Schochet, Kelley, & Landrym, 2004).

Reminiscent of the alcohol literature, adolescent rats have also been shown to differ from adults in their sensitivity to acute effects of nicotine. They often show greater locomotor stimulation and fewer signs of behavioral suppression following nicotine exposure than adults (Belluzzi, Lee, Oliff, & Leslie, 2004; Levin et al., 2003; Schochet et al., 2004; Vastola, Douglas, Varlinskaya, & Spear, 2002). Adolescents also appear more sensitive to the rewarding effects of nicotine and less sensitive to nicotine's aversive effects than adults. These effects have been observed when indexing rewarding effects via CPP (e.g., Belluzzi et al., 2004; Brielmaier, McDonald, & Smith, 2007; Shram, Funk, Li, & Le, 2006; Torres, Tejeda, Natividad, & O'Dell, 2008; Vastola et al., 2002) and aversive effects via conditioned place aversions (CPA—avoiding a place previously paired with drug exposure) or conditioned taste aversions (CTA—avoiding a flavor that was followed by drug exposure on one or more prior occasions) (Shram et al., 2006; Torres et al., 2008; Wilmouth & Spear, 2004). Aversive effects often emerge in CPA and CTA tests at somewhat higher nicotine doses than those supporting CPP, with adolescent-typical accentuated rewarding effects and attenuated aversive effects sometimes apparent in dose-response analyses within the same experimental series (see Shram et al., 2006; Torres et al., 2008). Reminiscent of the alcohol "hangover" data, adolescent rats have been found to be less sensitive to nicotine withdrawal-related aversive or anxiogenic effects under some but not all test circumstances (O'Dell, Torres, Natividad, & Tejeda, 2007; Shram, Siu, Li, Tyndale, & Le, 2008c; Wilmouth & Spear, 2006).

Other Drugs of Abuse

Although at lower prevalence rates than for alcohol and nicotine, some individuals initiate use of illicit substances during adolescence. Lifetime prevalence of use of one or more illicit drugs was about 25% in 12- to 17-year-olds and 57% in 18- to 25-year-olds, with past-month use peaking in 18- to 25-year-olds at levels higher than among younger or older individuals (2010 National Survey on Drug Use and Health, SAMHSA). Among the 18- to 25-year-old group, use of marijuana was most common (lifetime prevalence rate of 51%) followed by nonmedical use of psychotherapeutics (e.g., pain relievers, tranquilizers—29%) and cocaine and other stimulants (13% and 10%, respectively). Few studies have examined age differences in self-administration of illicit drugs in laboratory animals, and in those studies that have, few notable age differences have emerged. A number of studies have reported no differences in i.v. cocaine self-administration between adolescent and adult rats (Frantz, O'Dell, & Parsons, 2007; Harvey, Dembro, Rajagopalan, Mutebi, & Kantak, 2009; Kerstetter & Kantak, 2007; Li & Frantz, 2009). In other work, however, adolescents were found to exhibit more rapid acquisition and greater levels of amphetamine self-administration at a low infusion dose than adults (Shahbazi, Moffett, Williams, & Frantz, 2008) and to self-administer more heroin when response requirements were low, but not when response demands progressively increased (Doherty & Frantz, 2012).

Data reminiscent of that found with alcohol and nicotine emerge when assessing age differences in the rewarding and aversive properties of illicit drugs. Cocaine CPP generally appears stronger among adolescents than adults, with adolescents not only developing cocaine CPP at lower conditioning doses than adults (Badanich, Adler, & Kirstein, 2006; Brenhouse & Andersen, 2008; Brenhouse, Sonntag, & Andersen, 2008; Zakharova et al., 2009a, 2009b) but also extinguishing this conditioning more slowly (Brenhouse & Andersen, 2008) and showing a greater propensity for reinstatement when compared to adults (Brenhouse & Andersen, 2008; Shram & Lê, 2010). These findings are not ubiquitous, however, with some studies finding no difference in CPP to cocaine between adolescents and adults (Aberg, Wade, Wall, & Izenwasser, 2007; Campbell, Bliven, Silveri, Snyder, & Spear, 2000; Schramm-Sapyta, Pratt, & Winder, 2004). Again reminiscent of the data with alcohol and nicotine, when aversive drug effects are indexed via CTA or CPA, adolescents conversely have been reported to be less sensitive than adults to the aversive effects of amphetamine (Infurna & Spear, 1979), cocaine (Schramm-Sapyta, Morris, & Kuhn, 2006), and delta-9-tetrahydrocannabinol (THC) (Quinn et al., 2008; Schramm-Sapyta, Cha, Chaudhry, Wilson, Swartzwelder & Kuhn, 2007).

Summary/Reflections: Generalizability of Adolescent-Typical Acute Drug Sensitivities

As reviewed earlier, studies using basic animal models of adolescence have found adolescents to display greater sensitivities to the rewarding properties of a variety of drugs including alcohol, nicotine, and stimulants, as well as attenuated sensitivities to the aversive properties of these same drugs (and THC). This apparent shift in reward-aversive sensitivity between adolescents and adults may extend beyond drugs to nondrug stimuli as well. For instance, adolescents not only often show greater CPP to nicotine and cocaine than adults, but also to social stimuli and novelty under some circumstances. In a study of isolate-housed and socially housed adolescent and adult rats, adolescent male rats, even if not deprived of social stimuli prior to conditioning, demonstrated both social and novelty CPP, whereas conditioning to these stimuli was only evident in their adult counterparts if they had been isolate housed (and hence deprived of social and other enriching stimuli for some time before conditioning); similar age differences were evident in females for social, but not novelty CPP (Douglas, Varlinskaya, & Spear, 2003, 2004). In terms of aversive effects, adolescents have been found to be not only less sensitive than adults to the aversive properties of several drugs of abuse, but also to an illness-inducing agent, lithium chloride (Schramm-Sapyta et al., 2006; although see also O'Dell et al., 2007). Using a very different measure to index rewarding/aversive effects—that is, frame-by-frame analysis of appetitive and aversive oral reactions to different taste stimuli, adolescent rats were found to show both greater positive responses to some concentrations of pleasant (e.g., sweet) tastes than adults, as well as reduced negative taste reactions to an aversive taste stimulus, quinine (Wilmouth & Spear, 2009). Signs of adolescent-associated biases in the neural processing of reward and aversions toward enhanced rewarding and attenuated aversive biases are also evident in the human imaging literature as well (e.g., Ernst et al., 2005; see Spear, 2011, for review).

The story regarding the responses of adolescents to rewarding stimuli is a bit more complex, however, than reviewed thus far. For instance, while adolescents display more peer-directed social interactions than do adults, during these interactions they emit fewer ultrasonic calls at a frequency (50 kHz) thought to reflect positive affect (Willey et al., 2009). Moreover, in studies in both humans and laboratory animals, in contrast to the enhanced reactivity that adolescents sometimes show to the receipt of rewards (e.g., Cohen et al., 2010; Ernst et al., 2005; Galvan et al., 2006), they conversely often appear to express attenuated anticipatory neural and behavioral responses to cues predicting rewards (e.g., Anderson & Spear, 2011; Bjork et al., 2004; Doremus-Fitzwater & Spear; 2011; Geier, Terwilliger, Teslovich, Velanova, & Luna, 2010; see Doremus-Fitzwater et al., 2010; Spear, 2011, for review). For instance, adolescent rats are much less likely to approach a cue that predicts an upcoming, response-independent delivery of a food reward (termed "sign tracking") than are adults, even though they appear to learn the contingency, with animals of both ages directing similar amounts of attention to the location where the food will be delivered (i.e., "goal tracking") (Anderson & Spear, 2011; Doremus-Fitzwater & Spear, 2011). The overall picture that emerges from such studies is that, dependent on the specifics of the circumstances in which rewarding stimuli are provided, at the same time that adolescents often show greater sensitivity to natural and drug-related rewards, they may display attenuated anticipatory responses to cues predicting those rewards (see Doremus-Fitzwater et al., 2010; Spear, 2011).

Overall, the evidence to date is consistent with the suggestion that adolescence may be a time of unique sensitivity to natural rewards and aversive properties of meaningful stimuli, and that drugs of potential abuse, via tapping into very basic reward and motivational systems in brain, may exhibit comparable age-related sensitivity patterns. Indeed, there is substantial evidence that among the areas of brain undergoing considerable transformation during adolescence are a number of regions critical for the processing of rewarding and motivationally relevant stimuli, including forebrain DA projections and their targets such as the nucleus accumbens, PFC, and amygdala (see Doremus-Fitzwater et al., 2010, for review and references). Any age-associated biologically based bias toward enhanced positive drug effects and fewer aversive consequences likely to limit use would seemingly encourage initial drug use by adolescents, promote continued use, and permit relatively high levels of use when so inclined. Such high exposure levels, in turn, could potentially lead to lasting neurocognitive alterations and the emergence of abusive patterns of use among more vulnerable individuals. Indeed, evidence for long-lasting neurobehavioral consequences of repeated adolescent drug exposures is beginning to emerge in studies in laboratory animals, a topic to which we now turn.

Lasting Consequences of Adolescent Drug and Alcohol Use in Laboratory Animals

As discussed elsewhere in this volume, evidence is accumulating from human cross-sectional studies that youth with a history of adolescent substance use/abuse differ from other youth in their neuropsychological test performance and in certain regional neuroimaging characteristics, with initial longitudinal prospective studies suggesting that some of these alterations may predate drug use and represent risk factors for that use, whereas others may reflect consequences of that use (e.g., see Tapert & Schweinsburg, 2005). Prospective studies, however, are limited due to their cost and extended time commitment. Hence, the search for causal relationships may be aided by studies manipulating drug exposure during adolescence in laboratory animals, thereby allowing systematic evaluation of effects attributable to drug exposure per se, as well as the impact of drug dose, timing, and duration for production of these effects and their longevity. Yet this approach would only be useful to the extent that the generated findings have relevance for drug use in human adolescents. To a large extent, the jury is still out on this, given the limited amount of work to date in both laboratory animals and humans that assess lasting consequences of adolescent drug exposures. Yet in the *prenatal exposure* literature where there is an extensive across-species database, findings support the suggestion that "reliable and valid animal data predict human responses very well," with "the specific behavior disrupted in one species . . . linked to alterations in particular neurobiological substrates that also mediate a similar category of behavior in humans" (Adams et al., 2000, p. 524; see also Vorhees, 1987; Rice & Barone, 2000; Stanton & Spear, 1990). Whereas it is still largely an empirical question as to whether similar strong across-species comparability is evident following drug exposures during adolescence, rapid progress should be forthcoming with the current marked escalation of work in this area. This rising interest has been undoubtedly fueled in part by the increasing recognition of the notable transformations occurring in adolescent brain (e.g., see Spear, 2010), especially when coupled with the notion that the brain may be especially susceptible to lasting consequences of drug perturbations at times of rapid developmental change (e.g., see Adams et al., 2000).

To illustrate work in this area, the focus here will be on exposures to the three substances most commonly used by human adolescents: alcohol, nicotine, and the major active ingredients in marijuana—cannabinoids such as THC. One area of focus in these studies has been on exploring the early exposure effect—that is, the increase in drug use/abuse liability that has been associated (not necessarily causally) with early use of alcohol or other drugs in human studies (e.g., Clark, Kirisci, & Tarter, 1998). Indeed, because of such concerns and speculations that early use of "gateway" drugs might increase later propensity to use/abuse illicit drugs, some studies of lasting functional consequences of adolescent drug exposures have examined later responsiveness to and self-administration of that drug and others. It should be noted that, at this early stage in basic science research in this area, data are considerably limited in some areas and significant numbers of studies have not included other exposure periods that would ultimately be necessary to determine whether adolescence represents an especially vulnerable developmental period for induction of long-lasting drug effects.

Lasting Consequences of Adolescent Alcohol Exposure

Work exploring consequences of adolescent exposure to alcohol has escalated recently, and some common themes are beginning to emerge. Converging data from a number of laboratories support the idea that adolescent alcohol exposure may result in the maintenance of certain adolescent-typical alcohol sensitivities into adulthood, although observed alterations in later alcohol consumption are complex and defy easy summary. Reports of increases in anxiety after adolescent exposure to alcohol are rising. More complex cognitive tasks appear more likely to reveal lasting deficits than simple measures of conditioning. Evidence is also beginning to mount that neurotoxic consequences of alcohol exposure during adolescence differ from, and in some circumstances are more pronounced than, effects seen after adult exposures.

EFFECTS OF ADOLESCENT ALCOHOL EXPOSURE ON LATER ALCOHOL INGESTION

In studies in laboratory animals, access to self-administered or experimenter-administered alcohol during adolescence has sometimes been associated with increases in later alcohol consumption, effects often found to be adolescent specific in instances where an adult exposure comparison group was included. For instance, alcohol-preferring (P) rats given 24-hour free access to ethanol in their home cages throughout adolescence later acquired an operant self-administration task for alcohol more quickly than controls and showed greater resistance to extinction, more spontaneous recovery, and elevated levels of responding during reacquisition of

the operant task (Rodd-Henricks et al., 2002a). None of these effects were evident when the initial alcohol access period was delayed until adulthood (Rodd-Henricks et al., 2002b). Likewise, mice receiving voluntary home cage access to alcohol from weaning through adolescence and into adulthood consumed more alcohol than mice whose alcohol access did not begin until adulthood (Ho, Chin, & Dole, 1989). Intermittent intraperitoneal administration of ethanol during early-mid adolescence has also been observed to increased later voluntary intake of ethanol in 2 bottle choice tests (Alaux-Cantin, Warnault, Legastelois, Botia, Pierrefiche, Volpoux & Naassila, 2013; Pandey, Sakharkar, Tang & Zhang, 2015), an effect that was not observed after equivalent exposure late in adolescence (Alaux-Cantin et al, 2013). Subsequent elevations in intake after adolescent alcohol exposure, however, are not always evident. For instance, no increases in ethanol consumption in adulthood were found in animals exposed as adolescents to alcohol vapor (Slawecki & Betancourt, 2002) or given voluntary, 24-hour home cage access to ethanol throughout adolescence and into adulthood relative to those whose ethanol access was delayed into adulthood (Tambour, Brown, & Crabbe, 2008; Vetter et al., 2007). Rats allowed to operantly self-administer alcohol during adolescence showed no increase in baseline operant responding for alcohol in adulthood, although they did show exacerbated dependence-related increases in operant intake when compared with animals who did not receive alcohol access as adolescents (Gilpin, Karanikas, & Richardson, 2012).

Variables that likely influence whether adolescent alcohol exposure alters later intake include sex, genetic background, amount and mode of alcohol exposure during adolescence, and how intake is assessed in adulthood (see Blizard, Vandenbergh, Jefferson, Chatlos, Vogler, & McClearn, 2004; Siciliano & Smith, 2001; Strong et al, 2010; Walker & Ehlers, 2009). For instance, notable test context specificity was reported by Pascual and colleagues (2009) in a study where repeated injections of alcohol during adolescence were found not to influence ethanol consumption and preference in intake tests conducted early in adulthood, whereas both measures were increased in later consumption tests conducted in these same animals after 1 week of forced alcohol consumption (where the only fluid provided to the rats was 10% ethanol). When groups of rats were either given access to sweetened alcohol or the sweetened solution alone periodically during adolescence, both groups increased their later consumption of only the solution to which they were exposed as adolescents, and not to the alternative solution, suggesting that in some cases increases in alcohol intake after adolescent alcohol exposure may reflect enhanced solution acceptability rather than an alcohol-specific effect (Broadwater, Varlinskaya, & Spear, 2013). Most studies to date have not included controls for this possibility.

Thus, although these data overall support the conclusion that under some conditions increases in later alcohol preference and consumption are seen following adolescent alcohol drinking, work remains to determine the constraints and circumstances under which these intake-enhancing effects emerge.

EFFECTS OF ADOLESCENT ALCOHOL EXPOSURE ON LATER RESPONSIVENESS TO ALCOHOL: POSSIBLE "LOCK-IN" EFFECTS?

In a number of studies, adolescent exposure to alcohol was found to block normal developmental changes in alcohol sensitivity, thereby retaining adolescent-typical alcohol sensitivities into adulthood (see Spear & Swartzwelder, 2014, for review). This retention of specific adolescent phenotypes into adulthood was termed "lock-in" by Swartzwelder and colleagues (Fleming, Acheson, Moore, Wilson, & Swartzwelder, 2012). For instance, the attenuated sensitivity adolescents normally show to the sedative effects of alcohol relative to adults has been reported to be maintained into young adulthood following adolescent exposure to alcohol (Matthews, Tinsley, Diaz-Granados, Tokunaga, & Silvers, 2008; Quoilin, Didone, Tirelli, & Quertemont, 2012; Silvers, Tokunaga, Mittleman, & Matthews, 2003). Similar results were seen with CTA, with the adolescent-typical attenuation in aversive consequences of alcohol maintained into adulthood following chronic exposure to alcohol during adolescence (Diaz-Granados & Graham, 2007; Graham & Diaz-Granados, 2006; Saalfield & Spear, 2015). Likewise, adolescent exposure to alcohol has been found to disrupt normal developmental increases in sensitivity to the motor-impairing effects of ethanol (White et al., 2002) as well as to the developmental *declines* in sensitivity to ethanol-induced deficits in spatial working memory that typically emerge between adolescence and adulthood (White et al., 2000). When adolescent exposures were compared with comparable exposures in adulthood, this retention of adolescent-like phenotypes into adulthood was generally found to be specific to adolescent exposures (Diaz-Granados & Graham, 2007;

Graham & Diaz-Granados, 2006; White et al., 2002). Adolescent exposure effects were also found to be especially notable after episodic rather than continuous ethanol exposure (e.g., Diaz-Granados & Graham, 2007). Episodic exposure may be especially effective due to the production of multiple withdrawal episodes, with adolescents, for example, found to be more sensitive than adults to the exacerbation in withdrawal signs that emerge over repeated withdrawals (Wills, Knapp, Overstreet, & Breese, 2008, 2009).

Instances of attenuated insensitivities to alcohol that persist into adulthood following adolescent alcohol exposure could represent in part the emergence of persistent chronic tolerance (pharmacodynamic or metabolic) to alcohol (e.g., see Silvers et al., 2003), although there has yet been little investigation of the extent to which tolerance contributes to these results. Certainly tolerance is unlikely to play a role in the retention into adulthood of greater adolescent alcohol sensitivities that are seen to certain alcohol effects, including adolescent-typical enhanced sensitivities to the memory-impairing effects of alcohol (White et al., 2000), as well as to alcohol's locomotor stimulant and rewarding effects (Maldonado-Devincci, Badanich, & Kirstein, 2010; Quoilin et al., 2012; Toalston, et al., 2014).

COGNITIVE AND OTHER FUNCTIONAL CONSEQUENCES OF ADOLESCENT ALCOHOL EXPOSURE

A number of cognitive deficits, particularly in tasks thought to reflect aspects of "executive functions" have been observed in adulthood following adolescent alcohol exposure (Crews, He, & Hodge, 2007), including reversal learning deficits (Coleman, He, Lee, Styner, & Crews, 2011), delays in extinction and set-shifting (Gass et al., 2014), along with performance impairments on conditional discrimination and object recognition tasks (Pascual, Blanco, Cauli, Minarro, & Guerri, 2007). Greater risk preferences on a probability discounting task (Boutros, Semenova, Liu, Crews, Markou, 2014; Nasrallah, Yang, & Bernstein, 2009) along with increases in impulsivity and greater disinhibition (Acheson, Bearison, Risher, Abdelwahab, Wilson, & Swartzwelder, 2013; Desikan, Wills & Ehlers, 2014; Gass et al, 2014; Nasrallah, Yang, & Bernstein, 2009) have also been reported. Later performance deficits after adolescent alcohol exposure have generally not emerged on less cognitively challenging tasks such as passive avoidance (Popović,

Caballero-Bleda, Puelles, & Guerri, 2004) and delay conditioning (Yttri et al., 2004) tasks, although adolescent alcohol exposure was found to disrupt later trace conditioning, a hippocampal-dependent task (Yttri et al., 2004). On other tasks requiring hippocampal activity such as spatial memory tasks, the data are more mixed, with relatively long-lasting deficits in spatial memory performance occasionally (Sircar & Sircar, 2005) but not always (Silvers et al., 2006; White et al., 2000) observed after adolescent alcohol exposure.

Alterations in affect measures have also been reported. Long-lasting increases in general and social anxiety have been reported after adolescent ethanol exposure by several laboratories (Pandey et al, 2015; Popović et al., 2004; Slawecki, Thorsell & Ehlers, 2004; Varlinskaya, Truxell & Spear, 2014), although these effects are not ubiquitous (Ehlers, Criado, Wills, Liu, & Crews, 2011; Gilpin et al., 2012; Quoilin et al., 2012; White et al., 2000). Indices of depressive-like behavior in rodents (greater immobility in a forced swim task; decreases in sucrose preference thought to reflect anhedonia) have also been reported (Ehlers et al., 2011; Slawecki et al, 2004).

LASTING EFFECTS OF ADOLESCENT ALCOHOL EXPOSURE ON THE BRAIN

Evidence for long-lasting alterations in neural function after repeated exposure to alcohol during adolescence is rapidly accumulating. Although comparable adult exposure groups have not always been included, in instances when they have been, more pronounced effects have often been reported following adolescent exposures. Among the notable effects of adolescent alcohol exposure is the induction of neuroinflammation (Pascual et al, 2007; Pascual, Pla, Miñarro & Guerri, 2014; Vetreno & Crews, 2012). Reductions in neurogenesis and regionally specific increases in brain damage and cell death in areas such as frontal cortex, hippocampus (HPC), and cerebellum have also been reported (Broadwater, Liu, Crews & Spear, 2014; Crews, Braun, Hoplight, Switzer, & Knapp, 2000; Ehlers, Liu, Wills & Crews, 2013; Nixon, Morris, Liput, & Kelso, 2010; Vetreno & Crews, 2015). Although alcohol exposure in adulthood can also likewise produce brain damage, maximally affected brain regions vary with age, with regionally specific effects that are often more pronounced and that collectively produce an overall greater net effect after alcohol exposure during adolescence than during equivalent exposures in adulthood (e.g., see

Crews et al., 2000). Similarly, lasting disruptions in neurogenesis and increases in cell death were reported after adolescent, but not adult alcohol exposures (Broadwater et al, 2014). Induction of neuroinflammation may prove critical for production of lasting neurobehavioral consequences of adolescent alcohol exposure given that administration of an anti-inflammatory agent (indomethacin) during the alcohol exposure period was found to block both the cell death and lasting behavioral deficits associated with adolescent alcohol (Pascual et al., 2007).

Exposure to alcohol during adolescence has also been shown to influence epigenetic regulation via altering histone acetylation (Pandey et al, 2015; Pascual, Boix, Felipo, & Guerri, 2009; Pascual, Do Couto, Alfonso-Loeches, Aguilar, Rodriguez-Arias, & Guerri, 2012). Global expression of whole-brain mRNA is decreased (Coleman et al., 2011) as well as expression of genes related to functioning of cholinergic and several other neurotransmitter systems (Coleman et al., 2011). A number of neurotransmitter systems appear vulnerable to adolescent alcohol exposure, with effects that include decreases in the number of basal forebrain cholinergic neurons (Boutros et al., 2014; Coleman et al., 2011; Ehlers et al., 2011; Vetreno, Broadwater, Liu, Crews, & Spear, 2014), altered expression of $GABA_A$ receptors in dentate gyrus (Fleming et al., 2012) and increases in their sensitivity to alcohol (Fleming et al., 2012), increases in NMDA receptor binding and in expression of the NR2B subunit of this receptor, and alterations in NR2B subunit phosphorylation (Pascual et al., 2009; Sircar & Sircar, 2006). DA projections to reward-critical regions undergoing developmental transformation during adolescence also appear to be targeted, with reports of downregulated DA DRD2 receptors and increases in basal DA extracellular levels (Badanich, Maldonado, & Kirstein, 2007; Pascual et al., 2009) or basal levels of DA neurotransmission (Sahr, Thielen, Lumeng, Li, & McBride, 2004), along with exacerbated (i.e., elevated and/or prolonged) DA responses to alcohol challenges (Pascual et al., 2009; Philpot, Wecker, & Kirstein, 2009; Sahr et al., 2004). Evidence for long-lasting alterations in brain activity after adolescent alcohol exposure have also been reported in terms of decreases in time spent in slow-wave sleep and reductions in the P3 component of evoked potentials (Ehlers & Criado, 2010), as well in the functioning of neurocircuitry (e.g., hypothalamic, limbic, and noradrenergic regions) involved in orchestrating hormonal stress responses (Allen, Rivier, & Lee, 2011; Gilpin et al., 2012; Wills, Knapp, Overstreet, & Breese, 2010).

The Impact of Chronic Nicotine Exposure During Adolescence on Later Neurobehavioral Function

There has been substantial work in laboratory animals showing that adolescent nicotine exposure induces a variety of lasting neural consequences. Although less emphasized in the work to date, behavioral alterations have also been reported, including increases in later nicotine self-administration. Neural outcomes of adolescent nicotine exposure have been compared not only with consequences of comparable exposures in adulthood but also during the fetal period, studies that have led to the conclusion that adolescence is a unique developmental "period of vulnerability for nicotine-induced misprogramming of brain cell development and synaptic function" (Slotkin, 2002, p. 369).

BEHAVIORAL ALTERATIONS, INCLUDING RESPONSE TO DRUG CHALLENGES

Other than a few studies reporting behavioral differences such as altered baseline levels of locomotor activity, anxiety-related behavior, and fear conditioning (indexed via passive avoidance) (Faraday, Elliott, & Grunberg, 2001; Slawecki, Gilder, Roth, & Ehlers, 2003; Slawecki, Thorsell, Khoury, Mathé, & Ehlers, 2005; Trauth, Seidler, & Slotkin, 2000), the primary behavioral focus of the limited number of behavioral studies of adolescent nicotine exposure in laboratory animals to date has been on later responsiveness to (and self-administration of) nicotine and other drugs. Animals chronically exposed to nicotine as adolescents failed to develop nicotine adaptations that were evident after chronic nicotine exposure in adulthood, with adolescent-exposed animals not showing the sensitization to nicotine-induced locomotor activity and the development of tolerance to nicotine-induced increases in corticosterone levels that were evident in animals chronically exposed to nicotine as adults (Cruz, DeLucia, & Planeta, 2005). When assessing responsiveness to acute challenge with other drugs, exposure to nicotine during adolescence was found to enhance sensitivity to the locomotor stimulant effects of methylphenidate (Nolley & Kelley, 2007) and the locomotor-suppressing effects of cannabinoids (Werling, Reed, Wade, & Izenwasser, 2009). In contrast, nicotine exposure in adolescence has been reported to attenuate responsiveness to the rewarding effects of methylphenidate (Nolley

& Kelley, 2007) and cocaine (Kelley & Middaugh, 1999) when indexed via CPP and to decrease the ability of animals to discriminate the subjective effects of cocaine (Kelley & Middaugh, 1999). In a number of these studies, comparable adult exposure groups were not included, making it difficult to know if the effects observed were specific to adolescent exposure. Indeed, in a study where animals were challenged with alcohol after repeated nicotine exposure either during adolescence or in adulthood, similar exposure-related attenuations in the aversive and hypothermic effects of alcohol were seen after exposure at either age (Rinker et al., 2011).

It is a well-known pharmacological principle that decreases in drug reward sensitivity are generally associated with compensatory increases in drug self-administration under relatively low workloads (see Koob & LeMoal, 2006). Hence, the attenuated sensitivity to the rewarding properties of drugs after adolescent nicotine exposure noted earlier could contribute to increases in self-administration of the drug (see Kelley & Middaugh, 1999). Indeed, female rats that began self-administering nicotine in adolescence were observed to self-administer more nicotine in adulthood than females whose initial access was delayed into adulthood; this enhancement after adolescent exposure was not evident, however, in males—even though the males self-administered more nicotine as adolescents than did females (Levin et al., 2003, 2007, 2011). The findings are mixed with respect to whether enhanced self-administration after adolescent exposure to nicotine is seen when self-administering other drugs, with one study reporting that adolescent self-administration of nicotine did not enhance later self-administration of cocaine (Levin et al., 2011), whereas another found elevated cocaine self-administration following prior experimenter-administered nicotine exposure in adolescence that was not evident following comparable exposure in adulthood (Dao, McQuown, Loughlin, Belluzzi, & Leslie, 2011).

NEURAL ALTERATIONS

Reported neurotoxic effects of adolescent nicotine exposure include persistent cell loss (indexed via DNA reductions) along with an enlargement of remaining cells (indicated via elevated protein/DNA ratios); these effects were particularly notable in cortical regions and were generally more pronounced than comparable exposures given in early adulthood (Abreu-Villaça, Seidler, Tate, & Slotkin, 2003). Nicotine exposure in adolescence was also found to induce persistent alterations in gene regulation in the ventral tegmental area (where DA cell bodies projecting to reward-relevant forebrain regions are located). These changes involved different genes and were considerably more extensive than following adult nicotine exposure, with adolescent-vulnerable expression changes associated with developmental processes, neural plasticity, and various other neural functions (Doura, Luu, Lee, & Perry, 2010). Other vulnerable targets influenced by adolescent nicotine exposure include cellular signaling pathways (Slotkin et al., 2008a) and functioning of DA (Collins, Wade, Ledon, & Izenwasser, 2004), cholinergic (e.g., Abreu-Villaça, Seidler, Qiao, et al., 2003; Slotkin et al., 2008b), serotonergic (Collins et al., 2004; Slotkin & Seidler, 2009), and cannabinoid (Werling et al., 2009) systems. In instances where adult comparison groups were included, observed alterations after adolescent exposures were often found to differ from (e.g., Collins et al., 2004; Werling et al., 2009) and be longer lasting than (e.g., see Slotkin, 2002) those seen following comparable exposures in adulthood. Among the brain regions found to be particularly vulnerable to the effects of nicotine exposure during adolescence are regions such as the nucleus accumbens, amygdala, HPC, and frontal cortex that contribute to the processing of rewards, stressful/emotional situations, and learning and memory (Bergstrom, Smith, Mollinedo, & McDonald, 2010; Dao et al., 2011; Slawecki et al., 2005) and that have been shown to undergo considerable ontogenetic change during adolescence (e.g., see Spear, 2010, for review).

Long-Term Effects of Adolescent Exposure to Cannabinoids

Some of the most extensively studied illicit substances in animal studies of adolescent drug exposure are cannabinoids, including THC and a variety of synthetic cannabinoids. Although findings to date are sometimes mixed and in need of further confirmation and extension, relatively long-lasting behavioral and neural alterations have been reported in a number of domains following cannabinoid exposure during adolescence (see Jager & Ramsey, 2008; Malone, Hill, & Rubino, 2010; Realini, Rubino, & Parolaro, 2009, for review). Where studied, these adolescent exposures were often found to produce effects of greater magnitude than those seen with comparable exposures in adulthood, along with some sex-specific effects (Viveros et al., 2012). Included among these measures are

those thought to reflect endophenotypes of schizophrenia (for review, see Malone et al., 2010), an emphasis driven by reports from human studies suggesting that adolescent cannabis exposure may be one factor contributing to increased risk for later emergence of schizophrenia (e.g., Semple, McIntosh, & Lawrie, 2005).

COGNITIVE DEFICITS

Deficits in object recognition memory after adolescent cannabinoid exposure in animal studies have often been found to be greater than after comparable exposure in adulthood (O'Shea, Singh, McGregor, & Mallet, 2004; Quinn et al., 2008; Schneider & Koch, 2003; Schneider, Schömig, & Leweke, 2008), although these effects are not ubiquitous (O'Shea, McGregor, & Mallet, 2006). Such disruptions in working memory after adolescent cannabinoid exposure are even more pronounced after early lesions of the medial PFC, findings reminiscent of the "double-hit" notion—that is, that separate developmental perturbations may interact or synergize to exacerbate risk for later disruptions (see Schneider & Koch, 2007). Deficits in working memory have also been reported on a spatial memory task after adolescent THC exposure (Rubino et al., 2009a,b), although studies by another group that included adult exposure groups as well found no lasting spatial or nonspatial working memory deficits following chronic THC exposure at either age (Cha, Jones, Kuhn, Wilson, & Swartzwelder, 2007; Cha, White, Kuhn, Wilson, & Swartzwelder, 2006). Information processing deficits were observed after adolescent cannabinoid exposure when indexed via reductions in prepulse inhibition (PPI; a reduction in startle to a loud tone when that tone is preceded by a brief, soft tone) (Schneider & Koch, 2003; Wegener & Koch, 2009); such deficits were not evident following similar cannabinoid exposure in adulthood (Schneider & Koch, 2003). Assessment of PPI is of particular interest given that impairments in this index of sensory gating are prototypic of schizophrenia and hence often used as an index of this disorder in animal models.

SOCIAL BEHAVIOR, ANXIETY, AND DEPRESSION

Suppressed levels of social behavior perhaps reflecting increases in social anxiety have been reported following adolescent exposure to cannabinoids (O'Shea et al., 2004, 2006; Schneider et al., 2008). In some (O'Shea et al., 2004; Schneider et al., 2008) but not all instances (O'Shea et al., 2006), this suppression of social behavior was specific to adolescent exposure and was not apparent in animals whose cannabinoid exposure was delayed until adulthood (O'Shea et al., 2004; Schneider et al., 2008). Deficits in social behavior after cannabinoid exposure during adolescence were exacerbated by neonatal lesions of the medial PFC, additional data supporting "double-hit" views of developmental psychopathology (Schneider & Koch, 2005).

In contrast to the increased anxiety seen following adolescent cannabinoid exposure when indexed via suppression of social interactions, some studies have reported reduced anxiety when using nonsocial tests of anxiety (e.g., Biscaia et al., 2003; O'Shea et al. 2006; Wegener & Koch, 2009), along with some sex-specific effects (e.g., Biscaia et al., 2003). For instance, when using the elevated plus maze (EPM) to index anxiety via amount of time spent on (anxiety-provoking) open arms relative to the more protected closed arms, adult rats exposed to cannabinoids during adolescence have been found to be either less anxious than (Biscaia et al., 2003; Wegener & Koch, 2009) or not to differ from (Higuera-Matas et al., 2008; Rubino et al., 2008) their nonexposed counterparts. Sex-specific effects of adolescent cannabinoid exposure were found in the hole board test, with adolescent exposed females (but not males) showing greater activity and exploration, consistent with a reduced anxiety profile (Biscaia et al., 2003). Measures typically interpreted as reduced anxiety in these tests sometimes have been suggested to reflect a profile of "disinhibition" (for instance, see Desikan et al., 2014, and Gass et al., 2014, for examples with adolescent alcohol exposure).

Adolescent cannabinoid exposure has also been reported to induce signs of depression or behavioral "despair" when indexed via measures such as increased immobility in forced swim testing or via a reduced preference for sucrose (often used as an index of anhedonia) (Bambico, Nguyen, & Gobbi, 2010; Realini et al., 2011; Rubino et al., 2008). Some sex specificity again was evident, with adolescent cannabinoid-exposed females showing elevations in depression indices that were not apparent in males (Rubino et al., 2008). In work comparing adolescent with adult exposures, signs of "despair" were found to be specific to cannabinoid exposures during adolescence (Bambico et al., 2010).

LATER DRUG SELF-ADMINISTRATION

A few studies have used animal models to assess whether cannabinoids may serve as a "gateway drug"—that is, whether adolescent exposure to these substances would increase later propensity to use and abuse other illicit drugs. The results of these studies in general have found increases in self-administration of cocaine and opiates such as heroin and morphine in adults that had been exposed to cannabinoids during adolescence, although the effects observed were sometimes dependent on the subject's sex and on the specific self-administration test procedures (e.g., Biscaia et al., 2008; Ellgren, Spano, & Hurd, 2007; Higuera-Matas et al., 2008). For example, morphine self-administration was increased in male but not female rats after adolescent cannabinoid exposure when tested under low operant demands (a fixed ratio 1 [FR1] schedule where every response was rewarded with drug infusion) but not when animals had to work progressively harder to attain successive self-administrations (a progressive ratio [PR] schedule; Biscaia et al., 2008). It remains to be determined whether the enhancements of later drug self-administration seen after prior cannabinoid exposure are specific to experience with the drug during adolescence or whether similar effects would emerge after comparable exposures in adulthood.

NEURAL ALTERATIONS

Cannabinoid exposure during adolescence has been associated with alterations in the amygdala, PFC, HPC, nucleus accumbens, and other frontal brain regions that are critical for social/emotional responding, drug self-administration, information processing, working memory, and other aspects of cognition. Much remains to be discovered, however, regarding the relationship between specific behavioral consequences of adolescent cannabinoid exposure and their neural underpinnings.

Adolescent cannabinoid exposure has been linked to signs of compromised synaptic efficiency in PFC (when indexed via decreases in several critical synaptic proteins and in synaptic levels of proteins involved in energy metabolism—Rubino et al., 2009a) and in HPC (when indexed via measures such as decreases in numbers of dendrites and dendritic spines—Rubino et al., 2009b). Adolescent cannabinoid exposure has also been reported to disrupt the regulation of transcription factors induced by DA manipulations in amygdala, as well as to alter expression of transcription factors and opiate and cannabinoid system signaling cascades in DA terminal regions such as the nucleus accumbens (Ellgren et al., 2008; Rubino et al., 2008; Wegener & Koch, 2009). It largely remains to be determined, however, whether the adolescent brain is particularly susceptible to lasting neural consequences of chronic cannabinoid exposure, with most studies to date focused only on consequences of adolescent exposures. The few studies that have compared exposure periods are mixed, with, for instance, one study reporting that adolescent cannabinoid exposure induced more pronounced alterations in HPC protein expression than adult exposure (Quinn et al., 2008), whereas another conversely observed that repeated exposure to cannabinoids during adulthood but not in adolescence altered DA receptor densities in a number of forebrain DA terminal regions (Dalton & Zavitsanou, 2010).

Summary: Long-Term Consequences of Adolescent Drug Exposures

Although work in this area is limited, convincing data are beginning to emerge that exposure to drugs such as alcohol, nicotine, and cannabinoids during adolescence can exert relatively long-lasting alterations in later behavioral and neural functioning in neurocircuitry involved in reward and socioemotional processing, an in modulating more complex cognitive functions. Drug experience during adolescence has also been found under some conditions to increase later self-administration of that drug (or in the case of cannabinoids, other drugs of abuse), although increases are not seen under all circumstances. At this early stage of research in this area, however, significant numbers of the studies have only assessed consequences of adolescent exposures, thereby limiting the extent to which it can be concluded that adolescence is a vulnerable period for producing these consequences. Although dosing regimens have often been chosen to produce drug levels in the body that are roughly comparable to those seen with high-end human use, across-species comparability of exposure frequency, duration, and route is often less clear. While the effects discussed have been shown to persist for some time (days or weeks) following termination of the adolescent drug exposure, the long-term chronicity of effects is also largely unexplored territory. Reliable findings tend to be clustered within and across drugs, with, for example, alterations in DA systems and other reward system components commonly reported after adolescent exposure to each of the drugs reviewed. Other reliably observed effects appear somewhat drug specific (e.g., disruptions in tests thought to reflect endophenotypes of schizophrenia have been particularly reported after adolescent cannabinoid exposure). Whether such clustered and drug-specific effects are meaningful and reflect specific age- or drug-related vulnerabilities, or whether they merely represent areas where research has focused to date is unclear. Thus, while evidence is mounting that adolescent exposure to alcohol, nicotine, and cannabinoids can induce neurobehavioral toxicity, work remains to detail the nature and prevalence of these alterations as well as their underlying mechanisms, specificity for adolescent exposures, and usefulness in predicting and confirming findings obtained in studies of drug-abusing human adolescents.

Conclusion

Adolescence is being increasingly viewed as a time of enhanced brain plasticity—that is, a period hypothesized to be characterized by experience-related brain sculpting, with associated age-related vulnerabilities and opportunities (see Dahl & Spear, 2004; Spear, 2010, for discussion). Adolescent initiation of drug use may be facilitated by neural changes that influence their sensitivity to various drug effects in ways that promote use and abuse, with such drug exposure perhaps serving as one major type of experience-related event that could influence the brain sculpting of adolescence. Indeed, many neural systems that play important roles in developmental processes undergo change during adolescence, including cannabinoid, DA, cholinergic, GABA, and NMDA systems in brain regions such as the nucleus accumbens, PFC and amygdala. Alterations in activity of these systems induced by repeated drug use during adolescence may disrupt normal system maturation, with resultant long-term consequences for brain function and behavior. Particularly likely targets for long-term effects include disruptions in systems underlying normal developmental shifts in sensitivity to drug rewards and aversions between adolescence and adulthood, perhaps increasing probability of developing lasting problems with drug use and drug abuse that persist beyond adolescent drug use into adulthood. Evidence for adolescent drug exposures altering neurodevelopmental processes related to socioemotional functions and more advanced aspects of cognitive functioning is also mounting. Although still in its early stages, research using animal models to examine factors contributing to and consequences of adolescent drug use and abuse has uncovered initial evidence that adolescent drug exposures can influence sculpting of the adolescent brain, thereby exerting effects that long outlast adolescence.

Future Directions

Many questions require future study:

• What are the neural mechanisms underlying the enhanced reward and attenuated aversive sensitivities that adolescents often show to drugs and other substances, and to what extent does this reward/aversion bias contribute to the often enhanced drug self-administration shown by adolescents?

• To what extent does adolescent exposure to alcohol, nicotine, cannabinoids, and other drugs lead to lasting behavioral and cognitive consequences, and what are the similarities and differences in these effects across drugs?

• What are the neural mechanisms underlying the behavioral and cognitive consequences of adolescent drug exposures?

• Can lasting functional consequences of adolescent drug exposures be prevented or reversed by blocking drug-induced neural alterations?

• How reliable is the "stamping-in" effect with alcohol, what are its underlying mechanisms, and to what extent does adolescent exposure to other drugs induce a similar retention of immature, adolescent-typical drug sensitivities into adulthood?

• To what extent are consequences of adolescent exposure to drugs specific to exposure during adolescence and not evident following exposure in adulthood or at some other age?

• As data from human studies and using animal models of adolescence continue to accumulate, how effective will the animal data be in predicting findings obtained in substance-abusing human adolescents (i.e., what is the predictive validity of animal models of adolescence substance use/abuse)?

References

Aberg, M., Wade, D., Wall, E., & Izenwasser, S. (2007). Effect of MDMA (ecstasy) on activity and cocaine conditioned place preference in adult and adolescent rats. *Neurotoxicology and Teratology, 29*, 37–46.

Abreu-Villaça, Y., Seidler, F. J., Qiao, D., Tate, C. A., Cousins, M. M., Thillai, I., & Slotkin, T. A. (2003). Short-term adolescent nicotine exposure has immediate and persistent effects on cholinergic systems: Critical periods, patterns of exposure, dose thresholds. *Neuropsychopharmacology, 28*(11), 1935–1949.

Abreu-Villaça, Y., Seidler, F. J., Tate, C. A., & Slotkin, T. A. (2003). Nicotine is a neurotoxin in the adolescent brain: Critical periods, patterns of exposure, regional selectivity, and dose thresholds for macromolecular alterations. *Brain Research, 979*(1–2), 114–128.

Acheson, S., Stein, R., & Swartzwelder, H. S. (1998). Impairment of semantic and figural memory by acute alcohol: Age-dependent effects. *Alcoholism: Clinical and Experimental Research, 22*, 1437–1442.

Acheson, S. K., Bearison, C., Risher, M. L., Abdelwahab, S. H., Wilson, W. A., & Swartzwelder, H. S. (2013). Effects of acute or chronic ethanol exposure during adolescence on behavioral inhibition and efficiency in a modified water maze task. *PloS One, 8*(10), e77768.

Adams, J., Barone, S., Jr., LaMantia, A., Philen, R., Rice, D. C., Spear, L., & Susser, E. (2000). Workshop to identify critical windows of exposure for children's health: Neurobehavioral work group summary. *Environmental Health Perspectives, 108*, 535–544.

Allen, C., Rivier, C., & Lee, S. (2011). Adolescent alcohol exposure alters the central brain circuits known to regulate the stress response. *Neuroscience, 182*(19), 162–168.

Alaux-Cantin, S., Warnault, V., Legastelois, R., Botia, B., Pierrefiche, O., Vilpoux, C., & Naassila, M. (2013). Alcohol intoxications during adolescence increase motivation for alcohol in adult rats and induce neuroadaptations in the nucleus accumbens. *Neuropharmacology, 67*, 521–531.

Anderson, R. I., & Spear, L. P. (2011). Autoshaping in adolescence enhances sign-tracking behavior in adulthood: Impact on ethanol consumption. *Pharmacology, Biochemistry and Behavior, 98*, 250–260.

Anderson, R. L., & Spear, L. P. (2013). Age differences in ethanol discrimination: acquisition and ethanol dose generalization curves following multiple training conditions in adolescent and adult rats. *Alcoholism: Clinical and Experimental Research, 38*(1), 186–194.

Anderson, R. I., Varlinskaya, E. I., & Spear, L. P. (2010). Ethanol-induced conditioned taste aversion in male Sprague-Dawley rats: Impact of age and stress. *Alcoholism: Clinical and Experimental Research, 34*(12), 2106–2115.

Badanich, K. A., Adler, K. J., & Kirstein, C. L. (2006). Adolescents differ from adults in cocaine conditioned place preference and cocaine-induced dopamine in the nucleus accumbens septi. *European Journal of Pharmacology, 550*, 95–106.

Badanich, K., Maldonado, A., & Kirstein, C. (2007). Chronic ethanol exposure during adolescence increases basal dopamine in the nucleus accumbens septi during adulthood. *Alcoholism: Clinical and Experimental Research, 31*(5), 895–900.

Bambico, F. R., Nguyen, N. T., & Gobbi, G. (2010). Chronic exposure to cannabinoids during adolescence but not during adulthood impairs emotional behavior and monoaminergic neurotransmission. *Neurobiological Diseasem, 37*(3), 641–655.

Beck, K. H., Thombs, D. L., & Summons, T. G. (1993). The social context of drinking scales: Construct validation and relationship to indicants of abuse in an adolescent population. *Addictive Behaviors, 18*(2), 159–169.

Behar, D., Berg, C. J., Rapoport, J. L., Nelson, W., Linnoila, M., Cohen, M., . . . Marshall, T. (1983). Behavioral and physiological effects of ethanol in high-risk and control children: A pilot study. *Alcoholism: Clinical and Experimental Research, 7*(4), 404–410.

Bell, R. L., Rodd, Z. A., Sable, H. J. K., Schultz, J. A., Hsu, C. C., Lumeng, L., . . . McBride, W. J. (2006). Daily patterns of ethanol drinking in peri-adolescent and adult alcohol-preferring (P) rats. *Pharmacology, Biochemistry and Behavior, 83*(1), 35–46.

Belluzzi, J. D., Lee, A. G., Oliff, H. S., & Leslie, F. M. (2004). Age-dependent effects of nicotine on locomotor activity and conditioned place preference in rats. *Psychopharmacology*, *174*(3), 389–395.

Belluzzi, J., Wang, R., & Leslie, F. (2005). Acetaldehyde enhances acquisition of nicotine self-administration in adolescent rats. *Neuropsychopharmacology*, *30*, 705–712.

Bergstrom, H., Smith, R., Mollinedo, N., & McDonald, C. (2010). Chronic nicotine exposure produces lateralized, age-dependent dendritic remodeling in the rodent basolateral amygdala. *Synapse*, *64*(10), 754–764.

Berridge, K. C. (2007). The debate over dopamine's role in reward: The case for incentive salience. *Psychopharmacology*, *191*(3), 391–431.

Berridge, K. C., & Robinson, T. E. (2003). Parsing reward. *Trends in Neurosciences*, *26*(9), 507–513.

Biscaia, M., Fernández, B., Higuera-Matas, A., Miguéns, M., Viveros, M., Garcia-Lecumberri, C., & Ambrosio, E. (2008). Sex-dependent effects of periadolescent exposure to the cannabinoid agonist CP-55, 94- on morphine self-administration behaviour and the endogenous opioid system. *Neuropharmacology*, *54*(5), 863–873.

Biscaia, M., Marín, S., Fernández, B., Marco, E., Rubio, M., Guaza, C., . . . Viverso, M. P. (2003). Chronic treatment with CP 55,940 during the peri-adolescent period differentially affects the behavioural responses of male and female rats in adulthood. *Psychopharmacology*, *170*, 301–308.

Bjork, J. M., Knutson, B., Fong, G. W., Caggiano, D. M., Bennett, S. M., & Hommer, D. W. (2004). Incentive-elicited brain activation in adolescents: Similarities and differences from young adults. *Journal of Neuroscience*, *24*(8), 1793–1802.

Blizard, D., Vandenbergh, D., Jefferson, A., Chatlos, C., Vogler, G., & McClearn, G. (2004). Effects of periadolescent ethanol exposure on alcohol preference in two BALB substrains. *Alcohol*, *34*(2–3), 177–185.

Bogin, B. (1994). Adoleslcence in evolutionary perspective. *Acta Paediatrica*, *406*(Suppl.), 29–35.

Boileau, I., Assaad, J., Pihl, R., Benkelfat, C., Leyton, M., Diksic, M., . . . Dagher, A. (2003). Alcohol promotes dopamine release in the human nucleus accumbens. *Synapse*, *49*(4), 226–231.

Boutros, N., Semenova, S., Liu, W., Crews, F. T., & Markou, A. (2014). Adolescent intermittent ethanol exposure is associated with increased risky choice and decreased dopaminergic and cholinergic neuron markers in adult rats. *International Journal of Neuropsychopharmacology*, *18*(2). 10.1083/ijnp/pyu003.

Brasser, S. M., & Spear, N. E. (2002). Physiological and behavioral effects of acute ethanol hangover in juvenile, adolescent, and adult rats. *Behavioral Neuroscience*, *116*(2), 305–320.

Brenhouse, H. C., & Andersen, S. L. (2008). Delayed extinction and stronger reinstatement of cocaine conditioned place preference in adolescent rats, compared to adults. *Behavioral Neuroscience*, *122*(2), 460–465.

Brenhouse, H. C., Sonntag, K. C., & Andersen, S. L. (2008). Transient D1 Dopamine receptor expression on prefrontal cortex projection neurons: Relationship to enhanced motivational salience of drug cues in adolescence. *Journal of Neuroscience*, *28*(10), 2375–2382.

Brielmaier, J., McDonald, C., & Smith, A. (2007). Immediate and long-term behavioral effects of a single nicotine injection in adolescent and adult rats. *Neurotoxicology and Teratology*, *29*(1), 74–80.

Broadwater, M. A., Varlinskaya, E. I., & Spear, L. P. (2013). Effects of voluntary access to sweetened ethanol during adolescence on intake in adulthood. *Alcoholism: Clinical and Expeirmental Research*, *37*(6), 1048–1055.

Broadwater, M. A., Liu, W., Crews, F. T. & Spear, L. P. (2014). Persistent loss of hippocampal neurogenesis and increased cell death following adolescent, but not adult, chronic ethanol exposure. *Developmental Neuroscience*, *36*(3–4), 297–305.

Brunell, S. C., & Spear, L. P. (2005). Effect of stress on the voluntary intake of a sweetened ethanol solution in paired-house adolescent and adult rats. *Alcoholism: Clinical and Experimental Research*, *29*(9), 1641–1653.

Campbell, J. O., Bliven, T. D., Silveri, M. M., Snyder, K. J., & Spear, L. P. (2000). Effects of prenatal cocaine on behavioral adaptation to chronic stress in adult rats. *Neurotoxicology and Teratology*, *22*(6), 845–850.

Casey, B. J., & Jones, R. M. (2010). Neurobiology of the adolescent brain and behavior: Implications for substance use disorders. *Journal of the American Academy of Child and Adolescent Psychiatry*, *49*(12), 1189–1201.

Cha, Y., Jones, K., Kuhn, C., Wilson, W., & Swartzwelder, H. (2007). Sex differences in the effects of delta9-tetrahydrocannabinol on spatial learning in adolescent and adult rats. *Behavioural Pharmacology*, *18*(5–6), 563–569.

Cha, Y. M., White, A. M., Kuhn, C. M., Wilson, W. A., & Swartzwelder, H. S. (2006). Differential effects of delta9-THC on learning in adolescent and adult rats. *Pharmacology, Biochemistry and Behavior*, *83*(3), 448–455.

Chen, H., Matta, S., & Sharp, B. (2007). Acquisition of nicotine self-administration in adolescent rats given prolonged access to the drug. *Neuropsychopharmacology*, *32*, 700–709.

Clark, D. B., Kirisci, L., & Tarter, R. E. (1998). Adolescent versus adult onset and the development of substance use disorders in males. *Drug and Alcohol Dependence*, *49*, 115–121.

Cohen, J. R., Asarnow, R. F., Sabb, F. W., Bilder, R. M., Bookheimer, S. Y., Knowlton, B. J., & Poldrack, R. A. (2010). A unique adolescent response to reward prediction errors. *Nature Neuroscience*, *13*(6), 669–671.

Colby, S. M., Tiffany, S. T., Shiffman, S., & Niaura, R. S. (2000). Are adolescent smokers dependent on nicotine? A review of the evidence. *Drug and Alcohol Dependence*, *59*(Suppl. 1), S83–S95.

Collins, S., Wade, D., Ledon, J., & Izenwasser, S. (2004). Neurochemical alterations reduced by daily nicotine exposure in periadolescent vs. adult male rats. *European Journal of Pharmacology*, *502*, 75–85.

Coleman, L. G., Jr., He, J., Lee, J., Styner, M., & Crews, F. (2011). Adolescent binge drinking alters adult brain neurotransmitter gene expression, behavior, brain regional volumes, and neurochemistry in mice. *Alcoholism: Clinical and Experimental Research*, *35*(4), 671–688.

Conrod, P. J., Pihl, R., & Vassileva, J. (1998). Differential sensitivity to alcohol reinforcement in groups of men at risk for distinct alcoholism subtypes. *Alcoholism: Clinical and Experimental Research*, *22*(3), 585–597.

Crews, F. T., Braun, C. J., Hoplight, B., Switzer, R. C., III, & Knapp, D. J. (2000). Binge ethanol consumption causes differential brain damage in young adolescent rats compared with adult rats. *Alcoholism: Clinical and Experimental Research*, *24*(11), 1712–1723.

Crews, F., He, J., & Hodge, C. (2007). Adolescent cortical development: A critical period of vulnerability for addiction. *Pharmacology, Biochemistry and Behavior*, *86*(2), 189–199.

Cruz, F., DeLucia, R., & Planeta, C. (2005). Differential behavioral and neuroendocrine effects of repeated nicotine in adolescent and adult rats. *Pharmacology, Biochemistry and Behavior, 80*, 411–417.

Dahl, R., & Spear, L. P. (2004). Adolescent brain development: Vulnerabilities and opportunities. *Annals of the New York Adaemy of Sciences, 1021, 1–22.*

Dalton, V., & Zavitsanou, K. (2010). Differential treatment regimen-related effects of cannabinoids on D1 and D2 receptors in adolescent and adult rat brain. *Journal of Chemical Neuroanatomy, 40*(4), 272–280.

Dao, J., McQuown, S., Loughlin, S., Belluzzi, J., & Leslie, F. (2011). Nicotine alters limbic function in adolescent rat by a 5 -HT1A receptor mechanism. *Neuropsychopharmacology, 36*(7), 1319–1331.

Desikan, A., Wills, D. N., & Ehlers, C. L. (2014). Ontogeny and adolescent alcohol exposure in Wistar rats: open field conflict, light/dark box and forced swim test. *Pharmacology, Biochemistry and Behavior, 122*, 279–285.

Diaz-Granados, J. L., & Graham, D. (2007). The effects of continuous and intermittent ethanol exposure in adolescence on the aversive properties of ethanol during adulthood. *Alcoholism: Clinical and Experimental Research, 31*(12), 2020–2027.

Dickinson, S. D., Kashawny, S. K., Thiebes, K. P., & Charles, D. Y. (2009). Decreased sensitivity to ethanol reward in adolescent mice as measured by conditioned place preference. *Alcoholism: Clinical and Experimental Research, 33*(7), 1–6.

Doherty, J., & Frantz, K. (2012). Heroin self-administration and reinstatement of heroin-seeking in adolescent vs. adult male rats. *Psychopharmacology, 219*(3), 763–773.

Doremus, T. L., Brunell, S. C., Rajendran, P., & Spear, L. P. (2005). Factors influencing elevated ethanol consumption in adolescent relative to adult rats. *Alcoholism: Clinical and Experimental Research, 29*(10), 1796–1808.

Doremus-Fitzwater, T. L., & Spear, L. P. (2007). Developmental differences in acute ethanol withdrawal in adolescent and adult rats. *Alcoholism: Clinical and Experimental Research, 31*(9), 1–12.

Doremus-Fitzwater, T. L., & Spear, L. P. (2011). Amphetamine-induced incentive sensitization of sign-tracking behavior in adolescent and adult female rats. *Behavioral Neuroscience, 125*(4), 661–667.

Doremus-Fitzwater, T. L., Varlinskaya, E. I., & Spear, L. P. (2010). Motivational systems in adolescence: Possible implications for age differences in substance abuse and other risk-taking behaviors. *Brain and Cognition, 72*, 114–123.

Douglas, L. A., Varlinskaya, E. I., & Spear, L. P. (2003). Novel object place conditioning in adolescent and adult male and female rats: Effects of social isolation. *Physiology and Behavior, 80*, 317–325.

Douglas, L. A., Varlinskaya, E. I., & Spear, L. P. (2004). Rewarding properties of social interactions in adolescent and adult male and female rats: Impact of social versus isolate housing of subjects and partners. *Developmental Psychobiology, 45*, 153–162.

Doura, M., Luu, T., Lee, N., & Perry, D. (2010). Persistent gene expression changes in ventral tegmental area of adolescent but not adult rats in response to chronic nicotine. *Neuroscience, 170*(2), 503–513.

Ehlers, C., & Criado, J. (2010). Adolescent ethanol exposure: Does it produce long-lasting electrophysiological effects? *Alcohol, 44*(1), 27–37.

Ehlers, C., Criado, J., Wills, D., Liu, W., & Crews, F. (2011). Periadolescent ethanol exposure reduces adult forebrain ChAT+IR neurons: Correlation with behavioral pathology. *Neuroscience, 29*(199), 333–345.

Ehlers, C. L., Liu, W., Wills, D. M. & Crews, F. T. (2013). Periadolescent ethanol vapor exposure persistently reduces measures of hippocampal neurogenesis that are associated with behavioral outcomes in adulthood. *Neuroscience, 244*, 1–15.

Eissenberg, T., & Balster, R. (2000). Initial tobacco use episodes in children and adolescents: Current knowledge, future directions. *Drug and Alcohol Dependence, 59*(Suppl. 1), S41–S60.

Ellgren, M., Artmann, A., Tkalych, O., Gupta, A., Hansen, H. S., Hansen, S. H., . . . Hurd, Y. L. (2008). Dynamic changes of the endogenous cannabinoid and opioid mesocorticolimbic systems during adolescence: THC effects. *European Neuropsychopharmacology, 18*(11), 826–834.

Ellgren, M., Spano, S., & Hurd, Y. (2007). Adolescent cannabis exposure alters opiate intake and opioid limbic neuronal populations in adult rats. *Neuropsychopharmacology, 32*(3), 607–615.

Ernst, M., & Fudge, J. L. (2009). A developmental neurobiological model of motivated behavior: Anatomy, connectivity and ontogeny of the triadic nodes. *Neuroscience and Biobehavioral Reviews, 33*, 367–382.

Ernst, M., Nelson, E. E., Jazbec, S., McClure, E. B., Monk, C. S., Leibenluft, E., . . . Pine, D. S. (2005). Amygdala and nucleus accumbens in responses to receipt and omission of gains in adults and adolescents. *NeuroImage, 25*(4), 1279–1291.

Faraday, M. M., Elliott, B. M., & Grunberg, N. E. (2001). Adult vs. adolescent rats differ in biobehavioral responses to chronic nicotine administration. *Pharmacology, Biochemistry and Behavior, 70*(4), 475–489.

Fitch, T. E., & Roberts, D. C. S. (1993). The effects of dose and access restrictions on the periodicity of cocaine self-administration in the rat. *Drug and Alcohol Dependence, 33*, 119–128.

Fleming, R., Acheson, S., Moore, S., Wilson, W., & Swartzwelder, H. (2012). In the rat, chronic intermittent ethanol exposure during adolescence alters the ethanol sensitivity of tonic inhibition in adulthood. *Alcoholism: Clinical and Experimental Research, 36*(2), 279–285.

Frantz, K. J., O'Dell, L. E., & Parsons, L. H. (2007). Behavioral and neurochemical responses to cocaine in periadolescent and adult rats. *Neuropsychopharmacologoy, 32*, 625–637.

Galvan, A., Hare, T. A., Parra, C. E., Penn, J., Voss, H., Glover, G., & Casey, B. J. (2006). Earlier development of the accumbens relative to oribitofrontal cortex might underlie risk-taking behavior in adolescents. *Journal of Neuroscience, 26*(25), 6885–6892.

Gardner, E. (2011). Addiction and brain reward and antireward pathways. *Advances in Psychosomatic Medicine, 30*, 22–60.

Gass, J. T., Glen, W. B. Jr., McGonigal, J. T., Trantam-Davidson, H., Lopez, M. F., Randall, P. K., . . . Chandler, L. J. (2014). Adolescent alcohol exposure reduces behavioral flexibility, promotes disinhibition, and increases resistance to extinction of ethanol self-administration in adulthood. *Neuropsychopharmacology, 39*(11), 2570–2583.

Geier, C. F., Terwilliger, R., Teslovich, T., Velanova, K., & Luna, B. (2010). Immaturities in reward processing and its influence on inhibitory control in adolescence. *Cerebral Cortex, 20*, 1613–1629.

Gilpin, N. W., Karanikas, C. A., & Richardson, H. N. (2012). Adolescent binge drinking leads to changes in alcohol drinking, anxiety, and amygdalar corticotrophin releasing factor cells in adulthood in male rats. *PLoS One, 7*(2), 1–12.

Graham, D. L., & Diaz-Granados, J. L. (2006). Periadolescent exposure to ethanol and diazepam alters the aversive properties of ethanol in adult mice. *Pharmacology, Biochemistry and Behavior, 84*(3), 406–414.

Hargreaves, G., Monds, L., Gunasekaran, N., Dawson, B., & McGregor, I. (2009). Intermittent access to beer promotes binge-like drinking in adolescent but not adult Wistar rats. *Alcohol, 43*(4), 305–314.

Harvey, R., Dembro, K., Rajagopalan, K., Mutebi, M., & Kantak, K. (2009). Effects of self-administered cocaine in adolescent and adult male rats on orbitofrontal cortex-related neurocognitive functioning. *Psychopharmacology (Berlin), 206*(1), 61–71.

Higuera-Matas, A., Soto-Montenegro, M., del Olmo, N., Miguéns, M., Torres, I., Vaquero, J., . . . Ambrosio, E. (2008). Augmented acquisition of cocaine self-administration and altered brain glucose metabolism in adult female but not male rats exposed to a cannabinoid agonist during adolescence. *Neuropsychopharmacology, 33*(4), 806–813.

Ho, A., Chin, A. J., & Dole, V. P. (1989). Early experience and the consumption of alcohol by adult C57BL/6J mice. *Alcohol, 6*, 511–515.

Hollstedt, C., Olsson, O., & Rydberg, U. (1977). The effect of alcohol on the developing organism: Genetical, teratological and physiological aspects. *Medical Biology, 55*(1), 1–14.

Infurna, R. N., & Spear, L. P. (1979). Developmental changes in amphetamine-induced taste aversions. *Pharmacology, Biochemistry and Behavior, 11*(1), 31–35.

Jager, G., & Ramsey, N. (2008). Long-term consequences of adolescent cannabis exposure on the development of cognition, brain structure and function: An overview of animal and human research. *Current Drug Abuse Reviews, 1*, 114–123.

Kelley, B., & Middaugh, L. (1999). Periadolescent nicotine exposure reduces cocaine reward in adult mice. *Journal of Addictive Diseases, 18*(3), 27–39.

Kelly, S., Bonthius, D., & West, J. (1987). Developmental changes in alcohol pharmacokinetics in rats. *Alcoholism: Clinical and Experimental Research, 11*(3), 281–286.

Kerstetter, K. A., & Kantak, K. M. (2007). Differential effects of self-administered cocaine in adolescent and adult rats on stimulus-reward learning. *Psychopharmacology, 194*, 403–411.

Koob, G. F., & Le Moal, M. (2006). *Neurobiology of addiction.* San Diego, CA: Elsevier.

Levin, E. D., Lawrence, S., Petro, A., Horton, K., Rezvani, A., Seidler, F., & Slotkin, T. A. (2007). Adolescent vs. adult-onset nicotine self-administration in male rats: Duration of effect and differential nicotinic receptor correlates. *Neurotoxicology and Teratology, 29*(4), 458–465.

Levin, E. D., Rezvani, A. H., Montoya, D., Rose, J. E., & Swartzwelder, H. S. (2003). Adolescent-onset nicotine self-administration modeled in female rats. *Psychopharmacology, 169*(2), 141–149.

Levin, E. D., Slade, S., Wells, C., Cauley, M., Petro, A., Vendittelli, A., . . . Rezvani, A. H. (2011). Threshold of adulthood for the onset of nicotine self-administration in male and female rats. *Behavioural Brain Research, 225*, 473–481.

Li, C., & Frantz, K. (2009). Attenuated incubation of cocaine seeking in male rats trained to self-administer cocaine during periadolescence. *Psychopharmacology (Berlin), 204*(4), 725–733.

Little, P. J., Kuhn, C. M., Wilson, W. A., & Swartzwelder, H. S. (1996). Differential effects of ethanol in adolescent and adult rats. *Alcoholism: Clinical and Experimental Research, 20*(8), 1346–1351.

Maldonado-Devincci, A. M., Badanich, K. A., & Kirstein, C. L. (2010). Alcohol during adolescence selectively alters immediate and long-term behavior and neurochemistry. *Alcohol, 44*, 57–66.

Malone, D., Hill, M., & Rubino, T. (2010). Adolescent cannabis use and psychosis: Epidemiology and neurodevelopmental models. *British Journal of Pharmacology, 60*, 511–522.

Markwiese, B. J., Acheson, S. K., Levin, E. D., Wilson, W. A., & Swartzwelder, H. S. (1998). Differential effects of ethanol on memory in adolescent and adult rats. *Alcoholism: Clinical and Experimental Research, 22*(2), 416–421.

Matthews, D. B., Tinsley, K. L., Diaz-Granados, J. L., Tokunaga, S., & Silvers, J. M. (2008). Chronic intermittent exposure to ethanol during adoloescence produces tolerance to the hypnotic effects of ethanol in male rats: A dose-dependent analysis. *Alcohol, 42*(8), 617–621.

Mellanby, J. (1919). The influence of the nervous system on glycaemia and glycosuria. *Journal of Physiology, 53*(1–2), 1–16.

Moy, S. S., Duncan, G. E., Knapp, D. J., & Breese, G. R. (1998). Sensitivity to ethanol across development in rats: Comparison to [3H] zolpidem binding. *Alcoholism: Clinical and Experimental Research, 22*(7), 1485–1492.

Nasrallah, N., Yang, T., & Bernstein, I. (2009). Long-term risk preference and suboptimal decision making following adolescent alcohol use. *Proceedings of the National Academy of Sciences USA, 106*(41), 17600–17604.

Nixon, K., Morris, S., Liput, D., & Kelso, M. (2010). Roles of neural stem cells and adult neurogenesis in adolescent alcohol use disorders. *Alcohol, 44*, 39–56.

Nolley, E., & Kelley, B. (2007). Adolescent reward system perservation due to nicotine: Studies with methylphenidate. *Neurotoxicology and Teratology, 29*, 47–56.

O'Dell, L., Torres, O., Natividad, L., & Tejeda, H. (2007). Adolescent nicotine exposure produces less affective measures of withdrawal relative to adult nicotine exposure in male rats. *Neurotoxicology and Teratology, 29*(1), 17–22.

O'Shea, M., McGregor, I., & Mallet, P. (2006). Repeated cannabinoid exposure during perinatal, adolescent or early adult ages produces similar longlasting deficits in object recognition and reduced social interaction in rats. *Journal of Psychopharmacology, 20*(5), 611–621.

O'Shea, M., Singh, M., McGregor, I., & Mallet, P. (2004). Chronic cannabinoid exposure produces lasting memory impairment and increased anxiety in adolescent but not adult rats. *Journal of Psychopharmacology, 18*(4), 502–508.

Pandey, S. C., Sakharkar, A. J., Tang, L., & Zhang, H. (2015). Potential role of adolescent alcohol exposure-induced amygdaloid histone modifications in anxiety and alcohol intake during adulthood. *Neurobiology of Disease, 82*, 607–619.

Parvaz, M., Alia-Klein, N., Woicik, P., Volkow, N., & Gloldstein, R. (2011). Neuroimaging for drug addiction and related behaviors. *Reviews in the Neurosciences, 22*(6), 609–624.

Pascual, M., Blanco, A., Cauli, O., Minarro, J., & Guerri, C. (2007). Intermittent ethanol exposure induces inflammatory brain damage and causes long-term behavioural alterations in adolescent rats. *European Journal of Neuroscience, 25*(2), 541–550.

Pascual, M., Boix, J., Felipo, V., & Guerri, C. (2009). Repeated alcohol administration during adolescence causes changes in the mesolimbic dopaminergic and glutamatergic systems and promotes alcohol intake in the adult rat. *Journal of Neurochemistry, 108*(4), 920–931.

Pascual, M., Do Couto, B. R., Alfonso-Loeches, S., Aguilar, M. A., Rodriguez-Aris, M. & Guerri, C. (2012). Changes in histone acetylation in the prefrontal cortex of ethanol-exposed adolescent rats are associated with ethanol-induced place conditioning. *Neuropharmacology, 62*(7), 2309–2319.

Pascual, M., Pla, A., Miñarro, J., & Guerri, C. (2014). Neuroimmune activation and myelin changes in adolescent rats exposed to high-dose alcohol and associated cognitive dysfunction: a review with reference to human adolescent drinking. *Alcohol and Alcoholism, 49*(2), 187–192.

Pautassi, R. M., Myers, M., Spear, L. P., Molina, J. C., & Spear, N. E. (2008). Adolescent, but not adult, rats exhibit ethanol-mediated appetitive second-order conditioning. *Alcoholism: Clinical and Experimental Research, 32*(11), 1–12.

Pautassi, R. M., Myers, M., Spear, L. P., Molina, J. C., & Spear, N. E. (2011). Ethanol induces second-order aversive conditioning in adolescent and adult rats. *Alcohol, 45*(1), 45–55.

Philpot, R., Wecker, L., & Kirstein, C. (2009). Repeated ethanol exposure during adolescence alters the development trajectory of dopaminergic output from the nucleus accumbens septi. *International Journal of Developmental Neuroscience, 27*(8), 805–815.

Popovic, M., Caballero-Bleda, M., Puelles, L., & Guerri, C. (2004). Multiple binge alcohol consumption during rat adolescence increases anxiety but does not impair retention in the passive avoidance task. *Neuroscience Letters, 357*(2), 79–82.

Pyapali, G., Turner, D., Wilson, W., & Swartzwelder, H. (1999). Age and dose-dependent effects of ethanol on the induction of hippocampal long-term potentiation. *Alcohol, 19*(2), 107–111.

Quinn, H., Matsumoto, I., Callaghan, P., Long, L., Arnold, J., Gunasekaran, N., . . . McGregor, I. S. (2008). Adolescent rats find repeated Delta9-THC less aversive than adult rats but display greater residual cognitive deficits and changes in hippocampal protein expression following exposure. *Neurospychopharmacology, 33*, 1113–1126.

Quoilin, C., Didone, V., Tirelli, E., & Quertemont, E. (2012). Chronic ethanol exposure during adolescence alters the behavioral responsiveness to ethanol in adult mice. *Behavioural Brain Research, 299*(1), 1–9.

Ramirez, R. L., Varlinskaya, E. I., & Spear, L. P. (2011). Effect of the selective NMDA NR2B antagonist, ifenprodil, on acute tolerance to ethanol-induced motor impairment in adolescent and adult rats. *Alcoholism: Clinical and Experimental Research, 35*(6), 1149–1159.

Realini, N., Rubino, T., & Parolaro, D. (2009). Neurobiological alterations at adult age triggered by adolescent exposure to cannabinoids. *Pharmacological Research, 60*, 132–138.

Realini, N., Vigano, D., Guidali, C., Zamberletti, E., Rubino, T., & Parolaro, D. (2011). Chronic URB597 treatment at adulthood reverted most depressive-like symptoms induced by adolescent exposure to THC in female rats. *Neuropharmacology, 60*(203), 235–243.

Rice, D., & Barone, J., S (2000). Critical periods of vulnerability for the developing newvous system: Evidence from humans and animal models. *Environmental Health Perspectives, 108*(Suppl. 3), 511–533.

Rinker, J., Hutchison, M., Chen, S., Thorsell, A., Heilig, M., & Riley, A. (2011). Exposure to nicotine during periadolesecence or early adulthood alters aversive and physiological effects induced by ethanol. *Pharmacology, Biochemistry and Behavior, 99*(1), 7–16.

Ristuccia, R. C., & Spear, L. P. (2008). Adolescent and adult heart rate responses to self-administered ethanol. *Alcoholism: Clinical and Experimental Research, 32*(10), 1–9.

Rodd-Henricks, Z. A., Bell, R. L., Kuc, K. A., Murphy, J. M., McBride, W. J., Lumeng, L., & Li, T. K. (2002a). Effects of ethanol exposure on subsequent acquisition and extinction of ethanol self-administration and expression of alcohol-seeking behavior in adult alcohol-preferring (P) rats: I. Periadolescent exposure. *Alcoholism: Clinical and Experimental Research, 26*(11), 1632–1641.

Rodd-Henricks, Z. A., Bell, R. L., Kuc, K. A., Murphy, J. M., McBride, W. J., Lumeng, L., & Li, T. K. (2002b). Effects of ethanol exposure on subsequent acquisition and extinction of ethanol self-administration and expression of alcohol-seeking behavior in adult alcohol-preferring (P) rats: II. Adult exposure. *Alcoholism: Clinical and Experimental Research, 26*(11), 1642–1652.

Rubino, T., Realini, N., Braida, D., Alberio, T., Capurro, V., Vigano, D., . . . Parolaro, D. (2009a). The depressive phenotype induced in adult female rats by adolescent exposure to THC is associated with cognitive impairment and altered neuroplasticity in the prefrontal cortex. *Neurotoxicity Research, 15*, 291–302.

Rubino, T., Realini, N., Guidi, S., Capurro, V., Viganò, D., Guiladi, C., . . . Parolaro, D. (2009b). Changes in hippocampal morphology and neuroplasticity induced by adolescent THC treatment are associated with cognitive impairment in adulthood. *Hippocampus, 19*(8), 763–772.

Rubino, T., Vigano, D., Realini, N., Guidali, C., Braida, D., Capurro, V., . . . Parolaro, D. (2008). Chronic Delta(9)-tetrahydrocannabinol during adolescence provokes sex-dependent changes in the emotional profile in adult rats: Behavioral and biochemical correlates. *Neuropsychopharmacologoy, 33*(11), 2760–2771.

Saalfield, J., & Spear, L. P. (2015). Consequences of repeated ethanol exposure during early or late adolescence on conditioned taste aversions in rats. Developmental Cognitive Neuroscience, Dec.16, 174–182.

Sahr, A. E., Thielen, R. J., Lumeng, L., Li, T-K., & McBride, W. J. (2004). Long-lasting alterations of the mesolimbic dopamine system after periadolescent ethanol drinking by alcohol-preferring rats. *Alcoholism: Clinical and Experimental Research, 28*(5), 702–711.

Scheff, S. W., Price, D. A., & Sparks, D. L. (2001). Quantitative assessment of possible age-related change in synaptic numbers in the human frontal cortex. *Neurobiology of Aging, 22*, 355–365.

Schneider, M., & Koch, M. (2003). Chronic pubertal, but not adult chronic cannabinoid treatment impairs sensorimotor gating, recognition memory, and the performance in a progressive ratio task in adult rats. *Neuropsychopharmacology, 28*(10), 1760–1769.

Schneider, M., & Koch, M. (2005). Deficient social and play behavior in juvenile and adult rats after neonatal cortical lesion: Effects of chronic pubertal cannabinoid treatment. *Neuropsychopharmacology, 30*(5), 944–957.

Schneider, M., & Koch, M. (2007). The effect of chronic peripubertal cannabinoid treatment on deficient abject recognition memory in rats after neonatal mPFC lesion. *European Neuropsychopharmacology, 17*(3), 180–186.

Schneider, M., Schömig, E., & Leweke, F. (2008). Acute and chronic cannabinoid treatment differentially affects recognition memory and social behavior in pubertal and adult rats. *Addiction Biology, 13*(3–4), 345–357.

Schochet, T., Kelley, A., & Landrym, C. (2004). Differential behavioral effects of nicotine exposure in adolesecent and adult rats. *Psychopharmacology, 175*, 265–273.

Schramm-Sapyta, N. L., Cha, Y. M., Chaudhry, S., Wilson, W. A., Swartzwelder, H. S., & Kuhn, C. M. (2007). Differential anxiogenic, aversive, and locomotor effects of THC in adolescent and adult rats. *Psychopharmacology, 191*(4), 867–877.

Schramm-Sapyta, N. L., DiFeliceantonio, A. G., Foscue, E., Glowacz, S., Haseeb, N., Wang, N., . . . Kuhn, C. M. (2010). Aversive effects of ethanol in adolescent versus adult rats: Potential causes and implication for future drinking. *Alcoholism: Clinical and Experimental Research, 34*(12), 2061–2069.

Schramm-Sapyta, N. L., Morris, R. W., & Kuhn, C. M. (2006). Adolescent rats are protected from the conditioned aversive properties of cocaine and lithium chloride. *Pharmacology, Biochemistry and Behavior, 84*(2), 344–352.

Schramm-Sapyta, N. L., Pratt, A. R., & Winder, D. G. (2004). Effects of periadolescent versus adult cocaine exposure on cocaine conditioned place preference and motor sensitization in mice. *Psychopharmacology, 173*(1–2), 41–48.

Semple, D., McIntosh, A., & Lawrie, S. (2005). Cannabis as a risk factor for psychosis: systematic review. *Journal of Psychopharmacology, 19*(2), 187–194.

Shahbazi, M., Moffett, A., Williams, B., & Frantz, K. (2008). Age- and sex-dependent amphetamine self-administration in rats. *Psychopharmacology, 196*(1), 71–81.

Shram, M. J., Funk, D., Li, X., & Le, A. D. (2006). Periadolescent and adult rats respond differently in tests measuring the rewarding and aversive effects of nicotine. *Psychopharmacology, 186*, 201–208.

Shram, M., Funk, D., Li, Z., & Le, A. (2008a). Nicotine self-administration, extinction responding and reinstatement in adolescent and adult male rats: Evidence against a biological vulnerability to nicotine addiction during adolescence. *Neuropsychopharmacology, 33*, 739–748.

Shram, M., Li, Z., & Le, A. (2008b). Age differences in the spontaneous acquisition of nicotine self-administration in male Wistar and Long-Evans rats. *Psychopharmacology, 197*, 45–58.

Shram, M. J., & Le, A. (2010). Adolescent male Wistar rats are more responsive than adult rats to the conditioned rewarding effects of intravenously administered nicotine in the place conditioning procedure. *Behavioural Brain Research, 206*(2), 240–244.

Shram, M. J., Siu, E., Li, Z., Tyndale, R., & Le, A. (2008c). Interactions between age and the aversive effects of nicotine withdrawal under mecamylamine-precipitated and spontaneous conditions in male Wistar rats. *Psychopharmacology, 198*(2), 181–190.

Siciliano, D., & Smith, R. (2001). Periadolescent alcohol alters adult behavioral characteristics int he rat. *Physiology and Behavior, 74*(4–5), 637–643.

Siegmund, S., Vengeliene, V., Singer, M. V., & Spanagel, R. (2005). Influence of age at drinking onset on long-term ethanol self-administration with deprivation and stress phases. *Alcoholism: Clinical and Experimental Research, 29*(7), 1139–1145.

Silveri, M. M., & Spear, L. P. (1998). Decreased sensitivity to the hypnotic effects of ethanol early in ontogeny. *Alcoholism: Clinical and Experimental Research, 22*(3), 670–676.

Silveri, M. M., & Spear, L. P. (2000). Ontogeny of ethanol elimination and ethanol-induced hypothermia. *Alcohol, 20*(1), 45–53.

Silveri, M. M., & Spear, L. P. (2001). Acute, rapid and chronic tolerance during ontogeny: Observations when equating ethanol perturbation across age. *Alcoholism: Clinical and Experimental Research, 25*(9), 1301–1308.

Silveri, M. M., & Spear, L. P. (2004). The effects of NMDA and GABAA pharmacological manipulations on acute and rapid tolerance to ethanol during ontogeny. *Alcoholism: Clinical and Experimental Research, 28*, 884–894.

Silvers, J. M., Tokunaga, S., Mittleman, G., & Matthews, D. B. (2003). Chronic intermittent injections of high-dose ethanol during adolescence produce metabolic, hypnotic, and cognitive tolerance in rats. *Alcoholism: Clinical and Experimental Research, 27*(10), 1606–1612.

Silvers, J. M., Tokunaga, S., Mittleman, G., O'Buckley, T., Morrow, A. L., & Matthews, D. B. (2006). Chronic intermittent ethanol exposure during adolescence reduces the effect of ethanol challenge on hippocampal allopregnanolone levels and Morris water maze task performance. *Alcohol, 39*, 151–158.

Sircar, R., & Sircar, D. (2005). Adolescent rats exposed to repeated ethanol treatments show lingering behavioral impairments. *Alcoholism: Clinical and Experimental Research, 29*(8), 1402–1410.

Sircar, R., & Sircar, D. (2006). Repeated ethanol treatment in adolescent rats alters cortical NMDA receptor. *Alcohol, 39*(1), 51–58.

Slawecki, C., & Betancourt, M. (2002). Effects of adolescent ethanol exposure on ethanol consumption in adult rats. *Alcohol, 26*(1), 23–30.

Slawecki, C., Gilder, A., Roth, J., & Ehlers, E. (2003). Increased anxiety-like behavior in adult rats exposed to nicotine as adolescents. *Pharmacology, Biochemistry and Behavior, 75*(2), 355–361.

Slawecki, C. J., Thorsell, A. K., & Ehlers, C. L. (2004). Long-term neurobehavioral effects of alcohol or nicotine exposure in adolescent animal models. *Annuals of the New York Academy of Sciences, 1021*, 448–452.

Slawecki, C. J., Thorsell, A. K., Khoury, A. E., Mathé, A. A., & Ehlers, C. L. (2005). Increased CRF-like and NPY-like immunoreactivity in adult rats exposed to nicotine during adolescence: Relation to anxiety-like and depressive-like behavior. *Neuropeptides, 39*(4), 369–377.

Slotkin, T. A. (2002). Nicotine and the adolescent brain: Insights from an animal model. *Neurotoxicology and Teratology, 24*(3), 369–384.

Slotkin, T. A., Bodwell, B., Ryde, I., & Seidler, F. (2008b). Adolescent nicotine treatment changes the response of acetylcholine systems to subsequent nicotine administration in adulthood. *Brain Research Bulletin, 76*(1–2), 152–165.

Slotkin, T. A., Ryde, I. T., MacKillop, E. A., Bodwell, B. E., & Seidler, F. J. (2008a). Adolescent nicotine administration changes the responses to nicotine given subsequently in adulthood: Adenylyl cyclase cell signaling in brain regions during nicotine administration and withdrawal, and lasting effects. *Brain Research Bulletin, 76*, 522–530.

Slotkin, T., & Seidler, F. (2009). Nicotine exposure in adolescence alters the response of serotonin systems to nicotine administered subsequently in adulthood. *Developmental Neuroscience, 31*(1–2), 58–70.

Spear, L. P. (2000). The adolescent brain and age-related behavioral manifestations. *Neuroscience and Biobehavioral Reviews, 24*(4), 417–463.

Spear, L. P. (2007). The developing brain and adolescent-typical behavior patterns: An evolutionary approach. In E. Walker, J. Bossert, & D. Romer (Eds.), *Adolescent psychopathology and the developing brain: Integrating brain and prevention science* (pp. 9–30). New York, NY: Oxford University Press.

Spear, L. P. (2010). *The behavioral neuroscience of adolescence*. New York, NY: Norton.

Spear, L. P. (2011). Rewards, aversions and affect in adolescence: Emerging convergences across laboratory animal and human data. *Developmental Cognitive Neuroscience, 1*, 390–403.

Spear, L. P., & Swartzwelder, H. S. (2014). Adolescent alcohol exposure and persistence of adolescent-typical phenotypes into adulthood: a mini-review. *Neuroscience and Biobehavioral Reviews, 45*, 1–8.

Spear, L. P., & Varlinskaya, E. I. (2005). Adolescence: Alcohol sensitivity, tolerance, and intake. In M. Galanter (Ed.), *Recent developments in alcoholism, Vol. 17. Alcohol problems in adolescents and young adults* (pp. 143–159). New York, NY: Kluwer Academic/Plenum Publishers.

Stanton, M. E., & Spear, L. P. (1990). Workshop on the qualitative and quantitative comparability of human and animal developmental neurotoxicity, Work Group I report: Comparability of measures of developmental neurotoxicity in humans and laboratory animals. *Neurotoxicology and Teratology, 12*(3), 261–267.

Steinberg, L., & Belsky, J. (1996). *An evolutionary perspective on psychopathology in adolescence*. Rochester, NY: University of Rochester Press.

Strong, M., Yoneyama, N., Fretwell, A., Snelling, C., Tanchuck, M., & Finn, D. (2010). "Binge" drinking experience in adolescent mice shows sex differences and elevated ethanol intake in adulthood. *Hormones and Behavior, 58*(1), 82–90.

Substance Abuse and Mental Health Services Administration (SAMHSA). (2006). *Results from the 2005 National Survey on Drug Use and Health: National findings* (National Survey on Drug use and Health Series H-30, DHHS publication SMA 06-4194). Rockville, MD: Author.

Substance Abuse and Mental Health Services Administration (SAMHSA). (2010). Results from the 2010 National Survey on Drug Use and Health: Summary of national findings. In SAMHSA (Ed.), *Illicit drug use* (pp. 11–25). Rockville, MD: Author.

Tambour, S., Brown, L. L., & Crabbe, J. C. (2008). Gender and age at drinking onset affect voluntary alcohol consumption but neither the alcohol deprivation effect nor the response to stress in mice. *Alcoholism: Clinical and Experimental Research, 32*(12), 2100–2106.

Tapert, S. F., & Schweinsburg, A. D. (2005). The human adolescent brain and alcohol use disorders. In M. Galanter (Ed.), *Recent developments in alcoholism, Vol. 17. Alcohol problems in adolescents and young adults* (pp. 177–197). New York, NY: Kluwer Academic/Plenum.

Toalston, J. E., Deehan, G. A. Jr., Hauser, S. R., Engelman, E. A., Bell, R. L., Murphy, J. M., . . . & Rodd, Z. A. (2014). Reinforcing properties and neurochemical response of ethanol within the posterior ventral tegmental area are enhanced in adulthood by periadolescent ethanol consumption.

Journal of Pharmacology and Experimental Therapeutics, 351(2), 317–326.

Torres, O. V., Tejeda, H. A., Natividad, L. A., & O'Dell, L. E. (2008). Enhanced vulnerability to the rewarding effects of nicotine during the adolescent period of development. *Pharmacology, Biochemistry and Behavior, 90*, 658–663.

Trauth, J., Seidler, F., & Slotkin, T. (2000). Persistent and delayed behavioral changes after nicotine treatment in adolescent rats. *Brain Research, 880*, 167–172.

Varlinskaya, E. I., & Spear, L. P. (2002). Acute effects of ethanol on social behavior of adolescent and adult rats: Role of familiarity of the test situation. *Alcoholism: Clinical and Experimental Research, 26*(10), 1502–1511.

Varlinskaya, E. I., & Spear, L. P. (2004). Acute ethanol withdrawal (hangover) and social behavior in adolescent and adult male and female Sprague Dawley rats. *Alcoholism: Clinical and Experimental Research, 28*, 40–50.

Varlinskaya, E. I., Truxell, E. M., & Spear, L. P. (2014). Chronic intermittent ethanol during adolescence: effects on social behavior and ethanol sensitivity in adulthood. *Alcohol, 48*(5), 433–444.

Vastola, B. J., Douglas, L. A., Varlinskaya, E. I., & Spear, L. P. (2002). Nicotine-induced conditioned place preference in adolescent and adult rats. *Physiology and Behavior, 77*(1), 107–114.

Vetreno, R. P. & Crews, F. T. (2012). Adolescent binge drinking increases expression of the danger signal receptor agonist HMGB1 and Toll-like receptors in the adult prefrontal cortex. *Neuroscience, 226*, 475–488.

Vetreno, R. P. & Crews, F. T. (2015). Binge ethanol exposure during adolescence leads to a persistent loss of neurogenesis in the dorsal and ventral hippocampus that is associated with impaired adult cognitive functioning. *Fontiers of Neuroscience, 9*. doi:10.3389/fnins.2015.00035

Vetreno, R. P., Broadwater, M., Liu, W., Spear, L. P., & Crews, F. T. (2014). Adolescent, but not adult, binge ethanol exposure leads to persistent global reductions of choline acetyltransferase expressing neurons in brain. *PloS One, 9*(11), e113421.

Vetter, C. S., Doremus-Fitzwater, T. L., & Spear, L. P. (2007). Time-course of elevated ethanol intake in adolescent relative to adult rats under continuous, voluntary-access conditions. *Alcoholism: Clinical and Experimental Research, 31*(7), 1159–1168.

Vetter-O'Hagen, C. S., & Spear, L. P. (2011). Hormonal and physical markers of puberty and their relationship to adolescent-typical novelty-directed behavior. *Developmental Psychobiology*, doi:10.1002/dev.20610

Vetter-O'Hagen, C., Varlinskaya, E. I., & Spear, L. (2009). Sex differences in ethanol intake and sensitivity to aversive effects during adolescence and adulthood. *Alcohol and Alcoholism, 44*(6), 547–554.

Viveros, M., Llorente, R., Suarez, J., Llorente-Berzal, A., López-Gallardo, M., & Rodriguez de Fonseca, F. (2012). The endocannabinoid system in critical neurodevelopmental periods: Sex differences and neuropsychiatric implications. *Journal of Psychopharmacology, 26*, 164–176.

Volkow, N., Wang, G., Fowler, J., Tomasi, D., & Telang, F. (2011). Addiction: Beyond dopamine reward circuitry. *Proceedings of the National Academy of Sciences USA, 108*(37), 15037–15042.

Vorhees, C. V. (1987). Dependence on the stage of gestation: Prenatal drugs and offspring behavior as influenced by different periods of exposure in rats. In T. Fujii & P. M. Adams (Eds.), *Functional teratogenesis* (pp. 39–51). Tokyo, Japan: Teikyo University Press.

Walker, B. M., & Ehlers, C. L. (2009). Appetitive motivational experience during adolescence results in enhanced alcohol consumption during adulthood. *Behavioral Neuroscience, 124*(4), 926–935.

Wegener, N., & Koch, M. (2009). Behavioural disturbances and altered Fos protein expression in adult rats after chronic pubertal cannabinoid treatment. *Brain Research, 9,* 1253–1281.

Werling, L. L., Reed, S. C., Wade, D., & Izenwasser, S. (2009). Chronic nicotine alters cannabinoid-mediated locomotor activity and receptor density in periadolescent but not male rats. *International Journal of Developmental Neuroscience, 27,* 263–269.

White, A. M., Ghia, A. J., Levin, E. D., & Swartzwelder, H. S. (2000). Binge pattern ethanol exposure in adolescent and adult rats: Differential impact on subsequent responsiveness to ethanol. *Alcoholism: Clinical and Experimental Research, 24*(8), 1251–1256.

White, A. M., Bae, J. G., Truesdale, M. C., Ahmad, S., Wilson, W. A., & Swartzwelder, H. S. (2002) Chronic-intermittent ethanol exposure during adolescence prevents normal developmetal changes in sensitivity to ethanol-induced motor impairments. *Alcoholism: Clinical and Experimental Research, 26*(7), 960–968.

Willey, A. R., Varlinskaya, E. I., & Spear, L. P. (2009). Social interactions and 50 kHZ ultrasonic vocalizations in adolescents and adult rats. *Behavioural Brain Research, 202,* 122–129.

Willner, P. (1991). Methods of assessing the validity of animal models of human psychopathology. In A. Boulton, G. Baker, & M. Martin-Iverson (Eds.), *Neuromethods: Animal models in psychiatry* (Vol. 18, pp. 1–23). Clifton, NJ: Humana Press.

Wills, T., Knapp, D. J., Overstreet, D. H., & Breese, G. R. (2008). Differential dietary ethanol intake and blood ethanol levels in adolescent and adult rats: Effects on anxiety-like behavior and seizure thresholds. *Alcoholism: Clinical and Experimental Research, 32*(8), 1350–1360.

Wills, T., Knapp, D., Overstreet, D., & Breese, G. R. (2009). Sensitization, duration, and pharmacological blockade of anxiety-like behavior following repeated ethanol withdrawal in adolescent and adult rats. *Alcoholism: Clinical and Experimental Research, 33*(3), 455–463.

Wills, T., Knapp, D., Overstreet, D., & Breese, G. R. (2010). Interactions of stress and CRF in ethanol-withdrawal induced anxiety in adolescent and adult rats. *Alcoholism: Clinical and Experimental Research, 34*(9), 1603–1612.

Willuhn, I., Wanat, M., Clark, J., & Phillips, P. (2010). Dopamine signaling in the nucleus accumbens of animals self-administering drugs of abuse. *Current Topics in Behavioral Neuroscience, 3,* 29–71.

Wilmouth, C. E., & Spear, L. P. (2004). Adolescent and adult rats' aversion to flavors previously paired with nicotine. *Annals of the New York Academy of Sciences, 1021,* 462–464.

Wilmouth, C. E., & Spear, L. P. (2006). Withdrawal from chronic nicotine in adolescent and adult rats. *Pharmacology, Biochemistry and Behavior, 85*(3), 648–657.

Wilmouth, C. E., & Spear, L. P. (2009). Hedonic sensitivity in adolescent and adult rats: Taste reactivity and voluntary sucrose consumption. *Pharmacology, Biochemistry and Behavior, 92,* 566–573.

Yttri, E., Burk, J., & Hunt, P. (2004). Intermittent ethanol exposure in adolescent rats: Dose-dependent impairments in trace conditioning. *Alcoholism: Clinical and Experimental Research, 28*(10), 1433–1436.

Zakharova, E., Leoni, G., Kichko, I., & Izenwasser, S. (2009a). Differential effects of methamphetamine, cocaine on conditioned place preference and locomotor activity in adult and adolescent male rats. *Behavioural Brain Research, 198*(1), 45–50.

Zakharova, E., Wade, D., & Izenwasser, S. (2009b). Sensitivity to cocaine conditioned reward depends on sex and age. *Pharmacology, Biochemistry and Behavior, 92*(1), 131–134.

Zorzano, A., & Herrera, E. (1989). Decreased in vivo rate of ethanol metabolism in the suckling rat. *Alcoholism: Clinical and Experimental Research, 13*(4), 527–532.

Behavioral Genetics of Adolescent Substance Use and Abuse

Matt McGue *and* Brian M. Hicks

Abstract

We review behavioral and biometrical genetic research aimed at characterizing the nature of the familial aggregation of adolescent substance use and abuse. Twin and adoption studies have shown that genetic factors contribute to individual differences in adolescent substance use phenotypes. These studies have also documented the importance of the shared environment. Biometrical analyses of large samples of twins show that the contributions of genetic and shared environmental factors to substance use phenotypes change markedly between adolescence and early adulthood. The importance of genetic influence increases with age as the importance of shared environmental influences declines. Although only a small number of relevant genetic variants have been identified at this time, they show a similar pattern of increasing association with substance use behavior with age. A major question continues to be how genetic and environmental factors operate jointly to influence the development of complex behavioral phenotypes such as substance use.

Key Words: twin studies, adoption studies, heritability, biometrical genetics, candidate-gene associations, genome-wide association studies, gene–environment correlation, gene–environment interaction

Adolescence is a developmental period characterized by major transitions in nearly every major life domain, including physical, biological, emotional, social, and cognitive (Windle et al., 2008). It is also the stage in life when most individuals initiate substance use, even though in most cases it is illegal to do so (Schulenberg & Maggs, 2002). According to Monitoring the Future data from 2013, any use of alcohol increases from 22.1% among 8th graders to 62.0% among 12th graders, and any illicit drug use increases from 20.3% to 50.4% during the same period (Johnston, O'Malley, Miech, Bachman, & Schulenberg, 2014). For some, substance use experimentation in early or middle adolescence is followed by a period of rapid escalation into problematic and heavy substance use by late adolescence or early adulthood (Tucker, Ellickson, Orlando, Martino, & Klein, 2005). The period of late adolescence and early adulthood is not only when the first indications of problem use typically emerge; it is

also the time when the average number of substance abuse symptoms is at its maximal level (Vrieze, Hicks, Iacono, & McGue, 2012). Adolescence is clearly a critical period in the development of substance abuse.

Two features of the epidemiology of adolescent substance use are especially relevant to the behavioral genetic literature. First, adolescent substance use rarely occurs in isolation; that is, it is typically comorbid with other adolescent problem behavior (Donovan & Jessor, 1985). Adolescents who use one substance are more likely to use others, with polysubstance use being the norm rather than the exception (Conway et al., 2013). Moreover, adolescent substance use often co-occurs with other mental health disorders and behavioral problems. Most prominently, adolescent substance use has been associated with childhood disruptive disorders such as conduct disorder and oppositional defiant disorder (Armstrong & Costello,

2002). The associations among multiple substance use phenotypes as well as between substance use and childhood disruptive disorders have led several investigators to hypothesize the existence of a common liability that accounts for these comorbidities (Krueger et al., 2002; Young et al., 2009). This general liability is conceptualized as a broad temperament trait called behavioral disinhibition characterized by the inability or unwillingness to inhibit socially undesirable or restricted behavior. Behavioral disinhibition manifests phenotyically as externalizing psychopathology, which includes substance abuse, childhood disruptive disorders, and personality indicators of low impulse control. The behavioral disinhibition construct has provided a guiding structure for much behavioral genetic research on adolescent substance use. In particular, it has drawn behavioral genetic researchers' attention to the possibility that risk for the abuse of a substance is a combination of genetic and environmental influences that operate at the general level and so contribute to all forms of externalizing psychopathology, as well as at the specific level by influencing risk of the abuse of individual substances. The model is ecumenical in that it helps to explain both high rates of substance abuse co-occurrence as well as why some people develop certain substance use disorders and not others.

The second finding from epidemiological research on adolescent substance use that has influenced behavioral genetic research concerns the importance of developmental timing. Most individuals try nicotine and alcohol sometime during their lifetime, and a near-majority will try at least one illicit substance (Johnston, O'Malley, Bachman, & Schulenberg, 2006). Given the high rates of substance exposure, an important question concerns what differentiates those who go on to develop a substance use disorder from those who do not. One important factor appears to be the age at which substance use is initiated. In a highly cited study, Grant and Dawson (1997) reported that individuals who first tried alcohol before the age of 15 years were approximately four times more likely to develop alcohol dependence sometime during their lifetime than individuals who first tried alcohol after the age of 20 years. The association of early exposure with later problems is not specific to alcohol. For example, smoking early in adolescence is associated with increased risk of nicotine dependence (Breslau, Fenn, & Peterson, 1993), and early use of an illicit drug is associated with a substantially increased risk for later abuse of illicit drugs (Grant & Dawson,

1998). A major question concerning these associations between early adolescent substance use and adult substance abuse concerns whether they are causal. That is, do the associations arise because early use is a contributing cause for later abuse, as some have suggested (Dewit, Adlaf, Offord, & Ogborne, 2000), or are the associations spurious, arising because adolescent substance use and adult substance abuse are developmentally graded indicators of externalizing psychopathology (McGue, Iacono, Legrand, & Elkins, 2001)? As discussed later, behavioral genetic methods are particularly well suited to exploring these questions.

The current chapter provides an overview of behavioral genetic research on adolescent substance use and abuse. We begin with a review of the family, twin, and adoption studies that have shown that both genetic and environmental factors contribute to the familial aggregation of adolescent substance use and abuse. Although our focus is on adolescence, we next show how a developmental perspective has been critical in showing that the nature of genetic and environmental contributions to substance use and abuse changes across development and especially during the transition from late adolescence to early adulthood. One of the current challenges in genetic epidemiology is in identifying the specific genetic factors that underlie the heritability of complex phenotypes. As we will show, this is certainly the case for adolescent substance use and abuse where progress in identifying specific genetic risk factors has been slow. Finally, we describe models and associated research aimed at characterizing the interplay between genetic and environmental influences on the development of adolescent substance use and abuse.

Family, Twin, and Adoption Studies
Family Studies

Since Cotton's (1979) classic review of family studies of alcoholism, the existence of familial resemblance for substance use phenotypes has been widely recognized. In addition to alcoholism, evidence for strong familial aggregation has been reported for smoking (Avenevoli & Merikangas, 2003), cannabis use phenotypes (Merikangas et al., 2009), and other substance use disorders (Merikangas et al., 1998). Although most of the family studies of substance use and abuse have been based on adults, there are a large and growing number of family studies of adolescent substance use. Among the phenotypes of interest here, the most widely investigated in family studies is smoking initiation. For example, a recent meta-analysis of 58 studies reported that having a parent who smokes increases the odds of smoking by approximately a factor of 2 (Leonardi-Bee, Jere, & Britton, 2011). There have been fewer studies of parent–adolescent offspring resemblance for alcohol use, but these also suggest a moderate degree familial resemblance, with the correlation between parent and adolescent offspring drinking typically falling in the .1 to .25 range (Kendler, Gardner, et al., 2013; White, Johnson, & Buyske, 2000). Similarly, parent–offspring resemblance for cannabis-use phenotypes appears to be moderate, with correlations of approximately .30 being typical (Gfroerer, 1987). Several factors have been hypothesized to underlie the relationship between parent and adolescent offspring substance use, including modeling (White et al., 2000), qualities of the parent–offspring relationship (Latendresse et al., 2008), and genetics (McGue, 1999), an issue we return to later in this chapter.

Although the literature on sibling similarity for adolescent substance use phenotypes is less extensive than that for parent–offspring similarity, the findings are somewhat more consistent and the degree of sibling similarity for substance use phenotypes tends to be stronger than the degree of parent–offspring similarity. That is, sibling similarity has been found to be greater than parent–offspring similarity for smoking (Leonardi-Bee et al., 2011; Vuolo & Staff, 2013), drinking (Fagan & Najman, 2005; Scholte, Poelen, Willemsen, Boomsma, & Engels, 2008), cannabis use (Brook, Whiteman, Gordon, & Brenden, 1983), and other substance abuse (Hopfer, Stallings, Hewitt, & Crowley, 2003). Significantly, sibling resemblance for substance use is greater when the siblings are close in age and of the same gender as compared to distant in age and of different genders (Boyle, Sanford, Szatmari, Merikangas, & Offord, 2001; McGue, Sharma, & Benson, 1996; Trim, Leuthe, & Chassin, 2006), suggesting that social factors may contribute to sibling resemblance. Consistent with this interpretation, research suggests that older siblings may influence their younger siblings' substance use through modeling as well as direct facilitation (McGue & Iacono, 2009; Samek, McGue, Keyes, & Iacono, 2015).

Biometrics

A central tenet within behavioral genetics is that resemblance among relatives from intact families is potentially a function of the relatives' shared genes as well as their shared environment. Consequently, the parent–offspring and sibling studies reviewed earlier cannot be informative with respect to the origins of familial resemblance, even though they are critical to establishing the existence of that resemblance for substance use phenotypes. Behavioral geneticists have primarily relied on twin and adoption studies to resolve the separate contribution of genetic and environmental contributions to familial resemblance. The classical twin study is based on the existence of two types of twins. Monozygotic (MZ) twins are effectively genetically identical. Dizygotic (DZ) twins are genetically as similar as ordinary siblings; on average they share 50% of their segregating genetic material. The basic logic of the twin study is that genetic factors are implicated whenever MZ twin similarity is greater than DZ twin similarity. Clearly the validity of this comparison rests on several key assumptions, most notably that greater MZ than DZ twin similarity is not a consequence of greater environmental similarity (i.e., the so-called equal environmental similarity assumption; Felson, 2014). One way to address this assumption is to determine whether findings from twin studies are constructively replicated in other research designs. Adoption studies are the most common behavioral genetic design after twin studies. The logic of an adoption study is relatively straightforward, as they allow confirmation of both the importance of genetic factors, by documenting resemblance between adopted individuals and the biological relatives with whom they have had minimal contact, and the rearing environment, by documenting resemblance between adopted individuals and their adopted relatives.

The field of biometric genetics seeks to go beyond inferences about the existence of genetic and environmental influences made possible by simple comparisons in twin and adoption studies to quantify the magnitude of those influences through analysis of the similarity among twins and other familial pairings (Neale & Cardon, 1992). In a biometric analysis, individual differences are typically indexed by the phenotypic variance (P), which in the most basic (or ACE) biometric model is decomposed as

$$P = A + C + E$$

where A refers to the contribution of additive genetic factors to phenotypic variance, C refers to the contribution of shared environmental factors (i.e., those environmental factors shared by reared-together relatives and which thus potentially contribute to their phenotypic similarity), and E refers to the contribution of nonshared environmental factors (i.e., those environmental factors that reared-together relatives do not share and which thus potentially contribute to their phenotypic differences). In the classical twin study, it is often convenient to standardize the phenotypic variance to one and express the expected MZ and DZ correlations as

$$r_{MZ} = a^2 + c^2$$

$$r_{DZ} = 1/2a^2 + c^2$$

where a^2, c^2, and e^2 are, respectively, the proportion of phenotypic variance attributable to additive genetic ($a^2 = A/P$), shared environmental ($c^2 = C/P$), and nonshared environmental ($e^2 = E/P$) factors, so that $1 = a^2 + c^2 + e^2$. Simple algebraic manipulation of the expected twin correlations as well as the total normed variance gives the so-called Falconer or ACE estimates that are the outcome of the analysis of most twin studies:

$$a^2 = 2\left(r_{MZ} - r_{DZ}\right)$$

$$c^2 = 2r_{DZ} - r_{MZ}$$

$$e^2 = 1.0 - r_{mZ}$$

The basic biometric model for twins has been extended to various other relative pairings (Neale, Boker, Xie, & Maes, 2003), the most relevant for the discussion here being the extension to adopted (i.e., genetically unrelated) and nonadopted (i.e., full biological) sibling pairs. The adopted sibling correlation is a direct estimate of c^2, the proportion of variance in a trait that is associated with shared environmental factors; the nonadopted sibling correlation has the same expectation as that for DZ twins. Consequently an analysis of adopted and nonadopted sibling correlations can be used to generate ACE estimates in a way that is analogous to, and can thus test the replicability of findings from, twin studies (Matteson, McGue, & Iacono, 2013).

Twin and Adoption Studies of Substance Use Phenotypes

Table 13.1 provides an overview of the roughly dozen major twin studies on adolescent substance use phenotypes that have been published. The

table breaks down findings from these studies for three separate substances, tobacco, alcohol, and illicit drugs, and then within each substance for indicators of ever use/initiation, current use, and problematic use. Although the studies are diverse and there is clearly heterogeneity of findings across studies, several general patterns emerge. First, the MZ correlations are uniformly high; almost all are at least .70. By itself, a high MZ correlation cannot tell us the reason why MZ twins are so similar. Nonetheless, it does implicate the importance of some combination of genetic and shared environmental factors, and both these factors appear to be important in adolescent substance use. Second, the contribution of additive genetic factors is consistently moderate, with most estimates of a^2 falling between .30 and .60. Third, the contribution of shared environmental factors is generally comparable to that of additive genetic factors, with most estimates of c^2 falling between .30 and .50. Finally, there is no clear pattern of differences in the biometric estimates across the three substances as well as for the initiation, current use, and problem use phenotypes within each substance.

Table 13.2 provides a summary of adopted sibling studies of adolescent substance use. For comparison, included in the table are correlations for full biological siblings when those were also reported in the study. At a general level, the sibling studies are consistent with the twin studies. That is, correlations are generally higher for biological than adopted siblings, implicating the importance of genetic factors. Alternatively, most studies report a moderate level of adopted sibling similarity, implicating the importance of shared environmental factors. The magnitude of the shared environmental effect implied by the adoptive sibling correlation is, however, less than the typical estimate of c^2 from the twin studies reviewed earlier. Several factors may contribute to the lower estimates of shared environment influence from analysis of adoptive sibling correlations as compared to the twin correlations. Most important among these is that adopted sibling pairs differ in age and many of the studies reported in Table 13.2 pool like-sex adopted sibling pairs with a sizable number of unlike-sex pairs. In contrast, twins are necessarily the same age and most twin studies have included only like-sex DZ twin pairs. Several studies have found that adopted siblings are more correlated for substance use when they are near, as compared to distant, in age and of the same, as compared to different, sex (Buchanan, McGue, Keyes, & Iacono, 2009; McGue et al., 1996). The lower estimate from

Table 13.1 Twin Studies of Adolescent Substance Use

Substance Study	No. of Twin Pairs	Age Range (years)	Phenotype	Twin Correlations		Biometric Parameter Estimates		
				MZ	SS-DZ	a^2	c^2	e^2
Nicotine—Initiation								
Han et al. (1999)	501	17–18	Ever smoke	.81[a]	.63[a]	.36	.44	.21
Koopmans et al. (1999)	1,676	12–24	Ever smoke	.93[a]	.79[a]	.39	.54	.07
Korhonen et al. (2012)	1,459	14	Ever smoke	.95[a]	.85[a]	.20	.75	.05
Maes et al. (1999)	1,412	8–16	Ever smoke	.83[a]	.47[a]	.65	.18	.16
Rhee et al. (2003)	682	12–19	Ever smoke	.90	.71	.38	.34	.28
Weighted Average	**5,730**					**.40**	**.47**	**.13**
Nicotine—Use								
Korhonen et al. (2012)	1,459	14	Amount smoked	.95[a]	.85[a]	.20	.75	.05
Koopmans et al. (1999)	1,676	12–24	Amount smoked	.86[a]	.55[a]	.86	.00[b]	.14
Maes et al. (1999)	1,412	8–16	Currently smoke	.83[a]	.60[a]	.60	.21	.19
Rhee et al. (2003)	682	12–19	Nicotine use	.90	.71	.38	.34	.28
Young et al. (2006)	1,347	12–18	Ever use regularly	.89	.67	.43	.47[c]	.10
White et al. (2003)	414	13–18	Smoking involvement	.70	.62	.22	.52	.26
Weighted Average	**6,990**					**.50**	**.35**	**.15**
Nicotine—Problem Use								
McGue et al. (2000)	626	17–18	Nicotine dependence	.81[a]	.58[a]	.44	.37	.19
Rhee et al. (2003)	682	12–19	Nicotine dependence symptoms	.87	.51	.26	.48	.26
Young et al. (2006)	1,347	12–18	Problem use	.88	.61	.49	.38[c]	.13
Weighted Average	**1,973**					**.42**	**.41**	**.17**

(continued)

Table 13.1 Continued

Substance Study	No. of Twin Pairs	Age Range (years)	Phenotype	Twin Correlations		Biometric Parameter Estimates		
				MZ	SS-DZ	a^2	c^2	e^2
Alcohol—Initiation								
Han et al. (1999)	501	17–18	Ever drank	.82 [a]	.64 [a]	.35	.46	.19
Koopmans & Boomsma (1996)	403	15–16	Ever drank	.87 [a]	.84 [a]	.34	.58	.01
	805	17		.77 [a]	.58 [a]	.43	.37	.19
Meas et al. (1999)	1,412	8–16	Ever drank	.70 [a]	.45 [a]	.54	.17	.29
Rhee et al. (2003)	682	12–19	Ever drank	.70	.43	.39	.32	.29
Viken et al. (1999)	2,513	16	Ever drank	.93 [a]	.85 [a]	.14	.79	.07
Young et al. (2006)	1,347	12–18	Ever drank	.81	.75	.00 [b]	.78 [c]	.22
Weighted Average	**7,663**					**.27**	**.56**	**.17**
Alcohol—Use								
Hopfer et al. (2005)	751	13–21	Typical quantity	.55	.20	.52	.00 +	.22
Meas et al. (1999)	1,412	8–16	Current use	.73 [a]	.58 [a]	.56	.17	.27
Rhee et al. (2003)	682	12–19	Ever six or more drinks	.84	.79	.00 [b]	.82 [c]	.18
Viken et al. (1999)	2,513	16	Frequency of drinking	.73 [a]	.52 [a]	.37	.35	.27
Weighted Average	**5,358**					**.40**	**.31**	**.29**
Alcohol—Problems								
Rhee et al. (2003)	682	12–19	Alcohol abuse/ dependence Symptom	.75	.44	.78	.00 [b]	.22
Viken et al. (1999)	2,513	16	Frequency of intoxications	.57 [a]	.47 [a]	.28	.30	.42
Young et al. (2006)	1,347	12–18	Drinking symptom	.74	.48	.53	.21	.26
Weighted Average	**4,542**					**.43**	**.23**	**.34**

Table 13.1 Continued

Substance Study	No. of Twin Pairs	Age Range (years)	Phenotype	Twin Correlations		Biometric Parameter Estimates		
				MZ	SS-DZ	a^2	c^2	e^2
Illicit Drugs—Initiation								
Han et al. (1999)	501	17–18	Ever use illicit drug	.52 [a]	.41 [a]	.23	.29	.48
Korhonen et al. (2012)	1,459	14	Ever use illicit drug	.87 [a]	.72 [a]	.27	.60	.13
Meas et al. (1999)	1,412	8–16	Ever use marijuana	.88	.72	.22	.68	.09
Miles et al. (2001)	635	13–21	Ever use marijuana	NR	NR	.31	.47	.22
Rhee et al. (2003)	682	12–19	Ever use marijuana	.90	.65	.56	.34 [c]	.10
Young et al. (2006)	1,347	12–18	Ever use marijuana	.87	.66	.61	.27	.12
Weighted Average	6,036					.37	.48	.15
Illicit Drugs—Use								
Rhee et al. (2003)	682	12–19	Marijuana five or more times	.88	.69	.55	.33	.12
Illicit Drugs—Problems								
Rhee et al. (2003)	682	12–19	Symptoms of cannabis abuse/ dependence	.64	.63	.34	.36	.30
Young et al. (2006)	1,347	12–18	Marijuana problems	.76	.62	.55	.24	.21
Weighted Average	2,029					.48	.28	.24

Note: In some studies biometric parameters were estimated in a model that included data from nontwins (e.g., adopted siblings).

[a] Average of reported female and male twin correlations.

[b] Only fixed boundary value from "best-fitting" model reported.

[c] Includes twin specific environmental effect.

MZ, monozygotic; NR, correlation not reported; SS-DZ, same-sex dizygotic; a^2 = proportion of variance attributable to additive genetic factors; c^2 = proportion of variance attributed to shared environmental factors; and e^2 = proportion of variance attributed to nonshared environmental factors.

Table 13.2 Adoptive and Biological Sibling Correlations for Adolescent Substance Use

Substance Study	Age Range (years)s	Phenotype	Biological Siblings		Adopted Siblings	
			N	r	N	r
Nicotine—Initiation						
Rhee et al. (2003)	12–19	Ever use	306 [a]	.55	74 [a]	.36
Young et al. (2006)	12–18	Ever use	429 [a]	.36	96 [a]	.06
Nicotine—Use						
Rhee et al. (2003)	12–19	Nicotine use	306 [a]	.38	74 [a]	.08
Nicotine—Problems						
Hicks et al. (2013)	16–25	Nicotine dependence symptoms	208 [a]	.33	409 [a]	.07 [a]
Rhee et al. (2003)	12–19	Nicotine dependence symptoms	306 [a]	.44	74 [a]	.13
Young et al. (2006)	12–18	Problem use	429 [a]	.37	96 [a]	.21
Alcohol—Initiation						
Rhee et al. (2003)	12–19	Ever use	306 [a]	.64	74 [a]	.45
Young et al. (2006)	12–18	Ever use	429 [a]	.46	96 [a]	.45
Alcohol—Use						
McGue et al. (1996)	12–18	Alcohol involvement	NR	NR	99	.36
Rhee et al. (2003)	12–19	Ever use	306 [a]	.46	74 [a]	.46
Alcohol—Problems						
Hicks et al. (2013)	16–25	Alcohol dependence symptoms	208 [a]	.29	409 [a]	.06 [a]
Rhee et al. (2003)	12–19	Alcohol abuse/dependence symptoms	306 [a]	.47	74 [a]	.24
Young et al. (2006)	12–18	Drinking symptoms	429 [a]	.48	96 [a]	.14
Illicit Drugs—Initiation						
Rhee et al. (2003)	12–19	Ever use marijuana	306 [a]	.63	74 [a]	.08
Young et al. (2006)	12–18	Ever use marijuana	429 [a]	.56	96 [a]	.07
Illicit Drugs—Use						
McGue & Iacono (2009)	11–21	Drug involvement	130	.34	245	.19
Rhee et al. (2003)	12–19	Current use of marijuana	306 [a]	.60	74 [a]	.20
Illicit Drugs—Problems						
Hicks et al. (2013)	16–25	Drug dependence symptoms	208 [a]	.37	409 [a]	.12 [a]
Rhee et al. (2003)	12–19	Cannabis abuse/dependence symptom	306 [a]	.60	74 [a]	.13
Young et al. (2006)	12–18	Marijuana problems	429 [a]	.53	96 [a]	.03

[a] Sample includes both like-sex and unlike-sex sibling pairs.

NR, biological sibling sample not reported in study.

adopted sibling as compared to twin studies likely reflects that the overlap in siblings' substance-use environments is greatest when adolescents are close in age and of the same gender.

Are Genetic Influences on Adolescent Substance Use General or Substance Specific?

As noted previously, substance use disorders in adolescence are highly comorbid with each other as well as with other forms of externalizing psychopathology. Neale and Kendler (1995) have described 13 different models that might account for the comorbidity among multiple mental disorders, ranging from a chance model (i.e., disorder overlap is at chance levels) to causal models (i.e., having one disorder directly increases the likelihood of another), and showed how twin and family data can be used to test the relative fit of these models. In a clinical sample of 272 adolescents being treated for severe antisocial behavior and substance use disorders and 362 of their siblings, Rhee et al. (2006) investigated the fit of these models to comorbidity data between alcohol dependence and illicit drug dependence. In the best-fitting model, the comorbidity of alcohol dependence and illicit drug dependence was attributed to both being manifestations of the same underlying liability.

Palmer et al. (2012) extended these analyses by investigating genetic and environmental contributions to the comorbidity among symptoms of alcohol, nicotine, and cannabis dependence in a sample of 2,484 late-adolescent and early-adult twins from the University of Colorado's Center on Antisocial Drug Dependence. As in the previous study by Rhee and colleagues, they found that the associations among the three substance dependence scales could be accounted for by a single common substance dependence vulnerability factor that was highly heritable (64%). The common factor accounted for a large portion of the genetic effects underlying alcohol, nicotine, and cannabis dependence, although there was also evidence of specific genetic effects for each substance, which varied in magnitude by gender.

The Rhee et al. and Palmer et al. studies specifically investigated the associations among multiple indicators of adolescent substance abuse. Other studies have investigated comorbidity in samples that included both substance and non–substance use indicators of externalizing psychopathology (Krueger et al., 2002; Young et al., 2009; Young, Stallings, Corley, Krauter, & Hewitt, 2000). The

most comprehensive investigation of genetic and environmental contributions to the externalizing spectrum is provided by the study by Hicks et al. (2011). A sample of more than 4,300 adolescent twins, adopted and nonadopted offspring, and their parents was assessed on 17 facet measures of substance use (e.g., total number of lifetime uses of marijuana, binge drinking) and non–substance use disinhibited behavior (e.g., symptoms of conduct disorder). A hierarchical factor analysis of the 17 facets provided evidence for five common factors (Nicotine, Alcohol Use, Alcohol Dependence, Illicit Drugs, and Behavioral Disinhibition), which in turn all loaded on a general externalizing factor (Figure 13.1). A hierarchical biometric model was fit to the data to estimate genetic and environmental contributions at the general factor level (denoted by A_G, C_G, and E_G) as well as those that were specific to the five common factors (A_S, C_S, and E_S).

Table 13.3 summarizes the biometric analysis of the data from this study in terms of the genetic and environmental contributions to each of the five component phenotypes that are in common with the general externalizing factor and specific to each phenotype. The variance components estimates (95% confidence interval) for the externalizing factor were $a^2 = .62$ (.54, .70), $c^2 = .22$ (.14, .30), and $e^2 = .16$ (.14, .18). Each of the five component phenotypes is moderately heritable (heritability estimates, obtained by summing the common and specific contributions, ranged from .42 for Alcohol Use to .59 for Behavioral Disinhibition), with a significant shared environmental contribution that accounted for approximately 15%–25% of the variance in all components except Alcohol Dependence, where the shared environmental effect was estimated to be 0. Importantly, the common factor accounted for approximately 80% of the genetic and 90% of the shared environmental but only 50% of the nonshared environmental effects on the five component phenotypes.

An important question is whether the balance of common and specific contributions to substance abuse phenotypes differs with age. Vrieze et al. (2012) used a sample of 3,762 twins who were assessed for alcohol, nicotine, and marijuana abuse and dependence symptoms at ages 14, 17, 20, 24, and 29 years to answer this question. As in previous research, they found that a single common factor could account for the comorbidities that existed among the three symptom scales at any given age. But the strength of this factor declined markedly with age, accounting for on average more than 50%

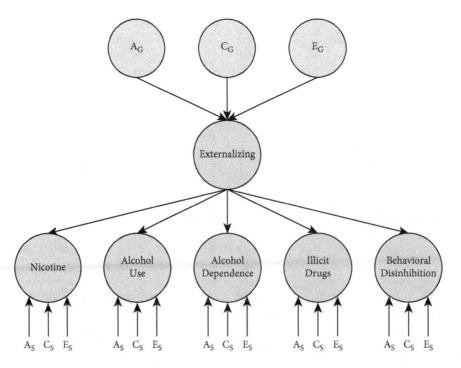

Figure 13.1 Hierarchical biometric factor model fit in the study by Hicks et al. (2011). Additive genetic (A), shared environmental (C), and nonshared environmental contributions (E) to the five component phenotypes are attributable to both a general externalizing factor (with parameter estimates denoted with the subscript G) and specific factors (denoted with the subscript S).

of the variance in adolescence but only about 30% of the variance in early adulthood (Figure 13.2). Due to the decline in importance of the general substance abuse factor, the contribution of general genetic influences declined with age as the contribution of specific genetic influences increased. These data suggest that as an individual gets older, he or she increasingly specializes in the substances he or she will use or abuse, so that substance-specific influences become increasingly important as nonspecific influences decline.

Table 13.3 Partition of Genetic and Environmental Contributions to Individual Indicators to Portions in Common With the General Externalizing Factor and Those Specific to That Indicator

	Genetic (A)		Shared Environment (C)		Nonshared Environment (E)	
	Common	Specific	Common	Specific	Common	Specific
Nicotine	.37	.11	.25	.00	.12	.15
Alcohol use	.30	.12	.29	.02	.16	.11
Alcohol dependence	.58	.08	.00	.00	.18	.16
Illicit drugs	.44	.12	.12	.04	.15	.13
Behavioral disinhibition	.50	.09	.18	.01	.12	.09

Note: Values give a partition of the total standardized variance, so that each row sums to 1.0. Common entry gives portion attributable to externalizing factor; specific entry gives portion not attributable to externalizing.

Source: Data are adapted from Hicks et al. (2011).

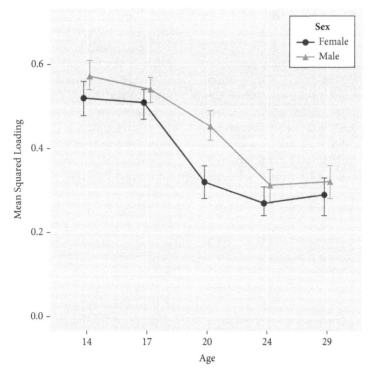

Figure 13.2 Decreasing importance of the common factor underlying abuse of nicotine, alcohol, and cannabis in the study by Vrieze et al. (2012). The vertical axis gives the average proportion of variance in the three substance abuse scales accounted for by the common factor. Error bars give 95% confidence intervals.

The Nature of Shared Environmental Influences

The shared environmental component of variance represents the collective effect of the nongenetic influences that reared-together individuals share. Adolescent substance use phenotypes are distinct from most other behavioral phenotypes in showing moderate to strong shared environmental influences. In searching for the specific factors that contribute to the shared environmental effect on adolescent substance use and abuse, two broad sources of shared environmental influences can be distinguished: (1) factors that operate within families, and (2) factors that are extra-familial but shared by reared-together relatives.

FAMILIAL SOURCES OF SHARED ENVIRONMENTAL EFFECTS

In searching for familial environmental factors that create similarities among reared-together relatives, it is natural to begin with parents. Parents have long been thought to represent the primary socialization agents of the children they rear (Collins, Maccoby, Steinberg, Hetherington, & Bornstein, 2000) and thus a likely source of shared environmental effects. There are three principal ways by which parents might environmentally affect the substance use behavior of their adolescent offspring (Hicks et al., 2013). First, parent substance use provides a model that may indirectly encourage substance use in their adolescent offspring. Second, parents may engage in harsh and inconsistent parenting, diminishing their ability as socialization agents. Finally, parents may have a permissive attitude concerning adolescent substance use or be lax in monitoring their adolescent offspring.

Most of the relevant behavioral genetic research on parent influences has focused on the extent to which both genetic and environmental factors contribute to parent–offspring similarity for substance use phenotypes. As discussed earlier, there is a moderate but consistent correlation between parent and offspring substance use, but this correlation may reflect both genetic and shared environmental influences. There are, however, several studies reporting significant parent–adolescent offspring substance use similarity in adopted as well as nonadopted families. The study by Keyes et al. (2008) is especially informative. This study investigated the effects of exposure to parent smoking on adolescent functioning in a sample of 463 adopted and 322 nonadopted adolescents. Exposure to parent smoking was associated with adolescent smoking in both nonadopted and adopted families, confirming the existence of a shared environmental effect. Exposure to parent smoking was also associated with other indicators of externalizing psychopathology, but only in the nonadopted families, indicating that these latter associations were predominantly genetically and not environmentally mediated. This study thus implicates two pathways by which parent smoking can impact adolescent offspring functioning (Figure 13.3). The first is a general pathway that is primarily genetically mediated and arises because parent smoking is a marker of parent externalizing, which has a general effect on offspring externalizing psychopathology. The second is a specific pathway that is primarily environmentally mediated and arises because parents who smoke have adolescent offspring who are specifically more likely to smoke.

Parents are not the only source of familial environmental influence. Indeed, some have argued that environmental transmission within families is stronger between horizontally related (i.e., siblings) than between vertically related (i.e., parent–offspring) relatives (Rowe & Gulley, 1992). The finding, discussed previously, that siblings are most similar in their levels of substance use when they are close in age and of the same gender supports the existence of sibling influences. As with parents, there are various ways by which siblings might influence each other. Samek et al. (2015) used a unique sample of adopted and nonadopted siblings to identify mechanisms of sibling influence. Consistent with the previous literature, these researchers reported a moderate correlation in the self-reported alcohol use of sibling pairs. This association was mediated entirely by two factors. First, older siblings facilitated the alcohol use of their younger siblings by making it easier for them to gain access to alcohol. Second, younger siblings' perception of the substance use of their older brothers and sisters was a better predictor of their alcohol use than their brothers' and sisters' self-reported use, indicating that perceptions of how much a sibling is using substances helps adolescents to develop a concept of what is normative adolescent behavior.

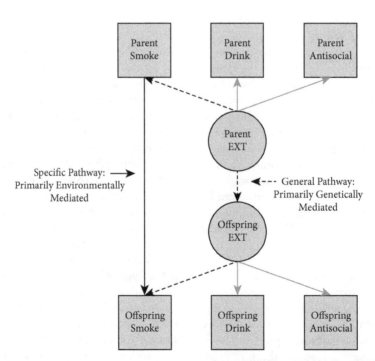

Figure 13.3 General and specific familial transmission of smoking as implicated in the adoption study by Keyes et al. (2008). The association of parent smoking with adolescent offspring functioning implicates two pathways of transmission. The first is a general pathway (highlighted by dashed lines), which is primarily genetically mediated and arises because both parent smoking and offspring smoking are markers of externalizing psychopathology. The second is a specific pathway (highlighted by bold solid lines), which is primarily environmentally mediated. EXT, externalizing.

EXTRA-FAMILIAL SOURCES OF SHARED ENVIRONMENTAL EFFECTS

Two extra-familial factors have been investigated as potential contributors to the shared environmental influence on adolescent substance use. Consistent with existing research, Walden et al. (2004) reported that 45% of the variance in a measure of overall substance use was attributable to shared environmental factors in a sample of 1,404 14-year-old twins. This study also included multiple measures of peer deviance (self- and teacher-rated) and found that twins had markedly similar peer groups. Twin correlations for peer group characteristics were generally between .60 and .70 regardless of zygosity, so that shared environmental factors were found to account for 49% to 65% of the variance in the different measures of peer deviance. Most significantly, peer group alone accounted for 77% of the shared environmental influence on adolescent substance use.

The second major extra-familial source of shared environmental influence that has been investigated is substance availability, a necessary prerequisite for adolescent substance use. In a sample of 1,722 adult male twins, Gillespie et al. (2009) investigated the overlap between retrospectively assessed cannabis use and cannabis availability. A moderate to strong shared environmental influence was found for both cannabis availability (accounting for 34% of the variance) and cannabis use initiation (41%), with over 95% of the shared environmental influence on the latter being attributable to cannabis availability. Clearly if substance availability accounts for 95% and peer group 77% of the shared environmental influence on adolescent substance use, the two factors must themselves overlap. Similarly, the shared environmental contributions associated with siblings and parents likely overlap those associated with peer group and substance availability. For example, siblings may be providing substance access and a conflicted parent–offspring relationship may amplify the influence of the peer group. Multivariate analyses are needed to characterize the various mediating pathways of shared environmental influence.

The Importance of a Developmental Perspective
Age Moderation of Genetic and Environmental Contributions to Substance Use and Abuse

One of the most consistent findings to emerge from the behavioral genetic literature is that the shared environment accounts for a relatively small proportion of phenotypic variance. For most behavioral traits, estimates of c^2, generally derived from twin studies, are small (Plomin, 1983; Turkheimer, 2000). The findings on adolescent substance use presented earlier are clearly not consistent with this general finding, raising the question of why these studies differ from those with other behavioral phenotypes. One possibility is that substance use is fundamentally different from the phenotypes (e.g., personality and cognitive ability) that have been the focus of most behavioral genetic research. Studies of substance use phenotypes in adult samples, however, do not report strong shared environmental effects (Goldman, Oroszi, & Ducci, 2005), suggesting developmental stage may be important. Indeed, meta-analyses of twin studies of diverse behavioral traits, including social attitudes, psychopathology, and cognitive ability, have shown that the magnitude of genetic influences on these traits increases with age while the importance of shared environmental influences declines (Bergen, Gardner, & Kendler, 2007). It may be that the strong shared environmental influences on substance use phenotypes found in adolescent samples do not persist into later developmental periods.

There are a limited number of longitudinal behavioral genetic studies on adolescent substance use, but these studies are consistent in showing that age is a powerful moderator of genetic and environmental effects. Rose et al. (2001) undertook a longitudinal study of the frequency of alcohol use in a sample of nearly 1,800 like-sex pairs of Finnish twins assessed three times, at ages 16, 17, and 18.5. The contribution of shared environmental factors decreased from 37% at age 16 to 14% at age 18.5, while the heritability increased from 33% to 50% over the same interval. Derringer et al. (2008) reported similar results in a second longitudinal study of 711 male and 675 female like-sex twin pairs. In this latter study the phenotype was a measure of overall substance use involvement (specifically the number of 11 possible substances used), and twins were assessed three times, at ages 11, 14, and 17 years. Figure 13.4 provides a summary of the findings from this study. In both the male and female samples, the proportion of phenotypic variance attributable to shared environmental factors decreased markedly across the assessment waves while the contribution of genetic factors increased.

In the only relevant longitudinal adoption study, McGue et al. (2014) investigated parent–offspring similarity for a composite quantity-frequency index of drinking in a sample of 689 adopted and 540 nonadopted offspring. The age of the offspring

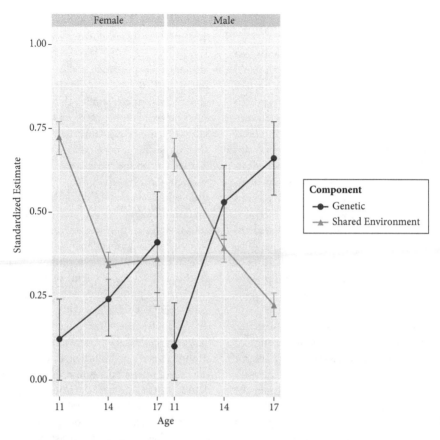

Figure 13.4 The increase in genetic influences and decrease in shared environmental influences with age in the longitudinal twin study by Derringer et al. (2007). Plotted is proportion of variance in substance use involvement accounted for by additive genetic and shared environmental factors. Errors bars give 95% confidence intervals.

sample spanned 11 to 28 years over the study's three longitudinal assessments. Consistent with a genetic influence, the parent–offspring drinking correlation was greater among the biologically related pairs than among pairs related only by adoption. Nonetheless, the adopted parent–offspring correlation was statistically significant albeit modest in magnitude (i.e., between .10 and .20). Both the adopted and nonadopted parent–offspring correlation increased with age up to age 21, suggesting that both genetic and shared environmental influences increase with age. After age 21, however, the two correlations diverged. The biological parent–offspring correlation continued to increase and reached its peak in the oldest age group at $r = .30$. The adopted parent–offspring correlation declined after age 21, equaling only .11 in the oldest age group. The divergence of the nonadopted and adopted parent–offspring correlations in the oldest age group supports findings from longitudinal twin studies showing the heritability of substance use phenotypes increases

with age while shared environmental influences declines.

Although not formally a longitudinal study, the retrospective study by Kendler et al. (2008) is relevant to the question of age moderation of genetic and environmental influences on substance use. The study involved a sample of nearly 1,800 pairs of male twins who were asked to retrospectively report on their use of nicotine, alcohol, and cannabis for every year of their life. Biometric analysis of the resulting data revealed that shared environmental influences for use of each of the three substances were maximal in adolescence but declined to zero by midlife. In contrast, heritability estimates for the three substances were near-zero in early adolescence but increased throughout life, reaching a peak in adulthood.

The shifting pattern of genetic and environmental contributions to substance use phenotypes over time could be a consequence of differences between substance use initiation and substance use progression. Specifically, with age, substance use phenotypes will increasingly reflect the progression of use rather than initial levels of use. Consequently, if the contribution of shared environmental factors is greater and genetic factors weaker on substance use initiation than on substance use progression, then aggregate measures of substance use should show increasing heritability and decreasing shared environmental influences with age. Although twin studies of adult samples do not consistently find these differences between substance use initiation and progression (Kendler, Karkowski, Corey, Prescott, & Neale, 1999; Kendler, Neale, et al., 1999), there is some preliminary support for this proposition in the limited relevant literature on adolescent substance use. For example, in an analysis of substance use in a sample of 1,214 adolescent twin pairs, Fowler et al. (2007) reported that genetic factors accounted for 26% of the variance in alcohol use initiation, and shared environmental factors accounted for 65%. In contrast, for alcohol use progression, genetic and shared environmental factors accounted for 35% and 47% of the variance, respectively. Similarly, genetic and shared environmental factors accounted for, respectively, 35% and 47% of the variance in marijuana use initiation but 64% and 0% for marijuana use progression.

The Importance of Age of Onset: Behavioral Genetic Perspectives

The observation that early initiation of substance use in adolescence is associated with increased risk for substance abuse in adulthood is robust and widely replicated (Breslau et al., 1993; Dewit et al., 2000; Grant & Dawson, 1997, 1998; McGue et al., 2001). Moreover, the association cannot be attributed simply to early substance users having a greater amount of time to progress to substance abuse as compared to late initiators (Anthony & Petronis, 1995). Nonetheless, the basis for the association is unclear. Guttmanova et al. (2012) described three alternative models for the association of early substance use with adult substance abuse (represented schematically in Figure 13.5). Under the marker hypothesis (Model A) the association is noncausal. It arises because both early substance use and adult substance abuse are indicators (i.e., markers) of a common vulnerability to externalizing psychopathology. This common liability can manifest as substance use experimentation in early adolescence but as a substance use disorder in later life. Under the compromised functioning hypothesis (Model B), the association is causal but indirect. That is,

substance use in early adolescence can result in compromised adolescent functioning in a way that increases the likelihood of adult substance abuse. This effect might be mediated socially by, for example, increasing exposure to high-risk social environments (Englund et al., 2013; Simons-Morton & Chen, 2006), or neurologically because the adolescent brain is especially susceptible to the neurotoxic effects of alcohol (Spear, 2013) and other drugs (Jacobus & Tapert, 2014). Finally, under the increased substance use hypothesis (Model C), the association is causal and direct. In this case, adolescents are seen to be especially vulnerable to overconsumption and rapid escalation in their drinking. As compared to adults, adolescents show reduced sensitivity to the negative effects of alcohol (e.g., sedation) (Cha, Li, Wilson, & Swartzwelder, 2006; Little, Kuhn, Wilson, & Swartzwelder, 1996; White et al., 2002) but an increased susceptibility to the positive effects (e.g., social facilitation, euphoria) (Varlinskaya & Spear, 2002). This divergence in negative and positive sensitivity contributes to adolescents adopting a pattern of periodic binging and an increased risk of developing abusive patterns of substance use (Sloan et al., 2011).

Behavioral genetic research provides support for the hypothesis that early substance use is a marker of a liability that in adulthood can manifest as externalizing psychopathology. In an early study of the question, Prescott and Kendler (1999) used a large sample of nearly 9,000 twins to investigate the basis for the association of early drinking with adult alcoholism. They concluded that the association was predominantly if not entirely noncausal, arising because the genetic and shared environmental factors that contributed to early drinking overlapped extensively with those influencing later alcoholism. In a subsequent study of over 5,000 twins, Sartor et al. (2009) corroborated this finding by showing that the association between age at first drink and alcohol dependence was due predominantly to common genetic influences. Building on this work, McGue et al. (2001) reported that early alcohol use was a nonspecific marker of risk, being associated not only with alcoholism but also drug abuse, antisocial personality disorder, personality markers of impulsivity, academic underachievement, and even P3 amplitude, a well-known psychophysiological marker of alcoholism risk (Iacono, Carlson, Malone, & McGue, 2002). The possibility that early use of alcohol is a marker of a general liability that manifests later in life in a broad array of externalizing disorders received additional support

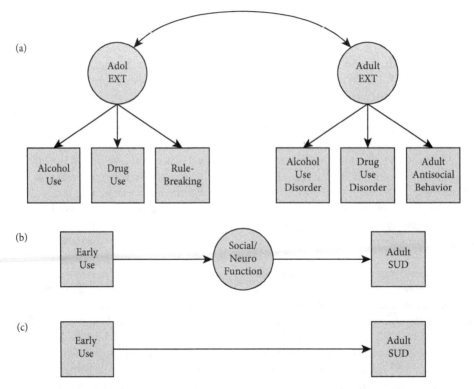

Figure 13.5 Alternative models relating early substance use involvement with adult substance abuse after Guttmannova et al. (2012). Model A is the marker hypothesis, Model B is the compromised functioning hypothesis, and Model C is the increased substance use hypothesis. EXT, externalizing; SUD, substance use disorder.

in a study by McGue and Iacono (2005). In this study, each of an array of early adolescent problem behaviors (e.g., drinking, police contact, sex) was associated with each of an array of adult externalizing disorders (e.g., antisocial personality disorder, drug abuse/dependence, nicotine dependence). The association between the two domains was largely accounted for by a correlation of .75 between a latent adolescent problem behavior factor and a latent adult externalizing factor.

Although behavioral genetic research is consistent in supporting the marker hypothesis, it does not entirely rule out the possibility that early substance use also has a causal influence on adult outcomes. The counterfactual model of causality (Winship & Morgan, 1999) provides one framework by which to leverage twin data to make stronger causal inferences with observational data (McGue, Osler, & Christensen, 2010). Given an outcome variable, the counterfactual model assumes an individual can only experience either exposure or nonexposure to a given variable that has an effect on the outcome. The key assumption is that regardless of an individual's actual exposure experience, he or

she has a potential status on the outcome variable in either state: the one that was actually experienced (observed) and the one that he or she could have but did not experience (unobserved). The advantage of investigating for associations within twin pairs discordant for an environmental exposure such as early substance use is that twins are perfectly matched on rearing environment and in the case of MZ twins also genotype. Consequently, in a within-pair analysis, the unexposed twin provides an approximation to the counterfactual model (i.e., what the outcome in the exposed twin might have been had she or he not been exposed). For example, if early substance use is causal, then we expect that within twin pairs discordant for early use the early-using twin will have higher rates of substance abuse than his or her cotwin.

Kendler et al. (2013) investigated the consequences of early smoking in a sample of 234 discordant MZ twin pairs. All twins had smoked sometime during their lifetime, but the two members of each pair differed by at least 2 years in the age at which they first smoked regularly. The earlier-smoking twin was more likely to be nicotine dependent in adulthood than the latter-smoking twin. Early smoking was not, however, associated with use or abuse of alcohol and illicit drugs within the discordant twin pairs, suggesting that early smoking was a specific liability for nicotine dependence rather than a general liability for substance abuse. Similar studies of MZ twins discordant for early drinking in Australian (Deutsch et al., 2013), Finnish (Rose, Winter, Viken, & Kaprio, 2014), and US (Irons, Iacono, & McGue, 2015) samples have all found that early use of alcohol in adolescence is associated with increased involvement with alcohol in adulthood but not consistently associated with other indicators of externalizing psychopathology.

Findings from MZ twins discordant for early use of nicotine and alcohol consequently appear largely inconsistent with one of the most venerable developmental models of substance abuse. The gateway model was introduced to account for the typical progression of adolescent substance use from "soft drugs" such as nicotine and alcohol to "hard drugs" such as cocaine and opioids. The gateway model sees this progression as causal; early use of nicotine and alcohol leads to the subsequent use of marijuana, which in turn increases the likelihood of cocaine and opioid use (Kandel, 2002). The gateway model has profound implications for prevention, as it suggests that "hard drug" use could be reduced by intervening early in the progression of substance use. Although the discordant MZ twin studies on early alcohol and nicotine use do not support the gateway model, a similar study of early cannabis use does.

Lynskey et al. (2003) studied a sample of 234 twin pairs where one member of each pair had used cannabis prior to age 18 and the other first used cannabis after age 17. The early-using twin was not only more likely to use and abuse cannabis as an adult; he or she was also more likely to use and abuse a range of illicit drugs, including sedatives, cocaine, and opioids. The early-using twin was even more likely to be alcohol dependent than the late-using cotwin. This study clearly supports the hypothesis that early use of softer drugs (in this case cannabis) increases the likelihood of later use of harder drugs, perhaps by facilitating access to these other drugs. Complicating interpretation of this study, however, is evidence that the cannabis-using twin in discordant MZ twin pairs had higher levels of sensation seeking, a known personality risk factor for substance abuse, than the nonusing cotwin (Vink, Nawijn, Boomsma, & Willemsen, 2007). It may be the personality risk factors that led to early cannabis use, rather than early cannabis use per se, that is causal of adult substance abuse.

Identifying the Specific Genetic Variants That Contribute to Adolescent Substance Use and Abuse

For much of the past 20 years, the search for the specific genetic variants that underlie the heritability of substance-use phenotypes has taken a candidate-gene approach. In this approach, researchers targeted for investigation variants in one or more genes hypothesized to be related to the disorder they were studying based either on what was known about the pathophysiology of the disorder or previous genetic linkage findings (Tabor, Risch, & Myers, 2002). Unfortunately, candidate-gene studies have had a poor record of replication, and progress in characterizing the nature of genetic risk for complex disorders has been slow (Ioannidis, Ntzani, Trikalinos, & Contopoulos-Ioannidis, 2001). Candidate-gene studies of substance-use phenotypes in adolescent samples have similarly struggled to produce replicable results (Corley et al., 2008; Verweij et al., 2012). Nonetheless, several gene systems have been implicated in adolescent substance use and abuse and, as we discuss later, the effects of the relevant variants appear to be developmentally moderated.

Within the past 5 years, the development of efficient genotyping technologies has led to the emergence of an alternative to the candidate-gene study approach. A genome-wide association study (GWAS) involves investigating the association of a phenotype with each of a large number of genetic variants (usually 500,000 or more). Because the genetic variants are selected to span the entire genome, a GWAS represents a hypothesis-free approach for searching the entire human genome for relevant variants (Visscher, Brown, McCarthy, & Yang, 2012). As we discuss later, even though this approach holds great promise, there has to date been a limited number of GWAS of substance-use related phenotypes.

Candidate-Gene Studies
GENETIC VARIANTS
IN ALCOHOL-METABOLIZING GENES

The primary metabolic pathway for the elimination of ethanol involves a two-step process. Ethanol is first oxidized to acetaldehyde by the enzyme alcohol dehydrogenase (ADH) and then acetaldehyde is oxidized to acetate by the enzyme aldehyde dehydrogenase (ALDH). High levels of acetaldehyde are toxic and can lead to the experience of nausea, headaches, and dizziness following drinking. Consequently, genetic variants that code for rapid ADH-mediated conversion to acetaldehyde or slow ALDH-mediated conversion to acetate would be expected to be protective against heavy drinking and alcohol dependence (Macgregor et al., 2009). Because the second step in the metabolic pathway is the rate-limiting step, however, genetic variation in ALDH is likely to have the greatest impact on drinking.

Consistent with this expectation, a genetic variant in the mitochondrial version of ALDH (designated ALDH2) has been consistently associated with drinking and alcoholism risk. Specifically, the ALDH2*2 variant, which is relatively common in East Asian populations but extremely rare in other population groups, codes for a deficient version of the enzyme and a markedly diminished capacity to eliminate the toxic substance acetaldehyde following drinking. East Asians who carry at least one copy of the ALDH2*2 allele are more likely to experience a flushing response following drinking and consequently less likely to drink heavily or become alcohol dependent (Luczak, Glatt, & Wall, 2006). Most of the research relating genetic variation in ALDH2 to drinking has been based on samples of adults and recent studies in adolescent samples suggest that the effect of the ALDH2 variant may differ markedly across development.

In a sample of 428 Chinese American first-year college students, Hendershot et al. (2005) reported that the ALDH2*2 allele was not associated with either current or heavy episodic drinking, suggesting that the ALDH2*2 allele may not be protective in a high-risk college environment. A longitudinal study by Kim et al. (2010) provides further support for the developmentally contingent nature of the ALDH2*2 effect. Consistent with the earlier study, these investigators reported that ALDH2 was not associated with the frequency of drinking or drinking problems in a sample of 551 Korean first-year college students. When this sample was followed up 6 years later, after they had completed college, however, a protective effect of ALDH2*2 was observed. In a second longitudinal study, Irons et al. (2012) extended these findings to the precollege adolescent years. In this study a sample of 356 adopted, Asian American adolescents were assessed over an age range that spanned early adolescence through the mid-20s. ALDH2 was not associated with alcohol consumption, drinking problems, or a diagnosis of alcohol dependence through age 19,

but after age 19 a protective effect of ALDH2*2 on drinking behavior was observed.

GENETIC VARIATION IN THE GABA SYSTEM

The primary neurotransmitter involved in inhibitory neurotransmission is γ -aminobutyric acid (GABA), and many of the neurological and behavioral effects of drugs, including ethanol, benzodiazepines, anesthetics, and barbiturates, are mediated either directly or indirectly by $GABA_A$ receptors (Krystal et al., 2006). Of the genes in the GABA system, the one that has been most strongly associated with substance use problems is GABRA2. In adult samples, genetic variation in GABRA2 has been shown to be significantly associated with risk of alcohol dependence (Covault, Gelernter, Hesselbrock, Nellissery, & Kranzler, 2004; Edenberg et al., 2004; Fehr et al., 2006; Lappalainen et al., 2005; Soyka et al., 2008), comorbid alcohol dependence and drug dependence (Agrawal et al., 2006), and general externalizing behavior (Dick et al., 2009). Other studies have, however, failed to find the expected associations of GABRA2 with alcohol dependence (Drgon, D'Addario, & Uhl, 2006; Matthews, Hoffman, Zezza, Stiffler, & Hill, 2007), drinking behavior (Irons et al., 2014), or other substance abuse (Drgon et al., 2006).

Only a small number of studies have explored whether genetic variants in GABRA2 are also associated with substance use behavior in adolescent samples. Corley et al. (2008) failed to observe any significant associations with GABRA2 in a comparison of 231 adolescent males with a diagnosis of antisocial drug dependence with a matched control sample of 231 unaffected male adolescents. Alternatively, using the offspring sample (N = 860) from the Consortium on the Genetics of Alcoholism (COGA) study, Dick et al. (2006) reported that GABRA2 was not associated with indicators of alcohol dependence in childhood or adolescence but was associated with symptoms of conduct disorder. By taking advantage of the longitudinal data available in COGA, however, these investigators were able to show a GABRA2 effect on drinking phenotypes that emerged after age 20. Similarly, Trucco, Villafuerte, Heitzeg, Burmeister, and Zucker (2014) reported an association between GABRA2 and alcohol abuse and drug use in late adolescence; an association that was mediated by rule breaking in early and middle adolescence.

GENETIC VARIANTS IN OTHER SYSTEMS

Genetic variation in two other systems has been investigated in adolescent samples, although the number of relevant studies is quite small. The endogenous opioid system has been extensively studied in addiction, with the mu-opioid receptor gene (*OPRM1*) being the focus of much of the genetic research (Koob & Kreek, 2007). A variant in the *OPRM1* gene (designated rs1799971) that changes the amino acid sequence of the receptor has been extensively investigated in studies of alcohol, cocaine, heroin, and nicotine in adult samples. Arias et al. (2006) undertook a meta-analysis of this literature and reported a nonsignificant pooled (across various forms of substance dependence) odds ratio of 1.01. Given the failure to find consistent evidence for an association of *OPRM1* with substance-use behavior in adults, it is not surprising that *OPRM1* has not been consistently associated with substance use phenotypes in adolescent samples (Corley et al., 2008; Kleinjan, Poelen, Engels, & Verhagen, 2013).

The cholinergic system, comprised of both nicotinic and muscarinic receptors, has been hypothesized to play an essential role in drug reward (Hyman, 2005). Genetic variation in the genes coding for nicotinic receptors has been associated specifically with smoking behavior and will be discussed later. Genetic variation in the muscarinic receptors has been associated more broadly with dependence on multiple different substances. In particular, variants in the gene coding for the cholinergic muscarinic receptor 2 (*CHRM2*) has been associated with alcohol dependence (Wang et al., 2004) and comorbid alcohol and drug dependence (Dick, Agrawal, et al., 2007). Although these findings suggest that CHRM2 might be a risk factor for general substance abuse, not every study of *CHRM2* has reported positive results (Luo et al., 2005). The limited investigation of *CHRM2* in adolescent samples suggests a similarly inconsistent pattern of results (Hendershot, Bryan, Ewing, Claus, & Hutchison, 2011).

Genome-Wide Association Studies

GWASs have led to the identification of several thousand genetic associations and revealed two fundamental characteristics of the genetic architecture of common disease (Visscher et al., 2012). First, for any specific heritable phenotype the number of relevant genetic variants is very large, numbering in the hundreds or more likely thousands. Second, the effect of any specific variant on phenotype is very small, accounting for much less than 1% of phenotypic variance for quantitative phenotypes or having an odds ratio less than 1.2 for categorical phenotypes. The small size of the genetic effects along with the need for a very small p-value threshold to correct for the large number of markers tested (usually $p < 5*10^{-8}$) means that very large samples are required for a GWAS to succeed. A recent review of GWAS studies in psychiatric genetics concluded that reliable identification of genetic variants requires samples of at least 30,000 cases (Gratten, Wray, Keller, & Visscher, 2014). To date, samples used in GWAS of most substance-related phenotypes have included far fewer than 30,000 participants, so it is not surprising that these GWASs have not as yet resulted in the identification of risk variants (Agrawal et al., 2011; Bierut et al., 2010; Edenberg et al., 2010; Kendler et al., 2011; McGue et al., 2013; Treutlein et al., 2009).

Smoking is the one substance use phenotype where researchers have been able to achieve very large GWAS samples (in excess of 100,000), and several genomic regions harboring risk variants for smoking have been identified (Liu et al., 2010; Thorgeirsson et al., 2010). The region most strongly implicated in smoking is the q25.1 region of chromosome 15, which contains a cluster of genes coding for *CHRNA5-CHRNA3-CHRNB4* nicotinic receptors (Chen et al., 2012). Although most of the research on genetic variation in this region has been based on adult samples, this region has also been implicated in samples of adolescent smokers (Rodriguez et al., 2011), perhaps because the genetic variants appear to be risk factors for early-onset heavy smoking (Hartz et al., 2012). The second region implicated by GWAS of smoking is the gene on chromosome 19 that codes for cytochrome P450 2A6 (*CYP2A6*), which plays a role in nicotine metabolism.

Rather than focus on the effect of any single genetic variant, several research groups have explored how the aggregate effect of multiple variants is related to smoking, and most important in the present context, whether this effect varied at different developmental stages. Vrieze et al. (2012) created an aggregate risk score from 92 genetic variants identified in large-scale GWASs of smoking in a sample of more than 3,000 individuals assessed longitudinally at ages 14, 17, 20, and 24 years. Although this score accounted for only a small amount of variance (~1%), the relationship of the score with smoking increased with age, being higher at ages 20 and 24 than at 14 and 17. These findings were extended in a study of 1,037 individuals from the

Dunedin longitudinal study by Belsky et al. (2013), who created a genetic risk score from six genetic variants, four from the nicotinic gene cluster on chromosome 15 and two from the *CYP2A6* region on chromosome 19. They found that the genetic risk score was not predictive of smoking initiation. However, among those who had initiated smoking, adolescents with a high genetic risk score were more likely to progress rapidly to heavy smoking and nicotine dependence than those who had a low genetic risk score.

Summary of Efforts to Identify Genetic Variants Associated With Adolescent Substance Use

Although only a small number of specific genetic variants have been identified to date, a consistent pattern of research findings is emerging from genetic research on adolescent substance use and abuse. First, contrary to expectations from a decade ago, variants with moderate or large effects on risk are unlikely to exist. Even when aggregated, genetic risk scores account for a very small percentage of phenotypic variance. As a consequence, the identification of the relevant genetic variants will require very large samples, much larger than has been achieved thus far with most substance-related phenotypes. Second, the effects of genetic variants are likely to be developmentally modulated. That is, whether it is the *ALDH2* effect on drinking, the *GABRA2* effect on substance abuse, or the genetic risk score association with smoking, the effects of specific genetic variants are diminished in adolescent relative to adult populations.

Models of Gene–Environment Interplay in Adolescent Substance Use and Abuse

Behavioral genetic research on adolescent substance use and abuse has documented the importance not only of genetic influences but also the contribution of environmental factors. Adoption studies have consistently reported correlations in the substance use patterns of reared-together relatives even when they are not genetically related, and the consistent lack of perfect concordance for substance use phenotypes in genetically identical MZ twins can only be explained by their environmental differences. There is a need to understand how genes and the environment combine to influence complex phenotypes such as substance use and abuse. Two forms of gene–environment interplay have received considerable theoretical

and empirical attention in the substance use field. First, gene–environment correlation arises because genetic factors are not likely to be independently distributed of environmental factors. The environments parents provide for the children they rear are likely correlated with the genes they transmitted to their children. Moreover, the manner in which an individual behaves helps to shape the environment he or she experiences, either by the reactions his or her behavior elicits from others or through the experiential choices the individual makes. To the extent an individual's behavior is genetically influenced, this will induce a gene–environment correlation. The second form of gene–environment interplay is gene–environment interaction. A gene–environment interaction occurs whenever the magnitude of a genetic influence varies as a function of the environment an individual is exposed to.

Gene–Environment Correlation

Passive gene–environment correlations arise because parents provide the children they rear with both their genes and their rearing environments. Hence, having a parent with a substance use disorder is an indicator not only of increased genetic risk but also increased environmental risk. For example, Buu et al. (2007) tracked the residential migration patterns of families with and without an alcoholic father over a 12-year period. Families with an alcoholic father were more likely to either remain in or move to a more disadvantaged neighborhood (high crime, poverty, and residential instability) relative to families not having an alcoholic father. As a consequence, these neighborhood characteristics predicted more symptoms of alcohol, nicotine, and marijuana dependence in the offspring of these men, as well as more symptoms of antisocial personality disorder and major depression in young adulthood (Buu et al., 2009). In a similar way, the dysfunctional family climates that substance-abusing parents are more likely to provide (Latendresse et al., 2008) create passive gene–environment correlations with the high-risk genetic variants these parents transmitted to their children.

As children transition into adolescence and gain greater autonomy in selecting their environments, active gene–environment correlations become more relevant in the development of substance use and abuse, which also emerge during the same developmental interval (Bergen et al., 2007; Scarr & McCartney, 1983). Active gene–environment correlations arise primarily because heritable traits increase exposure to complementary environments, which can then increase risk for substance use disorders. Hicks et al. (2013) used a longitudinal-twin design to delineate active gene–environment correlation processes over time by investigating the relationships among low socialization (i.e., failure to conform to adult supervision and internalize age-appropriate norms and values for behavior) at age 11, a nonspecific marker of risk; a composite of environmental liabilities at age 14 (e.g., parent–offspring conflict, peer group characteristics); and a composite of substance dependence symptoms at age 17 involving alcohol, nicotine, and marijuana disorders. Low socialization predicted substance dependence symptoms at age 17, but it was also strongly correlated with environmental risk at age 14. Moreover, low socialization at age 11 predicted greater environmental risk at age 14, even after controlling for the stability of environmental risk from ages 11 to 14. In turn, environmental risk at age 14 mediated some—but not all—of the effect of low socialization at age 11 on age 17 substance dependence. In fact, 78% of the genetic correlation between childhood socialization and adolescent SUDs was mediated by environmental risk at age 14. That is, to the extent that (under) socialization accounts for heritable risk in SUDs, the mechanism is indirect, via increased exposure to high-risk environments.

Gene–Environment Interaction

A gene–environment interaction occurs whenever the magnitude of the genetic influence varies as a function of the environment. Interactions can be established either using biometric methods, by showing that the heritability of a trait differs in different environments, or using a measured-gene approach, by showing that the effect of a specific gene variant varies as a function of the environment. Shanahan and Hofer (2005) have described different forms of gene–environment interaction, two of which are especially relevant to adolescent substance use. Under the *social control* form of interaction, the magnitude of the genetic effect is minimized in environments that limit the opportunity for behavioral expression through rigid social structure (Figure 13.6a). Under the *triggering* form of interaction, the dysfunctional nature of an environment can trigger the expression of an underlying genetic diathesis (Figure 13.6b).

Interactions involving social control have received consistent support in the adolescent substance use field. Thus, agents, institutions, and cultural practices that limit adolescent choice all serve to attenuate genetic influences on adolescent substance use. Using the biometric approach to detect gene–environment interaction, the heritability of adolescent substance use has been found to be reduced in religious homes (Button, Hewitt, Rhee, Corley, & Stallings, 2010; Koopmans, Slutske, van Baal, & Boomsma, 1999), when parents closely monitor their adolescent's behavior (Dick, Viken, et al., 2007), in rural settings that afford the opportunity for community control (Rose et al., 2001), and in states that prohibit smoking in public places (Boardman, Blalock, & Pampel, 2010) or tax cigarettes at a high rate (Boardman, 2009). Although there are only a limited number of relevant measured-gene tests for gene–environment interaction, these studies are also consistent in suggesting that genetic influences are diminished in environments characterized by high levels of social control. For example, high levels of parental monitoring diminish the effect of the high-risk allele (rs16969968) in the *CHRNA5* nicotinic receptor gene (Chen et al., 2009) and reduce the association of risk variants in both *GABRA2* (Dick et al., 2009) and *CHRM2* (Dick et al., 2011) with adolescent externalizing behavior.

There is also consistent support for the triggering form of gene–environment interaction, where high levels of environmental disorganization or dysfunction triggers a genetic diathesis for adolescent substance use and abuse. Much of the relevant research has involved peer group influences. For example, the heritability of substance use is higher among adolescents exposed to deviant peer groups as compared to those whose peer groups are not deviant (Agrawal et al., 2010; Harden, Hill, Turkheimer, & Emery, 2008). A systematic investigation of the triggering form of gene–environment interaction is provided by the study by Hicks et al. (2009). These investigators investigated how six different forms of environmental adversity (e.g., peer deviance, parent–offspring relationship problems, life stress) moderated the heritability of externalizing behavior (including substance abuse but also antisocial behavior) in a large sample of 17-year-old twins. For all six measures, genetic influences on externalizing increased in the context of greater levels of environmental adversity.

Conclusion and Future Directions

Behavioral genetic and biometrical research has shown that adolescent substance use and abuse differs in several important ways from adult substance use and abuse. First, whether as shown through

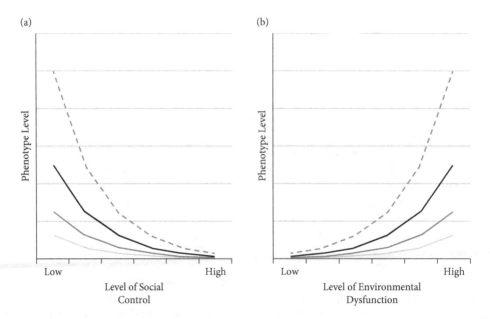

Figure 13.6 Plotted are hypothetical mean phenotypic values for three genotypes (each a separate curve) as a function of the environment (horizontal axis) under two alternative models of gene–environment interaction. (a) Social control model. (b) Triggering model. Each line represents the observed phenotypic reaction range associated with a specific genotype.

biometrical analysis of twin data or the exploration of associations with specific genetic variants, the importance of genetic influences is consistently weaker in adolescence than in adulthood. Alternatively, both twin and adoption studies have shown that the influence of the shared environment also changes between adolescence and early adulthood, with shared environmental influences being markedly more important in adolescence than in adulthood. These findings along with epidemiological research suggesting that the general substance abuse factor diminishes in importance with age suggest that an important developmental transition occurs between adolescence and early adulthood. During adolescence, genetic factors appear to have only a moderate influence on substance use behavior, and that influence appears to be largely general in that it is associated with increased risk for multiple substance abuse problems as well as with non-substance-related behavioral disinhibition. In early adulthood, genetic factors come to have a larger influence on substance use behavior, and the nature of that influence appears to be increasingly substance specific.

We believe that this characterization of existing behavioral genetic research on adolescent substance use and abuse motivates three major questions that we expect will guide future research in this area:

1. What are the specific genetic variants that contribute to risk of adolescent substance use and

abuse? Given everything we now know about the genetic architecture of complex behavioral phenotypes, we expect that answering this question will require large, collaborative efforts. We do not, however, expect that these efforts will result in the identification of all the relevant genetic variants, even with very large samples. Nonetheless, if findings with other psychiatric disorders be a guide (Gratten et al., 2014), the identification of even a small number of relevant variants is likely to lead to important insights into the biological nature of adolescent substance use.

2. Are the genetic variants that influence adolescent substance use behavior the same as those that influence adult substance use behavior? Existing research suggests that there are distinct genetic contributions to adolescent and adult substance use. We consequently expect that there will be some genetic variants that carry higher risk in adolescence (perhaps because they are associated with risk for general behavioral disinhibition) and other genetic variants that carry higher risk in adulthood (perhaps because they relate to the stimulus properties of specific substances.)

3. How do the specific genetic and specific environmental factors combine to influence the development of substance use behavior? We believe there are two important aspects to this question. First, gene–environment interaction research has shown that genetic risk can be modulated

by environmental circumstances. Most of this research is at an initial stage of inquiry, and there is a great need to better understand the underlying mechanisms in order to inform prevention and intervention efforts. Second, everything we know about adolescent substance use and abuse indicates that a developmental perspective is absolutely essential. Although undertaking the necessary longitudinal research is challenging, there is a pressing need to understand how the relevant genetic and environmental influences play out from prior to substance use initiation through to substance abuse onset.

References

Agrawal, A., Balasubramanian, S., Smith, E. K., Madden, P. A. F., Bucholz, K. K., Heath, A. C., & Lynskey, M. T. (2010). Peer substance involvement modifies genetic influences on regular substance involvement in young women. *Addiction, 105*(10), 1844–1853. doi: 10.1111/j.1360-0443.2010.02993.x

Agrawal, A., Edenberg, H. J., Foroud, T., Bierut, L. J., Dunne, G., Hinrichs, A. L., . . . Dick, D. M. (2006). Association of *GABRA2* with drug dependence in the collaborative study of the genetics of alcoholism sample. *Behavior Genetics, 36*(5), 640–650. doi: 10.1007/s10519-006-9069-4

Agrawal, A., Lynskey, M. T., Hinrichs, A., Grucza, R., Saccone, S. F., Krueger, R., . . . GENEVA Consortium. (2011). A genome-wide association study of DSM-IV cannabis dependence. *Addiction Biology, 16*(3), 514–518. doi: 10.1111/j.1369-1600.2010.00255.x

Anthony, J. C., & Petronis, K. R. (1995). Early-onset drug use and risk of later drug problems. *Drug and Alcohol Dependence, 40*, 9–15.

Arias, A., Feinn, R., & Kranzler, H. R. (2006). Association of an Asn40Asp (A118G) polymorphism in the mu-opioid receptor gene with substance dependence: A meta-analysis. *Drug and Alcohol Dependence, 83*(3), 262–268. doi: 10.1016/j.drugalcdep.2005.11.024

Armstrong, T. D., & Costello, E. J. (2002). Community studies on adolescent substance use, abuse, or dependence and psychiatric comorbidity. *Journal of Consulting and Clinical Psychology, 70*(6), 1224–1239.

Avenevoli, S., & Merikangas, K. R. (2003). Familial influences on adolescent smoking. *Addiction, 98*, 1–20.

Belsky, D. W., Moffitt, T. E., Baker, T. B., Biddle, A. K., Evans, J. P., Harrington, H., . . . Caspi, A. (2013). Polygenic risk and the developmental progression to heavy, persistent smoking and nicotine dependence: Evidence from a 4-decade longitudinal study. *JAMA Psychiatry, 70*(5), 534–542. doi: 10.1001/jamapsychiatry.2013.736

Bergen, S. E., Gardner, C. O., & Kendler, K. S. (2007). Age-related changes in heritability of behavioral phenotypes over adolescence and young adulthood: A meta-analysis. *Twin Research and Human Genetics, 10*(3), 423–433.

Bierut, L. J., Agrawal, A., Bucholz, K. K., Doheny, K. F., Laurie, C., Pugh, E., . . . GENEVA Consortium. (2010). A genome-wide association study of alcohol dependence. *Proceedings of the National Academy of Sciences USA, 107*(11), 5082–5087. doi: 10.1073/pnas.0911109107

Boardman, J. D. (2009). State-level moderation of genetic tendencies to smoke. *American Journal of Public Health, 99*(3), 480–486. doi: 10.2105/ajph.2008.134932

Boardman, J. D., Blalock, C. L., & Pampel, F. C. (2010). Trends in the genetic influences on smoking. *Journal of Health and Social Behavior, 51*(1), 108–123. doi: 10.1177/0022146509361195

Boyle, M. H., Sanford, M., Szatmari, P., Merikangas, K., & Offord, D. R. (2001). Familial influences on substance use by adolescents and young adults. *Canadian Journal of Public Health-Revue Canadienne De Sante Publique, 92*(3), 206–209.

Breslau, N., Fenn, N., & Peterson, E. L. (1993). Early smoking initiation and nicotine dependence in a cohort of young adults. *Drug and Alcohol Dependence, 33*, 129–137.

Brook, J. S., Whiteman, M., Gordon, A. S., & Brenden, C. (1983). Older brothers influence on younger siblings drug use. *Journal of Psychology, 114*(1), 83–90.

Buchanan, J. P., McGue, M., Keyes, M., & Iacono, W. G. (2009). Are there shared environmental influences on adolescent behavior? Evidence from a study of adoptive siblings. *Behavior Genetics, 39*(5), 532–540. doi: 10.1007/s10519-009-9283-y

Button, T. M. M., Hewitt, J. K., Rhee, S. H., Corley, R. P., & Stallings, M. C. (2010). The moderating effect of religiosity on the genetic variance of problem alcohol use. *Alcoholism: Clinical and Experimental Research, 34*(9), 1619–1624. doi: 10.1111/j.1530-0277.2010.01247.x

Buu, A., DiPiazza, C., Wang, J., Puttler, L. I., Fitzgerald, H. E., & Zucker, R. A. (2009). Parent, family, and neighborhood effects on the development of child substance use and other psychopathology from preschool to the start of adulthood. *Journal of Studies on Alcohol and Drugs, 70*(4), 489–498.

Buu, A., Mansour, M., Wang, J., Refior, S. K., Fitzgerald, H. E., & Zucker, R. A. (2007). Alcoholism effects on social migration and neighborhood effects on alcoholism over the course of 12 years. *Alcoholism: Clinical and Experimental Research, 31*(9), 1545–1551. doi: 10.1111/j.1530-0277.2007.00449.x

Cha, Y. M., Li, Q., Wilson, W. A., & Swartzwelder, H. S. (2006). Sedative and GABAergic effects of ethanol on male and female rats. *Alcoholism: Clinical and Experimental Research, 30*(1), 113–118.

Chen, L. S., Johnson, E. O., Breslau, N., Hatsukami, D., Saccone, N. L., Grucza, R. A., . . . Bierut, L. J. (2009). Interplay of genetic risk factors and parent monitoring in risk for nicotine dependence. *Addiction, 104*(10), 1731–1740. doi: 10.1111/j.1360-0443.2009.02697.x

Chen, L. S., Saccone, N. L., Culverhouse, R. C., Bracci, P. M., Chen, C. H., Dueker, N., . . . Bierut, L. J. (2012). Smoking and genetic risk variation across populations of European, Asian, and African American ancestry: A meta-analysis of chromosome 15q25. *Genetic Epidemiology, 36*(4), 340–351. doi: 10.1002/gepi.21627

Collins, W. A., Maccoby, E. E., Steinberg, L., Hetherington, E. M., & Bornstein, M. H. (2000). Contemporary research on parenting: The case for nature and nurture. *American Psychologist, 55*, 218–232.

Conway, K. P., Vullo, G. C., Nichter, B., Wang, J., Compton, W. M., Iannotti, R. J., & Simons-Morton, B. (2013). Prevalence and patterns of polysubstance use in a nationally representative sample of 10th graders in the United States. *Journal of Adolescent Health, 52*(6), 716–723. doi: 10.1016/j.jadohealth.2012.12.006

Corley, R. P., Zeiger, J. S., Crowley, T., Ehringer, M. A., Hewitt, J. K., Hopfer, C. J., . . . Krauter, K. (2008). Association of candidate genes with antisocial drug dependence in adolescents. *Drug and Alcohol Dependence, 96*(1–2), 90–98. doi: 10.1016/j.drugalcdep.2008.02.004

Cotton, N. S. (1979). The familial incidence of alcoholism: A review. *Journal of Studies on Alcohol, 40*(1), 89–116.

Covault, J., Gelernter, J., Hesselbrock, V., Nellissery, M., & Kranzler, H. R. (2004). Allelic and haplotypic association of *GABRA2* with alcohol dependence. *American Journal of Medical Genetics Part B-Neuropsychiatric Genetics, 129B*(1), 104–109.

Derringer, J., Krueger, R. F., McGue, M., & Iacono, W. G. (2008). Genetic and environmental contributions to the diversity of substances used in adolescent twins: A longitudinal study of age and sex effects. *Addiction, 103*, 1744–1751.

Deutsch, A. R., Slutske, W. S., Richmond-Rakerd, L. S., Chernyavskiy, P., Heath, A. C., & Martin, N. G. (2013). Causal influence of age at first drink on alcohol involvement in adulthood and its moderation by familial context. *Journal of Studies on Alcohol and Drugs, 74*(5), 703–713.

Dewit, D. J., Adlaf, E. M., Offord, D. R., & Ogborne, A. C. (2000). Age at first alcohol use: A risk factor for the development of alcohol disorders. *American Journal of Psychiatry, 157*, 745–750.

Dick, D. M., Agrawal, A., Wang, J. C., Hinrichs, A., Bertelsen, S., Bucholz, K. K., . . . Bierut, L. J. (2007). Alcohol dependence with comorbid drug dependence: genetic and phenotypic associations suggest a more severe form of the disorder with stronger genetic contribution to risk. *Addiction, 102*(7), 1131–1139.

Dick, D. M., Bierut, L., Hinrichs, A., Fox, L., Bucholz, K. K., Kramer, J., . . . Foroud, T. (2006). The role of *GABRA2* in risk for conduct disorder and alcohol and drug dependence across developmental stages. *Behavior Genetics, 36*(4), 577–590.

Dick, D. M., Latendresse, S. J., Lansford, J. E., Budde, J. P., Goate, A., Dodge, K. A., . . . Bates, J. E. (2009). Role of *GABRA2* in trajectories of externalizing behavior across development and evidence of moderation by parental monitoring. *Archives of General Psychiatry, 66*(6), 649–657.

Dick, D. M., Meyers, J. L., Latendresse, S. J., Creemers, H. E., Lansford, J. E., Pettit, G. S., . . . Huizink, A. C. (2011). *CHRM2*, parental monitoring, and adolescent externalizing behavior: Evidence for gene-environment interaction. *Psychological Science, 22*(4), 481–489. doi: 10.1177/0956797611403318

Dick, D. M., Viken, R., Purcell, S., Kaprio, J., Pulkkinen, L., & Rose, R. J. (2007). Parental monitoring moderates the importance of genetic and environmental influences on adolescent smoking. *Journal of Abnormal Psychology, 116*(1), 213–218.

Donovan, J. E., & Jessor, R. (1985). Structure of problem behavior in adolescence and young adulthood. *Journal of Consulting and Clinical Psychology, 53*, 890–904.

Drgon, T., D'Addario, C., & Uhl, G. R. (2006). Linkage disequilibrium, haplotype and association studies of a chromosome 4 *GABA* receptor gene cluster: Candidate gene variants for addictions. *American Journal of Medical Genetics Part B-Neuropsychiatric Genetics, 141B*(8), 854–860. doi: 10.1002/ajmg.b.30349

Edenberg, H. J., Dick, D. M., Xuei, X. L., Tian, H. J., Almasy, L., Bauer, L. O., . . . Begleiter, H. (2004). Variations in *GABRA2*, encoding the alpha 2 subunit of the GABA(A) receptor, are associated with alcohol dependence and with brain oscillations. *American Journal of Human Genetics, 74*(4), 705–714.

Edenberg, H. J., Koller, D. L., Xuei, X., Wetherill, L., McClintick, J. N., Almasy, L., . . . Foroud, T. (2010). Genome-wide association study of alcohol dependence implicates a region on chromosome 11. *Alcoholism: Clinical and Experimental Research, 34*(5), 840–852. doi: 10.1111/j.1530-0277.2010.01156.x

Englund, M. M., Siebenbruner, J., Oliva, E. M., Egeland, B., Chung, C. T., & Long, J. D. (2013). The developmental significance of late adolescent substance use for early adult functioning. *Developmental Psychology, 49*(8), 1554–1564. doi: 10.1037/a0030229

Fagan, A. A., & Najman, J. M. (2005). The relative contributions of parental and sibling substance use to adolescent tobacco, alcohol, and other drug use. *Journal of Drug Issues, 35*(4), 869–883.

Fehr, C., Sander, T., Tadic, A., Lenzen, K. P., Anghelescu, I., Klawe, C., . . . Szegedi, A. (2006). Confirmation of association of the *GABRA2* gene with alcohol dependence by subtype-specific analysis. *Psychiatric Genetics, 16*(1), 9–17.

Felson, J. (2014). What can we learn from twin studies? A comprehensive evaluation of the equal environments assumption. *Social Science Research, 43*, 184–199. doi: 10.1016/j.ssresearch.2013.10.004

Fowler, T., Lifford, K., Shelton, K., Rice, F., Thapar, A., Neale, M. C., . . . van den Bree, M. B. M. (2007). Exploring the relationship between genetic and environmental influences on initiation and progression of substance use. *Addiction, 102*(3), 413–422. doi: 10.1111/j.1360-0443.2006.01694.x

Gfroerer, J. (1987). Correlation between drug use by teenagers and drug use by older family members. *American Journal of Drug and Alcohol Abuse, 13*(1–2), 95–108. doi: 10.3109/00952998709001502

Gillespie, N. A., Neale, M. C., & Kendler, K. S. (2009). Pathways to cannabis abuse: A multi-stage model from cannabis availability, cannabis initiation and progression to abuse. *Addiction, 104*(3), 430–438. doi: 10.1111/j.1360-0443.2008.02456.x

Goldman, D., Oroszi, G., & Ducci, F. (2005). The genetics of addictions: Uncovering the genes. *Nature Reviews Genetics, 6*, 521–532.

Grant, B. F., & Dawson, D. A. (1997). Age at onset of alcohol use and its association with *DSM-IV* alcohol abuse and dependence: Results from the National Longitudinal Alcohol Epidemiologic Survey. *Journal of Substance Abuse, 9*, 103–110.

Grant, B. F., & Dawson, D. A. (1998). Age of onset of drug use and its association with DSM-IV drug abuse and dependence: Results from the National Longitudinal Alcohol Epidemiologic Survey. *Journal of Substance Abuse, 10*, 163–173.

Gratten, J., Wray, N. R., Keller, M. C., & Visscher, P. M. (2014). Large-scale genomics unveils the genetic architecture of psychiatric disorders. *Nature Neuroscience, 17*(6), 782–790. doi: 10.1038/nn.3708

Guttmannova, K., Hill, K. G., Bailey, J. A., Lee, J. O., Hartigan, L. A., Hawkins, J. D., & Catalano, R. F. (2012). Examining explanatory mechanisms of the effects of early alcohol use on young adult alcohol dependence. *Journal of Studies on Alcohol and Drugs, 73*(3), 379–390.

Han, C., McGue, M. K., & Iacono, W. G. (1999). Lifetime tobacco, alcohol, and other substance use in adolescent Minnesota twins: Univariate and multivariate behavioral genetic analyses. *Addiction*, 7, 981–993.

Harden, K. P., Hill, J. E., Turkheimer, E., & Emery, R. E. (2008). Gene-environment correlation and interaction in peer effects on adolescent alcohol and tobacco use. *Behavior Genetics*, 38(4), 339–347. doi: 10.1007/s10519-008-9202-7

Hartz, S. M., Short, S. E., Saccone, N. L., Culverhouse, R., Chen, L. S., Schwantes-An, T. H., . . . Bierut, L. J. (2012). Increased genetic vulnerability to smoking at *CHRNA5* in early-onset smokers. *Archives of General Psychiatry*, 69(8), 854–861. doi: 10.1001/archgenpsychiatry.2012.124

Hendershot, C. S., Bryan, A. D., Ewing, S. W. F., Claus, E. D., & Hutchison, K. E. (2011). Preliminary evidence for associations of *CHRM2* with substance use and disinhibition in adolescence. *Journal of Abnormal Child Psychology*, 39(5), 671–681. doi: 10.1007/s10802-011-9511-9

Hendershot, C. S., MacPherson, L., Myers, M. G., Carr, L. G., & Wall, T. L. (2005). Psychosocial, cultural and genetic influences on alcohol use in Asian American youth. *Journal of Studies on Alcohol*, 66(2), 185–195.

Hicks, B. M., Johnson, W., Durbin, C. E., Blonigen, D. M., Iacono, W. G., & McGue, M. (2013). Gene-environment correlation in the development of adolescent substance abuse: Selection effects of child personality and mediation via contextual risk factors. *Development and Psychopathology*, 25(1), 119–132. doi: 10.1017/s0954579412000946

Hicks, B. M., Schalet, B. D., Malone, S. M., Iacono, W. G., & McGue, M. (2011). Psychometric and genetic architecture of substance use disorder and behavioral disinhibition measures for gene association studies. *Behavior Genetics*, 41(4), 459–475. doi: 10.1007/s10519-010-9417-2

Hicks, B. M., South, S. C., DiRago, A. C., Iacono, W. G., & McGue, M. (2009). Environmental adversity and increasing genetic risk for externalizing disorders. *Archives of General Psychiatry*, 66(6), 640–648.

Hopfer, C. J., Stallings, M. C., Hewitt, J. K., & Crowley, T. J. (2003). Family transmission of marijuana use, abuse, and dependence. *Journal of the American Academy of Child and Adolescent Psychiatry*, 42(7), 834–841. doi: 10.1097/01.chi.0000046874.56865.85

Hopfer, C. J., Timberlake, D., Haberstick, B., Lessem, J. M., Ehringer, M. A., Smolen, A., & Hewitt, J. K. (2005). Genetic influences on quantity of alcohol consumed by adolescents and young adults. *Drug and Alcohol Dependence*, 78(2), 187–193.

Hyman, S. E. (2005). Addiction: A disease of learning and memory. *American Journal of Psychiatry*, 162(8), 1414–1422.

Iacono, W. G., Carlson, S. R., Malone, S. M., & McGue, M. (2002). P3 event-related potential amplitude and the risk for disinhibitory disorders in adolescent boys. *Archives of General Psychiatry*, 59(8), 750–757.

Ioannidis, J. P., Ntzani, E. E., Trikalinos, T. A., & Contopoulos-Ioannidis, D. G. (2001). Replication validity of genetic association studies. *Nature Genetics*, 29, 306–309.

Irons, D. E., Iacono, W. G., & McGue, M. (2015). Tests of the effects of adolescent early alcohol exposures on adult outcomes. *Addiction*, 110, 269–278.

Irons, D. E., Iacono, W. G., Oetting, W. S., Kirkpatrick, R. M., Vrieze, S. I., Miller, M. B., & McGue, M. (2014). Gamma-aminobutyric acid system genes: No evidence for a role in alcohol use and abuse in a community-based sample.

Alcoholism: Clinical and Experimental Research, 38(4), 938–947. doi: 10.1111/acer.12352

Irons, D. E., Iacono, W. G., Oetting, W. S., & McGue, M. (2012). Developmental trajectory and environmental moderation of the effect of *ALDH2* Polymorphism on alcohol use. *Alcoholism: Clinical and Experimental Research*, 36(11), 1882–1891. doi: 10.1111/j.1530-0277.2012.01809.x

Jacobus, J., & Tapert, S. F. (2014). Effects of cannabis on the adolescent brain. *Current Pharmaceutical Design*, 20(13), 2186–2193.

Johnston, L. D., O'Malley, P. M., Bachman, J. G., & Schulenberg, J. E. (2006). *Monitoring the Future national survey results on drug use, 1975-2005. Vol. 1. Secondary school students* (NIH Publication No. 06-5883). Bethesda, MD: National Institute on Drug Abuse.

Johnston, L. D., O'Malley, P. M., Miech, R. A., Bachman, J. G., & Schulenberg, J. E. (2014). *Monitoring the Future national results on drug use: 1975-2013: Overview, key findings on adolescent drug use*. Ann Arbor, Michigan: Institute for Social Research, University of Michigan.

Kandel, D. B. (2002). *Stages and pathways of drug involvement: Examining the gateway hypothesis*. New York, NY: Cambridge University Press.

Kendler, K. S., Gardner, C. O., Edwards, A., Hickman, M., Heron, J., Macleod, J., . . . Dick, D. M. (2013). Dimensions of parental alcohol use/problems and offspring temperament, externalizing behaviors, and alcohol use/problems. *Alcoholism: Clinical and Experimental Research*, 37(12), 2118–2127. doi: 10.1111/acer.12196

Kendler, K. S., Kalsi, G., Holmans, P. A., Sanders, A. R., Aggen, S. H., Dick, D. M., . . . Gejman, P. V. (2011). Genomewide association analysis of symptoms of alcohol dependence in the Molecular Genetics of Schizophrenia (MGS2) control sample. *Alcoholism: Clinical and Experimental Research*, 35(5), 963–975. doi: 10.1111/j.1530-0277.2010.01427.x

Kendler, K. S., Karkowski, L. M., Corey, L. A., Prescott, C. A., & Neale, M. C. (1999). Genetic and environmental risk factors in the aetiology of illicit drug initiation and subsequent misuse in women. *British Journal of Psychiatry*, 175, 351–356. doi: 10.1192/bjp.175.4.351

Kendler, K. S., Myers, J., Damaj, M. I., & Chen, X. G. (2013). Early smoking onset and risk for subsequent nicotine dependence: A monozygotic co-twin control study. *American Journal of Psychiatry*, 170(4), 408–413. doi: 10.1176/appi.ajp.2012.12030321

Kendler, K. S., Neale, M. C., Sullivan, P., Corey, L. A., Gardner, C. O., & Prescott, C. A. (1999). A population-based twin study in women of smoking initiation and nicotine dependence. *Psychological Medicine*, 29(2), 299–308. doi: 10.1017/s0033291798008022

Kendler, K. S., Schmitt, E., Aggen, S. H., & Prescott, C. A. (2008). Genetic and environmental influences on alcohol, caffeine, cannabis, and nicotine use from early adolescence to middle adulthood. *Archives of General Psychiatry*, 65(6), 674–682.

Keyes, M., Legrand, L. N., Iacono, W. G., & McGue, M. (2008). Parental smoking and adolescent problem behavior: An adoption study of general and specific effects. *American Journal of Psychiatry*, 165, 1338–1344.

Kim, S. K., Lee, S. I., Shin, C. J., Son, J. W., & Ju, G. (2010). The genetic factors affecting drinking behaviors of Korean young adults with variant Aldehyde Dehydrogenase

2 genotype. *Psychiatry Investigation*, *7*(4), 270–277. doi: 10.4306/pi.2010.7.4.270

Kleinjan, M., Poelen, E. A., Engels, R., & Verhagen, M. (2013). Dual growth of adolescent smoking and drinking: evidence for an interaction between the mu-opioid receptor (*OPRM1*) A118G polymorphism and sex. *Addiction Biology*, *18*(6), 1003–1012. doi: 10.1111/j.1369-1600.2011.00422.x

Koob, G. F., & Kreek, M. J. (2007). Stress, dysregulation of drug reward pathways, and the transition to drug dependence. *American Journal of Psychiatry*, *164*(8), 1149–1159. doi: 10.1176/appi.ajp.2007.05030503

Koopmans, J. R., & Boomsma, D. I. (1996). Familial resemblances in alcohol use: Genetic or cultural transmission? *Journal of Studies on Alcohol*, *57*(1), 19–28.

Koopmans, J. R., Slutske, W. S., van Baal, G. C., & Boomsma, D. I. (1999). The influence of religion on alcohol use initiation: Evidence for genotype X environment interaction. *Behavior Genetics*, *29*, 445–453.

Korhonen, T., Latvala, A., Dick, D. M., Pulkkinen, L., Rose, R. J., Kaprio, J., & Huizink, A. C. (2012). Genetic and environmental influences underlying externalizing behaviors, cigarette smoking and illicit drug use across adolescence. [Article]. *Behavior Genetics*, *42*(4), 614–625. doi: 10.1007/s10519-012-9528-z

Krueger, R. F., Hicks, B. M., Patrick, C. J., Carlson, S. R., Iacono, W. G., & McGue, M. (2002). Etiologic connections among substance dependence, antisocial behavior, and personality: Modeling the externalizing spectrum. *Journal of Abnormal Psychology*, *111*(3), 411–424.

Krystal, J. H., Staley, J., Mason, G., Petrakis, I. L., Kaufman, J., Harris, R. A., . . . Lappalainen, J. (2006). Gamma-Aminobutyric acid type A receptors and alcoholism: Intoxication, dependence, vulnerability, and treatment. *Archives of General Psychiatry*, *63*(9), 957–968.

Lappalainen, J., Krupitsky, E., Remizov, M., Pchelina, S., Taraskina, A., Zvartau, E., . . . Gelernter, J. (2005). Association between alcoholism and gamma-amino butyric acid alpha 2 receptor subtype in a Russian population. *Alcoholism-Clinical and Experimental Research*, *29*(4), 493–498.

Latendresse, S. J., Rose, R. J., Viken, R. J., Pulkkinen, L., Kaprio, J., & Dick, D. M. (2008). Parenting mechanisms in links between parents' and adolescents' alcohol use behaviors. *Alcoholism: Clinical and Experimental Research*, *32*(2), 322–330. doi: 10.1111/j.1530-0277.2007.00583.x

Leonardi-Bee, J., Jere, M. L., & Britton, J. (2011). Exposure to parental and sibling smoking and the risk of smoking uptake in childhood and adolescence: A systematic review and meta-analysis. *Thorax*, *66*(10), 847–855. doi: 10.1136/thx.2010.153379

Little, P. J., Kuhn, C. M., Wilson, W. A., & Swartzwelder, H. S. (1996). Differential effects of ethanol in adolescent and adult rats. *Alcoholism: Clinical and Experimental Research*, *20*(8), 1346–1351.

Liu, J. Z., Tozzi, F., Waterworth, D. M., Pillai, S. G., Muglia, P., Middleton, L., . . . Wellcome Trust Case Control. (2010). Meta-analysis and imputation refines the association of 15q25 with smoking quantity. *Nature Genetics*, *42*(5), 436–U475. doi: 10.1038/ng.572

Luczak, S. E., Glatt, S. J., & Wall, T. L. (2006). Meta-analyses of *ALDH2* and *ADH1B* with alcohol dependence in Asians. *Psychological Bulletin*, *132*(4), 607–621.

Luo, X. G., Kranzler, H. R., Zuo, L. J., Wang, S., Blumberg, H. P., & Gelernter, J. (2005). *CHRM2* gene predisposes to alcohol dependence, drug dependence and affective disorders: Results from an extended case-control structured association study. *Human Molecular Genetics*, *14*(16), 2421–2434. doi: 10.1093/hmg/ddi244

Lynskey, M. T., Heath, A. C., Bucholz, K. K., Slutske, W. S., Madden, P. A. F., Nelson, E. C., . . . Martin, N. G. (2003). Escalation of drug use in early-onset cannabis users vs. co-twin controls. *Journal of the American Medical Association*, *289*(4), 427–433.

Maes, H. H., Woodard, C. E., Murrelle, L., Meyer, J. M., Silberg, J. L., Hewitt, J. K., . . . Eaves, L. J. (1999). Tobacco, alcohol and drug use in eight- to sixteen-year-old twins: The Virginia Twin Study of Adolescent Behavioral Development. *Journal of Studies on Alcohol*, *60*(3), 293–305.

Macgregor, S., Lind, P. A., Bucholz, K. K., Hansell, N. K., Madden, P. A. F., Richter, M. M., . . . Whitfield, J. B. (2009). Associations of *ADH* and *ALDH2* gene variation with self report alcohol reactions, consumption and dependence: An integrated analysis. *Human Molecular Genetics*, *18*(3), 580–593. doi: 10.1093/hmg/ddn372

Matteson, L. K., McGue, M., & Iacono, W. G. (2013). Shared environmental influences on personality: A combined twin and adoption approach. *Behavior Genetics*, *43*(6), 491–504. doi: 10.1007/s10519-013-9616-8

Matthews, A. G., Hoffman, E. K., Zezza, N., Stiffler, S., & Hill, S. Y. (2007). The role of the *GABRA2* polymorphism in multiplex alcohol dependence families with minimal comorbidity: Within-family association and linkage analyses. *Journal of Studies on Alcohol and Drugs*, *68*(5), 625–633.

McGue, M. (1999). The behavioral genetics of alcoholism. *Current Directions in Psychological Science*, *8*(4), 109–115.

McGue, M., & Iacono, W. G. (2005). The association of early adolescent problem behavior with adult psychopathology. *American Journal of Psychiatry*, *162*(6), 1118–1124.

McGue, M., Elkins, I., & Iacono, W. G. (2000). Genetic and environmental influences on adolescent substance use and abuse. *American Journal of Medical Genetics (Neuropsychiatric Genetics)*, *96*, 671–677.

McGue, M., & Iacono, W. G. (2009). Siblings and the socialization of adolescent deviance: An adoption study approach. In K. McCartney & R. Weinberg (Eds.), *Experience and development: A festschrift to honor Sandra W. Scarr* (pp. 179–201). London, UK: Taylor & Francis.

McGue, M., Iacono, W. G., Legrand, L. N., & Elkins, I. (2001). The origins and consequences of age at first drink. I. Associations with substance-use disorders, disinhibitory behavior and psychopathology, and P3 amplitude. *Alcoholism: Clinical and Experimental Research*, *25*, 1156–1165.

McGue, M., Malone, S., Keyes, M., & Iacono, W. G. (2014). Parent-offspring similarity for drinking: A longitudinal adoption study. *Behavior Genetics*, *44*(6), 620–628.

McGue, M., Osler, M., & Christensen, K. (2010). Causal inference and observational aging research: The utility of twins. *Perspectives on Psychological Science*, *5*(5), 546–556.

McGue, M., Sharma, A., & Benson, P. (1996). Parent and sibling influences on adolescent alcohol use and misuse: Evidence from a U.S. adoption cohort. *Journal of Studies on Alcohol*, *57*, 8–18.

McGue, M., Zhang, Y. W., Miller, M. B., Basu, S., Vrieze, S., Hicks, B., . . . Iacono, W. G. (2013). A genome-wide association study of behavioral disinhibition. *Behavior Genetics*, *43*(5), 363–373. doi: 10.1007/s10519-013-9606-x

Merikangas, K. R., Li, J. J., Stipelman, B., Yu, K., Fucito, L., Swendsen, J., & Zhang, H. (2009). The familial aggregation of cannabis use disorders. *Addiction*, *104*(4), 622–629. doi: 10.1111/j.1360-0443.2008.02468.x

Merikangas, K. R., Stolar, M., Stevens, D. E., Goulet, J., Preisig, M. A., Fenton, B., . . . Rounsaville, B. (1998). Familial transmission of substance use disorders. *Archives of General Psychiatry*, *55*, 973–979.

Miles, D. R., van den Bree, M. B. M., Gupman, A. E., Newlin, D. B., Glantz, M. D., & Pickens, R. W. (2001). A twin study on sensation seeking, risk taking behavior and marijuana use. *Drug and Alcohol Dependence*, *62*(1), 57–68.

Neale, M. C., Boker, S. M., Xie, G., & Maes, H. H. (2003). *Mx: Statistical modeling* (6th ed.). Richmond: Department of Psychiatry, Virginia Commonwealth University.

Neale, M. C., & Cardon, L. R. (1992). *Methodology for genetic studies of twins and families*. Dordrecht, The Netherlands: Kluwer.

Neale, M. C., & Kendler, K. S. (1995). Models of comorbidity for multifactorial disorders. *American Journal of Human Genetics*, *57*, 935–953.

Palmer, R. H. C., Button, T. M., Rhee, S. H., Corley, R. P., Young, S. E., Stallings, M. C., . . . Hewitt, J. K. (2012). Genetic etiology of the common liability to drug dependence: Evidence of common and specific mechanisms for DSM-IV dependence symptoms. *Drug and Alcohol Dependence*, *123*, S24–S32. doi: 10.1016/j.drugalcdep.2011.12.015

Plomin, R. (1983). Developmental behavioral genetics. *Child Development*, *54*, 253–259.

Prescott, C. A., & Kendler, K. S. (1999). Age at first drink and risk for alcoholism: A noncausal association. *Alcoholism: Clinical and Experimental Research*, *23*, 101–107.

Rhee, S. H., Hewitt, J. K., Young, S. E., Corley, R. P., Crowley, T. J., Neale, M. C., & Stallings, M. C. (2006). Comorbidity between alcohol dependence and illicit drug dependence in adolescents with antisocial behavior and matched controls. *Drug and Alcohol Dependence*, *84*(1), 85–92. doi: 10.1016/j.drugalcdep.2005.12.003

Rhee, S. H., Hewitt, J. K., Young, S. E., Corley, R. P., Crowley, T. J., & Stallings, M. C. (2003). Genetic and environmental influences on substance initiation, use, and problem use in adolescents. *Archives of General Psychiatry*, *60*(12), 1256–1264.

Rodriguez, S., Cook, D. G., Gaunt, T. R., Nightingale, C. M., Whincup, P. H., & Day, I. N. M. (2011). Combined analysis of CHRNA5, CHRNA3 and CYP2A6 in relation to adolescent smoking behaviour. *Journal of Psychopharmacology*, *25*(7), 915–923. doi: 10.1177/0269881111405352

Rose, R. J., Dick, D. M., Viken, R. J., & Kaprio, J. (2001). Gene-environment interaction in patterns of adolescent drinking: Regional residency moderates longitudinal influences on alcohol use. *Alcoholism: Clinical and Experimental Research*, *25*(5), 637–643.

Rose, R. J., Winter, T., Viken, R. J., & Kaprio, J. (2014). Adolescent alcohol abuse and adverse adult outcomes: Evaluating confounds with drinking-discordant twins. *Alcoholism: Clinical and Experimental Research*, early view.

Rowe, D. C., & Gulley, B. L. (1992). Sibling effects on substance use and delinquency. *Criminology*, *30*, 217–233.

Samek, D. R., McGue, M., Keyes, M., & Iacono, W. G. (2015). Sibling facilitation mediates the association between older and younger sibling alcohol use in late adolescence. *Journal of Research in Adolescence*, *25*(4), 638–651.

Sartor, C. E., Lynskey, M. T., Bucholz, K. K., Madden, P. A. F., Martin, N. G., & Heath, A. C. (2009). Timing of first alcohol use and alcohol dependence: Evidence of common genetic influences. *Addiction*, *104*(9), 1512–1518. doi: 10.1111/j.1360-0443.2009.02648.x

Scarr, S., & McCartney, K. (1983). How people make their own environments: A theory of genotype => environment effects. *Child Development*, *54*, 424–435.

Scholte, R. H. J., Poelen, E. A. P., Willemsen, G., Boomsma, D. I., & Engels, R. (2008). Relative risks of adolescent and young adult alcohol use: The role of drinking fathers, mothers, siblings, and friends. *Addictive Behaviors*, *33*(1), 1–14. doi: 10.1016/j.addbeh.2007.04.015

Schulenberg, J. E., & Maggs, J. L. (2002). A developmental perspective on alcohol use and heavy drinking during adolescence and the transition to young adulthood. *Journal of Studies on Alcohol*, *54*, 70.

Shanahan, M. J., & Hofer, S. M. (2005). Social context in gene-environment interactions: Retrospect and prospect. *Journal of Gerontology*, *60B*, 65–76.

Simons-Morton, B., & Chen, R. S. (2006). Over time relationships between early adolescent and peer substance use. *Addictive Behaviors*, *31*(7), 1211–1223. doi: 10.1016/j.addbeh.2005.09.006

Sloan, F. A., Costanzo, P. R., Belsky, D., Holmberg, E., Malone, P. S., Wang, Y., & Kertesz, S. (2011). Heavy drinking in early adulthood and outcomes at mid life. *Journal of Epidemiology and Community Health*, *65*(7), 600–605. doi: 10.1136/jech.2009.102228

Soyka, M., Preuss, U. W., Hesselbrock, V., Zill, P., Koller, G., & Bondy, B. (2008). GABA-A2 receptor subunit gene (*GABRA2*) polymorphisms and risk for alcohol dependence. *Journal of Psychiatric Research*, *42*(3), 184–191.

Spear, L. (2013). The teenage brain: Adolescents and alcohol. *Current Directions in Psychological Science*, *22*(2), 152–157.

Tabor, H. K., Risch, N. J., & Myers, R. M. (2002). Candidate-gene approaches for studying complex genetic traits: Practical considerations. *Nature Reviews Genetics*, *3*(5), 391–397. doi: 10.1038/nrg796

Thorgeirsson, T. E., Gudbjartsson, D. F., Surakka, I., Vink, J. M., Amin, N., Geller, F., . . . Consortium, E. (2010). Sequence variants at CHRNB3-CHRNA6 and CYP2A6 affect smoking behavior. *Nature Genetics*, *42*(5), 448–U135. doi: 10.1038/ng.573

Treutlein, J., Cichon, S., Ridinger, M., Wodarz, N., Soyka, M., Zill, P., . . . Rietschel, M. (2009). Genome-wide association study of alcohol dependence. *Archives of General Psychiatry*, *66*(7), 773–784.

Trim, R. S., Leuthe, E., & Chassin, L. (2006). Sibling influence on alcohol use in a young adult, high-risk sample. *Journal of Studies on Alcohol*, *67*(3), 391–398.

Trucco, E. M., Villafuerte, S., Heitzeg, M. M., Burmeister, M., & Zucker, R. A. (2014). Rule breaking mediates the developmental association between GABRA2 and adolescent substance abuse. *Journal of Child Psychology and Psychiatry*, *55*, 1372–1379.

Tucker, J. S., Ellickson, P. L., Orlando, M., Martino, S. C., & Klein, D. J. (2005). Substance use trajectories from early adolescence to emerging adulthood: A comparison of smoking, binge drinking, and marijuana use. *Journal of Drug Issues, 35*(2), 307–331.

Turkheimer, E. (2000). Three laws of behavior genetics and what they mean. *Current Directions in Psychological Science, 9*, 160–164.

Varlinskaya, E. I., & Spear, L. P. (2002). Acute effects of ethanol on social behavior of adolescent and adult rats: Role of familiarity of the test situation. *Alcoholism: Clinical and Experimental Research, 26*(10), 1502–1511. doi: 10.1097/01.alc.0000034033.95701.e3

Verweij, K. J. H., Zietsch, B. P., Liu, J. Z., Medland, S. E., Lynskey, M. T., Madden, P. A. F., . . . Martin, N. G. (2012). No association of candidate genes with cannabis use in a large sample of Australian twin families. *Addiction Biology, 17*(3), 687–690. doi: 10.1111/j.1369-1600.2011.00320.x

Viken, R. J., Kaprio, J., Koskenvuo, M., & Rose, R. J. (1999). Longitudinal analyses of the determinants of drinking and of drinking to intoxication in adolescent twins. *Behavior Genetics, 29*(6), 455–461.

Vink, J. M., Nawijn, L., Boomsma, D. I., & Willemsen, G. (2007). Personality differences in monozygotic twins discordant for cannabis use. *Addiction, 102*(12), 1942–1946.

Visscher, P. M., Brown, M. A., McCarthy, M. I., & Yang, J. (2012). Five years of GWAS discovery. *American Journal of Human Genetics, 90*(1), 7–24. doi: 10.1016/j.ajhg.2011.11.029

Vrieze, S. I., Hicks, B. M., Iacono, W. G., & McGue, M. (2012). Decline in genetic influence on the co-occurrence of alcohol, marijuana, and nicotine dependence symptoms from age 14 to 29. *American Journal of Psychiatry, 169*(10), 1073–1081. doi: 10.1176/appi.ajp.2012.11081268

Vrieze, S. I., McGue, M., & Iacono, W. G. (2012). The interplay of genes and adolescent development in substance use disorders: Leveraging findings from GWAS meta-analyses to test developmental hypotheses about nicotine consumption. *Human Genetics, 131*(6), 791–801. doi: 10.1007/s00439-012-1167-1

Vuolo, M., & Staff, J. (2013). Parent and child cigarette use: A longitudinal, multigenerational study. *Pediatrics, 132*(3), E568–E577. doi: 10.1542/peds.2013-0067

Walden, B., McGue, M., Iacono, W. G., Burt, S. A., & Elkins, I. (2004). Identifying shared environmental contributions to early substance use: The respective roles of peers and parents. *Journal of Abnormal Psychology, 113*(3), 440–450. doi: 10.1037/0021-843x.113.3.440

Wang, J. C., Hinrichs, A. L., Stock, H., Budde, J., Allen, R., Bertelsen, S., . . . Bierut, L. J. (2004). Evidence of common and specific genetic effects: Association of the muscarinic acetylcholine receptor M2 (*CHRM2*) gene with alcohol dependence and major depressive syndrome. *Human Molecular Genetics, 13*(17), 1903–1911.

White, V. M., Hopper, J. L., Wearing, A. J., & Hill, D. J. (2003). The role of genes in tobacco smoking during adolescence and young adulthood: a multivariate behaviour genetic investigation. *Addiction, 98*(8), 1087–1100. doi: 10.1046/j.1360-0443.2003.00427.x

White, A. M., Truesdale, M. C., Bae, J. G., Ahmad, S., Wilson, W. A., Best, P. J., & Swartzwelder, H. S. (2002). Differential effects of ethanol on motor coordination in adolescent and adult rats. *Pharmacology Biochemistry and Behavior, 73*(3), 673–677.

White, H. R., Johnson, V., & Buyske, S. (2000). Parental modeling and parenting behavior effects on offspring alcohol and cigarette use: A growth curve analysis. *Journal of Substance Abuse, 12*(3), 287–310. doi: 10.1016/s0899-3289(00)00056-0

Windle, M., Spear, L. P., Fuligni, A. J., Angold, A., Brown, J. D., Pine, D., . . . Dahl, R. E. (2008). Transitions into underage and problem drinking: Developmental processes and mechanisms between 10 and 15 years of age. *Pediatrics, 121*, S273–S289. doi: 10.1542/peds.2007-2243C

Winship, C., & Morgan, S. L. (1999). The estimation of causal effects from observational data. *Annual Review of Sociology, 25*, 659–706. doi: 10.1146/annurev.soc.25.1.659

Young, S. E., Friedman, N. P., Miyake, A., Willcutt, E. G., Corley, R. P., Haberstick, B. C., & Hewitt, J. K. (2009). Behavioral disinhibition: Liability for externalizing spectrum disorders and its genetic and environmental relation to response inhibition across adolescence. *Journal of Abnormal Psychology, 118*(1), 117–130. doi: 10.1037/a0014657

Young, S. E., Rhee, S. H., Stallings, M. C., Corley, R. P., & Hewitt, J. K. (2006). Genetic and environmental vulnerabilities underlying adolescent substance use and problem use: General or specific? *Behavior Genetics, 36*(4), 603–615.

Young, S. E., Stallings, M. C., Corley, R. P., Krauter, K. S., & Hewitt, J. K. (2000). Genetic and environmental influences on behavioral disinhibition. *American Journal of Medical Genetics (Neuropsychiatric Genetics), 96*(5), 684–695.

The Neural Circuitry and Neurocognitive Development

Reagan R. Wetherill *and* Susan F. Tapert

Abstract

This chapter focuses on adolescent brain development and associated functional implications. We focus on changes in brain tissue composition, fiber architecture and circuitry, and neurochemistry and discuss how these maturational processes affect adolescent brain functioning, sleep, cognition, and behaviors. Given the substantial developments that occur during adolescence, the effects of puberty and sex hormones on brain structure and function are reviewed, and literature on the effects of substance use on the adolescent brain are covered. The chapter reports on recent neuroimaging studies suggesting that atypical and/or asynchronous maturation patterns may contribute to adolescents' proclivity for risk taking, heightened emotionality, and the emergence of psychopathology. Finally, future research opportunities are discussed.

Key Words: adolescence, development, neuromaturation, risk taking, functional connectivity, neural networks

Adolescence is a period of development between childhood and adulthood marked by complex physiological, psychological, and social transitions. Adolescents experience rapid physical growth, the onset of sexual maturation, emotional and motivational changes, and cognitive development (Forbes & Dahl, 2010). These changes are accompanied by the dynamic brain changes that typically result in more efficient and advanced cognitive and emotional processing (Bava & Tapert, 2010; Gogtay et al., 2004; Squeglia, Jacobus, & Tapert, 2009) and the development of skills and knowledge vital to adulthood (Blakemore, 2008; Dahl & Spear, 2004). During adolescence, brain maturation is most evident in the prefrontal cortex, limbic system, and white matter association and projection fibers, and it parallels advancements in cognition and behavior (Clark, Thatcher, & Tapert, 2008).

White Matter

White matter is brain tissue composed of myelinated axons, or nerve cells, that connect various brain regions together. The fatty substance, myelin, insulates the axons and improves signal transduction and thus, communication between brain regions (Sherman & Brophy, 2005). White matter volume increases in a steady, linear pattern throughout adolescence and well into adulthood (Paus et al., 1999). Compared with children, adolescents show greater white matter volume and lower gray matter volume in frontal and parietal cortices, as evidenced by early magnetic resonance imaging (MRI) studies (Giedd et al., 1999; Paus et al., 1999; Sowell et al., 1999). More recently, diffusion tensor imaging (DTI) has been used to better characterize age-related changes in microstructural organization of white matter. DTI is a neuroimaging technique that indirectly provides in vivo information about tissue microstructure by examining diffusion properties of water molecules in the brain (LeBihan et al., 2001). Two primary scalar values of DTI are fractional anisotropy (FA), a measure of directional diffusion motion, and mean diffusivity (MD), which describes the overall magnitude of diffusional motion. These

DTI-derived indices provide information about white matter microstructure and quality (Conturo et al., 1999; Shimony et al., 1999). High FA and low MD values suggest increased fiber organization, myelination, and white matter density (Alexander, Lee, Lazar, & Field, 2007; Roberts & Schwartz, 2007). In general, studies indicate that FA increases and MD decreases in a linear manner with age (Ashtari et al., 2007; Bonekamp et al., 2007; Giorgio et al., 2008). However, other data indicate that white matter quality and architecture change rapidly at first, and then slow and plateau during late adolescence and the early twenties (Lebel & Beaulieu, 2011; Lebel, Walker, Leemans, Phillips, & Beaulieu, 2008). These changes in white matter microstructure may indicate ongoing maturation of the axon and its myelin sheath.

Developmental DTI studies provide insight into white matter maturation schedules and how white matter maturation contributes to behaviors and cognitive capacities at various developmental stages. For example, the corticospinal tract, which contains fibers connecting cortical and brain stem regions, and several key long association tracts involved in intrahemispheric connections mature by adolescence (Asato, Terwilliger, Woo, & Luna, 2010; Lebel et al., 2008). During adolescence, white matter continues to mature in projection fibers associated with fronto-striatal and fronto-thalamic pathways and in association fiber tracts, such as the uncinate fasciculus and areas of the corpus callosum. In sum, developmental changes in white matter quality and architecture generally proceed in an inferior/posterior to superior/anterior fashion (Asato et al., 2010; Tamnes et al., 2010; Yakovlev & Lecours, 1967), which is similar to gray matter maturation patterns (Gogtay et al., 2004).

Gray Matter

Gray matter development follows an inverted parabolic curve, with cortical volume peaking around 12–14 years of age. At this time, the onset of puberty typically begins, and cortical gray matter gradually declines (Gogtay et al., 2004; Sowell et al., 2003). Gray matter and cortical thickness declines have been interpreted as evidence of synaptic pruning, where superfluous neuronal connections are eliminated (Purves, White, & Riddle, 1996). Longitudinal studies indicate significant regional variation in gray matter volume declines (Giedd et al., 1999; Gogtay et al., 2004; Sowell et al., 2003). In general, cortical gray matter maturation (in terms of gray matter loss) begins in the sensorimotor cortices (Gogtay et al., 2004; Shaw et al., 2008), followed by declines in the frontal poles and dorsolateral prefrontal and lateral temporal cortices (Jernigan & Tallal, 1990; Jernigan, Trauner, Hesselink, & Tallal, 1991; Sowell et al., 1999, 2004). Cortical thickness declines occur in a similar, nonlinear pattern with apparent attenuations in the parietal lobe, frontal regions, the cingulum, and occipital lobe (Tamnes et al., 2010). These cortical gray matter volume changes occur alongside axonal development and cortical refinement, and such changes likely optimize brain structure and function—leading to increased efficiency, integration, and specialization of the adolescent brain (Sowell et al., 2004; Yakovlev & Lecours, 1967).

Functional Brain Networks

Research provides insight into how physical brain structure changes alter brain network dynamics (He et al., 2007; Majewska & Sur, 2006). Functional brain networks adapt throughout life based on biological events, such as puberty and experience. Although brain networks have been examined in a variety of ways over the years, advancements in measuring physiological signals, such as functional magnetic resonance imaging blood oxygen level–dependent (fMRI BOLD) response, electroencephalography (EEG), magnetoencephalography (MEG), and positron emission tomography (PET) enable the investigation of brain networks during rest (Biswal, Yetkin, Haughton, & Hyde, 1995; Fair et al., 2007; Fox et al., 2005; Lowe, Mock, & Sorenson, 1998) and during a task (Friston, Harrison, & Penny, 2003; Horwitz, 2003). Resting-state functional connectivity (rs-fcMRI) provides important information about how brain regions are linked together and how efficiently brain regions communicate with each other (Bullmore & Sporns, 2009; Fox & Raichle, 2007). Similarly, task-dependent functional connectivity (fcMRI) gives insight into associations between brain regions and the directionality of influence of one brain region over another (Friston et al., 2003). Both rs-fcMRI and fcMRI describe functional network changes during adolescence (Fair et al., 2007, 2008, 2009; Hwang, Velanova, & Luna, 2010; Power, Fair, Schlaggar, & Petersen, 2010). Overall, functional connectivity increases within the default-mode network (DMN, the network of brain regions that activate during rest and deactivate during a task) during adolescence (Fair et al., 2008; Supekar et al., 2010) with increased long-range correlations and/

or decreased short-range correlations; however, the maturity of this network does not appear to be directly related to age (Power et al., 2010).

Functional connectivity studies also indicate that interactions between different networks change with age (Fair et al., 2007; Stevens et al., 2009). BOLD response strength during cognitive tasks increases in brain structures associated with task performance (Keulers, Stiers, & Jolles, 2011), while BOLD response strength in brain regions not correlated to task performance typically decreases or disappears with age (Rubia et al., 2006). Although age-related differences in task-related response strength are thought to be a consequence of maturational brain changes (Vogel, Power, Petersen, & Schlaggar, 2010), research examining the relationship between changes in functional brain organization and change in task-induced activation is in its early stages. In one of the studies evaluating the functional-structural connectivity development and task-induced activity, Keulers and colleagues (2012) examined maturation patterns in functional connectivity and task-related functional activation among 70 adolescents (approximately 12–21 years of age). Findings indicated that developmental differences in task activation are spatially distributed throughout the brain, and these distributed patterns generalize across tasks (Keulers, Goulas, Jolles, & Stiers, 2012). Task-related maturation was not associated with connectivity maturation. Although additional studies are needed to confirm these findings, functional connectivity studies provide clear evidence for functional brain network changes throughout the course of adolescence.

Puberty and Sex Differences

Puberty is an important period during adolescence when steroid hormones, such as testosterone, estrogens, and progesterone, increase and promote the maturation of secondary sex characteristics. Steroids also affect brain maturation (Sisk & Foster, 2004) and behavior (Forbes & Dahl, 2010). Specifically, research suggests that hormonal events of puberty start a second period of brain structure reorganization that is similar to the hormonal events that were active during infancy (Petanjek et al., 2011; Sisk & Foster, 2004). In recent years, MRI studies have examined the associations between sex steroids, brain structure, and sex-based brain differentiation in pubertal adolescents. For example, male adolescents show larger overall brain volume (Reiss, Abrams, Singer, Ross, & Denckla, 1996), more prominent gray matter reductions, and

a steeper slope of increase in white matter volume than female adolescents (Blanton et al., 2004; De Bellis et al., 2001; Lenroot & Giedd, 2010). DTI studies provide further evidence for sex differences in white matter microstructure. A DTI study of 106 children and adolescents between the ages of 5 and 18 years revealed that males had higher FA values in frontal, parietal, and occipito-parietal regions, whereas females showed higher FA values in the splenium of the corpus callosum (Schmithorst, Holland, & Dardzinski, 2008). Other findings suggest earlier white matter maturation in females compared to males (Asato et al., 2010). These discrepant findings may be due to differences in analytic approach (i.e., voxelwise comparison versus tractography methods), mean sample age, measures of pubertal maturation, and sample size, suggesting the need for additional research in this area.

Whereas sexual dimorphisms in brain structure have been identified, research has just begun to explore the effects of puberty and sex steroids on cortical maturation and white matter microstructure. Perrin and colleagues (2009) used magnetization-transfer ratio analysis, an indirect measure of myelin, to measure the effect of testosterone on white matter and found that increasing testosterone levels are associated with increased axonal diameter in males (Perrin et al., 2009). Similarly, higher levels of lutenizing hormone appear to influence greater white matter content (Peper et al., 2008). Herting and colleagues (Herting, Maxwell, Irvine, & Nagel, 2012) examined white matter microstructure and hormones among 77 adolescents (ages 10–16 years) and found that testosterone levels in males predicted white matter integrity; however, estradiol in females showed a negative association with white matter integrity. In general, sex steroids have been associated with increases in white volume and integrity, which in turn, may contribute to improvements in cognitive functioning.

Neurotransmitters

Concordant with other brain maturation processes, neurotransmitter systems undergo refinement during adolescence. Specifically, some neurotransmitter systems show significant growth, as evidenced by new connections between neurons and brain regions, while other neurotransmitter systems show loss of connections. Two primary neurotransmitter systems involved in neuronal communication, glutamate and gamma-aminobutyric acid (GABA), peak during early adolescence with significant declines thereafter (Frantz & Van

Hartesveldt, 1999; Yu, Wang, Fritschy, Witte, & Redecker, 2006). In animal studies, the binding potential and number of glutamatergic inputs decline most prominently in limbic regions during adolescence with reductions of 33% of one of glutamate's receptors, N-methyl-D-aspartate (NMDA) (Guilarte, 1998). The inhibitory GABAergic system continues to develop connections between subcortical structures and prefrontal regions during adolescence (Cunningham, Bhattacharyya, & Benes, 2002) with inputs to GABAergic interneurons in the prefrontal cortex declining from adolescence to adulthood (Lewis, 1997; Spear, 2000).

Whereas inputs from glutamate and GABA decline across adolescence, the dopamine (DA) neurotransmitter system shows significant growth. DA transmission contributes to several cognitive and physiological functions, including attention, reward, motivation, and movement. Given dopamine's varied uses, dopaminergic circuitry reorganization depends on several factors, including brain region, receptor type, and experience. For example, DA synthesis and turnover in prefrontal brain regions with subcortical projections increase from adolescence to adulthood (Andersen, Thompson, Rutstein, Hostetter, & Teicher, 2000), as does the density of dopaminergic connections to the prefrontal cortex (Lambe, Krimer, & Goldman-Rakic, 2000; Tunbridge et al., 2007). In reward and motor pathways, DA receptors decline by approximately one third during adolescence (Tarazi & Baldessarini, 2000; Teicher, Andersen, & Hostetter, 1995), perhaps suggesting maturation and stabilization of these pathways from adolescence to adulthood.

Serotoninergic transmission contributes to a wide range of behaviors, including sleep, mood, and anxiety. Alterations to the serotonergic system during adolescence are not well characterized. According to the animal literature, serotonin content, serotonin uptake sites, and serotonin receptor binding reach peak levels and decline prior to the onset of puberty (Murrin, Sanders, & Bylund, 2007; Rho & Storey, 2001); however, changes during adolescence are evident. For example, serotonin turnover rates are approximately four times lower in the nucleus accumbens during adolescence compared with turnover rates during childhood and adulthood (Teicher & Andersen, 1999). Given serotonin's role in development, sleep, and psychiatric disorders, additional research into changes in the serotonin system during adolescence is needed.

Functional Implications

The anatomical, functional, and organizational brain changes that occur during adolescence are accompanied by numerous functional adaptations, such as changes in cerebral blood flow, neurotransmission, and sleep, as well as behavior. Advances in neurophysiological techniques and neuropsychological assessments enhance our understanding of structure–function relationships during adolescent development and help identify neural circuitry underlying adolescent behavior and cognition.

Brain Function

With recent technological advances, research has begun to characterize adolescence-associated changes in brain metabolism, tissue perfusion, and neural transmissions rates. Understanding brain metabolism provides a measure of regional energy requirements for brain function and has important implications on overall brain tissue health and tissue perfusion. Historically, brain metabolism has been measured noninvasively using PET, which uses radiotracers to determine the metabolic rate of glucose and oxygen consumption. Closely coupled with glucose metabolism, tissue perfusion, or the measurement of cerebral blood flow (CBF), refers to the supply and removal of metabolic wastes via blood flow through microcirculation within brain tissue. Using magnetically labeled arterial water, arterial spin labeling (ASL) provides quantitative maps of CBF and has been used to further characterize structure-function relationships in the developing adolescent brain. In a study examining CBF during normal development using ASL (n = 44, ages 4-74) (Biagi et al., 2007), CBF decreased approximately 40% within gray matter and 23% within white matter from childhood to adulthood. Overall, CBF appeared to remain constant up to about 12 years of age followed by a significant decline during adolescence, most notably between ages 15 and 17. These findings are consistent with the limited number of PET studies of normal brain development (Chugani, 1998; Chugani, Phelps, & Mazziotta, 1987) and help clarify the metabolic changes underlying functional brain activity changes over time.

In addition to changes in brain metabolism and cerebral perfusion, neural transmission rates also change during adolescence. As previously described, dynamic structural maturation occurs between childhood and adulthood with increases in overall white matter volume and integrity. These microstructural changes include increased axonal diameter and thicker myelin sheaths around the axon, which allows for faster, more efficient flow of neural impulses along axons (Lebel & Beaulieu, 2011). Whereas DTI techniques provide evidence for structural maturation, EEG studies help characterize neural transmission via synaptic activity of neural networks. Spectral analyses of resting electrical activity in cortical networks reveal broad frequency bands described as delta (1–4 Hz), theta (4–7 Hz), alpha (8–12 Hz), beta (12–15 Hz), and gamma (>25 Hz). Across development, peak frequencies and the frequency composition of the EEG power spectra change (Katada, Ozaki, Suzuki, & Suhara, 1981; Marcuse et al., 2008). EEG studies indicate that there is a decrease in lower frequencies (e.g., delta) and an increase in higher frequencies (e.g., alpha) with age that begin over posterior brain regions (Clarke, Barry, McCarthy, & Selikowitz, 2001; Cragg et al., 2011), followed by changes in medial and frontal areas (Gasser, Jennen-Steinmetz, Sroka, Verleger, & Mocks, 1988; Katada et al., 1981). Although the exact mechanism underlying such neural transmission changes are not fully understood, the timing of these neural transmission changes coincides with decreases in gray matter and increases in white matter, and it may reflect such structural changes (Segalowitz, Santesso, & Jetha, 2010; Whitford et al., 2007).

Sleep Changes

Another domain affected by neuromaturation is sleep. In general, older adolescents go to bed later and sleep less than younger adolescents. Although external factors related to adolescence (e.g., academic, social, and extracurricular activities) contribute to these sleep changes, brain structure, organization, and other biological factors influence sleep behavior as well. EEG recordings allow for the examination of sleep architecture, and such studies indicate that sleep architecture changes during adolescence, with marked reductions in non–rapid eye movement (NREM) sleep (Feinberg, Higgins, Khaw, & Campbell, 2006; Gaudreau, Carrier, & Montplaisir, 2001). Longitudinal studies of sleep EEG among adolescent cohorts (i.e., one cohort with twice-yearly sleep EEG from ages 9–14 years; one cohort with twice-yearly sleep EEG from ages 12–17 years) indicate that NREM delta power decline begins at ages 11–12 years and decreases 66% by the age of 17 years (Campbell & Feinberg, 2009). The authors suggest that the decline in NREM power is related to synaptic pruning, as

the time course and regionally dependent pattern of gray matter volume declines parallels the timing and pattern of decline in delta power (Campbell & Feinberg, 2009).

Sleep behaviors also change during adolescence. Sleep behaviors, such as sleep timing and duration, have been related to a circadian timing system and a homeostatic drive for sleep. The circadian timing system affects sleep and arousal systems. The sleep homeostatic system, or the sleep-wake "pressure" system, favors sleep as hours of wakefulness increase and favors waking as hours of sleep are extended. These systems work together to regulate sleep. During adolescence, the biological regulation of sleep changes such that the circadian timing system undergoes a phase delay; that is, specific behaviors occur at a later time during the day (Feinberg & Campbell, 2010). Similarly, the homeostatic system shifts, and the physiological drive for sleep decreases as adolescents age and mature (Taylor, Jenni, Acebo, & Carskadon, 2005). Although sleep changes are a normative part of adolescence, reductions in NREM delta power and total sleep time contribute to daytime sleepiness (Carskadon et al., 1980) and may have a negative impact on mental health, well-being, school performance, and decision making (Colrain & Baker, 2011; Drake et al., 2003).

Cognitive and Behavior Implications

Typical adolescent neurodevelopment includes changes in brain volume, structure, and neurochemistry, which have important implications on adolescent behavior. Several studies of brain–structure relationships using DTI and fMRI suggest gray and white matter changes create more efficient neural networks that subserve complex cognitive skills (Royall et al., 2002). For example, working memory performance has been associated with frontoparietal white matter tract development (Nagy, Westerberg, & Klingberg, 2004). Visuospatial (e.g., copying complex drawings), psychomotor (e.g., responding in a coordinated manner to stimuli), and language skills improve with white matter changes in the corpus callosum (Fryer et al., 2008) and temporo-parietal tracts (Niogi & McCandliss, 2006). Intellectual functioning is associated with development of frontal, occipito-parietal, and occipito-temporo-parietal brain regions (Schmithorst, Wilke, Dardzinski, & Holland, 2005). Similarly, a longitudinal study examining white matter maturation and neuropsychological performance over 16 months during late adolescence found improved white integrity in the internal capsule was correlated with better complex attention and phonemic fluency, and changes in the inferior fronto-occipital fasciculus was associated with improved visuoconstruction ability, as well as learning and recall (Bava, Jacobus, Mahmood, Yang, & Tapert, 2010). Thus, increased myelination in white matter tracts and decreases in superfluous gray matter allows for smoother, more efficient communication between brain regions, allowing for improved neuropsychological functioning.

In the social and emotional domains, adolescence is a period of increased salience of social and peer interactions and heightened emotional reactivity (Arnett, 1999; Choudhury, Blakemore, & Charman, 2006). Developmental changes in the brain in concert with the refinement of higher order cognitive processes, including cognitive control and emotion discrimination skills, allow for increased emotion regulatory resources over time (Tottenham, Hare, & Casey, 2011). For example, brain regions involved in social information processing, such as the fusiform face area (FFA), superior temporal sulcus (STS), and occipital face area (OFA) undergo structural, functional, and connectivity changes that improve an adolescent's ability to process and respond to his or her social environment (Scherf & Scott, 2012). Emotion regulation, or the ability to modify experience and expression of emotion, typically improves across adolescence into early adulthood and is associated with age-related changes in prefrontal and amygdala activity (Pitskel, Bolling, Kaiser, Crowley, & Pelphrey, 2011).

Reward Sensitivity and Risk Taking

Risk-taking behavior and poor decision-making are salient characteristics of adolescence (Arnett, 1999; Steinberg, 2010) and may be related to differential development of subcortical and cortical regions (Casey et al., 2010). A recent model of adolescent brain development (Casey, Jones, & Somerville, 2011; Casey et al., 2010; Somerville, Jones, & Casey, 2010) suggests that subcortical circuitry and projections (e.g., ventral striatum, amygdala, orbitofrontal cortex) involved in motivation and reward develop early in adolescence relative to cortical (i.e., frontal) circuitry involved in top-down cognitive control, which results in an imbalance in adolescent frontolimbic circuitry. Indeed, adolescents exhibit heightened activation in limbic structures in anticipation and/or receipt of rewards (Galvan et al., 2006) and less activation in frontal regions during tasks involving decision making and

top-down cognitive control (Van Leijenhorst et al., 2010). Furthermore, the developmental imbalance between reward and cognitive control processing has been associated with an increased likelihood of engaging in behavioral risks (Galvan, Hare, Voss, Glover, & Casey, 2007; Somerville & Casey, 2010).

Pubertal maturation may also play a role in reward processing and risk-taking behaviors. Forbes and colleagues (2010) found that adolescents with more advanced pubertal maturation show less striatal and more medial prefrontal cortex activity in response to reward outcome compared with their less advanced counterparts. Given the role of the medial prefrontal cortex in social cognition, maturing adolescents may consider social factors when responding to reward (Forbes et al., 2010). Similarly, hormone levels may also affect reward sensitivity. Both male and female adolescents with higher testosterone levels showed reduced striatal activity to reward outcomes.

In sum, adolescents' heightened response and propensity for high-stakes rewards coupled with immature cognitive control abilities may be due to differential development of subcortical and cortical circuitry (Casey, Jones, & Hare, 2008; Galvan et al., 2006). Thus, findings suggest that adolescents may have limited capacity to assess potential reward outcomes and have heightened reactivity to rewards.

Substance Use and Substance-Related Problems

Adolescents' proclivity for risk taking is associated with increased drug and alcohol experimentation, with alcohol being the most widely used illegal substance among adolescents (Windle et al., 2008; Witt, 2010). National survey data indicate that past-year alcohol use rates increase from 29% to 65% between 8th and 12th grade, with similar increases in illicit drug use from 16% to 38% (Johnston, O'Malley, Bachman, & Schulenberg, 2010). By 8th grade, over a third (36%) of all adolescents have tried alcohol, increasing to 71% by the senior year of high school, and 21% and 48% of 8th and 12th graders, respectively, have at least tried illicit drugs (Johnston et al., 2010). Together, these findings highlight that substance use is normative during adolescence, yet this is a period of vulnerability for the emergence of substance use disorders (SUDs) (Rutherford, Mayes, & Potenza, 2010), as nearly 8% of adolescents ages 12 to 17 years and 21% of 18- to 25-year-olds meet diagnostic criteria for a SUD (Substance Abuse and Mental Health Services Administration [SAMHSA], 2011).

Early use of these substances reliably predicts SUD later in life (Li, Hewitt, & Grant, 2007). Youth who first used alcohol at age 14 years or younger have more than a five-time increased risk of alcohol use disorder compared to those who first used alcohol after their 21st birthday (SAMSHA, 2009). Substance use during adolescence has a myriad of negative effects on physiological, social, and psychological functioning (Newcomb & Locke, 2005; Tucker, Ellickson, Collins, & Klein, 2006), including risky sexual behaviors (Quinn & Fromme, 2010), hazardous driving (Lee, Maggs, Neighbors, & Patrick, 2011), and alterations in neurodevelopment (Squeglia, Jacobus, & Tapert, 2009).

Neural Consequences of Adolescent Substance Use

Although adolescents may be less sensitive to some behavioral effects of substance use (Spear & Varlinskaya, 2005; Wiley, Evans, Grainger, & Nicholson, 2008), exposure to such neurotoxins during this phase of brain maturation may interrupt neurodevelopment and key processes associated with cognitive and behavioral functioning. Neuroimaging studies of white matter microstructure (Bava et al., 2009; Jacobus et al., 2009; McQueeny et al., 2009); brain morphometry (Medina et al., 2008; Medina, Schweinsburg, Cohen-Zion, Nagel, & Tapert, 2007); brain functioning (Schweinsburg, Schweinsburg, Nagel, Eyler, & Tapert, 2011; Squeglia, Schweinsburg, Pulido, & Tapert, 2011; Tapert et al., 2007); and neuropsychological functioning among adolescent substance users (Medina, Hanson, et al., 2007; Squeglia, Spadoni, Infante, Myers, & Tapert, 2009; Tapert, Granholm, Leedy, & Brown, 2002) provide evidence of the potentially adverse effects of substance use on the developing adolescent brain.

Magnetic resonance imaging (MRI) has examined the effects of adolescent alcohol use on the hippocampus, a brain region involved in memory and learning. In this study, 12 adolescents diagnosed with adolescent alcohol use disorder (mean age = 17.2 years) and 24 healthy, age-matched controls (mean age = 17.0 years) underwent MRI scanning (De Bellis et al., 2000). Analyses revealed that youth with adolescent-onset alcohol use disorder had significantly smaller left and right hippocampal volumes compared with healthy, matched controls. Similarly, Medina, Schweinsburg, and colleagues (2007) found that increased alcohol abuse/dependency severity was associated with greater right-left asymmetry and smaller left hippocampal volumes among adolescent alcohol users compared with demographically matched controls and adolescents who consumed alcohol and used marijuana. Prefrontal volumes also appear smaller among adolescent substance users (De Bellis et al., 2005; Medina et al., 2008).

Studies examining the effects of adolescent substance use on white matter integrity consistently show that adolescent substance users have altered white matter organization. In a comparison between adolescents with heavy marijuana and alcohol use with demographically matched controls, substance-using youth showed poorer white matter integrity in several areas, including fronto-parietal circuitry and pathways connecting the frontal and temporal lobes (Bava et al., 2009). Compared to controls, adolescents diagnosed with a substance use disorder show poorer prefrontal and parietal white matter organization (Clark, Chung, Thatcher, Pajtek, & Long, 2012). McQueeny and colleagues (2009) compared white matter microstructure between adolescent binge drinkers and non-binge-drinking controls and found that binge drinkers exhibited altered anisotropy in frontal, cerebellar, temporal, and parietal regions. Furthermore, alcohol consumption appears to affect white matter quality in a dose-dependent manner where higher blood alcohol concentrations are associated with poorer white matter integrity in the corpus callosum, internal and external capsules, and superior corona radiata (McQueeny et al., 2009).

The implications of adolescent substance use on neural activity have been assessed using fMRI BOLD techniques. Squeglia and colleagues (2011) examined brain during a spatial working memory (SWM) task among binge-drinking adolescents and matched controls. Although groups performed similarly behaviorally, findings revealed that binge drinking during adolescence was associated with gender-specific alterations in brain activity with female binge drinkers showing less SWM-related activity than female controls, and male binge drinkers exhibiting greater SWM response than male controls. In another study, brain response during verbal learning was assessed among adolescents who use alcohol and marijuana (Schweinsburg et al., 2011). Participants were 74 adolescents (16- to 18-year-olds) who were classified as controls, binge drinkers, marijuana users, or binge-drinking marijuana users, and results indicate that adolescent substance users show altered brain response during verbal learning relative to nonusing controls with binge drinkers showing more differences that marijuana users, particularly in prefrontal regions (Schweinsburg et al., 2011). Other studies have shown that adolescent marijuana users exhibit increased activation during attentional control and inhibitory processing tasks compared with nonusing controls (Abdullaev, Posner, Nunnally, & Dishion, 2010; Tapert et al., 2007), suggesting that marijuana users exert more effort when trying to self-regulate (Dishion, Felver-Grant, Abdullaev, & Posner, 2011).

Adolescent substance use has also been linked to decrements in neuropsychological functioning. Studies indicate that adolescent substance users exhibit deficits in visuospatial and attentional performance (Squeglia, Spadoni, et al., 2009; Tapert et al., 2002), memory (Brown, Tapert, Granholm, & Delis, 2000), and executive functioning (Giancola & Moss, 1998; Thoma et al., 2011). A recent longitudinal study (Hanson, Medina, Padula, Tapert, & Brown, 2011) examined the long-term effects of adolescent substance use on neurocognition among individuals participating in a project following adolescents with and without substance use disorders who received neuropsychological examinations at baseline and semiannually for approximately 10 years. Findings indicated that adolescents who were diagnosed with a substance use disorder during adolescence showed decline in visuospatial and memory abilities 10 years later.

In summary, studies of adolescent substance use indicate that substance use is linked to changes in brain structure and function that include altered hippocampal and prefrontal volumes, reduced white matter organization and integrity, atypical brain activity, and weaknesses in neuropsychological functioning. Although the effects of substance use on the brain may be reversible with long-term abstinence (Delisi et al., 2006; Wang et al., 2011), additional studies are needed to better understand the neurotoxic effect of substance use on the developing adolescent brain.

Conclusion

Adolescence is a period of substantial physical, neurobiological, and behavioral change. Across this developmental period, the brain shows significant reorganization with changes in neurochemistry, fiber architecture, and overall tissue composition. Developmental neuroimaging studies indicate gray matter volume reductions, white matter volume increases, and improvements in functional brain networks associated with complex cognitive and behavioral skills. Although these changes are usually beneficial and enhance functioning, asynchronous maturation of prefrontal and limbic systems confer vulnerability to risk taking and affect regulation difficulties. As such, adolescence is a time when several psychiatric disorders emerge and substance use rates increase. Substance use during adolescence is particularly concerning given the potential neural consequences of use on the developing brain. Developmental research over the past 15 years has improved our understanding of adolescence and its associated changes; however, the integrative study of genetic, hormonal, neural, behavioral, and environmental characteristics is needed to explore how these factors interact and influence neurodevelopmental processes.

Future Directions

Despite our increased understanding of adolescent brain development, developmental neuroscience is still young and many questions remain. Adolescence is clearly a time of significant growth and development is several areas of one's life that help establish a foundation for the future. In this next section, we explore key areas for future research.

Research has only just begun to explore how brain structure and physiological development impact functional brain networks and associated behavior. Although researchers posit that synaptic pruning contributes to brain activity changes by fine-tuning connections and enabling specialized functional network development, direct evidence supporting this hypothesis is actually quite limited (see Paus, Keshavan, & Giedd, 2008), and structure–function relationships are likely more complex (Harris, Reynell, & Attwell, 2011). For example, the cellular and neurovascular coupling changes that underlie physiological changes remain unknown. A recent review (Harris et al., 2011) highlights the importance of examining microvascular and neurovascular coupling changes during adolescent brain development, as vascular changes may have confounding age-related effects on BOLD signal, a primary indirect measure of brain activity. Furthermore, it would be useful to know more about associations between brain structure (e.g., gray matter volume and white matter changes) and functional consequences. Although studies have attempted to correlate gray and white matter changes with functional development (Konrad et al., 2005; Lu et al., 2009; Olesen, Nagy, Westerberg, & Klingberg, 2003), structural changes do not account for all functional changes observed during development.

There is also a critical need to understand how puberty influences neural development. As described previously, the onset of puberty may trigger structural reorganization of the brain (Petanjek et al., 2011; Sisk & Foster, 2004).= MRI studies provide evidence for pubertal effects on gray and white matter volume (Herting et al., 2012; Neufang et al., 2009); however, the complex, reciprocal relationship between sex hormones, brain, and behavior remain poorly understood. To examine pubertal effects on adolescent brain development, important methodological procedures must be addressed. First, studies must evaluate the effects of sex steroids and/or pubertal status *independently* from chronological age. Disentangling puberty from age is an important concern because the correlation between age and pubertal status differs between males and females, and there are likely puberty-related changes that are independent of age-related brain and behavioral development. Second, measures of puberty should be accurate and reliable. Finally, replication of findings is needed. Although recent MRI studies provide some insight into the relationships between puberty and brain development, conflicting results, methodological issues, and the dearth of studies on this topic leave ample opportunity for additional research in this area.

Large individual variability in brain structure, function, and behavioral development calls for longitudinal studies that examine mechanisms underlying individual differences, as well as the protective and adverse factors influencing development. For example, adolescence is a time of vulnerability to psychopathology, with peak age of onset for having a mental health disorder at 14 years of age (Kessler, Chiu, Demler, Merikangas, & Walters, 2005). Several psychiatric disorders emerge during adolescence, including anxiety disorder, bipolar disorder, depression, eating disorder, and substance use disorder (Kessler et al., 2005). The emergence of psychopathology during adolescence is likely related to abnormalities in typical adolescent development, such as psychosocial, biological, and brain development processes that interact and contribute to cognitive, affective, and motivational disturbances (for review, see Paus et al., 2008). Furthermore, genetic factors likely play an important role in individual differences. Interindividual differences in genes have profound effects on brain development, cognition, and behavior. Such heritable individual differences interact with environmental factors and likely have a cumulative effect on brain structure and function; however, additional research on how genes interact with environment and affect brain development is needed.

A recent review (Blakemore, 2012) also highlights the importance of exploring how context and culture influence brain development. Given that the adolescent experience varies depending on one's culture (Choudhury, 2010), future research will need to explore how differences in culture might influence adolescent neurodevelopment. Specifically, cultural variations in puberty onset, traditions/activities, and dietary intake (Berkey, Gardner, Frazier, & Colditz, 2000) may have profound effects on adolescent development and neural circuitry.

References

Abdullaev, Y., Posner, M. I., Nunnally, R., & Dishion, T. J. (2010). Functional MRI evidence for inefficient attentional control in adolescent chronic cannabis abuse. *Behavioural Brain Research, 215*(1), 45–57.

Alexander, A. L., Lee, J. E., Lazar, M., & Field, A. S. (2007). Diffusion tensor imaging of the brain. *Neurotherapeutics, 4*(3), 316–329.

Andersen, S. L., Thompson, A. T., Rutstein, M., Hostetter, J. C., & Teicher, M. H. (2000). Dopamine receptor pruning in prefrontal cortex during the periadolescent period in rats. *Synapse, 37*(2), 167–169.

Arnett, J. J. (1999). Adolescent storm and stress, reconsidered. *American Psychologist, 54*(5), 317–326.

Asato, M. R., Terwilliger, R., Woo, J., & Luna, B. (2010). White matter development in adolescence: A DTI study. *Cerebral Cortex, 20*(9), 2122–2131.

Ashtari, M., Cervellione, K. L., Hasan, K. M., Wu, J., McIlree, C., Kester, H., . . . Kumra, S. (2007). White matter development during late adolescence in healthy males: A cross-sectional diffusion tensor imaging study. *NeuroImage, 35*(2), 501–510.

Bava, S., Frank, L. R., McQueeny, T., Schweinsburg, B. C., Schweinsburg, A. D., & Tapert, S. F. (2009). Altered white matter microstructure in adolescent substance users. *Psychiatry Research, 173*(3), 228–237.

Bava, S., Jacobus, J., Mahmood, O., Yang, T. T., & Tapert, S. F. (2010). Neurocognitive correlates of white matter quality in adolescent substance users. *Brain and Cognition, 72*(3), 347–354.

Bava, S., & Tapert, S. F. (2010). Adolescent brain development and the risk for alcohol and other drug problems. *Neuropsychology Review, 20*(4), 398–413.

Berkey, C. S., Gardner, J. D., Frazier, A. L., & Colditz, G. A. (2000). Relation of childhood diet and body size to menarche and adolescent growth in girls. *American Journal of Epidemiology, 152*(5), 446–452.

Biagi, L., Abbruzzese, A., Bianchi, M. C., Alsop, D. C., Del Guerra, A., & Tosetti, M. (2007). Age dependence of cerebral perfusion assessed by magnetic resonance continuous arterial spin labeling. *Journal of Magnetic Resonance Imaging, 25*(4), 696–702.

Biswal, B., Yetkin, F. Z., Haughton, V. M., & Hyde, J. S. (1995). Functional connectivity in the motor cortex of resting human brain using echo-planar MRI. *Magnetic Resonance in Medicine, 34*(4), 537–541.

Blakemore, S. J. (2008). The social brain in adolescence. *Nature Reviews. Neuroscience, 9*(4), 267–277.

Blakemore, S. J. (2012). Imaging brain development: The adolescent brain. *NeuroImage, 61*(2), 397–406.

Blanton, R. E., Levitt, J. G., Peterson, J. R., Fadale, D., Sporty, M. L., Lee, M., . . . Toga, A. W. (2004). Gender differences in the left inferior frontal gyrus in normal children. *NeuroImage, 22*(2), 626–636.

Bonekamp, D., Nagae, L. M., Degaonkar, M., Matson, M., Abdalla, W. M., Barker, P. B., . . . Horská, A. (2007). Diffusion tensor imaging in children and adolescents: Reproducibility, hemispheric, and age-related differences. *NeuroImage, 34*(2), 733–742.

Brown, S. A., Tapert, S. F., Granholm, E., & Delis, D. C. (2000). Neurocognitive functioning of adolescents: Effects of protracted alcohol use. *Alcoholism, Clinical and Experimental Research, 24*(2), 164–171.

Bullmore, E., & Sporns, O. (2009). Complex brain networks: Graph theoretical analysis of structural and functional systems. *Nature Reviews. Neuroscience, 10*(3), 186–198.

Campbell, I. G., & Feinberg, I. (2009). Longitudinal trajectories of non-rapid eye movement delta and theta EEG as indicators of adolescent brain maturation. *Proceedings of the National Academy of Sciences USA, 106*(13), 5177–5180.

Carskadon, M. A., Harvey, K., Duke, P., Anders, T. F., Litt, I. F., & Dement, W. C. (1980). Pubertal changes in daytime sleepiness. *Sleep, 2*(4), 453–460.

Casey, B. J., Jones, R. M., & Somerville, L. H. (2011). Braking and accelerating of the adolescent brain. *Journal of Research on Adolescence, 21*(1), 21–33.

Casey, B. J., Jones, R. M., & Hare, T. A. (2008). The adolescent brain. *Annals of the New York Academy of Sciences, 1124*, 111–126.

Casey, B. J., Jones, R. M., Levita, L., Libby, V., Pattwell, S. S., Ruberry, E. J., . . . Somerville, L. H. (2010). The storm and stress of adolescence: Insights from human imaging and mouse genetics. *Developmental Psychobiology, 52*(3), 225–235.

Choudhury, S. (2010). Culturing the adolescent brain: What can neuroscience learn from anthropology? *Social Cognitive and Affective Neuroscience, 5*(2–3), 159–167.

Choudhury, S., Blakemore, S. J., & Charman, T. (2006). Social cognitive development during adolescence. *Social Cognitive and Affective Neuroscience, 1*(3), 165–174.

Chugani, H. T. (1998). A critical period of brain development: Studies of cerebral glucose utilization with PET. *Preventive Medicine, 27*(2), 184–188.

Chugani, H. T., Phelps, M. E., & Mazziotta, J. C. (1987). Positron emission tomography study of human brain functional development. *Annals of Neurology, 22*(4), 487–497.

Clark, D. B., Chung, T., Thatcher, D. L., Pajtek, S., & Long, E. C. (2012). Psychological dysregulation, white matter disorganization and substance use disorders in adolescence. *Addiction, 107*(1), 206–214.

Clark, D. B., Thatcher, D. L., & Tapert, S. F. (2008). Alcohol, psychological dysregulation, and adolescent brain development. *Alcoholism, Clinical and Experimental Research, 32*(3), 375–385.

Clarke, A. R., Barry, R. J., McCarthy, R., & Selikowitz, M. (2001). Age and sex effects in the EEG: Development of the normal child. *Clinical Neurophysiology, 112*(5), 806–814.

Colrain, I. M., & Baker, F. C. (2011). Changes in sleep as a function of adolescent development. *Neuropsychology Review, 21*(1), 5–21.

Conturo, T. E., Lori, N. F., Cull, T. S., Akbudak, E., Snyder, A. Z., Shimony, J. S., . . . Raichle, M. E. (1999). Tracking neuronal fiber pathways in the living human brain. *Proceedings of the National Academy of Sciences USA, 96*(18), 10422–10427.

Cragg, L., Kovacevic, N., McIntosh, A. R., Poulsen, C., Martinu, K., Leonard, G., & Paus, T. (2011). Maturation of EEG power spectra in early adolescence: A longitudinal study. *Developmental Science, 14*(5), 935–943.

Cunningham, M. G., Bhattacharyya, S., & Benes, F. M. (2002). Amygdalo-cortical sprouting continues into early adulthood: Implications for the development of normal and abnormal function during adolescence. *Journal of Comparative Neurology, 453*(2), 116–130.

Dahl, R. E., & Spear, L. P. (2004). Adolescent brain development. *Annals of the New York Academy of Sciences, 1021*, 1–22.

De Bellis, M. D., Clark, D. B., Beers, S. R., Soloff, P. H., Boring, A. M., Hall, J., . . . Keshavan, M. S. (2000). Hippocampal volume in adolescent-onset alcohol use disorders. *American Journal of Psychiatry, 157*(5), 737–744.

De Bellis, M. D., Keshavan, M. S., Beers, S. R., Hall, J., Frustaci, K., Masalehdan, A., . . . Boring, A. M. (2001). Sex differences in brain maturation during childhood and adolescence. *Cerebral Cortex, 11*(6), 552–557.

De Bellis, M. D., Narasimhan, A., Thatcher, D. L., Keshavan, M. S., Soloff, P., & Clark, D. B. (2005). Prefrontal cortex, thalamus, and cerebellar volumes in adolescents and young adults with adolescent-onset alcohol use disorders and comorbid mental disorders. *Alcoholism, Clinical and Experimental Research, 29*(9), 1590–1600.

Delisi, L. E., Bertisch, H. C., Szulc, K. U., Majcher, M., Brown, K., Bappal, A., & Ardakani, B. A. (2006). A preliminary DTI study showing no brain structural change associated with adolescent cannabis use. *Harm Reduction Journal, 3*, 17.

Dishion, T. J., Felver-Grant, J. C., Abdullaev, Y., & Posner, M. I. (2011). Self-regulation and adolescent drug use: Translating developmental science and neuroscience into prevention practice. In M. T. Bardo, D. H. Fishbein, & R. Milch (Eds.), *Inhibitory control and drug abuse prevention: from research to translation* (pp. 281–301). New York, NY: Springer.

Drake, C., Nickel, C., Burduvali, E., Roth, T., Jefferson, C., & Pietro, B. (2003). The pediatric daytime sleepiness scale (PDSS): Sleep habits and school outcomes in middle-school children. *Sleep, 26*(4), 455–458.

Fair, D. A., Cohen, A. L., Dosenbach, N. U., Church, J. A., Miezin, F. M., Barch, D. M., . . . Schlaggar, B. L. (2008). The maturing architecture of the brain's default network. *Proceedings of the National Academy of Sciences USA, 105*(10), 4028–4032.

Fair, D. A., Cohen, A. L., Power, J. D., Dosenbach, N. U., Church, J. A., Miezin, F. M., . . . Petersen, S. E. (2009). Functional brain networks develop from a "local to distributed" organization. *PLoS Computational Biology, 5*(5), e1000381.

Fair, D. A., Schlaggar, B. L., Cohen, A. L., Miezin, F. M., Dosenbach, N. U., Wenger, K. K., . . . Petersen, S. E. (2007). A method for using blocked and event-related fMRI data to study "resting state" functional connectivity. *NeuroImage, 35*(1), 396–405.

Feinberg, I., & Campbell, I. G. (2010). Sleep EEG changes during adolescence: An index of a fundamental brain reorganization. *Brain and Cognition, 72*(1), 56–65.

Feinberg, I., Higgins, L. M., Khaw, W. Y., & Campbell, I. G. (2006). The adolescent decline of NREM delta, an indicator of brain maturation, is linked to age and sex but not to pubertal stage. *American Journal of Physiology, 291*(6), R1724–R1729.

Forbes, E. E., & Dahl, R. E. (2010). Pubertal development and behavior: Hormonal activation of social and motivational tendencies. *Brain and Cognition, 72*(1), 66–72.

Forbes, E. E., Ryan, N. D., Phillips, M. L., Manuck, S. B., Worthman, C. M., Moyles, D. L., . . . Dahl, R. E. (2010). Healthy adolescents' neural response to reward: Associations with puberty, positive affect, and depressive symptoms. *Journal of the American Academy of Child and Adolescent Psychiatry, 49*(2), 162–172 e161–e165.

Fox, M. D., & Raichle, M. E. (2007). Spontaneous fluctuations in brain activity observed with functional magnetic resonance imaging. *Nature Reviews. Neuroscience, 8*(9), 700–711.

Fox, M. D., Snyder, A. Z., Vincent, J. L., Corbetta, M., Van Essen, D. C., & Raichle, M. E. (2005). The human brain is intrinsically organized into dynamic, anticorrelated functional networks. *Proceedings of the National Academy of Sciences USA, 102*(27), 9673–9678.

Frantz, K., & Van Hartesveldt, C. (1999). The locomotor effects of MK801 in the nucleus accumbens of developing and adult rats. *European Journal of Pharmacology, 368*(2–3), 125–135.

Friston, K. J., Harrison, L., & Penny, W. (2003). Dynamic causal modelling. *NeuroImage, 19*(4), 1273–1302.

Fryer, S. L., Frank, L. R., Spadoni, A. D., Theilmann, R. J., Nagel, B. J., Schweinsburg, A. D., & Tapert, S. F. (2008). Microstructural integrity of the corpus callosum linked with neuropsychological performance in adolescents. *Brain and Cognition, 67*(2), 225–233.

Galvan, A., Hare, T., Voss, H., Glover, G., & Casey, B. J. (2007). Risk-taking and the adolescent brain: Who is at risk? *Developmental Science, 10*(2), F8–F14.

Galvan, A., Hare, T. A., Parra, C. E., Penn, J., Voss, H., Glover, G., & Casey, B. J. (2006). Earlier development of the accumbens relative to orbitofrontal cortex might underlie risk-taking behavior in adolescents. *Journal of Neuroscience, 26*(25), 6885–6892.

Gasser, T., Jennen-Steinmetz, C., Sroka, L., Verleger, R., & Mocks, J. (1988). Development of the EEG of school-age children and adolescents. II. Topography. *Electroencephalography and Clinical Neurophysiology, 69*(2), 100–109.

Gaudreau, H., Carrier, J., & Montplaisir, J. (2001). Age-related modifications of NREM sleep EEG: From childhood to middle age. *Journal of Sleep Research, 10*(3), 165–172.

Giancola, P. R., & Moss, H. B. (1998). Executive cognitive functioning in alcohol use disorders. *Recent Developments in Alcoholism, 14*, 227–251.

Giedd, J. N., Blumenthal, J., Jeffries, N. O., Castellanos, F. X., Liu, H., Zijdenbos, A., . . . Rapoport, J. L. (1999). Brain development during childhood and adolescence: A longitudinal MRI study. *Nature Neuroscience, 2*(10), 861–863.

Giorgio, A., Watkins, K. E., Douaud, G., James, A. C., James, S., De Stefano, N., . . . Johansen-Berg, H. (2008). Changes in white matter microstructure during adolescence. *NeuroImage, 39*(1), 52–61.

Gogtay, N., Giedd, J. N., Lusk, L., Hayashi, K. M., Greenstein, D., Vaituzis, A. C., . . . Thompson, P. M. (2004). Dynamic mapping of human cortical development during childhood through early adulthood. *Proceedings of the National Academy of Sciences USA, 101*(21), 8174–8179.

Guilarte, T. (1998). The N-methyl-D-aspartate receptor: Physiology and neurotoxicology in the developing brain. In W. Slikker, Jr. & L. W. Chang (Eds.), *Handbook of developmental neurotoxicology* (pp. 285–304). San Diego, CA: Academic Press.

Hanson, K. L., Medina, K. L., Padula, C. B., Tapert, S. F., & Brown, S. A. (2011). Impact of adolescent alcohol and drug use on neuropsychological functioning in young adulthood: 10-year outcomes. *Journal of Child and Adolescent Substance Abuse, 20*(2), 135–154.

Harris, J. J., Reynell, C., & Attwell, D. (2011). The physiology of developmental changes in BOLD functional imaging signals. *Developmental Cognitive Neuroscience, 1*(3), 199–216.

He, B. J., Snyder, A. Z., Vincent, J. L., Epstein, A., Shulman, G. L., & Corbetta, M. (2007). Breakdown of functional connectivity in frontoparietal networks underlies behavioral deficits in spatial neglect. *Neuron, 53*(6), 905–918.

Herting, M. M., Maxwell, E. C., Irvine, C., & Nagel, B. J. (2012). The impact of sex, puberty, and hormones on white matter microstructure in adolescents. *Cerebral Cortex, 22*(9), 1979–1992.

Horwitz, B. (2003). The elusive concept of brain connectivity. *NeuroImage, 19*(2 Pt 1), 466–470.

Hwang, K., Velanova, K., & Luna, B. (2010). Strengthening of top-down frontal cognitive control networks underlying the development of inhibitory control: A functional magnetic resonance imaging effective connectivity study. *Journal of Neuroscience, 30*(46), 15535–15545.

Jacobus, J., McQueeny, T., Bava, S., Schweinsburg, B. C., Frank, L. R., Yang, T. T., & Tapert, S. F. (2009). White matter integrity in adolescents with histories of marijuana use and binge drinking. *Neurotoxicology and Teratology, 31*(6), 349–355.

Jernigan, T. L., & Tallal, P. (1990). Late childhood changes in brain morphology observable with MRI. *Developmental Medicine and Child Neurology, 32*(5), 379–385.

Jernigan, T. L., Trauner, D. A., Hesselink, J. R., & Tallal, P. A. (1991). Maturation of human cerebrum observed in vivo during adolescence. *Brain, 114* (Pt 5), 2037–2049.

Johnston, L. D., O'Malley, P. M., Bachman, J. G., & Schulenberg, J. E. (2010). *Monitoring the Future national survey results on drug use, 1975–2009: Vol. 1, Secondary school students.* (NIH Publication No. 10-7584). Bethesda, MD: National Institute on Drug Abuse.

Katada, A., Ozaki, H., Suzuki, H., & Suhara, K. (1981). Developmental characteristics of normal and mentally retarded children's EEGs. *Electroencephalography and Clinical Neurophysiology, 52*(2), 192–201.

Kessler, R. C., Chiu, W. T., Demler, O., Merikangas, K. R., & Walters, E. E. (2005). Prevalence, severity, and comorbidity of 12-month DSM-IV disorders in the National Comorbidity Survey Replication. *Archives of General Psychiatry, 62*(6), 617–627.

Keulers, E. H., Goulas, A., Jolles, J., & Stiers, P. (2012). Maturation of task-induced brain activation and long range functional connectivity in adolescence revealed by multivariate pattern classification. *NeuroImage, 60*(2), 1250–1265.

Keulers, E. H., Stiers, P., & Jolles, J. (2011). Developmental changes between ages 13 and 21 years in the extent and magnitude of the BOLD response during decision making. *NeuroImage, 54*(2), 1442–1454.

Konrad, K., Neufang, S., Thiel, C. M., Specht, K., Hanisch, C., Fan, J., . . . Fink, G. R. (2005). Development of attentional networks: An fMRI study with children and adults. *NeuroImage, 28*(2), 429–439.

Lambe, E. K., Krimer, L. S., & Goldman-Rakic, P. S. (2000). Differential postnatal development of catecholamine and serotonin inputs to identified neurons in prefrontal cortex of rhesus monkey. *Journal of Neuroscience, 20*(23), 8780–8787.

Lebel, C., & Beaulieu, C. (2011). Longitudinal development of human brain wiring continues from childhood into adulthood. *Journal of Neuroscience, 31*(30), 10937–10947.

Lebel, C., Walker, L., Leemans, A., Phillips, L., & Beaulieu, C. (2008). Microstructural maturation of the human brain from childhood to adulthood. *NeuroImage, 40*(3), 1044–1055.

LeBihan, D., Mangin, J., Poupon, C., Clark, C., Papata, S., Molko, N., & Chabriat, H. (2001). Diffusion tensor imaging: Concepts and applications. *Journal of Magnetic Resonance Imaging, 13*, 534–546.

Lee, C. M., Maggs, J. L., Neighbors, C., & Patrick, M. E. (2011). Positive and negative alcohol-related consequences: Associations with past drinking. *Journal of Adolescence, 34*(1), 87–94.

Lenroot, R. K., & Giedd, J. N. (2010). Sex differences in the adolescent brain. *Brain and Cognition, 72*(1), 46–55.

Lewis, D. A. (1997). Development of the prefrontal cortex during adolescence: Insights into vulnerable neural circuits in schizophrenia. *Neuropsychopharmacology, 16*(6), 385–398.

Li, T. K., Hewitt, B. G., & Grant, B. F. (2007). Is there a future for quantifying drinking in the diagnosis, treatment, and prevention of alcohol use disorders? *Alcohol and Alcoholism, 42*(2), 57–63.

Lowe, M. J., Mock, B. J., & Sorenson, J. A. (1998). Functional connectivity in single and multislice echoplanar imaging using resting-state fluctuations. *NeuroImage, 7*(2), 119–132.

Lu, L. H., Dapretto, M., O'Hare, E. D., Kan, E., McCourt, S. T., Thompson, P. M., . . . Sowell, E. R. (2009). Relationships between brain activation and brain structure in normally developing children. *Cerebral Cortex, 19*(11), 2595–2604.

Majewska, A. K., & Sur, M. (2006). Plasticity and specificity of cortical processing networks. *Trends in Neurosciences, 29*(6), 323–329.

Marcuse, L. V., Schneider, M., Mortati, K. A., Donnelly, K. M., Arnedo, V., & Grant, A. C. (2008). Quantitative analysis of the EEG posterior-dominant rhythm in healthy adolescents. *Clinical Neurophysiology, 119*(8), 1778–1781.

McQueeny, T., Schweinsburg, B. C., Schweinsburg, A. D., Jacobus, J., Bava, S., Frank, L. R., & Tapert, S. F. (2009). Altered white matter integrity in adolescent binge drinkers. *Alcoholism, Clinical and Experimental Research, 33*(7), 1278–1285.

Medina, K. L., Hanson, K. L., Schweinsburg, A. D., Cohen-Zion, M., Nagel, B. J., & Tapert, S. F. (2007). Neuropsychological functioning in adolescent marijuana users: Subtle deficits detectable after a month of abstinence. *Journal of the International Neuropsychological Society, 13*(5), 807–820.

Medina, K. L., McQueeny, T., Nagel, B. J., Hanson, K. L., Schweinsburg, A. D., & Tapert, S. F. (2008). Prefrontal cortex volumes in adolescents with alcohol use disorders: Unique gender effects. *Alcoholism, Clinical and Experimental Research, 32*(3), 386–394.

Medina, K. L., Schweinsburg, A. D., Cohen-Zion, M., Nagel, B. J., & Tapert, S. F. (2007). Effects of alcohol and combined marijuana and alcohol use during adolescence on hippocampal volume and asymmetry. *Neurotoxicology and Teratology, 29*(1), 141–152.

Murrin, L. C., Sanders, J. D., & Bylund, D. B. (2007). Comparison of the maturation of the adrenergic and serotonergic neurotransmitter systems in the brain: Implications for differential drug effects on juveniles and adults. *Biochemical Pharmacology, 73*(8), 1225–1236.

Nagy, Z., Westerberg, H., & Klingberg, T. (2004). Maturation of white matter is associated with the development of cognitive functions during childhood. *Journal of Cognitive Neuroscience, 16*(7), 1227–1233.

Neufang, S., Specht, K., Hausmann, M., Gunturkun, O., Herpertz-Dahlmann, B., Fink, G. R., & Konrad, K. (2009). Sex differences and the impact of steroid hormones on the developing human brain. *Cerebral Cortex, 19*(2), 464–473.

Newcomb, M. D., & Locke, T. F. (2005). Childhood adversity and poor mothering: Consequences of polydrug abuse use as a moderator. *Addictive Behaviors, 30*(5), 1061–1064.

Niogi, S. N., & McCandliss, B. D. (2006). Left lateralized white matter microstructure accounts for individual differences in reading ability and disability. *Neuropsychologia, 44*(11), 2178–2188.

Olesen, P. J., Nagy, Z., Westerberg, H., & Klingberg, T. (2003). Combined analysis of DTI and fMRI data reveals a joint maturation of white and grey matter in a fronto-parietal network. *Brain Research, 18*(1), 48–57.

Paus, T., Keshavan, M., & Giedd, J. N. (2008). Why do many psychiatric disorders emerge during adolescence? *Nature Reviews. Neuroscience, 9*(12), 947–957.

Paus, T., Zijdenbos, A., Worsley, K., Collins, D. L., Blumenthal, J., Giedd, J. N., . . . Evans, A. C. (1999). Structural maturation of neural pathways in children and adolescents: In vivo study. *Science, 283*(5409), 1908–1911.

Peper, J. S., Brouwer, R. M., Schnack, H. G., van Baal, G. C., van Leeuwen, M., van den Berg, S. M., . . . Hulshoff Pol, H. E. (2008). Cerebral white matter in early puberty is associated with luteinizing hormone concentrations. *Psychoneuroendocrinology, 33*(7), 909–915.

Perrin, J. S., Leonard, G., Perron, M., Pike, G. B., Pitiot, A., Richer, L., . . . Paus, T. (2009). Sex differences in the growth of white matter during adolescence. *NeuroImage, 45*(4), 1055–1066.

Petanjek, Z., Judas, M., Simic, G., Rasin, M. R., Uylings, H. B., Rakic, P., & Kostovic, I. (2011). Extraordinary neoteny of synaptic spines in the human prefrontal cortex. *Proceedings of the National Academy of Sciences USA, 108*(32), 13281–13286.

Pitskel, N. B., Bolling, D. Z., Kaiser, M. D., Crowley, M. J., & Pelphrey, K. A. (2011). How grossed out are you? The neural bases of emotion regulation from childhood to adolescence. *Developmental Cognitive Neuroscience, 1*(3), 324–337.

Power, J. D., Fair, D. A., Schlaggar, B. L., & Petersen, S. E. (2010). The development of human functional brain networks. *Neuron, 67*(5), 735–748.

Purves, D., White, L. E., & Riddle, D. R. (1996). Is neural development Darwinian? *Trends in Neurosciences, 19*(11), 460–464.

Quinn, P. D., & Fromme, K. (2010). Self-regulation as a protective factor against risky drinking and sexual behavior. *Psychology of Addictive Behaviors, 24*(3), 376–385.

Reiss, A. L., Abrams, M. T., Singer, H. S., Ross, J. L., & Denckla, M. B. (1996). Brain development, gender and IQ in children. A volumetric imaging study. *Brain, 119*(Pt. 5), 1763–1774.

Rho, J. M., & Storey, T. W. (2001). Molecular ontogeny of major neurotransmitter receptor systems in the mammalian central nervous system: Norepinephrine, dopamine, serotonin, acetylcholine, and glycine. *Journal of Child Neurology*, *16*(4), 271–280; discussion 281.

Roberts, T. P., & Schwartz, E. S. (2007). Principles and implementation of diffusion-weighted and diffusion tensor imaging. *Pediatric Radiology*, *37*(8), 739–748.

Royall, D. R., Lauterbach, E. C., Cummings, J. L., Reeve, A., Rummans, T. A., Kaufer, D. I., . . . Coffey, C. E. (2002). Executive control function: A review of its promise and challenges for clinical research. A report from the Committee on Research of the American Neuropsychiatric Association. *Journal of Neuropsychiatry and Clinical Neurosciences*, *14*(4), 377–405.

Rubia, K., Smith, A. B., Woolley, J., Nosarti, C., Heyman, I., Taylor, E., & Brammer, M. (2006). Progressive increase of frontostriatal brain activation from childhood to adulthood during event-related tasks of cognitive control. *Human Brain Mapping*, *27*(12), 973–993.

Rutherford, H. J., Mayes, L. C., & Potenza, M. N. (2010). Neurobiology of adolescent substance use disorders: Implications for prevention and treatment. *Child and Adolescent Psychiatric Clinics of North America*, *19*(3), 479–492.

Scherf, K. S., & Scott, L. S. (2012). Connecting developmental trajectories: Biases in face processing from infancy to adulthood. *Developmental Psychobiology*, *54*(6), 643–663.

Schmithorst, V. J., Holland, S. K., & Dardzinski, B. J. (2008). Developmental differences in white matter architecture between boys and girls. *Human Brain Mapping*, *29*(6), 696–710.

Schmithorst, V. J., Wilke, M., Dardzinski, B. J., & Holland, S. K. (2005). Cognitive functions correlate with white matter architecture in a normal pediatric population: A diffusion tensor MRI study. *Human Brain Mapping*, *26*(2), 139–147.

Schweinsburg, A. D., Schweinsburg, B. C., Nagel, B. J., Eyler, L. T., & Tapert, S. F. (2011). Neural correlates of verbal learning in adolescent alcohol and marijuana users. *Addiction*, *106*(3), 564–573.

Segalowitz, S. J., Santesso, D. L., & Jetha, M. K. (2010). Electrophysiological changes during adolescence: A review. *Brain and Cognition*, *72*(1), 86–100.

Shaw, P., Kabani, N. J., Lerch, J. P., Eckstrand, K., Lenroot, R., Gogtay, N., . . . Wise, S. P. (2008). Neurodevelopmental trajectories of the human cerebral cortex. *Journal of Neuroscience*, *28*(14), 3586–3594.

Sherman, D. L., & Brophy, P. J. (2005). Mechanisms of axon ensheathment and myelin growth. *Nature Reviews: Neuroscience*, *6*(9), 683–690.

Shimony, J. S., McKinstry, R. C., Akbudak, E., Aronovitz, J. A., Snyder, A. Z., Lori, N. F., . . . Conturo, T. E. (1999). Quantitative diffusion-tensor anisotropy brain MR imaging: Normative human data and anatomic analysis. *Radiology*, *212*(3), 770–784.

Sisk, C. L., & Foster, D. L. (2004). The neural basis of puberty and adolescence. *Nature Neuroscience*, *7*(10), 1040–1047.

Somerville, L. H., & Casey, B. J. (2010). Developmental neurobiology of cognitive control and motivational systems. *Current Opinion in Neurobiology*, *20*(2), 236–241.

Somerville, L. H., Jones, R. M., & Casey, B. J. (2010). A time of change: Behavioral and neural correlates of adolescent sensitivity to appetitive and aversive environmental cues. *Brain and Cognition*, *72*(1), 124–133.

Sowell, E. R., Peterson, B. S., Thompson, P. M., Welcome, S. E., Henkenius, A. L., & Toga, A. W. (2003). Mapping cortical change across the human life span. *Nature Neuroscience*, *6*(3), 309–315.

Sowell, E. R., Thompson, P. M., Holmes, C. J., Batth, R., Jernigan, T. L., & Toga, A. W. (1999). Localizing age-related changes in brain structure between childhood and adolescence using statistical parametric mapping. *NeuroImage*, *9*(6 Pt. 1), 587–597.

Sowell, E. R., Thompson, P. M., Leonard, C. M., Welcome, S. E., Kan, E., & Toga, A. W. (2004). Longitudinal mapping of cortical thickness and brain growth in normal children. *Journal of Neuroscience*, *24*(38), 8223–8231.

Spear, L. P. (2000). The adolescent brain and age-related behavioral manifestations. *Neuroscience and Biobehavioral Reviews*, *24*(4), 417–463.

Spear, L. P., & Varlinskaya, E. I. (2005). Adolescence. Alcohol sensitivity, tolerance, and intake. *Recent Developments in Alcoholism*, *17*, 143–159.

Squeglia, L. M., Jacobus, J., & Tapert, S. F. (2009). The influence of substance use on adolescent brain development. *Clinical EEG and Neuroscience*, *40*(1), 31–38.

Squeglia, L. M., Schweinsburg, A. D., Pulido, C., & Tapert, S. F. (2011). Adolescent binge drinking linked to abnormal spatial working memory brain activation: Differential gender effects. *Alcoholism, Clinical and Experimental Research*, *35*(10), 1831–1841.

Squeglia, L. M., Spadoni, A. D., Infante, M. A., Myers, M. G., & Tapert, S. F. (2009). Initiating moderate to heavy alcohol use predicts changes in neuropsychological functioning for adolescent girls and boys. *Psychology of Addictive Behaviors*, *23*(4), 715–722.

Steinberg, L. (2010). A dual systems model of adolescent risk-taking. *Developmental Psychobiology*, *52*(3), 216–224.

Stevens, M. C., Pearlson, G. D., & Calhoun, V. D. (2009). Changes in the interaction of resting-state neural networks from adolescence to adulthood. *Human Brain Mapping*, *30*(8), 2356–2366.

Substance Abuse and Mental Health Services Administration. (2009). *Results from the 2008 National Survey on Drug Use and Health: National Findings*. (NSDUH Series H-36, HHS Publication No. SMA 09-4434). Rockville, MD: Author.

Substance Abuse and Mental Health Services Administration. (2011). *State estimates of substance use and mental disorders from 2008–2009 National Surveys on Drug Use and Health*. (NSDUH Series H-40, HHS Publication No. SMA 11-4641). Rockville, MD: Author.

Supekar, K., Uddin, L. Q., Prater, K., Amin, H., Greicius, M. D., & Menon, V. (2010). Development of functional and structural connectivity within the default mode network in young children. *NeuroImage*, *52*(1), 290–301.

Tamnes, C. K., Ostby, Y., Fjell, A. M., Westlye, L. T., Due-Tonnessen, P., & Walhovd, K. B. (2010). Brain maturation in adolescence and young adulthood: Regional age-related changes in cortical thickness and white matter volume and microstructure. *Cerebral Cortex*, *20*(3), 534–548.

Tapert, S. F., Granholm, E., Leedy, N. G., & Brown, S. A. (2002). Substance use and withdrawal: Neuropsychological functioning over 8 years in youth. *Journal of the International Neuropsychological Society*, *8*(7), 873–883.

Tapert, S. F., Schweinsburg, A. D., Drummond, S. P., Paulus, M. P., Brown, S. A., Yang, T. T., & Frank, L. R. (2007). Functional MRI of inhibitory processing in abstinent adolescent marijuana users. *Psychopharmacology, 194*(2), 173–183.

Tarazi, F. I., & Baldessarini, R. J. (2000). Comparative postnatal development of dopamine D(1), D(2) and D(4) receptors in rat forebrain. *International Journal of Developmental Neuroscience, 18*(1), 29–37.

Taylor, D. J., Jenni, O. G., Acebo, C., & Carskadon, M. A. (2005). Sleep tendency during extended wakefulness: Insights into adolescent sleep regulation and behavior. *Journal of Sleep Research, 14*(3), 239–244.

Teicher, M. H., & Andersen, S. L. (1999). *Limbic serotonin turnover plunges during puberty.* Paper presented at the Annual Meeting of the Society for Neuroscience, Miami, FL.

Teicher, M. H., Andersen, S. L., & Hostetter, J. C., Jr. (1995). Evidence for dopamine receptor pruning between adolescence and adulthood in striatum but not nucleus accumbens. *Brain Research. Developmental Brain Research, 89*(2), 167–172.

Thoma, R. J., Monnig, M. A., Lysne, P. A., Ruhl, D. A., Pommy, J. A., Bogenschutz, M., . . . Yeo, R. A. (2011). Adolescent substance abuse: The effects of alcohol and marijuana on neuropsychological performance. *Alcoholism, Clinical and Experimental Research, 35*(1), 39–46.

Tottenham, N., Hare, T. A., & Casey, B. J. (2011). Behavioral assessment of emotion discrimination, emotion regulation, and cognitive control in childhood, adolescence, and adulthood. *Frontiers in Psychology, 2,* 39.

Tucker, J. S., Ellickson, P. L., Collins, R. L., & Klein, D. J. (2006). Does solitary substance use increase adolescents' risk for poor psychosocial and behavioral outcomes? A 9-year longitudinal study comparing solitary and social users. *Psychology of Addictive Behaviors, 20*(4), 363–372.

Tunbridge, E. M., Weickert, C. S., Kleinman, J. E., Herman, M. M., Chen, J., Kolachana, B. S., . . . Weinberger, D. R. (2007). Catechol-o-methyltransferase enzyme activity and protein expression in human prefrontal cortex across the postnatal lifespan. *Cerebral Cortex, 17*(5), 1206–1212.

Van Leijenhorst, L., Gunther Moor, B., Op de Macks, Z. A., Rombouts, S. A., Westenberg, P. M., & Crone, E. A. (2010). Adolescent risky decision-making: Neurocognitive development of reward and control regions. *NeuroImage, 51*(1), 345–355.

Vogel, A. C., Power, J. D., Petersen, S. E., & Schlaggar, B. L. (2010). Development of the brain's functional network architecture. *Neuropsychology Review, 20*(4), 362–375.

Wang, X., Yu, R., Zhou, X., Liao, Y., Tang, J., Liu, T., . . . Hao, W. (2011). Reversible brain white matter microstructure changes in heroin addicts: A longitudinal study. *Addiction Biology, 18*(4), 727–728.

Whitford, T. J., Rennie, C. J., Grieve, S. M., Clark, C. R., Gordon, E., & Williams, L. M. (2007). Brain maturation in adolescence: Concurrent changes in neuroanatomy and neurophysiology. *Human Brain Mapping, 28*(3), 228–237.

Wiley, J. L., Evans, R. L., Grainger, D. B., & Nicholson, K. L. (2008). Age-dependent differences in sensitivity and sensitization to cannabinoids and "club drugs" in male adolescent and adult rats. *Addiction Biology, 13*(3–4), 277–286.

Windle, M., Spear, L. P., Fuligni, A. J., Angold, A., Brown, J. D., Pine, D., . . . Dahl, R. E. (2008). Transitions into underage and problem drinking: Developmental processes and mechanisms between 10 and 15 years of age. *Pediatrics, 121*(Suppl. 4), S273–S289.

Witt, E. D. (2010). Research on alcohol and adolescent brain development: Opportunities and future directions. *Alcohol, 44*(1), 119–124.

Yakovlev, P. I., & Lecours, A. R. (1967). The myelogenetic cycles of regional maturation of the brain. In A. Mikowski (Ed.), *Regional development of the brain in early life* (pp. 3–70). Oxford, UK: Blackwell Scientific.

Yu, Z. Y., Wang, W., Fritschy, J. M., Witte, O. W., & Redecker, C. (2006). Changes in neocortical and hippocampal GABAA receptor subunit distribution during brain maturation and aging. *Brain Research, 1099*(1), 73–81.

Behavioral Undercontrol: A Multifaceted Concept and Its Relationship to Alcohol and Substance Use Disorders

Michael Windle

Abstract

This chapter reviews research on alternative facets of behavioral undercontrol (e.g., disinhibition, impulsivity, sensation seeking) represented across rich and diverse literatures such as temperament, personality, childhood disorders, adolescent deviance, externalizing behaviors, and clinical disorders (e.g., substance abuse disorders, antisocial personality disorder). Research in the behavior genetic literature has focused on the identification of a common underlying general liability factor for behavioral undercontrol (or disinhibition) that is largely, but not exclusively, influenced by genetic variation. Research from other areas of study, including genomics and neuroscience, have identified some specificity of relationships between particular genes and neural circuits with different facets of behavioral undercontrol. A more integrative approach to the study of behavioral undercontrol is suggested that includes both general and specific factors within a multilevel, developmentally focused framework of behavioral, cognitive, and affective self-regulation.

Key Words: behavioral undercontrol, disinhibition, impulsivity, sensation seeking, substance use, externalizing behavior, childhood disorder, self-regulation

Behavioral undercontrol and related concepts (e.g., disinhibition, impulsivity, deviance proneness) have been widely used in the alcohol, substance use, and mental health literatures to refer to overt behavioral phenotypes (e.g., aggression, stealing), to latent dimensions or traits (e.g., impulsivity, sensation seeking), and to an underlying liability dimension for disorders (e.g., substance use disorders) influenced by genetic and environmental factors (Gorenstein & Newman, 1980; Iacono, Malone, & McGue, 2008; Zucker, 2006). Common across these approaches is that behavioral undercontrol is characterized by a spectrum of attributes that span features of poor behavioral, cognitive, and/or affective regulation. High levels of behavioral undercontrol have been hypothesized at the risk end of the liability dimension for childhood disorders such as attention-deficit/hyperactivity disorder (ADHD), oppositional defiant disorder (ODD), and conduct disorder, as well as later adolescent and adult alcohol and other substance abuse disorders and antisocial personality disorder. Given the wide range of research areas in which behavioral undercontrol and related constructs have been studied, it is not surprising that there is considerable variation in the conceptualization, measurement, and interpretation of findings related to behavioral undercontrol (DeWit, 2008; Dick et al., 2010; Nigg, 2002; Zucker, 2006). Hence, part of the variation in research on behavioral undercontrol stems from differences in focus from various disciplinary fields, with contributions from temperament and personality trait theories, neuropsychology, neurobiology, psychiatry, developmental psychopathology, sociology, clinical psychology, behavior genetics, genomics, and alcohol and substance use.

In addition, the multifaceted study of behavioral undercontrol is embedded in an ongoing dialectic between findings focused on a broader integration of literature supporting a postulated underlying *general*, largely genetic, liability dimension (Iacono et al., 2008; Tarter & Vanyukov, 1994) and findings that suggest that *specific* subdimensional relationships (rather than a general dimension) are consistent with empirical findings at the level of gene variants, neurobiology, and neurochemistry (Congdon & Canli, 2005; Winstanley, Eagle, & Robbins, 2006). Although these two approaches—general and specific—may appear antithetical, both continue to contribute to this emerging and integrative area of research on behavioral undercontrol that is cross-cutting with respect to disciplines, and core with regard to defining recent conceptualizations of behavioral undercontrol and alcohol and other substance use and abuse disorders (Hicks, Schalet, Malone, Iacono, & McGue, 2011; Iacono et al., 2008; Zucker, Heitzeg, & Nigg, 2011). Furthermore, a hybrid approach of having both general and specific influences for alcohol and substance use phenotypes (e.g., initiation, escalation of use, substance use–related problems, disorders) provides an integrative approach that may highlight strengths and limitations of solely general or solely specific influences, respectively, for making causal-explanatory inferences. For example, behavioral undercontrol may consist of a general genetic factor (or set of genes) that influences the developmental liability of alcohol and substance use disorders, along with other substance-specific factors (e.g., ethanol sensitivity, density and specificity of receptors for cocaine, cannabis, or nicotine), and environmental exposures (e.g., drug availability, parent and peer substance use exposure) that simultaneously may constitute features of a more comprehensive etiologic model, as well as provide multiple behavioral and pharmacologic targets for preventive interventions and treatment.

The goals of this chapter are threefold. First, because there has been considerable research completed in different areas and disciplines of research on what appears to be a common substrate, relevant literature will be reviewed regarding behavioral undercontrol *in relation to* alcohol and other substance abuse disorders. The intent of this brief review is not to be comprehensive, but rather to provide examples to illustrate critical points related to behavioral undercontrol as it relates to alcohol

and substance use phenotypes; there is an extensive literature on ADHD and other disruptive behavior disorders unrelated to alcohol and substance use that is not reviewed in this chapter (but see Barkley, 2006; Steinhausen, 2009). Second, alternative conceptual models related to the heterogeneity of alcohol disorders are discussed and conceptual links to behavioral undercontrol across some of the prior literature are provided. Third, some limitations of and challenges to the extant literature on behavioral undercontrol are presented to identify future research directions to advance this area of study.

Literature on Temperament and Personality as Facets of Behavioral Undercontrol

Several different substantial literatures have contributed to the identification of behavioral undercontrol as a significant factor in relation to substance use. Some of these literatures coexisted across time without necessarily directly impacting one another because of a different primary focus (e.g., emphasis on temperament and childhood disorders versus the identification of alcoholic subtypes in adults). Nevertheless, it is the consistency and integration of findings across these research areas that has spawned considerable interest in further pursuing research on behavioral undercontrol. In the following, studies related to Temperament and Personality as facets of behavioral undercontrol are presented in relation to alcohol and other substance use and disorders.

Temperament

Temperament refers to biogenetic dispositions that influence individual variation in emotional and behavioral styles. There is general agreement that temperament is manifested early in life, is highly heritable, and displays at least moderate stability over the life course. As mentioned previously, many theorists (Iacono et al., 2008; Tarter & Vanyukov, 1994; Zucker, 2006) describe temperament either as part of a general liability dimension or as a significant developmental precursor to the expression of alcohol and other substance use disorders. A number of studies have demonstrated both concurrent and short-term prospective associations between temperament characteristics and substance use and abuse. For example, Blackson, Tarter, Loeber, Ammerman, and Windle (1996) reported that temperamentally difficult features (e.g., high activity level, high distractibility) were associated among early adolescents with earlier disengagement from parents and the family and movement toward deviant peer groups. Hence, early behavioral undercontrol features of temperament influenced the timing of certain developmental events (e.g., movement away from parents and toward deviant peers) with regard to significant socialization agents who may influence subsequent antisocial and substance use behaviors. Similarly, findings by Wills et al. (2001) have indicated that behavioral undercontrol aspects of temperament (e.g., high activity level, low persistence) were associated with early-onset substance use by adolescents. Using a composite index of difficult temperament, which included behavioral undercontrol dimensions such as high activity level, high distractibility, and low persistence or perseverance, findings by Maziade et al. (1985) indicated that difficult temperament at age 7 years predicted psychiatric disorders at age 12 years. Tubman and Windle (1995) conducted a 1-year follow-up of adolescents that indicated that difficult temperament was significantly associated with substance use, and that increases in levels of difficult temperament across time were associated with significant increases in levels of substance use.

In addition to these cross-sectional and relatively short-term longitudinal findings of the relationships between features of temperamental behavioral undercontrol and childhood and adolescent behavior problems, there have also been a number of longer term longitudinal studies from childhood and adolescence to adulthood that support these relationships. For example, prospective findings by Caspi, Moffitt, Newman, and Silva (1996) indicated that children at age 3 years who manifested higher levels of behavioral undercontrol (i.e., were more impulsive, restless, and distractible) had an increased risk at age 21 years for the expression of antisocial personality disorder, alcohol-related problems, and criminal involvement. In a separate longitudinal study, Masse and Tremblay (1997) reported that higher novelty seeking (sensation seeking) and low fearfulness (disinhibition) in kindergarten significantly predicted early-onset substance use in middle childhood and early adolescence that carried forward to predict getting drunk and using other drugs in adolescence. Using data from the Avon Longitudinal Study of Parents and Children, Dick et al. (2013) reported that temperament prior to age 5 years significantly predicted adolescent alcohol and alcohol problems at age 15.5 years. Windle and Windle (2006) reported that temperament, measured during middle adolescence, predicted alcohol and other substance abuse disorders among a sample of 760 young adults

12 years later. Findings indicated that higher activity levels and lower task orientation (lower persistence and higher distractibility) in adolescence predicted alcohol and other substance use disorders in young adulthood.

Hence, findings from cross-sectional, short-term, and long-term longitudinal studies have converged in suggesting that early-onset features of temperament, including high activity levels, high distractibility, and low persistence, are associated with early-onset psychiatric disorders (e.g., conduct disorder, ADHD), an earlier onset of substance use, higher levels of substance use during adolescence, and externalizing behaviors and disorders in adulthood (e.g., alcohol and other substance abuse disorders, antisocial personality disorder, criminal behaviors). A methodological issue that frequently arises with regard to the measurement of temperament is the possible overlap, and thus confounding, of indicators of temperament and symptoms of psychiatric disorders and problem behaviors. However, several rigorous methodological studies have been completed that alleviate concerns about this potential measurement contamination (Lemery, Essex, & Smider, 2002; Lengua, West, & Sandler, 1998). For example, Lemery et al. concluded that the removal of item content from temperament scales that overlapped with problem behaviors did not alter the significant associations between temperament and behavior problems. Similarly, Windle (1992) removed temperament items that shared item content with those items measuring delinquency and depressive symptoms. Similar to the findings of Lemery et al., the removal of these items did not alter the significant associations between temperament and outcome variables (delinquency and depressive symptoms).

Personality: The Dimensions of Sensation Seeking and Impulsivity

There is a broad and extensive literature on personality correlates of alcohol and other substance use (Sher & Trull, 1994). However, for the more modest goals of this chapter focused on behavioral undercontrol during childhood and adolescence, the primary emphasis is on two exemplar personality constructs of behavioral undercontrol: sensation seeking and impulsivity. High sensation seeking and poor impulse control have been associated with child and adolescent risky behavior, including tobacco, alcohol, and other substance use. Both sensation seeking and impulsivity have been viewed commonly as temperament/personality traits associated with behavioral undercontrol (Iacono et al. 2008; Sher & Trull, 1994; Zucker, 2006).

Sensation seeking, as defined by Zuckerman (1994), is a trait characterized by the "seeking of varied, novel, complex, and intense sensations and experiences, and the willingness to take physical, social, legal, and financial risks for the sake of such experience" (p. 27). Underlying Zuckerman's theory of sensation seeking is the notion of individual differences in optimal levels of stimulation or arousal that serve to motivate people to prefer and engage in some activities rather than others. High sensation seekers have a tendency to be willing to engage in higher levels of risk behavior and more readily accept the attendant risks as a trade-off for the potential reward; hence, it is a reward-driven trait. Individuals high in sensation seeking tend to prefer and select activities and experiences (e.g., using substances, climbing mountains, parachute jumping) and to structure their environments (e.g., choice of peer groups) to match their levels of arousal associated with sensation seeking. Zuckerman proposed that sensation seeking consists of four subfactors of Thrill and Adventure Seeking, Experience Seeking, Disinhibition, and Boredom Susceptibility.

Zuckerman (1994) summarized findings regarding sensation seeking and substance use by noting that higher sensation seeking was associated with an earlier onset and more widespread use of tobacco, alcohol, and other drugs. Furthermore, among alcoholics, higher sensation seekers were more likely to have an earlier onset of alcohol abuse, were more aggressive, and engaged in more antisocial behaviors. Alcoholics lower on sensation seeking displayed a later onset of alcohol abuse, low levels of aggression and antisocial behavior, and higher levels of neuroticism. These distinct alcoholic subtypes identified via sensation seeking parallel other findings reported in the alcohol typology literature that have similarly identified antisocial and negative affect (neurotic) subtypes (Babor et al., 1992; Windle & Scheidt, 2004). Cloninger (1987) also proposed sensation seeking as an important component of his superordinate trait of novelty seeking, and research has supported associations between novelty seeking and substance use.

A unitary definition of *impulsivity* is elusive because research has indicated that impulsivity is a multidimensional trait (Coskunpinar, Dir, & Cyders, 2013; DeWit, 2008; Dick et al., 2010). For example, Miller, Joseph, and Tudway (2004) conducted a principal component analysis of 12 subscale-level responses to four prominent measures of impulsivity—the Eysenck Impulsiveness Scale (Eysenck, Pearson, Easting, & Allsopp, 1985), the Dickman Impulsiveness Scale (Dickman, 1990), Barratt's Impulsiveness Scale (Patton, Stanford, & Barratt, 1995), and the BIS/BAS scales (Carver & White, 1994). A three-component solution emerged with factors labeled (1) Nonplanning and dysfunctional impulsive behavior; (2) Functional venturesomeness; and (3) Reward responsiveness and drive. Similarly, Whiteside and Lynam (2001) conducted an exploratory factor analysis of several commonly used measures of impulsivity with 400 young adults and identified four distinct facets of impulsivity. One factor was labeled *Urgency* and was characterized by items such as "It is hard for me to resist acting on my feelings" and "Sometimes I do things on impulse that I later regret." A second factor was labeled *Premeditation* and contained items such as "I have a reserved and cautious attitude toward life" and "I usually think carefully before doing anything." A third factor was labeled *Sensation Seeking* and contained items such as "I generally seek new and exciting experiences and sensations" and "I quite enjoy taking risks." The fourth factor was labeled *Perseverance* and contained items such as "I finish what I start" and "I generally like to see things through to the end."

In addition to the Miller et al. (2004) and Whiteside and Lynam (2001) studies, others have also conducted factor analyses that have yielded multiple factors that are method specific (e.g., factors only for self-report scores or only for neuropsychological test performance scores). That is, self-report personality measures and neuropsychological test performance measures designed to assess features of impulsivity labeled identically have yielded zero or low and inconsistent correlations with regard to measures across these two methods of assessment. For example, Reynolds, Penfold, and Patak (2008) identified three dimensions of impulsivity via a principal components analysis with an adolescent sample using laboratory performance-based measures. The three factors were labeled Impulsive Decision Making, Impulsive Inattention, and Impulsive Disinhibition. A performance measure, the Go/Stop task (Dougherty, Mathias, & Marsh, 2003), was the only indicator of an impulsive disinhibition factor. The two self-report measures of impulsivity were significantly correlated with one another ($r = .407$, $p < .01$), but only one of these self-report measures correlated significantly (though of low magnitude) with any of the laboratory-based measures.

Winstanley et al. (2006) reviewed human and preclinical (animal) studies of impulsivity and, consistent with the previous research, concluded that impulsivity is not a unitary trait. By integrating neurobiological and neurochemical findings on different aspects of impulsivity, Winstanley et al. proposed that the two impulsivity dimensions of behavioral disinhibition and delay discounting (i.e., intolerance of delay of gratification) differ with regard to associations with dominant frontostriatal neurocircuitry. For instance, the dorsolateral prefrontal cortex appears to have a regulatory role with regard to inhibitory processes (i.e., behavioral disinhibition), but not with regard to impulsive choice (i.e., delay discounting). By contrast, the orbitofrontal cortex and basolateral amygdala are involved in the regulation of impulsive choice. Furthermore, different serotonergic manipulations in preclinical studies have produced different behavioral effects for distinct features of impulsivity. For example, through laboratory manipulations in rats, decreases in serotonin (5HT) were associated with increased impulsive responses (i.e., premature responding) on the acquisition and performance of the Go/No-Go task (Harrison, Everitt, & Robbins, 1999); however, no such influences were observed for impulsivity when a delay-discounting paradigm was used. These findings suggest that serotonin, dopamine, and other neurotransmitters and neuromodulators and their interactions are integrally involved in the various facets of impulsivity. The different features or facets of impulsivity likely share some common and some specific neural circuits associated with the underlying neurobiological bases of the multidimensional construct of impulsivity.

Relationship of Impulsivity and Sensation Seeking

Other investigators, such as Steinberg (2010), have drawn on findings in developmental neuroscience that suggest that impulsivity and reward seeking (more closely related to sensation seeking) have different developmental trajectories as well as different underlying neural influences that impact adolescent risk-taking behavior, including substance use. This "dual systems model" proposes that there is both a cognitive control system and a socioemotional system that are associated with different neurobiological regulatory systems. The cognitive control system is associated with functioning in the lateral prefrontal and parietal cortices and

components of the cingulated cortex to which they are interconnected. By contrast, the socioemotional system is localized in the limbic and paralimbic regions of the brain that include the amygdala, ventral striatum, orbitofrontal cortex, medial prefrontal cortex, and superior temporal sulcus.

According to the dual systems model, there are rapid and significant increases in dopaminergic activity in the socioemotional system around the time of puberty that are associated with increases in reward-seeking behavior and adolescent risk taking, including alcohol and other substance use. These changes in the socioemotional system precede the gradual unfolding of maturational and structural developmental processes associated with the cognitive control system in the dorsolateral prefrontal cortex that foster greater self-regulation and impulse control. In essence, developmental changes associated with the socioemotional reward-seeking system occur temporally prior to developmental changes in the cognitive control system that would serve to moderate, curb, or "put the break on" the reward-driven adolescent risky behaviors. Steinberg (2010) cites animal study findings that are consistent with this dual systems model, as well as data on humans, suggestive of associations between sensation seeking, which is highly correlated with reward seeking, and higher levels of the hormones of testosterone and estradiol among college-age students; there was also a finding suggestive of a negative correlation between age and impulsivity. In his study, Steinberg (2010) reported a linear pattern of decline for impulsivity from ages 10 to 30 years and a curvilinear pattern for reward seeking, with peak levels occurring between the ages of 12 and 15 years. Romer and Hennessy (2007) also reported a curvilinear pattern for sensation seeking with peak levels occurring among females around age 16 years and among males around age 19 years, though males reported higher levels of sensation seeking than females across all age levels from ages 14 to 22 years.

Importantly, although sensation seeking and impulsivity have been associated with higher risk for alcohol and substance use, findings influenced by neuroscience research suggest that the underlying neurobiological structures, developmental risk, and relative risk may differ for these two concepts (Romer, 2010; Steinberg, 2010). For example, Romer has proposed that certain forms of impulsivity, such as acting without thinking and impatience, are associated with risk-taking behavior in adolescence and have been associated with poor executive functioning (e.g., poor response inhi-bition and working memory). These findings are consistent with the idea of an age-related structural limitation associated with the lack of maturational development in the prefrontal cortex and frontostriatal regions that impacts adolescent risk-taking behaviors by failing to provide optimal decision-making skills and cognitive control (i.e., delayed maturation of the prefrontal cortex limits inhibitory control mechanisms). In contrast to this executive function-cognitive control system, Romer proposes that sensation seeking is mediated by an affective evaluation system of alternative behavioral choices. Accordingly, the more favorable, pleasant, or rewarding an activity is, the less risky is the affectively driven evaluation of the activity. Therefore, certain specific biases in making judgments and decisions (e.g., using alcohol and other drugs with adolescent peers) associated with sensation seeking are highly influenced by dominant affective reactions and behavioral options rather than by deficits in executive functioning and cognitive control mechanisms associated with development in the prefrontal cortex.

Others have also drawn upon findings in neuroscience to suggest that two brain functional response systems account for the more general concept of an undercontrol-disihibition pathway (Zucker et al., 2011). Zucker et al. suggest that the mechanistic structure underlying this pathway is driven by an effortful control system in dynamic tension with an incentive reactivity system. The effortful control system is associated with prefrontal circuitry, especially the lateral prefrontal cortex, which functions to suppress activity in limbic regions such as the ventral striatum/nucleus accumbens and amygdala. By contrast, the incentive reactivity system is relatively automatic and responds rapidly to novelty or incentive cues for potential near-term rewards or loss by interrupting behavior. Importantly, in contrast to primitive appetitive systems that are associated with drug response and addiction *after* drug ingestion, the incentive reactivity system activates incentive cues (e.g., relief from stress, pleasure) prior to or associated with drinking and therefore functions more as a liability marker for substance use problems.

In summary, this brief and selective review of temperament and personality traits suggests that behavioral undercontrol and related constructs (e.g., disinhibition, impulsivity, sensation seeking) are multidimensional. Furthermore, consistent with Block's (1995) description of the "jingle" and

"jangle" fallacies of constructs (measures), some constructs are identically labeled but display zero to low correlations ("jingle"), and other constructs are dissimilarly labeled but measure a similar construct ("jangle"). Clearly, method of assessment factors (e.g., self-report vs. neuropsychological test performance) are influential in this process, as are differences in conceptualization and measurement, such as whether sensation seeking is viewed as one facet of impulsivity or as an independent trait with neurobiological structures distinct from other facets of impulsivity (Romer, 2010). Despite the multidimensionality of these temperament and personality traits and their potential distinct underlying neurobiology and neurochemistry, they remain important components of a broader, more inclusive concept of a behavioral undercontrol spectrum (Iacono et al., 2008; Tarter, Kirisci, Habeych, Reynolds, & Vanyukov, 2003a; Tarter et al., 2003b; Zucker et al., 2011).

Conceptual Approaches to the Heterogeneity of Alcohol Disorders

A recognition of the heterogeneity of alcohol disorders was derived from consistent findings in the literature which indicated that alcoholics tended to differ with regard to important drinking-related parameters (e.g., intensity of problems, severity of withdrawal, individual variation in relapse rates), co-occurring psychiatric disorders, and specific etiologic factors (e.g., family history of alcoholism) (Leggio, Kenna, Fenton, Bonenfant, & Swift, 2009). For example, being a child of an alcoholic (COA) relative to not being a COA increases risk for the subsequent development of alcoholism by at least fourfold (up to a ninefold increase if the father also had an antisocial personality disorder; Russell, 1990). However, despite this significant increased risk for an alcohol disorder, the majority of COAs do not become alcoholics, and there are more non-COA alcoholics than COA alcoholics. Therefore, the literature suggested considerable heterogeneity as to who became an alcoholic and under what conditions. A few approaches that have attempted to address this heterogeneity issue are described now because of their support for the impact of behavioral undercontrol.

Alcoholic Subtypes

Alternative conceptual and data analytic approaches have been developed and applied in research that have been foundational in establishing the importance of behavioral undercontrol (Zucker,

2006). One such approach has been that of alcohol typologies that have distinguished subgroups of alcoholics based on clinical symptoms (e.g., age of onset, chronicity), time course, and treatment response (e.g., relapse). Cloninger, Bohman, and Sigvardsson (1981) differentiated two alcoholic subtypes: Type I and Type II. Type II alcoholics were typically males with early onset and persistent antisocial behaviors, an earlier onset of an alcohol disorder, and a high familial risk for alcoholism. Accordingly, Type II alcoholics were proposed to have a strong genetic diathesis toward alcohol disorders that was mediated by neurogenetic-influenced temperament characteristics (Cloninger, 1987). By contrast, Type I alcoholics consisted both of males and females, had a later onset of alcohol use, had a less severe alcoholic course, and were more strongly influenced by social factors.

A similar two-subgroup alcohol typology was also supported via cluster analyses of a range of risk factors and clinical characteristics in findings reported by Babor et al. (1992), though they referred to their two subtypes as Type A and Type B. Type B alcoholics were characterized by an earlier onset of alcoholism, more childhood risk factors (i.e., more externalizing problems), greater severity of alcohol dependence, and higher familial alcoholism. Type A alcoholics were characterized by a later onset of alcoholism, fewer childhood risk factors, and fewer (co-occurring) psychiatric symptoms. The findings for the early-onset, higher childhood antisocial behaviors, and high familial risk patterns of Cloninger et al.'s Type II alcoholics and Babor et al.'s Type B alcoholics influenced, and were consistent with, the notion of behavioral undercontrol being a significant component of a risk matrix for the development of early-onset alcohol disorders. Furthermore, a family history of alcoholism, a proxy for genetic influence, was more highly prevalent among the Type II and Type B alcoholics.

While these findings by Cloninger et al. (1981) and Babor et al. (1992) supported two alcoholic subtypes, one with an earlier onset and with childhood antisocial behaviors and high familial alcoholism, and the other a later onset and fewer childhood problem behaviors, other investigators have suggested that more than two subtypes are required to account for the heterogeneity of alcohol disorders. For example, based on the dominant comorbidity (co-occurrence) findings from the Epidemiologic Catchment Area study, Zucker (1987) proposed that there were four alcoholic subtypes: (1) antisocial alcoholics; (2) negative affect alcoholics; (3) mild course alcoholics; and (4) developmentally limited alcoholics. Findings by others (e.g., Del Boca & Hesselbrock, 1996; Windle & Scheidt, 2004) have largely supported the four alcoholic subtypes proposed by Zucker, and in particular, very strong support has been provided for the early-onset, childhood antisocial behaviors, and pervasiveness and chronicity of alcohol problems among (behaviorally undercontrolled) antisocial alcoholics. In addition, the idea that antisocial alcoholics are only men has been proven inaccurate, as has the idea that there is a "genetic" dominant form of alcoholism and an "environmental-social" form of alcoholism. Nevertheless, evidence for the role of behavioral undercontrol in influencing an antisocial alcohol subtype has been largely supported. The behavioral undercontrol, antisocial subtype has also been supported in examinations of dependence for other psychoactive substance abuse disorders, and thus there is generalizability across substances for this antisocial subtype (Basu, Ball, Feinn, Gelernter, & Kranzler, 2004).

Developmental Pathways

Another approach to addressing the heterogeneity of alcohol disorders that has been informed by prior research on alcohol subtypes and on psychiatric comorbidity has been the notion of different developmental pathways toward alcohol and other substance abuse disorders. According to this approach, there are both externalizing and internalizing pathways that may be distinguished with regard to antecedents, correlates, and the time course of alcohol and other substance abuse. The externalizing pathway is characterized by an earlier onset of alcohol use, childhood behavior problems (e.g., ADHD, conduct disorder), deviant substance-using peer groups, and a rapid escalation of substance abuse with adverse educational, occupational, interpersonal, and criminal outcomes. Consistent with the findings for the antisocial alcoholic described previously under alcoholic subtypes, there is substantial evidence supportive of the externalizing pathway (Hussong et al., 2007; King & Chassin, 2004; Zucker, 2006). For example, King and Chassin reported that behavioral undercontrol was a significant mediator of the influence of parental alcoholism on drug use disorders in early adulthood. Behavioral undercontrol and parental discipline mediated 58% of the prospective effect between parental alcoholism and young adult drug disorders. Hussong et al. used two different high-risk (COA) samples and reported that either an antisocial alcoholic parent, or two alcoholic parents, prospectively predicted higher rates of externalizing symptoms among offspring than among the offspring of non-COAs or COAs with a depressed alcoholic parent.

Although not discussed in-depth in this chapter, an alternative developmental pathway is the internalizing pathway, which is characterized by a somewhat later onset of alcohol use and alcohol-related problems, co-occurring major depression and anxiety disorders, and a greater reliance on using substances to self-medicate (or regulate) negative affective states (Hussong, Flora, Curran, Chassin, & Zucker, 2008). The internalizing pathway is consistent with the Negative Affect alcoholic subtype described in prior studies (Windle & Scheidt, 2004; Zucker, 1987). There have been far fewer studies of the internalizing pathway relative to the externalizing pathway, and to date findings supportive of this pathway have been mixed (Hussong et al., 2008). This is not to discount or dismiss epidemiologic research supportive of the high co-occurrence of alcohol disorders and major depressive disorders and anxiety disorders (Kushner, Sher, & Beitman, 1990), but rather to indicate that consistent empirical support for developmental features of this pathway has yet to be provided with the consistency reported for the externalizing pathway.

Distinctive Etiologic Influences on Alcohol Disorders

Yet another approach to address the heterogeneity of alcohol disorders has been to suggest that there are discrete, prominent etiologic factors associated with the differential expression of alcohol disorders. Sher and colleagues (Sher & Slutske, 2003; Sher, Grekin, & Williams, 2005) proposed four etiologic models of alcohol disorders. These included positive affect regulation, negative affect regulation, pharmacological vulnerability, and deviance proneness. The first two models emphasize the role of using alcohol to regulate affective states, in the first instance to regulate positive affect (e.g., to feel better, to enjoy activities more), and in the second instance to regulate negative affect (e.g., to cope with stressful events). The third model—the pharmacological vulnerability model—suggests that variation in specific biological (e.g., pharmacologic) responses, for instance intensity of response to alcohol or the "stress-dampening" response of alcohol, pose risk for the development of alcohol problems and disorders. The fourth model is the deviance proneness model, and it suggests that alcohol use is part of a more general pattern of deviance, consistent with Jessor and Jessor's (1977) problem behavior theory, that predicts subsequent heavier alcohol and substance use and associated alcohol- and substance-related adverse consequences.

According to the distinct etiologic influence approach, the central mechanisms accounting for differences in alcohol disorders may have different antecedents, correlates, and consequences, as well as different developmental trajectories. Of relevance to behavioral undercontrol, Sher et al. (2005) suggested that deviance proneness is a feature of personality that interacts with parenting and family socialization factors to influence risk factors associated with the development of alcohol disorders (e.g., deviant peer groups, conduct problems) and ultimately contributes to the expression of alcohol disorders. Importantly for this chapter, deviance proneness is conceptualized as a unitary, underlying personality characteristic that impacts, and is impacted by, salient environmental factors in the family (e.g., parents) and school (e.g., peers). Thus, the major factor contributing to alcohol disorders and the time course of such disorders is impacted significantly by the behavioral undercontrol manifestation in the form of deviance proneness. This notion of the significance of a major personality factor underlying behavioral undercontrol is similar to Jessor and Jessor's notion of an unconventional personality being central to the manifestation of the syndrome of problem behaviors during adolescence and young adulthood, and it is consistent with a general liability dimension advanced by others (Iacono et al., 2008; Tarter & Vanyukov, 1994).

Common Liability Model Approaches

Whereas previous approaches presented in this chapter have focused either on individual difference variables (e.g., temperament) or subgroup methods (e.g., identifying alcoholic subtypes), a number of investigators have also postulated common liability models to account for genetic and environmental contributions to the expression of behavioral undercontrol, including alcohol and other substance abuse disorders as manifestations of such undercontrol.

Among the early influences to the notion of a common liability were the seminal contributions of R. Jessor, S. Jessor, and Donovan (Donovan & Jessor, 1985; Jessor & Jessor, 1977) in their development of problem behavior theory. Jessor and Jessor proposed a theoretical model that cut across problem behavior domains and suggested that there was a unitary underlying dimension, factor, or syndrome that captured variation associated with multiple adolescent problem behaviors, such as alcohol and other substance use, cigarette use, poor school performance, delinquent behaviors, and precocious sexual activity. Donovan and Jessor further proposed and tested a number of hypothesized psychosocial predictors of problem behaviors and extended the framework to young adulthood. Although the research of Jessor and colleagues was not explicitly based on a common genetic liability framework, nor specifically on the concept of behavioral undercontrol, the notion of a single underlying factor that accounts for covariation among different problem behaviors is consistent with several behavior genetic theorists who have promulgated the idea of a general genetic liability factor referred to as behavioral undercontrol or disinhibition (Iacono et al., 2008; Tarter & Vanyukov, 1994; Vanyukov & Tarter, 2000).

Tarter and Vanyukov (1994) provided a developmental behavior genetic perspective on alcohol disorders in which they proposed that there was an underlying liability dimension for alcohol disorders that was influenced both by genetic and environmental components and gene–environment interactions and correlations. The liability dimension was described in a manner consistent with a multifactorial model of inheritance in which there is individual variation in a normally distributed liability trait (in this instance, behavioral undercontrol) that interacts with the environment and developmental processes in impacting the probability of exceeding a threshold for the expression of an alcohol disorder. Figure 14.1 provides an illustration of this general liability model and indicates that the liability dimension (trait) is normally distributed with mean liability in the middle of the distribution. However, individual variation in trait liability in interaction with the environment may contribute to individuals exceeding the threshold and developing abuse, psychological dependence, and physical dependence (American Psychiatric Association, 1994).

Importantly, as Tarter and Vanyukov (1994) elaborate in their article, the developmental features of this perspective emphasize that the endpoint of an alcohol disorder is preceded by intermediate phenotypes (behaviors) that are identifiable and expressed early in life in the form of temperament. Temperament characteristics (traits) of high behavior activity level and low attention span persistence were identified as early-onset, intermediate

phenotypes that pose risk for the future development of alcohol disorders. That is, deviations of these temperament dimensions toward the higher end of the liability dimension posed increased risk for an alcohol disorder because they, along with other temperament traits (e.g., heightened reactivity), in interaction with features of physical (neighborhood bar density) and social (alcohol and other substance use by family members and peers) environments across time, propel individual trajectories toward the alcohol disorder threshold along the liability dimension as portrayed in Figure 14.1.

The developmental (ontogenetic) processes have been elaborated subsequently by this research group to include intermediate steps such as increases in deviant and substance-using friends, poorer relationships with parents and other family members (e.g., higher conflict, lower emotional support), increases in disruptive behavior disorders (e.g., conduct disorder), poorer executive functioning, and early-onset substance use (Tarter et al., 2003a). Vanyukov and Tarter (2000) have also expanded this framework to other substances of abuse (beyond alcoholism) and have incorporated the assessment of genetic variants in their research program to identify major genetic polymorphisms associated with substance use phenotypes (e.g., onset, heavy use, disorders) using high-risk family samples (e.g., children of substance-abusing parents). In addition, Tarter et al. (2003a) have also proposed an expanded, integrated liability dimension referred to as *neurobehavioral disinhibition* measured in childhood that is hypothesized to increase the prediction of substance abuse disorders in later adolescence and adulthood. The neurobehavioral disinhibition dimension, which includes measures from cognitive (e.g., executive functioning), affective (e.g., temperament), and behavioral (e.g., disruptive behavior symptoms) domains, has demonstrated a unidimensional structure and has significantly predicted early age of onset to substance abuse disorder (Tarter et al., 2003b).

Iacono and colleagues (Hicks, Krueger, Iacono, McGue, & Patrick, 2004; Iacono et al., 2008; Krueger, Markon, Patrick, & Iacono, 2005) have developed a systematic research program on behavioral undercontrol that draws upon and extends the general liability notion of other investigators (Vanyukov & Tarter, 2000; Zucker, 2006). Iacono et al. proposed that behavioral disinhibition, or what is referred to in this chapter as behavioral undercontrol, refers to a common liability for a spectrum of traits characterized by "a propensity

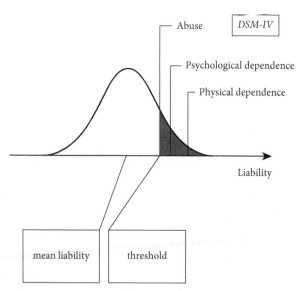

Abuse

DSM-IV

Psychological dependence

Physical dependence

Liability

mean liability

threshold

Figure 14.1. Overall liability phenotype upon surpassing the diagnosis threshold qualifies the person as affected (i.e., manifesting a clinical disorder of abuse or dependence). *Source*: Tarter, R. E., & Vanyukov, M. (1994). Alcoholism: A developmental disorder. *Journal of Consulting and Clinical Psychology, 62*(6), 1096–1107. Copyright 1994. Reprinted with permission of American Psychological Association (APA).

toward behavioral disinhibition, an inability to inhibit socially undesirable or restricted actions." They suggest that this general liability dimension is central to understanding one significant pathway to the development of early-onset substance abuse disorders. In support of their general liability dimension, Hicks et al. used structural equation modeling with data from the Minnesota Twin Family Study on symptoms of conduct disorder, alcohol and drug dependence, and antisocial personality disorder to evaluate whether family resemblance (using parent and twin offspring data) reflected the transmission of a general factor and not disorder-specific transmission. Their findings supported a general vulnerability factor that accounted for the underlying familial transmission of the externalizing behavior indicators (i.e., conduct disorder, alcohol and other substance dependence, antisocial personality disorder), thereby supporting the notion that parents transmit a vulnerability to a spectrum of disorders, with each disorder associated with an alternative expression of this general vulnerability. This is an important issue because prior research using non-twin, family and adoptee designs have tended to suggest that family resemblance for alcohol and substance use disorders is more specific than general; however, the family twin design offers some unique advantages in pursuing the generality-specificity issue for transmission associated with family resemblance.

Iacono et al. (2008) further summarized their research and that of others in the literature in the form of an integrated, developmental (or sequential) conceptual model presented in Figure 14.2. According to the model, the liability to behavioral disinhibition (undercontrol) influences the expression of several factors, including temperament (e.g., low levels of persistence; inattention), personality (e.g., impulsivity, aggressiveness), and endophenotypes (e.g., low-amplitude P300 electrophysiological responses), which in turn influence childhood disruptive disorders, the early onset of problem behaviors (e.g., substance use, academic difficulties), and environmental risks. These three intermediate variable domains (i.e., childhood disruptive disorders, early-onset problem behaviors, and environmental risks) influence one another through reciprocal feedback loops and, in turn, influence externalizing psychopathology directly, as well as partially mediate the relationships between the liability to the behavioral disinhibition dimension and externalizing psychopathology. Importantly, this conceptual model provides a time ordering for the sequence of manifestations leading toward externalizing psychopathology from pre-adolescence through late adolescence and early adulthood, and it is dynamic in the sense that it recognizes the bidirectionality of influences as development unfolds. This more comprehensive approach is of value for integrating research findings from different areas of study (e.g., parent–child

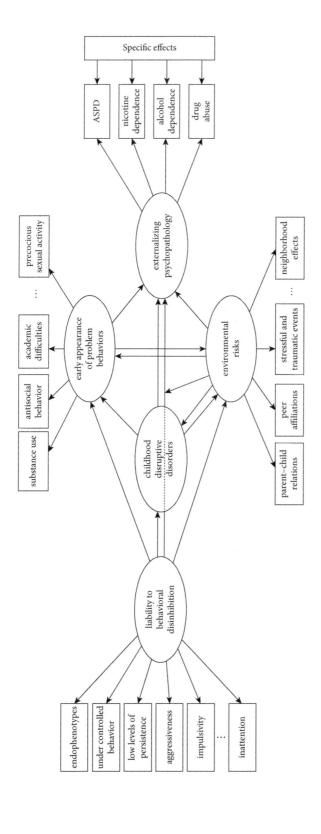

PRE-ADOLESCENCE   EARLY AND MID-ADOLESCENCE   LATE ADOLESCENCE/
                                                            EARLY ADULTHOOD

Figure 14.2. A conceptual model linking liability to behavioral disinhibition with the development of early-onset substance use disorders. ASPD, antisocial personality disorder. *Source:* Iacono, W. G., Malone, S. M., & McGue, M. (2008). Behavioral disinhibition and the development of early-onset addiction: Common and specific influences. *Annual Review of Clinical Psychology, 4,* 325–348. Reprinted with permission from Annual Reviews.

relations and externalizing behaviors, neighborhood influences on externalizing behaviors), for guiding the development of longitudinal statistical models and associated hypotheses, and for fostering ideas about focal targets for interventions at different portions of the life span.

In addition to the previous research programs that have supported a common liability dimension for externalizing (behaviorally undercontrolled) behaviors, there are other behavior genetic studies that also generally support this view. For example, disruptive behavior disorders in childhood and adolescence refer to the three disorders of ADHD, ODD, and conduct disorder. Although considered in the nomenclature of the *Diagnostic and Statistical Manual of Mental Disorders*, fourth edition (American Psychiatric Association, 1994) as distinct diagnostic entities, there is a high degree of comorbidity among these disorders such that they are commonly referred to as disruptive behavior disorders. In addition, there are high rates of covariation among the symptoms of these disorders such that they are commonly referred to as externalizing symptoms or behaviors. Furthermore, there have been some biometric models suggestive of a common genetic liability to account for a large portion of the covariation among the symptoms of these three disorders (Waldman, Rhee, Levy, & Hay, 2001; Young, Stallings, Corley, Krauter, & Hewitt, 2000). Features of behavioral undercontrol (i.e., disinhibition, impulsivity) have been commonly identified as central elements (phenotypes) associated with these childhood psychiatric disorders and have often been significantly related to adolescent and adult alcohol and other substance use and abuse.

Dick, Viken, Kaprio, Pulkkinen, and Rose (2005) used data from a Finnish twin study—the FinnTwin12, a population-based sample of five consecutive birth cohorts of twins born in Finland from 1983 to 1987—to examine genetic and environmental contributions to the co-occurrence of psychiatric symptoms of ADHD, ODD, and conduct disorder at age 14. They used the biometric ACE model that enabled quantitative estimates of additive genetic sources of variance (A), common (or shared) environmental sources of variance (C), and nonshared environmental (E) sources of variation (for further explication of the ACE model, see Neale & Cardon, 1992; Neale, Boker, Xie, & Maes, 1999). Similar to other behavior genetic studies that have addressed this research question (Waldman et al., 2001; Young et al.,

2000), additive genetic influences contributed most strongly to the covariation among the symptoms of the three disorders. However, in addition to the general A factor (i.e., additive genetic variance), there was also support for unique genetic influences for each disorder. This finding suggests that although common genetic influences largely account for covariance among symptoms of the disruptive behavior disorders, the disorder-specific components suggest both common and specific genetic factors. Furthermore, there were significant nonshared environmental influences that contributed to the covariation among the symptoms, especially for covariation among ADHD and ODD. Thus, while these findings do support the importance of a single genetic liability factor, they do not support the notion that the covariation among symptoms of these three disorders is fully accounted for by the same underlying genetic predisposition.

Using a similar modeling approach that also decomposed covariance relations into A, C, and E parameters, multivariate data from the Virginia Adult Twin Study of Psychiatric and Substance Use Disorders (VATSPSUD; $n > 5,600$ individuals) were analyzed (Kendler, Prescott, Myers, & Neale, 2003). A major question of interest in this research study pertained to the adequacy of a general, or common, additive variance model relative to a disorder-specific model in which genetic variation was better accounted for via unique genetic variance estimates associated with each indicator (i.e., each measured phenotype). Kendler et al. reported that the disorders of alcohol dependence, drug abuse/dependence, conduct disorder, and adult antisocial behavior could be plausibly represented by one common genetic factor, referred to as externalizing disorders. The additive genetic sources of variance (A) accounted for by this common factor ranged from 14% for conduct disorder to 42% for drug abuse/dependence. Common environmental sources of variance (C) were small (0 to 9%) except for conduct disorder, where the estimate was 25%. Nonshared environmental sources of variance (E) accounted for only 3%–4% for alcohol dependence and drug abuse/dependence, but for 42% of adult antisocial behavior and 10% of conduct disorder.

Kendler, Myers, and Prescott (2007) conducted another set of analyses with the VATSPSUD that included symptoms both of licit (alcohol, caffeine, nicotine) and illicit (cannabis, cocaine) substances to further investigate issues related to the structure of genetic and environmental risk factors for substance dependence disorders. In these analyses, the best-fitting model was one that consisted of two genetic factors—one for licit substances and one for illicit substances. Furthermore, a large portion of the variance for genetic influences was substance-specific rather than general, especially for nicotine and caffeine.

The findings by Kendler et al. (2003) suggest that neither the complete general (i.e., nonspecificity) model nor the complete specificity models optimally accounted for the observed patterns of covariation among these four externalizing phenotypes when decomposed using biometric methods with a large adult twin sample. Furthermore, the decomposition of the components by the ACE model suggested that there were some differences across the disorders with regard to the relative contributions of genetic and environmental sources (e.g., E accounted for 42% of the variance for antisocial behavior). The Kendler et al. (2007) study also indicated that two separate genetic factors were needed to account for covariation associated with licit and illicit drugs, and that large genetic specificity components were associated with nicotine and caffeine. Similar to the findings of Dick et al. (2005) with the FinnTwin12 study, these findings support the importance of a genetic liability dimension (or dimensions), but they do not support the notion that the covariation among symptoms of substance use disorders and antisocial behaviors are fully accounted for by one underlying genetic (liability) predisposition; rather, there are important disorder-specific influences and environmental sources of variation that contribute significantly to the observed covariation.

In summary, studies from behavior genetics using biometric models have been reasonably consistent in suggesting that behavioral undercontrol-disinhibition may best be characterized as having a common underlying liability dimension that is genetic (i.e., heritable) in origin, as well as genetic-specific dimensions, and (limited) shared and nonshared sources of environmental variation (Hicks et al., 2011; Kendler et al., 2003). Furthermore, some theorists (Iacono et al., 2008; Tarter et al., 2003a) have delineated developmental models that suggest early manifestations of characteristics (e.g., temperament) that influence mediators (e.g., parent and peer influences) that, in turn, influence substance use patterns.

Limitations, Challenges, and Future Directions for Research on Behavioral Undercontrol

Considerable progress has been made on the broad, integrative construct of behavioral undercontrol in relation to adolescent and adult alcohol and other substance abuse disorders. Simultaneously, this construct serves as a useful exemplar of challenging issues that need to be addressed in pursuing complex phenotypes in substance use and mental health. The next section will highlight some of these challenges and potential solutions by sequentially focusing on selective conceptual and methodological issues related to the study of behavioral undercontrol.

Which Genes Account for the Underlying Genetic Liability Factor?

Although there is support for a general genetic liability dimension for behavioral undercontrol, one major issue that arises if we "deconstruct" the extant literature pertains to the specific genes corresponding to this liability. A relatively large number of molecular genetic studies have been done on several of the specific disorders and dimensions associated with behavioral undercontrol, including ADHD (Faraone & Mick, 2010) and alcohol and other substance abuse disorders (Hodgkinson et al., 2008; Schuckit, 2009; Tabakoff et al., 2009). However, most of these studies have been conducted independent of one another and are therefore disorder-specific rather than focusing on common genetic polymorphisms across the common liability dimension of behavioral undercontrol. Findings across this broad set of studies have revealed a limited number of common genes; distinctiveness rather than commonality has been the more general finding. Nevertheless, Dick (2007) summarized molecular genetic findings on the externalizing (behavioral undercontrol) dimension and identified two promising genes: *GABRA2* and *CHRM2*. However, effect sizes of significant gene findings have typically been of low magnitude and collectively do not approach the high heritability estimates stemming from the behavior genetic literature.

Such findings for behavioral undercontrol are consistent with findings in the literature on other complex behavior phenotypes, such as height, HDL cholesterol, early-onset myocardial infarction, and fasting glucose, that have demonstrated high heritability estimates via traditional family-relatedness designs (e.g., twin studies) but have provided a limited yield with regard to variance coverage generated from molecular genomic studies (Manolio et al., 2009). For example, 40 genetic loci have been identified for the phenotype of height, but the proportion of heritability explained by these loci is approximately 5%. Goldstein (2009) extrapolated from these findings regarding the discrepancy between heritability estimates for human height, which is highly heritable (80%), to project (using an exponential function) the number of single nucleotide polymorphisms (SNPs) it would take to account for 80% of the population variance in height. The resulting number was 93,000 SNPs. The discrepancy between heritability estimates for complex phenotypes and findings from molecular genetic studies (e.g., family linkage studies, genome-wide association studies) has resulted in the term "missing heritability" to describe the unknown elements that account for this unexpectedly large discrepancy.

Research findings regarding the complex phenotypes associated with behavioral undercontrol have exhibited a similar pattern as the previously described complex phenotypes, with moderate to high heritability estimates, but low magnitude and often inconsistent findings generated from molecular genetic studies regarding chromosomal locations and SNPs. These findings are important when considering the notion of an underlying genetic liability dimension for behavioral undercontrol because it raises questions, such as how many SNPs are likely to underlie such a dimension if a presumably more clearly measured phenotype such as height would require 93,000 SNPs to account for the genetic population variance?

Current approaches in the molecular genomics of complex phenotypes are proposing alternative models to the common variant-common disease model that has guided much of the recent molecular genomics research, including the rare variant model that proposes that alleles of lower population frequency than common variants may have larger and more consistent effects on complex phenotypes. However, the applicability and scope of the rare variant model seem improbable for an underlying common genetic liability dimension for behavioral undercontrol in which individuals vary along a continuum and only when "pushed-pulled" beyond a threshold manifest problematic behaviors. That is, it is possible that a rare variant model may be applicable to some complex phenotypes and diseases, or even for a quite small subset of unique-cause cases, but it seems improbable for the phenotype of behavioral undercontrol because associated phenotypes

(e.g., sensation seeking, impulsivity) appear to have a long evolutionary history with normal distributions and conditions that foster advantages for these traits. These evolutionary characteristics are not consistent with a rare variant model.

Currently, it is also unknown if the same (cross-disorder), different, or overlapping genes are associated with phenotypes such as alcohol and substance use disorder, antisocial personality disorder, conduct disorder, impulsivity, and sensation seeking. Likewise, currently it is unknown if the same set of genes characterizing the general liability dimension are the same across development (e.g., childhood, adolescence, young adulthood) or equally influential across stages or phases of a disorder or phenotype (e.g., substance use initiation, escalation, heavy use, problem use). Furthermore, based on extant preclinical and human studies, there is evidence that different neurobiological (brain) systems are associated with different phenotypes (e.g., sensation seeking, impulsivity) that challenge the utility of a common genetic liability model representation (Romer, 2010; Steinberg, 2010), as do findings suggesting different interconnected brain systems that drive different sets of cognitive and affective processes (Rubia, 2011).

The Generality-Specificity Issue

As discussed previously, the behavioral undercontrol literature has progressed at a general level in psychometric and behavior genetic studies focused on issues of internal structure and variance-covariance decomposition to estimate parameters of the ACE model. While this literature has clearly suggested some commonality (a general liability dimension) for a broad set of externalizing disorders, symptoms, and behaviors, other studies focused on specificity have also contributed in advancing our understanding of behavioral undercontrol. Two examples from the specificity literature are provided next, with one focused on neuroimaging findings and the other on behavior symptoms. The examples illustrate that specificity can be studied at different levels of analysis (i.e., brain activation patterns, behavioral symptoms).

An example for the specificity orientation stems from a structural and functional neuroimaging review by Rubia (2011) regarding ADHD and conduct disorder. Based on her review, Rubia concluded that ADHD is associated with inferior frontal, striatal, parietotemporal, and cerebellar regions that are associated with "cool" cognitive functions (e.g., inhibitory, attention, and timing).

By contrast, conduct disorder is associated with the "hot" paralimbic system that is associated with the regulation of motivation and affect. The hot system includes the orbital and ventromedial prefrontal cortices, superior temporal lobes, and limbic structures, including the amygdala. Hence, based on findings from the neuroimaging literature, ADHD and conduct disorder represent distinct pathophysiologies and thus are disorder-specific rather than overlapping disorders with common etiologies. To the extent that these neuroimaging findings are disorder-specific, there are likely to be different prevention, intervention, and treatment targets that need to be considered in translating basic science findings from the laboratory to the clinic.

Yet another study that illustrates the importance of focusing on specific components of disorders was conducted by Elkins, McGue, and Iacono (2007) regarding the prospective association between ADHD, conduct disorder, and substance use and abuse in adolescence. The issue of the unique contribution of ADHD to adolescent substance use and abuse independent of conduct disorder has been a prominent issue in the literature for over 20 years (Biederman et al., 1997; Molina, Bukstein, & Lynch, 2002), with mixed findings across studies that have varied along a number of dimensions such as sample (clinic versus general population), measurement instrument, and longitudinal design issues (duration, number and spacing of intervals). Using both dimensional and categorical (diagnostic) scores, Elkins et al. reported that even when controlling for conduct disorder, hyperactivity/impulsivity significantly predicted adolescent initiation of several substances, nicotine dependence, and cannabis abuse/dependence. However, when conduct disorder and hyperactivity/impulsivity were controlled, inattention was not a significant predictor of adolescent substance use and abuse outcomes. As such, the broader, more general disorder of ADHD was a less sensitive predictor of adolescent substance initiation, use, and abuse than was the hyperactivity/impulsivity dimension; furthermore, the inattention dimension was not statistically significant.

These specificity findings highlight that more specific relationships are likely necessary to complement and extend the broader generality research that has been conducted. Furthermore, such specificity research is needed at, and across, multiple levels of analyses, given that causal structures are more likely to be matrix oriented (i.e., multilevel,

dynamic systems) rather than at any single level. In addition, new research methods such as imaging-genetic research designs will be particularly helpful both to map more precisely the gene-brain-behavior relationships and to systematically evaluate pharmacologic treatments for disorders and intermediate phenotypes associated with behavioral undercontrol and associated disorders (Pine, Ernst, & Leibenluft, 2010).

Sampling and Research Design Issues

A range of sampling designs has informed research on behavioral undercontrol, including population-based studies, high-risk designs, and randomly selected samples from clinical treatment settings. Each of these designs offers distinct strengths and limitations, but consistency of findings across these designs and associated samples can provide robustness to accrued findings on behavioral undercontrol. There are several other sampling and research designs that could further facilitate the study of behavioral undercontrol.

First, the use of discordant family twin designs with molecular genetic data and age-sensitive environmental measures could be quite useful in disentangling some of the gene, environment, and gene–environment relationships across time that may account for the discordant outcomes of monozygotic twins. The family portion of the design would permit critical, multiple informant, and multi-method assessments across time that could facilitate addressing research questions related to which environmental events in combination with what genes occurring when and under what conditions impacted discordant outcomes for twin pairs (e.g., one twin with a substance abuse disorder and one without such a disorder). Second, what could be described as enhanced imaging-genetic research designs, enhanced with age-sensitive environmental measures, would facilitate inquiry into the kinds of gene and environment research questions previously mentioned, but at the level of gene-brain-behavior-context relations.

Third, the use of cross-over prevention, intervention, and treatment research designs could also be helpful in determining if, for example, behavioral and/or pharmacologic treatments impact not only the targeted behavior (e.g., reduction in alcohol use) but also reductions in other behaviors, such as other drug use and level of antisocial behavior. To the extent that a common mechanism reflecting general features of behavior undercontrol exists, targeted interventions and treatments may influence more than one behavioral undercontrol phenotype or may have cross-disorder influences.

Fourth, a population that has been understudied from the perspective of mechanisms associated with behavioral undercontrol is that of resilient children and adults (Glantz & Johnson, 1999; Heitzeg, Nigg, Yau, Zubieta, & Zucker, 2008). In a standard high-risk research design with risk status (low versus high risk) crossed with outcome (e.g., disorder or no disorder), the resilient group is indicated by high risk but no disorder. A central research question to be addressed is what genetic and environmental factors and associated mechanisms contribute to the development of a resilient outcome across time given the set of at-risk conditions. Findings related to resilience are of importance not only to "natural history" etiologic research, but they may also identify targets for prevention and treatment.

Fifth, there may be value in studies that utilize common origin and founder populations. An example of the potential value of using a common origin and founder population for a feature (impulsivity) of behavioral undercontrol was reported by Bevilacqua et al. (2010) using a sample of native Finland convicts. This was a deep sequencing exon-focused study of 14 genes of dopamine or serotonin function in relation to a measure of severe impulsivity among a male convict population (n = 96). Severe impulsivity was assessed by an evaluation of criminal and clinical records on the degree of premediation and spontaneity of crimes committed—low premediation and high spontaneity of crimes was coded in the direction of higher impulsivity. One of the functional SNPs assessed was the HTR2B Q20* stop codon, which is common (minor allele frequency > 1%) but exclusive to Finnish people. In prior research the HTR2B gene has been associated with obsessive-compulsive disorder and illicit drug abuse. Research findings with the Finnish male convict population indicated that among the 17 violent offenders who carried the HTR2B Q20* stop codon, impulsivity was strongly associated with the commission of their violent crime, and 94% of their crimes were committed while under the influence of alcohol. While the HTR2B Q20* stop codon may be unique to the Finnish founder population, this kind of sampling strategy may be useful in identifying other candidate genes and rare alleles that influence facets of behavioral undercontrol.

Gene–Environment Interactions and Complex Behavioral Phenotypes

A unifying feature of behavioral undercontrol is that it reflects a developmental phenomenon that manifests itself early in life and may express itself differently across different portions of the life span (e.g., childhood, adolescence, adulthood) and different segments of, or transitions in, alcohol and other substance use (e.g., initiation, regular use, problem use, dependence) and antisocial behavior (early fighting and opposition to authority in childhood, criminal behavior and failures in social and occupational roles in adulthood). The incorporation of developmentally informed gene–environment and gene–gene models of behavioral undercontrol may be beneficial in understanding the heterogeneity of pathways and outcomes, and they may be of value to the plethora of potential intervention options (e.g., pharmacologic, behavioral interventions, combination therapies) and public health policies associated with these behavioral expressions that are so costly to individuals, families, and society.

For example, there is emerging evidence of potentially significant gene–environment interactions that affect phenotypes related to behavioral undercontrol. Several studies have been completed that indicate significant interactions between parenting behaviors (e.g., parental monitoring; harsh parenting) and specific genes (e.g., GABRA2, 5-HTTLPR) on substance use and other externalizing behaviors (Brody et al., 2009, 2014; Chen et al., 2009; Dick et al., 2014). Likewise, with an adolescent sample, Blomeyer et al. (2008) reported that stressful life events interacted with the CRHR1 gene in predicting heavy alcohol use.

Concerns have been expressed about limitations of human studies focused on gene–environment interactions of alcohol and other substance use phenotypes. One concern is that most human gene–environment studies rely on a candidate gene strategy, and that this strategy may provide quite limited coverage of potential SNPs and loci that may be significantly associated with the phenotype under investigation (Duncan & Keller, 2011). A second concern has been one of sample size, in that many human gene–environment studies typically have small sizes, relative to genome-wide association (GWA) studies, to obtain reliable interaction effects once statistical corrections are made; hence, an obtained significant interaction effect may be due to chance (Young-Wolf, Enoch, &

Prescott, 2011). Third, findings from GWA studies suggest that with respect to complex phenotypes, such as alcohol and substance use phenotypes, identified common variants are likely to have small effects; hence, single or even multiple loci are unlikely to account for large portions of variance for complex phenotypes. Fourth, a concern exists that there is no taxonomy or overarching framework for the environment or environmental exposures, thereby making the systematic study of a large number of genetic loci and an ill-defined set of environmental conditions quite daunting (Sher et al., 2010).

Although these are significant methodological challenges, there are strategies that can be used to minimize their impact. For example, replication of findings remains a viable scientific strategy, as does combining across-study findings in meta-analysis. The development of multilocus scores (Brody, Chen, & Beach, 2013) and polygenic indexes (i.e., summed or weighted SNP composites; Plomin & Simpson, 2013; Vrieze, Iacono, & McGue, 2012) may be useful in reducing the substantial burden of multiple comparison adjustments from testing a potentially substantially larger number of SNPs. The public accessibility of GWA datasets may facilitate both the identification of polygenic indexes and sets of tag SNPs that may be of particular relevance to the study of behavioral undercontrol or its facets and environmental factors. Also, promising efforts are underway to harmonize measures and data sets to permit meaningful pooling of samples to increase sample size to a respectable level. There are also efforts underway to encourage the assessment of common environmental measures among investigators conducting genome wide association studies and other large-scale genomic studies (e.g., next-generation sequencing studies) via the identification of a common set of measures across multiple domains that are compiled in Phenx (https://www.phenxtoolkit.org). Hence, the study of gene–environment interactions for behavioral undercontrol are challenging, but the barriers may be overcome through strategic planning and application.

Summary and Conclusions

There has been substantial progress in the study of behavioral undercontrol as a unifying, multifaceted construct that spans multiple areas of study. Findings from different disciplines and utilizing alternative methodological approaches have converged in suggesting that behavioral undercontrol

is significant in predicting and understanding adolescent substance use and abuse, as well as a number of other externalizing behaviors and disorders (e.g., antisocial personality disorder) in adolescence and adulthood. Emerging research in genomics and neuroimaging on behavioral undercontrol are providing methods of identifying more precise disinhibitory and inhibitory mechanisms that may serve as targets for behavioral and/or pharmacologic interventions.

A number of challenging issues remain to be addressed in future research. For instance, an alternative or expanded model needs to include specific genes or gene products (e.g., gene expression) in interaction with specific environments to maximize the potential clinical translation of findings to the fields of prevention science, interventions, and treatments. The use of recent technological developments in genomics and neuroimaging may facilitate these efforts by increasing the precision by which we can assess gene-brain-behavior-context relations and associated fundamental mechanisms, and to evaluate how interventions (behavioral or pharmacologic) may impact these dynamic, interrelated systems across time. In addition, we may begin to more fully explicate how cognitive, emotional, and behavioral systems develop across time and interact to produce self-regulation and self-control. While research on behavioral undercontrol provides an integrative framework for research and practice, there remain significant challenges ahead to increase the explanatory power of this framework and to maximize its translational value in applied settings.

References

American Psychiatric Association. (1994). *Diagnostic and statistical manual of mental disorders* (4th ed.). Washington, DC: Author.

Babor, T. F., Hofmann, M., DelBoca, F. K., Hesselbrock, V., Meyer, R. E., Dolinsky, Z. S., & Rounsaville, B. (1992). Types of alcoholics, I: Evidence for an empirically derived typology based on indicator of vulnerability and severity. *Archives of General Psychiatry, 49,* 599–608.

Barkley, R. A. (2006). *Attention deficit hyperactivity disorder: A handbook for diagnosis and treatment.* New York, NY: Guilford Press.

Basu, D., Ball, S. A., Feinn, R., Gelernter, J., & Kranzler, H. R. (2004). Typologies of drug dependence: comparative validity of a multivariate and four univariate models. *Drug and Alcohol Dependence, 73,* 289–300.

Bevilacqua, L., Doly, S., Kaprio, J., Yuan, Q., Tikkanen, R., Paunio, T., . . . Goldman, D. (2010). A population-specific HTR2B stop codon predisposes to severe impulsivity. *Nature, 468,* 1061–1068.

Biederman, J., Wilens, T., Mick, E., Faraone, S. V., Weber, W., Curtis, S., . . . Soriano, J. (1997). Is ADHD a risk factor for psychoactive substance use disorders? Findings from a four-year prospective follow-up study. *Journal of the American Academy of Child & Adolescent Psychiatry, 36* (1), 21–29.

Blackson, T. C., Tarter, R. E., Loeber, R., Ammerman, R. T., & Windle, M. (1996). The influence of paternal substance abuse and difficult temperament in fathers and sons on sons' disengagement from family to deviant peers. *Journal of Youth and Adolescence, 25*, 389–411.

Block, J. (1995). A contrarian view of the five-factor approach to personality description. *Psychological Bulletin, 117*, 187–215.

Blomeyer, D., Treutlein, J., Esser, G., Schmidt, M. H., Schumann, G., & Laucht, M. (2008). Interaction between CRHR1 gene and stressful life events predicts adolescent heavy alcohol use. *Biological Psychiatry, 63*, 146–151.

Brody, G. H., Beach, S. R. H., Philibert, R. A., Chen, Y. F., Lei, M. K., Murry, V. M., & Brown, A. (2009). Parenting moderates a genetic vulnerability factor in longitudinal increases in youths' substance use. *Journal of Consulting and Clinical Psychology, 77*(1), 1–11.

Brody, G. H., Yu, T., Beach, S. R. H., Kogan, S. M., Windle, M., & Philibert, R. A. (2014). Harsh parenting and adolescent health: A longitudinal analysis with genetic moderation. *Health Psychology, 33*, 401–409.

Brody, G. H., Chen, Y., & Beach, S. R. H. (2013). Differential susceptibility to prevention: GABAergic, dopaminergic, and mulitlocus effects. *Journal of Child Psychology & Psychiatry, 54*(8), 863–871.

Carver, C. S., & White, T. L. (1994). Behavioral inhibition, behavioral activation, and affective responses to impending reward and punishment: The BIS/BAS scales. *Journal of Personality and Social Psychology, 67*(2), 319–333.

Caspi, A., Moffitt, T. E., Newman, D. L., & Silva, P. A. (1996). Behavioral observations at age 3 years predict adult psychiatric disorders. *Archives of General Psychiatry, 53*, 1033–1039.

Chen, L. S., Johnson, E. O., Breslau, N., Hatsukami, D., Saccone, N. L, Grucza, R. A., . . . Bierut, L. J. (2009). Interplay of genetic risk factors and parent monitoring in risk for nicotine dependence. *Addiction, 104*(10), 1731–1740.

Cloninger, C. R. (1987). Neurogenetic adaptive mechanisms in alcoholism. *Science, 236*, 410–416.

Cloninger, C. R., Bohman, M., & Sigvardsson, S. (1981). Inheritance of alcohol abuse: Cross fostering analysis of adopted men. *Archives of General Psychiatry, 38*, 861–868.

Congdon, E., & Canli, T. (2005). The endophenotype of impulsivity: Reaching consilience through behavioral, genetic, and neuroimaging approaches. *Behavioral and Cognitive Neuroscience Reviews, 4*(4), 262–281.

Coskunpinar, A., Dir, A. L., & Cyders, M. A. (2013). Multidimensionality in impulsivity and alcohol use: A meta-analysis using the UPPS model of impulsivity. *Alcoholism: Clinical and Experimental Research, 37*(9), 1441–1450.

Del Boca, F. K., & Hesselbrock, M. N. (1996). Gender and alcoholic subtypes. *Alcohol Health and Research World, 20*, 56–62.

DeWit, H. (2008). Impulsivity as a determinant and consequence of drug use: A review of underlying processes. *Addiction Biology, 14*, 22–31.

Dick, D. M. (2007). Identification of genes influencing a spectrum of externalizing psychopathology. *Current Directions in Psychological Science, 16*(6), 331–335.

Dick, D. M., Aliev, F., Latendresse, S. L., Hickman, M., Heron, J., Macleod, J., . . . Kendler, K. S. (2013). Adolescent alcohol use is predicted by childhood temperament factors before age 5, with mediation through personality and peers. *Alcoholism: Clinical and Experimental Research, 37*(12), 2108–2117.

Dick, D. M., Cho, S. B., Latendresse, S. J., Aliev, F., Nurnberger, J. I., Edenberg, H. J., . . . Kuperman, S. (2014). Genetic influences on alcohol use across stages of development: *GABRA2* and longitudinal trajectories of drunkenness from adolescence to young adulthood. *Addiction Biology, 19*, 1055–1064.

Dick, D. M., Smith, G., Olausson, P., Mitchell, S. H., Leeman, R. F., O'Malley, S. S., & Sher, K. (2010). Understanding the construct of impulsivity and its relationship to alcohol disorders. *Addiction Biology, 15*, 216–226.

Dick, D. M., Viken, R. J., Kaprio, J., Pulkkinen, L., & Rose, R. J. (2005). Understanding the covariation among childhood externalizing symptoms: Genetic and environmental influences on conduct disorder, attention deficit hyperactivity disorder, and oppositional defiant disorder symptoms. *Journal of Abnormal Child Psychology, 33*(2), 219–229.

Dickman, S. J. (1990). Functional and dysfunctional impulsivity: Personality and cognitive correlates. *Journal of Personality and Social Psychology, 58*(1), 95–102.

Donovan, J. E., & Jessor, R. (1985). Structure of problem behavior in adolescence and young adulthood. *Journal of Consulting and Clinical Psychology, 33*(6), 890–904.

Dougherty, D. M., Mathias, C. W., & Marsh, D. M. (2003). *GoStop Impulsivity Paradigm (Version 1.0)* [Manual]. Neurobehavioral Research Laboratory and Clinic, University of Texas Health Science Center at Houston, Houston, TX.

Duncan, L. E., & Keller, M. C. (2011). A critical review of the first 10 years of candidate gene-by-environment interaction research in psychiatry. *American Journal of Psychiatry, 168*(10), 1041–1049.

Elkins, I. J., McGue, M., & Iacono, W. G. (2007). Prospective effects of attention-deficit/hyperactivity disorder, conduct disorder, and sex on adolescent substance use and abuse. *Archives of General Psychiatry, 64*(10), 1145–1152.

Eysenck, S. B. G., Pearson, P. R., Easting, G., & Allsopp, J. P. (1985). Age norms for impulsiveness, venturesomeness and empathy in adults. *Personality and Individual Differences, 6*, 613–619.

Faraone, S. V., & Mick, E. (2010). Molecular genetics of attention deficit hyperactivity disorder. *Psychiatric Clinics of North America, 33*, 159–180.

Glantz, M. D., & Johnson, J. L. (1999). *Resilience and development: Positive life adaptations*. New York, NY: Kluwer Academic/Plenum Publishers.

Goldstein, D. B. (2009). Common genetic variation and human traits. *New England Journal of Medicine, 360*(17), 1696–1698.

Gorenstein, E. E., & Newman, J. P. (1980). Disinhibitory psychopathology: A new perspective and a model for research. *Psychological Review, 87*, 301–315.

Harrison, A. A., Everitt, B. J., & Robbins, T. W. (1999). Central serotonin depletion impairs both the acquisition and performance of a symmetrically reinforced go/no-go conditional visual discrimination. *Behavioral Brain Research, 100*(1–2), 99–112.

Heitzeg, M. M., Nigg, J. T., Yau, W. Y., Zubieta, J. K., & Zucker, R. A. (2008). Affective circuitry and risk for alcoholism in late adolescence: Differences in frontostriatal responses between vulnerable and resilient children of alcoholic parents.

Alcoholism: Clinical and Experimental Research, 32(3), 414–426.

Hicks, B. M., Krueger, R. F., Iacono, W. G., McGue, M., & Patrick, C. J. (2004). Family transmission and heritability of externalizing disorders: A twin-family study. *Archives of General Psychiatry, 61*, 922–928.

Hicks, B. M., Schalet, B. D., Malone, S. M., Iacono, W. G., & McGue, M. (2011). Psychometric and genetic architecture of substance use disorder and behavioral disinhibition measures for gene association studies. *Behavior Genetics, 41*, 459–475.

Hodgkinson, C. A., Yuan, Q., Xu, K., Shen, P. H., Heinz, E., Lobos, E. A., . . . Goldman, D. (2008). Addictions biology: Haplotype-based analysis for 130 candidate genes on a single array. *Alcohol and Alcoholism, 43*(5), 505–515.

Hussong, A. M., Flora, D. R., Curran, P. J., Chassin, L. A., & Zucker, R. A. (2008). Defining risk heterogeneity for internalizing symptoms among children of alcoholic parents. *Development and Psychopathology, 20*, 165–193.

Hussong, A. M., Wirth, R. J., Edwards, M. C., Curran, P. J., Chassin, L. A., & Zucker, R. A. (2007). Externalizing symptoms among children of alcoholic parents: Entry points for an antisocial pathway to alcoholism. *Journal of Abnormal Psychology, 116*, 529–542.

Iacono, W. G., Malone, S. M., & McGue, M. (2008). Behavioral disinhibition and the development of early-onset addiction: Common and specific influences. *Annual Review of Clinical Psychology, 4*, 325–348.

Jessor, R., & Jessor, S. L. (1977). *Problem behavior and psychosocial development: A longitudinal study of youth.* New York, NY: Academic Press.

Leggio, L., Kenna, G. A., Fenton, M., Bonenfant, E., & Swift, R. M. (2009). Typologies of alcohol dependence. From Jellinek to genetics and beyond. *Neuropsychology Review, 19*, 115–129.

Lemery, K. S., Essex, M. J., & Smider, N. A. (2002). Revealing the relation between temperament and behavior problem symptoms by eliminating measurement confounding: expert ratings and factor analyses. *Child Development, 73*(3), 867–882.

Lengua, L. J., West, S. G., & Sandler, I. N. (1998). Temperament as a predictor of symptomatology in children: Addressing contamination of measures. *Child Development, 69*, 164–181.

Kendler, K. S., Myers, J., & Prescott, C. A. (2007). Specificity of genetic and environmental risk factors for symptoms of cannabis, cocaine, alcohol, caffeine, and nicotine dependence. *Archives of General Psychiatry, 64*(11), 1313–1320.

Kendler, K. S., Prescott, C. A., Myers, J., & Neale, M. C. (2003). The structure of genetic and environmental risk factors for common psychiatric and substance use disorders in men and women. *Archives of General Psychiatry, 60*, 929–937.

King, K. M., & Chassin, L. (2004). Mediating and moderated effects of behavioral undercontrol and parenting in the prediction of drug use disorders in emerging adulthood. *Psychology of Addictive Behaviors, 18*, 239–249.

Krueger, R. F., Markon, K. E., Patrick, C. J., & Iacono, W. G. (2005). Externalizing psychopathology in adulthood: A dimensional-spectrum conceptualization and its implications for DSM-V. *Journal of Abnormal Psychology, 114*, 537–550.

Kushner, M., Sher, K. J., & Beitman, B. (1990). The relation between alcohol problems and anxiety disorders. *American Journal of Psychiatry, 147*, 685–695.

Manolio, T. A., Collins, F. S., Cox, N. J., Goldstein, D. B., Hindorff, L. A., Hunter, D. J., . . . Visscher, P. M. (2009). Finding the missing heritability of complex diseases. *Nature, 461*(8), 747–753.

Masse, L. C., & Tremblay, R. E. (1997). Behavior of boys in kindergarten and the onset of substance use during adolescence. *Archives of General Psychiatry, 54*, 62–68.

Maziade, M., Caperaa, P., Laplante, B., Boudreault, M., Thivierge, J., Cote, R., & Boutin, P. (1985). Value of difficult temperament among 7-year-olds in the general population for predicting psychiatric diagnosis at age 12. *American Journal of Psychiatry, 142*, 943–946.

Miller, E., Joseph, S., & Tudway, J. (2004). Assessing the component structure of the four self-report measures of impulsivity. *Personality and Individual Differences, 37*, 349–358.

Molina, B. S. G., Bukstein, O. G., & Lynch, K. G. (2002). Attention-deficit/hyperactivity disorder and conduct disorder symptomatology in adolescents with alcohol use disorder. *Psychology of Addictive Behaviors, 16*(2), 161–164.

Neale, M. C., & Cardon, L. R. (1992). *Methodology for genetic studies of twins and families.* Dordrecht, The Netherlands: Kluwer Academic Publishers B.V.

Neale, M. C., Boker, S. M., Xie, G., & Maes, H. H. (1999). *Mx: Statistical modeling* (5th ed.). Richmond, VA: Medical College of Virginia, Department of Psychiatry.

Nigg, J. T. (2002). On inhibition/disinhibition in developmental psychopathology: Views from cognitive and personality psychology and a working inhibition taxonomy. *Psychological Bulletin, 126*(2), 220–246.

Patton, J. H., Stanford, M. S., & Barratt, E. S. (1995). Factor structure of the Barratt Impulsiveness Scale. *Journal of Clinical Psychology, 51*, 768–774.

Pine, D. S., Ernst, M., & Leibenluft, E. (2010). Imaging-genetics applications in child psychiatry. *Journal of the American Academy of Child and Adolescent Psychiatry, 49*(8), 772–782.

Plomin, R., & Simpson, M. A. (2013). The future of genomics for developmentalists. *Development and Psychopathology, 25*, 1263–1278.

Reynolds, B., Penfold, R. B., & Patak, M. (2008). Dimensions of impulsive behavior in adolescents: Laboratory behavioral assessments. *Experimental and Clinical Psychopharmacology, 16*(2), 124–131.

Romer, D. (2010). Adolescent risk taking, impulsivity, and brain development: Implications for prevention. *Developmental Psychobiology, 52*(3), 263–276.

Romer, D., & Hennessy, M. (2007). A biosocial-affect model of adolescent sensation seeking: The role of affect evaluation and peer-group influence in adolescent drug use. *Prevention Science, 8*(2), 89–101.

Rubia, K. (2011). "Cool" inferior frontostriatal dysfunction in attention-deficit/hyperactivity disorder versus 'hot' ventromedial orbitofrontal-limbic dysfunction in conduct disorder: A review. *Biological Psychiatry, 69*, e69–e87.

Russell, M. (1990). Prevalence of alcoholism among children of alcoholics. In M. Windle & J. S. Searles (Eds.), *Children of alcoholics: Critical perspectives* (pp. 9–38). New York, NY: Guilford Press.

Schuckit, M. A. (2009). An overview of genetic influences in alcoholism. *Journal of Substance Abuse Treatment, 36*(1), S5–14.

Sher, K. J., Dick, D. M., Crabbe, J. C., Hutchison, K. E., O'Malley, S. S., & Heath, A. C. (2010). Consilient research approaches in studying gene-environment interactions in alcohol research. *Addiction Biology, 15*, 200–216.

Sher, K. J., Grekin, E. R., & Williams, N. A. (2005). The development of alcohol use disorders. *Annual Review of Clinical Psychology, 1*, 493–523.

Sher, K. J., & Slutske, W. S. (2003). Disorders of impulse control. In G. Stricker & T. A. Widiger (Eds.), *Handbook of psychology, Vol. 8. Clinical psychology* (pp. 195–228). New York, NY: Wiley.

Sher, K. J., & Trull, T. J. (1994). Personality and disinhibitory psychopathology: Alcoholism and antisocial personality disorder. *Journal of Abnormal Psychology, 103*(1), 92–102.

Steinberg, L. (2010). A dual systems model of adolescent risk-taking. *Developmental Psychobiology, 52*(3), 216–224.

Steinhausen H. C. (2009). The heterogeneity of causes and courses of attention-deficit/hyperactivity disorder. *Acta Psychiatrica Scandinavica, 120*, 392–399.

Tabakoff, B., Saba, L., Printz, M., Flodman, P., Hodgkinson, C., Goldman, D., . . . WHO/ISBRA Study on State and Trait Markers of Alcoholism. (2009). Genetical genomic determinants of alcohol consumption in rats and humans. *BMC Biology, 7*, 70. doi:10.1186/1741-7007-7-70

Tarter, R. E., Kirisci, L., Habeych, M., Reynolds, M., & Vanyukov, M. (2003a). Neurobehavioral disinhibition in childhood predisposes boys to substance use disorders by young adulthood: direct and mediated etiologic pathways. *Drug and Alcohol Dependence, 73*, 121–132.

Tarter, R. E., Kirisci, L., Mezzich, A., Cornelius, J. R., Blackson, T., & Clark, D. (2003b). Neurobehavioral disinhibition in childhood predicts early age at onset of substance use disorder. *American Journal of Psychiatry, 160*, 1078–1085.

Tarter, R. E., & Vanyukov, M. (1994). Alcoholism: A developmental disorder. *Journal of Consulting and Clinical Psychology, 62*(6), 1096–1107.

Tubman, J. G., & Windle, M. (1995). Continuity of difficult temperament in adolescence: Relations with depression, life events, family support, and substance use across a one year period. *Journal of Youth and Adolescence, 24*, 133–153.

Vanyukov, M. M., & Tarter, R. (2000). Genetic studies of substance abuse. *Drug and Alcohol Dependence, 59*, 101–123.

Vrieze, S. I., Iacono, W. G., & McGue, M. (2012). Confluence of genes, environment, development, and behavior in a post Genome-Wide Association Study world. *Development and Psychopathology, 24*, 1195–1214.

Waldman, I., Rhee, S. H., Levy, F., & Hay, D. A. (2001). Causes of the overlap among symptoms of ADHD, oppositional defiant disorder, and conduct disorder. In F. Levy & D. A. Hay (Eds.), *Attention, genes, and ADHD* (pp. 115–138). New York, NY: Brunner-Routledge.

Whiteside, S. P., & Lynam, D. R. (2001). The Five-Factor Model and impulsivity: Using a structural model of personality to understand impulsivity. *Personality and Individual Differences, 30*(4), 669–689.

Wills, T. A., Cleary, S., Filer, M., Shinar, O., Mariani, J., & Spera, K. (2001). Temperament related to early onset substance use: Test of a developmental model. *Prevention Science, 2*, 145–163.

Windle, M. (1992). Temperament and social support in adolescence: Interrelations with depressive symptoms and delinquent behaviors. *Journal of Youth and Adolescence, 21*, 1–21.

Windle, M., & Scheidt, D. M. (2004). Alcoholic subtypes: Are two sufficient? *Addiction, 99*, 1508–1519.

Windle, M., & Windle, R. C. (2006). Adolescent temperament and lifetime psychiatric and substance abuse disorders assessed in young adulthood. *Personality and Individual Differences, 41*, 15–25.

Winstanley, C. A., Eagle, D. W., & Robbins, T. W. (2006). Behavioral models of impulsivity in relation to ADHD: Translation between clinical and preclinical studies. *Clinical Psychology Review, 26*, 379–395.

Young, S. E., Stallings, M. C., Corley, R. P., Krauter, K. S., & Hewitt, J. K. (2000). Genetic and environmental influences on behavior disinhibition. *American Journal of Medical Genetics, 96*, 684–695.

Young-Wolf, K. C., Enoch, M. A., & Prescott, C. A. (2011). The influence of gene-environment interactions on alcohol consumption and alcohol use disorders: A comprehensive review. *Clinical Psychology Review, 31*, 800–816.

Zucker, R. A. (1987). The four alcoholisms: A developmental account of the etiologic process. In P. C. Rivers (Ed.), *Nebraska symposium on motivation, 1986: Vol. 34. Alcohol and addictive behaviors* (pp. 27–84). Lincoln: University of Nebraska Press.

Zucker, R. A. (2006). Alcohol use and the alcohol use disorders: A developmental-biopsychosocial systems formulation covering the life course. In D. Cicchetti & D. J. Cohen (Eds.), *Developmental psychopathology, Vol. 3. Risk, disorder and adaptation* (2nd ed., pp. 620–656). New York, NY: Wiley.

Zucker, R. A., Heitzeg, M. M., & Nigg, J. T. (2011). Parsing the undercontrol-disinhibition pathway to substance use disorders: A multilevel developmental problem. *Child Development Perspectives, 5*(4), 248–255.

Zuckerman, M. (1994). *Behavioral expression and biosocial bases of sensation seeking*. Cambridge, UK: Cambridge University Press.

An Early Emerging Internalizing Pathway to Substance Use and Disorder

Andrea M. Hussong, Julia Shadur, Alison R. Burns, Gabriela Stein, Deborah Jones, Jessica Solis, *and* Laura G. McKee

Abstract

Accumulating evidence suggests that early emerging pathways to substance use and disorder may have identifiable markers in children as young as ages 3–6 years. Although most research has focused on the externalizing pathway, the current chapter describes an internalizing pathway to substance use and disorder. We consider potential mechanisms underlying early emerging risk related to this pathway that may emanate from responses to early stress exposure and the caregiving environment. We also discuss implications of the pathway for early prevention programming, particularly that targeting children of parents with substance use disorders.

Key Words: internalizing symptoms, alcohol, drug use, pathway, children, adolescence, substance use disorder

Adolescent substance use and disorder remain significant public health concerns. Substance use is associated with the three leading causes of death during this developmental period (i.e., suicide, homicide, and accidents; US DHHS, 2007) as well as with engaging in delinquent and criminal activity, poor school performance and retention, early and unplanned pregnancy, and mental health problems (Chassin, Hussong, & Beltran, 2009; Windle & Windle, 2006). Moreover, the use of substances in early adolescence (before age 14) is associated with an increased likelihood of having an adult alcohol use disorder (AUD) by as much as 35% (Grant & Dawson, 1997). The negative effect of adult alcohol and drug use disorders on public health and productivity loss are, in turn, well documented (Research Society on Alcoholism, 2011).

Emerging out of foundational work in the 1970s and 1980s, several developmental theories articulate mechanisms that shape the course of substance involvement in youth as they progress into adulthood (e.g., Baumrind, 1985; Brook, Whiteman, & Gordon, 1983; Jessor & Jessor, 1977). The majority of these theories point to risk processes that emerge in early adolescence or late childhood. However, substance use itself actually begins much earlier than once thought, with between 6% and 9% of 9-year-olds and as many as 18% of fourth graders having initiated drinking (Donovan, 2007). For some individuals, there is reason to believe that the origins of substance use may be found even earlier in childhood (Zucker, Donovan, Masten, Mattson, & Moss, 2008).

The concept of heterotypic continuity, a developmental psychopathology principle (Cicchetti, 2006; Cummings, Davies, & Campbell, 2000), states that many behaviors show continuity in function or the "core deficit" (a term from psychiatry) over time while also showing change in how the deficit is manifested at any given age (Caspi & Moffitt, 1995; Rutter, 1996). A classic example is that of antisocial behavior, which shows continuity in rebellious or disinhibited behaviors even when these behaviors change over time, looking more like biting and kicking in the 4-year-old and stealing and truancy in the 17-year-old. Given significant heterogeneity in substance use disorders (SUDs), many have hypothesized that there may be different core deficits for different subgroups of individuals with SUDs (SAMHSA, 2011). If we can identify a core deficit or deficits that drive substance use behavior, we can then move from this psychiatric question to one of development. Namely, if we can identify "what develops" (i.e., the core deficit), then we can pursue the study of "how it develops."

This shift from focusing on substance use behaviors to the underlying deficits that give rise to these behaviors is consist with research showing that symptomatology even in early childhood predicts substance use in late adolescence and early adulthood (Zucker et al., 2008). The leading example of this developmental approach is an early emerging externalizing pathway to SUDs. The core deficit of this pathway is commonly conceptualized as behavioral disinhibition, "an inability to inhibit socially undesirable or restricted actions" (p. 326, Iacono, Malone, & McGue, 2008), which is differentially expressed across development. As currently posited, the externalizing pathway first emerges as difficult temperament in infancy, which is followed in childhood by externalizing symptoms (e.g., aggression and conduct problems), an early onset of substance use, escalations in antisocial behavior, and the eventual onset of SUDs in late adolescence or early adulthood (Tarter et al., 1999; Zucker et al., 2006). Although multiple factors may account for how this pattern of behaviors develops, current models identify interactions between an underlying liability for behavioral disinhibition (e.g., genetic and neurobiological factors) and a high-risk environment (e.g., impaired parenting, disruptive or impoverished contexts, and deviant peer networks) as core to risk formation (e.g., Dick, 2011; Hussong, Curran, & Chassin, 1998; Iacono & Malone, 2011; Zucker et al., 2006; Zucker, Heitzeg, & Nigg, 2011).

Importantly, such developmental pathways facilitate earlier identification of risk processes that may contribute to eventual disorder. Such early identification has the potential to inform prevention programs designed to alter risk mechanisms early in the life course. For example, accumulating evidence already shows support for prevention programs that address early emerging risk and protective factors associated with the externalizing pathway (e.g., Henggeler, Clingempeel, Brondino, & Pickrel, 2002; Lochman, Wells, & Murray, 2007). Guidelines for the development of effective prevention programs emphasize the importance of developmental timing in matching risk mechanisms and the targets for intervention (e.g., Nation et al., 2003). This is an important contribution of developmental studies given that the treatment of substance use disorders is challenging and the typical course of recovery is marked by repeated relapse and multiple intervention attempts (Winters, Stinchfield, Latimer, & Stone, 2008). The current collective wisdom suggests that early prevention programs could prove more effective than later treatment programs (Zucker et al., 2008) because of their potential to alter risk considered more malleable early in life (e.g., Olds, Sadler, & Kitzman, 2007).

Although the externalizing pathway is more commonly studied, in the current chapter, we focus on a second early emerging pathway to SUDs that we term the internalizing pathway. Following we articulate the value in understanding multiple pathways to SUDs and define our use of the term "pathway" within a developmental psychopathology framework (Cicchetti, 2006; Cummings et al., 2000). We then describe the emergence of risk associated with an internalizing pathway to SUDs. Because the bulk of evidence regarding the internalizing pathway focuses on alcohol, rather than other drugs of abuse, we initially review studies accumulated from the study of alcohol use and then extend the model to include other drugs of abuse. Because we anticipate that this pathway may be more salient in high-risk youth in high-risk contexts, we discuss the relevance of the internalizing pathway for risk emergence among children of alcoholic parents (COAs). We then offer a description of mechanisms that place children at risk for entering and continuing on the internalizing pathway to SUDs. Finally, we end the chapter with a discussion of the implications of this theoretical model for future research.

A Developmental Psychopathology Perspective on Pathways

The ultimate "outcome variable" for the internalizing pathway is the pathway itself. By identifying the markers of progression along this pathway, we can then examine mechanisms that lead to engagement, entrenchment, or desistance associated with this pathway. First, however, it is important to understand our meaning of the term "developmental pathway." Although multiple definitions abound in the literature, we recognize a developmental pathway as identifiable by age-graded markers of progression that denote increasing entrenchment of the core deficit with ontogeny. Similar to historically emphasized stage theories (Kandel, 1975), such pathways are not deterministic; for example, we do not expect all children showing early indicators of risk associated with the internalizing pathway to eventually develop SUDs. Rather, the internalizing pathway includes the potential for moderating influences, which serve to propel children along the pathway either toward resilience or toward sustained or increasingly maladaptive behavior. These moderating influences thus continue to shape existing risk for negative outcomes through *protective* (reducing risk) and *vulnerability* (further entrenching or cascading this risk; Rutter, 1987) mechanisms. Moreover, mediating mechanisms articulate the processes through which early risk translates into outcomes (including both normal and abnormal behavior). Pathways can describe processes that result in both *equifinality* (describing why some individuals show large differences in early risk patterns and processes but reach the same outcome) as well as *multifinality* (describing why some individuals show similar early risk patterns but reach different outcomes; Cicchetti & Rogosch, 1996).

A point of frequent confusion is whether such pathways define mechanisms (sometimes discussed as variable-oriented approaches in a parallel methodological literature) or groups of homogeneous individuals (similarly, person-oriented approaches; Magnusson & Cairns, 1996). In our work, the two are somewhat less distinct. We define the internalizing pathway by the heterotypic expression of the core deficit in this pathway over maturation. To the extent that this internalizing mechanism is the sole or dominant contributor to substance use for a group of individuals, then the internalizing pathway defines both a risk mechanism and a risk group who experience this mechanism over time. However, for some individuals, the internalizing mechanism may be only one of the deficits underlying substance use over time, in which case the individuals who manifest the internalizing pathway will be rather heterogeneous depending on the other contributing core deficits that fuel their substance involvement. To best articulate the core deficit and resulting internalizing pathway in this chapter, we focus on the simplest case in which the internalizing pathway defines a risk mechanism that is the sole or dominant deficit contributing to SUDs over maturation, thereby defining a homogenous group of individuals with respect to the development of SUDs. We expect that the internalizing pathway we describe interacts in important ways with other core deficits (see Hussong et al., 2011, for a discussion

of potential interactions between the internalizing and externalizing pathways), but here we view such extrapolations as beyond the scope of the current discussion.

An Internalizing Pathway to Alcohol Use Disorders

Reflecting the focus of relevant research, we first narrow our presentation of this pathway to the literature on alcohol use and disorder before we consider evidence that the pathway may explain the use of other drugs of abuse as well. In this model, we identify markers of progression along the internalizing pathway across development, articulating the heterotypic expression of the core deficit associated with this pathway, namely poor emotion regulation. Although multiple definitions of emotion regulation reside in the literature, we adopt that of Thompson (1994), who characterizes emotion regulation as the "extrinsic and intrinsic processes responsible for monitoring, evaluating, and modifying emotional reactions, especially their intensive and temporal features, to accomplish one's goal" (pp. 27–28). The most widely cited etiological mechanism linking poor emotion regulation to AUDs is commonly referred to as self-medication, a negative reinforcement model in which drinking is a behavior motivated by a desire to reduce distress and negative affect, which is in turn reinforced in the short term through the pharmacological and situational consequences of drinking (Khantzian, 1997; see McCarthy, Curtin, Piper, & Baker, 2010, for history of the negative reinforcement model).

Defining the Outcome

A subtype of AUDs often associated with this negative reinforcement model is depressive or negative affect alcoholism. We anticipate that negative affect alcoholism is the most common outcome of a persistent internalizing pathway. Across the literature, this subtype is consistently identified by comorbidity between internalizing disorders (involving depression and anxiety) and AUDs, typically in which internalizing disorders are assumed to precede and motivate AUDs (Babor, 1996; Zucker, 2006).[1] Although studies of alcoholism subtypes often differentiate a subgroup of individuals with alcoholism who have this pattern of comorbidity, hypothesized correlates and characteristics of this subgroup are less consistently supported in the literature (Babor, 1996). The unsatisfying results of studies seeking to identify a coherent set of alcoholism subtypes likely contribute to reduced interest in defining separable pathways to AUDs, particularly based on comorbid symptomatology. Nonetheless, recent efforts to model and understand sources of comorbidity suggest that the distinction between internalizing and externalizing processes may indeed prove useful.

In their meta-analysis of 10 disorders, Krueger and Markon (2006) showed a hierarchical structure to liabilities for internalizing and externalizing disorders. Through a series of comparative structural equation models, the best-fitting structure identified two correlated, superordinate liabilities differentiating externalizing disorders (including alcohol use, drug use, conduct, and antisocial personality disorders) and internalizing disorders. In turn, internalizing disorders were further distinguished by two subordinate liabilities differentiating distress (major depression, dysthymia, and generalized anxiety disorders) and fear (agoraphobia, social phobia, simple phobia, and panic disorder). Thus, the work of these authors distinguishes internalizing and externalizing disorders as correlated yet distinct liabilities. Behavioral genetic analyses by Kendler and colleagues (2003) recover a similar hierarchical factor structure for externalizing and internalizing disorders. In this work, although alcohol dependence shares a common genetic liability with externalizing disorders, alcohol dependence shares unique environmental influences with internalizing disorders. These findings are consistent with those of other family linkage and twin studies which demonstrate modest co-transmission for internalizing disorders (primarily depression) and alcoholism (Kendler, Neale, Heath, & Kessler, 1994; Merikangas, Leckman, Prusoff, Pauls, & Weissman, 1985; Merikangas, Rounsaville, & Prusoff, 1992).

More recent work provides mixed results on the role of shared genetic influences on comorbid depression/anxiety and alcohol use/disorder, particularly in adolescent samples when such patterns of comorbidity may first be forming. For example, whereas some behavioral genetics studies of twin pairs show little impact of shared genetic liability for internalizing symptoms and alcohol intoxication frequency in adolescence (Edwards, Larsson, Lichtenstein, & Kendler, 2011), other behavioral genetics work does indicate that depressive symptoms and alcohol use share both genetic and environmental influences that vary in strength over the course of development and perhaps across gender (Edwards et al., 2011). Candidate gene studies of adolescence are also starting to identify potential shared genetic liabilities such as the role of the dopamine receptor (D4) polymorphism in predicting co-occurring marijuana abuse and depressive symptoms in the Add Health study (Bobadilla, Vaske, & Asberg, 2013). A review of shared genetic and nongenetic influences on co-occurring internalizing symptoms and alcohol problem use in adolescence indicated that as many as seven allele variants had been implicated in this comorbidity (Saraceno, Munafo, Heron, Craddock, & van den Bree, 2009). However, none of these findings were consistently replicated in the literature, and studies showing both positive and negative results could be cited for each of these variants. The current state of affairs provides consensus merely on the complexity of shared liabilities that may occur under comorbid internalizing and alcohol use problems. However, there is some promise that this may be a fruitful avenue for future research as studies begin to consider the complex underpinnings of dynamic gene–environment influences over development on the relation between internalizing symptoms and alcohol-related problems.

Following from these studies and the broader literature, we articulate an internalizing pathway likely to lead to negative affect AUDs, emphasizing what may be unique indicators of this pathway rather than indicators of early emerging risk for AUDs more generally (see Figure 15.1; Hussong et al., 2011). Specifically, we posit that the risk processes underlying the internalizing pathway are unique in that this pathway (a) emphasizes problems with emotion regulation as central to early risk for AUDs, (b) defines self-medication as a central process translating deficits in emotion regulation into alcohol-related behaviors and risk for addiction specifically, and (c) focuses on the negative affect form of AUDs as a salient outcome. With these emphases, the internalizing pathway defines markers of developmental progression along a trajectory to AUDs.

Beginning in Infancy

Based on theories of emotion regulation and internalizing disorders in young children and developmental formulations of AUDs (Fox, Henderson, Marshall, Nichols, & Ghera, 2005; Kagan, Reznick, & Gibbons, 1989; Rubin & Mills, 1991; Tarter et al., 1999), we posit that this pathway first manifests in infancy as a *behaviorally inhibited* temperament. Behavioral inhibition has been defined as "a restrained, cautious, avoidant reaction to unfamiliar persons, objects, events, or places" (p. 163;

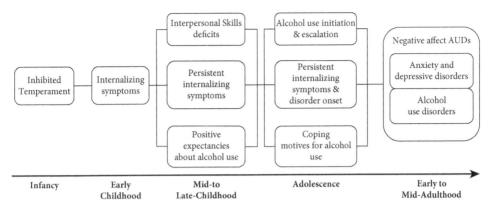

Figure 15.1 Internalizing pathway to negative affect alcohol use disorders. This pathway identifies markers of a risk process leading to negative affect alcohol use disorders, but it does not claim that this is the only pathway through which negative affect alcohol use disorders may be manifested. *Source*: Figure adapted from Hussong, Jones, Stein, Baucom, and Boeding (2011).

Kagan, 2008) and is considered an enduring, biologically mediated feature of temperament. Previous studies show a consistent link between behavioral inhibition in infancy and increased internalizing symptoms during childhood (Colder, Mott, & Berman, 2002; Eisenberg, Spinrad, & Eggum, 2010).

Studies showing that these early temperament markers predict later alcohol use further support the salience of early behavioral inhibition for the internalizing pathway to AUDs. For example, Caspi et al. (1996) found that inhibited (fearful, shy, and easily upset) 3-year-olds, compared to their peers, had higher rates of depression and, for boys, alcohol-related problems at age 21. Other studies also provide some support that indices of internalizing behavior between ages 3 and 10 are predictive of more alcohol-related problems and disorder in midadolescence to early adulthood (for review, see Zucker, 2006).

Obviously, not all behaviorally inhibited infants will progress toward alcohol use and eventual disorder. Rather, we expect that progression involves the emergence of internalizing symptoms in the preschool and early childhood years. Stable behavioral inhibition over time, particularly when paired with physiological indices of fear responses to novel stimuli, increases subsequent risk for internalizing symptoms (particularly anxiety but also depression) in childhood (Gladstone & Parker, 2006; Hirshfeld, Rosenbaum, Biederman, & Bolduc, 1992; Kagan, Snidman, Zentner, & Peterson, 1999). Thus, we posit that the early stages of the internalizing pathway to AUDs are marked by behavioral inhibition and emerging internalizing symptoms from infancy into early childhood.[2]

Early to Mid-Childhood

A growing literature identifies the concomitants of internalizing symptoms in early childhood (Graber & Sontag, 2009; Rubin & Mills, 1991). Notably, the social reticence accompanying behavioral inhibition in toddlers is associated with risk for peer rejection and self-perceptions of lower social competence in early childhood, particularly in girls (Nelson, Rubin, & Fox, 2005).[3] These temperament and social factors then set the stage for a self-defeating cognitive style about social events that further exacerbates risk for internalizing symptoms and leads to social withdrawal (see Abela & Hankin, 2008, for a review). As such, behaviorally inhibited infants are at a greater risk for *internalizing symptoms* as toddlers, which in turn increases their risk for social withdrawal and other forms of *interpersonal skill deficits* at the point of school entry.

Many of these concomitants are consistent with early risk markers for eventual alcohol use in adolescence, particularly those that indicate continued and even escalating problems with emotional and social adjustment. Challenges associated with social interaction in children with greater internalizing symptoms over time predict greater social rejection and isolation as they progress through the school years (Lillehoj, Trudeau, Spoth, & Wickrama, 2004). Although the relation between social withdrawal in early childhood and later alcohol use has not been directly explored in the literature, peer rejection in the grade school years is associated with later internalizing (as well as externalizing) symptoms in adolescence (Coie, Lochman, Terry, & Hyman, 1992). Moreover, the early emerging sociocognitive processing style associated with internalizing symptoms and social withdrawal may further entrench and even exacerbate risk for increasing internalizing symptoms through the middle childhood years. Based on these findings, we posit that early manifestations of the internalizing pathway to AUDs include high behavioral inhibition (in infancy), elevated internalizing symptoms (including both anxiety and depression, emerging with toddlerhood), and subsequent increases in peer rejection, social withdrawal, and disengagement (exacerbated at school entry).

Late Childhood and Adolescence

We expect that development toward negative affect AUDs more specifically, rather than AUDs more generally, occurs during late childhood and is marked by three factors, namely positive *expectations* for the effects of alcohol use, *interpersonal skill deficits* that lead to associations with deviant peers or to social withdrawal and the desire to self-medicate, and *coping motives* for substance use. The first of these indices concerns the growing expectation that alcohol use will reduce distress associated with internalizing symptoms. Although younger children generally endorse more beliefs about the undesirable than desirable or enhancing effects of alcohol, this balance of positive to negative beliefs changes both with age and drinking experience (Dunn & Goldman, 1998; O'Connor, Fite, Nowlin, & Colder, 2007). However, some youth indicate that they hold such tension reduction or coping expectations for alcohol use even as they enter adolescence (as consistent with evidence in Colder, Chassin, Stice, & Curran, 1997, and Cooper, Frone, Russell, & Mudar, 1995). Such beliefs, as with any positive expectation for drinking, are predictive of greater alcohol use in adolescence (Reese, Chassin, & Molina, 1994). Thus, the development of such positive expectancies for alcohol use, particularly for the reduction of negative affect, is posited to partially mediate the relation between early childhood internalizing symptoms and subsequent risk for alcohol use.

A second factor indicating progression along the internalizing pathway to AUDs during middle childhood and adolescence is interpersonal skill deficits. Specifically, the extent to which youth act upon their positive expectation about the effects of drinking by initiating and escalating alcohol use may in part be driven by their social context. Adolescents who are relatively more withdrawn or disengaged from their peers (perhaps as a function of prolonged internalizing symptoms) may actually initiate alcohol use somewhat later than their peers.

Consistent with this possibility are findings from Kaplow et al. (2001) showing that young teens with a separation anxiety disorder (often linked to lower peer interaction) delayed the onset of alcohol use compared to their peers, whereas teens with a generalized anxiety disorder (which may not pull youth out of a peer context) had an earlier onset of alcohol use. As such, social withdrawal may act to delay the onset of alcohol use into adolescence, given that many opportunities for alcohol use occur within a peer setting (Hussong, 2000).

Although social withdrawal could delay the onset of alcohol use, it may not decrease the overall risk for alcohol involvement by late adolescence. Motivated, distressed youth may instead find avenues for accessing and using alcohol. Adolescents who drink alone may indeed eventually show increased risk for AUDs because drinking alone in adolescence is associated with the motive of self-medication, or drinking to relieve stress, and with a greater risk for alcohol-related problems (Cooper, 1994; Cooper, Russell, Skinner, & Windle, 1992). Moreover, by late adolescence, social anxiety predicts greater risk for drinking, particularly heavy drinking (Sher, Grekin, & Gross, 2007).

These effects of social withdrawal may apply to just a subset of youth because not all teens with a history of internalizing symptoms will withdraw from their peers. Yet a history of internalizing symptoms may still leave children progressing along the internalizing pathway with the interpersonal skills deficits that they bring into adolescence. Rather than leading to social withdrawal, these interpersonal deficits may simply steer some youth away from mainstream peer associations, leaving them to find acceptance with more deviant peers. Due to shifting peer contexts, opportunities for social interaction in marginalized groups of peers engaging in deviant behavior provide these socially awkward youth with peer acceptance. At the same time, such groups increase risk for engaging in deviant activities, such as alcohol use (as articulated by self-derogation theory [Kaplan, 1980] and social context theory [Dishion, Duncan, Eddy, & Fagot, 1994]). For most youth, then, we expect to see the onset of drinking by midadolescence as social opportunities supportive of use expand and rates of depression are maintained (for boys) or increase (for girls; Angold, Costello, & Goodyer, 2001).

A third factor impacting whether adolescents progress along the internalizing pathway to AUDs is drinking motives. Specifically, adolescents following the internalizing pathway to AUDs may develop strong motives to drink as a means of coping or reducing tension. Such motives may emerge from earlier coping expectancies for alcohol use (Kuntsche, Knibbe, Engels, & Gmel, 2007). Two factors may in part impact the strength of these motives. First, coping motives are associated with internalizing symptoms (Rafnsson, Jonsson, & Windle, 2006; Tubman, Wagner, & Langer, 2003), and a long history of internalizing symptoms may underlie these motives in youth traveling the internalizing pathway and seeking to mitigate continued distress. Second, deviant peer groups may also reinforce these motives, given evidence for the social transmission and reinforcement of not only alcohol use but also coping motives associated with heavy drinking (Hussong, 2003).

Importantly, such coping motives for drinking predict a more problematic course of alcohol use in general (Carpenter & Hasin, 1999; Cooper et al., 1995). With progression from drinking to addiction, self-medication may be primarily motivated by the desire to avoid withdrawal (particularly the affective symptoms of withdrawal). In a reformulation of the classic negative reinforcement model, Baker and colleagues (Baker, Piper, McCarthy, Majeskie, & Fiore, 2004; McCarthy et al., 2010) offer three stipulations that account for inconsistent findings pertaining to this model of alcohol use. First, they state that the primary motive for substance use, including alcohol, is escape from these affective components of withdrawal. Second, motivation to use alcohol may occur outside of awareness and relate to interoceptive cues that precede affective symptoms of withdrawal. As such, salient cues for alcohol use may actually precede awareness of negative affect and internalizing symptoms but nonetheless remain linked to the anticipation of negative affect. And, third, such negative reinforcement learning may then generalize to other aversive states that are unrelated to withdrawal. These processes indicate how the relation between affective and alcohol use disorders may become entrenched, such that the two become interdependent in a single addictive cycle. Thus, with adolescence, we posit that progression along the internalizing pathway is marked by (a) increasing coping expectancies and motives for alcohol use, (b) initiation of use either with the goal of self-medication by drinking alone and/or with the goal of peer acceptance by drinking with deviant peers, and (c) escalation in use to AUDs in adulthood to the point of addiction. Collectively, these processes define an internalizing pathway that emerges at birth and continues, given supportive risk mechanisms, into adulthood. The markers of progression along this pathway emphasize internalizing symptoms and emotion regulation as related, eventually, to AUDs.

Extending the Internalizing Pathway to Other Substance Use Disorders

Fewer studies examine the associations between early risk markers in the internalizing pathway and drugs of abuse other than alcohol, likely due at least in part to its relatively wide availability for youth relative to other substances (e.g., Johnston, O'Malley, Miech, Bachman, & Schulenberg, 2014; SAMHSA, 2004). With that caveat in mind, we posit that the internalizing pathway likely also predicts drug use and disorder more broadly. Rigorous analyses testing the prospective prediction of various forms of substance use from early indicators of emotion regulation and internalizing symptoms are few, although existing studies indicate that this association may prove to be complex. For example, Ensminger, Juon, and Fothergill (2002) showed that first-grade boys classified as shy and aggressive had higher rates of marijuana and cocaine use in adulthood (age 32) than did their peers, though shyness alone did not predict these risk outcomes, and for women being a shy first-grader lowered risk for marijuana use in adulthood. Shedler and Block (1990) also showed that adolescents (age 18) classified as frequent users on a substance use index had more symptoms of emotional distress in childhood (ages 7 and 11) than did adolescents classified as experimenters, although adolescent abstainers also showed higher rates of inhibition, shyness, and anxious traits than did experimenters. (However, others do not replicate the finding of greater negative affect in abstainers than in experimenters; Tucker, Ellickson, Collins, & Klein, 2006). These findings indicate that inhibition and internalizing symptoms may play a role in early risk for later drug use, but the nature of this role, particularly relative to externalizing symptoms, remains unclear.

Colder, Chassin, Lee, and Villalta (2010) provide two ways of conceptualizing the relation between affective risk processes and substance use given heterogeneity in substance use behaviors. First, negative affect may be more strongly associated with substance use that reflects more problematic or severe forms of use. Although inconsistent, findings from studies of the predictors of drug use stages often find that early stages of use (i.e., initiation and experimentation) are unrelated or only weakly related to negative affect, whereas later stages of use are more strongly associated with affective predictors. Second, the relation between negative affect and substance use may depend on the class of drugs used, particularly the extent to which the drug is reinforcing or effective when used to alleviate negative affect.

Consistent with these possibilities, our own work shows differential prediction of drug use indicators by internalizing symptoms in adolescence. Using an integrative data analysis involving the simultaneous study of three longitudinal, community-based samples of children of alcoholic parents and matched controls (Curran & Hussong, 2009), we examined the unique and interactive effects of internalizing and externalizing symptoms in predicting alcohol use, heavy alcohol use, marijuana use, and other drug use between the ages of 11 and 22. Results replicate previous studies showing strong and consistent unique effects of externalizing symptoms, predicting both who is likely to use substances (i.e., between-person effects for all four substance use outcomes) as well as when youth are likely to use substances (i.e., within-person effects showing greater use of all four substances in years when youth show elevated externalizing symptoms). Internalizing symptoms also uniquely predicted both who used substances and when substance use occurred, but only for the use of drugs and not for alcohol or marijuana use. Thus, internalizing symptoms were a unique predictor only of more severe forms of substance use, after controlling for externalizing symptoms. These findings, however, do not distinguish between drugs of abuse relative to their anticipated ability to reduce negative affect, nor do they distinguish stages of use. These findings also do not define risk related to internalizing symptoms via a developmental pathway, as proposed here. Future research is needed to further explore these associations in analyses that consider differences among drugs related to their pharmacology and likelihood to provide reinforcement for use as a means of alleviating negative affect.

The Salience of the Internalizing Pathway for Children of Alcoholics

Although we believe that the internalizing pathway will be relevant for understanding processes leading to SUDs in a broad array of adolescents, we also believe that this pathway may be most evident within an established high-risk population, namely children of alcoholic parents (COAs).[4] COAs are among the highest risk groups for evidencing alcohol and other substance use disorders

(e.g., Chassin, Pitts, DeLucia, & Todd, 1999; Sher, 1991). COAs initiate substance use earlier, increase their rates of use more quickly, and show a faster escalation from initiation to AUDs than do children of nonalcoholic parents (Chassin, Curran, Hussong, & Colder, 1996; Chassin et al., 1999; Hussong, Bauer, & Chassin, 2008). Most notably, COAs show a substantially greater risk for alcohol and drug use disorders in young adulthood. By young adulthood, 53% of COAs evidence an AUD as compared to 25% of non-COAs (Chassin et al., 1999). Moreover, rates of drug abuse, mood, and anxiety disorders are approximately 21%, 24%, and 25% among COAs compared to 9%, 12%, and 18% among their peers, respectively.

We expect that COAs are particularly vulnerable to the internalizing pathway because they show elevated rates of all internalizing pathway indicators across development as compared to their peers. This is first evident with increased rates of difficult temperament (including behavioral inhibition) and internalizing symptoms in early childhood (Edwards, Leonard, & Das Eiden, 2001; Jansen, Fitzgerald, Ham, & Zucker, 1995). Although most studies rely on parental report to show this risk, observer ratings of child behavior also show greater behavioral inhibition among COAs than among their peers (Hill, Lowers, Locke, Snidman, & Kagan, 1999). Findings from observational ratings strengthen this conclusion because they indicate that parents from alcoholic families are not simply overreporting their children's behavioral inhibition, as might be hypothesized based on findings of biased parental reports of child behavior associated with other forms of parent psychopathology (e.g., Forehand et al., 1988).

This early childhood risk is evident among those children who experienced prenatal exposure to alcohol, tobacco, or other drugs, and the subsequent challenges associated with fetal alcohol effects/syndrome (Kodituwakku, Kalberg, & May, 2001; Streissguth et al., 2004; Testa, Quigley, & Eiden, 2003). However, research also shows an early pattern of risk behavior in young children of alcoholic parents who avoided prenatal exposure for their children. For example, analyses of two community samples showed that COAs (without prenatal exposure) began to evidence elevated internalizing symptoms and externalizing symptoms as early as age 2, with risk for symptomatology remaining high and stable into adulthood (Hussong et al., 2007; Hussong, Flora, Curran, Chassin, & Zucker, 2008). This same risk for greater internalizing symptoms is particularly marked in children of depressed and alcoholic parents (i.e., negative affect alcoholism) versus children of alcoholic parents without depression and children of nonalcoholic parents (Hussong et al., 2008).

We also have some evidence that COAs may show social deficits in comparison to their peers, although available research is sparse. COAs show higher rates of problems in school (e.g., poorer academic performance; McGrath, Watson, & Chassin, 1999) and in their peer relationships (e.g., lower rates of social competence and greater peer bullying in childhood, and greater risk of deviant peer affiliations in adolescence; Chassin et al., 1996; Eiden, Colder, Edwards, & Leonard, 2009; Eiden et al., 2010; Hussong, Zucker, Wong, Fitzgerald, & Puttler, 2005). Although whether COAs are more socially withdrawn in particular has not been examined in childhood, we expect that the effect of social withdrawal on risk for alcohol use may differ for these youth. Whereas social withdrawal may protect many youth from drinking because most adolescent alcohol use takes place within a peer context, this may not be true for socially withdrawn COAs who have easier access to alcohol in the home. Consistent with this hypothesis, COAs report drinking alone more frequently than do their peers (Chalder, Elgar, & Bennett, 2006).

Cognitive risk factors (i.e., expectations and motives) among children are also associated with parent alcoholism. Positive beliefs about drinking are stronger in children of alcoholic fathers (Colder et al., 1997) and may indeed mediate COAs' risk for substance involvement (Brown, Tate, Vik, Haas, & Aarons, 1999, though also see Colder et al., 1997). Moreover, tension reduction expectancies and motives are more strongly related to drinking among high school students from alcoholic versus nonalcoholic families (Mann, Chassin, & Sher, 1987).

These cognitions may be elevated in COAs due to their experiences with alcohol use. In alcohol challenge studies of young adults, COAs show a greater stress dampening response as a result of drinking than do their peers. That is, COAs experience greater reductions than do children of nonalcoholic parents in their physiological stress response when they use alcohol (particularly when they use heavily) in anticipation of stress versus when they remain sober in the same situations (Sher & Levenson, 1982; Sher et al., 2007). Alcohol, in particular, may then be a more effective short-term coping strategy for COAs, and this may in turn increase their coping motives for drinking.

In sum, we expect COAs to be a vulnerable risk group for processes outlined in the internalizing pathway to SUDs. Parent alcoholism is a broad risk factor for elevations in internalizing pathway markers, including early behavioral inhibition, internalizing symptoms, tension reduction expectancies, coping motives, negative affect disorders, SUDs, and to some extent interpersonal skills. Moreover, children of parents with negative affect alcoholism could show a specific vulnerability for this pathway given their increased risk for internalizing symptoms and depression/anxiety associated with parental depression (Hammen, 2009). The extent to which this form of parent alcoholism is particularly predictive of risk associated with the internalizing pathway, however, remains unexamined.

Early Emerging Risk Processes Associated With the Internalizing Pathway to Substance Use Disorders

Although individuals may evidence risk for SUDs associated with the internalizing pathway at any point over development, we posit that early childhood (between the ages of 2 and 5) is a potentially critical entry point for several reasons. First, the development of emotion regulation is a focal task of early childhood emerging around age 2 and showing rapid development in the preschool years (Blair & Diamond, 2008; Bronson, 2000). Given that such behaviors are emerging at this age, we anticipate that associated risk behaviors may be more malleable prior to school entry, when systemic repercussions of such behaviors (i.e., labeling, teacher expectations) may also reinforce and make these behaviors more difficult to change (Haring, Lovett, Haney, & Algozzine, 1992; Thurlow & Gilman, 1999).

Second, early risk markers for SUDs are first evident in this age period (for review, see Zucker, 2006). Studies by Zucker and colleagues (Zucker, Chermack, & Curran, 2000) of high-risk youth show that internalizing symptoms in children as young as ages 3–5 years predict substance use in early adolescence. Evidence from a community-based sample also showed that inhibited (fearful, shy, and easily upset) 3-year-old boys (though not girls) had higher rates of alcohol-related problems at age 21 compared to their peers (Caspi, Moffitt, Newman, & Silva, 1996). Although the effects of these correlates of internalizing symptoms on later substance use are sometimes moderated by other factors (Ensminger, Juon, & Fothergill, 2002), an emerging pattern suggests that for some youth such symptoms are a reliable marker of risk for later substance use and disorder.

Finally, as compared with their peers, children with known risk factors for later SUDs, namely COAs, show deficits in emotion regulation, which may predate internalizing symptomatology, that emerge in this age period. For example, Eiden, Lewis, Croff, and Young (2002) found that COAs exhibit less adaptive and less effective emotion regulation strategies compared to children of non-substance-abusing parents. Thus, although early childhood is not the only developmental period in which risk for the internalizing pathway may emerge, we argue that this is an important time for examining whether potential deficits in emotion regulation are forming as core to risk for the internalizing pathway.

As we noted earlier, we rely here on Thompson's (1994) definition of emotion regulation, which is particularly appropriate for early childhood because it focuses on both intrinsic (i.e., child-driven) and extrinsic (i.e., environmentally structured) processes to control emotion in pursuit of goal-directed behavior. In the early years, many of the ways in which children experience emotion regulation is through the efforts of their parents (Calkins & Hill, 2007). Although this is not the only means of emotion regulation for young children, the role of extrinsic processes in regulating emotion continues through the preschool years despite the increasing demands on young children to develop intrinsic processes for regulation. Moreover, we posit that the interaction between these intrinsic and extrinsic regulatory processes makes a fundamental contribution to risk formation in the vulnerable population of COAs.

In the following section, we review two mechanisms that may contribute to risk associated with the internalizing pathway via compromised emotion regulation skills in COAs.[5] The first concerns the cascading effect of stress exposure in these young children's risk profiles, and the second concerns caregiving environments that fail to account for the needs of these children. Because we view these mechanisms as working interactively, our treatment of them as distinct in the sections that follow is somewhat false. However, the parsing of risk processes into these two dominant mechanisms has clinical value, particularly in that psychoeducational and psychological interventions currently available or in development may be matched to each.

Stress Exposure and Response

Classically, stress models confer risk for substance use and other forms of psychopathology via a stress-diathesis mechanism (Sapolsky, 2007). These launch models suggest that stress exposure is a static baseline risk factor that only results in impairment among those who possess some intrinsic vulnerability. Current developmental psychobiological models, however, define stress influences as more dynamic and likely to change not only with development but also with different patterns of stress exposure, caregiving support, and genetic vulnerability (Gunnar & Quevedo, 2007). Early trauma and chronic stress, in particular, are posited to inhibit neurogenesis, and frequent activation of the stress response will tax finite resources, increasing overall allostatic load and resulting in disruptions of neuronal plasticity and neurotoxicity. As such, early severe or chronic stress exposure impacts not only the immediate stress response but also future neurobiological stress responding such that organisms with early stress exposure are more vulnerable to the detrimental effects of later stress exposure, forming a negative feedback loop over development.

We posit that such dynamic neurobiological models of the stress response are relevant for understanding the internalizing pathway to SUDs and, in particular, the development of poor emotion regulation during early childhood among COAs. Here, we invoke several lines of research showing that (a) parent alcoholism is associated with greater stress exposure, (b) increased stress exposure in young children has physiological implications for later stress responding and, in turn, emotion regulation, and (c) greater stress exposure also has psychological implications for children leading to emotional insecurity that impacts multiple aspects of functioning, including emotion regulation. Moreover, we expect that these stress-related mechanisms are particularly relevant for the internalizing pathway among COAs given (d) their altered stress responding and (e) susceptibility for stress response–dampening effects that reinforce the use of alcohol to cope with distress later in adolescence and young adulthood.

Across the first three decades of life, COAs differ from their peers in the greater number of life stressors they experience, particularly in the family domain (Hussong et al., 2008). These family-related stressors may come directly from the child's exposure to the alcoholic parent when she or he is impaired (e.g., violence, conflict, failure to fill expectations or role obligations), or they may be indirect (e.g., hearing others say bad things about the parent). Moreover, these stressors include crises related to the impaired parent's drinking episodes, which create both discrete stressors but also serve to disrupt the rituals and patterns that otherwise comprise family life. Alcoholic families that are able to maintain rituals (i.e., observing birthdays and holidays, eating evening meals together) have shown more positive outcomes than those for whom such rituals are disrupted (Wolin & Bennett, 1984). Previous studies show that COAs perceive the stressors they experience as more severe, even after controlling for the overall number of stressors experienced (Hussong et al., 2008). One possible explanation for this effect is that COAs may develop an altered stress response due to early and repeated exposure to stressors. Two such stressors that may be particularly important in this regard are child maltreatment and intense family conflict.

Although the specific level of risk varies to some extent across studies, research convincingly suggests that COAs are overrepresented in statistics on maltreatment, including physical, psychological, and sexual abuse, as well as neglect and witnessed violence (e.g., Besinger, Garland, Litrownik, & Landsverk, 1999; Freisthler, Holmes, & Wolf, 2014; Harrington, Dubowitz, Black, & Binder, 1995; Thomas, Leicht, Hughes, Madigan, & Dowell, 2003; Turner, Finkelhor, Hamby, & Shattuck, 2013; Walsh, MacMillan, & Jamieson, 2003). Studies estimate that between 10% and 20% of child maltreatment cases involve children of substance-abusing parents, with some estimates as high as 80% (US DHHS, 2012; also see Young, Boles, & Otero, 2007, for a review). Importantly, the wide range of estimates is likely the result of variations in whether and, if so, how states gather and use parental substance use data, as well as difficulties in disentangling the link between parental substance use and other co-occurring risk factors for child maltreatment, including poverty, overcrowding, other parental psychiatric issues, and health problems (see Krug, Dahlberg, Mercy, Zwi, & Lozano, 2002, for a review). Moreover, COAs are 2.7 times more likely to be physically or sexually abused and 4.2 times more likely to be neglected than children who do not live with a substance-abusing parent (Kelleher, Chaffin, Hollenberg, & Fischer, 1994; NCASA, 1999). Substance-abusing parents are also at greater risk for multiple child maltreatment allegations, being more likely than other parents to have a second child maltreatment report filed against them (Murphy, Jellinek, Quinn,

& Smith, 1991; Wolock & Magura, 1996), particularly parents of young children (Murphy et al., 1991; Wolock & Magura, 1996).

In addition to increasing the risk for maltreatment, substance use may also affect children's response to maltreatment experiences. For example, maltreated youth with substance-using parents demonstrate lower levels of resilience than youth with non-substance-using parents, particularly in those families in which substance use co-occurs with other risk factors like neighborhood crime (Jaffee, Caspi, Moffitt, Polo-Tomas, & Taylor, 2007). Beyond psychosocial outcomes, relatively recent data suggest that maltreated children with substance-abusing parents are also more likely than their peers to experience a maltreatment fatality (Douglas, 2013).

A growing literature documents the long-term deleterious effects of early maltreatment (and other forms of stress exposure) on the development of the neurobiological stress response (Gunnar & Quevedo, 2007). The nature of these changes is complex but may be profound, leading to prolonged dysregulation of the HPA axis that can be a risk factor for later psychiatric symptoms (McCrory, De Brito, & Viding, 2010). Research on the negative cascading effects of early stress exposure indicates that negative life stressors in young children can heighten subsequent stress reactivity to future life stressors, with this negative escalating cycle between neurobiological responsivity and environmental insult continuing into the adolescent years (Gunnar & Quevedo, 2007).

Studies of maltreatment specifically indicate that early experiences of abuse and neglect predict later neurobiological dysregulation, particularly LHPA dysregulation. However, whether reported dysregulation reflects a hypo- or hyperactive stress response varies across studies. As noted by Tarullo and Gunnar (2006), perhaps the most consistent findings are that maltreated children with internalizing problems have elevated morning basal cortisol, whereas adults who were maltreated as children (regardless of internalizing problems) often show low basal cortisol and elevated ACTH responses to psychological stressors. DeBellis (2001, 2002, for reviews) posits that cortisol levels that have been elevated for an extended period of time following trauma may result in downregulation of the HPA axis and, in turn, low cortisol levels. These stress responses reflect adaptation over time to a chronic stress or traumatic environment. Consistent with this theory, other studies of maltreatment and the

HPA axis find that participants exposed to stress have a blunted HPA response (e.g., Lovallo, Farag, Sorocco, Cohoon, & Vincent, 2012; MacMillan et al., 2009; Moss, Vanyukov, Yao, & Kirillova, 1999). Although some have suggested a blunted HPA response is due to comorbid psychiatric conditions that are associated with trauma exposure, a recent study by Lovallo and colleagues (2012) found that a greater number of traumatic stressors predicted a blunted HPA response in participants with no psychiatric diagnoses. Thus, despite the notable consensus regarding the dysregulating impact of trauma and chronic stress exposure on the neurobiological stress response, there is clearly less consensus regarding the mechanisms mediating the relation between stress and later adjustment problems (McCrory et al., 2010).

In addition to maltreatment, family conflict and violence have been associated with an increased stress response in studies of the emotional security hypothesis (offered by Davies & Cummings, 1994). This hypothesis posits that conflict within the family disrupts a child's most basic sense of individual and familial safety. Emotional insecurity is characterized by disruptions in children's feelings (e.g., anxiety, hypervigilance, sadness), behaviors (e.g., inappropriate attempts to regulate family arguments), and cognitions (e.g., skewed views of dangers within relationships; see Cummings & Davies, 2002; El-Sheikh, 2005, for reviews). In turn, prolonged and repeated exposure to marital conflict has been shown to effectively sensitize or increase children's behavioral and emotional reactivity to conflict in particular, as well as other stressors more generally (e.g., Cummings, 1998; Cummings & Davies, 2002). To date, well-established stress responses, including vagal tone, electrodermal responding, cortisol levels, and actigraphic measures of sleep, have all been shown to be compromised in children exposed to high levels of marital conflict (e.g., El-Sheikh, Keller, & Erath, 2007; El-Sheikh, 2005; Pendry & Adam, 2007). Over the long term, children exposed to higher levels of conflict between their parents are also more likely to evidence a relatively wide range of adjustment difficulties, including behavioral, emotional, cognitive, and sleep problems (e.g., Davies, Forman, Rasi, & Stevens, 2002; El-Sheikh, Harger, & Whitson, 2001).

Initial evidence supports the core prediction of the emotional security hypothesis relative to parent alcohol use such that family functioning (and marital interactions in particular) mediates the association between parental drinking and children's adjustment (El-Sheikh & Flanagan, 2001; Keller, Cummings, Davies, & Mitchell, 2008). For example, Keller, Gilbert, Koss, Cummings, and Davies (2011) showed that greater marital conflict mediated the association between parental problem drinking and children's negative emotional reactions (i.e., sad and anger reactions and negative expectations about the future) in a community sample of kindergarten children. More generally, chaotic home environments characterized by family stress and conflict have been found to directly impact children's emotion regulation abilities (El-Sheikh & Cummings, 1997). In addition, Cummings and Davies (1992, 1999) have used the emotional security hypothesis to characterize the impact of parental depression on children. The parenting style of depressed parents has been characterized by a lack of responsiveness, cooperation, and reciprocity, the same style that has been shown to interfere with the development of children's ability to self-regulate (Cummings, 1995). Not surprisingly, children of depressed parents experience a range of both internalizing and externalizing difficulties, which can be accounted for, at least in part, by emotional insecurity (e.g., Kouros, Merrilees, & Cummings, 2008). Cummings and colleagues (Kouros et al., 2008) found that children are most vulnerable to emotional insecurity associated with marital conflict in homes characterized by higher levels of parental depression. This model affords an ideal framework for conceptualizing how parental behaviors associated with alcohol use, including compromises in marital conflict, family violence, and maltreatment, may disrupt a child's most basic sense of safety and related stress responding.

The effects of these stressors on COAs specifically are speculative. Similar to the literature on the effects of maltreatment on neurobiology, studies of COAs provide some evidence of hypoactivity in LHPA response more generally for older youth and adults, but these results remain inconsistent. For example, when compared to those without a family history of addiction, both adolescents and adults with a positive family history demonstrate a persistent blunted stress response as measured by a lower cortical response to stressful events (Moss et al., 1995), lower basal ACTH plasma levels (Dai, Thavundayil, & Gianoulakis, 2002, Dai, Thavundayil, Santella, & Gianoulakis, 2007), and a smaller skin conductance response to a tone signaling delivery of an electric shock (Finn, Kessler, & Hussong, 1994). In a series of studies, Moss and colleagues (1999) attempted to disentangle chronic stress and genetic risk associated with family history of alcoholism as contributing factors to HPA dysregulation among COAs by examining whether the timing of the father's alcohol symptoms impacted child outcomes. They provide the following intriguing hypothesis that critical developmental periods govern when particular genetic or environmental factors are most influential in determining adverse outcomes. Specifically, these authors speculate that between the ages of 3 and 6 years the relation between paternal substance abuse and children's stress reactivity peaks. Summarizing their supportive data, they state that:

> prepubertal sons of fathers whose substance use disorders cease prior to the child's sixth year do not differ significantly in terms of externalizing and internalizing psychopathology from boys whose fathers never met diagnostic criteria for SUD [. . .]; however, when a paternal SUD extended into the child's sixth year, there was a significant increase in the boys' internalizing and externalizing problem behaviors. We now show that the offset of a paternal substance use disorder between the sons' ages of 3–6 years is associated with markedly diminished anticipatory cortisol stress reactivity between ages 10 and 12 years. Curiously, we have previously noted an association between internalizing and externalizing problem behavioral disposition and the salivary cortisol reactivity in anticipation to a stressor [. . .]. Thus, the sensitive period for cortisol reactivity formation may overlap with the sensitive period for the emergence of problem behaviors, and the significant environment stress of parental substance abuse may be a common factor (pp. 1297–1298).

DeBellis (2002) extends this link between environmental stress, physiological stress responding, and problem behavior in development. He underscores that dysregulation in the major biological stress response systems associated with childhood trauma and maltreatment have adverse influences on brain development that enhance vulnerability to later psychopathology, including posttraumatic stress disorder and depression, that precedes alcohol and substance use disorders. Given the heightened risk for trauma faced by COAs, altered stress regulatory responses early in development may indeed be one component of their elevated risk for SUDs as associated with the internalizing pathway.

Moreover, a consistent finding in adolescence and young adulthood is that alcohol serves to more strongly dampen peripheral indicators of physiological reactivity (e.g., heart rate, cortisol, prolactin) in response to stress among COAs as compared with their peers (Croissant, Demmel, Rist, & Olbrich, 2008; Finn, Earleywine, & Pihl, 1992; Sher & Levenson, 1982; Zimmermann et al., 2009). Indeed, studies of young adult men show that those from families with alcoholic fathers show greater stress reactivity in the absence of alcohol than do their peers (Finn et al., 1992). In turn, these heightened stress-dampening effects are more likely to occur only at high levels of drinking (Stewart, Finn, & Pihl, 1992), increasing risk for alcohol-related problems and disorder.

In sum, COAs show greater risk for negative life events that emanate from the family across the early life span (Hussong et al., 2008). In turn, these negative life events mediate the relation between parent alcoholism and children's internalizing symptoms and substance involvement (Chassin et al., 1996). Two of these stressors likely include child maltreatment and family violence and conflict. This stress exposure has implications for the development of neurobiological systems associated with future responses to stress (Gunnar & Quevedo, 2007) and for the development of emotional security in children (Cummings & Davies, 2010), both of which impact emotion regulation. The impact of early stressors and family conflict may be heightened among COAs due to increased exposure (Chassin, Pillow, Curran, Molina, & Barrera, 1993), less effective coping skills (Hussong & Chassin, 2004), and deficits in social competence and thus social resources (Hussong et al., 2005). Moreover, due to their greater susceptibility to the stress response–dampening effects of alcohol, COAs may be more likely to use substances as a means of coping with stress later in adolescence and adulthood.

The Caregiving Environment

Effective emotion regulation in children depends in part on a biological predisposition to functional regulatory capabilities but also on the extent to which the environment supports the development of adaptive regulation skills (Thompson, Lewis, & Calkins, 2008). In early childhood, the caregiving environment plays a fundamental role in supporting the development of emotion regulation (Calkins & Hill, 2007). Although there are many ways to characterize the nature of the early caregiving environment (Cox & Paley, 2003), we highlight two aspects of this environment that are posited to be particularly important for nurturing adaptive emotion regulation. These include parenting behaviors that promote a healthy parent–child attachment system more broadly (i.e., responsivity or sensitivity) as well as parenting that is specific to the socialization of emotion in children (i.e., parent emotion socialization). Although the two sets of parenting behaviors are related, the former refers to a more general style of parent–child interaction, whereas the latter is focused on how parents interact with their children specifically around the issue of emotion.

We posit that both responsive parenting styles and the specific ways in which parents socialize their children about emotion are relevant for understanding the internalizing pathway to SUDs and in particular the development of poor emotion regulation during early childhood among COAs. Here, we invoke several lines of research showing that (a) failure to develop secure attachments accounts for part of the association between insensitive parenting in early childhood and poor emotion regulation, (b) styles of parent emotion socialization that dismiss emotion rather than coach children in how to handle their emotions also predict poor emotion regulation, and (c) parent alcoholism is associated with both insecure attachments and insensitive parenting in early childhood. And, although limited work has considered parent alcoholism per se, (d) parent psychopathology is related to parent emotion socialization practices that are associated with poor child emotion regulation. Moreover, (e) initial evidence suggests that problematic parent emotion socialization is associated with greater risk for negative affect-cued drinking in adolescence.

Attachment theory posits that infants obtain an understanding of the world and what to expect from their relationships with others based on whether their caregivers are consistent, sensitive, and responsive to their needs (Ainsworth, 1979). Attachment styles reflect the nature of the parent–child relationship and are considered to be secure (i.e., children seek comfort from caregivers and respond positively when reunited with caregivers after a separation) or insecure (i.e., children may show no distress when caregivers leave and may show ambivalence or indifference when reunited with caregivers), and these patterns of behavior are evident in early childhood. Secure attachments are associated with a variety of positive outcomes for children, including the healthy development of emotion regulation (Brumariu, Kerns, & Seibert, 2012; Morris, Silk, Steinberg, Myers, & Robinson, 2007; Thompson, 2008). Thus, parenting that is sensitive and responsive to children's needs is linked to secure parent–child relationships that, in turn, predict adaptive emotion regulation (Calkins & Leerkes, 2011).

Alternatively, caregiving environments that are not characterized by appropriate titrations of sensitivity and responsivity have been associated with insecure attachment and decreased emotion regulation abilities in offspring (Leerkes & Wong, 2012). Some of the negative parenting behaviors demonstrated by caregivers who develop insecure caregiver–child relationships have also been documented in families of children with internalizing symptoms; similarities include high levels of negativity (i.e., criticism, hostility, harshness), detachment and withdrawal (i.e., lack of responsiveness or involvement), and control and conflict, as well as low levels of consistency or predictability and warmth (e.g., Brenning, Soenens, Braet, & Bal, 2012; Chorpita & Barlow, 1998; Garber & Horowitz, 2002; Ostrander & Herman, 2006). These negative parenting behaviors thus collectively increase risk for children's insecure attachment and poor emotion regulation in early childhood as well as internalizing symptoms as children mature.

These parenting behaviors could be particularly important for COAs who may receive less support for developing healthy emotion regulation strategies than do their peers. For example, alcoholic parents may engage in fewer behaviors that foster secure attachments in their children (Seifer et al., 2004). Previous studies show that parents who abuse substances are generally less engaged, less responsive, and exhibit less warmth, sensitivity, and encouragement while interacting with their children (e.g., Eiden, Edwards, & Leonard, 2002; Mayes & Bornstein, 1995; Salo & Flykt, 2013; Solis, Shadur, Burns, & Hussong, 2012), which compromises the extent to which they can support their children's regulation of emotion (Beeghly & Tronick, 1994). The direct effect that alcohol has on parents' functioning includes a compromised ability to attend to social cues, misattribution of children's behaviors (e.g., attributing negative intent), increased emotional arousal (Kerwin, 2005), and impaired memory and inhibition (Mayes & Bornstein, 1995), all of which may contribute to such compromised parenting behaviors. Current parental AUDs directly predict lower levels of parental warmth and sensitivity (Eiden, Edwards, & Leonard, 2004, 2007). These insensitive parenting styles are evident even in interactions with infants. For example, as compared to nonalcoholic fathers, alcoholic fathers' interactions with their infants are characterized by lower paternal sensitivity, responsiveness, positive affect, and verbalizations as well as higher negative affect and aggravation (Eiden, Chavez, & Leonard, 1999; Eiden & Leonard, 2000).

Clearly, parenting behaviors that lack supportiveness and sensitivity can compromise emotion regulation in COAs (e.g., Beeghly & Tronick, 1994). Importantly, such parenting behaviors have been shown to mediate the relations between parental alcohol problems and children's emotion regulation and attachment (Eiden et al., 2004, 2007; Seifer et al., 2004). In a longitudinal study, fathers' and mothers' sensitivity and warmth when their children were 2 years old was shown to mediate relations between fathers' AUDs when children were 12–18 months of age and children's self-regulation at 3 years of age (Eiden et al., 2004, 2007). Similar mediating effects were found among cocaine-exposed children, such that prenatal cocaine exposure predicted harsh maternal parenting behaviors at age 2, which, in turn, predicted poorer child self-regulation at age 3 (Eiden, Coles, Schuetze, & Colder, 2014). These findings emphasize the important role of the caregiving environment in linking parental AUDs and children's emotion regulation over time, though these behaviors are not necessarily specific to the context of emotions within the parent–child interaction.

A more specific parenting behavior that is likely to impact children's emotion regulation is parent emotion socialization. Parent emotion socialization broadly includes the ways in which parents explicitly and implicitly teach their children about if, when, and how it is appropriate to feel and express emotions, and how to manage or cope with emotions (Eisenberg, Cumberland, & Spinrad, 1998). Parents socialize their children around emotions in several key ways, including their reactions to their children's emotions, their own modeling of emotion and regulation, awareness and acceptance of emotions, and direct teaching about children's emotional expression (e.g., Eisenberg et al., 1998; Gottman, Katz, & Hooven, 1997). "Emotion-coaching" parents are aware of and accepting of children's emotions and respond supportively to children's expression of emotion through validation, teaching, and problem solving, whereas "emotion-dismissing" parents may minimize children's emotions and avoid teaching or problem solving around children's emotional experiences (Gottman et al., 1997). Parents' use of emotion-dismissing styles is associated with externalizing and internalizing symptoms (Lunkenheimer, Shields, & Cortina, 2007), whereas emotion-coaching styles are associated with more positive outcomes physically, socially, and academically (Gottman et al., 1997).

Parent emotion socialization practices may impact children's emotion regulation skills via their influence on children's regulatory functioning at a physiological level (Gottman, Katz, & Hooven, 1996). For example, children whose parents engage in emotion-coaching strategies have higher vagal tone (i.e., an indicator of more effective regulation; Gottman, 2001).

There is little empirical work that characterizes parent emotion socialization behaviors among substance-abusing parents or that examines the relation between parent emotion socialization and children's emotion regulation in substance-abusing families. Efforts to address these questions have been a focus of our work in which we found that the context of maternal drug use negatively impacted emotion socialization behaviors among mothers in addiction treatment (Shadur & Hussong, 2013). Specifically, mothers reported less supportive and less consistent emotion socialization practices during periods of problematic drug use compared to periods of sobriety. Moreover, we found support for cross-sectional mediation such that more severe impairment related to maternal drug use predicted higher levels of nonsupportive reactions to children's emotions, which, in turn, predicted poorer child emotion regulation.

Parent emotion socialization is an important predictor of children's emotion regulation in other at-risk samples as well, including low-income families (Brophy-Herb, Stansbury, Bocknek, & Horodynski, 2011), maltreated children (Shipman et al., 2007), and families impacted by maternal depression (Silk et al., 2011). Moreover, mothers who report physically abusing their children provide greater invalidating responses and fewer emotion-coaching behaviors in response to children's negative emotions compared to nonmaltreating mothers (Shipman et al., 2007; Shipman, Schneider, & Sims, 2005). Additionally, Garber and colleagues (Garber, Braafladt, & Zeman, 1991) demonstrated that depressed mothers responded to children's negative emotion with less supportive and problem-solving behaviors than nondepressed caregivers. Furthermore, mothers with a history of childhood-onset depression were more likely to respond to their young children's sadness, anger, and fear with neglect or punishment (behaviors that could be characterized as emotion dismissing) than mothers without such a history (Silk et al., 2011). Collectively, this work suggests that parent psychopathology is related to parent emotion socialization and, in turn, to emotion regulation.

Critical to the internalizing pathway, parent emotion socialization practices have also been shown to predict adolescent substance use as a means of coping with negative affect. In contrast to findings regarding symptomatology in younger children, Hersh and Hussong (2009) found that families characterized both by high levels of emotion-coaching and emotion-dismissing styles of parent emotion socialization, perhaps reflecting an overinvolved and critical interaction style, had adolescents who were more likely to use substances in a self-medicating manner. Although these findings are not based on an at-risk sample of COAs, these results suggest that parent emotion socialization practices can impact youth behaviors that are consistent with risk for progressing along the internalizing pathway.

In sum, COAs require unique coping efforts to achieve adaptive outcomes because they exhibit emotion regulation deficits and also face the unpredictable and uncontrollable nature of the stressor presented by having an alcoholic parent. Learning how to tailor emotion regulatory strategies to these complex and challenging stressors then creates a greater need for extrinsic regulatory processes. Despite this increased need, substance-abusing parents show compromised parenting behaviors that impact the security of the attachment relationship and negatively impact child emotion regulation. In addition to the impact of parenting deficits more broadly, specific emotion socialization practices have been associated with emotion regulation difficulties in children of substance-abusing parents. Trends from other at-risk families (i.e., parents who have experienced depression and who have maltreated their children) also suggest that parent psychopathology is related to parent emotion socialization practices that are associated with poor child emotion regulation. Finally, initial evidence suggests that problematic parent emotion socialization is associated with greater risk for negative affect-cued drinking in adolescence.

Implications and Future Directions

We have described an internalizing pathway that may be particularly applicable for understanding risk for SUDs associated with parent alcoholism, with early exposure to stress and impoverished child care environments serving to increase the likelihood that this pathway will begin to unfold in early childhood. Consistent with the dominant perspective in prevention science (Ialongo et al., 2006), we believe that the study of such early emerging pathways is critical to guide interventions for young children so as to reduce the need for later treatment of more entrenched problem behaviors in adolescence and beyond. Such developmental pathways inform important targets for prevention, including when intervention should occur, who should receive the intervention, and what factors should be altered by the intervention. In the case of the internalizing pathway, we believe that one implication for prevention is the need to target risk mechanisms associated with problems in the development of emotion regulation beginning in early childhood for those most likely to experience risk associated with the internalizing pathway, namely COAs. To further guide the potential factors to target in such prevention efforts, we described two mechanisms that may increase risk for COAs to show deficits in emotion regulation associated with engagement in the internalizing pathway. These include increased stress exposure (particularly that associated with trauma/maltreatment and family conflict/violence) and impoverished child care environments (characterized by insensitive parenting that leads to insecure attachments and poor parent emotion socialization practices).

In addition to these potential implications for prevention, we believe that the internalizing pathway also informs our understanding of etiological considerations in the study of SUDs over the life span. First, the question of the core deficit that underlies substance involvement opens the door for examining the early formation of risk even before substance use begins as well as for framing the problem of heterotypic continuity in SUDs over time. Second, by defining SUDs as a developmental disorder (Sher & Gotham, 1999), novel approaches to thinking about risk and protective processes may inform our etiological models by taking into account the importance of time and timing in how such processes impact the development of drinking and drug-taking behaviors. And, third, because the primary focus of early emerging pathways has considered externalizing or disinhibited behaviors as the defining feature of risk, the internalizing pathway offers an additional developmental mechanism that may capture risk for SUDs for some individuals either alone or in conjunction with other risk processes leading to SUDs.

Importantly, the mechanisms that we posit contribute to risk for the internalizing pathway in early childhood are supported by a small literature and are in need of direct evaluation. Thus, to guide future research, core hypotheses in need of evaluation regarding the risk mechanisms for the internalizing pathway include the following:

• Maltreatment and trauma in early childhood mediate an association between parent alcoholism and altered neurobiological stress responses, which in turn predict poor emotion regulation and internalizing symptoms across the early life span.
• Exposure to family violence and conflict accounts for increased risk for emotional insecurity among COAs, which is in turn associated with poor emotion regulation and risk for internalizing symptomatology in early childhood.
• Parental insensitivity and unpredictable, unresponsive styles mediate COAs' risk for insecure attachment formation, which in turns predicts poor emotion regulation and risk for internalizing symptoms in early childhood.
• Impoverished parent emotion socialization partially explains why COAs have poor emotion regulation skills, which make them vulnerable to later internalizing symptoms across the early life span.

Much remains to be learned about how parent alcoholism may impact these mechanisms, including the relative roles of prenatal and postnatal exposure to alcohol and of heterogeneity among COAs in susceptibility to these risk processes. Protective mechanisms that promote notable resilience observed among this at-risk population also deserve greater consideration.

Additionally, increased stress associated with exposure to parental substance abuse increases arousal and stress levels for children, making the development of self-regulatory skills more challenging but also making it more difficult to use such skills or to get support for emotion regulation within this type of unpredictable home environment (e.g., Söderström & Skårderud, 2009). There are several additional factors associated with increased risk for emotion regulation deficits among COAs, including confounding factors that often co-occur in substance-abusing families such as increased rates of comorbid maternal psychopathology (Mayes & Bornstein, 1996), in utero drug exposure (e.g., cocaine: Bendersky & Lewis, 1998; Schuetze, Eiden, & Danielewicz, 2009; cigarettes: Schuetze, Lopez, Granger, & Eiden, 2008), postnatal substance exposure (Eiden, Lewis, Croff, & Young, 2002; Hickey, Suess, Newlin, & Spurgeon, 1995), and

compromised parenting behaviors (e.g., Eiden et al., 2004, 2007). There is also clear support for the role of genetics in emotion regulation (Hariri & Forbes, 2007), and extensive research documents that substance abusers tend to have compromised emotion regulation abilities (Keller & Wilson, 1994; Taylor, Bagby, & Parker, 1997), especially for those with comorbid psychopathology (e.g., Litt, Hien, & Levin, 2003). Thus, COAs face the shared risk of environmental and genetic factors associated with compromised emotion regulation skills, and future research is needed to understand the integration of such influences.

Ethnic and racial influences on the internalizing pathway to substance use are another underdeveloped line of inquiry. Although specific racial and ethnic groups experience differential risk in adolescence regarding alcohol use and abuse (Grant et al., 2004; Patrick & Schulenberg, 2010), the internalizing pathway may be critically important to understand in the context of culturally based stressors (i.e., experiences of discrimination; acculturation stress). Experiences of culturally based stress have been linked concurrently and longitudinally to both negative affect and alcohol use (Williams & Mohammed, 2009), and a longitudinal meditational relationship between discrimination, negative affect, and substance use has been found in African American adolescents and their parents (Gibbons, Gerrard, Cleveland, Wills, & Brody, 2004). Future research should more carefully consider the interrelationship of this specific type of interpersonal stress, negative affect, and alcohol developmentally, particularly in the transition to adulthood when the risk for substance use increases.

In conclusion, the role of negative emotions and internalizing symptoms in drinking and drug-taking behavior has long been acknowledged (Kassel, 2010). However, we know very little about how problems with emotion regulation that may underlie such internalizing symptoms come to be associated with substance use and disorder and what mechanisms may predate the onset of substance use to increase the likelihood that such problematic patterns of use will emerge. We hope that the current theoretical model may offer one more step along the way to better understanding these clinically relevant issues.

Acknowledgments
The theoretical models presented in this chapter emerged out of discussions within the Family Stories

Program research group that included the coauthors as well as Dr. Don Baucom at the University of North Carolina at Chapel Hill.

Notes

1. Studies provide conflicting support for the validity of various subtypes of alcoholism. However, of those studies supporting subtypes, negative affect or depressive alcoholism is one of the most commonly found. The subtypes are often defined by reaching diagnostic levels of an affective disorder as well as an alcohol use disorder. Although reaching diagnostic levels of affective disorder may be likely for those ensnared in the internalizing pathway to AUDs, subthreshold levels of internalizing symptoms may be sufficient to create necessary risk for this pathway. As such, inconsistent support for distinct subtypes within the AUDs literature does not necessarily undermine the potential utility of an internalizing pathway.
2. Although greater levels of emotional reactivity in addition to lower regulation may be present in young children at risk for this pathway as well, we focus on emotion regulation specifically because we posit that it is the ability to regulate whatever level of affect is present in service of one's goals that is the key skill for adaptation here. We also posit that although risk for eventual negative affect AUDs is likely greatest for those who engage early and persistently in behaviors consistent with this pathway over time, entry into risk associated with the pathway may occur at any point over ontogeny.
3. The study of gender differences in the relations among internalizing symptoms, stress, and substance involvement has yielded a large and contradictory literature. Although we recognize the potential salience of gender differences within the internalizing pathway to AUDs that we posit here, we also recognize that integrating and applying this literature within the current model is beyond the scope of our paper.
4. This risk likely extends to children of parents who abuse other drugs as well, but the empirical basis for examining risk associated with indicators of the internalizing pathway in these children remains limited. For this reason, we limit our discussion of this high-risk population to children of alcoholic parents more specifically.
5. These risk mechanisms may also function to place children other than those of alcoholic parents at risk for the internalizing pathway (e.g., maltreated and traumatized children), but we restrict our discussion to COAs here due to scope.

References

Abela., J. R. Z., & Hankin, B. L. (2008). Cognitive vulnerability to depression in children and adolescents: A developmental psychopathology perspective. In J. R. Z. Abela & B. L. Hankin (Eds.), *Handbook of depression in children and adolescents* (pp. 35–78). New York, NY: Guilford Press.

Ainsworth, M. (1979). Infant-mother attachment. *American Psychologist, 34*(10), 932–937.

Angold, A., Costello, E. J., & Goodyer, I. M. (2001). The epidemiology of depression in children and adolescents. *The depressed child and adolescent* (2nd ed., pp. 143–178). New York, NY: Cambridge University Press.

Babor, T. F. (1996). The classification of alcoholics: Typology theories from the 19th century to the present. *Alcohol Health and Research World, 20*(1), 6–17.

Baker, T. B., Piper, M. E., McCarthy, D. E., Majeskie, M. R., & Fiore, M. C. (2004). Addiction motivation reformulated: An affective processing model of negative reinforcement. *Psychological Review, 111*(1), 33–51. doi:10.1037/0033-295X.111.1.33

Baumrind, D. (1985). Familial antecedents of adolescent drug use: A developmental perspective. In C. L. Jones & R. J. Battjes (Eds.), *Etiology of drug abuse: Implications for prevention* (NIDA Research Monograph No. 56, DHHS Publication No. [ADM] 85-1355, pp. 13–44). Rockville, MD: National Institute on Drug Abuse.

Beeghly, M., & Tronick, E. Z. (1994). Effects of prenatal exposure to cocaine in early infancy: Toxic effects on the process of mutual regulation. *Infant Mental Health Journal, 15*(2), 158–175. doi:10.1002/1097-0355(199422)15:2<158::AID-IMHJ2280150207>3.0.CO;2-7

Bendersky, M., & Lewis, M. (1998). Arousal modulation in cocaine-exposed infants. *Developmental Psychology, 34*(3), 555–564. doi:10.1037/0012-1649.34.3.555

Besinger, B. A., Garland, A. F., Litrownik, A. J., & Landsverk, J. A. (1999). Caregiver substance abuse among maltreated children placed in out-come-home care. *Child Welfare: Journal of Policy, Practice, and Program, 78*(2), 221–239.

Blair, C., & Diamond, A. (2008). Biological processes in prevention and intervention: The promotion of self-regulation as a means of preventing school failure. *Development and Psychopathology, 20*(3), 899–911. doi:10.1017/S0954579408000436

Bobadilla, L., Vaske, J., & Asberg, K. (2013). Dopamine receptor (D4) polymorphism is related to comorbidity between marijuana abuse and depression. *Addictive Behaviors, 38*, 2555–2562.

Brenning, K., Soenens, B., Braet, C., & Bal, S. (2012). The role of parenting and mother-adolescent attachment in the intergenerational similarity of internalizing symptoms. *Journal of Youth and Adolescence, 41*(6), 802–816.

Bronson, M. B. (2000). *Self-regulation in early childhood: Nature and nurture*. New York, NY: Guilford Press.

Brook, J. S., Whiteman, M., & Gordon, A. S. (1983). Stages of drug abuse in adolescence: Personality, peer, and family correlates. *Developmental Psychology, 19*(2), 269–277. doi:10.1037/0012-1649.19.2.269

Brophy-Herb, H., Stansbury, K., Bocknek, E., & Horodynski, M. A. (2011). Modeling maternal emotion-related socialization behaviors in a low-income sample: Relations with toddlers' self-regulation. *Early Childhood Research Quarterly*, doi:10.1016/j.ecresq.2011.11.005

Brown, S. A., Tate, S. R., Vik, P. W., Haas, A. L., & Aarons, G. A. (1999). Modeling of alcohol use mediates the effect of family history of alcoholism on adolescent alcohol expectancies. *Experimental and Clinical Psychopharmacology, 7*(1), 20–27. doi:10.1037/1064-1297.7.1.20

Brumariu, L. E., Kerns, K. A., & Seibert, A. (2012). Mother-child attachment, emotion regulation, and anxiety symptoms in middle childhood. *Personal Relationships, 19*(3), 569–585.

Calkins, S. D., & Hill, A. (2007). Caregiver influences in emerging emotion regulation: Biological and environmental transactions in early development. In J. J. Gross (Eds.), *Handbook on emotion regulation* (pp. 229–248). New York, NY: Guilford Press.

Calkins, S. D., & Leerkes, E. M. (2011). Early attachment processes and the development of emotional self-regulation. In K. D. Vohs & R. F. Baumeister (Eds.), *Handbook of* self-regulation: Research, theory, and applications (2nd ed., pp. 355–373). New York, NY: Guilford Press.

Carpenter, K. M., & Hasin, D. S. (1999). Drinking to cope with negative affect and DSM-IV alcohol use disorders: A test of three alternative explanations. *Journal of Studies on Alcohol, 60*, 694–704.

Caspi, A., & Moffitt, T. E. (1995). The continuity of maladaptive behavior: From description to understanding in the study of antisocial behavior. In D. CiCchetti & D. J. Cohen (Eds.), *Developmental psychopathology, Vol 2. Risk, disorder, and adaptation* (pp. 472–511). New York, NY: Wiley.

Caspi, A., Moffitt, T. E., Newman, D. L., & Silva, P. A. (1996). Behavioral observations at age 3 years predict adult psychiatric disorders: Longitudinal evidence from a birth cohort. *Archives of General Psychiatry, 53*(11), 1033–1039.

Chalder, M., Elgar, F. J., & Bennett, P. (2006). Drinking and motivations to drink among adolescent children of parents with alcohol problems. *Alcohol and Alcoholism, 41*(1), 107–113. doi:10.1093/alcalc/agh215

Chassin, L., Curran, P. J., Hussong, A. M., & Colder, C. R. (1996). The relation of parent alcoholism to adolescent substance use: A longitudinal follow-up study. *Journal of Abnormal Psychology, 105*(1), 70–80. doi:10.1037/0021-843X.105.1.70

Chassin, L., Hussong, A., & Beltran, I. (2009). Adolescent substance use. In R. M. Lerner & L. Steinberg (Eds.), *Handbook of adolescent psychology, Vol 1. Individual bases of adolescent development* (3rd ed., pp. 723–763). Hoboken, NJ: Wiley.

Chassin, L., Pillow, D. R., Curran, P. J., Molina, B. S. G., & Barrera, M., Jr. (1993). Relation of parental alcoholism to early adolescent substance use: A test of three mediating mechanisms. *Journal of Abnormal Psychology, 102*(1), 3–19. doi:10.1037/0021-843X.102.1.3

Chassin, L., Pitts, S. C., DeLucia, C., & Todd, M. (1999). A longitudinal study of children of alcoholics: Predicting young adult substance use disorders, anxiety, and depression. *Journal of Abnormal Psychology, 108*(1), 106–119. doi:10.1037/0021-843X.108.1.106

Chorpita, B. F., & Barlow, D. H. (1998). The development of anxiety: The role of control in the early environment. *Psychological Bulletin, 124*(1), 3–21. doi:10.1037/0033-2909.124.1.3

Cicchetti, D. (2006). Development and psychopathology. In D. Cicchetti & D. J. Cohen (Eds.), *Developmental psychopathology, Vol 1. Theory and method* (2nd ed., pp. 1–23). Hoboken, NJ: Wiley.

Cicchetti, D., & Rogosch, F. A. (1996). Equifinality and multifinality in developmental psychopathology. *Development and Psychopathology, 8*(4), 597–600. doi:10.1017/S0954579400007318

Coie, J. D., Lochman, J. E., Terry, R., & Hyman, C. (1992). Predicting early adolescent disorder from childhood aggression and peer rejection. *Journal of Consulting and Clinical Psychology, 60*(5), 783–792. doi:10.1037/0022-006X.60.5.783

Colder, C. R., Chassin, L., Lee, M. R., & Villalta, I. K. (2010). Developmental perspectives: Affect and adolescent substance use. In J. D. Kassel (Ed.), *Substance abuse and emotion* (pp. 109–135). Washington, DC: American Psychological Association. doi:10.1037/12067-005

Colder, C. R., Chassin, L., Stice, E. M., & Curran, P. J. (1997). Alcohol expectancies as potential mediators of parent alcoholism effects on the development of adolescent heavy

drinking. *Journal of Research on Adolescence, 7*(4), 349–374. doi:10.1207/s15327795jra0704_1

Colder, C. R., Mott, J. A., & Berman, A. S. (2002). The interactive effects of infant activity level and fear on growth trajectories of early childhood behavior problems. *Development and Psychopathology, 14*(1), 1–23. doi:10.1017/S0954579402001013

Cooper, M. L. (1994). Motivations for alcohol use among adolescents: Development and validation of a four-factor model. *Psychological Assessment, 6*(2), 117–128. doi:10.1037/1040-3590.6.2.117

Cooper, M. L., Frone, M. R., Russell, M., & Mudar, P. (1995). Drinking to regulate positive and negative emotions: A motivational model of alcohol use. *Journal of Personality and Social Psychology, 69*(5), 990–1005. doi:10.1037/0022-3514.69.5.990

Cooper, M. L., Russell, M., Skinner, J. B., & Windle, M. (1992). Development and validation of a three-dimensional measure of drinking motives. *Psychological Assessment, 4*(2), 123–132. doi:10.1037/1040-3590.4.2.123

Cox, M. J., & Paley, B. (2003). Understanding families as systems. *Current Directions in PsychologicalScience, 12*, 193–196.

Croissant, B., Demmel, R., Rist, F., & Olbrich, R. (2008). Exploring the link between gender, sensation seeking, and family history of alcoholism in cortisol stress-response dampening. *Biological Psychology, 79*(2), 268–274. doi:10.1016/j.biopsycho.2008.07.001

Cummings, E. M. (1995). Security, emotionality, and parental depression: A commentary. *Developmental Psychology, 31*(3), 425–427. doi:10.1037/0012-1649.31.3.425

Cummings, E. M. (1998). Stress and coping approaches and research: The impact of marital conflict on children. *Journal of Aggression, Maltreatment and Trauma, 2*(1), 31–50. doi:10.1300/J146v02n01_03

Cummings, M. E., & Davies, P. T. (1992). Parental depression, family functioning, and child adjustment: Risk factors, processes, and pathways. In D. Cicchetti & S. L. Toth (Eds.), *Developmental perspectives on depression* (pp. 283–322). Rochester, NY: University of Rochester Press.

Cummings, E. M., & Davies, P. T. (1999). Depressed parents and family functioning: Interpersonal effects and children's functioning and development. In T. Joiner & J. C. Coyne (Eds.), *The interactional nature of depression: Advances in interpersonal approaches* (pp. 299–327). Washington, DC: American Psychological Association. doi:10.1037/10311-011

Cummings, E. M., & Davies, P. T. (2002). Effects of marital conflict on children: Recent advances and emerging themes in process-oriented research. *Journal of Child Psychology and Psychiatry, 43*(1), 31–63. doi:10.1111/1469-7610.00003

Cummings, E. M., & Davies, P. T. (2010). *Marital conflict and children: An emotional security perspective*. New York, NY: Guilford Press.

Cummings, E. M., Davies, P. T., & Campbell, S. B. (2000). *Developmental psychopathology and family process: Theory, research, and clinical implications*. New York, NY: Guilford Press.

Curran, P. J., & Hussong, A. M. (2009). Integrative data analysis: The simultaneous analysis of multiple data sets. *Psychological Methods, Special Issue: Multi-Study Methods for Building a Cumulative Psychological Science, 14*, 81–100.

Dai, X., Thavundayil, J., & Gianoulakis, C. (2002). Response of the hypothalamic-pituitary-adrenal axis to stress in the absence and presence of ethanol in subjects at high and low risk of alcoholism. *Neuropsychopharmacology, 27*(3), 442–452. doi:10.1016/S0893-133X(02)00308-1

Dai, X., Thavundayil, J., Santella, S., & Gianoulakis, C. (2007). Response of the HPA-axis to alcohol and stress as a function of alcohol dependence and family history of alcoholism. *Psychoneuroendocrinology, 32,* 293–305.

Davies, P. T., & Cummings, E. M. (1994). Marital conflict and child adjustment: An emotional security hypothesis. *Psychological Bulletin, 116*(3), 387–411. doi:10.1037/0033-2909.116.3.387

Davies, P. T., Forman, E. M., Rasi, J. A., & Stevens, K. I. (2002). Assessing children's emotional security in the interparental relationship: The security in the interparental subsystem scales. *Child Development, 73*(2), 544–562. doi:10.1111/1467-8624.00423

De Bellis, M. D. (2001). Developmental traumatology: The psychobiological development of maltreated children and its implications for research, treatment, and policy. *Development and Psychopathology, 13*(3), 539–564. doi:10.1017/S0954579401003078

DeBellis, M. D. (2002). Developmental traumatology: A contributory mechanism for alcohol and substance use disorders. *Psychoneuroendocrinology, 27*(1–2), 155–170. doi:10.1016/S0306-4530(01)00042-7

Dick, D. M. (2011). Developmental changes in genetic influences on alcohol use and dependence. *Child Development Perspectives, 5*(4), 223–230. doi:10.1111/j.1750-8606.2011.00207.x

Dishion, T. J., Duncan, T. E., Eddy, J. M., & Fagot, B. I. (1994). The world of parents and peers: Coercive exchanges and children's social adaptation. *Social Development, 3*(3), 255–268. doi:10.1111/j.1467-9507.1994.tb00044.x

Donovan, J. E. (2007). Really underage drinkers: The epidemiology of children's alcohol use in the United States. *Prevention Science, 8*(3), 192–205. doi:10.1007/s11121-007-0072-7

Douglas, E. M. (2013). Case, service and family characteristics of households that experience a child maltreatment fatality in the United States. *Child Abuse Review, 22,* 311–326. doi: 10.1002/car.2236

Dunn, M. E., & Goldman, M. S. (1998). Age and drinking-related differences in the memory organization of alcohol expectancies in 3rd-, 6th-, 9th-, and 12th-grade children. *Journal of Consulting and Clinical Psychology, 66*(3), 579–585. doi:10.1037/0022-006X.66.3.579

Edwards, A. C., Larsson, H., Lichtenstein, P., & Kendler, K. (2011). Early environmental influences contribute to covariation between internalizing symptoms and alcohol intoxication frequency across adolescence. *Addictive Behaviors, 36,* 175–182.

Edwards, A. C., Sihvola, E., Korhonen, T., Pulkkinen, L., Moilanen, I., Kaprio, J., . . . Dick, D. M. (2011). Depressive symptoms and alcohol use are genetically and environmentally correlated across adolescence. *Behavioral Genetics, 41,* 476–487.

Edwards, E. P., Leonard, K. E., & Das Eiden, R. (2001). Temperament and behavioral problems among infants in alcoholic families. *Infant Mental Health Journal, 22*(3), 374–392. doi:10.1002/imhj.1007

Eiden, R. D., Chavez, F., & Leonard, K. E. (1999). Parent–infant interactions among families with alcoholic fathers. *Development and Psychopathology, 11*(4), 745–762. doi:10.1017/S0954579499002308

Eiden, R. D., Colder, C., Edwards, E. P., & Leonard, K. E. (2009). A longitudinal study of social competence among

children of alcoholic and nonalcoholic parents: Role of parental psychopathology, parental warmth, and self-regulation. *Psychology of Addictive Behaviors, 23*(1), 36–46. doi:10.1037/a0014839

Eiden, R. D., Coles, C. D., Schuetze, P., & Colder, C. R. (2014). Externalizing behavior problems among polydrug cocaine-exposed children: Indirect pathways via maternal harshness and self-regulation in early childhood. *Psychology of Addictive Behaviors, 28*(4), 139–153.

Eiden, R. D., Edwards, E. P., & Leonard, K. E. (2002). Mother-infant and father-infant attachment among alcoholic families. *Development and Psychopathology, 14,* 253–278. doi:10.1017/S0954579402002043

Eiden, R. D., Edwards, E. P., & Leonard, K. E. (2004). Predictors of effortful control among children of alcoholic and nonalcoholic fathers. *Journal of Studies on Alcohol, 65*(3), 309–319.

Eiden, R. D., Edwards, E. P., & Leonard, K. E. (2007). A conceptual model for the development of externalizing behavior problems among kindergarten children of alcoholic families: Role of parenting and children's self-regulation. *Developmental Psychology, 43,* 1187–1201.

Eiden, R. D., & Leonard, K. E. (2000). Paternal alcoholism, parental psychopathology, and aggravation with infants. *Journal of Substance Abuse, 11*(1), 17–29. doi:10.1016/S0899-3289(99)00016-4

Eiden, R. D., Lewis, A., Croff, S., & Young, E. (2002). Maternal cocaine use and infant behavior. *Infancy, 3*(1), 77–96. doi:10.1207/15250000252828253

Eiden, R. D., Ostroy, J. M., Colder, C. R., Leonard, K. E., Edwards, E. P., & Orrange-Torchia, T. (2010). Parent alcohol problems and peer bullying and victimization: Child gender and toddler attachment security as moderators. *Journal of Clinical Child and Adolescent Psychology, 39*(3), 341–350. doi:10.1080/15374411003691768

Eisenberg, N., Cumberland, A., & Spinrad, T. L. (1998). Parental socialization of emotion. *Psychological Inquiry, 9*(4), 241–273. doi:10.1207/s15327965pli0904_1

Eisenberg, N., Spinrad, T. L., & Eggum, N. D. (2010). Emotion-related self-regulation and its relation to children's maladjustment. *Annual Review of Clinical Psychology, 6,* 495–525. doi:10.1146/annurev.clinpsy.121208.131208

El-Sheikh, M. (2005). The role of emotional responses and physiological reactivity in the marital conflict-child functioning link. *Journal of Child Psychology and Psychiatry, 46*(11), 1191–1199. doi:10.1111/j.1469-7610.2005.00418.x

El-Sheikh, M., & Cummings, E. M. (1997). Marital conflict, emotional regulation, and the adjustment of children of alcoholics. In K. C. Barrett (Ed.), *The communication of emotion: Current research from diverse perspectives* (pp. 25–44). San Francisco, CA: Jossey-Bass.

El-Sheikh, M., & Flanagan, E. (2001). Parental problem drinking and children's adjustment: Family conflict and parental depression as mediators and moderators of risk. *Journal of Abnormal Child Psychology, 29,* 417–432.

El-Sheikh, M., Harger, J., & Whitson, S. M. (2001). Exposure to interparental conflict and children's adjustment and physical health: The moderating role of vagal tone. *Child Development, 72*(6), 1617–1636. doi:10.1111/1467-8624.00369

El-Sheikh, M., Keller, P. S., & Erath, S. A. (2007). Marital conflict and risk for child maladjustment over time: Skin conductance level reactivity as a vulnerability factor. *Journal of Abnormal Child Psychology, 35*(5), 715–727. doi:10.1007/s10802-007-9127-2

Ensminger, M. E., Juon, H. S., & Fothergill, K. E. (2002). Childhood and adolescent antecedents of substance use in adulthood. *Addiction*, *97*(7), 833–844. doi:10.1046/j.1360-0443.2002.00138.x

Finn, P. R., Earleywine, M., & Pihl, R. O. (1992). Sensation seeking, stress reactivity, and alcohol dampening discriminate the density of a family history of alcoholism. *Alcoholism: Clinical and Experimental Research*, *16*(3), 585–590. doi:10.1111/j.1530-0277.1992.tb01421.x

Finn, P. R., Kessler, D. N., & Hussong, A. M. (1994). Risk for alcoholism and classical conditioning to signals for punishment: Evidence for a weak behavioral inhibition system. *Journal of Abnormal Psychology*, *103*(2), 293–301. doi:10.1037/0021-843X.103.2.293

Forehand, R., Brody, G., Slotkin, J., Fauber, R., McCombs, A., & Long, N. (1988). Young adolescent and maternal depression: Assessment, interrelations, and family predictors. *Journal of Consulting and Clinical Psychology*, *56*(3), 422–426. doi:10.1037/0022-006X.56.3.422

Fox, N. A., Henderson, H. A., Marshall, P. J., Nichols, K. E., & Ghera, M. M. (2005). Behavioral inhibition: Linking biology and behavior within a developmental framework. *Annual Review of Psychology*, *56*, 235–262. doi:10.1146/annurev.psych.55.090902.141532

Freisthler, B., Holmes, M. R., & Price Wolf, J. (2014). The dark side of social support: Understanding the role of social support, drinking behaviors and alcohol outlets for child physical abuse. *Child Abuse and Neglect*, *38*, 1106–1119. doi:10.1016/j.chiabu.2014.03.011

Garber, J., Braafladt, N., & Zeman, J. (1991). The regulation of sad affect: An information-processing perspective. In J. Garber & K. A. Dodge (Eds.), *The development of emotion regulation and dysregulation* (pp. 208–240). New York, NY: Cambridge University Press.

Garber, J., & Horowitz, J. L. (2002). Depression in children. In I. H. Gotlib & C. L. Hammen (Eds.), *Handbook of depression* (pp. 510–540). New York, NY: Guilford Press.

Gibbons, F. X., Gerrard, M., Cleveland, M. J., Wills, T. A., & Brody, G. (2004). Perceived discrimination and substance use in African American parents and their children: a panel study. *Journal of Personality and Social Psychology*, *86*(4), 517.

Gladstone, G. L., & Parker, G. B. (2006). Is behavioral inhibition a risk factor for depression? *Journal of Affective Disorders*, *95*(1), 85–94. doi:10.1016/j.jad.2006.04.015

Gottman, J. (2001). Meta-emotion, children's emotional intelligence, and buffering children from marital conflict. In C. D. Ryff & B. H. Singer (Eds.), *Emotion, social relationships, and health* (pp. 23–40). New York, NY: Oxford University Press.

Gottman, J. M., Katz, L. F., & Hooven, C. (1996). Parental meta-emotion philosophy and the emotional life of families: Theoretical models and preliminary data. *Journal of Family Psychology*, *10*(3), 243–268. doi:10.1037/0893-3200.10.3.243

Gottman, J. M., Katz, L. F., & Hooven, C. (1997). *Meta-emotion: How families communicate emotionally*. Hillsdale, NJ: Erlbaum.

Graber, J. A., & Sontag, L. M. (2009). Internalizing problems in adolescence. In R. M. Lerner & L. Steinberg (Eds.), *Handbook of adolescent psychology, Vol. 1. Individual bases of adolescent development* (3rd ed., pp. 642–682). Hoboken, NJ: Wiley.

Grant, B. F., & Dawson, D. A. (1997). Age at onset of alcohol use and its association with DSM-IV alcohol abuse and dependence: Results from the National longitudinal alcohol epidemiologic survey. *Journal of Substance Abuse*, *9*, 103–110. doi:10.1016/S0899-3289(97)90009-2

Grant, B. F., Dawson, D. A., Stinson, F. S., Chou, S. P., Dufour, M. C., & Pickering, R. P. (2004). The 12-month prevalence and trends in DSM-IV alcohol abuse and dependence: United States, 1991–1992 and 2001–2002. *Drug and Alcohol Dependence*, *74*(3), 223–234.

Gunnar, M., & Quevedo, K. (2007). The neurobiology of stress and development. *Annual Review of Psychology*, *58*, 145–173. doi:10.1146/annurev.psych.58.110405.085605

Hammen, C. L. (2009). Children of depressed parents. In I. H. Gotlib & C. L. Hammen (Eds.), *Handbook of depression* (2nd ed., pp. 275–297). New York, NY: Guilford Press.

Haring, K. A., Lovett, D. L., Haney, K. F., & Algozzine, B. (1992). Labeling preschoolers as learning disabled: A cautionary position. *Topics in Early Childhood Special Education*, *12*(2), 151–173. doi:10.1177/027112149201200203

Hariri, A. R., & Forbes, E. E. (2007). Genetics of emotion regulation. In J. J. Gross (Ed.), *Handbook of emotion regulation* (pp. 110–132). New York, NY: Guilford Press.

Harrington, D., Dubowitz, H., Black, M. M., & Binder, A. (1995). Maternal substance use and neglectful parenting: Relationships with children's development. *Journal of Child Clinical Psychology*, *24*, 258–263.

Henggeler, S. W., Clingempeel, W., Brondino, M. J., & Pickrel, S. G. (2002). Four-year follow-up of multisystemic therapy with substance-abusing and substance-dependent juvenile offenders. *Journal of the American Academy of Child and Adolescent Psychiatry*, *41*(7), 868–874. doi:10.1097/00004583-200207000-00021

Hersh, M. A., & Hussong, A. M. (2009). The impact of observed parental emotion socialization on adolescent self-medication. *Journal of Abnormal Child Psychology*, *37*, 493–506. doi:10.1007/s10802-008-9291-z

Hickey, J. E., Suess, P. E., Newlin, D. B., & Spurgeon, L. (1995). Vagal tone regulation during sustained attention in boys exposed to opiates in utero. *Addictive Behaviors*, *20*(1), 43–59. doi:10.1016/0306-4603(94)00044-Y

Hill, S. Y., Lowers, L., Locke, J., Snidman, N., & Kagan, J. (1999). Behavioral inhibition in children from families at high risk for developing alcoholism. *Journal of the American Academy of Child and Adolescent Psychiatry*, *38*(4), 410–420. doi:10.1097/00004583-199904000-00013

Hirshfeld, D. R., Rosenbaum, J. F., Biederman, J., & Bolduc, E. A. (1992). Stable behavioral inhibition and its association with anxiety disorder. *Journal of the American Academy of Child and Adolescent Psychiatry*, *31*(1), 103–111. doi:10.1097/00004583-199201000-00016

Hussong, A. M. (2000). The settings of adolescent alcohol and drug use. *Journal of Youth and Adolescence*, *29*(1), 107–119. doi:10.1023/A:1005177306699

Hussong, A. M. (2003). Social influences in motivated drinking among college students. *Psychology of Addictive Behaviors*, *17*(2), 142–150. doi:10.1037/0893-164X.17.2.142

Hussong, A., Bauer, D., & Chassin, L. (2008). Telescoped trajectories from alcohol initiation to disorder in children of alcoholic parents. *Journal of Abnormal Psychology*, *117*(1), 63–78. doi:10.1037/0021-843X.117.1.63

Hussong, A. M., Bauer, D. J., Huang, W., Chassin, L., Sher, K. J., & Zucker, R. A. (2008). Characterizing the life stressors of children of alcoholic parents. *Journal of Family Psychology*, *22*(6), 819–832. doi:10.1037/a0013704

Hussong, A. M., & Chassin, L. (2004). Stress and coping among children of alcoholic parents through the young adult transition. *Development and Psychopathology*, *16*(4), 985–1006. doi:10.1017/S0954579404040106

Hussong, A. M., Curran, P. J., & Chassin, L. (1998). Pathways of risk for accelerated heavy alcohol use among adolescent children of alcoholic parents. *Journal of Abnormal Child Psychology*, *26*(6), 453–466. doi:10.1023/A:1022699701996

Hussong, A. M., Flora, D. B., Curran, P. J., Chassin, L. A., & Zucker, R. A. (2008). Defining risk heterogeneity for internalizing symptoms among children of alcoholic parents. *Development and Psychopathology*, *20*(1), 165–193. doi:10.1017/S0954579408000084

Hussong, A. M., Jones, D. J., Stein, G. L., Baucom, D. H., & Boeding, S. (2011). An internalizing pathway to alcohol use and disorder. *Psychology of Addictive Behaviors*, *25*(3), 390–404. doi:10.1037/a0024519

Hussong, A. M., Wirth, R. J., Edwards, M. C., Curran, P. J., Chassin, L. A., & Zucker, R. A. (2007). Externalizing symptoms among children of alcoholic parents: Entry points for an antisocial pathway to alcoholism. *Journal of Abnormal Psychology*, *116*(3), 529–542. doi:10.1037/0021-843X.116.3.529

Hussong, A. M., Zucker, R. A., Wong, M. M., Fitzgerald, H. E., & Puttler, L. I. (2005). Social competence in children of alcoholic parents over time. *Developmental Psychology*, *41*(5), 747–759. doi:10.1037/0012-1649.41.5.747

Iacono, W. G., & Malone, S. M. (2011). Developmental endophenotypes: Indexing genetic risk for substance abuse with the P300 brain event-related potential. *Child Development Perspectives*, *5*(4), 239–247. doi: 10.1111/j.1750-8606.2011.00205.x

Iacono, W. G., Malone, S. M., & McGue, M. (2008). Behavioral disinhibition and the development of early-onset addiction: Common and specific influences. *Annual Review of Clinical Psychology*, *4*, 325–348. doi:10.1146/annurev.clinpsy.4.022007.141157

Ialongo, N. S., Rogosch, F. A., Cicchetti, D., Toth, S. L., Buckley, J., Petras, H., & Neiderhiser, J. (2006). A developmental psychopathologyapproach to the prevention of mental health disorders. In D. Cicchetti, & D. Cohen (Eds.), *Developmental psychopathology, Vol. 1. Theory and method* (2nd ed., pp. 968–1018). Hoboken, NJ: Wiley.

Jaffee, S. R., Caspi, A., Moffitt, T. E., Polo-Tomás, M., Taylor, A. (2007). Individual, family, and neighborhood factors distinguish resilient from non-resilient maltreated children: A cumulative stressors model. *Child Abuse & Neglect*, *31*(3), 231–253.

Jansen, R. E., Fitzgerald, H. E., Ham, H. P., & Zucker, R. A. (1995). Pathways into risk: Temperament and behavior problems in three- to five-year-old sons of alcoholics. *Alcoholism: Clinical and Experimental Research*, *19*(2), 501–509. doi:10.1111/j.1530-0277.1995.tb01538.x

Jessor, R., & Jessor, S. L. (1977). *Problem behavior and psychosocial development: A longitudinal study of youth*. New York, NY: Academic Press.

Johnston, L. D., O'Malley, P. M., Miech, R. A., Bachman, J. G., & Schulenberg, J. E. (2014). *Monitoring the Future national results on drug use: 1975-2013: Overview, Key Findings on Adolescent Drug Use*. Ann Arbor: Institute for Social Research, University of Michigan.

Kagan, J. (2008). Behavioral inhibition as a risk factor for psychopathology. In T. P. Beauchaine & S. P. Hinshaw (Eds.), *Child and adolescent psychopathology* (pp. 157–179). Hoboken, NJ: Wiley.

Kagan, J., Reznick, J. S., & Gibbons, J. (1989). Inhibited and uninhibited types of children. *Child Development*, *60*(4), 838–845. doi:10.2307/1131025

Kagan, J., Snidman, N., Zentner, M., & Peterson, E. (1999). Infant temperament and anxious symptoms in school age children. *Development and Psychopathology*, *11*(2), 209–224. doi:10.1017/S0954579499002023

Kandel, D. (1975). Stages in adolescent involvement in drug use. *Science*, *190*(4217), 912–914.

Kaplan, H. B. (1980). *Deviant behavior in defense of self*. New York, NY: Academic Press.

Kaplow, J. B., Curran, P. J., Angold, A., & Costello, E. J. (2001). The prospective relation between dimensions of anxiety and the initiation of adolescent alcohol use. *Journal of Clinical Child Psychology*, *30*(3), 316–326. doi:10.1207/S15374424JCCP3003_4

Kassel, J. D. (2010). *Substance abuse and emotion*. Washington, DC: American Psychological Association. doi:10.1037/12067-000

Kelleher, K., Chaffin, M., Hollenberg, J., & Fischer, E. (1994). Alcohol and drug disorders among physically abusive and neglectful parents in a community-based sample. *American Journal of Public Health*, *84*(10), 1586–1590. doi:10.2105/AJPH.84.10.1586

Keller, D. S., & Wilson, A. (1994). Affectivity in cocaine and opiate abusers. *Psychiatry: Interpersonal and Biological Processes*, *57*(4), 333–347.

Keller, P. S., Cummings, E. M., Davies, P. T., & Mitchell, P. A. (2008). Longitudinal relations between parental drinking problems, family functioning, and child adjustment. *Development and Psychopathology*, *20*, 195–212.

Keller, P. S., Gilbert, L. R., Koss, K. J., Cummings, E. M., & Davies, P. T. (2011). Parental problem drinking: Marital aggression, and child emotional insecurity: A longitudinal investigation. *Journal of Studies on Alcohol and Drugs*, *72*(5), 711–722.

Kendler, K. S., Neale, M. C., Heath, A. C., & Kessler, R. C. (1994). A twin-family study of alcoholism in women. *American Journal of Psychiatry*, *151*(5), 707–715.

Kendler, K. S., Prescott, C. A., Myers, J., & Neale, M. C. (2003). The structure of genetic and environmental risk factors for common psychiatric and substance use disorders in men and women. *Archives of General Psychiatry*, *60*, 929–937.

Kerwin, M. E. (2005). Collaboration between child welfare and substance-abuse fields: Combined treatment programs for mothers. *Journal of Pediatric Psychology*, *30*(7), 581–597. doi:10.1093/jpepsy/jsi045

Khantzian, E. J. (1997). The self-medication hypothesis of substance use disorders: A reconsideration and recent applications. *Harvard Review of Psychiatry*, *4*(5), 231–244. doi:10.3109/10673229709030550

Kodituwakku, P. W., Kalberg, W., & May, P. A. (2001). The effects of prenatal alcohol exposure on executive functioning. *Alcohol Research and Health*, *25*(3), 192–198.

Kouros, C. D., Merrilees, C. E., & Cummings, E. M. (2008). Marital conflict and children's emotional security in the context of parental depression. *Journal of Marriage and Family*, *70*(3), 684–697. doi:10.1111/j.1741-3737.2008.00514.x

Krueger, R. F., & Markon, K. E. (2006). Reinterpreting comorbidity: A model-based approach to understanding and classifying psychopathology. *Annual Review of Clinical Psychology, 2*, 111–133.

Krug, E. G., Dahlberg, L. L., Mercy, J. A., Zwi, A. B., & Lozano, R. (2002). *Child abuse and neglect by parents and other caregivers. In* World report on violence and health (pp. 56–81). Geneva, Switzerland: World Health Organization.

Kuntsche, E., Knibbe, R., Engels, R., & Gmel, G. (2007). Drinking motives as mediators of the link between alcohol expectancies and alcohol use among adolescents. *Journal of Studies on Alcohol and Drugs, 68*(1), 76–85.

Leerkes, E. M., & Wong, M. S. (2012). Infant distress and regulatory behaviors vary as a function of attachment security regardless of emotion context and maternal involvement. *Infancy, 17*(5), 455–478.

Lillehoj, C. J., Trudeau, L., Spoth, R., & Wickrama, K. A. S. (2004). Internalizing, social competence, and substance initiation: Influence of gender moderation and a preventive intervention. *Substance Use and Misuse, 39*(6), 963–991. doi:10.1081/JA-120030895

Litt, L. C., Hien, D. A., & Levin, D. (2003). Adult antisocial behavior and affect regulation among primary crack/cocaine-using women. *Psychology of Women Quarterly, 27*(2), 143–152. doi:10.1111/1471-6402.00094

Lochman, J. E., Wells, K. C., & Murray, M. (2007). The Coping Power Program: Preventive intervention at the middle school transition. In P. Tolan, J. Szapocznik, & S. Sambrano (Eds.), *Preventing youth substance abuse: Science-based programs for children and adolescents* (pp. 185–210). Washington, DC: American Psychological Association. doi:10.1037/11488-008

Lovallo, W. R., Farag, N. H., Sorocco, K. H., Cohoon, A. J., & Vincent, A. S. (2012). Lifetime adversity leads to blunted stress axis reactivity: Studies from the Oklahoma Family Health Patterns Project. *Biological Psychiatry, 71*(4), 344–349. doi:10.1016/j.biopsych.2011.10.018

Lunkenheimer, E. S., Shields, A. M., & Cortina, K. S. (2007). Parental emotion coaching and dismissing in family interaction. *Social Development, 16*(2), 232–248. doi:10.1111/j.1467-9507.2007.00382.x

MacMillan, H. L., Georgiades, K., Duku, E. K., Shea, A., Steiner, M., Niec, A., . . . Schmidt, L. A. (2009). Cortisol response to stress in female youths exposed to childhood maltreatment: Results of the youth mood project. *Biological Psychiatry, 66*(1), 62–68. doi:10.1016/j.biopsych.2008.12.014

Magnusson, D., & Cairns, R. B. (1996). Developmental science: Toward a unified framework. In R. B. Cairns, G. R. Elder, & E. Costello (Eds.), *Developmental science* (pp. 7–30). New York, NY: Cambridge University Press.

Mann, L. M., Chassin, L., & Sher, K. J. (1987). Alcohol expectancies and the risk for alcoholism. *Journal of Consulting and Clinical Psychology, 55*(3), 411–417. doi:10.1037/0022-006X.55.3.411

Mayes, L. C., & Bornstein, M. H. (1995). Developmental dilemmas for cocaine-abusing parents and their children. In M. Lewis & M. Bendersky (Eds.), *Mothers, babies, and cocaine: The role of toxins in development* (pp. 251–272). Hillsdale, NJ: Erlbaum.

Mayes, L. C., & Bornstein, M. H. (1996). The context of development for young children from cocaine-abusing families. In P. M. Kato & T. Mann (Eds.), *Handbook of diversity issues in health psychology* (pp. 69–95). New York, NY: Plenum Press. doi:10.1007/978-0-585-27572-7_5

McCarthy, D. E., Curtin, J. J., Piper, M. E., & Baker, T. B. (2010). Negative reinforcement: Possible clinical implications of an integrative model. In J. Kassel (Ed.), *Substance abuse and emotion* (pp. 15–42). Washington, DC: American Psychological Association.

McCrory, E., De Brito, S. A., & Viding, E. (2010). Research review: The neurobiology and genetics of maltreatment and adversity. *Journal of Child Psychology and Psychiatry, 51*(10), 1079–1095. doi:10.1111/j.1469-7610.2010.02271.x

McGrath, C. E., Watson, A. L., & Chassin, L. (1999). Academic achievement in adolescent children of alcoholics. *Journal of Studies on Alcohol, 60*(1), 18–26.

Merikangas, K. R., Leckman, J. F., Prusoff, B. A., Pauls, D. L., & Weissman, M. M. (1985). Familial transmission of depression and alcoholism. *Archives of General Psychiatry, 42*(4), 367–372.

Merikangas, K. R., Rounsaville, B. J., & Prusoff, B. A. (1992). Familial factors in vulnerability to substance abuse. In M. D. Glantz & R. W. Pickens (Eds.), *Vulnerability to drug abuse* (pp. 75–97). Washington, DC: American Psychological Association. doi:10.1037/10107-003

Morris, A. S., Silk, J. S., Steinberg, L., Myers, S. S., & Robinson, L. R. (2007). The role of the family context in development of emotion regulation. *Social Development, 16*, 361–388. doi: 10.1111/j.1467-9507.2007.00389.x

Moss, H. B., Vanyukov, M. M., & Martin, C. S. (1995). Salivary cortisol responses and the risk for substance abuse in prepubertal boys. *Biological Psychiatry, 38*(8), 546–555. doi:10.1016/0006-3223(94)00382-D

Moss, H. B., Vanyukov, M., Yao, J. K., & Kirillova, G. P. (1999). Salivary cortisol responses in prepubertal boys: The effects of parental substance abuse and association with drug use behavior during adolescence. *Biological Psychiatry, 45*(10), 1293–1299. doi:10.1016/S0006-3223(98)00216-9

Murphy, J. M., Jellinek, M. S., Quinn, D., & Smith, G. (1991). Substance abuse and serious child mistreatment: Prevalence, risk, and outcome in a court sample. *Child Abuse and Neglect, 15*(3), 197–211. doi:10.1016/0145-2134(91)90065-L

Nation, M., Crusto, C., Wandersman, A., Kumpfer, K. L., Seybolt, D., Morrissey-Kane, E., & Davino, K. (2003). What works in prevention: Principles of effective prevention programs. *American Psychologist, 58*(6–7), 449–456. doi:10.1037/0003-066X.58.6-7.449

The National Center on Addiction and Substance Abuse at Columbia University. (1999). *No safe haven: Children of substance-abusing parents.* New York, NY: Author.

Nelson, L. J., Rubin, K. H., & Fox, N. A. (2005). Social withdrawal, observed peer acceptance, and the development of self-perceptions in children ages 4 to 7 years. *Early Childhood Research Quarterly, 20*(2), 185–200. doi:10.1016/j.ecresq.2005.04.007

O'Connor, R. M., Fite, P. J., Nowlin, P. R., & Colder, C. R. (2007). Children's beliefs about substance use: An examination of age differences in implicit and explicit cognitive precursors of substance use initiation. *Psychology of Addictive Behaviors, 21*(4), 525–533. doi:10.1037/0893-164X.21.4.525

Olds, D. L., Sadler, L., & Kitzman, H. (2007). Programs for parents of infants and toddlers: Recent evidence from randomized trials. *Journal of Child Psychology and Psychiatry, 48*(3–4), 355–391. doi:10.1111/j.1469-7610.2006.01702.x

Ostrander, R., & Herman, K. C. (2006). Potential cognitive, parenting, and developmental mediators of the relationship between ADHD and depression. *Journal of Consulting and Clinical Psychology*, *74*(1), 89–98. doi:10.1037/0022-006X.74.1.89

Patrick, M. E., & Schulenberg, J. E. (2010). Alcohol use and heavy episodic drinking prevalence and predictors among national samples of American eighth- and tenth-grade students. *Journal of Studies on Alcohol and Drugs*, *71*(1), 41–45.

Pendry, P., & Adam, E. K. (2007). Associations between parents' marital functioning, maternal parenting quality, maternal emotion and child cortisol levels. *International Journal of Behavioral Development*, *31*(3), 218–231. doi:10.1177/0165025407074634

Rafnsson, F. D., Jonsson, F. H., & Windle, M. (2006). Coping strategies, stressful life events, problem behaviors, and depressed affect. *Anxiety, Stress and Coping: An International Journal*, *19*(3), 241–257.

Reese, F. L., Chassin, L., & Molina, B. S. (1994). Alcohol expectancies in early adolescents: Predicting drinking behavior from alcohol expectancies and parental alcoholism. *Journal of Studies on Alcohol and Drugs*, *55*(3), 276–284.

Research Society on Alcoholism. (2011). Impact of alcoholism and alcohol induced disease on America. Retrieved March 2016, from http://www.rsoa.org/2011-04-11RSAWhitePaper.pdf

Rubin, K. H., & Mills, R. S. (1991). Conceptualizing developmental pathways to internalizing disorders in childhood. *Canadian Journal of Behavioural Science/Revue Canadienne Des Sciences Du Comportement*, *23*(3), 300–317.

Rutter, M. (1987). Psychosocial resilience and protective mechanisms. *American Journal of Orthopsychiatry*, *57*(3), 316–331.

Rutter, M. (1996). Developmental psychopathology: Concepts and prospects. In M. F. Lenzenweger & J. J. Haugaard (Eds.), *Frontiers of developmental psychopathology* (pp. 209–237). New York, NY: Oxford University Press.

Salo, S., & Flykt, M. (2013). The impact of parental addiction on child development. In N. E. Suchman, M. Pajulo, & L. C. Mayes (Eds.), *Parenting and substance abuse: Developmental approaches to intervention* (pp. 195–210). New York, NY: Oxford University Press.

Sapolsky, R. M. (2007). Stress, stress-related disease, and emotional regulation. In J. J. Gross (Ed.), *Handbook on emotion regulation* (pp. 606–615). New York, NY: Guilford Press.

Saraceno, L., Munafo, M., Heron, J., Craddock, N., & van den Bree, M. (2009). Genetic and non-genetic influences on the development of co-occurring alcohol problem use and internalizing symptoms in adolescence: A review. *Addiction*, *104*, 1110–1121.

Schuetze, P., Eiden, R. D., & Danielewicz, S. (2009). The association between prenatal cocaine exposure and physiological regulation at 13 months of age. *Journal of Child Psychology and Psychiatry*, *50*(11), 1401–1409. doi:10.1111/j.1469-7610.2009.02165.x

Schuetze, P., Lopez, F. A., Granger, D. A., & Eiden, R. D. (2008). The association between prenatal exposure to cigarettes and cortisol reactivity and regulation in 7 month-old infants. *Developmental Psychobiology*, *50*(8), 819–834. doi:10.1002/dev.20334

Seifer, R., LaGasse, L. L., Lester, B., Bauer, C. R., Shankaran, S., Bada, H. S., . . . Liu, J. (2004). Attachment status in children prenatally exposed to cocaine and other substances. *Child Development*, *75*, 850–868. doi: 0009-3920/2004/7503-0013

Shadur, J. M., & Hussong, A. M. (June, 2013). Parent emotion socialization and emotion regulation in substance abusing families. A paper presented at the 36th Annual Research Society on Alcoholism Scientific Meeting, Orlando, FL.

Shedler, J., & Block, J. (1990). Adolescent drug use and psychological health: A longitudinal inquiry. *American Psychologist*, *45*(5), 612–630. doi:10.1037/0003-066X.45.5.612

Sher, K. J. (1991). Psychological characteristics of children of alcoholics: Overview of research methods and findings. In M. Galanter (Ed.), *Recent developments in alcoholism, Vol. 9. Children of alcoholics* (pp. 301–326). New York, NY: Plenum Press.

Sher, K. J., & Gotham, H. J. (1999). Pathological alcohol involvement: A developmental disorder of young adulthood. *Development and Psychopathology*, *11*(4), 933–956. doi:10.1017/S0954579499002394

Sher, K. J., Grekin, E. R., & Gross, J. J. (2007). Alcohol and affect regulation. In J. Gross (Ed.), *Handbook of emotion regulation* (pp. 560–580). New York, NY: Guilford Press.

Sher, K. J., & Levenson, R. W. (1982). Risk for alcoholism and individual differences in the stress-response-dampening effect of alcohol. *Journal of Abnormal Psychology*, *91*(5), 350–367. doi:10.1037/0021-843X.91.5.350

Shipman, K. L., Schneider, R., Fitzgerald, M. M., Sims, C., Swisher, L., & Edwards, A. (2007). Maternal emotion socialization in maltreating and non-maltreating families: Implications for children's emotion regulation. *Social Development*, *16*(2), 268–285. doi:10.1111/j.1467-9507.2007.00384.x

Shipman, K., Schneider, R., & Sims, C. (2005). Emotion socialization in maltreating and non-maltreating mother-child dyads: Implications for children's adjustment. *Journal of Clinical Child and Adolescent Psychology*, *34*(3), 590–596. doi:10.1207/s15374424jccp3403_14

Silk, J. S., Shaw, D. S, Prout, J. P., O'Rourke, F., Lane, T. J., & Kovacs, M. (2011). Socialization of emotion and offspring internalizing symptoms in mothers with childhood-onset depression. *Journal of Applied Developmental Psychology*, *32*, 127–136. doi:10.1016/j.appdev.2011.02.001

Söderström, K., & Skårderud, F. (2009). Mentalization-based treatment in families with parental substance use disorder: Theoretical framework. *Nordic Psychology*, *61*(3), 47–65. doi:10.1027/1901-2276.61.3.47

Solis, J. M., Shadur, J. M., Burns, A. R., & Hussong, A. M. (2012). Understanding the diverse needs of children whose parents abuse substances. *Current Drug Abuse Reviews*, *5*(2), 135–147.

Stewart, S. H., Finn, P. R., & Pihl, R. O. (1992). The effects of alcohol on the cardiovascular stress response in men at high risk for alcoholism: A dose response study. *Journal of Studies on Alcohol*, *53*(5), 499–506.

Streissguth, A. P., Bookstein, F. L., Barr, H. M., Sampson, P. D., O'Malley, K., & Young, J. K. (2004). Risk factors for adverse life outcomes in fetal alcohol syndrome and fetal alcohol effects. *Journal of Developmental and Behavioral Pediatrics*, *25*(4), 228–238. doi:10.1097/00004703-200408000-00002

Substance Abuse and Mental Health Services Administration. (2004). *National Survey on Drug Use and Health (ICPSR04373-v1)*. Ann Arbor, MI: Inter-University Consortium for Political and Social Research. doi:10.3886/ICPSR04373.v1

Substance Abuse and Mental Health Services Administration. (2011). Results from the 2010 National Survey on Drug

Use and Health: Summary of national findings. Washington, DC: Author.

Tarter, R. E., Vanyukov, M., Giancola, P., Dawes, M., Blackson, T., Mezzich, A., & Clark, D. B. (1999). Etiology of early age onset substance use disorder: A maturational perspective. *Development and Psychopathology*, *11*(4), 657–683. doi:10.1017/S0954579499002266

Tarullo, A. R., & Gunnar, M. R. (2006). Child maltreatment and the developing HPA axis. *Hormones and Behavior*, *50*(4), 632–639. doi:10.1016/j.yhbeh.2006.06.010

Taylor, G. J., Bagby, R. M., & Parker, J. D. A. (1997). *Disorders of affect regulation: Alexithymia in medical and psychiatric illness*. New York, NY: Cambridge University Press. doi:10.1017/CBO9780511526831

Testa, M., Quigley, B. M., & Eiden, R. D. (2003). The effects of prenatal alcohol exposure on infant mental development: A meta-analytical review. *Alcohol and Alcoholism*, *38*(4), 295–304. doi:10.1093/alcalc/agg087

Thomas, D., Leicht, C., Hughes, C., Madigan, A., & Dowell, K. (2003). Maltreatment incidence, impact, and existing models of prevention. Retrieved from https://www.childwelfare.gov/pubPDFs/emerging_practices_report.pdf

Thompson, R. A. (1994). Emotion regulation: A theme in search of definition. *Monographs of the Society for Research in Child Development*, *59*(2–3), 25–52, 250–283. doi:10.2307/1166137

Thompson, R. (2008). Early attachment and later development: Familiar questions, new answers. In J. Cassidy & P. R. Shaver (Eds.) *Handbook of attachment: Theory, research, and clinical applications* (2nd ed., pp. 348–365). New York, NY: Guilford Press.

Thompson, R. A., Lewis, M. D., & Calkins, S. D. (2008). Reassessing emotion regulation. *Child Development Perspectives*, *2*(3), 124–131. doi:10.1111/j.1750-8606.2008.00054.x

Thurlow, M. L., & Gilman, C. J. (1999). Issues and practices in the screening of preschool children. In E. V. Nuttall, I. Romero, & J. Kalesnik (Eds.), *Assessing and screening preschoolers: Psychological and educational dimensions* (2nd ed., pp. 72–93). Needham Heights, MA: Allyn & Bacon.

Tubman, J. G., Wagner, E. F., & Langer, L. M. (2003). Patterns of depressive symptoms, drinking motives, and sexual behavior among substance abusing adolescents: Implications for health risk. *Journal of Child and Adolescent Substance Abuse*, *13*(1), 37–57. doi:10.1300/J029v13n01_03

Tucker, J. S., Ellickson, P. L., Collins, R. L., & Klein, D. J. (2006). Are drug experimenters better adjusted than abstainers and users? A longitudinal study of adolescent marijuana use. *Journal of Adolescent Health*, *39*(4), 488–494. doi:10.1016/j.jadohealth.2006.03.012

Turner, H. A., Finkelhor, D., Hamby, S, & Shattuck, A. (2013). Family structure, victimization, and child mental health in a nationally representative sample. *Social Science and Medicine*, *87*, 39–51. doi:10.1016/j.socscimed.2013.02.034

US Department of Health and Human Services. (2007). The surgeon general's call to action to prevent and reduce underage drinking. Washington, DC: US Department of Health and Human Services, Office of the Surgeon General.

US Department of Health and Human Services. (2012). Child maltreatment 2012. Washington, DC: US Department of Health & Human Services, Administration for Children and Families, Administration on Children, Youth and Families, Children's Bureau.

Walsh, C., MacMillan, H. L., & Jamieson, E. (2003). The relationship between parental substance abuse and child maltreatment: findings from the Ontario Health Supplement. *Child Abuse and Neglect*, *27*, 1409–1425.

Williams, D. R., & Mohammed, S. A. (2009). Discrimination and racial disparities in health: Evidence and needed research. *Journal of Behavioral Medicine*, *32*(1), 20–47.

Windle, M., & Windle, R. C. (2006). Alcohol consumption and its consequences among adolescents and young adults. In M. Galanter & M. Galanter (Eds.), *Alcohol problems in adolescents and young adults: Epidemiology, neurobiology, prevention, and treatment* (pp. 67–83). New York, NY: Springer Science + Business Media.

Winters, K. C., Stinchfield, R. D., Latimer, W. W., & Stone, A. (2008). Internalizing and externalizing behaviors and their association with the treatment of adolescents with substance use disorder. *Journal of Substance Abuse Treatment*, *35*(3), 269–278. doi:10.1016/j.jsat.2007.11.002

Wolin, S. J., & Bennett, L. A. (1984). Family rituals. *Family Process*, *23*(3), 401–420. doi:10.1111/j.1545-5300.1984.00401.x

Wolock, I., & Magura, S. (1996). Parental substance abuse as a predictor of child maltreatment re-reports. *Child Abuse and Neglect*, *20*(12), 1183–1193. doi:10.1016/S0145-2134(96)00114-7

Young, N. K., Boles, S. M., & Otero, C. (2007). Parental substance use disorders and child maltreatment: Overlaps, gaps, and opportunities. *Child Maltreatment*, *12*, 137–149. doi:10.1177/1077559507300322

Zimmermann, U. S., Buchmann, A. F., Spring, C., Uhr, M., Holsboer, F., & Wittchen, H. (2009). Ethanol administration dampens the prolactin response to psychosocial stress exposure in sons of alcohol-dependent fathers. *Psychoneuroendocrinology*, *34*(7), 996–1003. doi:10.1016/j.psyneuen.2009.01.015

Zucker, R. A. (2006). Alcohol use and the alcohol use disorders: A developmental- biopsychosocial systems formulation covering the life course. In D. Cicchetti & D. Cohen (Eds.), *Developmental psychopathology, Vol 3. Risk, disorder, and adaptation* (2nd ed., pp. 620–656). Hoboken, NJ: Wiley.

Zucker, R. A., Chermack, S. T., & Curran, G. M. (2000). Alcoholism: A life span perspective on etiology and course. In A. Sameroff, M. Lewis, & S. Miller (Eds.), *Handbook of developmental psychopathology* (2nd ed., pp. 569–587). New York, NY: Plenum Press.

Zucker, R. A., Donovan, J. E., Masten, A. S., Mattson, M. E., & Moss, H. B. (2008). Early developmental processes and the continuity of risk for underage drinking and problem drinking. *Pediatrics*, *121*(Suppl. 4), S252–S272. doi:10.1542/peds.2007-2243B

Zucker, R. A., Heitzeg, M. M., & Nigg, J. T. (2011). Parsing the undercontrol-disinhibition pathway to substance use disorders: A multilevel developmental problem. *Child Development Perspectives*, *5*(4), 248–255. doi:10.1111/j.1750-8606.2011.00172.x

Zucker, R. A., Wong, M. M., Clark, D. B., Leonard, K. E., Schulenberg, J. E., Cornelius, J. R., . . . Puttler, L. I. (2006). Predicting risky drinking outcomes longitudinally: What kind of advance notice can we get? *Alcoholism: Clinical and Experimental Research*, *30*(2), 243–252. doi:10.1111/j.1530-0277.2006.00033.x

Child and Adolescent Socialization into Substance Use

John E. Donovan

Abstract

This chapter reviews the literature on family, peer, and media influences on alcohol, tobacco, and other drug use among children and adolescents. Parental drinking and drug use are significant predictors of child and adolescent drinking, smoking, and marijuana use. Furthermore, parental substance use is associated with lower quality parenting and family management practices, which are, in turn, associated with greater offspring substance use. In addition, parental substance use and parenting practices are associated with adolescents' affiliation with substance-using friends. Parental nonuse and effective parenting practices buffer the relation between friends' modeling of substance use and adolescent offspring substance use. Sibling and friend substance use relate both concurrently and longitudinally to adolescent substance use. Lastly, child and adolescent exposure to alcohol and smoking on television and in films, and to alcohol and cigarette advertising, constitutes a third independent source of modeling and influence on child and adolescent substance use.

Key Words: alcohol use, smoking, marijuana use, children, adolescents, parents, peers, parenting, socialization, modeling

In the research literature on delinquency, socialization was long considered an outcome defining the opposite pole of a continuum from delinquency, a usage exemplified in the Socialization (So) Scale of the California Psychological Inventory (Gough, 1965; Stein, Gough, & Sarbin, 1966). Socialization is defined here not as an outcome but as a lifelong process through which an individual's personality, attitudes, and behaviors are shaped by agents in their evolving social environments of origin and selection.

In the present treatment, the social environment is conceptualized as a field of forces impacting the individual through a variety of mechanisms and processes (see Lewin, 1939). Social agents include the members of the adolescent's immediate family (parents, guardians, siblings); their extended family (grandparents, aunts, uncles, cousins); their close friends, classmates, and schoolmates; and their social-media peers, online video game competitors,

and the denizens of multiple intersecting subcultures and cultures inhabiting the Internet/blogosphere and the mass media of literature, magazines, art, advertising, television, movies, radio, and music. The following sections of this chapter review research on the roles of the family environment, the peer environment, and the social-representational environment in the socialization into substance use. The mix and relative influence of these interacting social environments will of course vary from one adolescent to another, as well as from one stage of adolescence to another.

Relevant Socialization Theories

A number of theories are relevant to an understanding of the socialization processes influencing adolescent involvement in substance use. I will only mention a few of the more important theories here. The most influential of these is social learning theory (SLT; Bandura, 1977) and its many offshoots. In their broadest form, social learning theories attend to the interaction between an individual and the social environment, and they focus on the various avenues through which behavior is shaped, including observational learning, imitation, and reinforcement. Briefly, SLT states that children learn about drinking, smoking, and drug use through observation of the behaviors of others in their social environment (including models observed on television and in the movies) and through their vicarious learning of the positive and negative consequences for these individuals of their substance use. According to the theory (Bandura, 1977, p. 88), responsiveness to modeling cues is determined by the characteristics of the models, the attributes of the observers, and the outcome expectancies associated with matching the modeled behavior. Important characteristics of the models include their high status, competence, and power. Based on these criteria, parents and close friends should be considered as highly salient models for substance use behavior.

Social control theories (also called bonding theories) generally derive from the sociological literature focused on delinquency (e.g., Hirschi, 1969). The underlying premise is that people will engage in such behavior unless they have a reason not to, specifically, strong bonds to conventional social agents and to the conventional institutions of society such as the family, religion, school systems, and the like.

Adolescent socialization theory (Kandel, 1980; Kandel & Andrews, 1987) encompasses aspects of both social learning and social control theories. Adolescent drug use behavior is considered to depend on intergenerational influences from parents as well as intragenerational influences from peers. Consistent with SLT, imitation of others' behavior as well as social reinforcement lead to the adoption of substance use behaviors and the internalization of definitions and values held by significant others. In addition, closeness to parents is seen as a control against involvement in deviant behavior, regardless of the parents' own behavior. It posits that parents are the primary source of socialization for the initiation of licit substance use in childhood and early adolescence, and that peer influence becomes more important in adolescence and for the escalation of substance use, including transitions into illicit drug use and misuse of licit substances.

Similarly, primary socialization theory (Oetting & Donnermeyer, 1998) states that adolescent drug use is socialized by three primary contexts of interaction—the family, schools, and peers—and focuses on the role of each context in transmitting norms concerning substance use. Where child bonding to the family or to the schools is low, children or adolescents are considered more likely to bond with deviant peers.

Interactional theory (Thornberry, 1987) also combines elements of both social control and social learning theories. The theory proposes that deviant behavior (e.g., drug use) results from both a weakening of the individual's bonds to conventional society and its agents, and from the individual's exposure to a social environment in which deviant behavior (including substance use) can be learned and reinforced.

The present chapter is organized around a framework that undergirds these theories of substance use socialization. The basic tenet of this general socialization framework is that there is a multiply moderated and mediated relationship between the model's and the child's substance use, in which exposure to social modeling influences the child's use if there is a positive relationship between them, leading to identification with the social agent, resulting in the internalization of substance-specific cognitions that are expressed in substance use if the adolescent is offered the substance, and in the context of low levels of parental control or monitoring. Parent control can be either direct behavioral control (such as rules or monitoring) or psychological control based on a positive relationship (as in bonding). There are three major pathways of social influence in this framework: a social control pathway; an identification pathway; and a bonding pathway (see Figure 16.1). In the following sections, I review the empirical support for the linkages between and among the variables comprising this general socialization framework.

Social models for drinking and drug use are often assessed in the literature by adolescent perceptions rather than by direct reports of these behaviors by the social agent in question. Kandel (1980) and others have warned of the dangers of relying solely on adolescent perceptions of parental and peer behavior as measures of their modeling behavior, citing the possibility of projection as a contributor to whatever relations are observed. On the other hand, it is difficult to understand how exposure to behavioral models is to be understood as an influence on child or adolescent behavior in the absence of their perceptions of that exposure. Strong arguments have been made for the primacy of the perceived social environment in the explanation of adolescent problem behavior (see Jessor & Jessor, 1973).

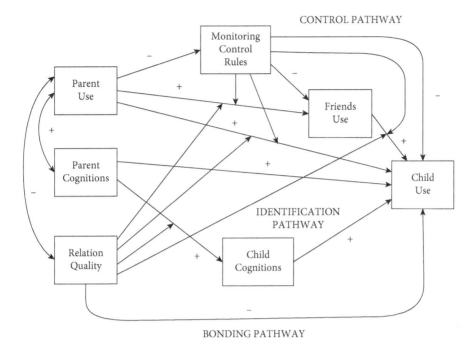

CONTROL PATHWAY

Figure 16.1. General socialization framework. (Single-headed arrows denote direction of influence; double-headed arrows denote correlation only; arrows intersecting other arrows denote moderation or buffering effects; plus or minus signs denote positive or negative relations.)

In the review that follows, I rely on child perceptions as well as parent reports of parental substance use, as these sources correlate strongly among both children (Barnett, O'Loughlin, Paradis, & Renaud, 1997; Dielman, Leech, & Loveland-Cherry, 1995; Murray, Kiryluk, & Swan, 1985; Smith, Miller, Kroll, Simmons, & Gallen, 1999) and adolescents (Aas, Jakobsen, & Anderssen, 1996; Gilman et al., 2009; Scholte, Poelen, Willemsen, Boomsma, & Engels, 2008; White, Johnson, & Buyske, 2000).

It is important to bear in mind that alcohol use, smoking, marijuana use, and other substance use correlate significantly in adolescence and tend to load on a single underlying factor (e.g., Catalano, White, Fleming, & Haggerty, 2011; Donovan & Jessor, 1985; Farrell, Danish, & Howard, 1992; Jessor & Jessor, 1977; Lynskey, Fergusson, & Horwood, 1998; McGee & Newcomb, 1992; McGue & Iacono, 2005; Palmer et al., 2009). These substances also constitute stages in a developmental sequence of progression in substance involvement in adolescence (see Kandel, 2002), generally starting with either alcohol or tobacco use, then marijuana use, followed by other illicit drug use (including nonmedical use of prescription drugs). These interrelations suggest that one could

generalize findings across substances to a certain extent.

The sections that follow are organized around the family environment, the peer environment, and the social-representational environment of the mass media and the Internet as sources of substance use socialization for children and adolescents. Within each of these social environments, I attend to research on the socialization of alcohol use, tobacco use, and marijuana or other drug use, generally in that order.

THE FAMILY ENVIRONMENT

Within the family environment, children and adolescents are exposed to parent, sibling, and other relatives' alcohol use, smoking, and other drug use and have their easiest access to these substances if family members use them.

Availability of Alcohol in the Home

According to the 2011 US National Survey on Drug Use and Health (NSDUH), approximately 90% of adults aged 26–54 years have ever drank, approximately 75% have had a drink in the past year, and about 62% have had a drink in the past month (Substance Abuse and Mental Health Administration [SAMHSA], 2012). Data from the

2005–2010 NSDUH show that 10.5% of all children live with a parent who had an alcohol use disorder in the past year (Center for Behavioral Health Statistics and Quality, 2011). The majority of children in the United States were thus likely exposed to parental alcohol use, and a substantial minority was exposed to parental alcohol abuse.

When children are asked where they got their first drink of alcohol, they overwhelmingly cite their parents or their home as the source of the alcohol (Johnson, Greenlund, Webber, & Berenson, 1997; Strycker, Duncan, & Pickering, 2003). The sources of alcohol change as children get older, with an increasing reliance on other adults and friends as sources as they move into and through adolescence (Center for Behavioral Health Statistics and Quality, 2011; Foley, Altman, Durant, & Wolfson, 2004; Hearst, Fulkerson, Maldonado-Molina, Perry, & Komro, 2007; SAMHSA, 2008).

Availability of Tobacco in the Home

Smoking is much less common among US parents than is drinking. National surveys show that among adults old enough to have children (aged 26–54 years), only 24%–34% smoked cigarettes in the past month, and many fewer used other tobacco products (SAMHSA, 2012). Thus, the availability of cigarettes and other tobacco products in the home, and hence, exposure to parental models for tobacco use, is much lower than for alcohol.

In contrast to alcohol use, fewer children had their first cigarette at home. In a study of third- to sixth-grade children (Greenlund, Johnson, Webber, & Berenson, 1997), only 40.5% of those who had ever tried cigarettes reported they first smoked with someone in the family. Access to cigarettes was significantly greater among children who had a parent who smoked. Among adolescent smokers, the most common sources of tobacco are friends, taking cigarettes from adults without their knowledge, purchases from stores, and purchases from vending machines (Robinson, Dalton, & Nicholson, 2006).

Availability of Other Drugs in the Home

There is also exposure to parental and other adult use of marijuana and other drugs in the home. National statistics from the 2011 NSDUH suggest that among adults aged 26 years and over, 6.3% had used an illicit drug in the past month, 4.8% had used marijuana, and 0.4% had used cocaine (SAMHSA, 2012). Estimates based on 2002–2007 NSDUH data indicate that 3% of children under the age of 18 lived with a parent who was dependent on or who abused illicit drugs (SAMHSA, 2009). A similar percentage (2.8%) of children in the United Kingdom lived with a drug-dependent parent in 2000 (Manning, Best, Faulkner, & Titherington, 2009).

Explicit parental socialization of illicit drug use has rarely been studied. Children in these households are nonetheless exposed to these drugs on a regular basis. News reports of kindergarten children innocently bringing baggies of marijuana, crack pipes, or dime bags of heroin to school for "show and tell" are unfortunately not uncommon.

The Influence of Parent Drinking on Child and Adolescent Drinking

A substantial literature has examined the influence of parental drinking on adolescent drinking. The following sections focus on parental alcoholism and parental drinking separately (although these obviously overlap).

Early adolescent children of alcoholics are more likely to have ever used alcohol, to have used it in the past 3 months, and to have ever had an alcohol- or drug-related social consequence or dependence symptom than are children of nonalcoholics (Chassin, Rogosch & Barrera, 1991; see also Chalder, Elgar, & Bennett, 2006; Cranford, Zucker, Jester, Puttler, & Fitzgerald, 2010; Mann, Chassin, & Sher, 1987). Parental alcoholism has also been shown to predict onset of alcohol use and of drunkenness by ages 12–14 years (Wong, Brower, Fitzgerald, & Zucker, 2004) as well as adolescent symptoms of alcohol use disorder (Buu et al., 2009).

Due to our interest in the socialization of child and adolescent drinking, we focus most of our attention on parent drinking rather than on parent alcoholism. This is not to suggest that modeling of alcohol use does not occur in families of alcoholics (see Brown, Tate, Vik, Haas, & Aarons, 1999), but to acknowledge that there are genetic factors that interact with environmental influence on socialization in such families.

Although there is not yet a large literature on alcohol use among children, research shows that child exposure to parental drinking is associated with both sipping or tasting of alcohol (Donovan & Molina, 2008, 2014; Jackson, Ennett, Dickinson, & Bowling, 2012, 2013; Quine & Stephenson, 1990) and drinking among elementary schoolchildren (Chen et al., 2011; Dielman et al., 1995; Felton et al., 1999; Iannotti & Bush, 1992; Jackson, 1997; Jackson, Henriksen, Dickinson, & Levine, 1997; Quine & Stephenson, 1990).

The literature also shows that parental drinking is associated with adolescent drinking frequency. This has been shown in numerous studies, including studies that relied on adolescent perceptions of parent drinking (for example, see recent studies by Beal, Ausiello, & Perrin, 2001; Epstein, Griffin, & Botvin, 2008; Hanewinkel, Tanski, & Sargent, 2007; Kelly et al., 2012), as well as studies utilizing parent reports of their own drinking (Aas et al., 1996; Casswell, Stewart, Connolly, & Silva, 1991; Duncan, Duncan, & Strycker, 2003, 2006; Latendresse et al., 2008; Ouellette, Gerrard, Gibbons, & Reis-Bergan, 1999; Shortt, Hutchinson, Chapman, & Toumbourou, 2007). In general, the magnitude of the correlation is modest (usually .10 to .24).

Parental drinking has also been shown to be an antecedent predictor of adolescents' initiation of drinking (e.g., Brook, Whiteman, Gordon, Nomura, & Brook, 1986; Ellickson & Hays, 1991; Fisher, Miles, Austin, Camargo, & Colditz, 2007; Hung, Yen, & Wu, 2009; Jackson, Henriksen, & Dickinson, 1999; Kandel & Andrews, 1987; Spijkerman et al., 2007), as well as an antecedent predictor of younger ages of onset of drinking (Hawkins et al., 1997; Hellandsjo Bu, Watten, Foxcroft, Ingebrigsen, & Relling, 2002; Pedersen & Skrondal, 1998; Stoolmiller et al., 2012) or early-onset drinking (Donovan & Molina, 2011; Hayatbakhsh et al., 2008; Rossow & Kuntsche, 2013). Furthermore, parental drinking has been found to be an antecedent predictor of adolescent alcohol misuse as well (Ellickson, Tucker, Klein, & McGuigan, 2001; Seljamo et al., 2006; van der Vorst, Engels, & Burk, 2010). (See also a review of longitudinal studies by Ryan, Jorm, & Lubman, 2010.)

It should be noted, however, that some studies report nonsignificant relations between parental and adolescent drinking (e.g., Andrews, Hops, Ary, Tildesley, & Harris, 1993; Dishion & Loeber, 1985; Prendergast & Schaefer, 1974; van der Vorst, Engels, Meeus, & Deković, 2006) or report (without including a correlation matrix) that parental drinking did not show a significant path coefficient to adolescent drinking in a path model or structural equation model (e.g., Bank et al., 1985; Biddle, Bank, & Marlin 1980; Hansen et al., 1987). Mediation of the effects of parental drinking by parenting practices and their influence on choice of friends may contribute to these findings of no relation and to the relatively modest levels of association found between parent and adolescent alcohol involvement.

Some of the variation in the magnitude of this relation between parent and adolescent alcohol involvement may be due to reliance on disparate indicators of parent drinking (including number of parents who drink, parental frequency of drinking, parental intake per occasion, parent binge drinking, and parent problem drinking). Additional variation may be a function of the time interval between the assessments of parent current drinking and adolescent current drinking. It may also be the case that different indicators of parental drinking may be more appropriate for examination at different child ages and for different stages of child/adolescent alcohol involvement.

The literature is somewhat mixed regarding the relative effects of father versus mother drinking. There are, however, a fair number of studies that found that *both* mother's and father's drinking relate to adolescent drinking (e.g., Aas et al., 1996; Epstein et al., 2008; Kelly et al., 2012; Rossow & Rise, 1994; Spijkerman et al., 2007; Thompson & Wilsnack, 1987). Several studies suggest that mother drinking is more important because children generally spend more time with their mothers, have better relationships with their mothers, and would therefore be more likely to model her behavior (Blanton, Gibbons, Gerrard, Conger, & Smith, 1997; Cranford et al., 2010; Macleod et al., 2008).

Relation of Parental Drinking to Parenting Styles and Practices

In the general socialization framework, parenting practices and relationship quality may serve as moderators of the relation between a child's observation of parental drinking and his or her own adoption of alcohol use. In addition, in social control theory, the emotional connection to parents is itself considered protective against involvement in underage drinking. There is some evidence in the literature for a linkage between parental drinking and parenting styles and practices. In this review, we distinguish between general parenting and alcohol-specific parenting. Alcohol-specific parenting refers to parental beliefs, attitudes, and rules that refer directly to child alcohol use.

Studies have shown that there is greater alcohol-impaired parenting, child abuse, and neglect in the households of alcoholic parents (Bijur, Kurzon, Overpeck, & Scheidt, 1992; Dube et al., 2001; Kelleher, Chaffin, Hollenberg, & Fischer, 1994). Sher (1991) proposed several models for the influence of parental alcoholism on offspring behavior.

The *deviance-proneness submodel* specifies that parental alcoholism impacts offspring behavior through deficits in parenting (e.g., failure to monitor child behavior) that impact child temperament, and that also moderate the relations between temperament and peer influence as well as between school failure and peer influence. In partial support of this model, Chassin, Pillow, Curran, Molina, and Barrera (1993) found that alcoholic fathers tend to monitor their children less than do nonalcoholic fathers (see also Clark, Kirisci, Mezzich, & Chung, 2008). Alcoholic parents were also rated by their children as being less consistent in their discipline and rule setting (King & Chassin, 2004).

Latendresse et al. (2008) showed that greater parental drinking at age 12 years for the child was associated with greater relational tension, fewer shared family activities, greater discipline, and less parental monitoring, but it did not relate consistently to parental warmth or autonomy granting. Other research has shown a relation between parent drinking and less relationship warmth, closeness, bonding, or support (Barnes, Reifman, Farrell, & Dintcheff, 2000; Gerrard, Gibbons, Zhao, Russell, & Reis-Bergan, 1999; Kuendig & Kuntsche, 2006; Zhang, Welte, & Wieczorek, 1999).

Parental drinking is associated as well with more permissive alcohol-specific parenting, including greater approval for adolescent drinking (Dielman, Butchart, & Shope, 1993; Webb et al., 1991; Yu, 2003) and fewer household rules against teen drinking (Pieters et al., 2012; van der Vorst et al., 2006; van Zundert et al., 2006; Yu, 2003; but see Koning et al., 2010). Reimuller, Hussong, and Ennett (2011) found that the more parents drank, the more permissive were their communications about alcohol with their children.

Importantly, most studies of the influence of parental drinking have failed to recognize that both parental drinking and parenting practices change as children move into and through adolescence (see Tildesley & Andrews, 2008; van der Zwaluw et al., 2008). Most studies have only examined the influence of baseline parental drinking (at various child/adolescent ages). There are a number of reasons to expect change in parent drinking, including more parent opportunities to have nights out once children are older, and the increases in stress that accompany their child's movement into adolescence.

Influence of Parenting Practices on Offspring Drinking

The third linkage of importance in the socialization framework is that between parenting and child or adolescent drinking. In studies of children, greater parental monitoring of child behavior was associated a year later with lower levels of drinking without parental permission, smoking, or use of marijuana or other drugs (Chilcoat, Dishion, & Anthony, 1995) and with later ages of initiation of alcohol, tobacco, or other drug use (Chilcoat & Anthony, 1996). Among fifth-grade children, less effective parenting practices were associated with child drinking (Jackson et al., 1997).

A recent review of the longitudinal literature on adolescent drinking (Ryan et al., 2010) concluded that less parental monitoring, lower parent–child relationship quality, and poorer general communication related to both earlier initiation of drinking and to higher levels of later adolescent alcohol use. This review also concluded that greater parental involvement related to delayed initiation of drinking but not to later levels of alcohol use; and that parent–child conflict did not show a consistent relationship.

With respect to alcohol-specific parenting, fourth- to sixth-grade children who had started to drink perceived their parents as being less likely to know if they were drinking with friends, as communicating with them less often about not drinking, and as less likely to react if they knew the child were drinking than did children who had not yet started drinking (Jackson, 1997). In a longitudinal follow-up study of fifth-grade children, Jackson et al. (1999) found that children's report of having had a drink of alcohol in the past 30 days in seventh grade was predicted by lower levels of alcohol use monitoring, greater permission to drink at home, and greater parental permissiveness at baseline. Interestingly, these alcohol-socialization variables partially mediated the effects of both earlier parental modeling and the child's fifth-grade alcohol use.

Ryan et al.'s (2010) review of the longitudinal adolescent research concluded that the alcohol-specific parenting variables of greater parental disapproval of drinking and parental support did not relate consistently to earlier onset of drinking, but they did relate to later alcohol use levels (see also Kelly, O'Flaherty, Toumbourou, et al., 2011). This review also concluded that having strict rules about adolescent drinking and having alcohol-specific communication showed no consistent longitudinal relation to adolescent drinking.

Parenting factors also relate to *growth* in adolescent alcohol involvement. Research has shown that there is slower growth in adolescent drinking when there is greater positive identification with parents (Gutman, Eccles, Peck, & Malanchuk, 2011), greater parental support (King, Molina, & Chassin, 2009), greater family cohesion and less family conflict (Bray, Adams, Getz, & Baer, 2001), and greater parental monitoring (Barnes et al., 2000; Barnes, Hoffman, Welte, Farrell, & Dintcheff, 2006). Capaldi, Stoolmiller, Kim, and Yoerger (2009) found that increases (or maintenance) in parental monitoring were associated with less growth in alcohol use. With respect to substance-specific parenting, Martino, Ellickson, and McCaffrey (2009) found that when parents maintained strong disapproval of substance use throughout adolescence, adolescents were more likely to abstain from heavy drinking across this life stage.

Parental Influences on Adolescent Smoking

As was true for alcohol use, research has shown that children and adolescents who have parents who smoke are more likely to start smoking themselves. A recent review and meta-analysis of 58 relevant studies (Leonardi-Bee, Jere, & Britton, 2011) concluded that the relative odds of initiation of smoking in children and adolescents were increased significantly if at least one parent smoked (see previous reviews: Avenevoli & Merikangas, 2003; Conrad, Flay, & Hill, 1992; Tyas & Pederson, 1998). There was also significant support for a dose–response relationship between the number of parents who smoked and child/adolescent smoking.

Children whose parents smoke are more likely to become smokers (Iannotti & Bush, 1992; Jackson, 1997; Jackson et al., 1997; Menezes, Gonçalves, Anselmi, Hallal, & Araújo, 2006). Children's exposure to parental smoking when in elementary school not only predicted initiation of smoking 1–2 years later (Jackson & Henriksen, 1997; Milton et al., 2004; O'Loughlin, Paradis, Renaud, & Sanchez Gomez, 1998; Wang, Ho, & Lam, 2011) but also increased their likelihood of smoking as adolescents (Bricker et al., 2006; Fleming, Kim, Harachi, & Catalano, 2002; Lynskey et al., 1998; O'Callaghan et al., 2006; Peterson et al., 2006).

In longitudinal research within adolescence, parental smoking has repeatedly been shown to predict initiation of smoking 1–3 years later (e.g., Forrester, Biglan, Severson, & Smolkowski, 2007; Gritz et al., 2003; Skinner, Haggerty, & Catalano, 2009; Titus-Ernstoff, Dalton, Adachi-Mejia, Longacre, & Beach, 2008; Wang et al., 1999; Wen, van Duker, & Olson, 2009). In a longitudinal study of adolescents from six European countries, smoking initiation over 1 year was predicted as well by perceived parental smoking as by perceived best friends' smoking (de Vries, Engels, Kremers, Wetzels, & Mudde, 2003; see also Hoving, Reubsaet, & de Vries, 2007; Morgenstern et al., 2013). Parents' smoking at child grade 7 was found to predict their escalation of smoking by grade 12 (Flay, Hu, & Richardson, 1998; Kim, Fleming, & Catalano, 2009).

Age at smoking initiation was predicted by parental smoking and by the duration of the adolescent's exposure to smoking parents (Gilman et al., 2009). This effect was equally strong for mother and father smoking, and it was stronger if exposure was before age 13, if both parents smoked, and if smoking fathers resided with the adolescent.

It should be noted that child and adolescent exposure to parental smoking is confounded with their exposure to secondhand smoke in the home and in the family automobile, which have also been shown to be risk factors for children's initiation of smoking (Wang et al., 2011).

In their meta-analysis of recent studies, Leonardi-Bee et al. (2011) concluded that while both mother smoking and father smoking increased the relative odds of child/adolescent smoking initiation, the effect was stronger for mother smoking than for father smoking. The analysis also found some support for stronger same-sex than opposite-sex socialization effects.

Parent Smoking, Parenting, and Child Smoking

There has been little research linking parental smoking to their general parenting practices. Parent smoking has nevertheless been found to relate to less positive parenting and inconsistent discipline (Kandel & Wu, 1995), lower levels of perceived authoritativeness (Mewse, Eiser, Slater, & Lea, 2004), and to less maternal responsiveness and demandingness (Wills, Sargent, Stoolmiller, Gibbons, & Gerrard, 2008).

Parents' use of antismoking socialization measures has been found to vary as a function of their history of smoking. Smoking parents had fewer household rules about child smoking (Harakeh, Scholte, de Vries, & Engels, 2005; Kodl & Mermelstein, 2004), a lower quality of communication about smoking issues (Harakeh, Scholte,

Vermulst, de Vries, & Engels, 2010), and weaker antismoking beliefs (Kodl & Mermelstein, 2004).

General parenting styles and practices have been found to relate to adolescent smoking in a number of studies. In cross-sectional research, adolescent smoking was associated with lower parental support (Brown & Rinelli, 2010; Simons-Morton, Haynie, Crump, Eitel, & Saylor, 2001), less closeness (Andrews, Hops, & Duncan, 1997; Foster et al., 2007; Kandel & Wu, 1995), lower family cohesion (Baer, McLaughlin, Burnside, Pokorny, & Garmezy, 1987), more parent–child conflict (Simons-Morton et al., 2001), less monitoring (Kandel & Wu, 1995; Simons-Morton et al., 2001), and harsh and inconsistent parenting (Melby, Conger, Conger, & Lorenz, 1993). Authoritative parenting, on the other hand, related to lower levels of adolescent smoking (Adamczyk-Robinette, Fletcher, & Wright, 2002; Mewse et al., 2004).

In longitudinal studies, parent–child attachment and parental involvement with the child's school in first or second grade predicted a lower likelihood of the child smoking in sixth grade (Fleming et al., 2002), and lower family cohesion at age 11–13 years predicted smoking 6 years later (Doherty & Allen, 1994). In short-term longitudinal studies within adolescence, less parental monitoring predicted cigarette use 6 months later (Biglan, Duncan, Ary, & Smolkowski, 1995), and mother responsiveness and mother demandingness among age 10–14 adolescent nonsmokers correlated negatively with their initiation of smoking 8 months later (Wills et al., 2008).

Several tobacco-specific parenting practices predict a lower likelihood of child or adolescent smoking, including antismoking communication (Harakeh et al., 2005; Jackson, 1997; Jackson & Henriksen, 1997), disapproval of child smoking (Sargent & Dalton, 2001), and having rules against smoking (Andersen, Leroux, Bricker, Rajan, & Peterson, 2004).

Parental Influences on Marijuana and Other Substance Use

There is much less recent research on the influence of parental use of marijuana or other illicit drugs on adolescents' initiation of use of such drugs. This may be partially due to the awkwardness of asking adolescents if their parents engage in illegal activities (and to school districts' reluctance to permit such questions in surveys performed in school), and partially due to the low prevalence of such behavior in adults who have children at home.

Consequently, much of the relevant research is somewhat dated.

Similar to alcohol and tobacco, when children were introduced to marijuana use during early elementary school, it was generally by a parent or close family friend, whereas in later elementary school and junior high school, it was generally by peers (Baumrind, 1985). Parental modeling of marijuana use has been found to be a significant correlate of child and adolescent use in several cross-sectional studies (Iannotti & Bush, 1992; Johnson, Shontz, & Locke, 1984; Smart & Fejer, 1972).

Longitudinal studies have demonstrated a linkage between parent-reported marijuana use and later child use, both between childhood and adolescence (Brook, Brook, Arencibia-Mireles, Richter, & Whiteman, 2001; Dishion, Capaldi, & Yoerger, 1999; Lynskey et al., 1998) and within adolescence for marijuana use (Andrews et al., 1997; Duncan, Tildesley, Duncan, & Hops, 1995; Ellickson, Tucker, Klein, & Saner, 2004) and for substance use more generally (Gibbons et al., 2004).

As was the case for drinking and smoking, parental substance use is associated with less optimal parenting practices, including poorer monitoring (Dishion, Patterson, & Reid, 1988; Dishion et al., 1999), poorer discipline (Dishion et al., 1999), less involvement (Dishion et al., 1988), and less mutual attachment with their son or daughter (Brook, Whiteman, Balka, & Cohen, 1995).

Generally, the same parenting practices and styles that relate to adolescent drinking and smoking also relate to adolescent marijuana use, including lower levels of behavioral control and monitoring (Brook, Whiteman, Nomura, Gordon, & Cohen, 1988; Cottrell, Li, Harris, et al., 2003; Dishion & Loeber, 1985; Loeber, Farrington, Stouthamer-Loeber, & van Kammen, 1998; Oxford, Harachi, Catalano, & Abbott, 2000), poor family management (Hemphill et al., 2011), lower quality parent–child relationship (Andrews et al., 1997; Brook et al., 1988), less family cohesion (Baer et al., 1987), less authoritative parenting (Baumrind, 1991; Lambourn, Mounts, Steinberg, & Dornbusch, 1991), and greater parental tolerance of child drug use (Brook et al., 1988; Ellickson et al., 2004; Hemphill et al., 2011; Olsson et al., 2003).

Moderation of Parental Modeling by Parenting Variables

There are two conflicting hypotheses in the socialization literature regarding the relation of parent–child bonding to child uptake of parental

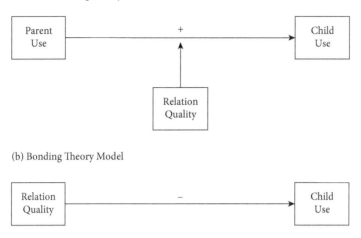

(a) Social Learning Theory Model

Parent
Use

+

Child
Use

Relation
Quality

(b) Bonding Theory Model

Relation
Quality

–

Child
Use

Figure 16.2. (*A*) Social learning theory model in contrast to (*B*) social bonding model.

use (see Figure 16.2). One hypothesis often attributed to social learning theory (SLT) is that children will model parent substance use only if they have a good relationship (usually tested as an interaction). In contrast, social control theory (SCT) states that positive parent–child bonding should result in low levels of child substance use, regardless of parent substance use. This latter hypothesis has been well supported in the preceding review of the literature.

Support for the hypothesized SLT interaction has been mixed. Yu (2003) found that the more time adolescents spent with alcohol-using parents, the more likely they were to use alcohol and to start drinking at an earlier age. Foshee and Bauman (1992) found that attachment to a parent resulted in smoking initiation if the parent was a smoker, but no initiation if the parent was not. Connectedness to nonsmoking parents predicted a lower likelihood of current adolescent smoking (Tilson, McBride, Lipkus, & Catalano, 2004). Two studies (Brook, Whiteman, Gordon, & Brook, 1984, 1986) found that greater identification with a drug-using father was associated with greater marijuana use by the late adolescent. Andrews et al. (1997) provided partial support, finding that parent–child relationship moderated the association of parent use to adolescent use for cigarettes and marijuana for mothers and for alcohol and marijuana use for fathers.

In contrast, studies examining bonding to parents who smoke or are heavy drinkers found that greater bonding is generally associated with *less* likelihood of adolescent imitation of parent behavior (Ennett et al., 2010; Foster et al., 2007; Kuendig

& Kuntsche, 2006; Wilson, McClish, Heckman, Obando, & Dahman, 2007; Zhang et al., 1999). Interestingly, in a study of families in which a parent was in methadone treatment for opiate addiction (Fleming, Brewer, Gainey, Haggerty, & Catalano, 1997), bonding to the parent was negatively related to child drug use if the parent had stopped using drugs, but it was positively related if the parent continued to use drugs.

Sibling Influences on Adolescent Substance Use

Parents are not the only family members whose substance use impacts adolescent use. Exposure to older siblings' substance use also influences younger siblings' use of the same substances.

In childhood, older sibling alcohol use is associated with the younger sibling's drinking (Chen et al., 2011; Quine & Stephenson, 1990). In adolescence, frequency of drinking correlates for older and younger siblings (Ary, Tildesley, Hops, & Andrews, 1993; Conger & Rueter, 1996; Fagan & Najman, 2005; Needle et al., 1986; van der Vorst et al., 2006). The relation between adolescent siblings' drinking levels depends on several factors, including biological relation, gender similarity, closeness in age, level of social contact, and mutual friendships (McGue, Sharma, & Benson, 1996; Rende, Slomkowski, Lloyd-Richardson, & Niaura, 2005; Scholte et al., 2008) (see Figure 16.3).

A meta-analysis of recent studies (2000–2009) shows that smoking by a sibling significantly increases the relative odds of smoking among adolescents (Leonardi-Bee et al., 2011). As was true

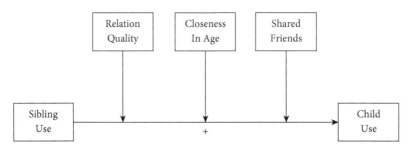

Figure 16.3. Relation of sibling substance use to child substance use. (Arrows intersecting other arrows denote moderation effects.)

for alcohol use, similarity in sibling smoking is a function of their levels of social contact and mutual friendships (Rende et al., 2005).

Longitudinal studies have found that childhood exposure to older sibling smoking predicted children's initiation of smoking, both within childhood (Milton et al., 2004; O'Loughlin et al., 1998) and years later as an adolescent (Bricker et al., 2006; Rajan et al., 2003). Sibling smoking also predicted initiation of smoking 18–24 months later among child or early adolescent nonsmokers (Forrester et al., 2007; Wills et al., 2007).

Exposure to older sibling marijuana use or illicit drug use in general is also associated with younger sibling use of the same substances (Duncan, Duncan, & Hops, 1996; Ellickson et al., 2004; Needle et al., 1986; Windle, 2000). Rowe and Gulley (1992) found that siblings were more similar in their frequency of substance use if they had a warm relationship or if they had mutual friends. Older sibling substance use correlated with the target's substance use both concurrently at target child age 11 and 3 years later (Low, Shortt, & Snyder, 2012).

Duncan et al. (1996) found that growth in older siblings' substance use over 3 years predicted growth in the younger siblings' use. They suggested that the older siblings were not only a continuing source of supply but also a source of encouragement, reinforcement, and companionship in the adolescents' substance use.

Cross-national studies replicate the finding of older sibling influence. Kokkevi et al. (2007) found not only that older sibling substance use (alcohol use, cannabis use, use of illegal drugs) related significantly to the target adolescent's use of the same substance but also that an older sibling's use of one substance was significantly associated with the adolescent's use of other substances as well.

A number of studies have suggested that sibling influence is in fact stronger in adolescence than the influence of parents (see Needle et al., 1986; Windle, 2000).

THE PEER ENVIRONMENT

The peer environment consists of a wide array of similarly aged individuals who vary in their degree of physical and socioemotional closeness to the adolescent, and hence in their potential level of influence on his or her behavior. The focus here is primarily on individuals with whom the adolescent interacts (best friends, close friends, acquaintances) or with whom they could interact if they so desired (classmates, other students at school). Peer involvement in substance use is commonly cited as the strongest risk factor for adolescent use of alcohol, tobacco, marijuana, and other drugs. The influence of peer use is apparent even in studies of children's drinking and smoking (Jackson, 1997; Quine & Stephenson, 1990). In general, the more friends an adolescent has who have used a substance (or the greater the proportion of friends), the more likely the adolescent is to also have used it. This has been shown with respect to alcohol use (e.g., Dal Cin et al., 2009; Dick et al., 2007; Grube, Morgan, & Seff, 1989; Kim & Neff, 2010; Webb et al., 1991), tobacco use (e.g., Kelly, O'Flaherty, Connor, et al., 2011; Kristjansson, Sigfusdottir, James, Allegrante, & Helgason, 2010; Liao et al., 2013), and marijuana or other drug use (Ellickson et al., 2004; Fleary, Heffer, McKyer, & Newman, 2010; Frauenglass et al., 1997; Guxens, Nebot, & Ariza, 2007; Windle, 2000). Cross-national studies replicate these associations between friend and target adolescent use (Farhat et al., 2012; Kokkevi et al., 2007).

When the predictive utility of adolescent perceptions of their friends' use is compared to that of friends' self-reported substance use, it is the child's or adolescent's perceptions that relate more strongly to own substance use (Bauman & Fisher, 1986; Iannotti & Bush, 1992; Kandel et al., 1978;

Urberg, Shyu, & Liang, 1990). Kandel (1996) has estimated that cross-sectional research relying on adolescent perceptions of friends' behavior has overestimated the predictive power of peer influence by a factor of five (see also Aseltine, 1995; Bauman & Ennett, 1996).

While reliance on adolescent perceptions of friends' substance use may exaggerate the influence of peers, there is nevertheless evidence of peer modeling in studies that relied instead on measures of nominated friends' self-reported substance use. Significant correlations were found in both cross-sectional and longitudinal research (over 1–2 years) between friends' alcohol use (Aikins, Simon, & Prinstein, 2010; Ali & Dwyer, 2010; Bauman & Fisher, 1986; Crosnoe, Erickson, & Dornbusch, 2002; Ennett et al., 2006), smoking (Adamczyk-Robinette et al., 2002; Aikins et al., 2010; Bauman & Fisher, 1986; Engels, Vitaro, den Exter Blokland, de Kemp, & Scholte, 2004; Ennett et al., 2006), marijuana use (Aseltine, 1995; Ennett et al., 2006), illicit drug use (Crosnoe et al., 2002), and substance use in general (Allen, Chango, Szwedo, Schad, & Marston, 2012; Mounts & Steinberg, 1995; Steinberg, Fletcher, & Darling, 1994).

There are two contrasting explanations for the similarity between adolescent and close friends' substance use: peer socialization or influence versus peer selection. Peer socialization refers to the situation in which the actions of the close friend bring about a change in the target adolescent's substance use to bring their behavior into correspondence. Peer selection refers to the situation in which the target adolescent chooses new friends based on their substance use. A third explanation is that both processes operate to bring about greater similarity in friends' substance use.

Longitudinal studies provide evidence that friend involvement in drug use is not just a correlate of one's own use but is also an antecedent risk factor for the initiation of substance use. In order to establish that a variable functions as a risk factor, it is necessary to demonstrate its longitudinal predictive utility among individuals who are abstainers or nonusers (see Donovan, 2004). Among alcohol abstainers, those with a close friend who drank were more likely to initiate drinking a year or so later (Fisher & Bauman, 1988; Spijkerman et al., 2007; Urberg, Değirmencioğlu, & Pilgrim, 1997). Similar results were found for smoking initiation (Forrester et al., 2007; Gritz et al., 2003; Milton et al., 2004; O'Loughlin et al., 1998; Urberg et al., 1997) and for marijuana use initiation (Ellickson et al., 2004).

Such results support the interpretation that substance use initiation results from peer socialization or influence.

Longitudinal studies have shown that the number of friends who drink or use marijuana in middle childhood or early adolescence is a significant predictor of a younger age of initiation of drinking or marijuana use, respectively (Brook, Kessler, & Cohen, 1999; Hawkins et al., 1997; Kosterman, Hawkins, Guo, Catalano, & Abbott, 2000; Pedersen & Skrondal, 1998). These findings are also consonant with a peer influence explanation.

In addition, friend modeling impacts growth in adolescent drinking and smoking over time. Parallel process models, which describe the association between the intercepts (initial levels) and slopes of two or more latent growth curves, have shown that growth in friends' drinking correlates with growth in the adolescents' own frequency of drinking (Curran, Stice, & Chassin, 1997; Simons-Morton, 2007). The analyses further show that initial level of adolescent alcohol use predicts growth in peer use (and vice versa). These results were interpreted as supporting both peer influence and peer selection processes as explanations for friends' similarity in alcohol use. With respect to smoking, parallel process analyses showed that as the number of friends who smoke increases across adolescence, so does the adolescents' own smoking involvement (Simons-Morton, 2007), and that initial level of adolescent smoking predicts growth in peer use (but *not* vice versa). These results imply that peer selection is more important than peer influence in regard to smoking.

Another approach to determining the relative influence of peer influence versus peer selection relies on social network analyses, in which all adolescents in a longitudinal study list their friends in order of closeness and all adolescents report their own substance use behavior (thus, no perceptions of peer behavior are relied upon). After a dozen studies, the clearest conclusion is that both processes operate on friend similarity in adolescent alcohol use (Burk, van der Vorst, Kerr, & Stattin, 2012; Ennett & Bauman, 1994; Kiuru, Burk, Laursen, Salmela-Aro, & Nurmi, 2010; Knecht, Burk, Weesie, & Steglich, 2010; Mercken, Steglich, Knibbe, & de Vries, 2012; Poulin, Kiesner, Pedersen, & Dishion, 2011; Sieving, Perry, & Williams, 2000) and smoking behavior (see Ennett & Bauman, 1994; Kiuru et al., 2010; Mercken, Snijders, Steglich, & de Vries, 2009; Poulin et al., 2011; Schaefer, Haas, & Bishop, 2012). There are no consistent differences between stages of adolescence within substance, or between substances at the same stage within adolescence.

With respect to friend similarity in marijuana use, Kandel (1978) found that peer influence and selection had approximately equal effect in a panel study of best friend dyads of high school students over an academic year (see also Poulin et al., 2011).

Consistent with SLT perspectives, adolescents were more likely to imitate the substance use of a more popular (higher status) substance-using peer whose friendship they desired (Allen et al., 2012; Bot, Engels, Knobbe, & Meeus, 2005; Laursen, Hafen, Kerr, & Stattin, 2012). Urberg, Luo, Pilgrim, and Degirmencioglu (2003) found that high peer acceptance and high friendship quality induced greater conformity to friends' substance use. Similarly, Cruz, Emery, and Turkheimer (2012) found that adolescents who were close to substance-using peers were involved in greater and more persistent alcohol use, whereas adolescents who were close to low-substance-using peers engaged in persistently low levels of drinking. Relevant to SLT's hypotheses concerning characteristics of the observer, modeling of peer substance use was greater among adolescents who were low in refusal self-efficacy (Allen et al., 2012; Stacy, Dent, Burton, & Flay, 1992).

Of importance in the interpretation of peer influence versus selection is the structured nature of the peer environment of opportunities to observe the use of novel (to the adolescent) substances, to meet users, to be offered new drugs, to learn about the mechanics and intricacies of their use, and to gain access to a supply. Generally, given the correlation among substances and the nature of stages of progression in drug use (Kandel, 2002), the adolescent is exposed to the use of marijuana and to offers to use through his or her friends who drink or smoke, and he or she is exposed to use of other drugs and to offers to use through friends who use marijuana (Wagner & Anthony, 2002).

FAMILY FACTORS AS MODIFIERS OF PEER INFLUENCE

An influential review of parenting research (Collins, Maccoby, Steinberg, Hetherington, & Bornstein, 2000) importantly stated: "Any psychological snapshot taken during adolescence, when peers are undeniably an important force in children's lives, rightly should be viewed as the end of a long process of socialization that began early in childhood and most likely has its origins in the family" (p. 227).

Parental modeling and parenting practices shape peer influence in at least three ways. First, they affect the child's internalization of parental attitudes toward drinking and drug use, which may counter the later influence of peers. Second, they reduce the likelihood of the child affiliating with substance-using peers, thereby reducing the child's overall risk for substance use. Third, they buffer the effects of peer modeling of substance use on the adolescent's own substance use (see Figure 16.1).

Parental Influences on the Internalization of Substance-Specific Beliefs

The influence of parental substance use on adolescents' use may be mediated by the influence of their use and parenting practices on the development of children's substance-specific cognitions, including their intentions to use substances and their substance-use outcome expectancies (the identification pathway in Figure 16.1).

Children or adolescents with parents who drink have greater intentions of drinking in the future (Collins, Ellickson, McCaffrey, & Hambarsoomians, 2007; Epstein et al., 1999; 2008; Glanton & Wulfert, 2013; Quine & Stephenson, 1990; Tildesley & Andrews; 2008), greater behavioral willingness to accept offers of alcohol (Dal Cin et al., 2009), and show faster growth in their intentions through the eighth grade (Tildesley & Andrews, 2008). Similarly, parental smoking is positively associated with child (Jackson & Henriksen, 1997) and adolescent intentions to smoke (Flay et al., 1994; Grube, Morgan, & McGree, 1986), and parental substance use significantly predicts adolescent intentions and behavioral willingness to try drugs approximately 2 years later (Gibbons et al., 2004).

Perceived parental drinking (Dal Cin et al., 2009) and perceived parental approval of drinking (Spijkerman et al., 2007) are associated with more positive adolescent prototypes of the typical drinker (but see Gerrard et al., 1999), as well as greater child susceptibility to peer pressure to use alcohol (Dielman et al., 1993).

Alcohol outcome expectancies (beliefs about the effects of alcohol) are also more positive among children of parents who drink (Chen et al., 2011; Cumsille, Sayer, & Graham, 2000; Dal Cin et al., 2009; Glanton & Wulfert, 2013; Martino et al., 2009; Ouellette et al., 1999; Pieters, van der Vorst, Engels, & Wiers, 2010). However, the relation between alcohol expectancies and parental alcoholism is less clear: Three studies show a positive relation

(Brown, Creamer, & Stetson, 1987; Brown et al., 1999; Colder, Chassin, Stice, & Curran, 1997); two studies show no relation (Cranford et al., 2010; Handley & Chassin, 2009); and two studies show a negative correlation (Campbell & Oei, 2010b; Wiers, Gunning, & Sergeant, 1998).

There are fewer studies of the relation between parental smoking and adolescent tobacco-specific cognitions. Parental smoking is associated with greater adolescent intentions to smoke (Flay et al., 1994; Harakeh, Scholte, Vermulst, de Vries, & Engels, 2004; Leatherdale, McDonald, Cameron, Jolin, & Brown, 2006; Mak, Ho, & Day, 2012), more positive attitudes toward smoking (Harakeh et al., 2004), more positive smoking expectancies (Chung, White, Hipwell, Stepp, & Loeber, 2010; Wills et al., 2008), perceptions of greater parent approval of adolescent smoking (Flay et al., 1994), and overestimation of the number of peers who smoke (Reid, Manske, & Leatherdale, 2008).

Direct examinations of the transmission of parental substance-specific cognitions to children are rare (see Campbell & Oei, 2010a). Brody and colleagues found that mother and father norms concerning the acceptability of child drinking predicted the norms held by their 10- to 12-year-old children, even after controlling for child temperament (Brody, Flor, Hollett-Wright, & McCoy, 1998), and that mother and father norms at child age 10–12 years significantly predicted the children's norms a year later (Brody, Ge, Katz, & Arias, 2000). Prins, Donovan, and Molina (2011) found that although both child and parent personal norms were disapproving of child sipping, drinking, and drunkenness at child ages 8–10 years, there was significant divergence in their norms as the children moved into early and middle adolescence. Handley and Chassin (2009), however, found no relation between mother or father expectancies and those of their adolescent child (which is consistent with the results found by Prins et al., 2011).

Studies have not explicitly addressed the mechanisms and processes involved in the transmission of substance-specific cognitions from parents to children. Nor has there been much attention to the later peer processes that presumably lead to the decay of previously internalized parental attitudes across adolescence and into emerging adulthood.

Family Influences on Choice of Friends

During childhood, parents are much more in control of the peers with whom their child interacts.

Parents can encourage greater interaction with some classmates and discourage greater interaction with others through their scheduling of play-dates and through their selection of after-school activities. With the movement into adolescence, however, parents frequently relinquish this level of control over the social life of their children. Parents may become increasingly clueless with respect to the composition of their child's peer group, especially given the explosion in teen's access to multiple avenues of peer interaction (texting, instant messaging online, Internet chat rooms, online gaming, etc.) that are outside of parental awareness or monitoring. Adolescents are also less dependent on parents for transportation to social events and venues, permitting further expansion of their opportunities to interact with peers of whom their parents might not approve.

One path through which parents can reduce their children's substance use is through their modeling of abstinence. Research has shown that parental abstinence can weaken the influence of peer modeling of substance use (Brook, 1993; Kandel, 1973; 1974; Li, Pentz, & Chou, 2002).

Parental and peer alcohol use are often positively related (Ary et al., 1993; Bush, Weinfurt, & Iannotti, 1994; Dielman et al., 1993; Gerrard et al., 1999; Hawkins et al., 1997; Huba & Bentler, 1980; Ouellette et al., 1999; Urberg, Goldstein, & Toro, 2005; Webb et al., 1991), as are parent and peer smoking (Bush et al., 1994; Flay et al., 1994; Liao et al., 2013; Wills et al., 2007) and family and friend marijuana use (Bush et al., 1994; Huba & Bentler, 1980). These correlations suggest that parental modeling of substance use may increase the likelihood that adolescents will choose to affiliate with peers who use substances.

Longitudinal studies provide stronger evidence for the impact of parental drinking and smoking on the selection of substance-using friends. Children who had heavy-drinking parents at age 11 years were more likely at age 15 years to affiliate with peers who used substances (Ferguson, Horwood, & Lynskey, 1995). Adolescents whose parents drank or smoked were more likely to associate with peers who drank or smoked, respectively, a year later (Blanton et al., 1997). Teenagers with a father who drank frequently were more willing to accept the offer of a drink from a peer (Gerrard et al., 1999). When choosing a new friend, adolescents having two smokers as parents tended to choose a smoker (Engels et al., 2004). Whether these friendship choices are a consequence of pro–substance use cognitions transmitted by their drinking or smoking parents has not yet been examined.

In addition to parental drinking and smoking, a number of other parenting variables also predict affiliation with deviant or substance-using peers. Greater parental monitoring (or knowledge) is associated with having fewer friends who drink (Frauenglass et al., 1997; Kim & Neff, 2010), smoke (Frauenglass et al., 1997), or use drugs (Bahr, Hoffmann, & Yang, 2005; Erickson, Crosnoe, & Dornbusch, 2000; Frauenglass et al., 1997; Mounts & Steinberg, 1995; Wang, Simons-Morton, Farhat, & Luk, 2009). In a parallel process model, Simons-Morton (2007) found that declines between grades 6 and 9 in parent monitoring, parent knowledge, and expected parental negative reactions to problem behavior were each associated with greater growth in the number of friends who drank or smoked. Blanton et al. (1997) found that a warm parent–child relationship was associated 1 year later with having fewer friends who drank or smoked.

There is also some evidence that peer modeling mediates the influence of positive parenting (Adamczyk-Robinette et al., 2002; Kelly, O'Flaherty, Toumbourou, et al., 2011; Walden, McGue, Iacono, Burt, & Elkin, 2004). While some might interpret this as evidence that peer influence is more important than parent influence, I prefer to see this as evidence of the importance of parent influence on the choice of peers and of the importance of peers as social support for or against substance use.

Parental Buffering of Peer Influence

Parenting variables have been shown to buffer or reduce the impact of peer modeling on adolescent substance use (usually demonstrated through significant interaction effects; see Figure 16.1). Among the family factors moderating the relation between peer models for substance use and the adolescents' own substance use are parental monitoring (Clark et al., 2012), positive parenting (Kung & Farrell, 2000), consistent discipline (Marshal & Chassin, 2000), perceived parental authoritativeness (Mounts & Steinberg, 1995), family support (Frauenglass et al., 1997; Marshal & Chassin, 2000), maternal support (Allen et al., 2012), a strong mother–adolescent relationship (Farrell & White, 1998), closeness to father, and the perception that parents would catch them if they broke family rules (Dorius, Bahr, Hoffmann, & Harmon, 2004).

Substance-specific parenting also has an effect. Sargent and Dalton (2001) found that the effect of peer smoking was reduced when both parents were seen as strongly against smoking. Greater perceived parental disapproval of teen drinking also accentuated the relations of positive parenting practices with greater self-efficacy to resist peer offers and with less peer approval and models for drinking (Nash, McQueen, & Bray, 2005).

Not only are parents effective in buffering the influence of peers, but there is evidence that other significant adults in the teen's environment can impact the teen's substance use as well. Fletcher, Darling, Steinberg, and Dornbusch (1995) found that the authoritative parenting style of the parents of an adolescent's friends contributed to lower levels of drug and alcohol use over and above the influence of their own parents' authoritative parenting (see also Cleveland, Feinberg, Osgood, & Moody, 2012; Shakya, Christakis, & Fowler, 2012).

THE SOCIAL REPRESENTATIONAL ENVIRONMENT

Beyond the social environments of family and friends is the wider world to which adolescents are exposed through their increasing multimedia access. Where once this consisted mainly of just newspapers, a few television networks, and films in theaters or on late-night television, there has been an explosion in media and online access to depictions of alcohol use, smoking, and other drug use. With the availability of on-demand movies on cable and satellite television channels, and with 24-hour access to online video resources such as YouTube, Tumblr, Hulu, and others, it is now possible for adolescents to observe drinking, smoking, and other drug use as much or as little as they want. According to a recent survey (Rideout, 2010), 8- to 18-year-olds on average spend 4.4 hours watching television, 2.3 hours listening to music, 1.3 hours on the computer, 1.1 hours playing video games, 38 minutes reading, and 25 minutes watching movies in a typical day. This is more time than they spend doing any other activity except for sleeping (Strasburger, Jordan, & Donnerstein, 2010).

Exposure to Advertisements and Adolescent Drinking and Smoking

A decade ago, the alcohol industry spent over $1.6 billion a year on advertising in radio, television, magazines, newspapers, billboards, and so on (Bonnie & O'Connell, 2004), and this expenditure is undoubtedly larger today. In 2005, tobacco advertising and promotion in the United States totaled more than $13.5 billion (National Cancer Institute, 2008).

Research has shown that exposure to alcohol advertisements has significant impact on children's and adolescents' attitudes toward drinking, intentions to drink, and on their initiation and escalation of drinking. This was true for exposure to ads on television (Austin & Meili, 1994; Collins et al., 2007; Grube & Wallach, 1994; Morgenstern, Isensee, Sargent, & Hanewinkel, 2011; Stacy, Zogg, Unger, & Dent, 2004), exposure to in-store beer displays (Ellickson, Collins, Hambarsoomians, & McCaffrey, 2005), and exposure to outdoor alcohol advertising near their schools (Pasch, Komro, Perry, Hearst, & Farbakhsh, 2007).

Similarly, greater exposure to smoking advertisements is associated with greater intentions to smoke among adolescents (Shadel, Tharp-Taylor, & Fryer, 2008) and with their smoking behavior (Botvin, Goldberg, Botvin, & Dusenbury, 1993; Hanewinkel, Isensee, Sargent, & Morgenstern, 2010; 2011; Henriksen, Schleicher, Feighery, & Fortman, 2010; Schooler, Feighery, & Flora, 1996).

Exposure to Television and Movie Portrayals of Substance Use

Children and adolescents are also exposed to depictions of drinking and smoking while watching television programs or going to the movies. Portrayals of alcohol use and its (lack of) consequences are common on television programs (see Christenson, Henriksen, & Roberts, 2000), as are portrayals of tobacco use (Cullen et al., 2011). Content analyses of top-grossing films, even children's animated films, show that a substantial percentage (especially of R-rated movies) contain scenes of people (or animals) drinking alcohol (Dal Cin, Worth, Dalton, & Sargent, 2008; Goldstein, Sobel, & Newman, 1999; Stern, 2005; Thompson & Yokota, 2001) or smoking (Glantz et al., 2011).

A recent review of the literature concluded that exposure to on-screen portrayals of alcohol use is associated with the initiation and escalation of alcohol involvement among adolescents (Koordeman, Anschutz, & Engels, 2012). Greater exposure to alcohol use in the movies is associated cross-sectionally with lifetime binge drinking in adolescents (Hanewinkel et al., 2012), and longitudinally with initiation of alcohol use (Hanewinkel & Sargent, 2009; Sargent, Wills, Stoolmiller, Gibson, & Gibbons, 2006), with initiation of binge drinking (Hanewinkel & Sargent, 2009), and with earlier onset of drinking and escalation to binge drinking (Stoolmiller et al., 2012).

Dal Cin et al. (2009) found that exposure to movie alcohol consumption was not only associated with greater alcohol consumption; it also had a direct influence on adolescents' alcohol prototypes, expectancies, and alcohol norms, and it was associated with an increase in the perceived number of friends who drank (see also Wills et al., 2009). These effects were stronger for White than for Black adolescents (Gibbons et al., 2010).

A recent meta-analysis concluded that exposure to tobacco marketing and media significantly increases the risk for positive attitudes toward smoking and doubles the risk for initiation of smoking (Wellman, Sugarman, DiFranza, & Winickoff, 2006). In addition, the National Cancer Institute has concluded that research indicates a *causal relation* between exposure to smoking portrayals in movies and adolescents' initiation of smoking (National Cancer Institute, 2008). Childhood and early adolescent exposure to movie smoking is predictive of smoking initiation (Titus-Ernstoff et al., 2008; Wills et al., 2007, 2008). This relation has been replicated in samples of early adolescents from six European countries (Morgenstern et al., 2013).

Interestingly, Dalton et al. (2003) found that the effect of movie cigarette smoking on initiation was larger among those adolescents who did not have parents who smoked (see also Tanski, Stoolmiller, Gerrard, & Sargent, 2012).

Exposure to Substance Use in Music and Music Videos

The lyrics of music and the images in music videos popular with adolescents commonly refer to substance use or drinking or depict paraphernalia reflecting alcohol, marijuana, and other drug use (see content analyses by Gruber, Thau, Hill, Fisher, & Grube, 2005; Johnson, Croager, Pratt, & Khoo, 2013; Primack, Dalton, Carroll, Agarwal, & Fine, 2008; Primack, Nuzzo, Rice, & Sargent, 2011). Greater exposure to music and music videos has been found to predict the initiation (Robinson, Chen, & Killen, 1998) and escalation of alcohol intake (van den Bulck & Beullens, 2005), as well as ever and current use of marijuana (Primack, Douglas, & Kraemer, 2009; Primack, Kraemer, Fine, & Dalton, 2009). Wingood et al. (2003) also found that greater exposure to rap music (mostly gangsta) videos was associated with greater escalation of alcohol and drug use over a year period among sexually active female African American adolescents.

Social Media and Alcohol and Drug Use

A recent national survey of adolescents ages 13–18 years found that 51% check their social networking sites more than once a day, and 22% check them more than 10 times a day; and that 33% visit sites with streaming TV or video more than once daily, and 13% visit such sites more than 10 times a day (Common Sense Media, 2009). Adolescents are exposed to a multitude of sources of imagery of alcohol use and abuse, smoking, and drug use on YouTube, Tumblr, Instagram, Facebook, Myspace, and others, as well as advertising for alcohol, cigarettes, and smokeless tobacco (Forsyth & Malone, 2010; Freeman, 2012; Moreno et al., 2010). There is no way to quantify the extent to which teens are exposed to drinking and drug use on the Internet because each adolescent navigates through the World Wide Web in his or her own way, pursuing individual interests.

Teens who spend any time on a social networking site are three times as likely to have ever drank, five times as likely to have smoked, and nearly twice as likely to have used marijuana (National Center on Addiction and Substance Abuse, 2011). In addition, Denniston, Swahn, Hertz, and Romero (2011) found that adolescents who use a computer more than 3 hours a day (not including schoolwork) are significantly more likely to have started using alcohol at age 13 years or younger. Ever drinkers access electronic social networks more frequently than never drinkers (Epstein, 2011). Quantifying child and adolescent exposure to models for substance use is only going to become more complicated with the continuing explosive growth in their access to electronic media.

CONCLUSIONS AND FUTURE DIRECTIONS

The most general conclusion of this review is that models for alcohol, tobacco, and other drug use in the family environment, in the peer environment, and in the social-representational environment are associated with greater child and adolescent involvement with these substances. Figure 16.4 summarizes the results of this review of the literature in terms of its support for the general socialization framework proposed at the beginning of the chapter.

When parental substance use (particularly drinking) is examined for predictive utility in multiple regression and structural equation models containing measures of family management practices or measures of substance-specific parenting, its significance diminishes, suggesting that its effect is mediated through these family environment variables (e.g., Dishion et al., 1999; Peterson et al., 1994). This conclusion is bolstered by the

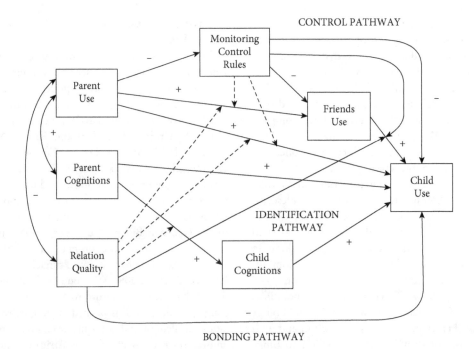

Figure 16.4. Support for the general socialization framework. (Solid lines represent paths for which there is support, while dotted lines represent paths for which support is equivocal or that have yet to be examined.)

array of research demonstrating the association of parental substance use to lower quality parent–child relationships and to less effective parenting practices, and research demonstrating the relation of these family factors to adolescent substance use. For the most part, however, the relations of parent substance use to general parenting and to substance-specific parenting have not been a major focus of study in the literature, particularly in US samples. Further knowledge in this arena could enhance the design of preventive interventions utilizing general parenting workshops and reduce the family consequences of parental excessive drinking or substance use.

Although there is support for children's imitation of parental substance use in general, there have been relatively few examinations of the moderating effect of parent–child relationship, and results have been somewhat inconsistent. There is as much support for greater imitation among adolescents having good parent–child relations as there have been failures to find this interaction effect. There are a variety of reasons why these analyses have not been supportive, including the fact that they are generally based on cross-sectional data and focused on the adolescent's current substance use (sometimes within a very narrow reference window, such as the past 30 days, which excludes many adolescent users) rather than lifetime or yearly involvement.

In contrast to the mixed support for social learning theory is the stronger support for social bonding explanations, in which greater attachment to parents results in less adolescent substance use, regardless of the level of parent modeling of the behavior. Examinations of more complex models of relevant interpersonal factors including identification with the parent have yet to be performed.

In contrast, the influence of peer modeling on adolescent substance use is more robust, and it is apparent not only for perceived peer use but also for peer self-reports of use. While its correlation to adolescent use is generally larger than that of parental modeling, its influence is diminished when family management and parent relationship variables are included in the predictive models. Family factors were found to influence both the choice of substance-using friends and to buffer their influence on the adolescent's own use. Such findings argue for more systematic attention to the interaction of parent and peer environments in the socialization of adolescent substance use.

The present review of media influences on adolescent drinking and smoking adds support to the characterization of the media as a "super-peer" (Brown et al., 2006). With an ever-increasing supply of portrayals of excessive drinking and drug use on the Internet, the only means of reducing their impact is through face-to-face, real-world relationships with parents.

As was recently pointed out in a review of the literature on parenting and peer relationships (Brown & Bakken, 2011), "time itself represents another variable largely neglected by researchers" (p. 162). This observation bears repeating in relation to the present review. For the most part, researchers have focused on relatively short intervals of time (1–3 years) within the life stage of adolescence. There has been little extension of research beyond a single phase of adolescence (e.g., early adolescence), nor have there been many efforts to address the impacts and outcomes of socialization processes across childhood and adolescence. Substance-specific attitudes, prototypes, and expectancies do not suddenly appear with puberty but are developed from about age 5 years onward. More research needs to be devoted to the childhood transmission from parents to children of these cognitive underpinnings of later substance use, and to the influence of peers and media in transforming these cognitions prior to initiation. Additionally, there has been little attention to the effects of progression in own substance use on further changes in these cognitions as a result of experience, or to how adolescent substance use affects parents' substance-use cognitions and parenting practices.

Another major problem in this research literature is the relatively long period of time that usually separates the waves of data collection, often a year or two. This makes it difficult to untangle the contributions of the various components of socialization, for example, the effect of modeling on attitudes and cognitions supportive of initiation of the behavior. By the time of the next longitudinal assessment, both the adolescent's behavior and his or her attitudes and expectancies may already have changed to bring the individual's personality and behavioral systems into balance. What is needed is highly focused longitudinal research in which assessments are repeated at shorter intervals.

A further problem is the failure to integrate qualitative and quantitative methods. Nearly all of the research reviewed is based on either questionnaires or computer-assisted interviews that fail to ask adolescents to tell their own story about the circumstances surrounding their first use of a substance or the factors impacting their escalation of use. Current research utilizing child narratives is generally based on very small samples (e.g., Eadie et al., 2010; McIntosh, MacDonald, & McKeganey, 2008; Milton et al., 2008).

In most adolescent research, variables are connected by paths in structural equation models supported oftentimes by conjecture rather than a theoretically justified cascade of psychosocial mediators. For example, little attention has been paid to personality and interpersonal factors mediating or moderating the influence of peer models on the adolescent's adoption or intensity of involvement in substance use. Exposure to peer models is often presumed sufficient to induce adoption of their behavior. While some research has identified family factors that moderate the influence of peers on adolescent substance use, these processes have yet to be modeled as a coherent theory of multiple-agent socialization recognizing that family factors in childhood may well set the stage for later, adolescent peer influence.

Given the importance of all three social environments (family, peer, and social-representational) for the socialization of substance use, it would be important for future research to attend to the interactions among these sources of social influence on child and adolescent substance use. An area of particular concern would be examination of the moderation of social media and mass media influences toward substance use by effective family management practices and by peer modeling of substance use abstinence or moderate involvement.

Although the present review documents many of the basic relationships within the domain of socialization research on substance use, it is clear that there are a multitude of directions for future research and elaboration in this arena.

References

Aas, H., Jakobsen, R., & Anderssen, N. (1996). Predicting 13-year-olds' drinking using parents' self-reported alcohol use and restrictiveness compared with offspring's perception. *Scandinavian Journal of Psychology, 37*, 113–120.

Adamczyk-Robinette, S. L., Fletcher, A. C., & Wright, K. (2002). Understanding the authoritative parenting—early adolescent tobacco use link: The mediating role of peer tobacco use. *Journal of Youth and Adolescence, 31*, 311–318.

Aikins, J. W., Simon, V. A., & Prinstein, M. J. (2010). Romantic partner selection and socialization of young adolescents' substance use and behavior problems. *Journal of Adolescence, 33*, 813–826.

Ali, M. M., & Dwyer, D. S. (2010). Social network effects in alcohol consumption among adolescents. *Addictive Behaviors, 35*, 337–342.

Allen, J. P., Chango, J., Szwedo, D., Schad, M., & Marston, E. (2012). Predictors of susceptibility to peer influence regarding substance use in adolescence. *Child Development, 83*, 337–350.

Andersen, M. R., Leroux, B. G., Bricker, J. B., Rajan, K. B., & Peterson, A. V., Jr. (2004). Antismoking parenting practices are associated with reduced rates of adolescent smoking. *Archives of Pediatrics and Adolescent Medicine, 158*, 348–352.

Andrews, J. A., Hops, H., Ary, D., Tildesley, E., & Harris, J. (1993). Parental influence on early adolescent substance use: Specific and nonspecific effects. *Journal of Early Adolescence, 13*, 285–310.

Andrews, J. A., Hops, H., & Duncan, S. C. (1997). Adolescent modeling of parent substance use: The moderating effect of the relationship with the parent. *Journal of Family Psychology, 11*, 259–270.

Ary, D. V., Tildesley, E., Hops, H., & Andrews, J. (1993). The influence of parent, sibling, and peer modeling and attitudes on adolescent use of alcohol. *International Journal of the Addictions, 28*, 853–880.

Aseltine, R. H., Jr. (1995). A reconsideration of parental and peer influences on adolescent deviance. *Journal of Health and Social Behavior, 36*, 103–121.

Austin, E. W., & Meili, H. K. (1994). Effects of interpretations of televised alcohol portrayals on children's alcohol beliefs. *Journal of Broadcasting and Electronic Media, 38*, 417–435.

Avenevoli, S., & Merikangas, K. R. (2003). Familial influences on adolescent smoking. *Addiction, 98*(Supp. 1), 1–20.

Baer, P. E., McLaughlin, R. J., Burnside, M. A., Pokorny, A. D., & Garmezy, L. B. (1987). Stress, family environment, and multiple substance use among seventh graders. *Psychology of Addictive Behaviors, 1*, 92–103.

Bahr, S. J., Hoffmann, J. P., & Yang, X. (2005). Parental and peer influences on the risk of adolescent drug use. *Journal of Primary Prevention, 2005*, 529–551.

Bandura, A. (1977). *Social learning theory*. Englewood Cliffs, NJ: Prentice-Hall.

Bank, B. J., Biddle, B. J., Anderson, D. S., Hauge, R., Keats, D. M., Keat, J. A., . . . Valentin, S. (1985). Comparative research on the social determinants of adolescent drinking. *Social Psychology Quarterly, 48*, 164–177.

Barnes, G. M., Hoffman, J. H., Welte, J. W., Farrell, M. P., & Dintcheff, B. A. (2006). Effects of parental monitoring and peer deviance on substance use and delinquency. *Journal of Marriage and Family, 68*, 1084–1104.

Barnes, G. M., Reifman, A. S., Farrell, M. P., & Dintcheff, B. A. (2000). The effects of parenting on the development of adolescent alcohol misuse: A six-wave latent growth model. *Journal of Marriage and Family, 62*, 175–186.

Barnett, T., O'Loughlin, J., Paradis, G., & Renaud, L. (1997). Reliability of proxy reports of parental smoking by elementary schoolchildren. *Annals of Epidemiology, 7*, 396–399.

Bauman, K. A., & Ennett, S. T. (1996). On the importance of peer influence for adolescent drug use: Commonly neglected considerations. *Addiction, 91*, 185–198.

Bauman, K. A., & Fisher, L. A. (1986). On the measurement of friend behavior in research on friend influence and selection: Findings from longitudinal studies of adolescent smoking and drinking. *Journal of Youth and Adolescence, 15*, 345–353.

Baumrind, D. (1985). Familial antecedents of adolescent drug use: A developmental perspective. In C. L. Jones & R. J.

Battjes (Eds.), *Etiology of drug abuse: Implications for prevention* [NIDA Research Monograph 56] (pp. 13–44). Rockville, MD: National Institute on Drug Abuse.

Baumrind, D. (1991). The influence of parenting style on adolescent competence and substance use. *Journal of Early Adolescence, 11*, 56–95.

Beal, A. C., Ausiello, J., & Perrin, J. M. (2001). Social influences on health-risk behaviors among minority middle school students. *Journal of Adolescent Health, 28*, 474–480.

Biddle, B. J., Bank, B. J., & Marlin, M. M. (1980). Social determinants of adolescent drinking: What they think, what they do and what I think and do. *Journal of Studies on Alcohol, 41*, 215–241.

Biglan, A., Duncan, T. E., Ary, D. V., & Smolkowski, K. (1995). Peer and parental influences on adolescent tobacco use. *Journal of Behavioral Medicine, 18*, 315–330.

Bijur, P. E., Kurzon, M., Overpeck, M. D., & Scheidt, P. C. (1992). Parental alcohol use, problem drinking, and children's injuries. *Journal of the American Medical Association, 267*, 3166–3171.

Blanton, H., Gibbons, F. X., Gerrard, M., Conger, K. J., & Smith, G. E. (1997). Role of family and peers in the development of prototypes associated with substance use. *Journal of Family Psychology, 11*, 271–288.

Bonnie, R. J., & O'Connell, M. E. (Eds.). (2004). *Reducing underage drinking: A collective responsibility*. Washington, DC: National Academies Press.

Bot, S. M., Engels, R. C. M. E., Knobbe, R. A., & Meeus, W. H. J. (2005). Friend's drinking behavior and adolescent alcohol consumption: The moderating role of friendship characteristics. *Addictive Behaviors, 30*, 929–947.

Botvin, G. J., Goldberg, C. J., Botvin, E. M., & Dusenbury, L. (1993). Smoking behavior of adolescents exposed to cigarette advertising. *Public Health Reports, 108*, 217–224.

Bray, J. H., Adams, G. J., Getz, J. G., & Baer, P. E. (2001). Developmental, family, and ethnic influences on adolescent alcohol usage: A growth curve approach. *Journal of Family Psychology, 25*, 301–314.

Bricker, J. B., Peterson, A. V., Jr., Leroux, B. G., Andersen, M. R., Rajan, K. B., & Sarason, I. G. (2006). Prospective prediction of children's smoking transitions: Role of parents' and older siblings' smoking. *Addiction, 101*, 128–138.

Brody, G. H., Flor, D. L., Hollett-Wright, N., & McCoy, J. K. (1998). Children's development of alcohol use norms: Contributions of parent and sibling norms, children's temperaments, and parent-child discussions. *Journal of Family Psychology, 12*, 209–219.

Brody, G. H., Ge, X., Katz, J., & Arias, I. (2000). A longitudinal analysis of internalization of parental alcohol-use norms and adolescent alcohol use. *Applied Developmental Science, 4*, 71–79.

Brook, J. (1993). Interactional theory: Its utility in explaining drug use behavior among African-American and Puerto Rican youth. In M. de la Rosa & J. R. Adrdos (Eds.), *Drug abuse among minority youth: Advances in research and methodology* [NIDA Research Monograph 130] (pp. 79–101). Rockville, MD: National Institute on Drug Abuse.

Brook, J. S., Brook, D. W., Arencibia-Mireles, O., Richter, L., & Whiteman, M. (2001). Risk factors for adolescent marijuana use across cultures and across time. *Journal of Genetic Psychology, 162*, 357–374.

Brook, J. S., Kessler, R. C., & Cohen, P. (1999). The onset of marijuana use from preadolescence and early adolescence to young adulthood. *Development and Psychopathology, 11*, 901–914.

Brook, J. S., Whiteman, M., Balka, E. B., & Cohen, P. (1995). Parent drug use, parent personality, and parenting. *Journal of Genetic Psychology, 156*, 137–151.

Brook, J. S., Whiteman, M., Gordon, A. S., & Brook, D. W. (1984). Identification with paternal attributes and its relationship to the son's personality and drug use. *Developmental Psychology, 20*, 1111–1119.

Brook, J. S., Whiteman, M., Gordon, A. S., & Brook, D. W. (1986). Father-daughter identification and its impact on her personality and drug use. *Developmental Psychology, 22*, 743–748.

Brook, J. S., Whiteman, M., Gordon, A. S., Nomura, C., & Brook, D. W. (1986). Onset of adolescent drinking: A longitudinal study of intrapersonal and interpersonal antecedents. *Advances in Alcohol and Substance Abuse, 5*, 91–110.

Brook, J. S., Whiteman, M., Nomura, C., Gordon, A. S., & Cohen, P. (1988). Personality, family, and ecological influences on adolescent drug use: A developmental analysis. *Journal of Chemical Dependency Treatment, 1*, 123–161.

Brown, B. B., & Bakken, J. P. (2011). Parenting and peer relationships: Reinvigorating research on family-peer linkages in adolescence. *Journal of Research on Adolescence, 21*, 153–165.

Brown, J. D., L'Engle, K. L., Pardun, C. J., Guo, G., Kenneavy, K., & Jackson, C. (2006). Sexy media matter: Exposure to sexual content in music, movies, television, and magazines predicts black and white adolescents' sexual behavior. *Pediatrics, 117*, 1018–1027.

Brown, S. A., Creamer, V. A., & Stetson, B. A. (1987). Adolescent alcohol expectancies in relation to personal and parental drinking patterns. *Journal of Abnormal Psychology, 96*, 117–121.

Brown, S. A., Tate, S. R., Vik, P. W., Haas, A. L., & Aarons, G. A. (1999). Modeling of alcohol use mediates the effect of family history of alcoholism on adolescent alcohol expectancies. *Experimental and Clinical Psychopharmacology, 7*, 20–27.

Brown, S. L., & Rinelli, L. N. (2010). Family structure, family processes, and adolescent smoking and drinking. *Journal of Research on Adolescence, 20*, 259–273.

Burk, W. J., van der Vorst, H., Kerr, M., & Stattin, H. (2012). Alcohol use and friendship dynamics: Selection and socialization in early-, middle-, and late-adolescent peer networks. *Journal of Studies on Alcohol and Drugs, 73*, 89–98.

Bush, P. J., Weinfurt, K. P., & Iannotti, R. J. (1994). Families versus peers: Developmental influences on drug use from grade 4-5 to grade 7-8. *Journal of Applied Developmental Psychology, 15*, 437–456.

Buu, A., DiPiazza, C., Wang, J., Puttler, L. I., Fitzgerald, H. E., & Zucker, R. A. (2009). Parent, family, and neighborhood effects on the development of child substance use and other psychopathology from preschool to the start of adulthood. *Journal of Studies on Alcohol and Drugs, 70*, 489–498.

Campbell, J. M., & Oei, T. P. (2010a). A cognitive model for the intergenerational transference of alcohol use behavior. *Addictive Behaviors, 35*, 73–83.

Campbell, J. M., & Oei, T. P. (2010b). The intergenerational transference of alcohol use behavior from parents to offspring: A test of the cognitive model. *Addictive Behaviors, 35*, 714–716.

Capaldi, D. M., Stoolmiller, M., Kim, H. K., & Yoerger, K. (2009). Growth in alcohol use in at-risk adolescent boys: Two-part random effects prediction models. *Drug and Alcohol Dependence, 105*, 109–117.

Casswell, S., Stewart, J., Connolly, G., & Silva, P. (1991). A longitudinal study of New Zealand children's experience with alcohol. *British Journal of Addiction, 86*, 277–285.

Catalano, R. F., White, H. R., Fleming, C. B., & Haggerty, K. P. (2011). Is nonmedical prescription opiate use a unique form of illicit drug use? *Addictive Behaviors, 36*, 79–86.

Center for Behavioral Health Statistics and Quality. (2011). *Data spotlight, National Survey on Drug Use and Health: Young alcohol users often get alcohol from family or home.* Rockville, MD: Substance Abuse and Mental Health Services Administration. Retrieved September 5, 2012, from http://oas.samhsa.gov

Chalder, M., Elgar, F. J., & Bennett, P. (2006). Drinking and motivations to drink among adolescent children of parents with alcohol problems. *Alcohol and Alcoholism, 41*, 107–113.

Chassin, L., Pillow, D. R., Curran, P. J., Molina, B. S. G., & Barrera, M., Jr. (1993). Relation of parental alcoholism to early adolescent substance use: A test of three mediating mechanisms. *Journal of Abnormal Psychology, 102*, 3–19.

Chassin, L., Rogosch, F., & Barrera, M. (1991). Substance use and symptomatology among adolescent children of alcoholics. *Journal of Abnormal Psychology, 100*, 449–463.

Chen, C., Storr, C. L., Liu, C., Chen, K., Chen, W. J., & Lin, K. (2011). Differential relationships of family drinking with alcohol expectancy among urban school children. *BMC Public Health, 11*, 87.

Chilcoat, H. D., & Anthony, J. C. (1996). Impact of parental monitoring on initiation of drug use through late childhood. *Journal of the American Academy of Child and Adolescent Psychiatry, 35*, 91–100.

Chilcoat, H. D., Dishion, T. J., & Anthony, J. C. (1995). Parent monitoring and the incidence of drug sampling in urban elementary school children. *American Journal of Epidemiology, 141*, 25–31.

Christenson, P. G., Henriksen, L., & Roberts, D. F. (2000). *Substance use in popular prime-time television.* Washington, DC: Office of National Drug Control Policy.

Chung, T., White, H. R., Hipwell, A. E., Stepp, S. D., & Loeber, R. (2010). A parallel process model of the development of positive smoking expectancies and smoking behavior during early adolescence in Caucasian and African American girls. *Addictive Behaviors, 35*, 647–650.

Clark, D. B., Kirisci, L., Mezzich, A., & Chung, T. (2008). Parental supervision and alcohol use in adolescence: Developmentally specific interactions. *Journal of Developmental and Behavioral Pediatrics, 29*, 285–292.

Clark, T. T., Belgrave, F. Z., & Abell, M. (2012). The mediating and moderating effects of parent and peer influences upon drug use among African American adolescents. *Journal of Black Psychology, 38*, 52–80.

Cleveland, M. J., Feinberg, M. E., Osgood, D. W., & Moody, J. (2012). Do peers' parents matter? A new link between positive parenting and adolescent substance use. *Journal of Studies on Alcohol and Drugs, 73*, 423–433.

Colder, C. R., Chassin, L., Stice, E. M., & Curran, P. J. (1997). Alcohol expectancies as potential mediators of parent alcoholism effects on the development of adolescent heavy drinking. *Journal of Research on Adolescence, 7*, 349–374.

Collins, R. L., Ellickson, P. L., McCaffrey, D., & Hambarsoomians, K. (2007). Early adolescent exposure to alcohol advertising and its relationship to underage drinking. *Journal of Adolescent Health, 40*, 527–534.

Collins, W. A., Maccoby, E. E., Steinberg, L., Hetherington, E. M., & Bornstein, M. H. (2000). Contemporary research on parenting: The case for nature versus nurture. *American Psychologist, 55*, 218–232.

Common Sense Media. (2009). Is social networking changing childhood? National poll reveals a disconnect between parents and teens on the role that social networking plays in their lives. Retrieved October 20, 2015, from http://www.commonsensemedia.org/about-us/news/press-releases/is-social-networking-changing-childhood

Conger, R. D., & Rueter, M. A. (1996). Siblings, parents, and peers: A longitudinal study of social influences in adolescent risk for alcohol use and abuse. In G. H. Brody (Ed.), *Sibling relationships: Their causes and consequences* (pp. 1–30). Norwood, NJ: Ablex.

Conrad, K. M., Flay, B. R., & Hill, D. (1992). Why children start smoking cigarettes: Predictors of onset. *British Journal of Addiction, 87*, 1711–1724.

Cottrell, L., Li, X., Harris, C., D'Alessandri, D., Atkins, M., Richardson, B., & Stanton, B. (2003). Parent and adolescent perceptions of parental monitoring and adolescent risk involvement. *Parenting: Science and Practice, 3*, 179–195.

Cranford, J. A., Zucker, R. A., Jester, J. M., Puttler, L. I., & Fitzgerald, H. E. (2010). Parental alcohol involvement and adolescent alcohol expectancies predict alcohol involvement in male adolescents. *Psychology of Addictive Behaviors, 24*, 386–396.

Crosnoe, R., Erickson, K. G., & Dornbusch, S. M. (2002). Protective functions of family relationships and school factors on the deviant behavior of adolescent boys and girls: Reducing the impact of risky friendships. *Youth and Society, 33*, 515–544.

Cruz, J. E., Emery, R. E., & Turkheimer, E. (2012). Peer network drinking predicts increased alcohol use from adolescence to early adulthood after controlling for genetic and shared environmental selection. *Developmental Psychology, 38*, 1390–1402.

Cullen, J., Sokol, N. A., Slaweh, D., Allen, J. A., Vallone, D., & Healton, C. (2011). Depictions of tobacco use in 2007 broadcast television programming popular among US youth. *Archives of Pediatrics and Adolescent Medicine, 165*, 147–151.

Cumsille, P. E., Sayer, A. G., & Graham, J. W. (2000). Perceived exposure to peer and adult drinking as predictors of growth in positive alcohol expectancies during adolescence. *Journal of Consulting and Clinical Psychology, 68*, 531–536.

Curran, P. J., Stice, E., & Chassin, L. (1997). The relation between adolescent alcohol use and peer alcohol use: A longitudinal random coefficients model. *Journal of Consulting and Clinical Psychology, 65*, 130–140.

Dal Cin, S., Worth, K. A., Dalton, M. A., & Sargent, J. D. (2008). Youth exposure to alcohol use and brand appearances in popular contemporary movies. *Addiction, 103*, 1925–1932.

Dal Cin, S., Worth, K. A., Gerrard, M., Gibbons, F. X., Stoolmiller, M., Wills, T. A., & Sargent, J. D. (2009). Watching and drinking: Expectancies, prototypes, and friends' alcohol use mediate the effect of exposure to alcohol use in movies on adolescent drinking. *Health Psychology, 28*, 473–483.

Dalton, M. A., Sargent, J. D., Beach, M. L., Titus-Ernstoff, L., Gibson, J. J., Ahrens, M. B., . . . Heatherton, T. F. (2003).

Effect of viewing smoking in movies on adolescent smoking initiation: A cohort study. *Lancet, 362*, 281–285.

Denniston, M. M., Swahn, M. H., Hertz, M. F., & Romero, L. M. (2011). Associations between electronic media use and involvement in violence, alcohol and drug use among United States high school students. *Western Journal of Emergency Medicine, 12*, 310–315.

De Vries, H., Engels, R., Kremers, S. Wetzels, J., & Mudde, A. (2003). Parents' and friends' smoking status as predictors of smoking onset: Findings from six European countries. *Health Education Research, 18*, 627–636.

Dick, D. M., Pagan, J. L., Holliday, C., Viken, R., Pulkkinen, L., Kaprio, J., & Rose, R. J. (2007). Gender differences in friends' influences on adolescent drinking: A genetic epidemiological study. *Alcoholism: Clinical and Experimental Research, 31*, 2012–2019.

Dielman, T. E., Butchart, A. T., & Shope, J. T. (1993). Structural equation model tests of patterns of family interaction, peer alcohol use, and intrapersonal predictors of adolescent alcohol use and misuse. *Journal of Drug Education, 23*, 273–316.

Dielman, T. E., Leech, S. L., & Loveland-Cherry, C. (1995). Parents' and children's reports of parenting practices and parent and child alcohol use. *Drugs and Society, 8*(3/4), 83–101.

Dishion, T. J., Capaldi, D. M., & Yoerger, K. (1999). Middle childhood antecedents to progressions in male adolescent substance use: An ecological analysis of risk and protection. *Journal of Adolescent Research, 14*, 175–205.

Dishion, T. J., & Loeber, R. (1985). Adolescent marijuana and alcohol use: The role of parents and peers revisited. *American Journal of Drug and Alcohol Abuse, 11*, 11–25.

Dishion, T. J., Patterson, G. R., & Reid, J. R. (1988). Parent and peer factors associated with drug sampling in early adolescence: Implications for treatment. In E. R. Rahdert & J. Grabowski (Eds.), *Adolescent drug abuse: Analyses of treatment research* [NIDA Research Monograph 77] (pp. 69–93). Rockville, MD: National Institute on Drug Abuse.

Doherty, W. J., & Allen, W. (1994). Family functioning and parental smoking as predictors of adolescent cigarette use: A six-year prospective study. *Journal of Family Psychology, 8*, 347–353.

Donovan, J. E. (2004). Adolescent alcohol initiation: A review of psychosocial risk factors. *Journal of Adolescent Health, 35*, 529.e7–529.e18.

Donovan, J. E., & Jessor, R. (1985). Structure of problem behavior in adolescence and young adulthood. *Journal of Consulting and Clinical Psychology, 53*, 890–904.

Donovan, J. E., & Molina, B. S. G. (2008). Children's introduction to alcohol use: Sips and tastes. *Alcoholism: Clinical and Experimental Research, 32*, 108–119.

Donovan, J. E., & Molina, B. S. G. (2011). Childhood risk factors for early-onset drinking. *Journal of Studies on Alcohol and Drugs, 72*, 741–751.

Donovan, J. E., & Molina, B. S. G. (2014). Antecedent predictors of children's initiation of sipping/tasting alcohol. *Alcoholism: Clinical and Experimental Research, 38*(9), 2488–2495.

Dorius, C. J., Bahr, S. J., Hoffmann, J. P., & Harmon, E. L. (2004). Parenting practices as moderators of the relationship between peers and adolescent marijuana use. *Journal of Marriage and the Family, 66*, 163–178.

Dube, S. R., Anda, R. F., Felitti, V. J., Croft, J. B., Edwards, V. J., & Giles, W. H. (2001). Growing up with parental alcohol abuse: Exposure to childhood abuse, neglect, and household dysfunction. *Child Abuse and Neglect, 25*, 1627–1640.

Duncan, S. C., Duncan, T. E., & Strycker, L. A. (2003). Family influences on youth alcohol use: A multiple-sample analysis by ethnicity and gender. *Journal of Ethnicity in Substance Abuse, 2*, 17–33.

Duncan, S. C., Duncan, T. E., & Strycker, L. A. (2006). Alcohol use from ages 9 to 16: A cohort-sequential latent growth model. *Drug and Alcohol Dependence, 81*, 71–81.

Duncan, T. E., Duncan, S. C., & Hops, H. (1996). The role of parents and older siblings in predicting adolescent substance use: Modeling development via structural equation latent growth methodology. *Journal of Family Psychology, 10*, 158–172.

Duncan, T. E., Tildesley, E., Duncan, S. C., & Hops, H. (1995). The consistency of family and peer influences on the development of substance use in adolescence. *Addiction, 90*, 1647–1660.

Eadie, D., MacAskill, S., Brooks, O., Heim, D., Forsyth, A., & Punch, S. (2010). *Pre-teens learning about alcohol: Drinking and family contexts*. York, UK: Joseph Rowntree Foundation. Retrieved October 25, 2012, from http://www.jrf.org.uk

Ellickson, P. L., Collins, R. L., Hambarsoomians, K., & McCaffrey, D. (2005). Does alcohol advertising promote adolescent drinking? Results from a longitudinal assessment. *Addiction, 100*, 235–246.

Ellickson, P. L., & Hays, R. D. (1991). Antecedents of drinking among young adolescents with different alcohol use histories. *Journal of Studies on Alcohol, 52*, 398–408.

Ellickson, P. L., Tucker, J. S., Klein, D. J., & McGuigan, K. A. (2001). Prospective risk factors for alcohol misuse in late adolescence. *Journal of Studies on Alcohol, 62*, 773–782.

Ellickson, P. L., Tucker, J. S., Klein, D. J., & Saner, H. (2004). Antecedents and outcomes of marijuana use initiation during adolescence. *Preventive Medicine, 39*, 976–984.

Engels, R. C. M. E., Vitaro, F., den Exter Blokland, E., de Kemp, R., & Scholte, R. H. J. (2004). Influence and selection processes in friendships and adolescent smoking behavior: The role of parental smoking. *Journal of Adolescence, 27*, 531–544.

Ennett, S. T., & Bauman, K. E. (1994). The contribution of influence and selection to adolescent peer group homogeneity: The case of adolescent cigarette smoking. *Journal of Personality and Social Psychology, 67*, 653–663.

Ennett, S. T., Bauman, K. E., Hussong, A., Faris, R., Foshee, V. A., & Cai, L. (2006). The peer context of adolescent substance use: Findings from social network analysis. *Journal of Research on Adolescence, 16*, 159–186.

Ennett, S. T., Foshee, V. A., Bauman, K. E., Hussong, A., Faris, R., Hipp, J. R., & Cai, L. (2010). A social contextual analysis of youth cigarette smoking development. *Nicotine and Tobacco Research, 12*, 950–962.

Epstein, J. A. (2011). Adolescent computer use and alcohol use: What are the role of quantity and content of computer use? *Addictive Behaviors, 36*, 520–522.

Epstein, J. A., Botvin, G. J., Baker, E., & Diaz, T. (1999). Impact of social influences and problem behavior on alcohol use among inner-city Hispanic and black adolescents. *Journal of Studies on Alcohol, 60*, 595–604.

Epstein, J. A., Griffin, K. W., & Botvin, G. J. (2008). A social influence model of alcohol use for inner-city adolescents: Family drinking, perceived drinking norms, and perceived social benefits of drinking. *Journal of Studies on Alcohol and Drugs, 69*, 397–405.

Erickson, K. G., Crosnoe, R., & Dornbusch, S. M. (2000). A social process model of adolescent deviance: Combining social control and differential association perspectives. *Journal of Youth and Adolescence, 29*, 395–425.

Fagan, A. A., & Najman, J. M. (2005). The relative contributions of parental and sibling substance use to adolescent tobacco, alcohol, and other drug use. *Journal of Drug Issues, 34*, 869–883.

Farhat, T., Simons-Morton, B. G., Kokkevi, A., van der Sluijs, W., Fotiou, A., & Kuntsche, E. (2012). Early adolescent and peer drinking homogeneity: Similarities and differences among European and North American countries. *Journal of Early Adolescence, 32*, 81–103.

Farrell, A. D., Danish, S. J., & Howard, C. W. (1992). Relationship between drug use and other problem behaviors in urban adolescents. *Journal of Consulting and Clinical Psychology, 60*, 705–712.

Farrell, A. D., & White, K. S. (1998). Peer influences and drug use among urban adolescents: Family structure and parent-adolescent relationship as protective factors. *Journal of Consulting and Clinical Psychology, 66*, 248–258.

Felton, G., Parsons, M. A., Ward, D. S., Pate, R. R., Saunders, R. P., Dowda, M., & Trost, S. (1999). Tracking of avoidance of alcohol use and smoking behavior in a fifth grade cohort over three years. *Public Health Nursing, 16*, 32–40.

Fergusson, D. M., Horwood, L. J., & Lynskey, M. T. (1995). The prevalence and risk factors associated with abusive or hazardous alcohol consumption in 16-year-olds. *Addiction, 90*, 935–946.

Fisher, L. A., & Bauman, K. E. (1988). Influence and selection in the friend-adolescent relationship: Findings from studies of adolescent smoking and drinking. *Journal of Applied Social Psychology, 18*, 289–314.

Fisher, L. B., Miles, I. W., Austin, B., Camargo, C. A., & Colditz, G. A. (2007). Predictors of initiation of alcohol use among U.S. adolescents. *Archives of Pediatrics and Adolescent Medicine, 161*, 959–966.

Flay, B. R., Hu, F. B., & Richardson, J. (1998). Psychosocial predictors of different stages of cigarette smoking among high school students. *Preventive Medicine, 27*, A9–A18.

Flay, B. R., Hu, F. B., Siddiqui, O., Day, L. E., Hedeker, D., Petraitus, J., . . . Sussman, S. (1994). Differential influence of parental smoking and friends' smoking on adolescent initiation and escalation of smoking. *Journal of Health and Social Behavior, 35*, 248–264.

Fleary, S. A., Heffer, R. W., McKyer, E. L. J., & Newman, D. A. (2010). Using the bioecological model to predict risk perception of marijuana use and reported marijuana use in adolescence. *Addictive Behaviors, 35*, 795–798.

Fleming, C. B., Brewer, D. D., Gainey, R. R., Haggerty, K. P., & Catalano, R. F. (1997). Parent drug use and bonding to parents as predictors of substance use in children of substance abusers. *Journal of Child and Adolescent Substance Abuse, 6*(4), 75–87.

Fleming, C. B., Kim, H., Harachi, T. W., & Catalano, R. F. (2002). Family processes for children in early elementary school as predictors of smoking initiation. *Journal of Adolescent Health, 30*, 184–189.

Fletcher, A. C., Darling, N. E., Steinberg, L., & Dornbusch, S. M. (1995). The company they keep: Relation of adolescents' adjustment and behavior to their friends' perceptions of authoritative parenting in the social network. *Developmental Psychology, 31*, 300–310.

Foley, K. L., Altman, D., Durant, R. H., & Wolfson, M. (2004). Adults' approval and adolescents' alcohol use. *Journal of Adolescent Health, 34*, 345.e17–345.e26.

Forrester, K., Biglan, A., Severson, H. H., & Smolkowski, K. (2007). Predictors of smoking onset over two years. *Nicotine and Tobacco Research, 12*, 1259–1267.

Forsyth, S. R., & Malone, R. E. (2010). "I'll be your cigarette—Light me up and get on with it": Examining smoking imagery on YouTube. *Nicotine and Tobacco Research, 12*, 810–816.

Foshee, V., & Bauman, K. E. (1992). Parental and peer characteristics as modifiers of the bond-behavior relationship: An elaboration of control theory. *Journal of Health and Social Behavior, 33*, 66–76.

Foster, S. E., Jones, D. J., Olson, A. L., Forehand, R., Gaffney, C. A., Zens, M. S., & Bau, J. J. (2007). Family socialization of adolescent's self-reported cigarette use: The role of parents' history of regular smoking and parenting style. *Journal of Pediatric Psychology, 32*, 481–493.

Frauenglass, S., Routh, D. K., Pantin, H. M., & Mason, C. A. (1997). Family support decreases influence of deviant peers on Hispanic adolescents' substance use. *Journal of Clinical Child Psychology, 26*, 15–23.

Freeman, B. (2012). New media and tobacco control. *Tobacco Control, 21*, 139–144.

Gerrard, M., Gibbons, F. X., Zhao, L., Russell, D. W., & Reis-Bergan, M. (1999). The effect of peers' alcohol consumption on parental influence: A cognitive mediational model. *Journal of Studies on Alcohol*, Supplement No. 13, 32–44.

Gibbons, F. X., Gerrard, M., Lune, L. S. V., Wills, T. A., Brody, G., & Conger, R. D. (2004). Context and cognitions: Environmental risk, social influence, and adolescent substance use. *Personality and Social Psychology Bulletin, 30*, 1048–1061.

Gibbons, F. X., Pomery, E. A., Gerrard, M., Sargent, J. D., Weng, C., Wills, T. A., . . . Yeh, H. (2010). Media as social influence: Racial differences in the effects of peers and media on adolescent alcohol cognitions and consumption. *Psychology of Addictive Behaviors, 24*, 649–659.

Gilman, S. E., Rende, R., Boergers, J., Abrams, D. B., Buka, S. L., Clark, M. A., . . . Niaura, R. S. (2009). Parental smoking and adolescent smoking initiation: An intergenerational perspective on tobacco control. *Pediatrics, 123*, e274–e281.

Glanton, C. F., & Wulfert, E. (2013). The relationship between parental alcohol use and college students' alcohol-related cognitions. *Addictive Behaviors, 38*, 2761–2767.

Glantz, S. A., Mitchell, S., Titus, K., Polansky, J. R., Kaufmann, R. B., & Bauer, U. E. (2011). Smoking in top-grossing movies—United States, 2010. *Morbidity and Mortality Weekly Report, 60*, 910–913.

Goldstein, A. O., Sobel, R. A., & Newman, G. R. (1999). Tobacco and alcohol use in G-rated children's animated films. *Journal of the American Medical Association, 281*(12), 1131–1136.

Gough, H. G. (1965). Cross-cultural validation of a measure of asocial behavior. *Psychological Reports, 17*, 379–387.

Greenlund, K. J., Johnson, C. C., Webber, L. S., & Berenson, G. S. (1997). Cigarette smoking attitudes and first use among third- through sixth-grade students: The Bogalusa Heart Study. *American Journal of Public Health, 87*, 1345–1348.

Gritz, E. R., Prokhorov, A. V., Hudmon, K. S., Jones, M. M., Rosenblum, C., Chang, C. C., . . . de Moor, C. (2003).

Predictors of susceptibility to smoking and ever smoking: A longitudinal study in a triethnic sample of adolescents. *Nicotine and Tobacco Research*, 5, 493–506.

Grube, J. W., Morgan, M., & McGree, S. T. (1986). Attitudes and normative beliefs as predictors of smoking intentions and behaviours: A test of three models. *British Journal of Social Psychology*, 25, 81–93.

Grube, J. W., Morgan, M., & Seff, M. (1989). Drinking beliefs and behaviors among Irish adolescents. *International Journal of the Addictions*, 24, 101–112.

Grube, J. W., & Wallach, L. (1994). Television beer advertising and drinking knowledge, beliefs, and intentions among schoolchildren. *American Journal of Public Health*, 84, 254–259.

Gruber, E. L., Thau, H. M., Hill, D. L., Fisher, D. A., & Grube, J. W. (2005). Alcohol, tobacco, and illicit substances in music videos: A content analysis of prevalence and genre. *Journal of Adolescent Health*, 37, 81–83.

Gutman, L. M., Eccles, J. S., Peck, S., & Malanchuk, O. (2011). The influence of family relations on trajectories of cigarette and alcohol use from early to late adolescence. *Journal of Adolescence*, 34, 119–128.

Guxens, M., Nebot, M., & Ariza, C. (2007). Age and sex differences in factors associated with the onset of cannabis use: A cohort study. *Drug and Alcohol Dependence*, 88, 234–243.

Handley, E. D., & Chassin, L. (2009). Intergenerational transmission of alcohol expectancies in a high-risk sample. *Journal of Studies on Alcohol and Drugs*, 70, 675–682.

Hanewinkel, R., Isensee, B., Sargent, J. D., & Morgenstern, M. (2010). Cigarette advertising and adolescent smoking. *American Journal of Preventive Medicine*, 38, 359–366.

Hanewinkel, R., Isensee, B., Sargent, J. D., & Morgenstern, M. (2011). Cigarette advertising and teen smoking initiation. *Pediatrics*, 127, e271–e278.

Hanewinkel, R., & Sargent, J. D. (2009). Longitudinal study of exposure to entertainment media and alcohol use among German adolescents. *Pediatrics*, 123, 989–995.

Hanewinkel, R., Sargent, J. D., Poelen, A. P., Scholte, R., Florek, E., Sweeting, H., . . . Morgenstern, M. (2012). Alcohol consumption in movies and adolescent binge drinking in 6 European countries. *Pediatrics*, 129, 709–720.

Hanewinkel, R., Tanski, S., & Sargent, J. D. (2007). Exposure to alcohol use in motion pictures and teen drinking in Germany. *International Journal of Epidemiology*, 36, 1068–1077.

Hansen, W. B., Graham, J. W., Sobel, J. L., Shelton, D. R., Flay, B. R., & Anderson, C. A. (1987). The consistency of peer and parent influences on tobacco, alcohol, and marijuana use among young adolescents. *Journal of Behavioral Medicine*, 10, 559–579.

Harakeh, Z., Scholte, R. H. J., de Vries, H., & Engels, R. C. M. E. (2005). Parental rules and communication: Their association with adolescent smoking. *Addiction*, 100, 862–870.

Harakeh, Z., Scholte, R. H. J., Vermulst, A. A., de Vries, H., & Engels, R. C. M. E. (2004). Parental factors and adolescents' smoking behavior: An extension of the Theory of Planned Behavior. *Preventive Medicine*, 39, 951–961.

Harakeh, Z., Scholte, R. H. J., Vermulst, A. A., de Vries, H., & Engels, R. C. M. E. (2010). The relations between parents' smoking, general parenting, parental smoking communication, and adolescents' smoking. *Journal of Research on Adolescence*, 20, 140–165.

Hawkins, J. D., Graham, J. W., Maguin, E., Abbott, R., Hill, K. G., & Catalano, R. F. (1997). Exploring the effects of

age of alcohol use initiation and psychosocial risk factors on subsequent alcohol misuse. *Journal of Studies on Alcohol*, 58, 280–290.

Hayatbakhsh, M. R., Mamun, A. A., Najman, J. M., O'Callaghan, M. J., Bor, W., & Alati, R. (2008). Early childhood predictors of early substance use and substance use disorders: Prospective study. *Australian and New Zealand Journal of Psychiatry*, 42, 720–731.

Hearst, M. O., Fulkerson, J. A., Maldonado-Molina, M. M., Perry, C. L., & Komro, K. A. (2007). Who needs liquor stores when parents will do? The importance of social sources of alcohol among young urban teens. *Preventive Medicine*, 44, 471–476.

Hellandsjø Bu, E. T., Watten, R. G., Foxcroft, D. R., Ingebrigsen, J. E., & Relling, G. (2002). Teenage alcohol and intoxication debut: The impact of family socialization factors, living area and participation in organized sports. *Alcohol and Alcoholism*, 37, 74–80.

Hemphill, S. A., Heerde, J. A., Herrenkohl, T. I., Patton, G. C., Toumbourou, J. W., & Catalano, R. F. (2011). Risk and protective factors for adolescent substance use in Washington State, the United States and Victoria, Australia: A longitudinal study. *Journal of Adolescent Health*, 49, 312–320.

Henriksen, L., Schleicher, N. C., Feighery, E. C., & Fortman, S. P. (2010). A longitudinal study of exposure to retail cigarette advertising and smoking. *Pediatrics*, 126, 232–238.

Hirschi, T. (1969). *Causes of delinquency*. Berkeley: University of California Press.

Hoving, C., Reubsaet, A., & de Vries, H. (2007). Predictors of smoking stage transitions for adolescent boys and girls. *Preventive Medicine*, 44, 485–489.

Huba, G. J., & Bentler, P. M. (1980). The role of peer and adult models for drug taking at different stages in adolescence. *Journal of Youth ad Adolescence*, 9, 449–465.

Hung, C., Yen, L., & Wu, W. (2009). Association of parents' alcohol use and family interaction with the initiation of alcohol use by sixth graders: A preliminary study in Taiwan. *BMC Public Health*, 9, 172.

Iannotti, R. J., & Bush, P. J. (1992). Perceived vs. actual friends' use of alcohol, cigarettes, marijuana, and cocaine: Which has the most influence? *Journal of Youth and Adolescence*, 21, 375–389.

Jackson, C. (1997). Initial and experimental stages of tobacco and alcohol use during late childhood: Relation to peer, parent, and personal risk factors. *Addictive Behaviors*, 22, 685–698.

Jackson, C., Ennett, S. T., Dickinson, D. M., & Bowling, J. M. (2012). Letting children sip: Understanding why parents allow alcohol use by elementary school children. *Archives of Pediatrics and Adolescent Medicine*, 166, 1053–1057.

Jackson, C., Ennett, S. T., Dickinson, D. M., & Bowling, J. M. (2013). Attributes that differentiate children who sip alcohol from abstinent peers. *Journal of Youth and Adolescence*, 42, 1687–1692.

Jackson, C., & Henriksen, L. (1997). Do as I say: Parent smoking, antismoking socialization, and smoking onset among children. *Addictive Behaviors*, 22, 107–114.

Jackson, C., Henriksen, L., & Dickinson, D. (1999). Alcohol-specific socialization, parenting behaviors and alcohol use by children. *Journal of Studies on Alcohol*, 60, 362–367.

Jackson, C., Henriksen, L., Dickinson, D., & Levine, D. W. (1997). The early use of alcohol and tobacco: Its relation to children's competence and parents' behavior. *American Journal of Public Health, 87,* 359–364.

Jessor, R., & Jessor, S. L. (1973). The perceived environment in behavioral science: Some conceptual issues and some illustrative data. *American Behavioral Scientist, 16,* 801–828.

Jessor, R., & Jessor, S. L. (1977). *Problem behavior and psychosocial development: A longitudinal study of youth.* New York, NY: Academic Press.

Johnson, C. C., Greenlund, K. J., Webber, L. S., & Berenson, G. S. (1997). Alcohol first use and attitudes among young children. *Journal of Child and Family Studies, 6,* 359–372.

Johnson, G. M., Shontz, F. C., & Locke, T. P. (1984). Relationships between adolescent drug use and parental drug behaviors. *Adolescence, 19*(74), 295–298.

Johnson, R., Croager, E., Pratt, I. S., & Khoo, N. (2013). Legal drug content in music video programs shown on Australian television on Saturday mornings. *Alcohol and Alcoholism, 48,* 119–125.

Kandel, D. B. (1973). Adolescent marijuana use: Role of parents and peers. *Science, 181,* 1067–1070.

Kandel, D. B. (1974). Inter- and intragenerational influences on adolescent marijuana use. *Journal of Social Issues, 30,* 107–135.

Kandel, D. B. (1978). Homophily, selection, and socialization in adolescent friendships. *American Journal of Sociology, 84,* 427–436.

Kandel, D. B. (1980). Drug and drinking behavior among youth. *Annual Review of Sociology, 6,* 235–285.

Kandel, D. B. (1996). The parental and peer contexts of adolescent deviance: An algebra of interpersonal influences. *Journal of Drug Issues, 26,* 289–315.

Kandel, D. B. (2002). (Ed.). *Stages and pathways of drug involvement.* New York, NY: Cambridge University Press.

Kandel, D. B., & Andrews, K. (1987). Processes of adolescent socialization by parents and peers. *International Journal of the Addictions, 22,* 319–342.

Kandel, D. B., Kessler, R. C., & Margulies, R. Z. (1978). Antecedents of adolescent initiation into stages of drug use: A developmental analysis. In D. B. Kandel (Ed.), *Longitudinal research on drug use* (pp. 73–99). Washington, DC: Hemisphere.

Kandel, D. B., & Wu, P. (1995). The contributions of mothers and fathers to the intergenerational transmission of cigarette smoking in adolescence. *Journal of Research on Adolescence, 5,* 225–252.

Kelleher, K., Chaffin, M., Hollenberg, J., & Fischer, E. (1994). Alcohol and drug disorders among physically abusive and neglectful parents in a community-based sample. *American Journal of Public Health, 84,* 1586–1590.

Kelly, A. B., Chan, G. C. K., Toumbourou, J. W., O'Flaherty, M., Homel, R., Patton, G. C., & Williams, J. (2012). Very young adolescents and alcohol: Evidence of a unique susceptibility to peer alcohol use. *Addictive Behaviors, 37,* 414–419.

Kelly, A. B., O'Flaherty, M., Connor, J. P., Homel, R., Toumbourou, J. W., Patton, G. C., & Williams, J. (2011). The influence of parents, siblings and peers on pre- and early-teen smoking: A multilevel model. *Drug and Alcohol Review, 30,* 381–387.

Kelly, A. B., O'Flaherty, M., Toumbourou, J. W., Connor, J. P., Hemphill, S. A., & Catalano, R. F. (2011). Gender differences in the impact of families on alcohol use: A lagged longitudinal study of early adolescents. *Addiction, 106,* 1427–1436.

Kim, M. J., Fleming, C. B., & Catalano, R. F. (2009). Individual and social influences on progression to daily smoking during adolescence. *Pediatrics, 124,* 895–902.

Kim, Y., & Neff, J. A. (2010). Direct and indirect effects of parental influence upon adolescent alcohol use: A structural equation modeling analysis. *Journal of Child and Adolescent Substance Abuse, 19,* 244–260.

King, K. M., & Chassin, L. (2004). Mediating and moderating effects of adolescent behavioral undercontrol and parenting in the prediction of drug use disorders in emerging adulthood. *Psychology of Addictive Behaviors, 18,* 239–249.

King, K. M., Molina, B. S. G., & Chassin, L. (2009). Prospective relations between growth in drinking and familial stressors across adolescence. *Journal of Abnormal Psychology, 118,* 610–622.

Kiuru, N., Burk, W. J., Laursen, B., Salmela-Aro, K., & Nurmi, J. (2010). Pressure to drink but not to smoke: Disentangling selection and socialization in adolescent peer networks and peer groups. *Journal of Adolescence, 33,* 801–812.

Knecht, A. B., Burk, W. J., Weesie, J., & Steglich, C. (2010). Friendship and alcohol use in early adolescence: A multilevel social network approach. *Journal of Research on Adolescence, 21,* 475–487.

Kodl, M. M., & Mermelstein, R. (2004). Beyond modeling: Parenting practices, parental smoking history, and adolescent cigarette smoking. *Addictive Behaviors, 29,* 17–32.

Kokkevi, A., Richardson, C., Florescu, S., Kuzman, M., & Stergar, E. (2007). Psychosocial correlates of substance use in adolescence: A cross-national study in six European countries. *Drug and Alcohol Dependence, 86,* 67–74.

Koning, I. M., Engels, R. C. M. E., Verdurmen, J. E. E., & Vollebergh, W. A. M. (2010). Alcohol-specific socialization practices and alcohol use in Dutch early adolescents. *Journal of Adolescence, 33,* 93–100.

Koordeman, R., Anschutz, D. J., & Engels, R. C. M. E. (2012). Alcohol portrayals in movies, music videos and soap operas and alcohol use of young people: Current status and future challenges. *Alcohol and Alcoholism, 47,* 612–623.

Kosterman, R., Hawkins, J. D., Guo, J., Catalano, R. F., & Abbott, R. D. (2000). The dynamics of alcohol and marijuana initiation: Patterns and predictors of first use in adolescence. *American Journal of Public Health, 90,* 360–366.

Kristjansson, A. L., Sigfusdottir, I. D., James, J. E., Allegrante, J. P., & Helgason, A. R. (2010). Perceived parental reactions and peer respect as predictors of adolescent cigarette smoking and alcohol use. *Addictive Behaviors, 35,* 256–259.

Kuendig, H., & Kuntsche, E. (2006). Family bonding and adolescent alcohol use: Moderating effect of living with excessive drinking parents. *Alcohol and Alcoholism, 41,* 464–471.

Kung, E. M., & Farrell, A. D. (2000). The role of parents and peers in early adolescent substance use: An examination of mediating and moderating effects. *Journal of Child and Family Studies, 9,* 509–528.

Lamborn, S. D., Mounts, N. S., Steinberg, L., & Dornbusch, S. M. (1991). Patterns of competence and adjustment among adolescents from authoritative, authoritarian, indulgent, and neglectful families. *Child Development, 62,* 1049–1065.

Latendresse, S. J., Rose, R. J., Viken, R. J., Pulkkinen, L., Kaprio, J., & Dick, D. M. (2008). Parenting mechanisms in links between parents' and adolescents' alcohol use behaviors. *Alcoholism: Clinical and Experimental Research, 32,* 322–330.

Laursen, B., Hafen, C. A., Kerr, M., & Stattin, H. (2012). Friend influence over adolescent problem behaviors as a function of relative peer acceptance: To be liked is to be emulated. *Journal of Abnormal Psychology, 121*, 88–94.

Leatherdale, S. T., McDonald, P. W., Cameron, R., Jolin, M. A., & Brown, K. S. (2006). A multi-level analysis examining how smoking friends, parents, and older students in the school environment are risk factors for susceptibility to smoking among non-smoking elementary school youth. *Prevention Science, 7*, 397–402.

Leonardi-Bee, J., Jere, M. L., & Britton, J. (2011). Exposure to parental and sibling smoking and the risk of smoking uptake in childhood and adolescence: A systematic review and meta-analysis. *Thorax, 66*, 847–855.

Lewin, K. (1939). Field theory and experiment in social psychology: Concepts and methods. *American Journal of Social Psychology, 44*, 873–884.

Li, C., Pentz, M. A., & Chou, C. (2002). Parental substance use as a modifier of adolescent substance use risk. *Addiction, 97*, 1537–1550.

Liao, Y., Huang, Z., Huh, J., Pentz, M. A., & Chou, C. (2013). Changes in friends' and parental influences on cigarette smoking from early through late adolescence. *Journal of Adolescent Health, 53*, 132–138.

Loeber, R., Farrington, D. P., Stouthamer-Loeber, M., & Van Kammen, W. B. (1998). *Antisocial behavior and mental health problems: Explanatory factors in childhood and adolescence*. Mahwah, NJ: Erlbaum.

Low, S., Shortt, J. W., & Snyder, J. (2012). Sibling influence on adolescent substance use: The role of modeling, collusion, and conflict. *Development and Psychopathology, 24*, 287–300.

Lynskey, M. T., Fergusson, D. M., & Horwood, L. J. (1998). The origins of the correlations between tobacco, alcohol, and cannabis use during adolescence. *Journal of Child Psychology and Psychiatry, 39*, 995–1005.

Macleod, J., Hickman, M., Bowen, E., Alati, R., Tilling, K., & Smith, G. D. (2008). Parental drug use, early adversities, later childhood problems and children's use of tobacco and alcohol at age 10: Birth cohort study. *Addiction, 103*, 1731–1743.

Mak, K., Ho, S., & Day, J. R. (2012). Smoking of parents and best friend—Independent and combined effects on adolescent smoking and intention to initiate and quit smoking. *Nicotine and Tobacco Research, 9*, 1057–1064.

Mann, L. M., Chassin, L., & Sher, K. J. (1987). Alcohol expectancies and the risk of alcoholism. *Journal of Consulting and Clinical Psychology, 55*, 411–417.

Manning, V., Best, D. W., Faulkner, N., & Titherington, E. (2009). New estimates of the number of children living with substance misusing parents: Results from UK national household surveys. *BMC Public Health, 9*, 377.

Marshal, M. P., & Chassin, L. (2000). Peer influence on adolescent alcohol use: The moderating role of parental support and discipline. *Applied Developmental Science, 4*, 80–88.

Martino, S. C., Ellickson, P. L., & McCaffrey, D. F. (2009). Multiple trajectories of peer and parental influence and their association with the development of adolescent heavy drinking. *Addictive Behaviors, 34*, 693–700.

McGee, L., & Newcomb, M. D. (1992). General deviance syndrome: Expanded hierarchical evaluation at four ages from early adolescence to adulthood. *Journal of Consulting and Clinical Psychology, 60*, 766–776.

McGue, M., & Iacono, W. G. (2005). The association of early adolescent problem behavior with adult psychopathology. *American Journal of Psychiatry, 162*, 1118–1124.

McGue, M., Sharma, A., & Benson, P. (1996). Parent and sibling influences on adolescent alcohol use and misuse: Evidence from a U.S. adoption cohort. *Journal of Studies on Alcohol, 57*, 8–18.

McIntosh, J., MacDonald, F., & McKeganey, N. (2008). Pre-teenage children's experiences with alcohol. *Children and Society, 22*, 3–15.

Melby, J. N., Conger, R. D., Conger, K. J., & Lorenz, F. O. (1993). Effects of parental behavior on tobacco use by young male adolescents. *Journal of Marriage and the Family, 55*, 439–454.

Menezes, A. M. B., Gonçalves, H., Anselmi, L., Hallal, P. C., & Araújo, C. L. P. (2006). Smoking in early adolescence: Evidence from the 1993 Pelotas (Brazil) birth cohort study. *Journal of Adolescent Health, 39*, 669–677.

Mercken, L., Snijders, T. A. B., Steglich, C., & de Vries, H. (2009). Dynamics of adolescent friendship networks and smoking behavior: Social network analyses in six European countries. *Social Science and Medicine, 69*, 1506–1514.

Mercken, L., Steglich, C., Knibbe, R., & de Vries, H. (2012). Dynamics of friendship networks and alcohol use in early and mid-adolescence. *Journal of Studies on Alcohol and Drugs, 73*, 99–110.

Mewse, A. J., Eiser, J. R., Slater, A. M., & Lea, S. E. G. (2004). The smoking behaviors of adolescents and their friends: Do parents matter? *Parenting Science and Practice, 4*, 51–72.

Milton, B., Cook, P. A., Dugdill, L., Porcatello, L., Springett, J., & Woods, S. E. (2004). Why do primary school children smoke? A longitudinal analysis of predictors of smoking uptake during pre-adolescence. *Public Health, 118*, 247–255.

Milton, B., Woods, S. E., Dugdill, L., Porcellato, L., & Springett, R. J. (2008). Starting young? Children's experiences of trying smoking during pre-adolescence. *Health Education Research, 23*, 298–309.

Moreno, M. A., Briner, L. R., Williams, A., Brockman, L., Walker, L., & Christakis, D. A. (2010). A content analysis of displayed alcohol references on a social networking web site. *Journal of Adolescent Health, 47*, 168–175.

Morgenstern, M., Isensee, B., Sargent, J. D., & Hanewinkel, R. (2011). Attitudes as mediators of the longitudinal association between alcohol advertising and youth drinking. *Archives of Pediatrics and Adolescent Medicine, 165*, 610–616.

Morgenstern, M., Sargent, J. D., Engels, R. C. M. E., Scholte, R. H. J., Florek, E., Hunt, K., . . . Hanewinkel, R. (2013). Smoking in movies and adolescent smoking initiation: Longitudinal study in six European countries. *American Journal of Preventive Medicine, 44*, 339–344.

Mounts, N. S., & Steinberg, L. (1995). An ecological analysis of peer influence on adolescent grade point average and drug use. *Developmental Psychology, 31*, 915–922.

Murray, M., Kiryluk, S., & Swan, A. V. (1985). Relation between parents' and children's smoking behavior and attitudes. *Journal of Epidemiology and Community Health, 39*, 169–174.

Nash, S. G., McQueen, A., & Bray, J. H. (2005). Pathways to adolescent alcohol use: Family environment, peer influence, and parental expectations. *Journal of Adolescent Health, 37*, 19–28.

National Cancer Institute. (2008). *The role of the media in promoting and reducing tobacco use* [Tobacco Control Monograph 19; NIH Pub. No. 07-6242]. Bethesda, MD: Author. Retrieved July 17, 2012, from http://www.cancercontrol.cancer.gov/tcrb/monographs/19/index.html

National Center on Addiction and Substance Abuse. (2011). *National survey of American attitudes on substance abuse XVI: Teens and parents.* New York, NY: Columbia University. Retrieved September 24, 2012 from http://www.casacolumbia.org/templates/publications_reports.aspx/ooc3hqnl.pdf

Needle, R., McCubbin, H., Wilson, M., Reineck, R., Lazar, A., & Mederer, H. (1986). Interpersonal influences in adolescent drug use—The role of older siblings, parents, and peers. *The International Journal of the Addictions, 21,* 739–766.

O'Callaghan, F. V., O'Callaghan, M., Najman, J. M., Williams, G. M., Bor, W., & Alati, R. (2006). Prediction of adolescent smoking from family and social risk factors at 5 years, and maternal smoking in pregnancy and at 5 and 14 years. *Addiction, 101,* 282–290.

Oetting, E. R., & Donnermeyer, J. F. (1998). Primary socialization theory: The etiology of drug use and deviance. I. *Substance Use and Misuse, 33,* 995–1026.

O'Loughlin, J., Paradis, G., Renaud, L., & Sanchez Gomez, L. (1998). One-year predictors of smoking initiation and of continued smoking among elementary schoolchildren in multiethnic, low-income, inner-city neighborhoods. *Tobacco Control, 7,* 268–275.

Olsson, C. A., Coffey, C., Toumbourou, J. W., Bond, L., Thomas, L., & Patton, G. (2003). Family risk factors for cannabis use: A population-based survey of Australian secondary school students. *Drug and Alcohol Review, 22,* 143–152.

Ouellette, J. A., Gerrard, M., Gibbons, F. X., & Reis-Bergan, M. (1999). Parents, peers, and prototypes: Antecedents of adolescent alcohol expectancies, alcohol consumption, and alcohol-related life problems in rural youth. *Psychology of Addictive Behaviors, 13,* 185–197.

Oxford, M. L., Harachi, T. W., Catalano, R. F., & Abbott, R. D. (2000). Preadolescent predictors of substance initiation: A test of both the direct and mediated effect of family social control factors on deviant peer associations and substance initiation. *American Journal of Drug and Alcohol Abuse, 27,* 599–616.

Palmer, R. H. C., Young, S. E., Hopfer, C. J., Corley, R. P., Stallings, M. C., Crowley, T. J., & Hewitt, J. K. (2009). Developmental epidemiology of drug use and abuse in adolescence and young adulthood: Evidence of generalized risk. *Drug and Alcohol Dependence, 102,* 78–87.

Pasch, K. E., Komro, K. A., Perry, C. L., Hearst, M. O., & Farbakhsh, K. (2007). Outdoor alcohol advertising near schools: What does it advertise and how is it related to intentions and use of alcohol among adolescents? *Journal of Studies on Alcohol and Drugs, 68,* 587–596.

Pedersen, W., & Skrondal, A. (1998). Alcohol consumption debut: Predictors and consequences. *Journal of Studies on Alcohol, 59,* 32–42.

Peterson, A. V., Jr., Leroux, B. G., Bricker, J., Kealey, K. A., Marek, P. M., Sarason, I. G., & Anderson, M. R. (2006). Nine-year prediction of adolescent smoking by number of smoking parents. *Addictive Behaviors, 31,* 788–801.

Peterson, P. L., Hawkins, J. D., Abbott, R. D., & Catalano, R. F. (1994). Disentangling the effects of parental drinking, family management, and parental alcohol norms on current drinking by black and white adolescents. *Journal of Research on Adolescence, 4,* 203–227.

Pieters, S., Burk, W. J., van der Vorst, H., Wiers, R. W., & Engels, R. C. M. E. (2012). The moderating role of working memory capacity and alcohol-specific rule-setting on the relation between approach tendencies and alcohol use in young adolescents. *Alcoholism: Clinical and Experimental Research, 36,* 915–922.

Pieters, S., van der Vorst, H., Engels, R. C. M. E., & Wiers, R. W. (2010). Implicit and explicit cognitions related to alcohol use in children. *Addictive Behaviors, 35,* 471–478.

Poulin, F., Kiesner, J., Pedersen, S., & Dishion, T. J. (2011). A short-term longitudinal analysis of friendship selection on early adolescent substance use. *Journal of Adolescence, 34,* 249–256.

Prendergast, T. J., & Schaefer, E. S. (1974). Correlates of drinking and drunkenness among high-school students. *Quarterly Journal of Studies on Alcohol, 35,* 232–242.

Primack, B. A., Dalton, M. A., Carroll, M. V., Agarwal, A. A., & Fine, M. J. (2008). Content analysis of tobacco, alcohol, and other drugs in popular music. *Archives of Pediatrics and Adolescent Medicine, 162,* 169–175.

Primack, B. A., Douglas, E. L., & Kraemer, K. L. (2009). Exposure to cannabis in popular music and cannabis use among adolescents. *Addiction, 105,* 515–523.

Primack, B. A., Kraemer, K. L., Fine, M. J., & Dalton, M. A. (2009). Media exposure and marijuana and alcohol use among adolescents. *Substance Use and Misuse, 44,* 722–739.

Primack, B. A., Nuzzo, E., Rice, K. R., & Sargent, J. D. (2011). Alcohol brand appearances in US popular music. *Addiction, 107,* 557–566.

Prins, J. C., Donovan, J. E., & Molina, B. S. G. (2011). Parent-child divergence in the development of alcohol use norms from middle childhood into middle adolescence. *Journal of Studies on Alcohol and Drugs, 72,* 438–443.

Quine, S., & Stephenson, J. A. (1990). Predicting smoking and drinking intentions and behavior of pre-adolescents: The influence of parents, siblings, and peers. *Family Systems Medicine, 8,* 191–200.

Rajan, K. B., Leroux, B. G., Peterson, A. V., Jr., Bricker, J. B., Andersen, M. R., Kealey, K. A., & Sarason, I. G. (2003). Nine-year prospective association between older siblings' smoking and children's daily smoking. *Journal of Adolescent Health, 33,* 25–30.

Reid, J. L., Manske, S. R., & Leatherdale, S. T. (2008). Factors related to adolescents' estimation of peer smoking prevalence. *Health Education Research, 23,* 81–93.

Reimuller, A., Hussong, A., & Ennett, S. T. (2011). The influence of alcohol-specific communication on adolescent alcohol use and alcohol-related consequences. *Prevention Science, 12,* 389–400.

Rende, R., Slomkowski, C., Lloyd-Richardson, E., & Niaura, R. (2005). Sibling effects on substance use in adolescence: Social contagion and genetic relatedness. *Journal of Family Psychology, 19,* 611–618.

Rideout, V. (2010). *Generation M2: Media in the lives of 8- to 18-year-olds.* Menlo Park, CA: Kaiser Family Foundation.

Robinson, L. A., Dalton, W. T., III, & Nicholson, L. M. (2006). Changes in adolescents' sources of cigarettes. *Journal of Adolescent Health, 39,* 861–867.

Robinson, T. N., Chen, H. L., & Killen, J. D. (1998). Television and music video exposure and risk of adolescent alcohol use. *Pediatrics, 102,* e54.

Rossow, I., & Kuntsche, E. (2013). Early onset of drinking and risk of heavy drinking in young adulthood—A 13-year prospective study. *Alcoholism: Clinical and Experimental Research, 37*(s1), e297–e304.

Rossow, I., & Rise, J. (1994). Concordance of parental and adolescent health behaviors. *Social Science and Medicine, 38,* 1299–1305.

Rowe, D. C., & Gulley, B. L. (1992). Sibling effects on substance use and delinquency. *Criminology, 30,* 217–233.

Ryan, S. M., Jorm, A. F., & Lubman, D. I. (2010). Parenting factors associated with reduced adolescent alcohol use: A systematic review of longitudinal studies. *Australian and New Zealand Journal of Psychiatry, 44,* 774–783.

Sargent, J. D., & Dalton, M. (2001). Does parental disapproval of smoking prevent adolescents from becoming established smokers? *Pediatrics, 108,* 1256–1262.

Sargent, J. D., Wills, T. A., Stoolmiller, M., Gibson, J., & Gibbons, F. X. (2006). Alcohol use in motion pictures and its relation with early-onset teen drinking. *Journal of Studies on Alcohol, 67,* 54–65.

Schaefer, D. R., Haas, S. A., & Bishop, N. J. (2012). A dynamic model of US adolescents' smoking and friendship networks. *American Journal of Public Health, 102,* e12–e18.

Scholte, R. H. J., Poelen, E. A. P., Willemsen, G., Boomsma, D. I., & Engels, R. C. M. E. (2008). Relative risks of adolescent and young adult alcohol use: The role of drinking fathers, mothers, siblings, and friends. *Addictive Behaviors, 33,* 1–14.

Schooler, C., Feighery, E., & Flora, J. A. (1996). Seventh graders' self-reported exposure to cigarette marketing and its relation to their smoking behavior. *American Journal of Public Health, 86,* 1216–1221.

Seljamo, S., Aromaa, M., Koivusilta, L., Rautava, P., Sourander, A., Helenius, H., & Silanpää, M. (2006). Alcohol use in families: A 15-year prospective follow-up study. *Addiction, 101,* 984–992.

Shadel, W. G., Tharp-Taylor, S., & Fryer, C. S. (2008). Exposure to cigarette advertising and adolescents' intentions to smoke: The moderating role of the developing self-concept. *Journal of Pediatric Psychology, 33,* 751–760.

Shakya, H. B., Christakis, N. A., & Fowler, J. H. (2012). Parental influence on substance use in adolescent social networks. *Archives of Pediatrics and Adolescent Medicine, 166,* 132–1139.

Sher, K. J. (1991). *Children of alcoholics: A critical appraisal of theory and research.* Chicago, IL: University of Chicago Press.

Shortt, A. L., Hutchinson, D. M., Chapman, R., & Toumbourou, J. W. (2007). Family, school, peer, and individual influences on early adolescent alcohol use: First-year impact of the Resilient Families programme. *Drug and Alcohol Review, 26,* 625–634.

Sieving, R. E., Perry, C. L., & Williams, C. L. (2000). Do friendships change behaviors, or do behaviors change friendships? Examining paths of influence in young adolescents' alcohol use. *Journal of Adolescent Health, 26,* 27–35.

Simons-Morton, B. (2007). Social influences on adolescent substance use. *American Journal of Health Behavior, 31,* 672–684.

Simons-Morton, B., Haynie, D. L., Crump, A. D., Eitel, P., & Saylor, K. E. (2001). Peer and parent influences on smoking and drinking among early adolescents. *Health Education and Behavior, 28,* 95–107.

Skinner, M. L., Haggerty, K. P., & Catalano, R. F. (2009). Parental and peer influences on teen smoking: Are white and black families different? *Nicotine and Tobacco Research, 11,* 558–563.

Smart, R. G., & Fejer, D. (1972). Drug use among adolescents and their parents: Closing the generation gap in mood modification. *Journal of Abnormal Psychology, 79,* 153–160.

Smith, G. T., Miller, T. L., Kroll, L., Simmons, J. R., & Gallen, R. (1999). Children's perceptions of parental drinking: The eye of the beholder. *Journal of Studies on Alcohol, 60,* 817–824.

Spijkerman, R., van den Eijnden, R. J. J. M., Overbeek, G., & Engels, R. C. M. E. (2007). The impact of peer and parental norms and behavior on adolescent drinking: The role of drinker prototypes. *Psychology and Health, 22,* 7–29.

Stacy, A. W., Dent, C. W., Burton, D., & Flay, B. R. (1992). Moderators of peer social influence in adolescent smoking. *Personality and Social Psychology Bulletin, 18,* 163–172.

Stacy, A. W., Zogg, J. B., Unger, J. B., & Dent, C. W. (2004). Exposure to televised alcohol ads and subsequent alcohol use. *American Journal of Health Behavior, 28,* 498–509.

Stein, K. B., Gough, H. G., & Sarbin, T. R. (1966). The dimensionality of the CPI Socialization Scale and an empirically derived typology among delinquent and nondelinquent boys. *Multivariate Behavioral Research, 1,* 197–208.

Steinberg, L., Fletcher, A., & Darling, N. (1994). Parental monitoring and peer influences on adolescent substance use. *Pediatrics, 93,* 1060–1064.

Stern, S. R. (2005). Messages from teens on the big screen: Smoking, drinking, and drug use in teen-centered films. *Journal of Health Communication, 10,* 331–346.

Stoolmiller, M., Wills, T. A., McClure, A. C., Tanski, S. E., Worth, K. A., Gerrard, M., & Sargent, J. D. (2012). Comparing media and family predictors of alcohol use: A cohort study of US adolescents. *BMJ Open, 2,* e000543.

Strasburger, V. C., Jordan, A. B., & Donnerstein, E. (2010). Health effects of media on children and adolescents. *Pediatrics, 125,* 756–767.

Strycker, L. A., Duncan, S. C., & Pickering, M. A. (2003). The social context of alcohol initiation among African American and white youth. *Journal of Ethnicity in Substance Abuse, 2,* 35–42.

Substance Abuse and Mental Health Services Administration, Office of Applied Studies. (2008). *The NSDUH Report: Underage alcohol use: Where do young people get alcohol?* Rockville, MD: Author.

Substance Abuse and Mental Health Services Administration, Office of Applied Studies. (2009). *The NSDUH Report: Children living with substance-dependent or substance-abusing parents: 2002 to 2007.* Rockville, MD: Author.

Substance Abuse and Mental Health Services Administration. (2012). *Results from the 2011 National Survey on Drug Use and Health: Summary of National Findings* [Office of Applied Studies, NSDUH Series H-44; HHS Publication No. SMA 12-4713]. Rockville, MD: Department of Health and Human Services.

Tanski, S. E., Stoolmiller, M., Gerrard, M., & Sargent, J. D. (2012). Moderation of the association between media exposure and youth smoking onset: Race/ethnicity, and parent smoking. *Prevention Science, 13,* 55–63.

Thompson, K. M., & Wilsnack, R. W. (1987). Parental influence on adolescent drinking: Modeling, attitudes, or conflict? *Youth and Society, 19,* 22–43.

Thompson, K. M., & Yokota, F. (2001). Depiction of alcohol, tobacco, and other substances in G-rated animated feature films. *Pediatrics, 107*(6), 1369–1374.

Thornberry, T. P. (1987). Toward an interactional theory of delinquency. *Criminology, 25,* 863–891.

Tildesley, E. A., & Andrews, J. A. (2008). The development of children's intentions to use alcohol: Direct and indirect effects of parent alcohol use and parenting behaviors. *Psychology of Addictive Behaviors, 22*, 326–339.

Tilson, E. C., McBride, C. M., Lipkus, I. M., & Catalano, R. F. (2004). Testing the interaction between parent-child relationship factors and parent smoking to predict youth smoking. *Journal of Adolescent Health, 35*, 182–189.

Titus-Ernstoff, L., Dalton, M. A., Adachi-Mejia, A. M., Longacre, M. R., & Beach, M. L. (2008). Longitudinal study of viewing smoking in movies and initiation of smoking by children. *Pediatrics, 121*, 15–21.

Tyas, S. L., & Pederson, L. L. (1998). Psychosocial factors related to adolescent smoking: A critical review of the literature. *Tobacco Control, 7*, 409–420.

Urberg, K. A., Değirmencioğlu, S. M., & Pilgrim, C. (1997). Close friend and group influence on adolescent cigarette smoking and alcohol use. *Developmental Psychology, 33*, 834–844.

Urberg, K., Goldstein, M. S., & Toro, P. A. (2005). Supportive relationships as a moderator of the effects of parent and peer drinking on adolescent drinking. *Journal of Research on Adolescence, 15*, 1–19.

Urberg, K. A., Luo, Q., Pilgrim, C., & Degirmencioglu, S. M. (2003). A two-stage model of peer influence in adolescent substance use: Individual and relationship-specific differences in susceptibility to influence. *Addictive Behaviors, 28*, 1243–1256.

Urberg, K. A., Shyu, S., & Liang, J. (1990). Peer influence in adolescent cigarette smoking. *Addictive Behaviors, 15*, 247–255.

Van den Bulck, J., & Beullens, K. (2005). Television and music video exposure and adolescent alcohol use while going out. *Alcohol and Alcoholism, 40*, 249–253.

Van der Vorst, H., Engels, R. C. M. E., & Burk, W. J. (2010). Do parents and best friends influence the normative increase in adolescents' alcohol use at home and outside the home? *Journal of Studies on Alcohol and Drugs, 71*(1), 105–114.

Van der Vorst, H., Engels, R. C. M. E., Meeus, W., & Deković, M. (2006). The impact of alcohol-specific rules, parental norms about early drinking and parental alcohol use on adolescents' drinking behavior. *Journal of Child Psychology and Psychiatry, 47*, 1299–1306.

Van der Zwaluw, C. S., Scholte, R. H. J., Vermulst, A. A., Buitelaar, J. K., Verkes, R. J., & Engels, R. C. M. E. (2008). Parental problem drinking, parenting, and adolescent alcohol use. *Journal of Behavioral Medicine, 31*, 189–200.

Van Zundert, R. M. P., van der Vorst, H., Vermulst, A. A., & Engels, R. C. M. E. (2006). Pathways to alcohol use among Dutch students in regular education and education for adolescents with behavioral problems: The role of parental alcohol use, general parenting practices, and alcohol-specific parenting practices. *Journal of Family Psychology, 20*, 456–467.

Wagner, F. A., & Anthony, J. C. (2002). Into the world of illicit drug use: Exposure opportunity and other mechanisms linking the use of alcohol, tobacco, marijuana, and cocaine. *American Journal of Epidemiology, 155*, 918–925.

Walden, B., McGue, M., Iacono, W. G., Burt, A., & Elkin, I. (2004). Identifying shared environmental contributions to early substance use: The respective roles of peers and parents. *Journal of Abnormal Psychology, 113*, 440–450.

Wang, J., Simons-Morton, B., Farhat, T., & Luk, J. W. (2009). Socio-demographic variability in adolescent substance use: Mediation by parents and peers. *Prevention Science, 10*, 387–396.

Wang, M. P., Ho, S. Y., & Lam, T. H. (2011). Parental smoking, exposure to secondhand smoke at home, and smoking initiation among young children. *Nicotine and Tobacco Research, 13*, 827–832.

Wang, M. Q., Fitzhugh, E. C., Green, B. L., Turner, L. W., Eddy, J. M., & Westerfield, R. C. (1999). Prospective social-psychological factors of adolescent smoking progression. *Journal of Adolescent Health, 24*, 2–9.

Webb, J. A., Baer, P. E., Caid, C. D., McLaughlin, R. J., & McKelvey, R. S. (1991). Concurrent and longitudinal assessment of risk for alcohol use among seventh graders. *Journal of Early Adolescence, 11*, 450–465.

Wellman, R. J., Sugarman, D. B., DiFranza, J. R., & Winickoff, J. P. (2006). The extent to which tobacco marketing and tobacco use in films contribute to children's use of tobacco. *Archives of Pediatrics and Adolescent Medicine, 160*, 1285–1296.

Wen, M., van Duker, H., & Olson, L. M. (2009). Social contexts of regular smoking in adolescence: Towards a multidimensional ecological model. *Journal of Adolescence, 32*, 671–692.

White, H. R., Johnson, V., & Buyske, S. (2000). Parental modeling and parenting behavior effects on offspring alcohol and cigarette use: A growth curve analysis. *Journal of Substance Abuse, 12*, 287–310.

Wiers, R. W., Gunning, W. B., & Sergeant, J. A. (1998). Do young children of alcoholics hold more positive or negative alcohol-related expectancies than controls? *Alcoholism: Clinical and Experimental Research, 22*, 1855–1863.

Wills, T. A., Sargent, J. D., Gibbons, F. X., Gerrard, M., & Stoolmiller, M. (2009). Movie exposure to alcohol cues and adolescent alcohol problems: A longitudinal analysis in a national sample. *Psychology of Addictive Behaviors, 23*, 23–35.

Wills, T. A., Sargent, J. D., Stoolmiller, M., Gibbons, F. X., & Gerrard, M. (2008). Movie smoking exposure and smoking onset: A longitudinal study of mediation processes in a representative sample of U.S. adolescents. *Psychology of Addictive Behaviors, 22*, 269–277.

Wills, T. A., Sargent, J. D., Stoolmiller, M., Gibbons, F. X., Worth, K. A., & Dal Cin, S. (2007). Movie exposure to smoking cues and adolescent smoking onset: A test for mediation through peer affiliations. *Health Psychology, 26*, 769–776.

Wilson, D. B., McClish, D. K., Heckman, C. J., Obando, P., & Dahman, B. A. (2007). Parental smoking, closeness to parents, and youth smoking. *American Journal of Health Behavior, 31*, 261–271.

Windle, M. (2000). Parental, sibling, and peer influences on adolescent substance use and alcohol problems. *Applied Developmental Science, 4*, 98–110.

Wingood, G. M., DiClemente, R. J., Bernhardt, J. M., Harrington, K., Davies, S. L., Robillard, A., & Hook, E. W., III (2003). A prospective study of exposure to rap music videos and African American female adolescents' health. *American Journal of Public Health, 93*, 437–439.

Wong, M. M., Brower, K. J., Fitzgerald, H. E., & Zucker, R. A. (2004). Sleep problems in early childhood and early onset of alcohol and other drug use in adolescence. *Alcoholism: Clinical and Experimental Research, 28*, 578–587.

Yu, J. (2003). The association between parental alcohol-related behaviors and children's drinking. *Drug and Alcohol Dependence, 69*, 253–262.

Zhang, L., Welte, J. W., & Wieczorek, W. F. (1999). The influence of parental drinking and closeness on adolescent drinking. *Journal of Studies on Alcohol, 60*, 245–251.

Application of the Expectancy Concept to Substance Use

Sarah J. Peterson *and* Gregory T. Smith

Abstract

This chapter provides an introduction to, and overview of, substance use expectancy theory, which offers one framework to explain why individuals approach and engage in substance use behaviors. We begin with an overview of basic behavioral science models of expectancy, noting that the capacity to anticipate outcomes of behaviors, and hence choose to engage in behaviors from which one expects benefits or rewards, is central to adaptive functioning. We note the importance of the insight that this anticipation/expectancy principle can be applied to substance use. We then review models of the development of learned anticipations or expectancies of reward from substance use and consider factors that influence substance use expectancy development. We observe that longitudinal data, documenting expectancies' prediction of subsequent addictive behaviors, and experimental data, documenting reductions in both drinking and eating disorder symptoms following expectancy reduction, speak to the functional role of expectancies in addictive behaviors.

Key Words: expectancy, learning, risk, adolescence, alcohol, smoking, disordered eating

The focus of this chapter is on applications of the expectancy concept to adolescent substance use, which constitutes one set of efforts to understand risk for substance use onset and the emergence of problematic substance use during the adolescent years. To understand the meaning and risk implications of the expectancy concept, it is necessary to review important developments in psychological science provided by both basic scientists and addiction researchers. We begin the chapter by highlighting, briefly, relevant scientific advances in order to place substance use expectancy theory in its proper context. Following this introduction, we discuss the development of substance use expectancies prior to, and during, the adolescent years. In doing so, we consider factors that influence the formation and strength of those expectancies. We then turn to the functional role of substance use expectancies for the prediction and treatment of problematic addictive behaviors.

Brief History of Substance Use Expectancy Theory
Anticipation as Key to Successful Functioning by Organisms

It is fundamentally adaptive for organisms to engage in behaviors that result in reward and avoid behaviors that result in punishment. Central to the capacity to do so is the ability to anticipate events and the outcomes of events. Without such an anticipatory capacity, organisms would have no basis for selecting rewarding versus punishing behaviors. The demonstration of such an anticipatory capacity, often referred to as expectancies, at the behavioral level goes at least as far back as the 1930s (Tolman, 1932; Tolman & Honzik, 1930). Using animal models, Tolman and his colleagues demonstrated that organisms formed expectancies concerning the relationships between stimuli and behaviors. Rats had memories, referred to as cognitive maps, based on their prior learning (Tolman & Honzik, 1930).

Once formed, the memories could be relied on to guide rats toward important rewards.

A crucial implication of the early Tolman research was that memory does not function primarily to look back in time. Rather, memory serves the function of facilitating effectiveness in looking forward in time. By virtue of memories formed from learning experiences, organisms can internally anticipate which behaviors produce which kinds of reward or punishment; they can then behave in ways to increase the likelihood of reward and decrease the likelihood of punishment. The capacity to anticipate behavioral outcomes is central to organized, adaptive behavior.

It is important to appreciate that learned, memory-based expectancies or anticipations of reward inherently include motivation and emotion components. For fundamental adaptive and survival reasons, organisms are motivated to pursue reward. As Holland and Gallagher (2004) described, expectancies reflect the associative activation of memory representations of reinforcers by the events that predict them. One forms expectancies about desired outcomes, that is, outcomes one is motivated to experience. The neuroscience of emotion similarly identifies the experience of emotion as a signal for outcomes to be pursued or avoided. To emote means literally to prepare for action (Maxwell & Davidson, 2007). Emotional experiences trigger the organism to attend to that which is important (that which relates to important rewards or threats). Consistent with this perspective (see Pinker, 1997), the motor cortex is activated during emotional experience (Morgenson, Jones, & Yim, 1980). The organism prepares to act to pursue desired reward or avoid threat or punishment. The direction of action to achieve a reward or avoid a punishment is based on memory-based associations between actions and their outcomes, or expectancies.

In recent years, the integration of neurocognitive and behavioral science has led to an increasingly full characterization of the neurobiological underpinnings of expectancy operation (Glimcher & Lau, 2005; Minamimoto, Hori, & Kimura, 2005: see review by Goldman & Reich, 2013). Neural signals that appear to indicate the reward is imminent have been identified, and the neurotransmitter dopamine appears central to that process (Berridge & Robinson, 1998; Montague & Berns, 2002). Essentially, neural activation in specified brain systems appears to communicate that rewards available in a particular context differ from the organism's prior anticipation of rewards. This

mechanism appears to serve to adjust ongoing behavior toward expected beneficial outcomes. This process is referred to as an expectancy process. For example, Kupfermann, Kandel, and Iversen (2000) described a process in which "dopaminergic neurons encode expectations about external rewards" (p. 1010).

The application of expectancy theory to risk for substance use represents an applied, clinical science adaptation of this basic functional process to increase understanding of engagement in one specific set of behaviors. An additional and very important preliminary step before substance use expectancy theory could develop was the insight that substance use behaviors are, in fact, behaviors that operate under the same principles of reward, punishment, and learning-based anticipation as other behaviors. Although this idea may be taken for granted by substance use researchers now, some of the key work demonstrating this reality took place only 40–50 years ago. We consider that work next.

Application of Basic Behavior Principles of Functioning to Substance Use

The crucial advances in this area were made with respect to the substance of alcohol, so we focus next on alcoholism. Because alcoholism has often been considered a disease, and thus assumed to operate in some different way from normal, everyday human functioning, it was not assumed that problematic drinking behavior could be understood using the same principles as other behaviors. The idea of expected or anticipated reward pursuit, which influences the wide range of human behavior, was not initially applied to the problem of alcoholism.

Seminal research in the 1970s, conducted largely by Peter Nathan, provided the scientific basis for a fundamental shift toward understanding problem drinking behavior in the same way other behaviors are understood. Drinking behavior follows the same operant principles of reward and punishment as other behaviors (Nathan & O'Brien, 1971; Silverstein, Nathan, & Taylor, 1974). As much as any set of scientific findings, these and other studies by Nathan and his colleagues pointed to the relevance of clinical psychological science for the problem of addictions. In fact, much of the content of this current volume reflects advances by psychological scientists that were made possible, directly or indirectly, by the insight that basic principles of behavior, learning, and memory shape drinking behavior just as they shape other human behaviors.

One clear implication of this early behavioral work on alcoholism is that, to understand drinking behavior, it is important to understand memory-based anticipations of reinforcing effects from drinking. Just as is true for other behaviors, individuals drink in part because they anticipate or expect desired reinforcement from the behavior (Brown, Goldman, Inn, & Anderson, 1980; Christiansen & Goldman, 1983; Darkes & Goldman, 1993; Marlatt & Rohsenow, 1980; Smith, Goldman, Greenbaum, & Christiansen, 1995). As we describe later in this chapter, numerous applied advances have accrued from this focus on anticipated reinforcement from substance use, both with respect to understanding risk and designing effective treatments.

Our focus in applying basic expectancy theory to the problem of substance use is, in part, to understand why individuals engage in behaviors that are, in the long term, harmful to the self. Thus, models to explain the approach toward addictive behaviors are essential. Understanding addictive behaviors as influenced by the same process of learned anticipation of reward as are other behaviors has led to the development of expectancy and expectancy-related risk models, which, as we describe later, have proven remarkably fruitful in efforts to understand addictive behaviors and intervene successfully.

Attempts to Measure Substance Use Expectancies

For a number of addictive behaviors, including drinking, smoking, marijuana use, cocaine use, and eating disorders, researchers have developed questionnaire measures of reinforcement expectancies (examples include Brandon & Baker, 1991; Fromme & D'Amico, 2000; Hohlstein, Smith, & Atlas, 1998; Schafer & Brown, 1991). These measures are designed to assess summaries of individuals' learning histories that result in expectancies for, or anticipations of, reinforcement from use of the substances. Of course, expectancies appear typically to operate on an internal level, influencing goal-directed behavior often without conscious thought. What is important for expectancy operation is the memory-based association of a behavior to a reward; that association is what influences subsequent behavioral choices. From the standpoint of basic science expectancy theory, whether the anticipations are experienced consciously is not highly relevant. Past experience shapes future behavior through the anticipation of reward. Given that theoretical context, by assessing content-specific learned expectancies in questionnaire form,

researchers hope to have a window into the day-to-day operation of anticipatory or expectancy processes.

Again from the basic science expectancy theory perspective we have described, a number of different terms are understood to capture anticipation of reward content. Perhaps the most widely used, other than "expectancy," is "motives." Cooper and her colleagues (see Cooper, 1994) have demonstrated that one can assess motives to use alcohol, and the motives predict future consumption (Read, Wood, Kahler, Maddock, & Palfai, 2003; Settles, Cyders, & Smith, 2010). Motives to drink, such as to cope with distress or enhance a positive mood, reflect anticipations of reinforcement from drinking behavior and thus tap into the same, basic anticipatory process referred to by the term "expectancy" (Reich & Goldman, 2015). Each term, be it "expectancy," "motive," or "anticipation," reflects an attempt to understand and measure the same underlying adaptive process of choosing behaviors that provide desired reinforcement.

CONTENT OF EXPECTANCY MEASURES

Expectancy measures have been constructed in different ways. For alcohol, Brown et al. (1980) used an inductive method, in which both drinkers and nondrinkers were asked what effects from drinking they anticipated. When the researchers no longer heard new anticipated effects, they constructed a questionnaire measure to reflect participants' expectancies. Hohlstein et al. (1998) took the same approach for eating disorders. Other researchers have developed expectancy measures using deductive, or theory-based approaches.

The addictive behavior for which the largest number of expectancy measures has been developed is alcohol use. Interestingly, regardless of the method of construction, largely the same content domains of expected effects from drinking have been identified. Typical expected reinforcement effects include that alcohol makes global, positive transformations of experience; it enhances a positive mood; it facilitates social behavior; it enhances sexuality; it provides tension reduction; it helps cope with subjective distress; it improves cognitive and motor abilities; it provides "liquid courage"; and it increases arousal (Christiansen & Goldman, 1983; Cooper, 1994; Fromme & D'Amico, 2000). Similar expected effects have been identified for other forms of addiction, such as that smoking facilitates social experience and reduces negative affect (Brandon & Baker, 1991) and eating helps manage negative affect, is pleasurable, and alleviates boredom (Hohlstein et al., 1998).

The best psychometric means for gaining a window into anticipatory or expectancy processes is, of course, an empirical question. Certainly explicit, questionnaire-based measurement of expectancy or motive content has proven quite useful and there is good evidence for its validity. First, individual differences in expectancies for reinforcement for many different addictive behaviors have been measured reliably (e.g., Brown et al., 1980; Fromme & D'Amico, 2000; Hohlstein et al., 1998). Second, expectancy measures correlate cross-sectionally with the relevant addictive behavior and typically account for a great deal of variance in the addictive behavior (Smith & Goldman, 1994). Third, youth variation in addiction-specific expectancy endorsement predicts the subsequent onset of, or increases in, the addictive behavior of interest. Examples of successful predictive tests include Smith et al. (1995), Read et al. (2003), and Colder et al. (2014) for drinking; Doran et al. (2013) and Guller, Zapolski, and Smith (2015a) for smoking; and Pearson, Combs, Zapolski, and Smith (2012) and Smith, Simmons, Flory, Annus, and Hill (2007) for disordered eating. Fourth, measured expectancies are behavior specific as they should be: Expectancies for reinforcement from drinking predict drinking, but not smoking or disordered eating; expectancies for reinforcement from smoking predict smoking, but not drinking or disordered eating; and expectancies for reinforcement from eating and from thinness predict disordered eating, but not the other behaviors (Fischer, Settles, Collins, Gunn, & Smith, 2012; Peterson & Smith, 2016). Fifth, explicitly measured expectancy assessment has been used successfully in intervention outcome studies for drinking (Darkes & Goldman, 1993) and disordered eating (Annus, Smith & Masters, 2008).

Even with that successful history, it is useful to consider whether a more implicit assessment of expectancies would be useful, particularly given the recognition that expectancies can operate outside of conscious reflection. Implicit expectancy measures for alcohol have been developed, and Reich, Below, and Goldman (2010) reported the results of a meta-analysis indicating that explicit and implicit measures were only weakly related to each other and the two approaches provided both shared and unique prediction of drinking

behavior. Explicit measures account for more variance in drinking than implicit measures, but both approaches appear to be useful.

An Alternative Expectancy Model

The expectancy model that we have described has its roots in basic behavioral theory and speaks to the mechanism by which learning and memory influence future behavior. A different expectancy model is represented in the theory of reasoned action (Ajzen & Fishbein, 1980). This model emphasized planned, deliberate, or conscious behavior. Part of what contributes to a drinking decision is the cognition that drinking provides a desired outcome, such as facilitating social experience. In models of this kind, individuals deliberate on expected outcomes, the likelihood of those outcomes, social norms, and other factors before forming behavioral intentions. The intentions then guide the behavior. From our point of view, although such deliberate, conscious processes no doubt occur, a more basic and broader focus on memory-based anticipations of reinforcement that can operate with or without conscious reflection captures the central role of anticipatory processing more fully.

Together, the basic science finding of learned expectancies playing a causal role in future behavior, the finding that substance use behaviors follow the same principles of reinforcement and punishment as other behaviors (Nathan & O'Brien, 1971), that measures of expectancy for reinforcement successfully predict the relevant addictive behavior, and that expectancy-based interventions have met with some success (Darkes & Goldman, 1993), all speak to the viability of expectancy models as part of the etiological matrix of substance use problems. Therefore, a crucial question concerns the emergence of learned expectancies over the course of development. We turn to findings on this topic next.

Developmental Emergence of Expectancies Over the Course of Development

Because measured substance use expectancies are understood to reflect summaries of individuals' learning histories relating substance use to desired outcomes, it is important to understand their development and formation over time. We next consider research on substance use expectancy formation, including research on factors that influence expectancy development. The bulk of this work has been done with respect to expectancies for reinforcement from drinking, so alcohol expectancy work will be strongly represented in this section of the chapter.

Expectancy Formation Through Modeling or Observation

There is good evidence that the process of forming expectancies regarding reinforcement from substance use begins much earlier than adolescence. For example, children as young as preschool age have conceptual knowledge of what alcohol is and how it exists in the social environment (Zucker, Donovan, Masten, Mattson, & Moss, 2008). These beliefs can be thought of as alcohol schemas, or a child's organization of knowledge and beliefs about alcohol (Zucker, Kincaid, Fitzgerald, & Bingham, 1995). Alcohol schemas, detectable in early childhood, have been conceptualized as precursors to alcohol expectancies (Zucker et al., 2008). At least by age 10, this knowledge includes developing perspectives regarding how alcohol produces changes in cognition, feeling, and behavior, as well as about who uses alcohol and why (Cameron, Stritzke, & Durkin, 2003; Dunn & Goldman, 1998; Miller, Smith, & Goldman, 1990). Associations between alcohol use and changes in thinking, feeling, or acting reflect anticipated consequences of, or expectancies from, alcohol consumption.

Most (but not all) children this young have yet to consume alcohol (Donovan, 2007). Therefore, youth expectancy formation seems not to depend on direct experience with drinking behavior. Instead, expectancy formation appears to function like other forms of learning, in which youth can learn to anticipate consequences of events through observation of models or awareness of societal knowledge. Consistent with this idea, there is evidence that alcohol schemas are more common in children of alcoholics, suggesting vicarious learning through experiences in the home (Zucker et al., 1995). Similarly, Smith (1994) found that a measure reflecting positive parental attitudes toward drinking, parental drinking level, and positive family history of alcoholism was associated with higher levels of alcohol reinforcement expectancies among early adolescents. More generally, researchers have documented increases in expectancies for reinforcement from drinking across pre-adolescent development (Dunn & Goldman, 1998; Miller et al., 1990), again implicating learning through some form of observation.

Drinking behavior is rare among elementary school children, but starting at the beginning of adolescence, the number of youth who drink increases in almost a linear fashion across the adolescent years. Similarly, use of other substances increases across these years (Chung & Jackson, this volume;

Patrick & O'Malley, this volume). Consistent with expectancy theory, expectancies for reinforcement from drinking, smoking, and binge eating that are formed prior to engagement in those behaviors predict the subsequent onset of, and increases in, the relevant addictive behavior (e.g., Guller et al., 2015b; Smith et al., 1995; Smith et al., 2007). It thus appears that those children who learn to anticipate reinforcement for engagement in a range of addictive behaviors before engaging in them are more likely to engage in those behaviors than other children.

Interestingly, there appears to be an important shift in expectancies during late childhood that precedes these adolescent increases in addictive behaviors. Concerning alcohol, children tend to have neutral perceptions of alcohol use at age 6, but the views of 10-year-olds are more negative about drinking (Fossey, 2005; Jahoda & Cramond, 1972). Attitudes then become increasingly positive between the ages of 10 and 14 as children grow into adolescence (Aitken, 1978). A study of youth ages 8–12 found evidence that positive and negative expectancies increase concurrently (Cameron et al., 2003), and a recent longitudinal study found that, from ages 10 through 15, perceived likely positive outcomes from drinking increased and perceived likely negative outcomes decreased (Colder et al., 2014). Because positive expectancies have been shown to predict the onset of drinking in adolescence, it may be that positive expectancies begin to carry more weight during late childhood and early adolescence (Bekman, Goldman, Worley, & Anderson, 2011; Zucker et al., 2008). Additionally, positive expectancy endorsement appears to increase with grade level (Bekman et al., 2011; Miller et al., 1990), as do subjective evaluations of outcomes from drinking (Corbin et al., 2014). Thus, there appears to be a shift from anticipating negative outcomes from drinking toward more anticipation of positive or reinforcing outcomes. Such a shift certainly appears to be consistent with societal messages that associate alcohol consumption with a range of positive outcomes (Smith & Goldman, 1994). This shift anticipates increased drinking rates during this developmental period.

It may be useful to consider this shift in terms of a characterization of expectancies that places them on two orthogonal dimensions representing positive-negative expectancies and arousal-sedation expectancies (Rather & Goldman, 1994; Rather, Goldman, Roehrich, & Brannick, 1992). Positive and/or arousal-related expectancies tend to predict heavier drinking patterns than negative and/or sedation-related expectancies (Reich & Goldman, 2005). A study done beginning in late elementary-aged children produced findings consistent with the hypothesis that there is a transition from an emphasis on the positive-negative dimension, with most expectancies on the negative pole, to an increase in focus on positive expectancies as well as an incorporation of the arousal-sedation dimension (Dunn & Goldman, 1996, 1998). This apparent shift in expectancies is thought to represent a differential gains model, in which expectancies of all types become incorporated into the learning history, but with one type increasing at a faster rate than another (Bekman et al., 2011; McCarthy, Pedersen, & D'Amico, 2009; Schell, Martino, Ellickson, Collins, & McCaffrey, 2005). Specifically, as youth progress into adolescence, children's expectancy networks likely become more elaborate across both dimensions. However, there may be a faster acquisition rate of positive and/or arousing expectancies, making them more salient and likely to be activated than the negative and/or sedating expectancies. The observation that positive expectancy endorsement increases more rapidly is again consistent with exposure to modeling and societal norms that communicate positive outcomes from alcohol consumption. Further research on the mechanisms of expectancy change during this developmental time period is warranted.

Expectancy Formation From Experience

Because expectancy measures are understood to represent summaries of learning histories regarding the anticipated consequences of engaging in a behavior, it follows that ongoing engagement in a behavior should influence subsequent expectancies for reinforcement from that behavior. Concerning alcohol, given the frequently replicated finding that adolescent alcohol expectancies predict subsequent drinking onset and drinking behavior (Christiansen, Smith, Roehling, & Goldman 1989; Goldberg, Halpern-Felsher, & Millstein, 2002; Ouellette, Gerrard, Gibbons, & Reis-Bergan, 1999; Settles, Zapolski, & Smith, 2014), the possibility that drinking behavior itself shapes subsequent expectancies raises the possibility of a reciprocal relationship between alcohol expectancies and drinking behavior. If this is true, an important question is whether drinking experience serves a corrective function, reducing expectations for reinforcement from drinking, or instead further enhances such expectations.

Research on three longitudinal samples of adolescents has shown that (a) drinking behavior does predict subsequent expectancies, controlling for prior expectancies; and (b) that prediction is positive, such that drinking experience leads to further increases in expectancies for reinforcement from drinking (Jester et al., 2015; Settles et al., 2014; Smith et al., 1995). Thus, there is replicated evidence for a reciprocal relationship, in the form of a positive feedback loop, between alcohol expectancies and adolescent drinking behavior. Expected reinforcement from drinking predicts both the onset of and increases in drinking behavior, which predicts subsequent increases in positive expectancies of drinking, which in turn predict further increases in drinking. Importantly, there was no evidence of a "corrective" feedback process in which drinking experiences served to reduce alcohol expectancies. This set of findings further highlights the risk associated with high levels of positive alcohol expectancies in youth.

Similar findings have emerged recently with respect to other addictive behaviors. Guller et al. (2015a) found positive, reciprocal prediction between expectancies for reinforcement from smoking and smoking behavior among early adolescents. Again, there was no evidence of a corrective process, in which smoking experience reduced expectancies for reinforcement. With respect to disordered eating, there is again evidence of a reciprocal prediction process between binge eating and expectancies for reinforcement from eating, and between purging and expectancies for reinforcement from dieting and thinness, over 12-month (Pearson et al., 2012) and 48-month (Davis, Riley, & Smith, 2016) intervals. As with the other behaviors, engagement in binge eating led to further increases in eating expectancies and engagement in purging led to further increases in dieting/thinness expectancies; there was no corrective process.

Expectancy Formation Influenced by Personality: The Acquired Preparedness Model of Risk

Although historically research on personality risk factors for substance use has proceeded along a separate track from research on experience-based, learning models of substance use, in recent years considerable support has accrued for a model integrating these two categories of risk factors. Personality traits are understood to represent stable, characteristic ways in which a person perceives the world and acts in it (Allport, 1937).

It follows, as recognized by person-environment transaction theory (Caspi, 1993), that individuals with different personalities can perceive a common event differently from each other. For example, an event such as turbulence on an airplane may be perceived as highly stressful for a person high in neuroticism but as inconsequential to a person who is not.

The acquired preparedness (AP) model proposed an additional implication of this understanding of the transactional relationship between personality and experience. If an objectively common environmental event may not be experienced in the same way by different people (Hartup & Van Lieshout, 1995), then two individuals may learn different things from the same event and thus develop different expectancies about that event (Davis, Riley, & Smith, in press). If individuals learn different things from the same event, it follows that they can form different expectancies from a common event, which can lead to different behavioral choices in the future. The model is referred to as the acquired preparedness model to reflect the concept that individuals are differentially prepared to acquire high-risk expectancies as a function of differences in their personality makeup.

Smith, Williams, Cyders, and Kelley (2006) conducted a longitudinal, laboratory-controlled study to test the viability of the AP model. They taught business students skills on how to invest in the stock market. Over several weeks after learning the skills, the students invested virtual money in (unnamed) stocks. They understood they were investing in a given stock based on its portfolio from a year in the past. The following week they "learned" how their stock performed over the 1-year period following their investment. The same process was repeated several times. The participants understood this procedure as designed to teach them the effectiveness of the different stock-trading skills they had learned. Unbeknownst to the participants, all students received the exact same rate of return on their investments. After several such learning trials, Smith et al. (2006) measured the students' expectancies concerning stock market investing. They found that, even though all students had the same learning experience, they formed different expectancies for future investment success, and their expectancies could be predicted in advance by the students' personality traits measured prior to the study. This study constitutes something of an existence proof for the AP process of differential learning

from a common event as a function of variation in personality.

Since the Smith et al. (2006) demonstration of the AP process, a number of studies have indicated the viability of the AP theory contention that individual differences in personality may influence expectancy formation and, in doing so, predict engagement in multiple addictive behaviors. Although there have been many cross-sectional studies testing the AP model, longitudinal tests of the model are the most useful, because they document the temporal sequence of predictive effects that must be present for the model to be viable. In this chapter, we focus on longitudinal studies.

Settles, Cyders, and Smith (2010) reported on the first longitudinal test of the AP model applied to drinking behavior. They found two AP pathways in their three-wave study of first-year college students. The trait of positive urgency (the disposition to act rashly when in an unusually positive mood), measured at the start of the first semester of college, predicted increased expectancies for positive arousing effects of alcohol at the start of the second semester (controlling for prior expectancies), and in turn this expectancy predicted subsequent increases in drinking quantity at the end of the second semester, again controlling for prior drinking quantity. Again controlling for prior levels of relevant variables, the trait of negative urgency (the disposition to act rashly when distressed) predicted increases in the motive to drink to cope with distress, which in part reflects the expectancy that drinking does help one manage distress, and the motive in turn predicted subsequent increases in drinking quantity (Settles et al., 2010). These prospective findings concerning drinking behavior were consistent with the laboratory findings of Smith et al. (2006).

In longer term studies with college students, expectancies for reinforcement from drinking mediated the predictive influence of trait disinhibition (measured as sensation seeking, novelty seeking, and lack of planning) on drinking behavior over a 4-year period (Corbin, Iwamoto, & Fromme, 2011) and the predictive influence of a trait reflecting the inclination to act in pursuit of reward (the behavioral activation system) on drinking over a 3-year period (Wardell, Read, Colder, & Merrill, 2012). These latter two findings suggest that the AP process is likely to operate for multiple impulsivity-related personality traits, not just for the urgency traits.

The AP model of drinking risk has also been supported in children making the transition from childhood to early adolescence. Settles, Zapolski, and Smith (2014) found that fifth graders' positive urgency scores predicted increased drinking frequency at the end of sixth grade, and the prediction was mediated by increases in expectancies for positive social effects of drinking measured at the beginning of sixth grade. In addition, laboratory research has provided evidence that personality does appear to bias the learning process, as proposed by the AP model (Scott & Corbin, 2014). Scott and Corbin (2014) used a between-subjects design in which young adult drinkers received alcohol or a placebo and were asked about their experience. They found that regardless of whether they received alcohol or placebo, participants high in the personality trait of sensation seeking reported a more positive experience.

Longitudinal findings consistent with the AP model have been found with other addictive behaviors. With respect to tobacco smoking, Doran and colleagues (2013) found that (a) expectancies for negative reinforcement from smoking mediated the predictive influence of negative urgency on smoking initiation, and (b) positive reinforcement expectancies mediated the predictive influence of sensation seeking on smoking initiation. As Settles et al. (2010) found with drinking, Doran et al. (2013) found that two different expectancies were predicted by two different personality traits. With respect to bulimic behaviors, Pearson, Combs, Zapolski, and Smith (2012) found that expectancies that eating helps one manage negative affect mediated the predictive influence of negative urgency on subsequent binge eating behavior in youth making the transition to middle school. Thus, the AP process appears to operate across behaviors; for each behavior studied to date, expectancies specific to that behavior mediate the influence of personality on engagement in the behavior.

Personality traits are broad dispositions that predict multiple behaviors. For example, the traits of positive and negative urgency prospectively predict drinking (Cyders, Flory, Rainer, & Smith, 2009; Settles et al., 2010, 2014), tobacco smoking (Doran et al., 2013; Guller et al., 2015a); drug use (Zapolski, Cyders, & Smith, 2009); gambling behavior (Cyders & Smith, 2008); disordered eating behavior (Fischer, Peterson, & McCarthy, 2013; Guller et al., 2015b; Pearson et al., 2012), risky sex (Zapolski et al., 2009); and nonsuicidal self-injury (Riley, Combs, Jordan, & Smith, 2015). In contrast, learned expectancies for reinforcement from a given behavior are understood to be specific to that behavior. Consistent with this distinction, negative urgency predicts drinking, smoking, and binge eating, but each of those behaviors is predicted only by the relevant expectancy (expectancies for reinforcement from drinking predict drinking but not the other behaviors: Fischer et al., 2012; Peterson & Smith, 2016).

The set of longitudinal findings we have reviewed, involving different addictive behaviors, different personality traits, and different expectancies, consistently supports the AP model of risk. Of course, the AP model is a causal model: The contention is that elevations in high-risk traits contribute to formation of high-risk expectancies, which in turn contribute to addictive behavior involvement. Longitudinal studies in which the predictors cannot be manipulated cannot demonstrate a causal process, but consistent prediction above and beyond relevant controls that is consistent with the AP model provides some basis for confidence in the model.

One important benefit of the AP model is that it helps identify an additional target of intervention. Whereas psychosocial learning models suggest expectancy-based interventions, which have proven useful (Scott-Sheldon, Terry, Carey, Garey, & Carey, 2012), the AP model suggest the potential value of also focusing on high-risk personality traits. We consider this issue further later in this chapter.

Sociodemographic Factors Influencing Expectancies

Other factors that may influence expectancy formation include gender and race/ethnicity. Rates of underage drinking tend to be highest for Whites, followed by Hispanics, and then African Americans, with males averaging higher frequency and quantity of drinking than females within racial/ethnic groups (Chen, Hsiao-ye, Williams, & Faden, 2009). Several studies have been done examining gender differences on alcohol expectancies. In general, the findings of this research tend to reveal mean differences in expectancy endorsement and expectancy content by gender. Research suggests that males have stronger expectancies regarding the tension-reducing and negative affect–reducing effects of alcohol (Brown et al., 2008), whereas females have stronger expectancies regarding physical and social pleasure (Baldwin, Oei, & Young, 1993). It has been hypothesized that these differences occur due to differential socialization of males and females (Lo & Globetti, 2000; Schulte, Ramo, & Brown, 2009).

Despite these mean differences, the risk process is thought to operate uniformly across gender, with greater expectancy endorsement predicting greater drinking behavior at the same magnitude of prediction (Chen, Grube, & Madden, 1994; Meier, Slutske, Arndt, & Cadoret, 2007). Indeed, tests of the AP model of risk are invariant across gender, meaning the predictive pathways do not differ for the two groups (McCarthy, Miller, Smith, & Smith, 2001; Peterson & Smith, 2016). Whereas the risk process appears to operate in a similar fashion for men and women, one study by Cooper, Russell, Skinner, Frone, and Mudar (1992) found that the relationship between positive alcohol outcome expectancies and drinking-related problems was stronger for men than women, suggesting more research is needed to clarify the nature of this relationship across genders.

Similarly, racial and/or ethnic differences have been shown in expectancy endorsement. One hypothesized reason for these differences is that they reflect differences in cultural practices and norms regarding drinking (O'Hare, 1995; Schweizer, Doran, Roesch, & Myers, 2011). In a study on smoking expectancies and behavior in 11- to 14-year-old Caucasian and African American girls, the average level of smoking expectancies was stable, but there was significant variability between races on initial level of endorsement and the rate of change in expectancy endorsement (Chung, White, Hipwell, Stepp, & Loeber, 2010). In this sample, African American girls initially had more positive expectancies but exhibited less rapid change, and Caucasian girls had greater positive expectancies by age 14.

With regard to alcohol, McCarthy and colleagues (2001) demonstrated that African American college students held significantly fewer alcohol expectancies and drank less than their Caucasian peers. However, as with gender, the relationship between expectancies and drinking behavior was invariant across race. Meier et al. (2007) had similar findings for Native American, Hispanic, and Asian youth. A similar study was done examining eating and dieting expectancies in Caucasian and African American college women (Atlas, Smith, Hohlstein, McCarthy, & Kroll, 2002), resulting in parallel findings such that African American women overall had fewer expectancies and symptoms than Caucasian women, but the magnitude of the expectancy–symptom association was the same across races. Overall, it appears that while expectancy endorsement may vary across race, the association between expectancies and addictive behaviors does not.

Functional Role of Expectancies in Addictive Behavior Involvement

We next summarize current findings regarding prediction of addictive behavior involvement from prior expectancy endorsement. As noted earlier, we will not consider the many cross-sectional studies relating expectancies to addictive behaviors.

Alcohol

LONGITUDINAL STUDIES OF ONSET AND INCREASES

Longitudinal studies have consistently documented that alcohol expectancies held by non-drinking youth predict the subsequent onset of drinking. This finding has been observed among adolescents (Christiansen et al., 1989; Smith et al., 1995) as well as in children as young as fifth and sixth grade (Goldberg et al., 2002; Settles et al., 2014).

Researchers have also examined the influence of alcohol expectancies on future levels of drinking behavior, controlling statistically for early levels of use. Many authors have found support for the hypothesis that, when controlling for prior levels of use, alcohol expectancies predict increases in drinking behavior (e.g., Christiansen et al., 1989; Colder et al., 2014; Goldberg et al., 2002; Jester et al., 2015; Ouellette et al., 1999; Settles et al., 2010, 2014; Smith et al., 1995). Each of these studies concerned preadolescents or adolescents. For the prediction of drinking onset, the expectancy that appears to be most predictive is the expectancy that drinking enhances social experience.

Alcohol expectancies' prediction of drinking behavior appears to mediate at least three different possible influences on alcohol-related learning. First, as noted earlier, drinking experience leads to increases in high-risk expectancies, particularly the expectancy that alcohol facilitates social experience (Jester et al., 2015; Smith et al., 1995). Second, expectancies for reinforcement from drinking appear to mediate the predictive effects of personality traits, such as positive and negative urgency, on subsequent drinking behavior. Third, there is some evidence that alcohol expectancies mediate the influence of family of origin drinking on adolescent drinking. Smith (1994) provided a partially longitudinal test, by measuring family drinking (positive parental attitudes, parental drinking, positive family history of alcoholism) and adolescent alcohol expectancies at one wave of a longitudinal study and predicting drinking behavior 1 year later. Family drinking did predict adolescent drinking and its predictive influence was partially explained by adolescent alcohol expectancies as a putative mediator.

EXPERIMENTAL AND LABORATORY MANIPULATIONS

Two studies have attempted to modify expectancies for reinforcement from alcohol in elementary school children. Kraus, Smith, and Ratner (1994) found that an expectancy modification intervention, designed to show how the actual effects of alcohol differ from expected positive effects, produced reductions on alcohol expectancies compared to control video and no-video conditions. The group differences were still present 4 weeks later. Cruz and Dunn (2003) conducted an expectancy manipulation with fourth-grade children. They compared two interventions, using an expectancy modification intervention condition and a traditional alcohol information condition. The expectancy modification intervention involved showing the fourth graders clips from parties and informing them of the prevalence of positive messages about drinking that are not true. Interactive games and quizzes were used to ensure material comprehension. The traditional alcohol information condition emphasized the dangerous and negative effects of alcohol (the predominant message schools send to children in alcohol use–prevention programs). Results revealed that changes in expectancies were greater in the expectancy-modification intervention condition than in the traditional alcohol education condition.

Turning to expectancy interventions with drinkers, Darkes and Goldman (1993) challenged male college students' positive alcohol expectancies using two methods. First, heavy-drinking students were to participate in a drinking party and, upon finding out that some people had been given alcohol and others had been given a placebo, told to identify those who had consumed alcohol. Results revealed that students were unable to tell which of their peers had consumed alcohol and which had not. The researchers then alerted them to this outcome and provided them with psychoeducation about expectancies and instructed them to record expectancy-relevant material they were exposed to from the media. This information communicated that many of the positive effects students thought were the results of alcohol were actually based on social expectations from drinking.

Outcome data revealed that students in the expectancy-treatment group showed (a) reduced positive alcohol expectancies and (b) a significantly greater reduction in alcohol consumption than did students in either an alcohol reduction program or a no-treatment control group. This intervention also appeared to be the strongest for the heavier drinkers in the expectancy-treatment group. Multisession experiential expectancy challenges similar to this one have also been shown to be successful in reducing positive expectancies and alcohol consumption in young women when compared to a control group (Wiers & Kummeling, 2004). The demonstration that experimental reduction of expectancies for reinforcement from drinking produces reductions in drinking constitutes direct evidence in support of the causal claims of alcohol expectancy theory.

A recent meta-analysis of alcohol expectancy challenge interventions with college students by Scott-Sheldon et al. (2012) identified 14 such studies. Although the reviewed studies differed in their intervention methods and in their outcomes, overall, participants exposed to expectancy challenges reported lower positive alcohol expectancies, reduced alcohol use, and reduced frequency of heavy drinking. These effects operated within individuals exposed to expectancy challenges, and they were not present in members of control groups. Thus, the laboratory support for alcohol expectancy theory has been present across results from multiple laboratories using different intervention methods.

As important as the experimental findings are, it is important to appreciate that the intervention effects were not maintained at follow-ups greater than 4 weeks. It may be that lasting interventions may need to target multiple risk factors, including causes of expectancy formation, such as personality. Another possibility is that intervening prior to the college years, perhaps among youth whose expectancies are perhaps most malleable, might produce longer lasting changes. It may also be the case that the specific nature of the expectancy challenge influences the durability of the effects.

The finding that experimental manipulation of alcohol expectancies has consistently been associated with reductions in drinking behavior provides important evidence in support of alcohol expectancy theory. These findings, along with basic science findings demonstrating expectancy effects on behavior dating back at least to the 1930s (Tolman & Honzik, 1930) and the existing, large body of longitudinal evidence that alcohol expectancies predict subsequent drinking (Christiansen et al., 1989; Colder et al., 2014; Goldberg et al., 2002; Jester et al., 2015; Ouellette et al., 1999; Settles et al., 2010, 2014; Smith et al., 1995), provide a strong basis for understanding expectancies or anticipations of reinforcement from drinking to be a central component of the alcohol use risk process.

Other Forms of Addictive Behavior

LONGITUDINAL STUDIES OF ONSET AND INCREASES

Although fewer longitudinal studies have been conducted assessing expectancy prediction of other addictive behaviors, the few that have been reported have provided evidence to support the same function role for expectancies. Doran et al. (2013), in his study of the acquired preparedness model of smoking, found that smoking expectancies predicted subsequent smoking behavior among college students. Guller et al. (2015a) found that smoking expectancies held by elementary school children predicted smoking onset and smoking increases over the following 12 months.

EXPERIMENTAL AND LABORATORY MANIPULATIONS

One expectancy experimental manipulation has been done in the field of eating disorders. A highly predictive expectancy for bulimic and anorexic behaviors is the expectancy for overgeneralized life improvement from thinness (Hohlstein et al., 1998; Pearson & Smith, 2015; Smith et al., 2007). Annus, Smith, and Masters (2008) created a series of videotaped "interviews on the street," some with men and some with women, designed to counteract expectancies that being thin increases (a) energy and strength, (b) attractiveness to men, and (c) success and popularity. Both college women and high school girls were exposed to the videotape expectancy challenges or a control condition that provided psychoeducation about healthy weight and healthy eating. The expectancy manipulation condition produced greater declines in expectancies for reinforcement from thinness and in the cognitive symptoms of eating disorders.

Conclusions About Expectancy's Functional Role in Addiction

Expectancy theory involves the claim that learned differences in the anticipated reinforcement associated with an addictive behavior increase the likelihood of engaging in that behavior. Similarly, the claim that expectancies mediate the effect of other variables on addictive behavior represents a hypothesized causal process. Using drinking as an example, our claim that expectancies for reinforcement from drinking mediate the influence of family drinking on adolescent drinking involves the claims that (a) family drinking predicts and influences adolescent alcohol expectancies; (b) adolescent alcohol expectancies predict and influence adolescent drinking; and (c) family drinking predicts and influences adolescent drinking at least in part through its influence on adolescent alcohol expectancies.

Two sets of findings provide support for the causal hypothesis of expectancy operation. The most direct support is provided by experimental studies of expectancy manipulation. For both alcohol and disordered eating, under conditions of strict laboratory control, manipulations of expectancies have produced changes in the targeted addictive behaviors. Longitudinal field research provides important additional information in support of the causal hypothesis. Multiply replicated findings, across three forms of addiction, that individual differences in measured expectancies predict the subsequent onset of, and increases in, addictive behavior—when controlling for important covariates, including prior engagement in addictive behavior—strengthen the basis for the inference of a causal process.

Summary

We have presented an overview of substance use expectancies as a risk factor for the onset of, and subsequent increase in, substance use and abuse in adolescence. Expectancies, when viewed in a neurocognitive framework, can be seen as markers of memory-based associative learning about behaviors and their outcomes. Detectable as schemas in children as young as preschool age, expectancies regarding substances develop over late childhood and shift from negative to positive in early adolescence. Their formation and strength appear to be influenced by modeling, direct experience with substances, and personality. Because longitudinal studies with relevant controls consistently demonstrate, across forms of addiction, that expectancies predict subsequent addictive behavior (including its onset), and because experimental manipulations of expectancy reduce addictive behavior, there is good reason to ascribe a causal, functional role to addition-related expectancies. In a very real sense, this finding is not at all surprising. It represents a straightforward applied extension of basic science findings demonstrating that anticipation of reinforcement plays an important role in guiding behavior. Among the important next steps in expectancy research is the task of further improving expectancy-based prevention and treatment interventions, in order to reduce problematic addictive behavior in youth.

References

Aitken, P. P. (1978). *Ten-to-fourteen-year-olds and alcohol: A developmental study in the central region of Scotland.* Edinburgh: HM Stationery Office.

Ajzen, I., & Fishbein, M. (1980). *Understanding attitudes and predicting social behavior.* Englewood Cliffs, NJ: Prentice Hall.

Allport, G. W. (1937). *Personality: A psychological interpretation.* New York, NY: Henry Holt and Company.

Annus, A. M., Smith, G. T., & Masters, K. (2008). Manipulation of thinness and restricting expectancies: Further evidence for a causal role of thinness and restricting expectancies in the etiology of eating disorders. *Psychology of Addictive Behaviors, 22*(2), 278–287.

Atlas, J. G., Smith, G. T., Hohlstein, L. A., McCarthy, D. M., & Kroll, L. S. (2002). Similarities and differences between Caucasian and African American college women on eating and dieting expectancies, bulimic symptoms, dietary restraint, and disinhibition. *International Journal of Eating Disorders, 32*(3), 326–334.

Baldwin, A. R., Oei, T. P., & Young, R. (1993). To drink or not to drink: The differential role of alcohol expectancies and drinking refusal self-efficacy in quantity and frequency of alcohol consumption. *Cognitive Therapy and Research, 17,* 511–530.

Bekman, N. M., Goldman, M. S., Worley, M. J., & Anderson, K. G. (2011). Pre-adolescent alcohol expectancies: Critical changes and associated maturational processes. *Experimental and Clinical Psychopharmacology, 19,* 420–432.

Berridge, K. C., & Robinson, T. E. (1998). What is the role of dopamine in reward: Hedonic impact, reward learning, or incentive salience? *Brain Research and Brain Research Reviews, 28,* 309–369.

Brandon, T. H., & Baker, T. B. (1991). The Smoking Consequences Questionnaire: The subjective expected utility of smoking in college students. *Psychological Assessment: A Journal of Consulting and Clinical Psychology, 3*(3), 484.

Brown, S. A., Goldman, M. S., Inn, A., & Anderson, L. R. (1980). Expectations of reinforcement from alcohol: Their domain and relation to drinking patterns. *Journal of Consulting and Clinical Psychology, 48*(4), 419–426.

Brown, S. A., McGue, M., Maggs, J. L., Schulenberg, J. E., Hingson, R. W., Swartzwelder, S., & Murphy, S. (2008). A developmental perspective on alcohol and youths 16 to 20 years of age. *Pediatrics, 121,* S290–S310.

Cameron, C. A., Stritzke, W. G., & Durkin, K. (2003). Alcohol expectancies in late childhood: An ambivalence perspective on transitions toward alcohol use. *Journal of Child Psychology and Psychiatry, 44,* 687–698.

Caspi, A. (1993). Why maladaptive behaviors persist: Sources of continuity and change across the life course. In D. C. Funder, R. D. Parke, C. Tomlinson-Keasey, & K. Widaman (Eds.), *Studying lives through time: Personality and development* (pp. 343–376). Washington, DC: American Psychological Association.

Chen, M. J., Grube, J. W., & Madden, P. A. (1994). Alcohol expectancies and adolescent drinking: Differential prediction of frequency, quantity, and intoxication. *Addictive Behaviors, 19,* 521–529.

Chen, C. M., Hsiao-ye, Y., Williams, G. D., & Faden, V. B. (2009). *Surveillance report #86: Trends in underage drinking in the United States, 1991–2007.* Bethesda, MD: National Institute on Alcohol Abuse and Alcoholism.

Christiansen, B. A., & Goldman, M. S. (1983). Alcohol-related expectancies versus demographic/background variables in the prediction of adolescent drinking. *Journal of Consulting and Clinical Psychology, 51*(2), 249–257.

Christiansen, B. A., Smith, G. T., Roehling, P. V., & Goldman, M. S. (1989). Using alcohol expectancies to predict adolescent drinking behavior after one year. *Journal of Consulting and Clinical Psychology, 57*(1), 93–99.

Chung, T., White, H. R., Hipwell, A. E., Stepp, S. D., & Loeber, R. (2010). A parallel process model of the development of positive smoking expectancies and smoking behavior during early adolescence in Caucasian and African American girls. *Addictive Behaviors, 35,* 647–650.

Colder, C. R., O'Connor, R. M., Read, J. P., Eiden, R. D., Lengua, L. J., Hawk, L. W., Jr & Wieczorek, W. F. (2014). Growth trajectories of alcohol information processing and associations with escalation of drinking in early adolescence. *Psychology of Addictive Behaviors, 28*(3), 659–670.

Cooper, H. L. (1994). Motivations for alcohol use among adolescents: Development and validation of a four-factor model. *Psychological Assessment, 6,* 117–128.

Cooper, M. L., Russell, M., Skinner, J. B., Frone, M. R., & Mudar, P. (1992). Stress and alcohol use: Moderating effects of gender, coping, and alcohol expectancies. *Journal of Abnormal Psychology, 101*(1), 139–152.

Corbin, W. R., Iwamoto, D. K., & Fromme, K. (2011). A comprehensive longitudinal test of the acquired preparedness model for alcohol use and related problems. *Journal of Studies on Alcohol and Drugs, 72*(4), 602–610.

Corbin, W. R., Zalewski, S., Leeman, R. F., Toll, B. A., Fucito, L. M., & O'Malley, S. S. (2014). In with the old and out with the new? A comparison of the old and new binge drinking standards. *Alcoholism: Clinical and Experimental Research, 38*(10), 2657–2663.

Cruz, I. Y., & Dunn, M. E. (2003). Lowering risk for early alcohol use by challenging alcohol expectancies in elementary school children. *Journal of Consulting and Clinical Psychology, 71*(3), 493–503.

Cyders, M. A., Flory, K., Rainer, S., & Smith, G. T. (2009). The role of personality dispositions to risky behavior in predicting first-year college drinking. *Addiction, 104*(2), 193–202.

Cyders, M. A., & Smith, G. T. (2008). Clarifying the role of personality dispositions in risk for increased gambling behavior. *Personality and Individual Differences, 45,* 503–508.

Darkes, J., & Goldman, M. S. (1993). Expectancy challenge and drinking reduction: experimental evidence for a mediational process. *Journal of Consulting and Clinical Psychology, 61*(2), 344–353.

Davis, H. A., Riley, E. N., & Smith, G. T. (2016). An integrative model of risk for high school disordered eating." Paper presented at the International Conference on Eating Disorders. San Francisco, CA.

Davis, H. A., Riley, E. N., & Smith, G. T. (in press). Transactions among personality and psychosocial learning risk factors for adolescent drinking: The acquired preparedness model of risk. In P. M. Monti, S. M. Colby, and T. A. O'Leary (Eds.). *Adolescents, Alcohol, and Substance Abuse: Reaching Teens through Brief Interventions* (2nd ed.). New York, NY: Guilford Press.

Donovan, J. E. (2007). Really underage drinkers: The epidemiology of children's alcohol use in the United States. *Prevention Science, 8*(3), 192–205.

Doran, N., Khoddam, R., Sanders, P. E., Schweizer, C. A., Trim, R. S., & Myers, M. G. (2013). A prospective study of the acquired preparedness model: The effects of impulsivity and expectancies on smoking initiation in college students. *Psychology of Addictive Behaviors, 27*(3), 714–722.

Dunn, M. E., & Goldman, M. S. (1996). Empirical modeling of an alcohol expectancy memory network in elementary school children as a function of grade. *Experimental and Clinical Psychopharmacology, 4*(2), 209–217.

Dunn, M. E., & Goldman, M. S. (1998). Age and drinking-related differences in the memory organization of alcohol expectances in 3rd-, 6th-, 9th-, and 12th-grade children. *Journal of Consulting and Clinical Psychology, 66*(3), 579–585.

Fischer, S., Peterson, C. M., & McCarthy, D. (2013). A prospective test of the influence of negative urgency and expectancies on binge eating and purging. *Psychology of Addictive Behaviors, 27*(1), 294–300.

Fischer, S., Settles, R., Collins, B., Gunn, R., & Smith, G. T. (2012). The role of negative urgency and expectancies in problem drinking and disordered eating: Testing a model of comorbidity in pathological and at-risk samples. *Psychology of Addictive Behaviors, 26*(1), 112.

Fossey, E. (2005). *Growing up with alcohol*. New York, NY: Routledge.

Fromme, K., & D'amico, E. J. (2000). Measuring adolescent alcohol outcome expectancies. *Psychology of Addictive Behaviors, 14*(2), 206–212.

Glimcher, P. W., & Lau, B. (2005). Rethinking the thalamus. *Nature Neuroscience, 8*, 983–984.

Goldberg, J. H., Halpern-Felsher, B. L., & Millstein, S. G. (2002). Beyond invulnerability: the importance of benefits in adolescents' decision to drink alcohol. *Health Psychology, 21*(5), 477–484.

Goldman, M. S., & Reich, R. R. (2013). The role of genetics in addiction and the expectancy principle. *Genetic Influences on Addiction: An Intermediate Phenotype Approach, 5*, 237–256.

Guller, L., Zapolski, T. C. B., & Smith, G. T. (2015a). Longitudinal test of a reciprocal model of smoking expectancies and smoking experience in youth. *Psychology of Addictive Behaviors, 29*(1), 201–210.

Guller, L., Zapolski, T. C. B., & Smith, G. T. (2015b). Personality measured in elementary school predicts middle school addictive behavior involvement. *Journal of Psychopathology and Behavioral Assessment, 37*, 523–532.

Hartup, W. W., & Van Lieshout, C. F. (1995). Personality development in social context. *Annual Review of Psychology, 46*(1), 655–687.

Hohlstein, L. A., Smith, G. T., & Atlas, J. G. (1998). An application of expectancy theory to eating disorders: Development and validation of measures of eating and dieting expectancies. *Psychological Assessment, 10*, 49–58.

Holland, P. C., & Gallagher, M. (2004). Amygdala-frontal interactions and reward expectancy. *Current Opinion in Neurobiology, 14*, 148–155.

Jahoda, G., & Cramond J. (1972). *Children and alcohol: A developmental study in Glasgow*. London, England: Her Majesty's Stationery Office.

Jester, J. M., Wong, M. M., Cranford, J. A., Buu, A., Fitzgerald, H. E., & Zucker, R. A. (2015). Alcohol expectancies in childhood: Change with the onset of drinking and ability to predict adolescent drunkenness and binge drinking. *Addiction, 110*(1), 71–79.

Kraus, D., Smith, G. T., & Ratner, H. H. (1994). Modifying alcohol-related expectancies in grade-school children. *Journal of Studies on Alcohol, 55*(5), 535–542.

Kupfermann, I., Kandel, E. R., & Iversen, S. (2000). Motivational and addictive states. In E. R. Kandel, J. H. Schwartz, & T. M. Jessell (Eds.), *Principles of neural science (998–1018)*. New York, NY: McGraw-Hill.

Lo, C. C., & Globetti, G. (2000). Gender differences in alcohol beliefs and usual blood-alcohol concentration. *Journal of Child & Adolescent Substance Abuse, 9*(3), 15–33.

Marlatt, G. A., & Rohsenow, D. J. (1980). Cognitive processes in alcohol use: Expectancy and the balanced placebo design. *Advances in Substance Abuse: Behavioral and Biological Research, 1*, 159–199.

Maxwell, J. S., & Davidson, R. J. (2007). Emotion as motion: Asymmetries in approach and avoidant actions. *Psychological Science, 18*, 1113–1119.

McCarthy, D. M., Miller, T. L., Smith, G. T., & Smith, J. A. (2001). Disinhibition and expectancy in risk for alcohol use: Comparing Black and White college samples. *Journal of Studies on Alcohol, 62*, 313–321.

McCarthy, D. M., Pedersen, S. L., & D'Amico, E. J. (2009). Analysis of item response and differential item functioning of alcohol expectancies in middle school youths. *Psychological Assessment, 21*, 444–449.

Meier, M. H., Slutske, W. S., Arndt, S., & Cadoret, R. J. (2007). Positive alcohol expectancies partially mediate the relation between delinquent behavior and alcohol use: Generalizability across age, sex, and race in a cohort of 85,000 Iowa schoolchildren. *Psychology of Addictive Behaviors, 21*, 25–34.

Miller, P. M., Smith, G. T., & Goldman, M. S. (1990). Emergence of alcohol expectancies in childhood: A possible critical period. *Journal of Studies on Alcohol, 51*(4), 343–349.

Minamimoto, T., Hori, Y., & Kimura, M. (2005). Complementary process to response bias in the centromedian nucleus of the thalamus. *Science, 308*(5729), 1798–1801.

Montague, P. R., & Berns, G. S. (2002). Neural economics and the biological substrates of valuation. *Neuron, 36*(2), 265–284.

Morgenson, G. J., Jones, D. L., & Yim, C. Y. (1980). From motivation to action: Functional interface between the limbic system and the motor system. *Progress in Neurobiology, 14*, 69–97.

Nathan, P. E., & O'Brien, J. S. (1971). An experimental analysis of the behavior of alcoholics and nonalcoholics during prolonged experimental drinking: A necessary precursor of behavior therapy? *Behavior Therapy, 2*(4), 455–476.

O'Hare, T. (1995). Differences in Asian and White drinking: Consumption level, drinking contexts, and expectancies. *Addictive Behaviors, 20*(2), 261–266.

Ouellette, J. A., Gerrard, M., Gibbons, F. X., & Reis-Bergan, M. (1999). Parents, peers, and prototypes: Antecedents of adolescent alcohol expectancies, alcohol consumption, and alcohol-related life problems in rural youth. *Psychology of Addictive Behaviors, 13*(3), 183–197.

Pearson, C. M., Combs, J. L., Zapolski, T. C., & Smith, G. T. (2012). A longitudinal transactional risk model for early eating disorder onset. *Journal of Abnormal Psychology, 121*(3), 707–718.

Pearson, C. M., & Smith, G. T. (2015). Bulimic symptom onset in young girls: A longitudinal trajectory analysis. *Journal of Abnormal Psychology*, *124*(4), 1003–1013.

Peterson, S. J., & Smith, G. T. (2016). The transactional nature of personality and learning to predict smoking and drinking in adolescence. Paper presented at the annual meeting of the Research Society on Alcoholism, New Orleans.

Pinker, S. (1997). *How the mind works*. New York, NY: Norton.

Rather, B. C., & Goldman, M. S. (1994). Drinking-related differences in the memory organization of alcohol expectancies. *Experimental and Clinical Psychopharmacology*, *2*(2), 167–183.

Rather, B. C., Goldman, M. S., Roehrich, L., & Brannick, M. (1992). Empirical modeling of an alcohol expectancy memory network using multidimensional scaling. *Journal of Abnormal Psychology*, *101*, 174–183.

Read, J. P., Wood, M. D., Kahler, C. W., Maddock, J. E., & Palfai, T. P. (2003). Examining the role of drinking motives in college student alcohol use and problems. *Psychology of Addictive Behaviors*, *17*, 13–23.

Reich, R. R., Below, M. C., & Goldman, M. S. (2010). Explicit and implicit measures of expectancy and related alcohol cognitions: A meta-analytic comparison. *Psychology of Addictive Behaviors*, *24*(1), 13–25.

Reich, R. R., & Goldman, M. S. (2005). Exploring the alcohol expectancy memory network: The utility of free associates. *Psychology of Addictive Behaviors*, *19*(3), 317–325.

Reich, R. R., & Goldman, M. S. (2015). Decision making about alcohol use: The case for scientific convergence. *Addictive Behaviors*, *44*, 23–28.

Riley, E. N., Combs, J. L., Jordan, C. E., & Smith, G. T. (2015). Negative urgency and lack of perseverance: Identification of differential pathways of onset and maintenance risk in the longitudinal prediction of non-suicidal self-injury. *Behavior Therapy*, *46*, 439–448.

Schafer, J., & Brown, S. A. (1991). Marijuana and cocaine effect expectancies and drug use patterns. *Journal of Consulting and Clinical Psychology*, *59*(4), 558–565.

Schell, T. L., Martino, S. C., Ellickson, P. L., Collins, R. L., & McCaffrey, D. (2005). Measuring developmental changes in alcohol expectancies. *Psychology of Addictive Behaviors*, *19*, 217–220.

Schulte, M. T., Ramo, D., & Brown, S. A. (2009). Gender differences in factors influencing alcohol use and drinking progression among adolescents. *Clinical Psychology Review*, *29*(6), 535–547.

Schweizer, C. A., Doran, N., Roesch, S. C., & Myers, M. G. (2011). Progression to problem drinking among Mexican American and White European first-year college students: A multiple group analysis. *Journal of Studies on Alcohol and Drugs*, *72*(6), 975–980.

Scott, C., & Corbin, W. R. (2014). Influence of sensation seeking on response to alcohol versus placebo: Implications for the Acquired Preparedness Model. *Journal of Studies on Alcohol and Drugs*, *75*(1), 136–144.

Scott-Sheldon, L. A., Terry, D. L., Carey, K. B., Garey, L., & Carey, M. P. (2012). Efficacy of expectancy challenge interventions to reduce college student drinking: A meta-analytic review. *Psychology of Addictive Behaviors*, *26*, 393–405.

Settles, R. E., Zapolski, T. C., & Smith, G. T. (2014). Longitudinal test of a developmental model of the transition to early drinking. *Journal of Abnormal Psychology*, *123*(1), 141–151.

Settles, R. F., Cyders, M., & Smith, G. T. (2010). Longitudinal validation of the acquired preparedness model of drinking risk. *Psychology of Addictive Behaviors*, *24*(2), 198–208.

Silverstein, S. J., Nathan, P. E., & Taylor, H. A. (1974). Blood alcohol level estimation and controlled drinking by chronic alcoholics. *Behavior Therapy*, *5*(1), 1–15.

Smith, G. T. (1994). Psychological expectancy as mediator of vulnerability to alcoholism. *Annals of the New York Academy of Sciences*, *708*(1), 165–171.

Smith, G. T., & Goldman, M. S. (1994). Alcohol expectancy theory and the identification of high-risk adolescents. *Journal of Research on Adolescence*, *4*(2), 229–247.

Smith, G. T., Goldman, M. S., Greenbaum, P. E., & Christiansen, B. A. (1995). Expectancy for social facilitation from drinking: The divergent paths of high-expectancy and low-expectancy adolescents. *Journal of Abnormal Psychology*, *104*(1), 32–40.

Smith, G. T., Simmons, J. R., Flory, K., Annus, A. M., & Hill, K. K. (2007). Thinness and eating expectancies predict subsequent binge eating and purging behavior among adolescent girls. *Journal of Abnormal Psychology*, *116*, 188–197.

Smith, G. T., Williams, S. F., Cyders, M. A., & Kelley, S. (2006). Reactive personality-environment transactions and adult developmental trajectories. *Developmental Psychology*, *42*(5), 877–887.

Tolman, E. C. (1932). *Purposive behavior in animals and men*. New York: Century/Random House.

Tolman, E. C., & Honzik, C. H. (1930). Introduction and removal of reward, and maze performance in rats. University of California, *Publications in Psychology*. Berkeley, CA.

Wardell, J. D., Read, J. P., Colder, C. R., & Merrill, J. E. (2012). Positive alcohol expectancies mediate the influence of the behavioral activation system on alcohol use: A prospective path analysis. *Addictive Behaviors*, *37*(4), 435–443.

Wiers, R. W., & Kummeling, R. H. (2004). An experimental test of an alcohol expectancy challenge in mixed gender groups of young heavy drinkers. *Addictive Behaviors*, *29*(1), 215–220.

Zapolski, T. C., Cyders, M. A., & Smith, G. T. (2009). Positive urgency predicts illegal drug use and risky sexual behavior. *Psychology of Addictive Behaviors*, *23*(2), 348–354.

Zucker, R. A., Donovan, J. E., Masten, A. S., Mattson, M. E., & Moss, H. B. (2008). Early developmental processes and the continuity of risk for underage drinking and problem drinking. *Pediatrics*, *121* (Suppl 4), S252–S272.

Zucker, R. A., Kincaid, S. B., Fitzgerald, H. E., & Bingham, C. R. (1995). Alcohol schema acquisition in preschoolers: Differences between children of alcoholics and children of nonalcoholics. *Alcoholism: Clinical and Experimental Research*, *19*(4), 1011–1017.

PART 5

Developmental Tasks and Substance Abuse

Linking Peer Relationships to Substance Use Across Adolescence

Kelly L. Rulison, Megan E. Patrick, *and* Jennifer L. Maggs

Abstract

The development of substance use during adolescence occurs against a backdrop of considerable changes in the social context, but these simultaneous changes alone are not conclusive evidence of a strong causal link between peers and drug use. Clarifying how peers shape the development of substance use is difficult because researchers often do not distinguish between different peer relationships (e.g., friendships, groups, networks), different social processes within these relationships (e.g., direct peer pressure, normative regulation, modeling), or adolescents' own social motives and perceptions. The chapter discusses how peer relationships change across adolescence, how social processes within different relationships might contribute to substance use, and the methodological challenges that researchers face when documenting these contributions. The chapter also highlights how studies could better match the complexity of research questions about peer influence with appropriate data collection and analytic strategies.

Key Words: friends, peer groups, social networks, social norms, peer influence, peer selection

The belief that peer influence is one of the strongest underlying causes of adolescents' drug use is pervasive. This assumption is promoted by mass media campaigns (e.g., *Just Say No, Above the Influence*) that encourage youth to resist peer pressure. The goals of many substance use prevention programs also imply that peer influence in the form of peer pressure is the primary cause of drug use. For example, Drug Abuse Resistance Education (D.A.R.E.) teaches youth "how to resist peer pressure" ("About D.A.R.E.," 2014). Despite the explicit causal role of peers assumed by these campaigns and programs, evidence from empirical studies is less decisive. Early studies often overestimated the strength of peer influence: They inferred influence based on cross-sectional similarity (e.g., youth who smoke have friends who smoke) and relied on adolescents' perceptions of their peers' behavior rather than on peers' own reports. Similarity alone, however, is not conclusive evidence of influence. Adolescents tend to view their friends as more similar to themselves than

they actually are, and similarity may also reflect peer selection or a shared environment (Cohen, 1977; Jussim & Osgood, 1989; Kandel, 1978a, 1996). After using proper statistical controls, some longitudinal studies find only modest evidence of peer influence (Berndt & Murphy, 2002). Yet studies using dynamic social network analysis often find strong evidence of peer influence even after controlling for peer selection (e.g., Kiuru, Burk, Laursen, Salmela-Aro, & Nurmi, 2010; Light, Greenan, Rusby, Nies, & Snijders, 2013; Osgood, Ragan, et al., 2013; Pearson, Steglich, & Snijders, 2006; Schaefer, Haas, & Bishop, 2012).

Studies of intervention programs also provide mixed evidence of peer influence on adolescent substance use. Programs that primarily emphasize refusal skills generally have little or no effect (Ennett, Tobler, Ringwalt, & Flewelling, 1994; Hansen & Graham, 1991). By contrast, programs that target social norms, passive social pressure, and interpersonal skills often prevent or reduce drug use (Botvin,

Baker, Dusenbury, Botvin, & Diaz, 1995; Ellickson, McCaffrey, Ghosh-Dastidar, & Longshore, 2003; Hansen & Graham, 1991; Hecht et al., 2003; Tobler et al., 2000). In addition, programs that group deviant youth together sometimes lead to *increases* in substance use (Dishion, McCord, & Poulin, 1999), highlighting that peer influence occurs in some contexts. Together, these findings suggest that peer influence occurs during adolescence, but that direct peer pressure is not the primary mechanism through which it operates. Instead, peers influence adolescent substance use in other ways, such as by shaping norms and modeling use.

Clearly, discrepant results across studies present a paradox: Some results are consistent with the hypothesis that peers play a causal role in the development of substance use, whereas other results suggest that peers play little, if any, role. One challenge to unraveling this paradox is that most theories and empirical studies focus on how "peers" contribute to substance use without regard to different types of peer relationships (e.g., friendships, groups, peer networks), the different social processes that occur within these relationships (e.g., direct peer pressure, normative regulation, modeling), or the individual characteristics and perceptions that adolescents bring to these relationships (e.g., their own perceptions of their peer context, their own social motives). In addition, peer relationships are complex, multilevel, and constantly changing, making them methodologically challenging to identify and study.

The goal of this review is thus threefold: (1) to integrate theory and findings across disciplines to clarify how peers contribute to the development of substance use during adolescence; (2) to review different levels of the peer context and describe the social processes within these relationships that might contribute to substance use; and (3) to discuss the methodological challenges that have limited our ability to document these contributions. We conclude with a discussion of several unanswered questions that future research could address.

The Link Between Peers and Substance Use

The initiation and escalation of alcohol, tobacco, and illicit drug use during adolescence (Miech, Johnston, O'Malley, Bachman, & Schulenberg, 2015) occurs against a backdrop of substantial changes in the social context. As youth transition into adolescence, they spend less time with families and more time with peers, often in unstructured, unsupervised activities (Brown, Dolcini, & Leventhal,

1997; Rubin, Bukowski, & Parker, 2006). Family management practices such as parental monitoring often decline, providing adolescents more opportunities to interact with deviant peers (e.g., Dishion, Nelson, & Bullock, 2004). At the same time, the transition into middle school and high school is often accompanied by structural changes in the school environment (e.g., several elementary schools feed into larger middle schools; students switch classes rather than remain with the same teacher all day). These changes, coupled with other changes that occur across the transition to adolescence, not only lead to a developmental mismatch between adolescents and their contexts (Eccles et al., 1993) but also weaken bonds with teachers and expose youth to a larger peer network (Brown, 1990; Felner, Ginter, & Primavera, 1982). Overall, the convergence of these rapid changes in the social context, along with adolescents' drive for exploration, risk taking, autonomy, and identity development (Lerner & Steinberg, 2009), suggest that adolescence is a particularly critical developmental period for studying the link between peers and substance use (Brown, McGue, et al., 2008; Patrick, Schulenberg, Maggs, & Maslowsky, 2014; Schulenberg & Maggs, 2002; Windle et al., 2008).

What is less clear, however, is whether peers play a causal, rather than incidental, role in the development of substance use. On the one hand, most adolescents initiate substance use when they are with their peers. For example, more than 70% of high school girls who smoked reported that they tried their first cigarette with a friend (Nichter, Vuckovic, Quintero, & Ritenbaugh, 1997). In addition, adolescents are often similar to their closest peers with respect to substance use (Alexander, Piazza, Mekos, & Valente, 2001; Brechwald & Prinstein, 2011; Elliott, Huizinga, & Ageton, 1985; Kandel, 1978b); indeed, associating with drug-using peers is one of the strongest predictors of adolescent substance use (Hawkins, Catalano, & Miller, 1992). On the other hand, however, this similarity could occur because drug-using adolescents seek out drug-using peers—and nonusing adolescents do the opposite—rather than through peer influence.

Furthermore, even though adolescents typically initiate and use drugs when they are with their peers and even though drug-using adolescents often affiliate with drug-using friends and groups, peers do not unilaterally provide a context that supports substance use. In many cases peers may even be more likely to encourage *nonuse* than to encourage substance use: The vast majority of adolescents report that their friends would *not* condone frequent drug use or experimenting with illicit drugs other than marijuana (Miech et al., 2015). Clarifying this complex, somewhat paradoxical role that peers play in the development of substance use thus requires a clearer understanding of peer relationships during adolescence and the social processes that occur within these relationships. We explore each topic in more detail next.

Peer Relations During Adolescence

Forming healthy relationships with peers is recognized as a central task of adolescence according to classic and contemporary developmental theories (Brown & Larson, 2009; Erikson, 1968; Hartup, 1996; Sullivan, 1953). Adolescents are often preoccupied with forming and maintaining friendships and trying to gain acceptance from their peers (e.g., Berndt, 1982; Brown, 1990; Crockett, Losoff, & Petersen, 1984). During adolescence, peer norms and values become more important even though they are sometimes at odds with those held by adults (Berndt, 1992; Brechwald & Prinstein, 2011; Brown et al., 1997; Rubin et al., 2006). As a result, adolescence is often considered to be the most peer-centered phase of the life course.

Although peer relationships are critical during adolescence, these relationships do not just suddenly emerge (Berndt, 2004; Hartup & Stevens, 1997). Friendships exist in preschool (e.g., Coplan & Arbeau, 2009), and early experiences with peers lay the foundation for adolescent peer relationships. Importantly, however, the *nature* of peer relationships changes across childhood and adolescence, and these changes set the stage for substance use. During middle childhood and preadolescence, children transition away from activity-based "play dates" and begin interacting with peers outside the direct supervision of adults (Rubin et al., 2006). The social skills that youth acquire through these interactions, the behavior that they exhibit during these interactions, and the social status that they earn impact which peers adolescents can befriend and which cliques and crowds they can join (Brown & Klute, 2003). Puberty and changes in social-cognitive abilities also lead to more complex social interactions: Reputationally defined crowds such as "jocks" and "brains" emerge (Brown, 1990), adolescents become more interested in cross-gender interactions, and dating relationships begin (Furman & Shaffer, 1999). Adolescents also begin to emphasize self-disclosure, intimacy, and social support as important qualities in their friendships (Berndt, 1982; Buhrmester & Furman, 1987; Hartup & Stevens, 1997; Sharabany, Gershoni, & Hofman, 1981).

At the same time that peers provide an important context for normative development, they also provide adolescents with the opportunity and the social context for substance use. Adolescents may actively seek out peers who engage in substance use: These peers may be fun to be around because of their risk-taking nature or because of their greater access to social resources and desirable adult roles (Gottfredson & Hirschi, 1990; Hawley, 2003; Moffitt, 1993, 2006). In addition, many social activities (e.g., parties, celebrations) occur in drinking contexts, and sociability expressed while drinking can facilitate successful peer relationships, bonding with peers, and developmental tasks such as making new friends (Brown, McGue, et al., 2008; Maggs, 1997; Newcomb & Bentler, 1989; Silbereisen & Noack, 1988). For example, Maggs and Hurrelmann (1998) found that adolescents who used alcohol and tobacco were more likely than their age-mates to spend time with friends, increase their perceptions of peer group closeness, and to have a romantic partner. These results illustrate the complex association between substance use and peer relationships during adolescence.

Theoretical Perspectives: Social Processes Within Peer Relationships

There is no single, unified "theory of peer relationships," so peer researchers often draw on theories from a range of disciplines to explain the association between peer relationships and substance use. For example, developmental theories suggest that individuals select themselves into specific contexts, or "ecological niches," based on the contexts that are available to them as well as their own personal characteristics, competencies, and interests; individuals are then influenced by the contexts they select, which in turn constrain their future opportunities for selection and socialization (Baltes, 1987; Elder, 1998; Lerner, 1982; Maggs, 1997; Nurmi, 1993; Scarr & McCartney, 1983; Schulenberg & Maggs, 2002). When applied to the study of peer relationships and adolescent substance use, these theories suggest that adolescents *select* themselves into a specific peer context (e.g., befriending peers who smoke). Once selected, these peers *influence* the adolescent (e.g., leading the adolescent to begin or continue smoking).

Within the context of this broad developmental perspective, more specific theories can be applied to clarify the social processes through which selection and influence may occur. These theories differ with respect to their emphasis on peer selection and influence. At one end, "social disability" (Hansell & Wiatrowski, 1981), "individual characteristics" (Vitaro, Brendgen, Pagani, Tremblay, & McDuff, 1999), or "intrapersonal" (Hoffman, Sussman, Unger, & Valente, 2006) theories argue that adolescents' own characteristics, not their peers' behavior, contribute to the development of substance use; thus, any similarity between adolescents and their peers is due to selection rather than influence. At the other end, "social ability" (Hansell & Wiatrowski, 1981), "peer facilitation" (Vitaro et al., 1999), or "interpersonal influence" (Hoffman et al., 2006) theories argue that deviant behavior is learned. From this perspective, the locus of the problem is external to the adolescent, in the form of peer, family, and media influences.

Both types of theories are overly simplistic, however. Social disability theories cannot explain why some adolescents who use drugs are popular (e.g., Allen, Porter, McFarland, Marsh, & McElhaney, 2005; Mayeux, Sandstrom, & Cillessen, 2008; Valente, Unger, & Johnson, 2005), why drug-using adolescents report more frequent peer involvement and higher perceived group closeness than their non-drug-using peers (Maggs & Hurrelmann, 1998), or how young adults who use drugs are able to form intimate, close friendships (e.g., Kandel & Davies, 1991). In turn, social ability theories cannot explain why some adolescents form relationships with drug-using peers in the first place. To address these concerns, integrated theories suggest that a combination of factors predicts deviant behavior directly and also leads youth to associate with deviant peers (Elliott et al., 1985), who in turn reinforce and encourage deviant behavior. Finally, interactional theories extend previous theories by incorporating bidirectional influences that develop over time (Dishion, Patterson, Stoolmiller, & Skinner, 1991; Patterson, DeBaryshe, & Ramsey, 1989; Patterson & Yoerger, 2002; Thornberry, 1987; Thornberry & Krohn, 1997).

Notably, most theories that attempt to explain the link between peers and substance use are not specific to substance use, and instead focus on how peers shape development of deviant behaviors more generally. In some cases, the theories go so far as to argue that the specific acts of deviant behavior are irrelevant, in that they reflect an underlying "syndrome" of problem behavior (Jessor & Jessor, 1977) or weak bonds to society (Hirschi, 1969). In other cases, the theories simply do not attempt to explain differences across specific behaviors. In many ways, this "generality of deviance" approach makes sense: Delinquency and substance use are positively correlated (e.g., Donovan & Jessor, 1985) and during adolescence, all substance use is illegal. Importantly, however, substance use and delinquency are far from perfectly correlated (e.g., Osgood, Johnston, O'Malley, & Bachman, 1988). Furthermore, as Maggs and Hurrelmann (1998) argue, delinquent behaviors are by their very nature *antisocial*, whereas smoking and drinking (in limited quantities) can actually be *prosocial*. Specifically, delinquent acts are aggressive and directed against people (e.g., fighting), property (e.g., arson), and institutions (e.g., shoplifting), whereas substance use frequently occurs in a social context, can increase contact and closeness with peers (e.g., Maggs & Hurrelmann, 1998), and is positively related to group cohesion and social status (e.g., Kreager, Rulison, & Moody, 2011).

Next, we review several theories and related empirical results about the twin processes of selection and influence, focusing on how adolescents' own substance use can shape their peer network (e.g., by impacting which peers they select as friends and which groups they select to join) and how peer networks can shape adolescents' own substance use. Although *both* selection and influence are tightly interwoven (see Brechwald & Prinstein, 2011, for a review), for organizational purposes, we describe the theories most relevant to each process separately.

Selection: "Birds of a Feather Flock Together"

Adolescents typically affiliate with peers who are similar to themselves with respect to a wide range of demographic features, attitudes, and behaviors (e.g., Kandel, 1978a; McPherson, Smith-Lovin, & Cook, 2001). One of the primary forces behind this homophily, or similarity, is the "proximity principle": Individuals who are in close proximity tend to affiliate (Verbrugge, 1977). In other words, adolescents form relationships with those who are in their class, grade, or school; those who live in the same neighborhood or dorm; those who participate in the same activities; and those who are similar to themselves with respect to a wide range of demographic and behavioral characteristics. Notably, proximity can be disrupted or reinforced during transitions (e.g., transition to high school, puberty), leading to changes in peer relationships.

Even if selection is a primary source of homophily, however, there are multiple selection mechanisms that could be at work (Bauman & Ennett, 1996; Cohen, 1977; Kandel, 1978a). Each process is described next and also summarized in the top half of Table 19.1.

1. Drug-using adolescents may actively seek other drug users as friends because these peers may positively reinforce their drug use.

2. Similarity with respect to drug use may be a by-product of selection with respect to other behaviors, characteristics, or activities, and it is this "third variable" that leads to similarity in drug use. For example, drug users may become friends because their drug use brings them into close proximity (e.g., a particular location off school grounds where smokers gather between classes) and by spending time together they become friends. Or adolescents with similar interests and propensities toward drug use (or nonuse) may join similar activities (e.g., particular clubs or sports teams) and become friends.

3. Groups dominated by drug use or groups dominated by nonuse may restrict membership to peers who are similar to existing group members. For example, social control theory (Gottfredson & Hirschi, 1990; Hirschi, 1969) argues that deviant youth can only form weak, shallow relationships and therefore deviant youth affiliate with each other by default. In the case of substance use, drug users—rejected by their non-drug-using peers—would be forced to affiliate with each other because they have no other options.

4. "De-selection" may occur, whereby relationships end when drug behavior becomes dissimilar between the parties involved.

Peer Influence: Beyond Peer Pressure— When Saying No Just Isn't Enough

Homophily can also reflect prior peer influence, in which adolescents have been socialized by their peers and became more similar to them over time. Peer influence can impact many attitudes and behaviors, ranging from clothing and music preferences to health risk behaviors such as substance use, delinquency, and aggression (Boivin & Vitaro, 1995; Dishion, Spracklen, Andrews, & Patterson, 1996; Elliott et al., 1985; Ennett & Bauman, 1994; Kiuru et al., 2010; Patterson, Dishion, & Yoerger, 2000; Pearson et al., 2006; Rulison, Gest, Loken, & Welsh, 2010; Steglich, Snijders, & West, 2006; Urberg, Degirmencioglu,

& Pilgrim, 1997). Importantly, there are multiple mechanisms through which peers influence each other (Bauman & Ennett, 1996; Brown, 2004; Hoffman et al., 2006; Kobus, 2003; Valente, Gallaher, & Mouttapa, 2004). Each process is described next and summarized in the bottom half of Table 19.1.

DIRECT PEER PRESSURE

Perhaps the most pervasive assumption about peer influence is that coercive, direct peer pressure (e.g., "Come on, just try it!") is the primary process through which peers influence each other. Many drug prevention approaches (e.g., *Just Say No*) are predicated on this assumption and thus devote considerable time teaching refusal skills to adolescents. Yet most studies find no evidence that direct peer pressure contributes significantly to adolescent substance use initiation (Alexander, Allen, Crawford, & McCormick, 1999; Berndt & Murphy, 2002; Nichter et al., 1997; Reed & Rountree, 1997; Urberg, Shyu, & Liang, 1990). Not only is direct peer pressure uncommon, when it does occur adolescents often perceive it as threatening their independence (Arnett, 2007; Denscombe, 2001). Furthermore, direct pressure on smokers *not* to smoke (Urberg et al., 1990) and on nonsmokers to remain nonsmokers is more common than pressure on nonsmokers *to begin* smoking (Lucas & Lloyd, 1999).

MODELING AND NORMATIVE REGULATION

Direct peer pressure may not strongly influence substance use initiation, but *indirect* peer pressure, in the form of modeling and normative regulation, may exert stronger, albeit more subtle, influences on adolescents. Differential association theory (Sutherland, 1947) and social learning theories (Akers, 1998; Bandura, 1978; Burgess & Akers, 1966) suggest that drug-using peers model and reinforce substance use behavior. More specifically, by watching parents, siblings, friends, and admired peers (among others), adolescents observe the potential punishments and rewards of substance use and decide whether to engage in, or refrain from, this behavior. Peers also convey specific norms, attitudes, and values through the process of normative regulation, which includes conversations among peers and teasing group members who do not conform to group norms (Brown, 2004). For example, Nichter and colleagues (1997) found that 10th- and 11th-grade girls rarely reported direct pressure to smoke, but they did report concerns of

Table 19.1 Social Processes Within Adolescents' Peer Relationships

Social Process	Example
Selection	
Active selection	Adolescents who smoke actively seek friendships with other adolescents who smoke
Selection on other traits	Adolescents who are highly stressed start smoking to cope, and it is their stress—rather than their smoking—that facilitates their friendship
Membership restriction	A friendship group of nonsmokers does not allow a smoker to join their group
De-selection	A friendship between two friends who do not smoke ends when one person starts smoking
Influence	
Direct peer pressure	An adolescent offers a cigarette to his friend and says, "Here, try this cigarette. What are you, a chicken?"
Modeling	An adolescent sees her friend smoking and observes the positive or negative consequences of that smoking (e.g., she thinks: "My friend smokes and everyone thinks she is cool. Smoking must make you cool")
Normative regulation	An adolescent worries her friends will make fun of her if she doesn't smoke. An adolescent notices (consciously or not) that his friends laugh when he tells a story about how crazy he acted when he was drunk.
Perceived norms	Descriptive norms—"Most kids my age smoke." Injunctive (approval) norms—"My friends would be okay with me smoking."
Social motives	Believing that drinking lets people have more fun with their friends
Structuring opportunities	Hanging out at a friend's house with no adults around

being ridiculed or excluded by their friends if they did not smoke. Further evidence of normative regulation comes from observations of boys and their friends (Dishion, Eddy, Haas, Li, & Spracklen, 1997; Dishion et al., 1996; Patterson et al., 2000). In these studies, antisocial dyads engaged in four times as much deviant talk as nondeviant dyads, and this talk was frequently followed by laughter. Exposure to this *deviancy training* predicted increases in substance use, delinquency, and risky sexual behavior.

PERCEIVED NORMS

All interpersonal social influences are filtered through the adolescent's own perceptions, personality, attitudes, and developmental stage (Hoffman et al., 2006). Thus, adolescents' *perceptions* of what their peers think and do may matter more than what their peers *actually* think or do (Bauman & Ennett, 1996). The theory of reasoned action (TRA; e.g., Fishbein & Ajzen, 1975) and the theory of planned behavior (TPB; e.g.,

Ajzen, 1991) support this conclusion, arguing that adolescents' decisions to use drugs are influenced by their expectations about the consequences of using (or not using) drugs, their perceptions of social norms toward drug use along with their willingness to conform to these norms, and—in TPB—their self-efficacy with respect to obtaining drugs, using drugs, and refusing drug offers (Petraitis, Flay, & Miller, 1995; Valente et al., 2004).

Perceptions of social norms come in different forms (see Cialdini, Reno, & Kallgren, 1990), including descriptive norms (e.g., whether adolescents believe most of their peers use drugs) and injunctive norms (e.g., whether adolescents believe their peers approve of drug use). Even though perceived norms are influenced by interacting with peers, these perceptions are often inaccurate. Prevention scientists have long recognized that adolescents tend to believe that drug use is more common than it actually is and that these misperceptions are linked to substance use, as adolescents try to fit in with perceived group behavior (Botvin, Botvin, Baker, Dusenbury, & Goldberg, 1992; Hansen & Graham, 1991; Sussman et al., 1988). This link between perceived norms and substance use continues beyond high school, with perceived social norms being one of the strongest predictors of substance use among college students (Neighbors, Lee, Lewis, Fossos, & Larimer, 2007; Perkins, Haines, & Rice, 2005). Importantly, because adolescents misperceive (i.e., overestimate) the prevalence of substance use among their peers, it is critical for research on peer influence to use peers' self-reports of their own behaviors, rather than rely on adolescents' own, often inaccurate, reports of their peers' behaviors.

SOCIAL MOTIVES

Another form of intrapersonal influence is adolescents' own motivations for substance use. For example, adolescents may choose to use drugs as a way to gain acceptance by a new peer group or to achieve or maintain status (Alexander et al., 1999; Barton, Chassin, Presson, & Sherman, 1982; Hurrelmann, 1990; Jessor, 1987; Leventhal & Cleary, 1980; Maggs, 1997; Semmer et al., 1987). In addition, adolescents commonly say that having a good time with their friends is a primary reason for substance use (Cooper, 1994; Cooper, Russell, Skinner, & Windle, 1992; Cox & Klinger, 1988; Johnston & O'Malley, 1986; Patrick & Schulenberg, 2011; Patrick, Schulenberg, O'Malley, Maggs, et al., 2011), and having these social motivations is associated with continued alcohol use across young adulthood (Patrick, Schulenberg, O'Malley, Johnston, & Bachman, 2011). Many adolescents believe that alcohol and other drug use will lead to positive social consequences, and these positive expectancies are strong predictors of alcohol use both concurrently and longitudinally (Bartholow, Sher, & Strathman, 2000; Patrick, Wray-Lake, Finlay, & Maggs, 2010; Sher, Wood, Wood, & Raskin, 1996; Zamboanga, Horton, Leitkowski, & Wang, 2006). This work suggests that many adolescents use substances because they believe it will facilitate social interactions or lead to positive social consequences.

STRUCTURING OPPORTUNITIES

Peers also provide the *opportunity* for substance use to occur. The routine activities perspective (Haynie & Osgood, 2005; Osgood, Wilson, O'Malley, Bachman, & Johnston, 1996) suggests that deviant behavior occurs when adolescents spend time socializing with peers in unstructured, unsupervised activities. These activities provide the opportunity and the situational motivation for deviant behavior because engaging in deviant behavior is both more rewarding and easier when peers are involved. The absence of adults also reduces the social control that can limit deviancy. The classic example is when adolescents throw an un-chaperoned party—complete with drinking and other drug use—but peers also provide the opportunity for substance use when they just hang around together after school without adults around. Not surprisingly, delinquent activity peaks between the hours of 3 pm, when school typically lets out, and 6 pm, when parents typically return home from work (see Osgood, Anderson, & Shaffer, 2005). Notably, parents may also unwittingly exacerbate deviant behavior by becoming less involved in their children's lives when they begin exhibiting problem behavior, thus leading to "premature adolescent autonomy" (Dishion et al., 2004).

Summary

In sum, there are multiple social processes within adolescent peer relationships that shape substance use (see Table 19.1). Adolescents select themselves into particular peer contexts that may facilitate, exacerbate, or hinder substance use. This selection takes different forms, such as actively selecting substance-using peers, selecting peers who are similar in other ways, being prohibited from joining certain groups, and ending relationships with dissimilar peers. These selection processes likely play an important role in the development of substance use as they govern which peers will be in a position to influence an adolescent. Despite assumptions that direct peer pressure to use drugs is pervasive, this form of peer influence is actually rare. Instead, peer pressure is usually indirect, in the form of modeling and normative regulation. In addition, adolescents' perceptions of how much their peers use or approve of substance use (regardless of whether these perceptions are accurate) exert a strong intrapersonal influence, as do adolescents' own expectations about the social benefits of substance use (e.g., having more fun with friends; making them look cool). Peers also provide opportunities for substance use to occur. Notably, despite the primary focus on the harmful effects of peer influence, influence is not universally negative (Berndt & Murphy, 2002): Adolescents also influence their peers *not* to use drugs.

Peer Contexts: Dyadic, Group, Network, and Distal Peer Influences

In addition to adolescents' own characteristics (e.g., their own social motives; their perceptions of their peers' behavior), their behavior is shaped by multiple levels of contextual factors or "systems." Specifically, adolescents are shaped by proximal interactions with peers and families (microsystems), connections between peers and parents (mesosystems), peers' families (exosystems), and cultural norms and policies (macrosystems; Bronfenbrenner, 1979; Bronfenbrenner & Morris, 1997). The peer microsystem itself is multilevel, with relationships at one level embedded in and shaped by relationships at other levels (Brechwald & Prinstein, 2011; Brown, 2004; Ennett, Foshee, et al., 2008; Kindermann & Gest, 2009; Rubin et al., 2006). At the *dyadic level*, adolescents engage with friends, enemies, and romantic partners. At the *group level*, adolescents are embedded in *cliques*, or groups of three or more peers who frequently interact with each other, and *social crowds*, or large, reputationally defined groups (e.g., jocks, brains, druggies). These cliques and crowds may include many (but rarely all) of the same peers that adolescents interact with at the dyadic level (e.g., Cairns, Leung, Buchanan, & Cairns, 1995; Molloy, Gest, & Rulison, 2011; Urberg, Degirmencioglu, Tolson, & Halliday Scher, 1995). These dyads and groups are shaped by *distal peer networks*, including everyone within a particular social context (e.g., all peers within a classroom, grade, school, or neighborhood) and influences transmitted through media and cultural norms.

Broadly speaking, social competence requires an adolescent to function effectively at each level of the peer context (Rubin et al., 2006). Peer relationships at each level may be shaped by different social processes and exert distinct influences on the individual (Brown, 2004; Cairns, Xie, & Leung, 1998; Kindermann & Gest, 2009; Urberg et al., 1997). Although there is a great deal of overlap in social processes that occur at each level, some processes play a stronger role at a given level as compared to others. For example, differential reinforcement for specific behaviors and attitudes as well as a desire to please the other person may be particularly influential within friendships, whereas perceived norms may be more influential within groups.

Despite these differences, most reviews addressing the links between peer relationships and substance use refer to broadly defined constructs such as peer pressure, social modeling, and peer selection rather than distinguishing between different levels of peer relationships. We believe, however, that it is important to clarify how each level of the peer system is linked with other levels, and to clarify when influences from each level are independent, synergistic, or even incompatible with influences at other levels. By articulating which processes are likely to operate at each level, it is possible to identify pertinent peer influence mechanisms and ideally improve existing (or develop new) substance use prevention programs. Thus, in what follows, we review each level of the peer context separately. For each level, we (1) identify the features of peer relationships at that level, (2) describe the methods that are typically used for studying relationships at that level, and (3) summarize the empirical literature connecting peer relationships at that level to substance use. We briefly define each level and summarize the key findings about the link between relationships at that level and substance use in Table 19.2.

Dyadic Relationships

Dyadic peer relationships, such as relationships with friends, romantic partners, and siblings, form the most basic building block of the adolescent peer context. All of these dyadic relationships may have important implications for adolescents' substance use (e.g., Duncan, Duncan, & Hops, 1996; Furman, Low, & Ho, 2009; Stormshak, Comeau, & Shepard, 2004), but we focus our review on dyadic friendships, as most studies on the link between dyadic peer relationships and substance use concentrate on friendships. Such a focus is warranted, as adolescents name friends as very important people in their lives much more often than they name siblings or romantic partners (Kerr, Stattin, & Kiesner, 2007) and by the end of high school students rank their best friend as more important than any other relationship (Brown et al., 1997). Readers may also wish to consult reviews of adolescent sibling relationships (Donovan, this volume) and sexual relationships (Norman, this volume).

FRIENDSHIP FEATURES

As noted in Table 19.2, friendships are voluntary relationships whose hallmark characteristics are equality and affection or "liking" (Berndt, 1982; Hartup, 1996; Hartup & Stevens, 1997). In addition to liking each other, friends often spend time together and help each other, although these characteristics are not considered necessary to define a relationship as a friendship (Berndt & McCandless, 2009). Friends differ from nonfriends across a range

Table 19.2 Defining Features and Key Findings for Different Levels of the Peer Context

Level	Defining Features	Key Findings
Dyadic friendships	• Defined by equality and affection or "liking" • Adolescents also tend to stress the importance of similar interests, intimacy, trust, honesty, and loyalty	• Friend selection may be more important than friend influence for smoking • Both friend selection and friend influence may be important for alcohol use, although friend influence may be stronger: for initiation of alcohol use, in early adolescence for drinking, and at later ages for drinking to intoxication • Fewer studies on marijuana use, but friend influence may be more important in early adolescence and friend selection may be more important in later adolescence
Groups Cliques	• Interaction based • Members are generally friends or "hang out together" a lot	• Selection is important for alcohol and smoking • Influence is important for alcohol, but inconsistent evidence of influence for smoking • Cliques may be more important for frequency of use and transitions to current use than either initiation or quitting
Crowds	• Reputation-based, generally based on appearance, interests and/ or behaviors (e.g., "jocks," "druggies") • Emerge during adolescence • Members do not necessarily know each other or interact	• Although substance use often defines crowd membership (e.g., adolescents who use drugs are viewed as part of the "druggie" crowd), crowd membership also appears to influence later use
Networks	• All the peers within a specific context (e.g., all peers who attend the same school; all peers in the same neighborhood)	• Students in networks with higher rates of substance use are more likely to use drugs, with the effects strongest for smoking and heavy alcohol use • Network-level substance use can modify the effects of social status, friends, and groups • Students in more cohesive networks less likely to smoke and use marijuana

Social status	• Includes dimensions of:
	  o Likeability (number of friends; being well-liked)
	  o Perceived popularity (being viewed as popular)
	  o Social dominance (having more power than others)
	• Also includes position in the network (e.g., bridge between multiple cliques; isolated from the network)
		• Being popular is risky: Popular adolescents often have the highest rates of substance use. Effect is likely bidirectional: adolescents who use drugs gain status over time and adolescents who are popular have more opportunities for use and increase use over time
		• Being unpopular is also risky: Isolated adolescents have higher rates of smoking although they are less likely to use alcohol
		• Alcohol use may be particularly associated with parties and other social experiences
		• Striving for status may also increase substance use

of dimensions, including the level of positive engagement (e.g., smiling, laughing) during interactions and their ability to manage conflict (see Newcomb & Bagwell, 1995, for a review). Children tend to view friends as peers who are fun to be around and their friendships are often activity and proximity based (Brown et al., 1997). By contrast, adolescents tend to emphasize shared values, similar interests, intimacy, trust, honesty, and loyalty as key features of friendship (Berndt, 1982, 1992; Buhrmester &

Furman, 1987; Cairns & Cairns, 1994; Hartup & Stevens, 1997). These developmental changes may reflect adolescents' increasing ability to understand the thoughts and feelings of others as well as the increasing amount of time that adolescents spend with their friends.

When asked, most adolescents will report at least one close friend, although the exact percentage varies across study and methodology used (e.g., number of nominations adolescents are allowed to provide, whether reciprocity is required to classify a relationship as a friendship, whether adolescents are asked to report friends or best friends). Most friendships are with peers who are in the same grade and attend the same school (Ennett & Bauman, 1993; Kandel, 1978a), but the proportion of outside-of-school friends increases with age (Kerr et al., 2007; Urberg et al., 1995). Notably, the *identity* of adolescents' friends can change, even over short periods of time (Brown & Klute, 2003; Cairns & Cairns, 1994), as personal preferences and opportunities to interact with particular friends fluctuate. Yet despite these changes, there is often stability in the *characteristics* of these friends (Dishion et al., 1997). Adolescents may sever ties with one friend who smokes and then befriend another peer who smokes, suggesting some continuity in the behaviors to which adolescents are exposed from friends over time.

METHODS FOR LINKING DYADIC FRIENDSHIPS TO ADOLESCENT SUBSTANCE USE

A common approach to assess friends' substance use is to directly ask adolescents about their friends' behaviors (e.g., "How many of your friends smoke?"). Unfortunately, adolescents are not reliable reporters of their friends' behavior because they often project their own behaviors onto their friends (e.g., Bauman & Ennett, 1996; Jussim & Osgood, 1989; Kandel, 1996). Therefore, these types of questions assess adolescents' *perceptions*, not *actual* behavior of friends.

Assessing actual behavior requires several steps. First, researchers must identify an adolescent's friends, typically by asking adolescents to name their friends or peers whom they like. There is general consensus among researchers that self-report should be used to determine friendship identities, instead of parent, teacher, or observer report (Rubin et al., 2006). There is less consensus, however, about the importance of reciprocity and about whether to limit friendship nominations and, if so, how many nominations to allow (Berndt & McCandless, 2009; Kindermann & Gest, 2009). Some researchers view

reciprocity as a defining characteristic of friendship and therefore require both adolescents to name each other as friends before classifying a relationship as a "friendship." Other researchers, however, view unreciprocated friendship nominations as an important reference group for shaping behavior. In addition, researchers who limit the number of friendship nominations should recognize that they are only capturing adolescents' closest friends, rather than the entire friendship continuum (Berndt & McCandless, 2009), and that this approach may exclude adolescents who do not have very close friends (especially when reciprocity is required). Studies also differ in whether they limit nominations to same-gender peers. Other-gender friendships can be qualitatively different than same-gender relationships (e.g., McDougall & Hymel, 2007), but other-gender relationships increase during adolescence (Furman & Shaffer, 1999; Kuttler, La Greca, & Prinstein, 1999; Poulin & Pedersen, 2007) and may be particularly important in the development of health-risk behaviors (Haynie, 2003; Molloy, Gest, Feinberg, & Osgood, 2014; Poulin, Denault, & Pedersen, 2011).

Next, researchers assess the extent to which an adolescent's friends use drugs. Involvement with substance-using friends can be operationalized in many ways, such as whether at least half of an adolescent's friends smoke, whether a best friend smokes, the proportion or number of friends who smoke, or the average level of smoking among friends.

Finally, researchers test whether involvement with substance-using friends is linked to the adolescent's own substance use. The most common analytic approaches are summarized as follows:

1. Correlate adolescents' drug use with the average drug use among their friends or use current friend characteristics to predict current substance use after adjusting for other factors (e.g., Alexander et al., 2001). Cross-sectional associations are straightforward to compute but difficult to interpret, as positive associations can reflect influence, selection, and shared environmental influences (Cohen, 1977; Jussim & Osgood, 1989; Kandel, 1978a, 1996).

2. Compare changes in substance use across different friendship dyads (e.g., Aloise-Young, Graham, & Hansen, 1994; Fisher & Bauman, 1988; Kandel, 1978a). For example, increases in similarity within stable dyads (i.e., adolescents who are friends at two time points) are assumed

to reflect influence, whereas similarity that exists between two adolescents before they become friends is assumed to reflect selection. This approach requires overly strict definitions of selection and influence and ignores the fact that adolescents are usually involved in many friendship dyads at the same time.

3. Predict later substance use (after controlling for earlier substance use) from involvement with substance-using friends at a previous point in time. This approach is a reasonable strategy for estimating influence, but it does not control for selection or structural features of the network (e.g., reciprocity, transitivity, hierarchy), which can bias estimates of influence.

4. Use actor-based models (e.g., Snijders, 1996; Snijders, Steglich, & Schweinberger, 2007; Steglich, Snijders, & Pearson, 2010) to estimate selection, influence, and network structure simultaneously. Actor-based models are built on the assumption that observations at any particular assessment are merely snapshots of a continuous latent process in which adolescents continually change their friendships and behavior. Estimating actor-based models requires extensive computer simulations to determine what factors most likely produced the observed changes in friendships and behavior between assessments. Initial adoption of actor-based modeling was limited, due to long computing times and model complexity; however, actor-based modeling is now used more widely (e.g., Veenstra, Dijkstra, Steglich, & Van Zalk, 2013) due to improvements in computing technology and the flexibility to test a wide range of conceptual hypotheses with these models.

Review of Empirical Literature Linking Dyadic Friendships to Substance Use

Friendship selection and influence from friends are intertwined in the development of adolescent substance use, but until recently, most studies only focused on influence. These studies often found that having drug-using friends predicted later initiation and escalation in smoking, drinking, and other drug use (e.g., Alexander et al., 2001; Ali & Dwyer, 2009; Kandel, 1978b; Steinberg, Fletcher, & Darling, 1994; Urberg et al., 1997). When both processes have been studied within the same study, peer selection is often stronger than peer influence (e.g., Aloise-Young et al., 1994; Fisher & Bauman, 1988). De-selection processes are also rarely tested, but when they are, most studies have found no

evidence that de-selection contributes to similarity between adolescents and their friends (e.g., Fisher & Bauman, 1988), which suggests that similarity is more important for friendship formation and less important for the maintenance of friendships.

More recently, several studies have used actor-based modeling (described earlier) to simultaneously test selection and influence processes. In terms of smoking, these studies have found strong evidence of selection but less consistent evidence of influence across samples from over a half dozen different European countries and the United States and among adolescents ranging from 12 to 17 years old (Huang, Soto, Fujimoto, & Valente, 2014; Kiuru et al., 2010; Mathys, Burk, & Cillessen, 2013; Mercken, Snijders, Steglich, Vartiainen, & De Vries, 2010; Mercken, Steglich, Sinclair, Holliday, & Moore, 2012; Pearson et al., 2006; Schaefer et al., 2012). For example, when the contributions of selection and influence to similarity in smoking behavior were compared, peer influence accounted for only 6%–23% of the similarity, whereas peer selection accounted for 17%–47% of the similarity (Mercken, Snijders, Steglich, & De Vries, 2009).

In terms of alcohol use, studies that have used actor-based modeling have generally found evidence of both selection and influence (Huang et al., 2014; Kiuru et al., 2010; Osgood, Ragan, et al., 2013; Pearson et al., 2006). One study of Dutch adolescents found more evidence of selection than influence with respect to drinking (Knecht, Burk, Weesie, & Steglich, 2011); however, this study used classroom-based friendships as opposed to friendships within the same grade or school, which may have limited the ability to detect influence effects if the most influential friends were not in the same classroom. Indeed, 45% of students in this study reported that they had more friends outside of their classroom than within it. Notably, results from other studies suggest that the role of friendship influence on drinking may depend on age and stage of substance use: There is stronger evidence of influence for initiating drinking (e.g., Light et al., 2013) and at earlier ages for alcohol use (e.g., Mercken, Steglich, Knibbe, & de Vries, 2012), but at later ages for drinking to intoxication (e.g., Burk, van der Vorst, Kerr, & Stattin, 2012).

Fewer studies have used actor-based modeling to test the role of marijuana use, and results from these studies are less consistent. One study found no evidence of either selection or influence for marijuana use after controlling for tobacco and alcohol use (Mathys et al., 2013), and two other studies made opposite conclusions about whether selection or influence was more important. Specifically, in a sample of younger adolescents, Pearson and colleagues (2006) found influence but not selection effects for marijuana use. By contrast, in a sample of older adolescents in two schools, de la Haye and colleagues (2013) found selection effects for marijuana initiation and current use in both schools, but influence effects only in one school and primarily for initiation. Taken together, these studies suggest that friend influence may play a stronger role for marijuana use in early adolescence, whereas friend selection may be more important in later adolescence. More work is needed, however, to elucidate the complex, dynamic link between adolescent friendships and different types of substance use.

Less common are studies of specific friendship processes, such as exposure to deviancy training during an interaction task (e.g., talking about drugs, discussing rule-breaking), time spent with deviant friends, and relative rate of reinforcement for deviant behavior. When studies have focused on these processes, they generally have found that deviant friendship processes can lead to later substance use (Dishion & Owen, 2002), particularly when coupled with decreasing family involvement (Dishion et al., 2004), and that deviancy training mediates the connection between involvement with deviant peers and growth in substance use (Patterson et al., 2000).

Beyond the Dyad: Cliques and Crowds

In addition to dyadic friendships, peer relationships at other levels also shape adolescent behavior (see Table 19.2). Some of the earliest studies of adolescents' peer relationships emphasized peer *groups* (e.g., Coleman, 1961), but because of the challenges of defining and measuring groups, most studies of peer relationships prior to the 1990s only assessed social status or dyadic friendships (Cairns et al., 1998). Although friendships are often nested within groups, these groups are more than simply a collection of dyadic relationships (Cairns et al., 1995; Molloy et al., 2011). Urberg and colleagues (1995) showed that, depending on the specific type of group examined (e.g., cliques, crowds), anywhere from 30% to 80% of an adolescents' friends were not in the same group as the adolescent. More important, some social processes (e.g., group norms) operate primarily at the group level and groups can possess properties, such as cohesiveness and hierarchy, that are not present in dyadic relationships (Rubin et al., 2006). Because of the

potentially important role that group processes can play in shaping adolescents' behavior, many recent studies have moved beyond the level of the dyad to study peer relationships at multiple levels, including *groups* and *networks*. Next, we explore two types of group relationships: cliques and crowds. We then explore peer networks in a later section.

FEATURES OF CLIQUES AND CROWDS
Cliques

Cliques are small, *interaction*-based groups, whose members are usually friends or peers who frequently "hang out" together (Kindermann & Gest, 2009). Across childhood and adolescence, clique membership is highly fluid (Brown & Klute, 2003). It is rare that everyone leaves a clique at the same time, but over longer periods, there can be complete turnover in clique membership. The fluidity of cliques makes them difficult to define and study. For example, how many adolescents can leave or join before a clique is considered to be a different clique? As with friendships, members of the same clique are often similar to each other with respect to demographic characteristics, attitudes, and behaviors (Cairns, Cairns, Neckerman, Gest, & Gariepy, 1988; Ennett & Bauman, 1994; Gest, Moody, & Rulison, 2007; Leung, 1996).

Crowds

Crowds are large, *reputation*-based groups, and crowd membership is generally defined by an adolescent's appearance, interests, and/or behaviors. Examples of typical crowds from the United States are "jocks," "brains," "druggies," and "preps" (Brown, 1990; Sussman, Pokhrel, Ashmore, & Brown, 2007; Urberg, 1992). Similar crowds generally exist among adolescents in Australia and Western Europe, albeit sometimes with slightly different labels, such as "hard people" and "sporty" (Heaven, Ciarrochi, & Vialle, 2008; Thurlow, 2001; Verkooijen, De Vries, & Nielsen, 2007). Crowds differ from cliques in several important ways (Brown, 1990). In contrast to cliques, members of the same crowd do not necessarily interact with, or even know, each other. In addition, crowd membership is determined by adolescents' *reputation* among their peers; therefore, adolescents do not always self-select their own crowd membership. Unlike cliques, which are present in elementary school, crowds typically do not emerge until adolescence, when youth are able to make the cognitive abstractions that are required to identify groups of peers who appear to share similar behaviors or characteristics (Brown & Klute, 2003). Although crowd membership is not as ubiquitous as friendship or clique membership, typically 40%–50% of adolescents are members of one crowd and 30% are members of two crowds (Brown, 2004).

METHODS FOR LINKING CLIQUES AND CROWDS TO ADOLESCENT SUBSTANCE USE

Cliques

By definition, cliques are comprised of individuals who frequently interact with each other. Information about who interacts with whom generally comes from one of three different sources: observations, self-reports, and peer reports (see Kindermann & Gest, 2009).

1. *Observations.* Observing how much time target youth spend interacting with specific peers is a valid source of information about interaction frequency, but as Kindermann and Gest (2009) note, observations require a lot of time and observers may only have limited access to settings in which adolescents interact with their peers. Thus, observations are more commonly used with preschoolers and elementary school children (e.g., Hanish, Martin, Fabes, Leonard, & Herzog, 2005; Strayer & Santos, 1996) rather than with adolescents.

2. *Self-reports.* Adolescents can list the peers with whom they hang around or like to spend time (e.g., Bagwell, Coie, Terry, & Lochman, 2000; Kiuru et al., 2010). These nominations are subject to self-enhancement bias, however, because youth often do not list unpopular peers who are in their clique (Leung, 1996). Some researchers have also used social network analytic tools to identify friendship cliques based on self-reported friendship nominations (Ennett & Bauman, 1994; Kreager et al., 2011; Urberg et al., 1995), but this approach somewhat blurs the distinction between dyadic friendships and group-based cliques.

3. *Peer reports.* Peers typically have more access than do observers to interactions that occur across many settings (e.g., in the locker room, on the bus, in neighborhood hangouts, on social media Web sites). The social cognitive map (SCM) approach uses peers as "expert participant-observers" and asks them to report groups of youth who "hang around together a lot" (Cairns et al., 1988; Killeya-Jones, Nakajima, & Costanzo, 2007; Kindermann, 1996). Gest and colleagues (2003) demonstrated

that peers can provide valid estimates of interaction frequency. They found that students interacted with same-clique classmates (as determined by SCM) four times more often than they interacted with other same-sex classmates. One advantage of peer reports is that, unlike self-reports, they are not subject to self-enhancement bias. A second advantage is that because cliques are compiled from peer reports, it is possible to efficiently determine which peers interact together even if some youth are absent on the day of data collection. A drawback of using this approach is that adolescents often disagree about who is a member of the same clique.

Once interaction frequency has been determined, the next step is to assign adolescents into cliques. Although researchers often discuss cliques as well-defined entities with clear boundaries, in reality, boundaries are fuzzy: Adolescents spend time interacting with members of their own clique as well as members of other cliques, so observers cannot always tell where one clique ends and another clique begins. Because of these fuzzy boundaries—and because of discrepancies between adolescents if peer reports are used—researchers must rely on statistical approaches to identify clique boundaries and decide who belongs to each clique. Different approaches can be used, such as SCM (Leung, 1996), factor analysis (Bagwell et al., 2000), recursive network means (Moody, 2001), NEGOPY (Richards, 1995), and UCINET (Borgatti, Everett, & Freeman, 2002); a full description of these approaches is beyond the scope of this chapter. Notably, when the same data are used, different analytic approaches typically reach similar (but not identical) conclusions about which adolescents belong in the same clique (Gest et al., 2007). Alternatively, some researchers identify each adolescent's clique members or interaction dyads (e.g., who they are named with more often than by chance) rather than identifying self-contained, nonoverlapping cliques (Kindermann, 1993).

Crowds

Crowd membership depends on how adolescents are viewed by their peers. The three most common approaches used to determine crowd membership are ethnography, self-report, and peer report (Cross & Fletcher, 2009; Kindermann & Gest, 2009). No matter which approach is used, researchers typically start by generating a list of crowds that are recognized by adolescents within a particular setting because specific crowd types and labels can vary across historical periods, schools, and communities. Generating this list often requires the researcher to conduct a pilot study or focus groups with students who are familiar with the particular setting (see La Greca, Prinstein, & Fetter, 2001; Verkooijen et al., 2007, for examples).

1. The *ethnographic approach* (e.g., Eckert, 1989; Michell & Amos, 1997) typically involves a series of observations, conversations with participants, and interviews (see Cross & Fletcher, 2009, for a review). Ethnographies and other qualitative data provide rich insight into adolescents' perceptions of which crowds exist and about who belongs to different crowds. Some disadvantages of this approach are that these methods require researchers to be accepted and trusted by their informants and often focus on one or two specific subgroups, such as students in one specific crowd, so the results are not always generalizable to larger populations (Cross & Fletcher, 2009).

2. The *self-report approach* asks adolescents to report their own crowd membership (e.g., La Greca et al., 2001; Prinstein & La Greca, 2002; Sussman, Unger, & Dent, 2004; Urberg et al., 1995). The specific prompt varies across studies (Cross & Fletcher, 2009): Some studies ask adolescents which crowd most of their classmates would say they belong to (Urberg, Degirmencioglu, Tolson, & Halliday-Scher, 2000), and other studies ask adolescents which crowd they identify with or want to be identified with. Self-reported crowd membership is relatively straightforward to obtain, but this approach has several limitations. Self-report bias is still a concern (Kindermann & Gest, 2009), and this approach is not consistent with a view of crowds as reputation-based because there is limited evidence that adolescents can accurately report how others see them (Cross & Fletcher, 2009).

3. *Peer reports* are arguably the most appropriate approach to determine crowd membership (Kindermann & Gest, 2009), because by definition, crowds are *reputation*-based groups. Peer reports are often gathered by asking representative students to go through a roster of classmates and indicate which crowd most people would say each classmate belonged to. These raters can be students suggested by school staff, students identified during the focus groups as leaders of each crowd, or students who receive the highest number of friendship nominations. Although peer reports are the most appropriate approach, they also have

some limitations (Cross & Fletcher, 2009). Raters often disagree about which crowd each person belongs to and researchers have to determine how to resolve these discrepancies; for example, one approach is to assign an adolescent to a crowd if at least half of the raters put him or her in that crowd and less than one third put them in a different crowd (e.g., Dolcini & Adler, 1994). In addition, which adolescents are selected as raters can impact crowd identification; for example, if only popular adolescents are selected, they may be unable to accurately assign unpopular peers into crowds.

REVIEW OF EMPIRICAL LITERATURE LINKING CLIQUES AND CROWDS TO SUBSTANCE USE

Compared with studies of friendship dynamics, fewer studies have focused on the link between cliques and substance use and those that do often have focused on friendship groups rather than interaction-based groups. In general, these studies have found that group selection and, to a lesser extent, group influence shape the development of substance use among adolescents in the United States (e.g., Ennett & Bauman, 1994; Urberg et al., 1997) and Europe (Kiuru et al., 2010). For example, Ennett and Bauman (1994) found that over time nonsmokers who belonged to smoking cliques were more likely to become current smokers than nonsmokers who belonged to nonsmoking cliques (i.e., influence). Nonsmokers were also more likely to leave smoking cliques than leave nonsmoking cliques (i.e., de-selection for nonsmokers); however, smokers did not appear to be differentially dropped from, or choose to leave, otherwise nonsmoking cliques. Another study (Kiuru et al., 2010) found evidence of active selection into groups: Adolescents were similar in terms of smoking and alcohol use to members of cliques they were about to join.

As with dyadic friendships, however, there is less consistent evidence about the extent to which peer groups influence their members. Although one study found evidence of influence for both alcohol use and smoking (Urberg et al., 1997), evidence from another study suggests that peer influence may play a stronger role for alcohol use than it does for smoking. Using data from a sample of Finnish adolescents, Kiuru and colleagues (2010) found that over the course of a year, stable cliques became more similar to each other with respect to alcohol use but not smoking. These results led the authors to conclude that there was "pressure to drink, but not to smoke." These mixed findings may indicate that friendship groups influence *frequency* of use and *transitions* from no recent use to recent use more so than either initiation of use or quitting. Instead, close friends may be more important than friendships groups for initiating alcohol use and smoking (Urberg et al., 1997), and addiction may be a stronger force than peer influence when it comes to quitting smoking (Ennett & Bauman, 1994).

Most empirical studies that explore the link between crowd membership and substance use focus on cross-sectional differences in level of substance use across crowds. In particular, members of some crowds, such as "dirts," "low-status," "troublemakers," and "hippies," are much more likely to use drugs than members of other peer crowds, such as "computer nerds," "religious," and "brains" (e.g., Dolcini & Adler, 1994; Kobus, 2003; La Greca et al., 2001; Mosbach & Leventhal, 1988; Verkooijen et al., 2007). In fact, engaging in health-related behaviors may be one of the driving forces behind crowd formation and identification (Brown et al., 1997). In their review of 44 studies, Sussman and colleagues (2007) found that adolescents who belonged to "deviant" crowds consistently had the highest level of smoking, marijuana, and alcohol use (compared to elites, athletes, academics, and other crowds).

Most studies of crowds assign adolescents to a single crowd. One exception is a study of Danish adolescents by Verkooijen and colleagues (2007), which found that adolescents who belonged to multiple "high-risk" crowds (i.e., crowds that had higher levels of substance use) reported the highest rates of substance use, whereas adolescents who belonged to multiple "low-risk" crowds reported the lowest rates of use, suggesting additive effects when adolescents are exposed to congruent norms. Belonging to mixed crowds with conflicting norms (e.g., one "high-risk" and one "low-risk" crowd) was associated with intermediate rates of substance use.

Notably, however, these cross-sectional studies cannot determine whether membership in a deviant crowd led to substance use (influence) or whether adolescents who engaged in substance use then joined—or were viewed as members of—substance-using crowds (selection). Of the few studies that have examined longitudinal associations between crowd membership and later outcomes, there appears to be more evidence of influence: Specifically, belonging to a high-risk crowd predicts later substance use both during adolescence (Barber, Eccles, & Stone, 2001) and into young adulthood (Sussman et al., 2004). Furthermore, in their study of alternative high school students,

Sussman and colleagues (1994) found that group identification in seventh grade predicted smoking in eighth grade, but smoking in seventh grade did not predict group identification in eighth grade. In other words, crowd identification appeared to lead to smoking rather than smokers selecting into a particular crowd after they had already begun smoking.

Stronger evidence of a *causal* link between group membership and substance use comes from randomized control studies that found harmful effects in targeted intervention programs that placed deviant youth in groups together. For example, high-risk participants who were randomly assigned to an adolescent group or an adolescent plus parent group had higher rates of tobacco use 3 years later than control participants and participants in parenting-only groups (Dishion et al., 1999; Dishion, Poulin, & Burraston, 2001). Notably, however, such iatrogenic effects are far from universal in group-based interventions (e.g., Handwerk, Field, & Friman, 2000). Instead, they are more likely when there are opportunities for unstructured interactions, such as time to hang out waiting for the intervention to start (Dishion, Dodge, & Lansford, 2006). Although these groups were experimentally created, the social processes that operated within them may be similar to those that operate within naturally occurring groups such as cliques and crowds. Thus, clarifying the conditions under which iatrogenic effects occur in intervention settings may shed light on factors that facilitate peer influence in natural contexts.

Beyond Close Relationships: Distal Peer Networks

Dyadic peer relationships, cliques, and crowds do not operate within a vacuum: They are nested within larger *peer networks*, which comprise all of an adolescent's peers within a specific context, such as all peers within the adolescent's school, neighborhood, sports team, or church group. These networks shape the norms around substance use, provide or limit opportunities to access drugs, model substance use and the consequences (or lack thereof) of this use, and shape the reinforcement that adolescents receive for substance use (Hawkins et al., 1992). Thus, even though influence *processes* are likely to be the same across different contexts, the *outcomes* of these influence processes may vary considerably (Snyder, 2002). For example, if school-wide norms (real or perceived) favor substance use, then more adolescents at that school may initiate substance use than adolescents at schools where the norms favor abstinence.

Notably, even more distal "peers" can shape the development of substance use. For example, some researchers have noted that the media can act as a powerful "best friend" or "superpeer," making risky behavior appear normative and glamorous, while also modeling different forms of substance use (e.g., Strasburger, Jordan, & Donnerstein, 2010). Although the media's role in shaping norms and modeling behavior is important, the focus of this chapter is on face-to-face peer relationships, and therefore a full review of the role of the media in shaping adolescent substance use is outside the scope of this chapter (see Donovan, this volume).

FEATURES OF PEER NETWORKS

Peer networks are defined as all of an adolescent's peers within a particular setting or context (see Table 19.2). Within schools, classroom-based networks may be the most relevant networks for children, whereas grade-wide or even school-wide networks may be more relevant for adolescents, because they often switch classes (and peers) throughout the day and have more opportunities to interact with peers outside of structured classroom activities. In particularly large schools, the most relevant network may be some subset of all students in the school (e.g., within same-ability tracks, co-participants in sports, arts, or other school activities), with that subset determined by school policies and practices as well as adolescents' own interests. Peers who live in the same neighborhood may also be an important peer network (Ennett, Foshee, et al., 2008; Kerr et al., 2007), and these peers may be especially relevant for adolescents who are disengaged from school or who drop out of school altogether.

Both the behavioral and structural features of peer networks can impact adolescents' behavior. Behavioral features generally capture the average behavior of individuals within the network (e.g., the average level of adolescent smoking in a school). For example, when a high proportion of adolescents in a peer network uses drugs, then there are more peers to model and reinforce substance use (modeling and normative regulation), it is easier for adolescents to access drugs (opportunity), the number of drug offers that adolescents receive may increase (direct peer pressure), and contextual norms may appear to, or actually, favor drug use (perceived norms). But behavioral features can also include other dynamics, such as which adolescents are selected as friends and

the degree to which peer influence occurs within that setting (Gest, Osgood, Feinberg, Bierman, & Moody, 2011). For example, if adolescents who use drugs are popular members of the network—indicated by a positive correlation between substance use and popularity—this would suggest that social norms within that setting favor substance use.

Structural features are the particular patterns of connections among all adolescents in the network. These connections, or "social ties," could represent specific friendship ties among all adolescents in the network, links between members of the same clique or crowd, or some estimate of how frequently each pair of adolescents in the network interacts with each other. These connections play a critical role in diffusion of innovations theory (e.g., Brown & Witherspoon, 2002; Rogers, 2003; Valente, 1995), which argues that the decision to adopt behavior typically involves five steps: a person (1) learns about, or is exposed to, the behavior, (2) forms an opinion about it, (3) decides whether to adopt it, (4) begins to engage in that behavior, and (5) seeks reinforcement for that decision. When individuals are connected to many people who adopt a behavior (e.g., begin smoking), they are more likely to be exposed to that behavior (step 1), form a favorable opinion about it (step 2), and be positively reinforced for engaging in the behavior if they adopt it (step 5). Thus, tightly connected, or socially integrated, networks might facilitate the spread of substance use once a few people begin using drugs. Yet social integration might simultaneously *lower* the risk of substance use; for example, social control theory (Hirschi, 1969) suggests that substance use would be less likely in socially integrated networks because social connections would reduce or control deviant impulses within these networks. Social integration might also promote the diffusion of intervention effects, such as promoting the spread of *un*favorable attitudes toward substance use, which could also lower the risk of substance use (Rulison, Gest, & Osgood, 2014). Notably, whether social integration facilitates or hinders the spread of substance use behavior may depend on the behavioral dynamics within the network, such as whether the most popular peers adopt favorable attitudes toward drug use or begin using drugs themselves.

METHODS FOR LINKING PEER NETWORKS TO ADOLESCENT SUBSTANCE USE

In studies of adolescent peer networks, researchers often define the boundaries of the network as all of the peers who are in the same grade or school as the adolescent. This decision is primarily based on logistics, due to the challenges of obtaining self-report data from all peers in non-school contexts, but it also makes sense theoretically, as adolescents spend a large percentage of their day in school. Some researchers, however, have argued that peer relationships outside of the school context might be particularly influential in the development of risky behaviors and should therefore be considered as well (e.g., Kerr et al., 2007; Kiesner, Kerr, & Stattin, 2004). Regardless of the particular boundary selected, it is important to recruit the majority of adolescents within that bounded network to provide self-reports of their own behavior, so as to avoid relying on adolescents' reports of their peers' behavior.

Once the boundaries of the network are established, the behavioral features are relatively straightforward to assess. These features are typically defined as the aggregate behavior across all individuals in the network (e.g., What is the average level of alcohol use among all of the peers in the network? What proportion of peers in the network smoke?). They could also include measures such as the correlation between substance use and popularity within the network to indicate the norms or influence potential within that context (Osgood, Feinberg, et al., 2013) or network-level estimates of peer influence obtained from actor-oriented models. The structural features of the network are more difficult to assess. Because structural features are defined by the patterns of connections among all peers in the network, measuring them requires first identifying which type of social ties to use. Typically, researchers use friendship ties, but other ties could also be used (e.g., nominations of peers the adolescent hangs around with, likes, or thinks are cool). Ideally, the type of tie should be selected based on theoretical considerations of which relationship is most important for the social processes or behaviors being studied. Once identified, these social ties are used to construct measures of different structural features of the network. Details about how to calculate these measures is beyond the scope of this chapter, but a partial list of commonly measured structures features is provided next (see Valente, 2010, for details about how to calculate these measures; see Gest et al., 2011, for a detailed description of how structural features can be linked to prevention efforts).

1. *Network density.* The proportion of all possible social ties that actually exist.

2. *Reciprocity.* The proportion of all ties in the network that are mutual (e.g., both adolescents name each other as friends).

3. *Transitivity.* The extent to which an adolescent's friends are also friends.

4. *Centralization.* The degree to which ties in the peer network are hierarchical.

5. *Clustering.* The degree to which the network is clustered into subgroups.

Once the behavioral and structural characteristics are identified, they can then be used to predict the adolescent's own substance use. Note that in this type of analysis, the key comparison focuses on comparing *networks* rather than *individuals*; thus, linking network characteristics to individual behavior requires researchers to obtain a large number of networks, such as networks from many different schools. Because individual adolescents are nested within networks, multilevel modeling is often used to account for the effect of the peer network on individual behavior (e.g., Botticello, 2009; Ennett et al., 2006; Mrug, Gaines, Su, & Windle, 2010).

REVIEW OF EMPIRICAL LITERATURE LINKING PEER NETWORKS TO SUBSTANCE USE

Studies of adolescent peer networks consistently demonstrate that students in school and neighborhood networks with a higher prevalence of substance use are more likely to use drugs (Alexander et al., 2001; Ali & Dwyer, 2009, 2010; Ennett, Faris, et al., 2008; Ennett, Foshee, et al., 2008), although interpreting the direction of the effect is challenging. Notably, these effects may be stronger for smoking and heavy alcohol use than moderate drinking or marijuana use (Botticello, 2009; Ennett et al., 2006; Mrug et al., 2010). Furthermore, one study found that higher rates of smoking among older students predicted higher rates of smoking among younger students at the same school (Leatherdale, Cameron, Brown, & McDonald, 2005), highlighting the importance of school-wide networks, at least in high school. In some cases, the effects of the wider peer network diminished or disappeared once friend use was added to the model (Mrug et al., 2010), suggesting that more proximal peers (e.g., friends, clique members) may have a stronger impact than distal peers. The effect of grade-level smoking on individual smoking also seems to fade as adolescents transition into adulthood, whereas the effect of friends' smoking persists (Ali & Dwyer, 2009), either because adolescents maintain these friendships into adulthood or because they select new friends with similar characteristics as their high school friends.

Importantly, network-level substance use not only has direct effects on adolescent substance use but can also modify the effects of social status, friends, and groups (Alexander et al., 2001; Leatherdale et al., 2005). For example, the effect of having friends who smoke or drink is greater in schools with higher rates of smoking and drinking (Ennett, Faris, et al., 2008; Ennett, Foshee, et al., 2008). In addition, adolescent-peer similarity is also greater for drinking in schools with higher rates of drug use compared to those with lower rates of drug use (Cleveland & Wiebe, 2003), which suggests that adolescents in networks with higher rates of drug use have more opportunities to select themselves into niches that support their own drug use attitudes and behaviors.

Until recently, the structural characteristics of the network were primarily neglected, but the rapid development of social network analytic tools has facilitated the ability to measure these characteristics. In one study, Ennett and colleagues (2006) found that adolescents who were in denser networks (i.e., networks with more friendship ties among students) were less likely to smoke and to use marijuana than students in less dense networks. Adolescents who were in networks with a higher reciprocation rate (i.e., relatively higher proportion of friendship ties that were mutual) were also less likely to use marijuana, although this effect was modest. In another study, Rulison and colleagues (2014) found that the diffusion of intervention effects from a substance use prevention program was greater in networks that were more connected and less clustered. These results suggest that not only do socially integrated networks promote less substance use (perhaps by providing some form of social control over adolescents' behavior); they can also facilitate the diffusion of *positive* effects from an intervention. More work is needed, however, to determine whether these results hold across contexts and how they interact with behavioral dynamics within the networks.

Social Status Within the Peer Network

In addition to different layers of the peer context, adolescents' *social status* within their peer context may shape their norms, social motives, and behavior. Clarifying the link between status and behavior may also shed some light on the relative strength of different peer influence mechanisms. For example, if influence occurs primarily through direct peer pressure from friends or group members

or through peers providing opportunities for use, then low-status or isolated adolescents should be *less* likely than their peers to use drugs. If, however, peer influence occurs more indirectly (e.g., via observational learning and pressure to conform to perceived group norms), then low-status adolescents may be *more* likely than their peers to use drugs, in an attempt to gain status or to become members of certain peer groups.

FEATURES OF SOCIAL STATUS WITHIN THE PEER NETWORK

Social status within the peer network is a multidimensional construct (see Table 19.2; see also Lease, Musgrove, & Axelrod, 2002) and includes dimensions such as *likeability* (i.e., how well liked adolescents are; how many friends an adolescent has), *perceived popularity* (i.e., whether peers view adolescents as "cool" or popular), and *social dominance* (i.e., whether adolescents have more power than their peers). These measures are related, but they are also uniquely associated with substance use, aggression, and sexual activity (Cillessen & Rose, 2005; LaFontana & Cillessen, 2002; Lease et al., 2002; Mayeux et al., 2008; Parkhurst & Hopmeyer, 1998). In addition to these reputational measures of status, *position* within the network is another important dimension of social status; position is typically defined by patterns of relationships among all of the adolescents within a network (Hanneman & Riddle, 2005; Scott, 2000; Wasserman & Faust, 1994). For example, some adolescents may be at the center of the network (e.g., friends or "friends of friends" with almost everyone in the network), other adolescents may "bridge" several different cliques rather than being solidly located within a single clique, and still other adolescents may be on the periphery of the network (e.g., have only a few friends who themselves only have a few friends) or isolated from the network altogether (i.e., have no friends in the network). As with specific types of peer relationships, status can be stable over the short term but also vary considerably over longer time frames (Moody, Brynildsen, Osgood, Feinberg, & Gest, 2011).

METHODS FOR STUDYING SOCIAL STATUS WITHIN THE PEER NETWORK

We review several measures of the different types of social status next.

Likeability (or "Sociometric Popularity")

The most common approach for assessing likeability is to ask adolescents to list which peers they "like the most" and which peers they "like the least," although friendship nominations (e.g., A. F. Newcomb & Bukowski, 1983) and other variations (e.g., "like to most spend time with on a Saturday night"; Allen et al., 2005) can also be used. Self-reports or teacher reports of status can be used, but self-reports do not capture actual reputation and teachers are often unreliable reporters of status (Cillessen, 2009). Allowing unlimited nominations may be best for research with adolescents, especially if the reference group is all peers in a grade or school, rather than only same-classroom peers (Cillessen, 2009). Once nominations are elicited, researchers can classify students as "popular" (many *liked most*, few *liked least* nominations), "rejected" (many *liked least*, few *liked most* nominations), "neglected" (rarely named), "controversial" (many nominations of both types), and "average" based on the total number of nominations and the balance of positive and negative nominations that each person receives (see Coie, Dodge, & Coppotelli, 1982). These categorical measures are useful for studying types of adolescents (e.g., "rejected youth"), but they have the disadvantage that boundaries are based on statistical cut-off scores rather than meaningful distinctions among groups. Alternatively, continuous scores can be created either by separately assessing *peer acceptance* (proportion of liked most nominations) and *peer rejection* (proportion of liked least nominations), or by standardizing liked most and liked least nominations and combining them into a single "social preference" score (Coie et al., 1982). Such continuous scores are more stable and preserve more information than categorical approaches (Cillessen & Mayeux, 2004).

Continuous data can also be collected through rating scales (e.g., Maassen, Van der Linden, Goossens, & Bokhorst, 2000). In this approach, respondents rate how they feel about every peer in that setting. For example, Maassen and colleagues asked students to rate each classmate on a −3 = very nasty to +3 = very nice scale, with the midpoint indicating an "ordinary classmate." Rating scales provide more detailed information than the nomination procedures described earlier; however, rating scales may not be appropriate for measuring sociometric popularity among adolescents because rating scales require that participants know each peer and collecting rating data takes more time in settings where there are many peers to rate.

Perceived Popularity

This status metric is assessed by asking adolescents to identify which peers they *think* are popular or cool and which peers they think are unpopular or not cool. For example, LaFontana and Cillessen (2002) asked students: "Who are the popular kids in your grade?" and "Who are the kids in your grade who are not very popular?" Typically, the number of times each adolescent is named as popular and the number of times each adolescent is named as unpopular are standardized within classroom or grade and combined to create a single, continuous "perceived popularity" score. Other studies, however, use just positive nominations (e.g., Rodkin, Farmer, Pearl, & Van Acker, 2000).

Centrality and Position Measures

Typically, centrality measures are calculated from students' friendship nominations, although they could be calculated from any type of nomination data (e.g., clique nominations). An in-depth review of all centrality measures is beyond the scope of this chapter (for more information about different available measures and how to calculate them, see Bonacich, 1987; Borgatti, 2005; Freeman, 1979; Hanneman & Riddle, 2005; Wasserman & Faust, 1994). It is also possible to use nomination data to compute categorical measures of position in the network (Osgood, Feinberg, Wallace, & Moody, 2014; Rodkin et al., 2000). For example, Ennett and Bauman (1994) identified *clique members* (i.e., adolescents who were solidly in one group), *liaisons* (i.e., adolescents who were connected to multiple groups), and *isolates* (i.e., adolescents with few or no connections to others in the group).

LINKING CHARACTERISTICS OF THE STATUS WITHIN THE PEER NETWORK TO SUBSTANCE USE

In the title of their article, Mayeux and colleagues (2008) asked: "Is being popular a risky proposition?" There is mounting evidence that the answer is "yes" for substance use (Balsa, Homer, French, & Norton, 2011; Becker & Luthar, 2007; Ennett et al., 2006; Moody et al., 2011): Popular adolescents often have the highest rates of substance use, regardless of the dimension of social status examined. One potential explanation for this association is that substance use may lead to social status. Adolescents who drink or use drugs may be desirable as friends due to their risk-taking nature and their perceived access to adult roles (Bukowski, Sippola, & Newcomb, 2000; Hawley, 2003; Moffitt, 1993, 2006). Alternatively, popularity may lead to substance use. Due to their popularity, high-status adolescents may frequently be invited to parties and other social events; because substance use often happens in these unstructured social contexts, these adolescents have more opportunities for substance use (Osgood, Ragan, et al., 2013). High-status adolescents may also feel pressure to conform—either to their friends or to perceived social norms—in order to maintain their status.

There is some support for both of these possibilities, suggesting that the link between substance use and status is likely bidirectional. In some cases, substance use predicted later social status, including being named more often as a friend (Huang et al., 2014; Kiuru et al., 2010; Mercken et al., 2009; Osgood, Ragan, et al., 2013; Schaefer et al., 2012), increased involvement with peers and romantic relationships, and increased self-perceptions of position in the peer group (Maggs & Hurrelmann, 1998). In addition, smoking, but not alcohol use, predicted *increased* perceived popularity for boys but *decreased* perceived popularity for girls (Mayeux et al., 2008). In other cases, social status predicted later substance use. For example, adolescents who were often named as a friend were more likely to use alcohol, cigarettes, and other drugs (Allen et al., 2005; Osgood, Ragan, et al., 2013; Valente et al., 2005). In addition, perceived popularity predicted increased alcohol use, but not smoking (Mayeux et al., 2008).

Notably, being *unpopular* may also be a risky proposition. Adolescents who are isolated from the peer network are more likely to smoke (Ennett & Bauman, 1993; Fang, Li, Stanton, & Dong, 2003; Valente et al., 2005), even after controlling for other demographic and behavioral characteristics that are related to smoking (Osgood et al., 2014). These low-status adolescents may feel pressure to conform so that they can gain access to friends or groups, or they may start smoking as an attempt to improve their social status. At the same time, isolated adolescents are *less* likely to use alcohol (Osgood et al., 2014), suggesting that peers may provide opportunities for alcohol use (e.g., at parties). Because isolated adolescents have few friends, they are excluded from these social events and thus are protected from alcohol use.

It is also possible that striving for popularity may increase the risk of substance use. Moody and colleagues (2011) found that adolescents who had considerable variability in their popularity over time—particularly those who started out as popular but lost popularity over time—also had high rates of substance use. The authors concluded that adolescents with highly variable popularity trajectories may use drugs to either regain or reinforce their past status.

Taken together, these studies suggest that average status adolescents may be least at risk for substance use (Ennett et al., 2006). Alcohol use in particular may be important to adolescent social experiences (Osgood et al., 2014), putting popular adolescents in a position to increase their alcohol use over time (Mayeux et al., 2008). Cigarette use may be less central to social experiences, but because of its link to perceived popularity, at least for boys (Mayeux et al., 2008), low-status adolescents may view smoking as a way to increase their social status. Notably, the results are not always consistent across studies and even sometimes within studies (e.g., isolation predicted smoking in sixth and eighth grade, but not tenth grade; Fang et al., 2003). Therefore, future research should continue to explore whether and how the link between substance use and social status varies across age, contexts, and types of substance use.

Future Directions

In sum, peers play a significant role in the development of substance use, but the patterns and underlying processes are complex and require further investigation. Next, we elaborate five questions that are important for future research to address.

How Do Peers Shape Substance Use Outside of School Contexts?

Most studies of adolescent peer relationships have focused on school-based relationships: Schools provide clearly bounded networks, and collecting data within schools allows researchers to more easily gather reports directly from peers rather than rely on often inaccurate self-reports of peers' behaviors. Despite these methodological conveniences, adolescents also interact with many peers outside of school (Kerr et al., 2007). Notably, drug use and antisocial behavior is often higher among adolescents who nominate more out-of-school friends (Ennett et al., 2006), among those who met their closest peers in their neighborhoods as opposed to school or other structured contexts (Kiesner et al., 2004), and among those who spend more time outside of school with drug-using friends (Ennett, Faris, et al., 2008; Kiesner, Poulin, & Dishion, 2010).

In addition to face-to-face interactions with peers outside of school, social networking sites now allow virtual interactions and increased exposure to indirect friends (i.e., "friends of friends"). Most adolescents have access to these online contexts: In 2012, 95% of 12- to 17-year-olds reported going online and 81% used online social networking sites (Madden et al., 2013). These sites not only serve as a context for peer interactions, but references to substance use on these sites are common (Moreno & Kolb, 2012) and can shape perceived norms: Adolescents tend to interpret images and text referring to drinking on social networking sites as representing actual alcohol use (Moreno, Briner, Williams, Walker, & Christakis, 2009). These perceptions may explain why adolescents who view experimentally manipulated social networking profiles displaying alcohol use are more willing to drink and have more positive attitudes toward alcohol use than adolescents who view profiles without alcohol displays (Litt & Stock, 2011). These perceptions may also explain why adolescents who reported that their friends posted pictures of themselves partying or drinking alcohol were more likely to smoke (Huang et al., 2014).

Future research must continue to explore how relationships with peers in nonschool contexts shape substance use. As the ubiquity of social media options and use grows, the number, importance, and influence of out-of-school relationships will likely increase, so researchers must find innovative ways to collect both rich snapshot and dynamically changing data that capture these important out-of-school relationships. In addition, clarifying how being part of an interactive, online social network where references to drug use are common affects adolescent substance use perceptions and behaviors is an important area for continued research.

Over What Time Frame Do Different Forms of Influence Occur?

There is little theoretical or empirical guidance to suggest the time frame over which different types of peer influence occur (i.e., minutes, days, weeks, months, or years). Most studies collect data only once or twice a year, due primarily to logistics, funding, and access to schools. Studies with these infrequent assessments may best capture cumulative influence arising from repeated exposure to peer interaction patterns (Brown, Bakken, Ameringer, & Mahon, 2008; Dishion et al., 1997; Dishion et al., 1996; Patterson et al., 2000). Yet observational studies of adolescents and their peers clearly document the importance of influence processes that occur within moment-by-moment interactions.

For example, rule-breaking talk met with laughter is frequently followed by more rule-breaking talk (Dishion et al., 1996). Capturing such unfolding processes of peer influence at the interactional level require more frequent data collection with very short intervals. Future studies should collect more real-time, frequent information about peer interactions (e.g., using smartphones) and link this information with longer term studies that capture cumulative influences on adolescents.

How Do Different Levels of the Peer Context Interact to Shape Substance Use?

Previous research on adolescents' salient social relationships has typically assessed these relationships at either the dyadic or social group level. Each level of the peer context, however, may involve a distinct social influence process (Brown, 2004; Cairns et al., 1998; Kindermann & Gest, 2009) and when different levels of the peer context are examined simultaneously, differential effects have been noted. For example, Urberg and colleagues (1997) found that even though adolescents were exposed to a greater number of substance-using peers within their friendship group, it was their closest friend, not their group, who predicted substance use initiation. Future work should explore the independent and perhaps interactive contributions of friendships, groups, and distal peer influences, particularly with respect to what happens when messages from popular peers, best friends, other friends, romantic partners, cliques, crowds, and the contextual norms pull adolescents in different directions (Brechwald & Prinstein, 2011).

Where Do Parents Fit Into the Peer Context During Adolescence?

Although adolescents spend more time with peers compared to time with their parents (Brown, 1990), parents still contribute to the development of substance use. In addition to their own important direct influences on adolescent substance use (e.g., modeling behavior; conveying attitudes about substance use), parents also contribute indirectly by shaping the peer context. For example, parents impact who their children can select as friends: By deciding where to live and where to send their children to school, parents limit the pool of potential friends (Kandel, 1996), and by shaping their children's academic achievement, self-reliance, and drug use, parents impact which crowds their children can join and which friends they select (Brown, Mounts, Lamborn, & Steinberg, 1993; Steinberg et al., 1994). Parental behaviors, such as discipline, social support, involvement, and monitoring, may also limit the number of drug-using peers that an adolescent selects (Dishion, Capaldi, Spracklen, & Li, 1995; Dishion et al., 2004; Simons-Morton, Chen, Abroms, & Haynie, 2004) and reduce the influence of drug-using peers by making adolescents less susceptible to influence (Marshal & Chassin, 2000; Simons-Morton, 2002) or limiting opportunities for adolescents to spend unsupervised time with drug-using peers. Despite the potentially interactive contribution of parents and peers, most studies focus on their independent contributions. Furthermore, few studies have considered the potential impact of *peers'* parents on an adolescent's substance use, but evidence from several recent studies (Cleveland, Feinberg, Osgood, & Moody, 2012; Ragan, Osgood, & Feinberg, 2014) suggests that peers' parents may shape an adolescent's substance use both directly (by monitoring their activities) and indirectly (by affecting the peer's substance use, which in turn impacts the adolescent's substance use). Future studies should focus on identifying how the roles of parents, peers, and peers' parents interact to promote (or hinder) substance use.

For Whom and Under What Conditions Does Peer Influence Occur?

Given abundant evidence that both selection and influence shape the development of substance use, research is now moving to determine the conditions under which these processes occur (Brechwald & Prinstein, 2011; Brown, Bakken, et al., 2008). Such moderating conditions, which can occur at multiple levels, are reviewed next.

WHO IS MOST SUSCEPTIBLE TO INFLUENCE?

Some adolescents are more susceptible than others to influence from their peers, and this susceptibility in turn predicts higher rates of substance use and other health-risk behaviors (Allen, Porter, & McFarland, 2006). Susceptibility to influence can vary depending on individual differences in demographic characteristics, personality, attitudes toward peers, social skills, and position in the peer network (Allen, Chango, Szwedo, Schad, & Marston, 2012; Brechwald & Prinstein, 2011; Dishion et al., 2006; Kerr, Van Zalk, & Stattin, 2011; Schulenberg et al., 1999; Urberg et al., 1997). For example, adolescents who are concerned about what their peers think and adolescents who are lower in centrality are more influenced by their friends' substance use

than other adolescents (Aloise-Young et al., 1994; Ennett, Faris, et al., 2008). Susceptibility to influence may increase during adolescence due to increased desires for autonomy, freedom from adult supervision, and major school transitions that expose adolescents to larger and more diverse peer networks, but whether and when susceptibility peaks in adolescence is controversial (Berndt & Murphy, 2002; Steinberg & Monahan, 2007; Steinberg & Silverberg, 1986; Urberg et al., 1997).

WHICH PEERS ARE MOST INFLUENTIAL?

Just as all adolescents are not equally susceptible to influence, not all peers are equally influential. For example, adolescents may value reinforcement by and approval from their high-status peers more than similar reinforcement from lower status peers. Until recently, however, research in this area was limited and primarily speculative based on conclusions from cross-sectional studies. A few recent studies, however, support the assumption that some peers are more influential than others. For example, adolescents are more influenced by friends who are well liked (Allen et al., 2012) and by friends who have higher perceived popularity than they do (Bot, Engels, Knibbe, & Meeus, 2005). In addition, peers who are high on psychopathic traits (e.g., callous-unemotional and grandiose-manipulative traits) may be more influential than peers who are lower on these traits with respect to delinquent behavior (Kerr et al., 2011).

WHAT TYPES OF RELATIONSHIP ARE MOST INFLUENTIAL?

Relationship quality, stability, and time spent together may facilitate influence, but support for the moderating role of these relationship characteristics is mixed. Urberg and colleagues (1997) found that stable relationships were not more influential than unstable relationships with respect to smoking or alcohol use. Thus, transient relationships may have enduring effects on use for self-reinforcing or addictive behavior, and influence may be at least as important before a friendship forms as during the course of a stable friendship (Aloise-Young et al., 1994). Other studies, however, suggest that the strength of influence depends on whether the relationship is reciprocated, although the *direction* of this effect varies across studies: Some studies found that reciprocated relationships are more influential (e.g., Burk, Steglich, & Snijders, 2007), other studies found that unilateral relationships are more influential (e.g., Bot et al., 2005), and still others found no effect of reciprocity (e.g., Mercken et al., 2010). These inconsistencies may reflect differences across studies in the type of behavior, type of relationship, and age of the participants; thus, more work is needed to clarify when and how relationship characteristics promote peer influence.

DO TYPE AND STAGE OF SUBSTANCE USE MATTER?

Many studies do not examine whether peers differentially impact the development of different *types* of substance use; instead, they either focus on a single drug or combine multiple drugs into a single "substance use" composite score. These composite scores might conceal important differences in social and biological processes across substances, such as social use of alcohol at parties and the addictive nature of tobacco (e.g., Osgood et al., 2014). Furthermore, consequences can also vary across different drugs. For example, alcohol use can lead to better social integration, whereas heavy hard drug use can lead to decreased psychological adaptation (e.g., Newcomb & Bentler, 1989). Indeed, studies that have separately documented the role of peers across different substances have found different social processes may operate for different substances at different points in development (e.g., Dishion & Owen, 2002). For example, both selection and influence may be important for drinking, whereas selection may be more important than influence for smoking, particularly during later adolescence once addiction comes into play (e.g., Huang et al., 2014; Kiuru et al., 2010; Pearson et al., 2006; Veenstra et al., 2013).

In addition, the role of peers may vary by *stage* of use (e.g., initiation, experimenting, maintenance, escalation, or quitting). For example, Fisher and Bauman (1988) found that friends had a bigger impact on quitting for smoking and on initiating for alcohol use. Stage of use may also interact with relationship type to impact the outcome. For example, close friends may be particularly important for the initiation of substance use, whereas groups may be more important for maintaining these behaviors (e.g., Urberg et al., 1997). Most studies, however, have focused on frequency of use or blurred the distinction between stages (e.g., by dichotomizing usage into never used / ever used), although a few studies have focused on a particular stage of use, such as initiation (e.g., Light et al., 2013). Future studies, particularly those with data collected multiple times within a single year, are needed to explore further the role of peers at each stage of use.

Conclusions

Popular culture suggests that direct peer pressure to use drugs is pervasive and conclusions based on early empirical work also suggested that adolescents were strongly influenced by their peers. Not surprisingly, then, many early substance use prevention programs primarily taught adolescents how to deflect or resist peer pressure. Disappointing findings from these prevention programs, coupled with mixed results from empirical studies that used stronger designs and statistical controls, demonstrate that the role of peers in the development of substance use is complex: Peer influence comes in many forms, operates simultaneously with other social processes such as selection, and comes from different sources (e.g., friendships, cliques, crowds, networks). More specifically, even though direct peer pressure does occur, it is rare. Peer influence more often occurs interpersonally through modeling and normative regulation, intrapersonally through perceived social norms and social motives, and by peers structuring the opportunities in which substance use can occur. Selection processes also shape network dynamics: Adolescents select peers who are similar to themselves as well as peers they believe can help them gain or maintain social status. In some cases, adolescents may even change their own behavior so as to gain access to certain friends, cliques, or crowds. Once these relationships form, peer influence continues, as peers model and reinforce certain behaviors.

The mixed pattern of findings across empirical studies underscores the complexity of the link between peers and substance use. To clarify when and how peers shape the development of substance use, researchers must attempt to match the complexity of their questions to appropriate data collection and analytic strategies. For example, future work must specify which social processes and level(s) of the peer context will be studied and justify these decisions, clearly operationalize each construct, and select appropriate measures of these constructs. Researchers should weigh the consequences of different measurement choices, such as whether to use adolescent, peer, or observer report for each construct; how many nominations to allow; and how often to assess peer relationships and behavior. Matching research questions, research designs, and analytic choices will lead to a better understanding of adolescent development and of the etiology of substance use and will allow program developers to design more effective interventions that prevent or reduce substance use and the negative consequences of this use.

References

"About D.A.R.E." (2014). Retrieved July 2014, from http://www.dare.org/about-d-a-r-e/

Ajzen, I. (1991). The theory of planned behavior. *Organizational Behavior and Human Decision Processes, 50*, 179–211.

Akers, R. L. (1998). *Social learning and social structure: A general theory of crime and deviance.* Boston, MA: Northeastern University Press.

Alexander, C., Allen, P., Crawford, M. A., & McCormick, L. K. (1999). Taking a first puff: Cigarette smoking experiences among ethnically diverse adolescents. *Ethnicity and Health, 4*, 245–257.

Alexander, C., Piazza, M., Mekos, D., & Valente, T. (2001). Peers, schools, and adolescent cigarette smoking. *Journal of Adolescent Health, 29*, 22–30.

Ali, M. M., & Dwyer, D. S. (2009). Estimating peer effects in adolescent smoking behavior: A longitudinal analysis. *Journal of Adolescent Health, 45*, 402–408.

Ali, M. M., & Dwyer, D. S. (2010). Social network effects in alcohol consumption among adolescents. *Addictive Behaviors, 35*, 337–342.

Allen, J. P., Chango, J., Szwedo, D., Schad, M., & Marston, E. (2012). Predictors of susceptibility to peer influence regarding substance use in adolescence. *Child Development, 83*, 337–350.

Allen, J. P., Porter, M. R., & McFarland, F. C. (2006). Leaders and followers in adolescent close friendships: Susceptibility to peer influence as a predictor of risky behavior, friendship instability, and depression. *Development and Psychopathology, 18*, 155–172.

Allen, J. P., Porter, M. R., McFarland, F. C., Marsh, P., & McElhaney, K. B. (2005). The two faces of adolescents' success with peers: Adolescent popularity, social adaptation, and deviant behavior. *Child Development, 76*, 747–760.

Aloise-Young, P. A., Graham, J. W., & Hansen, W. B. (1994). Peer influence on smoking initiation during early adolescence: A comparison of group members and group outsiders. *Journal of Applied Psychology, 79*, 281–287.

Arnett, J. J. (2007). The myth of peer influence in adolescent smoking initiation. *Health Education and Behavior, 34*, 594–607.

Bagwell, C. L., Coie, J. D., Terry, R. A., & Lochman, J. E. (2000). Peer clique participation and social status in preadolescence. *Merrill Palmer Quarterly, 46*, 280–305.

Balsa, A. I., Homer, J. F., French, M. T., & Norton, E. C. (2011). Alcohol use and popularity: Social payoffs from conforming to peers' behavior. *Journal of Research on Adolescence, 21*, 559–568.

Baltes, P. B. (1987). Theoretical propositions of life-span developmental psychology: On the dynamics between growth and decline. *Developmental Psychology, 23*, 611–626.

Bandura, A. (1978). Social learning theory of aggression. *Journal of Communication, 28*, 12–29.

Barber, B. L., Eccles, J. S., & Stone, M. R. (2001). Whatever happened to the jock, the brain, and the princess? *Journal of Adolescent Research, 16*, 429–455.

Bartholow, B. D., Sher, K. J., & Strathman, A. (2000). Moderation of the expectancy-alcohol use relation by private self-consciousness: Data from a longitudinal study. *Personality and Social Psychology Bulletin, 26*, 1409–1420.

Barton, J., Chassin, L., Presson, C. C., & Sherman, S. J. (1982). Social image factors as motivators of smoking initiation in early and middle adolescence. *Child Development, 53*, 1499–1511.

Bauman, K. E., & Ennett, S. T. (1996). On the importance of peer influence for adolescent drug use: Commonly neglected considerations. *Addiction, 91*, 185–198.

Becker, B. E., & Luthar, S. S. (2007). Peer-perceived admiration and social preference: Contextual correlates of positive peer regard among suburban and urban adolescents. *Journal of Research on Adolescence, 17*, 117–144.

Berndt, T. J. (1982). The features and effects of friendship in early adolescence. *Child Development, 53*, 1447–1460.

Berndt, T. J. (1992). Friendship and friends' influence in adolescence. *Current Directions in Psychological Science, 1*, 156–159.

Berndt, T. J. (2004). Children's friendships: Shifts over a half-century in perspectives on their development and their effects. *Merrill Palmer Quarterly, 50*, 206–223.

Berndt, T. J., & McCandless, M. A. (2009). Methods for investigating children's relationships with friends. In K. H. Rubin, W. M. Bukowski, & B. Laursen (Eds.), *Handbook of peer interactions, relationships, and groups* (pp. 63–81). New York, NY: Guilford Press.

Berndt, T. J., & Murphy, L. M. (2002). Influences of friends and friendships: Myths, truths, and research recommendations. In R. V. Kail (Ed.), *Advances in child development and behavior* (Vol. 30, pp. 275–310). San Diego, CA: Academic Press.

Boivin, M., & Vitaro, F. (1995). The impact of peer relationships on aggression in childhood: Inhibition through coercion or promotion through peer support. In J. McCord (Ed.), *Coercion and punishment in long-term perspectives* (pp. 183–197). New York, NY: Cambridge University Press.

Bonacich, P. (1987). Power and centrality: A family of measures. *American Journal of Sociology, 92*, 1170–1182.

Borgatti, S. P. (2005). Centrality and network flow. *Social Networks, 27*, 55–71.

Borgatti, S. P., Everett, M. G., & Freeman, L. C. (2002). *UCINET for Windows: Software for social network analysis.* Natick, MA: Analytic Technologies.

Bot, S. M., Engels, R. C. M. E., Knibbe, R. A., & Meeus, W. H. J. (2005). Friend's drinking behaviour and adolescent alcohol consumption: The moderating role of friendship characteristics. *Addictive Behaviors, 30*, 929–947.

Botticello, A. L. (2009). School contextual influences on the risk for adolescent alcohol misuse. *American Journal of Community Psychology, 43*, 85–97.

Botvin, G. J., Baker, E., Dusenbury, L., Botvin, E. M., & Diaz, T. (1995). Long-term follow-up results of a randomized drug abuse prevention trial in a white middle-class population. *Journal of the American Medical Association, 273*, 1106–1112.

Botvin, G. J., Botvin, E. M., Baker, E., Dusenbury, L., & Goldberg, C. J. (1992). The false consensus effect: Predicting adolescents' tobacco use from normative expectations. *Psychological Reports, 70*, 171–178.

Brechwald, W. A., & Prinstein, M. J. (2011). Beyond homophily: A decade of advances in understanding peer influence processes. *Journal of Research on Adolescence, 21*, 166–179.

Bronfenbrenner, U. (1979). *The ecology of human development: Experiments by nature and design.* Cambridge, MA: Harvard University Press.

Bronfenbrenner, U., & Morris, P. A. (1997). The ecology of developmental processes. In W. Damon (Ed.), *Handbook of child psychology* (5th ed., pp. 993–1028). New York, NY: Wiley.

Brown, B. B. (1990). Peer groups and peer cultures. In S. S. Feldman & G. R. Elliott (Eds.), *At the threshold: The developing adolescent* (pp. 171–196). Cambridge, MA: Harvard University Press.

Brown, B. B. (2004). Adolescents' relationships with peers. In R. M. Lerner & L. Steinberg (Eds.), *Handbook of adolescent psychology* (2nd ed., pp. 363–394). New York, NY: Wiley.

Brown, B. B., Bakken, J. P., Ameringer, S. W., & Mahon, S. D. (2008). A comprehensive conceptualization of the peer influence process in adolescence. In M. J. Prinstein & K. A. Dodge (Eds.), *Understanding peer influence in children and adolescents* (pp. 17–44). New York, NY: Guilford Press.

Brown, B. B., Dolcini, M. M., & Leventhal, A. (1997). Transformations in peer relationships at adolescence: Implications for health-related behavior. In J. E. Schulenberg, J. L. Maggs, & K. Hurrelmann (Eds.), *Health risks and developmental transitions during adolescence.* New York, NY: Cambridge University Press.

Brown, B. B., & Klute, C. (2003). Friendships, cliques, and crowds. In G. R. Adams & M. D. Berzonsky (Eds.), *Blackwell handbook of adolescence* (pp. 330–348). Malden, MA: Blackwell.

Brown, B. B., & Larson, J. (2009). Peer relationships in adolescence. In R. M. Lerner & L. Steinberg (Eds.), *Handbook of adolescent psychology* (3rd ed., pp. 74–103). Hoboken, NJ: Wiley.

Brown, B. B., Mounts, N., Lamborn, S. D., & Steinberg, L. (1993). Parenting practices and peer group affiliation in adolescence. *Child Development, 64*, 467–482.

Brown, J. D., & Witherspoon, E. M. (2002). The mass media and American adolescents' health. *Journal of Adolescent Health, 31*(6, Suppl.), 153–170.

Brown, S. A., McGue, M., Maggs, J. L., Schulenberg, J., Hingson, R., Swartzwelder, S., . . . Murphy, S. (2008). A developmental perspective on alcohol and youths 16 to 20 years of age. *Pediatrics, 121*(Suppl. 4), S290–S310.

Buhrmester, D., & Furman, W. (1987). The development of companionship and intimacy. *Child Development, 58*, 1101–1103.

Bukowski, W. M., Sippola, L. K., & Newcomb, A. F. (2000). Variations in patterns of attraction to same- and other-sex peers during early adolescence. *Developmental Psychology, 36*, 147–154.

Burgess, R. L., & Akers, R. L. (1966). A differential association-reinforcement theory of criminal behavior. *Social Problems, 14*, 128–147.

Burk, W. J., Steglich, C., & Snijders, T. A. B. (2007). Beyond dyadic interdependence: Actor-oriented models for co-evolving social networks and individual behaviors. *International Journal of Behavioral Development, 31*, 397–404.

Burk, W. J., van der Vorst, H., Kerr, M., & Stattin, H. (2012). Alcohol use and friendship dynamics: Selection and socialization in early-, middle-, and late-adolescent peer networks. *Journal of Studies on Alcohol and Drugs, 73*, 89–98.

Cairns, R. B., & Cairns, B. D. (1994). *Lifelines and risks: Pathways of youth in our time*. New York, NY: Cambridge University Press.

Cairns, R. B., Cairns, B. D., Neckerman, H. J., Gest, S. D., & Gariepy, J-L. (1988). Social networks and aggressive behavior: Peer support or peer rejection? *Developmental Psychology, 24*, 815–823.

Cairns, R. B., Leung, M. C., Buchanan, L., & Cairns, B. D. (1995). Friendships and social networks in childhood and adolescence: Fluidity, reliability, and interrelations. *Child Development, 66*, 1330–1345.

Cairns, R. B., Xie, H., & Leung, M-C. (1998). The popularity of friendship and the neglect of social networks: Toward a new balance. In W. M. Bukowski & A. H. Cillessen (Eds.), *Sociometry then and now: Building on six decades of measuring children's experiences with the peer group. New Directions for Child Development, No. 80* (pp. 25–53). San Francisco, CA: Jossey-Bass.

Cialdini, R. B., Reno, R. R., & Kallgren, C. A. (1990). A focus theory of normative conduct: Recycling the concept of norms to reduce littering in public places. *Journal of Personality and Social Psychology, 58*, 1015–1026.

Cillessen, A. H. N. (2009). Sociometric methods. In K. H. Rubin, W. M. Bukowski, & B. P. Laursen (Eds.), *Handbook of peer interactions, relationships, and groups* (pp. 82–99). New York, NY: Guilford Press.

Cillessen, A. H. N., & Mayeux, L. (2004). Sociometric status and peer group behavior: Previous findings and current directions. In J. B. Kupersmidt & K. A. Dodge (Eds.), *Children's peer relations: From development to intervention. Decade of behavior* (pp. 3–20). Washington, DC: American Psychological Association.

Cillessen, A. H. N., & Rose, A. J. (2005). Understanding popularity in the peer system. *Current Directions in Psychological Science, 14*, 102–105.

Cleveland, H. H., & Wiebe, R. P. (2003). The moderation of adolescent–to–peer similarity in tobacco and alcohol use by school levels of substance use. *Child Development, 74*, 279–291.

Cleveland, M. J., Feinberg, M. E., Osgood, D. W., & Moody, J. (2012). Do peers' parents matter? A new link between positive parenting and adolescent substance use. *Journal of Studies on Alcohol and Drugs, 73*, 423–433.

Cohen, J. M. (1977). Sources of peer group homogeneity. *Sociology of Education, 50*, 227–241.

Coie, J. D., Dodge, K. A., & Coppotelli, H. (1982). Dimensions and types of social status: A cross-age perspective. *Developmental Psychology, 18*, 557–570.

Coleman, J. S. (1961). *The adolescent society: The social life of the teenager and its impact on education*. New York, NY: Free Press.

Cooper, M. L. (1994). Motivations for alcohol use among adolescents: Development and validation of a four-factor model. *Psychological Assessment, 6*, 117–128.

Cooper, M. L., Russell, M., Skinner, J. B., & Windle, M. (1992). Development and validation of a three-dimensional measure of drinking motives. *Psychological Assessment, 4*, 123–132.

Coplan, R. J., & Arbeau, K. A. (2009). Peer interactions and play in early childhood. In K. H. Rubin, W. M. Bukowski, & B. Laursen (Eds.), *Handbook of peer interactions, relationships, and groups* (pp. 143–161). New York, NY: Guilford Press.

Cox, W. M., & Klinger, E. (1988). A motivational model of alcohol use. *Journal of Abnormal Psychology, 97*, 168–180.

Crockett, L., Losoff, M., & Petersen, A. C. (1984). Perceptions of the peer group and friendship in early adolescence. *Journal of Early Adolescence, 4*, 155–181.

Cross, J. R., & Fletcher, K. L. (2009). The challenge of adolescent crowd research: Defining the crowd. *Journal of Youth and Adolescence, 38*, 747–764.

de la Haye, K., Green, H. D., Kennedy, D. P., Pollard, M. S., & Tucker, J. S. (2013). Selection and influence mechanisms associated with marijuana initiation and use in adolescent friendship networks. *Journal of Research on Adolescence, 23*, 474–486.

Denscombe, M. (2001). Peer group pressure, young people and smoking: New developments and policy implications. *Drugs: Education, Prevention, and Policy, 8,* 7–32.

Dishion, T. J., Capaldi, D., Spracklen, K. M., & Li, F. (1995). Peer ecology of male adolescent drug use. *Development and Psychopathology, 7,* 803–824.

Dishion, T. J., Dodge, K. A., & Lansford, J. E. (2006). Findings and recommendations: A blueprint to minimize deviant peer influence in youth interventions and programs. In K. A. Dodge, J. E. Lansford, & T. J. Dishion (Eds.), *Deviant peer influences in programs for youth: Problems and solutions. Duke Series in Child Development and Public Policy* (pp. 366–394). New York, NY: Guilford Press.

Dishion, T. J., Eddy, M., Haas, E., Li, F., & Spracklen, K. M. (1997). Friendships and violent behavior during adolescence. *Social Development, 6,* 207–223.

Dishion, T. J., McCord, J., & Poulin, F. (1999). When interventions harm: Peer groups and problem behavior. *American Psychologist, 54,* 755–764.

Dishion, T. J., Nelson, S. E., & Bullock, B. M. (2004). Premature adolescent autonomy: Parent disengagement and deviant peer process in the amplification of problem behaviour. *Journal of Adolescence, 27,* 515–530.

Dishion, T. J., & Owen, L. D. (2002). A longitudinal analysis of friendships and substance use: Bidirectional influence from adolescence to adulthood. *Developmental Psychology, 38,* 480.

Dishion, T. J., Patterson, G. R., Stoolmiller, M., & Skinner, E. A. (1991). Family, school, and behavioral antecedents to early adolescent involvement with antisocial peers. *Developmental Psychology, 27,* 172–180.

Dishion, T. J., Poulin, F., & Burraston, B. (2001). Peer group dynamics associated with iatrogenic effects in group interventions with high-risk young adolescents. *New Directions for Child and Adolescent Development, 91,* 79–92.

Dishion, T. J., Spracklen, K. M., Andrews, D. W., & Patterson, G. R. (1996). Deviancy training in male adolescents friendships. *Behavior Therapy, 27,* 373–390.

Dolcini, M. M., & Adler, N. E. (1994). Perceived competencies, peer group affiliation, and risk behavior among early adolescents. *Health Psychology, 13,* 496.

Donovan, J. E., & Jessor, R. (1985). Structure of problem behavior in adolescence and young adulthood. *Journal of Consulting and Clinical Psychology, 53,* 890–904.

Duncan, T. E., Duncan, S. C., & Hops, H. (1996). The role of parents and older siblings in predicting adolescent substance use: Modeling development via structural equation latent growth methodology. *Journal of Family Psychology, 10,* 158–172.

Eccles, J. S., Midgley, C., Wigfield, A., Buchanan, C. M., Reuman, D., Flanagan, C., & MacIver, D. (1993). Development during adolescence: The impact of stage-environment fit on young adolescents' experiences in schools and in families. *American Psychologist, 48,* 90–101.

Eckert, P. (1989). *Jocks and burnouts: Social categories and identity in the high school.* New York, NY: Teachers College Press.

Elder, G. H. (1998). The life course and human development. In R. M. Lerner (Ed.), *Handbook of child psychology* (pp. 939–991). New York, NY: Wiley.

Ellickson, P. L., McCaffrey, D. F., Ghosh-Dastidar, B., & Longshore, D. L. (2003). New inroads in preventing adolescent drug use: Results from a large-scale trial of Project ALERT in middle schools. *American Journal of Public Health, 93,* 1830–1836.

Elliott, D. S., Huizinga, D., & Ageton, S. S. (1985). *Explaining delinquency and drug abuse.* Beverly Hills, CA: Sage.

Ennett, S. T., & Bauman, K. E. (1993). Peer group structure and adolescent cigarette smoking: A social network analysis. *Journal of Health and Social Behavior, 34,* 226–236.

Ennett, S. T., & Bauman, K. E. (1994). The contribution of influence and selection to adolescent peer group homogeneity: The case of adolescent cigarette smoking. *Journal of Personality and Social Psychology, 67,* 653–663.

Ennett, S. T., Bauman, K. E., Hussong, A., Faris, R., Foshee, V. A., Cai, L., & DuRant, R. H. (2006). The peer context of adolescent substance use: Findings from social network analysis. *Journal of Research on Adolescence, 16,* 159–186.

Ennett, S. T., Faris, R., Hipp, J., Foshee, V. A., Bauman, K. E., Hussong, A., & Cai, L. (2008). Peer smoking, other peer attributes, and adolescent cigarette smoking: A social network analysis. *Prevention Science, 9,* 88–98.

Ennett, S. T., Foshee, V. A., Bauman, K. E., Hussong, A., Cai, L., Reyes, H. L. M., . . . DuRant, R. (2008). The social ecology of adolescent alcohol misuse. *Child Development, 79,* 1777–1791.

Ennett, S. T., Tobler, N. S., Ringwalt, C. L., & Flewelling, R. L. (1994). How effective is Drug Abuse Resistance Education? A meta-analysis of Project DARE outcome evaluations. *American Journal of Public Health, 84,* 1394–1401.

Erikson, E. H. (1968). *Identity, youth, and crisis.* New York, NY: W.W. Norton.

Fang, X., Li, X., Stanton, B., & Dong, Q. (2003). Social network positions and smoking experimentation among Chinese adolescents. *American Journal of Health Behavior, 27,* 257–267.

Felner, R. D., Ginter, M., & Primavera, J. (1982). Primary prevention during school transitions: Social support and environmental structure. *American Journal of Community Psychology, 10,* 277–290.

Fishbein, M., & Ajzen, I. (1975). *Belief, attitude, intention, and behavior.* Reading, MA: Addison-Wesley.

Fisher, L. A., & Bauman, K. E. (1988). Influence and selection in the friend-adolescent relationship: Findings from studies of adolescent smoking and drinking. *Journal of Applied Social Psychology, 18,* 289–314.

Freeman, L. C. (1979). Centrality in social networks conceptual clarification. *Social Networks, 1,* 215–239.

Furman, W., Low, S., & Ho, M. J. (2009). Romantic experience and psychosocial adjustment in middle adolescence. *Journal of Clinical Child and Adolescent Psychology, 38,* 75–90.

Furman, W., & Shaffer, L. A. (1999). A story of adolescence: The emergence of other-sex relationships. *Journal of Youth and Adolescence, 28,* 513–522.

Gest, S. D., Farmer, T. W., Cairns, B. D., & Xie, H. (2003). Identifying children's peer social networks in school classrooms: Links between peer reports and observed interactions. *Social Development, 12,* 513–529.

Gest, S. D., Moody, J., & Rulison, K. L. (2007). Density or distinction? The roles of data structure and group detection methods in describing adolescent peer groups. *Journal of Social Structure, 6.* Retrieved October 2015, from http://www.cmu.edu/joss/content/articles/volume8/GestMoody/

Gest, S. D., Osgood, D. W., Feinberg, M. E., Bierman, K. L., & Moody, J. (2011). Strengthening prevention program theories and evaluations: Contributions from social network analysis. *Prevention Science, 12*, 349–360.

Gottfredson, M. R., & Hirschi, T. (1990). *General theory of crime*. Stanford, CA: Stanford University Press.

Handwerk, M. L., Field, C. E., & Friman, P. C. (2000). The iatrogenic effects of group intervention for antisocial youth: Premature extrapolations? *Journal of Behavioral Education, 10*, 223–238.

Hanish, L. D., Martin, C. L., Fabes, R. A., Leonard, S., & Herzog, M. (2005). Exposure to externalizing peers in early childhood: Homophily and peer contagion processes. *Journal of Abnormal Child Psychology, 33*, 267–281.

Hanneman, R. A., & Riddle, M. (2005). *Introduction to social network methods*. Riverside: University of California, Riverside. Retrieved October 2015, from http://faculty.ucr.edu/~hanneman/nettext/Introduction_to_Social_Network_Methods.pdf

Hansell, S., & Wiatrowski, M. D. (1981). Competing conceptions of delinquent peer relations. In G. F. Jensen (Ed.), *Sociology of delinquency: Current issues* (pp. 93–108). Beverly Hills, CA: Sage.

Hansen, W. B., & Graham, J. W. (1991). Preventing alcohol, marijuana, and cigarette use among adolescents: Peer pressure resistance training versus establishing conservative norms. *Preventive Medicine, 20*, 414–430.

Hartup, W. W. (1996). The company they keep: Friendships and their developmental significance. *Child Development, 67*, 1–13.

Hartup, W. W., & Stevens, N. (1997). Friendships and adaptation in the life course. *Psychological Bulletin, 121*, 355–370.

Hawkins, J. D., Catalano, R. F., & Miller, J. Y. (1992). Risk and protective factors for alcohol and other drug problems in adolescence and early adulthood: Implications for substance abuse prevention. *Psychological Bulletin, 112*, 64–105.

Hawley, P. H. (2003). Prosocial and coercive configurations of resource control in early adolescence: A case for the well-adapted Machiavellian. *Merrill Palmer Quarterly, 49*, 279–309.

Haynie, D. L. (2003). Contexts of risk? Explaining the link between girls' pubertal development and their delinquency involvement. *Social Forces, 82*, 355–397.

Haynie, D. L., & Osgood, D. W. (2005). Reconsidering peers and delinquency: How do peers matter? *Social Forces, 84*, 1109–1130.

Heaven, P. C. L., Ciarrochi, J., & Vialle, W. (2008). Self-nominated peer crowds, school achievement, and psychological adjustment in adolescents: Longitudinal analysis. *Personality and Individual Differences, 44*, 977–988.

Hecht, M. L., Marsiglia, F. F., Elek, E., Wagstaff, D. A., Kulis, S., Dustman, P., & Miller-Day, M. (2003). Culturally grounded substance use prevention: An evaluation of the Keepin' it REAL curriculum. *Prevention Science, 4*, 233–248.

Hirschi, T. (1969). *Causes of delinquency*. Berkeley: University of California Press.

Hoffman, B. R., Sussman, S., Unger, J. B., & Valente, T. W. (2006). Peer influences on adolescent cigarette smoking: A theoretical review of the literature. *Substance Use and Misuse, 41*, 103–155.

Huang, G. C., Soto, D., Fujimoto, K., & Valente, T. W. (2014). The interplay of friendship networks and social networking sites: Longitudinal analysis of selection and influence effects on adolescent smoking and alcohol use. *American Journal of Public Health, 104*, e51–e59.

Hurrelmann, K. (1990). Health promotion for adolescents: preventive and corrective strategies against problem behavior. *Journal of Adolescence, 13*, 231–250.

Jessor, R. (1987). Problem-behavior theory, psychosocial development, and adolescent problem drinking. *British Journal of Addiction, 82*, 331–342.

Jessor, R., & Jessor, S. L. (1977). *Problem behavior and psychological development: A longitudinal study of youth*. San Diego, CA: Academic Press.

Johnston, L. D., & O'Malley, P. M. (1986). Why do the nation's students use drugs and alcohol? Self-reported reasons from nine national surveys. *Journal of Drug Issues, 16*, 29–66.

Jussim, L., & Osgood, D. W. (1989). Influence and similarity among friends: An integrative model applied to incarcerated adolescents. *Social Psychology Quarterly, 52*, 98–112.

Kandel, D. B. (1978a). Homophily, selection, and socialization in adolescent friendships. *American Journal of Sociology, 84*, 427–436.

Kandel, D. B. (1978b). Similarity in real-life adolescent friendship pairs. *Journal of Personality and Social Psychology, 36*, 306–312.

Kandel, D. B. (1996). The parental and peer contexts of adolescent deviance: An algebra of interpersonal influences. *Journal of Drug Issues, 26*, 289–315.

Kandel, D. B., & Davies, M. (1991). Friendship networks, intimacy, and illicit drug use in young adulthood: A comparison of two competing theories. *Criminology, 29*, 441–469.

Kerr, M., Stattin, H. K., & Kiesner, J. (2007). Peers and problem behavior: Have we missed something? In R. C. M. E. Engels, M. Kerr, & H. Stattin (Eds.), *Friends, lovers, and groups: Key relationships in adolescence* (pp. 125–153). New York, NY: Wiley.

Kerr, M., Van Zalk, M., & Stattin, H. (2011). Psychopathic traits moderate peer influence on adolescent delinquency. *Journal of Child Psychology and Psychiatry, 53*, 826–835.

Kiesner, J., Kerr, M., & Stattin, H. (2004). "Very important persons" in adolescence: Going beyond in-school, single friendships in the study of peer homophily. *Journal of Adolescence, 27*, 545–560.

Kiesner, J., Poulin, F., & Dishion, T. J. (2010). Adolescent substance use with friends: Moderating and mediating effects of parental monitoring and peer activity contexts. *Merrill-Palmer Quarterly, 56*, 529–556.

Killeya-Jones, L. A., Nakajima, R., & Costanzo, P. R. (2007). Peer standing and substance use in early-adolescent grade-level networks: A short-term longitudinal study. *Prevention Science, 8*, 11–23.

Kindermann, T. A. (1993). Natural peer groups as contexts for individual development: The case of children's motivation in school. *Developmental Psychology, 29*, 970–977.

Kindermann, T. A. (1996). Strategies for the study of individual development within naturally-existing peer groups. *Social Development, 5*, 159–173.

Kindermann, T. A., & Gest, S. D. (2009). Assessment of the peer group: Identifying naturally occurring social networks and capturing their effects. In K. H. Rubin, W. M. Bukowski, & B. P. Laursen (Eds.), *Handbook of peer interactions, relationships, and groups* (pp. 100–117). New York, NY: Guilford Press.

Kiuru, N., Burk, W. J., Laursen, B., Salmela-Aro, K., & Nurmi, J. E. (2010). Pressure to drink but not to smoke: Disentangling selection and socialization in adolescent peer networks and peer groups. *Journal of Adolescence, 33*, 801–812.

Knecht, A. B., Burk, W. J., Weesie, J., & Steglich, C. (2011). Friendship and alcohol use in early adolescence: A multilevel social network approach. *Journal of Research on Adolescence, 21*, 475–487.

Kobus, K. (2003). Peers and adolescent smoking. *Addiction, 98*, 37–55.

Kreager, D. A., Rulison, K., & Moody, J. (2011). Delinquency and the structure of adolescent peer groupsgroups. *Criminology, 49*, 95–127.

Kuttler, A. F., La Greca, A. M., & Prinstein, M. J. (1999). Friendship qualities and social-emotional functioning of adolescents with close, cross-sex friendships. *Journal of Research on Adolescence, 9*, 339–366.

La Greca, A. M., Prinstein, M. J., & Fetter, M. D. (2001). Adolescent peer crowd affiliation: Linkages with health-risk behaviors and close friendships. *Journal of Pediatric Psychology, 26*, 131–143.

LaFontana, K. M., & Cillessen, A. H. N. (2002). Children's perceptions of popular and unpopular peers: A multimethod assessment. *Developmental Psychology, 38*, 635–647.

Lease, A., Musgrove, K. T., & Axelrod, J. L. (2002). Dimensions of social status in preadolescent peer groups: Likability, perceived popularity, and social dominance. *Social Development, 11*, 508–533.

Leatherdale, S. T., Cameron, R., Brown, K. S., & McDonald, P. W. (2005). Senior student smoking at school, student characteristics, and smoking onset among junior students: A multilevel analysis. *Preventive Medicine, 40*, 853–859.

Lerner, R. M. (1982). Children and adolescents as producers of their own development. *Developmental Review, 2*, 342–370.

Lerner, R. M., & Steinberg, L. D. (2009). *Handbook of adolescent psychology*. Hoboken, NJ: Wiley.

Leung, M. C. (1996). Social networks and self-enhancement in Chinese children: A comparison of self-reports and peer reports of group membership. *Social Development, 5*, 146–157.

Leventhal, H., & Cleary, P. D. (1980). The smoking problem: A review of the research and theory in behavioral risk modification. *Psychological Bulletin, 88*, 370–405.

Light, J. M., Greenan, C. C., Rusby, J. C., Nies, K. M., & Snijders, T. A. B. (2013). Onset to first alcohol use in early adolescence: A network diffusion model. *Journal of Research on Adolescence, 23*, 487–499.

Litt, D. M., & Stock, M. L. (2011). Adolescent alcohol-related risk cognition: The role of social norms and social networking sites. *Psychology of Addictive Behaviors, 25*, 708–713.

Lucas, K., & Lloyd, B. (1999). Starting smoking: Girls' explanations of the influence of peers. *Journal of Adolescence, 22*, 647–655.

Maassen, G. H., Van der Linden, J. L., Goossens, F., & Bokhorst, J. (2000). A ratings-based approach to two-dimensional sociometric status determination. *New Directions for Child and Adolescent Development, 2000*, 55–73.

Madden, M., Lenhart, A., Cortesi, S., Grasser, U., Duggan, M., Smith, A., & Beaton, M. (2013). Teens, social media, and privacy. Retrieved August 2014, from http://www.pewinternet.org/2013/05/21/teens-social-media-and-privacy/

Maggs, J. L. (1997). Alcohol use and binge drinking as goal-directed action during the transition to postsecondary education. In J. E. Schulenberg, J. L. Maggs, & K. Hurrelmann (Eds.), *Health risks and developmental transitions during adolescence* (pp. 345–371). New York, NY: Cambridge University Press.

Maggs, J. L., & Hurrelmann, K. (1998). Do substance use and delinquency have differential associations with adolescents' peer relations? *International Journal of Behavioral Development, 22*, 367–388.

Marshal, M. P., & Chassin, L. (2000). Peer influence on adolescent alcohol use: The moderating role of parental support and discipline. *Applied Developmental Science, 4*, 80–88.

Mathys, C., Burk, W. J., & Cillessen, A. H. N. (2013). Popularity as a moderator of peer selection and socialization of adolescent alcohol, marijuana, and tobacco use. *Journal of Research on Adolescence, 23*, 513–523.

Mayeux, L., Sandstrom, M. J., & Cillessen, A. H. N. (2008). Is being popular a risky proposition? *Journal of Research on Adolescence, 18*, 49–74.

McDougall, P., & Hymel, S. (2007). Same-gender versus cross-gender friendship conceptions: Similar or different? *Merrill-Palmer Quarterly, 53*, 347–380.

McPherson, M., Smith-Lovin, L., & Cook, J. M. (2001). Birds of a feather: Homophily in social networks. *Annual Review of Sociology, 27*, 415–444.

Mercken, L., Snijders, T. A. B., Steglich, C., & De Vries, H. (2009). Dynamics of adolescent friendship networks and smoking behavior: Social network analyses in six European countries. *Social Science and Medicine, 69*, 1506–1514.

Mercken, L., Snijders, T. A. B., Steglich, C., Vartiainen, E., & De Vries, H. (2010). Dynamics of adolescent friendship networks and smoking behavior. *Social Networks, 32*, 72–81.

Mercken, L., Steglich, C., Knibbe, R., & de Vries, H. (2012). Dynamics of friendship networks and alcohol use in early and mid-adolescence. *Journal of Studies on Alcohol and Drugs, 73*, 99–110.

Mercken, L., Steglich, C., Sinclair, P., Holliday, J., & Moore, L. (2012). A longitudinal social network analysis of peer influence, peer selection, and smoking behavior among adolescents in British schools. *Health Psychology, 31*, 450–459.

Michell, L., & Amos, A. (1997). Girls, pecking order and smoking. *Social Science and Medicine, 44*, 1861–1869.

Miech, R. A., Johnston, L. D., O'Malley, P. M., Bachman, J. G., & Schulenberg, J. E. (2015). *Monitoring the future: National survey results on drug use, 1975–2014, Vol. 1. Secondary school students*. Ann Arbor: Institute for Social Research, University of Michigan.

Moffitt, T. E. (1993). Adolescence-limited and life-course-persistent antisocial behavior: A developmental taxonomy. *Psychological Review, 100*, 674–701.

Moffitt, T. E. (2006). Life-course-persistent versus adolescence-limited antisocial behavior. In D. Cicchetti & D. J. Cohen (Eds.), *Developmental psychopathology, Vol. 3. Risk, disorder, and adaptation* (pp. 570–598). Hoboken, NJ: Wiley.

Molloy, L. E., Gest, S. D., Feinberg, M. E., & Osgood, D. W. (2014). Emergence of mixed-mixed sex friendship groups during adolescence: Developmental associations with substance use and delinquency. *Developmental Psychology, 50*(11), 2449–2461.

Molloy, L. E., Gest, S. D., & Rulison, K. L. (2011). Peer influences on academic motivation: Exploring multiple methods of assessing youths' most "influential" peer relationships. *Journal of Early Adolescence, 31*, 13–40.

Moody, J. (2001). Peer influence groups: Identifying dense clusters in large networks. *Social Networks, 23*, 261–283.

Moody, J., Brynildsen, W. D., Osgood, D. W., Feinberg, M. E., & Gest, S. D. (2011). Popularity trajectories and substance use in early adolescence. *Social Networks, 33,* 101–112.

Moreno, M. A., Briner, L. R., Williams, A., Walker, L., & Christakis, D. A. (2009). Real use or "real cool": Adolescents speak out about displayed alcohol references on social networking websites. *Journal of Adolescent Health, 45,* 420–422.

Moreno, M. A., & Kolb, J. (2012). Social networking sites and adolescent health. *Pediatric Clinics of North America, 59,* 601–612.

Mosbach, P., & Leventhal, H. (1988). Peer group identification and smoking: Implications for intervention. *Journal of Abnormal Psychology, 97,* 238–245.

Mrug, S., Gaines, J., Su, W., & Windle, M. (2010). School-level substance use: Effects on early adolescents' alcohol, tobacco, and marijuana use. *Journal of Studies on Alcohol and Drugs, 71,* 488–495.

Neighbors, C., Lee, C. M., Lewis, M. A., Fossos, N., & Larimer, M. E. (2007). Are social norms the best predictor of outcomes among heavy-drinking college students? *Journal of Studies on Alcohol and Drugs, 68,* 556–565.

Newcomb, A. F., & Bagwell, C. L. (1995). Children's friendship relations: A meta-analytic review. *Psychological Bulletin, 117,* 306–347.

Newcomb, A. F., & Bukowski, W. M. (1983). Social impact and social preference as determinants of children's peer group status. *Developmental Psychology, 19,* 856–867.

Newcomb, M. D., & Bentler, P. M. (1989). Substance use and abuse among children and teenagers. *American Psychologist, 44,* 242–248.

Nichter, M., Vuckovic, N., Quintero, G., & Ritenbaugh, C. (1997). Smoking experimentation and initiation among adolescent girls: Qualitative and quantitative findings. *Tobacco Control, 6,* 285–295.

Nurmi, J. E. (1993). Adolescent development in an age-graded context: The role of personal beliefs, goals, and strategies in the tackling of developmental tasks and standards. *International Journal of Behavioral Development, 16,* 169–189.

Osgood, D. W., Anderson, A. L., & Shaffer, J. N. (2005). Unstructured leisure in the after-school hours. In J. L. Mahoney, R. W. Larson, & J. S. Eccles (Eds.), *Organized activities as contexts of development: Extracurricular activities, after school and community programs* (pp. 45–64). Mahwah, NJ: Erlbaum.

Osgood, D. W., Feinberg, M. E., Gest, S. D., Moody, J., Ragan, D. T., Spoth, R., . . . Redmond, C. (2013). Effects of PROSPER on the influence potential of prosocial versus antisocial youth in adolescent friendship networks. *Journal of Adolescent Health, 53,* 174–179.

Osgood, D. W., Feinberg, M. E., Wallace, L. N., & Moody, J. (2014). Friendship group position and substance use. *Addictive Behaviors, 39,* 923–933.

Osgood, D. W., Johnston, L. D., O'Malley, P. M., & Bachman, J. G. (1988). The generality of deviance in late adolescence and early adulthood. *American Sociological Review, 53,* 81–93.

Osgood, D. W., Ragan, D. T., Wallace, L., Gest, S. D., Feinberg, M. E., & Moody, J. (2013). Peers and the emergence of alcohol use: Influence and selection processes in adolescent friendship networks. *Journal of Research on Adolescence, 23,* 500–512.

Osgood, D. W., Wilson, J. K., O'Malley, P. M., Bachman, J. G., & Johnston, L. D. (1996). Routine activities and individual deviant behavior. *American Sociological Review, 61,* 635–655.

Parkhurst, J. T., & Hopmeyer, A. (1998). Sociometric popularity and peer-perceived popularity: Two distinct dimensions of peer status. *Journal of Early Adolescence, 18,* 125–144.

Patrick, M. E., & Schulenberg, J. E. (2011). How trajectories of reasons for alcohol use relate to trajectories of binge drinking: National panel data spanning late adolescence to early adulthood. *Developmental Psychology, 47*(2), 311–317.

Patrick, M. E., Schulenberg, J. E., Maggs, J. L., & Maslowsky, J. (2014). Substance use and peers during adolescence and the transition to adulthood: Selection, socialization, and development. In K. Sher (Ed.), *Oxford handbook of substance use disorders.* New York, NY: Oxford University Press.

Patrick, M. E., Schulenberg, J. E., O'Malley, P. M., Johnston, L. D., & Bachman, J. G. (2011). Adolescents' reported reasons for alcohol and marijuana use as predictors of substance use and problems in adulthood. *Journal of Studies on Alcohol and Drugs, 72,* 106–116.

Patrick, M. E., Schulenberg, J. E., O'Malley, P. M., Maggs, J. L., Kloska, D. D., Johnston, L. D., & Bachman, J. G. (2011). Age-related changes in reasons for using alcohol and marijuana from ages 18 to 30 in a national sample. *Psychology of Addictive Behaviors, 25,* 330–339.

Patrick, M. E., Wray-Lake, L., Finlay, A. K., & Maggs, J. L. (2010). The long arm of expectancies: Adolescent alcohol expectancies predict adult alcohol use. *Alcohol and Alcoholism, 45,* 17–24.

Patterson, G. R., DeBaryshe, B. D., & Ramsey, E. (1989). A developmental perspective on antisocial behavior. *American Psychologist, 44,* 329–335.

Patterson, G. R., Dishion, T. J., & Yoerger, K. (2000). Adolescent growth in new forms of problem behavior: Macro- and micro-peer dynamics. *Prevention Science, 1,* 3–13.

Patterson, G. R., & Yoerger, K. (2002). A developmental model for early- and late-onset delinquency. In J. B. Reid, G. R. Patterson, & J. Snyder (Eds.), *Antisocial behavior in children and adolescents: A developmental analysis and model for intervention* (pp. 147–172). Washington, DC: American Psychological Association.

Pearson, M., Steglich, C., & Snijders, T. A. B. (2006). Homophily and assimilation among sport-active adolescent substance users. *Connections, 27,* 51–67.

Perkins, H. W., Haines, M. P., & Rice, R. (2005). Misperceiving the college drinking norm and related problems: A nationwide study of exposure to prevention information, perceived norms and student alcohol misuse. *Journal of Studies on Alcohol, 66,* 470–478.

Petraitis, J., Flay, B. R., & Miller, T. Q. (1995). Reviewing theories of adolescent substance use: Organizing pieces in the puzzle. *Psychological Bulletin, 117,* 67–86.

Poulin, F., Denault, A-S., & Pedersen, S. (2011). Longitudinal associations between other-othersex friendships and substance use in adolescence. *Journal of Research on Adolescence, 21,* 776–788.

Poulin, F., & Pedersen, S. (2007). Developmental changes in gender composition of friendship networks in adolescent girls and boys. *Developmental Psychology, 43,* 1484–1496.

Prinstein, M. J., & La Greca, A. M. (2002). Peer crowd affiliation and internalizing distress in childhood and adolescence: A longitudinal follow-followback study. *Journal of Research on Adolescence, 12,* 325–351.

Ragan, D. T., Osgood, D. W., & Feinberg, M. E. (2014). Friends as a bridge to parental influence: Implications for adolescent alcohol use. *Social Forces, 92,* 1061–1085.

Reed, M. D., & Rountree, P. W. (1997). Peer pressure and adolescent substance use. *Journal of Quantitative Criminology*, *13*, 143–180.

Richards, W. D. (1995). *NEGOPY 4.30 manual and user's guide.* Burnaby, BC: School of Communication, Simon Fraser University.

Rodkin, P. C., Farmer, T. W., Pearl, R., & Van Acker, R. (2000). Heterogeneity of popular boys: Antisocial and prosocial configurations. *Developmental Psychology, 36*, 14–24.

Rogers, E. M. (2003). *Diffusion of innovations.* New York, NY: Free Press.

Rubin, K. H., Bukowski, W., & Parker, J. G. (2006). Peer interactions, relationships, and groups. In W. Damon, R. M. Lerner, & N. Eisenberg (Eds.), *Handbook of child psychology, Vol. 3. Social, emotional, and personality development* (6th ed., pp. 571–645). New York, NY: Wiley.

Rulison, K. L., Gest, S. D., Loken, E., & Welsh, J. A. (2010). Rejection, feeling bad, and being hurt: Using multilevel modeling to clarify the link between peer group aggression and adjustment. *Journal of Adolescence, 33*, 787–800.

Rulison, K. L., Gest, S. D., & Osgood, D. W. (2014). Adolescent peer networks and the potential for the diffusion of intervention effects. *Prevention Science, 16(1), 133–144.*

Scarr, S., & McCartney, K. (1983). How people make their own environments: A theory of genotype→ environment effects. *Child Development, 54*(2), 424–435.

Schaefer, D. R., Haas, S. A., & Bishop, N. J. (2012). A dynamic model of US adolescents' smoking and friendship networks. *American Journal of Public Health, 102*, e12–e18.

Schulenberg, J. E., & Maggs, J. L. (2002). A developmental perspective on alcohol use and heavy drinking during adolescence and the transition to young adulthood. *Journal of Studies on Alcohol, 14*, 54–70.

Schulenberg, J. E., Maggs, J. L., Dielman, T. E., Leech, S. L., Kloska, D. D., Shope, J. T., & Laetz, V. B. (1999). On peer influences to get drunk: A panel study of young adolescents. *Merrill-Palmer Quarterly, 45*, 108–142.

Scott, J. (2000). *Social network analysis: A handbook.* Thousand Oaks, CA: Sage.

Semmer, N., Dwyer, J., Lippert, P., Fuchs, R., Cleary, P., & Schindler, A. (1987). Adolescent smoking from a functional perspective: The Berlin-Bremen Study. *European Journal of Psychology of Education, 2*, 387–401.

Sharabany, R., Gershoni, R., & Hofman, J. E. (1981). Girlfriend, boyfriend: Age and sex differences in intimate friendship. *Developmental Psychology, 17*, 800–808.

Sher, K. J., Wood, M. D., Wood, P. K., & Raskin, G. (1996). Alcohol outcome expectancies and alcohol use: A latent variable cross-lagged panel study. *Journal of Abnormal Psychology, 105*, 561.

Silbereisen, R. K., & Noack, P. (1988). On the constructive role of problem behavior in adolescence. In N. Bolger, A. Caspi, G. Downey, & M. Moorehouse (Eds.), *Persons in context: Developmental processes* (pp. 152–180). New York, NY: Cambridge University Press.

Simons-Morton, B. G. (2002). Prospective analysis of peer and parent influences on smoking initiation among early adolescents. *Prevention Science, 3*, 275–283.

Simons-Morton, B., Chen, R., Abroms, L., & Haynie, D. L. (2004). Latent growth curve analyses of peer and parent influences on smoking progression among early adolescents. *Health Psychology, 23*, 612.

Snijders, T. A. B. (1996). Stochastic actor-oriented dynamic network analysis. *Journal of Mathematical Sociology, 21*, 149–172.

Snijders, T. A. B., Steglich, C., & Schweinberger, M. (2007). Modeling the co-evolution of networks and behavior. In K. van Montfort, H. Oud, & A. Satorra (Eds.), *Longitudinal models in the behavioral and related sciences* (pp. 41–71). Mahwah, NJ: Erlbaum.

Snyder, J. (2002). Reinforcement and coercion mechanisms in the development of antisocial behavior: Peer relationships. In J. B. Reid, G. R. Patterson, & J. Snyder (Eds.), *Antisocial behavior in children and adolescents: A developmental analysis and model for intervention* (pp. 101–122). Washington, DC: American Psychological Association.

Steglich, C., Snijders, T. A. B., & Pearson, M. (2010). Dynamic networks and behavior: Separating selection from influence. *Sociological Methodology, 40*, 329–393.

Steglich, C., Snijders, T. A. B., & West, P. (2006). Applying SIENA: An illustrative analysis of the coevolution of adolescents' friendship networks, taste in music, and alcohol consumption. *Methodology, 2*, 48–56.

Steinberg, L., Fletcher, A., & Darling, N. (1994). Parental monitoring and peer influences on adolescent substance use. *Pediatrics, 93*, 1060–1064.

Steinberg, L., & Monahan, K. C. (2007). Age differences in resistance to peer influence. *Developmental Psychology, 43*, 1531.

Steinberg, L., & Silverberg, S. B. (1986). The vicissitudes of autonomy in early adolescence. *Child Development, 57*, 841–851.

Stormshak, E. A., Comeau, C. A., & Shepard, S. A. (2004). The relative contribution of sibling deviance and peer deviance in the prediction of substance use across middle childhood. *Journal of Abnormal Child Psychology, 32*, 635–649.

Strasburger, V. C., Jordan, A. B., & Donnerstein, E. (2010). Health effects of media on children and adolescents. *Pediatrics, 125*, 756–767.

Strayer, F. F., & Santos, A. (1996). Affiliative structures in preschool peer groups. *Social Development, 5*, 117–130.

Sullivan, H. S. (1953). *The interpersonal theory of psychiatry.* Oxford, UK: Norton.

Sussman, S., Dent, C. W., McAdams, L. A., Stacy, A. W., Burton, D., & Flay, B. R. (1994). Group self-identification and adolescent cigarette smoking: A 1-year prospective study. *Journal of Abnormal Psychology, 103*, 576–580.

Sussman, S., Dent, C. W., Mestel-Rauch, J., Johnson, C. A., Hansen, W. B., & Flay, B. R. (1988). Adolescent nonsmokers, triers, and regular smokers' estimates of cigarette smoking prevalence: When do overestimations occur and by whom? *Journal of Applied Social Psychology, 18*, 537–551.

Sussman, S., Pokhrel, P., Ashmore, R. D., & Brown, B. B. (2007). Adolescent peer group identification and characteristics: A review of the literature. *Addictive Behaviors, 32*, 1602–1627.

Sussman, S., Unger, J. B., & Dent, C. W. (2004). Peer group self-identification among alternative high school youth: A predictor of their psychosocial functioning five years later. *International Journal of Clinical and Health Psychology, 4*, 9–25.

Sutherland, E. H. (1947). *Principles of criminology* (4th ed.). Chicago, IL: J. B. Lippincott.

Thornberry, T. P. (1987). Toward an interactional theory of delinquency. *Criminology, 25*, 863–891.

Thornberry, T. P., & Krohn, M. D. (1997). Peers, drug use, and delinquency. In D. M. Stoff (Ed.), *Handbook of antisocial behavior* (Vol. *22*, pp. 218–233). New York, NY: Wiley.

Thurlow, C. (2001). The usual suspects? A comparative investigation of crowds and social-type labelling among young British teenagers. *Journal of Youth Studies, 4*, 319–334.

Tobler, N. S., Roona, M. R., Ochshorn, P., Marshall, D. G., Streke, A. V., & Stackpole, K. M. (2000). School-based adolescent drug prevention programs: 1998 meta-analysis. *Journal of Primary Prevention, 20*, 275–336.

Urberg, K. A. (1992). Locus of peer influence: Social crowd and best friend. *Journal of Youth and Adolescence, 21*, 439–450.

Urberg, K. A., Degirmencioglu, S. M., & Pilgrim, C. (1997). Close friend and group influence on adolescent cigarette smoking and alcohol use. *Developmental Psychology, 33*, 834–844.

Urberg, K. A., Degirmencioglu, S. M., Tolson, J. M., & Halliday Scher, K. (1995). The structure of adolescent peer networks. *Developmental Psychology, 31*, 540–547.

Urberg, K. A., Degirmencioglu, S. M., Tolson, J. M., & Halliday-Scher, K. (2000). Adolescent social crowds: Measurement and relationship to friendships. *Journal of Adolescent Research, 15*, 427–445.

Urberg, K. A., Shyu, S. J., & Liang, J. (1990). Peer influence in adolescent cigarette smoking. *Addictive Behaviors, 15*, 247–255.

Valente, T. W. (1995). *Network models of the diffusion of innovations.* Cresskill, NJ: Hampton Press.

Valente, T. W. (2010). *Social networks and health: Models, methods, and applications.* New York, NY: Oxford University Press.

Valente, T. W., Gallaher, P., & Mouttapa, M. (2004). Using social networks to understand and prevent substance use: A transdisciplinary perspective. *Substance Use and Misuse, 39*, 10–12.

Valente, T. W., Unger, J. B., & Johnson, C. A. (2005). Do popular students smoke? The association between popularity and smoking among middle school students. *Journal of Adolescent Health, 37*, 323–329.

Veenstra, R., Dijkstra, J. K., Steglich, C., & Van Zalk, M. (2013). Network-behavior dynamics. *Journal of Research on Adolescence, 23*, 399–412.

Verbrugge, L. M. (1977). The structure of adult friendship choices. *Social Forces, 56*, 576–597.

Verkooijen, K. T., De Vries, N. K., & Nielsen, G. A. (2007). Youth crowds and substance use: The impact of perceived group norm and multiple group identification. *Psychology of Addictive Behaviors, 21*, 55–61.

Vitaro, F., Brendgen, M., Pagani, L., Tremblay, R. E., & McDuff, P. (1999). Disruptive behavior, peer association, and conduct disorder: Testing the developmental links through early intervention. *Development and Psychopathology, 11*, 287–304.

Wasserman, S., & Faust, K. (1994). and *Social network analysis: Methods and applications.* New York, NY: Cambridge University Press.

Windle, M., Spear, L. P., Fuligni, A. J., Angold, A., Brown, J. D., Pine, D., . . . Dahl, R. E. (2008). Transitions into underage and problem drinking: Developmental processes and mechanisms between 10 and 15 years of age. *Pediatrics, 121*(Suppl. 4), S273–S289.

Zamboanga, B. L., Horton, N. J., Leitkowski, L. K., & Wang, S. C. (2006). Do good things come to those who drink? A longitudinal investigation of drinking expectancies and hazardous alcohol use in female college athletes. *Journal of Adolescent Health, 39*, 229–236.

Development of Sexual Relationships and Substance Use

Sonya B. Norman, Erin Harrop, Kendall C. Wilkins, Eric R. Pedersen, Ursula S. Myers, Aimee Chabot, *and* Carie Rodgers

Abstract

Sexual relationship development in adolescence can be affected by substance use. Substance use and risky sexual behavior frequently co-occur, and their co-occurrence is associated with short- and long-term negative consequences. The relationship appears to be bidirectional in nature, with substance use acting as a risk factor for risky sexual behavior and risky sexual behavior acting as a risk factor for substance use. Proposed mechanisms to explain this relationship include personality traits such as impulsivity or sensation-seeking tendencies, expectancies about how substances will affect sexual experiences, and effects of media messages that normalize substance use and sexual behavior for adolescents. Peer influence, family factors, and a constellation of problem behaviors that reinforce one another can also play a role. However, there are no integrative models to explain the relationship between substance use and sexual relationship development.

Key Words: substance use, sexual relationships, adolescence, risky behaviors, sexual relationship development

Substance use (i.e., alcohol and/or drug use) can play a pivotal role in the development of adolescent sexual relationships, particularly with regard to engagement in risky sexual behaviors such as early age of first intercourse, high number of sexual partners, inconsistent use of condoms, and contraction of sexually transmitted infections (STIs) (Schofield, Bierman, Heinrichs, & Nix, 2008; Wu, Witkiewitz, McMahon, & Dodge, 2010). The goal of this chapter is to synthesize knowledge of the relationship between substance use and the development of sexual relationships in adolescence in order to inform recommendations for future research. This relationship is examined from multiple angles. We first review the typical course of sexual relationship development among US adolescents, taking into account differences by gender, ethnicity, and socioeconomic status (SES). Next, we review the ways by which substance use can interact with and alter the typical course of development. We then move

to mechanisms of action that have been proposed to underlie the relationship between substance use and sexual risk behaviors in adolescence, specifically disinhibition, sex-related alcohol expectancies, and media exposure. We then turn attention to adolescent populations that are at particularly high risk for engaging in sexually risky behavior. Specifically, we discuss adolescents who experience early-onset puberty, youth who experienced childhood violence and/or fall victim to sexual aggression during adolescence, and adolescents who perpetrate sexual aggression. Finally, we attempt to integrate this large body of literature to inform recommendations for future research.

Typical Course of Sexual Relationship Development Among US Adolescents

The common course of most adolescents' romantic histories begin with a first kiss; later, a first date; and then, first sexual intercourse (Chandra,

2011; Regan, Durvasula, Howell, Ureno, & Rea, 2004). The average age of first kiss as reported by university students is approximately 15 years old, and first dates most often follow within a year. Several recent studies have found that the average age of American youth at first sexual intercourse is around 17 years old, and approximately 83% report using contraception at first intercourse (Chandra, 2011; Regan et al., 2004; Tapert, Aarons, Sedlar, & Brown, 2001). Most young adults report that their first serious relationships occurred approximately 1 year after first sex, at an average age of 18. By late adolescence (age 18–19), 72% report having experienced sexual contact with another person (Chandra, 2011).

The typical onset and course of sexual activity among adolescents can vary based on family/social environment, SES, and gender ethnic background. For example, adolescents living with both biological or adoptive (including same-sex) parents are less likely to endorse having experienced sexual intercourse, and sexually active youth living with both parents report less frequent sexual intercourse than those within other family structures (such as single parent, stepparent, or no parents; Martinez, Copen, & Abma, 2011; Patterson & Wainright, 2007). In addition, lower levels of parental education, lower income, lower socioeconomic status (SES), and having older friends are associated with earlier onset of sexual initiation and engagement in more high-risk sex behaviors (Little & Rankin, 2001; Manlove, Ryan, & Franzetta, 2007; Martinez et al., 2011).

In regard to gender differences, women reported that they first fell in love just prior to their first time having sex (age 17.58 "fell in love" vs. 17.61 first intercourse), whereas men reported that they had experienced sex before being in love (Regan et al., 2004). Women report slightly older average ages than men for sexual experiences, except serious relationships (Regan et al., 2004). Levels and type of sexual contact also appear to vary by gender. For instance, in the longitudinal National Survey of Family Growth (2009), males reported similar levels of opposite-sex sexual contact as females at age 15(34% vs. 32%), however, males reported higher levels by age 17(61% vs. 48%; Chandra et al., 2011). Female adolescents (aged 15–19) were more than four times as likely to endorse same-sex sexual experience than their male counterparts (11% vs. 2.5%). Of those females who endorsed same-sex sexual contact, more than 80% (9% of the total sample) also endorsed opposite-sex sexual contact,

as compared to 1.6% total males endorsing similar bisexual behaviors.

Differences by ethnicity have also been reported. For example, Caucasian/White students report the youngest initiation of romantic behaviors (age 14.5 at first kiss and first date). African American students are more likely to engage in sexual intercourse during high school and have the youngest comparative age at first sexual intercourse (around age 16; Regan et al., 2004). African American males are more than three times as likely to have multiple sex partners (39%) and more than five times to have had sex before age 13 (24%) than Caucasian/White males (Basile et al., 2011). Asian American students report an average age of first kiss 3 years later than their Caucasian/White classmates, as well as older average ages for all romantic firsts (except for falling in love) and significantly lower rates of romantic experiences. Asian American females are also the least likely to have multiple sex partners (2.8%) or sex before age 13 (2%).

Substance Use and Sexual Relationships in Adolescents
Substance Use and Risky Sexual Behavior

Substance use is often a pivotal component in adolescent risky sexual behavior, most often defined by factors such as early age of first intercourse, high number of sexual partners, inconsistent use of condoms, and contraction of sexually transmitted infections (STIs; Schofield et al., 2008; Wu et al., 2010). In a longitudinal study, participants in treatment for substance abuse reported initiating sexual intercourse more than 2 years earlier than average (approximately 13–14 years old; Tapert et al., 2001). This study also found that participants with a history of substance use engage in sex more frequently and casually, use condoms less frequently, and report much higher rates of pregnancy than a comparison group with no history of substance use. Similarly, Guo and colleagues (2005) found that adolescent binge drinkers and marijuana users used condoms less frequently compared to adolescent cigarette smokers and nonusers.

Several studies have found that substance use, especially early in adolescence, precedes early sexual debut and influences subsequent high-risk sex behaviors (Biglan, Brennan, Foster, & Holder, 2005; Caminis, Henrich, Ruchkin, Schwab-Stone, & Martin, 2007; French & Dishion, 2003; Santelli et al., 2004). A study on adolescents who reported never having had a sexual encounter found that those using at least one substance (alcohol, tobacco, or marijuana) were almost three times as likely than nonusers to have become sexually active 9 months later (Guo et al., 2005). The Youth Risk Behavior Survey (CDC, 2010) found that nearly a quarter (24.7%) of sexually active ninth graders report drinking alcohol or using drugs before last sexual intercourse, and this trend remained consistent for sexually active males throughout high school (CDC, 2010). An even larger proportion (29%) of 15- to 17-year-olds report drinking or drug use has influenced their decisions about sex (Kaiser Family Foundation, 2004).

While early substance use is fairly consistently associated with early and risky sex in adolescents, these relationships can be complex and vary in strength based on different mediating factors, including gender, development, and ethnicity. For example, in the National Survey of Adolescents and Young Adults (Hoff, Greene, & Davis, 2003), sexually active adolescents reported feeling significantly greater pressure to use alcohol and drugs than their non–sexually active counterparts, with males reporting the strongest feelings of pressure. Over a quarter of males report that mixing sex and substance use is "not a big deal" (Kaiser Family Foundation, 2004). Additionally, girls who experience early pubertal development are at greater risk for substance abuse and risky sexual behavior, though these negative effects are mostly time limited (see later section on early puberty; Copeland et al., 2010; Guo et al., 2005). Related to ethnicity, Caucasian males are the most likely to report having used alcohol or drugs prior to sexual intercourse (28%), while their Asian American peers are the least likely (12.6%; CDC, 2010).

Dating Relationships Influence Substance Use

Having a steady, romantic relationship has been shown to protect against heavy drinking behavior in both adolescent and young adult samples. For example, young adults in a relationship reported drinking about three fewer drinks per week than those actively dating multiple people (Pedersen, Lee, Larimer, & Neighbors, 2009). Having a steady relationship also appeared to protect recently graduated high school male and females students from heavy drinking behaviors compared to single individuals (Fleming, White, & Catalano, 2010). Upperclassmen women in steady relationships were less likely to use substances than young college students in non-committal relationships (Roberts & Kennedy,

2006). Although steady relationships may protect against heavy drinking and other substance use for some adolescents, patterns of alcohol use among adolescents in romantic relationships may also be influenced by the drinking behaviors of their partner and their partner's friends (Kreager & Haynie, 2011; Mushquash et al., 2013). Specifically, youths' drinking behavior may be influenced positively if the partner and his or her friends are light drinkers, while heavier drinking may influence youth to match their partner's/partners' friends higher use patterns.

Actively dating versus being in a monogamous romantic relationship may be a particular risk factor for increased drinking as adolescents and young adults seek to establish steady or casual dating relationships. Drinking while dating appears to be particularly risky in the early stages of relationships (Clapp & Shillington, 2001; Mongeau & Johnson, 1995), and high school students actively dating multiple partners were at greater risk for alcohol use increases over time than those not actively dating (Davies & Windle, 2000). Higher rates of alcohol use may be due to a variety of factors. For instance, alcohol may be used as a social lubricant with which to ease anxieties while on a date. Additionally, young people who are actively seeking partners may have greater exposure to situations involving drinking (e.g., parties) and thus have more access to alcohol. Attending parties may help individuals find partners; adolescents who engaged in drinking were more likely to report steady partners 3 years later (Engels & Knibbe, 2000). These complicated associations between sexual relationships and substance use highlight the need to understand mechanisms that may underlie these relationships.

Mechanisms Underlying Substance Use and Sexually Risky Behavior in Adolescence

Understanding the mechanisms that underlie the relationship between substance use and sexual relationship development is important given the strong evidence that substance use poses a risk for engagement in unsafe sexual behaviors among adolescents. This understanding is necessary to inform prevention and intervention efforts to reduce the risk of substance use and related unsafe sexual practices. Proposed mechanisms that have received a considerable amount of attention by researchers are disinhibition, sex-related alcohol expectancies, and exposure to mass media. The scientific literature regarding each of these is reviewed next.

Disinhibition

Disinhibition is a personality dimension characterized by a deficit in the ability to control response to novel and/or potentially rewarding stimuli (Sher & Trull, 1994; Windle & Windle, 1996). Disinhibition includes both impulsivity and sensation seeking. Impulsivity, defined as a trait or disposition to initiate behavior without forethought as to the consequences (Zuckerman, 1991), has been linked to poor attention, bad decisions, and weak inhibitory control (Crews & Boettiger, 2009). Complementary to impulsivity, sensation seeking is seeking assorted, new, and complex feelings and encounters, and being willingness to take risks to have such encounters (Zuckerman, 1994). As impulsivity and sensation seeking are related, some researchers have chosen to combine them into one construct (Zuckerman, 1996), whereas others see them as two separate constructs (Schalling, 1978). Regardless, impulsivity and sensation seeking are both important constructs to probe in the relationship between alcohol use and sexual behavior in adolescents.

DISINHIBITION AND THE ADOLESCENT BRAIN

Adolescence is a time when the brain is still maturing in areas associated with impulsivity and decision making, namely the frontal lobes and associated executive functional regions (Blakemore & Choudhury, 2006). With respect to neurobiological changes, the frontal lobes and the associated executive functions that are related to social/emotion behavior undergo dramatic changes that continue until early adulthood (Yurgelun-Todd, 2007). Likely because of this ongoing maturation, impulsivity generally peaks during adolescence (Monti et al., 2005; Tapert & Schweinsburg, 2005). Research also suggests that adolescents may be more sensitive to the effects of alcohol, including social disinhibition (Varlinskaya & Spear, 2006). The fact that areas of the brain related to impulsive behavior and/or impaired judgment are still maturing during adolescence and that adolescents are especially sensitive to the effects of alcohol may help to explain why adolescents exhibit less inhibition with regard to sexual cues while under the influence of alcohol.

DISINHIBITION AND SUBSTANCE USE

Research with adolescent and young adult samples shows that disinhibition is associated with both alcohol abuse and alcohol dependence (see review by Dick et al., 2010). For example, different studies of individuals meeting *DSM-IV* alcohol dependence criteria have demonstrated high impulsivity scores on laboratory tasks in college-age participants (Kollins, 2003) and on self-report measures in both college-age and adolescent participants (Baker & Yardley, 2002; Trull, Waudby, & Sher, 2004). Multiple studies have shown that individuals with disinhibited traits have a higher risk for the development of future alcohol dependence. In one study, Sher et al. (2000) found that among a college-aged sample disinhibited traits prospectively predicted future alcohol use disorders.

Studies examining meditating factors have documented a complex relationship between disinhibition and alcohol use in college samples (Magid, MacLean, & Colder, 2007; Simons, Gaher, Correia, Hansen, & Christopher, 2005). One such study reported that sensation seeking had a direct effect on alcohol use, while impulsivity did not (Magid et al., 2007). This same study reported that the relationship between impulsivity and alcohol-related problems was partially mediated by reported drinking to cope with stressful situations, whereby individuals with high impulsivity had high levels of drinking to cope, which in turn were associated with high levels of alcohol-related problems.

DISINHIBITION AND SEXUAL DECISION MAKING

High impulsivity has been associated with high levels of sexually risky behavior (Breakwell, 1996; Kahn, Kaplowitz, Goodman, & Emans, 2002). Breakwell (1996) reported that higher levels of impulsivity in females were associated with an earlier age of first sexual intercourse and a higher number of sexual partners. Additionally, higher levels of impulsivity have been associated with STIs, nonuse of condoms, and number of sexual partners (Brown, DiClemente, & Park, 1992; Kahn et al., 2002). A number of studies have examined the role of either sensation seeking or impulsivity in risky sexual behavior among adolescents, with only a small number of studies incorporating both aspects of disinhibition simultaneously. One study that incorporated both aspects of disinhibition identified that sensation seeking and impulsivity had a synergistic effect on risky sexual behavior, in which adolescents that possessed either characteristic were more likely to take sexual health risks, and adolescents that possessed both were the most likely to engage in risky sex (Donohew et al., 2000).

Frequent co-occurrence of impulsivity, substance use, and risky sexual behavior has been well documented in literature on adults (McCoul & Haslam, 2001). As noted earlier, a number of studies have also shown a link between high impulsivity and both risky sexual behaviors in youth (e.g., younger first sexual intercourse, higher number of sexual partners, less use of condoms/contraception, early sexually transmitted infections) and alcohol/drug use (e.g., earlier use; Brown et al., 1992; Kahn et al., 2002). Studies have also examined all three variables together (i.e., substance use, sexual behavior, disinhibition). For instance, Wu et al., (2010) conducted a longitudinal study beginning in fifth grade and reported that higher conduct/impulsivity problems and more alcohol problems (i.e., binge drinking) were both associated with higher frequency of early sexual intercourse, infrequent condom use, odds of ever contracting an STI, and receiving money for sexual services. Bailey, Gao, and Clark (2006) examined the connection between sensation seeking, alcohol, and condom use in adolescents and reported that while there was not a significant association among alcohol use and condom use, there was a significant association between higher levels of sensation-seeking behavior and nonuse of condoms. Additionally, adolescents reporting alcohol use and higher levels of impulsivity were more likely to have casual sexual partners (Bailey et al., 2006). Another study examining the role of impulsivity and alcohol and/or marijuana use in adolescents showed that as levels of impulsivity increased, levels of alcohol/marijuana use and unprotected sexual behaviors under the influence also increased (Dévieux et al., 2002).

Although frequently co-occurring with one another, the relationships between disinhibition, substance use, and sexual decision making are complex with both mediating and moderating factors. For instance, a number of studies have reported that the relationship between risky sexual behavior and substance use in adolescents may be moderated by impulsivity (Bryan, Ray, & Cooper, 2007; Cooper, Wood, Orcutt, & Albino, 2003; Justus, Finn, & Steinmetz, 2000; Kalichman & Cain, 2004; Kalichman, Cain, Zweben, & Swain, 2003; Kalichman, Heckman, & Kelly, 1996). For example, Cooper et al. (2003) showed that sensation seeking partially moderated the relationship between risky sexual behavior and alcohol use, but only for Caucasian (and not African American)

adolescents in their sample. A smaller number of studies have examined meditational models, in which disinhibited personality traits predicted drinking motives, which then predicted alcohol use and risky sexual behavior. Looking solely at sensation seeking, Cooper, Frone, Russell, and Mudar (1995) reported that alcohol use and enhancement motives for drinking fully mediated the relationship between sensation-seeking and alcohol-related problems, including risky sexual behavior. Taken together, these findings indicate that disinhibition at least partially underlies both alcohol use and sexual behavior in adolescence.

The social lubricating effect of alcohol may interact with impulsivity to even further increase the likelihood of sexually risky behavior. As noted previously, alcohol can act as a social lubricant, a tool that helps ease anxiety and nervousness in social interactions, which may result in individuals engaging in behaviors they would not otherwise do (Monahan & Lannutti, 2000). In adults, social lubrication has been associated with high-risk sexual behavior, lower condom use, and sexual aggression (Griffin, Umstattd, & Usdan, 2010). Few studies have examined alcohol's social lubricating effects in adolescents. One study with criminally involved adolescents (adolescents on probation or going through criminal proceedings) identified latent classes of adolescents in regard to alcohol use and risky sexual behavior. Three classes emerged: for 25% of the sample, alcohol use did not predict risky sex outcomes; for 38%, alcohol use negatively predicted condom use and positively predicted frequency of intercourse; and for the rest of the sample, alcohol use negatively predicted condom use but not frequency of intercourse. These classes were then distinguished on the basis of five covariates previously associated with alcohol use, risky sexual behavior, or the relationship between the two: self-esteem, gender, age, relationship status, and impulsivity/sensation seeking. The classes did not differ based on impulsivity/sensation-seeking characteristics. High self-esteem, being female, being older, and being in a relationship predicted membership in the class with no observed relationship between alcohol use and risky sexual behavior (Schmiege, Levin, & Bryan, 2009). The authors posited that for this 25% of adolescents, alcohol did not have a social lubricating effect. This study suggests that alcohol may provide "social lubrication" for some but not all adolescents in regard to sexual behavior.

The relationship between alcohol and impulsivity appears to be moderated by gender, as this relationship affects male and female adolescent sexuality differently. Cooper and Orcutt (1997) reported that adolescent male alcohol consumption on a first date was associated with increased likelihood of sexual contact, but adolescent female alcohol consumption was not. The authors posited that males responded more strongly to the instigating cues of desire when alcohol lowered their inhibition (increasing impulsivity), while females did not view these instigating cues as strongly as males, making the disinhibitory effects of alcohol less salient.

Another correlate of the interaction of alcohol use and impulsivity is sexual aggression. Adolescents who had perpetrated sexual aggression reported higher impulsivity and greater alcohol consumption than adolescents who had not perpetrated sexually aggressive acts (Young, King, Abbey, & Boyd, 2009).

DISINHIBITION: SUMMARY AND RECOMMENDATIONS

Disinhibition and alcohol use appear to have a bidirectional relationship, with adolescents who are more disinhibited reporting earlier alcohol initiation, and adolescents with alcohol histories endorsing impulsive/sensation-seeking behavior, in particular sexual behavior. Adolescents with greater alcohol use and higher impulsivity have been shown to have lower rates of condom use, with potential for negative consequences such as unwanted pregnancies, STIs, and HIV/AIDS. This relationship between alcohol use and impulsivity on adolescent sexual behavior varies according to gender.

Studies that gather genetic and neuroimaging data in addition to self-report and behavioral observation data can further understanding of the neurobiological mechanisms that drive disinhibited behavior. In addition, many studies have used adult and college student samples. However, studies with adolescents are important given the brain development that occurs in regions associated with disinhibition during this unique period of development. Information is needed about potential long-term consequences, such as psychopathology, of disinhibition and alcohol use in adolescence. The relationships among alcohol use, disinhibition, and sexual relationships with adolescents are complex, with a number of factors still needing further elucidation.

Sex-Related Expectancies, Substance Use, and Sexual Relationships in Adolescence

Adolescents may have expectations or beliefs that alcohol will enhance or disinhibit sexual activity that can impact decision making around alcohol use and sexual behavior (Dermen & Cooper, 1994a; Fromme, Stroot, & Kaplan, 1993). These "sex-related alcohol expectancies" have been measured in large samples of adolescents and college students and typically assess three domains: enhancement, sexual risk taking, and disinhibition. Enhancement refers to beliefs that using alcohol will enhance sex by increasing enjoyment, boosting confidence, and reducing anxiety related to performance (e.g., "I enjoy sex more," "I am a better lover," "I am less nervous about sex"). Sexual risk taking refers to the belief that alcohol may impair decisions around prevention of unplanned pregnancy and sexually transmitted infections (e.g., "I am less likely to (ask a partner to) use a condom during sex," "I am less likely to use birth control"). Disinhibition refers to increased sexual responding and less restraint over sexual behaviors (e.g., "I am more likely to do sexual things that I wouldn't do when sober," "I am more likely to have sex on a first date"). Adolescents who believe alcohol negatively impacts sexual behavior (e.g., sexual risk taking such as not wearing a condom) may drink less than those who believe alcohol acts positively to enhance and disinhibit sex (Dermen & Cooper, 1994b). However, risky sex (e.g., not using a condom with a casual partner) was predicted by alcohol use among those with higher sex-related alcohol expectancies around risk taking during sex (e.g., alcohol makes it less likely to use a condom; Derman, Cooper, & Acocha, 1998).

Young adults of different relationship statuses (e.g., steady partner, dating multiple partners) report varying levels of sex-related alcohol expectancies, and this effect may be moderated by gender. For example, male adolescents have greater sex-related alcohol expectancies than females (Dermen & Cooper, 1994b; Mongeau & Johnson, 1995). Whereas young men who were actively dating reported higher sex-related alcohol expectancies than men in relationships and those not dating, young women in relationships reported similar levels of sex-related alcohol expectancies to women who were actively dating (Pedersen et al., 2009). Upon further exploration, however, increased risk of drinking for women was apparent for those with high sex-related alcohol expectancies who were actively dating. Thus, actively dating women with high sex-related expectancies may be most at risk for increased drinking. Similarly, Mongeau and Johnson (1995) found that young adults with higher sex-related alcohol expectancies drank more and initiated sex more frequently on first dates, and adolescents who believed alcohol would impair their judgment drank more while on dates (Dermen & Cooper, 1994b). Thus, the "negative" expectancies of drinking alcohol may exacerbate risk for early sexual encounters while dating. In an event-level study (i.e., one that looks at specific occasions rather than global behaviors) with college women, Brown and Vanable (2007) found over half of all sexual encounters with casual partners involved alcohol, compared with approximately one fifth of sexual encounters with steady partners.

SEX-RELATED EXPECTANCIES RESEARCH: SUMMARY AND RECOMMENDATIONS

The research on sex-related alcohol expectancies and dating relationships among adolescents and young adults has yielded inconsistent results, which makes drawing conclusions about these factors in predicting drinking difficult. The research generally suggests young people with high sex-related expectancies may be at risk for heavier drinking behavior while dating, while a steady relationship may protect against heavy drinking if partners are light/moderate drinkers themselves. More research is needed to better understand what types of partners may influence heavier (or reduced) drinking and how partner types (e.g., steady, casual) interact with one's sex-related alcohol expectancies to increase or protect against alcohol use.

Media Exposure, Substance Use, and Sexual Relationships in Adolescence

Adolescent exposure to mass media has received increasing attention in addictive behaviors research. Adolescents encounter television, movies, music, computers, the Internet, advertisements, videogames, and magazines on a daily basis, and many adolescents use multiple types of media simultaneously (Roberts, 1999). According to Flay and Sobel (1983), a typical American child will spend more time watching television than engaging in any other daily activity, including school and peer socialization. Often these habits begin before age 2 (Villani, 2001), and by adolescence the average American spends 6–7 hours a day with media (Roberts, 1999). In addition, the type of media exposure varies by gender, race, and class. For example, male adolescents have higher preference for television and Internet compared to females, whereas females more often prefer magazines (Hawk, Vanwesenbeeck, de Graaf, & Bakker, 2006); similarly, African American adolescents often have more media contact compared to White adolescents (Brown et al., 2006).

The frequent, positive portrayals of sexual and drug behaviors—with few negative consequences—found within this mass media is concerning (DuRant et al., 1997; McEwen & Hanneman, 1974; Robinson et al., 1998). Despite the ban of direct television advertisements for cigarettes in 1971, tobacco and other drugs are commonplace in the media, with alcohol being the most commonly depicted substance on television (Flay & Sobel, 1983). Often drug use is portrayed as humorous, harmless, and socially beneficial (McEwen & Hanneman, 1974). In addition, the media frequently references sexual behaviors with varying degrees of explicitness (DuRant et al., 1997; Hawk et al., 2006). Escobar-Chaves and colleagues (2005) reviewed literature on modern mass media and found that sexual content was commonplace across all media subtypes. Likewise, in a study of over 500 music videos, Durant and colleagues (1997) found that sexual situations were frequently paired with alcohol use, potentially leading to glamorized views of sex under the influence of alcohol.

Due to the pervasive nature of mass media, the effects are difficult to study (Flay, 2000). However, given the multitude of sexual and drug-related messages conveyed in mass media, researchers have begun to focus on the effects of media exposure on substance use and sexual behavior outcomes. In a recent review of this literature, Villani and colleagues (2001) concluded that the primary effects of media exposure are as follows: increased alcohol and tobacco use, earlier onset of sexual activity, and increased violent and aggressive behavior. Researchers have also observed positive correlations between exposure to media and levels of substance use (Iannotti, Kogan, Janssen, & Boyce, 2009; Robinson, Chen, & Killen, 1998; Sargent et al., 2001). Various theories have been posited to explain these correlations, many of which involve the modeling and normalization of risky health behaviors (DuRant et al., 1997; Escobar-Chaves et al., 2005; Flay & Sobel, 1983).

Robinson and colleagues (1998) surveyed over 1,500 ninth-grade students at baseline and then reassessed them after 18 months. Nondrinking students reporting higher levels of media exposure at baseline were more likely to initiate drinking within the 18-month study period. However, drinking students demonstrated no associations between media and alcohol use. Thus, it appears that media influences on the initiation of drinking are particularly important. Sargent and colleagues (2001) report similar findings with tobacco initiation among middle schoolers. These researchers reviewed a list of 50 films commonly viewed by adolescent populations and found that they contained an average of five occurrences of smoking per film. The prevalence of having ever tried a cigarette increased with the number of films viewed; only 4.9% of students with lowest media exposure reported smoking initiation compared to 31.3% of students with the highest media exposure (Sargent et al., 2001). In another, larger study, Iannotti and colleagues (2009) found similar relationships between media exposure and substance use. In this study, 20,000 students grades 6–10 reported on media use and health behaviors. Iannotti et al. (2009) found that increased exposure to screen-based media (i.e., computers and television) was negatively related to adolescents' physical health, overall quality of life, and quality of familial relationships (Iannotti et al., 2009). Additionally, media exposure was positively correlated with physical aggression, cigarette smoking, alcohol use, and drunkenness.

Media exposure has also been linked to earlier ages of onset of sexual behavior (Brown et al., 2006) and increased rates of risky sexual behaviors (Escobar-Chaves et al., 2005). In a recent longitudinal survey of 1,017 middle-school students, Brown and colleagues (2006) examined the connection between baseline media use and subsequent sexual behavior 2 years later. For White adolescents, increased exposure to sexual content in music, movies, television, and magazines was positively associated with earlier age of intercourse initiation. Furthermore, in a review of recent literature on the effects of media exposure on the sexual behavior of adolescents, increased exposure to television, movies, and music videos each resulted in increased sexual behaviors (Escobar-Chaves et al., 2005). Specifically, exposure to music videos was associated with more permissive attitudes toward sex among adolescents, and viewing X or NC-17 rated videos was associated with riskier sexual behavior (Escobar-Chaves et al., 2005).

Despite the negative associations between media exposure and adolescent drug/sexual behavior, researchers are attempting to utilize mass media for the prevention of substance use problems. Most of these interventions involve antidrug advertisements (Flay, 2000). Many early campaigns were unsuccessful or showed mixed results (Fray, 1983; Hawkins & Catalano, 1992); however, some researchers have found successful mass media interventions (Flay, 2000). For example, Flynn and colleagues (1992, 1994) found that a mass media intervention paired with a school intervention resulted in greater decreases in student smoking, compared to the school intervention alone. Other researchers found that recall of antidrug campaigns was associated with lower marijuana use (Block, Morwitz, Putsis Jr, & Sen, 2002), with another study indicating that similar campaigns may be particularly effective among high-sensation-seeking adolescents (Palmgreen, Donohew, Lorch, Hoyle, & Stephenson, 2001). In a review of this media intervention literature, Flay (2000) concludes that successful campaigns utilize several key factors: multiple, novel messages targeted at specific issues repeated over long periods, high-quality materials, and the modeling of attitudinal/behavior alternatives.

Another intervention that seems to hold promise is training in media literacy skills (Durham, 1999; Flay, 2000; Hawk et al., 2006). Training students to critically analyze the overt and subtle messages of media content can serve as a protective factor against harmful media messages (Flay, 2000). Further research in this area may serve to circumvent the harmful media messages that adolescents encounter on a daily basis.

MEDIA EXPOSURE: SUMMARY AND RECOMMENDATIONS

Research about the impact of media exposure is still in its infancy. Many studies that address these issues fail to deal directly with behavioral effects (Escobar-Chaves et al., 2005). In regard to understanding the effects of mass media on sexual relationships and substance use, more information is needed with regard to gender, racial, and SES differences in media exposure and media effects. Additionally, since most research has focused on television, new studies should address the impact of more modern media sources, including video games, Internet, multiplayer online computer games, and online social networks (Escobar-Chaves et al., 2005; Villani, 2001), particularly with regard to sexual attitudes and behaviors. Overall, controlled, longitudinal trials are needed to understand both short- and long-term effects of media on behavior. In regard to interventions, much more work is needed to develop and evaluate widespread media literacy skills training programs. More information on when developmentally to introduce such media literacy training programs is needed. For example, it is possible that some studies did not find that media literacy training programs had positive effects on initiation of sexual behaviors because the students had already initiated sexual behaviors. Given the vast capacity of mass media to effectively convey negative—and positive—messages, it is imperative that researchers partner with policy makers and educators to promote adolescent health.

At-Risk Populations

Although the negative consequences of substance use on adolescent sexual development are evident among all populations that have been studied, certain populations appear to be at particularly high risk for negative consequences or the consequences appear to be particularly dire. Adolescents with early-onset puberty are at high risk for both engagement in substance use and risky sexual behaviors. Prevalence of substance use and risky sex are particularly high among adolescents who experienced sexual or physical abuse during childhood or adolescence. Use of substances and unsafe sex are also highly prevalent among adolescents who perpetrate sexual aggression. As these special populations likely need prevention and intervention efforts targeted to their particular risks and characteristics, findings regarding substance use and sexual relationship development for each of these groups are reviewed next. Particular attention is paid to proposed mechanisms underlying the relationship between substance use and sexual relationship development specific to these populations.

Early Puberty, Substance Use, and Sexual Relationships

Puberty marks a critical transition period for children and adolescents. Changes occur concurrently spanning multiple realms of development—biologically, physically, socially, psychologically, and cognitively. This signifies a period of adjustment for adolescents, their families, and their peers. Children and adolescents must adapt not only to their changing bodies and minds but also to the changing expectations of society. Not surprisingly, these changes have a plethora of consequences for the development of the individual, including implications for substance use and sexual relationship development.

For Westernized countries, pubertal development typically begins between ages 8.5 and 13 among females, 9 and 14 in males (Murphy & Elias, 2006). Biological effects include multiple physical developments, including the maturation of hormonal and reproductive systems. The onset of these changes is largely individual and is predominantly determined by genetics, which accounts for 57%–100% of the variation in pubertal timing (Biro, Wolff, & Kushi, 2009; Mustanski, Viken, Kaprio, Pulkkinen, & Rose, 2004). Other factors influencing pubertal timing include nutrition, weight, race, ethnicity, migration, and familial stress (Belsky, Steinberg, & Draper, 1991; Herman-Giddens et al., 1997; Parent et al., 2003; Sun et al., 2002). Each of these factors interacts to determine the specific timing of pubertal onset for each individual.

Occasionally, pubertal onset occurs outside the normal range of development. Precocious puberty is a condition defined by pubertal onset prior to age 8 in girls and 9 in boys (Kaplowitz & Oberfield, 1999). Some studies suggest these limits be lowered to age 7 in White American girls and age 6 in African American girls (Herman-Giddens et al., 1997; Kaplowitz & Oberfield, 1999). Prevalence rates for precocious puberty range from 2 to 28 per 10,000, depending on gender and country (Cesario & Hughes, 2007; Teilmann, Pedersen, Jensen, Skakkebæk, & Juul, 2005), with girls representing about 80% of the cases (Teilmann et al., 2005). Though precocious puberty may be caused by abnormalities within the central nervous system or the periphery (Brito, Latronico, Arnhold, & Mendonça, 2008; Partsch & Sippell, 2001), most cases show no specific organic cause (Parent et al., 2003). Precocious puberty is associated with multiple medical consequences, including a higher body mass index (Gaudineau et al., 2010), shorter stature (Brito et al., 2008; Partsch & Sippell, 2001), and increased incidences of obesity, breast cancer, type II diabetes, and cardiovascular disease (Golub et al., 2008).

This untimely advent of puberty is also associated with medical, academic, psychological, social, and sexual consequences (Brito et al., 2008; Gaudineau et al., 2010; Golub et al., 2008; Mendle, Turkheimer, & Emery, 2007; Reardon, Leen-Feldner, & Hayward, 2009; Sonis et al., 1985). Though not all early maturers reach clinical levels of precocious puberty, the earlier a child begins puberty, the more problems occur in adolescence and early adulthood (Lynne-Landsman, 2010; Wise et al., 2009). Studies that define early puberty more broadly (frequently the earliest quintile of adolescents) observe similar associations between early pubertal timing and negative outcomes (Caspi & Moffitt, 1991; Gaudineau et al., 2010; Lynne-Landsman, 2010).

In Mendle and colleagues' (2007) recent review of this literature, several theories were proposed to explain the preponderance of negative outcomes associated with early puberty: psychological and biological theories and the theory of selection effects. The psychological processes theory posits that early developing children have more negative outcomes because they are not developmentally ready for pubertal changes. Early puberty artificially aborts preadolescent development, leaving these adolescents less equipped to deal with normal adolescent experiences. Of particular importance is the adolescent's likely association with older peers, whose physical appearance resembles the precocious individual's more than same-age peers (Mezzich et al., 1997; Money & Walker, 1971; Wichstrøm, 2001). Such fraternization results in the younger individual being prematurely exposed to more risky situations such as sexual activities and drug use (Mezzich et al., 1997; Money & Walker, 1971; Wichstrøm, 2001).

The theory of biological processes suggests that the biological changes of puberty lead to behavioral consequences (Mendle et al., 2007). Indeed, early maturers not only experience changes earlier, but they also have higher hormonal concentrations and develop at faster rates, leaving them less time to adjust (Apter & Vihko, 1985). Additionally, early maturers have increased levels of sex steroids, which result in more aggressive behavior (Sonis et al., 1985), potentially mediating later behavioral problems.

Finally, the theory of selection effects highlights that many of the associations between pubertal development and outcomes may be bidirectional. For example, household stress (which often increases for early maturers) is thought to contribute to early pubertal onset in girls (Belsky et al., 1991; Mendle et al., 2007). Additional environmental factors such as sexual abuse (Wise, Palmer, Rothman, & Rosenberg, 2009) and parental substance abuse (Kirillova, Vanyukov, Kirisci, & Reynolds, 2008) are also thought to contribute to early menarcheal age. This convergence of predisposing genetic and environmental factors with later problematic behaviors results in cyclic patterns of behavior spanning generations. Summarizing the literature on this point, Mendle and colleagues (2007) assert that an early-maturing mother is more likely to produce an early-maturing daughter—not only because of genetic factors but also because of predisposing environmental factors. Due to the hodgepodge of converging problematic behaviors and the bidirectional relationship of these factors, it is difficult to perceive causal relationships. Thus, it is clear that no single theory accounts for all outcomes; multiple theories must be considered.

Cognitively, there is little difference between early maturers and on-time or late maturers; IQ scores are similar for both groups (Erhardt, 1986). However, early maturures are more likely to perform poorly academically compared to later-maturing peers (Mendle et al., 2007). It has been proposed that behavioral outcomes, such as delinquency, sexual initiation, and substance use, may explain this discrepancy between academic potential (as reflected in IQ score) and performance (Mendle et al., 2007).

Psychologically, early maturers face increased vulnerabilities for internalizing and externalizing psychopathologies (Erhardt, 1986; Ge et al., 1996; Graber et al., 1997; Sonis et a., 1985). According to Graber, Seeley, Brooks-Gunn, and Lewinsohn (2004), increased pathology persists into adulthood, resulting in higher rates of lifetime psychological disorders. More specifically, rates of anxiety are higher among early-maturing girls; the literature on boys is less clear (Reardon et al., 2009). Rates of depression are increased for both genders, with a stronger association for girls (Ge, Conger, & Elder Jr, 2001; Stice, Presnell, & Bearman, 2001). However, researchers also note that negative life events may mediate these psychological effects (Brooks-Gunn & Warren, 1989). Puberty may simply be accentuating symptoms in predisposed individuals (Ge et al., 2001).

Socially, early maturers tend to be more withdrawn among same-age peers (Golub et al., 2008; Sonis et al., 1985). This could be partly due to their altered physical appearances, which may foster a sense of alienation (Golub et al., 2008). Additional biological factors may also play a part; increased hormonal levels may lead to more aggressive and hyperactive behaviors, which further isolate the individual (Caspi & Moffitt, 1991; Sonis et al., 1985). Instead of same-age peers, early maturing adolescents tend to associate with older peers, who more closely resemble their physique. These peer relationships are particularly important, because as a result of these relationships, early maturers are also more vulnerable to deviant peer pressures (Ge, Conger, & Elder Jr, 1996), and these relationships appear to mediate the effects of pubertal status on sexual initiation (French & Dishion, 2003; Mezzich et al., 1997), increased substance use, and conduct disorder (Kirillova et al., 2008; Wichstrom, 2001).

Behaviorally, early puberty is associated with a plethora of negative outcomes, including risky behaviors such as substance use. Early maturers show increased delinquency rates for both genders (Flannery, Rowe, & Gulley, 1993; Negriff & Trickett, 2010). In a longitudinal study of boys and their parents, Kirillova and colleagues (2008) found that early maturation was also associated with increased rates of conduct disorder—which increased the chances of that individual developing a substance use disorder by a factor of 9. In a larger, longitudinal study of girls, Caspi and Moffitt (1991) found that early pubertal timing was associated with stealing, truancy, drug use, and aggression. However, childhood behavioral problems proved to be more indicative of later adolescent behavior problems than pubertal timing (Caspi & Moffitt, 1991).

Sexually, early maturers experience sexual milestones at earlier ages (Erhardt, 1986; Meyer-Bahlburg et al., 1985). Not only are early-maturing girls more interested in sex, they are also exposed to sexual content more often (Brown, Halpern, & L'Engle, 2005). Early-maturing females initiate masturbation younger (Meyer-Bahlburg et al., 1985), and they are more likely to begin dating earlier (Mendle et al., 2007). Once dating, they are more likely to date older boys (Mezzich et al., 1997) and initiate behaviors such as kissing and petting sooner (Mendle et al., 2007). Importantly, they are more likely to initiate intercourse at earlier ages (Flannery et al., 1993; French & Dishion, 2003; Gaudineau et al., 2010; Magnusson, 2001). Early intercourse is associated with increased rates of pregnancy, sexual assault, and sex under the influence (O'Donnell, O'Donnell, & Stueve, 2001). Thus, age of initiation has many potentially life-altering consequences. But again, pubertal status is not the strongest predictor of initiation. French and Dishion (2003) found that deviant peer relationships predicted age of initiation more strongly. Thus, the importance of peer environment is highlighted again.

Early maturers are also at greater risk for practicing risky sexual behaviors (Mezzich et al., 1997) and being sexually assaulted or abused (Golub et al., 2008; Wise et al., 2009). Again, peer relationships are particularly important. In Mezzich and colleagues' (1997) study of female adolescents, association with an adult boyfriend completely accounted for the relationship between age and sexually risky behavior. Additionally, in a large study of over 35,000 women, early menarche was associated with an increase of sexual abuse, with the earliest maturers reporting the most abuse (Wise et al., 2009). To explain this finding, Golub and colleagues (2008) posit that the precocious development of breasts may attract attention from abusive adults. Given that negative life events appear to mediate relationships between early pubertal onset and negative outcomes (Brooks-Gunn & Warren, 1989), these findings on abuse are important. Sexual abuse may be a mediating factor for adolescent risk behaviors.

Finally, it is important to consider the association between early pubertal onset and substance use outcomes. Advanced pubertal status creates opportunities for younger adolescents to engage not only in sexual experiences at younger ages but also to engage in substance use (Gaudineau et al., 2010). Multiple studies have shown that early-maturing boys and girls initiate cigarette (Negriff & Trickett, 2010; Westling, Andrews, Hampson, & Peterson, 2008), alcohol (Costello, Sung, Worthman, & Angold, 2007; Westling et al., 2008), and other substance use (Patton et al., 2004; Tschann et al., 1994) sooner than same-age peers. The timing of initiation is particularly important in substance use outcomes, because early initiation is associated with higher rates of later substance abuse and dependence (Feldstein & Miller, 2006).

For early maturers, social environment plays a crucial role in substance initiation—particularly the presence of deviant peers (Westling et al., 2008; Wichstrøm, 2001). Of similar importance is the role of familial environment. In a longitudinal study of over 1,000 elementary students, Lynne-Landsman and colleagues (2010) found that early onset of puberty was associated with substance use only for those students whose households exhibited high levels of risk during the student's childhood. Thus, early pubertal onset was not a risk factor for those in low-risk households. Similarly, positive social environments have been found to moderate the relationship between early pubertal onset and problem behavior (Crockett, Raymond Bingham, Chopak, & Vicary, 1996; Westling et al., 2008). Similar to findings from other studies of US adolescents, among early maturers, those with both biological parents present show lower rates of early sexual initiation (Crockett et al., 1996), and those with greater parental monitoring show lower rates of substance initiation (Westling et al., 2008). Similarly, regular participation in church and academic clubs had a protective influence (Crockett, 1994). Thus, social environment can be a liability for a vulnerable adolescent or serve a protective function.

Early-maturing adolescents not only initiate use sooner but also report drinking more alcohol per episode, increased drinking frequency, and more incidences of alcohol intoxication (Gaudineau et al., 2010; Wichstrøm, 2001); each of these associations was found to be mediated by peer environment (Wichstrøm, 2001). In Feldstein and Miller's (2006) summary of normal adolescent drinking, they note that though most adolescent substance use does not progress to pathological levels, certain factors increase this risk: earlier drinking initiation, earlier binge drinking, drinking more alcohol per episode, and comorbid psychopathology. It is interesting to note that early pubertal onset is associated with each of these risk factors (Ehrhardt & Meyer-Bahlburg, 1986; Gaudineau et al., 2010; Ge et al., 1996; Graber, Lewinsohn, Seeley, & Brooks-Gunn, 1997; Sonis et al., 1985; Westling et al., 2008; Wichstrøm, 2001). Not surprisingly, early pubertal onset is also associated with increased rates of alcohol use disorder (Costello et al., 2007), substance abuse (Stice et al., 2001), and later substance use disorder (Graber, Seeley, Brooks-Gunn, & Lewinsohn, 2004; Kirillova et al., 2008).

Gaudineau and colleagues (2010) posit two theories to explain increased levels of substance use and earlier sexual initiation among early maturers. First, these associations could be due to affiliation with older peers who are more likely to be sexually active, delinquent, and have access to substances. Second, the increased psychopathology associated with early pubertal onset could increase risk-taking behaviors. Ultimately, early pubertal onset appears to function as a trigger for maladaptive behaviors in predisposed adolescents. Specific vulnerabilities include a history of familial/household risk (Lynne-Landsman et al., 2010); childhood behavioral problems (Caspi & Moffitt, 1991); an unconscientious, open or disagreeable personality (Markey, Markey, & Tinsley, 2003); negative life events (Brooks-Gunn & Warren, 1989); conduct disorder (Costello et al., 2007); and initial levels of psychopathology (Ge et al., 1996).

EARLY PUBERTAL ONSET: SUMMARY
AND RECOMMENDATIONS

Though it is clear that early maturers have increased pathological symptoms and higher rates of substance use, the exact role played by early pubertal onset is unclear. Other factors, such as peer and family environment, may explain these associations. For all negative outcomes, girls experience an increased level of severity compared to boys; it is unclear the extent to which findings generalize to both genders. Most studies to date have used primarily female samples. More studies are needed to understand if findings regarding early puberty generalize to boys. Also, it is unclear if these findings generalize to different cultures, races, and ethnicities (Mendle et al., 2007). This is particularly important in order to understand why non-Westernized cultures do not have the same negative outcomes associated with early pubertal onset.

Early Victimization and Substance Use in Adolescence

Certain forms of early psychological trauma, such as childhood abuse (i.e., sexual abuse, physical abuse) and/or adolescent dating violence, increase the likelihood of substance use and may divert the normative development of sexual relationships. Unfortunately, prevalence research suggests these traumatic events are not uncommon. It is estimated that 1 in 4 girls and 1 in 10 boys will experience childhood sexual abuse (Finkelhor, 1993). Additionally, conservative estimates of dating violence suggest that approximately 1 in 5 youth will be victims of some type of dating violence, with 1 in 10 experiencing more severe forms of abuse (Eaton et al., 2008; Silverman, Raj, Mucci, & Hathaway, 2001; Temple, Weston, & Marshall, 2010). Concerning prevalence rates and the possible negative impact of childhood abuse and teen dating violence make it important to examine the influence of these experiences when discussing adolescent sexual relationships. Research examining the consequences of childhood abuse and teen dating violence have identified numerous negative consequences and suggest increased risk for concerning problem behaviors, particularly in regard to substance use, sexual activity, and revictimization (e.g., Butt et al., 2011; Simpson & Miller, 2002; Tyler, 2002).

Numerous community-based and clinical investigations report an association between childhood sexual abuse and some aspect of substance use, including higher rates of alcohol and illicit drug use, earlier initiation of use, greater frequency of use, intravenous drug use, increased likelihood of substance use disorders, and more substance use–related problems when compared to nonabused peers (e.g., Butt, Chou, & Browne, 2011; Chandy, Blum, & Resnick, 1996; Dinwiddie et al., 2000; Fergusson, Horwood, & Lynskey, 1996; Harrison, Edwall, Hoffman, & Worthen, 1990; Harrison,

Fulkerson, & Beebe, 1997; Huang & Feng, 2008; Kilpatrick et al., 2000; Molnar, Berkman, & Buka, 2001; Plant, Miller, & Plant, 2007; Simpson & Miller, 2002).

There is also a well-established relationship between childhood sexual abuse and risky sexual behavior in later childhood and adolescence. Victims of sexual abuse have been found to initiate sexual activity at earlier ages, appear less likely to use contraceptives and protection, and are more likely to report multiple sex partners when compared to nonabuse peers (Boyer & Fine, 1992; Buzi et al., 2003; Fergusson, Horwood, & Lynskey, 1997; Luster & Small, 1997; Mason, Zimmerman, & Evans, 1998; Raj, Silverman, & Amaro, 2000). CSA has also been linked to higher rates of teen pregnancy (Fergusson et al., 1997; Raj et al., 2000; Zierler et al., 1991).

A relationship also exists between both physical and sexual dating violence and substance use and related problems, including higher prevalence of alcohol use, drug use, and binge drinking (e.g., Ackard, Eisenberg, & Neumark-Sztainer, 2007; Coker et al., 2000; Eaton, Davis, Barrios, Brener, & Noonan, 2007; Howard, Qi Wang, & Yan, 2007; Kim-Godwin, Clements, McCuiston, & Fox, 2009; Kreiter et al., 1999; Silverman, Raj, Mucci, & Hathaway, 2001).

Physical and sexual forms of dating violence also increase the risk of teen pregnancy, increased vulnerability to STDs, early initiation of sexual relationships, multiple sex partners, and unprotected sex (Coker et al., 2000; Eaton et al., 2007; Howard et al., 2007; Howard, Griffin, & Boekeloo, 2008; Kim-Godwin et al., 2009; Roberts, Auinger, & Klein, 2005; Silverman, Raj, & Clemens, 2004; Silverman et al., 2001; Wingood, DiClemente, & McCree, 2001).

These forms of trauma continue to be risk factors well into adulthood. For instance, it is estimated that youth who experience childhood abuse and/or teen dating violence are at significant risk for physical or sexual revictimization as adults (e.g., Classen, Palesh, & Aggarwal, 2005; Humphrey & Kahn, 2000; McGee, Garavan, de Barra, Byrne, & Conroy, 2002; Messman-Moore & Long, 2003; Steel & Herlitz, 2005; Whitfield, Anda, Dube, & Felitti, 2003). Additionally, experiencing sexual or physical violence in childhood and adolescence appears to increase the likelihood of substance use and related problems in adulthood (e.g., Butt et al., 2011; Dube et al., 2005; Simpson, 2002), with higher lifetime prevalence of substance use disorders found in

adult survivors of childhood sexual abuse (i.e., in community samples, abuse survivors 14% to 31% versus nonabused 3% to 12%; in clinical samples, abuse survivors 21% to 57% versus nonabused 2%–27%; Polusny & Follette, 1995; Simpson & Miller, 2002). In addition, childhood abuse has been linked to a greater number of sexual partners and prostitution in adulthood (Steel & Herlitz, 2005; Widom & Kuhns, 1996; Zierler et al., 1991).

There are three proposed pathways to explain the relationships between trauma and negative outcomes such as substance use and risky sexual behavior: (1) trauma provokes negative consequence (e.g., Secondary A/SUD), (2) negative consequence provokes trauma (e.g., Secondary Trauma), and (3) a third variable gives rise to both trauma and negative consequence (i.e., Common Factor; Goodwin, Fergusson, & Horwood, 2004; Kushner, Abrams, & Borchardt, 2000; Simpson & Miller, 2002). It is important to note that more than one process may be driving and influencing these relationships (Simpson & Miller, 2002). While review of all proposed explanations for the relationships described here is outside the scope of this chapter, some of the more frequently proposed mechanisms are briefly reviewed here.

The self-medication hypothesis provides one theory of how trauma may directly contribute to increased substance use and risky sexual behaviors (i.e., trauma provokes negative consequence). Specifically, in the wake of a traumatic event, children and adolescents may struggle to cope with and manage intense negative emotions and reactions elicited by their trauma. Those who experience difficulty with this task may turn to maladaptive and potentially dangerous coping methods in an attempt to reduce or avoid negative emotions (i.e., self-medicate), such as substance use and other risky behaviors (e.g., Fals-Stewart, 2003; Felitti et al., 1998; Garnefski & Arends, 1998; Kilpatrick et al., 2000; Ouimette & Brown, 2003; Stewart, 1996; Triffleman, Marmar, Delucchi, & Ronfeldt, 1995).

Another mechanism proposed to explain the relationship between trauma and increased substance use, risky behavior, and revictimization involves the possible effect of trauma on cognitive and emotional development. For example, trauma exposure may negatively affect cognitive development in a way that reduces the adolescent's ability to appraise danger and learn from consequences (De Bellis, 2001; De Bellis & Keshavan, 2003; De Bellis et al., 1999). Similarly, it has been suggested that childhood abuse may disrupt the development of affect regulation and social development (e.g., ability to relate to others) in a way that minimizes one's awareness of danger (e.g., Arata, 2002; National Child Traumatic Stress Network, 2008).

In addition, substance use may increase the likelihood of risky behaviors (i.e., negative consequence provokes trauma) through the potentially dangerous behaviors youth engage in to obtain and/or while under the influence of drugs (e.g., impaired decision making, impulsivity). These actions may increase one's risk for trauma exposure, including dating violence and revictimization (e.g., Giaconia et al., 2000; Kann et al., 2000; Simpson & Miller, 2002). For example, a longitudinal study of adolescent girls indicated that sexual victimization occurring in adolescence most often followed the onset of heavy drinking, possibly due in part to increases in exposure to dangerous situations (Pedersen & Skrondal, 1996; Simpson & Miller, 2002). Substance use may also play a role in dating violence, with one study finding at least 30% of adolescents reported using alcohol prior to an incident of dating violence (Rhynard, Krebs, & Glover, 1997). It is important to note that these findings suggest substance use might serve as both a negative outcome of trauma as well a mediator between trauma and other negative outcomes such as risky sexual behavior and revictimization.

A variety of factors can increase one's risk for childhood abuse, dating violence, substance use, risky sexual behavior, and revictimization. Thus, it is possible that the relationships seen between childhood abuse/dating violence and these negative outcomes are a result of these common factors. Possible common factors include other forms of childhood abuse and neglect, family history of substance use, family violence/instability, parental monitoring, parental support, community violence, low socioeconomic status/poverty, and peer influences (e.g., Banyard & Cross, 2008; Butt et al., 2011; Clark, Lesnick, & Hegedus, 1997; Glass et al., 2003; Holt & Espelage, 2005; Huang & Feng, 2008; Luster & Small, 1997; Pedersen & Skrondal, 1996; Roche, Runtz, & Hunter, 1999; Simpson & Miller, 2002). Research examining the role of parental substance use highlights how one factor could be responsible for substance use, trauma, and risky sexual behavior (Gelles, Finkelhor, Gelles, Hotaling, & Straus, 1983; McCurdy & Daro, 1994; Yama, Fogas, Teegarden, & Hastings, 1993). Specifically, parental substance use is a known risk factor for substance use and use disorders in offspring. Parental

substance use has also been linked to increased perpetration of child abuse (Famularo, Kinscherff, & Fenton, 1992). Further, parental substance has been linked with poor parental monitoring (Chassin, Curran, Hussong, & Colder, 1996), which may increase a child's risk for abuse outside the family (see Harrison, Hoffmann, & Edwall, 1989; Simpson & Miller, 2002). In addition, poor parental monitoring is associated with increases in adolescent risky behaviors, including risky sexual behaviors and substance use (Howard, Qiu, & Boekeloo, 2003; Luster & Small, 1997).

The relationships between childhood abuse, dating violence, and substance use and its negative outcomes may also be due in part to mediating and/or moderating factors. In fact, many potential common factors may function in this capacity. For example, while childhood abuse may have a direct relationship with substance use, a family history of substance use may moderate this relationship such that those with family histories of substance use report more severe substance use outcomes. Other variables that have been proposed include mediating psychological symptoms or disorders and moderating factors including severity of abuse, gender, and ethnicity (Boyer & Fine, 1992; Dembo, Williams, Schmeidler, & Wothke, 1993; Mezzich et al., 1997; Simpson & Miller, 2002; Steel & Herlitz, 2005).

While childhood abuse and dating violence are generally linked to substance use and related problems as well as risky sexual behaviors, these results are not always consistent. Specifically, variability exists in the aspects of substance use and risky sexual behaviors found to have significant relationships with these forms of trauma (e.g., Butt et al., 2001; Glass, Chan, & Rentz, 2000; Simpson, 2002). For example, Mason and colleagues (1998) found significant differences between adolescent victims of childhood sexual abuse and nonabused peers with regard to contraceptive use but failed to find differences in number of sexual partners or age of first intercourse. Conversely, Buzi and colleagues (2003) did find significant differences between adolescent childhood abuse survivors and nonabused peers with regard to early initiation of sexual activity but not with regard to teenage pregnancy. Some investigations fail to detect these associations at all. A recent review of the childhood sexual abuse literature using male populations highlights this point. Two out of eight studies of community samples and two out of nine studies involving clinical samples failed to find an association between childhood sexual abuse and some aspect of substance use (Butt et al., 2011).

The negative consequences of childhood abuse and dating violence include increased risk of substance use and related problems, risky behavior, and revictimization. These relationships are both acute and long term, as many negative consequences continue well into adulthood. Due to inconsistencies in the literature and methodological limitations, firm conclusions about the relationships between these variables cannot be drawn. At best, the current literature supports the existence of some relationship between childhood abuse, dating violence, substance use, risky sexual behaviors, and revictimization. Knowledge of the temporal sequencing and causal relationships between these variables is quite limited, and it remains possible that a common factor is responsible for the relationships seen. Research addressing these limitations is needed to better understand the impact of sexual and/or physical victimization on sexual relationship development and addiction. Future endeavors would benefit from prospective designs to establish temporal precedence and causality and evaluation of mechanisms, including examination of mediation variables, moderating factors, and model testing to better understand the relationships found. More research is needed using male and ethnic minority samples to allow for comparisons across gender and ethnic groups.

Perpetration of Sexual Aggression and Substance Use in Adolescence

Unfortunately the perpetration of dating violence in adolescence is far too common. Data from community samples suggest that from 12% to 57% of adolescents report perpetrating physical abuse in a dating relationship (Foshee et al., 2009; O'Donnell et al., 2006; Rothman et al., 2011), and approximately 2% to 5% report perpetrating sexual assault (Foshee et al., 2009; Stappenbeck & Fromme, 2010).

Alcohol use is linked to the perpetration of interpersonal violence in both adults and adolescents. Adolescents who report using alcohol in the past 30 days are more likely to report the perpetration of dating violence than those who have not used alcohol in the same time period (Foshee, Linder, MacDougall, & Bangdiwala, 2001; Young et al., 2009). In addition, problematic, frequent, or heavy

alcohol use is related not only to initiating partner violence (Locke & Mahalik, 2005; McNaughton Reyes, Foshee, Bauer, & Ennett, 2011; Young et al., 2009) but also to the level of severity of the violence (Testa & Parks, 1996; Ullman, Karabatsos, & Koss, 1999). Although the relationship between the regular use of alcohol and the perpetration of interpersonal violence is well established, it is likely partially explained by other variables, such as antisocial behavior or impulsivity (Fals-Stewart, 2003; Herrera, Wiersma, & Cleveland, 2011). This explanation, however, does not fully account for the data implicating the immediate effect of alcohol on the perpetration of dating violence.

Alcohol use by perpetrators *at the time* of dating violence is common (Muehlenhard & Linton, 1987; Stappenbeck & Fromme, 2010; Testa & Livingston, 1999). Testa and Livingston (1999) interviewed young adult women who were victims of sexual violence. These late adolescents reported that 70% of their perpetrators had used alcohol at the time of the assault. Perpetrators also report this pattern. Moore and colleagues (2011) asked late adolescents to rate their daily alcohol use and the perpetration of dating violence on handheld computers. They found that alcohol consumption significantly increased the likelihood of interpersonal violence perpetration on the same day. In addition, the number of drinks consumed before the incident was also a significant predictor of dating violence.

The connection between dating violence and alcohol use may at least partially result from impaired cognitive abilities due to alcohol intoxication (Chermack & Giancola, 1997; Giancola, 2000). Intoxicated individuals may be less able to attend to multiple situational cues, thereby increasing the likelihood that they will misinterpret or simply not attend to information that would hinder partner violence (Noel, Maisto, Johnson, & Jackson Jr, 2009). It has also been posited that the use of alcohol has a disinhibitory effect whereby the more alcohol that is consumed the less likely an individual is able to inhibit aggressive behaviors. Noel and colleagues (2009) tested these theories in a laboratory setting and found that, in response to videotaped vignettes, young male adults who had consumed alcohol were more likely than those who had not consumed alcohol to rate sexually aggressive behavior as acceptable.

Another factor that may explain why alcohol use is a risk factor for dating violence is perpetrators' expectations about the effects of drinking alcohol.

Specifically, there appears to be a relationship between perpetrating sexual assault and having high expectations that alcohol will enhance sexual experiences. Wilson and colleagues (2002) found that sexually coercive young adult males had higher expectations that alcohol would have a positive impact on sexual behavior and feelings than their non-coercive peers. In their sample, sex-related alcohol expectancies moderated the relationship between alcohol consumption and sexual coercion, such that alcohol expectancies impacted the relationship between alcohol consumption and sexually coercive behavior only for men with high alcohol expectancies. Zawacki and colleagues (2003) compared three groups of young men: those who reported perpetrating alcohol-involved sexual assault to those who denied committing assault to those who reported perpetrating sexual assault without consuming alcohol. They found that alcohol-involved perpetrators held stronger sex-related alcohol expectancies than men in the other two groups.

LONG-TERM CONSEQUENCES

Only a small body of research has examined the relationship between alcohol and perpetration of sexually aggressive acts longitudinally in adolescents and the results of the few studies that do exist do not establish a clear picture. Foshee et al. (2001) examined the relationship between regular alcohol use and dating violence both cross-sectionally and longitudinally. In their cross-sectional analysis of eighth and ninth graders the regular use of alcohol (number of days consumed in past 30 days) predicted both mild and serious dating violence in males but not females. To examine whether regular alcohol use predicted the initiation of dating violence longitudinally, adolescents who had not reported perpetrating dating violence at baseline were then assessed 1 ½ years later. Their data suggest that engaging in regular alcohol use at the baseline assessment predicted perpetration of dating violence 1 ½ years later for females but not for males. O'Donnell and colleagues (2006) looked at longitudinal risk factors for the perpetration of violence over a 6-year period beginning when adolescents were in the eighth grade. They found that the early initiation of substance use was a risk factor for the perpetration of partner violence 6 years later for both genders. However, McNaughton Reyes et al. (2011) found that while high levels of alcohol use in early adolescence did predict perpetration of relationship violence in early and middle adolescence, it did not predict later perpetration of partner violence.

PERPETRATION OF SEXUAL VIOLENCE: SUMMARY AND RECOMMENDATIONS

It is clear that there is a relationship between alcohol use and dating violence in adolescents due in part to expectations as well as the physiological effects of using alcohol. It is also likely that both the use of alcohol and the perpetration of dating violence are related to other variables, such as antisocial traits or impulse control difficulties. We know very little, however, about the impact of alcohol use on later sexual violence. Most studies have been with older adolescents or college students. However, perpetration of sexual violence can start much earlier in adolescence as can substance use and sexual behavior. Longitudinal studies including younger samples are needed to understand the long-term relationships between substance use and perpetration of sexual violence. In large part, such studies are needed to inform intervention efforts targeted at offenders.

Conclusions

This review documents the highly prevalent co-occurrence of substance use and risky sexual behavior and associated negative outcomes in adolescence. The relationship appears to be bidirectional with substance use acting as a risk factor for future risky sexual behavior and risky sexual behavior acting as a risk factor for substance use. In seeking to explain this relationship, researchers have theorized and data suggest that this relationship may be the result of a number of factors, including (1) personality traits such as impulsivity or sensation-seeking tendencies that may be exaggerated in adolescents whose brains are not yet fully mature (Schofield et al., 2008; Zimmer-Gembeck, Siebenbruner, & Collins, 2004); (2) expectancies about how alcohol will affect sexual experiences; and (3) media effects. In addition, a number of other factors likely contribute to this co-occurrence, including a number of problem behaviors that reinforce one another (Jessor & Jessor, 1977; Kotchick et al., 2001) and/or the influence of family factors and deviant peer groups or perceived peer attitudes (Miller, Alberts, Hecht, Trost, & Krizek, 2000; Scaramella, Conger, Simons, & Whitbeck, 1998; Schofield et al., 2008). However, as of yet, there are no integrative models to explain the relationship between substance use and sexual relationship development. Differences seen between genders and ethnic groups in relation to substance use and sexual behavior highlight the need for research delineating the unique risk and protective factors of different groups. Subgroups such as early maturers, sexual aggression victims, and sexual aggression perpetrators further underscore the need to understand and target interventions to the unique needs and characteristics of specific high-risk populations.

Future Directions
Integrative Models

Biological, psychological, and cultural processes rarely operate in isolation; understanding interactions between biological, psychological, and cultural factors is paramount. There is also a need for integrative models to understand the mechanisms for specific high-risk groups. For example, why does early maturation lead to increased negative outcomes in multiple domains? More research is needed to understand the mechanisms of action, including genetic and neurobiological factors that lead to negative outcomes and how various risk factors interact with each other. There is also a need to understand the role of protective factors such as stable dating relationships and potentially others such as resilience, as not all substance users go on to experience negative sexual outcomes. Use of multivariate analyses would allow for further identification of groups of adolescents who may benefit from tailored interventions. For example, through simultaneous examination of sensation-seeking, impulsivity, alcohol use, and sexual behavior, different groups of adolescents may emerge. Some adolescents may show a strong relationship involving the sensation-seeking traits and need to be targeted by interventions stressing different "thrilling" options for adolescents, whereas adolescents showing a stronger association with impulsivity may need interventions targeting "thinking consequences through." Information about mechanisms of action, including both risk and protective factors, can help guide prevention and/or intervention programs that target all adolescents or specific at-risk groups such as early maturers, possibly starting as early as elementary school. Without integrative models, prevention and intervention efforts may miss important factors that underlie both substance use and risky sexual behaviors.

Prospective Longitudinal Studies

One of the greatest limitations of the research is the dearth of prospective evaluations (Lewis & Fremouw, 2001; Simpson & Miller, 2002). For example, for studies of childhood abuse and dating violence survivors, trauma cannot be experimentally manipulated, prospective designs become essential to determine temporal sequencing and causality. Without longitudinal studies, little is known about the long-term consequences of substance use on sexual relationship development. Although immediate consequences of risky sex are extremely concerning, long-term consequences may be as concerning or more so if associations with long-term relationship impairment, psychiatric illness, and physical illness exist. The cross-sectional and correlational nature of the majority of the current literature greatly limits our awareness of long-term patterns and consequences and conclusions that can be drawn. Future studies should focus on longitudinal designs.

Understanding Differences by Gender, Ethnicity, and Religion

Sexual behavior among adolescents cannot be fully understood unless it is examined in a framework that includes cultural norms based on gender, ethnicity, religion, and so on. Of note, while research involving males and ethnic minorities is becoming increasingly available, the majority of early research focused predominantly on females and Caucasian samples (Butt et al., 2011; Tyler, 2002). The little information available suggests a great deal of variability based on demographic and ethnic differences. For example, Caucasian males and Hispanic/Latina females report the lowest rates of consistent condom use (CDC, 2010). Rates of newly reported STIs are highest among adolescents who are racial/ethnic minorities and men who have sex with men (CDC, 2010). No studies were found examining religious affiliation or religiosity, yet most religions have clear delineations regarding appropriate sexual conduct. Factors such as gender, ethnicity, and religion may also cause noise in analyses if not controlled. The degree to which background factors and other possibly important confounding variables are considered in analyses (e.g., matching groups, statistically controlling for confounders) varies by investigation (Butt et al., 2011). As a result, it remains difficult to fully understand and establish the relationship between some of the proposed mechanisms, substance use, and sexual development. To more fully understand sexual decision making in adolescence, including the role of substance use, differences by gender, ethnicity, and religiosity need to be better understood.

Clearly Defined Variables of Interest

Variable definitions and subsequent measurement often vary by study. For example, various definitions are used for teen dating violence (e.g., verbal abuse, physical violence, sexual violence; Jackson, 1999; Lewis & Fremouw, 2001). Consistent use of terms and measurement will allow for replication of previous results when appropriate and more definitive understanding of the co-occurrence of substance use and sexual relationship development.

Expand Definition of Sex

Although clearer definitions are important, the definitions many studies have used for sex may in fact be too narrow. Most studies use vaginal intercourse as the only marker of sexual activity. Not only does this ignore other risky sexual behaviors (i.e., oral or anal sex), which can result in negative outcomes such as STIs or HIV, but this also ignores sexual activity within same-sex sexual relations. With 11% of adolescent girls endorsing such behavior, and men who sleep with men among the highest at risk for contracting STIs, more sensitive measures and continuous data collection on sexual experience should be implemented. Although current research is moving away from indiscriminately framing all adolescent sexual experiences as "risky" (e.g., Wu et al., 2010), the majority of extant literature on adolescent sexuality has classified all sexual behavior during adolescence as problematic (Kotchick, Shaffer, Miller, & Forehand, 2001). Referring to work done by Miller et al. (1997) demonstrating that adolescent sexual risk behaviors exist along a continuum, Kotchick et al. (2001) concludes that dichotomous classifications of sexual activity are inadequate, and that behaviors such as early sex initiation should not be considered a risk behavior in itself, but instead a risk factor for later sexual risk taking.

Delineating Age and Developmental Stage

Much of the literature reviewed was with older adolescents, even college students. Yet the prevalence of substance use and sexual behavior among younger adolescents is increasing. Given changes in brain maturation, education, and social norms that occur throughout adolescence, more research is needed to delineate differences between younger and older adolescents.

Prevention and Intervention Efforts

Overall, this review shows that evaluations of prevention and intervention efforts targeting the link between substance use and sexual behavior have been scarce. The culmination of the recommendations mentioned herein can lead to the development of prevention and intervention efforts targeted at adolescents at risk for substance use, risky sexual behavior, and their associated negative outcomes. The findings of this review highlight that efforts to break the cycle between substance use and risky sexual behavior need to occur on multiple levels, including personal (targeting unique factors such as age, ethnicity, possible trauma background), community, and national-level campaigns using multiple forms of media. Considering the complex intersection of factors responsible for substance use and sexual risk trajectories, researchers have recommended seeking a multidimensional system approach to interrupt this progression, such as targeting sexual risk behaviors through substance use prevention efforts (Kotchick et al., 2001). Such efforts need to undergo vigorous evaluation to ensure their efficacy and effectiveness. Only with such stringent efforts do we have the greatest likelihood of breaking the link.

References

Ackard, D. M., Eisenberg, M. E., & Neumark-Sztainer, D. (2007). Long-term impact of adolescent dating violence on the behavioral and psychological health of male and female youth. *The Journal of Pediatrics, 151*(5), 476–481.

Apter, D., & Vihko, R. (1985). Premenarcheal endocrine changes in relation to age at menarche. *Clinical Endocrinology, 22*(6), 753–760.

Arata, C. M. (2002). Child sexual abuse and sexual revictimization. *Clinical Psychology: Science and Practice, 9*(2), 135–164.

Bailey, S. L., Gao, W., & Clark, D. B. (2006). Diary study of substance use and unsafe sex among adolescents with substance use disorders. *Journal of Adolescent Health, 38*(3), 297, e213–297, e220.

Baker, J. R., & Yardley, J. K. (2002). Moderating effect of gender on the relationship between sensation seeking-impulsivity and substance use in adolescents. *Journal of Child & Adolescent Substance Abuse, 12*(1), 27–43.

Banyard, V. L., & Cross, C. (2008). Consequences of teen dating violence. *Violence Against Women, 14*(9), 998–1013.

Basile, K. C., Black, M. C., Breiding, M. J., Chen, J., Merrick, M. T., Smith, S. G., . . . Walters, M. L. (2011). *National intimate partner and sexual violence survey: 2010 summary report*. Atlanta, GA: Centers for Disease Control and Prevention, National Center for Injury Prevention and Control, Division of Violence Prevention.

Belsky, J., Steinberg, L., & Draper, P. (1991). Childhood experience, interpersonal development, and reproductive strategy: An evolutionary theory of socialization. *Child Development, 62*(4), 647–670.

Biglan, A., Brennan, P. A., Foster, S. L., & Holder, H. D. (2005). *Helping adolescents at risk: Prevention of multiple problem behaviors*. New York, NY: Guilford Press.

Biro, F. M., Wolff, M. S., & Kushi, L. H. (2009). Impact of yesterday's genes and today's diet and chemicals on tomorrow's women. *Journal of Pediatric and Adolescent Gynecology*, 22(1), 3.

Blakemore, S. J., & Choudhury, S. (2006). Development of the adolescent brain: Implications for executive function and social cognition. *Journal of Child Psychology and Psychiatry*, 47(3–4), 296–312.

Block, L. G., Morwitz, V. G., Putsis, W. P., Jr, & Sen, S. K. (2002). Assessing the impact of antidrug advertising on adolescent drug consumption: Results from a behavioral economic model. *American Journal of Public Health*, 92(8), 1346.

Boyer, D., & Fine, D. (1992). Sexual abuse as a factor in adolescent pregnancy and child maltreatment. *Family Planning Perspectives*, 24(1), 4–19.

Breakwell, G. M. (1996). Risk estimation and sexual behaviour. *Journal of Health Psychology*, 1(1), 79.

Brito, V. N., Latronico, A. C., Arnhold, I. J. P., & Mendonça, B. B. (2008). Update on the etiology, diagnosis and therapeutic management of sexual precocity. *Arquivos Brasileiros de Endocrinologia & amp; Metabologia* 52(1), 18–31.

Brooks-Gunn, J., & Warren, M. P. (1989). Biological and social contributions to negative affect in young adolescent girls. *Child Development*, 60(1), 40–55.

Brown, J. D., L'Engle, K. L., Pardun, C. J., Guo, G., Kenneavy, K., & Jackson, C. (2006). Sexy media matter: Exposure to sexual content in music, movies, television, and magazines predicts black and white adolescents' sexual behavior. *Pediatrics*, 117(4), 1018.

Brown, J. D., Halpern, C. T., & L'Engle, K. L. (2005). Mass media as a sexual super peer for early maturing girls. *Journal of Adolescent Health*, 36(5), 420–427.

Brown, J. L., & Vanable, P. A. (2007). Alcohol use, partner type, and risky sexual behavior among college students: Findings from an event-level study. *Addictive Behaviors*, 32(12), 2940–2952.

Brown, L. K., DiClemente, R. J., & Park, T. (1992). Predictors of condom use in sexually active adolescents. *Journal of Adolescent Health*, 13(8), 651–657.

Bryan, A., Ray, L. A., & Cooper, M. L. (2007). Alcohol use and protective sexual behaviors among high-risk adolescents. *Journal of Studies on Alcohol and Drugs*, 68(3), 327–335.

Butt, S., Chou, S., & Browne, K. (2011). A rapid systematic review on the association between childhood physical and sexual abuse and illicit drug use among males. *Child Abuse Review*, 20(1), 6–38.

Buzi, R. S., Tortolero, S. R., Roberts, R. E., Ross, M. W., Addy, R. C., & Markham, C. M. (2003). The impact of a history of sexual abuse on high-risk sexual behaviors among females attending alternative schools. *Adolescence-San Diego*, 38(152), 595–606.

Caminis, A., Henrich, C., Ruchkin, V., Schwab-Stone, M., & Martin, A. (2007). Child and Adolescent Psychiatry and Mental Health. *Child and Adolescent Psychiatry and Mental Health*, 1(14), 14.

Caspi, A., & Moffitt, T. E. (1991). Individual differences are accentuated during periods of social change: The sample case of girls at puberty. *Journal of Personality and Social Psychology*, 61(1), 157–168.

Centers for Disease Control and Prevention (CDC). (2010, June 4). Youth risk behavior surveillance—United States, 2009. *MMWR. Morbidity and Mortality Weekly Reports*. Retrieved from https://www.cdc.gov/mmwr/pdf/ss/ss5905.pdf.

Center for Disease Control and Prevention. (2011). *2006-2010 National survey of family growth*. Retrieved from https://www.cdc.gov/nchs/nsfg/nsfg_2006_2010_puf.htm.

Cesario, S. K., & Hughes, L. A. (2007). Precocious puberty: A comprehensive review of literature. *Journal of Obstetric, Gynecologic, & Neonatal Nursing*, 36(3), 263–274.

Chandra, A. (2011). *Sexual behavior, sexual attraction, and sexual identity in the United States: Data from the 2006–2008 National Survey of Family Growth*. Washington, DC: US Department of Health and Human Services, Centers for Disease Control and Prevention, National Center for Health Statistics.

Chandy, J. M., Blum, R. W., & Resnick, M. D. (1996). History of sexual abuse and parental alcohol misuse: Risk, outcomes and protective factors in adolescents. *Child and Adolescent Social Work Journal*, 13(5), 411–432.

Chassin, L., Curran, P. J., Hussong, A. M., & Colder, C. R. (1996). The relation of parent alcoholism to adolescent substance use: A longitudinal follow-up study. *Journal of Abnormal Psychology*, 105(1), 70–80.

Chermack, S. T., & Giancola, P. R. (1997). The relation between alcohol and aggression: An integrated biopsychosocial conceptualization. *Clinical Psychology Review*, 17(6), 621–649.

Clapp, J. D., & Shillington, A. M. (2001). Environmental predictors of heavy episodic drinking. *The American Journal of Drug and Alcohol Abuse*, 27(2), 301–313.

Clark, D. B., Lesnick, L., & Hegedus, A. M. (1997). Traumas and other adverse life events in adolescents with alcohol abuse and dependence. *Journal of the American Academy of Child & Adolescent Psychiatry*, 36(12), 1744–1751.

Classen, C. C., Palesh, O. G., & Aggarwal, R. (2005). Sexual revictimization. *Trauma, Violence, & Abuse*, 6(2), 103–129.

Coker, A. L., McKeown, R. E., Sanderson, M., Davis, K. E., Valois, R. F., & Huebner, E. S. (2000). Severe dating violence and quality of life among south carolina high school students. *American Journal of Preventive Medicine*, 19(4), 220–227.

Cooper, M. L., Frone, M. R., Russell, M., & Mudar, P. (1995). Drinking to regulate positive and negative emotions: A motivational model of alcohol use. *Journal of Personality and Social Psychology*, 69(5), 990.

Cooper, M. L., & Orcutt, H. K. (1997). Drinking and sexual experience on first dates among adolescents. *Journal of Abnormal Psychology*, 106(2), 191.

Cooper, M. L., Wood, P. K., Orcutt, H. K., & Albino, A. (2003). Personality and the predisposition to engage in risky or problem behaviors during adolescence. *Journal of Personality and Social Psychology*, 84(2), 390.

Copeland, W., Shanahan, L., Miller, S., Costello, E. J., Angold, A., & Maughan, B. (2010). Outcomes of early pubertal timing in young women: A prospective population-based study. *American Journal of Psychiatry*, 167(10), 1218–1225.

Costello, E. J., Sung, M., Worthman, C., & Angold, A. (2007). Pubertal maturation and the development of alcohol use and abuse. *Drug and Alcohol Dependence*, 88, S50–S59.

Crews, F. T., & Boettiger, C. A. (2009). Impulsivity, frontal lobes and risk for addiction. *Pharmacology Biochemistry and Behavior*, 93(3), 237–247.

Crockett, L. J., Raymond Bingham, C., Chopak, J. S., & Vicary, J. R. (1996). Timing of first sexual intercourse: The role of social control, social learning, and problem behavior. *Journal of Youth and Adolescence*, 25(1), 89–111.

Davies, P. T., & Windle, M. (2000). Middle adolescents. *Merrill-Palmer Quarterly, 46*(1), 90–118.

De Bellis, M. D. (2001). Developmental traumatology: The psychobiological development of maltreated children and its implications for research, treatment, and policy. *Development and Psychopathology, 13*(3), 539–564.

De Bellis, M. D., & Keshavan, M. S. (2003). Sex differences in brain maturation in maltreatment-related pediatric post-traumatic stress disorder. *Neuroscience & Biobehavioral Reviews, 27*(1–2), 103–117.

De Bellis, M. D., Keshavan, M. S., Clark, D. B., Casey, B., Giedd, J. N., Boring, A. M., Frustaci, K., & Ryan, N. D. (1999). Developmental traumatology, Part II: Brain development. *Biological Psychiatry, 45*(10), 1271–1284.

Dembo, R., Williams, L., Schmeidler, J., & Wothke, W. (1993). A longitudinal study of the predictors of the adverse effects of alcohol and marijuana/hashish use among a cohort of high risk youths. *Substance Use & Misuse, 28*(11), 1045–1083.

Derman, K., Cooper, M., & Acocha, V. (1998). Sex-related alcohol ex ectancies as moderators of the use relationship between alcohol use and risky sex in adolescent. *Journal of Studies on Alcohol, 59,* 71–77.

Dermen, K. H., & Cooper, M. L. (1994a). Sex-related alcohol expectancies among adolescents: I. Scale development. *Psychology of Addictive Behaviors, 8*(3), 152.

Dermen, K. H., & Cooper, M. L. (1994b). Sex-related alcohol expectancies among adolescents: II. Prediction of drinking in social and sexual situations. *Psychology of Addictive Behaviors, 8*(3), 161.

Dévieux, J., Malow, R., Stein, J. A., Jennings, T. E., Lucenko, B. A., Averhart, C., & Kalichman, S. (2002). Impulsivity and HIV risk among adjudicated alcohol-and other drug-abusing adolescent offenders. *AIDS Education and Prevention: Official Publication of the International Society for AIDS Education, 14*(5 Suppl B), 24.

Dick, D. M., Smith, G., Olausson, P., Mitchell, S. H., Leeman, R. F., O'Malley, S. S., & Sher, K. (2010). Review: Understanding the construct of impulsivity and its relationship to alcohol use disorders. *Addiction Biology, 15*(2), 217–226.

Dinwiddie, S., Heath, A. C., Dunne, M. P., Bucholz, K. K., Madden, P. A. F., Slutske, W. S., Bierut, L. J., Statham, D. B., & Martin, N. G. (2000). Early sexual abuse and lifetime psychopathology: A co-twin-control study. *Psychological Medicine, 30*(1), 41–52.

Donohew, L., Zimmerman, R., Cupp, P. S., Novak, S., Colon, S., & Abell, R. (2000). Sensation seeking, impulsive decision-making, and risky sex: Implications for risk-taking and design of interventions. *Personality and Individual Differences, 28*(6), 1079–1091.

Dube, S. R., Anda, R. F., Whitfield, C. L., Brown, D. W., Felitti, V. J., Dong, M., & Giles, W. H. (2005). Long-Term consequences of childhood sexual abuse by gender of victim. *American Journal of Preventive Medicine, 28*(5), 430–438.

DuRant, R. H., Rome, E. S., Rich, M., Allred, E., Emans, S. J., & Woods, E. R. (1997). Tobacco and alcohol use behaviors portrayed in music videos: A content analysis. *American Journal of Public Health, 87*(7), 1131.

Durham, M. G. (1999). Girls, media, and the negotiation of sexuality: A study of race, class, and gender in adolescent peer groups. *Journalism and Mass Communication Quarterly, 76,* 193–216.

Eaton, D. K., Davis, K. S., Barrios, L., Brener, N. D., & Noonan, R. K. (2007). Associations of dating violence victimization with lifetime participation, co-occurrence, and early initiation of risk behaviors among U.S. high school students. *Journal of Interpersonal Violence, 22*(5), 585–602.

Eaton, D. K., Kann, L., Kinchen, S., Shanklin, S., Ross, J., Hawkins, J., Harris, W. A., Lowry, R., McManus, T., & Chyen, D. (2008). Youth risk behavior surveillance—United States, 2007. *MMWR. Surveillance Summaries: Morbidity and Mortality Weekly Report. Surveillance summaries/CDC, 57*(4), 1.

Ehrhardt, A. A., & Meyer-Bahlburg, H. F. L. (1986). Idiopathic precocious puberty in girls: Long-term effects on adolescent behavior. *Acta Endocrinologica, 113*(4 Suppl), S247.

Engels, R. C. M. E., & Knibbe, R. A. (2000). Alcohol use and intimate relationships in adolescence* 1,* 2,* 3:: When love comes to town. *Addictive Behaviors, 25*(3), 435–439.

Escobar-Chaves, S. L., Tortolero, S. R., Markham, C. M., Low, B. J., Eitel, P., & Thickstun, P. (2005). Impact of the media on adolescent sexual attitudes and behaviors. *Pediatrics, 116*(Supplement), 303.

Fals-Stewart, W. (2003). The occurrence of partner physical aggression on days of alcohol consumption: A longitudinal diary study. *Journal of Consulting and Clinical Psychology, 71*(1), 41.

Famularo, R., Kinscherff, R., & Fenton, T. (1992). Psychiatric diagnoses of maltreated children: Preliminary findings. *Journal of the American Academy of Child & Adolescent Psychiatry, 31*(5), 863–867.

Feldstein, S. W., & Miller, W. R. (2006). Substance use and risk-taking among adolescents. *Journal of Mental Health, 15*(6), 633–643.

Felitti, V. J., Anda, R. F., Nordenberg, D., Williamson, D. F., Spitz, A. M., Edwards, V., Koss, M. P., & Marks, J. S. (1998). Relationship of childhood abuse and household dysfunction to many of the leading causes of death in adults: The Adverse Childhood Experiences (ACE) Study. *American Journal of Preventive Medicine, 14*(4), 245–258.

Fergusson, D. M., Horwood, L., & Lynskey, M. T. (1996). Childhood sexual abuse and psychiatric disorder in young adulthood: II. Psychiatric outcomes of childhood sexual abuse. *Journal of the American Academy of Child & Adolescent Psychiatry, 35*(10), 1365–1374.

Fergusson, D. M., Horwood, L. J., & Lynskey, M. T. (1997). Childhood sexual abuse, adolescent sexual behaviors and sexual revictimization. *Child Abuse & Neglect, 21*(8), 789–803.

Finkelhor, D. (1993). Epidemiological factors in the clinical identification of child sexual abuse. *Child Abuse & Neglect, 17*(1), 67–70.

Flannery, D. J., Rowe, D. C., & Gulley, B. L. (1993). Impact of pubertal status, timing, and age on adolescent sexual experience and delinquency. *Journal of Adolescent Research, 8*(1), 21–40.

Flay, B. R. (2000). Approaches to substance use prevention utilizing school curriculum plus social environment change. *Addictive Behaviors, 25*(6), 861–885.

Flay, B. R., & Sobel, J. L. (1983). The role of mass media in preventing adolescent substance abuse. In *Preventing adolescent drug abuse: Intervention strategies* (pp. 5–35). Washington, DC: National Institute on Drug Abuse.

Fleming, C. B., White, H. R., & Catalano, R. F. (2010). Romantic relationships and substance use in early adulthood. *Journal of Health and Social Behavior*, *51*(2), 153–167.

Flynn, B. S., Worden, J. K., Secker-Walker, R. H., Badger, G. J., Geller, B. M., & Costanza, M. C. (1992). Prevention of cigarette smoking through mass media intervention and school programs. *American Journal of Public Health*, *82*(6), 827.

Flynn, B. S., Worden, J. K., Secker-Walker, R. H., Pirie, P. L., Badger, G. J., Carpenter, J. H., & Geller, B. M. (1994). Mass media and school interventions for cigarette smoking prevention: Effects 2 years after completion. *American Journal of Public Health*, *84*(7), 1148.

Foshee, V. A., Benefield, T., Suchindran, C., Ennett, S. T., Bauman, K. E., Karriker-Jaffe, K. J., Reyes, H. L. M. N., & Mathias, J. (2009). The development of four types of adolescent dating abuse and selected demographic correlates. *Journal of Research on Adolescence*, *19*(3), 380–400.

Foshee, V. A., Linder, F., MacDougall, J. E., & Bangdiwala, S. (2001). Gender differences in the longitudinal predictors of adolescent dating violence. *Preventive Medicine*, *32*(2), 128–141.

French, D. C., & Dishion, T. J. (2003). Predictors of early initiation of sexual intercourse among high-risk adolescents. *The Journal of Early Adolescence*, *23*(3), 295–315.

Fromme, K., Stroot, E. A., & Kaplan, D. (1993). Comprehensive effects of alcohol: Development and psychometric assessment of a new expectancy questionnaire. *Psychological Assessment*, *5*(1), 19.

Garnefski, N., & Arends, E. (1998). Sexual abuse and adolescent maladjustment: Differences between male and female victims. *Journal of Adolescence*, *21*(1), 99–107.

Gaudineau, A., Ehlinger, V., Vayssiere, C., Jouret, B., Arnaud, C., & Godeau, E. (2010). Factors associated with early menarche: Results from the French Health Behaviour in School-aged Children (HBSC) study. *BMC Public Health*, *10*(1), 175.

Ge, X., Conger, R. D., & Elder, G. H., Jr (1996). Coming of age too early: Pubertal influences on girls' vulnerability to psychological distress. *Child Development*, *67*(6), 3386–3400.

Ge, X., Conger, R. D., & Elder, G. H., Jr (2001). Pubertal transition, stressful life events, and the emergence of gender differences in adolescent depressive symptoms. *Developmental Psychology*, *37*(3), 404.

Gelles, R. J. (1983). An exchange/social control theory. In D. Finkelhor, R. J. Gelles, G. T. Hotaling, & M. A. Straus (Eds.), *The dark side of families: Current family violence research* (pp. 151–165). Beverly Hills, CA: Sage.

Giancola, P. R. (2000). Executive functioning: a conceptual framework for alcohol-related aggression. *Experimental and Clinical Psychopharmacology*, *8*(4), 576.

Giaconia, R. M., Reinherz, H. Z., Hauf, A. C., Paradis, A. D., Wasserman, M. S., & Langhammer, D. M. (2000). Comorbidity of substance use and post-traumatic stress disorders in a community sample of adolescents. *American Journal of Orthopsychiatry*, *70*(2), 253–262.

Glass, N., Fredland, N., Campbell, J., Yonas, M., Sharps, P., & Kub, J. (2003). Adolescent dating violence: Prevalence, risk factors, health outcomes, and implications for clinical practice. *Journal of Obstetric, Gynecologic, & Neonatal Nursing*, *32*(2), 227–238.

Glass, R. J., Chan, G., & Rentz, D. (2000). Cognitive impairment screening in second offense DUI programs. *Journal of Substance Abuse Treatment*, *19*(4), 369–373.

Golub, M. S., Collman, G. W., Foster, P., Kimmel, C. A., Rajpert-De Meyts, E., Reiter, E. O., Sharpe, R. M., Skakkebaek, N. E., & Toppari, J. (2008). Public health implications of altered puberty timing. *Pediatrics*, *121*(Supplement 3), S218.

Goodwin, R. D., Fergusson, D. M., & Horwood, L. J. (2004). Association between anxiety disorders and substance use disorders among young persons: Results of a 21-year longitudinal study. *Journal of Psychiatric Research*, *38*(3), 295–304.

Graber, J. A., Lewinsohn, P. M., Seeley, J. R., & Brooks-Gunn, J. (1997). Is psychopathology associated with the timing of pubertal development? *Journal of the American Academy of Child & Adolescent Psychiatry*, *36*(12), 1768–1776.

Graber, J. A., Seeley, J. R., Brooks-Gunn, J., & Lewinsohn, P. M. (2004). Is pubertal timing associated with psychopathology in young adulthood? *Journal of the American Academy of Child & Adolescent Psychiatry*, *43*(6), 718–726.

Griffin, J. A., Umstattd, M. R., & Usdan, S. L. (2010). Alcohol use and high-risk sexual behavior among collegiate women: A review of research on alcohol myopia theory. *Journal of American College Health*, *58*(6), 523–532.

Guo, J., Stanton, B., Cottrell, L., Clemens, R. L., Li, X., Harris, C., Marshall, S., & Gibson, C. (2005). Substance use among rural adolescent virgins as a predictor of sexual initiation. *Journal of Adolescent Health*, *37*(3), 252–255.

Harrison, P. A., Edwall, G. E., Hoffman, N. G., & Worthen, M. D. (1990). Correlates of sexual abuse among boys in treatment for chemical dependency. *Journal of Child & Adolescent Substance Abuse*, *1*(1), 53–67.

Harrison, P. A., Fulkerson, J. A., & Beebe, T. J. (1997). Multiple substance use among adolescent physical and sexual abuse victims. *Child Abuse & Neglect*, *21*(6), 529–539.

Harrison, P. A., Hoffmann, N. G., & Edwall, G. E. (1989). Sexual abuse correlates. *Journal of Adolescent Research*, *4*(3), 385–399.

Hawk, S. T., Vanwesenbeeck, I., de Graaf, H., & Bakker, F. (2006). Adolescents' contact with sexuality in mainstream media: A selection-based perspective. *Journal of Sex Research*, *43*(4), 352–363.

Hawkins, J. D., & Catalano, R. F., Jr. (1992). *Communities that care: Action for drug abuse prevention* Jossey-Bass, San Francisco, CA. Retrieved from https://search.proquest.com/docview/618228113?accountid=14524.

Herman-Giddens, M. E., Slora, E. J., Wasserman, R. C., Bourdony, C. J., Bhapkar, M. V., Koch, G. G., & Hasemeier, C. M. (1997). Secondary sexual characteristics and menses in young girls seen in office practice: A study from the Pediatric Research in Office Settings network. *Pediatrics*, *99*(4), 505.

Herrera, V. M., Wiersma, J. D., & Cleveland, H. H. (2011). Romantic partners' contribution to the continuity of male and female delinquent and violent behavior. *Journal of Research on Adolescence*, *21*(3), 608–618.

Hoff, T., Greene, L., & Davis, J. (2003). National survey of adolescents and young adults: Sexual health knowledge, attitudes and experiences. Menlo Park, California, Henry J. Kaiser Family Foundation, 2003. 136 p.

Holt, M. K., & Espelage, D. L. (2005). Social support as a moderator between dating violence victimization and depression/anxiety among African American and Caucasian adolescents. *School Psychology Review*, *34*(3), 309.

Howard, D. E., Griffin, M. A., & Boekeloo, B. O. (2008). Prevalence and psychosocial correlates of alcohol-related sexual assault among university students. *Adolescence*, *43*(172), 733.

Howard, D. E., Qi Wang, M., & Yan, F. (2007). Psychosocial factors associated with reports of physical dating violence among U.S. adolescent females. *Adolescence, 42*(166), 311.

Howard, D. E., Qiu, Y., & Boekeloo, B. (2003). Personal and social contextual correlates of adolescent dating violence. *Journal of Adolescent Health, 33*(1), 9–17.

Huang, T. Y., & Feng, J. Y. (2008). Dating violence among college students in Taiwan. Poster presentation at the 19th International Nursing Research Congress Focusing on Evidence-Based Practice, 2008, Singapore

Humphrey, S. E., & Kahn, A. S. (2000). Fraternities, athletic teams, and rape. *Journal of Interpersonal Violence, 15*(12), 1313–1320.

Iannotti, R. J., Kogan, M. D., Janssen, I., & Boyce, W. F. (2009). Patterns of adolescent physical activity, screen-based media use, and positive and negative health indicators in the US and Canada. *Journal of Adolescent Health, 44*(5), 493–499.

Jackson, S. M. (1999). Issues in the dating violence research: A review of the literature. *Aggression and Violent Behavior, 4*(2), 233–247.

Jessor, R., & Jessor, S. L. (1977). *Problem behavior and psychosocial development: A longitudinal study of youth.* New York: Academic Press.

Justus, A. N., Finn, P. R., & Steinmetz, J. E. (2000). The influence of traits of disinhibition on the association between alcohol use and risky sexual behavior. *Alcoholism: Clinical and Experimental Research, 24*(7), 1028–1035.

Kahn, J. A., Kaplowitz, R. A., Goodman, E., & Emans, S. J. (2002). The association between impulsiveness and sexual risk behaviors in adolescent and young adult women. *Journal of Adolescent Health, 30*(4), 229–232.

Kaiser Family Foundation. (2004). *Health insurance survey.* Retrieved from https://kaiserfamilyfoundation.files.wordpress.com/2013/01/2003-health-insurance-survey-summary-and-chartpack.pdf.

Kalichman, S. C., & Cain, D. (2004). The relationship between indicators of sexual compulsivity and high risk sexual practices among men and women receiving services from a sexually transmitted infection clinic. *Journal of Sex Research, 41*(3), 235–241.

Kalichman, S. C., Cain, D., Zweben, A., & Swain, G. (2003). Sensation seeking, alcohol use and sexual risk behaviors among men receiving services at a clinic for sexually transmitted infections. *Journal of Studies on Alcohol, 64*(4), 564–569.

Kalichman, S. C., Heckman, T., & Kelly, J. A. (1996). Sensation seeking as an explanation for the association between substance use and HIV-related risky sexual behavior. *Archives of Sexual Behavior, 25*(2), 141–154.

Kann, L., Kinchen, S. A., Williams, B. I., Ross, J. G., Lowry, R., Grunbaum, J. A., & Kolbe, L. J. (2000). Youth risk behavior surveillance—United States, 1999. *Journal of School Health, 70*(7), 271–285.

Kaplowitz, P. B., & Oberfield, S. E. (1999). Reexamination of the age limit for defining when puberty is precocious in girls in the United States: Implications for evaluation and treatment. *Pediatrics, 104*(4), 936–941.

Kilpatrick, D. G., Acierno, R., Saunders, B., Resnick, H. S., Best, C. L., & Schnurr, P. P. (2000). Risk factors for adolescent substance abuse and dependence: Data from a national sample. *Journal of Consulting and Clinical Psychology, 68*(1), 19.

Kim-Godwin, Y. S., Clements, C., McCuiston, A. M., & Fox, J. A. (2009). Dating violence among high school students in southeastern North Carolina. *The Journal of School Nursing, 25*(2), 141–151.

Kirillova, G. P., Vanyukov, M. M., Kirisci, L., & Reynolds, M. (2008). Physical maturation, peer environment, and the ontogenesis of substance use disorders. *Psychiatry Research, 158*(1), 43–53.

Kollins, S. H. (2003). Delay discounting is associated with substance use in college students. *Addictive Behaviors, 28*(6), 1167–1173.

Kotchick, B. A., Shaffer, A., Miller, K. S., & Forehand, R. (2001). Adolescent sexual risk behavior: A multi-system perspective. *Clinical psychology review, 21*(4), 493–519.

Kreager, D. A., & Haynie, D. L. (2011). Dangerous liaisons? Dating and drinking diffusion in adolescent peer networks. *American Sociological Review, 76*(5), 737–763.

Kreiter, S. R., Krowchuk, D. P., Woods, C. R., Sinal, S. H., Lawless, M. R., & DuRant, R. H. (1999). Gender differences in risk behaviors among adolescents who experience date fighting. *Pediatrics, 104*(6), 1286–1292.

Kushner, M. G., Abrams, K., & Borchardt, C. (2000). The relationship between anxiety disorders and alcohol use disorders: A review of major perspectives and findings. *Clinical Psychology Review, 20*(2), 149–171.

Lewis, S. F., & Fremouw, W. (2001). Dating violence: A critical review of the literature. *Clinical Psychology Review, 21*(1), 105–127.

Little, C. B. & Rankin, A. (2001). Why do they start it? Explaining reported early-teen sexual activity. *Sociological Forum, 16*(4), 703–729.

Locke, B. D., & Mahalik, J. R. (2005). Examining masculinity norms, problem drinking, and athletic involvement as predictors of sexual aggression in college men. *Journal of Counseling Psychology, 52*(3), 279.

Luster, T., & Small, S. A. (1997). Sexual abuse history and number of sex partners among female adolescents. *Family Planning Perspectives, 29*(5), 204–211.

Lynne-Landsman, S. D., Graber, J. A., & Andrews, J. A. (2010). Do trajectories of household risk in childhood moderate pubertal timing effects on substance initiation in middle school? *Developmental Psychology, 46*(4), 853.

Magid, V., MacLean, M. G., & Colder, C. R. (2007). Differentiating between sensation seeking and impulsivity through their mediated relations with alcohol use and problems. *Addictive Behaviors, 32*(10), 2046–2061.

Magnusson, C. (2001). Adolescent girls' sexual attitudes and opposite-sex relations in 1970 and in 1996. *Journal of Adolescent Health, 28*(3), 242–252.

Manlove, J. S., Ryan, S., & Franzetta, K. (2007). Risk and protective factors associated with the transition to a first sexual relationship with an older partner. *Journal of Adolescent Health, 40*(2), 135–143.

Markey, C. N., Markey, P. M., & Tinsley, B. J. (2003). Personality, puberty, and preadolescent girls' risky behaviors: Examining the predictive value of the Five-Factor Model of personality. *Journal of Research in Personality, 37*(5), 405–419.

Martinez, G., Copen, C., & Abma, J. (2011). Teenagers in the United States: Sexual activity, contraceptive use, and child-bearing, 2006–2010 national survey of family growth. *Vital and Health Statistics. Series 23, Data from the National Survey of Family Growth, 31*, 1.

Mason, W. A., Zimmerman, L., & Evans, W. (1998). Sexual and physical abuse among incarcerated youth: Implications for sexual behavior, contraceptive use, and teenage pregnancy1. *Child Abuse & Neglect, 22*(10), 987–995.

McCoul, M. D., & Haslam, N. (2001). Predicting high risk sexual behaviour in heterosexual and homosexual men: The roles of impulsivity and sensation seeking. *Personality and Individual Differences, 31*(8), 1303–1310.

McCurdy, K., & Daro, D. (1994). Child maltreatment. *Journal of Interpersonal Violence, 9*(1), 75.

McEwen, W. J., & Hanneman, G. J. (1974). The depiction of drug use in television programming. *Journal of Drug Education, 4*(3), 281–293.

McGee H., Garavan R., De Barra M., Byrne J. & Conroy R. (2002). *The SAVI Report: Sexual Abuse and Violence in Ireland*. Dublin: The Liffey Press, p. 22.

McNaughton Reyes, H. L., Foshee, V. A., Bauer, D. J., & Ennett, S. T. (2011). The role of heavy alcohol use in the developmental process of desistance in dating aggression during adolescence. *Journal of Abnormal Child Psychology, 39*(2), 239–250.

Mendle, J., Turkheimer, E., & Emery, R. E. (2007). Detrimental psychological outcomes associated with early pubertal timing in adolescent girls. *Developmental Review, 27*(2), 151–171.

Messman-Moore, T. L., & Long, P. J. (2003). The role of childhood sexual abuse sequelae in the sexual revictimization of women: An empirical review and theoretical reformulation. *Clinical Psychology Review, 23*(4), 537–571.

Meyer-Bahlburg, H. F. L., Ehrhardt, A. A., Bell, J. J., Cohen, S. F., Healey, J. M., Feldman, J. F., Morishima, A., Baker, S. W., & New, M. I. (1985). Idiopathic precocious puberty in girls: Psychosexual development. *Journal of Youth and Adolescence, 14*(4), 339–353.

Mezzich, A. C., Tarter, R. E., Giancola, P. R., Lu, S., Kirisci, L., & Parks, S. (1997). Substance use and risky sexual behavior in female adolescents. *Drug and Alcohol Dependence, 44*(2), 157–166.

Miller, K. S., Clark, L. F., Wendell, D. A., Levin, M. L., Gray-Ray, P., Velez, C. N., & Webber, M. P. (1997). Adolescent heterosexual experience: A new typology. *Journal of Adolescent Health, 20*(3), 179–186.

Miller, M. A., Alberts, J. K., Hecht, M. L., Trost, M. R., & Krizek, R. L. (2000). *Adolescent relationships and drug use* Lawrence Erlbaum Associates Publishers, Mahwah, NJ.

Molnar, B. E., Berkman, L., & Buka, S. L. (2001). Psychopathology, childhood sexual abuse and other childhood adversities: Relative links to subsequent suicidal behaviour in the US. *Psychological Medicine, 31*(6), 965–977.

Monahan, J. L., & Lannutti, P. J. (2000). Alcohol as social lubricant. *Human Communication Research, 26*(2), 175–202.

Money, J., & Walker, P. A. (1971). Psychosexual development, maternalism, nonpromiscuity, and body image in 15 females with precocious puberty. *Archives of Sexual Behavior, 1*(1), 45–60.

Mongeau, P. A., & Johnson, K. L. (1995). Predicting cross-sex first-date sexual expectations and involvement: Contextual and individual difference factors. *Personal Relationships, 2*(4), 301–312.

Monti, P. M., Miranda, R., Jr, Nixon, K., Sher, K. J., Swartzwelder, H. S., Tapert, S. F., White, A., & Crews, F. T. (2005). Adolescence: Booze, brains, and behavior. *Alcoholism: Clinical and Experimental Research, 29*(2), 207–220.

Moore, T. M., Elkins, S. R., McNulty, J. K., Kivisto, A. J., & Handsel, V. A. (2011). Alcohol use and intimate partner violence perpetration among college students: Assessing the temporal association using electronic diary technology. *Psychology of Violence, 1*(4), 315.

Muehlenhard, C. L., & Linton, M. A. (1987). Date rape and sexual aggression in dating situations: Incidence and risk factors. *Journal of Counseling Psychology, 34*(2), 186.

Murphy, N. A., & Elias, E. R. (2006). Sexuality of children and adolescents with developmental disabilities. *Pediatrics, 118*(1), 398.

Mushquash, A. R., Stewart, S. H., Sherry, S. B., Mackinnon, S. P., Antony, M. M., & Sherry, D. L. (2013). Heavy episodic drinking among dating partners: A longitudinal actor–partner interdependence model. *Psychology of Addictive Behaviors, 27*(1), 178–183.

Mustanski, B. S., Viken, R. J., Kaprio, J., Pulkkinen, L., & Rose, R. J. (2004). Genetic and environmental influences on pubertal development: Longitudinal data from Finnish twins at ages 11 and 14. *Developmental Psychology, 40*(6), 1188.

National Survey of Family Growth (2009). Retrieved on December 5, 2017, from https://www.cdc.gov/nchs/data/series/sr_23/sr23_030.pdf.

National Child Traumatic Stress. (2008). Retrieved December 04, 2017, from http://nctsnet.org/.

Negriff, S., & Trickett, P. K. (2010). The relationship between pubertal timing and delinquent behavior in maltreated male and female adolescents. *The Journal of Early Adolescence, 30*(4), 518.

Noel, N. E., Maisto, S. A., Johnson, J. D., & Jackson, L. A., Jr (2009). The effects of alcohol and cue salience on young men's acceptance of sexual aggression. *Addictive Behaviors, 34*(4), 386–394.

O'Donnell, L., O'Donnell, C. R., & Stueve, A. (2001). Early sexual initiation and subsequent sex-related risks among urban minority youth: The reach for health study. *Family Planning Perspectives, 33*(6), 268–275.

O'Donnell, L., Stueve, A., Myint-U, A., Duran, R., Agronick, G., & Wilson-Simmons, R. (2006). Middle school aggression and subsequent intimate partner physical violence. *Journal of Youth and Adolescence, 35*(5), 693–703.

Ouimette, P. E., & Brown, P. J. (2003). *Trauma and substance abuse: Causes, consequences, and treatment of comorbid disorders*. Washington, DC: American Psychological Association.

Palmgreen, P., Donohew, L., Lorch, E. P., Hoyle, R. H., & Stephenson, M. T. (2001). Television campaigns and adolescent marijuana use: Tests of sensation seeking targeting. *American Journal of Public Health, 91*(2), 292.

Parent, A. S., Teilmann, G., Juul, A., Skakkebaek, N. E., Toppari, J., & Bourguignon, J. P. (2003). The timing of normal puberty and the age limits of sexual precocity: Variations around the world, secular trends, and changes after migration. *Endocrine Reviews, 24*(5), 668–693.

Partsch, C. J., & Sippell, W. G. (2001). Pathogenesis and epidemiology of precocious puberty: Effects of exogenous oestrogens. *Human Reproduction Update, 7*(3), 292.

Patterson, C. J., & Wainright, J. L. (2007). *Adolescents with same-sex parents: Findings from the National Longitudinal Study of Adolescent Health: Lesbian and gay adoption: A new American reality*. New York, NY: Oxford University Press.

Patton, G. C., McMorris, B. J., Toumbourou, J. W., Hemphill, S. A., Donath, S., & Catalano, R. F. (2004). Puberty and the onset of substance use and abuse. *Pediatrics, 114*(3), e300.

Pedersen, E. R., Lee, C. M., Larimer, M. E., & Neighbors, C. (2009). Gender and dating relationship status moderate the association between alcohol use and sex-related alcohol expectancies. *Addictive Behaviors*, *34*(9), 786–789.

Pedersen, W., & Skrondal, A. (1996). Alcohol and sexual victimization: a longitudinal study of Norwegian girls. *Addiction*, *91*(4), 565–581.

Plant, M., Miller, P., & Plant, M. (2007). Sexual abuse in childhood, alcohol consumption and relationships with a partner. *Journal of Substance Use*, *12*(1), 49–57.

Polusny, M. A., & Follette, V. M. (1995). Long-term correlates of child sexual abuse: Theory and review of the empirical literature. *Applied and Preventive Psychology*, *4*(3), 143–166.

Raj, A., Silverman, J. G., & Amaro, H. (2000). The relationship between sexual abuse and sexual risk among high school students: Findings from the 1997 Massachusetts Youth Risk Behavior Survey. *Maternal and Child Health Journal*, *4*(2), 125–134.

Reardon, L. E., Leen-Feldner, E. W., & Hayward, C. (2009). A critical review of the empirical literature on the relation between anxiety and puberty. *Clinical Psychology Review*, *29*(1), 1–23.

Regan, P. C., Durvasula, R., Howell, L., Ureno, O., & Rea, M. (2004). Gender, ethnicity, and the developmental timing of first sexual and romantic experiences. *Social Behavior and Personality: An International journal*, *32*(7), 667–676.

Rhynard, J., Krebs, M., & Glover, J. (1997). Sexual assault in dating relationships. *Journal of School Health*, *67*(3), 89–93.

Roberts, D. F. (1999). *Kids and Media@ the New Millennium: A comprehensive national analysis of children's media use*. Darby, PA Diane Publishing.

Roberts, S. T., & Kennedy, B. L. (2006). Why are young college women not using condoms? Their perceived risk, drug use, and developmental vulnerability may provide important clues to sexual risk. *Archives of Psychiatric Nursing*, *20*(1), 32–40.

Roberts, T. A., Auinger, P., & Klein, J. D. (2005). Intimate partner abuse and the reproductive health of sexually active female adolescents. *Journal of Adolescent Health*, *36*(5), 380–385.

Robinson, T. N., Chen, H. L., & Killen, J. D. (1998). Television and music video exposure and risk of adolescent alcohol use. *Pediatrics*, *102*(5), e54.

Roche, D. N., Runtz, M. G., & Hunter, M. A. (1999). Adult attachment. *Journal of Interpersonal Violence*, *14*(2), 184–207.

Rothman, E. F., Stuart, G. L., Greenbaum, P. E., Heeren, T., Bowen, D. J., Vinci, R., Baughman, A. L., & Bernstein, J. (2011). Drinking style and dating violence in a sample of urban, alcohol-using youth. *Journal of Studies on Alcohol and Drugs*, *72*(4), 555–566.

Santelli, J. S., Abma, J., Ventura, S., Lindberg, L., Morrow, B., Anderson, J. E., Lyss, S., & Hamilton, B. E. (2004). Can changes in sexual behaviors among high school students explain the decline in teen pregnancy rates in the 1990s? *Journal of Adolescent Health*, *35*(2), 80–90.

Sargent, J. D., Beach, M. L., Dalton, M. A., Mott, L. A., Tickle, J. J., Ahrens, M. B., & Heatherton, T. F. (2001). Effect of seeing tobacco use in films on trying smoking among adolescents: cross sectional study. *British Medical Journal*, *323*(7326), 1394.

Schalling D. Psychopathy-related personality variables and the psychophysiology of socialization. In: Hare RD, Schalling D, editors. *Psychopathic behavior: Approaches to research*. Chichester: Wiley; 1978. pp. 85–106.

Scaramella, L. V., Conger, R. D., Simons, R. L., & Whitbeck, L. B. (1998). Predicting risk for pregnancy by late adolescence: A social contextual perspective. *Developmental Psychology*, *34*(6), 1233–1245.

Schmiege, S. J., Levin, M. E., & Bryan, A. D. (2009). Regression mixture models of alcohol use and risky sexual behavior among criminally-involved adolescents. *Prevention Science*, *10*(4), 335–344.

Schofield, H. L. T., Bierman, K. L., Heinrichs, B., & Nix, R. L. (2008). Predicting early sexual activity with behavior problems exhibited at school entry and in early adolescence. *Journal of Abnormal Child Psychology*, *36*(8), 1175–1188.

Sher, K. J., Bartholow, B. D., & Wood, M. D. (2000). Personality and substance use disorders: A prospective study. *Journal of Consulting and Clinical Psychology*, *68*(5), 818.

Sher, K. J., & Trull, T. J. (1994). Personality and disinhibitory psychopathology: Alcoholism and antisocial personality disorder. *Journal of Abnormal Psychology*, *103*(1), 92.

Silverman, J. G., Raj, A., & Clements, K. (2004). Dating violence and associated sexual risk and pregnancy among adolescent girls in the United States. *Pediatrics*, *114*(2), 220–225.

Silverman, J. G., Raj, A., Mucci, L. A., & Hathaway, J. E. (2001). Dating violence against adolescent girls and associated substance use, unhealthy weight control, sexual risk behavior, pregnancy, and suicidality. *JAMA: The Journal of the American Medical Association*, *286*(5), 572.

Simons, J. S., Gaher, R. M., Correia, C. J., Hansen, C. L., & Christopher, M. S. (2005). An affective-motivational model of marijuana and alcohol problems among college students. *Psychology of Addictive Behaviors*, *19*(3), 326.

Simpson, T. L., & Miller, W. R. (2002). Concomitance between childhood sexual and physical abuse and substance use problems: A review. *Clinical Psychology Review*, *22*(1), 27–77.

Sonis, W. A., Comite, F., Blue, J., Pescovitz, O. H., Rahn, C. W., & Hench, K. D. (1985). Behavior problems and social competence in girls with true precocious puberty+. *The Journal of Pediatrics*, *106*(1), 156–160.

Stappenbeck, C. A., & Fromme, K. (2010). A longitudinal investigation of heavy drinking and physical dating violence in men and women. *Addictive Behaviors*, *35*(5), 479–485.

Steel, J. L., & Herlitz, C. A. (2005). The association between childhood and adolescent sexual abuse and proxies for sexual risk behavior: A random sample of the general population of Sweden. *Child Abuse & Neglect*, *29*(10), 1141–1153.

Stewart, S. H. (1996). Alcohol abuse in individuals exposed to trauma: A critical review. *Psychological Bulletin*, *120*(1), 83.

Stice, E., Presnell, K., & Bearman, S. K. (2001). Relation of early menarche to depression, eating disorders, substance abuse, and comorbid psychopathology among adolescent girls. *Developmental Psychology*, *37*(5), 608.

Sun, S. S., Schubert, C. M., Chumlea, W. C., Roche, A. F., Kulin, H. E., Lee, P. A., Himes, J. H., & Ryan, A. S. (2002). National estimates of the timing of sexual maturation and racial differences among US children. *Pediatrics*, *110*(5), 911.

Tapert, S. F., Aarons, G. A., Sedlar, G. R., & Brown, S. A. (2001). Adolescent substance use and sexual risk-taking behavior. *Journal of Adolescent Health*, *28*(3), 181–189.

Tapert, S. F., & Schweinsburg, A. D. (2005). The human adolescent brain and alcohol use disorders. *Recent Developments in Alcoholism*, *17*, 177–197.

Teilmann, G., Pedersen, C. B., Jensen, T. K., Skakkebæk, N. E., & Juul, A. (2005). Prevalence and incidence of precocious pubertal development in Denmark: An epidemiologic study based on national registries. *Pediatrics, 116*(6), 1323.

Temple, J. R., Weston, R., & Marshall, L. L. (2010). Long term mental health effects of partner violence patterns and relationship termination on low-income and ethnically diverse community women. *Partner Abuse, 1*(4), 379.

Testa, M., & Livingston, J. A. (1999). Qualitative analysis of women's experiences of sexual aggression. *Psychology of Women Quarterly, 23*(3), 573.

Testa, M., & Parks, K. A. (1996). The role of women's alcohol consumption in sexual victimization. *Aggression and Violent Behavior, 1*(3), 217–234.

Triffleman, E. G., Marmar, C. R., Delucchi, K. L., & Ronfeldt, H. (1995). Childhood trauma and posttraumatic stress disorder in substance abuse inpatients. *Journal of Nervous and Mental Disease, 183*(3), 172–176.

Trull, T. J., Waudby, C. J., & Sher, K. J. (2004). Alcohol, tobacco, and drug use disorders and personality disorder symptoms. *Experimental and Clinical Psychopharmacology, 12*(1), 65.

Tschann, J. M., Adler, N. E., Irwin, C. E., Millstein, S. G., Turner, R. A., & Kegeles, S. M. (1994). Initiation of substance use in early adolescence: The roles of pubertal timing and emotional distress. *Health Psychology, 13*(4), 326.

Tyler, T. R. (2002). A national survey for monitoring police legitimacy. *Justice Research and Policy, 4*(1), 71–86.

Ullman, S. E., Karabatsos, G., & Koss, M. P. (1999). Alcohol and sexual aggression in a national sample of college men. *Psychology of Women Quarterly, 23*(4), 673.

Varlinskaya, E. I., & Spear, L. P. (2006). Ontogeny of acute tolerance to ethanol-induced social inhibition in Sprague–Dawley rats. *Alcoholism: Clinical and Experimental Research, 30*(11), 1833–1844.

Villani, S. (2001). Impact of media on children and adolescents: A 10-year review of the research. *Journal of the American Academy of Child & Adolescent Psychiatry, 40*(4), 392–401.

Westling, E., Andrews, J. A., Hampson, S. E., & Peterson, M. (2008). Pubertal timing and substance use: The effects of gender, parental monitoring and deviant peers. *Journal of Adolescent Health, 42*(6), 555–563.

Whitfield, C. L., Anda, R. F., Dube, S. R., & Felitti, V. J. (2003). Violent childhood experiences and the risk of intimate partner violence in adults. *Journal of Interpersonal Violence, 18*(2), 166–185.

Wichstrøm, L. (2001). The impact of pubertal timing on adolescents' alcohol use. *Journal of Research on Adolescence, 11*(2), 131–150.

Widom, C. S., & Kuhns, J. B. (1996). Childhood victimization and subsequent risk for promiscuity, prostitution, and teenage pregnancy: A prospective study. *American Journal of Public Health, 86*(11), 1607.

Wilson, A. E., Calhoun, K. S., & McNair, L. D. (2002). Alcohol consumption and expectancies among sexually coercive college men. *Journal of Interpersonal Violence, 17*(11), 1145.

Windle, M., & Windle, R. C. (1996). Coping strategies, drinking motives, and stressful life events among middle adolescents: Associations with emotional and behavioral problems and with academic functioning. *Journal of Abnormal Psychology, 105*(4), 551.

Wingood, G. M., DiClemente, R. J., & McCree, D. H. (2001). Dating violence and the sexual health of black adolescent females. *Pediatrics, 107*(5), 72.

Wise, L. A., Palmer, J. R., Rothman, E. F., & Rosenberg, L. (2009). Childhood abuse and early menarche: Findings from the Black Women's Health Study. *American Journal of Public Health, 99*(S2), S460.

Wu, J., Witkiewitz, K., McMahon, R. J., & Dodge, K. A. (2010). A parallel process growth mixture model of conduct problems and substance use with risky sexual behavior. *Drug and Alcohol Dependence, 111*(3), 207–214.

Yama, M. F., Fogas, B. S., Teegarden, L. A., & Hastings, B. (1993). Childhood sexual abuse and parental alcoholism: Interactive effects in adult women. *American Journal of Orthopsychiatry, 63*(2), 300–305.

Young, A. M., King, L., Abbey, A., & Boyd, C. J. (2009). Adolescent peer-on-peer sexual aggression: Characteristics of aggressors of alcohol and non-alcohol-related assault. *Journal of Studies on Alcohol and Drugs, 70*(5), 700.

Yurgelun-Todd, D. (2007). Emotional and cognitive changes during adolescence. *Current Opinion in Neurobiology, 17*(2), 251–257.

Zawacki, T., Abbey, A., Buck, P. O., McAuslan, P., & Clinton-Sherrod, A. M. (2003). Perpetrators of alcohol-involved sexual assaults: How do they differ from other sexual assault perpetrators and nonperpetrators? *Aggressive Behavior, 29*(4), 366–380.

Zierler, S., Feingold, L., Laufer, D., Velentgas, P., Kantrowitz-Gordon, I., & Mayer, K. (1991). Adult survivors of childhood sexual abuse and subsequent risk of HIV infection. *American Journal of Public Health, 81*(5), 572.

Zimmer-Gembeck, M., Siebenbruner, J., & Collins, W. A. (2004). A prospective study of intraindividual and peer influences on adolescents' heterosexual romantic and sexual behavior. *Archives of Sexual Behavior, 33*(4), 381–394.

Zuckerman, M. (1991). *Psychobiology of personality.* Cambridge, UK: Cambridge University Press.

Zuckerman, M. (1994). *Behavioral expressions and biosocial bases of sensation seeking.* Cambridge, UK: Cambridge University Press.

Zuckerman, M. (1996). Impulsive unsocialized sensation seeking: A comparative approach. *Neuropsychobiology, 34,* 125–129.

Substance-Impaired Driving in Adolescence

Kayleigh N. McCarty *and* Denis M. McCarthy

Abstract

Driving while impaired by alcohol and other substances is a substantial problem for adolescents. This chapter provides an overview of the current state of the literature on adolescent substance-impaired driving (SID), including trends in the rate of engagement by gender, race, and ethnicity, and the effect of specific policies in reducing these rates. Factors that affect adolescent risk for SID are also discussed, including social and parental influences, personality traits, and cognitive factors. Interventions and prevention methods for reducing SID in adolescents are reviewed. The chapter concludes by highlighting future directions for research on this topic, including an increased focus on marijuana-impaired driving; the development of adolescent-specific theoretical models; and the examination of proximal, event-level influences on SID.

Key Words: substance-impaired driving, adolescence, intervention, policy, marijuana, alcohol

For many adolescents, obtaining a license to drive independently is a significant event. In addition to social and personal advantages, learning to drive and driving independently can also involve the navigation of key issues in adolescent development, such as gaining autonomy and independence from parents (Laird, 2011). Learning to drive also involves the acquisition of a complex set of cognitive and motor skills, many of which adolescents are not well suited to master. Motor vehicle accidents are typically a leading cause of death for people ages 13–18 years in the United States (Heron, 2016), and the majority (>75%) of motor vehicle crashes involving youth are attributable to driving error by the adolescent (Curry, Hafetz, Kallan, Winston, Winston, & Durbin 2011). The high risk associated with teen driving is thought to result from a combination of inexperience and the physical, cognitive, psychosocial, and neurological aspects of adolescence.

In addition to the inherent risks of driving during this period, the initiation and use of alcohol and other substances are also common during adolescence (Degenhardt et al., 2008). Adolescents are therefore simultaneously working to develop the skills needed to drive safely and learning to negotiate decisions about driving after use of substances or riding with a driver who has done so. Encouragingly, there is some evidence that adolescents are actually less likely than older drivers to choose to drive while intoxicated (Hingson & Winter, 2003; Royal, 2003). However, due in part to their relative inexperience with both driving and substance use, adolescents are more susceptible to substance-related impairment of driving skill. For example, risk of fatal car accidents is higher for young drivers at all blood alcohol concentration (BAC) levels, and risk increases faster for youth as BAC increases (Voas, Torres, Romano, & Lacey, 2012; Zador, Krawchuk, & Voas, 2000). Youth also tend to consume a greater amount of alcohol before driving and consider it safe to drive at higher BACs than older drivers (Hingson & Winter, 2003).

In this chapter, we provide a review of the current state of the literature on adolescent substance-impaired driving (SID), covering epidemiology, policy, risk factors for SID (familial and peer influences, individual difference factors), and treatment/intervention. We then review what we see as important future directions for SID research, including an increased emphasis on understanding the prevalence of and risk associated with marijuana-impaired driving, the need for developmentally informed theoretical models specific to SID, and finally the need for improving our understanding of proximal, event-level influences on the decision to engage in SID.

Adolescent Engagement in Substance-Impaired Driving

Estimates of adolescent engagement in SID are influenced by a number of methodological factors. Differences in the source of the data (self-report, biological screening, traffic records, roadside surveys; Romano, Voas, & Lacey, 2010), the time frame assessed (weekend driving, past 2 weeks, past year), and the substance(s) targeted can result in varying estimates of adolescent SID. For substances other than alcohol, there is also considerable variability in the accuracy of biological indicators (oral fluid test, blood test) and their ability to correctly quantify current intoxication or to disentangle current intoxication from recent use. Despite this methodological variability, some general conclusions about the prevalence of adolescent SID emerge from the literature.

Although the percent of adolescents who engage in SID is lower than other age groups (Hingson & Winter, 2003; Royal, 2003), it is still alarmingly high. Recent data from the Monitoring the Future (MTF) study indicate that 16% of high school seniors report SID in the past 2 weeks (O'Malley & Johnston, 2013). Estimates of SID from the 2013 National Survey on Drug Use and Health (NSDUH) were lower, with 8.7% of 17 year olds and 12.6% of 18 years olds reporting past-year SID (Substance Abuse and Mental Heealth Services Administration, 2014). Data from the 2007 National Roadside Survey (NRS: Lacey et al., 2009) found that 7.9% of adolescent drivers had a positive BAC on weekend nights. The same study (Lacey et al., 2009) found that 16.1% of adolescent nighttime drivers tested positive for a potentially impairing substance other than alcohol on oral fluid test (oral fluid tests may reflect recent use rather than acute impairment, so it may overestimate impaired drivers).

Trends over time indicate that, for alcohol-impaired driving (AID), there was a steady decline in both overall rates and traffic crashes from 1980 and 1996 (Hingson & Winter, 2003). This trend extended to adolescents, who in fact showed the largest drop in rates of AID (Voas et al., 2007). Adolescents also showed the greatest decline in traffic crashes following use of alcohol (Royal, 2003) and marijuana (Terry-McElrath, O'Malley, & Johnston, 2014). Since 2000, adolescent rates of accidents, tickets, and warnings for driving after alcohol and marijuana use have remained relatively stable (Terry-McElrath et al., 2014).

Historically, adolescents have been more likely to use alcohol than other substances prior to driving, consistent with their rate of use of these substances (O'Malley & Johnston, 2003). However, recent trends have indicated an increase in driving after use of marijuana, such that the percentage of adolescents reporting driving after use of marijuana was higher (12.4%) than for alcohol (8.7%; O'Malley & Johnston, 2013). Although the NSDUH does not examine driving after marijuana separately from other illegal substances, a similar pattern has emerged in recent years, with higher rates of driving following illicit drug use than alcohol consumption for 16–18 year olds (SAMHSA, 2014). Recent data on fatally injured drivers suggest that nearly 20% of individuals under the age of 25 years tested positive for cannabinol (Brady & Li, 2013, a higher rate than reported for any other age group).

Demographic differences in SID are fairly consistent across studies. The percent of youth engaging in SID increases with age across late adolescence (SAMHSA, 2014; Walker, Treno, Grube, & Light, 2003). Male adolescents are more likely to engage in SID than females (e.g., alcohol 12% males vs. 7.8% females, Kann et al., 2014; marijuana 14.5% males vs. 8.6% females, O'Malley & Johnston, 2013). White and Latino adolescents are more likely than other racial/ethnic groups to report driving after drinking alcohol (Kann et al., 2014 O'Malley & Johnston, 2013). There is evidence that differences in SID rates across ethnicity, but not gender, may be due to differences in rates of substance use. For example, when alcohol use is controlled for, Latino youth were more likely than White youth to report AID (Walker et al., 2003).

Data regarding SID and urbanicity remain inconclusive. In the United States, studies suggest no difference in SID between adolescents in rural and urban settings (O'Malley & Johnston, 2013). Estimates from European countries and Canada indicate that SID and riding with an intoxicated driver are more common in rural settings (Font-Ribera et al., 2013; Poulin, Boudreau, & Asbridge, 2006). In contrast, urban youths in Australia were more likely to engage in AID than those living in rural communities (Dunsire & Baldwin, 1999).

Although rates of SID are high, rates of riding with a driver who has used alcohol or other substances are even higher. Recent data from MTF suggest that the percentage of high school seniors who reported riding (in the past year) with a driver who had used marijuana is the highest, at 21.9% (O'Malley & Johnston, 2013). Riding with a driver who had used alcohol is the second most common at 15.2%, while riding with a driver who had used an illicit drug (other than marijuana) was comparatively low at 3.7% (O'Malley & Johnston, 2013). Ethnic/racial differences emerge in riding with an intoxicated driver as well. Latino adolescents were more likely to ride with a driver who had been drinking alcohol than their White or Black counterparts (Kann et al., 2013). Although the decision to drive while impaired by substances and to ride with someone who is impaired are distinct behaviors (Yu & Shacket, 1999), recent data from the NEXT Generation Study suggest that youth reporting riding with an intoxicated driver were also more likely to report driving while intoxicated (Li, Simons-Morton, Vaca, & Hingson, 2014).

Policy and Substance-Impaired Driving

There is ample evidence that the rate of SID and SID-related crashes in adolescents has been significantly affected by the implementation of specific legal policies. Laws that have been shown to reduce adolescent SID, particularly AID, include those directly focused on adolescent SID (e.g., zero tolerance laws), on SID in general (e.g., per se laws), on adolescent use (e.g., increasing the minimum legal drinking age [MLDA]), or adolescent driving (e.g., graduated licensing).

The clearest evidence for the effect of policy on SID is for the increase in the MLDA. Multiple streams of evidence indicate that increases in the MLDA lead to the reduction of alcohol use, AID behavior, crashes, and fatalities. Reviews of the literature (Shults et al., 2001; Wagenaar & Toomey, 2002) have found that the vast majority of studies in the United States and Canada observe an inverse relationship between MLDA and both alcohol consumption and crash risk for adolescents. Data from the 1996 NRS indicated that adolescents showed the largest drop in rates of AID from earlier roadside surveys in 1986 and 1973 (Voas et al., 2007). Adolescents also showed the greatest decline in

alcohol-related fatal crashes from 1982 to 2003 (Royal, 2003).

Despite the weight of empirical evidence, there are occasional calls for reducing the MLDA in the United States (Choose Responsibility, n.d.). Several rationales have been provided for reducing the MLDA, including potential reductions in hazardous drinking and other (non-AID) alcohol-related negative consequences, that alternative methods for preventing adolescent AID are available (e.g., interlock devices for all vehicles; Pitts, Johnson, & Eidson, 2014), and that lowering the MLDA would not produce increases in AID in adolescents. A natural experiment addressing this last issue was conducted in New Zealand (Kypri et al., 2006), which lowered its minimum age for purchasing alcohol from 20 to 18 years in 1999. Results of this study suggest that lowering the drinking age would have a negative effect on AID. Although AID rates did not increase, the age groups both directly (18–19 year olds) and indirectly (15–17 year olds) affected by the change exhibited much lower rates of decline in alcohol-related traffic injuries, compared to those not affected by the change (20–24 year olds).

The establishment of per se laws for defining impairment by alcohol is another example of a highly effective policy in reducing SID. Reviews of the evidence in both the United States (Tippetts, Voas, Fell, & Nichols, 2005) and comparisons across countries (Mann et al., 2001) indicate that both the introduction of per se standards and the reduction of those standards (e.g., to .08 BAC in the United States) have produced reductions in alcohol-related crashes, and this reduction has been shown to extend to adolescents (Fell, Fisher, Voas, Blackman, & Tippetts, 2009).

Starting in the 1980s, US states began to implement specific (lower) BAC limits for adolescent drivers. An early review suggested that the implementation of these laws was effective in reducing nighttime single-vehicle fatal crashes involving adolescents (Hingson, Heeren, & Winter, 1994). This review also suggested that a limit of .00 or .02 BAC was more effective than lesser reductions (e.g., .05). This lower limit, typically described as zero tolerance (ZT), was increasingly adopted and, by 1997, over 80% of adolescents in the United States were covered by such laws (Voas, Tippetts, & Fell, 2003). Analyses of the effects of ZT laws have generally supported their effect on reducing self-reported AID (Wagenaar, Malley, & Lafond, 2001) and alcohol-related fatal crashes (Fell et al., 2009; Voas et al., 2003). However, a study using the

Behavioral Risk Factor Surveillance System found that ZT laws reduced self-reported alcohol use in males, but not females, and did not support an effect of ZT on self-reported AID (Carpenter, 2004).

Laws that place restrictions on adolescent driving behavior in general have been found to reduce adolescent traffic accidents, including fatal crashes (e.g., Shope, 2007; Shope, Molnar, Elliott, & Waller, 2001). These restrictions, generally referred to as graduated driver licensing (GDL), are designed to introduce adolescent drivers to low-risk driving situations for a set period of time before allowing increased autonomy as driving skills/experience increases. GDL laws often have three stages—a supervised stage, which requires an older, licensed passenger at all times; a limited driving stage, which allows unsupervised driving but with restrictions (nighttime driving, number of passengers; Hartling, Wiebe, Petruk, Spinola, & Klassen, 2009); and finally an unrestricted stage. Despite differences in these laws across jurisdictions, particularly in the second stage, the evidence is clear that these policies are successful in reducing crashes and fatalities for adolescent drivers (Hartling et al., 2009; Shope, 2007). However, it is less clear whether these laws have a specific effect on SID behavior or crash risk (Fell et al., 2009).

Policies that influence the availability and cost of legal substances can influence use of those substances, and in the case of alcohol, reduce the likelihood of AID. These polices typically do not specifically target adolescents, but nevertheless may have an outsized effect on adolescent AID. For example, policies that increase the price of alcohol through increased taxes, limiting competition, or prohibiting price promotions have been found to decrease alcohol consumption and alcohol-related negative consequences, including AID (Wagenaar, Tobler, & Komro, 2010) and this effect has been found to extend to adolescents (Elder et al., 2010; Xu & Chaloupka, 2011).

The availability of alcohol in a community, indicated by metrics such as outlet density, is consistently associated with alcohol use (Gruenewald, Ponicki, & Holder, 1993) and alcohol-related negative consequences, including AID and crash risk (Gruenewald et al., 1996; Gruenewald, Johnson, & Treno, 2002). This association has been extended to adolescents, with increased outlet density associated with increased AID and riding with a driver who has been drinking (Treno, Grube, & Martin, 2003). The fact that there are legal restrictions on the sale of alcohol to adolescents suggests that the

mechanisms by which outlet density influences alcohol use and AID likely differs for adolescents and adults. For example, the association between alcohol outlet density and availability for youth may be due to increased locations to complete underage purchases and increased availability of alcohol in an adolescent's social network (Chen, Gruenewald, & Remer, 2009). Data on adults suggest that the type of outlet has a complex relationship with AID. For example, there is some evidence that restaurant outlets are associated with increased AID, but bar density is inversely related to AID (Gruenewald et al., 2002). Given the unique role that outlets play in the availability of alcohol to youth, the role of outlet type in determining adolescent AID is less clear.

Policies for regulating driving after use of marijuana and other impairing substances have been enacted in all US states and many other countries (Asbridge, Duff, Marsh, & Erickson, 2014). The specifics of these policies are more variable than those for alcohol. For example, some states have per se marijuana laws, either with a defined blood concentration limit or zero tolerance, whereas others have per se laws either for all drivers or specifically for those under 21 (Lacey, Brainard, & Snitow, 2010). The effectiveness of these policies at reducing marijuana-intoxicated driving remains unclear.

Social-Environmental Influences on Substance-Impaired Driving
Familial Influences

An adolescent's risk for engaging in SID is also influenced by elements of his or her social environment, including familial and peer influences. For familial factors, adolescent engagement in SID has been found to be influenced by aspects of the family structure, parental monitoring, and parental modeling of both substance use and SID behavior.

Parental substance use and SID behavior have a large impact on adolescent risk for engaging in SID. Recent evidence suggests that parental alcohol use is prospectively predictive of AID in adolescence, even after controlling for a number of individual-level covariates (Maldonado-Molina, Reingle, Delcher, & Branchini, 2011). Parental substance use can also moderate the influence of peers. When parents do not report drinking, peer alcohol use is prospectively predictive of AID in adolescence; however, this effect disappears for youth whose parents do report use (Maldonado-Molina et al., 2011). There is also some evidence for gender differences in the effect of parental behavior. Parental drinking is associated with experiencing more serious driving offenses (including but not limited to SID) in girls, but with fewer serious driving offenses among boys (Shope, Waller, Raghunathan, & Patel, 2001). Similar patterns emerge for parental modeling of SID specifically. Adolescents with fathers who engage in AID were more likely to report engaging in AID (Chen, Grube, Nygaard, & Miller, 2008). Parental modeling of AID also appears to be related to increased rates of riding with a drinking driver (Chen et al., 2008).

Overall parental monitoring, as well as driving-specific parental monitoring, is associated with adolescent risky driving behavior and SID (Hartos, Eitel, Haynie, & Simons-Morton, 2000). Low parental monitoring in adolescence is prospectively associated with increased likelihood of AID (Bingham, Shope, & Raghunathan, 2006) and higher rates of serious driving offenses (Shope, Waller, et al., 2001) in young adulthood. Conversely, increased parental monitoring, particularly by fathers, is associated with decreased rates of SID in adolescents (Li, Simons-Morton, Brooks-Russell, Ehsani, & Hingson, 2014). Parental attitudes toward driving and substance use in general are also related to adolescent risky driving practices. Parental limits on youth driving have been found to reduce youth driving behaviors related to crash risk (Simons-Morton & Ouimet, 2006). Similarly, lenient parental attitudes toward drinking (e.g., parents allowing children to drink or get drunk at parties) were prospectively associated with increased rates of serious driving offenses in boys (Shope, Waller, et al., 2001).

Familial structure and closeness have also been found to play an important role in adolescent risky driving behavior. Among adolescent girls, living with a single parent or a biological parent and a step-parent was prospectively related to higher rates of serious driving offenses (Shope, Waller, et al., 2001). Living with a parent and step-parent was also prospectively associated with higher serious crash rates in girls (Shope, Waller, et al., 2001). This pattern was not observed among boys. For AID, there is no evidence for an effect of familial structure, but having two parents in the home appears to be protective against driving following marijuana use (O'Malley & Johnston, 2013). Familial connectedness and parental nurturing also appear to be protective against serious driving offenses (Shope, Waller, et al., 2001). Adolescents who report more family connectedness (e.g., relying on parents for advice when experiencing a problem) and/or more parental nurturing (e.g., parental affection or praise) experienced fewer serious driving offenses and fewer serious crashes (Shope, Waller, et al., 2001).

Peers

Like families, peers are another important element of an adolescent's social environment that can influence risk of engagement in SID. The peer influences most consistently associated with SID are peer substance use, peer SID behaviors, and peer attitudes about both substance use and SID. The social contexts in which substance use occurs are also associated with risk for SID.

Peer attitudes about general substance use and SID have been consistently found to be related to adolescent SID behavior. Being involved with peers who support drinking is associated with rates of alcohol-related crashes and offenses (Shope, Raghunathan, & Patil, 2003). Similarly, adolescents who perceive their peers to be disapproving of AID are less likely to engage in AID or ride with a driver who had been drinking (Chen et al., 2008; Shope et al., 2003). Adolescents also differ in their susceptibility to peer attitudes, and those with higher susceptibility to peer pressure are more likely to experience an alcohol-related driving offense in their first 3 years of driving (Shope et al., 2003). Adolescents susceptible to peer pressure are also more likely ride with an intoxicated driver (Kim & Kim, 2012).

Peer modeling of substance use and SID behavior can have a substantial impact on adolescent behavior. Being involved with peers who use alcohol is prospectively associated with an increased likelihood of experiencing serious driving offenses (Elliot, Shope, Raghunathan, & Waller, 2006). This effect is not specific to alcohol-related offenses, and the effect appears to be stronger for girls (Elliot et al., 2006). Peer modeling of SID behaviors has stronger effects on adolescent SID. Adolescents exposed to peer models who engage in AID are more likely to engage in AID themselves (Chen et al., 2008). Observation of peer AID also increases the likelihood of riding with a driver who had been drinking (Chen et al., 2008). Active exposure to peer SID (e.g., being a passenger in an intoxicated driver's car) impacts rates of SID both cross-sectionally (Leadbeater, Foran, & Grove-White, 2008) and prospectively (Gulliver & Begg, 2004). Adolescents who rode with an alcohol-impaired driver had higher rates of AID, and a similar pattern was observed for riding with a marijuana-impaired driver and later driving after use of marijuana (Leadbeater et al.,

2008). This association appears to be reciprocal, as rates of riding with a marijuana-using driver are also higher among those who report driving after using marijuana (Whitehill, Rivara, & Moreno, 2014). Adolescents who report riding with an intoxicated peer were more likely to report AID upon turning 21 (Gulliver & Begg, 2004). This effect was only observed for male adolescents.

The social and environmental context of adolescent substance use is another important risk factor for SID. Consuming alcohol with friends, rather than with parents, is associated with an increased risk of AID, as well as an increased risk of riding with an intoxicated driver (Reboussin, Song, & Wolfson, 2012). Drinking alcohol supplied by friends, especially friends that are over the age of 21, is also related to an increased frequency of AID (Dent, Grube, & Biglan, 2005). The environments in which substance use occurs are differentially related to risk for SID. For instance, drinking away from home in general is associated with increased rates of AID (Tin et al., 2008). Drinking in unstructured social settings (e.g., parties, informal gathering) or while outdoors is also associated with AID and riding with an intoxicated driver (Chen et al., 2008; Lee, Jones-Webb, Short, & Wagenaar, 1997). In each of these settings, parents are less likely to be present, increasing an adolescent's risk for SID (Dent et al., 2005; Reboussin et al., 2012). In addition, these settings are associated with fewer rules and regulations than more structured drinking environments (e.g., bars, restaurants), thus incurring less risk of legal consequences for underage drinking. Consuming substances in these settings can also increase the need for transportation back to the adolescents' home, potentially contributing to an increased risk for SID.

Personality Influence on Substance-Impaired Driving

Individual differences in personality characteristics are an important component of models of substance use and other health risk behaviors (Caspi et al., 1997; Elkins, King, McGue, & Iacono, 2006; Flory, Lynam, Milich, Leukefeld, & Clayton, 2002; Zuckerman & Kuhlman, 2000). The domains of personality associated with risk for externalizing behavior in general and SID specifically are impulsivity/disinhibition, negative affectivity/emotionality, and extraversion/sociability.

The impulsivity/disinhibition domain of personality has the most consistent evidence for association with engagement in SID. High scores on general measures of impulsivity have been found to be related to higher rates of SID (Hampson, Severson, Burns, Slovic, & Fisher, 2001; Pedersen & McCarthy, 2008). Similar patterns are observed for specific facets of impulsivity. Adolescents who are higher in measures of sensation seeking, the tendency to seek out novelty or stimulation, and urgency, the tendency to act rashly when experiencing strong emotions, engage in higher rates of AID (Greene, Krcmar, Walters, Rubin, & Hale, 2000; Pedersen & McCarthy, 2008; Quinn & Fromme, 2012; Treloar, Morris, Pedersen, & McCarthy, 2012). Longitudinal data suggest that impulsive personality traits prospectively predict SID behavior. For instance, adolescents who scored low on measures on constraint, indicating a tendency to act on impulses, were more likely to engage in AID at age 21 (Caspi et al., 1997).

There is some evidence that traits related to emotion regulation are associated with rates of SID. High negative emotionality refers to a proneness to experiencing anger or anxiety. Adolescents high in negative emotionality exhibit increased rates of AID as adults (Caspi et al., 1997). A tendency to act on these negative emotions is also associated with SID. Adolescents scoring high on measures of aggression or hostility report higher rates of AID, both cross-sectionally and longitudinally (Caspi et al., 1997; Gulliver & Begg, 2007; McMillen, Pang, Wells-Parker, & Anderson, 1992).

The role of extraversion and sociability traits has been studied in the realm of risk-taking behaviors more broadly. In general, adolescents high on extraversion are more likely to engage in risk-taking behaviors (Raynor & Levine, 2009) in general, but whether this association extends to SID is unclear.

Expectancies and Substance-Impaired-Driving-Related Perceptions

Consistent with theoretical models of health risk behaviors (e.g., theory of planned behavior, Ajzen, 1985; health belief model, Janz & Becker, 1984), cognitive factors are significant influences on adolescent SID. Expectancies, attitudes, and normative beliefs have each been found to predict engagement in SID (we discussed normative beliefs and SID in the "Peers" section). Although there is a large empirical literature on substance use outcome expectancies and related problem behaviors (Treloar, Pedersen, & McCarthy, 2015), comparatively few studies have examined substance use expectancies as predictors of SID specifically (e.g., Arterberry et al., 2013).

Many efforts to reduce SID (e.g., sobriety checkpoints and high-profile enforcement; NHTSA, 2007) are intended, in part, to alter expectancies about SID by emphasizing the perceived severity and likelihood of negative consequences. Studies in adult samples have clearly indicated that greater perceived negative consequences of SID are associated with reduced likelihood of engagement in the behavior (Turrisi, Jaccard, & McDonnell, 1997) and reduced risk for recidivism among offenders (Freeman & Watson, 2006; Watling, Palk, Freeman, & Davey, 2010). Studies of adolescents indicate that perceived negative consequences of SID (e.g., injury, arrest, getting pulled over) are associated with engagement in the behavior (Hampson et al., 2001; McCarthy, Lynch, & Pederson, 2007), although there is some evidence that this variable predicts riding with an impaired driver, but not personal AID (Grube & Voas, 1996). Low perceived risk of AID in adolescents is also prospectively related to higher rates of AID during college (Quinn & Fromme, 2012).

In the literature on substance use expectancies, positive expectancies are generally more consistently associated with the behavior than negative expectancies (Treloar et al., 2015). However, relatively little research has examined positive expectancies of SID, or the perceived benefits of engaging in this behavior. Studies have demonstrated that perceived benefits are significant predictors of a range of adolescent risk behaviors, including SID (Fromme, Katz, & Rivet, 1997; Maslowsky, Buvinger, Keating, Steinberg, & Cauffman, 2011), but often SID-specific results are not reported. Studies of AID have found that perceived benefits are associated with intentions and engagement in the behavior (Dhami, Mandel, & Garcia-Retamero, 2011; Greening & Stoppelbein, 2000). A measure of positive expectancies for AID in adolescents and young adults (Positive Expectancies for Drinking and Driving—Youth; McCarthy, Pedersen, Thompsen, & Leuty, 2006) has been used to demonstrate that youth who hold expectancies that AID allows them to avoid consequences (e.g., telling their parents they were drinking) or is more convenient (e.g., getting home faster) than alternatives are more likely to engage in AID (Espada, Griffin, Carballo, & McCarthy, 2012; McCarthy et al., 2006; Treloar et al., 2012).

Attitudes about SID are also strong predictors of SID behavior. Adolescents who report disapproving of SID, or who perceive SID as negative or dangerous, are less likely to report driving while impaired by alcohol or marijuana (Arterberry et al., 2013; Labrie, Kenney, Mirza, & Lac, 2011; Marcil, Bergeron, & Audet, 2001; McCarthy et al., 2007). Attitudes toward AID have also been shown to prospectively predict engagement in the behavior (McCarthy & Pedersen, 2009).

Prevention/Intervention

A number of programs have been enacted with the goal of reducing SID. Some of these programs have been developed specifically to target adolescents, including school-based programs (e.g., Students Against Destructive Decisions), mass media campaigns (e.g., Highway Safety Mass Media Youth Project), and recidivism prevention programs (e.g., Preventing Alcohol Related Convictions). Others are focused broadly, affecting rates of SID across all age groups, such as sobriety checkpoints and increasing penalties associated with SID.

School-based programs targeting both adolescents and younger students are designed to increase awareness about consequences of and alternatives to AID (Elder et al., 2005). School-based programs can be divided into the broad categories of peer organizations and instructional programs. Peer organizations, such as Students Against Destructive Decisions (SADD), consist of groups of students and faculty advisors who encourage other students to avoid SID, AID, or riding with an impaired driver (Elder et al., 2005). SADD specifically includes a number of activities designed to increase knowledge and challenge social norms and attitudes. SADD and similar programs have a number of benefits to those participating and to the broader school community, including stronger attitudes about AID and increased access to substance free events (Elder et al., 2005). Although these programs appear to have beneficial effects on the school community, there is a lack of well-designed studies testing the effectiveness of peer organizations on reducing AID.

School-based instructional programs are heterogeneous and vary widely in content. Some, such as the Risk Skills Training Program, target the consequences of substance use in general (D'Amico & Fromme, 2000). Others focus specifically on driving under the influence (e.g., One for the Road; Singh, 1993). Still others focus on unsafe driving practices in general (e.g., Stay Alive from Education [SAFE]; Wilkins, 2000). There is strong evidence to suggest that these programs are related to decreased rate of riding with an intoxicated driver (Elder et al., 2005). The evidence for SID is less promising. Any initial reductions in SID observed following these programs dissipate over time. To date, there is insufficient evidence to determine the effectiveness of instructional programs on reducing SID (Elder et al., 2005).

Educational programs have also been developed targeting recidivism in young first-time DUI offenders. Preventing Alcohol-Related Convictions (PARC) is an example of one of these educational curricula (Rider et al., 2006). This program does not focus on controlling drinking behavior (e.g., abstain from alcohol, control drinking while driving). Instead, the program aims to reduce future AID by encouraging students to not drive their car to drinking events. This novel program is being implemented in Florida, and follow-up studies suggest that participants in the program are more likely to plan ahead and avoid driving to drinking venues or events (Rider et al., 2006). Future research will need to evaluate the effectiveness of this approach in other environments.

An alternate method of preventing AID is through population-based campaigns disseminated via mass media (Elder et al., 2004). These campaigns are typically developed with the goal of encouraging individuals to avoid AID or to prevent others from engaging in AID. The effects of mass media campaigns can be difficult to measure, as they are often implemented in a way that makes it difficult to isolate any effects of the campaign. There is some evidence to suggest that mass media campaigns are related to reductions in AID and alcohol-related crashes, particularly in the presence of other enforcement efforts that reinforce the messages of the campaigns (Elder et al., 2004). Mass media campaigns can also have indirect effects on AID by influencing public perception of these behaviors.

Among the most successful preventive measures for SID/AID generally are sobriety checkpoints and random breath testing (RBT). Sobriety checkpoints involve stopping every vehicle or every nth vehicle that passes a set location on a public road to determine if the driver is impaired (Elder et al., 2002). As noted, one goal of such checkpoints is to reduce SID by increasing the perceived risk of arrest. Sobriety checkpoints also serve as a method for strengthening the enforcement of laws outlined earlier (see section on "Policy and Substance-Impaired Driving"). Recent meta-analyses have suggested that sobriety checkpoints are associated with a 20% decrease in fatal crashes in the general population (Elder et al., 2002; Shults et al., 2001). Despite

their effectiveness, sobriety checkpoints are not without weaknesses. Specifically, those who have previously experienced a sobriety checkpoint might believe the likelihood of arrest is actually relatively low, as there is evidence to suggest that police miss as many as 50% of drivers with BACs greater than 0.10% (McKnight & Voas, 2001). Nevertheless, there is substantial evidence to suggest that sobriety checkpoints are cost-effective programs, decreasing rates of SID and leading to fewer alcohol-related deaths, crashes, and arrests, particularly among younger drivers (Bergen et al., 2014).

Random breath testing is a similarly effective enforcement method practiced in New Zealand, Australia, and some European countries. Also known as compulsory breath testing, RBT involves drivers being stopped at random by police to take a breath test, even if they are not suspected of any other offense (Watson & Freeman, 2007). RBT is most effective when it is highly visible and widely publicized. In countries that utilize RBT, the chances of being stopped are usually quite high, and drivers that have been stopped typically report greater concern about AID (Watson & Freeman, 2007). RBT seems to be an effective strategy for reducing AID and related harms. Meta-analytic work suggests that RBT is associated with a 22% decline in crash fatalities and a 24% decline in drivers with BACs greater than 0.08% (Shults et al., 2001). However, the effectiveness of RBT at reducing AID in adolescents specifically is yet to be determined.

The punishments and penalties associated with SID can serve as deterrents as well. There is evidence to suggest that more severe penalties are more effective than those that are less severe (Paternoster, 1987). Severity for AID penalties can be adjusted by changing maximum penalties or by introducing mandatory minimum penalties. However, the evidence for increased severity of AID penalties is mixed. For instance, mandatory jail sentences are one method of increasing the severity of AID penalties. Some studies have found that mandatory jail sentences are related to decreased alcohol-related fatalities (Stout, Sloan, Liang, & Davies, 2000), but others have failed to find an effect (Benson, Rasmussen, & Mast, 1999). Imposing mandatory fines is an alternate method of adjusting penalty severity. There is some evidence to suggest that mandatory fines are related to a reduction in fatal crashes involving drivers with BACs greater than 0.08% (Wagenaar et al., 2007). These results are inconsistent, and effects may vary by level of drinking. For instance, Stout and colleagues (2000) found that increased fines were related to lower self-reported AID among moderate drinkers but not heavy drinkers. In sum, increasing the severity of punishment seems to have limited effect on AID or alcohol-related crashes, and little research has tested the effect of punishment severity on adolescent SID.

Penalties for SID are incurred following some length of delay. Based on the learning theory principle that penalties are more effective when immediate than when delayed, efforts have been made to increase the immediacy of SID penalties. For example, preconviction administrative license revocation is permitted in most states in the United States (NHTSA, 2008). This form of license revocation involves the suspension of a driver's license without a court hearing and is initiated either at the time of the offense or shortly thereafter. Enforcement of this penalty can be problematic, however, as nearly 75% of offenders continue to drive following license suspension (Voas & DeYoung, 2002). Despite its drawbacks, administrative license revocation is a cost-effective strategy that has consistently positive effects on alcohol-related crashes. However, the effects of administrative license revocation have not been studied specifically in adolescents.

Conclusions and Future Directions

In this chapter, we provide an overview of the state of the literature on adolescent SID, reviewing what is currently known about the prevalence of SID; family, peer, and individual factors that influence adolescent risk for engaging in SID; and policy, prevention, and intervention methods that are effective in reducing adolescent SID. Despite the significant empirical database on adolescent SID, there remain a number of important gaps in our knowledge. In this section, we highlight what we consider three important future directions for research on adolescent SID: (1) increasing our understanding of marijuana-impaired driving in adolescents; (2) the development of theoretical models specific to adolescent SID; and (3) increased research on the role of within-person and event-level influences on SID decisions.

Marijuana-Impaired Driving

As is clear from much of our review, the majority of adolescent SID research has focused specifically on AID, rather than SID more generally. One important future direction is to improve our understanding of adolescent SID, particularly marijuana-impaired driving, as recent data suggest an increase in the prevalence of adolescent engagement

in this behavior (O'Malley & Johnston, 2013). There is a relative dearth of research on the role of marijuana in adolescent driving, including the acute effects of marijuana on adolescent driving skill, the contribution of marijuana to vehicle crash risk, and factors that increase the likelihood of driving while impaired by marijuana. A review of the overall literature (Sewell, Poling, & Sofuoglu, 2009) found that evidence for the contribution of marijuana to crash risk was inconsistent. Sewell et al. (2009) noted that, while marijuana impairs driving-related skills, there is considerably more variability in this impairment than typically observed with alcohol, in part due to differences in experience with marijuana. This pattern of results suggests the importance of further research on marijuana and driving in adolescents to determine the extent to which marijuana impairs driving skill in individuals who are both relatively novice drivers and novice marijuana users. Given recent increases in marijuana use and driving in adolescents (O'Malley & Johnston, 2013) and the potential for future increases in this behavior (Wright, 2015), additional focus on this area is imperative.

Theory Development and Adolescent Substance-Impaired Driving

In our view, an essential future direction for adolescent SID research is the development of theoretical models specific to adolescent SID risk. There have been a number of applications of more general theoretical models to adolescent SID, including models of behavioral decision making (e.g., theory of reasoned action; Armitage, Norman, & Conner, 2002), criminal behavior (e.g., deterrence theory; Piquero & Pogarsky, 2002; Pogarsky & Piquero, 2003), and adolescent health risk behavior (e.g., problem behavior theory; Shope & Bingham, 2002, 2008). Theoretical models specific to adolescent SID present a unique challenge, as they would require the integration of perspectives from adolescent development, substance use risk, adolescent driving behavior, and traffic safety. In addition to the inherent complexity in developing this type of integrated theoretical model, we outline next what we see as three additional challenges to the development of adolescent SID-specific theories.

One challenge is that, in contrast to developmental models of adolescent substance use (Arnett, 2005; Wills et al., 2001), there is a relative lack of extant developmental work focused on adolescent driving behavior. As Laird (2011) has argued, driving behavior is an important developmental milestone, and learning to drive shares common features with other developmental tasks. The examination of developmental processes, such as parent–adolescent autonomy negotiation and information management, can be fruitfully applied to driving behavior and both shed new light on these processes and provide new information on how to reduce risks for novice drivers. A number of studies have examined the role of such processes in adolescent risky driving (e.g., Beck, Hartos, & Simons-Morton, 2005; Hsieh et al., 2015) and SID (e.g., Bingham et al., 2006). However, we are aware of only one theoretical model that focuses on the role of adolescent driving behavior in adolescent development, the transition teens theory (TTT; Voas & Kelley-Baker, 2008). The TTT focuses on how environmental, peer, and parent influences on adolescent health risk behaviors are affected by the transition to licensed driver. For example, the TTT posits that this transition reduces the influence of the home environment and increases the influence of peer and extended environment (Voas & Kelley-Baker, 2008).

An additional difficulty facing both empirical and theoretical models of adolescent SID is that SID is an intersection of two health risk behaviors: risky driving and substance-related negative consequences. It therefore shares commonalities with behaviors in each domain but also has unique elements that have implications for models of SID risk. One such implication is that, because both driving and substance use are required for SID, research and intervention efforts focused on one domain (e.g., driver education, brief motivational interviewing for substance use) must account for the other. For example, empirical studies seeking to identify risk factors for substance-related negative consequences must condition on driving to understand risk specific to SID. In other words, risk estimates for other substance-related problems cannot be extended to SID without accounting for driving exposure. The converse is also true: Studies examining adolescent risk factors for engaging in risky driving behavior must condition on substance use in predicting SID. Youth at risk for other dangerous driving behaviors (e.g., texting and driving) will not engage in SID if they do not use substances. Despite the clear importance of measuring and accounting for both substance use and driving exposure in modeling risk for SID, this is often not done in large-scale studies where SID is not a primary focus (Voas & Kelley-Baker, 2007).

A related challenge for developing models of adolescent SID risk is the question of what model should be used to account for substance involvement. Although SID requires both driving and substance use, their status is not symmetrical. Despite the relatively high crash risk in adolescence, driving is not itself a health risk behavior—many youth are expected or even required to drive and do so relatively safely under most conditions. Adolescent substance involvement, in contrast, is itself an important target of health research. Models of adolescent SID must be able to identify risk that is specific to SID, separate from risk for substance use. Bingham and colleagues (Bingham, Elliott, & Shope, 2007) pose three potential models of how substance involvement may function in the prediction of SID risk. Substance use can be (1) unconfounded with other risk factors, meaning that their association with use and SID is independent; (2) partially confounded; or (3) completely confounded, where the association between the other risk factors and SID is only due to their association with substance use. In their study, by using population-attributable risk to adjust for level of alcohol use, they found that all AID risk factors (e.g., personality traits, risk perceptions) were at least partially confounded with alcohol use (Bingham et al., 2007). From a prevention standpoint, confounded risk factors do not provide unique information on SID risk—although they may contribute to risk of heavy substance use, they do not tell us anything additional about SID risk. From an intervention standpoint, confounded factors are unlikely to be fruitful targets of intervention for SID; interventions that target substance use directly would likely be more appropriate.

Microlevel Understanding of Causal Structure: Proximal Influences on Decision Making in Substance-Impaired Driving

A final direction we would highlight for future work is the examination of prospective, event-level contributors to SID. Although there has been considerable longitudinal work on risk for adolescent SID, these studies have examined SID behavior in the aggregate—examining factors that predict who will engage in SID or exhibit changes in the frequency of SID over a given period, rather than examine specific SID decisions. Event-level studies, such as roadside surveys or on-location interviews, have been used to examine factors associated with a single SID event (Lacey et al., 2009), intentions to engage in SID (Rossheim et al., 2015; Thombs et al., 2010), and even changes in SID decision making over a given evening (Voas et al., 2013). To date, however, we are aware of only one study that has prospectively examined event-level data, allowing for the examination of the influence of both within-subject variability and event-level predictors of AID (Quinn & Fromme, 2012). Using a repeated daily diary methodology in a sample of college students, Quinn and Fromme found that exceeding one's typical alcohol consumption was associated with a small increase in likelihood of driving. More importantly, this effect was moderated by subjective intoxication, such that higher consumption had a large effect on likelihood of AID when subjective intoxication was low. In other words, AID was most likely on drinking occasions with high discrepancy between subjective intoxication and objective alcohol consumption. Findings from this study illustrate the important role that intraindividual variability plays across drinking occasions, in this case variability in both alcohol consumption and subjective intoxication in determining AID decisions.

The lack of prospective, event-level studies of SID has left a significant gap in our understanding of the role of within-subject variability, and its potential interaction with contextual factors, in SID risk. For example, one of the strongest predictors of AID at the between subjects level is impulsivity, which has consistently been shown to predict AID both cross-sectionally (Ryb, Dischinger, Kufera, & Read, 2006) and prospectively (Pedersen & McCarthy, 2008). But there is considerable intraindividual variability in impulsive processes, both over time (Tomko et al., 2014) and as a function of intoxication (McCarthy, Niculete, Treloar, Morris, & Bartholow, 2012). Prospective examination of within-subjects and event-level influences on SID will allow for the examination of interactions between psychological and environmental factors that determine risk for adolescent SID in a specific instance. Perhaps more important for potential interventions, this type of research is also necessary to identify individual- and event-level factors that mitigate an adolescent's risk for SID.

References

Ajzen, I. (1985). From intentions to actions: A theory of planned behavior. In J. Kuhl & J. Beckmann (Eds.), *Action control: From cognition to behavior* (pp. 11–39). Berlin, Germany: Springer Berlin Heidelberg.

Armitage, C. J., Norman, P., & Conner, M. (2002). Can the theory of planned behaviour mediate the effects of age, gender and multidimensional health locus of control ? *British Journal of Health Psychology*, 7, 299–316.

Arnett, J. J. (2005). The developmental context of substance use in emerging adulthood. *Journal of Drug Issue, 35*(2), 235–254.

Arterberry, B. J., Treloar, H. R., Smith, A. E., Martens, M. P., Pedersen, S. L., & McCarthy, D. M. (2013). Marijuana use, driving, and related cognitions. *Psychology of Addictive Behaviors, 27*(3), 854–860. doi:10.1037/a0030877

Asbridge, M., Duff, C., Marsh, D. C., & Erickson, P. G. (2014). Problems with the identification of 'problematic' cannabis use: Examining the issues of frequency, quantity, and drug use environment. *European Addiction Research, 20*, 254-267.

Beck, K. H., Hartos, J. L., & Simons-Morton, B. G. (2005). Parent-teen disagreement of parent-imposed restrictions on teen driving after one month of licensure: Is discordance related to risky teen driving? *Prevention Science, 6*(3), 177–185. doi:10.1007/s11121-005-0001-6

Benson, B. L., Rasmussen, D. W., & Mast, B. D. (1999). Deterring drunk driving fatalities: An economics of crime perspective. *International Review of Law and Economics, 19*, 205-225.

Bergen, G., Pitan, A., Qu, S., Shults, R. A., Chattopadhyay, S. K., Elder, R. W., . . . the Community Preventive Services Task Force. (2014). Publicized sobriety checkpoint programs: A community guide systematic review. *American Journal of Preventive Medicine, 46*(5), 529–539.

Bingham, C. R., Elliott, M. R., & Shope, J. T. (2007). Social and behavioral characteristics of young adult drink/drivers adjusted for level of alcohol use. *Alcoholism, Clinical and Experimental Research, 31*(4), 655–664. doi:10.1111/j.1530-0277.2007.00350.x

Bingham, C. R., Shope, J. T., & Raghunathan, T. (2006). Patterns of traffic offenses from adolescent licensure into early young adulthood. *Journal of Adolescent Health, 39*(1), 35–42. doi:10.1016/j.jadohealth.2005.10.002

Brady, J. E., & Li, G. (2013). Prevalence of alcohol and other drugs in fatally injured drivers. *Addiction, 108*(1), 104–114.

Carpenter, C. (2004). How do zero tolerance drunk driving laws work? *Journal of Health Economics, 23*(1), 61–83. doi:10.1016/j.jhealeco.2003.08.005

Caspi, A., Begg, D., Dickson, N., Harrington, H., Langley, J., Moffitt, T. E., & Silva, P. A. (1997). Personality differences predict health-risk behaviors in young adulthood: Evidence from a longitudinal study. *Journal of Personality and Social Psychology, 73*(5), 1052–1063.

Chen, M-J., Grube, J. W., Nygaard, P., & Miller, B. A. (2008). Identifying social mechanisms for the prevention of adolescent drinking and driving. *Accident Analysis and Prevention, 40*(2), 576–585.

Chen, M-J., Gruenewald, P. J., & Remer, L. G. (2009). Does alcohol outlet density affect youth access to alcohol? *Journal of Adolescent Health, 44*(6), 582–589. doi:10.1016/j.jadohealth.2008.10.136

Curry, A. E., Hafetz, J., Kallan, M. J., Winston, F. K., & Durbin, D. R. (2011). Prevalence of teen driver errors leading to serious motor vehicle crashes. *Accident Analysis and Prevention, 43*, 1285–1290.

D'Amico, E. J., & Fromme, K. (2000). Implementation of the risk skills training program: A brief intervention targeting adolescent participation in risk behaviors. *Cognitive and Behavioral Practice, 7*, 101–117.

Degenhardt, L., Chiu, W. T., Sampson, N., Kessler, R. C., Anthony, J. C., Angermeyer, M., . . . Wells, J. E. (2008). Toward a global view of alcohol, tobacco, cannabis, and cocaine use: Findings from the WHO World Mental Health surveys. *PLoS Medicine*, *5*(7), 1053–1067. doi:10.1371/journal.pmed.0050141

Dent, C. W., Grube, J. W., & Biglan, A. (2005). Community level alcohol availability and enforcement of possession laws as predictors of youth driving. *Preventive Medicine, 40*, 355–362.

Dhami, M., Mandel, D., & Garcia-Retamero, R. (2011). Canadian and Spanish youths' risk perceptions of drinking and driving, and riding with a drunk driver. *International Journal of Psychology, 46*(2), 81–90. doi:10.1080/00207594.2010.526121

Dunsire. M., & Baldwin, S. (1999). Urban-rural comparisons of drink-driving behavior among late teens: A preliminary investigation. *Alcohol & Alcoholism, 34*(1), 59-64.

Elder, R. W., Lawrence, B., Ferguson, A., Naimi, T. S., Brewer, R. D., Chattopadhyay, S. K., . . . Fielding, J. E. (2010). The effectiveness of tax policy interventions for reducing excessive alcohol consumption and related harms. *American Journal of Preventive Medicine, 38*(2), 217–229. doi:10.1016/j.amepre.2009.11.005

Elder, R. W., Nichols, J. L., Shults, R. A., Sleet, D. A., Barrios, L. C., Compton, R., & Task Force on Community Preventive Services. (2005). Effectiveness of school Based programs for reducing drinking and driving and riding with drinking drivers: A systematic review. *American Journal of Preventive Medicine, 28*(5S), 288-304.

Elder, R. W., Shults, R. A., Sleet, D. A., Nichols, J. L., Thompson, R. S., Rajab, R., & Task Force on Community Preventive Services. (2004). Effectiveness of mass media campaigns for reducing drinking and driving and alcohol-involved crashes: A systematic review. *American Journal of Preventive Medicine, 27*(1), 57–65.

Elder, R. W., Shults, R. A., Sleet, D. A., Nichols, J. L., Zaza, S., & Thompson, R. S. (2002). Effectiveness of sobriety checkpoints for reducing alcohol-involved crashes. *Traffic Injury Prevention, 3*, 266-274.

Elkins, I. J., King, S. M., McGue, M., & Iacono, W. G. (2006). Personality traits and the development of nicotine, alcohol, and illicit drug disorders: Prospective links from adolescence to young adulthood. *Journal of Abnormal Psychology, 115*(1), 26–39.

Elliot, M. R., Shope, J. T., Raghunathan, T. E., & Waller, P. F. (2006). Gender differences among young drivers in the association between high-risk driving and substance use/environmental influences. *Journal of Studies on Alcohol, 67*, 252–260.

Espada, J. P., Griffin, K. W., Carballo, J. L., & McCarthy, D. M. (2012). Spanish version of the positive expectanceis for drinking and driving for youth. *Spanish Journal of Psychology, 15*, 1495–1502. doi:10.5209/rev

Fell, J. C., Fisher, D. A., Voas, R. B., Blackman, K., & Tippetts, A. S. (2009). The impact of underage drinking laws on alcohol-related fatal crashes of young drivers. *Alcoholism: Clinical and Experimental Research, 33*(7), 1208–1219. doi:10.1111/j.1530-0277.2009.00945.x

Flory, K., Lynam, D., Milich, R., Leukefeld, C., & Clayton R. (2002). The relations among personality, symptoms of alcohol and marijuana abuse, and symptoms of comorbid psychopathology: Results from a community sample. *Experimental and Clinical Psychopharmacology, 10*(4), 425–434.

Font-Ribera, L., Garcia-Continente, X., Pérez, A., Torres, R., Sala, N., Espelt, A., & Nebot, M. (2013). Driving under the influence of alcohol or drugs among adolescents: The role of urban and rural environments. *Accident Analysis and Prevention, 60*, 14.

Freeman, J., & Watson, B. (2006). An application of Stafford and Warr's reconceptualisation of deterrence to a group of recidivist drink drivers. *Accident Analysis and Prevention, 38*(3), 462–471. doi:10.1016/j.aap.2005.11.001

Fromme, K., Katz, E. C., & Rivet, K. (1997). Outcome expectancies and risk-taking behavior. *Cognitive Therapy and Research, 21*(4), 421–442.

Greene, K., Krcmar, M., Walters, L. H., Rubin, D. L., & Hale, J. L. (2000). Targeting adolescent risk-taking behaviors: The contributions of egocentrism and sensation-seeking. *Journal of Adolescence, 23*(4), 439-461.

Greening, L., & Stoppelbein, L. (2000). Young drivers' health attitudes and intentions to drink and drive. *Journal of Adolescent Health, 27*(2), 94–101. doi:10.1016/S1054-139X(99)00114-7

Grube, J. W. & Voas, R. B. (1996). Predicting underage drinking and driving behaviors. *Addiction, 91*(12), 1843–1857.

Gruenewald, P. J., Johnson, F. W., & Treno, A. J. (2002). Outlets, drinking and driving: A multilevel analysis of availability. *Journal of Studies on Alcohol, 63*(4), 460–468.

Gruenewald, P. J., Millar, A. B., Treno, A. J., Yang, Z., Ponicki, W. R., & Roeper, P. (1996). The geography of availability and driving after drinking. *Addiction, 91*(7), 967–983. doi:10.1111/j.1360-0443.1996.tb03594.x

Gruenewald, P. J., Ponicki, W. R., & Holder, H. D. (1993). The relationship of outlet densities to alcohol consumption: A time series cross-sectional analysis. *Alcoholism: Clinical and Experimental Research, 17*(1), 38–47. doi:10.1111/j.1530-0277.1993.tb00723.x

Gulliver, P., & Begg, D. (2004). Influences during adolescence on perceptions and behavior related to alcohol use and unsafe driving as young adults. *Accident Analysis and Prevention, 36*, 773–781.

Gulliver, P., & Begg, D. (2007). Personality factors as predictors of persistent risky driving behavior and crash involvement among young adults. *Injury Prevention, 13*, 376-381.

Hampson, S. E., Severson, H. H., Burns, W. J., Slovic, P., & Fisher, K. J. (2001). Risk perception, personality factors and alcohol use among adolescents. *Personality and Individual Differences, 30*, 167–181.

Hartling, L., Wiebe, N., Kf, R., Petruk, J., Spinola, C., & Klassen, T. P. (2009). Graduated driver licensing for reducing motor vehicle crashes among young drivers. *Cochrane Database of Systematic Reviews*, (2), CD003300.

Hartos, J. L., Eitel, P., Haynie, D. L., & Simons-Morton, B. G. (2000). Can I take the car? Relations among parenting practices and adolescent problem-driving practices. *Journal of Adolescent Research, 15*(3), 352–367.

Hingson, R., Heeren, T., & Winter, M. (1994). Lower legal blood alcohol limits for young drivers. *Public Health Reports, 109*(6), 738–744.

Hingson, R., & Winter, M. (2003). Epidemiology and consequences of drinking and driving. *Alcohol Research and Health, 27*(1), 63–78.

Hsieh, H-F., Heinze, J. E., Aiyer, S. M., Stoddard, S. A., Wang, J-L., & Zimmerman, M. A. (2015). Cross-domain influences on youth risky driving behaviors: A developmental cascade analysis. *Journal of Applied Developmental Psychology, 38*, 11–21. doi:10.1016/j.appdev.2015.03.002

Heron, M. (2016). Deaths: Leading Causes for 2013. *National Vital Statistics Reports, 65*(2), 1-95.

Janz, N. K., & Becker, M. H. (1984). The health belief model: A decade later. *Health Education Quarterly, 11*(1), 1-47.

Kann, L., Kinchen, S., Shanklin, S. L., Flint, K. H., Kawkins, J., Harris, W. A., . . . Zaza, S. (2014). Youth risk behavior surveillance—United States, 2013. *MMWR Surveillance Summaries, 63* (4, Suppl. 4), 1–168.

Kim, J., & Kim, K. S. (2012). The role of sensation seeking, perceived peer pressure, and harmful alcohol use in riding with an alcohol-impaired driver. *Accident Analysis and Prevention, 48*, 326-334.

Kypri, K., Voas, R. B., Langley, J. D., Stephenson, S. C. R., Begg, D., Tippetts, S., & Davie, G. S. (2006). Minimum purchasing age for alcohol and traffic crash injuries among 15- to 19-year-olds in New Zealand. *American Journal of Public Health, 96*(1), 126–131.

LaBrie, J. W., Kenney, S. R., Mirza, T., & Lac, A. (2011). Identifying factors that increase the likelihood of driving after drinking among college students. *Accident Analysis and Prevention, 43*(4), 1371–1377. doi:10.1016/j.aap.2011.02.011

Lacey, J., Brainard, K., & Snitow, S. (2010). *Drug per se laws: A review of their use in states.* Washington, DC: National Highway Traffic Safety Administration.

Lacey, J. H., Kelley-Baker, T., Voas, R. B., Romano, E., Furr-Holden, C. D., Torres, P., & Berning, A. (2009). Alcohol- and drug-involved driving in the United States: Methodology for the 2007 National Roadside Survey. *Evaluation Review, 35*(4), 319–353. doi:10.1177/0193841X11422446

Laird, R. D. (2011). Teenage driving offers challenges and potential rewards for developmentalists. *Child Development Perspectives, 5*(4), 311–316. doi:10.1111/j.1750-8606.2011.00203.x

Leadbeater, B. J., Foran, K., & Grove-White, A. (2008). How much can you drink before driving? The influence of riding with impaired adults and peers on the driving behaviors of urban and rural youth. *Addiction, 103*, 629–637.

Lee, J. A., Jones-Webb, R. J., Short, B. J., & Wagenaar, A. C. (1997). Drinking location and risk of alcohol-impaired driving among high school seniors. *Addictive Behaviors, 22*(3), 387–393.

Li, K., Simons-Morton, B. G., Brooks-Russell, A., Ehsani, J., & Hingson, R. (2014). Drinking and parenting practices as predictors of impaired driving behaviors among U.S. adolescents. *Journal of Studies on Alcohol and Drugs, 75*(1), 5–15.

Li, K., Simons-Morton, B. G., Vaca, F. E., & Hingson, R. (2014). Association between riding with an impaired driver and driving while impaired. *Pediatrics, 133*(4), 620-626.

Maldonado-Molina, M. M., Reingle, J. M., Delcher, C., & Branchini, J. (2011). The role of parental alcohol consumption on driving under the influence of alcohol: Results from a longitudinal, nationally representative sample. *Accident Analysis and Prevention, 43*(6), 2182-2187.

Mann, R. E., Macdonald, S., Stoduto, G., Bondy, S., Jonah, B., & Shaikh, A. (2001). The effects of introducing or lowering legal per se blood alcohol limits for driving: An international review. *Accident Analysis and Prevention, 33*(5), 569–583. doi:10.1016/S0001-4575(00)00077-4

Marcil, I., Bergeron, J., & Audet, T. (2001). Motivational factors underlying the intention to drink and drive in young male drivers. *Journal of Safety Research, 32*(4), 363–376. doi:10.1016/S0022-4375(01)00062-7

Maslowsky, J., Buvinger, E., Keating, D. P., Steinberg, L., & Cauffman, E. (2011). Cost-benefit analysis mediation of the relationship between sensation seeking and risk behavior among adolescents. *Personality and Individual Differences, 51*(7), 802–806. doi:10.1016/j.paid.2011.06.028

McCarthy, D. M., Lynch, A. M., & Pederson, S. L. (2007). Driving after use of alcohol and marijuana in college students. *Psychology of Addictive Behaviors, 21*, 425–430. doi:10.1037/0893-164X.21.3.425

McCarthy, D. M., Niculete, M. E., Treloar, H. R., Morris, D. H., & Bartholow, B. D. (2012). Acute alcohol effects on impulsivity: Associations with drinking and driving behavior. *Addiction, 107*(12), 2109-2114.

McCarthy, D. M., & Pedersen, S. L. (2009). Reciprocal associations between drinking and driving behavior and cognitions in adolescents. *Journal of Studies on Alcohol and Drugs, 70*, 536-542.

McCarthy, D. M., Pedersen, S. L., Thompsen, D. M., & Leuty, M. E. (2006). Development of a measure of drinking and driving expectancies for youth. *Psychological Assessment, 18*(2), 155–164. doi:10.1037/1040-3590.18.2.155

McKnight, A. J., & Voas, R. B. (2001). Prevention of alcohol related crashes. In Heather, N., Peters, T. J., & Stockwell, T. (Eds.), *International Handbook of Alcohol Dependence and Problems,* pp.741–770. Chichester, England: John Wiley & Sons.

McMillen, D. L., Pang, M. G., Wells-Parker, E., & Anderson, B. J. (1992). Alcohol, personality traits, and high risk driving: A comparison of young, drinking driver groups. *Addictive Behaviors, 17*(6), 525–532.

National Highway Traffic Safety Administration [NHTSA]. (2007). *Countermeasures that work: A highway safety countermeasure guide for state highway safety offices* (2nd ed.). Washington, DC: US Department of Transportation.

NHTSA (2008). *Administrative license revocation.* DOT HS 810 878. Washington, DC: National Highway Traffic Safety Administration.

O'Malley, P. M., & Johnston, L. D. (2003). Unsafe driving by high school seniors: National trends from 1976 to 2001 in tickets and accidents after use of alcohol, marijuana and other illegal drugs. *Journal of Studies on Alcohol, 64*(3), 305–312.

O'Malley, P. M., & Johnston, L. D. (2013). Driving after drug or alcohol use by US high school seniors, 2001-2011. *American Journal of Public Health, 103*(11), 2027–2034. doi:10.2105/AJPH.2013.301246

Paternoster, R. (1987). The deterrent effect of the perceived certainty and severity of a punishment: A review of the evidence and issues. *Justice Quarterly, 4*(2), 173–217.

Pedersen, S. L., & McCarthy, D. M. (2008). Person-environment transactions in youth drinking and driving. *Psychology of Addictive Behaviors, 22*(3), 340–348. doi:10.1037/0893-164X.22.3.340

Piquero, A. R., & Pogarsky, G. (2002). Beyond Stafford and Warr's reconceptualization of deterrence: Personal and vicarious experiences, impulsivity, and offending behavior. *Journal of Research in Crime and Delinquency, 39*(2), 153–186. doi:10.1177/002242780203900202

Pitts, J. R., Johnson, I. D., & Eidson, J. L. (2014). Keeping the case open: Responding to DeJong and Blanchette's "Case Closed" on the minimum legal drinking age in the

United States. *Journal of Studies on Alcohol and Drugs, 75,* 1047–1049.

Pogarsky, G., & Piquero, A. R. (2003). Can punishment encourage offending? Investigating the "resetting" effect. *Journal of Research in Crime and Delinquency, 40*(1), 95–120. doi:10.1177/0022427802239255

Poulin, C., Boudreau, B., & Asbridge, M. (2006). Adolescent passengers of drunk drivers: A multi-level exploration into the inequities of risk and safety. *Addiction, 102,* 51–61.

Quinn, P. D., & Fromme, K. (2012). Event-level associations between objective and subjective alcohol intoxication and driving after drinking across the college years. *Psychology of Addictive Behaviors, 26*(3), 384–392. doi:10.1037/a0024275

Raynor, D. A., & Levine, H. (2009). Associations between the five-factor model of Personality and health behaviors among college students. *Journal of American College Health, 58*(1), 73-81.

Reboussin, B. A., Song, E., & Wolfson, M. (2012). Social influences on the clustering of underage risky drinking and its consequences in communities. *Journal on Studies of Alcohol and Drugs, 73,* 890–898.

Rider, R., Kelley-Baker, T., Voas, R. B., Murphy, B., McKnight, A. J., & Levings, C. (2006). The impact of a novel educational curriculum for first-time DUI offenders on intermediate outcomes relevant to DUI recidivism. *Accident Analysis and Prevention, 38*(3), 482–489. doi:10.1016/j.aap.2005.11.004

Romano, E., Voas, R. B., & Lacey, J. C. (2010). *Alcohol and highway safety: Special report on race/ethnicity and impaired driving.* Washington, DC: National Highway Traffic Safety Administration.

Rossheim, M. E., Weiler, R. M., Barnett, T. E., Suzuki, S., Walters, S. T., Barry, A. E., . . . Thombs, D. L. (2015). Self-efficacy to drive while intoxicated: Insights into the persistence of alcohol-impaired driving. *Alcoholism: Clinical and Experimental Research, 39*(8), 1547–1554. doi:10.1111/acer.12795

Royal, D. (2003). *National Survey of Drinking and Driving Attitudes and Behavior: 2001, Vol. 1. Summary Report (No. HS-809 549).* Washington, DC: National Highway Traffic Safety Administration, US Department of Transportation.

Ryb, G. E., Dischinger, P. C., Kufera, J. A., & Read, K. M. (2006). Risk perception and impulsivity: Association with risky behaviors and substance abuse disorders. *Accident Analysis and Prevention, 38*(3), 567–573. doi:10.1016/j.aap.2005.12.001

Sewell, R. A., Poling, J., & Sofuoglu, M. (2009). The effect of cannabis compared with alcohol on driving. *American Journal on Addictions, 18*(3), 185–193. doi:10.1080/10550490902786934

Shope, J. T. (2007). Graduated driver licensing: Review of evaluation results since 2002. *Journal of Safety Research, 38*(2), 165–175. doi:10.1016/j.jsr.2007.02.004

Shope, J. T., & Bingham, C. R. (2002). Drinking-driving as a component of problem driving and problem behavior in young adults. *Journal of Studies on Alcohol, 63*(1), 24–33.

Shope, J. T., & Bingham, C. R. (2008). Teen driving: Motor-vehicle crashes and factors that contribute. *American Journal of Preventive Medicine, 35*(3 Suppl.), S261–S271. doi:10.1016/j.amepre.2008.06.022

Shope, J. T., Molnar, L. J., Elliott, M. R., & Waller, P. F. (2001). Graduated driver licensing in Michigan. *Journal of the American Medical Association, 286*(13), 1593–1598.

Shope, J. T., Raghunathan, T. E., & Patil, S. M. (2003). Examining trajectories of adolescent risk factors as predictors of subsequent high-risk driving behavior. *Journal of Adolescent Health, 32*(3), 214–224.

Shope, J. T., Waller, P. F., Raghunathan, T. E., & Patil, S. M. (2001). Adolescent antecedents of high-risk driving behavior into young adulthood: Substance use and parental influences. *Accident Analysis and Prevention, 33,* 649-658.

Shults, R. A., Elder, R. W., Sleet, D. A., Nichols, J. L., Alao, M. O., Carande-Kulis, V. G., . . . Thompson, R. S. (2001). Reviews of evidence regarding interventions to reduce alcohol-impaired driving. *American Journal of Preventive Medicine, 21*(4, Suppl. 1), 66–88. doi:10.1016/S0749-3797(01)00381-6

Simons-Morton, B., & Ouimet, M. C. (2006). Parent involvement in novice teen driving: A review of the literature. *Injury Prevention, 12*(Suppl. 1), i30–37. doi:10.1136/ip.2006.011569

Singh, A. (1993). Evaluation of the four films on drinking and driving known as "One for the Road" series. *Journal of Traffic Medicine, 21*(2), 65–72.

Stout, E. M., Sloan, F. A., Liang, L., & Davies, H. H. (2000). Reducing harmful alcohol related behaviors: Effective regulatory methods. *Journal of Studies on Alcohol, 61,* 402–412.

Substance Abuse and Mental Health Services Administration. (2014). Results from the 2012 National Survey on Drug Use and Health: Summary of National Findings. Rockville, MD: US Department of Health and Human Services.

Terry-McElrath, Y. M., O'Malley, P. M., & Johnston, L. D. (2014). Alcohol and marijuana use patterns associated with unsafe driving among U.S. high school seniors: High use frequency, concurrent use, and simultaneous use. *Journal of Studies on Alcohol and Drugs, 75,* 378–389.

Thombs, D. L., O'Mara, R. J., Tsukamoto, M., Rossheim, M. E., Weiler, R. M., Merves, M. L., & Goldberger, B. A. (2010). Event-level analyses of energy drink consumption and alcohol intoxication in bar patrons. *Addictive Behaviors, 35*(4), 325–330. doi:10.1016/j.addbeh.2009.11.004

Tin, S. T., Ameratunga, S., Robinson, E., Crengle, S., Schaaf, D., & Watson, P. (2008). Drink driving and the patterns and context of drinking among New Zealand adolescents. *Acta Paediatrica, 97,* 1433–1437.

Tippetts, A. S., Voas, R. B., Fell, J. C., & Nichols, J. L. (2005). A meta-analysis of .08 BAC laws in 19 jurisdictions in the United States. *Accident Analysis and Prevention, 37*(1), 149–161. doi:10.1016/j.aap.2004.02.006

Tomko, R. L., Solhan, M. B., Carpenter, R. W., Brown, W. C., Jahng, S., Wood, P. K., & Trull, T. J. (2014). Measuring impulsivity in daily life: The Momentary Impulsivity Scale. *Psychological Assessment, 26*(2), 339–349. doi:10.1037/a0035083

Treloar, H. R., Morris, D. H., Pedersen, S. L., & McCarthy, D. M. (2012). Direct and indirect effects of impulsivity traits on drinking and driving in young adults. *Journal of Studies on Alcohol and Drugs, 73*(5), 794–803.

Treloar, H. R., Pedersen, S. L., & McCarthy, D. M. (2015). The role of expectancy in substance abuse progression. In C. Kopetz & C. Lejuez (Eds.), *Addictions: A Social Psychological Perspective* (pp. 120–147). New York, NY: Routledge

Treno, A. J., Grube, J. W., & Martin, S. E. (2003). Alcohol availability as a predictor of youth drinking and driving: A hierarchical analysis of survey and archival data. *Alcoholism: Clinical and Experimental Research, 27*(5), 835–840. doi:10.1097/01.ALC.0000067979.85714.22

Turrisi, R., Jaccard, J., & McDonnell, D. (1997). An examination of the relationships between personality, attitudes, and cognitions relevant to alcohol-impaired driving tendencies. *Journal of Applied Social Psychology, 27*(15), 1367–1394. doi:10.1111/j.1559-1816.1997.tb01811.x

Voas, R. B. & DeYoung, D. J. (2002). Vehicle action: Effective policy for controlling drunk and other high-risk drivers? *Accident Analysis and Prevention, 34*, 263-270.

Voas, R. B., Johnson, M. B., & Miller, B. A. (2013). Alcohol and drug use among young adults driving to a drinking location. *Drug and Alcohol Dependence, 132*(1–2), 69–73. doi:10.1016/j.drugalcdep.2013.01.014

Voas, R. B., & Kelley-Baker, T. (2007). Alcohol and other drug use and the transition from riding to driving. *Addiction, 102*(1), 8–10. doi:10.1111/j.1360-0443.2006.01707.x

Voas, R. B., & Kelley-Baker, T. (2008). Licensing teenagers: Nontraffic risks and benefits in the transition to driving status. *Traffic Injury Prevention, 9*(2), 89–97. doi:10.1080/15389580701813297

Voas, R. B., Tippetts, A. S., & Fell, J. C. (2003). Assessing the effectiveness of minimum legal drinking age and zero tolerance laws in the United States. *Accident Analysis and Prevention, 35*(4), 579–587. doi:10.1016/S0001-4575(02)00038-6

Voas, R. B., Torres, P., Romano, E., & Lacey, J. H. (2012). Alcohol-related risk of driver fatalities: An update using 2007 data. *Journal of Studies on Alcohol and Drugs, 73*(3), 341–350. Retrieved from

Wagenaar, A. C., Maldonado-Molina, M. M., Erickson, D. J., Ma, L., Tobler, A. L., & Komro, K. A. (2007). General deterrence effects of U.S. statutory DUI fine and jail penalties: Long-term follow-up in 32 states. *Accident Analysis and Prevention, 39*, 982–994.

Wagenaar, A. C., Malley, P. M. O., & Lafond, C. (2001). Lowered legal blood alcohol limits for young drivers : Effects on drinking, driving, and driving-after-drinking behaviors in 30 states. *American Journal of Public Health, 91*(5), 801–804.

Wagenaar, A. C., Tobler, A. L., & Komro, K. A. (2010). Effects of alcohol tax and price policies on morbidity and mortality: A systematic review. *American Journal of Public Health, 100*(11), 2270–2278. doi:10.2105/AJPH.2009.186007

Wagenaar, A. C., & Toomey, T. L. (2002). Effects of minimum drinking age laws: Review and analyses of the literature from 1960 to 2000. *Journal of Studies on Alcohol, S14*, 206–225.

Walker, S., Treno, A. J., Grube, J. W., & Light, J. M. (2003). Ethnic differences in driving after drinking and riding with drinking drivers among adolescents. *Alcoholism: Clinical and Experimental Research, 27*(8), 1299–1304. doi:10.1097/01.ALC.0000080672.05255.6C

Watling, C. N., Palk, G. R., Freeman, J. E., & Davey, J. D. (2010). Applying Stafford and Warr's reconceptualization of deterrence theory to drug driving: Can it predict those likely to offend? *Accident Analysis and Prevention, 42*(2), 452–458. doi:10.1016/j.aap.2009.09.007

Watson, B., & Freeman, J. (2007). Perceptions and experiences of random breath testing in Queensland and the self-reported deterrent impact on drunk driving. *Traffic Injury Prevention, 8*(1), 11–19.

Whitehill, J. M., Rivara, F. P., & Moreno, M. A. (2014). Marijuana-using drivers, alcohol-using drivers, and their passengers. *JAMA Pediatrics, 168*(7), 618–624.

Wilkins, T. T. (2000). The "Stay Alive From Education" (SAFE) program: Description and preliminary pilot testing. *Journal of Alcohol and Drug Education, 45*(2), 1-11.

Wills, T. A., Cleary, S., Filer, M., Shinar, O., Mariani, J., & Spera, K. (2001). Temperament related to early-onset substance use: Test of a developmental model. *Prevention Science, 23*(3), 145–163.

Wright, M. J. (2015). Legalizing marijuana for medical purposes will increase risk of long-term, deleterious consequences for adolescents. *Drug and Alcohol Dependence, 149*, 298–303. doi:10.1016/j.drugalcdep.2015.01.005

Xu, X., & Chaloupka, F. J. (2011). Trends in alcoholic beverage taxes and prices. *Alcohol Research and Health, 34*, 236–245.

Yu, J., & Shacket, R. W. (1999). Drinking-driving and riding with drunk drivers among young adults: An analysis of reciprocal effects. *Journal of Studies on Alcohol, 60*(5), 615–621.

Zador, P. L., Krawchuk, S. A., & Voas, R. B. (2000). Alcohol-related relative risk of driver fatalities and driver involvement in fatal crashes in relation to driver age and gender: An update using 1996 data. *Journal of Studies on Alcohol, 61*(3), 387–395.

Zuckerman, M., & Kuhlman, D. M. (2000). Personality and risk-taking: Common biosocial factors. *Journal of Personality, 68*(6), 999–1029.

Self-Regulation and Decision Making

Kristen G. Anderson *and* Kristen E. L. Briggs

Abstract

Adolescence involves a complex interplay of biological, cognitive, emotional, and psychosocial changes when normative transitions in self-regulation, reward sensitivity, and decision making occur. As behavioral and cognitive systems mature at differing rates in adolescence, teens may be more vulnerable to the emergence of emotional and behavioral problems in the context of greater autonomy, independence, and responsibility. Youth develop more complex association networks pertaining to alcohol and other drug use across childhood and adolescence in concert with the development of more nuanced decision-making capabilities. As such, self-regulation of alcohol and other drug use behaviors may be particularly challenging for teens. In this chapter, we review the literature on the growth of self-regulation and decision-making abilities, their influence on the initiation and maintenance of alcohol and drug use in adolescence, and potential implications for prevention and intervention.

Key Words: Self-regulation, Decision making, Human development, Alcohol, Drugs

Underage drinking arises not in a passive organism but in one that is thinking, motivated, self-regulating, and in many other ways actively and dynamically interacting with people and objects within the environment. The development of self-regulation, planning, motivation, decision-making, risk-taking, friendship, and other manifestations of agency are important aspects of an understanding of the development of alcohol use and its consequences

—*Masten, Faden, Zucker, and Spear (2008, p. 5247)*

Although the opening quotation speaks to the processes underlying underage drinking in particular, the developmental perspective portrayed is appropriate to our broader consideration of adolescent substance use and other behavioral dependencies. The pathways leading to the abuse of alcohol and other drugs are multifaceted and multiply determined (Brown, Ramo & Anderson, 2011) and need to be considered within the adolescent developmental context (Cichetti & Cohen,

1995; Masten et al., 2008). Adolescence is a period when decision-making abilities, and the neural structures that underlie them, undergo significant change (Steinberg, 2008; Chapter 13, this volume). Although a preponderance of adolescent substance use models reflect a deficit perspective (i.e., alcohol and drug use result from self-regulatory or decision-making failures), we should consider the broader developmental significance of alcohol and drug use for adolescents (Casey & Caudle, 2013; Percy, 2008; Chapter 2, this volume). In this chapter, we review the literature on the development of self-regulation and decision-making skills, their influence on initiation and maintenance of alcohol and drug use in adolescence, and potential implications of this work for prevention and intervention during this period.

Of note, much of the research in this area suffers from definitional issues; a heterogeneous group of terms (e.g., self-regulation, self-control) are used to capture similar, but perhaps distinct, constructs in this area (Eisenberg, 2015; Gladwin, Figner, Crone,

& Wiers, 2011). In our attempts to bridge disparate literatures in this review, we will default to the term "self-regulation" when considering this class of processes and behaviors. To begin, we will summarize some dominant models of self-regulation and perspectives on the development of these capabilities.

Self-Regulation

Self-regulation has been defined as "the capacity to override one's thoughts, emotions, impulses, and automatic or habitual behaviors," and it is considered to be a vital capacity across the life span (Gaillot, Mead, & Baumeister, 2010, p. 472). The ability to self-monitor and enact self-control allows for responsible social behavior and greater care of the self and others (Doerr & Baumeister, 2010). Self-regulation involves the ability to inhibit predispositions toward negative actions, thoughts, and moods, as well as the capacity for self-improvement and implementation of new, more beneficial patterns of thinking and behaving. Effortful exertions of self-control are intended to help bring the individual into accord with the environment (Doerr & Baumeister, 2010). As humans are social animals, the motivation to succeed in the social sphere justifies the task of controlling natural responses and sacrificing self-centered desires. Self-regulation has been called the "master virtue" because it "empowers us to overcome selfish impulses" in order to better serve the greater good (Doerr & Baumeister, 2010, p. 71). Self-regulatory strength affords the short-term benefits of behavioral self-improvement and smoother social interactions as well as facilitating the achievement of long-term goals (Baumeister, Zell, & Tice, 2007). Self-control provides the ability to resist temptations that provide immediate rewards in the short term but that may lead to negative consequences in the future, thus affording the ability to seek delayed rather than immediate gratification (Casey & Caudle, 2013; Mischel, 1974, 1996).

Self-regulatory activity can occur in behavior, thought, and emotion. *Behavioral regulation* is the ability to inhibit, activate, or modify behavior willfully as appropriate (Eisenberg, Smith, & Spinrad, 2011). The voluntary inhibition of negative behaviors to meet social demands or to reach a standard is called *inhibitory control. Activation control*, on the other hand, is the effortful activation of positive behaviors to more closely match environmental expectations (Eisenberg et al., 2004; Kochanska, Murray, & Harlan, 2000). Activation control and inhibitory control can occur simultaneously during

the same self-regulatory act. *Emotion regulation*, or the ability to alter mood states to match environmental or personal standards, represents a separate subclass of general self-regulatory skills (Baumeister, Zell, & Tice, 2007; Eisenberg, 2015). Behavioral regulation and emotional regulation often occur in concert. The self-regulation of negative emotion may require the inhibition of impulses toward detrimental behaviors and the activation of more positive behavioral strategies for mood improvement (Eisenberg, Smith, & Spinrad, 2011). However, emotion regulation may take precedence when there is a greater perceived need for emotion regulation, particularly when distressed (Baumeister, Zell, & Tice, 2007). Emotional regulation may be detrimental to behavioral self-regulation when individuals feel they have control over their current mood state and anticipate improvement in affect as a result of their efforts (Baumeister, Zell, & Tice, 2007).

Models of Self-Regulation

A number of explanatory models have been posed for self-regulation. The four-factor model views self-regulation as resulting from a system composed of standards, monitoring, capacity for change, and motivation (Doerr & Baumeister, 2010). For an individual to initiate behavior change, they must first have a standard for the behavioral goal she wants to achieve. This *standard* can be an ideal, goal, or other specification of a desired state and reflects what the individual thinks is right or correct. Self-regulatory standards are often based on expectations or values imposed by the social environment. Higgins (1987) suggests that there may be two types of standards: ideal standards and ought standards. Ideal standards reflect hopes and aspirations, whereas ought standards reflect duties and obligations. Self-regulation is undermined when individuals set standards that are vague or ambiguous (Gaillot, Mead, & Baumeister, 2010), and conflicts can arise when multiple standards exist concurrently. Effective self-regulation cannot occur if two mutually exclusive standards are simultaneous goals.

In the *monitoring* process, individuals compare the current behavior with the goals dictated by the behavioral standards set previously. This monitoring must be both consistent and accurate to promote successful self-regulation. Failures to assess accurately the difference between the current state and the standard, or a lapse in monitoring altogether, can lead to ineffective self-regulation (Doerr & Baumeister, 2010). The capacity for change, also referred to as *self-regulatory strength*, is the ability to change and actively put forth effort to achieve behavioral goals (Gaillot, Mead, & Baumeister, 2010). The strength and endurance necessary to initiate and sustain preceding self-regulatory efforts must be present for successful self-regulation. Even if individuals evidence sufficient self-regulatory capacity, they still must be motivated to behave in concert with their standards (Doerr & Baumeister, 2010). Insufficient motivation can lead to self-regulatory failures, and high motivation can serve as a facilitating factor in the maintenance of self-regulatory strength (Muraven & Slessareva, 2003). For the four-part self-regulatory system to function effectively, each component must be represented sufficiently within the individual. However, in some cases, if one of the four factors is lacking, an unusual strength in another area may compensate (Doerr & Baumeister, 2010). For example, if an individual lacks sufficient self-regulatory strength as a general trait or within a particular context, it is possible that an extremely high amount of motivation may compensate. However, no amount of motivation or capacity for change can save self-regulatory efforts when standards set by the individual are hopelessly conflicting or unrealistic.

Self-regulatory failures can result from insufficiencies in standard setting, monitoring, self-regulatory strength, or motivation. Research suggests that self-regulatory failures, regardless of origin, fall into three main categories: underregulation, overregulation, and misregulation (Doerr & Baumeister, 2010). Underregulation, or poor self-control, can result from insufficient efforts at any of the four levels of the self-regulation model. This type of self-regulatory failure is commonly associated with substance use (Sayette & Griffin, 2010). Overregulation is a form of rigid self-regulation, where self-regulatory goals take priority over other important life goals. Individuals who are overregulating have sufficient self-regulatory strength, but they need a more flexible approach. Effective self-regulators monitor and moderate their self-regulatory efforts appropriately to avoid overregulation. Misregulation occurs when sufficient self-regulatory energy is expended, but the efforts are misguided or ineffective. Misregulation is frequently due to competition between conflicting standards. Sayette and Griffin (2010) provide the example of a smoker who uses cigarettes as a method of weight control; the long-term costs

associated with smoking far outweigh any short-term benefit of controlling weight gain (p. 506).

The limited resource model of self-regulation and ego depletion (e.g., Baumeister & Vohs, 2007) likens self-regulation to a muscle, which can be exhausted by use. This theory asserts that all self-regulatory skills rely on a single, limited resource. Self-regulatory exertion in one domain can cause transient deficits in future self-regulation across conceptually related domains (Baumeister, Gailliot, & Tice, 2009; Muraven, Tice, & Baumeister, 1998). This exhaustion of self-regulatory resources across subdomains is termed "ego depletion" (Doerr & Baumeister, 2010). Self-regulatory resources can be exhausted by making conscious choices (Baumeister, Bratslavsky, Muraven, & Tice, 1998; Vohs et al., 2008), engaging in effortful thinking (Schmeichel, Vohs, & Baumeister, 2003), controlling thought (Gailliot, Schmeichel, & Baumeister, 2006; Muraven et al., 1998), and maintaining desired mood states (Tice & Bratslavsky, 2000). Deficits in the body's glucose levels have been associated with self-regulatory deficits, and drinking glucose-sweetened beverages has been shown to reduce ego depletion on laboratory tasks (Doerr & Baumeister, 2010). Sleep and rest may be another source of energy for self-regulatory processes. Individuals who are more tired and fatigued have shown greater tendencies toward self-regulatory failures (Baumeister, Stillwell, & Heatherton, 1994; Peper & Dahl, 2013), and certain types of meditation that mimic rest replenish self-regulatory strength after ego depletion (Doerr & Baumeister, 2010).

Development of Self-Regulation

From a very young age, individuals are physiologically equipped and socially expected to self-regulate, yet the capability for self-control changes substantially over the course of development. Temperamental self-regulatory capacity, otherwise known as *effortful control*, is the "ability to inhibit a dominant response and/or activate a subdominant response" (Eisenberg, Smith, & Spinrad, 2011, p. 263) and is subsumed under the general umbrella of executive functioning. Effortful control is a central part of voluntary action, including the intentional shifting of attention, or attentional control, and the regulation of behavior, or behavioral control (Eisenberg, Smith, & Spinrad, 2011; Eisenberg, 2015). A neuroscience account of self-regulation, or self-control, suggests that these abilities rely on interactions between multiple structures within the brain and a network of transactions between appetitive, inhibitory, and motivational processes (Casey & Caudle, 2013; Gladwin et al., 2011). For example, the regulation of attention has been linked to the anterior cingulate cortex (Posner & Fan, 2008), while the behavioral inhibition portion of effortful control is believed to be grounded in the anterior cingulate gyrus and areas of the prefrontal cortex (Eisenberg, Smith, & Spinrad, 2011; Eisenberg 2015). The ability to inhibit habitual responses is associated with activation in the ventrolateral prefrontal cortex, showing increases in activation as a function of age, while the ventral striatum shares a role when emotionally salient stimuli or rewarding stimuli are present (Casey & Caudle, 2013; Galvan, 2013). Integrated functioning of these two systems, inhibitory and reward based, enable goal-directed behavior and demonstrate age-related differences (Luna, Paulsen, Padmanabhan, & Geier, 2013).

Children's self-regulatory growth begins with attention control as a largely reactive means of coping with emotional distress in the first 2 or so years of life, and then follows with the development of more voluntarily controlled behavioral regulation in the later years (Blair & Ursache, 2010; Eisenberg, Smith, & Spinrad, 2011). Behavioral inhibition and related markers of true effortful control (like complying with parental demands and controlling one's own actions even in the absence of adult monitoring) do not fully appear on the developmental stage until about age 3 (Rothbart, Ellis, & Posner, 2010). Between the ages of 3 and 4, toddlers develop more adult-like abilities to inhibit behavior, often testing and practicing these skills in childhood games like Simon Says (Eisenberg, Smith, & Spinrad, 2011). Self-regulatory skill is thought to increase dramatically in the preschool years, and neural connectivity in brain regions related to effortful control continues to grow at least into late childhood (Rueda, Posner, & Rothbart, 2010). Neurodevelopmental work suggests that the basics of cognitive control are fully formed by childhood, while developmental shifts in adolescence improve executive functioning. Across adolescence, specific aspects of self-regulation, particularly those related to performance monitoring and controlled responding across contexts, improve and become more adult-like (Luna et al., 2013). Given increased reward sensitivity found in adolescence, however, self-regulation within certain rewarding contexts, particularly involving peers, may be more challenging and recruit greater resources (Galvan, 2013; van Duijvenvoorde & Crone, 2013).

The development of effortful control may be influenced by many factors. Evidence suggests that effortful control has a genetic, temperamental basis (Goldsmith, Pollack, & Davidson, 2008) and that parent–child relationships have a strong effect, as children need external support to develop functional self-regulatory skills (Eisenberg, Smith, & Spinrad, 2011; Eisenberg, 2015). Although genetic markers predict effortful control in children, these effects are often mediated by parenting quality (Rueda, Posner, & Rothbart, 2010), such that poor parenting (Sheese et al., 2008) and insecure attachment in infancy (Kochanska, Philibert, & Barry, 2009) can inhibit self-regulation development in children at genetic risk for poor effortful control.

Warm, responsive, and supportive parenting has been linked with greater effortful control abilities in infancy (Calkins, Dedmon, Gill, Lomax, & Johnson, 2002), toddlerhood (Kochanska, Aksan, Prisco, & Adams, 2008), and even in later childhood (Belsky, Fearon, & Bell, 2007). Conversely, harsh, authoritarian parenting styles, characterized by high levels of control and low levels of warmth, have been found to be detrimental to the development of effortful control in children (Kochanska, Aksan, Prisco, & Adams, 2008), especially in those children already exhibiting lower than average levels of self-control (Calkins, 1994). Parents' responses to their children's emotional expressions (Spinrad et al., 2007) and the type/intensity of mothers' own emotional expressions (Eisenberg et al., 2005) also influence the development of effortful control. These personal emotional expressions and responses to child emotions act as either positive or negative models of emotion regulation and influence self-regulation from preschool through adolescence (Eisenberg, Cumberland, & Spinrad, 1998). Although many aspects of parenting may predict effortful control development, some studies have proposed a bidirectional relationship, where children's regulatory abilities may also induce changes in parenting tactics (Belsky et al., 2007; Bridgett et al., 2009; Eisenberg, 2015).

Environmental influences outside of parenting styles may also have the power to affect the development of self-regulation. Lengua, Bush, Long, Trancik, and Kovacs (2008) found that effortful control in 8- to 12-year-old children was predicted by a multitude of factors, including family income, parent education, neighborhood, negative life events, family conflict, and maternal depression (Rothbart, Ellis, & Posner, 2010). Interestingly, these factors only predicted growth in the development of effortful control between the ages of 3 and 3.5 years, when the most significant changes in self-regulational abilities occur (Rothbart, Ellis, & Posner, 2010). Research has focused specifically on elucidating the developmental pathway through which poverty negatively affects the development of self-regulation (Noble, McCandliss, & Farah, 2007). Stress physiology may be the mediating factor between the experience of poverty and effortful control deficits in both preschool-aged children and older adolescents (Evans & Schamberg, 2009). Both highly stressful and understimulating social environments can cause misregulation in children's stress hormones, directly limiting effortful control development, and in parents' stress hormones, indirectly affecting self-regulation development by means of greater likelihood of parental neglect (Blair & Ursache, 2010).

Although much of the research on factors impacting the development of self-regulation has focused on childhood (Eisenberg, 2015), self-regulation has substantive impacts on decision making in adolescence as greater refinement and integration of brain structures impact youth ability to make decisions associated with long-term consequences.

Adolescent Development, Self-Regulation, and Decision Making

Adolescence involves a complex interplay of biological, cognitive, emotional, and psychosocial changes where normative transitions in self-regulation, particularly emotional regulation, occur (Albert, Chein, & Steinberg, 2013; Albert & Steinberg, 2011; Spear, 2010). During this period, youth increase their ability to inhibit, control, and modulate behavior as a function of neuromaturation: The prefrontal cortex becomes more efficient and better able to communicate with other brain structures throughout adolescence and into adulthood, allowing for higher level abstract thinking and improved executive functioning (Chapters 11 and 13, this volume; Spear, 2010). To function adaptively, individuals need to self-regulate emotions and behavior to attain long-term goals (Baumeister, Zell, & Tice, 2007). As behavioral and cognitive systems mature at different rates in adolescence, teens may be more vulnerable to the emergence of emotional and behavioral problems within the context of greater autonomy, independence, and responsibility (Reyna & Farley, 2006; Steinberg, 2005).

Adolescents actively explore their environment and develop skills necessary to function as independent adults (Spear, 2010). The transition from childhood to young adulthood incorporates developmental changes in cognitive abilities, emotional regulation, autonomy, and a shift from greater familial influence to peer influence. During this time period, youth's declarative, procedural, and conceptual knowledge increases; deductive and inductive reasoning abilities advance; explicit and implicit memory further develops (Byrnes, 2006); processing speed, or the fluidity by which youth can access and interpret information, and long- and short-term memory capacities improve (Spear, 2010). Emotional development in adolescence is closely allied with shifts in cognitive ability, hormonal changes, and life experiences: Emotions can be influenced by abstract ideas, a greater ability to introspect, and greater empathy for the viewpoints of others; emotions may be more intense and negative in tone than before; and teens experience a host of new life challenges brought about by the assumption of a more adult-like physique, transitions to more independent school environments, and the need for more sophisticated coping skills to face these challenges (Crone et al., 2009; Peper & Dahl, 2013; Rosenblum & Lewis, 2006).

A hallmark of adolescence is greater autonomy and independence from parents and caregivers. Adolescent development within this area is characterized by "socially responsible and optimal autonomous functioning following from the continuing maintenance of connections to social partners, while becoming increasingly self-regulating, self-motivating and independent" (Zimmer-Gembeck & Collins, 2006, p. 176). In the context of continued influence by the family of origin and a normative developmental shift to greater peer influence (Brown, Bakken, Ameringer, & Mahon, 2008), adolescents must balance needs for independence and positive interpersonal relationships for optimal development (Zimmer-Gembeck & Collins, 2006). Romantic interests increase through the process of attaining sexual maturity, and youth must learn to manage autonomy and interpersonal intimacy in both romantic and friendship contexts (Bouchey & Furman, 2006). Peers and romantic partners exert significant influences on youth, aiding in the determination of behavioral expectations and goals as well as conferring greater exposure to mores and values that may differ from that of their parents (Zimmer-Gembeck & Collins, 2006). Although the development of identity and adult-like social relationships have often been considered hallmarks of adolescence, recent work suggests that this task may continue into emerging adulthood (ages 18–24) in Western industrialized societies (Arnett, 2001).

Embedded within this developmental context, adolescents continue to advance their decision-making abilities. *Decision making* has been defined as the underlying processes that allow us to attain a particular goal (Byrnes, 2006). Classic models of decision making focus on deliberative processes, involving a view of human behavior governed by principles of rational action (Reyna & Farley, 2006). Rationality, in this context, refers to decisions based upon the orderly consideration of current beliefs and the individual's goals. Behavior, from these perspectives, is governed by systematic consideration of the possible outcomes of the act. Rational decision making can result in unhealthy behavior or lead to negative outcomes for the decision maker. It is assumed that healthy decision making will result if underlying attitudes and beliefs are supportive of such decisions (Reyna & Farley, 2006). Other models suggest that much of human behavior is governed by automatic or heuristic-based processes (Jacobs & Klaczynski, 2002; Tversky & Kahneman, 1974), particularly helpful in understanding why individuals often make decisions that seem counterintuitive in terms of the net costs and benefits. Contradictions in the literature on rational and automatic process models have led to a cadre of dual-process models, proposed to integrate both aspects of decision making (Bickel, Quisenberry, Moody, & Wilson, 2014; Gladwin et al., 2011; Klaczynski, 2005; Reyna, Adam, Poirier, LeCroy, & Brainerd, 2005; Strack & Deutsch, 2004), that allow for greater flexibility in understanding the situational or contextual features impacting information processing (Albert & Steinberg, 2011). Because a thorough review of the decision-making literature is beyond the scope of this chapter, interested readers are referred to Reisberg (2013).

Developmental research often focuses on comparing the decision-making abilities of adolescents to that of younger children or adults. Adult decision making is often the gold standard (although this metric is questionable given the sufficient number of errors adults evidence in this realm; Jacobs & Klaczynski, 2002; Males, 2009; Reyna & Farley, 2006). Laboratory tasks and performance in hypothetical situations suggest that teens anticipate the consequences of their actions and learn from their successes and failures better than younger children (Byrnes, 2006). Older adolescents seem to comprehend the distinction between choices satisfying just one goal as compared to multiple goals at once, and they are better able to make inferences, perceive risk, and consider consequences when planning compared to younger teens (Byrnes, 2006; Jacobs & Klaczynski, 2002). Adolescents perform similarly to adults on tasks requiring searching for and attending to relevant information and generating solutions in the laboratory decision-making environments (Jacobs & Klaczynski, 2002). Interestingly, adolescents may engage in more rational decision making about risk than adults (Casey & Caudle, 2013). Whereas youth are more likely to weigh the pros and cons of a risky situation before responding, adults may rely on the gist of a risky situation and react in risk-adverse ways (Chick & Reyna, 2012; Reyna et al., 2005). Despite this deliberative processing of contingencies, youth may continue to make more risky decisions than adults as a function of developmental differences in reactions to situational contexts involving peers, novelty, high emotionality, or pressures for rapid decision making (Albert et al., 2013; Albert & Steinberg, 2011; van Duijvenvoorde & Crone, 2013). Neuroimaging findings suggest that adolescents' difficulties in applying self-control within emotional salient contexts, in particular those with positive emotional cues, are associated with greater activation in the ventral striatum, an area associated with learning about novel or rewarding cues; as such, teens exaggerated response to appetitive cues "may serve to 'hijack' a less fully mature prefrontal control response" (Casey & Caudle, 2013, p. 85).

Normative risk taking and a focus on peer relationships within this period provide youth the opportunity to develop skills and relationships needed to move from the sphere of the family of origin toward greater independence (Casey & Caudle, 2013; Spear, 2010). This context seems particularly important as it relates to adolescent decision making and self-regulatory ability (Chein, Albert, O'Brien, Uckert, & Steinberg, 2011). Despite some differences, adolescents and adults perform similarly on a number of domains of cognitive performance around age 15 (Reyna & Farley, 2006). However, decision-making contexts may differentiate adult and adolescent abilities. While adults and teens tend to generate similar responses in risk assessments in *cold* situations ("thinking processes under conditions of low emotion and/or arousal"), differences emerge in *hot* contexts ("conditions of strong feelings or high arousal"; Steinberg, 2005, p. 72), whereby youth evidence a reward bias in information processing and shifts toward more impulsive/risky decision making (Albert & Steinberg, 2011; Chick & Reyna, 2012; Galvan, 2012). Peer contexts can be particularly activating for adolescents given their focus on peer relationships and need for affiliation (Albert et al., 2013). Adolescents often face novel situations when engaging in decision making unaided by adult influence; the adaptive pressures engendered in novel situations may tax youths' self-regulatory capacity, potentially supporting more impulsive responding when compared to adults.

Unpleasant emotional states disrupt self-regulation and subsequent decision making as emotional distress shifts individual priorities to coping with the current negative emotional state, away from distal goals (Baumeister, Zell, & Tice, 2007). As adolescents tend to experience higher levels of negative affectivity than children or adults, a greater propensity for self-regulatory failures may be evidenced. Pubertal maturation influences aspects of emotional intensity and reactivity in early adolescence (Albert & Steinberg, 2011). As connections between the limbic system, underlying emotional regulation, and frontal executive structures develop across adolescence, this inability to self-regulate in the face of negative emotion may be potentiated (Spear, 2010). Given changes in the sleep-wake cycle and evidence of greater sleep deprivation in adolescents, sleep status may impact self-regulation (Carskadon, Acebo, & Jenni, 2004; Peper & Dahl, 2013), also influencing emotional and behavioral regulation for teens.

Novelty and requirements for in-the-moment decisions may engender risky decision making for teens (Reyna & Farley, 2006). Developmental changes in reward neurocircuitry are believed to underlie a rise in disinhibition, sensation seeking, and impulsivity in adolescence (Galvan, 2013; Spear, 2013; Steinberg, 2005). Although some see impulsivity and risk taking as a hallmark of adolescence (Albert & Steinberg, 2011; Reyna et al., 2005), others have been critical of such characterization (Hollenstein & Lougheed, 2013), noting that much of adult behavior can also be considered risky (Males, 2009). Despite this debate, a preponderance of evidence suggests that high-risk behavior in adolescence corresponds to negative developmental outcomes across a variety of domains, including hazardous alcohol and drug use, problematic gambling, and high-risk sexual behavior (Steinberg, 2008; Chassin, 2015).

Self-Regulation and Adolescent Substance Use Decision Making

Self-regulatory skills develop and are refined in the period of adolescence and emerging adulthood. These changes are often contemporaneous with the initiation of alcohol and drug use behaviors (Masten et al., 2008; Percy, 2008). Given that alcohol and drug use peaks within emerging adulthood (ages 18–24 years), adolescence is often associated with initiation of alcohol, tobacco, and marijuana and, to some degree, other drug use (SAMHSA, 2015). Understanding the interplay of nascent self-regulation skills and transitions in substance use behavior is needed as rates of alcohol and drug use disorders peak subsequent to adolescence, particularly for boys (Masten et al., 2008; SAMHSA, 2015).

In framing our discussion of the intersection of self-regulation and youth decision making about initiating substance use as well as transitions in consumption, it is important to consider the social/cultural context in which these decisions are being made. Although late adolescent experimentation with alcohol, tobacco, and to some extent, cannabis, may be common in the United States, an important distinction is made between normative and acceptable behavior within society. The determination of deviant behavior within this realm may be on the basis of timing (i.e., earlier vs. later) or in terms of societal or cultural acceptance (Masten et al., 2008). If we consider self-regulation as altering individual responses in order to attain long-term benefits (Sayette & Griffin, 2010), youth understanding of the societal context of these decisions is important. If engagement in alcohol and drug use is viewed by society as expected/normative and approved, the potential long-term consequences for use may be evaluated differently by youth than when engagement in these behaviors is unexpected/nonnormative and disapproved by society (Masten et al., 2008). The mixed cultural messages that youth receive surrounding these behaviors, particularly within the United States and the United Kingdom (Percy, 2008), may have marked impacts on youth goal setting and motivation around alcohol and drug use and subsequent self-regulation in substance use contexts.

Self-Regulation Capacity and Adolescent Substance Use

Commonly, self-regulation deficits have been seen as precursors to the initiation of problematic alcohol and other drug use for youth (Gladwin et al., 2011; Wiers et al., 2007; Wills & Ainette, 2009), and disordered substance use has been characterized as failure of self-regulation (Peeters et al., 2013; Sayette & Griffin, 2010). From this perspective, youth are at greatest risk for the development of alcohol and other drug use disorders as a function of immature self-regulation abilities (Chambers, Taylor, & Potenza, 2003) or trait-like predispositions to poor self-regulation (Hoyle, 2006). Although we addressed developmental patterns in self-regulation earlier, a number of chapters within this volume provide trait- or temperament-based etiological models for adolescent substance use, many associated with self-regulatory capacity (Hoyle, 2006; Wills, Pokhrel, Morehouse, & Fenster, 2011). Temperamental traits such as attentional control (e.g., Rueda, Posner, & Rothbart, 2010), behavioral inhibition (Chapter 15, this volume), effortful control (e.g., Eisenberg, 2015; Rothbart, Ellis, & Posner, 2010), and resilience (e.g., Wong et al., 2006) as well as personality constructs such as impulsivity, and disinhibition (Chapter 14, this volume; Sher & Slutske, 2004) are involved in an individual's ability to self-regulate their consumption of illicit substances. Although developmental differences in self-regulation are important considerations, the range of individual differences among adolescents on these traits (Casey & Caudle, 2013) and subsequent substance use should not be minimized. For example, behavioral control, both in terms of baseline differences and rate of development, and resiliency (defined here as the ability to appropriately adapt levels of control in response to the environment) in early childhood (~age 4 years) predicted the onset of drinking, drunkenness, alcohol-related problems, and other drug use in adolescence, with greater control and resilience delaying the onset or limiting engagement with substances of abuse (Wong et al., 2006). In early and middle adolescence, behavioral and emotional aspects of self-regulation have been implicated in complex models of adolescent substance use and problems (Wills et al., 2011; Wills, Walker, Mendoza, & Ainette, 2006). The interaction of individual characteristics, development, and environmental context are central to the timing and course of substance use (Chassin, 2015).

For youth who initiate alcohol and drug use in adolescence, behavioral self-regulation skills may be promoted or disrupted as a function of the timing or intensity of use (Percy, 2008). Experimental or moderate use of alcohol or other

drugs within adolescence may be a precursor to the regulation of these behaviors in adulthood. Although adolescent alcohol and drug initiation is not a necessary precursor for the development of these skills, normative experimentation during this period may provide opportunities for youth to hone the specific skills needed for behavioral regulation within this domain (for a contrasting view, see Reyna & Farley, 2006). The timing of use within this developmental period may be a significant factor as to whether this opportunity for self-regulatory development engenders more positive outcomes. Early-onset substance use may also disrupt, versus foster, the development of self-regulatory skill; use prior to age 14 may occur at a time when youth are unable to self-regulate substance use and may result in greater negative developmental consequences. However, successes and failures in behavioral regulation during the phases of experimental and moderate use later in adolescence may be a "preliminary stage in the acquisition of self-regulatory mastery" in the consumption of these agents (Percy, 2008, p. 452).

The development of alcohol and drug dependence in adolescence can be seen as developmentally mediated poor regulation of an appetitive, approach-oriented system that is sensitive to the acute and protracted use of alcohol and other drugs (Chambers et al., 2003; Gladwin et al., 2011). The progression from use to dependence moves from early phases when youth are able to regulate tendencies toward cue-related responding, but may lack the necessary motivation to do so, to later phases when motivation to inhibit these responses is evident, but they are unable to do so. The notion is that this imbalance between self-regulation capacity and motivation is a hallmark of transition from experimental to more problematic or disordered use for adolescents (Gladwin et al., 2011; Wiers et al., 2007).

Expectancies and Substance-Specific Motivation

As depicted by the four-part self-regulation model, standards, self-regulation capacity, monitoring, and motivation are central to the ability to self-regulate (Doerr & Baumeister, 2010). Self-regulation capacity is a necessary but not sufficient condition for adaptive alcohol and drug use decision making. Expectancies, central to goal or standard setting, and substance-specific motivations are important aspects to consider within this context (Hull & Slone, 2004). Expectancies and motives are believed to stem from biological, cultural, and environmental considerations (Cox & Klinger, 1988). Across child and adolescent development, changes occur in the form and function of youth cognitions about alcohol and other drugs, reciprocally influencing substance use decisions. As alcohol is the most commonly used agent, much of the research on child and adolescent cognitions has been alcohol specific. However, a growing body of work has examined these constructs related to other drug use.

Outcome expectancies are if-then statements that summarize our learning history about certain behaviors (Chapter 17, this volume). In the case of alcohol expectancies, these are paired associations between drinking and its consequences (Goldman, Brown, Christiansen, & Smith, 1991), and many investigators have examined the nature and influence of these cognitions on drinking (e.g., Brown, Christiansen, & Goldman, 1987; Jones, Corbin, & Fromme, 2001; Rohsenow & Marlatt, 1981). Whereas traditional conceptualizations of alcohol expectancies focused on the positive-negative dimension, later work specified an additional arousal-sedation dimension, and a developmental progression from childhood to adulthood whereby the positive-negative dimension is more dominant (with negative being particularly strong) to a more nuanced interplay of both positive-negative and arousal-sedation expectancies (Dunn & Goldman, 1996; 2000). Expectancies' influence on use patterns has been shown for other substances of abuse, such as cannabis (Hayakia et al., 2010), stimulants (Labbe & Maisto, 2010), and opioids (Powell, Bradley, & Gray, 1992). *Drinking motives*, or reasons endorsed for drinking (Cooper, Russell, Skinner, & Windle, 1992; Kuntsche, Knibbe, Gmel, & Engels, 2005; Newcomb, Chou, Bentler, & Huba, 1988), seemingly evidence a developmental progression from a unidimensional drinking motive in late childhood/early adolescence to more nuanced motives to drink by late adolescence and adulthood (Kuntsche et al., 2005). Research on motives for cannabis use (Comeau, Stewart, & Loba, 2001; Simons, Correia, Carey, & Borsari, 1998; Zvolensky et al., 2009) and nonmedical use of prescription drugs (McCabe, Boyd, Cranford, & Teter, 2009; McCabe, Cranford, Boyd, & Teter, 2007) suggest differentiation and developmental differences across adolescence.

Although the majority of research has focused on cognitions associated with use, a growing literature has emerged on *expectancies and motives for abstinence or moderation*, or anticipated outcomes from not using and reasons for limiting or abstaining from use. Global and social expectancies for not drinking have been associated with alcohol consumption; youth with more alcohol use experience (moderate and heavy drinkers) showed greater differentiation in abstention expectancies than lighter drinkers. For youth with greater alcohol consumption, these expectancies predicted cessation efforts (Metrik, McCarthy, Frissell, MacPherson, & Brown, 2004). Motives to limit or abstain from drinking also change qualitatively and quantitatively from childhood through emerging adulthood (Epler, Sher & Piasecki, 2009; Greenfield, Guydish, & Temple, 1989; Maggs & Schulenberg, 1998). From late childhood to mid-adolescence (grades 6–10), youth endorse fewer motives not to drink, contemporaneous with increases in drinking motives (Maggs & Schulenberg, 1998), a finding consistent with cross sectional work with middle and high school students (Anderson, Grunwald, Bekman, Brown, & Grant, 2011). Transitions in adolescents' alcohol use patterns correspond with the relative influence of expectancies for use, cessation, and motivation for abstinence (Bekman et al., 2011). Motives to abstain from alcohol (Anderson, Briggs, & White, 2013) and cannabis (Anderson, Sitney, & White, 2015; Patrick, Schulenberg, O'Malley, Johnston, & Bachman, 2011) show prospective relations with use of these agents from adolescence through emerging adulthood, and findings suggest a complex interplay of motives to use and abstain on decision making.

Developmentally, we would expect greater differentiation of cognitions surrounding substance use as youth age and garner greater experience with alcohol and other drugs (Donovan, Molina, & Kelly, 2009; Dunn & Goldman, 1996; Miller, Smith, & Goldman, 1990). Consistent with models whereby information-processing networks demonstrate less consolidation and sophistication earlier in development or with less experience (Bekman, Goldman, Worley, & Anderson, 2011; Donovan et al., 2009), a progression from lesser to greater integration of expectancies and motives for use and abstention would be anticipated. In the context of decision making, if these competing expectations and motives are not successfully integrated, holding mutually exclusive goals for use, abstinence, or moderation may hinder effective self-regulation of these behaviors. If individuals feel they have control over their current mood state and anticipate improvement in affect as a result of drinking or using, as in the case of expectancies and motives for coping, they may be more likely to consume alcohol or other drugs rather than abstain.

The work depicted earlier focuses on aspects of cognition characterized by the more deliberative route of decision making. The area of implicit cognitions relating to alcohol and drug use has grown in the past decade. Implicit alcohol- and drug-related cognition captures the more automatic, heuristic-based processing discussed earlier (Ames, Franken, & Coronges, 2006; Wiers, Houben, Smulders, Conrod, & Jones, 2006). Dual-process models integrate both automatic and deliberative aspects of decision making to understand substance use and behavioral dependencies (Evans & Coventry, 2006; Wiers et al., 2006), with work articulating the interaction of these processes in adolescent decision making (Gladwin et al., 2011; O'Conner & Colder, 2015). Theory and research suggest that both explicit and implicit processes are important considerations when examining the motivational processes outlined earlier (Cox, Fadardi, & Klinger, 2006; Gladwin et al., 2011). Associative memory, reaction time, and attentional bias tasks suggest that implicit alcohol- and drug-related cognitions demonstrate both concurrent and prospective relations with use behaviors and consequences and discriminate those with use-related problems (Ames et al., 2006; Wiers, Gladwin, Hofman, Salemink, & Ridderinkhof, 2013). Similar to findings with explicit alcohol expectancies, implicit cognitions regarding alcohol seem to follow the valence versus arousal dimensions depicted earlier (Wiers et al., 2006). Whether these dimensions demonstrate developmental changes across adolescence, similar to the progression for explicit cognitions, requires further study. Implicit cognitions pertaining to alcohol (Thush & Wiers, 2007) and cannabis use (Stacy, Ames, Sussman, & Dent, 1996) predict later use in teens. Prospectively, young adolescents with stronger automatic approach tendencies evidenced increased alcohol consumption a half a year later, but only for youth with the poorest self-regulation skills (Peeters et al., 2013). O'Conner and Colder (2015) demonstrated that a complex interplay of implicit cognitions about alcohol, self-regulation, and motivation to self-regulate predicted alcohol use across one year in early adolescents. Cross-sectionally, relations between implicit cognition and use have been found in children (Pieters, van der Vorst, Burk, Wiers, & Engels, 2010) and young and middle adolescents (Thush & Wiers, 2007). Work with samples of youth (ages 12–24 years) suggests a complex relation between implicit and explicit cognitions, parental consumption patterns, and current and future alcohol consumption (Belles, Budde, Moesgen, & Klein, 2011). As work within this area continues to proliferate, the developmental progression of these cognitions and their interaction with self-regulation capacities will become more apparent.

Historically, most expectancy and motives assessment has focused on the immediate rewards or punishments associated with use (Cooper, 1994; Goldman et al., 1991). The recent emphasis on expectancies and motives to limit or abstain from use is important, allowing researchers to assess expectancy and motivational structures associated with the pursuit of both immediate and delayed rewards (Settles & Smith, 2011). This conceptual overlap with self-regulation is compelling. Aspects of adolescent development, particularly a bias toward reward, may influence youth evaluation of the proximal benefits of alcohol and other drug use over more distal rewards associated with moderation or abstention (Albert & Steinberg, 2011; Smith & Anderson, 2001). Given that youth develop more complex association networks pertaining to alcohol and other drug use across childhood and adolescence (Donovan, Molina, & Kelly, 2009; Dunn & Goldman, 1996), in concert with the development of more nuanced decision-making networks (Reyna & Farley, 2006), self-regulation of these behaviors may be particularly challenging for youth. If, as a function of immature self-regulation and decision-making capabilities, adolescents are at greater risk for problems associated with alcohol and other drug use, how can we use this knowledge to design better prevention and intervention efforts?

Implications for Prevention and Intervention

A review of prevention and intervention strategies that target self-regulation and adolescent decision making is well beyond the bounds of this chapter (see Chapters 29–34). However, the framework provided here can provide some direction in the implementation of developmentally relevant prevention and intervention programs for youth.

1. Although poor self-regulation has been targeted as a risk factor for the early initiation of substance use (Masten et al., 2008; Wiers et al., 2007), prevention programs need not focus solely on alcohol or other drug use. Self-regulatory improvements in one domain can

enhance self-regulation overall (Oaten & Cheng, 2006), and consistently practicing self-regulation in a single domain seems to produce relatively long-term improvements in overall abilities to self-regulate (Muraven et al., 1999), suggesting that early intervention on general self-regulation capacity may impact later abilities to regulate in contexts involving alcohol and other drugs (Chassin, 2015; Pentz, Riggs, & Warren, 2016).

2. Self-regulation has been compared to a muscle in that it relies upon a limited source of energy that can be exhausted in the short term (Bickel et al., 2014; Muraven & Baumeister, 2000; Muraven et al., 1998). Greater attention to issues of sleep hygiene, nutrition, and overall health promotion may benefit adolescents' abilities to self-regulate and foster better self-care across the life span.

3. Adolescents approach intervention and treatment differently than children and emerging adults; developmentally sensitive programs will address issues related to adolescent autonomy, need for peer affiliation, motivation, and cognitive development (D'Amico, McCarthy, Metrik, & Brown, 2004). Programs using developmentally tailored, self-referral formats in the middle and high school setting have promise for alcohol and other drug use prevention (D'Amico et al., 2006; D'Amico & Edelen, 2007; Garcia et al., 2015).

4. Given neural maturation and refinement of cognitive function in adolescence, prevention and intervention programs should consider how developmental changes might influence service provision for teens (Steinberg, 2008). Interventions including multiple foci—the family, the individual, and institutions—may evidence the greatest success in terms of skill retention as a function of these neurocognitive changes (Lopez, Schwartz, Prado, Campo, & Pantin, 2008). Work suggests that certain family-centered interventions may prevent escalations in antisocial behaviors, including substance use, across middle school by increasing self-regulatory abilities in youth (Fosco, Frank, Stormshak, & Dishion, 2013).

5. Substance use prevention and intervention have generally focused on explicit aspects of self-regulation and substance-related cognitions, but they have often ignored the importance of implicit processes (Krank & Goldstein, 2006; Palfai, 2006). Given our growing understanding of the dual processes underlying decision making, integrating these two modes of processing within

prevention and intervention programs should be further examined (Bickel et al., 2014; Gladwin et al., 2011) and be integrated into multilevel interventions with youth (Chassin, 2015; Peeters et al., 2013).

Summary

Processes underlying self-regulation continue to develop across childhood and adolescence, contemporaneous with changes in decision-making abilities (Albert et al., 2013; Steinberg, 2008). Adolescents may be at greater risk for diminished self-regulatory capacity as a function of developmental differences in stress tolerance, negative emotionality, sleep deprivation, and immature coping skills (Spear, 2010). Differences in adolescent and adult decision-making capability are seemingly context dependent; youth seem prone to impulsive or risky decision making in contexts involving novelty, high emotion, peers, or the need for in-the-moment decisions (Chein et al., 2011; Reyna & Farley, 2006). These situational characteristics show remarkable similarity to contexts where youth typically use alcohol or other drugs, increasing the likelihood that underregulation or misregulation of these behaviors will occur (Albert & Steinberg, 2011). The broader social context involving expectations for adolescent experimentation with alcohol (Masten et al., 2008) and, to some extent, other drug use (Percy, 2008), as well as cognitive changes in the integration of substance-specific expectancy and motivational networks (Anderson et al., 2011, 2013; Bekman, Goldman et al., 2011), may influence adolescent self-regulation of substance use. In aggregate, the existent literature supports a developmentally specific liability for poor regulation of alcohol and other drug use if these behaviors are initiated early in adolescence, consistent with data showing rapid progressions from use to dependence within adolescent samples (DeWit, Adlaf, Offord, & Ogborne, 2000).

We must remember that the majority of youth do not evidence problems associated with alcohol and drug use. The adolescent developmental context may provide ample opportunities for dysregulated alcohol and drug use, but many youth demonstrate adequate self-regulation of these behaviors (Albert & Steinberg, 2011). Important individual differences in temperament/personality, parenting practices, peer networks, and the environment, particularly issues of availability and access, will influence whether youth initiate substance use or make important transitions to problematic or dependent patterns of use (Brown, McGue et al., 2008; Chassin, 2015). By better understanding the processes underlying effective self-regulation within the adolescent developmental context, we will have a more comprehensive and nuanced view of the developmental progression of alcohol and other drug use from childhood to adulthood.

References

Albert, D., Chein, J., & Steinberg, L. (2013). The teenaged brain: Peer influences on adolescent decision making. *Current Directions in Psychological Science, 22*(2), 114–120.

Albert, D., & Steinberg, L. (2011). Judgment and decision making in adolescence. *Journal of Research on Adolescence, 21*(1), 211–224.

Ames, S. L., Franken, I. H. A., & Coronges, K. (2006). Implicit cognition and drugs of abuse. In R. W. Wiers & A. W. Stacy (Eds.), *Handbook of implicit cognition* (pp. 363–378). Thousand Oaks, CA: Sage Publishing.

Anderson, K. G., Briggs, K. M., White, H. R. (2013). Motives to drink or not to drink: Longitudinal relations among personality, motives and alcohol use across adolescence and early adulthood. *Alcoholism: Clinical and Experimental Research, 37*(5), 860–867.

Anderson, K. G., Grunwald, I., Bekman, N. M., Brown, S. A., & Grant, A. (2011). To drink or not to drink: Motives and expectancies for use and nonuse in adolescence. *Addictive Behaviors, 10*, 972–979.

Anderson, K. G., Sitney, M., & White, H. R. (2015). Marijuana motivations across adolescence: Impacts on use and consequences. *Substance Use and Misuse, 50*(3), 292–301.

Arnett, J. J. (2001). Conceptions of the transition to adulthood: Perspectives from adolescence through midlife. *Journal of Adult Development, 8*(2), 133–143.

Baumeister, R. F., Bratslavsky, E., Muraven, M., & Tice, D. M. (1998). Ego depletion: Is the active self a limited resource? *Journal of Personality and Social Psychology, 74*, 1252–1265.

Baumeister, R. F., Gailliot, M. T., & Tice, D. M. (2009). Free willpower: A limited resource theory of volition, choice, and self-regulation. In E. Morsella, J. A. Bargh, & P. M. Gollwitzer (Eds.), *The Oxford handbook of human action.* New York, NY: Oxford University Press.

Baumeister, R. F., Stillwell, A. M., & Heatherton, T. F. (1994). Guilt: An interpersonal approach. *Psychological Bulletin, 115*, 243–267.

Baumeister, R. F., & Vohs, K. D. (2007). Self-regulation, ego depletion, and motivation. *Social and Personality Psychology Compass, 1*, 1–14.

Baumeister, R. F., Zell, A. L., & Tice, D. M. (2007). How emotions facilitate and impair self-regulation (pp. 408–426). In J. J. Gross (Ed.), *Handbook of emotion regulation.* New York, NY: Guilford Press.

Bekman, N. M., Anderson, K. G., Trim, R. S., Metrik, J., Diulio, A. R., Myers, M. G., & Brown, S. A. (2011). Thinking and drinking: Alcohol-related cognitions across stages of adolescent alcohol involvement. *Psychology of Addictive Behaviors, 25*(3), 415–425.

Bekman, N. M., Goldman, M. S., Worley, M. J., & Anderson, K. G. (2011). Pre-adolescent alcohol expectancies: Critical shifts and associated maturational processes. *Experimental and Clinical Psychopharmacology, 19*(6), 420–432.

Belles, S., Budde, A., Moesgen, D., & Klein, M. (2011). Parental problem drinking predicts implicit alcohol expectancy in adolescents and young adults. *Addictive Behaviors, 36*(11), 1091–1094.

Belsky, J., Fearon, R. M. P., & Bell, B. (2007). Parenting, attention, and externalizing problems: Testing mediation longitudinally, repeatedly and reciprocally. *Journal of Child Psychology and Psychiatry, 48*, 1233–1242.

Bickel, W. K., Quisenberry, A. J., Moody, L., & Wilson, A. G. (2014). Therapeutic opportunities for self-control repair in addiction and related disorders: Change and the limits of change in trans-disease processes. *Clinical Psychological Science*, 1–14.

Blair, C., & Ursache, A. (2010). A bidirectional model of executive functions and self-regulation (pp. 300–320). In K. D. Vohs & R. F. Baumeister (Eds.), *Handbook of self-regulation: Research, theory, and applications* (2nd ed.). New York, NY: Guilford Press.

Bouchey, H. A., & Furman, W. (2006). Dating and romantic experiences in adolescence. In G. R. Adams & M. D. Berzonsky (Eds.), *Blackwell handbook of adolescence* (pp. 313–329). Malden, MA: Blackwell.

Bridgett, D. J., Gartstein, M. A., Putnam, S. P., McKay, T., Iddins, E., Robertson, C., et al. (2009). Maternal and contextual influences and the effect of temperament development during infancy on parenting and toddlerhood. *Infant Behavior and Development, 32*, 103–116.

Brown, B. B., Bakken, J. P., Ameringer, S. W., & Mahon, S. D. (2008). Comprehensive conceptualization of the peer influence process in adolescence. In K. A. Dodge and M. Putallaz (Eds.), *Understanding peer influence in children and adolescence* (pp. 17–44). New York, NY: Guilford Press.

Brown, S. A., Christiansen, B. A., & Goldman, M. S. (1987). The Alcohol Expectancy Questionnaire: An instrument for the assessment of adolescent and adult alcohol expectancies. *Journal of Studies on Alcohol, 48*(5), 483–491.

Brown, S. A., McGue, M. K., Maggs, J., Schulenberg, J. E., Hingson, R., Swartzwelder, H. S., et al. (2008). A developmental perspective on alcohol and youth ages 16–20. *Pediatrics, 121*, S290–S310.

Brown, S. A., Ramo, D. E., & Anderson, K. G. (2011). Long-term trajectories of adolescent recovery. In J. Kelly and W. L. White (Eds.), *Addiction recovery management: Theory, research & practice* (pp. 127–142). New York, NY: Springer Science.

Byrnes, J. P. (2006). Cognitive development during adolescence. In G. R. Adams & M. D. Berzonsky (Eds.), *Blackwell handbook of adolescence* (pp. 227–246). Malden, MA: Blackwell.

Calkins, S. D. (1994). Origins and outcomes of individual differences in emotion regulation. *Monographs of the Society for Research in Child Development, 59* (240), 53–72.

Calkins, S. D., Dedmon, S. E., Gill, K. L., Lomax, L. E., & Johnson, L. M. (2002). Frustration in infancy: Implications for emotion regulation, physiological processes, and temperament. *Infancy, 3*, 175–197.

Carskadon, M. A., Acebo, C., & Jenni, O. G. (2004). Regulation of adolescent sleep: Implications for behavior. *Annals of the New York Academy of Sciences, 1021*, 276–291.

Casey, B. J., & Caudle, K. (2013). Teenaged brain: Self-control. *Current Directions in Psychological Science, 22*(2), 82–87.

Chassin, L. (2015). Self-regulation and adolescent substance use. In G. Ottingen & P. M. Gollwitzer (Eds.), *Self-regulation in adolescence* (pp. 266–287). New York, NY: Cambridge University Press.

Chambers, R. A., Taylor, J. R., & Potenza, M. N. (2003). Developmental neurocircuitry of motivation in adolescence: A critical period of addiction vulnerability. *American Journal of Psychiatry, 160*(6), 1041–1052.

Chein, J., Albert, D., O'Brien, L., Uckert, K., & Steinberg, L. (2011). Peers increase adolescent risk taking by enhancing activity in the brain's reward circuitry. *Developmental Science, 14*(2), F1–F10.

Chick, C. F., & Reyna, V. F. (2012). A fuzzy trace theory of adolescent risk taking: Beyond self- control and sensation seeking. In V. F. Reyna, S. B. Chapman, M. R. Dougherty, and J. Confrey (Eds.), *The adolescent brain: Learning, reasoning, and decision making* (pp. 379–428). Washington, DC: American Psychological Association.

Cichetti, D., & Cohen, D. J. (1995). Perspectives on developmental psychopathology. In D. Cicchetti & D. J. Cohen (Eds.), *Developmental psychopathology* (Vol. 1, pp. 13–20). New York: Wiley & Sons, Inc.

Comeau, N., Stewart, S. H., & Loba, P. (2001). The relations of trait anxiety, anxiety sensitivity, and sensation seeking to adolescents' motivations for alcohol, cigarette, and marijuana use. *Addictive Behaviors, 26*(6), 803–825.

Cooper, M. L. (1994). Motivations for alcohol use among adolescents: Development and validation of a four-factor model. *Psychological Assessment, 6*, 117–128.

Cooper, M. L., Russell, M., Skinner, J. B., & Windle, M. (1992). Development and validation of a three-dimensional measure of drinking motives. *Psychological Assessment, 4*, 123–132.

Cox, M., Fadardi, J. S., & Klinger, E. (2006). Motivational processes underlying implicit cognition in addiction. In R. W. Wiers & A. W. Stacy (Eds.), *Handbook of implicit cognition* (pp. 253–266). Thousand Oaks, CA: Sage Publishing.

Cox, W. M., & Klinger, E. (1988). A motivational model of alcohol use. *Journal of Abnormal Psychology, 97*(2), 168–180.

Crone, E. A., Wendelken, C., van Leijenhorst, L., Honomichl, R. D., Christoff, K., & Bunge, S. A. (2009). Neurocognitive development of relational reasoning. *Developmental Science, 12*(1), 55–66.

D'Amico, E. J., Anderson, K. G., Metrik, J., Frissell, K. C., Ellingstad, T., & Brown, S. A. (2006). Adolescent self-selection of service formats: Implications for secondary interventions targeting alcohol use. *American Journal on Addictions, 15*: 58–66.

D'Amico, E. J., & Edelen, M. O. (2007). Pilot test of project CHOICE: A voluntary afterschool intervention for middle school youth. *Psychology of Addictive Behaviors, 21*(4), 592–598.

D'Amico, E. J., McCarthy, D. M., Metrik, J., & Brown, S. A. (2004). Alcohol-related services: Prevention, secondary intervention, and treatment preferences of adolescents. *Journal of Child & Adolescent Substance Abuse, 14*(2), 61–80.

DeWit, D. J., Adlaf, E. M., Offord, D. R., & Ogborne, A. C. (2000). Age at first alcohol use: A risk factor for the development of alcohol disorders. *American Journal of Psychiatry, 157*(5), 745–750.

Doerr, C. E., & Baumeister, R. F. (2010). Self-regulatory strength and psychological adjustment: Implications of the limited resource model of self-regulation (pp. 71–83). In J. E. Maddux & J. P. Tangney (Eds.), *Social psychological foundations of clinical psychology*. New York, NY: Guilford Press.

Donovan, J. E., Molina, B. S. G., & Kelly, T. M. (2009). Alcohol outcome expectancies as socially shared and socialized beliefs. *Psychology of Addictive Behaviors, 23*, 248–259.

Dunn, M. E., & Goldman, M. S. (1996). Empirical modeling of an alcohol expectancy memory network in elementary school children as a function of grade. *American Psychologist, 4*, 209–217.

Dunn, M. E., & Goldman, M. S. (2000). Validation of multidimensional scaling-based modeling of alcohol expectancies in memory: Age and drinking related differences in expectancies of children assessed as first associates. *Alcoholism: Clinical and Experimental Research, 24*, 1639–1646.

Eisenberg, N., Cumberland, A., & Spinrad, T. L. (1998). Parental socialization of emotion. *Psychological Inquiry, 9*, 241–273.

Eisenberg, N., Smith, C. L., & Spinrad, T. L. (2011). Effortful control: Relations with emotion regulation, adjustment, and socialization in childhood (pp. 263–283). In K. D. Vohs & R. F. Baumeister (Eds.), *Handbook of self-regulation: Research, theory, and applications* (2nd ed.). New York, NY: Guilford Press.

Eisenberg, N., Spinrad, T. L, Fabes, R. A., Reiser, M., Cumberland, A., Shepard, S. A., et al. (2004). The relations of effortful control and impulsivity in children's resiliency and adjustment. *Child Development, 75*, 25–46.

Eisenberg, N., Zhou, Q., Spinrad, T. L., Valiente, C., Fabes, R. A., & Liew, J. (2005). Relations among positive parenting, children's effortful control, and externalizing problems: A three-wave longitudinal study. *Child Development, 76*, 1055–1071.

Eisenberg, N. (2015). Self-regulation: Conceptual issues and relations to developmental outcomes in childhood and adolescence. In G. Ottingen & P. M. Gollwitzer (Eds.), *Self-regulation in adolescence* (pp. 55–77). New York, NY: Cambridge University Press.

Epler, A. J., Sher, K. J., & Piasecki, T. M. (2009). Reasons for abstaining or limiting drinking: A perspective. *Psychology of Addictive Behavior, 23*, 428–442.

Evans, S. B. T., & Coventry, K. (2006). A dual process approach to behavioral addictions: The case for gambling. In R. W. Wiers & A. W. Stacy (Eds.), *Handbook of implicit cognition* (pp. 29–43). Thousand Oaks, CA: Sage Publishing.

Evans, G. W., & Schamberg, M. A. (2009). Childhood poverty, chronic stress, and adult working memory. *Proceedings of the National Academy of Sciences USA, 106*(16), 6545–6549.

Fosco, G. M., Frank, J. L., Stormshak, J. A., & Dishion, T. A. (2013). Opening the "black box": Family check-up intervention effects on self-regulation that preventions growth in problem behavior and substance use. *Journal of School Psychology, 51*, 455–468.

Gailliot, M. T., Mead, N. L., & Baumeister, R. F. (2010). Self-regulation. In O. P. John, R. W. Robins, & L. A. Pervin (Eds.), *Handbook of personality: Theory and research* (3rd ed., pp. 472–491). New York, NY: Guilford Press.

Gailliot, M. T., Schmeichel, B. J., & Baumeister, R. F. (2006). Self-regulatory processes defend against the threat of death: Effects of self-control depletion and trait self-control on thoughts and fears of dying. *Journal of Personality and Social Psychology, 91*, 49–62.

Galvan, A. (2012). Risky behavior in adolescence: The role of the developing brain. In V. F. Reyna, S. B. Chapman, M. R. Dougherty, and J. Confrey (Eds.), *The adolescent brain: Learning, reasoning, and decision making* (pp.

267–289). Washington, DC: American Psychological Association.

Galvan, A. (2013). Teenaged brain: Sensitivity to rewards. *Current Directions in Psychological Science, 22*(2), 88–93.

Garcia, T. A., Bacio, G. A., Tomlinson, K., Ladd, B. O., & Anderson, K. G. (2015). Effects of sex composition on group processes in alcohol prevention groups for teens. *Experimental and Clinical Psychopharmacology, 23*(4), 275–283.

Gladwin, T. E., Figner, B., Crone, E. A., & Wiers, R. W. (2011). Addiction, adolescence, and the integration of control and motivation. *Developmental Cognitive Neuroscience, 1*, 364–376.

Goldman, M. S., Brown, S. A., Christiansen, B. A., & Smith, G. T. (1991). Alcoholism and memory: Broadening the scope of alcohol-expectancy research. *Psychological Bulletin, 10*, 137–146.

Goldsmith, H. H., Pollack, S. D., & Davidson, R. J. (2008). Developmental neuroscience perspectives on emotion regulation. *Child Development Perspectives, 2*, 132–140.

Greenfield, T. K., Guydish, J., & Temple, M. T. (1989). Reasons students give for limiting drinking: A factor analysis with implications for research and practice. *Journal of Studies on Alcohol, 50*, 108–115.

Hayakia, J., Hagerty, C. E., Herman, D. S., de Diosb, M. A., Anderson, B. J., & Stein, M. D. (2010). Expectancies and marijuana use frequency and severity among young females. *Addictive Behaviors, 35*(11), 995–1000.

Higgins, E. T. (1987). Self-discrepancy: A theory relating self and affect. *Psychological Review, 94*, 319–340.

Hollenstein, T., & Lougheed, H. P. (2013). Beyond storm and stress: Typicality, transactions, timing, and temperament to account for adolescent change. *American Psychologist, 68*(6), 444–448.

Hoyle, R. H. (2006). Personality and self-regulation: Trait and information processing perspectives. *Journal of Personality, 74*(6), 1507–1526.

Hull, J. G., & Slone, L. B. (2004). Alcohol and self-regulation. In R. F. Baumeister & K. D. Vohs (Eds.), *Handbook of self-regulation* (pp. 466–491). London, UK: the Guilford Press.

Jacobs, J. E., & Klaczynski, P. A. (2002). The development of judgment and decision making during childhood and adolescence. *Current Directions in Psychological Science, 11*(4), 145–147.

Jones, B. T., Corbin, W., & Fromme, K. (2001). Conceptualizing addiction: A review of expectancy theory and alcohol consumption. *Addiction, 96*, 57–72.

Klaczynski, P. A. (2005). Metacognition and cognitive variability: A dual-process model of decision making and its development. In J. E. Jacobs & P. A. Klaczynski (Eds.), *The development of judgment and decision making in children and adolescents* (pp. 39–106, 303–326). Mahwah, NJ: Lawrence Erlbaum Associates.

Kochanska, G., Aksan, N., Prisco, T. R., & Adams, E. E. (2008). Mother-child and father-child mutually responsive orientation in the first 2 years and children's outcomes at preschool age: Mechanisms of influence. *Child Development, 79*, 30–44.

Kochanska, G., Murray, K. L., & Harlan, E T. (2000). Effortful control in early childhood: Continuity and change, antecedents, and implications for social development. *Developmental Psychology, 36*, 220–232.

Kochanska, G., Philibert, R. A., & Barry, R. A. (2009). Interplay of genes and early mother-child relationship in the development of self-regulation from toddler to preschool age. *Journal of Child Psychology and Psychiatry, 5*, 1331–1338.

Krank, M. D., & Goldstein, A. L. (2006). Adolescent changes in implicit cognitions and prevention of substance abuse. In R. W. Wiers & A. W. Stacy (Eds.), *Handbook of implicit cognition* (pp. 439–453). Thousand Oaks, CA: Sage Publishing.

Kuntsche, E., Knibbe, R., Gmel, G., & Engels, R. (2005). Why do young people drink? A review of drinking motives. *Clinical Psychology Review, 25*, 841–861.

Labbe, A. K., & Maisto, S. A. (2010). Development of the Stimulant Medication Outcome Expectancies Questionnaire for college students. *Addictive Behaviors, 35*(7), 726–729.

Lengua, L. J., Bush, N., Long, A. C., Trancik, A. M., & Kovacs, E. A. (2008). Effortful control as a moderator of the relation between contextual risk and growth in adjustment problems. *Development and Psychopathology, 20*, 509–528.

Lopez, B., Schwartz, S. J., Prado, G., Campo, A. E., & Pantin, H. (2008). Adolescent neurological development and its implications for adolescent substance use prevention. *Journal of Primary Prevention, 29*, 5–35.

Luna, B., Paulsen, D. J., Padmanabhan, A., & Geier, C. (2013). Teenaged brain: Cognitive control and motivation. *Current Directions in Psychological Science, 22*(2), 94–100.

Maggs, J. L., & Schulenberg, J. (1998). Reasons to drink and not to drink: Altering trajectories of drinking through an alcohol misuse prevention program. *Applied Developmental Science, 2*(1), 48–60.

Males, M. (2009). Does the adolescent brain make risk taking inevitable? A skeptical appraisal. *Journal of Adolescent Research, 24*(11), 3–20.

Masten, A. S., Faden, V. B., Zucker, R. A., & Spear, L. P. (2008). Underage drinking: A developmental framework. *Pediatrics, 121*, S235–S251.

McCabe, S. E., Boyd, C. J., Cranford, J. A., & Teter, C. J. (2009). Motives for nonmedical use of prescription opioids among high school seniors in the United States: self-treatment and beyond. *Archives of Pediatric Adolescent Medicine, 163*(8), 739–744.

McCabe, S. E., Cranford, J. A., Boyd, C. J., & Teter, C. J. (2007). Motives, diversion and routes of administration associated with nonmedical use of prescription opioids. *Addictive Behaviors, 32*(3), 562–575.

Metrik, J., McCarthy, D. M., Frissell, K. C., MacPherson, L., & Brown, S. A. (2004). Adolescent alcohol reduction and cessation expectancies. *Journal of Studies on Alcohol, 65*, 217–226.

Miller, P. M., Smith, G. T., & Goldman, M. S. (1990). Emergence of alcohol expectancies in childhood: A possible critical period. *Journal of Studies on Alcohol, 51*, 343–349.

Mischel, W. (1974). Processes in delay of gratification. In L. Berkowitz (Ed.), *Advances in experimental social psychology, vol. 7* (pp. 249–292). San Diego, CA: Academic Press.

Mischel, W. (1996). From good intentions to willpower. In P. Gollwitzer & J. Bargh (Eds.), *The psychology of action.* (pp. 197–218). New York, NY: Guilford Press.

Muraven, M., & Baumeister, R. F. (2000). Self-regulation and depletion of limited resources: Does self-control resemble a muscle? *Psychological Bulletin, 126*(2), 247–259.

Muraven, M., Baumeister, R. F., & Tice, D. M. (1999). Longitudinal improvement of self-regulation through practice: Building self-control strength through repeated exercise. *The Journal of Social Psychology, 139*(4), 446–457.

Muraven, M., & Slessareva, E. (2003). Mechanism of self-control failure: Motivation and limited resources. *Personality and Social Psychology Bulletin, 29,* 894–906.

Muraven, M., Tice, D. M., & Baumeister, R. F. (1998). Self-control as a limited resource: Regulatory depletion patterns. *Journal of Personality and Social Psychology, 74,* 774–789.

Newcomb, M. D., Chou, C. P., Bentler, P. M., & Huba, G. J. (1988). Cognitive motivations for drug use among adolescents: Longitudinal tests of gender differences and predictors of change in drug use. *Journal of Counseling Psychology, 35,* 426–438.

Noble, K. G., McCandliss, B. D., & Farah, M. J. (2007). Socioeconomic gradients predict individual differences in neurocognitive abilities. *Developmental Science, 10*(4), 464–480.

Oaten, M., & Cheng, K. (2006). Improved self-control: The benefits of a regular program of academic study. *Basic and Applied Social Psychology, 28*(1), 1–16.

O'Connor, R. M. & Colder, C. R. (2015). The prospective joint effects of self-regulation and impulsive processes on early adolescence alcohol use. *Journal of Studies on Alcohol and Drugs, 76*(6), 884-894.

Palfai, T. P. (2006). Automatic processes in the self-regulation of addictive behaviors. In R. W. Wiers & A. W. Stacy (Eds.), *Handbook of implicit cognition* (pp. 411–424). Thousand Oaks, CA: Sage Publishing.

Patrick, M. E., Schulenberg, J. E., O'Malley, P. M., Johnston, L. D., & Bachman, J. G. (2011). Adolescents' reported reasons for alcohol and marijuana use as predictors of substance use and problems in adulthood. *Journal of Studies on Alcohol and Drugs, 72,* 106–116.

Peeters, M., Monshouwer, K., van de Schoot, R. A., Janssen, T., Vollebergh, W. A., & Wiers, R. W. (2013). Automatic processes and the drinking behavior in early adolescence: A prospective study. *Alcoholism: Clinical and Experimental Research, 37*(10), 1737–1744.

Pentz, M. A., Riggs, N. R., & Warren, C. M. (2016). Improving substance use prevention efforts with executive function training. *Drug and Alcohol Dependence, 163,* 554–559.

Percy, A. (2008). Moderate adolescent drug use and the development of substance use self-regulation. *International Journal of Behavioral Development, 32*(5), 451–458.

Peper, J. S., & Dahl, R. E. (2013). The teenage brain: Surging hormones—brain-behavior interactions during puberty. *Current Directions in Psychological Science, 22*(2), 134–139.

Pieters, S., van der Vorst, H., Burk, W. J., Wiers, R. W., & Engels, R. C. E. (2010). Puberty-dependent sleep regulation and alcohol use in early adolescents. *Alcoholism: Clinical and Experimental Research, 34*(9), 1512–1518.

Posner, M. I., & Fan, J. (2008). Attention as an organ system. In J. Pomerantz (Ed.), *Neurobiology of perception and communication: From synapse to society: The 4th De Lange Conference* (pp. 31–61). Cambridge, UK: Cambridge University Press.

Powell, J., Bradley, B., & Gray, J. (1992). Classical conditioning and cognitive determinants of subjective craving for opiates: An investigation of their relative contributions. *British Journal of Addictions, 87*(8), 1133–1144.

Reisberg, D. (2013). *Cognition: Exploring the science of the mind* (5th ed.). New York, NY: W.W. Norton & Co.

Reyna, V. F., Adam, M. B., Poirier, K., LeCroy, C. W., & Brainerd, C. J. (2005). Risky decision-making in childhood and adolescence: A fuzzy-trace theory approach. In J. Jacobs & P. Klaczynski (Eds.), *The development of children's and adolescents' judgment and decision-making* (pp. 77–106). Mahwah, NJ: Erlbaum.

Reyna, V. F., & Farley, F. (2006). Risk and rationality in adolescent decision making: Implications for theory, practice, and public policy. *Psychological Science in the Public Interest, 7*(1), 1–44.

Rohsenow, D. J., & Marlatt, G. A. (1981). The balanced placebo design: Methodological considerations. *Addictive Behaviors, 6*(2), 107–122.

Rosenblum, G. D., & Lewis, M. (2006). Emotional development during adolescence. In G. R. Adams & M. D. Berzonsky (Eds.), *Blackwell handbook of adolescence* (pp. 270–289). Malden, MA: Blackwell.

Rothbart, M. K., Ellis, L. K., & Posner, M. L. (2010). Temperament and self-regulation (pp. 441–460). In K. D. Vohs & R. F. Baumeister (Eds.), *Handbook of self-regulation: Research, theory, and applications* (2nd ed.). New York, NY: Guilford Press.

Rueda, M. R., Posner, M. I., & Rothbart, M. K. (2010). Attentional control and self-regulation In K. D. Vohs & R. F. Baumeister (Eds.), *Handbook of self-regulation: Research, theory, and applications* (2nd ed., pp. 284–298). New York, NY: Guilford Press.

Sayette, M. A., & Griffin, K. M. (2010). Self-regulatory failure and addiction. In K. D. Vohs & R. F. Baumeister (Eds.), *Handbook of self-regulation: Research, theory, and applications* (2nd ed., pp. 505–521). New York, NY: Guilford Press.

Schmeichel, B. J., Vohs, K. D., & Baumeister, R. F. (2003). Intellectual performance and ego depletion: Role of the self in logical reasoning and other information processing. *Journal of Personality and Social Psychology, 85,* 33–46.

Settles, R., & Smith, G. T. (2011). *College student motivations to limit alcohol consumption.* In K. G. Anderson (Chair), *Weighing the pros and cons: Understanding the interplay of cognitions to drink and not to drink across development.* Scientific Meeting of the Research Society on Alcoholism Annual Meeting. Atlanta, Georgia.

Sheese, B. E., Rothbart, M. K., Posner, M. I., White, L. K., & Fraundorf, S. H. (2008). Executive attention and self-regulation in infancy. *Infant Behavior and Development, 31,* 501–510.

Sher, K. J., & Slutske, W. S. (2004). Disorders of impulse control. In G. Stricker & T. A. Widiger (Eds.), *Handbook of psychology* (Vol. 8, pp. 195–228). Hoboken, NJ: John Wiley & Sons.

Simons, J., Correia, C. J., Carey, K. B., & Borsari, B. E. (1998). Validating a five-factor marijuana motives measure: Relations with use, problems, and alcohol motives. *Journal of Counseling Psychology, 45,* 265–273.

Smith, G. T., & Anderson, K. G. (2001). Adolescent risk for alcohol problems as acquired preparedness: A model and suggestions for intervention. In P. M. Monti, S. M. Colby, & T. A. O'Leary (Eds.). *Adolescents, alcohol, and substance abuse: Reaching teens through brief interventions* (pp. 109–144). New York, NY: Guilford Press.

Spear, L. (2010). *The behavioral neuroscience of adolescence.* New York: W.W. Norton & Company.

Spear, L. (2013). Teenaged brain: Adolescents and alcohol. *Current Directions in Psychological Science, 22*(2), 152–157.

Spinrad, T. L., Eisenberg, N., Gaertner, B., Popp, T., Smith, C. L., Kupfer, A., et al. (2007). Relations of maternal socialization and toddlers' effortful control to children's adjustment and social competence. *Developmental Psychology, 43,* 1170–1186.

Stacy, A. W., Ames, S. L., Sussman, S., & Dent, C. W. (1996). Implicit cognition in adolescent drug use. *Psychology of Addictive Behaviors, 10*(3), 190–203.

Steinberg, L. (2005). Cognitive and affective development in adolescence. *TRENDS in Cognitive Sciences, 9*(2), 69–74.

Steinberg, L. (2008). A social neuroscience perspective on adolescent risk-taking. *Developmental Review, 28*, 78–106.

Strack, F., & Deutsch, R. (2004). Reflective and impulsive determinants of social behavior. *Personality and Social Psychology Review, 8*(3), 220–247.

Substance Abuse and Mental Health Services Administration (2015). *Results from the 2014 National Survey on Drug Use and Health: Summary of National Findings,* NSDUH Series H-50, HHS Publication No. (SMA) 15–4927. Rockville, MD: Substance Abuse and Mental Health Services Administration.

Thush, C., & Wiers, R. W. (2007). Explicit and implicit alcohol-related cognitions and the prediction of future drinking in adolescents. *Addictive Behaviors, 32*, 1367–1383.

Tice, D. M., & Bratslavsky, E. (2000). Giving in to feel good: The place of emotion regulation in the context of general self-control. *Psychological Inquiry, 11*, 149–159.

Tversky, A., & Kahneman, D. (1974). Judgment under uncertainty: Heuristics and biases. *Science, 185*(4157), 1124–1131.

van Duijvenvoorde, A. C. K., & Crone, E. A. (2013). Teenage brain: A neuroeconomic approach to adolescent decision making. *Current directions in Psychological Science, 22*(2), 108–113.

Vohs, K. D., Baumeister, R. F., Schmeichel, B. J., Twenge, J. M., Nelson, N. M., & Tice, D. M. (2008). Making choices impairs subsequent self-control: A limited resource account of decision making, self-regulation, and active initiative. *Journal of Personality and Social Psychology, 94*, 883–898.

Wiers, R. W., Bartholow, B. D., van den Wildenberg, Thush, C., Engels, R. C., Sher, K. J., Grenard, J., Ames, S. L., & Stacy, A. W. (2007). Automatic and controlled processes and the development of addictive behaviors in adolescents: A review and a model. *Pharmacology, Biochemistry, & Behavior, 86*, 263–283.

Wiers, R. W., Gladwin, T. E., Hofmann, W., Salemink, E., & Ridderinkhof, K. R. (2013). Cognitive bias modification and cognitive control training in addiction and related psychopathology: Mechanisms, clinical perspectives, and ways forward. *Clinical Psychological Science, 1*(2), 192–212.

Wiers, R. W., Houben, K., Smulders, F. T. Y., Conrod, P. J., & Jones, B. T. (2006). To drink or not to drink: The role of automatic and controlled cognitive processes in the etiology of alcohol-related problems. In R. W. Wiers & A. W. Stacy (Eds.), *Handbook of implicit cognition* (pp. 339–361). Thousand Oaks, CA: Sage Publishing.

Wills, T. A., & Ainette, M. G. (2009). Temperament, self-control and adolescent substance use: A two-factor model of etiological processes. In L. M. Scheier (Ed.), *Handbook of drug use etiology: Theory, methods, and empirical findings* (pp. 127–146). Washington, DC: American Psychological Association.

Wills, T. A., Pokhrel, P., Morehouse, E., & Fenster, B. (2011). Behavioral and emotional regulation and adolescent substance use problems: A test of moderation effects in a dual-process model. *Psychology of Addictive Behaviors, 25*(2), 279–292.

Wills, T. A, Walker, C., Mendoza, D., & Ainette, M. G. (2006). Behavioral and emotional self-control: Relations to substance use in samples of middle and high school students. *Psychology of Addictive Behaviors, 20*(3), 265–278.

Wong, M. M., Nigg, J. T., Zucker, R. A., Puttler, L. I., Fitzgerald, H. E., Jester, J. M., Glass, J. M., & Adams, K. (2006). Behavioral control and resiliency in the onset of alcohol and illicit drug use: A prospective study from preschool to adolescence. *Child Development, 77*(4), 1016–1033.

Zimmer-Gembeck, M. J., & Collins, W. A. (2006). Autonomy development during adolescence. In G. R. Adams & M. D. Berzonsky (Eds.), *Blackwell handbook of adolescence* (pp. 175–204). Malden, MA; Blackwell.

Zvolensky, M. J., Marshall, E. C., Johnson, K., Hogan, J., Bernstein, A., & Bonn-Miller, M. O. (2009). Relations between anxiety sensitivity, distress tolerance, and fear reactivity to bodily sensations to coping and conformity marijuana use motives among young adult marijuana users. *Experimental and Clinical Psychopharmacology, 17*(1), 31–42.

Identity Development and Substance Use in Adolescence

Thomas A. Wills, Steve Sussman, *and* Meghan McGurk

Abstract

This chapter considers how identity-related variables operate as risk or protective factors for substance use/dependence in adolescence. We discuss theoretical work that has distinguished between identity and self-concept and present a model of personal identity as a second-order concept based on self-perceptions in specific areas. We then consider research on identity development in adolescence, including self-esteem, gender identity, religious identification, ethnic identity, and identification with particular peer groups or "crowds." Finally, we discuss the relation of each aspect of identity to substance use and the probable mediators and moderators of the relationship. A final section summarizes the implications of our model of adolescent identity for prevention and treatment and provides suggestions for further research in this area.

Key Words: identity, substance use, adolescents, self-esteem, gender, ethnicity, religiosity, peer group, mediation, moderation

This chapter discusses how identity development in adolescence is related to substance use or dependence. Identity is a complex topic, encompassing several different psychological domains that are relevant for personal identity (Cote, 2009). Also there are large changes in the developmental tasks that confront adolescents, who must depart from a simple, largely parent-centered world in childhood, through the beginnings of personal identity development and peer-group formation in early adolescence, moving on from small same-sex peer groups to heterosexual crowds and romantic dyads. This culminates in late adolescence in a more mature individual who is managing both parental and peer relationships and is on the verge of assuming his or her own responsibility for further educational and vocational development (Cote, 2006; Sussman & Ames, 2008). This is a large set of developmental tasks by any measure, and in retrospect we can stand in awe of the many young persons who have weathered this voyage successfully and assumed vocational and parental responsibilities. However there is a small but not trivial proportion of persons who run into trouble on the journey, getting far off course (e.g., dropping out of high school) or running up on the rocks of substance abuse. Here we consider how identity development may serve as an area of either weakness or strength in helping to steer young persons on their voyage.

In considering identity formation, it has been noted that the developmental tasks of adolescence involve getting along simultaneously in several worlds, including the family, the school, and the peer-group context (Compas & Reeslund, 2009; Wills, Resko, Ainette, & Mendoza, 2004). Adolescents face implicit or explicit pressures to do well in school; get along well (or at least not get along badly) with parents and other family members; and gain acceptance in peer relationships. During this period a teen is learning gender-linked sex roles, acquiring an ethnic/cultural identity, and trying to develop an integrated self-concept involving teen-central attributes such as physical attractiveness and athletic ability (Harter, 2012a). Some youth may begin to develop a religious identity, which will have implications for their risk for substance use (Jessor & Jessor, 1977; King & Roeser, 2009). Also through decision (or indecision) the young person is gravitating toward one of the peer subcultures in the school environment (Sussman, Pokhrel, Ashmore, & Brown, 2007). Whether a teen takes up with groups of peers who are oriented toward academic achievement and other adaptive behaviors, versus peers who are more inclined to deviant and antisocial behavior, this creates a structured environment that will be conducive toward adjustment or maladjustment (Bryant, Schulenberg, O'Malley, Bachman, & Johnston, 2003; Mounts & Steinberg, 1995; Wills & Cleary, 1999). An adolescent's experiences in each of these areas will likely have profound implications for his or her developing identity as a person. Across these areas there is undoubtedly variation in the extent to which family, peers, and social institutions explicitly aim to shape a person's identity versus providing a context within which an adolescent may experiment with various roles and values and ultimately arrive at an integrated self-concept. But whatever the types of influences that operate in these various contexts, there will be an impact on the adolescent's identity.

The construct of identity has been considered from several different research perspectives. From the perspective of identity researchers, the concept of *personal identity* is based on a set of social roles and a commitment to certain values and beliefs (Cote, 1996; Erikson, 1968; Waterman, 1999). This organized set of roles and values is assumed to be stable within a developmental period (though it can change as a result of an identity crisis) and provides a sense of continuity in functioning, so that a youth perceives himself or herself as the same person across time periods and social contexts. In recent years the overall construct of personal identity has begun to be divided into more specific aspects, such as ethnic identity (Phinney & Rosenthal, 1992).

From the perspective of self psychology (Baumeister, 1997; Harter, 2012a), the *self-concept* is an organized cognitive schema of the attributes one possesses (e.g., intelligence, physical appearance, social competence). Self-concept is usually defined as the content of the various attributes and role areas; self-esteem is the evaluation of the quality of one's functioning in each of the areas that provide the basis for the self-concept. While previous research in the area focused on global self-esteem, recent research has tended to view self-esteem as based on an assessment of one's competencies in various areas (e.g., academics, athletics) and a salience hierarchy in which the centrality of each area for the individual is weighted (Dusek & McIntyre, 2003). The psychological function of the self-concept is assumed to be providing a sense of consistency and predictability about how one perceives himself or herself and how others perceive him or her, and the stored self-schema helps provide a cognitive screen for attending to information from the environment according to its self-relevance.

Reviewers have noted that identity and self-concept have been studied independently by different groups of researchers, but there has not been much convergence between the two areas (Cote, 2009; Schwartz, 2001). Identity researchers have tended to focus on identity development during late adolescence and emerging adulthood, whereas self-concept researchers tend to focus on younger ages. In this chapter we will be focusing primarily on research deriving from the self-psychology tradition, as traditional identity measures have not shown good reliability at younger ages (Cote, 2006; Kroger, 2000), whereas measures of self-esteem have good reliability, with both strengthening and differentiation during early adolescence (Harter, 2012a). Research so far has not generally studied how changes in identity are related to substance abuse, focusing instead on how specific aspects of self-concept are related to substance use either cross-sectionally or longitudinally. We will include suggestions about how these constructs develop during adolescence, but our approach here will focus on exploring *how* various aspects of identity are related to substance use.

As Cote (2009) has discussed, identity is a multidimensional construct and can be considered at several different levels of analysis. The working model that we use for this chapter is summarized in Figure 22.1. This suggests that a higher order construct of identity is based on an aggregate of identifications, including self-concept, gender identity, and peer-group identification, and for some persons their self-identity with regard to ethnicity and religiosity.[1] It is plausible that the self-concept level of analysis is nested within the other, such that an individual's identity is impacted by the micro and macro social worlds within which one is embedded (i.e., the nested self; Hobfoll, 2001).

In this chapter, we will use this model to discuss how self-esteem derived from specific areas of

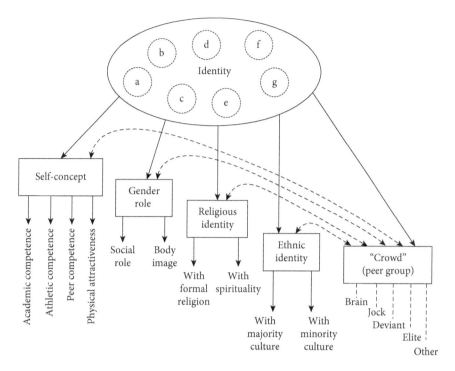

Figure 22.1 Second-order model of multidimensional identity construct. Lower level has four aspects of competence and three specific identifications (gender, religion, and ethnicity) together with peer-group identification. Upper level has multidimensional construct of identity with contributions from different aspects at lower level. Straight single-headed arrows are contributions from particular indicators. Curved double-headed arrows indicate possible reciprocal relationships, with particular identifications influencing initial peer-group membership and one's peer group then serving to further consolidate the identity.

competence is related to adolescent substance use. Additionally, we will discuss how gender identity, religious identification, and ethnic identity are related to risk for substance use or abuse during the adolescent period. Finally, we will consider how identification with a defined peer group may shape the consolidation of identity and the progression of substance use.

Self-Esteem and Substance Use

The self-concept is defined as an individual's cognitive schema based on his or her perception of the attributes he or she possesses (i.e., content or self-concept), an evaluation of his or her competence in each of these areas (i.e., quality or self-esteem), and in more recent theoretical versions, an individual's weighting of the centrality of each attribute for self-esteem (Harter, 2012a). It is generally posited that self-esteem develops from a combination of early temperamental characteristics and parental reactions to those attributes (Harter, 2006; Wills, Sandy, & Yaeger, 2000). When the child enters the school environment, relationships with teachers and peers will further shape the development of self-esteem (Wills et al., 2004).

Research on adolescents has generally proceeded from the assumption that high self-esteem should be a protective factor for substance use.[2] Discussing research on self-esteem and substance use is potentially complex because self-esteem is related to other entities. Low self-regard is certainly going to be correlated with negative affect, but affective variables have not generally been considered in self-concept research. This area constitutes a substantial body of literature in itself (see, for example, Kassel et al., 2010), but the role of affective variables in adolescent substance use will not be discussed here. Similarly, psychopathology in the form of depressive disorder has low self-esteem as one of its defining attributes; but since diagnosable psychopathology requires extreme levels and involves other attributes as well, we will not consider this in detail (see Chapter 15 by Hussong et al., and Chapter 24 by Wilson & Janoff, this volume). Our review will consider research that has included one of the commonly used measures of self-esteem with a general population of adolescents and has studied its relation to substance use or abuse.

Several methodological issues are particularly relevant for research on self-esteem and substance use. One is the issue of measuring both positive and negative self-perceptions. Self-esteem is often defined as positive self-regard, but empirical studies of adolescents have shown that self-esteem measures factor into a positive or self-esteem scale (e.g., "I think I am a good person") and a negative or self-derogation scale (e.g., "I feel pretty useless at times"). These make independent contributions (in opposite directions) to liability for substance use in multivariate analyses (e.g., Corte & Zucker, 2008; Wills, 1994). Thus, it is desirable for research on self-esteem and substance use to consider both dimensions of self-esteem. Another issue, derived from the competence model, is that self-esteem should be related to perceived control, as persons with more developed competencies are better able to control, and obtain rewards from, school and social environments. Because positive self-esteem is related to perceived control, it is desirable to consider this covariation in research on self-esteem, and several studies have shown that positive perceived control shows a unique inverse contribution to substance use, whereas other dimensions of self-esteem and lack of control are sometimes nonsignificant (Adalbjarnardottir & Rafnsson, 2001; Auerbach, Tsai, & Abela, 2010; Engels, Hale, Noom, & De Vries, 2005; Kim, 2005). Thus, it is relevant for research to consider perceived control as a possible covariate in studies on self-esteem. Finally, theoretical models have emphasized that self-esteem is based on a weighting of perceived competence in several areas (e.g., academics, athletics, peer relationships), with the weighting of these attributes posited to vary considerably across individuals. However, studies using global measures of self-esteem typically don't indicate what the relative weightings are or account for the fact that subdimensions (e.g., academic and peer competence) may be related to substance use in different directions (e.g., Swaim & Wayman, 2004; Wills et al., 2004). Thus, it is important in self-esteem research to consider the specific dimensions that contribute to an individual's overall self-concept.

Selected Findings on Self-Esteem and Substance Use

We now discuss selected findings on the relation of self-esteem to adolescent substance use. We focus on research mostly conducted since 2000 as it has sometimes (though not invariably) addressed the methodological issues discussed previously. There are studies indicating global self-esteem is a protective factor, particularly at younger ages and over shorter time periods (e.g., Glendinning, 2002; Otten, van Lier, & Engels, 2011) but sometimes over longer periods as well (Trzesniewski et al., 2006). A protective effect for self-esteem has been demonstrated in several national populations (e.g., Brook, Rubenstone, Zhang, Morolele, & Brook, 2011; Kim, 2001, 2005; Li, Mao, Stanton, & Zhao, 2010). US studies have shown self-esteem to be a protective factor most consistently in samples with minority-group adolescents, where issues of ethnic identity and ethnicity-based self-esteem may be more central than they are for majority adolescents (Carvajal, Evans, Nash, & Getz, 2002; Wills et al., 2007).

POSITIVE AND NEGATIVE DIMENSIONS

A study of middle school students using multidimensional measures (Wills, 1994) showed that positive and negative self-scales were inversely but modestly correlated, and a multivariate analysis showed two independent effects, with positive self-esteem inversely related to adolescent substance use while self-derogation was positively related to substance use. A study with a high-risk sample (Corte & Zucker, 2008) formed positive and negative self-scales from the Harter inventory and used an analysis based on subgroups that were more versus less vulnerable to substance use. Results showed that adolescents who perceived fewer positive attributes and more negative attributes were at increased risk for early onset of alcohol use and drunkenness. In two other studies it was found that negative self-schemas demonstrated a significant risk effect (Epstein, Griffin, & Botvin, 2004; Veselska et al., 2009), whereas positive self-schemas showed several buffering effects, reducing the impact of risk factors on substance use.

ACADEMIC SELF-ESTEEM

Academic competence is an important component of self-esteem and is one of the proximal pathways to adolescent substance use, often mediating the effect of more distal variables such as temperament (e.g., Wills et al., 2001) or self-regulation (Wills, Simons, Sussman, & Knight, 2016). Several studies have examined the academic component of self-esteem and generally found inverse relations with substance use. Bergen et al. (2005) related perceived academic competence to substance use in a mixed (middle- and high-school) sample controlling for global self-esteem. Perception of low academic competence was related to weekly use of alcohol, tobacco, and marijuana, and supplementary analyses suggested this was partly mediated by antisocial behavior. Wheeler (2010) found in an analysis of AdHealth data that high global self-esteem and good academic competence were both inversely related to illicit substance use among girls (though not for boys). Some studies have compared academic self-esteem with other areas and generally have found independent effects. Donnelly et al. (2008) compared peer, family, and academic esteem in a mixed sample and found high academic esteem inversely related to a range of substance use behaviors, with academic esteem making the largest multivariate contribution. Wild et al. (2004) in a mixed South African sample compared academic, peer, family, and athletic esteem and body image and found that only academic esteem showed an (inverse) unique relation to substance use and sexual risk behavior when controlling for other dimensions. Low body-image esteem showed unique relations to tobacco, alcohol, and illicit drug use among girls though not among boys.

PEER SELF-ESTEEM

Same-age peers are important models for adolescents in the development of an identity, and peers can be an important source of support and confiding (Wills & Ainette, 2011). However, peers tend to hold different values than parents and some peer groups tend more to encourage substance use than to discourage it (Hoffman, Sussman, Unger, & Valenti, 2006; Wills et al., 2004). Social acceptance by peers, then, carries a mixed message as far as substance use is concerned. Swaim and Wayman (2004) addressed this issue in a mixed (Mexican American and Anglo) sample of adolescents with a measure that indexed three different dimensions of self-esteem. Their results showed that a measure of perceived competence (e.g., "I am able to do things well") and a measure of self-esteem ("I am proud of myself") were both inversely related to adolescent alcohol use, whereas a measure of social acceptance ("People like to be with me") was positively related to substance use. This pattern of findings has been conceptually replicated in several other studies (e.g., Donnelly, Young, Pearson, Penhollow, & Hernandez, 2008), and Karatzias et al. (2001) found in a sample of Scottish adolescents that substance use was predicted only by peer self-esteem. Wild et al. (2004) found that high esteem in the peer domain was positively related to substance use and several other risk behaviors; similarly, McKay et al. (2012) and Veselska et al. (2009) showed that adolescent substance use was positively related

to social competence but inversely related to academic competence and efficacy. Wills et al. (2004) showed that a positive multivariate relation of peer support to substance use occurred as a suppression effect because of its complex relations to both good self-control and poor behavioral regulation (cf. Tomcikova, Geckova, van Dijk, & Reijneveld, 2011). Thus, the effect of peer acceptance should be considered for research on aspects of self-esteem.

MEDIATION AND MODERATION EFFECTS

Studies have examined self-esteem as a mediator of environmental stressors (Brook et al., 2011; Zamboanga, Schwartz, Jarvis, & van Tyne, 2009), but there is little research on how effects of self-esteem on substance use are mediated. Bergen et al. (2005) noted that the effect of low academic esteem on marijuana use was mediated through higher antisocial behavior. DuBois and Silverthorn (2004) also demonstrated that an inverse relation of global self-esteem with adolescent substance use, and a positive relation of peer self-esteem with substance use, each were mediated through level of affiliation with deviant peers. Aside from studies showing larger effects of self-esteem for younger adolescents, we noted only one other moderation study. Lazuras, Eiser, and Rodafinos (2009) showed that persons with low self-esteem were more susceptible to social influence, a finding that has implications for prevention programs. Evidence on mediation and moderation effects is intriguing but limited at present.

Summary

There has been a sizable amount of research on self-esteem and adolescent substance use, and in recent years studies have begun to include both positive and negative aspects of self-esteem and to use multidimensional measures. Findings have generally shown high global self-esteem to be a protective factor for substance use in adolescence. However, this research does include some null findings and studies that have examined specific facets of self-concept have produced more consistent results. Negative perceptions of the self seem to be more prominent as predictors of substance use than positive self-perceptions, and academic esteem is a protective factor whereas esteem based on peer acceptance tends to be a risk factor for substance use. Other aspects such as athletic competence and body image have been less studied, but some research suggests that body-image disturbances may be a risk factor (Kaufman & Augustson, 2008; Lisha & Sussman, 2010; Wild, Fisher, Bhana, & Lombard,

2004). We have not provided detailed discussion of higher order interactions but when significant they tend to suggest that self-esteem variables are most prominently related to substance use among females and minority-group adolescents.[3]

The Role of Gender Identity in Adolescent Substance Use

Gender identity is a person's concept of being male or female as it is defined by biological sex traits, social norms of attributes and behaviors, and cultural conceptions of gender roles (Galambos, Berenbaum, & McHale, 2009, Kulis, Marsiglia, & Hecht, 2002). Much of the research on gender identity development focuses on childhood development because gender awareness and gender roles develop significantly during this time (Galambos et al., 2009). Children are aware of gender role stereotypes as early as age 3 years through family, peer, cultural, and ethnic influences (Weinraub et al., 1984). However, changes occur during adolescence that may profoundly impact a person's gender self-concept.

Sexual maturation makes a person's body image and biological gender more salient, and therefore his or her gender identity more distinct. Cognitive and intellectual changes allow teens to conceptualize gender differences in a more egalitarian way. These factors, in combination with the expansion of peer groups to include members of the opposite sex, the increased independence afforded to adolescents as they age, and the onset of dating, play a significant role in gender identity conceptualization. These profound physical, cognitive, and social changes that occur during adolescence make it an important period of time to examine gender identity development, especially as to how it relates to substance use.

The complexity of these changes and the paucity of research on gender identity development during this time create methodological issues that can limit our understanding of the associations between gender identity and substance use. As with self-concept, the multitude of factors that interact to create a person's concept of his or her gender identity makes studying the impact of gender identity on substance use quite complex. Gender identity is more than being biologically male or female; it is a person's subjective sense of what it means to be male or female, based on social constructions of masculine or feminine personality traits and behaviors and cultural gender roles (Kulis et al., 2002; Kulis, Marsiglia, Lingard, Nieri, & Nagoshi,

2008). However, much of the research in this area tends to focus on gender labels, not gender identity, as a predictor for adolescent substance use.

Empirical Findings on Gender and Adolescent Substance Use

GENDER DIFFERENCES IN RATES OF USE

Research on gender differences in adolescent substance use has shown mixed results. While historically there has been a male differential for tobacco and alcohol use among US adolescents, differences in rates have decreased in recent years and at present some research finds no significant gender differences. Findings from current cross-sectional and longitudinal studies indicate that males more frequently use smokeless tobacco, steroids, and crystal methamphetamine at all ages (Johnston, O'Malley, Bachman, & Schulenberg, 2011). Females are more frequent users of inhalants and drugs other than marijuana in eighth grade (Centers for Disease Control [CDC], 2010; Johnston et al., 2011). Some substances, such as alcohol, cigarettes, Vicodin, Oxycontin, Ritalin, and cocaine have little gender difference at eighth and tenth grades but are more often used by males in twelfth grade (Johnston et al., 2011). Despite this variability in findings of male and female substance use, in general, by the time adolescents reach twelfth grade, males exceed females in rates of use for most substances (Johnston et al., 2011; Rodham, Hawton, Evans, & Weatherall, 2005). These explorations into gender differences in use are important because they show that for some age groups and some substances, gender differences do exist, and because they track changes in social norms about gender use over time. Furthermore, they track societal changes over time in gender use. However, there is less exploration of the causal pathways for these differences, leaving researchers to speculate on the associations discovered. Some possible mechanisms for understanding of gender disparities in adolescent substance use will be discussed briefly in the last part of this section.

GENDER IDENTITY AND SUBSTANCE USE

More detailed studies of gender differences in adolescent substance use examine the role that gender identity and cultural gender roles play in gender differences in use. In fact, gender identity has been found to mediate gender differences in drug use (Huselid & Cooper, 1992) and has been found to be a better predictor of drug use than gender alone (Kulis, Marsiglia, & Hurdle, 2003). This research is based on two common conceptions of gender identity: masculine and feminine personality attributes and cultural gender roles. Those studying gender identity personality traits have found that one individual can express both masculine and feminine attributes, assembling a spectrum of gender identity rather than a dichotomous concept of gender (Bem, 1974; Koestner & Aube, 1995; Kulis et al., 2002, 2008). Through this research, socially "desirable" and "undesirable" attributes have been identified for both masculinity and femininity. "Desirable" masculine traits include being assertive, confident, independent, and instrumental, whereas "undesirable" traits include being aggressive, emotionally repressed, controlling, and dominant (Athenstaedt, Mikula, & Bredt, 2009; Huselid & Cooper, 1992; Kulis et al., 2008). Likewise, "desirable" feminine traits include being warm, showing concern for others, and being emotionally expressive, whereas "undesirable" traits include being submissive and whiny. These gender identity traits have various implications for adolescent substance use. Research has shown that both male and female adolescents who express aggressive or dominant characteristics show higher substance use than other gender identity traits (Athenstaedt, Mikula, & Bredt, 2009; Huselid & Cooper, 1992; Kulis et al., 2002, 2003). Higher nurturance or expressive characteristics tend to be inversely related to substance use, implying a protective effect for these attributes (Huselid & Cooper, 1992; Kulis et al., 2008). In addition, confident or assertive traits lead to more refusals of drug offers in females but more frequent drug use in males (Kulis et al., 2002).

IDENTITY-RELATED VARIABLES

The associations between masculine and feminine personality traits and substance use raise questions of the impact that general personality types have on substance use. It is possible that these trends in substance use are due not to masculinity traits themselves, but to the gender-neutral personality traits that put both adolescent genders at risk for substance use: power seeking, defying, risk taking, and controlling (Huselid & Cooper, 1992). Both males and females with typically masculine traits could be using substances as part of general personality coping mechanisms, not based on gender conceptions. In particular, a person who copes with problems through demonstrating assertiveness or dominance (instrumentality) may be more likely to use substances than a person who copes by seeking or providing nurturance (Sussman

& Ames, 2008). Despite these personality trait assertions, it is evident in the mere labeling of confident and assertive characteristics as masculine and nurturing and caring characteristics as feminine, that cultural values, gender roles, and social norms play a significant role in adolescent conceptions of their gender identity. It is thus necessary to examine the role that cultural social norms and gender roles play in adolescent substance use.

CULTURAL GENDER ROLES

Culture and ethnicity play significant roles in conceptualizations of what is acceptable behavior for males and females. It is not only limited to interests, activities, and professions, but includes substance use as well. Western cultural ideals generally encourage males to consume alcohol as rite of passage into manhood, while females, to some degree, are discouraged from substance use (Kulis et al., 2002). The social acceptability of male substance use may be further explained in a study by Moon, Hecht, Jackson, and Spellers (1999), which found that boys reported getting drug offers from parents and other male relatives at a young age. In addition, boys are given more freedom at a younger age, which may lead them to earlier explorations with a variety of substances (Moon et al., 1999). Additional evidence of the cultural impact on substance use can be seen in studies which show that when adolescents identify strongly with cultural gender roles, their drinking habits reflect those cultural norms. Huselid and Cooper (1992) found that identification with traditional gender roles was positively associated with alcohol consumption in males but negatively associated with alcohol consumption in females.

GENDER ROLES IN OTHER POPULATIONS

Cultural gender roles and concepts of masculinity and femininity are commonly studied in Hispanic populations, due to the influential and distinct cultural constructs of machismo and marianismo. Machismo is the concept that men are emotionally controlled, aggressive, hard-working, courageous, dignified, and dominant, much like the masculine characteristics of Western cultures (Kulis et al., 2008; Soto et al., 2011). Marianismo defines women as being nurturing, submissive, devoted to the family, and self-sacrificing (Kulis et al, 2008; Soto et al., 2011). When adolescents adhere strictly to these cultural gender norms, they show stereotypical substance use behavior patterns, with males having higher levels of alcohol consumption and females having lower levels (Soto et al., 2011). Evidence from other countries with traditional gender roles further supports a cultural influence on gender differences in substance use. For example, in China, males are more likely to smoke than females, and in Mexico, there are higher smoking and drinking rates for males than females (Arpawong et al., 2010; Johnson et al., 2006).

Additional Areas of Study

Much has been done to study gender differences in adolescent substance use. However, why there are gender differences in the rates of substance use is not well understood and needs further research. Puberty itself may have an impact on the differences between male and female adolescent substance use. More frequent use of substances by younger females may indicate a developmental link, in which females mature faster than males and date older males who, as studies have shown, are more likely to use substances than younger males (Galambos et al., 2009; Johnston et al., 2011; Rodham et al., 2005). This is further confirmed by one study which found that females commonly experience drug offers from their boyfriends, in addition to female peers (Moon et al., 1999). Additionally, females who mature early have been shown to have more emotional distress, substance use, delinquency, and earlier sexual behaviors than those who mature later (Galambos et al., 2009).

Differences in the types of substances used by male and female adolescents could also be based on the differing motivations that they have for use. Adolescent girls report more body dissatisfaction and engage in more weight control behaviors in general than adolescent (Galambos et al., 2009). Therefore, female use of cigarettes and amphetamines could be due to weight-control behaviors and body-image factors (cf. Wild et al., 2004). For example, when the Monitoring the Future study modified its amphetamine question to eliminate over-the-counter weight-loss drugs, the rate of female use dropped significantly (Johnston et al., 2011). In addition, girls with a positive body image have a lower likelihood of alcohol or prescription drug use than those with lower body satisfaction (Schinke, Fang, & Cole, 2008).

Body image–related motivations for female substance use are not typically shared by males; male motivations for substance use have been found to be more related to mood and creativity enhancement instead (Newcomb, Chou, Bentler, & Huba,

1988). While there are differences in substance use motivations, there are findings of similar motivations for use between males and females. For example, it was found that alcohol use was motivated by affect regulation and socialization among both males and females, and both male and female smoking was motivated by boredom relief and affect regulation (Piko, Wills, & Walker, 2007). These findings show an area for further study of potential mediating factors for gender differences in substance use.

One final area in need of study for gender differences is the association between depression and substance use (Colder et al., 2010; Kassel et al., 2010). Studies have shown that females have higher rates of depression than males during adolescence (Galambos et al., 2009). However, there are mixed findings for how depression and gender interact depending on age and substance used. One study showed positive associations between depression and methamphetamine use for eleventh-grade males (Embry, Hankins, Biglan, & Boles, 2009), while another showed that high levels of depression are associated with more alcohol consumption in females than males, but that males, over time, more quickly progress to alcohol problems at the same levels of depression (Marmorstein, 2009). These mixed findings show a significant need for more research on the interactions between gender, substance use, and depression (Galaif, Sussman, Chou, & Wills, 2003). Also, research needs to study gender differences in specific emotions (e.g., depression, anxiety, anger, embarrassment, guilt, and shame) and determine whether there are different mechanisms for coping with emotional distress, possibly linked to gender differences in substance use.

Summary

Examining gender differences in adolescent substance use can enable more tailored interventions and more effective drug-prevention programs. However, merely examining the differences in substance use by males and females ignores the significant role that an adolescent's conceptualization of his or her gender identity plays in substance use. Whether gender identity is formed through masculine and feminine personality traits or through cultural norms, it most certainly plays a role in adolescent substance use. Further study of gender identity is necessary to better understand how it contributes to substance use or abuse.

Religiosity and Adolescent Substance Use

Religiosity can be a salient part of identity for those who have a connection with a religious faith. National surveys show that the majority of adolescents say that they have some degree of involvement in religion (Benson et al., 2003; King & Roeser, 2009), and a significant proportion of adolescents endorse religious coping as part of their ways of dealing with life problems (Pargament, 1997). Religiosity among adolescents has been conceptualized and measured in several different ways (Cotton, McGrady, & Rosenthal, 2010). Some measures ask whether the participant is a member of a church, temple, mosque, or other formal religious organization; and, if so, how often he or she attends services. Other measures ask about the personal importance of religion in one's life and attachment to religious values, as in the Value on Religion Scale (Jessor & Jessor, 1977). Another type of measure indexes nonreligious spirituality, recognizing that a person may hold spiritual beliefs aside from membership in a formal religious organization (Hill & Pargament, 2003; Ritt-Olson et al., 2004; Underwood & Teresi, 2002). These various scales are correlated and recent studies have used several types of measures to tap a broad spectrum of religious identification and coping (e.g., Walker, Ainette, Wills, & Mendoza, 2007).

Religiosity has become a theme in substance use research because initial studies showed religiosity was positively related to mental health and inversely related to use of tobacco, alcohol, and other substances (Wallace & Williams, 1997), although drug use–related spirituality may also exist (Sussman et al., 2006). A substantial body of recent research has shown that while measures of belonging or attendance tend to have erratic effects, measures indexing personal importance, religious values, and sometimes nonreligious spirituality show consistent inverse relations to substance use (Cotton, Zebracki, Rosenthal, Tsevat, & Drotar, 2006; Rew & Wong, 2006). This effect has been found in both longitudinal and cross-sectional studies (e.g., Mason & Spoth, 2011; Spears, Stein, & Koniak-Griffin, 2010; Windle, Mun, & Windle, 2005) and a protective effect for adolescent risk behavior has been found across a range of US religious faiths; hence, it is not limited to a subgroup of adolescents belonging to a particular religion (Chitwood, Weiss, &

Leukefeld, 2008; Ghandour, Karam, & Maalouf, 2009; el Marroun et al., 2008). A protective effect for religiosity has also been noted for adolescents in other countries (e.g., Sanchez et al., 2011; Spein, Melhus, Kristiansen, & Kvernmo, 2011).

Investigators have noted that research on the development of religious identity has been underdeveloped in comparison with other areas of adolescent research (Benson, 2006; King & Roeser, 2009). What is known suggests that children initially acquire religious beliefs through parents who belong to a religious organization (Boyatzis, Dollahite, & Marks, 2006; Laird, Marks, & Marrero, 2011) and their connection with religion may be developed through family rituals and attendance at religious services, even though this participation may not be entirely voluntary (Benson, Roehlkepartain, & Rude, 2003). Religious organizations have formal means for instruction in religious faith and beliefs, such as brief schooling held alongside religious services, and there are formal rituals that recognize more advanced development of beliefs and acceptance into the community of believers (e.g., first Communion, Bar/Bat Mitzvah). In addition to family influences, peers may contribute to the development of religious identity; through congruity and selection processes, adolescents tend to have peers who share their religious beliefs (King & Roeser, 2009; Regnerus, Smith, & Smith, 2004). Although some data suggest that degree of religiosity tends to decline during adolescence, a substantial proportion of older adolescents still perceive religion as an important influence and part of a search for purpose and meaning in their lives (Damon, Menon, & Bronk, 2003; King & Benson, 2006), and this may continue into adulthood (Levenson, Aldwin, & D'Mello, 2005).

Research Issues

Recognizing that religion may not be part of identity for all adolescents, we discuss several aspects of research on religiosity and substance use that are particularly germane to the theme of the present chapter. We do not consider methodological issues in detail because while there are different approaches to assessing religiosity, empirical findings are fairly consistent across measures and research designs. Current questions concern different aspects of religiosity, moderating effects of religiosity for drug use risk factors, and mediation of religiosity effects.

DIFFERENT ASPECTS OF RELIGIOSITY

Earlier research generally found that structural aspects of religiosity (e.g., whether or not one belonged to a religious organization) showed inconsistent relations with tobacco and alcohol use, whereas personal aspects (e.g., importance of religion) were more consistently related to substance use (Cotton et al., 2006). Recent research has examined some different aspects of religiosity. For example, Nonnemaker et al. (2006) found that private religiosity (akin to perceived importance) was protective against smoking initiation and transition to regular smoking, but not related to cessation once a person was addicted. Intrinsic religiosity (i.e., internalizing religious values) has generally been found to have protective effects compared with extrinsic religiosity (e.g., conforming to an external influence) (Brown et al., 2007; Galen & Rogers, 2004). In addition, the communal aspect, perceiving oneself to be a member of a community of faith, may have a protective effect net of other aspects of religiosity (Ellison, Bradshaw, Rote, Storch, & Trevino, 2008; Good & Willoughby, 2006; Hill & McCullough, 2008).

MODERATION EFFECTS OF RELIGIOSITY

Prior research has concentrated on investigating main effects of religiosity, but moderation effects (i.e., reducing the effect of a risk factor) can also be important. For example, a longitudinal study by Wills, Yaeger, and Sandy (2003) with a general-population sample demonstrated that the effect of life stress on growth in substance use over time was reduced among adolescents who scored higher on viewing religion as important in their lives. A similar effect was reported for an African American sample by Belgrave et al. (2010), who found that the impact of perceived stress on tobacco use was lower among those who scored higher on a measure of personal religiosity, and by Laird et al. (2011), who found that the impact of poor self-control on antisocial behavior was reduced among adolescents who scored higher on personal importance of religion. Moderation of peer influences has been found by several investigators. Two studies using different indices of peer influence have found that peers have less effect on tobacco, alcohol, and marijuana use among adolescents who are religious (Desmond, Soper, & Kraus, 2011; Nasim, Belgrave, Jagers, Wilson, & Owens, 2007). Moreover, an analysis using twin data found that perceived importance of religion reduced the impact of genetic influences on smoking initiation, whereas an organizational

measure (e.g., belonging to a church) did not have a moderation effect (Timberlake et al., 2006).

MEDIATION OF RELIGIOSITY EFFECTS

Both religiosity and substance use are complex constructs with cultural and social dimensions, so it is relevant to study how the effect of religiosity on adolescent substance use is mediated. Several studies have tested attitudinal variables and have found evidence for mediation effects. For example, Chawla et al. (2007) studied mediation using a single-item measure on perceived importance of religion; their analyses showed significant mediation effects for personal attitudes about drinking and perceived peer attitudes about drinking, but also showed a significant direct effect of religiosity on alcohol use, similar to findings by Gryczynski and Ward (2011) for smoking and by Vaughan et al. (2011) for alcohol use. Bahr and Hoffmann (2010) used a composite measure of religious attendance and importance and found a significant indirect effect of religiosity through (less) peer alcohol use but also noted an inverse direct effect on adolescents' alcohol use. Johnson, Sheets, and Kristeller (2008) used a composite measure including intrinsic religiosity, nonreligious spirituality, religious coping, and religious support. Their results showed religiosity had significant indirect effects through both peer affiliations and negative alcohol expectancies, but it had no direct effects. For other religion measures, Search for Meaning had an overall protective effect, whereas Religious Struggle had a risk-promoting effect. Related results were noted by Galen and Rogers (2004) in a study that also included motives for alcohol use and found similar indirect pathways as well as an inverse direct effect. Thus, some of the effect of religiosity on adolescent substance use is accounted for by its relation to attitudes and affiliations, but direct effects are also noted.

RELIGIOSITY AND SELF-CONTROL

Self-control constructs have recently been investigated as mediators for religiosity. Walker et al. (2007) tested this formulation with two samples of urban adolescents. They found that a composite measure of religiosity based on personal importance, forgiveness, and nonreligious spirituality had a substantial positive relation to more good self-control and less tolerance for deviance; these variables in turn had paths to proximal risk and protective factors (negative attitudes about substances, coping motives for use, and peer user affiliations). There was no path from religiosity to poor regulation.

McCullough and Willoughby (2009) noted that several alternative explanations for religiosity effects have been ruled out through covariate analyses and longitudinal research, and suggested from a variety of evidence that an effect of religiosity on self-control was a plausible mechanism for the protective effect of religious involvement on health. Recent studies by Abar et al. (2009) and Laird et al. (2011) have shown results consistent with this formulation for other indices of adolescent risk behavior.

Summary

A body of research has shown religiosity to be a protective factor with regard to adolescent substance use and, in a few studies, substance abuse. In addition, several studies have shown that a higher level of religiosity serves as a buffering agent, reducing the impact of life stress and adverse social influences on adolescents' involvement in substance use. Moreover, a growing body of studies indicates the existence of mediating constructs in pathways from religiosity to substance use. Despite the substantial body of research showing religiosity to be inversely related to substance use, however, there is almost no research showing how religiosity becomes incorporated into personal identity (King & Roeser, 2009). Beyond a few studies showing that adolescent girls have higher levels of religiosity and that religious affiliations vary across ethnic groups, there is little understanding of how religiosity is structurally related to self-esteem, gender roles, or ethnic identity.

Ethnic Identity and Substance Use

In addition to other aspects of personal identity, ethnic identity has emerged in recent years as a focus of detailed study. Ethnic identity is defined as the extent to which a person attaches importance to his or her membership in a particular racial/ethnic group and its cultural values; identifies with the accomplishments of group members; and participates in cultural activities (e.g., food, art, special celebrations) that help to define the group as distinctive. This construct has often been measured by the Multidimensional Ethnic Identity Measure (MEIM; Phinney, 1992; Phinney & Alipuria, 1990), which includes subscales for belongingness, ethnic affirmation, and ethnic identity achievement. More recent measures have been developed for specific ages and ethnic groups (e.g., Scottham, Sellers, & Nguyen, 2008). In contrast to other identity measures, which tend to be present focused, ethnic identity measures may include content on learning about the group's history. While an ethnic group's historical experiences may not always have been positive ones, an individual can gain a unique aspect of identity through understanding how prior group members persevered through oppression and discrimination to bring about a better future for the present members of the group (e.g., Evans-Campbell, 2008; Kaholokula, 2007; Murry, 2000).

It should be noted that ethnic identification does not have to be exclusive, as minority-group members can identify to some extent with the majority culture as well as with the culture and values of their own group (Oetting & Beauvais, 1991; Phinney, Cantu, & Kurtz, 1997). Some studies in fact suggest that adaptation is enhanced through identifying with both the minority and the majority culture (Berry, Phinney, Sam, & Vedder, 2006; Kaholokula et al., 2008). It should also be noted that ethnic identity processes may not be similar for males and females, and studies have shown that both the content of ethnic identity and its linkage with more general aspects of self-esteem can differ for adolescent boys and girls (Cote, 2009; Hughes, Hagelskamp, Way, & Foust, 2009; Mandara, Gaylord-Harden, Richards, & Ragsdale, 2009).

It is posited that ethnic identity develops through processes analogous to those outlined in the Eriksonian model of identity development (Phinney & Rosenthal, 1992). From an initial vague conception of ethnicity and its implications, a child becomes acquainted with group differences, observes the distinctive characteristics of his or her own ethnic group, and begins to identify the self with the group. Ethnic identification typically increases during adolescence (French, Seidman, Allen, & Aber, 2006; Huang & Stormshak, 2011). Having an early experience of discrimination may stimulate an exploration of ethnic identity through learning about the history of the group and talking with other group members about their experiences (Fuligni, Hughes, & Way, 2009; Pahl & Way, 2006). It is suggested that this type of identity development is completed by late adolescence though empirical data indicate that in late adolescence, only about a quarter of individuals meet the criteria for having a fully resolved identity (Cote, 2009).

The methodological issues for studying the relation of ethnic identity to adolescent substance use are similar in some ways to those for self-esteem, as ethnic identity is multidimensional and can vary in salience across social contexts (Ashmore, Deaux, & McLaughlin-Volpe, 2004; Yip & Fuligni, 2002). However, there are additional dimensions because minority-group adolescents are susceptible to ethnic/racial discrimination, which is a risk factor for elevated stress and for problem behaviors (e.g., Gibbons, Gerrard, Cleveland, Wills, & Brody, 2004; Williams, Spencer, & Jackson, 1999), and minority-group parents may explicitly socialize their children about race in order to prepare them for possible discrimination (Fuligni et al., 2009; Hughes & Chen, 1997). Although evidence is not totally consistent, several studies suggest that parental communication about cultural and racial issues is related to better adjustment (Hughes et al., 2006; Wills et al., 2007) and to the formation of a resolved ethnic identity (Neblett et al., 2009). Accordingly, research needs to recognize the development of ethnic identity within a context of experiencing discrimination, considering how racial socialization from parents and psychological resources help to buffer the impact of discrimination on substance use (e.g., Fuligni et al., 2009; Gibbons et al., 2010). Also, it is noted empirically that positive ethnic identity is correlated with generalized self-esteem (e.g., Rowley, Sellers, Chavous, & Smith, 1998). It has been suggested that this correlation occurs because individuals who have competencies for dealing with various life problems are able to achieve more developed identities in both domains, although this question has not been totally clarified (Cote, 2009; Fuligni et al., 2009).

Ethnic Identity and Adolescent Substance Use

A number of studies have explored how ethnic identity is related to substance use, frequently though not exclusively with samples of African American adolescents. The assumption has been that, like self-esteem, a positive ethnic identity serves as a psychological resource that promotes positive self-regard and makes adolescents less vulnerable to stress and to adverse social pressures from other adolescents. The following sections discuss selected aspects of this work.

PROTECTIVE EFFECTS AMONG AFRICAN AMERICANS

Ethnic identity was originally studied in relation to adolescent substance use among African American populations (Belgrave, Ridley-Brome, & Hampton, 2000; Brook, Balka, Brook, Win, & Gursen, 1998; Scheier, Botvin, Diaz, & Ifill-Williams, 1997). For example, Brook et al. (1998) studied a version of Phinney's scale in relation to categories of drug use and mainly found interactive effects for belonging and racial pride; these buffered

the effects for some risk factors and enhanced the effects of some protective factors. A study by Wallace and Fisher (2007) with a sample of African American high school students used one subscale from the Phinney inventory analyzed together with a number of subscales from Stevenson's racial socialization measure. Analyses with disapproval of substance use as the criterion showed the Affirmation and Belonging scale was positively correlated with drug disapproval but was not significant when entered together with the other scales on racial pride. However, Pugh and Bry (2007) did find inverse relations of the Affirmation and Belonging scale to alcohol and marijuana use in a sample of Black college students. A study with a different measure of Black identity found that positive regard for one's racial group was inversely associated with alcohol use among adolescents for whom racial identification was a central part of their self-definition (Caldwell, Sellers, Bernat, & Zimmerman, 2004). Corneille and Belgrave (2007) found that strong ethnic identity was a significant moderator for the effect for neighborhood risk on drug use among female African American adolescents, and Nasim et al. (2007) found that Africentric values (e.g., communalism and interdependence) had a main effect for promoting later age of onset, while ethnic identity reduced the impact of peer risk behavior on substance use. Finally, two laboratory studies by Stock et al. (2011) examined moderation effects for the MEIM Affirmation and Belonging scale in response to visualized racial discrimination scenarios. Main effects for ethnic identity were marginal, but a significant interaction indicated that higher ethnic identity reduced the impact of perceived discrimination on willingness to use drugs. Thus, buffering effects for ethnic identity have been found in both observational and experimental studies.

ETHNIC IDENTITY AND SUBSTANCE USE AMONG LATINO ADOLESCENTS

Results among Latinos have been more variable. A brief scale assessing ethnic pride was administered by Castro et al. (2009) to a Southwestern sample of Latino middle school students. Results showed that ethnic pride was inversely related to substance use, though correlations were larger and significant for girls but were nonsignificant for boys. A structural model showed that ethnic pride was positively related to self-efficacy for avoiding substance use and inversely related to perceiving benefits of smoking, and these variables mediated the association of ethnic identity with tobacco/alcohol use. Schwartz et al. (2009) examined the relation of the MEIM and Eriksonian measures of identity coherence and confusion to several problem behaviors indices in a Southeastern sample of Hispanic adolescents. Their results showed ethnic identity was positively correlated with identity coherence, but neither had a significant pathway to substance use; in contrast, identity confusion was significantly related to conduct problems and substance use. Zamboanga et al. (2009) studied a Midwestern sample of younger Hispanic students and found the ethnic identity score was positively related to substance use. The authors suggested that their results reflected the stresses of trying to fit in with the majority culture in a small and largely monocultural community. Their results do parallel findings by Marsiglia et al. (2004), who found in a mixed Southwestern sample that ethnic identity was inversely related to substance use in the whole sample but this effect was more characteristic of Whites and non-Mexican Latinos, whereas ethnic identity was positively related to alcohol use for some Mexican American groups. These authors noted that the present results differed from their own previous findings indicating ethnic identity to be a protective factor for minority adolescents (Marsiglia, Kulis, & Hecht, 2001) and suggested that large changes in school systems (toward majority Hispanic enrollment) could be implicated in the differing results, as White adolescents in these schools now found themselves in the position of being the minority group.

OTHER POPULATIONS

Studies have generally found ethnic identity to have protective effects in other ethnic populations. Galliher, Jones, and Dahl (2011), with a sample of Navajo adolescents, found the MEIM Affirmation and Belonging scale was related to better adaptive functioning, as did Gazis, Connor, and Ho (2010) with a multiethnic sample that included Australian indigenous adolescents. Galliher et al. (2011) also found that connection with Navajo culture buffered the effect of discrimination on substance use; they noted that, independently, connection with White culture also had a buffering effect. Spein, Sexton, and Kvemmo (2007) found stronger ethnic identity was inversely related to drinking in a sample of indigenous Sami in Northern Norway, and J. Brook et al. (2006) found ethnic identification protective with regard to cigarette smoking in a South African multiethnic sample that included White, Black, and Indian adolescents. Though research on ethnic identity in Polynesian populations is limited, a protective effect for substance use and related problem behavior has been suggested in studies of Native Hawaiian adolescents (Austin, 2004) and Samoan adolescents (Fiaui & Hishinuma, 2009).

MEDIATION EFFECTS

It is of interest to determine how the association of ethnic identity with substance use is mediated. With a sample of African American adolescents, Wills, Murry, et al. (2007) tested for mediation of the effect of a Black identity scale (Sellers, Rowley, Chavous, Shelton, & Smith, 1997). Results from a structural model showed the ethnic pride construct was related to less deviance-prone attitudes, more unfavorable prototypes of substance users, and higher substance resistance efficacy; these pathways constituted indirect protective effects for substance use. This is similar to the study by Castro et al. (2009), who found indirect effects through self-efficacy and negative expectancies about smoking, and that by Salazar et al. (2004), who found indirect effects through assertive communication skills. Long-term evidence was found by Brook et al. (2010) with samples of African Americans and Puerto Ricans interviewed during adolescence and followed up during their twenties. Their results showed weak ethnic identity in adolescence was related to antisocial behavior and more affiliation with friends who smoked or used illicit drugs, which in turn were related to smoking in adulthood; this is similar to results from Schwartz et al. (2009), who found conduct problems to be a mediator for personal identity confusion.

Summary

In summary, there is fairly consistent evidence for ethnic identity as a protective factor for adolescent substance use, though results for main effects are less marked and findings of moderation effects are more prominent. There is evidence of protective effects in several populations; however, results for US Hispanic adolescents are more variable and seem to depend more on local contexts, according to the proportion of Latinos. The concept that a strong ethnic identity decreases vulnerability to social pressure is supported by mediation studies that have shown pathways from ethnic identity to higher resistance efficacy and better communication skills, and by moderation studies that have shown ethnic identity to buffer the impact of several types of risk factors, including discrimination and peer risk behavior.

Peer-Group Identification

As part of solidifying a sense of identity, youth may identify themselves conceptually (through social comparison) or literally (through social affiliation) with specific groups of peers (Brown & Lohr, 1987). The various peer groups or "crowds" that have been identified in adolescent research differ considerably in their general values; in their health-related behaviors, including smoking and alcohol use (e.g., Sussman et al., 1990; La Greca, Prinstein, & Fetter, 2001); and in other attributes, including psychiatric symptomatology (e.g., Conway, Rancourt, Adelman, Burk, & Prinstein, 2011; Prinstein & La Greca, 2002). The groups tend to have specific names such as "Populars," "Athletes," "Brains," or "Burnouts," which are similar across different studies of adolescent populations (Sussman, Pokhrel, Ashmore, & Brown, 2007), and evidence suggests that most adolescents tend to identify with one or more of the peer group types. The same types of groups have been identified among adolescents in multiple countries, including the United States, England, the Netherlands, and the Russian Federation (e.g., Sussman et al., 2010), and similar group types have been noted among US college students (e.g., Ashmore et al., 2007). Findings also suggest that a social hierarchy exists among adolescent groups, with Elites or Athletes at the top, and that this hierarchy is associated with level of social involvement, social acceptance, and self-esteem (Brown & Larson, 2009; Sussman, Pokhrel, & Moran, 2011).

Identification with a peer-group type may occur in at least two ways. First, adolescents may conceptually identify themselves with a group that delineates a particular reputation or lifestyle that they wish to adopt, so one way to define peer groups is as *reputation-based collectives* of adolescents with which they may or may not have direct contact. Such conceptual peer groups tend to be based on shared beliefs, interests in clothes and music, and preference for specific activities (Sussman et al., 2007). Second, youth may actively participate in a specific peer group, directly interacting and developing friendships with others in the group, making this an *affiliation-based collective*. If youth actively interact with others from the same group, interpersonal processes (e.g., group cohesiveness, social interactional skills) can operate, above and beyond simply identifying with the norms of a particular group type that one perceives to exist.

The posited psychological function of peer-group identification is similar to what has been suggested for other aspects of identity processes, namely to build positive self-regard and a coherent view of the self. There are several mechanisms through which this may occur. A social comparison mechanism is that incorporating a peer reference group into one's personal identity can help develop a positive self-concept because the adolescent can gain esteem through "reflected glory" from the status and behavior of other group members (Brown & Larson, 2009; Gibbons, Gerrard, & Lane, 2003). A group-process mechanism is that adolescents tend to self-select into groups of peers with similar attributes, and peer members can then provide reinforcement for the adolescent's attitudes and behaviors—even if the values and behaviors tend to be deviant ones by the standards of the larger society (Granic & Dishion, 2003). Affiliation with members of a peer group can also help adolescents achieve autonomy in the larger world through gaining "strength in numbers" for their behavioral goals, whether the goal is a conventional one such as academic accomplishment (Steinberg, Dornbusch, & Brown, 1992) or a deviant one such as acquiring and using drugs (Dishion, Capaldi, Spracklen, & Li, 1995). These mechanisms are not mutually exclusive and theorists have suggested that peer-group identity development is an interactive process: Group members coalesce through shared interests and behaviors and then socialize each other toward the core of the group's values (Brown & Larson, 2009). Recent research, using social network analysis of friendships suggests that both processes may operate.

Peer-group identification differs in two important respects from the other identity processes that have been discussed previously. One difference is that deviant peer groups are regarded as a "final common pathway" to substance use, providing social situations in which initial experimentation with tobacco and alcohol occurs and an attitudinal context that encourages further experimentation and escalation of use (e.g., Hoffman, Sussman, Unger, & Valente, 2006; Wills & Cleary, 1999). Not only are peer groups involved in adolescent identity processes, but as noted previously, identification and/or affiliation with substance-using peers is one of the primary mediators for more distal variables, including attributes such as negative self-regard or positive ethnic identity (Brown, Herman, Hamm, & Heck, 2008; DuBois & Silverthorn, 2004; Wills et al., 2007). Another difference is that peer group membership may serve to consolidate other aspects of identity processes because younger adolescents tend to associate with peers who are of the same gender, who have similar levels of self-esteem (even if it is low), and who share similar religious or non-religious values (Brown & Larson, 2009). Although ethnic aspects have not been widely explored, there is evidence that minority adolescents tend to select same-race peers for friends and that ethnic identity development may also be bolstered through these affiliations (Brown, Herman, Hamm, & Heck, 2008; Rock, Cole, Houshyar, Lythcott, & Prinstein, 2011).

General Group Types and Characteristics

In their review of 44 group identification studies, Sussman et al. (2007) noted four basic ways of assessing adolescents' crowd affiliation: (1) adolescents' self-report on their own peer crowd affiliation (i.e., self-identification); (2) classification of adolescents into peer crowds by the researchers based on ethnographic methods; (3) peer ratings of adolescents into groups according to the perceived "social types" prevalent at their schools (i.e., social-type rating); and (4) researchers' classification of adolescents into peer crowds based on their behavioral characteristics (e.g., aggression), social aspiration among peers, and social involvement (see also Sussman, Pokhrel, & Moran, 2011). There are several approaches taken to conceptualizing and categorizing peer-crowd affiliation and incorporating the issue of whether perceived membership in a peer crowd is reciprocated by other members (Brown, Von Bank, & Steinberg, 2008; Fujimoto & Valente, 2012; Piehler & Dishion, 2007; Urberg et al., 2000). However, it has been found that different measurement approaches tend to yield similar outcome results, and as illustrated in the review by Sussman et al. (2007), the convergence of findings related to peer-crowd names and characteristics across a methodologically varying set of studies suggests a consensus among researchers and participants regarding the nature of the peer-crowd construct.

The review by Sussman et al. (2007) indicates that youth tend to identify with one of five general categories: Elites, Athletes, Deviants, Academics, and Others. The Elites (also labeled "populars" or "hot-shots") are high in peer status and social involvement, and are somewhat involved in academics. An elite-type group is the leading group at school and is composed of members who generally are successful in academic and extracurricular activities, hold a high opinion of themselves, and are high in both other perceived and self-perceived social competence. In a few studies, but not the majority, members of elite groups have been found to be relatively likely to smoke or drink alcohol (Dolcini & Adler, 1994; La Greca et al., 2001; Mosbach & Leventhal, 1988; Valente, Unger, & Johnson, 2005).

Athletes (also called "jocks") are high in peer status and social involvement but somewhat less involved in academics, and in some studies they are merged with the Elite group. These youth tend to be interested in school and participate in sports and school athletic activities. Athletes in general are not involved in drug use but in a few studies are found to be relatively likely to drink alcohol (Barber, Eccles, & Stone, 2001; Miller et al., 2003; see also Lisha & Sussman, 2010).

Deviants (variously called "burnouts," "stoners," "gangsters," "greasers," or "dirts") are sometimes in the middle on peer status and social involvement (because of controversial status or split ratings) but rebel against school, having poor grades and very low academic involvement. They tend to be relatively low in self-esteem and life satisfaction. They are the group most likely to smoke, drink, use marijuana, and use hard drugs (La Greca et al., 2001; Mosbach & Leventhal, 1988; Sussman et al., 1990; Urberg et al., 2000).

Academics are high in academic involvement, in the middle on peer status, and relatively low on social involvement (e.g., "brains," "nerds"). Academics are least likely to engage in various problem behaviors. Finally, Others (with labels such as "outsiders") tend to be relatively low in peer status, social involvement, and academic involvement. They may be involved in small school groups (e.g., "card" clubs). On average, Others tend to be somewhat elevated in level of risky behaviors, but are not as high as Deviants.

There is agreement about the general categories of peer crowds: Elites, Athletes, Academics, Deviants, and Others (Sussman et al., 2007), as well as the lifestyle that their names depict. The Deviants are perhaps the most distinct among the groups. Self-identification as part of a Deviant peer group shows the greatest stability over time, and identification as a deviant versus any other group is an important long-term predictor of drug abuse (Sussman, Dent, & McCullar, 2000).

Research Issues

While studies of peer crowds have consistently identified groups with low or high risk for substance use, two issues relevant for identity research remain to be clarified. The first question is how, within a particular peer group, the adolescent's identity is crystallized and elaborated. Beyond a few studies showing that members of various peer groups differ in ethnicity or self-esteem, there has been little research focused on understanding how adolescent identities develop and change for a given group type (B. Brown & Larson, 2009).

The second issue concerns the understanding of the nature of peer influence. How do peers actually influence each other's identity and behavior? There is no debate about the fact that adolescents' problem behavior is strongly related to the behavior of their peers. There are also general empirical findings indicating that, at the behavioral level, both peer selection and peer influence processes operate (e.g., Hoffman, Monge, Chou, & Valente, 2007; Poulin, Kiesner, Pederson, & Dishion, 2011; Wills & Cleary, 1999). Beyond these propositions, however, it is not at all clear what the nature of peer influence processes actually is. The lay conception is that teen substance use is simply due to "peer pressure," usually taken to mean explicit influence attempts. However, evidence from process studies does not generally support overt social pressure as a primary factor in adolescent substance use (e.g., Urberg, Shyu, & Liang, 1990; Urberg, Degirmencioglu, & Pilgrim, 1997), and other processes have been identified as influential; for example, perceiving that substance use is common in the school population has an effect for promoting substance use onset independent of the actual level of use by one's peers (Graham, Marks, & Hansen, 1991; Sussman et al., 1988).

Current activity in the field is trying to build a comprehensive theoretical understanding of peer influence and the best methods for studying peer-group processes (Brechwald & Prinstein, 2011; Brown, Bakken, Ameringer, & Mahon, 2008; Dishion et al., 2008, Dishion & Tipsord, 2011). For example, the recent model of Brown et al. (2008) builds on prior work by outlining different models of peer influence for adolescent substance use. Peers may display a behavior that others can then model if they wish; they can verbally reinforce statements favorable toward the behavior; they can explicitly pressure a person to perform the behavior; or they can structure opportunities where the behavior can occur (e.g., inviting someone to a gathering where alcohol is available). It is possible that behavioral modeling is influenced by a desire to be like high-status peers (Cohen & Prinstein, 2006), and social-cognitive theories suggest that overt peer pressure may not even be necessary because some adolescents are predisposed to perceive substance use as prevalent among their age-mates (Graham et al., 1991; Sussman et al., 1988) and have relatively favorable images of substance users (Brechwald & Prinstein, 2011; Gerrard, Gibbons, Houlihan, Stock, & Pomery, 2008; Gibbons et al., 2003). There is also evidence that images of "superpeers" derived from media presentations may be as influential as actual peer interactions (Brown et al., 2006; Wills et al., 2008). Each of these models has some supporting evidence. There is currently much ferment in the field, and new findings about the nature of peer influence should emerge from this.

General Discussion

In this chapter we have outlined a working model of personal identity and have discussed five aspects of identity that are relevant to adolescent substance use or abuse. Our view is that identity is a higher order construct based on specific dimensions, including self-concept, gender identity, religious identity, and ethnic identity. These various aspects may be reflected in affiliation with a defined peer group that helps first to develop an identity and then to consolidate and strengthen it. We think it is evident that identity is a multidimensional construct and that each aspect of identity is salient to some proportion of the adolescent population, though the different aspects are not equally salient for everyone.

The research discussed in this chapter has predominantly been conducted with younger adolescents and with criterion variables representing frequency of substance use. Only a few studies have specifically focused on growth in substance use (e.g., Wills et al., 2003), stages of involvement in drug use (e.g., Brook et al., 2006), or differential relationships to substance use problems (e.g., Johnson et al., 2008). It is known that level of substance use is a predictor of substance use problems (e.g., Simons, Carey, & Wills, 2009; Wills et al., 2011), but the correlation between level and problems is moderate and differential relations to symptoms of abuse and dependence may occur. In the area of personal identity, this question is underrepresented and there is a need for more research testing different aspects of identity in relation to risk for level of use and risk for problematic use. Some aspects of personal identity (e.g., gender identity, ethnic identity) may have specific effects for preventing progression from substance use to substance abuse, but such issues remain to be studied in detail at the present time.

We think the material discussed in this chapter supports five general conclusions. These are summarized in the following sections together with suggestions for further research.

IDENTITY IS IMPORTANT FOR SUBSTANCE USE

The research we have discussed indicates that each aspect of identity is related to risk or protection for substance use in adolescence. The size and consistency of effects varies across areas, being perhaps less consistent for self-esteem and most consistent for religiosity, but in each case there is a body of research showing a significant relationship with tobacco, alcohol, and marijuana use, sometimes (though not invariably) with extensive covariates included in the analyses. There is some evidence also for relations to illicit drug use and sexual risk behavior. The studies discussed show significant relations to drug use for various aspects of identity from early adolescence to late adolescence; moreover, we have noted that effects of identity are found across gender and racial/ethnic groups and in several different national populations. Thus, we conclude that personal identity is quite relevant for substance use researchers.

SPECIFIC DIMENSIONS OF IDENTITY ARE CRUCIAL

We have discussed how predictive effects vary considerably for different subdimensions of self-esteem. This is especially marked for academic esteem and peer esteem, where correlations with substance use can be opposite in direction, and for negative vs. positive aspects of self-regard, where the former are influential but the latter are often nonsignificant in multivariate analyses. Similar conclusions can be drawn for ethnic identity, where scales on belongingness and racial pride are consistently predictive of substance use, and for religiosity, where organizational measures tend to be nonsignificant whereas personal importance of religion is consistently significant. In the area of peer-group identification, most research has concentrated on risk effects, but there is evidence that some adolescents primarily affiliate with peers who are interested in academics, and this decision has significant beneficial effects as far as grades and substance use are concerned (Mounts & Steinberg, 1995; Sussman et al., 2007). Thus, identity does not operate as an amorphous global variable, but rather it is the case that different facets of identity can have quite different effects. This concept should be recognized in further research.

THE EFFECTS OF IDENTITY VARIABLES ARE PROBABLY NOT DIRECT ONES

The bulk of the literature we have discussed consists of studies that have demonstrated there is a statistical relation between identity and substance use, but some researchers have tested for mediation and generally have found it. The most consistent evidence is for affiliation with substance-using peers as a mediator of risk for substance use, a pathway that may be both a consequence of an identity variable (e.g., negative view of the self) and an incubator of further changes in personal identity and behavior (e.g., escalation of substance use). However, other variables have been identified as mediators (e.g., substance-related attitudes), and in the area of religiosity, recent research is showing indirect effects mediated through self-control (McCullough & Willoughby, 2009). Thus, further research should continue to investigate the mediators of identity effects.

IDENTITY CAN ACT AS A MODERATOR

There is substantial evidence indicating that a strong ethnic identity can buffer the impact of general life stressors and a specific stressor, racial discrimination, on adolescents' substance use. Some studies also show that ethnic identity buffers the impact of peer risk behavior. For religious identity there is evidence that persons for whom religion is important show less effect of life stress and, in a few studies, lower impact of deviance-prone peers. The way in which the moderation operates has not been explicated in detail and may not always occur through an intuitively obvious mechanism (see Wills et al., 2011, for a discussion of upstream and downstream effects), but the consistency of the observed buffering effects suggests that these should be explored for possible clinical application among persons who are struggling with stress and addiction.

HOW DIFFERENT ASPECTS OF IDENTITY ARE INTEGRATED IS NOT WELL UNDERSTOOD

It is generally recognized that there are multiple aspects of identity. But how these various aspects (specific competencies, gender, ethnicity, religiosity, and peer crowd identification) are integrated has not been studied much, if at all (Cote, 2009; Oyserman, Elmore, & Smith, 2012; Swann & Buhrmester, 2012). There has been little research on whether adolescents perceive different parts of their identity as congruent or conflicting--and if the latter, what they do about it. And while theorists have generally suggested that personal identity is an organized structure, there is little empirical information on this issue; in contrast, to give one example, the linkages among cognitive networks for alcohol expectancies have been extensively studied (e.g., Stacy, Ames, Wiers, & Krank, 2010). Considering all the dimensions discussed in this chapter, do adolescents perceive that they have an organized, coherent personal identity? If it is not organized, how disorganized is it? And if an individual's identity is pretty disorganized, what are the implications for his or her behavior? These questions need to be addressed in further research.

Implications for Prevention and Treatment

Research on identity and substance use has several implications for prevention and treatment. We discuss three issues derived from the theoretical perspective of the present chapter, which as far as we know have not been well developed in the clinical literature.

IDENTITY ISSUES AS A LEVERAGE POINT FOR CHANGE

Theory on identity development suggests that persons seek coherence and consistency in their self-concept. Though there is little direct evidence for this, it seems plausible and is consistent with social-psychological theory on cognitive consistency (Swann & Buhrmester, 2012). The question for treatment research is whether discrepancies among different parts of the self-concept can be used therapeutically to motivate change in self-destructive behavior. For example, consider an adolescent female who is abusing drugs but also has a connection with a religious faith that emphasizes self-control; or an adolescent male who is addicted to cigarettes but maintains a value on physical strength and athletic competence as part of a masculine self-image. More examples could be constructed, but the point is that identity conflicts are probably quite individualized (and not well understood in the first place). Our argument is that if such discrepancies were systematically assessed, they could provide a point of entry into disrupting a self-destructive behavior pattern through focusing on cognitive consistency processes, analogous to some elements of motivational interviewing approaches (e.g., Barnett, Monti, & Wood, 2001). Consistency of course can be a double-edged sword, as persons with low self-esteem may strive to maintain a negative view of the self (Kwang & Swann, 2010; Swann, 2004), but it would be interesting for clinical research to explore identity conflicts as an approach for motivating change.

COMPETENCE AND SELF-ESTEEM

Low self-esteem is common among persons presenting for psychological treatment, and certainly this can be in part a reaction to having caused oneself and others a great deal of trouble through drug use. However, our presentation has noted that negative self-regard predates the progression to drug abuse, being noted in early adolescence among persons who are just beginning to experiment with tobacco and alcohol (Corte & Zucker, 2008; Wills, 1994). Current models of self-esteem focus on the relation of self-concept and competence in relevant life domains. It is intuitive to suspect that persons who perceive they have low competence in academics, interpersonal relationships, or other important life domains will feel bad about themselves. However, the identity model carries the clinical implication that self-esteem could be enhanced the most through skill training in the life domains that are most central for a person's self-concept (Harter, 2012a). It is probably a rare therapist who does not try in some ways to increase a client's competence, but our theoretical model of self-processes points out the additional element of centrality as a target for assessment and intervention. Sending a drug-abusing adolescent to reading and writing courses (on top of one-to-one therapy sessions) might sound a bit odd, but from the perspective of the current literature on etiology of substance problems, where low academic competence is a major part of the risk profile, then it does look more sensible if academics is a central part of the adolescent's self-concept.

PEER INFLUENCE IN AND OUT OF TREATMENT

Addiction therapists have their hands full dealing with the tangled life problems and psychodynamic complexities of the individual client who sits in front of them. However, we have emphasized the role of peer groups in risk for substance use. Drug use in most cases begins in a peer group, escalates in this group (Wills & Cleary, 1999), and in all likelihood transitions to drug abuse in such a group (Sussman et al., 2000). While a group of alienated, antisocial, and uncontrolled peers are not likely to respond to an invitation to join with the focal client in therapy, still they are out there and a significant therapy goal is to keep the client from rejoining this group after the end of treatment. The framework of the present chapter, however, points out that it is quite likely that the peer group has become incorporated into the client's identity. Whether it is a group of friends who get together in the park after school to drink a few beers, or later a group of "shooting buddies" to do hard drugs with, in either case they help to shape the person's identity.

Also we have suggested that there are different facets of peer influence. The peers do not have to be there physically to exert some kind of influence; rather, it is the perception that drug use is relatively common in the population, that many people think using drugs isn't so bad, and that the drug-using peer group has positive aspects, being perceived as fun-loving people, friendly (as long as you have drugs on hand), and providing an element of acceptance, excitement, and thrill seeking that is lacking in the youth's everyday life. Our theoretical perspective suggests that one goal of individual therapy is to "get the peer group out of the client's head," building an alternative self-concept based on different types of reference groups and assessing changes in the types and centralities of various alternative peer groups in the client's life space. We recognize that the therapeutic and psychometric tools to do this mostly aren't available at this point, but the development of such techniques seems a plausible direction for the future.

Notes

1. There are other aspects of identity that may be relevant as (e.g., national or political identity) so this presentation is not meant to be exhaustive.
2. This is based on the assumption that for the majority of adolescents, a behavior such as cigarette smoking is seen as undesirable (or at least not very desirable); hence, higher self-esteem enables them to steer closer to mainstream values and avoid pressures for deviant behavior. The situation could change when a person is immersed in a group where the majority sees substance use as a positive (or at least not very negative) behavior, such as a group of heavy-drinking college students; then persons with higher self-esteem could take a leading role in the behavior.
3. This has been interpreted in terms of different gender roles for minority males and females, a possible differential impact of discrimination for boys and girls in some racial groups, and a higher centrality of ethnic identity for minority adolescents in general (see, for example, Cote, 2009; Fuligni et al., 2009; Gibbons, Pomery, & Gerrard, 2010). Theoretical interpretations for observed ethnic/racial differences in self-esteem (which typically show African Americans having higher self-esteem compared with Caucasians or with other minority groups) have focused on cultural explanations (Gray-Little & Hafdahl, 2000; Twenge & Crocker, 2002), but this remains a topic of active debate (Crocker & Park, 2012; Harter, 2012b; Sedikides, 2012).

References

Abar, B., Carter, K., & Winsler, A. (2009). Effects of maternal parenting style and religious commitment on self-regulation, academic achievement, and risk behavior among African-American college students. *Journal of Adolescence, 32,* 259–273.

Adalbjarnardottir, S., & Rafnsson, F. D. (2001). Perceived control in adolescent substance use: Concurrent and longitudinal analyses. *Psychology of Addictive Behaviors, 15,* 25–32.

Arpawong, T. E., Sun, P., Chang, C. C., Gallaher, P., Pang, Z., Johnson, C. A., & Unger, J. (2010). Family and personal protective factors moderate the effects of adversity on smoking among Chinese adolescents. *Substance Use and Misuse, 45,* 1367–1389.

Ashmore, R. D., Deaux, K., & McLaughlin-Volpe, T. (2004). An organizing framework for collective identity: Articulation of multidimensionality. *Psychological Bulletin, 130,* 80–114.

Ashmore, R. D., Griffo, R., Green, R., & Moreno, A. H. (2007). Dimensions and categories underlying college student types. *Journal of Applied Social Psychology, 37,* 2922–2950.

Athenstaedt, U., Mikula, G., & Bredt, C. (2009). Gender role self-concept and leisure activities of adolescents. *Sex Roles, 60,* 399–409.

Auerbach, R. P., Tsai, B., & Abela, J. R. Z. (2010). Temporal relationships among depressive symptoms, risky behavior engagement, and perceived control, and gender in a sample of adolescents. *Journal of Research on Adolescence, 20,* 726–747.

Austin, A. A. (2004). Alcohol, tobacco, other drug use, and violent behavior among Native Hawaiians: Ethnic pride and resilience. *Substance Use and Misuse, 39,* 721–746.

Bahr, S. J., & Hoffmann, J. P. (2010). Parenting style, peers, and adolescent heavy drinking. *Journal of Studies on Alcohol and Drugs, 71,* 539–543.

Barber, B. L., Eccles, J. S., & Stone, M. R. (2001). Whatever happened to the jock, the brain, and the princess? Young adult pathways linked to adolescent activity involvement and social identity. *Journal of Adolescent Research, 16,* 429–455.

Barnett, N. P., Monti, P. M., & Wood, M. D. (2001). Motivational interviewing for alcohol-using adolescents in the emergency room. In E. Wagner & H. Waldron (Eds.), *Innovations in adolescent substance abuse interventions* (pp. 143–168). New York, NY: Pergamon.

Baumeister, R. F. (1997). The self and society: Changes, problems, and opportunities. In R. D. Ashmore & L. Jussim (Eds.), *Self and identity: Fundamental issues* (pp. 191–217). New York, NY: Oxford University Press.

Belgrave, F. Z., Johnson, J., Nguyen, A., Hood, K., Tademy, R., Clark, T. & Nasim, A. (2010). Stress and tobacco use among African American adolescents: The buffering effect of cultural factors. *Journal of Drug Education, 40,* 173–188.

Belgrave, F. Z., Ridley-Brome, D., & Hampton, C. (2000). The contribution of Afrocentric values and racial identity to the prediction of drug knowledge, attitudes, and use among African American youth. *Journal of Black Psychology, 26,* 386–401.

Bem, S. L. (1974). The measurement of psychological androgyny. *Journal of Consulting and Clinical Psychology, 42,* 155–162.

Benson, P. L. (2006). The science of child and adolescent spiritual development. In E. Roehlkpartain, P. King, L. Wagener, & P. Benson (Eds.), *Handbook of spiritual development in childhood and adolescence* (pp. 484–497). Thousand Oaks, CA: Sage.

Benson, P. L., Roehlkepartain, E. C., & Rude, S. P. (2003). Spiritual development in childhood and adolescence: A field of inquiry. *Applied Developmental Science, 7*, 205–213.

Bergen, H. A., Martin, G., Roeger, L., & Allison, S. (2005). Perceived academic performance and alcohol, tobacco and marijuana use: Longitudinal relationships in young community adolescents. *Addictive Behaviors, 30*, 1563–1573.

Berry, J. W., Phinney, J. S., Sam, D. L., & Vedder, P. (2006). Immigrant youth: Acculturation, identity, and adaptation. *Applied Psychology, 55*, 303–332.

Boyatzis, C. J., Dollahite, D. C., & Marks, L. D. (2006). The family as a context for religious and spiritual development in children and youth. In E. Roehlkepartain, P. King, L. Wagener, & P. Benson (Eds.), *Handbook of spiritual development in childhood and adolescence* (pp. 297–309). Thousand Oaks, CA: Sage.

Brechwald, W. A., & Prinstein, M. J. (2011). Beyond homophily: A decade of advances in understanding peer influence processes. *Journal of Research on Adolescence, 21*, 166–179.

Brook, D. W., Rubenstone, E., Zhang, C., Morolele, N. K., & Brook, J. S. (2011). Environmental stressors, low well-being, and smoking and alcohol use among South African adolescents. *Social Science and Medicine, 72*, 1447–1453.

Brook, J. S., Balka, E., Brook, D., Win, P., & Gursen, M. (1998). Drug use among African Americans: Ethnic identity as a protective factor. *Psychological Reports, 83*, 1427–1446.

Brook, J. S., Morojele, N. K., Brook, D. W., Zhang, C., & Whiteman, M. (2006). Personal, interpersonal, and cultural predictors of stages of cigarette smoking among adolescents in Johannesburg, South Africa. *Tobacco Control, 15*, 148–153.

Brook, J. S., Zhang, C., Finch, S. J., & Brook, D. W. (2010). Adolescent pathways to adult smoking: Ethnic identity, peer substance use, and antisocial behavior. *American Journal on Addictions, 19*, 178–186.

Brown, B. B., Bakken, J. P., Ameringer, S. W., & Mahon, S. D. (2008). A comprehensive conceptualization of the peer influence process in adolescence. In M. Prinstein & K. Dodge (Eds.), *Understanding peer influence in children and adolescents* (pp. 17–44). New York, NY: Guilford Press.

Brown, B. B., Herman, M., Hamm, J. V., & Heck, D. J. (2008). Ethnicity and image: Correlates of crowd affiliation among ethnic minority youth. *Child Development, 79*, 529–546.

Brown, B. B., & Larson, J. (2009). Peer relationships in adolescence. In R. Lerner & L. Steinberg (Eds.), *Handbook of adolescent psychology, Vol. 2. Contextual influences in adolescent development* (3rd ed., pp. 74–103). Hoboken, NJ: Wiley.

Brown, B. B., & Lohr, M. J. (1987). Peer-group affiliation and adolescent self-esteem: An integration of ego-identity and symbolic-interaction theories. *Journal of Personality and Social Psychology, 52*, 47–55.

Brown, B. B., Von Bank, H., & Steinberg, L. (2008). Smoke in the looking glass: Effects of discordance between self- and peer-rated crowd affiliation on adolescent anxiety, depression, and self-feelings. *Journal of Youth and Adolescence, 37*, 1163–1177.

Brown, J., L'Engle, K., Pardun, C., Guo, G., Kenneavy, K., & Jackson, C. (2006). Exposure to sexual content in media predicts adolescents sexual behavior. *Pediatrics, 117*, 1018–1027.

Brown, T., Salsman, J., Brechtinb, E., & Carlson, C. (2007). Religiousness, spirituality, and social support: How are they related to underage drinking? *Journal of Child and Adolescent Substance Abuse, 17*, 15–39.

Bryant, A. L., Schulenberg, J., O'Malley, P. M., Bachman, J. G., & Johnston, L. D. (2003). How academic achievement and attitudes relate to the course of substance use during adolescence. *Journal of Research on Adolescence, 13*, 361–397.

Caldwell, C. H., Sellers, R. M., Bernat, D. H., & Zimmerman, M. A. (2004). Racial identity, parental support, and alcohol use in a sample of at-risk African American high school students. *American Journal of Community Psychology, 34*, 71–82.

Carvajal, S. C., Evans, R. I., Nash, S. G., & Getz, J. G. (2002). Global positive expectancies of the self and adolescents' substance use avoidance. *Journal of Personality, 70*, 421–442.

Castro, F. G., Stein, J. A., & Bentler, P. M. (2009). Ethnic pride, traditional family values, and acculturation in early cigarette and alcohol use among Latino adolescents. *Journal of Primary Prevention, 30*, 265–292.

Centers for Disease Control and Prevention. (2010). Youth Risk Behavior Surveillance-United States, 2009: Surveillance summaries. *Morbidity and Mortality Weekly Report Surveillance Summaries, 59*, SS-5.

Chawla, N., Neighbors, C., Lewis, M., Lee, C., & Larimer, M. (2007). Attitudes and perceived approval of drinking as mediators of the relation between religiosity and alcohol use. *Journal of Studies on Alcohol and Drugs, 68*, 410–418.

Chitwood, D. D., Weiss, M. L., & Leukefeld, C. G. (2008). A systematic review of recent literature on religiosity and substance use. *Journal of Drug Issues, 38*, 653–688.

Cohen, G. L., & Prinstein, M. J. (2006). Peer contagion of aggression and health risk behavior among adolescent males: An experimental investigation on public conduct and private attitudes. *Child Development, 77*, 967–983.

Colder, C. R., Chassin, L., Lee, M. R., Villalta, I. K., & Kassel, J. D. (2010). Developmental perspectives: Affect and adolescent substance use. In J. D. Kassel (Ed.), *Substance abuse and emotion* (pp. 109–135). Washington, DC: American Psychological Association.

Compas, B. E., & Reeslund, K. L. (2009). Processes of risk and resilience during adolescence. In R. M. Lerner & L. Steinberg (Eds.), *Handbook of adolescent psychology, Vol. 1. Individual bases of adolescent development* (3rd ed., pp. 561–588). Hoboken, NJ: Wiley.

Conway, C. C., Rancourt, D., Adelman, C. B., Burk, W. J., & Prinstein, M. J. (2011). Depression socialization within friendship groups in adolescence: The roles of gender and group centrality as moderators of peer influence. *Journal of Abnormal Psychology, 120*, 857–867.

Corneille, M. A., & Belgrave, F. Z. (2007). Ethnic identity, neighborhood risk, and adolescent drug and sex attitudes and refusal efficacy: The urban African American girls experience. *Journal of Drug Education, 37*, 177–190.

Corte, C., & Zucker, R. A. (2008). Self-concept disturbances: Cognitive vulnerability for early drinking and early drunkenness in adolescents at high risk for alcohol problems. *Addictive Behaviors, 33*, 1282–1290.

Cote, J. E. (1996). Identity: A multidimensional analysis. In G. Adams, R. Montemayor, & T. Giulotta (Eds.), *Psychosocial development during adolescence* (pp. 130–180). Thousand Oaks, CA: Sage.

Cote, J. E. (2006). Emerging adulthood as an institutionalized moratorium: Risks and benefits to identity formation. In J. Arnett & J. Tanner (Eds), *Emerging adults in America* (pp. 85–116). Washington, DC: American Psychological Association.

Cote, J. E. (2009). Identity formation and self-development in adolescence. In R. M. Lerner & L. Steinberg (Eds.), *Handbook of adolescent psychology, Vol. 1. Individual bases of adolescent development* (3rd ed., pp. 266–304). Hoboken, NJ: Wiley.

Cotton, S., McGrady, M., & Rosenthal, S. (2010). Measurement of religiosity/spirituality in adolescent health outcomes research: Trends and recommendations. *Journal of Religion and Health, 49*, 414–444.

Cotton, S., Zebracki, K., Rosenthal, S. L., Tsevat, J., & Drotar, D. (2006). Religion-spirituality and adolescent health outcomes. *Journal of Adolescent Health, 38*, 472–480.

Crocker, J., & Park, L. E. (2012). Contingencies of self-worth. In M. R. Leary & J. P. Tangney (Eds.), *Handbook of self-and identity* (2nd ed., pp. 309–326). New York, NY: Guilford Press.

Damon, W., Menon, J., & Bronk, K. C. (2003). The development of purpose during adolescence. *Applied Developmental Science, 7*, 119–128.

Desmond, S., Soper, S., & Kraus, R. (2011). Does religiosity reduce the effect of peers on delinquency? *Sociological Spectrum, 31*, 665–694.

Dishion, T. J., Capaldi, D., Spracklen, K. M., & Li, F. (1995). The peer ecology of male adolescent drug use. *Development and Psychopathology, 7*, 803–824.

Dishion, T. J., Piehler, T. F., & Myers, M. W. (2008). Dynamics and ecology of adolescent peer influence. In M. Prinstein & K. Dodge (Eds.), *Understanding peer influence in children and adolescents* (pp. 72–93). New York, NY: Guilford Press.

Dishion, T. J., & Tipsord, J. M. (2011). Peer contagion in child and adolescent social and emotional development. *Annual Review of Psychology, 62*, 189–214.

Dolcini, M. M., & Adler, N. E. (1994). Perceived competencies, peer group affiliation, and risk behavior among early adolescents. *Health Psychology, 13*, 496–506.

Donnelly, J., Young, M., Pearson, R., Penhollow, T. M., & Hernandez, A. (2008). Area-specific self-esteem and adolescent substance use. *Journal of Drug Education, 38*, 389–403.

DuBois, D. L., & Silverthorn, N. (2004). Do deviant peer associations mediate the contribution of self-esteem to problem behavior during early adolescence? A 2-year longitudinal study. *Journal of Clinical Child and Adolescent Psychology, 33*, 382–388.

Dusek, J. B., & McIntyre, J. G. (2003). Self-concept and self-esteem development. In G. R. Adams & M. D. Berzonsky (Eds.), *Blackwell handbook of adolescence* (pp. 290–309). Malden, MA: Blackwell.

Ellison, C., Bradshaw, M., Rote, S., Storch, J., & Trevino, M. (2008). Exploring the role of domain-specific religious salience in alcohol use. *Journal of Drug Issues, 38*, 821–846.

Embry, D., Hankins, M., Biglan, A., & Boles, S. (2009). Behavioral and social correlates of methamphetamine use in a population-based sample of early and later adolescents. *Addictive Behaviors, 34*, 343–351.

Engels, R. C. M. E., Hale, W. W., Noom, M., & De Vries, H. (2005). Self-efficacy and emotion as precursors of smoking in adolescence. *Substance Use and Misuse, 40*, 1883–1893.

Epstein, J. A., Griffin, K. W., & Botvin, G. (2004). Efficacy, self-derogation, and alcohol use among inner-city adolescents. *Journal of Youth and Adolescence, 33*, 159–166.

Erikson, E. H. (1968). *Identity: Youth and crisis*. New York, NY: Norton.

Evans-Campbell, T. (2008). Historical trauma in American Indian/Alaska Native communities: A multilevel framework for exploring impact on individuals, families, and communities. *Journal of Interpersonal Violence, 23*, 316–338.

Fiaui, P. A., & Hishinuma, E. S. (2009). Samoan adolescents in American Samoa and Hawaii: Comparison of youth violence and development indicators. *Aggression and Violent Behavior, 14*, 478–487.

French, S. E., Seidman, E., Allen, L., & Aber, J. L. (2006). The development of ethnic identity during adolescence. *Developmental Psychology, 42*, 1–10.

Fujimoto, K., & Valente, T. W. (2012). Decomposing the components of friendship and friends' influence on adolescent drinking and smoking. *Journal of Adolescent Health*. doi: 10.1016/j.jadohealth.2011.11.013.

Fuligni, A. J., Hughes, D. L., & Way, N. (2009). Ethnicity and immigration. In R. M. Lerner & L. Steinberg (Eds.), *Handbook of adolescent psychology, Vol. 2. Contextual influences in adolescent development* (3rd ed., pp. 527–569). Hoboken, NJ: Wiley.

Galaif, E., Sussman, S., Chou, C-P., & Wills, T. A. (2003). Longitudinal relations among depression, stress, and coping in high-risk youth. *Journal of Youth and Adolescence, 32*, 243–258.

Galambos, N. L., Berenbaum, S. A., & McHale, S. M. (2009). Gender development in adolescence. In R. Lerner & L. Steinberg (Eds.), *Handbook of adolescent psychology, Vol. 1. Individual bases of development* (3rd ed., pp. 305–357). Hoboken, NJ: Wiley.

Galen, L. W., & Rogers, W. M. (2004). Religiosity, expectancies, and drinking motives in the prediction of drinking among college students. *Journal of Studies on Alcohol, 65*, 469–476.

Galliher, R. V., Jones, M. D., & Dahl, A. (2011). Concurrent and longitudinal effects of ethnic identity and experiences of discrimination on psychosocial adjustment of Navajo adolescents. *Developmental Psychology, 47*, 509–526.

Gazis, N., Connor, J. P., & Ho, R. (2010). Cultural identity and peer influences as predictors of substance use among culturally diverse Australian adolescents. *Journal of Early Adolescence, 30*, 345–368.

Gerrard, M., Gibbons, F. X., Houlihan, A. E., Stock, M. L., & Pomery, E. A. (2008). A dual-process approach to health risk decision making. *Developmental Review, 28*, 29–61.

Ghandour, L., Karam. E., & Maalouf, W. (2009). Lifetime alcohol use, abuse and dependence among university students in Lebanon: Exploring the role of religiosity in different religious faiths. *Addiction, 104*, 940–948.

Gibbons, F. X., Etcheverry, P., Stock, M., Gerrard, M., Weng, C-Y., Kiviniemi, M., & O'Hara, R. (2010). Exploring the link between racial discrimination and substance use: What mediates? What buffers? *Journal of Personality and Social Psychology, 99*, 785–801.

Gibbons, F. X., Gerrard, M., Cleveland, M. J., Wills, T. A., & Brody, G. (2004). Perceived discrimination and substance use in African-American parents and their children: A panel study. *Journal of Personality and Social Psychology, 86*, 517–529.

Gibbons, F. X., Gerrard, M., & Lane, D. (2003). A social reaction model of adolescent health risk. In J. Suls & K. A. Wallston (Eds.), *Social psychological foundations of health and illness* (pp. 107–136). Malden, MA: Blackwell.

Gibbons, F. X., Pomery, E., & Gerrard, M. (2010). Racial discrimination and substance abuse: Risk and protective factors in African American adolescents. In L. Scheier (Ed.), *Handbook of drug use etiology* (pp. 341–361). Washington, DC: American Psychological Association.

Glendinning, A. (2002). Self-esteem and smoking in youth: Muddying the waters? *Journal of Adolescence, 25,* 415–425.

Good, M., & Willoughby, T. (2006). The role of spirituality versus religiosity in adolescent psychosocial adjustment. *Journal of Youth and Adolescence, 35,* 41–55.

Graham, J. W., Marks, G., & Hansen, W. B. (1991). Social influence processes affecting adolescent substance use. *Journal of Applied Psychology, 76,* 291–298.

Granic, I., & Dishion, T. J. (2003). Deviant talk in adolescent friendships: A step toward measuring a pathogenic attractor process. *Social Development, 12,* 314–334.

Gray-Little, B., & Hafdahl, A. R. (2000). Factors influencing racial comparisons of self-esteem: A quantitative review. *Psychological Bulletin, 126,* 26–54.

Gryczynski, J., & Ward, B. (2011). The relation between cigarette use and religiosity among adolescents in the United States. *Health Education and Behavior, 38,* 39–48.

Harter, S. (2006). Development of self-esteem. In D. Mroczek & T. Little (Eds.), *Handbook of personality development* (pp. 311–334). Mahwah, NJ: Erlbaum.

Harter, S. (2012a). *The construction of the self: Developmental and sociocultural foundations (2nd ed.).* New York, NY: Guilford Press.

Harter, S. (2012b). Emerging self-processes during childhood and adolescence. In M. Leary & J. Tangney (Eds.), *Handbook of self and identity* (2nd ed., pp. 680–715). New York, NY: Guilford Press.

Hill, P. C., & Pargament, K. I. (2003). Advances in the conceptualization and measurement of religion and spirituality. *American Psychologist, 58,* 64–74.

Hill, T. D., & McCullough, M. E. (2008). Religious involvement and the alcohol involvement trajectories of low-income urban women. *Journal of Drug Issues, 38,* 847–862.

Hobfoll, S. E. (2001). The influence of culture, community, and the nested-self in the stress process. *Applied Psychology, 50,* 337–370.

Hoffman, B. R., Monge, P. R., Chou, C-P., & Valente, T. W. (2007). Perceived peer influence and peer selection on adolescent smoking. *Addictive Behaviors, 32,* 1546–1554.

Hoffman, B. R., Sussman, S., Unger, J., & Valente, T. W. (2006). Peer influences on adolescent cigarette smoking: A review of the literature. *Substance Use and Misuse, 41,* 103–155.

Huang, C. Y., & Stormshak, E. A. (2011). A longitudinal examination of early adolescence ethnic identity trajectories. *Cultural Diversity and Ethnic Minority Psychology, 17,* 261–270.

Hughes, D., & Chen, L. (1997). When and what parents tell children about race: An examination of race-related socialization among African American families. *Applied Developmental Science, 1,* 200–214.

Hughes, D., Hagelskamp, C., Way, N., & Foust, M. D. (2009). The role of mothers' and adolescents' perceptions of ethnic-racial socialization in shaping ethnic-racial identity among early adolescent boys and girls. *Journal of Youth and Adolescence, 38,* 605–626.

Hughes, D., Rodriguez, J., Smith, E. P., Johnson, D. J., Stevenson, H. C., & Spicer, P. (2006). Parents' ethnic-racial socialization practices: A review of research and directions for future study. *Developmental Psychology, 42,* 747–770.

Huselid, R. F., & Cooper, M. L. (1992). Gender roles as mediators of sex differences in adolescent alcohol use and abuse. *Journal of Health and Social Behavior, 33,* 348–362.

Jessor, R., & Jessor, S. (1977). *Problem behavior and psychosocial development.* New York, NY: Academic Press.

Johnson, C. A., Palmer, P. H., Chou, C. P., Zengchang, P., Zhou, D., Dong, L., . . . Unger, J. (2006). Tobacco use among youth and adults in mainland, China: The China seven cities study. *Journal of the Royal Institute of Public Health, 120,* 1156–1169.

Johnson, T. J., Sheets, V. L., & Kristeller, J. L. (2008). Identifying mediators of the relation between religiosity and alcohol use. *Journal of Studies on Alcohol and Drugs, 69,* 160–170.

Johnston, L. D., O'Malley, P. M., Bachman, J. G., & Schulenberg, J. E. (2011). *Monitoring the Future national survey results on drug use, 1975-2010, Vol. 1. Secondary students.* Ann Arbor: Institute for Social Research, University of Michigan.

Kaholokula, J. K. (2007). Colonialism, acculturation, and depression among Kanaka Maoli of Hawaii. In P. Culbertson, M. Agee, & C. Makasiale (Eds.), *Confronting challenges in mental health for Pacific peoples* (pp. 180–195). Honolulu: University of Hawaii Press.

Kaholokula, J. K., Grandinetti, A., Nacapoy, A. H., & Chang, H. K. (2008). Association of acculturation and Type 2 diabetes among Native Hawaiians. *Diabetes Care, 31,* 698–700.

Karatzias, A., Power, K. G., & Swanson, V. (2001). Predicting use and maintenance of use of substances in Scottish adolescents. *Journal of Youth and Adolescence, 30,* 465–484.

Kassel, J. D., Hussong, A. M., Wardle, M. C., Veilleux, J. C., Heinz, A., Greenstein, J. E., & Evatt, D. P. (2010). Affective influences in drug use etiology. In L. Scheier (Ed.), *Handbook of drug use etiology* (pp. 183–205). Washington, DC: American Psychological Association.

Kaufman, A., & Augustson, E. (2008). Predictors of cigarette smoking in adolescent females: Does body image matter? *Nicotine and Tobacco Research, 10,* 1301–1309.

Kim, Y-H. (2001). Korean adolescents' health risk behaviors and their relationships with selected psychological constructs. *Journal of Adolescent Health, 29,* 298–306.

Kim, Y-H. (2005). Korean adolescents' smoking behavior and its correlation with psychological variables, *Addictive Behaviors, 30,* 343–350.

King, P. E., & Benson, P. L. (2006). Spiritual development and adolescent well-being. In E. Roehlkpartain, P. King, L. Wagener, & P. Benson (Eds.), *Handbook of spiritual development in childhood and adolescence* (pp. 384–398). Thousand Oaks, CA: Sage.

King, P. E., & Roeser, R. W. (2009). Religion and spirituality in adolescent development. In R. M. Lerner & L. Steinberg (Eds.), *Handbook of adolescent psychology, Vol. 1. Individual bases of adolescent development* (3rd ed., pp. 435–478). Hoboken, NJ: Wiley.

Koestner, R., & Aube, J. (1995). A multifactorial approach to the study of gender characteristics. *Journal of Personality, 63,* 681–710.

Kroger, J. (2000). Ego identity research in the new millennium. *International Journal of Behavioral Development, 24,* 145–148.

Kulis, S., Marsiglia, F. F., & Hecht, M. (2002). Gender labels and gender identity as predictors of drug use among ethnically diverse middle school students. *Youth and Society, 33,* 442–475.

Kulis, S., Marsiglia, F. F., & Hurdle, D. (2003). Gender identity, ethnicity, acculturation, and drug use: Exploring differences among adolescents in the southwest. *Journal of Community Psychology, 31,* 167–188.

Kulis, S., Marsiglia, F. F., Lingard, E., C., Nieri, T., & Nagoshi, J. (2008). Gender identity and substance use among students in two high schools in Monterrey, Mexico. *Drug and Alcohol Dependence, 95*, 258–268.

Kwang, T., & Swann, W. B. (2010). Do people embrace praise even when they feel unworthy? A review of critical tests of self-enhancement versus self-verification. *Personality and Social Psychology Review, 14*, 263–280.

La Greca, A., Prinstein, M., & Fetter, M. (2001). Adolescent crowd affiliation: Linkages with health-risk behaviors and close friendships. *Journal of Pediatric Psychology, 26*, 131–143.

Laird, R. D., Marks, L. D., & Marrero, M. D. (2011). Religiosity, self-control, and antisocial behavior. *Journal of Applied Developmental Psychology, 32*, 78–85.

Lazuras, L., Eiser, J. R., & Rodafinos, A. (2009). Predicting Greek adolescents' intentions to smoke: A focus on normative processes. *Health Psychology, 28*, 770–778.

Levenson, M. R., Aldwin, C. M., & D'Mello, M. (2005). Religious development from adolescence to middle adulthood. In R. Paloutzian & C. Park (Eds.), *Handbook of the psychology of religion and spirituality* (pp. 144–160). New York, NY: Guilford Press.

Li, X., Mao, R., Stanton, B., & Zhao, Q. (2010). Parental and individual factors associated with smoking among students in Nanjing. *Journal of Child and Family Studies, 19*, 308–317.

Lisha, N. E., & Sussman, S. (2010). Relation of high school and college sports participation with alcohol, tobacco, and illicit drug use: A review. *Addictive Behaviors, 35*, 399–407.

Mandara, J., Gaylord-Harden, N. K., Richards, M. H., & Ragsdale, B. L. (2009). The effect of changes in racial identity and self-esteem on changes in African American adolescents' mental health. *Child Development, 80*, 1660–1675.

Marmorstein, N. R. (2009). Longitudinal associations between alcohol problems and depressive symptoms. *Alcoholism: Clinical and Experimental Research, 33*, 49–59.

el Marroun, H., Tiemeier, H., Jaddoe, V., Hofman, A., Machenbach, J., Steegers, E., . . . Huizink, A. (2008). Demographic and social determinants of cannabis use in early pregnancy: The Generation R Study. *Drug and Alcohol Dependence, 98*, 218–226.

Marsiglia, F. F., Kulis, S., & Hecht, M. L. (2001). Ethnic labels and ethnic identity as predictors of drug use among middle school students in the Southwest. *Journal of Research on Adolescence, 11*, 21–48.

Marsiglia, F. F., Kulis, S., Hecht, M. L., & Sills, S. (2004). Ethnicity and ethnic identity as predictors of drug norms and drug use among preadolescents in the US Southwest. *Substance Use and Misuse, 39*, 1061–1094.

Mason, W. A., & Spoth, R. L. (2011). Thrill seeking and religiosity in relation to adolescent substance use: Interactive influences. *Psychology of Addictive Behaviors, 25*, 683–696.

McCullough, M. E., & Willoughby, B. L. B. (2009). Religion, self-regulation, and self-control: Associations, explanations, and implications. *Psychological Bulletin, 135*, 69–93.

McKay, M. T., Sumnall, H. R., Cole, J. C., & Percy, A. (2012). Self-esteem and self-efficacy: Associations with alcohol consumption in a sample of adolescents in Northern Ireland. *Drug Education, Prevention, and Policy, 19*, 72–80.

Miller, K. E., Hoffman, J. H., Barnes, G. M., Farrrell, M. P., Sabo, D., & Melnick, M. J. (2003). Jocks, gender, race, and adolescent drug use. *Journal of Drug Education, 33*, 445–462.

Moon, D. G., Hecht, M. L., Jackson, K. M., & Spellers, R. E. (1999). Ethnic and gender differences and similarities in adolescent drug use and refusals of drug offers. *Substance Use and Misuse, 34*, 1059–1083.

Mosbach, P., & Leventhal, H. (1988). Peer group identification and smoking. *Journal of Abnormal Psychology, 97*, 238–245.

Mounts, N. S., & Steinberg, L. (1995). An ecological analysis of peer influence on adolescent grade point average and drug use. *Developmental Psychology, 31*, 915–922.

Murry, V. M. (2000). Extraordinary challenges and ordinary life experiences of black American families. In P. C. McKenry & S. H. Price (Eds.), *Family stress and change* (2nd ed., pp. 333–358). Thousand Oaks, CA: Sage.

Nasim, A., Belgrave, F. Z., Jagers, R. J., Wilson, K. D., & Owens, K. (2007). The moderating effects of culture on peer deviance and alcohol use among high-risk African-American adolescents. *Journal of Drug Education, 37*, 335–363.

Neblett, E. W., Smalls, C. P., Ford, K. R., Nguyen, H. X., & Sellers, R. M. (2009). Racial socialization and racial identity: African American parents' messages about race as precursors to identity. *Journal of Youth and Adolescence, 38*, 189–203.

Newcomb, M. D., Chou, C. P., Bentler, P. M., & Huba, G. J. (1988). Cognitive motivations for drug use among adolescents: Longitudinal tests of gender differences and predictors of change in drug use. *Journal of Counseling Psychology, 35*, 426–438.

Nonnemaker, J., McNeely, C., & Blum, R. (2006). Public and private domains of religiosity and adolescent smoking transition. *Social Science and Medicine, 62*, 3084–3095.

Oetting, G. R., & Beauvais, F. (1991). Orthogonal cultural identification theory: The cultural identification of minority adolescents. *International Journal of the Addictions, 25*, 655–685.

Otten, R., van Lier, P. A. C., & Engels, R. C. M. E. (2011). Disentangling underlying processes in the initial phase of substance use. *Addictive Behaviors, 36*, 237–240.

Oyserman, D., Elmore, K., & Smith, G. (2012). Self, self-concept, and identity. In M. Leary & J. Tangney (Eds.), *Handbook of self and identity* (2nd ed., pp. 69–104). New York, NY: Guilford Press.

Pahl, K., & Way, N. (2006). Longitudinal trajectories of ethnic identity among urban black and Latino adolescents. *Child Development, 77*, 1403–1415.

Pargament, K. I. (1997). *Psychology of religion and coping: Theory, research, and practice*. New York, NY: Guilford Press.

Phinney, J. S. (1992). The multigroup ethnic identity measures: A scale for use with diverse groups. *Journal of Adolescent Research, 7*, 156–176.

Phinney, J. S., & Alipuria, L. (1990). Ethnic identity in college students from four ethnic groups. *Journal of Adolescence, 13*, 171–183.

Phinney, J. S., Cantu, C. L., & Kurtz, D. A. (1997). Ethnic and American identity as predictors of self-esteem among African American, Latino, and White adolescents. *Journal of Youth and Adolescence, 26*, 165–185.

Phinney, J. S., & Rosenthal, D. A. (1992). Ethnic identity in adolescence: Process, context, and outcome. In G. R. Adams, T. Giulotta, & R. Montemayor (Eds.), *Psychosocial development during adolescence* (pp. 145–172). Thousand Oaks, CA: Sage.

Piehler, T. F., & Dishion, T. J. (2007). Interpersonal dynamics within adolescent friendships: Deviant talk, and patterns of antisocial behavior. *Child Development, 78*, 1611–1624.

Piko, B. F., Wills, T. A., & Walker, C. (2007). Motives for smoking and drinking: Country and gender differences in samples of Hungarian and US high school students. *Addictive Behaviors, 32*, 2087–2098.

Poulin, F., Kiesner, J. Pederson, S., & Dishion, T. J. (2011). A longitudinal analysis of friendship selection processes on early adolescent substance use. *Journal of Adolescence, 34*, 249–256.

Prinstein, M., & La Greca, A. (2002). Peer crowd affiliation and internalizing distress in childhood and adolescence. *Journal of Research on Adolescence, 12*, 325–351.

Pugh, L. A., & Bry, B. H. (2007). The protective effect of ethnic identity for alcohol and marijuana use among black young adults. *Cultural Diversity and Ethnic Minority Psychology, 13*, 187–193.

Regnerus, M. D., Smith, C., & Smith, B. (2004). Social context in the development of adolescent religiosity. *Applied Developmental Science, 8*, 27–38.

Rew, L., & Wong, Y. J. (2006). A review of associations among religiosity-spirituality and adolescent health attitudes and behaviors. *Journal of Adolescent Health, 38*, 433–442.

Ritt-Olson, A., Milam, J., Unger, J. B., Trinidad, D., Teran, L., Dent, C. W., & Sussman, S. (2004). The protective influence of spirituality and 'health-as-a-value" against substance use among adolescents varying in risk. *Journal of Adolescent Health, 34*, 192–199.

Rock, P. F., Cole, D. J., Houshyar, S., Lythcott, M., & Prinstein, M. J. (2011). Peer status in an ethnic context: Association with African American adolescents' ethnic identity. *Journal of Applied Developmental Psychology, 32*, 163–169.

Rodham, K., Hawton, K., Evans, E., & Weatherall, R. (2005). Ethnic and gender differences in drinking, smoking and drug taking among adolescents in England: A self-report school-based survey of 15 and 16 year olds. *Journal of Adolescence, 28*, 63–73.

Rowley, S. J., Sellers, R. M., Chavous, T. M., & Smith, M. A. (1998). The relation between racial identity and self-esteem in African American college and high school students. *Journal of Personality and Social Psychology, 74*, 715–724.

Salazar, L. F., DiClemente, R. J., Wingood, G. M., Crosby, R. A., Harrington, K., Davies, S., . . . Oh, M. K. (2004). Self-concept and adolescents' refusal of unprotected sex: A test of mediating mechanisms among African American girls. *Prevention Science, 5*, 137–149.

Sanchez, Z., Martins, S., Opaleye, E., Moura, Y., Locatelli, D., & Noto, A. (2011). Social factors associated to binge drinking among Brazilian students. *BMC Public Health, 11*, doi: 10.1186/1471-2458-201.

Scheier, L. M., Botvin, G. J., Diaz, T., & Ifill-Williams, M. (1997). Ethnic identity as a moderator of psychosocial risk and adolescent alcohol and marijuana use: Concurrent and longitudinal analyses. *Journal of Child and Adolescent Substance Abuse, 6*, 21–47.

Schinke, S. P., Fang, L., & Cole, K. C. A. (2008). Substance use among early adolescent girls: Risk and protective factors. *Journal of Adolescent Health, 43*, 191–194.

Schwartz, S. J. (2001). Integration of Eriksonian and neo-Eriksonian identity theory and research. *Identity, 1*, 7–58.

Schwartz, S. J., Mason, C. A., Pantin, H., Wang, W., Brown, C. H., Campo, A. E., & Szapocznik, J. (2009). Relationships of social context and identity to problem behavior among high-risk Hispanic adolescents. *Youth and Society, 40*, 541–570.

Scottham, K. M., Sellers, R. M., & Nguyen, H. X. (2008). A measure of racial identity in African American adolescents. *Cultural Diversity and Ethnic Minority Psychology, 14*, 297–306.

Sedikides, C. (2012). Self-protection. In M. R. Leary & J. P. Tangney (Eds.), *Handbook of self and identity* (2nd ed., pp. 327–353). New York, NY: Guilford Press.

Sellers, R. M., Rowley, S. J., Chavous, T. M., Shelton, J. N., & Smith, M. A. (1997). The Multidimensional Inventory of Black Identity: Investigation of reliability and construct validity. *Journal of Personality and Social Psychology, 73*, 805–815.

Simons, J. S., Carey, K. B., & Wills, T. A. (2009). Alcohol abuse and dependence symptoms: A multidimensional model of common and specific etiology. *Psychology of Addictive Behaviors, 23*, 415–427.

Soto, C., Unger, J. B., Ritt-Olson, A., Soto, D. W., Black, D. S., & Baezconde-Garbanati, L. (2011). Cultural values associated with substance use among Hispanic adolescents in southern California. *Substance Use and Misuse, 46*, 1223–1233.

Spears, G., Stein, J., & Koniak-Griffin, D. (2010). Latent growth trajectories of substance use among pregnant/parenting adolescents. *Psychology of Addictive Behaviors, 24*, 322–332.

Spein, A., Melhus, M., Kristiansen, R., & Kvernmo, S. (2011). The influence of religious factors on drinking behavior among young indigenous Sami and non-Sami peers in Northern Norway. *Journal of Religion and Health, 50*, 1024–1039.

Spein, A. R., Sexton, H., & Kvemmo, S. (2007). Substance use in young indigenous Sami: An ethnocultural and longitudinal perspective. *Substance Use and Misuse, 42*, 1379–1400.

Stacy, A. W., Ames, S. L., Wiers, R. W., & Krank, M. D. (2010). Associative memory in appetitive behavior: Framework and relevance to epidemiology and prevention. In L. Scheier (Ed.), *Handbook of drug use etiology* (pp. 165–182). Washington, DC: American Psychological Association.

Steinberg, L., Dornbusch, S. M., & Brown, B. B. (1992). Ethnic differences in adolescent achievement: An ecological perspective. *American Psychologist, 47*, 723–729.

Stock, M. L., Gibbons, F. X., Walsh, L. A., & Gerrard, M. (2011). Racial identification, racial discrimination, and substance use vulnerability among African American young adults. *Personality and Social Psychology Bulletin, 37*, 1349–1361.

Sussman, S., & Ames, S. L. (2008). *Drug abuse: Concepts, prevention, and cessation.* Cambridge, GB: Cambridge University Press.

Sussman, S., Dent, C. W., Mestel-Rauch, J., Johnson, C. A., Hansen, W. B., & Flay, B. R. (1988). Adolescent nonsmokers, triers, and regular smokers' estimates of cigarette smoking prevalence: When do overestimations occur and by whom? *Journal of Applied Social Psychology, 18*, 537–551.

Sussman, S., Dent, C. W., & McCullar, W. J. (2000). Group self-identification as a prospective predictor of drug use and violence in high-risk youth. *Psychology of Addictive Behaviors, 14*, 192–196.

Sussman, S., Dent, C. W., Stacy, A. W., Burciaga, C., Raynor, A., Turner, G. E., . . . Flay, B. R. (1990). Peer-group association and adolescent cigarette smoking. *Journal of Abnormal Psychology, 99*, 349–352.

Sussman, S., Pokhrel, P., Ashmore, R. D., & Brown, B. B. (2007). Adolescent peer group identification and characteristics: a review. *Addictive Behaviors, 32*, 1602–1627.

Sussman, S., Pokhrel, P., & Moran, M. B. (2011). Group identification. In R. J. R. Levesque (Ed.), *Encyclopedia of adolescence* (pp. 1237–1240). New York, NY: Springer.

Sussman, S., Skara, S., Rodriguez, Y., & Pokhrel, P. (2006). Non drug use- and drug use-specific spirituality as one-year predictors of drug use among high-risk youth. *Substance Use and Misuse, 41*, 1801–1816.

Sussman, S., Sun, P., Gunning, M., Moran, M. B., Pokhrel, P., Rohrbach, L. A., . . . Masagutov, R. (2010). Peer group self-identification in samples of Russian and U.S. adolescents. *Journal of Drug Education, 40*, 203–215.

Swaim, R. C., & Wayman, J. C. (2004). Multidimensional self-esteem and alcohol use among Mexican-American and white Non-Latino adolescents: Concurrent and prospective effects. *American Journal of Orthopsychiatry, 74*, 559–570.

Swann, W. B. (2004). The trouble with change: Self-verification and allegiance to the self. In R. Kowalski & M. Leary (Eds.), *The interface of social and clinical psychology: Key readings* (pp. 349–356). New York, NY: Psychology Press.

Swann, W. B., & Buhrmester, M. (2012). Self-verification: The search for coherence. In M. Leary & J. Tangney (Eds.), *Handbook of self and identity* (2nd ed., pp. 405–424). New York, NY: Guilford Press.

Timberlake, D., Rhee, S., Haberstick, B., Hopfer, C., Ehringer, M., Lessem, J., . . . Hewitt, J. (2006). Moderating effect of religiosity on the genetic and environmental determinants of smoking initiation. *Nicotine and Tobacco Research, 8*, 123–133.

Tomcikova, Z., Geckova, A. M., van Dijk, J. P., & Reijneveld, S. A. (2011). Characteristics of adolescent excessive drinkers. *Drug and Alcohol Review, 30*, 157–165.

Trzesniewski, K. H., Donnellan, M. B., Moffitt, T. E., Robins, R. W., Poulton, R., & Caspi, A. (2006). Low self-esteem during adolescence predicts poor health, criminal behavior, and limited economic prospects during adulthood. *Developmental Psychology, 42*, 381–390.

Twenge, J. M., & Crocker, J. (2002). Race and self-esteem: Meta-analyses comparing whites, blacks, Hispanics, Asians, and American Indians. *Psychological Bulletin, 128*, 371–408.

Underwood, L. G., & Teresi, J. A. (2002). The Spiritual Experience Scale: Reliability and preliminary construct validity. *Annals of Behavioral Medicine, 24*, 22–33.

Urberg, K. A., Degirmencioglu, S. M., & Pilgrim, C. (1997). Close friend and group influence on adolescent cigarette smoking. *Developmental Psychology, 33*, 834–844.

Urberg, K. A., Degirmencioglu, S. M., Tolson, J. M., & Halliday-Scher, K. (2000). Adolescent social crowds: Relation to friendships. *Journal of Adolescent Research, 15*, 427–445.

Urberg, K. A., Shyu, S. J., & Liang, J. (1990). Peer influence in adolescent cigarette smoking. *Addictive Behaviors, 15*, 247–255.

Valente, T. W., Unger, J. B., & Johnson, C. A. (2005). Do popular students smoke? The association between popularity and smoking among middle school students. *Journal of Adolescent Health, 37*, 323–329.

Vaughan, E., de Dios, M., Steinfeldt, J. & Kratz, J. (2011). Religiosity, attitudes, and alcohol use in a national sample of adolescents. *Psychology of Addictive Behaviors, 25*, 547–553.

Veselska, Z., Geckova, A. M., Orosova, O., Gajdosova, B., van Dijk, J. P., & Reijneveld, S. A. (2009). Self-esteem, resilience, and risky behavior among adolescents. *Addictive Behaviors, 34*, 287–291.

Walker, C., Ainette, M. G., Wills, T. A., & Mendoza, D. (2007). Religiosity and substance use: Test of a mediation model in adolescence. *Psychology of Addictive Behaviors, 21*, 84–96.

Wallace, J. M., & Williams, D. R. (1997). Religion and adolescent health-compromising behavior. In J. Schulenberg, J. Maggs, & K. Hurrelmann (Eds.), *Health risks and developmental transitions during adolescence* (pp. 444–468). New York, NY: Cambridge University Press.

Wallace, S. A., & Fisher, C. B. (2007). Substance use attitudes among black adolescents: The role of peer and cultural factors. *Journal of Youth and Adolescence, 36*, 441–451.

Waterman, A. S. (1999). Identity, the identity statuses, and identity status development: A contemporary perspective. *Developmental Review, 19*, 591–621.

Weinraub, M., Clemens, L. P., Sockloff, A., Ethridge, T., Gracely, E., & Myers, B. (1984). The development of sex role stereotypes in the third year. *Child Development, 55*, 1493–1503.

Wheeler, S. B. (2010). Effects of self-esteem and academic performance on early sexual intercourse and illegal substance use. *Journal of Adolescent Health, 47*, 582–590.

Wild, L. G., Fisher, A. J., Bhana, A., & Lombard, C. (2004). Associations of risk behavior and self-esteem in six domains. *Journal of Child Psychology and Psychiatry, 45*, 1454–1467.

Williams, D. R., Spencer, M. S., & Jackson, J. S. (1999). Race, stress, and physical health. In R. J. Contrada & R. D. Ashmore (Eds.), *Self, social identity, and physical health* (Vol. 2, pp. 71–100). New York, NY: Oxford University Press.

Wills, T. A. (1994). Self-esteem and perceived control in adolescent substance use: Comparative tests. *Psychology of Addictive Behaviors, 8*, 223–234.

Wills, T. A., & Ainette, M. G. (2011). Social networks and social support. In A. Baum, T. Revenson, & J. Singer (Eds.), *Handbook of health psychology* (2nd ed., pp. 461–489). New York, NY: Psychology Press.

Wills, T. A., & Cleary, S. D. (1999). Peer and adolescent substance use among 6th-9th graders: Influence versus selection mechanisms. *Health Psychology, 18*, 453–463.

Wills, T. A., Cleary, S. D., Filer, M., Shinar, O., Mariani, J., & Spera, K. (2001). Temperament related to early-onset substance use. *Prevention Science, 2*, 145–163.

Wills, T. A., Murry, V. M., Brody, G. H., Gibbons, F. X., Gerrard, M., Walker, C., & Ainette, M. G. (2007). Ethnic pride and self-control related to protective and risk factors in the Strong African American Families Program. *Health Psychology, 26*, 50–59.

Wills, T. A., Pokhrel, P., Morehouse, E., & Fenster, B. (2011). Behavioral and emotional regulation and adolescent substance use problems: A test of moderation effects in a dual-process model. *Psychology of Addictive Behaviors, 25*, 279–292.

Wills, T. A., Resko, J., Ainette, M., & Mendoza, D. (2004). The role of parent and peer support in adolescent substance use. *Psychology of Addictive Behaviors, 18*, 122–134.

Wills, T. A., Sandy, J. M., & Yaeger, A. (2000). Temperament and adolescent substance use: An epigenetic approach to risk and protection. *Journal of Personality, 68*, 1127–1152.

Wills, T. A., Sargent, J. D., Stoolmiller, M., Gibbons, F. X., & Gerrard, M. (2008). Movie smoking exposure and smoking onset. *Psychology of Addictive Behaviors, 22*, 269–277.

Wills, T. A., Simons, J. S., Sussman, S., & Knight, R. A. (2016). Emotional self-control and dysregulation: A dual-process analysis of pathways to externalizing and internalizing symptomatology and positive well-being in younger adolescents. *Drug and Alcohol Dependence.*

Wills, T. A., Yaeger, A. M., & Sandy, J. M. (2003). Buffering effect of religiosity for adolescent substance use. *Psychology of Addictive Behaviors, 17,* 24–31.

Windle, M., Mun, E. Y., & Windle, R. C. (2005). Adolescent to young adulthood heavy drinking trajectories and their prospective predictors. *Journal of Studies on Alcohol, 66,* 313–322.

Yip, T., & Fuligni, A. J. (2002). Daily variation in ethnic identity and psychological well-being among American adolescents of Chinese descent. *Child Development, 77,* 1557–1572.

Zamboanga, B. L., Schwartz, S. J., Jarvis, L. H., & van Tyne, K. (2009). Acculturation and substance use among Hispanic early adolescents: Investigating the mediating roles of acculturative stress and self-esteem. *Journal of Primary Prevention, 30,* 315–333.

Adolescent Resilience: Promoting More Positive Outcomes Among Youth at Risk of Using and Abusing Substances

Noelle Hurd *and* Marc Zimmerman

Abstract

Resilience refers to positive adjustment among youth who have been exposed to one or more risk factor(s). In this chapter, we review articles published within the past two decades that have included a focus on resilience processes among adolescents at risk of using substances. The review is organized by the level of promotive factor investigated (individual, family, and community), followed by a review of studies that have focused on exposure to cumulative risk and promotive factors. Prior to reviewing these studies, we provide a brief overview of resilience theory, including key terms and models of resilience. The chapter concludes by addressing the limitations of the research on resilience and adolescent substance use and makes recommendations for future research.

Key Words: resilience, substance use, adolescents, risk factors, promotive factors

Until the last two decades, researchers interested in the study of adolescent substance use focused most of their efforts on identifying factors that could be implicated in the etiology of drug use and abuse. While these efforts improved our understanding of risk factors for adolescent substance use and informed us of which risk factors to target in substance use interventions, these investigations taught us little about the factors that enable youth to avoid using and abusing substances. Furthermore, although study results have pointed to specific factors that may increase the likelihood of substance use, they have not explained why some youth who face these risks do not use substances. Growing interest in researching the factors that promote more positive outcomes among at-risk youth was spurred by the resilience movement that was rapidly gaining popularity among researchers interested in taking a strengths-based approach to the prevention of problem behaviors. Thus, over the past 20 years, a number of researchers have employed a resilience framework to the study of adolescent substance use

and abuse. In this chapter, our review of the literature only includes studies conducted within the past two centuries where a resilience model was used to identify factors that have been found to counteract or protect against risk factors of substance use. Prior to reviewing these studies, we provide a brief overview of resilience theory, including key terms and models of resilience. We conclude this chapter by addressing the limitations of the research on resilience and adolescent substance use and make recommendations for future research.

Resilience Theory

Resilience theory emerged as researchers became increasingly interested in understanding why some youth who experience hardship or trauma are able to overcome this adversity and avoid negative outcomes associated with risk (Fergus & Zimmerman, 2005; Luthar & Cicchetti, 2000; Zimmerman & Arunkumar, 1994). Resilience theory differs from deficit-focused theories such as problem behavior theory (Jessor & Jessor, 1977) in that its purpose is to explain the absence of negative developmental outcomes and/or the presence of positive outcomes in the face of risk, whereas the primary intent of problem behavior theory is to understand factors that contribute to the presence of negative adolescent outcomes. Thus, resilience theory is oriented toward the positive aspects of adolescents' lives and adjustment as opposed to risk and negative outcomes. Yet resilience theory builds on problem behavior theory in that it focuses on factors in adolescents' lives that promote more positive outcomes among adolescents who have been exposed to adversity (Fergus & Zimmerman, 2005).

Resilience theory also relates to positive youth development theory (Damon, 2004) in that both of these approaches place emphasis on youth's strengths and offer alternative models for youth intervention. The positive youth development approach promotes youth engagement in prosocial activities (e.g., extracurricular activities), which provide a context for healthy development for all youth (Damon, 2004). This idea of creating contexts where youth can flourish relates to efforts to develop and enhance adolescents' preexisting strengths to promote healthier adolescent outcomes underscored by resilience theory. According to both approaches, interventions that build on youth's strengths (as opposed to solely focusing on remediating their weaknesses) hold promise for helping youth to realize their full potential and develop into capable and contributing members of society. Resilience theory is a useful approach for estimating outcomes among at-risk populations because it allows researchers to focus on factors that may predict positive development within these populations. Thus, a resilience approach is unique because it is applicable to youth facing adversity, yet it focuses on strengths within the youth and their environment.

Resilience Terms

It is necessary to underscore that resilience is a process as opposed to a trait or attribute of an adolescent (Fergus & Zimmerman, 2005; Luthar & Cicchetti, 2000). *Resilience* refers to positive adjustment among youth who have been exposed to one or more risk factor(s) (Fergus & Zimmerman, 2005). *Risk factors* increase the likelihood of developing negative outcomes. A risk factor may be a traumatic event (e.g., crime victimization, a car accident) or a circumstance (e.g., being raised by a mentally ill parent, living in substandard housing). Thus, exposure could be limited to one occasion or could involve chronic exposure. Risk factors can be experienced at multiple levels, including individual, family, school, community, or societal. *Positive adaptation* has typically been used to indicate the absence of negative outcomes or an achieved competence in a certain domain (e.g., developmental or social). What constitutes positive adaptation may vary depending on the nature of the risk factor(s) to which the adolescent was exposed (Luthar & Cicchetti, 2000). *Vulnerability* is a term commonly used in resilience research to refer to an adolescent's susceptibility to negative developmental outcomes based on exposure to risk. Thus, vulnerability indicates a heightened probability of maladaptive development among youth exposed to a risk situation (Zimmerman & Arunkumar, 1994). *Promotive factors*, on the other hand, contribute positively to youth outcomes and/or buffer youth from negative consequences associated with risk (Fergus & Zimmerman, 2005; Sandler, Wolchik, Davis, Haine, & Ayers, 2003). Promotive factors may be *assets*, positive factors within individual youth that help them overcome adversity (e.g., self-efficacy), or *resources*, external factors that promote more positive outcomes among youth exposed to risk (e.g., adult mentors).

Resilience Models

A number of models have been proposed for the study of resilience processes. The models that have received the most empirical study include the compensatory model, the protective model, and to a lesser degree the challenge model (Garmezy, Masten, & Tellegen, 1984; Rutter, 1985; Zimmerman & Arunkumar, 1994). In the *compensatory model*, a risk factor and a promotive factor (in this model labeled a compensatory factor) both contribute to an outcome in additive but opposite ways. In other words, the compensatory model includes direct effects of the risk factor and the compensatory factor on the outcome of interest. Thus, the compensatory factor works to neutralize exposure to risk or counteract the negative effects of the risk factor on the outcome of interest (Garmezy et al., 1984; Masten et al., 1988). Exposure to peers who use substances, for example, may be associated with higher levels of adolescent substance use; however, living in a neighborhood with norms against substance use may counter these negative peer influences, leading to lower levels of adolescent substance use. Researchers have tested compensatory models using hierarchical multiple-regression analyses (Hurd, Zimmerman, & Xue, 2009; Zimmerman, Bingenheimer, & Notaro, 2002) as well as structural equation modeling

(SEM; Hurd, Zimmerman, & Reischl, 2011). Both approaches allow the investigator to test for main effects of the compensatory factor on the outcome of interest after accounting for the direct effects of the risk factor.

The *protective model* differs from the compensatory model in that it involves an interaction between the risk and promotive factor (in this model labeled a protective factor). Thus, rather than exploring main effects of a risk and promotive factor on a particular outcome, the protective model includes a protective factor that moderates the negative influence of the risk factor to reduce the likelihood of a negative outcome (Rutter, 1985). While protective factors may also exert a main effect on the dependent variable, their primary function is to buffer an individual from the negative effects of risk exposure (i.e., moderate the relationship between a risk factor and an outcome). Researchers have differentiated between two different types of protective models: risk-protective and protective-protective (Brook, Whiteman, Gordon, & Cohen, 1986; Luthar, Cicchetti, & Becker, 2000). The *risk-protective model* includes a protective factor that functions to diminish or completely remove the relationship between a risk factor and a negative outcome. An example would be a model where lower school engagement related to higher levels of adolescent substance use; however, this relationship was diminished or nonexistent among youth who reported receiving higher levels of parental monitoring. The *protective-protective model* includes a protective factor that enhances the positive effects of another promotive factor on adolescent outcomes (Brook et al., 1986). Yet, because resilience models require overcoming adversity, the protective-protective model is only a true resilience model when it is applied to a population that is considered to be at elevated risk for developing a particular negative outcome. Thus, we might look at such models in a sample of youth living in poverty or who have been incarcerated. Otherwise, the protective-protective model would just be a study of positive youth development. Therefore, an example of this model would be a negative relationship between involvement in prosocial activities and substance use among adolescents living in impoverished neighborhoods that is stronger for youth who have adult mentors in their communities. As with the compensatory model, hierarchical multiple regression and SEM are appropriate statistical methods for testing the protective model of resilience. In hierarchical multiple regression, the researcher must

create an interaction term (risk × protective factor) to test the potential protective effects of a variable. In SEM, the researcher conducts a multigroup analysis to test whether or not the relationship between a risk factor (or a promotive factor) and outcome differs depending on the level of protective factor (i.e., low vs. high). Hierarchical linear modeling (HLM) may also be used to investigate interactions between risk and protective factors across multiple levels of analyses.

The *challenge model* suggests a curvilinear relationship between a risk factor and an outcome (Garmezy et al., 1984). This model of resilience has received comparatively less attention in resilience research; however, it may most accurately fit the nature of the relationship between certain risk factors and outcomes. According to this model, exposure to low or high levels of a risk factor contributes to negative outcomes; however, exposure to moderate levels of risk provides the adolescent with a challenge that can be overcome (Luthar & Zelazo, 2003). Where levels of risk that are too low do not allow for a challenge and levels of risk that are too high create a sense of helplessness, moderate levels of risk allow adolescents the opportunity to successfully meet this challenge. By overcoming this challenge, adolescents' competence can be strengthened, leaving them better prepared to face future obstacles (Zimmerman & Arunkumar, 1994). This process has been referred to as *steeling* or *inoculation* (Rutter, 1987). Testing this model would require longitudinal data involving multiple exposures to risk over time to determine if adolescents who experience moderate levels of risk are becoming more successful in overcoming future risk exposures. Challenge models of resilience can be tested using HLM or SEM.

Adolescent Substance Use

Although adolescents' experimentation with alcohol, cigarettes, and marijuana is considered by some to be a normative part of adolescent development (Clark & Winters, 2002), distinguishing substance abuse and dependence from nonproblematic use among adolescents has proven difficult (Baer, MacLean, & Marlatt, 1998). Statistics from Monitoring the Future, a nationally representative longitudinal study of adolescent substance use (Johnston, O'Malley, Bachman, & Schulenberg, 2010), reflect fairly widespread use of substances during adolescence. Specifically, results of this study indicate that almost half (45%) of all adolescents have tried cigarettes by 12th grade and 20% of 12th graders are current smokers. Furthermore, almost three fourths (72%) of adolescents have consumed alcohol by the end of high school, and over half (55%) of 12th graders report having been drunk at least once in their life. Forty-seven percent of 12th graders reported having tried an illicit substance at least once, and 25% reported having tried an illicit substance other than marijuana. Although distinguishing problematic levels of use has been a challenge, researchers have successfully identified a host of negative outcomes associated with adolescents' substance use. These negative outcomes include neglecting responsibilities, attenuated motivation, poor performance at school or work, psychological or physical impairment, driving under the influence, interpersonal problems, unprotected or coercive sexual activity, suicidal behavior, and victimization (Baer et al. 1998; Hawkins, Catalano, & Miller, 1992; O'Malley, Johnston, & Bachman, 1998; Windle, 1994; Windle, Miller-Tutzauer, & Domenico, 1992). Cigarettes, alcohol, and marijuana are the most prevalent drugs used among adolescents (Johnston et al., 2010). Thus, much of adolescent substance use research conducted to date has focused on one or all of these substances. Beyond the frequency with which these substances are used by adolescents, researchers have noted the potential for the use of these substances to lead to other illegal drug use (i.e., gateway theory; Kandel, Yamaguchi, & Chen, 1992). Given the negative outcomes associated with adolescent substance use, efforts to better understand the etiology and methods of prevention of adolescent substance use and abuse are needed.

Resilience and Adolescent Substance Use

Initially, much of the research on adolescent substance use focused on identifying risk factors that may contribute to the initiation of substance use or the maintenance of use over time (Jessor & Jessor, 1977). More recently, however, researchers have included a focus on promotive factors that mitigate or counteract the effects of risk exposure on adolescent substance use (Newcomb & Felix-Ortiz, 1992). The emergence of a prevention science paradigm has upheld the importance of further exploration and identification of both risk and promotive factors as they can inform prevention interventions (Arthur, Hawkins, Pollard, Catalano, & Baglioni, 2002). Despite the increasing amount of research being conducted on resilience and adolescent substance use, primary causal or prevention factors have not

emerged and some studies have yielded discrepant findings (Newcomb, 1995). Rather than taking these findings as an indication of elusive risk and promotive factors, researchers have suggested that these results reflect multiple pathways to both substance use and prevention. Thus, some researchers have postulated that an investigation of cumulative risk and promotive factors may be a more appropriate approach to understanding the etiology and prevention of adolescent substance use and abuse (Ostaszewski & Zimmerman, 2006; Sameroff, Bartko, Baldwin, Baldwin, & Seifer, 1998). This approach operates under the assumption that risk and promotive factors are varied and complex, and it also allows for the integration of diverse theories and findings (Sullivan & Farrell, 1999).

Much of the research on resilience and adolescent substance use has been organized by the triarchic framework of resilience (Seifer, Sameroff, Baldwin, & Baldwin, 1992; Wyman, Cowen, Work, & Parker, 1991). According to this framework, risk and promotive factors occur at three broad levels: the individual, family, and community levels (Luthar et al., 2000). Notably, researchers have varied in how they have measured these variables and how they have defined risk and promotive factors. In some cases, higher levels of a variable (e.g., IQ) have been defined as a promotive factor, whereas lower levels of the same variable have been considered a risk factor (Adlaf & Smart, 1985; Newcomb & Felix-Ortiz, 1992). Thus, risk and promotive factors are different ends of the same continuum. Although this may make sense for some variables, lower levels of promotive factors do not automatically constitute risk nor do lower levels of risk equate to protection. For example, though more frequent church attendance may be a promotive factor, less frequent church attendance may not be a risk factor. Moreover, higher levels of parental substance use might be a risk factor, but lower levels of parental substance use are not necessarily promotive. Therefore, researchers have created resilience models where risk and promotive factors are separate variables and higher levels of a risk variable are hypothesized to contribute to higher levels of substance use while higher levels of a promotive factor are expected to contribute to lower levels of substance use or exert a stronger moderation effect on the relationship between a specific risk factor and substance use/abuse (Bryant & Zimmerman, 2002; Newcomb & Felix-Ortiz, 1992).

Considering how risk and promotive factors interact as a process over time is essential to the study of adolescent resilience (Rutter, 1985). In addition, considering how these factors interact with adolescent developmental processes is essential. This is particularly relevant when considering the role of substance use in adolescent development and changing biological, emotional, social, and environmental factors that may moderate the influences of risk or promotive factors on adolescents' substance use. Including a theoretical focus on interactions between adolescents and their ecological context is consistent with both Bronfenbrenner's (1977) ecological theory and Sameroff and Chandler's (1975) transactional model. These paradigms underscore the need to understand how context shapes adolescent development, risk, and resilience. Furthermore, they account for the interplay between individuals and their environment, specifically focusing on the adaptive nature of the relationship between the individual and her/his context (Sameroff & Mackenzie, 2003). Building on these two perspectives, Cicchetti and Lynch (1993) proposed an integrative ecological-transactional model of development. This model includes layers of context that are nested within each other (each with varying levels of proximity to the individual). In addition, this model addresses the tendency of these levels to transact with each other over time as they shape adolescents' development and adaption. Models that account for the complex interactions between developing adolescents and their contexts facilitate the study of resilience among adolescents at-risk for substance use and abuse. In the following sections, we will review the recent literature on resilience and adolescent substance use. This review is organized by promotive factors at multiple levels, including those that occur at the individual, family, and community levels.

Individual-Level Promotive Factors

A number of intrapersonal and interpersonal promotive factors have been identified by researchers interested in identifying factors that counter or buffer the negative effects of risk exposure on adolescent substance use. Examples of promotive factors at the individual level include religiosity, academic achievement, temperament characteristics, positive affect, behavioral control, personal competence, and racial identity.

Regarding religiosity, interest in exploring this as a promotive factor among adolescents at risk for substance use emerged after epidemiologic studies indicated protective effects of religiosity on health status (Levin, 1996) and research findings demonstrated a relationship between religious involvement and lower rates of substance use among adolescents (Bahr, Maughan, Marcos, & Li, 1998; Wallace & Williams, 1997). To examine the potential of religiosity to serve as a protective factor among at-risk youth, Wills, Yaeger, and Sandy (2003) conducted cross-sectional and longitudinal analyses with a sample of 1,182 ethnically diverse, urban and suburban middle schoolers (47% female) whom they followed from 7th through 10th grade. They defined religiosity as adolescents' perceived importance of religion and used Jessor's Value on Religion Scale (Jessor & Jessor, 1977) to assess this construct. They found that higher levels of religiosity buffered youth from the adverse effects of negative life events on cigarette, alcohol, and marijuana use. These buffering effects held for the initial level of substance use and for growth in use of these substances over time. Steinman and Zimmerman (2004) also found promotive effects of religiosity against age-related increases in substance use among 705 African American urban high school students. Students who endorsed more frequent attendance of church or other religious services during the ninth grade demonstrated lower increases in substance use throughout high school (less frequent marijuana use during the past month among males and less frequent cigarette use during the past month among females) in comparison to their less religious peers.

Academic attitudes and achievement have also been studied using a resilience framework. Theories such as problem behavior theory (Jessor & Jessor, 1977) and the social development model (Hawkins & Weis, 1985) implicate adolescents' academic performance with substance use. Yet researchers have primarily focused on the role of school failure in substance use (Eccles, Lord, Roeser, Barber, & Jozefowicz, 1997; Schulenberg, Bachman, O'Malley, & Johnston, 1994), as opposed to investigating the potential of academic success to prevent substance use among at-risk youth. Bryant et al. (2003) used longitudinal nationally representative panel data (Monitoring the Future study) to investigate the relationships between risk, academic attitudes and achievement, and adolescents' substance use over time. Results of this study indicated that academic achievement (operationalized as adolescents' grade point averages [GPAs]) may have protected against age-related increases in substance use over time such that adolescents with higher grades in early adolescence were less likely to demonstrate an increase in cigarette or marijuana use over time. Additionally, among youth who were at increased risk of substance use due to lower academic achievement, feeling bonded to their school and having college plans counteracted the negative effects of academic underachievement on concurrent alcohol use.

Scal, Ireland, and Borowsky (2003) found that academic achievement (i.e., self-reported GPA) was protective against transitioning to smoking among 7th- through 12th-grade youth from the National Study of Adolescent Health (Add Health), who faced a number of risk factors (e.g., using alcohol, marijuana, and other illicit substances; having friends who smoke). Wright and Fitzpatrick (2004) suggest that academic achievement may be an especially potent protective factor among adolescents of color as they may see doing well in school as a way to increase their opportunities for future academic and occupational success and thus be less likely to engage in potentially destructive behaviors (e.g., substance use) that could interfere with these future opportunities. In their study of 1,494 African American adolescents in grades 5 through 12, Wright and Fitzpatrick (2004) found that among youth who were at increased risk of substance use due to experiences with domestic violence, gang affiliation, or peers who held tolerant attitudes toward substance use, those with higher reported GPAs reported lower incidences of recent alcohol, cigarette, and marijuana use. In a study with 785 urban, predominantly African American, older adolescents, Bryant and Zimmerman (2002) found that high grades alone did not inoculate against substance use risks. Rather, they found that the combination of high grades and high achievement-related motivational beliefs and values protected 10th-grade adolescents from age-related increases in cigarette use throughout high school. These findings suggest that, at least for some youth, academic achievement may need to be coupled with high expectations and values in order to serve a protective function against substance use risks. Related to academic achievement, school bonding has also demonstrated potential promotive effects among adolescents experiencing increased risk of substance use. Dickens, Dieterich, Henry, and Beauvais (2012) investigated the potential of school bonding to counter the negative influence of peer alcohol use on frequency and amount of alcohol use among a sample of 2,582 American Indian adolescents. Their findings were consistent with the compensatory model in that higher levels of school bonding

countered the negative influence of peer alcohol use on adolescents' lifetime alcohol use and level of use among alcohol users.

Other intrapersonal factors that have been found to promote more positive outcomes among youth at risk of using substances include temperament and affect. Researchers have conjectured that temperament characteristics can influence how susceptible youth are to the effects of certain experiences (Wachs, 1992). In addition, Rutter et al. (1997) have underscored the role of transactions between a child's temperament and her/his family environment in the development of problem behavior among youth. Wills, Sandy, Yaeger, and Shinar (2001) investigated the potential of several temperament dimensions to moderate the association between family and peer risk factors and adolescents' substance use over time among a sample of 1,810 ethnically diverse middle-schoolers. They found that the relationship between parental risk factors (i.e., parent–child conflict and parental substance use) and peer risk factors (i.e., peer substance use) and growth in adolescents' substance use over time were weaker among adolescents with higher task attentional orientation (e.g., being able to focus on tasks, persisting on a task until finished) and positive emotionality (e.g., generally being in a cheerful mood, smiling frequently). In another study using the same longitudinal data, Wills, Sandy, Shinar, and Yaeger (1999) focused specifically on the relationships between adolescents' positive and negative affect and their substance use. They found that positive affect (e.g., feeling happy, interested, relaxed) moderated the relationship between negative affect (e.g., feeling tense, sad, and nervous) and substance use (i.e., frequency of tobacco, alcohol, and marijuana use) among adolescents over the transition from middle to high school. They suggest that activities geared at enhancing positive mood among adolescents with high emotional distress may help prevent substance use in this group.

Other researchers have suggested that regulatory processes may prevent problem behavior among youth who are prone to experiencing negative emotions (Eisenberg et al., 1997). In an effort to test this hypothesis in a sample of 514 White children of alcoholics and matched controls (Michigan Longitudinal Study), Wong et al. (2006) examined whether rates of increase in behavioral control (defined as the tendency to express or contain one's impulses and behaviors and assessed in this study using the California Child Q-Sort) over time influenced the association between negative emotionality and participants' substance use. They found that among youth who were at increased risk of substance use due to high negative emotionality, those with a faster rate of increase in behavioral control reported fewer alcohol-related problems (e.g., getting in trouble with teachers or principal because of drinking, losing friends because of drinking).

Others have posited that succeeding at developmental tasks throughout adolescence and developing a sense of competence (i.e., skills and abilities that enable youth to successfully meet the challenges of adolescence) may lead to more effective decision making and task persistence and, thus, be protective against the risk factors of substance use (Griffin, Botvin, Scheier, Epstein, & Doyle, 2002). Furthermore, highly competent youth may experience high levels of personal achievement and as a result feel less enticed to use substances or see substance use as more problematic in comparison to their less competent peers. Griffin et al. (2001, 2002) explored the role of personal competence in adolescent substance use among their samples of 849 suburban predominantly White seventh graders and 1,184 urban, ethnically diverse adolescents. They found that through increasing adolescents' psychological well-being, competence skills (defined in this study as the skills related to cognitive and behavioral self-regulation) countered the negative effects of previous substance use (seventh grade) on current substance use (ninth grade). In their study, substance use was a composite variable composed of frequency and quantity of tobacco, alcohol, and marijuana use. Scheier, Botvin, and Miller (1999) also found promotive effects of competence (defined in their study as a composite of grades, decision-making skills, and self-efficacy for academic tasks) in their sample of 1,419 urban, ethnic minority early adolescents such that higher levels of individual competence countered the negative influences of neighborhood stress on adolescents' alcohol use. The findings of these studies indicate that promoting resistance, behavioral-management, decision-making, and social skills, as well as academic self-efficacy and achievement, may be effective strategies for preventing adolescents' substance use.

Among African American youth, racial identity may counter substance use risk factors. Given lower documented rates of substance use among African American adolescents in comparison to their White peers (Johnston et al., 2010), some researchers have cited cultural factors as protective against risks of substance use (Brook, Balka, Brook, Win, & Gursen, 1998; Scheier, Botvin, Diaz, & Ifill-Williams, 1998).

These assertions are reflected in findings that ethnic minority youth with higher levels of ethnic identity and ethnic pride demonstrate lower levels of substance use than their ethnic minority counterparts with lower levels of ethnic identity and pride and their White peers (Brook et al., 1998; Marsiglia, Kulis, & Hecht, 2001). Caldwell, Sellers, Bernat, and Zimmerman (2004) explored whether two dimensions of racial identity (i.e., racial centrality and private regard) may contribute to lower levels of alcohol use among their sample of 488 academically at-risk African American 12th graders. Although lower levels of academic achievement may increase adolescents' risk of using substances, Caldwell et al. (2004) hypothesized that higher levels of racial centrality (defined as the importance of race to one's identity) and private regard (defined as the extent to which one feels positively about one's race) would offset these risks. They found that a higher level of regard for one's racial group (private regard) was associated with less alcohol use. Furthermore, they found that the magnitude of the effect of private regard on alcohol use was greater among adolescents who also endorsed higher levels of racial centrality (i.e., felt that race was a central part of their identity). Due to experiences with racism and other race-related stressors, African American adolescents may face a number of additional risk factors that may lead them to use substances as a way to cope. These findings suggest that holding race as central to their identity and feeling positively about their racial group may counteract the substance use risks African American adolescents face. Thus, including materials that teach youth about the significance of their race and foster a sense of racial/ethnic pride in substance use prevention interventions may yield added benefits for African American and potentially other ethnic minority adolescents. Relatedly, Unger et al. (2014) explored how orientation toward Hispanic culture may counter the negative influence of perceived discrimination on tobacco, alcohol, and marijuana use over time among a sample of 2,722 Hispanic (predominantly Mexican-origin) high-school students. They found that participants who reported having experienced greater discrimination during the ninth grade also reported greater substance use during the ninth grade; however, they found that holding greater orientation toward Hispanic culture predicted less escalation in substance use over time. These findings underscore the potential of heritage-culture retention efforts to ward off growth in substance use over time among Hispanic youth. These efforts may be especially warranted in light of the noxious effects of discrimination on polysubstance use among Hispanic and other racial/ethnic minority adolescents.

These studies have identified a variety of factors at the individual level that may contribute to resilience among adolescents at risk of using substances. Strengths of these studies include the use of both cross-sectional and longitudinal research designs, the inclusion of diverse samples of adolescents (as well as nationally representative samples), and researchers' attention to the ways in which these findings could inform substance use prevention efforts with at-risk adolescents. Although these studies included complex analyses of the role of individual-level promotive factors in countering or protecting against substance use risk factors at multiple levels (e.g., individual, peer, parent, neighborhood), researchers did not explore how individual-level promotive factors may have been shaped by other factors at various levels of adolescents' social ecologies. Although interventions at the individual level geared at teaching adolescents additional skills or modifying their behavior may be somewhat effective in reducing or preventing adolescents' substance use, interventions that address social and structural factors that foster more positive individual outcomes (e.g., academic achievement, behavioral management) may be more likely to yield sustainable reductions in adolescents' substance use.

Familial/Parental Promotive Factors

The role of family factors, particularly parental influences, in adolescents' substance-using behaviors has been studied extensively. Yet a disproportionate majority of this work has focused on identifying familial risk factors for adolescent substance use (e.g., familial substance use, family conflict, ineffective parenting; Abdelrahman, Rodriguez, Ryan, French, & Weinbaum, 1999; Doherty & Allen, 1994; Jackson & Henriksen, 1997), as opposed to promotive factors that may foster healthier adolescent outcomes. In this section, we will review familial promotive factors pertaining to adolescent substance use, including parental attachment, involvement, relations, support and monitoring, effective parenting, and family functioning.

In regard to parental attachment, family interaction theory (Brook, Brook, Gordon, Whiteman, & Cohen, 1990) indicates that a strong attachment between a parent and her/his child can help prevent substance use among at-risk youth. One reason for this may be that children who are more attached to their parents may be more influenced by their parents' objections to substance use. Additionally, youth with strong attachments to their parents may be less likely to affiliate with deviant peer groups (Brody & Forehand, 1993; Mason, Cauce, Gonzales, & Hiraga, 1994). Hahm, Lahiff, and Guterman (2003) explored the potential protective nature of parental attachment among a sample of 714 Asian American middle and high school students (taken from the Add Health data set) who were at increased risk of substance use due to higher levels of acculturation and a resulting acculturation gap between them and their parents. Although they found that the most acculturated group in their sample (US-born adolescents who reported using English at home) had a higher risk of using alcohol over time than the least acculturated group (foreign-born adolescents who did not use English at home), adolescents' reports of parental attachment (i.e., parents are warm and loving, feel close to parents, communicate well, feel parents' care, satisfied with relationship with parents) moderated their alcohol use. Thus, higher levels of parental attachment protected Asian American adolescents against the risks of high levels of acculturation on substance use such that acculturation was only a risk factor for adolescents' substance use when accompanied by low levels of parental attachment.

In another longitudinal study, 810 predominantly White second and third graders were followed over time to see if family processes during early elementary school predicted smoking initiation in middle school (Fleming, Kim, Harachi, & Catalano, 2002). Fleming et al. (2002) found that higher levels of parental attachment and more frequent parental contact with the child's school both countered the negative effects of antisocial behavior, childhood depression, and exposure to parental smoking on smoking initiation during middle school. This finding suggests that even when parents are modeling substance use, having a close family bond and supporting children in areas outside of the home may allow parents to discourage their children from smoking in the future. Continued investigation into the mediating pathways between parental attachment and reduced substance use among adolescents may promote a better understanding of how parental attachment may predict lower levels of substance use among adolescents whose parents model substance use.

Researchers have also documented the potential of higher quality youth–parent relations (similar to parental attachment) to buffer against substance use risks. Kim, Zane, and Hong (2002), for example, found that higher quality youth–parent relations contributed to lower levels of adolescent substance use (frequency of alcohol and tobacco use within past 30 days) by decreasing participants' vulnerability to negative peer pressure (i.e., likelihood they would be influenced by their peers to engage in substance use or other risk behaviors) among their sample of 164 Asian American early adolescents. Kim et al. (2002) postulate that family norms and sanctions may have a powerful influence on Asian Americans' susceptibility to peer influence due to collectivist cultural values that prioritize the goals of the collective (e.g., the family) over personal goals.

In another study on negative peer influences and adolescent substance use, Farrell and White (1998) tested whether the parent–child relationship could be protective against peer pressure for drug use among their sample of 630 predominantly African American, urban 10th graders. They found that family structure (living in a home with a father or step-father) and low levels of distress in their relationships with their mothers (based on being able to use appropriate problem-solving skills to resolve conflict, positive communication skills, and warm affect) diminished the relationship between peer pressure to use drugs and adolescents' frequency of alcohol, cigarette, and marijuana use in the past 30 days. It is unclear whether the finding of a protective effect of father presence in the home was due to something about the relationship with the father or additional resources that having a father in the home provided. It is possible, for example, that having a father in the home provided more support to mothers and thus facilitated more positive mother–child relationships. It is worth noting that Zimmerman, Salem, and Maton (1995) did not find differences in past 6-month frequency of alcohol, cigarette, or marijuana use between urban, African American, male adolescents whose fathers resided with them and their counterparts living in single-mother households. They did find that emotional support from fathers was associated with less marijuana use, suggesting that paternal support is more predictive of adolescents' substance use than family structure. Likewise, Salem, Zimmerman, and Notaro (1998) did not find differences in substance use outcomes (frequency of alcohol, cigarette, and marijuana use) among urban, African American adolescents (*n* = 679; 50% female) living with or without their fathers, but they did find that time spent with fathers and the significance of their father in their lives were associated with cigarette and marijuana use among males and alcohol and

cigarette use among females. Overall, the findings of these studies suggest that interventions aimed at reducing parent–adolescent conflicts and fostering more positive parent–child relationships may help prevent and reduce adolescent substance use.

Familial support has also been identified as both a mediating and moderating variable in models of adolescent substance use. Familial support may counteract or buffer against substance use risks by contributing to adolescents' decision-making skills, promoting improved behavioral coping and academic competence, and encouraging less tolerance of deviance (Wills & Cleary, 1996). Duncan, Duncan, and Strycker (2000) found compensatory effects of familial support (i.e., having parents they can talk to about anything, doing things with family members, parents who comfort them when they are unhappy, celebrate their accomplishments, and with whom they get along well) and time spent with family among 1,044 predominantly White adolescents from the National Youth Survey. They found that time spent with family and family support countered the negative influences of deviant peers on adolescents' problem behavior (including alcohol and marijuana use) over time (data were collected annually over 4 years). Newcomb, Heinz, and Mustanski (2012) investigated the potential promotive effects of family support in reducing alcohol consumption among 246 lesbian, gay, bisexual, and transgender (LGBT) youth (a demographic group that has demonstrated increased risk for alcohol misuse) followed for 2.5 years. Family support was measured using the family support subscale of the *Multidimensional Scale of Perceived Social Support* (Zimet, Powell, Farley, Werkman, & Berkoff, 1990). Though they found variation in risk factors for alcohol use as a function of gender and race/ethnicity, they found that family support was negatively associated with alcohol use for all LGBT adolescents across all study waves.

In light of lower rates of substance use among African American adolescents in comparison to their White peers, some researchers suggest that family processes (e.g., familial support) that occur within the African American family system may be instrumental in explaining these lower rates (Johnson & Johnson, 1999). Caldwell et al. (2004) explored whether more parental support may contribute to less alcohol use in a sample of 488 academically at-risk African American older adolescents. They found that paternal support, but not maternal support, predicted lower levels of alcohol use among participants. They suggest that their null findings regarding maternal support may be due to limited variance in this variable (almost all participants reported strong maternal support). Additionally, their findings indicate that support from fathers may provide African American adolescents with additional coping resources that may diminish their likelihood of using substances. Taken together, these findings suggest that increased support from families (parents in particular) may promote more positive outcomes among White and African American youth who may be at increased risk of using substances.

Other researchers have focused on parental monitoring as a factor that may contribute to the resilience process among youth at risk of substance use. Rai et al. (2003) found that parental monitoring (as reported by adolescents) reduced the relationship between exposure to peer substance use (cigarette smoking, marijuana and alcohol use) and adolescents' probability of using substances. They included in their analyses 2,619 predominantly African American adolescents taken from six community-based risk-reduction or risk-assessment studies. Parental monitoring was assessed by asking adolescents about their perceptions of how much their parents tended to be aware of where they were, what they were doing, and who they were with. These findings suggest that open communication between adolescents and their parents and a vested interest on behalf of adolescents' caregivers in knowing what their children are doing, where they are, and who they are associating with may discourage substance use among those at risk of using.

Griffin, Botvin, Scheier, Diaz, and Miller (2000) also tested the potential of parental monitoring as well as other parent–child relationship variables to counter or protect against the risks associated with male gender and residence in a single-parent home on substance use. They found that males and youth living in single-parent homes were more likely to consume alcohol and smoke cigarettes; however, parental monitoring was related to marginally less smoking across all participants and was most strongly associated with lower levels of alcohol use among males. Participants in this study included 228 urban, predominantly African American sixth graders. Cigarette and alcohol use were measured by frequency of use "in general," and parental monitoring was measured by parents' reports regarding their knowledge of their children's whereabouts after school and on the weekends, as well as details about their children's peer networks and social activities.

In another study of parental monitoring and substance use, Wright and Fitzpatrick (2004) found that among youth who were at increased risk of substance use due to experiences with domestic violence, gang affiliation, or having peers who held tolerant attitudes toward substance use, those who experienced higher levels of parental monitoring reported lower incidences of recent alcohol, cigarette, and marijuana use. They included 1,494 African American fifth through twelfth graders in their study and measured parental monitoring by asking the youth participants how frequently their parents knew where they were going with their friends. In a study with 227 racially/ethnically diverse adolescents recruited from a hospital emergency department, McManama O'Brien, Hernandez, and Spirito (2014) found that parental monitoring reduced associations between depressed mood and alcohol-related problems. Depressed mood was measured with the Center for Epidemiologic Studies Depression Scale (Harrell & Wirtz, 1989), and alcohol-related problems were measured with the Adolescent Drinking Inventory (Radloff, 1977). Adolescents reported on parental monitoring by indicating the extent to which their parents knew about the adolescent's whereabouts and friendships. Findings of this study suggest that parental monitoring may serve a critical function in reducing the link between depressed mood and problematic drinking. In light of consistent findings regarding the promotive effects of parental monitoring on adolescents' substance use outcomes, researchers have suggested that prevention efforts may include parent training in an effort to improve parents' monitoring and communication skills. Adding a parenting-training component to preexisting substance use intervention programs may be another strategy for preventing and reducing adolescents' substance use.

Positive parenting styles have been associated with lower levels of adolescent substance use (Conger & Rueter, 1996; Li, Stanton, & Feigelman, 2000) and reduced affiliation with substance-using peers (Bogenschneider, Wu, Raffaelli, & Tsay, 1998). Gibbons et al. (2004) examined the potential of effective parenting to reduce African American early adolescents' vulnerability to substance use and affiliation with peers who use substances. In their sample of 684 children and their primary caregivers, they found that effective parenting countered the harmful effects of experiencing discrimination on young adolescents' willingness to use substances and positive perceptions of others who use substances (both of which were related to later substance use and affiliation with substance-using peers).

Substance use was a composite measure of cigarette, alcohol, and marijuana use. They defined effective parenting as parenting characterized by warmth and support, open communication, and monitoring of the child's activities. They assessed the extent to which youth felt connected and supported by their caregivers (items inquired about child's perceptions of the frequency of receiving caring messages and loving acts from the caregiver and feeling understood by the caregiver), as well as the child's report of the quality of communication between the child and caregiver (adolescents' perceptions of the frequency with which their caregivers communicated with them about drugs and alcohol). Perceived parental monitoring was assessed by both child and caregiver report (items pertained to adolescents' and caregivers' perceptions of the frequency with which caregivers knew where their children were and what they were doing).

Family functioning has also been found to counter and reduce adolescents' risk of substance use. Rosenblum et al. (2005) investigated the associations between family functioning, psychosocial factors, and substance use among a sample of 77 predominantly African American (53%) and Hispanic (30%) early adolescents (11–15 years old) who had an HIV-infected parent and lived in an area with high HIV prevalence. Substance use was measured by lifetime use of cigarettes, alcohol, or any other drugs. Family functioning consisted of five scales: parental attachment, family discipline, family conflict, family management, and parental permissiveness. They found that more positive family functioning (i.e., higher reported parental attachment, family discipline and family management, and lower reported family conflict and parental permissiveness) directly related to lower levels of substance use when included in a model that accounted for risk factors of substance use such as older age and association with deviant peers. In addition, they found that more positive family functioning was indirectly related to less substance use through its relation to higher levels of *resiliency* (defined in this study as lower levels of internalizing and externalizing problems, higher levels of perceived competence and prosocial skills, and lower levels of moral disengagement), which was related to less association with deviant peers, which was, in turn, associated with higher levels of substance use. This study highlights the complexities with which multiple parent and family influences may combine to directly and indirectly affect adolescents' use of substances.

As a whole, studies that have investigated familial promotive factors have considered a range of familial processes and included youth from differing backgrounds and at various stages of adolescence. In addition, a diverse set of risk factors were considered as researchers modeled resilience processes occurring at multiple levels. While researchers measured a variety of family processes, they largely depended on adolescents' reports of these processes (for exception, see Gibbons et al., 2004). Studies that incorporate responses from multiple sources (e.g., parents, siblings, extended kin) may strengthen findings related to the potential promotive effects of family processes, such as parental monitoring, parenting style, and disciplinary practices. In addition, relationships with siblings and extended family members have largely been excluded from this body of research, and inquiry into their role in promoting adolescents' resilience to risk factors associated with substance use could broaden our perspective on the ways family factors may reduce adolescents' susceptibility to substance use. Furthermore, future studies that consider how various parental and family forces interact with each other as well as the transactional nature with which family factors and adolescent outcomes may influence each other (i.e., bidirectional paths of influence) over time are needed to further our understanding of how parental and family processes may contribute to substance use prevention or reduction among at-risk adolescents.

Community-Level Promotive Factors

Community-level factors that may promote more positive outcomes among youth at risk of substance use include both social (e.g., positive peer influences, positive relationships with neighborhood adults, role models in the community) and structural (e.g., community resources, aspects of the built environment) influences. Few researchers have studied community-level promotive factors specific to adolescent substance use, electing instead to focus on individual- and family-level promotive factors. Although some resilience researchers have considered community-level factors in their models, they have almost exclusively focused on community-level risk factors of substance use (e.g., exposure to deviant peer groups, access to drugs and alcohol, poverty, and neighborhood crime rates). Furthermore, of those who have elected to consider community-level promotive factors, they have exclusively studied social influences. In this section, we will review recent studies that have considered how promotive social influences may contribute to the reduction or prevention of substance use among at-risk youth.

Researchers have theorized about the salience of peer influences, particularly during the adolescent years when youth are becoming more autonomous and less dependent on their parents (Marcia, 1980). In addition, research findings have indicated that peers may exert a stronger influence on adolescents' substance use in comparison to parental influences (Kandel & Andrews, 1987). Given that peer groups are often selected by adolescents, associating with peers who share adolescents' experiences and values can help to confirm and strengthen adolescents' own beliefs and behavior. Thus, researchers have hypothesized that affiliating with peers who use substances will increase adolescents' likelihood of using substances. Yet it is also reasonable to expect that belonging to peer groups where academics are valued over substance use may decrease adolescents' inclination to use substances.

Bryant and Zimmerman (2002) included positive peer influences in their study of risk and protective factors of substance use (cigarette, alcohol, and marijuana use) over time. Their study included 785 urban, predominantly African American, older adolescents. They asked participants to indicate how many of their friends had positive school experiences (e.g., good grades) and whether or not their friends would think it was cool if the respondent did well in school or participated in school activities. They found that adolescents who reported that their friends had more positive school experiences were less likely to smoke cigarettes or drink alcohol and that participants who thought their friends would think it was cool if the participant was doing well in school or participating in school activities were protected against age-related increases in cigarette and marijuana use over time. These findings suggest that raising high school students' awareness of the positive academic attitudes and aspirations of their peers may increase their motivation to do well in school and make them less likely to increase their use of substances over time (Bryant & Zimmerman, 2002). Vest and Simpkins (2013) investigated peer influence on adolescent alcohol use in the context of sports participation among a large, nationally representative sample of adolescents. They found that whether sports friends contributed to or countered risk of alcohol use depended on the amount of their sports peers' alcohol use. Having sports peers who had low alcohol use predicted lower alcohol use among adolescent athletes. Students who did not participate in sports were influenced by the level of alcohol use of their non-sports-participating peers in similar ways. Interestingly, adolescent athletes were influenced by the alcohol use of their sports peers but were not influenced by the alcohol use of their non-sports-participating friends. Thus, research findings indicate that peer influences may serve as either risk or promotive factors for adolescent substance use and that targeting peer norms may be an effective strategy for both reducing risk and enhancing protection against substance use.

Although more research has focused on parental as opposed to nonparental adult influences on adolescents' substance use, relationships with important nonparental adults have also been investigated in the context of resilience and adolescent substance use (DuBois & Silverthorn, 2005; Hurd & Zimmerman, 2010b). Researchers have speculated that the additional support that these relationships provide may help buffer youth against the substance use risks they face. Furthermore, researchers have documented health-protective effects of these relationships for a number of adolescent health outcomes (Greenberger, Chen, & Beam, 1998; Hurd & Zimmerman, 2010a; Rhodes, Contreras, & Mangelsdorf, 1994; Rhodes, Ebert, & Fischer, 1992). Zimmerman, Bingenheimer, and Notaro (2002) found that mentoring relationships with adults from adolescents' preexisting social networks (i.e., natural mentors) countered the risk of having friends who used substances and engaged in other problem behaviors on adolescents' problem behavior (including alcohol and marijuana use, as well as violence and nonviolent delinquency). They also found that adolescents who perceived peer group norms that were favorable to substance use and deviant behavior were more likely to engage in problem behavior; however, having a relationship with a natural mentor partially offset this risk. They also found that relationships with natural mentors may have indirect effects on adolescents' problem behavior through encouraging adolescents to avoid associating with peers who engage in deviant behavior. Notably, other researchers have also investigated whether a relationship with a natural mentor may serve as a compensatory or protective factor among youth at-risk of using substances, yet the promotive effects of natural mentors for adolescent substance use were not found (DuBois & Silverthorn, 2005; Hurd & Zimmerman, 2010b). Given that relationships with natural mentors have demonstrated health-protective effects for other outcomes (e.g., mental health, risk taking), further research is needed to understand conflicting findings regarding relationships with natural mentors and adolescent substance use.

Given the limited amount of research that has been conducted on community-level promotive factors and adolescent substance use, there is a clear need for further investigation into factors beyond individual- and family-level factors that can counteract or protect against adolescents' risks of using substances. Moreover, a diverse focus on both social and structural community-level factors will advance our understanding of the ways in which social and physical contexts may contribute to the resilience process. Researchers have documented the beneficial effects of participation in structured activities, civic engagement, and prosocial behavior in community settings on a variety of adolescent psychosocial outcomes (Barber, Abbott, Blomfield, & Eccles, 2009; Ramirez-Valles, Zimmerman, Newcomb, 1998; Roth & Brooks-Gunn, 2003; Zimmerman & Maton, 1992). Thus, in addition to further inquiry into peer and nonparental adult influences, researchers may want to explore how opportunities for participation in organized community activities and prosocial involvement in the community may promote resistance to substance use among at-risk adolescents. Also, potential promotive factors in the built environment such as proximity to youth programs and youth-centered organizations, the availability of adult-supervised recreational sites, and safe neighborhoods warrant empirical investigation as study findings can expand our approaches to substance use prevention with at-risk adolescents.

Cumulative Promotive Factors

Although identifying specific factors that may counter or protect against specific risks is important for improving our understanding of which factors matter for the prevention and reduction of adolescent substance use, researchers have argued that risk and promotive factors do not occur in isolation, and improving our understanding of how combined or cumulative promotive factors influence substance use outcomes among at-risk adolescents may be a fruitful line of investigation.

Oman and colleagues (2004) considered the salubrious effects of multiple individual-, family-, and community-level assets and resources on adolescent alcohol and drug use. They included 1,255 ethnically diverse, urban adolescents in their study. Alcohol and drug (e.g., marijuana, inhalants, cocaine, heroin) use were measured by adolescents' self-reported use over the past 30 days. Promotive factors (referred to as "youth assets" by study authors) assessed in this study included nonparental adult role models, peer role models, positive family communication, participation in sports or other organized activities, participation in religious activities, community involvement, aspirations for the future, responsible choices, and good health practices. Oman et al. (2004) used participants' mean responses to the variable to dichotomously code whether assets were present or absent. While most of these promotive factors were individually associated with a lower likelihood of having used alcohol and all nine of these factors were individually associated with a lower likelihood of having used drugs, Oman and colleagues found that the collective influence of these assets on adolescents' substance use behavior was greater than that of any individual asset. Specifically, they found that youth who had peer role models, participated in religious activities, endorsed positive family communication, and reported making responsible choices were 4.44 times more likely to report that they had not consumed alcohol in the past 30 days in comparison to their counterparts with 3 or fewer assets. Also, youth who had peer role models, participated in religious activities, and reported making responsible choices were 5.41 times more likely to report that they had not used drugs in the past 30 days in comparison to their counterparts with 2 or fewer assets.

In addition to focusing on cumulative promotive factors, other researchers have also considered cumulative risk factors and the potential interactions between cumulative risk and promotive factor indices. Newcomb and Felix-Ortiz (1992), for example, explored how facing increasing amounts of risk may contribute to higher levels of substance use (frequency of use in past 30 days of cigarettes, alcohol, cannabis, cocaine, and hard drugs) and problems related to substance use, and how exposure to a greater number of protective factors may reduce adolescents' use and problems related to substance use over time. In their longitudinal study including 896 late adolescents (68% female; 63% White, 17% African American, 10% Hispanic, 10% Asian) followed over the transition to adulthood, Newcomb and Felix-Ortiz used 14 variables to create risk and protective factor indices and tested out associations between these indices and participants' reported substance use and problems with substance use. They used cutoff points to designate the upper 20% or lower 20% of each variable distribution as risk or protective, yielding 14 potential risk and 14 potential protective factors. Hypothesized risk and protective variables (based on cutoff points) were then correlated with the substance use outcome variables and whichever correlation was higher for the variable (risk vs. protective end of the spectrum) determined whether that variable was deemed a protective factor and included in the protective factor index (PFI) or a risk factor and included in the risk factor index (RFI). High GPA, low symptoms of depression, having supportive relationships with parents and family, perceiving a lot of sanctions against drug use, high religiosity, high self-acceptance, and high law abidance were all deemed protective factors that contributed to the PFI. Low educational aspirations, high perceived adult and peer drug use, a high number of deviant behaviors, high perceptions of community and important adult support of drug use, higher availability of drugs, and low perceived opportunities for the future were deemed risk factors that contributed to the RFI. Thus, seven variables each contributed to the RFI and the PFI and each index ranged from 0 to 7. Findings indicated that both the RFI and the PFI accounted for moderate amounts of variance in all substances, but particularly alcohol, cannabis, and cocaine. Beyond the additive main effects of the PFI when included in the model with the RFI, the PFI also moderated the relationship between the RFI and hard drug use, such that the effects of high risk on hard drug use were exacerbated by low protection and buffered by high protection. These same moderation effects of the PFI were found for the relationship between the RFI and alcohol problems over time.

In another study of cumulative risk and promotive factors, Costa, Jessor, and Turbin (1999) found that psychosocial risk and protective factors accounted for cross-sectional variation in adolescents' problem drinking (frequency of drunkenness and negative consequences of drinking in past 6 months) as well as the timing of transition into problem drinking during adolescence. They found that higher risk and lower protection contributed independently to greater alcohol problems and increased the likelihood that youth who were not problem drinkers would become problem drinkers during the transition from middle to high school. While protective factors moderated the impact of risk on problem drinking in their cross-sectional analysis, this moderation effect was not replicated in their longitudinal analysis of the transition into problem drinking. Their cross-sectional analyses included 1,525 White, African American, and Hispanic 10th through 12th graders, and their longitudinal analyses included 1,188 participants from the larger sample who were not problem drinkers at Wave 1 and who had participated in four waves of data spanning their transition from middle to high school. They included in their analyses eight psychosocial risk factors (low expectations for success, low self-esteem, hopelessness, friends as models for using alcohol and other drugs, greater orientation to friends than parents, high stress, low academic achievement, and proneness for dropping out of school) and eight psychosocial protective factors (positive orientation to school, attitudinal intolerance of deviance, religiosity, positive orientation to health, positive relationships with adults, perception of strong regulatory controls against transgression, friends as models for conventional behavior, and involvement in prosocial activities). Each of these variables was entered into the multiple regression equation for the cross-sectional analyses; however, a composite measure of risk and a composite measure of protection were computed by adding the standardized scores of the seven respective risk and protective variables, and these composite measures were used in the longitudinal analyses.

Sullivan and Farrell (1999) identified seven risk and seven protective factors (with minimal overlap) that were associated with substance use in their sample of 994 African American, urban eighth graders. They found associations between the total number of risk factors and adolescents' cigarette, alcohol, and marijuana use, and a composite measure of polysubstance use (lifetime and use during the past month). They also found that their protective factor index (PFI) moderated the relationship between cumulative risk and participants' alcohol, marijuana, and polydrug use. Longitudinal analyses focusing on changes in past-month drug use during the 1-year transition from middle to high school also demonstrated a moderating effect of the PFI on the association between cumulative risk and cigarette use. Risk factors included in this study were intentions to use any drugs (e.g., marijuana, cocaine, injected drugs), any history of sexual intercourse, any history of alcohol use, any history of cigarette use, high delinquent behavior (scores in the upper quartile of the Delinquent Behavior Scale), feeling pressured by friends to drink or use drugs during past 30 days, and having any friends who had an alcohol or drug problem or used drugs at least once per month. The risk factor index (RFI) was calculated by adding the number of risk factors present (0–7). Protective factors in this study were intolerant attitudes toward deviance (scored in the upper quartile of the Attitudes Toward Deviance

Scale), high family support (reported that most of the time they felt free to talk to parents about personal problems and parents showed interest in their ideas, feelings, and plans), high commitment to school (reported they had not skipped school in past month, completed their homework 10–19 times in the past month, and studied for a test 3–5 times in the past month), good school attendance (scored in the upper quartile for school attendance), parents' positive expectations for academic achievement (reported that it was very important to their parents that they get good grades in school), no adult models for problem or illicit drug use, and involvement in extracurricular activities (scored in Upper Quartile of Behavior Frequency Scale for activities such as playing sports and attending school clubs). Similar to the RFI, the PFI was computed by adding the number of protective factors present (0–7).

Pollard, Hawkins, and Arthur (1999) also considered multiple risk and promotive factors for adolescent substance use (alcohol and marijuana use in the past 30 days). They used aggregated risk and protective factor scores in their analyses, which were created by averaging each participant's standardized scores across the risk and protective factor scales so that aggregated scores reflected participants' relative levels of risk and protection. They included 20 risk factors in their analyses: low neighborhood attachment, community disorganization, high mobility, laws and norms favoring drug use, high perceived availability of drugs, low commitment to school, poor supervision by family, poor family discipline, high degree of family conflict, family history of antisocial behavior, parental attitudes that promote antisocial behavior, parental attitudes that promote drug use, high degree of rebelliousness, early initiation of antisocial behavior, attitudes that favor drug use, peer antisocial behavior, peer drug use, rewards for antisocial behavior, and high degree of sensation seeking. The eight protective factors they included in their study were high perceived rewards for community involvement, many opportunities for school involvement, high perceived rewards for school involvement, high degree of family attachment, high perceived opportunities for family involvement, belief in moral order, and high degree of social problem-solving skills. Pollard et al. organized participants into quintiles (each containing 20% of participants) based on higher versus lower levels of risk and higher versus lower levels of protection. They found that higher levels of risk exposure were exponentially associated with more alcohol and marijuana use. Yet they found that higher levels of protection moderated the negative effects of exposure to risk. They found the greatest moderation effects at the highest level of risk exposure. Their study sample consisted of 78,710 predominantly White sixth through twelfth graders who resided in Kansas, Maine, Oregon, South Carolina, or Washington.

In their sample of 4,851 African American (71%) and Hispanic (29%) seventh graders from inner-city schools, Epstein, Botvin, Griffin, and Diaz (2001) found that higher levels of cumulative risk were associated with more alcohol use while higher levels of cumulative protection were associated with less alcohol use. In addition, they found that among participants with moderate to higher levels of risk, those who reported higher protection reported less alcohol use than their counterparts with low protection. They assessed current alcohol use with four items: frequency of consumption of alcoholic beverages (e.g., less than once a month, daily), frequency of getting drunk, quantity of alcoholic drinks they have at a time, and intentions to consume alcohol during the next year. Epstein et al. assigned variables to risk or protection status based on intuition and also whether or not the factor was something that could reasonably be intervened upon. Factors that appeared to be amenable to change through some form of intervention were assigned to the protective index. The risk factor index (RFI) included the following nine factors: receiving free lunch in school, getting grades that were mostly Ds or lower, being absent from school 7 or more days during the past year, having a mother or step-mother who drinks or used to drink alcohol, having a father or step-father who drinks or used to drink alcohol, having an older sibling who drinks or used to drink alcohol, having friends who drink alcohol, reporting that half or more of one's peers drink alcohol, and finding it easy or very easy to acquire alcohol. Participants received one point for each risk factor present, making the range for the RFI 0 to 9. Protective factors consisted of the following six factors: living in a two-parent household, attending church six or more times a year, scoring above the median on antialcohol attitudes, having a high level of alcohol knowledge, alcohol refusal assertiveness (high likelihood of saying "no" if offered alcohol), and alcohol refusal skills (high likelihood of employing a variety of refusal skills if offered alcohol). As with the RFI, each factor present awarded the participant one point on the protective factor index (PFI).

Other researchers interested in understanding cumulative risk and protection have organized their analyses by context. Beam, Gil-Rivas, Greenberger, and Chen (2002), for example, investigated whether protective factors from one context (e.g., family) could buffer adolescents against the risks they encountered in another context (e.g., community). Their study sample comprised 243 ethnically diverse eleventh graders. They included adolescent problem behavior as an outcome variable in their study. Adolescent problem behavior included substance use as well as risk taking, school-related deviance, status offenses, physical aggression, vandalism, theft, and other problem behaviors (e.g., forgery). Participants were asked about the frequency with which they had done these things during the past 6 months. They measured risk in three different contexts: family, peer, and a very important adult person (VIP) in adolescents' lives. Family risk factors included lower parental education, family structure (biological family not intact), negative family life events (e.g., severe arguing between parents, serious illness or death of a parent), higher frequency of adolescent–parent conflict, perceptions of parental engagement in problem behavior, and perceptions of sibling involvement in problem behavior. Peer risk factors included negative peer events (e.g., a close friend moved away), higher reported childhood aggression toward peers (frequency of arguments and physical fights during elementary school), fewer friendships during childhood, and perceptions of peer involvement in problem behavior. VIP risk was assessed with one item: perceptions of VIP involvement in problem behavior. Participants received cumulative risk scores for each context derived from the mean of their standardized scores for each of the component risk factors. Protective factors were organized similarly; however, they assessed fewer of these variables (i.e., only three). They assessed participants' perceptions of parents', peers', and VIPs' sanctions of problem behaviors. These questions asked participants how these sources would react (e.g., be upset, disapprove) to participants' involvement in any of the problem behaviors listed earlier. Perceiving upset or disapproving reactions was considered protective. Interaction terms included a risk context by a protective factor (i.e., perceived parental, peer, or VIP sanctions). They found that aggregated peer risk and VIP risk predicted greater problem behavior among participants, and perceived parental and peer sanctions countered the effects of these risks on adolescents' problem behavior. Although they only found one significant interaction effect in their within-context analyses (perceiving higher peer sanctions moderated the relationship between peer risk and adolescent problem behavior), they found four cross-context interaction effects. Higher perceived peer sanctions were protective against the negative effects of family risk and VIP risk on adolescents' problem behavior. Higher perceived parental sanctions were protective against the negative effects of exposure to peer risk, and higher perceived VIP sanctions protected adolescents from the negative effects of peer risk on their engagement in problem behavior.

Ostaszewski and Zimmerman (2006) studied the effects of cumulative risk and promotive factors on polydrug use among 624 urban, predominantly African American (80%) ninth graders. Polydrug use was a composite measure computed by summing z-scores for five items inquiring about tobacco, alcohol, and marijuana use during the past month and alcohol and marijuana use during the past year. Ostaszewski and Zimmerman found compensatory and protective effects of cumulative promotive factors in their cross-sectional analysis. They found that the moderating effect of cumulative promotive factors on the relationship between cumulative risk and polydrug use was strongest among participants exposed to the most risk. Additionally, incorporating data from participants' twelfth-grade year ($n = 531$), they found that the cumulative promotive factor index exerted a compensatory effect on change in adolescents' polydrug use from ninth to twelfth grade. They measured risk and promotive factors at multiple levels. Individual risk factors included approval of violence to solve problems, observed violence, being the victim of violence, perpetration of violence, early substance use, having been held back a grade, skipping whole days of school, and skipping classes. Peer risk factors included having friends who use alcohol or drugs, having friends who engage in aggressive or delinquent behavior, and having friends who have skipped school, been suspended from school, or dropped out of school. Family-level risk factors included drug and alcohol use by adults raising the adolescent, family conflict, and weapons possession by adults raising the adolescent. Individual-level promotive factors were positive attitudes about school, perceiving school as interesting and relevant, future orientation, self-acceptance, high-effort coping, church attendance, participation in church activities, and religious coping. Peer promotive factors consisted of support from friends, friends' participation in prosocial activities, and closeness and satisfaction with friends. Familial promotive factors included involvement in family decision making, closeness with family, parental support, spending time in shared activities with mother or father, and participating in fun activities with one's family. Ostaszewski and Zimmerman designated the upper 25% of the distribution of the variables as either a risk or promotive factor when possible and when not possible (due to limited variance), a priori criteria were used to find natural cutoff points. Scores equal to or above the cutoff points were assigned a value of 1 and then risk and protective factors were summed to yield their respective risk factor and promotive factor indices.

Kliewer and Murrelle (2007) considered risk and promotive factors for substance use across Central American adolescents' social ecologies. Their study included 17,215 adolescents aged 12–20 years from Panama, Costa Rica, and Guatemala. Outcome variables of their analyses were lifetime use of alcohol, tobacco, marijuana, and other drugs, as well as problems with drugs and alcohol. Risk factors included in the study were dysregulated affect, behavior, and cognition; family problems with drugs and alcohol; negative family interactions and communication; school disengagement; peer deviance; and exposure to serious violence. Protective factors were having a belief in God, positive family interaction and communication, parent religiosity, and positive student–teacher interactions. Participants scoring at or above one standard deviation above the mean for a given risk or protective variable were assigned a value of 1 for that factor, and then factors were summed accordingly to yield risk factor and protective factor indices. They found that risk factors were associated with more substance use and problems with substance use, while protective factors were associated with less substance use and problems with substance use. In addition, risk and promotive factor indices interacted to predict lifetime drunkenness and marijuana use, as well as drug and alcohol problems. These interactions indicated that cumulative protective factors may mitigate the negative effects of cumulative risk on adolescents' substance use and problems with substance use.

Most recently, Cleveland, Feinberg, and Jones (2012) investigated cumulative risk and protective factors for alcohol use by the following four domains: family, peer, school, and community. Their study included 7,819 adolescents from rural communities in Iowa and Pennsylvania. This sample was predominantly White (85%) and participants were followed across 5 years. Their study also included 8,051 adolescents from urban public school districts in Detroit, Houston, Los Angeles, Newark, New Orleans, and St. Louis. This sample was racially/ethnically diverse (40% White, 15% Black, 18% Hispanic/Latino, 8% American Indian, 5% Asian). Average age at Time 1 was 12.3 and 12.5 for the two samples, and data were collected from participants in both samples over a 5-year period. Recent alcohol use was the outcome of interest and was measured with one item assessing frequency of use within the past month. Individual risk was a composite of positive attitudes toward alcohol and tobacco use; perceived risks of alcohol, tobacco, and other drug use; and sensation seeking. Individual protection was not measured. Peer risk included friends' delinquent behavior, peer rewards for antisocial behavior, and peer substance use. Peer protection was not measured. Family risk was a single item measuring parental attitudes favorable to alcohol, tobacco, and other drug use. Family protection included family attachment, family opportunities for prosocial involvement, family supervision, and parents' use of consistent discipline. School risk was not measured. School protection included school commitment, school opportunities for prosocial involvement, and school rewards for prosocial involvement. Community risk was not measured. Community protection was measured by community rewards for prosocial involvement, community opportunities for prosocial involvement, and lower perceived availability of drugs and firearms. Findings indicated that the influence of individual risk on adolescents' alcohol use increased over time and the influence of family protection on adolescents' alcohol use decreased over time among both samples. Findings also indicated that the influence of family risk, community protection, and school protection on adolescents' alcohol use remained constant over time. Lastly, findings indicated that peer risk had an increasingly stronger influence on adolescents' alcohol use through ninth grade followed by a subsequent decrease in its strength of influence. Given developmental variation in the strength of influence of various levels of risk and protective factors, Cleveland et al. recommend that prevention efforts target risk and protective factors at differing levels (e.g., individual, family, community) depending on the age of the adolescents.

Taken together, the findings of these studies indicate that multiple risk and promotive factors may accumulate and interact to predict adolescents' substance use. The authors of many of these studies have recommended continued research in this area to improve our understanding of the complexities of the resilience process and the role of context in shaping adolescent substance use. Of note, all of these studies demonstrated greater effects of cumulative risk factors than cumulative promotive factors on adolescent substance use. Results indicated that in comparison to the PFIs, the RFIs accounted for much more of the variance in substance use outcomes. In addition, findings suggest that very few participants with high RFIs also had high PFIs. Furthermore, moderation effects, when found, were modest at best. In no instance did high levels of protection eliminate substance use among those at the highest risk levels, and some findings indicated that low protection exacerbated risk more so than high protection mitigated risk.

Yet it is worth noting that RFIs are often entered into statistical equations prior to PFIs, thus leaving less statistical variance for the PFIs to explain. Also, RFIs may demonstrate stronger associations with adolescents' substance use in comparison to the associations between PFIs and substance use because risk measures tend to be more specific to substance use behavior (e.g., parental or peer substance use modeling, personal history of substance use, intentions to use drugs, laws and norms favoring drug use), whereas promotive factors tend to be more general (e.g., community involvement, supportive family relationships, belief in a moral order). Another potential explanation of the stronger associations between RFIs (in comparison to PFIs) and adolescent substance use outcomes is that researchers have conducted substantially more research on risk factors of substance use as opposed to promotive factors. Thus, risk measures may be more sensitive because researchers understand them better. In addition, researchers may be inclined to include more risk factors in their models. In fact, many of the cumulative risk and promotive studies included a disproportionate amount of risk factors in comparison to promotive factors, reflecting researchers' relatively lower levels of familiarity with positive factors that have the potential to counter or moderate the effects of risk on adolescents' substance use. It may be unreasonable to expect one promotive factor or a PFI composed of a few promotive factors to be potent enough to completely counter the negative effects of or substantially reduce the strong relationship between an RFI composed of 10 or more risk factors and adolescents' substance use.

Despite explaining less variance than cumulative measure of risk, the compensatory and protective effects of PFIs found in these studies indicate that these variables are relevant and worthy of continued attention. In light of these findings, researchers have suggested that combined efforts to reduce risk and support asset development and resource promotion will be more effective in reducing adolescent substance use as opposed to focusing on either in isolation (Newcomb & Felix-Ortiz, 1992; Pollard et al., 1999). Moreover, the results of these studies suggest that there are a range of systems and contexts in the resilience process, indicating that prevention efforts that account for and address factors across adolescents' social ecologies will likely yield more positive results than unidimensional prevention efforts that ignore the multitude of influences adolescents experience across multiple contexts.

Limitations and Directions for Future Research

Collectively, the studies reviewed in this chapter point to a number of factors that individually or combined have the potential to promote resilience among adolescents at risk of substance use. Yet important limitations of this work and directions for future research must be noted. As a whole, this body of research has included greater attention to individual- and family-level promotive factors, with relatively little focus on promotive influences beyond these domains. This may be problematic for a number of reasons. First, this greater emphasis on individual- and family-level factors could be interpreted by some to mean that individuals and families are solely responsible for facilitating at-risk adolescents' resilience. This may lead to a greater focus on interventions that aim to bolster individual and familial strengths while neglecting opportunities to reinforce or promote resources in the larger community. Thus, this heavy focus on individual and family promotive factors may inadvertently send the message to academics, practitioners, and policymakers that resilience has to occur at these levels and that prevention efforts should be targeted at helping adolescents and their families better adapt to environmental risks as opposed to addressing environmental risk and supporting environmental resources. Therefore, it is possible that this unbalanced research focus on factors that promote resilience may undermine substance use prevention efforts aimed at affecting change at larger levels.

Second, the emphasis on individual and family interventions may exaggerate the role of individual assets and family factors in countering or reducing adolescents' experiences with substance use risk and result in researchers and practitioners ignoring the potential for other foci of change. A number of developmental contexts where promotive factors likely exist have yet to be fully examined, including schools, churches or other religious organizations, peer networks, and neighborhoods. Although some of these factors have received substantial attention as risk factors for adolescent substance use (e.g., peer influences), researchers have not considered how these factors may counter or protect against adolescents' substance use risks with the same fervor (for exceptions see Bryant & Zimmerman, 2002; Beam et al., 2002; Oman et al., 2004; Ostaszewski & Zimmerman, 2006). Moreover, educational and religious settings have yet to be explored as contexts that may promote resilience to substance use among at-risk youth. Although researchers have investigated academic attitudes and behaviors and religiosity as individual-level factors that may protect youth against risks of using substances, there have been limited investigations into the roles of settings or organizations in directly or indirectly fostering adolescents' resilience to substance use. Without further understanding what factors in adolescents' diverse social ecologies may counteract or protect against risks of substance use, we will not be able to support or encourage resilience in these domains through programs or social policies.

Third, focusing primarily on these person- and family-specific variables may perpetuate confusion in the literature that resilience is a characteristic or trait as opposed to a dynamic process (Luthar et al., 2000). This risk may be heightened when the promotive factors under investigation are related to adolescents' temperament or affect, particularly when researchers do not acknowledge how these factors are influenced by adolescents' environments. As Luthar and Cicchetti (2000, p. 863) stated, "these attributes are not indelibly implanted in children; rather, they are substantially shaped by life circumstances." Thus, researchers may benefit from not only broadening contexts of investigation but also acknowledging how more distal factors can influence proximal factors to promote resilience. While it is understandable that researchers are drawn to study variables that are perceived to have the most proximal influence, ignoring the larger contexts within which adolescents and their families are situated may prevent an advanced understanding of the complex pathways that lead to resilience. Testing mediation and moderation models that account for multiple contexts may help

to advance the study of resilience and adolescent substance use.

This point relates to an additional limitation of the resilience work reviewed in this chapter, which is a lack of consideration of bidirectional effects between adolescents and their environments (Sameroff & Mackenzie, 2003). While adolescents are shaped by their environments, they also shape their environments, and attempts to model these transactions over time could add to our conceptualizations of adolescent resilience. Although studies employing transactional models have historically emphasized transactions between children and their parents, Sameroff and Mackenzie (2003) argue for more attention paid to multiple sources of bidirectional influence, including peer interactions and school involvement, which can occupy more of adolescents' time. This suggests that youth may be useful resources in our intervention efforts as opposed to the foci of our strategies to fix them. Thus, interventions that involve youth as part of the solution may have the benefit of creating social norms of prosocial action, improving the environment, and enhancing individual sense of control and empowerment. The Youth Empowerment Solutions (YES) curriculum, for example, provides an example of an after-school program for middle-school youth that is designed to help them become change agents to improve their community (Franzen, Morrel-Samuels, Reischl, & Zimmerman, 2009; Zimmerman, Stewart, Morrel-Samuels, Reischl, & Franzen, 2011).

Another major limitation of the studies reviewed in this chapter is the manner with which promotive factors were identified and selected for study inclusion. While a number of study authors cited theoretical underpinnings and prior empirical findings for their selections, it was less obvious in other studies why certain promotive factors were selected. Family structure, for example, was included in several studies; however, the theoretical justification for considering this a risk or promotive factor was not specified by study authors (Beam et al., 2002; Farrell & White, 1998). It is possible that authors expected living in a two-parent household to be an indication of greater access to resources, more monitoring, and more support; however, investigations of the promotive effects of family structure suggest that this assumption may not hold for diverse groups of adolescents (Salem et al., 1998; Zimmerman et al., 1995). Whereas an assessment of utilization of family resources, parental monitoring, or parental support could generate opportunities to explore how specific family processes contribute to risk or resilience, generic assessments of family structure may fail to capture the complex familial mechanisms that contribute to resilience. Furthermore, considering a nonintact biological family as a universal risk factor for all study participants (Beam et al., 2002) is value-laden and inconsistent with findings that African American adolescents living in single-mother households have reported receiving higher levels of parental support in comparison to their peers living in other family constellations (Zimmerman et al., 1995). Continued research that considers a more nuanced approach to identifying risk and promotive factors among diverse groups of adolescents might help highlight important family factors that have been largely neglected in the literature. Moreover, although it can be tempting, particularly in studies of cumulative risk and protection, to include a hodgepodge of risk and promotive variables that intuitively seem related to substance use, selecting variables for study inclusion that are not informed by theory and previous research can detract from the overall study of resilience (Luthar et al., 2000).

In addition to having a theoretical basis for the inclusion of specific variables in resilience models, researchers may want to consider opportunities to incorporate participants' perceptions of risk and promotive factors in their lives. Through qualitative investigation with adolescents and their families, similar to that conducted by Werner and Smith (1982) almost 30 years ago, new theories could emerge that could shape our understanding of factors that have the potential to promote resilience among adolescents at risk of using substances. These types of investigations could also inform our understanding of resilience outcomes. At this point, researchers have not reached consensus in defining resilience in terms of substance use outcomes other than a general acknowledgment that lower levels of use are considered more positive.

Conclusions

Despite the limitations of this literature, the field of adolescent substance use research has largely benefited from an increased focus on positive factors in adolescents' lives that may reduce their risk of using substances. Historically, investigations of the etiology of adolescent substance use exclusively considered risk factors. Although an emphasis on risk still remains, this ever-burgeoning study of resilience has encouraged substance use researchers to move beyond the deficit-focused models of

adolescent substance use to more complex models of use that account for deficits, strengths, and interactions between the two. By acknowledging multiple, simultaneously occurring positive and negative influences, studies of cumulative risk and promotive factors also have helped to paint a more complete picture of risk and resilience processes affecting adolescent substance use. Furthermore, these studies have created opportunities for the identification of positive factors that may mitigate substance use among adolescents who are experiencing adversity. This work has provided useful information that can help guide innovative prevention efforts that focus on building assets and strengthening resources for positive youth development. As this area of study continues to expand and grow, researchers, practitioners, and policymakers will benefit from understanding the positive factors in youths' lives and communities that help them overcome adversity and risks they face. Critiques notwithstanding, continued study of resilience processes among adolescents at risk of using and abusing substances holds promise for advancing our understanding of the complex etiology of adolescent substance use, as well as shaping practice and policy in this domain.

References

Abdelrahman, A. I., Rodriguez, G., Ryan, J. A., French, J. F., & Weinbaum, D. (1999). The epidemiology of substance use among middle school students: The impact of school, familial, community and individual risk factors. *Journal of Child and Adolescent Substance Abuse, 8*, 55–75.

Adlaf, E. M., & Smart, R. G. (1985). Drug use and religious affiliation, feelings, and behavior. *British Journal of Addiction, 80*, 163–171.

Arthur, M. W., Hawkins, J. D., Pollard, J. A., Catalano, R. F., & Baglioni, A. J. (2002). Measuring risk and protective factors for substance use, delinquency, and other adolescent problem behaviors: The communities that care youth survey. *Evaluation Review, 26*, 575–601.

Baer, J., MacLean, M., & Marlatt, G. (1998). Linking etiology and treatment for adolescent substance abuse: Toward a better match. In R. Jessor (Ed.), *New perspectives on adolescent risk behavior* (pp. 182–220). New York, NY: Cambridge University Press.

Bahr, S. J., Maughan, S. L., Marcos, A. C., & Li, B. (1998). Family, religiosity, and the risk of adolescent drug use. *Journal of Marriage and the Family, 60*, 979–992.

Barber, B. L., Abbott, B. D., Blomfield, C. J., & Eccles, J. S. (2009). Secrets of their success: Activity participation and positive youth development. In R. Gilman, M. J. Furlong, & E. S. Huebner (Eds.), *Handbook of positive psychology in schools* (pp. 273–289). New York, NY: Routledge.

Beam, M. R., Gil-Rivas, V., Greenberger, E., & Chen, C. S. (2002). Adolescent problem behavior and depressed mood: Risk and protection within and across social contexts. *Journal of Youth and Adolescence, 31*, 343–357.

Bogenschneider, K., Wu, M., Raffaelli, M., & Tsay, J. C. (1998). Parent influences on adolescent peer orientation and substance use: The interface of parenting practices and values. *Child Development, 69*, 1672–1688.

Brody, G. H., & Forehand, R. (1993). Prospective associations among family form, family processes, and adolescents' alcohol and drug use. *Behaviour Research and Therapy, 31*, 587–593.

Bronfenbrenner, U. (1977). Toward an experimental ecology of human development. *American Psychologist, 32*, 513–531.

Brook, J. S., Balka, E. B., Brook, D. W., Win, P. E., & Gursen, M. D. (1998). Drug use among African Americans: Ethnic identity as a protective factor. *Psychological Reports, 83*, 1427–1446.

Brook, J. S., Brook, D. W., Gordon, A. S., Whiteman, M., & Cohen, P. (1990). The psychosocial etiology of adolescent drug use: A family interactional approach. *Genetic, Social, and General Psychology Monographs, 116*, 111–267.

Brook, J. S., Whiteman, M., Gordon, A. S., & Cohen, P. (1986). Dynamics of childhood and adolescent personality traits and adolescent drug use. *Developmental Psychology, 22*, 401–414.

Bryant, A. L., Schulenberg, J. E., O'Malley, P. M., Bachman, J. G., & Johnston, L. D. (2003). How academic achievement, attitudes, and behaviors relate to the course of substance use during adolescence: A 6-year multiwave national longitudinal study. *Journal of Research on Adolescence, 13*, 361–397.

Bryant, A. L., & Zimmerman, M. A. (2002). Examining the effects of academic beliefs and behaviors on changes in substance use among urban adolescents. *Journal of Educational Psychology, 94*, 621–637.

Caldwell, C. H., Sellers, R. M., Bernat, D. H., & Zimmerman, M. A. (2004). Racial identity, parental support, and alcohol use in a sample of academically at-risk African American high school students. *American Journal of Community Psychology, 34*, 71–82.

Cicchetti, D., & Lynch, M. (1993). Toward an ecological/transactional model of community violence and child maltreatment: Consequence for children's development. *Psychiatry, 56*, 96–118.

Clark, D. B., & Winters, K. C. (2002). Measuring risks and outcomes in substance use disorders prevention research. *Journal of Consulting and Clinical Psychology, 70*, 1207–1223.

Cleveland, M. J., Feinberg, M. E., & Jones, D. E. (2012). Predicting alcohol use across adolescence: Relative strength of individual, family, peer, and contextual risk and protective factors. *Psychology of Addictive Behaviors, 26*, 703–713.

Conger, R. D., & Rueter, M. A. (1996). Siblings, parents, and peers: A longitudinal study of social influences in adolescent risk for alcohol use and abuse. In G. H. Brody (Ed.), *Sibling relationships: Their causes and consequences* (pp. 1–30). Norwood, NJ: Alex Publishing.

Costa, F. M., Jessor, R., & Turbin, M. S. (1999). Transition into adolescent problem drinking: The role of psychosocial risk and protective factors. *Journal of Studies on Alcohol, 60*, 480–490.

Damon, W. (2004). What is positive youth development? *Annals of the American Academy of Political and Social Science, 591*, 13–24.

Dickens, D. D., Dieterich, S. E., Henry, K. L., & Beauvais, F. (2012). School bonding as a moderator of the effect of peer influences on alcohol use among American Indian adolescents. *Journal of Studies on Alcohol and Drugs, 73*, 597–603.

Doherty, W. J., & Allen, W. (1994). Family functioning and parental smoking as predictors of adolescent cigarette use: A six-year prospective study. *Journal of Family Psychology, 8*, 347–353.

DuBois, D. L., & Silverthorn, N. (2005). Natural mentoring relationships and adolescent health: Evidence from a national study. *American Journal of Public Health, 95*, 518–524.

Duncan, S. C., Duncan, T. E., & Strycker, L. A. (2000). Risk and protective factors influencing adolescent problem behavior: A multivariate latent growth curve analysis. *Annals of Behavioral Medicine, 22*, 103–109.

Eccles, J. S., Lord, S. E., Roeser, R. W., Barber, B. L., & Jozefowicz, D. M. (1997). The association of school transitions in early adolescence with developmental trajectories through high school. In J. Schulenberg, J. Maggs, & K. Hurrelmann (Eds.), *Health risks and developmental transitions during adolescence* (pp. 283–320). New York, NY: Cambridge University Press.

Eisenberg, N., Guthrie, I. K., Fabes, R. A., Reiser, M., Murphy, B. C., Holgren, R., . . . Losoya, S. (1997). The relations of regulation and emotionality to resiliency and competent social functioning in elementary school children. *Child Development, 68*, 295–311.

Epstein, J. A., Botvin, G. J., Griffin, K. W., & Diaz, T. (2001). Protective factors buffer effects of risk factors on alcohol use among inner-city youth. *Journal of Child and Adolescent Substance Abuse, 11*, 77–90.

Farrell, A. D., & White, K. S. (1998). Peer influences and drug use among urban adolescents: Family structure, and parent-adolescent relationship as protective factors. *Journal of Consulting and Clinical Psychology, 66*, 248–258.

Fergus, S., & Zimmerman, M. A. (2005). Adolescent resilience: A framework for understanding healthy development in the face of risk. *Annual Review of Public Health, 26*, 399–419.

Fleming, C. B., Kim, H., Harachi, T. W., & Catalano, R. F. (2002). Family processes for children in early elementary school as predictors of smoking initiation. *Journal of Adolescent Health, 30*, 184–189.

Franzen, S., Morrel-Samuels, S., Reischl, T. M., & Zimmerman, M. A. (2009). Using process evaluation to strengthen intergenerational partnerships in the Youth Empowerment Solutions Program. *Journal of Prevention and Intervention in the Community, 37*, 289–301.

Garmezy, N., Masten, A. S., & Tellegen, A. (1984). The study of stress and competence in children: A building block for developmental psychopathology. *Child Development, 55*, 97–111.

Gibbons, F. X., Gerrard, M., Cleveland, M. J., Wills, T. A., & Brody, G. (2004). Perceived discrimination and substance use in African American parents and their children: A panel study. *Journal of Personality and Social Psychology, 86*, 517–529.

Greenberger, E., Chen, C., & Beam, M. R. (1998). The role of "very important" nonparental adults in adolescent development. *Journal of Youth and Adolescence, 27*, 321–343.

Griffin, K. W., Botvin, G. J., Scheier, L. M., Diaz, T., & Miller, N. L. (2000). Parenting practices as predictors of substance use, delinquency, and aggression among urban minority youth: Moderating effects of family structure and gender. *Psychology of Addictive Behaviors, 14*, 174–184.

Griffin, K. W., Botvin, G. J., Scheier, L. M., Epstein, J. A., & Doyle, M. M. (2002). Personal competence skills, distress, and well-being as determinants of substance use in a predominantly minority urban adolescent sample. *Prevention Science, 3,* 23–33.

Griffin, K. W., Scheier, L. M., Botvin, G. J., & Diaz, T. (2001). The protective role of personal competence skills in adolescent substance use: Psychological well-being as a mediating factor. *Psychology of Addictive Behaviors, 15,* 194–203.

Hahm, H. C., Lahiff, M., & Guterman, N. B. (2003). Acculturation and parental attachment in Asian-American adolescents' alcohol use. *Journal of Adolescent Health, 33,* 119–129.

Harrell, A., & Wirtz, P. M. (1989). Screening for adolescent problem drinking: Validation of a multidimensional instrument for case identification. *Psychological Assessment, 1,* 61–63.

Hawkins, J. D., Catalano, R. F., & Miller, J. Y. (1992). Risk and protective factors for alcohol and other drug problems in adolescence and early adulthood: Implications for substance abuse prevention. *Psychological Bulletin, 112,* 64–105.

Hawkins, J. D., & Weis, J. G. (1985). The social development model: An integrated approach to delinquency prevention. *Journal of Primary Prevention, 6,* 73–97.

Hurd, N. M., & Zimmerman, M. A. (2010a). Natural mentoring relationships among adolescent mothers: A study of resilience. *Journal of Research on Adolescence, 20,* 789–809.

Hurd, N. M., & Zimmerman, M. A. (2010b). Natural mentors and health outcomes: A longitudinal analysis of African American adolescents transitioning into adulthood. *American Journal of Community Psychology, 46,* 36–48.

Hurd, N. M., Zimmerman, M. A., & Reischl, T. M. (2011). Role model behavior and youth violence: A study of positive and negative effects. *Journal of Early Adolescence, 31,* 323–354.

Hurd, N. M., Zimmerman, M. A., & Xue, Y. (2009). Negative adult influences and the protective effects of role models: A study with urban adolescents. *Journal of Youth and Adolescence, 38,* 777–789.

Jackson, C., & Henriksen, L. (1997). Do as I say: Parent smoking, anti-smoking socialization, and smoking onset among children. *Addictive Behaviors, 22,* 107–114.

Jessor, R., & Jessor, S. L. (1977). *Problem behavior and psychosocial development: A longitudinal study of youth.* New York, NY: Academic Press.

Johnson, P. B., & Johnson, H. L. (1999). Cultural and familial influences that maintain the negative meaning of alcohol. *Journal of Studies on Alcohol, 13,* 79–83.

Johnston, L. D., O'Malley, P. M., Bachman, J. G., & Schulenberg, J. E. (2010). *Monitoring the Future national results on adolescent drug use: Overview of key findings, 2009* (NIH Publication No. 10-7583). Bethesda, MD: National Institute on Drug Abuse.

Kandel, D. B., & Andrews, K. (1987). Processes of adolescent socialization by parents and peers. *International Journal of Addictions, 22,* 319–342.

Kandel, D. B., Yamaguchi, K., & Chen, K. (1992). Stages of progression in drug involvement from adolescence to adulthood: Further evidence for the gateway theory. *Journal of Studies on Alcohol, 53,* 447–457.

Kim, I. J., Zane, N. W. S., & Hong, S. (2002). Protective factor against substance use among Asian American youth: A test

of the peer cluster theory. *Journal of Community Psychology, 30,* 565–584.

Kliewer, W., & Murrelle, L. (2007). Risk and protective factors for adolescent substance use: Findings from a study in selected Central American countries. *Journal of Adolescent Health, 40,* 448–455.

Levin, J. S. (1996). How religion influences morbidity and health: Reflections on natural history, salutogenesis and host resistance. *Social Science and Medicine, 43,* 849–864.

Li, X., Stanton, B., & Feigelman, S. (2000). Impact of perceived parental monitoring on adolescent risk behavior over 4 years. *Journal of Adolescent Health, 27,* 49–56.

Luthar, S. S., & Cicchetti, D. (2000). The construct of resilience: Implications for interventions and social policies. *Development and Psychopathology, 12,* 857–885.

Luthar, S. S., Cicchetti, D., & Becker, B. (2000). The construct of resilience: A critical evaluation and guidelines for future work. *Child Development, 71,* 543–562.

Luthar, S. S., & Zelazo, L. B. (2003). Research on resilience: An integrative review. In S. S. Luthar (Ed.), *Resilience and vulnerability: Adaptation in the context of childhood adversities* (pp. 510–550). New York, NY: Cambridge University Press.

Marcia, J. E. (1980). Identity in adolescence. In J. Adelson (Ed.), *Handbook of adolescent psychology* (pp. 109–137). New York, NY: Wiley.

Marsiglia, F. F., Kulis, S., & Hecht, M. L. (2001). Ethnic labels and ethnic identity as predictors of drug use among middle school students in the Southwest. *Journal of Research on Adolescence, 11,* 21–48.

Mason, C. A., Cauce, A. M., Gonzales, N., & Hiraga, Y. (1994). Adolescent problem behavior: The effect of peers and the moderating role of father absence and the mother-child relationship. *American Journal of Community Psychology, 22,* 723–743.

Masten, A. S., Garmezy, N., Tellegen, A., Pelligrini, D. S., Larkin, K., & Larsen, A. (1988). Competence and stress in school children: The moderating effects of individual and family qualities. *Journal of Child Psychology and Psychiatry, 29,* 745–764.

McManama O'Brien, K. H., Hernandez, L., & Spirito, A. (2014). Parental monitoring affects the relationship between depressed mood and alcohol-related problems in adolescents. *Substance Abuse.* doi:10.1080/08897077.2014.934417

Newcomb, M. D. (1995). Identifying high-risk youth: Prevalence and patterns of adolescent drug abuse. In E. Rahdert, D. Czechowicz, and I. Amsel (Eds.), *Adolescent drug abuse: Clinical assessment and therapeutic intervention* (pp. 7–38). Rockville, MD: National Institute on Drug Abuse.

Newcomb, M. D., & Felix-Ortiz, M. (1992). Multiple protective and risk factors for drug use and abuse-cross-sectional and prospective findings. *Journal of Personality and Social Psychology, 63,* 280–296.

Newcomb, M. E., Heinz, A. J., & Mustanski, B. (2012). Examining risk and protective factors for alcohol use in lesbian, gay, bisexual, and transgender youth: A longitudinal multilevel analysis. *Journal of Studies on Alcohol and Drugs, 73,* 783–793.

O'Malley, P. M., Johnston, L. D., & Bachman, J. G. (1998). Alcohol use among adolescents. *Alcohol Health and Research World, 22,* 85–93.

Oman, R. F., Vesely, S., Aspy, C. B., McLeroy, K. R., Rodine, S., & Marshall, L. (2004). The potential protective effect of youth assets on adolescent alcohol and drug use. *American Journal of Public Health, 94*, 1425–1430.

Ostaszewski, K., & Zimmerman, M. A. (2006). The effects of cumulative risk and promotive factors on urban adolescent alcohol and other drug use: A longitudinal study of resiliency. *American Journal of Community Psychology, 38*, 237–249.

Pollard, J. A., Hawkins, J. D., & Arthur, M. W. (1999). Risk and protection: Are both necessary to understand diverse behavioral outcomes in adolescence? *Social Work Research, 23*, 145–158.

Radloff, L. S. (1977). The CES-D scale: A self-report depression scale for research in the general population. *Applied Psychological Measurement, 1*, 385–401.

Rai, A. A., Stanton, B., Wu, Y., Li, X., Galbraith, J., Cottrell, L., . . . Burns, J. (2003). Relative influences of perceived parental monitoring and perceived peer involvement on adolescent risk behaviors: An analysis of six cross-sectional data sets. *Journal of Adolescent Health, 33*, 108–118.

Ramirez-Valles, J., Zimmerman, M. A., & Newcomb, M. D. (1998). Sexual risk behavior among youth: Modeling the influence of prosocial activities and socioeconomic factors. *Journal of Health and Social Behavior, 39*, 237–253.

Rhodes, J. E., Contreras, J. M., & Mangelsdorf, S. C. (1994). Natural mentor relationships among Latina adolescent mothers: Psychological adjustment, moderating processes, and the role of early parental acceptance. *American Journal of Community Psychology, 22*, 211–238.

Rhodes, J. E., Ebert, L., & Fischer, K. (1992). Natural mentors: An overlooked resource in the social networks of young, African American mothers. *American Journal of Community Psychology, 20*, 445–461.

Rosenblum, A., Magura, S., Fong, C., Cleland, C., Norwood, C., Casella, D., et al. (2005). Substance use among young adolescents in HIV-affected families: Resiliency, peer deviance, and family functioning. *Substance Use and Misuse, 40*, 581–603.

Roth, J. L., & Brooks-Gunn, J. (2003). Youth development programs: Risk, prevention and policy. *Journal of Adolescent Health, 32*, 170–182.

Rutter, M. (1985). Resilience in the face of adversity: Protective factors and resistance to psychiatric disorder. *British Journal of Psychiatry, 147*, 598–611.

Rutter, M. (1987). Psychosocial resilience and protective mechanisms. *American Journal of Orthopsychiatry, 57*, 316–331.

Rutter, M., Dunn, J., Plomin, R., Simonoff, E., Pickles, A., Maughan, B., . . . Eaves, L. (1997). Integrating nature and nurture: Implications of person-environment correlations and interactions for developmental psychopathology. *Development and Psychopathology, 9*, 335–364.

Salem, D. A., Zimmerman, M. A., & Notaro, P. C. (1998). Effects of family structure, family process, and father involvement on psychosocial outcomes among African-American adolescents. *Family Relations, 47*, 331–341.

Sameroff, A. J., Bartko, W. T., Baldwin, A., Baldwin, C., & Seifer, R. (1998). Family and social influences on the development of child competence. In M. Lewis & C. Feiring (Eds.) *Families, risk, and competence* (pp. 161–185). Mahwah, NJ: Erlbaum.

Sameroff, A. J., & Chandler, M. J. (1975). Reproductive risk and the continuum of caretaking casualty. In F. D. Horowitz, M. Hetherington, S. Scarr-Salapatek, & G. Siegel (Eds.), *Review of child development research* (pp. 187–243). Chicago, IL: University of Chicago Press.

Sameroff, A. J., & Mackenzie, M. J. (2003). Research strategies for capturing transactional models of development: The limits of the possible. *Development and Psychopathology, 15*, 613–640.

Sandler, I., Wolchik, S., Davis, C., Haine, R., & Ayers, T. (2003). Correlational and experimental study of resilience in children of divorce and parentally bereaved children. In S. S. Luthar (Ed.), *Resilience and vulnerability: Adaptation in the context of childhood adversities* (pp. 213–243). New York, NY: Cambridge University Press.

Scal, P., Ireland, M., & Borowsky, I. W. (2003). Smoking among American adolescents: A risk and protective factor analysis. *Journal of Community Health, 28*, 79–97.

Scheier, L. M., Botvin, G. J., Diaz, T., & Ifill-Williams, M. (1998). Ethnic identity as a moderator of psychosocial risk and adolescent alcohol and marijuana use: Concurrent and longitudinal analyses. *Journal of Child and Adolescent Substance Abuse, 6*, 21–47.

Scheier, L. M., Botvin, G. J., & Miller, N. L. (1999). Life events, neighborhood stress, psychosocial functioning, and alcohol use among urban minority youth. *Journal of Child and Adolescent Substance Abuse, 9*, 19–50.

Schulenberg, J., Bachman, J. G., O'Malley, P. M., & Johnston, L. D. (1994). High school educational success and subsequent substance use: A panel analysis following adolescents into young adulthood. *Journal of Health and Social Behavior, 35*, 45–62.

Seifer, R., Sameroff, A. J., Baldwin, C., & Baldwin, A. (1992). Child and family factors that ameliorate risk between 4 and 13 years of age. *Journal of American Academy of Child and Adolescent Psychiatry, 31*, 893–903.

Steinman, K. J., & Zimmerman, M. A. (2004). Religious activity and risk behavior among African American adolescents: Concurrent and developmental effects. *American Journal of Community Psychology, 33*, 151–161.

Sullivan, T. N., & Farrell, A. D. (1999). Identification and impact of risk and protective factors for drug use among urban African American adolescents. *Journal of Clinical Child Psychology, 28*, 122–136.

Unger, J. B., Schwartz, S. J., Huh, J., Soto, D. W., & Baezconde-Garbanati, L. (2014). Acculturation and perceived discrimination: Predictors of substance use trajectories from adolescence to emerging adulthood among Hispanics. *Addictive Behaviors, 39*, 1293–1296.

Vest, A. E., & Simpkins, S. D. (2013). When is sport participation risky or protective for alcohol use? The role of teammates, friendships, and popularity. In J. A. Fredricks & S. D. Simpkins (Eds.), *Organized out-of-school activities: Settings for peer relationships. New Directions for Child and Adolescent Development, 140*, 37–55.

Wachs, T. D. (1992). *The nature of nurture*. Newbury Park, CA: Sage.

Wallace J. M., Jr., & Williams, D. R. (1997). Religion and adolescent health-compromising behavior. In J. Schulenberg, J. L. Maggs, & K. Hurrelmann (Eds.), *Health risks and developmental transitions during adolescence* (pp. 444–468). New York, NY: Cambridge University Press.

Werner, E. E., & Smith, R. S. (1982). *Vulnerable but invincible*. New York, NY: McGraw-Hill.

Wills, T. A., & Cleary, S. D. (1996). How are social support effects mediated? A test with parental support and adolescent substance use. *Journal of Personality and Social Psychology, 71,* 937–952.

Wills, T. A., Sandy, J. M., Shinar, O., & Yaeger, A. (1999). Contributions of positive and negative affect to adolescent substance use: Test of a bidimensional model in a longitudinal study. *Psychology of Addictive Behaviors, 13,* 327–338.

Wills, T. A., Sandy, J. M., Yaeger, A., & Shinar, O. (2001). Family risk factors and adolescent substance use: Moderation effects for temperament dimensions. *Developmental Psychology, 37,* 283–297.

Wills, T. A., Yaeger, A., & Sandy, J. M. (2003). Buffering effect of religiosity for adolescent substance use. *Psychology of Addictive Behaviors, 17,* 24–31.

Windle, M. (1994). Substance use, risky behaviors, and victimization among a US national adolescent sample. *Addiction, 89,* 175–182.

Windle, M., Miller-Tutzauer, C., & Domenico, D. (1992). Alcohol use, suicidal behavior, and risky activities among adolescents. *Journal of Research on Adolescence, 2,* 317–330.

Wong, M. M., Nigg, J. T., Zuker, R. A., Puttler, L. I., Fitzgerald, H. E., Jester, J. M., . . . Adams, K. (2006). Behavioral control and resiliency in the onset of alcohol and illicit drug use: A prospective study from preschool to adolescence. *Child Development, 77,* 1016–1033.

Wright, D. R., & Fitzpatrick, K. M. (2004). Psychosocial correlates of substance use behaviors among African American youth. *Adolescence, 39,* 653–667.

Wyman, P. A., Cowen, E. L., Work, W. C., & Parker, G. R. (1991). Developmental and family milieu interview correlates of resilience in urban children who have experienced major life-stress. *American Journal of Community Psychology, 19,* 405–426.

Zimet, G. D., Powell, S. S., Farley, G. K., Werkman, S., & Berkoff, K. A. (1990). Psychometric characteristics of the multidimensional scale of perceived social support. *Journal of Personality Assessment, 55,* 610–617.

Zimmerman, M. A., & Arunkumar, R. (1994). Resiliency research: Implications for schools and policy. *Social Policy Report, 8,* 1–18.

Zimmerman, M. A., Bingenheimer, J. B., & Notaro, P. C. (2002). Natural mentors and adolescent resiliency: A study with urban youth. *American Journal of Community Psychology, 30,* 221–243.

Zimmerman, M. A., & Maton, K. I. (1992). Lifestyle and substance use among male African-American urban adolescents: A cluster analytic approach. *American Journal of Community Psychology, 20,* 121–138.

Zimmerman, M. A., Salem, D. A., & Maton, K. I. (1995). Family structure and psychosocial correlates among urban African-American adolescent males. *Child Development, 66,* 1598–1613.

Zimmerman, M. A., Stewart, S., Morrel-Samuels, S., Reischl, T., & Franzen, S. (2011). Youth empowerment solutions for peaceful communities: Combining theory and practice in a community-level violence prevention curriculum. *Health Promotion Practice, 12,* 425–439.

PART 6

Comorbidity in Adolescent Substance Abuse

Adolescent Substance Use and Co-Occurring Disorders

Jeffrey J. Wilson *and* Megan Janoff

Abstract

Adolescents with substance use disorders (SUDs) have the highest proportion of co-occurring psychiatric disorders (CODs) compared to other age cohorts. Externalizing psychiatric disorders, such as conduct disorder, oppositional defiant disorder, and attention-deficit disorders, are most commonly associated with adolescent SUDs compared to older adults with SUD. The developmental psychopathology of SUD is reviewed. Categories of COD are reviewed, in turn, beginning with externalizing or disruptive behavior disorders. Disruptive behavior disorders are critical to the developmental psychopathology of adolescent SUD. Studies of co-occurring depressive and bipolar disorders are then considered in detail, examining the relationship between SUD and these particular CODs. Finally, the relationships between anxiety, thought, eating and personality disorders, and adolescent SUD are examined.

Key Words: adolescent substance abuse, developmental psychopathology, disruptive behavior disorders, epidemiology, etiology, mood disorders, personality disorders, psychiatric comorbidity, substance abuse treatment

The Substance Abuse and Mental Health Services Administration ([SAMSHA], 2007) estimates that 8.9 million individuals in the United States struggle with co-occurring psychiatric disorders (CODs) and substance use disorders (SUDs). Few (7.4%) of these individuals find help for both of these disorders: Some are treated for psychiatric disorders or SUDs, and 55.8% receive no treatment whatsoever. These complex patients with CODs and SUDs have chronic debilitating illnesses that can destroy lives. Failing to address COD during SUD treatment may contribute to treatment failure. By the time they obtain help, individuals have a panoply of psychiatric disorders and life problems that are very difficult to treat. The significance of CODs for individuals suffering with SUDs, their families, and their health care providers cannot be overstated. Obviously, these problems did not start in adulthood, and the focus of this chapter is those younger

individuals who are already symptomatic in this way or are on their way to becoming so. Youth with SUDs and CODs are more difficult to treat, have more difficulty obtaining abstinence, and are more likely to relapse (Tomlinson, Brown, & Abrantes, 2004). The increased prevalence of COD in adolescents and young adults often contributes to their treatment resistance (American Academy of Child and Adolescent Psychiatry, 2005).

It is estimated that three quarters of all psychiatric disorders begin before the age of 24 years, and one half before the age of 14 years (SAMSHA, 2007). As substance use also begins in adolescence and peaks in young adulthood, this developmental period is critical for the study and treatment of CODs. Earlier intervention may prevent the development of further comorbidity and maladaptation. For youth with CODs, access to care is complicated by a number of factors, including a fragmented health care system with a lack of continuing care across behavioral health care, primary care, and substance abuse treatment providers (American Academy of Child and Adolescent Psychiatry, 2005; Riggs & Davies, 2002). Youth also struggle within their family systems, educational systems, cultural systems, and peer systems to get the help that they need. The stigma of being an "addict" is further complicated by the stigma of being "crazy," and the combination presents a formidable obstacle for youth with CODs. Moreover, as presented next, most youth with SUD have a COD, and many youth (perhaps a quarter) with psychiatric disorders use drugs; these youth are, not surprisingly, at an increased risk for developing an SUD (SAMSHA, 2007).

As pictured in Figure 24.1, it is estimated that about four out of five adolescents with SUD (79%) have a comorbid psychiatric disorder, with the most common disorders being conduct disorder (CD) and attention-deficit/hyperactivity disorder (ADHD), which themselves are commonly comorbid. Relative to adults with SUD, CODs are more common in adolescents with SUD. Children receiving mental health services more commonly use drugs (27% vs. 17%) than children not receiving such services, and hence they are at an increased risk of developing life course–persistent SUD.

In child psychiatry and psychology, a major hope for the future of children is early intervention and treatment, prior to the relative hard-wiring of psychiatric problems and their co-related troubles. Several psychiatric disorders place youth at higher risk for SUDs, especially ADHD, oppositional defiant disorder (ODD), and CD. As the most common psychiatric disorders among adolescents with SUD, they delineate one of the principal developmental pathways leading to SUD. Disruptive behavior disorders usually present prior to the onset of SUD, often early in childhood, and dramatically increase the risk of SUD, as will be discussed next (American Academy of Child and Adolescent Psychiatry, 2005).

Historically, child behavior health researchers and providers have distinguished between externalizing (includes disruptive behavior disorders) and internalizing disorders (includes anxiety and depression). Externalizing disorders (including CD, ODD, and attention-deficit disorders) have long been associated with the development of SUD, particularly in children and adolescents. As will be seen, the role of internalizing disorders in the development of SUD is also significant. Many youth with externalizing disorders also have co-occurring internalizing disorders, and the combination places such youth at even higher risk than either disorder alone. Some studies suggest that a combination of internalizing and externalizing pathology predicts a variety of adult outcomes, including ADHD, mood, SUD, and suicidality (Holtmann et al., 2011).

Chan et al. (2008) pooled multisite data from 77 substance abuse treatment studies using the Global Assessment of Individual Need (GAIN). A total of 4,930 adolescents and 1,956 adults in substance abuse treatment were included. The highest proportion of CODs (75.6%) is found in the youngest age group, those under 15 years. Notably, the relative prevalence of co-occurring externalizing and internalizing disorders differs with age: Externalizing disorders are more common in younger age groups,

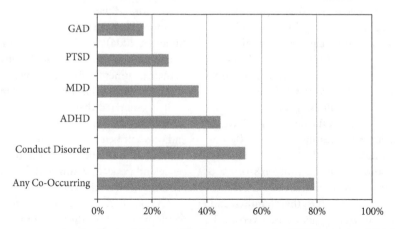

Figure 24.1 Common co-occurring disorders in adolescents with substance use disorder. ADHD, attention-deficit/hyperactivity disorder; GAD, generalized anxiety disorder; MDD, major depressive disorder; PTSD, posttraumatic stress disorder. *Source*: Adapted from SAMSHA/CSAT 2006.

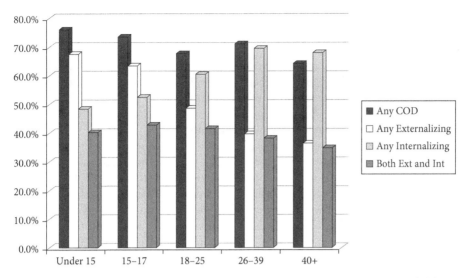

Figure 24.2 Externalizing and internalizing disorders among clients in substance use disorder treatment across the life span. *Source*: Data summarized from Chan et al. (2008). Prevalence and comorbidity of externalizing and internalizing problems among adolescents and adults presenting to substance abuse treatment.

and internalizing disorders more predominant in older age groups. These proportions are presented in Figure 24.2. It is also notable that a substantial proportion has co-occurring externalizing and internalizing disorders.

Figure 24.3 presents the psychiatric problems, rather than the general categories of externalizing and internalizing problems. As can be seen, depression, anxiety, and traumatic distress increase with age, eventually overcoming both ADHD and

conduct problems as the most common COD with SUD in adults. In contrast, conduct problems and ADHD decrease as the age of the patients in SUD increase.

Chan et al.'s (2008) description of COD across the life span in treatment-seeking adolescents and adults suggests a changing general pattern of COD among younger versus older individuals with COD (i.e., younger individuals with COD tend to have more externalizing disorders and older

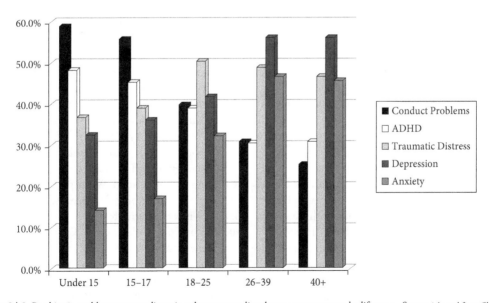

Figure 24.3 Psychiatric problems among clients in substance use disorder treatment across the life span. *Source*: Adapted from Chan et al. (2008). Prevalence and comorbidity of externalizing and internalizing problems among adolescents and adults presenting to substance abuse treatment.

individuals with COD tend to have more internalizing disorders). This study elucidates changes in patterns of COD across the life span, but there are limitations in the generalizability of these data, given the cross-sectional nature of the study and that the patients included are in treatment. However, since these observations are consistent with clinical observations of working with adolescents and adults in SUD treatment, and because they involve treatment seekers, they are of particular interest to clinicians treating SUD and COD.

Clearly there are a substantial and relatively consistent number of individuals with both externalizing and internalizing disorders across the developmental span studied, but there is a shift from a preponderance of externalizing disorders in younger individuals and a preponderance of internalizing disorders among older individuals with COD. As a cross-sectional study, it does not address the causal relationship between SUD and COD; nor can it address when these disorders began. There are many yet unanswered questions. Were there seeds of depression and anxiety during youth that were subclinical, undiagnosed, and went untreated? Do these youth develop depression and anxiety secondary to their delinquent or antisocial behaviors? Is the reduction in externalizing disorders developmental as many adults with antisocial personality disorder desist from antisocial behavior as they age, or is it a change related to the age of onset of SUD and COD (i.e., early vs. late onset)? While there are limitations to what questions these data can answer, these cross-sectional snapshots suggest a remarkable degree of heterogeneity. Furthermore, they suggest these differences merit further prospective studies to better understand these developmental trajectories, particularly the relationship between SUD and in particular COD.

Adolescents with SUD are a heterogeneous group. Research continues to develop and illuminate these heterogeneous patterns, and over the past 10 years research into adolescent-specific comorbidity has improved our understanding of CODs in adolescents with SUD. It is hoped that by parsing out the CODs we can develop a better understanding of the developmental pathways that lead to SUD. We will explore what is known regarding categories of CODs in turn, beginning with the categories with the strongest relationships with SUD. Each category of disorders will be considered in terms of the degree of co-occurrence, relevance to the developmental psychopathology of SUD, and implications for treatment of youth

with SUD. In many areas, understanding of adult psychopathology and its relationship to SUD will exceed our particular understanding of adolescent SUD. In such cases, we will extrapolate from the adult literature where necessary to provide direction for further study.

Etiology

Substance use commonly begins in adolescence and young adulthood. This chapter will predominantly focus on CODs, but multiple risk and protective factors have been found in relation to early-onset substance use and the transition to early-onset SUD. These include parent–child relations, peer relations, sibling relations, childhood attributes, adolescent individuation, adolescent neurobiology, and interactions between many of these variables (Brook, Brook, Richter, & Whiteman, 2003). Multiple prevention strategies have been used for adolescent SUDs, but no single theoretical or conceptual model takes precedent at present (Commission on Adolescent Substance Use and Alcohol Abuse, 2005).

Government policy intentionally delays the legal use of alcohol until 21 years of age to prevent the high degree of abuse and problems associated with the use of alcohol during adolescence and early adulthood. The 2013 Monitoring the Future Study estimates that in the 12th grade, 40.3% of students reported using an illicit drug at least once in their lifetime and 62.0% reported using alcohol at least once (Johnson, O'Malley, Miech, Bachman, & Schulenberg 2014). However, illicit drug use appears to be on the rise, and this increase is due to increased cannabis use. For example, 36.4% of adolescents reported having used marijuana in the past year, which is a significant increase from the 31.7% of adolescents who reported use in the Monitoring the Future survey in 2007. Illicit use other than cannabis, however, decreased moderately to its 2013 level of 17.3% from 18.5% in 2007.

It appears that most adolescents will use substances (most often alcohol, nicotine, or cannabis) prior to adulthood. While prevention appears to have an impact on substance use, it remains a fact that it is normative for many adolescents to use alcohol or drugs at least once. Early-onset alcohol use alone does not necessarily predict alcohol dependence, but patterns of use, particularly binge drinking and frequent use of alcohol, predict alcohol use disorder (Bonomo, Bowes, Coffey, Carlin, & Patton, 2004). It has been estimated that 27% of young adults who have used drugs six or more times progress to daily substance use, and approximately half of these daily users develop an SUD (Robins & Regier 1991). Since earlier exposure appears to convey increased risk of SUD, it seems reasonable to hypothesize that the incidence of SUD in adolescents who use substances six or more times may be higher. Nonetheless, the majority of youth who use substances are not likely to develop SUD, even among high-risk populations such as children of alcohol- or drug-dependent parents (Wilson, Beckman, & Nunes, 2007).

Several hypotheses have been proposed to explain the development of SUD, which have various degrees of support on a population level. These hypotheses are often useful on an individual level as well. These include the gateway hypothesis, the genetic vulnerability hypothesis, the behavioral dysregulation hypothesis, self-medication hypothesis, and the common liability model (Van Leeuwen et al., 2011; also see Table 24.1). In terms of understanding the developmental psychopathology of an individual's development of SUD, these hypotheses are often helpful in determining the underlying causes of SUD and may have implications for treatment on an individual level. For example, among youth with few conduct problems, self-medication appears to contribute to substance use, while among youth with more conduct problems, the influence of self-medication on substance use behavior is moderated (Hussong, Gould, & Hersh, 2008). On an individual level, several of these hypotheses may explain an individual's unique developmental psychopathology.

The use of so-called gateway substances such as nicotine (Chen et al., 2002), alcohol (Kirby & Barry, 2012), and marijuana are correlated positively with use of other illicit substances, and earlier onset use is associated with both progression to other substances and with increased risk of the development of an SUD (Fiellin, Tetrault, Becker, Fiellin, & Hoff, 2012). Some studies have even evaluated these relationships within particular groups of youth with SUD and COD. For example, cigarette smoking among ADHD youth is a robust predictor of SUD, perhaps even a stronger "gateway" substance in this high-risk group of youth (Biederman et al., 2006). It is hypothesized that earlier exposure to drugs may itself promote the development of SUD because of neurodevelopmental immaturity, lower prefrontal cortex volumes, lower or higher hippocampal volumes, and a vulnerable reward system (e.g., the mesocorticolimbic system)

that is particularly sensitive during this period of development (Rutherford, Mayes, & Potenza, 2010). Molecular changes in gene expression following exposure to gateway substances such as nicotine have also been reported (Levine et al., 2001). It is also possible that the neuropsychological profile of early-onset substance users itself promotes both early use and the development of SUD (Tarter, Kirisci, Habeych, Reynolds, & Vanyukov, 2004).

Toxic effects from exposure to substances during this vulnerable developmental period may also contribute to differences between youth with and without SUD, and they may even exacerbate pre-exposure vulnerabilities. Moreover, certain neuropsychological profiles and environments may promote risk of additional risk factors for SUD, and the risk conferred may be more dimensional in nature, such as a more general degree of behavioral dysregulation (Holtmann et al., 2011). These fundamental differences may increase the risk for COD; indeed, fundamental differences in neuroanatomy or neurophysiology may underlie the observed association between SUD and particular COD, for example, the associations between SUD, ADHD, and CD or antisocial personality disorder. New research domain criteria proposed by the National Institute of Mental Health (NIMH) may further our understanding of the relationship between neuroanatomy and function and particular domains that mechanistically underlie our phenomenological descriptions of behavior, per the *Diagnostic and Statistical Manual of Mental Disorders* (*DSM*).

As development proceeds, it is clear that each risk (genetic, neurodevelopmental, and environmental) compounds further risk, and risks often synergistically transact at each stage to promote the development of SUD; perhaps they also further contribute to the development of some degree of sociopathy, vis-à-vis ODD and then CD. Drug use itself also contributes to the sociopathic trajectory. As will be seen, the association between disruptive behavior disorders (especially conduct and adult antisocial personality disorder) and early-onset SUD is compelling and appears to indicate the most robust developmental trajectory toward early-onset SUD. Early drug use in the context of a youth with CD places youth at high risk of life course–persistent SUD (Fergusson, Boden, & Horwood, 2008). Risk factors tend to be found more often together than in isolation; they transact and enhance their individual risks synergistically to promote the development of SUD (Rutter, 1990).

Table 24.1 Hypotheses for the Development of Substance Use Disorder

Behavioral disinhibition hypothesis	Dysregulated impulse and behavioral control promotes early-onset use, impulsivity promotes more use, and failure to consider long-term consequences promotes further use and dependence.
Common liability model	There are common factors that underlie both licit and illicit substance use; that is, the same underlying liability is responsible for the use of gateway and other drugs.
Gateway hypothesis	Early-onset use primes the reward system for further drug use and promotes development of dependence. Exposure to gateway drugs increases risk of subsequent use in a stage-like sequence.
Genetic vulnerability hypothesis	Individuals have biochemical sensitivities to particular substances that promote their development of dependence. For example, persons who have a higher tolerance to alcohol, that is, metabolize it better, have a higher chance of developing an alcohol use disorder.
Route of administration model	Similarities in the route of administration account for progression between substances; that is, when an adolescent smokes cigarettes, he or she is at risk for smoking cannabis, or when an athlete injects steroids, he or she is at risk for injecting heroin.
Self-medication hypothesis	Individuals who develop substance use disorders have an emotional vulnerability that they actively seek to treat with a particular substance. For example, a socially anxious individual finds that alcohol reduces his or her anxiety and promotes more social interaction. The pattern of using alcohol to self-medicate anxiety is likely to increase and lead to dependence.

When considering developmental psychopathology, in our case, the relationship between SUD and COD, it is imperative to appreciate both the diversity of process and the diversity of outcome (Wills & Dishion, 2004). In order to conceptualize the unique developmental pathways in this diverse group, that is, youth with SUD (most of which have COD), the concepts of multifinality and equifinality can help an investigator to explain the diversity in starting points and outcomes (Cicchetti & Rogosch, 1999). Equifinality is defined as a common outcome obtained from various starting points, emphasizing diversity in the processes that cause the shared outcome. Multifinality is defined as diverse outcomes that are likely to emerge from any original starting point. Individuals who share common characteristics at a particular starting point will not have the same developmental outcome.

While these concepts are central to research aimed at understanding the transactional interplay between risk and resilience, these concepts are also useful in the individual psychiatric treatment of adolescents and young adults. A central question in the developmental psychopathology of early-onset SUD is why do some children of parents with SUD, or even some siblings of youth with SUD, turn completely away from substances of abuse? Why do some persons, with few or no risk factors, become addicted to heroin?

Disruptive Behavior Disorders

Disruptive behavior disorders have historically included attention-deficit disorders, ODD, and CD (Wilson & Levin, 2005). Young children with disruptive behavioral problems in preschool and kindergarten are at substantially greater risk for developing early-onset SUD (Mayzer, Fitzgerald, & Zucker, 2009). Externalizing problems in early adolescence are prospectively associated with substance use in later adolescence, and greater intensity of externalizing problems predicts greater substance use in a dose-dependent fashion (Goodman, 2010). Similarly, the intensity of behavioral dysregulation, as measured by a subscale of the CBCL–Externalizing Scale, also predicts SUD in young adulthood (Holtmann et al., 2011). This general behavioral dysregulation early in childhood is not captured by a single disease process and may be a marker of persistent deficits in self-regulation (Holtmann et al., 2011). This may explain to some extent the variety of particular CODs and the frequency of multiple CODs in adolescents with SUD.

In other words, fundamental deficits in behavioral and/or emotional dysregulation may increase the risk for a variety of child/adolescent psychiatric disorders and thereby SUD. As development proceeds into adulthood, more specific phenotypes may emerge; for example, antisocial personality disorder, bipolar disorders, and so on.

ADHD increases the risk of developing an SUD. A recent meta-analysis of prospective cohort studies of children with ADHD who were followed into young adulthood were at increased risk of alcohol (OR 1.35), cannabis (OR 1.51), and illicit drug use disorders (OR 3.48) in young adulthood and increased risk of nicotine use (OR 2.36) in mid-adolescence (Charach, Yeung, Climans, & Lillie, 2011). There is some evidence that the Hyperactive/Impulsive Subtype of ADHD is more strongly associated with SUD in adolescence than the Inattentive Subtype (Tamm, Adinoff, Nakonezny, Winhusen, & Riggs, 2012). Among disruptive behavior disorders, ADHD is often identified earliest, followed by the development of ODD in approximately 40% of youth with ADHD. Most longitudinal studies of children with ADHD treated with stimulants appear to suggest that treatment of ADHD is unlikely to increase the risk of SUD, and some studies suggest there may be a protective effect. Since ADHD itself is associated with SUD independent of stimulants, studies of stimulant use which fail to include control groups of youth with ADHD are confounded by the high rate of SUD in ADHD in general (Wilson & Levin, 2005).

ODD places youth at risk for CD, which may in turn lead to the development of SUD and/or antisocial personality disorder (Steiner & Wilson, 1999). CD is the most robust predictor of SUD among youth with ADHD. In fact, the development of CD appears to mediate the relationship between ADHD and early-onset SUD, which itself may represent a unique genetic subtype of youth with ADHD (Faraone, 2004). It is estimated that about a third of youth with CD go on to have antisocial personality disorder, but among youth with SUD and CD, one 4-year prospective study found that almost two thirds (61%) met criteria for antisocial personality disorder at follow-up (Myers, Brown, & Mott, 1995).

As the developmental bridge between CD and ADHD, ODD is of particular interest in the developmental psychopathology of SUD. There is particular interest in identifying youth with the greatest risk of developing antisocial personality disorder, and some studies have demonstrated

that youth with callous-unemotional traits and youth with early-onset CD are at high risk for life course–persistent antisocial personality disorder. In fact, Jester et al. (2008) demonstrated that children with ADHD and high levels of aggression had the greatest risk for SUD.

Recent research expands on the types of psychopathology predicted by ODD during childhood and adolescence. Stringaris and Goodman (2009) further parse ODD into three subtypes: irritable, headstrong, and hurtful. These three categories are based upon *DSM-IV* criteria for ODD. A total of 7,912 children (5–16 years) are followed for 3 years, and at follow-up those children with ODD whose symptoms are defined as irritable have more distress disorders (i.e., anxiety and depression), even after controlling for baseline psychopathology. ADHD, however, is predicted only by the headstrong ODD symptomatology. CD is predicted by both headstrong and harmful subtypes, although only headstrong symptoms predict CD once baseline CD is controlled for. However, regarding aggressive CD symptoms, only the hurtful symptomatology is predictive of aggressive CD symptomatology. Hence, both of these phenotypes of ODD have prognostic importance in predicting the most aggressive youth with CD. The role of the harmful phenotype suggests a developmental link of aggression: between the ODD criterion of spitefulness/vindictiveness and the most aggressive symptoms of CD. These may increase the risk of a more violent phenotype of antisocial personality disorder. Stringaris et. al. (2012) further described phenotypic associations and genetic links between irritability (as opposed to hurtful/headstrong subtypes) and depressed mood. More longitudinal research is needed to assess the risk of SUD among these three subphenotypes of ODD.

Depressive Disorders

Depressive disorders, now including disruptive mood dysregulation disorder in *DSM-5*, are among the most common CODs. Approximately a third of adolescents with SUD have co-occurring depression (32.7% under 15 years, 36.2% 16–17 years; Chan et al., 2008). Among young psychiatric patients, youth under 13 years old may have an even higher co-occurrence at 56.7% (Wu, Gersing, Burchett, Woody, & Blazer, 2011), and adults over 40 also have a high co-occurrence rate at 56.2% (Chan et al., 2008). Among inpatients with SUD, the co-occurrence of depression has also been reported to be over 50% (i.e., 56%). On the other hand, as many as a third of depressed adolescents may turn to substance abuse (Deas, 2006; Rao et al., 1999).

During adolescence, the presence of disruptive behavior disorders appears to be the strongest predictor of SUDs; however, a large group (40%) of youth has co-occurring externalizing and internalizing disorders. Not surprisingly, adolescents with co-occurring conduct problems and depression appear to have greater maladjustment in young adulthood (Capaldi & Stoolmiller, 1999). Moreover, youth with baseline depression may have a greater chance of relapse following residential treatment (Subramaniam et al., 2007). Among adolescent girls, initial depression can also promote eating disorder behaviors, antisocial behaviors, and the development of SUD (Measelle, Stice, & Hogansen, 2006).

In any case, self-medication is commonly reported among both adolescents and adults with depression. Depression is a predictor of alcohol use, illicit drug use (Lansford et al., 2008), and alcohol-related problems and alcohol dependence in young adulthood (Crum et al., 2008). There may be some gender differences; some studies have suggested that alcohol use is associated with depression in girls but not boys (Saraceno, Heron, Munafo, Craddock, & van den Bree, 2012). Co-occurring depression may also contribute to treatment resistance among depressed individuals, and it is clinically significant in many cases (Birmaher & Brent, 2007). In one large study, 28% of depressed adolescents reported using substances for self-medication of depressive symptoms (Goldstein et al., 2009). Other studies have reported similar rates among depressed adults, and higher rates among those with co-occurring bipolar disorder (Bolton, Robinson, & Sareen, 2009).

Some studies suggest that depression is a consequence of SUD more so than a cause of SUD (Fergusson, Boden, & Horwood, 2009). The neurotoxic effects of the abuse of substances may also contribute to depressive psychopathology (Brady & Sinha, 2005). Substance use during adolescence and young adulthood is strongly associated with externalizing disorders (Lansford et al., 2008). Although the magnitude of association is much stronger for externalizing disorders, for some youth, depressive disorders are also associated with substance use in adolescence and young adulthood. Interestingly, among adolescents, there is some suggestion that depression may play a larger role in the development of SUD in girls than in boys (Saraceno et al., 2012). Therefore, on an individual level, the developmental

sequence of psychopathology is an important aspect of treatment planning. Failing to identify this may impact treatment of the SUD (Kratochvil, Wilens, & Upadhyaya, 2006).

As depression more clearly becomes a risk factor for SUD, and for relapse, it is recommended that youth with co-occurring depression and SUD be treated for both conditions, as the depression can prevent effective SUD treatment just as SUD can promote depression (American Academy of Child and Adolescent Psychiatry, 2007). Increasingly, the literature suggests that there are multiple pathways to early-onset SUD, and while the majority may be associated with primary externalizing disorders such as CD, for some adolescents internalizing disorders such as depression may play a significant role (Crum et al., 2008, Hadland et al., 2011; Saraceno et al., 2012).

The *DSM-5* defines a new diagnosis in the depressive disorders section, disruptive mood dysregulation disorder (DMDD), that includes nonepisodic irritability, which may prove upon further study to also convey risk for SUD (American Psychiatric Association, 2014). Presently, little is known regarding the relationship between DMDD and SUD. These youth appear more prone to unipolar depression and anxiety, more so than bipolar disorder. Ninety percent of these youth have ODD, and the *DSM-5* requires that if a practitioner makes the diagnosis of DMDD, then ODD is excluded (American Psychiatric Association, 2014). Others argue that this is more properly a variant of ODD, while the recommendation for including a new diagnosis in the *DSM-5* argues that the mood component defines a different trajectory than that typically implied by ODD; that is, these youth are at risk for CD and thereby SUD. It may turn out that chronic or nonepisodic irritability is a ticking time bomb for later onset SUD, possibly associated with depressive psychopathology, but the research remains to be done to test this hypothesis.

A Comment on Irritability, Depression, and Broad-Phenotype "Bipolarity"

The definition of bipolar disorders in children and adolescents is a complex and controversial subject beyond the scope of the present chapter (Althoff, 2010). However, given the frequency of this diagnosis among children and adolescents and adolescents with SUD, some commentary is indicated. In brief, part of the controversy involves the definition of bipolar disorder with narrow versus broad phenotype bipolar disorder. Broad phenotype bipolar disorder includes a broader spectrum beyond what is diagnosable as bipolar disorder in *DSM-IV* or *DSM-5*. The controversy also includes whether to include nonepisodic irritability as a bipolar spectrum disorder. As was seen earlier, the *DSM-5* defines DMDD as a depressive disorder. How much this diagnosis will account for youth with severe mood dysregulation who do not meet *DSM* criteria for bipolar disorder remains speculative at the time of the writing of this chapter. For the sake of this review, *DSM-5* criteria will be used to define bipolar disorder; in other words, the narrow phenotype of bipolar affective disorder, which is consistent through development, will be used to define bipolar disorder.

Irritability is commonly encountered in child and adolescent psychiatry, and over the past few decades it has increasingly been associated with bipolar disorders. Nonepisodic irritability or severe mood dysregulation is among the more common psychiatric symptoms among both children and adolescents that parents often seek help for, but substantial division and controversy remain as to how to categorize it (Carlson, 2012). ADHD is often associated with irritability, and this is most often associated with the co-occurrence of ODD and depression (Ambrosini, Bennett, & Elia, 2013). Many psychiatric diagnoses in childhood include irritability, but there has been relatively less research into this dimensional characteristic and its prognostic significance. The differential of irritability is broad and psychiatric diagnostic constructs often overlap.

Perhaps youth with severe mood dysregulation or disruptive mood dysregulation represent a variant of ODD that has a strong mood component. Another possibility is that this irritability and high levels of oppositionality may predict borderline personality development (Burke & Stepp, 2012). Irritability then may indicate risk for depression, and perhaps for later onset SUDs, which appear more related to depression/anxiety than to more externalizing or disruptive disorders (which in adulthood are typified by antisocial personality disorder). Irritability may indicate a variety of problems later in adult development, including unipolar depression, anxiety, bipolar mood, and perhaps borderline personality disorders. It appears this childhood irritability is most commonly associated with later depression, but in some cases it may be associated with SUD and in others may indicate bipolar disorder. Accurate diagnosis is critical to effective treatment, as the underlying cause of the observed irritability will fail to be given evidence-based treatment if misdiagnosed. Moreover, the wrong treatment can exacerbate the irritability (in the case of bipolarity treated with antidepressants or in the case of depression treated with mood stabilizers.) In other cases, ADHD/ODD irritability may be masked if misdiagnosed as bipolar disorder and treated with mood stabilizers, and in some cases it may also be aggravated by worsening attention due to cognitive side effects. These are complex issues in child psychiatry, made even more complicated by an adolescent who continues to abuse drugs or alcohol.

The stakes are high in terms of diagnosis: False-positive diagnoses of bipolar disorder can cause youth to take medications that are not only ineffective but toxic. False-negative diagnoses can fail to prevent the progression of a devastating disease process. Of course, substance intoxication and particularly withdrawal can also contribute to irritability among youth with CODs. Careful psychiatric diagnosis can help discern the phenomenology of an individual's irritability in the majority of cases, but there remains a degree of unreliability in our diagnostic systems on an individual level. More research is sorely needed to determine the relationship between DMDD and SUD, as well as to better understand the relationship between irritability and SUD during development. How we define these disorders is to an extent semantic; however, how we define these disorders also has broad implications for the youth so diagnosed, from prognosis to treatment. Moreover, the definition of these disorders has substantial implications for future research of mood dysregulation in youth and its relationship to SUD.

Bipolar Mood Disorders

Bipolar disorders are commonly associated with SUD among adults, but the existing evidence in adolescents suggests a lower degree of comorbidity. There are limited data on the lifetime prevalence of narrow phenotype bipolar disorder among adolescents with SUDs. The available data are inconsistent, with Lubman et al. (2007) finding a prevalence of 7% of adolescents with bipolar disorder while Wilens et al. (1997) found a prevalence of 32% (Wilens et al., 1997). There are somewhat more data on the lifetime prevalence of SUD among adolescents with bipolar disorder, with various studies presenting disparate values between 16% and 34% (Goldstein et al., 2008; Lewinsohn, Klein, & Seeley, 1995; Wilens et al., 2004, 2008).

It is widely reported that adolescent-onset as opposed to childhood-onset bipolar disorder confers a greater risk of developing SUD (Goldstein et al., 2008; Wilens et al., 2004, 2008). One study found that adolescent-onset bipolar disorder confers nearly nine times the risk for developing SUD compared to childhood-onset bipolar disorder. Studies have not yet elucidated reasons for this pattern. Whether childhood-onset and adolescent-onset bipolar disorder are different phenotypes with different associated risks, or the onset of bipolar disorder in adolescence confers a particular vulnerability to the development of SUD, is unclear (Wilens et al., 1999). Bipolar disorder tends to precede the development of SUD with between 60% and 83% of adolescents developing bipolar disorder before SUD (Goldstein et al., 2008; Wilens et al., 1999, 2004). Some of this pattern may be explained by self-medication of mood symptoms. One study found that youth with bipolar disorder were more likely to report initiating drug use to attenuate mood than those without bipolar disorder. Thirty percent of substance-using youth with bipolar disorder initiated or continued to use substances specifically to change their mood (Lorberg, Wilens, Martelon, Wong, & Parcell, 2010).

The combination of bipolar disorder with SUD appears to be associated with greater comorbidity and worse outcomes. Bipolar adolescents with SUD have a higher prevalence of suicide attempts, CD, and posttraumatic stress disorder (PTSD). Those with SUD are more likely to report trouble with law enforcement, a history of pregnancy and abortion, and a greater prevalence of physical and sexual abuse (Goldstein et al., 2009). Severe bipolar disorder confers a greater risk of SUD than more mild forms of the illness (Wilens et al., 2004).

CD and PTSD also appear to be particularly intertwined with the development of SUD among adolescents with bipolar disorder. Studies have found that adolescents with CD comorbid with bipolar disorder are more likely to go on to develop SUD than those with bipolar disorder alone (Goldstein et al., 2008; Wilens et al., 1999). Another study found that among bipolar adolescents, those with SUD had a greater risk of CD (Wilens et al., 1999). Bipolar disorder with comorbid PTSD also confers a greater risk of developing SUD than bipolar disorder alone, with the onset of PTSD and bipolar disorder occurring prior to the onset of SUD in the majority of cases (Steinbuchel, Wilens, Adamson, & Sgambati, 2009).

While the exact prevalence of these disorders is inconclusive, it is clear that adolescents with SUD have a disproportionate risk of carrying a bipolar diagnosis and vice-versa. Youth with adolescent onset bipolar disorder have a greater risk of developing SUD than those with childhood onset, and bipolar disorder precedes the development of SUD in the majority of cases. Bipolar disorder and SUD are associated with poor psychosocial outcomes and greater psychiatric comorbidity, particularly CD and PTSD. Clinical research is needed to determine whether effective treatment of bipolar disorder during childhood or adolescence reduces the risk of SUD or otherwise improves outcomes for youth with bipolar disorder and SUD. Clinically it is recommended that both disorders are treated, and the treatment is integrated as much as possible (Nunes, Selzer, Levounis, & Davies, 2010). In the case of multiple CODs, mood stabilization is recommended prior to treatment of other psychiatric disorders.

Anxiety Disorders

Anxiety disorders are a heterogeneous group that currently include disorders as varied as specific phobia, panic disorder with or without agoraphobia, PTSD, obsessive-compulsive disorder (OCD), social phobia or social anxiety disorder, and generalized anxiety disorder (GAD), as well as separation anxiety disorder in childhood (American Psychiatric Association, 2000). Anxiety disorders are reported among youth with SUD, although with the exception of PTSD (which DSM-5 categorizes as a trauma and stressor-related disorder, not as an anxiety disorder), epidemiologically they are not more common than in youth without SUD. It should be noted that these disorders themselves are often co-occurring and have a complex and highly variable pattern of co-occurrence (American Academy of Child and Adolescent Psychiatry, 2007). Studies of adults suggest that these disorders should be considered separately (Alegria et al., 2010). As will be suggested from the available literature, these disorders may have different effects on the risk of substance use and the development of SUD in particular. Moreover, they may have differential effects at different stages of development. At this stage of research of adolescents and SUD, we have found relatively little specific research on anxiety disorders and SUD. As a result, we will review the available research in the context of adult research on SUD and anxiety disorders, extrapolating where possible and making suggestions for further research of this important topic.

PTSD is found in approximately a quarter of adolescents with SUD. Among adults with PTSD, it is estimated that over 40% meet criteria for SUD (Jacobsen, Southwick, & Kosten, 2001). Evidence-based treatment of PTSD among adults with SUD has been shown to improve substance use as well as PTSD outcomes (Hien et al., 2010). PTSD appears to contribute an independent risk for cannabis use disorders after controlling for the effect of conduct disorders or delinquency (Cornelius et al., 2010). Trauma with and without PTSD is associated with adverse treatment outcomes. For example, traumatic history without PTSD is associated with higher rates of dropout from treatment (Jaycox, Ebener, Damesek, & Becker, 2004). Young adults entering college with PTSD have higher rates of substance use and higher rates of substance-related problems (Read et al., 2012). In treatment-seeking adolescents with bipolar disorder, 8% meet full criteria for PTSD and 8% meet partial criteria for PTSD (Steinbuchel et al., 2009). Interestingly, in this study 39% of adolescents with PTSD in treatment at the bipolar disorder clinic had co-occurring SUD; hence, it may be that youth with co-occurring PTSD and bipolar affective disorders have higher risk for SUD than either disorder alone.

There are indications that social anxiety disorder in particular may be positively associated with alcohol dependence in adults, but perhaps may be protective (negatively correlated) for adolescents. For example, in a community study of over 40,000 adults, the odds ratio for having alcohol abuse given social anxiety disorder was 1.2, and the odds ratio for having alcohol dependence given social anxiety disorder was 2.8. Note that the risk for alcohol dependence, the more severe phenotype, was much greater than for alcohol abuse given a diagnosis of social anxiety (Schneier et al., 2010). In this study, approximately 80% of the subjects reported having social anxiety prior to the development of substance use. It is also noteworthy that adults with these CODs were at substantially higher risks for additional psychopathology, in particular, personality disorders and other SUDs as well as compulsive gambling.

In contrast, Frojd et al. (2011) found that social phobia in mid-adolescence may have a protective effect regarding SUD, and it may reduce the risk of substance use in later adolescence. Longer prospective study would be needed to see if these youth had similar risks for SUD later in life. It may be

that the protective effect diminishes once a person uses substances in adulthood. This research has not yet been done. On the other hand, GAD appears to have a greater role during mid-adolescence in predicting substance use than social phobia, although this may be mediated by depression (Frojd, Ranta, Kaltiala-Heino, & Marttunen, 2011). Alegria et al. (2010) reported that as many as half of all individuals with GAD have a co-occurring SUD in adulthood. Adults with co-occurring GAD and SUD have more complex psychiatric histories than with either disorder alone, greater incidence of new Axis I disorders, and greater self-reported drug use at follow-up 3 years later (Magidson, Liu, Lejuez, & Blanco, 2012).

Substances may also differ in their relationship with anxiety. For example, cannabis in particular seems to be associated with anxiety and mood disorders, and indeed it has been reported that frequent, moderate, and infrequent users of cannabis report higher levels of anxiety than controls, suggesting a complex relationship between anxiety and cannabis (Cheung et al., 2010). This is not surprising given the behavioral pharmacology of cannabis, which is a stimulant and increases heart rate. Cannabis is also associated with developing depression, but since the acute effects include euphoria, adolescents can be caught in a spiral of worsening depression (Harder, Stuart, & Anthony, 2008; Reece, 2009).

Blom et al. (2011) found that among adult men, SUD is more strongly associated with OCD than other (*DSM-IV*) anxiety disorders. No studies of OCD and SUD in adolescents were found to review.

Lansford et al. (2008) suggested that anxiety itself may act as a protective factor, which may delay exposure to substances of abuse. However, the relationship may be complex. Anxiety could theoretically decrease the risk of use, but once a person uses, this might trigger a substance use disorder through a self-medication mechanism. On a developmental level, anxiety may also increase risk of substance use and/or disorder vis-à-vis social impairment, which has been associated with the prospective development of SUD, after common predictors of SUD are controlled for (Greene et al., 1999). Anxiety disorders are also likely to change during development, and earlier onset anxiety disorders may increase the risk of a broad spectrum of problems. Childhood anxiety manifested by (retroactive reports of) separation anxiety disorder during mid-adolescence is predictive of adult psychiatric problems, including panic disorder and depression (Lewinsohn et al., 2008). The presence of anxiety during childhood and adolescence might be related to the later development of SUD through complex mechanisms, including the development of potentially mediating disorders such as generalized anxiety disorder that appear as risk factors for adult SUD. More research is needed to test these hypotheses.

Another study demonstrated that alcohol dependence was increased in adults with combined anxiety and depression, while alcohol abuse did not differ from controls. Other risk factors for alcohol dependence in this group of individuals with anxiety and depressive disorders included being male, family history of alcohol dependence or anxiety/depression, childhood trauma, and childhood onset of depression or anxiety (Boschloo et al., 2011). While this study reports on adults, retrospectively it considered the role of child-onset disorders and the relationships between primary versus secondary alcohol use disorders. Interestingly, they found that introverted lonely and neurotic individuals were more likely to develop alcohol dependence secondarily to their anxiety disorders, while extroverted males were more likely to have primary alcohol dependence.

The existing literature suggests the relationship between SUD and anxiety disorders is complex. Individuals with anxiety or depressive disorders may have a high risk of developing alcohol and other SUD during adulthood, but these same disorders during adolescence may be protective in regard to early-onset SUD (Liang & Chikritzhs, 2011). Clinically it is imperative to recognize that youth with anxiety disorders have high rates of comorbidity with other psychiatric disorders, for example, ODD, which also may further augment risk for developing early-onset SUD (Manassis & Monga, 2001). Identifying and treating anxiety disorders during adolescence may be preventative of adult-onset SUD, but again, more research is necessary to better understand the relationship between anxiety in its various forms and early- versus late-onset SUD. Moreover, research parsing out the heterogeneity in various anxiety disorders and particular forms of SUD (alcohol, cannabis, cocaine, etc.) is necessary to better prevent and treat individuals with co-occurring anxiety and substance use disorders. Study indicates that the relationships are complex, and at particular periods of development specific anxiety disorders may be protective (e.g. social phobia in adolescence) and at other times are positively associated with SUD (i.e., GAD

in adolescents and adults with SUD.) Moreover, anxiety may result from the consequences of addiction, and its role in recovery from SUD merits further study.

Thought Disorders

Although thought disorders are relatively uncommon among adolescents in contrast to adults, thought disorders often begin in young adulthood, especially for young men. Exposure to cannabis during this developmental period can lead to prolonged subsyndromal psychosis (van Gastel et al., 2012). Moreover, for youth who develop cannabis use disorders at 14 years of age or younger, the age at onset of first-episode psychosis has been shown to be significantly younger (Schimmelmann et al., 2011). Cannabis use has been associated with a younger age of onset for both schizophrenia and bipolar disorder (De Hert et al., 2011).

Both cannabis and amphetamines can induce psychosis, and hallucinogens are associated with psychosis-like symptoms, including de-realization, depersonalization, and illusions. Amphetamine-induced psychosis can last up to 12 months, making it difficult at times to ascertain the relationship between the psychosis and the substance use, particularly if the individual continues to relapse on amphetamines (Marshall & Werb, 2010). A vulnerable brain that is still developing at a time when many individuals begin to experiment with drugs is a major concern. Cannabis in particular is particularly problematic because of its relative legalization across the United States and its actual legalization in Washington and Colorado during the November 2012 election. Cannabis use as well as cannabinomimetic drugs or synthetic cannabinoids is on the rise in adolescents. On the front lines of the war on drugs, adolescents are barraged with a variety of messages regarding the safety of drug use. Hence, it is critical for health care and substance use professionals to be aware of and convey the real risks associated with these drugs. In our opinion it is critical that the information be accurate and neither over- nor understated since in the age of information technology, a variety of sources are available at the click of a mouse or touch of an iPhone.

One concern that is clear in the literature is the risk of psychosis associated with cannabis use (Dragt et al., 2012; Hides et al., 2009). While many studies focus on adults, adolescence is a critical period of developmental vulnerability where many youth first use cannabis. In one retrospective study, cannabis use significantly decreased the age of onset of psychosis (Gonzalez-Pinto et al., 2008). In a prospective study of young people, cannabis use moderately increased the risk of psychosis, a risk that was substantially increased in youth with a predisposition toward psychosis such as a positive family history of psychosis (Henquet et al., 2005). There is some suggestion from imaging studies that cannabis use disorders may mediate the development of early-onset schizophrenia, which is associated with reduced left superior parietal lobe volumes (Kumra et al., 2012). In early-onset schizophrenia, diffuse white matter and gray matter deficits in a variety of areas (including the ventral striatum, right middle temporal gyrus, insular cortex, and paracingulate gyrus) are associated with cannabis use (James et al., 2011).

One of the most vexing considerations in COD is how many risk factors overlap, and in some instances combine, to dramatically increase risk. Childhood symptoms of inattention-hyperactivity appear to independently predict first-onset psychosis, even after ODD and CD symptoms are controlled for (Cassidy, Joober, King, & Malla, 2011). It is interesting to note that desistance in cannabis use is associated with reduced psychosis (Baeza et al., 2009). Childhood trauma and cannabis use may also interact to promote risks for developing psychosis (Harley et al., 2010).

Clinically, adolescents with SUD should be screened for drugs of abuse such as cannabis and amphetamines and cocaine, since they can contribute to the development and maintenance of psychosis. Hallucinogens such as LSD may also promote risk of psychosis. Children at risk for psychosis because of a family history of schizophrenia or bipolar disorder, or with a trauma history, should be counseled regarding the risk of triggering a psychotic disorder through the use of these drugs.

Eating Disorders

Eating disorders are also present among a minority of youth in treatment for SUDs. Some studies have demonstrated an elevated rate of SUDs in adults with eating disorders, bulimia nervosa in particular (Holderness, Brooks-Gunn, & Warren, 1994). As a high-risk behavior, disordered eating in adolescence is associated with elevated frequencies of substance misuse, including binge drinking and drug use, in a dose-dependent fashion (Unikel, Root, Vonholle, Ocampo, & Bulik, 2011). Elevated use of tobacco and other drugs is also reported among clinical samples of adolescents with eating disorders (Pisetsky, Chao,

Dierker, May, & Striegel-Moore, 2008). There is some suggestion that substance misuse is even more relevant among boys than in girls with disordered eating behaviors (Pisetsky et al., 2008). Eating disorders themselves are associated with substantial co-occurring psychopathology, particularly depression (Lewinsohn, Striegel-Moore, & Seeley 2000). The relationship between disordered eating behaviors and substance use has been explained by a variety of factors, including mutual association with other CODs such as depression or conduct problems or other impulse control disorders such as ADHD (Ackard, Fulkerson, & Neumark-Sztainer, 2011). Substances such as tobacco, cocaine, and amphetamines may be particularly appealing to some given their anorectic propensities. Other substances such as steroids or growth hormones may be appealing because of their performance enhancement or anabolic properties. Body builders and ballet dancers are at particular risk for eating disorders and related drug use.

Personality Disorders

It is estimated that 15% of adults in the community have a personality disorder. It is notable that identifying "character defects" is a core aspect of the 12 steps (steps 4–7) in self-help programs such as Alcoholics Anonymous or Narcotics Anonymous. While character defects do not equate to personality disorders, character defects are synonymous with personality traits to a large extent (Alcoholics Anonymous, 1939).

Personality disorders often begin in adolescence, although many clinicians are reluctant to diagnose personality disorders at this stage of development (Bleiberg, 2001). Three personality disorders in particular are associated with SUD in adulthood; these include antisocial (OR 2.46–3.51), borderline (OR 2.04–2.78), and schizotypal (OR 1.65–5.90) personality disorders (Hasin et al., 2011). While the phenomenology of particular personality disorders may differ between adults and adolescents, there is evidence of prognostic validity to the diagnosis of borderline personality disorder in adolescents (Chanen et al., 2004). Antisocial personality disorder by definition is not diagnosed until age 18 (American Psychiatric Association, 2014), but as has been reviewed, CD, a precursor of antisocial personality disorder, is the most common COD in adolescents with SUD. Little is known about the relationship of the schizotypal personality disorder to SUD in adolescents (Bleiberg, 2001; Western, Shedler, Durett, Glass, & Martens, 2003).

In one well-designed study of psychiatric outpatients, approximately a third (31%) meet criteria for *DSM-IV* personality disorders, and when the category of personality disorder NOS is included, close to half have a personality disorder (45.5%; Zimmerman, Rothschild, & Chelminski, 2005). Borderline and antisocial personality disorders were both strongly associated with alcohol use disorders in that study. In one study of adolescent inpatients, the highest co-occurring psychiatric disorders with SUD were CD and borderline personality disorder (Daudin et al., 2010). A recent longitudinal study of twins demonstrated that the co-occurrence of SUD and borderline personality disorder was accounted for by shared environmental factors at 14, but at 18 genetic factors accounted for the association, suggesting that the co-occurrence of these conditions may be because of common risk factors across the conditions (Bornovalova, Hicks, Iacono, & McGue, 2013). Some studies suggest that the borderline personality construct in adolescents may be more variable than in adults; indeed, this is an issue for personality disorders in general, with the most common diagnosis often personality disorder NOS (Becker, McGlashan, & Grilo, 2006).

Although once controversial, the diagnosis of borderline personality disorder during adolescence is increasingly recognized to be critical to accurate assessment and treatment (Kaess, Brunner, & Chanen, 2014). Given that there are evidence-based treatments for adolescents that may be useful in treating borderline personality disorder or potentially for preventing the development of borderline personality disorder, failing to diagnose even a prodromal borderline or antisocial personality disorder deprives the youth of potentially preventative or curative treatment at a relatively malleable stage of development. The application of treatments such as dialectical behavior therapy has been effectively applied to adolescents who have borderline characteristics such as self-injury, mood lability, and chronic suicidal ideation. Indeed, DBT and similar treatments such as mentalizing therapy are evidence-based mainstays of many adolescent inpatient and residential programs (Katz, Cox, Gunasekara, & Miller, 2004; Rossouw & Fonagy, 2012).

Personality disorders are present in an estimated 30% of completed suicides and 40% of suicide attempts; when alcohol or drug use disorders are co-occurring with personality disorders, suicide and a variety of other serious problems are terribly likely (Oldham, 2006). Hence, since most adults with personality disorder recall developing the symptoms in childhood, and given their prospective validity as well as effective treatments, a compelling argument can be made for the diagnosis and treatment of personality disorders in adolescents in general, and in adolescents with SUDs in particular (Kernberg, Weiner, & Bardenstein, 2000) This is particularly the case for antisocial and borderline personality disorders because of their high prevalence and strong associations with SUDs in adulthood.

It may be that fundamental deficits in socioemotional processing may place youth at risk for developing antisocial and borderline personality disorders (Bleiberg, 2001; Western et al., 2003). Cluster B personality disorders in particular share characteristics such as mood lability, which also may contribute to their proclivity to substance abuse. Studying the dimension of irritability developmentally may prove to better elucidate the developmental psychopathology of borderline personality disorders (Burke & Stepp, 2012). Parsing out these developmental pathways may have meaning for prevention and treatment of both personality disorders and SUDs. Moreover, SUD themselves may promote irregular socioemotional processing in relationships, further "hardwiring" such socioemotional irregularities. In psychodynamic terms, basic deficits in socioemotional processing may in turn promote defense mechanisms characteristic of various types of character psychopathology: schizotypal, avoidant, borderline, and antisocial in particular.

Through developing ever better diagnostic descriptions of behavioral phenomenology, developmental psychopathology can improve our characterizations of behavior and prognostic pitfalls. The current tendency to diagnose severe mood dysregulation or irritability on a sometimes vague bipolar spectrum may dilute this information (Carlson, 2012). On the other hand, parsing out significant prognostic information may assist family and health care providers to develop more useful plans to help the youth grow. For example, irritability associated with early childhood ODD predicts depression and anxiety in middle childhood, not bipolar disorder. This distinction can help to develop more specific and theoretically more effective treatment. Including personality disorders, or even prodromal personality disorders in our consideration of CODs in adolescents, in our opinion further adds to our formulation of individual cases and provides valuable guidance in developing an effective recovery plan for youth with CODs. Unfortunately, their complexity often requires extensive treatment in a controlled environment.

Clinical Implications
Case Example: Garrett

Garrrett is a 15-year-old, socially anxious youth who uses cannabis with his peers to fit in, and the euphoric effects of cannabis initially overcome some of his social anxiety. However, as he becomes tachycardic due to the effects of cannabis and as the euphoria remits, he may be prone to panic attacks and increased social anxiety. Lacking other means of overcoming his social anxiety, he is likely to resist abstinence from cannabis, especially if his sole peer group primarily gets together to smoke cannabis. In this situation the anxiety disorder predated the cannabis use, but the cannabis use also exacerbates his anxiety in a complex manner which is not clear to him. Furthermore, his unique social system also promotes cannabis use and without cannabis he is quite alone. Understanding these relationships, and perhaps, more important, helping him to see these relationships, is critical to effecting recovery from cannabis use disorder.

One of the more vexing problems in the clinical management of adolescent comorbidity is discerning the etiology of a COD, specifically whether the observed COD is primary (i.e., occurred independently) or secondary to the abuse of a particular substance. For example, cannabis is associated with depression, psychosis, inattention, learning problems, and anxiety; when adolescents with cannabis use disorder present with any of these symptoms, it is imperative to consider cannabis as a potential causative agent for any of these problems. As clinicians, our first approach is simply to remove the potential causative agent, but at times the co-occurring problems interfere with our ability to do so. At such times the systems supporting use of cannabis within an individual adolescent conspire against our best efforts. The belief system of the adolescent may be that the cannabis treats her anxiety, or that the cannabis facilitates learning, or in other cases inattention and hyperactivity may conspire against change by interfering with the learning required of a particular recovery program. In such cases failing to treat the COD may interfere with the treatment of SUD. Our approach to adolescents with substance use and CODs is to focus primarily on stabilizing the adolescent's addiction, preferably through achieving abstinence for a period. However, when we are not able to accomplish abstinence, we may need to settle for stabilizing or minimizing use and providing the adolescent with alternative tools to address his or her co-occurring symptoms.

Clinical Observations and Commentary

SUDs can be responsible for the development and maintenance of CODs just as CODs can be responsible for the maintenance and development of SUDs. Moreover, these relationships can be interactive and dynamic. The interactive relationship between substance misuse and particular psychiatric symptoms is the next layer in understanding a particular individual struggling with SUD and COD. The clinician's task would be to understand the development of SUD in this particular individual. Understanding the etiology of the SUD and its relationship to COD is a critical step in developing a reasonable plan of recovery for any particular individual.

We have reviewed a broad spectrum of CODs that may be seen in relation to SUDs. The risks these youth face cannot be overstated, particularly for suicide, violence, trauma, accidents, and victimization. Since the majority of youth have some degree of psychiatric comorbidity, to some extent the terms "dual diagnosis" or "comorbidity" or even "co-occurring disorders" is unnecessary since most youth have such COD. The relevance of describing COD, however, cannot be overstated because we believe that the comprehensive understanding of the specific developmental pathways by which youth develop SUDs is a critical, central process to developing treatments for any particular youth. The relationships between SUD and COD can be complex and are often associated with life-threatening risks. As a result, it is often not as simple as sequencing treatment by sobering up an individual to see if he or she still has the disorder, in order to determine if he or she can engage effectively in treatment. Few individuals with COD receive adequate treatment for both types of disorders. To make matters worse, COD often involves multiple disorders and hence even fewer receive treatment for all of these disorders. Treatment of these complex youth requires integrated treatment modalities that utilize evidence-based strategies for SUDs as well as each of the CODs. A major concern in working with youth with COD is their safety, and in particular their risk for suicide, self-injury, and other comorbid problems. Youth with SUD and particularly youth with COD are at significant risk for suicide, self-injury, motor vehicle accidents, unintentional overdose, sexual victimization and trauma, and a variety of other types of violence, including homicide and assault.

Regarding suicide in adolescents, there are two general categories: (1) depressed and (2) impulsive (Shaffer et al., 1996). Most commonly in early-onset SUD the impulsive explanation is most relevant; this is best explained by the relationship between early-onset SUD and disruptive behavior disorders, particularly CD. However, as has been seen, many youth have co-occurring disruptive behavior disorders and mood disorders, suggesting the need to apply both of these general categories for suicides. Moreover, even after controlling for externalizing behaviors, substance use appears to contribute independently to impulsivity and suicide attempts. It is important to note that youth with SUD are at particularly high risk of suicidality because of impulsivity as well as depression. Some youth struggle with depression and impulse control disorders, and when SUD is added, a deadly cocktail is mixed. It can be challenging for the clinician to become aware of the emotional pain experienced by some antisocial youngsters who only seem to hate, but hate themselves most of all.

Although we tend to focus on CODs that have a higher frequency than the general population, youth can also have these CODs at the same frequency as the general population. For example, although self-injurious behavior is not particularly associated with SUD, youth with self-injurious behavior still have the same risk of SUD. Therefore, the SUD becomes an important aspect of the behavioral complex of individual patients. Thus, on an individual level, this is a particular risk combination for the child, irrespective of its frequency of association in the general population. Being aware of such associations is useful at a macro level, but on a micro level all of the possible relationships and consequential risks need consideration. At a clinical level there appear a multitude of pathways that can lead to SUD in adolescents, and on an individual level understanding these developmental relationships is critical to maximizing the chances for recovery from SUD. Understanding the relationship between pre-substance use psychiatric disorders and the development of SUD is critical to designing a particular individual's plan of recovery. Failing to do so will lead a recovering adolescent vulnerable to significant risk factors that reduce the rate of recovery.

Context is critical when considering any particular risk factor in a particular individual. In individual cases, one can often discern developmental trajectories that lead to the development of a particular individual's SUD that appear not to follow the dominant pattern. A complete developmental history including a variety of sources—involving the patient, family, teachers, pediatricians, probation officers, and so on—can be helpful in this regard. With individual patients, we have found that a "Time Line Follow Back" approach is the most useful in discerning relationships between psychiatric symptoms and SUD (Epstein-Ngo et al., 2012; Nunes et al., 2010). This method of interviewing does not emphasize the relationship between SUD and the COD, as many patients can be biased against admitting any relationship. Instead of focusing on the relationship (e.g., "Do you think using cannabis in high school caused you to hear voices?"), the alternative is to focus on the individual behavior and its appearance (e.g., "Tell me about when the voices began" and "When did you begin using cannabis?"). This method allows the clinician to discern relationships by creating timelines of each symptom and considering associations. As more than an academic exercise, this information is critical in developing an understanding of a particular youth's substance use and how it developed into a disorder.

A major concern remains that substance use and psychiatric treatment services tend to be separated when it is clear that these two types of problems are often intricately interrelated for the majority of adolescents with COD. The more such services can be integrated, the more likely we are to be successful in treating both conditions in any particular individual. Case management and communication between professionals across care services bridges the gap at times, but too often in our experience, the child ends up in one service or the other when both types of problems need treatment simultaneously (Nunes et al., 2010). Psychiatric services are uncomfortable with actively substance-using youth, just as substance abuse providers are uncomfortable with kids who are too "psychiatric." So-called dual-diagnosis programs begin to provide simultaneous treatment but are much less common in adolescent as opposed to adult populations. Yet as has been seen, the heterogeneity of this population of youth with COD is complex and multitiered. Youth more often than not have multiple CODs and can also have multiple SUDs. Treatment of some conditions may reduce substance use, while treatment of other disorders may have no effect; similarly, reduced substance use may improve or exacerbate psychiatric disorders. More research is sorely needed to ferret out these relationships to inform clinical practice. At present, the best approach is careful evaluation by adolescent providers skilled at substance use and psychiatric treatment.

In the past several years, research has expanded the understanding of the complex realm of CODs and SUDs. Investigators are beginning to make inroads in evaluating the treatment of specific types of CODs, such as depression with cognitive-behavioral therapy (Curry, Wells, Lochman, Craighead, & Nagy, 2003) and combined medication with cognitive-behavioral therapy (Riggs & Davies, 2002) and are also developing clinical models for their treatment (Pettinati et al., 2010). These studies are highly valuable to the treatment of depressed youth with SUDs. However, clinicians will need to continue to evaluate each child carefully and comprehensively, discerning the relationships between CODs and SUDs in order to develop unique treatment plans for this complex group of youth. In this age of restrictions on health care through cost control, it is increasingly difficult to treat youth long enough and comprehensively enough. This is particularly troubling for the treatment of CODs because assessing the impact of the SUD on the individual's psychology and vice-versa is complex, and it involves discerning whether the relationships are substance-induced, either via abuse or withdrawal. It is often the case that the condition persists or worsens without substance use, but it is nonetheless critical to determine even if in a minority of cases the condition desists. Over the past few decades, clinicians have become increasingly aware of CODs, although integration of treatment is still out of reach for this population of youth. With awareness of the variability and at times complex presentations of these youth, clinicians in substance use and in adolescent mental/behavioral health can continue to develop better access to comprehensive treatment. This in our opinion is critical to improving outcomes. Many times we have heard from colleagues in behavioral health that they do not treat SUD, and reflectively in substance abuse treatment, that they do not treat psychiatric problems. CODs are too common in substance abuse treatment and vice-versa for this to be a viable approach. The stakes are too high for these youth for us to fail to treat them as whole individuals.

References

Ackard, D. M., Fulkerson, J. A., & Neumark-Sztainer, D. (2011). Psychological and behavioral risk profiles as they relate to eating disorder diagnoses and symptomatology among a school-based sample of youth. *International Journal of Eating Disorders*, 44(5), 440–446.

Alegria, A. A., Hasin, D. S., Nunes, E. V., Liu, S. M., Davies, C., Grant, B. F., & Blanco, C. (2010). Comorbidity of generalized anxiety disorder and substance use disorders: Results from the National Epidemiologic Survey on Alcohol and Related Conditions. *Journal of Clinical Psychiatry*, 71(9), 1187–1195.

Althoff, R. R. (2010). Dysregulated children reconsidered. *American Academy of Child and Adolescent Psychiatry*, 49(4), 302–305.

Ambrosini, P. J., Bennett, D. S., & Elia, J. (2013). Attention deficit hyperactivity disorder characteristics II. Clinical correlates of irritable mood. *Journal of Affective Disorders*, 145(1), 70–76.

Alcoholics Anonymous. (1939). Alcoholics Anonymous. Retrieved October 2015, from http://www.aa.org/pages/en_US/alcoholics-anonymous

American Academy of Child and Adolescent Psychiatry. (2007). Practice parameter for treatment of depression. *Journal of the American Academy of Child and Adolescent Psychiatry*, 66(11), 1503–1526.

American Academy of Child and Adolescent Psychiatry. (2005). Practice parameter for the assessment and treatment of children and adolescents with substance use disorders. *Journal of the American Academy of Child and Adolescent Psychiatry*, 44(6), 609–621.

American Academy of Child and Adolescent Psychiatry. (2007). Practice parameter for the assessment and treatment of children and adolescents with anxiety disorders. *Journal of the American Academy of Child and Adolescent Psychiatry*, 46(2), 267–283.

American Psychiatric Association. (2000). *Diagnostic and statistical manual of mental disorders (4th ed., text rev.)*. Arlington, VA: Author.

American Psychiatric Association. (2014). *Diagnostic and statistical manual of mental disorders (5th ed.)*. Arlington, VA: Author.

Becker, D. F., McGlashan, T. H., & Grilo, C. M. (2006). Exploratory factor analysis of borderline personality disorder criteria in hospitalized adolescents. *Comprehensive Psychiatry*, 47(2), 99–105.

Biederman, J., Monuteaux, M. C., Mick, E., Wilens, T. E., Fontanella, J. A., Poetzl, K. M., . . . Faraone, S. V. (2006). Is cigarette smoking a gateway to alcohol and illicit drug use disorders? A study of youth with and without attention deficit hyperactivity disorder. *Biological Psychiatry*, 59, 258–264.

Birmaher, B., Brent, D., AACAP Work Group on Quality Issues, Bernet, W., Bukstein, O., Walter, H., . . . Medicus, J. (2007). Practice parameter for the assessment and treatment of children and adolescents with depressive disorders. *Journal of the American Academy of Child and Adolescent Psychiatry*, 46(11), 1503–1526.

Bleiberg, E. (2001). *Treating personality disorders in children and adolescents*. New York, NY: Guilford Press.

Blom, R. M., Koeter, M., van den Brink, W., de Graaf, R., Ten Have, M., & Denys, D. (2011). Co-occurrence of obsessive-compulsive disorder and substance use disorder in the general population. *Addiction*, 106, 2178–2185.

Bonomo, Y. A., Bowes, G., Coffey, C., Carlin, J. B., & Patton, G. C. (2004). Teenage drinking and the onset of alcohol dependence: A cohort study over seven years. *Addiction, 99*, 1520–1528.

Bornovalova, M. A., Hicks, B. M., Iacono, W. G., & McGue, M. (2013). Longitudinal twin study of borderline personality disorder traits and substance use in adolescence: Developmental change, reciprocal effects, and genetic and environmental influences. *Personality Disorders, 4*(1), 23–32.

Brady, K. T., & Sinha, R. (2005). Co-occurring mental and substance use disorders: The neurobiological effects of chronic stress. *American Journal of Psychiatry, 162*(8), 1483–1493.

Baeza, I., Graell, M., Moreno, D., Castro-Fornieles, J., Parellada, M., Gonzalez-Pinto, A., . . . Arango, C. (2009). Cannabis use in children and adolescents with first episode psychosis: Influence on psychopathology and short-term outcome (CAFEPS study). *Schizophrenia Research, 113*(2–3), 129–137.

Bolton, J. M., Robinson, J., & Sareen, J. (2009). Self-medication of mood disorders with alcohol and drugs in the National Epidemiologic Survey on Alcohol and Related Conditions. *Journal of Affective Disorders, 115*, 367–375.

Boschloo, L., Vogelzangs, N., Smit, J. H., van den Brink, W., Veltman, D. J., Beekman, A. T., & Penninx, B. W. (2011). Comorbidity and risk indicators for alcohol use disorders among persons with anxiety and/or depressive disorders: Findings from the Netherlands Study of Depression and Anxiety (NESDA). *Journal of Affective Disorders, 131*(1–3), 233–242.

Brook, J. S., Brook, D. W., Richter, L., & Whiteman, M. (2003). Risk and protective factors of adolescent drug use: Implications for prevention programs. In Z. Sloboda & W. J. Bukoski (Eds.) *Handbook of drug abuse prevention* (pp. 265–287). New York, NY: Kluwer Academic/Plenum Publishers.

Burke, J. D., & Stepp, S. D. (2012). Adolescent disruptive behavior and borderline personality symptoms in young adult men. *Journal of Abnormal Child Psychology, 40* (1), 35–44.

Capaldi, D. M., & Stoolmiller, M. (1999). Co-occurrence of conduct problems and depressive symptoms in early adolescent boys: III. Prediction to young-adult adjustment. *Developmental Psychopathology, 11*, 59–84.

Carlson, G. (2012). Who are the children with severe mood dysregulation, a.k.a. "rages"? *American Journal of Psychiatry, 164*(8), 1140–1142.

Cassidy, C. M., Joober, R., King, S., & Malla, A. K. (2011). Childhood symptoms of inattention-hyperactivity predict cannabis use in first episode psychosis. *Schizophrenia Research, 132*(2–3), 171–176.

Charach, A., Yeung, E., Climans, T., & Lillie, E. (2011). Childhood attention-deficit/hyperactivity disorder and future substance use disorders: Comparative meta-analyses. *Journal of the American Academy of Child and Adolescent Psychiatry, 50*(1), 9–21.

Chanen, A. M., Jackson, H. J., McGorry, P. D., Allot, K. A., Clarkson, V., & Yuen, H. P. (2004). Two-year stability of personality disorder in older adolescent outpatients. *Journal of Personality Disorders, 18*(6), 526–541.

Chen, X., Ungera, J. B., Palmera, P., Weinera, M. D., Johnson, C. A., Mamie, M., . . . Austin, G. (2002). Prior cigarette smoking initiation predicting current alcohol use: Evidence for a gateway drug effect among California adolescents from eleven ethnic groups. *Addictive Behaviors, 27*, 799–817.

Cheung, J. T., Mann, R. E., Ialomiteanu, A., Stoduto, G., Chan, V., Ala-Leppilampi, K., & Rehm, J. (2010). Anxiety and mood disorders and cannabis use. *American Journal of Drug Alcohol Abuse, 36*(2), 118–122.

Cicchetti, D., & Rogosch, F. A. (1999). Psychopathology as a risk factor for adolescent substance use disorders: A developmental psychopathology perspective. *Journal of Consulting and Clinical Psychology, 28*(3), 355–365.

Commission on Adolescent Substance and Alcohol Abuse. (2005). Prevention of substance use disorders. In D. L. Evans, E. B. Foa, R. E. Gur, H. Hendin, C. P. O'Brien, M. E. P. Seligman & B. T. Walsh (Eds.), *Treating and preventing mental health disorders: What we know and what we don't know* (pp. 412–426). New York, NY: Oxford University Press.

Cornelius, J. R., Kirisci, L., Reynolds, M., Clark, D. B., Hayes, J., & Tarter, R. (2010). PTSD contributes to teen and young adult cannabis use disorders. *Addictive Behaviors, 35*(2), 91–94.

Chan, Y., Dennis, M. L., & Funk, R. R. (2008). Prevalence and comorbidity of major externalizing and internalizing problems among adolescents and adults presenting to substance abuse treatment. *Journal of Substance Abuse and Treatment, 34*, 14–24.

Crum, R. M., Green, K. M, Storr, C. L., Chan, Y., Ialongo, N., Stuart, E. A., & Anthony, J. C. (2008). Depressed mood in childhood and subsequent alcohol use through adolescence and young adulthood. *Archives of General Psychiatry, 65*(6), 702–712.

Curry, J. F., Wells, K. C., Lochman, J. E., Craighead, W. E., & Nagy, P. D. (2003). Cognitive-behavioral intervention for depressed, substance-abusing adolescents: Development and pilot testing. *Journal of the American Academy of Child and Adolescent Psychiatry, 42*(6), 656–665.

Daudin, M., Cohen, D., Edel, Y., Bonnet, N., Bodeau, N., Consoli, A., & Guile, J. M. (2010). Psychosocial and clinical correlates of substance use disorder in an adolescent inpatient psychiatric population. *Journal of the Canadian Academy of Child and Adolescent Psychiatry, 19*(4), 264–273.

Deas, D. (2006). Adolescent substance abuse and psychiatric comorbidities. *Journal of Clinical Psychiatry, 67*(S7), 18–23.

De Hert, M., Wampers, M., Jendricko, T., Franic, T., Vidovic, D., De Vriendt, N., . . . van Winkel, R. (2011). Effects of cannabis use on age at onset in schizophrenia and bipolar disorder. *Schizophrenia Research, 126*(1–3), 270–276.

Dragt, S., Nieman, D. H., Schultze-Lutter, F., van der Meer, F., Becker, H., de Haan, L., . . . Linszen, D. H. (2012). Cannabis use and age at onset of symptoms in subjects at clinical high risk for psychosis. *Acta Psychiatrica Scandinavica, 125*(1), 45–53.

Epstein-Ngo, Q. M., Cunningham, R. M., Whiteside, L. K., Chermack, S. T., Booth, B. M., Zimmerman, M. A., & Walton, M. A. (2012). A daily calendar analysis of substance use and dating violence among high risk urban youth. *Drug and Alcohol Dependency, 130* (1–3), 194–200.

Faraone, S. V. (2004). Genetics of adult attention-deficit/hyperactivity disorder. *Psychiatric Clinics of North America, 27*, 303–322.

Fergusson, D. M., Boden, J. M., & Horwood, L. J. (2008). The developmental antecedents of illicit drug use: Evidence from a 25-year longitudinal study. *Drug and Alcohol Dependency, 96*, 165–177.

Fergusson, D. M., Boden, J. M., & Horwood, L. J. (2009). Tests of causal links between alcohol abuse or dependence and major depression. *Archives of General Psychiatry*, 66(3), 260–266.

Fiellin, L. E., Tetrault, J. M., Becker, W. C., Fiellin, D. A., & Hoff, R. A. (2012). Previous use of alcohol, cigarettes, and marijuana and subsequent abuse of prescription opioids in young adults. *Journal of Adolescent Health*, 52(2), 158–163.

Frojd, S., Ranta, K., Kaltiala-Heino, R., & Marttunen, M. (2011). Associations of social phobia and general anxiety with alcohol and drug use in a community sample of adolescents. *Alcohol and Alcoholism*, 46(2), 192–199.

Goldstein, B. I., Shamsedeen, W., Spirito A., Emslie, G., Clarke, G., Wagner, K. D., . . . Brent, D. A. (2009). Substance use and the treatment of resistant depression in adolescents. *Journal of the American Academy of Child and Adolescent Psychiatry*, 48(12), 1182–1192.

Goldstein, B. I., Strober, M. A., Birmaher, B., Axelson, D. A., Esposito-Smythers, C., Goldstein, T. R., . . . Keller, M. B. (2008). Substance use disorders among adolescents with bipolar spectrum disorders. *Bipolar Disorder*, 10(4), 469–478.

Gonzalez-Pinto, A., Vega, P., Ibanez, B., Mosquera, F., Barbeito, S., Gutierrez, M., . . . Vieta, E. (2008). Impact of cannabis and other drugs on age at onset of psychosis. *Journal of Clinical Psychiatry*, 69(8), 1210–1216.

Goodman, A. (2010). Substance use and common child mental health problems: Examining longitudinal associations in a British sample *Addiction*, 105, 1484–1496.

Greene, R. W., Biederman, J., Faraone, S. V., Wilens, T. E., Mick, E., & Blier, H. K. (1999). Further validation of social impairment as a predictor of substance use disorders: Findings from a sample of siblings of boys with and without ADHD. *Journal of Clinical Child Psychology*, 28(3), 349–354.

Hadland, S. E., Marshall, B. D., Kerr, T., Qi, J., Montaner, J. S., & Wood, E. (2011). Depresseed symptoms and patterns of drug use among street youth. *Journal of Adolscent Health*, 48, 585–590.

Harder, V. S., Stuart, E. A., & Anthony, J. C. (2008). Adolescent cannabis problems and young adult depression: Male-female stratified propensity score analyses. *American Journal of Epidemiology*, 168, 592–601.

Harley, M., Kelleher, I., Clarke, M., Lynch, F., Arseneault, L., Connor, D., . . . Cannon, M. (2010). Cannabis use and childhood trauma interact additively to increase the risk of psychotic symptoms in adolescence. *Psychological Medicine*, 40(10), 1627–1634.

Hasin, D., Fenton, M. C., Skodol, A., Krueger, R., Keyes, K., Geier, T., & Grant, B. (2011). Personality disorders and the 3-year course of alcohol, drug, and nicotine use disorders. *Archives of General Psychiatry*, 68(11), 1158–1167.

Henquet, C., Krabbendam, L., Spauwen, J., Kaplan, C., Lieb, R., Wittchen, H. U., & van Os, J. (2005). Prospective cohort study of cannabis use, predisposition for psychosis, and psychotic symptoms in young people. *British Medical Journal*, 330(7481), 11.

Hides, L., Lubman, D. I., Buckby, J., Yuen, H. P., Cosgrave, E., Baker, K., & Yung, A. R. (2009). The association between early cannabis use and psychotic-like experiences in a community adolescent sample. *Schizophrenia Research*, 112(1–3), 130–135.

Hien, D. A., Jiang, H., Campbell, A. N., Hu, M. C., Miele, G. M., Cohen, L. R., . . . Nunes, E. V. (2010). Do treatment improvements in PTSD severity affect substance use outcomes? A secondary analysis from a randomized clinical trial in NIDA's Clinical Trials Network. *American Journal of Psychiatry*, 167(1), 95–101.

Holderness, C. C., Brooks-Gunn, J., & Warren, M. P. (1994). Co-morbidity of eating disorders and substance abuse review of the literature. *International Journal of Eating Disorders*, 16(1), 1–34.

Holtmann, M., Buchmann, A. F., Esser, G., Schmidt, M. H., Banaschewski, T., & Laucht, M. (2011). The CBCL child dysregulation profile predicts substance use, suicidality and functional impairment. *Journal of Child Psychology and Psychiatry*, 52(2), 139–147.

Hussong, A. M., Gould, L. A., & Hersh, M. A. (2008). Conduct problems moderate self-medication and mood-related drinking consequences in adolescents. *Journal of the Study of Alcohol and Drugs*, 69, 296–307.

Jacobsen, L. K., Southwick, S. M., & Kosten, T. R. (2001). Substance use disorders in patients with posttraumatic stress disorder: A review of the literature. *American Journal of Psychiatry*, 158(8), 1184–1190.

James, A., Hough, M., James, S., Winmill, L., Burge, L., Nijhawan, S., . . . Zarei, M. (2011). Greater white and grey matter changes associated with early cannabis use in adolescent-onset schizophrenia (AOS). *Schizophrenia Research*, 128(1–3), 91–97.

Jaycox, L. H., Ebener, P., Damesek, L., & Becker, K. (2004). Trauma exposure and retention in adolescent substance abuse treatment. *Journal of Trauma and Stress*, 17(2), 113–121.

Jester, J. M., Nigg, J. T., Buu, A., Puttler, L. I., Glass, J. M., Heitzeg, M. M., . . . Zucker, R. A. (2008). Trajectories of childhood aggression and inattention/hyperactivity: Differential effects on substance abuse in adolescence. *Journal of the American Academy of Child and Adolescent Psychiatry*, 47(10), 1158–1165.

Johnson, L. D., O'Malley, P. M., Miech, R. A., Bachman, J. G., & Schulenberg, J. E. (2014). Monitoring the future: national survey results on drug use 1975–2013. Retrieved October 2015, from http://www.monitoringthefuture.org//pubs/monographs/mtf-vol1_2013.pdf

Kaess, M., Brunner, R., & Chanen, A. (2014). Borderline personality disorder in adolescence. *Pediatrics*, 134, 782–793.

Katz, L. Y., Cox, B. J., Gunasekara, S., & Miller, A. L. (2004). Feasibility of dialectical behavior therapy for suicidal adolescent inpatients. *Journal of the American Academy of Child and Adolescent Psychiatry*, 43(3), 276–282.

Kernberg, P., Weiner, A. S., & Bardenstein, K. K. (2000). *Personality disorders in children and adolescents*. New York: Basic Books.

Kirby, T., & Barry, A. E. (2012). Alcohol as a gateway drug: A study of US 12th graders. *Journal of the Sch Health*, 82(8), 371–379.

Kratochvil, C. J., Wilens, T. E., & Upadhyaya, H. (2006). Pharmacological management of a youth with ADHD, marijuana use, and mood symptoms. *Journal of the American Academy of Child and Adolescent Psychiatry*, 45(9), 1138–1141.

Kumra, S., Robinson, P., Tambyraja, R., Jensen, D., Schimunek, C., Houri, A., . . . Lim, K. (2012). Parietal lobe volume deficits in adolescents with schizophrenia and adolescents with cannabis use disorders. *Journal of the American Academy of Child and Adolescent Psychiatry, 51*(2), 171–180.

Lansford, J. E., Erath, S., Yu, T., Pettit, G. S., Dodge, K. A., & Bates, J. E. (2008). The developmental course of illicit substance use from age 12 to 22: Links with depressive, anxiety, and behavior disorders at age 18. *Journal of Child Psychology and Psychiatry, 49*(8), 877–878.

Levine, A., Huang, Y. Y., Drisaldi, B., Griffin, B., Pollak, D. D., Xu, S. Y., . . . Kandel, E. R. (2001). Molecular mechanism for a gateway drug: Epigenetic changes initiated by nicotine prime gene expression by cocaine. *Science Translational Medicine, 3*(107), 107–109.

Lewinsohn, P. M., Holm-Denoma, J. M., Small, J. W., Seeley, J. R., & Joiner, T. E., Jr. (2008). Separation anxiety disorder in childhood as a risk factor for future mental illness. *Journal of the American Academy of Child and Adolescent Psychiatry, 47*(5), 548–555.

Lewinsohn, P. M., Klein, D. N., & Seeley, J. R. (1995). Bipolar disorders in a community sample of older adolescents: Prevalence, phenomenology, comorbidity, and course. *Journal of the American Academy of Child and Adolescent Psychiatry, 34*(4), 454–463.

Lewinsohn, P. M., Striegel-Moore, R. H., & Seeley, J. R. (2000). Epidemiology and natural course of eating disorders in young women from adolescence to young adulthood. *Journal of the American Academy of Child and Adolescent Psychiatry, 39*(10), 1284–1292.

Liang, W., & Chikritzhs, T. (2011). Affective disorders, anxiety disorders and the risk of alcohol dependence and misuse. *British Journal of Psychiatry, 199*(3), 219–224.

Lorberg, B., Wilens, T. E., Martelon, M., Wong, P., & Parcell, T. (2010). Reasons for substance use among adolescents with bipolar disorder. *American Journal of Addict, 19*(6), 474–480.

Lubman, D. I., Allen, N. B., Rogers, N., Cementon, E., & Bonomo, Y. (2007). The impact of co-occurring mood and anxiety disorders among substance-abusing youth. *Journal of Affective Disorders, 103*(1–3), 105–112.

Magidson, J. F., Liu, S. M., Lejuez, C. W., & Blanco, C. (2012). Comparison of the course of substance use disorders among individuals with and without generalized anxiety disorder in a nationally representative sample. *Journal of Psychiatric Research, 46*(5), 659–666.

Manassis, K., & Monga, S. (2001). A therapeutic approach to children and adolescents with anxiety disorders and associated comorbid conditions. *Journal of the American Academy of Child and Adolescent Psychiatry, 40*(1), 115–117.

Marshall, B. D., & Werb, D. (2010). Health outcomes associated with methamphetamine use among young people: A systematic review. *Addiction, 105*(6), 991–1002.

Mayzer, R., Fitzgerald, H. E., & Zucker, R. A. (2009). Anticipating problem drinking risk from preschoolers' antisocial behavior: Evidence for a common delinquency-related diathesis model. *Journal of the American Academy of Child and Adolescent Psychiatry, 48*(8), 820–827.

Measelle, J. R., Stice, J. R., & Hogansen, J. M. (2006). Developmental trajectories of co-occurring depressive, eating, antisocial, and substance abuse problems in female adolescents. *Journal of Abnormal Psychology, 115*(3), 524–538.

Myers, M. G., Brown, S. A., & Mott, M. A. (1995). Preadolescent conduct disorder behaviors predict relapse and progression of addiction for adolescent alcohol and drug

abusers. *Alcohol: Clinical and Experimental Research, 19*(6), 1528–1536.

Nunes, E. V., Selzer, J., Levounis, P., & Davies, C. A. (2010). *Substance dependence and co-occurring disorders: Best practices for diagnosis and clinical treatment.* Kingston, NJ: Civic Research Institute.

Oldham, J. M. (2006). Borderline personality disorder and suicidality. *American Journal of Psychiatry, 163*(1), 20–26.

Pettinati, H. M., Oslin, D. W., Kampman, K. M., Dundon, W. D., Xie, H., Gallis, T. L., . . . O'Brien, C. P. (2010). A double-blind, placebo-controlled trial combining sertraline and naltrexone for treating co-occurring depression and alcohol dependence. *American Journal of Psychiatry, 167*(6), 668–675.

Pisetsky, E. M., Chao, Y. M., Dierker, L. C., May, A. M., & Striegel-Moore, R. H. (2008). Disordered eating and substance use in high-school students: Results from the Youth Risk Behavior Surveillance System. *International Journal of Eating Disorders, 41*(5), 464–470.

Rao, U., Ryan, N. D., Dahl, R. E., Birmaher, B., Rao, R., Williamson, D. E., & Perel, J. M. (1999). Factors associated with the development of substance use disorder in depressed adolescents. *Journal of the American Academy of Child and Adolescent Psychiatry, 38*(9), 1109–1117.

Read, J. P., Colder, C. R., Merrill, J. E., Ouimette, P., White, J., & Swartout, A. (2012). Trauma and posttraumatic stress symptoms predict alcohol and other drug consequence trajectories in the first year of college. *Journal of Consulting and Clinical Psychology, 80*(3), 426–439.

Reece, A. S. (2009). Chronic toxicology of cannabis. *Chronic Toxicology, 47*, 517–524.

Riggs, P., & Davies, A. (2002). A clinical approach to integrating treatment for adolescent depression and substance abuse. *Journal of the American Academy of Child and Adolescent Psychiatry, 41*(10), 1253–1255.

Robins, L., & Regier, D. (1991). *Psychiatric disorders in America: The epidemiological catchment area study.* New York, NY: The Free Press.

Rossouw, T. I., & Fonagy, P. (2012). Mentalization-based treatment for self-harm in adolescents: A randomized controlled trial. *Journal of the American Academy of Child and Adolescent Psychiatry, 51*(12), 1304–1313.

Rutter, M. (1990). Psychosocial resilience and protective mechanisms. In J. Rolf, A. Masten, D. Cicchetti, K. Nuechterlein, & S. Weintraub (Eds.), *Risk and protective factors in the development of psychopathology* (pp. 181–214). New York, NY: Cambridge University Press.

Rutherford, H. J. V., Mayes, L. C., & Potenza, M. N. (2010). Neurobiology of adolescent substance use disorders: Implications for prevention and treatment. *Child and Adolescent Psychiatric Clinics of North America, 19*, 479–492.

Saraceno, L., Heron, J., Munafo, M., Craddock, N., & van den Bree, M. B. (2012). The relationship between childhood depressive symptoms and problem alcohol use in early adolescence: Findings from a large longitudinal population-based study. *Addiction, 107*(3), 567–577.

Schimmelmann, B. G., Conus, P., Cotton, S. M., Kupferschmid, S., Karow, A., Schultze-Lutter, F., . . . Lambert, M. (2011). Cannabis use disorder and age at onset of psychosis—a study in first-episode patients. *Schizophrenia Research, 129*(1), 52–56.

Schneier, F. R., Foose, T. E., Hasin, D. S., Heimberg, R. G., Liu, S. M., Grant, B. F., & Blanco, C. (2010). Social anxiety disorder and alcohol use disorder co-morbidity in the National Epidemiologic Survey on Alcohol and Related Conditions. *Psychological Medicine*, *40*(6), 977–988.

Shaffer, D., Gould, M. S., Fisher, P., Trautman, P., Moreau, D., Kleinman, M., & Flory, M. (1996). Psychiatric diagnosis in child and adolescent suicide. *Archives of General Psychiatry*, *53*(4), 339–348.

Steinbuchel, P. H., Wilens, T. E., Adamson, J. J., & Sgambati, S. (2009). Posttraumatic stress disorder and substance use disorder in adolescent bipolar disorder. *Bipolar Disorders*, *11*(2), 198–204.

Steiner, H., & Wilson, J. J. (1999). Conduct disorder. In R. Hendren (Ed.), *Disruptive behavior disorders* (pp. 47–98). Washington, DC: American Psychiatric Press.

Stringaris A, Goodman R (2009). Longitudinal outcome of youth oppositionality: irritable, headstrong, and hurtful behaviors have distinctive predictions. *Journal of the American Academy of Child & Adolescent Psychiatry* 48(4), 404–412.

Stringaris, A., Zavos, H., Leibenluft, E., Maughan, B., & Eley, T. (2012). Adolescent irritability: Phenotypic associations and genetic links with depressed mood. *American Journal of Psychiatry*, *169*, 47–54.

Subramaniam, G. A., Stitzer, M. A., Clemmey, P., Kolodner, K., & Fishman, M. J. (2007). Baseline depressive symptoms predict poor substance use outcome following adolescent residential treatment. *Journal of the American Academy of Child and Adolescent Psychiatry*, *46*(8), 1062–1069.

Substance Abuse and Mental Health Services Administration. (2007). *Results from the 2006 National Survey on Drug Use and Health: National Findings* [Office of Applied Studies, NSDUH Series H-32, DHHS Publication No. SMA 07-4293]. Rockville, MD: Author.

Tamm, L., Adinoff, B., Nakonezny, P. A., Winhusen, T., & Riggs, P. (2012). Attention-deficit/hyperactivity disorder subtypes in adolescents with comorbid substance-use disorder. *American Journal of Drug Alcohol Abuse*, *38*, 93–100.

Tarter, R. E., Kirisci, L., Habeych, M., Reynolds, M., & Vanyukov, M. (2004). Neurobehavior disinhibition in childhood predisposes boys to substance use disorder by young adulthood and mediated etiologic pathways. *Drug Alcohol Depend*, *73*, 121–132.

Tomlinson, K. L., Brown, S. A., & Abrantes, A. (2004). Psychiatric comorbidity and substance use treatment outcomes of adolescents. *Psychology of Addictive Behaviors* *18*, 160–169.

Unikel, C., Root, T., Vonholle, A., Ocampo, R., & Bulik, C. M. (2011). Disordered eating and substance use among a female sample of Mexican adolescents. *Substance Use and Misuse*, *46*(4), 523–534.

van Gastel, W. A., Wigman, J. T., Monshouwer, K., Kahn, R. S., van Os, J., Boks, M. P., & Vollebergh, W. A. (2012). Cannabis use and subclinical positive psychotic experiences in early adolescence: Findings from a Dutch survey. *Addiction*, *107*(2), 381–387.

Van Leeuwen, A. P., Verhulst, F. C., Reijneveld, S. A., Vollebergh, W. A. M., Ormel, J., & Huizink, A. C. (2011) Can the gateway hypothesis, the common liability model and/or, the route of administration model predict initiation of cannabis use during adolescence? A survival analysis—The TRAILS Study. *Journal of Adolescent Health, 48*, 73–78.

Western, D., Shedler, J., Durett, C., Glass, S., & Martens, A. (2003). Personality diagnoses in adolescence: DSM-IV Axis II diagnoses and an empirically derived alternative. *American Journal of Psychiatry, 160*, 952–966.

Wills, T. A., & Dishion, T. J. (2004). Temperament and adolescent substance use: A transactional analysis of emerging self-control. *Journal of Clinical Child and Adolescent Psychology, 33*(1), 69–81.

Wilens, T. E., Biederman, J., Abrantes, A. M., & Spencer, T. J. (1997). Clinical characteristics of psychiatrically referred adolescent outpatients with substance use disorder. *Journal of the American Academy of Child and Adolescent Psychiatry, 36*(7), 941–947.

Wilens, T. E., Biederman, J., Adamson, J. J., Henin, A., Sgambati, S., Gignac, M., & Monuteaux, M. C. (2008). Further evidence of an association between adolescent bipolar disorder with smoking and substance use disorders: A controlled study. *Drug and Alcohol Dependcy, 95*(3), 188–198.

Wilens, T. E., Biederman, J., Kwon, A., Ditterline, J., Forkner, P., Moore, H., & Faraone, S. V. (2004). Risk of substance use disorders in adolescents with bipolar disorder. *Journal of the American Academy of Child and Adolescent Psychiatry, 43*(11), 1380–1386.

Wilens, T. E., Biederman, J., Millstein, R. B., Wozniak, J., Hahesy, A. L., & Spencer, T. J. (1999). Risk for substance use disorders in youth with child- and adolescent-onset bipolar disorder. *Journal of the American Academy of Child and Adolescent Psychiatry, 38*(6), 680–685.

Wilson, J. J., Beckman, L., & Nunes, E. V. (2007). The identification, prevention, and treatment of vulnerabilities among children of alcohol- or drug-dependent parents. In P Vostanis (Ed.), *Mental health interventions and services for vulnerable children and young people (*pp. 203–217). London, UK: Jessica Kinsgsley.

Wilson, J. J., & Levin, F. R. (2005). Attention deficit and early onset substance use disorders. *Journal of the Child Adolescent Psychopharmacology, 15*(5), 751–763.

Wu, L-T., Gersing, K., Burchett, B., Woody, G. E., & Blazer, D. G. (2011). Substance use disorders and comorbid Axis I and II psychiatric disorders among young psychiatric patients: Findings from a large electronic health records database. *Journal of the Psychiatr Research, 45*, 1453–1462.

Zimmerman, M., Rothschild, L., & Chelminski, I. (2005). The prevalence of DSM-IV personality disorders in psychiatric outpatients. *American Journal of Psychiatry, 162*(10), 1911–1918.

Alcohol and Drug Use as Risk Factors for Delinquent Behavior Among Adolescents

Helene Raskin White, Courtney Cronley, *and* Padmini Iyer

Abstract

This chapter examines alcohol and drug use as risk factors for delinquency during adolescence. There is strong evidence for comorbidity between substance use and delinquency for individuals. Users, compared to nonusers, are more likely to be delinquent; and delinquents, compared to nondelinquents, are more likely to use substances. Conversely, substance use and delinquency follow different developmental patterns from adolescence into young adulthood, and trends in adolescent substance use and delinquency from 1980 through 2009 do not converge well. Alcohol, compared to drugs, has a stronger acute effect on adolescent aggression/violence. Developmentally, there appears to be a reciprocal association between substance use and delinquency, although findings differ across samples and time frames. There are several alternative models that explain why alcohol and drug use are risk factors for adolescent delinquency.

Key Words: alcohol, marijuana, drugs, substance use, violence, aggression, delinquency

Adolescent delinquency and aggression are public health issues of significant concern. Arrest statistics show that 2.11 million individuals under the age of 18 years were arrested in 2008 and juveniles accounted for 16% of all arrests for violent crimes and 26% of all arrests for property crimes (Puzzanchera, 2009). Survey data from 2003 indicate that approximately 9 million US juveniles (aged 12 to 17 years) had engaged in at least one delinquent act in the past year (Substance Abuse and Mental Health Services Administration, 2005). Urban community samples, such as the Pittsburgh (PA) Youth Survey (PYS; Loeber, Farrington, Stouthamer-Loeber, & White, 2008), the Rochester (NY) Youth Survey (Thornberry & Krohn, 2003), and the Denver (CO) Youth Survey (Huizinga, Weiher, Espiritu, & Esbensen, 2003) show even higher levels of self-reported adolescent delinquency. For example, in the PYS, which oversampled high-risk boys, but for which we weighted the data back to the original sample of public school attendees in Pittsburgh,

54% of the boys had committed minor theft (defined as stealing less than $5 outside the home or shoplifting) between ages 12 and 18 years (during the mid-1980s through the mid-1990s). Half had committed moderate theft (larceny or dealing in stolen property), and 18% had committed serious theft (burglary or motor vehicle theft) between ages 12 and 18 years. Violent delinquency is especially problematic. In 2008, 16% of all violent crime was committed by juveniles, with 1,280 juveniles arrested for murder, 3,340 for forcible rape, and 56,000 for aggravated assault (Puzzanchera, 2009). In the PYS using weighted data, we found that 29% of the boys had engaged in gang fighting between ages 12 and 18 years, and 21% had committed a serious violent act (defined as forcible robbery, assault, sexual coercion, or rape).

Violence and other forms of delinquency are often related to substance use, but it is unclear whether the use of substances directly affects delinquent behavior (White & Gorman, 2000). While it is possible that substance use may lead to aggression and delinquency, it is also likely that involvement in illegal behaviors puts adolescents at risk for substance use or that substance use and delinquency are related through common causes such as poverty, family structure and parental behaviors, peer influence, and individual factors (e.g., school achievement and temperament). This chapter addresses these alternative explanations.

Specifically, this chapter examines alcohol and drug use as risk factors for delinquency during adolescence. First, we briefly discuss the comorbidity of substance use and delinquency at the individual and macro levels. We next discuss the alternative models that explain the connection between delinquency and substance use. Finally, we summarize research on acute and developmental associations between substance use and delinquency during adolescence.

There are several methodological issues when studying the association between substance use and delinquency that make it difficult to compare results across studies. For example, there are large inconsistencies in the definition of drug-related delinquency, in measures of delinquency and substance use, and in samples studied (for a discussion of these issues, see Roizen, 1993; White, 1990; White & Gorman, 2000). In this chapter, alcohol and illicit drug (e.g., marijuana, cocaine, heroin, psychedelics, etc.) use are sometimes differentiated and are collectively referred to as substance use (see Chapters 4 and 6–8 for details on rates of substance use among adolescents). We treat aggression as a type of delinquent behavior unless discussed specifically. Delinquency is characterized by rule-breaking behavior and used to refer to both illegal offenses, such as assault and theft, as well as generally noncriminal behaviors like fighting. Drug dealing and gang membership are considered distinct from other types of illegal behaviors given their inherent connection with drug use and each other (Esbensen & Huizinga, 1993; Inciardi & Pottieger, 1991; Thornberry, Krohn, Lizotte, Smith, & Tobin, 2003).

Substance Use and Delinquency Comorbidity

In this section we examine the comorbidity of substance use and delinquency at the individual level as well as at the macro level by examining trends in behaviors over time. It is important to note that correlations between substance use and delinquency vary by type of substance and by type of delinquent behavior.

Individual-Level Associations

Most studies find that adolescents who use substances are more likely than nonusers to commit delinquent acts. Additionally, delinquents are more likely to be substance users compared to nondelinquents (White & Gorman, 2000). For example, in one large regional sample, youth who reported drinking one ounce of alcohol a day were delinquent during the school year a total of 57 days compared to 9.2 days among youth who reported no alcohol consumption (Barnes, Welte, & Hoffman, 2002). In addition, rates of substance use differentiate delinquents from nondelinquents. In 2005, 17.3% of those who reported being in a fight in the past year reported past-month illicit drug use compared to 7.6% of those who did not fight; 38.9% of those who stole something worth more than $50 reported past-month illicit drug use compared to 8.5% who did not steal (Substance Abuse and Mental Health Services Administration, 2005). (For additional examples, see White, 1990.) There is also a high degree of synchrony in progression through substance use and delinquency stages during adolescence. Abstainers and alcohol-only users are most likely to be nondelinquents; those who use both alcohol and marijuana are more likely to be delinquent than those who only use alcohol; and those who progress to the use of other drugs, compared to those who do not, are most likely to have also progressed to involvement in more serious forms of delinquency (White, 1990).

Drug dealing is also associated with substance use and criminal activity (Inciardi & Pottieger, 1991; Van Kammen & Loeber, 1994). Similarly, gang membership is strongly related to other types of delinquency and substance use, as well as to drug dealing (Esbensen & Huizinga, 1993; Thornberry, Krohn, Lizotte, Smith, & Tobin, 2003). We discuss the associations among drug dealing, gang membership, drug use, and delinquency in a separate section later in the chapter.

Despite the high degree of overlap between substance use and delinquency, it must be noted that the strength of the relationship varies among adolescents; for some, substance use and delinquency are closely related, and for others they are independent of each other (White & Labouvie, 1994). In addition, the strength of the associations between substance use and delinquency depends on the severity of the delinquency and the amount and types of substances used (Eklund & Klinteberg, 2009), as well as the sex, age, and composition of the study sample (Huizinga & Jakob-Chien, 1998).

Not only has the substance-delinquency nexus been supported in community samples of adolescents, but it has also received strong support in samples of adjudicated delinquents (Mulvey, Schubert, & Chassin, 2010). Data from the Arrestee Drug Abuse Monitoring (ADAM) program show very high rates of drug use among arrested youth, although these rates vary according to geographic region (National Institute of Justice, 2003). In 2000, 56% of all male juvenile arrestees and 40% of all female juvenile arrestees tested positive for at least one of five illicit drugs (marijuana, cocaine, methamphetamine, PCP, and opiates). More than half (53%) the male juveniles and a third (33%) of the female juveniles tested positive for marijuana, which was the most commonly identified drug. Urine samples at the time of arrest do not provide evidence of whether drugs were used at the time that the youths committed the offense. Rather, these data simply indicate that juvenile arrestees report high levels of recent drug use. Data from the year 2000 compiled from multiple national sources show that those adolescents who had been arrested once in the past year, compared to those who were not arrested, were more than twice as likely to have used alcohol, more than three and a half times as likely to have used marijuana, more than three times as likely to have used prescription drugs for nonmedical purposes, more than nine times as likely to have used cocaine, and twenty times as likely to have used heroin (Horowitz, Sung, & Foster, 2006). In a US study of serious juvenile offenders ages 14–17 years in 2000–2003, 85% reported lifetime marijuana use, 80% lifetime alcohol use, and 27% lifetime use of other illegal drugs (i.e., cocaine, hallucinogens, ecstasy, sedatives, opiates, inhalants, amyl nitrate odorizers, or "other") (Mulvey et al., 2010). Furthermore, 48% reported having used more than one substance in the past 6 months. In addition, 37% of the males and 35% of the females met the criteria for drug or alcohol abuse/dependence, which was about three to four times higher than rates found for their same-age peers in community samples (Mulvey et al., 2010; see also McClelland, Elkington, & Teplin, 2004; Ramchand, Morral, & Becker, 2009). Nationally, more than half the incarcerated youth in the United States in 2006 met the clinical criteria for alcohol or drug abuse or dependence (The National Center on Addiction and Substance Abuse at Columbia University, 2010). Across studies, substance use dependence prevalence rates are 62% to 81% among youth in the juvenile justice system, compared to 6% to 10% in community and school samples (Doran, Luczak, Bekman, Koutsenok, & Brown, 2012).

The association between substance use and delinquency is not unique to American adolescents. In a study of eighth-grade students in Sweden, male and female adolescents committing the most serious forms of delinquency reported the highest rates of alcohol use and drunkenness compared to their peers who showed well-adjusted behavior or committed only minor offenses (Eklund & Klinteberg, 2009). Similarly, in a study of more than 5,000 primarily 15- and 16-year-old Swedish youth, Felson, Savolainen, Aaltonen, and Moustgaard (2008) found that those who drank were more likely than nondrinkers to commit delinquent offenses when sober. Furthermore, among drinkers, those who drank more frequently were also more likely to commit sober offenses.

Studies often find gender, age, and racial/ethnic differences in the comorbidity of substance use and delinquency (White & Gorman, 2000). For example, Barnes et al. (2002) found that the positive relationship between heavy drinking and delinquency was stronger for males than females, as well as for younger than older adolescents. Whereas Felson, Teasdale, and Burchfield (2008) did not find sex differences in the association between fighting and alcohol use (see also Eklund & Klinteberg, 2009), they did find that the alcohol–violence association was much stronger for White than Black adolescents, and it was stronger for older than younger adolescents.

In sum, the empirical evidence shows a strong association of adolescent substance use to delinquency and aggression. It is important to note, however, that some adolescents who engage in delinquent behaviors do not use alcohol or drugs, and many adolescents who use alcohol and drugs do not engage in delinquent behavior (White, 1990). Nevertheless, many studies indicate a considerable overlap between substance use and delinquency (White & Labouvie, 1994).

Trends in Adolescent Substance Use and Delinquency

In the preceding section, we discussed the putative individual associations between substance use and delinquency; here, we examine these associations on a macro level by looking at trends in delinquency in relation to trends in substance use over time. Figure 25.1 shows theft and violent offense arrest statistics for juveniles (ages 10 to 17 years) from 1980 to 2009 (National Center for Juvenile Justice,

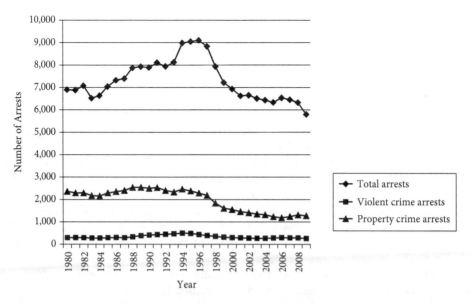

Figure 25.1 Rates of arrests per 100,000 adolescents ages 10–17 years, 1980–2009. Total crime index includes violent crime, property crime, vandalism, weapons carrying, drug abuse violations, driving under the influence, drunkenness, disorderly conduct, liquor laws, curfew and loitering law violations, and runaways. Violent crime index includes murder and nonnegligent manslaughter, forcible rape, robbery, and aggravated assault. Property crime index includes burglary, larceny-theft, motor vehicle theft, and arson. *Source*: Adapted from the National Center for Juvenile Justice (2011).

2011). Figure 25.2 shows annual prevalence rates for alcohol, marijuana, and cocaine use for high school seniors from the Monitoring the Future (MTF) study during the same time period (Johnston, O'Malley, Bachman, & Schulenberg, 2003, 2011). For the most part, the trends in property and violent offenses among adolescents do not match the trends in substance use. For example, both marijuana and cocaine showed significant decreases between the mid-1980s and 1992. Marijuana use returned to

relatively high levels by the mid-1990s and declined somewhat since then, but cocaine showed a relative increase in the late 1990s and early 2000s. Alcohol use has been declining since the late 1980s with a slight increase in the late 1990s followed by a continual decline. In contrast, property offenses were relatively high in the early 1990s and then declined considerably through the 2000s, whereas violent offenses peaked in the mid-1990s and have declined somewhat since then.

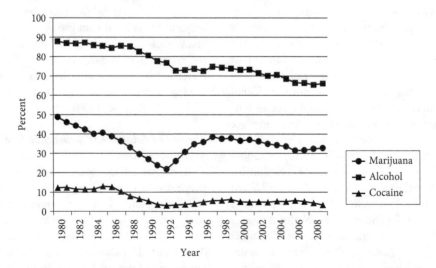

Figure 25.2 Trends in annual prevalence of drug use among high school seniors, 1980–2009. *Source*: Adapted from Johnston et al. (2003) and Johnston et al. (2011).

These figures demonstrate that, at the macro level, trends in substance use do not converge well with arrest trends for violent and property offenses among adolescents. However, many factors in addition to rates of delinquency affect arrest decisions and rates (e.g., demographic characteristics of offenders, national and local government policy etc.; see Hirschfield, Maschi, White, Goldman-Traub, & Loeber, 2006). In addition, the data presented earlier on substance use relied on self-reports, whereas the arrest data were compiled from official FBI statistics. It is important to note that many offenders escape getting arrested, and delinquency does not necessarily involve activities that are punishable by arrest. Arrest statistics may also reflect a lag because offenders may be arrested more than a year after committing the offense.

Therefore, we also examined trends in self-reported delinquency in relation to the MTF substance use trends. The data on self-reported delinquency come from the Centers for Disease Control and Prevention's (2011) Youth Risk Behavior Surveillance System (YRBSS) and are shown in Figure 25.3. The YRBSS has been administered biannually since 1991 and is intended to monitor priority health-risk behaviors, including tobacco and alcohol use, sexual behaviors, and behaviors that contribute to injury and violence. Generally, trends for the delinquent behaviors shown here (i.e., getting into physical fights and carrying a weapon) followed a pattern similar to the arrest rates shown in Figure 25.1. They showed a marked decline throughout the 1990s and then

began to level off around 2000. Both violent offenses (Figure 25.1) and getting into physical fights (Figure 25.3) actually showed a slight increase in the early 2000s. These self-reported delinquent behavior trends did not follow substance use trends. Prevalence trends for use of alcohol, marijuana, and cocaine (Figure 25.2) showed more incremental declines in the 1990s compared to self-reported delinquency (Figure 25.3). In addition, when we compared YRBSS rates of self-reported delinquency to the YRBSS rates of self-reported substance use (alcohol, marijuana, and cocaine) over time, the trends were also quite divergent (not shown but available from the authors upon request).

Within-individual developmental courses of substance use and delinquency also do not converge well. Heavy drinking peaks in the late teens and early 20s (Johnston et al., 2011), and initiation to illicit drugs other than marijuana may be as late as 25 years (Chen & Kandel, 1995). Initiation of property offenses occurs predominantly in early adolescence, and violent offending peaks in middle to late adolescence (Elliott, 1994; Loeber et al., 2008). Whereas most youth mature out of delinquency and aggressive behavior by age 18 years (Elliott, 1994), substance use continues to increase after high school (White, Labouvie, & Papadaratsakis, 2005).

Overall, the trend data discussed earlier would argue against a direct causal association between substance use and delinquency during adolescence, at least on a macro level. Next we briefly discuss causal and noncausal models that have been

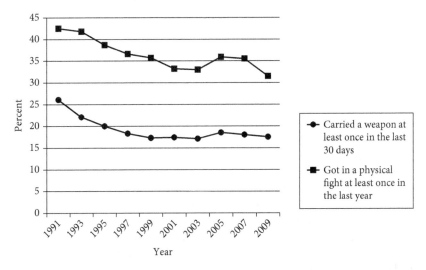

Figure 25.3 Trends in self-reported delinquency and substance use, 1980–2008. *Source*: Adapted from Center for Disease Control and Prevention (2011).

proposed to explain the association between substance use and delinquency.

Explanatory Models

There are three basic explanatory models for the relationship between substance use and delinquent behavior: (1) substance use "causes" delinquent behavior; (2) delinquent behavior leads to substance use; and (3) the relationship is explained by a set of common causes (White, 1990). Each model may be applicable to different subgroups of the population of substance-using offenders or to different incidents of substance use–related offending. These three basic models represent simplistic models, which can be expanded into reciprocal, mediation, and moderation models (see D'Amico, Edelen, Miles, & Morral, 2008; Pernanen, 1993; White, 2016). In the following sections the three basic models are briefly described.

Substance Use "Causes" Delinquency

The tripartite model has been used to explain a causal connection between substance use and violence predominantly among adults (Goldstein, 1985). This model postulates that there are three ways in which substance use could cause violence: (1) through psychopharmacological effects of alcohol and drugs on the individual, (2) by generating predatory crime to get money to pay for drugs, and (3) because of systemic violence involved in the illegal drug market. The tripartite model has received some criticism (e.g., MacCoun, Kilmer, & Reuter, 2003; Parker & Auerhahn, 1998) and may not generalize well to adolescents or to offenders outside the United States (White & Gorman, 2000).

THE PSYCHOPHARMACOLOGICAL MODEL

This model proposes that the effects of intoxication cause violent behavior. Acute use of alcohol and some drugs impairs cognitive processes that in turn affect perceptions of and attention to cues, interpersonal communication, awareness of consequences, behavioral inhibition, and judgment; this impairment increases the likelihood for violence and risk taking (for greater detail, see Fagan, 1990; Miczek et al., 1994; Parker & Auerhahn, 1999). In addition, heavy use of alcohol and drugs by adolescents can lead to cognitive impairments (Medina & Tapert, 2011), which can increase delinquent and, especially, violent behavior (Ostrowsky, 2011). Furthermore, research suggests that the effect of alcohol and some drugs on aggression may be mediated through their effects on neurotransmitter

systems (see Boles & Miotto, 2003, for greater detail).

The pharmacological model has received most of its support from laboratory studies examining the effects of alcohol intoxication on aggressive responding. Adolescents have not been included in this research, given restrictions on providing alcohol to minors. However, many studies of college students support the fact that alcohol intoxication in the laboratory increases aggressive responding (Giancola, 2002). The psychopharmacological explanation has received less support for most illicit drugs (e.g., marijuana and heroin) than it has for alcohol. In contrast, some anxiolytic drugs, such as sedatives and tranquilizers, may have effects on aggression similar to those of alcohol. (For a review of specific drug effects on aggression, see Boles & Miotto, 2003; Miczek et al., 1994; Ostrowsky, 2011; Parker & Auerhahn, 1998.)

Alcohol's impact on aggressive responding in laboratory studies appears to depend on other factors that facilitate or inhibit aggression, including subject characteristics, experimental design conditions, and beverage characteristics (Ito, Miller, & Pollock, 1996; Leonard, 2008). It has also been suggested that expectancies that alcohol use causes violence may actually account for some of the observed relationship between alcohol use and aggressive behavior (Pihl & Ross, 1987), although one meta-analysis of laboratory studies refuted this explanation (Bushman, 1997). Very few expectancy studies, however, have been conducted on adolescents as opposed to college students. One study compared children's (ages 6–14 years) expectations of aggression in videotaped vignettes depicting disputes between adults in sober and intoxicated states (El-Sheikh & Elmore-Staton, 2007). Children expected men and women to be verbally and physically aggressive when intoxicated, regardless of whether or not the other member of the dispute was intoxicated. (For more detail on expectancy research, see Chapter 17 in this volume.)

In sum, the psychopharmacological model appears relevant for explaining a potential causal relationship between alcohol and aggressive behavior, but it is less relevant for explaining the relationship between illicit drugs and aggression. Overall, it appears that the relationship depends on individual and environmental factors rather than solely on the pharmacological properties of alcohol. Research testing the pharmacological model among adolescents has had to rely on self-reports of crimes committed under the influence of alcohol.

This research is reviewed in the section on "Acute Associations."

THE ECONOMIC MOTIVATION MODEL

This model assumes that drug users engage in predatory crimes, such as robbery, to acquire drugs or the money to buy drugs. Support for the economic motivation model comes mostly from literature on adult heroin addicts (e.g., Anglin & Perrochet, 1998; Nurco, Shaffer, Ball, & Kinlock, 1984). Self-report data from US adolescents do not provide strong support that economic motivation accounts for much drug-related violence (White, 1997a). Overall, the economic motivation model, while supported in studies of adult drug addicts, appears less applicable for adolescents, perhaps because most adolescents are not dependent on drugs, especially addictive drugs such as heroin (Menard & Mihalic, 2001; White, 1990).

THE SYSTEMIC MODEL

This model posits that the system of drug distribution and use is inherently connected with violent crime (Goldstein, 1985). Studies conducted in the 1980s suggested that the systemic model was not applicable to the majority of youthful drug users because few were involved in distribution at a high enough level (see White, 1990). Later research suggested that the systemic model accounted for a significant amount of drug-related violence among youths in inner cities during the late 1980s and the 1990s because the crack market attracted a younger group of sellers than previous drug markets (Fagan & Chin, 1990; Inciardi & Pottieger, 1991).

Nevertheless, studies of adolescents have found that individuals drawn to dealing were already violent and delinquent, although once involved in drug use and dealing their level of violent behavior increased (see also Fagan & Chin, 1990; Inciardi & Pottieger, 1991; Johnson, Natarajan, Dunlap, & Elmoghazy, 1994; Van Kammen & Loeber, 1994). Thus, it is not likely that drug selling *causes* individuals to become offenders; rather, the association of drug use and delinquency among dealers is probably accounted for by a common cause model (see later discussion). (Drug dealing is discussed in greater detail later in the chapter.)

Delinquency Leads to Substance Use

Although this chapter focuses on alcohol and drug use as risk factors for delinquency, the possibility that delinquency may also be a risk factor for alcohol and drug use cannot be overlooked.

Longitudinal studies have consistently found that aggressive behavior developmentally precedes alcohol and drug use and that early aggressive and delinquent behavior is a predictor of later alcohol and drug use and problems (Farrington, 1995; Mason et al., 2010; White, Brick, & Hansell, 1993; see section on "Developmental Associations"). Furthermore, aggressive and hostile individuals may use drugs to self-medicate (Khantzian, 1985) or to give themselves an excuse to commit an illegal act (Collins, 1993). In addition, deviant individuals often tend to have peer groups and lifestyles that promote alcohol and drug use (Collins & Messerschmidt, 1993).

Therefore, it is likely that delinquency and substance use are reciprocally related, with each type of behavior reinforcing the other (see section on "Developmental Associations"). For example, adolescent gang members often drink before a fight to give themselves courage and then drink after the fight to celebrate (Fagan, 1993). Furthermore, the connection between delinquency and substance use results, at least in part, from the fact that both types of behavior are predicted by the same set of risk and protective behaviors rather than the fact that either behavior *causes* the other. Next we discuss some of these common predictors.

The Common Cause Model

The common cause model postulates that substance use and delinquency do not have a direct causal link; rather, they are related because they are predicted by a similar underlying set of risk factors (Jessor & Jessor, 1977). Overall, the common cause model appears to explain a great deal of the connection between substance use and delinquency during adolescence (White, 1997a, 1997b).

Jessor and Jessor (1977) argued that delinquency, substance use, and other deviant behaviors cluster together in adolescence as part of a "problem behavior syndrome" predicted by an underlying set of risk factors. They found that these factors included lower value on academic achievement, lower intolerance of deviance, greater friends' approval, and models for problem behavior, among others (see also Donovan, Jessor, & Costa, 1999). More recently, Noyori-Corbett and Moon (2010) tested a multifaceted model of risk (e.g., community disorganization, family socioeconomic status, peer delinquency) and protective (e.g., extracurricular activities and parental involvement) factors for adolescent deviant behavior. Their results indicated that adolescent violence and illicit substance use were related to each other and to a common set of putative risk and protective factors. Although there is support for substance use and delinquency clustering together during adolescence, studies have also found unique factors that determine whether an adolescent will become a heavy drinker/drug user, a delinquent, or both (e.g., White & Labouvie, 1994). Next we focus on a few common risk and protective factors (for greater detail on correlates of substance use, see Chapters 14–16 and 19, 21 in this volume).

COMMON CORRELATES

The World Health Organization has identified several individual-level predictors of violence among adolescents, including hyperactivity, impulsiveness, poor behavioral control, attention problems, and low educational achievement (Krug, Mercy, Dahlberg, Zwi, & Lozano, 2002; see also Marcus, 2007; Martel et al., 2009; Reiss & Roth, 1993). Many of these same variables are related to general delinquent behavior and have also been shown to predict adolescent heavy drinking and drug use in studies conducted in the United States and Europe (Doran et al., 2012; European Monitoring Centre for Drugs and Drug Addiction, 2003; Hawkins, Catalano, & Miller, 1992). For example, sensation seeking, which is defined as the "need for varied, novel and complex sensations and experiences and the willingness to take physical and social risks for the sake of such experience" (Zuckerman, 1979, p. 10), is a temperamental or personality trait that is one of the best predictors of adolescent substance use (Bates, Labouvie, & White, 1986; Zuckerman, 1994) and is also linked strongly to delinquency (Greene et al., 2000; White, Labouvie, & Bates, 1985). Similarly, school achievement problems have been associated with substance use (Fleming, Catalano, Haggerty, & Abbott, 2010; Henry, 2010), delinquency (Maguin & Loeber, 1996), and delinquent recidivism (Katsiyannis, Ryan, Zhang, & Spann, 2008).

In addition to individual-level characteristics, peer relationships are important predictors of substance use (Ennett et al., 2006; Pandina, Johnson, & White, 2009) and delinquency (Gorman & White, 1995). During adolescence, youth spend more time with their peers than their families, and therefore these interactions can be highly influential. In fact, several studies have found that substance-using and deviant peers are among the strongest predictors of adolescent substance use (e.g., Ennett & Bauman, 1996; Pandina et al., 2009; Trucco, Colder, & Wieczorek, 2011) and that delinquent peer

affiliation is one of the strongest predictors of adolescent delinquency (e.g., Gorman & White, 1995). However, youth are just as likely to choose friends whose behavior matches their own (selection) as to be socialized by their peers into both types of deviant behavior (Gorman & White, 1995; Pandina et al., 2009).

Family structure and interactions are also strongly correlated with adolescent substance use (Hemovich, Lac, & Crano, 2011; Kramer et al., 2008) and delinquent behavior (Demuth & Brown, 2004). Parental substance use and substance use disorders have been shown to be significant predictors of substance use in offspring (Andrews, Hops, Ary, Tildesley, & Harris, 1993; Brook et al., 2010; Sher, 1991; White, Johnson, & Buyske, 2000), as well as of adolescent aggression and other forms of conduct problems (e.g., lying and stealing) (Fuller et al., 2003; Johnson, Sher, & Rolf, 1991; Marmorstein, Iacono, & McGue, 2009; Ritter, Stewart, Bernet, Coe, & Brown, 2002). Positive parenting behaviors, such as setting limits and monitoring, can act as protective factors against substance use (Simons-Morton & Chen, 2005; Substance Abuse and Mental Health Services Administration, 2009) and delinquency (Simons & Conger, 2007), whereas negative parenting behaviors, such as harsh discipline and abuse/neglect, can act as risk factors (Loeber et al., 2008; Widom & Hiller-Sturmhèfel, 2001). In addition, single-parent households and family transitions, such as divorce, have been associated with an increased risk of substance use (Doherty & Needle, 1991; Paxton, Valois, & Drane, 2007) and delinquency (Petts, 2009; Snyder & Sickmund, 2006).

At the larger, structural level, school and neighborhood context also influences adolescent delinquency (for a review, see Sampson, Morenoff, & Gannon-Rowley, 2002) and substance use (for a review, see Gardner, Barajas, & Brooks-Gunn, 2010). Neighborhood factors, including residential mobility, population heterogeneity, high proportion of single-parent households, and concentrated poverty, all contribute to greater opportunities for delinquency (Sampson et al., 2002) and are often related to drug availability and exposure for adolescents (Ensminger, Anthony, & McCord, 1997; Freisthler, Lascala, Gruenewald, & Treno, 2005).

THEORETICAL EXPLANATIONS

Deviance theories, which have received strong empirical support for explaining delinquency, have been applied to substance use as well. These include (among others) differential association (Sutherland, 1947), social learning (Akers, 1985), social control (Hirschi, 1969), strain (Agnew, 1992), and social disorganization (Shaw & McKay, 1942) theories. Differential association/social learning theory, operationalized primarily by friends' deviance or friends' approval of deviance, has been found to be the strongest theoretical predictor of adolescent substance use (White, Johnson, & Horwitz, 1986). General strain theory, which focuses on negative relationships with others and the negative affective states (e.g., anger) that result from these relationships, has also garnered some support as a predictor of adolescent substance use (Agnew & White, 1992). Social disorganization theory posits that disadvantaged characteristics of a neighborhood, such as poverty and high residential mobility, contribute to deviance by reducing supervision and socialization among neighbors (Sampson & Raudenbush, 1997). Although studies have found that substance use patterns vary across neighborhoods, the findings are mixed as to whether neighborhood social disadvantage is related to increased substance use (Karriker-Jaffe, 2011; Sampson et al., 2002). Social control theory (Hirschi, 1969) posits that deviance arises when youth lack sufficient ties to conventional groups such as families and schools. This theory has received some support in studies of adolescent substance use (e.g., Marcos & Bahr, 1995).

Some theorists have integrated the aforementioned theories in order to more fully explain deviant behavior. For example, Elliott, Huizinga and Ageton (1985) integrated strain, control, and social learning theories to explain adolescent drug use (marijuana and other illicit drug use) and delinquency (general delinquency, index offenses, and minor offenses). They found that increases in strain at home led to decreases in family and school involvement and increased school alienation; additionally, increases in school strain led to decreased school involvement and increased alienation. Decreased conventional bonding, in turn, led to increased involvement with delinquent peers, which had a direct positive effect on all types of delinquency and drug use. Prior delinquency and involvement with delinquent peers were the major factors that directly affected drug use and delinquency. Overall, the effects of the bonding and strain variables were weak and indirect.

Similarly Catalano and Hawkins (1996) combined differential association, social learning, and control theories into the social development model (SDM). The SDM posits that an individual's behavior will be shaped by the amount of association with various types of individuals, as well as by the level of involvement in prosocial and antisocial activities. The SDM, which has been shown to predict adolescent violence (Huang, White, Kosterman, Catalano, & Hawkins, 2001), has also been found to predict substance use during adolescence (Catalano, Kosterman, Hawkins, Newcomb, & Abbott, 1996). Likewise, Thornberry's (1987) interactional theory, which combines elements of social control and learning theories, has predicted adolescent delinquency (Thornberry, Lizotte, Krohn, Farnworth, & Jang, 1991) and adolescent substance use (Krohn, Lizotte, Thornberry, Smith, & McDowall, 1996).

DIFFERENTIAL RISK FACTORS

In contrast to the common causes and theoretical explanations identified earlier, demographic correlates, such as sex, race, and ethnicity, differentially affect rates of substance use and delinquent behavior (Johnston et al., 2011; Snyder & Sickmund, 2006). For instance, the 2010 MTF data show that although males tend to report slightly higher prevalence rates for illicit substance use and heavy drinking than females by the 12th grade, these sex differences are less obvious at younger ages, and females actually report higher annual prevalence rates for some substances in the 8th grade (Johnston et al., 2011). In contrast, there are large differences in prevalence rates for delinquency between the sexes, with males reporting significantly higher levels across adolescence (Marcus, 2007; Miller, Malone, & Dodge, 2010). In addition, males accounted for 70% of all juvenile arrests in 2008 (Puzzanchera, 2009). However, the discrepancy between male and female rates of delinquency might be declining, as evidenced by a 20% decline in arrests for male juveniles between 1980 and 2003 compared to a 22% increase for females (Snyder & Sickmund, 2006).

Whereas Whites are more likely than Blacks to drink alcohol and use most hard drugs during adolescence, Blacks report comparable or higher rates of marijuana use (Lee, Mun, White, & Simon, 2010). In contrast, rates of delinquency, especially violent delinquency, are higher for Blacks than Whites even when only self-report data are compared (Elliott, 1994; Snyder & Sickmund, 2006). Overall, arrest rates are proportionally higher for Black than White youth, although they vary depending on the nature of the offense (Snyder & Sickmund, 2006). Loeber and colleagues (2008) argued, however, that racial disparities in delinquency are due most likely to other risk factors that are correlated with race, such as high peer delinquency, low academic achievement, and low socioeconomic status.

Summary

Both substance use and delinquency are multilevel phenomena that have been explained at different levels of analysis, ranging from individual models to macro or social models. At the same time, within each level, there are alternative causal models, and within them, some are even further differentiated. Across all of these levels, a large array of common risk and protective factors has been found to predict adolescent substance use and delinquency. Therefore, youth exposed to the same types of risk factors are expected to engage in both behaviors. This overlapping set of predictors provides strong support for a common cause model, especially in adolescence when substance use and delinquency represent different forms of deviant behavior. Thus far, we have provided a background for understanding the comorbidity of substance use and delinquency. In the following sections, we summarize the empirical literature on alcohol and drugs as risk factors for adolescent delinquency.

Empirical Research on the Direct Associations Between Substance Use and Delinquency

To better understand the connection between substance use and delinquency, both acute effects and longer-term developmental associations require consideration. Whereas studies of acute effects elucidate the association between consumption of substances and immediate delinquent behavior, developmental studies help to elucidate the temporal associations and to delineate longer-term effects (Huang et al., 2001).

Acute Associations

As discussed earlier, it is not possible to directly test the effects of alcohol or drug consumption on delinquency among adolescents. Instead, researchers rely on self-reports of substance use immediately prior to engaging in delinquent acts. In a study in Ireland, 42% of juvenile suspected offenders were under the influence of alcohol, 17% drugs, and 4% both at the time of their offense (Millar, O'Dwyer, & Finnegan, 1998, as cited in European Monitoring Centre for Drugs and Drug Addiction, 2003). Alcohol was more often related to public

order offenses (e.g., public intoxication, nuisance), whereas drug use was most often associated with robberies. In contrast, in the mid-1990s, US adolescent arrestees' reports of crime commission under the influence were fairly equal for alcohol and drugs (Bureau of Justice Statistics, 1994). In a study of US adolescents who were adjudicated for a violent crime, over half of the youths said that taking alcohol (29%) or drugs (33%) contributed to their acting violently, and about half had used either alcohol (17%) or drugs (34%) immediately prior to the offense (Hartstone & Hansen, 1984). The rates, as shown earlier, were higher for drugs than for alcohol.

Given the high rates of multiple-substance use among adolescents (Jackson, Sher, & Schulenberg, 2008), it may be difficult to isolate the effects of specific drugs. Nevertheless, a study of incarcerated youth in New South Wales found that the most frequently used substance prior to committing a violent offense was alcohol, followed by cocaine (Lennings, Copeland, & Howard, 2003). In a study of juvenile offenders in Australia, 70% were under the influence of alcohol or drugs at the time of their last offense, and almost one third of those charged with assault reported being drunk or high at the time of the offense (Prichard & Payne, 2005).

Data from community and high-risk samples of adolescents provide mixed support for substance use directly affecting delinquency (Ostrowsky, 2011; White, 1997a). In one large community interview study, researchers found that most of the delinquent incidents occurred while adolescents were not using alcohol or drugs and, in fact, most adolescents reported that they moderated their use before committing a crime (Carpenter, Glassner, Johnson, & Loughlin, 1988). In a national sample of adolescents, Elliott, Huizinga, and Menard (1989) examined self-reports of the use of alcohol and drugs immediately prior to commission of Uniform Crime Report index offenses (violent index offenses include aggravated assault, forcible rape, robbery, and murder, whereas property index offenses include arson, burglary, larceny-theft, and motor vehicle theft). They found no relationship between acute drug use and property or violent crime. On the other hand, they found a definite relationship between alcohol and sexual assault (forcible rape) and a probable relationship between alcohol and aggravated assault. However, the association between alcohol use and violent crime was stronger in young adulthood than in adolescence, suggesting that the nature of the relationship may change over the life course. Using these same data, Menard and Mihalic (2001) found support for an acute association between alcohol use, but not drug use, and violent index offending during adolescence. Overall, alcohol's pharmacological effects were strongest for violent offenses, vandalism, and public disorder offenses but were not significant for most other offenses during adolescence.

White and Hansell (1998) examined the acute effects of alcohol, marijuana, and cocaine use on fighting and acting mean from adolescence (ages 12–18 years) into young adulthood (ages 25–31 years). They found that acute incidents of alcohol- and drug-related fighting were reported more often by users of alcohol than by users of marijuana and cocaine, especially as they approached young adulthood. White, Tice, Loeber, and Stouthamer-Loeber (2002) also examined self-reported proximal associations between substance use and illegal activities from age 16 through 19 in a high-risk sample of young men. Proportionally, the most frequent illegal acts reported to be committed under the influence of alcohol or drugs were strong-arming, gang fighting, attacking, vandalism, and throwing things at others. For each of these offenses, more than one third of those who committed the offense committed their most serious offense under the influence of alcohol or drugs. Overall, White and colleagues found that violent offenses, as opposed to property offenses, were more strongly related to acute incidents of alcohol and drug use. Although they could not separate the effects of alcohol from other drugs, when they limited their analyses to only alcohol users, the results were almost identical. In addition, results indicated that more adolescents engaged in fighting while using alcohol than while using marijuana. Their results also suggested that impulsivity might either mediate or moderate the effects of alcohol on violent offending.

Using individual-level analyses with a representative sample of US high school students, Felson, Teasdale, and colleagues (2008) found that drinkers were more likely to engage in fighting than nondrinkers even when they were sober. Thus, the researchers concluded that the association between prevalence of drinking (i.e., use vs. no use) and fighting was spurious. When they limited the analyses to only drinkers and examined fighting when sober and when drinking, results indicated that frequency and quantity of drinking had a "causal" effect on fighting. Their analyses demonstrated that the association between drinking and fighting was stronger for those youth who were more violence prone, for Whites versus Blacks, and for older versus younger adolescents. In a similar study of Finnish adolescents, Felson, Savolainen, and colleagues (2008) found that the association between alcohol use and certain types of offenses (i.e., violence, vandalism, car theft, and graffiti writing) was "causal" (i.e., it could not be explained by common risk factors), whereas for other types (i.e., petty theft, shoplifting, and stealing from home), the relationship was purely spurious. A plausible reason for this difference might be that the former types of offenses are more impulsive in nature. Felson and colleagues (Felson, Savolainen, et al., 2008; Felson, Teasdale, et al., 2008) suggested that the routine activities theory might explain part of the spurious relationship between drinking and delinquency. That is, drinkers may be more likely than nondrinkers to associate with other youth in unsupervised activities, which can increase the risk for delinquent behavior.

A study investigating the impact of alcohol use on adolescent violence in 30 European countries found regional variations in drinking patterns and their relationships to violence. Adolescents from Nordic countries had a higher incidence of intoxication than those from Mediterranean countries (Felson, Savolainen, Bjarnason, Anderson, & Zohra, 2011). Moreover, in Nordic countries, and to a lesser extent Eastern European countries, drinking was shown to have a strong effect on adolescent violence (i.e., fighting), whereas in Mediterranean countries drinking had little to no effect on violence. The authors concluded that the direct effects of alcohol on violence depend on the drinking culture of the country.

Based on a review of the literature on alcohol, drugs, and violence among youth, Osgood (1994, p. 33) concluded that there was little evidence that substance use makes an independent contribution to adolescent violence because both violence and substance abuse have the same underlying risk factors. Nevertheless, several of the more recent studies reviewed earlier suggest that acute alcohol use may contribute to aggressive delinquency during adolescence.

Developmental Associations

As stated earlier, an examination of developmental associations sheds light on the temporal order of, and long-term associations between, substance use and delinquency. Most studies have found that, in terms of life course development, aggression and minor delinquent behavior precede alcohol and drug use (Farrington, 1995; White et al., 1993; Windle, 1990), and others have found that serious violent offending precedes illicit drug use (e.g., White, Loeber, & Farrington, 2008). One problem with assessing temporal order is that some youth do not initiate some of the behaviors being assessed and thus data are often right censored. To overcome this problem, White and colleagues (2008) assessed the temporal order among different types of substance use and serious offending among young men who engaged in all of the behaviors. They found that although the onset of alcohol use generally preceded the onset of serious theft and violence, youth were equally likely to either first use illicit drugs or to first engage in serious violence (i.e., strong-arming, rape, and assault). The mean age of onset of serious violence preceded the mean age of onset of illicit drug use by a few months. In addition, the onset of serious theft (breaking and entering and auto theft) preceded the onset of illicit drug use.

Although the data indicate that, for most youth, delinquent behavior precedes initiation into substance use, chronic use of substances can have an effect on subsequent offending (Elliott et al., 1989) and can impede desistance from delinquency (e.g., Farrington & Hawkins, 1991). For example, Welte, Barnes, Hoffman, Wieczorek, and Zhang (2005) found that drug use interfered with an early maturation out of delinquency; they attributed this interference to involvement with deviant peers or involvement in drug dealing. Because of the evidence that aggression developmentally precedes alcohol and drug use in many adolescents, it is difficult to establish a developmental causal effect of substance use on delinquency. Next we review longitudinal studies that have examined substance use as a predictor of later delinquency, delinquency as a predictor of later substance use, and the reciprocal relationship between delinquency and substance use over time.

PREDICTING DELINQUENCY FROM SUBSTANCE USE

Several studies have found that heavy drinking in adolescence is related to violent and property offending in later adolescence and adulthood (Fergusson & Horwood, 2000; Menard & Mihalic, 2001; Popovici, Homer, Fang, & French, 2012; Swahn & Donovan, 2004). In complement, Kaplan and Damphousse (1995) showed that drug use in

adolescence predicted increased aggression in adulthood, although the predictive utility was relatively weak (see also Kandel, Simcha-Fagan, & Davies, 1986). Welte and colleagues (2005) demonstrated that alcohol use and dependence were strongly related to an increasing trajectory of delinquency. A study of youths from 30 countries (in Europe, Latin America, and elsewhere) revealed that marijuana use, compared to alcohol or hard drug use, was a better predictor of delinquency (Steketee, 2011). In contrast, Kuhns (2005) found that drug use was not a consistent positive predictor of serious violent offending among adolescents over time (for a review, see Ostrowsky, 2011). In general, however, trajectory analyses have shown that substance use trajectories distinguished by high levels of use and early onset are associated with later delinquency and conduct disorder (Hill, White, Chung, Hawkins, & Catalano, 2000; Marti, Stice, & Springer, 2010; Orlando, Tucker, Ellickson, & Klein, 2005; Tucker, Orlando, & Ellickson, 2003).

PREDICTING SUBSTANCE USE FROM DELINQUENCY

Childhood and adolescent aggression, especially among males, has been consistently related to heavy drinking in adolescence and adulthood (Farrington, 1995; White et al., 1993; White & Hansell, 1996). White and colleagues (White et al., 1993; White & Hansell, 1996) examined the longitudinal associations among alcohol use, aggression, and alcohol-related aggression during adolescence and young adulthood. They found that aggression in early adolescence predicted increases in later alcohol use, but alcohol use did not predict increases in aggression. Furthermore, early aggression was a better predictor of later alcohol-related aggression for males, whereas among females, alcohol use was found to be a better predictor (White & Hansell, 1996). Overall, the data indicated that early aggression was stable over the life cycle and set the stage for later heavy drinking and alcohol-related aggression (White et al., 1993). In a longitudinal study of juvenile offenders, Dembo, Wareham, and Schmeidler (2007) found that delinquency exacerbated alcohol and marijuana use over time. Furthermore, a longitudinal study of Black youth followed from childhood to age 42 years found that serious adolescent delinquency had a positive impact on drug use initiation that extended into middle adulthood (Doherty, Green, & Ensminger, 2008).

Studies have also found that trajectories of offending predict later alcohol and drug use and abuse. For example, Hill, Chung, Herrenkohl, and

Hawkins (2000 as reported in Weisner, Kim, and Capaldi, 2005) found that adolescent chronic property offenders were more likely than nonoffenders to exhibit drug, but not alcohol, dependence in emerging adulthood (age 21 years), whereas chronic violent offenders, compared to nonoffenders, were more likely to exhibit later alcohol dependence. Weisner and colleagues (2005) found that high-level offending from ages 12 to 24 years predicted greater drug use at ages 23 – 26 years. Using latent growth curve models, Loeber, Stepp, Chung, Hipwell, and White (2010) examined the prospective associations between conduct problems and alcohol use for girls followed from ages 11 to 15 years. Their results indicated that conduct disorder prospectively predicted alcohol use, but alcohol use did not prospectively predict conduct disorder. However, the timing of the associations differed by race. Among White girls, conduct problems prospectively predicted alcohol use at ages 11–13 years but not later. In contrast, among Black girls, prospective prediction was not observed until ages 13–14 years. Mason and colleagues (2010) used latent growth curve modeling to examine the development of delinquency and alcohol use from late childhood into young adulthood. Late childhood delinquency predicted young adult crime and alcohol use disorders as mediated through adolescent delinquency. These associations were significantly stronger for those youths from low- versus middle-income backgrounds. Lynne-Landsman, Graber, Nichols, and Botvin (2011) examined associations among joint trajectories of aggression, delinquency, and substance use in an urban, middle-school sample. Overall, they found that individuals following more problematic trajectories of aggression and delinquency had a higher probability of also following a problematic trajectory of substance use. However, information about an individual's trajectory of delinquency was more informative for predicting his or her trajectory of substance use than vice versa. The researchers concluded that externalizing behaviors may be one pathway to early substance use (see also Martel et al., 2009).

RECIPROCAL RELATIONSHIPS

Several studies have examined cross-lagged associations between substance use and delinquency and have found that the association is reciprocal. For example, Mason and Windle (2002) tested a cross-lagged model of substance use (latent variable of alcohol, marijuana, and tobacco) and delinquency (latent variable of property damage, aggression,

and theft) over four waves during adolescence. They found that there was a significant positive association between substance use and delinquency, such that changes in delinquency were associated with small but consistent changes in substance use across all waves. However, the effect of substance use on delinquency was significant only in the earlier waves of the study. The results varied for boys and girls; among boys, bidirectional effects between the latent variables were observed, while no such effects were found for girls. In contrast, whereas a study of British adolescents also found a strong reciprocal relationship between offending and drug use, this association was stronger for girls than boys (Estévez & Emler, 2011). Findings from a study of juvenile offenders in a large US metropolitan area indicated a reciprocal association between delinquency and substance use, even when controlling for age, ethnicity, and sex (D'Amico et al., 2008). Welte, Zhang, and Wieczorek (2001) found that early delinquency moderated the effects of substance use on crime in a sample of young men aged 16–19 years. For those who reported early onset of delinquency (i.e., before age 12 years), there was no significant relation between delinquency and substance use. However, for those who reported later onset of delinquency (i.e., after age 13 years), there were significant bidirectional associations between substance use and delinquency.

White, Loeber, Stouthamer-Loeber, and Farrington (1999) examined cross-lagged associations of alcohol and marijuana use with violent offending in a high-risk sample of young men from ages 13 to 18 years. Heavy drinking in one year predicted violent offending in the next, even while controlling for current violence; violent offending in one year predicted alcohol use in the next controlling for current alcohol use (see also Weisner et al., 2005). The relationship between marijuana and violence was also reciprocal. When the researchers controlled for common risk factors (temperament, family, and neighborhood variables) and violence at age 13 years, alcohol and marijuana use at age 13 years remained strong predictors of violent offending in later adolescence. Wei, Loeber, and White (2004) replicated these analyses with another cohort studied from ages 11 to 20 years and found similar reciprocal relationships between alcohol and violence and between marijuana and violence. However, frequent marijuana use, compared to frequent alcohol use, was more strongly related to later violence. When common risk factors, specifically race/ethnicity and hard drug use, were controlled, the relationship between frequent marijuana use and violence (and vice-versa) was no longer significant, suggesting a spurious relationship. Therefore, the researchers argued that the developmental associations between drug use and delinquency may simply reflect a common cause model, in which both behaviors are predicted by the same underlying risk factors. White, Jackson, and Loeber's (2009) trajectory analyses indicated that the developmental associations between alcohol frequency and prevalence of serious violence depended on the age period studied. They found moderate associations between trajectories of drinking and violence during adolescence (ages 13–18 years), but no significant associations during emerging adulthood (ages 18–25 years) (see also White, Lee, Mun, & Loeber, 2012). In addition, adolescent trajectories of violence did not predict emerging adult drinking, and adolescent trajectories of drinking did not predict emerging adult violent offending.

In a latent growth model analysis, Dembo and Sullivan (2009) reported significant positive correlations in growth trajectories of cocaine use and delinquent behavior among justice-involved youths between the ages of 11 and 18 years. Mulvey and colleagues (2010) also found that substance use and offending were significantly related to each other across time in a sample of serious juvenile offenders. Their preliminary analyses suggested, however, that substance use predicted offending over time more consistently than offending predicted substance use over time. In summary, the research evidence indicates that delinquency and substance use are often reciprocally related during adolescence and that both are related to many of the same underlying factors.

Drug Dealing and Gang Membership

We have chosen to treat drug dealing and gang membership as unique types of delinquency given their inherent connection to substance use and each other. Rates of drug use vary considerably among dealers. Although at the lower levels of the drug-selling business most dealers use drugs, those at higher levels do not necessarily use (Hunt, 1990). In fact, studies of adolescent crack dealers suggested that drug selling was an economic opportunity rather than a means of financing their own drug use (Harrison & Freeman, 1998). Although many serious drug users are involved in dealing activities at some point in time, many high-frequency dealers also engage in other criminal activities (Inciardi &

Pottieger, 1994; Lipton & Johnson, 1998). For instance, adolescent dealers, compared to adolescents who do not deal, are more likely to carry weapons, be truant, engage in violence and other problem behaviors, and engage in high-risk sexual behaviors (Centers & Weist, 1998; Li & Feigelman, 1994; Li, Priu, & MacKenzie, 2000; Vaughn, Shook, Perron, Abdon, & Ahmedani, 2011).

Van Kammen and Loeber (1994) demonstrated that previous involvement in violent crime increased the risk of drug dealing for male adolescents, as did previous involvement in property crime. Thus, individuals drawn to dealing were already violent and delinquent, and once involved in dealing, their level of violent behavior (including weapons possession) increased (see also Fagan & Chin, 1990; Johnson et al., 1990). Inciardi and Pottieger (1991) found that crack dealers, compared to those with little or no involvement in crack sales, were younger when they began their criminal careers and had been involved in criminal activity (including sale of marijuana) prior to becoming crack dealers. However, involvement in dealing accelerated their involvement in delinquent activity. Overall, the literature on dealing suggests that deviant youths are attracted to drug selling rather than drug selling leading them to delinquency or drug use. In fact, many of the correlates of dealing are similar to those found for delinquency and drug use (Altschuler & Brounstein, 1991; Centers & Weist, 1998; Li et al., 2000; Little & Steinberg, 2006; Van Kammen & Loeber, 1994).

A great deal of research has explored the associations among drug use, drug dealing, and gang membership. Research generally indicates that gang membership starts in early adolescence, around the time of entry into middle school (Peterson, Taylor, & Esbensen, 2004; Thornberry et al., 2003). Data from the 1997 National Longitudinal Survey of Youth indicate that 8% of the youth belonged to a gang at some point between the ages of 12 and 17 years (Snyder & Sickmund, 2006) and that the annual prevalence rate of gang membership was 2.3% for youth ages 12 to 16 years and declined to 1% for the same youth followed 5 years later (Bellair & McNulty, 2009). Gang membership is even higher (ranging from 15% to 32%) among youth living in high-risk areas of large cities (Howell, 2010). In the Rochester Youth Study, Thornberry et al. (2003) found that nearly one third of the sample reported some gang involvement between approximately ages 14 and 17 years. Additionally, gang membership was higher among non-Whites than Whites, but there were no sex differences in the prevalence of gang membership. Esbensen and Winfree (1998) found that, although females were underrepresented as gang members, at younger ages a large proportion of gang members were female.

In the Thornberry et al. (2003) study, boys who had ever been gang members reported significantly higher rates of involvement in general delinquency (98.1%) and violence (90.6%) than those who never joined a gang (68.4% and 46.4%, respectively). Male gang members were also more likely than male nonmembers to deal drugs (39.5% vs. 9.5%, respectively) and use drugs (65.1% vs. 23.3%). Prevalence rates of drug use were similar for both male and female gang members. Gang members were responsible for 69.8% of all reported drug sales. In addition, for both boys and girls, frequencies of delinquency and drug use were significantly higher among gang members than nonmembers.

Using data from the Denver Youth Study, Esbensen and Huizinga (1993) found much higher frequency rates for delinquency among male, compared to female, gang members. However, they found that both male and female gang members reported significantly higher prevalence rates for all types of delinquency, drug selling, alcohol use, and drug use than their same-sex, nonmember peers. Male gang members, compared to male nonmembers, also reported significantly higher individual offending rates, although offending rates did not differ significantly among female gang members versus nonmembers.

Gang membership is not a stable phenomenon (Esbensen & Huizinga, 1993; Thornberry et al., 2003). Two thirds of the gang members in the Denver study were members for only 1 out of the 4 years studied, and only 9% belonged to a gang for more than 2 years (Esbensen & Huizinga, 1993). In fact, findings from several studies indicate that most youth belong to a gang for less than a year (Bendixen, Endresen, & Olweus, 2006; Peterson et al., 2004; Thornberry et al., 2003). Girls tend to mature out of gang membership earlier than boys (Esbensen & Huizinga, 1993; Thornberry et al., 2003).

This short period of membership makes it possible for longitudinal studies to examine substance use and delinquency prior to and after gang membership. For example, Esbensen and Huizinga (1993) found significantly higher rates of delinquency among gang members prior to membership, compared to their peers who did not become gang members. However, rates of offending were much higher during the years of being an active gang member than before joining. Thus, the data supported both a selection model (i.e., a youth who would eventually join a gang is already involved in delinquency prior to membership) and a facilitation (or socialization) model (i.e., a youth joining a gang would show an increase in delinquent behavior by virtue of participation in the gang's activities) for delinquent behavior (Thornberry et al., 2003). Furthermore, rates of delinquency dropped considerably after leaving the gang. Esbensen and Huizinga also found that drug use was significantly higher for gang members, compared to nonmembers, during the years that they were involved with the gang. However, differences between gang members and nonmembers in drug use prior to joining and after leaving the gang were not significant.

In the Rochester study, Thornberry et al. (2003) found that the differences in delinquency and drug use between gang members and nonmembers were only evident during the active years of gang membership. They suggested that their data provide stronger support for a facilitation effect than a selection effect. Similarly, there were significant increases in drug selling during the first year of joining a gang. Active gang members reported higher levels of drug use than nonmembers, but most of these differences were not statistically significant. Furthermore, drug use and drug selling did not predict joining a gang. Thus, the results from this study combined with those from the earlier Esbensen and Huizinga (1993) study suggest that drug use and dealing do not predict involvement in gangs.

Esbensen, Peterson, Taylor, and Freng (2009) compared the predictors of gang membership to those of violence. They found that several predictors (such as low guilt, use of neutralizations, association with and commitment to delinquent peers, spending time where drugs and/or alcohol are available, and negative school environment) were similar for both behaviors, but that low guilt and commitment to negative peers had stronger effects on gang membership than on violence. Several variables were related to violence, which were not related to gang membership (such as impulsivity, risk-seeking tendencies, few conventional peers, and unsupervised, unstructured socializing with peers), but there were no unique predictors of gang membership. It should be noted, however, that definitions of gangs vary considerably across studies, which may account for a general lack of consistency in identifying predictors and correlates of membership (Esbensen & Huizinga, 1993; Klein & Maxson, 1989).

Conclusion

In summary, the literature reviewed in this chapter shows substantial evidence of both acute and developmental associations between adolescent substance use and delinquency. In terms of acute associations, there may be a unique relationship between alcohol consumption and aggressive behavior, which supports a psychopharmacological model. On the other hand, studies examining developmental associations indicate that substance use and delinquency are reciprocally related over time, and these studies tend to support a common cause model (i.e., that both substance use and delinquency are predicted by the same risk and protective behaviors). The numerous shared risk factors would suggest that, for most adolescents, the relationship is correlational rather than causal. Nevertheless, prior delinquency is a strong predictor of dealing and gang membership, and involvement in substance use, dealing, and gangs (at least during the period of active involvement) increases delinquent behavior.

It is therefore evident from the research reviewed herein that a single model cannot account for the substance use–delinquency nexus among all youths, and there are multiple pathways to each behavior as well as to their co-occurrence. Furthermore, there appear to be distinctions among types of substances in the nature of their associations with illegal offending. For some adolescents, the psychopharmacological effects of heavy drinking promote aggressive behavior on certain occasions. In addition, chronic use of drugs may lead to longer-term cognitive impairments that increase risky behavior. For other adolescents, delinquent behavior weakens bonds to conventional norms and increases involvement with deviant peers. In turn, these involvements provide opportunities and reinforcement for increased substance use and offending. Finally, for many youths, individual factors (e.g., temperament) and early experiences in the family along with socioenvironmental factors increase the risk for involvement in both substance use and delinquency.

It is especially clear that early exposure to risk and protective factors plays an instrumental role in both types of deviant behavior. Due to the extent of common causes, a focus on risk and protective factors for substance use would potentially help alleviate delinquent behavior and vice versa. It would be best to institute prevention approaches that focus on reducing risk factors and enhancing protective factors during childhood and early adolescence, prior to the onset of substance use and serious delinquency (for a review of evidence-based interventions for adolescent aggression and substance use involvement, see Doran et al., 2012). These programs may include preventive interventions that teach parenting skills and increase school involvement and commitment (see Hawkins, Catalano, Kosterman, & Hill, 1999; Henggeler, Schoenwald, Borduin, Rowland, & Cunningham, 1998; see also Chapters 29 and 31 in this volume), as well as those that target children with high-risk temperaments (i.e., overly aggressive or impulsive children) (Cunningham & Henggeler, 2001; see also Chapter 30 in this volume). Community approaches to prevention can also be used to reduce problems of substance use and delinquency (Hawkins et al., 2008). Community interventions may prove to be particularly effective in addressing the reciprocal associations of substance use and delinquency to dealing and gang membership (see Howell, 2010, for a review of effective gang prevention programs).

Future Directions

Future research should continue to move toward developing and testing prevention and treatment programs for adolescent substance use and delinquency that are multifaceted and that focus on early developmental influences (e.g., parenting skills and cognitive development) as well as later, more proximal influences (e.g., peers, schools, and neighborhood context). This research should concentrate on identifying mechanisms of change as well as moderators of intervention efficacy.

In addition to more research on interventions, there are still etiological questions, which merit additional research. It is important to better understand adolescents' motivations for engaging in delinquent behavior and whether these motivations are similar to their reasons for using alcohol and drugs. We recommend that this research take into account sex, age, and race/ethnicity differences in these motivations. A better understanding of what motivates adolescents may help in the design of effective interventions. Similarly, we need more research on desistance from substance use and delinquency, which could provide clues for accelerating the desistance process. It is also essential to develop more effective screening tools to identify at-risk youth. The earlier we can identify such youth, the sooner they can receive interventions to prevent the onset or escalation of delinquency and substance use. Whereas several studies have examined the acute and developmental associations between substance use and delinquency during adolescence, few studies have examined how these associations are moderated by individual and contextual factors. An overall research agenda focused on moderators for onset, escalation, and desistance of substance use and delinquency, as well as for prevention and intervention efficacy, will help move the field forward in reducing the serious costs associated with adolescent substance use and delinquency.

References

Agnew, R. (1992). Foundation for a general strain theory of crime and delinquency. *Criminology*, 30(1), 47–87.

Agnew, R., & White, H. R. (1992). An empirical test of general strain theory. *Criminology*, 30(4), 475–499.

Akers, R. L. (1985). *Deviant behavior: A social learning approach (Vol. 3)*. Belmont, CA: Wadsworth.

Altschuler, D. M., & Brounstein, P. J. (1991). Patterns of drug use, drug trafficking, and other delinquency among inner-city adolescent males in Washington, D.C. *Criminology*, 29(4), 589–622.

Andrews, J. A., Hops, H., Ary, D., Tildesley, E., & Harris, J. (1993). Parental influence on early adolescent substance use. *Journal of Early Adolescence*, 13(3), 285–310.

Anglin, M. D., & Perrochet, B. (1998). Drug use and crime: A historical review of research conducted by the UCLA drug abuse research center. *Substance Use and Misuse*, 33(9), 1871–1914.

Barnes, G. M., Welte, J. W., & Hoffman, J. H. (2002). Relationship of alcohol use to delinquency and illicit drug use in adolescents: Gender, age, and racial/ethnic differences. *Journal of Drug Issues*, 32(1), 153–178.

Bates, M. E., Labouvie, E. W., & White, H. R. (1986). The effect of sensation seeking needs on alcohol and marijuana use in adolescence. *Society of Psychologists in Addictive Behaviors Bulletin*, 5(1), 29–36.

Bellair, P. E., & McNulty, T. L. (2009). Gang membership, drug selling, and violence in neighborhood context. *Justice Quarterly*, 26(4), 644–669.

Bendixen, M., Endresen, I. M., & Olweus, D. (2006). Joining and leaving gangs: Selection and facilitation effects on self-reported antisocial behaviour in early adolescence. *European Journal of Criminology*, 3(1), 85–114.

Boles, S. M., & Miotto, K. (2003). Substance and violence: A review of the literature. *Aggression and Violent Behavior*, 8(2), 155–174.

Brook, J. S., Balka, E. B., Crossman, A. M., Dermatis, H., Galanter, M., & Brook, D. W. (2010). The relationship between parental alcohol use, early and late adolescent alcohol use, and young adult psychological symptoms: A longitudinal study. *The American Journal on Addictions*, 19(6), 534–542.

Bureau of Justice Statistics. (1994). *Fact sheet: Drug data summary*. Washington, DC: US Department of Justice.

Bushman, B. J. (1997). Effects of alcohol on human aggression: Validity of proposed explanations. In M. Galanter (Ed.), *Recent developments in alcoholism, Vol. 13. Alcohol and violence* (pp. 227–243). New York, NY: Kluwer Academic.

Carpenter, C., Glassner, B., Johnson, B. D., & Loughlin, J. (1988). *Kids, drugs, and crime*. Lexington, MA: Lexington Publications.

Catalano, R. F., & Hawkins, J. D. (1996). The social development model: A theory of antisocial behavior. In J. D. Hawkins (Ed.), *Delinquency and crime: Current theories* (pp. 149–197). New York, NY: Cambridge University Press.

Catalano, R., F., Kosterman, R., Hawkins, J. D., Newcomb, M. D., & Abbott, R. (1996). Modeling the etiology of adolescent alcohol use: A test of the social development model. *Journal of Drug Issues*, 26(2), 429–455.

Centers, N. L., & Weist, M. D. (1998). Inner city youth and drug dealing: A review of the problem. *Journal of Youth and Adolescence*, 27(3), 395–411.

Centers for Disease Control and Prevention. (2011). Trends in the prevalence of behaviors that contribute to violence-National YRBS: 1991—2011. Retrieved on November 10, 2015 from http://www.cdc.gov/HealthyYouth/yrbs/pdf/us_violence_trend_yrbs.pdf.

Chen, K., & Kandel, D. B. (1995). The natural history of drug use from adolescence to the mid-thirties in a general population sample. *American Journal of Public Health*, 85(1), 41–47.

Collins, J. J. (1993). Drinking and violence. An individual offender focus. In S. E. Martin (Ed.), *Alcohol and interpersonal violence: Fostering multidisciplinary perspectives* (pp. 221–235). Rockville, MD: National Institutes of Health.

Collins, J. J., & Messerschmidt, P. M. (1993). Epidemiology of alcohol-related violence. *Alcohol Health and Research World*, 17(2), 93–100.

Cunningham, P. B., & Henggeler, S. W. (2001). Implementation of an empirically based drug and violence prevention and intervention program in public school settings. *Journal of Clinical Child Psychology*, 30(2), 221–232.

D'Amico, E. J., Edelen, M. O., Miles, J. N. V., & Morral, A. R. (2008). The longitudinal association between substance use and delinquency among high-risk youth. *Drug and Alcohol Dependence*, 93(1), 85–92.

Dembo, R., & Sullivan (2009). Cocaine use and delinquent behavior among high-risk youths: A growth model of parallel processes. *Journal of Child and Adolescent Substance Abuse*, 18, 274–301.

Dembo, R., Wareham, J., & Schmeidler, J. (2007). Drug use and delinquent behavior: A growth model of parallel processes among high-risk youths. *Crime Justice and Behavior*, 34(5), 680–696.

Demuth, S., & Brown, S. L. (2004). Family structure, family processes, and adolescent delinquency: The significance of parental absence versus parental gender. *Journal of Research in Crime and Delinquency*, 41(1), 58–81.

Doherty, E. E., Green, K. M., & Ensminger, M. E. (2008). Investigating the long-term influence of adolescent delinquency on drug use initiation. *Drug and Alcohol Dependence*, 93(1–2), 72–84.

Doherty, W. J., & Needle, R. H. (1991). Psychological adjustment and substance use among adolescents before and after a parental divorce. *Child Development*, 62(2), 328–337.

Donovan, J. E., Jessor, R., & Costa, F. M. (1999). Adolescent problem drinking: Stability of psychosocial and behavioral correlates across a generation. *Journal of Studies on Alcohol, 60*(3), 352–361.

Doran, N., Luczak, S. E., Bekman, N., Koutsenok, I., & Brown, S. A. (2012). Adolescent substance use and aggression: A review. *Criminal Justice and Behavior, 39*(6), 748–769.

Eklund, J. M., & Klinteberg, B. (2009). Alcohol use and patterns of delinquent behaviour in male and female adolescents. *Alcohol and Alcoholism, 44*(6), 607–614.

Elliott, D. S. (1994). Serious violent offenders: Onset, developmental course, and termination: The American Society of Criminology 1993 Presidential Address. *Criminology, 32*(1), 1–21.

Elliott, D. S., Huizinga, D., & Ageton, S. S. (1985). *Explaining delinquency and drug use.* New York, NY: Springer-Verlag.

Elliott, D. S., Huizinga, D., & Menard, S. W. (1989). *Multiple problem youth: Delinquency, substance abuse, and mental health problems.* New York, NY: Springer-Verlag.

El-Sheikh, M., & Elmore-Staton, L. (2007). The alcohol–aggression link: Children's aggression expectancies in marital arguments as a function of the sobriety or intoxication of the arguing couple. *Aggressive Behavior, 33*(5), 458–466.

Ennett, S. T., & Bauman, K. E. (1996). Adolescent social networks: School, demographic and longitudinal considerations. *Journal of Adolescent Research, 11*(2), 194–215.

Ennett, S. T., Bauman, K. E., Hussong, A., Faris, R., Foshee, V. A., Cai, L., & DuRant, R. H. (2006). The peer context of adolescent substance use: Findings from social network analysis. *Journal of Research on Adolescence, 16*(2), 159–186.

Ensminger, M. E., Anthony, J. C., & McCord, J. (1997). The inner city and drug use: Initial findings from an epidemiological study. *Drug and Alcohol Dependence, 48*(3), 175–184.

Esbensen, F. A., & Huizinga, D. (1993). Gangs, drugs, and delinquency in a survey of urban youth. *Criminology, 31*(4), 565–589.

Esbensen, F. A., Peterson, D., Taylor, T. J., & Freng, A. (2009). Similarities and differences in risk factors for violent offending and gang membership. *Australian and New Zealand Journal of Criminology, 42*(3), 310–335.

Esbensen, F. A., & Winfree, L. T. (1998). Race and gender differences between gang and nongang youths: Results from a multisite survey. *Justice Quarterly, 15*(3), 505–526.

Estévez, E., & Emler, N. P. (2011). Assessing the links among adolescent and youth offending, antisocial behaviour, victimization, drug use, and gender. *International Journal of Clinical and Health Psychology, 11*, 269–289.

European Monitoring Centre for Drugs and Drug Addiction [EMCDDA]. (2003). *2003 Annual report on the drug situation in the EU & Norway.* Lisbon, Portugal: EMCDDA.

Fagan, J. (1990). Intoxication and aggression. In M. Tonry & J. Q. Wilson (Eds.), *Drugs and crime* (pp. 241–320). Chicago, IL: University of Chicago Press.

Fagan, J. (1993). Set and setting revisited: Influence of alcohol and illicit drugs on the social context of violent events. In S. E. Martin (Ed.), *Alcohol and interpersonal violence: Fostering multidisciplinary perspectives* (pp. 161–191). Rockville, MD: National Institutes of Health.

Fagan, J., & Chin, K. (1990). Violence as regulation and social control in the distribution of crack. In M. De La Roda, E. Y. Lambert, & B. Gropper (Eds.), *Drugs and violence: Causes, correlates, and consequences.* Rockville, MD: US Department of Health and Human Services, National Institute on Drug Abuse.

Farrington, D. P. (1995). The development of offending and antisocial behaviour from childhood: Key findings from the Cambridge study in delinquent development. *Journal of Child Psychology and Psychiatry and Allied Disciplines, 36*(6), 929–964.

Farrington, D. P., & Hawkins, J. D. (1991). Predicting participation, early onset, and later persistence in officially recorded offending. *Criminal Behaviour and Mental Health, 1*(1), 1–33.

Felson, R., Savolainen, J., Aaltonen, M., & Moustgaard, H. (2008). Is the association between alcohol use and delinquency causal or spurious? *Criminology, 46*(3), 785–808.

Felson, R., Savolainen, J., Bjarnason, T., Anderson, A. L., & Zohra, I. T. (2011). The cultural context of adolescent drinking and violence in 30 European countries. *Criminology, 49*(3), 699–728.

Felson, R. B., Teasdale, B., & Burchfield, K. B. (2008). The influence of being under the influence. *Journal of Research in Crime and Delinquency, 45*(2), 119–141.

Fergusson, D. M., & Horwood, L. J. (2000). Alcohol abuse and crime: A fixed-effects regression analysis. *Addiction, 95*(10), 1525–1536.

Fleming, C., Catalano, R., Haggerty, K., & Abbott, R. (2010). Relationships between level and change in family, school, and peer factors during two periods of adolescence and problem behavior at age 19. *Journal of Youth and Adolescence, 39*(6), 670–682.

Freisthler, B., Lascala, E. A., Gruenewald, P. J., & Treno, A. J. (2005). An examination of drug activity: Effects of neighborhood social organization on the development of drug distribution systems. *Substance Use and Misuse, 40*(5), 671–686.

Fuller, B. E., Chermack, S. T., Cruise, K. A., Kirsch, E., Fitzgerald, H. E., & Zucker, R. A. (2003). Predictors of aggression across three generations among sons of alcoholics: Relationships involving grandparental and parental alcoholism, child aggression, marital aggression and parenting practices. *Journal of Studies on Alcohol, 64*(4), 472–483.

Gardner, M., Barajas, R. G., & Brooks-Gunn, J. (2010). Neighborhood influences on substance use etiology: Is where you live important? In L. M. Scheier (Ed.), *Handbook of drug use etiology: Theory, methods, and empirical findings* (pp. 423–441). Washington, DC: American Psychological Association.

Giancola, P. R. (2002). Alcohol-related aggression during the college years: Theories, risk factors, and policy implications. *Journal of Studies on Alcohol*, Supplement 14, 129–139.

Goldstein, P. J. (1985). The drugs/violence nexus: A tripartite conceptual framework. *Journal of Drug Issues, 15*(4), 493–506.

Gorman, D., & White, H. R. (1995). You can choose your friends, but do they choose your crime? Implications of differential association theories for crime prevention policy. In H. Barlow (Ed.), *Criminology and public policy: Putting theory to work* (pp. 131–155). Boulder, CO: Westview Press.

Greene, K., Krcmar, M., Walters, L. H., Rubin, D. L., Jerold, & Hale, L. (2000). Targeting adolescent risk-taking behaviors: The contributions of egocentrism and sensation-seeking. *Journal of Adolescence, 23*(4), 439–461.

Harrison, L., & Freeman, C. (1998, November). The drug-violence nexus among youth. Paper presented at the American Society of Criminology, Washington, DC.

Hartstone, E., & Hansen, K. V. (1984). Violent juvenile offender—an empirical portrait. In R. A. Mathias, P. DeMuro, & R. S. Allison (Eds.), *Violent juvenile offenders: An anthology* (pp. 83–112). San Francisco, CA: National Council on Crime and Delinquency.

Hawkins, J. D., Brown, E. C., Oesterle, S., Arthur, M. W., Abbott, R. D., & Catalano, R. F. (2008). Early effects of communities that care on targeted risks and initiation of delinquent behavior and substance use. *Journal of Adolescent Health, 43*(1), 15–22.

Hawkins, J. D., Catalano, R. F., Kosterman, A. R., & Hill, K. G. (1999). Preventing adolescent health-risk behaviors by strengthening protection during childhood. *Archives of Pediatrics and Adolescent Medicine, 153*(3), 226–234.

Hawkins, J. D., Catalano, R. F., & Miller, J. Y. (1992). Risk and protective factors for alcohol and other drug problems in adolescence and early adulthood: Implications for substance abuse prevention. *Psychological Bulletin, 112*(1), 64–105.

Hemovich, V., Lac, A., & Crano, W. D. (2011). Understanding early-onset drug and alcohol outcomes among youth: The role of family structure, social factors, and interpersonal perceptions of use. *Psychology, Health, and Medicine, 16*(3), 249–267.

Henggeler, S. W., Schoenwald, S. K., Borduin, C. M., Rowland, M. D., & Cunningham, P. B. (1998). *Multisystemic treatment of antisocial behavior in children and adolescents*. New York, NY: Guilford Press.

Henry, K. L. (2010). Academic achievement and adolescent drug use: An examination of reciprocal effects and correlated growth trajectories. *Journal of School Health, 80*(1), 38–43.

Hill, K. G., Chung, I. J., Herrenkohl, T. I., & Hawkins, J. D. (2000, November). Consequences of trajectories of violent and non-violent offending. Paper presented at the Annual Meeting of the American Society of Criminology. San Francisco, CA.

Hill, K. G., White, H. R., Chung, I-J., Hawkins, J. D., & Catalano, R. F. (2000). Early adult outcomes of adolescent binge drinking: Person- and variable-centered analyses of binge drinking trajectories. *Alcoholism: Clinical and Experimental Research, 24*(6), 892–901.

Hirschfield, P., Maschi, T., White, H. R., Goldman-Traub, L., & Loeber, R. (2006). The effects of mental health problems on juvenile arrests: Criminality, criminalization, or compassion? *Criminology, 44*, 593–630.

Hirschi, T. (1969). *Causes of delinquency*. Berkeley: University of California Press.

Horowitz, H., Sung, H. E., & Foster, S. E. (2006). The role of substance abuse in US juvenile justice systems and populations. *Corrections Compendium, 31*(1), 1–4.

Howell, J. C. (2010). *Gang prevention: An overview of research and programs*. Washington, DC: US Department of Justice, Office of Justice Programs, Office of Juvenile Justice and Delinquency Prevention.

Huang, B., White, H. R., Kosterman, R., Catalano, R. F., & Hawkins, J. D. (2001). Developmental associations between alcohol and aggression during adolescence. *Journal of Research in Crime and Delinquency, 38*(1), 64–83.

Huizinga, D., & Jakob-Chien, C. (1998). The contemporaneous co-occurrence of serious and violent juvenile offending and other problem behaviors. In R. Loeber & D. P. Farrington (Eds.), *Serious and violent juvenile offenders* (pp. 47–67). Thousand Oaks, CA: Sage.

Huizinga, D., Weiher, A. W., Espiritu, R., & Esbensen, F. A. (2003). Delinquency and crime: Some highlights from the denver youth survey. In T. P. Thornberry & M. D. Krohn (Eds.), *Taking stock of delinquency: An overview of findings from contemporary longitudinal studies* (pp. 47–91). New York, NY: Kluwer/Plenum.

Hunt, D. E. (1990). Drugs and consensual crimes: Drug dealing and prostitution. *Crime and Justice, 13*, 159–202.

Inciardi, J. A., & Pottieger, A. E. (1991). Kids, crack, and crime. *Journal of Drug Issues, 21*(2), 257–270.

Inciardi, J. A., & Pottieger, A. E. (1994). Crack-cocaine use and street crime. *Journal of Drug Issues, 24*(1–2), 273–292.

Ito, T. A., Miller, N., & Pollock, V. E. (1996). Alcohol and aggression: A meta-analysis on the moderating effects of inhibitory cues, triggering events, and self-focused attention. *Psychological Bulletin, 120*(1), 60–82.

Jackson, K. M., Sher, K. J., & Schulenberg, J. E. (2008). Conjoint developmental trajectories of young adult substance use. *Alcoholism: Clinical and Experimental Research, 32*(5), 723–737.

Jessor, R., & Jessor, S. L. (1977). *Problem behavior and psychosocial development: A longitudinal study of youth*. New York, NY: Academic Press.

Johnson, B. D., Natarajan, M., Dunlap, E., & Elmoghazy, E. (1994). Crack abusers and noncrack abusers: Profiles of drug use, drug sales and nondrug criminality. *Journal of Drug Issues, 24*(1–2), 117–141.

Johnson, B. D., Williams, T., Dei, K. A., Sanabria, H., Tonry, M., & Wilson, J. Q. (1990). Drug abuse in the inner city: Impact on hard-drug users and the community. *Drugs and Crime, 13*, 9–67.

Johnson, J. L., Sher, K. J., & Rolf, J. E. (1991). Models of vulnerability to psychopathology in children of alcoholics: An overview. *Alcohol Health and Research World, 15*(1), 33–42.

Johnston, L. D., O'Malley, P. M., Bachman, J. G., & Schulenberg, J. E. (2003). *Monitoring the future national survery results on drug use, 1975-2003, Vol. 1. Secondary school students*. Bethesda, MD: National Institute on Drug Abuse.

Johnston, L. D., O'Malley, P. M., Bachman, J. G., & Schulenberg, J. E. (2011). *Monitoring the future national survey results on drug use, 1975-2010, Vol. 1. Secondary school students*. Ann Arbor: Institute for Social Research, University of Michigan.

Kandel, D., Simcha-Fagan, O., & Davies, M. (1986). Risk factors for delinquency and illicit drug use from adolescence to young adulthood. *Journal of Drug Issues, 16*(1), 67–90.

Kaplan, H. B., & Damphousse, K. R. (1995). Self-attitudes and antisocial personality as moderators of the drug use-violence relationship. In H. B. Kaplan (Ed.), *Drugs, crime, and other deviant adaptations: Longitudinal studies* (pp. 187–210). New York, NY: Plenum Press.

Karriker-Jaffe, K. (2011). Areas of disadvantage: A systematic review of effects of area level socioeconomic status on substance use outcomes. *Drug and Alcohol Review, 30*, 84–95.

Katsiyannis, A., Ryan, J. B., Zhang, D., & Spann, A. (2008). Juvenile delinquency and recidivism: The impact of academic achievement. *Reading and Writing Quarterly, 24*(2), 177–196.

Khantzian, E. J. (1985). The self-medication hypothesis of addictive disorders: Focus on heroin and cocaine dependence. *American Journal of Psychiatry, 142*(11), 1259–1264.

Klein, M. W., & Maxson, C. L. (1989). Street gang violence. In N. A. Weiner & M. E. Wolfgang (Eds.), *Violent* crime, violent criminals (pp. 489–512). Thousand Oaks, CA: Sage.

Kramer, J. R., Chan, G., Dick, D. M., Kuperman, S., Bucholz, K. K., Edenberg, H. J., ... Bierut, L. J. (2008). Multiple-domain predictors of problematic alcohol use in young adulthood. *Journal of Studies on Alcohol and Drugs, 69*(5), 649–659.

Krohn, M. D., Lizotte, A. J., Thornberry, T. P., Smith, C., & McDowall, D. (1996). Reciprocal causal relationships among drug use, peers, and beliefs: A five-wave panel model. *Journal of Drug Issues, 26*(2), 405.

Krug, E. G., Mercy, J. A., Dahlberg, L. L., Zwi, A. B., & Lozano, R. (2002). *The world report on violence and health.* Geneva, Switzerland: World Health Organization.

Kuhns, J. B. (2005). The dynamic nature of the drug use/serious violence relationship: A multi-causal approach. *Violence and Victims, 20*(4), 433–454.

Lee, C., Mun E. Y., White, H. R., & Simon, P. (2010). Substance use trajectories of black and white young men from adolescence to emerging adulthood: A two-part growth curve analysis. *Journal of Ethnicity in Substance Abuse, 9*, 301–319.

Lennings, C. J., Copeland, J., & Howard, J. (2003). Substance use patterns of young offenders and violent crime. *Aggressive Behavior, 29*(5), 414–422.

Leonard, K. E. (2008). The role of drinking patterns and acute intoxication in violent interpersonal behaviors. In *International Center for Alcohol Policies, Alcohol and violence: Exploring patterns and responses* (pp. 29–55). Washington, DC: International Center for Alcohol Policies.

Li, S. D., Priu, H. D., & MacKenzie, D. L. (2000). Drug involvement, lifestyles, and criminal activities among probationers. *Journal of Drug Issues, 30*(3), 593–619.

Li, X., & Feigelman, S. (1994). Recent and intended drug trafficking among male and female urban African-American early adolescents. *Pediatrics, 93*(6), 1044.

Lipton, D. S., & Johnson, B. D. (1998). Smack, crack, and score: Two decades of NIDA-funded drugs and crime research at NDRI 1974-1994. *Substance Use and Misuse, 33*(9), 1779–1815.

Little, M., & Steinberg, L. (2006). Psychosocial correlates of adolescent drug dealing in the inner city. *Journal of Research in Crime & Delinquency, 43*(4), 357–386.

Loeber, R., Farrington, D. P., Stouthamer-Loeber, M., & White, H. R. (2008). *Violence and serious theft: Developmental course and origins from childhood to adulthood.* New York, NY: Routledge Press.

Loeber, R., Stepp, S. D., Chung, T., Hipwell, A., & White, H. R. (2010). Time-varying associations between conduct problems and alcohol use in adolescent girls: The moderating role of race. *Journal of Studies on Alcohol and Drugs, 71*(4), 544–553.

Lynne-Landsman, S. D., Graber, J. A., Nichols, T. R., & Botvin, G. J. (2011). Trajectories of aggression, delinquency, and substance use across middle school among urban, minority adolescents. *Aggressive Behavior, 37*, 161–176.

MacCoun, R., Kilmer, B., & Reuter, P. (2003). Research on drugs-crime linkages: The next generation. In *Towards a drugs and crime research agenda for the 21st century* (pp. 65–95). Washington, DC: National Institute of Justice.

Maguin, E., & Loeber, R. (1996). Academic performance and delinquency. *Crime and Justice, 20*, 145–264.

Marcos, A. C., & Bahr, S. J. (1995). Drug progression model: A social control test. *International Journal of the Addictions, 30*(11), 1383–1405.

Marcus, R. F. (2007). *Aggression and violence in adolescence.* Cambridge, UK: Cambridge University Press.

Marmorstein, N. R., Iacono, W. G. &. McGue, M. (2009). Alcohol and illicit drug dependence among parents: Associations with offspring externalizing disorders. *Psychological Medicine, 39*, 149–155.

Martel, M. M., Pierce, L., Nigg, J. T., Jester, J. M., Adams, K. M., Puttler, L. I., ... Zucker, R. A. (2009). Temperament pathways to childhood disruptive behavior and adolescent substance abuse: Testing a cascade model. *Journal of Abnormal Child Psychology, 37*, 363–371.

Marti, C. N., Stice, E., & Springer, D. W. (2010). Substance use and abuse trajectories across adolescence: A latent trajectory analysis of a community-recruited sample of girls. *Journal of Adolescence, 33*(3), 449–461.

Mason, W. A., Hitch, J. E., Kosterman, R., McCarty, C. A., Herrenkohl, T. I., & Hawkins, J. D. (2010). Growth in adolescent delinquency and alcohol use in relation to young adult crime, alcohol use disorders, and risky sex: A comparison of youth from low- versus middle-income backgrounds. *Journal of Child Psychology and Psychiatry, 51*(12), 1377–1385.

Mason, W. A., & Windle, M. (2002). Reciprocal relations between adolescent substance use and delinquency: A longitudinal latent variable analysis. *Journal of Abnormal Psychology, 111*, 63–76.

McClelland, G. M., Elkington, K. S., & Teplin, L. A. (2004). Multiple substance use disorders in juvenile detainees. *Journal of the American Academy of Child and Adolescent Psychiatry, 43*(10), 1215–1224.

Medina, K. M., & Tapert, S. (2011). Chronic effects of heavy alcohol and marijuana use on the brain and cognition in adolescents and young adults. In H. R. White & D. L. Rabiner (Eds.), *College drinking and drug use* (pp. 63–82). New York, NY: Guilford Press.

Menard, S., & Mihalic, S. (2001). The tripartite conceptual framework in adolescence and adulthood: Evidence from a national sample. *Journal of Drug Issues, 31*(4), 905–940.

Miczek, K. A., DeBold, J. F., Haney, M., Tidey, J., Vivian, J., & Weerts, E. M. (1994). Alcohol, drugs of abuse, aggression, and violence. In A. J. Reiss & J. A. Roth (Eds.), *Understanding and preventing violence, Vol. 3. Social influences* (pp. 377–468). Washington, DC: National Academy Press.

Millar, D., O'Dwyer, K., & Finnegan, M. (1998). *Alcohol and drugs as factors in offending behaviour: Garda Survey.* Tipperary, Ireland: Garda Research Unit.

Miller, S., Malone, P. S., & Dodge, K. A. (2010). Developmental trajectories of boys' and girls' delinquency: Sex differences and links to later adolescent outcomes. *Journal of Abnormal Child Psychology, 38*, 1021–1032.

Mulvey, E. P., Schubert, C. A., & Chassin, L. (2010). *Substance use and delinquent behavior among serious adolescent offenders.* Washington, DC: US Department of Justice, Office of Justice Programs, Office of Juvenile Justice and Delinquency Prevention.

National Center for Juvenile Justice. (2011). Juvenile arrest rates by offense, sex, and race. Retrieved October 2015, from http://www.ojjdp.gov/ojstatbb/crime/excel/JAR_2009.xls

National Institute of Justice. (2003). *Towards a drug and crime research agenda for the 21st century.* Washington, DC: US Department of Justice, Office of Justice Programs.

Noyori-Corbett, C., & Moon, S. (2010). Multifaceted reality of juvenile delinquency: An empirical analysis of structural theories and literature. *Child and Adolescent Social Work Journal*, 27(4), 245–268.

Nurco, D. N., Shaffer, J. W., Ball, J. C., & Kinlock, T. W. (1984). Trends in the commission of crime among narcotic addicts over successive periods of addiction and nonaddiction. *American Journal of Drug and Alcohol Abuse*, 10(4), 481–489.

Orlando, M., Tucker, J. S., Ellickson, P. L., & Klein, D. J. (2005). Concurrent use of alcohol and cigarettes from adolescence to young adulthood: An examination of developmental trajectories and outcomes. *Substance Use and Misuse*, 40(8), 1051–1069.

Osgood, D. W. (1994, November). Drugs, alcohol, and adolescent violence. Paper presented at the Annual Meeting of the American Society of Criminology, Miami, FL.

Ostrowsky, M. K. (2011). Does marijuana use lead to aggression and violent behavior? *Journal of Drug Education*, 41, 369–389.

Pandina, R. J., Johnson, V. L., & White, H. R. (2009). Peer influences on substance use during adolescence and emerging adulthood. In L. M. Scheier (Ed.), *Handbook of drug use etiology* (pp. 383–401). Washington, DC: American Psychological Association.

Parker, R. N., & Auerhahn, K. (1998). Alcohol, drugs, and violence. *Annual Review of Sociology*, 24, 291–311.

Parker, R. N., & Auerhahn, K. (1999). *Drugs, alcohol, and homicide: Issues in theory and research*. Beverly Hills, CA: Sage.

Paxton, R. J., Valois, R. F., & Drane, J. W. (2007). Is there a relationship between family structure and substance use among public middle school students? *Journal of Child and Family Studies*, 16, 593–605.

Pernanen, K. (1993). Alcohol-related violence: Conceptual models and methodological issues. In S. E. Martin (Ed.), *Alcohol and interpersonal violence: Fostering multidisciplinary perspectives* (pp. 149–159). Rockville, MD: National Institute of Health.

Peterson, D., Taylor, T. J., & Esbensen, F. A. (2004). Gang membership and violent victimization. *Justice Quarterly*, 21(4), 793–815.

Petts, R. J. (2009). Family and religious characteristics' influence on delinquency trajectories from adolescence to young adulthood. *American Sociological Review*, 74(3), 465–483.

Pihl, R. O., & Ross, D. (1987). Research on alcohol related aggression: A review and implications for understanding aggression. *Drugs and Society*, 1(4), 105–126.

Popovici, I., Homer, J. F., Fang, H., & French, M. T. (2012). Alcohol use and crime: Findings from a longitudinal sample of U.S. adolescents and young adults. *Alcoholism: Clinical and Experimental Research*, 36(3), 532–543.

Prichard, J., & Payne, J. (2005). *Alcohol, drugs and crime: A study of juveniles in detention*. Canberra, Australia: Australian Institute of Criminology.

Puzzanchera, C. (2009). *Juvenile arrests 2008 (Juvenile justice bulletin)*. Washington, DC: Office of Justice Programs.

Ramchand, R., Morral, A. R., & Becker, K. (2009). Seven-year life outcomes of adolescent offenders in Los Angeles. *American Journal of Public Health*, 99(5), 863–870.

Reiss, A. J., Jr., & Roth, J. A. (1993). *Understanding and preventing violence (Vol. 1)*. Washington, DC: National Academy Press.

Ritter, J., Stewart, M., Bernet, C., Coe, M., & Brown, S. A. (2002). Effects of childhood exposure to familial alcoholism and family violence on adolescent substance use, conduct problems, and self-esteem. *Journal of Traumatic Stress*, 15(2), 113–122.

Roizen, J. (1993). Issues in the epidemiology of alcohol and violence. In S. E. Martin (Ed.), *Alcohol and interpersonal violence. Fostering multidisciplinary perspectives* (pp. 3–36). Rockville, MD: National Institute of Health.

Sampson, R. J., Morenoff, J. D., & Gannon-Rowley, T. (2002). Assessing "neighborhood effects:" Social processes and new directions in research. *Annual Review of Sociology*, 28, 444–478.

Sampson, R. J., & Raudenbush, S. W. F. (1997). Neighborhoods and violent crime: A multilevel study of collective efficacy. *Science*, 277(5328), 918–924.

Shaw, C. R., & McKay, H. D. (1942). Juvenile delinquency and urban areas. *Journal of Criminal Psychopathology*, 4(3), 569.

Sher, K. J. (1991). Characteristics of children of alcoholics: Putative risk factors, substance use and abuse, and psychopathology. *Journal of Abnormal Psychology*, 100(4), 427–448.

Simons, L. G., & Conger, R. D. (2007). Linking mother-father differences in parenting to a typology of family parenting styles and adolescent outcomes. *Journal of Family Issues*, 28(2), 212–241.

Simons-Morton, B., & Chen, R. (2005). Latent growth curve analyses of parent influences on drinking progression among early adolescents. *Journal of Studies on Alcohol*, 66(1), 5–13.

Snyder, H. N., & Sickmund, M. (2006). *Juvenile offenders and victims: 2006 National report*. Washington, DC: US Department of Justice, Office of Justice Programs, Office of Juvenile Justice and Delinquency Prevention.

Steketee, M. (2011). Substance use of young people in 30 countries. In J. Junger-Tas, I. Haen-Marshall, D. Enzmann, M. Killias, M. Steketee, & B. Gruszczynska (Eds.), *The many faces of youth crime: Contrasting theoretical perspectives on juvenile delinquency across countries and cultures* (pp.117–141). New York, NY: Springer.

Substance Abuse and Mental Health Services Administration. (2005). *The National Survey on Drug Use and Health report: Alcohol use and delinquent behaviors among youth*. Rockville, MD: Author.

Substance Abuse and Mental Health Services Administration. (2009). *Results from the 2008 National Survey on Drug Use and Health: National findings*. Rockville, MD: Office of Applied Studies.

Sutherland, E. H. (1947). *Principles of criminology*. Philadelphia, PA: Lippincott.

Swahn, M. H., & Donovan, J. E. (2004). Correlates and predictors of violent behavior among adolescent drinkers. *Journal of Adolescent Health*, 34(6), 480–492.

The National Center on Addiction and Substance Abuse at Columbia University. (2010). Behind bars II: Substance abuse and America's prison population. Retrieved October 2015, from http://www.casacolumbia.org/templates/publications_reports.aspx

Thornberry, T. P. (1987). Toward an interactional theory of delinquency. *Criminology*, 25(4), 863–892.

Thornberry, T. P., & Krohn, M. D. (2003). *Taking stock of delinquency: An overview of findings from contemporary longitudinal studies*. New York, NY: Kluwer Academic/Plenum.

Thornberry, T. P., Krohn, M. D., Lizotte, A. J., Smith, C. A., & Tobin, K. (2003). *Gangs and delinquency in developmental perspective*. Cambridge, UK: Cambridge University Press.

Thornberry, T. P., Lizotte, A. J., Krohn, M. D., Farnworth, M., & Jang, S. J. (1991). Testing interactional theory: An examination of reciprocal causal relationships among family, school, and delinquency. *Journal of Criminal Law and Criminology*, 82(1), 3–35.

Trucco, E. M., Colder, C. R., & Wieczorek, W. F. (2011). Vulnerability to peer influence: A moderated mediation study of early adolescent alcohol use initiation. *Addictive Behaviors*, 36, 729–736.

Tucker, J. S., Orlando, M., & Ellickson, P. L. (2003). Patterns and correlates of binge drinking trajectories from early adolescence to young adulthood. *Health Psychology*, 22(1), 79–87.

Van Kammen, W. B., & Loeber, R. (1994). Are fluctuations in delinquent activities related to the onset and offset in juvenile illegal drug use and drug dealing? *Journal of Drug Issues*, 24(1–2), 9–24.

Vaughn, M. G., Shook, J. J., Perron, B. E., Abdon, A., & Ahmedani, B. (2011). Patterns and correlates of illicit drug selling among youth in the USA. *Substance Abuse and Rehabilitation*, 2, 103–111.

Wei, E. H., Loeber, R., & White, H. R. (2004). Teasing apart the developmental associations between alcohol and marijuana use and violence. *Journal of Contemporary Criminal Justice*, 20(2), 166–183.

Weisner, M., Kim, H. K., & Capaldi, D. M. (2005). Developmental trajectories of offending: Validation and prediction to young adult alcohol use, drug use, and depressive symptoms. *Development and Psychopathology*, 17(1), 251–270.

Welte, J., Barnes, G., Hoffman, J., Wieczorek, W., & Zhang, L. (2005). Substance involvement and the trajectory of criminal offending in young males. *American Journal of Drug and Alcohol Abuse*, 31(2), 267–284.

Welte, J. W., Zhang, L., & Wieczorek, W. F. (2001). The effects of substance use on specific types of criminal offending in young men. *Journal of Research in Crime and Delinquency*, 38(4), 416–438.

White, H. R. (1990). The drug use-delinquency connection in adolescence. In R. A. Weisheit (Ed.), *Drugs, crime and the criminal justice system* (pp. 215–256). Cincinnati, OH: Anderson.

White, H. R. (1997a). Alcohol, illicit drugs, and violence. In D. M. Stoff, J. Breiling, & J. D. Maser (Eds.), *Handbook of antisocial behavior* (pp. 511–523). New York, NY: Wiley.

White, H. R. (1997b). Longitudinal perspective on alcohol use and aggression during adolescence. *Recent Developments in Alcoholism: Alcohol and Violence*, 13, 81–103.

White, H. R. (2016). Substance Use and crime. In K.J. Sher (Ed.). *The Oxford handbook of substance use and substance use disorders, Volume 2* (pp. 347–378). New York, NY: Oxford University Press.

White, H. R., Brick, J., & Hansell, S. (1993). A longitudinal investigation of alcohol use and aggression in adolescence. *Journal of Studies on Alcohol*, Suppl. 11, 62–77.

White, H. R., & Gorman, D. M. (2000). Dynamics of the drug-crime relationship. In G. LaFree (Ed.), *Criminal justice 2000. The nature of crime: Continuity and change* (pp. 151–218). Washington, DC: US Department of Justice.

White, H. R., & Hansell, S. (1996). Longitudinal predictors of serious substance use and delinquency. *Journal of Research in Crime and Delinquency*, 33(4), 450–470.

White, H. R., & Hansell, S. (1998). Acute and long-term effects of drug use on aggression from adolescence into adulthood. *Journal of Drug Issues*, 28, 837–858.

White, H. R., Jackson, K., & Loeber, R. (2009). Developmental sequences and comorbidity of substance use and violence. In M. Krohn, A. M. Lizotte, & G. P. Hall (Eds.), *Handbook of deviance and crime* (pp. 433–486). New York, NY: Springer.

White, H. R., Johnson, V., & Buyske, S. (2000). Parental modeling and parenting behavior effects on offspring alcohol and cigarette use—a growth curve analysis. *Journal of Substance Abuse*, 12(3), 287–310.

White, H. R., Johnson, V., & Horwitz, A. (1986). An application of three deviance theories to adolescent substance use. *International Journal of the Addictions*, 21(3), 347.

White, H. R., & Labouvie, E. W. (1994). Generality versus specificity of problem behavior: Psychological and functional differences. *Journal of Drug Issues*, 24(1–2), 55–74.

White, H. R., Labouvie, E. W., & Bates, M. E. (1985). The relationship between sensation seeking and delinquency: A longitudinal analysis. *Journal of Research in Crime and Delinquency*, 22(3), 197–211.

White, H. R., Labouvie, E. W., & Papadaratsakis, V. (2005). Changes in substance use during the transition to adulthood a comparison of college students and their noncollege age peers. *Journal of Drug Issues*, 35(2), 281–305.

White, H. R., Lee, C., Mun, E. Y., & Loeber, R. (2012). Developmental co-occurrence of alcohol use and persistent serious violent offending among African American and Caucasian young men. *Criminology*, 50, 391–426.

White, H. R., Loeber, R., & Farrington, D. P. (2008). Substance use, drug dealing, gang membership, and gun carrying and their predictive associations with serious violence and serious theft. In R. Loeber, D. P. Farrington, M. Stouthamer-Loeber, & H. R. White (Eds.), *Violence and serious theft: Development and prediction from childhood to adulthood* (pp. 137–166). New York, NY: Routledge Taylor and Francis Group.

White, H. R., Loeber, R., Stouthamer-Loeber, M., & Farrington, D. P. (1999). Developmental associations between substance use and violence. *Development and Psychopathology*, 11, 785–803.

White, H. R., Tice, P. C., Loeber, R., & Stouthamer-Loeber, M. (2002). Illegal acts committed by adolescents under the influence of alcohol and drugs. *Journal of Research in Crime and Delinquency*, 39(2), 131–152.

Widom, C. S., & Hiller-Sturmhèfel, S. (2001). Alcohol abuse as a risk factor for and consequence of child abuse. *Alcohol Research and Health*, 25(1), 52–57.

Windle, M. (1990). A longitudinal study of antisocial behaviors in early adolescence as predictors of late adolescent substance use: Gender and ethnic group differences. *Journal of Abnormal Psychology*, 99(1), 86–91.

Zuckerman, M. (1979). *Sensation seeking: Beyond the optimal level of arousal*. Hillsdale, NJ: Erlbaum.

Zuckerman, M. (1994). *Behavioral expressions and biosocial bases of sensation seeking*. New York, NY: Cambridge University Press.

Medical Issues in Adolescent Substance Use: Background and Role of the Primary Care Physician

Miriam Schizer, Elissa R. Weitzman, *and* Sharon Levy

Abstract

Use of psychoactive substances is both common during adolescence and highly associated with acute and chronic health risks. Routine health care provides an opportunity to provide a range of interventions— from primary prevention to assisting adolescents with substance use disorders in accessing treatment. In particular, primary care offers a unique opportunity to intervene with adolescents who have developed substance use problems but do not meet criteria or are unwilling to enter specific treatment for a substance use disorder, and thus provide a level of service for adolescents who would otherwise likely receive no intervention. This chapter reviews the evidence base for primary care interventions and explores the role for primary care providers.

Key Words: screening, brief intervention, alcohol, marijuana, office-based intervention, brief advice, motivational intervention

Adolescent substance use is a ubiquitous public health problem, causing significant morbidity and mortality among adolescents as well as contributing to substance use disorders later in life. Pediatricians play a vital longitudinal role in the lives of adolescents and, as such, are uniquely positioned to influence their adolescent patients. Relating to substance use, ideally this guidance could take many forms—preventing or delaying onset, discouraging ongoing use and reducing harm, or guiding patients that have developed a severe substance use disorder to long-term treatment.

Adolescent Brain Development

As any clinician who has worked with adolescents can attest, the management of adolescent substance use is a challenging proposition. Adolescence is a period that includes puberty with its remarkable physical changes that are well known and studied (Stuart, Shock, Breckenridge, & Vincent, 1953).

This period also includes astounding development and maturation of the brain with associated profound changes in the expression of emotions, behaviors, and cognition. Research in the last decade has demonstrated that the brain is still developing well into the third decade of life, with the prefrontal areas that control "executive functions" (attention, organization, planning, response inhibition, and regulation of emotions) the final areas to mature (Chambers, Taylor, & Potenza, 2003).

New research using functional magnetic resonance imaging (fMRI) techniques has begun to elucidate the progression of anatomical changes that correlate with maturation from adolescence to young adulthood and finally to fully mature adulthood. One important observation is that different structures in the brain develop at different rates. Of note, the subcortical limbic system, which encompasses the brain's reward system, matures earlier than the prefrontal cortex (Dahl, 2004), which is responsible for rational decision making and impulse control. Neurobiological models predict that because of this imbalance, particularly in highly emotional contexts, adolescents would be more likely than adults to choose immediately rewarding behaviors despite risks and the potential for adverse consequences subsequently (Di Chiara, 1999). Studies using fMRI to monitor neural activation have also shown that the presence of peers leads adolescents, but not adults, to increase risk-taking behaviors (Becker, Curry, & Yang, 2011).

Adolescents are biologically "wired" to seek stimulation. This drive manifests itself in many ways, including the use of psychoactive substances, which peaks during adolescence and young adulthood. Adolescents are much more likely to engage in heavy, episodic ("binge") drinking than adults (Miller, Naimi, Brewer, & Jones, 2007) Studies in animals have demonstrated that compared to adults, who are much more susceptible to the depressant effects of alcohol, adolescents become more active when intoxicated (White et al., 2002). In human adolescents, heavy drinking disproportionately impairs memory and judgment, while sparing gross motor function. This means that, compared to adults, teens are more likely to remain awake, to wander about, or to drive a car, while having a much greater degree of mental impairment. The natural proclivity to risk taking and the increased vulnerability to both acute and long-term consequences of substance use make the use of psychoactive substances one of the most important health risks of adolescence.

Epidemiology

In the United States, the prevalence of adolescent substance use remains high. The Monitoring the Future Study (MTFS), which began in 1975, examines trends in drug use among 8th, 10th, and 12th graders nationwide. According to the 2013 MTFS, 20.3% of 8th graders and 50.4% of 12th graders have used an illicit drug (Johnston, O'Malley, Bachman, Schulenberg, & Miech, 2014). Although marijuana use had declined over the past decade, the 2013 study showed an increase in marijuana use among 10th and 12th graders, including a notable increase in the number of daily marijuana smokers. Among 12th graders, 6.5% use marijuana on a daily basis. One third of 8th graders and 70% of 12th graders have used alcohol in their lifetime. Nearly one in six 12th graders (16%) is a current cigarette smoker (Johnston, O'Malley, Bachman, et al., 2014).

Delaying the initiation of substance use is critically important. Several studies have shown a correlation between early age of onset of substance use and lifetime risk of developing dependence. In one study, 47% of adolescents who began drinking before age 13 years developed an alcohol use disorder during their lifetime. In contrast, only 9% of people who started drinking after their 21st birthday developed a disorder (Hingson, Heeren, & Winter, 2006). Individuals who begin drinking early are more likely to injure themselves or others in alcohol-related accidents compared to their peers, even if they never meet criteria for a substance use disorder (Hingson & Zha, 2009). A similar pattern has been observed for marijuana use (Winters & Lee, 2008). Adolescents, particularly young teens, who use alcohol or drugs are a particularly high-risk group, though ironically, substance use in this age group may be "written off" by parents and even professionals as benign "experimentation" or a developmental "phase." Public health messaging is a possible avenue for correcting these misconceptions, though these messages compete with industry marketing, which often portrays young adults enjoying alcohol. "Legalizaton" will likely result in similar messaging around marijuana and may further contribute to the problem.

The Psychosocial Interview

Conducting a psychosocial interview is considered a routine component of quality pediatric primary care. By adolescence, the psychosocial interview is conducted entirely with the adolescent. The "HEEADSSS" (Goldenring & Cohen, 1988) is a mnemonic acronym serving as a framework to guide the physician in asking about life at home, school functioning, and mood, as well as high-risk behaviors such as substance use and sexual activity. The SSHADESS (Ginsburg, 2007) covers similar topics and includes questions about strengths, which can help promote self-esteem. Inquiring about an adolescent's strengths also provides a platform upon which brief advice can be based.

Regardless of framework, a psychosocial interview with adolescents should include a discussion of tobacco, alcohol, and other drug use (as triggered by the "D" in both HEEADSSS and SSHADESS) (see Table 26.1).

Traditionally, interventions for substance use have focused on the small percentage of individuals with the most serious problems. More recently, the toll of substance use on the large group of individuals with more moderate use

Table 26.1 HEEADSSS and SSHADESS Psychosocial Interviews

HEEADSSS		SSHADESS	
H	**H**ome environment	S	**S**trengths
E	**E**ducation and employment	S	**S**chool
E	**E**ating	H	**H**ome
A	Peer-related **A**ctivities	A	**A**ctivities
D	**D**rugs	D	**D**rugs/substance use
S	**S**exuality	E	**E**motions/depression
S	**S**uicide/depression	S	**S**exuality
S	**S**afety from injury and violence	S	**S**afety

has received attention. The Center for Substance Abuse Treatment (CSAT) recommends that physicians screen all patients for substance use, make brief interventions for those who can be treated in primary care, and refer to treatment those with the most serious disorders (Substance Abuse and Mental Health Services Administration [SAMHSA], 2009a). This treatment framework is referred to as Screening, Brief Intervention, and Referral to Treatment (SBIRT). An evaluation of 15 studies found SBIRT with adults to be cost-effective, with the most favorable cost–benefit ratio in primary care (Kraemer, 2007). In concordance with CSAT, the American Academy of Pediatrics and other professional organizations (American Academy of Pediatrics, 2002) recommend that physicians screen all adolescents at yearly health maintenance visits to identify substance use. Because patients with substance use disorders might not present for regular well visits, substance use screening may also be useful during "urgent care" appointments, particularly when the chief complaint might be linked to high-risk behavior. Examples include visits for trauma or sexually transmitted infections.

Adolescent drug and alcohol consumption patterns, and problems associated with use, are distinct. Unlike adult patients whose chronic use of alcohol or other substances often results in tangible medical consequences, use of substances by adolescents is primarily associated with risk, which may be less motivating for behavior change. "Scare tactics" that present extreme consequences of long-term substance use are not effective (Butterworth, 2008). Thus, a particular challenge is both refining the tools that accurately assess risk

and finessing the salient messages delivered to this age group.

Screening Tools for Substance Use

The goal of screening is to determine an individual's risk level in order to determine the appropriate level of intervention. While experienced providers may feel confident in their ability to detect substance use–related problems, a study by Wilson et al. found that providers significantly underestimate the risk level associated with substance use when they rely on their clinical impressions alone (Wilson, Sherritt, Gates, & Knight, 2004). Despite the obvious advantage, many physicians do not use validated tools (Harris et al., 2011); the primary reason cited for this omission is lack of time (Van Hook et al., 2007). Very brief screens or screens that can be self-administered may present significant advantages.

The ideal screening tool would be brief, easy to administer and score, screen for all psychoactive substances (including tobacco) simultaneously, and accurately triage youth of different ages into actionable categories. A number of extant screening tools have been validated with adolescents (Table 26.2) and can accurately distinguish between low-risk and high-risk alcohol and drug use (Dennis, Chan, & Funk, 2006; Grisso, Barnum, Fletcher, Cauffman, & Peuschold, 2001; Knight, Sherritt, Harris, Gates, & Chang, 2003; Martino, Grilo, & Fehon, 2000; Miller, 1990; Willner, 2000; Winters, 1992), though these tools all have limitations and have not been popular in the primary care setting. Within the past few years, the National Institutes of Health has developed newer tools in an attempt to ameliorate these problems.

Table 26.2 Substance Abuse Screening and Assessment Tools for Use With Adolescents

Brief Screens	
S2BI	• Two-question frequency screen • Screens for tobacco, alcohol, marijuana, and other illicit drug use • Discriminates between no use, no SUD, moderate SUD, and severe SUD, based on *DSM-5* diagnoses
BSTAD	• Brief Screener for Tobacco, Alcohol, and Other Drugs • Identifies problematic tobacco, alcohol, and marijuana use in pediatric settings.
NIAAA Youth Alcohol Screen	• Two-question screen • Screens for friends' use and own use

Brief Assessments	
CRAFFT	Car, Relax, Alone, Friends/Family, Forget, Trouble • The CRAFFT is a good tool for quickly identifying problems associated with substance use • Not a diagnostic tool
GAIN	• Global Appraisal of Individual Needs • Assesses for both substance use disorders and mental health disorders
AUDIT	• Alcohol Use Disorders Identification Test • Assesses risky drinking • Not a diagnostic tool

SUD, substance use disorder.

In 2011 the National Institute on Alcohol Abuse and Alcoholism published a youth alcohol screening guide (National Institute on Alcohol Abuse and Alcoholism, 2011a) which includes an empirically based two-question screen and guidance for brief intervention (see Table 26.3). The screen distinguishes between no use, "lower," "moderate," and "highest" risk alcohol use. The screen is quick and relatively simple to use and has been designed for children as young as 9 years old to facilitate screening *before* most children start drinking regularly. Because it focuses on alcohol, it may be easier to employ clinically and hence useful in situations where clinical time is limited. The basic steps and brief intervention recommendations remain the same regardless of which tool is chosen.

The National Institute on Drug Abuse also funded development of two new brief tools, BSTAD and S2BI, which are compatible with the electronic medical record (Kelly et al., 2014; Levy et al., 2014). BSTAD uses the questions from the NIAAA screening tool with added questions for tobacco and "drugs" to quickly discriminate between high and low risk for substance use disorder. The tool found that regarding past-year use, the optimal cut points for identifying a substance use disorder

were ≥6 days of tobacco use (sensitivity = 0.95; specificity = 0.97); ≥2 days of alcohol use (sensitivity = 0.96; specificity = 0.85); and ≥2 days of marijuana use (sensitivity = 0.80; specificity = 0.93). S2BI uses three past-year frequency questions, one each for tobacco, alcohol, and marijuana, to triage adolescents into four risk categories based on *DSM-5* categories: no past-year use, use but no substance use disorder (SUD), mild–moderate SUD, and severe SUD (Table 26.4).

S2BI offers distinct advantages for office-based screening (see Table 26.5). It is very brief, easy to administer, and accurately maps to *DSM-5* criteria for alcohol, marijuana, and tobacco use disorders. Notably, it is the only tool validated for use with adolescents that can distinguish adolescents with a severe substance use disorder, who would most likely benefit from specific treatment for substance use disorders.

Managing Confidentiality

Protecting an appropriate level of confidentiality of adolescents' health care information is an essential determinant of whether adolescents will access care and answer questions honestly, and whether a therapeutic alliance between doctor and patient can

Table 26.3 National Institute on Alcohol Abuse and Alcoholism Screening Questions and Risk Assessment

Elementary School (ages 9–11 years)

1. Do you have any friends who drank beer, wine, or any drink containing alcohol in the past year?
2. How about you—have you ever had more than a few sips of beer, wine, or any drink containing alcohol?

Middle School (ages 11–14 years)

1. Do you have any friends who drank beer, wine, or any drink containing alcohol in the past year?
2. How about you—in the past year, on how many days have you had more than a few sips of beer, wine, or any drink containing alcohol?

High School (ages 14–18 years)

1. In the past year, on how many days have you had more than a few sips of beer, wine, or any drink containing alcohol?
2. If your friends drink, how many drinks do they usually drink on an occasion?

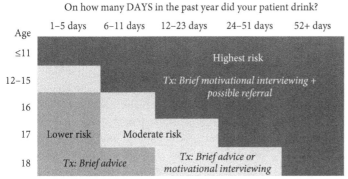

Estimated risk levels by age and frequency in the past year

SUD, substance use disorder.

Source: National Institute on Alcohol Abuse and Alcoholism (2011a, b).

Table 26.4 *DSM-5* Criteria

Criteria		Severity
1	Use in larger amounts or for longer periods of time than intended	Severity is designated according to the number of symptoms endorsed:
2	Unsuccessful efforts to cut down or quit	• 0–1: No diagnosis • 2–3: mild SUD
3	Excessive time spent taking the drug	• 4–5: moderate SUD • 6 or more: Severe SUD
4	Failure to fulfill major obligations	
5	Continued use despite problems	
6	Important activities given up	
7	Recurrent use in physically hazardous situations	
8	Continued use despite problems	
9	Tolerance	
10	Withdrawal	
11	Craving	

SUD, substance use disorder.

Source: American Psychiatric Association. (2013). *Diagnostic and Statistical Manual of Mental Disorders,* fifth edition. Arlington, VA: American Psychiatric Association.

Table 26.5 S2BI

Frequency of Using Tobacco, Alcohol, or Marijuana	Risk Level	Brief Intervention
Never	No use	Positive reinforcement
Once or twice	No SUD	Brief advice
Monthly	Mild/moderate SUD	Further assessment, brief motivational intervention, referral

SUD, substance use disorder.

Source: Levy, S., Weiss, R., Sherritt, L., Ziemnik, R., Spalding, A., Van Hook, S., & Shrier, L. A. (2014). An electronic screen for triaging adolescent substance use by risk levels. *Journal of the American Medical Association Pediatrics, 168*(9), 822–828. doi:10.1001/jamapediatrics.2014.774

be maintained (Ford, Millstein, Halpern-Felsher, & Irwin, 1997). Adolescents who are concerned that clinicians will reveal private information to their parents or other adults may delay obtaining health care for even serious medical problems or forgo preventative health care entirely. Health care professional organizations guiding best practices in adolescent and young adult medical care, including the American Medical Association, the American Academy of Pediatrics, the American College of Obstetricians and Gynecologists, the American Academy of Family Physicians, and the Society for Adolescent Medicine, have established positions and recommendations supporting confidentiality and informed consent in this age group and addressing the medical, legal, and ethical ramifications that face patients and clinicians alike ("Confidential health services for adolescents. Council on Scientific Affairs, American Medical Association," 1993; Society for Adolescent Medicine, 2004).

Best practice recommendations include introducing confidentiality provisions prior to the first time that the teen or "tween" is interviewed without a parent present or during the initial visit for adolescents new to a practice. An adolescent's confidentiality may be maintained unless his or her health or safety, or the health or safety of another individual, is acutely in danger. Determining when confidentiality must be breached for safety is a matter of clinical judgment. In general, occasional use of alcohol or marijuana per se can be kept confidential, though heavy binge drinking, any indication for acute hospitalization, including medical supervision of withdrawal, or mixing drugs—particularly sedatives—justifies informing parents. Situations such as a suicide threat clearly warrant breaking confidentiality, but other situations, including many issues related to substance

use, are not so clear. Older adolescents generally may be afforded more confidentiality than younger teens, given their generally higher risk for both the acute and chronic consequences of substance use, and because of the importance of sustaining a trusting relationship with their doctor within which the possibility for effecting change can occur.

Explaining confidentiality provisions—including limits—to patient and parent(s) simultaneously is a practice that can help to minimize subsequent misunderstandings. Parents can be reassured that they will receive any information involving the immediate safety of their child, while adolescents can be reassured that details discussed will remain confidential. Even when sensitive information such as suicidal or homicidal ideation needs to be revealed, a preliminary, private conversation with the adolescent discussing what information will be revealed and how it will be presented may help maintain the therapeutic alliance despite the confidentiality breach. In many instances adolescents will be relieved that their parents will be informed of serious problems, though they may have preferences as to how information is presented. For example, an adolescent may prefer the phrase "addicted to opiates" over "addicted to heroin." Adolescents may also request that details such as who supplied substances and where and when they used them not be shared with parents; these requests should be honored if they are not directly related to the safety concern. By strategizing with the adolescent ahead of time, a clinician can transmit necessary information to parents while simultaneously protecting the physician–patient bond.

Even in situations where there is not an acute safety risk, adolescents typically benefit from support from their parents in accessing recommended services because completion rates are low when adolescents are given referrals without parental involvement (Macaulay, Griffin, Gronewold, Williams, & Botvin, 2005). Teen participation in confidential health services should not overshadow the desirability of parental involvement. The Society for Adolescent Health and Medicine's position statement on the delivery of confidential health services to adolescents specifically enumerates that "health care professionals should support effective communication between adolescents and their parents or other caretakers. Participation of parents in the health care of their adolescents should usually be encouraged, but not mandated" (Society for Adolescent Medicine, 2004).

In many cases by the time an adolescent has developed a serious substance use disorder, parents are already aware of their drug use, though they may underestimate the seriousness of the problem (Fisher et al., 2006). When this is the case, an adolescent may be willing to invite parents into the conversation. This can be a rewarding experience for the adolescent, particularly if the clinician focuses on points of mutual agreement. For example, a clinician may say to a parent, "Your son has been very honest in discussing his use of marijuana with me. I recommended that he quit smoking entirely in order to protect his health. It is clear that he has been thinking about the role that marijuana plays in his life, and he has agreed to return to discuss it further with one of the social workers in our office. In the meantime, he has agreed *never* to drive a car after smoking or ride with a driver who has been using alcohol or drugs. He has also agreed that he will not smoke marijuana on weekdays. He knows that you do not allow marijuana in your home, and that you will be checking his room and removing any drugs and/or paraphernalia that you find. You can support him by ensuring that he follows through and returns for the appointments with the counselor."

Interventions

"Brief intervention" can be viewed as an umbrella term referring to any interaction between a clinician and an adolescent that is intended to decrease, defer, or delay substance use. Because all US adolescents are at risk for substance use, brief interventions are appropriate for all teens. Even those who report no substance use can receive a prevention message from their provider.

Adolescents consider physicians an authoritative source of knowledge about alcohol and drugs, and they are receptive to discussing substance use

as long as they feel respected (Yoast, Fleming, & Balch, 2007). Brief interventions for adolescents at "high risk" for a substance use disorder are based on the principles of motivational interviewing, in which the clinician aims to enhance an individual's own arguments for reducing substance use while respecting the patient's autonomy rather than persuading, coercing, or demanding behavior change (Burke, O'Sullivan, & Vaughan, 2005). Formative work has found that physician-implemented brief interventions are acceptable to both teens (Hagan, Shaw, & Duncan, 2008) and clinicians (Buckelew, Adams, Irwin, Gee, & Ozer, 2008). Because adolescents are even more susceptible to acute and long-term consequences of substance use than adults (Chambers et al., 2003), counseling this age group offers promise in reducing the public health burden of morbidity and mortality related to substance use.

Adolescents with more serious problems and disorders may either be identified by screening or, perhaps more commonly, by presenting to the primary care setting with substance use–related problems. In either case, the resulting intervention to reduce substance use is identical. To be efficient and cost effective, the brief intervention should be appropriate to the level of risk as determined by screen results (see Table 26.6).

Brief Advice for No Use

The effectiveness of positive reinforcement as a behavioral technique to reinforce desired behaviors is well established (Beck, Daughtridge, & Sloane, 2002; Elder, Ayala, & Harris, 1999). A quasi-experimental study set in primary care settings that included educational materials and positive reinforcement for adolescents who reported no past-year substance use found that the intervention reduced alcohol initiation rates up to 12 months later (Harris et al., 2012). Examples used in this study include statements such as "Choosing not to use alcohol or drugs is a very good decision. For the sake of your health, I hope that you will keep it up."

Screening even young children for alcohol use has never been shown to *increase* substance use. However, the NIAAA recommends adding a statement about use norms to avoid creating the misperception that drinking is common, which might be implied by administering a screen for children under age 12. Statements such as "I am glad that you do not drink—of course, most kids your age don't drink!" may avert unintended implications.

Discussions that "leave the door open" for future conversations with statements such as "You can

Table 26.6 Substance Use Spectrum and Goals for Office Intervention

Stage	Description	Intervention Goal
Abstinence	The time before an individual has ever used drugs or alcohol more than a few sips	Prevent or delay initiation of substance use through positive reinforcement and patient/parent education.
Substance use without a disorder	Limited use, generally in social situations, without related problems. Typically, use occurs at predictable times, such as on weekends.	Advise to stop. Provide counseling regarding the medical harms of substance use. Promote patient strengths.
Mild–moderate substance use disorder	Use in high-risk situations, such as when driving or with strangers. Use associated with a problem, such as a fight, arrest, or school suspension. Use for emotional regulation, such as to relieve stress or depression. Defined in *DSM-5* as meeting 2–5 of the 11 SUD criteria.	Brief assessment to explore patient-perceived problems associated with use. Give clear, brief advice to quit. Provide counseling regarding the medical harms of substance use. Negotiate a behavior change to quit or cut down. Close patient follow-up. Consider referral to SUD treatment. Consider breaking confidentiality.
Severe substance use disorder	Loss of control or compulsive drug use associated with neurologic changes in the reward system of the brain. Defined as meeting 6 or more SUD criteria in *DSM-5*.	As above. Involve parents in treatment planning whenever possible. Refer to the appropriate level of care. Follow up to insure compliance with treatment and to offer continued support.
Acute risk	Use associated with acute risk of overdose or in a situation that is physically risky	Intervention for safety

SUD, substance use disorder.

always ask me any questions you may have about drugs and alcohol" may reassure adolescents that substance use is a legitimate topic for conversation and help establish the primary care clinician as a subject matter expert.

No Substance Use Disorder

Adolescents who have initiated substance use but have not yet begun to experience problems are nonetheless at high risk for escalating use over the next few years, according to national statistics (Johnston, O'Malley, Miech, Bachman, & Schulenberg, 2014). While little research has specifically targeted this group, one quasi-experimental trial found that adolescents in this risk category benefitted from brief, medically oriented advice to quit. Examples of this type of advice include statements such as "I recommend that you quit smoking marijuana, and now is the best time. Marijuana is bad for your lungs, makes it harder for you to concentrate, and can even make you feel paranoid." Brief physician advice, combined with psychoeducation, reduced

rates of alcohol initiation for up to 12 months after the intervention (Harris et al., 2012).

To take advantage of the medical setting, advice should be medically grounded in meaningful health consequences; knowledge of the patient as is often available in primary care can be used to select the most relevant and meaningful advice. A strengths-based approach focusing on positive reasons for quitting is also recommended. For example, a statement such as "You are such a good student/athlete/big brother/etc. I would hate to see anything interfere with your future." Or "I hope that you don't let anything threaten your goal of joining the military/earning a scholarship, etc." may be particularly motivating because they focus on positive attributes. Adolescents for whom drug use is not yet an established pattern should be able to quit without the hardships experienced by individuals with severe substance use disorders.

In addition to medical advice, counseling to avoid driving or riding in a car with an impaired driver is vital, as this behavior is common (Hingson,

Zha, & Weitzman, 2009) and dangerous. The Contract for Life (SADD, 2005) is a document whose purpose is to facilitate communication between adolescents and their parents about "potentially destructive decisions" made by adolescents. In the Contract, the adolescent promises to avoid driving while intoxicated or riding with an intoxicated driver, and the parent promises to provide or arrange "sober" transportation in such circumstances and to postpone discussion until the next morning when both parent and child are calm. More generally, adolescents who have driven while impaired should have a follow-up after the initial discussion. Continued risk through repeated instances of riding with an intoxicated driver may require breach of confidentiality in order to protect the adolescent (Levy, Williams, & Knight, 2008).

Mild–Moderate Substance Use Disorder

Substance use disorders form a continuum from mild to severe. Typically adolescents with mild substance use disorders are beginning to have consequences and problems associated with their use, while those who have progressed to severe substance use disorders have lost control over use and use compulsively. Use tends to escalate as adolescents age into young adulthood and the severity of a substance use disorder may also progress.

Individuals with mild–moderate substance use disorders have most often been the targets of primary care interventions, though to date, most studies have been small and inconclusive. The most promising studies have used structured approaches based on motivational interviewing. Studies conducted with adolescents presenting for Emergency Department care found that brief interventions administered by non-MD behavioral counselors *can* reduce alcohol use (Monti et al., 1999, 2007; Spirito et al., 2004) and marijuana use (Bernstein et al., 2009). Studies conducted in primary care using trained behavioral counselors have found brief motivational interventions are acceptable and feasible in this setting for high risk alcohol (Stern, Meredith, Gholson, Gore, & D'Amico, 2007) and marijuana use (Shrier, Rhoads, Burke, Walls, & Blood, 2014). A study comparing behavioral counselors to computerized interventions found that both were effective in reducing some risks, although neither reduced quantity or frequency of marijuana use (Walton et al., 2013). A study conducted in Switzerland found that adolescents and young adults with heavy

alcohol and marijuana use reduced their use after consultation with a family physician, although there were no differences between control and intervention physicians who had received specific training in using a structured, motivational intervention (Haller et al., 2014).

Based on this nascent literature, brief interventions based on motivational interviewing are recommended for adolescents that have begun to use substances regularly (American Academy of Pediatrics, 2002). Teens that report monthly or more use are likely to have begun to experience problems (Levy et al., 2014) that are often associated with ambivalence, setting the stage for a brief motivational intervention, based on the principles of motivational interviewing. A detailed discussion of the motivational interviewing technique is beyond the scope of this chapter; readers interested in more information are referred to *Motivational Interviewing* by Miller and Rollnick (2013).

Three key pillars of brief motivational interventions (Miller & Rollnick, 2013) are to (1) develop a discrepancy by discovering and exploring the negative consequences associated with substance use, (2) acknowledge individual autonomy—only the adolescent can control his or her own behavior, and (3) use a respectful, empathetic, and engaging approach. While not a standard motivational technique, we recommend including brief advice for abstinence with each intervention (see later discussion).

Table 26.7 demonstrates a sample framework for a brief motivational intervention involving four steps: engagement, assessment for areas of ambivalence around substance use, brief advice, and planning.

Engagement

Engagement involves asking permission to discuss a personal topic with the adolescent, who may be cautious, particularly with an unfamiliar clinician. This invitation demonstrates respect for the adolescent from the start and communicates that the adolescent is "in charge." Formative work has found that the majority of adolescents are willing to speak with their clinician about their substance use if they feel respected (Yoast et al., 2007), and most will agree to the conversation. However, refusal should be respected unless the adolescent's substance use is acutely dangerous or his or her safety is otherwise at risk. In these unusual cases, the clinician may need to make an acute intervention

Table 26.7 Sample Framework for Brief Motivational Intervention

Process	Description
Engagement	Request permission to discuss substance use.
	Sample statement:
	Thank you for completing the screening tool. I would like to invite you to discuss your results with me. Is now a good time for a conversation?
Assessment and summary	Targeted assessment for areas of ambivalence to establish rapport and develop a discrepancy between current status and future goals.
	Sample questions:
	• *What problems have you had, if any, related to your use of substances?*
	• *What regrets do you have, if any, related to your use of alcohol?*
	• *What trouble have you had, if any, related to your use of marijuana?*
Brief advice	Offer specific medical advice to quit or cut down substance use as a means for decreasing the types of problems reported during the assessment.
	Sample statement:
	• *Only you can decide whether or not to drink alcohol. In regard to your health, I recommend you quit.*
	• *Having a blackout means that you have had enough alcohol to poison your brain cells, at least temporarily.*
	• *Kids often make bad choices, like the decision to have sex without a condom, when they are drinking.*
	• *What are your thoughts on this?*
Planning	Engage patient in setting personal goals and agenda for change and link to follow-up.
	Sample statement:
	• *It sounds like you really enjoy drinking but don't want to have another blackout. What could you do to protect yourself?*

(see later discussion) rather than engaging the adolescent in a brief motivational intervention.

Assessment and Summary

The purpose of the assessment step is twofold: (1) to identify adolescents whose substance use presents an acute risk to their health or safety and (2) to build a discrepancy or identify ambivalence as a step in a motivational intervention. The CRAFFT tool, which asks six questions about problems associated with substance use (Table 26.8), may be used as an assessment guide. The CRAFFT questions are closed-ended (i.e., "yes/no"). Any "yes" response triggers follow-up with open-ended questions that explore the nature of the problem and generally yield the most relevant information.

Questions about whether the adolescent has ever made a quit attempt and, if so, why may help the adolescent to explore the negative side of ambivalence and allow him or her to hear the perceived negative consequences in his or her own words— a standard motivational interviewing technique (Miller & Rollnick, 2013). For example, an adolescent who quits marijuana during sports season

likely has concerns about the impact of smoking on lung function, although he or she may not have considered the implications of this statement. "Connecting the dots" to make this relationship explicit may be helpful in increasing ambivalence and moving toward behavior change.

Brief Advice

Including brief advice to quit in a motivational intervention may help reduce the risk of an adolescent misinterpreting "risk reduction" as tacit endorsement of continued substance use. Advice can be given while acknowledging the patient's own autonomy in order to keep a patient from becoming resistant. This type of directive is not typically associated with motivational interviewing, but it is unlikely to provoke resistance in the adolescent if expressed as the clinician's advice rather than a "command."

Planning

A key component of office-based brief interventions is discussing an explicit behavior change plan. Questions such as "What do you want

Table 26.8 The CRAFFT Questions

During the past 12 months have you:	
C	Ridden in a **CAR** driven by someone, including yourself, who was high or had been using alcohol or drugs?
R	Used alcohol or drugs to **RELAX**, feel better about yourself, or fit in?
A	Used alcohol or drugs while you are by yourself, **ALONE**?
F	**FORGOTTEN** things you did while using alcohol or drugs?
F	Had your **FAMILY** or **FRIENDS** tell you that you should cut down on your drinking or drug use?
T	Gotten into **TROUBLE** while you were using alcohol or drugs?

Source: Knight, Sherritt, Harris, Gates, and Chang (2002).

to do about it?" after a summary of the negative aspects of substance use challenge the adolescent to consider behavior change and allow the clinician to work with the adolescent in designing and implementing a plan.

Some adolescents will be willing to cut down their use, even if they are not willing to quit. The clinician can guide a behavior change plan by encouraging the adolescent to focus on highest risk behaviors.

Follow-Up

Follow-up is recommended whenever an adolescent makes a change plan. If available and amenable to the adolescent and his or her parents, short-term counseling with an allied mental health professional such as a psychologist or social worker is recommended. Adolescents who refuse to allow their parents to participate are unlikely to follow through with a referral, and they may not be willing or able to return to the primary care office for further discussion. A notation in the medical record can help to alert the clinician to follow up the next time the patient presents to the office for any reason.

Severe Substance Use Disorder

Severe substance use disorder (American Psychiatric Association, 2013), or addiction, is a chronic, relapsing disorder that requires long-term treatment. Adolescents who report weekly or more use of a substance are likely to have developed a severe substance use disorder (Patrick et al., 2013). A study of a primary care network in New England found that approximately 3% of 12- to 18-year-old adolescents presenting for routine medical care met criteria for dependence to one or more substances (Knight et al., 2007). While effective treatment for substance use disorders is available (Deas &

Thomas, 2001), fewer than 10% of adolescents with a substance use disorder receive any specific treatment. The majority of referrals originate in the judicial system, with the medical home contributing very few (SAMHSA, 2009b). Motivational strategies may be useful in encouraging the adolescent to accept a referral, using the strategy described earlier. The planning phase should target getting the adolescent to accept a referral and follow-through. An adolescent who is willing to honestly report his or her substance use and related problems may also be willing to participate in treatment; having a good experience with a brief motivational intervention may make the adolescent more willing to enter treatment. Work done with adolescents seen in an Emergency Department found that those who received a brief motivational intervention were more likely to engage in treatment than those who received treatment as usual (Tait, Hulse, Robertson, & Sprivulis, 2005). Including parents whenever possible may help facilitate referral completion.

Various different counseling styles and levels of intensity are available to treat patients with substance use disorders (see Table 26.9). Specialists or programs designed specifically for adolescents with substance use disorders are recommended by the Center for Substance Abuse Treatment (CSAT) (1999a) as well as the American Academy of Pediatrics (Committee on Substance Abuse, 2011). Teens may not engage in treatment or, worse, may be exposed to more dangerous behaviors if mixed in with adults with more chronic problems. Adolescents whose behavior is unstable may need to take a leave of absence from school, although long-term residential treatment programs for adolescents should always include an educational component.

Adolescents who enter specialty addiction treatment should continue to be followed by their

Table 26.9 Substance Use Treatment

Outpatient

Group therapy	Group therapy is a mainstay of substance abuse treatment for adolescents with substance use disorders. It is a particularly attractive option because it is cost effective and takes advantage of the developmental preference for congregating with peers. However, group therapy has not been extensively evaluated as a therapeutic modality for this age group, and existing research has produced mixed results.[1,2]
Family therapy	Family-directed therapies are the best validated approach for treating adolescent substance abuse. A number of modalities have all been demonstrated effective. Family counseling typically targets domains that figure prominently in the etiology of substance use disorders in adolescents—family conflict, communication, parental monitoring, discipline, child abuse/neglect, and parental substance use disorders.[1]
Intensive outpatient program	Intensive outpatient programs (IOPs) serve as an intermediate level of care for patients who have needs that are too complex for outpatient treatment but do not require inpatient services. These programs allow individuals to continue with their daily routine and practice newly acquired recovery skills both at home and at work. IOPs generally comprise a combination of supportive group therapy, educational groups, family therapy, individual therapy, relapse prevention and life skills, 12-step recovery, case management, and aftercare planning. The programs range from 2–3 hours, 2–5 days per week, and last 1–3 months. These programs are appealing, because they provide a plethora of services in a relatively short period of time.[3]
Partial hospital program	Partial hospitalization is a short-term, comprehensive outpatient program in affiliation with a hospital that is designed to provide support and treatment for patients with substance use disorders. The services offered at these programs are more concentrated and intensive than regular outpatient treatment; they are structured throughout the entire day and offer medical monitoring in addition to individual and group therapy. Participants typically attend sessions for 7 or 8 hours per day, at least 5 days per week, for 1–3 weeks. As with IOPs, patients return home in the evenings and have a chance to practice newly acquired recovery skills.[4]

Inpatient/Residential

Detoxification	Detoxification refers to the medical management of symptoms of withdrawal. Medically supervised detoxification is indicated for any adolescent who is at risk of withdrawing from alcohol or benzodiazepines and might also be helpful for adolescents withdrawing from opioids, cocaine, or other substances. Detoxification may be an important first step but is not considered definitive treatment. Patients who are discharged from a detoxification program should then begin either an outpatient or residential substance abuse treatment program.[2,5]
Acute residential treatment	Acute residential treatment (ART) is a short-term (days-to-weeks) residential placement designed to stabilize patients in crisis, often before entering a longer term residential treatment program.[5] ART programs typically target adolescents with co-occurring mental health disorders.
Residential treatment	Residential treatment programs are highly structured live-in environments that provide therapy for those with severe substance abuse, mental illness, or behavioral problems that require 24-hour care. The goal of residential treatment is to promote the achievement and subsequent maintenance of long-term abstinence and equip each patient with both the social and coping skills necessary for a successful transition back into society. Residential programs are classified by length of stay; some are short term (<30 days) or long term (≥30 days). Residential programs generally comprise individual and group therapy sessions, plus medical, psychological, clinical, nutritional, and educational components. Residential facilities aim to simulate real living environments with added structure and routine to prepare patients with the framework necessary for their lives to continue drug- and alcohol-free after completion of the program.[6]

Table 26.9 Continued

Inpatient/Residential

Therapeutic boarding school	Therapeutic boarding schools are educational institutions that provide constant supervision for their students by a professional staff. These schools offer a highly structured environment with set times for all activities, smaller more specialized classes, and social and emotional support. In addition to the regular services offered at traditional boarding schools, therapeutic schools also provide individual and group therapy for adolescents with mental health or substance use disorders.[7]

[1] Bukstein, O. G., Bernet, W., Arnold, V., Beitchman, J., Shaw, J., Benson, R. S., . . . Ptakowski, K. K. (2005). Practice parameter for the assessment and treatment of children and adolescents with substance use disorders. *Journal of American Academy of Child and Adolescent Psychiatry, 44*(6), 609–621. doi:00004583-200506000-00020 [pii]

[2] Vaughan, B. L., & Knight, J. R. (2009). Intensive drug treatment. In L. S. Neinstein, C. Gordon, D. Katzman, E. R. Woods, & D. Rosen (Eds.), *Adolescent healthcare: A practical guide* (5th ed., pp. 671–675). Philadelphia, PA: Lippincott Williams & Wilkins.

[3] Center for Substance Abuse Treatment. (2006). Services in intensive outpatient treatment programs. In *Substance abuse: Clinical issues in intensive outpatient treatment*. Rockville, MD: Substance Abuse and Mental Health Services Administration. Retrieved October 2015, from http://www.ncbi.nlm.nih.gov/books/NBK64094/

[4] Nemeck, D., & Lopez, W. (Eds.). (2010). *CIGNA level of care guidelines for behavioral health and substance abuse*. Retrieved October 2015, from http://www.cignabehavioral.com/web/basicsite/provider/pdf/levelOfCareGuidelines.pdf

[5] Fournier, M. E., & Levy, S. (2006). Recent trends in adolescent substance use, primary care screening, and updates in treatment options. *Current Opinion in Pediatrics, 18*(4), 352–358. doi:10.1097/01.mop.0000236381.33907.9d 00008480-200608000-00003 [pii]

[6] Center for Substance Abuse Treatment. (1999b). Triage and placement in treatment services. In *SAMHSA/CSAT Treatment Improvement Protocols*. Rockville, MD: Substance Abuse and Mental Health Services Administration.

[7] Center for Substance Abuse Treatment. (1999c). Therapeutic communities. In *SAMHSA/CSAT treatment improvement protocols*. Rockville, MD: Substance Abuse and Mental Health Services Administration. Retrieved October 2015, from http://www.ncbi.nlm.nih.gov/books/NBK64342//

primary care clinician. As with patients with other chronic disorders, they should continue to receive routine health maintenance. Encouraging patients to return to primary care may also help to destigmatize addiction treatment, and it indicates unconditional regard for the adolescent. Primary care follow-up also provides the opportunity to inquire about services and encourage long-term addiction treatment.

Immediate Intervention for Adolescents at Acute Risk

Adolescents who put themselves at acute risk of morbidity or mortality related to their substance use require immediate intervention, which includes breaking confidentiality and informing parents. While uncommon in primary care, behaviors such as mixing sedatives, consuming large quantities of alcohol for age and gender, or consuming unidentified "pills" (which is a popular activity at "pharming" parties) threaten life and limb and require immediate intervention. Teens at risk for medical complications of withdrawal can be referred to a detoxification program, which can be accessed through an emergency department. Safety plans that can be monitored by adults should be

implemented for all teens who report a history of reckless substance use. These adolescents should be referred to an addiction or mental health specialist as soon as possible for further evaluation, treatment, and monitoring.

Some adolescents with serious substance use disorders refuse to engage in treatment. In these cases, mandated treatment may be advisable if a teen's life is at risk, though it is a last resort. Parents can encourage their adolescents to agree to treatment by eliminating enabling behaviors—such as providing money and other resources that can help teens to access drugs. Parent guidance that teaches parents to avoid enabling by withdrawing resources, including cars, cash, and cell phones, may be helpful. Parents should be encouraged to monitor their children closely and avoid unsupervised contact with other teens until treatment has begun and the adolescent is more stable. Adolescents in need of treatment for substance use disorders often have co-occurring mental health disorders, school problems, and other behavioral problems that should be assessed and treated.

Parents may use legal mechanisms to mandate treatment for adolescents who are at serious risk of injuring themselves or others due to substance use but refuse to engage in treatment. Adolescents who use intravenous drugs or sleep on the streets or in unsafe homes may be candidates for mandated treatment, and we recommend that clinicians familiarize themselves with state laws in order to be prepared to support parents in this endeavor if necessary. The primary benefit of mandated treatment is keeping the adolescent safe and allowing initial phases of detoxification to occur in a structured setting. Long-term abstinence or even significant long-term improvements are rarely achieved with brief mandated treatment for serious drug disorders, and working with the adolescent to accept voluntary treatment is preferred whenever possible.

SBIRT for Youth With Chronic Medical Conditions

One in four youth in the United States grows up with a chronic medical condition such as diabetes, asthma, or arthritis that requires long-term follow-up by a clinical care team (Van Cleave, Gortmaker, & Perrin, 2010). Screening these adolescents for substance use and attending to special risks given their condition are recommended.

Youth with chronic medical conditions (YCMCs) may differ in the type of specific diagnoses they carry and, with that, follow varying disease management and treatment regimens. Common to this group is the need for adhering to medication regimens, clinical monitoring protocols, self-management plans, and control of health behaviors essential to disease control, including sleep, diet/meals, and activities. Use of alcohol and other substances may adversely impact any of these issues and heighten risks for poor health outcomes, making them vital topics to discuss and potential anchor points for screening and brief intervention. Physicians may have substantial opportunity to discuss these issues with YCMCs given the high frequency with which these youth interact with the health care system. Long-term rapport with specialty providers may increase the salience of health guidance and messages.

The Need to Tailor Screening Tools and Guidance to Youth With Chronic Medical Conditions

Available screening tools for YCMCs have been developed from population data about healthy youth, which may underestimate risks from substance use to youth with special vulnerabilities related to chronic disease. For example, even "lower risk" alcohol or other drug use may expose youth to co-occurring risks that generally worsen health—such as inadequate sleep, skipped meals, exposure to smoke, and unprotected sex (a particular hazard for youth taking teratogenic or immunity-suppressing medicines). While these factors are generally well tolerated by healthy youth, they can lead to disease exacerbation and serious complications among the chronically ill. Alcohol and other drugs may pose unique risks to the validity of diagnostic test interpretation, impacting treatment protocols derived from them, and undermine the safety of prescription medications. To the extent that screens underestimate risks from substance use, physicians may miss important opportunities to give relevant medical advice and promote intervention or treatment when warranted. Given the absence of validated screening tools for use with this special population, we recommend use of extant tools coupled with additional probes to elicit reports of problems that healthy youth might encounter as well as complications related to substance use or problems with a disease management plan, program, or medication regimen. Salient points for brief intervention can include those points suitable for discussion with healthy youth and also points that reflect the unique and often near-term potential for harms, complications, or exacerbations associated with poor disease management, medication adherence, and behavioral health risks. Positive as well as negative messages may be persuasive because many YCMCs are acutely attuned to goals of staying healthy, keeping their symptoms under control, and avoiding unnecessary procedures, treatments, and visits. Hence, emphasizing goals of disease management and symptom quiescence may counterbalance messages to avoid/delay and cut back on substance use.

Follow-Up and Coordination With Specialty Care

Many YCMCs use a specialty care setting as their medical home, so coordination between primary care and this setting may be an effective frame for SBIRT. The specialty care setting offers a number of advantages for SBIRT implementation. Strong bonds and frequent (semiannually or quarterly) interactions characterize relationships between YCMCs and specialists—ideal conditions for screening, brief intervention, and follow-up as patients mature and gain exposure to and experience with alcohol and other drugs. The multidisciplinary team approach of many pediatric specialty care settings may facilitate follow-up and internal or external referral to a mental health or addiction specialist, if needed. To date, however, very few YCMCs are screened in subspecialty programs; only 4.2% of adolescents in treatment for rheumatic conditions were screened for alcohol use, despite significant risks of adverse interactions between alcohol and common medications (Britto, Rosenthal, Taylor, & Passo, 2000). As with programs serving healthy youth, better care and effective SBIRT implementation rests on improved tools, better integration of services, and more behavioral health services as well as clinician activation and awareness.

Conclusion

Adolescence should be a period of excellent health. Psychiatrist and pediatrician Ronald Dahl describes the following paradox: Adolescents are in many ways more robust than younger children, with better immune function, capacity to withstand injury, and other relative strengths, and yet their overall morbidity and mortality rates increase 200% compared to their younger counterparts over a comparable time period (Dahl, 2004). The major causes of death and disability in adolescents are strikingly behavioral in origin, versus the more organic etiologies seen in adults. Adolescent substance use is a formidable and relentless contributor to this health paradox. Clinicians who care for adolescents must be familiar with the extent of this problem, and they should have an appropriate armamentarium of tools to combat substance use in their individual patient population.

Given the enormity of the problem of adolescent substance use, both in the United States and worldwide, it is critical that ongoing research target all aspects of the problem. Ongoing neurobiological research continues to shed new light on the intricacies of adolescent brain development. Research is also well underway looking at the successes of various interventions targeting adolescent substance abuse. In the United States, experts are looking at medical education and residency training, with ambitious and well-substantiated goals to increase the amount of training given in substance use. The hope is that a generation of better trained clinicians will emerge, more capable of recognizing and treating the sequelae—early and late—of substance use among their patients, and even, more important, preventing its initiation.

Future Directions

In 2012, the US Preventive Services Task Force (2013) officially recommended brief motivational interventions, or brief clinician–patient interactions that use motivational interviewing techniques, as effective in reducing "at-risk" alcohol use by adults, although evidence for effectiveness with adolescents was insufficient for formal recommendation at this time. However, noting their safety (Baer, Kivlahan, Blume, McKnight, & Marlatt, 2001), low cost (Dennis et al., 2004), and suggestive evidence from work done with this age group in the emergency setting, the American Academy of Pediatrics does recommend brief motivational interventions for "high-risk" substance use in teens. Future studies determining the efficacy of brief motivational interventions with adolescents in the medical home should guide widespread implementation.

The Affordable Care Act requires that treatment for substance use disorders be reimbursed similar to other chronic medical conditions and *requires* screening and brief intervention implementation in general medical settings, providing opportunities for implementation science. Electronic screening tools that can be incorporated into electronic medical records, self-administered tools, and screening algorithms that guide the clinician to the appropriate level of intervention all may help to improve screening in practice. Both the National Institute on Alcohol Abuse and Alcoholism and the National Institute on Drug Abuse address these areas in their research portfolios (i.e., National Institute on Drug Abuse, 2008; National Institute on Alcohol Abuse and Alcoholism, 2011b).

AcknowledgmentWe would like to thank Ms. Rosemary Ziemnik for assistance with preparation of this manuscript.

References

American Academy of Pediatrics. (2002). Make time to screen for substance use during office visits (Committee on Substance Abuse). *AAP News*, *21*(1), 14, 34. Retrieved October 2015, from http://www.aappublications.org/content/aapnews/21/1/14.full.pdf

American Psychiatric Association. (2013). *Diagnostic and statistical manual of mental disorders* (5th ed.). Arlington, VA: Author.

Baer, J. S., Kivlahan, D. R., Blume, A. W., McKnight, P., & Marlatt, G. A. (2001). Brief intervention for heavy-drinking college students: 4-year follow-up and natural history. *American Journal of Public Health*, *91*(8), 1310–1316. Retrieved October 2015, from http://www.ncbi.nlm.nih.gov/entrez/query.fcgi?cmd=Retrieve&db=PubMed&dopt=Citation&list_uids=11499124

Beck, R. S., Daughtridge, R., & Sloane, P. D. (2002). Physician-patient communication in the primary care office: a systematic review. *Journal of the American Board of Family Practice*, *15*(1), 25–38. Retrieved October 2015, from http://www.jabfm.org/content/15/1/25.short

Becker, S. J., Curry, J. F., & Yang, C. (2011). Factors that influence trajectories of change in frequency of substance use and quality of life among adolescents receiving a brief intervention. *Journal of Substance Abuse Treatment, 41*(3), 294–304. doi:S0740-5472(11)00082-1 [pii] 10.1016/j.jsat.2011.04.004

Bernstein, E., Edwards, E., Dorfman, D., Heeren, T., Bliss, C., & Bernstein, J. (2009). Screening and brief intervention to reduce marijuana use among youth and young adults in a pediatric emergency department. *Academic Emergency Medicine, 16*(11), 1174–1185. doi:ACEM490 [pii] 10.1111/j.1553-2712.2009.00490.x

Britto, M. T., Rosenthal, S. L., Taylor, J., & Passo, M. H. (2000). Improving rheumatologists' screening for alcohol use and sexual activity. *Archives of Pediatrics and Adolescent Medicine, 154*(5), 478–483.

Buckelew, S. M., Adams, S. H., Irwin, C. E., Jr., Gee, S., & Ozer, E. M. (2008). Increasing clinician self-efficacy for screening and counseling adolescents for risky health behaviors: Results of an intervention. *Journal of Adolescent Health, 43*(2), 198–200. doi:S1054-139X(08)00098-0 [pii] 10.1016/j.jadohealth.2008.01.018 [doi]

Burke, P. J., O'Sullivan, J., & Vaughan, B. L. (2005). Adolescent substance use: Brief interventions by emergency care providers. *Pediatric Emergency Care, 21*(11), 770–776. doi:00006565-200511000-00014 [pii]

Butterworth, S. W. (2008). Influencing patient adherence to treatment guidelines. *Journal of Managed Care Pharmacy, 14*(6 Suppl. B), 21–24. Retrieved October 2015, from http://www.ncbi.nlm.nih.gov/pubmed/18693785

Center for Substance Abuse Treatment. (1999a). *Treatment of adolescents with substance abuse disorders. CSAT Treatment Improvement Protocol Series, No. 32.* Rockville, MD: DHHS. Retrieved October 2015, from http://adaiclearinghouse.org/downloads/TIP-32-Treatment-of-Adolescents-with-Substance-Use-Disorders-62.pdf

Center for Substance Abuse Treatment. (1999b). Triage and placement in treatment services. In *SAMHSA/CSAT treatment improvement protocols.* Rockville, MD: Substance Abuse and Mental Health Services Administration.

Center for Substance Abuse Treatment. (1999c). Therapeutic communities. In *SAMHSA/CSAT treatment improvement protocols.* Rockville, MD: Substance Abuse and Mental Health Services Administration. Retrieved October 2015, from http://www.ncbi.nlm.nih.gov/books/NBK64342/

Chambers, R. A., Taylor, J. R., & Potenza, M. N. (2003). Developmental neurocircuitry of motivation in adolescence: a critical period of addiction vulnerability. *American Journal of Psychiatry, 160*(6), 1041–1052.

Committee on Substance Abuse. (2011). Substance use screening, brief intervention, and referral to treatment for pediatricians. *Pediatrics, 128*(5), e1330–e1340. doi:10.1542/peds.2011-1754

"Confidential health services for adolescents. Council on Scientific Affairs, American Medical Association." (1993). *Journal of the American Medical Association, 269*(11), 1420–1424. Retrieved October 2015, from http://www.ncbi.nlm.nih.gov/entrez/query.fcgi?cmd=Retrieve&db=PubMed&dopt=Citation&list_uids=8441220

Dahl, R. E. (2004). Adolescent brain development: A period of vulnerabilities and opportunities. Keynote address. *Annals of the New York Academy of Science, 1021*, 1–22. doi:10.1196/annals.1308.001 1021/1/1 [pii]

Deas, D., & Thomas, S. E. (2001). An overview of controlled studies of adolescent substance abuse treatment. *American Journal on Addictions, 10*(2), 178–189. doi:10.1080/105504901750227822

Dennis, M., Godley, S. H., Diamond, G., Tims, F. M., Babor, T., Donaldson, J., . . . Funk, R. (2004). The Cannabis Youth Treatment (CYT) Study: Main findings from two randomized trials. *Journal of Substance Abuse Treatment, 27*(3), 197–213. doi:S0740-5472(04)00087-X [pii] 10.1016/j.jsat.2003.09.005

Dennis, M. L., Chan, Y. F., & Funk, R. R. (2006). Development and validation of the GAIN Short Screener (GSS) for internalizing, externalizing and substance use disorders and crime/violence problems among adolescents and adults. *American Journal of Addiction, 15*(Suppl. 1), 80–91. doi:G007886P85267424 [pii] 10.1080/10550490601006055

Di Chiara, G. (1999). Drug addiction as dopamine-dependent associative learning disorder. *European Journal of Pharmacology, 375*(1–3), 13–30. Retrieved October 2015, from http://www.sciencedirect.com/science/article/pii/S0014299999003726

Elder, J. P., Ayala, G. X., & Harris, S. (1999). Theories and intervention approaches to health-behavior change in primary care. *American Journal of Preventive Medicine, 17*(4), 275–284. Retrieved October 2015, from http://www.sciencedirect.com/science/article/pii/S074937979900094X

Fisher, S. L., Bucholz, K. K., Reich, W., Fox, L., Kuperman, S., Kramer, J., . . . Bierut, L. J. (2006). Teenagers are right—parents do not know much: An analysis of adolescent-parent agreement on reports of adolescent substance use, abuse, and dependence. *Alcoholism: Clinical and Experimental Research, 30*(10), 1699–1710. doi:ACER205 [pii] 10.1111/j.1530-0277.2006.00205.x

Ford, C. A., Millstein, S. G., Halpern-Felsher, B. L., & Irwin, C. E., Jr. (1997). Influence of physician confidentiality assurances on adolescents' willingness to disclose information and seek future health care. A randomized controlled trial. *Journal of the American Medical Association, 278*(12), 1029–1034. Retrieved October 2015, from http://www.ncbi.nlm.nih.gov/entrez/query.fcgi?cmd=Retrieve&db=PubMed&dopt=Citation&list_uids=9307357

Ginsburg, K. R. (2007). Viewing our adolescent patients through a positive lens. *Contemporary Pediatrics, 24*, 65–76.

Goldenring, J. M., & Cohen, G. (1988). Getting into adolescent heads. *Contemporary Pediatrics, 5*(7), 75–90.

Grisso, T., Barnum, R., Fletcher, K. E., Cauffman, E., & Peuschold, D. (2001). Massachusetts Youth Screening Instrument for mental health needs of juvenile justice youths. *Journal of the American Academy of Child and Adolescent Psychiatry, 40*(5), 541–548. doi:S0890-8567(09)60684-5 [pii] 10.1097/00004583-200105000-00013

Hagan, J. F., Shaw, J. S., & Duncan, P. (2008). *Bright Futures guidelines for health supervision of infants, children, and adolescents (3rd ed.).* Elk Grove Village, IL: American Academy of Pediatrics.

Haller, D. M., Meynard, A., Lefebvre, D., Ukoumunne, O. C., Narring, F., & Broers, B. (2014). Effectiveness of training family physicians to deliver a brief intervention to address excessive substance use among young patients: A cluster randomized controlled trial. *Canadian Medical Association*

Journal, *186*(8), E263–E272. Retrieved October 2015, from http://www.ncbi.nlm.nih.gov/pubmed/24616136

Harris, S. K., Csemy, L., Sherritt, L., Starostova, O., Van Hook, S., Bacic, J., . . . New England Partnership for Substance Abuse Research. (April 30–May 3, 2011). Computer-facilitated screening and physician brief advice to reduce substance use among adolescent primary care patients: A multi-site international trial. Poster Symposium at the 2011 Pediatric Academic Societies Annual Meeting, Denver, CO.

Harris, S. K., Csemy, L., Sherritt, L., Starostova, O., Van Hook, S., Johnson, J., . . . Knight, J. R. (2012). Computer-facilitated substance use screening and brief advice for teens in primary care: an international trial. *Pediatrics*, *129*(6), 1072–1082. doi:peds.2011-1624 [pii] 10.1542/peds.2011-1624

Hingson, R. W., Heeren, T., & Winter, M. R. (2006). Age at drinking onset and alcohol dependence: Age at onset, duration, and severity. *Archives of Pediatric and Adolescent Medicine*, *160*(7), 739–746. Retrieved October 2015, from http://www.ncbi.nlm.nih.gov/entrez/query.fcgi?cmd=Retrieve&db=PubMed&dopt=Citation&list_uids=16818840

Hingson, R. W., & Zha, W. (2009). Age of drinking onset, alcohol use disorders, frequent heavy drinking, and unintentionally injuring oneself and others after drinking. *Pediatrics*, *123*(6), 1477–1484. doi:123/6/1477 [pii] 10.1542/peds.2008-2176

Hingson, R. W., Zha, W., & Weitzman, E. R. (2009). Magnitude of and trends in alcohol-related mortality and morbidity among U.S. college students ages 18-24, 1998-2005. *Journal of Studies on Alcohol and Drugs Supplement*, 16, 12–20. Retrieved October 2015, from http://www.ncbi.nlm.nih.gov/entrez/query.fcgi?cmd=Retrieve&db=PubMed&dopt=Citation&list_uids=19538908

Johnston, L. D., O'Malley, P. M., Bachman, J. G., Schulenberg, J. E., & Miech, R. A. (2014). *Monitoring the Future national survey results on drug use, 1975–2013, Vol. 1. Secondary school students*. Retrieved October 2015, from http://www.monitoringthefuture.org/pubs/monographs/mtf-vol1_2013.pdf

Johnston, L. D., O'Malley, P. M., Miech, R. A., Bachman, J. G., & Schulenberg, J. E. (2014). *Monitoring the Future national results on drug use: 1975-2013: Overview, key findings on adolescent drug use*. Retrieved October 2015, from http://www.monitoringthefuture.org/pubs/monographs/mtf-overview2013.pdf

Kelly, S. M., Gryczynski, J., Mitchell, S. G., Kirk, A., O'Grady, K. E., & Schwartz, R. P. (2014). Validity of brief screening instrument for adolescent tobacco, alcohol, and drug use. *Pediatrics*, *133*(5), 819–826. Retrieved October 2015, from http://www.ncbi.nlm.nih.gov/pubmed/24753528

Knight, J. R., Sherritt, L., Harris, S. K., Gates, E. C., & Chang, G. (2003). Validity of brief alcohol screening tests among adolescents: a comparison of the AUDIT, POSIT, CAGE, and CRAFFT. *Alcoholism: Clinical and Experimental Research*, *27*(1), 67–73. doi:10.1097/01.alc.0000046598.59317.3a

Knight, J. R., Harris, S. K., Sherritt, L., Van Hook, S., Lawrence, N., Brooks, T., . . . Kulig, J. (2007). Prevalence of positive substance abuse screen results among adolescent primary care patients. *Archives of Pediatrics and Adolescent Medicine*, *161*(11), 1035.

Kraemer, K. L. (2007). The cost-effectiveness and cost-benefit of screening and brief intervention for unhealthy alcohol use in medical settings. *Substance Abuse*, *28*(3), 67–77.

Levy, S., Williams, J. F., & Knight, J. R. (2008). Screening, brief intervention, and referral to treatment for adolescents: Companion clinical case. *Journal of Addiction Medicine*, *2*(4), 222–226. Retrieved October 2015, from http://familymed.uthscsa.edu/sstart/documents/SBIRT Adolescent Case.pdf

Levy, S., Weiss, R., Sherritt, L., Ziemnik, R., Spalding, A., Van Hook, S., & Shrier, L. A. (2014). An electronic screen for triaging adolescent substance use by risk levels. *Journal of the American Medical Association Pediatrics*, *168*(9), 822–828. Retrieved October 2015, from http://www.ncbi.nlm.nih.gov/pubmed/25070067

Macaulay, A. P., Griffin, K. W., Gronewold, E., Williams, C., & Botvin, G. J. (2005). Parenting practices and adolescent drug-related knowledge, attitudes, norms and behavior. *Journal of Alcohol and Drug Education*, *49*(2), 67–83.

Martino, S., Grilo, C. M., & Fehon, D. C. (2000). Development of the drug abuse screening test for adolescents (DAST-A). *Addictive Behaviors*, *25*(1), 57–70. doi:S0306-4603(99)00030-1 [pii]

Miller, G. (1990). *The Substance Abuse Subtle Screening Inventory—Adolescent Version*. Bloomington, IN: SASSI Institute.

Miller, J. W., Naimi, T. S., Brewer, R. D., & Jones, S. E. (2007). Binge drinking and associated health risk behaviors among high school students. *Pediatrics*, *119*(1), 76–85. Retrieved October 2015, from http://www.ncbi.nlm.nih.gov/entrez/query.fcgi?cmd=Retrieve&db=PubMed&dopt=Citation&list_uids=17200273

Miller, W. R., & Rollnick, S. (2013). *Motivational interviewing: Helping people change* (3rd ed.). New York, NY: Guilford Press.

Monti, P. M., Colby, S. M., Barnett, N. P., Spirito, A., Rohsenow, D. J., Myers, M., . . . Lewander, W. (1999). Brief intervention for harm reduction with alcohol-positive older adolescents in a hospital emergency department. *Journal of Consulting and Clinical Psychology*, *67*(6), 989–994. Retrieved October 2015, from http://www.ncbi.nlm.nih.gov/entrez/query.fcgi?cmd=Retrieve&db=PubMed&dopt=Citation&list_uids=10596521

Monti, P. M., Barnett, N. P., Colby, S. M., Gwaltney, C. J., Spirito, A., Rohsenow, D. J., & Woolard, R. (2007). Motivational interviewing versus feedback only in emergency care for young adult problem drinking. *Addiction*, *102*(8), 1234–1243. doi:10.1111/j.1360-0443.2007.01878.x

National Institute on Alcohol Abuse and Alcoholism. (2011a). *Alcohol screening and brief intervention for youth: A practitioner's guide*. (NIH Publication No. 11-7805). Retrieved October 2015, from http://pubs.niaaa.nih.gov/publications/Practitioner/YouthGuide/YouthGuide.pdf

National Institute on Alcohol Abuse and Alcoholism. (2011b). *RFA-AA-12-008: Evaluation of NIAAAs alcohol screening guide for children and adolescents (R01)*. Retrieved October 2015, from http://grants.nih.gov/grants/guide/rfa-files/RFA-AA-12-008.html

National Institute on Drug Abuse (NIDA). (2008). *RFA-DA-08-021: Screening, brief intervention and referral to treatment (SBIRT) for drug abuse in general medical settings (R01)*. Retrieved October 2015, from http://grants.nih.gov/grants/guide/rfa-files/RFA-DA-08-021.html

Patrick, M. E., Schulenberg, J. E., Martz, M. E., Maggs, J. L., O'Malley, P. M., & Johnston, L. D. (2013). Extreme binge drinking among 12th-grade students in the United

States: Prevalence and predictors. *Journal of the American Medical Association Pediatrics, 167*(11), 1019–1025. doi:10.1001/jamapediatrics.2013.2392

Students Against Destructive Decisions (SADD). (2005). *Contract for life: A foundation for trust and caring.* Marlborough, MA: Author. Retrieved October 2015, fromhttps://www.stopdui.org/contract_for_life.pdf

Shrier, L. A., Rhoads, A., Burke, P., Walls, C., & Blood, E. A. (2014). Real-time, contextual intervention using mobile technology to reduce marijuana use among youth: A pilot study. *Addictive Behaviors, 39*(1), 173–180. doi:10.1016/j.addbeh.2013.09.028

Society for Adolescent Medicine. (2004). Access to health care for adolescents and young adults. *Journal of Adolescent Health, 35*(4), 342–344. Retrieved October 2015, from http://www.ncbi.nlm.nih.gov/entrez/query.fcgi?cmd=Retrieve&db=PubMed&dopt=Citation&list_uids=15481116

Spirito, A., Monti, P. M., Barnett, N. P., Colby, S. M., Sindelar, H., Rohsenow, D. J., . . . Myers, M. (2004). A randomized clinical trial of a brief motivational intervention for alcohol-positive adolescents treated in an emergency department. *Journal of Pediatrics, 145*(3), 396–402. Retrieved October 2015, from http://www.jpeds.com/article/S0022-3476(04)00378-6/pdf

Stern, S. A., Meredith, L. S., Gholson, J., Gore, P., & D'Amico, E. J. (2007). Project CHAT: A brief motivational substance abuse intervention for teens in primary care. *Journal of Substance Abuse Treatment, 32*(2), 153–165. Retrieved October 2015, from http://www.ncbi.nlm.nih.gov/pubmed/17306724

Stuart, H. C., Shock, N. W., Breckenridge, M. E., & Vincent, E. L. (1953). Physical growth and development. In J. M. Seidman (Ed.), *The adolescent: A book of readings* (xviii, pp. 88–153). Forth Worth, TX: The Dryden Press. Retrieved October 2015, from http://psycnet.apa.org/books/11402/004

Substance Abuse and Mental Health Services Administration. (2009a). *About screening, brief intervention, and referral to treatment (SBIRT)* Rockville, MD: Center for Substance Abuse Treatment. Retrieved October 2015, from http://www.samhsa.gov/sbirt/about

Substance Abuse and Mental Health Services Administration. (2009b). *The TEDS report: Substance abuse treatment admissions referred by the criminal justice system.* Rockville, MD: Author. Retrieved October 2015, from http://www.samhsa.gov/data/2k9/211/211CJadmits2k9.pdf

Tait, R. J., Hulse, G. K., Robertson, S. I., & Sprivulis, P. C. (2005). Emergency department-based intervention with adolescent substance users: 12-month outcomes. *Drug and Alcohol Dependence, 79*(3), 359–363. Retrieved October 2015, from http://www.sciencedirect.com/science/article/pii/S0376871605000943

US Preventive Services Task Force. (2013). *Screening and behavioral counseling interventions in primary care to reduce alcohol misuse: Recommendation statement (AHRQ Publication No. 12-05171-EF-3).* Retrieved October 2015, from http://www.uspreventiveservicestaskforce.org/uspstf12/alcmisuse/alcmisuserfinalrs.htm

Van Cleave, J., Gortmaker, S. L., & Perrin, J. M. (2010). Dynamics of obesity and chronic health conditions among children and youth. *Journal of the American Medical Association, 303*(7), 623–630. doi:303/7/623 [pii] 10.1001/jama.2010.104

Van Hook, S., Harris, S. K., Brooks, T., Carey, P., Kossack, R., Kulig, J., & Knight, J. R. (2007). The "six T's": Barriers to screening teens for substance abuse in primary care. *Journal of Adolescent Health, 40*(5), 456–461. Retrieved October 2015, from http://www.ncbi.nlm.nih.gov/entrez/query.fcgi?cmd=Retrieve&db=PubMed&dopt=Citation&list_uids=17448404

Walton, M. A., Bohnert, K., Resko, S., Barry, K. L., Chermack, S. T., Zucker, R. A., . . . Blow, F. C. (2013). Computer and therapist based brief interventions among cannabis-using adolescents presenting to primary care: One year outcomes. *Drug and Alcohol Dependence, 132*(3), 646–653. Retrieved October 2015, from http://www.ncbi.nlm.nih.gov/pubmed/23711998

White, A. M., Truesdale, M. C., Bae, J. G., Ahmad, S., Wilson, W. A., Best, P. J., & Swartzwelder, H. S. (2002). Differential effects of ethanol on motor coordination in adolescent and adult rats. *Pharmacology Biochemistry and Behavior, 73*(3), 673–677. doi:S0091305702008602 [pii]

Willner, P. (2000). Further validation and development of a screening instrument for the assessment of substance misuse in adolescents. *Addiction (Abingdon, England), 95*(11), 1691–1698. Retrieved October 2015, from http://www.ncbi.nlm.nih.gov/pubmed/11219372

Wilson, C. R., Sherritt, L., Gates, E., & Knight, J. R. (2004). Are clinical impressions of adolescent substance use accurate? *Pediatrics, 114*(5), e536–e540. doi:114/5/e536 [pii] 10.1542/peds.2004-0098

Winters, K. C. (1992). Development of an adolescent alcohol and other drug abuse screening scale: Personal Experience Screening Questionnaire. *Addictive Behaviors, 17*(5), 479–490. doi:0306-4603(92)90008-J [pii]

Winters, K. C., & Lee, C-Y. S. (2008). Likelihood of developing an alcohol and cannabis use disorder during youth: association with recent use and age. *Drug and Alcohol Dependence, 92*(1–3), 239–247. Retrieved October 2015, from http://www.pubmedcentral.nih.gov/articlerender.fcgi?artid=2219953&tool=pmcentrez&rendertype=abstract

Yoast, R. A., Fleming, M., & Balch, G. I. (2007). Reactions to a concept for physician intervention in adolescent alcohol use. *Journal of Adolescent Health, 41*(1), 35–41. doi:S1054-139X(07)00100-0 [pii] 10.1016/j.jadohealth.2007.02.008

Sleep Impairment

Mairav Cohen-Zion *and* Natali Svirsky

Abstract

Sleep is a vital physiological state, and it is essential for optimal daytime function. Sleep patterns undergo tremendous quantitative and structural changes throughout the maturational process from infancy to late adolescence. These universal alterations in sleep and sleep patterns reflect the essential need for optimal sleep during normal healthy development. Unfortunately, sleep loss has become omnipresent in modern adult culture and has also become a widespread phenomenon among children, particularly with respect to adolescents. Specifically, sleep loss in adolescence is a function of multiple normative endogenous changes often amplified by exogenous influences. Substance abuse has also achieved epidemic proportions among today's adolescents, with well-documented negative functional outcomes. This chapter summarizes objective and subjective studies examining the bidirectional links between alcohol and substance use and inadequate sleep and/or sleep patterns in adolescents.

Key Words: adolescence, sleep, sleep loss, delayed sleep phase, alcohol, marijuana, substance use, risk behaviors

Extensive research indicates that neurobiological sleep-regulatory systems continually mature throughout late adolescence (Crowley, Acebo, & Carskadon, 2007; Taylor, Jenni, Acebo, & Carskadon, 2005). It has also been proposed that altered sleep patterns during adolescence are not solely organic in nature. They could derive from the multiple psychosocial and behavioral changes that youth undergo during this critical developmental period (Feinberg & Campbell, 2010). Sleep, a vital biological function, has been shown to play a crucial role in healthy adolescent development by impacting upon daytime behavior, emotional regulation, and cognitive performance (Beebe, 2011; Wolfson & Carskadon, 2003). Unfortunately, in terms of both time and quality, many teenagers do not get sufficient sleep. Survey data in the last decade suggest the vast majority of adolescents today suffer from chronic sleep loss and associated pathological sleepiness (Colten, Altevogt, & Institute of Medicine, 2006; National Sleep Foundation, 2006; Wolfson & Carskadon, 1998). Under conditions of sleep debt, otherwise healthy youth are at high risk of developing sleep-related problems, that is, "downs" or irritable moods, performing below standard at school, and/or exercising poor judgment. They may also be more prone to risk-taking behavior, involving alcohol and substance abuse, physical violence, unprotected sexual activity, and/or drunken/irresponsible driving (McKnight-Eily et al., 2011; O'Brien & Mindell, 2005). Furthermore, a contemporary view of the implications of poor sleep for adolescent clinical populations suggests disturbed sleep patterns may not only help sustain medical or psychiatric conditions but also trigger them (Brand & Kirov, 2011). Given the widespread occurrence of both sleep loss and alcohol and substance use among today's youth, this chapter will review the

Healthy and Unhealthy Sleep Patterns in Adolescence

There are several well-established, sleep-related developmental changes in adolescence. Probably, the most dramatic universal change, consistently observed in the transition from childhood to adolescence, is the significant decline in slow-wave sleep (SWS) or deep sleep and its replacement with lighter sleep stages (primarily stage 2) (Ohayon, Carskadon, Guilleminault, & Vitiello, 2004). A more modest but well-documented decline also occurs in rapid eye movement (REM) sleep (Ohayon et al., 2004). Perhaps the most observable hallmark of adolescent sleep-related behavior is the intrinsic delay in circadian (24-hour) sleep/wake rhythm, which has been hypothesized to occur due to altered melatonin secretion and/or increased sensitivity of the circadian pacemaker to light during adolescence (Carskadon, Acebo, Richardson, Tate, & Seifer, 1997; Crowley et al., 2007; Taylor et al., 2005). This endogenous delay in circadian sleep phase results in adolescents often not feeling physiologically tired enough to fall asleep until late at night, and thus the sleep period often continues into the late morning. Thus, even if teens were to go to bed at a more normative bedtime (often requested by their parents), it would likely take them an extended period of time to fall asleep; thus, their natural sleep period would remain approximately the same. This tendency for delayed sleep/wake schedules, that is, delayed bedtimes and wake times, becomes significantly more prominent with age and pubertal maturation (from early to late adolescence) (Gradisar, Gardner, & Dohnt, 2011; Wolfson & Carskadon, 1998) and seems stable across genders (Wolfson & Carskadon, 1998), cultures (Gradisar et al., 2011), and certain environmental characteristics (e.g., urban vs. rural areas) (Loessl et al., 2008).

These intrinsic changes in sleep/wake regulatory mechanism interact with a wide range of environmental influences. The adolescent years are known for increases in academic demands, after-school employment, and an abundance of extracurricular activities and/or social pressures and demands. Many teenagers report staying up later to complete homework and communicate with peers (Shochat, Flint-Bretler, & Tzischinsky, 2010), which has been made more accessible in the nighttime hours by the availability of Internet and electronic communication devices, such as online social networks and mobile phones. These behavioral and environmental stimuli intensify the typical adolescent's predisposition toward evening preference, resulting in a more extreme sleep outcome.

The collective shift in sleep/wake patterns in adolescence is likely the result of the combined effects of intrinsic delays in sleep regulatory mechanisms (homeostatic and circadian systems) and simultaneous extrinsic academic, social, economic, and other environmental demands (Carskadon & Acebo, 2002; Colrain & Baker, 2011). The additive and interactive effects of these internal and external influences on sleep results in the aforementioned preference for a delayed sleep-wake schedule but also a natural propensity to maintain this delayed nocturnal schedule when permitted (e.g., weekend and holidays). It is therefore not surprising that among Westernized cultures, we often label our teenagers as "night owls."

The need for sleep declines by about 40% from infancy through the onset of adolescence, that is, from about 16 hours to approximately 9 hours per night (Jenni, Achermann, & Carskadon, 2005). Unlike the gradual decrease in sleep amounts seen across earlier developmental stages, the required 9-hour sleep need remains stable over the course of adolescence (Carskadon et al., 1980). Despite this biological need, most adolescents (approximately 80%–90%) are unable to consistently achieve adequate sleep (National Sleep Foundation, 2006; Noland, Price, Dake, & Telljohann, 2009). Several environmental issues are known to influence the adolescent's sleep schedule and ability to achieve adequate sleep quantity. For example, the delayed sleep pattern during adolescence becomes problematic during the school year, when societal norms and expectations require teens to wake up early for morning classes, resulting in an average weeknight sleep duration of about 6–7 hours per night in teens 13 to 19 years old (Gradisar et al., 2011; Wolfson & Carskadon, 1998). This unhealthy sleep pattern results in a chronic state of partial sleep loss that intensifies with age and grade level (Gibson et al., 2006; Loessl et al., 2008), may be more pronounced for girls than boys (i.e., girls tend to have earlier self-imposed wake times), and may be intensified by cultural norms and expectations (e.g., bedtimes are significantly later among Asian than North American or European teens) (Gradisar et al., 2011). This accumulated sleep loss is particularly apparent during the week when academic demands

bidirectional effects of these health-related problems and their associated functional and behavioral outcomes.

are at their greatest. This sleep loss is also associated with highly erratic sleep/wake schedules with significant night-to-night variability (i.e., short nights are followed by compensatory long nights), excessive daytime sleepiness (particularly during early-morning classes), and longer and more delayed weekend sleep. Despite many adolescents' attempts to compensate for sleep loss (e.g., after-school napping or "catch-up" weekend sleep), most teens rapidly accrue a significant sleep debt (up to 2 hours per night), which rapidly accumulates over time.

Effects of Alcohol and Marijuana Use on Objective Sleep Parameters

The vast majority of research examining links between sleep and substance use in youth has utilized survey or self-report data. Unfortunately, research using objective measures of sleep assessment (e.g., polysomnography [PSG]) has primarily been conducted in younger and older adult populations. Therefore, our understanding of the effects of alcohol on electroencephalographic (EEG) activity during sleep is based primarily on the adult literature. These data have consistently shown acute and heavy alcohol intake leads to reduced REM sleep, increased SWS, sleep fragmentation (particularly in the second half of the night), and reduced sleep time (Stein & Friedmann, 2005). Although these effects become more moderate with chronic use, a clear "REM rebound" and co-occurring inhibition of SWS is reliably seen with alcohol withdrawal (Stein & Friedmann, 2005), suggesting sleep architecture and sleep quality remain disturbed during ongoing alcohol use and cessation.

Similar to the aforementioned findings, research data on PSG-recorded sleep and marijuana (MJ) use has also been primary conducted in adult populations. Moreover, these studies are limited in number and fraught with methodological limitations, such as small sample sizes, heterogeneity of samples (e.g., chronicity of use, psychiatric comorbidity), and type and dosage of cannabis administration, among other concerns (Jacobus, Bava, Cohen-Zion, Mahmood, & Tapert, 2009; Schierenbeck, Riemann, Berger, & Hornyak, 2008). Nonetheless, a few higher quality studies in adults have linked acute heavy MJ use with decreased REM sleep, mild increases in SWS, and shorter sleep-onset latencies (SOL; time taken to fall asleep) (Jacobus et al., 2009; Schierenbeck et al., 2008). Frequent and chronic users have been shown to continue to show these alterations in sleep architecture as well as a gradual SWS stabilization (Jacobus et al., 2009; Schierenbeck et al., 2008). As is the case with alcohol withdrawal, abrupt cessation of chronic MJ use causes a reversal of EEG sleep activity (i.e., SWS suppression coupled with REM overexpression). Furthermore, sleep initiation difficulties and greater reports of vivid dreaming (consistent with elevated REM sleep time) continue up to 45 days of abstinence (Budney, Hughes, Moore, & Novy, 2001; Budney, Moore, Vandrey, & Hughes, 2003).

Despite the scarcity of PSG data in chronic marijuana- and alcohol-using youth, three highly controlled studies, two in young adults (ages 18–30 years) (Bolla et al., 2008, 2010) and one in adolescents (ages 16–21 years) (Cohen-Zion et al., 2009), demonstrated substantial sleep disruption following abrupt cessation of both heavy alcohol and marijuana use (all participants screened positive for marijuana use prior to MJ cessation). When compared to 14 young adult nonusers, 17 heavy users showed a dramatic initial reduction in SWS (27 vs. 70 min/night) (Bolla et al., 2008), which improved but did not return to healthy nonusing levels in 18 heavy MJ users over a 14-day abstinence period (Bolla et al., 2010). In contrast to adult data, REM suppression was not visible initially in this young sample; however, with abstinence, REM suppression was more apparent (34 min/night less than baseline measures) (Bolla et al., 2010). Although it is impossible to completely disentangle the effects of these substances on sleep, Cohen-Zion and colleagues (2009) showed that in 29 chronic and heavy adolescent users, past-month alcohol use predicted REM sleep alterations, while past-month marijuana use predicted SWS changes (immediately following cessation). In regard to sleep quantity and continuity measures, progressive reductions in sleep duration and elevations in both time taken to fall asleep and time spent awake at night occur starting immediately following cessation (Bolla et al., 2008). The objective sleep disturbances seen in these young samples seemed to persist for at least the first 2 weeks of abstinence (Bolla et al., 2010); however, most seem to abate within a 1-month period (Cohen-Zion et al., 2009). Due to the scarcity of PSG data in substance-using adolescents, additional objective studies are needed to confirm these results.

The aforementioned findings suggest a clear reaction of sleep regulatory mechanisms in response to alcohol and MJ use and cessation during adolescence. These findings are particularly disconcerting given the typical adolescent's substance use patterns, which are often erratic in nature (i.e., variable frequency, type intake, and dosage), such that most teens tend to use a substance for one to a few days and then stop for several days and so forth. These intermittent use patterns result in a constant flux of sleep mechanisms responding to these chemical changes. In addition, teens often engage in illicit drug use, other than alcohol and MJ use, as well as polysubstance use, which may exponentially deregulate sleep processes and patterns; however, due to the extreme shortage of PSG studies examining these issues, no clear insights can be made at this time. Additional objective sleep studies are sorely needed to confirm the summarized findings in alcohol- and MJ-using teens and reveal unknown effects of a wide range of other substances on the adolescent sleep mechanisms. The adolescent brain and specifically neurobiological sleep/wake systems continue to mature during this developmental period. Deregulation of these crucial functions may interfere with healthy physiological and neurological development, the behavioral and functional consequences of which we are only now beginning to identify.

Bidirectional Links Between Self-Reported Sleep Loss and Substance Use

Both inadequate sleep and substance use have achieved epidemic proportions in the United States and worldwide (Colten et al., 2006; Johnson & Breslau, 2001). Descriptive studies and survey data have primarily attempted to examine how substance use may affect self-reported sleep disturbances in adolescence and alternatively how inadequate or insufficient sleep and associated fatigue may contribute to the development and maintenance of use patterns. One of the main questions of interest is whether sleep loss and/or premorbid sleep disturbances and associated outcomes, such as daytime sleepiness, irritability, and other negative behavioral outcomes, may put youth at heightened risk for substance use as a means of increasing alertness (e.g., nicotine, caffeine, illicit or prescription stimulants) or increasing the ability to sleep (e.g., alcohol, marijuana). Regular use of these substances may increase the adolescent's vulnerability to a positive feedback loop of escalating sleep difficulties and problems in daytime functioning, temporarily masked by increasing substance use. Another central question is whether teens with histories of alcohol and substance use may suffer from sleep disruptions as a function of withdrawal, thereby increasing their chances for relapse as a means of self-medication. Following is an overview of the research findings attempting to answer these important questions.

Descriptive studies have consistently shown that during adolescence sleep deprivation increases the likelihood of engaging in a wide range of risky behaviors, including alcohol and illicit drug use (O'Brien & Mindell, 2005). A large representative survey of over 12,000 private and public high school students (grades 9–12) from the 1997 US Youth Risk Behavior Survey found that close to 70% of teens do not get the required amount of nightly sleep hours and that those getting under 8 hours of sleep per night had greater odds of caffeine (OD = 1.1), nicotine (OD = 1.7), alcohol (odds ratio 1.6), and marijuana use (OD = 1.5), among other high-risk behaviors, such as current sexual activity and physical violence (McKnight-Eily et al., 2011).

Similar results were found in a study using a more comprehensive and standardized measure of sleep in adolescents, the School Sleep Habits Survey (SSHS), the most widely used instrument for the subjective assessment of adolescent sleep pattern (Wolfson et al., 2003). In this study of 388 high school students, living in rural, suburban, and urban areas, less than 10% of teens reported getting a sufficient amount of nightly sleep (O'Brien & Mindell, 2005). Moreover, those students reporting exceptionally short weeknight sleep durations (44%; <6.75 hours/night) endorsed greater alcohol use than those who were well rested (9%; >8.25 hours/night) (O'Brien & Mindell, 2005). Moreover, students whose bedtimes were significantly later on weekend nights when compared to school nights (more delta sleep between weekday and weekend bedtime) also showed greater alcohol use (O'Brien & Mindell, 2005). Interestingly, several studies have shown that longer weekend sleep durations do not seem to significantly influence overall alcohol consumption or drunkenness (O'Brien & Mindell, 2005; Pasch, Laska, Lytle, & Moe, 2010), suggesting that sleep overextension on weekends does not protect teens from the cumulative effects of weekday sleep loss. One potential explanation for these results may be that sleep insufficiency and potential weekday misalignment between extrinsically imposed sleep patterns and intrinsic sleep/wake circadian rhythms may lead to more erratic sleep/wake schedules (i.e., greater variability in bedtimes and wake times) and varying levels of sleepiness across the day and night, which in turn may make teens more susceptible to alcohol use and other risk behaviors.

International studies examining this relationship suggest the aforementioned data are not culture specific. Based on past-month self-reported sleep durations, over 8,000 Taiwanese junior high and high school students were classified as "shorter" sleepers (13%; <6 hours/night), "average" sleepers (79%; 6–8 hours/night), or "longer" sleepers (8%; >8 hours/night) (Yen, King, & Tang, 2010). After controlling for sociodemographic factors and depression, shorter sleepers were more likely to use psychoactive substances, when compared to the "average and longer sleepers," with this relationship being most apparent among the older adolescents (Yen et al., 2010). Supporting data have been published across numerous countries, including but not limited to France (Vignau et al., 1997), Italy (Giannotti, Cortesi, Sebastiani, & Ottaviano, 2002), Norway (Pallesen et al., 2011), Finland (Tynjala, Kannas, & Levalahti, 1997), Korea (Yang, Kim, Patel, & Lee, 2005), and South Africa (Fakier & Wild, 2011), suggesting this phenomenon has become a significant worldwide public health issue.

Despite the multitude of international, cross-sectional studies linking sleep insufficiency and alcohol/substance use in adolescence, it remains unclear which of these related behaviors constitutes the cause and which the consequence. Most recently, a handful of prospective studies have attempted to answer this important question (Catrett & Gaultney, 2009; Roberts, Roberts, & Duong, 2008, 2009). In a large follow-up study of over 3,000 representative community-based adolescents (ages 11–17 years) living in an urban area, teen sleep, health factors, and daytime functioning were tracked for two waves occurring 1 year apart (Roberts, Roberts, & Chan, 2008; Roberts et al., 2009). Consistent with studies showing less sleep time with age, from wave I to wave II, the percentage of teens sleeping less than 6 hours per night on weeknights (in past month) increased from 20% to 25%, while those getting 9 or more hours decreased from 27% to 22%. Interestingly, they also found that teens suffering from sleep loss (<6 hours/night) or from at least one insomnia symptom (e.g., trouble initiating or maintaining sleep, nonrestorative sleep) and co-occurring tiredness were at greater risk of future alcohol and/or substance use problems (OR 0.9–2.6) (Roberts, Roberts, & Duong, 2008; Roberts et al., 2009). Similar data were found in another follow-up study of a representative US sample of over 4,000 7th- to 12th-grade students, which found self-reported insomnia, defined as troubled sleep and morning tiredness in the past year,

predicted cigarette smoking and drunken driving 1 year later. Interestingly, both studies found that in general the effects of sleep loss on subsequent substance use remained stable, even after controlling for the effects of school grade, gender, depressive symptoms (Catrett & Gaultney, 2009), other sociodemographic factors, pubertal status, insomnia, and overall baseline functioning (Roberts et al., 2009). In the most recent and longest prospective study examining sleep and substance use, Pasch, Latimer, Cance, Moe, and Lytle (2012) tracked 705 US teens for 2 years (across three overlapping cohorts between 2007 and 2010) and examined possible causal relationships using structural equation modeling. Similar to previous data, these researchers found that reduced sleep duration (both weekday and whole week) predicted greater cigarette and marijuana use 2 years later (Pasch et al., 2012). Not surprisingly, these relationships were found to be bidirectional, with higher baseline cigarette use leading to less weekend and overall sleep duration, whereas greater alcohol use at baseline predicted reduced weekend sleep and weekend oversleep (Pasch et al., 2012). Although limited in number and length, longitudinal data suggest a clear causal link between sleep loss and alcohol/substance use in adolescents. Additional longer term data are sorely needed in order to further elucidate these relationships.

In addition to the examination of the direct effects of sleep loss substance use, a few studies have attempted to examine its indirect effects via moderators or mediators, such as gender or perceived sense of sleepiness (Pasch et al., 2010; Tynjala et al., 1997). Excessive daytime sleepiness is one of the most unpleasant physiological outcomes of poor or insufficient sleep. In a large Finnish study, coordinated by the World Health Organization, of over 4,000 adolescents (11–15 years), Tynjala et al. (1997) attempted to understand the interrelationships between sleep patterns, subjective sleepiness, and psychoactive substance use (alcohol, tobacco, and caffeine). They found that self-reported daily sleepiness (primarily in morning hours) increased dramatically with age and was considerably more common in older adolescents. Moreover, using structural equation modeling, the authors found that among older adolescents (age 15 years), sleep habits (primarily delayed bedtimes and to a lesser degree weekend bedtime delay) and perceived sleepiness (particularly in morning hours) accounted for 26% of the variance in alcohol and nicotine intake in boys and 12% of the variance in girls. Conversely, substance use and perceived sleepiness explained 42% and 16% of the variance, respectively, for boys and girls, in the adolescents' sleep patterns (Tynjala et al., 1997). These findings suggest sleepiness, sleep patterns, and substance use are highly intertwined during adolescence and that these interrelationships may strengthen with age and with male gender. Adolescents are experiencing chronic daily tiredness, which in combination with erratic sleep schedules and frequent use of substances suggests an unhealthy lifestyle, which may greatly affect their well-being.

In line with these data, several other studies have suggested the relationship between sleep and substance use in adolescence may differ as a function of gender. In a report of 242 high school students (9th–11th grade), Pasch et al. (2010) found that past month alcohol use and drunkenness were significantly associated with shorter weeknight sleep duration, however, when gender was included in this model, the relationship was significant for boys but not for girls. However, they did find that past month alcohol use was associated with later weekend bedtimes/weekend oversleep in girls but not in boys. (Pasch et al., 2010). These gender differences may in part reflect the known differences in substance use and sleep deficiency between girls and boys, with boys being more extreme in both. However, it may also suggest the relationship between sleep insufficiency and risk behaviors in adolescents may be more complex and multifactorial and in need of more investigation. In an attempt to categorize and elucidate these behavioral patterns, Laska, Pasch, Lust, Story, and Ehlinger (2009) performed a latent class analysis of health risk behaviors in 2,025 older adolescents and young adults (ages 18–25 years) attending a public university in the United States. Based on the identified risk behaviors, they found four distinctive "classes" or health-related homogeneous behavioral profiles per gender. The "high-risk" group was similar for males and females, 33% and 24% of sample, respectively, and was characterized as the greatest likelihood of reporting insufficient sleep (approximately 80% probability) and of engaging in high-risk behaviors (e.g., smoking cigarettes, binge drinking, having sex while intoxicated, and driving under the influence) (Laska et al., 2009). Although these data describe slightly older youth in living situations different to that of the typical high school student, nonetheless, these findings paint a coherent clustering of health-related risk behaviors and high-risk lifestyles among youth, which may have significant real-world

consequences and utility when identifying these at-risk populations and designing long-term intervention and prevention programs.

Although the majority of research in adolescent sleep and risk behaviors has focused on sleep quantity or sleep loss (mostly a consequence of too little opportunity for sleep), more recently the focus has also turned to adolescent insomnia (the inability to generate good sleep despite ample opportunity) as well as sleep quality (Johnson & Breslau, 2001; Ohayon, Roberts, Zulley, Smirne, & Priest, 2000) and how these sleep difficulties may impact and be impacted by risk behaviors. A recent study found the lifetime prevalence of insomnia (based on *DSM-IV* criteria) in community-dwelling adolescents (ages 13–16 years) was approximately 10% with 11 years being the median age of onset (Johnson & Roth, 2006). Interestingly, of those reporting past history of insomnia, 88% indicated they are currently suffering from insomnia symptoms, suggesting chronic insomnia may be common during adolescence (Johnson & Roth, 2006). Other studies have confirmed that the point prevalence of insomnia in adolescence is approximately 9% among US teens (Roane & Taylor, 2008) and about 4% among European adolescents (Ohayon et al., 2000).

A large survey of close to 14,000 adolescents (ages 12–17 years) from the 1994–1996 US National Household Survey of Drug Abuse found extensive evidence supporting the link between substance use and sleep problems (Johnson & Breslau, 2001). After controlling for sociodemographic and socioeconomic factors, teens who report troubles with sleep in the last 6 months were also more likely to smoke cigarettes (OR 1.5–3.2), drink alcohol (OR 2.4–3.7), or use other drugs (OR 2.6–3.7). Moreover, longer self-reported duration of alcohol and illicit substance use were associated with higher risk for sleep difficulties (Johnson & Breslau, 2001). Importantly, the relationship between substance use and sleep was attenuated when externalizing and internalizing problems were included in the model (Johnson & Breslau, 2001). Other epidemiologic studies indicate that a large percentage (25% to 52%) of teens suffering from insomnia suffer from a comorbid psychiatric disorder as well (Johnson & Roth, 2006; Ohayon et al., 2000). These studies therefore suggest these relationships of health issues and behaviors may be more complex and that the link between sleep and substance abuse problems may occur more commonly in the context of other behavioral and/or psychiatric problems.

In addition to survey and cross-sectional data, a couple of longitudinal studies have also attempted to examine the link between insomnia and risk behaviors in adolescence (Catrett & Gaultney, 2009; Roane & Taylor, 2008). A prospective study examining adolescent health in a representative US sample of over 4,300 middle and high school students found that after controlling for grade, gender, and current depression, self-reported insomnia (defined as troubled sleep and morning tiredness in the past year) was significantly associated with current tobacco use and predicted driving while intoxicated 2 years later (Catrett & Gaultney, 2009). Moreover, in a longer 7-year prospective study of over 3,500 adolescents (ages 12–18 years) who were followed up in young adulthood (ages 18–25 years), Roane and Taylor (2008) found that adolescents with insomnia were more likely to use alcohol, marijuana, and other drugs at baseline; and they were at increased risk for depression (OD = 1.5–3.0) and suicidal ideation (OD = 1.2–6.5) 7 years later (as young adults), even after controlling for psychopathology (Roane & Taylor, 2008). In sum, these studies suggest adolescent-onset insomnia seems to be pervasive and chronic in adolescence and may have significant and lasting negative health-related outcomes.

Both sleep restriction and sleep problems may significantly affect risk-related behavior, specifically psychoactive substance use, which in turn seems to further exacerbate sleep problems and reduce sleep amounts. These behavioral health profiles may place certain teens at heightened risk for a wide range of negative physical, behavioral, and psychiatric outcomes, both in the short and long term, and may ultimately affect adolescent and young adult health and quality of life. Furthermore, these studies suggest outcomes research should focus on developing and testing targeted treatment programs for sleep difficulties and substance use in order to examine the efficacy and effectiveness of these interventions on these physical, emotional, and behavioral outcomes.

Circadian Preference in Adolescence and Substance Use

Many human functions, including body temperature, melatonin secretion, sleepiness/alertness cycles, and morningness/eveningness (M/E) tendencies (a measure of sleep/wake preference) follow a 24-hour circadian rhythm. Morning (M) types, often called "morning larks," are phase advanced, with a preference for "normative" bedtimes and

relatively early wake times. In contrast, evening (E) types, or "night-owls," are phase delayed with a preference for later bedtimes and typically have difficulty with earlier more socially acceptable wake times. Infants and children (thorough preadolescence) are more commonly M types. However, starting in early adolescence, a large proportion of these M types gradually become E types. This progressively increasing evening preference occurs with advancing pubertal development and age (until young adulthood). Adolescent E types tend to report having shorter weekday sleep durations, more napping, more daytime sleepiness, and more dissatisfaction with their sleep (Gau et al., 2007; Giannotti et al., 2002). Moreover, in a large study of 1,747 Italian adolescents, E types used caffeinated beverages, nicotine, and alcohol more frequently than M types, with this tendency strengthening with increasing age (Giannotti et al., 2002). Several large studies also evidenced similar links between eveningness and habitual nicotine and alcohol use among young and older adolescents (ages 11–17 years), even after controlling for gender, education, and internalizing and externalizing problems (Gau et al., 2007; Negriff, Dorn, Pabst, & Susman, 2011; Pieters, Van Der Vorst, Burk, Wiers, & Engels, 2010), suggesting emotional or behavioral problems alone account for the observed link between evening preference and substance use.

Melatonin is an endogenous hormone, secreted by the pineal gland. Circulating levels of this hormone follow a circadian (24-hour) rhythm of secretion (high during the night and low during the day), which allows for the entrainment of many biological functions, including the sleep/wake cycle. Melatonin secretion is suppressed by light exposure and promoted by darkness. Dim-light melatonin onset (DLMO; onset of melatonin secretion) is one biological marker of circadian phase, and it can be used in combination with other sleep variables as an objective measure of M/E preference. The vast majority of studies (summarized earlier) examining circadian preference have used self-report measures to estimate sleep phase; however, one study of 21 adolescents (14–19 years) with past histories of substance abuse and current sleep difficulties found that teens with late salivary-based DLMO (i.e., E types) reported greater severity of substance abuse, dependence, and related problems, in comparison to teens with earlier DLMOs (Hasler, Bootzin, Cousins, Fridel, & Wenk, 2008). Moreover, in an elegant path analysis of over 700 young adolescents, Pieters et al. (2010) found puberty was both directly related to alcohol use, and indirectly related vis-à-vis changes in sleep regulation (e.g., delayed sleep phase and associated sleep problems), even after controlling for age, education, and psychopathology. In other words, early-maturing teens who tend to be E types may be at higher risk for substance use than their later maturing peers (irrespective of age). This finding was later supported by another study that found Caucasian and African American girls (ages 11–17 years), with earlier puberty timing (based on early onset of menarche) and eveningness preference, were more frequent cigarette smokers than girls with later puberty timing (Negriff et al., 2011), again suggesting early-maturing girls with marked eveningness tendencies may be at greater risk for substance use at the young age.

This association between puberty, eveningness tendencies, and substance use seems intuitive; however, direction and causality remain unclear. Thus, do teenagers whose biological tendency for later bedtimes (eveningness) have increased availability of substances (often taken at night) and substance-using friends, which, in combination with internal and external factors known to affect use patterns, leads to more substance use? It is also a known fact that teens readily and easily delay their bedtimes. This occurs in part because the circadian timing system is naturally adaptable to delays (Dahl & Lewin, 2002). Hence, it is also possible that teens interested in illicit substances artificially delay their bedtimes (irrespective of their natural inclination), in order participate in unsanctioned risk-taking behaviors. Furthermore, as previously mentioned, these delayed sleep/wake patterns often lead to chronic sleep loss and sleepiness (Gradisar et al., 2011), which once again are associated with more risk-taking behavior, including substance use (McKnight-Eily et al., 2011; O'Brien & Mindell, 2005). Further research is needed in order to clarify the causal nature of these relationships.

Treatment of Sleep and Substance Abuse During Adolescence

There are several potential causal pathways for sleep disturbance to increase the vulnerability for substance use; however, as detailed earlier, the exact nature of this relationship has yet to be well defined. Several potential causal factors have been identified, such as childhood sleep problems, maturational changes in the circadian timing system, environmental influences during adolescence, and emotional conditions (Wong, Brower, Fitzgerald, & Zucker, 2004; Wong, Brower, Nigg, & Zucker, 2010; Wong, Brower, & Zucker, 2009; Zhang et al., 2011). Additionally, adolescents may use alerting substances (e.g., coffee, caffeinated sodas, and energy drinks) to counteract the chronic fatigue and cognitive deficits due to insufficient or poor sleep, and/or they may ingest depressants (e.g., alcohol and marijuana) to induce drowsiness and sleep, and lessen mood difficulties at night. It has also been established that cessation of use in chronic substance users may cause significant decline in self-assessed sleep quality and observable sleep disturbances in teens and young adults, particularly in the first days and weeks of abstinence (Bolla et al., 2008, 2010; Cohen-Zion et al., 2009). These sleep-related side-effects may make teens particularly vulnerable to alcohol and substance use as a means of self-medicating for sleep problems. All these potential pathways suggest possible sleep psychoeducation and intervention at critical junctures in adolescence may be beneficial in reducing this inappropriate and harmful self-medication with psychoactive substances.

Nonetheless, despite the pervasiveness and scope of these problems, there are almost no studies examining possible interventions. A series of studies conducted by Bootzin and colleagues examined the effects of a six-session cognitive-behavioral-oriented sleep intervention, including cognitive, meditation, and educational components in a sample of 55 adolescents (13–19 years) who also underwent outpatient substance abuse treatment in the past year (Britton et al., 2010; Haynes et al., 2006). At posttreatment, completers (n = 23) improved on all sleep measures, including sleep duration, sleep onset time, number and duration of night-time awakenings, and sleep efficiency and quality, but no change in substance abuse frequency was observed. Although the overall treatment did not show significant differences between completers and noncompleters, follow-up data in a subgroup of 18 participants indicated frequency of at-home mindfulness meditation (10-minute sessions) was correlated with longer sleep duration (on average 1.25 hours/night) at posttreatment (6 weeks), which in turn was linked to lowered substance-related problems at follow-up (20 weeks) (Britton et al., 2010). These data suggest some components of cognitive-behavioral therapies may improve sleep and substance use outcomes in teens; however, additional treatment approaches and their mechanisms of action should be evaluated and long-term efficacy determined.

Conclusions

Sleep mechanisms continue to develop and mature through adolescence. These biological changes interact and are amplified by environmental influences and demands common in adolescence, resulting in pervasive and systematic sleep loss and disrupted sleep in this population. Alcohol and substance use, another highly problematic and widespread public health issue, has been consistently shown to have significant detrimental effects on sleep. This is of particular concern during this critical developmental period across which sensitive neurological changes continue to occur. The individual and combined effects of sleep insufficiency and substance use often place teens at risk for multiple other negative functional consequences, such as academic problems, somatic health problems, mental or emotional stress, and other risk behaviors.

Although the causal pathways of sleep difficulties and co-occurring substance use are not yet known, there is sufficient evidence to suggest that the relationship between these health issues is bidirectional. Specifically, healthy adolescents with delayed sleep preference and teens with excessive daytime fatigue and/or accumulating sleep debt are at increased risk for substance use; whether this is due to increased access to illicit substances at nighttime hours, a means of inducing alertness and/or drowsiness, or a combination of both remains unclear. In addition, chronic substance users, with or without comorbid mental health conditions, may be using psychoactive substances to regulate sleep difficulties or insomnia and may be at heightened risk for relapse due to the effects of cessation of use on sleep. Both scenarios are likely to lead to positive feedback loops of increasing sleep problems followed by heightened use in attempts to maintain sleep ability, which often leads to even more impoverished sleep patterns and sleep quality.

These findings in combination with the extensiveness of these problems in youth today suggest that targeted interventions should be systematically investigated and implemented. Intervention goals may include educating teens and their family members on healthy sleep and related circadian processes and the benefits of maintaining healthy sleep practices. In addition, in substance-using teens suffering from insomnia or other sleep disorders, treating the sleep difficulties may break the positive feedback loop, thereby possibly reducing future substance use or relapse.

Future Directions

• To conceptualize underlying causal mechanisms linking sleep loss, insomnia, and substance use in adolescent populations.

• To develop prospective longitudinal studies to better the understand alterations in sleep patterns of substance-using adolescents and the resulting negative functional outcomes.

• To develop and implement behavioral interventions designed at promoting balanced sleep practices in adolescents as well as targeted treatments for teens suffering from clinical sleep difficulties, which may be affecting their use patterns.

References

Beebe, D. W. (2011). Cognitive, behavioral, and functional consequences of inadequate sleep in children and adolescents. *Pediatric Clinics of North America, 58*(3), 649–665. doi: 10.1016/j.pcl.2011.03.002

Bolla, K. I., Lesage, S. R., Gamaldo, C. E., Neubauer, D. N., Funderburk, F. R., Cadet, J. L., & Benbrook, A. R. (2008). Sleep disturbance in heavy marijuana users. (Research Support, N.I.H., Extramural Research Support, N.I.H., Intramural). *Sleep, 31*(6), 901–908.

Bolla, K. I., Lesage, S. R., Gamaldo, C. E., Neubauer, D. N., Wang, N. Y., Funderburk, F. R., . . . Cadet, J. L. (2010). Polysomnogram changes in marijuana users who report sleep disturbances during prior abstinence. *Sleep Medicine, 11*(9), 882–889. doi: 10.1016/j.sleep.2010.02.013

Brand, S., & Kirov, R. (2011). Sleep and its importance in adolescence and in common adolescent somatic and psychiatric conditions. *International Journal of Genetic Medicine, 4*, 425–442. doi: 10.2147/IJGM.S11557

Britton, W. B., Bootzin, R. R., Cousins, J. C., Hasler, B. P., Peck, T., & Shapiro, S. L. (2010). The contribution of mindfulness practice to a multicomponent behavioral sleep intervention following substance abuse treatment in adolescents: A treatment-development study. *Substance Abuse, 31*(2), 86–97. doi: 10.1080/08897071003641297

Budney, A. J., Hughes, J. R., Moore, B. A., & Novy, P. L. (2001). Marijuana abstinence effects in marijuana smokers maintained in their home environment. *Archives of General Psychiatry, 58*(10), 917–924.

Budney, A. J., Moore, B. A., Vandrey, R. G., & Hughes, J. R. (2003). The time course and significance of cannabis withdrawal. *Journal of Abnormal Psychology, 112*(3), 393–402.

Carskadon, M. A., & Acebo, C. (2002). Regulation of sleepiness in adolescents: Update, insights, and speculation. *Sleep, 25*(6), 606–614.

Carskadon, M. A., Acebo, C., Richardson, G. S., Tate, B. A., & Seifer, R. (1997). An approach to studying circadian rhythms of adolescent humans. *Journal of Biological Rhythms, 12*(3), 278–289.

Carskadon, M. A., Harvey, K., Duke, P., Anders, T. F., Litt, I. F., & Dement, W. C. (1980). Pubertal changes in daytime sleepiness. *Sleep, 2*(4), 453–460.

Catrett, C. D., & Gaultney, J. F. (2009). Possible insomnia predicts some risky behaviors among adolescents when controlling for depressive symptoms. *Journal of Genetic Psychology, 170*(4), 287–309. doi: 10.1080/00221320903218331

Cohen-Zion, M., Drummond, S. P., Padula, C. B., Winward, J., Kanady, J., Medina, K. L., & Tapert, S. F. (2009). Sleep architecture in adolescent marijuana and alcohol users during acute and extended abstinence. *Addiction Behavior, 34*(11), 976–979. doi: 10.1016/j.addbeh.2009.05.011

Colrain, I. M., & Baker, F. C. (2011). Changes in sleep as a function of adolescent development. *Neuropsychology Review, 21*(1), 5–21. doi: 10.1007/s11065-010-9155-5

Colten, H. R., Altevogt, B. M., & Committee on Sleep Medicine and Research, Institute of Medicine. (2006). *Sleep disorders and sleep deprivation: An unmet public health problem.* Washington, DC: National Academies Press.

Crowley, S. J., Acebo, C., & Carskadon, M. A. (2007). Sleep, circadian rhythms, and delayed phase in adolescence. *Sleep Medicine, 8*(6), 602–612. doi: 10.1016/j.sleep.2006.12.002

Dahl, R. E., & Lewin, D. S. (2002). Pathways to adolescent health sleep regulation and behavior. *Journal of Adolescent Health, 31*(6 Suppl.), 175–184.

Fakier, N., & Wild, L. G. (2011). Associations among sleep problems, learning difficulties and substance use in adolescence. *Journal of Adolescence, 34*(4),717–726. doi: 10.1016/j.adolescence.2010.09.010

Feinberg, I., & Campbell, I. G. (2010). Sleep EEG changes during adolescence: An index of a fundamental brain reorganization. *Brain and Cognition, 72*(1), 56–65. doi: 10.1016/j.bandc.2009.09.008

Gau, S. S., Shang, C. Y., Merikangas, K. R., Chiu, Y. N., Soong, W. T., & Cheng, A. T. (2007). Association between morningness-eveningness and behavioral/emotional problems among adolescents. *Journal of Biological Rhythms, 22*(3), 268–274. doi: 10.1177/0748730406298447

Giannotti, F., Cortesi, F., Sebastiani, T., & Ottaviano, S. (2002). Circadian preference, sleep and daytime behaviour in adolescence. *Journal of Sleep Research, 11*(3), 191–199.

Gibson, E. S., Powles, A. C., Thabane, L., O'Brien, S., Molnar, D. S., Trajanovic, N., . . . Chilcott-Tanser, L. (2006). "Sleepiness" is serious in adolescence: Two surveys of 3235 Canadian students. *BMC Public Health, 6,* 116. doi: 10.1186/1471-2458-6-116

Gradisar, M., Gardner, G., & Dohnt, H. (2011). Recent worldwide sleep patterns and problems during adolescence: A review and meta-analysis of age, region, and sleep. *Sleep Medicine, 12*(2), 110–118. doi: 10.1016/j.sleep.2010.11.008

Hasler, B. P., Bootzin, R. R., Cousins, J. C., Fridel, K., & Wenk, G. L. (2008). Circadian phase in sleep-disturbed adolescents with a history of substance abuse: A pilot study. *Behavioral Sleep Medicine, 6*(1), 55–73. doi: 10.1080/15402000701796049

Haynes, P. L., Bootzin, R. R., Smith, L., Cousins, J., Cameron, M., & Stevens, S. (2006). Sleep and aggression in substance-abusing adolescents: Results from an integrative behavioral sleep-treatment pilot program. *Sleep, 29*(4), 512–520.

Jacobus, J., Bava, S., Cohen-Zion, M., Mahmood, O., & Tapert, S. F. (2009). Functional consequences of marijuana use in adolescents. *Pharmacology, Biochemistry and Behavior, 92*(4), 559–565. doi: 10.1016/j.pbb.2009.04.001

Jenni, O. G., Achermann, P., & Carskadon, M. A. (2005). Homeostatic sleep regulation in adolescents. *Sleep, 28*(11), 1446–1454.

Johnson, E. O., & Breslau, N. (2001). Sleep problems and substance use in adolescence. *Drug Alcohol Depend, 64*(1), 1–7.

Johnson, E. O., & Roth, T. (2006). An epidemiologic study of sleep-disordered breathing symptoms among adolescents. *Sleep, 29*(9), 1135–1142.

Laska, M. N., Pasch, K. E., Lust, K., Story, M., & Ehlinger, E. (2009). Latent class analysis of lifestyle characteristics and health risk behaviors among college youth. *Prevention Science, 10*(4), 376–386. doi: 10.1007/s11121-009-0140-2

Loessl, B., Valerius, G., Kopasz, M., Hornyak, M., Riemann, D., & Voderholzer, U. (2008). Are adolescents chronically sleep-deprived? An investigation of sleep habits of adolescents in the Southwest of Germany. *Child: Care, Health and Development, 34*(5), 549–556. doi: 10.1111/j.1365-2214.2008.00845.x

McKnight-Eily, L. R., Eaton, D. K., Lowry, R., Croft, J. B., Presley-Cantrell, L., & Perry, G. S. (2011). Relationships between hours of sleep and health-risk behaviors in US adolescent students. *Preventive Medicine, 53*(4–5), 271–273. doi: 10.1016/j.ypmed.2011.06.020

National Sleep Foundation. (2006). 2006 Sleep in America poll: Teens and Sleep: National Sleep Foundation. https://sleepfoundation.org/sleep-polls-data/sleep-in-america-poll/2006-teens-and-sleep

Negriff, S., Dorn, L. D., Pabst, S. R., & Susman, E. J. (2011). Morningness/eveningness, pubertal timing, and substance use in adolescent girls. *Psychiatry Research, 185*(3), 408–413. doi: 10.1016/j.psychres.2010.07.006

Noland, H., Price, J. H., Dake, J., & Telljohann, S. K. (2009). Adolescents' sleep behaviors and perceptions of sleep. *Journal of School Health, 79*(5), 224–230. doi: 10.1111/j.1746-1561.2009.00402.x

O'Brien, E. M., & Mindell, J. A. (2005). Sleep and risk-taking behavior in adolescents. *Behavioral Sleep Medicine, 3*(3), 113–133. doi: 10.1207/s15402010bsm0303_1

Ohayon, M. M., Carskadon, M. A., Guilleminault, C., & Vitiello, M. V. (2004). Meta-analysis of quantitative sleep parameters from childhood to old age in healthy individuals: Developing normative sleep values across the human lifespan. *Sleep, 27*(7), 1255–1273.

Ohayon, M. M., Roberts, R. E., Zulley, J., Smirne, S., & Priest, R. G. (2000). Prevalence and patterns of problematic sleep among older adolescents. *Journal of the American Academy of Child and Adolescent Psychiatry, 39*(12), 1549–1556. doi: 10.1097/00004583-200012000-00019

Pallesen, S., Saxvig, I. W., Molde, H., Sorensen, E., Wilhelmsen-Langeland, A., & Bjorvatn, B. (2011). Brief report: Behaviorally induced insufficient sleep syndrome in older adolescents: Prevalence and correlates. *Journal of Adolescence, 34*(2), 391–395. doi: 10.1016/j.adolescence.2010.02.005

Pasch, K. E., Laska, M. N., Lytle, L. A., & Moe, S. G. (2010). Adolescent sleep, risk behaviors, and depressive symptoms: Are they linked? *American Journal of Health Behavior, 34*(2), 237–248.

Pasch, K. E., Latimer, L. A., Cance, J. D., Moe, S. G., & Lytle, L. A. (2012). Longitudinal bi-directional relationships between sleep and youth substance use. *Journal of Youth and Adolescence.* doi: 10.1007/s10964-012-9784-5

Pieters, S., Van Der Vorst, H., Burk, W. J., Wiers, R. W., & Engels, R. C. (2010). Puberty-dependent sleep regulation and alcohol use in early adolescents. *Alcoholism: Clinical and Experimental Research, 34*(9), 1512–1518. doi: 10.1111/j.1530-0277.2010.01235.x

Roane, B. M., & Taylor, D. J. (2008). Adolescent insomnia as a risk factor for early adult depression and substance abuse. *Sleep*, *31*(10), 1351–1356.

Roberts, R. E., Roberts, C. R., & Chan, W. (2008). Persistence and change in symptoms of insomnia among adolescents. *Sleep*, *31*(2), 177–184.

Roberts, R. E., Roberts, C. R., & Duong, H. T. (2008). Chronic insomnia and its negative consequences for health and functioning of adolescents: A 12-month prospective study. *Journal of Adolescent Health*, *42*(3), 294–302. doi: 10.1016/j.jadohealth.2007.09.016

Roberts, R. E., Roberts, C. R., & Duong, H. T. (2009). Sleepless in adolescence: Prospective data on sleep deprivation, health and functioning. *Journal of Adolescence*, *32*(5), 1045–1057. doi: 10.1016/j.adolescence.2009.03.007

Schierenbeck, T., Riemann, D., Berger, M., & Hornyak, M. (2008). Effect of illicit recreational drugs upon sleep: Cocaine, ecstasy and marijuana. *Sleep Medicine Review*, *12*(5), 381–389. doi: 10.1016/j.smrv.2007.12.004

Shochat, T., Flint-Bretler, O., & Tzischinsky, O. (2010). Sleep patterns, electronic media exposure and daytime sleep-related behaviours among Israeli adolescents. *Acta Paediatrica*, *99*(9), 1396–1400. doi: 10.1111/j.1651-2227.2010.01821.x

Stein, M. D., & Friedmann, P. D. (2005). Disturbed sleep and its relationship to alcohol use. *Substance Abuse*, *26*(1), 1–13.

Taylor, D. J., Jenni, O. G., Acebo, C., & Carskadon, M. A. (2005). Sleep tendency during extended wakefulness: Insights into adolescent sleep regulation and behavior. *Journal of Sleep Research*, *14*(3), 239–244. doi: 10.1111/j.1365-2869.2005.00467.x

Tynjala, J., Kannas, L., & Levalahti, E. (1997). Perceived tiredness among adolescents and its association with sleep habits and use of psychoactive substances. *Journal of Sleep Research*, *6*(3), 189–198.

Vignau, J., Bailly, D., Duhamel, A., Vervaecke, P., Beuscart, R., & Collinet, C. (1997). Epidemiologic study of sleep quality and troubles in French secondary school adolescents. *Journal of Adolescent Health*, *21*(5), 343–350. doi: 10.1016/S1054-139X(97)00109-2

Wolfson, A. R., & Carskadon, M. A. (1998). Sleep schedules and daytime functioning in adolescents. *Child Development*, *69*(4), 875–887.

Wolfson, A. R., & Carskadon, M. A. (2003). Understanding adolescents' sleep patterns and school performance: A critical appraisal. *Sleep Medicine Review*, *7*(6), 491–506.

Wolfson, A. R., Carskadon, M. A., Acebo, C., Seifer, R., Fallone, G., Labyak, S. E., & Martin, J. L. (2003). Evidence for the validity of a sleep habits survey for adolescents. *Sleep*, *26*(2), 213–216.

Wong, M. M., Brower, K. J., Fitzgerald, H. E., & Zucker, R. A. (2004). Sleep problems in early childhood and early onset of alcohol and other drug use in adolescence. *Alcoholism: Clinical and Experimental Research*, *28*(4), 578–587.

Wong, M. M., Brower, K. J., Nigg, J. T., & Zucker, R. A. (2010). Childhood sleep problems, response inhibition, and alcohol and drug outcomes in adolescence and young adulthood. *Alcoholism: Clinical and Experimental Research*, *34*(6), 1033–1044. doi: 10.1111/j.1530-0277.2010.01178.x

Wong, M. M., Brower, K. J., & Zucker, R. A. (2009). Childhood sleep problems, early onset of substance use and behavioral problems in adolescence. *Sleep Medicine*, *10*(7), 787–796. doi: 10.1016/j.sleep.2008.06.015

Yang, C. K., Kim, J. K., Patel, S. R., & Lee, J. H. (2005). Age-related changes in sleep/wake patterns among Korean teenagers. *Pediatrics*, *115*(1 Suppl.), 250–256. doi: 10.1542/peds.2004-0815G

Yen, C. F., King, B. H., & Tang, T. C. (2010). The association between short and long nocturnal sleep durations and risky behaviours and the moderating factors in Taiwanese adolescents. *Psychiatry Research*, *179*(1), 69–74. doi: 10.1016/j.psychres.2009.02.016

Zhang, J., Lam, S. P., Li, S. X., Li, A. M., Lai, K. Y., & Wing, Y. K. (2011). Longitudinal course and outcome of chronic insomnia in Hong Kong Chinese children: A 5-year follow-up study of a community-based cohort. *Sleep*, *34*(10), 1395–1402. doi: 10.5665/SLEEP.1286

PART 7

Assessment and Intervention

Assessing Adolescent Alcohol and Other Drug Abuse

Ken C. Winters, Tamara Fahnhorst, Andria Botzet, Randy Stinchfield, *and* Ali Nicholson Stockness

Abstract

This chapter addresses several assessment and measurement issues relevant to adolescent drug abuse. Both researchers and clinicians working with youth suspected of problems associated with drug involvement are considered as the following topics are discussed: principles of assessment, validity of self-report, clinical domains of interest, instrumentation, clinical considerations when assessing youth, and assessing treatment outcome. Despite some research gaps, the field consists of several psychometrically sound screening and comprehensive assessment tools to assist researchers and clinicians when measuring drug use, drug problems, symptoms of substance use disorders, and behavioral problems that commonly coexist with drug involvement. Future research needs are also discussed, including the need for more psychometric data on sub-populations of young people defined by age and ethnicity/race.

Key Words: adolescent drug abuse, screening, assessment, measurement, substance use disorders, substance abuse

Precise and developmentally specific measurement of adolescent alcohol and other drug use and related variables, such as risk variables, is essential to provide an accurate understanding of the nature and extent of adolescent drug use, to measure the effectiveness of interventions and treatment and what predicts effectiveness, and to gauge the health service delivery needs of communities. The assessment plan also needs to consider the developmental periods of those being assessed, adjustments for longitudinal evaluation, and plans for statistical analyses. Given that this chapter cannot comprehensively address the wide-ranging goals suggested by this topic, some constraints and resulting compromises are acknowledged. In this light, the chapter will focus on practical measurement and evaluation issues faced by those in research and clinical settings. Specifically, the following issues will be discussed: principles of assessment, self-report, clinical content, instrumentation, clinical considerations, and assessing treatment outcome.

Principles of Assessment
Two Types of Assessment

Broadly speaking, there are two distinct types of assessment: screening and comprehensive assessment (Allen, 2003). The goal of screening is to identify accurately youth who will benefit from a full and complete assessment. Screening determines the need for a comprehensive assessment; it does not establish definitive information about diagnosis and possible treatment needs. A screening should take no longer than 30 minutes, and ideally it may be shorter. Screening questions may inquire about recent drug use quantity and frequency (e.g., How often did you use drugs in the past 6 months?), the presence of adverse consequences of use (e.g., Has your drug use led to problems with your parents?), and contextual factors (e.g., Do your friends use alcohol or other drugs?).

If there are positive indications of a problem, then a comprehensive assessment follows. This process confirms the presence of a diagnosis, helps illuminate other problems connected with the adolescent's drug involvement, and helps the assessor in determining if treatment is warranted and, if so, at what level and for what specific problems. A detailed assessment needs to be conducted by a well-trained professional experienced with adolescent substance use issues, such as a psychologist or mental health professional, school counselor, social worker, or a substance abuse counselor. A comprehensive assessment can include a detailed inquiry into the age of onset and progression of use for specific substances, the context of use (e.g., the usual times and places of drug use), the attitudes and use patterns of the adolescent's peers, typical behavioral and social antecedents that are associated with his or her drug use, and the direct and indirect personal consequences of use (e.g., school, social, family, psychological functioning, and physical functioning).

Self-Report Method

Research and clinical assessment rely heavily on the self-report method, due to this method's convenience, ease of administration, and the expectation that the individual is the most knowledgeable source of information (Martin & Winters, 1998). This method includes several variants—self-administered questionnaire (SAQ), interview, Timeline Follow Back (TLFB; Sobell & Sobell, 1992), and computer-assisted interview (CAI). SAQs are completed independently by the individual and traditionally via paper-and-pencil or computer-version formats. An interview (varying in degree of structure) is completed by a trained individual; this format is typically used when diagnostic data are obtained. The TLFB is a type of assisted interview in which a detailed history of a person's drug use over a specified time (up to a year) is assessed. This method uses specific dates and events (e.g., birthdays, holidays, and vacations) to enhance the respondent's recollection of his or her recent drug use. The CAI method involves the respondent completing an interview independently on a computer; a version of this has the questions delivered audibly via headphones. Research on the concordance of SAQ, interview, TLFB, and CAI formats in clinical and epidemiological samples is not conclusive, although the data suggest that, for the most part, the various formats yield similar levels of disclosure (e.g., Dillon, Turner, Robbins, & Szapocznik, 2005; Newman et al., 2002; Sarrazin, Hall, Richards, & Carswell, 2002).

Validity of Self-Report

The validity of the self-report method for assessing adolescent drug use and related problems continues to be debated in the literature (Allen, 2003; Babor Stephens, & Marlatt, 1987; Watson, Tilleskjor, Hoodecheck-Show, Pucel, & Jacobs, 1984). In addition to purposely distorting the truth, an adolescent's self-report may be distorted due to lack of insight, inattentiveness, or misunderstanding of the question. Also, the validity of self-report by adolescents can be affected by developmental factors. Substance-abusing youth have been characterized as developmentally delayed in terms of their cognitive, social, and ego functioning (Masten, Faden, Zucker, & Spear, 2008; Noam & Houlihan, 1990), which may alter perception of personal problems and how these problems are characterized in the self-disclosure process. Researchers are beginning to identify factors that may contribute to compromised self-report. Underreporting likely occurs more often when the respondent is reporting on less socially acceptable drugs, such as cocaine or heroin, rather than marijuana or alcohol (Harrison, 1995; Williams & Nowatzki, 2005). When adolescents are asked about past drug use that was sporadic or infrequent, significant inconsistencies have been observed (Bailey, Flewelling, & Rachal, 1992). In clinical settings, inconsistency has been observed. Stinchfield (1997) compared self-reports of drug use problems obtained from adolescents at two points in time: at drug assessment intake and after completion of treatment 1 month later. In both instances, subjects were instructed to base their self-reports on the same historical time frame, namely, 1 year prior to treatment. When test scores were compared, the scores at discharge were significantly higher than the scores at intake.

Nonetheless, there are several lines of evidence that provide support for the validity of self-report (e.g., Brown et al., 1998; Johnston & O'Malley, 1997; Maisto, Connors, & Allen, 1995): (1) a large proportion of respondents in clinic-referred settings admit to illicit drug use; (2) as expected, youth in clinical settings report much higher rates of drug involvement and accompanying problems compared to nonclinical samples; (3) youth report low rates of faking tendencies; (4) there is a general pattern of convergence when self-report is compared to other informants (e.g., parents and teachers) and archival records; and (5) there is a general consistency of disclosures across time, although stability has been shown to be higher for lifetime use reports than other reports of other drug use behaviors, such as the age of drug use onset (Shillington, Clapp, & Reed, 2011). Invalid responding can be minimized by using standardized questionnaires and structured or semistructured interviews (examples of which are provided later in the chapter). Standardized instruments have several advantages, such as minimizing bias from the assessor and the inclusion of scales designed to assess response bias. Interviews can promote the validity of self-report in at least three ways. First, the interviewer has an opportunity to express concern about the client's situation. When a client feels intimidated by the assessment or is resistant to questioning, expressions of empathy may improve the respondent's willingness to self-disclose. Second, general information may be gained by observing nonverbal clues such as emotional and physical characteristics. Finally, follow-up questioning may elicit information that would have been difficult to obtain through the forced-choice format of a questionnaire.

ALTERNATIVES TO SELF-REPORT

Regardless of how accurate one may view the self-report method, there are numerous instances in which a person's report needs to be verified with other sources. We provide a brief summary of these sources: biological testing, reports from others, and clinical observation.

Biological Testing

Four biologically based tests (urine, hair, saliva, and sweat) are currently utilized to detect drugs in the body (Allen, Sillanaukee, Strid, & Litten, 2003; Dolan, Rouen, & Kimber, 2004). The main aspect that distinguishes these specimens is the period or window of time for which the drug can be detected. In addition, cost, access, tampering vulnerability, invasiveness, and reliability/validity are other factors that differentiate these biological sampling procedures.

Urinalysis is the most commonly used biological procedure to detect drug use and validate self-report. The window of detection varies considerably for illicit drugs; the detection period for alcohol is only about 8 hours. What interpretations can be inferred from urinalysis? A positive result on a urinalysis indicates that the identified drug was in the adolescent's urine. Yet a positive result does not provide specific information about the person's use. Also, research findings have indicated a low association between substance use self-report and drug test findings (McLaney, Del-Boca, & Babor,

1994; Williams & Nowatzki, 2005). The discordance in the McLaney et al. study (1994) was largely the result of negative drug screens and concurrent positive self-report of recent drug use, which was primarily alcohol and/or marijuana use. Yet the type of drug—and perhaps the stigma associated with it—may be related to reporting bias. When hair analyses for cocaine, opiates, and marijuana were compared to confidential adolescent self-report, substantial underreporting of recent cocaine and opiate use was observed. For recent marijuana, the underreporting pattern was not found (Delaney-Black et al., 2010).

Analysis of hair is a method to detect exposure to drugs over a longer period of time than afforded by urine testing (Allen et al., 2003; Dolan et al., 2004). Unfortunately, several variables affect the concentrations of drugs in the hair, including chemical processing; differences in hair structure, growth, porosity, and hygiene; and exposure to drugs in the air (see Kidwell & Blank, 1996; Rohrich, Zorntlein, Pötsch, Skopp, & Becker, 2000). The testing of saliva and sweat to detect drug exposure is still being refined; their advantages include a noninvasive collection process and the detection of very recent drug use (12–24 hours) (Allen et al., 2003).

Reports From Others

Parents can be relatively valid in identifying and describing many mental health problems in their son or daughter, particularly externalizing disorders such as attention-deficit/hyperactivity disorder (ADHD) and conduct problems (Ivens & Rehm, 1988; Rey, Schrader, & Morris-Yates, 1992). Clinical experience and research indicate that parents generally do not provide meaningful details about their child's drug use. For example, diagnostic agreement between mothers' and children's reports of substance use disorders has shown a considerable range. Edelbrock and colleagues (Edelbrock, Costello, Dulcan, Conover, & Kala, 1986) reported an average mother–child agreement of 63% for substance use disorder symptoms; Weissman's research team reported an average agreement between mothers' and sons' reports of only 17% (Weissman et al., 1987). A recent agreement study examined drug-clinic adolescents' and mothers' reports on a wide range of drug use behaviors and consequences (Winters, Anderson, Bengston, Stinchfield, & Latimer, 2000). They found that mothers concurred at a 78% level with their child with respect to the broad question of whether use has or has not occurred with various drugs. However, when mothers were asked about specific details about the child's substance involvement, about 15% responded "do not know," and concordance with child data was only moderate when mothers did respond to the specific questions. Chung and colleagues (Chung, Sealy, Maisto, Winters, & Bukstein, unpublished manuscript,) examined two self-report baseline measures and found parent–adolescent agreement of the adolescent substance involvement in both community and clinical samples was positively correlated (range of *r* values, .27–.64). It is likely that peers are a more accurate source of drug use about a teenager, although it is not realistic to expect a friend to participate in an assessment.

Clinical Observation

Direct observation by the assessor for behavioral and psychological indicators of drug use can be an objective and useful supplement to the assessment process. A simple checklist of items, such as the presence of needle marks, unsteady gate, slurred or incoherent speech, shaking of hands or twitching of eyelids, and so on, can indicate problematic use. A 14-item checklist of observable signs that may indicate a drug problem is contained in the Simple Screening Instrument for Alcohol and Other Drug Abuse (Winters & Zenilman, 1994).

Clinical Content

A comprehensive assessment of adolescent drug abuse requires attention to a wide range of variables. We will focus on two main domains here. The first area pertains to the details of a person's drug abuse problem severity and resulting problems; the second domain is the biopsychosocial factors that are presumed to have contributed to the onset, maintenance, and progression of the drug involvement, and may have a role in determining level and nature of treatment.

Drug Abuse Problem Severity

Several factors pertinent to drug abuse problem severity have been identified as important to assess comprehensively: age of onset of first and regular drug use; lifetime and more recent (e.g., prior 6 months) pattern of use, including frequency, quantity, and duration for individual drugs; which drug or drugs are preferred; the functional value of the drug use for the adolescent (e.g., social benefits, psychological benefits); and the presence of *DSM*-based symptoms of a substance use disorder. The latter component merits further discussion.

SUBSTANCE USE DISORDER

Drug use that goes beyond experimentation and progresses into problematic involvement is formally delineated by various classification systems, with the primary system the *Diagnostic and Statistical Manual of Mental Disorders*, fourth edition (*DSM-IV*; American Psychiatric Association, 1994). *DSM-IV* identifies criteria for two disorders within the substance use disorder (SUD) category—abuse and dependence. The four abuse symptoms pertain to negative social and personal consequences as a result of repetitive use of a substance; the seven dependence symptoms refer to symptoms associated with the continued use of substances in the face of negative consequences. The differential diagnosis of adolescent substance use disorders requires consideration that the symptoms of drug use are not due to premorbid or concurrent problems, such as conduct disorder or family issues. Given the frequent comorbidity of SUDs and other psychiatric disorders (Grella, Hser, Joshi, & Rounds-Bryant, 2001), it is important that the assessor comprehensively review via a timeline the past and present history of psychiatric symptoms. This type of detailed interview can help sort out the course of the onset of SUD symptoms and symptoms related to a mental or behavior illness (Riggs & Davies, 2002).

DSM-5 and Its Applicability to Adolescents

The new *DSM-5* criteria offer both continuity and changes to the *DSM* system (American Psychiatric Association, 2013). Similar to *DSM-IV*, a feature of the *DSM-5* is that none of the criteria directly refer to onset, quantity, and frequency variables. This is not to say that these variables are not important to assess. Indeed, consumption history does produce important information, particularly when data are compared with regularly updated norms of use. But in the *DSM-5*, a single SUD for various substance classes is proposed, using a set of 11 symptoms for all substances. Ten of these symptoms are in the current *DSM-IV* abuse and dependence group of symptoms, and the eleventh symptom is a new one—persistent drug use craving. Individuals would be assigned a diagnosis based on how many symptoms on that list the individual met: no disorder (0–1), moderate (2–3), or severe (4 or more) (www.dsm5.org).

Recent commentary pieces have discussed the pros and cons of the proposed *DSM-5* criteria for adolescents (Kaminer & Winters, 2012; Winters, Martin, & Chung, 2011). Two positives were noted: (1) the use of a combined criterion set to diagnose a single SUD, given that abuse and dependence as defined by *DSM-IV* have overlapping conceptual content (Martin & Winters, 1998) and that factor and latent class analyses indicate a single dimension of substance problems (Chung & Martin, 2001); and (2) the elimination of the "legal problems" symptom as this symptom tends to be less relevant for female and younger teenagers and is significantly related to coexisting conduct disorder (Martin, Chung, Kirisci, & Langenbucher, 2006).

Nonetheless, the authors argue that four of the draft criteria have questionable validity when applied to adolescent drug users. We briefly review them. *Tolerance*: Tolerance to substances, particularly to alcohol, can be a mild symptom and may occur without significant harm or distress. Also, neurodevelopmental changes during adolescence (Giedd, 2004a, b) may contribute to variability of developmental sensitivity to substances among teenagers and thus falsely produce signs that mimic legitimate tolerance (Spear, 2000). *Withdrawal*: Withdrawal symptoms, which typically emerge after years of heavy drug use, are present in a very low percentage of drug-abusing adolescents (Langenbucher et al., 2000). Whereas withdrawal symptoms may have prognostic significance in those few adolescents who report it, alcohol withdrawal is only moderately associated with levels of problem severity (Chung & Martin, 2001). *Hazardous Use*: This symptom is most certainly more relevant to adults than adolescents. For example, adolescents have less access to automobiles than adults (a common way for individuals to meet this criterion) (Hasin, Paykin, Endicott, & Grant, 1999). *Craving*: The value of including the craving criteria when diagnosing adolescents is uncertain. There are clinical observations that many youth who have escalated to regular use report strong cravings (Martin, Chung, & Langenbucher, 2008), but it is not clear as to the best way to assess signs of continued appetitive urges and behaviors in this age group.

Then there is the problem of the two-symptom threshold. The impact to youth of the 2/11 threshold for the "mild" version of an SUD category merits further research. Some of the proposed *DSM-5* symptoms may be developmentally normative for teenagers and could be easily misunderstood and overendorsed (e.g., tolerance), and thus the proposed taxonomy may include many mild cases who are false positives. A related problem is that the proposed low threshold for SUD may identify a very heterogeneous group of adolescents.

Biopsychosocial Risk and Protective Factors

Biopsychosocial factors refer to the range of personal, environmental, and biological factors that influence the onset, development, and maintenance of drug use behaviors. These factors work together to increase (risk) or decrease (protective) an individual's propensity to use drugs (Clark & Winters, 2002; Petraitis, Flay, & Miller, 1995). For youth already using drugs, identifying and addressing these factors can help to personalize interventions and treatments and, thus, optimize effectiveness of behavior change efforts (Shoham & Insel, 2011). Also, these factors may reflect the likelihood of a young person who is not using drugs yet; too many risk factors and too few asset factors provide a biopsychosocial profile that is a harbinger of future drug use.

We provide a list of biopsychosocial factors that have received prominent attention in the research literature as being significant contributors to the likelihood of a drug use (Clark & Winters, 2002; Clayton, 1992; Hawkins, Catalano, & Miller, 1992). The list is organized according to risk or asset factors, although most factors are bimodal and can be defined either way. Following the list, we briefly describe a core set of these factors.

RISK FACTORS
- Family history of a substance use disorder
- Sibling drug use
- Deviant behavior; legal problems
- Coexisting behavioral/mental disorders (e.g., conduct disorders, ADHD, affective disorders, learning disorders)
- School failure
- Peer drug use; peer delinquency
- Poor impulse control or frustration tolerance
- Expectation that drug use has social benefits
- Community population density and level of crime

ASSET FACTORS
- Psychological well-being
- Positive parenting practices
- Social connectedness to caring adults and institutions
- Goal directedness in school or vocation
- Association with non-drug-using peers
- Academic achievement
- Problem-solving and coping skills
- Motivation to change
- Involvement in religion

ELABORATION OF SELECT FACTORS

It is our contention that a select group of four biopsychosocial factors are among the strongest contributors to adolescent drug use onset and the progression from use to a substance use disorder. We provide a brief overview of these four domains: family history of an SUD, parenting practices, peer influences, and coexisting mental/behavioral disorders.

Family History of a Substance Use Disorder

The children of parents with SUD have increased liability for SUD (McGue, 1999; Zucker, Donovan, Masten, Mattson, & Moss, 2008), and this liability represents both a heritable risk as well as an environmental risk, both directly and through effects on family functioning. Many phenotypic characteristics relevant to developing an SUD likely have a significant heritable component, such as disinhibitory traits (Elkins, McGue, & Iacono, 2007; Nestler & Landsman, 2001). Family discord, as evidenced by poor parental monitoring of the teenager or by parental mental illness, particularly parental antisocial behavior history (e.g., Cadoret, Yates, Troughton, Woodworth, & Stewart, 1995), will contribute to environmental risk. Poor global family functioning and poor quality of parent–child relationships are associated with more alcohol and drug involvement among adolescents (Bahr & Hoffmann, 2010). We address parenting practices next, given that this issue is an important psychosocial factor.

Parenting Practices

Specific parenting practices are among the most important influences on child development, and numerous studies have shown that parents continue to exert considerable influence on their child's drug use during adolescence and young adulthood (Abar & Turrisi, 2008). Parental support and connectedness to the child, and monitoring of his or her whereabouts, are associated with reduced drug use, whereas lack of nurturance and poor monitoring are linked to increased drug involvement (LaBrie & Cail, 2011). A well-cited conceptualization of parenting is based on Baumrind's identification of different degrees of parental involvement, support, and monitoring (Baumrind, 1991). A *permissive* parenting style is characterized by high nurturance, but excessive leniency and lack of guidance; an *authoritarian* parent is one who displays high expectations for obedience without sufficient communication; and the optimal parenting style is *authoritative*, described as a parent who communicates high expectations to the adolescent, is responsive to his or her needs, and displays warmth and interpersonal connectedness.

Parenting practices can positively affect the adolescent in profound ways, such as by providing security and emotional support for the child and by supporting the teenager's psychosocial development and competency to cope with everyday life stressors. For example, research has shown that youth with authoritative parents, as compared to permissive or authoritarian parents, reveal greater psychosocial and academic proficiency (Steinberg, 2004), better self-regulation of emotions (Patock-Peckham et al., 2001), and a more optimistic outlook on life (Baldwin, McIntyre, & Hardaway, 2007).

Peer Effects

There is an extensive body of literature establishing the importance of peer influences on child risk behaviors (Ary et al., 1999; Oetting & Beauvais, 1986). Early studies suggested that the more reliance on peers over parents, the greater the risk of alcohol and other drug use (Barnes & Windle, 1987). More recent literature using longitudinal study designs supports the notion that aspects of the parent–child relationship and parental behaviors influence the child's peer choices and affiliation with deviant peers, which, in turn, will raise the risk for underage drinking and drug use (Brook, Brook, Zhang, & Cohen, 2009; Simons-Morton & Chen, 2005; Svensson, 2003). There is also evidence to suggest that deviant peer affiliation occurs as a result of active rejection of negative parental influences (Gerrard, Gibbons, Zhao, Russell, & Reis-Bergan, 1999).

Peer drug use is another peer variable that has been researched. Adolescents who report being affiliated with drug-using friends report higher levels of drug use compared to those who deny having drug-using friends (Farrell & Danish, 1993). Other drug-peer related factors that have been linked to adolescent drug involvement are pro-drug attitudes among peers and extent of peer attachment to peer groups with a pro-drug attitude (Dishion, Capaldi, Spracklen, & Fuzhong, 1995; Hawkins, Catalano, & Miller, 1992; Patterson, Forgatch, Yoerger, & Stoolmiller, 1998).

The mechanisms that account for why peer influences are a risk factor are likely varied and complex (Fujimoto & Valente, 2012). The individual–peer drug use connection may be related to several factors: shared propensity toward delinquency and other habits that support drug involvement; cohesive peer groups making drugs available to each other; drug use being modeled by friends within the group; and peer group support and norms that support drug use. Also, drug involvement in a peer group has been found to be reciprocally influential. Curran and colleagues (Curran, Stice, & Chassin, 1997) found that the initial status of peer alcohol use was predictive of later increases in adolescent alcohol use, and the initial status on adolescent alcohol use was predictive of later increases in peer alcohol use.

Coexisting Behavioral/Mental Disorders

The behavioral and mental disorders that commonly coexist with a SUD represent complex constructs that are relevant to understanding the etiology of drug involvement and also provide insights into the prevention and treatment of SUD (Clark & Winters, 2002). One major category of coexisting disorders may be conceptualized as externalizing disorders. These disorders are characterized by disruptive-type behavioral features readily observed in the person's environment; examples include conduct disorder (CD), oppositional defiant disorder (ODD), and ADHD. Another prominent category is referred to as internalizing disorders, which includes anxiety and depression. A common feature among this group of disorders is that the person's emotional states compromise his or her level of functioning.

The aforementioned coexisting disorders, as well as others (e.g., PTSD, learning disability, eating disorders), have been shown from cross-sectional research to be highly prevalent among youth with SUD (Clark et al., 1997). Yet prospective research provides more clues as to the nature of the association. As an example, let us turn to the prospective data on externalizing behaviors (CD, ODD, and ADHD) and SUD. Although exceptions exist, there are converging findings indicating that externalizing behaviors, particularly antisocial behaviors, that onset in late childhood are highly linked to the initiation of substance use in early adolescence and to the development of later SUD (Lee, Humphreys, Flory, Liu, & Glass, 2011; Mirza & Bukstein, 2011). How early onset of externalizing disorders contributes to the subsequent elevated risk for drug involvement and SUD has been widely discussed in the literature. For example, it has been hypothesized that externalizing features contribute to increased affiliation with delinquent peers, fewer social rewards, greater frustration

with school, and less influence from parenting, and that these risk factors increase the individual's likelihood of drug use (Burke, Loeber & Lahey, 2007; Marshal, Molina, & Pelham, 2003; Molina, Marshal, Pelham, & Wirth, 2005).

From an assessment standpoint, the presumed connection of externalizing behaviors and subsequent SUD provides a good illustration of the necessity for both developmentally appropriate measurement across developmental stages as well as the need to assess etiologically related variables. The constellation of behavioral and cognitive characteristics of externalizing disorders and the related variables is complex regardless of age. Yet when age of the youth is also a consideration, one has to make sure that the assessment measures have been constructed to measure the constructs at the age of the respondent and that the tool takes into account who is the most suitable reporter. Also at issue here is the decision to use categorical, dimensional, or both types of measures. It is conventional in research to use a categorical measure when assessing disorders or diagnostic categories, and yet preferable to use dimensional measures when assessing underlying, etiologic factors.

Instrumentation

Significant advances have occurred since the mid 1980s in the development and evaluation of adolescent assessment instruments for epidemiological and clinical purposes (Winters, Fahnhorst, Botzet, & Stinchfield, 2009). Some tools are designed to screen youth at risk for drug problems, whereas other measures provide extensive, diagnostically related information. Several detailed summaries and descriptions of these tools have been published: a report by CSAT (*Screening and Assessment of Adolescents with a Substance Use Disorder* [Winters, 1999]); the adolescent chapter in a handbook published by the National Institute on Alcohol Abuse and Alcoholism (*Screening and Assessing Youth for Drug Involvement* [Winters, 2003]); journal articles (e.g., Leccese & Waldron, 1994; Martin & Winters, 1998; Winters & Kaminer, 2008), and book chapters (e.g., Winters et al., 2009; Winters, Newcomb, & Fahnhorst, 2004).

A new source of measures is the PhenX Toolkit (Hamilton et al., 2011). This resource provides standard measures related to up to 15 complex diseases, phenotypic traits, and environmental exposures. Use of PhenX measures facilitates combining data from a variety of studies and makes it easy for investigators to expand a study design beyond the primary research focus. All the measures, which were selected by a panel of research experts, are of the highest psychometric standards and are in public domain. The substance abuse section of the toolkit consists of measures for tobacco, alcohol, and other substances that cover age of initiation, 30-day use, lifetime use, lifetime dependence (tobacco), and abuse and dependence (alcohol and other substances). The kit includes measures for adolescents and adults.

Assessment Standards

There are several principles that have been identified by experts as a guide for the appropriate use of questionnaires and interviews (e.g., American Psychological Association, 1999; Eyde, Moreland & Robertson, 1988). We briefly discuss next a set of key principles.

1. *Knowledge of the Test's Psychometric Properties*. Test users need to have knowledge about the test's reliability and validity. Reliability refers to the capacity of an instrument to measure a relatively enduring trait with some level of consistency over time, across settings, and between raters. Validity refers to the accuracy of the test in measuring what it intends to measure. These psychometric data need to be relevant for the intended use of the test (e.g., data were collected on subjects and in the setting similar to the use of the test). If its use does not match the conditions under which the test was psychometrically evaluated, then results need to be interpreted with caution. Also, when scales or domains are to be used as part of a pre-post comparison, the standard error of measurement needs to be acceptable for use in this manner.

2. *Proper Test Use*. A related standard of test use is to ensure that the test actually measures what it is supposed to be measuring. This can be determined by reviewing the test's manual, which should describe the traits and characteristics of the test's content, the types of respondents it is intended to measure, and in what settings the use of the test is appropriate.

3. *Appropriate Use of Norms and Criterion Data*. Most self-administered tests that measure continuous variables (e.g., personality traits) are norm based. It is important that the norms associated with such tests are appropriate for the given samples being tested. For criterion-based tests (e.g., diagnostic interviews), it is important to make sure that all criterion measures which

were established in the development of the test are appropriate for the patients being tested. For both types of tests, the condition and setting under which the norms and criterion data were collected need to be similar to the present application of the test.

4. *Scoring Accuracy*. For hand-scored tests, the test user has the responsibility for checking scoring accuracy. Computerized score reports that provide standardized scores, narrative summaries, and recommendations for treatment should be interpreted cautiously because they are based on generalities.

5. *Interpretative Feedback*. The user should have clinical skills and formal training in the interpretation of tests in order to understand test results, to communicate them to clients and other professionals, and to provide appropriate services and referrals to the individual being tested.

Then there is the issue of the extent to which adolescent drug treatment programs use standardized tools. A somewhat discouraging report was published by Gans and colleagues on this issue (Gans, Falco, Schackman, & Winters, 2010). They surveyed 120 programs that were rated as exemplary treatment programs. Although the programs recognized the importance of screening and assessment, the quality of such practices varied significantly. A large number of different tools were used, and many of them were developed in house; such nonstandardized tools have questionable standards of reliability and validity. Also, numerous programs were using assessment instruments that were not specifically designed for adolescents.

Specific Tools

Next we provide an overview of the instrumentation field. For a measure or tool to be included here, several requirements had to be met: the instrument was developed specifically for adolescents; its psychometric properties have been reported in a peer-reviewed publication; user information is available in print (e.g., manual, scoring information); and the instrument's author(s) or publisher is accessible to answer user questions. We have organized the overview into screening and comprehensive instruments, and Tables 29.1 (screening) and 2 (comprehensive) provide additional information for a select group of them.

SCREENING INSTRUMENTS

Clinicians and researchers working with adolescents have access to a wide range of screening instruments, most commonly self-report questionnaires, to determine the possible or probable presence of a drug problem. Four categories of screening tools are described: alcohol, all drugs (including alcohol), nonalcohol drugs, and multiscreens (see Table 28.1).

Alcohol Screens

There are three contemporary screening tools that focus exclusively on alcohol use. One is the *Adolescent Drinking Inventory* (ADI; Harrell & Wirtz, 1989). The ADI's 24 items examine adolescent problem drinking by measuring psychological symptoms, physical symptoms, social symptoms, and loss of control. Scoring to the ADI provides a single score with cutoffs and two research subscale scores (self-medicating drinking and rebellious drinking). This screen is associated with very favorable psychometrics (e.g., high internal consistency reliability and an impressive hit rate of 82% in classification accuracy). The second measure in this group is the 23-item *Rutgers Alcohol Problem Index* (RAPI; Martens et al., 2007; White & Labouvie, 1989). The RAPI measures alcohol use problems in multiple areas of functioning—family life, social relations, psychological adjustment, delinquency, physical problems, and neuropsychological adjustment. The RAPI was found to have high internal consistency (.92) in a general population; among binge drinkers, the RAPI showed a strong correlation with *DSM-III-R* criteria for substance use disorders (.75–.95) (White & Labouvie, 1989). A recent study provided psychometric evidence when the instrument is dichotomously scored (Martens et al., 2007). The third tool is the *Alcohol Screening Protocol for Youth* (National Institute on Alcohol Abuse and Alcoholism, 2011). This empirically derived tool was based on a collaborative effort with NIAAA, American Academy of Pediatrics, clinical researchers, and health practitioners. The tool consists of just two questions; one focuses on drinking frequency and the other on drinking frequency by the teenager's friends.

Drug Screens

A second group of screening tools nonspecifically cover all drug categories, including alcohol. The 14-item *Adolescent Alcohol and Drug Abuse Involvement Scale* (AADAIS; Moberg, 2003) measures drug abuse problem severity; a range of reliability and validity evidence for this screen has been reported (Moberg, 2003). The *CRAFFT* (Kelly, Donovan, Chung, Cook, & Delbridge, 2004; Knight, Sherritt, Shrier, Harris, & Chang, 2002) is a specialized six-item screen designed to be administered verbally during a primary care interview to address both alcohol and drug use. Its name is a mnemonic device to assist physicians to incorporate six questions during their primary care exams. Based on a study in a large hospital-based adolescent clinic, scores from the *CRAFFT* were found to be highly correlated with scores from several existing and valid measures, and a cutoff score of 2 has been found to be highly predictive of a drug problem (Knight et al., 2002, 2003). The *GAIN-Short Screener* (GSS; Dennis, Chan, & Funk, 2006) is a 3- to 5-minute screener to quickly identify those who would likely have a disorder based on the full companion instrument, the Global Appraisal of Individual Needs (GAIN; Dennis, 1999). The screener has very favorable internal consistency (alpha of .96 on total screener), and it is highly correlated (r, .84 to .94) with the longer scales in the full GAIN. The 40-item *Personal Experience Screening Questionnaire* (PESQ; Winters, 1992) consists of a problem severity scale (coefficient alpha, .91–.95), drug use history, select psychosocial problems, and response distortion tendencies ("faking good" and "faking bad"). Norms for normal, juvenile offender, and drug-abusing populations are available (Winters, 1992; Winters, DeWolfe, Graham, & St. Cyr, 2006). The 81-item adolescent version of the *Adolescent Substance Abuse Subtle Screening Inventory-2* (SASSI-A2; Miller, 2002) yields scores for several scales, including face-valid alcohol, face-valid other drug, obvious attributes, subtle attributes, and defensiveness. Validity data indicate that SASSI scale scores are highly correlated with MMPI scales and that its cut score for "chemical dependency" corresponds highly with intake diagnoses of substance use disorders (Risberg, Stevens, & Graybill, 1995). However, claims that the SASSI can accurately detect *unreported* drug use and related problems have been questioned (Feldstein & Miller, 2006).

Screens for Nonalcohol Drugs

The third category of screening tools pertains to those that screen only nonalcohol drugs. Only one screen falls into this group: the *Drug Abuse Screening Test for Adolescents* (DAST-A; Martino, Grilo, & Fehon, 2000). This tool was adapted from Skinner's (1982) adult tool, the Drug Abuse Screening Test. This 27-item questionnaire is associated with favorable reliability data and is highly predictive of *DSM-IV* drug-related disorder when tested among adolescent psychiatric inpatients (Yudko, Lozhkina, & Fouts, 2007).

Table 28.1 Screening Instruments

Instrument	Purpose	Source	Group Used	Norms	Normed Groups	Format	Time (min.)
Adolescent Alcohol & Drug Involvement Scale (AADIS)	Screen for drug abuse problem severity	Moberg, 2003	Adolescents referred for emotional or behavioral disorders	Yes	Substance abusers	14 items, qx	5
Adolescent Drinking Inventory (ADI)	Screen for alcohol use problem severity	Harrell & Wirtz, 1989	Adolescents suspected of alcohol use problems	Yes	Normals; substance abusers	24 items, qx	5
CRAFFT	Screen for drug use problem severity	Knight, Sherritt, Harris, Gates, & Chang, 2003	Adolescents referred for emotional or behavioral disorders	Yes	Normals; substance abusers	6 items, qx	5
Drug Abuse Screening Test-Adolescents (DAST-A)	Screen for drug use problem severity	Martino, Grilo, & Fehon, 2000	Adolescents referred for emotional or behavioral disorders	Yes	Substance abusers	27 items, qx	5
Drug Use Screening Inventory-Revised (DUSI-R)	Screen for substance use problem severity and related problems	Kirisci, Mezzich, & Tarter, 1995	Adolescents referred for emotional or behavioral disorders	Yes	Substance abusers	159 items, qx	20
GAIN-Short Screener (GSS)	Screen for drug use problem severity and related problems	Dennis, Chan, & Funk, 2006	Adolescents referred for emotional or behavioral disorders	Yes	Substance abusers	20 items, qx	5
Personal Experience screening Questionnaire (PESQ)	Screen for substance use problem severity	Winters, 1992	Adolescents referred for emotional or behavioral disorders	Yes	Normals; substance abusers	40 items, qx	10
Problem Oriented Screening Instrument for Teenagers (POSIT)	Multiscreen for substance use problem severity and related problems	Latimer, Winters, & Stinchfield, 1997; Rahdert, 1991	Adolescents referred for emotional or behavioral disorders	Yes	Normals; substance abusers	139 items, qx	20–25
Rutgers Alcohol Problem Index (RAPI)	Screen for alcohol use problem severity	White & Labouvie, 1989	Adolescents at risk for alcohol use problems	Yes	Normals; substance abusers	23 items, qx	10
Substance Abuse Subtle Screening Inventory-Adolescents (SASSI-A)	Screen for substance use problem severity and related problems	Miller, 2002	Adolescents referred for emotional or behavioral disorders	Yes	Normals; substance abusers	81 items, qx	10–15

Multiproblem Screens

The final group of screening measures consists of two "multiscreen" instruments that examine several domains in addition to drug involvement. The 139-item *Problem Oriented Screening Instrument for Teenagers* (POSIT; Rahdert, 1991) is part of the Adolescent Assessment and Referral System developed by the National Institute on Drug Abuse. It tests for 10 functional adolescent problem areas: substance use, physical health, mental health, family relations, peer relationships, educational status, vocational status, social skills, leisure and recreation, and aggressive behavior/delinquency. Cut scores for determining the need for further assessment have been rationally established, and some have been confirmed with empirical procedures (Latimer, Winters, & Stinchfield, 1997). Convergent and discriminant evidence for the POSIT has been reported by several investigators (e.g., Dembo, Schmeidler, Borden, Chin-Sue, & Manning, 1997; McLaney, Del-Boca, & Babor, 1994). The *Drug Use Screening Inventory-Revised* (DUSI-R) is a 159-item instrument that describes drug use problem severity and related problems. It produces scores on 10 subscales and one lie scale. Domain scores were shown to be significantly related to *DSM-III-R* substance use disorder criteria in a sample of adolescent substance abusers (Tarter, Laird, Bukstein, & Kaminer, 1992). Additional publications provide further psychometric evidence for this tool (Kirisci, Mezzich, & Tarter, 1995; Tarter et al., 2003).

COMPREHENSIVE ASSESSMENT INSTRUMENTS

When a more detailed assessment is needed, there are numerous diagnostic interviews, problem-focused interviews, and multiscale questionnaires from which to choose (see Table 28.2). This group of tools provides information that can more definitively assess the nature and severity of the drug involvement (e.g., whether a substance use disorder is present or not); identify the psychosocial factors that may predispose, perpetuate, and maintain the drug involvement; and assist with treatment placement and planning.

Diagnostic Interviews

Diagnostic interviews focus on *DSM*-based criteria for SUDs, and in some instances, all psychiatric disorders relevant to adolescents, and many include measures for other clinical information (e.g., treatment history, level of functioning). The majority of the diagnostic interviews in the adolescent drug abuse field are structured. This format directs the interviewer to read verbatim a series of questions in a decision-tree format, and the answers to these questions are restricted to a few predefined alternatives. The respondent is assigned the principal responsibility of interpreting the question and deciding on a reply.

There are two well-researched psychiatric diagnostic interviews that address SUDs as well as the full range of child and adolescent psychiatric disorders. The *Diagnostic Interview for Children and Adolescents* (DICA-R; Reich, Shayla, & Taibelson, 1992) is a structured interview and is used widely among researchers and clinicians. Psychometric evidence specific to substance use disorders has not been published on the DICA, but many sections have been evaluated for reliability and validity (de la Osa, Ezpeleta, Domenech, Navarro, & Losilla, 1997; Welner, Reich, Herjanic, Jung, & Amado, 1987). An instrument that has undergone several adaptations is the *Diagnostic Interview Schedule for Children* (DISC-C; Costello, Edelbrock, & Costello, 1985; Shaffer et al., 1993). Its *DSM-IV* version is the DISC-R (Shaffer, Fisher, & Dulcan, 1996; Shaffer, Fisher, Lucas, Dulcan, & Schwab-Stone, 2000). Separate forms of the interview exist for the child and the parent. As part of a larger study focusing on several diagnoses, Fisher and colleagues (1993) found the *DSM-IV*-based DISC-C to be highly sensitive in correctly identifying youth who had received a hospital diagnosis of any substance use disorder ($n = 8$). Both interview forms (parent and child) had a sensitivity of 75%. For the one parent–child disagreement case, the parent indicated that he or she did not know any details about their child's substance use.

The second subgroup of diagnostic interviews focuses on diagnostic criteria for SUDs. The *Adolescent Diagnostic Interview* (ADI; Winters & Henly 1993) assesses *DSM-5* diagnostic symptoms associated with SUDs. Other sections provide an assessment of substance use consumption history, psychosocial stressors, level of functioning and screens for several adolescent psychiatric disorders. The interview's psychometric properties have been published (Chung, Martin, Winters, & Langenbucher, 2001; Winters & Henly 1993; Winters, Latimer, & Stinchfield, 1999; Winters, Stinchfield, Fulkerson, & Henly, 1993). Another substance use disorder–focused interview is the *Customary Drinking and Drug Use Record* (CDDR; Brown et al., 1998). The CDDR measures alcohol and other drug use consumption, *DSM-IV* substance dependence symptoms (including a detailed

Table 28.2 Comprehensive Assessment Instruments

Instrument	Purpose	Source	Examples Group Used	Norms	Normed Groups	Format	Time (min.)
Diagnostic Interviews							
Adoles. Diagnostic Interview (ADI)	Assess *DSM-5* substance use disorders and problems	Winters & Henly, 1993	Adolescents suspected of drug use problems	NA	NA	Structured interview	45–60
Customary Drinking and Drug Use Record (CDDR)	Assess *DSM-5* substance use disorders and problems	Brown et al., 1998	Adolescents suspected of drug use problems	NA	NA	Structured interview	10–30
Diagnostic Interview for Children & Adolescents (DICA-R)	Assess *DSM-5* child/adol. disorders	Reich, Shayla, & Taibelson, 1992	Youth suspected mental, behavioral problems	NA	NA	Structured interview	45–60
Diagnostic Interview Schedule for Children (DISC-R)	Assess *DSM-5* child/adol. disorders	Shaffer, Fisher, & Dulcan, 1996	Youth suspected mental, behavioral problems	NA	NA	Structured interview	45–60
Global Appraisal of Individual Needs (GAIN)	Assess *DSM-5* substance use disorders and problems	Dennis, 1999	Adolescents suspected of drug use problems	NA	NA	Structured interview	60–90
Problem-Focused Interviews							
Compre-hensive Adolescent Severity Inventory (CASI)	Assess drug use and other life problems	Meyers, McLellan, Jaeger, & Pettinati, 1995	Adolescents suspected of drug use problems	NA	NA	Semistructured interview	45–55
Teen Severity Index (T-ASI)	Assess drug use and other life problems	Kaminer, Bukstein, & Tarter, 1991	Adolescents at risk for drug use problems	NA	NA	Semistructured interview	20–45
Multiscale Questionnaires							
Adolescent Self-Assessment Profile (ASAP)	Multiscale measure of drug use and related problems	Wanberg, 1998	Adolescents suspected of substance use problems	Yes	Normals; substance abusers	225 items, qx	45–60
Hilson Adolescent Profile (HAP)	Multiscale measure of drug use and related problems	Inwald, Brobst, & Morissey, 1986	Adolescents suspected of substance use and related problems	Yes	Normals; substance abusers	310 items, qx	45

Table 28.2 Continued

Instrument	Purpose	Source	Examples Group Used	Norms	Normed Groups	Format	Time (min.)
Juvenile Automated Substance Abuse Evaluation (JASAE)	Multiscale measure of drug use and related problems	Ellis, 1987	Adolescents suspected of substance use problems	Yes	Normals; substance abusers	108 items	20
Personal Experience Inventory (PEI)	Multiscale measure of drug use and related problems	Winters & Henly, 1994	Adolescents suspected of substance use problems	Yes	Normals; substance abusers	276 items, qx	45–60

assessment of withdrawal symptoms), and several types of consequences of drug involvement. There are both lifetime and prior 2-years versions of the CDDR. Psychometric studies provide supporting evidence for this instrument's reliability and validity (Brown et al., 1998). The third instrument in this subgroup is the *Global Appraisal of Individual Needs* (GAIN; Dennis, 1999). The GAIN has eight core sections: Background, Substance Use, Physical Health, Risk Behaviors and Disease Prevention, Mental and Emotional Health, Environment and Living Situation, Legal, and Vocational. This instrument is associated with very favorable psychometric properties (Dennis et al., 2004).

Problem-Focused Interviews

The second major group of comprehensive instruments—problem-focused interviews—measure several problem areas associated with adolescent drug involvement but do not provide a specific diagnostic assessment of SUDs. These interviews assess drug use history and related consequences, as well as several functioning difficulties often experienced by drug-abusing adolescents.

The *Comprehensive Adolescent Severity Inventory* (CASI; Meyers, McLellan, Jaeger, & Pettinati, 1995) measures education, substance use, use of free time, leisure activities, peer relationships, family (including family history and intrafamilial abuse), psychiatric status, and legal history. At the end of several major topics, space is provided for the assessor's comments, severity ratings, and quality ratings of the respondent's answers. The interview incorporates observations from the assessor. Psychometric studies on the CASI support the instrument's reliability and validity and factor structure (Meyers et al., 1995, 2006). The *Teen*

Severity Index (T-ASI; Kaminer, Bukstein, & Tarter, 1991) consists of seven content areas: chemical use, school status, employment-support status, family relationships, legal status, peer-social relationships, and psychiatric status. A medical status section was not included because it was deemed to be less relevant to adolescent drug abusers. Adolescent and interviewer severity ratings are elicited on a five-point scale for each of the content areas. Psychometric data indicate favorable interrater agreement and validity evidence (Brodey et al., 2005; Kaminer, Wagner, Plummer, & Seifer, 1993). Kaminer has also developed a health service utilization tool that compliments the T-ASI, the *Teen Treatment Services Review* (T-TSR; Kaminer, Blitz, Burleson, & Sussman, 1998). This interview examines the type and number of services that the youth received during the treatment episode.

Multiscale Questionnaires

The third group of comprehensive instruments consists of self-administered, multiscale questionnaires. Whereas these instruments range considerably in terms of administration length (some as short as 20 minutes), they share several characteristics: Scales are provided for both drug use problem severity and psychosocial risk factors; strategies are included for detecting response distortion tendencies; norms are provided; and the option of computer administration and scoring is available. Four examples of instruments in this group are briefly summarized. The *Adolescent Self-Assessment Profile-II* (ASAP-II) was developed on the basis of a series of multivariate research studies by Wanberg (1998). The 225-item instrument provides an in-depth assessment of drug involvement, including drug use frequency, drug use consequences and benefits, and major risk factors associated with such involvement (e.g., deviance, peer influence). Supplemental scales, which are based on common factors found within the specific psychosocial and problem severity domains, can be scored as well. Extensive reliability and validity data based on several normative groups are provided in the manual. The *Hilson Adolescent Profile* (HAP; Inwald, Brobst, & Morissey, 1986), a 310-item questionnaire (true/false) has 16 scales, two of which measure alcohol and drug use. The other content scales correspond to characteristics found in psychiatric diagnostic categories (e.g., antisocial behavior, depression) and psychosocial problems (e.g., home life conflicts). Normative and psychometric data have been collected from clinical patients, juvenile offenders, and normal adolescents (Inwald et al., 1986; Streeter & Franklin, 1991). Another questionnaire is the 108-item *Juvenile Automated Substance Abuse Evaluation* (JASAE; Ellis, 1987). The JASAE is a computer-assisted instrument that produces a five-category score, ranging from no use to drug abuse (including a suggested *DSM-IV* classification), as well as a summary of drug use history, measure of life stress, and a scale for test-taking attitude. The JASAE has been shown to discriminate clinical groups from non-clinical groups. The *Personal Experience Inventory* (PEI; Winters & Henly, 1994) consists of several scales that measure chemical involvement problem severity, psychosocial risk, and response distortion tendencies. Supplemental problem screens measure eating disorders, suicide potential, physical/sexual abuse, and parental history of drug abuse. The scoring program provides a computerized report that includes narratives and standardized scores for each scale, as well as other various clinical information. Normative and psychometric data are available (Henly & Winters, 1988, 1989; Winters, Stinchfield, & Henly, 1996; Winters, Stinchfield, Latimer, & Stone, 2008).

Clinical Considerations
Establishing Confidentiality

The assessment process should not formally begin until the assessor has established with the adolescent client and parent the rules and guidelines for confidentiality. This includes explicitly informing them of your professional requirements for disclosing and protecting information. In most instances, detailed information can be held confidential. This includes not releasing and sharing of information—including drug use and drug selling—unless the adolescent grants consent (although states vary to

some degree on this issue). Important exceptions to this principle are when a client discloses threats of danger to oneself or others, or evidence of sexual or physical abuse, and when assessment information is gathered during a court-ordered evaluation and the assessor is obligated to report all self-disclosed information.

The Clinical Interview

The importance of the initial assessment interview with the adolescent requires that we discuss it in some detail. We provide next some key issues related to conducting a productive and therapeutic initial interview with a teenager:

• Decide up front who will be present for the initial interview. In most instances, it is preferable to begin with the teenager alone; the parent portion of the interview can follow.

• It is advisable to situate oneself out from behind the desk. Maintain as much eye contact as possible and avoid too much note taking during the interview.

• Spend the first part of the interview building rapport. Begin with small talk and nonthreatening openers. Also, focus early in the interview on the present situation; withhold historical issues until later in the interview. (Many of the comprehensive interviews reviewed earlier provide questions to guide this type of opening.)

• Acknowledge that you are aware that the current situation may be difficult for the teenager. But level with the teenager that your job is to help to assess the situation and work with him or her to determine a course of action.

• Act as the teenager's advocate as much as possible; highlight positive behaviors; when offering criticism, criticize the activity, not the person.

• Acknowledge the functional (and positive) value of drug use; for example, drugs have social and psychological benefits for the user. Acknowledgment does not mean you are approving drug use.

• Be aware of your own biases and "resentments" so they do not interfere with your judgment. Avoid pontificating, lecturing, and admonishing.

Assessing Treatment Outcome

A basic strategy when evaluating treatment outcome is to have, at minimum, a comprehensive intake assessment tool and a parallel version for the follow-up assessment(s). The intake instrument would provide measures for treatment-related questions, including what diagnostic symptoms and related psychosocial problems to target, what assets the youth and family can utilize to promote the treatment goals, what are the obstacles to treatment success, and how to best manage recovery. Follow-up measures provide the basis for evaluating the effectiveness of treatment. They can be based on intake instruments by making adjustments in the time frame (e.g., "since you were discharged from the treatment program") and content (e.g., "How have you made changes in your social life to promote recovery?") of the intake questionnaire. Additional questions unique to the follow-up period can be added (e.g., use for aftercare services). Two noteworthy examples of a battery of intake-follow-up measures are the ADI (Adolescent Diagnostic Interview-Youth Follow-Up; Winters, Stinchfield, Botzet, & Fahnhorst, 2010) and the Global Appraisal of Individual Needs—Monitoring 90 Days (GAIN-M90; Chestnut Health Systems, 2008).

Outcome Variables

Outcome variables are routinely associated with the core problems of the client that are targeted by treatment and for which treatment effects are expected. These are considered primary outcomes because clinically there is a rationale for expecting effects on these outcomes or problems. In the case of treatment for alcohol and other drug problems or disorders, it is important to measure changes in quantity and frequency of drug use, problems associated with drug involvement, status of any comorbid disorders, and psychosocial outcomes, such as family functioning, school behavior, and delinquency.

Summary

Drug use is still prevalent among American teenagers. The 2012 Monitoring the Future study found that over 20% of high school seniors reported at least one binge drinking episode in the prior 2 weeks, nearly half have tried an illicit drug (primarily marijuana), and more than 20% have used a prescription drug for a nonmedical purpose (Johnston, O'Malley, Bachman, & Schulenberg, 2013).

Not only do youth have the highest prevalence of drug users within its age group compared to older age groups (Substance Abuse and Mental Health Services Administration (SAMHSA), 2005), drug use during adolescence greatly increases the likelihood of developing a later addiction (Winters &

Lee, 2008). To further complicate the issue, adolescent drug use frequently co-occurs with other behavioral or mental disorders (Clark & Winters, 2002), making the assessment process even more complex. Also, drug use does not equate to diagnostic symptoms, and thus there is a need for accurate assessment tools. Fortunately, the field consists of numerous psychometrically sound screening and comprehensive measures to assess not only level of use but also patterns of use, accompanying drug use behaviors, SUDs, and comorbidity.

Future research needs to address current measurement gaps. For some instruments, there are no reports of psychometric data on subpopulations of young people defined by age and ethnicity/race, and most measures have not been formally tested to determine their adequacy as a measure of change (Stinchfield & Winters, 1997). A good measure of change should meet the condition that its standard error of measurement is sufficiently minimal to permit its use in detecting small to medium change over time (Jacobson & Truax, 1991). Also there is a need to improve our measurement of individual substance use disorder criteria for youth, given that some criteria in the *DSM* system have questionable relevance when applied to young people (Winters et al., 2011). A related unresolved area is the need for more precise identification of related psychosocial problems that may contribute to the onset and maintenance of drug involvement. Many existing tools assess psychosocial risk factors historically, which is not optimal for more precisely understanding which risk factors recently preceded the drug use or are current consequences of it. Another need on the horizon is to advance the utility of mobile technology for use in momentary assessment strategies (Heron & Smyth, 2010). This technique has great potential to advance our understating of the nature of relapse, and such knowledge can importantly inform treatment approaches.

References

Abar, C., & Turrisi, R. (2008). How important are parents during the college years? A longitudinal perspective of indirect influences their parents yield on their college teens' alcohol use. *Addictive Behaviors, 33*, 1360–1368.

Allen, J. P. (2003). Assessment of alcohol problems: An overview (pp. 1–11). In J. P. Allen and & V. B. Wilson (Eds.), *Assessing alcohol problems: A guide for clinicians and researchers* (2nd ed., pp. 1–11). Rockville, MD: National Institute on Alcohol Abuse and Alcoholism.

Allen, J. P., Sillanaukee, P., Strid, N., & Litten, R. Z. (2003). Biomarkers of heavy drinking. In J. P. Allen & V. B. Wilson

(Eds.), *Assessing alcohol problems: A guide for clinicians and researchers* (2nd ed., pp. 37–53). Rockville, MD: National Institute on Alcohol Abuse and Alcoholism.

American Psychological Association. (1999). *Standards for educational and psychological testing.* Washington, DC: Author.

American Psychiatric Association. (1994). *Diagnostic and statistical manual of mental disorders* (4th ed.). Washington, DC: Author.

American Psychiatric Association. (2013). *Diagnostic and statistical manual of mental disorders* (5th ed.). Washington, DC: Author.

Ary, D. V., Duncan, T. E., Biglan, A., Metzler, C. W., Noell, J. W., & Smolkowski, K. (1999). Development of adolescent problem behavior. *Journal of Abnormal Child Psychology, 27,* 141–150.

Babor, T. F., Stephens, R. S., & Marlatt, G. A. (1987). Verbal report methods in clinical research on alcoholism: Response bias and its minimization. *Journal of Studies on Alcohol, 48,* 410–424.

Bahr, S. J., & Hoffmann, J. P. (2010). Parenting style, religiosity, peers, and adolescent heavy drinking. *Journal of Studies on Alcohol and Drugs, 71,* 539–543.

Bailey, S. L., Flewelling, R. L., & Rachal, J. V. (1992). The characterization of inconsistencies in self-reports of alcohol and marijuana use in a longitudinal study of adolescents. *Journal of Studies on Alcohol, 53,* 636–647.

Baldwin, D. R., McIntyre, A., & Hardaway, E. (2007). Perceived parenting styles on college students' optimism. *College Student Journal, 43,* 550.

Barnes, G. M., & Windle, M. (1987). Family factors in adolescent alcohol and drug abuse. *Pediatrician, 14,* 13–28.

Baumrind, D. (1991). The influence of parenting style on adolescent competence and substance use. *The Journal of Early Adolescence, 11,* 56–95.

Brodey, B. B., Rosen, C. S., Winters, K. C., Brodey, I. S., Sheetz, B. M., Steinfeld, R. R., & Kaminer, Y. (2005). Conversion and validation of the Teen-Addiction Severity Index (T-ASI) for internet and automated telephone self-report administration. *Psychology of Addictive Behaviors, 19,* 54–61.

Brook, J. S., Brook, D. W., Zhang, C., & Cohen, P. (2009). Pathways from adolescent parent-child conflict to substance use disorders in the fourth decade of life. *American Journal on Addictions, 18,* 235–242.

Brown, S. A., Myers, M. G., Lippke, L., Tapert, S. F., Stewart, D. G., & Vik, P. W. (1998). Psychometric evaluation of the customary drinking and drug use record (CDDR): A measure of adolescent alcohol and drug involvement. *Journal of Studies on Alcohol, 59,* 427–438.

Burke, J. D., Loeber, R., & Lahey, B. B. (2007). Adolescent conduct disorder and interpersonal callousness as predictors of psychopathy in young adults. *Journal of Clinical Child and Adolescent Psychology, 36,* 334–346.

Cadoret, R. J., Yates, W. R., Troughton, E., Woodworth, G., & Stewart, M. A. (1995). Adoption study demonstrating two genetic pathways to drug abuse. *Archives of General Psychiatry, 52,* 42–52.

Chestnut Health Systems. (2008). *Global appraisal of individual needs—Monitoring 90 days.* Normal, IL: Author.

Chung, T., & Martin, C. S. (2001). Classification and course of alcohol problems among adolescents in addictions treatment programs. *Alcohol and Clinical Experimental Research, 25,* 1734–1742.

Chung, T., Martin, C. S., Winters, K. C., & Langenbucher, J. W. (2001). Assessment of alcohol tolerance in adolescents. *Journal of Studies on Alcohol, 62,* 687–695.

Clark, D. B., Moss, H., Kirisci, L., Mezzich, A. C., Miles, R., & Ott, P. (1997). Psychopathology in preadolescent sons of substance abusers. *Journal of the American Academy of Child and Adolescent Psychiatry, 36,* 495–502.

Clark, D., & Winters, K. C. (2002). Measuring risks and outcomes in substance use disorders prevention research. *Journal of Consulting and Clinical Psychology, 70,* 1207–1223.

Clayton, R. R. (1992). Transitions in drug use: Risk and protective factors. In M. D. Glantz & R. W. Pickens (Eds). *Vulnerability to drug abuse* (pp. 15–51). Washington, DC: American Psychological Association.

Costello, E. J., Edelbrock, C., & Costello, A. J. (1985). Validity of the NIMH Diagnostic Interview Schedule for Children: A comparison between psychiatric and pediatric referrals. *Journal of Abnormal Child Psychology, 13,* 570–595.

Curran, P. J., Stice, E., & Chassin, L. (1997). The relation between adolescent alcohol use and peer alcohol use: A longitudinal random coefficients model. *Journal of Consulting and Clinical Psychology, 65,* 130–140.

de la Osa, N., Ezpeleta, L., Domenech, J. M., Navarro, J. B., & Losilla, J. M. (1997). Convergent and discriminant validity of the Structured Diagnostic Interview for Children and Adolescents (DICA-R). *Psychology in Spain, 1,* 37–44.

Delaney-Black, V., Chiodo, L. M., Hannigan, J. H., Greenwald, M. K., Janisse J, Patterson, G., . . . Sokol, R. J. (2010). Just say "I don't:" Lack of concordance between teen report and biological measures of drug use. *Pediatrics, 126,* 887–893.

Dembo, R., Schmeidler, J., Borden, P., Chin Sue, C., & Manning, D. (1997). Use of the POSIT among arrested youths entering a juvenile assessment center: A replication and update. *Journal of Child and Adolescent Substance Abuse, 6,* 19–42.

Dennis, M. L. (1999). *Global Appraisal of Individual Needs (GAIN): Administration Guide for the GAIN and Related Measures.* Normal, IL: Chestnut Health Systems.

Dennis, M. L., Chan, Y. F., & Funk, R. (2006). Development and validation of the GAIN Short Screener (GSS) for internalizing, externalizing, and substance use disorders and crime/violence problems among adolescents and adults. *American Journal on Addictions, 15,* s80–s91.

Dennis, M. L, Funk, R., Godley, S. H., Godley, M. D, & Waldron, H. (2004). Cross-validation of the alcohol and cannabis use measures in the Global Appraisal of Individual Needs (GAIN) and Timeline Followback (TLFB; Form 90) among adolescents in substance abuse treatment. *Addiction, 99*(Suppl. 2), 120–128.

Dillon, F., Turner, C., Robbins, M., & Szapocznik, J. (2005). Concordance among biological, interview, and self-report measures of drug use among African American and Hispanic adolescents referred for drug abuse treatment. *Psychology of Addictive Medicine, 19*(4), 404–413.

Dishion, T. J., Capaldi, D., Spracklen, K. M., & Fuzhong, L. (1995). Peer ecology and male adolescent drug use. *Development and Psychopathology, 7,* 803–824.

Dolan, K., Rouen, D., & Kimber, J. (2004). An overview of the use of urine, hair, sweat, and saliva to detect drug use. *Drug and Alcohol Review, 23,* 213–217.

Edelbrock, C., Costello, A. J., Dulcan, M. K., Conover, N. C., & Kala, R. (1986). Parent-child agreement on child psychiatric symptoms assessed via structured interview. *Journal of Child Psychology and Psychiatry, 27*, 181–190.

Elkins, I. J., McGue, M., & Iacono, W. G. (2007). Prospective effects of ADHD, conduct disorder, and sex on adolescent substance use and abuse. *Archives of General Psychiatry, 64*, 1145–1152.

Ellis, B. R. (1987). *Juvenile Automated Substance Abuse Evaluation (JASAE).* Clarkston, MI: ADE.

Eyde, L. D., Moreland, K. L., & Robertson, G. J. (1988). *Test user qualifications: A data-based approach to promoting good test use.* American Psychological Association.

Farrell, A. D., & Danish, S. J. (1993). Peer drug associations and emotional restraint: Causes and consequences of adolescents' drug use? *Journal of Consulting and Clinical Psychology, 61*, 327–334.

Feldstein, S. W., & Miller, W. R. (2006). Does subtle screening for substance abuse work? A review of the Substance Abuse Subtle Screening Inventory (SASSI). *Addiction, 102*, 41–50.

Fisher, P., Shaffer, D., Piacentini, J. C., Lapkin, J., Kafantaris, V., Leonard, H., & Herzog, D. B. (1993). Sensitivity of the Diagnostic Interview Schedule for Children, 2nd edition (DISC-2.1) for specific diagnoses of children and adolescents. *Journal of the American Academy of Child and Adolescent Psychiatry, 32*, 666–673.

Fujimoto, K., & Valente, T. W. (2012). Social network influences on adolescent substance use: Disentangling structural equivalence from cohesion. *Social Science and Medicine, 74*, 1952–1960.

Gans, J., Falco, M., Schackman, B., & Winters, K. C. (2010). An in-depth survey of the screening and assessment practices of highly regarded adolescent substance abuse treatment programs. *Journal of Child and Adolescent Substance Abuse, 19*, 33–47.

Gerrard, M., Gibbons, F. X., Zhao, L., Russell, D. W., & Reis-Bergan, M. (1999). The effect of peers' alcohol consumption on parental influence: A cognitive mediational model. *Journal of Studies on Alcohol Supplement, 13*, 32–44.

Giedd, J. (2004a). Structural magnetic resonance imaging of the adolescent brain. In R. E. Dahl & L. P. Spear (Eds.), *Adolescent brain development: Vulnerabilities and opportunities* (pp. 77–85). New York, NY: New York Academy of Sciences.

Giedd, J. N. (2004b). Structural magnetic resonance imaging of the adolescent brain. *Annals of the New York Academy of Sciences, 1021*, 77–85.

Grella, C., Hser, Y-I., Joshi, V., & Rounds-Bryant, J. (2001). Drug treatment outcomes for adolescents with comorbid mental and substance use disorders. *Journal of Nervous and Mental Disease, 189*, 384–392.

Hamilton, C. M., Strader, L. C., Pratt, J. G., Maiese, D., Hendershot, T., Kwok, R. K., . . . Haines, J. (2011). The PhenX Toolkit: Get the most from your measures. *American Journal of Epidemiology, 174*(3), 253–260.

Harrell, A., & Wirtz, P. M. (1989). Screening for adolescent problem drinking: Validation of a multidimensional instrument for case identification. *Psychological Assessment, 1*, 61–63.

Harrison, L. D. (1995). The validity of self-reported data on drug use. *Journal of Drug Issues, 25*, 91–111.

Hasin, D., Paykin, A., Endicott, J., & Grant, B. (1999). The validity of DSM-IV alcohol abuse: Drunk drivers versus all others. *Journal of Studies on Alcohol, 60*, 746–755.

Hawkins, J. D., Catalano, R. F., & Miller, J. Y. (1992). Risk and protective factors for alcohol and other drug problems in adolescence and early adulthood: Implications for substance abuse prevention. *Psychological Bulletin, 112*, 64–105.

Henly, G. A., & Winters, K. C. (1988). Development of problem severity scales for the assessment of adolescent alcohol and drug abuse. *International Journal of the Addictions, 23*, 65–85.

Henly, G. A., & Winters, K. C. (1989). Development of psychosocial scales for the assessment of adolescent alcohol and drug involvement. *International Journal of the Addictions, 24*, 973–1001.

Heron, K. E., & Smyth, J. M. (2010). Ecological momentary interventions: Incorporating mobile technology into psychosocial and health behaviour treatments. *British Journal of Health and Psychology, 15*, 1–39.

Inwald, R. E., Brobst, M. A., & Morissey, R. F. (1986). Identifying and predicting adolescent behavioral problems by using a new profile. *Juvenile Justice Digest, 14*, 1–9.

Ivens, C., & Rehm, L. P. (1988). Assessment of childhood depression: Correspondence between reports by child, mother, and father. *Journal of the American Academy of Child and Adolescent Psychiatry, 27*, 738–747.

Jacobson, N. S., & Truax, P. (1991). Clinical significance: A statistical approach to defining meaningful change in psychotherapy research. *Journal of Consulting and Clinical Psychology, 59*, 12–19.

Johnston, L. D., & O'Malley, P. M. (1997). The recanting of earlier reported drug use by young adults. *NIDA Research Monograph, 167*, 59–80.

Johnston, L. D., O'Malley, P. M., Bachman, J. G., & Schulenberg, J. E. (2013). *Monitoring the Future national results on adolescent drug use: Overview of key findings, 2012.* Ann Arbor: Institute for Social Research, University of Michigan.

Kaminer, Y., Blitz, C., Burleson, J. A., & Sussman, J. (1998). The Teen Treatment Services Review (T-TSR). *Journal of Substance Abuse Treatment, 15*, 291–300.

Kaminer, Y., Bukstein, O. G., & Tarter T. E. (1991). The Teen Addiction Severity Index (T-ASI): Rationale and reliability. *International Journal of Addiction, 26*, 219–226.

Kaminer, Y., Wagner, E., Plummer, B., & Seifer, R. (1993). Validation of the Teen Addiction Severity Index (T-ASI): Preliminary findings. *American Journal on Addiction, 2*, 221–224.

Kaminer, Y., & Winters, K. C. (2012). Proposed DSM-5 substance use disorders for adolescents: If you build it will they come? (NIHMSID #467309). *American Journal on Addiction, 21*, 280–281.

Kelly, T. M., Donovan, J. E., Chung, T., Cook, R. L., & Delbridge, T. R. (2004). Alcohol use disorders among emergency department–treated older adolescents: A new brief screen (RUFT-Cut) using the AUDIT, CAGE, CRAFFT, and RAPS-QF. *Alcoholism: Clinical and Experimental Research, 28*, 746–753.

Kidwell, D. A., & Blank, D. L. (1996). Environmental exposure: The stumbling block of hair testing. In P. Kintz (Ed.), *Drug testing in hair* (pp. 17–68). Boca Raton, FL: CRC Press.

Kirisci, L., Mezzich, A., & Tarter, R. (1995). Norms and sensitivity of the adolescent version of the drug use screening inventory. *Addictive Behaviors, 20*, 149–157.

Knight, J., Sherritt, L., Harris, S. K., Gates, E., & Chang, G. (2003). Validity of brief alcohol screening tests among adolescents: A comparison of the AUDIT, POSIT, CAGE and CRAFFT. *Alcoholism: Clinical and Experimental Research, 27,* 67–73.

Knight, J. R, Sherritt, L., Shrier, L. A., Harris, S. K., & Chang, G. (2002). Validity of the CRAFFT substance abuse screening test among adolescent clinic patients. *Archives of Adolescent Medicine, 156,* 607–614.

LaBrie, J. W., & Cail, J. (2011). The moderating effect of parental contact on the influence of perceived peer norms on drinking during the transition to college. *Journal of College Student Development, 52,* 610–621.

Langenbucher, J., Martin, C., Labouvie, E., Sanjuan, P., Bavley, L., & Pollock, N. (2000). Toward the DSM-V: A withdrawal-gate model of alcohol dependence. *Journal of Consulting and Clinical Psychology, 68,* 799–809.

Latimer, W. W., Winters, K. C., & Stinchfield, R. D. (1997). Screening for drug abuse among adolescents in clinical and correctional settings using the Problem Oriented Screening Instrument for Teenagers. *American Journal of Drug and Alcohol Abuse, 23,* 79–98.

Lee, S. S., Humphreys, K. L., Flory, K., Liu, R., & Glass, K. (2011). Prospective association of childhood Attention-Deficit/Hyperactivity Disorder (ADHD) and substance use and abuse/dependence: A meta-analytic review. *Clinical Psychological Review, 32,* 328–341.

Leccese, M., & Waldron, H. B. (1994). Assessing adolescent substance use: A critique of current measurement instruments. *Journal of Substance Abuse Treatment, 11,* 553–563.

Maisto, S. A., Connors, G. J., & Allen, J. P. (1995). Contrasting self-report screens for alcohol problems: A review. *Alcoholism: Clinical and Experimental Research, 19,* 1510–1516.

Marshal, M. P., Molina, B. S., & Pelham, W. E., Jr. (2003). Childhood ADHD and adolescent substance use: An examination of deviant peer group affiliation as a risk factor. *Psychology of Addictive Behaviors, 17,* 293–302.

Martens, M. P., Neighbors, C., Dams-O'Connor, K., Lee, C. M., & Larimer, M. E. (2007). The factor structure of a dichotomously scored Rutgers Alcohol Problems Index. *Journal of Studies on Alcohol and Drugs, 68,* 597–606.

Martin, C. S., Chung, T., Kirisci, L., & Langenbucher, J. W. (2006). Item response theory analysis of diagnostic criteria for alcohol and cannabis use disorders in adolescents: Implications for DSM-V. *Journal of Abnormal Psychology, 115,* 807–814.

Martin, C. S., Chung, T., & Langenbucher, J. W. (2008). How should we revise diagnostic criteria for substance use disorders in the DSM-V? *Journal of Abnormal Psychology, 117,* 561–575.

Martin, C. S., & Winters, K. C. (1998). Diagnosis and assessment of alcohol use disorders among adolescents. *Alcohol Health and Research World, 22,* 95–105.

Martino, S., Grilo, C. M., & Fehon, D. C. (2000). The development of the drug abuse screening test for adolescents (DAST-A). *Addictive Behaviors, 25,* 57–70.

Masten, A. S., Faden, V. B., Zucker, R. A., & Spear, L. P. (2008). Underage drinking: A developmental framework. *Pediatrics, 121* (Suppl. 4), S235–S251.

McGue, M. (1999). Behavioral genetics models of alcoholism and drinking. In K. E. Leonard & H. T. Blane (Eds.), *Psychological theories of drinking and alcoholism* (2nd ed., pp. 372–421). New York, NY: Guilford Press.

McLaney, M. A., Del-Boca, F., & Babor, T. (1994). A validation study of the Problem Oriented Screening Instrument for Teenagers (POSIT). *Journal of Mental Health- United Kingdom, 3,* 363–376.

Meyers, K., Hagan, T. A., McDermott, P., Webb, A., Randall, M., & Frantz, J. (2006). Factor structure of the Comprehensive Adolescent Severity Inventory (CASI): Results of reliability, validity, and generalizability analyses. *American Journal of Drug and Alcohol Abuse, 32,* 287–310.

Meyers, K., McLellan, A. T., Jaeger, J. L., & Pettinati, H. M. (1995). The development of the Comprehensive Addiction Severity Index for Adolescents (CASI-A): An interview for assessing multiple problems of adolescents. *Journal of Substance Abuse Treatment, 12,* 181–193.

Miller, G. (2002). *Adolescent Substance Abuse Subtle Screening Inventory-2.* Springville, IN: SASSI Institute.

Mirza, K. A. H., & Bukstein, O. G. (2011). Attention-disruptive behavior disorders and substance use disorders in adolescents. In Y. Kaminer & K. C. Winters (Eds.), *Clinical manual of adolescent substance abuse treatment* (pp. 283–306). Washington, DC: American Psychiatric Association.

Moberg, D. P. (2003). Screening for alcohol and other drug problems using the Adolescent Alcohol and Drug Involvement Scale (AADIS). Madison: Center for Health Policy and Program Evaluation, University of Wisconsin-Madison.

Molina, B. S., Marshal, M. P., Pelham, W. E., Jr., & Wirth, R. J. (2005). Coping skills and parent support mediate the association between childhood attention-deficit/hyperactivity disorder and adolescent cigarette use. *Journal of Pediatric Psychology, 30,* 345–357.

National Institute on Alcohol Abuse and Alcoholism (NIAAA). (2011). *Alcohol screening and brief intervention for youth: A practitioner's guide.* Rockville, MD: Author.

Nestler, E. J., & Landsman, D. (2001). Learning about addiction from the genome. *Nature, 409,* 834–835.

Newman, J. C., Des Jarlais, D. C., Turner, C. F., Gribble, J., Cooley, P., & Paone, D. (2002). The differential effects of face-to-face and computer interview modes. *American Journal of Public Health, 92,* 294–297.

Noam, G. G., & Houlihan, J. (1990). Developmental dimensions of DSM-III diagnoses in adolescent psychiatric patients. *American Journal of Orthopsychiatry, 60,* 371–378.

Oetting, E. R., & Beauvais, F. (1986). Peer cluster theory: Drugs and the adolescent. *Journal of Counseling and Developement, 65,* 17–22.

Patock-Peckham, J. A., Cheong, J., Balhorn, M. E., & Nagoshi, C. T. (2001). A social learning perspective: A model of parenting styles, self-regulation, perceived drinking control, and alcohol use and problems. *Alcoholism: Clinical and Experimental Research, 25,* 1284–1292.

Patterson, G. R., Forgatch, M. S., Yoerger, K. L., & Stoolmiller, M. (1998). Variables that initiate and maintain an early-onset trajectory for juvenile offending. *Development and Psychopathology, 10,* 531–548.

Petraitis, J., Flay, B. R., & Miller, T. Q. (1995). Reviewing theories of adolescent substance abuse: Organizing pieces in the puzzle. *Psychological Bulletin, 117,* 67–86.

Rahdert, E. (Ed.). (1991). *The Adolescent Assessment/Referral System Manual.* (DHHS Pub. No. [ADM] 91-1735). Rockville, MD: US Department of Health and Human Services, ADAMHA, National Institute on Drug Abuse.

Reich, W., Shayla, J. J., & Taibelson, C. (1992). *The Diagnostic Interview for Children and Adolescents-Revised (DICA-R).* St. Louis, MO: Washington University.

Rey, J. M., Schrader, E., & Morris-Yates, A. (1992). Parent-child agreement on children's behaviours reported by the Child Behaviour Checklist (CBCL). *Journal of Adolescence, 15,* 219–230.

Riggs, P. D., & Davies, R. (2002). A clinical approach to treatment of depression in adolescents with substance use disorders and conduct disorder. *Journal of the American Academy of Child and Adolescent Psychiatry, 41,* 1253–1255.

Risberg, R. A., Stevens, M. J., & Graybill, D. F. (1995). Validating the adolescent form of the Substance Abuse Subtle Screening Inventory. *Journal of Child and Adolescent Substance Abuse, 4,* 25–41.

Rohrich, J., Zorntlein, S., Pötsch, L., Skopp, G., & Becker, J. (2000). Effect of the shampoo Ultra Clean on drug concentrations. *International Journal of Legal Medicine, 113,* 102–106.

Sarrazin, M. S., Hall, J. A., Richards, C., & Carswell, C. (2002). The comparison of computer-based versus pencil-and-paper assessment of drug use. *Research on Social Work Practice, 12*(5) 669–683.

Shaffer, D., Fisher, P., & Dulcan, M. (1996). The NIMH Diagnostic Interview Schedule for Children (DISC 2.3): Description, acceptability, prevalence, and performance in the MECA study. *Journal of the American Academy of Child and Adolescent Psychiatry, 35,* 865–877.

Shaffer, D., Fisher, P., Lucas, C. P., Dulcan, M. K., & Schwab-Stone, M. E. (2000). NIMH Diagnostic Interview Schedule for Children Version IV (NIMH DISC-IV): Description, differences from previous versions, and reliability of some common diagnoses. *Journal of the American Academy of Child and Adolescent Psychiatry, 39,* 28–38.

Shaffer, D., Schwab-Stone, M., Fisher, P., Cohen, P., Placentini, J., Davies, M., . . . Regier, D. (1993). The diagnostic interview schedule for children-revised version (DISC-R): I. Preparation, field testing, interrater reliability, and acceptability. *Journal of the American Academy of Child & Adolescent Psychiatry, 32,* 643–650.

Shillington, A. M., Clapp, J. D., & Reed, M. B. (2011). The stability of self-reported marijuana use across eight years of the National Longitudinal Survey of Youth. *Journal of Child and Adolescent Substance Abuse, 20,* 407–420.

Shoham, V., & Insel, T. R. (2011). Rebooting for whom? Portfolios, technology, and personalized intervention. *Perspectives on Psychological Science, 6,* 478–482.

Simons-Morton, B., & Chen, R. (2005). Latent growth curve analyses of parent influences on drinking progression among early adolescents. *Journal of Studies on Alcohol, 66,* 5–13.

Skinner, H. (1982). *Development and Validation of a Lifetime Alcohol Consumption Assessment Procedure.* (Substudy No. 1248). Toronto, ON: Addiction Research Foundation.

Sobell, L. C., & Sobell, M. B. (1992). Time-line follow-back: A technique for assessing self-reported alcohol consumption. In R. Z. Litten & J. P. Allen (Eds.), *Measuring alcohol consumption* (pp. 73–98). Totowa, NJ: Humana Press.

Spear, L. P. (2000). The adolescent brain and age-related behavioral manifestations. *Neuroscience and Biobehavioral Review, 24,* 417–463.

Steinberg L. (2004). Risk taking in adolescence: What changes and why? *Annals of the New York Science Academy, 1021,* 269–309.

Stinchfield, R. D., & Winters, K. C. (1997). Measuring change in adolescent drug misuse with the Personal Experience Inventory (PEI). *Substance Use and Misuse, 32,* 63–76.

Stinchfield, R. D. (1997). Reliability of adolescent self-reported pretreatment alcohol and other drug use. *Substance Use and Misuse, 32,* 63–76.

Streeter, C. L., & Franklin, C. (1991). Psychological and family differences between middle class and low income dropouts: A discriminant analysis. *High School Journal, 74,* 211–219.

Substance Abuse and Mental Health Services Administration (SAMHSA). (2005). *Results from the 2004 national survey on drug use and health: National findings.* (DHHS Publication No. SMA 05-4062). Rockville, MD: Author.

Svensson, R. (2003). Gender differences in adolescent drug use: The impact of parental monitoring and peer deviance. *Youth and Society, 34*(3), 300–329.

Tarter, R. E., Kirisci, L., Mezzich, A., Cornelius, J. R., Pajer, K., Vanyukov, M. . . . Clark, D. (2003). Neurobehavioral disinhibition in childhood predicts early age at onset of substance use disorder. *American Journal of Psychiatry, 160,* 1078–1085.

Tarter, R. E., Laird, S. B., Bukstein, O., & Kaminer, Y. (1992). Validation of the adolescent drug use screening inventory: Preliminary findings. *Psychology of Addictive Behaviors, 6,* 233–236.

Wanberg, K. (1998). *User's guide to the Adolescent Self-Assessment Profile-II (ASAP-II).* Arvada, CO: Center for Addictions Research and Evaluation.

Watson, C. G., Tilleskjor, C., Hoodecheck-Schow, E. A., Pucel, J., & Jacobs L. (1984). Do alcoholics give valid self-reports? *Journal of Studies on Alcohol, 45,* 344–348.

Weissman, M. M., Wickramaratne, P., Warner, V., John, K., Prusoff, B. A., Merikangas, K. R., & Gammon, G. D. (1987). Assessing psychiatric disorders in children. Discrepancies between mothers' and children's reports. *Archives of General Psychiatry, 44*(8), 747–753.

Welner, Z., Reich, W., Herjanic, B., Jung, K., & Amado, K. (1987). Reliability, validity and parent-child agreement studies of the Diagnostic Interview for Children and Adolescents (DICA). *Journal of American Academy of Child Psychiatry, 26,* 649–653.

White, H. R., & Labouvie, E. W. (1989). Towards the assessment of adolescent problem drinking. *Journal of Studies on Alcohol, 50,* 30–37.

Williams, R., & Nowatzki, N. (2005). Validity of adolescent self-report of substance use. *Substance Use and Misuse, 40,* 299–311.

Winters, K. C. (1992). Development of an adolescent alcohol and other drug abuse screening scale: Personal experience screening questionnaire. *Addictive Behaviors, 17*(5), 479–490.

Winters, K. C. (1999). Screening and assessing adolescents for substance use disorders (Treatment Improvement Protocol (TIP) Series 31). *Rockville, MD: Center for Substance Abuse Treatment,* b7.

Winters, K. C. (2003). Screening and assessing youth for drug involvement. *Assessing alcohol problems: A guide for clinicians and researchers, 2,* 101–124.

Winters, K. C., Anderson, N., Bengston, P., Stinchfield, R. D., & Latimer, W. W. (2000). Development of a parent questionnaire for the assessment of adolescent drug abuse. *Journal of Psychoactive Drugs, 32,* 3–13.

Winters, K. C., DeWolfe, J., Graham, D., & St. Cyr, W. (2006). Screening American Indian youth for referral to drug abuse prevention and intervention services. *Journal of Child and Adolescent Substance Abuse, 16,* 39–52.

Winters, K. C., Fahnhorst, T., Botzet, A. M., & Stinchfield, R. D. (2009). Assessing adolescent drug use. In R. Reis, D. Fiellin, S. Miller, & R. Saitz (Eds.), *Principles of addiction medicine* (4th ed., pp. 1429–1443). Baltimore, MD: Wolters Kluwer.

Winters, K. C., & Henly, G. A. (1993). *Adolescent Diagnostic Interview Schedule and Manual.* Los Angeles, CA: Western Psychological Services.

Winters, K. C., & Henly, G. A. (1994). *Personal Experience Inventory and Manual.* Los Angeles, CA: Western Psychological Services.

Winters, K. C., & Kaminer, Y. (2008). Screening and assessing adolescent substance use disorders in clinical populations. *Journal of the Academy of Child and Adolescent Psychiatry, 47,* 740–744.

Winters, K. C., Latimer, W. W., & Stinchfield, R. D. (1999). The DSM-IV criteria for adolescent alcohol and cannabis use disorders. *Journal of Studies on Alcohol, 60,* 337–344.

Winters, K. C., & Lee, S. (2008). Likelihood of developing an alcohol and cannabis use disorder during youth: Association with recent use and age. *Drug and Alcohol Dependence, 92,* 239–247.

Winters, K. C., Martin, C. S., & Chung, T. (2011). Commentary on O'Brien: Substance use disorders in DSM-5 when applied to adolescents. *Addiction, 106,* 882–884.

Winters, K. C., Newcomb, M., & Fahnhorst, T. (2004). Substance use disorders. In M. Hersen (Ed.), *Psychological assessment in clinical practice: A pragmatic guide* (pp. 393–408). New York, NY: Brunner-Routledge.

Winters, K. C., Stinchfield, R. D., Botzet, A., & Fahnhorst, T. (2010). *Adolescent Diagnostic Interview Schedule follow-up.* Minneapolis: Department of Psychiatry, University of Minnesota.

Winters, K. C., Stinchfield, R. D., Fulkerson, J., & Henly, G. A. (1993). Measuring alcohol and cannabis use disorders in an adolescent clinical sample. *Psychology of Addictive Behaviors, 7,* 185–196.

Winters, K. C., Stinchfield, R. D., & Henly, G. A. (1996). Convergent and predictive validity of the Personal Experience Inventory. *Journal of Child and Adolescent Substance Abuse, 5,* 37–55.

Winters, K. C., Stinchfield, R. D., Latimer, W. W., & Stone, A. (2008). Internalizing and externalizing behaviors and their association to the treatment of adolescents with a substance use disorder. *Journal of Substance Abuse Treatment, 35,* 269–278.

Winters, K. C., & Zenilman, J. (1994). *Simple screening for infectious diseases and drug abuse* (Treatment Improvement Protocol Series). Rockville, MD: Center for Substance Abuse Treatment.

Yudko, E., Lozhkina, O., & Fouts, A. (2007). A comprehensive review of the psychometric properties of the Drug Abuse Screening Test. *Journal of Substance Abuse Treatment, 32,* 189–198.

Zucker, R. A., Donovan, J. E., Masten, A. S., Mattson, M. M., & Moss, H. B. (2008). Early developmental processes and the continuity of risks for underage drinking and problem drinking. *Pediatrics, 121,* s252–s272.

Prevention in School, Primary Care, and Community-Based Settings

Elizabeth J. D'Amico *and* Sarah W. Feldstein Ewing

Abstract

Across all races and ethnicities, alcohol, tobacco, and other drug (ATOD) use increases during the middle school and high school years. The current chapter discusses ATOD use and adolescent development, cultural considerations for ATOD use, and factors that may affect ATOD use during this developmental period. It also reviews the prevention and intervention work with this population across a variety of settings, including schools, primary care settings, homeless shelters, and juvenile justice. Overall, the research in this area emphasizes the importance of identifying adolescence as a distinct neurodevelopmental period, with its own set of specific prevention and intervention needs.

Key Words: development, adolescence, culture, alcohol, drugs, prevention, intervention, motivational interviewing

Across all races and ethnicities, alcohol, tobacco, and other drug (ATOD) use increases during the middle school and high school years (Johnston, O'Malley, Bachman, & Schulenberg, 2013; Shih, Miles, Tucker, Zhou, & D'Amico, 2010). Specifically, rates of alcohol and marijuana use triple from sixth to eighth grade (D'Amico, Ellickson, Wagner, et al., 2005). By the 12th grade, not only have most youth tried alcohol, marijuana, and tobacco at least once (alcohol = 79%, marijuana = 48.9%, and cigarettes = 54.5%), many youth use these substances fairly regularly (Eaton et al., 2012). In fact, in one cross-national survey, 48.4% of American high school seniors drank alcohol in the past month, with 31.5% engaging in heavy drinking (defined for adolescents as drinking at least 3 drinks per drinking occasion for girls, and at least 4 drinks per drinking occasion for boys). In addition, 28% of seniors reported using marijuana in the past month and 25.1% described themselves as current cigarette smokers (CDC, 2014). Importantly, many youth are not restricting their use to simply one substance. Rather, most American

adolescents tend toward polysubstance use, meaning that those who are drinking also tend to be smoking cigarettes and using marijuana (Chung & Maisto, 2006; Moss, Chen, & Yi, 2014).

Given that this is an important developmental period when incredible changes are taking place socially, and in the brain and body (Paus, Keshavan, & Giedd, 2008), age of initiation of ATOD can have dramatic effects on functioning across many areas, particularly if youth initiate at younger ages. Surveys indicate that before eighth grade, 1 in 5 youth have initiated alcohol use, 1 in 12 have initiated marijuana use, and 1 in 10 have initiated cigarette smoking (Eaton et al., 2012). Age of initiation has been linked to a number of serious health risk factors, including greater rates of accidents, interpersonal violence, and unintentional injuries (Hingson, Heeren, Jamanka, & Howland, 2000; Kuntsche, Rossow, et al., 2014; Scholes-Balog, Hemphill, Kremer, & Toumbourou, 2013); earlier age of sexual debut and related sexual risk behavior (French & Dishion, 2003; Oshri, Handley, Sutton, Wortel, & Burnette, 2014); and increased likelihood of continued substance use disorders into late adolescence and adulthood (D'Amico, Ellickson, Collins, Martino, & Klein, 2005; Hingson, Heeren, & Winter, 2006; Marshall, 2014). And emerging data are suggesting the critical interplay between genetic risk factors (e.g., CDH13), parent/peer variables, and the age of alcohol use initiation and sexual debut (Feldstein Ewing, Magnan, Houck, Morgan, & Bryan, 2014). Furthermore, among adults who first tried marijuana before age 14, 12.7% developed abuse or dependence of illicit drugs compared to 2.0% of adults who initiated marijuana use after age 18. Similarly, 14.8% of adults who first drank alcohol before age 14 developed alcohol abuse or dependence compared to 3.5% who started drinking after age 18 (SAMHSA, 2012).

ATOD Use and Adolescent Development

Some research has argued that experimentation with ATOD during adolescence is normative (Chassin & DeLucia, 1996; Guilamo-Ramos, Turrisi, Jaccard, & Gonzalez, 2004; Hurrelmann, 1990), and it may potentially even be socially indicated. For example, during this developmental period, many youth aspire to be popular among their peers, which may involve minor levels of ATOD use and delinquency (Allen, Porter, McFarland, McElhaney, & Marsh, 2005), and achieving this social status is commonly viewed as both desirable and an indicator of positive youth development (Tucker et al., 2011, 2013). There is stronger evidence, however, that abstaining youth have better health outcomes and fewer alcohol and drug problems in young adulthood than youth who experiment with ATOD during this time (Ellickson, Martino, & Collins, 2004; Lisdahl, Gilbert, Wright, & Shollenbarger, 2013; Tucker, Ellickson, Orlando, Martino, & Klein, 2005; Tucker, Ellickson, Collins, & Klein, 2006).

It is important to note that numerous major developmental changes occur in the brain and the body throughout adolescence (Giedd, 2012; Paus, 2005), and some of these changes may affect the choices that youth make related to ATOD use (Geier, 2013; Steinberg, Cauffman, Woolard, Graham, & Banich, 2009; Steinberg, 2007). Although we are only still beginning to understand the nature of the brain-based changes that take place throughout adolescence (Casey, Getz, & Galvan, 2008; Paus et al., 2008), consistent with the "dual-process" model (Somerville, 2010; Steinberg, 2010), data have reliably indicated the relatively greater activation of brain-based reward regions during this developmental period (e.g., Ernst, Pine, & Hardin, 2006; Galvan et al., 2006). For example, motivation for seeking social stimuli and novelty is enhanced during adolescence compared to adulthood (Doremus-Fitzwater, Varlinskaya, & Spear, 2010). Findings with human adolescents are consistent with rodent models (Laviola, Macri, Morley-Fletcher, & Adriani, 2003). Previous imaging studies (Ernst & Fudge, 2009), suggest, for example, enhanced nucleus accumbens activity in response to rewards during adolescence, relative to other developmental periods (childhood and adulthood). Practically, this means that risk-taking behaviors, such as engaging in ATOD use, may in fact, *feel* much more exciting, frightening, and fun during adolescence (Dahl, 2011; Galvan, Hare, Voss, Glover, & Casy, 2007). Following adolescence, there is a substantial decline in risk taking. This may be because connectivity and processing improve throughout areas such as the prefrontal cortex, thereby enhancing planning ability and self-regulation during emerging adulthood (Ernst, 2014; Ernst & Fudge, 2009; Sebastian, Burnett, & Blakemore, 2008; Steinberg, 2008b).

Despite the increased reward area activation in the brain during adolescence, ATOD use during this developmental period can adversely affect neurocognitive functioning across several different areas, and it can result in serious consequences during adolescence and into early and late adulthood. For example, substance use may disrupt the brain maturation process and impair brain function over the long term (Chambers, Taylor, & Potenza, 2003; Feldstein Ewing, Blakemore, & Sakhardande, 2014; Jacobus & Tapert, 2013; Tapert, Caldwell, & Burke, 2004; Welch, Carson, & Lawrie, 2013; White, 2009). Empirical studies have consistently found that adolescents who use alcohol and marijuana regularly process information differently compared to adolescents who do not use these substances (Padula, Schweinsburg, & Tapert, 2007; Tapert & Schweinsburg, 2005; Tapert, Granholm, Leedy, & Brown, 2002; Tapert et al., 2007); many of these youth also exhibit modest but significant neurocognitive deficits by late adolescence (Schweinsburg, Brown, & Tapert, 2008; Schweinsburg et al., 2005; Tapert & Brown, 1999, 2000; Tapert & Schweinsburg, 2006).

ATOD use during adolescence can also affect interpersonal, occupational, and educational functioning during adolescence, young adulthood, and adulthood. Specifically, adolescents who use ATOD regularly report lower functioning across all of these areas compared to youth who do not use regularly (Brown, D'Amico, McCarthy, & Tapert, 2001; van Gastel et al., 2013). For example, use of alcohol in adolescence has been associated with interpersonal consequences such as physical fights and injuries (Bonomo et al., 2001; Kuntsche, Rossow, et al., 2014) and more problems with school and employment (Berg et al., 2013; Ellickson, Tucker, & Klein, 2003). Similarly, marijuana use during adolescence is associated with lower educational achievement, lower life satisfaction, and poorer educational outcomes (Broman, 2009; Fergusson & Boden, 2008; Lynskey & Hall, 2000; van Gastel et al., 2013). Furthermore, early adolescent ATOD use has been associated with increased risk of major depression and psychiatric vulnerability in late adolescence and the late 20s (Brook, Brook, Zhang, Cohen, & Whiteman, 2002; Griffith-Lendering et al., 2013; Grigsby, Forster, Baezconde-Garbanati, Soto, & Unger, 2014), and suicidal ideation attempts and crime during adulthood (Chabrol, Chauchard, & Girabet, 2008; Fergusson, Horwood, & Swain-Campbell, 2002; Green, Doherty, Stuart, & Ensminger, 2010).

In sum, ATOD use during this critical developmental period is associated with a wide range of problems that can last into young adulthood and adulthood. Prevention and intervention programs must therefore address initiation of use, particularly early initiation, and escalation of use that can occur as youth transition from early adolescence to middle and late adolescence. Programs must also take into account how existing prevention/intervention models may fit for youth across these different age groups.

Cultural Considerations for ATOD Use

Research related to ATOD use among youth has tended to focus on the patterns and prevalence of use within Caucasian samples, with few studies focused on understanding transitions in ATOD use among diverse ethnic and racial samples (D'Amico, Tucker, Shih, & Miles, 2014; Jackson & Sartor, in press). However, the United States is on its way to becoming a minority majority country, where racial/ethnic minority groups will predominate, and current mainstream groups (Caucasian) will be less prominent. During the next 15 years, Asian American, Hispanic American, African American, and Native American populations are expected to rapidly grow in size, with each of these cultures subsequently comprising a significant proportion of the nation (Campbell, 1996). Currently, Hispanics represent the nation's largest minority group, and this group is expected to triple in size, accounting for most of the nation's population growth from 2005 through 2050. Similarly, the Asian population is expected to triple, and the African American population to double during this same period (Passel & Cohn, 2008). Due to the increase in minority populations over the next four decades, it is important to examine ATOD among minority youth because understanding initiation and escalation among these groups can help clinicians and providers know the best time and way to intervene.

Despite the growing presence of minority groups within the United States, significant health disparities still exist (Carter-Pokras & Baquet, 2002). In particular, the effects of ATOD use are not equitable across groups (Lowman & Le Fauve, 2003; Russo, Purohit, Foudin, & Salin, 2004), with minority populations bearing a substantially greater burden of social and health-related consequences from ATOD use (Caetano, 2003; Galea & Vlahov, 2002; Mulia, Ye, Greenfield, & Zemore, 2009; Mulia, Ye, Zemore, & Greenfield, 2008), despite the fact that minority youth typically evidence a number of important protective factors, including higher parental monitoring and more consistent family interactions compared to Caucasian youth (Fulkerson, Story, & Mellin, 2006). Among adults, these consequences take the form of greater levels of ATOD-related morbidity and mortality, including cancer, cirrhosis, driving under the influence (DUI) arrests, and intimate partner violence (Trujillo, Castaäneda, Martâinez, & Gonzalez, 2006). Among adolescents, despite equivalent (if not lower) rates of ATOD use among minority youth (Feldstein Ewing, Venner, Mead, & Bryan, 2011), minority adolescents typically experience greater levels of substance-related consequences, including drinking and driving, riding with a drinking driver, violence (physical fighting and relationship violence), and sexual risk behaviors (Centers for Disease Control and Prevention, 2010; Hellerstedt, Peterson-Hickey, Rhodes, & Garwick, 2006; Walker, Treno, Grube, & Light, 2003).

Several factors may contribute to the relatively greater levels of substance-related consequences observed among minority youth. For example, among minority adolescents, higher visibility of and exposure to substances, perceived ease of obtaining substances, and higher levels of community policing in the youths' community may play a role in their experience of greater substance-related consequences (Wallace, 1999). In addition, greater rates of poverty, and greater rates of being underinsured or uninsured may also contribute to existing health disparities. For example, Hispanic families have been found to earn an annual income at 71% of the median for Caucasian families, and Native American families typically earn even less than that (DeNavas-Walt, Proctor, & Lee, 2006). Furthermore, one third of Hispanic and Native American families do not have insurance, which is double the uninsurance rate of Caucasian families (DeNavas-Walt et al., 2006).

Another important factor that may contribute to greater social and health consequences among minority youth is that there may be a differential pattern of treatment and referral, with minority youth more likely to be referred to justice settings rather than treatment settings (Aarons, Brown, Garland, & Hough, 2004; Feldstein Ewing, Venner, & May, 2006). Ultimately, at this time, minority adolescents are less likely than Caucasian youth to receive prevention and intervention for ATOD use (Garland et al., 2005; Wu, Woody, Yang, Pan, & Blazer, 2011) and also typically have lower levels of treatment engagement and completion once they are enrolled (Alegria, Carson, Goncalves, & Keefe, 2011). Thus, clinicians and providers may need to work harder to ensure that these groups receive needed services and are retained in services.

In terms of concrete differences in rates of use, although evidence remains slightly mixed (Shih et al., 2010; Shih, Miles, Tucker, Zhou, & D'Amico, 2012), Hispanic and Caucasian youth generally report comparable rates of alcohol, marijuana, and tobacco use (Eaton et al., 2012; Feldstein Ewing, Filbey, Sabbineni, Chandler, & Hutchison, 2011). Whereas Caucasian youth appear to have greater co-occurring psychopathology (Feldstein Ewing, Venner, Mead, & Bryan, 2011), Hispanic youth initiate ATOD use earlier and show greater rates of ATOD-related consequences than Caucasian youth (Eaton et al., 2012). Furthermore, according to the largest national-based study to date, Native American youth report the highest rates of ATOD use, greatest frequency and intensity of ATOD use, earliest first ATOD use, and much higher alcohol-related mortality than other racial/ethnic groups surveyed (Office of Applied Studies, 2006, 2007; Szlemko, Wood, & Thurman, 2006). In contrast to these patterns, there are two groups that reliably demonstrate lower rates of risk than Caucasian youth; African American and Asian American youth report the lowest rates of adolescent substance use as well as the lowest levels of related risk behaviors (Feldstein Ewing, Venner, et al., 2011; Shih et al., 2010, 2012).

Thus, based on these data, we recommend that efforts to improve existing health disparities for adolescent ATOD use must incorporate the following into their investigations: First, investigators need to specifically evaluate how ATOD use may (or may not) differ across youth of different races/ethnicities. Second, investigators must evaluate how individual, social, and environmental contexts may differentially affect ATOD use rates for these different racial/ethnic groups. Better understanding of how these contexts interact to predict ATOD use rates during this important developmental period can provide salient information for prevention and intervention efforts.

Reasons for Substance Use During This Developmental Period

There are many theories that attempt to explain ATOD use during this developmental period. There are biological, behavioral, psychological, and demographic explanations for why adolescents may initiate ATOD use or escalate their use (Frisher, Crome, Macleod, Bloor, & Hickman, 2007; Petraitis, Flay, & Miller, 1995; Sher, Grekin, & Williams, 2005; Weinberg, 2001; World Health Organization, 2004–2005). In addition to the developmental changes that occur in the brain during this time (e.g., increased reward sensitivity), other biological factors, such as hyperactivity, aggression, depression, withdrawal, anxiety (Ensminger, Juon, & Fothergill, 2002; Fuemmeler et al., 2013; Heron, Maughan, et al., 2013; Maslowsky, Schulenberg, & Zucker, 2014; Zucker, Wong, Puttler, & Fitzgerald, 2003), rebelliousness (Hall & Degenhardt, 2007; Voelkl & Frone, 2000), difficulty avoiding harm or harmful situations (Blanco et al., 2014; Castellanos-Ryan, Parent, Vitaro, Tremblay, & Séguin, 2013; Sussman, McCuller, & Dent, 2003), and neurobehavioral disinhibition (Anderson, Briggs, & White, 2013; Colder & O'Connor, 2002; Wills, Walker, Mendoza, & Ainette, 2006; World Health Organization, 2004–2005) can also affect ATOD use. In addition, genetic factors include an important subset of salient biological factors. More specifically, being biologically related to first-degree relatives who struggle with alcohol dependence (Carlson, Iacono, & McGue, 2002; Chassin, Flora, & King, 2004; Donovan, 2004; Hartman, Lessem, Hopfer, Crowley, & Stallings, 2006; Sher, Walitzer, Wood, & Brent, 1991) or drug abuse or dependence (Gil, Vega, & Turner, 2002; Hopfer, Stallings,

Hewitt, & Crowley, 2004; Yule, Wilens, Martelon, Simon, & Biederman, 2013) is associated with greater rates of ATOD use during adolescence, along with less response to the expected subjective side effects of use (Quinn & Fromme, 2011). Unfortunately, this genetic predisposition actually places youth at much greater risk for abusing ATOD because they need more alcohol in order to feel the physiological effects (Schuckit, 2009).

Emotional Factors

Adolescence is not only a time of substantial biological change; it is also a time of significant emotional and social change. For example, early adolescence is a critical developmental window for the attainment of mature self-regulatory processes. Silvers and colleagues (Silvers et al., 2012) found that emotional self-regulatory skills increased from age 10 to age 16 and then tapered off. They also found that situational factors affected emotional regulation success, whereby younger adolescents were less effective at regulating emotional responses to social stimuli compared to older youth. The authors hypothesized that this may be due to older adolescents having more experience with reappraising social situations and regulating emotions compared to younger adolescents, or that the older adolescents' prefrontal control regions are more developed (Sebastian et al., 2008; Steinberg, 2008b). Overall, findings highlight that developmental processes during this time period are highly likely to affect the choices that youth make.

Social Factors

One very important social change that takes place during adolescence is that youth become more involved with their peers. Peer influence has been shown to increase substantially during middle school and high school (Steinberg & Monahan, 2007) and is often associated with adolescent ATOD use (Brook, Pahl, & Ning, 2006; Chein, Albert, O'Brien, Uckert, & Steinberg, 2010; D'Amico & McCarthy, 2006; Poelen, Engels, Scholte, Boomsma, & Willemsen, 2009; Steinberg & Monahan, 2007; Thai, Connell, & Tebes, 2010; Wood, Read, Mitchell, & Brand, 2004). One study found that both selection and influence of friends played an important role in initiating and maintaining smoking behavior (Mercken, Steglich, Sinclair, Holliday, & Moore, 2012). Over time, however, peer selection became more important for continuing this behavior, underscoring what other work has shown: As adolescents grow older, they strive for independence, become more autonomous, and conformity to peers decreases (Spear & Kulbok, 2004; Steinberg, 2008a). In fact, there is strong evidence that shows that across all demographic groups, resistance to peer influence increases linearly between ages 14 and 18, and that middle adolescence is a period in which youth develop the capacity to stand up for what they believe in and to resist the pressure they may feel from their peers (Steinberg & Monahan, 2007).

Family Factors

Although peers can influence both initiation and escalation of substance use during adolescence, family can serve a crucial protective role, as parents still have significant influence over whether or not their child chooses to use ATOD. For example, one study found that family supervision and family attachment were strongly associated with younger compared to older adolescents' substance use (Cleveland, Bontempo, & Greenberg, 2008); thus, parents may have more influence over youth's initiation of substance use, and/or their substance use during early adolescence. In addition, other studies have shown that across different races and ethnicities, parental monitoring, involvement, having a strong parent–child relationship, and disapproval of substance use are all associated with a lower likelihood of drinking (Mrug & McCay, 2013; Wood et al., 2004), smoking cigarettes (Simons-Morton, Abroms, Haynie, & Chen, 2004; Whitesell et al., 2014), using marijuana (Lac, Alvaro, Crano, & Siegel, 2009; Pinchevsky et al., 2012), and risky sexual behavior (DiClemente et al., 2001; Johnson, 2013; Ramirez et al., 2004; van der Vorst, Engels, Meeus, Dekovic, & Vermulst, 2006).

Parent substance use is also strongly associated with an adolescent's choice to use substances (Harrier, Lambert, & Ramos, 2001; Johnson & Johnson, 2001; Jones & Magee, 2014; Li, Pentz, & Chou, 2002; Patrick, Maggs, Greene, Morgan, & Schulenberg, 2014). Teens who have nonusing parent(s) are less likely to use (Peterson, Leroux, et al., 2006); thus, parental nonuse appears to be protective. In contrast, parental drinking is strongly associated with adolescent drinking (Alati et al., 2014; Chassin, Pillow, Curran, Molina, & Barrera, 1993; Latendresse et al., 2008; Rose, Kaprio, Winter, Koskenvuo, & Viken, 1999), and youth who report that their parent(s) use marijuana are twice as likely to smoke cigarettes, drink alcohol, and use marijuana (Li et al., 2002). Across groups, having a parent who has or is using ATOD significantly increases the odds that an adolescent will use (Ehlers, Slutske, Gilder, Lau, & Wilhelmsen, 2006; Heron, Barker, et al., 2013; Kilpatrick et al., 2003; Miller, Siegel, Hohman, & Crano, 2013; Richardson, Newcomb, Myers, & Coombs, 2002).

Other family members, such as siblings, can also play a role in adolescent ATOD use. When older siblings report a higher willingness to use substances, younger siblings are more likely to report substance use (Pomery et al., 2005). Work in this area has also consistently shown that both actual older sibling substance use (Chan et al., 2013; Fagan & Najman, 2005; Fisher, Miles, Austin, Camargo, & Colditz, 2007) as well as perceived older sibling ATOD use (Ary, Tildesley, Hops, & Andrews, 1993; D'Amico & Fromme, 1997; Windle, 2000) are strongly associated with drinking behavior and positive beliefs about drugs. Of adolescents entering treatment, 11%–23% had someone living in their home (parent, sibling, or other family member) using substances at least weekly (Tims et al., 2002). Moreover, adolescents with substance-using family members evidenced more severe SUD diagnoses, with higher rates of cannabis dependence (14%) versus abuse (8%) (Tims et al., 2002).

Finally, family conflict can affect ATOD use during this period. Across all cultures, adolescents in households characterized by conflict, including family disruption, marital conflict, and low family harmony, are at higher risk for ATOD use (Best et al., 2014; Hayatbakhsh, Najman, Jamrozik, Mamun, & Alati, 2006; Richardson et al., 2002; Zhou, King, & Chassin, 2006) as well as externalizing disorders, internalizing disorders, trauma, and distress (Diamond et al., 2006; Skeer, McCormick, Normand, Buka, & Gilman, 2009). When looking across cultures, in a sample of adolescents entering substance abuse treatment, American Indian/Alaska Native adolescents reported the highest levels of experienced family conflict (Campbell, Weisner, & Sterling, 2006). Notably, while SES may overlap with many family stressors and may be believed to be a source of family conflict, family income has not consistently predicted adolescents' substance use behaviors (Hayatbakhsh et al., 2006; Radin et al., 2006).

Individual-Level Factors

Numerous cross-sectional and longitudinal studies over the past three decades have shown that adolescents' attitudes and beliefs about ATOD use are strong predictors of their subsequent ATOD use (Bot, Engels, & Knibbe, 2005; Brown, 1993;

Fromme & D'Amico, 2000; Goldman, Brown, & Christiansen, 1987; Kuntsche, Gabhainn, et al., 2014; Martino, Collins, Ellickson, Schell, & McCaffrey, 2006; McCarthy & Thompsen, 2006). Outcome expectancies, the positive and negative beliefs that one holds about the effects of alcohol or drugs, are one type of belief that has been consistently and strongly associated with adolescent cigarette, alcohol, and marijuana use (Brown, 1990; Fulton, Krank, & Stewart, 2012; McCarthy, Pedersen, & D'Amico, 2009; Schafer & Brown, 1991; Skenderian, Siegel, Crano, Alvaro, & Lac, 2008). Some examples of positive outcome expectancies are, "If I drink . . .,": "I will be more social" or "I will be brave and daring" (Fromme, Stroot, & Kaplan, 1993). Some examples of negative outcome expectancies are, "If I drink . . . ": "I would feel dizzy" or "I would act aggressively" (Fromme et al., 1993). Adolescents with strong positive outcome expectancies for ATOD are more likely to use compared to youth who do not hold these strong positive beliefs (Colder et al., 2014; Fisher et al., 2007; Skenderian et al., 2008; Smith, Goldman, Greenbaum, & Christiansen, 1995). In contrast, youth with strong negative outcome expectancies typically drink less (Colder et al., 2014; Jones & McMahon, 1993) and use drugs less (Aarons, Brown, Stice, & Coe, 2001; Alfonso & Dunn, 2009; Fulton et al., 2012; Galen & Henderson, 1999).

Cultural Factors

Several researchers (e.g., Vega & Gil, 1999; Wagner, 2003) have suggested evaluating acculturation factors, including preferred language of the adolescent and parents; however, the influence of acculturation on ATOD outcomes has yielded mixed results across many groups, including Hispanic youth and adults (Arroyo, Miller, & Tonigan, 2003; Delva et al., 2005; Fosados et al., 2007; Gil, Wagner, & Tubman, 2004; Guilamo-Ramos, Jaccard, Johansson, & Turrisi, 2004; Shih et al., 2010, 2012). Two potentially important indicators of family relationships, familism and parental respect, have been investigated as protective factors for adolescents' ATOD use (Unger et al., 2002). High familism (*familismo*), or strength of family relationships, is often seen as a traditionally Hispanic value, whereas high parental respect is often associated with traditionally Asian values (Kaplan, Nápoles-Springer, Stewart, & Pérez-Stable, 2001; Unger et al., 2002). Perhaps due to the importance placed on parental respect, work in this area has shown that Asian Americans may be reluctant to disobey family rules regarding ATOD use (Unger et al., 2002). Similarly, Hispanic adolescents who place a higher weight on familism have shown decreased risk for cigarette initiation (Kaplan et al., 2001) and heavy drinking (Wahl & Eitle, 2010). A recent study of approximately 10,000 middle school youth found that parental respect was associated with lower rates of ATOD use among Asian American youth; however, familism was unrelated to ATOD among Hispanic youth. The authors observed a ceiling effect within this diverse sample, whereby average familism scores were high with limited variability, potentially contributing to the inability to detect a significant relationship (Shih et al., 2010).

In sum, there are many factors that can influence whether an adolescent chooses to initiate or escalate ATOD use. To strengthen prevention and intervention program success, we recommend that programs targeting this age group specifically address at least one of these salient factors, such as focusing on misperceptions of use, discussing peer influence and family ATOD use, and working with youth to develop skills that are relevant for their developmental stage to help them make a healthy choice.

Prevention Programming for Adolescents

Despite the high levels of substance use observed within this age group, many youth report actively making efforts to reduce or abstain from ATOD use (Centers for Disease Control and Prevention, 2012). However, most youth may not know how to successfully limit their use, and/or where to seek intervention to gain information and support. Furthermore, particularly for minority youth, there may be other social and environmental factors (e.g., proximity to care, peer perception, family factors, financial concerns, underinsurance and uninsurance) that may influence their ability to effectively seek services.

Importance of Ensuring Developmental and Cultural Relevance

Prevention programs need to account for youth's developmental status along with relevant sociocultural factors. For example, our work has shown that the needs of middle and high school youth are very different, requiring articulated presentation styles to engage youth. Specifically, younger adolescents enjoy doing role plays to act out potential high-risk situations, whereas older youth prefer to just discuss these situations and how they would respond (D'Amico, Ellickson, Wagner, et al., 2005).

Prevention and intervention programming aimed at non-treatment-seeking youth must also attempt to engage high-risk and high-need youth who would otherwise not receive intervention. For example, because minority youth may be less likely to successfully engage in, receive, or complete programs, innovative and creative approaches are needed to reach these high-need and underserved youth.

One approach that has demonstrated particular promise with youth of different ages and races/ethnicities (cultures) is motivational interviewing (MI) (Miller & Rollnick, 2012; Rollnick, Miller, & Butler, 2008). The brevity and transportability of this intervention has made it ideal in reaching youth across a variety of settings, including juvenile justice, medical clinics, homeless shelters, and schools (Cushing, Jensen, Miller, & Leffingwell, 2014; Jensen et al., 2011; Lundahl, Kunz, Brownell, Tollefson, & Burke, 2010). Not only is this brief (1–2 session), empathic, and strength-based intervention highly transportable, it is also highly effective across a number of substance use and health risk behaviors (Hettema, Steele, & Miller, 2005; Jofre-Bonet & Sindelar, 2001; Lundahl et al., 2010). Moreover, it is particularly good at facilitating therapeutic alliance with wary recipients, such as non-treatment-seeking youth who report at-risk levels of ATOD use (D'Amico, Miles, Stern, & Meredith, 2008; McCambridge, Slym, & Strang, 2008; Peterson, Baer, Wells, Ginzler, & Garrett, 2006). Additionally, qualitative studies have suggested that the approach of MI resonates with adolescents across all ages, with high percentages of youth reporting that they liked the MI intervention and would recommend it to a friend (D'Amico, Hunter, Miles, Ewing, & Osilla, 2013; D'Amico, Osilla, & Hunter, 2010; D'Amico, Tucker, et al., 2012; Martin & Copeland, 2008; Stern, Meredith, Gholson, Gore, & D'Amico, 2007). This is likely due to the nonjudgmental, empathic, and collaborative approach of MI (Miller, Villanueva, Tonigan, & Cuzmar, 2007), whereby adolescents' own values, opinions, and arguments for change are the most valued and reflected part of the therapeutic discussion.

MI has been actively promoted as an intervention for use with minority youth (Kirk, Scott, & Daniels, 2005). Because there are aspects of MI that appear to be a good fit with minority youth, but also aspects that make it potentially less efficacious, it is critical to specifically determine how to evaluate and improve the efficacy of interventions like MI with minority youth (Feldstein Ewing, Wray,

Mead, & Adams, 2012). Specifically, as of 2011 there were 21 MI outcome trials conducted with adolescents for substance use. Only five of these studies included samples with more than 50% non-White youth (Jensen et al., 2011), and very few explicitly evaluated the role of race, ethnicity, or culture in prevention and intervention outcomes. This area deserves attention, because preliminary evidence suggests that cultural factors (e.g., level of ethnic mistrust, cultural orientation, ethic pride) may influence adolescents' response to MI-based interventions (Gil et al., 2004). More research is needed to highlight factors that may differentially influence outcomes by group, in order to identify culturally relevant variables that may be important to include in the adaptation of this intervention (Feldstein Ewing et al., 2012).

School-Based Programs

There are many school-based prevention programs that have been successful in decreasing adolescent ATOD use (see D'Amico, Osilla, & Stern, in press, for a review). In this chapter we describe three classroom-based programs and two voluntary after-school programs that have shown promise.

Project ALERT (Ellickson & Bell, 1990) was designed to teach middle school youth skills to resist influences to use drugs, promote social skills, and help youth understand how drug use affects them. The curriculum requires eleven 45-minute sessions across both seventh (eight sessions) and eighth grade (three sessions). In the initial test of ALERT, 30 control and treatment schools from California and Oregon were chosen to reflect a diverse range of school and community environments, including urban, suburban, and rural areas. Nine of the schools had a minority population of 50% or more, and 18 drew from neighborhoods with household incomes below the median for their state. In this study, the investigators found that at the 15-month follow-up, students who had participated in Project ALERT were less likely to initiate cigarette and marijuana use, and they had lower current use of these substances than students in the control schools. Although intervention effects were found for alcohol use at the 3-month follow-up, these were no longer significant at the 15-month follow-up (Ellickson & Bell, 1990). Based on these findings, the ALERT curriculum was revised to put more emphasis on curbing alcohol misuse and was tested in a large-scale, randomized trial with 55 schools in South Dakota (Ellickson, McCaffrey, Ghosh-Dastidar, & Longshore, 2003).

Three additional lessons were added in seventh grade. The program continued to curb marijuana and cigarette use. It also decreased alcohol misuse and alcohol-related problems at 18-month follow-up (Ellickson, McCaffrey, et al., 2003). The authors suggested that the program could be improved further by focusing more on adolescents' perception of peers' attitudes toward alcohol and the prevalence of alcohol use (Orlando, Ellickson, McCaffrey, & Longshore, 2005).

St. Pierre and colleagues (St Pierre, Osgood, Mincemoyer, Kaltreider, & Kauh, 2005) conducted an independent evaluation of Project ALERT in eight Pennsylvania middle schools and conducted four waves of posttests over the 2-year program and 2-year follow-up. They did not find any effects of ALERT on AOD use or on any of the mediators at any time point. Despite some differences in the research design from the original study of ALERT, the authors conclude that their null findings were not due to modifications in research design, sample size, or data analysis approaches (St Pierre et al., 2005). In 2009, Ringwalt and colleagues (Ringwalt, Clark, Hanley, Shamblen, & Flewelling, 2010) tested the Project ALERT curriculum in a randomized controlled trial in 34 schools in sixth–eighth grades across 11 states. They implemented ALERT in sixth grade and examined effects on 30-day use of cigarettes, alcohol, marijuana, and inhalants 1 year after curriculum implementation. They found that substance use increased over time for all substances and did not support the long-term effectiveness of ALERT when delivered to sixth graders (Ringwalt et al., 2010). Overall, it appears that additional effectiveness studies are needed to assess this program in different contexts (Gorman & Conde, 2010).

One of the few culturally grounded, school-based prevention programs is Keepin' it REAL (Gosin, Marsiglia, & Hecht, 2003), a drug resistance curriculum tailored for Mexican American youth in the Southwest. Keepin' it REAL is comprised of ten 40- to 45-minute lessons with five videos. The program teaches cognitive and communication skills for use with four "REAL" resistance strategies: Refuse, Explain, Avoid, and Leave (Gosin et al., 2003). Three curricula were developed: one targeting Hispanic students (Mexican American version), another targeting non-Latino students (African American and Caucasian version), and a multicultural version combining the previous two. The program was effective such that increases in alcohol, marijuana, and cigarette use were less substantial among intervention students compared to control students. The Hispanic version of the program generated more positive outcomes overall; however, in this particular study, there was little evidence that matching the message to the ethnicity of participants enhanced the program's effectiveness. Specifically, when analyses limited the sample to those youth who reported Mexican/Mexican American identity, the Hispanic version did not generate better outcomes than the non-Hispanic version (Hecht et al., 2003; Kulis et al., 2005).

ASSIST (A Stop Smoking in Schools Trial) is a peer-led program for high school youth that took place in England and Wales. Two days of peer training helped peer leaders develop communication skills, listening skills, ways of giving and receiving information, and learn how to talk effectively with other students about the short-term risks of smoking and the benefits of remaining smoke-free (Campbell et al., 2008). The intervention took place over 10 weeks during which peer leaders had informal conversations about smoking with their peers in a variety of situations (e.g., lunchtime, breaks, to and from school), and peers logged a record of these conversations into a diary. The evaluation involved a cluster randomized trial of 10,730 students aged 12–13 years in 59 schools. Data were gathered at baseline, immediately following the intervention, and at 1-year and 2-year follow-ups. Examination of baseline characteristics between the intervention and control schools indicated that more students at the control schools reported smoking each week compared to students in the intervention schools. After controlling for all baseline differences, results indicated that prevalence of smoking was lower in the intervention schools compared to the control schools at all three follow-up time points, with some attenuation of these effects over time (Campbell et al., 2008).

ASSIST was reanalyzed as part of the European Union–funded TEENAGE project to examine the effects on smoking in different socioeconomic categories, and ASSIST showed the strongest results for youth in the lowest socioeconomic category (Mercken, Moore, et al., 2012). An important part of the ASSIST intervention is choosing peer leaders, who are nominated by fellow students. The peer nomination process in the 2008 study resulted in a mix of students, with both genders and different ethnicities represented. Despite some student and teacher misgivings about the process, results from the trial suggest that the intervention was effective, indicating that the broad range of youth who were nominated as peer supporters and delivered

the intervention contributed to the success of the program (Starkey, Audrey, Holliday, Moore, & Campbell, 2009). A recent cost-effectiveness analysis of ASSIST indicated that the cost of the program per student was modest at approximately 32 GBP or 50 dollars (Hollingworth et al., 2013).

In contrast to the many mandated in-class programs that address ATOD use, there are few voluntary programs available for youth that specifically target ATOD, and even fewer that take place outside of class time (Little & Harris, 2003). Voluntary ATOD programs may appeal to youth because they can decide to go based on interest and/or need. Research has shown that providing youth with a choice can increase the likelihood that they choose to obtain additional services (e.g., Baer, Garrett, Beadnell, Wells, & Peterson, 2007) or make changes in their ATOD use (D'Amico et al., 2008; Monti et al., 2007; Spirito et al., 2004).

To date, there are only two voluntary programs that specifically target ATOD use. One intervention called Project Options was implemented in several high schools (Brown, Anderson, Schulte, Sintov, & Frissell, 2005) and was available via individual (four sessions), group (six sessions), or website (unlimited access) format (Brown, 2001). Individual and group sessions took place either during lunch or after school. Curriculum content across all three options focused on coping, behavioral management, communication, addressing outcome expectancies, and receiving normative feedback about ATOD. One important component of this research was to better understand which students would voluntarily choose the different intervention formats. Findings indicated that 5 out of 6 participants chose to participate in the group format and that minority and biracial/multiracial youth disproportionately sought the individual context for services (D'Amico et al., 2006). Overall, students reported greater satisfaction with the group and individual formats compared to the website (Kia-Keating, Brown, Schulte, & Monreal, 2008). Brown and colleagues (Brown et al., 2005) conducted a one-semester follow-up of Project Options, focusing on adolescents' efforts to change their drinking. Although actual changes in drinking behavior were not examined, the authors found that the heaviest drinking students who attended at least one session (individual, group, or web format) reported more attempts to cut down or quit drinking compared to heavy drinking adolescents who did not attend the program (Brown et al., 2005).

In 2010, Schulte and colleagues examined the effects of Project Options on intervention youth

(N = 327) in three high schools who reported life-time drinking by comparing them to a matched sample of control youth from these schools who also reported lifetime drinking (N = 1,728). They measured perceptions of peer drinking and alcohol use in the fall and spring. Project Options participants reported more accurate estimates of peer alcohol use; however, there was no effect of the intervention on adolescents' actual alcohol use (Schulte, Monreal, Kia-Keating, & Brown, 2010). A cross-sectional examination of youth who self-selected into Project Options in the second semester of the 2006–2007 school year (6.3%) found that compared to youth who did not attend, attendees were more likely to be male, report heavier drinking, and were more likely to report experiences of victimization or bullying, suggesting that this program attracted youth with some risk characteristics (McGee, Valentine, Schulte, & Brown, 2011).

The only other voluntary intervention targeted middle school youth. D'Amico and colleagues implemented CHOICE in a small pilot trial in two schools (D'Amico & Edelen, 2007) and then in a larger cluster randomized controlled trial in 16 schools (D'Amico, Tucker, et al., 2012). CHOICE took place for a half hour after school once a week. There were five sessions, which repeated throughout the course of the school year. The sessions focused on providing normative feedback, discussing unrealistic positive beliefs about ATOD, resisting pressure to use ATOD through the use of role plays, walking through the potential benefits of both continuing use and cutting down, and discussion of risky situations and coping strategies, such as getting social support or learning how to avoid certain high-risk situations (D'Amico, Ellickson, Wagner, et al., 2005). CHOICE also utilized an MI approach; sessions were collaborative and interactive, with discussion focused on how students could make healthier choices.

In the small pilot trial of CHOICE, approximately 13% of students came to the after-school program. Those who attended CHOICE reported less alcohol use and lower perceptions of alcohol, marijuana, and cigarette use than a matched sample of control students. In addition, a 2-year comparison of the CHOICE and control school indicated that actual alcohol and marijuana use, and perceptions of friends' alcohol and marijuana use, increased more sharply among control school students relative to CHOICE students (effect sizes = 0.21 to 0.52; D'Amico & Edelen, 2007). The large randomized controlled trial of CHOICE with 16 middle schools

replicated the pilot results (D'Amico, Tucker, et al., 2012). Across the eight CHOICE schools, similar to other after-school programs (Afterschool Alliance, 2009), 15% of consented students voluntarily attended CHOICE during the year. In contrast to other after-school programs, CHOICE reached those youth who typically do not obtain services (Harvard Family Research Project, 2007; Sterling, Weisner, Hinman, & Parthasarathy, 2010; Wu, Hoven, Tiet, Kovalenko, & Wicks, 2002), including minority youth and youth who reported regular use of alcohol and marijuana (D'Amico, Green, et al., 2012). Furthermore, across CHOICE schools, 1 adolescent out of 15 was prevented from initiating alcohol use during the academic year (D'Amico, Tucker, et al., 2012). A cost analysis of the CHOICE program found that the median cost per enrolled student was approximately $21 per student (Kilmer, Burgdorf, D'Amico, Tucker, & Miles, 2011).

Hospital and Primary Care Settings

There are several MI interventions for youth that occur in hospital settings after a "teachable moment," where an adolescent receives services in an Emergency Department (ED) due to some type of consequence from drinking or drug use (Colby et al., 1998, 2005; Gwaltney et al., 2011; Horn, Dino, Hamilton, Noerachmanto, & Zhang, 2008; Monti et al., 1999, 2007; Spirito et al., 2011). Many of these interventions have been conducted by Drs. Monti, Spirito, and Colby and the Brown University research group. These studies have focused on prevention and intervention approaches with adolescent alcohol-related behaviors (Becker et al., 2012; Gwaltney et al., 2011; Linakis et al., 2013; Monti et al., 1999, 2007; Spirito et al., 2004, 2011) and tobacco use behaviors (Colby et al., 1998, 2005, 2012), with initial explorations into the role of marijuana in participant outcomes (Magill, Barnett, Apodaca, Rohsenow, & Monti, 2009). In terms of alcohol use behaviors, in their prior work (Monti et al., 1999; Spirito et al., 2004), this research team found that both middle (13–17) and late (18–19) adolescent ED patients were responsive to a single individualized MI intervention targeting drinking reductions. Building upon these findings, in their more recent exploration, Spirito and colleagues (Spirito et al., 2011) recruited newly admitted adolescent ED patients who either tested positive for alcohol (blood, breath, saliva) or reported alcohol use within 6 hours prior to the ED visit. To determine the critical role that parents/families may play in alcohol use outcomes, participants (ages 13–17) were randomized to receive either one 45-minute individualized MI approach (comparable to their prior interventions) or an individualized MI plus a family-checkup (FCU; Dishion et al., 2008) that was comprised of an hour videotaped family assessment task and a 1-hour feedback session. Due to extenuating circumstances (time of night, blood alcohol level), most youth did not receive their interventions within the context of the ED, but rather returned to the hospital to participate within a few days of their ED visit. All youth were followed at 3, 6, and 12 months post intervention. Whereas both groups evidenced significant reductions in quantity, frequency, and high-risk alcohol use throughout the follow-up periods, the effects were particularly robust at 3 months. Furthermore, although the outcomes appeared to be slightly better for the MI + FCU group relative to the MI-only condition, perhaps due to sample size (N = 125), group differences were not statistically significant.

In addition to providing a salient moment to discuss alcohol use, accessing youth through the ED also provides an opportunity to reach youth that may be ambivalent about their tobacco use and/or reluctant to seek treatment. Building upon their series of adolescent smoking interventions (Colby et al., 1998), Colby and colleagues (2005) recruited 85 adolescents (ages 14–19) from ED and clinic settings. All interventions were scheduled to take place within 2 weeks of their medical visit. Youth were randomized to receive either brief advice (BA), where clinicians informed youth of the importance of quitting smoking and provided them with a pamphlet on smoking cessation along with relevant local treatment sources, or a single-session MI, which focused on discussing the pros and cons of smoking, identifying/exploring ambivalence, and walking through a personalized feedback sheet. Youth in the MI condition additionally received a 15- to 20-minute booster MI session by telephone 1 week after their first MI intervention. All youth were recontacted at 1, 3, and 6 months to evaluate progress. Youth in both conditions evidenced improved smoking behaviors across all follow-up periods, with youth in the MI condition showing better outcomes relative to the BA group at 3 months (reduced cotinine levels). At 6 months, both groups demonstrated comparable cotinine outcomes. However, the MI group reported greater abstinence from tobacco. Importantly, similar to the alcohol studies, whereas many youth reported reductions in tobacco use, few transitioned into total cessation.

Similar to the work of Colby and colleagues, Horn et al. (2008) also explored the acceptability and feasibility of an MI-based intervention to reduce tobacco use among pediatric ED attendees. Seventy-four youth (ages 14–19) received either an MI or BA condition. Despite nonsignificant cessation rates, the authors found medium effects for reduction in smoking and large effects for percent reduction (Cohen's h = 0.38 and 0.69, respectively). In addition, the MI intervention was found to be highly acceptable to the providers, adolescent patients, and their parents. However, the authors reported that the major obstacle in this intervention paradigm was "reach," or their ability to enroll eligible youth within this setting.

In contrast to the work in the ED, there is a critical gap in providing and evaluating preventive services for at-risk adolescents in the primary care (PC) setting. PC settings provide a practical and efficient opportunity to screen and intervene with youth who use alcohol, tobacco, and marijuana because 66% of 12- to 17-year-old teens visit a PC provider at least once every 6 months (Bloom & Cohen, 2009), and most adolescents report willingness to discuss ATOD use with their PC provider (Brown & Wissow, 2009; Ford, Millstein, Halpern-Felsher, & Irwin, 1997; Klein et al., 2001; Stern et al., 2007; Yoast, Fleming, & Balch, 2007).

Recognizing this opportunity, AMA guidelines propose that providers integrate preventive services into routine medical care for teens (Elster & Levenberg, 1997) by screening for ATOD use and providing brief counseling and referrals where appropriate (Elster & Kuznets, 1993). Furthermore, the American Academy of Pediatrics released a policy statement in 2010 recommending that doctors screen all pediatric patients for alcohol use starting in middle school (American Academy of Pediatrics Committee on Substance Abuse, 2010). Unfortunately, integration of AOD preventive services in PC is rare (Chung, Lee, Morrison, & Schuster, 2006; Klein et al., 2001; Ozer et al., 2001). Notably, early adolescents (e.g., age 11–14) (Ellen, Franzgrote, Irwin, & Millstein, 1998; Millstein & Marcell, 2003) and youth from lower-income or disadvantaged backgrounds are even less likely to be screened or receive prevention services in the PC setting (Stevens & Shi, 2003).

Some brief, office-based AOD interventions have focused on providing information before the PC appointment. For example, Boekeloo and colleagues (2004) conducted a randomized controlled trial of 409 adolescents (44% male; 79%

African American) to evaluate a 15-minute audio intervention program. The audio program modeled an adolescent going to a PC provider for a check-up, asking about confidentiality, and being encouraged to discuss risk behaviors with the provider. There were also testimonials by youth who wished they had avoided drinking. The audio program ended with youth discussing fun alcohol-free activities. Youth in the intervention group received this audio program before their PC appointment. Those who received this program reported higher intentions to drink and were more likely to report heavy drinking at 6-month follow-up compared to the control group. The authors suggested that this may have been because the audio program emphasized discussing alcohol use with the PC provider. As a result, they posit that these youth were more honest in their self-reports about their drinking compared to the control adolescents (Boekeloo et al., 2004).

Recently, Ozer and colleagues (2011) conducted a study with 904 youth (49% male; 47% Caucasian, 19% Hispanic, 10% African American, 12% Asian American, and 4% Native American) to determine whether delivering preventive services in PC settings would reduce risk behaviors across ATOD use, sexual behavior, and use of seat belts and bike helmets. The authors trained the providers, helped providers integrate screening and charting tools into their PC practices, and provided additional resources for the health educator in each clinic. Each youth visit was approximately 24–30 minutes and focused on the "Four A's": Ask, Advise, Assist, Arrange. If the adolescent reported the behavior, the provider was encouraged to address severity, express concern, and provide information about the consequences. Intervention youth were compared to population-based samples. Interestingly, they found that the intervention had the strongest effects on helmet use and seat belt use, but they had no effects on sexual activity or ATOD use (Ozer et al., 2011).

In a recent meta-analytic review of MI interventions with adolescents (Jensen et al., 2011), only 3 of the 21 studies reviewed were conducted with adolescents in a PC setting. One of these studies was the Colby and colleagues (2005) study (reviewed earlier). Second, Hollis and colleagues (2005) conducted a large randomized controlled trial with adolescents (n = 2,542; 80% Caucasian), examining whether a tobacco intervention that included (1) a 30-second clinician advice message by the provider, (2) a 10-minute computer activity program, (3) a 5-minute MI intervention by the provider, and (4) two 10-minute booster sessions during the following 11 months decreased tobacco use. They compared this intervention to a single 5-minute MI intervention to promote increased consumption of fruits and vegetables. They found strong effects for baseline smokers, with those in the MI group targeting tobacco reporting greater abstinence rates at 2 years than those in the MI group targeting increased fruit/vegetable intake. Third, D'Amico and colleagues (2008) developed a 15-minute MI intervention for youth in PC provided by a health care worker. In a small pilot trial of at-risk and predominantly Hispanic youth (48% male; 86% Hispanic, 10% African American, 4% Caucasian), they found that their MI intervention led to reductions in intentions to use marijuana (d = .86) and alcohol (d = .62), frequency of marijuana use (d = .79), and affiliation with substance-using peers (ds = .34 and .61, for alcohol-using and marijuana-using peers, respectively).

In sum, given that most teens visit a PC provider, brief interventions have the potential to reach many at-risk teens who would not otherwise be reached through more conventional interventions. Unfortunately, many PC providers do not have the requisite training or resources available to be comfortable in routinely screening and addressing ATOD use among adolescents in the PC setting (Babor et al., 2008; Gordon, Ettaro, Rodriguez, Mocik, & Clark, 2011; Halpern-Felsher et al., 2000; Marcell, Halpern-Felsher, Coriell, & Millstein, 2002; Ozer et al., 2004). Clearly, greater work is needed to improve brief ATOD service provision in the PC setting and to understand how these services may affect adolescents' long-term ATOD use.

Other Community Programs
Juvenile Justice and Teen Court Settings

Many clinical/research groups have found that MI interventions targeting ATOD are a particularly good fit within the juvenile justice and teen court contexts. Because recent research has indicated that there may be disproportionately more minority youth within justice settings (Feldstein Ewing, Venner, et al., 2011), it is particularly important to examine how these interventions work with minority samples.

Teen Court is a setting that was created for youth who receive a first-time misdemeanor offense. In the Teen Court setting, youth are offered the opportunity to participate in a program in lieu of formal processing in the juvenile justice system. As part of this program, youth who commit an alcohol or drug offense are sentenced to receive six alcohol and drug education groups, along with other sanctions (e.g., community service, peer groups, serve on the Teen Court jury, fees). One of the major benefits of Teen Court participation is that adolescents who successfully complete their Teen Court sentence have their AOD offense expunged from their juvenile probation record. Working in conjunction with this existing Teen Court system, D'Amico et al. (2010) developed a six-session MI group intervention called Free Talk. They examined client acceptance and intervention feasibility, and conducted a preliminary outcome evaluation of Free Talk. Free Talk teens reported higher quality and satisfaction ratings, and MI integrity scores were higher for Free Talk groups. AOD use and delinquency decreased for both groups at 3 months, and 12-month recidivism rates were lower but not significantly different for the Free Talk group compared to UC (D'Amico et al., 2013). Sequential analysis of the Free Talk groups found that youth who participated in groups that expressed more change talk, or self-expressed speech that is an argument for change (Miller & Rollnick, 2012), were more likely to report decreased alcohol intentions, alcohol use, and heavy drinking 3 months later. Change talk in this setting was influenced by both the facilitators' reflections of change talk and by positive peer responses to change talk, emphasizing the importance of the group process in helping youth make healthier choices (D'Amico et al., 2015).

There have been several studies with youth who have offended more than one time and are therefore placed in a juvenile justice setting. For example, in a preliminary analysis of an ongoing research protocol evaluating MI across a sample of Hispanic American and Caucasian youth on probation (Feldstein Ewing, 2012), Hispanic American youth who received an MI intervention targeting ATOD use reported liking the MI intervention ($n = 68$; $M = 4.5$ on a scale of 1–5) and stated that they would recommend it to a friend ($M = 4.46$ on a scale of 1–5). Furthermore, Gil and colleagues (Gil et al., 2004) conducted an MI-based intervention with a sample of predominantly high-risk, African American and Hispanic youth who were involved in the justice system. They found that post intervention, these youth decreased their frequency of marijuana use and alcohol use. Additionally, with a sample of Hispanic and African American youth residing in detention, Schmiege and colleagues (Schmiege, Broaddus, Levin, & Bryan, 2009) demonstrated that adding an MI component targeting

alcohol use to a sexual risk prevention program reduced the likelihood of having sex while drinking ($d = .13$, $d = .40$) when compared with sex risk prevention without alcohol and information control conditions, respectively.

Stein and colleagues (Stein et al., 2011) randomized a diverse sample of detained youth (33% Caucasian; 29% Hispanic; 28% African American; 4% Native American; and 3% Asian American) to receive an MI versus relaxation training (RT) condition. Compared with youth in the RT condition, MI youth demonstrated lower rates of alcohol and marijuana use at the 3-month follow-up. In Walton and colleagues' evaluation of MI with a sample of urban African American youth in an emergency department setting (Walton et al., 2010), the authors found a 32.2% reduction in alcohol-related consequences at the 6-month follow-up (OR = 0.56). Finally, in an innovative translational study aimed at using a neurodevelopmental approach to deconstruct the active ingredients of MI with justice-involved adolescents, Feldstein Ewing and colleagues (Feldstein Ewing et al., 2013) evaluated the efficacy of an MI intervention with regular cannabis users who were in a diversion program, aimed at having youth with lower-level arrests (e.g., minor in possession) participate in a one-time education class in lieu of further justice involvement. Integrating functional magnetic resonance imaging (fMRI) with a standard two-session MI intervention targeting reductions in cannabis use behaviors, client statements in favor of changing their cannabis use behavior (change talk; e.g., I need to cut down my marijuana use) and in favor of sustaining cannabis behavior (sustain talk; e.g., Marijuana use is not a problem for me) were directly taken from the first MI session. Client statements were then re-presented to youth auditorally and visually within an fMRI paradigm immediately prior to exposure to a tactile cannabis (marijuana pipe) or control cue. Youth reported significant changes in cannabis use, problems, and dependence 1 month following the intervention. Furthermore, brain activation (blood oxygen level–dependent; BOLD response) during change talk significantly predicted posttreatment cannabis use, particularly in areas involved in introspection (posterior cingulate, precuneus), indicating the key role of brain activation during an important aspect of MI (client change talk) and its association with better treatment outcomes for youth. Overall, these data continue to support the efficacy of MI with justice-involved youth, as well as highlight the importance of salient neurodevelopmental processes during an active ingredient of MI.

In addition to the strong set of MI prevention and intervention efforts, there are a number of impressive multifaceted interventions that have been found to be successful in reducing justice-involved youth's ATOD use. Perhaps one of the best-known multifaceted intervention approaches is multisystemic therapy (MST; Henggeler & Borduin, 1990). As detailed in a recent meta-analysis (van der Stouwe, Asscher, Stams, Deković, & van der Laan, 2014), MST proposes that justice-involved adolescents' ATOD use stems from a complex interplay of youth, family, peer, school, and neighborhood risk factors (Henggeler, 2011). With particular attention to the importance of facilitating and supporting family-directed change, MST tries to remove standard barriers to treatment accessibility in order to successfully work with youth toward positive change. For example, intervention sessions are often conducted at home at the family's convenience with a team of specialized providers (more than one per family) who have purposefully low-level caseloads (often fewer than five). Ultimately, empirical evidence from the past several decades has strongly indicated that juvenile justice–involved samples (youth with delinquent behaviors, youth with substance use disorders, violent/chronically offending youth, adolescent sexual offenders) receiving MST evidence improved behaviors across family relations, behavior/emotional problems, recidivism, externalizing behaviors, and substance use up to 24 months post recruitment (Henggeler, 2011).

Liddle and colleagues (Henderson, Dakof, Greenbaum, & Liddle, 2010; Liddle, 1999; Liddle et al., 2009) also developed a multilevel intervention for high-risk, substance-using adolescents: multidimensional family therapy (MDFT). Similar to MST, MDFT is an approach that focuses on what are considered to be four interdependent treatment domains: the adolescent domain, the parent domain, the family interaction domain, and the extrafamilial domain (Hogue, Dauber, Samuolis, & Liddle, 2006). Through multi-informant clinical assessments, MDFT providers determine where youth evidence areas of strength, and what areas may be contributing to the youth's ATOD use (e.g., association with deviant peers, school failure, absence of prosocial activities/involvement). Three recent studies support positive outcomes for MDFT with justice-involved adolescents who report ATOD use. Liddle et al. (2009) found that compared with a peer group intervention, MDFT youth evidenced reduced substance use frequency, substance related problems, delinquency, distress, and family/peer/school risk (ds = 0.27–0.77) at 12 months. Furthermore, in a second study MDFT was compared with cognitive-behavioral therapy (Henderson et al., 2010). Whereas the two interventions performed comparably for youth with lower levels of substance use severity, more severe youth (defined as youth with greater substance use frequency and/or greater comorbid diagnoses) had better outcomes when receiving MDFT compared to CBT. Finally, in a randomized controlled trial for adolescent cannabis users across five locations within Europe (the International Need for Cannabis Treatment Study; INCANT), Rigter and colleagues (2013) found positive outcomes for both MDFT and individual psychotherapy (IP). However, adolescents in the MDFT condition were more likely to stay in treatment, as well as reduce their cannabis dependence over time (Rigter et al., 2013).

Homeless Shelters

In terms of reaching difficult-to-reach adolescent populations, the group of youth with the greatest need and least accessibility is likely to be homeless youth. Across the board, research is lacking on interventions that meet the health care needs of homeless adolescents (Hwang, Tolomiczenko, Kouyoumdjian, & Garner, 2005; Xiang, 2013). There are only a few published studies that have evaluated individual- or group-based risk reduction interventions for homeless youth. In terms of design, these interventions have tended to either require substantial time and resources to deliver, are incredibly brief intervention approaches, or focus on supporting street outreach efforts.

The more intensive interventions include the Street Smart program (Rotheram-Borus, Koopman, Haignere, & Davies, 1991; Rotheram-Borus et al., 2003) and the Adolescent Community Reinforcement Approach (A-CRA) (Slesnick & Kang, 2008; Slesnick, Prestopnik, Meyers, & Glassman, 2007). Street Smart is a group-based HIV/STI prevention intervention designed for 11- to 18-year-old runaway and homeless youth. Based on social learning theory, the program consists of eight 1.5- to 2-hour group sessions, one individual session, and one visit to a community-based organization resource. Information on reducing ATOD use is integrated throughout the sessions. In terms of outcomes, in the initial evaluation with 145 runaway youth, the intervention was associated with an increase in condom use at 3 months and a decrease in high-risk sexual behavior at 6 months (Rotheram-Borus et al., 1991). A second evaluation involved 187 youth followed over a 2-year period. The authors found that compared to control youth, females who received the program showed significant health risk reduction across the board (e.g., 24 months = reductions in unprotected sexual acts; 12 months = reductions in alcohol use, marijuana use, and number of drugs used), and males who received the intervention significantly reduced marijuana use at 6 months (Rotheram-Borus et al., 2003).

Slesnick and colleagues (Slesnick et al., 2007) evaluated a program that included 16 individual sessions of the adolescent-community reinforcement approach (A-CRA) (Godley et al., 2001; Meyers & Smith, 1995), a comprehensive behavioral program for addressing substance-abuse problems and HIV prevention. Youth (n = 180) were followed for 6 months, with intervention youth reporting less substance use (Slesnick et al., 2007) and more condom use (Slesnick & Kang, 2008) compared to the treatment-as-usual control group. Both of these intensive interventions demonstrated promising results. However, the involved resources (e.g., manpower, establishing a site to deliver interventions, cost of supporting resource delivery) required to provide these types of programs can be a major obstacle for many community-based settings.

To date, brief interventions for homeless youth have tended to focus either on ATOD or HIV/STI prevention. For example, two studies by Baer and colleagues evaluated MI interventions to reduce ATOD use among homeless youth. One study evaluated a single individualized MI intervention, which included an MI-congruent provision of personalized feedback about youth's ATOD use and associated risk (Peterson, Leroux, et al., 2006). Compared to the control groups, homeless youth who received the MI intervention (n = 92) reduced illicit drug use other than marijuana at the 1-month follow-up (ns = 94 and 99); however, this effect was not sustained by the 3-month follow-up. Furthermore, no effects were observed at the 1- and 3-month follow-ups for alcohol or marijuana use. The second evaluation of an MI intervention involved 127 homeless youth, with the opportunity to receive up to four individualized sessions. The sessions followed the general model of a substance use check-up where information

about patterns and risks related to AOD use are provided, along with personal feedback (Baer et al., 2007). Total treatment exposure across all four sessions averaged 73 minutes. Homeless youth rated their experience in the program quite positively; however, there were no statistically significant effects on their ATOD use at 3-month follow-up.

In general, these types of brief interventions for homeless youth have met with little success. A recent review of ATOD and sexual risk reduction interventions for runaway and homeless youth concluded that programs need to be both intensive enough to address the multiple and interrelated risk behaviors that most homeless youth exhibit *and* feasible to integrate into settings such as drop-in resource centers where these youth routinely seek services (Slesnick, Dashora, Letcher, Erdem, & Serovich, 2009). Additional work is needed in this area to ensure that programs meet the needs of these youth.

Conclusion

Together, these studies underscore the importance of identifying adolescence as a distinct neurodevelopmental period, with its own set of specific prevention and intervention needs. Specifically, most neurodevelopmental research emphasizes that adolescence is a distinct (Luna, Padmanabhana, & O'Hearn, 2010; Paus et al., 2008; Sturman & Moghaddam, 2011) and highly vulnerable period, which may be particularly sensitive to ATOD exposure (Ashtari, Cervellione, Cottone, Ardekani, & Kumra, 2009; Jager & Ramsey, 2008; Schweinsburg et al., 2008). Furthermore, key factors, including emotional development (capacity for self-regulation and control), social networks (whether youth are nested within a set of prosocial or substance-using peers), family practices and behaviors (parent/sibling use and level of family conflict), individual attitudes and beliefs (positive and negative expectancies), and cultural identification and practices (preferred language, parental respect, familism) have been shown to be particularly salient to ATOD use during this developmental period. To improve effectiveness in reducing youth ATOD use, prevention and intervention programs are encouraged to pay particular attention to the developmentally specific influence of these factors in adolescent ATOD use, potentially by incorporating and articulating intervention content focused on helping adolescents navigate these issues.

Future Directions

There are many challenges that the field faces as we continue our work to prevent ATOD use among adolescents of all backgrounds across a variety of settings. One important issue is making sure that we reach youth at all ages and developmental stages with our prevention messages. Clinicians, medical providers, justice personnel, and schools must be prepared to address ATOD use across early, middle, and late adolescence, realizing that youth of different ages are going to have different milestones they are trying to reach and thus different concerns. Ultimately, our message is that "one size does not fit all." Yet this leads to an important question: To be effective, how do we ensure that prevention and intervention programming is developmentally appropriate?

Another challenge that we must address is reaching minority youth and those at-risk youth who may already have initiated ATOD use because both of these groups are less likely to access available resources and to be retained in services. Efforts must therefore focus on improving outreach and intervention programming for these groups, particularly as many at-risk youth may initiate at a very young age (Feldstein Ewing, Magnan, et al., 2014). Moreover, emerging work suggests that providers may conduct interventions in different ways with minority versus majority (e.g., Hispanic vs. Caucasian youth), in the direction of providing less skillful intervention work with minority youth. And this has been shown to affect treatment outcomes, particularly for alcohol-related problems (Feldstein Ewing, Gaume, Ernst, Rivera, & Houck, 2015). The field must also better understand why minority youth tend to have poorer ATOD outcomes when they typically have equivalent or lower rates of ATOD use; we must begin to address how to resolve these health disparities.

Finally, many community-based organizations face difficulty in implementing prevention programs with fidelity and quality, along with matching the significant outcomes reported in the work of prevention researchers. This gap between research and practice (e.g., Green, 2001; Wandersman & Florin, 2003) is often the result of limited training and implementation resources in these real-world settings. To improve effective dissemination, organizations need support. This involves providing the knowledge and skills, along with a clear delineation of the resources that will be needed to conduct the steps required, including needs assessment, setting priorities, and understanding what program delivery will pragmatically look like across these settings. Program implementation can be improved if organizations can obtain buy-in from the stakeholders in their communities (Chinman et al., 2008; D'Amico, Chinman, Stern, & Wandersman, 2009).

Many research groups have taken active steps to reduce the gap between research and practice (Biglan, Mrazek, Carnine, & Flay, 2003; Liddle et al., 2002); however, the support and resources available to on-the-ground community adolescent ATOD organizations may not be comparable to those available within a protected research protocol. As a result, despite interest and investment in improving adolescent ATOD outcomes, organizations may be challenged in providing even well-supported evidence-based practices (McGovern, Fox, Xie, & Drake, 2004), especially during tough economic times. Thus, innovative efforts by the research community to work directly with community-based partners to provide accessible and affordable training and support may offer one avenue to help transition effective prevention programs into the community; ultimately, better communication and support between research and clinical providers can only benefit youth. Closing the gap between research and practice can help expand the range of services available to this age group and reach youth across a variety of settings.

References

Aarons, G., Brown, S. A., Stice, E., & Coe, M. (2001). Psychometric evaluation of the marijuana and stimulant effect expectancy questionnaire for youth. *Addictive Behaviors, 26,* 219–236.

Aarons, G. A., Brown, S. A., Garland, A. F., & Hough, R. L. (2004). Racial/ethnic disparity and correlates of substance abuse service utilization and juvenile justice involvement among adolescents with substance use disorders. *Journal of Ethnicity in Substance Abuse, 3,* 47–64.

Afterschool Alliance. (2009). American after 3pm: The most in-depth study of how America's children spend their afternoons. Retrieved February 2016, from http://www.afterschoolalliance.org/AA3_Full_Report.pdf

Alati, R., Baker, P., Betts, K. S., Connor, J. P., Little, K., Sanson, A., & Olsson, C. A. (2014). The role of parental alcohol use, parental discipline and antisocial behaviour on adolescent drinking trajectories. *Drug and Alcohol Dependence, 134*(1), 178–184.

Alegria, M., Carson, N. J., Goncalves, M., & Keefe, K. (2011). Disparities in treatment for substance use disorders and co-occurring disorders for ethnic/racial minority youth. *Journal of the American Academy of Child and Adolescent Psychiatry, 50*(1), 22–31.

Alfonso, J., & Dunn, M. E. (2009). Differences in the marijuana expectancies of adolescents in relation to marijuana use. *Substance Use and Misuse, 42,* 1009–1025.

Allen, J. P., Porter, M. R., McFarland, F. C., McElhaney, K. B., & Marsh, P. (2005). The two faces of adolescents' success with peers: Adolescent popularity, social adaptation, and deviant behavior. *Child Development, 76,* 747–760.

American Academy of Pediatrics Committee on Substance Abuse. (2010). Policy statement—Alcohol use by youth and adolescents: A pediatric concern. *Pediatrics 125,* 1078–1087.

Anderson, K. G., Briggs, K. E. L., & White, H. R. (2013). Motives to drink or not to drink: Longitudinal relations among personality, motives, and alcohol use across adolescence and early adulthood. *Alcoholism: Clinical and Experimental Research, 37*(5), 860–867.

Arroyo, J. A., Miller, W. R., & Tonigan, J. S. (2003). The influence of Hispanic ethnicity on long-term outcome in three alcohol-treatment modalities. *Journal of Studies on Alcohol, 64,* 98–104.

Ary, D. V., Tildesley, E., Hops, H., & Andrews, J. (1993). The influence of parent, sibling, and peer modeling and attitudes on adolescent use of alcohol. *International Journal of the Addictions, 28,* 853–880.

Ashtari, M., Cervellione, K., Cottone, J., Ardekani, B. A., & Kumra, S. (2009). Diffusion abnormalities in adolescents and young adults with a history of heavy cannabis use. *Journal of Psychiatric Research, 43*(3), 189–204.

Babor, T. F., McRee, B. G., Kassebaum, P. A., Grimaldi, P. L., Ahmed, K., & Bray, J. (2008). Screening, brief intervention, and referral to treatment (SBIRT): Toward a public health approach to the management of substance abuse. *Substance Abuse, 28*(3), 7–30.

Baer, J. S., Garrett, S. B., Beadnell, B., Wells, E. A., & Peterson, P. L. (2007). Brief motivational intervention with homeless adolescents: Evaluating effects on substance use and service utilization. *Psychology of Addictive Behaviors, 21,* 582–586.

Becker, S. J., Spirito, A., Hernandez, L., Barnett, N. P., Eaton, C. A., Lewander, W., . . . Monti, P. M. (2012). Trajectories of adolescent alcohol use after brief treatment in an emergency department. *Drug and Alcohol Dependence, 125,* 103–109.

Berg, N., Kiviruusu, O., Karvonen, S., Kestilä, L., Lintonen, T., Rahkonen, O., & Huurre, T. (2013). A 26-year follow-up study of heavy drinking trajectories from adolescence to midadulthood and adult disadvantage. *Alcohol and Alcoholism, 48*(4), 452–457.

Best, D. W., Wilson, A. S., MacLean, S., Savic, M., Reed, M., Bruun, A., & Lubman, D. I. (2014). Patterns of family conflict and their impact on substance use and psychosocial outcomes in a sample of young people in treatment. *Vulnerable Children and Youth Studies, 9*(2), 114–122.

Biglan, A., Mrazek, P. J., Carnine, D., & Flay, B. R. (2003). The integration of research and practice in the prevention of youth problem behaviors. *American Psychologist, 58,* 6–7.

Blanco, C., Rafful, C., Wall, M. M., Ridenour, T. A., Wang, S., & Kendler, K. S. (2014). Towards a comprehensive developmental model of cannabis use disorders. *Addiction, 109*(2), 284–294.

Bloom, B., & Cohen, R. A. (2009). Summary health statistics for U.S. children: National Health Interview Survey, 2007. *Vital Health Statistics, 10,* 1–80.

Boekeloo, B. O., Jerry, J., Lee-Ougo, W. I., Worrell, K. D., Hamburger, E. K., Russek-Cohen, E., & Snyder, M. H. (2004). Randomized trial of brief office-based interventions to reduce adolescent alcohol use. *Archives of Pediatric and Adolescent Medicine, 158*(7), 635–642.

Bonomo, Y., Coffey, C., Wolfe, R., Lynskey, M., Bowes, G., & Patton, G. (2001). Adverse outcomes of alcohol use in adolescents. *Addiction, 96*(10), 1485–1496.

Bot, S. M., Engels, R. C. M. E., & Knibbe, R. A. (2005). The effects of alcohol expectancies on drinking behaviour in peer groups: Observations in a naturalistic setting. *Addiction, 100,* 1270–1279.

Broman, C. L. (2009). The longitudinal impact of adolescent drug use on socioeconomic outcomes in young adulthood. *Journal of Child and Adolescent Substance Abuse, 18,* 131–143.

Brook, D. W., Brook, J. S., Zhang, C., Cohen, P., & Whiteman, M. (2002). Drug use and the risk of major depressive disorder, alcohol dependence, and substance use disorders. *Archives of General Psychiatry, 59,* 1039–1044.

Brook, J. S., Pahl, K., & Ning, Y. (2006). Peer and parental influences on longitudinal trajectories of smoking among African Americans and Puerto Ricans. *Nicotine and Tobacco Research, 8*(5), 639–651.

Brown, J. D., & Wissow, L. S. (2009). Discussion of sensitive health topics with youth during primary care visits: Relationship to youth perceptions of care. *Journal of Adolescent Health, 44*(1), 48–54.

Brown, S. A. (1990). Adolescent alcohol expectancies and risk for alcohol abuse. *Addiction and Recovery, 10,* 16–19.

Brown, S. A. (1993). Drug effect expectancies and addictive behavior change. *Experimental and Clinical Psychopharmacology, 1*(1–4), 55–67.

Brown, S. A. (2001). Facilitating change for adolescent alcohol problems: A multiple options approach. In E. F. Wagner & H. B. Waldron (Eds.), *Innovations in adolescent substance abuse intervention* (pp. 169–187). Oxford, UK: Elsevier Science.

Brown, S. A., Anderson, K., Schulte, M. T., Sintov, N. D., & Frissell, K. C. (2005). Facilitating youth self-change through school-based intervention. *Addictive Behaviors, 30,* 1797–1810.

Brown, S. A., D'Amico, E. J., McCarthy, D. M., & Tapert, S. F. (2001). Four year outcomes from adolescent alcohol and drug treatment. *Journal of Studies on Alcohol, 62,* 381–388.

Caetano, R. (2003). Alcohol-related health disparities and treatment-related epidemiological findings among whites, blacks, and Hispanics in the United States. *Alcoholism: Clinical and Experimental Research, 27,* 1337–1339.

Campbell, C. I., Weisner, C., & Sterling, S. (2006). Adolescents entering chemical dependency treatment in private managed care: Ethnic differences in treatment initiation and retention. *Journal of Adolescent Health, 38,* 343–350.

Campbell, P. R. (1996). *Population projections for states by age, sex, race and Hispanic origin: 1995-2025.* Washington, DC: US Census Bureau.

Campbell, R., Starkey, F., Holliday, J., Audrey, S., Bloor, M., Parry-Langdon, N., . . . Moore, L. (2008). An informal school-based peer-led intervention for smoking prevention in adolescence (ASSIST): A cluster randomized trial. *Lancet, 371,* 1595–1602.

Carlson, S. R., Iacono, W. G., & McGue, M. (2002). P300 amplitude in adolescent twins discordant and concordant for alcohol use disorders. *Biological Psychology, 61,* 203–227.

Carter-Pokras, O., & Baquet, C. (2002). What is a "health disparity?" *Public Health Reports, 117,* 426–434.

Casey, B. J., Getz, S., & Galvan, A. (2008). The adolescent brain. *Developmental Review, 28*(1), 62–77.

Castellanos-Ryan, N., Parent, S., Vitaro, F., Tremblay, R. E., & Séguin, J. R. (2013). Pubertal development, personality, and substance use: A 10-year longitudinal study from childhood to adolescence. *Journal of Abnormal Psychology, 122*(3), 782–796.

Centers for Disease Control and Prevention. (2010). Youth risk behavior surveillance survey. *Morbidity and Mortality Weekly Report, 59*(SS-5), 1–142.

Centers for Disease Control and Prevention. (2012). Youth Risk Behavior Surveillance Survey. *Morbidity and Mortality Weekly Report, 61*, SS-162.

Centers for Disease Control and Prevention. (2014). Youth Risk Behavior Surveillance Survey. *Morbidity and Mortality Weekly Report, 63*, SS-172.

Chabrol, H., Chauchard, E., & Girabet, J. (2008). Cannabis use and suicidal behaviors in high-school students. *Addictive Behaviors, 33*(1), 152–155.

Chambers, R. A., Taylor, J. R., & Potenza, M. N. (2003). Developmental neurocircuitry of motivation in adolescence: A critical period of addiction vulnerability. *American Journal of Psychiatry, 160*, 1041–1052.

Chan, G. C. K., Kelly, A. B., Toumbourou, J. W., Hemphill, S. A., Haynes, M. A., & Catalano, R. F. (2013). Predicting steep escalations in alcohol use over the teenage years: Age-related variations in key social influences. *Addiction, 108*(11), 1924–1932.

Chassin, L., & DeLucia, C. (1996). Drinking during adolescence. *Alcohol Health and Research, 20*, 175–180.

Chassin, L., Flora, D. B., & King, K. M. (2004). Trajectories of alcohol and drug use and dependence from adolescence to adulthood: The effects of familial alcoholism and personality. *Journal of Abnormal Psychology, 113*(4), 483–498.

Chassin, L., Pillow, D. R., Curran, P. J., Molina, B. S. G., & Barrera, M. (1993). Relation of parental alcoholism to early adolescent substance use: A test of three mediating mechanisms. *Journal of Abnormal Psychology, 102*, 3–19.

Chein, J., Albert, D., O'Brien, L., Uckert, K., & Steinberg, L. (2010). Peers increase adolescent risk taking by enhancing activity in the brain's reward circuitry. *Developmental Science, 2010*, F1-F10.

Chinman, M., Hunter, S., Ebener, P., Paddock, S. M., Stillman, L., Imm, P., & Wandersman, A. (2008). The Getting to Outcomes demonstration and evaluation: An illustration of the prevention support system. *American Journal of Community Psychology, 41*(3–4), 206–224.

Chung, P. J., Lee, T. C., Morrison, J. L., & Schuster, M. A. (2006). Preventive care for children in the United States: Quality and barriers. *Annual Review of Public Health, 27*, 491–515.

Chung, T., & Maisto, S. A. (2006). Relapse to alcohol and other drug use in treated adolescents: Review and reconsideration of relapse as a change point in clinical course. *Clinical Psychology Review, 26*, 149–161.

Cleveland, M. J., Bontempo, D. E., & Greenberg, M. T. (2008). The role of risk and protective factors in substance use across adolescence. *Journal of Adolescent Health, 43*, 157–164.

Colby, S. M., Monti, P. M., Barnett, N. P., Rohsenow, D. J., Weissman, K., Spirito, A., . . . Lewander, W. J. (1998). Brief motivational interviewing in a hospital setting for adolescent smoking: A preliminary study. *Journal of Consulting and Clinical Psychology, 66*, 574–578.

Colby, S. M., Monti, P. M., Tevyaw, T. O., Barnett, N. P., Spirito, A., Rohsenow, D. J., . . . Lewander, W. (2005). Brief motivational intervention for adolescent smokers in medical settings. *Addictive Behaviors, 30*(5), 865–874.

Colby, S. M., Nargiso, J., Tevyaw, T. O., Barnett, N. P., Metrik, J., Lewander, W., . . . Monti, P. M. (2012). Enhanced motivational interviewing versus brief advice foradolescent smoking cessation: Results from a randomized clinical trial. *Addictive Behaviors, 38*(7), 817–823.

Colder, C. R., & O'Connor, R. (2002). Attention biases and disinhibited behavior as predictors of alcohol use and enhancement reasons for drinking. *Psychology of Addictive Behaviors, 16*(Part 4), 325–332.

Colder, C. R., O'Connor, R. M., Read, J. P., Eiden, R. D., Lengua, L. J., Hawk, L. W., Jr., & Wieczorek, W. F. (2014). Growth trajectories of alcohol information processing and associations with escalation of drinking in early adolescence. *Psychology of Addictive Behaviors*, Epub ahead of print. doi:10.1037/a0035271.

Cushing, C. C., Jensen, C. D., Miller, M. B., & Leffingwell, T. R. (2014). Meta-analysis of motivational interviewing for adolescent health behavior: Efficacy beyond substance use. *Journal of Consulting and Clinical Psychology, 82*(6), 1212–1218.

D'Amico, E. J., Anderson, K. G., Metrik, J., Frissell, K. C., Ellingstad, T., & Brown, S. A. (2006). Adolescent self-selection of service formats: Implications for secondary interventions targeting alcohol use. *American Journal on Addictions, 15*, 58–66.

D'Amico, E. J., Chinman, M., Stern, A., & Wandersman, A. (2009). Community prevention handbook on adolescent substance abuse prevention and treatment. In C. Leukefeld, T. Gullotta, & M. S. Tindall (Eds.), *Adolescent substance abuse: Evidence-based approaches to prevention and treatment* (pp. 73–96). New York, NY: Springer Science + Business Media.

D'Amico, E. J., & Edelen, M. (2007). Pilot test of Project CHOICE: A voluntary after school intervention for middle school youth. *Psychology of Addictive Behaviors, 21*(4), 592–598.

D'Amico, E. J., Ellickson, P. L., Collins, R. L., Martino, S. C., & Klein, D. J. (2005). Processes linking adolescent problems to substance use problems in late young adulthood. *Journal of Studies on Alcohol, 66*, 766–775.

D'Amico, E. J., Ellickson, P. L., Wagner, E. F., Turrisi, R., Fromme, K., Ghosh-Dastidar, B., . . . Wright, D. (2005). Developmental considerations for substance use interventions from middle school through college. *Alcoholism: Clinical and Experimental Research, 29*, 474–483.

D'Amico, E. J., & Fromme, K. (1997). Health risk behaviors of adolescent and young adult siblings. *Health Psychology, 16*(5), 426–432.

D'Amico, E. J., Green, H. D., Jr., Miles, J. N. V, Zhou, A. J., Tucker, J. A., & Shih, R. A. (2012). Voluntary after school alcohol and drug programs: If you build it right, they will come. *Journal of Research on Adolescence, 22*(3), 571–582.

D'Amico, E. J., Houck, J. M., Hunter, S. B., Miles, J. N. V., Osilla, K. C., & Ewing, B. A. (2015). Group motivational interviewing for adolescents: Change talk and alcohol and marijuana outcomes. *Journal of Consulting and Clinical Psychology, 83*(1), 68–80.

D'Amico, E. J., Hunter, S. B., Miles, J. N. V., Ewing, B. A., & Osilla, K. C. (2013). A randomized controlled trial of a group motivational interviewing intervention for adolescents with a first time alcohol or drug offense. *Journal of Substance Abuse Treatment, 45*(5), 400–408.

D'Amico, E. J., & McCarthy, D. M. (2006). Escalation and initiation of younger adolescents' substance use: The impact of perceived peer use. *Journal of Adolescent Health, 39*, 481–487.

D'Amico, E. J., Miles, J. N. V., Stern, S. A., & Meredith, L. S. (2008). Brief motivational interviewing for teens at risk of substance use consequences: A randomized pilot study in a primary care clinic. *Journal of Substance Abuse Treatment, 35*, 53–61.

D'Amico, E. J., Osilla, K. C., & Hunter, S. B. (2010). Developing a group motivational interviewing intervention for adolescents at-risk for developing an alcohol or drug use disorder. *Alcoholism Treatment Quarterly, 28*, 417–436.

D'Amico, E. J., Osilla, K. C., & Stern, S. A. (in press). Prevention and intervention in the school setting. In K. J. Sher (Ed.), *The Oxford handbook of substance use disorders*. New York, NY: Oxford University Press. doi:10.1093/oxfordhb/9780199381708.013.008

D'Amico, E. J., Tucker, J. S., Miles, J. N. V., Zhou, A. J., Shih, R. A., & Green, H. D., Jr. (2012). Preventing alcohol use with a voluntary after school program for middle school students: Results from a cluster randomized controlled trial of CHOICE. *Prevention Science, 13*(4), 415–425.

D'Amico, E. J., Tucker, J. S., Shih, R. A., & Miles, J. N. V. (2014). Does diversity matter? The need for longitudinal research on adolescent alcohol and drug use trajectories. *Substance Use and Misuse, 49*(1), 1069–1073.

Dahl, R. (2011). Understanding the risky business of adolescence. *Neuron, 69*(5), 837–839.

Delva, J., Wallace, J. M., Jr., O'Malley, P. M., Bachman, J. G., Johnston, L. D., & Schulenberg, J. E. (2005). The epidemiology of alcohol, marijuana, and cocaine use among Mexican American, Puerto Rican, Cuban American, and other Latin American eighth-grade students in the United States: 1991–2002. *American Journal of Public Health, 95*(4), 696–702.

DeNavas-Walt, C., Proctor, B. D., & Lee, C. H. (2006). *U.S. Census Bureau, current population reports: Income, poverty, and health insurance coverage in the United States: 2005*. Washington, DC: US Government Printing Office.

Diamond, G., Panichelli-Mindel, S. M., Shera, D., Dennis, M., Tims, F., & Ungemack, J. (2006). Psychiatric syndromes in adolescents with marijuana abuse and dependency in outpatient treatment. *Journal of Child and Adolescent Substance Abuse, 15*(4), 37–52.

DiClemente, R. J., Wingood, G. M., Crosby, R., Sionean, C., Cobb, B. K., Harrington, K., . . . Oh, M. K. (2001). Parental monitoring: Association with adolescents' risk behaviors. *Pediatrics, 107*(6), 1363–1368.

Dishion, T. J., Shaw, D. S., Connell, A., Gardner, F., Weaver, C., & Wilson, M. (2008). The Family Check-Up with high-risk indigent families: Preventing problem behavior by increasing parents' positive behavior support in early childhood. *Child Development, 79*(5), 1395–1414.

Donovan, J. E. (2004). Adolescent alcohol initiation: A review of psychosocial risk factors. *Journal of Adolescent Health, 35*(6), 529.e7–18.

Doremus-Fitzwater, T. L., Varlinskaya, E. I., & Spear, L. P. (2010). Motivational systems in adolescence: Possible implications for age differences in substance abuse and other risk-taking behaviors. *Brain and Cognition, 72*(1), 114–123.

Eaton, D. K., Kann, L., Kinchen, S., Shanklin, S., Flint, K. H., Hawkins, J., . . . Wechsler, H. (2012). Youth risk behavior surveillance—United States, 2011. *Morbidity and Mortality Weekly Report Surveillance Summaries, 61*, 1–162.

Ehlers, C. L., Slutske, W. S., Gilder, D. A., Lau, P., & Wilhelmsen, K. C. (2006). Age of first intoxication and alcohol use disorders in southwestern California Indians. *Alcoholism: Clinical and Experimental Research, 30*(11), 1856–1865.

Ellen, J. M., Franzgrote, M., Irwin, C. E., Jr., & Millstein, S. G. (1998). Primary care physicians' screening of adolescent patients: A survey of California physicians. *Journal of Adolescent Health, 22*(6), 433–438.

Ellickson, P. L., & Bell, R. M. (1990). Drug prevention in junior high: A multi-site, longitudinal test. *Science, 247*, 1299–1305.

Ellickson, P. L., Martino, S. C., & Collins, R. L. (2004). Marijuana use from adolescence to young adulthood: Multiple developmental trajectories and their associated outcomes. *Health Psychology, 23*, 299–307.

Ellickson, P. L., McCaffrey, D. F., Ghosh-Dastidar, B., & Longshore, D. L. (2003). New inroads in preventing adolescent drug use: Results from a large-scale trial of Project ALERT in middle schools. *American Journal of Public Health, 93*, 1830–1836.

Ellickson, P. L., Tucker, J. S., & Klein, D. J. (2003). Ten-year prospective study of public health problems associated with early drinking. *Pediatrics, 111*, 949–955.

Elster, A. B., & Kuznets, N. K. (1993). *Guidelines for adolescent preventive services (GAPS): Recommendations and rationale*. Baltimore, MD: Williams & Wilkins.

Elster, A. B., & Levenberg, P. (1997). Integrating comprehensive adolescent preventive services into routine medicine care. *Adolescent Medicine, 44*, 1365–1377.

Ensminger, M. E., Juon, H. S., & Fothergill, K. E. (2002). Childhood and adolescent antecedents of substance use in adulthood. *Addiction, 97*, 833–844.

Ernst, M. (2014). The triadic model perspective for the study of adolescent motivated behavior. *Brain and Cognition, 89*, 104–111.

Ernst, M., & Fudge, J. L. (2009). A developmental neurobiological model of motivated behavior: Anatomy, connectivity and ontogeny of the triadic nodes. *Neuroscience and Biobehavioral Reviews, 33*, 367–382.

Ernst, M., Pine, D. S., & Hardin, M. (2006). Triadic model of the neurobiology of motivated behavior in adolescence. *Psychological Medicine, 36*(3), 299–312.

Fagan, A. A., & Najman, J. M. (2005). The relative contributions of parental and sibling substance use to adolescent tobacco, alcohol, and other drug use. *Journal of Drug Issues, 35*, 869–883.

Feldstein Ewing, S. W. (2012). *Assessing the fit of motivational interviewing across cultures with adolescents*. Albuquerque, NM: NIH/NIAAA.

Feldstein Ewing, S. W., Blakemore, S-J., & Sakhardande, A. (2014). The effect of alcohol consumption on the adolescent brain: A systematic review of MRI and fMRI studies of alcohol-using youth. *Neuroimage: Clinical, 5*, 420–437.

Feldstein Ewing, S. W., Filbey, F. M., Sabbineni, A., Chandler, L. D., & Hutchison, K. E. (2011). How psychosocial alcohol interventions work: A preliminary look at what fMRI can tell us. *Alcoholism: Clinical and Experimental Research, 35*(4), 643–651.

Feldstein Ewing, S. W., Gaume, J., Ernst, E. B., Rivera, L., & Houck, J. M. (2015). Do therapist behaviors differ with Hispanic youth? A brief look at within-session therapist behaviors and youth treatment response. *Psychology of Addictive Behaviors, 29*(3), 779–786.

Feldstein Ewing, S. W., Magnan, R. E., Houck, J., Morgan, M., & Bryan, A. D. (2014). Associations between CDH13 variants and the initiation of alcohol use and sexual intercourse with high-risk Hispanic and Caucasian youth. *Online Journal of Rural and Urban Research*. Retrieved February 2016, from http://ojs.jsumurc.org/ojs/index.php?journal=ojrur&page=article&op=view&path%5B%5D=124

Feldstein Ewing, S. W., McEachern, A. D., Yezhuvath, U., Bryan, A. D., Hutchison, K. E., & Filbey, F. M. (2013). Integrating brain and behavior: Evaluating adolescents' response to a cannabis intervention. *Psychology of Addictive Behaviors, 27*(2), 510–525.

Feldstein Ewing, S. W., Venner, K. L., & May, P. A. (2006). American Indian/Alaska Native alcohol-related incarceration and treatment. *American Indian and Alaska Native Mental Health Research, 13*, 1–22.

Feldstein Ewing, S. W., Venner, K. L., Mead, H., & Bryan, A. B. (2011). Exploring racial/ethnic differences in substance use: A preliminary theory-based investigation with juvenile justice-involved youth. *BMC Pediatrics, 11*, 71.

Feldstein Ewing, S. W., Wray, A. M., Mead, H. K., & Adams, S. K. (2012). Two approaches to tailoring treatment for cultural minority adolescents. *Journal of Substance Abuse Treatment, 43*, 190–213.

Fergusson, D. M., & Boden, J. M. (2008). Cannabis use and later life outcomes. *Addiction, 103*(6), 969–976.

Fergusson, D. M., Horwood, L. J., & Swain-Campbell, N. (2002). Cannabis use and psychosocial adjustment in adolescence and young adulthood. *Addiction, 97*, 1123–1135.

Fisher, L. B., Miles, I. W., Austin, S. B., Camargo, C. A., & Colditz, G. A. (2007). Predictors of initiation of alcohol use among US adolescents: Findings from a prospective cohort study. *Archives of Pediatric and Adolescent Medicine, 161*, 959–966.

Ford, C. A., Millstein, S. G., Halpern-Felsher, B. L., & Irwin, C. E. (1997). Influence of physician confidentiality assurances on adolescents' willingness to disclose information and seek future health care. *Journal of the American Medical Association, 278*, 1029–1034.

Fosados, R., McClain, A., Ritt-Olson, A., Sussman, S., Soto, D., Baezconde-Garbanati, L., & Unger, J. B. (2007). The influence of acculturation on drug and alcohol use in a sample of adolescents. *Addictive Behaviors, 32*(12), 2990–3004.

French, D. C., & Dishion, T. J. (2003). Predictors of early initiation of sexual intercourse among high-risk adolescents. *Journal of Early Adolescence, 23*(3), 295–315.

Frisher, M., Crome, I., Macleod, J., Bloor, R., & Hickman, M. (2007). *Predictive factors for illicit drug use among young people: A literature review*. London, UK: Home Office. Retrieved February 2015, from http://dera.ioe.ac.uk/6903/1/rdsolr0507.pdf

Fromme, K., & D'Amico, E. J. (2000). Measuring adolescent alcohol outcome expectancies. *Psychology of Addictive Behaviors, 14*, 206–212.

Fromme, K., Stroot, E., & Kaplan, D. (1993). Comprehensive effects of alcohol: Development and psychometric assessment of a new expectancy questionnaire. *Psychological Assessment, 5*(1), 19–26.

Fuemmeler, B., Lee, C-T., Ranby, K. W., Clark, T., McClernon, F. J., Yang, C., & Kollins, S. H. (2013). Individual- and community-level correlates of cigarette-smoking trajectories from age 13 to 32 in a U.S. population-based sample. *Drug and Alcohol Dependence, 132*(1–2), 301–308.

Fulkerson, J. A., Story, M., & Mellin, A. (2006). Family dinner meal frequency and adolescent development: Relationships with developmental assets and high-risk behaviors. *Journal of Adolescent Health, 39*(3), 337–345.

Fulton, H. G., Krank, M. D., & Stewart, S. H. (2012). Outcome expectancy liking: A self-generated, self-coded measure predicts adolescent substance use trajectories. *Psychology of Addictive Behaviors, 26*(4), 870–879.

Galea, S., & Vlahov, D. (2002). Social determinants and the health of drug users: Socioeconomic status, homelessness, and incarceration. *Public Health Reports, 117*, S135–S144.

Galen, L. W., & Henderson, M. J. (1999). Validation of cocaine and marijuana effect expectancies in a treatment setting. *Addictive Behaviors, 24*, 719–724.

Galvan, A., Hare, T. A., Parra, C. E., Penn, J., Voss, H., Glover, G., & Casey, B. J. (2006). Earlier development of the accumbens relative to orbitofrontal cortex might underlie risk-taking behavior in adolescents. *Journal of Neuroscience, 26*(25), 6885–6892.

Galvan, A., Hare, T. A., Voss, H., Glover, G., & Casy, B. J. (2007). Risk-taking and the adolescent brain: Who is at risk. *Developmental Science, 10*, F8–F14.

Garland, A. F., Lau, A. S., Yeh, M., McCabe, K. M., Hough, R. L., & Landsverk, J. A. (2005). Racial and ethnic differences in utilization of mental health services among high-risk youths. *American Journal of Psychiatry, 162*(7), 1336–1343.

Geier, C. F. (2013). Adolescent cognitive control and reward processing: Implications for risk taking and substance use. *Hormones and Behavior, 64*, 333–342.

Giedd, J. N. (2012). The digital revolution and adolescent brain evolution. *Journal of Adolescent Health, 51*, 101–105.

Gil, A. G., Vega, W. A., & Turner, R. J. (2002). Early and mid-adolescence risk factors for later substance abuse by African Americans and European Americans. *Public Health Reports, 117*(Suppl. 1), S15–S29.

Gil, A. G., Wagner, E. F., & Tubman, J. G. (2004). Culturally sensitive substance abuse intervention for Hispanic and African American adolescents: Empirical examples from the Alcohol Treatment Targeting Adolescents in Need (ATTAIN) project. *Addiction, 99*(Suppl. 2), 140–150.

Godley, S. H., Meyers, R. J., Smith, J. E., Karvinen, T., Titus, J. C., & Godley, M. D. (2001). *The adolescent community reinforcement approach for adolescent cannabis users* (DHHS Publication No. SMA 01–3489). Washington, DC: US Department of Health and Human Services.

Goldman, M. S., Brown, S. A., & Christiansen, B. A. (1987). Expectancy theory: Thinking about drinking. In H. T. Blane & K. E. Leonard (Eds.), *Psychological theories of drinking and alcoholism* (pp. 181–266). New York, NY: Guilford Press.

Gordon, A. J., Ettaro, L., Rodriguez, K. L., Mocik, J., & Clark, D. B. (2011). Provider, patient, and family perspectives of adolescent alcohol use and treatment in rural settings. *Journal of Rural Health, 27*, 81–90.

Gorman, D. M., & Conde, E. (2010). The making of evidence-based practice: The case of Project ALERT. *Children and Youth Services Review, 32*(2), 214–222.

Gosin, M., Marsiglia, F. F., & Hecht, M. L. (2003). Keepin' it R.E.A.L.: A drug resistance curriculum tailored to the strengths and needs of pre-adolescents of the southwest. *Journal of Drug Education, 33*, 119–142.

Green, K. M., Doherty, E. E., Stuart, E. A., & Ensminger, M. E. (2010). Does heavy adolescent marijuana use lead to criminal involvement in adulthood? Evidence from a multiwave longitudinal study of urban African Americans. *Drug and Alcohol Dependence, 112*(1–2), 117–125.

Green, L. W. (2001). From research to "best practices" in other settings and populations. *American Journal of Health Behavior, 25*(3), 165–178.

Griffith-Lendering, M. F. H., Wigman, J. T. W., van Leeuwen, A. P., Huijbregts, S. C. J., Huizink, A. C., Ormel, J., . . . Vollebergh, W. A. M. (2013). Cannabis use and vulnerability for psychosis in early adolescence—A TRAILS study. *Addiction, 108*(4), 733–740.

Grigsby, T. J., Forster, M., Baezconde-Garbanati, L., Soto, D. W., & Unger, J. B. (2014). Do adolescent drug use consequences predict externalizing and internalizing problems in emerging adulthood as well as traditional drug use measures in a Hispanic sample? *Addictive Behaviors, 39*(3), 644–651.

Guilamo-Ramos, V., Jaccard, J., Johansson, M., & Turrisi, R. (2004). Binge drinking among Latino youth: Role of acculturation-related variables. *Psychology of Addictive Behaviors, 18*(2), 135–142.

Guilamo-Ramos, V., Turrisi, R., Jaccard, J., & Gonzalez, B. (2004). Progressing from light experimentation to heavy episodic drinking in early and middle adolescence. *Journal of Studies on Alcohol, 65*, 494–500.

Gwaltney, C. J., Magill, M., Barnett, N. P., Apodaca, T. R., Colby, S. M., & Monti, P. M. (2011). Using daily drinking data to characterize the effects of a brief alcohol intervention in an emergency room. *Addictive Behaviors, 36*(3), 248–250.

Hall, W., & Degenhardt, L. (2007). Prevalence and correlates of cannabis use in developed and developing countries. *Current Opinion in Psychiatry, 20*(4), 393–397.

Halpern-Felsher, B., Ozer, E. M., Millstein, S. G., Wibbelsman, C. J., Fuster, C. D., Elster, J., & Irwin, C. E. (2000). Preventive services in a health maintenance organization: How well do pediatricians screen and educate adolescent patients? *Archives of Pediatric and Adolescent Medicine, 154*, 173–179.

Harrier, L. K., Lambert, P. L., & Ramos, V. (2001). Indicators of adolescent drug users in a clinical population. *Journal of Child and Adolescent Substance Abuse, 10*, 71–87.

Hartman, C. A., Lessem, J. M., Hopfer, C. J., Crowley, T. J., & Stallings, M. C. (2006). The family transmission of adolescent alcohol abuse and dependence. *Journal of Studies on Alcohol, 67*, 657–664.

Harvard Family Research Project. (2007). *Findings from HFRP's study of predictors of participation in out-of-school time activities: Fact sheet.* Cambridge, MA: Harvard Graduate School of Education.

Hayatbakhsh, M. R., Najman, J. M., Jamrozik, K., Mamun, A. A., & Alati, R. (2006). Do parents' marital circumstances predict young adults' DSM-IV cannabis use disorders? A prospective study. *Addiction, 101*, 1778–1786.

Hecht, M. L., Marsiglia, F. F., Elek, E., Wagstaff, D. A., Kulis, S., Dustman, P., & Miller-Day, M. (2003). Culturally grounded substance use prevention: An evaluation of the keepin' it R.E.A.L. curriculum. *Prevention Science, 4*, 233–248.

Hellerstedt, W. L., Peterson-Hickey, M., Rhodes, K. L., & Garwick, A. (2006). Environmental, social, and personal correlates of having ever had sexual intercourse among American Indian youths. *American Journal of Public Health, 96*(12), 2228–2234.

Henderson, C. E., Dakof, G. A., Greenbaum, P. E., & Liddle, H. A. (2010). Effectiveness of multidimensional family therapy with higher severity substance-abusing adolescents: Report from two randomized controlled trials. *Journal of Consulting and Clinical Psychology, 78*(6), 885–897.

Henggeler, S. W. (2011). Efficacy studies to large-scale transport: The development and validation of Multisystemic Therapy Programs. *Annual Review of Clinical Psychology, 7*, 351–381.

Henggeler, S. W., & Borduin, C. M. (1990). *Family therapy and beyond: A multisystemic approach to treating the behavior problems of children and adolescents.* Pacific Grove, CA: Brooks/Cole.

Heron, J., Barker, E. D., Joinson, C., Lewis, G., Hickman, M., Munafò, M., & Macleod, J. (2013). Childhood conduct disorder trajectories, prior risk factors andcannabis use at age 16: Birth cohort study. *Addiction, 108*(12), 2129–2138.

Heron, J., Maughan, B., Dick, D. M., Kendler, K. S., Lewis, G., Macleod, J., . . . Hickman, M. (2013). Conduct problem trajectories and alcohol use and misuse in mid to late adolescence. *Drug and Alcohol Dependence, 133*(1), 100–107.

Hettema, J., Steele, J., & Miller, W. R. (2005). Motivational Interviewing. *Annual Review of Clinical Psychology, 1*(1), 91–111.

Hingson, R. W., Heeren, T., Jamanka, A., & Howland, J. (2000). Age of drinking onset and unintentional injury involvement after drinking. *Journal of the American Medical Association, 284*, 1527–1533.

Hingson, R. W., Heeren, T., & Winter, M. R. (2006). Age of alcohol-dependence onset: Associations with severity of dependence and treatment seeking. *Pediatrics, 118*, e755–e763.

Hogue, A., Dauber, S., Samuolis, J., & Liddle, H. A. (2006). Treatment adherence and differentiation in individual versus family therapy for adolescent substance abuse. *Journal of Family Psychology, 20*, 535–543.

Hollingworth, W., Cohen, D., Hawkins, J., Hughes, R. A., Moore, L. A., Holliday, J. C., . . . Campbell, R. (2013). Reducing smoking in adolescents: Cost-effectiveness results from the cluster randomized ASSIST (A Stop Smoking in Schools Trial). *Nicotine and Tobacco Research, 14*(2), 161–168.

Hollis, J. F., Polen, M. R., Whitlock, E. P., Lichtenstein, E., Mullooly, J. P., Velicer, W. F., & Redding, C. A. (2005). Teen reach: Outcomes from a randomized, controlled trial of a tobacco reduction program for teens seen in primary medical care. *Pediatrics, 115*(4), 981–989.

Hopfer, C. J., Stallings, M. C., Hewitt, J. K., & Crowley, T. J. (2004). Family transmission of marijuana use, abuse, and dependence. *Journal of the American Academy of Child and Adolescent Psychiatry, 42*, 834–841.

Horn, K., Dino, G., Hamilton, C., Noerachmanto, N., & Zhang, J. (2008). Feasibility of a smoking cessation intervention for teens in the emergency department: Reach, implementation fidelity, and acceptability. *American Journal of Critical Care, 17*, 205–216.

Hurrelmann, K. (1990). Health promotion for adolescents: Preventive and corrective strategies against problem behavior. *Journal of Adolescence, 13*(3), 231–250.

Hwang, S. W., Tolomiczenko, G., Kouyoumdjian, F. G., & Garner, R. E. (2005). Interventions to improve the health of the homeless: A systematic review. *American Journal of Preventive Medicine, 29*, 311–319.

Jackson, K. M., & Sartor, C. E. (in press). The natural course of substance use and dependence. In K. J. Sher (Ed.), *The Oxford handbook of substance use disorders.* New York,

NY: Oxford University Press. doi:10.1093/oxfordhb/9780199381708.013.008

Jacobus, J., & Tapert, S. F. (2013). Neurotoxic effects of alcohol in adolescence. *Annual Review of Clinical Psychology*, 9, 703–721.

Jager, G., & Ramsey, N. F. (2008). Long-term consequences of adolescent cannabis exposure on the development of cogntion, brain structure and function: An overview of animal and human research. *Current Drug Abuse Reviews*, 1(2), 114–123.

Jensen, C. D., Cushing, C. C., Aylward, B. S., Craig, J. T., Sorell, D. M., & Steele, R. G. (2011). Effectiveness of motivational interviewing interventions for adolescent substance use behavior change: A meta-analytic review. *Journal of Consulting and Clinical Psychology*, 79(4), 433–440.

Jofre-Bonet, M., & Sindelar, J. L. (2001). Drug treatment as a crime fighting tool. *Journal of Mental Health Policy and Economics*, 4, 175–188.

Johnson, M. D. (2013). Parent–child relationship quality directly and indirectly influences hooking up behavior reported in young adulthood through alcohol use in adolescence. *Archives of Sexual Behavior*, 42(8), 1463–1472.

Johnson, P. B., & Johnson, H. L. (2001). Reaffirming the power of parental influence on adolescent smoking and drinking decisions. *Adolescent and Family Health*, 2, 37–43.

Johnston, L. D., O'Malley, P. M., Bachman, J. G., & Schulenberg, J. E. (2013). *Monitoring the Future national survey results on drug use, 1975–2012, Vol. 1 Secondary school students*. Ann Arbor, MI: Institute for Social Research, University of Michigan.

Jones, B. T., & McMahon, J. (1993). Alcohol motivations as outcome expectancies. In W. R. Miller & N. Heather (Eds.), *Treating addictive behaviors* (pp. 75–91). New York, NY: Plenum Press.

Jones, S. C., & Magee, C. A. (2014). The role of family, friends and peers in Australian adolescent'salcohol consumption. *Drug and Alcohol Review*, 33(3), 304–313.

Kaplan, C. P., Nápoles-Springer, A., Stewart, S. L., & Pérez-Stable, E. J. (2001). Smoking acquisition among adolescents and young Latinas: The role of socioenvironmental and personal factors. *Addictive Behaviors*, 26, 531–550.

Kia-Keating, M., Brown, S. A., Schulte, M. T., & Monreal, T. K. (2008). Adolescent satisfaction with brief motivational enhancement for alcohol abuse. *Journal of Behavioral Health Services and Research*, 36, 385–395.

Kilmer, B., Burgdorf, J., D'Amico, E. J., Tucker, J. S., & Miles, J. N. V. (2011). A multi-site cost analysis of a school-based voluntary alcohol and drug prevention program. *Journal of Studies on Alcohol and Drugs*, 72(5), 823–832.

Kilpatrick, D. G., Ruggiero, K. J., Acierno, R., Saunders, B. E., Resnick, H. S., & Best, C. L. (2003). Violence and risk of PTSD, major depression, substance abuse/dependence, and comorbidity: Results from the National Survey of Adolescents. *Journal of Consulting and Clinical Psychology*, 71(4), 692–700.

Kirk, S., Scott, B. J., & Daniels, S. R. (2005). Pediatric obesity epidemic: Treatment options. *Journal of the American Dietetic Association*, 105(5), S44–S51.

Klein, D. J., Allan, M. J., Elster, A. B., Stevens, D., Cox, C., Hedberg, V. A., & Goodman, R. A. (2001). Improving adolescent preventive care in community health centers. *Pediatrics*, 107, 318–327.

Kulis, S., Marsiglia, F. F., Elek, E., Dustman, P., Wagstaff, D. A., & Hecht, M. L. (2005). Mexican/Mexican American adolescents and keepin' it REAL: An evidence-based substance use prevention program. *Children and Schools*, 27(3), 133–145.

Kuntsche, E., Gabhainn, S. N., Roberts, C., Windlin, B., Vieno, A., Bendtsen, P., . . . Wicki, M. (2014). Drinking motives and links to alcohol use in 13 European countries. *Journal of Studies on Alcohol and Drugs*, 75(3), 428–437.

Kuntsche, E., Rossow, I., Simons-Morton, B., Bogt, T., Kokkevi, A., & Godeau, E. (2014). Not early drinking but early drunkenness is a risk factor for problem behaviors among adolescents from 38 European and North American countries. *Alcoholism: Clinical and Experimental Research*, 37(2), 308–314.

Lac, A., Alvaro, E. M., Crano, W. T., & Siegel, J. T. (2009). Pathways from parental knowledge and warmth to adolescent marijuana use: An extension to the theory of planned behavior. *Prevention Science*, 10, 22–32.

Latendresse, S. J., Rose, R. J., Viken, R. J., Pulkkinen, L., Kaprio, J., & Dick, D. M. (2008). Parenting mechanisms in links between parents' and adolescents' alcohol use behaviors. *Alcoholism: Clinical and Experimental Research*, 32, 322–330.

Laviola, G., Macri, S., Morley-Fletcher, S., & Adriani, W. (2003). Risk-taking behavior in adolescent mice: Psychobiological determinants and early epigenetic influence. *Neuroscience and Biobehavioral Reviews*, 27(1–2), 19–31.

Li, C., Pentz, M. A., & Chou, C-P. (2002). Parental substance use as a modifier of adolescent substance use risk. *Addiction*, 97, 1537–1550.

Liddle, H. A. (1999). Theory development in a family-based therapy for adolescent drug abuse. *Journal of Clinical Child Psychology*, 28(4), 521–532.

Liddle, H. A., Rowe, C. L., Dakof, G. A., Quille, T. J., Henderson, C. E., & Greenbaum, P. E. (2009). Multidimensional family therapy for young adolescent substance abuse: Twelve-month outcomes of a randomized controlled trial. *Journal of Consulting and Clinical Psychology*, 77(1), 12–25.

Liddle, H. A., Rowe, C. L., Quille, T. J., Dakof, G. A., Mills, D. S., Sakran, E., & Biaggi, H. (2002). Transporting a research-based adolescent drug treatment into practice. *Journal of Substance Abuse Treatment*, 22(4), 231–243.

Linakis, J. G., Bromberg, J., Baird, J., Nirenberg, T. D., Chun, T. H., Mello, M. J., . . . Spirito, A. (2013). Feasibility and acceptability of a pediatric emergency department alcohol prevention intervention for young adolescents. *Pediatric Emergency Care*, 11, 1180–1188.

Lisdahl, K. M., Gilbert, E. R., Wright, N. E., & Shollenbarger, S. (2013). Dare to delay? The impacts of adolescent and alcohol and marijuana use onset on cognition, brain structure, and function. *Front Psychiatry*, 4, 53.

Little, P. M. D., & Harris, E. (2003). A review of out-of-school time program quasi-experimental and experimental evaluation results. In Harvard Family Research Project (Ed.), *Out-of-school time evaluation snapshot* (Vol. 1, pp. 1–12). Cambridge. MA: Harvard Graduate School of Education.

Lowman, C., & Le Fauve, C. E. (2003). Health disparities and the relationship between race, ethnicity, and substance abuse treatment outcomes. *Alcoholism: Clinical and Experimental Research*, 27, 1324–1326.

Luna, B., Padmanabhana, A., & O'Hearn, K. (2010). What has fMRI told us about the development of cognitive control through adolescence? *Brain and Cognition*, 72(1), 101–113.

Lundahl, B. W., Kunz, C., Brownell, C., Tollefson, D., & Burke, B. L. (2010). A meta-analysis of motivational interviewing: Twenty-five years of empirical studies. *Research on Social Work Practice, 20*(2), 137–160.

Lynskey, M., & Hall, W. (2000). The effects of adolescent cannabis use on educational attainment: A review. *Addiction, 95*, 1621–1630.

Magill, M., Barnett, N. P., Apodaca, T. R., Rohsenow, D. J., & Monti, P. M. (2009). The role of marijuana use in brief motivational intervention with young adult drinkers treated in an emergency department. *Journal of Studies on Alcohol and Drugs, 70*, 409–413.

Marcell, A. V., Halpern-Felsher, B., Coriell, M., & Millstein, S. G. (2002). Physicians' attitudes and beliefs concerning alcohol abuse prevention in adolescents. *American Journal of Preventive Medicine, 22*, 49–55.

Marshall, E. J. (2014). Adolescent alcohol use: Risks and consequences. *Alcohol and Alcoholism, 49*(2), 160–164.

Martin, G., & Copeland, J. (2008). The adolescent cannabis check-up: Randomized trial of a brief intervention for young cannabis users. *Journal of Substance Abuse Treatment, 34*(4), 407–414.

Martino, S. C., Collins, L. M., Ellickson, P. L., Schell, T. L., & McCaffrey, D. (2006). Socio-environmental influences on adolescents' alcohol outcome expectancies: A prospective analysis. *Addiction, 101*, 971–983.

Maslowsky, J, Schulenberg, J. E., & Zucker, R. A. (2014). Influence of conduct problems and depressive symptomatology on adolescent substance use: Developmentally proximal versus distal effects. *Developmental Psychology, 50*(4), 1179–1189.

McCambridge, J., Slym, R. L., & Strang, J. (2008). Randomized controlled trial of motivational interviewing compared with drug information and advice for early intervention among young cannabis users. *Addiction, 103*(11), 1809–1818.

McCarthy, D. M., Pedersen, S. L., & D'Amico, E. J. (2009). Analysis of item response and differential item functioning of alcohol expectancies in middle school youth. *Psychological Assessment, 23*, 444–449.

McCarthy, D. M., & Thompsen, D. M. (2006). Implicit and explicit measures of alcohol and smoking cognitions. *Psychology of Addictive Behaviors, 20*, 436–444.

McGee, E., Valentine, E, Schulte, M. T., & Brown, S. A. (2011). Peer victimization and alcohol involvement among adolescents self-selecting into a school-based alcohol intervention. *Journal of Child and Adolescent Substance Abuse, 20*, 253–269.

McGovern, M. P., Fox, T. S., Xie, H., & Drake, R. E. (2004). A survey of clinical practices and readiness to adopt evidence-based practices: Dissemination research in an addiction treatment system. *Journal of Substance Abuse Treatment, 26*(4), 305–312.

Mercken, L., Moore, L., Crone, M. R., De Vries, H., De Bourdeaudhuij, I., Lien, N., . . . Van Lenthe, F. J. (2012). The effectiveness of school-based smoking prevention interventions among low- and high-SES European teenagers. *Health Education Research, 27*(3), 459–469.

Mercken, L., Steglich, C., Sinclair, P., Holliday, J., & Moore, L. (2012). A longitudinal social network analysis of peer influence, peer selection, and smoking behavior among adolescents in British schools. *Health Psychology, 31*(4), 450–459.

Meyers, R. J, & Smith, J. E. (1995). *Clinical guide to alcohol treatment: The community reinforcement approach.* New York, NY: Guilford Press.

Miller, S. M., Siegel, J. T., Hohman, Z., & Crano, W. D. (2013). Factors mediating the association of the recency of parent's marijuana use and their adolescent children's subsequent initiation. *Psychology of Addictive Behaviors, 27*(3), 848–853.

Miller, W. R., & Rollnick, S. (2012). *Motivational interviewing: Helping people change* (3rd ed.). New York, NY: Guilford Press.

Miller, W. R., Villanueva, M., Tonigan, J. S., & Cuzmar, I. (2007). Are special treatments needed for special populations? *Alcoholism Treatment Quarterly, 25*(4), 63–78.

Millstein, S. G., & Marcell, A. V. (2003). Screening and counseling for adolescent alcohol use among primary care physicians in the United States. *Pediatrics, 111*(1), 114–122.

Monti, P. M., Colby, S. M., Barnett, N. P., Spirito, A., Rohsenow, D. J., Myers, M., . . . Lewander, W. (1999). Brief intervention for harm reduction with alcohol-positive older adolescents in a hospital emergency department. *Journal of Consulting and Clinical Psychology, 67*, 989–994.

Monti, P. M., Barnett, N. P., Colby, S. M., Gwaltney, C. J., Spirito, A., Rohsenow, D. J., & Woolard, R. (2007). Motivational interviewing versus feedback only in emergency care for young adult problem drinking. *Addiction, 102*(8), 1234–1243.

Moss, H. B., Chen, C. M., & Yi, H. Y. (2014). Early adolescent patterns of alcohol, cigarettes, and marijuana polysubstance use and young adult substance use outcomes in a nationally representative sample. *Drug and Alcohol Dependence, 136*, 51–62.

Mrug, S., & McCay, R. (2013). Parental and peer disapproval of alcohol use and its relationship to adolescent drinking: Age, gender, and racial differences. *Psychology of Addictive Behaviors, 27*(3), 604–614.

Mulia, N., Ye, Y., Greenfield, T. K., & Zemore, S. E. (2009). Disparities in alcohol-related problems among white, black, and Hispanic Americans. *Alcoholism: Clinical and Experimental Research, 33*, 654–662.

Mulia, N., Ye, Y., Zemore, S. E., & Greenfield, T. K. (2008). Social disadvantage, stress, and alcohol use among black, Hispanic, and white Americans: Findings from the 2005 U.S. National Alcohol Survey. *Journal of Studies on Alcohol and Drugs, 69*, 824–833.

Office of Applied Studies. (2006). Native Americans/American Indians in California and nationwide: Substance use prevalence and comparison with other ethnic groups. Retrieved February 2016, from http://www.adp.cahwnet.gov/oara/pdf/na_substance_prevalence.pdf

Office of Applied Studies. (2007). Substance use and substance use disorders among American Indians and Alaska Natives. Retrieved February 2016, from http://oas.samhsa.gov/2k7/AmIndians/AmIndians.htm

Orlando, M., Ellickson, P. L., McCaffrey, D. F., & Longshore, D. L. (2005). Mediation analysis of a school-based drug prevention program: Effects of Project ALERT. *Prevention Science, 6*, 35–46.

Oshri, A., Handley, E. D., Sutton, T. E., Wortel, S., & Burnette, M. L. (2014). Developmental trajectories of substance use among sexual minority girls: Associations with sexual victimization and sexual health risk. *Journal of Adolescent Health Care, 55*(1), 100–106.

Ozer, E. M., Adams, S. H., Gardner, L. R., Mailloux, D. E., Wibbelsman, C. J., & Irwin, C. E. (2004). Provider self-efficacy and the screening of adolescents for risky health behaviors. *Journal of Adolescent Health, 35*(101), 101–107.

Ozer, E. M., Adams, S. H., Lustig, J. L., Millstein, S. G., Camfield, K., El-Diwany, S., . . . Irwin, C. E. (2001). Can it be done? Implementing adolescent clinical preventive services. *Health Services Research, 36*(6, Pt. 2), 150–165.

Ozer, E. M., Adams, S. H., Orrell-Valente, J. K., Wibbelsman, C. J., Lustig, J. L., Millstein, S. G., . . . Irwin, C. E. (2011). Does delivering preventive services in primary care reduce adolescent risky behavior? *Journal of Adolescent Health, 49*(5), 476–482.

Padula, C. B., Schweinsburg, A. D., & Tapert, S. F. (2007). Spatial working memory performance and fMRI activation interaction in abstinent adolescent marijuana users. *Psychology of Addictive Behaviors, 21*, 478–487.

Passel, J. S., & Cohn, D. (2008). *U.S. population projections: 2005–2050.* Washington, DC: Pew Research Center.

Patrick, M. E., Maggs, J. L., Greene, K. M., Morgan, N. R., & Schulenberg, J. E. (2014). The link between mother and adolescent substance use: Intergenerational findings from the British cohort study. *Longitudinal Life Course Studies, 5*(1), 56–63.

Paus, T. (2005). Mapping brain maturation and cognitive development during adolescence. *Trends in Cognitive Science, 9*(2), 60–68.

Paus, T., Keshavan, M., & Giedd, J. N. (2008). Why do many psychiatric disorders emerge during adolescence? *Nature Reviews Neuroscience, 9*(12), 947–957.

Peterson, A. V., Jr., Leroux, B. G., Bricker, J., Kealey, K. A., Marek, P. M., Sarason, I. G., & Andersen, M. R. (2006). Nine-year prediction of adolescent smoking by number of smoking parents. *Addictive Behaviors, 31*, 788–801.

Peterson, P. L., Baer, J. S., Wells, E. A., Ginzler, J. A., & Garrett, S. B. (2006). Short-term effects of a brief motivational intervention to reduce alcohol and drug risk among homeless adolescents. *Psychology of Addictive Behaviors, 20*, 254–264.

Petraitis, J., Flay, B. R., & Miller, T. Q. (1995). Reviewing theories of adolescent substance use: Organizing pieces in the puzzle. *Psychological Bulletin, 117*(1), 67–86.

Pinchevsky, G. M., Arria, A. M., Caldeira, K. M., Garnier-Dykstra, L. M., Vincent, K. B., & O'Grady, K. E. (2012). Marijuana exposure opportunity and initiation during college: Parent and peer influences. *Prevention Science, 13*(1), 43–54.

Poelen, E. A. P., Engels, R. C. M. E., Scholte, R. H. J., Boomsma, D. I., & Willemsen, G. (2009). Predictors of problem drinking in adolescence and young adulthood: A longitudinal twin-family study. *European Child and Adolescent Psychiatry, 18*(6), 345–352.

Pomery, E. A., Gibbons, F. X., Gerrard, M., Cleveland, M. J., Brody, G. H., & Wills, T. A. (2005). Families and risk: Prospective analyses of familial and social influences on adolescent substance use. *Journal of Family Psychology, 19*(4), 560–570.

Quinn, P. D., & Fromme, K. (2011). Subjective response to alcohol challenge: A quantitative review. *Alcoholism: Clinical and Experimental Research, 35*(10), 1759–1770.

Radin, S. M., Neighbors, C., Walker, P. S., Walker, R. D., Marlatt, G. A., & Larimer, M. E. (2006). The changing influences of self-worth and peer deviance on drinking problems in urban American Indian adolescents. *Psychology of Addictive Behaviors, 20*(2), 161–171.

Ramirez, J. R., Crano, W. D., Quist, R., Burgoon, M., Alvaro, E. M., & Grandpre, J. (2004). Acculturation, familism, parental monitoring, and knowledge as predictors of marijuana and inhalant use in adolescents. *Psychology of Addictive Behaviors, 18*(1), 3–11.

Richardson, M. A., Newcomb, M. D., Myers, H. F., & Coombs, R. H. (2002). Psychosocial predictors of recent drug use among Anglo and Hispanic children and adolescents. *Journal of Child and Adolescent Substance Abuse, 12*(2), 47–76.

Rigter, H., Henderson, C. E., Pelc, I., Tossmann, P., Phan, O., Hendriks, V., . . . Rowe, C. L. (2013). Multidimensional family therapy lowers the rate of cannabis dependence in adolescents: A randomised controlled trial in Western European outpatient settings. *Drug and Alcohol Dependence, 130*(1–3), 85–93.

Ringwalt, C. L., Clark, H. K., Hanley, S., Shamblen, S. R., & Flewelling, R. L. (2010). The effects of Project ALERT one year past curriculum completion. *Prevention Science, 11*(2), 172–184.

Rollnick, S., Miller, W. R., & Butler, C. C. (2008). *Motivational interviewing in health care: Helping patients change behavior.* New York, NY: Guilford Press.

Rose, R. J., Kaprio, J., Winter, T., Koskenvuo, M., & Viken, R. J. (1999). Familial and socioregional environmental effects on abstinence from alcohol at age sixteen. *Journal of Studies on Alcohol Supplement, 13*, 63–74.

Rotheram-Borus, M. J., Koopman, C., Haignere, C., & Davies, M. (1991). Reducing HIV sexual risk behaviors among runaway adolescents. *Journal of the American Medical Association, 266*, 1237–1241.

Rotheram-Borus, M. J., Song, J., Gwadz, M., Lee, M., Van Rossem, R., & Koopman, C. (2003). Reductions in HIV risk among runaway youth. *Prevention Science, 4*, 173–187.

Russo, D., Purohit, V., Foudin, L., & Salin, M. (2004). Workshop on alcohol use and health disparities 2002: A call to arms. *Alcohol, 32*, 37–43.

Substance Abuse and Mental Health Services Administration. (2012). *Results from the 2011 National Survey on Drug Use and Health: Summary of national findings. (NSDUH Series H-44, HHS Publication No. [SMA] 12-4713).* Rockville, MD: Substance Abuse and Mental Health Services Administration.

Schafer, J., & Brown, S. A. (1991). Marijuana and cocaine effect expectancies and drug use patterns. *Journal of Consulting and Clinical Psychology, 59*(4), 558–565.

Schmiege, S. J., Broaddus, M. R., Levin, M., & Bryan, A. D. (2009). Randomized trial of group interventions to reduce HIV/STD risk and change theoretical mediators among detained adolescents. *Journal of Consulting and Clinical Psychology, 77*(1), 38–50.

Scholes-Balog, K. E., Hemphill, S. A., Kremer, P., & Toumbourou, J. W. (2013). A longitudinal study of the reciprocal effects of alcohol use and interpersonal violence among Australian young people. *Journal of Youth and Adolescence, 42*(12), 1811–1823.

Schuckit, M. A. (2009). An overview of genetic influences in alcoholism. *Journal of Substance Abuse Treatment, 36*, S5–S14.

Schulte, M. T., Monreal, T. K., Kia-Keating, M., & Brown, S. A. (2010). Influencing adolescent social perceptions of alcohol use to facilitate change through a school-based intervention. *Journal of Child and Adolescent Substance Abuse, 19*(5), 371–390.

Schweinsburg, A. D., Brown, S. A., & Tapert, S. F. (2008). The influence of marijuana use on neurocognitive functioning in adolescents. *Current Drug Abuse Reviews, 1*(1), 99–111.

Schweinsburg, A. D., Schweinsburg, B. C., Cheung, E. H., Brown, G. G., Brown, S. A., & Tapert, S. F. (2005). fMRI response to spatial working memory in adolescents with comorbid marijuana and alcohol use disorders. *Drug and Alcohol Dependence, 79*, 201–210.

Sebastian, C., Burnett, S., & Blakemore, S-J. (2008). Development of the self-concept during adolescence. *Trends in Cognitive Sciences, 12*(11), 441–446.

Sher, K. J., Grekin, E. R., & Williams, N. A. (2005). The development of alcohol use disorders. *Annual Review of Clinical Psychology, 1*, 493–523.

Sher, K. J., Walitzer, K. S., Wood, P. K., & Brent, E. E. (1991). Characteristics of children of alcoholics: Putative risk factors, substance use and abuse, and psychopathology. *Journal of Abnormal Psychology, 100*, 427–448.

Shih, R. A., Miles, J. N. V., Tucker, J. S., Zhou, A. J., & D'Amico, E. J. (2010). Racial/ethnic differences in adolescent substance use: Mediation by individual, family, and school factors. *Journal of Studies on Alcohol and Drugs, 71*, 640–651.

Shih, R. A., Miles, J. N. V., Tucker, J. S., Zhou, A. J., & D'Amico, E. J. (2012). Racial/ethnic differences in the influence of cultural values, alcohol resistance self-efficacy and expectancies on risk for alcohol initiation. *Psychology of Addictive Behaviors, 26*(3), 460–470.

Silvers, J. A., McRae, K., Gabrieli, J. D. E., Gross, J. J., Remy, K. A., & Ochsner, K. N. (2012). Age-related differences in emotional reactivity, regulation, and rejection sensitivity in adolescence. *Emotion, 12*(6), 1235–1247. doi:10.1037/a0028297

Simons-Morton, B., Abroms, L., Haynie, D. L., & Chen, R. (2004). Latent growth curve analyses of peer and parent influences on smoking progression among early adolescents. *Health Psychology, 23*, 612–621.

Skeer, M., McCormick, M. C., Normand, S-L. T., Buka, S. L., & Gilman, S. E. (2009). A prospective study of familial conflict, psychological stress, and the development of substance use disorders in adolescence. *Drug and Alcohol Dependence, 104*(102), 65–72.

Skenderian, J. J., Siegel, J. T., Crano, W. D., Alvaro, E. E., & Lac, A. (2008). Expectancy change and adolescents' intentions to use marijuana. *Psychology of Addictive Behaviors, 22*, 563–569.

Slesnick, N., Dashora, P., Letcher, A., Erdem, G., & Serovich, J. (2009). A review of services and interventions for runaway and homeless youth: Moving forward. *Children and Youth Services Review, 31*, 732–742.

Slesnick, N., & Kang, M. (2008). The impact of an integrated treatment on HIV risk reduction among homeless youth: A randomized controlled trial. *Journal of Behavioral Medicine, 38*, 45–99.

Slesnick, N., Prestopnik, J. L., Meyers, R. J., & Glassman, M. (2007). Treatment outcome for street-living, homeless youth. *Addictive Behaviors, 32*, 1237–1251.

Smith, G. T., Goldman, M. S., Greenbaum, P. E., & Christiansen, B. A. (1995). Expectancy for social facilitation from drinking: The divergent paths of high-expectancy and low-expectancy adolescents. *Journal of Abnormal Psychology, 104*, 32–40.

Somerville, L. H., Jones, R., & Casey, B. J. (2010). A time of change: Behavioral and neural correlates of adolescent sensitivity to appetive and aversive environmental cues. *Brain and Cognition, 72*, 124–133.

Spear, H. J., & Kulbok, P. (2004). Autonomy and adolescence: A concept analysis. *Public Health Nursing, 21*(2), 144–152.

Spirito, A., Monti, P. M., Barnett, N. P., Colby, S. M., Sindelar, H., Rohsenow, D., . . . Myers, M. (2004). A randomized clinical trial of a brief motivational intervention for alcohol-positive adolescents treated in an emergency department. *Journal of Pediatrics, 145*, 396–402.

Spirito, A., Sindelar-Manning, H., Colby, S. M., Barnett, N. P., Lewander, J. W., Rohsenow, D., & Monti, P. M. (2011). Individual and family motivational interventions for alcohol-positive adolescents treated in an emergency department: Results of a randomized clinical trial. *Archives of Pediatric Adolescent Medicine, 165*(3), 269–274.

St Pierre, T. L., Osgood, D. W., Mincemoyer, C. C., Kaltreider, D. L., & Kauh, T. J. (2005). Results of an independent evaluation of Project ALERT delivered in schools by Cooperative Extension. *Prevention Science, 6*(4), 305–317.

Starkey, F., Audrey, S., Holliday, J., Moore, L., & Campbell, R. (2009). Identifying influential young people to undertake effective peer-led health promotion: The example of A Stop Smoking in Schools Trial (ASSIST) *Health Education Research, 24*(6), 977–988.

Stein, L. A., Clair, M., Lebeau, R., Colby, S. M., Barnett, N. P., Golembeske, C., & Monti, P. M. (2011). Motivational interviewing to reduce substance-related consequences: Effects for incarcerated adolescents with depressed mood. *Drug and Alcohol Dependence, 118*(2–3), 475–478.

Steinberg, L. (2007). Risk taking in adolescence: New perspectives from brain and behavioral science. *Current Directions in Psychological Science, 16*(2), 55–59.

Steinberg, L. (2008a). *Adolescence* (8th ed.). New York, NY: McGraw Hill.

Steinberg, L. (2008b). A social neuroscience perspective on adolescent risk-taking. *Developmental Review, 28*(1), 78–106.

Steinberg, L. (2010). A dual systems model of adolescent risk-taking. *Developmental Psychobiology 52*, 216–224.

Steinberg, L., Cauffman, E., Woolard, J., Graham, S., & Banich, M. (2009). Are adolescents less mature than adults? *American Psychologist, 64*(7), 583–594.

Steinberg, L., & Monahan, K. C. (2007). Age differences in resistance to peer influence. *Developmental Psychology, 43*, 1531–1543.

Sterling, S., Weisner, C., Hinman, A., & Parthasarathy, S. (2010). Access to treatment for adolescents with substance use and co-occurring disorders: Challenges and opportunities. *Journal of the American Academy of Child and Adolescent Psychiatry, 49*, 637–646.

Stern, S. A., Meredith, L. S., Gholson, J., Gore, P., & D'Amico, E. J. (2007). Project CHAT: A brief motivational substance abuse intervention for teens in primary care. *Journal of Substance Abuse Treatment, 32*, 153–165.

Stevens, G. D., & Shi, L. (2003). Racial and ethnic disparities in the primary care experiences of children: A review of the literature. *Medical Care Research and Review, 60*, 3–30.

Sturman, D. A., & Moghaddam, B. (2011). The neurobiology of adolescence: Changes in brain architecture, functional dynamics, and behavioral tendencies. *Neuroscience and Biobehavioral Reviews, 35*(8), 1704–1712.

Sussman, S., McCuller, W. J., & Dent, C. W. (2003). The associations of social self-control, personality disorders, and demographics with drug use among high-risk youth. *Addictive Behaviors, 28*, 1159–1166.

Szlemko, W. J., Wood, J. W., & Thurman, P. J. (2006). Native Americans and alcohol: Past, present, and future. *Journal of General Psychology, 133*(4), 435–451.

Tapert, S. F., & Brown, S. A. (1999). Neuropsychological correlates of adolescent substance abuse: Four year outcomes. *Journal of the International Neuropsychological Society, 5,* 475–487.

Tapert, S. F., & Brown, S. A. (2000). Substance dependence, family history of alcohol dependence and neuropsychological functioning in adolescence. *Addiction, 95*(7), 1043–1053.

Tapert, S. F., Caldwell, L., & Burke, M. A. (2004). Alcohol and the adolescent brain—Human studies. *Alcohol Research and Health, 28,* 205–212.

Tapert, S. F., Granholm, E., Leedy, N. G., & Brown, S. A. (2002). Substance use and withdrawal: Neuropsychological functioning over 8 years in youth. *Journal of the International Neuropsychological Society, 8,* 873–883.

Tapert, S. F., & Schweinsburg, A. D. (2005). The human adolescent brain and alcohol use disorders. *Recent Developments in Alcoholism, 17,* 177–197.

Tapert, S. F., & Schweinsburg, A. D. (2006). The human adolescent brain and alcohol use disorders. In M. Galanter (Ed.), *Alcohol problems in adolescents and young adults: Epidemiology, neurobiology, prevention, and treatment* (pp. 177–197). New York, NY: Springer Science + Business Media.

Tapert, S. F., Schweinsburg, A. D., Drummond, S. P. A., Paulus, M. P., Brown, S. A., Yang, T. A., & Frank, L. R. (2007). Functional MRI of inhibitory processing in abstinent adolescent marijuana users. *Psychopharmacology, 194,* 173–183.

Thai, N. D., Connell, C. M., & Tebes, J. K. (2010). Substance use among Asian American adolescents: Influence of race, ethnicity, and acculturation in the context of key risk and protective factors. *Asian American Journal of Psychology, 1,* 261–274.

Tims, F. M., Dennis, M. L., Hamilton, N., Buchan, B. J., Diamond, G., Funk, R., & Brantley, L. B. (2002). Characteristics and problems of 600 adolescent cannabis abusers in outpatient treatment. *Addiction, 97*(Suppl. 1), 46–57.

Trujillo, K. A., Castaäneda, E., Martâinez, D., & Gonzalez, G. (2006). Biological research on drug abuse and addiction in Hispanics: Current status and future directions. *Drug and Alcohol Dependence, 84*(Suppl. 1), S17–S28.

Tucker, J. S., Ellickson, P. L., Collins, R. L., & Klein, D. J. (2006). Are drug experimenters better adjusted than abstainers and users? A longitudinal study of adolescent marijuana use. *Journal of Adolescent Health, 39,* 488–494.

Tucker, J. S., Ellickson, P. L., Orlando, M., Martino, S. C., & Klein, D. J. (2005). Substance use trajectories from early adolescence to emerging adulthood: A comparison of smoking, binge drinking, and marijuana use. *Journal of Drug Issues, 35,* 307–332.

Tucker, J. S., Green, H., Zhou, A. J., Shih, R. A., Miles, J. N., & D'Amico, E. J. (2011). Substance use among middle school students: Associations with self-rated and peer-nominated popularity. *Journal of Adolescence, 34,* 513–519.

Tucker, J. S., Miles, J. N. V., D'Amico, E. J., Zhou, A. J., Green, H. D., & Shih, R. A. (2013). Temporal associations of popularity and alcohol use among middle school students. *Journal of Adolescent Health, 52*(1), 108–115.

Unger, J. B., Ritt-Olson, L. T., Teran, L., Huang, T., Hoffman, B. R., & Palmer, P. (2002). Cultural values and substance use in a multiethnic sample of California adolescents. *Addiction Research, 10,* 257–279.

van der Stouwe, T., Asscher, J. J., Stams, G. J., Deković, M., & van der Laan, P. H. (2014). The effectiveness of Multisystemic Therapy (MST): A meta-analysis. *Clinical Psychology Review, 34*(6), 468–481.

van der Vorst, H., Engels, R. C. M. E., Meeus, W., Dekovic, M., & Vermulst, A. (2006). Parental attachment, parental control, and early development of alcohol use: A longitudinal study. *Psychology of Addictive Behaviors, 20*(2), 107–116.

van Gastel, W. A., Tempelaar, W., Bun, C., Schubart, C. D., Kahn, R. S., & Plevier, C. (2013). Cannabis use as an indicator of risk for mental health problems in adolescents: A population-based study at secondary schools. *Psychological Medicine, 43*(9), 1849–1856.

Vega, W. A., & Gil, A. G. (1999). A model for explaining drug use behavior among Hispanic adolescents. *Drugs and Society, 14*(1–2), 57–74.

Voelkl, K., & Frone, M. (2000). Predictors of substance use at school among high school students. *Journal of Educational Psychology, 92,* 583–592.

Wagner, E. F. (2003). Conceptualizing alcohol treatment research for Hispanic/Latino adolescents. *Alcoholism: Clinical and Experimental Research, 27*(8), 1349–1352.

Wahl, A., & Eitle, T. M. (2010). Gender, acculturation and alcohol use among Latina/o adolescents: A multi-ethnic comparison. *Journal of Immigrant and Minority Health, 12*(2), 153–165.

Walker, S., Treno, A. J., Grube, J. W., & Light, J. M. (2003). Ethnic differences in driving after drinking and riding with drinking drivers among adolescents. *Alcoholism: Clinical and Experimental Research, 27*(8), 1299–1304.

Wallace, J. M., Jr. (1999). The social ecology of addiction: Race, risk, and resilience. *Pediatrics, 103,* 1122–1127.

Walton, M. A., Chermack, S. T., Shope, J. T., Bingham, C. R., Zimmerman, M. A., Blow, F. C., & Cunningham, R. M. (2010). Effects of a brief intervention for reducing violence and alcohol misuse among adolescents: A randomized controlled trial. *Journal of the American Medical Association, 304*(5), 527–535.

Wandersman, A., & Florin, P. (2003). Community interventions and effective prevention: Bringing researchers/evaluators, funders and practitioners together for accountability. *American Psychologist, 58,* 441–448.

Weinberg, N. Z. (2001). Risk factors for adolescent substance abuse. *Journal of Learning Disabilities, 34,* 342–351.

Welch, K. A., Carson, A., & Lawrie, S. M. (2013). Brain structure in adolescents and young adults with alcohol problems: Systematic review of imaging studies. *Alcohol and Alcoholism, 48*(4), 433–444.

White, A. (2009). Understanding adolescent brain development and its implications for the clinician. *Adolescent Medicine, 20,* 73–90.

Whitesell, N. R., Asdigian, N. L., Kaufman, C. E., Big Crow, C., Shangreau, C., Keane, E. M., . . . Mitchell, C. M. (2014). Trajectories of substance use among young American Indian adolescents: Patterns and predictors. *Journal of Youth and Adolescence, 43*(3), 437–453.

Wills, T. A., Walker, C., Mendoza, D., & Ainette, M. G. (2006). Behavioral and emotional self-control: Relations to substance use in samples of middle and high school students. *Psychology of Addictive Behaviors, 20,* 265–278.

Windle, M. (2000). Parental, sibling, and peer influences on adolescent substance use and alcohol problems. *Applied Developmental Science Special Issue: Familial and Peer Influences on Adolescent Substance Use, 4,* 98–110.

Wood, M. D., Read, J. P., Mitchell, R. E., & Brand, N. H. (2004). Do parents still matter? Parent and peer influences on alcohol involvement among recent high school graduates. *Psychology of Addictive Behaviors, 18*, 19–30.

World Health Organization. (2004–2005). Psychosocial processes and mechanisms of risk and protection. *Alcohol, Health and Research World, 28*, 143–154.

Wu, L. T., Woody, G. E., Yang, C., Pan, J. J., & Blazer, D. G. (2011). Racial/ethnic variations in substance-related disorders among adolescents in the United States. *Archives of General Psychiatry, 68*(11), 1176–1185.

Wu, P., Hoven, C. W., Tiet, Q., Kovalenko, P., & Wicks, J. (2002). Factors associated with adolescent utilization of alcohol treatment services. *American Journal of Drug and Alcohol Abuse, 28*, 353–369.

Xiang, X. (2013). A review of interventions for substance use among homeless youth. *Research on Social Work Practice, 23*(1), 34–45.

Yoast, R. A., Fleming, M., & Balch, G. I. (2007). Reactions to a concept for physician intervention in adolescent alcohol use. *Journal of Adolescent Health, 41*(1), 35–41.

Yule, A. M., Wilens, T. E., Martelon, M. K., Simon, A., & Biederman, J. (2013). Does exposure to parental substance use disorders increase substance use disorder risk in offspring? A 5-year follow-up study. *American Journal on Addictions, 22*(5), 460–465.

Zhou, Q., King, K. M., & Chassin, L. (2006). The roles of familial alcoholism and adolescent family harmony in young adults' substance dependence disorders: Mediated and moderated relations. *Journal of Abnormal Psychology, 115*(2), 320–331.

Zucker, R. A., Wong, M. A., Puttler, L. I., & Fitzgerald, H. E. (2003). Resilience and vulnerability among sons of alcoholics: Relationships to developmental outcomes between early childhood and adolescence. In S. S. Luthar (Ed.), *Resilience and vulnerability: Adaptation in the context of childhood adversities* (pp. 76–103). New York, NY: Cambridge University Press.

Targeted Prevention Approaches

Eric F. Wagner *and* Nehama Lewis

Abstract

This chapter reviews the current literature on targeted prevention approaches for adolescent alcohol and other drug (AOD) use. We open the chapter by examining both the historical and current use of the term "targeted prevention" in regard to teen AOD use. We then provide a review of existing targeted prevention work from a health communication perspective and offer recommendations for future areas for research on targeting in health campaigns. This is followed by a review of existing targeted prevention work from a clinical intervention perspective, with attention to both selective and indicated prevention strategies. This includes recommendations for future areas for research on targeting in early intervention programs. We conclude the chapter with a brief recapitulation of its contents.

Key Words: targeted prevention, message tailoring, selective prevention, indicated prevention, clinical intervention perspective

To be sure of hitting the target, shoot first, and call whatever you hit the target

—Ashleigh Brilliant

Just what, exactly, do prevention scientists mean by targeted prevention for adolescent alcohol and other drug (AOD) use? It turns out there is no simple answer to this question. Despite more than half a century of rigorous attempts to reach consensus about what defines prevention, much semantic fuzziness remains (Kutash, Duchnowski, & Lynn, 2006; Mrazek & Haggerty, 1994). In the following introductory section, we review both the historical and current use of the term "targeted prevention."

A Brief History of Attempts to Define the Term "Targeted Prevention"

The first prevention intervention definitional system was proposed by the Commission on Chronic Illness (1957), which distinguished three

types of prevention: (1) primary prevention, which seeks to decrease the number of new cases of a disorder; (2) secondary prevention, which seeks to lower the rate of established cases of a disorder in the population (prevalence); and (3) tertiary prevention, which seeks to decrease the amount of disability associated with an existing disorder. It should be noted that the notion of "targeted prevention" was not included in the Commission on Chronic Illness's prevention definitions.

Three decades later, Gordon (1987) proposed a prevention typology integrating a "risk-benefit" perspective, with an emphasis on specifying populations and subpopulations toward which different types of prevention should be directed. Gordon's prevention classification included three types of preventive measures, with "measures" defined as actions applied to persons who are not suffering discomfort or disability due to the disorder being prevented. Essentially, defining measures in this way eliminates from consideration most of what was encompassed in the Commission on Chronic Illness's tertiary prevention category. Gordon's typology included (1) universal measures, which are desirable for everyone because the benefits outweigh the costs at the population level; (2) selective measures, which are desirable only for persons belonging to a subgroup at above-average risk of contracting a disorder; and (3) indicated measures, which are desirable only for persons already manifesting a disorder. The notion of targeted prevention, while never explicitly invoked by Gordon, is suggested in his use of the terms "selective" and "indicated."

The next important development in refining prevention definitions came in the form of the Institute on Medicine's (IOM) report on prevention research for mental disorders (Mrazek & Haggerty, 1994). The IOM used Gordon's prevention classification system as its model, though improved upon it by (a) redefining "measures" as "prevention interventions" and (b) explicitly specifying targets for each class of preventive interventions. The IOM classification system included (1) universal preventive interventions, targeted to the general public or population, not based on individual risk, and desirable for everyone; (2) selective preventive interventions, targeted to individuals or a subgroup of the population at above-average imminent or lifetime risk for a disorder; and (3) indicated preventive interventions, targeted to individuals having minimal but detectable signs or symptoms foreshadowing meeting diagnostic criteria for a disorder. In the strictest sense, all three levels of intervention were targeted prevention approaches, distinguished from one another by their target recipients. However, universal approaches, just as in Gordon's system, are designed for an entire population, whereas selected and indicated approaches target only subpopulations with elevated odds of developing a disorder.

A recent development in honing prevention definitions comes from Weisz, Sndler, Durlak, and Anton (2005), who (a) substituted the term "strategy" in place of Gordon's "measure" and the IOM's "intervention;" (b) made health promotion programs their own category of prevention strategies; and (c) reintroduced treatment ("tertiary prevention" as per the Commission on Chronic Illness) as its own category in the typology. Weisz et al.'s (2005) resulting five-tiered integrative classification included (1) health promotion/positive development strategies, targeted to enhance protective factors, or increase prospects for positive development, for an entire population; (2) universal prevention strategies, targeted to address risk factors for an entire population; (3) selective prevention strategies, targeted to address risk factors among specific subgroups at elevated risk for a disorder; (4) indicated prevention strategies, targeted to individuals with significant symptoms of a disorder, but not meeting diagnostic criteria for that disorder; and (5) treatment interventions, targeted to those presenting with diagnosable disorders. Like Gordon and the IOM, Weisz et al. define each level of prevention strategies by the specific (and increasingly narrow) subgroups for which they are appropriate. Weisz et al. also maintain the distinction between selected prevention strategies and indicated prevention strategies; such strategies have smaller subgroup targets than do health promotion/positive development or universal prevention strategies, and larger subgroup targets than do treatment interventions. Moreover, primary targets-for-change are risk factors for disorder in selected prevention strategies, versus symptoms of disorder as in indicated prevention strategies.

Current Use of the Term "Targeted Prevention" in the Adolescent Alcohol and Other Drug Use Literature

To delineate further what prevention scientists mean by the term "targeted prevention," we conducted a literature search based on the term "targeted prevention." We looked for the term in both titles and abstracts, concentrating on the publications from the past decades in order to gauge current usage. Our literature search identified a dozen evidence-based published articles that, in one way or another, reported on targeted AOD prevention approaches with teenagers. The operative phrase in the previous sentence is "in one way or another." As it turns out, targeted prevention means different things to different people dedicated to preventing AOD use problems among adolescents. From our literature search, we identified seven different current specifications of what the adjective "targeted" means when applied to the noun "prevention" (see Table 30.1).

Koning et al. (2009) used "targeted" to describe *broad demographic qualities of the intended recipients* of a prevention program. For Koning et al., adolescents, their parents, or simultaneously adolescents and their parents were examples of three different prevention targets in their targeted prevention approach. From the Koning et al. perspective, a targeted prevention approach might include distributing informational pamphlets about positive parenting approaches to parents of middle school–aged

Table 30.1 In regard to adolescent alcohol and drug use behavior, "targeted prevention" can mean *targeted . . .*

1.	to broad demographic qualities of the intended recipients (e.g., parents of teenagers)
2.	toward adolescents at elevated risk (e.g., eighth graders who report underage drinking)
3.	deployment of prevention program content (e.g., individualized content based on individual profiles)
4.	to affect mediators of program effects (e.g., social influences on underage drinking)
5.	to affect specific AOD outcomes (e.g., the initiation of smoking)
6.	toward a specific developmental cohort (e.g., eighth graders)
7.	toward a specific developmental transition (e.g., moving from high school to college)

children. This targets the broad demographic group of parents of middle school–aged children, but not the children themselves, despite having the goal of preventing AOD use problems among the children. Targeting in this case refers to whom the prevention program was applied.

Stewart et al. (2005) apply the label "targeted" only to AOD prevention programs geared *toward adolescents at elevated risk* for problematic substance use. Using Stewart et al.'s definition, teens who are early initiators of substance use, or teens with family histories of substance use problems, are examples of appropriate targets for a targeted prevention approach. Our own research group's NIH-supported Adolescent Behavior and Lifestyle Evaluation (ABLE) projects, which evaluated the efficacy of school-based brief motivational intervention, conformed to Stewart et al.'s definition of a targeted prevention program. In the first ABLE randomized controlled trial (R01 AA013825; PI: Wagner), we targeted public high school sophomores and juniors who reported six or more drinking occasions during the past 90 days. In the second ABLE study (R01 DA025640; PI: Wagner), we targeted public high school sophomores who reported three or more marijuana use occasions during the past year. As these examples demonstrate, targeting in this case refers to directing prevention efforts toward subgroups of teenagers at above-average risk for using or abusing substances, commensurate with Selective and Indicated Prevention Strategies as defined by Weisz et al. (2005).

Coffman, Patrick, Palen, Rhoades, and Ventura (2007) offer a third variation on defining targeted prevention. These investigators used "targeted" to describe the tailored *deployment of prevention program content* such that it is "molded to each participant's needs based on tailoring variables and individual characteristics" (p. 246). From the Coffman et al.

perspective, targeting means tailoring program content so as to best fit a particular participant's presenting or baseline profile; this profile is derived from one or more tailoring variables. For Coffman et al., adolescents' motivations for drinking (i.e., Experimentation, Thrill-seeking, Multi-reasons, & Relaxing) are an especially promising tailoring variable for targeted prevention. In this case, targeting involves systematically varying prevention program content according to motivations for drinking particular to individual adolescents (or according to other tailoring variables, singularly or in combination with one another), with the ultimate goal of improving the effectiveness of preventive efforts.

Stephens et al. (2009) used "targeted" to describe prevention programs that attempt to *directly affect constructs* associated with adolescent AOD initiation and use. The constructs may be *mediators* of the association between program participation and AOD outcomes (i.e., mechanisms of change) or the *AOD outcomes* themselves. For example, Stephens and colleagues examined the effectiveness of a universal prevention approach that targeted the constructs of social influences and competence, both of which are thought to account for program effectiveness. These targets were selected because of their (a) significant associations with the initiation and use of substances by youth and (b) amenability to intervention. To make matters a bit more complicated, Stephens et al. also use targeted to describe prevention approaches designed for *specific drugs*. In this case, a universal prevention approach specifically focusing on adolescent cigarette smoking could be defined as a targeted prevention approach. Thus, targeting in Stephens et al.'s sense involves orienting prevention efforts toward specific skills and competencies believed to be protective against the use of specific drugs.

A final variation on the definition of targeted prevention is developmental in nature. Prevention approaches may define "targeted" as (a) designed for a *specific developmental cohort* (e.g., middle school students) or (b) focused on a *specific developmental transition* (e.g., the transition from high school to college). For example, Stephens et al. point out that universal school-based substance abuse prevention programs are generally administered in middle school and the first 2 years of high school. In this case, targeting involves directing prevention efforts toward a specific developmental cohort experiencing a specific (and normative) developmental transition. Both the targeted developmental cohort (e.g., 8th graders) and the targeted developmental transition (e.g., moving from middle to senior high school) were selected because of their association with risk for AOD initiation and use. This risk is not subgroup specific; rather, it is population-level risk based on developmental level, making it commensurate with Universal Prevention Strategies as defined by Weisz et al. (2005). This developmental angle is yet another semantic slant to the term "targeted prevention" as currently used in the adolescent AOD prevention literature.

Our Use of the Term "Targeted Prevention": Differences Between Disciplines

So . . . what, exactly, do the authors of this chapter mean by targeted prevention for adolescent AOD use? Both of us have spent considerable time working on the targeted prevention of adolescent AOD use, and we had assumed that our definitions of the term would line up. However, that was not the case. N. L., who is trained in health communication, applies the term "targeted prevention" to media campaigns aimed at influencing secular trends in the amount and veracity of information available on a given topic, with the ultimate goal of health promotion. For her, targeted prevention involves the tailored deployment of prevention messages so as to best fit a particular participant's presenting or baseline profile, similar to Coffman et al.'s (2007) use of the term. E. F. W., who is trained as a clinical psychologist, defines targeted prevention as interventions designed for adolescents at elevated risk for substance use problems, similar to Stewart et al.'s (2005) use of the term. In speaking with our colleagues, we realized that they too were roughly equally divided in defining targeted prevention as either (a) message targeting or tailoring in health

campaigns or (b) providing specialized intervention to select high-risk individuals. Agreeing to disagree, we chose for the purposes of this chapter to use both definitions. The next section reviews the empirical literature on targeted prevention as defined as the tailored deployment of AOD prevention messages to youth, which represents the health communication perspective on targeted prevention. The section after that reviews the empirical literature on targeted prevention as defined as intervening with youth at elevated risk for AOD use problems, which represents the clinical intervention perspective on targeted prevention.

Targeted Prevention: Health Communication Perspective

Mass media campaigns, because of their wide reach, appeal, and cost-effectiveness, have been major tools in health promotion and are often the primary or sole component in a variety of public health campaigns (Backer, Rogers, & Sopory, 1992; Flay, 1987; Randolph & Viswanath, 2004; Rice & Atkin, 1989). In particular, campaigns directed at the prevention of substance abuse and other risk behaviors have often relied on the mass media as the primary vehicle for disseminating prevention messages (Flay & Sobel, 1983; Rogers & Storey, 1987; Schilling & McAllister, 1990). Mass media campaigns have been described as exercises in information control (Viswanath, Finnegan, Hannan, & Luepker, 1991). Targeted interventions utilizing mass media channels usually are aimed at influencing the secular trend in the amount of information available on a given topic in a system. This occurs through attempting to increase the amount of information available on a particular topic, or by also redefining or framing the issue as a public health problem to make it salient, engage the attention of the target audience, and suggest a solution to resolving a problem (Randolph & Viswanath, 2004; Viswanath et al., 1991; Wallack & Dorfman, 1996). Typical campaigns have placed messages in media that reach large audiences, most frequently via television or radio but also outdoor media (billboards and posters) and print media (magazines and newspapers) (Wakefield, Loken, & Hornik, 2010). One of the benefits of mass media campaigns lies in their ability to disseminate well-defined, behaviorally focused messages to large audiences repeatedly, over time, in a cost-effective manner (Wakefield et al., 2010).

Mass media campaigns can work through direct and indirect pathways to change the behavior of a population (Hornik & Yanovitzky, 2003). Media campaigns can influence behavior through three paths—institutional diffusion, social diffusion, and the individual path, which involves direct exposure of individuals to the persuasive messages generated by the campaign, whether through ads placed in the media, educational programs, or other forms of messages (Hornik & Yanovitzky, 2003). The individual path of media effects is the path of effects most commonly conceptualized and tested in the design and evaluation of many targeted health communication campaigns. This path is derived directly from influential theories of health behavior change. A great deal of evidence exists of successful campaigns that applied guiding theoretical frameworks such as social learning theory, diffusion of innovations, the theory of reasoned action, the health belief model, the elaboration likelihood model, and protection motivation theory (Flora, Maibach, & Maccoby, 1989; Maibach & Parrott, 1995; McAlister, Ramirez, Galavotti, & Gallion, 1989; Petty, Baker, & Gleicher, 1991; Rogers, 1995; Rosenstock, 1990; Schilling & McAllister, 1990; Zimmerman & Vernberg, 1994).

Using Behavioral Theory in Substance Abuse Prevention Campaigns

Theory can be used to carefully identify a set of determinants that influence cognitions, affect, and behaviors. For example, the Integrated Model of Behavior Change (Fishbein, 2000; Fishbein, Cappella, et al., 2002; Fishbein & Ajzen, 2010) provides guidance for message strategies. According to this approach, if the target population has formed intentions to perform the behavior, for example, to reduce their alcohol intake, but are not acting on it, possibly due to a lack of skills or the presence of environmental constraints, the strategy will be directed at skill building or at helping people to overcome environmental constraints (Fishbein & Yzer, 2003). In contrast, if formative research indicates that the target population has not formed strong intentions to reduce their alcohol intake, a message might address one or more of the primary determinants of intention—attitude toward performing the behavior, perceived norms concerning performing the behavior, and self-efficacy with respect to performing the behavior (Fishbein & Yzer, 2003, p. 167). The message strategy will depend both upon the behavior and the population being targeted. Once a researcher determines, in a given population, which factors determine a particular behavior, they can identify specific beliefs

that discriminate between people who do or do not engage in the behavior in question, that is, beliefs that are highly correlated with behavioral intention (Fishbein & Yzer, 2003, p. 172). Beliefs that are most amenable to change are those for which most of the population do not already hold the belief in question. For example, if the targeted belief is that "*alcohol does not make you feel good*," an individual's own direct experience with alcohol may make this belief more difficult to change than other less common beliefs.

Message Effects Theories

Although the application of behavioral theory and exposure to the message is a critical element in the success of any media-based campaign, the content and format of a message is also an important factor. Message effects theories can be used to design messages for target audience, which can enhance the probability of a campaign's success. There are a number of studies which provide evidence that theoretically based messages addressing the beliefs and values of a specific population can significantly change behavior (CDC AIDS Community Demonstration Projects Research Group, 1999; Fishbein, 1997; Fishbein et al., 1997; Kamb et al., 1998, among others). For example, theory on the use of narratives in persuasion could suggest whether a message in the form of a narrative may be more persuasive for a particular population, compared with an informational message (Berger, 2013; Green & Brock, 2000). The Extended-ELM (E-ELM: Slater, 2002; Slater & Rouner, 1997, 2002) is a useful theoretical framework with which to examine the effects of narrative and nonnarrative (expository) messages. The E-ELM proposes that interest in the plot (transportation) and identification with protagonists facilitate persuasion in the context of narrative messages (Cohen, 2001; Green & Brock, 2000; Slater & Rouner, 1997, 2002). Among audiences who are likely to resist overt attempts at persuasion, such as high-risk adolescents, the use of narratives may help overcome various kinds of resistance to persuasion, particularly through reducing message counterarguing, a key obstacle to persuasion and attitude change (Petty & Cacioppo, 1986; Slater & Rouner, 2002). A substance abuse prevention campaign focused on prevention of alcohol abuse among a high-risk population should, according to this approach, adopt narrative messages emphasizing the benefits of reducing alcohol intake or illustrating the risks of alcohol abuse. Message effects theories such as the E-ELM (Slater, 2002; Slater & Rouner, 1997, 2002) can be applied to encourage a new viewpoint or to alter the current view of a public health issue among the target audience. Messages designed to address substance abuse can be conceptualized in an infinite number of different ways. In this section we will review a number of approaches to media-based substance abuse prevention messages, highlighting examples from recent campaigns.

Targeted Substance Abuse Prevention Campaigns: A Review

Although media-based substance abuse campaigns play an important role by providing information and education, generally, these and other public information campaigns have not been found to be effective in reducing alcohol-related outcomes (Babor et al., 2003) and have shown modest or mixed effects on drug-related outcomes (Block, Morwitz, Putsis, & Sen, 2002; Fishbein, Hall-Jamieson, Zimmer, Haefter, & Nabi, 2002). It is difficult for a campaign to lead to sustained changes in behavior in an environment in which individuals are surrounded by many competing messages in the form of marketing and social norms supporting drinking, and in which alcohol and other substances are readily acceptable (Anderson, Chisholm, & Fuhr, 2009).

However, when properly designed, public information media campaigns can be effective in changing beliefs, attitudes, intentions, and even behaviors (e.g., Beck et al., 1990; Flay, 1987; Flynn, Worden, Seeker-Walker, Badger, & Geller, 1995; Hornik, 2002; McDivitt, Zimick, & Hornik, 1997). Derzon and Lipsey (2002) conducted a meta-analysis of 72 antidrug media campaigns targeting young people and found that effects, while small overall, were larger for campaigns using a series of ads rather than a "one shot" treatment, and they were larger for campaigns that were supplemented with other activities (e.g., peer advocacy or community-based programs) to reinforce and provide greater depth to the media messages (Longshore, Ghosh-Dastidar, & Ellickson, 2006).

Public health campaign literature outlines four important principles that underscore campaign success: (a) interventions based on well-tested social and behavioral theories are more likely to be successful (Donohew, Lorch, & Palmgreen, 1991; Flay, 1987; Maibach & Parrott, 1995; McAlister et al., 1989; Rogers, 1995; Rosenstock, 1990; Schilling & McAllister, 1990; Zimmerman & Vernberg, 1994, among others); (b) obtaining sufficient (i.e.,

widespread, frequent, and prolonged) exposure to messages to achieve measurable impact is vital to campaign success (Flay, 1987; Hornik, 2002); (c) audience segmentation is required to target messages to at-risk audiences (Backer et al., 1992; Slater, 1996); and (d) formative research should be employed throughout the audience segmentation, message design, and channel selection phases (Atkin & Freimuth, 1989), in particular identifying message strategies that can achieve the desired impact given adequate exposure (Pechmann, Zhao, Goldberg, & Reibling, 2003; Worden, 1999).

Some substance abuse prevention campaigns have applied these principles, but others have failed to do so. There have been relatively few controlled mass-media based campaigns which have applied these principles and can establish campaign exposure effects on behavioral outcomes. One campaign that successfully did so was a two-city antismoking advertising campaign conducted by Palmgreen, Donohew, Lorch, Hoyle, and Stephenson (2001). This prevention campaign illustrates the critical roles of careful message construction and choice of messages reflecting an underlying model or theory about how communication is to influence behavior (Hornik, 2002). The campaign also successfully employed audience targeting, which employs variables kinked both to the behavior of interests and to the communication channels and message styles most preferred by the target audience (Slater, 1996).

Palmgreen and colleagues' prevention approach was called SENTAR (sensation-seeking targeting). The SENTAR approach can be summarized by four principles: (a) employ sensation seeking as a major audience segmentation variable; (b) conduct formative research with high sensation-seeking members of the target audience; (c) design prevention messages high in sensation value; and (d) place campaign messages in high–sensation value contexts (e.g., TV programs). Sensation seeking is a personality trait with a relatively high degree of temporal stability, and it is associated both with drug risk as well as with the need for novel, complex, ambiguous, and emotionally intense stimuli and the willingness to take risks to obtain such stimulation (Zuckerman, 1979, 1994). Sensation seeking is a moderate to strong predictor of drug use and earlier onset of use, with high sensation seekers at greater risk than low sensation seekers (Kilpatrick, Sutker, & Smith, 1976; Pedersen, 1991; Segal, Huba, & Singer, 1980; Zuckerman, 1979, 1994). High sensation seekers have distinct preferences for certain types of message characteristics based on their need for messages that are novel, usual and intense (Donohew et al., 1991; Zuckerman, 1994). Messages that appeal to this group elicit strong sensory, affective, and arousal responses (Palmgreen et al., 1991) and tend to be novel, dramatic, emotionally powerful or physically arousing, graphic or explicit, somewhat ambiguous, unconventional, fast-paced, or suspenseful (Palmgreen, Donohew, Lorch, Hoyle, & Stephenson, 2002).

Focus groups of 8th through 12th graders, scoring above and below the median on a sensation-seeking scale for adolescents, expressed opinions on existing antidrug public service announcements varying in sensation value and discussed salient risks and consequences associated with marijuana use (Palmgreen et al., 2002). Feedback from these focus groups guided the creation of five 30-second TV ads, which were shown together with several public service announcements provided by the Partnership for a Drug-Free America (PDFA), which were judged high in sensation value. These ads were aired on local TV station and cable companies, and had high exposure among the target audience; at least 70% of the targeted age group was exposed to a minimum of three campaign ads per week.

The campaign was evaluated using a 32-month controlled, interrupted time-series with switching replications (Cook & Campbell, 1979) in Fayette County, Kentucky, and Knox County, Tennessee, in 1997 and 1998. Interviews were conducted using systematic random sampling of 32 monthly pools of potential respondents from 7th to 10th graders attending public schools in 1996. The campaign showed declines in marijuana use among high sensation seekers with each wave of their campaign (Hornik, 2002; Palmgreen et al., 2002). The results indicate that mass media–based substance abuse campaigns can affect drug behavior, but only in the context of carefully targeted campaigns that achieve high levels of reach and frequency, and with messages designed specifically for the target audience on the basis of social scientific theory and formative research (Palmgreen et al., 2002, p. 52).

Another successful media-based substance abuse prevention campaign applied social marketing principles, in combination with a participatory, community-based media effort, to reduce marijuana, alcohol, and tobacco use among middle school students (Slater et al., 2006). This program was developed over 5 years of formative research and testing (Kelly, Swaim, & Wayman, 1996; Kelly, Stanley, & Edwards, 2000; Kelly, Comello, & Slater, 2006). This was a randomized controlled trial (RCT) conducted in 16 middle schools, with 8 schools randomly assigned to media treatment and 8 schools serving as controls. Eight communities received the in-school and community media campaign and eight did not. Within each community, two middle schools were recruited, one of which received a classroom-based intervention and one that did not (Slater, Kelly, Lawrence, Stanley, & Comello, 2011). The media program was conducted through several channels (print, posters, T-shirts, book covers, water bottles) with the positive theme of "Be Under Your Own Influence" in combination with related community activities. This theme was intended to emphasize the inconsistency of substance use (and, to a lesser extent, smoking), with the aspirations of an adolescent to attain greater independence and autonomy (Oman et al., 2004). The campaign aimed to reframe substance use as a choice that impairs rather than enhances personal autonomy (Williams, Cox, Kouides, & Deci, 1999). In addition, the campaign messages incorporated images that were intended to be appealing to risk-oriented, sensation-seeking youth, similar to the approach used by Palmgreen et al. (2001).

Results of the evaluation of this campaign provided support for the effectiveness of in-school media efforts combined with participatory communication efforts at the community level. The intervention was found to reduce uptake trajectories for several substance outcomes, and in particular for marijuana and alcohol use (Slater et al., 2006). Compared with the control group, youth in the intervention communities had fewer users at final posttest for marijuana (OR = .50, $p < .05$), alcohol (OR = .40, $p < .01$), and cigarettes (OR = .49, $p < .05$). These results suggest that the focus on autonomy and personal aspirations was seen as applicable to both substances (Slater et al., 2006, p. 164). The "Be Under Your Own Influence" campaign's success illustrates the importance of aligning substance abuse prevention measures with developmentally appropriate goals (Slater et al., 2011; Wagner, Brown, Monti, Myers, & Waldron, 1999).

In contrast to these examples of successful media-based campaigns, the Office of National Drug Control Policy's (ONDCP) 5-year, $2 billion National Youth Anti-Drug Media Campaign is an example of a media-based substance abuse campaign for which there was high hopes, but which failed to show positive effects, and even, it is argued, led to negative effects on some outcomes among high-risk youth. The National Youth Anti-Drug Media Campaign was the largest drug abuse prevention effort in history. The campaign was a multimedia effort that tried to stimulate community-based programs, but its central component was the targeted dissemination of televised antidrug ads and public service announcements (Palmgreen et al., 2002). The messages reflected three themes of the campaign's community strategy—resistance self-efficacy, antidrug norms, and negative consequences of use—and were aired in paid and donated advertising on a full range of media (Longshore et al., 2006). The 5-year campaign, initiated in 1998, was designed to be a comprehensive social marketing effort that aimed antidrug messages through a range of media channels at youths aged 9 to 18 years, their parents, and other influential adults. In addition, the campaign established partnerships with civic, professional, and community groups and outreach programs with the media, entertainment, and sports industries (Hornik, Jacobsohn, Orwin, Piesse, & Kalton, 2008).

The evaluation of this campaign was supervised by the National Institute on Drug Abuse and undertaken by Westat and the Annenberg School for Communication at the University of Pennsylvania. The primary evaluation tool was the National Survey of Parents and Youth (NSPY), an in-home survey of youths and their parents living in households in the United States (Hornik et al., 2008). Results showed substantial exposure to antidrug advertising, but no change in prevalence of marijuana use among those aged 12.5 to 18 years between 2000 and 2004, and no association between exposure to antidrug ads and any of the outcomes, after adjusting for confounders. In lagged analyses, results indicated the possible presence of *pro-marijuana effects* of ad exposure on intentions to use marijuana; examination of the 80 subgroup analyses reveals 20 significant effects, with 19 of those in a pro-marijuana direction, an overriding pattern of unfavorable lagged exposure effects.

One explanation for these findings is that youth who saw the campaign perceived that their peers were using marijuana. In turn, those who came to believe that their peers were using marijuana were more likely to initiate use themselves (Hornik et al., 2008). Evidence consistent with this explanation is that more ad exposure was associated with the belief that other youths were marijuana users, and this belief was predictive of subsequent initiation of marijuana use (Hornik et al., 2008; Orwin et al., 2006). Jacobsohn (2007) studied possible explanations for the campaign's boomerang effect. Findings from the research pointed to mass communication's role in influencing perceived norms; results suggested that the campaign ads cumulatively delivered an implicit "meta-message" that marijuana use was widespread among youth, which in turn, negatively affected youth behavior. Future substance abuse campaigns would be well advised to empirically test the effects of ads among members of the target population prior to launching a full-scale campaign in order to avoid undesirable boomerang effects such as appear to have occurred in the ONDCP campaign.

Following public release of the negative findings for the "My Anti-drug" campaign, the ONDCP campaign was rebid and the contract was assigned to a new advertising firm, which launched a rebranded marijuana prevention campaign, "Above the Influence," in 2005 (Slater et al., 2011). No formal external evaluation of the rebranded campaign was funded. However, internal rolling cross-sectional surveys conducted weekly over the course of the campaign show significant positive associations between exposure to the new campaign and antidrug attitudes (White, 2008).

Fear appeals are a widely used message strategy in media-based substance abuse prevention campaigns. A review by Witte and Allen (2000) suggested that strong fear appeals increase perception of susceptibility, and that, combined with messages suggestive of skills and actions, fear appeals can be an effective way to change behavior. However, when strong fear appeals are not accompanied by self-efficacy information, the effects of messages on substance abuse outcomes can be undermined. One recent example of the challenges posed by using this form of appeal is the Montana Meth Project (MMP), a large-scale methamphetamine prevention program in Montana in 2005. The campaign used extremely graphic ads featuring the effects of methamphetamine use, portraying users as unhygienic, dangerous, untrustworthy, and exploitive (Erceg-Hurn, 2008). Users are depicted killing their parents, being raped, and prostituting themselves to support their drug habit (Erceg-Hurn, 2008). The project was lauded as a resounding success by the nonprofit organization MMP, media, and politicians, who have argued that the campaign has dramatically increased antimethamphetamine attitudes and reduced drug use in Montana. However, these claims have been called into question by Erceg-Hurn (2008), who reviews the evidence for effects and finds that the empirical support for the campaign is weak, and not supported by data. Erceg-Hurn (2008) further argues that the MMP misrepresented campaign data, allegedly selecting data for presentation that is consistent with its claims of positive campaign effects. Erceg-Hurn's (2008) argument is that teens exposed to these ads are likely to believe that the risks of methamphetamine use are exaggerated, and that the use of scary, graphic images in public health campaigns such as the Montana Meth Project is an ineffective strategy to bring about behavior change, based on existing research into this approach (Ringold, 2002; Ruiter, Abraham, & Kok, 2001; Witte & Allen, 2000).

Future Directions in Research on Targeted Health Communication Campaigns

In recent years, with advances in communication technologies, the transformation of the public communication environment has led to a fragmentation of what was formerly perceived as a mass public, to increasingly distinct subgroups, each with a varied pattern of media use. This change has made it more challenging to reach large numbers of people with effective messages. Given that exposure to a message is vital to a campaign's success (Hornik, 2002; McGuire, 1989), this can present a significant obstacle for practitioners and theorists working in the area of substance abuse interventions.

In response to audience fragmentation, researchers have begun to use audience segmentation and message targeting and tailoring in behavior change interventions. Segmentation and targeting practices focus on identifying group-level similarities and designing messages that are hypothesized to resonate with the particular group or subgroup (Noar, Harrington, & Aldrich, 2009). Audience segments are homogenous subgroups that are internally similar yet differ from one another. The rationale for audience segmentation is that, when audiences are divided into groups with more similar than different members, research suggests that they react similarly (and positively) to a campaign message designed for the segment (Noar et al., 2009). Audience segmentation can be done on an almost infinite number of variables, including demographic, geographic, psychographic, attitudinal, cultural, and behavioral characteristics (Albrecht & Bryant, 1996; Hornikx & O'Keefe, 2009; Slater, 1996).

Recent research has examined engagement with drug-related information as a potential indicator of increased risk of substance use, and thus a potentially important variable for segmentation in targeted substance use prevention programs. This project, supported by the European Union (Marie Curie Career Integration Grant 333605; PI: Lewis), investigates the role of active and passive (scanning)

drug-related information seeking among young adults in transition to college, and their effects in shaping drug use trajectories (Lewis, Martinez, Agbarya, & Piatok-Vaisman, 2016). Results of on-line surveys show direct associations between information seeking and (nonmedical) marijuana use intention among young adults in the United States and in Israel. Furthermore, drug-related information seeking was shown to indirectly impact intentions through changes in attitude and perceived norms (Martinez & Lewis, 2016). These preliminary findings offer evidence to suggest that information seeking may serve as an earlier indicator of drug-use risk, which may provide a tool for earlier identification of subgroups of young adults who are at greater need of targeted intervention.

Message Tailoring

Message tailoring refers to the practice of designing messages at the individual level (see Kreuter, Farrell, Olevitch, & Brennan, 2000; Kreuter & Skinner, 2000; Kreuter & Wray, 2003). Messages that are tailored are customized to fit the interests and values of the individual target, enhancing the perceived relevance of the message for the recipient, and consequently the likelihood that the message will be attended to and processed, necessary conditions for long-term persuasion. The elaboration likelihood model (ELM; Petty & Cacioppo, 1981) provides the most common explanation for the mechanism of effects. The ELM suggests that tailored messages are perceived as personally relevant more often than generic ones, thus increasing the chance that central processing of the message will occur, and that the result will be attitude and/or behavior change (Noar et al., 2009). The majority of reviews of tailored interventions support this claim; participants perceive tailored messages as more relevant, and they are also more likely to read and recall such messages (Noar et al., 2009). Tailored messages also have been shown to be more effective at influencing health behavior change as compared with targeted interventions or no-treatment control conditions (see meta-analyses by Noar et al., 2009; Sohl & Moyer, 2007, and Kreuter et al., 2000; Kroeze, Werkman, & Brug, 2006; Richards et al., 2007; Rimer & Glassman, 1999; Skinner, Campbell, Rimer, Curry, & Prochaska, 1999). This practice has the potential for stronger direct effects of media-based health communication campaigns, for example, sending personal reminders to moderate alcohol intake on one's birthday or prior to a holiday party. Tailoring has been used successfully in commercial operations like Amazon.com and Netflix, where suggestions for products are based on past preferences or matches to related items. The Internet lends itself very well to tailored messaging, as does the smart phone. However, message tailoring also raises concerns about intrusion and privacy (Cohen-Almagor, 2007), and the exploitation of personal information for persuasion purposes through database marketing (McAllister & Turow, 2002).

Research on tailored health interventions is currently being developed to test the efficacy of matching health messages to preassessed characteristics of the target population. For example, a team of researchers from the University of Pennsylvania's Annenberg and Engineering schools have recently been awarded a $1 million Exceptional Unconventional Research Enabling Knowledge Acceleration (EUREKA) grant from the National Institutes of Health (NIH) to develop a new way of evaluating effective antismoking appeals. The team at the University of Pennsylvania, headed by Joseph Cappella, from the Annenberg School for Communication, and Michael Kearns from the School of Engineering and Applied Science, Department of Computer and Information Science, are developing descriptors for a large number of smoking cessation advertisements, and compiling preference data from smokers to develop and test algorithms that can be used to recommend antismoking appeals that are effective for individual smokers. A similar approach could be applied to substance abuse interventions, and it has been applied in a few studies (Neumann et al., 2006; Simon-Arndt, Hurtado, & Patriarca-Troyk, 2006; Weitzel, Bernhardt, Usdan, Mays, & Glanz, 2007; Werch et al., 2005). As noted earlier in the chapter, adolescents' motivations for drinking (i.e., Experimentation, Thrill-seeking, Multi-reasons, & Relaxing) may be particularly helpful in tailoring alcohol prevention messages in order to make them more effective.

Targeted Prevention: Clinical Intervention Perspective

In regard to adolescent AOD use, universal prevention typically involves educating a youth population about the harms associated with substance use. The underlying premise is that better educated youth (i.e., those who come to know more about the negative consequences of AOD use) will make better decisions (i.e., not initiate AOD use). While well intentioned, most universal prevention

programs have not fared well when subjected to rigorous evaluation (Foxcroft, Ireland, Lister-Sharp, Lowe, & Breen, 2003; Monti et al., 1999; Stewart et al., 2005; Wagner et al., 1999). To date, the only universal programs showing any promise in preventing adolescent AOD are multifaceted, multiyear, school-based programs, which involve skills training for teachers, parents, and young (preteen) children, and which require ongoing professional and peer support (Conrod, Stewart, Comeau, & Maclean, 2006). This state of affairs has led many researchers and practitioners to advocate instead for targeted prevention approaches, which by definition prioritize the allocation of limited prevention intervention resources to those who need it most. Targeted prevention programs need only one half to one third of the usual number of students that universal prevention programs need to produce a significant preventive effect on adolescent drinking behavior (Conrod et al., 2006).

Targeted prevention involves intervening with youth subpopulations at above-average risk for using or abusing substances. The targeted subpopulations may be "selected" based on risk factor profiles, or "indicated" based on disorder symptom profiles. Therapeutic processes (e.g., changing distorted perceptions about drinking or drugging norms, increasing self-confidence to resist substance use, increasing motivation to change), rather than increased knowledge, are responsible for preventive effects. Meta-analyses of school-based AOD prevention studies find targeted prevention programs generally produce stronger effects than do universal prevention programs (Gottfredson & Wilson, 2003). Although some existing selective prevention programs have proved effective, rigorous empirical studies of their efficacy are rare, and the full range of putative intervention targets (e.g., underlying motivations for alcohol misuse among teenagers who are at greatest risk) has not been explored (Conrod, Castellanos, & Mackie, 2008; Stewart et al., 2005). Several other studies have examined the efficacy of indicated prevention strategies targeting teenage alcohol and/or marijuana users. Particularly in regard to motivational interviewing (Miller & Rollnick, 2013), indicated prevention strategies appear to yield clinically meaningful reductions with teen substance users. The following sections review targeted prevention from a clinical intervention perspective, focusing first on selective prevention strategies and next on indicated prevention strategies.

Targeted Prevention: Selective Prevention Strategies

For more than a decade, Patricia Conrod and colleagues have been systematically investigating the efficacy of a school-based selective prevention program targeting personality risk factors for adolescent alcohol use problems. As a selective prevention strategy, their approach targets precursors to alcohol use problems, rather than symptoms of alcohol use problems. Their manualized, personality-matched intervention strategies are designed to target anxiety sensitivity, hopelessness, or sensation seeking, and have been tested in three recent randomized controlled trials (RCTs) described next.

Conrod and colleagues (2006) conducted an RCT of their personality-matched intervention strategies with 297 Canadian high school students (56% girls; mean age, 16 years). Participants were selected through school-wide screenings; selection was based on (a) reporting at least one episode of underage drinking during the previous 4 months and (b) scoring at least one standard deviation above the mean on measures of sensation seeking, anxiety, and/or hopelessness. Participants were assigned to either personality-matched interventions or a no-treatment control group, and they were assessed at preintervention and at 4 months postintervention. Interventions were conducted with groups of two to seven adolescents during two 90-minute sessions spread across 2 weeks, with a between-session homework exercise. Interventions (a) relied on motivational and cognitive-behavioral behavior change principles, (b) had main three components (psychoeducation, behavioral coping skills training, and cognitive coping skills training), and (c) throughout incorporated personality-specific content (i.e., sensation seeking, anxious, or hopeless). Participants were matched to interventions based on the personality variables assessed during screening. It was hypothesized that students in the personality-targeted intervention condition would show reductions in overall drinking levels, binge drinking, and drinking problems relative to students in the no-treatment condition.

In regard to 4-month follow-up abstinence rates, there was a trend for a greater proportion of the intervention group to report being abstinent relative to the control group (22% vs. 14%; $p < .08$). Rates of binge drinking at the 4-month follow-up were significantly lower for the intervention group relative to the control group (42% vs. 60%; $p < .01$). For drinking quantity, the intervention group demonstrated lower levels of alcohol consumption at follow-up relative to the control group (3–4 drinks per drinking occasion vs. 5–6 drinks per drinking occasion; $p < .05$). The frequency of drinking, however, did not differ between groups at follow-up. Finally, problem drinking symptoms at the 4-month follow-up were significantly less common among the intervention group relative to the control group (63% vs. 78%; $p < .01$). In sum, relative to no intervention, the personality-matched interventions were shown to facilitate abstinence and significantly reduce binge drinking rates, drinking quantity, and alcohol problems in selected groups of high-risk youth.

Conrod and colleagues (2008) conducted a second RCT of their personality-matched intervention strategies with 368 English secondary school students (68% girls; median age, 14 years). The study's procedures and design paralleled those used in Conrod and colleagues (2006), with three notable exceptions: (1) the targeting of negative thinking as a fourth personality risk factor for adolescent alcohol use problems; (2) the use of 6- and 12-month follow-up assessments; and (3) the omission of a measure of drinking problems. It was hypothesized that students in the personality-targeted intervention condition would show reductions in overall drinking levels and binge drinking relative to students in the no-treatment condition.

Conrod and colleagues (2008) found abstinence rates did not differ between the intervention and control groups at either the 6- or 12-month follow-up assessment. Rates of binge drinking at the 6-month follow-up were significantly lower for the intervention group relative to the control group (41.1% vs. 64.6%; $p = .009$), though by the 12-month follow-up, these differences had disappeared. Finally, a significant personality by intervention interaction effect was documented for sensation seeking. Sensation-seeking drinkers in the intervention group were 45% less likely to report drinking at the 6-month follow-up, and 50% less likely to report binge drinking at the 12-month follow-up, compared to sensation-seeking drinkers in the control group.

Findings from a third RCT of Conrad and colleagues' personality-matched intervention strategies were recently published. Conrod and colleagues (2013) studied the long-term effectiveness of their targeted prevention approach with 1,210 high-risk and 1,433 low-risk English students enrolled in the ninth grade (unspecified gender distribution, mean age = 13.7 years). High-risk youth were assigned to personality-matched interventions or treatment as usual (i.e., the regular national statutory drug education curriculum provided in England). Low-risk youth received no intervention—they were included in the study in order to assess for secondary school–level "herd effects" from the interventions.

Procedures and design were generally the same as Conrod and colleagues (2008), though in this study, impulsivity, rather than negative thinking, was used as a fourth personality risk factor for adolescent alcohol use problems. Also, school personnel (teachers, mentors, counselors, and educational specialists), rather than master's-level therapists with cofacilitators, were trained in and administered the personality-matched intervention strategies. Finally, participants were assessed every 6 months over the course of 24 months of follow-up. It was hypothesized that the personality-matched intervention strategies would prevent the growth and severity of alcohol misuse among the targeted high-risk youth.

Latent growth modeling analyses indicated significant long-term effects of the intervention on abstinence ($p = .03$), binge drinking ($p = .03$), and drinking quantity ($p = .04$). The personality-matched interventions also significantly slowed growth over 24 months in binge drinking ($p = .009$), binge drinking frequency ($p = .047$), drinking quantity ($p = .02$), and problem drinking ($p = .02$) for high-risk youth. Among low-risk youth in schools with active intervention, some mild herd effects were observed. These youth demonstrated higher abstinence rates ($p = .049$) and slower growth of binge drinking ($p = .001$) during the 24-month follow-up relative to low-risk youth in schools in the treatment-as-usual condition. These findings offer additional support for the long-term benefits of Conrod et al.'s personality-targeted approach to alcohol. High-risk youth who received the intervention reported 29% reduced odds of drinking, 43% reduced odds of binge drinking, and 29% reduced odds of problem drinking relative to high-risk youth receiving only treatment as usual.

Targeted Prevention: Indicated Prevention Strategies

Recently, several investigators have begun to systematically investigate the efficacy of brief motivational interventions for preventing substance use problems among teenagers already in the early stages of developing problems. As indicated prevention strategies, these prevention programs target individuals with significant symptoms of a disorder, but not meeting diagnostic criteria for that disorder. Recently, motivational interviewing (Miller & Rollnick, 2013) has been an especially popular choice in RCTs of indicated prevention strategies targeting youth with early indications of substance use problems. This literature is reviewed next in separate sections devoted to alcohol use and to marijuana use.

MOTIVATIONAL INTERVIEWING AND ADOLESCENT ALCOHOL USE PROBLEMS

A small empirical literature exists concerning the effectiveness of motivational interviewing with adolescent drinkers. Marlatt et al. (1998) conducted a randomized controlled clinical trial comparing the effectiveness of a brief motivational intervention (assessment plus a subsequent motivational interview feedback session) with assessment-only for reducing heavy drinking among college students reporting high-risk drinking behavior ($n = 348$). The feedback included attention to (a) self-reported drinking rate vis-à-vis college averages, (b) perceived current and future risks of drinking, (c) beliefs about real and imagined alcohol effects, (d) the biphasic effects of alcohol, and (e) methods for risk reduction. Each motivational interview participant left the interview with a printed personalized summary concerning self-reported drinking, along with a generic tips page concerning the biphasic effects of alcohol, imagined (placebo) alcohol effects, and suggestions for alcohol risk reduction.

At 6-month postintervention follow-up, motivational interview participants demonstrated significantly lower drinking frequency, quantity, and peak quantity than did assessment-only participants (standardized effect size of .15 on a composite drinking pattern score). These differences remained through the 24-month postintervention follow-up, with effect sizes for individual drinking outcomes ranging from .14 to .20. Putative moderator variables, including gender, parental history of alcoholism, and conduct disorder history, did not interact with treatment condition, indicating the motivational interview was effective independent of individual risk factors. Roberts, Neal, Kivlahan, Baer, and Marlatt (2000) reanalyzed these findings using clinical significance methodology and confirmed the previous results. Motivational interview participants were more likely to improve and less likely to worsen than assessment-only participants over the 2 years of follow-up. Finally, Burke, Arkowitz, and Menchola's (2003) reanalysis of the Marlatt et al. (1998) study using unit-free, bias-corrected effect size calculations documented effects of .23 for drinking frequency at 26 weeks posttreatment, .34 for drinking consequences at 52 weeks posttreatment, and .28 for drinking consequences at 208 weeks posttreatment.

Borsari and Carey (2000) conducted a randomized controlled clinical trial comparing the effectiveness of a brief motivational intervention with assessment-only for reducing alcohol use and related consequences among college student binge drinkers ($n = 60$). The motivational interviewing intervention consisted of five components: (1) self-reported drinking rate vis-à-vis campus and national averages; (2) personal negative consequences of drinking; (3) the influence of positive and negative expectancies on personal alcohol use including perceived risks and benefits; (4) accurate information about alcohol and its effects; and (5) options for decreasing drinking and avoiding high-risk drinking situations. At 6 weeks postintervention follow-up, motivational interviewing participants reported fewer drinks consumed per week (ES = .21), fewer alcohol use occasions per month (ES = .28), and fewer binge drinking episodes (ES = .12). Burke et al.'s (2003) reanalysis of the Bosari and Carey study documented a unit-free, bias-corrected effect size of .57 for standard ethanol content consumed per week at 6 weeks posttreatment.

Larimer et al. (2001) conducted an RCT comparing the effectiveness of a brief motivational intervention (assessment plus a subsequent 1-hour individually tailored feedback session) with assessment-only for reducing drinking and drinking-related consequences among first-year college student fraternity members ($n = 120$). The feedback session included attention to (a) individual drinking patterns, (b) training in estimating blood alcohol concentration, (c) comparing typical alcohol use patterns and perceived norms to actual college-wide norms, (d) the biphasic effects of alcohol, (e) identifying and challenging alcohol-related expectancies, (f) personalized review of drinking-related consequences, and (g) reviewing strategies to encourage moderate drinking. At their fraternity houses, participants in both conditions received a 1-hour didactic group presentation about drinking and drinking-related problems; this presentation included motivational feedback in the intervention condition but not in the control condition. At 1-year postintervention follow-up, motivational interview participants demonstrated significant reductions in average drinks per week (ES = .42) and typical peak blood alcohol content (ES = .38), but not in quantity per occasion,

frequency of alcohol consumption, or alcohol-related negative consequences. Putative moderator variables, including family history of alcoholism, motivation to change alcohol use, and desire to avoid the risks associated with drinking, did not interact with treatment condition, indicating the motivational interview was effective independent of individual risk factors.

Monti, Colby, et al. (1999) conducted an RCT comparing the effectiveness of a brief motivational intervention (assessment followed immediately by a motivational interviewing session) with assessment-only for reducing alcohol use and related consequences among adolescents treated in an emergency room following an alcohol-related event. The motivational interviewing session included five sections: (1) introduction and review of event circumstances; (2) exploration of motivation to change (e.g., pros and cons); (3) personalized and computerized assessment feedback; (4) imagining the future; and (5) establishing goals. Participants in both the motivational interviewing and assessment-only conditions received a handout on avoiding drinking and driving and a list of local treatment agencies. At a 6-month postintervention follow-up, motivational interviewing participants were significantly less likely to report drinking and driving (OR = 3.92), alcohol-related injuries (OR = 3.94), and alcohol-related problems (standardized effect size [ES] of .23). Moreover, putative moderator variables including gender and stage of change did not interact with treatment condition, indicating the motivational interview was effective independent of individual risk factors. Burke et al.'s (2003) reanalysis of the Monti et al. (1999) study documented a unit-free, bias-corrected effect size of .43 for alcohol-related problems at 52 weeks posttreatment.

MOTIVATIONAL INTERVIEWING AND ADOLESCENT MARIJUANA USE

Clinical trials concerning the effectiveness of motivational interviewing with adolescent marijuana users have been conducted in Australia, Great Britain, and the United States. Martin, Copeland, and Swift (2005) conducted a nonrandomized pretest/posttest feasibility study of 73 young Australian cannabis users (aged 14–19 years; mean age = 16.4 years; 81% Australian nonindigenous). These investigators' four-session Adolescent Cannabis check-up (ACCU) was adapted from Stephens et al.'s (2004) Marijuana Checkup (MCU) for adults, and it included (1) an initial session with concerned others (e.g., parents), (2) a second session devoted to assessment, (3) a third session focused on personalized feedback, and (4) a final optional session addressing pragmatic strategies for reducing cannabis use. Personalized feedback covered the topics of amount of cannabis used, comparison of each individual's cannabis use with age specific normative data, the pros and cons of using cannabis, and perceived interactions between cannabis use and individual goals. Results provided preliminary support for this adolescent-focused adaptation of the MCU. Days using cannabis in the past 90 days declined from the mean of 56.6 days at baseline to 42.6 days at 3 months, and amount of cannabis used declined from 512.5 cones at baseline to 358.3 cones at 3 months. Moreover, three quarters (77.7%) of the follow-up sample reported voluntarily reducing or stopping their cannabis use at some time during the follow-up period. In addition, high levels of consumer satisfaction with the ACCU were reported, including lengths of the session (68% satisfied, 28% neutral), the clinician (98.5% moderately or very satisfied; 96.9% described the clinician as moderately or extremely helpful), and receiving feedback on cannabis use and its consequences (86.9% believed it was helpful; 10.8% were neutral). Martin et al.'s study indicated that the ACCU was both feasible and effective, though these researchers caution "[a] more rigorous design and a larger sample size are required to demonstrate that participation in the check-up is causally related to reductions in quantity and frequency of cannabis use and cannabis-related problems."

McCambridge and Strang (2004) randomized a sample of 200 young British drug users (aged 16–20 years; mean age = 17.6 years; 88% non-Hispanic White or Black) to either (a) a single 60-minute session of motivational interviewing or (b) "education as usual." Those randomized to motivational interviewing reduced their use of cigarettes, alcohol, and cannabis (effect sizes of 0.37, 0.34, and 0.75, respectively), mainly through moderation of ongoing drug use rather than cessation. Three months postintervention, the mean frequency of cannabis use declined by 66% in the MI group (from 15.7 to 5.4 times per week); in contrast, there was a cannabis use increase of 27% in the education-as-usual group (from 13.3 to 16.9 times per week). In analyses restricted to ongoing cannabis smokers only, the mean weekly frequency of cannabis use in the intervention group reduced from 18.0 to 6.6 times per week, while the control group increased from 13.9 to 18.2 times per

week. In a subsequent report, McCambridge and Strang (2005) describe 12-month outcomes, many of which no longer differed between the MI and control groups. These researchers ruled out selective attrition as explaining their dissipated results, given no differences between their original sample and the 81% successfully contacted at 1-year follow-up. Instead, they suggest two additional explanations: assessment reactivity or simple deterioration of effects over time.

A dissemination study of McCambridge and Strang's intervention also has been conducted. Gray, McCambridge, and Strang (2005) trained college-based youth work practitioners in the MI intervention and examined its effectiveness in a nonrandomized comparison of 59 intervention recipients and 103 nonintervention controls. Over the 3-month study period, there was no change in the prevalence of current cannabis smoking in either group. Moreover, the groups did not differ in attempts to cut down or stop smoking cannabis. Finally, McCambridge and Strang (2004) examined the ability of practitioner ratings to predict outcome among the MI participants from McCambridge and Strang (2004, 2005). Clinician reports of (a) discussing readiness-to-change-related issues including the pros and cons of using and making changes in use, (b) being directive, and (c) conducting intervention in college interview rooms versus more informal settings (e.g., cafés) were associated with greater participant improvement.

Stein et al. (2006) assigned 105 American substance-using incarcerated adolescents (72.4% non-Hispanic White or Black; 89.5% male) to either motivational interviewing (MI) or relaxation training (RT) and examined how depressed mood might moderate treatment response. Key outcomes included DUI (alcohol and/or marijuana) and being a passenger with a driver under the influence (PUI). Adolescents who received MI had lower rates of drinking and driving, and being a passenger in a car with someone who had been drinking; MI and RT participants did not differ on any of the marijuana-related outcomes. There was a significant treatment by depressive symptom interaction for driving under the influence of marijuana (η^2 = .043). Post-hoc analyses revealed this resulted from high-depressive adolescents responding better to RT. Stein et al.'s results suggest that among incarcerated teenagers marijuana-related risk behaviors may be more resistant to MI intervention than are alcohol-related risk behaviors.

Walker, Roffman, Stephens, Berghuis, and Kim (2006) examined the effectiveness of motivational interviewing with adolescent marijuana abusers in Washington State. Walker et al. (2006) randomized 97 adolescent marijuana users (mean age = 15.6 years, 5% Hispanic/Latino, 52% female), recruited through classroom presentations, advertisements, and referrals, to either an immediate two-session MI intervention (i.e., an assessment session followed 1 week later by a personalized feedback session) or to a 3-month delay condition. The MI intervention was called the Teen Marijuana Check-Up (TMCU), derived directly from Stephens et al.'s (2004) Marijuana Check-up (MCU), and took place entirely at school. Over the 3-month study period, both groups significantly reduced their marijuana use (e.g., past 60 days mean of 38.2 days at baseline to 32.0 days at 3 months), but did not differ from one other in amount of change. The investigators speculated that assessment reactivity may have influenced their findings and cautioned that their findings were preliminary, based on a small sample, and in need of replication.

D'Amico, Miles, Stern, and Meredith (2008) published a small pilot study evaluating a very brief MI intervention in a primary care clinic with teens (n = 42; 85.7% Hispanic/Latino; 48% male). Patients between 12 and 18 years of age who scored positively on a substance abuse screening questionnaire were randomly assigned to usual care or MI. The 15-minute MI session focused on assessing motivation to change, enhancing motivation for change, and making a plan. At the 3-month follow-up, adolescents assigned to MI reported less marijuana use (standardized ES = .79), lower perceived prevalence of marijuana use (ES = .79), fewer friends who used marijuana (ES = .61), and lower intentions to use marijuana in the next 6 months (ES = .86), as compared to adolescents assigned to usual care. This preliminary works suggests that even very brief MI interventions, in specialized contexts like primary care clinics, can positively impact marijuana use outcomes among teenagers.

Future Directions in Targeted Selective and Indicated Prevention

Conrod and colleagues' work supports the effectiveness of personality-matched interventions as targeted prevention strategies for adolescents at risk for the development of substance use problems. The effects they documented were larger than effect sizes obtained in other effective prevention and early intervention programs; effect sizes for the group at greatest risk for binge drinking, sensation-seeking drinkers, were found to be double that typically seen in prevention and early intervention programs (Conrod et al., 2008). Spurred on by their success, these researchers have identified several paths down which future research in personality-matched indicated prevention strategies should go.

First, RCTs need to compare the personality-based approach to an attention-only control; thus far, only no-treatment or treatment-as-usual comparison conditions have been used. Second, the relative efficacy of the personality-based approach should be compared with established effective prevention programs. In making such comparisons, both behavioral outcomes and cost-effectiveness of the programs need to be taken into account. Third, research needs to explicitly test hypotheses about the role of matching in the efficacy of personality-based approaches; to this end, Conrod and colleagues suggest future studies include nonmatched intervention comparison groups in which youth are provided interventions that target a personality dimension irrelevant to their own personality profile. Fourth, studies need to begin to investigate putative mechanisms of intervention effects by measuring potential mediators of intervention impact such as changes in drinking motives and coping strategies. Finally, in regard to the herd effects documented in Conrod et al. (2013), social network analyses may help to test whether intervention effects on high-risk youth prospectively influenced the behavior of low-risk youth attending the same school at the same time intervention is taking place.

A growing empirical literature also supports the effectiveness of motivational interviewing (MI) as targeted prevention strategies for adolescents with indications of alcohol or marijuana use problems. Relatively large intervention effects, sustained as much as 208 weeks postintervention, have been documented. Treatment effects have been independent of putative moderator variables (i.e., amenability to treatment variables), including gender, parental history of alcoholism, history of conduct disorder, and stage of change. However, RCTs of target prevention strategies that have relied on MI have the following limitations: (a) limited diversity of samples (to date, studies have included predominantly non-Hispanic White, older adolescents), (b) no direct examination of putative mechanisms of change, (c) absence of no-assessment (or minimal assessment) control conditions, which prevents the estimation of reactivity-to-assessment effects, and (d) absence of research designs incorporating booster sessions. All four of these areas remain fertile and important topics for additional inquiry.

Conclusion

Targeted prevention strategies offer great promise in efforts to reduce substance use problems among adolescents. They appear to be more clinically effective and more cost-effective than nontargeted universal prevention strategies, which require intensive labor and resources and at best produce only modest AOD prevention effects. Conceptual fuzziness about what exactly is meant by "targeted prevention" has slowed development of the field, but things are gradually improving. Currently, two definitions of targeted prevention in regard to adolescent AOD use predominate: (1) message tailoring in health campaigns (the health communication definition), and (2) specialized intervention to select high- risk individuals (the clinical intervention perspective). Recent empirical work from both of these perspectives has supported the efficacy of targeting prevention, and it argues persuasively for increased research devoted to refining and testing targeted prevention strategies for adolescent substance use.

References

Albrecht, T. L., & Bryant, C. (1996). Advances in segmentation modeling for health communication and social marketing campaigns. *Journal of Health Communication, 1*, 65–83.

Anderson, P., Chisholm, D., & Fuhr, D. C. (2009). Effectiveness and cost-effectiveness of policies and programmes to reduce the harm caused by alcohol. *Lancet, 373*, 2234–2246.

Atkin, C. K., & Freimuth, V. (1989). Formative evaluation research in campaign design. In R. E. Rice & C. K. Atkin (Eds.), *Public communication campaigns* (pp. 131–150). Newberry Park, CA: Sage.

Babor, T. F., Caetano, R., Casswell, S., Edwards, G., Giesbrecht, N., Graham, K., . . . Rossow, I. (2003). *Alcohol: No ordinary commodity. Research and public policy.* Oxford, England: Oxford University Press.

Backer, T. E., Rogers, E. M., & Sopory, R. (1992). *Designing health communication campaigns: What works?* Newbury Park, CA: Sage.

Beck, E. J., Donegan, C., Kenny, C., Cohen, C. S., Moss, V., Terry, R., . . . Cunningham, D. G. (1990). Update on HIV-testing at a London sexually transmitted disease clinic: Long-term impact of the AIDS media campaigns. *Genitourinary Medicine, 66*, 142–147.

Berger, J. (2013). *Contagious: Why things catch on.* New York, NY: Simon & Schuster.

Block, L. G., Morwitz, V. G., Putsis, W. P., & Sen, S. K. (2002). Assessing the impact of antidrug advertising on adolescent drug consumption: Results from a behavioral economic model. *American Journal of Public Health, 92*, 1346–1351.

Borsari, B., & Carey, K. B. (2000). Effects of a brief motivational intervention with college student drinkers. *Journal of Consulting and Clinical Psychology, 68*, 728–733.

Burke, B. L., Arkowitz, H., & Menchola, M. (2003). The efficacy of motivational interviewing: A meta-analysis of controlled clinical trials. *Journal of Consulting and Clinical Psychology, 71*, 843–861.

The CDC AIDS Community Demonstration Projects Research Group. (1999). Community-level HIV intervention in 5 cities: Final outcome data from the CDC AIDS Community Demonstration Projects. *American Journal of Public Health, 89*, 36–345.

Coffman, D. L., Patrick, M. E., Palen, L. A., Rhoades, B. L., & Ventura, A. K. (2007). Why do high school seniors drink? Implications for a targeted approach to intervention. *Prevention Science, 8*(4), 241–248.

Cohen, J. (2001). Defining identification: A theoretical look at the identification of audiences with media characters. *Mass Communication and Society, 4*, 245–264.

Cohen-Almagor, R. (2007). Conceptualizing the right to privacy: Ethical and legal considerations. In R. Wilson & M. Blondheim (Eds.), *The Toronto School of Communication Theory: Interpretations, extensions, applications* (pp. 305–336). Toronto and Jerusalem: University of Toronto Press and Magnes Press.

Commission on Chronic Illness (1957). *Chronic illness in the United States, Volume I: Prevention of chronic illness.* Cambridge, MA: Harvard University Press.

Conrod, P. J., Castellanos, N., & Mackie, C. J. (2008). Personality-targeted interventions stem the growth of adolescent drinking and binge drinking. *Journal of Child Psychology and Psychiatry, 49*, 181–190.

Conrod, P. J., O'Leary-Barrett, M., Newton, N., Topper, L., Castellanos-Ryan, N., Mackie, C., & Girard, A. (2013). Effectiveness of a selective, personality-targeted prevention program for adolescent use and misuse. A cluster-randomized controlled trial. *JAMA Psychiatry, 70*(3), 334–342.

Conrod, P. J., Stewart, S. H., Comeau, M. N., & Maclean, M. (2006). Efficacy of cognitive behavioral interventions targeting personality risk factors for youth alcohol misuse. *Journal of Clinical Child and Adolescent Psychology, 35*, 550–563.

Cook, T. D., & Campbell, D. T. (1979). *Quasi experimentation: Design and analytical issues for field settings.* Chicago, IL: Rand McNally.

D'Amico, E. J., Miles, J. N. V., Stern, S. A., & Meredith, L. S. (2008). Brief motivational interviewing for teens at risk of substance use consequences: A randomized pilot study in a primary care clinic. *Journal of Substance Abuse Treatment, 35*, 53–61.

Derzon, J. H., & Lipsey, M. W. (2002). A meta-analysis of the effectiveness of mass-communication for changing substance use knowledge, attitudes, and behavior. In W. D. Crano (Ed.), *Mass media and drug prevention: Classic and contemporary theories and research* (pp. 231–258). Mahwah, NJ: Lawrence Erlbaum.

Donohew, L., Lorch, E. P., & Palmgreen, P. (1991). Sensation seeking and targeting of televised anti-drug PSAS. In L. Donohew, H. E. Sypher, & W. J. Bukoski (Eds.), *Persuasive communication and drug abuse prevention* (pp. 209–226). Hillsdale, NJ: Lawrence Erlbaum.

Erceg-Hurn (2008). Drugs, money and graphic ads: A critical review of the Montana Meth Project. *Prevention Science*, 9, 256–263.

Fishbein, M. (1997). Predicting, understanding, and changing socially relevant behaviors: Lessons learned. In C. McGarty & S. A. Haslam (Eds.), *The message of social psychology* (pp. 77–91). Oxford, England: Blackwell.

Fishbein, M. (2000). The role of theory in HIV prevention. *AIDS Care*, 12, 273–278.

Fishbein, M., & Ajzen, I. (2010). *Predicting and changing behavior: The reasoned action approach*. New York, NY: Psychology Press (Taylor & Francis).

Fishbein, M., Cappella, J. N., Hornik, R., Sayeed, S., Yzer, M. C., & Ahern, R. K. (2002). The role of theory in developing effective anti-drug public service announcements. In W. D. Crano & M. Burgoon (Eds.), *Mass media and drug prevention: Classic and contemporary theories and research* (pp. 89–111). Mahwah, NJ: Erlbaum.

Fishbein, M., Guenther-Grey, C., Johnson, W., Wolitski, R. J., McAlister, A., Rietmeijer, C. A., . . . The AIDS Community Demonstration Projects (1997). Community intervention to reduce AIDS risk behaviors: The CDC's AIDS Community Demonstration Projects. In M. E. Goldberg, M. Fishbein, & S. E. Middlestadt (Eds.), *Social marketing: Theoretical and practical perspectives* (pp. 123–146). Mahwah, NJ: Lawrence Erlbaum.

Fishbein, M., Hall-Jamieson, K., Zimmer, E., Haefter, I. V., & Nabi, R. (2002). Avoiding the boomerang: Testing the relative effectiveness of antidrug public service announcements before a national campaign. *American Journal of Public Health*, 92, 238–245.

Fishbein, M., & Yzer, M. C. (2003). Using theory to design effective health behavior interventions. *Communication Theory*, 13, 164–183.

Flay, B. R. (1987). Mass media and smoking cessation: A critical review. *American Journal of Public Health*, 77, 153–160.

Flay, B. R., & Sobel, J. L. (1983). The role of mass media in preventing adolescent substance abuse. NIDA Research Monograph 47. In T. J. Glynn, C. G. Leukefeld, & J. P. Ludford (Eds.), *Preventing adolescent drug abuse: Intervention strategies* (pp. 5–35). Rockville, MD: National Institute on Drug Abuse.

Flora, J. A., Maibach, E. W., & Maccoby, N. (1989). The role of media across four levels of health promotion intervention. *Annual Review of Public Health*, 10, 181–201.

Flynn, B. S., Worden, J. K., Seeker-Walker, R. H., Badger, G. J., & Geller, B. M. (1995). Cigarette smoking prevention effects of mass media and school interventions targeted to gender and age groups. *Journal of Health Education*, 26, 45–51.

Foxcroft, D. R., Ireland, D., Lister-Sharp, D. J., Lowe, G., & Breen, R. (2003). Longer-term primary prevention for alcohol misuse in young people: A systematic review. *Addiction*, 98, 397–411.

Gordon, R. (1987). An operational classification of disease prevention. In J. A. Steinberg & M. M. Silverman (Eds.) *Preventing mental disorders* (pp. 20–26). Rockville, MD: Department of Health and Human Services.

Gottfredson, D. C., & Wilson, D. B. (2003). Characteristics of effective school-based substance abuse prevention. *Prevention Science*, 4, 27–38.

Gray, E., McCambridge, J., & Strang, J. (2005). The effectiveness of motivational interviewing delivered by youth workers in reducing drinking, cigarette and cannabis smoking among young people: Quasi-experimental pilot study. *Alcohol & Alcoholism*, 40, 535–539.

Green, M. C., & Brock, T. C. (2000). The role of transportation in the persuasiveness of public narratives. *Journal of Personality and Social Psychology*, 79, 701–721.

Hornik, R. C. (2002). Evaluation design for public health communication programs. In R. C. Hornik (Ed.), *Public health communication* (pp. 385–408). Mahwah, NJ: Lawrence Erlbaum.

Hornik, R. C., Jacobsohn, L., Orwin, R., Piesse, A., & Kalton, G. (2008). Effects of the National Youth Anti-Drug Media Campaign on youths. *American Journal of Public Health*, 98, 2229–2236.

Hornik, R. C., & Yanovitzky, I. (2003). Using theory to design evaluations of communication campaigns: The case of the National Youth Anti-Drug Media Campaign. *Communication Theory*, 13, 204–224.

Hornikx, J., & O'Keefe, D. J. (2009). Adapting consumer advertising appeals to cultural values: A meta-analysis review of effects on persuasiveness and ad liking. In C. S. Beck (Ed.), *Communication yearbook 33* (pp. 39–71). New York, NY: Lawrence Erlbaum.

Jacobsohn, L. S. (2007). Explaining the boomerang effect of the National Youth Anti-Drug Media Campaign (Unpublished doctoral dissertation). Annenberg School for Communication, University of Pennsylvania, Philadelphia, PA.

Kamb, M. L., Fishbein, M., Douglas, J. M., Rhodes, F., Rogers, J., Bolan, G., . . . Peterman, T. A. (1998). Efficacy of risk-reduction counseling to prevent human immunodeficiency virus and sexually transmitted diseases: A randomized controlled trial, *Journal of the American Medical Association*, 280, 1161–1167.

Kelly, K. J., Comello, M. L. G., & Slater, M. D. (2006). Development of an aspirational campaign to prevent youth substance use: "Be Under Your Own Influence." *Social Marketing Quarterly*, 12, 14–27.

Kelly, K. J., Stanley, L. R., & Edwards, R. W. (2000). The impact of a localized anti-alcohol and tobacco media campaign on adolescent females. *Social Marketing Quarterly*, 1, 39–43.

Kelly, K. J., Swaim, R. C., & Wayman, J. C. (1996). The impact of a localized antidrug media campaign on targeted variables associated with adolescent drug use. *Journal of Public Policy & Marketing*, 15, 238–251.

Kilpatrick, D. G., Sutker, P. B., & Smith, A. D. (1976). Deviant drug and alcohol use: The role of anxiety, sensation seeking, and other personality variables. In M. Zuckerman & C. D. Spielberger (Eds.), *Emotions and anxiety: New concepts, methods, and application* (pp. 247–278). Hillsdale, NJ: Erlbaum.

Koning, I. M., Vollebergh, W. A. M., Smit, F., Verdurmen, J. E. E., van den Eijnden, R. J. J. M., . . . Engels, R. C. M. E. (2009). Preventing heavy alcohol use in adolescents (PAS): Cluster randomized trial of a parent and student intervention offered separately and simultaneously. *Addiction*, 104(10), 1669–1678.

Kreuter, M. W., Farrell, D., Olevitch, L., & Brennan, L. (2000). *Tailoring health messages: Customizing communication with computer technology*. Mahwah, NJ: Erlbaum.

Kreuter, M. W., & Skinner, C. S. (2000). Tailoring: What's in a name? *Health Education Research*, 15, 1–4.

Kreuter, M. W., & Wray, R. J. (2003). Tailored and targeted health communication: Strategies for enhancing information relevance. *American Journal of Health Behavior*, 27, S227–S232.

Kroeze, W., Werkman, A., & Brug, J. (2006). A systematic review of randomized trials on the effectiveness of computer-tailored education on physical activity and dietary behaviors. *Annals of Behavioral Medicine, 31*, 205–223.

Kutash, K., Duchnowski, A. J., & Lynn, N, (2006). *School-based mental health: An empirical guide for decision-makers*. Tampa, FL: University of South Florida, The Louis de la ParteFlorida Mental Health Institute, Department of Child & Family Studies, Research and Training Center for Children's Mental Health.

Larimer, M. E., Turner, A. P., Anderson, B. K., Fader, J. S., Kilmer, J. R., Palmer, R. S., & Cronce, J. M. (2001). Evaluating a brief alcohol intervention with fraternities. *Journal of Studies on Alcohol, 62*, 370–380.

Lewis, N., Martinez, L., Agbarya, A., & Piatok-Vaisman, T. (2016). Examining patterns and motivations for drug-related information seeking and scanning behavior: A cross-national comparison of American and Israeli college students, *Communication Quarterly, 64*(2), 145–172.

Longshore, D., Ghosh-Dastidar, B., & Ellickson, P. L. (2006). National Youth Anti-Drug Media Campaign and school-based drug prevention: Evidence for a synergistic effect in ALERT Plus. *Addictive Behaviors, 31*, 496–508.

Maibach, E., & Parrott, R. L. (1995). *Designing health messages: Approaches from communication theory and public health practice*. Thousand Oaks, CA: Sage.

Marlatt, G. A., Baer, J. S., Kivlahan, D. R., Dimeff, L. A., Larimer, M. E., Quigley, L. A., . . . Williams, E. (1998). Screening and brief intervention for high-risk college student drinkers: Results from a 2-year follow-up assessment. *Journal of Consulting and Clinical Psychology, 66*(4), 604–615.

Martin, G., Copeland, J., & Swift, W. (2005). The Adolescent Cannabis Check-Up: Feasibility of a brief intervention for young cannabis users. *Journal of Substance Abuse Treatment, 29*, 207–213.

Martinez, L., & Lewis, N. (2016). A mediation model to explain the effects of information seeking from media and interpersonal sources on young adults' intention to use marijuana. *International Journal of Communication, 10*, 1–24.

McAlister, A., Ramirez, A. G., Galavotti, C., & Gallion, K. J. (1989). Anti-smoking campaigns: Progress in the application of social learning theory. In R. E. Rice & C. K. Atkin (Eds.), *Public communication campaigns* (pp. 291–307). Newbury Park, CA: Sage.

McAllister, M. P., & Turow, J. (2002). New media and the commercial sphere: Two intersecting trends, five categories of concern. *Journal of Broadcasting and Electronic Media, 46*, 505–514.

McCambridge, J., & Strang, J. (2004). The efficacy of single-session motivational interviewing in reducing drug consumption and perceptions of drug-related risk and harm among young people: Results from a multi-site cluster randomized trial. *Addiction, 99*, 39–52.

McCambridge, J., & Strang, J. (2005). Deterioration over time in effect of Motivational Interviewing in reducing drug consumption and related risk among young people. *Addiction, 100*, 470–478.

McDivitt, J. A., Zimick, S. & Hornik, R. C. (1997). Explaining the impact of a communication campaign to change vaccination knowledge and coverage in the Philippines. *Health Communication, 9*, 95–118.

McGuire, W. J. (1989). Theoretical foundations of campaigns. In R. Rice & C. Atkin (Eds.), *Public communication campaigns* (pp. 43–65). Newbury Park, CA: Sage.

Miller, W. R., & Rollnick, S. (2013). *Motivational interviewing: Helping people change* (3rd ed.). New York, NY: Guilford Press.

Monti, P. M., Colby, S. M., Barnett, N. P., Spirito, A., Rohsenow, D. J., Myers, M., . . . Lewander, W. (1999). Brief intervention for harm reduction with alcohol-positive older adolescents in a hospital emergency department. *Journal of Consulting and Clinical Psychology, 67*, 989–994.

Mrazek, P. J., & Haggerty, R. J. (Eds.). (1994). *Reducing risks for mental disorders: Frontiers for preventive intervention research*. Washington, DC: National Academy Press.

Neumann, T., Neuner, B., Weiss-Gerlach, E., Tønnesen, H., Gentilello, L. M., Wernecke, K. D., . . . Spies, C. D. (2006). The effect of computerized tailored brief advice on at-risk drinking in subcritically injured trauma patients. *The Journal of Trauma Injury, Infection, and Critical Care, 61*, 805–814.

Noar, S. M, Harrington, N. G., & Aldrich, R. S. (2009). The role of message tailoring in the development of persuasive health communication messages. *Communication Yearbook, 33*, 73–133.

Oman, R. F., Vesely, S., Aspy, C. B., McLeroy, K. R., Rodine, S., & Marshall, L. (2004). The potential protective effect of youth assets on adolescent alcohol and drug use. *American Journal of Public Health, 94*, 1425–1430.

Orwin, R., Cadell, D., Chu, A., Kalton, G., Maklan, D., Morin, C., . . . Tracy, E. (2006). *Evaluation of the national youth anti-drug media campaign: 2004 Report of findings*. Washington, DC: National Institute of Drug Abuse.

Palmgreen, P., Donohew, L., Lorch, E. P., Hoyle, R. H., & Stephenson, M. T. (2001). Television campaigns and adolescent marijuana use: Tests of sensation seeking targeting. *American Journal of Public Health, 91*, 292–296.

Palmgreen, P., Donohew, L., Lorch, E. P., Hoyle, R. H., & Stephenson, M. T. (2002). Television campaigns and sensation seeking targeting of adolescent marijuana use: a controlled time-series approach. In R. C. Hornik (Ed.), *Public health communication: Evidence for behavior change* (pp. 35–56). Mahwah, NJ: Erlbaum.

Palmgreen, P., Donohew, L., Lorch, E. P., Rogus, M., Helm, D., & Grant, N. E. (1991). Sensation seeking, message sensation value, and drug use as mediators of PSA effectiveness. *Health Communication, 3*, 217–227.

Pechmann, C., Zhao, G., Goldberg, M., & Reibling, E. T. (2003). What to convey in antismoking advertisements for adolescents: The use of protection motivation theory to identify effective message themes. *Journal of Marketing, 67*, 1–18.

Pedersen, W. (1991). Mental health, sensation seeking and drug use patterns: A longitudinal study. *British Journal of Addiction, 86*, 195–204.

Petty, R. E., Baker, S. M., & Gleicher, F. (1991). Attitudes and drug abuse prevention: Implications of the elaboration likelihood model of persuasion. In L. Donohew, H. E. Sypher, and W. J. Bukoski (Eds.), *Persuasive communication and drug abuse prevention* (pp. 71–90). Hillsdale, NJ: Lawrence Erlbaum.

Petty, R. E., & Cacioppo, J. T. (1981). *Attitudes and persuasion: Classic and contemporary approaches*. Dubuque, IA: Brown.

Petty, R. E., & Cacioppo, J. T. (1986). *Communication and persuasion: Central and peripheral routes to attitude change*. New York, NY: Springer-Verlag.

Randolph, W., & Viswanath, K. (2004). Lessons learned from public health mass media campaigns: marketing health in a crowded media world. *Annual Review of Public Health, 25,* 419–437.

Rice, R. E., & Atkin, C. K. (Eds., 1989). *Public communication campaigns* (2nd ed.). Newbury Park, CA: Sage.

Richards, K. C., Enderlin, C. A., Beck, C., McSweeney, J. C., Jones, T. C., & Roberson, P. K. (2007). Tailored biobehavioral interventions: A literature review and synthesis. *Research and Theory for Nursing Practice, 21,* 271–285.

Rimer, B. K., & Glassman, B. (1999). Is there a use for tailored print communications in cancer risk communication? *Journal of the National Cancer Institute Monographs, 25,* 140–148.

Ringold, D. J. (2002). Boomerang effects in response to public health interventions: Some unintended consequences in the alcoholic beverage market. *Journal of Consumer Policy, 25,* 27–63.

Roberts, L. J., Neal, D. J., Kivlahan, D. R., Baer, J. S., & Marlatt, G. A. (2000). Individual drinking changes following a brief intervention among college students: Clinical significance in an indicated preventive context. *Journal of Consulting and Clinical Psychology, 68*(3), 500–505.

Rogers, E. M. (1995). *Diffusion of innovations.* New York, NY: Free Press.

Rogers, E. M., & Storey, J. D. (1987). Communication campaigns. In C. R. Berger & S. H. Chaffee (Eds.), *Handbook of communication science* (pp. 817–846). Beverly Hills, CA: Sage.

Rosenstock, I. M. (1990). The health belief model: Explaining health behavior through expectancies. In K. Glanz, F. Lewis, & B. Rimer (Eds.), *Health behavior and health education: Theory, research, and practice* (pp. 39–62). San Francisco, CA: Jossey-Bass.

Ruiter, R. A. C., Abraham, C., & Kok, G. (2001). Scary warnings and rational precautions: A review of the psychology of fear appeals. *Psychology and Health, 16,* 613–630.

Schilling, R. F. & McAllister, A. L. (1990) Preventing drug use in adolescents through media interventions. *Journal of Consulting and Clinical Psychology, 58,* 415–424.

Segal, B., Huba, G. J., & Singer, J. L. (1980). *Drugs, daydreaming, and personality: A study of college youth.* Hillsdale, NJ: Lawrence Erlbaum.

Simon-Arndt, C. M., Hurtado, S. L., & Patriarca-Troyk, L. A. (2006). Acceptance of web based personalized feedback: User ratings of an alcohol misuse prevention program targeting U.S. Marines. *Health Communication, 20,* 13–22.

Skinner, C. S., Campbell, M. K., Rimer, B. K., Curry, S., & Prochaska, J. O. (1999). How effective is tailored print communication? *Annals of Behavioral Medicine, 21,* 290–298.

Slater, M. D. (1996). Theory and method in health audience segmentation. *Journal of Health Communication, 1,* 267–283.

Slater, M. D. (2002). Involvement as goal-directed, strategic processing: The extended ELM. In J. Dillard & M. Pfau (Eds.), *The persuasion handbook: Developments in theory and practice* (pp. 175–194). Thousand Oaks, CA: Sage.

Slater, M. D., Kelly, K. J., Edwards, R. W., Plested, B. A., Thurman, P. J., Keefe, T. J., . . . Henry, K. L. (2006). Combining in-school social marketing and participatory, community-based media efforts: Reducing marijuana and alcohol uptake among younger adolescents. *Health Education Research, 21,* 157–167.

Slater, M. D., Kelly, K. J., Lawrence, F. R., Stanley, L. R., & Comello, M. L. G. (2011). Assessing media campaigns linking marijuana non-use with autonomy and aspirations: "Be Under Your Own Influence" and ONDCP's "Above the Influence." *Prevention Science, 12,* 12–22.

Slater, M. D., & Rouner, D. (1997). The processing of narrative fiction containing persuasive content about alcohol use: Effects of gender and outcome. Paper presented at the annual meeting of the International Communication Association, May 1997, Montreal, Canada.

Slater, M. D., & Rouner, D. (2002). Entertainment–education and elaboration likelihood: Understanding the processing of narrative persuasion. *Communication Theory, 12,* 173–191.

Sohl, S. J., & Moyer, A. (2007). Tailored interventions to promote mammography screening: A meta-analytic review. *Preventive Medicine, 45,* 252–261.

Stein, L. R., Colby, M. S., Barnett, P. N., Monti, M. P., Golembeske, C., Lebeau-Craven, R., & Robert, M. (2006). Enhancing substance abuse treatment engagement in incarcerated adolescents. *Psychological Services, 3*(1), 25–34.

Stephens, P. C., Sloboda, Z., Stephens, R. C., Teasdale, B., Grey, S. F., Hawthorne, R. D., & Williams, J. (2009). Universal school-based substance abuse prevention programs: Modeling targeted mediators and outcomes for adolescent cigarette, alcohol and marijuana use. *Drug and Alcohol Dependence, 102*(1–3), 19–29.

Stephens, R. S., Roffman, R. A., Fearer, S. A., Williams, C., Picciano, J. F., & Burke, R. S. (2004). The Marijuana Check-Up: Reaching users who are ambivalent about change. *Addiction, 99,* 1323–1332.

Stewart, S. H., Conrod, P. J., Marlatt, G. A., Comeau, M. N., Thush, C., & Krank, M. (2005). New developments in prevention and early intervention for alcohol abuse in youths. *Alcoholism: Clinical and Experimental Research, 29,* 278–286.

Viswanath, K., Finnegan, J. R., Hannan, P. J., & Luepker, R. V. (1991). Health and knowledge gaps: Some lessons from the Minnesota Heart Health Program. *American Behavioral Scientist, 34,* 712–726

Wagner, E. F., Brown, S. A., Monti, P. M., Myers, M. G., & Waldron, H. B. (1999). Innovations in adolescent substance abuse intervention. *Alcoholism: Clinical and Experimental Research, 23,* 236–249.

Wakefield, M. A., Loken, B., & Hornik, R. C. (2010). Use of mass media campaigns to change health behavior. *Lancet, 376,* 1261–1271.

Walker, D. D., Roffman, R. A., Stephens, R. S., Berghuis, J., & Kim, W. (2006). Motivational enhancement therapy for adolescent marijuana users: A preliminary randomized controlled trial. *Journal of Consulting and Clinical Psychology, 74,* 628–632.

Wallack, L., & Dorfman, L. (1996). Media advocacy: A strategy for advancing policy and promoting health. *Health Education Quarterly, 23,* 293–317.

Weisz, J. R., Sndler, I. N., Durlak, J. A., & Anton, B. S. (2005). Linking prevention and treatment within an integrated model. *American Psychologist, 60*(6), 628–648.

Weitzel, J. A., Bernhardt, J. M., Usdan, S., Mays, D., & Glanz, K. (2007). Using wireless handheld computers and tailored text messaging to reduce negative consequence of drinking alcohol. *Journal of Studies on Alcohol and Drugs, 68,* 534–537.

Werch, C., Jobli, E., Moore, M. J., DiClemente, C. C., Dore, H., & Brown, C. H. (2005). A brief experimental alcohol beverage-tailored program for adolescents. *Journal of Studies on Alcohol, 66,* 284–290.

White T. (2008). Innovative analytic approaches to measure the impact of a drug prevention social marketing campaign. Paper presented at the International Communication

Association, Health Communication Division; Montreal, Canada, May 2008.

Williams, G. C., Cox, E. M., Kouides, R., & Deci, E. L. (1999) Presenting the facts about smoking to adolescents—effects of an autonomy-supportive style. *Archives of Pediatrics, 153,* 959–964.

Witte, K., & Allen, M. (2000). A meta-analysis of fear appeals: Implications for effective public health campaigns. *Health Education & Behavior, 27,* 591–615.

Worden, J. K. (1999) Research in using mass media to prevent smoking. *Nicotine and Tobacco Research, 1,* S117–S121.

Zimmerman, R. S., & Vernberg, D. (1994). Models of preventive health behavior: Comparison, critique, and meta-analysis. In G. Albrecht (Ed.), *Advances in medical sociology, volume 4: Health behavior models: A reformulation* (pp. 45–67). Greenwich, CT: JAI Press.

Zuckerman, M. (1979). *Sensation seeking: Beyond the optimal level of arousal.* Hillsdale, NJ: Erlbaum.

Zuckerman, M. (1994). *Behavioral expressions and biological bases of sensation seeking.* New York, NY: Cambridge University Press.

Family-Based Treatments for Adolescent Substance Abuse: Advances Yield New Developmental Challenges

Maya M. Boustani, Craig E. Henderson, *and* Howard A. Liddle

Abstract

Adolescent drug and alcohol abuse remains a serious health problem. Family-based treatments are recognized as among the most effective interventions for youth with drug and alcohol problems. This chapter presents the state of the science of the family-based adolescent substance abuse treatment field, summarizing the advances, methodological features, and outcomes of 36 randomized controlled trials, representing 18 distinct models of family-based therapies for youth substance abuse. The chapter reviews developments and gaps in this specialty, including theory issues, treatment development, research, and services for referred youths. The chapter also discusses the unknowns of the field, including the topic of treatment mechanisms and moderators, and deliberates on the complicated topic of implementing evidence-based therapies in usual care settings.

Key Words: adolescent substance abuse, family-based treatment, adolescent treatment research, evidence-based therapies, treatment development

Adolescent drug and alcohol abuse continue to pose global public health challenges (Toumbourou et al., 2007). Epidemiological studies, expert-authored reports from private and government agencies, media coverage, and accumulating research all reveal a consistent concern with the consequences and costs of substance misuse and related problems among adolescents (Armstrong & Costello, 2002; CASA, 2011; Costello, Foley, & Angold, 2006; Meier et al., 2012; O'Connor, 2013; World Health Organization [WHO], 2009). Scientific advances in the youth substance abuse specialty are numerous, and these are summarized in basic science reviews (Squeglia, Jacobus, & Tapert, 2009; Steinberg, Fletcher, & Darling, 1994) and the increasing number of intervention-focused reviews (Akram & Copello, 2013; Winters, Tanner-Smith, Bresani, & Myers, 2014). Scholars in developmental psychology and developmental psychopathology have specified the continuing importance of developmental considerations (Brown, 2004; Brown et al., 2008; Windle & Zucker, 2010), positive and long-term relationships, and a youth's family relationships in particular to short and long-term developmental outcomes (Cranford, Zucker, Jester, Puttler, & Fitzgerald, 2010). Longitudinal studies about risk and protective factors that influence the development of drug and alcohol problems (Corte & Zucker, 2008; Cranford et al., 2010; Zucker, 2008; Zucker, Donovan, Masten, Mattson, & Moss, 2008) have created a clinically relevant knowledge base unavailable in youth treatment's earliest days.

Family-based conceptual frameworks, theories of change, and intervention programs have been specified over the past four or so decades and influenced the major disciplines and sectors of clinical care (Akram & Copello, 2013). Ecological, contextual, developmental, and dynamic systems theories and research have all been represented in the family-based therapies for youth substance abuse, and the research base of these treatments has grown in size and quality over the years.

Amid these accomplishments, vexing clinical puzzles and numerous scientific gaps remain. Most youth in need of treatment do not receive it (Kessler et al., 2003); the treatment retention (Grella, Hser, Joshi, & Douglas Anglin, 1999) and outcomes of usual care (Weisz, Jensen-Doss, & Hawley, 2006) remain inconsistent compared to those achieved by evidence-based treatments. Clinicians across sectors of care have inadequate opportunity to learn how to provide evidence-based therapies, and those responsible for training new generations of clinicians seem to be lackadaisical about incorporating evidence-based therapies into their training (Weissman, Brown, & Talati, 2011).

Family-Based Treatments

The number of stand-alone family-based treatment models that specialize in adolescent substance abuse treatment has increased significantly since the specialty's formative days (Catalano, Hawkins, Wells, & Miller, 1990; Stanton & Shadish, 1997). Initially, approaches were more standard classic family therapy models with the aim of changing family interaction per se as the most important—and in some cases the only—therapeutic target. Gradually, as the influence of ecological theory and research grew, and in response to changes in family therapy thinking as well, the therapeutic models tended to become more comprehensive. The more recent clinical models try to change family interaction but may also focus on extrafamilial sources of influence as change targets as well. But several approaches today retain behavioral roots and feature contingency management methods as primary methods. Parents are included, but extensive targeting of social ecological settings is generally avoided in the behavioral models.

This chapter presents a state of the science characterization of the family-based adolescent substance abuse treatment specialty. We review the scientific advances, methodological features, and outcomes of 36 randomized controlled trials, representing 18 distinct models of family-based therapies for youth substance abuse. We discuss a variety of developments and gaps in this specialty—gaps that touch on theory, clinical work, research, services for referred youths, and the complicated topic of implementing evidence-based therapies (Fixsen, Blase, Metz, & Naoom, 2014) in usual care settings.

Signs of the Times

More complex and rigorous methodological standards for reporting randomized controlled trials (RCTs) have come from diverse sources (e.g., Lindstrom, Rasmussen, Kowalski, Filges, & Klint Jorgensen, 2013). For instance, the Consolidated Standards of Reporting Trials (CONSORT) guidelines were developed by researchers and editors of medical journals to serve as "an evidence-based minimum set of recommendations for reporting RCTs" (see http://www.consort-statement.org/home). They address issues such as participant eligibility, randomization, sample size, and other similar methodological features. Their purpose was to enable readers to understand a trial's design, conduct, analysis, and interpretation, and to assess the validity of its results. CONSORT guidelines have resulted in more consistent reporting of core methodological details, yet their use frequently hinges on whether journals require authors to follow the standards (Hopewell, Ravaud, Baron, & Boutron, 2012; Turner, Shamseer, Altman, Schulz, & Moher, 2012). At the same time, Ladd, McCrady, Manuel, and Campbell (2010) found that authors had increased their reporting of CONSORT items in alcohol treatment research regardless of whether or not the journal required it. Tools to evaluate methodology (Miller & Wilbourne, 2002), an increase in meta-analyses (Baldwin, Christian, Berkeljon, Shadish, & Bean, 2012), and *quality of evidence* reviews (Becker & Curry, 2008; Hogue, Henderson, Ozechowski, & Robbins, 2014; Miller & Wilbourne, 2002; Sprenkle, 2012; Waldron & Turner, 2008) are other examples of attention to the methodological aspects of this specialty's science. Overall, the major and most consistent improvements in the research base have been in reporting participant characteristics, obtaining more reliable measurements of key outcome variables, specifying and monitoring intervention delivery, and conducting more appropriate and sophisticated data analytic methods.

Defining the Evidence Base

Potential studies to discuss in this chapter were identified by searching Medline, *PsychInfo*, and the aggregated Social Sciences database on ISI Thompson's Web of Knowledge. We created a set of search items based on a variety of addictive behaviors as well as addictive products such as marijuana, cannabis, and alcohol. Another set of terms was formed to include different types of treatment, including family therapy. We then combined these two sets and limited the search to studies of treatment outcomes published in English that examined adolescents as a target age group and involved families in treatment. Our final set of articles consisted of papers that (a) used a family-based model as either a stand-alone treatment or was combined with features of another type of treatment in an integrative model; (b) participants were between the ages of 11 and 18 years; (c) random assignment to a family/integrative treatment or an intervention intended to produce a decrease in substance use (in contrast to a no-treatment control condition or placebo treatment) occurred; (d) the study sample was drawn from a clinically referred population with adolescent substance abuse as a presenting problem; (e) substance use was a main outcome variable in the study; and (f) have a minimum of two time points (usually pre intervention and post intervention).

For some studies, more than one outcome paper was published from the same sample. In such cases, we included the most recent publication. The final sample included 36 RCTs. The comparison treatments were categorized as "active treatment" or "nonactive treatment." To meet criteria for active treatment, treatments had to meet more stringent criteria than previous reviews to make it consistent with current standards. Active treatment is defined as (1) using a treatment manual in the study, (2) following stated supervision procedures where therapists received feedback on treatment delivery, and (3) using an instrument to conduct fidelity checks on treatment delivery.

Of the 36 studies, 12 (33%) compared the family-based treatment to an active treatment, including cognitive-behavioral therapy (CBT) (group and individual), CBT with motivational enhancement treatment, Chestnut's Bloomington outpatient treatment, family process, functional family therapy, motivational interviewing, joint family and individual therapy, adolescent group therapy, individual CBT, residential treatment, and The 7 Challenges program/strengths-oriented family therapy (compared to each other without specification of which is the experimental condition). The other 14 studies compared the family-based therapy to nonactive comparisons. These comparison treatments were interventions described as group counseling/group therapy, individual psychotherapy/individual counseling, usual continuing care, treatment as usual/services as usual, community referral, traditional family therapy, individual cognitive problem-solving therapy, extended

services, parent group, group care, and training in parenting skills.

The 36 studies occurred in diverse settings and used multiple designs—efficacy, effectiveness, and hybrid studies that blended elements of efficacy and effectiveness studies (Carroll & Rounsaville, 2003). Five of the studies are considered effectiveness studies. They were conducted within community settings, with community-based therapists providing the experimental condition within agencies. These studies are strong in external validity and provide new information about the feasibility of delivering evidence-based interventions in usual care settings. Twenty-one of the studies are considered efficacy studies. Clinicians hired specifically for the study usually provided these interventions. Generally speaking, these therapists receive high-quality supervision and have lower caseloads than they might have in a standard clinic position. Furthermore, participants (youth and families) recruited for these studies frequently need to meet certain criteria (such as diagnosis or severity of symptoms). In hybrid studies (n = 10), the intervention is delivered in a community setting, but it typically had involvement from the developer and/or affiliated researchers. Finally, six studies were independent replications, undertaken by a separate group of researchers, with no affiliation with the developers.

Finally, the 36 studies varied in the frequency and intervals of their research follow-up interviews. To be a part of this review, studies had to have a minimum of two time points (usually pre intervention and post intervention). Seven of the 36 studies met this minimum requirement, with other studies exceeding it (M = 4.34, SD = 1.06). Most studies had between three (n = 7) and seven (n = 2) follow-ups, with most having four (n = 9) or five (n = 11). Those with the most follow-ups assessed families up to 24 (Slesnick, Erdem, Bartle-Haring, & Brigham, 2013) and 48 months (Dembo, Wothke, Livingston, & Schmeidler, 2002; Henggeler, Clingempeel, Brondino, & Pickrel, 2002; Liddle et al., 2012).

Table 31.1 provides definitions for the methodological attributes used to evaluate the research quality of the included studies.[1] Table 31.2 provides a description of every family therapy model included in this chapter. Table 31.3 gives details on the studies included and summarizes the study outcomes. It also includes a methodological "score" consisting of a percentage of the number of methodological attributes included in the study divided by the total number of methodological attributes.

Table 31.1 Definitions of Methodological Attributes

Attribute	Criteria
1. Specific hypotheses	Specific hypotheses are explicitly established.
2. Sample description	Description of participants' baseline demographics and clinical characteristics is given in sufficient detail that a determination regarding the generalization of the findings can be made, or the study could be replicated.
3. Adequate sample size	Process for determining sample size is discussed, and the study is sufficiently powered to detect differences between treatment groups.
4. Active comparison	Experimental condition is compared to at least one active evidence-based treatment or a comparison treatment with sufficient bases for determining it was active (e.g., standardized treatment, clear supervision, and fidelity checks).
5. Random sequence	Process for generating a random sequence is described with sufficient detail to confirm that each participant had an unpredictable, independent chance of receiving each intervention.
6. Allocation concealed	Process of assigning participants to groups described with sufficient detail to confirm that investigators recruiting and conducting the initial assessment could not discern the participant's treatment group.
7. Manual	At least one treatment condition was guided by a manual.
8. Treatment ratings	Treatment adherence monitored with scales, checklists, or rating forms completed by therapist, supervisor, independent observer, and/or patient.
9. Collateral report	At least one outcome is a collateral report (e.g., parent, caregiver, teacher).
10. Objective measure	At least one outcome is an objective measure (e.g., urine, blood samples, paper records).
11. Intent-to-treat	All subjects analyzed in groups to which they were assigned, even if they did not complete assessments or treatment.
12. Blind assessment	Follow-up assessments completed by treatment-blind evaluator.
13. Effect sizes	Effect sizes are reported.
14. Clinical significance	Clinical significance outcomes are reported.
15. Therapist training	Description of therapist training procedures is provided.
16. Therapist characteristics	Description of therapist characteristics is provided.
17. Independent replication	Study is an independent replication not involving the treatment developer.

Source: Adapted from Becker and Curry (2008).

The following sections summarize the state of the science, focusing on attributes that are *frequently reported*, attributes that are *infrequently reported* (noting biases nonattendance to these issues may introduce), and attributes *reported more frequently in recent versus older studies*.

Frequently Reported Attributes

Studies adequately described the background and clinical characteristics of treatment samples (89%), specified treatments using a treatment manual (89%), used a self-report or objectively rated measure of treatment fidelity (78%), and provided information on the background of the therapists providing the treatment (72%). Although all studies were RCTs, only 69% of them described the random sequence process in enough detail to guarantee that all participants had an equal chance of receiving the intervention. In 67% of studies, researchers are reporting the procedures they used

Table 31.2 Description of Treatment Models

Treatment	Description
1. Adolescent-Community Reinforcement Approach (ACRA) Assertive Continuing Care (ACC)	ACRA is a 12-week behavioral intervention that seeks to increase positive prosocial activities in substance-abusing adolescents. ACRA's philosophy is to use the community to reward nonusing behaviors and encourage prosocial behaviors. The program begins with rapport building and a functional analysis of substance abuse behaviors and social behaviors. Client self-assessments are used to develop and monitor treatment goals. Techniques used include prosocial priming and reinforcing. Skills taught include relapse prevention, problem solving, and communication. Initially, caregivers and adolescents are seen separately and then join together. Optional modules include coping with relapse, anger management, and finding a job. Case management services are included in the ACC program (Godley et al., 2010, 2002, 2007). Assertive Continuing Care (ACC) is a 12- to 14-week home-based continuing care program. It is often offered following residential treatment. ACC uses an operant reinforcement and skills training model to help adolescents and their families develop prosocial skills and access community services. ACC is a combination of ACRA and case management services (Godley et al., 2007, 2010).
2. Brief Strategic Family Therapy (BSFT)	BSFT is a 12-week manual-based intervention that integrates strategic and structural family therapy theory techniques. The goal is to reduce problematic adolescent behavior by improving relationships with the family and other important systems such as school and peers. BSFT is problem-focused, directive, practical, and follows a prescribed format delivered in treatment phases that have specific goals. Initial sessions are focused on establishing therapeutic alliance, identifying family strengths and weaknesses, and developing a treatment plan. Sessions then address negative family interaction and implement restructuring strategies that will improve family relations (Robbins et al., 2011).
3. Contingency Management	The abstinence-based contingency management program (duration may vary) is an intervention that uses classic behavioral theory. Contingency management offers teenagers financial incentives for documented abstinence and participation in treatment. Parent participation and compliance is also rewarded via participation in a draw to win gift cards. Behaviors that are reinforced include attending therapy, attending urine testing appointments, implementing the Substance Monitoring Contract, completing homework, and administering breathalyzers.
4. Culturally Informed and Flexible Family-Based Treatment for Adolescents (CIFTA)	CIFTAA is a 14-week program that has its foundations in structural family therapy and integrates themes relevant to Hispanic families. It is delivered using a modular and flexible approach that includes about half of the sessions alone with the adolescent, and the other half with the parent alone or the family together. The family work integrates individual interventions such as motivational interviewing and skills training along with psychoeducation modules that include parenting, drug education, risky sexual behavior, and acculturation stress (Santisteban, Mena, & McCabe, 2011; Santisteban & Mena, 2009).
5. Ecologically Based Family Therapy (EBFT)	EBFT is a 15-session treatment used for runaway substance-abusing youth. It is based on crisis intervention theory, which postulates that families are most open to change when they are faced with a crisis, and their normal modes of coping no longer work. Individual sessions with the adolescent focus on engagement, HIV prevention, and outlining clinical tasks. With the family, the focus is on preparing the parents to come together with the adolescent to develop a new kind of relationship. Finally, family members are brought together to work on specific dysfunctional interactions using training in communication and problem-solving skills.

(*continued*)

Table 31.2 Continued

Treatment	Description
6. Family Behavior Therapy (FBT)	FBT is a 15-session, multicomponent program based on classic behavior therapy, which addresses cognitive, verbal, social, and familial factors, in addition to variables that influence drug use and antisocial behaviors. Techniques used include therapist modeling, rehearsal for each procedure, self-recording, homework assignments, and therapist praise at signs of progress. The primary interventions used are behavioral contracting, stimulus control, urge control, and communication training. Secondary procedures include anger prevention, positive request procedure, relationship enhancement, and problem-solving training (Azrin et al, 2001).
7. Family Empowerment Intervention (FEI)	FEI is a 10-week home-based intervention which provides families with personal in-home visits from project field consultants to work on the following goals: restore the family hierarchy; restructure boundaries between parents and children; encourage parents to take greater responsibility for family functioning; increase family structure through implementation of rules and consequences; enhance parenting skills; have parents set limits, expectations, and rules that increase the likelihood the target youth's behavior will improve; improve communication skills among all family members; improve problem-solving skills, particularly in the target youth; and where needed, connect the family to other systems—"system-fit" (e.g., school, church, community activities) (Dembo et al., 2002).
8. Family Support Network (FSN)	FSN is a 12-session treatment that uses cognitive-behavioral treatment to provide adolescents with substance-abuse treatment. In addition, six parent education group meetings are offered to improve parent knowledge and skills relevant to adolescent problems and family functioning. Four therapeutic home visits are also provided along with referral to self-help support groups and case management services (Dennis et al., 2004).
9. Family Systems Therapy (FST)	FST is a 12-week treatment that integrates structural and strategic family therapy. The goal is to use the family system to influence change in the individual adolescent (Joanning et al., 1992).
10. Functional Family Therapy (FFT)	FFT is a 24-week, systems-oriented, behaviorally based model of structured family therapy. The goal is to change dysfunctional family patterns that contribute to adolescent substance abuse. The first phase focuses on engaging families and motivating them for change. The second phase focuses on effecting behavioral changes in the family. Behavioral interventions such as contingency management, communication, problem-solving, and behavioral contracting are used (Waldron et al., 2001).
11. Integrated Family and Cognitive-Behavioral Therapy (IFCBT)	IFCBT is a 16-week intervention comprised of 16 individual family therapy sessions, based on structural family therapy, and 32 peer group cognitive-behavioral sessions. The primary goal of the problem-focused family therapy component is to promote youth abstinence by fostering adaptive family communication, age-appropriate familial roles, and effective parenting skills. The cognitive-behavioral component initially introduces youth to rational-emotive and problem-solving behavior change principles, the goal of which is to promote rational beliefs that are associated with psychiatric well-being and drug abstinence (Latimer, Winters, D'Zurilla, & Nichols, 2003).
12. Integrated Cognitive-Behavioral Therapy (I-CBT)	I-CBT is a 12-month intervention grounded in social cognitive learning theory and integrates CBT techniques to remediate maladaptive cognitions and behaviors found to underlie both adolescent suicidality and substance use disorders. Problems targeted include cognitive distortions as well as poor coping, communication, and parenting skills. In the acute (6 months) treatment phase, adolescents attended weekly sessions and parents attended weekly to biweekly sessions. In the continuation (3 months) treatment phase, adolescents attended biweekly sessions and parents attended biweekly to monthly sessions. In the maintenance treatment phase (3 months), adolescents attended monthly sessions and parents attended monthly sessions as needed.

Table 31.2 Continued

Treatment	Description
13. Multidimensional Family Therapy (MDFT)	MDFT is a 4- to 5-month treatment system. MDFT focuses on four interdependent treatment domains: the adolescent domain, the parent domain, the interactional domain, and the extrafamilial domain. The adolescent domain helps youths communicate effectively with parents and other adults; develop coping, emotion regulation, and problem-solving skills; improve social competence and school or work functioning; and establish alternatives to substance use and delinquency. The parent domain increases behavioral and emotional involvement with the adolescents; improves parenting skills, especially monitoring, clarifying adolescent expectations, limit setting and consequences; and addresses their individual psychosocial functioning. The interactional domain focuses upon decreasing family conflict and improving emotional attachments, communication, and problem-solving skills. The extrafamilial domain fosters family competency within all social systems in which the youth participates (e.g., school, juvenile justice, recreational) (Liddle et al., 2008).
14. Multidimensional Treatment Foster Care	MTFC is a 6- to 9-month intensive intervention, based on social learning theory. MTFC is an alternative to group home treatment or state training facilities for youths who have been removed from their home due to conduct and delinquency problems, substance use, and/or involvement with the juvenile justice system. MTFC places youth with highly trained foster parents, while also preparing their family to provide effective parenting and support that will facilitate a positive reunification. Four key elements are targeted: providing a consistent reinforcing environment where they are mentored and encouraged to develop academic and positive living skills; providing daily structure with clear expectations, limits, and consequences; providing close supervision; and helping youth to avoid deviant peer associations while providing them with the support and assistance needed to establish prosocial peer relationships.
15. Multisystemic Therapy (MST)	MST is a 16-week treatment based on pragmatic, problem-focused treatments such as strategic family therapy, structural family therapy, behavioral parent training, and cognitive-behavioral therapies. MST addresses the multiple determinants of youth and family problems by targeting factors at the individual, family, peer, school, and community levels. The MST therapist identifies the strengths and weaknesses of these systems to establish treatment goals in collaboration with the family. Families are encouraged to produce changes in the problem behaviors and in the adolescent's social ecology—such as the peer network—to promote long-term therapeutic gains. Intervention modalities are based on Henggeler (1999).
16. Parent Skills Training (PST)	PST is an eight-session coping skills parent training program. The first session focuses on general parenting principles, stress and coping, general problem-solving skills, and the "do's" and "don'ts" of parenting. The second through eighth sessions focus on individualized problem solving, modeling, and rehearsal, and a specific skills training such as replacing negative thoughts with positive thoughts, psychoeducation about drugs and alcohol, communication skills, using positive and negative consequences, establishing and maintaining house rules, and issues related to adolescent's treatment and post treatment planning (McGillicuddy et al., 2001).
17. Purdue Brief Family Therapy Model	PBFT is a 12-session program that combines evidence-based components of structural, strategic, functional, and behavioral family therapies. The goal is to establish rapport with the family and assist in modifying family dynamics so that the adolescent will reduce substance abuse by decreasing resistance, redefining drug use as a family problem, reestablishing appropriate parental influence, interrupting dysfunctional family behavior, implementing change strategies, and providing assertion skills training for the adolescent (Lewis, Piercy, Sprenkle, & Trepper, 1990).
18. Strengths-Oriented Family Therapy (SOFT)	SOFT is a 15-session treatment that uses solution-focused language and techniques to enhance parent–adolescent communication skills. The first session focuses on a family-based assessment and motivational feedback. Then, the therapist works with individual families followed by multifamily groups. Finally, case management is provided as needed (Smith & Hall, 2007).

to train therapists and specify testable hypotheses. Researchers are also taking steps to get a strong measurement of their primary outcomes with 61% of studies including an objective measure of substance use (such as use of urinalysis) and 64% using collateral report to substantiate participants' self-reports (usually parent report).

Infrequently Reported Attributes

Keeping investigators blind to the randomization sequence (31%) and keeping assessors blind to the treatment condition of participants (22%) are reported in less than one third of studies. While entirely conceivable that these are simple omissions—that is, researchers followed these procedures but did not document them in their manuscripts—particulars of this nature may be helpful to establish transparency of research conduct. Some research suggests that allocation concealment and blind outcome assessment can guard against effect size inflation (Brouwers et al., 2005; Jüni, Altman, & Egger, 2001; Moja et al., 2005). With that said, it is possible that some of the attributes most recently emphasized in the research methodology literature, including the dimension of allocation concealment and blind assessment of outcomes, may not always be possible in certain types of clinical outcome research. In community-based studies, for example, it may be unethical or impossible—given the setting (e.g., juvenile justice)—to withhold information regarding treatment assignment from community collaborators, which would also make it impossible to keep the research staff blind to treatment assignment.

The least frequently occurring attributes are (a) providing explicit justification for sample sizes (17%) and (b) a lack of independent replications (17%). Some researchers may consider the former superfluous if their studies are adequately powered; however, less than half of the studies met this criterion (44%). With respect to independent replication, Wampold (2013) discussed how researcher allegiances can influence outcome. As stated by Sprenkle (2012), "even though researchers are only very rarely intentionally deceptive, certain biases may creep into research about models favored by the investigators. Biases include using alternatives (control groups) to the experimental treatment that are less well organized, which have less invested therapists or have other characteristics which suggest they are less valued by the researchers" (p. 9).

Attributes Reported More Frequently in Recent Studies

Interestingly, the four attributes that seem to be reported more frequently in recent years—justifying sample size (17%), adequate statistical power (44%), intent-to-treat (ITT, 53%) analyses, and effect sizes (69%)—all concern statistical reporting. These developments might be seen as co-occurring alongside parallel requirements of publications such as the *Journal of Consulting and Clinical Psychology* (Odgaard & Fowler, 2010), more accessible methods for deriving effect sizes from more advanced analytic procedures (Feingold, 2009), and, in the case of ITT, advanced procedures for handling missing data and their implementation in statistical software such as Mplus (Muthén & Muthén, 1998–2013) and hierarchical linear modeling (HLM) (Raudenbush & Bryk, 2002). Developments such as the CONSORT statement and related procedures are changing the nature of publications and thus the available knowledge base in clinical science.

Summarizing the Scientific Advances of Family Interventions

Summarizing these data, there can be no doubt that the methodological quality of family-based RCTs for adolescent substance abuse has improved considerably over the years (Catalano et al., 1990; Deas & Thomas, 2001; Liddle & Dakof, 1995). Criticisms from these and other reviews (i.e., incomplete reporting of sample characteristics, inadequate comparison treatments, missing follow-up data, use of invalidated outcome measures or solely using participant self-reports) have by and large been addressed, as Table 32.3 shows. Furthermore, in a recent methodological review of couple and family therapy, Sprenkle (2012) rated RCTs conducted in 10 substantive research domains[2] on 12 dimensions of methodological quality focused on the maturation of couple and family therapy research over the past decade. On Sprenkle's rating system, the strength of the research base for substance abuse research ranked just below conduct disorder with 11 of 12 dimensions of methodological strengths being represented. Notably, a number of RCTs have been conducted in community settings using samples representative of what is seen in clinical practice (e.g., comorbid conditions) and employing active comparison treatments. Family treatments have performed well against a variety of comparison treatments—evidence-based

Table 31.3 Study Details and Outcomes

Study	Sample	Family-Based Treatment Details	Comparison Treatment Details	Follow-Up	Treatment Outcomes and Effect Sizes
Assertive Continuing Care					
Godley et al. (2002) *Efficacy Trial* *Attribute score: 33%*	N = 114, 76.3% male, ages 15–18, 16.6% African American, 73.7% Caucasian, 57.1% alcohol dependence, 90.3% marijuana dependence, 77.2% prior substance use treatment, 52.6% prior mental health treatment, 82% juvenile justice system	Usual continuing care (UCC): variable duration and locations) + Assertive continuing care (ACC): 90 days, home-based	Usual continuing care (UCC)	2 TOTAL: Baseline and post treatment (3 months)	• No group differences in number of sessions attended • Median days to marijuana use: 90 days vs. 31 days—64% decrease for ACC and 18% decrease for UCC • Median days to marijuana use significantly longer for ACC (90 days vs. 31 days, d = .39) • ACC more likely to be abstinent from marijuana (52% vs. 31%, d = .43) • ACC more likely than UCC to receive continuing care services (92% vs. 59%, d = .86) • ACC more continuing care sessions (M = 14.4 vs. M = 7.6, d = .48)
Dennis et al. (2004) *Hybrid Trial* *Attribute score: 94%*	Trial 2 only: N = 300, 81% male, ages 12–17, 49% White, 47% African American, 82% juvenile justice system, 76% weekly or daily substance use	Adolescent community reinforcement approach (ACRA): 12–14 weeks, location not specified Therapists: All conditions: 20% doctorates, 30% bachelors, 50% masters. Average 7 years of experience. First time using manual-guided therapy	*ACTIVE* Motivational enhancement treatment/cognitive-behavioral therapy 5 session (MET/CBT5): 6–7 weeks, location not specified *and* multidimensional family therapy (MDFT): 12–41 weeks, location not specified	5 TOTAL: Baseline, 3 months, 6 months, 9 months, 12 months follow-ups	• Total days of abstinence not significantly different by site or treatment • Percent in recovery not significantly different by condition across sites, but small trend (Cohen's f = 0.16) for ACRA (34%) higher percent of participants in recovery than MET/CBT5 (23%) and MDFT (19%) • Drug use reduced similarly across treatment conditions. (f = 0.06) • Trend for ACRA participants higher percent in recovery (34%) compared to MET/CBT5 23%) and MDFT (19%) with moderate effects (f = 0.16), but no statistically significant differences • Cost-effectiveness of treatments significantly differed (f = 0.22) with A-CRA being the most cost-effective for cost per day abstinent (ACRA = \$6.62, MET/CBT5 = \$9.00, MDF = \$10.38)

(continued)

Table 31.3 Continued

Study	Sample	Family-Based Treatment Details	Comparison Treatment Details	Follow-Up	Treatment Outcomes and Effect Sizes
Godley et al. (2007) *Hybrid Trial* *Attribute score: 56%*	N = 183, 71% male, mean age 16.2, 73% Caucasian, 18% African American, 100% substance use dependence, 82% juvenile justice system	Assertive continuing care (including ACRA): 12 weeks, home-based	Usual continuing care: duration not specified, outpatient clinic	4 TOTAL: Baseline, 3, 6, and 9 months follow-ups	• No significant between-group differences in overall alcohol and other drugs abstinence (19% to 28% UCC and 28% to 38% ACC), and alcohol abstinence (26% to 44% UCC and 31% to 50% ACC) • ACC more effective linking clients to continuing care (*d* = 1.07) • ACC clients received more days of continuing care (*d* = 0.64) • ACC more likely to meet with parents (72% vs. 49%) and follow-up on referrals (89% vs. 68%) • ACC resulted in significantly greater marijuana abstinence at 9 months (*d* = 0.32)
Godley et al. (2010) *Hybrid Trial* *Attribute score: 83%*	N = 320, 76% male, mean age 15.9, 73% Caucasian, 13% African American, 75% cannabis abuse or dependence, 49% alcohol abuse or dependence, 35% both cannabis and alcohol disorders,, 56% co-occurring psychological problems, 73% involved in criminal justice	CBOP with assertive continuing care (ACC): duration and location not specified; therapists: 12.5% bachelors, 87.5% masters, 87.5% Caucasian, 12.5% African American, 62.5% females	*ACTIVE:* Chestnut's Bloomington Outpatient Treatment (CBOP) without ACC—AND—MET/ CBT 17 without ACC vs. MET/CBT 17 with ACC: 12–14 weeks, home based; therapists: 25% bachelors, 75% masters, 100% Caucasian, 75% females	5 TOTAL: Baseline, 3, 6, 9, and 12 months follow-ups	• No statistical differences in urine test results or recovery status across conditions • Percent of days abstinent from alcohol or other drugs increased from 74.4% to 81% across groups • Percent of days abstinent from alcohol decreased from 95.2% to 94.1% across groups • Percent of days abstinent higher for both CBOP conditions (10.6 and 10.9%) than MET/CBT7 conditions (5% and 6.1%) (*f* = .08). ACC did not add incremental benefits • CBOP with ACC received significantly more treatment than MET/CBT7 with ACC • Most cost-effective intervention was MET/CBT7 without ACC

Brief Strategic Family Therapy (BSFT)

Szapocznik et al. (1986) *Efficacy Trial* *Attribute score: 11%*	N = 35 families, 100% Hispanic, middle to lower class, 21% arrested	Conjoint family therapy (CFT): duration and location not specified; 1 doctoral level, over 15 years' experience	One-person family therapy (OPFT); duration and location not specified	3 TOTAL: Baseline, discharge, and 6 to 12 months follow-up	• There was a main effect for time, with improved psychiatric symptoms, behavior problems, and observational ratings of family functioning • OPFT was marginally more effective in improving psychiatric symptoms
Santisteban et al. (2003) *Efficacy Trial* *Attribute score: 61%*	N = 126, 75% male, mean age 15.6, 100% Hispanic, 94% two or more behavior problems, 52% alcohol or drug use in past month	Brief strategic family therapy (BSFT): 4 to 20 weeks at clinic or research center; 1 child psychiatric trainee and 6 clinical psychologists	Group control (GC): 6 to 16 sessions, school-based; two child psychiatric trainee, one clinical psychologist, and one masters-level counselor	2 TOTAL: Pre and Post	• No group differences on behavior, family, age, gender, nationality • BSFT resulted in greater behavioral improvements than GGT; η² = .10 • BSFT resulted in greater reductions in marijuana use than GGT η² = .09 • Substantially larger proportion of family therapy cases demonstrated clinically significant improvement in behavior problems (43% vs. 11%) and marijuana use (60% vs. 17%) • Family cohesion improved to a greater extent with BSF; η² = .08
Robbins et al. (2008) *Efficacy Trial* *Attribute score: 56%*	N = 190, 78% male, mean age: 15.57, 59% Hispanic, 41% African American, mean days marijuana use in past month: 6.49; 86% co-occurring psychiatric disorder, 80% juvenile justice, 41% annual household income below $15,000	Structural ecosystems therapy (SET): 24 sessions, in multiple locations; therapists 2 females, 1 male. From Colombia, Cuba (Afro-Cuban), and African American. 0–7 years experience. 1 postdoctoral psychologist and 2 masters psychologists	*ACTIVE*—family process-only (FAM): 12–16 sessions, location not specified) AND Community Services Control (CS): duration and location not specified	5 TOTAL: Baseline, 3, 6, 12, and 18 months follow-ups	• There was a main effect for ethnicity • More ecosystemic therapy sessions were provided in SET than in FAM, η² = .41 • CS received more services at community agencies than FAM and SET, η² = .07 • SET focused more on changing ecosystemic interactions than FAM therapists, η² = .05 • FAM therapists focused more on changing within family interactions than SET, η² = .04 • No main effects for treatment conditions in reducing drug use • SET reduced substance use more than CS and FAM *among Hispanic adolescents only*, p = 0.32 • SET was more efficacious at producing a linear decline in drug use over 18 months follow-up than FAM and CS • No effect sizes reported for treatment outcomes

(continued)

Table 31.3 Continued

Study	Sample	Family-Based Treatment Details	Comparison Treatment Details	Follow-Up	Treatment Outcomes and Effect Sizes
Robbins et al. (2011) *Effectiveness Trial* *Attribute score: 67%*	N = 480, 79% male, mean age: 15.5, 44% Hispanic, 30% White, and 22.9% Black; 67% marijuana abuse, 25.9% marijuana dependence, 6.7% other drug abuse, 14.6% other drug dependence; 72% juvenile justice; 60% family income below 30K	Brief strategic family therapy (BSFT): 12–16 weeks, flexible location: home, clinic, school, work or other. Both conditions: 49 therapists at community agencies, randomly assigned to treatment conditions	Treatment as usual: duration varied, community-based	4 TOTAL: Baseline, 4, 8, 12 months follow-ups	• No overall differences between conditions were observed in the trajectories of self-reports of adolescent drug use • Median number of days of self-reported drug use was significantly higher in TAU than BSFT at 12 months following randomization (*Mdn* = 3.5 vs. 2 occasions of use). • BSFT was significantly more effective than TAU in engaging (Risk Ratio = 0.43) and retaining adolescents (Risk Ratio = 0.71) and in improving parent reports of family functioning • No effect sizes reported
Valdez et al. (2013) *Hybrid Trial* *Attribute score: 61%*	N = 200, 49% male; mean age: 15.25; 100% Hispanic (Mexican-American); 55% alcohol use (40% 5 + drinks), 76.5% marijuana use, 22% crack cocaine, 13.5% heroin, 10.5% barbiturates; 55% single-parent household, 39.4% public housing; 80% family member in a gang	Brief strategic family therapy (BSFT): 16 weeks standard BSFT + gang diversion training 3 sessions for youth, 1 session for parents, + 1 HIV/STD prevention session; flexible location: home, clinic, school, work, or other; 2 licensed trained therapists	Control: referral to substance abuse counseling, duration varied, community-based	3 TOTAL: Baseline, treatment exit at 16 weeks, and 6 months follow-up	• At 6 months following randomization, BSFT more effective in reducing days of alcohol use *d* = 0.50 • At 6-month follow-up, BSFT parents report fewer conduct problems, *d* = 0.57 • No treatment differences in marijuana use, other illicit drugs, gang identification, family functioning, or other parent reports

Contingency Management (CM)

Stanger et al. (2009) *Efficacy Trial* *Attribute score:* 72%	N = 69; 82.5% male; mean age: 16; 91.5% Caucasian, 6% African American, 3% Hispanic; 45% marijuana dependence, 44.5% marijuana abuse, 21.5% alcohol abuse, 52% mental health services in past year; 31.5% juvenile justice; 7.0 mean SES (9-step scale)	Motivational enhancement/cognitive-behavioral therapy + abstinence CM + family management: 14 weeks, clinic-based Both conditions: 3 masters-level (1 male and 2 females) and 1 female postdoctoral fellow. 100% European American) *ACTIVE* MET/CBT + attendance CM + parent psychoeducation: 14 weeks, clinic-based	5 TOTAL: Baseline + treatment exit, 3, 6, and 9 months follow-ups	• No group differences in attendance and provision of urine samples • Results of urine testing indicated that youth receiving MET/CBT + CM + Parent Training (EXP) had more weeks of continuous marijuana abstinence during treatment than youth receiving MET/CBT + parent psychoeducation (CON) (7.6 vs. 5.1, d = .48) • No treatment x time interaction significant abstinence post treatment • Both groups show decreased drug and alcohol use during treatment, increase post treatment, and stabilization to lower than pretreatment levels • EXP youth more likely to achieve ≥8 weeks of continuous abstinence (53% vs. 30%) • Both groups reported improved parenting (positive involvement, monitoring) • Parents of EXP youth reported less negative discipline (d = .25), and youth reported less externalizing behavior than CON (d = .30)
Henggeler et al. (2012) *Effectiveness Trial* *Attribute score:* 61%	N = 104; 83% male; mean age: 15.4; 57% White, 40% African American, 3% biracial; 80% cannabis abuse, 24% cannabis dependence, 38% alcohol abuse, 25% alcohol dependence, 16% abuse and 8% dependence of other drugs; 65% co-occurring psychiatric disorder; 70% single-parent family; median annual household income: 20K–30K; 47% of families on financial assistance	Juvenile drug court with contingency management and family engagement strategies (CM-FAM): 4 months, office-base Juvenile drug court as usual AND usual services (US) (4 months), office-based Both conditions: community-based therapists, 76% male, 61% White, 39% African American. Mean age: 41.7 years. 29% bachelors, 69% masters, 2% doctorate. Average 11 years clinical experience, 44% certified addiction counselors	4 TOTAL: Baseline, 3, 6, 9 months follow-ups	• Rapid decrease in marijuana use and delinquency throughout treatment for both groups, significant differences between groups did note emerge until final assessment • At final assessment, the odds of a positive marijuana result per drug screen for US youths increased 94% (odds ratio = 1.94) and decreased for CM-FAM youths 18% (odds ratio = 0.82) • At final assessment, general delinquency a increased 14% for US youths (event rate ratio = 1.14) and decreased 53% for CM-FAM youths (event rate ratio = 0.47) • At final assessment, person offense decreased 34% for US youths (event rate ratio = 0.66) and decreased significantly more for CM-FAM youth: 85% (event rate ratio = 0.15) • At final assessment, property offense *increased* 91% for US youths (event rate ratio = 0.48) and decreased for CM-FAM youth: 52% (event rate ratio = 0.34) • Significant moderators not observed

(continued)

Table 31.3 Continued

Study	Sample	Family-Based Treatment Details	Comparison Treatment Details	Follow-Up	Treatment Outcomes and Effect Sizes
Culturally Informed and Flexible Family-Based Treatment for Adolescents					
Santisteban et al. (2011) *Efficacy Trial* *Attribute score: 22%*	N = 28; Ages 14–17 (gender and mean age not specified); 100% Hispanic; Referred by a local juvenile justice. (Clinical and SES information not provided)	The Culturally Informed and Flexible Family-Based Treatment for Adolescents (CIFFTA): 16 weeks, location not specified; experienced family therapists	Traditional family therapy. Youth and families (TFT): 16 weeks, location not specified; therapists experienced in structural family therapy and adolescent drug abuse treatment	2 TOTAL: Baseline & 8 months follow-up	• At baseline, TFT significantly more externalizing problems (added as covariate) • No treatment differences in parent reports of adolescent behavior problems, but large time effect on child-reported externalizing behaviors over time for both groups ($\eta^2 = .27$) • CIFTAA reduced substance use ($\eta^2 = .33$) and improved parenting practices ($\eta^2 = .29$, teen report and $\eta^2 = .10$, parent report) more
Ecologically-Based Family Therapy					
Slesnick and Prestopnik (2005) *Efficacy Trial* *Attribute score: 44%*	N = 124; 41% male; mean age = 14.8; 44% Hispanic, 37% Anglo, 7% African America, 4% Native American. IV drug use, 10.6%. Use of baseline alcohol or drugs, 50%. Mean lifetime runs = 3.1., 52% in school, 31% sexually abused, 55% physically abused, 37% attempted suicide	Ecologically based family therapy (EBFT): 15 sessions, home-based; master's-level licensed counselors with 2–5 years experience and trained in substance abuse treatment using cognitive-behavioral and behavioral family systems approaches	Services as usual (SAU): mean no. of sessions: 4; office-based	4 TOTAL: Baseline, 3, 6, 12 months follow-ups	• No treatment differences with intent-to-treat analyses • Among adolescents who completed 4 or more sessions, substance use was reduced for both groups ($\eta^2 = .10$) • Significant time main effects for HIV knowledge, psychological functioning, and family functioning • Among youth who had experienced sexual abuse, EBFT decreased substance use more than SAU
Slesnick and Prestopnik (2009) *Hybrid Trial* *Attribute score: 67%*	N = 119; mean age: 15.1; 45% males; 44% Hispanic, 29% Anglo, 11% Native American, 5% African American; 45% alcohol and drug abuse. Runaway shelters with alcohol problems. Mean runs = 4.79; mean arrests = 3.3. 50% enrolled	Ecologically based family therapy (EBFT) (mean 10.31 sessions, home-based); Both conditions: 2 therapists. Both females, master's level, licensed, with 2–5 years experience	Functional family therapy (*ACTIVE*): mean 6.51 sessions, office-based) AND Services as Usual: duration not specified, shelter-based	4 TOTAL: Baseline, 3, 9, and 15 months follow-ups	• Significant time main effects for substance use measures, for number of psychiatric diagnoses, externalizing behaviors, delinquent behaviors, verbal aggression, family cohesion, and family conflict • EBFT and FFT reduced substance use more than SAU (EBFT: $\eta^2 = .20$; FFT: $\eta^2 = .25$) • Youth in EBFT attended more sessions (M = 10.31) than FFT (M = 6.51). SAU was not included in these analyses.

	in school, 39% sexually, 36% physically abused, 48% suicide attempts; median income = 25K			
Slesnick et al. (2013) *Hybrid Trial* *Attribute score: 67%*	N = 179; 47.5% male; mean age: 15.4; 65.9% African American, 26% Caucasian; 3.2 mean number of runs	Ecologically based family therapy: home-based, average 6.5 sessions. All conditions: therapists are 7 females, 1 male. 4 masters-level counselors, or social workers, 4 graduate students in couple and family therapy. *ACTIVE* Motivational Intervention: home-based, average 1.6 sessions AND Community Reinforcement Approach: home-based, average 5.3 sessions	7 TOTAL: Baseline, 3, 6, 9, 12, 18, and 24 months follow-ups.	• All groups significantly decreased substance use over time, with increase at follow-up; no between treatment differences • Teens in EBFT more likely to receive intervention than CRA and MI condition, Chi Square(2) = 7.50, $p < .05$ • No between-group differences in treatment attendance or attrition • LTPA identified three classes (Decreasing, Fluctuating High, U Shaped). In the decreasing use class, MI produced more rapid changes but faster relapse than EBFT • No effect sizes reported

Family Behavior Therapy (FBT)

Azrin et al. (2001) *Efficacy Trial* *Attribute score: 44%*	N = 56; 82% male; mean age: 15.4; 21% ethnic minority; 40% special education, 76% dual diagnosis of conduct disorder and substance dependence, 100% marijuana use history, most had also used alcohol or other "hard" drugs; 71% externally mandated to treatment; 77% previously arrested	Family behavioral therapy (FBT): 15 sessions, location not specified Both conditions: doctoral graduate students, 10 females, 9 males ages 24–33 Individual-cognitive problem-solving therapy: 15 sessions, location not specified	3 TOTAL: Baseline, treatment exit (approx.3 months), 6 months follow-up	• Significant time main effects indicate reductions in substance use and conduct problems in both treatments through 6-month follow-up • No between-treatment differences on any measures • No effect sizes reported

(continued)

Table 31.3 Continued

Study	Sample	Family-Based Treatment Details	Comparison Treatment Details	Follow-Up	Treatment Outcomes and Effect Sizes
Family Empowerment Intervention (FEI)					
Dembo et al. (2002) *Efficacy Trial* *Attribute score:* 22%	N = 278; 56% male; mean age: 14.5; 56% Anglo, 41% African American; 26% Hispanic; 44% special Ed; 50% repeated a grade. Prior mental health treatment (16%) or substance use treatment (4%); 100% juvenile justice	Family empowerment intervention (FEI) (10 weeks, home-based); field consultants not trained as therapists	Extended services intervention (ESI) (monthly phone contacts)	5 TOTAL: Baseline, 12 months, 24 months, 36 months, 48 months follow-ups	• ITT analyses showed no differences between FEI and ESI on getting very high or drunk on alcohol. • Treatment completer analyses showed FEI reduced getting very high or drunk more than ESI [critical ratio: −1.56; .10 > p >.05] • No effect sizes reported
Family Support Network (FSN)					
Dennis et al. (2004) *Hybrid Trial* *Attribute score:* 83%	(Trial 1) N = 300; 84% male, ages 12–17; 84% male; 73% White, 13% African American, 6% Hispanic; 84% juvenile justice system; 75% weekly or daily substance use; 83% started using drugs or alcohol before the age of 15, 27% past substance abuse treatment, 28% past mental health treatment; 57% from single-parent families	Family support network (FSN) (12 group sessions + 6 parent education + 4 home visits, mixed location, including home-based) All conditions: 20% doctorates, 30% bachelors, 50% masters. Average 7 years of experience. First time using manual-guided therapy	*ACTIVE* (Trial 1) motivational enhancement treatment/cognitive-behavioral therapy 5 session (MET/CBT5), 6–7 weeks, location not specified AND motivational enhancement treatment/cognitive-behavioral therapy 12 session (MET/CBT12), location not specified	5 TOTAL: Baseline, 3 months, 6 months, 9 months, 12 months follow-ups	• Total days of abstinence not significantly different by site or treatment • Percentage in recovery at the end of the study highest in MET/CBT5 (27%) followed by FSN (22%) and MET/CBT12 (17%), Cohen's $f = 0.12$ • Cost per day of abstinence significantly differed by condition with MET/CBT5 = $4.91, MET/CBT12 = $6.15, and FSN = $15.13, $f = 0.48$

Family Systems Therapy (FST)

Study	Sample	Treatment	Comparison	Timepoints	Results
Joanning et al. (1992) *Efficacy Trial* *Attribute score: 33%*	N = 134; mean age = 15.4; 68% White, 29% Mexican American, Black 2% (mothers ethnicity); substance use and delinquency	Family systems therapy (FST): 12 weeks, clinic-base); 3 male advanced graduate students, 28–33 years, with prior experience in marriage and family therapy, 5 years experience.	Adolescent group therapy (AGT) (12 weeks, hospitals and mental health centers) AND family drug education (FDE): biweekly for 6 sessions, location not specified). Clinic-based: male and 1 female advanced graduate students ages 26–43, with prior work experience, with the senior therapist (age 43) having 10 years prior experience	2 TOTAL: Pretest, posttest (12 weeks)	• At posttest, 54% of FGT not using, 28% of FDE not using, 16% of GT not using • Adolescent drug use at posttest was significantly different between FST and AGT and between FST and FDE. No differences between AGT and FDE • More FST adolescents reported abstaining from drugs at posttest than AGT and FDE • Family functioning improved for all groups, no significant differences • No effect sizes reported

Functional Family Therapy (FFT)

Study	Sample	Treatment	Comparison	Timepoints	Results
Friedman et al. (1989) *Efficacy Trial* *Attribute score: 22%*	N = 135; 60.5% male, Mean age = 17.9 89% White; Low SES; 33% arrested	Family therapy (FT): 24 weeks, location not specified; 4–17 years in family therapy	Parent group (PG): 24 weeks, location not specified	3 TOTAL: Baseline, Post treatment (approx. 6 months), and 9-months follow-up	• Similar significant decreases over time in substance use in both treatment groups: 50% reduction on drug severity index score • Similar significant within-treatment improvements in youth psychiatric symptoms and family functioning • Both groups satisfied with treatment • No effect sizes reported
Barrett et al. (2001) *Hybrid Trial* *Attribute score: 61%*	N = 114; 80% male; Mean age = 15.6 years; 49% Hispanic, 40% White; 29.7% anxious/depressed, 27.3% attention difficulties, 47.7% externalizing behaviors, 45.3% internalizing behaviors; 43% referred by juvenile justice; mean annual income 38.5K	Functional family therapy: FFT; 8 to 12 weeks, clinic and office based All conditions: 2 doctorates, 7 masters-level graduate student. Experience 4–10 years	*ACTIVE* Joint family and individual therapy (Joint): 24 sessions AND group counseling (GC): 8 to 12 weeks AND cognitive-behavioral therapy (CBT): 8 to 12 weeks.	3 TOTAL: Baseline, 4, 7 months follow-up.	• Nonsignificant main effect for treatment condition • Significant main effect for time (η^2 = .101), significant for FFT (η^2 = .226), for joint (η^2 = .183), and for group (η^2 = .176), but not for CBT (η^2 = .001) • Significant interaction between time and condition η^2 = .072 • From pre to 4 months, youth in FFT (η^2 = .422) and joint (η^2 = .229) significantly reduced marijuana use, but not CBT or group • From pre to 7 months, youth in joint maintained reduced marijuana use (η^2 = .243), but not FFT (η^2 = .102). Youth in group reduced from pre to 7 months (η^2 = .216), but not CBT (η^2 = .001)

(*continued*)

Table 31.3 Continued

Study	Sample	Family-Based Treatment Details	Comparison Treatment Details	Follow-Up	Treatment Outcomes and Effect Sizes
Integrated Family and Cognitive Behavioral Therapy (IFCBT)					
Latimer et al. (2003) *Efficacy Trial* *Attribute score: 28%*	N = 43; 76.7% male; mean age = 16.07; 86% White; 7% Native American, 4.6% Hispanic; 97.7% marijuana use; 86% alcohol use; 85% diagnosed with substance use disorder	Integrated family and cognitive-behavioral therapy (IFCBT): 16, family therapy sessions and 32 cognitive-behavioral group session	Drugs harm psychoeducation curriculum (DHPE): 16 group sessions, location not specified	4 TOTAL: Baseline, 3, and 6 months follow-ups	• 50% of youth receiving IFCBT provided clean urine samples at and 6 months follow-ups • FCBT attended more sessions—added as a control variable • IFCBT reduced alcohol (d = .56) and drug use (d = .79) more than DHPE • IFCBT improved rational problem solving (d = .59) and learning strategy skills (d = .58) more than DHPE • IFCBT parents: stronger increases in communication (d = .54), involvement (d = .75), control (d = .63), and values/norms (d = .61)
Esposito-Smythers et al. (2011) *Efficacy Trial* *Attribute score: 72%*	N = 40; 33.3% male; mean age = 15; 89% White; 13.9% Hispanic.	Integrated outpatient cognitive-behavioral intervention for co-occurring AOD and suicidality (I-CBT): 3 PhD, 8 postdoctoral trainees, 1 masters-level clinician with prior training and experience using CBT	Enhanced treatment as usual; community agency therapists	5 TOTAL: Baseline, 3, 6, 12, and 18 months follow-ups.	• I-CBT attended more sessions than E-TAU • No group differences on number of youth prescribed medication • I-CBT resulted in lower rates of substance use disorders than E-TAU (27% vs. 77%, Cohen's h = 1.10) • I-CBT associated with lower rates of mood disorder (7% vs. 31%, h = 0.65) and disruptive behavior disorders (0% vs. 40%, h = 1.31) • ICBT had fewer suicide attempts (b = 0.82), inpatient hospital visits (b = 0.81), and arrests (b = 0.94)
Multidimensional Family Therapy (MDFT)					
Liddle et al. (2001) *Efficacy Trial* *Attribute score: 50%*	N = 182; 80% male; mean age: 16; 51% White, non-Hispanic; 18% African American; 15% Hispanic; 6% Asian; 10% other; 61% juvenile justice involved	Multidimensional family therapy (MDFT): 16 weeks, home & office-based All conditions: experienced community clinicians trained to competence	*ACTIVE* Adolescent group therapy (AGT): (14 to 16 weeks, office-based AND multifamily educational intervention (MEI): 16 weeks, office-based	4 TOTAL: Baseline, Discharge (approx. 4 months), 6 months and 12 months follow-ups	• Significant effect for time on drug use (η^2 = .36) and acting out behaviors (η^2 = .12), but not for family competence or GPA • Significant time x condition interaction for drug use (η^2 = .12) and family competence (η^2 = .11) = not for acting out or GPA

Study	Sample	MDFT / Therapists	Active comparison	Assessments	Outcomes
	and supervised. 80% White, non-Hispanic. 50% female. 80% masters-level, 20% doctoral-level. Average 7 years' work with teens, 3 years with substance abusers, 6 years within their modality				• MDFT decreased substance use more than AGT and MEI ($\eta^2 = 0.12$) • MDFT improved family competence more, ($\eta^2 = 0.11$) • 45% of MDFT youth reported clinically significant change at 12 month follow-up compared to 32% in AGT and 26% in MEI • MDFT resulted in better school outcomes with 76% of youth MDFT reported GPAs of 2.0 or more vs.60% AGT and 40% MEI
Dennis et al. (2004) *Hybrid Trial* *Attribute score: 83%*	Trial 2 only: N = 300, 81% male, ages 12–17, 49% White, 47% African American, 82% juvenile justice system, 76% weekly or daily substance use	Multidimensional family therapy (MDFT): 12-41 weeks, location not specified All conditions (both trials): 20% doctorates, 30% bachelors, 50% masters. Average 7 years of experience. First time using manual-guided therapy	*ACTIVE* motivational enhancement treatment/cognitive-behavioral therapy 5 session (MET/ CBT5): 6–7 weeks, location not specified AND adolescent community reinforcement approach (ACRA): 12–14 weeks, location not specified	5 TOTAL: Baseline, 3 months, 6 months, 9 months, 12 months follow-ups	Trial 2 only: • Total days of abstinence not significantly different by site or treatment • Percent in recovery not significantly different by condition across sites, but small trend (Cohen's $f = 0.16$) for ACRA (34%) higher percent of participants in recovery than MET/CBT5 (23%) and MDFT (19%) • Drug use reduced similarly across treatment conditions. ($f = 0.06$) • Trend for ACRA participants higher percent in recovery (34%) compared to MET/CBT5 23%) and MDFT (19%) with moderate effects ($f = 0.16$), but no statistically significant differences • Cost-effectiveness of treatments significantly differed ($f = 0.22$) with A-CRA being the most cost-effective for cost per day abstinent (ACRA = $6.62, MET/ CBT5 = $9.00, MDF = $10.38)
Liddle et al. (2008) *Efficacy Trial* *Attribute score: 56%*	*N = 224;* mean age, 15 (range: 12–17.5); 81% male; 72% African American, 18% White, non-Hispanic, 10% Hispanic; all drug users: 75% cannabis dependence 13% cannabis abuse; 58% single-parent home, 13K family income	MDFT (4–6 months office-based); 4 masters, 2 doctoral-level therapists Both conditions: 12 therapists, 6 in each condition. 50% White non-Hispanic, 50% African American, ages 29–54 (M = 40)	*ACTIVE* Individual cognitive-behavioral therapy (4–6 months, office-based; 3 masters, 3 doctoral therapists	4 TOTAL: Baseline, termination (approx. 4 months), 6 and 12 months post termination	• Both treatments reduced substance use severity and 30 day frequency of cannabis use • MDFT resulted in greater reductions in substance use problem severity between intake and 6 months ($d = 0.39$) and intake to 12 months ($d = 0.59$) than CBT • No treatment effects for 30-day frequency of cannabis use • MDFT resulted in greater decreases in hard drug use ($d = 0.32$) • MDFT led to greater proportion of youth reporting abstinence from substance use at 12-month follow-up

(continued)

Table 31.3 Continued

Study	Sample	Family-Based Treatment Details	Comparison Treatment Details	Follow-Up	Treatment Outcomes and Effect Sizes
Liddle et al. (2009) *Effectiveness Trial* *Attribute score: 67%*	$N = 83$; mean age: 13.73 (range: 11–15); 74% male; 42% Hispanic, 38% African American; 47% juvenile justice, 47% substance abuse; 16% substance dependence, 38% conduct disorder, 29% ADHD. 47% juvenile justice involved. 53% single-parent homes, median family income: 19K	MDFT: 12 to 16 weeks, home-based, twice per week for 90 min. Both conditions: masters in counseling, social work, or family therapy. Mean: 2 years experience. Ages 26–47 (mean = 33). 71% female. 57% Hispanic, 29% Black, 14% White non-Hispanic	Adolescent group therapy (12 to 16 weeks, clinic-based, twice per week for 90 min)	5 TOTAL: Baseline, 6 weeks after Baseline, Discharge, 6 months, 12-months follow-ups	• MDFT better treatment completion rates • Both groups showed reductions in substance use at 1 year (*pseudo z* = −4.29) and substance use related problems (pseudo z = −8.35) • Among those reporting at least some substance use, MDFT resulted in greater decreases in: substance use (*d* = 0.77); substance use problems (*d* = 0.74), and delinquency (*d* = 0.31) • MDFT less internalized distress (*d* = 0.54) and greater improvements in family, peer, and school domains (*d* = 0.27, 0.67, and 0.35).
Rigter et al. (2013) *Effectiveness Trial* *Attribute score: 83%*	$N = 450$; 85% male; mean age: 16.3; Youth from European countries: Belgium, Germany, France, Netherlands, Switzerland but 40% of foreign descent. 40% alcohol use disorder; 33% arrested in past 3 months. 84% dependent on cannabis	Multidimensional family therapy (MDFT): 5–7 months, office and clinic based Both conditions: 41 therapists. 3–20 years experience, average 39.6 years old, 66% female, advanced degrees in psychology, psychiatry, counseling, or social work	Individual psychotherapy (IP): 5–7 months, duration not specified	5 TOTAL: Baseline, 3 month, 6 months, 9 months, and 12 months follow-ups	• At baseline 66% to 97% of MDFT youth and 69% to 97% of IP youth cannabis dependence • At 12 months, 29% to 44% of MDFT youth and 38% to 71% of IP youth cannabis dependence • MDFT youth retained in treatment more effectively than IP (Odds Ratio = 9.8) • MDFT resulted in greater decreases in proportion of youth with cannabis use disorders (*d* = .65) and cannabis dependence symptoms (*d* = 1.27) than IP. • No treatment differences in frequency of cannabis use overall, but in a subgroup of adolescents reporting more use, MDFT had more decreased substance use (*d* = .60). No treatment differences in youth reporting less frequent use

Study	Sample	Treatment conditions	Assessments	Outcomes
Liddle et al. (2012) *Efficacy Trial* *Attribute score: 89%*	N = 113; mean age, 15; 75% male; 68% Hispanic; 81% juvenile justice involved; 100% cannabis use disorder, 71% alcohol use disorder, 33% other substance use disorder; mean family income: 19K	MDFT (home-multidimensional family therapy (MDFT): 4 months, weekly, clinic and home-based Residential Treatment (RT) (6–9 months, inpatient)	7 TOTAL: Baseline, 4, 12, 18, 24, 36, and 48 months	• EARLY OUTCOMES: Both treatment decreased substance use. No significant treatment differences in frequency or severity of substance use, or externalizing problems • MDFT youth decreased internalizing more than RT ($d = .42$) • 18 months OUTCOMES: MDFT maintained treatment gains while RT increased substance use problem severity ($d = 0.51$) • Among youth remaining in community, RT youth increased substance use and delinquency more than MDFT (substance use: $d = 1.18$; delinquency: $d = .42$)
Dakof et al. (in press) *Hybrid Trial* *Attribute score: 78%*	N = 112; 89% male; mean age: 16; 59% Hispanic, 36% African American; Alcohol: 24%; cannabis abuse 61%; cannabis dependence 30%; conduct disorder: 52%; anxiety disorder: 41%. Lifetime arrests: 2.89. 51% single-parent family homes. Median family income: 19.5K	Multidimensional family therapy (MDFT) (2–3 times weekly for 4–6 months, home based) Adolescent group therapy (AGT). (office-based, 3 times per week, duration not specified Both conditions: Masters degrees in counseling, social work or related fields. Similar experience and educational backgrounds	5 TOTAL: Baseline, 6, 12, 18, & 24 months	• Both treatments significant improvement across all outcomes from baseline to 6 months • From 6 months—24 months: increase in substance use for both treatments (lower than baseline), with slightly less increase for MDFT: $d = .54$ (nonsignificant) • From 6 months—24 months, both treatments reduced externalizing problems, with MDFT reporting more reductions than AGT on externalizing symptoms ($d = .39$), serious crimes ($d = .38$), and felony arrests ($d = .96$)
Multidimensional Treatment Foster Care (MTFC)				
Smith et al. (2010) *Efficacy Trial* *Attribute score: 44%*	N = 79; 100% male; mean age: 14.9; 85% Caucasian, 6% African American, 6% Latino, 3% Native American; Average 13.5 criminal referrals, more than 4 felonies; average 76 days in detention in past year; 56% single-parent homes, 70% have 1 parent convicted of a crime	Multidimensional treatment foster care (MTFC): inpatient placement with a family, 6–9 months Group care (GC): outpatient, duration not specified	3 TOTAL: Baseline, 12 and 18 months follow-ups	• At 12-month follow-up, MTFC reduced substance use more than GC (largest effect: $\beta = -.26$ for drugs other than alcohol and marijuana). • At 18-month follow-up, MTFC also reduced substance use more than GC (largest effect: $\beta = -.31$ for marijuana use)

(continued)

Table 31.3 Continued

Study	Sample	Family-Based Treatment Details	Comparison Treatment Details	Follow-Up	Treatment Outcomes and Effect Sizes
Multisystemic Therapy (MST)					
Henggeler et al. (1991) *Efficacy Trial* *Attribute score: 22%*	*MDP* N = 200; 67% male; mean age: 14; 70% White, 30% African American; mean number of arrests: 4.2; 65% low SES *FANS* N = 47; 72% male; mean age: 15.1; 74% African American, 26% White; 71% Low SES (Strata IV or V of Hollingshead); 33% of household heads unemployed	*MDP:* Multisystemic therapy (MST) (16 weeks, home or community-based); 6 graduate students in clinical psychology, mean age: 26, 50% female *FANS:* Multisystemic therapy (MST) (16 weeks, home or community-based); 3 community-based professionals, masters degrees in education, 2 females, 1.5 years experience	*MDP:* Individual counseling (IC) (duration and location not specified); 6 masters-level therapists, mean age: 28, 50% female. *FANS:* Usual Services (US) (duration and location not specified—court orders monitored by probation officer)	2 TOTAL: Pre & Post (approx. 4 months)	• *MDP:* MST youths had fewer drug-related arrests than IC (4% vs 16%) • MST reduced alcohol and marijuana use more than UC • No effect sizes reported
Henggeler et al. (2002) *Efficacy Trial* *Attribute score: 39%*	N = 118; mean age: 15.7, 79% male; 50% African American, 47% White. 56% abuse, 44% dependence, 50% polysubstance abuse, 87% alcohol abuse, 67% marijuana abuse. Median annual income: 15K–20K	Multisystemic therapy (MST): 4–6 months, home-based; masters-level therapists	Usual community services (UCS) (weekly—duration not specified, office-based)	4 TOTAL: Baseline, post treatment (approx. 4 months), 6 months, and 4 year follow-ups	• Results from urine testing indicated that MST increased abstinence from marijuana more than UCS at 4-year follow-up (55% MDFT and 28% UCS) • No group differences in cocaine abstinence at 4-year follow-up (53% MDFT and 40% UCS) • MST reduced aggressive crimes more than UCS at 4 years. No treatment differences in property crimes • No treatment differences in psychiatric symptoms at 4 years • No significant moderators • No effect sizes reported

Study	Sample	Treatment	Design	Findings
Henggeler et al. (2006) *Hybrid Trial* Attribute score: 50%	N = 161; mean age: 15.2, 83% male. 67% African American, 31% White. 35% prior mental health or substance abuse treatment. 52% live with single parent, family income 10–15K	Drug court with multisystemic therapy (DC/MST): 12 months drug court based Drug court with multisystemic therapy enhanced with contingency management (DC/MST/CM); 6 masters-level therapists with degrees in social work, psychology, or education. Ages 25–50. 3 African American, 3 European American. All females. Average 5 years post-masters experience. 2 of the 6 had previous MST experience.	Family court with usual community services (FC); 12 months drug court based Drug court with usual community services (DC) FC & DC: 10 community-based therapists. 8 masters-level therapists with degrees in social work): 12 months drug court based; 2 bachelors-level. 5 African American, 5 European American. 6 females. Ages 25–59. Average 10 years experience	3 TOTAL: Baseline, 4 months, 12 months	• Simple linear time effects or all groups on marijuana use • DC + MST + CM and DC + MST decreased substance use more than FC (effect sizes range from 0.38 to 2.48) • DC + MST + CM (d = 0.82 to 2.05), and DC + MST (d = 1.2 to 1.8) had fewer positive urine screens than DC alone • DC + MST + CM and DC decreased status offenses and crimes against person more than FC
Sundell et al. (2008) *Effectiveness Trial* Attribute score: 56%	N = 156; mean age: 15, 61% male. 47% not of Swedish heritage. 67% arrested at least once. 67% single-parent home, 61% living on social welfare	Multisystemic therapy (MST) vs. home-based (mean length 212 days); 20 therapists with education equivalent to masters or bachelors level in social work, psychology, or education. 12 therapists had additional training in family therapy or CBT	Treatment as usual (TAU) (office-based, mean length 212 days); variety of services, therapist info not provided	2 TOTAL: Baseline, 7 months follow-ups	• Youths in both treatments decreased their alcohol and drug use, but no treatment differences (30% decrease for MST; 36% for TAU) • Youths in both treatments decreased their delinquent behaviors, increased their social skills, improved school attendance, and decreased their psychiatric symptoms • Parents reported similar between-treatment improvements in parenting skills and mothers' mental health. No treatment differences • Some evidence that outcomes are better when adherence is higher • No significant treatment x time effects (effect sizes range –.52 to .24)

(continued)

Table 31.3 Continued

Study	Sample	Family-Based Treatment Details	Comparison Treatment Details	Follow-Up	Treatment Outcomes and Effect Sizes
Parent Skills Training (PST)					
McGillicuddy et al. (2001) *Efficacy Trial* *Attribute score: 39%*	N = 22 families 71% male; mean age = 16; 86% current alcohol problems, 79% current drug problems; 86% single-parent households	Parent skills training (8 sessions, 2 hours per week)	Waitlist control	2 TOTAL: Baseline and post treatment (approx. 4 months)	• PST more improvement in parent coping skills than control ($\eta^2 = .34$) • PST more improvement in parent depression than control ($\eta^2 = .18$) • PST more improvement in family functioning than control ($\eta^2 = .17$) • Effect sizes of parent report teen's the use favored PST ($\eta^2 = 0.08$)
Purdue Brief Family Therapy (PBFT)					
Lewis et al. (1990) *Efficacy Trial* *Attribute score: 28%*	N = 84; 81% male; mean age: 16; 96% White; 51.2% juvenile justice; 35.5% single families	Purdue brief family therapy (PBFT) (12 weeks, office-based)	Training in parenting skills (TIPS) (12 weeks, office-based)	2 TOTAL: Baseline & post treatment (approx. 3 months)	• PBFT resulted in a greater proportion of youth reducing their drug use to a clinically reliable extent than TIPS (55% vs. 38%) • 44% of "hard drug" users in PBFT moved to no drug use compared to 25% in TIPS • No effect sizes reported

Strengths-Oriented Family Therapy (SOFT)

| Smith et al. (2006)
Efficacy Trial
Attribute score: 39% | N = 98; 71% male; mean age = 15.8; 24% minority; 39% single families; 71% juvenile justice system; 90% substance abuse, 47% substance dependence, 68% history of abuse. 80% 3 or more past year substance related problems | Strengths-oriented family therapy (SOFT) (15 sessions over 3 months, office-based); 3 masters-level, 1 male, 2 females, 1 therapist 6 years experience, other 2 no adolescent substance abuse treatment experience | *ACTIVE*
The Seven Challenges (7C) (15 sessions over 3 months, office-based); 4 therapists. 2 masters-level, 2 bachelors-level. 1 male, 3 females. Average 2 years experience with substance-abusing teens | 5 TOTAL:
Baseline, 3, 6, 9, 12 months follow-ups | • 54% of PBFT and 37.5% of TIPS youth report improvement in drug use
• 13.6% of PBFT and 27.5% of TIPS youth report drug use is the same
• 31.8% of PBFT and 35% of TIPS youth report worsened drug use
• Both treatments increased abstinence from substance use, but no treatment differences (at 6 months SOFT: 31%, 7C: 39%)
• Both treatments resulted in high percentages of symptom-free youth at 6 months but no treatment differences (SOFT: 60%, 7C: 61%)
• Both treatments reduced frequency of substance use at 6 months, but no treatment differences
• Baseline to 6 months both treatments significantly decrease substance use frequency (7C: $\beta = -2.97$, SOFT: $\beta = -3.06$) and substance use problems (7C: $\beta = -1.16$, SOFT: $\beta = -1.44$ |

Notes. Study Reference is most recent publication for that study. Attribute score refers to percentage of methodological attributes (Table 31.1) fulfilled.

therapies (Barrett, Slesnick, Brody, Turner, & Peterson, 2001; Dembo et al., 2002; Hendriks, van der Schee, & Blanken, 2012; Liddle, Dakof, Turner, Henderson, & Greenbaum, 2008), treatment modalities frequently seen in clinical practice (e.g., adolescent group therapy, individual psychotherapy), and treatment as usual (TAU)/ TAU-enhanced conditions. Although family treatments have outperformed some evidence-based comparisons, effect sizes are typically not as strong as when other comparisons are utilized. That said, a way in which the research base can be improved is in reporting more details to specify TAU comparison conditions. In some studies, it is difficult to determine the type and amount of services youth randomized to TAU conditions received, and this issue has not necessarily improved in recent studies. Godley's work (Godley, Godley, Dennis, Funk, & Passetti, 2002, 2007) in this regard is notable, as these researchers have described "usual continuing care" quite well, along with describing how much of the types of interventions included they received. Hogue, Henderson, Ozechowski, and Robbins (2014) update the Waldron and Turner (2008) summary of adolescent substance abuse treatment research and note that the majority of the methodologically strong studies conducted in the past 5 years are family-based treatment trials, and of six well-established treatments for adolescent substance abuse, three either consist of or incorporate family interventions: ecologically based family therapies, behavioral family therapies, and contingency management plus family integrative treatments.

Comparative Effectiveness of Family Interventions

As noted in recent reviews (Hogue & Liddle, 2009; Rowe, 2012) and summarized in Table 31.4, several manual-guided versions of family therapy have established records of treatment efficacy for adolescent substance use (see also NREPP, 2014). These models are defined in Table 31.2. Beyond substance use, family interventions have achieved favorable and durable effects on co-occurring externalizing and internalizing problems, and other key outcomes such as academic/school and peer relations. These studies usually include diverse samples with large proportions of racial/ethnic minority groups (López-Viets, Aarons, Ellingstad, & Brown, 2003), and recently with international samples (Hendriks, van der Schee, & Blanken, 2011; Rigter et al., 2013; Sundell et al., 2008). These outcomes are noteworthy in light of some family-based

prevention interventions' failure to transfer due to cultural fit issues.

Two recent meta-analyses of outpatient treatment studies targeting adolescent substance use describe favorable results for family interventions. Baldwin et al. (2012) reviewed the impact of four family interventions—brief strategic family therapy (BSFT), functional family therapy (FFT), multidimensional family therapy (MDFT), and multisystemic therapy (MST)—on substance use, delinquency, or both. Collectively, these models resulted in a significant, albeit modest, effect size when compared to TAU or an active, manualized comparison treatment; and a large effect size when compared to no-treatment control. There were no differences found between the treatment models, although the statistical power of the comparison was limited. In a larger meta-analysis including both family treatments and other interventions, Tanner-Smith, Jo Wilson, and Lipsey (2013) found that family treatments demonstrated superior outcomes in almost every group comparison in which they were tested, including tests against other manualized treatments. Other research-supported interventions, including CBT, behavioral models, and motivational interviewing, also demonstrated favorable outcomes, though not with the consistency of results of the family interventions.

Few studies involve head-to-head comparisons of research-supported interventions (n = 9), and the results of these studies are mixed, with some studies suggesting family-based treatments have outperformed research-supported interventions using other modalities (individual, group), and other studies indicating they have been similarly effective. MDFT is more effective than individual CBT in reducing symptoms of drug dependence and promoting abstinence and sustaining treatment effects (Liddle et al., 2008). Furthermore, Barrett et al. (2001) showed that FFT and an intervention combining FFT with CBT resulted in superior substance use outcomes to individual- and group-delivered CBT alone. On the other hand, Slesnick et al. (2013) found no differences between ecologically based family therapy, motivational interviewing, and the community-reinforcement approach. Likewise, Azrin et al. (2001) found that behavioral family therapy and CBT showed similar effects in decreasing substance use and conduct problems. Independent replications of MDFT have suggested that its outcomes are similar to CBT interventions, including motivational enhancement therapy/CBT and the adolescent–community

Table 31.4 Conclusions From Major Reviews/Meta-Analyses on the Effectiveness of Family-Based Therapies

Review	Conclusions
Baldwin et al. (2012), JMFT	1. Family therapy—specifically BSFT, FFT, MDFT, and MST—appear to modestly exceed effects of TAU and alternative therapies. 2. Literature is not yet sufficiently large to answer questions pertaining to whether one treatment is more effective than the others and on what outcomes the family therapies have the biggest effect. 3. On average, families and their troubled adolescents get better when treated with one of the four approaches above than if treated using TAU or alternative therapy such as group therapy or psychoeducation. 4. These findings provide reliable evidence for the value of family-based treatments over individual-only therapy approaches. 5. The four models above have been tested and found to be effective across various levels of delinquency severity and in relation to a number of specific behavior problems (e.g., sexual offenses, serious drug use, bullying). 6. All the models have been examined for application to populations of color and some international samples so they can be viewed as generalizable beyond the White, European American majority. 7. There is not a clear answer to the question of how the models will perform when implemented outside the direct supervision of program developers. 8. The most significant limitation (of these treatments) is that training in these models is not readily accessible for most practicing clinicians and interested trainees. • The models are not easily transportable to typical clinical settings. • Access to these and other ESTs is hampered by significant dissemination difficulties. • Training programs currently have little incentive to train students in these approaches because the majority of their graduating students will not be working for agencies that use these modalities.
Huey and Polo (2008)	1. EBTs exist for ethnic minority youth with diverse mental health problems. These treatments produced treatment effects of medium magnitude. 2. MDFT only *probably* efficacious treatment for substance use with ethnic minority populations. MST also *possibly* efficacious with substance-abusing African American adolescents.
Stanton and Shadish (1997)	1. Studies that compared family-couples therapy with non-family modalities showed superior results for family therapy. 2. Comparisons of family therapy with other forms of family intervention give an edge to family therapy over family education. 3. As with the field of family-couples therapy as a whole, comparisons between different schools of family therapy are not conclusive. 4. Compared with other studies and approaches to psychotherapy with drug abusers, family therapy conditions have attained relatively high rates of engagement and retention in treatment.
Austin, Macgowan, and Wagner (2005)	1. MST, MDFT, FFT, and BSFT had adequate power. 2. Only MST, MDFT, and FFT included ethnically heterogeneous samples. 3. The primary target of intervention was substance use, but all studies assessed multiple areas of adolescent and family functioning. 4. The clinical significance of changes in substance use differed substantially across the studies. MDFT is the only intervention that demonstrated substance use changes that were clinically significant according to Kendall and Flannery-Schroeder's (1998) criterion of 1.5 SD from the baseline DV value. 5. MDFT and BSFT met Chambless's criteria for *probably* efficacious. However, only the MDFT study reported follow-up assessments. 6. Overall, MDFT emerges as the only family-based intervention with empirical support for changes in substance use behaviors that are both statistically significant and clinically significant immediately following treatment and at 1 year post treatment.

(continued)

Table 31.4 Continued

Review	Conclusions

Becker and Curry (2008)	1. 9 of 14 methodological attributes were reported in fewer than 50% of studies:
	  • Techniques utilized to ensure random sequence
	  • Techniques used to conceal allocation schedule
	  • Sample sizes small and rarely justified
	  • Studies rarely established a priori hypotheses or primary outcomes
	  • Studies didn't report blinding of outcome assessment
	2. Models that had evidence of immediate treatment superiority in two or more methodologically stronger studies included ecological family therapy, brief motivational intervention, and CBT.
	3. Family therapy models were the most frequently tested, yet ecological family therapy was the only family approach tested in two or more studies using methodologically stronger designs.
	4. Higher levels of methodological quality were not necessarily associated with stronger evidence in support of an intervention.

Catalano, Hawkins, Wells, and Miller (1990)	1. Some treatment is better than no treatment. 2. Post treatment relapse is high. 3. No clear superiority of specific treatment techniques. 4. Worse results were obtained for marijuana and alcohol use. 5. More controlled studies of adolescent drug treatment are needed.
Vaughn and Howard (2004)	Two interventions, MDFT and CBT group, met highest category ("A") of evidentiary support.
Waldron and Turner (2008)	1. MDFT, FFT and CBT-Group produced significantly greater reductions in marijuana use than minimal treatment controls. CBT-Individual did not. 2. Studies with higher proportions of Hispanic adolescents had smaller effect sizes.
Weinberg et al. (1997)	1. Little research done on natural course of substance use disorders. 2. Epidemiology of adolescent substance use has increased in the early 1990s. 3. Biological factors and family environment are being studied as etiological factors. 4. More research is needed on psychiatric comorbidity. 5. Family-based interventions have received the most study and have shown superior outcomes, while patient-centered approaches have received less research attention. 6. Science-based prevention programs have been developed but have yet to be disseminated and implemented.
Williams and Chang (2000)	1. Because treatment appears preferable to no treatment, programs should strive to be readily accessible and able to provide treatment for large numbers of people. 2. Programs should develop procedures to minimize treatment dropout and to maximize treatment completion. 3. Programs should attempt to provide or arrange for post treatment aftercare. 4. Programs should attempt to provide comprehensive services in areas other than just substance abuse. 5. Family therapy should be a component of treatment. 6. Programs should encourage and develop parent and peer support, especially regarding nonuse of substances. 7. Adolescent conduct problems: Family therapy appears particularly effective
Deas and Thomas (2001)	1. Family systems-based treatments have been reported more extensively in the literature than other treatments, and for the most part, findings suggest that family-based therapies may be effective for the treatment of adolescent SUD. 2. Few of these studies utilize validated measures of substance use. 3. Most of these studies report findings from early post treatment. 4. Most of these studies fail to include measures other than self-reported frequency of use and/or urinalysis.

Table 31.4 Continued

Review	Conclusions
	5. Family-based treatment studies would benefit by including assessment instruments that assess multiple domains as well as instruments that guard against a respondent "faking good."
	6. The most progress [since Catalano et al.'s (1990) review] has been made in the area of family therapy interventions, although sufficient inclusion of substance sue outcome measures other than collateral or self-reported frequency of use and/or urinalysis remains a major limitation.
Diamond and Josephson (2005)	1. Family treatments have proven effective with externalizing disorders, particularly conduct and substance abuse disorders. In the past decade four treatment models have received the most programmatic attention: FFT, MDFT, MST, and SFT.
	• MDFT is the most systematically developed family treatment specifically for substance abuse.
	2. With the exception of MST and MDFT, few family based treatments qualify as empirically supported treatment.
	3. The field needs more investigations that match treatment approach to clinical condition. For a child with a given disorder, different types of durations of family interventions may be necessary. Studies need to investigate which treatment type is most effective at a given stage of a disorder for a patient with given characteristics.
	4. Children with psychiatric impairment often interact with multiple social systems and agencies. Given the underlying systemic perspective, family treatments lend themselves to multisystem-level intervention.
	5. Our brief review of family risk factors suggest that some negative family processes may be common across disorders.
	6. Dissemination of empirically supported treatments is one of the greatest challenges facing family treatment researchers. The process of exporting empirically validated treatments to real world clinical settings has proven far more complicated than anticipated.
	7. Incorporating findings from family developmental psychopathology and family intervention research can only improve the theory, research and treatment of mental disorders in children and adolescents.
Galanter, Glickman, and Singer (2007)	Family-based and particularly multisystem therapy, adapted for substance using adolescents, show great promise and appear to be the future direction for the most effective treatment of adolescents.
Hawkins (2009)	1. Co-occurring disorders are highly prevalent and are to be expected in every adolescent service setting.
	2. Youth with co-occurring disorders tend to have severe symptoms, multiple psychosocial and family issues, and are often engaged in numerous systems such as specialized education services, child welfare, and juvenile justice.
	3. Co-occurring disorders among adolescents are associated with difficulties in treatment engagement and retention, poor treatment outcomes, high relapse rates, and a chronic and persistent course that often continues into adulthood.
	4. Comprehensive integrated treatment programs appear to be the most effective method of treating co-occurring disorders in adolescents.
	5. Critical clinical, administrative, financial, and policy changes are necessary to support effective systems of care for youth with co-occurring disorders and improve their outcomes.

(continued)

Table 31.4 Continued

Review	Conclusions
Hogue and Liddle (2009)	1. Assessment designs should extend beyond substance use patterns, psychiatric problems, and behavioral coping skills to routinely include indicators of positive youth development that provide a fuller picture of developmental functioning and adult role-taking. 2. FBT research should renew its early intentions to examine processes of family change during the course of treatment. • The research area known as implementation science offers a world of exciting new challenges and opportunities. Indeed, given the lack of widespread use of family-based therapies in regular clinical practice settings, this research area has more urgency than it might have if such dissemination were widespread.

Liddle (2004)	1. Family-based interventions have provided a developmentally and contextually oriented conceptual framework and corresponding set of therapies. Family-based therapies are the most-tested approach for adolescent drug misuse.
	2. Family-based therapies can reduce drug abuse and correlated problem behaviors and can change multiple areas of functioning related to the genesis and continuation of drug problems, including connection to deviant peers, school-related difficulties and dysfunctional family environments.
	3. Process studies have found evidence for particular theory-based aspects of family-oriented treatment, such as the mechanism that links changes in family environment to changes in drug problems . . . Process studies are also illuminating therapy's interior and pointing to probable in-session and in-treatment processes that associate with desired short- and longer-term outcomes.
	4. Yet, we are far from realizing the benefits of these many positive developments. Barriers to widespread dissemination and adoption of effective family-based treatments are in no short supply.
	   • Most clinicians have no access to training in empirically supported [family-based] therapies
	   • Although the interventions themselves may not be optimally constructed for transportation, current data on existing services for adolescents present a gloomy picture.
	   • In the most comprehensive study of contemporary drug treatment, Grella, Joshi, and Hser (2004) notes that the greatest gap in needed and received services occurs in the family intervention area.
	   • Clinician work-force development remains a fundamental but virtually neglected area.
	   • Although studies are emerging and templates are being produced that can guide our actions, we know too little about training methods and circumstances that are optimal to helping therapists learn and practice empirically supported treatments.
	   • Powerful systemic factors, most notably reimbursement schemes that effectively block clinicians from conducting family-based interventions, must also be changed for progress to be made.

Liddle and Dakof (1995)	1. In controlled clinical trials, family therapy has been found to be more effective than other treatments in engaging and retaining adolescents in treatment and reducing their drug use. 2. Although a blanket endorsement of family treatment of drug abuse cannot be offered, on the basis of studies to date, the adolescent treatment specialty evidences considerable potential for major breakthroughs. 3. Overall, though, considering the adolescent and adult areas together, there is promising but not definitive efficacy evidence. 4. Eight issues or limitations are given detailed discussion because of their importance to the scientific evaluation of family-based intervention.

Table 31.4 Continued

Review	Conclusions
	• Incomplete or unclear reporting of experimental procedures and sample characteristics • Comorbidity and diagnosis • Follow-up data • Therapist factors, treatment manuals, and treatment integrity • Forms of bias (inadequate comparison treatments, investigator bias) • Moderators of treatment outcome • Assessment of family interaction patterns • Processes of change in family therapy
Muck et al. (2001)	1. Although many questions still remain, it is clear that much progress has been made to identify effective models of adolescent substance abuse treatment. 2. As communities begin to adopt best practices and develop systems of care for adolescents in need of substance abuse treatment, they are likely to converge in some localities with ongoing restorative justice programs. Given the preponderance of justice-involved youth in the treatment system, it is extremely important that these two fields communicate and maximize their service delivery. 3. Community-based treatment that involves establishing or supplementing a continuum of seamless care is a natural nexus for application of adolescent substance abuse treatment and restorative justice practices.
Ozechowski and Liddle (2000)	1. Known Outcomes of Treatment: • Engagement in treatment • Retention in treatment • Significant reductions in drug use • Significant reductions in behavioral problems associated with drug use • Decreases in psychiatric comorbidity • Improvements in school attendance and performance • Improvements in family functioning • In session processes associated with change 2. Unknown Outcomes of Treatment: • Risky sexual behavior • Association with drug using and delinquent peers • Long-term outcomes • Clinical significance of treatment effects • Mechanisms of change • Moderators • Gender • Ethnicity • Psychiatric comorbidity • Motivation for treatment • Parental and sibling substance use • Transportability • Cost-effectiveness 3. Solid empirical support exists for the efficacy of family-based therapy in ameliorating drug abuse, externalizing and internalizing behaviors, and symptoms of psychiatric comorbidity among drug-abusing adolescents. 4. Empirical support has been obtained for hypothesized mechanisms of change; process studies have illuminated ingredients of intervention effectiveness within key stages of treatment. 5. Dismantling and constructive research designs are needed to compare the effectiveness of different versions of family-based therapy and pinpoint the effects of specific treatment components.

(continued)

Table 31.4 Continued

Review	Conclusions
	6. Parametric strategies are needed to identify the amount, frequency, duration, and intensity of family-based therapy necessary for producing particular outcomes. 7. Therapist variables merit more focused attention . . . In particular, factors related to the quality of the therapist-adolescent/family relationship and its association with treatment retention and outcome . . . In addition, levels of therapist adherence and competence should be studied as mechanisms of treatment effectiveness and of outcomes in their own right. 8. Family-based therapy development for adolescent drug abuse can be advanced by returning to a foundational measurement and research in family-based research—observation-based details about changes in family functioning. • More than ever, family-based treatment development research requires collaborative partnerships among researchers, administrators, and providers within clinical service delivery systems.

Rowe (2012)	1. Reviews of both adolescent and adult drug abuse now consistently include family-based models among the most highly regarded and most strongly supported approaches.
	2. In the adolescent field, there has been consistent focus on validating these models and examining therapy processes with racial and ethnic minority groups.
	3. Adolescent-focused, family-based treatment research has also made strides during the last decade in examining mechanisms of change, long-term effects, and dissemination of models into practice settings.
	4. There are limitations inherent in much of the research despite considerable methodological advances.
	  • Small sample sizes still plague the field
	  • Most studies examine change up to 12 to 18 months at the most, yet drug abuse is now considered a chronic relapsing condition . . . thus, examining long-term outcomes and continuing care models are important areas of focus for research on family-based drug treatments.
	  • Additionally, much more work is needed to close the research-practice gap by elucidating the active ingredients of these models and their mechanisms of change, and to identify moderators of treatment effects so that clinicians may be better informed about which moderators are most effective for specific client populations.
	  • Perhaps the area of most consistent and urgent concern is in the dissemination of evidence-based approaches into practice.
	5. Dissemination itself needs to be an individualized, iterative and adaptive process considering many factors in integrating EBTs in usual care settings.

reinforcement approach (A-CRA) (Dennis et al., 2004; Hendriks et al., 2011). However, in Hendriks et al. (2011), MDFT was more effective in reducing substance use in more severely impaired youth, consistent with previous MDFT research (Henderson, Dakof, Greenbaum, & Liddle, 2010). The mixed findings from studies involving direct comparisons of research-supported treatments suggest a further need for research indicating under which circumstances family-based treatments are preferred over other research-supported interventions.

Another question regarding the treatment research literature to date is how family interventions compare against treatments regularly used in clinical practice. Group treatment remains the predominant treatment modality for treating adolescent substance use in regular treatment settings (Kaminer, 2005). However, note that more recent analyses of the Dennis et al. (2004) study through 30-month follow-ups have shown that the initial effectiveness of motivational enhancement therapy (MET)/CBT was not sustained (Dennis, 2005). Although the group-based MET/CBT approach achieved outcomes similar to family interventions (Dennis, 2005; Dennis et al., 2004; S. H. Godley et al., 2010), family treatments generally outperform group interventions (Barrett et al., 2001; Dakof et al., 2015; Liddle & Hogue, 2001;

Liddle, Rowe, Dakof, Henderson, & Greenbaum, 2009). In the studies that used an active group treatment comparison (Barrett et al., 2001; Dennis et al., 2004; S. H. Godley et al., 2010; Liddle & Hogue, 2001; Liddle et al., 2009; Stanger, Budney, Kamon, & Thostensen, 2009), family treatments outperformed group treatments in four out of six studies (Barrett et al., 2001; Liddle & Hogue, 2001; Liddle et al., 2009; Stanger et al., 2009). Likewise, results from the Tanner-Smith et al. (2013) meta-analysis indicated that non-CBT group/mixed treatments and TAU fared poorly in comparison to family treatments and were not demonstrably superior to no-treatment control. But studies in real-world settings do not always break in favor of the family therapy models. In the largest family therapy effectiveness study to date (Robbins et al., 2011), a high-profile and well-funded study, part of NIDA's Clinical Trials Network, Robbins and colleagues found no differences between BSFT and TAU in substance abuse outcomes. Based on those and other outcomes (e.g., Valdez, Cepeda, Parrish, Horowitz, & Kaplan, 2013), an independent scientific evaluation (The Campbell Collection) of BSFT concluded that the research base for BSFT is modest, the available studies have methodological problems, and definitive conclusions about effectiveness are "difficult, if not impossible" to make (Lindstrom et al., 2013, p. 53). We now turn our attention to some of the more notable knowledge gaps in the family treatment studies conducted to date.

Mechanisms of Action

First, although it is clear that family treatments work, our understanding of how they work is limited. Research on MST (Huey, Henggeler, Brondino, & Pickrel, 2000) and MDFT (Henderson, Rowe, Dakof, Hawes, & Liddle, 2009; Schmidt, Liddle, & Dakof, 1996), as examples, indicate that changes in family functioning—specifically parenting practices and parental monitoring—are related to changes in substance use. More research is needed, however, as mechanisms of change for most research-supported family treatments have not been tested, leaving the theoretical tenets of this specialty supported primarily by conjecture. Recent work by Deković, Asscher, Manders, Prins, and van der Laan (2012), however, points in a direction that could be replicated with other treatment models. To our knowledge, Deković et al. (2012) are the first to examine mediators of intervention effects directly during treatment. These researchers found that MST led

to improvements in parental sense of competence, which led to more effective discipline strategies, and, in turn, to decreased externalizing problems. The use of observational data has a long history in family therapy and intervention research, and more work of this nature would be welcome

Moderators of Treatment Effects

Closely aligned with mechanisms-of-change research is the need to identify groups of participants who appear to differentially benefit from or, conversely, not respond to family-based treatments. Almost all previous reviews have identified the need to study this further, yet much work remains to be done in this area. Recent work with MDFT (Henderson et al., 2010; Hendriks et al., 2011; Rigter et al., 2013) suggests that family-based treatments may be differentially effective for more severely impaired adolescents. Ryan, Stanger, Thostenson, Whitmore, and Budney (2013) report a similar finding with an integrative MET + contingency management + parent training intervention that was more effective for adolescents with disruptive behavior disorders than an MET + parent psychoeducation comparison.

A moderator of treatment that warrants further exploration is the benefit (or not) of ethnic matching between families and therapists. There is evidence that ethnic matching may improve outcomes for minority youth. For example, youth receiving multisystemic therapy from therapists of the same ethnicity as their own had a greater decrease in symptoms, stayed in treatment longer, and were more likely to be discharged for meeting their therapeutic goals (Halliday-Boykins, Schoenwald, & Letourneau, 2005). In a separate study, Flicker, Waldron, Turner, Brody, and Hops (2008) found that the benefit of ethnic matching held up for Hispanic teenagers receiving functional family therapy, when they were matched with Hispanic therapists. However, Anglo teenagers matched with Anglo therapists did not experience the same enhanced benefit. Chapman and Schoenwald (2011) examined ethnic matching and adherence in long-term outcomes for 1,979 served by 429 therapists across 45 sites. They found that, if you take adherence into account, the only outcome that was independently related to ethnic matching was the reduction of externalizing behaviors. Interestingly, adherence ratings were higher for therapists who were ethnically matched to their clients, leading to slightly better outcomes for youth in internalizing and externalizing behaviors at 1 year post treatment, and in youth criminal charges at 4 years post treatment. Taking it a step further, when taking into account problem severity and adherence in the context of ethnic matching, the outcome varies depending on the youth's ethnicity. For Caucasian and Hispanic youth receiving multisystemic therapy, levels of youth problem behaviors disrupted the therapeutic process, leading to decreased adherence, and, for Hispanic youth, decreased emotional bonding with the therapist. For African American youth, however, higher externalizing behaviors and drug use was associated with increased bonding between the youth and the therapist (Ryan, Cunningham, et al., 2013). Clearly, the issue of ethnic matching is a complex process, with ethnicity, therapist adherence, and severity of youth's problems interacting to predict youth outcomes.

Independent Replications

There are few independent replications of RCTs testing evidence-based family treatments (Sprenkle, 2012). Independent replications are needed to separate the potency of the treatments themselves from the well-functioning teams of investigators testing them. In addition to extending the generalizability of research-supported treatments to European samples, recent international studies are notable because they have been conducted by independent research teams, albeit training, certification, and supervision are provided by the treatment developers (Hendriks et al., 2011; Rigter et al., 2013; Sundell et al., 2008). The Rigter et al. (2013) study used individual therapy conducted by experienced therapists under well-defined, ongoing training and supervision (Rowe et al., 2013). An interesting paradox exists with respect to independent replications; although they are necessary to move the science forward, they may not be seen as innovative by review committees, leading to a situation in which such studies are not funded with the resources necessary to conduct the evaluations. Because international studies test treatments supported by research conducted in the United States with new populations, research conducted by independent international research teams offers the opportunity to combine tests of treatments' generalizability while also mitigating the potential of investigator allegiance bias. Therefore, such collaborations may be perceived as having more potential significance and innovation than independent replications conducted in the United States. Along this line, studies conducted in non-European nations are needed in this specialty.

Research Synthesis Across Studies and Outcomes

More work also remains on research synthesis. This issue has implications for outcome studies using multiple measures of the same construct as well as synthesizing research findings across multiple trials. While meta-analysis was once hailed as an analytic technique that would support the creation of a cumulative knowledge within the social sciences (Hunter & Schmidt, 1994), it rests on some clear limitations. Meta-analysis relies on the synthesis of summary statistics and is most useful when the original data are not available. However, given the numerous trials that have been conducted with family-based treatments, and greater expectations for data sharing and more effective options for data storage and retrieval, it is now possible to enjoy the advantages of synthesizing data provided by individual adolescents in a methodology Curran and Hussong (2009) have termed "integrative data analysis" (IDA). IDA is the "the statistical analysis of a single data set that consists of two or more separate samples that have been pooled into one" (p. 82). Kan et al. (2012) have demonstrated that IDA, as compared to meta-analysis, resulted in more powerful intervention effects while avoiding the ecological fallacy inherent in traditional meta-analysis; that is, attributing relations observed in groups to the individuals comprising those groups (Cooper & Patall, 2009). Furthermore, IDA using modern latent variable modeling methods has the potential for combining multiple outcomes both within a given study as well as across studies that may not even use the same measures (Bauer & Hussong, 2009). Greenbaum et al. (2015) have applied IDA methods to MDFT trials and found that male, African American, and White, non-Hispanic adolescents decrease their substance use (defined as a latent variable comprised of urinalysis results, timeline followback method, and self-report measures) more when receiving MDFT than active comparison treatments. Previous moderator analyses conducted in individual MDFT trials have been underpowered to discover these effects, and these results are among the first directly demonstrating ethnicity/gender subgroup differences with family-based treatments. Because several of the family treatments we have reviewed have been tested in multiple RCTs, it is quite feasible for the methods used by Greenbaum and colleagues to be extended to other family-based treatments examining other potential moderators which may be underpowered in individual studies.

Innovations and Future Directions in Family Intervention Research

The number of RCTs testing family treatments for adolescent drug abuse has rapidly expanded since the earliest trials published in the 1980s. Using the metric of the number of studies included in the current review in comparison to the first meta-analysis on the topic (Stanton & Shadish, 1997) reveals a 414% increase, from 7 to 36 studies. This growth in research is resulting in more effective treatments. While family-based treatments have historically been, and currently are, among the most effective treatments available, treatments originating from other research strains have integrated well-specified family intervention modules into their treatments and have met the field's standard for being either "well established" (Dennis et al., 2004; Esposito-Smythers, Spirito, Kahler, Hunt, & Monti, 2011) or "probably efficacious" (Henggeler, McCart, Cunningham, & Chapman, 2012; Stanger et al., 2009) treatments. Such cross-fertilization works both ways, in that contingency management was successfully integrated with MST (Henggeler, Halliday-Boykins, et al., 2006; Henggeler et al., 2012).

These developments have led us to take a more comprehensive view of family interventions in this chapter. Family treatments continue to produce notable innovations. For instance, Robbins et al. (2011) have added another level of control for allegiance effects by randomly assigning therapists to treatment conditions, and greatly enhancing the external validity of the study by conducting it in eight community substance abuse treatment agencies. But this study yielded poor outcomes for the BSFT model compared to some other BSFT studies, and this occurrence is consistent with Henggeler, Melton, Brondino, Scherer, and Hanley (1997), who found decreased effect sizes with therapists delivering MST in community settings, relative to the more carefully controlled settings of previous trials. Achieving strong effects in naturalistic settings remains a formidable challenge for family treatment researchers.

RCTs in recent years have also extended the boundaries of intervention impact by situating them in unique settings (e.g., drug courts; Dakof et al., 2015; Henggeler, Halliday-Boykins, et al., 2006) and bridging contexts such as detention and community treatment settings (Liddle, Dakof, Henderson, & Rowe, 2011). Other research has adapted treatments developed to address delinquency and substance abuse to other adolescent clinical problems such as Type I diabetes (Ellis et al., 2007), juvenile sex offending (Borduin, Schaeffer, & Heiblum, 2009), and HIV prevention (Marvel, Rowe, Colon-Perez, Diclemente, & Liddle, 2009; Prado et al., 2007).

A second example of innovative work that we hope spurs similar studies is Glisson et al. (2010), who integrated MST in the context of a broad-based implementation trial examining the impact of an organizational intervention (Availability, Responsiveness, Continuity [ARC]) designed to integrate MST into community-based mental health centers. These researchers used two levels of randomization: (1) counties receiving ARC or not, and (2) delinquent youth receiving MST or usual services, and found that the MST + ARC intervention produced the best outcomes.

Integrating Family Interventions in Routine Clinical Practice

Despite the continual growth of the field of family interventions and its notable achievements, a remaining issue facing family interventions, as well as other evidence-based approaches, is the lack of widescale use by community agencies. The predominant model for integrating evidence-based treatments into clinical practice is the training and certification model in which expert trainers train teams or an entire clinical staff in an evidence-based treatment and provide ongoing monitoring, feedback, and coaching (Miller, Yahne, Moyers, Martinez, & Pirritano, 2004). The drawbacks to this model are clinician turnover (Garner, Hunter, Modisette, Ihnes, & Godley, 2012; Knudsen, Ducharme, & Roman, 2008) and economic barriers, as achieving a critical mass of expert clinicians in an agency requires considerable resources devoted to training. It seems that additional models for achieving high-quality family treatment in routine clinical practice are necessary. An alternate model that has not yet been fully examined is training clinicians in key family interventions responsible for good outcomes that span across evidence-based approaches. Indeed, Stanger et al. (2009) demonstrated the feasibility of this model with respect to contingency management combined with parent training and in their integration of CM and MST. Henggeler et al. (2012) confine the MST interventions to engaging families in treatment. Furthermore, as mentioned earlier, well-designed implementation studies (Glisson et al., 2010) hold promise in integrating organizational and therapeutic change and thus may promote sustainability of research-supported interventions in routine clinical practice by effectively addressing organizational barriers to their existence. Therefore, it is likely that as the field of family treatment for adolescent substance abuse continues to mature, we will continue to see an expansion of such research, along with other innovations designed to impact routine clinical practice. It is our hope that future reviews will be able to highlight research expanding the reach of effective family interventions in clinical practice settings.

Conclusions

Kazdin's (1993) recommendations to devise and evaluate broadband and comprehensive interventions have been followed, as well as the NIDA behavioral therapies development framework (Kazdin, 1993; Onken, Blaine, & Boren, 1993; Rounsaville, Carroll, & Onken, 2001). But articles have criticized the nature of the substance abuse treatment development research strategy (Morgenstern & McKay, 2007) and the limitations of what has been called an FDA model in treatment research (Stiles, 1994; Stiles & Shapiro, 1989; Yeaton & Sechrest, 1981). The comprehensive treatments recommended by Kazdin and others have been referred to as "kitchen sink" approaches (Rohrbaugh, Shoham, & Racioppo, 2002). A variegated pushback is discernible against evidence-based family therapies ("acronym therapies" per Dattilio, Piercy, & Davis, 2014; Michenbaum, 2014) about their "business models" (i.e., dissemination practices) (Hogue et al., 2014) and commercialization (Rowe, 2012). Others critique the field's affection for brand names (Dattilio et al., 2014; Eisler, 2007) and "our sacred models" (vs. therapy principles, common factors) (Sprenkle & Blow, 2004). An alternative to whole evidence-based therapy models, the modular approach of Chorpita, Weisz, Daleiden, and colleagues, has empirical support for some child and adolescent disorders (Chorpita et al., 2013), including anxiety and depression, but not for substance abuse disorders, as far as we know.

Controversies have erupted about the correct conclusions to be drawn from family-based treatment research. The expansion and influence of independent scientific entities and the judgments contained in their reports have, on occasion, collided with the growth of dissemination organizations that conduct training in particular evidence-based therapies. For example, numerous other reviews have concluded otherwise. The Cochrane Collaboration (Littell, Popa, & Forsythe, 2005) concluded that

MST is not consistently more effective than other alternatives for youth with social, emotional, or behavioral problems. The review challenged the well-established effectiveness of MST, as well as asserting that the decision to adopt MST in real-world settings must be made for reasons other than its empirically demonstrated effectiveness in comparison to other services. The response of MST developer Henggeler and colleagues (Henggeler, Schoenwald, Borduin, & Swenson, 2006) was fierce and instructive in several ways. Other papers also notable for their candidness kept the discussion alive and broadened it as well (Gambrill & Littell, 2010; Henggeler, 2004; Littell, 2005, 2006).

In another report addressing evidence-based practice dissemination, the Campbell Collaboration report on BSFT (Lindstrom et al., 2013) concludes that "The current landscape of family therapy approaches for treatment of youth drug use shows that many initiatives have been tried. A certain inconsistency seems to be developing: while existing BSFT programs have not yet been evaluated properly, new BSFT interventions continue to surface. This is not only costly, it is also risky, as initiatives backed only by unclear research could ultimately be damaging" (Lindstrom et al., 2013, p. 53). On the basis of these reports alone, the conflict level within the referenced landscape has increased considerably. Whether or not the events and publications we refer to here will influence dissemination practices remains to be seen. As noted, there are now many national and international evidence-based practice registries that are evaluating and creating lists of evidence-based models. One bottom line is that future reviews will have additional content to cover in addition to the methodological strengths and weaknesses of available studies.

Notes

1. A table summarizing the presence or absence of these attributes, as well as the proportion of studies reporting these attributes, may be obtained by visiting www.oxfordhandbooks.com
2. The specific domains were conduct disorder, drug abuse, psychoeducation for major mental illness, couple distress, alcoholism, relationship education, depression, childhood and adolescent disorders (other), chronic illness, and interpersonal violence.

References

Akram, Y., & Copello, A. (2013). Family-based interventions for substance misuse: A systematic review of reviews. *Lancet*, *382*, S24.

Armstrong, T. D., & Costello, E. J. (2002). Community studies on adolescent substance use, abuse, or dependence and psychiatric comorbidity. *Journal of Consulting and Clinical Psychology*, *70*(6), 1224.

Austin, A. M., Macgowan, M. J., & Wagner, E. F. (2005). Effective family-based interventions for adolescents with substance abuse problems: A systematic review. *Research on Social Work Practice, 15*, 67-83.

Azrin, N. H., Donohue, B., Teichner, G. A., Crum, T., Howell, J., & DeCato, L. A. (2001). A controlled evaluation and description of individual-cognitive problem solving and family-behavior therapies in dually-diagnosed conduct-disordered and substance-dependent youth. *Journal of Child and Adolescent Substance Abuse, 11*(1), 1–43. doi:10.1300/J029v11n01_01

Baldwin, S. A., Christian, S., Berkeljon, A., Shadish, W. R., & Bean, R. (2012). The effects of family therapies for adolescent delinquency and substance abuse: A meta-analysis. *Journal of Marital and Family Therapy, 38*(1), 281–304. doi:10.1111/j.1752-0606.2011.00248.x

Barrett, H., Slesnick, N., Brody, J. L., Turner, C. W., & Peterson, T. R. (2001). Treatment outcomes for adolescent substance abuse at 4- and 7-month assessments. *Journal of Consulting and Clinical Psychology, 69*(5), 802–813. doi:10.1037/0022-006X.69.5.802

Bauer, D. J., & Hussong, A. M. (2009). Psychometric approaches for developing commensurate measures across independent studies: Traditional and new models. *Psychological Methods, 14*(2), 101–125. doi:10.1037/a0015583

Becker, S. J., & Curry, J. F. (2008). Outpatient interventions for adolescent substance abuse: A quality of evidence review. *Journal of Consulting and Clinical Psychology, 76*(4), 531–543. doi:10.1037/0022-006X.76.4.531

Borduin, C. M., Schaeffer, C. M., & Heiblum, N. (2009). A randomized clinical trial of multisystemic therapy with juvenile sexual offenders: Effects on youth social ecology and criminal activity. *Journal of Consulting and Clinical Psychology, 77*(1), 26–37. doi:10.1037/a0013035

Brouwers, M. C., Johnston, M. E., Charette, M. L., Hanna, S. E., Jadad, A. R., & Browman, G. P. (2005). Evaluating the role of quality assessment of primary studies in systematic reviews of cancer practice guidelines. *BMC Medical Research Methodology, 5*(1), 8.

Brown, S. A. (2004). Measuring youth outcomes from alcohol and drug treatment. *Addiction, 99*(Suppl. 2), 38–46. doi:10.1111/j.1360-0443.2004.00853.x

Brown, S. A., McGue, M., Maggs, J., Schulenberg, J., Hingson, R., Swartzwelder, S., . . . Murphy, S. (2008). A developmental perspective on alcohol and youths 16 to 20 years of age. *Pediatrics, 121*(Suppl. 4), S290–S310. doi:10.1542/peds.2007-2243D

Carroll, K. M., & Rounsaville, B. J. (2003). Bridging the gap: A hybrid model to link efficacy and effectiveness research in substance abuse treatment. *Psychiatric Services, 54*(3), 333–339. doi:10.1176/appi.ps.54.3.333

CASA. (2011). Adolescent substance use: America's # 1 public health problem. In *National Center on Alcohol and Substance Abuse* (Ed.), New York, NY: Columbia University Press.

Catalano, R. F., Hawkins, J. D., Wells, E. A., & Miller, J. L. (1990). Evaluation of the effectiveness of adolescent drug abuse treatment, assessment of risks for relapse, and promising approaches for relapse prevention. *International Journal of the Addictions, 25*(9A–10A), 1085–1140.

Chapman, J. E., & Schoenwald, S. K. (2011). Ethnic similarity, therapist adherence, and long-term multisystemic therapy outcomes. *Journal of Emotional and Behavioral Disorders, 19*(1), 3–16. doi:10.1177/1063426610376773

Chorpita, B. F., Weisz, J. R., Daleiden, E. L., Schoenwald, S. K., Palinkas, L. A., Miranda, J., . . . Gibbons, R. D. (2013). Long-term outcomes for the Child STEPs randomized effectiveness trial: A comparison of modular and standard treatment designs with usual care. *Journal of Consulting and Clinical Psychology, 81*(6), 999–1009. doi:10.1037/a0034200

Cooper, H., & Patall, E. A. (2009). The relative benefits of meta-analysis conducted with individual participant data versus aggregated data. *Psychological Methods, 14*(2), 165–176. doi:10.1037/a0015565

Corte, C., & Zucker, R. A. (2008). Self-concept disturbances: Cognitive vulnerability for early drinking and early drunkenness in adolescents at high risk for alcohol problems. *Addictive Behaviors, 33*(10), 1282–1290. doi:10.1016/j.addbeh.2008.06.002

Costello, E. J., Foley, D. L., & Angold, A. (2006). 10-year research update review: The epidemiology of child and adolescent psychiatric disorders: II. Developmental epidemiology. *Journal of the American Academy of Child and Adolescent Psychiatry, 45*(1), 8–25.

Cranford, J. A., Zucker, R. A., Jester, J. M., Puttler, L. I., & Fitzgerald, H. E. (2010). Parental alcohol involvement and adolescent alcohol expectancies predict alcohol involvement in male adolescents. *Psychology of Addictive Behaviors, 24*(3), 386–396. doi:10.1037/a0019801

Curran, P. J., & Hussong, A. M. (2009). Integrative data analysis: The simultaneous analysis of multiple data sets. *Psychological Methods, 14*(2), 81–100. doi:10.1037/a0015914

Dakof, G. A., Henderson, C. E., Rowe, C. L., Boustani, M., Greenbaum, P. E., Wang, W., . . . Liddle, H. A. (2015). A randomized controlled trial of Multidimensional Family Therapy in juvenile drug court. *Journal of Family Psychology, 29*, 232-241. doi: 10.1037.fam0000053

Dattilio, F. M., Piercy, F. P., & Davis, S. D. (2014). The divide between "evidenced-based" approaches and practitioners of traditional theories of family therapy. *Journal of Marital and Family Therapy, 40*(1), 5–16. doi:10.1111/jmft.12032

Deas, D., & Thomas, S. E. (2001). An overview of controlled studies of adolescent substance abuse treatment. *American Journal on Addictions, 10*(2), 178–189. doi:10.1080/105504901750227822

Deković, M., Asscher, J. J., Manders, W. A., Prins, P. J. M., & van der Laan, P. (2012). Within-intervention change: Mediators of intervention effects during multisystemic therapy. *Journal of Consulting and Clinical Psychology, 80*(4), 574–587. doi:10.1037/a0028482

Dembo, R., Wothke, W., Livingston, S., & Schmeidler, J. (2002). The impact of a family empowerment intervention on juvenile offender heavy drinking: A latent growth model analysis. *Substance Use and Misuse, 37*(11), 1359–1390. doi:10.1081/JA-120014082

Dennis, M. L. (2005). Cannabis Youth Treatment (CYT) Trials: 12 and 30 month main findings. Paper presented at the Presentation for the Adolescent Training Initiative, Bloomington, IL.

Dennis, M. L., Godley, S. H., Diamond, G., Tims, F. M., Babor, T., Donaldson, J., . . . Funk, R. (2004). The Cannabis Youth Treatment (CYT) Study: Main findings from two randomized trials. *Journal of Substance Abuse Treatment, 27*(3), 197–213. doi:10.1016/j.jsat.2003.09.005

Diamond, G., & Josephson, J. (2005). Family-based treatment research: A 10-year update. *Journal of the American Academy of Child and Adolescent Psychiatry, 44,* 872-887.

Eisler, I. (2007). Treatment models, brand names, acronyms and evidence-based practice. *Journal of Family Therapy, 29*(3), 183–185.

Ellis, D. A., Podolski, C-L., Frey, M., Naar-King, S., Wang, B., & Moltz, K. (2007). The role of parental monitoring in adolescent health outcomes: Impact on regimen adherence in youth with type 1 diabetes. *Journal of Pediatric Psychology, 32*(8), 907–917. doi:10.1093/jpepsy/jsm009

Esposito-Smythers, C., Spirito, A., Kahler, C. W., Hunt, J., & Monti, P. (2011). Treatment of co-occurring substance abuse and suicidality among adolescents: A randomized trial. *Journal of Consulting and Clinical Psychology, 79*(6), 728–739. doi:10.1037/a0026074

Feingold, A. (2009). Effect sizes for growth-modeling analysis for controlled clinical trials in the same metric as for classical analysis. *Psychological Methods, 14*(1), 43–53. doi:10.1037/a0014699

Fixsen, D. L., Blase, K. A., Metz, A. J., & Naoom, S. F. (2014). Producing high levels of treatment integrity in practice: A focus on preparing practitioners. In L. M. Sanetti & T. R. Kratochwill (Eds.) *Treatment integrity: A foundation for evidence-based practice in applied psychology* (pp. 185-201). Washington, DC: American Psychological Association.

Flicker, S. M., Waldron, H. B., Turner, C. W., Brody, J. L., & Hops, H. (2008). Ethnic matching and treatment outcome with Hispanic and Anglo substance-abusing adolescents in family therapy. *Journal of Family Psychology, 22*(3), 439–447. doi:10.1037/0893-3200.22.3.439

Friedman, A. S. (1989). Family therapy vs. parent groups: Effects on adolescent drug abusers. *American Journal of Family Therapy, 17,* 335-347.

Galanter, M., Glickman, L., & Singer, D. (2007). An overview of outpatient treatment of adolescent substance abuse. *Substance Abuse, 28,* 51-58.

Gambrill, E., & Littell, J. H. (2010). Do haphazard reviews provide sound directions for dissemination efforts? *American Psychologist, 65*(9), 927.

Garner, B. R., Hunter, B. D., Modisette, K. C., Ihnes, P. C., & Godley, S. H. (2012). Treatment staff turnover in organizations implementing evidence-based practices: Turnover rates and their association with client outcomes. *Journal of Substance Abuse Treatment, 42*(2), 134–142. doi:10.1016/j.jsat.2011.10.015

Glisson, C., Schoenwald, S. K., Hemmelgarn, A., Green, P., Dukes, D., Armstrong, K. S., & Chapman, J. E. (2010). Randomized trial of MST and ARC in a two-level evidence-based treatment implementation strategy. *Journal of Consulting and Clinical Psychology, 78*(4), 537–550. doi:10.1037/a0019160

Godley, M. D., Godley, S. H., Dennis, M. L., Funk, R., & Passetti, L. L. (2002). Preliminary outcomes from the assertive continuing care experiment for adolescents discharged from residential treatment. *Journal of Substance Abuse Treatment, 23*(1), 21–32.

Godley, M. D., Godley, S. H., Dennis, M. L., Funk, R. R., & Passetti, L. L. (2007). The effect of assertive continuing care on continuing care linkage, adherence and abstinence following residential treatment for adolescents with substance use disorders. *Addiction, 102*(1), 81–93.

Godley, S. H., Garner, B. R., Passetti, L. L., Funk, R. R., Dennis, M. L., & Godley, M. D. (2010). Adolescent outpatient treatment and continuing care: Main findings from a randomized clinical trial. *Drug and alcohol dependence, 110*(1–2), 44–54. doi:10.1016/j.drugalcdep.2010.02.003

Greenbaum, P. E., Wang, W. W., Henderson, C. E., Kan, L., Hall, K., Dakof, G. A., & Liddle, H. A. (2015). Integrative data analysis of Multidimensional Family Therapy randomized clinical trials: Moderator effects of sex and ethnicity. *Journal of Family Psychology.* doi:10.1037/fam0000127

Grella, C. E., Hser, Y-I., Joshi, V., & Douglas Anglin, M. (1999). Patient histories, retention, and outcome models for younger and older adults in DATOS. *Drug and Alcohol Dependence, 57*(2), 151–166.

Grella, C. E., Johsi, V., & Hser, Y-I. (2004). Effects of comorbidity on treatment processes and outcomes among adolescents in Drug Treatment Programs. *Journal of Child & Adolescent Substance Abuse, 13,* 13-31.

Halliday-Boykins, C. A., Schoenwald, S. K., & Letourneau, E. J. (2005). Caregiver-therapist ethnic similarity predicts youth outcomes from an empirically based treatment. *Journal of Consulting and Clinical Psychology, 73*(5), 808–818. doi:10.1037/0003-066X.42.1.37

Hawkins, E. H. (2009). A tale of two systems: Co-occurring mental health and substance abuse disorders treatment for adolescents. *Annual Review of Psychology, 60,* 197-227.

Henderson, C. E., Dakof, G. A., Greenbaum, P. E., & Liddle, H. A. (2010). Effectiveness of multidimensional family therapy with higher severity substance-abusing adolescents: Report from two randomized controlled trials. *Journal of Consulting and Clinical Psychology, 78*(6), 885–897. doi:10.1037/a0020620

Henderson, C. E., Rowe, C. L., Dakof, G. A., Hawes, S. W., & Liddle, H. A. (2009). Parenting practices as mediators of treatment effects in an early-intervention trial of multidimensional family therapy. *American Journal of Drug and Alcohol Abuse, 35*(4), 220–226. doi:10.1080/00952990903005890

Hendriks, V., van der Schee, E., & Blanken, P. (2011). Treatment of adolescents with a cannabis use disorder: Main findings of a randomized controlled trial comparing multidimensional family therapy and cognitive behavioral therapy in The Netherlands. *Drug and Alcohol Dependence, 119*(1–2), 64–71. doi:10.1016/j.drugalcdep.2011.05.021

Hendriks, V., van der Schee, E., & Blanken, P. (2012). Matching adolescents with a cannabis use disorder to multidimensional family therapy or cognitive behavioral therapy: Treatment effect moderators in a randomized controlled trial. *Drug and Alcohol Dependence, 125*(1), 119–126.

Henggeler, S. W. (1999). Multisystemic therapy: An overview of clinical procedures, outcomes, and policy implications. *Child Psychology & Psychiatry Review, 4,* 2-10.

Henggeler, S. W. (2004). Decreasing effect sizes for effectiveness studies-implications for the transport of evidence-based treatments: comment on Curtis, Ronan, and Borduin (2004). *Journal of Family Psychology, 18*(3), 420–423.

Henggeler, S. W., Borduin, C. M., Melton, G. B., & Mann, B. J. (1991). Effects of multisystemic therapy on drug use and abuse in serious juvenile offenders: A progress report from two outcome studies. *Family Dynamics of Addiction Quarterly, 1,* 40-51.

Henggeler, S. W., Clingempeel, W. G., Brondino, M. J., & Pickrel, S. G. (2002). Four-year follow-up of multisystemic therapy with substance-abusing and substance-dependent juvenile offenders. *Journal of the American Academy of Child and Adolescent Psychiatry, 41*(7), 868–874. doi:10.1097/00004583-200207000-00021

Henggeler, S. W., Halliday-Boykins, C. A., Cunningham, P. B., Randall, J., Shapiro, S. B., & Chapman, J. E. (2006). Juvenile drug court: Enhancing outcomes by integrating evidence-based treatments. *Journal of Consulting and Clinical Psychology*, 74(1), 42–54. doi:10.1037/0022-006X.74.1.42

Henggeler, S. W., McCart, M. R., Cunningham, P. B., & Chapman, J. E. (2012). Enhancing the effectiveness of juvenile drug courts by integrating evidence-based practices. *Journal of Consulting and Clinical Psychology*, 80(2), 264–275. doi:10.1111/j.1752-0606.2011.00244.x

Henggeler, S. W., Melton, G. B., Brondino, M. J., Scherer, D. G., & Hanley, J. H. (1997). Multisystemic therapy with violent and chronic juvenile offenders and their families: The role of treatment fidelity in successful dissemination. *Journal of Consulting and Clinical Psychology*, 65(5), 821–833. doi:10.1037/0022-006X.65.5.821

Henggeler, S. W., Schoenwald, S. K., Borduin, C. M., & Swenson, C. C. (2006). Methodological critique and meta-analysis as Trojan horse. *Children and Youth Services Review*, 28(4), 447–457.

Hogue, A., Henderson, C. E., Ozechowski, T. J., & Robbins, M. S. (2014). Evidence base on outpatient behavioral treatments for adolescent substance use: Updates and recommendations 2007-2013. *Journal of Clinical Child and Adolescent Psychology*, 43(5), 695–720.

Hogue, A., & Liddle, H. A. (2009). Family-based treatment for adolescent substance abuse: Controlled trials and new horizons in services research. *Journal of Family Therapy*, 31(2), 126–154. doi:10.1111/j.1467-6427.2009.00459.x

Hopewell, S., Ravaud, P., Baron, G., & Boutron, I. (2012). Effect of editors' implementation of CONSORT guidelines on the reporting of abstracts in high impact medical journals: Interrupted time series analysis. *British Medical Journal*, 345(7864), 1–7.

Huey, S. J., Jr., Henggeler, S. W., Brondino, M. J., & Pickrel, S. G. (2000). Mechanisms of change in multisystemic therapy: Reducing delinquent behavior through therapist adherence and improved family and peer functioning. *Journal of Consulting and Clinical Psychology*, 68(3), 451–467. doi:10.1037/0022-006X.68.3.451

Huey, S. J., Jr., & Polo, A. J. (2008). Evidence-based psychosocial treatments for ethnic minority youth. *Journal of Clinical Child and Adolescent Psychology*, 262-301.

Hunter, J. E., & Schmidt, F. L. (1994). *Correcting for sources of artificial variation across studies*. New York, NY: Russell Sage Foundation.

Joanning, H., Quinn, W., Thomas, F., & Mullen, R. (1992). Treating adolescent drug abuse: A comparison of family systems therapy, group therapy, and family drug education. *Journal of marital and family therapy*, 18(4), 345–356.

Jüni, P., Altman, D. G., & Egger, M. (2001). Assessing the quality of controlled clinical trials. *British Medical Journal*, 323(7303), 42–46.

Kaminer, Y. (2005). Challenges and opportunities of group therapy for adolescent substance abuse: A critical review. *Addictive Behaviors*, 30(9), 1765–1774. doi:10.1016/j.addbeh.2005.07.002

Kan, L., Henderson, C. E., Wevodau, A., Greenbaum, P. E., Wang, W., & Liddle, H. A. (2012, May). A comparison of meta-analytic and integrative data analysis approaches to evaluating multidimensional family therapy substance use outcomes. Poster presented at the Annual Meeting of the Society for Prevention Research, Washington, DC.

Kazdin, A. E. (1993). Psychotherapy for children and adolescents: Current progress and future research directions. *American Psychologist*, 48(6), 644.

Kendall, P. C., & Flannery-Schroeder, E. C. (1998). Methodological issues in treatment research for anxiety disorders in youth. *Journal of Abnormal Child Psychology*, 26, 27-38.

Kessler, R. C., Merikangas, K. R., Berglund, P., Eaton, W. W., Koretz, D. S., & Walters, E. E. (2003). Mild disorders should not be eliminated from the DSM-V. *Archives of general psychiatry*, 60(11), 1117–1122. doi:10.1001/archpsyc.60.11.1117

Knudsen, H. K., Ducharme, L. J., & Roman, P. M. (2008). Clinical supervision, emotional exhaustion, and turnover intention: A study of substance abuse treatment counselors in the Clinical Trials Network of the National Institute on Drug Abuse. *Journal of Substance Abuse Treatment*, 35(4), 387–395. doi:10.1016/j.jsat.2008.02.003

Ladd, B. O., McCrady, B. S., Manuel, J. K., & Campbell, W. (2010). Improving the quality of reporting alcohol outcome studies: Effects of the CONSORT statement. *Addictive Behaviors*, 35(7), 660–666. doi:10.1016/j.addbeh.2010.02.009

Latimer, W. W., Winters, K. C., D'Zurilla, T., & Nichols, M. (2003). Integrated family and cognitive-behavioral therapy for adolescent substance abusers: A stage I efficacy study. *Drug and Alcohol Dependence*, 71(3), 303–317.

Lewis, R. A., Piercy, F. P., Sprenkle, D. H., & Trepper, T. S. (1990). Family-based interventions for helping drug-abusing adolescents. *Journal of Adolescent Research*, 5(1), 82–95.

Liddle, H. A. (2004). Family-based therapies for adolescent alcohol and drug abuse: Research contributions and future research needs. *Addiction*, 99(Suppl 2), 76-92.

Liddle, H. A., & Dakof, G. A. (1995). Efficacy of family therapy for drug abuse: Promising but not definitive. *Journal of Marital and Family Therapy*, 21(4), 511–543.

Liddle, H. A., Dakof, G. A., Henderson, C. E., & Rowe, C. L. (2011). Implementation outcomes of multidimensional family therapy-detention to community: A reintegration program for drug-using juvenile detainees. *International Journal of Offender Therapy and Comparative Criminology*, 55(4), 587–604. doi:10.1177/0306624X10366960

Liddle, H. A., Dakof, G. A., Parker, K., Diamond, G. S., Barrett, K., & Tejeda, M. (2001). Multidiminsional family therapy for adolescent drug abuse: Results of a randomized clinical trial. *The American Journal of Drug and Alcohol Abuse*, 27, 651-688.

Liddle, H. A., Dakof, G. A., Rowe, C. L., Henderson, C. E., Greenbaum, P., & Alberga, L. (2012, April). Is it possible to create an effective outpatient alternative to residential treatment? Paper presented at the 2012 Joint Meeting on Adolescent Treatment Effectiveness, Washington, DC.

Liddle, H. A., Dakof, G. A., Turner, R. M., Henderson, C. E., & Greenbaum, P. E. (2008). Treating adolescent drug abuse: A randomized trial comparing multidimensional family therapy and cognitive behavior therapy. *Addiction*, 103(10), 1660–1670. doi:10.1111/j.1360-0443.2008.02274.x

Liddle, H. A., & Hogue, A. (2001). Multidimensional family therapy for adolescent substance abuse. In E. Wagner & H. Waldron (Eds.), *Innovations in adolescent substance abuse interventions* (pp. 229–261). Amsterdam, The Netherlands: Pergamon/Elsevier Science.

Liddle, H. A., Rowe, C. L., Dakof, G. A., Henderson, C. E., & Greenbaum, P. E. (2009). Multidimensional family therapy for young adolescent substance abuse: Twelve-month outcomes of a randomized controlled trial. *Journal of Consulting and Clinical Psychology, 77*(1), 12–25. doi:10.1037/a0014160

Lindstrom, M., Rasmussen, P. S., Kowalski, K., Filges, T., & Klint Jorgensen, A-M. (2013). Family behavior therapy for young people in treatment for illicit non-opioid drug use. *The Campbell Collaboration, 9*(7). http://www.campbellcollaboration.org/lib/project/210/

Littell, J. H. (2005). Lessons from a systematic review of effects of multisystemic therapy. *Children and Youth Services Review, 27*(4), 445–463.

Littell, J. H. (2006). The case for multisystemic therapy: Evidence or orthodoxy? *Children and Youth Services Review, 28*(4), 458–472.

Littell, J. H., Popa, M., & Forsythe, B. (2005). Multisystemic therapy for social, emotional, and behavioural problems in youth aged 10-17. *Cochrane Database of Systematic Reviews*, (4), CD004797.

López-Viets, V. C., Aarons, G. A., Ellingstad, T. P., & Brown, S. A. (2003). Race and ethnic differences in attempts to cut down or quit substance use in a high school sample. *Journal of Ethnicity in Substance Abuse, 2*(3), 83–103. doi:10.1300/J233v02n03_05

Marvel, F., Rowe, C. L., Colon-Perez, L., Diclemente, R. J., & Liddle, H. A. (2009). Multidimensional family therapy HIV/STD risk-reduction intervention: An integrative family-based model for drug-involved juvenile offenders. *Family Process, 48*(1), 69–84. doi:10.1111/j.1545-5300.2009.01268.x

McGillicuddy, N. B., Rychtarik, R. G., Duquette, J. A., & Morsheimer, E. T. (2001). Development of a skill training program for parents of substance-abusing adolescents. *Journal of Substance Abuse Treatment, 20*(1), 59–68.

Meier, M. H., Caspi, A., Ambler, A., Harrington, H., Houts, R., Keefe, R. S., . . . Moffitt, T. E. (2012). Persistent cannabis users show neuropsychological decline from childhood to midlife. *Proceedings of the National Academy of Sciences USA, 109*(40), E2657–E2664.

Michenbaum, D. (2014). Workshop description. *The Psychotherapy Networker*.

Miller, W. R., & Wilbourne, P. L. (2002). Mesa Grande: A methodological analysis of clinical trials of treatment for alcohol use disorders. *Addiction, 97*(3), 265–277. doi:10.1046/j.1360-0443.2002.00019.x

Miller, W. R., Yahne, C. E., Moyers, T. B., Martinez, J., & Pirritano, M. (2004). A randomized trial of methods to help clinicians learn motivational interviewing. *Journal of Consulting and Clinical Psychology, 72*(6), 1050–1062. doi:10.1037/0022-006X.72.6.1050

Moja, L. P., Telaro, E., D'Amico, R., Moschetti, I., Coe, L., & Liberati, A. (2005). Assessment of methodological quality of primary studies by systematic reviews: Results of the metaquality cross sectional study. *British Medical Journal, 330*(7499), 1053. doi:10.1136/bmj.38414.515938.8F

Morgenstern, J., & McKay, J. R. (2007). Rethinking the paradigms that inform behavioral treatment research for substance use disorders. *Addiction, 102*(9), 1377–1389.

Muck, R., Zempolich, K. A., Titus, J. C., Fishman, M., Godley, M. D., & Schwebel, R. (2001). An overview of the effectiveness of adolescent substance abuse treatment models. *Youth & Society, 33*, 143-168.

National Registry of Evidence-Based Programs and Practices (NREPP). (2014). Mental Health Services Administration.

The national registry of evidence-based programs and practices (NREPP): Retrieved from http://www.nrep.samhsa.gov/.

O'Connor, A. (2013, December 18). Increasing marijuana use in high school is reported. *The New York Times*. Retrieved October 2015, from http://well.blogs.nytimes.com/2013/12/18/growing-marijuana-use-among-teenagers-spurs-concerns/?_r=0

Odgaard, E. C., & Fowler, R. L. (2010). Confidence intervals for effect sizes: Compliance and clinical significance in the Journal of Consulting and Clinical Psychology. *Journal of Consulting and Clinical Psychology, 78*(3), 287–297. doi:10.1037/a0019294

Onken, L. S., Blaine, J. D., & Boren, J. J. (1993). Behavioral treatments for drug abuse and dependence: Progress, potential, and promise. *Behavioral Treatments for Drug Abuse and Dependence, 137*, 1-4.

Ozechowski, T. J., & Liddle, H. A. (2000). Family-based therapy for adolescent drug abuse: Knowns and unknowns. *Clinical Child and Family Psychology Review, 3*, 269-298.

Prado, G., Pantin, H., Briones, E., Schwartz, S. J., Feaster, D., Huang, S., . . . Szapocznik, J. (2007). A randomized controlled trial of a parent-centered intervention in preventing substance use and HIV risk behaviors in Hispanic adolescents. *Journal of Consulting and Clinical Psychology, 75*(6), 914–926. doi:10.1037/0022-006X.75.6.914

Raudenbush, S. W., & Bryk, A. S. (2002). *Hierarchical linear models: Applications and data analysis methods* (Vol. 1). Thousand Oaks, CA: Sage.

Rigter, H., Henderson, C. E., Pelc, I., Tossmann, P., Phan, O., Hendriks, V., . . . Rowe, C. L. (2013). Multidimensional family therapy lowers the rate of cannabis dependence in adolescents: A randomised controlled trial in Western European outpatient settings. *Drug and Alcohol Dependence, 130*(1–3), 85–93. doi:10.1016/j.drugalcdep.2012.10.013

Robbins, M. S., Feaster, D. J., Horigian, V. E., Rohrbaugh, M., Shoham, V., Bachrach, K., . . . Szapocznik, J. (2011). Brief strategic family therapy versus treatment as usual: Results of a multisite randomized trial for substance using adolescents. *Journal of Consulting and Clinical Psychology, 79*(6), 713–727. doi:10.1037/a0025477

Robbins, M. S., Szapocznik, J., Dillon, F. R., Turner, C. W., Mitrani, V. B., & Feaster, D. J. (2008). The efficacy of structural ecosystems therapy with drug-abusing/dependent African American and Hispanic American adolescents. *Journal of Family Psychology, 22*(1), 51.

Rohrbaugh, M. J., Shoham, V., & Racioppo, M. W. (2002). Toward family level attributex treatment interaction research. In H. A. Liddle, D. A. Santisteban, R. F. Levant, & J. H. Bray (Eds.), *Family psychology: Science-based interventions* (pp. 215–237). Washington, DC: American Psychological Association.

Rounsaville, B. J., Carroll, K. M., & Onken, L. S. (2001). A stage model of behavioral therapies research: Getting started and moving on from stage I. *Clinical Psychology: Science and Practice, 8*(2), 133–142.

Rowe, C. L. (2012). Family therapy for drug abuse: Review and updates 2003–2010. *Journal of Marital and Family Therapy, 38*(1), 59–81. doi:10.1111/j.1752-0606.2011.00280.x

Rowe, C. L., Rigter, H., Henderson, C. E., Gantner, A., Mos, K., Nielsen, P., & Phan, O. (2013). Implementation fidelity of multidimensional family therapy in an international trial. *Journal of Substance Abuse Treatment, 44*(4), 391–399. doi:10.1016/j.jsat.2012.08.225

Ryan, S. R., Cunningham, P. B., Foster, S. L., Brennan, P. A., Brock, R. L., & Whitmore, E. (2013). Predictors of therapist adherence and emotional bond in multisystemic therapy: Testing ethnicity as a moderator. *Journal of Child and Family Studies, 22*(1), 122–136. doi:10.1007/s10826-012-9638-5

Ryan, S. R., Stanger, C., Thostenson, J., Whitmore, J. J., & Budney, A. J. (2013). The impact of disruptive behavior disorder on substance use treatment outcome in adolescents. *Journal of Substance Abuse Treatment, 44*(5), 506–514. doi:10.1016/j.jsat.2012.11.003

Santisteban, D. A., Coatsworth, J. D., Perez-Vidal, A., Kurtines, W. M., Schwartz, S. J., LaPerriere, A., & Szapocznik, J. (2003). Efficacy of brief strategic family therapy in modifying Hispanic adolescent behavior problems and substance use. *Journal of Family Psychology, 17*(1), 121.

Santisteban, D. A., & Mena, M. P. (2009). Culturally informed and flexible family-based treatment for adolescents: A tailored and integrative treatment for Hispanic youth. *Family Process, 48*, 253-268.

Santisteban, D. A., Mena, M. P., & McCabe, B. E. (2011). Preliminary results for an adaptive family treatment for drug abuse in Hispanic youth. *Journal of Family Psychology, 25*(4), 610.

Schmidt, S. E., Liddle, H. A., & Dakof, G. A. (1996). Changes in parenting practices and adolescent drug abuse during multidimensional family therapy. *Journal of Family Psychology, 10*(1), 12–27. doi:10.1037/0893-3200.10.1.12

Slesnick, N., Erdem, G., Bartle-Haring, S., & Brigham, G. S. (2013). Intervention with substance-abusing runaway adolescents and their families: Results of a randomized clinical trial. *Journal of Consulting and Clinical Psychology, 81*(4), 600–614. doi:10.1037/a0033463

Slesnick, N., & Prestopnik, J. L. (2005). Ecologically based family therapy outcome with substance abusing runaway adolescents. *Journal of Adolescence, 28*(2), 277–298.

Slesnick, N., & Prestopnik, J. L. (2009). Comparison of family therapy outcome with alcohol-abusing, runaway adolescents. *Journal of Marital and Family Therapy, 35*(3), 255–277.

Smith, D. C., Hall, J. A., Williams, J. K., An, H., & Gotman, N. (2006). Comparative efficacy of family and group treatment for adolescent substance abuse. *American Journal on Addictions, 15*(s1), s131–s136.

Smith, D. K., Chamberlain, P., & Eddy, J. M. (2010). Preliminary support for multidimensional treatment foster care in reducing substance use in delinquent boys. *Journal of Child and Adolescent Substance Abuse, 19*(4), 343–358.

Smith, D. C., & Hall, J. A. (2007). Strengths-oriented referrals for teens (SORT): Giving balanced feedback to teens and families. *Health & Social Work, 32*, 69-72.

Sprenkle, D. H. (2012). Intervention research in couple and family therapy: A methodological and substantive review and an introduction to the special issue. *Journal of Marital and Family Therapy, 38*(1), 3–29. doi: 10.1111/j.1365-2214.2007.00747.x10.1111/j.1752-0606.2011.00271.x

Sprenkle, D. H., & Blow, A. J. (2004). Common factors and our sacred models. *Journal of Marital and Family Therapy, 30*(2), 113–129.

Squeglia, L. M., Jacobus, J., & Tapert, S. F. (2009). The influence of substance use on adolescent brain development. *Clinical EEG and Neuroscience, 40*(1), 31–38.

Stanger, C., Budney, A. J., Kamon, J. L., & Thostensen, J. (2009). A randomized trial of contingency management for adolescent marijuana abuse and dependence. *Drug and Alcohol Dependence, 105*(3), 240–247. doi:10.1016/j.drugalcdep.2009.07.009

Stanton, M. D., & Shadish, W. R. (1997). Outcome, attrition, and family–couples treatment for drug abuse: A meta-analysis and review of the controlled, comparative studies. *Psychological Bulletin, 122*(2), 170–191. doi:10.1037/0033-2909.122.2.170

Steinberg, L., Fletcher, A., & Darling, N. (1994). Parental monitoring and peer influences on adolescent substance use. *Pediatrics, 93*(6), 1060–1064.

Stiles, W. B. (1994). Drugs, recipes, babies, bathwater, and psychotherapy process-outcome relations. *Journal of Consulting and Clinical Psychology, 62*(5), 955-959.

Stiles, W. B., & Shapiro, D. A. (1989). Abuse of the drug metaphor in psychotherapy process-outcome research. *Clinical Psychology Review, 9*(4), 521–543.

Szapocznik, J., Kurtines, W. M., Foote, F., Perez-Vidal, A., & Hervis, O. (1986). Conjoint versus one-person family therapy: Further evidence for the effectiveness of conducting family therapy through one person with drug-abusing adolescents. *Journal of Consulting and Clinical Psychology, 54*, 395-397.

Sundell, K., Hansson, K., Löfholm, C. A., Olsson, T., Gustle, L-H., & Kadesjö, C. (2008). The transportability of multisystemic therapy to Sweden: Short-term results from a randomized trial of conduct-disordered youths. *Journal of Family Psychology, 22*(4), 550–560. doi:10.1037/a0012790

Tanner-Smith, E. E., Jo Wilson, S., & Lipsey, M. W. (2013). The comparative effectiveness of outpatient treatment for adolescent substance abuse: A meta-analysis. *Journal of Substance Abuse Treatment, 44*(2), 145–158. doi:10.1016/j.jsat.2012.05.006

Toumbourou, J. W., Stockwell, T., Neighbors, C., Marlatt, G. A., Sturge, J., & Rehm, J. (2007). Interventions to reduce harm associated with adolescent substance use. *Lancet, 369*(9570), 1391–1401.

Turner, L., Shamseer, L., Altman, D. G., Schulz, K. F., & Moher, D. (2012). Does use of the CONSORT Statement impact the completeness of reporting of randomised controlled trials published in medical journals? A Cochrane review. *Systematic Reviews, 1*(1), 60.

Valdez, A., Cepeda, A., Parrish, D., Horowitz, R., & Kaplan, C. (2013). An adapted brief strategic family therapy for gang-affiliated Mexican American adolescents. *Research on Social Work Practice, 23*(4), 383–396. doi:10.1177/1049731513481389

Vaughn, M. G., & Howard, M. O. (2004). Adolescent substance abuse treatment: A synthesis of controlled evaluations. *Research on Social Work Practice, 14*, 325-335.

Waldron, H. B., Slesnick, N., Brody, J. L., Turner, C. W., & Peterson, T. R. (2001). Treatment outcomes for adolescent substance abuse at 4- and 7-month assessments. *Journal of Consulting and Clinical Psychology, 69*, 802-813.

Waldron, H. B., & Turner, C. W. (2008). Evidence-based psychosocial treatments for adolescent substance abuse. *Journal of Clinical Child and Adolescent Psychology, 37*(1), 238–261. doi:10.1080/15374410701820133

Wampold, B. E. (2013). *The great psychotherapy debate: Models, methods, and findings* (Vol. 9). New York, NY: Routledge.

Weissman, M. M., Brown, A. S., & Talati, A. (2011). Translational epidemiology in psychiatry: Linking population to clinical and basic sciences. *Archives of General Psychiatry, 68*(6), 600–608. doi:10.1001/archgenpsychiatry.2011.47

Weinberg, N. Z., Rahdert, E., Colliver, J. D., & Glantz, M. D. (1997). Adolescent substance sbuse: A review of the past 10 years. *Journal of the American Academy of Child and Adolescent Psychiatry, 37*, 252-261.

Weisz, J. R., Jensen-Doss, A., & Hawley, K. M. (2006). Evidence-based youth psychotherapies versus usual clinical care: A meta-analysis of direct comparisons. *American Psychologist, 61*(7), 671–689. doi:10.1037/0003-066X.61.7.671

Williams, R. J., Chang, S. Y., and Addiction Centre Adolescent Research Group. (2000). A comprehensive and comparative review of adolescent substance abuse treatment outcome. *Clinical Psychology: Science and Practice, 7*, 138-166.

World Health Organization. (2009). *Global health risks: Mortality and burden of disease attributable to selected major risks.* Geneva, Switzerland: World Health Organization.

Windle, M., & Zucker, R. A. (2010). Reducing underage and young adult drinking: How to address critical drinking problems during this developmental period. *Alcohol Research and Health, 33*(1–2), 29–44.

Winters, K., C., Tanner-Smith, E., Bresani, E., & Myers, K. (2014). Current advances in the treatment of adolescent substance use. *Adolescent Health, Medicine and Therapeutics, 5*, 199–210.

Yeaton, W. H., & Sechrest, L. (1981). Meaningful measures of effect. *Journal of Consulting and Clinical Psychology, 49*(5), 766–767. doi:10.1037/0022-006X.49.5.766

Zucker, R. A. (2008). Anticipating problem alcohol use developmentally from childhood into middle adulthood: What have we learned? *Addiction, 103*(Suppl. 1), 100–108. doi:10.1111/j.1360-0443.2008.02179.x

Zucker, R. A., Donovan, J. E., Masten, A. S., Mattson, M. E., & Moss, H. B. (2008). Early developmental processes and the continuity of risk for underage drinking and problem drinking. *Pediatrics, 121*(Suppl. 4), S252–S272. doi:10.1111/j.1469-7610.2004.00387.x

Adolescent Cultural Contexts for Substance Use: Intergroup Dynamics, Family Processes, and Neighborhood Risks

Seth J. Schwartz, Sabrina E. Des Rosiers, Jennifer B. Unger, *and* José Szapocznik

Abstract

This chapter reviews the role of cultural processes in substance use and other health problems among adolescents. The chapter focuses on Hispanics because of their status as both a minority group and an immigrant group, and because Hispanics have been a "lightning rod" for political discourse about immigration and US national identity. The core argument is that intergroup processes such as social dominance and system justification are responsible, at the population level, for unequal allocation of social resources—which, in turn, creates health disparities. These intergroup processes compound the effects of more proximal contexts such as individual, family, and neighborhood. It is argued that interventions to combat the social/cultural determinants of health disparities should be multilevel, including individual-, family-, community-, and population-level strategies.

Key Words: culture, Hispanic, social dominance, system justification, intergroup, family, intervention, health disparities

In this chapter we propose that the effects of cultural processes on substance use (and other health outcomes) operate at multiple levels of analysis—individual, family, and population. First, we review the epidemiology of adolescent substance use across racial/ethnic groups and conclude that Hispanics are among the racial/ethnic groups that are at considerable risk for drug and alcohol use in adolescence. We next define what we mean by "culture" and review culturally based social-psychological theories that may help to account for disparities in substance use (and other outcomes) across racial/ethnic groups. Third, we discuss health disparities as influenced by intergroup social dominance and system justification processes. We argue that, to reduce health disparities, prevention scientists might consider augmenting individual, family, or policy intervention programs with comprehensive population-level interventions targeting

social dominance and system justification processes; and we discuss ways in which individual-level and family-level interventions can be (and have been) used to complement population-based interventions targeting health disparities (or to counter deleterious population-level processes).

Epidemiology of Adolescent Substance Use Across Ethnicity: Culture as a Context for Development

Examining the epidemiology of adolescent substance use and its consequences across racial/ethnic groups strongly suggests a cultural basis for disparities in drug and alcohol use.[1] Compared to White Americans, Hispanic 8th and 10th graders are more likely to have initiated substance use, whereas African American and Asian American adolescents are least likely to report having initiated drug and alcohol use (Johnston, O'Malley, Miech, Bachman, &

Schulenberg, 2016). Specifically, 15% of Hispanic 8th graders, and 31% of Hispanic 10th graders, had used marijuana in 2010. Corresponding rates for alcohol were 36% and 59%. Rates of use among Whites and African Americans were at least 5 percentage points lower than those for Hispanics in both 8th and 10th grades. Although the Monitoring the Future study does not report separate rates for Asian Americans, the 2008 National Study on Drug Use and Health indicates that the percentage of Asian Americans aged 12 and older who use substances (3.6%) was 1.75 times lower than the percentage for any other ethnic group (Hong, Huang, Sabri, & Kim, 2011).

Overall prevalence rates across ethnicity do not tell the entire story—there are also ethnic differences in the ages at which substance use initiation occurs. In the 2005 through 2008 National Surveys of Drug Use and Health, the percentages of Hispanic and White adolescents who reported using various substances were comparable (Wu, Woody, Yang, Pan, & Blazer, 2011). However, compared to their White American counterparts, Hispanic adolescents tend to initiate substance use at earlier ages (Johnston et al., 2016), and Hispanic adolescents tend to experience disproportionately negative consequences of substance use (e.g., arguments with family and friends, car accidents, legal and health problems; Mulia, Ye, Greenfield, & Zemore, 2009). African Americans, although they tend to initiate substance use in emerging adulthood rather than in adolescence, are also more likely to experience negative consequences (e.g., HIV) when they do use drugs and alcohol (Adimora et al., 2003). These ethnic differences suggest that culture is important in understanding the etiology of substance use and related health problems.

Defining Culture

The term "culture" has been defined in a number of ways (see Hofstede, 2001 and Kroeber & Kluckhohn, 1952 for discussions of the definitions of culture that have been used over the past 200 years in numerous academic disciplines). These definitions usually include a set of basic assumptions, values, and behaviors that are shared by and transmitted within a group of people (Sam & Berry, 2010). For example, peer groups have cultures, religions have cultures, neighborhoods have cultures, and countries and regions have cultures. Indeed, culture is a fundamental aspect of the human experience, in that it helps people to make sense of the world and of their relationships with each other (Baumeister,

2010). At national, ethnic, and other large-group levels, culture dictates the extent to which individuals are expected to value their own individual autonomy versus the needs and desires of the groups to which they belong (e.g., family, community, nation, religion; Triandis, 1995). Culture also specifies both prescribed and proscribed behaviors and beliefs in specific settings and relationships.

The culture of a group is both (a) an aggregation of the cultural orientations of the individuals within that group (Berry, 2003) and (b) a larger entity that evolves over time, sometimes separately from the individuals who endorse it (Matsumoto, 2003). Although culture originates as a social construction among the individuals belonging to a given group, some subgroups may evolve away from this shared meaning (or may never endorse it in the first place). For example, as a whole, "American culture" can be characterized as self-focused and individualistic (Hofstede, 2001), despite the fact that many US residents, and many cultural subgroups within the United States, do not hold these values.[2] However, the culture of a larger group—such as a national or racial/ethnic group—will influence its members, regardless of whether they subscribe to the values and ideals of that group. Larger forces such as media, social trends, and even built structures convey and transmit the culture of the larger group in which these forces are situated (Al-Sayyad, 2001; Kellner, 2011).

Culture refers not only to macro-level societal units (e.g., countries or regions) but also to values and beliefs endorsed by subgroups of people within these regions. Within the United States, for instance, racial/ethnic groups are assumed to be associated with specific cultural streams. African American culture is posited as being associated with strong religiosity and with valuing relationships with both blood and nonblood kin (e.g., pastors, neighbors, and close friends may be regarded and treated as family members; Constantine, Wilton, Gainor, & Lewis, 2002). Hispanic culture is presumed to be associated with respect for and interdependence with family members, and with not disagreeing openly with others (Santisteban, Muir-Malcolm, Mitrani, & Szapocznik, 2002). Asian American culture is assumed to be linked with modesty, saving face, and deference toward family elders (Kim, Lee, & Ng, 2005). In contrast, White American culture (which is often viewed as synonymous with American culture in general; Devos & Heng, 2009) is often viewed as individualistic and competitive. Thus, many racial/ethnic minority and traditional cultures are viewed as largely collectivistic, whereas "mainstream-modern" White American culture is viewed as largely individualistic (see Oyserman, Coon, & Kemmelmeier, 2002, for a review of empirical evidence regarding these assumptions).

Culture may be important vis-à-vis substance use and other health problems in some ways but not others. Research has found that the effects of neighborhood and family processes on substance use are similar across racial/ethnic groups (Choi, Harachi, & Catalano, 2006)—suggesting that context–outcome relations are at least somewhat universal. However, cultural processes may also exert direct effects on substance use and other health outcomes for minority groups. We provide two examples here. First, acculturation, which is generally used as an umbrella term for a set of cultural processes that are assumed to change as a result of international migration or as a result of growing up in an immigrant family (Sam & Berry, 2010), has been found to predict health outcomes in some immigrant and minority groups (Lopez-Class, Castro, & Ramirez, 2011).[3] We review the literature on acculturation and substance use in more detail later in this chapter.

Second, discriminatory or "institutionally racist" policies or procedures may be enacted toward specific racial/ethnic or cultural groups (Krieger, 2012), especially those that are devalued and/or regarded as "threatening" by the cultural majority group. These policies often have the effect of marginalizing members of devalued or "threatening" groups to positions of social and economic disadvantage— and often relegating them to impoverished, high-crime, and underresourced communities (Sidanius, Pratto, van Laar, & Levin, 2004). Socioeconomic marginalization may then be predictive of a host of negative health outcomes, including higher rates of substance use and related problematic behavior (US Department of Health and Human Services, 2011). The unequal distribution of health problems across racial/ethnic and socioeconomic lines is referred to as health disparities—and these disparities have been the focus of a great deal of public health scholarship and policy since the early 1980s (LaVeist, 2005). As we argue in the next section, negative intergroup processes (both intentional and unintentional) are important determinants of health disparities (Gee, Walsemann, & Brondolo, 2012; Krieger, 2012). Through their effects on socioeconomic disadvantage, these negative intergroup processes create risk in the neighborhood, family, peer, and school contexts that then increases the likelihood that adolescents will be involved in substance use and related problem behaviors (Chuang, Ennett, Bauman, & Foshee, 2005; Smedley, 2012). Although some families, neighborhoods, and communities are able to offset the effects of these negative contextual processes through collective efforts (a) to promote policing and supervision of neighborhood public spaces and (b) to monitor adolescent and young adult activities (Sampson, Raudenbush, & Earls, 1997), many neighborhoods are not able to carry out these protective functions.

Population-Level Cultural Contributors to Health Disparities in Substance Use and Other Outcomes: Social Dominance and System Justification Processes

In most ethnically diverse societies, one racial/ethnic group controls the majority of social and physical resources—such as government positions, prestigious occupations, gentrified and clean communities and housing, and access to amenities (e.g., reliable transportation, access to healthy and varied food). This "dominant" racial/ethnic group is generally either the group that is most well established (as is the case in many European countries) or the group that colonized or conquered land that once belonged to others (as is the case in the Americas and Oceania, and in parts of Africa and Asia). In many cases, many other racial/ethnic groups are in a "one-down" position, where their members tend to be poorer, less well educated, and more likely to be more heavily burdened with disease (LaVeist, 2005). Indeed, in the United States, health disparities are most closely associated with the neighborhood in which one resides—which in turn is closely associated with concentration of members of specific racial/ethnic groups (LaVeist, Pollack, Thorpe, Fesahazion, & Gaskin, 2011). Nevertheless, as LaVeist et al. (2011) have demonstrated, neighborhood physical and cultural conditions (e.g., socioeconomic status, built environment, neighborhood social cohesion), and not necessarily race/ethnicity per se, appear to be responsible for the greater prevalence of physical and mental health problems among members of specific ethnic or cultural groups. It must be emphasized that population-level intergroup biases operate largely by creating socioeconomic disadvantage and/or decreasing social capital, such that differences in socioeconomic resources and social capital may help to explain disparities in substance use and other social and health problems across ethnic groups (LaVeist et al., 2011; Sampson et al., 1997). The bottom line here is that it may be effective to address health disparities "from the top"—that is, by focusing on the intergroup processes that create and maintain health disparities (Smedley, 2012)—as well as from other angles (e.g., by targeting individual, family, and community determinants of substance use and other health behaviors).

The finding that health disparities are rooted in social, more than biological, processes (Krieger, 2012) suggests that these disparities can be reduced by addressing the social, economic, political, and cultural factors that underlie health problems. Although we focus on drug and alcohol use in this chapter, the principle that health disparities are underlain by cultural processes likely applies to other health conditions as well.

It is relatively straightforward to understand how health disparities develop in "disease" outcomes such as cancer, diabetes, and cardiovascular disease. Although there are strong behavioral determinants of these diseases, substandard housing conditions and lack of access to competent medical care also increase the likelihood that individuals will be exposed to dangerous chemicals and that health problems will go undetected. However, disparities in more overtly behavioral health indices, such as drug and alcohol use, may be more difficult to understand. Furthermore, because many disease outcomes are rooted in behavioral and lifestyle factors (e.g., poor diet is linked with diabetes and cardiovascular disease), behaviorally based interventions may represent one promising way of addressing disease outcomes as well as more overtly behavioral outcomes such as drug and alcohol use (Jenum et al., 2006; Toumbourou et al., 2007).

Behaviorally based interventions, however, allow us to address only part of the problem. One of the key principles underlying the social/cultural understanding of health disparities is that these disparities are rooted in intergroup social processes as well as in individual behaviors (Krieger, 2012; Major, Mendes, & Dovidio, 2013). Social dominance theory (Pratto, Sidanius, & Levin, 2006) and system justification theory (Jost, Banaji, & Nosek, 2004) represent two social-psychological approaches, both rooted in intergroup relations, that attempt to explain how systematic inequities and disparities develop, and are maintained, between dominant and nondominant racial/ethnic groups. Social dominance theory maintains that the cultural majority group systematically (and often unconsciously) prevents members of certain minority and socioeconomic groups from gaining access to educational and employment opportunities that would allow

them to improve their socioeconomic standing. Social-psychological research indicates that, given the chance to do so, members of a given group tend to allocate resources primarily toward fellow ingroup members (Hodson, Dovidio, & Esses, 2003). Although members of other groups may not be intentionally discriminated against, the end result is that they are more likely to be subjected to "substandard housing, disease, underemployment, dangerous and distasteful work, disproportionate punishment, stigmatization, and vilification" (Pratto et al., 2006, p. 272). Social dominance theory is similar to institutional racism (see Haney Lopez, 2000, and Krieger, 2012, for comprehensive reviews), where certain minority group members are blocked from, or fail to get the support needed to obtain, the skills or credentials required to make progress in one's education and career.

At the societal level, health disparities then result—at least in part—from the systematic and disproportionate allocation of physical and cultural resources to members of the majority cultural group (e.g., White Americans in the United States; Phelan, Link, & Tehranifar, 2010), which then leaves members of other groups with fewer—and often insufficient—resources. These disparities are then self-perpetuating, not necessarily because any given majority member specifically intends to discriminate against members of other racial/ethnic groups, but most intergroup processes occur automatically and without conscious intent (Brewer, 1999). In some cases, majority group members are unconsciously threatened by the presence of specific "threatening" minority groups—especially when those minority groups are large in size (Tip, Zagefka, González, Brown, & Cinnirella, 2012)—and this threat leads individuals to identify more strongly with their ingroups and to allocate resources toward those groups.

Under these types of conditions, why do minority group members not "fight back" against the disparities between themselves and members of the dominant group? Perhaps the answer can be explained in part by system justification theory (Jost et al., 2004). This theory is based on the "just world hypothesis," where lower status individuals and groups tend to accept and legitimize the discrepancy in status between themselves and members of the dominant group. Experimental research indicates that members of lower status groups tend not to challenge the status quo and to accept their groups' social position (Jost & Burgess, 2000). Members of racial/ethnic minority groups may quietly blame the dominant racial/ethnic group for the health disparities that they experience, but in relatively few cases do they actually attempt to publicly challenge the legitimacy of these disparities. Indeed, as Ogbu and colleagues (see Ogbu & Simons, 1998, for a comprehensive review) have found, the social structures in many societies are configured such that minority group members are marginalized (rather than served) by mainstream institutions such as schools, and these social structures actively discourage minority individuals from voicing or expressing their concerns. In response to being blocked from achieving success through normative pathways such as education and employment, some minority individuals may develop identities based on opposition to "mainstream" society. Although some of these "oppositional" identities, and the behaviors they engender, may be transformative and positive (such as becoming a politician or community leader), many such identities are negative—often based on antisocial behaviors and substance use (Destin & Oyserman, 2010).

Each society designates—either formally or informally—some racial/ethnic groups as "preferred" and others as "devalued." In the United States, many Hispanic groups—especially Mexicans, Puerto Ricans, Dominicans, and Central Americans—are regarded as unwanted or devalued (Alba et al., 2010); and some Asian groups, such as Chinese, Japanese, and Koreans, are regarded (at least at the group level) as preferred because they tend to be well educated and/or upwardly mobile (Steiner, 2009).[4] Although they are not immigrants, African Americans have had an extremely difficult history in the United States; they were brought involuntarily from Africa as slave labor and continued to be devalued and marginalized long after slavery was outlawed (Wilson, 2002). Perhaps among the most devalued groups are the Native Americans, who bravely fought the White invasion and lost.

Although Hispanic and Asian cultural contexts espouse similar values of familism and filial piety, respectively (Kao, McHugh, & Travis, 2007; Schwartz, Weisskirch, et al., 2010), and although Hispanic and Asian adolescents both report that their parents strongly value success in school and upwardly mobile career paths (Fuligni & Witkow, 2004), Asian children and adolescents are most likely among US racial/ethnic groups to complete high school, whereas Hispanics are least likely (Chapman, Laird, & KewalRamani, 2010). In turn, school dropout, as well as disengagement from school, represents risks for drug and alcohol misuse (Aloise-Young & Chavez, 2002).

These divergent paths for Hispanics versus Asians may be rooted in differences in the socioeconomic backgrounds and educational credentials that many Hispanic and Asian immigrants have traditionally brought with them to the United States. Many Mexican immigrants arrive with minimal formal education and/or without permission to work in the United States; as a result, the only employment available to them may be unskilled manual labor or housekeeping jobs (Henderson, 2011). Similarly, the original wave of Puerto Ricans migrating to the US mainland also sought low-wage labor (Acosta-Belen & Santiago, 2006). White Americans' perceptions of Mexicans and Puerto Ricans (the two largest Hispanic groups in the United States) gave rise to stereotypes about Hispanics in general. Hispanics are often stereotyped as uneducated, as uninterested in learning English and becoming American, and as seeking unskilled and low-wage jobs (Jimeno-Ingrum, Berdahl, & Lucero-Wagoner, 2009). Immigrants from some Asian countries, in contrast, are overrepresented among scientists and professionals who obtain permission to immigrate through educational or employment opportunities and through immigration quotas based on abilities. Although many Asian immigrants are not scientists or professionals, they are often nonetheless stereotyped as intelligent, hardworking, upwardly mobile, and eager to assimilate into American culture (i.e., the "model minority myth"; Leong & Okazaki, 2009). This "model minority" stereotype persists despite the tendency for some Asian groups—such as Hmong and Cambodians—to evidence outcomes that are more similar to those of Hispanics (Ngo & Lee, 2007). In turn, these pan-ethnic stereotypes may exacerbate the effects of socioeconomic and educational disparities between Hispanics and Asians. Because Asians are seen as an asset to the United States (whereas Hispanics are often viewed as a drain on the country), and because Asians are viewed as eager to become American (whereas Hispanics are viewed as wanting to remain separate from the American mainstream), Hispanics are regarded as a threat to American national identity. In particular, the Spanish language, which is spoken by the vast majority of Hispanic immigrants, is viewed by many Americans as a threat to the status of English as a core component of American national identity (Huntington, 2004). Perhaps as a result, most Hispanic groups—especially those who tend to be socioeconomically disadvantaged—have become targets for social dominance processes that keep them in subservient social positions. Asian Americans, because they do not share a common language and are generally viewed as contributing to the progress of the United States, are perceived as less of a threat. Social dominance and system justification processes clearly do not impact all ethnic minority groups equally.

Perhaps because of these stereotypes, many Americans therefore maintain positive views of the "typical" Asian immigrant or Asian American (largely because of the "model minority" stereotype; Leong & Okazaki, 2009), but negative views of Hispanic immigrants and their descendants (Cornelius, 2002). In fact, two treatises on American national identity, one published by a well-renowned Harvard University political science professor (Huntington, 2004) and another published by a prominent conservative commentator (Buchanan, 2006), specifically targeted Hispanics as the primary threat to the American national fabric. Is it not possible, however, that many Hispanic adolescents and families would adapt more favorably if they had access to some of the same resources (e.g., advanced training in mathematics and a cultural focus on achievement and discipline)? Many South American immigrants, for example, arrive in the United States with advanced degrees and professional careers, and they often do not experience many of the same disparities as Mexicans, Puerto Ricans, Central Americans, and Dominicans (see Sabogal, 2005, for an example). The original cohort of Cubans in Miami also were fairly socioeconomically advantaged (Stepick & Dutton Stepick, 2002), although subsequent cohorts of Cuban immigrants have been less so. The role of skin tone is also important to note: Many Cubans and South Americans in the United States are Caucasian, whereas the majority of Mexicans, Central Americans, Puerto Ricans, and Dominicans in the United States are visible minorities.

When a racial/ethnic or cultural group is perceived as a threat, the dominant group takes defensive steps to separate itself from the "threatening" minority group and to limit that group's influence (Tip et al., 2012).[5] Two prime examples of this dynamic are the various English-only movements in the United States (Barker et al., 2001) and the 2009 "racial profiling" law passed in Arizona that allows police officers to detain anyone whom they suspect might be in the country illegally (Pew Research Center, 2010). Although some attempts were made to frame these initiatives as applying to the public in general, public discourse clearly indicated that they were intended to apply specifically to Hispanics—and to reduce the threat that they present (Schwartz, Vignoles, Brown, & Zagefka, 2014). In turn, through unequal allocation of resources and marginalization of "threatening" groups to underserved areas, these intergroup threat processes are likely to underlie disparities in many health outcomes, including drug and alcohol use (Pratto et al., 2006). Where social dominance processes do predict disparities in substance use and other health outcomes, these processes are likely to work indirectly (a) through macro-level social processes such as inequitable distribution of socioeconomic resources and (b) through institutional and individual discrimination (Krieger, 2012; Sidanius & Pratto, 2001). Note that the threats experienced by members of the dominant group can be real, perceived, or both, and that the primary mediators between threats perceived by the dominant group and health outcomes (including substance use) in minority groups involve discriminatory overtures—intentional or otherwise—directed toward members of threatening or devalued minority groups (Major et al., 2013).

Social dominance theory is based on social-psychological and intergroup processes, and as such it applies primarily to groups that are placed into a subservient position (Sidanius, Pratto, van Laar, & Levin, 2004). Of course, more proximal determinants of substance use are also relevant. For example, Hispanics in southern Florida report high rates of illicit drug use despite not being socially marginalized. However, southern Florida is an important point of entry for drugs shipped from Latin America (US Department of Justice, 2011)—indicating that drugs are likely to be more available in this area than in other areas where drug smuggling is not taking place. Although social dominance processes may be an important predictor of disparities in drug/alcohol use and other health outcomes, they are certainly not the only important predictor.

But again, what explains health disparities in health *behaviors* such as substance use? Because family closeness tends to protect against alcohol and drug use (Kelly et al., 2011), the family closeness that is often valued within both Hispanic and Asian families suggests that both of these groups should report the lowest levels of alcohol and drug use. However, in early adolescence, Hispanics actually have the *highest* rates of use of alcohol, marijuana, and most other drugs. Although there are multiple explanations for this trend, including the overrepresentation of Latin American countries among sources and exporters of illicit drugs (US Department of Justice, 2011), another potential answer may involve returning to resource allocation within social dominance theory and other perspectives on intergroup relations (Phelan et al., 2010; Pratto et al., 2006). Social dominance and system justification processes tend to be self-reinforcing—unequal distribution of resources tends to create poverty in minority communities, and this poverty results in social, economic, and political marginalization. In turn, being marginalized from "mainstream" culture creates more poverty—and the social dominance/system justification cycle continues. As noted earlier in this chapter, the deleterious community, family, peer, and school influences within poor minority communities are often associated with substance use and preclude access to quality health care, which reinforces the cycle of substance use–related problems and poor health (Dovidio & Fiske, 2012). Of course, access to advanced educational credentials and professional careers can help to mitigate this marginalization.

The Statistical Abstract of the United States (US Census Bureau, 2011) demonstrates that non-Hispanic Whites report higher incomes than other racial/ethnic groups, especially African Americans and Hispanics. Because of these disparities in income, disproportionate numbers of African Americans and Hispanics are often marginalized into poorer neighborhoods with higher rates of crime, violence, and drug and alcohol misuse (LaVeist et al., 2011). Because of the disparities in socioeconomic resources between Whites and other ethnic groups in the United States (as well as in other Western nations), disparities in substance use and other health problems likely result from some combination of socioeconomic and cultural factors. For example, Mulia et al. (2009) found that racial/ethnic disparities in alcohol use and its consequences were partially explained by social disadvantage—that is, lower incomes and personal and institutionalized discrimination. We focus on both of these types of influences in the present chapter, given that health disparities reflect a "social determinants of health" perspective focusing on inequalities at the population level (Marmot, 2005).

In the present chapter, we focus primarily on Hispanics as an example of the effects of cultural processes on substance use and other health outcomes, for two primary reasons. First, the concept of "culture" carries an entirely different meaning for immigrant groups such as Hispanics than it does for involuntarily subjugated minority groups such as

African Americans and Native Americans. The concept of acculturation, which is central to our framework on culture as a determinant of substance use, is used primarily with reference to immigrants and their immediate descendants (Sam & Berry, 2010). Second, involuntarily subjugated groups often hold strong grievances against the dominant ethnic group—grievances that can help to define the culture of the minority group (for example, the identities of many young Palestinians are centered on opposition to Israel; Hammack, 2011).[6] We therefore focus on Hispanics as a way of exemplifying the micro-level and macro-level cultural processes that can influence drug and alcohol use, as well as other health outcomes, in immigrant groups—especially those that are devalued or viewed as threatening to the national identity of the receiving society.[7]

At the macrosocial level, health disparities in substance use, and in many other health behaviors, lie at the intersection of social psychology and sociology (which explain how health disparities come into being) with public health (which focuses on understanding the determinants of health and on strategies for reducing or eliminating health disparities). It is important, therefore, to draw on (and integrate) both social-psychological and public health understandings of health disparities so that we can be most successful in addressing these disparities. It is also essential to keep in mind that a reciprocal-causal loop exists between socioeconomic disadvantage and social dominance and system justification processes (through unequal distribution of resources and marginalization of certain groups to undesirable areas; Pratto et al., 2006). One must also be mindful that socioeconomic disadvantage is strongly predictive of many health disparities—including disparities in consequences of drug and alcohol use (Aguirre-Molina, Borrell, Muñoz-Laboy, & Vega, 2010).

Intergroup Dynamics and Substance Use: Mechanisms of Influence

Understanding the ways in which intergroup processes—specifically the social dominance and system justification processes that lead to health disparities—affect substance use in Hispanic adolescents is an important but complex endeavor. First, these processes most strongly affect individuals and families who reside in low-income, resource-poor communities (LaVeist et al., 2011). Although the majority of Hispanics in the United States reside in these types of neighborhoods, some subgroups of Hispanics do not fit this profile.

Mexicans, Puerto Ricans, Central Americans, and Dominicans are most likely to reside in poor and underresourced areas (Alba et al., 2010)—but Cubans and South Americans are less likely to reside in poor neighborhoods (Sabogal, 2005; Stepick & Dutton Stepick, 2002). Indeed, Cubans, and most recently many South American groups such as Colombians, Argentinians, and Venezuelans, have defied the "poor and uneducated" Hispanic stereotype. Cubans became a major presence in the United States, and especially in southern Florida, following the rise of the Castro regime in Cuba (Stepick & Dutton Stepick, 2002). The first Cuban arrivals in Miami were wealthy and highly educated, and they helped to establish Miami as a racial/ethnic enclave where Cubans maintain the majority of political and economic power (Stepick, Grenier, Castro, & Dunn, 2003). Additional waves of Cubans followed, many of whom were not wealthy but entered the cultural context that was being (or had been) established by the original cohort of Cubans. Many other Hispanic groups followed as well, including Central American refugees (who generally reside in low-income neighborhoods) beginning in the 1980s and South American professionals (who generally reside in middle- or upper-middle-class areas; Sabogal, 2005) largely in the first decade of the 21st century. South American professionals have also settled in the greater New York City, Washington, D.C., and Boston metropolitan areas (Ennis, Rios-Vargas, & Albert, 2011). It appears that socioeconomic status in one's country of origin tends to predict socioeconomic status following arrival in the United States, because the intellectual, financial, and social capital that immigrants bring with them helps them to secure employment and resources in the United States. However, it should be noted that children of poor immigrants sometimes fare better than their parents did in their countries of origin.

Because social dominance processes are based on the unequal allocation of resources (Sidanius et al., 2004), these processes manifest themselves largely in terms of neighborhood and socioeconomic conditions. Poverty in the country of origin often reproduces itself as poverty in the receiving country—and as a result, it is not surprising that, according to the National Survey of Drug Abuse and Health, Cubans and South Americans, who may be better off than other Hispanic groups, may be less likely than other Hispanic groups to manifest disparities in heavy alcohol use (Lipsky & Caetano, 2009): 3.0% of Cuban men and 0.6% of Cuban women, and 6.2% of South American men and

1.5% of South American women, as compared to 12.4% of Mexican men and 2.2% of Mexican women, reported heavy alcohol use (at least 5–6 drinks per day for men and at least 3–4 drinks per day for women). Heavy drinking rates for Puerto Ricans were also elevated (8.6% of men and 4.3% of women). Similar statistics have been reported for adolescents (Delva et al., 2005).

West et al. (2010) found that, among Hispanic adolescents in California, proximity to alcohol retailers was predictive of the amount of alcohol consumed by a given adolescent. The concentration of dedicated liquor stores within lower socioeconomic areas is predictive of violent crime (Gruenewald, Freisthler, Remer, LaScala, & Treno, 2006). This finding may help to explain the links among social dominance processes, marginalization to poor and underresourced neighborhoods, and alcohol misuse and criminal perpetration as well as victimization among Hispanics—especially Mexicans, Puerto Ricans, Dominicans, and Central Americans. Because social dominance processes are less likely to operate among individuals who have greater socioeconomic and social capital resources, Cubans and South Americans are likely underrepresented among individuals affected by urban poverty, high crime rates, and high rates of substance misuse (Alba et al., 2010; Lipsky & Caetano, 2009). Although Hispanics are characterized by the highest high school dropout rates among US racial/ethnic groups (Chapman et al., 2010), individuals of Mexican descent, who represent both the largest and the most stigmatized Hispanic subgroup, are largely responsible for this dropout rate. Indeed, in Mexico, especially in small villages, the majority of people are provided with only 7–8 years of formal education (Santibañez, Vernez, & Razquin, 2005). Mexican immigrant parents may therefore experience difficulty guiding their children in their schoolwork and directing them toward higher education—and lack of parental involvement in schoolwork is a predictor of academic underperformance and school dropout, especially in economically disadvantaged families (Cooper & Crosnoe, 2007). In turn, underperformance in school often predicts involvement in drug and alcohol use (Townsend, Flisher, & King, 2007).

Family-Level Cultural Predictors of Adolescent Substance Use

Social dominance and system justification theories are based on group-level phenomena, such as the intergroup dynamics (e.g., threat, unequal allocation of resources, and defensive attitudes and policies directed toward "threatening" minority groups) underlying health disparities. Public health research on health disparities focuses on population-level differences in health behaviors and outcomes, both within and across subgroups. These theories and approaches do not, however, explain individual differences in health outcomes. Put another way, the fact that Hispanic adolescents are disproportionately represented among alcohol and drug users does not allow us to predict whether a *specific* Hispanic adolescent will engage in substance use. Similar to the statistical assumptions underlying multilevel modeling (Raudenbush & Bryk, 2002), population-level predictors are most suited to explain how groups vary at the population level, whereas individual-level and family-level predictors are most suited to explain variations in individual outcomes. Indeed, individual-level and family-level cultural orientations, as well as more proximal individual-level variables (such as decision-making processes), may be most predictive of individual differences in substance use (Romano & Netland, 2008; Schwartz et al., 2011). Although the present chapter focuses on cultural processes, interested readers are directed to other sources (e.g., Palmer et al., 2009) for reviews of other individual-level predictors of substance use among adolescents and young adults.

Consistent with our strategy of mapping influences beginning from the macrosocial level and moving inward, we first focus on family-level cultural factors and then focus on individual-level cultural factors. Cultural risk factors operating within the family may predispose Hispanic adolescents toward drug and alcohol use. We define acculturation in greater depth in the section on individual-adolescent cultural predictors of substance use, but we will state briefly here that acculturation represents the process of adapting to a new cultural context following immigration or as a result of growing up in an immigrant-headed home. A number of writers (e.g., Berry, 1980; Phinney, 2003) have proposed that acculturation consists of separate dimensions for receiving-culture acquisition and heritage-culture retention. Schwartz, Unger, Zamboanga, and Szapocznik (2010) suggested that each of these dimensions operates within at least three domains: cultural practices, values, and identifications. Again, this conceptualization is discussed further under the section on "Individual-Level Cultural Determinants of Substance Use."

Whereas the majority of research on acculturation and substance use has examined the confluence of acculturation and drug/alcohol use within the individual adolescent, it has been increasingly recognized that acculturation is—at least in part—a family-level phenomenon (Santisteban & Mitrani, 2003). A great deal of research has been conducted on effects of family cultural processes on adolescent substance use and other problem behaviors (see Smokowski & Bacallao, 2010, for a recent review). In general, this research can be subdivided into two general themes: (a) effects of parents' cultural orientations (with or without also considering adolescents' cultural orientations), and (b) effects of differential parent–adolescent acculturation on adolescent substance use. We cover each of these themes in more detail in the following sections.

Parent Acculturation, Adolescent Acculturation, and Adolescent Substance Use

Because acculturation is a family phenomenon, it is important to examine effects of parental acculturation, as well as of adolescent acculturation, on adolescent substance use. Some research (e.g., Prado et al., 2010) has suggested that parents' own acculturation (in this case, U.S. cultural practices) predicts family functioning both (a) directly and (b) indirectly through parents' receipt of social support and their perceptions of family functioning. Other research suggests that Hispanic adolescents' acculturation may predict cigarette smoking through perceptions of discrimination (Lorenzo-Blanco, Unger, Ritt-Olson, Soto, & Baezconde-Garbanati, 2011) or through perceptions of peers' substance use (Myers et al., 2009).

More research is needed, however, on specific parental values that may be related to adolescent substance use indirectly through the ways in which parents relate to their children and adolescents. For example, parental familism has been found to be negatively related to adolescent externalizing problems (Santiago & Wadsworth, 2011). However, the extent to which this effect operates through parenting is not clear. Because many Hispanic parents retain their culture-of-origin practices and values (Smokowski & Bacallao, 2010), the extent to which these heritage-cultural influences affect adolescent outcomes through parenting processes and interactions is in need of study. Indeed, the effects of parental heritage-culture retention may depend on the acculturation approaches that adolescents employ. To the extent that adolescents remain oriented toward their cultures of origin, parental familism (as well as other Hispanic values, such as respeto and simpatía) may exert protective effects on adolescent outcomes. However, for adolescents who assimilate—that is, those who discard their cultural heritage and essentially become American—parental endorsement of familism and other traditional Hispanic values may be viewed as overly controlling (Kurtines & Szapocznik, 1996). Martinez, McClure, Eddy, and Wilson (2011) found that many Hispanic adolescents continue to adopt American behaviors with increasing time in the United States, but that many Hispanic parents do not appear to change their parenting practices over time.

Although most immigrant adolescents increase over time in their endorsement of American cultural practices, perhaps more important is the extent to which they retain their cultural heritage. Intervention implications may be very different for those adolescents who retain their Hispanic cultural heritage versus those who do not. For example, it is possible that interventions aimed at improving parenting, and at connecting parents with the school system and with the adolescent's peer network (e.g., Pantin, Schwartz, Sullivan, Prado, & Szapocznik, 2004), may be most efficacious in preventing or reducing substance use for youth who remain connected to their cultural heritage and are willing to accept their parents' traditional values and behaviors. For families in which adolescents are more resistant to their parents' traditional Hispanic cultural orientations, additional parent–adolescent dyadic intervention modules to promote biculturalism in both parents and adolescents (e.g., Smokowski & Bacallao, 2010; Szapocznik et al., 1989) may be needed. In any case, however, interventions may be needed to help parents and adolescents to improve their relationships with each other, as well as to help immigrant parents to adapt to life in the United States and to obtain the support that they need to guide their adolescents effectively.

Differential Parent–Adolescent Acculturation and Adolescent Substance Use

Indeed, Szapocznik and Kurtines (1980, 1993) have suggested that differential levels of acculturation between parents and adolescents may predispose adolescents toward drug and alcohol use. The logic behind this hypothesis was that, when adolescents underwent rapid Americanization while parents remained faithful to their cultures of origin,

parents would regard the adolescents' overly individualist and independent values and behaviors as disrespectful, and adolescents would regard parents' collectivist and traditional values and behaviors as overly controlling, old-fashioned, or nonnormative. Indeed, Smokowski, Rose, and Bacallao (2008) found that parent–adolescent differences in American cultural behaviors were negatively predictive of family cohesion and adaptability and positively predictive of family conflict; and Smokowski, Rose, and Bacallao (2009) found that parent–adolescent acculturation discrepancies were predictive of adolescent aggression. Unger, Ritt-Olson, Wagner, Soto, and Baezconde-Garbanati (2009) found that family cohesion *mediated* the effect of parent–adolescent discrepancy in American cultural practices on cigarette, alcohol, and marijuana use.

The availability of an expanded, multidimensional model of acculturation (Schwartz, Unger, Zamboanga, & Szapocznik, 2010)—consisting of heritage and receiving cultural practices, values, and identifications—suggests that *multiple* types of acculturation gaps may exist (see Telzer, 2010, for an extended discussion). First, following Smokowski et al. (2008, 2009) and Unger et al. (2009), gaps may exist in American cultural orientation, Hispanic cultural orientation, or both. Second, gaps may exist in cultural values and identifications as well as in cultural practices—and gaps in heritage-cultural orientation may be more harmful than gaps in American-cultural orientation (Telzer, 2010). For example, Schwartz, Unger, Baezconde-Garbanati, et al. (in press) found that parent–adolescent gaps in all three domains of Hispanic cultural orientation (Hispanic practices, collectivist values, and ethnic identity—with parents scoring higher than adolescents) were indirectly and positively predictive of depressive symptoms, aggressive behavior, and binge drinking indirectly through adolescent reports of family relationships.

Notwithstanding the findings reported here regarding significant effects of parent–adolescent acculturation discrepancies on substance use, a number of arguments have been furthered against the differential acculturation hypothesis. First, not all studies have found acculturation gaps to be predictive of adolescent risk outcomes (for examples of studies that have not found significant effects, see Gil et al., 2000; Lau et al., 2005). Second, Gil et al. (2000) argue that the absolute levels of cultural orientations are more important than the magnitude of the gap between parent and adolescent reports. For example, if on a measure of American practices with values ranging from 0 to 10, a family where the adolescent reports a 10 and the parent reports a 7 is quite different than a family where the adolescent reports a 3 and the parent reports a 0. Even though the gap is three points in each of these scenarios, the first family appears to be relatively highly Americanized, whereas the second family appears low on the American practices scale. Knowing only the magnitude of the acculturation gap does not provide this information—so one recommendation might be to model both the absolute level (as a linear combination of the parent and adolescent scores) and the gap (as an observed or latent difference score) as predictors of family functioning and of adolescent outcomes (see Newsom, 2012, for related data analytic examples). In this way, the contributions of absolute levels of, and gaps in, acculturation-related variables can be examined.

Individual-Level Cultural Determinants of Substance Use: Cultural Practices, Values, and Identifications

Because almost two thirds of US Hispanic children and adolescents are either immigrants or children of immigrants, cultural orientations are often studied in Hispanics in the form of acculturation. Although acculturation is an individual-difference construct (Berry, 2003), it represents a response to one's cultural context (Berry, 2006)—and as a result, acculturation may represent a conduit between the cultural context and a given individual's risk for drug and alcohol use. In turn, effects of acculturation on substance use may be mediated by decision making, peer affiliations, and other more proximal factors (e.g., Des Rosiers, Schwartz, Zamboanga, Ham, & Huang, 2013; Gil et al., 2000; Myers et al., 2009).

Early views of acculturation were unidimensional, in that immigrants and their immediate descendants were assumed to discard their cultural heritage as they acquired American culture (Gordon, 1964)—and a great deal of health-related research still relies on unidimensional acculturation models (Lopez-Class, Castro, & Ramirez, 2011). With regard to substance use, studies have suggested that greater degrees of "acculturation" are associated with higher likelihood of alcohol (Caetano, Ramisetty-Mikler, & Rodriguez, 2009) and drug (Myers et al., 2009) misuse. Gil et al. (2000) also found that decreases in familism (orientation toward family) were predictive of greater alcohol use in Hispanic adolescents. The conclusion drawn from this line of research was that the larger American society increased risks for problematic outcomes among Hispanics by exposing them to risky influences within American culture or by pulling them away from their cultural heritage.

Biculturalism and Substance Use

A key conceptual problem with unidimensional acculturation models, however, is that it is not possible to disentangle the effects of heritage-culture retention from the effects of American-culture acquisition. That is, an adolescent who reports speaking primarily English in social situations is assumed to have both "become American" and discarded Hispanic culture, but this need not be the case. Most principally, unidimensional approaches do not acknowledge the possibility of biculturalism—where the person endorses both the heritage and receiving cultures. Literature suggests that biculturalism is often the most favorable approach to acculturation (e.g., Phinney, Berry, Vedder, & Liebkind, 2006). Indeed, some bicultural individuals are able to navigate well within both their heritage and receiving cultural contexts, and to be comfortable within both of these contexts.

With biculturalism defined as endorsing both the heritage and receiving cultures, evidence is mixed regarding the extent to which biculturalism is associated with the lowest likelihood of drug and alcohol use in adolescents from immigrant families (Fosados et al., 2007; Unger, Baezconde-Garbanati, Shakib, Palmer, Nezami, & Mora, 2004). However, in many cases, biculturalism may be "more than the sum of its parts"—that is, it is more than simply the combination of receiving-culture retention with heritage-culture acquisition. In the biculturalism and bilingualism literatures, for example, there is evidence that individuals engage in "code switching"—that is, responding to specific cultural prompts in culturally syntonic ways (Benet-Martínez, Leu, Lee, & Morris, 2002). For example, bicultural adolescents may behave in "American ways" in school and with peers, but in more "traditional ways" with family members. There may be considerable individual differences in the extent to which this code-switching process is used successfully—in cases where the code switching is not successful, biculturalism may actually cause more stress than it alleviates (see Rudmin, 2003, for further discussion).

Following Rudmin's suggestion, a number of studies (e.g., Benet-Martínez & Haritatos, 2005; Des Rosiers et al., 2013; Schwartz & Zamboanga, 2008) have identified multiple types of biculturalism. Most broadly, bicultural individuals can be subdivided into (a) those who are able to integrate their two cultural streams into an individualized cultural mosaic and (b) those who prefer to keep their two cultural streams separate and do not attempt to integrate them. Research has suggested that "integrated" bicultural individuals score higher on self-esteem, and lower on symptoms of anxiety and depression, compared to "compartmentalized" bicultural individuals (Chen et al., 2008)—but thus far no published research has compared these two types of biculturalism in terms of susceptibility to drug and alcohol use. However, Benet-Martínez et al. (2002) found that individuals utilizing a more compartmentalized type of biculturalism tended to invoke the "wrong" set of cultural schemata in a given situation. That is, they adopted a heritage-cultural mindset when exposed to receiving cultural primes, and vice versa. Although the reasons for this mismatch of responses with contexts are not clear, the mismatch clearly suggests that compartmentalized biculturalism is associated with a discomfort with the task of balancing one's two cultural worlds. More broadly, the identification of multiple variants of biculturalism may help to explain the inconsistent findings regarding the link between biculturalism and substance use. It is important for further research to compare different subtypes of biculturalism in terms of likelihood and extent of drug and alcohol use.

A further nuance is the appropriateness of biculturalism within different cultural contexts. Flannery, Reise, and Yu (2001) used the term *ethnogenesis* to refer to "hybrid" cultural contexts created by the intersection of multiple cultural streams. For example, Miami Cuban culture represents a blend of Cuban and American cultures—and as such, it is likely unfamiliar both to people from Cuba and to people from other parts of the United States. Similar statements might be made about "Chicano" cultural contexts in the Southwest and in California, and about "Niyorican" culture in Upper Manhattan and the South Bronx. In hybrid cultural contexts such as these, a hybrid bicultural approach to acculturation might be most adaptive, whereas such hybridity might be less adaptive in parts of the Midwest, Plains, and Deep South where cultural diversity is less prominent or has a shorter history. An approach where the person appears—at least outwardly—to "conform" to the receiving cultural context might be more accepted in less diverse areas. So an interactionist approach to acculturation (Schwartz, Vignoles, et al., 2014; van Oudenhoven, Ward, & Masgoret, 2006) might more accurately predict who is most at risk for substance use given their acculturation profile.

Substance Use Within a Multidimensional Model of Acculturation

Much of the research linking acculturation with drug and alcohol use has utilized measures of behavioral acculturation. However, recent theorizing suggests that acculturation encompasses multiple domains of cultural functioning, including values and identifications as well as behaviors (e.g., Abraido-Lanza, Armbrister, Florez, & Aguirre, 2006; Lopez-Class et al., 2011; Schwartz, Unger, et al., 2010). The effects of acculturation on substance use may therefore be more varied and nuanced than may have been previously realized (see Schwartz, Unger, Des Rosiers, et al., 2014, for an empirical example).

Some research has examined links between cultural *values* and substance use. Unger and Schwartz (2012) and Unger et al. (2006) found that respect for others and deference to parents were protective against cigarette smoking and alcohol use across racial/ethnic groups. However, broader transcultural values, such as individualism and collectivism (i.e., the extent to which one's own needs are prioritized above those of others, or vice versa), have only recently been examined as correlates or predictors of drug and alcohol use in the published literature (Schwartz et al., 2011). Given that individualism represents concern primarily for oneself and one's own needs (Triandis, 1995), one would expect endorsement of individualist values to be associated with family conflicts, which in turn may predict drug and alcohol use. On the other hand, because collectivism represents prioritizing others ahead of oneself, one would anticipate that collectivist values would protect against substance use—perhaps because the person would not want others (especially parents and other family members) to worry about (or to be ashamed of or adversely affected by) her or his behavior (cf. Schwartz et al., 2011).

Especially given that most Hispanic cultural contexts are centered on the importance of family relationships and obligations (Santisteban et al., 2002), in Hispanic adolescents, collectivism should be strongly contraindicative of risk-taking behaviors in general. Moreover, it has been hypothesized that *parents'* collectivist values may influence how they guide their children and adolescents (Cox, Burr, Blow, & Parra Cardona, 2011; Santisteban, Coatsworth, Briones, Kurtines, & Szapocznik,

2012). As we discuss in the next subsection, to understand Hispanic adolescent substance use, we must understand not only the adolescent's own cultural orientation, but also the cultural context within the family and community.

A body of research has developed around the role of cultural *identifications* on substance use in Hispanic adolescents, and this research has generally not been connected to the literature on acculturation (Lopez-Class et al., 2011). The literature on cultural identifications and substance use has focused largely on racial/ethnic identity (Unger, 2012), with scarce attention to the role of American identity. Findings in this literature have been mixed, with some studies suggesting that racial/ethnic identity protects against drug and alcohol use in Hispanic adolescents (Marsiglia, Kulis, Hecht, & Sills, 2004) and other studies suggesting that racial/ethnic identity represents a *risk* for substance use in this population (Schwartz et al., 2011; Zamboanga, Schwartz, Jarvis, & Van Tyne, 2009).

Although it is not entirely clear what is responsible for these discrepant findings across studies, definitional issues might provide at least a partial explanation. In the vast majority of studies on its effects on substance use, racial/ethnic identity has been studied as a singular construct. However, racial/ethnic identity—and perhaps cultural identifications in general—has been proposed as a multidimensional construct (Phinney & Ong, 2007; Umaña-Taylor et al., 2014). Specifically, racial/ethnic identity exploration, resolution, and affirmation have been proposed as separate components. *Exploration* refers to consideration of what it means to be a member of one's racial/ethnic or cultural group. For example, adolescents and emerging adults might talk to other members of their racial/ethnic group, think about different representations of their racial/ethnic group in the media, or consult books or Web sites about their racial/ethnic group's history in the United States. *Resolution* refers to settling on a set of ideas about one's racial/ethnic group and about the meaning of membership in that group. For example, a Mexican American person might decide that being Mexican American means taking pride in one's indigenous Mexican heritage while defying the stereotypes of Mexican Americans as poor, uneducated, and uninterested in integrating themselves into American society. *Affirmation* refers to feeling positively about one's racial/ethnic group and deriving self-esteem from this group membership. Although no published research has been conducted on the contributions of these different components of racial/ethnic identity to risk for drug and alcohol use, the three components have been found to predict other outcomes (e.g., self-esteem) in different ways (e.g., Umaña-Taylor, Gonzales-Backen, & Guimond, 2009; Umaña-Taylor, Vargas-Chanes, Garcia, & Gonzales-Backen, 2008). Ethnic identity is a component of acculturation, which is itself multidimensional. Given this multidimensionality, it is possible that different racial/ethnic identity components may have been responsible for the discrepant associations of racial/ethnic identity with drug and alcohol use across studies. Moreover, given the hypothesis that exploration, resolution, and affirmation represent a developmental sequence (Phinney, 1990), the effect of racial/ethnic identity on substance use may differ according to where one is on that developmental sequence. Further research is necessary to examine this, and other, possibilities.

Let us return now to the larger model of acculturation that we (Schwartz et al., 2010) have proposed. Whereas past research has examined cultural practices, values, and identifications *separately* as predictors of substance use outcomes, a major step forward for the study of acculturation and substance use would be to include all three of these domains *together* as predictors (Unger & Schwartz, in press). A small number of studies (e.g., Schwartz et al., 2011; Schwartz, Unger, Des Rosiers, et al., 2014) have adopted such an approach, such that the unique contributions of each cultural domain to substance use outcomes can be evaluated. For both adolescents and emerging adults, ethnic identity served as a risk for alcohol and drug use, whereas American identity was largely protective.

In those studies where racial/ethnic identity was identified as a positive correlate or predictor of drug and alcohol use among Hispanic adolescents and emerging adults (e.g., Schwartz et al., 2011; Zamboanga et al., 2009), cultural practices were also used in analysis. Given that Hispanic cultural practices and racial/ethnic identity were at least moderately correlated (correlation coefficients ranged from .34 to .47), the contribution of racial/ethnic identity to substance use was estimated controlling for the effects of Hispanic practices. When racial/ethnic behaviors (e.g., engaging in activities as a way of exploring one's ethnicity, or as a way of demonstrating one's commitment to of affirmation of that ethnicity) are factored out of the racial/ethnic identity construct, what remains is largely defensive identification with one's racial/ethnic group. Indeed, drawing in part on Ogbu's work (see Ogbu & Simons, 1998, for a review), Rumbaut

(2008) has coined the term "reactive ethnicity" to refer to increases in racial/ethnic identification that occur in response to discrimination or other negative intergroup events. When effects of Hispanic cultural practices are taken into account, the unique effects of Hispanic racial/ethnic identity may reflect a reactive racial/ethnic identification—which may then positively predict drug and alcohol use. The finding that this reactive ethnicity effect emerged only for Hispanics—and not for any of the other five ethnic groups studied—in Schwartz et al.'s (2011) national multisite study is not surprising given that Hispanics are at the center of American national debates about immigration (Stepick, Dutton Stepick, & Vanderkooy, 2011), language (Tran, 2010), and national identity (Buchanan, 2006; Huntington, 2004). Nonetheless, additional research is necessary to more clearly understand the role of racial/ethnic identity in substance use among Hispanic adolescents—including measuring reactive ethnicity and/or reactions to being targeted as a "threat" to the national fabric of the United States.

So the effects of acculturation on substance use and other health behaviors are likely moderated by reactive ethnicity, which by definition is a product of discrimination. Moreover, reactive ethnicity can be viewed as a system justification response—in that individuals distance themselves from (rather than challenging) the larger social structure from which they are marginalized or excluded. However, as Steiner (2009) emphasizes, some racial/ethnic groups (or subgroups within a single racial/ethnic group) are stereotyped and subjected to social dominance processes to a greater extent than other racial/ethnic groups or subgroups are.

Specifically, the probability of experiencing negative intergroup dynamics—including discrimination and other social dominance reactions—is likely linked with socioeconomic status, skin color and other physical traits, and the circumstances surrounding one's (or one's family's) immigration to the United States. Immigrants who are phenotypically White, who have more financial resources, who are well educated, and/or who immigrated legally are likely to be welcomed and accepted more readily compared to people of color, poorer and uneducated people, and undocumented immigrants (Steiner, 2009). Some Asian subgroups, although they may experience some personal discrimination, may not be blocked from advancing themselves because they are viewed as an asset to the United States (Leong & Okazaki, 2009).

Given that stereotypes tend to be activated based on first impressions, in many cases, darker skinned Hispanics and those working in lower paying jobs—especially those stereotypically associated with uneducated or undocumented individuals— may be most likely to experience discrimination and social dominance processes (cf. Espino & Franz, 2002). Not coincidentally, acculturation options for socially marginalized individuals and groups— including poor individuals and those stereotyped as being from devalued minority groups—may be more limited. Indeed, discrimination, social dominance processes, and reactive ethnicity may steer many impoverished individuals away from socially desirable goals and options and toward countercultural life paths (Pratto et al., 2006; Sidanius et al., 2004). Social dominance processes are also largely responsible for the continued relegation of many African Americans and Hispanics to poor inner-city neighborhoods. Not surprisingly, poverty is by far the strongest predictor of health disparities in substance use and other outcomes (Barr, 2008), likely because of high unemployment and high school dropout rates that lead residents to pursue antisocial activities as a way of generating income, and because of built-environment features (e.g., liquor stores, abandoned buildings, and cigarette kiosks) that encourage substance use (Bernstein, Galea, Ahern, Tracy, & Vlahov, 2007; Henriksen et al., 2008; West et al., 2010).

Substance Use Within an Intergroup Context of Acculturation

Let us return briefly to the larger intergroup context in which Hispanics find themselves in the United States. Schwartz and colleagues (Schwartz, Unger, et al., 2010; Schwartz, Vignoles, et al., 2014) have outlined the intergroup processes that constrain and direct the acculturation process. Most principally, they have argued that acculturation operates quite differently for "valued" and "devalued" immigrant groups (see Steiner, 2009, for further discussion). Of course, who is valued and who is devalued depends on the receiving society in question—as well as on the historical epoch in which immigration is occurring. For example, groups that were devalued in the early 20th century, such as Jews and Italians, are now valued by many other Americans—due in large part to the fact that the flow of these immigrants has stopped, allowing their descendants to become part of the "American mainstream" (Stepick et al., 2011). Hispanics are now perceived as the most threatening immigrant group, both because of their growing political power and because they share a common language that is seen as a threat to the status of English as a pillar of American national identity (Huntington, 2004).

As a largely devalued group in the United States—due to threat and subsequent social dominance and system justification processes—Hispanics are likely to be constrained in the ways in which they can acculturate. For example, assimilating to American culture has been shown to be more consistently detrimental (and risk inducing) for Hispanics (Cook, Alegría, Lin, & Guo, 2009) than for Asians (John, de Castro, Martin, Duran, & Takeuchi, 2012). One possible reason for this disparity in effects of acculturation between immigrant groups is that Asians are stereotyped as "wanting" to learn English and to fit in with American culture, whereas Hispanics are not (Steiner, 2009). Indeed, when members of groups that are stereotyped as "threatening" appear to assimilate to the receiving society, they are often rejected and discriminated against by members of the majority group (Guimond, De Oliveira, Kamiesjki, & Sidanius, 2010). In turn, experiences of discrimination are linked with drug and alcohol use (Lo & Cheng, 2012; Pascoe & Smart Richman, 2009). As a result, as we noted earlier, intergroup processes between Whites and Hispanics may determine the extent to which health disparities emerge in alcohol and drug use between Hispanics and other racial/ethnic groups, as well as the extent to which specific acculturation profiles may be linked with these disparities. Moreover, we need to understand *how* and *why* discrimination is predictive of drug and alcohol use. Is the explanation due to other ecological influences, self-medication, engagement in "oppositional" activities in response to being rejected by mainstream society, or some other explanation? Knowledge of the mechanisms responsible for the discrimination-substance use link can help us to design interventions to offset and disrupt this effect.

Social dominance and system justification theories proceed from the assumption that group identities have been activated, and these theories outline the intergroup events that occur subsequently and that produce disparities in wealth, living conditions, incarceration, risk-taking behavior, and physical and mental health (among other outcomes) between dominant and nondominant groups (Jost et al., 2004; Sidanius et al., 2004). Baum (2008) and Moshman (2007) describe a number of steps that occur between the activation of group identities and the unequal distribution of tangible and intangible resources across groups. Perhaps the steps that are most relevant to the genesis of health disparities are dichotomization and dehumanization, and we describe these steps in detail immediately next.

Dichotomization is the act of grouping individuals into two basic categories—"us" and "them." "We" (ingroup members) are deserving of unwarranted favoritism and of unequal and unbalanced distribution of resources (Brewer, 1999). "They" do not matter as long as they are not a threat to "us," but if they are a threat, then ingroup members are justified in taking whatever actions are necessary to neutralize the outgroup and the threat that it poses. According to these principles, when meeting an unfamiliar person, one of the first steps one will take is to determine whether that person is "one of us" or "one of them," and stereotyped first impressions (e.g., physical appearance, speech) are often used to make these judgments. For example, Devos, Gavin, and Quintana (2010) found that, using implicit measures, such as asking participants to respond as quickly as possible and without stopping to think, prototypically Anglo-American last names (e.g., Johnson, Smith, or Jones) were more quickly and consistently classified as "American," whereas prototypically Hispanic last names (e.g., Rodriguez, Sanchez, or Hernandez) were more quickly and consistently classified as "foreign." In that same set of studies, both White and Hispanic participants took significantly less time to match Hispanic themes with the heading of "foreign," and to match White American themes with the heading of "American," than vice versa. Given that ingroup-outgroup judgments are made implicitly and without deliberate thought (Spears, 2011), the take-home message from the Devos et al. (2010) study is that Hispanics are excluded from the larger heading of "Americans." That is, for many Americans, Hispanics are viewed as an outgroup, rather than as part of the larger national ingroup—suggesting that they may, in many cases, be victimized by unequal distribution of resources in the United States. This conclusion may be further bolstered by the fact that Devos et al.'s study was conducted in Southern California, where Hispanics comprise nearly 40% of the population (Ennis et al., 2011).

Furthermore, there is evidence that Hispanics—and members of other racial/ethnic minority groups—classify *themselves* as an outgroup relative to the United States (although they may think of themselves as an ingroup relative to one another). The construct of stereotype threat (Steele, 1997) refers to a self-fulfilling prophecy whereby minority individuals internalize commonly held negative beliefs about their groups and come to believe that these stereotyped outcomes are inevitable for them. In effect, individuals lower their expectations of themselves so that the stereotype is ultimately supported (see Madon, Willard, Guyll, & Scherr, 2011, for a review). For example, in many areas of the United States, Hispanic children and adolescents, especially those whose physical features identify them as Hispanic, may struggle in school largely because of the belief that Hispanics are uneducated and not capable of performing as well as Whites (Guyll, Madon, Prieto, & Scherr, 2010). Indeed, Osborne (2001) found that anxiety—possibly reflecting the fear of confirming a negative stereotype about one's ethnic group—explained nearly 40% of differences in standardized test scores between Hispanics and Whites. Moreover, in their series of studies using implicit measures, Devos et al. (2010) found that Hispanic individuals were more likely to characterize other Hispanics as foreigners than as Americans. Indeed, the complicity of many Hispanics in their own marginalization from the American "ingroup" may underlie system justification processes where most Hispanics do not challenge—and may actually endorse—unequal distribution of resources in favor of Whites. Perhaps more ominously, minority individuals who do *not* endorse system justification beliefs may experience cardiovascular stress and reactivity immediately following episodes of discrimination; and those who *do* endorse system justification beliefs may be so accustomed to experiencing discrimination that they experience cardiovascular stress and reactivity following episodes where discrimination is expected but does not occur (Townsend, Major, Sawyer, & Mendes, 2010; see also Krieger, 2012).

Dichotomization of others into ingroup versus outgroup members appears to occur in most situations where multiple groups occupy different roles (e.g., dominant versus minority) in the status hierarchy or are competing for the same set of resources. In one of the earliest studies of intergroup relations, Tajfel (1970) randomly assigned adolescent boys into two meaningless groups and found that the boys proposed allocating resources unfairly to ingroup members—even though the groups were artificially created. Haney, Banks, and Zimbardo (1973), in the Stanford Prison Experiment, randomly assigned young men to serve either as prisoners or as guards in a mock prison. The two groups assumed their roles so quickly that the study was discontinued within 6 days because of extreme torture that the

guards were inflicting on the prisoners. The remarkable effects of such artificial group memberships suggest that intergroup processes may be even more entrenched in the context of groups defined by ethnicity, nationality, or other demographic characteristics. Put differently, ingroup/outgroup distinction and competition is a strong tendency in humans and becomes even more entrenched as groups interact with one another over decades or centuries.

Dehumanization may occur once individuals have been classified into ingroups versus outgroups. Dehumanization is the process whereby the outgroup is viewed as a single entity rather than as a group of people with varying individual characteristics (Moshman, 2007). Outgroup members and subgroups (e.g., people from different countries, or from different migration waves originating from the same country) may also maintain tensions with one another, which in turn may further decrease the likelihood of their banding together against the ingroup. Dehumanization is likely responsible for the unequal allocation of resources to the ingroup—given that the welfare of individual outgroup members is not considered when decisions about resource allocation are made. The relevance of dehumanization to health disparities is clear—if more members of the dominant racial/ethnic or cultural group thought carefully about the living conditions of poor minority families, then the increased risk taking, disease, and mortality rates among minority groups would likely not be tolerated. The disparate concentration of liquor stores, cigarette kiosks, and abandoned buildings—all of which are known to facilitate substance use (Bernstein et al., 2007; Henriksen et al., 2008; West et al., 2010)—in low-income minority areas would not be permitted if the plight of each child or adolescent living in these communities was considered. Even if the liquor stores or cigarette kiosks are owned by minority group members, it is the social-structural allocation of resources that encourages these outlets to be concentrated in poor minority areas. Viewing "minorities" at the group level allows members of the dominant racial/ethnic group to avoid considering the plight of minority individuals who directly experience health disparities in substance use and other health outcomes.

Implications for Intervention: Ways to Address Culturally Driven Disparities in Substance Abuse

Now that we have outlined a number of social and cultural risk factors associated with the problem of Hispanic drug and alcohol use, and explained their rootedness using a sociological, psychological, and population-level perspective, how do we address the problem? How do we reduce health disparities in substance use—and by extension, in many other undesirable outcomes (e.g., crime and violence, diseases related to alcohol and drug use)?

The answer to this question likely involves interventions at all three levels that we have covered in this chapter—systemic/structural, individual, and family. Let us illustrate this principle using the terminology of multilevel modeling, a statistical technique designed to analyze datasets where variability occurs at multiple levels of organization (e.g., individuals within families and families within communities). One of the fundamental principles of multilevel modeling is that individual-level or family-level variability should be explained using individual-level or family-level predictors, whereas population-level variability should be explained using population-level predictors (Raudenbush & Bryk, 2002). A second principle is that population-level predictors can explain individual-level or family-level variability through their effects on population-level outcomes, but that individual-level or family-level predictors cannot explain population-level variability. If we extrapolate this principle back to the problem of health disparities, it suggests that addressing health disparities requires simultaneous intervention at all three levels. Although individual-level and family-level substance use interventions have been designed, evaluated, and disseminated, interventions to change population-level intergroup dynamics have not been systematically implemented. Indeed, one of the reasons why health disparities have persisted despite our best attempts to eradicate them is that *there are determinants of these disparities to which we have not yet attended.*

Thus far, family-based interventions (some of which also include individual-level components) have been shown to be quite efficacious in preventing or reducing substance use, especially in racial/ethnic minority groups (see Szapocznik, Prado, Burlew, Williams, & Santisteban, 2007; van Ryzin, Stormshak, & Dishion, 2012, for reviews). The efficacy and effectiveness of family-based intervention strategies are likely due to the important role of positive family processes in lowering risk for substance use and related problems. There is abundant research that family strengths can help to offset the effects of neighborhood dangerousness. For example, parental limit setting and management of adolescent activities can counter the effects of

neighborhood crime (e.g., Gayles, Coatsworth, Pantin, & Szapocznik, 2009) and of deviant peer affiliations (Dishion, Nelson, & Bullock, 2004) on adolescent problem behavior and substance use. Indeed, although family-based interventions are appropriate and efficacious for adolescents from many racial/ethnic backgrounds, they are particularly well suited for racial/ethnic minority adolescents, who tend to come from cultural backgrounds that emphasize family connectedness and interdependence.

Beyond promoting positive family processes, it is also important for family-based interventions for immigrant and minority adolescent substance use to promote biculturalism (or multiculturalism) in both parents and adolescents (Smokowski & Bacallao, 2010; Szapocznik et al., 1989). Promoting biculturalism—endorsement of both American culture and the family's heritage culture—has the potential to reduce risks for alcohol and drug use associated with differential parent–adolescent acculturation and with adolescents drifting away from their cultural heritage. Although large-scale studies have not yet investigated the efficacy and effectiveness of adding a biculturalism component to a family-based intervention modality, this is a promising direction for future substance use prevention and treatment research.

Nonetheless, regardless of how widely they are implemented, family-based interventions can only impact family-level and individual-level risks for adolescent drug and alcohol abuse. Intergroup social dominance and system justification processes, which operate at the population level, are unlikely to be affected by *any* intervention delivered to individual adolescents or families. The emerging field of implementation science, which focuses on overcoming barriers to—and facilitating—widespread adoption of effective interventions (e.g., Chamberlain et al., 2008), may help to increase the number of individuals and families who can benefit from a given intervention program. However, the extent to which implementing interventions targeting individual- and family-level processes can offset the deleterious effects of harmful intergroup processes is not yet known.

Even structural and policy interventions delivered at the population level may only partially reduce the disparities in alcohol and drug use—and the consequences of these behaviors—among racial/ethnic groups. Structural and policy interventions, such as raising prices of and taxes on alcohol and tobacco (Wagenaar, Tobler, & Komro, 2009), enforcing bans on alcohol and tobacco sales to minors

(Treno, Gruenewald, Lee, & Remer, 2007; Tutt, Bauer, & DiFranza, 2009), restricting alcohol and tobacco advertising and special sales promotions in low-socioeconomic neighborhoods (Henriksen, 2012), and lowering the blood-alcohol level criterion that is considered indicative of intoxication (Wagenaar, Maldonado-Molina, Ma, Tobler, & Komro, 2007), appear to have some effects on substance use rates and consequences. However, it should be noted that the same minority groups are characterized by disparities in a large number of outcomes—including not only substance use but also related outcomes such as incarceration and other health problems (e.g., cancer, heart disease, stroke) that may occur as a consequence of tobacco, alcohol, and illicit drug use (US Department of Health and Human Services, 2011). As a result, intervention efforts are needed to directly target the intergroup processes responsible for these health disparities. Targeting large numbers of health disparities one at a time may not be effective and is likely to overlook the common causes of the various disparities.

However, targeting and changing social dominance, system justification, and other population-level intergroup processes is likely an extremely difficult endeavor. Intergroup processes are especially intractable, largely because they operate outside of conscious awareness (Pratto et al., 2006; Spears, 2011), and because groups in power may be reluctant to give up their power. Indeed, perceptions of threat from minority groups, and the strategies adopted to minimize (or distance oneself or one's group from) these groups, operate almost automatically (Tip et al., 2012). When a group identity is activated as a result of a perceived threat, the individual thinks and acts as a group member rather than as an individual person (Spears, 2011). To disrupt the potentially destructive dynamics that result from intergroup conflicts, we must disrupt—or reverse—the activation of group identities and the processes that occur as an immediate result of activating these group identities. But to do this, we must first understand how intergroup processes proceed.

Some theorizing and research has attempted to elucidate solutions to intergroup conflicts and dynamics. Proposed methods of reducing ingroup biases and of reducing social dominance and system justification beliefs include facilitating intergroup contact (Hammack, 2006), encouraging majority group members to advocate on behalf of minority groups (Subašić, Reynolds, & Turner, 2008), and emphasizing similarities (rather than differences) between ingroup and outgroup members (Danso, Sedlovskaya, & Suanda, 2007). We discuss each of these methods briefly next.

Facilitating intergroup contact involves bringing together individuals from different racial/ethnic or national groups and promoting informal social interactions among them. In many cases, spending time with someone from an outgroup may counter the dehumanization process and may help people from different groups to see one another as human beings rather than as members of a competing or devalued social group. Direct contact with people from other groups is most desirable (Hammack, 2006), and at the population level, strategies such as school desegregation and neighborhood ethnic mixing may—if utilized effectively—help to facilitate such direct contact (Dixon & Rosenbaum, 2004). Where direct contact is not possible or feasible, experimental research suggests that simulated intergroup contact, through methods such as storytelling or role playing, may also help to reverse dichotomization, dehumanization, and ingroup favoritism (Cameron, Rutland, Brown, & Douch, 2006). Indeed, seeing and spending time with people from other groups is likely to facilitate regarding them as peers rather than as enemies or competitors. Once unconscious intergroup processes are brought into conscious awareness, they become amenable to change. Indeed, it may be possible to create a "common enemy" (even an imaginary one—such as terrorism from the outside or a public health epidemic such as Ebola) that can bring members of competing groups together in support of a common set of goals. Such a strategy may help to create an ingroup to which everyone belongs.

Recruiting majority group members to serve as advocates for minority groups may be effective because the advocates come from the same racial/ethnic group as the individuals who are threatened by the growing influence of minorities. However, the "black sheep effect," whereby ingroup members are judged especially harshly for betraying the ingroup's interests (e.g., Pinto, Marques, Levine, & Abrams, 2010), represents an important caution with regard to majority-group advocacy. Indeed, prominent ingroup members may be evaluated most critically, suggesting that there may be a price to be paid for advocating on behalf of minorities whose interests are viewed as being in conflict with those of the majority racial/ethnic group. However, if the advocacy approach is used in combination with efforts to reduce ingroup biases, social dominance beliefs, and system justification beliefs, the black sheep effect may represent less of an obstacle. Indeed, majority-group advocates might be recruited to lead efforts to reduce intergroup biases among fellow majority-group members—including (and especially) those in positions of political or economic power.

A third strategy is to target social dominance and system justification beliefs directly. Evidence suggests that, among majority group members, social dominance beliefs can be reduced by focusing attention on individual values and beliefs rather than on intergroup distinctions (Danso et al., 2007). That is, because social dominance is an intergroup process that operates after group identities have been activated and dichotomization has taken place, reactivating individual identity may reduce social dominance beliefs. Highlighting areas of commonality between majority and minority individuals may also help to reduce dichotomization and dehumanization (Dovidio & Fiske, 2012). Additionally, role-plays where individuals high on social dominance beliefs adopt supporting (rather than dominant) roles may help to decrease social dominance orientation (Pratto, Tatar, & Conway-Lanz, 1999).

System justification beliefs may be reduced by helping minority-group members to view the status quo as changeable (Johnson & Fujita, 2012) and to develop a sense of perceived control over their own life course (Kay & Friesen, 2011). However, it stands to reason that, for system justification beliefs to be legitimately challengeable, the majority group would need to be at least somewhat supportive of increased self-determination and rights for minority group members. As a result, interventions to reduce or change majority-minority intergroup dynamics would need to target both the majority group (under the assumption that the majority group must give up power in order for minority groups to obtain power) and minority groups (so that they can effectively use their power to improve health outcomes, such as reducing drug and alcohol use and associated consequences). Such a philosophy stands in contrast to most approaches to reducing health disparities, which focus on changing health outcomes in minority group members.

Specifically, it may be necessary to target both the majority group (in terms of addressing intergroup biases and reducing social dominance beliefs) and minority groups (in terms of reducing system justification beliefs and in terms of implementing family- and community-based interventions to improve health outcomes and care in minority populations). Such an approach would bring together strengths from social psychology and public health and would suggest a blending of (a) theoretically driven interventions aimed at the intergroup dynamics that underlie health disparities with (b) practically driven, public health interventions aimed at the specific health behaviors and outcomes through which health disparities are manifested.

In the case of adolescent alcohol and drug use, prevention and treatment programs would target contextual, social-ecological, and biological risk and protective factors known to be associated with higher incidence and prevalence of substance use. For example, family-based interventions are designed to increase family support, parental supervision, and parent–adolescent communication—all of which are known to protect against adolescent substance use in low-risk as well as high-risk adolescents (Prado, Szapocznik, Maldonado-Molina, Schwartz, & Pantin, 2008). At the same time, interventions should be aimed at the population-based intergroup processes that result in unequal allocation of resources across racial/ethnic groups and the disproportional marginalization of minorities (especially Hispanics and African Americans) to poor, dangerous, and underresourced neighborhoods. Such interventions will likely be difficult to develop and implement at the population level, but if our goal is to reduce health disparities in a lasting way, we will need to take up this challenge. Most critically, systematic and lasting efforts must be devoted to preventing or reversing the activation of group identities in interethnic situations and conflicts. As reviewed in this chapter, some potential ways to accomplish this include facilitating intergroup contact (face-to-face or simulated), highlighting individual differences among ingroup and outgroup members to offset dichotomization and dehumanization, and engaging a critical mass of majority-group individuals to serve as advocates for minority health. Indeed, given that health disparities in substance use are likely a microcosm of health disparities in many other health-related outcomes (US Department of Health and Human Services, 2011), the intergroup processes that would be targeted for intervention are likely quite similar across a range of health-disparity indices.

Conclusion

In this chapter, we have reviewed the state of the science on the cultural context of adolescent substance use. Cultural processes predict and affect substance use at multiple levels, including individual, family, and population-intergroup.

Although individual-level interventions may be somewhat efficacious in preventing or treating adolescent substance use, family-based interventions are especially well suited for preventing or treating adolescent substance use—especially in racial/ethnic minority groups. Widespread implementation of effective family-based prevention and treatment interventions is important to offset family-level and individual-level risks—though incorporating cultural concerns directly into these interventions (in the form of modules to promote biculturalism in parents and adolescents) may also help to reduce risks for drug and alcohol use. Perhaps the most novel contribution that we offer in this chapter, however, is the connection between (a) intergroup-based social dominance and system justification processes and (b) racial/ethnic disparities in substance use and any number of other health outcomes. Given that minority groups—especially African Americans and Hispanics—experience disparities in a large array of health and quality-of-life indices, it is likely that these various disparities share a common set of causes. These causes include social dominance processes, which result in the unequal allocation of resources away from devalued minority groups; and system justification processes, which prevent minority groups from directly challenging the status quo and instead prompt them to develop countercultural identities. Because substance use is multiply determined at various levels of the biological, intrapersonal, social, and cultural context, a number of intervention strategies are likely necessary to effectively prevent and reduce substance use among Hispanic adolescents and those from other ethnic minority groups. Such strategies include individual- and family-based interventions, policy changes, and interventions into population-level intergroup processes. Of all of these potential intervention targets, intergroup processes may be among the most difficult to change because they operate on a largely automatic basis.

Nonetheless, these intergroup processes need to be targeted for intervention if we are to be successful in reducing or eliminating health disparities in a range of outcomes (rather than targeting these health outcomes one at a time). Social-psychological research has suggested ways for addressing these intergroup processes, but translational research that moves this knowledge from the laboratory to the design and implementation of interventions at the population level is likely to be quite challenging. We have suggested some potential directions for intervention here, and we hope that researchers and policy makers will follow these suggestions so that we can identify promising ways to reduce the negative intergroup dynamics that underlie disparities in substance use and other health outcomes. It is through such steps that we can help to improve the health of our population.

AcknowledgmentWe thank Byron L. Zamboanga for his helpful feedback on earlier drafts of this chapter.

Notes

1. Although a large number of health disparities operate for African Americans, in this chapter we focus specifically on adolescent substance use—for which Hispanics evidence the greatest disparities.
2. Although the term "American" can be used to refer to countries and groups throughout North, Central, and South America, we use this term here to refer to the United States and its residents.
3. The term "minority" refers to the amount of social, political, and economic power controlled by a given group, rather than to the size of the group. For example, in apartheid-era South Africa, Whites held the majority of power even though they were a distinct numerical minority.
4. Although social dominance and system justification theories assume that the majority group is responsible for the unequal allocation of resources, minority groups also often discriminate against each other.
5. It should be emphasized that we are referring to population-level intergroup processes, and that not every member of the dominant group will hold these views.
6. It should be recognized that some immigrants may have been involuntarily subjugated in their countries of origin, and that they may bring these experiences of subjugation with them into their experiences in the United States.
7. Note that the term "immigrant group" refers to groups that are perceived as consisting primarily of immigrants and their immediate descendants—even if many members of these groups have been in the receiving society for many generations (e.g., Japanese Americans and some Mexican Americans).

References

Abraido-Lanza, A. E., Armbrister, A. N., Florez, K. R., & Aguirre, A. N. (2006). Toward a theory-driven model of acculturation in public health research. *American Journal of Public Health, 96*, 1342–1346.

Acosta-Belen, E., & Santiago, C. E. (2006). *Puerto Ricans in the United States: A contemporary portrait*. Boulder, CO: Westview.

Adimora, A., Schoenbach, V. J., Martinson, F. E. A., Donaldson, K. H., Stancil, T. R., & Fullilove, R. E. (2003). Concurrent partnerships among rural African Americans with recently reported heterosexually transmitted HIV infection. *Journal of Acquired Immune Deficiency Syndromes, 34*, 423–429.

Aguirre-Molina, M., Borrell, L. N., Muñoz-Laboy, M., & Vega, W. A. (2010). Introduction: A social-structural framework for the analysis of Latino males' health. In M. Aguirre-Molina, L. N. Borrell, & W. A. Vega (Eds.), *Health issues* in *Latino males: A social and structural approach* (pp. 1–16). Piscataway, NJ: Rutgers University Press.

Al-Sayyad, N. (Ed.). (2001). *Hybrid urbanism: On the identity discourse and the built environment.* Westport, CT: Praeger.

Alba, R., Denton, N. A., Hernandez, D. J., Disha, I., McKenzie, B., & Napierala, J. (2010). Nowhere near the same: The neighborhoods of Latino children. In N. S. Landale, S. McHale, & A. Booth (Eds.), *Growing up Hispanic: Health and development of children of immigrants* (pp. 3–48). Washington, DC: Urban Institute Press.

Aloise-Young, P. A., & Chavez, E. L. (2002). Not all school dropouts are the same: Racial/ethnic differences in the relation between reason for leaving school and adolescent substance use. *Psychology in the Schools, 39,* 539–547.

Barker, V., Giles, H., Noels, K., Duck, J., Hecht, M., & Clément, R. (2001). The English-only movement: A communication analysis of changing perceptions of language vitality. *Journal of Communication, 51,* 3–37.

Barr, D. A. (2008). *Health disparities in the United States: Social class, race, ethnicity, and health.* Baltimore, MD: Johns Hopkins University Press.

Baum, S. K. (2008). *The psychology of genocide: Perpetrators, bystanders, and rescuers.* Cambridge, England: Cambridge University Press.

Baumeister, R. F. (2010). Understanding free will and consciousness on the basis of current research findings in psychology. In R. F. Baumeister, A. R. Mele, & K. D. Vohs (Eds.), *Free will and consciousness: How might they work?* (pp. 24–42). Oxford, England: Oxford University Press.

Benet-Martínez, V., & Haritatos, J. (2005). Bicultural identity integration (BII): Components and psychosocial antecedents. *Journal of Personality, 73,* 1015–1050.

Benet-Martínez, V., Leu, J., Lee, F., & Morris, M. (2002). Negotiating biculturalism: Cultural frame switching in biculturals with oppositional versus compatible cultural identities. *Journal of Cross-Cultural Psychology, 33,* 492–516.

Bernstein, K. T., Galea, S., Ahern, J., Tracy, M., & Vlahov, D. (2007). The built environment and alcohol consumption in urban neighborhoods. *Drug and Alcohol Dependence, 91,* 244-252.

Berry, J. W. (1980). Acculturation as varieties of adaptation. In A. M. Padilla (Ed.), *Acculturation: Theory, models, and some new findings* (pp. 9-25). Boulder: Westview Press.

Berry, J. W. (2003). Conceptual approaches to understanding acculturation. In K. M. Chun, P. B. Organista, & G. Marín (Eds.), *Acculturation: Advances in theory, measurement, and applied research* (pp. 17–38). Washington, DC: American Psychological Association.

Berry, J. W. (2006). Contexts of acculturation. In D. L. Sam & J. W. Berry (Eds.), *Cambridge handbook of acculturation psychology* (pp. 27–42). Cambridge, England: Cambridge University Press.

Brewer, M. B. (1999). The psychology of prejudice: Ingroup love or outgroup hate? *Journal of Social Issues, 55,* 429–444.

Buchanan, P. J. (2006). *State of emergency: The Third World invasion and conquest of America.* New York, NY: St. Martin's Press.

Caetano, R., Ramisetty-Mikler, S., & Rodriguez, L. A. (2009). The Hispanic Americans Baseline Alcohol Survey (HABLAS): The association between birthplace, acculturation and alcohol abuse and dependence across Hispanic national groups. *Drug and Alcohol Dependence, 99,* 215–221.

Cameron, L., Rutland, A., Brown, R., & Douch, R. (2006). Changing children's intergroup attitudes toward refugees: Testing different models of extended contact. *Child Development, 77,* 1208–1219.

Chamberlain, P., Brown, C., Saldana, L., Reid, J., Wang, W., Marsenich, L., . . . Bouwman, G. (2008). Engaging and recruiting counties in an experiment on implementing evidence-based practice in California. *Administration and Policy in Mental Health and Mental Health Services Research, 35,* 250–260.

Chapman, C., Laird, J., & KewalRamani, A. (2010). *Trends in high school dropout and completion rates in the United States: 1972–2008* (National Center for Education Statistics report 2011-012). Washington, DC: US Department of Education. Retrieved April 12, 2016 from http://nces. ed.gov/pubs2011/2011012.pdf

Chen, S. X., Benet-Martínez, V., & Bond, M. H. (2008). Bicultural identity, bilingualism, and psychological adjustment in multicultural societies: Immigration-based and globalization-based acculturation. *Journal of Personality, 76,* 803-838.

Choi, Y., Harachi, T. W., & Catalano, R. F. (2006). Neighborhoods, family, and substance use: Comparisons of the relations across racial and ethnic groups. *Social Science Review, 80,* 675–704.

Chuang, Y-C., Ennett, S. T., Bauman, K. E., & Foshee, V. A. (2005). Neighborhood influences on adolescent cigarette and alcohol use: Mediating effects through parent and peer behaviors. *Journal of Health and Social Behavior, 46,* 187–204.

Constantine, M. G., Wilton, L., Gainor, K. A., & Lewis, E. L. (2002). Religious participation, spirituality, and coping among African American college students. *Journal of College Student Development, 43,* 605–613.

Cook, B., Alegría, M., Lin, J. Y., & Guo, J. (2009). Pathways and correlates connecting Latinos' mental health with exposure to the United States. *American Journal of Public Health, 99,* 2247–2254.

Cooper, C. E., & Crosnoe, R. (2007). The engagement in schooling of economically disadvantaged parents and children. *Youth and Society, 38,* 372–391.

Cornelius, W. (2002). Ambivalent reception: Mass public responses to the "new" Latino immigration to the United States. In M. M. Suárez-Orozco & M. M. Páez (Eds.), *Latinos: Remaking America* (pp. 165–189). Berkeley: University of California Press.

Cox, R. B., Jr., Burr, B., Blow, A., & Parra Cardona, J. R. (2011). Latino adolescent substance use in the United States: Using the bioecodevelopmental model as an organizing framework for research and practice. *Journal of Family Theory and Review, 3,* 96–123.

Danso, H. A., Sedlovskaya, A., & Suanda, S. H. (2007). Perceptions of immigrants: Modifying the attitudes of individuals higher in social dominance orientation. *Personality and Social Psychology Bulletin, 33,* 1113–1123.

Delva, J., Wallace, J. M., Jr., O'Malley, P. M., Bachman, J. G., Johnston, L. D., & Schulenberg, J. E. (2005). The epidemiology of alcohol, marijuana, and cocaine use among Mexican American, Puerto Rican, Cuban American, and other Latin American eighth-grade students in the United States: 1991–2002. *American Journal of Public Health, 95,* 696–702.

Destin, M., & Oyserman, D. (2010). Incentivizing education: Seeing schoolwork as an investment, not a chore. *Journal of Experimental Social Psychology, 46,* 846-849.

Des Rosiers, S. E., Schwartz, S. J., Zamboanga, B. L., Ham, L. S., & Huang, S. (2013). A cultural and social-cognitive model of differences in acculturation orientations, alcohol expectancies, and alcohol risk behaviors among Hispanic college students. *Journal of Clinical Psychology, 69,* 319–340.

Devos, T., Gavin, K., & Quintana, F. J. (2010). Say "adios" to the American Dream? The interplay between racial/ethnic and national identity among Latino and Caucasian Americans. *Cultural Diversity and Ethnic Minority Psychology, 16,* 37–49.

Devos, T., & Heng, L. (2009). Whites are granted the American identity more swiftly than Asians: Disentangling the role of automatic and controlled processes. *Social Psychology, 40,* 192–201.

Dishion, T. J., Nelson, S. E., & Bullock, B. M. (2004). Premature adolescent autonomy: Parent disengagement and deviant peer process in the amplification of problem behavior. *Journal of Adolescence, 27,* 515–530.

Dixon, J. C., & Rosenbaum, M. S. (2004). Nice to know you? Testing contact, cultural, and group threat theories of anti-black and anti-Hispanic stereotypes. *Social Science Quarterly, 85,* 257–280.

Dovidio, J. F., & Fiske, S. T. (2012). Under the radar: How unexamined biases in decision-making processes in clinical interactions can contribute to health care disparities. *American Journal of Public Health, 102,* 945–952.

Ennis, S. R., Rios-Vargas, M., & Albert, N. G. (2011). *The Hispanic population: 2010* (Current Population Report C2010BR-04). Washington, DC: US Census Bureau.

Espino, R., & Franz, M. M. (2002). Latino phenotypic discrimination revisited: The impact of skin color on occupational status. *Social Science Quarterly, 83,* 612–623.

Flannery, W. P., Reise, S. P., & Yu, J. (2001). A comparison of acculturation models. *Personality and Social Psychology Bulletin, 27,* 1035–1045.

Fosados, R., McClain, A., Ritt-Olson, A., Sussman, S., Soto, D., Baezconde-Barbanati, L., & Unger, J. B. (2007). The influence of acculturation on drug and alcohol use in a sample of adolescents. *Addictive Behaviors, 32,* 2990–3004.

Fuligni, A. J., & Witkow, M. (2004). The postsecondary educational progress of children from immigrant families. *Journal of Research on Adolescence, 14,* 159–183.

Gayles, J. G., Coatsworth, J. D., Pantin, H., & Szapocznik, J. (2009). Parenting and neighborhood predictors of youth problem behaviors within Hispanic families: The moderating role of family structure. *Hispanic Journal of Behavioral Sciences, 31,* 277–296.

Gee, G. C., Walsemann, K. M., & Brondolo, E. (2012). A life course perspective on how racism may be related to health inequities. *American Journal of Public Health, 102,* 967–974.

Gil, A. G., Wagner, E. F., & Vega, W. A. (2000). Acculturation, familism, and alcohol use among Latino adolescent males: Longitudinal relations. *Journal of Community Psychology, 28,* 443–458.

Gordon, M. (1964). *Assimilation in American life.* New York, NY: Oxford University Press.

Gruenewald, P. J., Freisthler, B., Remer, L., LaScala, E. A., & Treno, A. (2006). Ecological models of alcohol outlets and violent assaults: Crime potentials and geospatial analysis. *Addiction, 101,* 666–677.

Guimond, S., De Oliveira, P., Kamiesjki, R., & Sidanius, J. (2010). The trouble with assimilation: Social dominance and the emergence of hostility against immigrants. *International Journal of Intercultural Relations, 34,* 624–650.

Guyll, M., Madon, S., Prieto, L., & Scherr, K. C. (2010). The potential roles of self-fulfilling prophecies, stigma consciousness, and stereotype threat in linking Latino/a race/ethnicityand educational outcomes. *Journal of Social Issues, 66,* 113–130.

Hammack, P. L., (2006). Identity, conflict, and coexistence: Life stories of Israeli and Palestinian adolescents. *Journal of Adolescent Research, 21,* 323–369.

Hammack, P. L. (2011). *Narrative and the politics of identity: The cultural psychology of Israeli and Palestinian youth.* Oxford, England: Oxford University Press.

Haney, C., Banks, C., & Zimbardo, P. G. (1973). Interpersonal dynamics in a simulated prison. *International Journal of Criminology and Penology, 1,* 69–97.

Haney Lopez, I. F. (2000). Institutional racism: Judicial conduct and a new theory of racial discrimination. *Yale Law Journal, 109,* 1717–1884.

Henderson, T. J. (2011). *Beyond borders: A history of Mexican migration to the United States.* Malden, MA: Wiley-Blackwell.

Henriksen, L. (2012). Comprehensive tobacco marketing restrictions: Promotion, packaging, price, and place. *Tobacco Control, 21,* 147–153.

Henriksen, L., Feighery, E. C., Schleicher, N. C., Cowling, D. W., Kline, R. S., & Fortmann, S. P. (2008). Is adolescent smoking related to the density and proximity of tobacco outlets and retail cigarette advertising near schools? *Preventive Medicine, 47,* 210–214.

Hodson, G., Dovidio, J. F., & Esses, V. M. (2003). Ingroup identification as a moderator of positive-negative asymmetry in social discrimination. *European Journal of Social Psychology, 33,* 215–233.

Hofstede, G. (2001). *Culture's consequences* (2nd ed.). London, England: Sage.

Hong, J. S., Huang, H., Sabri, B., & Kim, J. (2011). Substance abuse among Asian American youth: An ecological review of the literature. *Children and Youth Services Review, 33,* 669–677.

Huntington, S. P. (2004). *Who are we? The challenge to America's national identity.* New York, NY: Simon & Schuster.

Jenum, A. K., Anderssen, S. A., Birkeland, K. I., Holme, I., Graff-Iversen, S., Lorentzen, C., . . . Bahr, R. (2006). Promoting physical activity in a low-income multiethnic district: Effects of a community intervention study to reduce risk factors for type 2 diabetes and cardiovascular disease. *Diabetes Care, 29,* 1605–1612.

Jimeno-Ingrum, D., Berdahl, J. L., & Lucero-Wagoner, B. (2009). Stereotypes of Latinos and whites: Do they guide evaluations in diverse work groups? *Cultural Diversity and Ethnic Minority Psychology, 15,* 158–164.

John, D. A., de Castro, A. B., Martin, D. P., Duran, B., & Takeuchi, D. T. (2012). Does an immigrant health paradox exist among Asian Americans? Associations of nativity and occupational class with self-rated health and mental disorders. *Social Science and Medicine, 75,* 2085–2098.

Johnson, I. R., & Fujita, K. (2012). Change we can believe in: Using perceptions of changeability to promote system-change motives over system-justification motives in information search. *Psychological Science, 23,* 133–140.

Johnston, L. D., O'Malley, P. M., Miech, R. A., Bachman, J. G., & Schulenberg, J. E. (2016). *Monitoring the future national survey results on drug use, 1975-2015.* Ann Arbor, MI: University of Michigan Institute for Social Research.

Jost, J. T., Banaji, M. R., & Nosek, B. A. (2004). A decade of system justification theory: Accumulated evidence of conscious and unconscious bolstering of the status quo. *Political Psychology*, *25*, 881–919.

Jost, J. T., & Burgess, D. (2000). Attitudinal ambivalence and the conflict between group and system justification motives in low status groups. *Personality and Social Psychology Bulletin*, *26*, 293–305.

Kao, H. F., McHugh, M. L., & Travis, S. S. (2007). Psychometric tests of expectations to filial piety scale in a Mexican-American population. *Journal of Clinical Nursing*, *16*, 1460–1467.

Kay, A. C., & Friesen, J. (2011). On social stability and social change: Understanding when system justification does and does not occur. *Current Directions in Psychological Science*, *20*, 360–364.

Kellner, D. (2011). Cultural studies, multiculturalism, and media culture. In G. Dines & J. M. Humez (Eds.), *Gender, race, and class in media: A critical reader* (3rd ed., pp. 7–18). Thousand Oaks, CA: Sage.

Kelly, A. B., O'Flaherty, M., Toumbourou, J. W., Connor, J. P., Hemphill, S. A., & Catalano, R. F. (2011). Gender differences in the impact of families on alcohol use: a lagged longitudinal study of early adolescents. *Addiction*, *106*, 1427–1436.

Kim, B. S. K., Lee, L. C., & Ng, G. (2005). The Asian American Values Scale—Multidimensional: Development, reliability, and validity. *Cultural Diversity and Ethnic Minority Psychology*, *11*, 187–201.

Kroeber, A., & Kluckhohn, F. (1952). *Culture: A critical review of concepts and definitions*. Cambridge, MA: Harvard Business Review.

Krieger, N. (2012). Methods for the study of discrimination and health: An ecosocial approach. *American Journal of Public Health*, *102*, 936–945.

Kurtines, W. M., & Szapocznik, J. (1996). Structural family therapy in contexts of cultural diversity. In E. Hibbs & R. Jensen (Eds.), *Psychosocial treatment research with children and adolescents* (pp. 671–697). Washington, DC: American Psychological Association.

Lau, A. S., McCabe, K., Yeh, M., Garland, A. F., Wood, P. A., & Hough, R. L. (2005). The acculturation gap-distress hypothesis among high-risk Mexican American families. *Journal of Family Psychology*, *19*, 367–375.

LaVeist, T. A. (2005). *Minority populations and health: An introduction to health disparities in the United States*. San Francisco, CA: Jossey-Bass.

LaVeist, T. A., Pollack, K. Thorpe, R., Jr., Fesahazion, R., & Gaskin, D. (2011). Place, not race: Disparities dissipate in Southwest Baltimore when blacks and whites live under similar conditions. *Health Affairs*, *30*, 1880–1887.

Leong, F. T. L., & Okazaki, S. (2009). History of Asian American psychology. *Cultural Diversity and Ethnic Minority Psychology*, *15*, 352–362.

Lipsky, S., & Caetano, R. (2009). Epidemiology of substance abuse among Latinos. *Journal of Ethnicity in Substance Abuse*, *8*, 242-260.

Lo, C. C., & Cheng, T. C. (2012). Discrimination's role in minority groups' rates of substance use disorder. *American Journal on Addictions*, *21*, 150–156.

Lopez-Class, M., Castro, F. G., & Ramirez, A. G. (2011). Conceptions of acculturation: A review and statement of critical issues. *Social Science and Medicine*, *72*, 1555–1562.

Lorenzo-Blanco, E. I., Unger, J. B., Ritt-Olson, A., Soto, D. W., & Baezconde-Garbanati, L. (2011). Acculturation, gender, depression, and cigarette smoking among U.S. Hispanic youth: The mediating role of perceived discrimination. *Journal of Youth and Adolescence*, *40*, 1519-1533.

Madon, S., Willard, J., Guyll, M., & Scherr, K. C. (2011). Self-fulfilling prophecies: Mechanisms, power, and links to social problems. *Social and Personality Psychology Compass*, *5*, 578–590.

Major, B., Mendes, W. B., & Dovidio, J. F. (2013). Intergroup relations and health disparities: A social psychological perspective. *Health Psychology*, *32*, 514–524.

Marmot, M. (2005). Social determinants of health inequalities. *Lancet*, *365*, 1099–1104.

Marsiglia, F. F., Kulis, S., Hecht, M. L., & Sills, S. (2004). Ethnicity and ethnic identity as predictors of drug norms and drug use among preadolescents in the U.S. Southwest. *Substance Use and Misuse*, *39*, 1061–1094.

Martinez, C. R., Jr., McClure, H. H., Eddy, J. M., & Wilson, D. M. (2011). Time in US residency and the social, behavioral, and emotional adjustment of Latino immigrant families. *Hispanic Journal of Behavioral Sciences*, *33*, 323-349.

Matsumoto, D. (2003). The discrepancy between consensual-level culture and individual-level culture. *Culture and Psychology*, *9*, 89–95.

Moshman, D. (2007). Us and them: Identity and genocide. *Identity: An International Journal of Theory and Research*, *7*, 115–135.

Mulia, N., Ye, Y., Greenfield, T. K., & Zemore, S. E. (2009). Disparities in alcohol-related problems among white, black, and Hispanic Americans. *Alcoholism: Clinical and Experimental Research*, *33*, 654–662.

Myers, R., Chou, C-P., Sussman, S., Baezconde-Garbanati, L., Pachon, H., & Valente, T. W. (2009). Acculturation and substance use: Social influence as a mediator among Hispanic alternative school youth. *Journal of Health and Social Behavior*, *50*, 164–179.

Newsom, J. T. (2012). Basic longitudinal analysis approaches for continuous and categorical variables. In J. T. Newsom, R. N. Jones, & S. M. Hofer (Eds.), *Longitudinal data analysis: A practical guide for researchers in aging, health, and social sciences* (pp. 143–180). New York, NY: Taylor & Francis.

Ngo, B., & Lee, S. J. (2007). Complicating the image of model minority success: A review of Southeast Asian American education. *Review of Educational Research*, *77*, 415–453.

Ogbu, J. U., & Simons, H. D. (1998). Voluntary and involuntary minorities: A cultural-ecological theory of school performance with some implications for education. *Anthropology and Education Quarterly*, *29*(2), 155–188.

Osborne, J. W. (2001). Testing stereotype threat: Does anxiety explain race and sex differences in achievement? *Contemporary Educational Psychology*, *26*, 291–310.

Oyserman, D., Coon, H. M., & Kemmelmeier, M. (2002). Rethinking individualism and collectivism: Evaluation of theoretical assumptions and meta-analyses. *Psychological Bulletin*, *128*, 3–72.

Palmer, R. H. C., Young, S. E., Hopfer, C. J., Corley, R. P., Stallings, M. C., Crowley, T. J., & Hewitt, J. K. (2009). Developmental epidemiology of drug use and abuse in adolescence and young adulthood: Evidence of generalized risk. *Drug and Alcohol Dependence*, *102*, 78–87.

Pantin, H., Schwartz, S. J., Sullivan, S., Prado, G., & Szapocznik, J. (2004). Ecodevelopmental HIV prevention programs for Hispanic immigrant adolescents. *American Journal of Orthopsychiatry*, *74*, 545–558.

Pascoe, E. A., & Smart Richman, L. (2009). Perceived discrimination and health: A meta-analytic review. *Psychological Bulletin, 135*, 531–554.

Pew Research Center. (2010). Public supports Arizona immigration law. Retrieved August 4, 2011 from http://pewresearch.org/pubs/1591/public-support-arizona-immigration-law-poll

Phelan, J. C., Link, B. G., & Tehranifar, P. (2010). Social conditions as fundamental causes of health inequalities: Theory, evidence, and policy implications. *Journal of Health and Social Behavior, 51S*, S28–S40.

Phinney, J. S. (1990). Ethnic identity in adolescents and adults: A review of research. *Psychological Bulletin, 108*, 499–514.

Phinney, J. S. (2003). Ethnic identity and acculturation. In K. M. Chun, P. B. Organista, & G. Marín (Eds.), *Acculturation: Advances in theory, measurement, and applied research* (pp. 63-82). Washington, DC: American Psychological Association.

Phinney, J. S., Berry, J. W., Vedder, P., & Liebkind, K. (2006). The acculturation experience: Attitudes, identities, and behaviors of immigrant youth. In J. W. Berry, J. S. Phinney, D. L. Sam, & P. Vedder (Eds.), *Immigrant youth in cultural transition* (pp. 71–116). Mahwah, NJ: Erlbaum.

Phinney, J. S., & Ong, A. D. (2007). Conceptualization and measurement of racial/ethnic identity: Current status and future directions. *Journal of Counseling Psychology, 54*, 271–281.

Pinto, I. R., Marques, J. M., Levine, J. M., & Abrams, D. (2010). Membership status and subjective group dynamics: Who triggers the black sheep effect? *Journal of Personality and Social Psychology, 99*, 107–119.

Prado, G., Huang, S., Maldonado-Molina, M., Bandiera, F., Schwartz, S. J., de la Vega, P., . . . Pantin, H. (2010). An empirical test of ecodevelopmental theory in predicting HIV risk behaviors among Hispanic youth. *Health Education and Behavior, 37*, 97–114.

Prado, G., Szapocznik, J., Maldonado-Molina, M. M., Schwartz, S. J., & Pantin, H. (2008). Drug use/abuse prevalence, etiology, prevention, and treatment in Hispanic adolescents: A cultural perspective. *Journal of Drug Issues, 38*, 5–36.

Pratto, F., Sidanius, J., & Levin, S. (2006). Social dominance theory and the dynamics of intergroup relations: Taking stock and looking forward. *European Review of Social Psychology, 17*, 271–320.

Pratto, F., Tatar, D. G., & Conway-Lanz, S. (1999). Who gets what and why: Determinants of social allocations. *Political Psychology, 20*, 127–150.

Raudenbush, S. M., & Bryk, A. S. (2002). *Hierarchical linear models: Applications and data analysis methods.* Thousand Oaks, CA: Sage.

Romano, J. L., & Netland, J. D. (2008). The application of the theory of reasoned action and planned behavior to prevention science in counseling psychology. *Counseling Psychologist, 36*, 777–806.

Rudmin, F. W. (2003). Critical history of the acculturation psychology of assimilation, separation, integration, and marginalization. *Review of General Psychology, 7*, 3–37.

Rumbaut, R. G. (2008). Reaping what you sow: Immigration, youth, and reactive ethnicity. *Applied Developmental Science, 12*(2), 108–111.

Sabogal, E. (2005). Viviendo en la sombra: The immigration of Peruvian professionals to South Florida. *Latino Studies, 3*, 113–131.

Sam, D. L., & Berry, J. W. (2010). Acculturation: When individuals and groups of different cultural backgrounds meet. *Perspectives on Psychological Science, 5*, 472–481.

Sampson, R. J., Raudenbush, S. W., & Earls, F. (1997). Neighborhoods and violent crime: A multilevel study of collective efficacy. *Science, 277*, 918–924.

Santiago, C. D., & Wadsworth, M. E. (2011). Family cultural influences on low-income Latino children's adjustment. *Journal of Clinical Child and Adolescent Psychology, 40*, 332–337.

Santibañez, L., Vernez, G., & Razquin, P. (2005). *Education in Mexico: Challenges and opportunities.* Santa Monica, CA: RAND Corporation.

Santisteban, D. A., Coatsworth, J. D., Briones, E., Kurtines, W. M., & Szapocznik, J. (2012). Beyond acculturation: An investigation of the relationship of familism and parenting to behavior problems in Hispanic youth. *Family Process, 51*, 470–482.

Santisteban, D. A., & Mitrani, V. B. (2003). The influence of acculturation processes on the family. In K. M. Chun, P. B. Organista, & G. Marín (Eds.), *Acculturation: Advances in theory, measurement, and applied research.* Washington, DC: American Psychological Association.

Santisteban, D. A., Muir-Malcolm, J. A., Mitrani, V. B. & Szapocznik, J. (2002). Integrating the study of ethnic culture and family psychology intervention science. In H. A. Liddle, R. F. Levant, D. A. Santisteban, & J. H. Bray (Eds.), *Family psychology: Science-based interventions* (pp. 331–352). Washington, DC: American Psychological Association.

Schwartz, S. J., Unger, J. B., Baezconde-Garbanati, L., Córdova, D., Lorenzo-Blanco, E., Huang, S., . . . Szapocznik, J. (in press). Testing the parent-adolescent acculturation discrepancy hypothesis: A five-wave longitudinal study. *Journal of Research on Adolescence.*

Schwartz, S. J., Unger, J. B., Des Rosiers, S. E., Lorenzo-Blanco, E. I., Zamboanga, B. L., Huang, S., . . . Szapocznik, J. (2014). Domains of acculturation and their effects on substance use and sexual behavior in Hispanic recent immigrant adolescents. *Prevention Science, 15*, 385–396.

Schwartz, S. J., Unger, J. B., Zamboanga, B. L., & Szapocznik, J. (2010). Rethinking the concept of acculturation: Implications for theory and research. *American Psychologist, 65*, 237–251.

Schwartz, S. J., Vignoles, V. L., Brown, R., & Zagefka, H. (2014). The identity dynamics of acculturation and multiculturalism: Situating acculturation in context. In V. Benet-Martínez & Y-Y. Hong (Eds.), *Oxford handbook of multicultural identity* (pp. 57–92). Oxford, UK: Oxford University Press.

Schwartz, S. J., Weisskirch, R. S., Hurley, E. A., Zamboanga, B. L., Park, I. K., Kim, S., . . . Greene, A. D. (2010). Communalism, familism, and filial piety: Are they birds of a collectivist feather? *Cultural Diversity and Ethnic Minority Psychology, 16*, 548–560.

Schwartz, S. J., Weisskirch, R. S., Zamboanga, B. L., Castillo, L. G., Ham, L. S., Huynh, Q-L., . . . Cano, M. A. (2011). Dimensions of acculturation: Associations with health risk behaviors among college students from immigrant families. *Journal of Counseling Psychology, 58*, 27–41.

Schwartz, S. J., & Zamboanga, B. L. (2008). Testing Berry's model of acculturation: A confirmatory latent class approach. *Cultural Diversity and Ethnic Minority Psychology, 14*, 275–285.

Sidanius, J., & Pratto, F. (2001). *Social dominance: An intergroup theory of social hierarchy and oppression.* Cambridge, UK: Cambridge University Press.

Sidanius, J., Pratto, F., van Laar, C., & Levin S. (2004). Social dominance theory: Its agenda and method. *Political Psychology, 25,* 845–880.

Smedley, B. D. (2012). The lived experience of race and its health consequences. *American Journal of Public Health, 102,* 933–935.

Smokowski, P. R., & Bacallao, M. L. (2010). *Becoming bicultural: Risk, resilience, and Latino youth.* New York, NY: New York University Press.

Smokowski, P. R., Rose, R., & Bacallao, M. L. (2008). Acculturation and Latino family processes: How cultural involvement, biculturalism, and acculturation gaps influence family dynamics. *Family Relations, 57,* 295–308.

Smokowski, P. R., Rose, R., & Bacallao, M. L. (2009). Acculturation and aggression in Latino adolescents: Modeling longitudinal trajectories from the Latino acculturation and health project. *Child Psychiatry and Human Development, 40,* 589–608.

Spears, R. (2011). Group identities: The social identity perspective. In S. J. Schwartz, K. Luyckx, & V. L. Vignoles (Eds.), *Handbook of identity theory and research* (pp. 201–224). New York, NY: Springer.

Steele, C. M. (1997). A threat in the air: How stereotypes shape intellectual identity and performance. *American Psychologist, 52,* 613–629.

Steiner, N. (2009). *International migration and citizenship today.* New York, NY: Routledge.

Stepick, A., & Dutton Stepick, C. (2002). Power and identity: Miami Cubans. In M. M. Suárez-Orozco & M. Páez (Eds.), *Latinos: Remaking America* (pp. 75–92). Cambridge, MA: Harvard University Press.

Stepick, A., Dutton Stepick, C., & Vanderkooy, P. (2011). Becoming American. In S. J. Schwartz, K. Luyckx, & V. L. Vignoles (Eds.), *Handbook of identity theory and research* (pp. 867–894). New York, NY: Springer.

Stepick, A., Grenier, G., Castro, M., & Dunn, M. (2003). *This land is our land: Immigrants and power in Miami.* Berkeley: University of California Press.

Subašić, E., Reynolds, K. J., & Turner, J. C. (2008). The political solidarity model of social change: Dynamics of self-categorization in intergroup power relations. *Personality and Social Psychology Review, 12,* 330–352.

Szapocznik, J., & Kurtines, W. M. (1980). Acculturation, biculturalism and adjustment among Cuban Americans. In A. M. Padilla (Ed.), *Psychological dimensions on the acculturation process: Theory, models, and some new findings* (pp. 139–159). Boulder, CO: Westview.

Szapocznik, J., & Kurtines, W. M. (1993). Family psychology and cultural diversity: Opportunities for theory, research and application. *American Psychologist, 48,* 400–407.

Szapocznik, J., Prado, G., Burlew, A. K., Williams, R. A., & Santisteban, D. A. (2007). Drug abuse in African American and Hispanic adolescents: Culture, development, and behavior. *Annual Review of Clinical Psychology, 3,* 155–183.

Szapocznik, J., Santisteban, D., Rio, A., Perez-Vidal, A., Santisteban, D. A., & Kurtines, W. M. (1989). Family Effectiveness Training: An intervention to prevent drug abuse and problem behavior in Hispanic adolescents. *Hispanic Journal of Behavioral Sciences, 11,* 3–27.

Tajfel, H. (1970). Experiments in intergroup discrimination. *Scientific American, 223,* 96–102

Telzer, E. H. (2010). Expanding the acculturation gap-distress model: An integrative review of research. *Human Development, 53,* 313–340.

Tip, L., Zagefka, H., González, R., Brown, R., & Cinnirella, M. (2012). Is the biggest threat to multiculturalism . . . threat itself? *International Journal of Intercultural Relations, 36,* 22–30.

Toumbourou, J. W., Stockwell, T., Neighbors, T., Marlatt, G. A., Sturge, J., & Rehm, J. (2007). Interventions to reduce harm associated with adolescent substance use. *Lancet, 369,* 1391–1401.

Townsend, L., Flisher, A. J., & King, G. (2007). A systematic review of the relationship between school dropout and substance use. *Clinical Child and Family Psychology Review, 10,* 295–317.

Townsend, S. S. M., Major, B., Sawyer, P. J., & Mendes, W. B. (2010). Can the absence of prejudice be more threatening than its presence? It depends on one's worldview. *Journal of Personality and Social Psychology, 99,* 933–947.

Tran, V. C. (2010). English gain vs. Spanish loss? Language assimilation among second-generation Latinos in young adulthood. *Social Forces, 89,* 257–284.

Treno, A. J., Gruenewald, P. J., Lee, J. P., & Remer, L. G. (2007). The Sacramento Neighborhood Alcohol Prevention Project: Outcomes from a community prevention trial. *Journal of Studies on Alcohol and Drugs, 68,* 197–207.

Triandis, H. C. (1995). *Individualism and collectivism.* Boulder, CO: Westview.

Tutt, D., Bauer, L., & DiFranza, J. (2009). Restricting the retail supply of tobacco to minors. *Journal of Public Health Policy, 30,* 68–82.

Umaña-Taylor, A. J., Gonzales-Backen, M., & Guimond, A. B. (2009). Latino adolescents' racial/ethnic identity: Is there a developmental progression and does growth in racial/ethnic identity predict growth in self-esteem? *Child Development, 80,* 391–405.

Umaña-Taylor, A. J., Quintana, S. M., Lee, R. M., Cross, W. E., Jr., Rivas-Drake, D., Schwartz, S. J., . . . Ethnic and Racial Identity in the 21st Century Study Group. (2014). Ethnic and racial identity revisited: An integrated conceptualization. *Child Development, 85,* 21–39.

Umaña-Taylor, A. J., Vargas-Chanes, D., Garcia, C. D., & Gonzales-Backen, M. (2008). A longitudinal examination of Latino adolescents' racial/ethnic identity, coping with discrimination, and self-esteem. *Journal of Early Adolescence, 28,* 16–50.

Unger, J. B. (2012). The most critical unresolved issues associated with race, ethnicity, culture, and substance use. *Substance Use and Misuse, 47,* 390–395.

Unger, J. B., Baezconde-Garbanati, L., Shakib, S., Palmer, P. H., Nezami, E., & Mora, J. (2004). A cultural psychology approach to "drug abuse" prevention. *Substance Use and Misuse, 39,* 1779–1820.

Unger, J. B., Ritt-Olson, A., Wagner, K. D., Soto, D. W., & Baezconde-Garbanati, L. (2009). Parent–child acculturation discrepancies as a risk factor for substance use among Hispanic adolescents in Southern California. *Journal of Immigrant and Minority Health, 11,* 149–157.

Unger, J. B., & Schwartz, S. J. (2012). Measuring cultural influences: Quantitative approaches. *Preventive Medicine, 55,* 353-355.

Unger, J. B., Shakib, S., Gallagher, P., Ritt-Olson, A., Mouttapa, M., Palmer, P. H., & Johnson, C. A. (2006). Cultural/interpersonal values and smoking in an ethnically diverse sample of Southern California adolescents. *Journal of Cultural Diversity, 13*, 55–63.

US Census Bureau. (2011). *2011 statistical abstract of the United States.* Retrieved June 20, 2011 from https://www.census.gov/prod/2011pubs/11statab/pop.pdf.

US Department of Health and Human Services. (2011). *HHS action plan to reduce racial and racial/ethnic health disparities: A nation free of disparities in health and health care.* Washington, DC: Author. Retrieved April 20, 2012 from http://minorityhealth.hhs.gov/npa/templates/content.aspx?lvl=1&lvlid=33&ID=285

US Department of Justice. (2011). *National drug threat assessment, 2011.* Retrieved May 7, 2012 from www.justice.gov/ndic/pubs44/44849/44849p.pdf

van Oudenhoven, J. P., Ward, C., & Masgoret, A.-M. (2006). Patterns of relations between immigrants and host societies. *International Journal of Intercultural Relations, 30*, 637–651.

Van Ryzin, M. J., Stormshak, E. A., & Dishion, T. J. (2012). Engaging parents in the family check-up in middle school: Longitudinal effects on family conflict and problem behavior through the high school transition. *Journal of Adolescent Health, 50*, 627–633.

Wagenaar, A. C., Maldonado-Molina, M. M., Ma, L., Tobler, A. L., & Komro, K. A. (2007). Effects of legal BAC limits on fatal crash involvement: Analyses of 28 states from 1976 through 2002. *Journal of Safety Research, 38*, 493–499.

Wagenaar, A. C., Tobler, A. L., & Komro, K. A. (2009). Effects of alcohol tax and price policies on morbidity and mortality: A systematic review. *American Journal of Public Health, 100*, 2270–2278.

West, J. H., Blumberg, E. J., Kelley, N. J., Hill, L., Sipan, C. L., Schmitz, K. E., . . . Hovell, M. H. (2010). Does proximity to alcohol retailers influence alcohol and tobacco use among Latino adolescents? *Journal of Immigrant and Minority Health, 12*, 626–633.

Wilson, J. Q. (2002). Slavery and the black family. *National Affairs, 147*, 3–23.

Wu, L-T., Woody, G. E., Yang, C., Pan, J-J., & Blazer, D. (2011). Racial-ethnic variations in substance-related disorders among adolescents in the United States. *Archives of General Psychiatry, 68*, 1176–1185.

Zamboanga, B. L., Schwartz, S. J., Jarvis, L. H., & Van Tyne, K. (2009). Acculturation and substance use among Hispanic early adolescents: Investigating the mediating roles of acculturative stress and self-esteem. *Journal of Primary Prevention, 30*, 315–333.

Twelve-Step Approaches

John F. Kelly, Matthew J. Worley, *and* Julie Yeterian

Abstract

Twelve-step approaches to addressing substance use disorder (SUD) are unique in the treatment field in that they encompass professionally led, as well as peer-led, intervention methods. Also, in contrast to most professional treatments that have emerged from scientific theories and empirical data (e.g., cognitive-behavioral treatments), 12-step approaches have been derived, in large part, from the collective addiction and recovery experiences of laymen. Despite this, 12-step approaches have become influential in tackling SUD, with research demonstrating the clinical utility of employing such approaches among adults, and increasingly, among youth. Findings among adolescent samples indicate community 12-step mutual-help organizations, in particular, may provide a beneficial recovery-supportive social context during a life stage where such support is rare.

Key Words: Alcoholics Anonymous, Narcotics Anonymous, Marijuana Anonymous, 12-step, groups, recovery, addiction, adolescents, young adults, emerging adults

Twelve-step approaches to addressing substance use disorder (SUD) are unique in the treatment field in that they encompass professionally led, as well as peer-led, intervention methods. In contrast to most professional treatments that have emerged from sound scientific theories and empirical data (e.g., cognitive-behavioral treatments), 12-step approaches have been derived, in large part, from the collective addiction and recovery experiences of laymen. Despite this, 12-step approaches have become very influential in tackling SUD, and rigorous research has demonstrated the clinical utility of employing such approaches among adults, and increasingly, among adolescents and emerging adults.

Twelve-step approaches began in the early post–Prohibition era of 1935 America when two severely alcohol-dependent adults—a New York City stockbroker by the name of Bill Wilson ("Bill W.") and an Akron, Ohio, surgeon by the name of Robert Smith ("Dr. Bob")—founded the mutual-help organization (MHO) Alcoholics Anonymous (AA).

The organization was established on the founding principle that by helping others with the same problem, notably by offering tangible support and through communicating one's personal addiction and recovery experiences, the compulsion to drink was attenuated and longer periods of abstinence and remission could be achieved. The publication of AA's first book documenting its recovery program, *Alcoholics Anonymous* (Alcoholics Anonymous, 1939), helped spread AA's message across the United States and later, internationally (Mäkela, 1996). A subsequent publication, *Twelve Steps and Twelve Traditions* (Alcoholics Anonymous, 1953), provided a more detailed account of AA's 12-step process, but more important, documented AA's early growth experience, including operational guidelines ("Twelve Traditions") on how AA groups might optimally function. As other psychoactive drugs became more accessible after the 1950s, addiction to drugs other than alcohol became more prevalent, leading to the growth of other substance-specific MHOs that were based on AA's steps and traditions. Some of the largest of these are Narcotics Anonymous (NA), Cocaine Anonymous (CA), and Marijuana Anonymous (MA) (Kelly & White, 2011).

As the influence and perceived success of AA grew, professional treatment programs, beginning with Hazelden in Minnesota (McElrath, 1997), began to incorporate 12-step philosophy and practices into their formal treatment protocols. This hybrid "Minnesota Model," established in 1949, began to be adopted across the United States and gradually became the standard for residential SUD treatment nationally (White, 1998).

Professional programs available today in the United States and in many other countries, often utilize at least some aspects of 12-step philosophy and practices, including attempting to facilitate patients' participation in community 12-step MHOs, such as AA or NA, during and following treatment (Kelly, Myers, & Rodolico, 2008; Kelly, Yeterian, & Myers, 2008; Knudsen, Ducharme, Roman, & Johnson, 2008; Roman & Blum, 1999, 2004). These 12-step community MHOs are a *nonprofessional*, peer-led, system of mutual aid intended to address SUD and enhance recovery that runs completely independent of professional agencies and are not affiliated in any way (AA, 1953). In this chapter we examine the utility and benefit of both the professionally led, formal 12-step interventions as well as mutual aid-based, peer-led, 12-step organizations as they apply to adolescents and emerging adults.

Professional Versus Nonprofessional 12-Step Interventions

Twelve-step approaches to the treatment of SUD among adolescents are more common in the United States, where the 12-step model originated, than in other developed countries (Knudsen et al., 2008; Mäkela, 1996). While most professional adolescent treatment programs in the United States are not based solely on a 12-step model of care, the vast majority of programs (84%) link adolescents to 12-step organizations to help patients sustain treatment gains over the long term (Kelly, Yeterian, & Myers, 2008; Knudsen et al., 2008). Thus, most professional treatment agencies appear to view non-professional community 12-step organizations as important continuing care resources and encourage patients' participation in these groups. Professional adolescent treatment programs that are based on a 12-step model (mostly residential programs) often emphasize understanding and completing the first 5 steps of the 12-step program and provide education about and exposure to 12-step meetings during treatment (Jaffe & Kelly, 2010; see Table 33.1 for a list of the 12 steps, followed by interpretations of the broader themes on which each step is based and of the steps themselves, and the therapeutic outcomes that should result from successfully completing each step). Professional interventions also include the more recently developed twelve-step facilitation (TSF) treatments, which have been validated among adults (e.g., Kahler et al., 2004; Kaskutas, Subbaraman, Witbrodt, & Zemore, 2009; Litt, Kadden, Kabela-Cormier, & Petry, 2009; Manning et al., 2012; Project MATCH Research Group, 1997; Timko, Debenedetti, & Billow, 2006; Walitzer, Dermen, & Barrick, 2009). The main aim of TSF approaches is to promote patients' involvement in 12-step organizations through ongoing education, facilitation (e.g., active linkage), and support.

Nonprofessional 12-step interventions occur in the peer-led community group meetings and associated social fellowship (Humphreys, 2004; Kelly, 2003). The primary tenets of community-based 12-step mutual-help organizations include frequent attendance at meetings, having regular contact with a 12-step mentor or "sponsor," connecting with other peers in recovery, engaging in service activities in the organization (e.g., making coffee, setting up the meeting space, helping newer members), and reading relevant 12-step literature. Involvement and participation in a group fellowship of individuals in recovery is seen as a crucial aspect of maintaining sobriety (Alcoholics Anonymous, 2001; Humphreys, 2004; Kelly & McCrady, 2008).

Developmental Issues Related to Adolescents' Participation in 12-Step Groups

Despite the potential of 12-step resources to aid in the recovery from SUD among youth, adolescents appear to participate in 12-step meetings at a lower rate than adults. One study found that 88% of adult patients attended at least one 12-step meeting in the first 90 days after treatment, with an average of 36 meetings, while only 65% of adolescents attended a meeting, with 12 meetings on average (Godley, Godley, Dennis, Funk, & Passetti, 2007). Younger patients are less likely than older patients to consider themselves members of AA (Mason & Luckey, 2003), and adults are more likely to endorse the incorporation of 12-step resources into their treatment than adolescents (Aromin, Galanter, Solhkhah, Bunt, & Dermatis, 2006). However,

Table 33.1 Interpretation and Potential Therapeutic Outcome of AA's 12-Step Process

AA Step	AA Theme	Youth-Focused Interpretation	Therapeutic Outcome
1. We admitted we were powerless over alcohol—that our lives had become unmanageable	Honesty	I've got an alcohol/ drug problem	Liberation/relief
2. Came to believe that a Power greater than ourselves could restore us to sanity	Open-mindedness	Help is available; change is possible	Instillation of hope
3. Made a decision to turn our will and our lives over to the care of God, *as we understood him*	Willingness	Decide to get help	Self-efficacy
4. Made a searching and fearless moral inventory of ourselves	Self-assessment and appraisal	Take a look at what's bothering you and why	Insight
5. Admitted to God, to ourselves, and to another human being the exact nature of our wrongs	Self-forgiveness	Talk about what's bothering you and why with someone you trust and who can help you	Reduced shame and guilt
6. Were entirely ready to have God remove all these defects of character	Readiness to change	Start to make the necessary changes	Cognitive consonance
7. Humbly asked Him to remove our shortcomings	Making changes	Continue to make the necessary changes	Cognitive consonance
8. Made a list of all persons we had harmed and became willing to make amends to them all	Taking responsibility and forgiveness of others	Attempt to rectify sources of guilt/shame	Peace of mind; diminution of guilt
9. Made direct amends to such people whenever possible except when to do so would injure them or others	Restitution to others	Talk to those concerned and make amends where necessary	Peace of mind; diminution of guilt self-esteem
10. Continued to take personal inventory and when we were wrong promptly admitted it	Emotional balance	Keep on taking a look at yourself and correct mistakes as you go	Affect- and self-regulation
11. Sought through prayer and meditation to improve our conscious contact with God, *as we understood Him*, praying only for knowledge of his will for us and the power to carry that out	Connectedness and emotional balance	Stay connected; stay mindful	Awareness; psychological well-being
12. Having had a spiritual awakening as the result of these steps, we tried to carry this message to alcoholics and to practice these principles in all our affairs	Helping others achieve recovery	Continue to access help, work on yourself and try to help others	Self-esteem; confidence and mastery

youth treated in 12-step inpatient programs attend 12-step meetings at much higher rates. One study found that approximately 90% of youth attended 12-step meetings in the first 6 months post discharge, with 83% attending monthly, and 65% weekly. However, these high rates of attendance did attenuate rapidly during the 8-year follow-up period (Kelly, Brown, Abrantes, Kahler, & Myers, 2008).

Young people make up a small percentage of overall 12-step group membership, as only 4.6% of MHO participants are between the ages of 12 and 17 (Substance Abuse and Mental Health Services Administration, 2008) and only 1% of AA members are under the age of 21 (Alcoholics Anonymous, 2015). Having fewer young people at meetings may mean that the substance-related problems experienced by adolescents (e.g., school expulsion, conflict with parents) are not regularly discussed in meetings, which could negatively influence adolescents' sense of connection with other members, at least in mostly adult-attended meetings. Even if teens are willing and able to attend 12-step groups, the adult composition of most groups may provide a barrier to affiliation and continued attendance. However, NA and AA have meetings that are specifically geared toward young people and beginners of all ages, which may help to mitigate this barrier. One study revealed that teens who attended AA and NA meetings with a substantial proportion of teenagers had superior substance use outcomes 3 and 6 months posttreatment compared to those who attended predominantly adult meetings (Kelly, Myers, & Brown, 2005). Given these findings, it is important to consider developmentally relevant factors that may affect adolescents' level of engagement in and benefit experienced from 12-step MHOs, which include recovery motivation, substance use patterns and addiction severity, spirituality, and relapse precursors.

Recovery Motivation

Adolescents entering treatment have been found to differ from adults in their motivation to stop using alcohol and/or drugs, since they rarely enter treatment due to an intrinsic desire to stop using (Tims et al., 2002). Youth often have more extrinsic motivations for treatment entry, as they are usually coerced into treatment to some degree, as a result of school, legal, or familial/interpersonal problems (Brown, Vik, & Creamer, 1989; Wu, Pilowsky, Schlenger, & Hasin, 2007). This presumably results in lower levels of motivation for recovery. Decreased recovery motivation may affect adolescents' level

of participation in unstructured, informal treatment approaches such as 12-step meetings, which usually require that individuals be self-motivated to attend. Lower levels of intrinsic motivation may make adolescents less likely to endorse certain tenets of the 12-step model, such as the need to work on the 12 steps or to be completely abstinent from all substances. Importantly, low recovery motivation could be expected to negatively impact adolescents' response to any treatment, not just 12-step approaches. The relative influence of motivation on 12-step-specific interventions has yet to be determined.

Substance Use Patterns and Addiction Severity

A major driver of SUD recovery motivation and help-seeking is perceived addiction severity (Finney & Moos, 1995). Compared to adults, teenagers in treatment report less frequent substance use, display fewer dependence symptoms, and have fewer medical complications and withdrawal symptoms, on average (e.g., Brown, 1993; Stewart & Brown, 1995; Kelly, Stout, Greene, & Slaymaker, 2014). Those adolescents who are less severely dependent or who have not yet experienced medical consequences of substance use may be less likely to identify with the 12-step ideas of "powerlessness" over a substance and the need for complete abstinence. In addition, adolescents are likely to be polysubstance users and often have multiple SUD diagnoses when presenting for treatment. In a sample of adolescents presenting for inpatient treatment, rates of alcohol and marijuana dependence were 72% and 86% (Winters, Stinchfield, Latimer, & Lee, 2007). In a separate study, 54% of adolescents were using both alcohol and drugs at intake and more than half were using multiple drugs (Campbell, Chi, Sterling, Kohn, & Weisner, 2009). As many 12-step meetings are structured around the discussion of one particular substance (e.g., alcohol in AA, cocaine in CA), polysubstance-using adolescents may find these substance-specific meetings to be less tailored to their needs.

Spirituality

Twelve-step organizations have a spiritual orientation and focus. The 12-step literature abounds with references to spirituality and a self-defined "God" or "Higher Power" and meetings often start and/or end with a prayer, such as the Serenity Prayer (Alcoholics Anonymous, 2015). Although religiousness has been found to be a protective factor against the onset of SUD (Miller, Davies, & Greenwald, 2000; Ouimette et al., 2001; Vaughan, de Dios, Steinfeldt, & Kratz, 2011) and is predictive of a better treatment response among adolescents treated for SUD (Kelly, Pagano, Stout, & Johnson, 2011), this aspect of 12-step fellowships does not appear to be appealing to most adolescents treated for SUD (Kelly, Myers, et al., 2008), and the overtly spiritual language and content of some meetings may constitute a further barrier for young people who may be more preoccupied and interested with more terrestrial pursuits and social factors.

Adolescent Relapse Contexts

Another major difference between adolescents and adults is the context in which relapse typically occurs. Whereas in adults, the precursors to relapse often involve negative affect (e.g., boredom, depression, anger) and interpersonal conflict (e.g., disagreements or quarrels with a partner), the vast majority of relapse among adolescents and young adults occurs in social contexts where alcohol and other drugs are present (Brown, 1993; Chung & Maisto, 2006). In a sample of adolescents who completed inpatient treatment, 44% of initial relapses occurred when socializing with friends, and the majority of relapses occurred in response to direct offers to use (Brown et al., 1989). Adolescent patients have reported extremely high rates (94%) of alcohol and marijuana use by their closest friends (Alford, Koehler, & Leonard, 1991) and peer alcohol and drug use is a consistent predictor of patients' own abstinence following treatment (Campbell et al., 2009). Adolescents may be more likely to engage in heavy substance use in social contexts and in an episodic fashion, as opposed to adults who typically have more chronic patterns of use (Deas, Riggs, Langenbucher, Goldman, & Brown, 2000).

While this could be expected to deter adolescent participation in 12-step groups, research with adults has found that 12-step facilitation interventions are especially effective for patients with social networks that are supportive of substance use (Longabaugh, Wirtz, Zweben, & Stout, 1998; Wu & Witkiewitz, 2008) and that mobilizing changes in social network ties and social activities appears to be one of the major mechanisms through which 12-step organizations help to sustain remission and recovery (Kelly, Magill, & Stout, 2009; Kelly, Stout, Magill, Tonigan, & Pagano, 2010; Litt et al., 2009). If adolescents engage in 12-step groups and successfully make changes to their social networks, these interventions may be particularly effective.

Twelve-step MHOs may provide a rare and concentrated source of supportive peers with whom young people can socialize and lower the influence of this potent relapse risk (Kelly, Brown, et al., 2008). To some extent, research supports this notion. Yet, although 12-step MHO participation appears to confer recovery benefits (Kelly, Stout, Slaymaker, 2013), and may reduce negative high-risk network members (Kelly et al., 2014), these MHOs may be unable to provide new social network member friends in recovery because there are fewer young people attending 12-step MHOs (Hoeppner, Hoeppner, & Kelly, 2014; Kelly et al., 2014).

What Do Adolescents Think About 12-Step Organizations?

Studies have only recently sought to assess adolescents' own perceptions of their 12-step experiences. There are some indications that some aspects of these treatments do appeal to younger patients. In a young adult sample (age 20–29), participants in 12-step meetings reported a sense of connectedness, gaining new friendships, receiving support, and learning through others' experiences as key factors in maintaining their involvement in 12-step activities (Dadich, 2010). Another study with 300 young adult patients (18–24 years) followed for 1 year after residential SUD treatment found that a sense of belonging/universality, cohesion, and instillation of hope for change were the main facets that these patients reported they found most helpful about attending 12-step MHOs. Similar results were found with adolescents, who reported liking the sense of universality and belonging, positive encouragement and support, and instillation of hope gained through 12-step meetings (Kelly, Myers, et al., 2008). However, it is also notable that one fourth of adolescents in this study liked "nothing" about AA/NA. This suggests that a substantial proportion of adolescents do not respond positively to 12-step community resources. Whether this is due to individual characteristics (e.g., low motivation) or contextual factors related to specific meetings (e.g., older members) is currently unclear, and it is an important topic for future inquiry.

In general, these developmental differences could potentially explain adolescents' somewhat lower sustained rates of participation in community 12-step mutual-help meetings, but few have been evaluated directly in empirical research. Studies directly comparing adults to adolescents are rare, and it is unclear which developmental factors may negatively impact adolescents' participation specifically.

Next, we examine what is currently known about adolescent participation rates.

Adolescent Participation in 12-Step Groups
Rates of Adolescent Participation

In a national survey of public and private adolescent SUD treatment centers, 49% of the centers required attendance at 12-step meetings during treatment and 85% linked adolescents to community 12-step meetings at discharge (Knudsen et al., 2008). Studies of individual treatment settings also show high rates (73%–92%) of clinician referral to community 12-step meetings, with an average referral rate across sites of 86% (Kelly, Dow, Yeterian, & Kahler, 2010; Kelly, Yeterian, et al., 2008). Thus, there is reason to believe that most adolescents who engage in SUD treatment are aware of and have been referred to 12-step resources. However, only a portion of these patients actually utilize these resources after treatment.

Two studies of adolescents in 12-step-oriented inpatient programs showed high rates of 12-step meeting attendance immediately following treatment, with declining rates of attendance over time. Kelly, Myers, and Brown (2005) found that 72% of adolescent inpatients (N = 74) attended at least one 12-step meeting during the first 3 months after discharge, with an average attendance rate of two times per week. During the next 3 months (i.e., 4–6 months post discharge), the attendance rate dropped to 54%, with average attendance around once per week. In an 8-year follow-up of adolescent inpatients (N = 166), rates of 12-step meeting attendance were very high in the first 6 months post treatment (91% attended at least once, 83% at least monthly, 65% at least weekly), but rates dropped off in the next 6-month period (i.e., 6–12 months post treatment; 59% attended at least once, 48% at least monthly, 33% at least weekly) and continued to decline steadily across the 8-year follow-up period. By 6–8 years after treatment, only 31% attended at least once, 19% at least monthly, and 6% at least weekly (Kelly, Brown, et al., 2008). High rates of postdischarge 12-step MHO participation have been found also with young adult samples, especially from 12-step-oriented treatments (Kelly, Stout, & Slaymaker, 2013).

In contrast, studies of adolescents in outpatient programs have shown lower rates of attendance. For instance, a 3-year follow-up of 357 adolescents in intensive outpatient treatment found that at 1-year post intake, 29% reported having attended 10 or more 12-step meetings in the past 6 months.

At 3 years post intake, this number dropped to 14%, although a total of 19% had gone to at least one 12-step meeting in the prior 6 months (Chi, Kaskutas, Sterling, Campbell, & Weisner, 2009). In a 6-month follow-up of 127 adolescents in low-intensity outpatient treatment, just over one quarter of patients (28%) attended at least one 12-step meeting during the 3 months post intake, whereas from 4–6 months post intake, that figure dropped to just under one quarter (24%). At intake, less than half (43%) of participants had ever been to a 12-step meeting (Kelly, Dow, et al., 2010).

Affiliation with prescribed 12-step activities (e.g., having a sponsor, reading literature, calling a member for help), measured separately from group meeting attendance, has been recognized as an important and unique component of 12-step involvement (e.g., Kelly, 2003; Montgomery, Miller, & Tonigan, 1995; Weiss et al., 2005). Yet studies have rarely reported levels of adolescent active 12-step involvement in addition to attendance. Studies that have examined these variables have generally found somewhat low levels of involvement. In one study, only 38% of adolescents had a sponsor during the first 3 months after inpatient treatment, and only 34% had engaged in any 12-step social activity outside of meetings (Kelly, Myers, & Brown, 2002). At a 3-year follow-up of outpatient adolescents, only 14% had engaged in a 12-step-related activity (e.g., having a sponsor, reading 12-step literature; Chi et al., 2009). A recent year-long longitudinal study conducted with adolescent outpatients reported more detail regarding both attendance and eight indices of 12-step involvement (Kelly & Urbanoski, 2012). This study found that between a quarter and one third of adolescents attended AA/NA over the 12-month follow-up period and that the proportion of these youth that engaged in contact with a sponsor or other fellowship members, reading the AA/NA literature, volunteering to help out or speak during meetings, or participate in other ways ranged from about 20% up to nearly 70%. Separate measurement and investigation of 12-step attendance and active 12-step involvement has become somewhat standard in adult 12-step research, and integration of this practice into adolescent studies may provide insight into the unique role of active involvement with adolescent patients.

An increasingly recognized developmental stage that is gaining attention is the period of emerging adulthood (18–25 years old). Less research is available on rates of AA attendance among young adults in this age range. One study found that among 98 young adults (ages 18–25) currently receiving managed care treatment for alcohol use disorder (AUD), 68% reported that they had ever attended an AA meeting (Mason & Luckey, 2003). Another study of 270 young adult problem or dependent drinkers drawn from treatment settings and the general population found that just 35% of the total sample had attended AA at baseline (Delucchi, Matzger, & Weisner, 2008). The authors did not break down the attendance rates by treatment status, but it may be reasonable to assume that this overall lower rate was due to the inclusion of a general population subsample, given reports of very low rates of treatment service use (including AA) among those with AUD in the general population (Wu et al., 2007).

Most studies have only reported the rates of short- and long-term 12-step attendance and involvement and have focused less on potential explanations for reduced attendance at meetings and participation in activities. It is possible that some less severe patients do not find meetings to be relevant and stop attending. Others may relapse and subsequently stop attending meetings, as reported in qualitative research (Kelly, Myers, et al., 2008). Some individuals may remain abstinent and be confident enough in their recovery to maintain sobriety without continued meeting attendance, becoming "nonattending participators" (Weiss et al., 2005). Studies investigating the correlates of nonattendance have the potential to increase our understanding of the reasons for low or declining rates of adolescent participation over time.

Predictors of Adolescent Attendance at 12-Step Meetings

There is clear clinical utility in determining the most consistent predictors of posttreatment 12-step involvement for adolescents. Despite reportedly high rates of 12-step referral, many adolescents do not engage in 12-step resources following formal treatment. Gaining a clearer picture of the malleable and fixed characteristics that are predictive of posttreatment engagement in 12-step organizations could help clinicians focus more efficiently on clinical subgroups of patients who may be more resistant to 12-step engagement post discharge.

Consistent with the health beliefs model (HBM; Rosenstock, 1974), one important common predictor of 12-step participation across both adolescent and adult samples is the degree of substance involvement or addiction severity; those with more substance-related problems tend to become more involved in 12-step organizations (the same

is true of professional treatment; Chi et al., 2009; Delucchi et al., 2008; Finney & Moos, 1995; Kelly, Brown, et al., 2008; Kelly, Dow, et al., 2010; Kelly, Myers, & Brown, 2000; Kelly et al., 2002). This finding is not surprising, as young people who face more severe problems are likely to be more motivated to engage in treatment, be more accepting of an abstinence-based model, and more likely to benefit. Providing confirmation of this idea is the finding that the perception of having an alcohol problem predicts greater long-term AA/NA attendance, while a perception of having the ability to use alcohol/drugs in moderation predicts less involvement (Kelly, Brown, et al., 2008). This pattern of results is quite consistent with what would be expected given the 12-step emphasis on problem recognition and complete abstinence. Because 12-step treatments evolved as a recovery approach for addiction, it has been suggested that adolescents with subdiagnostic levels of substance use problems may be less appropriate for referral to 12-step meetings and may benefit more from family therapy or other interventions (Jaffe & Kelly, 2010). However, there are no relevant studies testing the comparative efficacy of treatments under these conditions.

Prior treatment engagement has been found to predict 12-step meeting attendance in samples drawn from inpatient and outpatient settings (Kelly, Dow, et al., 2010; Kelly, Myers, et al., 2008), suggesting that adolescents with more experience engaging in treatment may be more comfortable in 12-step group settings or that these individuals may have more severe or chronic problems than nonattendees. Social factors may also play a role, as adolescents with more drug-using friends have been found to be less likely to be currently attending AA after residential treatment for SUD (Hohman & LeCroy, 1996). As this evidence comes from a cross-sectional study, the temporal relations behind this finding are somewhat unclear. Future studies might investigate whether reengagement with substance-using friends negatively impacts future 12-step meeting attendance.

Somewhat surprisingly, parents' expectations of 12-step meeting attendance did not predict meeting attendance in their adolescent children (Kelly, Dow, et al., 2010), suggesting that adolescent patients' own expectations and motivation may be more important than parental beliefs about 12-step involvement.

Adolescents have cited the age of other group attendees as an important factor when deciding whether to attend a particular aftercare group

(Winters et al., 2007). Among adolescents and emerging adults who attended AA/NA meetings after inpatient treatment, those attending meetings with a greater level of youth involvement had higher rates of meeting attendance and rated meetings as being more important to their recovery (Kelly et al., 2005; Labbe et al., 2013). Furthermore, there was a trend for these patients to have lower future substance use early posttreatment, providing preliminary evidence that adolescents benefit from 12-step meetings where at least some other young members are in attendance. The findings here are more nuanced, however. Findings suggest that attendance at youth-focused meetings initially may aid engagement and enhance abstinence, but over time this may produce diminishing returns. Specifically, failing to branch out and attend meetings where older, longer sober, members may also be in attendance may reduce the recovery benefits (Kelly et al., 2005; Labbe et al., 2013). The relative benefit of attending *pro*-youth versus youth-*only* 12-step meetings remains an unaddressed area and is an important topic for further inquiry.

From this limited research, it may be concluded that, at least for professionally treated youth, those who self-select into community-based 12-step mutual-help organizations (a) tend to have more severe substance use problems and (b) have greater compatibility with 12-step model concepts of having an abstinence goal and recognizing a problem with drugs or alcohol. In addition, for these treated individuals, a more extensive history of prior formal treatment for either substance use or mental health issues also seems to be related to 12-step meeting attendance (Grella, Joshi, & Hser, 2003). From a theoretical standpoint, this fits well with the HBM (Rosenstock, 1974), in terms of the construct of "perceived severity." The more severely impaired someone perceives himself or herself to be, the more likely he or she is to seek help for drug or alcohol use.

Effects of 12-Step Treatment on Substance Use Outcomes
Effectiveness of 12-Step-Based Treatment Programs

Early studies of 12-step treatments for adolescents with SUD examined long-term outcomes of patients in 12-step-based inpatient treatment programs and found that completion of the treatment program predicted better substance use outcomes. One of the earliest studies of 12-step-based treatment for adolescents found

greater 6-month rates of abstinence (males = 71%, females = 79%) for treatment "completers," with abstinence rates for males declining to noncompleter levels at the 1- (48%) and 2-year (40%) follow-ups (Alford et al., 1991). Other studies of inpatient/residential 12-step treatments found similar 1-year abstinence rates, ranging from 47% to 53% (Hsieh, Hoffmann, & Hollister, 1998; Kennedy & Minami, 1993; Winters et al., 2007). Due to the absence of a comparison condition in these studies, it is not possible to determine whether these 12-step treatments were superior to other treatments or no treatment. Generally, the available evidence suggests that about half of adolescent patients who complete a 12-step-based inpatient residential program can be expected to remain abstinent up to 1 year following treatment.

One study attempted to address the limitations of these noncontrolled studies by assessing adolescents who received a "Minnesota Model" of inpatient/outpatient 12-step treatment and a separate "wait-list" group that was evaluated but received no treatment during the study (Winters et al., 2007; Winters, Stinchfield, Opland, Weller, & Latimer, 2000). At the 1-year follow-up, 53% of treatment patients were abstinent or had experienced only a minor lapse, compared to 28% of wait-list adolescents (Winters et al., 2000). However, these differences were substantially greater at a 5.5-year follow-up, when improvements on substance use were sustained by approximately one third of the treatment sample (35%) but almost none of the wait-list sample (5%). While the lack of randomization still limits conclusions from this quasi-experimental study, the groups were not statistically different at intake on any variables examined, including socioeconomic status. In the absence of more rigorous randomized controlled trials, the results from these studies provide some preliminary evidence for the effectiveness of 12-step-based formal treatment.

Relation of Posttreatment 12-Step Mutual-Help Group Attendance to Outcomes

Evidence for the benefits of 12-step MHO attendance on substance use outcomes has come from studies examining short- and long-term follow-up of inpatient/residential treatment samples. These studies generally find that greater 12-step involvement predicts superior substance use outcomes over time. Adolescents who were abstinent at 3 and 6 months post treatment had attended twice as many 12-step meetings in the prior 3 months as nonabstinent adolescents (Kelly et al., 2000). A separate study found that when examining intake, during-treatment, and posttreatment characteristics as predictors of abstinence, posttreatment attendance at 12-step groups was the most powerful predictor at 6- and 12-month follow-up (Hsieh et al., 1998). Studies examining longer-term follow-ups have found similar results. At a 1-year follow-up, adolescent patients who were not attending AA/NA were 4 times more likely to have relapsed than regular attenders (Kennedy & Minami, 1993). Similarly, a 1-year follow-up with a multisite sample of over 800 youth found that adolescents with more severe addiction/mental problems benefitted from AA and NA participation the most, and 12-step participation was the strongest predictor of abstinence (Grella et al., 2003). A longer follow-up with inpatient youth found that 84% of adolescents with high frequency of AA/NA attendance were abstinent, compared to 31% of patients with no attendance (Alford et al., 1991). Studies that have examined long-term outcomes into young adulthood have found similar relationships. Greater participation in aftercare (including 12-step attendance) following professionally led 12-step-based treatment predicted better 4- to 5-year follow-up outcomes (Winters et al., 2007), and more frequent AA/NA attendance consistently predicted less future alcohol/drug use across an 8-year posttreatment follow-up, even when controlling for important confounding variables, such as prior alcohol/drug use, gender, and receipt of formal treatment services (Kelly, Brown, et al., 2008). By meeting especially stringent criteria (Hill, 1965; Kazdin & Nock, 2003), including establishing temporal precedence and accounting for potentially confounding explanatory variables, this latter study, in particular, helps build confidence in the beneficial effects of 12-step meeting attendance for more severely substance-involved adolescents treated in 12-step-oriented inpatient settings.

Although studies of youth in outpatient treatment have been less frequent, the findings in these samples have been similar. Greater 12-step attendance was found to be associated concurrently and prospectively with better short-term (3 months) substance use outcomes, even when controlling for important confounds such as baseline substance use severity, abstinence goals, self-efficacy, pretreatment 12-step attendance, and outpatient therapy attendance (Kelly, Stout, et al., 2010; Kelly & Urbanoski, 2012). In these analyses, abstinence rates were markedly higher among patients attending 12-step meetings more than once a week, with percent days abstinent (PDA) around 85%, as compared to those attending zero meetings, who had less than 50% PDA. Another outpatient study found similar benefits of 12-step attendance at a 3-year follow-up, with abstinence rates near 60% for patients attending at least 10 meetings in the past 6 months (Chi et al., 2009). The treatments delivered in these outpatient studies were primarily cognitive-behavioral in orientation, and it is unknown if outpatient treatments based on 12-step principles would be successful at eliciting higher rates of posttreatment AA/NA attendance and improving the derived benefit. Studies of adult samples suggest this could be the case (Humphreys, Huebsch, Finney, & Moos, 1999; Longabaugh et al., 1998). On the other hand, these studies also indicate that continued 12-step meeting attendance may extend the benefits of formal treatments of various types, and they may constitute a key component of effective continuing care regardless of the theoretical orientation of the formal treatment approach.

Although few adolescent studies have specifically examined the effects of active involvement in 12-step activities, one study found that participation in at least three activities (e.g., having a sponsor, reading literature, calling a member for help) in the prior 6 months predicted greater likelihood of abstinence at 3 years post treatment (Chi et al., 2009). The outpatient adolescent study by Kelly and Urbanoski (2012) also found an incremental benefit (over and above the effects of attendance alone) on outcomes for contacting a sponsor outside of meetings and verbally participating during 12-step meetings. However, a prior adolescent study found no independent effects of active 12-step involvement (above and beyond the effects of 12-step meeting attendance) on substance use outcomes, possibly because the two constructs in that study were so highly correlated (Kelly et al., 2002). Future studies should seek to clarify the unique and potentially incremental benefits derived from active involvement in specific 12-step activities for maintaining long-term recovery among adolescents.

One important question is whether there is a "dose–response" relationship between 12-step involvement and alcohol/drug use or whether there is a "threshold" level of participation that is necessary to have any effect. When examining AA/NA attendance at 6-month posttreatment follow-up, one study identified a linear relationship, with significant benefits attained by attending as few as one meeting per week. However, attending three meetings per week was associated with complete abstinence (Kelly, Brown, et al., 2008). This study also focused on the importance of AA/NA attendance early (first 6 months) after treatment and found that greater early attendance consistently predicted higher PDA across 8 years posttreatment. Similar lasting effects of early 12-step attendance have also been found with adults (Moos & Moos, 2004). Given these consistent findings, it appears that immediate and frequent 12-step attendance may have particularly strong effects on reducing the likelihood of future substance use. Effective referral strategies should emphasize the importance of early engagement in community 12-step MHOs, immediately after the end of formal treatment.

Another important aspect of 12-step MHO referral and participation for patients suffering from SUD is that that they can help extend treatment benefits, increase abstinence and remission rates, and simultaneously reduce health care use and related costs in adults (Humphreys & Moos, 2001, 2007) and adolescents (Mundt, Parthasarathy, Chi, Sterling, & Campbell, 2012). A 7-year prospective study with adolescents found that adolecents who participated in 12-step MHOs following the index treatment episode had significantly better substance use outcomes, and for every 12-step meeting these youth attended they saved approximately $145 in health care costs (Mundt et al., 2012).

In sum, the available evidence consistently shows a relation between 12-step meeting attendance and better substance use outcomes in adolescents. Studies that have controlled for other pertinent predictors of abstinence have found that AA/NA attendance still predicts abstinence above and beyond these other factors. However, conclusions should be made somewhat cautiously from the available evidence, which is limited by the mostly (although not exclusively) inpatient nature of the samples studied and observational, nonexperimental designs. Whereas a number of clinical trials examining professional 12-step facilitation (TSF) interventions have been conducted with adult samples (Kaskutas, 2009; Kelly & Yeterian, 2012), to our knowledge, there have been no experimental studies of adolescent participation in AA/NA or TSF treatment for youth, which decreases the ability to draw firm conclusions about causal effects of 12-step treatments and mutual-help group participation on outcomes for adolescents. That said, there appears to be sufficient evidence to suggest that AA, NA, and other 12-step groups can be of help to young people, especially those youth with more severe

substance involvement. As we note later, there are now well-delineated TSF methods validated with adults that might be adapted to help engage young people with NA or AA.

How Does 12-Step Mutual Help Group Participation Aid Youth Recovery?
Studies of Mediational Effects

Mediating variables are third variables that explain the association between a predictor (e.g., treatment) and outcome (e.g., substance use), and can help identify the explanatory mechanisms underlying treatment effects (Baron & Kenny, 1986; Nock, 2007). Several MHO mechanisms have been proposed and studied (Kelly et al., 2009; Kelly, Hoeppner, Stout, & Pagano, 2012; McCrady, 1994), mostly with adult samples. When examining potential mediators, these investigations have looked at both common psychological processes (e.g., abstinence-focused coping, self-efficacy, abstinence motivation, social network changes) and 12-step-specific variables (e.g., working the 12 steps, increasing spirituality; Kelly, Pagano, et al., 2011; Robinson, Krentzman, Webb, & Brower, 2011; Zemore, 2007). In most, but not all, of these studies, the outcome and mediator variables are appropriately lagged in time behind the measurement of the 12-step participation variables to ensure temporal precedence and enhance causal attribution (Hill, 1965; Kazdin & Nock, 2003). In temporally lagged mediational studies of 12-step participation with adolescents that examined common process variables (i.e., coping, motivation, self-efficacy), the effects of 12-step meeting attendance on future substance use were found to be mediated by maintaining and enhancing motivation for abstinence, but not by abstinence-focused coping or self-efficacy, during the follow-up period (Kelly et al., 2000). In a separate study of the same sample, motivation for abstinence also mediated the effects of 12-step involvement on posttreatment substance use (Kelly et al., 2002), suggesting that both continued attendance and active involvement helps adolescents reduce substance use by maintaining their motivation for abstinence over time following discharge from inpatient care. This recovery motivation may be maintained by the ongoing recounting of one's personal "story" that occurs at AA and NA meetings as well as through the exposure to others' stories. This process may help attendees stay more cognizant of the memories of past negative consequences from alcohol/ drug use—memories that may decay over time or be suppressed—while simultaneously instilling hope by providing exposure to real-life examples of the kinds of progress and success that is attainable if one continues in recovery. A separate study also found evidence for social support as a mediator of the effects of 12-step attendance and activities on 3-year alcohol and drug use outcomes (Chi et al., 2009). Religious service attendance was also a mediator of 12-step attendance, but only for drug use outcomes. Although this study did not employ a lagged design to examine mediation, findings support results from research with adults that has recently found social network and spirituality factors to mediate the effects of AA on abstinence (Kelly, Pagano, et al., 2011; Kelly, Stout, et al., 2010). Although there are many potential mediators at different levels of scale (e.g., social, psychological, neurobiological), it appears that both intrinsic (e.g., motivation) and extrinsic (e.g., social support) factors can at least partially explain the relationship between 12-step attendance and improved substance use outcomes among young people. As mediation studies help explain how and why treatments work (Longabaugh, 2007), future work in this area will be helpful to understand how AA/NA participation benefits young people over time and how such beneficial elements inherent in AA and NA might be obtained from other resources.

Moderators of Outcomes

Moderating variables are those that affect the strength of relations between two other variables, such as treatment and outcome (Baron & Kenny, 1986). Discovery of moderating variables in this context is important, as these variables could help identify adolescents who may derive less benefit from participation in 12-step organizations and thus require other/additional forms of intervention or continuing care. Conversely, 12-step resources might be particularly effective for some adolescent patients based on some predisposing variables. Characteristics of particular 12-step meetings (e.g., age composition) could also moderate their positive influence on adolescents who attend.

No known studies have examined moderators of 12-step treatment effects in adolescents, but there are some candidate moderators for future study. Age of the patient may be a potential moderating variable, as one study found younger adolescents were more likely to report negative experiences with 12-step meetings, and they were shown to attend meetings less frequently during and following formal outpatient treatment (Kelly, Stout, Magill, & Tonigan, 2011). Comorbid mental health problems may be a moderator of outcome for professionally led, 12-step-based treatment. In one study of long-term 12-step-oriented inpatient treatment (Winters, Stinchfield, Latimer, & Stone, 2008), adolescents with greater externalizing symptoms had poorer outcomes up to 5 years post treatment, a finding that was independent of gender or "completion" of the original index treatment episode. Other long-term studies found that adolescents with conduct disorder were more likely to return to substance use following 12-step-based treatment (Tomlinson, Brown, & Abrantes, 2004). However, these studies did not examine 12-step mutual-help group participation in relation to outcome either during or post treatment. In contrast, a large, multisite US study, with more than 800 adolescents from 23 treatment programs examined the effects of comorbidity on treatment outcomes in relation to 12-step participation. The study found that those with comorbid psychiatric disorders (62% of the entire sample) were the most likely to participate and benefit from 12-step participation (Grella et al., 2003). In fact, 12-step participation was the strongest predictor of abstinence for the comorbid group, but it did not predict outcome for the noncomorbid group. Specifically, 12-step participants in the comorbid group were three times more likely to be abstinent. This group may have had a higher density and severity of substance use and psychiatric problems that motivated them to seek further support in AA/NA groups. The authors noted that 12-step participation may have helped provide a buffer against the negative social peer influences that are strongly implicated in youth relapse (Brown et al., 1989; Grella et al., 2003). As noted earlier, adult studies suggest also that 12-step-based interventions can be particularly effective for patients with a greater proportion of heavy drinkers in their social networks (Longabaugh et al., 1998; Stout, Kelly, Magill, & Pagano, 2012; Wu & Witkiewitz, 2008). Another study with emerging adults following residential treatment found that those with a comorbid psychiatric illness (e.g., mood/anxiety disorders at treatment intake) had worse substance use outcomes in the year following discharge, but those comorbid patients who became more involved with 12-step MHOs had outcomes that were on par with their SUD-only counterparts (Bergman et al., 2014).

Further investigation of potential variables that may moderate the benefit of 12-step participation among youth is needed, but some likely candidates to explore are addiction severity, age, gender, and specific types of psychiatric conditions (e.g., social anxiety, major depression, conduct disorder).

Facilitating Youth Involvement in 12-Step Groups

As mentioned earlier, TSF is a professionally delivered intervention wherein the therapist works to educate the patient about 12-step meetings and promote his or her active engagement in such groups. No experimental studies of TSF have been conducted specifically with adolescent or young adult populations, but it is reasonable to assert that this form of treatment could be effective with a younger population, especially when age-specific concerns and barriers to meeting attendance are addressed. In the existing adolescent literature, there are hints that a greater focus on 12-step meetings in professional treatment is associated with more 12-step meeting participation. For instance, Kelly, Dow, et al. (2010) found a significant correlation between the degree to which adolescents reported that treatment staff encouraged them to attend AA/NA and their actual rates of AA/NA attendance. There are also higher overall rates of 12-step attendance among young people treated in inpatient programs, which are more likely to be 12-step-oriented, as compared to young people in outpatient treatment, which are more likely to have a cognitive-behavioral or eclectic orientation. However, findings such as these are confounded with factors like severity, which is a robust and independent predictor of AA/NA attendance. However, the evidence to date suggests that these free community resources have clinical utility and benefit and that use of adult-derived TSF strategies are likely to result in enhanced attendance and improved outcomes (see Table 33.2 for descriptions of how TSF can be implemented in professional treatment). Several experimental studies have tested interventions designed specifically to facilitate 12-step involvement with adults (Kaskutas et al., 2009; Manning et al., 2012; Timko & DeBenedetti, 2007; Walitzer et al., 2009). One preliminary pilot TSF study has been reported for adolescents (Passetti, Godley, & Godley, 2012).

There has been some research examining characteristics of clinicians that relate to greater facilitation of youth involvement in 12-step meetings. In one study of several adolescent SUD treatment settings, 44% of clinicians referred all of their patients to 12-step meetings, and nearly all had referred at least one patient (Passetti & Godley, 2008). Clinicians cited such factors as greater perceived severity of SUD and perceived maturity level as contributing to increased chances of making a referral to 12-step groups. Many clinicians tended to steer patients toward youth-specific or "youth-friendly" meetings, and nearly all made efforts to provide schedules of meetings and identify specific meetings that were accessible and convenient. Sites with the highest rates of 12-step meeting attendance used a variety of engagement strategies, including screening potential 12-step sponsors and inviting them to meetings, conducting meetings at the treatment center, and encouraging youth participation in sober social activities. These sites also engaged in active monitoring of meeting attendance, and even facilitated transportation to local meetings. Another study conducted similar, qualitative work, and found that clinicians who perceived AA/NA as more helpful, more important, and safe for adolescents had higher rates of referral to meetings (Kelly, Yeterian, et al., 2008). For these clinicians, the most salient barriers for adolescent participation in AA/NA were the mostly adult age composition of members, and expecting that adolescents did not want complete abstinence from all substances. Successful engagement strategies identified in these studies might be incorporated into more formal protocols aimed at facilitating youth involvement, and reducing biases and misperceptions about youth attendance at 12-step meetings. Assertive continuing-care protocols have been shown to improve both short-and long-term abstinence for adolescents after residential treatment (Godley et al., 2007), but it remains to be seen whether intensive 12-step facilitation would exert similar effects.

Limitations and Future Directions

In this chapter examining 12-step approaches for adolescents, a number of limitations and suggestions for future research can be identified. First, most of the studies reviewed limited their attention to attendance at 12-step meetings, with very few (Chi et al., 2009; Kelly et al., 2002; Kelly & Urbanoski, 2012; Kelly, Stout, Slaymaker, 2013) measuring and examining the impact of active 12-step involvement as a separate and uniquely important variable. Studies with adults suggest these hypothesized 12-step "mechanisms" have distinct effects (Weiss et al., 2005), with possible differences in their relative degree of importance over time. The effects of active 12-step involvement among adolescent patients

Table 33.2 Ways for Clinicians to Implement 12-Step Facilitation (TSF) Strategies

Method	How It Might Be Implemented	Studies Using the Approach
Stand-alone treatment	Individual therapy devoted entirely to facilitating AA attendance by promoting an abstinence goal, increasing willingness to use AA as a tool to help achieve abstinence, and monitoring reactions to AA	Project MATCH Research Group (1997) Compared TSF as a stand alone treatment to CBT and MET
Integrated with other treatment	Within an existing treatment, such as CBT, incorporating encouragement to attend AA, getting patient to agree to attend specific meetings, and discussing AA literature, meetings, and sponsorship	Walitzer et al. (2009): Compared treatment as usual (5% of time spent discussing AA), motivational AA facilitation (20% AA-related), and directive AA facilitation (38% AA-related)
Component of a treatment package	Group education and discussion about AA separate from other treatment, with homework assignments to attend meetings, talk to other AA members outside of sessions, and get a sponsor	Kaskutas et al. (2009): "Making AA Easier," a group intervention to help encourage participation, minimize resistance, and provide education about AA
Modular add-on	Assertive linkage to specific groups, review of 12-step program and common concerns, direct connection to current AA members, review of client attendance and experiences	Timko et al. (2006): Compared standard AA referral to intensive referral

need further study, as does the relative importance of different markers (e.g., having a sponsor, contact with other members) of involvement.

There has been virtually no research into the effectiveness of 12-step facilitation or intensive 12-step referral treatments, which can be delivered as outpatient psychotherapies. In the adult literature these treatments have usually been at least as effective as other evidence-based interventions, and they may be more effective under certain conditions (Wu & Witkiewitz, 2008). Among adolescent patients greater treatment staff encouragement of AA/NA meetings does predict greater meeting attendance (Kelly, Yeterian, et al., 2008), and integration of 12-step programs into formal treatment (e.g., facilitation and monitoring of attendance) may be superior to passive referrals to 12-step meetings (Kelly & Yeterian, 2011). Future research might investigate standardized 12-step facilitation protocols that could be tested and disseminated into a broad range of treatment settings.

A major limitation of this body of research is the lack of true experimental studies. Randomized clinical trials for adolescents have most often tested cognitive-behavioral, motivational enhancement, or family interventions (Dennis et al., 2004; Waldron, Miller, & Tonigan, 2001), with 12-step protocols largely ignored. Given the potential of

12-step treatment protocols to engage adolescent patients with a readily accessible and cost-free support network over the long term, it is important to test the relative effectiveness of these protocols in scientifically rigorous research. Similarly, studies have not tested the potential utility of combining treatments or particular components of therapies with 12-step-based treatments. Perhaps the most effective adolescent treatments will be those that best match treatment components with patient needs (McWhirter, 2008), but sound empirical research has not examined these questions to this date.

Further investigation of factors currently limiting adolescent participation in 12-step treatment would help guide development of resources specifically geared toward the treatment of adolescent patients. Although we discussed developmental factors that could be limiting youth participation, few of these have been investigated in empirical studies. Furthermore, there is little known about the conditions under which these factors become less relevant. For example, one perception is that adolescents would not benefit from 12-step meetings because of the primarily adult composition, but there is some evidence that attending meetings where at least some other youth are present would counteract this effect at least early post treatment (Kelly et al., 2005; Labbe et al., 2014).

Summary

Treatment providers working with adolescents recognize that younger patients with SUD have specific developmental needs and challenges that distinguish them from their older adult counterparts. In general, adolescents on average may be less intrinsically motivated for treatment, less likely to have an abstinence goal, and less severe in their substance use and related problems, all of which may act as barriers to engagement with continuing care and 12-step recovery resources. However, research on treated samples has shown that many adolescents do attend AA/NA and that beneficial outcomes are consistently related to attendance and active involvement. These effects have been replicated in numerous studies and settings. Definitive causal conclusions about the effects of AA/NA on substance use outcomes cannot yet be drawn, as no experimental research studies have been conducted with these populations, but longitudinal studies that control for various factors that also predict abstinence have shown that AA/NA attendance predicts abstinence above and beyond these other factors. As with adults, AA/NA is not likely to be helpful to every young person, particularly those who have less severe problems or who are explicitly ideologically opposed to 12-step content and philosophy. However, current evidence suggests that good clinical practice would be to inquire about prior AA/NA participation and to encourage substance-dependent or more severely substance-involved patients to at least sample some 12-step meetings during treatment, and to discuss their experiences and perceptions of 12-step meetings during treatment. Doing this could help young people take advantage of this free, widely available, and supportive recovery resource. With the current lack of adolescent-specific studies of TSF, adapting

Table 33.3 Barriers to 12-Step Facilitation and Strategies to Overcome These

TSF Barrier	TSF Strategy
Our youth have problems mostly with cannabis and not alcohol or opiates.	Try to match adolescents' primary substance (e.g., cannabis, alcohol, opiates) with attendance at the appropriate organization (e.g., Marijuana Anonymous [MA], Alcoholics Anonymous [AA], Narcotics Anonymous [NA]).
There are no Young Persons' AA or NA meetings in my area.	Consider starting a young person's NA or AA meeting at your own facility. The local AA or NA office can help facilitate this.
Youth won't go to their first AA/NA meeting alone.	Try to actively facilitate a personal linkage with an existing NA or AA member by developing lists of personal contacts through local NA or AA offices or with your own treatment program alumni. Also, invite the Hospital and Institutions branch of NA/MA/AA to come and speak to patients during a group treatment session.
I am worried about whether adolescents will be welcomed at some NA and AA meetings.	Visit and investigate "open" AA or NA meetings, especially Young Persons' meetings, to find youth-friendly meetings.
I don't know where Young Persons' meetings are located.	Almost all cities and regions have a Web site for AA and NA meetings; there are likely to be local phone contacts via the national Web site for smaller 12-step organizations, such as Marijuana Anonymous.
Transportation is going to be an issue. How will they get there?	Educate parents about the potential value and importance of having their child try some AA and NA meetings. Parents tend to be the major direct or indirect facilitator of transportation to meetings for adolescents.
Most of our youth have never been to AA or NA before and have no clue about what to expect.	Take some time during treatment to discuss things like what happens in meetings, what a sponsor is, and what the 12 steps are. Adapt some empirically supported content such as Kaskutas's "Making AA Easy (MAAEZ)" treatment manual, which can be downloaded free of charge from http://arg.org/wp-content/uploads/2015/02/MAAEZ.Manual.pdf.

TSF methods that have been found effective among older adult samples may be helpful at this stage (see Table 33.3).

Organizations such as NA and AA may be some of the very few concentrated sources of recovery-specific support available to adolescents as they enter the challenging transitional life stage of emerging adulthood where the prevalence of substance use and related problems is higher than at any other time across human development.

References

Alcoholics Anonymous. (1939). *Alcoholics Anonymous: The story of how thousands of men and women have recovered from alcoholism* (3 ed.). New York, NY: Alcoholics Anonymous World Services.

Alcoholics Anonymous. (1953). *Twelve steps and twelve traditions.* New York, NY: Alcoholics Anonymous World Services.

Alcoholics Anonymous. (2001). *Alcoholics Anonymous: The story of how thousands of men and women have recovered from alcoholism* (4 ed.). New York, NY: Alcoholics Anonymous World Services.

Alcoholics Anonymous. (2015). *2014 Membership Survey.* New York, NY: Alcoholics Anonymous World Services.

Alford, G. S., Koehler, R. A., & Leonard, J. (1991). Alcoholics Anonymous–Narcotics Anonymous model inpatient treatment of chemically dependent adolescents: A 2-year outcome study. *Journal of Studies on Alcohol and Drugs, 52*(2), 118–126.

Aromin, R. A., Galanter, M., Solhkhah, R., Bunt, G., & Dermatis, H. (2006). Preference for spirituality and twelve-step-oriented approaches among adolescents in a residential therapeutic community. [Comparative Study; Research Support, Non-U.S. Gov't]. *Journal of Addictive Diseases, 25*(2), 89–96. doi: 10.1300/J069v25n02_12

Baron, R. M., & Kenny, D. A. (1986). The moderator-mediator variable distinction in social psychological research: Conceptual, strategic, and statistical considerations. *Journal of Personality and Social Psychology, 51*(6), 1173–1182.

Bergman, B. G., Greene, M. C., Hoeppner, B. B., Slaymaker, V., & Kelly, J. F. (2014). Psychiatric comorbidity and 12-step participation: A longitudinal investigation of treated young adults. *Alcoholism: Clinical and Experimental Research, 38*(2), 501–510.

Brown, S. A. (1993). Recovery patterns in adolescent substance abuse. In G. A. Marlatt & J. S. Baer (Eds.), *Addictive behaviors across the life span: Prevention, treatment, and policy issues* (pp. 161–183). Newbury Park, CA: Sage Publications, Inc.

Brown, S. A., Vik, P. W., & Creamer, V. A. (1989). Characteristics of relapse following adolescent substance abuse treatment. *Addictive Behaviors, 14*(3), 291–300.

Campbell, C. I., Chi, F., Sterling, S., Kohn, C., & Weisner, C. (2009). Self-initiated tobacco cessation and substance use outcomes among adolescents entering substance use treatment in a managed care organization. [Research Support, N.I.H., Extramural; Research Support, Non-U.S. Gov't]. *Addictive Behaviors, 34*(2), 171–179. doi: 10.1016/j.addbeh.2008.10.002

Chi, F. W., Kaskutas, L. A., Sterling, S., Campbell, C. I., & Weisner, C. (2009). Twelve-Step affiliation and 3-year substance use outcomes among adolescents: Social support and religious service attendance as potential mediators. *Addiction, 104*(6), 927–939. doi: ADD2524 [pii] 10.1111/j.1360-0443.2009.02524.x

Chung, T., & Maisto, S. A. (2006). Relapse to alcohol and other drug use in treated adolescents: Review and reconsideration of relapse as a change point in clinical course. [Research Support, N.I.H., Extramural Review]. *Clinical Psychology Review, 26*(2), 149–161. doi: 10.1016/j.cpr.2005.11.004

Dadich, A. (2010). Expanding our understanding of self-help support groups for substance use issues. *Journal of Drug Education, 40*(2), 189–202.

Deas, D., Riggs, P., Langenbucher, J., Goldman, M., & Brown, S. (2000). Adolescents are not adults: developmental considerations in alcohol users. *Alcoholism: Clinical and Experimental Research, 24*(2), 232–237.

Delucchi, K. L., Matzger, H., & Weisner, C. (2008). Alcohol in emerging adulthood: 7-year study of problem and dependent drinkers. *Addictive Behaviors, 33*(1), 134–142. doi: S0306-4603(07)00126-8 [pii] 10.1016/j.addbeh.2007.04.027

Dennis, M., Godley, S. H., Diamond, G., Tims, F. M., Babor, T., Donaldson, J., . . . Funk, R. (2004). The Cannabis Youth Treatment (CYT) Study: Main findings from two randomized trials. *Journal of Substance Abuse and Treatment, 27*(3), 197–213. doi: S0740-5472(04)00087-X [pii] 10.1016/j.jsat.2003.09.005

Finney, J. W., & Moos, R. H. (1995). Entering treatment for alcohol abuse: A stress and coping model. *Addiction, 90*(9), 1223–1240.

Godley, M., Godley, S., Dennis, M., Funk, R., & Passetti, L. (2007). The effect of assertive continuing care on continuing care linkage, adherence and abstinence following residential treatment for adolescents with substance use disorders. *Addiction, 102*(1), 81–93.

Grella, C. E., Joshi, V., & Hser, Y. I. (2003). Followup of cocaine-dependent men and women with antisocial personality disorder. [Multicenter Study; Research Support, U.S. Gov't, P.H.S.]. *Journal of Substance Abuse and Treatment, 25*(3), 155–164.

Hill, A. B. (1965). The environment and disease: Association or causation? *Proceedings of the Royal Society of Medicine, 58*(5), 295–300.

Hoeppner, B. B., Hoeppner, S. S., & Kelly, J. F. (2014). Do young people benefit from AA as much, and in the same ways, as adult aged 30+? A moderated multiple mediation analysis. *Drug and Alcohol Dependence, 143*, 181–188. doi: 10.1016/j.drugalcdep.2014.07.023

Hohman, L., & LeCroy, C. W. (1996). Predictors of adolescent AA affiliation. *Adolescence, 31*(122), 339–352.

Hsieh, S., Hoffmann, N. G., & Hollister, C. D. (1998). The relationship between pre-, during-, post-treatment factors, and adolescent substance abuse behaviors. *Addictive Behaviors, 23*(4), 477–488. doi: S0306-4603(98)00028-8 [pii]

Humphreys, K. (2004). *Circles of recovery: Self-help organizations for addictions.* Cambridge, UK: Cambridge University Press.

Humphreys, K., Moos, R. (2001). Can encouraging substance abuse patients to participate in self-help groups reduce demand for health care? A quasi-experimental study. *Alcoholism: Clinical and Experimental Research, 25*(5), 711–716.

Humphreys K., Moos R. H. (2007). Encouraging posttreatment self-help group involvement to reduce demand for continuing care services: two-year clinical and utilization outcomes. *Alcoholism: Clinical and Experimental Research, 31*(1), 64–68.

Humphreys, K., Huebsch, P. D., Finney, J. W., & Moos, R. H. (1999). A comparative evaluation of substance abuse treatment: V. Substance abuse treatment can enhance the effectiveness of self-help groups. *Alcoholism: Clinical and Experimental Research, 23*(3), 558–563. doi: 00000374-199903000-00026 [pii]

Jaffe, S., & Kelly, J. F. (2010). Twelve-step mutual help programs for adolescents—A guide for clinicians. In Y. Kaminer & K. Winters (Eds.), *Handbook of clinical interventions for adolescents*. Washington, DC: American Psychiatric Association Press.

Kahler, C. W., Read, J. P., Ramsey, S. E., Stuart, G. L., McCrady, B. S., & Brown, R. A. (2004). Motivational enhancement for 12-step involvement among patients undergoing alcohol detoxification. *Journal of Consulting and Clinical Psychology, 72*(4), 736–741. doi: 10.1037/0022-006X.72.4.736 2004-16970-020 [pii]

Kaskutas, L. A. (2009). Alcoholics anonymous effectiveness: Faith meets science. *Journal of Addictive Diseases, 28*(2), 145–157. doi: 910142603 [pii] 10.1080/10550880902772464

Kaskutas, L. A., Subbaraman, M. S., Witbrodt, J., & Zemore, S. E. (2009). Effectiveness of Making Alcoholics Anonymous Easier: A group format 12-step facilitation approach. *Journal of Substance Abuse Treatment, 37*(3), 228–239. doi: S0740-5472(09)00010-5 [pii] 10.1016/j.jsat.2009.01.004

Kazdin, A. E., & Nock, M. K. (2003). Delineating mechanisms of change in child and adolescent therapy: Methodological issues and research recommendations. *Journal of Child Psychology and Psychiatry, 44*(8), 1116–1129.

Kelly, J. F. (2003). Mutual-help for substance use disorders: History, effectiveness, knowledge gaps & research opportunities. *Clinical Psychology Review, 23*(5), 639–663.

Kelly, J. F., Brown, S. A., Abrantes, A., Kahler, C. W., & Myers, M. (2008). Social recovery model: An 8-year investigation of adolescent 12-step group involvement following in-patient treatment. *Alcoholism: Clinical and Experimental Research, 32*(8), 1468–1478. doi: ACER712 [pii] 10.1111/j.1530-0277.2008.00712.x

Kelly, J. F., Dow, S. J., Yeterian, J. D., & Kahler, C. (2010). Can 12-step group participation strengthen and extend the benefits of adolescent addiction treatment? A prospective analysis. *Drug and Alcohol Dependence, 110*(1–2), 117–125.

Kelly, J. F., Hoeppner, B., Stout, R. L., & Pagano, M. (2012). Determining the relative importance of the mechanisms of behavior change within Alcoholics Anonymous: a multiple mediator analysis. *Addiction, 107*(2), 289–299. doi: 10.1111/j.1360-0443.2011.03593.x

Kelly, J. F., Magill, M., & Stout, R. L. (2009). How do people recover from alcohol dependence? A systematic review of the research on mechanisms of behavior change in Alcoholics Anonymous. *Addiction Research & Theory, 17*(3), 236–259.

Kelly, J. F., & McCrady, B. S. (2008). Twelve-step facilitation in non-specialty settings. In M. Galanter & L. A. Kaskutas (Eds.), *Recent developments in alcoholism (vol. 18): Research on Alcoholics Anonymous and spirituality in addiction recovery* (pp. 321–346). Totowa, NJ: Springer.

Kelly, J. F., Myers, M. G., & Brown, S. A. (2000). A multi-variate process model of adolescent 12-step attendance and substance use outcome following inpatient treatment. *Psychology of Addictive Behaviors, 14*(4), 376–389.

Kelly, J. F., Myers, M. G., & Brown, S. A. (2002). Do adolescents affiliate with 12-step groups? A multivariate process model of effects. *Journal of Studies in Alcohol, 63*(3), 293–304.

Kelly, J. F., Myers, M. G., & Brown, S. A. (2005). The effects of age composition of 12-step groups on adolescent 12-step participation and substance use outcome. *Journal of Child and Adolescent Substance Abuse, 15*(1), 63–72. doi: 10.1300/J029v15n01_05

Kelly, J. F., Myers, M. G., & Rodolico, J. (2008). What do adolescents exposed to Alcoholics Anonymous think about 12-step groups? *Substance Abuse, 29*(2), 53–62.

Kelly, J. F., Pagano, M. E., Stout, R. L., & Johnson, S. M. (2011). Influence of religiosity on 12-step participation and treatment response among substance-dependent adolescents. [Research Support, N.I.H., Extramural Research Support, Non-U.S. Gov't]. *Journal of Studies in Alcohol and Drugs, 72*(6), 1000–1011.

Kelly, J. F., Stout, R. L., Greene, M. C., & Slaymaker, V. (2014). Young adults, social networks, and addiction recovery: Post treatment changes in social ties and their role as a mediator of 12-step participation. *PloS One, 9*(6), e100121.

Kelly, J. F., Stout, R. L., Magill, M., & Tonigan, J. S. (2011). The role of Alcoholics Anonymous in mobilizing adaptive social network changes: A prospective lagged mediational analysis. *Drug and Alcohol Dependence, 114*(2–3), 119–126. doi: S0376-8716(10)00323-6 [pii] 10.1016/j.drugalcdep.2010.09.009

Kelly, J. F., Stout, R. L., Magill, M., Tonigan, J. S., & Pagano, M. E. (2010). Mechanisms of behavior change in alcoholics anonymous: Does Alcoholics Anonymous lead to better alcohol use outcomes by reducing depression symptoms? *Addiction, 105*(4), 626–636. doi: ADD2820 [pii] 10.1111/j.1360-0443.2009.02820.x

Kelly, J. F., Stout, R. L., & Slaymaker, V. (2013). Emerging adults' treatment outcomes in relation to 12-step mutual-help attendance and active involvement. *Drug and Alcohol Dependence, 129*(1–2), 151–157. doi: 10.1016/j.drugalcdep.2012.10.005

Kelly, J. F., & Urbanoski, K. (2012). Youth recovery contexts: The incremental effects of 12-step attendance and involvement on adolescent outpatient outcomes. *Alcoholism: Clinical and Experimental Research*. doi: 10.1111/j.1530-0277.2011.01727.x

Kelly, J. F., & White, W. L. (Eds.). (2011). *Addiction recovery management*. New York, NY: Springer.

Kelly, J. F., & Yeterian, J. D. (2011). The role of mutual-help groups in extending the framework of treatment. *Alcohol Research and Health, 33*(4), 350–355.

Kelly, J. F., & Yeterian, J. D. (2012). Empirical awakening: The new science on mutual help and implications for cost containment under health care reform. *Substance Abuse, 33*(2), 85–91. doi: 10.1080/08897077.2011.634965

Kelly, J. F., Yeterian, J. D., & Myers, M. G. (2008). Treatment staff referrals, participation expectations, and perceived benefits and barriers to adolescent involvement in 12-step groups. *Alcoholism Treatment Quarterly, 26*(4), 427–449.

Kennedy, B. P., & Minami, M. (1993). The Beech Hill Hospital/Outward Bound adolescent chemical dependency treatment program. *Journal of Substance Abuse Treatment, 10*(4), 395–406.

Knudsen, H. K., Ducharme, L. J., Roman, P. M., & Johnson, J. A. (2008). Service delivery and use of evidence-based treatment practices in adolescent substance abuse treatment settings: Project report: Robert Wood Johnson Foundation's Substance Abuse Policy Research Program (Grant No. 53130).

Labbe, A. K., Greene, C., Bergman, B. G., Hoeppner, B., & Kelly, J. F. (2013). The importance of age composition of 12-step meetings as a moderating factor in the relation between young adults' 12-step participation and abstinence. *Drug and Alcohol Dependence, 133*(2), 541–547.

Litt, M. D., Kadden, R. M., Kabela-Cormier, E., & Petry, N. M. (2009). Changing network support for drinking: Network support project 2-year follow-up. *Journal of Consulting and Clinical Psychology, 77*(2), 229–242. doi: 2009-03774-004 [pii] 10.1037/a0015252

Longabaugh, R. (2007). The search for mechanisms of change in behavioral treatments for alcohol use disorders: A commentary. *Alcoholism: Clinical and Experimental Research, 31*(10 Suppl), 21s–32s. doi: ACER490 [pii] 10.1111/j.1530-0277.2007.00490.x

Longabaugh, R., Wirtz, P. W., Zweben, A., & Stout, R. L. (1998). Network support for drinking, Alcoholics Anonymous and long-term matching effects. *Addiction, 93*(9), 1313–1333.

Mäkela, K. (1996). *Alcoholics Anonymous as a mutual-help movement: A study in eight societies*. Madison, WI: University of Wisconsin Press.

Manning, V., Best, D., Faulkner, N., Titherington, E., Morinan, A., Keaney, F., . . . Strang, J. (2012). Does active referral by a doctor or 12-Step peer improve 12-Step meeting attendance? Results from a pilot randomised control trial. *Drug and Alcohol Dependency*. doi: 10.1016/j.drugalcdep.2012.05.004

Mason, M. J., & Luckey, B. (2003). Young adults in alcohol-other drug treatment: An understudied population. *Alcoholism Treatment Quarterly, 21*(1), 17–32.

McCrady, B. S. (1994). Alcoholics Anonymous and behavior therapy: Can habits be treated as diseases? Can diseases be treated as habits? *Journal of Consulting and Clinical Psychology, 62*(6), 1159–1166.

McElrath, D. (1997). The Minnesota Model. *Journal of Psychoactive Drugs, 29*(2), 141–144.

McWhirter, P. T. (2008). Enhancing adolescent substance abuse treatment engagement. [Case Reports; Research Support, N.I.H., Extramural]. *Journal of Psychoactive Drugs, 40*(2), 173–182.

Miller, L., Davies, M., & Greenwald, S. (2000). Religiosity and substance use and abuse among adolescents in the National Comorbidity Survey. [Comparative Study; Research Support, Non-U.S. Gov't; Research Support, U.S. Gov't, P.H.S.]. *Journal of the American Academy of Child and Adolescent Psychiatry, 39*(9), 1190–1197. doi: 10.1097/00004583-200009000-00020

Montgomery, H. A., Miller, W. R., & Tonigan, J. S. (1995). Does Alcoholics Anonymous involvement predict treatment outcome? *Journal of Substance Abuse and Treatment, 12*(4), 241–246. doi: 074054729500018Z [pii]

Moos, R. H., & Moos, B. S. (2004). Long-term influence of duration and frequency of participation in alcoholics anonymous on individuals with alcohol use disorders. *Journal of Consulting and Clinical Psychology, 72*(1), 81–90. doi: 10.1037/0022-006X.72.1.81 2004-10364-008

Mundt, M. P., Parthasarathy, S., Chi, F. W., Sterling, S., & Campbell, C. I. (2012). 12-Step participation reduces medical use costs among adolescents with a history of alcohol and other drug treatment. *Drug and Alcohol Dependence*. doi: 10.1016/j.drugalcdep.2012.05.002

Nock, M. K. (2007). Conceptual and design essentials for evaluating mechanisms of change. *Alcoholism: Clinical and Experimental Research, 31*(10 Suppl), 4s–12s. doi: ACER488 [pii] 10.1111/j.1530-0277.2007.00488.x

Ouimette, P., Humphreys, K., Moos, R. H., Finney, J. W., Cronkite, R., & Federman, B. (2001). Self-help group participation among substance use disorder patients with posttraumatic stress disorder. *Journal of Substance Abuse Treatment, 20*(1), 25–32.

Passetti, L. L., Godley, M., & Godley, S. H. (2012). Youth participation in mutual support groups: History, current knowledge, and areas for future research. *Journal of Groups in Addiction Recovery*.

Passetti, L. L., & Godley, S. H. (2008). Adolescent substance abuse treatment clinicians' self-help meeting referral practices and adolescent attendance rates. [Comparative Study; Research Support, N.I.H., Extramural Research Support, U.S. Gov't, P.H.S.]. *Journal of Psychoactive Drugs, 40*(1), 29–40.

Project MATCH Research Group. (1997). Matching alcoholism treatments to client heterogeneity: Project MATCH posttreatment drinking outcomes. *Journal of Studies on Alcohol, 58*(1), 7–29.

Robinson, E. A., Krentzman, A. R., Webb, J. R., & Brower, K. J. (2011). Six-month changes in spirituality and religiousness in alcoholics predict drinking outcomes at nine months. [Research Support, N.I.H., Extramural]. *Journal of Studies on Alcohol and Drugs, 72*(4), 660–668.

Roman, P. M., & Blum, T. C. (1999). *National Treatment Center Study (Summary 3)*. Athens, GA: University of Georgia.

Roman, P. M., & Blum, T. C. (2004). *National Treatment Center Study (Summary 3)*. Athens, GA: University of Georgia.

Rosenstock, I. (1974). Historical origins of the health belief model. *Health Education Monographs, 2*(4), 328–335.

Stewart, D. G., & Brown, S. A. (1995). Withdrawal and dependency symptoms among adolescent alcohol and drug abusers. *Addiction, 90*(5), 627–635.

Stout, R. L., Kelly, J. F., Magill, M., & Pagano, M. E. (2012). Association between social influences and drinking outcomes across three years. [Research Support, N.I.H., Extramural]. *Journal of Studies on Alcohol and Drugs, 73*(3), 489–497.

Substance Abuse and Mental Health Services Administration. (2008). *The NSDUH Report: Participation in Self-Help Groups for Alcohol and Illicit Drug Use: 2006 and 2007*. Rockville, MD: Office of Applied Studies.

Timko, C., & DeBenedetti, A. (2007). A randomized controlled trial of intensive referral to 12-step self-help groups: one-year outcomes. *Drug and Alcohol Dependence, 90*(2–3), 270–279. doi: S0376-8716(07)00176-7 [pii] 10.1016/j.drugalcdep.2007.04.007

Timko, C., Debenedetti, A., & Billow, R. (2006). Intensive referral to 12-step self-help groups and 6-month substance use disorder outcomes. *Addiction, 101*(5), 678–688. doi: ADD1391 [pii] 10.1111/j.1360-0443.2006.01391.x

Tims, F. M., Dennis, M. L., Hamilton, N., B, J. B., Diamond, G., Funk, R., & Brantley, L. B. (2002). Characteristics and problems of 600 adolescent cannabis abusers in outpatient treatment. *Addiction, 97* (Suppl 1), 46–57. doi: add08 [pii]

Tomlinson, K. L., Brown, S. A., & Abrantes, A. (2004). Psychiatric comorbidity and substance use treatment outcomes of adolescents. [Research Support, U.S. Gov't,

P.H.S.]. *Psychology of Addictive Behaviors, 18*(2), 160–169. doi: 10.1037/0893-164X.18.2.160

Vaughan, E. L., de Dios, M. A., Steinfeldt, J. A., & Kratz, L. M. (2011). Religiosity, alcohol use attitudes, and alcohol use in a national sample of adolescents. *Psychology of Addictive Behaviors, 25*(3), 547–553. doi: 10.1037/a0024660

Waldron, H., Miller, W. R., & Tonigan, J. S. (2001). Client Anger as a predictor to treatment response. In R. H. Longabaugh & P. W. Wirtz (Eds.), *Project MATCH hypotheses: Results and causal chain analyses. NIAAA Project MATCH Monograph Series, Vol. 8.* Rockville, MD: NIAAA.

Walitzer, K. S., Dermen, K. H., & Barrick, C. (2009). Facilitating involvement in Alcoholics Anonymous during out-patient treatment: A randomized clinical trial. *Addiction, 104*(3), 391–401. doi: ADD2467 [pii] 10.1111/j.1360-0443.2008.02467.x

Weiss, R. D., Griffin, M. L., Gallop, R. J., Najavits, L. M., Frank, A., Crits-Christoph, P., . . . Luborsky, L. (2005). The effect of 12-step self-help group attendance and participation on drug use outcomes among cocaine-dependent patients. *Drug and Alcohol Dependence, 77*(2), 177–184. doi: S0376-8716(04)00227-3 [pii] 10.1016/j.drugalcdep.2004.08.012

White, W. L. (1998). *Slaying the dragon: The history of addiction treatment and recovery in America.* Bloomington, IL: Chestnut Health Systems.

Winters, K. C., Stinchfield, R., Latimer, W. W., & Lee, S. (2007). Long-term outcome of substance-dependent youth following 12-step treatment. [Controlled Clinical Trial; Research Support, N.I.H., Extramural]. *Journal of Substance Abuse and Treatment, 33*(1), 61–69. doi: 10.1016/j.jsat.2006.12.003

Winters, K. C., Stinchfield, R. D., Latimer, W. W., & Stone, A. (2008). Internalizing and externalizing behaviors and their association with the treatment of adolescents with substance use disorder. [Research Support, N.I.H., Extramural]. *Journal of Substance Abuse and Treatment, 35*(3), 269–278. doi: 10.1016/j.jsat.2007.11.002

Winters, K. C., Stinchfield, R. D., Opland, E., Weller, C., & Latimer, W. W. (2000). The effectiveness of the Minnesota Model approach in the treatment of adolescent drug abusers. [Comparative Study Research Support, U.S. Gov't, P.H.S.]. *Addiction, 95*(4), 601–612.

Wu, J., & Witkiewitz, K. (2008). Network support for drinking: an application of multiple groups growth mixture modeling to examine client-treatment matching. [Research Support, N.I.H., Extramural]. *Journal of Studies on Alcohol and Drugs, 69*(1), 21–29.

Wu, L. T., Pilowsky, D. J., Schlenger, W. E., & Hasin, D. (2007). Alcohol use disorders and the use of treatment services among college-age young adults. *Psychiatric Services, 58*(2), 192–200. doi: 58/2/192 [pii] 10.1176/appi.ps.58.2.192

Zemore, S. E. (2007). A role for spiritual change in the benefits of 12-step involvement. *Alcoholism: Clinical and Experimental Research, 31*(10 Suppl), 76s–79s. doi: ACER499 [pii] 10.1111/j.1530-0277.2007.00499.x

Effective Inpatient and Outpatient Models of Treatment for Adolescents With Substance Use Disorders

Marianne Pugatch, John R. Knight, Sarah Copelas, Tatiana Buynitsky, *and* J. Wesley Boyd

Abstract

This chapter provides an overview of the physical, psychological, and brain development of the adolescent, establishing the need for treatment tailored to their unique developmental needs. It also defines the goals and phases of treatment, describes the continuum of care and contextualizes the body of effectiveness treatment research. The chapter reviews the evidence based literature on inpatient and outpatient settings including short-term detoxification, acute and long-term residential care, sober houses, therapeutic schools, day hospitals, intensive outpatient as well as outpatient approaches. Overall, studies indicate that treatment in youth has small to moderate effects. The chapter concludes with recommendations for what professionals and parents should look for in treatment programs for adolescent clients and discusses future research and policy recommendations.

Key Words: adolescence, substance use disorders, treatment effectiveness, evidence-based, inpatient treatment, outpatient treatment

Addiction is a pediatric disorder, with typical onset during adolescence. The younger a child is when he initiates alcohol, marijuana, or other substance use, the more likely he is to develop an addiction later in life (Grant & Dawson, 1998; Hingson, Heeren, & Winter, 2006; McGue, Iacono, Legrand, Malone, & Elkins, 2001; Substance Abuse and Mental Health Services Administration, 2010) and to have generally poor outcomes in young adulthood (Patton et al., 2007). Adolescent substance use is a major public health problem (Feinstein, Richter, & Foster, 2012) that has great costs to society—both financial (Bouchery, Harwood, Sacks, Simon, & Brewer, 2011; Hon, 2003) and years of life lost (Borse, Rudd, Dellinger, & Sleet, 2012). Although limited, the body of evidence indicates that substance use treatment for adolescents works, with a small to moderate effect size.

Developmental Science of Adolescence

Adolescence describes the period of development that occurs as individuals leave childhood to become independent, contributing members of adult society (Steinberg, 2014). Adolescents experiment, explore, take risks, test limits, and question established rules and authority. Although these behaviors are functional, they can lead to serious injury and illness when combined with alcohol or drug use. Simple warnings about associated risks may be insufficient: All too often, warnings elicit the classic response, "Don't worry, that will never happen to me."

Adolescence can be a very positive developmental period as interpersonal relationships transform and new cognitive abilities emerge. In social relationships, there is movement from predominant family influence (preconformist), to peer influence (conformist), to independent thinking (postconformist) (Petersen & Leffert, 1995). Cognitively, the development of formal operations leads to the ability to think in the abstract (Piaget & Inhelder, 1958). Propositional logic, that is, the formation of hypotheses and consideration of a variety of solutions, emerges. Adolescents also develop metacognition, or the ability to think about the thought process itself. These new abilities are essential for the establishment of therapeutic provider–patient relationships and for counseling interventions such as cognitive-behavioral therapy and motivational enhancement therapy.

Problem-behavior theory and social cognitive theory provide a conceptual framework for understanding risk behaviors during adolescence. Problem-behavior theory defines "risk behavior" as anything that can interfere with successful psychosocial development and "problem behavior" as risk behaviors that elicit either formal or informal social responses designed to control them (Jessor & Jessor, 1977). These may cluster to form a "risk behavior syndrome" when they serve a common social or psychological developmental function (e.g., affirming individuation from parents, helping to achieve adult status, gaining acceptance from peers). These behaviors may help the adolescent cope with failure, boredom, social anxiety, unhappiness, rejection, social isolation, low self-esteem, or a lack of self-efficacy. Adolescents, for example, may use substances as a way of achieving social status among their peers.

Social cognitive theory posits a "triadic reciprocal causation," in which behavior, personal determinants, and environmental influences all interact to determine behavior (Bandura, 1977). According to this theory, individuals learn how to behave through a process of modeling and reinforcement, imitating behaviors observed in others that are perceived to have positive consequences. Therefore, exposure to successful, high-status role models who use drugs will likely influence adolescents. Health risk and problem behaviors are both purposeful and functional. Peer influences may suggest to adolescents that drug use and sexual behaviors are necessary if one is to become popular, cool, sexy, grown-up, sophisticated, macho, or tough.

Scientists now know that the human brain continues to undergo critical development in structure and function well into the mid-twenties (Casey, Getz, & Galvan, 2008). The first decade of life is a time of exponential growth in neurons, comprising the gray matter of the brain. Brain development progresses from back to front, with areas in the back, such as those involved in vision and physical coordination, developing more quickly than areas in the front (Gogtay et al., 2004). The prefrontal cortex, which is responsible for higher level functions such as organization, planning, self-control, emotional regulation, and judgment, is the last to finish maturing (Rubia et al., 2000).

During the teens and early twenties, white matter grows exponentially as the brain establishes connectivity among the various neuronal processing areas of activity (Giorgio et al., 2008). For the prefrontal cortex to function well, its connections to other parts of the brain involved in emotional and impulsive behavior need to be strengthened so that impulse control can be quickly applied when needed (Nagy, Westerberg, & Klinbgerg, 2004). This brain connectivity is still developing in adolescence, so a teen's ability to control her emotions and impulses, or make sound decisions, is not the same as that of an adult. Teens are thus more likely to impulsively try dangerous pursuits, such as speeding on a motorcycle or experimenting with alcohol or drugs.

Connectivity is critical to higher order thinking (Liston et al., 2005). Today's teens face a challenging and competitive world, and they need their brains to be as healthy as possible to develop their maximum potential. One cannot function at the college level in reading, writing, or complex task management without the ability to connect many centers within the brain. And connectivity is dramatically affected by exogenous psychoactive substances, such as cannabinoids (Dekker et al., 2010; Yucel et al., 2008).

Exposure to exogenous psychoactive substances during the critical adolescent years causes longstanding changes in brain structure and function, which can persist for years even after an individual stops using (Meier et al., 2012; Squeglia, Jacobus, & Tapert, 2009). The receptors of the brain's "cannabinoid system" are for the endogenous neurotransmitter anandamide that shapes how brain cells grow and connect to each other and helps the brain monitor and regulate itself, calming brain cells when they become overexcited (Wilson & Nicoll, 2002). The active chemical in marijuana, THC, is a chemical imposter that binds to the same receptor sites as anandamide (Devane et al., 1992). However, THC causes a much stronger, longer effect on brain cells and interferes with anandamide's function (Ameri, 1999). The same interference occurs with most other psychoactive substances of abuse: They are counterfeit near-copies of the naturally occurring neurotransmitters, which fool brain receptors in the nucleus accumbens and ventral tegmental area (VTA) into triggering the brain's very powerful reward pathway (Koob & Volkow, 2010).

The neuroscience implications of substance use are profound. The hippocampus, critical for learning and memory, tends to be smaller in heavy-drinking adolescents compared to those who did not drink (De Bellis et al., 2000). A study measuring the effect of marijuana use on IQ showed that at age 13, before starting marijuana use, everyone in the study had about the same IQ. However, 25 years later, those who smoked marijuana heavily for 3 or more years showed a significant drop in their IQ. Also, those who started before age 18 had a bigger drop than those who started after age 18 (Meier et al., 2012).

Teen brains respond differently to alcohol—they are less sensitive to its sedative and motor impairment effects (Silveri & Spear, 1998; White et al., 2002). When adults drink too much, their judgment becomes impaired and they tend to become slower and sleepier. When teens drink too much, their judgment is also impaired, but they are more likely to stay awake, active, and social. Thus, teens are at far greater risk for injuring themselves or others while drunk. They are more likely to drive drunk or ride with an impaired driver, or to become a victim or perpetrator of physical or sexual violence.

Addiction is a phenotypical behavioral disorder that is determined by an intersection of genotype and experiential influences and exogenous neuroactive substances at critical points in time. The earlier the exposure, the more devastating the effect (Hingson, Heeren, & Winter, 2006). Someone who starts drinking at age 21 has a lifetime alcoholism risk of 9%, while someone who starts drinking at 13 or younger faces a lifetime risk of nearly 50%, a five-fold increase (Hingson et al., 2006; Substance Abuse and Mental Health Services Administration, 2010). If a family member has alcoholism, the risk is even greater. Someone who starts smoking marijuana at 21 has about a 4% chance of developing addiction. Someone who starts at 13 has a risk greater than 16%, a four-fold increase (Substance Abuse and Mental Health Services Administration, 2010).

Marijuana has powerful effects on the brain's reward system (Gardner, 2005; Lupica, Riegel, & Hoffman, 2004) as well as on motor coordination, vision, memory, sensation, movement, and judgment (Asbridge, Hayden, & Cartwright, 2012;

Castle & Solowij, 2004; Crean, Crane, & Mason, 2011). Marijuana impairs driving, and its effects last longer than those of alcohol (Grant, Gonzalez, Carey, Natarajan, & Wolfson, 2003). More 15- to 17-year-olds are in treatment for marijuana addiction than for all other drugs combined (Substance Abuse and Mental Health Services Administration Office of Applied Studies, 2009). Starting regular marijuana use early greatly increases the risk of developing major depression, an anxiety disorder, and psychosis (Bossong & Niesink, 2010). Smoking marijuana regularly causes a five-fold increase in the risk of having depression or an anxiety disorder (de Graaf et al., 2010). Smoking marijuana more than 50 times increases the risk of developing psychotic disorders like schizophrenia almost seven-fold (Andreasson, Allebeck, Engstrom, & Rydberg, 1987). If a family member has mental illness, the risk is even greater and the symptoms often appear earlier (Bayer, Falkai, & Maier, 1999; Sugranyes et al., 2009).

Given the immediate and long-term neurotoxic effects on the developing brain's structure and function, it is best for teens' development and future success to remain alcohol and drug-free until their brains have fully matured.

Goals of Treatment and Research

The primary goal of adolescent substance abuse treatment is abstinence from substances with a secondary goal of harm reduction. Typically, there are two phases of treatment for substance abuse care; the first phase is focused on supporting the adolescent in achieving abstinence, and the second phase of treatment centers on the adolescent maintaining abstinence while integrating back into the community. Reintegration to the community is a process in which an adolescent plans with caregivers to gradually regain privileges such as socializing time with peers, managing an allowance, and other freedoms—one contingency at a time. In this systematic way, ideally the adolescent learns of his particular challenges in the environment and develops skills to contend with them in the service of maintaining a drug-free state. There is some consensus that an adolescent should remain abstinent for at least 90 days within an environment without substances before he "steps down" to a less restrictive setting to begin the process of reintegrating in the community. It takes 90 days for an adolescent to become physically free from the symptomatic effects of alcohol and other drugs as well as desensitized to external drug and alcohol triggers. If an adolescent remains in a cloistered environment for 90 days, away from his peer social system, he increases his receptivity to new coping skills, including resisting situations with peers who are using and reconnecting with hobbies in lieu of using alcohol and drugs. Although some adolescents require removal from their social system to achieve abstinence—in part due to the developmental importance of the peer network—this is not true for all adolescents. Additionally, the concept of recovery goes beyond sobriety to encompass holistic health and wellness, including biopsychosocial and spiritual markers of functioning for the adolescent and family system. These particular markers are dependent on the phase of adolescence: early, middle, or late. These biopsychosocial and spiritual markers of "recovery" are pertinent to multiple facets of effective treatment: type of placement, development of treatment goals, readiness for discharge, and the kind of continuing care services. The goals of an adolescent's treatment include increasing the patient's protective factors while decreasing risk factors. Due to the individual nature of each adolescent's physiology, psychology, social, culture, and ethnic make-up, the recovery process is unique to an individual. Abstinence is not the only marker of recovery—the health and well-being of an adolescent are the ultimate goals of treatment as measured by meeting normative developmental tasks and functioning optimally across life domains. Recovery includes gains from treatment, other than abstinence or reduction in use, that contribute to the adolescent's unique development and wellness and, ultimately, the determination of whether treatment has been effective (Substance Abuse and Mental Health Services Administration, 2009). Recovery-oriented outcomes for adolescent treatment effectiveness include improved school performance, reduced criminal involvement, increased school attendance and employment functioning, a decrease in the number of incidents of driving and riding while intoxicated, and markers of physical and psychological health (Godley, Passetti, & White, 2006). The improvement in function of an adolescent's family and peer network is also an indication of treatment success—a change to a sober peer group, feelings of social connectedness, improved relationships with parents, and engagement in extracurricular activities are examples. Given that the neurobiology of substance use indicates that addiction is represented by a change in the structure of the brain—the association between psychological change and biological markers

as well as brain imaging may ultimately provide the most reliable measurements of the effectiveness of substance use treatments for adolescents (Feldstein Ewing & Chung, 2013).

Adolescent Treatment Gap

The treatment gap for adolescents who need but do not receive treatment is wide; in 2011 the National Survey on Drug Use and Health (NSDUH) reports that only about 12% of adolescents with a past-year substance use disorder have received treatment in the past year (Substance Abuse and Mental Health Services Administration, 2013). The inability of parents to identify when their teen is misusing substances (Fisher et al., 2006) may contribute to the treatment gap, as well as other factors such as a fragmented substance abuse treatment system (Steenrod, 2009); the medical and mental health as well as substance use services developed separately (Grob & Howard, 2006) and have remained for the most part in silos. Adolescents are typically referred to treatment through the mental health or juvenile justice system as well as from the teachers, providers, and parents. At times, they may self-refer. Most often, adolescents are mandated to treatment by one or more systems. Contingencies support maintenance of treatment. Not all adolescents who use substances require formal treatment; a percentage of youth "recover" with no treatment. Many adolescents stop using substances on their own in their mid-twenties; this is also known as natural recovery. This change in use patterns in early adulthood may be due to the commencement of maturity in brain development and/or new priorities of adulthood. There are adolescents who also report feeling traumatized in treatment. Despite these concerns, there is evidence that treatment works—mandated or not. Due to the high risk of morbidity and mortality, as well as biopsychosocial risk factors of continued substance use, delaying treatment or opting out of recommended treatment should be an individual/family decision following a complete diagnostic assessment.

Once a provider, such as a primary care pediatrician, nurse practitioner, guidance counselor, or even a parent, teacher, or friend is concerned about an adolescent's use of substances, a screening or evaluation is recommended. A valid and reliable screening tool yields accurate information about level of risk of the adolescent in regard to his substance use as well as whether a referral to treatment is indicated. If the adolescent does not require detoxification or supervision for psychiatric or medical reasons, and/or he is not at risk in the home or community environment, an outpatient setting will be the first line of treatment. The reason why outpatient treatment is preferred for the adolescent is that it is the least restrictive setting and allows the adolescent to recover naturally within the context of family. An adolescent who can maintain abstinence and work toward treatment goals while living in a home is ready for outpatient care. An adolescent is referred to an outpatient setting in two ways—either in the initial assessment or upon discharge to the community after completing a residential or an inpatient treatment episode. In this second circumstance, the adolescent and his family, the treatment team as well as treatment funders, ideally work together to determine how best to support the adolescent to return to the community while maintaining treatment gains. An adolescent who meets criteria for an outpatient level of care would ideally live in a community setting that provides adequate levels of supervision in order to minimize risks of further substance use, encourage engagement in educational pursuits, and support development of a sober support network that includes healthy peer relationships based on positive activities away from common triggers of a culture of drugs and alcohol. With this type of containment and structure in place, the adolescent can focus on developing healthy competencies including but not limited to the task of individuation and separation. This particular developmental task, one hallmark of adolescence, contributes to the need for the specialization of care for the adolescent as separate from the treatment of an adult. The flexibility and structure required to develop and maintain quality treatment for the adolescent requires a provider team that is trained in case management, motivational interviewing, adolescent development, family systems theory, policy, and advocacy, to name a few. A clinician or team of clinicians who can coordinate an adolescent's care and maintain relationships with the family within and across systems and levels of care is imperative to the health and well-being of the adolescent who uses substances.

Adolescent Addiction Treatment Continuum of Care

In the 1980s the federal government set up a collaborative team of specialists to develop national guidelines for outcome and research-based addiction treatment (Mee-Lee, 2013). Presently the American Society of Addiction Medicine (ASAM) has established criteria for the continuum of care that are a staple and a resource for professionals to describe the nomenclature for addiction treatment. Additionally, ASAM criteria are used to place patients along the continuum of care for addiction treatment; there are differential criteria for adults and adolescents. Varying levels of treatment intensity for adolescents exist; each level of treatment has a different set of principles and guidelines that conform to best practices and are frequently updated and in alignment with the best evidence. ASAM utilizes six dimensions to assess and place adolescents: withdrawal potential; biomedical conditions and complications; emotional, behavioral, or cognitive complications; readiness to change; relapse or continued use potential; and recovery or living environment (Mee-Lee, 2013). Additionally, addiction treatment facilities are required to follow certain criteria in order to meet licensure and credentialing specifications on a state-by-state basis. Adolescents should be referred to licensed or credentialed facilities if possible.

Evidence

In tracing the history of effectiveness studies for adolescent substance use, it is important to examine the first important study for adult alcohol use disorders, Project Match. Project Match was a banner study and a turning point in the treatment of alcoholism for adults. It examined whether people with alcohol use disorders had better outcomes when matched to a type of treatment based on their psychosocial profile. Findings indicated a marginal differential impact of abstinence; basically, use reduction was the same in the three treatment groups. Project Match showed that treatment works and any treatment was better than no treatment.

Adolescent Treatment

The most well-known comparative effectiveness trial for adolescent substance use is the Cannabis Youth Treatment (CYT) project. This research consisted of two trials of adolescent patients in four sites representing three regions of the United States (Dennis et al., 2004). All patients in these two trials had cannabis use disorders, were more likely to be male (83% vs. 73%), white (61% vs. 70%), and had current involvement in the juvenile justice department (Dennis et al., 2004). The study tested different promising treatments, including motivational enhancement therapy (MET), a brief manualized version of motivational interviewing, and cognitive-behavioral therapy (CBT) and several family therapies. The study employed psychoeducation of certain recovery topics to test outcomes; specifically, adolescents were taught and practiced refusal skills, as well as how to develop a supportive peer network, develop a plan for alternate social activities, and establish a plan of how to manage high-risk situations, solve problems, and deal with relapse (Dennis et al., 2004). The first trial, MET/CBT5, tested brief treatment in the form of a combination of two individual sessions of MET and three group sessions of CBT; this arm mimicked community treatment for adolescents (Dennis et al., 2004). The second treatment arm included family treatment, which tested the hypothesis that more "comprehensive treatment" for the adolescent was best practice. Several types of family therapy were tested. One model of treatment was called "family support network" and consisted of six parent education group meetings, four therapeutic home visits, a referral to self-help support groups, and case management. The six parent education meetings had the goal of improving parent knowledge and skills in regard to adolescent substance use and to improve family functioning (Dennis et al., 2004). Groups for the parents or caregivers of these adolescents included information on adolescent development and family roles, substance use diagnoses, recovery and signs of relapse, family systems theory, and organization/communication (Dennis et al., 2004). Case management was also employed to help with adolescent/parent engagement in the treatment process (Dennis et al., 2004). Results of this study were similar to results of Project Match indicating that one treatment arm was as effective as the other; one treatment was not superior to another.

A second trial in the CYT, called MET/CBT12, consisted of testing an additional seven group sessions of CBT designed to teach adolescents coping skills for problems including but not limited to managing thoughts about cannabis and depression management (Dennis et al., 2004). In addition, in the second trial, another arm of the study tested a family therapy called the Adolescent Community Reinforcement Approach (ACRA). Finally, a third arm tested the comparative effectiveness of multidimensional family therapy (MDFT). MDFT is more time intensive and consists of more hours of family therapy then the other approaches. Results were promising in that all combinations of outpatient treatment were found to have a small but significant effect on outcomes, and one treatment was not considered better then another. Although there are methodological limitations to this study and

the results are not generalizable to all adolescents, especially a diverse ethnic and cultural population of adolescents, the results supported the findings from Project MATCH. Additionally, finding that a briefer treatment course was just as effective as a more extensive treatment course, the results may have implications for implementation in other treatment settings like primary care, where new models of co-location with mental health providers may be adequate delivery systems for the integration of the treatment of substance use disorders with health care.

Although adolescent treatment, like adult treatment for substance use, has been found to be better than no treatment, and many specific treatments are promising, there may be treatments that are not effective for adolescents. We do not know if psychoanalysis leads to reductions in substance use or has positive effects for adolescents who use alcohol; in the absence of evidence, caution is recommended. It makes sense to practice and implement what we know works.

Meta-Analytic and Systematic Reviews of Adolescent Treatment

Early systematic reviews of adolescent treatment for substance use included few experiments. Due to the paucity of randomized controlled trials testing adolescent substance use treatment, conclusions in these early reviews suffer from methodological weaknesses. In 2000, Williams and colleagues completed one of the first reviews of adolescent treatment that included controlled trials (Williams & Chang, 2000); studies included in this meta-review were found through a systematic search of a limited number of databases. Exclusion criteria from this review included adolescents younger than 13 years of age, older than 19 years of age, and a study sample size of 20 or fewer. Inclusion criteria in this review were noncontrolled research in sites offering differing levels of treatment: outpatient, inpatient, wilderness programs, and therapeutic communities (Williams & Chang, 2000). Studies had a homogenous population of mostly White (89%) males (96%) and 90% were between the age of 15 and 17 years (Williams & Chang, 2000). Whereas 53 studies were found, only 21 studies were included in the results in an attempt to bolster rigor of findings. The results in this review excluded studies that did not report an intent-to-treat analysis, had follow-up rates that were less than 75%, had only parental report used to establish substance use, or had average age at follow-up as 21 years old or greater (Williams & Chang, 2000). Williams and colleagues found that the average rate of sustained abstinence after adolescent treatment was 38% with a range of 30%–55% at 6 months and 32% with a range of 14%–47% at 12 months (Williams & Chang, 2000). The variables related to successful outcomes at posttreatment included treatment completion, low use of substances before treatment, peer/parental support of nonuse of substances and school functioning, attendance in aftercare, and peer/parental support (Williams & Chang, 2000). Findings supported that treatment was superior to no treatment, but there was not enough evidence (studies completed) at this time to compare the relative effectiveness of types of treatment with the exception that the review indicated that at an outpatient level of care, family therapy seemed superior in terms of outcomes to other therapies for adolescents (Williams & Chang, 2000). This makes good sense given the importance of the caregivers in terms of adolescent development. Treatment variables consistently related to successful outcomes in this review include treatment completion, programs that provide comprehensive services, programs with experienced therapists, and larger programs with more funds (Williams & Chang, 2000). Although there was not enough power to compare outcomes in different treatment types, there were also serious problems in methodology due to lack of controlled experiments at this time (Williams & Chang, 2000). This makes it impossible to know if the effect was due to treatment or natural recovery, regression to the mean, or other factors. Other more rigorous reviews found similar evidence: that treatment was superior to no treatment and the one treatment was not necessarily superior in effectiveness to another. The more rigorous reviews that include only randomized control trials have created a formal evidence base of literature that more confidently supports these findings. Waldron synthesized findings from 17 studies of adolescent treatment facilities and concluded that the effect of functional family therapy, multidimensional family therapy, and group CBT were "well established" and produced a small effect that was significant. Additionally, none of these three methods of intervention were clearly superior for treating adolescents with substance use disorders (Waldron & Turner, 2008). They also concluded that other treatment approaches are "probably efficacious" as well. Inclusion criteria for this review included randomized trials, larger sample sizes, more accurate substance use measures and longer term post-treatment substance use measures. Furthermore, the treatment population is less homogenous. Population examined was 75% male, 45% White, 25% Hispanic, 25% African American, and 5% other groups (Waldron & Turner, 2008). The studies included in this review took place in treatment settings, excluding community-based settings such as schools, emergency rooms, juvenile justice settings (Waldron & Turner, 2008, p. 6). It is important to mention that the terms "well established" and "probably efficacious" are based on rigorous nomenclature that includes, but is not limited to, a specified client sample, manualized treatments, and an experimental design with one or more comparison groups. (Waldron & Turner, 2008).

A more recent meta-analysis of adolescent outpatient treatment outcomes substantiates previous findings that many types of treatment are effective. Yet this review adds scientific rigor and weight to supporting programs with a family therapy component as having the strongest evidence for effectiveness in this population (Tanner-Smith, Wilson, & Lipsey, 2013).

Inpatient Treatment

In this section of the chapter, we will describe inpatient treatment and the evidence base for inpatient level of care. There are many forms of inpatient treatment for adolescents that range from short-term detox admission to acute or long-term residential care in a residential treatment. Other long-term settings might include a sober house or a therapeutic school. In addition, we will clarify what each of these types of treatment entails: Which of these options might be best for any given individual depends on various factors, including the extent and severity of drug use; whether the individual is physically dependent on a drug, and, if so, if the individual might be at risk of seizure or death if he were to suddenly stop using the substance; whether the individual is willing to enter a treatment program or will need to be compelled to go there; and whether previous attempts at treatment have been tried and failed.

Determining the actual success rates of any single option for treatment can be difficult, since much of the research on outcomes has been funded or carried out by treatment facilities themselves, and because there are few case control studies. Because the market for services of the kind we describe in this section can be quite competitive, individual programs and entities might have significant motivation to overestimate or overstate their actual success rates. This point leads to another, namely, the definitions of "success" might differ, sometimes substantially, from one published report to another, further complicating any effort to draw significant conclusions about efficacy. Because of these kinds of issues—as well as a general lack of consistent standards between many of these programs and options, the US Federal Trade Commission weighed in several years ago and issued a warning that although "some programs make specific success claims in their advertising materials . . . to date, there is no systematic, independently collected descriptive or outcome data on these programs" (US Federal Trade Commission, 2008).

Acute Medical Stabilization (Detox)

Acute medical stabilization, often simply referred to as detoxification (or detox for short), is typically the initial option for treatment for individuals who are actively abusing specific substances. Individuals who are dependent on substances often require a detox admission to be able to safely withdraw from the substance of abuse. Withdrawing from some substances, such an opiates or cocaine, can be uncomfortable but generally not life threatening, whereas withdrawing from benzodiazepines or alcohol in rare instances can be life threatening given the risk of experiencing withdrawal seizures. In these latter instances the safest option is to enter a detox facility to withdraw from the substance.

The goal of a detox admission is to have the individual safely and, as comfortably as possible, withdraw from the substance. Detox facilities accomplish these goals by monitoring the individual's vital statistics and utilizing medications to facilitate safe withdrawal from the drug of choice. Some of the medications used are intended to be substituted for their drug of choice and allow measured withdrawal from the substituted substance. An example of this is when detox facilities prescribe chlordiazepoxide—a long-acting benzodiazepine—to individuals who come in seeking withdrawal off of alcohol or other benzodiazepines. Chlordiazepoxide has a long half-life—much longer than alcohol or the benzodiazepines that are frequently abused—and can safely and slowly be prescribed and then tapered and discontinued over a period of time. Doing so hopefully allows the individual to feel as little discomfort as possible. Some facilities will utilize other benzodiazepines as well, including diazepam, clonazepam, oxazepam, and lorazepam, among others.

In addition to safety, comfort is another key component of detox admissions. Various reports have concluded that the extent to which an individual feels comfortable during a detox admission is the single most important ingredient that predicts whether that individual will enter detox again in the future.

Not surprisingly, detox facilities can vary widely in their styles and comfort levels, with some being more or less inpatient medical wards, often with few frills (whether attached to a hospital or not) beyond a bed in a dorm room type setting with routine checks of vital signs, medications administered at a nursing window, and minimal staffing. Other detox units in essence try to mimic luxury hotels, with comfortable homey living quarters, fine dining (perhaps with a celebrity chef creating meals), and highly attentive medical staffs. Still others can be religiously or spiritually based—irrespective of the luxury of the environs—emphasizing faith in God while also providing medical support as necessary.

Several factors appear to predict better outcomes in detox admissions. One older study found that predictors of success included "slow detoxification, full-time employment, positive motivation for detoxification, and high degree of assimilation into the nondrug world" (Cushman, 1974, p. 393).

A detox admission can be vitally important for many individuals, but detox alone is almost always not sufficient for most individuals to successfully kick a drug habit; although detox helps the individual safely and as comfortably as possible withdraw from the substances of abuse, in and of itself it is not sufficient to lay down the habits of healthy, drug-free living for most individuals. Thus, detox might be a starting point for remaining clean and sober, but detox alone is rarely sufficient for doing so. As such, many detox admissions are followed by intensive rehabilitation work, either in an inpatient facility or on an outpatient basis.

Acute Residential Treatment

Acute residential treatment, often referred to by its acronym ART, provides lower intensity inpatient treatment than does a detox admission because generally individuals who enter an ART either do not warrant a detox admission or have already successfully withdrawn physically from whatever their drug of choice is. It is generally accepted that "acute" means that treatment in the inpatient stay was 30 days or fewer in duration.

Residential treatment is seen as an alternative to hospitalizing individuals and generally is far less expensive than hospitalizations. Residential treatment settings—whether shorter or longer term—are generally clinically focused and thus keep an emphasis on educating individuals about substance use and reinforcing sobriety. If the individual appears unsure about the need to remain sober, motivational interviewing might be indicated. If the individual is already sober and trying to remain so but a bit unsure about how exactly to do so, then perhaps relapse prevention would be stressed. These techniques, along with behavioral therapy and treatment more generally, are often mainstays of treatment in residential settings.

Given that in ART settings individuals are generally beyond the acute withdrawal phases of drug dependence (which is the norm in detox settings), in ART settings individuals might receive psychiatric medications if they were indicated, but generally they are not prescribed medications such as benzodiazepines, which are used to ameliorate the physical symptoms of acute withdrawal and are mainstays of detox admissions. Indeed, many residential treatment settings actually prohibit medications of this sort entirely given their significant potential for abuse. And given that individuals in ART settings are not in the throes of drug withdrawal, medications that provide symptomatic relief of withdrawal symptoms would be far less often used in ART settings compared with detox settings but might be prescribed for anxiety and other psychiatric symptoms.

Studies suggest that ART placements are cost-effective compared with full hospital admissions, even though their outcomes are comparable. For example, one study compared veterans who were treated in either a hospital or an ART program and found that both groups showed significant improvement between admission, discharge, and 2-month follow-up and, additionally, that there were few statistically significant differences between the groups in symptoms and functioning. Thus, this study showed not only that ART admissions proved beneficial but also that despite their lower cost they were not significantly different with respect to outcomes than regular hospital admissions (Hawthorne et al., 2005). We cannot say definitively whether or not these findings are generalizable to adolescents.

So which types of drug users do best in ART settings? A study published in 2009 found that treatment completion was highest among those who primary substance of abuse was alcohol at 66% and lowest for those who primarily abused stimulants at 46% (Substance Abuse and Mental Health Services Administration & Office of Applied Studies, 2005).

Long-Term Residential Treatment

As its name implies, long-term residential treatment is inpatient treatment that lasts longer than 30 days. A long-term residential treatment is different from short-term residential treatment in that stays are longer than 30 days and might last as long as 2 years. The goal of these longer term stays is to reinforce and support all of the tools individuals need in order live sober, while hopefully discovering that life is not only possible without drugs or alcohol but, in fact, might even be preferable without them. Some studies have shown that residential treatment leads to improved outcomes not just with respect to substance abuse but also with respect to crime (Borse et al., 2012). However, to our knowledge, these studies looked at adults and not adolescents.

One study that compared short- and long-term residential treatment among adults using data from 2005 found that found that "clients discharged from short-term residential treatment were more likely to complete treatment than clients discharged from long-term residential treatment (57 vs. 38%) and less likely to drop out of treatment (15 vs. 31%). Similar percentages of clients discharged from short-term residential and long-term residential treatment were terminated by the facility (7 and 9%)" (Substance Abuse and Mental Health Services Administration & Office of Applied Studies, 2005), presumably for noncompliance. These findings are not too surprising, given that individuals obviously spend more time in long-term treatment and thus have more opportunity to be either discharged early or to drop out prior to completion.

The report went on to conclude that among those discharged from long-term residential facilities, "treatment completion was highest among those reporting primary alcohol abuse (46%); treatment completion was lowest among those reporting primary cocaine abuse (33%) or primary opiate abuse (35%)." Additionally, "clients discharged from long-term residential treatment who reported primary stimulant abuse were less likely than those who reported other primary substances to be terminated by the facility (4 vs. 9 to 13%)" (Substance Abuse and Mental Health Services Administration & Office of Applied Studies, 2005).

One of this study's conclusions was that in either acute or long-term residential treatment, "certain client characteristics, such as primary alcohol abuse and higher educational level, were associated with treatment completion regardless of the type of residential treatment received" (Substance Abuse and Mental Health Services Administration & Office of Applied Studies, 2005). We cannot be certain that this study's findings are applicable to adolescents.

The research literature to date has been limited in terms of examining the effectiveness of residential settings for adolescents with substance use disorders. However, it is possible to examine reviews of residential treatment centers in general and establish whether those that implement evidence-based practices with known effectiveness for the treatment of substance use disorders in teens can be implemented effectively in residential settings. A recent systematic review from 1990 to 2012 identified 10 types of evidence-based treatment and 13 studies conducted in youth residential care services (RCS) and examined the evidence of intervention effectiveness within a residential center setting (James, Alemi, & Zepeda, 2013). In this review RCS is defined as short- or long-term group homes or residential centers (James et al., 2013). Populations examined include substance use disorders and teenagers. This systematic review is atypical in that it identified types of interventions rather than specific studies to review. All evidence-based practices included in the review have prior proven efficacy or effectiveness. Some of the limitations of these studies are that most of the participants were White. Six of the studies used randomization. All of the substance use treatment programs in this review were randomized controlled trials or quasi-experimental designs (considered promising). The populations examined in these studies do not represent the entire population who are served in the RCS's, which limits their generalizability. In the context of many limitations, including study sample size and representativeness, the studies on Adolescent Community Reinforcement Approach (ACRA) found a medium effect size (James et al., 2013). However, in this same review, studies on Multi modal Substance Abuse Prevention (MSAP) had mixed results—whereas adolescents' decreased drug use and drug selling following MSAP, other behaviors were not found to be significantly reduced. Another study found Ecologically Based Family Therapy (EBFT) more effective than functional family therapy (FFT) in reducing drug use, and both were more effective then treatment as usual. These findings should be considered cautiously, however, given the weaknesses in study design.

Therapeutic Communities

Therapeutic communities encompass a wide swath of treatment modalities that are usually residential, group-based, and participatory in nature. Therapeutic communities have historically been milieu based—that is, observant of the various interactions between all of the members of the community—and have involved group activities in general and group therapy in particular.

When a therapeutic community is focused on substance abuse, many of the activities will be centered on substance use issues. Given the breadth of treatment options, a "therapeutic community" can include long-term residential placements that generally could fall under this rubric (assuming they focus on group interaction and dynamics), as well as other longer term treatment options.

We could find no scientific literature addressing treatment outcomes and efficacy for youths who choose a therapeutic community for treatment of their substance misuse.

Therapeutic Schools

Therapeutics schools are educational facilities where the focus is on emotional and academic recovery. These schools provide structure and supervision for physical, emotional, behavioral, family, social, intellectual, and academic development. A therapeutic school is a special residential school designed to help troubled children, typically teenagers, with a variety of emotional and other problems. As a rule, the child cannot get the consistent treatment he needs in a local school and at home. As a result, it makes sense in many cases to send the child away to a highly structured environment where he will receive the treatment he needs 24/7. Most schools also work with their students to get the academics back on track as well. The kinds of problems that children face who might benefit from a therapeutic school include those with substance use disorders as well as those who perpetually defy authority, those who are threatening to or violent toward others, and those who simply can't abide by school rules or are otherwise significant disciplinary problems.

Although each one is unique, therapeutic schools generally provide a highly structured program with a lot of focus on the individual. The goal is to provide education, support, and guidance in learning new, more productive study and life habits. Given that many of these schools restrict access to the world at large, procuring drugs or engaging in dangerous behaviors otherwise can be difficult. Hopefully, therapeutic schools provide the encouragement and support necessary to establish new, health-inducing behavior. Although there is no defined length of stay, generally youths will stay in these programs for a year, although some stays are much shorter (especially if a child proves unable to adhere to the rules and structure), and many are longer.

We could find no scientific literature addressing treatment outcomes and efficacy for youths who choose to attend therapeutic schools.

Halfway House

Halfway houses are transitional residential facilities, which are sometimes called sober houses, which individuals often enter when they are transitioning from prison, rehab, or some other facility back into ordinary life. Many individuals will be discharged from jail or have parole requirements that mandate halfway house placement, whereas others will avoid jail altogether and have halfway house placement as part of their probation requirements. Others enter halfway houses voluntarily, on their own, perhaps because they feel that they need the added structure that a halfway house adds in order to remain sober. Halfway houses usually have some kind of staffing, although perhaps only for daytime hours. Halfway houses often have Alcoholics Anonymous or Narcotics Anonymous (AA/NA) meetings on site and usually have some kind of sobriety support in place otherwise. Apart from these elements, they often offer some structure and occasionally will offer counseling on site as well. Halfway houses will generally drug test individuals when they are entering the facility because they don't have detox capabilities and, if someone were to test positive upon entry, he or she might be referred to a detox facility with an invitation to return afterward. Halfway houses usually have strict requirements to remain clean and sober and will randomly drug test individuals throughout their stay.

Most states have halfway houses. They range in size from a handful of beds to over 100. The average length of stay is 12 weeks (Allen, Carlson, Parks, & Seiter, 1978).

Halfway houses may or might not be regulated through local and state agencies. Many of the best ones will seek out such review and regulation in order to guarantee others about their quality, something that is important given the very loose oversight of many of these programs.

Sober House

Although the terms "halfway house" and "sober house" are often used interchangeably, when there is a distinction between these two terms, a sober house will offer fewer services, it is often entirely voluntary as opposed to mandatory the way many halfway house placements are, and it might not have anyone staffing the facility. A sober house might or might not have any form of drug testing as part of its residency requirements. Sober houses often are little more than a large house with individual rooms rented out to individuals who voice a desire to live a clean and sober life—and also might not offer any programming on site, such as AA/NA meetings in-house or counseling services. Individuals might or might not take meals together. The idea behind a sober house is that the individuals residing there can be mutually supportive of one another in their efforts to live a drug-free life and, as such, individuals might attend AA meetings together, assist one another in getting to appointments, and so on, but the structure of sober houses is often minimal.

Wilderness Program/Boot Camp

Wilderness programs can have various names, with the "boot camp" approach being among the most popular, although there is no standard definition of these programs. These programs, as their names imply, are often based out of doors in rustic or rural settings, often with spartan living quarters and offerings. At times, adolescents do not even know that their parents or caregivers are considering these programs and some of them will actually arrive at the clients' place of residence unbeknownst to the adolescent, compel (including by force if necessary) the adolescent to come with them, and then transport the adolescent to a rustic location. At that point the focus often is living in a drug-free environment that requires physical participation in various activities—perhaps including food gathering or meal preparation. Some will have hikes of various lengths and other physically stressful activities. All encourage full sobriety and are often located in such rural settings that even accessing drugs or alcohol would be all but impossible.

These programs are often utilized by parents as a last measure, utilized only after many other efforts at achieving sobriety have failed, and also often after family, work, and school relationships are incredibly strained or simply broken.

Thus, when families consider these programs for the adolescents, they are often emotionally drained, desperate, and as such, fairly vulnerable. Because of this, these families might be vulnerable to sales pitches for programs that might not be either effective or particularly safe. This dynamic is particularly problematic because the federal government does not generally regulate these programs, and many are not regulated by any state either.

Because of this general lack of regulation and oversight for many of these programs, the FTC developed 15 questions that it advises families to ask these programs prior to enrolling a teen in them. Among the questions are the following:

• Are you licensed by the state?

If the answer is yes, find out what aspects of the program the license covers: educational, mental/behavioral health, and/or residential?

• Do you provide an academic curriculum?

• Do you provide accreditation?

• Do you have a clinical director? What are his or her credentials?

• What are the credentials of the staff, especially the counselors and therapists, who will be working with my child? (The FTC encourages families to ask to see copies of relevant documents and consider contacting the certifying or licensing organization to confirm the staff credentials.)

• How experienced is your staff? Have they worked at other residential treatment programs? If yes, where and for how long?

• Do you conduct background checks on your employees?

• How do you handle medical issues like illness or injury? Is there a nurse or doctor on staff? On the premises?

• How do you discipline program participants?

• Can I contact/speak with my child when I want?

• What are the costs? What do they cover? What is your refund policy? These questions are especially important since insurance rarely covers the cost of a wilderness camp.

Although some programs might bristle when asked these questions, any legitimate program should welcome these questions and, obviously, be prepared to answer them in a forthright manner (Commission, 2008; Hubbard, Rachal, Harwood, Cavanaugh, & Ginzburg, 1989).

It bears noting that these programs are certainly not for everyone, and research has shown that for some individuals, approaches such as "scared straight," boot camp interventions, and other potentially scary programs will likely harm some youth (Lilienfield, 2007). Therefore, although we stop short of advising against ever enrolling a youth in a boot camp, we advise an abundance of caution prior to doing so.

Outpatient Level of Care

There are varying levels of intensity of outpatient treatment for adolescents who experience problems with substance use. These levels of treatment exist along a continuum of care ranging from intensive day treatment to regular outpatient meetings. Three levels of outpatient treatment will be discussed in this part of the chapter: partial hospitalization, intensive outpatient, and outpatient treatment (Mee-Lee, 2013). Each level of outpatient treatment has a different set of guidelines that conform to best practices for outpatient level of care; credentialed and/or licensed facilities are required to follow these criteria. Adolescent outpatient substance abuse treatment has been found to have a small effect in meta-analyses (Williams & Chang, 2000). Given the fact that effects have not been shown to last post-treatment—a few studies have begun to look on the promising effects of continuing care also known as aftercare (Godley, Godley, Dennis, Funk, & Passetti, 2002; Godley, Coleman-Cowger, Titus, Funk, & Orndorff, 2010).

Research Findings and Empirical Evidence of Behavioral Therapies

To date, there have been few published randomized controlled trials of psychosocial substance abuse treatments, including behavioral treatments for adolescents. The studies conducted have shown promising effects of behavioral therapies, including but not limited to motivational interviewing (MI) (D'Amico, Miles, Stern, & Meredith, 2008; de Dios et al., 2012; Knight et al., 2005; Macgowan & Engle, 2010; Monti et al., 2007; Spirito et al., 2004, 2011), contingency management (CM) (Kaminer, 2000; Stanger, Budney, Kamon, & Thostensen, 2009; Stanger & Budney, 2010), CBT (Azrin et al., 2001; Waldron & Kaminer, 2004), and different types of family therapy (Austin, Macgowan, & Wagner, 2005; Garner et al., 2009; Godley et al., 2001; Henggeler, Clingempeel, Brondino, & Pickrel, 2002; Liddle, 2002a, 2002b, 2004). Additionally, there have been a few promising experiments examining combined behavioral and pharmacotherapy for adolescents with opioid dependence (Marsch, 2007; Marsch et al., 2005a, 2005b; Woody et al., 2008).

MI is a client-centered and directive counseling style that seeks to support a client making behavioral change. MI was initially developed to address adult alcohol use but has been applied to many types of addictive behaviors and other unhealthy behaviors in patients across the lifespan, including for self-management of diabetes care. MI has been found to be effective when used as an adjunct to other therapies, within the context of a brief intervention, or alone.

MI is conceptually promising for adolescents who strive to meet the psychosocial task of independence, in part because MI supports adolescents in exercising the development of propositional logic. MI has been tested with adolescents who are using different substances, including alcohol, marijuana, tobacco, and other drugs, and within a variety of settings on different adolescent populations. MI has been shown to successfully reduce substance use, (Rubak, Sandbaek, Lauritzen, & Christensen, 2005), decrease the negative consequences of use (Knight et al., 2005), enhance engagement in treatment with incarcerated youth (Stein et al., 2006), and in combination with CBT enhance readiness to change in a brief group therapy for adolescents when compared to no treatment (Bailey, Baker, Webster, & Lewin, 2004; Grenard et al., 2007) as well as a brief intervention of MI for at-risk youth (Grenard et al., 2007). Several individual studies indicate that MI as a brief intervention is more effective than usual care for different-age adolescents with alcohol or substance use issues in a variety of settings (D'Amico et al., 2008; Monti et al., 1997, 1999; Spirito et al., 2004, 2011). One meta-analysis of 14 experiments testing MI from 1998 to 2008 for adolescents age 12–25 years old found that one session of MI might be more effective than other brief interventions; additionally, it indicates that across different age groups, in disparate settings with varying lengths of intervention, MI had a small but significant posttreatment effective, $d = .173$ (Jensen et al., 2011). Despite the evidence, it is challenging to provide conclusive evidence of the size and length of the treatment effect because MI has been conducted with different dosages of MI, across different adolescent population groups, in disparate settings and some studies suffer from small sample sizes and other methodological limitations (Wachtel & Staniford, 2010, p. 618). Furthermore, most of the studies examining MI have not included a racially diverse sample and thus cannot be generalized as a treatment until more treatment on representative samples is conducted.

CM is a type of treatment that is based on the behavioral theory of operant conditioning; it utilizes relatively immediate rewards for positive behaviors such as abstinence from alcohol and drugs. Contingencies are also offered for process measures like engagement in the process of treatment as indicated by kept appointments and medication adherence. CM can be a stand-alone therapy or it can be used with another therapy liked CBT, MI, or family treatment (Stanger & Budney, 2010). In this technique, monetary-based rewards like small prizes, a dose of medication, and vouchers provide immediate and concrete benefit to the patient. It is theorized, although not yet proven, that these intermediate outcomes could lead to long-term outcomes like better grades in school, improved relationships with family, better health, and other socially productive behavior.

CM has been tested and found effective in reducing use with adults for different types of drugs (cocaine, marijuana, opioids, and alcohol). Relatively few studies of CM have been completed with teens, yet of those completed, the results have been promising in terms of reduction of use during treatment and engagement and retention in treatment (Grob & Howard, 2006). One experiment for adolescents with marijuana use found that CM as an adjunctive treatment for 69 adolescents age 14–18 years old who received MET/CBT and twice weekly drug testing improved more marijuana abstinence 7.6 versus 5.1 weeks and 50% versus 18% reached more than 10 weeks of abstinence. Improvements in parenting and youth psychopathology in the treatment condition suggest that CM when added to other outpatient substance abuse interventions provides an increased effect (Stanger et al., 2009). A voucher-based contingency management study in adults (Ledgerwood, Alessi, Hanson, Godley, & Petry, 2008) and a meta-analysis found that this method improved engagement and retention in treatment (Lussier, Heil, Mongeon, Badger, & Higgins, 2006). Because teens are challenging to engage and retain in treatment, CM is particularly promising for this age group.

CBT is based on cognitive restructuring; the idea is that through identifying faulty cognitions, clients can change their feelings and behaviors. this is the case for CBT has been found to be effective in a variety of therapy modalities with adolescents; this is the case for CBT alone and in combination with other treatment techniques. In fact, several randomized controlled trials of adolescent substance use at an outpatient level have included CBT. Perhaps the most well-known study is the Cannabis Youth Treatment (CYT) study that consisted of two trials of adolescent patients in various regions of the United States (Dennis et al., 2004). Despite a lack of efficacy research, clinical judgment of trained providers with supervision is essential. In the following sections we review some of the practice wisdom for formal and informal treatments for adolescent substance use at an outpatient level.

Day Hospital

A day hospital, also called a "partial hospitalization" program, provides a structured setting for an adolescent in the community. Typically, a day hospital is defined as treatment that lasts "20 hours a week" (Mee-Lee, 2013), but this may vary depending on the facility. A day hospital usually includes medical and psychiatric services within the setting for the adolescent. In addition to these services, day hospitals provide psychosocial treatments through individual, group, and family treatment modalities, random drug screening, and adjunctive services, including vocational and educational support. The benefit of a day hospital is that this setting provides an adolescent with medical supervision for substance use or co-occurring psychiatric disorders during this period of time.

A day hospitalization could be initiated as a step down from a residential or inpatient facility. In this situation the day hospital provides a patient who has been discharged from an inpatient level of care, with a relatively secure and monitored day treatment setting while living in a home environment, in the community. Alternatively, the day hospital setting could serve as a higher level of care for a patient who is already living in the community and receiving outpatient treatment. In this situation it might be that the adolescent and caregiver require intensive services related to improvement of adolescent monitoring; a less intensive setting may not be sufficient in meeting the adolescent's treatment goals in this instance, which could include adolescent improving skill deficits and the provision of parent education. In this context the adolescent would typically spend part of each day up to 3 days a week in the day hospital.

We found no randomized controlled trials to date of adolescent patients in partial hospitalization or day hospital settings and thus advise using best practices to guide effective treatment.

Intensive Outpatient Treatment

Intensive outpatient programs (IOPs) are less intensive then a day hospital setting. IOPs are typically 9 hours a week (Mee-Lee, 2013) and typically last several weeks. Similar to day hospitals, IOPs can provide treatment that is a step down from a higher level of care or as a first line of treatment. IOPs often offer flexible hours and multiple meeting times per week in the day and/or evening. They typically provide a core set of services like individual and group therapy. Because IOPs are short term, the group therapy is typically open ended, with multiple groups that are topic focused, and membership in these groups can include adolescents at differing stages of change. Unlike day treatment, an IOP traditionally does not have as much family involvement, and its medical and psychiatric services are typically not on site and are variable in intensity from none to weekly. An IOP may include pharmacotherapy and medication management. IOPs typically have case management that includes assessment, planning, linkage monitoring, and advocacy. IOPs also typically require that an adolescent actively participate in self-help groups and 12-step programs. There is little empirical evidence showing the effectiveness of IOPs for adolescents (Center for Substance Abuse Treatment & Substance Abuse and Mental Health Services Administration, 2006).

Sobriety Schools

Sobriety schools, also known as recovery high schools, are educational settings typically funded by the educational system that provide a recovery-oriented setting for adolescents with substance use disorders who are returning to the community from inpatient treatment or are in need of a sober educational setting that meets an outpatient level of care. Most sobriety schools require drug testing and have 12-step recovery meetings on site, yet they are not considered treatment facilities.

The first sobriety school started in 1987 in Minnesota. The Association of Recovery Schools (ARS) began in 2002 and developed criteria for schools (D'Amico et al., 2008). Recovery high schools are considered to be a part of a "continuing care model" (Moberg & Finch, 2008). Recovery schools are intended for adolescents who have completed an intensive treatment program, have achieved abstinence, and are ready to return to the community or for those adolescents who have adequate motivation to stop using substances and enough supervision to support this goal. According to Moberg and Finch, a continuing care community should prevent relapse (Moberg & Finch, 2008). Typically, adolescents transfer to recovery high schools upon discharge from a residential treatment program or completion of an IOP; a recovery school, in theory, is one which can limit the potential triggers and increase the sober support network during an adolescent's return to the community (Moberg & Finch, 2008). There have been single-site case studies of recovery high schools as well as an evaluation of recovery high schools (Moberg & Finch, 2008). One descriptive study that included 18 recovery schools found that these schools were more publically than privately funded, had more voluntary than involuntary enrollment, emphasized maintenance of recovery and support as opposed to primary treatment, balanced academics with therapy, offered an eclectic recovery model that included 12-step recovery, and was integrated with another school program rather than freestanding, including sharing facilities and staff (Moberg & Finch, 2008). Students who attended these schools were mostly male (54%), White (78%), with about 50% from two-parent homes (Moberg & Finch, 2008). There have only been retrospective pre/posttest analyses of recovery high schools. These studies suggest a significant reduction in substance use as well as an improvement in mental health (Moberg & Finch, 2008). In general, students have been less enthusiastic about the educational program and more supportive of its therapeutic value (Moberg & Finch, 2008). However, to date this research is quite limited in its rigor and generalizability. Additionally, a lack of understanding currently exists about what tools recovery schools utilize to serve their students, who the students are, whether they show effects for students significantly different from those attained by recovering students attending nonrecovery schools, and how student and programmatic differences affect outcomes.

Individual Counseling

Individual counseling is a type of treatment in which an adolescent meets with a trained master's- or doctoral-level clinician for psychosocial treatment that typically lasts for a 45- to 50-minute period and could either be brief or longer term treatment depending on the goals of the treatment plan. This type of treatment is often covered by insurance. Few studies to date have been completed for adolescents in individual therapy, but several

meta-analyses point to certain types of individual treatment that produce a small but significant effect on adolescent treatment outcomes that are retained over time, including behavioral treatments (BTs), CBT, and MI.

Psychotherapy

Psychotherapy for the adolescent is a general term for a type of treatment whose goal is to increase the well-being and health of the individual. A range of techniques are used to improve health, including behavioral, cognitive-behavioral, family systems, and psychodynamic therapy, to name a few. Each form of psychotherapy can be practiced in a variety of settings utilizing different treatment modalities such as individual, group, or family. Whereas most studies testing psychotherapy indicate that one type of psychotherapy is not better than any other, psychodynamic psychotherapy, which has the goal of a deeper understanding and knowledge of the self, like psychoanalysis has no known effectiveness studies for adolescent substance use.

Group Therapy

Although not yet fully described or studied (Engle & Macgowan, 2009), group therapy has been a core treatment modality for adolescents with addiction. While most groups take place in a clinic, hospital setting, or in the community, some groups are led in schools. "Group therapy" may include any number of treatment modalities, including therapist-led or co-led psychoeducational, behavioral, or psychodynamic discussion groups, 12-step or other peer support groups, and task-centered groups. Group therapy is often considered the treatment of choice for adolescents due to the developmental change process and the importance of peers in influencing behavior during this stage of development. Group treatment for adolescents who misuse substances and have addictive disorders has the same goals as other addiction therapies—to achieve abstinence, reduce use and harm, and to increase protective factors and reduce risk factors. The group may be a place for adolescents to build new social support networks through practicing refusal skills and other behavioral coping skills with peers. One study that compared a behavioral group to a discussion-based supportive group found superior outcomes in the behavioral group (Azrin et al., 1994). Cognitive-behavioral group therapy is also an effective group treatment for adolescents with substance use disorders (Jensen et al., 2011; Macgowan & Engle, 2010; Waldron & Kaminer, 2004).

Groups for adolescents with substance use should be highly structured, time limited, and led by a trained clinician(s) who utilizes manuals from evidence-informed treatment. It is important for adolescents to have treatment goals that relate to use of addictive substances as well as goals based on the adolescents' strengths. Both voluntary and involuntary participation in these groups have a positive effect. Implementing a group in treatment practice requires several clinical steps that include developing a group of adolescent members that work well together—creating a therapeutic group composition. The group leader typically interviews potential group members and matches him to a group. This typically involves a pregroup screening meeting in which the individual adolescent and provider consider the adolescent's motivation to be a member of the group and prepare the patient for the group content and process by reviewing the group rules. Additionally, in the group screen meeting, the clinician works with the adolescent to create individual and group goals. Often this includes signing contractual agreements that lay out expectations for behavior in the group and outside of the group—that includes no outside contact with other group members. In this meeting, the clinician and potential group member review the process of what happens if rules are broken. In this way all members are prepared for an experience that is as structured and safe as possible while providing room for therapeutic change. Given that many members may have co-occurring issues, including trauma histories, clinicians need to carefully assess their potential adolescent group member during the group screen to ensure that the group will be a therapeutic one for all patients involved. Including the parent in the screening process is typical to obtain family history and support engagement.

Typically a therapy group for adolescents who misuse substances or have addiction includes three to eight members. Groups are often co-ed, and they could include patients with different levels of use as well as types of substances used and co-occurring mental health issues. These differences in group membership become important when developing group composition because the members learn from each other, and it is important to protect and nurture the members, not expose them to further risk. A group member usually becomes acclimated to the group within four sessions (including the group screen); it is important to contract with the member to attend the group for at least three sessions before making a decision about final membership. Additionally, girls and boys engage in the group process differently; girls typically taking their time to form positive relationships, whereas boys will often vie for status outright. There has been much discussion about these groups having negative outcomes—meaning that groups lead to more use due to contagion (Dishion, Poulin, & Burraston, 2001). To prevent negative contagion in groups, skilled group leaders and research-informed group therapy should be conducted. Furthermore, groups that are led by highly trained clinicians that are evidence informed and highly structured usually have agreements/contracts which group members agree to contractually prior to engagement with other members; when group contract is broken, there are contingencies and additional opportunities for a corrective experience. The CYT study found that groups were just as effective as other models of treatment, and there were no iatrogenic effects (Burleson, Kaminer, & Dennis, 2006).

Although there has been speculation that gender-only treatment groups might be beneficial to meet the needs of girls, especially with trauma, evidence has not yet substantiated this. In fact, mixed-gender groups have been found to be equally successful (Greenfield, Trucco, McHugh, Lincoln, & Gallop, 2007). Additionally, one small trial of a curriculum called Seeking Safety has been found to be effective with adolescent girls only (Najavits, Gallop, & Weiss, 2006). Replication is needed. Another promising group is for opioid-dependent patients. In one small pilot study, data indicate that this specific research-informed group curriculum may teach parents of opioid-dependent adolescents to recognize when their adolescent patient is using substances (Pugatch, Knight, McGuiness, Sherritt, & Levy, 2014). This manualized psychoeducational with 13 sessions has two entry points with parallel and coordinated treatment tracks for adolescents and parents. Parents play an integral part in adolescent growth and development as well as the treatment for adolescents. For this reason we recommend family-centered care when providing group and other modalities of treatment for adolescents.

Family Therapy

Family therapy usually involves some portion of a family or an entire family meeting together with a clinician whose job is to ensure that each person within the family system has an opportunity to be heard and to offer observations about the group dynamic along with suggestions for improvement. Because the addicted adolescent patient exists within a family system, this type of treatment has been conceptually promising. Early research of family therapy for adolescent substance use suggested that it was more effective for adolescents than other forms of treatment. However, more recent research suggests that family therapy is no more effective than other modalities of psychosocial treatment; in one review of 17 studies of adolescent substance abuse treatment, multidimensional family therapy and functional family therapy as well as group CBT were considered established models of substance abuse treatment, yet not superior in their treatment effect to other types of treatment (Waldron & Turner, 2008).

Support Groups

Support groups are often a key part of substance use treatment during the outpatient phase of treatment. Support groups typically have peer leaders, are open ended, have no limit on the number of members, and are open to all adolescents whose qualifications for membership in the group depend on their own use of alcohol or drugs coupled with a desire to stop using drugs addictively. Most support groups are not adolescent age specific, although some meetings are "young persons' meetings." Membership in 12-step support groups is often an expectation as an adjunct to substance use treatment in adolescents otherwise and sometimes is their only treatment. Because anonymity is a major principle of 12-step programs, there have been few rigorous experiments completed. However, there have been recent data that strongly suggest the effectiveness of 12-step groups as adjunctive treatment for adolescents (Kelly, Brown, Abrantes, Kahler, & Myers, 2008; Kelly, Dow, Yeterian, & Kahler, 2010; Kelly, Myers, & Brown, 2000, 2005; Kelly & Urbanoski, 2012).

"Treatment wisdom" indicates that an adolescent, especially a young adolescent, attends his or her first meeting with a parent or known person who is familiar with the program and has experience with recovery within the context of the group. We recommend that adolescents who are in recovery attend their first 12-step meeting with a peer who is affiliated in the program and has a sponsor with at least a year of abstinence and who is working his or her "program" consistently. Because the 12-step approach suggests that the adolescent is powerless over his or her addiction, without support from a seasoned person in recovery or a trained professional,

this first step of the program may appear to be at odds with the normative adolescent developmental task of individuation, competency, and self-efficacy. There is a delicate balance between admitting powerlessness while developing competence; both are needed for full recovery and wellness.

Complementary and Alternative Medicine Approaches

Complementary and alternative medicine (CAM) is an emerging area of interest for individuals who need assistance in remaining clean and sober. In a review of the evidence for adults and adolescents, the effect of this modality to date has been mixed. Because the topic is so new at this time, there exist multiple weaknesses to this body of effectiveness literature. However, stress and anxiety may be alleviated by alternative therapies, including mindfulness. Including CAM approaches with adolescents who use substances has not yet been tested rigorously. One small pilot study of mindfulness-based therapy in combination with MI for young adult females who use marijuana showed a greater reduction of days of marijuana use at 1, 2, and 3 months post treatment than assessment only (de Dios et al., 2012). More research is needed to indicate if CAM has efficacy and in what contexts it is effective with adolescents.

Strengths and Limitations

Although evidence exists for the effectiveness of treatment for adolescents, the evidence is limited by methodological and other challenges. The gold standard psychosocial interventions for addiction lead to moderate effects post treatment. It is clear that the field of addiction needs to understand the components of sustained behavioral change for addiction before modeling interventions after the components. Feldstein and colleagues (2013) propose that we examine how neurobiological mechanisms and behavior change interact to create positive change in psychosocial addictions treatment. Because the majority of adolescent patients with substance use disorders have co-occurring conditions, efficacy trials that address comorbidity in adolescence are important. Although not the subject of this chapter, examining this literature is germane. There are promising treatments for adolescents with comorbid conditions like "Seeking Safety," a treatment for female adolescents who have alcohol and posttraumatic stress disorders (Najavits et al., 2006). Large-scale randomized controlled trials testing different mental health and substance use conditions, including anxiety and alcohol, and depression and alcohol, are important to build foundational evidence for our understanding of an adequate treatment system of care for adolescents with substance use conditions. However, until the research is completed, clinicians may want to look toward evidence of treatments that work across conditions and tailor these to clients' needs.

Most adolescent substance use effectiveness studies examine the adolescents who have access to treatment—the majority of whom are male and white. Given the wide gap between those adolescents who are at risk for a substance use problem and those receiving services, examining how to increase access and decrease health disparities is essential. Either casting a wider net by screening adolescents in other settings like schools and/or increasing cultural competency is essential. Given the current prevention mandate and the Patient Protection and Affordable Care Act, from now on referred to as the Affordable Care Act (ACA), reaching minority, at-risk youth may be more feasible. We found one study on culturally competent treatment for adolescents with substance use (Santisteban et al., 2003). A growing and needed area of effectiveness research for adolescents with substance use issues is in the area of health disparities for African American, Hispanic and immigrant populations. Researching adolescents with different sexual identity and preferences is also essential given what is known about risk for suicide among this population. In the abstinence of evidence best practices around treatment that is racially, ethnically, and culturally competent should be followed.

There has been some attention to female-only treatment in the substance abuse outcome literature for adults and adolescents (Acharyya & Zhang, 2003; Najavits et al., 2006; Toray, Coughlin, Vuchinich, & Patricelli, 1991). Findings initially suggested that women and girls have different treatment needs than men and boys. In Christine Grella's chapter in *Adolescent Substance Abuse* entitled "The Drug Abuse Treatment Outcomes Studies: Outcomes With Adolescent Substance Abusers," she reports that adolescent girls have higher rates of internalizing symptoms than adolescent boys (2006). However, more recently, some studies have found the contrary. In the presence of mixed evidence, culturally competent clinical care with experienced trained clinicians is essential.

Primary Care

Perhaps one of the most promising outpatient settings for future identification and treatment for adolescents includes the primary care office. With the advent of Parity 2008 and the Affordable Care Act (Abrams, Nuzum, Mika, & Lawlor, 2011), treatment within a primary care center for addiction and mental health concerns is covered at an equal amount to coverage for health conditions. Furthermore, preventive services for Medicaid and other populations will be covered. The patient-centered medical home (PCMH) is one type of primary care center that has its roots in pediatrics (Monti et al., 2007) and holds promise for the delivery of effective therapies (Cooley, McAllister, Sherrieb, & Kuhlthau, 2009; Crabtree et al., 2010; Croghan & Brown, 2010; Ernst, Miller, & Rollnick, 2007; Friedberg, Safran, Coltin, Dresser, & Schneider, 2009; Grumbach & Grundy, 2010; Nielsen, Langner, Zema, Hacker, & Grundy, 2012). Although there are several models of PCMHs, they include co-located or integrated models, and they represent a new frontier for adolescent substance abuse treatment. The PCMH is particularly promising due to emphasis on the child and family building strong and trusting relationships with their providers. This principle of the PCMH has its roots in the American Academy of Pediatrics (AAP), and pediatricians are trained to provide family-centered care. The PCMH is a potential context for nonstigmatized care for adolescents with substance use as well as mental health concerns when care is integrated. Primary care and in particular the PCMH are optimal centers for the prevention, treatment, and/or referral for adolescents with substance misuse or addiction. Screening, brief interventions, and referral to treatment (SBIRT) may be effective in reducing the disease burden of addiction that develops during the adolescent years. The evidence for SBIRT for adolescents holds promise (De Micheli, Fisberg, & Formigoni, 2004; Harris et al., 2012), yet few effectiveness trials exist. Due to the lack of evidence, it is challenging to form conclusions from existing evidence (Mitchell, Gryczynski, O'Grady, & Schwartz, 2013). In many primary care settings that do not yet have the capacity to deliver effective substance use treatment for an adolescent, it is necessary to send a referral to an appropriate specialty agency that will conduct a developmentally appropriate substance abuse assessment and match to the appropriate level of care. Resources for treatment are available in most states and should be on hand and referrals to treatment supported.

Practical Considerations

Because addiction is now framed as a chronic condition, substance abuse treatment should be seen as a chronic care model that includes prevention and long-term monitoring. In this model, relapse is considered to be normative (Tripodi, Bender, Litschge, & Vaughn, 2010). Given this reconceptualization of addiction as a chronic condition, patients require care management like that in other chronic disease models and will benefit most from integrated and coordinated care over their lifetime (Humphreys & McLellan, 2010; McLellan, Lewis, O'Brien, & Kleber, 2000; McLellan & McKay, 2005). The scope and severity of fragmentation in the substance abuse treatment system in the United States are widespread (Institute of Medicine, 2001, 2006; Waldron & Turner, 2008) and can interfere with the delivery of effective treatment. Implementation research is a new area that can help provide benchmarks to treatment fidelity as well as identify and begin to overcome barriers of translation science.

When considering the types of facilities available to adolescents, it is useful to consider the funding source: Some treatment facilities are publically funded, others accept health insurance, some are private pay only, and many have a mixture of funding sources. Some facilities have inpatient and outpatient treatment located within the same facility. When differing levels of care exist within one facility or group, transitioning from higher to lower intensity levels of treatment is typically facile. However, more often than not, different levels of outpatient treatment are not located at the same site or within the same corporation or government agency. In this case, transitioning from one level of care to another has added complexity, and even when effective treatment is known, implementation of a particular model of care can be compromised. Patients, caregivers and referring providers should work together to examine the quality of a treatment facility through reviewing quality measures while utilizing principles of adolescent treatment to guide decision making.

Within the context of a shifting system of care with mixed evidence, it is vital that stakeholders utilize certain principles to guide them in choosing treatment. The National Institute on Drug Abuse (NIDA) has developed 13 principles of drug addiction treatment (National Institute on Drug Abuse, 2009), and Brannigan et al. (2004) has listed the attributes of quality adolescent treatment.

1. Drug and alcohol addiction like other chronic conditions have high rates of relapse and optimal outcomes for treatment often require multiple interventions over time; some of these are overlapping.

2. Facilities should be accredited and have qualified staff that are trained in adolescent development, family systems, substance use and addiction, and co-occurring disorders.

3. A complete biopsychosocial assessment and treatment matching are needed.

4. Continuing care should follow a treatment episode and this should include relapse prevention training, aftercare, and referrals for community resources and follow-up.

5. Adolescence can be divided into three phases: early, middle, and late adolescence. Typically, treatment should not mix these age groups without careful clinical consideration that includes the patient and family. Different age groups have varying developmental needs. Adolescents should not be treated with an adult or young adult population.

6. Treatment should take place in the least restrictive setting that will provide treatment success.

7. Provide a comprehensive and integrated approach to treatment; treatment should include evidence-based therapies in a setting that addresses the whole person using a comprehensive range of core and adjunct services tailored to meet the individual needs of the adolescent patient and his or her family.

8. Programs should be licensed and engage in ongoing evaluation that regularly reports performance measures of initiation, engagement, and continuity of care.

9. Programs should be tailored to meet the racial and ethnic needs of an adolescent; culturally competent care is essential.

10. Programs should address the needs of sexual minority youth competently.

11. Because the length of time in treatment is correlated with better outcomes for teens, and due to high treatment dropout rates, keeping adolescents engaged in treatment is important and building positive relationships between therapist and patient is primary. Programs that utilize contingencies and pay for performance may implement care more effectively.

12. Both voluntary and mandated treatments have favorable outcomes.

13. Adolescent treatment should incorporate parental or caregiver involvement.

14. Treatment providers should work across systems and agencies to coordinate care.

15. Comprehensive case management and family support should be provided.

Policy Implications

Although more research on the effectiveness of substance use treatment for adolescents is needed to bolster the evidence base, the current research indicates that treatment works and is better than no treatment. With the advent of new policies, there are recent changes in funding streams for substance abuse treatment that may alter the nature of the settings in which effective treatments will be delivered. Additionally, within the context of two parity laws (1996 and 2008), treatment for adolescents with substance use disorders is now covered at the same rate as other medical conditions. Furthermore, with the advent of the ACA (2010), a universal mandate and an essential benefit package encourage the likelihood of coverage for adolescents and therefore access for more at-risk populations. Screening and treatment for adolescents in settings like primary care may be a wave of the future. And it is vital that we focus on prevention of adolescent substance use disorders. If adolescents are identified often and early, their health and well-being will improve. Additionally, it is essential to fund, promote, and prioritize research to support optimal health of adolescents to secure our future.

Acknowledgments

We thank Sion Kim Harris, PhD, and Melissa Weiksnar, MBA.

References

Abrams, M., Nuzum, R., Mika, S., & Lawlor, G. (2011). *Realizing health reform's potential: How the Affordable Care Act will strengthen primary care and benefit patients, providers and payers.* New York, NY: The Commonwealth Fund.

Acharyya, S., & Zhang, H. (2003). Assessing sex differences on treatment effectiveness from the drug abuse treatment outcome study (DATOS). *American Journal of Drug and Alcohol Abuse, 29*(2), 415–444.

Allen, E. H., Carlson, E. W., Parks, E. C., & Seiter, R. P. (1978). Halfway Houses, 111 pp. *US Department of Justice, National Institute of Law Enforcement and Criminal Justice,* Washington, DC, 20531.

Ameri, A. (1999). The effects of cannabinoids on the brain. *Progress in Neurobiology, 58,* 315–348.

Andreasson, S., Allebeck, P., Engstrom, A., & Rydberg, U. (1987). Cannabis and schizophrenia: A longitudinal study of Swedish conscripts. *Lancet, 26,* 1483–1486.

Asbridge, M., Hayden, J. A., & Cartwright, J. L. (2012). Acute cannabis consumption and motor vehicle collision risk: Systematic review of observational studies and meta-analysis. *British Medical Journal, 344,* doi:10.1136/bmj.e536

Austin, A. M., Macgowan, M. J., & Wagner, E. F. (2005). Effective family-based interventions for adolescents with substance use problems: A systematic review. *Research on Social Work Practice, 15*(2), 67–83.

Azrin, N., Donohue, B., Teichner, G. A., Crum, T., Howell, J., & DeCato, L. A. (2001). A controlled evaluation and description of individual-cognitive problem solving and family-behavior therapies in dually-diagnosed conduct-disordered and substance-dependent youth. *Journal of Child and Adolescent Substance Abuse, 11*(1), 1–43.

Azrin, N., McMahon, P. T., Donohue, B., Besalel, V. A., Lapinski, K. J., Kogan, E. S., . . . Galloway, E. (1994). Behavior therapy for drug abuse: A controlled treatment outcome study. *Behavior Research and Therapy, 32*(8), 857–866. Retrieved from http://www.ncbi.nlm.nih.gov/pubmed/7993330

Bailey, K. A., Baker, A. L., Webster, R. A., & Lewin, T. J. (2004). Pilot randomized controlled trial of a brief alcohol intervention group for adolescents. *Drug and Alcohol Review, 23*(2), 157–166. doi:10.1080/09595230410001704136

Bandura, A. (1977). *Social learning theory.* Englewood Cliffs, NJ: Prentice Hall.

Bayer, T. A., Falkai, P., & Maier, W. (1999). Genetic and non-genetic vulnerability factors in schizophrenia: The basis of the "two hit hypothesis." *Journal of Psychiatric Research, 33,* 543–548.

Borse, N., Rudd, R., Dellinger, A., & Sleet, D. (2012). Years of potential life lost from unintentional injuries among persons aged 0–19 years—United States, 2000–2009. *Morbidity and Mortality Weekly Report, 61*(41), 830–833.

Bossong, M. G., & Niesink, R. J. M. (2010). Adolescent brain maturation, the endogenous cannabinoid system and the neurobiology of cannabis-induced schizophrenia. *Progress in Neurobiology, 92,* 370–385.

Bouchery, E. E., Harwood, H. J., Sacks, J. J., Simon, C. J., & Brewer, R. D. (2011). Economic costs of excessive alcohol consumption in the U.S., 2006. *American Journal of Preventive Medicine, 41*(5), 516–524. doi:10.1016/j.amepre.2011.06.045

Brannigan, R., Schackman, B. R., Falco, M., & Millman, R. B. (2004). The quality of highly regarded adolescent substance abuse treatment programs: Results of an in-depth national survey. *Archives of Pediatric and Adolescent Medicine, 158*(9), 904–909. doi:10.1001/archpedi.158.9.904

Burleson, J. A., Kaminer, Y., & Dennis, M. L. (2006). Absence of iatrogenic or contagion effects in adolescent group therapy: Findings from the Cannabis Youth Treatment (CYT) study. *American Journal of Addiction, 15* (Suppl. 1), 4–15. doi:10.1080/10550490601003656

Casey, B. J., Getz, S., & Galvan, A. (2008). The adolescent brain. *Developmental Review, 28*(1), 62–77.

Castle, D. J., & Solowij, N. (2004). *Acute and subacute psychomimetic effects of cannabis in humans.* Marijuana and madness: Psychiatry and neurobiology, pp 41–53. New York: Cambridge University Press.

Center for Substance Abuse Treatment, & Substance Abuse and Mental Health Services Administration. (2006).

Clinical issues in intensive outpatient treatment. Rockville, MD: Author.

Commission, U. F. T. (2008). Evaluating private residential treatment programs for troubled teens [Press release]. Retrieved from https://www.ftc.gov/news-events/press-releases/2008/07/evaluating-private-residential-treatment-programs-troubled-teens

Cooley, W. C., McAllister, J. W., Sherrieb, K., & Kuhlthau, K. (2009). Improved outcomes associated with medical home implementation in pediatric primary care. *Pediatrics, 124*(1), 358–364. doi:10.1542/peds.2008-2600

Crabtree, B. F., Nutting, P. A., Miller, W. L., Stange, K. C., Stewart, E. E., & Jaen, C. R. (2010). Summary of the National Demonstration Project and recommendations for the patient-centered medical home. *Annals of Family Medicine, 8* (Suppl. 1), S80–S90; S92. doi:10.1370/afm.1107

Crean, R. D., Crane, N. A., & Mason, B. J. (2011). An evidence based review of acute and long-term effects of cannabis use on executive cognitive functions. *Journal of Addiction Medicine, 5*(1), 1–8. doi:10.1097/ADM.0b013e31820c23fa

Croghan, T., & Brown, J. (2010). *Integrating mental health treatment into the patient centered medical home*. Rockville, MD: US Department of Health and Human Services.

Cushman, P., Jr. (1974). Detoxification of rehabilitated methadone patients: frequency and predictors of long-term success. *American Journal of Drug and Alcohol Abuse, 1*(3), 393–408.

D'Amico, E. J., Miles, J. N. V., Stern, S. A., & Meredith, L. S. (2008). Brief motivational interviewing for teens at risk of substance use consequences: A randomized pilot study in a primary care clinic. *Journal of Substance Abuse Treatment, 35*(1), 53–61. doi:http://dx.doi.org/10.1016/j.jsat.2007.08.008

De Bellis, M. D., Clark, D. B., Beers, S. R., Soloff, P. H., Boring, A. M., Hall, J., . . . Keshavan, M. S. (2000). Hippocampal volume in adolescent-onset alcohol use disorders. *American Journal of Psychiatry, 157*, 737–744.

de Dios, M. A., Herman, D. S., Britton, W. B., Hagerty, C. E., Anderson, B. J., & Stein, M. D. (2012). Motivational and mindfulness intervention for young adult female marijuana users. *Journal of Substance Abuse Treatment, 42*(1), 56–64. doi:10.1016/j.jsat.2011.08.001

de Graaf, R., Radovanovic, M., van Laar, M., Fairman, B., Degenhardt, L., Auguilar-Gaxiola, S., . . . Anthony, J. C. (2010). Early cannabis use and estimated risk of later onset of depression spells: epidemiologic evidence from the population-based World Health Organization World Mental Health Survey Initiative. *American Journal of Epidemiology, 172*(2), 149–159.

De Micheli, D., Fisberg, M., & Formigoni, M. L. (2004). Study on the effectiveness of brief intervention for alcohol and other drug use directed to adolescents in a primary health care unit. *Revista da Associação Médica Brasileira, 50*(3), 305–313.

Dekker, N., Schmitz, N., Peters, B. D., van Amelsvoort, T. A., Linszen, D. H., & de Haan, L. (2010). Cannabis use and callosal white matter structure and integrity in recent-onset schizophrenia. *Psychiatry Research, 181*(1), 51–56.

Dennis, M., Godley, S. H., Diamond, G., Tims, F. M., Babor, T., Donaldson, J., . . . Webb, C. (2004). The Cannabis Youth Treatment (CYT) study: Main findings from two randomized trials. *Journal of Substance Abuse Treatment, 27*(3), 197–213. Retrieved from http://www.sciencedirect.com/science/article/pii/S074054720400087X

Devane, W. A., Hanus, L., Breuer, A., Pertwee, R. G., Stevenson, L. A., Griffin, G., . . . Mechoulam, R. (1992). Isolation and structure of a brain constituent that binds to the cannabinoid receptor. *Science, 258*, 1946–1949.

Dishion, T. J., Poulin, F., & Burraston, B. (2001). Peer group dynamics associated with iatrogenic effects in group interventions with high-risk young adolescents. *New Directions for Child and Adolescent Development, 91*, 79–92. doi:10.1002/cd.6

Engle, B., & Macgowan, M. J. (2009). A critical review of adolescent substance abuse group treatments. *Journal of Evidence-Based Social Work, 6*(3), 217–243.

Ernst, D., Miller, W. R., & Rollnick, S. (2007). Treating substance abuse in primary care: a demonstration project. *Internations Journal of Integrative Care, 7*, e36.

Feinstein, E. C., Richter, L., & Foster, S. E. (2012). Addressing the critical health problem of adolescent substance use through health care, research, and public policy. *The Journal of Adolescent Health: Official Publication of the Society for Adolescent Medicine, 50*(5), 431–436.

Feldstein Ewing, S. W., & Chung, T. (2013). Neuroimaging mechanisms of change in psychotherapy for addictive behaviors: Emerging translational approaches that bridge biology and behavior. *Psychology of Addictive Behaviors, 27*(2), 329–335. doi:10.1037/a0031491

Fisher, S. L., Bucholz, K. K., Reich, W., Fox, L., Kuperman, S., Kramer, J., . . . Laura, J. (2006). Teenagers are right—parents do not know much: An analysis of adolescent-parent agreement on reports of adolescent substance use, abuse, and dependence. *Alcoholism: Clinical and Experimental Research, 30*(10), 1699–1710.

Friedberg, M. W., Safran, D. G., Coltin, K. L., Dresser, M., & Schneider, E. C. (2009). Readiness for the patient-centered medical home: Structural capabilities of Massachusetts primary care practices. *Journal of General Internal Medicine, 24*(2), 162–169. doi:10.1007/s11606-008-0856-x

Gardner, E. L. (2005). Endocannabinoid signaling system and brain reward: Emphasis on dopamine. *Pharmacology Biochemistry and Behavior, 81*, 263–284.

Garner, B. R., Godley, S. H., Funk, R. R., Dennis, M. L., Smith, J. E., & Godley, M. D. (2009). Exposure to Adolescent Community Reinforcement Approach treatment procedures as a mediator of the relationship between adolescent substance abuse treatment retention and outcome. *Journal of Substance Abuse Treatment, 36*(3), 252–264. Retrieved from http://www.ncbi.nlm.nih.gov/pmc/articles/PMC2675944/pdf/nihms103459.pdf

Giorgio, A., Watkins, K. E., Douaud, G., James, A. C., James, S., De Stefano, N., . . . Johansen-Berg, H. (2008). Changes in white matter microstructure during adolescence. *NeuroImage, 39*, 52–61.

Godley, M. D., Godley, S. H., Dennis, M. L., Funk, R., & Passetti, L. L. (2002). Preliminary outcomes from the assertive continuing care experiment for adolescents discharged from residential treatment. *Journal of Substance Abuse Treatment, 23*(1), 21–32.

Godley, M. D., Coleman-Cowger, V. H., Titus, J. C., Funk, R. R., & Orndorff, M. G. (2010). A randomized controlled trial of telephone continuing care. *Journal of Substance Abuse Treatment, 38*(1), 74–82. Retrieved from http://www.ncbi.nlm.nih.gov/pmc/articles/PMC2789918/ http://www.ncbi.nlm.nih.gov/pmc/articles/PMC2789918/pdf/nihms135678.pdf

Godley, S. H., Meyers, R., Smith, J., Karvinen, T., Titus, J., Godley, D., . . . Kelberg, P. (2001). *The adolescent community reinforcement approach for adolescent cannabis users.* Washington, DC: US Department of Health and Human Services.

Godley, S. H., Passetti, L. L., & White, M. K. (2006). Employment and adolescent alcohol and drug treatment and recovery: An exploratory study. *The American Journal on Addictions, 15*(s1), s137–s143.

Gogtay, N., Giedd, J., Lusk, L., Hayashi, K. M., Greenstein, D., Vaituzis, A. C., . . . Thompson, P. M. (2004). Dynamic mapping of human cortical development during childhood through early adulthood. *Proceedings of the National Academy of Sciences, 101*, 8174–8179.

Grant, B. F., & Dawson, D. A. (1998). Age of onset of drug use and its association with DSM-IV drug abuse and dependence: Results from the National Longitudinal Alcohol Epidemiologic Survey. *Journal of Substance Abuse, 10*(2), 163–173.

Grant, I., Gonzalez, R., Carey, C. L., Natarajan, L., & Wolfson, T. (2003). Non-acute (residual) neurocognitive effects of cannabis use: A meta-analytic study. *Journal of the International Neuropsychology Society, 9*(5), 679–689. doi:10.1017/s1355617703950016

Greenfield, S. F., Trucco, E. M., McHugh, R. K., Lincoln, M., & Gallop, R. J. (2007). The Women's Recovery Group Study: A Stage I trial of women-focused group therapy for substance use disorders versus mixed-gender group drug counseling. *Drug and Alcohol Dependence, 90*(1), 39–47. doi:10.1016/j.drugalcdep.2007.02.009

Grella, C. (2006). The Drug Abuse Outcome Studies: Outcomes with Adolescent Substance Abusers. In H. A. Liddle, Rowe, C. L., (Ed.), *Adolescent Substance Abuse: Research and Clinical Advances* (pp. 148–173). New York: Cambridge University Press.

Grenard, J. L., Ames, S. L., Wiers, R. W., Thush, C., Stacy, A. W., & Sussman, S. (2007). Brief intervention for substance use among at-risk adolescents: A pilot study. *Journal of Adolescent Health, 40*(2), 188–191. doi:10.1016/j.jadohealth.2006.08.008

Grob, G. N., & Howard, G. H. (2006). *The dilemma of federal mental health policy radical reform or incremental change?* New Brunswick, NJ: Rutgers University Press.

Grumbach, K., & Grundy, P. (2010). *Outcomes of implementing patient-centered medical home interventions.* Washington, DC: Patient-Centered Primary Care Collaborative.

Harris, S. K., Csemy, L., Sherritt, L., Starostova, O., Van Hook, S., Johnson, J., . . . Knight, J. R. (2012). Computer-facilitated substance use screening and brief advice for teens in primary care: An international trial. *Pediatrics, 129*(6), 1072–1082. doi:10.1542/peds.2011-1624

Hawthorne, W. B., Green, E. E., Gilmer, T., Garcia, P., Hough, R. L., Lee, M., . . . Lohr, J. B. (2005). A randomized trial of short-term acute residential treatment for veterans. *Psychiatry Services, 56*(11), 1379–1386. doi:10.1176/appi.ps.56.11.1379

Henggeler, S. W., Clingempeel, W. G., Brondino, M. J., & Pickrel, S. G. (2002). Four-year follow-up of multisystemic therapy with substance-abusing and substance-dependent juvenile offenders. *Journal of the American Academy of Child & Adolescent Psychiatry, 41*(7), 868–874.

Hingson, R. W., Heeren, T., & Winter, M. R. (2006). Age at drinking onset and alcohol dependence. *Archives of Pediatric and Adolescent Medicine, 160*, 739–746.

Hon, J. (2003). *A sound investment: Identifying and treating alcohol problems.* Ensurig Solutions to Alcohol Problems. Washington, DC: The George Washington University Medical Center.

Hubbard, R., Rachal, J., Harwood, H., Cavanaugh, E., & Ginzburg, H. (1989). *Drug abuse treatment: A national study of effectiveness* (Vol. 213). Chapel Hill, NC: University of North Carolina Press.

Humphreys, K., & McLellan, A. T. (2010). Brief intervention, treatment, and recovery support services for Americans who have substance use disorders: An overview of policy in the Obama administration. *Psychological Services, 7*(4), 275–284. doi:10.1037/a0020390

Institute of Medicine. (2001). *Crossing the quality chasm: A new health system for the 21st century.* Washington, DC: National Academics Press.

Institute of Medicine. (2006). *Improving the quality of health care for mental health and substance abuse.* Washington, DC: National Academics Press.

James, S., Alemi, Q., & Zepeda, V. (2013). Effectiveness and implementation of evidence-based practices in residential care settings. *Children and Youth Service Review, 35*(4), 642–656. doi:10.1016/j.childyouth.2013.01.007

Jensen, C. D., Cushing, C. C., Aylward, B. S., Craig, J. T., Sorell, D. M., & Steele, R. G. (2011). Effectiveness of motivational interviewing interventions for adolescent substance use behavior change: A meta-analytic review. *Journal of Consulting and Clinical Psychology, 79*(4), 433–440. doi:10.1037/a0023992

Jessor, R., & Jessor, S. L. (1977). *Problem behavior and psychosocial development.* New York, NY: Academic Press.

Kaminer, Y. (2000). Contingency management reinforcement procedures for adolescent substance abuse. *Journal of the American Academy of Child & Adolescent Psychiatry, 39*(10), 1324–1326.

Kelly, J. F., Brown, S. A., Abrantes, A., Kahler, C. W., & Myers, M. (2008). Social recovery model: An 8-year investigation of adolescent 12-step group involvement following inpatient treatment. *Alcoholism: Clinical and Experimental Research, 32*(8), 1468–1478. doi:10.1111/j.1530-0277.2008.00712.x

Kelly, J. F., Dow, S. J., Yeterian, J. D., & Kahler, C. W. (2010). Can 12-step group participation strengthen and extend the benefits of adolescent addiction treatment? A prospective analysis. *Drug and Alcohol Dependence, 110*(1–2), 117–125. doi:10.1016/j.drugalcdep.2010.02.019

Kelly, J. F., Myers, M. G., & Brown, S. A. (2000). A multivariate process model of adolescent 12-step attendance and substance use outcome following inpatient treatment. *Psychology of Addictive Behaviors, 14*(4), 376–389. Retrieved from http://www.ncbi.nlm.nih.gov/pubmed/11130156 http://graphics.tx.ovid.com/ovftpdfs/FPDDNCFBHGJGKB00/fs047/ovft/live/gv024/00011970/00011970-200012000-00008.pdf

Kelly, J. F., Myers, M. G., & Brown, S. A. (2005). The effects of age composition of 12-step groups on adolescent 12-step participation and substance use outcome. *Journal of Children and Adolescent Substance Abuse, 15*(1), 63–72. doi:10.1300/J029v15n01_05

Kelly, J. F., & Urbanoski, K. (2012). Youth recovery contexts: The incremental effects of 12-step attendance and involvement on adolescent outpatient outcomes. *Alcoholism: Clinical and Experimental Research, 36*(7), 1219–1229. doi:10.1111/j.1530-0277.2011.01727.x

Knight, J. R., Sherritt, L., Van Hook, S., Gates, E. C., Levy, S., & Chang, G. (2005). Motivational interviewing for adolescent substance use: A pilot study. *Journal of Adolescent Health*, *37*(2), 167–169. Retrieved from http://www.ncbi.nlm.nih.gov/entrez/query.fcgi?cmd=Retrieve&db=PubMed&dopt=Citation&list_uids=16026730

Koob, G. F., & Volkow, N. D. (2010). Neurocircuitry of addiction. *Neuropsychopharmacology*, *35*, 217–238.

Ledgerwood, D. M., Alessi, S. M., Hanson, T., Godley, M. D., & Petry, N. M. (2008). Contingency management for attendance to group substance abuse treatment administered by clinicians in community clinics. *Journal of Applied Behavior Analysis*, *41*(4), 517–526.

Liddle, H. (2002a). *Advances in family-based therapy for adolescent substance abuse*. Paper presented at the L. S. Harris (ed.), *Problems of drug dependence 2001: Proceedings of the 63rd annual scientific meeting*. Bethesda, Maryland: The College on Problems of Drug Dependence.

Liddle, H. (2002b). *Multidimensional Family Therapy (MDFT) for adolescent cannabis users*. Rockville, MD: Center for Substance Abuse Treatment, Substance Abuse and Mental Health Services Administration.

Liddle, H. (2004). Family-based therapies for adolescent alcohol and drug use: research contributions and future research needs. *Addiction*, *99*(s2), 76–92.

Lilienfield, S. (2007). Psychological treatments that cause harm. *Perspectives on Psychological Science*, *2*(1), 53–70. doi:10.1111/j.1745-6916.2007.00029x

Liston, C., Watts, R., Tottenham, N., Davidson, M. C., Niogi, S., Ulug, A. M., & Casey, B. J. (2005). Frontostriatal microstructure modulates efficient recruitment of cognitive control. *Cerebral Cortex*, *16*, 553–560.

Lupica, C. R., Riegel, A. C., & Hoffman, A. F. (2004). Marijuana and cannabinoid regulation of brain reward circuits. *British Journal of Pharmacology*, *143*, 227–234.

Lussier, J. P., Heil, S. H., Mongeon, J. A., Badger, G. J., & Higgins, S. T. (2006). A meta-analysis of voucher-based reinforcement therapy for substance use disorders. *Addiction*, *101*(2), 192–203. doi:10.1111/j.1360-0443.2006.01311.x

Macgowan, M. J., & Engle, B. (2010). Evidence for optimism: Behavior therapies and motivational interviewing in adolescent substance abuse treatment. *Child and Adolescent Psychiatric Clinics of North America*, *19*(3), 527–545. Retrieved from http://www.ncbi.nlm.nih.gov/pmc/articles/PMC2916874/pdf/nihms-189541.pdf

Marsch, L. A. (2007). Combined behavioral and pharmacological treatment of opioid dependent adolescents: A randomized, controlled trial. *Progress in Neurotherapeutics and Neuropsychopharmacology*, *2*(1), 251–264.

Marsch, L. A., Bickel, W. K., Badger, G. J., Stothart, M. E., Quesnel, K. J., Stanger, C., & Brooklyn, J. (2005a). Comparison of pharmacological treatments for opioid-dependent adolescents: A randomized controlled trial. *Archives of General Psychiatry*, *62*(10), 1157–1164. Retrieved from http://www.ncbi.nlm.nih.gov/entrez/query.fcgi?cmd=Retrieve&db=PubMed&dopt=Citation&list_uids=16203961

Marsch, L. A., Bickel, W. K., Badger, G. J., Stothart, M. E., Quesnel, K. J., Stanger, C., & Brooklyn, J. (2005b). Comparison of pharmacological treatments for opioid-dependent adolescents: A randomized controlled trial. *Archives of General Psychiatry*, *62*(10), 1157–1164. doi:10.1001/archpsyc.62.10.1157

McGue, M., Iacono, W. G., Legrand, L. N., Malone, S., & Elkins, I. (2001). Origins and consequences of age at first drink. I. Associations with substance-use disorders, disinhibitory behavior and psychopathology, and P3 amplitude. *Alcoholism: Clinical & Experimental Research*, *25*(8), 1156–1165.

McLellan, A., Lewis, D. C., O'Brien, C. P., & Kleber, H. D. (2000). Drug dependence: A chronic medical illness implications for treatment, insurance, and outcomes evaluation. *JAMA: The Journal of the American Medical Association*, *284*(13), 1639–1699.

McLellan, A., & McKay, J. (2005). *Appendix D, The treatment of addiction: What can research offer practice*. Washington, DC: Institute of Medicine, National Academy Press.

Mee-Lee, D. (Ed.) (2013). *The ASAM criteria: Treatment criteria for addictive, substance-related, and co-occurring conditions*. Carson City, NV: The Change Companies.

Meier, M. H., Caspi, A., Ambler, A., Harrington, H., Houts, R., Keefe, R. S. E., . . . Moffitt, T. E. (2012). Persistent cannabis users show neuropsychological decline from childhood to midlife. *Proceedings of the National Academy of Sciences*, *109*(40), E2657–E2664. doi:10.1073/pnas.1206820109

Mitchell, S. G., Gryczynski, J., O'Grady, K. E., & Schwartz, R. P. (2013). SBIRT for adolescent drug and alcohol use: Current status and future directions. *Journal of Substance Abuse and Treatment*, *44*(5), 463–472. doi:10.1016/j.jsat.2012.11.005

Moberg, D. P., & Finch, A. J. (2008). Recovery high schools: A descriptive study of school programs and students. *Journal of Groups in Addiction and Recovery*, *2*, 128–161. doi:10.1080/15560350802081314

Monti, P. M., Barnett, N. P., Colby, S. M., Gwaltney, C. J., Spirito, A., Rohsenow, D. J., & Woolard, R. (2007). Motivational interviewing versus feedback only in emergency care for young adult problem drinking. *Addiction*, *102*(8), 1234–1243. doi:10.1111/j.1360-0443.2007.01878.x

Monti, P. M., Colby, S. M., Barnett, N. P., Spirito, A., Rohsenow, D. J., Myers, M., . . . Lewander, W. (1999). Brief intervention for harm reduction with alcohol-positive older adolescents in a hospital emergency department. *Journal of Consulting and Clinical Psychology*, *67*(6), 989–994. Retrieved from http://www.ncbi.nlm.nih.gov/pubmed/10596521 http://graphics.tx.ovid.com/ovftpdfs/FPDDNCJCFDDCMM00/fs046/ovft/live/gv023/00004730/00004730-199912000-00018.pdf

Nagy, Z., Westerberg, H., & Klingberg, T. (2004). Maturation of white matter is associated with the development of cognitive functions during childhood. *Journal of Cognitive Neuroscience*, *16*, 1227–1233.

Najavits, L. M., Gallop, R. J., & Weiss, R. D. (2006). Seeking safety therapy for adolescent girls with PTSD and substance use disorder: A randomized controlled trial. *Journal of Behavioral Health Services Research*, *33*(4), 453–463. doi:10.1007/s11414-006-9034-2

Nielsen, M., Langner, B., Zema, C., Hacker, T., & Grundy, P. (2012). *Benefits of implementing the primary care patient-centered medical home*. Washington, DC: Patient-Centered Primary Care Collaborative.

Patton, G. C., Coffey, C., Lynskey, M. T., Reid, S., Hemphill, S., Carlin, J. B., & Hall, W. (2007). Trajectories of adolescent alcohol and cannabis use into young adulthood. *Addiction*, *102*, 607–615.

Petersen, A., & Leffert, N. (1995). Developmental issues influencing guidelines for adolescent health research: A review. *Journal of Adolescent Health*, *17*, 298–305.

Piaget, J., & Inhelder, B. (1958). *The growth of logical thinking from childhood to adolescence*. New York, NY: Basic Books.

Pugatch, M., Knight, J. R., McGuiness, P., Sherritt, L., & Levy, S. (2014). A group therapy program for opioid-dependent adolescents and their parents. *Substance Abuse, 35*(4), 435–441. doi:10.1080/08897077.2014.958208

Rubak, S., Sandbaek, A., Lauritzen, T., & Christensen, B. (2005). Motivational interviewing: A systematic review and meta-analysis. *British Journal of General Practice, 55*(513), 305–312.

Rubia, K., Overmeyer, S., Taylor, E., Brammer, M., Williams, S. C., Simmons, A., . . . Bullmore, E. T. (2000). Functional frontalisation with age: Mapping neurodevelopmental trajectories with fMRI. *Neuroscience and Biobehavioral Reviews, 24*, 13–19.

Santisteban, D. A., Coatsworth, J. D., Perez-Vidal, A., Kurtines, W. M., Schwartz, S. J., LaPerriere, A., & Szapocznik, J. (2003). Efficacy of brief strategic family therapy in modifying Hispanic adolescent behavior problems and substance use. *Journal of Family Psychology, 17*(1), 121. Retrieved from http://graphics.tx.ovid.com/ovftpdfs/FPDDNCJCFDDCMM00/fs046/ovft/live/gv025/00012003/00012003-200303000-00010.pdf

Silveri, M. M., & Spear, L. P. (1998). Decreased sensitivity to the hypnotic effects of ethanol early in ontogeny. *Alcoholism: Clinical and Experimental Research, 22*, 670–676.

Spirito, A., Monti, P. M., Barnett, N. P., Colby, S. M., Sindelar, H., Rohsenow, D. J., . . . Myers, M. (2004). A randomized clinical trial of a brief motivational intervention for alcohol-positive adolescents treated in an emergency department. *The Journal of Pediatrics, 145*(3), 396–402. doi:http://dx.doi.org/10.1016/j.jpeds.2004.04.057

Spirito, A., Sindelar-Manning, H. Colby, S. M., Barnett, N. P, Lewander, W., Rohsenow, D. J., & Monti, P. M. (2011). Individual and family motivational interventions for alcohol-positive adolescents treated in an emergency department: Results of a randomized clinical trial. *Archives of Pediatrics & Adolescent Medicine, 165*(3), 269–274. doi:10.1001/archpediatrics.2010.296

Squeglia, L. M., Jacobus, J., & Tapert, S. F. (2009). The influence of substance use on adolescent brain development. *Clinical EEG and Neuroscience Journal, 40*(1), 31–38.

Stanger, C., Budney, A. J., Kamon, J. L., & Thostensen, J. (2009). A randomized trial of contingency management for adolescent marijuana abuse and dependence. *Drug and alcohol dependence, 105*(3), 240–247.

Stanger, C., & Budney, A. (2010). Contingency management approaches for adolescent substance use disorders. *Child and Adolescent Psychiatric Clinics of North America, 19*(3), 547–562. Retrieved from http://getit.brandeis.edu/sfx_local?sid=Entrez%3APubMed&id=pmid%3A20682220 http://www.ncbi.nlm.nih.gov/pmc/articles/PMC2916869/pdf/nihms189542.pdf

Steenrod, S. A. (2009). The interface between community-based and specialty substance abuse treatment sectors: Navigating the terrain in social work. *Journal of Social Work Practice in the Addictions, 9*(1), 4.

Stein, L. A., Monti, P. M., Colby, S. M., Barnett, N. P., Golembeske, C., Lebeau-Craven, R., & Miranda, R. (2006). Enhancing substance abuse treatment engagement in incarcerated adolescents. *Psychology Services, 3*(1), 25–34. Retrieved from http://www.ncbi.nlm.nih.gov/pubmed/20617117 http://www.ncbi.nlm.nih.gov/pmc/articles/PMC2898284/pdf/nihms-134912.pdf

Steinberg, L. (2014). *Adolescence* (10th ed.). New York, NY: McGraw-Hill.

Substance Abuse and Mental Health Services Administration, & Office of Applied Studies. (2005). *Treatment outcomes among clients discharged from residential substance abuse treatment*. Rockville, MD: Author.

Substance Abuse and Mental Health Services Administration Office of Applied Studies. (2009). *The NSDUH report: Young adults' need for and receipt of alcohol and illicit drug use treatment: 2007*. Rockville, MD: Author.

Substance Abuse and Mental Health Services Administration. (2009). *Designing a recovery oriented care model for adolescents and transition age youth with substance use or co-occurring mental health disorders*. Rockville, MD: Author.

Substance Abuse and Mental Health Services Administration. (2010). *Results from the 2009 National Survey on Drug Use and Health: Volume I. Summary of national findings*. Rockville, MD: Author.

Substance Abuse and Mental Health Services Administration. (2013). *Behavioral health, United States, 2012*. HHS Publication No. (SMA) 13-4797. Rockville, MD: Author.

Sugranyes, G., Flamarique, I., Parellada, E., Baeza, I., Goti, J., Fernandez-Egea, E., & Bernardo, M. (2009). Cannabis use and age of diagnosis of schizophrenia. *European Journal of Psychiatry, 24*, 282–286.

Tanner-Smith, E. E., Wilson, S. J., & Lipsey, M. W. (2013). The comparative effectiveness of outpatient treatment for adolescent substance abuse: A meta-analysis. *Journal of Substance Abuse Treatment, 44*(2), 145–158. Retrieved from http://www.ncbi.nlm.nih.gov/pmc/articles/PMC3477300/pdf/nihms-383158.pdf

Toray, T., Coughlin, C., Vuchinich, S., & Patricelli, P. (1991). Gender differences associated with adolescent substance abuse: Comparisons and implications for treatment. *Family Relations, 40*(3), 338–344. doi:10.2307/585021

Tripodi, S. J., Bender, K., Litschge, C., & Vaughn, M. G. (2010). Interventions for reducing adolescent alcohol abuse: A meta-analytic review. *Archives of Pediatrics & Adolescent Medicine, 164*(1), 85–91. doi:10.1001/archpediatrics.2009.235

US Federal Trade Commission. (2008). Residential treatment programs for teens. Retrieved from https://www.consumer.ftc.gov/articles/0185-residential-treatment-programs-teens

US Department of Health and Human Services. National Institute on Drug Abuse (2009). Principles of drug addiction treatment: A research-based guide. *NIH Publication*, (09-4180). https://www.drugabuse.gov/publications/principles-drug-addiction-treatment-research-based-guide-third-edition/principles-effective-treatment

Wachtel, T., & Staniford, M. (2010). The effectiveness of brief interventions in the clinical setting in reducing alcohol misuse and binge drinking in adolescents: A critical review of the literature. *Journal of Clinical Nursing, 19*(5–6), 605–620.

Waldron, H. B., & Kaminer, Y. (2004). On the learning curve: The emerging evidence supporting cognitive-behavioral therapies for adolescent substance abuse. *Addiction, 99*(s2), 93–105. Retrieved from http://www.ncbi.nlm.nih.gov/pmc/articles/PMC1781376/

Waldron, H. B., & Turner, C. W. (2008). Evidence-based psychosocial treatments for adolescent substance abuse. *Journal of Clinical Child & Adolescent Psychology, 37*(1), 238–261.

White, A. M., Truesdale, M., Bae, J., Ahmad, S., Wilson, W. A., Best, P., & Swartzwelder, H. S. (2002). Differential effects of alcohol on motor coordination in adolescent and adult rats. *Pharmacology Biochemistry and Behavior, 73*, 673–677.

Williams, R. J., & Chang, S. Y. (2000). A comprehensive and comparative review of adolescent substance abuse treatment outcome. *Clinical Psychology: Science and Practice, 7*(2), 138–166.

Wilson, R. I., & Nicoll, R. A. (2002). Endocannabinoid signaling in the brain. *Science, 296*, 678–682.

Woody, G. E., Poole, S. A., Subramaniam, G., Dugosh, K., Bogenschutz, M., Abbott, P., . . . Fudala, P. (2008). Extended vs. short-term buprenorphine-naloxone for treatment of opioid-addicted youth: A randomized trial. *Journal of the American Medical Association, 300*(17), 2003–2011.

Yucel, M., Solowij, N., Respondek, C., Whittle, S., Fornito, A., Pantelis, C., & Lubman, D. I. (2008). Regional brain abnormalities associated with long-term heavy cannabis use. *Archives of General Psychiatry, 65*, 694–701. Retrieved from http://archpsyc.jamanetwork.com/data/Journals/PSYCH/11863/yoa80004_694_701.pdf

PART 8

Social Policy

Public Health Policy and Prevention of Alcohol, Tobacco, and Drug Problems

Harold D. Holder *and* Lawrence W. Green

Abstract

The misuse of alcohol, tobacco, and illicit drugs by youth and young adults is a major public health challenge across nations and the world. This chapter reviews the extensive international research concerning the use of public policy approaches to reducing these problems associated with the use and misuse of alcohol, tobacco, and illicit drugs. In general, wide differences arise in public policies both in the type of research undertaken and the practical application of policy approaches to reduce harm. For illegal drugs and for alcohol, research concerning public health effects has been associated with policies addressing specific control mechanisms, whereas many public health policy approaches for tobacco harm prevention have been multifaceted. Overall, the cumulative international evidence offers public health policy approaches with demonstrated potential to reduce harm from and use of alcohol, tobacco, and illicit drugs and can have specific effects for adolescents and young adults.

Key Words: substance abuse, public health policy, alcohol, tobacco and illicit drugs, prevention

The misuse of alcohol, tobacco, and illicit drugs by youth and young adults is a major public health challenge across nations and the world. While alcohol and tobacco have legal standing for adults in most countries, limits or restrictions on youth purchase and consumption occur in most of them. Illicit drugs are defined as substances banned or prohibited in most countries for all ages (even though alcohol is banned in some Islamic countries), but special emphasis has been placed on children and youth. Typically, such bans include cannabis, heroin, cocaine, stimulants, and/or a host of synthetic substances, including LSD or Ecstasy. The challenge most jurisdictions face is to implement those public health approaches that have the greatest potential to reduce harm in general and for children and youth in particular. This potential is based on generalizable international research concerning effects of prevention strategies. A major strategy for reducing youth problems associated with the use

and misuse of alcohol, tobacco, and illicit drugs is public policy, which is the focus here.

There are important differences in public health policies specific to substance abuse both in the manner and type of research undertaken and the practical application of policy approaches to reduce harm. For illegal drugs and for alcohol, research concerning public health effects has been associated with specific policies, for example, minimum drinking age, random breath testing for drink driving, and drug supply interdiction and punishment. In contrast, most of the public health policy approaches, besides taxation, for tobacco harm prevention have been multifaceted policy efforts, and these have been successful. Such multicomponent public health policy approaches for tobacco do not have a clear counterpart in alcohol or illegal drugs, as reflected in the summary of policy research here.

Another important difference is that deadly acute effects (especially for adolescents) accompany alcohol and illicit drugs, while tobacco effects are typically more long term in their lethal effects. Of course, addiction to alcohol and illicit drugs can begin in adolescence, as can dependence on tobacco, which can certainly have longer term health effects, including liver cirrhosis, physical addiction with associated health decline, and lung cancer. Such differences also shape the manner in which public health policy effects are presented and discussed in the following sections for alcohol, tobacco, and illicit drugs.

Public Policy as a Prevention Strategy

The primary goals of prevention are (a) to delay or prevent the onset of use, that is, the age at which alcohol, tobacco, or illicit drugs are first used; and (b) to reduce the associated problems related to alcohol, tobacco, and illicit drug use. The first goal is important because early initiation of substance use (illicit drugs, tobacco, or alcohol) by children or youth is both illegal in most cultures and often associated with later problems surrounding this substance. The earlier one begins to use alcohol, tobacco, or illicit drugs, the more one develops later dependency on any of these substances, and the greater the lifetime risks associated with the substance.

The second goal has two aspects. First is the prevention of acute problems or those immediately associated with the substance and uses of it, such as binge drinking. This is best illustrated by alcohol intoxication and associated problems of drunk-driving crashes, falls, and violence but also by overdose of drugs resulting in death or disablement. The second aspect relates to chronic effects—that is, the long-term exposure to the harmful toxins in substances such as tobacco or alcohol as well as the increased dependence on illicit drugs, for example, heroin or cocaine. Here the concern is to prevent physical effects of long-term (often dependent) use, including illness and early death, requiring abstinence or moderate use.

To force, facilitate, or encourage changes in social, economic, or physical environments to reduce substance abuse, public policies are utilized. A policy is any established process, priority, or structure that is purposefully sustained over time. Thus, policy, at whatever level it is promulgated or implemented, is an environmental response to specific substance abuse or associated problems. National, state, or provincial laws often establish the base for local policies, including legal drinking or smoking ages, regulation of alcohol and tobacco prices and retail outlets, smoking or drinking in certain public places, the legal blood alcohol level for drinking and driving, advertising restrictions, and alcohol service to obviously intoxicated persons and underage persons. In some instances, a groundswell of local laws, such as restraining smoking in public places and even in homes, has the effect of prompting state or federal laws to harmonize differences among jurisdictions or to preempt stronger laws at the local level than a state law would allow. This chapter will review policy strategies according to substances (alcohol, tobacco, and illicit drugs) as well as the major policy levers shown by international research to be effective, including price, retail availability by limiting legal age of purchase, and other limits on access or use such as hours and/or days of sale and licensing restrictions, and bans on smoking or drinking in selected environments.

Public policy effects can provide a means to fast-forward or leap-frog the incremental process; that is, what has occurred in some countries may be informative for others just beginning a similar process to streamline it. For example, alcohol or tobacco policies that stimulate the development of commercially produced alcohol and importing or manufacturing cigarettes in some less industrialized countries can be informed by the public health consequences (both positive and negative) observed from more developed countries and their policies.

Alcohol

Alcohol contributes to problems of public health and safety in two ways; that is, drinking can have acute or immediate as well as chronic or long-term consequences. Alcohol is a psychoactive substance that affects one's ability to carry out complex tasks and/or to make socially appropriate or safe decisions, especially in a stressful situation. For example, an automobile driver who has been drinking, even one drink of alcohol, has a reduced ability to operate the vehicle and impaired decision-making ability. The more drinks consumed, the greater the driver's impairment. Secondly, alcohol, consumed regularly in high amounts, can have a direct harmful effect on the body. This is the aspect of drinking that most affects adolescents.

Alcohol Policies

Insofar as alcohol is a legal product in most countries, the regulation of these products through policies has usually, in industrialized countries, been a part of a public health approach to limit the damage associated with drinking, as well as to increase tax revenues. Government policies can in some cases actually determine the retail price of beverages, the opening hours or days for retail sales, the number and location of retail outlets, how the alcohol can be advertised and promoted, and restrictions on who may sell or purchase alcohol. Restricting alcohol availability through law has been a key policy in many parts of the world. Because all policy occurs within an individual society and reflects the unique attitudes and values of that society, the potential effectiveness of any policy is directly related to public acceptability and compliance with these policies, and the associated willingness of the jurisdiction to enforce the policy. The extreme example of an alcohol policy that exceeded public acceptability and enforceability and was eventually repealed was Prohibition in the United States. Acceptability of a minimum age of legal drinking, possession, or purchase of alcohol has also varied with regional cultures across countries, states, and municipalities while enacted in some form in every US state. Considerable evidence demonstrates the sensitivity of adolescents to their social, economic, and geographical environments (see Paschall, Lipperman-Kreda, & Grube, 2014).

Alcohol policy strategies are designed to alter these environments for drinkers, especially adolescents. These policies have been shown to be consistently effective over time and in two or more countries or cultural settings include the following general policies used in public health efforts to reduce alcohol-related harm:

(a) Economic access—the price of alcohol and its relationship to disposable income or ability to purchase. The consumption of alcohol, tobacco, and other drugs is related to the product's retail price; that is, all other things being equal, the higher the price, the lower the consumption. This sensitivity called price elasticity differs by age, income, and country.

(b) Physical access—the ability of adolescents to obtain alcohol; that is, its convenience to purchase alcohol and the barriers (policies) that reduce retail access.

(c) Alcohol promotion and advertising restrictions—policy efforts to reduce the attractiveness of alcohol to youth and demand, which could occur through alcohol advertising.

(e) Social access—the availability of alcohol to adolescents from social sources, including friends and family members, and in social settings such as parties and informal gatherings.

(f) Harm reduction—drinking and driving-specific policies to reduce harm related to drinking while driving.

ECONOMIC ACCESS

The sensitivity of drinking to retail alcohol price has been demonstrated in a dozen or more countries, as shown in reviews by Gallet (2007), and Wagenaar, Salois, and Komro (2009). Furthermore, alcohol tax increases have the potential to reduce the rate of fatal car accidents involving alcohol; for example, it is estimated that a 10% increase in the price of alcoholic beverages in the United States could reduce the probability of drinking and driving by about 7% for males and 8% for females, with even larger reductions among those 21 years and under because of their lower disposable income. One example of increasing retail price as a part of policy occurred in the Northern Territory of Australia under a Living With Alcohol Program (LAP), which increased the cost of standard drinks by five cents in 1992 followed by other problem reduction strategies in 1996, including lowering the legal blood alcohol content (BAC) limit and a special levy on case wine (Stockwell et al., 2001). Over the years of this program, there were statistically significant reductions in acute conditions such as road deaths (34.5%) and other mortality (23.4%) as well as traffic crashes requiring hospitalization (28.3%).

Adolescents who drink weekly or are heavy drinkers (typically defined as five or more drinks per occasion) have more sensitivity to price than do other youth (Coate & Grossman, 1988). Tax increases may influence not only consumption but also other alcohol-related outcomes, and youth again appear to be more price responsive than adults in terms of these outcomes. Increased price appears to reduce drinking and driving among youth more than among adults (Chaloupka, Saffer, & Grossman, 1993, 2002).

Dee and Evans (2001) reported that price increases would reduce motor vehicle crash fatalities among 18- to 20-year-olds. Sorenson and Berk (2001) after statistically controlling for potential confounder variables found that beer sales and handgun sales in California (from 1972 through 1993) generally predicted homicides during one year, particularly among young men, and that reducing beer sales and handguns sold could reduce the number of homicides. Grossman and Markowitz (2001) examined the effect of beer price on violence among students from 191 colleges and universities from 29 states and found that higher prices for beer were associated with lower incidences of (1) getting into trouble with police or college authorities, (2) damaging property, (3) fighting or arguing, and (4) being taken advantage of or taking advantage of someone sexually. The principal finding is that the incidence of each of these four acts of violence is inversely related to the price of beer in the state in which the student attends college. Markowitz (2001) concluded that higher beer taxes would reduce the likelihood of teens engaging in physical fights. In summarizing its systematic review and weighing of the evidence, the Task Force on Community Preventive Services (2010a) and Elder et al. (2010) have recommended increasing alcohol taxes as a policy to reduce excess alcohol consumption and alcohol-associated problems.

PHYSICAL ACCESS

Another class of alcohol policies particularly relevant to youth consists of policy approaches to reduce the ability of adolescents to obtain alcohol from retail sources.

Minimum Legal Drinking Age or Alcohol Purchase Age

One notable public policy has involved establishing a minimum legal drinking or retail purchase age to reduce the consumption of alcohol by youth. There are legal ages of alcohol purchase in many countries, but most often they are ignored or not enforced. One example of a national policy to reduce youth drinking using minimum age occurred in the United States in the 1980s with a minimum purchase or drinking age of 21 years for all alcoholic beverages. Wagenaar and Toomey (2002) in their extensive summary of international research on the effects of the minimum legal drinking age (MLDA) studied the effects of changes in the MLDA on incidents of drunk driving and traffic crashes (e.g., fatal crashes, drink-driving crashes, or self-reported driving after drinking); a clear majority found that raising the MLDA reduced crashes and associated problems and lowering the MLDA increased crashes. Raising the MLDA in the United States has been associated with a 47% decrease in fatal crashes involving young drivers with BACs $\geq 0.08\%$ and a 40% decrease in such crashes involving young drivers with BACs $\geq 0.01\%$ (Dang, 2008). Conversely, a review of research indicated that the

trend to decrease the MLDA in the United States from 21 to 18 years during the 1970s was associated with a 7% increase in traffic fatalities for the affected age groups (Cook, 2007). The US National Highway Traffic Safety Administration (NHTSA) estimated that with a drinking age of 21 years across all 50 states cumulatively through 2000, over 20,000 lives have been saved (US Department of Transportation, 2001). In Australia, Smith (1986) and Smith and Burvill (1987) found that the lowering of the drinking age from 21 to 18 years in three Australian states resulted in increases in traffic-related hospital admissions, other accident-related hospital admissions, and rates of juvenile crime. More recently, the lowering of the drinking age in New Zealand from 20 to 18 years was related to increases in traffic injuries among 15- to 19-year-olds (Kypri et al., 2006) and in prosecutions for disorder offences among 14- to 15-year-olds (Huckle, Pledger, & Casswell, 2006). A systematic review of 33 evaluations of MLDA laws in the United States, Canada, and Australia found a median decline of 16% in crash-related outcomes for the targeted age groups following passage of laws to increase the MLDA (Shults et al., 2001).

Hours and Days of Retail Sale

The number of hours and days of a week in which alcohol is available for retail sales is a policy that affects both drinking and associated harm. Thus, reducing the days and hours of retail alcohol availability restricts the opportunities for alcohol purchases both in bars and restaurants as well as alcohol outlets. A recent study by Rossow and Norström (2012) analyzed the effects of local policy in18 Norwegian cities that extended or restricted the closing hours for on-premise alcohol sales. Outcomes suggested that each 1-hour extension of closing hours was associated with an assault increase of about 17% or 5.0 assaults per 100,000 inhabitants and that the effects were symmetrical; that is, assaults change proportionally up or down whether hours were increased or decreased. One policy change in Western Australia permitted extended trading permits (ETPs), which enabled longer opening hours. It was found that these extended hours, which stimulated greater sales of high-alcohol-content beer, wine, and spirits, also significantly increased monthly assault rates associated with those hotels with ETPs (Chikritzhs & Stockwell, 2002, 2006). Kelly-Baker et al. (2000) found temporary bans on the sales of alcohol from midnight Friday through 10 a.m. Monday because of federal elections in Mexico reduced cross-border drinking in Mexico by young Americans. A local policy in Diadema, Brazil, limited opening hours for alcohol sales and produced a significant decrease in murders (Duailibi et al., 2007). Stockwell and Chikritzhs (2009) completed a review of 48 international studies of the effects of changes in hours and days of sale and concluded that the balance of reliable evidence suggests that extended late-night trading hours leads to increased consumption and related harms. Thus, from a policy perspective, restricting hours and specific days of sale can have considerable impact on acute alcohol-related problems such as traffic crashes, violence, and heavy drinking, which is also the conclusion reached by the Hahn et al. (2010) and the Task Force on Community Preventive Services (2010b).

Retail Monopolies

Retail alcohol government-operated monopolies are a public policy means to reduce drinking. Elimination of a private profit interest typically facilitates the enforcement of rules against selling to minors. Rossow, Karlsson, and Raitasalo (2008), in a study in Norway and Finland in which underage-appearing 18-year-olds attempted to purchase alcohol in off-premise outlets, found that they were more likely to be requested to present an ID and less likely to succeed in purchasing alcohol in alcohol retail monopoly outlets as compared to other types of outlets. They concluded that such monopoly outlets can facilitate enforcement of minimum legal age for purchase of alcohol. Miller et al. (2006) found that underage drinking rates, including heavy drinking as well as youth-involved traffic crashes, were lower in US states that had retail sale monopolies controlling for other factors. The Task Force on Community Preventive Services (2012a) also concluded that sufficient evidence supports policies that should discourage jurisdictions from ending retail alcohol government monopolies.

Enforcement of Alcohol Laws and Policies

The systematic checking by law enforcement of whether a licensed establishment actually sells alcohol to underage persons or "underage-looking persons" represents a key factor in policy effectiveness. Even moderate increases in enforcement can reduce sales of alcohol to minors by as much as 35% to 40%, especially when combined with media and other community and policy activities (Grube & Nygaard, 2001). There is some evidence that enforcement primarily affects the specific establishments

targeted in compliance checks with limited diffusion and that any effects on sales may decay relatively quickly (Wagenaar, Toomey, & Erickson, 2005a, b). In one study, enforcement of underage sales laws increased compliance with alcohol sales laws from 11% to 39% (Scribner & Cohen, 2001). Dent, Grube, and Biglan (2005) found that perceived compliance and enforcement of underage drinking laws at the community level was inversely related to individual heavy drinking, drinking at school, and drinking and driving and to the use of commercial sources for alcohol by adolescents. Similarly, compliance rates as determined by surveys in which youth attempted to purchase alcohol have been found to be inversely related to frequency of use of commercial sources for alcohol by minors (Paschall, Grube, Black, Flewelling, et al., 2007). Paschall, Grube, Black, and Ringwalt (2007) found that the alcohol sales rate was positively related to students' use of commercial alcohol sources and perceived alcohol availability. Another policy version of enforcement is establishing legal liability for providing alcohol to underage persons, especially if alcohol-involved harms occur; for example, when an intoxicated minor is involved in a traffic crash. Sloan et al. (2000) analyzed traffic fatalities across all US states and found that imposing legal liability on commercial services resulted in reduced fatality rates for those drivers 15 to 20 years, controlling for other dependent variables.

Results from a randomized community trial in one US state (Oregon) found significant associations between the level of law enforcement of underage drinking in the intervention communities and reductions in both 30-day use of alcohol and binge drinking. The enforcement level included all types of enforcement, including drunk driving, youth possession of alcohol, underage age purchase violations, and provision of alcohol to minors (Flewelling et al., 2013). This is further explored in Paschall et al. (2012) and Paschall, Lipperman-Kreda, and Grube (2014).

Number and Densities of Alcohol Outlets

Adolescents, like adults, can potentially obtain alcohol from any retail alcohol outlets that sell alcohol. The geographical concentration of outlets in neighborhoods and communities can either enhance or reduce total alcohol availability. Gruenewald, Ponicki, and Holder (1993), using a time-series cross-sectional analysis of alcohol consumption and density of alcohol outlets over 50 US states, found a 10% reduction in the density of alcohol outlets would reduce consumption of spirits from 1% to 3% and consumption of wine by 4% across all ages. Similar findings have been reported in other countries (see Babor, Caulkins, et al., 2010). Treno, Grube, and Martin (2003) found that higher density of outlets was positively related to drinking and driving among licensed youth drivers and negatively related to riding with drinking drivers among youth who did not have driver's licenses. Alcohol outlet density was found to be related to both perceived ease of access to alcohol and to consumption among youth in 50 zip codes in California (Treno et al., 2008). There is consistent evidence that outlet density is related to rates of heavy episodic drinking by youths and young adults (Huckle, Huakau, Sweetsur, Huisman, & Casswell, 2008; Scribner et al., 2008; Weitzman, Folkman, Folkman, & Wechsler, 2003). Treno et al. (2003) found evidence that outlet density was positively associated with frequency of underage drinking and driving and with riding with drinking drivers. Based on reviews of the scientific evidence, the Task Force on Community Preventive Services (2009) and Campbell et al. (2009) confirm the potential of limiting alcohol outlet density as a means to reduce excessive consumption and alcohol-related harms. Drinking context and outlet density have been associated with intimate partner violence (Mair, Cunradi, Gruenewald, Todd, & Remer, 2013) and neighborhood violence including adolescents (Mair, Gruenewald, Ponicki, & Remer, 2013).

ALCOHOL PROMOTION AND ADVERTISING RESTRICTIONS

Restrictions and outright bans of alcohol promotion and commercial advertising have been employed as part of public health policy. The evidence of the effects of advertising bans has been mixed, but recent research suggests that limits on point-of-purchase advertising and promotion could have specific effects on youth drinking. Promotion of alcohol and its effect on youth drinking has been a significant public health issue. Studies have examined the relationship between exposure to different forms of alcohol advertising and subsequent drinking among adolescents and youth. Erickson et al. (2014) examined the relationship to subsequent drinking among US adolescents. They found that for seventh-grade nondrinkers, exposure to in-store beer displays predicted drinking onset by grade 9; for seventh-grade drinkers, exposure to magazines with alcohol advertisements and to beer concession stands at sports or music events predicted

frequency of grade 9 drinking, and that for 12-year-old children exposure to in-store beer displays predicted drinking onset by age 14 years. Similar research concluded that exposure to magazines with alcohol advertisements and to beer concession stands at sports or music events for 12-year-olds predicted frequency of drinking at age 14 years (see also Ellickson, Collins, Hambarsoomians, & McCaffrey, 2005). Snyder et al. (2006) found that youth who saw more alcohol advertisements drank more on average (each additional advertisement seen increased the number of drinks consumed by 1%). These researchers found that restrictions on point-of-purchase price advertising at liquor stores reduced the probability of drinking and driving among all drinkers and when price advertising is permitted, prices may be expected to fall, thereby leading to increases in overall consumption. They found that drinkers who lived in locations with policies permitting grocery stores to sell beer and wine had a significantly higher probability of drinking and driving and concluded that advertising and availability of alcohol promote drinking.

SOCIAL ACCESS

Around the world, a substantial amount of alcohol obtained by underage persons is not directly from retail sources but from social sources (friends, parties, homes, etc.) and other persons who purchase alcohol and provide it to underage persons (both persons themselves under the legal purchase age and persons who themselves are of legal age) (Harrison, Fulkerson, & Park, 2000).

Curfews for Youth

Curfews establish a time when children and young people below certain ages must be home. While this policy was not initially considered an alcohol-problem prevention strategy, research has shown positive effects in reducing alcohol-involved traffic crashes for adolescents as a result of reducing social access to alcohol away from home (Preusser, Williams, Zador, & Blomberg, 1984; Williams, Lund, & Preusser, 1984).

Social Host Liability

Under social host liability, adults who provide alcohol to a minor or serve intoxicated adults in social settings can be sued through civil action for damages or injury caused by that minor or intoxicated adult (Grube & Nygaard, 2005). In one study in the United States, social host liability laws were associated with decreases in alcohol-related traffic fatalities among adults, but not among minors (Whetten-Goldstein, Sloan, Stout, & Liang, 2000). In a second study, social host liability laws were associated with decreases in reported heavy drinking and in decreases in drinking and driving by lighter drinkers (Stout et al., 2000). Although social host liability may send a powerful message, that message must be effectively disseminated, implemented, and enforced before it can have a deterrent effect.

Third-Party Provision of Alcohol to Youth

Adults or young adults of legal age can purchase alcohol on behalf of an underage person who approaches a stranger outside of an alcohol establishment and asks this person to purchase alcohol for him or her. Toomey et al. (2007) in one US study found that 19% of young males over the age of 21 years were willing to purchase alcohol for youth who appeared to be underage when "shoulder-tapped" outside a convenience or liquor store. Refusal of sales to adults who are believed to be purchasing alcohol for underage persons is enforced in many retail monopoly stores, including in Norway, Iceland, Finland, and Sweden (see Rossow et al., 2008).

Social Availability Enforcement

Key aspects of potential effectiveness of policies to reduce social availability of alcohol include using law enforcement to (a) enforce laws prohibiting adult provision of alcohol to minors and underage drinking at private parties and (b) disrupt one of the highest risk settings for alcohol availability and misuse, that is, private drinking parties, by conducting weekend and nighttime patrols of areas known to be regular drinking locations. There is limited empirical evidence of effectiveness. One example occurred in Oregon where a local community implemented a weekend drunk driving and party patrol program. An unpublished evaluation of this program revealed that arrests of youth for possession of alcohol increased in 1 year with a corresponding decrease of 35% in underage drunk driving crashes (Little & Bishop, 1998; Radecki, 1993).

HARM REDUCTION POLICIES—DRINKING AND DRIVING

Public policies concerning alcohol as described earlier are typically concerned with reducing retail and social access to alcohol in order to reduce drinking by youth and thus reduce alcohol problems. There are some policies that focus specifically on the reduction of alcohol-involved harm.

A major policy approach to reducing alcohol-involved harm is drinking and driving enforcement.

Policies that discourage drinking before or while driving can reduce alcohol-related crashes and the injuries and deaths that result from them. Strategies for reducing alcohol-related traffic crashes include increased and highly visible law enforcement (e.g., sobriety checkpoints and random breath testing) and the level of legal BAC at which a driver is considered legally drunk or impaired.

Random Breath Testing

Random breath testing (RBT) involves extensive and continuous random stops of drivers who are required to take a breath test to establish their BAC. Tests of RBT in Australia, Canada, and Great Britain show that RBT can reduce traffic crashes. Shults et al. (2001) reviewed 23 studies of RBT and intensive enforcement and found a median decline of 22% (range 13%–36%) in fatal crashes, with slightly lower decreases for noninjury and other crashes for such strategies. A limited version of RBT, called sobriety checkpoints, is often implemented in individual US states. There is strong evidence that they reduce drinking and driving and related traffic crashes (Shults et al., 2001). In both Australia and the United States, the preventive effect of enforcement is enhanced if accompanied by publicity and news attention (see Shults et al., 2009). No studies have evaluated the specific effects of these strategies on adolescent drinking and driving, but there is little reason to believe that youthful drivers would not be affected by such policies.

Lowering Blood Alcohol Concentration Limits

BAC limits are public laws that legally define drunk driving using a BAC at or above a prescribed level for the whole population (e.g., from 0.08 to as low as 0.02). A review of both US and Australian studies (Shults et al., 2001) found reductions between 9% and 24% in fatal crashes associated with the implementation of zero-tolerance laws. Similarly, a review of Canadian studies concluded that lower BAC levels for young drivers were related to a 25% reduction in reported drinking and driving among young males in Ontario and an 8.9% reduction in single-vehicle nighttime crashes in Quebec (Chamberlain & Solomon, 2008). Some countries have set specific BAC limits for young drivers and commonly invoke penalties such as automatic license revocation. A study of all 50 US states and the District of Columbia found a net decrease of 24% in the number of young drivers with positive BACs as a result of the implementation of lower BAC limits for these ages (Voas, Tippetts, & Fell, 2003), and Wagenaar, O'Malley, and LaFond (2001) found similar results in 30 US states.

Graduated Licensing Places Special Limits on New or Young Drivers

Graduated licenses establish unique driving restrictions for young or novice drivers (e.g., restricts nighttime driving and/or prohibits driving with other adolescents). The policy effects appear to also be related to adolescent drinking and driving. A graduated licensing program in Connecticut led to a 14% net reduction in crash involvement among the youngest drivers; similarly, in New Zealand, a 23% reduction in car crash injuries among novice drivers was found after implementation of a graduated licensing system (Langley, Wagenaar, & Begg, 1996). Similar findings were reported by Goodwin et al. (2005).

Driver's education was challenged in the 1970s for its qualifying and placing of younger drivers at risk behind the wheel; it was then replaced with graduated licensing in the 1980s. Eventually, the combination of policy restraints and driver's education demonstrated significant improvements in teen auto injury and death rates. This illustrates a principle that many of the innovations in alcohol-related policy described earlier have established. The lesson has been that educational or mass media strategies alone, or policies alone, do not work as well as the combination of the two. Sobriety checkpoints, as noted earlier, depend for their best effect on strong media coverage and public information. Driver's education by itself, with its qualifying of younger drivers to get licensed to drive, only produced more young, inexperienced drivers. But when combined with graduated licensing, the combination had dramatic effects (Green & Gielen, 2015).

Recommendations About Policies and Alcohol

Policies for which there is the greatest experience and evidence include (a) retail price of alcohol; (b) minimum age for drinking or purchase of alcohol; (c) drinking/driving deterrence, especially via regular and highly visible enforcement such as random breath testing and sobriety checkpoints; (d) hours and days of alcohol sales; (e) responsible beverage service—alcohol serving and sales policies, training, and enforcement; (f) lower BAC limits for driving; (g) density and concentration of alcohol outlets; and (h) public retail monopolies. All of these are either targeted at the retail availability of alcohol or at drink driving. Most of the evidence concerning effects on adolescents is concentrated in minimum purchase/drinking age and retail price, though there is no reason that adolescents are impacted by the policies which target all drinkers as well. Much less policy evidence is available for potential effects on social availability of alcohol and on restrictions on promotion and advertising of alcohol to youth.

Tobacco

Tobacco accounted for an increasing number of cancer, cardiovascular, and respiratory illnesses and deaths in Western countries through the first two thirds of the 20th century. Efforts to control tobacco advertising and consumption that began most earnestly in the mid-1960s in English-speaking countries of North America, Europe, and Australia have resulted in dramatic reductions in most tobacco-related diseases in those countries and other jurisdictions with the most aggressive and effective policies and programs. Their cancer deaths continued to rise even after successfully reduced smoking because the incidence and mortality from cancer has a 20- to 30-year lag time between smoking and cancer. Despite the 50% reductions in smoking among adults, some one in five continue to smoke in the United States. Most promising for the future health of Americans, the current smoking rate of US high school students declined from 39% to 22% between 1976 and 2006. We will examine particularly the US experience in bringing this dramatic decline about, with lessons drawn also from studies of specific policy interventions in other countries.

More detailed accounts of European trends in policies related to tobacco control are contained in a document commissioned by the European Union's Directorate-General for Health and Consumer Protection (Tiessen et al., 2010).

European tobacco control policies encompass a wide range of policy measures, including restrictions on cross-border advertising, harmonization of tobacco excise duties, initiatives to reduce exposure to secondhand smoke, recommendations for comprehensive tobacco control policies across EU Member States, and tobacco product regulation. One of the key instruments is the Tobacco Products Directive (2001/37/EC), which establishes maximum tar, nicotine, and carbon monoxide (TNCO) yields for cigarettes, specifies the labeling provisions, bans the use of misleading descriptors—such as "mild," "light," and so on—and bans the marketing of oral tobacco in the European Union (except in Sweden).

The status of policies and programs in other countries around the world is documented in annual reports of the World Health Organization's MPOWER program of guidance and technical assistance to countries seeking to implement the Framework Convention on Tobacco Control (WHO, 2004, 2008; Yach & Wipfli, 2006).

Policy Directed at Adolescent and Young Adult Smoking

Most adult tobacco users initiated their use during adolescence. Some 80% of adult smokers began smoking before 18 years of age. Adolescent smokeless tobacco users also tend to be more likely than nonusers to become adult cigarette smokers (Centers for Disease Control and Prevention, 2003, 2007; Johnson, O'Malley, Bachman, & Schulenberg, 2011). Youth cigarette use in the United States declined sharply during 1997–2003; rates have remained relatively stable in more recent years (Centers for Disease Control and Prevention, 2010b). Smokeless tobacco use by youth also declined in the late 1990s and early 2000s, but an increasing number of US high school students have reported using smokeless tobacco products in recent years through 2010 (Centers for Disease Control and Prevention, 2010a). The late 1990s declines in adolescent tobacco use nationally, and sharp declines at other times in some states and cities hold important lessons about policy influences, advocacy, and enforcement strategies.

Factors Associated With Adolescent Tobacco Use

Like most other substance abuse by youth, adolescent tobacco use has been found widely associated with socioeconomic status; use and approval of tobacco use by peers or siblings; limited skills to resist influences to use tobacco; smoking by parents or guardians; lack of parental support or involvement; availability, accessibility, and price of tobacco products (Task Force on Community Preventive Services, 2014); perceptions that tobacco use is the norm among peers and the general population; low levels of academic achievement; low self-image or self-esteem; and aggressive behavior (e.g., fighting, carrying weapons).

Price: Higher Costs for Tobacco Products Through Increased Excise Taxes

Price proved to be the most powerful and independent predictor of tobacco consumption rates, especially among youth, because of their more limited disposable income and the lower price elasticity for them. Taxation on tobacco was the main policy lever for increasing prices, because government could not dictate the industry's pricing. Increased taxes on tobacco were partially offset by industry lowering their prices. Taxation also produced revenue that supported, in part, state-wide comprehensive tobacco control programs.

The Community Preventive Services Task Force (2014) has established from its systematic reviews that the effects of price increases are multiple and substantial.

TOTAL DEMAND (CHANGES IN USE AND CONSUMPTION OF TOBACCO PRODUCTS)

A 20% increase in tobacco unit price would be associated with a 7.4% median reduction in demand among adults (16 studies, median price elasticity estimate: −0.37; interquartile interval [IQI]: −0.47 to −0.29) and a 14.8% median reduction in demand among young people (13 studies, median elasticity of −0.74; IQI: −1.13 to −0.57).

PREVALENCE OF TOBACCO USE

A 20% increase in tobacco unit price would be associated with 3.6% median reduction in the proportion of adults who use tobacco (26 studies, median elasticity of −0.18; IQI: −0.31 to −0.11) and a 7.2% median reduction in the proportion of young adults who use tobacco (22 studies, median elasticity of −0.36; IQI: −0.73 to −0.24).

CESSATION OF TOBACCO USE

A 20% increase in tobacco unit price would be associated with a 6.5% increase in cessation among adults (one study, elasticity = 0.375) and an 18.6% median increase in cessation among young people (five studies, median elasticity of 0.93; IQI: 0.37 to 1.00).

INITIATION OF TOBACCO USE

A 20% increase in tobacco unit price would be associated with an 8.6% median reduction in initiation among young people (seven studies, median elasticity of −0.43; IQI: −0.90 to −0.0).

The specific health-risk behaviors associated with tobacco use include high-risk sexual behavior, use of alcohol, and use of other drugs. How much of these associations are attributable to causation in one direction or the other, with tobacco use as a gateway drug or as a consequence of exposure to the other risk behaviors, cannot be conclusively answered and varies with contexts. The most plausible explanation for the associations is the covariance of both tobacco consumption and the other risk behaviors with common social influences, including environmental conditions conducive to smoking or nonsmoking behavior. Many of these influences are susceptible to modification or control through policy.

Counteradvertising Mass-Media Campaigns

Television and radio commercials, posters, and other media messages targeted toward youth to counter pro-tobacco marketing have been a particularly notable feature of comprehensive programs credited with reductions in adolescent tobacco use (Mukherjea & Green, 2015). One way such efforts have been found to achieve these successes is to raise broad awareness of the tactics used by the tobacco industry to "dupe" teenagers and other demographic groups into smoking (Campaign for Tobacco Free Kids, 2012a, b, c; Tobacco Education and Research Oversight Committee, 2014). The "Truth" campaign of Florida, later taken to scale nationally by the Legacy Foundation, presented youth with messages showing how deceptive and duplicitous tactics of the tobacco industry were seducing young people into desires to use tobacco. These counteradvertising tactics were shown to be effective in reducing teen smoking and engaging adolescents actively in supporting antitobacco campaigns and advocacy (Legacy Foundation, 2014).

In 2002, New York City launched a multipronged, phased initiative to reduce adult and youth smoking rates that included increasing the state's tobacco excise tax, making workplaces smoke-free, expanding cessation services, providing tobacco education, and implementing an extensive television-based media campaign based in part on the "Truth" campaign model from Florida. Counteradvertising messages were broadcast at varying levels for 10 months. The state conducted a simultaneous antitobacco campaign for 12 months. From 2002 to 2006, adult smoking rates in the city declined 19% overall (see Figure 35.1). Among young adults aged 18 to 24 years, smoking declined 17% in the year after the implementation of the media campaign and 35% from the start of the broader initiative in 2002 (Centers for Disease Control and Prevention, 2007). Statistics on the New York City high school students show a 52% decrease in smoking in between 1997 and 2005 (CDC, 2007, 2010b, 2014a; http://www.nyc.gov/html/doh/downloads/pdf/survey/survey-2006teensmoking.pdf).

Strategies recommended for countermarketing and related mass communication campaigns are compiled in various federal government publications, including the Centers for Disease Control and Prevention (2003); Green et al. (2000); Schar et al. (2006) and National Cancer Institute (2002, 2005); and Sparks and Green (2000).

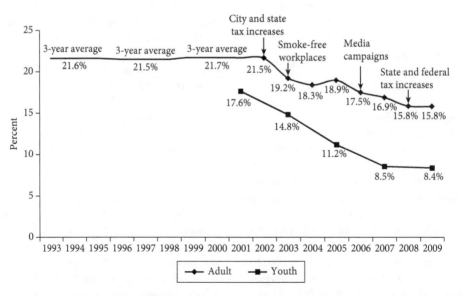

Figure 35.1 New York City's dramatic drop in tobacco consumption following initiation.

Comprehensive School-Based Tobacco-Use Prevention Policies and Programs (e.g., Tobacco-Free Campuses)

Systematic reviews have been inconclusive to negative on the singular effectiveness of school-based curricula or classroom interventions by themselves to prevent tobacco experimentation or uptake among youth. When adopted or tested without the support of school-wide smoke-free policies, classroom curricular interventions have been disappointing, but they appear to have been vindicated as a component of comprehensive school health and comprehensive school-based tobacco control (Centers for Disease Control and Prevention, 2014b; Green et al., 1985). Smoke-free schools have been the vanguard of local smoke-free legislation protecting youth, often in concert with smoke-free workplaces, restaurants, and public buildings to protect adults from secondhand smoke (Green & Gielen, 2015). These, together with mass media campaigns, have contributed to the "denormalization" of smoking, which has been a conscious strategy of some state programs, including the pioneer program of California (Rogers, 2010).

Policies and Programs to Increase Smoking Cessation

Another policy effort within comprehensive tobacco control programs has been to reduce barriers to access to and use of smoking cessation programs and supports. These have notably targeted the reduction of out-of-pocket costs of smoking cessation programs, including the costs of nicotine replacement drugs. The Community Preventive Task Force Services (2012b) has recently updated its previous review (Hopkins et al., 2001) of studies testing the effectiveness of policy or program changes that reduce tobacco users' out-of-pocket costs and that make evidence-based treatments, including medication, counseling, or both, more affordable for people interested in quitting (Community Preventive Task Force Services, 2012b); also see similar reviews by Fiore et al. (2008) and the Cochrane Collaboration (Reda, Kotz, Evers, & van Schayck, 2009). Policies sought to achieve this either by providing new benefits or by changing the level of benefits offered to reduce costs or co-payments. These policies or interventions may also include promoting to tobacco users and health care providers the benefit of increased awareness and interest in quitting and use of evidence-based treatments. Of the 18 new studies reviewed (1999–2011), three were from Europe, including the United Kingdom (Dey et al.,

1999), the Netherlands (Kaper et al., 2005, 2006), and Germany (Twardella & Brenner, 2007), nine had controlled trial designs, and nine had other evaluation designs. The studies showed a median increase of 2.8% in quit attempts. This outcome is considered important despite its limited assurance of effective quitting on the particular attempt because successful quitting is known to increase with the number of quit attempts. Twelve studies with 20 arms showed a median effective quitting rate of a 4.3 percentage point increase. Though modest, these improvements are particularly significant in relation to a major barrier to access and quitting among low-income and underserved populations.

Community, State, and National Interventions That Reduce Commercial Promotion and Availability of Tobacco Products

Besides the federal and state laws seeking to constrain advertising of tobacco products to youth, and commercial access to such products, communities have taken additional policy and program steps in these directions. These have included more aggressive enforcement of penalties for sales to minors younger than the state minimum age, laws removing cigarettes from vending machines, laws locking tobacco products behind counters, and laws restricting the proximity to schools of retail tobacco sales. The enforcement of sales-to-minors laws have included state and community "sting" operations in which younger-appearing adults are hired to request cigarettes in retail stores to determine whether they ask to see identification before making the sale.

The most sweeping US national policies on tobacco promotion following the Surgeon General's Report (US Department of Health and Human Services, 1994) declaring the health hazards of smoking were the fair broadcasting doctrine of the late 1960s, which required equal time for counter-advertising of tobacco, and the Surgeon General's warning statement on each package of tobacco. Nothing in tobacco control has approached the pervasive influence of these federal communication mandates (with the exception of increased taxes on tobacco) until the 2010 Congressional Act giving the Food and Drug Administration the authority to label all tobacco products with graphically explicit messages about the horrors of harm done by tobacco consumption. As the FDA moved toward field testing of graphic images and messages to implement this law, US District Court Judge Richard Leon ruled twice (after appeal of the first ruling) for tobacco companies and issued a permanent injunction blocking implementation of FDA's new graphic health warnings.

The Campaign for Tobacco Free Kids has issued a statement saying:

> It is incomprehensible that Judge Leon would conclude that the warnings are "neither factual nor accurate" when they unequivocally tell the truth about cigarette smoking—that it is addictive, harms children, causes fatal lung disease, cancer, strokes and heart disease, and can kill you. What isn't factual or accurate about these warnings? Not even the tobacco industry disputes these facts.
> *(see http://www.tobaccofreekids.org/press_releases/post/2012_02_29_ruling)*

To read more about this court decision, see, among news reports in February 2012: http://abcnews.go.com/US/wireStory/judge-blocks-graphic-images-cigarette-packages-15821958. See also on the general subject of warning labels and their impact in tobacco, Freeman et al. (2010) and Tiessen et al. (2010).

Global Tobacco Policy Initiatives

In the international context, the United States has had some important innovations and successes that have been emulated elsewhere, but it lags in other respects (Green et al., 2000; Tiessen et al., 2010). The World Health Organization (WHO) Report on the Global Tobacco Epidemic (2011) documents that in the previous 2 years, more than 1 billion people around the world had been newly protected by tobacco control interventions, including mass media campaigns, graphic health warnings, and various policies, including smoke-free public spaces. In addition, there has been significant progress toward protecting children and adults from tobacco in countries throughout the world, with policies controlling industry advertising and other marketing practices, and controls on smuggling, pricing, and sales.

Gruesomely graphic warning labels and hard-hitting mass media campaigns have proven effective in reducing tobacco use and encouraging people to quit. According to the report, more than 1 billion people now live in countries with legislation requiring large graphic health warnings on every cigarette pack sold in their countries, and 1.9 billion people live in the 23 countries that have aired high-quality national antitobacco mass media campaigns within the past 2 years. During this time in the United States, Congress authorized the Food and Drug Administration to issue requirements for more prominent, graphic cigarette health warnings on all cigarette packaging and advertisements in the United States.

According to the WHO report, 16 countries with a total of 385 million people have newly enacted national-level, smoke-free laws covering all public places and workplaces. Comprehensive smoke-free laws at the subnational level newly protect an additional 100 million people. In the United States over the past decade, 25 states and the District of Columbia enacted laws for smoke-free workplaces, bars, and restaurants. However, despite increased adoption of state and local smoke-free laws, approximately 88 million nonsmoking Americans aged 3 years and older are still exposed to secondhand smoke each year. More than half of children over age 3 years are exposed to secondhand smoke.

Unfortunately, the report also noted that though global governments collect nearly $133 billion in tobacco excise tax revenue, less that $1 billion is actually spent on tobacco control. In the United States, between 2000 and 2009, states collected $203.5 billion from tobacco settlement funds and tobacco taxes. Yet only 2% of annual tobacco-generated revenues ($25.3 billion) are being dedicated to state tobacco prevention and cessation programs; 14.6% would be needed to fund state tobacco control programs fully at CDC-recommended levels (Centers for Disease Control and Prevention, 2014a).

Tobacco use is the leading preventable cause of premature disease and death in the world. About half of all current smokers will die prematurely from smoking-related causes. In the 20th century, the tobacco epidemic killed 100 million people worldwide; during the 21st century, it will kill more than 1 billion unless urgent action is taken. Containing this epidemic is one of the most important public health priorities of our time.

Other highlights of this report include the following:

• The greatest progress in tobacco control in terms of population coverage has been in countries adopting health warnings on tobacco packaging; three more countries with a total population of 458 million have enacted recent pack labeling laws.

• An additional 115 million people are living in countries with the recommended minimum tobacco taxes, and 26 countries and one territory now have taxes constituting the recommended minimum of 75% of retail price.

• Low- and middle-income countries have been in the forefront of developing anti-tobacco mass media campaigns, showing that countries can successfully implement this intervention regardless of income classification.

To combat the tobacco epidemic, the Centers for Disease Control and Prevention and the World Health Organization recommend MPOWER, a set of six proven strategies: *m*onitoring tobacco use and prevention policies; *p*rotecting people from tobacco smoke; *o*ffering help to quit tobacco use; *w*arning about the dangers of tobacco; *e*nforcing bans on tobacco advertising, promotion and sponsorship; and *r*aising taxes on tobacco.

The Centers for Disease Control and Prevention oversees the Global Adult Tobacco Survey, which produces national and subnational estimates on tobacco use and key tobacco control indicators among adults aged 15 years and older, and the Global Youth Tobacco Survey, a school-based survey designed to monitor tobacco use and key tobacco control indicators among youth aged 13–15 years (Warren et al., 2000). Data from both surveys were used in compiling the Global Tobacco Epidemic 2011 report (Frieden, 2011).

Successful Reductions in Adolescent Tobacco Use

Some efforts have been made to rate the components of tobacco control efforts (e.g., Lipperman-Kreda, Friend, & Grube, 2014), but the conventional wisdom is that policies and programs must be interdependent and synergistic. If they fail to support and reinforce each other, they undermine or even cancel each other out. If they have the slightest inconsistency or contradictions, teenagers are quick to see hypocrisy in them and to dismiss them as adult propaganda and an excuse to act out their objection to adult control. Other reasons that the CDC's Office on Smoking and Health (Centers for Disease Control and Prevention, 2014a) and others have concluded from the experience of statewide and community programs that "comprehensive" tobacco control must coordinate policies and programs is that they depend on each other for success, they must emanate from different levels of organizations and government, and each component of comprehensive programs differentially reaches different segments of the population (see Eriksen et al., 2010).

As seen in the drug control policy and practice (Reuter, 2013), tobacco policies are made more politically possible with an informed electorate, and they are more expediently passed with an outraged, or at least very concerned, public. These are facilitated by informational, educational, and motivational messages through various media and channels. For youth there is a need for mass media to provide a backdrop of messages and images that are consistent with those they receive from family and teachers, rather than inconsistent. Hollywood film images of smokers who are protagonists and magazine advertisements with images of glamorous models smoking, for example, send an inconsistent message about smoking from those presented in school by teachers or at home by concerned parents. Adolescents sometimes defiantly mock rules for nonsmoking in schools and other public places when they see them as adult control on behavior they perceive to be fashionable, cool, or even normative in the adult world to which they aspire.

A particular challenge to coordinated policies and programs is that the tobacco industry outspends state tobacco control programs at least $10 to $1, and up to $20 to $1 on media and marketing during political campaigns to raise taxes on cigarettes (because that alone among policies has a known independent effect on tobacco consumption, especially on adolescents who have less disposable income). Most political efforts to ban smoking in public places were successfully beaten back by tobacco industry lobbying at state and federal levels in the 1970s, but they were passed during those periods in most of the city and county initiatives because the industry could not put out the multiplicity of "brush fires" at the local level. Coordinating local and state policy and program efforts has been key to the notable successes of California and other states and municipalities. Localities, for example, cannot afford the high costs of mass media placements, and states cannot tailor all aspects of programs and policies to every jurisdiction where wide diversity exists. When each level of government and voluntary agency action coordinates and divides the labor of comprehensive programs and policies, the synergy produces more successful outcomes.

Drugs

Based upon the 2012 US National Survey on Drug Use and Health (NSDUH), an estimated 23.9 million Americans aged 12 years or older had used at least one illicit drug within the past 30 days of their interview. Among American youth (ages 12–17 years), approximately 10% had used an illicit drug within the past month (Substance Abuse and Mental Health Services Administration, 2014).

Public policies concerning illicit drugs and adolescence are typically concerned with drug use, possession, retail sale, and production. While some of the same policy strategies exist (at least in name), drug policies are largely based upon deterrence and most often involve extensive use of law enforcement in most countries.

Retail Price and Illegal Drug Use

Although illegal, retail price of illegal drugs also affects the demand. Pacula et al. (2001) estimated that the price elasticity for use of marijuana in the last 30 days ranged from –0.002 to –0.69 such that a 10% increase in the cost of marijuana could produce as much as a 6.9% decrease in the number of youth who used in the last month. Other studies have also found that an increase in price yields decreased use of marijuana (De Simone & Farrelly, 2001; Pacula et al., 2001), cocaine (Caulkins, 1995), and heroin (Saffer & Chaloupka, 1999). The underlying assumption for law enforcement is that it will reduce supplies and costs to suppliers and thus increase retail prices. However, massive increases in drug enforcement during the past two decades in the United States have not had the expected effect; that is, prices for cocaine and heroin have fallen substantially without an evident decrease in demand (Caulkins, Reuter, & Taylor, 2006). Rydell and Everingham (1994) concluded, employing a series of mathematical models, that supply costs increase as producers replace seized product and assets, compensate drug traffickers for the risk of arrest and imprisonment, and devote resources to avoiding seizures and arrests. However, as drug researchers have noted (Caulkins et al., 2006; Reuter, 2001), retail drug markets are influenced by factors such as addiction, product illegality, and the role of violence. They point out that prohibition plus some modest but nontrivial level of enforcement can drive up drug prices beyond what they would be if drugs were legal. In summary, efforts to increase the price of illicit drugs through interdiction would appear to affect their use, although it is not clear that this will affect drug abuse. In that adolescents have less disposable funds than other age groups, the potential price effects for illicit drugs could be more significant for youth.

Retail and Social Availability of Illicit Drugs

All illicit drugs are retail products that are affected by both supply and demand factors. Illegal sales are accomplished more through social networks, especially for methamphetamine rather than cocaine or heroin sales. Methamphetamine dealers are more likely than cocaine and heroin dealers to sell out of single-family homes and to sell out of areas with fewer security measures (Eck, 1995; Rodriguez, Katz, Webb, & Schaefer, 2005). Drugs change hands multiple times between import (or production in the case of domestically manufactured drugs) and final sale to the user (Caulkins, 1997a, 1997b). As one moves down through the distribution hierarchy, transaction size gets smaller and the price per unit increases.

For example, methamphetamine sold in US drug markets is supplied by domestic labs and foreign producers, most notably the large "super labs" in Mexico that have become an increasingly important source in recent years. Analyses on the spatial relations between drug sales and use, however, suggest that associations may be more complex with drug sales occurring across neighborhoods (i.e., use is higher among residents of surrounding areas compared to those living in communities with drug markets; Freisthler, LaScala, Gruenewald, & Treno, 2005).

One implication of the substantial differential between the replacement cost of drugs and their retail value is that law enforcement efforts that remove drugs at the higher levels of the distribution system (where the replacement costs are relatively low) are less damaging to the drug trade than seizures made at the lower levels of the distribution hierarchy. Freisthler, Gruenewald, et al. (2005) examined the geographic relationships between availability and self-reported drug use. Use of illegal drugs was significantly positively related to sales of drugs in surrounding geographic areas for both youth (aged 12 to 18 years) and adults (those 19 years old and older). Interestingly, drug sales within any given area were unrelated to self-reported use among youth and negatively associated with use among adults. Thus, areas of greatest access—at least for adults— are not necessarily the areas of greatest use. Because drug markets are more likely to be located in places immediately adjacent to high drug use areas, prevention efforts may need to be located within different areas of communities to address the issues of sales, use, and related problems.

A unique version of cannabis retail distribution is the public policy to permit sale if a physician's prescription is submitted. While often debated, there is concern that such availability increases adolescent use of cannabis. A recent study analyzed adolescent cannabis use from 2003 to 2011 comparing states which had a medical marijuana policy to those without such policies and found that there was no evidence of an increase in adolescent use associated with this policy (Lynne-Landsman, Livingston, & Wagenaar, 2013).

High-Level Law Enforcement to Disrupt Drug Importation and Distribution Operations

Efforts to interdict illicit drugs, including methamphetamine, are undertaken at various levels of government. The long-term effects of such interdiction efforts are tempered by several factors, including the relatively cheap replacement costs of drugs seized high in the distribution system and the adaptability of drug traffickers to modify their operations and find new supply routes and new sources of drugs.

Civil Remedies to Disrupt Local Drug Markets

While police crackdowns focus primarily on individuals (i.e., dealers and users), a number of civil remedies use actions targeted at drug selling locations to try to reduce the quantity of drugs sold by making it more difficult for buyers and sellers to engage in the drug trade. Eck and Wartell (1998) reported the results of a randomized study of abatement actions, with rental properties where drug sales had occurred being assigned to one of three conditions (letter sent to property owners informing them of drug sales and warning of fines or closure of the building if the problem continued; warning letter plus a request for a meeting between police and property owner; no abatement notice). Follow-up over the next 30 months indicated that significantly fewer crimes were reported in the two abatement conditions than in the control condition (see Eck, 2002). Another form of civil remedy, code enforcement, involves community groups using enforcement of local building codes, zoning laws, or health codes to pressure property owners to stop drug sales from being conducted inside or in front of residences. Little is known about the effectiveness of code enforcement in reducing drug activity. However, a study by Mazerolle et al. (2000) used a randomized experiment with 100 drug hotspots assigned to traditional police enforcement (surveillance, arrests, and field interrogation) or traditional police enforcement plus civil enforcement (abatement actions and code enforcement). The properties subject to the civil actions showed a decrease in drug sales and a decline in signs of disorder relative to the properties assigned to traditional police enforcement only.

Altering the Physical Environment to Hinder Drug Selling

Some community groups have used various strategies to alter the physical environment where drug sales are occurring (e.g., boarding up abandoned houses, cutting back shrubbery in parks, improving lighting) to deny drug dealers a safe haven for conducting business. Green (1996) found that not only did a program of code enforcement combined with police crackdowns not lead to displacement effects, but it resulted in diffused benefits to the surrounding area. Davis and Lurigio (1996) noted that while displacement is a serious possibility when local retail drug markets are disrupted, it often does not occur or the displaced activities are of a lesser magnitude such that benefits associated with a local intervention may accrue to the surrounding areas.

Summary of Drug Policies

Drug policies and public health approaches to prevention have not been evaluated as extensively as those concerning alcohol and tobacco. The Committee on Data and Research for Policy on Illegal Drugs of the United States (2001) points to the need for data and research information that policymakers lack in order to create effective national policy concerning illicit drugs. The Drugs and Public Policy Group (2010) summarized key points concerning international evidence on drug policy to include the following: (1) there is scientific evidence that can inform drug policy development, especially concerning health services for drug dependency but that policies with little evidence of effectiveness are most preferred in many countries, (2) no single policy can solve the drug problem in any country, (3) increasing law enforcement efforts against drug dealers has diminishing returns and does not result in large price increases beyond which might occur with routine enforcement, (4) opiate treatment has the ability to reduce drug problems related to that use, (5) there is limited scientific evidence to guide law enforcement policies of interdiction against drug supply and related incarnation of offenders, and (6) drug policies should be not evaluated only in terms of their intended effects but also in terms of the unintended effects (which might in some situations be worse than the status quo). An international review of drug policies conducted by Greenfield and Paoli (2012) found a number of contradictions and inefficiencies in supply-side policies and suggested a harm reduction policy approach, thus marking clearer distinction between the two policy approaches.

The most recent change in drug policy in the United States is the unprecedented legalization of the production and retail sale of cannabis to adults in 11 states by 2018, though still illegal by federal law. This follows a number of states that have established the policy for medical marijuana. In an editorial, Hawken et al. (2013) expressed concern about the unknown impacts and public health and safety consequences of these policies and the limited research knowledge about the associated risks. Such research concerning these drug policies will be needed over upcoming years for a complete evaluation.

Evidence About Public Policies—Practice Evidence and Research Evidence

Substances and products used by adolescents, including alcohol, tobacco, and illicit drugs, are produced, distributed, and sold by a substantial domestic and international collection of establishments, organizations, informal consortiums, and companies. The increased expansion of this multifaceted industry has been discussed for alcohol by Babor, Caulkins, et al. (2010), for tobacco by The World Health Organization (WHO) Report on the Global Tobacco Epidemic (2011), and for drugs by Babor, Caetano, et al. (2010). This expansion has unique effects on countries that have fewer historical traditions and experiences with commercially produced and distributed substances of abuse. While indigenous (often informal, family or small group) based alcohol and illicit drug production have typically existed in such countries, they are often displaced with more modern and cost-effective production and distribution technologies. Such countries as well as more industrially developed nations can take advantage of public policies that seek to reduce harm. In terms of the effects of public policies on alcohol, tobacco, and drug use and related problems, there is substantial evidence from scientific studies or evaluations from many countries, especially on tobacco control, from North America (Partos et al., 2013), Europe (Tiessen et al., 2010), Australia (Freeman, Gartner, Hall, & Chapman, 2010), and New Zealand (Salmond, Crampton, Atkinson, & Edwards, 2012). Thus, there is guarded confidence in the potential of many of the public policies described in this chapter to reduce adolescent

use and associated alcohol problems. Examples of efforts to summarize international evidence on alcohol policy effects include Babor, Caetano, et al. (2010), which provides a summary of research as well as indications of evidence weakness or limitations, and Casswell et al. (2012). The book by Babor and colleagues is the fourth such book written by a collection of international alcohol researchers from many countries, which began with the first such publication (Bruun et al., 1975). Other such reports were Edwards et al. (1994, 1995) and Babor et al. (2003). A specific review of evidence concerning adolescents and public policy can be found in Grube and Nygaard (2005). An important international summary of policy research concerning illicit drugs is provided by Babor, Caulkins, et al. (2010).

Another effort to independently evaluate the overall weight of evidence concerning policies has been carried out by the US Centers for Disease Control via its program "Using Evidence for Public Health Decision Making: Preventing Excessive Alcohol Consumption and Related Harms," which summarizes recommended strategies for reducing alcohol problems.

Conclusion

The cumulative international evidence is that public health policy approaches have demonstrated potential to reduce harm from and use of alcohol, tobacco, and illicit drugs, and in many instances such policies have specific effects for adolescents. This evidence can increase the confidence for policymakers that evidence-based policies have strong potential to reduce substance abuse problems in the 21st century.

Future Directions

Further research on the effects of public policies to reduce the harms associated with alcohol, tobacco, and drugs will always be useful and welcomed. However, an essential challenge for policies concerning substances in the future will be examining the barriers and opportunities for the implementation of policies to reduce the harm related these substances. Such challenges most certainly include political, cultural, and economic issues.

References

Babor, T. F., Caetano, R., Casswell, S., Edwards, G., Giesbrecht, N., Graham, K., . . . Rossow, I. (2003). *Alcohol: No ordinary commodity: Research and public policy*. New York, NY: Oxford University Press.

Babor, T. F., Caetano, R., Casswell, S., Edwards, G., Giesbrecht, N., Graham, K., . . . Rossow, I. (2010). *Alcohol: No ordinary commodity: Research and public policy* (2nd ed.). New York, NY: Oxford University Press.

Babor, T. F., Caulkins, J. P., Edwards, G., Fischer, B., Foxcroft, D. R., Humphreys, K., . . . Strang, J. (2010). *Drug policy and the public good*. New York, NY: Oxford University Press.

Bruun, K., Edwards, G., Lumio, M., Mäkelä, K., Pan, L., Popham, R. E., . . . Österberg, E. (1975). *Alcohol control policies in public health perspective*. Helsinki, Finland: The Finnish Foundation for Alcohol Studies.

Campaign for Tobacco-Free Kids. (2012a). *The path to smoking addiction starts at very young ages*. Washington, DC: Campaign for Tobacco-Free Kids. Retrieved from http://www.tobaccofreekids.org/research/

Campaign for Tobacco-Free Kids. (2012b). *Tobacco company marketing to kids*. Retrieved December 2015, from Campaign for Tobacco-Free Kids.

Campaign for Tobacco-Free Kids. (2012c.) *How parents can protect their kids from becoming addicted smokers*. Retrieved December 2015, from http://www.tobaccofreekids.org/research/factsheets/pdf/0152.pdf

Campbell, C. A., Hahn, R. A., Elder, R., Brewer, R., Chattopadhyay, S., Fielding, J., . . . Task Force on Community Preventive Services. (2009). The effectiveness of limiting alcohol outlet density as a means of reducing excessive alcohol consumption and alcohol-related harms. *American Journal of Preventive Medicine, 37*(6), 556–569.

Casswell, S., Meier. P., Mackintosh, A. M., Brown, A., Hastings, G., Thamarangsi, T., . . . You, R. Q. (2012). The International Alcohol Control (IAC) Study—Evaluating the impact of alcohol policies. *Alcoholism: Clinical and Experimental Research, 36*(8), 1462–1467.

Caulkins, J. P. (1995). Domestic geographic variation in illicit drug prices. *Journal of Urban Economics, 37*(1), 38–56.

Caulkins, J. P. (1997a). Are mandatory minimum drug sentences cost-effective? (*RAND Research Briefs*). Retrieved December 2015, from http://www.rand.org/pubs/research_briefs/RB6003/index1.html

Caulkins, J. P. (1997b). Modeling the domestic distribution network for illicit drugs. *Management Science, 43*(10), 1364–1371.

Caulkins, J. P., Reuter, P., & Taylor, L. J. (2006). Can supply restrictions lower price? Violence, drug dealing and positional advantage. *Contributions to Economic Analysis and Policy, 5*(1), 1–18.

Centers for Disease Control and Prevention. (2003). *Designing and implementing an effective tobacco counter-marketing campaign*. Atlanta, GA: US Department of Health and Human Services. Retrieved from http://www.cdc.gov/tobacco/stateandcommunity/counter_marketing/manual/pdfs/chapter6.pdf

Centers for Disease Control and Prevention. (2007). Decline in smoking prevalence—New York City, 2002–2006. *Morbidity and Mortality Weekly Report, 56*(24), 604–608.

Centers for Disease Control and Prevention. (2010a). Cigarette use among high school students—United States, 1991–2009. *Morbidity and Mortality Weekly Report, 9*(26), 797–801.

Centers for Disease Control and Prevention. (2010b). Tobacco use among middle and high school students—United States, 2000–2009. *Morbidity and Mortality Weekly Report, 59*(33), 1063–1068.

Centers for Disease Control and Prevention. (2014a). *Best practices for comprehensive tobacco control programs—2014* (3rd ed.). Atlanta, G: US Department of Health and Human Services, Centers for Disease Control and Prevention, National Center for Chronic Disease Prevention and Health Promotion, Office on Smoking and Health. Retrieved December 2015, from http://www.cdc.gov/tobacco/stateandcommunity/best_practices/index.htm

Centers for Disease Control and Prevention. (2014b). *Comprehensive school health programs*. Retrieved from http://www.nap.edu/catalog/9084/defining-a-comprehensive-school-health-program-an-interim-statement

Chaloupka, F. J., Grossman, M., & Saffer, H. (2002). The effects of price on consumption and alcohol-related problems. *Alcohol Research and Health, 26*(1), 22–34.

Chaloupka, F. J., Saffer, H., & Grossman, M. (1993). Alcohol control policies and motor vehicle fatalities. *Journal of Legal Studies, 22*(1), 161–186.

Chamberlain, E., & Solomon, R. (2008). Zero blood alcohol concentration limits for drivers under 21: Lessons from Canada. *Injury Prevention, 14*(2), 123–128.

Chikritzhs, T., & Stockwell, T. (2002). The impact of later trading hours for Australian public houses (hotels) on levels of violence. *Journal of Studies on Alcohol, 63*, 591–599.

Chikritzhs, T., & Stockwell, T. (2006). The impact of later trading hours for hotels on levels of impaired driver road crashes and drive breath alcohol levels. *Addiction, 101*, 1254–1264

Coate, D., & Grossman, M. (1988). Effects of alcoholic beverages prices and legal drinking ages on youth alcohol use. *Journal of Law and Economics, 31*(1012), 145–171.

Committee on Data and Research for Policy on Illegal Drugs. (2001). *Informing America's policy on illegal drugs: What we don't know keeps hurting us*. Washington, DC: The National Research Council, National Academic Press.

Cook, P. J. (2007). *Paying the tab: The costs and benefits of alcohol control*. Princeton, NJ: Princeton University Press.

Dang, J. N. (2008). *Statistical Analysis of Alcohol-Related Driving Trends, 1982–2005* (DOT HS 810 942). Washington, DC: National Highway Traffic Safety Administration. Available at: http://wwwnrd.nhtsa.dot.gov/Pubs/810942.pdf.

Davis, R. C., & Lurigio, A. J. (1996). *Fighting back: Neighborhood antidrug strategies*. Thousand Oaks, CA: Sage.

De Simone, J., & Farrelly, M. C. (2001). Price and enforcement effects on cocaine and marijuana demand. *Economic Inquiry, 41*(1), 98–115.

Dee, T. S., & Evans, W. N. (2001). Teens and traffic safety. In J. Gruber (Ed.), *Risky behavior among youth: An economic perspective* (pp. 121–165). Chicago, IL: University of Chicago Press.

Dent, C., Grube, J., & Biglan, T. (2005). Community level alcohol availability and enforcement of possession laws as predictors of youth drinking. *Preventive Medicine, 40*(3), 355–362.

Dey, P., Foy, R., Woodman, M., Fullard, B., & Gibbs, A. (1999). Should smoking cessation cost a packet? A pilot randomized controlled trial of the cost-effectiveness of distributing nicotine therapy free of charge. *British Journal of General Practice, 49*(439), 127–128.

Drugs and Public Policy Group. (2010). Drug policy and the public good: A summary of the book. *Addiction, 105*, 1137–1145.

Duailibi, S., Ponicki, W., Grube, J., Pinsky, I., Laranjeira, R., & Raw, M. (2007). The effect of restricting opening hours on alcohol-related violence. *American Journal of Public Health, 97*(12), 2276–2280.

Eck, J. E. (1995). A general model of the geography of illicit drug marketplaces. In J. E. Eck & D. Weisburd (Eds.), *Crime prevention studies, Vol. 4. Crime and place* (pp. 67–94). Monsey, NY: Criminal Justice Press.

Eck, J. E. (2002). Preventing crime at places. In L. Sherman, D. P. Farrington, B. Welsh, & D. Mackenzie (Eds), *Evidence-based crime prevention* (pp. 9241–9294). London, UK: Routledge.

Eck, J. E., & Wartell, J. (1998). Improving the management of rental properties with drug problems: A randomized experiment. In I. G. Mazerolle & J. R. Roehl (Eds.), *Crime prevention studies, Vol. 9. Civil remedies and crime prevention* (pp. 161–185). New York, NY: Criminal Justice Press.

Edwards, G., Anderson, P., Babor, T. F., Casswell S., Ferrence, R., Giesbrecht, N., . . . Skog O-J. (1994). *Alcohol policy and the public good*. New York, NY: Oxford University Press.

Edwards, G., Anderson, P., Babor, T. F., Casswell S., Ferrence, R., Giesbrecht, N., . . . Skog O-J. (1995). *A summary of alcohol policy and the public good, a guide for action*. EUROCARE (Advocacy for the Prevention of Alcohol Related Harm in Europe) and WHO Europe Office, Copenhagen.

Elder, R. W., Lawrence, B., Ferguson, A., Naimi, T. S., Brewer, R. D., Chattopadhyay, S. K., . . . Task Force on Community Preventive Services. (2010). The effectiveness of tax policy interventions for reducing excessive alcohol consumption and related harms. *American Journal of Preventive Medicine, 38*(2), 217–229.

Ellickson, P., Collins, R. C., Hambarsoomians, K., & McCaffrey, D. F. (2005). Does alcohol advertising promote adolescent drinking? Results from a longitudinal assessment. *Addiction, 100*(2), 235–246.

Erickson, D. J, Lenk, K. M., Toomey, T. L., Nelson, T. F., Jones-Webb, R., & Mosher, J. F. (2014). Measuring the strength of state-level alcohol control policies. *World Medical and Health Policy, 6*(3), 171–186.

Eriksen, M. P., Green, L. W., Husten, C. G., Pederson, L. L., & Pechacek, T. F. (2010). Thank you for not smoking: The public health response to tobacco-related mortality in the United States. In J. W. Ward & C. S. Warren (Eds.), *Silent victories: The history and practice of public health in twentieth-century America* (pp. 423–436). New York, NY: Oxford University Press.

Fiore, M. C., Jaén, C. R., Baker, T. B., Bailey, W. C., Benowitz, N. L., Curry, S. J., . . . Wewers, M. E. (2008). *Treating tobacco use and dependence: 2008 update. Clinical practice guideline*. Rockville, MD: US Department of Health and Human Services, Public Health Service. Retrieved December 2015, from http://bphc.hrsa.gov/buckets/treatingtobacco.pdf

Flewelling, R., Grube, J. W., Paschall, M. J., Biglan, A., Kraft, A., Black, C., . . . Ruscoe, J. (2013). Reducing youth access to alcohol: Findings from a community-based randomized trial. *American Journal of Community Psychology, 51*(1-2), 264–277.

Freeman, B., Gartner, C., Hall, W., & Chapman, S. (2010). Forecasting future tobacco control policy: Where to next? *Australian and New Zealand Journal of Public Health, 34*(5), 447–450.

Freisthler, B., Gruenewald, P. J., Johnson, F. W., Treno, A. J., & LaScala, E. A. (2005). An exploratory study examining the spatial dynamics of illicit drug availability and rates of drug use. *Journal of Drug Education, 35*(1), 15–27.

Freisthler, B., LaScala, E. A., Gruenewald, P. J., & Treno, A. J. (2005). An examination of drug activity: Effects of neighborhood social organization on the development of drug distribution systems. *Substance Use and Misuse, 40*(5), 671–686.

Frieden, T. (2011). CDC Office of the Director, July 11, 2011. Retrieved from <https://www.highbeam.com>

Gallet, C. A. (2007). The demand for alcohol: A meta-analysis of elasticities. *Australian Journal of Agricultural and Resource Economics, 51*(2), 121–135.

Goodwin, A. H., Wells, J. K., Foss, R. D., & Williams, A. F. (2005). *Encouraging compliance with graduated driver licensing restrictions*. Washington, DC: Insurance Institute for Highway Safety.

Green, L. A. (1996). *Policing places with drug problems*. Newbury Park, CA: Sage.

Green, L. W., Cook, T., Doster, M. E., Fors, S. W., Hambleton, R., Smith, A., & Walberg, H. J. (1985). Thoughts from the School Health Education Evaluation Advisory Panel. *Journal of School Health, 55*(8), 300.

Green, L. W., & Gielen, A. C. (2015). Evidence and ecological theory in two public health successes for health behavior change. In S. Kahan, A. C. Gielen, P. Fagen, & L. W. Green (Eds.), *Behavioral approaches to population health* (pp. 26–43). Baltimore, MD: Johns Hopkins University Press.

Green, L. W., Pappas, A., Eriksen, M., & Fishburn, B. (2000). Le role de la legislation dans la lutte contre le tabagisme aux Etats-Unis [Tobacco control legislative experience in the United States]. *Promotion and Education: International Journal of Health Promotion and Education, 7*(3), 38–42.

Greenfield, V. A., & Paoli, L. (2012). If supply-oriented drug policy is broken, can harm reduction help fix it? Melding disciplines and methods to advance international drug-control policy. *International Journal on Drug Policy, 23*(1), 6–15.

Grossman, M., & Markowitz, S. (2001). Alcohol regulation and violence on college campuses. In M. Grossman & C. R. Hsieh (Eds.), *The economics of substance use and abuse: The experiences of developed countries and lessons for developing countries* (pp. 169–198). London, UK: Edward Elgar.

Grube, J. W., & Nygaard, P. (2001). Adolescent drinking and alcohol policy. *Contemporary Drug Problems, 28*(1), 87–132.

Grube, J. W., & Nygaard, P. (2005). Alcohol policy and youth drinking: Overview of effective interventions for young people. In T. Stockwell, J. Tournbourou, & W. Loxley (Eds.), *Preventing harmful substance use: The evidence base for policy and practice* (pp. 113–127). New York, NY: Wiley.

Gruenewald, P. J., Ponicki, W. R., & Holder, H. D. (1993). The relationship of outlet densities to alcohol consumption: A time series cross-sectional analysis. *Alcoholism: Clinical and Experimental Research, 17*(1), 38–47.

Hahn, R. A., Kuzara, J. L., Elder, R., Brewer, R., Chattopadhyay, S., Fielding, J., . . . Task Force on Community Preventive Services. (2010). Effectiveness of policies restricting hours of alcohol sales in preventing excessive alcohol consumption and related harms. *American Journal of Preventive Medicine, 39*(6), 590–604.

Harrison, P. A., Fulkerson, J. A., & Park, E. (2000). The relative importance of social versus commercial sources in youth access to tobacco, alcohol, and other drugs. *Preventive Medicine, 31*(1), 39–48.

Hawken, A., Caulkins, J. P., Kilmer, B., & Kleiman, M. A. R. (2013). Quasi-legal cannabis in Colorado and

Washington: Local and national implications. *Addiction, 108*(5), 837–838.

Hopkins, D. P., Briss, P. A., Ricard, C. J., Husten, C. G., Carande-Kulis, V. G., Fielding, J. E., . . . Task Force on Community Preventive Services. (2001). Reviews of evidence regarding interventions to reduce tobacco use and exposure to environmental tobacco smoke. *American Journal of Preventive Medicine, 20*(2S), 16–66.

Huckle, T., Pledger, M., & Casswell, S. (2006). Trends in alcohol-related harms and offences in a liberalized alcohol environment. *Addiction, 101*(2), 232–240.

Huckle, T., Huakau, J., Sweetsur, P., Huisman, O., & Casswell, S. (2008). Density of alcohol outlets and teenage drinking: Living in an alcogenic environment is associated with higher consumption in a metropolitan setting. *Addiction, 103*(10), 1614–1621.

Johnston, L. D., O'Malley, P. M., Bachman, P. M., & Schulenberg, J. E. (2011). *Monitoring the Future—National results on adolescent drug use: Overview of key findings, 2010.* Ann Arbor: University of Michigan, Institute for Social Research.

Kaper, J., Wagena, E. J., Willemsen, M. C., & van Schayck, C. P. (2005). Reimbursement for smoking cessation treatment may double the abstinence rate: Results of a randomized trial. *Addiction, 100*(7), 1012–1020.

Kaper, J., Wagena, E. J., Willemsen, M. C., & van Schayck, C. P. (2006). A randomized controlled trial to assess the effects of reimbursing the costs of smoking cessation therapy on sustained abstinence. *Addiction, 101*(11), 1656–1661.

Kelly-Baker T., Johnson, M. B., Voas, R. B., & Lange, J. E. (2000). Reduce youthful binge drinking: Call an election in Mexico. *Journal of Safety Research, 31*(2), 61–69.

Kypri, K., Voas, R. B., Langley, J. D., Stephenson, S. C. R., Begg, D. J., Tippetts, A. S., & Davie, G. S. (2006). Minimum purchasing age for alcohol and traffic crash injuries among 15- to 19-year-olds in New Zealand. *American Journal of Public Health, 96*(1), 126–131.

Langley, J. D., Wagenaar, A. C., & Begg, D. J. (1996). An evaluation of the New Zealand graduated driver licensing system. *Accident Analysis and Prevention, 28*(2), 139–146.

Legacy Foundation. (2014). *Truth®: Youth and young adult tobacco prevention.* Retrieved from http://legacyforhealth.org/what-we-do/national-education-campaigns/keeping-young-people-from-using-tobacco

Lipperman-Kreda, S., Friend, K. B., & Grube, J. W. (2014). Rating the effectiveness of local tobacco policies for reducing youth smoking. *Journal of Primary Prevention, 35*(2), 85–91.

Little, B., & Bishop, M. (1998). Minor drinkers/major consequences: Enforcement strategies for underage alcoholic beverage violators. *Impaired Driving Update, 2*(6), 88.

Lynne-Landsman, S. D., Livingston, M. D., & Wagenaar, A. C. (2013). Effects of state medical marijuana laws on adolescent marijuana use. *American Journal of Public Health, 103*(8), 1500–1506.

Mair, C., Cunradi, C., Gruenewald, P. G., Todd, M., & Remer, L. (2013). Drinking context specific associations between intimate partner violence and frequency and volume of alcohol consumption. *Addiction, 108*(12), 2102–2111.

Mair, C., Gruenewald, P. G., Ponicki, W. R., & Remer, L. (2013). Varying impacts of alcohol outlet densities on violent assaults: Explaining differences across neighborhoods. *Journal of Studies on Alcohol and Drugs, 74*(1), 50–58.

Markowitz, S. (2001). The role of alcohol and drug consumption in determining physical fights and weapon carrying by teenagers. *Eastern Economic Journal, 27*(4), 409–432.

Mazerolle, L., Green, J. F., Price, J., & Roehl, J. (2000). Civil remedies and drug control: A randomized field trial in Oakland, CA. *Evaluation Review, 24*(2), 211–239.

Miller, T., Snowden, C., Birckmayer, J., & Hendrie, D. (2006). Retail alcohol monopolies, underage drinking, and youth impaired driving deaths. *Accident Analysis and Prevention, 38*(6), 1162–1167.

Mukherjea, A., & Green, L. W. (2015). Tobacco and behavior change. In S. Kahan, A. C. Gielen, P. Fagen, & L. W. Green (Eds.), *Behavioral approaches to population health (pp. 153–187).* Baltimore, MD: Johns Hopkins University Press.

National Cancer Institute. (2002). *Making health communication programs work.* Washington, DC: National Institutes of Health.

National Cancer Institute. (2005). *Theory at a glance: A guide for health promotion practice.* Washington, DC: National Institutes of Health.

Pacula, R. L., Grossman, M., Chaloupka, F. J., O'Malley, P., Johnston, L. D., & Farrelly, M. C. (2001). Marijuana and youth. In J. Gruber (Ed.), *Risky behavior among youth: An economic analysis (pp. 271–326).* Chicago, IL: University of Chicago Press.

Partos, T. R., Borland, R., Yong, H. H., Thrasher, J., & Hammond, D. (2013). Cigarette packet warning labels can prevent relapse: Findings from the international tobacco control 4-country policy evaluation cohort study. *Tobacco Control, 22*(e1), 43–50. doi:.10.1136/tobaccocontrol-2011-050254

Paschall, M. J., Grube, J. W., Black, C., Flewelling, R. L., Ringwalt, C. L., & Biglan, A. (2007). Alcohol outlet characteristics and alcohol sales to youth: Results of alcohol purchase surveys in 45 Oregon communities. *Prevention Science, 8*(2), 153–159.

Paschall, M. J., Grube, J. W., Black, C., & Ringwalt, C. L. (2007). Is commercial alcohol availability related to adolescent alcohol sources and alcohol use? Findings from a multilevel study. *Journal of Adolescent Health, 41*(2), 168–174.

Paschall, M. J., Grube, J. W., Thomas, S., Cannon, C., & Treffers, R. (2012). Relationships between local enforcement, alcohol availability, drinking norms, and adolescent alcohol use in 50 California cities. *Journal of Studies on Alcohol and Drugs, 73*(4), 657–665.

Paschall, M. J., Lipperman-Kreda, S., & Grube, J. W. (2014). Effects of the local alcohol environment on adolescents' drinking behaviors and beliefs. *Addiction, 109*(3), 407–416.

Preusser, D., Williams, A., Zador, P., & Blomberg, R. (1984). The effect of curfew laws on motor vehicle crashes. *Law and Policy, 6*(1), 115–128.

Radecki, T. (1993). *Compliance checks and other enforcement methods to deter underage drinking.* Rockville, MD: US Department of Health and Human Services, Center for Substance Abuse Prevention.

Reda, A. A., Kotz, D., Evers, S. M., & van Schayck, C. P. (2009). Healthcare financing systems for increasing the use of tobacco dependence treatments. *Cochrane Database of Systematic Reviews, 2,* CD004305.

Reuter, P. H. (2001). The limits of supply-side drug control. *The Milken Institute Review, First Quarter,* 14–23.

Reuter, P. H. (2013). Can tobacco control endgame analysis learn anything from the U.S. experience with illegal drugs? *Tobacco Control, 22*(Suppl. 1), i49–i51.

Rodriguez, N., Katz, C., Webb, V. J., & Schaefer, D. R. (2005). Examining the impact of individual, community, and market factors on methamphetamine use: A tale of two cities. *Journal of Drug Issues, 35*(4), 665–694.

Rogers, T. (2010). The California tobacco control program: Introduction to the 20-year retrospective. *Tobacco Control, 19*(2, Suppl. 1), i1–i2.

Rossow, I., Karlsson, T., & Raitasalo, K. (2008). Old enough for a beer? Compliance with minimum legal age for alcohol purchases in monopoly and other off-premise outlets in Finland and Norway. *Addiction, 103*(9), 1468–1473.

Rossow, I., & Norström, T. (2012). The impact of small changes in bar closing hours on violence. The Norwegian experience from 18 cities. *Addiction, 107*(3), 530–537.

Rydell, C., & Everingham, S. (1994). *Controlling cocaine: Supply versus demand programs.* Santa Barbara, CA: RAND.

Saffer, H., & Chaloupka, F. J. (1999). The demand for illicit drugs. *Economic Inquiry, 37*(3), 401–411.

Salmond, C., Crampton, P., Atkinson, J., & Edwards, R. (2012). A decade of tobacco control efforts in New Zealand (1996-2006): Impacts on inequalities in census-derived smoking prevalence. *Nicotine and Tobacco Research, 14*(6), 664–673.

Schar, E., Gutierrez, K., Murphy-Hoefer, R., & Nelson, D. E. (2006). *Tobacco use prevention media campaigns: Lessons learned from youth in nine countries.* Atlanta, GA: US Department of Health and Human Services, Centers for Disease Control and Prevention, National Center for Chronic Disease Prevention and Health Promotion, Office on Smoking and Health.

Scribner, R. A., & Cohen, D. A. (2001). The effect of enforcement on merchant compliance with the minimum legal drinking age law. *Journal of Drug Issues, 31*(4), 857–866.

Scribner, R. A., Mason, K., Theall, K., Simonsen, N., Schneider, S. K., Towvim, G. L., & DeJong, W. (2008). The contextual role of alcohol outlet density in college drinking. *Journal of Studies on Alcohol and Drugs, 69*(1), 112–120.

Shults, R. A., Elder, R. W., Sleet, D. A., Nichols, J. L., Alao, M. O., Carande-Kulis, V. G., . . . Task Force on Community Preventive Services. (2001). Reviews of evidence regarding interventions to reduce alcohol-impaired driving. *American Journal of Preventive Medicine, 21*(4), 66–88.

Shults, R. A., Elder, R. W., Nichols, J. L., Sleet, D. A., Compton, R., Chattopadhyay, S. K., & Task Force on Community Preventive Services. (2009). Effectiveness of multicomponent programs with community mobilization for reducing alcohol-impaired driving. *American Journal of Preventive Medicine, 37*(4), 360–371.

Sloan, F. A., Stout, E. M., Whetten-Goldstein, K., & Liang, L. (2000). *Drinkers, drivers, and bartenders: Balancing private choices and public accountability.* Chicago, IL: University of Chicago Press.

Smith, D. I. (1986). Effect on non-traffic accident hospital admissions of lowering the drinking age in two Australian states. *Contemporary Drug Problems, 13*(4), 621–639.

Smith, D. I., & Burvill, P. (1987). Effect on juvenile crime of lowering the drinking age in three Australian states. *Addiction, 82*(2), 181–188.

Snyder, L., Milici, F. F., Slater, M., Sun, H., & Strizhakova, Y. (2006). Effects of alcohol advertising exposure on drinking among youth. *Archives of Pediatrics and Adolescent Medicine, 160*(1), 18–24.

Sorenson, S. B., & Berk, R. A. (2001). Handgun sales, beer sales, and youth homicide, California, 1972–1993. *Journal of Public Health Policy, 22*(2), 182–197.

Sparks, R. E., & Green, L. W. (2000). Mass media in support of smoking cessation. In National Cancer Institute (Ed.), *Population-based smoking cessation: Proceedings of a conference on what works to influence cessation in the general population. Smoking and Tobacco Control Monograph, No.12.* (NIH Publication 00-4892, pp. 199-216). Bethesda, MD: US Department of Health and Human Services, National Institutes of Health, National Cancer Institute.

Stockwell, T., & Chikritzhs, T. (2009). Do relaxed trading hours for bars and clubs mean more relaxed drinking? A review of international research on the impacts of changes to remitted hours of drinking. *Crime Prevention and Community Safety, 11*(3), 153–170.

Stockwell, T., Chikritzhs, T., Hendrie, D., Fordham, R., Ying, F., Phillips, M., . . . O'Reilly, B. (2001). The public health and safety benefits of the Northern Territory's Living with Alcohol programme. *Drug and Alcohol Review, 20*(2), 167–180.

Stout, E. M., Sloan, F. A., Liang, L., & Davies, H. H. (2000). Reducing harmful alcohol-related behaviors: Effective regulatory methods. *J of Studies on Alcohol, 61*(3), 402–412.

Substance Abuse and Mental Health Services Administration. (2014). *Results from the 2012 National Survey on Drug Use and Health: Detailed tables.* Retrieved December 2015, from http://www.samhsa.gov/data/NSDUH/2012SummNatFindDetTables/Index.aspx

Task Force on Community Preventive Services. (2009). Recommendations for reducing excessive alcohol-related harms by limiting alcohol outlet density. *American Journal of Preventive Medicine, 37*(6), 570–571.

Task Force on Community Preventive Services. (2010a). Increasing alcoholic beverage taxes is recommended to reduce excessive alcohol consumption and related harms. *American Journal of Preventive Medicine, 38*(2), 230–232.

Task Force on Community Preventive Services. (2010b). Recommendations on maintaining limits on days and hours of sale of alcoholic beverages to prevent excessive alcohol consumption and related harms. *American Journal of Preventive Medicine, 39*(6), 605–606.

Task Force on Community Preventive Services. (2012a). Recommendations on privatization of alcohol retail sales and prevention of excessive alcohol consumption and related harms. *American Journal of Preventive Medicine, 42*(4), 428–429.

Task Force on Community Preventive Services. (2012b). *Reducing tobacco users out-of-pocket costs for evidence-based tobacco cessation treatments.* www.thecommunityguide.org/tobacco/outofpocketcosts.html. Retrieved February 14, 2016.

Task Force on Community Preventive Services. (2014). *Reducing tobacco use and secondhand smoke exposure: Interventions to increase the unit price for tobacco products.* Retrieved December 2015, from http://www.thecommunityguide.org/tobacco/increasingunitprice.html

Tiessen, J., Hunt, P., Celia, C., Fazekas, M., de Vries, H., Staetsky, L., . . . Ling, T. (2010). *Assessing the impacts of revising the tobacco products directive.* Cambridge, UK: RAND Europe Westbrook Centre.

Tobacco Education and Research Oversight Committee. (2014). *Master plan for California tobacco control program.* Sacramento: California Department of Public Health.

Toomey, T. L., Fabian, L. E., Erickson, D. J., & Lenk, K. M. (2007). Propensity for obtaining alcohol through shoulder tapping. *Alcoholism: Clinical and Experimental Research, 31*(7), 1218–1223.

Treno, A. J., Grube, J. W., & Martin, S. E. (2003). Alcohol availability as a predictor of youth drinking and driving: A hierarchical analysis of survey and archival data. *Alcoholism: Clinical and Experimental Research, 27*(5), 835–840.

Treno, A. J., Ponicki, W. R., Remer, L. G., & Gruenewald, P. J. (2008). Alcohol outlets, youth drinking and self-reported ease of access to alcohol: A constraints and opportunities approach. *Alcoholism: Clinical and Experimental Research, 32*(8), 1372–1379.

Twardella, D., & Brenner, H. (2007). Effects of practitioner education, practitioner payment and reimbursement of patients' drug costs on smoking cessation in primary care: A cluster randomised trial. *Tobacco Control, 16*(1), 15–21.

US Department of Health and Human Services. (1994). *Preventing tobacco use among young people: A report of the surgeon general.* Atlanta, GA: US Department of Health and Human Services, Centers for Disease Control and Prevention, Coordinating Center for Health Promotion, National Center for Chronic Disease Prevention and Health Promotion, Office on Smoking and Health. Retrieved December 2015, from http://www.cdc.gov/tobacco/data_statistics/sgr/1994/index.htm

US Department of Transportation. (2001). *Traffic safety facts 2000.* (DOT HS 809 323). Washington, DC: National Highway Traffic Safety Administration.

Voas, R. B., Tippetts, A. S., & Fell, J. C. (2003). Assessing the effectiveness of minimum legal drinking age and zero tolerance laws in the United States. *Accident Analysis and Prevention, 35*(4), 579–587.

Wagenaar, A. C., O'Malley, P. M., & LaFond, C. (2001). Very low legal BAC limits for young drivers: Effects on drinking, driving, and driving-after-drinking behaviors in 30 states. *American Journal of Public Health, 91*(5), 801–804.

Wagenaar, A. C., Salois, M. J., & Komro, K. A. (2009). Effects of beverage alcohol taxes and prices on consumption: A systematic review and meta-analysis of 1003 estimates from 112 studies. *Addiction, 104*(2), 179–190.

Wagenaar, A. C., & Toomey, T. L. (2002). Effects of minimum drinking age laws: Review and analyses of the literature from 1960 to 2000. *Journal of Studies on Alcohol, 14*, 206–225.

Wagenaar, A. C., Toomey, T. L., & Erickson, D. J. (2005a). Complying with the minimum drinking age: Effects of enforcement and training interventions. *Alcoholism: Clinical and Experimental Research, 29*(2), 255–262.

Wagenaar, A. C., Toomey, T. L., & Erickson, D. J. (2005b). Preventing youth access to alcohol: Outcomes from a multi-community time-series trial. *Addiction, 100*(3), 335–345.

Warren, C. W., Riley, L. A., Asma, S., Eriksen, M. P., Green, L. W., & Yach, D. (2000). Tobacco use by youth: A surveillance report from the Global Youth Tobacco Survey project. *Bulletin of the World Health Organization, 78*(7), 868–876.

Weitzman, E. R., Folkman, A., Folkman, K. L., & Wechsler, H. (2003). The relationship of alcohol outlet density to heavy and frequent drinking and drinking-related problems among college students at eight universities. *Health and Place, 9*(1), 1–6.

Whetten-Goldstein, K., Sloan, F. A., Stout, E., & Liang, L. (2000). Civil liability, criminal law, and other policies and alcohol-related motor vehicle fatalities in the United States, 1984-1995. *Accident Analysis and Prevention, 32*(6), 723–733.

Williams, A. F., Lund, A. K., & Preusser, D. F. (1984). *Night driving curfews in New York and Louisiana: Results of a questionnaire survey.* Washington, DC: Insurance Institute for Highway Safety.

World Health Organization. (2004). *Building blocks for tobacco control: A handbook.* Geneva, Switzerland: World Health Organization.

World Health Organization. (2008). *WHO report on the global tobacco epidemic, 2008: The MPOWER Package.* Geneva, Switzerland: World Health Organization.

World Health Organization. (2011). *WHO report on the global tobacco epidemic: Warning about the dangers of tobacco.* Geneva, Switzerland: World Health Organization.

Yach, D., & Wipfli, H. (2006). A century of smoke. *Annals of Tropical Medicine and Parasitology, 100*(5–6), 465–479.

Agenda for Future Research and Concluding Comments

Sandra A. Brown *and* Robert A. Zucker

Abstract

This concluding chapter highlights issues we see as especially important next-step agendas for the field. The issues we have highlighted concern (a) the implications that a developmental frame of reference provides in characterizing and parsing the etiology and course of addictive behavior; (b) the relevance of event-level predictors occurring in microtime and the extent to which they will supercede the more summative indicators that currently dominate the substance abuse field; (c) the increasing awareness, and characterization of drug-specific influences, and the degree to which these influences are useful in evaluating the vulnerability potential of drugs of abuse; (d) the differences in characterization of clinical symptomatology and course that have the potential to occur when evaluation of psychopathology and the details of intervention methods are unpacked with a specifically developmental lens; (e) the insights that new big data collection programs will create in understanding the cross-domain causal structure of substance abuse.

Key Words: developmental frame of reference, event-level prediction, drug-specific influences, big data, cross-level influences

The discourse of this *Handbook* covers an age period just prior to adulthood, when the majority of substance use begins, and when it escalates close to its peak level by the time of early adulthood (Jackson, this volume; McCabe et al., 2016). The volume covers 34 discrete areas of work, grouped within eight sections that were selected to describe the major domains of the field. It has a specifically developmental focus for several reasons. For one, substance use is a moving target that changes dramatically over the course of adolescence and has linkages extending far beyond the use of the substances themselves. Because this is a time frame when powerful physical, social, and biological changes are all taking place, it demands treatment at many levels of analysis that cut across a number of scientific disciplines. The dynamic nature of the process, means explanations and understanding are needed at multiple points in time. Despite these complexities, the period is often regarded as a

unitary one, of "adolescence," and by so explaining it, the nuances and the shifts in process are not seen. Our intent in this work is to focus a lens that destroys this unitary characterization, and that at the same time provides the insights that allow the reader to discern these different levels of process with greater understanding.

The *Handbook*'s chapters were selected to address these multiple levels of causal structure and also to summarize the applied work that has evolved to prevent and/or treat the clinical and social problems that result from substance abuse. In addition to summarizations of the literature in each of the areas, the authors were requested to comment on where the work needed to go next. Here we highlight the issues we see as especially important for the next generation of research to address. Our grouping of issues is organized based on evaluation about their salience, and about the extent to which they share commonalities across multiple content areas.

We also make some observations, based upon our reading of the full set of contributions, about what some of the overarching issues are that are essential next-step agendas for the field.

Implications of a Developmental Frame of Reference for Characterization of the Etiology and Course of Addictive Behavior

Two principles have organized the content of this *Handbook*. One, already noted earlier, is that adolescent substance abuse is a developmental phenomenon. This is more than a truism; it is a statement calling a major body of work into play which articulates that the passage of time is a dynamic process, involving multiple systems operating on the organism simultaneously, and which also articulates that outcomes from these multiple systems operating together produce distinctive, differentiated pathways of behavior over time. The operation of these multiple systems requires both scientists and clinicians to be cognizant of the fact that onset and course of substance use (or alternatively, substance nonuse while the majority of others have started using) is a moving target occurring at different developmental waypoints. The impact of surrounding systems is likely to be different because they also are changing. For this reason, the possibility of producing different outcomes is large; these influences occur at different times and operate on subsystems that are differentially developed.

A good example of this is the development of nicotine dependence, wherein different patterns of symptomatology show up at different stages in the emergence of the disorder, and unique social and biological factors predict attainment of different points in the dependence trajectory (see Myers & MacPherson, this volume; also Flay et al., 1998; Jester et al., in press; Kandel et al., 2009; Strong et al., 2012.) A similar pattern has been shown for the development of alcohol dependence (Buu et al., 2012a, 2012b). Another example pertaining to risk and protective factors for substance use is the recent work showing developmental changes in serotonin signaling which increase sensitivity to risky home environments but also amplify positive response to a nurturing environment (Brummelte et al., 2017). Perhaps the clearest illustration of developmental variations in risk is Dodge et al.'s (2008) dynamic cascade analysis of the development of severe violence. That work demonstrates the impact of developmentally adjacent influences, each of which has the potential to turn what begins early on as a trajectory to severe violence into one which has a number of developmentally shaped bifurcations along the way. Some of the influences move the developmental path "off-track" from the risky outcome, and some strengthen it.

There are two larger implications of this work. One is that the etiologic trajectory of drug involvement is not likely to involve a single pathway, although the multiple pathways that flow from the effects of these influences at different developmental time points is not infinite. The second is that the time has come to incorporate developmentally informed gene-environment and gene-gene models in studies focusing on substance use and substance abuse risk. Windle (this volume) articulates some of the challenges such translational research faces, including the need to characterize the specific mediational role that genetic influences play, as well as detailing the manner in which such influences express themselves—through brain and endocrine systems. A parallel challenge involves characterizing the specific environments which maximize or mitigate such influences. Our field is only in the very early stages of embracing such comprehensive models, with advances focusing upon understanding parts of the full model while ignoring others.

Event-Level Predictors: Action and Predictability in Microtime

The developmental perspective typically involves fairly long swaths of time. The variables examined within this framework are primarily within-person factors such as personality and temperament. Measurement of these factors involves summating behavioral expression in different situations and relationships. At the contextual or environmental level, assessment of the parallel factors also involves summative measurement of what happens—in a variety of specific situations that have a common environmental feature/attraction/threat. In both these spheres, what is sought is a marker index that averages across a variety of circumstances and that also shows a range of variation across these circumstances. But what is a useful tool from one perspective becomes a source of error from another. If one wishes to know precisely what will take place at a particular point in time (e.g., whether one will choose to take marijuana at a particular party on a particular evening; whether one decides to drive after having drunk), utilization of these measures provides only a loose approximation of what will take place. To address this gap, one needs to characterize what goes on at the event level, whether it be about decisions to use or not use a drug at a particular event, engaging in sexual behavior with a particular partner on a particular night, acting on an aggressive thought, and so on (e.g., Borodovsky et al., 2018; Moore et al., 2011).

Several *Handbook* authors have addressed this gap, including Peterson and Smith in their chapter on expectancies, and McCarty and McCarthy in their chapter on substance-impaired driving (SID). The expectancy studies make it very clear that it is the event-related evocation of memories, sometimes well formed and conscious, sometimes rudimentary and present as part of the cognitive background, that serves as the mediator between opportunity for use and actual use, and that this is one of the critical elements in the action chain that tends to be overlooked by behavioral researchers, whose focus is personality–behavior or temperament–behavior relationships. Similarly, McCarty and McCarthy note the need for work which will examine the specific decision-making process related to the choice to use a drug at a particular time. To do such work, one needs to turn to field-based data sampling in high-risk situations (e.g., in bars, at roadside stops), or—in the worst-case scenario—use timeline-follow-back methodology to approximate it. The timeline-follow-back methodology has been used to evaluate the event-level connections between alcohol, marijuana, cigarette use, and partner violence in dating and nondating situations (e.g., Epstein-Ngo et al., 2013). Smartphones have been used to assess current feelings in peer group situations (e.g., Kenny et al., 2016) and in prevention/treatment contexts, where monitoring of the symptomatology of the moment (e.g., anxiety, suicidal ideation, depression) can become the basis of help signals to an on-call treatment provider. Such assessments, utilizing social media, become very effective methodologies to reduce the problematic behavior (cf. Jander et al., 2014; Theedele et al., 2017).

McCarty and McCarty also make the more general point that all behavior is ultimately an interaction between contextual variations in risk and within-subject variability in intent/expectancy to use a drug, or conversely, intent/expectancy to avoid risk. They appropriately emphasize the need for "prospective examination of within-subjects and event-level influences on substance use, which would allow for the examination of interactions between psychological, physiological and environmental factors that determine risk for . . . (substance use) in a specific instance." We note that an understanding of near real-time subjective experience/action that is taking place at this micro level

provides the closest parallel to what is taking place at the neural level. Ultimately, these microtime variations are the building blocks of precision mechanistic cross-level models of the networks that organize behavior. Although this work is presently restricted to the computational neuroscience, which probes the networks of function in brain, it ultimately has extensions to behavioral variation. The precision for that work is currently far beyond behavioral measurement capability of, but this level of understanding ultimately will be achieved, and when it does it will have implications for preventive intervention at a level of focused attack that is well beyond our current treatment capabilities (Menossi et al., 2013; Steele et al., 2018).

Drug-Specific Influences: Vulnerability Potential and Potency Differences for Specific Drugs of Abuse

Although drug "addiction" is most often referred to as a singular phenomenon, the clinical evidence indicates that the addictive potential of pharmacological agents varies considerably across the drugs of abuse, and the evidence in this volume shows that their course, their effects upon behavior, and their vulnerability to influence by the social environment are by no means monolithic. The effort to understand these differentiating attributes requires multiple levels of analysis, ranging from the behavioral, to the physiological, to the neural, to the genetic. However, the key parameters that would link this variation together are currently unknown, so the field is left with a conceptual framework that is either monolithic (lumped under the rubric of "addictive drugs") or that addresses characteristics of each of the drugs individually. The ability to integrate their disparate characteristics in a way that would have direct clinical relevance is only in its very early stages of development (Heilig et al., 2016). We briefly review some of the drug-specific features, and commonalities, that have been discussed in a number of chapters, with the intent to stimulate efforts toward this integration.

One powerful and discriminatory index of addictive potential is catch rate, the probability that addiction will result once use has been initiated. A number of epidemiologic studies, ranging as far back as 1994 (Anthony, Warner, & Kessler) and as recently as 2015 (Lopez-Quintero & Neumark), have noted major across-drug differences in this probability. Among the common drugs of abuse, cannabis is the drug with the lowest catch rate, with only 8.9% of those who begin use moving thereafter into dependence. Nicotine is the highest, with 67% eventually becoming dependent. Speed of progression from first use to dependence among those who eventually become dependent has a substantially different profile, with cocaine initiators being the most rapid in progression (half have become dependent in 4 years) and nicotine users being the slowest (27 years from onset) (Lopez-Quintero & Neumark, 2015; Wagner & Anthony, 2002). These differences in addiction potential are driven to a very substantial degree by differences in the pharmacologic action of each of the drugs as well as differences in their site of action (Koob & Volkow, 2010; Volkow & Morales, 2015). At the same time, although these drugs all have addictive potential, there are clear differences in neural signature and subsequent potential to ensnare. Different neuroadaptations are present among the common drugs of abuse (Badiani et al., 2011), and different behavioral and molecular alterations are produced after abstinence from cocaine vis-à-vis morphine, nicotine, cannabis, and alcohol (Becker, Kiefer, & LeMerrer, 2017). These variations are not sufficiently accounted for by either a dopaminergic model or a stress surfeit disorder model (Badiani et al., 2018).

Moreover, the epidemiologic evidence also indicates that once use has begun, the developmental course varies across classes of drugs over the interval between adolescence and early adulthood. Nonmedical use of opioids, sedatives, stimulants, and tranquilizers all shows peak use in late adolescence, with a consistent descending linear path of use into the mid-20s for nonmedical use of opioids and sedatives, and a much flatter pathway of use for stimulants and tranquilizers (McCabe et al., 2016). Level of use and pattern of decline vary by both sex and racial/ethnic group status, indicating that the social ecology of use has some impact upon the addictive characteristics of these significantly addictive substances. In addition, personality factors, in particular internalizing and externalizing behavior, predict patterns of drug use for some drugs but not others, and in some instances predict protection from engagement for some drugs, but not others (Colder et al., 2013). There are also noted drug–drug interactions that influence trajectory course. Binge drinking at age 18 is consistently associated with a slower rate of decline in frequency of nonmedical use of all classes of prescription drugs; conversely, marijuana use was only associated with a slower rate of decline in sedative and tranquilizer use (McCabe et al., 2016).

Genetic influences across the drugs of abuse also vary substantially, both in terms of type of influence on the phenotype and developmental phase of action. This is an issue that the field has struggled to understand for well over 20 years. In the 1990s, genetic studies suggested that the mechanisms of addiction involved a common genetic core, which accounted for the largest single component of variance in addiction potential (Tsuang et al., 1996). The underlying genetic disposition appeared to be common to both licit (alcohol and tobacco) and illicit (marijuana) drugs, and it involved a vulnerability to disinhibitory or externalizing behavior (Iacono et al., 2008; Kendler et al., 2003). Although the data indicated that the genetic contribution was large, the proportion of genetic factors influencing the pathway from use to abuse to addiction appeared to be stage specific (Agrawal & Lynskey, 2006). In short, the evidence indicated that there was also developmental variation in the mechanistic structures operating at each of these stages.

Time-dependent differences in genetic influence have suggested that the issue of drug vulnerability differences is not going to be accounted for by a single metric. Moreover, research involving a broader swath of substances of abuse has indicated that the genetic disposition for licit and illict drugs is not a common one when a broader array of drugs is included in the analyses (cf. Kendler et al., 2007). As noted by Windle (this volume), "recent findings support the notion that there are important disorder-specific influences and environmental sources of variation that contribute significantly to the observed covariation." Recent work has also demonstrated the interaction of environmental, developmental, and allelic variation that is drug specific (Trucco et al., 2018).

Taken together, the weight of this evidence across multiple domains strongly advocates for a differentiated view of "substance" abuse and "drug" addiction, and it indicates the need for drug-specific modifiers for our understanding of the mechanistic structure of this family of disorders. In a broader sense, the questions about the developmental course of use for these drugs; their specific genetic, neurophysiological, and sociocultural etiology; and the different requirements (special needs) involved in treatment and prevention for each of them raise a larger challenge that the chapters in this *Handbook* echo in many multiple ways. What the field needs is a more delineated understanding of what the drug-specific and non-drug-specific elements are among the drugs of abuse, as well as an understanding of the specific targets that differentiate the intervention/prevention strategies for each of these substances of abuse. To put this another way, given knowledge of the critical components and timing that lead to substance use, abuse, and addiction, our goal needs to be identification of which components are most central in advancement of the dependence process, and specificity as to when, developmentally, is the most sensitive time where such advancement can be halted. The field is now sufficiently differentiated, and the science is sufficiently elaborated such that this challenge is a feasible one to take on.

Clinical Implications of a Developmental Frame of Reference

There are also direct clinical implications stemming from a developmental frame of reference. Being able to characterize development more precisely will sharpen our ability to identify the time points of greatest vulnerability, and hence time points of greatest sensitivity to change. By ignoring developmental time, a core piece of the matrix of causation is overlooked, yet the ability to understand it is to take advantage of natural points of stability and transition as points of opportunity, albeit requiring different strategies to have impact (see, for example, the classic work on turning points by Rutter, 1996, and a recent and more articulated version by Schulenberg and colleagues (this volume). At the moment, both clinical practice and prevention programming remain largely ignorant about these issues. The ability to begin to quantify these developmental locations has the potential to make intervention much more powerful, as an insulator against the impact of risk, on the one hand, and as a tool with greater potency for change. Moreover, the points of change are not just about timing; they typically imply a shift in activity and attention. To the extent these modality shifts can be woven into the intervention they have the potential for greater effect. To provide but one example, the shifts in adolescent brain responsivity to reward would suggest that more affectively framed messaging will have greater impact at this time.

Above and beyond the ability to identify time points of greatest vulnerability, there are other clinical practice implications stemming from an understanding of the developmental nature of substance use disorder (SUD). These implications are sketched out in a number of the *Handbook* chapters. Wilson and Janoff (this volume) emphasize that comorbidity means multiple etiologies,

and that to address only the substance abuse in the presenting adolescent is likely to be ineffective in the long term for the treatment. For this reason, just as is the obverse case with SUD, understanding the course of the comorbidity and addressing it in the initial evaluation as well as in treatment is critical.

Understanding the developmental phase within which the adolescent makes the connection with treatment is also critical. Contexts are different, goals for the adolescent are different, and significant influences are likely to be different, at various points in adolescence. Different modalities of treatment are called for under these circumstances. A related clinical question is the time sequencing of onset and course for adolescents with SUD and one or more co-occurring clinical disorders. Wilson and Janoff make the case for an in-depth developmental understanding of the emergence of symptomatology for both clinical problems. They point to the commonly used treatment strategy of working to make the patient substance abuse free in order to ascertain the linkage between the co-occuring disorder and the SUD, and note that this involves an at-best crude understanding of the interrelationship. Although the diagnostic system implies that there are two separate entities, this is simply a labeling of categories to indicate the multiple symptomatologies that are present. From an individual standpoint, it is much more likely that the two disorders are woven together in their development. Without understanding this, and documentation of the patient's account of what emerged when, one will not be able to identify the nodal points of the symptomatic course and will likewise not be able to devise an effective treatment plan with the potential to address the patient's idiosyncratic etiology. Although Wilson and Janoff's account is very practical, it simultaneously embraces a sophisticated developmental view of the clinical picture that goes far beyond a cross-sectional assessment of what presents at time of treatment entry. As they describe, this strategy is much more likely to lead to the design of an effective plan of recovery that has the potential to create long-term resolution of these complex cases.

White, Cronley, and Iyer (this volume) also focus on the dynamics of comorbidity issues in their review of the evidence for direction of effects in the relationship between delinquency and substance use. That work is most commonly focused on etiologic questions rather than clinical ones—that is, which is the causal agent and which the outcome—but the reality is that once the relationship is established, the behaviors ("symptoms") coexist. Or to put the matter differently, each is comorbid with the other. The authors point out that the evidence for developmental complexity of this relationship is considerable. Comorbidity that originated by an effect in one direction can reverse causal flow at a later developmental way point; in other instances, the influences are reciprocal across both types of behavior. They review the studies showing these multiple directions of effect, and their conclusions offer a tantalizing invitation for clinical researchers to use this multidirectional developmental model to facilitate understanding of other clinical symptomatology as it is embedded in context. Their findings also provide an invitation for clinicians to probe more deeply the issues of timing of first symptom appearance and tracking direction of effect as they relate both to etiology and current treatment. Finally, we note that adolescent drug use is newer and less practiced, and hence the behavior should be easier to modify.

At the same time, the clinician's fallacy—shared as well in the field of medicine more generally—is that all trouble is ultimately addressable at the individual level. For some types of problems this may be impossible. As noted by Schwartz and colleagues (this volume), some problems are the result of forces impacting the individual from macro-level influences, such as racial prejudice, socio-economic deprivation, and so on. These influences both create elevated stress and also, via a process of system justification, result in the discriminated group accepting its "inferior" status. It is likely that addressing these problems only at the individual level will ultimately lead to relapse, except for the most resilient. And even for those who are resilient, the macro-level processes create great stress. Unless macro-level effects can be loosened (e.g., by moving to another part of the community, and perhaps even in some instances, by migration) the same or other symptomatology is likely to appear. To address such issues, the clinician's efforts need to move more toward public health action, with a special focus on social policy change (see especially Holder and Green, this volume).

Cross-Domain Causal Structure of Substance Abuse and the Challenge for New Data Collection Methodologies

The multiple empirical studies reviewed in this book utilize a very large number of methods to assess the variables hypothesized to lead to, or correlate with, the development of substance abuse. The variation being assessed covers multiple domains,

crossing multiple levels of analysis. Understanding the relationships between these levels of function and how they affect one another is in its infancy, but the effort to establish these connections is driven by increasing sensitivity to the fact that mechanistic variation at any one level of analysis can explain only a small portion of the predictive variance (Karmiloff-Smith et al., 2014; McEwen & Akil, 2011). This volume's authors indicate an awareness of this issue to varying degrees, with the acknowledgment being most obvious in the chapters that utilize a developmental psychopathology conceptual framework, a cross-species perspective, or are characterizing the mechanistic structure of substance abuse etiology at the extremes of the social neuroscience continuum (i.e., genetics and neuroimaging on the one hand and sociocultural influence on the other). Creation of a methodology to handle this diversity of causal influences is a daunting enterprise, but comprehensive templates are slowly emerging. The National Institutes of Health (NIH) collection of assessment methods for Research Domain Criteria (RDoC) Constructs (2016, RDoC) is one such broad-ranging array of instruments that was constructed with the goal to cover these domains. The PhenX Toolkit (Conway et al., 2014; Hendershot et al., 2015) is another.

Concurrent to the need to develop a suitably broad-ranging methodology is the challenge to create studies that would be able to assess and then manage this extraordinarily large set of measures, and that likewise will have the expertise to take on the major analytic challenges such a massive, cross-domain matrix will present. At the time most of these chapters were written, such a project did not exist, although two were in fact either in the launch stage or in the planning stage. They are the National Consortium on Alcohol and Neurodevelopment in Adolescence (NCANDA) Study (2015) and the Adolescent Brain Neurocognitive Development (ABCD) Study (Garavan et al., 2018; Jernigan & Brown, 2018; Volkow et al., 2017). NCANDA, currently in its fifth year of operation, is following 831 adolescents between the ages of 12 and 21, The ABCD study, currently in its third year of operation, is the largest developmental neuroimaging study worldwide, beginning at ages 9–10 and following a nationally representative sample of approximately 11,900 study participants for a period of 10 years. In was conceptualized using a population neuroscience perspective (Falk et al., 2013) and involves a high-dimensional data collection endeavor that utilizes assessments of structural and functional brain imaging, bioassay of key biological processes for genetic and epigenetic analysis, neurocognition, physical and mental health, substance use, social and emotional functions, culture, and environment. It is out of these longitudinal, cross-level matrices of data that new levels of understanding of the causes and course of substance use and abuse are most likely to emerge. Because they are multidomain as well as developmental, it is hard to predict what the shape of those understandings will be. But it is very clear that we are entering a new era of science that not only cuts across disciplines but also seeks to integrate them. In so doing, we will be constructing new models of the emergence of risk as well as the evolution of resilience.

References

Agrawal, A., & Lynskey, M. T. (2006). The genetic epidemiology of cannabis use, abuse and dependence. *Addiction, 101*, 801–812.

Anthony, J. C., Warner, L. A., & Kessler, R. C. (1994). Comparative epidemiology of dependence on tobacco, alcohol, controlled substances, and inhalants: Basic findings from the National Comorbidity Survey. *Experimental and Clinical Psychopharmacology, 2*(3), 244.

Badiani, A., Belin, D., Epstein, D., Calu, D., & Shaham, Y. (2011). Opiate versus psychostimulant addiction: The differences do matter. *Nature Reviews Neuroscience, 12*(11), 685.

Badiani, A., Berridge, K. C., Heilig, M., Nutt, D. J., & Robinson, T. E. (2018). Addiction research and theory: A commentary on the Surgeon General's Report on alcohol, drugs, and health. *Addiction Biology, 23*(1), 3–5.

Becker, J. A., Kieffer, B. L., & Le Merrer, J. (2017). Differential behavioral and molecular alterations upon protracted abstinence from cocaine versus morphine, nicotine, THC and alcohol. *Addiction Biology, 22*(5), 1205–1217.

Borodovsky J. T., Marsch L. A., & Budney A. J. (2018). Studying cannabis use behaviors with Facebook and Web surveys: Methods and insights. *JMIR Public Health Surveillance, 4*(2), e48. doi:10.2196/publichealth.9408

Brummelte, S., McGlanaghy, E., Bonnin, A., & Oberlander, T. F. (2017). Developmental changes in serotonin signaling: Implications for early brain function, behavior and adaptation. *Neuroscience, 7*(342), 212–231. doi:10.1016/j.neuroscience.2016.02.037

Buu, A., Wang, W., Schroder, S. A., Kalaida, N. L., Puttler, L. I., & Zucker, R. A. (2012a). Developmental emergence of alcohol use disorder symptoms and their potential as early indicators for progression to alcohol dependence in a high-risk sample: A longitudinal study from childhood to early adulthood. *Journal of Abnormal Psychology, 121*(4), 897.

Buu, A., Wang, W., Schroder, S. A., Kalaida, N. L., Puttler, L. I., & Zucker, R. A. (2012b). Correction to Buu et al. (2012a). *Journal of Abnormal Psychology, 122*(1), 25. doi:10.1037/a0025961. PMID: 21842966. PMCID: PMC3560403

Colder, C. R., Scalco, M., Trucco, E. M., Read, J. P., Lengua, L. J., Wieczorek, W. F., & Hawk, L. W. (2013). Prospective associations of internalizing and externalizing problems and

their co-occurrence with early adolescent substance use. *Journal of Abnormal Child Psychology, 41*(4), 667–677.

Conway, K. P., Vullo, G. C., Kennedy, A. P., Finger, M. S., Agrawal, A., Bjork, J. M., . . . Huggins, W. (2014). Data compatibility in the addiction sciences: An examination of measure commonality. *Drug & Alcohol Dependence, 141*, 153–158. doi:10.1016/j.drugalcdep.2014.04.029

Dodge, K. A., Greenberg, M. T., Malone, P. S., & Conduct Problems Prevention Research Group. (2008). Testing an idealized dynamic cascade model of the development of serious violence in adolescence. *Child Development, 79*(6), 1907–1927.

Epstein-Ngo, Q. M., Cunningham, R. M., Whiteside, L. K., Chermack, S. T., Booth, B. M., Zimmerman, M. A., Walton, M. A. (2013). A daily calendar analysis of substance use and dating violence among high risk urban youth. *Drug and Alcohol Dependence, 130*(1–3), 194–200.

Falk, E. B., Hyde, L. W., Mitchell, C., Faul, J., Gonzalez, R., Heitzeg, M. M., . . ., Morrison, F. J. (2013). What is a representative brain? Neuroscience meets population science. *Proceedings of the National Academy of Sciences, 110*(44), 17615–17622.

Flay, B. R., Phil, D., Hu, F. B., & Richardson, J. (1998). Psychosocial predictors of different stages of cigarette smoking among high school students. *Preventive Medicine, 27*(5), A9–A18.

Garavan, H., Bartsch, H., Conway, K., Decastro, A., Goldstein, R. Z., Heeringa, S., . . . Zahs, D. (2018). Recruiting the ABCD sample: Design considerations and procedures. *Developmental Cognitive Neuroscience, 32*,16–22. doi:10.1016/j.dcn.2018.04.004

Heilig, M., Epstein, D. H., Nader, M. A., & Shaham, Y. (2016). Time to connect: Bringing social context into addiction neuroscience. *Nature Reviews. Neuroscience, 17*(9), 592–599. doi:10.1038/nrn.2016.67

Hendershot, T., Pan, H., Haines, J., Harlan, W. R., Marazita, M. L., McCarty, C. A., Ramos, E. M., & Hamilton, C. M. (2015). Using the PhenX Toolkit to add standard measures to a study. *Current Protocols in Human Genetics, 86*(1), 1–21.

Iacono, W. G., Malone, S. M., & McGue, M. (2008). Behavioral disinhibition and the development of early-onset addiction: Common and specific influences. *Annual Review of Clinical Psychology, 4*(1), 325–348.

Jander, A., Crutzen, R., Mercken, L., & De Vries, H. (2014). A Web-based computer-tailored game to reduce binge drinking among 16 to 18 year old Dutch adolescents: Development and study protocol. *BMC Public Health, 14*(1), 1054.

Jernigan, T. L., Brown, S. A., & ABCD Consortium Coordinators. (2018). Introduction. *Developmental Cognitive Neuroscience 32*, 1–3.

Jester, J. M., Glass, J. M., Bohnert, K., Nigg, J. T., Wong, M., & Zucker, R. A. (in press). Child and adolescent influences predicting degree of smoking involvement in emerging adulthood. *Health Psychology*.

Kandel, D. B., Griesler, P. C., & Schaffran, C. (2009). Educational attainment and smoking among women: Risk factors and consequences for offspring. *Drug & Alcohol Dependence, 104*, S24–S33.

Karmiloff-Smith, A., Casey, B. J., Massand, E., Tomalski, P., & Thomas, M. S. C. (2014). Environmental and genetic influences on neurocognitive development: The importance of multiple methodologies and time-dependent intervention. *Clinical Psychological Science, 2*(5), 628–637.

Kendler, K. S., Myers, J., & Prescott, C. A. (2007). Specificity of genetic and environmental risk factors for symptoms of cannabis, cocaine, alcohol, caffeine, and nicotine dependence. *Archives of General Psychiatry, 64*(11), 1313–1320.

Kendler, K. S., Prescott, C. A., Myers, J., & Neale, M. C. (2003). The structure of genetic and environmental risk factors for common psychiatric and substance use disorders in men and women. *Archives of General Psychiatry, 60*, 929–937.

Kenny, R., Dooley, B., & Fitzgerald, A. (2016). Ecological momentary assessment of adolescent problems, coping efficacy, and mood states using a mobile phone app: An exploratory study. *JMIR Mental Health, 3*(4), e51. doi:10.2196/mental.6361

Koob, G. F., & Volkow, N. D. (2010). Neurocircuitry of addiction. *Neuropsychopharmacology, 35*(1), 217–238.

Lopez-Quintero, C., & Neumark, Y. (2015). Prevalence and determinants of resistance to use drugs among adolescents who had an opportunity to use drugs. *Drug & Alcohol Dependence, 149*, 55–62.

McCabe, S. E., Kloska, D. D., Veliz, P., Jager, J., & Schulenberg, J. E. (2016). Developmental course of non-medical use of prescription drugs from adolescence to adulthood in the United States: National longitudinal data. *Addiction, 111*(12), 2166–2176.

McEwen, B. S., & Akil, H. (2011). Introduction to social neuroscience: Gene, environment, brain, body. *Annals of the New York Academy of Sciences, 1231*, vii–ix.

Menossi, H. S., Goudriaan, A. E., Périco, C. D. A. M., Nicastri, S., de Andrade, A. G., D'Elia, Li, C. S., & Castaldelli-Maia, J. M. (2013). Neural bases of pharmacological treatment of nicotine dependence—Insights from functional brain imaging: A systematic review. *CNS Drugs, 27*(11), 921–941.

Moore, T. M., Elkins, S. R., McNulty, J. K., Kivisto, A. J., & Handsel, V. A. (2011). Alcohol use and intimate partner violence perpetration among college students: Assessing the temporal association using electronic diary technology. *Psychology of Violence, 1*, 315–328. doi:10.1037/a0025077

National Institutes of Health. (2016). Research Domain Criteria (RDoC) Matrix. Retrieved from https://www.nimh.nih.gov/research-priorities/rdoc/constructs/rdoc-matrix.shtml

Rutter, M. (1996). Transitions and turning points in developmental psychopathology: As applied to the age span between childhood and mid-adulthood. *International Journal of Behavioral Development, 19*, 603–626.

Steele, V. R., Maurer, J. M., Arbabshirani, M. R., Claus, E. D., Fink, B. C., Rao, V., Calhoun, V. D., & Kiehl, K. A. (2018). Machine learning of functional magnetic resonance imaging network connectivity predicts substance abuse treatment completion. *Biological Psychiatry: Cognitive Neuroscience and Neuroimaging, 3*(2), 141–149. doi:10.1016/j.bpsc.2018.07.003

Strong, D. R., Schonbrun, Y. C., Schaffran, C., Griesler, P. C., & Kandel, D. (2012). Linking measures of adult nicotine dependence to a common latent continuum and a comparison with adolescent patterns. *Drug & Alcohol Dependence, 120*(1), 88–98.

Theedele D. A., Cushing C. C., Fritz A., Amaro C. M., & Ortega A. (2017). Mobile health interventions for improving health outcomes in youth: A meta-analysis. *JAMA Pediatrics, 171*(5), 461–469. doi:10.1001/jamapediatrics.2017.0042

Trucco, E., Villafuerte, S., Hussong, A., Burmeister, M., & Zucker, R. A. (2018). Biological underpinnings of an internalizing pathway to alcohol, cigarette, and marijuana use. *Journal of Abnormal Psychology, 127*(1), 79–91.

Tsuang, M. T., Lyons, M. J., Eisen, S. A., Goldberg, J., True, W., Lin, N., . . . Eaves, L. J., (1996). Genetic influences on abuse of illicit drugs: A study of 3,297 twin pairs. *American Journal of Medical Genetics, 67*, 473–477.

Volkow, N. D., Koob, G. F., Croyle, R. T., Bianchi, D. W., Gordon, J. A., Koroshetz, W. J., . . . Deesds, B. G. (2017). The conception of the ABCD study: From substance use to a broad NIH collaboration. *Developmental Cognitive Neuroscience, 32*, 4–7.

Volkow, N. D., & Morales, M. (2015). The brain on drugs: From reward to addiction. *Cell, 162*(4), 712–725.

Wagner, F. A., & Anthony, J. C. (2002). From first drug use to drug dependence: Developmental periods of risk for dependence upon marijuana, cocaine, and alcohol. *Neuropsychopharmacology, 26*, 479–488.

INDEX

Tables and figures are indicated by an italic *t* and *f* following the page number.